D0031187
VDQS
AISNE
Aisne
Oise
Reims
Épernay
MARNE
SEINE-ET-MARNE
CHAMPAGNE
MOSELLE
EST
MEURTHE-ET-MOSELLE
Toul
BAS-RHIN
Strasbourg
ALSACE
AUBE
Aube
Troyes
les Riceys
Marne
HAUTE-MARNE
YONNE
Auxerre
Chablis
Seine
BOURGOGNE
Colmar
HAUT-RHIN
CÔTE-D'OR
Dijon
Saône
Besançon
Sancerre
CHER
NIÈVRE
Beaune
BOURGOGNE
VALLÉE
LA LOIRE
Loire
Arbois
JURA
JURA
SAÔNE-ET-LOIRE
ALLIER
Saint-Pourçain-sur-Sioule
Mâcon
AIN
HAUTE-SAVOIE
Annecy
Villefranche-sur-Saône
BEAUJOLAIS
Rhône
SAVOIE
Roanne
Clermont-Ferrand
CENTRE
RHÔNE
Lyon
Chambéry
SAVOIE
PUY-DE-DÔME
LOIRE
Vienne
Allier
Loire
VALLÉE
Rhône
Valence
DU
Die
ARDÈCHE
DRÔME
Lot
Montélimar
RHÔNE
Durance
AVEYRON
Orange
ALPES-DE-HAUTE-PROVENCE
ALPES-MARITIMES
GARD
VAUCLUSE
Avignon
Nîmes
LANGUEDOC
BOUCHES-DU-RHÔNE
PROVENCE
Nice
Montpellier
HÉRAULT
Aix-en-Provence
Draguignan
VAR
Patrimonio
Bastia
HAUTE-CORSE
Marseille
Toulon
Ajaccio
CORSICA
CORSE DU-SUD
Perpignan
Banyuls
MEDITERRANEAN SEA

HACHETTE WINE GUIDE

THE FRENCH WINE BIBLE

HACHETTE WINE GUIDE

Editorial Director: Catherine Montalbetti

With the help of: Christian Asselin, INRA, *Vigne et Vin research unit*; Jean-François Bazin; Claude Bérenguer; Richard Bertin, *Oenologists*; Pierre Bidan, *Lecturer at ENSA, Montpellier*; Jean Bisson, *former Director of the INRA Viticultural Centre*; Jacques Blouin, *Oenologist*; Jean-Pierre Callède, *Oenologist*; Pierre Casamayor, *Conference Director at the Science Faculty, Toulouse*; Béatrice de Chabert, *Oenologist*; Robert Cordonnier, *Director of Research at INRA*; Jean-Pierre Deroudille; Michel Dovaz; Michel Feuillat, *Lecturer at the Science Faculty, Dijon*; Pierre Huglin, *Research Director at INRA*; Robert Lala, *Oenologist*; Antoine Lebègue; Michel Le Seac'h; Jean-Pierre Martinez, *Chamber of Agriculture, Loir-et-Cher*, Mariska Pezzutto, *Oenologist*; Jacques Puisais, *honorary President of the Union Française des Oenologues*; Pascal Ribéreau-Gayon, *Former Dean of the Oenology Faculty, Bordeaux University II*; André Roth, *Agricultural Engineer*, Alex Schaeffer, *INRA, Director of the Vigne et Vin Research Centre*; Anne Seguin; Bernard Thévenet, *Agricultural Engineer*, Pierre Torrès, *Director of the Vine and Wine-growing Centre, Roussillon.*

Also: Patricia Abbou; Evelyne Azzola; Sylvie Chambadal; Nicole Crémer; Sylvie Hano; Micheline Martel; François Merveilleau; Diane Meur; Evelyne Werth; **Assistant editor:** Christine Cuperly; **Editorial secretary:** Anne Le Meur; **Computer processing:** Marie-Line Gros-Desormeaux; Sylvie Clochez; Martine Lavergne.

We should like to express our very grateful thanks to the 800 members of wine-tasting committees who met specially to help produce this guide, and who, as is customary, remain anonymous, and also to the organisations who kindly gave their support to the book or took part in general research: the Institut National des Appellations d'Origine, INAO; the Institut National de la Recherche Agronomique, INRA; the board of Consumption and Fraud Prevention; the Office National Interprofessionel des Vins and its regional delegations, ONIVINS; the CFCE; the DGDDI; the various professional committees, councils, federations and unions; the Institut des Produits de la Vigne of Montpellier and ENSAM; the Paul Sabatier University, Toulouse; the wine-growing unions and wine-growers' associations; the unions and federations for the Grands Crus; the wine-merchants' unions; the Confédération des Caves Particulières and their regional federations; the Confédération Nationale des Caves Coopératives and the Fédérations des Caves Coopératives; the chamber of agriculture; the departmental analytical laboratories; the agricultural colleges of Amboise, Avize, Blanquefort, Bommes, Montagne-Saint-Emilion, Montreuil-Bellay and Nîmes-Rodilhan, the hotelier's college of Tain l'Hermitage, the CFPPA at Hyères; the Institut Rhodanien; the Union Française des Oenologues and the Fédérations Régionale des Oenologues; the wine-brokers' unions; the Union de la Sommellerie Française and the Associations Régionales de Sommeliers; the Chartreuse de Villeneuve-lès-Avignon; in Switzerland, the Office Fédéral de l'Agriculture, the Commission Fédérale du Contrôle du Commerce des Vins, the officers of the cantonal wine-growing services, the OVV, OPAV and OPAGE; in the Grand Duchy of Luxembourg, the Institut Viti-Vinicole Luxembourgeois; the Marque Nationale du Vin Luxembourgeois; the Fonds de Solidarité.

Layout: François Huertas; **Cartography:** Fabrice Le Goff; **Illustrations:** Véronique Chappée; **Photo credits:** p. 13; p. 17 and p. 27 all © Scope/M. Guillard.

First published in the United Kingdom in 2000 by Hachette UK

Distributed in the United States of America by Sterling Publishing Co., Inc.
387 Park Avenue South, New York, NY 10016-8810

A CIP catalogue for this book is available from the British Library

ISBN 1 84202 067 6

English translation by Translate-A-Book, Oxford
Typeset by WestKey Ltd, Falmouth, Cornwall
Printed and bound in Spain

Hachette UK
Cassell & Co
Wellington House
125 Strand
London
WC2R 0BB

HACHETTE

WINE GUIDE

THE FRENCH WINE BIBLE

HACHETTE

CONTENTS

CONTENTS

A selection of the best French wines

SYMBOLS

SYMBOLS USED IN THIS GUIDE

A photo of the label signifies that the wine is strongly recommended by the committee.

★★★ exceptional wine
★★ excellent wine
★ good wine

1999 vintage or year of wine tasted

□ still white wine
◪ still rosé wine
■ still red wine
○ sparkling white wine
◕ sparkling rosé wine
● sparkling red wine

50,000, 12,500 . . . average number of bottles on offer

4 ha (10 acres): area of vineyard for this wine (in hectares and acres)

- aged in vat
- aged in cask
- temperature regulation
- address
- for sale on the premises
- conditions of visit or tasting
- name of owner, if different from that mentioned in address

n.c. information not supplied

PRICES

THE PRICES are given as a guide only (average price of a bottle in France per case of 12). The equivalent in Euros is given below.

– FF20	FF20 to 29	FF30 to 49	FF50 to 69	FF70 to 99
– €3.04	€3.04 – 4.57	€4.57 – 7.62	€7.62 – 10.67	€10.67 – 15.24
FF100 to 149	FF150 to 199	FF200 to 249	FF250 to 299	300 to 499FF
€15.24 – 22.87	€22.87 – 30.49	€30.49 – 38.11	€38.11 – 45.73	€45.73 – 76.07
FF+500				
€+76.22				

Where the price is highlighted in red, this indicates good value for money –30F

VINTAGES (82) 83 |(85)| |86| 89 (90) 91 |92| 93 **95** **96** |97| **98**

83 91 the vintages marked in red are ready to drink

93 95 the vintages marked in black should be kept

|86| |92| the vintages marked in black between two vertical lines are ready to drink but can be kept

83 95 the best vintages are in bold

(90) exceptional vintages are circled

The vintages mentioned are not necessarily for sale at the property but can be found at wine-merchants and restaurants.

CONVERSIONS

Length		**Weight**		**Volume**	
1mm	0.0394 in	1gm	0.035 oz	1 cu cm	0.061 cu in
1cm	0.394 in	1kg	2.2 lb	1 cu m	35.3 cu ft
1m	39.4 in	1kg	0.001 ton	1 cu m	1.31 cu yd
1m	1.09 yd	1 tonne	2200 lb		
1km	0.621 miles				
Area		**Liquid Capacity**			
1sq cm	0.155 sq in	1ml	0.035 fl oz		
1sq m	10.76 sq ft	1l	0.53 pt (US pint = 16 fl oz)		
1sq m	1.2 sq yd	1hl (100 litre)	26.4 gal		
1ha	2.47 acre	1hl/ha	10.8 gal/acre		
1sq km	247 acres				
1sq km	0.386 sq miles				
1a	0.25 acre	Note: Conversions are into US measurements.			

HOW THE GUIDE WORKS

A brand new selection of wines

This guide contains details of the 9,000 best wines from France, Switzerland and Luxembourg, all tasted in the year 2000. This is an entirely new selection, focusing on the latest bottled vintage. The wines have been chosen for you by 800 experts from more than 28,000 wines from every appellation during the course of blind tastings held by the *Hachette Wine Guide*. Some thousand wines are mentioned in bold type in the index that lists producers' most highly rated wines.

An objective guide

The absence of any financial or promotional involvement by the producers, wine-merchants or co-operatives mentioned ensures the impartiality of the book, the sole aim of which is to be a wine-buying guide for consumers. The tasting notes should be used only to draw comparisons within the same appellation; it is, in fact, impossible to judge different appellations according to exactly the same criteria.

The tasting process and classification

Each unlabelled wine is examined by a jury. The colour, aroma and taste are described, and it is given a mark between 0 and 5.

0 faulty wine: eliminated
1 poor or mediocre wine: eliminated
2 wine typical of the area: worth a mention but not starred
3 good wine: **one star**
4 excellent wine: **two stars**
5 exceptional wine and a perfect example of the appellation: **three stars**.

Our choice

The wines whose labels are reproduced in the guide represent the 'coups de coeur'. These are wines that inspired our tasters to 'love at first sip', wines that are so good that they are particularly recommended to readers. References to wines being successful in previous years refer to previous editions of the French guide. We have kept them in to acknowledge the wine's status as a previously successful wine.

User friendly

The structure of this guide is very simple.
A special chapter is dedicated to the history of French vineyards over the last hundred years
The 'What's New?' section gives up-to-date information on French vineyards, an analysis of the 2000 vintage and regional economic information.
A practical section, 'Wine – General', explains the techniques of cultivating the vine and wine-production.

A 'Consumer's Guide' gives advice on buying, keeping and tasting wine and suggests the best food–wine combinations.

The selected wines are listed alphabetically by region, followed by three sections dedicated to Vins Doux Naturels (sweet fortified wines), Vins de Liqueurs and Vins de Pays (country wines). There is also a chapter on a selection of wines from Luxembourg and another on Swiss wines.They are also listedby appellation, presented geographically within each region, and alphabetically within each appellation.

There are four indexes at the back of the book listing the appellations, communes, producers and wines.

There are 49 original maps showing the geographical situation of the vineyards.

Weights and measurements are given in both metric and imperial for ease of use.

Omissions

Some well-known and reputable wines are missing from this guide, either because the producers did not take part in, or were eliminated from, the tastings. Some wines were tasted and favourably assessed but additional information was not supplied; next to these wines you will see 'nc' (information not supplied).

Elsewhere, it is not surprising that there is no vintage or year for Vins d'Assemblage (mixed wines – for example, non-vintage champagnes), nor for liqueurs or sweet fortified wines, nor for those wines that are offered by different producers, supplied by wine-merchants or co-operatives.

Reader's guide

Because the object of this book is to advise the consumer on choosing wines, according to his or her individual taste, and to advise on the best value for money (the price range is indicated in red), everything has been done to make this guide practical and easy to read.

It is important to read the general introduction as well as the ones to the regions and the appellations, because information common to all the wines is not repeated in each section.

Prices

The price range (average price per bottle for a case of 12) is subject to market trends and is given as a guide only. All prices are given in French francs only to avoid fluctuating exchange rates, for practicability of use and for consistency Prices for wines from Switzerland and Luxembourg are also given in French francs.

Telephone numbers

In France telephone numbers have ten digits. If you want to phone or fax a French producer from abroad you need to dial the international code (00 from the UK and 011 from the USA) followed by the country code, which is 33 for France, and then the number, omitting the first zero. To telephone Switzerland and Luxembourg, the procedure is the same but the country code for Switzerland is 41 and for Luxembourg 352. E-mail addresses are also given where appropriate.

A HUNDRED YEARS OF FRENCH WINE PRODUCTION

French viticulture has been blessed with many advantages. Well established and prosperous, today it is one of the flagships of a world-wide industry. Despite the various adjustments it has had to make to suit fluctuating market conditions, it is currently flourishing and enjoying one of the very best periods in its entire history.

At the beginning of the 21st century, wine-growing has never been quite as prosperous nor wine so universally recognised and appreciated as a cultural product as well as simply something to drink. Today there are more enlightened consumers buying and tasting good wines and showing an in-depth knowledge of wine than ever before. The lowering of production costs in some regions and the stepping-up of competition at a global level are changes that had to be made in the wake of several years of overheating in the French economy, fuelled by a healthy export market and speculation.

It would doubtless be easy to find some golden age with which to counter this statement – 15th century Burgundy under Philip the Good, perhaps, or Champagne during the Belle Époque – but just a handful shared in this prosperity and only a privileged few actually tasted these great wines. As for the great vintages of the past, they were mainly happy accidents of nature. The wine-growers, although undoubtedly knowledgeable and full of good common sense, were often ignorant of the scientific principles of wine-making and not able to use them on a regular basis to their advantage. The 1899 and 1900 vintages are two such examples. Combining quality and quantity, they left some fabulous bottles, notably those of the Médoc Grands Crus. Nevertheless, it would be wrong to make a general rule from a few memorable exceptions.

Oidium, mildew and phylloxera: the three scourges

In 1899 French wine-growing was in crisis. Phylloxera, the most serious disease that wine-growers had ever had to deal with, had devastated almost all French vineyards and was about to complete its work the following year in Champagne, the last bastion of resistance. The slump was beginning to affect Languedoc, the Bordeaux region, Charentes, the Garonne and Rhône valleys and Provence. As for the vineyards

ce que nous voulons

around Paris, they had been practically wiped off the map, with the exception once again of Champagne. Everything was conspiring to transform the face of the French wine-growing world, which was barely recognisable by the second half of the 19th century.

Two other diseases had accompanied phylloxera: in 1851 oidium (powdery mildew) and, worse still, in 1878 mildew. By 1900 the French had learned how to combat these three parasites: powdery mildew could be treated with sulphur, mildew with copper sulphate, and phylloxera by replanting with European vines that had been grafted on to parasite-resistant American rootstocks. But these treatments were expensive and time consuming – indeed, the vine remains one of the costliest plants to cultivate even today and none of these parasites has been totally eradicated.

The immense financial effort required when the industry was in crisis was a hard burden to bear. The vineyards whose wine was not highly rated enough to warrant the expense disappeared, and those farmers who were able to do so converted permanently to other products. The remaining vineyards were weakened for a considerable time. In *L'Histoire de la France Paysanne* (*History of Rural France*),[1] Gabriel Désert and Robert Specklin have detailed the extent of the upheaval. They calculated the shrinkage of large wine-growing areas between 1870 and 1912. The Mediterranean area (Provence and Languedoc) lost 22% of its surface area, Aquitaine 38%, the Loire valley 17%, Burgundy and the Rhône valley 20%, Charentes 72% and Champagne, which was affected only from 1900, 58%. In total, France was cultivating only 1,624,000 ha (4,011,280 acres) in 1912 compared with 2,874,000 ha (7,098,780 acres) at its peak in 1874, according to reliable statistics obtained from taxation figures. More than half the production was concentrated in the four *départements* of Languedoc, as opposed to less than 20% in 1874.

The repercussions of this crisis have been felt almost up to the present. A great many vineyards, even in the best appellations, remained planted with hybrid American vines (more robust and more productive but of a mediocre quality) right up to the 1960s. In some regions they still remember the Noah variety, while Bacco, used in the distillation of Armagnac, is a rarity now. Elsewhere, appellations like Cahors, very popular today, had almost disappeared, and some, such as Gaillac, had been transformed into Vin de Table areas. These unsettling changes were not entirely due to natural catastrophes, but they were intensified and speeded up by them. In spite of these crises, the influence of technology and industry was changing production conditions, and the arrival of urbanisation and general prosperity were changing consumer habits too.

Regional specialisation

The spread of the railways throughout France gave southern vineyards a comparatively new advantage before the practice of chaptalisation (adding sugar before fermentation) became general. Languedoc, sunnier and with fewer large industrial centres, had proved too competitive for the northern vineyards, with the exception of the quality strongholds: Champagne, Burgundy, the Loire valley, and also Alsace, which at that time was part of the German Empire and so not subject to this north–south rivalry.

In its turn, however, the south had to face new competition from vineyards that were even better placed geographically. France's defeat by Prussia in 1870 relaunched French colonialism, and Algeria, a country new to wine production, threw itself wholeheartedly into the venture. By 1904 it was already exporting nearly 7 million hl (184,800,000 gal) of wine to mainland France, wine that was stronger and of a more reliable quality than most of the French national products. The Bordeaux region was quick to import Algerian wine in order to improve its own Vins de Négoce (wines blended and sold by wine-merchants). The consistent quality of the Algerian product was much appreciated, even more so because the quality of Bordeaux wines varied depending on climatic conditions.

These imports were the much-needed answer to demand from the internal market, which France itself could no longer satisfy. Industrialisation had changed the structure of French society, and wine now featured on the tables of the working classes as well as on those of the bourgeoisie. Wine was becoming increasingly popular and was even catching up on local drinks such as cider and beer. However, despite these regional differences, the greatest challenge facing the vineyards at the turn of the century was fraud.

Fraud

Advances in chemistry made it easy to produce wine from a variety of substitutes, with the help of sugar, selected acids and manufactured aromas. These substitute wines masqueraded as whatever the counterfeiters felt the public required at the time – anything from Burgundy, Bordeaux to Côtes du Rhône. Fraud, which made a mockery of the quality of the genuine article and the work of the grower, had become wine's greatest enemy. Today, when the wine authorities rightly complain if a wine-producer is a little heavy-handed with the sugar or mixes two appellations, we cannot begin to imagine what unmentionable concoctions were served up in the bistros of the 1900s.

However, at the turn of the century, with the two great vintages of 1899 and 1900 safely in the cellars, wine-growers already possessed the scientific knowledge necessary to revitalise oenology and the wine-growing economy. Unfortunately, however, there were still several decades of misery to come. The 20th century had events in store for mankind of far greater concern than the perfecting of wine production.

Advances in wine-making

Two factors that helped in the renaissance of wine production – science and technology – had already progressed sufficiently to solve most of the technical problems. The main vine diseases were now treatable. It was exactly a hundred years since the French scientist Chaptal had shown how fermentation transformed sugar into alcohol and, consequently, how to offset any deficiencies in the ripeness of the grape. At the request of Napoleon III, Pasteur turned his attention to wine diseases and discovered a previously unknown microscopic environment in which tiny organisms were responsible for good and bad wine alike. The even more mysterious process of fermentation was soon to be mastered, too, and from the 1880s onwards sulphur was routinely used to get rid of undesirable bacteria or to clarify the wine.

Chemical analysis also had its role to play in combating fraud, whether it was in measuring the amounts of tartaric acid or, much later in the 1990s, the use of nuclear magnetic resonance to detect the origin of the sugar in the wine. As they were developed, these techniques came to be more widely known, although while progress was rapid so far as saving vines was concerned, it was a longer and more delicate process for scientific analysis to be accepted in the *chai* or cellar, where vinification takes place. In his book *Vins et Jours* (*Wine and Days*),[2] Emile Peynaud fondly remembers the difficulties he encountered in trying to get rational and scientific evidence accepted by wine-makers, even as late as the 1960s.

Bacteria: the new discoveries

Following in the footsteps of Pasteur, Ulysse Gayon (1845–1929) founded the Bordeaux oenological research station, which has since become a university, directed first by his son, Jean, and then his grandson, Pascal. Here, little by little the vinification of fine wines was first understood, then codified into practice; traditional methods were tested scientifically and those proven to work were retained, while methods that proved worthless were discarded. A Swiss scientist, Hermann Müller, known for his work on the selection of vinestocks, showed the effectiveness of spraying with sulphur at harvest time. He also demonstrated the effects of bacteria on wine: acescency (souring), oily disease, lactic fermentation of tartaric acid and glycerol and especially malolactic fermentation. It was not until the 1950s and 1960s that malolactic fermentation was applied to all red wines, and even then against considerable resistance, mainly from the Languedoc region. The results of malolactic fermentation were clear: wine became less acidic and more supple. Later still, Denis Dubourdieu's work on white wines revealed the role that biochemistry plays in the development of aroma and quality.

Overall, these discoveries led to better working methods. The growing importance of hygiene led to new materials being used (stainless steel vats, for example) and new practices being employed (in sorting and pressing grapes, in the precise determination of date of ripeness and in the use of selected yeasts and of less brutal treatments such as cold stabilisation, etc). However, in 1900 this quest for quality was by no means universally followed.

A need for regulation

The growing awareness of wine-producers, who were becoming less dependent on wine-merchants, led them to protest against commercial blending, demanding that the origin of their wines be protected. The wine-producers' *syndicat* (a professional association or union) of Saint-Emilion was created in 1885, and quickly threw itself into the defence of its appellation. In 1900 79 wine-growers from Chablis formed a group to defend the origin of their wine, and in 1901 the owners of the Médoc Grands Crus created their own *syndicat*.
Pressure began to mount for a regulatory code that would protect wine-growers and consumers and would also clean up the market. There had already been some unco-ordinated attempts at this in the past. The Ancien Régime, which disappeared in the Revolution of 1789, had previously maintained a certain number of rules governing wine-production and business. Long before this Philip the Bold regulated wine production in Burgundy. In the Bordeaux region a committee fixed the dates of the harvest, and elsewhere this task fell to local lords of the manor. However, by the 19th century these rules, perceived as symbols of arbitrary power, had fallen into disuse, and craft corporations, which had previously set and maintained professional standards, were banned by law as old-style instruments of oppression used by skilled workers to dominate their co-workers. It was several decades before the right to create unions and to formulate certain laws to protect workers was re-established, and it was only later that the needs to regulate competition and to protect the consumer were recognised.
More recently, urbanisation, which has severed the French from their rural roots (in 1900 80% of the French population lived in rural areas and 20% in towns or cities, whereas today the reverse is true), has made many people yearn for the honesty and quality of country life. Nowadays they find it by touring wine-growing areas – the *Hachette Wine Guide* in the glove compartment of their cars – or in the supermarkets and specialist warehouses that are now the main distributors of wines, and where row upon row of bottles can be found within easy reach. No aristocrat of the Ancien Régime or 19th-century gentleman, no matter how rich he might have been, would have had access to such a choice of wines, from the finest Grand Cru to the humblest Vin de Pays. Nevertheless, progress from those times to these has not been altogether smooth.

The long road to AOC

It has already been explained that in the past wine fraud affected everyone, but the effects were most keenly felt in Languedoc, where in 1900 the price of wine fell to FF10 per hl (26.4 gal), well below the cost of production, then about FF15 per hl.
The law against wine fraud passed on 1 August 1905 was the first step along the path. Even today, it constitutes the framework for all regulations governing wine-making ingredients and has been used as a basis for all laws in this context ever since. However, it was still not precise enough for the authorities to implement it in practical fashion.
In September 1907 a decree defined wine as deriving 'exclusively from the alcoholic fermentation of fresh grapes or fresh grape-juice'. It was such a simple statement that no one had thought of writing it down in black and white before. The International Wine Bureau (OIV, Office International du Vin), followed by the European Union, adopted this definition. However, this alone was not enough to enable wine-growers to increase their prices. The old Vin Naturel wine that was produced in the Languedoc was neither well known nor appreciated, which was why the wine wholesalers were able to blend it with Algerian wine. Fraud certainly did not help the situation, but urban consumers were also demanding better quality wines, although they were not prepared to pay the price.

Revolt in the Midi . . .

In 1906 the unrest began to be more visible, centring around a café owner, Marcelin Albert, and Antoine Marty from Argeliers in the Aude. Their newspaper, *Le Tocsin*, gave voice to the campaign and a defence committee organised demonstration after demonstration in all the towns of the south. Their biggest triumph was the demonstration in Montpellier on 9 June 1907, which brought together at least 500,000 people. However, it was difficult to tackle a government that at the time did not have the means to intervene in the market and to which the very idea of doing so was quite foreign (except for taxing imports, which they had already been doing for a long time).

The mayors and councillors of 300 communes resigned, but socialist deputy-mayor of Narbonne, Dr Ferroul, took up the challenge. (In Narbonne, five people died during the riots.) A little later, the 17th Territorial Regiment from Languedoc, stationed at Béziers, laid down their arms during manoeuvres so that they would not have to suppress a wine-growers' demonstration.

The radical Clemenceau, then president of France, managed to ease the tension by discrediting Marcelin Albert, but the government understood that they had to produce some effective anti-fraud legislation. Establishing a definition for wine was a beginning, but it was to take another 30 years to perfect.

A new law of 5 August 1908 made provision for the marking out, by decree, of the wine-growing areas, based on 'local, loyal and consistent usage'. If the 1905 law and the 1907 decrees suppressed the manufacture of false wine, the 1908 law left the door wide open for conflict over the limits of the appellations. Its first decree, which concerned Champagne, appeared on 17 December 1908. For once the government had acted quickly and did not slacken its efforts. In 1909 it was the turn of Cognac, Armagnac and Banyuls, and in 1910 of Clairette de Die. Preparations were in hand for defining the wine areas of Bordeaux when the storm broke – where it was least expected.

... And in Champagne

In 1910, after a catastrophic harvest, there were mass demonstrations in the Marne region, involving attacks on Champagne houses. Barrels were emptied, bottles were broken and the streets of Aÿ ran with champagne. Some houses and even vineyards were burned, and 40,000 troops were needed to restore order. The wine-growers from the Marne and Aisne accused the Champagne houses of acquiring wine illegally from Aube, a department that, although excluded from the administrative zone, had traditionally supplied them with wine. In the spring of 1911 the wine-growers of the Aube responded with violent riots, and they refused to accept that they had been excluded from the Champagne area.

Debates about delimitation

The shortcomings of an administrative delimitation were beginning to show, as was shortly to be further demonstrated in Bordeaux. In 1907 a commission was set up under the prefect (the senior administrative official of the department) which included representatives not only from Gironde but also from Dordogne and Lot-et-Garonne. At that time it was felt strongly that the vineyards of Bergerac (Dordogne), Duras, Marmande and Buzet (all Lot-et-Garonne) should be included in the Bordeaux appellation, which was still in the process of being defined. The argument was carried, and the first delimitation approved by the Council of State included 41 Dordogne communes and 22 from Lot-et-Garonne.

In the face of growing resentment, the government decided to review its decision, and a new, smaller commission recommended limiting the appellation to the department of Gironde. The decree of 18 February 1911 confirmed this wise suggestion before trouble and unrest of a similar nature to that experienced in Champagne had the chance to erupt.

To cut short the inevitable debates, the minister of agriculture, Jules Pams, presented a bill to the French Parliament on 30 June 1911 that aimed to change the method by which the appellation boundaries were decided. Administrative regulations, which took not just usage but also the quality of the wine into account, were due to become law and thus no longer open to debate. However, although voted through by the chamber after bitter discussions, the bill was never adopted because, the moment it arrived at the Senate, war was declared. The government and Parliament had other things to worry about, while the wine-growers themselves died in their tens of thousands in the trenches as this terrible conflict took its toll, first and foremost, of the young men from the rural areas.

The Great War cancels out surpluses

Those wine-growers who were not at the front temporarily forgot problems of origin and outlets. The army became their best client, generously distributing rations to those who were in action. Prices gradually increased. It was in the trenches that red wine (*pinard* or 'plonk') became the definitive French national drink, even in regions such as Brittany and Normandy that did not traditionally drink wine. Between 1900 and 1926 the annual national consumption of wine went from 100 litres (22 gal) to 135 litres (30 gal) per person. The price of a hectolitre (220 gal) in the south rose to FF98 in 1921 and as high as FF190 in 1926 (compared with FF10 in 1900).

On 24 April 1919 a law defining the appellations was adopted, however, taking as its basis the bill proposed by Pams. In the wake of war, the wine-growers, who had contributed to the victory with their lives and to the morale of the troops with their products, were not forgotten by the government of the day. The law, finally passed on 6 May 1919, remains at the core of the present system and the legal boundaries that it laid down are in force today. It defined 'appellation' as a collective property belonging to interested parties. It also recognised the *syndicats* 'associations defending the appellations as the legal representatives of the wine-growers' and made it obligatory to mention the appellation in the declaration of the harvest for those who wished to claim it. Lastly, going beyond purely geographical matters, it began to establish definitions for cultivation and wine-making methods for Champagne. The concept of the Appellation d'Origine Contrôlée was getting closer.

It was at this stage that Joseph Capus, from the Gironde region, who was to be the real 'father' of the AOC, became involved. Agronomist, professor of agriculture and director of the plant pathology research station at Cadillac (in Gironde), he had had, during his professional career plenty of time to evaluate the disadvantages of the different legislative responses, from their beginnings in 1905 to this latest request for protection of both origin and quality. As a deputy (elected member of Parliament) from 1919 to 1928, then a senator from 1930 to 1941, he managed to get a new law passed on 22 July 1927.

This laid down that the use of an appellation should be linked to the cultivation of vines approved by 'local, loyal and consistent usage' and forbade the use of hybrids. So, no more Gamay in Burgundy – as Duke Philip the Bold had decreed in 1395! It also stipulated that, even within the area defined by law, only those lands best suited to producing the appellation wine should be retained. It was another step in the direction towards 'plot delimitation' that the INAO (Institut National des Appellations d'Origine) finally achieved only very recently.

However, once again, even though great progress had been made, the ultimate goal had still not been achieved. Because production rules were not defined precisely enough, the door was still open to lax practices.

THE BIG SLUMP OF THE 1930s

With the regulations still so imprecise, the catastrophic economic crisis of the 1930s hit the main appellations as hard as it did the table wines of the south, where prices fell from FF154 a hl (26.4 gal) in 1929 to FF128 in 1932 and to FF64 in 1935. In the case of Vin de Consommation Courante, as table wine was known at that time, the government had started to intervene by distilling the surplus and encouraging the setting-up of co-operatives. These were beginning to appear in the Bordeaux region, too, during the same period; the first mention of one such co-operative was in the early 1930s.

In Bordeaux some of the largest châteaux were for sale for next to nothing. The owner of a Grand Cru Classé recalls happily how his baker grandfather acquired the family estate. Wine-merchants from Corrèze were able to buy the pick of the bunch, and that is how, in 1935, the lowest point of the slump, Haut-Brion passed into the hands of an extremely rich American financier and diplomat called Clarence Dillon.

In Burgundy the great landowners sold their estates strip by strip to the wine-growers who worked on the land. Already fragmented, the vineyards of this region became even more so. A prime example is the Clos de Vougeot – 55 adjacent ha (136 acres) belonging to some 80 wine-growers (no one dares to give a precise figure).

A few owners tried to protect their labels at all costs. This was the case with the courageous Philippe de Rothschild, who decided in 1924 to insist on bottling his Premier Grand Cru Classé, Château Mouton-Rothschild, in his own cellars. There was no better way of protecting the brand.

Government decrees of 1935: birth of the AOC

The situation remained at an impasse. In March 1935 Joseph Capus again brought a bill before the Senate to try to find a way out of the situation. At the same time, Pierre Laval, who seven years later would become prime minister under Philippe Pétain, had just formed an emergency government to try to get the country out of economic crisis. He had obtained from Parliament the power to legislate swiftly by government decree, which is how Joseph Capus's bill was implemented immediately, without having to go before the deputies again.

The government decree of 30 July 1935 created the CNAO (Comité National des Appellations d'Origine, which became an institute in 1947, the present INAO), an inter-professional body, which served as a model for most subsequent French agricultural associations (such as those for cereals, milk, beef, flowers, etc). It is this body that examines all requests to create appellations, and its committee then submits the propositions to the minister of agriculture, who cannot change the content or terms of the application. All professions and all wine-growing areas are represented through the unions for the defence of the various appellations. The principle of the method remains unchanged to this day. The same government decree is responsible for the creation of Appellations d'Origine Contrôlée, the end result of all the tentative regulatory and legislative steps taken since 1919. With only a few small differences, it still governs French wine-growing. The decrees instituting these various appellations define not only the production areas but also the *encépagement* (the detailing of grape varieties used in any given area), cultivation techniques (especially pruning) and, for the first time, the yield, the minimum natural sugar content of the grapes, as well as a minimum and maximum limit for the degrees of alcohol in the wine.

On 17 May 1936, various Appellations d'Origine Contrôlée (those of Arbois, Cassis, Châteauneuf-du-Pape and Monbazillac) were officially recognised. By the end of the year 70 AOCs had been created, and by 1939 the essentials of the wine-growing landscape had been established.

The system proved to be successful. Responsibility for defining production rules now lay with the producers, leaving implementation and control in the hands of the state.

The Second World War and the Occupation were not appropriate times to put the new system to the test, as throughout this dark period there was no chance of over-production. The German occupying forces helped themselves to as much as they wanted. On the other hand, the AOCs escaped rationing and the taxation that was levied on Vins de Consommation Courante. Prices climbed rapidly during this time of shortage, and it was during the Occupation that the category of 'quality wines' or Vins Réglementés made its appearance. These wines, without being AOCs, could claim a degree of authenticity and quality. They also escaped taxation and in 1945 became reclassified as Vins Délimités de Qualité Supérieure or VDQS, now AOVDQS. The new VDQS wines were successfully regulated by the wine-growing *syndicats*.

The system is extended to the Common Market

In 1970, when the wine market was at last organised at European level (some eight years after cereal crops), the member states recognised the specific nature of the appellations and used them as their inspiration for drawing up two new regulations. The first of these, No. 816/70, applied exclusively to table wines and stipulated compulsory distillations of surplus wine to limit quantities and sustain the market price. The second, No. 817/70, instituted VQPRD (Vins de Qualité Produits dans les Régions Déterminées), which fitted the categories of AOC and VDQS perfectly, leaving them with a free hand. Regulation No. 817/70 has since been modified several times, the last occasion being in 1999. The OCM (Organisation Commune du Marché), adopted by the 15 countries of the European Union, still respects the hard-won autonomy of the Appellations d'Origine. The only concession that the French wine-growers have been forced to make is that they are no longer free to accord new planting rights, which is hard when demand is growing as rapidly as it has done during the last decade. The effects of this on prices have not always been well received, but it is no doubt prudent to grant planting rights sparingly. The life-span of a vine is 40–50 years, and the vagaries of the market have a much shorter impact. During the last 30 years, Bordeaux, the largest producer of fine wines, has seen the greatest price fluctuations: first, a slump in the mid-1970s, followed by a small crisis due to inflated prices in 1985, another gloomy period caused by the 1991 frosts, which pushed prices to peak levels in a recession, and finally the exaggerated prices of 1997. However, the long-term tendency is towards a consistent rise of AOC production and price, in response to ever-increasing demand.

A NEW-FOUND TASTE FOR QUALITY

In 1926 the average annual consumption of wine per person in France was 135 litres. In 1955 it had risen to 140 litres, in 1973 it had gone down to 103 litres, and today it is 60 litres. However, the profile of consumption has changed completely. Table wine with no indication of provenance, other than the country or countries of origin, is now in a minority, overtaken by the vins de pays and the Appellations d'Origine. In 1998 in France out of 11 million hl (290,400,000 gal) sold in supermarkets and specialist warehouses (65% of the total market) table wine represented only 30.5% of the volume and 15% of the value. Wines that indicated their origins represented more than two-thirds of the total consumed, 19.5% of which were vins de pays and 48.5% AOC and AOVDQS (72% in value); the remaining 1.5% were wines from outside France. If you add to this the turnover from wine-merchants, restaurants and direct sales, the French now consume more Vins d'Appellation than vins de table and vins de pays put together, which is a complete reversal of the situation 20 years ago.

A FALL IN CONSUMPTION LEADS TO FEWER VINEYARDS

French wine consumption has declined overall, and with yields becoming more regular and falling into line with those of the better years, the total area of French vineyards has continued to decrease gradually, as it did at the end of the 19th century. In 1912 there were 1,624,000 ha (4,011,280 acres) under vines (excluding Alsace), in 1965 there were still 1,340,000 ha (3,309,800 acres), but only 872,773 ha (2,155,749 acres) at the declaration of the harvest in 1998. Meanwhile, many hundreds of thousands of hectares (several million acres) have been uprooted with the help of EU subsidies. Not that long ago, at the beginning of the 1980s, about 30% of income from the production of table wine in the south was made up of revenue from distilling. It took at least two decades (the 1960s and 1970s) to the changes in consumption and to implement the necessary adjustments. In 1976, at Montredon (Aude), the last large-scale revolts by wine-growers resulted in two deaths, tragedies that signalled that it was time for something to be done. Subsidies were provided to destroy surpluses, and help was given towards improving quality; this was followed by a massive uprooting programme. In its Agenda 2000 (drawn up in 1998) proposing a reform of the Common Agricultural Policy and its structural funding, the European Commission acknowledge that the internal balance of the market has been achieved. The standard litre bottle (AFNOR) decorated with six stars and capped rather than corked – the symbol of Vin de Consommation Courante in 1960 – has all but disappeared. The 1.5 litre (1.32 quart) plastic bottles that replaced it for a while are no longer popular, even if the bottles are now made of a newer material. Tetra-Paks (the bag-in-a-box product) replaced these, but their success is not widespread. Today, wine must provide evidence of its provenance and is sold in 75 cl (1.3 pint) corked bottles, although the cork may sometimes be artificial. The advantage that wine has over, say, chickens is that wine-growers and the state have been working for nearly a century on its 'traceability' – a new word, but an old concept in viticulture. The example given by Philippe de Rothschild, who decided to bottle all his production at the château, has been widely followed. While wholesaler-bottlers (*négoces distributeurs*) can still buy wine in tanks and blend for their own labels, it is rare for them to do so with wines from outside the vineyard production area. The traditional scenario, of a wholesaler based in the production area selling on wine in bulk to other wholesalers in the cities, no longer exists.

NEW BUSINESS, NEW LABELS

The largest French wine business is now Castel Frères, a company from the Bordeaux region, which bought the largest maker of table wine, the Société des Vins de France (SVF), based at Châteauneuf-lès-Martigues (Bouches-

du-Rhône) and Gennevilliers. It was the result of a good 20 years of whittling away at the small inter-regional and inter-departmental businesses. The large companies in the trade are now based in the production areas: in Champagne (from the start), but also in Bordeaux (La Baronnie, Ginestet, CVBG, GVG, Yvon Mau), in Burgundy and in the Loire valley. Some new traders have appeared in Burgundy, the most important of whom, Jean-Claude Boisset, has emerged in the last few decades, much to the displeasure of the more traditional trading houses. It is the same thing in Champagne, where companies like Vranken and Paillard have recently joined the upper echelons. In the Languedoc, new arrivals, such as Jeanjean and Skalli, have concentrated on Vins d'Origine (wines of specific origin) and Vins de Cépage (wines made from one particular variety), while all over France, co-operatives have created their own labels or subsidiaries. Val d'Orbieu in the Aude, Jacquard in Champagne, Producta in the Bordeaux region, Sieur d'Arques in Limoux and Wolfberger in Alsace have representatives throughout the world. In this way, they are in direct contact with the consumer, can better serve the interests of their shareholders and can ensure that they are not left with just the bulk market.
The role of bottler at the consumer end of the business has almost disappeared, as there is now practically no demand for blended table wines. Only a few buying centres still practise this, but they also work on non-French wines, as well as vins de pays and Vins d'Appellations bought in bulk.

Changes in the export market

The metamorphosis of French consumption has also had an influence on the French export market. In 1900 France imported large quantities of table wine to improve its own products, in the order of 7–10 million hl (185–264 million gal) per year, and exported a few wines to enlightened wine-lovers, Champagne and Bordeaux Grands Crus alone accounting for 80% of these export sales.
The defining of the AOCs and the efforts of the trade allowed so much progress to be made that French exporters managed to convince the rest of the world of the pleasures of imbibing good wines, although the French consumer, in the words of Christian Bonnet, minister of agriculture in 1975, continued to gulp down 'dishwater'. Thus, between 1965 and 1997, the average wine consumption per head (in those countries that are the main importers of French wine) went up from 17 litres (3.4 gal) to 23 litres (5.06 gal) in Germany, from 3.35 litres (2.95 quarts) to 17.5 litres (3.85 gal) in the Netherlands, from 2.2 litres (3.87 pints) to 14.3 litres (3.15 gal) in the United Kingdom, from 11.2 litres (2.46 gal) to 25 litres (5.5 gal) in Belgium, from 3.7 litres (3.25 quarts) to 7.4 litres (1.96 US gal) in the United States and from 0.3 litre (0.53 pint) to 1.1 litres (1.94 pints) in Japan.[3]
In 1950 and 1951, France was still importing 9.8 million hl (259,000,000 gal) of Algerian wine. Even though its own production had increased, 14.3 million hl (378,000,000 gal) of Algerian wine crossed the Mediterranean between 1957 and 1958. The establishment of the Common Market had an effect on the origin of imports but did not immediately affect quantities. In 1974 and 1975 France imported 8 million hl (211,000,000 gal) of table wine, 7 million hl (185,000,000 gal) of which came from Italy (this figure dropped to 4.1 million hl (108,000,000 gal) in 1985–6), but during the last ten years the situation has improved considerably.

Export records

In 1998 France exported FF34.7 billion worth of wine (6.5% of total exports) – a good deal more than would have been obtained from the sale of 100 Airbuses – and imported FF3 billion worth. Of this total, Champagne sales accounted for FF9.3 billion, the other AOCs for FF19 billion and table wines and vins de pays for FF5.6 billion. Even more remarkable is the fact that French wine exports are no longer limited to neighbouring European countries but are now world-wide. It is almost as if access to the world of wine is a sign of belonging to a world culture, in which wine plays a part, largely due to its endorsement by the English-speaking world.
Even so, table wine imports to France have reached 4.4 million hectolitres (more than 108 million gallons), over half from Italy, the rest from Spain and Portugal, but only account for FF1.45 billion. This may be a legacy from previous years, and we can envisage an increase in imports of non-French VQPRD, linked to a growing

curiosity on the part of French consumers. Leisure activities, notably travel, have led the French to experiment with different types of food and consequently drinks that complement them. They are also sometimes curious to try their own familiar varieties cultivated in the countries of the southern hemisphere, New Zealand, Australia and Chile.

THE ENVIRONMENT – A CURRENT PREOCCUPATION

French wine production is well established today, based as it is on increasingly professional and specialised family businesses, with largely competitive production costs, the only exception being the price of land in the great vineyards. Its hard-won reputation for quality and reliability, acquired particularly during the 20th century, is well known, and it has also learned to respond to demand. The 1980s saw a world-wide demand for ecologically sound practices, and viticulture, with its many preventative treatments and chemical pesticides, was hardly a good role model. Wine-growers have begun to convert to organic methods of cultivation, and scientific research is taking into account people's very real concerns about the environment. For a decade now, wine-growers have been advised to carry out treatments only when necessary, and a global approach towards environmental matters is being adopted. This applies to the wineries and cellars as well, where, on occasion, chemical products used to protect woodwork have been in too close proximity to the wine.

Scientific research in France, focusing mainly on quality, is world-class. Wine merchandising, which has been restructured to a great extent during the last 20 years, is a powerful force on an international scale. Obviously, nothing can shelter French wine from the vagaries of the market, but when there is an imbalance, as there was at the end of the last decade, things are soon evened out – a few suppliers disappear and prices return to normal. The 2001 vintage may turn out to be promising, mediocre or even disastrous – nature will always have the final say. All that the wine-growers can do is reduce the risks and make the best of it. Whatever the pessimists think, the 20th century has been a privileged period in the history of wine-making, quite unlike any that has gone before. It is no doubt this that has brought new enthusiasts to the world of wine – the refinements of which can be endlessly assessed and appreciated. As a product, wine is forever evolving and changing, but always – if a way can be found – for the better.

Jean-Pierre Deroudille

1. Gabriel Désert and Robert Specklin, *Histoire de la France rurale* (Seuil, 1976), under the direction of Georges Duby and Armand Wallon.
2. Emile Peynaud, *Le vin et les jours* (Dunod, 1988).
3. Source: French Centre of External Commerce.

NEWS FROM WINE-GROWING FRANCE

1999: A year of change

Although competition intensified on the international market, 1999 showed that France has maintained its position as a leading wine producer. The Appellations d'Origine have worked to display their individual characters, offering consumers not only authenticity but also a product of traceable provenance, without ignoring the necessity of adapting to modern oenology. Never has research been so preoccupied with the environment, and with the support of French public bodies such as the universities, the National Institute of Agricultural Research (INRA), the Institute of Wine-growing Technology (ITV) and the Ministry of Agriculture, the French wine-growing industry will continue to reconcile fidelity to tradition with the need to adapt to modern demands.

WHAT'S NEW IN ALSACE?

In general, strong optimism generated by the market performance of Alsace wines has been combined with the need to take on board a new approach to the regulatory system governing the Alsace Grand Cru. A summary of the 1999 season follows.

Despite very wet and often stormy weather, climatic conditions in the winter and spring of 1999 were quite good. The first leaves began to appear around 13 April, and the growing season was marked by a fine May. Three weeks of intense sunshine and high temperatures preceded the harvest. The grapes ripened reasonably well. However, there was a great deal of rain between April and August – one day in two, in fact. There were storms over Rouffach, Dambach and Ribeauvillé and around Colmar; a mudslide on the Altenberg by Bergheim; and hail over Schoenenbourg (in the Riquewihr region). Harvesting of the Crémants began on 20 September, of Alsace AOC on 4 October, of Alsace Grand Cru on 7 October and of the late-harvest grades and the noble grape selections on 18 October.

YIELDS: A STEP TOWARDS COMMON SENSE

The grapes were in a good, clean state, but disparities in ripening were observed according to area and vine-stock (notably in the Gewurztraminer variety) because of capricious weather conditions in October. Mildew was sometimes rife, notably in Gueberschwihr. Wines were for the most part balanced, but the Sylvaners proved particularly successful. The Pinot Blanc grapes yielded excellent sparkling whites (Crémants). Among the Grand Crus, the Riesling had a marked *goût de terroir*. The Muscats, the Pinots Gris and the Gewurztraminers all produced the aromas expected of them, while the Pinots Noirs showed excellent colour and are well structured and have good staying power.

A fine, late autumn allowed a yield of more than 21,000 hl (554,400 gal) in late-harvested and 'grains nobles' selections, but the complexity of aroma was often modest because of a widespread lack of noble rot.

The 1999 vintage was the first to be produced under the new regulations of the Alsace AOC. Recent criticisms concerning excess yields, coupled with a slight reduction in quality, have effectively led the Alsace wine authorities to define a ceiling for yields per grape variety rather than, as previously, give a global yield for each vineyard. These upper limits make good sense, but nevertheless the ceilings often remain high – between 82.5 hl and 100 hl per ha (891 gal and 1080 gal per acre) according to the grape variety.

The volume announced for 1999 AOC wines is 1.8% less than that of the preceding vintage, the 1999 figure being 1,239,161 hl (32.7 million gal), of which 42,349 hl (1.1 million gal) are in Grand Cru wines. The production of Crémants established a record with

173,245 hl (4.6 million gal). The sparkling whites are enjoying a growing commercial success.

The Year of the Century for the Market

The sales of Alsace wines in 1999, mixing all markets and labels, have attained an unprecedented level. They point up an advance of 6% in relation to 1998, with more than 160 million bottles sold throughout the year, for a turnover of 2.9 billion French Francs.
Home sales reached 878,000 hl (23.2 million gal), a rise of 5% and exports 313,000 hl (8.3 million gal), a rise of 10%. Alsace is thus one of the rare wine-growing regions of France to produce AOC wines that have increased their export volume.
The best breakthroughs in the market were made in Finland (+38%), in Switzerland (+35%), in the United States (+31%), in Britain (+22%), in Holland, the principal customer for Alsace wines (+14%) and in Sweden (+16%). On the other hand, the German market has fallen to second place, despite having been the leading customer for the past 30 years. The Japanese and Canadian markets also experienced marked downturns.

Alsace Grand Cru: Towards New Regulations

Alsace wine-growers have always promoted Alsace Grand Cru wines. Experiments in the local management of the Grand Cru varieties at Altenberg de Bergheim and Bruderthal de Molsheim bear recent witness to this fact. Given the interest in such work, new wine legislation concerning the Grand Cru wines of Alsace is currently being drafted. It aims at more prescriptive regulations that will confer the right to bear the label AOC Alsace Grand Cru, and that will govern minimum planting distances, minimum foliar surface, reduced pruning and an increase in the minimum number of steps necessary to gain approval.
Above all, it introduces the principle of local management, a measure likely to emphasise the particular qualities of each vineyard. It will be up to local *syndicats*' 'professional associations of growers' to define their own standards. For example, nothing will prohibit the exclusion of chaptalisation or the imposition of a minimum alcohol content, which could be higher than those fixed by the regulations. The list of authorised vinestocks can also vary according to the vineyard, which would permit, for example, Sylvaners or Pinots Noirs to carry the label of Grand Cru. Similar flexibility will apply to the process of combining wines and to mixed plantings. 'Local management is a formidable trump card in giving a distinct character to each Grand Cru,' believes Marcel Blanck, one of the 'founding fathers' of the 1975 regulations.
This new policy will allow ratification of the differing styles followed by individual vineyards. If there are plans to give greater leeway to the *syndicats*, their proposals will nevertheless have to be accepted by the Council of Experts (Comité d'experts) and thereafter by the National Council of the INAO, which will define the conditions of production of each Grand Cru.

WHAT'S NEW IN BEAUJOLAIS?

Currently, the major issue in Beaujolais – and one that deeply divides opinion is – whether or not mechanical harvesting should be authorized.

At the moment the mechanical grape-picker is banned in this area, because the regulation concerning labelling of origin states precisely that harvesting should be of the whole bunch of grapes, that is it should include the woody stems.
The problem is that a machine will harvest single grapes and not bunches. On 13 March 2000, by 31 votes 'for', 19 'against' and 1 'void', the officers of the Beaujolais Wine-growers Union (L'Union Viticole de Beaujolais) pronounced themselves in favour of mechanical harvesting. However, there remains the need to obtain the consent of the different branches of the wine-growing community, as well as official ratification from the INAO and the actual rewording of the regulation itself.

MECHANICAL HARVESTING: 1,000 HA (2,470 ACRES) IN EVERY 22,000 HA (54,340 ACRES)?

Why has this revolution happened? The reasons put forward include the difficulties of hiring workers, the expense of harvesting by hand, administrative constraints and the possibility of more flexible harvesting. Comparative trials have been made over four years. Some experts are of the opinion that mechanical harvesting does not have any negative consequences for the wine.

This change does not involve very young wines (such as Beaujolais nouveau), whose specific qualities would be unfavourably affected by mechanical harvesting. Nor does it apply to traditionally goblet-pruned vine-stocks (Beaujolais-Villages and Crus) or vines growing on slopes.

In effect, the harvesting machine would be used for trellissed and guyot-trained vines growing on the southern plains – that is, about 1,000 in the 22,000 ha (2,470 in 54,340 acres) that make up the Beaujolais vineyard as a whole. But from now until 2005 this surface area could multiply threefold. Quite strict production specifications have been drawn up, particularly on the subject of thermal regulation.

Understandable as the wishes of the wine-growers may be, the effect on the public of such a step is still open to question. Harvesting by hand contributes not only to an image of quality and of tradition, but also to the festive atmosphere associated with harvest-time itself. Has a grape-picking machine ever been heard to break into song?

CO-ORDINATED RIPENING

In 1999, although slow to start, the ripening process accelerated very quickly. Flowers appeared early. The favourable weather conditions prevailing at the end of August and the beginning of September stabilized acidity, allowing an exceptional increase in the sugar content. The only negative factors were hailstorms on 2 June and 9 August, which were quite violent. The absence of rain explains the high concentration of fruit, while the grapes (particularly those exposed to the south) diminished in size. Significant rains at the end of September lowered potential alcohol content in the late-ripening sectors, which are in fact, few in number.

All in all, the early ripening was comparable to that of 1995, with harvesting beginning on 7 September. It is worth noting the average rate of ripening that has been recorded for eight years across 200 parcels in 73 communes and that has proved a reliable technique. Full bodied and fleshy, the new Beaujolais '99 resembles those of '91 and '95 with a fairly supple character and aromas of soft fruits (cherry, strawberry). The '98 Beaujolais was deep purple, the '99 more garnet-coloured. The '99 Crus have a clearly defined structure, designated for longer maturing.

PRODUCTION AND SALES: FROM A SLIGHT DIP TO A HIGH

What of production? It was slightly lower than in 1998 (1,390,820 hl against 1,403,062 hl/36.7 million gal against 37 million gal) but still giving about 185 million bottles. Green harvesting, by which an excess yield of grapes is prevented before full ripening, has begun to bear fruit here. The Crus make up 369,709 hl (9.8 million gal), the Villages 353,793 hl (9.3 million gal) and the Beaujolais AOC 667,318 hl (17.6 million gal). White Beaujolais has diminished in volume – 11,154 hl against more than 12,000 hl in preceding years (0.3 million gal against more than 0.32 million gal).

Sales of 'nouveau' or *en primeur* wines followed a growth curve in 1999 after a season that saw the sale of 62 million bottles (+13%). Volume released was up by 5%, young wine making up two-thirds of the volume of Beaujolais AOC and 35% of the output of the Beaujolais vineyard as a whole. (In all, 45% of Beaujolais production was exported, for sale in 192 countries!)

And what of exports? The 800,000 hl (21.1 million gal) of 1998 is considered atypical, and in 1999 exports returned with 680,000 hl (18 million gal), figures more comparable with the 684,000 hl (18.1 million gal) of 1997. As always, Germany headed the list of export markets, followed by Switzerland (on a downward trend), Japan (up by 91%) and Britain.

WHAT'S NEW IN BORDEAUX?

Promising at the outset to be a splendid affair, the 1999 vintage turned out, in fact, to be a mixed bag, despite some terrific successes. With bigger stocks than Bordeaux has known for a long time, the record harvest of 1999 is unlikely to help matters. However the Bordeaux region will soldier on and will not be deflected from the true path by falling prices.

It's no secret in Bordeaux that the 1999 vintage is a source of worry. There were unprecedented yields for red wines, but the quality was mixed, factors fully recognised by responsible professionals. At the end of June 1999, Jean-Louis Roumage, president of the association of Bordeaux appellations, announced a tightening-up of approval procedures for the production of each grower on the register, with two possible appeals before the obligatory tasting. He justified himself vigorously, stating: 'If we allow ourselves to get slack, what will become of those who remain resistant to all progress and tarnish our image by spoiling the efforts of their betters?'

An early budding season

However, 1999 started off well. For the first time in a decade the end of winter was mild and rather short on rain, as noted by Pascal Ribereau-Gayon and Guy Guimberteau of the Faculty of Oenology at Bordeaux's University of Victor-Segalen in their annual report on the vintage. From January to March each month showed higher temperatures and lower rainfall than normal. As a result, budding took place early, as is often the case for great vintages, and the initial grape clusters were extremely abundant, which is far from incompatible with quality. April and May were also extremely warm (1°C above normal in April and 2.9°C above normal in May), but very humid, which contributed to mildew. By chance, flowering took place in a window of fine weather at the end of May, putting the year, forward as it was, alongside the great vintages such as 1989 and even 1990. When the rain returned at the end of June, it was too late to affect fertilisation and it seemed certain at that time that production would be abundant. But parasites remained a constant problem, forcing the growers to maintain constant vigilance and to use multiple pesticide treatments. The summer itself (June, July, August) was again a hot one, with a total temperature of 1946°C against an average of 1826°C. Hours of sunshine were also higher than normal, with showers occurring around the beginning of June and the end of July. Pascal Ribereau-Gayon and Guy Guimberteau place the half-way ripening point at 4 August, which is the same date as in 1989, which is a good point of reference. The other parameters, such as sugar content and acidity, were also a good sign – with, however, one reservation, the size of the grapes, which were 15–20% above average with abundant foliage. The weight of the heavy fruit encourages attack by parasites, and dilution occurs when the rainfall is high. This was, unfortunately, a threat that was to materialize. Mildew and botrytis (grey rot) led the wine-growers a merry dance, and they did not know where to spray next. By this stage, the different styles of management of the vines were already apparent: those who pruned back hard and who thinned in July experienced less difficulty in overcoming the problem.

The disappointments of autumn

After a magnificent start to September, the rains came. A week from the theoretical date of harvest, a great vintage for red wines it was possible to hope for with probable sugar and alcohol contents superior to the '90 vintage and hardly lower than '89, which are still the best references for the decade. Acidity levels, on the other hand, were quite low, a sign of lesser balance than in the two great vintages. The first ten days of September were still very beautiful and very hot. For the white wine varieties, which had benefited from the forward conditions, the harvest could begin under favourable auspices therefore, with nicely ripened grapes and stunning aromas. But everything went wrong in the second part of September: record downpours (three times more than in 1998, and five times more than in 1989) combined with very mild temperatures to create the perfect conditions for grey rot. The dry whites, harvested from mid-September, suffered accordingly, with faint aromas and a certain amount of dilution.

When hard work pays off

Red grapes are traditionally more resistant to these kinds of difficult conditions. Their constitution, as we have seen, was robust. In the well-managed vineyards the earliest ripening grapes were were sufficiently forward to be harvested in time. This was particularly the case with the Merlot, always early in the Bordelais area. Most of the Crus Classics were not affected, and the smaller vineyards, where the owners are fully aware of the work involved in producing good wines, also avoided the worst. It will not be impossible to find some classic bottles in the 1999 vintage, because the climatic conditions were good for those who had worked hard. On the other hand, the weather did no favours for those winegrowers satisfied with approximate timings and who (subsequently) were disagreeably surprised to find that their wines failed in the approval procedures (15.7% in the first instance for the regional wine-growers union of Bordeaux).

Pascal Ribereau-Gayon and Guy Guimberteau admit that 'We cannot pretend that all the red wines have been successful,' but as they also make clear, 'once again, it is the big vineyards have put up the best fight'.

A last word about the very sweet whites. It was noted that mushrooms were doing very well and *Botrytis cinerea*, which is responsible for noble rot, showed itself early. As the grapes were saturated with sugar, it was possible to pick highly concentrated grapes of quality very early, but there would have had to be no delay, as the rains made quick work of diluting even these choice grapes. Unlike 1998, when a renewal of good weather in October favoured the late-harvested very sweet whites, 1999 is the vintage for early sweet white wines.

Record quantities and stocks

Vines in full vigour, no frost, no hail, a perfect flowering season, optimal temperatures and hours of summer sunshine, and showers at the end of the cycle, all these factors came together for a record harvest, which duly happened, with 6,855,711 hl (181 million gal) of wines produced in the Gironde in 1999, of which 6,806,674 hl (180 million gal) were ratified by the AOC. A similar figure had been achieved in 1990, but because 800,000 hl (21.1 million gal) of table wine were produced above this, production of AOC wines hardly passed the 6 million hl (158 million gal) mark. However, the sheer quality of the vintage made up for this short fall. With its huge harvest and mixed quality, the 1999 vintage proved to be harder to sell than its predecessors. And to make things more difficult, stocks were at their highest at the beginning of the season, with 6,937,576 hl (183 million gal), a rise of 13%. This was because the sales of 1998–1999 had themselves dropped by 15%, the major reason being that price levels were previously judged too high by the majority of consumers. A substantial increase in sales in April 1998, at the end of the season, happened too late for an upturn in the market, since the average price for the season 1998–1999 was fixed at FF9,066 per 900 l (238 gal) compared with, FF9,292 in 1997–1998. At the beginning of the season therefore the wine-growing industry of the Gironde had the equivalent of two very big harvests in its *chais*, a situation that had, on other occasions, led to a landslide collapse in prices. Nothing of the kind happened, despite a persistent slackness in prices, in relation to the preceding year, of around FF8,500 a barrel. The Bordeaux wine trade did not panic.

The season for *en primeur* sales, which is very particular to Bordeaux and which consists – for the Grands Crus and some Crus Bourgeois – of selling the year's production *en barrique* (in barrel) a year before the end of maturation and bottling, was very significant. Pessimists predicted a catastrophe if the châteaux did not substantially lower their expectations. Traders were asking for a discount of 15–30% compared with the vintage of 1998, and the first to come out, Gruaud Larose, prudently accepted a 15% reduction on the previous year's prices.

In spite of comments and in view of the success, others reacted by making moderate cuts (5% only), keeping prices unchanged or even putting up prices. This was the case with Mouton-Rothschild, which came out with FF459, a 6% rise, thus stealing a march on its fellow Grands Crus classés in Graves and the Médoc. The rise of the dollar and of the pound sterling effectively favoured those who sold substantial quantities outside the Euro zone, a currency that had depreciated 15% in comparison with the pound sterling since the spring of 1998.

Thus the season of the *en primeur* wines closed with a reduction in activity, estimated at between 15 and 30%, but with nothing apparently catastrophic. As far as the major labels are concerned demand is world-wide and expanding and sufficiently dispersed to compensate for changes in individual markets.

For most Bordeaux wines the tale is different, and one should remember the distinction between expensive big labels and unpretentious bottles (the average price per bottle in the main supermarkets is around FF28). Some 60% of the volume of wine from the Bordeaux region is consumed in France. In 1999 exports fell by 12% in volume but only 2% in value, which still represents FF8.08 billion francs (FF52 per 75 cl bottle on average in the dollar zone and in Switzerland, FF33 outside the European Union). Against this, the French market for Bordeaux wine remained stable in volume and even went up by 5% in value. The French market, therefore, appears to be less sensitive to economic circumstances. It seems that the bottle of Bordeaux belongs in the housewife's shopping basket as did the vin de table of 30 years ago! This is not a reason for the wine-growers to make the same mistakes as in the past and their professional managers seem to be keeping a watchful eye.

Changes of ownership

The period of uncertainty does not seem to have inspired investors. Whereas the 1990s saw the best Grands Crus spiralling and selling at the peak of their value, it would be interesting to cash in on the present downturn. However, owners can wait and always hope for a new boom in which to get the best prices, whereas potential buyers think that the present slack period should be reflected in the prices of wine properties.

One event that stands out in Bordeaux is the sale of the Château Loudenne in Médoc. Although it produces only a straightforward Saint-Yzans Cru Bourgeois, there is associated with it a whole Anglo-French story such as they love in Gironde. Owned by the London-based Gilbey family (gin producers) since the 1880s, it has recently been taken over by the Diageo group, which commands an estate of 18.6 ha (120 acres), of which half are vineyards, where not so long ago they lived a life modelled on British polite society. The wine-merchant Jean-Paul Lafragette of the Syndicate of Cognac and Speciality Wines (Comptoir des Cognacs et Spécialités), producer of, among other things, the Alizé cocktail, has acquired it.

A more important brand – since we are talking now of the classified Médoc Grand Cru – has changed hands. The property is the La Tour-Carnet Château in Saint-Laurent, whose owner, M. Pelegrin died about ten years ago as the result of a terrible accident at harvesting time. His wife courageously took over from him. It is a vast estate of 126 ha (316 acres), of which 48 ha (118.6 acres) acres are given over to vineyards, with medieval buildings dating back to the 14th century and another more 'recent' addition dating from the 17th century. The buyer,

Bernard Magrez, is the owner of William Pitters, a business that sells Malesan, the top Bordeaux brand-name in France. Bernard Magrez also owns Château Pape-Clement in Pessac (Pessac-Léognan) and Fombrauge (St-Emilion Grand Cru).
Finally, a small real estate transaction for the town of Talence, in the suburbs of Bordeaux, made it possible for the Château at La Mission Haut-Brion to acquire 6,800 sq m (8160 sq yd) of territory – that is, a little more than half a hectare (1.23 acres) – for the tidy sum of FF3.6 million. Hope is not lost in Bordeaux, and the success of the 2nd Wine Festival on 30 June and 2 July 2000 has shown that the wine-growing culture is shared by a great many people. (These wine festivals take place alternatively with Vinexpo; the first one was in 1998.) Such occasions act as magnets for other economic activities, from establishing industry subject to scientific meetings!
On this subject, the creation of a scientific institute for wine and the vine (Institut des sciences de la vigne et du vin), which was intended to bring together the specialised laboratories of four Bordeaux universities on to the site of the INRA, will ensure that wine and wine-growing activities in Bordeaux are solidly anchored in the 21st century. Finally, the registration of the Jurisdiction of Saint-Émilion (the wine-producing communes and their vineyards) as a UNESCO world heritage site on 2 December, 1999 is a symbolic distinction that has, for the first time, been conferred on an entire wine-growing area.

WHAT'S NEW IN BURGUNDY?

This was an excellent vintage. The only fly in the ointment has been the prices, which overall have climbed by nearly 20% in a year, particularly in the case of the most sought-after labels, which have become unobtainable on the French market. The standard is good, however, and some bottles of the 1999 vintage will be outstanding.

Rarely has nature shown itself so benign. Except in June, the temperatures in 1999 were higher than average, resulting in a brilliant flowering season. Rainfall was sufficient on the whole. Fertilisation was extremely good: this is becoming a regular occurrence, which will have to be corrected by green harvesting and by sorting at the vat house. With full sun by August and during the first two weeks of September, the maturing process took place under the twin good omens of dry weather and sunshine. The rains came on 18 September, interfering a little with the harvesting, but the clean state of the grapes was remarkable, with a good natural degree of alcohol. The harvest was notably early and abundant.

THREE TIMES MORE BURGUNDY WINE IN 30 YEARS

In 1969 Burgundy wine yielded 458,000 hl (12.1 million gal). In 1979 it totalled 1 million hl (26.4 million gal). In 1999 it reached 1,598,789 hl (42.2 million gal) and has therefore tripled in 30 years. The strongest growth was during the 1970s. From the 1998 vintage to the 1999 vintage the volume has increased by 13% and by 11% in relation to the 1995–9 average. It is true that the vintage of 1999 was a gift of nature. Only the Mâcon Blancs and the Mâcon Villages saw their volumes decrease a little. The AOC Villages reds from the Côtes de Nuits and Côtes de Beaune have increased by some 15–18%, the AOC Villages whites from the Côte de Beaune by 22%, and Chablis by 11%. That makes a total for 1999 of 950,410 hl (25.1 million gal) for the white wines (+11%) and a total of 648,379 hl (17.1 million gal) for the reds an increase of almost 19%, all of high quality. Some Côte de Nuits reds and some from the north of the Côte de Beaune – are truly great. These wines are full, round, firm and chewy in character: with their good acidity, they should keep well. The whites, fleshy and fruity, can lack finesse, and they have been found to be somewhat thin, and buyers should stick to vineyards that monitor quality closely.

WHO DRINKS IT?

In a market of between 160 and 170 million bottles of Burgundy wine sold each year, the French consume 45%, of which 5.5% is bought direct from the grower, 6% through traditional outlets, 16% in the CHR sector (cafés, hotels and restaurants), and 18% in the mass market. The EU consumes 34% (Britain ahead of Germany and Belgium), the rest of the world 21% (the US leading, followed by Japan, Switzerland and Canada). A recent downturn of 6% in volume on the French market can be ascribed to the rise in prices and the increased scarcity of supply.

Exports represented 700,000 hl (18.5 million gal) in 1999 – that is, nearly one half of the yield – for a turnover of FF3.5 billion. These figures are slightly behind the phenomenal results of the preceding year. Large reserve stocks in Japan help to explain the situation, as does stockpiling in the German and Dutch markets. Even accounting for the strength of the US dollar, Americans bought in some 13.5 million bottles, taking the first place among non-EU importing countries (13%).

The sale of the 1999 wines from the Hospices de Beaune produced FF31 million or 4.5 million Euros. Red wines gained 3% in value against 1998, while white wines lost 9%. The situation remains stable, but it is worth noting that there were 577 barrels sold in 1998 (with 300 bottles per barrel) as against 730 in 1999. This is the first time that the Euro has been placed in the glare of such a spotlight. At the Hospices de Nuits-Saint-Georges a few months later, the tendency to weaker prices was reaffirmed (down 12.6% by value). Yet for the first time a white wine, Les Terres Blanches Premier Cru, was put up for auction. It reached FF46,000 a barrel!

News in brief from the vineyards

Jean-Francois Vandroux is the director of Anima Vinum, the new organisation created by the co-operative at Saint-Marie-la-Blanche (near Beaune) to market its 60 ha (148 acres) of vines and its jewel, Château Bligny-les-Beaune (ex- GMF, Suntory, etc), recently acquired by the intermediary of the SAFER of Burgundy. Roland Masse left the Bertagna vineyard to take up the management of the Hospices de Beaune estate and was replaced at Vougeot by Claire Forestier. Pierre-Henry Gagey (Louis Jadot) became president of the Federation of the Merchant-Growers Unions of Grand Bourgogne (the regions of Burgundy and Beaujolais). Louis Trebuchet (Chartron and Trebuchet) is back in the presidency of the BIVB, with Hubert Camus (Gevrey Chambertin) as vice-president. The Union of the Grand Crus de Chablis was established, with Michel Laroche as president. (In reality there is a single Grand Cru vineyard, divided into seven plots.)

The Bacardi group has handed over its aperitifs and liqueurs (Casarus, Raptia, etc) to the Jean-Claude Boisset group (Nuits-Saint-Georges), which has taken over the Hardy Cognac and settled in Canada near the Niagara Falls in the Jordan vineyard (first harvest in 2005; 17 ha/42 acres planted). Jacques Bollinger (Ay-en-Champagne) has taken control of Chanson Père et Fils (Beaune). The barrel-makers François Frères (Saint Romain) have set up in Hungary. The next Saint-Vincent travelling wine fair will take place at Meursault on 27 and 28 January 2001.

The inauguration ceremony took place at Loche (in the Mâconnais) of Vigneroscope, which was founded by Philippe Bérard and conceived as a journey through the world of vine and wine.

One sad loss was that of Raymond Dumay at the age of 83 years. Born near Mâcon, he was one of the greatest of French wine-writers, having published works of reference on all the vineyards of the world. On the subject of appellations, Pierre Tchernia (former pupil of Auxerre grammar school) brought a new AOC, named Irancy, into the world on 7 May 2000. Elsewhere in Burgundy few changes were in view, with the exception of some 10 ha (24.7 acres) that are to be classified as Premier Cru: Ladoix-Serrigny sur les Grechons, Les Buis, En Naget, Le Bois Roussot, Les Hautes-Mourottes and Rognet-et-Corton (currently classified as Bourgogne Villages). In June 2000 about 20 big vineyards in Burgundy (Romanée-Conti, Leflaive, Bonneau du Martray, Louis Latour, etc) took a stand on the OGM (regulations relating to genetically modified vines and subsequent changes in vinification) to demand a moratorium of 10 years and a scientific approach in conformity with the goals of quality and protection of the vineyard.

WHAT'S NEW IN CHAMPAGNE?

The two New Year's Eves of 1999–2000 and 2000–2001 have seen and will see champagne greeting the new century and the new millennium. It is surely too early to make a full judgement on the vintage of 1999. If the preceding year was considered miraculous, this year is at a momentous point in the millennium.

A record for volume was established in 1998. In 1999 production was maintained at a very high level 2,349,993 hl (62 million gal) despite a small decrease of 3.58%. The year started quite mildly, in spite of night and morning frosts, and continued under a fickle sky, but spring arrived with a flourish, with March being rather warm. Rain, fine hail and snow occurred from time to time, with the first leaves appearing in April. Frost caused some damage – the temperature fell to -4°C, (24.8°F) on the night of 17 April among the lower areas of some slopes. Flowering was very early in a storm-ridden May, which saw hail falling on about 60 villages. About 3,000 ha (7400 acres) were affected, and 450 ha (99 acres) of vines destroyed. The eclipse of 11 August attracted 500,000 observers, who were able to confirm that the rains at the beginning of July had done nothing to spoil the vineyards. Harvesting took place during the second fortnight of September. Temperatures were exceptionally high, and the average for the year was clearly passed (comparable temperatures were in 1956, 1990, 1994 and 1995). There was little in the way of a failure of pollination or malformation of grapes.

A PROLIFIC HARVEST

Rarely have the vines of Champagne known such a prolific harvest, even though it took place under incessant rain. It averaged 19,000 kg (19 tons) of grapes per hectare (2.47 acres). This yield per hectare may be compared with 100 kg (220 lb) in 1910 and 3,680 kg (3.7 tons) in 1978, but it comes close to 1973's 13,000 kg (13 tons), 1982's 14,300 kg (14.3 tons) and 1993's 15,200 kg (15.2 tons). A potential 460,000 hl (12.1 million gal) has been declared as being beyond the volume capable of being harvested. Thus, 1999 saw disproportionate volume but very acceptable quality: the base yield is in principle 10,400 kg (10.4 tons) per hectare, with an authorized maximum of 13,000 kg (13 tons), a range first permitted in 1998. If consensus on this point was quickly reached in Champagne, it was still necessary to get the go-ahead from the INAO, which was granted in a realistic and logical manner. The average yield in Champagne was therefore established as 12,984 kg (13 tons) per hectare in 1999. Grapes harvested elsewhere constituted a surplus that did not benefit from the AOC label and was destined for the distilling industry, a volume amounting to nearly 430,000 hl (11.4 million gal). In the event, a figure of 1.2 million barrels of AOC wines was achieved.

VINTAGES

The best of 1999 should be given the Vintage label. The alcohol content of 10% is higher than the average for the last 20 years but the same as for the 1959. There is thus an atypical ratio of alcohol content – acidity, less remarkable than that in 1996 and 1990, but comparable to that in 1992 and 1989. The Pinots Meuniers have brought compliments. The Chardonnays are forceful, the Pinot Noirs lively. A number of names, such as Deutz and probably Bollinger, will produce Vintage wines, while others, such as Michel Arnould et Fils, will not.

The vintage as a whole should come close to 1982 and 1988. Adding the 1999 to the reserves of the three previous harvests will give a good volume of production, a little higher than 300 million bottles at the end of the first half-year in 2001. Stock will then increase to 900 million bottles, giving a possible annual turnover of 280 million bottles in 2001 and 2002, after the explosion of 1999 (when 327 million bottles were sold at the peak).

Of the total, 67% will have been sold by the Champagne houses, 32.9% by the growers and the cooperatives. The French market represents 58.2%, bought in equal parts between the two main groups, whereas exports (41.8%) are for the most part made up from the houses, with Britain in first place, followed by the United States, Germany, Belgium, Italy, Switzerland and Japan.

NEWS IN BRIEF FROM THE VINEYARDS

Bertrand Gautherot has taken over the presidency of the Association of Young Wine-growers from Jerome Prevost. Philippe Pascal (Veuve Clicquot) has become president of the Association of Wines and Spirits of LVMH. Guy Bizot has become director-general of Champagne Bollinger, which has taken over the management in Beaune of Chanson Père et Fils. Pascal Ferat is now president of the Federation of the Wine-growers' Co-operatives of Champagne, succeeding Sylvain Delaunois, who now chairs the Centre Vinicole for Champagne, in place of Alain Robert.

J.-J. Frey has sold Champagne Binet and the Collery name to the family group Prin. Louis Roederer has taken over the management of the house of Jean Descaves, specialists in the best Bordeaux Crus.

The group Marne & Champagne issued 396 million Euro bonds based on its stock. Bernard de Nonancourt (Laurent-Perrier), one of the great figures in the Champagne world, received the medal of honour of the CIVC on the occasion of his eighty-fourth birthday. In March 2000 wine-growers and the major Champagne houses started new negotiations regarding future contractual relationships.

WHAT'S NEW IN THE JURA?

Clean, ripe grapes, good yields and high quality what more could one want? The vintage of 1999 is on a par with 1979 and 1989, almost as if all the years ending in 9 are alike.

From the beginning of May, 1999 was warm. But with the rains came attacks of mildew that persisted until the middle of July. The flowering season dragged on somewhat in fresh, humid weather. There was little rain, on the other hand, during the last heat-wave of August, which, as we knew, was 'making the must'.

Until mid-September the vines had their heads in the sun. Harvesting started in September, a week earlier than usual, on 13 for the sparkling whites (Crémants), towards the 20–22 for still wines, and finally 25 September for the Château-Chalon wines. There was no worry about rot, just a bit of mildew in the plains, and the clean state of the grapes was encouraging. Showers did not really occur until 23 September, when rains and storms followed hard on each other's heels until the first days of October.

THE POULSARD TAKES PRIDE OF PLACE

Where the yield was controlled, the 1999 *trousseau* was excellent. If the Pinot Noir was reasonable, the Poulsard variety showed itself delightfully generous in its ripeness and clean condition. The 1999 Chardonnay is freshly acidic,

and has great finesse. The Savagnin is explosive, and its blending with the Chardonnay grape augurs well. It is a true *vin jaune*, already promising, and will perform well in a few years. The vintage of '99 was ratified at 110,150 hl (2.9 million gal).

NEWS IN BRIEF FROM THE VINEYARDS

At the presidential residence of the Inter-professional Council of Jura Wines (Comité interprofessionnel des vins du Jura), Luc Boilley has handed over to Marie-Christine-Tarby-Maire, director-general of La Sainte Henri-Maire at Arbois.

WHAT'S NEW IN SAVOY?

It has been called an exemplary success. The description is perhaps excessive, but it is true that 1999 went by reasonably well for the Mondeuse and Roussette grape varieties.

Weather conditions were favourable throughout the whole year, in spite of a few frosts and hailstorms, which were very localized. The summer stayed dry, lasting into mid-September, with a great deal of sunshine during the last days, before a series of storms in October. In general, harvesting started early, which allowed the grapes to be picked in a clean condition. The volume of the harvest remained stable in relation to the preceding years, and production reached 100,774 hl (2.7 million gal) of white wine and 37,524 hl (0.99 million gal) of red and rosé wine.

The best tastings were to be had from the Savoy Roussette, which was in excellent form in the 1999 vintage, as well as the red Mondeuse, which was judged to be particularly well knit. Some of the wines are more full bodied than those of the preceding year.

MORE VINES

The area of land under vine is growing slightly but steadily: from 1% to 2% a year. The new planting is on the higher slopes, and a great deal of work has gone into the battle against erosion, a particularly acute problem in mountainous areas.

The market is doing well, regularly expanding from a basis of restricted supply. The consumption of Savoy wines is essentially regional, closely associated with the winter sports season, and drunk to accompany fondues and other cheese dishes, such as raclettes (cheese melted over vegetables), but the market is developing in the Paris region through better distribution and the enthusiasm of a number of wine-merchants. A tourist circuit of the vineyards of Savoy has been planned, passing around the Lac du Bourget, around Bonneville to Lake Geneva and from there Chambéry and Fréterive. The culinary combination of Brittany oysters and Savoy wines is regaining popularity.

WHAT'S NEW IN LANGUEDOC AND ROUSSILLON?

The year 1999 was one of suspense and catastrophe. Yet, even though there was none of the euphoria of 1998, the vintage turned out to be very reasonable. Alas, the floods of November ensued, and despite the heroism and solidarity showed by the population at the time, the wine-growing economy could take five years to recover

The year began with cold, dry weather, with a relatively quick budding. The only disaster was a violent hailstorm that swept over a good part of Roussillon on 21 April. Spring was never really cheerful, with cloudy skies, frequent showers and a warm atmosphere, which encouraged parasites and diseases. May was wet, and flowering came early. These conditions continued throughout a summer that was punctuated by hail showers, which did not prevent the grapes from ripening but did mean that harvests were spread out from the end of August throughout September, sometimes in storms or showers, sometimes under a clear blue sky. Despite these contrasting conditions, there was little dilution to worry about, and the results, for whites as much as the reds, were very reasonable. The whole vintage proved suitable for medium-term keeping, with some bottles even for long-term laying down. Such difficulties as arose were more to do with the evolution of the country wines and the associated problems of commercialisation. For the VQPRD wines, on the other hand, in 1999 Languedoc-Rousillon constituted the fourth-ranking region of production by volume (behind Bordeaux, the Loire and the Rhône), with 2,427,590 hl (5.8 million gal) in AOC labels from an area of 63,053 ha (155,740 acres) and 30,097 hl (0.79 million gal) in VDQS from 513 ha (1267 acres). Exports of Languedoc-Roussillon during the first nine months of 1999 showed an increase of 8% in value for a slightly lower volume against the previous year.

Harvesting in Languedoc

The AOC wines of Languedoc had to face up to a very hot end of season and very changeable weather conditions in the course of the year. A green harvest and sorting made all the difference between mediocrity and excellence. The reasonable conditions in spring and winter favoured growth and encouraged flowering. At the beginning of July the cold slowed down ripening, but from the end of this month and during the whole of the month of August the weather became exceptional, with a total absence of northerly winds, but with a warm, humid wind from the sea. These unstable weather conditions weakened the grapes, which promised to be abundant in quantity. Fortunately, the month of September restored the situation, thanks to very hot and dry weather. The ripeness and concentration of the grapes were therefore satisfactory.

The Corbières, benefiting from favourable weather at the crucial period of the harvest, showed a good, even quality. At 47 hl per ha (508 gal per acre), markedly higher than that of 1998, the yield nevertheless remained modest compared with many northern AOC wines. For the same reason the Fitou managed to maintain 41 hl per ha (443 gal per acre) and to produce a good vintage. Minervois wines kept their promise, while in the hands of the best growers the Faugères showed evidence of lots of bouquet and solidity. As for Saint-Chignan wines, they are a notch below the 1998 vintage but are nevertheless satisfactory. On the whole, the phenolic potential of the grapes allowed a strong and easy extraction of must, with shorter maceration than usual.

The national committee of the INAO has ratified the special qualities of the Côtes de la Malepère wines by recognising Merlot as the main variety for the appellation (50% minimum): Cabernet Franc will eventually make up 20%, together with the Cot variety if necessary. Cabernet-Sauvignon, Cinsault and Grenache may now be added to the assembly, with Syrah permitted in rosé wines. In June 2000 the AOC committee for Corbières invited its 2,300 wine-growers to prepare targets for the vineyards for the next three years. Alongside the ratification of the Crus, there are high hopes for an award of a regional appellation. Worthy of note is the Côteaux du Languedoc AOC, newly given to the Haut Larzac region.

Harvesting in Roussillon

The vintage of 1999 proved to be a delicate and complex affair. The storm of 21 April, which affected 5,000 ha (12,350 acres) of vines (Agly, Têt, Fenouillèdes) caused losses to local harvests. For most of the area, however, the quantity was generally good, despite problems with flowering for Grenache and grape malformation in the Muscat variety.

The tendencies seen in preceding years were confirmed in 1999. The Côtes du Roussillon wines registered the biggest production since their introduction in 1977, with acceptable quality on the whole. The sweet, unsugared whites continue to decrease in volume (down 12% compared with 1998) and also in area of cultivation. The Muscat de Rivesaltes have gone from strength to strength since 1994 and make up the main AOC for this type of wine, yielding almost 150,000 hl (3.96 million gal) for 5,000 ha (12,350 acres) in 1999. The Muscat variety is definitely back in the ascendant. The Rivesaltes AOC, producing less than 100,000 hl (2.64 million gal) from 7,400 ha (18,278 acres), continues to decline. Banyuls, similarly reducing in volume and in area of cultivation since 1994, gave 28,500 hl (752,400 gal) this season. Output is expected to stabilize soon however.

Disaster in November

During the night of 12 and 13 November Languedoc-Roussillon was devastated by a truly biblical deluge: 500 mm (19.7 in) of rain fell in 36 hours, the equivalent of the entire annual rainfall for the region (the Aude department was the most affected). The effect of these downpours, unprecedented in living memory, was further worsened by a storm at sea that blocked the natural drainage, turning little streams into treacherous torrents. The human cost was savage: in the Aude department alone, 25 people died and one disappeared, 100 villages were cut off, 30 bridges were destroyed, 21 roads were rendered impossible and 50 vinification cellars wiped out. As to plant and machinery, the ministry of agriculture of the Aude department estimated losses at FF350 million: 600 ha (1480 acres) of vineyards were destroyed, and 2,600 ha (6422) were damaged. Soil washed away from vineyards and roads totalled 780,000 cu m (more than 1 million cu yd). The toll continued: 350 km (217.3 miles of field tracks were destroyed 58,000 cu m (75,980 cu yd) of walls and 750 km (466 miles) of ditches were obliterated; and some 3,300 plantations were devastated. To all this could be added the damage caused to the rural infrastructure. Supported by the ministry of agriculture and the professional agricultural organizations, the population demonstrated enormous solidarity, initially in emergency aid, then in agricultural reconstruction. Individual farmers, as well as agricultural organizations in France and from Europe at large, came to bring their support. But it will take the vineyards, still in the midst of reconstruction, five years to heal their wounds.

News from the vineyards

Is Languedoc-Roussillon really the new California? To judge by the lively discussions on the subject one might be excused for thinking this to be true. Aniane (Hérault) is waiting for Robert Mondavi to take up ownership of 50 ha (124 acres) of about to be classified vineyard. The plantation rights should be awarded to him, which has aroused some dissatisfaction among those producers who will receive no benefit from the contract. Robert Mondavi will invest some FF55 million (FF20 million for the purchase of the land, FF30 million for the construction of the winery) and is waiting for the hue and cry to die down in order to raise his flag in France. Vinisud, an exhibition that is normally held in Montpellier, will 'emigrate' for the second time to New York on the 6 and 7 February 2001 under the name of 'Mediterranean Lifestyle Show'. Meanwhile, the exhibition Innovigne was instituted at the Narbonne Branch of INRA. In June 2000 the town of Limoux hosted the 11th National Competition for Sparkling White Wines.

WHAT'S NEW IN PROVENCE?

There was a surprise in store at the end of a rather dry growing season for some areas: the 1999 vintage was distinguished by a high level of production.

The vine-growing season progressed satisfactorily in spring, with normal budding and good weather conditions for flowering. There was no hail or frost to worry about. The summer period was marked by a lack of rain in the coastal areas, where the vines on the edge of the region showed signs of leaf loss, but other areas benefited from widespread showers. After normal ripening, harvesting started in the first few days of September. A few attacks of third-generation grape-worm (a very rare event) led to a spoilt harvest in some areas, notably in the north.

The harvest was characterised by a high sugar content, and also by a polyphenolic ripening, which was delayed or, at the very least, was out of step with the sugar balance. The big surprise lay in the high level of production. In these conditions the vintage of 1999 could be defined as the 'year of the wine-grower', so delicate was the matter of balancing quantity with maturity. The qualitative range of white wines and rosés is wide, while the richness of the reds depends on the mastery of the polyphenolic maturity.

News of the Côtes de Provence wines

The harvest rose to 950,000 hl (25 million gal), a sign both of an abundant year and of the continued increase in the productive capacity of the appellation. The rosé wines dominated as usual, making up 80% of the output. Then came the reds with 15%, while the whites remained at a low but stable level. The rosé wines displayed an attractive palette of colours, from salmon to clear pink, with fruity aromas ranging from classical to exotic. On the nose, these rosé wines offer finesse rather than aromatic power, while on the palate they are rich and generous. The presence of Cinsault and Grenache give lingering aromas of rose and acacia. For the most part these are wines to enjoy with a meal rather than simply to drink. In general, the red wines should keep really well: they offer a good natural alcohol content of around 12.5% by volume, consistent colour, aromas of the, garrigue and good structure. The procedures for revising the delimitation of plots of land in the appellation have entered their final phase now that the complaints that were put forward during the course of inquiry are being scrutinised. The professional association for the protection of the appellation has recognised sub-regional classifications in order to emphasise the diversity of the AOC vineyards without, threatening the standard of the regional appellation by creaming off the best. The idea is to allow the reputation of the rosé to develop by emphasising the link between the individuality of the product and the *terroir*. A commission of inquiry has been nominated by the INAO, and it has already sat several times to consider the claims presented by the Haut Bassin district de l'Arc (Saint-Victoire) and the Bay of Fréjus. The commission has given its comments to the wine-growers so that they can sharpen up their proposals. The German market for Côtes de Provence wines is stagnating, especially for the rosés, although Germany has hitherto been the main export outlet for the appellation.

THE APPELLATIONS

The production of 1999 Bandol (red, white and rosé) is at about the 53,000 hl (1.4 million gal) mark and is growing slightly. The rosés are well knit, and the reds are solidly structured, all due to the patience of the wine-growers during the harvesting of the Mourvèdre grape variety. The red wines of the 1998 harvest finished their period of 18 months (minimum) of ageing in wood and are now redolent of the autumn scents of the woods of Provence.

In Baux-de-Provence the harvest of 1999 confirms the regional abundance of reds, with a volume of 9,179 hl (0.24 million gal). The reds of 1998, after 12 months of maturation in the barrel, are distinguished by their aromas of the garrigue, the fragrant, high, stony moorland of the region. The local professional association of wine-growers has initiated seminars focusing on the local appellations (Bandol, Bellet, Cassis and Palette). The Bellet AOC has continued to produce consistent quality. The 1999 whites – 328.45 hl (8,670 gal) – are full, round wines with undertones of lemon and hints of lime; the red wines – 479 hl (12,645 gal) – have the whimsical and extravagant character of the Folle Noire variety, typical Niçois qualities.

Cassis AOC, with a production of 7,300 hl (0.193 million gal), continues to exhibit the consistency that is its keynote, with some wines that have delicate floral and balsamic aromas. Wines from Aix-en-Provence continue to make progress, with a 1999 harvest of 198,000 hl (5.3 million gal). For reds and rosés alike, quality is improving, and this has been greatly helped by a strong local economy. The 1999 vintage offers the chance of discovering the wine-growing areas that stretch across the chalky foothills of lower Provence.

In 1999 the volume of Côteaux Varois AOC grew to 85,000 hl (2.2 million gal), an increase matched in quality. The rosés showed consistent colour and fruity bouquet. The white wines, still not released, are floral and fresh. The reds are full of agreeable surprises, with fine tannins that bode well for the future.

In the wake of the renascent Château Simone, the Château de Cremade and three other producers have on offer 1,500 hl (39,600 gal) of Palette, not yet released, but with great keeping potential.

NEWS IN BRIEF FROM THE VINEYARDS

Towards the end of 1999 Provence's Centre for Research and Experimentation on rosé wines completed its first programme of work under the auspices of a scientific committee. All the links in the chain leading to a quality product – from the vineyard and the vine to the techniques of wine-making – have been explored.

The *syndicat* for the Côtes de Provence appellation, chaired by Guy Gasperini, a wine-grower from La Crau, and the interprofessional committee thoroughly discussed their appellation during the course of a two-day winter seminar. The quality of the vineyard, of the vines, improvement of production, oenological techniques, and the future economic development of the AOC were high on the agenda of the seminar, which was well attended. Areas of discussion included vineyards and wine, lines of enquiry as to how conditions of production should be monitored and claims for recognition from sub-regional denominations. In addition, the idea was floated of enlarging the interprofessional committee to embrace neighbouring appellations. The validity of this enlarged committee seems to have been agreed by consensus, even though questions of denomination, organisation and sharing of funds must still be resolved.

WHAT'S NEW IN CORSICA?

The year 1999 started with rain, but then there was hot, dry weather, which continued right up to the harvest, which was quite early. On the whole, the grapes were in good condition. It was necessary to harvest promptly because storms had broken out around the region from 20 September. The Nielluciu variety was then just coming up to full maturity, but the Sciacarellu had already been harvested.

The vineyards of Ajaccio and Calvi came out well and produced a reasonable volume of reds and whites. The Patrimonio vineyard showed best results in the whites and from the Muscat du Cap Corse. Of the Corsican AOC wines, the red Sartène wines proved rather light, while the white wines are already drinking well. In Porto-Vecchio the situation was the other way round, and the red wines now appear to be more successful than the whites.

After a large increase in 1998, Corsica saw a return to the production levels of 1997, with a declared volume of 92,640 hl (2.4 million gal) for the 1999 vintage, of which 8,731 hl (0.23 million gal) were dry white wines and 1,983 hl (52, 350 gal) were Muscat du Cap Corse (VDN). Ajaccio accounted for only 6,902 hl (0.18 million gal), of which 778 hl (20,539 gal) were white wines. Patrimonio produced 13,290 hl (0.35 million gal), of which 1,895 hl (50,000 gal) were whites.

WHAT'S NEW IN THE SOUTH WEST?

In spite of Bordeaux's commercial difficulties, the wines of the hinterland and the high country continued to prosper. The harvest was, nevertheless, rather mixed for most of the region, because 1999 proved to be fertile but wet.

It is not every year that a new *appellation d'origine* is created, but you have to take your hat off to this one. It is the AOVDQS wine Côteaux de Quercy. The area of production (which covers the province of Bas Quercy) straddles the departments of the Lot and the Tarn-et-Garonne, to the south of Cahors. There is nothing odd about that, because the area is culturally and geographically uniform, something the revolutionaries of 1790 understood when they created one big department covering Haut Quercy and Bas Quercy, although it was later separated by Napoleon. The wine-growing map often proves to have more of a memory than either politicians or administrative divisions. The grape varieties, of which the principal one is the Cabernet Franc, are native to the region. The complementary varieties are more classical: Merlot, Cot (as in neighbouring Cahors), Gamay (as planted in Gaillac) and Tannat.

From Vin de Pays to AOC

For many years confined to the category 'vin de pays', today the appellation Côteaux du Quercy, with its distinctive *goût de terroir*, has 400 ha (988 acres) in production. This has involved a rigorous selection of the vines that were already planted and claiming the VDP classification. Nowadays the INAO is very vigilant when it creates a new appellation, and it will not do so without the new AOC vineyard having been completely marked out and defined. It will, moreover, follow matters in the region much more closely, because its original south-west delegation, previously situated in Bordeaux, has now been divided to cover three sites: Cahors, Gaillac and Pau. In the south west many appellations co-exist in an enormous area, giving rise both to mixed quality and economic difficulties. The new AOVDQS, created by a ministerial decree on 28 December 1999, is addressing that problem. In order to take account of efforts already long since achieved, not only will the harvest of 1999 be able to display the appellation but wines in stock from the vintages of 1997 and 1998 will also be included. This is a way of instantly creating a small market that might otherwise have been difficult to get off the ground with the production of a single year, which might not figure among the best.

A MIXED VINTAGE

Just as in the Bordeaux region, the vintage of 1999 will remain in people's memories chiefly for its abundance. As in Bordeaux, all production records were broken. In Bergerac the AOCs of the area claimed 680,347 hl (17.9 million gal), of which 265,649 hl (7 million gal) were dry, sweet and very sweet white wines, a hitherto unprecedented volume of production. Even in 1997, a historic year, the declaration of production had reached a ceiling of 625,221 hl (16.5 million gal).

The appellations of Bordeaux and Bergerac, whose destinies are linked by the climate and the varieties they have in common, were thus stars in the same year, although not for the best of reasons.

In Bergerac as in Bordeaux, early flowering had been followed by over-abundant growth, and then by diseases encouraged by hot summer weather punctuated by heavy rains. Finally, the rains at the end of September swelled the grapes, which were already larger than average, to bursting point. Only those sensible wine-growers who routinely cut back their yield at the winter pruning succeeded in producing quality. In Cahors, on the limestone plateaux and slopes of the Lot valley, where the climate is a little drier and the soil rather poorer, the same phenomenon was not recorded. There, only 243,911 hl (6.4 million gal) of AOC wines were declared in 1999, as against 248,228 hl (6.6 million gal) for the preceding year, which had been very abundant. The appellations of the Garonne valley, such as Buzet and Côtes du Marmandais, benefited from an earlier flowering. The harvest was more abundant than in 1998 and suffered less from rains at the end of September. The smaller surface area of these AOC vineyards also helps to quicken the process of harvesting. The production of Lot-et-Garonne has increased by 5%. Madiran, on the other hand, suffered from a freak severe weather event, a sort of tornado mixed with hail just before the harvest. This seriously damaged those grapes that were ready for harvesting. In an annual production which had peaked at 70,000 hl (1.8 million gal) because of difficulties in obtaining new planting rights, the shortfall due to this calamity could be estimated at 3,000–4,000 hl (79,300–105,600 gal).

At Gaillac it is difficult to find one's bearings, so used are the wine-growers to juggling the declarations of harvest among AOC wines, vins de pays and vins de table, depending on financial expediency. The Tarn department saw a significant increase in production by 5.6%, from 613,127 hl (16.2 million gal) to 649,459 hl (17.1 million gal). At the same time the declaration of volume for AOC red wines increased by 9%.

The overheated market in the Bordeaux region, where wine-growers at first reduced quantities in order to maintain prices right up to the middle of 1999, was seen as a godsend by the south-west. The system whereby wine from the hinterland is sold in Bordeaux is not new, but it is not about to disappear either.

The most convincing example is that of Bergerac. Although the harvests of 1996, 1997 and 1998 were the largest in the history of wine-making until that of 1999, stocks of wine in that vineyard have not stopped decreasing: 501,682 hl (13.2 million gal) on 30 August 1997, 459,153 hl (12.1 million gal) in 1998 and 431,639 hl, (7.1 million gal), hardly two-thirds of one year's consumption, in 1999! Moreover, the joint trade organisation of Bergerac wants to have, and is negotiating for, an institutional rapprochement with Bordeaux.

Of course, the subsequent fall in prices of Bordeaux wines, beginning in late 1999 and accentuated in, the spring of 2000, make the situation a delicate one. Those appellations with a reputation for inconsistency have suffered most. Monbazillac, for example, is at a crisis unprecedented for 20 years. On the other hand, the solidly classified appellations, such as Madiran, Cahors and Buzet, have experienced hardly any difficulties.

The wine-growers of Charentes are undergoing a grave economic crisis. In addition, growers in Ségonzac were hit by a hailstorm in July, which cut a swathe 15 km (9¼ miles) long and 1.5 km (1 mile) wide through their vines.

Plaimont-Crousseilles: A new power in the South

In the Madiran sector – a new co-operative association has proved itself equal to that of Buzet in Lot-et-Garonne. This is the dynamic Plaimont Union, based in Saint-Mont, which is a veritable conglomerate. Practically controlling the AOVDQS Côtes de Saint-Mont and already with a foothold in Madiran and Pacherenc du Vic-Bilh AOC wines, the union has just completed a twofold deal. First of all, it bought the emblematic Château Aricau-Bordes and its vineyard. The château building itself was sold to Dutch owners who were less concerned with the cultivation of the vineyard than in its historic interest. Thus the Plaimont Union finds itself in charge of 11 richly historic hectares (27 acres). Moreover, André Dubose, the tireless organizer of the Union, has had yet another new idea: a commercial union with the wine-growers' cooperative at Crouseilles, the principal producer of Madiran, with a third of the volume of sales. Plaimont, with a turnover of FF295 million, compared with FF47 million at Crouseilles, represents the commercial strike force with the most powerful marketing, while Crouseilles is the pillar of tradition. The association will no doubt be a talking point.

WHAT'S NEW IN THE LOIRE VALLEY?

Like the châteaux of the Loire valley, the wines of the Loire have a family likeness, although each has its own personality. That personality is often a product of heavenly whim, as in the vintage of 1999. Weather conditions were marked, as elsewhere, by a distinctly early start to the growing season and by hot, sunny weather at the end of summer, which helped ripening. However, rains in mid-September affected the production of the sweet and very sweet white wines. For the other types of wines, the year of 1999 is a year of contrasts.

In the vineyards overall, acidity is weak, but fruit is very much to the fore. The red wines are pleasant, the best lacking neither richness nor character. Many of the dry white wines have good body and fruit and are very pleasant. As everywhere, the sweet wines are rather thin on the ground, but careful wine-growers have achieved some undeniable successes. The overall production for this region reached 2,743,542 hl (72.4 million gal) in AOC wines and 319,948 hl (8.4 million gal) in AOVDQS.

In the Nantes area

If 1999 was a difficult year for most of the Loire valley, the Muscadet vintage was, by contrast, excellent. Indeed, in the area of Nantes, the harvest, which had started on 6 September, was three-

quarters finished by mid-September. Good-quality grapes and uneventful weather produced a fairly fruity, supple and well-balanced wine, low in acid. Gros Plant and the Fiefs Vendéens also did well, but, in contrast, the rains affected Côteaux d'Ancenis wines.

At 935,526 hl (24.7 million gal) the Nantais harvest, was about 6% higher than that of 1998. Muscadet AOC accounted for most of the increase, whereas, for a few years now, the volume of better quality Muscadet wines defined by geographical area (mainly Muscadet Côteaux de la Loire, but also Muscadet Sèvre-et-Maine) has tended either to stagnate or to decrease; it has been the same story for Muscadet *sur lie* wines.

This move towards the bottom end of the market is obviously a response to economic anxieties. Indeed, the market remains difficult, but the demand is certainly there, for example, in the commercial sector where it outstrips production. But prices, which had risen after their steep fall in 1996–7, have tended to go backwards since the summer of 1999. This has done little to smooth relations between producers and wine-wholesalers, who provide 80% of the commercial market.

Faced with this situation, the professionals have not relaxed their efforts. It is currently being decided whether or not to set up a 'third-tier' level of AOC wines. This third level already exists *de facto* in terms of quality, but now it is a question of a more rigorous definition of the 'third tier' and tying this definition in to *terroir*. Moreover, work continues on delimiting the vineyards of the Muscadet appellation. This was, in fact, finished in May 2000 for communes outside the Sèvre-and-Maine, Côteaux de la Loire and Côtes de Grand-Lieu appellations. A redefinition of boundaries is under way for the Côteaux d'Ancenis. The new rules for the *sur lie* designation, meaning wine left for a defined period 'on the lees', are equally strictly controlled: 30,000 hl (0.79 million gal), which had not been bottled in time, did not qualify in 1999. Although the area planted has stabilized around 2,300 ha (5,680 acres), as against more than 3,000 ha (7,410) acres in 1989, consumption has been slightly higher than production for two years and stocks are at their lowest.

In Anjou-Saumur

René Renou (of Bonnezeaux), a native of this region of the Loire valley, has been nominated president of the Comité des Vins de l'INAO. In Anjou-Saumur, the spring was hot and humid. The vines performed well and did not suffer from dryness and flowering and ripening occurred under the very best conditions. Ripening of the Cabernet grapes was complete by the end of August, something never seen before. Unfortunately, late autumn was very wet, with particularly heavy precipitation at the end of September and for the month of October. During the four or five weeks of harvesting, rainfall reached 300 mm (11.8 in), more than half the annual rainfall.

Grolleau and Gamay (for rosés) and Chardonnay (for whites) performed well. It was the same for the red varieties, which maintained good colour with low acidity. In contrast, Chenin caused more difficulties. Preparation work – sowing with grass, thinning out leaves, pruning back and spreading out branches to allow light and space to the grapes – along with harvesting by hand were decisive factors in the achievement of quality. Elsewhere, the sorting of grapes was complicated by the prevalence of botrytis, even on vines that had been well managed until then. Thus 1999 does not seem a lucky year for the very sweet white wines. In Quarts de Chaume and Côteaux de l'Aubance, wines will henceforth be subjected to a monitoring process using magnetic nuclear resonance. This technique should avoid the need for excessive chaptalisation and should, therefore, encourage a return to the natural purity of sweet white.

In Touraine

As has been pointed out by Etienne Carre, director of the Analysis and Research Unit of the Touraine Laboratory, according to the data given out by the French Meteorological Board, 1999 was an exceptionally hot year, with unusual rainfall levels. With a mild, late winter and spring, the year was a forward one: flowering started between 10 and 15 days in advance of normal.

If the beginning of the summer proved to be rainy, with heavy rainfall particularly at the end of July and at the beginning of August, ripening and maturation proceeded under optimal conditions, with sun and high temperatures, which led to hopes for a superb harvest of overripe grapes. In fact, 1999 was one of the hottest of the past 40 years. By mid-September, the situation was exceptional, with full ripening as much as three weeks in advance. Early varieties, such as Gamay, and Sauvignon, got the full benefit of these favourable conditions and produced ample, generous wines, low in acid, with full *terroir* character. Unfortunately, from mid-September, heavy rains slowed down the ripening process and obliged the wine-growers to harvest cautiously between downpours: 100 mm (3.9 in) of rain fell during the last ten days of September, and October brought its own share.

The Cabernet Franc grapes came out of all this well, producing supple, full wines with good structure, and the Chinon, Bourgeuil and Saint-Nicholas-de-Bourgeuil varieties will be good for laying down. On the other hand, there are few sweet or medium-dry wines, because the selection process for the Chenin grape variety could not be undertaken under suitable conditions. The dry whites and the base wines for the sparkling AOCs were pleasant enough at early tastings.

In the Central Region

The Central Region shared similar weather conditions with those found in the rest of the Loire valley: forwardness in the early part, tremendous heat during the ripening period and autumn rains. As luck would have it, the aforementioned rains did not come until relatively late, with the result that the vintage of 1999 was very acceptable. Budding (from 6–10 April), flowering (from 10–20 June) and ripening (from the 15–25 August) were all early. Summer storms brought on attacks of mildew and grape-worm, which made spraying necessary. Hot, dry weather from the end of August to mid-September quickened the pace of ripening, and when the harvest started, the grapes were very healthy. Harvesting proceeded from 13 September for Pinot Gris at Reuilly and from 27 September at Châteaumeillant. For Sancerre, Menetou-Salon and Côteaux du Giennois harvesting began on 22 September. Rainstorms occurred locally from 20th September, but the grapes had ripened nicely and harvesting took place quickly, before the grapes could be affected. The whites turned out to be supple, with elegant aromas and pronounced fruit, all with good *terroir* character. The reds offer balanced tannins, more or less concentrated according to their vineyard of origin and the choice of wine-making process. The aromas, with their note of soft red fruit, are very typical of the region.

In the Central Region of the Loire, the international market is stable (13% of the volume from the Loire valley as a whole, a share worth nearly 30% in value for a turnover of some FF250 million). The market in the United States is growing (+20%), is breaking through in Ireland, is decreasing in Japan (-40%), as in Germany, but is stable in Britain and Belgium. A third of the wines of the region are exported. A tourist wine route through the vineyards will be available in 2001.

News in brief from the Loire

The Joint Trade Council of the Wines of Nantes (Conseil Interprofessional des Vins de Nantes) is continuing its campaign to promote Muscadet *sur lie*, which started in 1997. After the 'Dance Hall Years' and the 'Impressionist Moments', the campaign is now organized around the theme of operetta tunes from the Belle Epoque (roughly 1890–1914). A street spectacle, with 27 singers from the Nantes Opera was organised across six towns in Europe and in five big North American cities. For Gros-Plant, on the other hand, the CIVN has concentrated its activities on the slopes of the Loire-Atlantique department and the Vendée on the theme 'the wine nearest the ocean'. The decree inaugurating the Inter-trade Organisation of the Wines of the Loire valley (L'Interprofession des vins du val de Loire) was published in the trade journal of 18 January, 2000. This new organisation joins Touraine with Anjou-Saumur. The consitutional general assembly of InterLoire took place on 26 January in Angers, with Dominique Amirault as president, Marc Morgat and Jacques Couly. The group of unions making up the BIVC (Centre) will decide by vote at the end of the year 2001 if the vineyards of the Centre Loire will integrate into this structure. The winegrowers of Saint-Pourçain (VDQS) have put in an application for the promotion of their vineyard to AOC status. Their case is 15 years old. New regulations of production are in progress.

From 1–4 June 2000 French Minister of Culture Jack Lang hosted the festival of Arts and Crafts of the Vine at Blois, which put on an educational and cultural wine-fair. The Quincy AOC will join the Inter-trade Organisation of the Vins du Centre in September 2000. The *syndicat* (professional association) for the Vins de Pays du Jardin de la France, sponsored by Onivins, intends to substitute the name Jardin de la Loire for Jardin de la France. The AOC labels already carry the word Loire (as in Crémant de Loire, Rosé de Loire). The request has been submitted to the Conseil d'Etat.

WHAT'S NEW IN THE RHÔNE VALLEY?

Take all the time you need to taste it: the vintage of 1999 promises to be one for laying down. It might sing like a cricket, but it has enough power and drive to walk squarely into the 21 century.

As ever, of course, there is the contrast between north and south. The northern vineyards experienced a highly inconsistent start to the year with alternating heat and cold, as well as humidity and dryness. Then, from March dry, hot weather allowed a favourable budding. A little frost was experienced on the right bank, but nothing serious. A shadow fell over flowering in the first days of June, as hail and storms hit the Côte Rôtie and Saint-Joseph. The summer was perfectly satisfactory, producing grapes in an excellent clean state. Harvesting started on 6 September on the seasonally advanced vineyards such as Crozes-Hermitage and Saint Peray and continued until mid-October, according to area and ripeness of the grapes. On the whole, the weather in the second half of September was fine weather, but mixed in with a few showers.

In the south they enjoyed a warmer than average winter in 1998–9, a dry spring with flowering at the end of May, a very sunny July, beneficial rain at the beginning of August, followed by a return to dry weather. The harvest proceeded from the end of August and through September. Conditions were very satisfactory from the northern to the southern AOC areas. The yield surpassed that of 1998 by some 3,661,000 hl (96.6 million gal), of which 2,208,953 hl (58.3 million gal) were Côtes du Rhône AOC, and 317,685 hl (8.4 million gal) Côtes du Rhône-Villages (a net increase).

A GREAT YEAR

Across the entire valley, the red wines have proved to have exceptional tone. Rich to the point of opulence, with a natural degree of alcohol blessed by the sun, they possess a demonstrative maturity and exceptionally deep colours. The aromas too, were potent and ripe from a very young age. The tannins are impressive. These are truly wines for long maturing.

The whites are a different story, mediocre in the south and mixed in the north. The *vins doux naturels* have already established themselves as superb, with a fascinating complexity and considerable ageing potential. They are best tasted in the wine-cellars where they really know the delicate art of getting the best out of a great year.

THE MARKET IS MAKING GOOD PROGRESS

During the season of 1998–9 the market for Rhône wines beat all records. It increased by 29%, surpassing 40 million bottles (314,000 hl/8.3 million gal) for Côtes du Rhône-Villages, which have now truly got the wind in their sails. Turnover for the whole of the region, has grown by 7%, and the volume output by 3.2%, to a total of 500 million bottles or 3.75 million hl (99 million gal). Exports have increased by 2%, thanks notably to new appellations, such as Côtes du Ventoux (+10%).

NEWS IN BRIEF FROM THE VINEYARD

To commemorate the millennium a pyramid of 120 barrels was built in Saint-Pantaléon-les-Vignes. It measured 8.86 m (29 ft) high, weighed 5 tonnes (4.9 tons) and displayed the flags of the European Union.

At Lirac an 'open cellar' (allowing retail business) was established. This groups together 90% of the wine-growers of the AOC. Not far from there, at Tavel, a 15 km (9.3 miles) tourist route through the vineyard was opened. Clearly marked with 21 signposts, the route takes tourists via the main vineyards in this appellation. In the same area the wine-growers of Pujaut have built new cellars, costing FF20 million with a capacity of 49,000 hl (12.9 million gal). On the other bank of the Rhône the co-operative of Vacqueyras is continuing with the fitting out of its new cellars, designed to produce the best conditions in which to carry out consistent vinification policies for its wines. At Châteauneuf-du-Pape, the museum devoted to Père Anselme is getting larger. Part of the 500 sq m (600 sq yds) of floor space is given over to the history of the AOC wines as well as to the people who made and developed them.

Turning to business affairs, it is worth noting that David Chagny is the new commercial director of the Cave de pain-l'Hermitage, where the president has also changed, Amaury Cornut-Chauvinc (Saint-Joseph and Saint Peray) having taken over from Jacques Lechenard. The new director-general is Julie Campos, until now at the helm of Maison Moreau at Chablis (taken over by Jean-Claude Boisset). Michel Courtial has gone to Maison Mousset at Châteauneuf-du-Pape, a branch of Cellier des Dauphins.

Marc Chapoutier, who brought such distinction to the vineyard that bears his name, has died at the age of 92 years. The business has long since been managed by his son Michel Chapoutier, who has recently taken over his brother's share. The firm has expanded into Australia, the Lebanon and, of course, within France itself (in Languedoc-Roussillon, notably in Banyuls, Côteaux d'Aix, Côteaux du Tricastin), investing in the Conseil en Agronomie and the provision of services.

Maison Jaboulet has started construction work on its new cellars at Châteauneuf-sur-Isère, in the ancient sandstone quarries there, which have been worked since Roman times. This promises to be a veritable subterranean cathedral of wine.

The Grands Vins Gabriel Meffre (Gigondas) issued FF20 million of convertible bonds to fund expansion.

Paul Avril, of Clos des Papes (Châteauneuf-du-Pape), and long-time member of the INAO, acceded to the presidency of the permanent committee of the INAO. This committee unanimously voted through a motion against the AOC Côte Rôtie's plan to build a major truck-route ring road to the west of Lyon. A new inter-trade branch came into being at Inter-Rhône. The vineyards of Beaumes-de-Venise and Rasteau joined the inter-trade organisation of the Rhône after leaving the inter-trade organisation of *vins doux naturels*, the CIVDN, having requested its merger with the GIP, an interprofessional group of Côtes du Roussillon and Côtes du Roussillon-Villages.

Finally, Vinsobres and Beaumes-de-Venise have asked to be granted the local appellation: Beaumes-de-Venise for the three colours, red, white and rosé, and Vinsobres for the red and the white.

WINE

Wine is defined as 'the product obtained exclusively from partial or total alcoholic fermentation of grape must or fresh grapes, which can be pressed or whole'.
All legal definitions require wine to have a minimum alcohol content of 8.5% vol or 9.5% vol, depending on the wine-growing area. The degree of alcohol is expressed in the percentage of the volume consisting of pure alcohol; 17 grams of sugar are needed for the must to produce 1% vol of alcohol by fermentation.

THE DIFFERENT TYPES OF WINE

European regulations, which incorporate French usage, distinguish between table wine and VQPRD. The Vins de Qualité Produits dans une Région Déterminée (VQPRD) are subject to certain controls. In France, they correspond to Appellations d'Origine Vins Délimités de Qualité Supérieure (AOVDQS) and to Vins d'Appellation d'Origine Contrôlée (AOC). It is worth noting that young vines (those under four years old) are excluded from appellations, because the wines they produce are too light to represent the appellation.

— Dry wines and sweet wines (*demi-secs, moelleux* and *doux*) are characterised by varying amounts of sugar. The production of sweet wine requires very ripe grapes, rich in sugar, of which only a part is transformed into alcohol by fermentation. Sauternes, for example, are particularly rich wines obtained from grapes whose sugar has been concentrated by *pourriture noble* (noble rot). They are often termed Grands Vins Liquoreux, not to be confused with Vins de Liqueurs, which are defined by European legislation (see below).

— Sparkling wines differ from still wines by the escape of carbon dioxide (the familiar 'pop') on opening – this comes from a second fermentation known as *prise de mousse*. In the traditional method, which used to be known as *méthode champenoise*, this is achieved in the bottle; if it is carried out in the vat, it is called the *cuve close* method.

— Vins Mousseux Gazéifiés also give off carbon dioxide on opening, but with these wines it has been added, either partially or totally. Vins Pétillants (lightly sparkling wines) have a carbon dioxide pressure of between 1 and 2.5 bars and need contain only 7% of alcohol. Pétillant de Raisin is obtained from the partial fermentation of grape must, and its alcohol content is low, the minimum being 1% vol.

— *Vins de Liqueur* (sweet fortified wines) are obtained by adding – before, during and after fermentation – pure alcohol, eau-de-vie de vin (brandy), concentrated grape must or a mixture of these products. The term 'mistelle' is not included in the European regulations, which refer to 'fresh grape must mixed with alcohol', the result of alcohol or brandy being added to the grape must (without fermentation). Pineau des Charentes, Floc de Gascogne and Macvin du Jura belong in this category.

CULTIVATING THE VINE

The vine belongs to the genus *Vitis*, in which there are many species. Traditionally, wine is produced from different varieties of *Vitis vinifera*, which originated on the European continent. There are however, other species that originated on the American continent. Some of these are infertile, others produce wines with very particular organoleptic qualities (known as *foxé* or foxy), and these are not very popular. However, these 'American' varieties have a greater resistance to disease than *Vitis vinifera*. In the 1930s attempts were made to create hybrids that would be resistant to disease, like the American species, but would also produce wines of the same quality as *Vitis vinifera*. Unfortunately, these were a complete failure.

— *Vitis vinifera* is susceptible to phylloxera, an insect that attacks the roots of the vine and that caused terrible devastation at the end of 19th century. The development of a graft onto an American rootstock that was resistant to phylloxera led to a vinestock that had the properties of its own grape family but roots that could not be infected by the insect.

— The species *Vitis vinifera* includes many varieties, known as *cépages*.

REGIONS	VARIETIES	CHARACTERISTICS
All the red Burgundy AOCs	Pinot	Fine wines to lay down
All the white Burgundy AOCs	Chardonnay	Fine wines to lay down
Beaujolais	Gamay	'Nouveau' or 'Primeur' wines or wines for rapid consumption
Northern Rhône (red)	Syrah	Fine wines to lay down
Northern Rhône (white)	Marsanne, Roussanne	Wines for medium to long-term maturing
Northern Rhône (white)	Viognier	Full-bodied wines to lay down
Southern Rhône, Languedoc, Côtes de Provence	Grenache, Cinsault Mourvèdre, Syrah	Copious wines for medium to long-term maturing
Alsace (each variety, vinified separately, lends its name to the wine)	Riesling, Pinot Gris, Gewurztraminer, Sylvaner, Muscat . . .	Aromatic wines to be drunk quickly except for Grands Crus, late-harvest or selected grains nobles (noble berries)
Champagne	Pinot, Chardonnay	Can be drunk on purchase
Loire (white)	Sauvignon	Aromatic wines to be drunk rapidly
Loire (white)	Muscadet	To be drunk quickly
Loire (white)	Chenin	Improve with age
Loire (red)	Cabernet Franc (Breton)	Short to long-term maturing
All the red Bordeaux, Bergerac and south-western AOCs	Cabernet-Sauvignon, Cabernet Franc, Merlot	Fine wines to lay down
Madiran	Tannat, Cabernets	Fine wines to lay down
Bordeaux (white), Bergerac, Montravel, Monbazillac, Duras	Sémillon, Sauvignon, Muscadelle	Dry: for short to long-term maturing; Sweet dessert wines: for laying down;
Jurançon	Petit Manseng	Dry: short-term maturation;
	Gros Manseng	Sweet: long-term maturation

Each wine-growing region has chosen the most suitable variety for its area, but economic conditions and the tastes of consumers can also play a part in modifying what is planted. Some vineyards produce wine from a single variety (for example, Pinot Noir and Chardonnay in Burgundy and Riesling in Alsace). In other regions (for example, in Champagne and Bordeaux) the greatest wines are the result of mixing several varieties with complementary characteristics. The varieties are themselves made up of 'individuals' (clones), which do not have identical characteristics (of productivity, rate of ripening, resistance to disease). The search is always on for the best stock. At the moment, research is being carried out into creating disease-resistant vines by genetic modification.

— Growing conditions have a decisive effect on the quality of wine. It is possible to increase yields considerably by changing fertilisation and pruning methods, choosing different stock and altering the density of the plants. It is not possible However, to increase yields dramatically without affecting quality, except when nature intervenes; then quality is rarely compromised, and some of the greatest vintages have been produced from abundant harvests.

— In recent years the increase in yields has been linked to better growing conditions. The advisable limit depends on the style of the wine: for good red wines the maximum advisable yield is between 45 and 60 hl per ha (486 and 648 gal per acre) and a little more for dry white wines. To produce very good wines, you also need vines that are ten years old or more, with a well-developed root system.

— The vine is susceptible to numerous diseases, various types of mildew and rot, which deplete the harvest and give the grapes a nasty taste, which is detectable in the wine. Wine-growers now have the means to treat these diseases effectively and this has certainly contributed to the general improvement in quality. In the past, a concern for security has probably led to an over-zealous use of chemical pesticides, but today they are used more prudently. In general, these chemical treatments are used only when absolutely necessary, and research within agricultural biology is now focusing on soil biodynamics, with the aim of creating natural conditions that will make the vine less susceptible to disease.

SOILS FOR WINE-GROWING: THE ADAPTATION OF VARIETIES TO SOIL AND CLIMATE

Taken in its broadest sense, the notion of 'soils for wine-growing', often referred to as *terroir*, brings together several different factors: biological (choice of variety), geographical, climatic, geological and pedological (types of soil). Added to these are the human, historical and commercial aspects: for example, the existence of the port at Bordeaux and its commerce with Scandinavian countries encouraged the wine-growers of the 18th century to improve the quality of their wines.

— In the northern hemisphere the vine is cultivated between the latitudes of 35° and 50°; it therefore has to adapt to very different climates. However, the most northerly vineyards usually cultivate only white varieties, which ripen slowly and whose grapes are resistant to early autumn frosts. In warmer climates, later fruiting varieties with high yields are grown. To make good wine you need well-ripened grapes, but the maturation process should not be too rapid nor too advanced because this leads to a loss in aroma; thus varieties are chosen with close attention paid to the maturation period. For the vineyards that are situated at the edges of climatic zones, the big problem is inconsistency of climatic conditions during the maturation period.

— Excessive dryness or humidity also play a part. The soil plays an essential role in the irrigation of the plant; in spring, during the growing period, it supplies the vines with water and allows any excess rain during maturation to drain away. Gravelly and chalky soils are particularly suited to this, but there are also highly reputable Crus that are grown on sandy and even clayey soils. Artificial drainage is sometimes used, and this accounts for the existence of high-quality Crus being grown on different types of soil, while neighbouring vineyards, with the same soil type, produce wine of varying quality.

— The different types of soil and subsoil can affect the colour, aroma and taste of wines from the same variety and growing in the same climatic conditions. Wines can vary depending on whether the soil is chalky, clayey, sandy or gravelly or a combination of any of these. An increase in the proportion of clay in Graves makes the wine more acidic, more tannic and full bodied and less refined; a white Sauvignon takes on more flowery notes when grown on chalky, gravelly or marly soils. In any case, the vine is not particular about the quality of the soil on which it grows. In fact, poor soil is often a contributory factor in good wines, as the yield is limited and characteristics, such as colour, aroma and taste, are subsequently advanced.

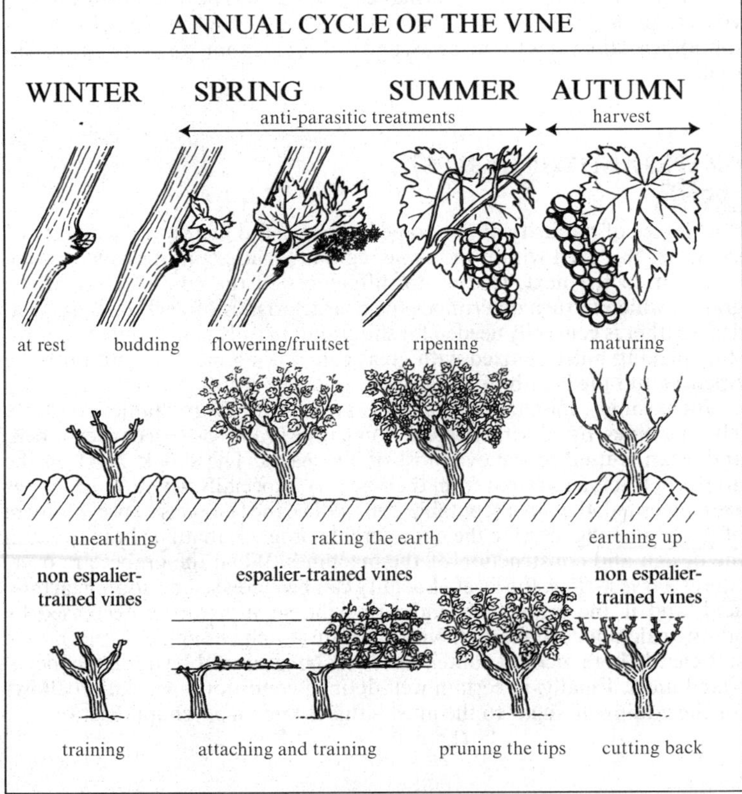

THE CYCLE OF WORK IN THE VINEYARD

Annual pruning, aimed at limiting excessive growth of the woody stem and giving a balanced yield, normally takes place between December and March. The potential number of buds is determined by the strength of the plant, and this has a direct effect on the size of the harvest. In spring the work consists of 'unearthing' the vines – the soil is raked into the middle of the row, creating a loose layer that should stay relatively dry.

— The ground is tended throughout the whole growing cycle, according to need: self-propagating plants are destroyed, the loose topsoil is maintained and loss of moisture through evaporation is prevented. Sometimes chemical herbicides are used for weeding; if they are applied to the whole vineyard, this is usually done at the end of winter and all ploughing is halted. This is known as 'non-cultivation' and represents a considerable saving. However, some environmentally aware producers prefer not to weed the rows, as the weeds act to limit the growth of the vines naturally.

— During the growing cycle, several different procedures are employed to limit excessive growth: *épamprage*, thinning out selected branches; *rognage*, pruning the tips; *effeuillage*, the removal of leaves, which allows the grapes to be more exposed to the sun; and *accolage*, training the shoots along wire espaliers. The wine-grower also has to protect the vines from disease, and to help him the Service for the Protection of Plants distributes information about various treatments, mainly sprays made from either natural or chemical products.

— Finally, in autumn, after the harvest, the earth is heaped up around the vines to protect them from the winter frosts; a furrow in the middle of the row allows rain water to run away, and fertiliser is sometimes dug in here as well.

GRAPES AND THE HARVEST

The degree of maturity of the grape is an essential factor in the quality of the wine. But even within the same region climatic conditions vary from one year to the next, leading to differences in the composition of the grapes, which in turn determines the characteristics of each vintage. Hot, dry weather is generally needed for the grapes to fully ripen, and the date to start picking must be fixed with great care, taking into account both the ripeness and the health of the grapes.

— Increasingly, manual harvesting is giving way to mechanical picking. The machines, fitted with 'beaters', knock the grapes on to a conveyor belt, and a fan is used to remove most of the leaves. The shock effect on the grapes detracts somewhat from their quality, especially where white grapes are concerned; the most reputable Crus will be the last ones to use this form of grape-picking, despite the considerable progress that has been made in the design and construction of the machines. When the grapes are over-ripe at harvest-time, the level of acidity can be increased by adding tartaric acid, and if the grapes are under-ripe the acidity can be decreased by adding calcium carbonate. A wine that is not rich enough may not have a sufficiently high alcohol content and can be improved by adding concentrated must. Finally, in certain well-defined conditions, legislation allows for the adding of sugar to the must – this is known as 'chaptalisation'.

THE WINEGROWER'S CALENDAR

JANUARY

St Vincent's Day is the feast day of the patron saint of wine growers.

FEBRUARY

Wine contracts with the cold. Barrels need to be checked periodically and topped up if necessary. Malolactic fermentation should now be completed.

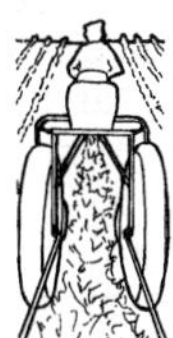

MARCH

Clear heaped-up earth away from the vines to let air circulate between them. Pruning should now be finished. Wines for early drinking should now be bottled.

APRIL

Before phylloxera, vines were trained on sticks. Nowadays, vines are trained along wire espaliers (except at l'Hermitage, Côte Rôtie and Condrieu).

MAY

This is the time to watch out for and protect against spring frosts. The spaces between the rows are raked.

JUNE

Vines are trained and the stems are pruned. The way the fruits set, known as the flowering, will determine the volume of the harvest.

JULY

Anti-parasitic treatments continue and the vines are studied carefully; this is a time when temperatures can vary enormously, and there is a risk of summer hail storms.

AUGUST

Disturbing the soil could be harmful to the vines, but a close look-out must be kept for parasites. In early-ripening regions, the vats and casks are prepared.

SEPTEMBER

Grapes are picked and tested regularly for maturation in order to set a date for the harvest; harvest begins in Mediterranean areas.

OCTOBER

In most vineyards, it is harvest-time and wine-making begins. Wines for laying down are put in casks to mature.

NOVEMBER

Young wines ready for drinking *en primeur* are bottled now. Progress of the nouveau wines is checked. The autumn cutback begins.

DECEMBER

The temperature in the wine-cellar is monitored to ensure alcoholic and malolactic fermentation.

THE MAKING OF WINE

The essential microbiological phenomenon that creates wine is alcoholic fermentation. The development of a type of yeast (*Saccharomyces cerevisae*), which is not exposed to the air, breaks down the sugar into alcohol and carbon dioxide; numerous by-products appear (glycerol, succinic acid, ethyl esters etc), and these enhance the aroma and taste of the wine. The process of fermentation produces heat, and the vat may need to be cooled down by refrigeration.

— In some cases, malolactic fermentation occurs after alcoholic fermentation; with the aid of certain bacteria, the malic acid is broken down into lactic acid and carbon dioxide. This results in a lowering of acidity, a smoothing out and refining of the aroma and a more stable wine. Red wines are always improved by this process, but it is not always so for white wines. Yeast and bacteria exist naturally on the grapes; they develop during the procedures carried out in the wineries, and often they are all that is needed to start fermentation. However, the use of dried commercial yeast is becoming more common because it allows more control of the fermentation process and avoids certain defects (odours caused by reduction or lack of aeration) associated with some naturally occurring yeast varieties. In some cases, a modified stock allows dormant aromas specific to a particular variety (Sauvignon) to be released from non-aromatic characteristics already existing in the grape. In any case, the quality and the character of the wine depend not wholly on the quality of the grape but also on natural factors, such as exposure and soil.

— Yeast always develops before the bacteria, which begin to grow only when the yeast has stopped fermenting. If the yeast stops fermenting before all the sugar has been transformed into alcohol, the residual sugar can be broken down by the bacteria, producing acetic acid (volatile acid); this is a serious setback, known as *piqûre*. A recently discovered procedure allows toxic substances formed from the yeast itself to be eliminated. During the ageing process, bacteria are still present in the wine and could lead to serious problems, such as the decomposition of fruit elements of the wine, oxidation and the formation of acetic acid (a process in the making of vinegar). Today, however, the precautions used in vinification can help to avoid these risks.

THE DIFFERENT WINE-MAKING PROCESSES

Making red wine

In most cases, the grapes are first detached from their stalks and then crushed; the mixture of pulp, pips and skins is put into the fermenting vat along with a small dose of sulphur dioxide, which helps to protect against bacteria and oxidation. Once fermentation has started, the carbon dioxide lifts all the solid particles to the top of the vat where they form a solid mass called *chapeau* or *marc*.

— Alcoholic fermentation takes place in the vat at the same time as the maceration of the skins and pips in the juice. It usually takes a minimum of five to eight days for the sugar to ferment completely; this is helped by allowing air in to increase the growth of the yeast and by controlling the temperature (at around 30°C/86°F) to avoid killing off the yeast. The maceration gives red wine its colour and much of its tannic structure. Wines that are to be aged should be rich in tannin and need a long period of

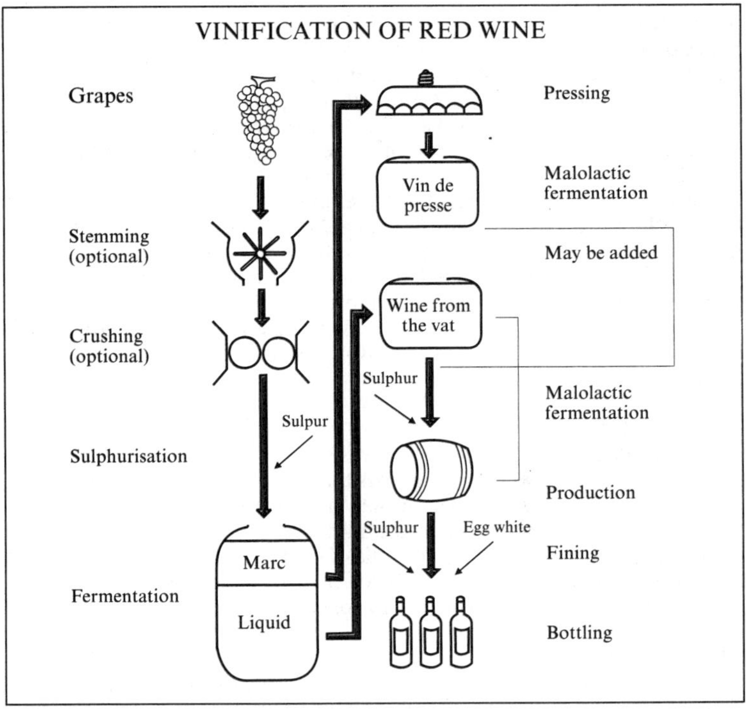

VINIFICATION OF RED WINE

Grapes

Stemming (optional)

Crushing (optional)

Sulpur

Sulphurisation

Marc

Liquid

Fermentation

Pressing

Vin de presse

Malolactic fermentation

May be added

Wine from the vat

Sulphur

Malolactic fermentation

Production

Sulphur

Egg white

Fining

Bottling

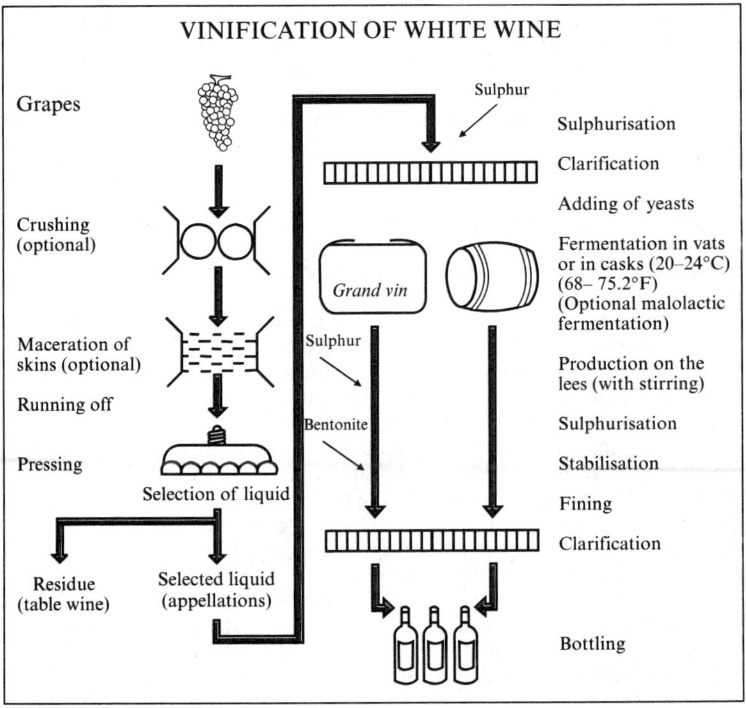

VINIFICATION OF WHITE WINE

Grapes

Crushing (optional)

Maceration of skins (optional)

Running off

Pressing

Selection of liquid

Residue (table wine)

Selected liquid (appellations)

Sulphur

Sulphurisation

Clarification

Adding of yeasts

Grand vin

Fermentation in vats or in casks (20–24°C) (68– 75.2°F) (Optional malolactic fermentation)

Sulphur

Production on the lees (with stirring)

Bentonite

Sulphurisation

Stabilisation

Fining

Clarification

Bottling

maceration (two or three weeks) at 25–30°C (77–86°F). On the other hand, wines that are to be drunk young, such as Vins Nouveaux, should be fruity and not very tannic; these need to be macerated for only a few days.

— The liquid part of the mixture is then separated from the residue or *marc*. The liquid part is known as *vin de goutte* (wine from the vat) or *grand vin*. The *marc* is then pressed and this gives what is known as *vin de presse*. *Vin de presse* is sometimes blended with *vin de goutte*, depending on defined criteria for taste and analysis. The wines are put into separate vats for the final settling and for malolactic fermentation to take place. With expensive, hand-made wines it is becoming more and more common for the liquid to be run off directly into small oak barrels in which malolactic fermentation takes place. Red wines thus acquire a more consistently complex character.

— This is the basic method, but other vinification procedures are of special interest, including thermovinifaction, continuous vinification and carbonic maceration.

Making rosé wine

Rosé, *clairet* (deep rosé) or *gris* (light rosé) wines are obtained by macerating, for varying lengths of time, grapes that are either strongly coloured or very lightly coloured. More often than not, they are vinified by pressing black grapes or by a short maceration process. For the latter, the vat is filled, as it is for the vinification of a classic red wine, then after a few hours a certain amount of juice is run off to ferment separately. The vat is then refilled to make red wine, which is, in consequence, more concentrated.

Making white wine

There is a wide variety of types of white wine, each one with its own particular vinification technique and appropriate harvesting method. In most cases white wine results from the fermentation of grape juice, without the skins, which occurs after pressing. In some cases, however, the skins are macerated for a short time before fermentation in order to extract their aroma. To achieve this you need perfectly healthy and ripe grapes in order to avoid defects in taste and aroma, such as bitterness and unpleasant odours. The juice is extracted by crushing the grapes, running off the juice and pressing. The *jus de presse* is fermented separately because it is inferior in quality. The white must, which is very susceptible to oxidation, is protected by the addition of sulphur dioxide. After the juice has been extracted, it will be clarified by a process known as *débourbage* (removing the sediment from the wine). During the whole fermentation process the vat has to be maintained at a temperature of between 20° and 24°C (68°F and 75.2°F) to protect the aroma.

— The Grands Vins Blancs are vinified in barrels and consequently take on a succulent, woody character. This method also allows, among other things, an ageing on the yeast lees or sediments, which increases the richness and flavour of the wine. This development is accentuated by stirring the wine with a pole to keep the lees in suspension.

— In many cases malolactic fermentation is not required for white wines, which have a fresher more acid taste, and a second fermentation can often reduce the characteristic aromas of the variety. However, those white wines that have a fairly long ageing in casks (for example, white Burgundies) develop richness and volume during this second fermentation. They are also more stable biologically once bottled.

— Grapes very rich in sugar are needed for the vinification of Vins Doux. Part of the sugar is transformed into alcohol, but the fermentation is stopped before it is completed by the addition of sulphur dioxide, and the yeast is eliminated by decanting, by centrifuge or by pasteurisation.

Sauternes and Barsacs, which are particularly rich in both alcohol (13 to 15% vol) and in sugar (50 to 100 g per litre), need very ripe grapes, which cannot be obtained by the normal ripening process. This requires the action on the grape of a fungus, *Botrytis cinerea*, to produce noble rot; the grapes are also harvested in successive stages according to the development of the noble rot.

THE DIFFERENT STAGES OF PRODUCTION

New wine is rough, cloudy and full of carbon dioxide. It needs *élevage* (clarification, stabilisation and refining) to prepare it for the next stage, that of bottling. The time this takes varies according to the type of wine: Vins Nouveaux are bottled a few weeks after vinification, whereas wines for laying down are aged for two or more years.

— If the wine is kept in small containers, such as 225-litre oak barrels, clarification can be obtained by decanting the wine (*soutirage*) and removing the sediments. If the wine is kept in large vats, however, centrifugation or other methods of filtration have to be used.

— Because of its complexity, cloudiness and deposits can occur in the wine. These are totally natural phenomena of microbiological or chemical origin. When this happens in the bottle, it can be very serious, which is why stabilisation should take place beforehand.

— Microbiological accidents (acescency caused by bacteria or refermentation) can be avoided by preventing exposure to air and by keeping the container full. A topping-up process, or ullage, is carried out to prevent contact with air. Sulphur dioxide, which is both an antioxidant and an antiseptic, is often added, as is sorbic acid (an antiseptic) and ascorbic acid (an antioxidant).

— The treatment of wines is born from necessity; the products added are relatively few, they do not affect the quality of the wine, and they have been proved to be harmless. Laboratory tests help to predict risks of instability and to limit treatments to what is absolutely essential. However, the modern tendency is towards taking action immediately after vinification in order to limit the need for later treatments and the handling operations that these involve.

— Refrigeration can help to prevent deposits of tartar before bottling. Metatartaric acid, which inhibits crystallisation, has an immediate but not a long-lasting effect. Fining consists of adding a protein, such as egg white or gelatine, to the wine. This has a coalescent action, taking out suspended particles that are liable to make the wine cloudy or to leave deposits at a later stage. The adding of substances (usually egg white) to red wine is an ancient practice, indispensable for getting rid of excess colouring matter that would otherwise line the inside of the bottle. Gum arabic has a similar effect and is used for table wines that are to be consumed soon after bottling. The coagulation of natural proteins in white wines is avoided by adding bentonite which is a protective colloid. An excess of certain metals such as iron or copper, can also lead to cloudiness; they can be eliminated by adding potassium ferrocyanide.

— *Élevage* also contains a refining stage. First of all there is the elimination of any excess carbon dioxide that has been produced during fermentation. How this is done depends on the type of wine, for while it gives freshness to dry white wines and young wines, it has a coarsening effect on wines to be laid down, especially good red wines. The carefully controlled introduction of oxygen acts on the tannins of young red wines and is indispensable for their later ageing in bottles. Controlled aeration happens naturally in oak casks, but it is possible to introduce precise amounts of oxygen; the technique is known as *microbullage*.

— When the wood is new, oak casks give wines tones of vanilla and toastiness, which harmonise perfectly with the aromas of the fruit. Allier oak (from the Tronçais forest) is more suitable than Limousin oak. The wood must be split and dried in the open air for three years before it is used. This is all part of the traditional method used for Grands Vins, but it is very expensive in terms of the cost of the casks, the manual labour involved and the loss of wine through evaporation. In addition, when the casks are old they can be a source of microbiological contamination and can sometimes do more harm than good. This type of ageing should be reserved for wines that are sufficiently rich for the oakiness not to dominate the fruity aromas of the wine and mask its typical characteristics. The contribution that oak can make depends on the structure of the wines (taking into account the length of ageing and the proportion of new casks), and care must be taken that the wine does not become too dry. Attempts have been made to simplify the process by, for example, macerating the wine with oak shavings or wood chips, but this is forbidden in the production of AOC wines.

AGEING

The word 'ageing' is specifically reserved for the slow transformation of wine in the bottle, with no exposure to the oxygen in the air. Bottling must be carried out with great care in very hygienic conditions. By this stage the wine has been thoroughly clarified and must not be contaminated. Care must also be taken to fill the bottles with the right quantity. Because of its elasticity and imperviousness to liquids, cork still remains the first choice for sealing bottles. However, it is advisable to re-cork bottles every 25 years or so, as cork is degradable. There are also two risks of contamination connected with corks: leaky bottles and a 'corky' taste.

— The changes that occur in the bottle are many and complex. There is, first of all, a change in colour, which is most evident in red wines. The bright red colour of young wines evolves into a more yellowy shade, resembling the colour of tiles or bricks. In very old wines the red is replaced by tones of brown and orange. This process of change is responsible for the deposits that are often present in very old wines. Bottle age also 'softens' the general structure of the wine by reducing the tannic element.

— It is during the ageing process in the bottle that aromas and the individual 'bouquets' of old wines develop. These developments are due to complex chemical changes that are still not fully understood but that do not involve esterification.

QUALITY CONTROL

Good wine is not necessarily great wine. A wine of quality can be anything from a table wine to a Grand Cru or any permutation in between. A distinction also has to be made between the human factors and natural factors that contribute to the quality of the wine. The first category is indispensable for a good wine, but a great wine requires very specific environmental conditions of soil and climate.

— Chemical analysis has helped to point out anomalies and defects, but it has its limitations when it comes to defining quality: in the final analysis, taste is the essential criterion. However, considerable progress has been made over the last 20 years in sensory analytical techniques, giving us a better understanding and knowledge of the physiology of odour and taste and of practical tasting conditions. Tasting expertise is playing an increasingly large part in gauging quality, in particular in the registration of AOC wines and in legal cases.

— In fact, quality control has been subject to regulation for some time. The first official text was the French wine law of 1 August 1905 concerning commercial transactions. Regulations have progressed in step with developments in the understanding of the composition of wine and the changes that occur. With the help of chemical analysis, regulations define a minimum level of quality, thus eliminating major defects; they also encourage ways of improving this minimum level. The Consumers and Fraud Association is responsible for checking the analytical standards that have been established.

— Added to this is the work carried out by the National Institute of Appellations d'Origine (INAO), which, in consultation with the *syndicats* concerned, lays down and controls production conditions, including production zones, varieties, planting and pruning methods, cultivation techniques, vinification, composition of musts and wines, and yields. This body is also responsible for representing AOC wines within France and abroad.

— Finally, in every region, wine-growing *syndicats* defend the interests of their members, especially when it comes to matters concerning appellations. This work is often co-ordinated by councils, bodies or interprofessional committees that bring together representatives from various unions and from groups of producers and wine-merchants, as well as people from the professional and administrative worlds.

Pascal Ribéreau-Gayon

A CONSUMER'S GUIDE TO BUYING WINE

Buying wine is the easiest thing in the world; choosing wisely is the most difficult. If you were to consider everything that is on offer, you would find that there are several hundreds of thousands of different wines to choose from.

France alone produces tens of thousands of wines, each of which has its own individuality and characteristics. What distinguishes them in appearance, apart from their colour, is their label, hence the importance and care that the public and professional authorities attach to controlling the use and presentation of labelling. It is also important for the buyer to understand a label's many 'mysteries'.

THE LABEL

The label fulfils several functions.

— The first is a legal one. It indicates who is responsible for the wine in case of any dispute. This could be a wine-merchant or the grower himself. In some cases this information is also indicated on the top of the cap or capsule.

— The second function of the label is very important, because it establishes the category to which the wine belongs: vin de table, vin de pays, AOVDQS or AOC; the last two of these have been assimilated into the European term Vin de Qualité Produit dans des Régions Déterminées (VQPRD).

AOC

This is the top class, the category for all the great wines. The label has to have 'XXXX Appellation Contrôlée' or 'Appellation XXXX Contrôlée' on it. This mentions the precise region, town or commune or even sometimes the Cru (or *climat*, a part of a Cru) where the vineyard is situated. To have the right to an AOC, a wine must have been produced according to 'local, loyal and consistent usage'– that is, it is from approved 'noble' varieties planted in specific vineyards and vinified according to regional traditions. The yield per hectare and alcoholic content (minimum and sometimes maximum) are also fixed by law. The wines are approved every year by a tasting committee.

— National regulations are supplemented by the institutionalised application of local customs. Thus, in Alsace the letters indicating the regional appellation are nearly always double the size of the name of the variety. In Burgundy on the other hand, only the Premiers Crus can be printed in letters that are the same size as those used for the appellation of the commune; the *climats* that are not in the highest classification can be mentioned only in small letters, half the size of the characters indicating the appellation. In addition, the communes of the Grands Crus do not appear on the labels, because these wines have their own individual appellations. These requirements are all given in detail in current French wine law.

HOW TO READ A LABEL

The label must identify the wine and indicate who is responsible for it. The last person in the production process is the bottler, and his name must also appear on the label. Each category of wine is subject to its own specific labelling regulations. The first duty of the label is to inform the consumer and to indicate which category the wine belongs to:

– Vin de table (origin, alcohol content, volume, name and address of bottler must all be mentioned; vintages, or years, are forbidden).
– Vins de pays.
– Appellation d'Origine Vin Délimité de Qualité Supérieure (AOVDQS).
– Appellation d'Origine Contrôlée (AOC).

alcohol content in degrees (compulsory)

Alsace AOC

green fiscal stamp (on cap)
wine category (compulsory)
variety (only allowed if grapes are from one single variety)
volume (compulsory)
all other compulsory indications
necessary for export to certain countries

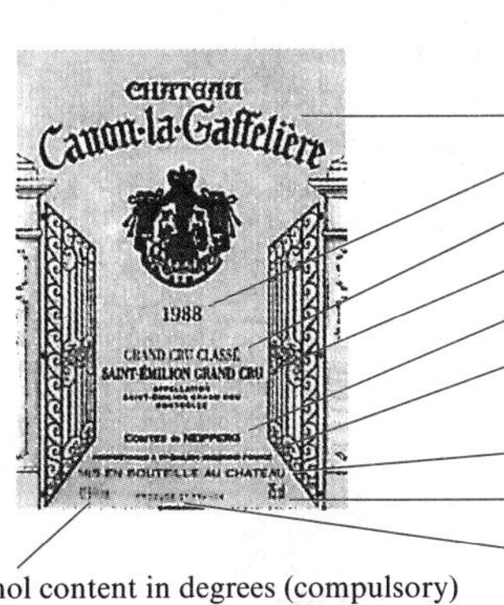

alcohol content in degrees (compulsory)

Bordeaux AOC

green fiscal stamp
brand (optional)
vintage (optional)
class of category (optional)
category (compulsory)
name and address of bottler (compulsory)
the word 'owner' (optional) fixes the status of the vineyard
optional
volume (compulsory)
necessary for export to certain countries

volume (compulsory)

Burgundy AOC

green fiscal stamp
the vintage is often on a label around the neck of the bottle (optional)
name of the Cru (optional); if the letters are the same size as those of the appellation, it is a Premier Cru
category (compulsory)
alcohol content (compulsory)
name and address of bottler (compulsory); also indicates that it is bottled at the property not by a wine-merchant
necessary for export to certain countries

Champagne AOC

green fiscal stamp

of no great significance (optional)

compulsory

all Champagne is AOC, so this does not figure on the label; this is the only exception to the rule that requires a reference to the category of wine

brand and address (compulsory; it is taken as read that it is bottled at the same address)

volume (compulsory)

status of the vineyard and its professional identification number (optional)

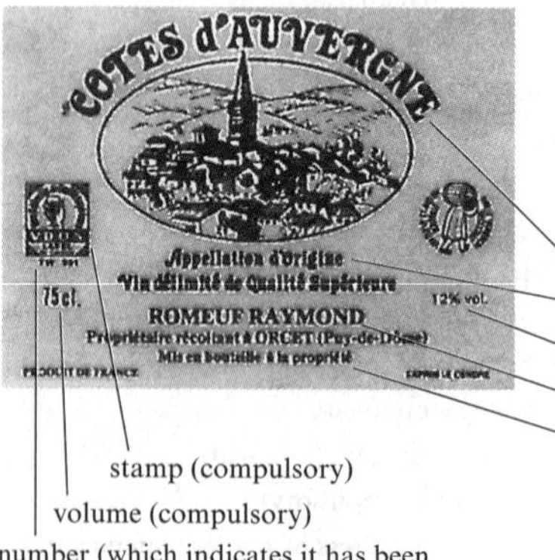

stamp (compulsory)

volume (compulsory)

number (which indicates it has been checked), compulsory in France

AOVDQS

green fiscal stamp

vintage (optional)

variety (optional, only allowed if grapes are from one single variety)

name of the appellation (compulsory)

category (compulsory)

alcohol content (compulsory)

name and address of bottler (compulsory)

indicates whether bottled on premises (optional)

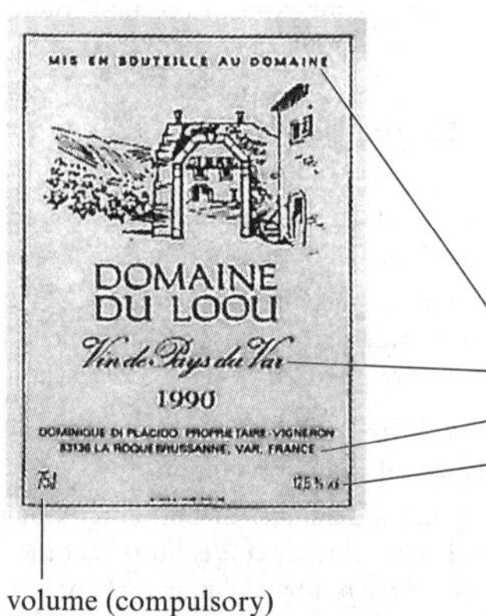

volume (compulsory)

Vins de Pays

blue fiscal stamp

table wines are subject to the same regulations. The words 'Vin de Pays' must be followed by the name of the region (compulsory)

'au domaine' optional

geographical area (compulsory)

name and address of bottler (compulsory)

alcohol content in degrees (compulsory)

Appellation d'Origine Vin Délimité de Qualité Supérieure (AOVDQS)

The 'antechamber' of AOC, this category is sensibly subject to the same rules. AOVQDS wines are labelled after they have been tasted. The label must include the words 'Appellation d'Origine Vin Délimité de Qualité Supérieure' and its corresponding stamp. These are not wines for laying down, but some of them improve after being kept in cellars for a while.

Vins de pays

The labels for Vins de pays indicate which region the wine comes from, so you will see 'Vin de Pays de . . .' followed by the name of the region.

— Wines in this category come from a legally defined list of more or less 'noble' grape varieties grown in large regional areas that are nevertheless 'limited'. Their alcoholic content, acidity and acidic volatility are all subject to controls. These are fresh, fruity and lively wines, to be drunk young. They are not suitable for laying down, and they can, in fact, deteriorate if kept.

— Labels can contain other information that is not compulsory, unlike the above requirements, but is nevertheless subject to regulations. The terms 'Clos', 'Château' and 'Cru Classé', for example, can be used only in accordance with traditional usage and only if they refer to something that actually exists. What labels might lose in creativity they make up for in honesty, and the buyer should feel reassured that the information on labels is more credible nowadays than in times past.

Vintages and bottling

Two non-compulsory pieces of information on the bottle will interest the wine-lover: first, the vintage, which will either be on the label (which is the best option) or on another label attached to the neck of the bottle, and, second, the exact location of the bottling.

— A keen wine-lover will be satisfied only with a label that indicates that bottling has taken place at the estate, property or château. Any other indication that does not establish a direct link between the place where the wine was vinified and where it was bottled is not of any great interest. No matter how accurate such phrases as 'bottled in the region of production', 'bottled by ourselves', 'bottled in our cellars', 'bottled by X (X being an intermediary)' may be, they do not have the same guarantee of origin as 'bottled at the property'.

— The concern of the public authorities and of professional committees has always been twofold: first, to encourage producers to improve the quality of their wine and to check this by tasting before labelling and second to make sure that the wine described on the label is indeed the wine that is in the bottle, without any mixing, additions or substitutions. However, despite all sorts of precautions, including possible checks during transportation, the best guarantee of authenticity remains 'bottled at the property' (*mis en bouteille à la propriété*). This is because a wine-grower does not have the right to purchase other wine to store in his commercial cellar, which can contain only wine that he has produced himself.

— Note that a co-operative that bottles its own wine can use the term 'bottled at the property'.

Caps

Most bottles are topped with a cap or capsule. Sometimes the cap bears a French government fiscal stamp, which is proof that all legal requirements have been fulfilled for its distribution. This clearance certificate is known colloquially as a *congé*, and that is why the caps are often referred to as *capsules congés*. When the bottles are not stamped, they have to be accompanied by a receipt or certificate issued by the nearest tax office (see the section on transporting wine).

The stamp shows the status of the producer (owner or wine-merchant) and the region of production. The caps do not officially have to be stamped or personalised, but in general one or the other is usually done.

Stamping corks

The producers of quality wine have felt the need to confirm the information on their labels by marking the corks as well. A label can become unstuck but a cork cannot; that is why the vintage and the origin of the wine are stamped on the cork. It is also a way of discouraging potential fraudsters who can no longer just replace the labels. Note that the appellation of AOC sparkling wines, must be mentioned on the cork.

HOW TO BUY WINE AND FROM WHOM

The ways in which wine is distributed are complex and vary from the very simple to the most convoluted, each method having its advantages and disadvantages. The ways in which wine is sold also take different forms according to the method of presentation (whether it is in containers or in bottles) and when it is bought for example, if it is bought *en primeur* (before it is bottled).

Wines to drink and wines to keep

The procedures for buying wine to drink and buying wine for laying down are not the same: there are different methods for different purposes. Wines destined for immediate consumption are ready to drink as they are; these are 'nouveau' wines or vins de pays, of 'small' or 'medium' origin and modest vintages, which do not require much ageing. Or they may be great wines that have reached their peak (but these are practically impossible to find on the market).

In every case, but obviously more importantly for fine wines, it is essential that there is a rest period of two days to two weeks between purchasing (including transportation) and consumption. Old bottles should be transported with great care, in a vertical position and protected from knocks, to avoid any stirring up of sediments.

Wines for keeping or laying down should be bought young with the aim of ageing them. Always choose the best possible wines from the finest vintages; these are not only less likely to deteriorate over time but will improve over the years.

Buying in containers

Wine that is not bought in bottles is bought *en vrac* (in bulk, ie in containers). The term *en cercle* is reserved for wines in barrels, whereas *vrac* means containers of any kind, from a 220 hl steel tank on a truck to a 5-litre plastic container or glass demijohn.

Wine is sold in containers by co-operatives, by some wine-growers and wine-merchants, and even by some retailers. It is sometimes called wine sold *à la tireuse* or 'drawn by hand'. Usually, table wines or wines of medium quality are sold in this way; it is rare to find a good-quality wine sold in a container. In fact, in certain areas, it is forbidden – for example, Bordeaux Crus Classés cannot be sold in this way.

The wine-lover should be aware that even when a wine-grower says that the wine he is selling in containers is the same as the one that he is selling in bottles, this is not strictly true. He will always choose the best batches for the wine that he bottles himself.

— Buying wine in containers can represent a saving of about 25%, as it is common practice to pay, at most, the same price for a litre as you would pay for a 75cl bottle.

— The purchaser can also save on transport costs, but will have to buy corks and bottles if he or she does not have any to hand. If the transaction is made by the barrel, the costs (not very high in France) of returning the cask have also to be taken into account.

These are the most commonly used containers:

Bordeaux barrique	225 litres
Burgundy pièce	228 litres
Mâconnais pièce	216 litres
Chablis pièce	132 litres
Champagne pièce	205 litres

— Bottling, which can be fun when it is done with a group of friends, does not pose too many problems, whatever anyone might say, provided that certain elementary rules (see below) are adhered to.

Buying by the bottle

In France bottles can be bought from the wine-grower, from a co-operative, at a wine-merchant or at any of many other outlets.

— Where should a wine-lover in France go to get the best deal? For wines that are not widely distributed the best option is to go to the wine-grower, and there are many of these. To avoid paying the ever-increasing costs of transport for small quantities of wine, co-operatives are a good choice. In other cases, such a strategy is not as simple as it seems. It should be borne in mind that wine-growers and wine-merchants are not in competition with their distributors, and they are not going to sell their bottles more cheaply. In fact, a number of Bordeaux châteaux that do very little direct selling sell their bottles at an even higher price than retailers to discourage buyers who, through ignorance or for whatever other reason, persist in buying directly from the owners. For wines of repute prices are bound to be lower at the retailers, which can obtain much better deals by placing large orders, than an individual can obtain by buying a single case.

— A general rule can be drawn from this: it is not worth buying widely distributed wines direct from famous domains and châteaux, except when it is a rare vintage or a special reserve.

Buying *en primeur*

This method of buying wine, practised for several years in the Bordeaux region, was very successful during the 1980s. Today, it is probably better to talk about buying or selling by subscription. The principle is simple: you buy a wine before it has been aged or bottled at a lower price than it would be sold at when it is ready to be delivered.

— Subscriptions are available for a limited time and for specified quantities, usually in the spring or the beginning of the summer that follows the harvest. The purchaser pays a deposit of half the total cost when he or she orders and the rest on delivery, ie 15 months later. In this way, the producer has ready cash and the buyer can make a profit if prices increase. This was the case from 1974–5 to the end of the 1980s. This type of transaction is similar to what, on the Stock Exchange, is known as a forward-exchange transaction.

— If, because of overproduction or an economic crisis, the price goes down between subscription and delivery, the subscribers pay more for their bottles than those who did not subscribe. This has happened in the past and could well happen again. In fact, some leading wine-merchants have been ruined in the past by trying to guarantee their supplies with this type of speculation. It is true that such speculators run more risks if their contract spans several years.

Under normal circumstances, buying wine *en primeur* is undoubtedly the only way to buy wine for less than its normal price (between 20% and 40% less). Opportunities to buy *en primeur* are organised by the wine-growers themselves, and also by wine-merchants and wine clubs.

Buying directly from the producer

Apart from the rather technical aspects described above, a visit to the producer, which is indispensable if the wine is not very widely distributed, gives the wine-lover a different kind of satisfaction from that of simply getting a bargain. Only by visiting the producers, the true 'fathers' of their wines, can oenophiles fully understand the meaning of *terroir* and its characteristics, appreciate the art of vinification, which brings out the very essence of the grape, and, finally, see the strong links that exist between a wine-grower and his wine, – between a creator and his creation. It is a stage that needs to be experienced in order to 'drink well and drink better', as the French say. To truly appreciate a wine, nothing can replace a visit to the grower.

Buying from a co-operative

The quality of wines sold by co-operatives is improving all the time. They are well equipped for selling wines, either in containers or in bottles, at prices that are usually slightly lower than those of other sales outlets offering similar quality.

The principle underlying co-operatives is well known. The members bring in their harvested grapes, and those responsible for the technical side (usually oenologists) take care of the pressing, vinification and, in some appellations, the ageing and selling.

The fact that they usually produce several types of wine gives co-operatives an opportunity of either using the best grapes (by separating them out from the others) or of highlighting certain *terroirs* through separate vinifications. For the best co-operatives, the system of special payments for the ripest and noble grapes, coupled with the possibility of making and selling wines according to the quality of each individual delivery of grapes, opens up opportunities to produce quality wines or even wines for laying down. Other co-operatives remain suppliers of table wines and vins de pays that are not intended for ageing or laying down.

Buying from a wine-merchant

In France a wine-merchant, by definition, buys wines for resale. In addition, he or she may often be a vineyard owner. Such a merchant–owner may thus produce and sell his or her own wine, sell wine from independent producers without having to do anything other than arrange transportation (this is the case for Bordeaux wine-merchants who sell wines that have been château bottled) or may even have an exclusive contract with a single production unit. A merchant may be a *négociant-éleveur*, producing wines by assembling or mixing wines from the same appellation, but supplied by different growers; such a practice influences the final product twice: once by the choice of purchase and second by mixing the wines. Wine-merchants are usually located in the larger wine-growing areas, but there is, of course, nothing to stop a Burgundian wine-merchant from selling wine from Bordeaux or vice versa. The main purpose of a wine-merchant is to distribute and feed the retail network rather than to sell wines at much lower prices than retailers.

Buying from a cellarman (*caviste*) or a retailer
This is the easiest and quickest way of buying wine, and it is also the safest if the cellarman is sufficiently expert. Over the last few years, a number of shops specialising in the sale of quality wines have appeared. A good cellarman is someone who stores wines in good conditions but who also knows how to choose original wines from producers who love their work. In addition, a good retailer or cellarman should be able to advise clients, helping them to discover new wines and to choose appropriate wines to complement different types of food.

Supermarkets
In France buying quality wines in supermarkets has become a widespread practice, compared with the 1970s when it was rare. Whatever the location, the presentation in this type of shop is not always of the best, with problems such as too high a temperature, harsh neon lighting and the vertical storage of bottles. However, these oversights are becoming increasingly rare. Today in France, and elsewhere, many establishments possess specialised, well-equipped shelves where the bottles are stored horizontally and are classified by appellation. In France especially the wine-lover will find not only ordinary wines in supermarkets but also prestigious Crus. The only wines not represented in supermarkets are appellations that are not widely distributed and wines from smaller vineyards. Contrary to common belief, it can be advantageous for the visitor to buy a prestigious bottle of French wine from a French supermarket.

Clubs
All over the world wine is delivered directly to wine-lovers, by the bottle or by the case, by so-called 'wine clubs', which offer their members a certain number of advantages, including serious and informed critiques. Often, the wines on offer are chosen by wine experts and well-known and competent personalities. There is a wide choice, which sometimes includes little-known wines. However, it is worth noting that many such 'clubs' are, in reality, wine-merchants.

Auction sales
In France, sales by auction, which are becoming increasingly fashionable and popular, are organised by auctioneers with the help of wine experts. Wherever the sale takes place, it is extremely important to know the origin of the bottles. If they have come from a good restaurant or from the cellar of a wine-lover who has had to relinquish some bottles for personal reasons, it is probable that they have been kept in very good condition. If they consist of smaller lots that have been brought together from various sources, there is nothing to guarantee that the wine has been kept properly.

— The appearance of the wine is the only indicator. The alert wine-lover will not bid for a bottle that is not filled to the correct level, nor for a white wine that is veering towards a darkish bronze colour, nor for red wine that looks 'tired'.

— It is rare to be able to buy great appellations that restaurateurs are interested in having on their lists at a bargain price; however, the lesser appellations, which are not so sought keenly after by professionals, are sometimes more affordable.

Bordeaux
Champagne
Burgundy
Alsace
Côtes du Rhône
Clavelin (Jura)
Provence
Burgundy
Bordeaux
Champagne
Alsace
INAO
Red wines
Sparkling wines
White wines
Young red and rosé wines
Old red wines

The Hospices de Beaune wine auction and similar auctions
Wines sold during these charity events are sold in casks and have to be aged for 12 to 14 months. They are therefore reserved for professionals.

Transporting wine
Once the problem of choosing wine has been resolved and you know that there is somewhere to store the bottles in good condition (see below), the next step is transporting them. The transportation of quality wines requires that several precautions be taken and in France, it is also subject to strict regulations.

— Whether you transport the wine yourself by car or use the services of a shipper, the height of summer and the depths of winter are not the best times to undertake it. The wine must be protected from extremes of temperature, especially from high temperatures, which not only affect wine in the short term but also in the long term, no matter how long a rest period (even years) it may be given and no matter what its colour, type or origin may be.

— Once they are at their destination, the bottles should be stored in the cellar without delay. If the wine has been bought in containers, it should be stored where it is going to be bottled as soon as possible – in the cellar if space allows – in order to avoid having to move it again. Plastic containers should be placed 80 cm (32 in) from the ground (at table height), and casks 30 cm (12 in) from the ground, so that the wine can be drawn to the very last drop without changing its position, which is essential.

Regulations governing shipping wine in France
In France shipping alcoholic drinks is subject to a special regime and incurs taxes. These take the form of either a capsule (known as a *capsule fiscalisée* or a *capsule congé*), which is found on the top of each bottle, or an accompanying document issued by the tax office nearest to the sales point or by the wine-grower, if empowered to do so. Wine in containers must always be accompanied by the relevant permit.

— The name of the seller, the Cru, the volume and number of containers, the recipient, the method of transport and length of journey must all appear on this document. If the journey takes longer than predicted, the length of the validity of the permit must be altered accordingly by the nearest tax office.

— In France shipping wine without clearance is considered to be fiscal fraud and is punishable as such. It is advisable to keep relevant fiscal documents in case the wine is moved again, because they can be used to establish a new *congé*.

— The taxes that are levied are in proportion to the volume of wine and are divided into one of two categories: table wine or appellation wine.

Exporting wine
Like all products made or manufactured in France, wine is subject to a certain number of taxes. When these products or objects are exported, it is possible to obtain tax exemptions or rebates. Wine is exempt from VAT and transport tax (but not from the *taxe parafiscale*, a special tax assigned to the national fund for the development of agriculture). When a visitor wishes to benefit from tax exemption on exports, the wine that he or she buys must be accompanied by its *titre de mouvement* (a green form No. 8102 for appellation wines, and a blue form No. 8101 for table wines), which will be accepted by the customs office that oversees the export of the merchandise. If the bottles have fiscal stamps the tax cannot be reclaimed. In order to benefit from a tax rebate, therefore, it is advisable to indicate to

the seller that the wine is intended for export at the time of purchase. It is also advisable to find out about importing wines and other alcoholic drinks into the countries concerned, as each country has its own regulations, which can range from import taxes to quotas to a blanket ban. Potential exporters of French wines should always contact their own customs authorities to clarify relevant regulations.

KEEPING WINE

Building up a good wine cellar involves a lot more than simply accumulating bottles. In addition to the principles already described, there are a number of important factors. One useful approach is to try to acquire wines of similar character and style, which need different lengths of time to age, so that they do not all reach their peak at the same time. It is also best to select wines that stay at their peak for the maximum possible period and so do not all need to be consumed within a short space of time. Choose a wide variety of wines so that you do not always have to drink the same sort, even if they are of the best, and so that you can be sure that there is always something appropriate to every occasion and to accompany all sorts of different food. Finally, there are two constraints that condition all other requirements – your budget and the size of the cellar space itself.

— A good cellar space should be enclosed, dark, free from vibration, noise and smells, and protected from draughts. At the same time it should be airy, not too dry nor too damp (a humidity level of about 75%). Most importantly, it should have a constant temperature of about 11°C (52°F).

— Cellars in towns rarely have all these characteristics. It is, therefore, important to try to improve the cellar before storing the wine by increasing or decreasing the ventilation as required. For example, it is possible to adjust the humidity of a too-dry cellar by introducing a basin of water and charcoal. If a cellar is too damp, dry it out by putting a layer of gravel on the floor and increasing the ventilation. If necessary the temperature can be regulated with the help of insulating panels, and, if vibration is a problem, by placing the racks on rubber blocks. If there is a central heating boiler nearby giving off oil fumes, the future will be less than bright for your wine.

— It is possible that a cellar may not be available or even if there is, that it may not be fit for use. In this case, there are two options: either buy a specially made unit that can store between 50 and 500 bottles, whose temperature and humidity are automatically regulated, or build a unit from scratch, somewhere at the back of your house or apartment. You will need a store-room in which the temperature is fairly constant and, if possible, does not rise above 16°C (60.8°F). Bear in mind that the higher the temperature the more quickly a wine ages and that it is not true, as was once commonly thought, that a wine that reaches its peak quickly in bad conditions is of the same quality as one that has matured slowly in a good cool cellar. Thus, fine wines that need to mature slowly should not be aged in a cellar, or any other type of store, that is too warm. Wine-lovers should plan their purchases and storage according to the premises that they have at their disposal.

Establishing a good cellar

Experience has shown that a cellar is always too small. The storage of the bottles has to be organised logically. A wine-rack with one or two rows has several advantages: it is not expensive, it can be installed straight away, and it gives easy access to the bottles. Unfortunately, it takes up a lot of room for the number of bottles stored. To gain extra space, the only way is to store the bottles in piles. In order to separate the stacks and have access to different wines you need to build, or have built, 'bins', which are made from breeze-blocks and which can contain 24, 36 or 48 bottles in stacks on two levels.

— If there is enough room it is possible to raise the bins on planks. However, these will need to be checked regularly for rot as well as for the presence of insects that might attack the corks.

— Two pieces of apparatus will complete the cellar: a maximum-and-minimum thermometer and a hygrometer to measure the humidity. Regular readings will help to correct any variations in temperature or humidity and to maintain the long-term requirements for ageing wines to best effect.

Bottling

If the wine has been transported in a container, it should be bottled as soon as possible; if it has been shipped by barrel, it is essential that it should rest for two weeks before bottling. This general advice needs to be tempered in light of the atmospheric conditions prevailing on the day chosen for bottling. Ideally, the weather should be mild, with high barometric pressure and no threat of rain or storms. In practice, the wine-lover will have to compromise between the ideal and the possible. However, no compromises should be made with the necessary equipment. First of all, the bottles should be the appropriate ones for the wine. As a rule, Bordeaux bottles should be used for all wines from the south-west and, possibly, from the Midi too, and Burgundy bottles for wines from the south-east, Beaujolais and Burgundy (always bearing in mind that there are other types of regional bottles for specific appellations).

— If the bottles are to be stored in stacks, it should be noted that, whether they are Bordeaux or Burgundy in style, bottles are of varying thickness (some bottles have flat, or nearly flat, bases). As well as weight, the height and diameter also vary.

— All bottles are suitable for keeping wine in, but the lighter bottles are less suitable for storing wine in stacks over a long period of time. In addition, if lighter gauge bottles are over-filled they can sometimes explode when the cork is forced into place.

— Generally, it is better to use the heavier gauge bottles. It is almost as incongruous to bottle a great wine in light glass as it would be to use a clear glass bottle for a red wine. Custom dictates that these bottles should be used only for certain white wines, so that the colour can be clearly seen. However, white wines are particularly sensitive to the light, and this custom should be ignored. Their sensitivity to light is so great that Champagne houses that sell wine in clear bottles always protect them with opaque paper or with a box.

— Whichever type of bottle is chosen, it is essential that there are sufficient bottles and corks available before bottling is begun, because once under way this operation should be completed rapidly. If the cask or container is left open, the remaining wine may become oxidised and develop acescency, making the wine unfit to drink. Cleanliness is also essential, and the bottles should be scrupulously rinsed and dried before they are used.

Corks

Despite extensive research, cork remains the only material suitable for sealing bottles. Corks are not identical, differing in diameter, length and quality.

— The diameter of the cork is always 6 mm (¼ in) larger than the bottleneck.

— The better the wine, the longer the cork required. This is necessary for long-term ageing and is no more than due consideration for the wine and for those who will one day enjoy it.

— The quality of a cork is more difficult to assess. It needs to be about ten years old to have the necessary suppleness. Good corks should not have those little cracks that are sometimes blocked up with cork powder – these are known as 'improved' corks. It is also possible to buy corks that have been stamped (or to have them stamped) with the vintage of the wine that is to be bottled.

— Today, it is possible to buy ready-to-use corks, which are available in ozone-sterilised packaging. They are no longer moistened, but inserted dry, as this has proved to be the most successful method.

Filling the bottles

The ideal apparatus for filling bottles is a pump. There are two types: a piston pump and a vane pump, both of which are available in DIY stores for a modest price.

— The bottle should be slightly tilted to let the wine run down the whole length of the side, to minimise the amount of oxidation and stirring up. This precaution is even more necessary for white wines. In no circumstances should a scum be allowed to appear on the surface of the liquid. The bottles should be filled as full as possible, so that the cork is in contact with the wine when the bottle is in an upright position. The cork should be inserted with the help of a special corking device that compresses the cork width-wise before insertion. There is a wide range of equipment available at varying prices for this purpose.

Labels

These can be attached with wallpaper paste or a mixture of flour and water. Simpler still, the labels can be moistened with milk and stuck on the bottles. The bottom edge of the label should be 3 cm (about 1 in) from the base of the bottle.

— Perfectionists will add ready-made capsules to the top of the bottle with the aid of a little machine, or they will seal the tops with melted coloured wax, which can be bought from a cork merchant.

Storing wine in the cellar

As far as possible, the following rules should be observed: white wines should be stored close to the ground with the red wines on top; wines for long-term keeping should be stored on the less-accessible racks at the back, with bottles ready for drinking near the front.

— Bottles bought or delivered in cardboard boxes should not be left in this type of packaging, unlike those delivered in wooden crates. Buyers who envisage reselling the wine should leave it in the crate, but others should not for two reasons: it takes up a lot of room, and it is a prime target for thieves. In any case, a cataloguing system (numerical, for example) will help to identify racks and bottles. This system can be logged in the most useful tool of the wine-cellar, the cellar book.

Three suggestions for your cellar

Everyone stocks his or her own cellar according to personal taste. The collections described on the following page are only suggestions and the main theme is diversity. Vins Nouveau, and wines that gain nothing from being aged in the cellar do not feature in these lists. The fewer the bottles, the greater the need to maintain stocks. The prices in brackets are, of course, applicable only to France and are given as a guide only.

A 50-bottle cellar (FF4000)

25 bottles of Bordeaux	17 red (Graves, Saint-Emilion, Médoc, Pomerol, Fronsac) 8 white: 5 dry (Graves), 3 sweet (Sauternes-Barsac)
20 bottles of Burgundy	12 red (Côte de Nuits Crus, Côte de Beaune Crus) 8 white (Chablis, Meursault, Puligny)
10 bottles of Vallée du Rhône	7 red (Côte-Rôtie, Hermitage, Châteauneuf-du-Pape) 3 white (Hermitage, Condrieu)

A 150-bottle cellar (about FF13,000)

Region		Red	White
40 Bordeaux	30 red 10 white	Fronsac Pomerol Saint-Émilion Graves Médoc (Crus Classés, Crus Bourgeois)	5 good, dry white wines 5 Sainte-Croix-du-Mont Sauternes-Barsac
30 Burgundy	15 red 15 white	Côte de Nuits Crus Côte de Beaune Crus Côte Chalonnaise	Chablis Meursault Puligny-Montrachet
25 Vallée du Rhône	19 red 6 white	Côte-Rôtie Hermitage (red) Cornas Saint-Joseph Châteauneuf-du-Pape Gigondas Côtes-du-Rhône Villages	Condrieu Hermitage (white) Châteauneuf-du-Pape (white)
15 Vallée de la Loire	8 red 7 white	Bourgueil Chinon Saumur-Champigny	Pouilly-Fumé Vouvray Coteaux du Layon
10 South-west	7 red 3 white	Madiran Cahors	Jurançon (sweet and dry)
8 South-east	6 red 2 white	Bandol Palette (red)	Cassis Palette (white)
7 Alsace	(white)		Gewurztraminer Riesling Tokay
5 Jura	(white)		Vins jaunes (yellow wines) Côtes du Jura-Arbois
10 Champagne and sparkling wines (readily accessible, as these wines do not improve with age)			Crémant de Loire Burgundy Alsace Various types of Champagne

A 300-bottle cellar

To create such a cellar an investment of about FF25,000 is needed. You double the numbers required for the 150-bottle cellar but should bear in mind that the more bottles you have, the longer the life of the wine has to be. This usually means, unfortunately, that despite discounts the wine is going to be more expensive.

The cellar book

This is the record, guide, judge and jury of the wine-lover. The following information should be recorded in the book: date acquired, number of bottles of each Cru, precise identification details, price, presumed peak date, location in cellar and, possibly, tasting notes and details of ideal culinary accompaniments.

THE ART OF DRINKING

If drinking is a physiological necessity, drinking wine is a pleasure. This pleasure varies in intensity depending on the wine, the tasting conditions and the sensitivity of the taster.

Tasting

There are several types of wine-tasting, each suited to a particular end. The technical, analytical, comparative, triangular and so forth types of tasting are reserved for professionals. The wine-lover practises tasting purely for pleasure, to discover the quintessence of a wine, to learn how to put this into words and to improve the sensitivity of the nose and palate.

— Tasting and, more generally, consumption of wine, should not take place anywhere and in any fashion. The location should be pleasant, well lit natural light or 'daylight' lighting, which does not alter colours, preferably with light-coloured walls and free from any stray odours, such as perfume, smoke (tobacco and fire), cooking smells or flowers. The temperature should be between 18 and 20°C (64 to 68°F).

— The choice of an appropriate glass is extremely important. It should be clear, so that the colour of the wine can be clearly seen, and if possible not too thick. It should have a tulip shape – that is it should not turn outwards at the top, which is often the case, but should in fact turn slightly inwards. The body of the glass should be separated from the foot by a stem. This prevents the glass from being warmed when it is held (by the stem) and makes it easier to swirl the wine; this is done in order to oxygenate the wine and to release its bouquet.

— The shape of the glass is so important and has such an influence on the olfactory appreciation of wine (both taste and smell) that the Association Française de Normalisation (AFNOR) and the Instances Internationales de Normalisation (ISO) have, as a result of a study, adopted a glass that is eminently suitable for both taster and consumer. This type of glass, which is commonly referred to in France as 'the INAO glass', is not just for professionals but can be found in France in specialist shops. Over the last few years, French, German and Austrian glassmakers have considerably extended the choice of wine glasses available.

Tasting techniques

Tasting involves sight, smell, taste and touch – not touching with the fingers, of course, but with the mouth, which is sensitive to 'mechanical' effects of wine, such as temperature, consistency and fizz.

SIGHT

The first contact that a consumer has with wine is with the eye. Examining the visual appearance of the wine, which includes assessing its distinguishing colour, can reveal a lot of information. This is the first test. Whatever the colour and tint of the wine, it should be clear, not cloudy. Any trace of streaks or cloudiness is a sign of disease and the wine should be rejected. Only small insoluble tartaric crystals (*gravelle*), which occur when there is a sudden cold spell, should be accepted; the quality of the wine is not affected by them.

The clarity of a wine can be tested by placing the glass between the eye and a source of light that should, if possible, be at the same height. The transparency of red wine can be determined by looking at it against a white background, such as a tablecloth or a piece of paper. The glass should be tilted and the surface, or 'disc', should form an ellipse; the shape can say a

Wine	Shade of colour	Interpretation
White	Almost colourless	Very young, well protected from oxidisation. Modern vinification in vat
	Very light yellow with hints of green	Young to very young. Vinified and aged in vat
	Straw yellow, golden yellow	Matured. Perhaps aged in wood
	Coppery gold, bronze gold	Already old
	Amber to black	Oxidised, too old
Rosé	Flecked white, partridge eye (soft corn colour) with hints of pink	Rosé obtained by pressing and light young rosés
	Very light, clear salmon-pink to red	Young, fruity rosé, ready to drink
	Pink with shades of yellow to onion skin	Beginning to be old for its type
Red	Purple	Very young. Good shade for nouveau Gamay and Beaujolais Nouveau (6 to 18 months)
	Pure red (cherry)	Neither young nor old. Peak period for wines which are neither nouveau nor for laying down (2–3 years)
	Red with bands of orange	Mature wine (short-term keeping). Beginning of ageing (3–7 years)
	Brownish red to brown	Only great wines have reached their peak when they are this colour. For others, it is too late.
Too light	Not pressed enough Rainy year Too large a yield Young vines Grapes not sufficiently ripe Rotten grapes Too short a time in vat Fermentation at low temperature	Light wines for short-term keeping Unexceptional vintages
Dark	Well pressed Low yield Old vines Successful vinification	Good or great wines Good future

lot about the age of the wine and how it has been kept. The next thing to examine is the actual shade of the colour. All young wines should be transparent, which is not the case with old, quality wines.

— The brilliance or luminosity of a wine is also important. If a wine is luminous it is lively; a dull wine will be lifeless. The intensity of colour, which is not to be confused with shade or tone, should also be taken into account.

— The intensity of the colour of red wines, which is the easiest to see, is the most telling.

— 'Legs' or 'tears', formed on the side of the glass when it is swirled around to breathe in the bouquet (see below) are also part of the visual aspect of wine. They are related to the alcoholic content: cognac always produces these, vins de pays rarely do so.

Examples of vocabulary used when talking about the appearance of wine:

Shades: purple, garnet, ruby, violet, cherry, peony
Intensity: light, strong, dark, deep, intense
Brilliance: matt, dull, sad, sparkling, brilliant
Clarity and transparency: opaque, hazy, veiled, crystalline, flawless

SMELL

Olfactory examination is the next test that wine has to undergo during tasting. Certain odours, such as volatile acidity (acescency, vinegar), and a corky smell discount wines straight away, but in most cases the bouquet – that is, the combination of odours released from the glass – is a new voyage of discovery each time.

— The aromatic components of the bouquet are expressed according to their volatility. What takes place is a kind of evaporation, and that is why the temperature at which wine is served is so important. If the wine is too cold, there will be no bouquet; too hot, and the result is too rapid evaporation, marked by aromas joining together, oxidation, the loss of highly volatile aromas and the release of abnormally heavy aromatic elements.

— The bouquet of a wine is like a kaleidoscope of scents that is forever changing; they emerge one after another depending on temperature and exposure to the air. This is why the way the glass is handled is important. First of all, the aromas released from a still glass are breathed in, then the glass is swirled around, and exposure to the air releases yet other scents.

— The quality of a wine is a function of the intensity and complexity of its bouquet. Mediocre wines have a small bouquet, if any; they usually have one note only and can be summed up very simply, in one word. On the other hand, great wines have full, deep bouquets, and their complexity is constantly changing.

— The vocabulary used to describe bouquets is almost infinite, because it uses analogy. Several classifications to describe them been put forward, but to simplify matters we will use the following characteristics: floral, fruity, vegetable (or herbaceous), spicy, balsamic, gamey, woody, smoky or burnt and chemical.

Examples of vocabulary used to describe the bouquet:

Flowers: violets, linden flowers, jasmine, elderflower, acacia, iris, peony
Fruits: raspberry, blackcurrant, cherry, Morello cherry, gooseberry, apricot, apple, banana, prune
Vegetable: grassy, fern, moss, undergrowth, damp ground, chalky, various mushrooms
Balsamic: resin, pine, terebinth (turpentine tree)
Gamey: meat, well-hung meat, game, civet, musk, fur
Burnt: burnt, grilled, toasted, tobacco, dried hay, all roasted aromas (coffee etc).

TASTE

Having triumphantly passed through the two examinations of sight and smell, a wine's final test is that of taste.

— A small amount of wine is taken into the mouth, where it is held, and a breath of air is also taken in and diffused throughout the oral cavity. If this is not possible, the wine is just swirled around the mouth. As the wine warms up in the mouth, it releases new aromas that are captured by the retronasal passage. The papillae (taste buds) on the tongue can detect only the four basic flavours – bitter, acidic, sweet and salty – which is why a person with a cold cannot taste wine (or food) because the retronasal passage is blocked.

— In addition to the four flavours mentioned above, the mouth is also sensitive to the temperature of the wine, its viscosity, the presence or absence of carbon dioxide and astringency (the effect of astringency is the contraction of mucous membranes in response to tannin, which is felt as the absence of lubrication from the saliva glands).

— It is by tasting that the balance and harmony of a wine is revealed or, conversely, that the characteristics of a badly constructed wine, which is not to be bought, are discovered.

White wines, light rosés and rosés are characterised by a good balance between acidity and sweetness.

Too much acidity: the wine is aggressive; not acidic enough, it is flat
Too sweet: the wine is heavy and thick; not sweet enough, it is thin and dull

In red wines there should be a balance between acidity, sweetness and tannin.

Excess acidity:	wine is too vigorous and often thin
Excess tannin:	wine is hard and astringent
Excess sweetness (rare):	heavy wine
Lack of acidity:	flabby wine
Lack of tannin:	unstructured, undefined wine
Lack of sweetness:	wine will dry out

A good wine balances the three components acidity, sweetness and tannin. These elements give it its richness of aroma. A great wine can be distinguished from a good wine by its rigorous, powerful but harmonious structure and the fullness of its aromatic complexity.

Examples of vocabulary used to describe the actual tasting of wine:

Minus points: unstructured, flabby, flat, thin, watery, limited, transparent, poor, heavy, massive, coarse, thick, unbalanced

Plus points: structured, well-built, well-constructed, balanced, fleshy (or full-bodied), elegant, fine, good texture, rich

After this analysis in the mouth, the wine is swallowed. The wine-lover then concentrates on measuring the persistence of its aromas, known familiarly as 'length in the mouth'. This estimation is expressed in caudals, one unit being equal quite simply, to one second. The 'longer' a wine is, the better the quality. The 'length in the mouth' alone is the only method of grading wines from the poorest to the greatest.

— This measuring in seconds is very simple and at the same time very complicated. It concerns only the length of the aromas, not the structure of the wine (acidity, bitterness, sweetness or alcohol content), which cannot be measured in this way.

Identifying wine

Tasting, like consuming, is a way of appreciating wine. It involves tasting it fully and deciding whether it is of average, good or excellent quality. Often, it is a matter of deciding whether it conforms to its type, so its origin also needs to be identified.

— Tasting to identify – that is recognition – is a sport, a kind of parlour game, but it is an impossible game to play without a minimum of information. It is easy enough to identify a variety such as a Cabernet-Sauvignon, but to know whether it comes from Italy, Languedoc, California, Chile, Argentina, Australia or South Africa is another matter. If the range is limited to France, it is possible to identify the larger regions, but being more precise presents serious problems. If there were six glasses representing six Médoc appellations (Listrac, Moulis, Margaux, Saint-Julien, Pauillac, Saint-Estèphe), how many people would be able to guess which was which without making any mistakes?

— A classic experiment that anyone can try proves how difficult tasting can be: the taster, blindfolded, tastes in random order red wines with very little tannin and non-aromatic white wines, preferably oak-aged. The taster has simply to distinguish between red and white (and vice versa); it is very rare not to make a mistake! Paradoxically, it is much easier to recognise a very characteristic wine whose memory and taste lingers on in your memory – but what are the chances of being offered the same wine?

Tasting with a view to purchasing

When you visit a vineyard with a view to purchasing wine, the first step towards choosing the wine is to taste it. Tasting is an act both of appreciation and of comparison. It is easy to compare two or three wines, but the situation becomes more complicated when price has to be taken into account. With a fixed budget – and budgets are invariably fixed – purchases are automatically eliminated. The tasting is further complicated when the purpose of the wine (for example, as an accompaniment to different kinds of food) is considered. To guess what you might be eating in ten years' time, and consequently to buy an appropriate wine for the occasion, has something of the magician's art about it. Comparative tasting, easy and simple in principle, becomes a delicate matter when the buyer has to guess the necessary length of ageing and peak periods of various wines. Wine-growers themselves sometimes make mistakes when they try to envisage the future of their wines and it is not unknown for wine-growers to buy back their own wine, originally sold at cut-price, because they had thought wrongly, that it would age badly.

— Nevertheless, some general principles can help in the appreciation of wine. To age well, wines must have a solid structure. They must have a sufficient degree of alcohol, and chaptalisation (the adding of sugar, regulated by law) can be a contributory factor if necessary. It is also advisable to pay attention to the levels of acidity and tannin. A wine that is too supple because its acidity is low or very low (which can, nevertheless, taste very pleasant), will be fragile and its longevity uncertain. A wine that is low in tannin will also not have much of a future. In the first example, the grapes will have been over-exposed to the sun and heat; in the second, the grapes will not have ripened sufficiently, will have been attacked by rot or will have suffered an inappropriate vinification.

— These two components of wine, acidity and tannin, can be measured. Acidity can be calculated by its equivalence in sulphuric acid, in grams per litre or in pH, and tannin can be measured according to the Folain scale, but this needs to be carried out in a laboratory.

— A wine with less than three grams per litre of acidity does not have much of a future. It is more difficult to give an exact estimation of the level of tannin below which long-term keeping would be problematic, but it is

Peak (in years)

W = White; R = Red	
Alsace (W): within the year Alsace Grand Cru (W): 1–4 Alsace (late harvest) (W): 8–12 Jura (W): 4; (R): 8 Jura, rosé: 6 Vin jaune (W): 20 Savoie (W): 1–2; (R): 2–4 Burgundy (W): 5 (R): 7 Burgundy, Grand (W): 8–10; (R): 10–15 Mâcon (W): 2–3; (R): 1–2 Beaujolais (R): within the year Beaujolais Crus (R): 1–4 Vallée du Rhône, Northern (W): 2–3; (R): 4–5 Côte-Rôtie, Hermitage etc. (W): 8; (R): 8–15	Vallée du Rhône, Southern (W): 2; (R): 4–8 Loire (W): 1–5; (R): 3–10 Loire, sweet, rich (W): 10–15 Périgord wines (W): 2–3; (R): 3–4 Périgord wines, sweet (W): 6–8 Bordeaux (W): 2–3; (R): 6–8 Grands Bordeaux (W): 4–10; (R): 10–15 Bordeaux, sweet (W): 10–15 Jurançon, dry (W): 2–4 Jurançon, sweet, rich (W): 6–10 Madiran (R): 5–12 Cahors (R): 3–10 Gaillac (W): 1–3; (R): 2–4 Languedoc (W): 1–2; (R): 2–4 Côtes de Provence (W): 1–2; (R): 2–4 Corsican (W): 1–2; (R): 2–4

NB:
Do not confuse peak period with maximum longevity.
A warm cellar or one with a variable temperature accelerates the ageing process.

useful to know what the scale is, as very ripe, smooth tannins are sometimes underestimated on tasting and are not always revealed.

— In any case, wine should be tasted in good conditions, without the ambience of the wine-cellar taking over. Avoid tasting immediately after a meal or after consuming a liqueur, coffee, chocolate or mints, or after smoking. Beware if a wine-grower offers nuts, because they make any wine taste better! Beware also of cheese, as this changes the sensitivity of the palate; if absolutely necessary, eat a piece of plain bread.

Practising tasting

Like any other technique, tasting can be learned. It can be practised at home following the guidelines above or, if you are very keen, you can enrol on one of the ever-increasing number of courses offered by various private organisations. The best of such courses cover a whole range of topics in addition to just tasting, including food and wines, the discovery of the larger wine-producing areas (not only French regions) through tasting, an analysis of the influence of grape varieties, vintages and soils, the effect of vinification techniques and organised visits to wine estates in the company of the vineyard owner.

Serving wine

In a restaurant serving wine is the responsibility of the wine waiter. At home no wine waiter will be available, and it pays to learn some of the tricks of the trade. There are many of these, starting with choosing the bottles that are best suited to the dishes making up the meal and those that have reached their peak.

— Individual taste does come into matching food and wine, but, centuries of experience have made it possible to establish some general principles, ideal combinations and major incompatibilities.

— The rate at which wines age varies tremendously. The wine-lover who wants nothing but the best will be interested only in the wine's peak period. Depending on the appellation, variety, soil and vinification, this could be any time between one and twenty years. Depending on the year on the label, the same wine could age two or three times more rapidly. However, it is possible to establish average times that can be used as a basis and that can be adapted to the cellar and the information on the vintage cards.

Methods of serving

Care must be taken with the wine from its selection in the cellar to its arrival in the glass. The older the wine, the more care should be taken. The bottle should be taken from its stack and gently returned to an upright position, ready to be taken to table, unless it is going to be put straight into a special pouring basket.

Wines of average quality should be served simply. A very old and consequently very delicate wine should be poured from the basket, where it has been carefully placed in the same position as it was in the stack. Younger wines and robust wines should be decanted, either to oxygenate them because they still contain gas left over from fermentation or to start oxidisation, which improves the taste of the wine, or simply to separate clear wine from sediment at the bottom of the bottle. In the last case, the wine must be decanted with care and should be done in front of a light source, traditionally a candle – a custom that predates the arrival of electric lighting and has no particular advantage – to allow the sediments and cloudy wine to stay in the bottle.

Opening the bottle and serving

Professor Peynaud, France's leading scientific authority on wine-tasting, maintains that it is not necessary to open a bottle a long time before drinking the wine, because the surface area of the wine that is exposed to the air (at the neck of the bottle) is too small to make a difference. However, the table on the following page summarises traditional usage that, if it does not always improve the wine, never spoils it.

Opening

The capsule should be cut below the ring or in the middle of it. The wine should never come into contact with the metal of the capsule. If the neck is sealed with wax, chip the wax away gently or, better still, remove the wax from the top part of the neck with a knife; this method is preferable because it does not disturb the wine or the bottle.

To remove the cork, a traditional-style corkscrew (or one with arms, if handled gently) should be used. Theoretically, the cork should not be pierced all the way through. Once removed, it should be smelt to make sure that there are no bacterial odours present and that there is no corky smell. Afterwards, as a final test, the wine should be tasted before it is served.

White aromatic wines Red or white nouveau wines Red and white young wines Rosé wines	Open, drink straight away Bottle vertical
White Loire wines Sweet white wines	Open, wait an hour Bottle vertical
Young red wines Red wines at their peak	Decant half an hour to 2 hours before drinking
Old delicate red wines	Open in pouring basket and serve immediately; in some cases, decant and drink immediately

The right temperature

A wine can be completely spoiled by serving it at the wrong temperature; conversely a wine can be improved by being served at the right temperature. It is rare to achieve this without the help of a wine thermometer – a pocket version is handy for taking to restaurants and for dipping in the wine when at home. The temperature for serving wine depends on its appellation (its type), its age and, in a few cases, the temperature of the room. It should be remembered that wine warms up in the glass.

Bordeaux Grands Vins, red	16–17°C	60.8–62.6°F
Burgundy Grands Vins, red	15–16°C	59–60.8°F
Quality red wines, red Grands Vins before their peak	14–16°C	57.2–60.8°F
White, dry Grands Vins	14–16°C	57.2–60.8°F
Light, fruity, young red wines	11–12°C	51.8–53.6°F
Rosé wines, nouveau wines	10–12°C	50–53.6°F
Dry white wines, red vins de pays	10–12°C	50–53.6°F
Average white wines, white vins de pays	8–10°C	46.4–50°F
Champagne, sparkling	7–8°C	44.6–46.4°F
Sweet	6°C	42.8°F

These temperatures should be increased by one or two degrees if the wine is old.

__ There is a tendency to serve wines slightly more chilled when they are offered as an apéritif and warmer when they are to accompany a meal. Similarly, the climate of the area and the temperature of the room should be taken into account; in very hot weather a wine drunk at 11°C (51.8°F) can seem icy and it is therefore advisable to serve it at 13° or even 14°C (55.4° or 57.2°F).

__ Nevertheless, the 20°C (68°F) mark should not be passed because physico-chemical phenomena, independent of the environment, can cause irreversible changes, altering the qualities of the wine and the pleasure that we expect from it.

Glasses

Each region has its own particular glass. In practice, and to avoid being excessively purist, it is best to use either a universal-style glass (a tasting glass) or the two sorts most commonly used, the Bordeaux and the Burgundy. Whichever glass is used, it should be filled in moderation, nearer one-third full rather than half full.

In the restaurant

In the restaurant the wine waiter looks after the bottle and examines the cork but allows the person who ordered the wine to taste it. Before this, the wine waiter will have recommended wines to accompany the dishes.

__ Reading the wine list is instructive, not only because it reveals the secrets of the cellar, which is its function, but because it is also indicative of the level of competence of the wine waiter, the cellar-master or the manager. A good wine list should definitely include the following information for each wine: appellation, vintage, place where it was bottled and the name of the wine-merchant or owner responsible for the wine. This last piece of information is often omitted – for no good reason.

__ A good wine list should offer a wide range of appellations and a variety of vintages of different qualities (some restaurateurs have the annoying habit of offering only average quality vintages). An intelligent list should be adapted to the style or specialities of the cuisine and should offer a good selection of local wines.

— Sometimes, house wine is on offer. It is possible to buy a pleasant wine that does not benefit from an AOC, but these wines are never great wines.

Wine bistros and wine bars

In France there have always been wine bistros selling good-quality wine by the glass, often wines selected by the bistro owner on personal visits to vineyards. Selections of cold meat and cheese are usually on offer to customers in these establishments.

— In the 1970s a new generation of French wine bistros appeared, often referred to as 'wine bars'. The perfecting of an apparatus that protects wine in open bottles with a layer of nitrogen (*le cruover*) has allowed these establishments to offer customers very good wines with prestigious vintages. More sophisticated menus have been developed to accompany these wines.

VINTAGES

All quality wines have vintages. The only exceptions to this rule are a few particular wines and some Champagnes, whose own individual production involves the blending of several different years.

— Having said this, what should we make of a bottle that does not have a vintage? There are two possible reasons for the omission: either the year is inadmissible because its reputation is so tarnished within the appellation, or it cannot be given a year because it is a mixture of several years blended together (known among professionals as *vins de plusieurs années*). The quality of the product depends on the talent of the blender; generally, a blended wine is superior to each of its individual components, but it is not advisable to age this type of bottle. A wine from a great year is concentrated and balanced and is usually, but not always, the result of small yields, harvested early.

— In every case, great vintages come only from perfectly healthy grapes, untainted by rot. To obtain a great vintage, it does not matter what the weather is like at the beginning of the vegetative cycle. It can even be said that a few mishaps such as frost or *coulure* (the falling of young grapes before maturation) are a good thing, as they reduce the number of grapes per bunch, thus reducing the volume. On the other hand, the period between 15 August to harvest time (end of September) is crucial; a maximum of sun and heat are necessary. The year 1961, *the* year of the 20th century, was exemplary; everything happened as it should. On the other hand, 1963, 1965 and 1968 were disastrous years, because they suffered from a combination of cold and rain, which meant that the grapes did not mature properly. There was a glut and the grapes were swollen with water. The combination of rain and heat is not much better as warm water invites rot. This was the stumbling-block that tripped up the potentially great 1976 vintage in the south west. Progress in the development of treatments to protect grapes, in particular from the grape worm and from rot, have led to quality harvests that previously would have been spoiled. These treatments also make it possible to wait with equanimity for the grapes to ripen fully (which improves the quality) even if the immediate meteorological conditions are not encouraging. From 1978 onwards, there have been some excellent late-harvested vintages.

— It is customary to record and grade the quality of vintages in table form. These grades are averages only and do not take into account microclimates, or the heroic efforts of hand sorting the grapes at harvest time or the vagaries of the wine-making process. For example, a Graves, Domaine de

Chevalier from 1965 – which elsewhere was a terrible year – proves that a great wine can be produced even during a year that is ranked at zero!

Vintage table (from 0 to 20)

	Bordeaux Red	Bordeaux White, Sweet	Bordeaux White, dry	Burgundy Red	Burgundy White	Champagne	Loire	Rhône	Alsace
1900	19	19	17	13		17			
1901	11	14							
1902									
1903	14	7	11						
1904	15	17		16		19		18	
1905	14	12							
1906	16	16		19	18				
1907	12	10		15					
1908	13	16							
1909	10	7							
1910									
1911	14	14		19	19	20	19	19	
1912	10	11							
1913	7	7							
1914	13	15				18			
1915		16		16	15	15	12	15	
1916	15	15		13	11	12	11	10	
1917	14	16		11	11	13	12	9	
1918	16	12		13	12	12	11	14	
1919	15	10		18	18	15	18	15	15
1920	17	16		13	14	14	11	13	10
1921	16	20		16	20	20	20	13	20
1922	9	11		9	16	4	7	6	4
1923	12	13		16	18	17	18	18	14
1924	15	16		13	14	11	14	17	11
1925	6	11		6	5	3	4	8	6
1926	16	17		16	16	15	13	13	14
1927	7	14		7	5	5	3	4	
1928	19	17		18	20	20	17	17	17
1929	20	20		20	19	19	18	19	18
1930							3	4	3
1931	2	2		2	3		3	5	3
1932				2	3	3	3	3	7
1933	11	9		16	18	16	17	17	15
1934	17	17		17	18	17	16	17	16

1935	7	12		13	16	10	15	5	14
1936	7	11		9	10	9	12	13	9
1937	16	20		18	18	18	16	17	17
1938	8	12		14	10	10	12	8	9
1939	11	16		9	9	9	10	8	3
1940	13	12		12	8	8	11	5	10
1941	12	10		9	12	10	7	5	5
1942	12	16		14	12	16	11	14	14
1943	15	17		17	16	17	13	17	16
1944	13	11	12	10	10		6	8	
1945	20	20	18	20	18	20	19	18	20
1946	14	9	10	10	13	10	12	17	9
1947	18	20	18	18	18	18	20	18	17
1948	16	16	16	10	14	11	12		15
1949	19	20	18	20	18	17	16	17	19
1950	13	18	16	11	19	16	14	15	14
1951	8	6	6	7	6	7	7	8	8
1952	16	16	16	16	18	16	15	16	14
1953	19	17	16	18	17	17	18	14	18
1954	10			14	11	15	9	13	9
1955	16	19	18	15	18	19	16	15	17
1956	5						9	12	9
1957	10	15		14	15		13	16	13
1958	11	14		10	9		12	14	12
1959	19	20	18	19	17	17	19	15	20
1960	11	10	10	10	7	14	9	12	12
1961	20	15	16	18	17	16	16	18	19
1962	16	16	16	17	19	17	15	16	14
1963					10				
1964	16	9	13	16	17	18	16	14	18
1965			12				8		
1966	17	15	16	18	18	17	15	16	12
1967	14	18	16	15	16		13	15	14
1968									
1969	10	13	12	19	18	16	15	16	16
1970	17	17	18	15	15	17	15	15	14
1971	16	17	19	18	20	16	17	15	18
1972	10		9	11	13		9	14	9
1973	13	12		12	16	16	16	13	16
1974	11	14		12	13	8	11	12	13
1975	18	17	18		11	18	15	10	15

1976	15	19	16	18	15	15	18	16	19
1977	12	7	14	11	12	9	11	11	12
1978	17	14	17	19	17	16	17	19	15
1979	16	18	18	15	16	15	14	16	16
1980	13	17	18	12	12	14	13	15	10
1981	16	16	17	14	15	15	15	14	17
1982	18	14	16	14	16	16	14	13	15
1983	17	17	16	15	16	15	12	16	20
1984	13	13	12	13	14	5	10	11	15
1985	18	15	14	17	17	17	16	16	19
1986	17	17	12	12	15	9	13	10	10
1987	13	11	16	12	11	10	13	8	13
1988	16	19	18	16	14	15	16	18	17
1989	18	19	18	16	18	16	20	16	16
1990	18	20	17	18	16	19	17	17	18
1991	13	14	13	14	15	11	12	13	13
1992	12	10	14	15	17	12	14	12	12
1993	13	8	15	14	13	12	13	13	13
1994	14	14	17	14	16	12	14	14	12
1995	16	18	17	14	16	16	17	16	12
1996	15	18	16	17	18	19	17	14	12
1997	14	18	14	14	17	15	16	14	13
1998	15	16	14	15	15	13	14	18	13
1999	14	17	13	13	12	15	12	16	10

The areas encircled with a thick line indicate wines that should be cellared.
Sweet wines from the Loire were given 20 for the year 1990.

Which vintages should be drunk now?
Wines evolve differently according to whether they are created during a gloomy year or a sunny year and also according to their appellation, their position in the hierarchy within the appellation, their vinification and their ageing, the latter stages of which depend also on the cellar in which they have been stored.

— The vintage table includes only good wines from recent years, which are therefore available, provided they have been looked after correctly. It does not include exceptional wines or exceptional Cuvées. Wines are graded at their peak, and the table does not include the current evolution of old vintages.

COOKING WITH WINE

Cooking with wine is not a recent phenomenon. The Roman gourmet Apicius gave us a recipe for suckling pig in wine sauce (it was a *Vin de Paille*, the grapes being ripened on a layer of straw). Wine is used in cooking for the flavour it brings to the dishes and for its digestive properties, which are due to the glycerine and tannin it contains. Even non-drinkers may approve, as alcohol all but disappears on cooking.

— The history of cooking can be traced through wine. Wine marinades were invented to preserve pieces of meat – today we use them for their taste – and the reduction of marinades that took place during cooking was the origin of sauces. Sometimes, meat was actually cooked in wine marinades, a method that gave rise to the development of such dishes as stews, casseroles, court-bouillons and *oeufs en meurette* (eggs in red wine sauce).

Recommendations

Do not waste old vintages in cooking. It is expensive, ineffective and can be detrimental.

Never use vins ordinaires or very light wines in cooking; their reduction only brings out their lack of presence.

A corky taste disappears in cooking, so use bottles that have this defect.

Drink the same wine that has been used in the preparation of the dish or one that has the same origin as an accompaniment.

WINE VINEGAR

Wine is man's friend, but vinegar is wine's enemy. However, it would be wrong to conclude that vinegar is man's enemy too – wines and vinegars each have their roles to play in the range of flavours that people enjoy. To throw away quality wines that are a little musty, corky or oxidised would be a shame as they can easily be turned into vinegar. A domestic vinegar-maker is a 3- to 5-litre receptacle, made of wood or, even better, glazed earthenware, with a tap. The acidity of vinegar acts as a counterbalance to other flavours. To keep its fieriness in check, gourmet-style aromatic vinegars have been developed. Many strong flavours blend harmoniously together, including garlic, shallots, pickled onions, mustard grains, peppercorns, cloves, elderflower, chicory, rose petals, bay leaves, thyme, parsley and so on.

Recommendations

Never leave a vinegar-maker in a cellar.

Whenever the so-called *mère du vinaigre* or 'vinegar mother' (a viscous mass) develops in the vinegar, it should be quickly removed.

Place the vinegar-maker in a warm room at 20°C (68°F).

Never hermetically seal it because the acetic bacteria, which transform the alcohol in the wine into acetic acid, cannot live without air.

Never put herbs or spices in the vinegar-maker. The vinegar needs to be extracted from the vinegar-maker and placed with the seasoning in another receptacle, this time preferably hermetically sealed.

Never use wine that has no stated origin in the vinegar-maker.

The vinegar-maker must be in constant use. Each time vinegar is withdrawn from the vinegar-maker, an equivalent volume of wine should be added.

A vinegar that is left for more than two or three months will taste bitter. It will lose its wine flavour and will be of no use.

FOOD AND WINE

Nothing is more difficult than finding an ideal wine to accompany a dish. But should there be such a thing? The marrying of wine and food should not be a monogamous affair; the variety that French wines offer should be an opportunity to experiment, and a good cellar should allow us to experiment with different combinations in order to extend our range of eating and drinking pleasure.

HORS D'OEUVRE

ANCHOVY PURÉE ON TOAST
- Côtes du Roussillon, rosé
- Coteaux d'Aix-en-Provence, rosé
- Alsace, Sylvaner

ASPARAGUS WITH CREAMY HOLLANDAISE SAUCE
- Alsace, Muscat

AVOCADO PEAR
- Champagne
- Bugey, white
- Bordeaux, dry

FOIE GRAS
- Barsac
- Corton-Charlemagne
- Listrac
- Banyuls Rimage

FOIE GRAS IN BRIOCHE
- Alsace Tokay, selection of quality wines
- Montrachet
- Pécharmant

FROGS' LEGS
- Corbières, white
- Entre-Deux-Mers
- Touraine Sauvignon

GRILLED FOIE GRAS
- Jurançon
- Graves, red
- Condrieu

GRILLED RED PEPPERS IN VINAIGRETTE
- Clairette de Bellegarde
- Muscadet
- Mâcon Lugny, white

PROVENÇALE ARTICHOKES
- Coteaux d'Aix-en-Provence, rosé
- Loire, rosé
- Bordeaux, rosé

SALADE NIÇOISE
- Alsace Sylvaner
- Côtes du Rhône, red
- Coteaux d'Aix-en-Provence, rosé

SNAILS À LA BOURGUIGNONNE
- Bourgogne Aligoté
- Alsace Riesling
- Touraine Sauvignon

SOYA BEAN SALAD
- Alsace Tokay
- Clairette du Languedoc
- Muscadet

COLD MEATS

BAYONNE HAM
- Côtes du Rhône-Villages
- Bordeaux, clairet
- Corbières, rosé

BRAISED HAM
- Alsace Tokay
- Côtes du Rhône, red
- Côtes du Roussillon, rosé

CHICKEN LIVER TERRINE
- Meursault-Charmes
- Saint-Nicolas de Bourgueil
- Morgon

COLD COOKED SAUSAGE
- Côtes du Rhône-Villages
- Beaujolais
- Côtes de Roussillon, rosé

HAM FLAVOURED WITH PARSLEY
- Chassagne Montrachet, white
- Coteaux de Tricastin, red
- Beaujolais, red

HARE PÂTÉ
- Côtes de Duras, red
- Saumur-Champigny
- Moulin à Vent

RILLETTES (POTTED PORK)
- Burgundy, red
- Alsace Pinot Noir
- Touraine Gamay

RILLONS (CUBES OF PORK)
- Touraine Cabernet
- Beaujolais-Villages
- Loire, rosé

SMOKED HAM (WILD BOAR)
- Côtes de Saint-Mont, red
- Bandol, red
- Sancerre, white

SHELLFISH

BROCHETTE OF SCALLOPS
- Graves, white
- Alsace Sylvaner
- Beaujolais-Villages, red

CHARENTAIS MUSSEL STEW
- Saint-Véran
- Bergerac, dry
- Haut-Poitou, Chardonnay

CLAMS WITH GRILLED CHEESE TOPPING
- Pacherenc du Vic-Bilh
- Rully, white
- Beaujolais, white

CRAB COCKTAIL
- Jurançon, dry
- Fiefs Vendéens, white
- Bordeaux Sauvignon, dry

CRAYFISH IN COURT-BOUILLON
- Sancerre, white
- Côtes du Rhône, white
- Gaillac, white

CRAYFISH WITH MAYONNAISE
- Patrimonio, white
- Alsace Riesling
- Savoie Apremont

DUBLIN BAY PRAWNS IN COGNAC
- Chablis, Premier Cru
- Graves, white
- Muscadet de Sèvres-et-Maine

FRESH RAW MUSSELS
- Coteaux du Languedoc, white
- Muscadet de Sèvre-et-Maine
- Coteaux d'Aix-en-Provence, white

GRILLED LOBSTER
- Hermitage, white
- Pouilly-Fuissé
- Savennières

LOBSTER IN TOMATO AND WHITE WINE SAUCE
- Arbois, jaune
- Juliénas

MOULES MARINIÈRES
- Burgundy, white
- Alsace Pinot
- Bordeaux Sauvignon, dry

MUSSELS WITH SPINACH
- Muscadet
- Bouzeron Bourgogne Aligoté
- Coteaux Champenois, white

OYSTERS
- Muscadet
- Bourgogne Aligoté
- Alsace Sylvaner
- Chablis
- Beaujolais Nouveau, red

OYSTERS IN CHAMPAGNE
- Burgundy, Hautes-Côtes de Nuit, white
- Coteaux Champenois, white
- Roussette de Savoie

PRAWNS WITH MAYONNAISE
- Burgundy, white
- Alsace Riesling
- Haut-Poitou Sauvignon

SEAFOOD PLATTER
- Chablis
- Muscadet
- Alsace Sylvaner

SHELLFISH SALAD WITH CUCUMBER
- Graves, white
- Muscadet, white
- Alsace Klevner

STUFFED CLAMS
- Graves, white
- Montagny
- Anjou, white

STUFFED SQUID
- Mâcon-Villages
- Good-quality Côtes de Bordeaux
- Gaillac, rosé

FISH

BARQUETTES GIRONDINES (PASTRY SHELLS FILLED WITH A SELECTION OF SEA-FOOD)
- Bâtard-Montrachet
- Good-quality Graves,
- Quincy

BOUILLABAISSE (FISH STEW)
- Côtes du Roussillon, white
- Coteaux d'Aix-en-Provence, white
- Muscadet des Coteaux de la Loire

BOURRIDE (CREAMY FISH SOUP WITH AÏOLI)
- Coteaux d'Aix-en-Provence, white
- Loire, rosé
- Bordeaux, rosé

BRILL WITH WHITE WINE AND SHELLFISH SAUCE
- Graves, white
- Puligny-Montrachet
- Coteaux de Languedoc, white

COD IN GARLIC SAUCE (AÏOLI)
- Coteaux d'Aix-en-Provence, rosé
- Bordeaux, rosé
- Haut-Poitou, rosé

COLD HAKE WITH MAYONNAISE
- Pouilly-Fuissé
- Savoie
- Chignin
- Bergeron
- Alsace Klevner

COQUILLES DE POISSON (SELECTION OF FISH SERVED IN SCALLOP SHELLS)
- Saint-Aubin, white
- Saumur, dry white
- Crozes-Hermitage, white

DEEP-FRIED WHITING
- Alsace Gutedal
- Entre-Deux-Mers
- Seyssel

FILLET OF SOLE BONNE FEMME
- Graves, white
- Chablis, Grand Cru
- Sancerre, white

FILLET OF TURBOT IN FLAKY PASTRY
- Chevalier-Montrachet
- Crozes-Hermitage, white

FISH STEW
- Chablis, Premier Cru
- Arbois, white
- Alsace Riesling

FRESHWATER FISH STEW WITH WHITE WINE
- Meursault
- L'Étoile
- Mâcon-Villages

GRILLED COD
- Gros Plant du Pays Nantais
- Loire, rosé
- Coteaux d'Aix-en-Provence, rosé

GRILLED RED MULLET
- Chassagne-Montrachet, white
- Hermitage, white
- Bergerac

GRILLED SALMON STEAK
- Chassagne-Montrachet,white
- Cahors
- Côtes du Rhône, rosé

GRILLED SARDINES
- Clairette de Bellegarde
- Jurançon, dry
- Bourgogne Aligoté

GRILLED SEA-BASS
- Auxey-Duresses, white
- Bellet, white
- Bergerac, dry

LAMPREY IN RED WINE SAUCE
- Graves, red
- Bergerac, red
- Bordeaux, rosé

MACKEREL IN WHITE WINE
- Alsace Sylvaner
- Haut-Poitou Sauvignon
- Quincy

MONKFISH
- Mâcon-Villages
- Châteauneuf-de-Papes, white
- Bandol, rosé

OYSTERS FROM ARCACHON IN WINE SAUCE
- Graves, white
- Bordeaux, dry
- Jurançon, dry

PAN-FRIED EEL WITH GARLIC AND PARSLEY
- Corbières, rosé
- Gros Plant du Pays Nantais
- Blaye, white

PIKE QUENELLES (DUMPLINGS) IN WINE SAUCE
- Montrachet
- Pouilly-Vinzelles
- Beaujolais-Villages, red

RED TUNA WITH ONIONS
- Coteaux d'Aix, white
- Coteaux du Languedoc, white
- Côtes de Duras Sauvignon

ROUILLE SÉTOISE (SELECTION OF SEA-FOOD IN SPICY GARLIC SAUCE)
- Clairette du Languedoc
- Côtes du Roussillon, rosé
- Loire, rosé

SALMON IN PASTRY
- Pouilly-Vinzelles
- Graves, white
- Loire, rosé

SALMON ROE
- Haut-Poitou, rosé
- Graves, red
- Côtes du Rhône, red

SALT COD
- Haut-Poitou, rosé
- Bandol, rosé
- Corbières, rosé

SHAD WITH SORREL
- Anjou, white
- Loire, rosé
- Haut-Poitou, Chardonnay

SMALL FRIED FISH (WHITEBAIT)
- Beaujolais, white
- Béarn, white
- Fiefs Vendéens, white

SMOKED SALMON
- Puligny-Montrachet, Premier Cru
- Pouilly-Fumé
- Bordeaux Sauvignon, dry

SOLE MEUNIÈRE
- Meursault, white
- Alsace Riesling
- Entre-Deux-Mers

SOUFFLÉ WITH CRAYFISH SAUCE
- Bâtard-Montrachet
- Crozes-Hermitage, white
- Bergerac, dry

STUFFED CARP
- Montagny
- Touraine, Azay-le-Rideau, white
- Alsace, Pinot

STUFFED CRAB
- Premières Côtes de Bordeaux, white
- Burgundy, white
- Muscadet

TROUT WITH ALMONDS
- Chassagne-Montrachet, white
- Alsace Klevner
- Côtes du Roussillon

TURBOT WITH HOLLANDAISE SAUCE
- Graves, white
- Saumur, white
- Hermitage, white

WHITE TUNA IN BASQUE SAUCE
- Graves, white
- Pacherenc de Vic-Bilh
- Gaillac, white

ZANDER (PIKE PERCH) IN BUTTERY SAUCE
- Muscadet
- Saumur, white
- Saint-Joseph, white

RED AND WHITE MEAT

Lamb

COLD LAMB WITH MAYONNAISE
- Saint-Aubin, white
- Bordeaux, red
- Entre-Deux-Mers

FILLET OF LAMB EN CROÛTE
- Pomerol
- Mercurey
- Coteaux du Tricastin

LAMB CARBONADE
- Graves de Vayres, red
- Fitou
- Crozes-Hermitage, red

LAMB CURRY
- Montagne Saint-Émilion
- Alsace Tokay
- Côtes du Rhône

LAMB STEW (DAUBE)
- Patrimonio, red
- Côtes du Rhône-Villages, red
- Morgon

LAMB STEW (NAVARIN)
- Anjou, red
- Bordeaux Côtes-de-Francs, red
- Bourgogne Marsannay, red

LAMB STEW FLAVOURED WITH THYME
- Châteauneuf-du-Pape, red
- Saint-Chinian
- Fleurie

MARLY LAMB CHOPS (FROM BEST END OF NECK)
- Saint-Julien
- Ajaccio
- Coteaux du Lyonnais

ROAST BARON OF LAMB
- Haut-Médoc
- Savoie-Mondeuse
- Minervois

ROAST LAMB
- Morey-Saint-Denis
- Saint-Émilion
- Côte de Provence, red

SADDLE OF LAMB FLAVOURED WITH HERBS
- Vin de Corse, red
- Côtes du Rhône, red
- Coteaux de Giennois, red

SAUTÉED LAMB PROVENÇALE STYLE
- Gigondas
- Côtes de Provence, red
- Bourgogne Passetoutgrain, red

SHOULDER OF LAMB IN ONION SAUCE
- Hermitage, red
- Côtes de Bourg, red
- Moulin à Vent

STUFFED BREAST OF LAMB
- Côtes de Jura, red
- Graves, red
- Haut-Poitou Gamay

Beef

BEEF FONDUE BURGUNDY-STYLE
- Bordeaux, red
- Côtes du Ventoux, red
- Burgundy, rosé

BEEF STEW
- Buzet, red
- Côtes du Vivrais, red
- Arbois, red

BEEF STEW WITH RED WINE
- Lirac, red
- Côtes du Luberon, red
- Costières de Nîmes, red

BOEUF BOURGUIGNON
- Rully, red
- Saumur, red
- Côte du Marmandais, red

ENTRECOTE STEAK WITH BORDELAISE SAUCE
- Saint-Julien
- Saint-Joseph, red
- Côtes du Roussillon-Villages

FILLET OF BEEF DUCHESSE
- Côte-Rôtie
- Gigondas
- Graves, red

FILLET STEAK WITH BÉARNAISE SAUCE
- Listrac
- Saint-Aubin, red
- Touraine Amboise, red

POT-AU-FEU
- Anjou, red
- Bordeaux, red
- Beaujolais, red

ROAST BEEF (COLD)
- Madiran
- Beaune, red
- Cahors

ROAST BEEF (HOT)
- Moulis
- Aloxe-Corton
- Côtes du Rhône, red

STEAK CHATEAUBRIAND
- Margaux
- Alsace Pinot
- Coteaux du Tricastin

STEAK MAÎTRE D'HÔTEL (WITH PARSLEY AND LEMON SAUCE)
- Bergerac, red
- Arbois, rosé
- Chénas

Pork

ANDOUILLETTE (CHITTERLING SAUSAGE) WITH CREAM SAUCE
- Touraine, white
- Burgundy, white
- Saint-Joseph, white

CASSOULET (CASSEROLE OF WHITE BEANS AND PORK, GOOSE OR DUCK MEAT)
- Côtes du Frontonnais, red
- Minervois, red
- Bergerac, red

CHOUCROUTE
- Alsace Riesling
- Alsace Sylvaner

COLD ROAST PORK
- Burgundy, white
- Lirac, red
- Bordeaux, dry

CONFIT
- Tursan, red
- Corbières, red
- Cahors

COUNTRY-STYLE SOUP WITH CABBAGE
- Côtes du Luberon
- Côte de Brouilly
- Bourgogne Aligoté

GRILLED ANDOUILLETTE
- Coteaux Champenois, white
- Petit Chablis
- Beaujolais, red

GRILLED TOULOUSE SAUSAGE
- Saint-Joseph or Bergerac, red
- Côtes du Frontonnais, rosé

PORK CHOP WITH ONION AND WHITE WINE SAUCE
- Burgundy, white
- Côtes d'Auvergne, red
- Bordeaux, clairet

ROAST PORK FLAVOURED WITH SAGE
- Rully, white
- Côtes du Rhône, red
- Minervois, rosé

SHOULDER OF PORK WITH SAUVIGNON
- Bergerac, dry
- Menetou-Salon
- Bordeaux, rosé

STUFFED CABBAGE
- Côtes du Rhône, red
- Touraine Gamay
- Bordeaux Sauvignon, dry

SUCKLING PIG EN GELÉE
- Graves de Vayres, white
- Costières du Gard, rosé
- Beaujolais-Villages, red

Veal

BRAISED TOPSIDE OF VEAL
- Mâcon-Villages, white
- Côtes de Duras, red
- Brouilly

CALVES LIVER À L'ANGLAISE
- Médoc
- Coteaux d'Aix-en-Provence, red
- Haut-Poitou, rosé

GRILLED VEAL CHOP
- Côtes du Rhône, red
- Anjou, white
- Burgundy, rosé

KIDNEY BROCHETTES
- Cornas
- Beaujolais-Villages
- Coteaux du Languedoc, rosé

SAUTÉED KIDNEYS IN VIN JAUNE
- Arbois, white
- Gaillac, Vin de Voile
- Bourgogne Aligoté

VEAL ESCALOPE IN BREADCRUMBS
- Côtes du Jura, white
- Corbières, white

Côtes du Ventoux, red

VEAL KIDNEYS WITH MARROW-BONE
- Saint-Émilion
- Saumur-Champigny
- Coteaux d'Aix-en-Provence, rosé

VEAL MARENGO (TOMATO AND WINE SAUCE)
- Côtes de Duras Merlot
- Alsace Klevner
- Coteaux du Tricastin, rosé
- Lirac, rosé

VEAL PARCELS
- Anjou Gamay
- Minervois, rosé
- Costières de Nîmes, white

VEAL STEW IN WHITE SAUCE À L'ANCIENNE
- Arbois, white
- Alsace Riesling, Grand Cru
- Côtes de Provence, rosé

VEAL SWEETBREADS WITH LANGOUSTINES
- Graves, white
- Alsace Tokay
- Bordeaux, rosé

POULTRY, RABBIT

BARBARY DUCK WITH OLIVES
- Savoie-Mondeuse, red
- Canon-Fronsac
- Anjou Cabernet, red

BREAST OF DUCK WITH GREEN PEPPER
- Saint-Joseph, red
- Bourgueil, red
- Bergerac, red

CHICKEN COOKED WITH SALT CRUST
- Listrac
- Mâcon-Villages, white
- Côtes du Rhône, red

CHICKEN CURRY
- Montagne Saint-Émilion
- Alsace Tokay
- Côtes du Rhône

CHICKEN WITH TRUFFLE SAUCE
- Chevalier-Montrachet
- Arbois, white
- Juliénas

COQ AU VIN
- Ladoix
- Côte de Beaune
- Châteauneuf-du-Pape, red
- Touraine Cabernet

DUCK HEART BROCHETTES
- Saint-Georges-Saint-Émilion
- Chinon
- Côtes du Rhône-Villages

DUCK WITH ORANGE
- Côtes du Jura, jaune
- Cahors
- Graves, red

DUCK WITH TURNIPS
- Puisseguin Saint- Émilion
- Saumur-Champigny
- Coteaux d'Aix-en-Provence, red

DUCKLING WITH PEACHES
- Banyuls
- Chinon, red
- Graves, red

GUINEA-FOWL WITH ARMAGNAC
- Saint-Estèphe
- Chassagne-Montrachet, red
- Fleurie

PIGEON WITH DICED VEGETABLES
- Crozes-Hermitage, red
- Bordeaux, red
- Touraine Gamay

POULET BASQUAISE
- Côtes de Duras, Sauvignon
- Bordeaux, dry
- Coteaux du Languedoc, rosé

RABBIT FRICASEE
- Touraine, rosé
- Côtes de Blaye, white
- Beaujolais-Villages, red

ROAST CAPON
- Burgundy, white
- Touraine-Mesland
- Côtes du Rhône, rosé

ROAST RABBIT WITH MUSTARD
- Sancerre, red
- Tavel
- Côtes de Provence, white
- Graves, white
- Châteaumeillant, rosé

SAUTÉED CHICKEN WITH MOREL MUSHROOMS
- Savigny-lès-Beaune, red
- Arbois, white
- Sancerre, white

SPIT-ROASTED TURKEY
- Monthélie

STUFFED DUCK
- Saint-Émilion, Grand Cru
- Bandol, red
- Buzet, red

STUFFED GOOSE
- Anjou Cabernet, red
- Côtes du Marmandais, red
- Beaujolais-Villages

TURKEY WITH CHESTNUTS
- Saint-Joseph, red
- Sancerre, red
- Meursault, white

TURKEY ESCALOPES WITH ROQUEFORT
- Côtes du Jura, white
- Bourgogne Aligoté
- Coteaux d'Aix-en-Provence, rosé

GAME

BRAISED WILD BOAR
- Fronsac
- Châteauneuf-du-Pape, red
- Moulin à Vent

FILLET OF WILD BOAR WITH BORDELAISE SAUCE
- Pomerol
- Bandol
- Gigondas

FLAMBÉED WOODCOCK
- Pauillac
- Musigny
- Hermitage

HARE À LA ROYALE
- Saint-Joseph, red
- Volnay
- Pécharmant

HAUNCH OF WILD BOAR WITH VENISON SAUCE
- Chambertin
- Montage Saint-Émilion
- Corbières, red

JUGGED HARE
- Canon-Fronsac
- Bonnes-Mares
- Minervois, red

PARTRIDGE À LA CATALANE
- Maury
- Côtes du Roussillon, red
- Beaujolais-Villages

PARTRIDGE WITH CABBAGE
- Burgundy, Irancy
- Arbois, rosé
- Cornas

PHEASANT IN CHARTREUSE
- Moulis
- Pommard
- Saint-Nicolas de Bourgeuil

ROAST PARTRIDGE
- Haut-Médoc
- Vosne-Romanée
- Bourgueil

ROAST RABBIT
- Auxey-Duresses, red
- Puisseguin Saint-Émilion
- Crozes-Hermitage, red

ROAST WILD DUCK
- Saint-Émilion, Grand Cru
- Côte Rotie
- Faugères

SADDLE OF HARE WITH JUNIPER
- Chambolle, Musigny
- Savoie-Mondeuse
- Saint-Chinian

VENISON CHOPS CONTI STYLE
- Lalande-de-Pomerol
- Côtes de Beaune, red
- Crozes-Hermitage, red

VENISON GRAND VENEUR
- Hermitage, red
- Corton, red
- Côtes de Roussillon, red

WILD DUCK IN RED WINE SAUCE
- Côte Rôtie
- Chinon, red
- Bordeaux, superior quality

WOODCOCK IN RED WINE SAUCE
- Saint-Julien
- Côte de Nuits-Villages
- Patrimonio

VEGETABLES

BRAISED CELERY
- Côtes de Ventoux, red
- Alsace Pinot Noir
- Touraine Sauvignon

DAUPHINOIS POTATOES
- Bordeaux Côtes de Castillon
- Châteauneuf-du-Pape, white
- Alsace Riesling

FRIED AUBERGINES
- Burgundy, red
- Beaujolais, red
- Bordeaux, dry

GREEN BEANS
- Côte de Beaune, white
- Sancerre, white
- Entre-Deux-Mers

MANGETOUT PEAS
- Graves, white
- Côtes du Rhône, red
- Alsace Riesling

MUSHROOMS
- Beaune, white
- Alsace Tokay
- Coteaux de Giennois, red

PASTA
- Côtes du Rhône, red
- Coteaux d'Aix, rosé

PETITS POIS
- Saint-Romain, white
- Côtes du Jura, white
- Touraine Sauvignon

SAUTÉED MUSHROOMS MARBLED WITH PARSLEY
- Beaune, white
- Alsace Tokay
- Coteaux du Giennois, red

STUFFED PEPPERS
- Mâcon-Villages
- Côtes du Rhône, rosé
- Alsace Tokay

CHEESE

Made with cow's milk

BEAUFORT
- Arbois, jaune
- Meursault
- Vin de Savoie
- Chignin
- Bergeron

BLEU D'AUVERGNE
- Côtes de Bergerac, sweet
- Beaujolais
- Touraine Sauvignon

BLEU DE BRESSE
- Côtes du Jura, white
- Macon, red
- Côtes de Bergerac, white

BRIE
- Beaune, red
- Alsace Pinot Noir
- Coteaux du Languedoc, red

CAMEMBERT
- Bandol, red
- Côtes du Roussillon-Villages
- Beaujolais-Villages

CANTAL
- Coteaux du Vivrais, red
- Côtes de Provence, rosé
- Lirac, white

CARRÉ DE L'EST
- Saint-Joseph, red
- Coteaux d'Aix-en-Provence, red
- Brouilly

CARRÉ FRAIS
- Cahors
- Côtes du Roussillon, rosé
- Côtes du Rhône, white

CHAOURCÉ
- Montagne Saint-Émilion
- Cadillac
- Chénas

CÎTEAUX
- Aloxe-Corton
- Coteaux Champenois, red
- Fleurie

COMTÉ
- Graves, Château-Chalon, white
- Côtes du Luberon, white

EDAM DEMI-ÉTUVE
- Pauillac
- Fixin
- Costières de Nîmes, red

ÉPOISSES
- Savigny
- Côtes du Jura, red
- Côte de Brouilly

FOURME D'AMBERT
- L'Étoile, jaune
- Cérons
- Banyuls Rimage

GOUDA DEMI-ÉTUVE
- Saint-Estèphe
- Chinon
- Coteaux du Tricastin

LIVAROT
- Bonnezeaux
- Sainte-Croix-du-Mont
- Alsace Gewurztraminer

MAROILLES
- Jurançon
- Alsace, Gewurztraminer, late harvests

MIMOLETTE DEMI-ÉTUVE
- Graves, red
- Santenay
- Côtes du Rhône, red

MORBIER
- Gevrey-Chambertin
- Madiran
- Côtes du Ventoux, red

MUNSTER
- Coteaux du Layon-Villages
- Loupiac
- Alsace Gewurztraminer

CHEESE FONDUE
- Alsace Riesling
- Haut-Poitou Sauvignon
- Côtes du Rhône-Villages

PONT L'ÉVÊQUE
- Côtes de Saint-Mont
- Bourgueil
- Nuit Saint-Georges

RACLETTE
- Vin de Savoie
- Apremont
- Côtes de Duras Sauvignon
- Juliénas

REBLOCHON
- Mercurey
- Lirac, red
- Touraine Gamay

RIGOTTE
- Bourgogne Hautes-Côtes de Nuits, red
- Côte du Forez
- Saint-Amour

SAINT MARCELLIN
- Faugères
- Tursan, red
- Chiroubles

SAINT-NECTAIRE
- Fronsac
- Burgundy, red
- Mâcon-Villages, white

VACHERIN
- Corton
- Bordeaux, Premières Côtes
- Barsac

Made with goat's milk

CABEÇOU
- Burgundy, white
- Tavel
- Gaillac, white

CORSICAN GOAT'S CHEESE
- Patrimonio, white
- Cassis, white
- Costières de Nîmes, white

CROTTIN DE CHAVIGNOL
- Sancerre, white
- Bordeaux, dry
- Côte Roannaise

FRESH GOAT CHEESE
- Champagne
- Montlouis, medium dry
- Crémant d'Alsace

PELARDON
- Condrieu
- Roussette de Savoie
- Coteaux du Lyonnais, red

SAINTE-MAURE
- Rivesaltes, white
- Alsace Tokay
- Cheverny Gamay

SELLES-SUR-CHER
- Coteaux de l'Aubance
- Cheverny
- Romorantin
- Sancerre, rosé

VALENÇAY
- Vouvray, sweet
- Haut-Poitou, rosé
- Valençay, Gamay

Made with ewe's milk

CORSICAN EWE'S CHEESE
- Bourgogne, Irancy
- Ajaccio
- Côtes du Roussillon, red

EISBARECH
- Lalande-de-Pomerol
- Cornas
- Marcillac

ROQUEFORT
- Côtes du Jura, jaune
- Sauternes
- Muscat de Rivesaltes

LARUNS
- Bordeaux, Côtes de Castillon
- Gaillac, red
- Côtes de Provence, red

DESSERTS

ALMOND CAKE
- Maury
- Bonnezeaux
- Muscat de Lunel

BRIOCHE
- Rivesaltes, red
- Muscat de Beaumes-de-Venise
- Alsace, late harvest

CHOCOLATE CAKE
- Banyuls, Grand Cru
- Pineau des Charentes, rosé

CHRISTMAS LOG
- Champagne, medium dry
- Clairette de Die Tradition

CRÈME RENVERSÉE
- Coteaux du Layon-Villages
- Sauternes
- Muscat de Saint-Jean de Minervoios

ÎLE FLOTTANTE
- Loupiac
- Rivesaltes, white
- Muscat de Rivesaltes

KOUGLOF (CAKE FROM ALSACE)
- Quarts de Chaume
- Alsace, late harvests
- Muscat de Mireval

LEMON TART
- Alsace, various good quality wines
- Cérons
- Rivesaltes, white

ORANGE FRUIT SALAD
- Sainte-Croix-du-Mont
- Rivesaltes, white
- Muscat de Rivesaltes

PRUNE FLAN
- Pineau des Charentes
- Anjou, Coteaux de la Loire
- Cadillac

STRAWBERRIES

- Muscat de Rivesaltes
- Maury

TARTE TATIN

- Pineau des Charentes
- Arbois, Vin de Paille
- Jurançon

VANILLA ICE-CREAM WITH RASPBERRY SAUCE

- Loupiac
- Coteaux du Layon

Alsace

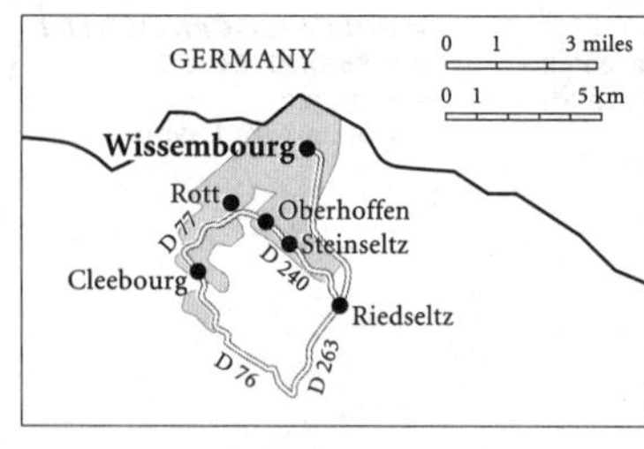
GERMANY
0 1 3 miles
0 1 5 km
Wissembourg
Rott
Oberhoffen
Steinseltz
Cleebourg
Riedseltz
D 77
D 240
D 76
D 263

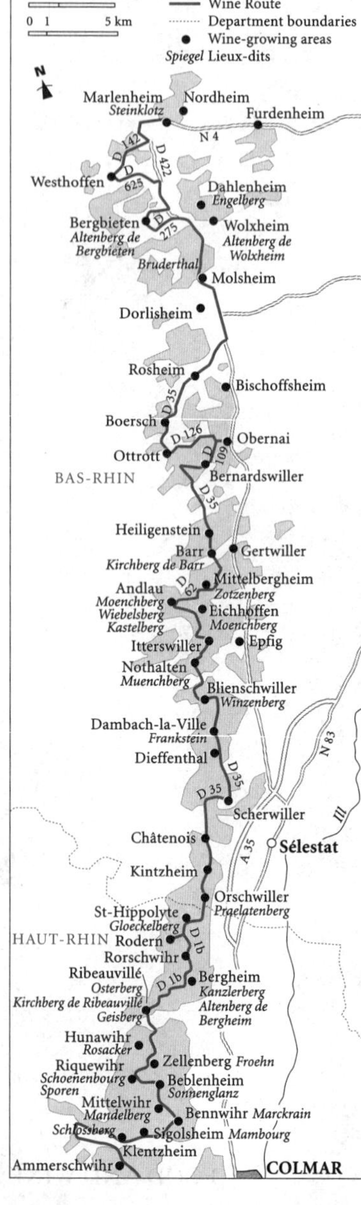
0 1 3 miles
0 1 5 km
Alsace AOC Area
Wine Route
Department boundaries
Wine-growing areas
Spiegel Lieux-dits
N
Marlenheim
Steinklotz
Nordheim
Furdenheim
N 4
D 142
D 422
Westhoffen
D 625
Dahlenheim
Engelberg
Bergbieten
Altenberg de Bergbieten
D 275
Wolxheim
Altenberg de Wolxheim
Bruderthal
Molsheim
Dorlisheim
Rosheim
Bischoffsheim
D 35
Boersch
D 126
Obernai
Ottrott
D 109
Bernardswiller
BAS-RHIN
D 35
Heiligenstein
Barr
Kirchberg de Barr
Gertwiller
Andlau
Moenchberg
Wiebelsberg
Kastelberg
D 62
Mittelbergheim
Zotzenberg
Eichhoffen
Moenchberg
Itterswiller
Epfig
Nothalten
Muenchberg
Blienschwiller
Winzenberg
Dambach-la-Ville
Frankstein
Dieffenthal
D 35
N 83
Scherwiller
Ill
Châtenois
Sélestat
A 35
Kintzheim
Orschwiller
Praelatenberg
St-Hippolyte
Gloeckelberg
HAUT-RHIN
Rodern
D 1b
Rorschwihr
Ribeauvillé
Osterberg
Kirchberg de Ribeauvillé
Geisberg
Bergheim
Kanzlerberg
Altenberg de Bergheim
Hunawihr
Rosacker
Zellenberg *Froehn*
Riquewihr
Schoenenbourg
Sporen
Beblenheim
Sonnenglanz
Mittelwihr
Mandelberg
Bennwihr *Marckrain*
Schlossberg
Sigolsheim *Mambourg*
Klentzheim
Ammerschwihr
COLMAR

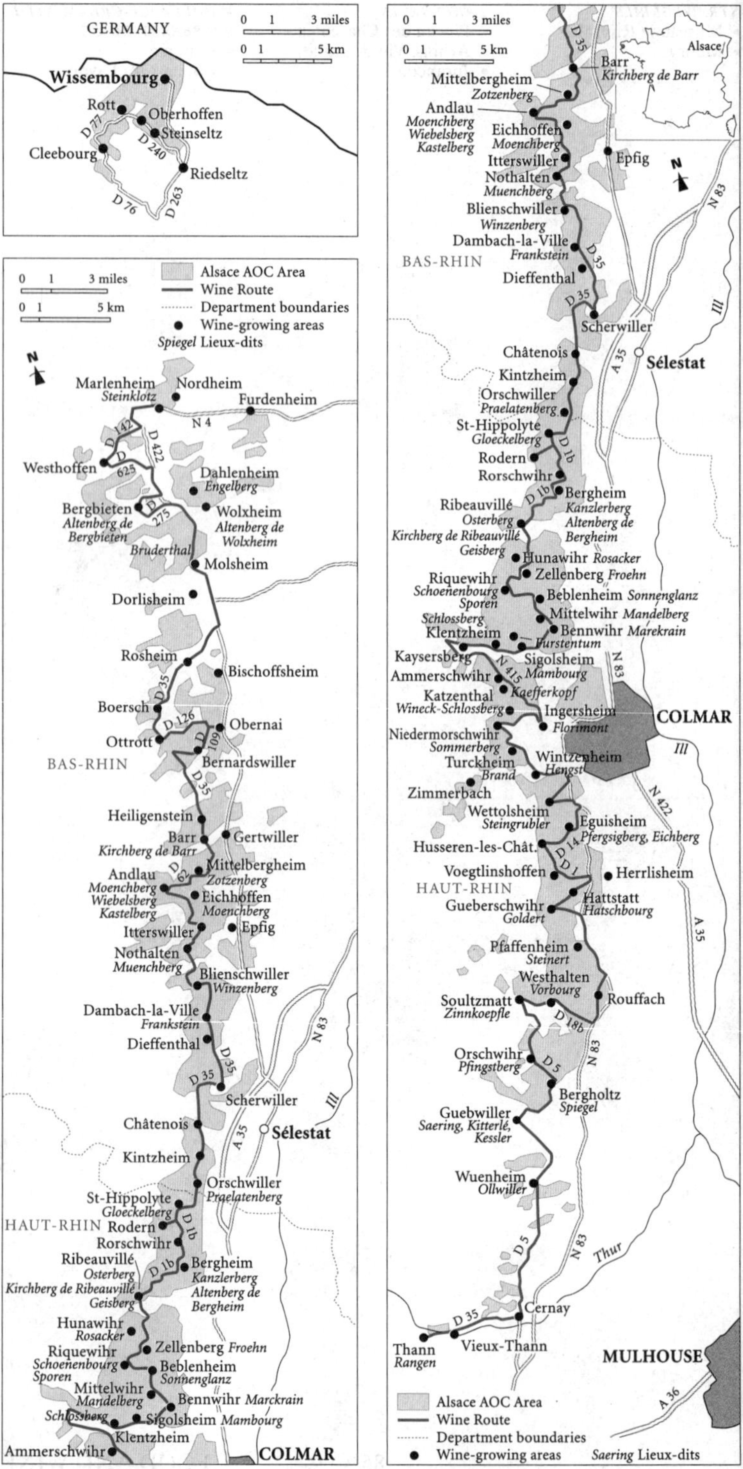

0 1 3 miles
0 1 5 km
Alsace
D 35
Barr
Kirchberg de Barr
Mittelbergheim
Zotzenberg
Andlau
Moenchberg
Wiebelsberg
Kastelberg
Eichhoffen
Moenchberg
Itterswiller
Epfig
N
Nothalten
Muenchberg
N 83
Blienschwiller
Winzenberg
Dambach-la-Ville
Frankstein
BAS-RHIN
D 35
Dieffenthal
D 35
Ill
Scherwiller
Châtenois
A 35
Sélestat
Kintzheim
Orschwiller
Praelatenberg
St-Hippolyte
Gloeckelberg
D 1b
Rodern
Rorschwihr
Ribeauvillé
D 1b
Bergheim
Osterberg
Kanzlerberg
Altenberg de Bergheim
Kirchberg de Ribeauvillé
Geisberg
Hunawihr *Rosacker*
Zellenberg *Froehn*
Riquewihr
Schoenenbourg
Sporen
Beblenheim *Sonnenglanz*
Schlossberg
Mittelwihr *Mandelberg*
Klentzheim
Bennwihr *Marckrain*
Furstentum
Kaysersberg
Sigolsheim
Mambourg
N 83
Ammerschwihr
N 415
Katzenthal
Kaefferkopf
Wineck-Schlossberg
Ingersheim
COLMAR
Florimont
Niedermorschwihr
Sommerberg
Ill
Turckheim
Brand
Wintzenheim
Hengst
Zimmerbach
N 422
Wettolsheim
Steingrubler
Eguisheim
Pfergsigberg, Eichberg
Husseren-les-Chât.
D 14
Voegtlinshoffen
D 1
Herrlisheim
HAUT-RHIN
Hattstatt
Hatschbourg
Gueberschwihr
Goldert
A 35
Pfaffenheim
Steinert
Westhalten
Vorbourg
Rouffach
Soultzmatt
Zinnkoepfle
D 18b
N 83
Orschwihr
Pfingstberg
D 5
Bergholtz
Spiegel
Guebwiller
Saering, Kitterlé, Kessler
Wuenheim
Ollwiller
D 5
N 83
Thur
Cernay
D 35
Thann
Rangen
Vieux-Thann
MULHOUSE
A 36
Alsace AOC Area
Wine Route
Department boundaries
Wine-growing areas
Saering Lieux-dits

ALSACE AND THE EAST

Alsace

Most of the Alsace wine region is on the hills that rise at the foot of the Vosges mountains and run eastward to the Rhine plain. The Vosges form a natural barrier between Alsace and the rest of France and help to create the region's individual climate. Because the moisture absorbed over the Atlantic falls as rain on the mountains, it leaves the eastern slopes only lightly watered. The average annual rainfall in the Colmar region is the lowest in France, less than 500 mm (19.7 in) a year. In summer the mountains also provide some protection from the cool Atlantic winds. Most importantly, however the undulating relief of the hills creates the minute variations in the micro-climates that ultimately contribute to the variety and quality of the vineyards.

The Alsace vineyards are also characterised by a great diversity in soil types. Some fifty million years ago, the recent past in geological terms, the Vosges and the Black Forest formed a single mass, created by a sequence of geological activity during the Tectonic era – floods, erosion and the folding of the earth's crust. From the Tertiary era, the central part of the mountains began to subside, creating, over time, a plain. As a result of this compression, nearly all the strata (layers of soil that had accumulated over different geological periods) were exposed along the line of schism. This is the area where the vineyards are located. In most of the wine-growing communes there are at least four or five different geological structures to the terrain.

The origins of the Alsatian vineyards are lost in the mists of time, but it is thought that the early inhabitants of the region probably harvested grapes, although organised cultivation did not take place until after the Roman conquest. In the wake of Germanic invasions in the 5th century, vine-growing fell into decline for a period, although manuscripts show the vineyards soon began to flourish again under powerful centres of Christianity such as bishoprics, abbeys and convents. Documents from before AD 900 cite more than 160 places where vines were cultivated.

The development of the vineyards continued uninterrupted until the 16th century, the period when wine-growing in Alsace was at its peak. The magnificent Renaissance-style houses that can be seen in the wine villages bear witness to the undoubted prosperity of the times, when great quantities of Alsatian wines were exported to every country in Europe. But the Thirty Years' War was devastating: pillage, famine, plague and destruction had catastrophic consequences for wine-growing and were ruinous for economic activity in the region.

When peace was restored cultivating vines and wineproduction were gradually put back on a stable footing and began again to flourish and expand. The areas of vineyards increased, but they were mainly planted with ordinary grape varieties, which meant wine was produced in quantity but was not necessarily of high quality. In 1731 a royal edict attempted to put a stop to this situation, but without much success. The expansion of the vineyards continued unabated after the Revolutions and by 1808 more than 23,000 ha (56,810 acres) were under vines, an area that increased to 30,000 ha (74,100 acres) by 1828. There was significant over-production of wine and the situation was made worse when the export market collapsed and the consumption of wine dropped as beer-drinking increased. At the same time, wines from southern France offered stiff competition, and they could now easily be shipped to the rest of France on the new railways. In Alsace the vines suffered from a variety of diseases, vine worm and phylloxera, which compounded the difficulties. From 1902 the once-extensive vineyards gradually diminished, and by 1948 the area of vine cultivation had fallen to 9,500 ha (23,456 acres), of which 7,500 ha (18,525 acres) was given the Alsace appellation.

The post-war economic boom and the increased professionalism of the wine-growers combined to drive the revival and redevelopment of the Alsace vineyards. They now cover an area of about 14,500 ha (35,815 acres) with a potential average annual production of some 1,228,000 hl (32,419,200 gal) – 42,000 hl (1,119,360 gal) of Grands Crus and 163,000 hl (4,303,200 gal) of Crémant d'Alsace – and the wine is marketed throughout France and abroad. Exports represent about a quarter of total sales. The widespread improvements in the production and quality of Alsace wines were the collaborative work of the various professional groups which all agreed to limit the quantities of wine on the market. These groups included the wine-making wine-growers, co-operatives and *négociants* (local wine wholesalers), who were often also wine-growers themselves and who also bought large quantities of grapes from growers who did not vinify their own harvest.

The villages and towns along the Route du Vin hold wine festivals throughout the year. These are great tourist attractions and important cultural events for the region. The annual wine fair, held at Colmar in August, is undoubtedly the most important festival, and the ones held earlier in Guebwiller, Ammerschwihr, Ribeauvillé, Barr and Molsheim are also worth visiting. The most prestigious event is organised by the Confrérie Saint-Étienne, which was first established in the 14th century and revived in 1947.

The most distinctive attribute of Alsace wines is their aromatic perfume, which is at its best from grapes grown in cool, temperate areas where they ripen slowly and over a long time. The particular flavours naturally depend on the grape variety, and in Alsace wines are almost always labelled and sold under their grape variety, as distinct from most other French AOC wines which, as a rule, are named after the region or particular geographical location where the grapes are grown.

The grapes are harvested in October and transported as quickly as possible to the wine store for first pressing. Sometimes the grapes are stripped from the stalks, then they undergo a second pressing. The must that flows from the press is full of residual particles from pressing, such as fragments of grape flesh, pips, skins and stalks, which must be removed as quickly as possible by sedimentation or centrifugation. The clarified must then starts its fermentation. During this crucial phase enormous care has to be taken to avoid excessive temperatures. The young wine is often murky, and the wine-maker can use a variety of methods to clarify it, including racking, adding sulphur dioxide and fining. The developing wine is kept in vats or barrels until late spring when most of it is bottled. This method of production makes the dry white wines, which represent more than 90% of Alsace wine production.

The Alsace wines made from late-harvested grapes and the *sélection de grains nobles*, (wines made from late-harvested grapes that are individually selected from the bunch for their ripeness and sweetness) have had their own official appellation only since 1984. These wines are made under strictly regulated production guidelines, the most rigorous concerning the amount of sugar in the grapes. These wines are in a class of their own and, in addition to being very expensive, cannot be produced every year. Only certain grape varieties qualify for late harvesting, mainly Gewurztraminer, Pinot Gris and Riesling, but also Muscat, though more rarely.

Alsace wines are generally considered to be better when drunk young, and this is mostly true for the Sylvaner, Chasselas, Pinot Blanc varieties and Edelzwicker, a blend of varieties. But their youthfulness can mature and Riesling, Gewurztraminer and Pinot Gris often benefit from being kept for at least two years. There is no hard and fast rule, but some Grands Vins, made in years when the grapes are very ripe, can keep longer, sometimes for decades.

The Alsace appellation applies to all of the 110 areas of communal production and is restricted to the use of 11 grape varieties: Gewurztraminer, Riesling Rhénan, Pinot Gris, Muscat Blanc à Petits Grains and Rosé à Petits Grains, Muscat Ottonel, Pinot Blanc, Auxerrois Blanc, Pinot Noir, Sylvaner and Chasselas Blanc and Rosé.

Alsace Klevener de Heiligenstein

Klevener de Heiligenstein is no different from Vieux Traminer (or Savagnin Rose), which have been known in Alsace for centuries.

Mostly it has given way over time to the spicy 'Gewurztraminer' variant but has remained popular in Heiligenstein and five neighbouring communes.

Its rarity and elegance are what make it original. The wines are very well balanced and discreetly aromatic.

CAVE VINICOLE D'ANDLAU-BARR Cuvée Ehret-Wantz 1998★

☐ n.c. 40,000 50–69 F

This Klevener has an attractive colour with orangey lights and is remarkable for its intense aromas. The taste of this 1998 wine combines full ripeness with a fresh citrus flavour that helps to give it persistence.

Cave vinicole d'Andlau et environs, 15, av. des Vosges, 67140 Barr, tel. 03.88.08.90.53, fax 03.88.08.41.79 by appt.

Alsace Sylvaner

It is not clear where the Sylvaner originated, but it has customarily been grown only in vineyards in Germany and the Lower Rhine in France, to which it is eminently suited. In Alsace this variety is particularly successful and regularly produces a large and reliable yield.

Sylvaner makes remarkably fresh, quite acid wines, which have a delicate fruitiness. There are two different types of Sylvaner on the market. The first, by far the better, comes from the well-exposed vineyards that do not produce over-large quantities of grapes. The second type is for those who like a particularly appealing, unpretentious, thirst-quenching wine. Sylvaner is an excellent accompaniment to sauerkraut, and is often drunk with shellfish and seafood. It goes particularly well with oysters.

PIERRE ET FRANCOIS KOCH
Zellberg 1998

☐ 1 ha 4,500 30–49 F

The Koch estate comprises 12 ha (30 acres) of vines around Nothalten, a commune with terroir ideal for making wine from the Sylvaner grape, such as the chalky hillside of Zellberg. With its fine, intense aromas, this 1998 wine contains a subtle blend of floral and buttery notes. It is quite lively as it hits the palate, developing honey and apricot flavours in the mouth which bode well for good ageing.

Pierre et François Koch, 2, rte du Vin, 67680 Nothalten, tel. 03.88.92.42.30, fax 03.88.92.62.91 ☑ Y by appt.

KUMPF ET MEYER
Vieilles vignes 1998★★

☐ 0.5 ha 4,500 20–29 F

Sophie Kumpf and Philippe Meyer linked their destinies – and their respective family estates – in 1997. The couple now run an estate of 15 ha (37 acres). This Sylvaner from their chalky-clay soil is a most definite success. Its intense nose, marked by notes of citrus and white flowers, is matched by a lively, well-balanced and persistent taste. A very harmonious wine which can be recommended for fish or seafood.

Kumpf et Meyer, 34, rte de Rosenwiller, 67560 Rosheim, tel. 03.88.50.20.07, fax 03.88.50.26.75 ☑ Y ev. day 8.30am–12 noon 1.30pm–7pm

Sophie et Philippe Meyer

DOM. LOEW Vérité de Sylvaner 1998★

☐ 0.26 ha 1000 30–49 F

Now 23 years old, Etienne Loew inherited the vineyard from his grandparents in 1996, and is giving his youthful talents a free rein. An advocate of traditional wine-making methods, Etienne has taken his cue from the hermit Clauss, who worked in the district in 1280, giving him his due place on the label! The Sylvaner he offers has a nose marked by notes of overripeness; the taste is very complex and well-balanced despite a hint of roundness. A real gourmet wine.

Etienne Loew, 135, rue Birris, 67310 Westhoffen, tel. 03.88.50.30.34, fax 03.88.50.59.19 ☑ Y by appt.

JULES MULLER Réserve 1998

☐ 3 ha 20,000 20–29 F

People tend to think of Alsace in terms of a few clichés, too often forgetting that every village, like Bergheim, contains treasures of medieval architecture. Jules Muller's business has been a success for more than a century. The nose of this Sylvaner is fairly intense, with strong aromas of ripe fruits and mineral notes. The latter characteristic also emerges in its lively and well-balanced taste.

Jules Muller, 91, rue des Vignerons, 68750 Bergheim, tel. 03.89.73.22.21, fax 03.89.73.30.49 ☑ Y ev. day except Sun. 10am–12 noon 2pm–6.30pm

Gustave Lorentz

GILBERT RUHLMANN 1998

☐ 0.8 ha 7,500 20–29 F

Guy Ruhlmann has run this 10-ha (25-acre) vineyard since 1997. Coming from a silty-sandy soil, his Sylvaner has very intense aromas of flowers and hazelnuts. Rather lively as it hits the palate, this is a light wine suitable for first courses.

Gilbert Ruhlmann Fils, 31, rue de l'Ortenbourg, 67750 Scherwiller, tel. 03.88.92.03.21, fax 03.88.82.30.19 ☑ Y by appt.

Guy Ruhlmann

MARTIN SCHAETZEL
Vieilles vignes 1998★

☐ 0.2 ha n.c. 30–49 F

Jean Schaetzel took over his uncle's estate more than ten years ago. He remains a teacher of viticulture and is now able to combine theory with practice – and he continues to surprise us! This time it is with a very opulent Sylvaner made from overripe grapes. The nose is marked by intense aromas of citrus and crystallised fruits, while the wine seems very round in taste when it attacks the palate, then reveals its well-balanced structure. An atypical wine, but very interesting, best drunk as an aperitif.

SARL Martin Schaetzel, 3, rue de la 5nd-Division-Blindée, 68770 Ammerschwihr, tel. 03.89.47.11.39, fax 03.89.78.29.77 by appt.

Béa et Jean Schaetzel

SIFFERT

Coteau du Haut-Koenigsbourg Vieilles vignes 1998★★

0.72 ha 7,000 30–49 F

The Siffert estate, with its 10 ha (25 acres) on the slopes of the Haut-Koenigsbourg, enjoys a solid reputation which this Sylvaner will only enhance. Elegant and intense to the nose, with a fruity character and good attack, it is cool, well-balanced and persistent. In short, this is a ripe and rounded Sylvaner.

SCEA Dom. Siffert, 16, rte du Vin, 67600 Orschwiller, tel. 03.88.92.02.77, fax 03.88.82.70.02, e-mail Siffert@rmcnet.fr ev. day 9am–12 noon 1.30pm–7pm; Sun. by appt.; cl. 15 Jan.–15 Feb.

THIERRY-MARTIN 1998★

4 ha 3,000 30–49 F

Thierry Unterreiner and Martin Lorentz joined forces in 1998 to found this new enterprise which sells direct. They have made an encouraging start, judging from this very expressive Sylvaner with its distinctive nose containing a slight hint of minerals. Well-balanced on the palate, it finishes on a light note of lemon which makes it ideal for drinking with seafood.

Thierry-Martin, rte de Westhoffen, 67520 Wangen, tel. 03.88.04.11.22, fax 03.88.04.11.21, e-mail alsacethierrymartin@minitel.net by appt.

BERNARD WEBER 1998★★

1 ha 2,000 20–29 F

The origins of this estate are lost in the mists of time, and it hardly needs any introduction now. Bernard Weber, who has been in charge since 1974, greets every year's wine with the same enthusiasm. Marked by the chalky-clay ground in which it is grown, his Sylvaner has a very evolved aroma dominated by scents of mint and lemon. It hits the palate with length and balance, which makes it a model of harmony. Exactly what is needed to accompany a platter of seafood.

Bernard Weber, 49, rue de Saverne, 67120 Molsheim, tel. 03.88.38.52.67, fax 03.88.38.58.81, e-mail info@bernard-weber.com by appt.

Alsace Pinot or Klevner

Wine labelled with either of these names (the second is the old Alsace name) can be a blend of grape varieties, usually Pinot Blanc Vrai or Auxerrois Blanc. These two varieties are not too hard to cultivate and can produce excellent wines on mediocre soil. The wines are pleasantly fresh as well as having body and suppleness. In ten years the area given over to cultivating these two varieties has practically doubled, from 10% to 18% of the total vineyard.

In the range of Alsace wines, Pinot Blanc ranks just about in the middle, and it can outclass some Rieslings. When it comes to food, it goes well with a great range of dishes, although it is not especially good with cheese or desserts.

A L'ANCIENNE FORGE 1998★

0.19 ha 1,450 30–49 F

Occupying the village's former forge dating from 1720, the Brandner estate is widely known despite its small size (5 ha/12 acres). It offers a 1998 Pinot Blanc which is very typical of the variety with a very subtle nose and notes of ripe fruits and liquorice. It has middling persistence, but its chief attraction lies in the freshness with which it hits the palate, its fullness and perfect balance.

Jérôme Brandner, 51, rue Principale, 67140 Mittelbergheim, tel. 03.88.08.01.89, fax 03.88.08.94.92 ev. day 9am–12 noon 1.30pm–7pm; groups by appt.

DOM. BARMES-BUECHER

Auxerrois 1998★★

1.2 ha 8,000 30–49 F

The Barmès-Buecher estate, born of the union of two long-established wine-growing families, today comprises 15 ha (37 acres) of vines near Colmar and is regularly praised by wine-writers. This year, it offers an Auxerrois grown on gravelly soils. It has a very intense nose with a hint of overripeness. Very strong on the palate, it is fruity and persistent. Its overripe character, rare in a Pinot Blanc, means that this 1998 wine can be served not just with white meats but also with foie gras.

Dom. Barmès-Buecher, 30, rue Sainte-Gertrude, 68920 Wettolsheim, tel. 03.89.80.62.92, fax 03.89.79.30.80, e-mail barmes-buecher@terre-net.fr by appt.

BECK-DOM. DU REMPART

Auxerrois Cuvée de l'Ours Armoriée An 2000 1998★

☐ 0.5 ha 4,000 30–49 F

Having headed an estate of 8 ha (20 acres) since 1978, Gilbert Beck in 1995 established the Maison des Grands Crus at Dambach, where a rich range of products can be discovered. His Pinot Blanc grown on sandy marl soils surprises with its scents of flowers and hints of apricot. Vigorous on the palate, it has length and liveliness and can accompany a variety of dishes.

Beck, Dom. du Rempart, 5, rue des Remparts, 67650 Dambach-la-Ville, tel. 03.88.92.62.03, fax 03.88.92.49.40 Y by appt.

Gilbert Beck

CAMILLE BRAUN

Auxerrois Vieilles vignes Cuvée Marguerite-Anne 1998★

☐ 0.58 ha 6,000 30–49 F

Camille Braun's plantation of more than 8 ha (20 acres) of vines lies within the first major wine-growing village encountered coming into the wine country from the south. Grown on a chalky-clay soil, his Marguérite-Anne vintage has a nose of white flowers and fruits. Smoky notes are evident to the palate, and contribute to the wine's persistence. This is a straightforward and well- balanced product.

Camille Braun, 16, Grand-Rue, 68500 Orschwihr, tel. 03.89.76.95.20, fax 03.89.74.35.03 Y ev. day except Sun. 8am–12 noon 1.30pm–7pm

DREYER Eguisheim 1998★★

☐ 0.8 ha 6,000 20–29 F

On the heights of Eguisheim, the famous medieval town, the Dreyers today cultivate almost 10 ha (25 acres) of vines. Despite originating on chalky-clay soils, this 1998 wine already reveals a nose of strong intensity and great subtlety, with aromas of spices and roasted meats. Lively as it comes on to the palate, this is a very well-balanced wine, rather rich and powerful, a fact which doubtless reflects careful control of the yield from the vineyard.

GAEC Robert Dreyer et Fils, 17, rue de Hautvillers, 68420 Eguisheim, tel. 03.89.23.12.18, fax 03.89.41.61.45 Y by appt.

PAUL GINGLINGER

Clevner 1998★★★

☐ 2.5 ha 15,000 30–49 F

Grand Master of the Confrérie Saint-Etienne, Paul Ginglinger is the worthy heir of a line of wine-growers going back to 1636. This Pinot of chalky-marl origin is one of the best. The nose is very intense, and the rich, bewitching aromas linger in the mouth to the very end. This wine is made with excellent fruit and has a rare harmony and remarkable persistence. A gourmet might see it as an apt

accompaniment to escargots with vegetable broth.

Paul Ginglinger, 8, pl. Charles-de-Gaulle, 68420 Eguisheim, tel. 03.89.41.44.25, fax 03.89.24.94.88 Y by appt.

W. GISSELBRECHT 1998★

☐ 3 ha 25,000 30–49 F

Willy Gisselbrecht's house is one of the gems of the Alsatian wine-trade. He nevertheless remains attached to his own estate, which comprises 17 ha (42 acres)of vines. His Pinot Blanc, grown on granite, has already developed an excellent nose marked by elegant flowery notes. It attacks the palate well and is a fresh-tasting wine, characteristic of its type. Its persistence makes it equally suitable with seafood, fish and white meat.

Willy Gisselbrecht et Fils, 5, rte du Vin, 67650 Dambach-la-Ville, tel. 03.88.92.41.02, fax 03.88.92.45.50, e-mail W.Gisselbrecht@wanadoo.fr Y ev. day except Sun. 8am–12 noon 2pm–6pm

HASSENFORDER Auxerrois 1998★

☐ n.c. 1,950 20–29 F

Gilbert Hassenforder has been in charge since 1977 at Nothalten, a small village not far from Barr entirely devoted to viticulture. His Pinot Auxerrois, grown on sandy soil, has a nose characterised by aromas both of fruit and slight smokiness. It arrives on the palate with freshness and liveliness and the same fruitiness and smokiness reappear in the taste. A very well-balanced product that will go well with exotic specialities or white meat.

Gilbert Hassenforder, 57, rte des Vins d'Alsace, 67680 Nothalten, tel. 03.88.92.41.81, fax 03.88.92.41.81 Y by appt.

HEIM Strangenberg Réserve 1998★

☐ 2.66 ha n.c. 30–49 F

This long-established Westhalten firm now belongs to the Bestheim group. All the same it has kept its individuality and continues to gather grapes from surrounding hillsides reputed for their Mediterranean flora. The nose of this Pinot is very intense, marked by notes of ripe fruits and honey which betray a touch of overripeness. The palate is well-structured, balanced and persistent. A gourmet wine to accompany white meats or salads with foie gras.

Heim, 53, rte de Soultzmatt, 68250 Westhalten, tel. 03.89.78.09.08, fax 03.89.49.09.20

CHARLES SCHLERET 1998★★

☐ 0.37 ha 3,000 30–49 F

Established at Turckheim since 1950, Charles Schleret enjoys an excellent reputation both inside and outside France – more than half of his production is exported. This Pinot Blanc, grown on gravelly soil, is proof of his reputation. The nose of this 1998, with its notes of yellow fruits, is already very open. Its balanced structure, power and exceptional length are impressive.

Charles Schleret, 1–3, rte d'Ingersheim, 68230 Turckheim, tel. 03.89.27.06.09 ev. day 9am–7pm; Sun. 9am–12 noon

MICHEL SCHOEPFER 1998★

☐ 0.5 ha 4,000 20–29 F

Visitors to Eguisheim can imbibe a thousand years of history! Michel Schoepfer's property has its headquarters in the former tithe court of the Augustinian monastery in Marbach (1212). Made from high-quality grapes, this Pinot is redolent of ripe fruits and overripeness. The touch of roundness evident to the palate quickly merges into the structure of the wine, which is a model of power and harmony.

Michel Schoepfer, 43, Grand-Rue, 68420 Eguisheim, tel. 03.89.41.09.06, fax 03.89.23.08.50 ev. day 8am–12 noon 2pm–6pm

JEAN-VICTOR SCHUTZ 1998★

☐ n.c. 30,000 20–29 F

Jean-Victor Schutz started out in 1997, and immediately sought to export his production. His wines almost all go abroad, currently to Belgium, Holland and Denmark. Grown on alluvial soil, his Pinot Blanc has a nose that is already well developed, with aromas of flowers and honey. On the palate it is quite round and fat, the result of using high-quality grapes which have given it the desired harmony.

Jean-Victor Schutz, 34, rue du Mal.-Foch, 67650 Dambach-la-Ville, tel. 03.88.92.41.86, fax 03.88.92.61.86 by appt.

SEILLY Les Coteaux d'Obernai 1998★

☐ 0.96 ha 7,040 30–49 F

Though established in 1865, the Seilly estate is entirely up to date, being equipped with a temperature-controlled winery. A keen oenologist, Marc Seilly keeps his wines on the lees for eight months. He offers a Pinot with a full and expressive nose with notes of apricot and hazelnut. The wine is beautifully fresh as it hits the palate and finishes in a burst of flavours. This very well-balanced wine will go well with first courses and white meats.

Dom. Seilly, 18, rue du Gal-Gouraud, 67210 Obernai, tel. 03.88.95.55.80, fax 03.88.95.54.00, e-mail info@seilly.fr by appt.

DOM. MICHELE ET JEAN-LUC STOECKLE Cuvée réservée 1998

☐ 1 ha 5,000 30–49 F

The former firm of Klur-Stoecklé, a successful business at Katzenthal, has become the estate of Michèle and Jean-Luc Stoecklé. It is a fair bet that this new generation will manage to serve the cause of Alsatian wine with no less passion than their forebears. This Pinot, grown on granite soils, already has a beautifully mature nose, combining aromas of ripe fruits and smokiness. Clean-tasting as it hits the palate, this is a full, rich wine still dominated by a hint of residual sugar. It should be given a little more time.

Michèle et Jean-Luc Stoecklé, 9, Grand-Rue, 68230 Katzenthal, tel. 03.89.27.05.08, fax 03.89.27.33.61 ev. day except Sun. afternoon 8am–12 noon 1pm–7pm

WINTZER ET FILS 1998★

☐ 0.77 ha 1000 20–29 F

Established since 1978 at Soultz, beneath the Grand Ballon, the Wintzer family, currently growing some 8 ha (20 acres) of vines, have continued to increase the proportion of their wine sold by the bottle. Their Pinot Blanc has an intense nose dominated by notes of white flowers. The attack on the palate is good, and this is a fairly rich, well-balanced wine, ideal for accompanying a light meal.

GAEC Louis Wintzer et Fils, 53, rue du Mal-de-Lattre-de-Tassigny, 68360 Soultz, tel. 03.89.76.80.79, fax 03.89.76.80.41 by appt.

FERNAND ZIEGLER 1998★★★

☐ 0.9 ha 8,190 20–29 F

This estate is built upon more than 350 years of wine-growing tradition, and Fernand Ziegler has drawn upon more than 35 years' experience of bottling his own wine to produce a Pinot Blanc that has charmed the jury. The nose is very expressive with its aromas of peach and citrus. The palate is enlivened by an unambiguous acidity and reveals a concentration brought on by noble rot. A full, well-balanced and unusually persistent wine.

EARL Fernand Ziegler et Fils, 7, rue des Vosges, 68150 Hunawihr, tel. 03.89.73.64.42, fax 03.89.73.71.38 ev. day 8.30am–12 noon 1.30pm–6.30pm; Sun. by appt.

ZIEGLER-MAULER 1998★

□ 0.5 ha 3,500 20–29 F

After a long period working with his son Philippe, Jean-Jacques Ziegler-Mauler handed over the reins of this 4.5-ha (11-acre) estate in 1996. Despite its chalky-clay origins, this Pinot Blanc is already very open with notes of citrus fruits and bergamot very evident in the nose. Lively when it hits the palate, this is a long, well-balanced wine that is suitable for pork and white meats.

EARL J.-J. Ziegler-Mauler et Fils, 2, rue des Merles, 68630 Mittelwihr,
tel. 03.89.47.90.37, fax 03.89.47.98.27
by appt.

DOM. VALENTIN ZUSSLIN ET FILS

l'Auxerrois du Printemps Vieilles vignes 1998★★

□ 0.68 ha 6,300 30–49 F

This family vineyard of 12 ha (30 acres) has been passed down from father to son since 1691. Still young to the nose, with very subtle floral notes, this Pinot is true to its chalky-clay soil. Hints of spices are evident on the palate, facilitating a marvellous conjunction of power and elegance. A remarkable wine.

Dom. Valentin Zusslin et Fils, 57, Grand-Rue, 68500 Orschwihr,
tel. 03.89.76.82.84, fax 03.89.76.64.36
by appt.

Alsace Edelzwicker

Edelzwicker occupies a special place among the Alsace appellations. Its name, which is extremely old, designates a wine that is a blend of several grape varieties. It is worth noting that up to a hundred years ago it was rare for Alsace vineyards to be planted with only one grape variety. The main grapes used for Edelzwicker are Pinot Blanc, Auxerrois, Sylvaner and Chasselas. Some Edelzwickers are of poor quality, so the reputation of this wine has been somewhat tarnished, but it is very popular with the Alsatians, and for many restaurant and café owners it is a matter of pride to serve some quite good-quality Edelzwicker wines by the carafe. It is high time that the reputation of this appellation was reappraised.

COMTE D'ANDLAU-HOMBOURG

Château d'Ittenwiller 1998

□ n.c. n.c. 30–49 F

Originally a monastic vineyard, this estate passed to the bishopric of Strasbourg and was subsequently sold as a nationalised asset in 1792. It has belonged to the same family since 1806. Their Edelzwicker results from combining Auxerrois, Pinot Gris and Muscat varieties. Still very young, it is pleasantly fruity to the nose. It is a forthright, lively and light wine that will suit charcuterie or fish.

Comte d'Andlau-Hombourg, SCI Dom. d'Ittenwiller, 67140 Saint-Pierre,
tel. 03.88.08.92.63, fax 03.88.08.13.30
by appt.

Alsace Riesling

Riesling is *the* grape variety of the Rhineland, and the Rhine valley is where it originated and flourished. It matures later than other varieties in the region and can be relied on to produce both quality and quantity. About 22% of the Alsace vineyard is planted with Riesling.

The Alsace Riesling is made in a dry style compared with the sweeter German Rieslings. Typically, there is a harmonious balance between its delicately fruity bouquet, good body and finely pronounced acidity. To fulfil its promise it must come from a sunny, sheltered *terroir*.

Riesling is planted in many other wine-growing countries, and there are at least ten other varieties that carry the Riesling name. Unless you specify Riesling Rhénan, the wines can be disappointing. On the gastronomic front, Riesling is particularly good when it is drunk with fish dishes, seafood and, naturally enough, a good Alsace sauerkraut or, alternatively, *coq au Riesling*. When the late-harvested grapes do not contain sufficient sugar, they are used as blending wines for *vins blancs liquoreux*.

A L'ANCIENNE FORGE Stein 1998★

☐ 0.32 ha 2,700 30–49 F

This vineyard of 5 ha is located at the former forge at Mittelbergheim. Its Stein Riesling has a very elegant nose, blending mineral notes with those of blackcurrant buds. Rather lively on its first impression, this is a wine with structure, possessing the balance classic to this vintage. (Residual sugar: 1.8 g/l.)

Jérôme Brandner, 51, rue Principale, 67140 Mittelbergheim, tel. 03.88.08.01.89, fax 03.88.08.94.92 ☒ Y ev. day 9am–12 noon 1.30pm–7pm; groups by appt.

AMBERG Damgraben Vieilles vignes 1998

☐ n.c. 5,000 30–49 F

In charge of this ten-hectare (25-acre) estate since 1987, Yves Amberg presses the grapes whole to maximise the extraction of aromas. His Riesling, grown on sandy soil, already possesses a nose in which a small mineral note is detectable. Supple on the palate, it goes on to reveal a fine structure and good persistence. (Residual sugar: 7 g/l.)

Yves Amberg, 19, rue Fronholz, 67680 Epfig, tel. 03.88.85.51.28, fax 03.88.85.52.71 ☒ Y by appt.

RENE BARTH Rebgarten 1998★

☐ 0.2 ha 1,500 30–49 F

An oenologist by training, Michel Fonné took over his uncle's vineyard of 5 ha (12 acres) in 1989. Bearing the stamp of its silty and sandy soil of origin, the nose of this Riesling combines power and elegance. Lively and well-balanced on the palate, it will go well with fish. (Residual sugar: 5 g/l.)

Dom. René Barth succ. Michel Fonné, 24, rue du Gal-de-Gaulle, 68630 Bennwihr, tel. 03.89.47.92.69, fax 03.89.49.04.86 ☒ Y by appt.

DOM. JEAN-PIERRE BECHTOLD Suessenberg Sélection de grains nobles 1997★

☐ 0.6 ha 1,100 250–299 F

Only in exceptional years are *Sélection de Grains Nobles* Rieslings successful. One such year was 1997. Add to this the wine-grower's skill, and here is an attractive straw-yellow wine with a nose of quince jelly and honey. Fresh and lemony as it hits the palate, it has a well-structured finish and is a wine for the future, when it will suit foie gras, Roquefort, or apple or lemon tart. (Half-litre bottles)

Dom. Jean-Pierre Bechtold, 49, rue Principale, 67310 Dahlenheim, tel. 03.88.50.66.57, fax 03.88.50.67.34 ☒ Y by appt.

DOM. BERNHARD-REIBEL Vendanges tardives 1997★★

☐ 0.45 ha 1,623 70–99 F

Cécile Bernhard-Reibel has been running a wine-growing estate of 12 ha (30 acres) since 1981. This is a late-harvest wine that gets everyone's vote. Its strong golden yellow

colour is instantly appetising. The nose, which is extremely subtle, mixes citrus (lemon), passionfruit, honey and acacia flowers. It makes one impatient to sample the taste, which is superb. Some aromatic elements need only a little more time to burst into life. (Half-litre bottles.)

Dom. Bernhard-Reibel, 20, rue de Lorraine, 67730 Châtenois, tel. 03.88.82.04.21, fax 03.88.82.59.65, e-mail bernhard-reibel@wanadoo.fr ☒ Y by appt.

BESTHEIM Rebgarten 1998

☐ 12 ha n.c. 30–49 F

The Bennwihr cellar has recently merged with that of Westhalten to establish the Bestheim group, but the firm has faithfully retained separate vinification in the locality of Rebgarten. Still very young, the nose of this Riesling is developing lemony aromas that mingle with mineral notes. Quite lively on the palate, this is a well-balanced, very delicate wine, typical of the variety.

Cave de Bestheim-Bennwihr, 3, rue du Gal-de-Gaulle, 68630 Bennwihr, tel. 03.89.49.09.29, fax 03.89.49.09.20 ☒ Y ev. day 9am–12 noon 2pm–6pm

PATRICK BEYER Pflanzer 1998

☐ 0.89 ha 3,500 30–49 F

Epfig, with its church perched on a spur is an easy place for visitors to find, and is one of the leading vineyards in the Alsace wine-growing region. Patrick Beyer has around 7 ha (17 acres) of vines there. The nose of his Pflanzer Riesling, grown on sandy-clay soil, mingles hints of fruits and plants. This wine, which attacks the palate well, is lively and could accompany trout au bleu, for example.

Patrick Beyer, 27, rue des Alliés, 67680 Epfig, tel. 03.88.85.50.21, fax 03.88.57.81.46 ☒ Y ev. day 9am–11.30am 2pm–7pm

JOSEPH ET CHRISTIAN BINNER Kaefferkopf Sélection de grains nobles 1997★

☐ 0.3 ha 1000 300–499 F

A wine-grower to the core, Joseph Binner is also a technical enthusiast. He is a developer of vinification equipment and has founded a company, Binner-Innovations, to market his own design for a tasting-glass. This wine is the work of his son Christian, who joined him on the estate three years ago. Yellow with amber

lights, its nose is not yet fully developed, but is already yielding some quite intense candied notes. Harmonious in the mouth, it comes over as full, powerful and rich.
⊶ Joseph et Christian Binner, 2, rue des Romains, 68770 Ammerschwihr, tel. 03.89.78.23.20, fax 03.89.78.14.17 ☒ Y ev. day 9am–12.30pm 2pm–6pm

DOM. CLAUDE BLEGER

Coteaux du Haut-Kœnigsbourg 1998*

☐ 0.35 ha 3,000 30–49 F

Claude Bléger's forebears established themselves at the foot of the Haut-Koenigsbourg over 350 years ago. Claude Bléger, who heads a seven-hectare (17-acre) estate, offers a Riesling grown on granite soils. This very complex 1998 wine is developing a nose with aromas of honey and overripeness. The touch of roundness and fatness in the mouth is well counterbalanced by the acidity, which suggests that the wine will keep well. A strong, persistent wine. (Residual sugar: 6 g/l.)
⊶ Dom. Claude Bléger, 23, Grand-Rue, 67600 Orschwiller, tel. 03.88.92.32.56, fax 03.88.82.59.95 ☒ Y ev. day 9am–12.15 1.15–7.30pm

HENRI BLEGER

Coteau du Haut-Kœnigsbourg 1998*

☐ 0.6 ha 5,600 30–49 F

Wine-growers from father to son for generations, the Blégers welcome visitors to their cellar, located beneath the Haut-Koenigsbourg, which dates from 1562. Reflecting its chalky-clay origins, this Riesling remains in its youthful phase. The nose is characterised by discreet aromas of green almonds. On the palate the wine has good balance and long persistence. A wine of character. (Residual sugar: 5 g/l.)
⊶ Henri Bléger, 2, rue Saint-Fulrade, 68590 Saint-Hippolyte, tel. 03.89.73.00.08, fax 03.89.73.05.93 ☒ Y by appt.

E. BOECKEL Brandluft 1998*

☐ 1 ha 8,500 30–49 F

Established at Mittelbergheim in 1530, the Boeckel family today cultivates 20 ha (49 acres) of vines. With a nose characterised by notes of citrus fruits and overripeness, their Brandluft Riesling is the quintessential product of its chalky soil of origin. Given its remarkable structure and length, this is a wine to keep. (Residual sugar: 5 g/l.)
⊶ Emile Boeckel, 2, rue de la Montagne, 67140 Mittelbergheim, tel. 03.88.08.91.91, fax 03.88.08.91.88 ☒ Y by appt.

JUSTIN BOXLER

Vendanges tardives Cuvée Jean-Louis 1997*

☐ 0.2 ha 1,100 100–149 F

Nestling in its valley west of Colmar and on the road to the health resort of Les Trois Epis, Niedermorschwihr has a church with a curious twisted steeple. Justin Boxler, who cultivates 11 ha (27 acres) of vines there, has produced a very successful 1997 late-harvest wine with a firm golden colour, very complex candied nose, and full, rich, fat, generous taste, which is developing aromas of ripe and exotic fruits.
⊶ GAEC Justin Boxler, 15, rue des Trois-Epis, 68230 Niedermorschwihr, tel. 03.89.27.11.07, fax 03.89.27.01.44 ☒ Y ev. day 8am–12 noon 2pm–7pm; groups by appt.

JOSEPH CATTIN 1998*

☐ 5 ha 48,000 30–49 F

Jacques Cattin is never daunted. Witness the new ultra-modern vathouse with its 3,000-hectolitre (79,200-gallon) capacity, designed to exploit the diversity of soils on the vast family estate (39 ha/96 acres). Marked by its chalky-clay origin, his Riesling is still very young in the nose but its full potential is already evident on the palate. A fruity, well-balanced, persistent wine, which will go very well with white meats. (Residual sugar: 5 g/l.)
⊶ Joseph Cattin, 18, rue Roger-Frémeaux, 68420 Voegtlinshoffen, tel. 03.89.49.30.21, fax 03.89.49.26.02 ☒ Y ev. day 8am–12 noon 2pm–6pm; Sun. by appt.
⊶ Jacques et Jean-Marie Cattin

DOM. VITICOLE DE LA VILLE DE COLMAR 1998*

☐ 1 ha 8,000 50–69 F

Managed by Jean-Rémy Haeffelin since 1980, the 24 ha (59 acres) of the Domaine Viticole de la Ville de Colmar have a special place in Alsace, having in effect taken over from the famous Institut Oberlin. With its very open fragrance, this Riesling, grown on the gravelly soil of Colmar, is dominated by hints of overripeness. The palate reflects the high quality of the grapes used. The slight sweetness should fade after several years of keeping. (Residual sugar: 3.3 g/l.)
⊶ Dom. viticole de la ville de Colmar, 2, rue du Stauffen, 68000 Colmar, tel. 03.89.79.11.87, fax 03.89.80.38.66 ☒ Y ev. day except Sun. 8am–12 noon 2pm–6pm; cl. Aug.

COMTE DE BEAUMONT 1998*

☐ 4 ha 32,000 50–69 F

Preiss-Zimmer run a successful business in the famous village of Riquewihr. Grown on gravelly soils, this Riesling has a nose of great finesse that mixes scents of honey and white flowers (hawthorn). Delightfully lively in the mouth, it promises to be a wine to keep: a thoroughbred that will gain in harmony as the years go by. (Residual sugar: 4.2 g/l.)
⊶ SARL Preiss-Zimmer, 40, rue du Gal-de-Gaulle, 68340 Riquewihr, tel. 03.89.47.86.91, fax 03.89.27.35.33

EBLIN-FUCHS Zellenberg 1998*

☐ 1 ha 8,000 30–49 F

This eight-hectare (20-acre) estate is the result of two families, both established for hundreds of years in Zellenberg, coming together in the 1950s. This Riesling, made from 50-year-old vines planted on chalky-sandstone soils, already has a well-developed nose, with mineral notes moderating its fruity character. Its freshness hits the palate, announcing a full, dry wine with good structure.

🔑 Christian et Joseph Eblin, 75, rte des Vins, Schlossreben, 68340 Zellenberg, tel. 03.89.47.91.14, fax 03.89.49.05.12 ☒ 🍷 by appt.

DOM. ANDRE EHRHART

Herrenweg 1998★★

☐ 0.5 ha 3,500 30–49 F

Established at Wettolsheim, a village very close to Colmar, André Ehrhart has reached the pinnacle of his art and wins two stars for this 1998 Riesling from Herrenweg. Grown on gravelly soils, it has a nose marked by aromas of flowers and fruit. Lively, well-balanced, distinctive, long and harmonious, it has a great future before it. (Residual sugar: 2 g/l.)

🔑 André Ehrhart et Fils, 68, rue Herzog, 68920 Wettolsheim, tel. 03.89.80.66.16, fax 03.89.79.44.20 ☒ 🍷 ev. day except Sun. 8am–12 noon 1.30pm–7pm

DOM. ENGEL 1998

☐ 2 ha 6,000 30–49 F

With its 18 ha (44 acres) of vines, The Engel estate is an important Alsatian vineyard. Active in most of the markets of northern Europe, the firm is now in its third generation and since 1998 has adopted a rational approach to agriculture. This Riesling reveals notes of white flowers and overripeness in the nose. It arrives on the palate with a hint of roundness, and has a lively finish. (Residual sugar: 5.5 g/l.)

🔑 Dom. Christian et Hubert Engel, 1, rue des Vignes, 67600 Orschwiller, tel. 03.88.92.01.83, fax 03.88.82.25.09 ☒ 🍷 ev. day 9am–11.30am 2pm–6pm

F. ENGEL ET FILS

Clos des Anges 1998★

☐ 0.94 ha 7,500 50–69 F

Located at Rorschwihr, this estate has modern equipment and uses it to get the best out of the soil. With more than 35 ha (86 acres) of vines it is one of the most extensive vineyards in the region. Marked by its chalky origin, the Clos des Anges Riesling still has a very young nose. Fresh and well-structured in flavour, it is elegant and has great promise. This wine would go well with white meats. (Residual sugar: 13 g/l.)

🔑 Fernand Engel et Fils, 1, rte du Vin, 68590 Rorschwihr, tel. 03.89.73.77.27, fax 03.89.73.63.70 ☒ 🍷 by appt.

DOM. FLEISCHER Breitling 1998★

☐ 1.29 ha 5,300 30–49 F

The Fleischer estate began bottling in 1990 with 3.5 ha (nine acres) of vines. Ten years later, there are now 8 ha (20 acres) – a measure of their ambition. This Riesling, grown on silty-sandy soil, has a characteristically lemony nose. Clean-tasting as it hits the palate, it swiftly betrays a slight touch of sweetness that is well balanced by the acid structure. A harmonious wine. (Residual sugar: 7 g/l.)

🔑 Dom. Fleischer, 28, rue du Moulin, 68250 Pfaffenheim, tel. 03.89.49.62.70, fax 03.89.49.50.74 ☒ 🍷 by appt.

RENE FLEITH-ESCHARD

Vendanges tardives 1997★

☐ 1 ha 5,400 70–99 F

In charge since 1995, Vincent Fleith represents the 11th generation of his family on this estate. He has taken all due care to make this late-harvest wine a success, pressing the grapes pneumatically in view of their physical condition and, in particular, keeping the wine on the lees for six months to refine its aroma. This 1997 wine is straw-coloured with an open nose yielding fine scents of grapes dried on the vine together with a hint of liquorice. The impression of candied fruits is emphasised in the fat, well-balanced taste, which has a most pleasing persistence.

🔑 René Fleith-Eschard, lieu-dit Lange Matten, 68040 Ingersheim, tel. 03.89.27.24.19, fax 03.89.27.56.79 ☒ 🍷 by appt.

GEORGES ET CLAUDE FREYBURGER

Goldesch de Bergheim 1998★

☐ 0.35 ha 3,300 30–49 F

Founded in 1956 by Georges Freyburger, this estate has been run since 1988 by his son Claude, who cultivates 12 ha (30 acres) of vines. The style of viticulture practised is environmentally friendly and aims to get the best out of the soil. The Goldesch de Bergheim Riesling, of chalky-clay provenance, has a very expressive nose, with notes of citrus fruits. Lively and well-balanced on the palate, this is an elegant wine. (Residual sugar: 19 g/l.)

🔑 Georges et Claude Freyburger, rte des Vins, 68750 Bergheim, tel. 03.89.73.63.78, fax 03.89.73.82.91, e-mail cfreyburger@terre-net.fr ☒ 🍷 ev. day except Sun. 8am–12 noon 1.30pm–6pm

PIERRE FRICK

Vendanges tardives 1997★

☐ 0.65 ha 3,000 100–149 F

Pierre Frick is a specialist in biodynamics, which he has practised since 1981, having used organic methods since 1970. His wines have become extremely well-known both in France and elsewhere. His late-harvest Riesling, with its intense straw-yellow colour, is especially noteworthy for its very complex nose combining gunflint with citrus. The taste, which would have benefited from a touch more freshness, is nonetheless well-balanced and elegant.

🔑 Pierre Frick, 5, rue de Baer, 68250 Pfaffenheim, tel. 03.89.49.62.99, fax 03.89.49.62.99 ☒ 🍷 ev. day except Sun. 9am–11.30am 1.30pm–6.30pm

PIERRE-HENRI GINGLINGER

1998★

☐ 1.3 ha 11,000 30–49 F

Coming from a long line of wine-growers going back to 1684, Pierre-Henri Ginglinger cultivates 9 ha (22 acres) of vines. His Riesling, grown on chalky-clay soil, has a nose that is still not fully formed but with delicate oaky and spicy aromas. Marked by notes of undergrowth on the palate, it is a fleshy and well-balanced wine, the product of excellent fruit. (Residual sugar: 4 g/l.)

Pierre-Henri Ginglinger, 33, Grand-Rue, 68420 Eguisheim, tel. 03.89.41.32.55, fax 03.89.24.58.91, e-mail gingling@terre-net.fr by appt.

MICHEL GOETTELMANN 1998

☐ 0.21 ha 2,150 30–49 F

Established at Châtenois since 1991, Michel Goettelmann has wasted no time. He made his first wine in 1992 and began bottling in 1994. His Riesling, grown on gravelly soil, has a nose with nuances of flowers and fruit, and good attack on the palate. Its structure and persistence make this a very harmonious wine which will go well with fish. (Residual sugar: 3.9 g/l.)

Michel Goettelmann, 27, rue des Goumiers, 67730 Châtenois, tel. 03.88.82.12.40, fax 03.88.82.12.40 ev. day 8am–12 noon 1pm–7pm

JOSEPH GSELL 1998★★

☐ 1 ha 8,000 30–49 F

The very picturesque wine-making village of Orschwihr is a special place with high standards of quality, borne out by the fine skills of Joseph Gsell. Characterised by notes of citrus and exotic fruits, the nose of his Riesling is remarkably true to type. Fresh and well balanced on the palate, this is a persistent, distinguished, well-balanced wine, suitable for fish served with a sauce and seafood.

Joseph Gsell, 26, Grand-Rue, 68500 Orschwihr, tel. 03.89.76.95.11, fax 03.89.76.20.54 ev. day 9am–7pm

BERNARD ET DANIEL HAEGI

Brandluft Cuvée Prestige 1998★★

☐ 0.45 ha 3,400 30–49 F

In Mittelbergheim, where Bernard and Daniel Haegi grow 8 ha (20 acres) of vines, every cellar is a minor architectural marvel. The same could be said of this Riesling, grown on the famous chalky Brandluft soil. The nose is fruity with a tiny hint of Muscat, while the palate has structure and ideal balance. A distinguished, persistent wine that will go well with a creamy fish dish. (Residual sugar: 5 g/l.)

Bernard et Daniel Haegi, 33, rue de la Montagne, 67140 Mittelbergheim, tel. 03.88.08.95.80, fax 03.88.08.91.20 ev. day except Sun. 8am–12 noon 1pm–6pm

DOM. PIERRE HAGER

Weingarten 1998★★

☐ 0.75 ha 5,000 50–69 F

Pierre Hager is located in Orschwihr, a picturesque village in the south of the wine-growing area and an important centre for direct sales. His Weingarten Riesling, grown on gravelly soil, is very open. The nose is intense and the taste powerful and harmonious. This wine reflects the excellence of the fruit from which it is made. Serve with shellfish à l'américaine or a goat's cheese. (Residual sugar: 6 g/l.)

Dom. Pierre Hager, 26, rue de Soultzmatt, 68500 Orschwihr, tel. 03.89.76.11.19, fax 03.89.74.36.76 ev. day 9am–12 noon 2pm–6pm; Sun. by appt.

ANDRE HARTMANN

Armoirie Hartmann 1998★

☐ 0.66 ha n.c. 50–69 F

Wine-growers from father to son since the 17th century, the Hartmann family have stayed true to traditional wine methods. Their Armoirie Riesling, which comes from chalky marl soils, is still young and is developing a nose with aromas of overripeness. It opens well on the palate, revealing a very concentrated taste with a hint of roundness. A well-bred wine with a great future before it. (Residual sugar: 10 g/l.)

André Hartmann, 11, rue Roger-Frémeaux, 68420 Voegtlinshoffen, tel. 03.89.49.38.34, fax 03.89.49.26.18 ev. day except Sun. 9am–12 noon 1.30pm–6pm

LOUIS HAULLER

Vendanges tardives 1997★

☐ 0.5 ha 2,400 100–149 F

Having been coopers from father to son since 1775, the Haullers took up wine-growing at the beginning of the 20th century. Louis and his son Claude today tend some 10 ha (25 acres) of vines. Their late-harvest Riesling, brilliant gold in colour, mixes scents of lemon and honey. Passionfruit makes an appearance in a palate that is extremely complex, rich, fat and very long. The fresh finish is particularly agreeable. This wine would suit fish in sauce or a hot apple tart.

Louis et Claude Hauller, La Cave du Tonnelier, rue du Mal-Foch, 67650 Dambach-la-Ville, tel. 03.88.92.41.19, fax 03.88.92.47.10, e-mail claude.hauller@wanadoo.fr by appt.

VICTOR HERTZ 1998★★

☐ 0.65 ha 5,300 30–49 F

As the head of a renowned vineyard within the communes of Herrlisheim, Wettolsheim and Wintzenheim near Colmar, Victor Hertz has become an advocate of making specific wines from specific soils. He offers a Riesling grown on chalky clay, which has an intense and elegant nose with floral and fruity notes. Full in the mouth, this is a well-balanced, persistent and very distinguished wine which will keep for a long time and will go well with cooked fish. (Residual sugar: 9 g/l.)

Dom. Victor Hertz, 8, rue Saint-Michel, 68420 Herrlisheim, tel. 03.89.49.31.67, fax 03.89.49.22.84 by appt.

CHARLES JUX Réserve 1998★

☐ 1.1 ha 24,000 30–49 F

Riquewihr is not just the most famous medieval town in Alsace, it is also one of the region's wine centres. This Riesling marries mineral nuances and lemon notes in splendid harmony. Quite lively on the palate, structured and persistent, it will go well with Alsatian specialities and with fish and seafood. (Residual sugar: 4.5 g/l.)

Charles Jux, B.P. 3, 68340 Riquewihr, tel. 03.89.47.80.55 by appt.

DOM. KEHREN DENIS MEYER

Cuvée réservée Ulrich Meyer 1998

☐ 0.35 ha 2,400 30–49 F

Located at the entrance to the elevated village of Voegtlinshoffen, Denis Meyer's estate overlooks the Alsatian plain. Marked by its chalky origins, this Riesling remains youthful. It regales the nose with the perfumes of many fruits, including peaches. Well structured in the mouth, it is a well-balanced and persistent wine. (Residual sugar: 4 g/l.)

Denis Meyer, 2, rte du Vin, 68420 Voegtlinshoffen, tel. 03.89.49.38.00, fax 03.89.49.26.52 by appt.

KIEFFER 1998

☐ 1 ha 6,000 20–29 F

Located on the wine route in the Bas-Rhin department, Itterswiller is a wine-growing village decked with flowers and favoured by tourists, where visitors will find an abundance of hotels and restaurants. Jean-Charles Kieffer's business was founded in 1737. Bright and limpid in the glass, his lightish Riesling already has an element of mineral in the aroma.. This is carried through to the taste which has the vigour typical of the variety. (Residual sugar: 7 g/l.)

Jean-Charles Kieffer, 7, rte des Vins, 67140 Itterswiller, tel. 03.88.85.59.80, fax 03.88.57.81.44 by appt.

GEORGES KLEIN 1998★

☐ 1 ha 10,000 30–49 F

Located close to the Haut-Koenigsbourg, on the edge of the Bas-Rhin department, Saint-Hippolyte has kept a fair proportion of its medieval fortifications. The Georges Klein estate, established in 1958 with 3 ha (7 acres) of vines, now has 9 ha (22 acres). Marked by its granite origins, his Riesling has an expressive nose mingling notes of lemon, vegetation and minerals. In the mouth it is well-structured, powerful, long and well-balanced. (Residual sugar: 8 g/l.)

EARL Georges Klein et Fils, 10, rte du Vin, 68590 Saint-Hippolyte, tel. 03.89.73.00.28, fax 03.89.73.06.28, e-mail a.klein@rmcnet.fr by appt.

Auguste Klein

KLEIN AUX VIEUX REMPARTS

Schlossreben 1998★

☐ 0.45 ha 4,000 30–49 F

The estate's name evokes the old ramparts of Saint-Hippolyte and the wine name the Château of Haut-Koenigsbourg which dominates the village. Françoise and Jean-Marie Klein, both oenologists, have been in charge since 1973. They are both very keen on grape-quality. Despite its granite origins, this Riesling still seems young and its aromas are discreet. The nose is elegant, the taste powerful and well-balanced. A promising wine, it is suitable for fish or a chicken in white sauce. (Residual sugar: 3 g/l.)

Françoise et Jean-Marie Klein, rte du Haut-Koenigsbourg, 68590 Saint-Hippolyte, tel. 03.89.73.00.41, fax 03.89.73.04.94 ev. day 9am–11.30am 1.30pm–7pm; Sun. and groups by appt.

PIERRE ET FRANCOIS KOCH

Zellberg 1998

☐ 1 ha 4,000 30–49 F

At Nothalten, a village entirely devoted to viticulture, Pierre and François Koch have an estate of 12 ha (30 acres) of vines, which is quite substantial in Alsatian terms. Grown on chalk, their Zellberg Riesling is still in its youthful phase. The nose is rather discreet; the taste has a remaining hint of sugar that should fade with time. (Residual sugar: 5.5 g/l.)

Pierre et François Koch, 2, rte du Vin, 67680 Nothalten, tel. 03.88.92.42.30, fax 03.88.92.62.91 by appt.

PIERRE ET FRANCOIS KOCH

1998★

☐ 1.3 ha 5,500 30–49 F

The Koch estate offers a second Riesling, grown on granite and very clearly showing its origins. The nose is intense and complex, dominated by aromas of flowers and ripe fruits. Fairly supple and round in the mouth, it shows the full ripeness of the grapes. (Residual sugar: 4.1 g/l.)

Pierre et François Koch, 2, rte du Vin, 67680 Nothalten, tel. 03.88.92.42.30, fax 03.88.92.62.91 by appt.

KROSSFELDER 1998★

☐ n.c. 10,000 30–49 F

With nearly a century behind it, the Dambach Cave Coopérative is one of the oldest in Alsace, and indeed France, and belongs to the Wolfberger group. This beautifully

intense Riesling has a nose dominated by aromas of mature fruits. Powerful and well-balanced on the palate, it is a thoroughbred wine true to its type. (Residual sugar: 6 g/l.)
⊶ Krossfelder, 37, rue de La Gare, 67650 Dambach-la-Ville, tel. 03.88.92.40.03, fax 03.88.92.42.89 Y by appt.

KUENTZ Vendanges tardives 1997★

☐ 0.15 ha 1,300 70–99 F

On the wine route to the south of Colmar, Pfaffenheim stands where two great vintages meet, the Hatschbourg to the north and the Steinert to the south-west. Its position explains the special role the town has played in developing late-harvest wines. This particular wine is light yellow in colour, a sign of its youth. Nevertheless, the nose is already very expressive and yields most gratifying aromas of dried fruits. The palate subtly reveals a definite roundness and a good concentration of flavours. Will benefit from longer keeping.
⊶ R. Kuentz et Fils, 22–24, rue du Fossé, 68250 Pfaffenheim, tel. 03.89.49.61.90, fax 03.89.49.77.17 ☑ Y ev. day 9am–12 noon 2pm–7pm; Sun. by appt.

FREDERIC KUHLMANN
Muhlforst 1998★

☐ 0.18 ha n.c. 30–49 F

Frédéric Kuhlmann is not simply a wine-grower; he is also a music-lover, a fact confirmed by his many contacts in the world of music. His Riesling too is a symphony of sensations. The nose is marked by a fine harmony of floral and mineral notes. The taste is powerful and perfectly balanced. A persistent wine, very characteristic of the grape variety. (Residual sugar: 2 g/l.)
⊶ Frédéric Kuhlmann et Fils, 8, rue de la Fontaine, 68150 Hunawihr, tel. 03.89.73.60.33, fax 03.89.47.81.92, e-mail info@fkuhlmann.com ☑ Y by appt.
⊶ Willy Kuhlmann

MEISTERMANN 1998★

☐ 0.4 ha 4,000 30–49 F

The modernity of Pfaffenheim's bell-tower is deceptive, for the town has retained some of its heritage despite the destruction wrought by the Second World War, and wine-making is a continuing part of its deeply-rooted history. Grown on a chalky-clay soil, this Riesling has aromas of fruits. Notes of liquorice appear on the palate; the attack is dry and the finish long. The very thing to accompany *choucroute*, fish or seafood.
⊶ Michel Meistermann, 37, rue de l'Eglise, 68250 Pfaffenheim, tel. 03.89.49.60.61 ☑ Y by appt.

GILBERT MEYER
Cuvée Saint-Michel 1998★★

☐ n.c. 2,400 30–49 F

Voegtlinshoffen is a picturesque village perched up high, overlooking the plain of Colmar. Gilbert Meyer cultivates some 6 ha (15 acres) of vines there. With the Saint-Michel vintage, he offers a Riesling in full bloom. There is a positive explosion of aromas in the nose, citrus mingling with pineapple and crystallised fruits. Its fullness in the mouth gives the wine an element of softness, but the tasters thought its structure would bring it quickly to a perfect balance. A remarkable creation. (Residual sugar: 8 g/l.)
⊶ Gilbert Meyer, 5, rue du Schauenberg, 68420 Voegtlinshoffen, tel. 03.89.49.36.65, fax 03.89.86.42.45 ☑ Y by appt.

CAVE D'OBERNAI 1998

☐ n.c. 50,000 30–49 F

Lying in the plain, the town of Obernai is the ritual point of departure towards the Mont Sainte-Odile, the promontory dedicated to Alsace's eighth-century patroness. This co-operative, together with the Turckheim cellar, forms one of the main groups in the region. The Riesling offered is already quite developed, its nose bursting with aromas. Light and well-balanced on the palate, it finishes on a note of almond, making it suitable for serving with grilled fish. (Residual sugar: 5.4 g/l.)
⊶ Cave vinicole d'Obernai, 30, rue du Gal-Leclerc, 67210 Obernai, tel. 03.88.47.60.20, fax 03.88.47.60.22 ☑ Y by appt.

CH. D'ORSCHWIHR Enchenberg 1998★★

☐ 0.8 ha 2,500 30–49 F

In a very few years, Hubert Hartmann has breathed new life into the Château of Orschwihr, which has become a place not to be missed. His Enchenberg Riesling, grown on glacial conglomerate soils, is the product of exceptional fruit. While the nose has a concentration due to overripeness, the taste is dry, lively and very well structured. A wine with length, extraordinary in every sense. (Residual sugar: 3 g/l.)
⊶ Ch. d'Orschwihr, M. Hartmann, 68500 Orschwihr, tel. 03.89.74.25.00, fax 03.89.76.56.91, e-mail chateau-orschwihr@rmcnet.fr ☑ Y by appt.

LA CAVE DU ROI DAGOBERT
Vendanges tardives 1997

☐ 3 ha 10,000 100–149 F

Covering the whole of the region of Molsheim, the Roi Dagobert co-operative has become a force to reckon with, sometimes offering wines of great distinction. This late-harvest Riesling has a nose of imposing potential, with powerful and complex aromas of exotic fruits. Though still immature, the taste is nonetheless harmonious and has good length.
⊶ La cave du Roi Dagobert, 1, rte de Scharrachbergheim, 67310 Traenheim, tel. 03.88.50.69.00, fax 03.88.50.69.09 ☑ Y by appt.

WILLY ROLLI-EDEL
Silberberg de Rorschwihr 1998★★★

☐ 0.79 ha 1,623 50–69 F

Located in the south of the Haut-Koenigsbourg, in the small wine-making

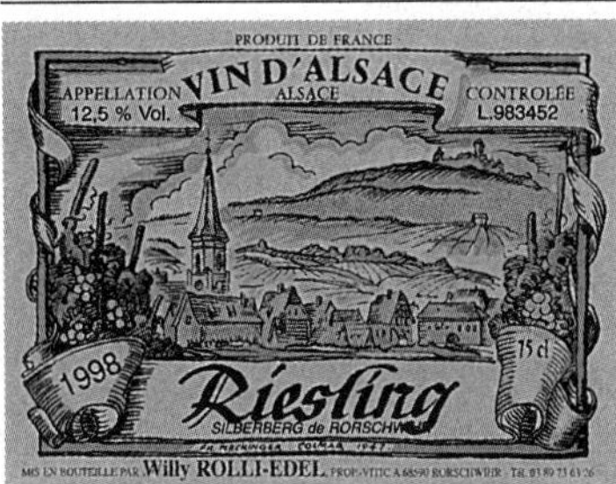

town of Rorschwihr, Willy Rolli tends the vines on his 11 ha (27 acres) with the hand of a master. Proof lies in this Riesling, grown on marly sand, which quite simply conquered the jury – 'Makes you want to drink it in great gulps' is how one taster's notes read. The nose of this 1998 wine is elegant, with notes of citrus and vanilla; it is structured, powerful and perfectly harmonious on the palate. Serve with the most elegant dishes. (Residual sugar: 14 g/l.)

⊶ Willy Rolli-Edel, 5, rue de l'Eglise, 68590 Rorschwihr, tel. 03.89.73.63.26, fax 03.89.73.83.50 ☑ Y by appt.

GILBERT RUHLMANN

Vendanges tardives 1997★

☐ 0.38 ha 1,000 70–99 F

Gilbert Ruhlmann has 10 ha (25 acres) of vines at Scherwiller, a commune with siliceous soils of granite origin especially good for Riesling. This wine has golden lights and an intense nose strongly marked by noble rot with overtones of crystallised fruits. It is perfectly balanced on the palate, its flavours slightly less pronounced than in the nose. It shows good potential for development.

⊶ Gilbert Ruhlmann Fils, 31, rue de l'Ortenbourg, 67750 Scherwiller, tel. 03.88.92.03.21, fax 03.88.82.30.19 ☑ Y by appt.

⊶ Guy Ruhlmann

DOM. RUNNER 1998★★

☐ 1 ha 10,000 30–49 F

With its 12 ha (30 acres) of vines, this vineyard offers a whole range of Alsatian wines. Francis Runner, who has just taken over, represents the third generation on the estate. Grown on chalky clay, his Riesling is already very expressive in the nose, with notes of citrus, particularly lime. It attacks the palate well and is a totally well-balanced and harmonious wine. Its persistence makes it good for serving with fish in sauce. (Residual sugar: 7 g/l.)

⊶ Dom. François Runner et Fils, 1, rue de la Liberté, 68250 Pfaffenheim, tel. 03.89.49.62.89, fax 03.89.49.73.69 ☑ Y ev. day 9am–12 noon 1pm–6pm

SAULNIER 1998★★

☐ 0.55 ha 4,800 30–49 F

Marco Saulnier began his career in Alsace as cooper to the Chambre d'Agriculture and was tempted to turn his knowledge to practical use, setting up in 1982. This Riesling, grown on a gravelly, loess-enriched soil, entirely fulfils expectation. The nose is intense, mixing hints of flowers and vanilla. The excellent first impressions give way to a palate that is fairly rounded, with a very concentrated and encompassing finish. (Residual sugar: 6 g/l.)

⊶ Marco Saulnier, rte de Saint-Marc, 68420 Gueberschwihr, tel. 03.89.86.42.02 ☑ Y by appt.

LOUIS SCHERB ET FILS

Vendanges tardives 1997★

☐ 0.28 ha 2,800 100–149 F

Gueberschwihr is a wine-making village 12 km (seven miles) from Colmar, which is worth stopping at to see the church with its Romanesque bell-tower and its old houses. Joseph and André Scherb cultivate more than 10 ha (25 acres) of vines there. Their bright golden-yellow late-harvest Riesling has complex citrus aromas with a touch of gunflint and *pain d'épice* (a kind of spicy loaf). On the palate it is full and warm. A very generous wine, which can be drunk now.

⊶ EARL Joseph et André Scherb, 1, rte de Saint-Marc, 68420 Gueberschwihr, tel. 03.89.49.30.83, fax 03.89.49.30.65 ☑ Y ev. day 8am–12 noon 1pm–7pm; Sun. 9am–12 noon

THIERRY SCHERRER

Vendanges tardives 1997★

☐ 0.21 ha 1,700 70–99 F

Having started out as a wine-specialist within trade firms, Thierry Scherrer took over the family holding at Ammerschwihr in 1993. Ammerschwihr is the largest wine-growing commune in the Haut-Rhin department; its Confrérie Saint-Etienne has been revived. The golden yellow colour immediately points to this being a quality product. It has a clear concentration of exotic and citrus fruits in the nose. The quite strong impression of sweetness in the mouth tends to balance the acidity. The wine is thus assured of a long life. The concentration of citrus-like aromas and great persistence also guarantee it. A splendid wine.

⊶ Thierry Scherrer, 1, rue de la Gare, 68770 Ammerschwihr, tel. 03.89.47.15.86, fax 03.89.47.15.86, e-mail thierry.scherrer@wanadoo.fr ☑ Y by appt.

MICHEL SCHOEPFER

Vieilles vignes d'Eguisheim 1998★

☐ 0.3 ha 2,000 30–49 F

Eguisheim is an incomparable medieval town. Michel Schoepfer energetically plies his art in the tithe court of the Abbey of Marbach, the history of which goes back to 1212. Grown on a chalky clay, his Riesling, with its very complex nose, is still blossoming. Well structured on the palate, this is a balanced wine distinguished by a small touch of roundness at the finish. (Residual sugar: 4 g/l.)

🔑 Michel Schoepfer, 43, Grand-Rue, 68420 Eguisheim, tel. 03.89.41.09.06, fax 03.89.23.08.50 ☒ 𝐘 ev. day 8am–12 noon 2pm–6pm

LOUIS SIPP Réserve personnelle 1998★

☐ 1.5 ha 12,700 50–69 F

Begun by Louis Sipp in 1920, the estate now belongs to the fourth generation. Although the firm has developed an extensive wine-merchant's business, it still jealously cares for its 32 ha (79 acres) of vines. Despite its chalky-clay soil of origin, this Riesling is already well open to the nose, judging by its lemony aromas. It attacks the palate well, is balanced and true to type. It will go well with regional specialities. (Residual sugar: 5 g/l.)

🔑 Louis Sipp Grands Vins d'Alsace, 5, Grand-Rue, 68150 Ribeauvillé, tel. 03.89.73.60.01, fax 03.89.73.31.46, e-mail louis@sipp.com ☒ 𝐘 by appt.

SPITZ ET FILS Vieilles vignes 1998★★

☐ 0.6 ha 6,400 30–49 F

Spitz et Fils have become a name to rely on. This 1998 Riesling demonstrates their skill yet again. It has a very seductive nose with citrus aromas enhanced by overripeness, and seems especially opulent in the mouth. Lively as it hits the palate, it reveals a fleshiness that will go wonderfully well with fish in sauce. A great wine. (Residual sugar: 4 g/l.)

🔑 Spitz et Fils, 2/4, rte des Vins, 67650 Blienschwiller, tel. 03.88.92.61.20, fax 03.88.92.61.26 ☒ 𝐘 by appt.

🔑 Dominique et M.-Claude Spitz

ANDRE STENTZ Rosenberg 1998★★

☐ 0.75 ha 3,300 50–69 F

André Stentz runs a nine-hectare (22-acre) estate established more than three centuries ago, and plunged into organic cultivation in 1982. Despite its chalky-clay soil of origin, his Rosenberg Riesling already has a very intense nose, with floral notes mingling with aromas of overripeness. Power and elegance unite on the palate to make it a wine of high class with a great future ahead of it. (Residual sugar: 12 g/l.)

🔑 André Stentz, 2, rue de la Batteuse, 68920 Wettolsheim, tel. 03.89.80.64.91, fax 03.89.79.59.75 ☒ 𝐘 by appt.

STENTZ-BUECHER Ortel 1998★

☐ 0.22 ha 850 50–69 F

Located at Wettolsheim, a small wine-making town close to Colmar, the Stentz-Buecher estate grows 14 ha (35 acres) of vines reputedly on the best soils around. Their Riesling has a nose characterised by complexity and overripeness. Very ample and structured on the palate and fairly round, this is a persistent wine that will go well with cooked fish. (Residual sugar: 15 g/l.)

🔑 Dom. Stentz-Buecher, 21, rue Kleb, 68920 Wettolsheim, tel. 03.89.80.68.09, fax 03.89.79.60.53 ☒ 𝐘 by appt.

DOMAINE STOEFFLER Kronenbourg 1998★★

☐ 0.4 ha 3,000 50–69 F

Martine and Vincent Stoeffler are both oenologists, and took over the family estate in 1986, committing all their skills to serving the wine-growing environment. The result is stunning. This Riesling, grown on chalky-marl soils, has a very open nose mixed with notes of citrus and hints of over-ripeness. Beautifully full on the palate, it is well-balanced, fleshy and persistent, and deserves every superlative. (Residual sugar: 6.8 g/l.)

🔑 Dom. Martine et Vincent Stoeffler, 1, rue des Lièvres, 67140 Barr, tel. 03.88.08.52.50, fax 03.88.08.17.09, e-mail vins.stoeffler@wanadoo.fr ☒ 𝐘 ev. day except Sun. 8am–12 noon 1.30pm–6.30pm

ACHILLE THIRION 1998★

☐ n.c. 18,000 30–49 F

With its vineyards scattered over the slopes of the Haut-Koenigsbourg, the Achille Thirion estate goes back to 1760. Blending mineral, floral, and lemony notes, the nose of their Riesling is highly characteristic of the variety. The same is true of the taste, which is well-balanced and long. A wine to drink beside the sea. (Residual sugar: 5 g/l.)

🔑 Dom. Achille Thirion, 69, rte du Vin, 68590 Saint-Hippolyte, tel. 03.89.73.00.23, fax 03.89.73.06.46 ☒ 𝐘 by appt.

THOMANN Clos du Letzenberg 1998★

☐ 0.32 ha 1,908 50–69 F

The Thomann family have undertaken the immense task of restoring the hillside of the Letzenberg, which was abandoned after the First World War owing to the steepness of the site. Grown in a propitious south-facing location, this Riesling has a nose marked by aromas of citrus and honey. Frank and lively in approach, the wine is well-balanced and persistent on the palate. A very high-quality wine. (Residual sugar: 7 g/l.)

🔑 Vins Le Manoir, 56, rue de la Promenade, 68040 Ingersheim, tel. 03.89.27.23.69, fax 03.89.27.23.69 ☒ 𝐘 by appt.

🔑 Thomann

CAVE DE TURCKHEIM

Heimbourg 1998★

☐ 3.5 ha 23,900 50–69 F

Established in 1955 and covering the best hillsides of the district, the wine cellar of Turckheim has gained a solid reputation which this 1998 Riesling will do nothing to dislodge. Despite its chalky origins, it already displays a well-developed nose, with mineral aromas mingling with notes of overripeness. It has a good attack and is a lively wine, well equipped for laying down, and finishes on notes of ripe fruits. (Residual sugar: 5.2 g/l.)

Cave de Turckheim, 16, rue des Tuileries, 68230 Turckheim, tel. 03.89.30.23.60, fax 03.89.27.35.33, e-mail brandt@cave-turckheim.com ☒ by appt.

LAURENT VOGT

Rothstein Vendanges tardives 1997★

☐ 0.5 ha 3,000 100–149 F

Thomas Vogt joined his father on the family vineyard of 11 ha (27 acres) in 1998. Their late-harvest Riesling is a great success with its brilliant green golden colour, its harmonious and complex nose, mingling honey with nuances of butter and passionfruit, and its palate in which all the aromatic richness perceived in the nose is tasted in the mouth. Full and rich, this wine is dominated by residual sugar which tends to balance the acidity. Good potential for future improvement.

EARL Laurent Vogt, 4, rue des Vignerons, 67120 Wolxheim, tel. 03.88.38.50.41, fax 03.88.38.50.41 ☒ by appt.

VORBURGER 1998★★★

☐ n.c. n.c. 30–49 F

This family concern was founded in 1958 at Voegtlinshoffen, a charming village from which one can view the Alsace wine region. Their Riesling, grown on chalky-clay, is outstanding. While the nose mixes notes of citrus, honey, and overripeness, the palate possesses remarkable structure and length with just the right amount of richness. A wine worthy of the best cooked fish. (Residual sugar: 3 g/l.)

EARL Jean-Pierre Vorburger et Fils, 3, rue de la Source, 68420 Voegtlinshoffen, tel. 03.89.49.35.52, fax 03.89.49.35.52 ☒ ev. day except Sun. 8am–12 noon 1.30pm–6pm

JEAN WACH 1998

☐ 1.5 ha 6,000 30–49 F

Andlau, a small town owing its existence to an abbey founded at the end of the ninth century, is dedicated exclusively to the cult of the vine and possesses a variety of terrains. Jean Wach cultivates nearly 20 ha (25 acres) there. His Riesling has a nose marked by a mineral note and the wine attacks the palate well. Well-structured, this wine is both true to type and persistent. (Residual sugar: 6.2 g/l.)

Jean Wach, 16A, rue du Mal-Foch, 67140 Andlau, tel. 03.88.08.09.73, fax 03.88.08.09.73 ☒ ev. day except Sun. 8am–12 noon 2pm–7pm

ANDRE WANTZ

Riesling de Mittelbergheim 1998★

☐ 2 ha 1,800 30–49 F

Established in Mittelbergheim for over four hundred years, the Wantz family cultivate 10 ha (25 acres) of vines. They offer us a Riesling of chalky-clay origin very true to its terroir. Although the nose is still young, this 1998 wine nevertheless releases floral and mineral notes and attacks the palate very cleanly. It has the balance and persistence necessary to accompany *choucroute* or fish. (Residual sugar: 4.12 g/l.)

André Wantz, 41, rue des Vosges, 67140 Mittelbergheim, tel. 03.88.08.44.52, fax 03.88.08.46.32 ☒ ev. day 8am–12 noon 1pm–7pm; Sun. 8am–12 noon

ALBERT WINTER Muhlforst 1998★

☐ 0.11 ha 1,200 30–49 F

Near the famous fortified church of Hunawihr, Albert Winter cultivates an estate that is modest in size (4 ha/10 acres) but of interest for the quality of its production. He offers a very intense Riesling, grown on chalky-clay soil. The nose of this 1998 wine is dominated by aromas of grapefruit. The first impression on the palate is quite supple, and the wine very quickly reveals its whole structure. A thoroughbred wine with great aromatic persistence. (Residual sugar: 6 g/l.)

Albert Winter, 17, rue Sainte-Hune, 68150 Hunawihr, tel. 03.89.73.62.95, fax 03.89.73.62.95 ☒ by appt.

WUNSCH ET MANN

Vendanges tardives Collection Joseph Mann 1997★

☐ 0.9 ha 4,200 100–149 F

Founded in 1948, the firm is famous throughout the Alsace wine region, Monsieur Mann being Grand Master of the Confrérie Saint-Etienne. The company are wine-merchants and cultivate their own 20 ha (49 acres) of vines. As yet this brilliant light-yellow wine has a discreet nose, though it nonetheless releases hints of candied fruits and spices. In the mouth, the wine's fullness and richness are already perceptible, even if it remains for the moment austere and immature. A shy wine that will open up in time.

🔑 Wunsch et Mann, 2, rue des Clefs, 68920 Wettolsheim, tel. 03.89.22.91.25, fax 03.89.80.05.21, e-mail wunsch-mann@wanadoo.fr ☒ 🍷 by appt.

DOM. XAVIER WYMANN

Steinacker de Ribeauvillé 1998★★

□ 0.4 ha n.c. 🍾 30–49 F

When your name is Wymann ('wine-man' in Alsatian), it can only mean one thing: you were born into the business. So it was with this young, 30-year-old winemaker, who in 1996 took over the family vineyard. Grown on a soil of chalky shingle, this Riesling has a very elegant nose with notes of white flowers and retains all its youth. Dry and harmonious on the palate, it definitely bears the stamp of its terroir. A wine of great class. (Residual sugar: 4.71 g/l.)

🔑 Xavier Wymann, 41, rue de la Fraternité, 68150 Ribeauvillé, tel. 03.89.73.66.83, fax 03.89.73.66.83 ☒ 🍷 by appt.

PAUL ZINCK Prestige 1998★

□ 0.9 ha 6,000 🍾 🌡 30–49 F

Paul Zinck has more than one string to his bow. Not satisfied with cultivating the family estate of 8 ha (20 acres) handed down through the generations, in 1990 he opened an Alsatian restaurant in which his wines could be sampled. Grown on chalky-clay soil, his Prestige wine is developing aromas of great ripeness in the nose. Its lovely structure means that it can tolerate the hint of sweetness that rounds off the finish, making it a suitable accompaniment to, for example, a seafood vol-au-vent. (Residual sugar: 6 g/l.)

🔑 Paul Zinck, 18, rue des Trois-Châteaux, 68420 Eguisheim, tel. 03.89.41.19.11, fax 03.89.24.12.85, e-mail phz@p-zinck.fr ☒ 🍷 ev. day except Sun. 8am–12 noon 2pm–6pm; cl. Jan.

ZOELLER Vendanges tardives 1997

□ n.c. n.c. 🍾🍾 100–149 F

Established in 1700, this firm has been bottling its wines for a hundred years or so. Pale gold with green lights, their late-harvest Riesling offers a grapefruit-dominated nose, indicating great freshness. There is an excellent acid-alcohol-sugar balance, and the palate is young but promising.

🔑 GAEC Maison Zoeller, 14, rue de l'Eglise, 67120 Wolxheim, tel. 03.88.38.15.90, fax 03.88.38.15.90, e-mail vins.Zoeller@wanadoo.fr ☒ 🍷 ev. day except Sun. 8.30am–12 noon 1.30pm–7pm; cl. during the grape harvest season

Alsace Muscat

Two varieties of Muscat are used to make this dry, aromatic white wine, which is reminiscent of the burst of flavour you get when biting into a fresh grape. One variety, traditionally called Muscat d'Alsace, is more accurately known as the Muscat de Frontignan. It is a late-maturing variety so it is planted on slopes with the best aspect. The second variety, which develops earlier and so is more widely grown, is the Muscat Ottonel. The two varieties are planted on 340 ha (840 acres), 2.4% of the Alsace vineyard. The Muscat d'Alsace is a pleasing and sometimes surprising speciality. It makes a good aperitif and is a good wine to serve at drinks parties. It goes well with cakes or salty nibbles like pretzels.

JOSEPH FREUDENREICH 1998

□ 0.28 ha 3,000 🍾 🌡 30–49 F

The Freudenreich family have been settled in Eguisheim since 1566. Their headquarters are located a hundred metres or so from the château in which the 11th-century Pope Leo IX was born. Grown on a chalky-clay soil and made from equal proportions of Muscat Ottonel and Muscat d'Alsace, this wine has a very intense nose and a supple, fruity taste; it is a typical example of its appellation. Drink as an aperitif. (Residual sugar: 3 g/l.)

🔑 Joseph Freudenreich et Fils, 3, cour Unterlinden, 68420 Eguisheim, tel. 03.89.41.36.87, fax 03.89.41.67.12, e-mail info@joseph-freudenreich.fr ☒ 🍷 ev. day 8am–12 noon 1.30pm–7pm; groups by appt.; cl. Sun. in winter

HARTWEG Cuvée Prestige 1998

□ 0.4 ha 2,100 🍾 50–69 F

With its 8 ha (20 acres) of vines, this vineyard is now being worked by the fourth generation, represented by son Frank's arrival in 1996. Grown on chalky-clay, the Muscat is still a young wine in which the character of the grape mixes with spicy notes in the nose. Fairly rich and well structured on the palate, this is a persistent wine. (Residual sugar: 26 g/l.)

🔑 Jean-Paul et Frank Hartweg, 39, rue Jean-Macé, 68980 Beblenheim, tel. 03.89.47.94.79, fax 03.89.49.00.83 ☒ 🍷 ev. day except Sun. 8am–11.30am 1.30pm–6pm

LEON HEITZMANN 1998★★

☐ 0.63 ha 7,000 30–49 F

Endowed with its 11 ha (27 acres) of vines and a long tradition, this vineyard is an aspect of Ammerschwihr which is not to be missed. Despite the chalky-clay soil of origin, this very Alsatian Muscat is a particularly elegant wine with notes of fresh grapes and is already blossoming well in the nose. The same explosive aromatic character is even more evident in the mouth. A very distinguished wine, very full and persistent. (Residual sugar: 3 g/l.)

Léon Heitzmann, 2, Grand-Rue, 68770 Ammerschwihr, tel. 03.89.47.10.64, fax 03.89.78.27.76 ev. day except Sun. 8am–12 noon 1.30pm–6pm

DOM. DE LA SINNE

Sélection de Grains nobles 1997★

☐ 0.25 ha 1,000 150–199 F

In Ammerschwihr, one of the cradles of Alsatian viticulture, the Geschickt family have a vineyard of about 10 ha (25 acres). A number of specialities, like this *Sélection de Grains Nobles* Muscat wine, demonstrate the oenological expertise of these growers. The brilliant straw-yellow colour and the candied nose with its acute notes of noble rot make for a good beginning. And the taste lives up to expectation, having good balance, harmony, great richness and good length. (Half-litre bottles)

GAEC Jérôme Geschickt et Fils, 1, pl. de la Sinne, 68770 Ammerschwihr, tel. 03.89.47.12.54, fax 03.89.47.34.76 by appt.

ROLLY GASSMANN

Moenchreben de Rorschwihr 1998★★★

☐ 0.89 ha 6,000 70–99 F

Rolly-Gassmann is a concern whose reputation for excellence has come down through the generations. Once again, it has achieved perfection with this great Muscat. Grown on a chalky-marl soil, it has a very intense nose; notes of linden-flowers mingle with fruitiness, giving it an exceptionally high quality. The wine is beautifully full on the palate, and there is an element of roundness which, assisted by the structure, produces real harmony. (Residual sugar: 12 g/l.)

Rolly Gassmann, 2, rue de l'Eglise, 68590 Rorschwihr, tel. 03.89.73.63.28, fax 03.89.73.33.06 by appt.

JEAN-LOUIS SCHOEPFER

Vendanges tardives 1997★★

☐ 0.15 ha 700 70–99 F

The Schoepfer family have been winegrowers at Wettolsheim since 1656. Gilles joined Jean-Louis in the business in 1997. Yellow with green lights, their late-harvest Muscat has a very attractive nose combining a certain fleshiness with scents of Muscat and lilac. Its contact with the palate is soft, velvety and full. It is redolent of dry Muscat grapes. A charming wine with great persistence.

EARL Jean-Louis Schoepfer, 35, rue Herzog, 68920 Wettolsheim, tel. 03.89.80.71.29, fax 03.89.79.61.35 by appt.

WINTER 1998★

☐ 0.13 ha 1,200 30–49 F

Although Albert Winter's terrain has remained on a human scale (4 ha/10 acres), he nevertheless manages to cultivate all the Alsatian varieties. His Muscat, grown on chalky-clay soil, is already open to the nose and true to type. Although the attack on the palate is softish, it still has good balance owing to its acid structure. A promising wine. (Residual sugar: 18 g/l.)

Albert Winter, 17, rue Sainte-Hune, 68150 Hunawihr, tel. 03.89.73.62.95, fax 03.89.73.62.95 by appt.

Alsace Gewurztraminer

The grape variety used to make this wine is a particularly aromatic member of the Traminer family. In a treatise published in 1551 it was already being acknowledged as a variety that was typical of Alsace. Ideally suited to the Alsace *terroir*, it has been adapted over the centuries to create top-quality wines with a worldwide reputation.

It makes full-bodied, well-structured wines, which are basically dry but with some softness and have a marvellous, characteristic bouquet, which varies in power depending on the year and on where the grapes are grown. Gewurztraminer is an early-fruiting variety and has a limited and unreliable yield, but it produces very ripe grapes. About 2,500 ha (6,175 acres) are planted with Gewurztraminer, 17.6% of the Alsace wine region. It is often served as an aperitif or at drinks parties, and it is a good accompaniment to desserts, as well as being an excellent foil, particularly when full and rich in character, for strongly flavoured cheeses, such as Roquefort and Munster.

DOM. PIERRE ADAM

Kaefferkopf 1998★★

☐ 0.5 ha 3,500 50–69 F

Ammerschwihr, with 400 ha (988 acres) of vines, is without doubt one of the major wine-growing communes of the Alsace region. Pierre Adam has 11 ha (27 acres) of these, notably in Le Kaefferkopf, a locality which has made the village's reputation for over sixty years and in which this Gewurztraminer is grown. The nose is a mix of delicate notes of honey, acacia and citrus, and there is a similar, well-balanced complexity of sensations in the mouth. It will be well worth waiting a year or two to really enjoy this wine. (Residual sugar: 20 g/l.)

Dom. Pierre Adam, 8, rue du Lt-Louis-Mourier, 68770 Ammerschwihr, tel. 03.89.78.23.07, fax 03.89.47.39.68, e-mail domaine.pierre.adam@wanadoo.fr ev. day 8am–12 noon 1pm–7pm

LUCIEN ALBRECHT

Cuvée Martine Albrecht 1998

☐ 7 ha 50,000 50–69 F

Established in 1772, this family estate extends a warm welcome to private customers. In addition to discovering the estate's wines, it is possible during the summer months to see the work of Alsatian artists exhibited in the 18th-century cellar. Their Martine Albrecht Gewurztraminer receives regular praise. Floral and fruity, the 1998 version is beginning to open out. Best advice is to wait a few more months to allow it to acquire greater length and fruitiness. (Residual sugar: 15 g/l.)

Lucien Albrecht, 9, Grand-Rue, 68500 Orschwihr, tel. 03.89.76.95.18, fax 03.89.76.20.22, e-mail lucien.albrecht@wanadoo.fr ev. day 8am–7pm; cl. Sun. from Jan. until June

Jean Albrecht

DOM. ALLIMANT-LAUGNER

Sélection de grains nobles 1997★★

☐ 0.15 ha 600 100–149 F

This estate, beneath the Château of the Haut-Koenigsbourg, is regularly mentioned in wine books. Its Sélection de Grains Nobles received much praise from the tasters. It has an intense golden-yellow colour with orangey glints. Its nose, though still rather discreet, gives off the odd note of dried apricot and other crystallised fruits. The palate, however, is exquisite, fleshy, rich and powerful, finishing on aromas of apricot jam. It is, to borrow the terms of one delighted taster, 'a really liqueur-like wine'. A very great wine that needs to be kept a little longer.

Allimant-Laugner, 10, Grand-Rue, 67600 Orschwiller, tel. 03.88.92.06.52, fax 03.88.82.76.38, e-mail alaugner@terre-net.fr ev. day except Sun. 9am–7pm

Hubert Laugner

LAURENT BANNWARTH

Bildstoecklé 1998★

☐ 1.8 ha 9,500 30–49 F

At Obermorschwihr is a half-timbered church which, although it is the only one of its kind in the department, might symbolise historic, unchanging Alsace. This wine-grower is no less committed to traditional ways: he practises natural fermentation, keeps the wine on fine lees, and bottles in September. His wines often figure in wine books. Chosen here is his Bildstoecklé Gewurztraminer. The appeal of the 1998 version lies in its characteristic golden-yellow colour and powerful, fruity, spicy nose. A little light at the finish, it is round and honey-like in the mouth. (Residual sugar: 15 g/l.)

Laurent Bannwarth et Fils, 9, rte du Vin, 68420 Obermorschwihr, tel. 03.89.49.30.87, fax 03.89.49.29.02, e-mail bannwarth@rmcnet.fr by appt.

DOM. BARMES-BUECHER

Wintzenheim 1998

☐ 0.6 ha 2,400 70–99 F

This 15-hectare (37-acre) estate, resulting from the union of two wine-growing families, has a number of different terroirs, which explains how it can produce 30 different wines. The Wintzenheim terrain, a chalky marl, yielded wonderful wines in 1994, 1996 and 1997. The 1998 version is perhaps a little lacking in complexity, but was still adjudged a handsome wine, having a very expressive nose, a well-balanced and long taste with savours of fruits and spices. (Residual sugar: 30 g/l.)

Dom. Barmès-Buecher, 30, rue Sainte-Gertrude, 68920 Wettolsheim, tel. 03.89.80.62.92, fax 03.89.79.30.80, e-mail barmes-buecher@terre-net.fr by appt.

LEON BAUR

Vendanges tardives Cuvée 2000 1997★★

☐ 0.78 ha 3,200 100–149 F

This well-known vineyard was established in 1738 in the picturesque village of Eguisheim. Its very limpid golden-yellow wine is a credit to the district in which it was grown. It has a pleasing nose with scents of rose, lily of the valley and crystallised fruits, and on the palate displays a delightful smoothness with elegant aromas, richness, fullness and persistence.

Jean-Louis Baur, 22, rue du Rempart-Nord, 68420 Eguisheim, tel. 03.89.41.79.13, fax 03.89.41.93.72 by appt.

HUBERT BECK

Vendanges tardives 1997★

☐ 0.57 ha 3,000 ▮▮ 100–149 F

This concern specialises in sales to wine professionals, like specialist wine shops and wine-importers – three-quarters of its production is drunk outside France. Their golden-yellow late-harvest Gewurztraminer has a discreet nose which nevertheless reveals a beautiful range of aromas when given time to breathe. The palate is delicate, combining honey with crystallised fruit (apricots). The wine already has remarkable persistence, sustained by its fresh acidity. The 1996 version was awarded a *coup de coeur* by the jury.

Hubert Beck, 25, rue du Gal-de-Gaulle, 67650 Dambach-la-Ville, tel. 03.88.92.45.90, fax 03.88.92.61.28 ☑ Y ev. day except Sun. 8am–12 noon 1.30pm–6pm

EMILE BEYER

Cuvée de l'Hostellerie Au Cheval blanc 1998

☐ 0.88 ha 8,000 ▮▮ 50–69 F

The former hostelry *Au Cheval Blanc* is the headquarters of this family concern which goes back to 1580. Only a stone's throw from the château, the cellar is also one of the oldest in the region and great wines are still kept there. This particular wine is beginning to open up with aromas of fruits and a hint of orange blossom. On the palate, the wine is smooth, rich and spicy. An excellent example. (Residual sugar: 32 g/l.)

Maison Emile Beyer, 7, pl. du Château, 68420 Eguisheim, tel. 03.89.41.40.45, fax 03.89.41.64.21, e-mail info@émile-beyer.fr ☑ Y ev. day 9am–12 noon 2pm–6pm

PATRICK BEYER 1998

☐ 0.4 ha 2,400 30–49 F

A traditional, rural peasant scene – a couple of wine-growers in costume before a village and vine-clad hillsides – adorns the label on this 1998 wine. Left to breathe, its aromas open up to yield notes of fresh fruits. It surprises the palate with its dual character, combining the freshness of youth with the richness of slowly fading residual sugar. (Residual sugar: 23 g/l.)

Patrick Beyer, 27, rue des Alliés, 67680 Epfig, tel. 03.88.85.50.21, fax 03.88.57.81.46 ☑ Y ev. day 9am–11.30am 2pm–7pm

BOTT FRERES

Réserve personnelle Vin de Prestige 1998★

☐ 1 ha 7,000 ▮▮ 100–149 F

As the traveller enters Ribeauvillé, he or she should visit this cellar, both to see its large wooden casks, which are more than 100 years old, and to discover well-chosen wines like this Réserve Personnelle Gewurztraminer. Initially closed, the nose opens to reveal a wide range of aromas: the same medley is repeated on the palate, where the fruit will assert itself further with time. A wine to be drunk as an aperitif or to accompany a sweet-and-savoury dish. (Residual sugar: 12 g/l.)

Bott Frères, 13, av. du Gal-de-Gaulle, 68150 Ribeauvillé, tel. 03.89.73.22.50, fax 03.89.73.22.59, e-mail vinsbott-freres.fr ☑ Y ev. day 9am–12 noon 2pm–6pm; groups by appt.

Laurent Bott

CAMILLE BRAUN Uffholtz 1998★★

☐ 0.35 ha 2,500 30–49 F

A 'witches' chapel' overlooks the Orschwihr wine-growing district. Is that why this straw-yellow Gewurztraminer is so bewitching? It has an aromatic nose offering nuances of rose, acacia flowers and honey, indicating a good mature product with perfect balance. The finish is a bouquet of flowers with long-lingering aromas. (Residual sugar: 17 g/l.)

Camille Braun, 16, Grand-Rue, 68500 Orschwihr, tel. 03.89.76.95.20, fax 03.89.74.35.03 ☑ Y ev. day except Sun. 8am–12 noon 1.30pm–7pm

BUECHER-FIX

Cuvée Sainte-Gertrude 1998★★

☐ 0.8 ha 9,200 ▮ 🌡 30–49 F

Established in 1934, this vineyard is in the lee of the foothills of the Vosges, dominated by châteaux of the 12th and 13th centuries. The mastery of recent techniques has led to some great wines being produced in the cellar, like this intensely fruity 1998 Gewurztraminer. The attack is beautiful, anticipating the fullness of the wine and the rich medley of aromas: flowers, fruits and spices. The subtle finish rounds off its harmony. 'Lots of class,' observed one taster. (Residual sugar: 8 g/l.)

Buecher-Fix, 21, rue Sainte-Gertrude, 68920 Wettolsheim, tel. 03.89.80.64.93, fax 03.89.79.61.56 ☑ Y by appt.

Buecher

BUTTERLIN 1998★

☐ 1.15 ha 5,200 ▮ 30–49 F

Jean Butterlin took the estate over from his father in 1980. He cultivates 8 ha (20 acres) of vines. His Gewurztraminer has a nose that begins discreetly, then strengthens to reveal a fruity character. The wine's fullness in the mouth is accentuated by a certain sweetness. There is a peppery note in addition to the exotic fruits. Though of middling persistence, the wine is nevertheless very easy to like. (Residual sugar: 9 g/l.)

Jean Butterlin, 27, rue Herzog, 68920 Wettolsheim, tel. 03.89.80.60.85, fax 03.89.80.58.61, e-mail info@butterlin.fr ☑ Y by appt.

CAVE DE CLEEBOURG 1998★

☐ 22 ha 60,000 ▮ 🌡 30–49 F

Established in 1946 in the northern part of the Alsace wine-making district, the Cléebourg co-operative makes wine from 170 ha (420 acres) of vines. Their golden-yellow Gewurztraminer has a very expressive nose, mixing notes of roses and exotic fruits which develop as the wine is exposed to the air. The palate is full, well-balanced and long,

combining the earlier aromatic elements of mango and rose with peaches, (Residual sugar: 7.5 g/l.)
Cave vinicole de Cléebourg, rte du Vin, 67160 Cléebourg, tel. 03.88.94.50.33, fax 03.88.94.57.08, e-mail cave.cleebourg@wanadoo.fr ev. day 10am–12 noon 2pm–6pm; groups by appt.

ANDRE DOCK

Vendanges tardives 1997★★

n.c. 2,000 70–99 F

This estate, not far from Barr, one of the wine centres of the Bas-Rhin department, hosts a wine fair every Bastille Day involving all the villages in southern Bas-Rhin. Its own late-harvest Gewurztraminer, golden-yellow in colour with green lights, has a nose of flowers, musk and vanilla. These elements, with an admixture of citrus, are also active in the fruit-dominated taste, which has warmth sustained by good acidity. (Half-litre bottles)
André et Christian Dock, 20, rue Principale, 67140 Heiligenstein, tel. 03.88.08.02.69, fax 03.88.08.19.72 ev. day 8am–12 noon 1pm–6pm

ANDRE DUSSOURT

Réserve Prestige 1998

0.4 ha 2,150 70–99 F

Coming from a long line of Blienschwiller wine-growers, André Dussourt established himself in 1964 at Scherwiller, a pretty village dominated by the ruins of the château of Ortenbourg. Today he has 10 ha (25 acres). This wine displays aromatic nuances typical of Gewurztraminer. The substance is admittedly average, but the full, intense, round and lightly spiced palate has good harmony. (Residual sugar: 23 g/l.)
André Dussourt, 2, rue de Dambach, 67750 Scherwiller, tel. 03.88.92.10.27, fax 03.88.92.18.44 ev. day except Sun. 8am–12 noon 1.30pm–6pm
Paul Dussourt

FAHRER-ACKERMANN

Silbergrube 1998

0.4 ha 2,100 50–69 F

After working for Michel Fahrer for eight years, Vincent Ackermann has taken over these 7.5 ha (19 acres) of vines, which lie below the Château of the Haut-Koenigsbourg. His Silbergrube Gewurztraminer, grown on silty-clay soil, needs time for its fresh, fine aromas to open. Similarly, on the palate, the wine is full and true to type, but has not yet developed fully. It would be better opened around 2002. (Residual sugar: 24 g/l.)
Fahrer-Ackermann, 15, rte du Vin, 67600 Orschwiller, tel. 03.88.92.90.23, fax 03.88.92.90.23 by appt.
Vincent Ackermann

SYLVIE FAHRERŒŒ

Bruchwegreben 1998★

0.52 ha 1,200 30–49 F

Sylvie Fahrer took over the reins of the family vineyard, currently 6 ha (15 acres) of vines, in 1995. Her Bruchwegreben wine is golden with amber lights. The nose is lively and spicy with a hint of bergamot. Honey aromas play on the palate, thereby enhancing the impression of richness and roundness left by this lovely wine. (Residual sugar: 27 g/l.)
Sylvie Fahrer, 24, rte du Vin, 68590 Saint-Hippolyte, tel. 03.89.73.00.40, fax 03.89.73.00.40 by appt.

ALBERT FALLER

Vendanges tardives Cuvée Théo 1997★

0.3 ha 1,600 70–99 F

This 7.6-ha (19-acre) estate is located at Itterswiller, a pretty village full of flowers from spring onwards. Its golden late-harvest Cuvée Théo has an attractive, delicate nose which marries apricot and quince. The same fruits, joined by honey, are to be found on the palate. Persistence is middling, but the wine is beautifully subtle. (Half-litre bottles)
EARL André Faller, 2, rte du Vin, 67140 Itterswiller, tel. 03.88.85.53.55, fax 03.88.85.51.13 by appt.

DOM. FLEISCHER

Vendanges tardives 1997★

0.31 ha 3,600 100–149 F

Established in 1990, this young estate has gone from 3.5 to 8 ha (9 to 20 acres). It markets around 60,000 bottles a year. This late-harvest Gewurztraminer has a discreet nose which nevertheless hints at crystallised fruits. Its good, clean-tasting attack is the mark of a wine that is already pleasing and has good potential.
Dom. Fleischer, 28, rue du Moulin, 68250 Pfaffenheim, tel. 03.89.49.62.70, fax 03.89.49.50.74 by appt.

JEAN GEILER

Vendanges tardives Cuvée An 2000 1997

3 ha 25,000 70–99 F

Founded in 1926, the Ingersheim co-operative sells its top-quality wines under the name of Jean Geiler. The colour of this late-harvest wine is a bright, intense golden yellow. The nose is discreet, with a hint of toasted bread. Supple and clean-tasting on hitting the palate, the wine has persistence. It is already fairly well balanced, and will become totally harmonious in a short time. (Half-litre bottles)
Cave vinicole Jean Geiler, 45, rue de la République, 68040 Ingersheim, tel. 03.89.27.05.96, fax 03.89.27.51.24 by appt.

HENRI GROSS ET FILS

Vendanges tardives 1996★

0.2 ha 1,300 70–99 F

Ten years ago, Rémy Gross took over the family concern. His late-harvest Gewurztraminer impressed the jury with its straw-yellow colour and glistering lights, its intense nose combining notes of citrus and noble rot, and its well-balanced, full-bodied, rich, complex palate, the product of high-quality grapes. (Half-litre bottles)

🔑 EARL Henri Gross et Fils, 11, rue du Nord, 68420 Gueberschwihr, tel. 03.89.49.24.49, fax 03.89.49.33.58 ☑ 𝐈 by appt.
🔑 Rémy Gross

JOSEPH GRUSS ET FILS

Cuvée du Millénaire 1998

☐ 1 ha 6,000 50–69 F

In 1997, after studying oenology, André Gruss joined his father on the family vineyard of 13 ha (32 acres). Their golden Millennium wine has a fruitiness that develops slightly on exposure to air. Though fairly powerful, the taste remains quite balanced. (Residual sugar: 15 g/l.)
🔑 Joseph Gruss et Fils, 25, Grand-Rue, 68420 Eguisheim, tel. 03.89.41.28.78, fax 03.89.41.76.66, e-mail gruss@hotmail.com ☑ 𝐈 ev. day 8am–12 noon 1.30pm–6pm

HENRI GSELL

Vendanges tardives 1997★

☐ 0.5 ha 5,000 70–99 F

This property, which dates from the early 19th century, lies in the heart of Eguisheim. The cellar walls, 1.2 metres (4 ft) thick, were once part of the town's fortifications. From there comes this intense golden-yellow late-harvest wine. The nose is expressive, mixing aromas of stewed fruits and spices with a hint of the exotic. On the palate the quality and power of the wine's raw materials are revealed; on the finish there are notes of honey and acacia. (Half-litre bottles)
🔑 Henri Gsell, 22, rue du Rempart-Sud, 68420 Eguisheim, tel. 03.89.41.96.40, fax 03.89.41.58.46 ☑ 𝐈 by appt.

ANDRE HARTMANN

Terrasses du Hagelberg 1998★

☐ 0.3 ha n.c. 50–69 F

This estate, a favourite with wine-writers, is proud of its Hagelberg terraces. Reconstructed in 1991, they adorn the landscape as well as favouring the overripening of aromatic grape varieties. Overripeness is the key to this Gewurztraminer which, with its golden-yellow colour, exotic and candied aromas, and fleshy, long taste hinting at dried fruits, is virtually a late-harvest wine. 'An excellent profile,' observed one taster. (Residual sugar: 30 g/l; half-litre bottles.)
🔑 André Hartmann, 11, rue Roger-Frémeaux, 68420 Voegtlinshoffen, tel. 03.89.49.38.34, fax 03.89.49.26.18 ☑ 𝐈 ev. day except Sun. 9am–12 noon 1.30pm–6pm

HAULLER Cuvée Saint-Sébastien 1998

☐ 4 ha 30,000 30–49 F

Run by René Hauller since 1977, this vineyard was established at Dambach-la-Ville in 1830. Today there are 19 ha (47 acres) of vines, and the family also act as wine-merchants. The Chapelle Saint-Sébastien, once the parish church of a village that disappeared towards the end of the 13th century, towers over the surrounding vines above Dambach. The wine to which it has given its name has a discreet nose and a well-balanced, expressive palate. (Residual sugar: 16 g/l.)
🔑 J. Hauller et Fils, 3, rue de la Gare, 67650 Dambach-la-Ville, tel. 03.88.92.40.21, fax 03.88.92.45.41 ☑ 𝐈 by appt.
🔑 René Hauller

J.-V. HEBINGER ET FILS

Vendanges tardives 1997★

☐ 0.5 ha 3,500 100–149 F

Located on the main thoroughfare of Eguisheim, close to the town-hall, this concern has vines on some of the best soils in the commune, notably those of the Eichberg and Pfersigberg Grand Crus. In the field of late-harvest wines, their superb 1994 Pinot Gris received much praise. This current Gewurztraminer is light in colour and possesses aromatic complexity and delicacy (roses, fruits and mineral notes) that inform both nose and palate. A really subtle wine that needs to be given more time.
🔑 Jean-Victor Hebinger et Fils, 14, Grand-Rue, 68420 Eguisheim, tel. 03.89.41.19.90, fax 03.89.41.15.61 ☑ 𝐈 ev. day except Sun. 8am–12 noon 2pm–6pm

HERTZOG Cuvée Sainte-Cécile 1998★★

☐ 0.5 ha 5,000 50–69 F

There are records of wine-growing in Obermorschwir going back to the tenth century, involving numerous monasteries, such as the Abbey of Marbach, as well as the Bishop of Basle. This consistently good wine demonstrates the quality of the terroirs here. Its colour is gold, the nose overripe, mingling aromas of roses, spices and honey, and the concentrated, rich taste admirably extends the whole olfactory experience. Would suit pan-fried foie gras or a dessert. (Residual sugar: 25 g/l.)
🔑 EARL Sylvain Hertzog, 18, rte du Vin, 68420 Obermorschwihr, tel. 03.89.49.31.93, fax 03.89.49.28.85 ☑ 𝐈 by appt.

E. HORCHER ET FILS

Sélection de grains nobles 1997★

☐ 0.27 ha 1,500 150–199 F

This vineyard, a feature of Mittelwihr for generations, has some excellent terroirs which have helped it to make some wines of excellent quality. The firm receives regular praise in wine books, notably for its Gewurztraminers. This wine is a clear light-yellow colour, and has a lively, somewhat floral nose with hints of citrus and spices. The intensely aromatic taste has an ideal suppleness and uncommon length, with a finish on notes of dried apricot. A great wine with an excellent future. (Half-litre bottles)
🔑 Ernest Horcher et Fils, 6, rue du Vignoble, 68630 Mittelwihr, tel. 03.89.47.93.26, fax 03.89.49.04.92 ☑ 𝐈 ev. day except Sun. 8am–12 noon 2pm–7pm

CLAUDE ET GEORGES HUMBRECHT

Vendanges tardives 1997★★★

☐ 0.3 ha 2,000 100–149 F

Gueberschwihr has a church with a very tall Romanesque bell-tower and houses dating from the Renaissance. It also has good terroirs for producing wines from overripe grapes. This wine, which has an intense straw-gold colour, immediately delights with its scents of various spices (pepper especially) and overripe fruits. The palate is no less beautiful, powerful and elegant. Fruitiness, concentration, freshness and smoothness: it has everthing. 'Faultless,' was how one taster described it, adding: 'I'll buy it!' A wine to enjoy for its own sake or with foie gras.

EARL Claude et Georges Humbrecht, 31, rue de Pfaffenheim, 68420 Gueberschwihr, tel. 03.89.49.31.51 Y by appt.

HUNOLD Vendanges tardives 1997★

☐ 0.4 ha 3,000 100–149 F

This major vineyard of 12 ha (30 acres) is a fixture in Rouffach, the chief town in the canton and a wine-growing centre. Regularly praised by wine-writers, the vineyard has produced a late-harvest wine which is yellow with straw-coloured lights and has the most beautiful perfumes: acacia honey, crystallised fruits and spices. The aromatic range of the powerful, rich, harmonious taste includes flowers, dried fruits (figs) and honey.

EARL Bruno Hunold, 29, rue aux Quatre-Vents, 68250 Rouffach, tel. 03.89.49.60.57, fax 03.89.49.67.66 Y ev. day except Sun. 8am–12 noon 1pm–7pm

DOM. JUX Prestige 1998★★

☐ n.c. 2,000 70–99 F

This estate, west of Colmar, is part of the Wolfberger group. It has, however, retained its individuality. Its Prestige Gewurztraminer is noteworthy for its aromatic complexity, offering a basket of flowers and exotic fruits. The well-balanced taste reveals the overripe ingredients and the finish is long. This wine is already agreeable, but can equally be kept for four or five years. (Residual sugar: 17 g/l.)

Dom. Jux, chem. de la Fecht, 68000 Colmar, tel. 03.89.79.13.76, fax 03.89.79.62.93 Y by appt.

CAVE DE KIENTZHEIM-KAYSERSBERG

Altenburg 1998★

☐ 12.08 ha 32,000 50–69 F

At Kientzheim, visitors can study the region's viticultural history in the Musée du Vignoble et des Vins d'Alsace. The co-operative cellar, established in 1955, makes wine from some 180 ha (445 acres) of vines. Good quality is a priority, as this pure-yellow 98 wine demonstrates, with its spicy, fruity aromas typical of the grape variety. The palate brings together suppleness, finesse and freshness. A well-balanced wine suitable as an aperitif. (Residual sugar: 12 g/l.)

Cave de Kientzheim-Kaysersberg, 10, rue des Vieux-Moulins, 68240 Kientzheim, tel. 03.89.47.13.19, fax 03.89.47.34.38 Y by appt.

KLEE FRERES 1998

☐ 0.4 ha 2,400 30–49 F

This small concern, barely 2 ha (5 acres) in size, has been run by the Klée brothers for a good dozen years. In their cellar, they favour spontaneous fermentation and keep their wines on fine lees. This wine has a lovely freshness and opens on spicy notes which are followed by a more complex fruitiness. (Residual sugar: 12 g/l.)

Klée Frères, 18, Grand-Rue, 68230 Katzenthal, tel. 03.89.47.17.90 Y by appt.

CLEMENT KLUR

Vieilles vignes 1998★

☐ 0.7 ha 5,000 50–69 F

Clément Klur established himself here in 1999 after the Klur-Stoecklé estate was dissolved. The new, highly unusual cellar is built in the round: large wooden casks and vats are placed in a circle. No wonder, as the tasters discovered, this Gewurztraminer has such a beautiful rounded finish. Finesse and elegance similarly characterise its spicy aromas and good structure in the mouth. (Residual sugar: 25 g/l.)

Clément Klur, 105, rue des Trois-Epis, 68230 Katzenthal, tel. 03.89.80.94.29, fax 03.89.27.30.17, e-mail katz@newel.net Y by appt.

CLEMENT KLUR Vendanges tardives 1997★

☐ 0.5 ha 3,500 100–149 F

A strong yellow colour, a nose redolent of roses, spices and fruits (pineapple), and a beautifully fresh, powerful, well-balanced taste hinting at spices and quince: these are all features of a great wine with an assured future.

Clément Klur, 105, rue des Trois-Epis, 68230 Katzenthal, tel. 03.89.80.94.29, fax 03.89.27.30.17, e-mail katz@newel.net Y by appt.

FRANCOIS LICHTLE

Sélection Vieilles vignes 1998★

☐ 0.15 ha 1000 70–99 F

South-west of Colmar is the village of Husseren-les-Châteaux, named after the three châteaux that dominate it. François Lichtlé has been tending 6 ha (15 acres) of vines there since 1992. His Sélection Vieilles Vignes (made from old vines) has character, a golden colour and an intense and complex nose that is both floral and fruity (citrus, mango, lychee). After a good attack on the palate, the taste is fruity with a touch of botrytis. Despite its moderate persistence, this is still an imposing wine. (Residual sugar: 15 g/l.)

Dom. François Lichtlé, 17, rue des Vignerons, 68420 Husseren-les-Châteaux, tel. 03.89.49.31.34, fax 03.89.49.37.52 ☑ Y by appt.

MADER Cuvée Théophile 1998★★

☐ 0.25 ha 1,800 ▮ 50–69 F

Hunawihr has many attractions: a tropical butterfly house, a stork park, a fortified church and vineyards. Jean-Luc Mader, who has distinguished himself more than once, now has another success with this bright yellow wine. The nose is expressive, mixing fresh and crystallised fruits. The palate is well-balanced, full-bodied, and has a long, fresh and very successful finish. (Residual sugar: 43 g/l.)

🔑 EARL Jean-Luc Mader, 13, Grand-Rue, 68150 Hunawihr, tel. 03.89.73.80.32, fax 03.89.73.31.22 ☑ Y by appt.

JEAN-LOUIS ET FABIENNE MANN

Vieilles vignes Cuvée Fabienne et Jean-Louis 1998★

☐ 0.39 ha 2,800 70–99 F

The 'old stones' of Alsace are much in evidence on the region's wine-labels. This particular wine shows them in close-up, with the wine-name printed on a photograph of chalky marl, a nice warm yellow-ochre colour. The spicy, peachy nose is a lovely introduction to this Gewurztraminer and similarly adorns its finish. The richness of the palate, its excellent balance between sugar and alcohol, and its long finish make it a very successful wine. (Residual sugar: 40 g/l.)

🔑 EARL Jean-Louis Mann, 6 A, rue de Colmar, 68420 Eguisheim, tel. 03.89.24.26.47, fax 03.89.24.09.41 ☑ Y by appt.

METZ-GEIGER 1998

☐ 0.63 ha 2,000 ▮ 50–69 F

At Epfig, south of Barr, the Romanesque chapel of Sainte-Marguerite is worth a visit. Epfig is the birthplace, too, of this Gewurztraminer which has an open, floral, spicy nose and a well-structured, rich, intense, long taste. (Residual sugar: 22 g/l.)

🔑 Louis Metz-Geiger, 9, rue Fronholz, 67680 Epfig, tel. 03.88.85.55.21, fax 03.88.85.55.21 ☑ Y by appt.

DOM. RENE MEYER

La Croix du Pfoeller Vieilles vignes 1998★

☐ 0.35 ha 4,100 🛢 50–69 F

Nestling in a small peaceful valley, Katzenthal is dominated by the Donjon du Wineck. The chalky soil yields well-structured Gewurztraminers, like this one. Its intense nose breathes dried fruits and spices; its taste is elegant, powerful and long. Its creator invites visitors to try it with another speciality of the region: Munster cheese. (Residual sugar: 13 g/l.)

🔑 EARL Dom. René Meyer et Fils, 14, Grand-Rue, 68230 Katzenthal, tel. 03.89.27.04.67, fax 03.89.27.50.59 ☑ Y by appt.

JEAN-LUC MEYER

Cuvée Vieilles vignes 1998★

☐ 0.4 ha 3,500 ▮ 30–49 F

At Eguisheim, the streets that run in three concentric circles round the castle recall the town's rich medieval history. Today there are a number of producers with successful businesses, like Jean-Luc Meyer with his 10 ha (25 acres) of vines. His Sélection Vieilles Vignes (made from old vines) was appreciated for its conformity to type, with its aroma of roses characteristic of the grape variety, good attack, balance, freshness and quality. A beautiful, dryish Gewurztraminer. (Residual sugar: 8 g/l.)

🔑 Jean-Luc Meyer, 4, rue des Trois-Châteaux, 68420 Eguisheim, tel. 03.89.24.53.66, fax 03.89.41.66.46 ☑ Y by appt.

MEYER-FONNE

Kaefferkopf Vendanges tardives 1997★★★

☐ 0.3 ha 1,600 🛢 100–149 F

The Kaefferkopf at Ammerschwihr, a renowned environment for growing vines with its gritty clay soils, and a family concern which in recent years has attracted notice for its expertise. Not surprisingly, this wine gets everyone's vote. Its brilliant yellow colour and golden lights attract the eye before its floral and fruity perfumes charm the nose, adding an exotic touch that lends complexity. As for the taste, its fullness, richness, fleshiness, balance (sustained by good supporting acidity) and harmonious finish make it quite simply superb.

🔑 Meyer-Fonné, 24, Grand-Rue, 68230 Katzenthal, tel. 03.89.27.16.50, fax 03.89.27.34.17 ☑ Y by appt.

🔑 François Meyer

DOM. DU MOULIN DE DUSENBACH Kaefferkopf 1998

☐ 0.6 ha 5,300 ▮ 🌡 70–99 F

This family estate comprises some 20 ha (49 acres) of vines divided over several communes, some of them distant from the headquarters in Ribeauvillé. The Gewurztraminer offered comes from the Kaefferkopf at Ammerschwihr. The nose is somewhat dominated by the alcohol. The palate reveals notes of overripeness, a rich structure and marked

sweetness. This wine, evocative of late-harvest wines, will need time to attain harmony.
🔑 Bernard Schwach, 25, rte de Sainte-Marie-aux-Mines, 68150 Ribeauvillé, tel. 03.89.73.72.18, fax 03.89.73.30.34 ☑ Y by appt.

CAVE D'OBERNAI 1998

☐ n.c. 50,000 30–49 F

With its lovely 15th- and 16th-century houses and remnants of town walls, Obernai is a typically Alsatian town. It is also a centre of wine-growing, holding both a wine-fair and a grape-harvest festival. The co-operative offers a fairly light but pleasing Gewurztraminer with complex savours of fruit, spices and, above all, roses, which are a feature both of the nose and the taste. (Residual sugar: 9.3 g/l.)
🔑 Cave vinicole d'Obernai, 30, rue du Gal-Leclerc, 67210 Obernai, tel. 03.88.47.60.20, fax 03.88.47.60.22 ☑ Y by appt.

OTTER Vendanges tardives 1997★

☐ 0.36 ha 2,500 100–149 F

In 1998 Jean-François Otter took over the family estate at Hattstatt, a village south of Colmar bordering on the RN 83. His late-harvest Gewurztraminer has an intense golden-yellow colour and an open nose redolent of fruits and spices. The taste has yet to mature, but its assets are already evident: aromas of figs with a hint of liquorice, plus robustness and power. Needs a little more time to develop.
🔑 Dom. François Otter et Fils, 4, rue du Muscat, 68420 Hattstatt, tel. 03.89.49.33.00, fax 03.89.49.38.69, e-mail ottjef@nucleuv.fr ☑ Y by appt.
🔑 Jean-François Otter

DOM. FRANCOIS RUNNER ET FILS

Bergweingarten 1998

☐ 0.45 ha 4,000 30–49 F

François Runner took over the reins of the family estate in 1997, representing the third generation on these 12 ha (30 acres). He offers a wine grown in a chalky-clay locality. This respectable wine has a finish marked by a certain power, adorned with complex spicy aromas. A good harmonious entity. (Residual sugar: 10 g/l.)
🔑 Dom. François Runner et Fils, 1, rue de la Liberté, 68250 Pfaffenheim, tel. 03.89.49.62.89, fax 03.89.49.73.69 ☑ Y ev. day 9am–12 noon 1pm–6pm

CLOS SAINTE-APOLLINE

Bollenberg Cuvée sélectionnée Fût de chêne 1998★

☐ 3 ha 8,000 50–69 F

Located on the heights of the Bollenberg, the hill overlooking the village of Westhalten, this estate, founded in 1887, comprises 24 ha (59 acres) of vines. Its Bollenberg wine marries notes of roses and hints of fruits, particularly peach, kiwi-fruit, and clementine. This profusion of aromas is also evident on the palate, and a note of overripeness comes as an added bonus. (Residual sugar: 8 g/l.)
🔑 A. et D. Meyer, Clos Sainte-Apolline, Dom. du Bollenberg, 68111 Westhalten, tel. 03.89.49.67.10, fax 03.89.49.76.16 ☑ Y ev. day 8am–8pm

CLOS SAINTE-ODILE 1998★

☐ n.c. 10,000 50–69 F

This firm, located on the heights of Obernai, uses vines grown on south-facing terraces. Their Gewurztraminer has a golden-yellow colour and a subtle, particularly fruity nose, signalling the excellent quality of the fruit used. The taste is gratifyingly well-balanced and full, with elegant exotic notes. One taster suggested the wine as an accompaniment to *canard à l'orange*. (Residual sugar: 8.7 g/l.)
🔑 Sté vinicole Sainte-Odile, 3, rue de la Gare, 67210 Obernai, tel. 03.88.47.60.20, fax 03.88.47.60.22 ☑ Y by appt.

SAULNIER

Vendanges tardives Vieilles vignes 1997★★

☐ 0.3 ha 1,800 100–149 F

Although a relatively new enterprise (1982), it has quickly established a reputation among Alsace wine-growers. This late-harvest 1997 wine is evidence of its expertise. The amber colour, the utterly gorgeous nose dominated by scents of candied fruit and bergamot with hints of dried hay, and the harmonious taste, remarkably well-balanced, rich without being excessively so, and sustained by a dissolving acidity – all these are signs of a great wine in the making.
🔑 Marco Saulnier, rte de Saint-Marc, 68420 Gueberschwihr, tel. 03.89.86.42.02 ☑ Y by appt.

MARTIN SCHAETZEL

Kaefferkopf Cuvée Catherine 1998★

☐ 0.5 ha n.c. 50–69 F

Jean Schaetzel and his wife run an enterprise of nearly 8 ha (20 acres). This Gewurztraminer from the famous Kaefferkopf Cru has been named after their daughter Catherine. The 1998 version has a subtle, intense nose, which is true to type with hints of dried fruits and *pain d'épice* (a kind of spicy loaf). This is confirmed in the mouth, where the wine finishes with a lovely persistence. (Residual sugar: 25 g/l.)
🔑 SARL Martin Schaetzel, 3, rue de la 5nd-Division-Blindée, 68770 Ammerschwihr, tel. 03.89.47.11.39, fax 03.89.78.29.77 ☑ Y by appt.
🔑 Béa et Jean Schaetzel

PAUL SCHERER Vieilles vignes 1998★

☐ 0.24 ha n.c. 50–69 F

The three famous castles seem to watch over the vines of Husseren, where the Scherer family have been making wine for five generations. Their Vieilles Vignes wine (made from old vines) reveals a contrast between a subtle, delicately floral nose and a rich – or rather, massive – taste, which is strong both at the

start and finish. This wine left a very good impression. (Residual sugar: 18 g/l.)
🔑 EARL Paul Scherer et Fils, 40, rue Principale, 68420 Husseren-les-Châteaux, tel. 03.89.49.30.34, fax 03.89.86.41.67 ☑ 🍷 by appt.

DOM. PIERRE SCHILLE 1998★★★

☐ 0.49 ha 5,500 ▮ 🌡 30–49 F

VIN D'ALSACE
APPELLATION ALSACE CONTROLEE
DOMAINE
PIERRE SCHILLÉ
Gewurztraminer
13% vol
750 ml
PIERRE & CHRISTOPHE SCHILLÉ

Founded in 1954 by Pierre Schillé, this estate was taken over by his son Christophe in 1990. The vineyard comprises a good range of terroirs spread over several communes. Grown on chalky-clay soils, this wine has a charming and unmistakably powerful nose of fruits and honey. Superby well-balanced, intense and coherent on the palate, the wine's finish is silky, clean and long, with remarkably persistent aromas. An exceptional wine, it can be enjoyed for its own sake, and could be laid down for four or five years if you can wait that long. (Residual sugar: 19 g/l.)
🔑 Pierre Schillé et Fils, 14, rue du Stade, 68240 Sigolsheim, tel. 03.89.47.10.67, fax 03.89.47.39.12 ☑ 🍷 by appt.

DOM. SCHIRMER

Vendanges tardives 1997

☐ 0.2 ha 1,000 ▮ 🌡 100–149 F

Established since 1865 at Soulzmatt in the Noble valley, the Schirmer family cultivate 7 ha (17 acres) of vines, a part of which is located in the Zinnkoepflé Grand Cru area. Their late-harvest Gewurztraminer is a very bright golden-yellow colour, and the nose declares the wine's richness with aromas of overripeness – raisins and crystallised fruits. The rounded, supple taste is very full-bodied, and needs more time to develop.
🔑 Dom. Lucien Schirmer et Fils, 22, rue de la Vallée, 68570 Soultzmatt, tel. 03.89.47.03.82, fax 03.89.47.02.33 ☑ 🍷 ev. day 8am–12 noon 1pm–7pm

DOMAINES SCHLUMBERGER

Sélection de grains nobles Cuvée Anne 1997★

☐ 2.6 ha 10,000 ▮ 🛢 250–299 F

With 145 ha (358 acres) of vines, this estate is the largest in Alsace. This Sélection de Grains Nobles has a deep golden-yellow colour which inspires confidence. Intense and complex, mixing apricot and spices, the nose confirms the visual impression. The taste strikes the same note, being both powerful and yet subtle. A wine of great class, which lives up to its promise. (Half-litre bottles)
🔑 Domaines Schlumberger, 100, rue Théodore-Deck, 68501 Guebwiller Cedex, tel. 03.89.74.27.00, fax 03.89.74.85.75, e-mail jvschlum@aol.com ☑ 🍷 by appt.

FRANCOIS SCHMITT

Cuvée Marie-France 1998

☐ 0.67 ha 5,300 ▮ 30–49 F

François Schmitt and his son Frédéric keep 11 ha (27 acres) of vines on a variety of soils. Their Marie-France wine has surprisingly restrained aromas. The palate, after a powerful attack, continues in lighter vein. Well balanced overall. (Residual sugar: 20 g/l.)
🔑 Cave François Schmitt, 19, rte de Soultzmatt, 68500 Orschwihr, tel. 03.89.76.08.45, fax 03.89.76.44.02 ☑ 🍷 by appt.

ALBERT SCHOECH Letzenberg 1998★

☐ 8.4 ha 30,000 ▮ 🌡 30–49 F

This is a wine-trading firm in Ammerschwihr, a township already flourishing in the 14th century whose medieval remains, such as the Tour des Voleurs, the Tour des Bourgeois and the Porte-Haute, are famous images in the region. Coming from a chalky-clay locality, this Gewurztraminer gradually opens out with fruity notes when left to breathe. A pleasant attack contributes to the harmony of the taste, which has a lovely fruitiness. (Residual sugar: 10.2 g/l.)
🔑 Albert Schoech, pl. du Vieux-Marché, 68770 Ammerschwihr, tel. 03.89.78.23.17, fax 03.89.27.51.24

DOM. FRANCOIS SCHWACH ET FILS Vendanges tardives 1997★★

☐ 1.3 ha 7,000 ▮ 🌡 70–99 F

This large estate of 20 ha (49 acres) looks abroad for business, exporting half the wines from its modern cellars. Golden-yellow in colour, this late-harvest wine has a charmingly subtle, deep nose blending flowers and crystallised fruits. The taste combines finesse and concentration. It is already beautifully balanced. A great wine. (Half-litre bottles)
🔑 Dom. François Schwach et Fils, 28, rte de Ribeauvillé, 68150 Hunawihr, tel. 03.89.73.62.15, fax 03.89.73.37.84, e-mail schwach@rmcnet.fr ☑ 🍷 by appt.

CHRISTIAN SCHWARTZ

Sélection de grains nobles Collection Marine 1997★

☐ 0.3 ha 900 ▮ 150–199 F

This family enterprise of 6.5 ha (16 acres) is located at Blienschwiller, a pretty village on the wine route which was already growing vines in Carolingian times. They offer a very well-made 1997 Sélection de Grains Nobles wine, which has a straw-yellow, near-golden colour and an intense nose dominated by dried apricots and accompanying notes of lychee and spices tinged with liquorice in the mouth. The taste also has good balance, fullness and length. (Half-litre bottles)

🔑 Christian Schwartz, 8, rue de l'Ungersberg, 67650 Blienschwiller, tel. 03.88.92.41.73, fax 03.88.92.63.06 ☑ Y by appt.

EMILE SCHWARTZ

Vendanges tardives Cuvée Maxime 1997*

☐ 0.3 ha 1,700 100–149 F

This Cuvée Maxime comes from Husseren-les-Châteaux, a commune with the highest vineyards on the wine route, nearly 400 m (1,300 ft) above sea-level. Straw-yellow with golden lights, it is distinguished by the highly developed and complex aromas of honey and lychee evident in both the nose and mouth. The rich and yet fresh taste is given class by the wine's fine attack.

🔑 EARL Emile Schwartz et Fils, 3, rue Principale, 68420 Husseren-les-Châteaux, tel. 03.89.49.30.61, fax 03.89.49.27.27 ☑ Y ev. day except Sun. 8am–12 noon 2pm–7pm; cl. 1–15 Sep.

JEAN-PAUL SIMONIS

Kaefferkopf 1998

☐ 0.27 ha 2,000 50–69 F

Jean-Marc Simonis took over the family business in 1993 and is enthusiastically exploiting a plot on the Kaefferkopf planted with 45-year-old vines. The soil is chalky clay. This 1998 wine is characterised by a note of honey and a gentle attack. The taste is supple, dominated by the sugar. Not for drinking straight away. (Residual sugar: 15 g/l.)

🔑 EARL Jean-Paul Simonis et Fils, 1, rue du Chasseur-M.-Besombes, 68770 Ammerschwihr, tel. 03.89.47.13.51, fax 03.89.47.13.51 ☑ Y by appt.

🔑 Jean-Marc Simonis

RENE SIMONIS Vieilles vignes 1998*

☐ 0.15 ha 600 70–99 F

The other Simonis family in Ammerschwihr (Etienne, who took over in 1996) offer a Sélection Vieilles Vignes wine (made from old vines) that bears the stamp of its granite origins. The nose is quite open, dominated by spicy notes with fruity touches. On the palate there are hints of overripeness. Its rich, smooth character emphasises the impressions of honey which linger at the finish. Almost a late-harvest wine. (Residual sugar: 46 g/l.)

🔑 René et Etienne Simonis, 2, rue des Moulins, 68770 Ammerschwihr, tel. 03.89.47.30.79, fax 03.89.78.24.10 ☑ Y by appt.

THIERRY-MARTIN

Vieilles vignes 1998

☐ 4 ha 3,000 70–99 F

This new concern, born of the association between Thierry Unterreiner and Martin Lorentz in 1998, has already been praised in print. Their pale-yellow wine has an aroma of fruit with a touch of honey. The fresh taste reveals a note of alcohol which has yet to blend in. (Residual sugar: 18.9 g/l.)

🔑 Thierry-Martin, rte de Westhoffen, 67520 Wangen, tel. 03.88.04.11.22, fax 03.88.04.11.21, e-mail alsacethierrymartin@minitel.net ☑ Y by appt.

ACHILLE THIRION 1998

☐ 2.35 ha 8,000 30–49 F

The Thirion family, whose forebears were involved in wine as early as 1760, combine tradition and modern techniques to produce fine, expressive wines. This 1998 offering is neither very complex nor very powerful, but nevertheless has a delicate aroma of roses and its light harmony makes it very pleasant. (Residual sugar: 12.8 g/l.)

🔑 Dom. Achille Thirion, 69, rte du Vin, 68590 Saint-Hippolyte, tel. 03.89.73.00.23, fax 03.89.73.06.46 ☑ Y by appt.

CAVE DU VIEIL-ARMAND

Armorie 1998

☐ n.c. 10,000 70–99 F

This wine-producing cellar contains a wine and vine museum. It also has this 1998 wine, endowed with sharp, intense aromas of overripeness. The well-balanced, long taste extends the perceptions of the nose, with notes of botrytis and a balance dominated by sweet smoothness. (Residual sugar: 25 g/l.)

🔑 Cave vinicole du Vieil-Armand, 3, rte de Cernay, 68360 Soultz-Wuenheim, tel. 03.89.76.73.75, fax 03.89.76.70.75 ☑ Y by appt.

VORBURGER 1998

☐ n.c. n.c. 30–49 F

Established during the 1950s, this business is located in Voegtlinshoffen, a charming village overlooking the wine-growing area and plain of Alsace. Its Gewurztraminer has a nose of clean, fine, spicy aromas. The palate is supple and has good structure, fruitiness and agreeable persistence. (Residual sugar: 20 g/l.)

🔑 EARL Jean-Pierre Vorburger et Fils, 3, rue de la Source, 68420 Voegtlinshoffen, tel. 03.89.49.35.52, fax 03.89.49.35.52 ☑ Y ev. day except Sun. 8am–12 noon 1.30pm–6pm

CH. WAGENBOURG

Vendanges tardives 1997

☐ 0.5 ha 3,000 100–149 F

The Château of Wagenbourg, where this estate was established in 1905, is the only one to survive intact out of the seven châteaux formerly listed in the Noble valley. Jacky and Mireille Klein, who took over in 1995, are the heirs to a long line of wine-growers which goes back to 1605. They offer a late-harvest wine that is yellow in colour with amber lights. Its nose is of ripe fruits (cherry plum) and grapes dried on the vine, with hints of dried apricot at the finish. This 1997 is not very powerful, but should develop favourably.

🔑 Joseph et Jacky Klein, Ch. Wagenbourg, 25, rue de la Vallée, 68570 Soultzmatt, tel. 03.89.47.01.41, fax 03.89.47.65.61 ☑ Y ev. day except Sun. 8am–12 noon 2pm–7pm

JEAN-MICHEL WELTY 1998★

☐ 1.42 ha 9,000 30–49 F

This concern has its headquarters in a former tithe court dating from 1576. Jean-Michel Welty has been in charge since 1984. His Gewurztraminer is rich and elegant both in the nose and on the palate. The wine has a lovely balance between power and freshness, as well as good persistence.

EARL Jean-Michel Welty, 22–24, Grand-Rue, 68500 Orschwihr, tel. 03.89.76.09.03, fax 03.89.76.16.80 ev. day 8.30am–11.30am 2pm–6.30pm; Sun. by appt.

JEAN-MICHEL WELTY

Cuvée Aurélie 1998★★

☐ 0.82 ha 5,800 50–69 F

A very original wine-label – congratulations to the artist, but what about the wine? An intense golden colour and a nose of spices, overripe fruits and a taste of great substance adorned by rich nuances of dried and crystallised fruits. Remarkable length. Congratulations to the wine-grower too! (Residual sugar: 21 g/l.)

EARL Jean-Michel Welty, 22–24, Grand-Rue, 68500 Orschwihr, tel. 03.89.76.09.03, fax 03.89.76.16.80 ev. day 8.30am–11.30am 2pm–6.30pm; Sun. by appt.

DOM. DU WINDMUEHL 1998★

☐ 1.1 ha 7,000 30–49 F

Claude Bléger is established at Saint-Hippolyte, a wine-growing village dominated by the Château of Haut-Koenigsbourg, without doubt the region's most visited monument. Grown on granitic clay, his Gewurztraminer is true to its origins: its unambiguous aromas mix honey, spices, fruits and flowers (roses). The residual sugar is evident (20 g/l.), but is well-absorbed in a rounded, powerful wine.

EARL Claude Bléger, Dom. du Windmuehl, 92, rte du Vin, 68590 Saint-Hippolyte, tel. 03.89.73.00.21, fax 03.89.73.04.22 by appt.

BERNARD WURTZ

Vieilles vignes 1998

☐ 1 ha 5,000 70–99 F

This young wine-grower 'prefers quality to quantity' and aims at wines expressive of their environment. His 70-year-old vines have yielded this 1998 wine whose golden-yellow colour betokens a dense wine. The nose confirms the impression of overripeness, but remains closed. The taste reveals a rich, supple substance; the sweet finish is marked by a well-integrated touch of bitterness. Similar to a late-harvest wine, this Gewurztraminer should go well with a fruit tart. (Residual sugar: 10 g/l.)

Bernard Wurtz, 12, rue du Château, 68630 Mittelwihr, tel. 03.89.47.93.24, fax 03.89.86.01.69 by appt.

Jean-Michel Wurtz

JULES ET REMY ZIMMERMANN

Vallée Noble 1998★

☐ n.c. n.c. 30–49 F

As golden as the Noble valley in autumn, this Gewurztraminer distils the fruits of summer – 'with a hint of citronella', remarked one of the tasters. Here are fullness, balance, persistence and harmony.

Rémy Zimmermann, 13, rue des Prêtres, 68570 Soultzmatt, tel. 03.89.47.08.13, fax 03.89.47.04.84 by appt.

Alsace Tokay-Pinot Gris

Pinot Gris has been known locally as Tokay d'Alsace for over four centuries. This is quite astonishing, because it is a variety that has never been grown in eastern Hungary (famous for Tokay). Legend has it, however, that Tokay was brought back to Alsace by General L. de Schwendi, who was the owner of a substantial vineyard in Alsace. The original area in which it was grown belonged to the historic Duchy of Burgundy, as did all the areas where Pinot is grown.

Pinot Gris is planted on only 1,300 ha (3,211 acres) and produces a full-bodied, heavy, fine wine, which can easily be substituted for red wine to accompany meat dishes. At its most sumptuous, as it was in 1983, 1989 and 1990, which were exceptional vintages, it is one of the best possible accompaniments for foie gras.

J.B. ADAM

Letzenberg Cuvée Jean-Baptiste 1998★★

☐ 1.1 ha 6,500 70–99 F

The wine-grower and merchant J.-B. Adam heads an undertaking that has been in business for more than 380 years. He offers a most promising Pinot Gris. Golden yellow with bright glints, it has a subtle yet already very agreeable nose of white-flesh fruits (peaches), and an aromatic taste with strong persistence and a remarkable balance between sugar and acidity. All are signs of a great wine which will become more expressive as time passes. (Residual sugar: 15 g/l.)

Jean-Baptiste Adam, 5, rue de l'Aigle, 68770 Ammerschwihr, tel. 03.89.78.23.21, fax 03.89.47.35.91, e-mail adam@jb-adam.com ▣ Y ev. day except Sun. 8am–12 noon 2pm–6.30pm; groups by appt.

DOM. PIERRE ADAM

Katzenstegel Cuvée Théo 1998★★

☐ 1 ha 7,000 50–69 F

Another family called Adam, established like the last at Ammerschwihr, look after 11 ha (27 acres) of vines. This year, they offer a praiseworthy Pinot Gris grown in the locality of Katzenstegel. The beautifully bright, light-yellow colour and very expressive nose of crystallised fruits were instant charmers. Powerful, rich, balanced and very mature, the taste confirmed the excellent first impression. (Residual sugar: 18 g/l.)

Dom. Pierre Adam, 8, rue du Lt-Louis-Mourier, 68770 Ammerschwihr, tel. 03.89.78.23.07, fax 03.89.47.39.68, e-mail domaine.pierre.adam@wanadoo.fr ▣ Y ev. day 8am–12 noon 1pm–7pm

DOM. ALLIMANT-LAUGNER

Au Puits des Moines 1998★★

☐ 0.55 ha 4,400 50–69 F

This 11-ha (27-acre) estate close to the Haut-Koenigsbourg is regularly praised by wine-writers. It offers a Pinot Gris grown on chalky-clay soil. This golden-yellow 1998 version has an extremely subtle nose of honey and crystallised fruits. The taste, which is candied yet light, has remarkable balance. A wine with imposing presence, which will reach full maturity in about five years' time. Excellent with foie gras. (Residual sugar: 34 g/l.)

Allimant-Laugner, 10, Grand-Rue, 67600 Orschwiller, tel. 03.88.92.06.52, fax 03.88.82.76.38, e-mail alaugner@terre-net.fr ▣ Y ev. day except Sun. 9am–7pm

Hubert Laugner

ANDRE ANCEL 1998★

☐ 0.24 ha 2,100 30–49 F

A vineyard established in 1885 and comprising nearly 9 ha (22 acres) of vines. This 1998 wine, grown on chalky-clay soils, is deep yellow in colour with brilliant lights. On the nose it seems already very mature, with aromas of smokiness, roasted almonds and dried fruits. After coming on to the palate with a delightful fruitiness, it continues in a somewhat rustic vein, though full-bodied and long. It should get smoother with age. (Residual sugar: 8 g/l.)

André Ancel, 3, rue du Collège, 68240 Kaysersberg, tel. 03.89.47.10.76, fax 03.89.78.13.78 ▣ Y ev. day 8am–12 noon 1.30pm–7pm; cl. Sat. Sun. winter from Jan.

VIGNOBLE FREDERIC ARBOGAST

Vendanges tardives 1996★★

☐ 0.3 ha 2,400 70–99 F

This vineyard, which is regularly praised by wine-writers, wins a particularly distinguished mention for this straw-yellow late-harvest wine, which has a nose of violets, crystallised fruits and honey. The honey is also perceptible in the mouth, where the wine has intensity and great complexity, including notes of coffee and chocolate. This is a high-class wine.

Frédéric Arbogast, 135, pl. de l'Eglise, 67310 Westhoffen, tel. 03.88.50.30.51, fax 03.88.50.30.51 ▣ Y by appt.

PIERRE ARNOLD

Vendanges tardives 1996★★★

☐ 0.2 ha 1,200 70–99 F

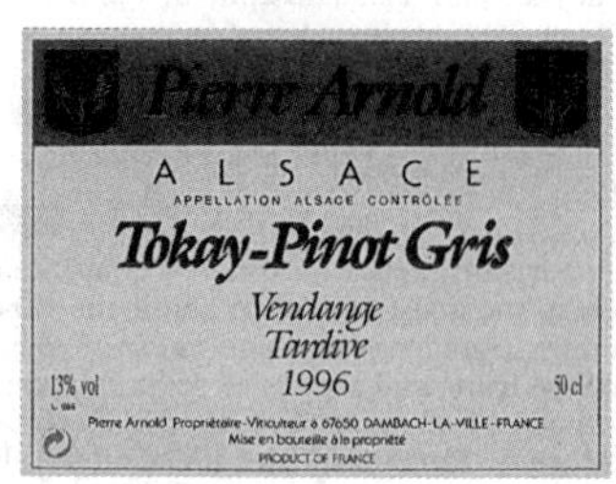

This plot, currently 6.5 ha (16 acres) has been handed down from father to son since 1711 – although the ears of wheat on its emblem should now really be a vine! Pierre Arnold spent a year in Burgundy before joining his family's estate, yet this truly Alsatian Pinot Gris turns out to be his best achievement. Yellow with nuances of amber, his 1996 wine has an extremely attractive nose, mixing scents of undergrowth and liquorice. Both rich and aromatic in the mouth, the wine releases intense exotic notes and has a well-balanced freshness. That it is good value for money is an added bonus. (Half-litre bottles)

Pierre Arnold, 16, rue de la Paix, 67650 Dambach-la-Ville, tel. 03.88.92.41.70, fax 03.88.92.62.95 ▣ Y ev. day 9am–7pm; Sun. by appt.

DIDIER BECK Réserve 1998★

☐ 0.6 ha 3,000 30–49 F

Although Didier Beck began marketing his wine under his own name only in 1996, the estate he has inherited goes back to 1596. Today there are 7.5 ha (19 acres) of vines. The 1998 Réserve was grown on granitic sand, which has given the wine a certain lightness. Light yellow with green lights and wonderfully brilliant, it has a quite intense nose that mingles aromas of mint, vanilla and honey. Fat and spicy in the mouth, with notes of pepper and cloves, the taste of this wine has characteristics of overripeness and a good length. (Residual sugar: 5 g/l.)

Didier Beck, 14, rte du Vin, 67650 Dambach-la-Ville, tel. 03.88.92.40.17, fax 03.88.92.60.40 ▣ Y by appt.

DOM. CLAUDE BLEGER

Coteaux du Haut-Kœnigsbourg 1998★

☐ 0.55 ha 4,700 30–49 F

Claude Bléger grows 7 ha (17 acres) of vines at the foot of the Haut-Koenigsbourg, like his ancestors who settled there during the Thirty Years' War. His intense yellow 1998 wine has a nose that mixes aromas of violets, dried hay and toast. The same delicate range of aromas continues in the mouth, where the wine is beautifully long and slightly smoky. (Residual sugar: 9 g/l.)

🔑 Dom. Claude Bléger, 23, Grand-Rue, 67600 Orschwiller, tel. 03.88.92.32.56, fax 03.88.82.59.95 ☑ 🍷 ev. day 9am–12.15 1.5–7.30pm

FRANCOIS BLEGER

Kappellreben 1998★★

☐ 0.27 ha 2,400 ⊕ 30–49 F

Swiss in origin, the Bléger family settled in Saint-Hippolyte in 1562. A 17th-century cellar testifies to the age of this vineyard, run by François Bléger since 1996. He offers a clear yellow Tokay with a nose of spices and exotic fruits. The taste is also richly aromatic. A rich and powerful wine with great length and elegance. (Residual sugar: 20 g/l.)

🔑 François Bléger, 63, rte du Vin, 68590 Saint-Hippolyte, tel. 03.89.73.06.07, fax 03.89.73.06.07 ☑ 🍷 by appt.

FRANCOIS BRAUN Bollenberg Cuvée

Vieilles vignes 1998★★

☐ n.c. 4,700 🍾 🌡 50–69 F

Yet another vineyard over 400 years old. Today it comprises 21 ha (52 acres) of vines. The Bollenberg Pinot Gris instantly attracts with its beautiful straw-yellow colour and green lights. The nose is intense, musky and smoky: the taste is rich, expressive, powerful, well structured and already has good balance. A really great wine. (Residual sugar: 20 g/l.)

🔑 EARL François Braun et Fils, 19, Grand-Rue, 68500 Orschwihr, tel. 03.89.76.95.13, fax 03.89.76.10.97 ☑ 🍷 ev. day except Sun. 8am–11.30am 1.30pm–6pm

DOM. BURGHART-SPETTEL

Réserve 1998★

☐ 0.32 ha 2,800 ⊕ 30–49 F

Established in 1948, this estate has more than 8 ha (20 acres) of vines. It is located at Mittelwihr, a commune well known to wine-lovers for its Mandelberg Grand Cru. Though not from that precise spot, this Tokay Réserve is nevertheless a quality product. Brilliant yellow in colour with green lights, it has a subtly fruity but still somewhat immature nose. Very rich and powerful, the taste is marked by residual sugar: it still requires time to reach perfect balance. It might well suit sweet-and-savoury dishes like filet of duck with fruit. (Residual sugar: 10 g/l.)

🔑 Dom. Burghart-Spettel, 9, rte du Vin, 68630 Mittelwihr, tel. 03.89.47.93.19, fax 03.89.49.07.62 ☑ 🍷 by appt.

BUTTERLIN 1998

☐ 0.6 ha 5,400 🍾 30–49 F

Jean Butterlin keeps 8 ha (20 acres) of vines in the little wine-growing commune of Wettelsheim, to the west of Colmar. A very clear straw-yellow in colour, his Pinot Gris has smoky aromas, which are characteristic of this grape variety. It is rich and full in the mouth and contains a large amount of residual sugars, which need to fade. It is best kept until it has had time to gain in balance, (Residual sugar: 20 g/l.)

🔑 Jean Butterlin, 27, rue Herzog, 68920 Wettolsheim, tel. 03.89.80.60.85, fax 03.89.80.58.61, e-mail info@butterlin.fr ☑ 🍷 by appt.

CLOS DES CHARTREUX 1998

☐ 1 ha 4,500 ⊕ 50–69 F

Molsheim is close to Strasbourg, where the Bruche valley opens out beneath the foothills of the Vosges. Named after the Carthusian monks who settled there in the 16th century, this beautiful 17-ha (42-acre) estate is well known to wine-writers. Its 1998 Tokay has an elegant golden yellow colour, a fine, characteristic nose, a very sweet first impression on the palate and pleasant aromas. It is dominated by sugars in the mouth, and is not yet completely balanced. Best kept for a while. (Residual sugar: 12 g/l.)

🔑 Robert Klingenfus, 60, rue de Saverne, 67120 Molsheim, tel. 03.88.38.07.06, fax 03.88.49.32.47 ☑ 🍷 by appt.

DONTENVILLE

Hahnenberg de Châtenois 1998

☐ 0.6 ha 5,000 ⊕ 50–69 F

Located in the extreme south of the Bas-Rhin department, to the west of Sélestat and at the foot of the crystalline slopes of the Hahnenberg, Châtenois takes its name from the chestnut trees which used to grow high up on the mountain and provided the wine-makers with stakes for their vines. Gilbert Dontenville has a vineyard of 10 ha (25 acres) here, most of it on granite soils, the source of this light-yellow Pinot Gris with glints of green and a nose of uncomplicated smoky aromas. Slightly sweet in the mouth, it has good length and should develop well.

🔑 Gilbert Dontenville, 2, rte de Kintzheim, 67730 Châtenois, tel. 03.88.82.03.48, fax 03.88.82.23.81 ☑ 🍷 ev. day 9am–6pm

DOPFF AU MOULIN

Vendanges tardives 1997★

☐ 2.5 ha 7,600 🍾 🌡 100–149 F

This family concern is probably as well known as the town in which it has enjoyed prosperity and respect for more than 350 years. It played a part in the development of the traditional method of wine-growing in Alsace, and now exports its produce as far afield as Finland and Japan. This late-harvest wine is yellow-green in colour with brilliant lights. Its nose is subtle, but does release some hints of exotic fruits. It hits the palate fully, with a mellow, almost syrupy body and lingering flavours of crystallised quince and liquorice, which delight the taste buds.

🔑 SA Dopff au Moulin, 2, av. Jacques-Preiss, 68340 Riquewihr, tel. 03.89.49.09.69, fax 03.89.47.83.61 ☑ 🍷 ev. day 9am–12 noon 2pm–6pm

MICHEL FAHRER

Vendanges tardives 1996★

☐ 0.3 ha 2,000 100–149 F

After working for the Michel Fahrer firm for eight years, Vincent Ackermann purchased this vineyard of 7.5 ha (19 acres), located at the foot of the Haut-Koenigsbourg. He offers a characteristic late-harvest wine which is golden yellow in colour, has a noble-rot nose with hints of undergrowth, and is pleasantly full, fleshy and round on the palate. An excellent wine which needs more time to develop. (Half-litre bottles.)

Fahrer-Ackermann, 15, rte du Vin, 67600 Orschwiller, tel. 03.88.92.90.23, fax 03.88.92.90.23 ☑ Y by appt.
Vincent Ackermann

ANDRE FALLER ET FILS

Vendanges tardives Cuvée Robin 1997★

☐ 0.27 ha 1,500 70–99 F

The Faller family in Itterswiller serves the needs of gastronomic tourism; the grower's mother runs a hotel there, his brother and sister have a restaurant, and his grandfather founded this estate before the Second World War. This late-harvest wine has a delightful golden colour which suggests a certain richness from the start. With a nose combining quince and dried and crystallised fruits, and growing power in the mouth – where although perhaps not as long as some, it is luscious and pleasant – this is a delightful wine. (Half-litre bottles.)

EARL André Faller, 2, rte du Vin, 67140 Itterswiller, tel. 03.88.85.53.55, fax 03.88.85.51.13 ☑ Y by appt.

RENE FLECK Vendanges tardives 1997★

☐ n.c. 2,100 100–149 F

In Soultzmatt, vine and wine live happily alongside the mineral water which is also produced there – surely a sign of harmony and good quality of life. It is certainly well worth taking a stroll around the village and giving this excellent 1997 late-harvest wine a try; to look at, it is pure bottled gold. The nose is still immature, and all its best points are in the mouth, where it has a rich, full attack on the palate, a superb final note of liquorice and a touch of mineral flavour, which adds complexity.

René Fleck et Fille, 27, rte d'Orschwihr, 68570 Soultzmatt, tel. 03.89.47.01.20, fax 03.89.47.09.24 ☑ Y by appt.

PIERRE FRICK Rot-Murlé 1998★

☐ 0.6 ha 3,600 70–99 F

This vineyard, which has been using organic methods successfully for a long time now, is often praised by wine-writers. Its Tokay is yellow with a touch of gold, and has a distinct trace of crystallised fruits in the nose and also in the mouth, where there is an additional taste of *pain d'épice* (a kind of spicy loaf). Its fine, subtle savours, harmony and freshness combine to form a very attractive overall impression. (Residual sugar: 12 g/l.)

Pierre Frick, 5, rue de Baer, 68250 Pfaffenheim, tel. 03.89.49.62.99, fax 03.89.49.62.99 ☑ Y ev. day except Sun. 9am–11.30am 1.30pm–6.30pm

PIERRE-HENRI GINGLINGER

1998★★

☐ 0.58 ha 5,000 30–49 F

This is an old wine-making family which has been established for more than three centuries in the venerable town of Eguisheim. Their 1998 Tokay immediately attracts attention with its colour, which is an intense golden yellow with brilliant lights, and its very ripe nose of dried fruits (dates and banana), quince and exotic fruits. Sweet and distinctly fruity in the mouth, it is dense and fills the palate well. A wine which is already mature and can be served as an aperitif. (Residual sugar: 8 g/l.)

Pierre-Henri Ginglinger, 33, Grand-Rue, 68420 Eguisheim, tel. 03.89.41.32.55, fax 03.89.24.58.91, e-mail gingling@terre-net.fr ☑ Y by appt.

GOCKER Vieilles vignes 1998★

☐ 0.4 ha 2,500 50–69 F

Philippe Gocker keeps 7 ha (17 acres) of vines in Mittelwihr. This 1998 Vieilles Vignes is not bad at all: it is a beautiful golden-yellow colour, its nose offers a profusion of dried fruits and spices, and in the mouth it is already superb, balanced, well-structured, full and delightfully harmonious. A promising wine which needs to be kept for a while. Ideal to drink with foie gras and after dessert. (Residual sugar: 20 g/l.)

Philippe Gocker, 1, pl. des Cigognes, 68630 Mittelwihr, tel. 03.89.49.01.23, fax 03.89.49.04.72 ☑ Y by appt.

GOCKER Vendanges tardives 1997★

☐ 0.45 ha 1,800 100–149 F

Philippe Gocker's late-harvest Pinot Gris is also a great success. A bright old-gold in colour, this 1997 has scents of liquorice, wax and honey, with shades of toast and dried fruits (apricots). Along with a hint of citrus fruits, the liquorice and toast return in the mouth, which is fleshy, full, long and well-structured.

Philippe Gocker, 1, pl. des Cigognes, 68630 Mittelwihr, tel. 03.89.49.01.23, fax 03.89.49.04.72 ☑ Y by appt.

HENRI GROSS

Cuvée Christine 1998★★★

☐ 0.2 ha 2,000 50–69 F

Established at Gueberschwihr, between Colmar and Rouffach, this is a 'small vineyard which does its best to promote the produce of our family's inheritance', as Henri Gross junior modestly defines it, having taken over the estate in 1990. With wines like these, he should have no difficulty in achieving his aims. This 1998 offering has everything it takes to please: a beautiful straw colour, long, powerful, full-bodied and superbly structured flavours in the mouth, following an excellent nose combining hints of toast with the smoky aroma that is typical of this grape variety. A wine to be drunk with foie gras. (Residual sugar: 10 g/l.)
🔑 EARL Henri Gross et Fils, 11, rue du Nord, 68420 Gueberschwihr,
tel. 03.89.49.24.49, fax 03.89.49.33.58 ☑ Y by appt.
🔑 Rémy Gross

JOSEPH GRUSS ET FILS

Cuvée Frohnenberg 1998★

☐ 1.35 ha 6,000 ⫴ 30–49 F

This wine is pale yellow with glints of green, and has an attractive yet subtle nose of peach and acacia. It hits the palate cleanly and is complex and well-balanced in the mouth. Although the tasters agree that this 1998 wine is a little young, they all predict a highly successful future for it. This should encourage André Gruss, who after studying oenology has been helping his father Bernard and grandfather Joseph on the family vineyard since 1997. (Residual sugar: 15 g/l.)
🔑 Joseph Gruss et Fils, 25, Grand-Rue, 68420 Eguisheim, tel. 03.89.41.28.78, fax 03.89.41.76.66, e-mail gruss@hotmail.com ☑ Y ev. day 8am–12 noon 1.30pm–6pm

DOM. HENRI HAEFFELIN ET FILS

Le Silex 1998★★

☐ 0.5 ha 4,000 ⫴ 50–69 F

Guy Haeffelin keeps an estate of 15 ha (37 acres) at Wettolsheim near Colmar. His 'Silex' has made an excellent impression, with its golden-yellow colour with glints of green, and a nose combining fruits and spices which is already powerful and distinguished. The flavours in the mouth are second to none: slightly sweet, complex, long and extremely well-balanced. (Residual sugar: 5 g/l.)
🔑 Dom. Henri Haeffelin, 13, rue d'Eguisheim, 68920 Wettolsheim,
tel. 03.89.80.76.81, fax 03.89.79.67.05 ☑ Y by appt.
🔑 Guy Haeffelin

DOM. PIERRE HAGER

Vieilles vignes 1998★

☐ 0.66 ha 2,000 ▮ ♁ 50–69 F

This vineyard is located in the southern part of the Alsatian wine-country, on chalky-clay soils which are well sheltered from the west wind by the highest peaks of the Vosges. It offers a straw-yellow 1998 wine, which some tasters felt could have been fresher at the finish. Apart from that it is a very good wine with an attractive nose of exotic and citrus fruits, and a sweet attack on the palate with continued notes of exotic fruits. Best left to age for a while. (Residual sugar: 12.5 g/l.)
🔑 Dom. Pierre Hager, 26, rue de Soultzmatt, 68500 Orschwihr,
tel. 03.89.76.11.19, fax 03.89.74.36.76 ☑ Y ev. day 9am–12 noon 2pm–6pm; Sun. by appt.

BRUNO HERTZ 1998★

☐ 0.17 ha 1,300 ⫴ 30–49 F

Bruno Hertz is an wine specialist who has taken over and developed his parents' vineyard. Bottled under a colourful and far from traditional label, his Tokay is golden or even amber yellow, with brilliant lights. The nose combines aromas of undergrowth, barley sugar and honey, which continue on the palate. After a fresh attack it becomes supple in the mouth. Already a very mature wine. (Residual sugar: 6 g/l.)
🔑 Bruno Hertz, 9, pl. de l'Eglise, 68420 Eguisheim, tel. 03.89.41.81.61,
fax 03.89.41.68.32, e-mail bruno.hertz@libertysurf.fr ☑ Y by appt.

JOSMEYER Le Fromenteau 1998

☐ 2 ha 9,000 ⫴ 50–69 F

Founded in 1854, the Josmeyer firm keeps 23 ha (57 acres) of vines on its own account, and also deals in wines purchased from other wine-growers. It produces highly characteristic dry wines, such as this 1998 offering which has a strong yellow colour with silvery glints, and intense aromas of violets and plums, both in the nose and in the mouth. The palate is supple and has good balance, structure and length. Best kept for a while. (Residual sugar: 3 g/l.)
🔑 Josmeyer, 76, rue Clemenceau, 68920 Wintzenheim, tel. 03.89.27.91.90,
fax 03.89.27.91.99,
e-mail josmeyer@wanadoo.fr ☑ Y by appt.
🔑 Jean Meyer

ROBERT KARCHER Harth 1998

☐ 0.23 ha 4,000 ⫴ 30–49 F

This vineyard of about 10 ha (25 acres) was founded in 1953 by Robert Karcher. Since 1991, his son Georges has been running the estate. His visitors are received right in the centre of old Colmar, in this old farmhouse dating back to 1602. Here they will find a Tokay which is a brilliant golden-yellow in colour with glints of silver. With its very fruity nose and elegance in the mouth, where a structure sustained by a plenty of acidity gives it freshness, and aromas of fruit with hints of spices, this wine deserves its place in the Guide. (Residual sugar: 5 g/l.)
🔑 Dom. Robert Karcher et Fils, 11, rue de l'Ours, 68000 Colmar, tel. 03.89.41.14.42,
fax 03.89.24.45.05,
e-mail domaine.karcherrobert@wanadoo.fr
☑ Y ev. day 8am–12 noon 2pm–7pm; groups by appt.

KLEIN AUX VIEUX REMPARTS
Geissberg 1998

☐ 0.7 ha 5,100 50–69 F

Described on the label as 'winemakers-oenologists', the Kleins cultivate 8 ha (20 acres) of vines at Saint-Hippolyte, at the foot of the Haut-Koenigsbourg. The Pinots from this estate, Gris or Noir depending on their preference at the time, have an excellent reputation. This 1998 wine is golden-yellow with green lights and fresh and sweet in the mouth. Its aromas and flavours have a great deal of charm, with an already mature nose of dried fruits (figs and dried banana) and a peppery, mandarin finish. (Residual sugar: 7 g/l.)

Françoise et Jean-Marie Klein, rte du Haut-Kœnigsbourg, 68590 Saint-Hippolyte, tel. 03.89.73.00.41, fax 03.89.73.04.94 ☑ Y ev. day 9am–11.30am 1.30pm–7pm; Sun. and groups by appt.

KLEIN-BRAND 1998★

☐ 0.7 ha 6,500 30–49 F

The village of Soultzmatt is located to the south of Colmar and at the heart of the Noble Valley, where there are fine wine-growing soils along the banks of the Ohmbach. This estate, founded in 1950, offers a really excellent 1998 Tokay. Golden yellow with brilliant lights, it has an intense nose of spices (cloves) and dried fruits. Delightfully subtle and elegant, but with plenty of body and structure as well. To complete the list of its good qualities, it has freshness and length. (Residual sugar: 12 g/l.)

Klein-Brand, 96, rue de la Vallée, 68570 Soultzmatt, tel. 03.89.47.00.08, fax 03.89.47.65.53 ☑ Y ev. day except Sun. 8am–12 noon 1.30pm–6pm

KROSSFELDER Armorié 1998★

☐ n.c. n.c. 70–99 F

There is no shortage of good things to be said about this 1998 wine from one of the oldest co-operatives in the region, founded at the beginning of the 20th century: a pleasant appearance with a straw-yellow colour, and an expressive nose with pronounced notes of dried fruits which contribute to its complexity. It has delightful balance and harmony in the mouth, where it combines roundness and power. (Residual sugar: 20 g/l.)

Krossfelder, 37, rue de La Gare, 67650 Dambach-la-Ville, tel. 03.88.92.40.03, fax 03.88.92.42.89 ☑ Y by appt.

MADER Cuvée Théophile 1998★★

☐ 0.3 ha 2,000 30–49 F

Jean-Luc Mader keeps 6.5 ha (16 acres) of vines at Hunawihr, a village famous for its church with a fortified cemetery; a picture of this appears on the label. This wine comes very close to winning a *coup de coeur*. Its colour (golden-yellow with green-gold glints), and complex nose dominated by fruit (pineapple, mango and dried apricot) with added hints of menthol, herald a follow-through which is just as rich. A perfect balance and excellent length complete this picture of a remarkable wine. (Residual sugar: 17 g/l.)

EARL Jean-Luc Mader, 13, Grand-Rue, 68150 Hunawihr, tel. 03.89.73.80.32, fax 03.89.73.31.22 ☑ Y by appt.

MEISTERMANN 1998

☐ 0.5 ha 4,000 30–49 F

This is an estate of 4.5 ha (11 acres), the classic family vineyard. Coming from a chalky-clay soil which is particularly well suited to it, this Pinot Gris has a golden-yellow colour very much in keeping with a nose which is honeyed, smoky and fruity. It is powerful and conforms well to type in the mouth, where it develops flavours of quince. (Residual sugar: 5 g/l.)

Michel Meistermann, 37, rue de l'Eglise, 68250 Pfaffenheim, tel. 03.89.49.60.61 ☑ Y by appt.

GUY MERSIOL Vendanges tardives 1997★

☐ 0.4 ha 2,600 70–99 F

This ten-hectare (25-acre) estate, formed 40 years ago by the marriage of two wine-growers, is established at Dambach-la-Ville, the largest wine-producing commune in Alsace, and no doubt the one with the greatest number of wine-makers who market their own produce. This brilliant straw-yellow Tokay has a nose which as yet is unforthcoming, combining ashy and smoky notes with touches of quince. The initial attack on the palate is straightforward, after which it develops a beautifully subtle, velvety impression of delicate pear flavours and shades of citrus fruits. A promising wine. (Half-litre bottles.)

Guy Mersiol, 13, rte du Vin, 67650 Dambach-la-Ville, tel. 03.88.92.40.43, fax 03.88.92.48.73 ☑ Y by appt.

LES VIGNERONS DE PFAFFENHEIM ET GUEBERSCHWIHR
Cuvée Rabelais Grande Réserve 1998★

☐ 0.72 ha 6,400 50–69 F

The wine cellar in Pfaffenheim, founded about forty years ago, has made a name for itself in the world of Alsatian wine-production, not least thanks to the efforts of its chief cellarman, Michel Kueny. Golden-yellow with bronze glints, in the nose this Cuvée Rabelais develops scents of roasted hazelnuts, butter and smoke. It hits the palate roundly, and the flavours in the mouth are similar to the aromas in the nose. Already a well-balanced wine. (Residual sugar: 13.7 g/l.)

Cave vinicole de Pfaffenheim, 5, rue du Chai, B.P. 33, 68250 Pfaffenheim, tel. 03.89.78.08.08, fax 03.89.49.71.65, e-mail cave@pfaffenheim ☑ Y ev. day 8am–12 noon 2pm–6pm

WILLY ROLLI-EDEL 1998★

☐ 0.34 ha 2,032 50–69 F

This 11-hectare (27-acre) vineyard has been established for generations at Rorschwir, a small town located on the Route des Vins to the north of Ribeauvillé. An intense yellow in colour, its Tokay has a smoky nose. It hits the palate cleanly, and is silky and heady in the mouth, with very good length. An excellent wine which still needs to become more assertive. (Residual sugar: 18 g/l.)

🗝 Willy Rolli-Edel, 5, rue de l'Eglise, 68590 Rorschwihr, tel. 03.89.73.63.26, fax 03.89.73.83.50 ☑ Y by appt.

ROLLY GASSMANN

Vendanges tardives 1996★

☐ 1.13 ha 8,200 100–149 F

This is a major vineyard, which enjoys a wealth of experience gained over more than three centuries, and appears not only in the wine guides but on the tables of the best restaurants. Yellow with orangey glints, its late-harvested Tokay shows great potential as soon as it hits the nose. Fleshy, rich, and sustained by a plenty of acidity, the palate is characterised by flavours of dried fruits.

🗝 Rolly Gassmann, 2, rue de l'Eglise, 68590 Rorschwihr, tel. 03.89.73.63.28, fax 03.89.73.33.06 ☑ Y by appt.

RUHLMANN

Cuvée des Amoureux 1998★

☐ 0.35 ha 3,000 50–69 F

This firm was founded more than three centuries ago and has about 15 ha (37 acres) of vines. It has grown considerably over the last twenty years, mainly because of its exports, which represent 45 % of its sales. This Cuvée des Amoureux has a light-yellow colour in the glass and an elegantly fruity nose. Its structure in the mouth is very harmonious. Both rich and robust, this is a pleasant wine which will no doubt become even better with time. (Residual sugar: 20 g/l.)

🗝 Ruhlmann, 34, rue du Mal-Foch, 67650 Dambach-la-Ville, tel. 03.88.92.41.86, fax 03.88.92.61.81 ☑ Y ev. day except Sun. 8am–12 noon 1.30pm–7pm

CLOS SAINTE-ODILE 1998★

☐ n.c. 5,000 50–69 F

This wine-merchant's products are developed by its technical director Jean-Pierre Bergeret, who is an oenologist. This Tokay promises great things for the future. A strong yellow in colour, it holds the attention with a complex nose of fruits (apricots, pineapple and mango), mingled with undergrowth and flowers. The same rich flavours reappear in the mouth, where freshness and roundness combine in a long finish. (Residual sugar: 15 g/l.)

🗝 Sté vinicole Sainte-Odile, 3, rue de la Gare, 67210 Obernai, tel. 03.88.47.60.20, fax 03.88.47.60.22 ☑ Y by appt.

THIERRY SCHERRER

Réserve particulière 1998★

☐ 0.21 ha 1,700 30–49 F

Thierry Scherrer refers to himself as an 'oenologist-winegrower'. At the start of his career he gave the benefit of his knowledge to great wine firms in Alsace and Champagne, then a few years ago took over the family estate on which he set up a vathouse and a wine-press. He offers an excellent Tokay, with a strong golden-yellow colour, a fine, already somewhat developed nose of crystallised fruits with a touch of menthol, and a very well-balanced palate. This is a pleasant wine with good presence, elegance and length. It will go well with any foie gras dish. (Residual sugar: 30 g/l.)

🗝 Thierry Scherrer, 1, rue de la Gare, 68770 Ammerschwihr, tel. 03.89.47.15.86, fax 03.89.47.15.86, e-mail thierry.scherrer@wanadoo.fr ☑ Y by appt.

CAVE DE SIGOLSHEIM

Vendanges tardives 1997★★

☐ n.c. n.c. 150–199 F

This co-operative was set up in 1945 to enable wine-growers to get back to work in a region which had been completely devastated by the fighting in the Colmar Pocket. It seems that the arts of wine-making have been well and truly mastered, if this remarkable Tokay is anything to go by. With its golden-yellow appearance and intense nose of crystallised fruits, it has virtually reached its full potential. The first impression on the palate is rich and full, and this is reinforced by deep flavours of liquorice, violets and spices. A robust wine with good length.

🗝 La Cave de Sigolsheim, 11–15, rue Saint-Jacques, 68240 Sigolsheim, tel. 03.89.78.10.10, fax 03.89.78.21.93 ☑ Y ev. day 8am–12 noon 1.30pm–5.30pm

JEAN SIPP Trottacker 1998★★

☐ n.c. 5,000 70–99 F

This concern cultivates 20 ha (49 acres) of vines which used to be part of the Ribeaupierre estate owned by the lords of Ribeauvillé. The Trottacker has a chalky clay soil and is located on hillsides which face east-south-east. It has yielded a very great Tokay which is bright straw-yellow in colour and manifestly rich and powerful, both in the nose and in the mouth. Intense yet subtle aromas of crystallised fruits in the nose are followed by a finely spiced palate with good length. This is a wine to be drunk with foie gras. (Residual sugar: 18 g/l.)

🗝 Dom. Jean Sipp, 60, rue de la Fraternité, 68150 Ribeauvillé, tel. 03.89.73.60.02, fax 03.89.73.82.38 ☑ Y ev. day 9am–11.30am 2pm–6pm; Sun. by appt.

🗝 Jean-Jacques Sipp

JEAN SIPP Clos Ribeaupierre 1998★★

☐ 1 ha 2,500 150–199 F

The year 1998 was evidently a good one for Jean Sipp, whose Ribeaupierre walled vineyard, the jewel of an estate dating back to the 13th century, has yielded a Tokay which is every bit as finely developed as the previous one. Coming from a granite soil, this wine impresses from the start by its strong golden-yellow colour with amber glints. After that comes a captivating, concentrated nose consisting of honey and candied fruits, and finally a candied flavour in the mouth, which is rich and very long. Somewhat reminiscent of a late-harvest wine. (Residual sugar: 25 g/l.)

🗝 Dom. Jean Sipp, 60, rue de la Fraternité, 68150 Ribeauvillé, tel. 03.89.73.60.02, fax 03.89.73.82.38 ☑ 𝕐 ev. day 9am–11.30am 2pm–6pm; Sun. by appt.

SIPP-MACK

Vendanges tardives Cuvée Amélie 1997★★

☐ 0.3 ha 2,500 ▮ 70–99 F

This estate is both venerable – it has been in existence for over four centuries – and dynamic, exporting over 55% of its produce. Its Cuvée Amélie is delectable, with a brilliant pale-gold colour and a delightful nose combining cocoa, hazelnuts and quince. To crown it all, it is full, luscious and powerful in the mouth, with slight hints of aniseed and liquorice and good length. Full of charm and character, with just a touch of wildness about it. (Half-litre bottles.)

🗝 Dom. Sipp-Mack, 1, rue des Vosges, 68150 Hunawihr, tel. 03.89.73.61.88, fax 03.89.73.36.70, e-mail sippmack@rmcnet.fr ☑ 𝕐 ev. day except Sun. 9am–11.30am 1pm–6pm

SPECHT Réserve 1998★

☐ 0.15 ha 1,100 30–49 F

Established since 1978 at Mittelwihr, a commune which is well-known for its Grand Cru, Jean-Paul and Denis Specht keep 8 ha (20 acres) of vines. With its beautiful light-yellow colour, its expressive nose of roses mingled with honey, and an attack on the palate which is both sweet and fresh, their Réserve has everything it needs to develop well. It is long in the mouth and will reach its full potential before long. (Residual sugar: 11 g/l.)

🗝 Jean-Paul et Denis Specht, 2, rue des Eglises, 68630 Mittelwihr, tel. 03.89.47.90.85, fax 03.89.49.04.22 ☑ 𝕐 by appt.

STRAUB 1998

☐ 0.37 ha 3,300 ⦀ 30–49 F

The Blienschwiller vineyard is located mainly on granitic sands which seem to impart their lightness to the wines which come from them. This one has golden-yellow lights and an expressive nose which is already well developed. Rich and assertive on the palate, it then becomes round and well-balanced. It will be good to drink with a *galette des Rois* (a traditional cake) at the New Year in 2001. (Residual sugar: 10 g/l.)

🗝 Jean-Marie Straub, 61, rte du Vin, 67650 Blienschwiller, tel. 03.88.92.40.42, fax 03.88.92.40.42 ☑ 𝕐 by appt.

ACHILLE THIRION 1998★

☐ n.c. 9,000 ▮ 🌡 30–49 F

This family business, established since 1760 at Saint-Hippolyte, can be found by visitors to the Château du Haut-Koenigsbourg. Its Tokay created a very good impression. A strong golden-yellow colour with green glints, it has a rich, intense nose containing aromas of toast and stewed fruit. Undergrowth is the dominant flavour in a palate that is long, rich and well-balanced. A wine that conforms well to type. (Residual sugar: 12.2 g/l.)

🗝 Dom. Achille Thirion, 69, rte du Vin, 68590 Saint-Hippolyte, tel. 03.89.73.00.23, fax 03.89.73.06.46 ☑ 𝕐 by appt.

CAVE DE TURCKHEIM

Herrenweg 1998★★

☐ 5 ha 33,200 ▮ 🌡 50–69 F

Founded in 1955, this co-operative cellar is a recognised Alsatian wine-producer. Its Herrenweg Tokay charmed the jury with its beautiful harmony. The first impression is magnificent: a strong golden colour and subtle scents of apricots and citronella. Full and well-structured, the palate has a freshness which gives it real elegance. A wine which will go well with meat en croûte and white meats. (Residual sugar: 12 g/l.)

🗝 Cave de Turckheim, 16, rue des Tuileries, 68230 Turckheim, tel. 03.89.30.23.60, fax 03.89.27.35.33, e-mail brandt@cave-turckheim.com ☑ 𝕐 by appt.

WACKENTHALER 1998★

☐ 0.38 ha 3,000 ⦀ 30–49 F

This family business has been established since the mid-18th century at Ammerschwihr, the commune where the Confrérie Saint-Etienne has its headquarters today. A strong, very brilliant yellow in colour, this Tokay has a beautifully expressive nose of honeyed and smoky aromas. Full-bodied and powerful with a pronounced roundness, it has a delightfully supple finish in the mouth. (Residual sugar: 8 g/l.)

🗝 EARL François Wackenthaler, 8, rue du Kaefferkopf, 68770 Ammerschwihr, tel. 03.89.78.23.76, fax 03.89.47.15.48, e-mail wackenthal@wanadoo.fr ☑ 𝕐 ev. day except Sun. 10am–12 noon 2pm–7pm

DOM. WEINBACH

Cuvée Laurence 1998★★

☐ 0.8 ha 4,200 150–199 F

The vast, beautiful estate run by Colette Faller and her daughters now has too well-established a reputation to need any introduction. This Cuvée Laurence is an intense golden yellow with amber glints, and offers a nose which is discreet but of great finesse. The structure is concentrated and gives way to a long finish with notes of dried fruits (currants). (Residual sugar: 48 g/l.) A great wine in the making.

🗝 Colette Faller et ses Filles, Dom. Weinbach, Clos des Capucins, 68240 Kaysersberg, tel. 03.89.47.13.21, fax 03.89.47.38.18 ☑ 𝕐 by appt.

JEAN WEINGAND 1998★

☐ n.c. n.c. ▮ 🌡 30–49 F

Jacques and Jean-Marie Cattin are wine-merchants who have taken over the Jean Weingand estate from the Weingand family. Their Tokay has a brilliant yellow colour with glints of gold. Its intense, complex scents are

dominated by fruit (apricots and mango), with touches of mint. With a round attack on the palate and good length, its flavours in the mouth are the same as its aromas in the nose. An agreeable overall impression. (Residual sugar: 13 g/l.)
🗝 Jean Weingand, 19, rue Roger-Frémeaux, 68420 Voegtlinshoffen, tel. 03.89.49.30.21, fax 03.89.49.26.02 ☑ 𝕐 ev. day except Sun. 8am–12 noon 2pm–6pm
🗝 Jacques et Jean-Marie Cattin

W. WURTZ Vendanges tardives 1996★★

□ 0.1 ha 800 70–99 F

Mittelwihr stretches out along the Route du Vin. Ravaged by the fighting in 1945, this commune quickly got back on its feet. One of the many talented winemakers there is W. Wurtz, whose late-harvested Tokay delighted the jury. This is a pale-yellow wine, with a floral nose which also has some fern and a touch of mandarin. The structure is superb, centred on freshness with flavours of kiwi-fruit and a hint of grapefruit. A remarkable wine with excellent prospects. (Half-litre bottles.)
🗝 Willy Wurtz et Fils, 6, rue du Bouxhof, 68630 Mittelwihr, tel. 03.89.47.93.16, fax 03.89.47.89.01 ☑ 𝕐 by appt.

DOM. XAVIER WYMANN

Réserve 1998★

□ 0.3 ha 2,300 30–49 F

Jean-Luc Schaerlinger comes from an old Ribeauvillé family, and in 1996 he took over an estate of about 5 ha (12 acres) from his uncle. Judging by this 1998 wine, he has made a promising start. It is light gold in colour, and has an attractive candied nose with some added floral touches. The candied note reappears in the taste, which is silky, long, and still distinctly sweet at the finish. This is a wine which will assert itself after a while. (Residual sugar: 27 g/l.)
🗝 Jean-Luc Schaerlinger, 41, rue de la Fraternité, 68150 Ribeauvillé, tel. 03.89.73.66.83 ☑ 𝕐 by appt.

Alsace Pinot Noir

Alsace is particularly renowned for its white wines, but it is not widely known that in the Middle Ages red grapes were widely grown. Pinot Noir then virtually disappeared from the area – it is the best red-wine grape variety in regions further south – but it has been reintroduced and is now cultivated in 1,225 ha (3,026 acres), some 8.5% of the Alsace area. It is principally used to make a pleasant rosé that is dry and fruity, and, like other rosés, it can be drunk with a variety of different dishes. Increasing efforts are being made to produce red wines with Pinot Noir, and this is a welcome development.

PIERRE BECHT

Cuvée Frédéric 1998★★★

■ 0.3 ha 2,500 50–69 F

This Cuvée Fréderic wins three stars. It has a superb, deep-red colour, and a nose which combines touches of fresh fruit with crystallised cherries and a well-integrated oakiness. The attack on the palate is clean and very fruity, and it has a soft richness and perfect balance in the mouth. The finish is still marked by tannins, but it will become more harmonious in a few months' time.
🗝 Pierre et Frédéric Becht, 26, fg des Vosges, 67120 Dorlisheim, tel. 03.88.38.18.22, fax 03.88.38.87.81 ☑ 𝕐 by appt.

HUBERT BECK

Réserve du Chevalier 1998

■ 0.5 ha 4,000 30–49 F

Founded in 1985, this firm of winemaker-merchants markets its produce mainly through cellarmen, importers and other wine professionals. Its Réserve du Chevalier has some orangey glints. Its nose is still quite discreet, and is characteristic of this grape variety. On the palate it seems light and fairly round. A pleasant, straightforward wine.
🗝 Hubert Beck, 25, rue du Gal-de-Gaulle, 67650 Dambach-la-Ville, tel. 03.88.92.45.90, fax 03.88.92.61.28 ☑ 𝕐 ev. day except Sun. 8am–12 noon 1.30pm–6pm

PAUL BUECHER

Les Terrasses Elevé en barrique 1998★★★

■ 1 ha 4,500 70–99 F

As descendants from a line of wine-makers which goes back to the 17th century, the prime concern of Henri and Jean-Marc Buecher is to bring out the particular qualities of their terroir, whether by growing techniques or during the wine-making process and maturation stage. Their Rouge d'Alsace

is more than worthy of its name; it is a real red wine, with a remarkably deep-purple colour and a nose in which fruit merges into a fine oaky aroma. It has excellent substance on the palate, where notes of vanilla persist at the finish. A wine which needs to be kept patiently for two or three years before being served with red meat or game.
🗝 Paul Buecher, 15, rue Sainte-Gertrude, 68920 Wettolsheim, tel. 03.89.80.64.73, fax 03.89.80.58.62 ☒ Y ev. day except Sun. 9am–12 noon 2pm–6pm

JEAN DIETRICH

Côtes de Kaysersberg 1998

■ 0.38 ha 3,500 ⫼ 50–69 F

The setting for this business is a picture postcard of traditional Alsace: an old, half-timbered house which, standing next to a fortified bridge, is one of the most photographed spots in Kaysersberg. The cellar offers a Pinot Noir with a pleasing light-red colour. Its fruity, fresh nose bodes well for a good overall impression. A wine which conforms to type and is lively and easy to drink.
🗝 Jean Dietrich, 4, rue de l'Oberhof, 68240 Kaysersberg, tel. 03.89.78.25.24, fax 03.89.47.30.72 ☒ Y ev. day 10am–12 noon 2pm–6pm

ANDRE DUSSOURT

Rouge de Blienschwiller Réserve prestige 1998★

■ 0.45 ha 4,470 ⫼ 50–69 F

The 1998 Rouge de Blienschwiller has been matured for eight months in large oak casks. This excellent Pinot Noir has a deep, dark-red colour and a fruity, clean, expressive nose. Balanced, well-structured and quite long, it is powerful and delightfully harmonious. One taster suggests serving it as an accompaniment to meat cooked with fruit.
🗝 André Dussourt, 2, rue de Dambach, 67750 Scherwiller, tel. 03.88.92.10.27, fax 03.88.92.18.44 ☒ Y ev. day except Sun. 8am–12 noon 1.30pm–6pm
🗝 Paul Dussourt

HARTWEG

Elevé en fût de chêne 1998★★★

■ 0.2 ha 1,200 ⫼ 30–49 F

In 1996 Frank Hartweg took over the family vineyard of 8 ha (20 acres), which was founded in 1930. Ruby in colour with dark purple glints, his Pinot Noir has notes of vanilla and spices, which it has acquired over ten months of maturing in barrels. Rich, powerful, supple and well-structured, it has a long finish with spicy, peppery flavours. 'I wish I had some in my cellar,' writes one spellbound taster.
🗝 Jean-Paul et Frank Hartweg, 39, rue Jean-Macé, 68980 Beblenheim, tel. 03.89.47.94.79, fax 03.89.49.00.83 ☒ Y ev. day except Sun. 8am–11.30am 1.30pm–6pm

LEON HEITZMANN

Rouge d'Alsace 1998★

■ 0.68 ha 3,400 ⫼ 50–69 F

At the head of the family business since 1987, Léon Heitzmann is a passionate, meticulous wine-grower whose Pinot Noir is often praised. This 1998 version has a fine oaky aroma which opens out into flowery fragrances. It comes from very good stock and is built on a full, solid structure. The dense flavours confirm that it has a certain potential, which will be achieved in two or three years.
🗝 Léon Heitzmann, 2, Grand-Rue, 68770 Ammerschwihr, tel. 03.89.47.10.64, fax 03.89.78.27.76 ☒ Y ev. day except Sun. 8am–12 noon 1.30pm–6pm

JEAN HIRTZ ET FILS

Rouge de Mittelbergheim 1998

■ 0.4 ha 2,000 ▮ 30–49 F

Listed as 'one of the most beautiful villages in France', Mittelbergheim is better known for its Grands Blancs than for its red wines. A dark ruby red colour, this 1998 wine opens out gradually into notes of fruit. After an initial roundness in the mouth, the structure is dominated by tannins; there is a slightly peppery finish, which gives it a persistent character.
🗝 Jean Hirtz et Fils, 13, rue Rotland, 67140 Mittelbergheim, tel. 03.88.08.47.90, fax 03.88.08.47.90 ☒ Y by appt.

ARMAND HURST Vieilles vignes 1998

■ 0.36 ha 3,000 ⫼ 50–69 F

Armand Hurst cultivates some 8 ha (20 acres) of vines in Turckheim, a commune whose ramparts and gates are a reminder of its past as a free town in the 16th century. He offers a Pinot Noir which has been produced in large oak casks, and whose nose is characterised by oaky notes along with hints of undergrowth. It has a satisfying structure, but is still dominated by oak which masks the fruit: this one needs more time to mature.
🗝 Armand Hurst, 8, rue de la Chapelle, 68230 Turckheim, tel. 03.89.27.40.22, fax 03.89.27.47.67 ☒ Y by appt.

JACQUES ILTIS

Rouge de Saint-Hippolyte Schlossreben 1998★

■ 0.7 ha 3,500 ⫼ 30–49 F

This family business's cellar bears the stamp of a grandfather who was a cooper. Needless to say, the wines here are matured in traditional oak barrels. Brick-red in colour, this Pinot Noir has some floral notes, and above all a fruity aroma of raspberry and blackcurrant. Supple and fresh, this wine is

rich, generous, aromatic and persistent.
Jacques Iltis, 1, rue Schlossreben, 68590 Saint-Hippolyte, tel. 03.89.73.00.67, fax 03.89.73.01.82 ev. day 8am–12 noon 2pm–6pm

J.-CH. ET D. KIEFFER

Rouge d'Itterswiller 1998*

0.3 ha 2,000 30–49 F

Founded in 1737, this business is run from a house with a remarkable half-timbered façade. It offers a Pinot Noir with an intense, dark ruby colour, and aromas of soft fruits. After a supple, even slightly round attack on the palate, it has a good structure with well-blended tannins. Forthcoming and harmonious, this 1998 wine has a long finish which brings the tasting to an agreeable conclusion.
Jean-Charles Kieffer, 7, rte des Vins, 67140 Itterswiller, tel. 03.88.85.59.80, fax 03.88.57.81.44 by appt.

PHILIPPE KIRMANN 1998**

0.78 ha 5,800 30–49 F

This vineyard probably dates back to 1630, when Alsace was on the eve of the Thirty Years' War. Its Pinot Noir really is a bowl of Morello cherries! Its fresh, fruity, cherry aroma, good attack on the palate and clean, balanced, pleasant content, make it a typical representative of the appellation. Will go well with red meat or duck.
Philippe Kirmann, 2, rue du Gal-de-Gaulle, 67560 Rosheim, tel. 03.88.50.43.01, fax 03.88.50.22.72 by appt.

GEORGES KLEIN

Rouge de Saint-Hippolyte 1998

0.5 ha 3,500 30–49 F

This firm, which was founded in 1997, complements the activities of the G. Klein estate. It specialises in sales to individual customers. The Rouge de Saint-Hippolyte tends towards a brick-red colour, and opens with a fruity aroma punctuated with hints of spice. It finds its balance within a supple structure, with velvety flavours and very good length.
SARL Georges Klein, 10, rte du Vin, 68590 Saint-Hippolyte, tel. 03.89.73.00.28, fax 03.89.73.06.28, e-mail a.klein@rmcnet.fr by appt.
Auguste Klein

KOEBERLE KREYER

Vieilles vignes 1998

0.3 ha 2,000 50–69 F

Rodern, where this vineyard has been established since the 18th century, is without doubt one of the cradles of Alsace Pinot Noir. This one offers a nose of red berries with hints of vanilla. Its sustained structure is marked by tannins, on which the opinions of the tasters varied. They all agreed that it had excellent fullness and would keep well.
Koeberlé Kreyer, 28, rue du Pinot-Noir, 68590 Rodern, tel. 03.89.73.00.55, fax 03.89.73.00.55 by appt.

DOM. DE L'ANCIEN MONASTERE

Rouge de Saint-Léonard Cuvée des Trois Filles du vigneron 1998**

3 ha 9,333 30–49 F

The marquetries at Saint-Léonard have enjoyed a great reputation for several decades. As for its wine-growing, this 1998 Cuvée produced by the Hummel family will do a great deal to promote it. Deep red in colour, it has hints of oakiness that quickly give way to aromas of well-ripened soft fruits. On the palate it is dense and well structured yet velvety. Here again there is an oaky flavour, with touches of pepper and leather, which contribute to an impression of richness, all of this in an almost silky harmony.
B. Hummel et Filles-Dom. L'Ancien Monastère, 4, cour du Chapître-Saint-Léonard, 67530 Boersch, tel. 03.88.95.81.21, fax 03.88.48.11.21 ev. day 8am–12 noon 2pm–7pm

DOM. DE LA TOUR

Cuvée Xavière 1998*

0.8 ha 5,000 30–49 F

Wine has been made here for almost half a millennium. In the estate's period cellar, the wine-lover will find this delightful Pinot Noir with notes of spices and soft fruits. A full, rich, fleshy wine, whose good balance indicates some potential to improve with maturity.
Jean-François Straub, Dom. de la Tour, 35 rte du Vin, 67650 Blienschwiller, tel. 03.88.92.48.72, fax 03.88.92.62.90 ev. day 8am–12 noon 2pm–6pm; Sat. Sun. by appt.

FRANCOIS LICHTLE 1998*

n.c. 3,000 30–49 F

This vineyard has conserved many traditional wine-growing practices. On its 6 ha (15 acres) it cultivates all the grape varieties of the region. Its Pinot Noir is almost black in colour, and red and fruity in the nose. It hits the palate cleanly, is slightly supple, and shows a good balance. The fairly long finish makes it a promising wine, which only needs longer to mature.
Dom. François Lichtlé, 17, rue des Vignerons, 68420 Husseren-les-Châteaux, tel. 03.89.49.31.34, fax 03.89.49.37.52 by appt.

RUHLMANN DIRRINGER

A fleur de roche 1998*

0.5 ha 3,000 30–49 F

Visitors are received in the former residence of the Counts of Mullenheim, where they can enjoy the privilege of tasting wines in a 1578 cellar with beautiful barrel vaults and a stained-glass window. Call it ruby or purple, the colour of this 1998 is noble indeed! Its fine aromas are dominated by a subtle oakiness. Full in the mouth with well-blended tannins, it finishes on an agreeable note.
Ruhlmann-Dirringer, 3, rue de

Mullenheim, 67650 Dambach-la-Ville, tel. 03.88.92.40.28, fax 03.88.92.48.05 ☑ Y by appt.

SCHOENHEITZ

Côte du Val Saint-Grégoire 1998*

■ 1 ha 5,000 ▮ 30–49 F

During the 20th century, this old wine-making family contributed a great deal to the revival of the vineyard located at the entrance to the Munster Valley. It offers a Pinot Noir which comes from a granite soil. Dark red in colour, this 1998 wine has a slight oakiness which gives way to aromas of fruits and spices. Supple and fresh, it has richness and good concentration. A pleasant finish.

🗝 Henri Schoenheitz, 1, rue de Walbach, 68230 Wihr-au-Val, tel. 03.89.71.03.96, fax 03.89.71.14.33 ☑ Y by appt.

J. ET L. SCHWARTZ 1998

■ 0.5 ha 4,800 (D 30–49 F

The village of Itterswiller, where this family business is established, lies on the old Roman road which used to run along the foothills of the Vosges. No doubt this route contributed to the development of the Alsatian vineyards from the third century on. This 1998 wine has a purple colour with a touch of redcurrant, which harmonises well with its discreet aromas of small soft fruits. In the mouth it is full, with a fairly powerful attack on the palate, after which it becomes more balanced. The tannins are still pronounced and leave a somewhat austere final impression and a feeling that this wine needs to be kept for a while.

🗝 Dom. Justin et Luc Schwartz, rte Romaine, 67140 Itterswiller, tel. 03.88.85.51.59, fax 03.88.85.59.16 ☑ Y ev. day 9am–1pm; Sat. 9am–6pm

J. SIEGLER 1998*

■ 0.5 ha 3,600 (D 30–49 F

Purple-red in colour, this 1998 wine makes no attempt to conceal its maturation in oak, whose aromas dominate in the nose. In the mouth it has a good, balanced structure and flavours of soft fruits which have a certain finesse.

🗝 EARL Jean Siegler Père et Fils, Clos des Terres-Brunes, 68630 Mittelwihr, tel. 03.89.47.90.70, fax 03.89.49.01.78, e-mail siegler@caveparticuliere.com Y ev. day 8am–12 noon 2pm–7pm

J.-M. SOHLER

Les terrasses du Bubenberg 1998*

■ 0.18 ha 1,400 (D 30–49 F

With 64 plots of vines on very varied soils, a cellar dating back to 1563 and high-quality, large oak casks, the Sohlers have everything they need to develop distinctive wines. This Pinot Noir, coming from a granite soil, is discreet in the nose at first, then opens out into notes of raspberry. Well-balanced tannins in the mouth give it great suppleness, albeit with quite a powerful finish.

🗝 Jean-Marie et Hervé Sohler, 16, rue du Winzenberg, 67650 Blienschwiller, tel. 03.88.92.42.93, fax 03.88.92.42.93 ☑ Y by appt.

PHILIPPE SOHLER

Rouge de Nothalten 1998*

■ 0.29 ha 2,400 ▮ 🌡 30–49 F

Philippe Sohler created this estate in 1997 by taking over the family vineyard, which now adds up to 5 ha (12 acres). His Rouge de Nothalten comes from a sandstone soil. The richness of its fruity aromas lives up to its intense ruby colour. Once again there is a pleasant fruitiness on the palate, harmonising with a structure which is both rich and velvety. The tasting ends on a note of finesse, with an aromatic finish and good length.

🗝 Philippe Sohler, 80A, rte du Vin, 67680 Nothalten, tel. 03.88.92.49.89, fax 03.88.92.48.20 ☑ Y by appt.

THOMANN

Clos du Letzenberg Elevé et vieilli en barrique de chêne 1998*

■ 0.45 ha 2,580 (D 50–69 F

M. Thomann runs a vineyard of some 7 ha (17 acres), where he has endeavoured to bring back into use some south-facing hillsides which had been abandoned since the First World War. His 1998 Pinot Noir is clearly very young, and is still dominated by oaky notes which mask fruity aromas with hints of cherry. In the mouth the structure is full, but the tannins are very much in evidence. For this reason it is recommended that this wine should be kept for two or three years.

🗝 Vins Le Manoir, 56, rue de la Promenade, 68040 Ingersheim, tel. 03.89.27.23.69, fax 03.89.27.23.69 ☑ Y by appt.

🗝 Thomann

LAURENT VOGT

Elevé en fût de chêne 1998

■ 0.2 ha 1,200 (D 30–49 F

This Pinot Noir is the first wine produced by Thomas Vogt, who has joined his father in the vineyard. Both father and son deserve great encouragement. Notes of cherry with added touches of vanilla give a very well-defined nose. The combination of tannins and dark berries in the mouth is in keeping with a very good, fresh balance, which will be fully apparent as early as 2001.

🗝 EARL Laurent Vogt, 4, rue des Vignerons, 67120 Wolxheim, tel. 03.88.38.50.41, fax 03.88.38.50.41 ☑ Y by appt.

CH. WANTZ Réserve particulière 1998

■ n.c. 5,000 ▮ 🌡 30–49 F

This wine-maker/merchant is established at Barr, whose 17th-century town hall and Folie-Marco museum are well worth a visit. The first impression of his Réserve Particulière is an intense, purplish colour with beautiful glints. The nose is not yet mature but nevertheless bodes well for a good, full content.

There is a combination of roundness and fullness in the mouth, where the finish still has the imbalance of youth.
🔑 SA Charles Wantz, 36, rue Saint-Marc, 67140 Barr, tel. 03.88.08.90.44, fax 03.88.08.54.61 ☑ 🍷 by appt.

WASSLER 1998

■ 0.37 ha 3,300 30–49 F

A new generation has just taken over this estate, which was created in 1962 and now has more than 6.5 ha (16 acres). Ruby-red in colour, this Pinot Noir remains discreet in the nose. In the mouth it has a most engaging attack on the palate; the finish is dominated by a tannic structure which reveals its youth.
🔑 EARL Henri Wassler Successeurs, 71, rte du Vin, 67140 Itterswiller, tel. 03.88.57.82.19, fax 03.88.57.83.98 ☑ 🍷 by appt.
🔑 Sohler

Alsace Grand Cru

As a way of promoting the best situated vineyards, a new appellation, Alsace Grand Cru, was established by decree in 1975. Strict limits were set on the quantity that the designated vineyards qualifying for this appellation could produce, and the sugar content of the wine was also limited. They were to be vineyards growing only Gewurztraminer, Pinot Gris, Riesling and Muscat. Along with wines labelled with the seal of the Confrérie Saint-Étienne and some notable vintages, the vineyards that qualify produce the *nec plus ultra* of Alsace wines.

In 1983 a decree identified a group of 25 vineyards that qualified for the appellation, but the decree was rescinded and superseded by a new one on 17 December 1992. There are 50 official Grands Crus from 47 communes, although the decree mentions only 46, Rouffach having been omitted in error. Each vineyard covers an area of between 3.23 ha and 80.28 ha (8 and 198 acres), and each had to meet certain geological criteria appropriate to Grands Crus. The volume of wine produced by the Grands Crus is still modest: only 42,403 hl (1,119,440 gal in 1999.

New regulations were put in place after the 1987 harvest. They increased the minimum alcoholic content from 11 to 12 in Gewurztraminers and Tokay-Pinot Gris. At the same time, there were new requirements for labels to show the specific vineyard alongside the grape variety and the year, and this information also had to be shown on all administrative and commercial documentation.

Alsace Grand Cru Altenberg de Bergbieten

FREDERIC MOCHEL Riesling 1998★

□ 1.1 ha 7,000 50–69 F

Located in the northern part of the Alsatian vineyards and on a gypseous marly-clay soil, the Altenberg has been recognised for nearly a millennium. The Riesling and Gewurztraminer grape varieties take pride of place there. This Riesling is quite rich and complex, with nuances of citrus fruits accompanied by a slight mineral aroma. The citrus fruits are in evidence again on the palate, where their freshness ensures good balance and makes for an attractive finish. This wine will gain in balance in one or two years. (Residual sugar: 5 g/l.)
🔑 Frédéric Mochel, 56, rue Principale, 67310 Traenheim, tel. 03.88.50.38.67, fax 03.88.50.56.19 ☑ 🍷 ev. day except Sun. 9am–12 noon 1.30pm–6pm

Alsace Grand Cru Altenberg de Bergheim

LORENTZ Gewurztraminer 1998

□ 6 ha 20,000 100–149 F

Founded in 1836, the Lorentz firm is in Bergheim, a picturesque village located to the east of Ribeauvillé. The Altenberg cru, one of

its finest jewels, is characterised by red, very stony marly-clay soils which produce excellent Gewurztraminers. This one is a very brilliant gold-yellow in the glass, and of great aromatic complexity. It is powerful, vinous, heady and round in the mouth: a very agreeable overall impression, but as yet a little unbalanced. Needs some time to mature. (Residual sugar: 32 g/l.)
🔑 Gustave Lorentz, 35, Grand-Rue, 68750 Bergheim, tel. 03.89.73.22.22, fax 03.89.73.30.49 ☒ Y ev. day except Sun. 10am–12 noon 2pm–6.30pm
🔑 Charles Lorentz

Alsace Grand Cru Brand

JUSTIN BOXLER Riesling 1998

☐ 0.28 ha 2,000 30–49 F

Originally from St-Gallen in Switzerland, Justin Boxler's ancestors settled in 1672 at Niedermorschwihr, west of Colmar. To the south of the village, on the southern face of a hillside with granite soils and, according to legend, a dragon hiding on it, is the Brand Grand Cru, which in general yields very expressive wines. This one is dominated by floral aromas, with additional hints of citrus fruits. The content is good, fresh and harmonious. The slightly mineral finish is characteristic of the terroir. (Residual sugar: 6 g/l.)
🔑 GAEC Justin Boxler, 15, rue des Trois-Epis, 68230 Niedermorschwihr, tel. 03.89.27.11.07, fax 03.89.27.01.44 ☒ Y ev. day 8am–12 noon 2pm–7pm; groups by appt.

PAUL BUECHER Riesling 1998★★

☐ 0.53 ha 4,000 70–99 F

Heirs to more than three centuries of wine-growing experience, Henri and Jean-Marc Buecher do their utmost to develop wines which reflect their terroir and their vintage. The result is convincing, if this 1998 wine is anything to go by. Its nose is discreet at first, then opens out into notes of white flowers, with a slight touch of iodine. With a good attack and no excessive freshness, the palate has excellent harmony. A very great Riesling. (Residual sugar: 5 g/l.)
🔑 Paul Buecher, 15, rue Sainte-Gertrude, 68920 Wettolsheim, tel. 03.89.80.64.73, fax 03.89.80.58.62 ☒ Y ev. day except Sun. 9am–12 noon 2pm–6pm

EMILE HERZOG

Tokay-Pinot gris 1998

☐ 0.18 ha 1,300 70–99 F

The golden glints in this Tokay are the fruits of the sun on the Brand Cru. It has a very mature nose which develops notes of grapes, smoke and toast. The straightforward, slightly harsh attack in the mouth comes as a surprise. Still an immature wine which will need to wait until its flavours become more distinct. (Residual sugar: 4 g/l.)
🔑 Emile Herzog, 28, rue du Florimont, 68230 Turckheim, tel. 03.89.27.08.79, fax 03.89.27.08.79 ☒ Y by appt.

PREISS-ZIMMER Riesling 1998★

☐ 5 ha 37,000 70–99 F

The Brand Cru, whose name suggests a 'land of fire' is located in the Turckheim area. Its wines are sought after by all good wine-merchants, such as this one in Riquewihr, who offers a pale-yellow Riesling with the characteristic aromas of the grape variety, and a slight mineral note as well. There is a lively, elegant attack on the palate, after which it becomes fuller. A frisky, harmonious wine. (Residual sugar: 4 g/l.)
🔑 SARL Preiss-Zimmer, 40, rue du Gal-de-Gaulle, 68340 Riquewihr, tel. 03.89.47.86.91, fax 03.89.27.35.33

PREISS-ZIMMER

Gewurztraminer 1998★

☐ 3 ha 23,000 70–99 F

From the same Grand Cru, Preiss-Zimmer has also produced a very successful Gewurztraminer. Golden-yellow in colour, this 1998 has powerful, spicy scents. There are similar spicy flavours in the mouth, which is round and well-balanced. This wine will achieve its full potential in two to three years. (Residual sugar: 13 g/l.)
🔑 SARL Preiss-Zimmer, 40, rue du Gal-de-Gaulle, 68340 Riquewihr, tel. 03.89.47.86.91, fax 03.89.27.35.33

DOM. SAINT-REMY

Tokay-pinot gris 1998★

☐ 0.5 ha 2,700 50–69 F

The Saint-Remy estate has done very well indeed with its Pinot Gris from the Brand Grand Cru. It has an unusual, complex nose which shows a good level of maturity. After a round, full, assertive attack on the palate, this wine offers a fine, fresh finish. Needs to be kept for a while. It will be equally good to serve as an aperitif or with gourmet dishes such as foie gras or quails with grapes. (Residual sugar: 28 g/l.)
🔑 Dom. François Ehrhart et Fils, 6, rue Saint-Remy, 68920 Wettolsheim, tel. 03.89.80.60.57, fax 03.89.79.74.00, e-mail domaine.st-remy@wanadoo.fr ☒ Y ev. day except Sun. 8am–12 noon 1.30pm–7pm

Alsace Grand Cru Bruderthal

PHILIPPE HEITZ

Riesling Vendanges tardives 1997★

☐ 0.15 ha 1000 70–99 F

Thanks to its marly-clay soil which enables the grapes to mature completely over a prolonged period, the Bruderthal is perfectly suited to late-harvest wines. Light-yellow in the glass, this one has a slightly mineral nose with a good degree of intensity, while there are notes of lemon and blackcurrant in the mouth. The palate is balanced and long, and well sustained by a fresh acidity. A wine which conforms well to type, and will be a good accompaniment to fish served in a sauce.

Philippe Heitz, 4, rue Ettore-Bugatti, 67120 Molsheim, tel. 03.88.38.25.38, fax 03.88.38.82.53 ev. day 9am–12 noon 2pm–7pm; Sun. by appt.

GERARD NEUMEYER

Gewurztraminer 1998

☐ 0.64 ha 4,400 70–99 F

The commune of Molsheim is located about 20 km (12 miles) to the south-west of Strasbourg. Its wine-producers have set up a charter of quality which enables people to obtain top-class wines. Golden-yellow and brilliantly clear, this one offers some as yet rather undeveloped aromas of exotic fruit (mango) and overripeness. After a clean attack on the palate, it is sustained by a fresh acidity; this balances the residual sugar which is still very much in evidence. (Residual sugar: 25 g/l.)

Dom. Gérard Neumeyer, 29, rue Ettore-Bugatti, 67120 Molsheim, tel. 03.88.38.12.45, fax 03.88.38.11.27, e-mail domaine.neumeyer@wanadoo.fr ev. day except Sun. 9am–12 noon 2pm–7pm

Alsace Grand Cru Eichberg

CHARLES BAUR

Gewurztraminer 1998★

☐ 0.29 ha n.c. 50–69 F

Oenologist Armand Baur has produced a Gewurztraminer from the Eichberg Grand Cru which has a crystalline yellow colour with brilliant glints, and great finesse in the nose. Powerful, very fruity and well-balanced, this 1998 wine shows excellent length. A good wine to drink with foie gras, cheese or even desserts, or indeed as an aperitif. (Residual sugar: 16 g/l.)

Charles Baur, 29, Grand-Rue, 68420 Eguisheim, tel. 03.89.41.32.49, fax 03.89.41.55.79 by appt.

Armand Baur

CHARLES BAUR

Gewurztraminer Vendanges tardives 1997★

☐ 0.29 ha 2,000 100–149 F

The late-harvest Gewurztraminer developed by the same firm is excellent. Its colour is a strong yellow; scents of quince and crystallised fruits break through in a nose which is not yet mature; in the mouth it is full and long, releasing interesting notes of orange peel. A wine which should gain in harmony with time.

Charles Baur, 29, Grand-Rue, 68420 Eguisheim, tel. 03.89.41.32.49, fax 03.89.41.55.79 by appt.

ALBERT HERTZ

Gewurztraminer Cuvée de l'An 2000 1998★

☐ 0.25 ha 2,000 50–69 F

Founded in 1843, this Eguisheim concern exports 40% of its produce. Its 'Year 2000' Gewurztraminer is golden yellow with brilliant glints, and draws attention with a nose which offers a well-balanced mixture of smoky and peppery notes. It is well-structured, and marked by the presence of a strong residual sugar content, which will need to fade. It will acquire greater maturity after a while. (Residual sugar: 13 g/l.)

Albert Hertz, 3, rue du Riesling, 68420 Eguisheim, tel. 03.89.41.30.32, fax 03.89.23.99.23 by appt.

ALBERT HERTZ

Tokay-pinot gris 1998★

☐ 0.37 ha 3,000 50–69 F

Albert Hertz has also produced a Pinot Gris which satisfies every requirement. Still young, this 1998 has the characteristic aromas of the grape variety: smokiness accompanied by notes of toast and over-ripeness. After a supple attack on the palate, it becomes both powerful and thoroughbred, with no excessive roundness. (Residual sugar: 12 g/l.)

Albert Hertz, 3, rue du Riesling, 68420 Eguisheim, tel. 03.89.41.30.32, fax 03.89.23.99.23 by appt.

PAUL SCHNEIDER Riesling 1998

☐ 0.27 ha 2,000 50–69 F

This family business is established in the old tithe court which used to belong to the Grand Provost of Strasbourg Cathedral. Coming from a mixture of chalky and marly soils, their 1998 Riesling is of lesser calibre than the previous vintage, which was awarded a *coup de coeur* in the same Grand Cru. It is still rather immature, and a certain warmth is perceptible in the finish. Even so there are discreet notes of white flowers and vanilla which conform well to type, and it has good balance, length and character, exuding an impression of richness. (Residual sugar: 6.5 g/l.)

🔑 Paul Schneider et Fils, 1, rue de l'Hôpital, 68420 Eguisheim, tel. 03.89.41.50.07, fax 03.89.41.30.57 ☑ Y ev. day 10am–12 noon 1.30pm–6.30pm; Sun. by appt.

WOLFBERGER Tokay-pinot gris 1998★

☐ n.c. n.c. 50–69 F

Known since the Middle Ages, this locality, whose delimited area is now 57 ha (140 acres), usually yields opulent wines. This one is no exception: dominated by overripening, it has intense notes of wax, honey and dried fruits. Its roundness and richness in the mouth give it a luscious quality which is reminiscent of a late-harvest wine. Will go well with foie gras or dessert. (Residual sugar: 20 g/l.)

🔑 Wolfberger, 6, Grand-Rue, 68420 Eguisheim, tel. 03.89.22.20.20, fax 03.89.23.47.09 ☑ Y by appt.

PAUL ZINCK Gewurztraminer 1998★

☐ 0.8 ha 4,500 50–69 F

With its ramparts and castle, Eguisheim is well worth a visit. There are many well-respected and prosperous wine producers here, such as this family business, which has also opened a restaurant. The Eichberg Grand Cru soils are a mixture of chalk and marl, which lends itself extremely well to Gewurztraminer. This one has a very brilliant, strong yellow colour, and a nose that mingles aromas of overripening and toast with some hints of butter. The palate is very full and rich, combining both sweetness and complexity. Good general balance. (Residual sugar: 10 g/l.)

🔑 Paul Zinck, 18, rue des Trois-Châteaux, 68420 Eguisheim, tel. 03.89.41.19.11, fax 03.89.24.12.85, e-mail phz@p-zinck.fr ☑ Y ev. day except Sun. 8am–12 noon 2pm–6pm; cl. Jan.

Alsace Grand Cru Engelberg

DOM. JEAN-PIERRE BECHTOLD

Gewurztraminer Vendanges tardives 1997★

☐ 0.3 ha 1,400 100–149 F

Located in Dahlenheim to the south-east of Strasbourg, this estate has more than 18 ha (44 acres) of vines, which makes it large by Alsatian standards. Coming from a marly chalk soil, its golden-yellow, late-harvest Gewurztraminer has a complex array of aromas, ranging from white flowers, toast and apricots to bergamot orange. The flavour in the mouth is of crystallised fruits with a touch of undergrowth. An excellently-balanced wine, well sustained by an acidity, which gives it freshness.

🔑 Dom. Jean-Pierre Bechtold, 49, rue Principale, 67310 Dahlenheim, tel. 03.88.50.66.57, fax 03.88.50.67.34 ☑ Y by appt.

🔑 Jean-Marie Bechtold

DOM. JEAN-PIERRE BECHTOLD

Gewurztraminer 1998★★

☐ 0.65 ha 4,200 50–69 F

With its southern aspect and very stony marly-chalk soil, the Engelberg Grand Cru, or 'Angels' Hill', is a particularly favourable site for producing well-ripened grapes. This Gewurztraminer shows itself worthy of such a poetic locality. A pronounced yellow in colour, it delights with a nose of great finesse which conjures up exotic fruits. Very rich on the palate, it has a harmonious structure thanks to good acid support. A great wine, to be enjoyed as an aperitif, or with foie gras or dessert. (Residual sugar: 40 g/l.)

🔑 Dom. Jean-Pierre Bechtold, 49, rue Principale, 67310 Dahlenheim, tel. 03.88.50.66.57, fax 03.88.50.67.34 ☑ Y by appt.

Alsace Grand Cru Frankstein

BECK-DOMAINE DU REMPART

Riesling 1998★

☐ 0.6 ha 3,000 50–69 F

Located on the heights of Dambach-la-Ville, the Frankstein consists of four zones, which face south-east. The soils are essentially granitic. Delicate, fruity and above all floral, this Riesling is well-balanced, fresh, pleasant and persistent. You can taste it at the cellar on this estate, and also at the Maison des Grands Crus d'Alsace, which was set up by Gilbert Beck in 1995. (Residual sugar: 5 g/l.)

🔑 Beck, Dom. du Rempart, 5, rue des Remparts, 67650 Dambach-la-Ville, tel. 03.88.92.62.03, fax 03.88.92.49.40 ☑ Y by appt.

🔑 Gilbert Beck

ANDRE HERRBACH Riesling 1997★

☐ 0.13 ha 1,066 30–49 F

The Frankstein's reputation dates back to the Middle Ages: several abbeys grew vines there as early as 1320. This vineyard on the other hand is very recent, having been founded in 1982. That does not prevent this Riesling from giving complete satisfaction, with a fine nose bordering on citrus fruits. Similar fruity flavours recur on the palate. A full wine which is already mature. (Residual sugar: 7.01 g/l.)

🔑 GAEC Herrbach, 3, rue du Bernstein, 67650 Dambach-la-Ville, tel. 03.88.92.45.56, fax 03.88.92.40.45 ☑ Y by appt.

P. KIRSCHNER ET FILS

Riesling 1998★★

□ 0.3 ha 2,100 50-69 F

This estate was founded at the beginning of the nineteenth century, and shortly afterwards started to sell its wines under its own label, as we can see from surviving examples of its oldest bottles. Light golden in the glass, this 1998 has a seductively fruity nose of great finesse. It has a clean, pleasant attack on the palate, with the same fruitiness as before on the palate, and also elegance and good length. A great Riesling which confirms this vineyard's *savoir-faire*. (Residual sugar: 10 g/l.)
Pierre Kirschner, 26, rue Théophile-Bader, 67650 Dambach-la-Ville, tel. 03.88.92.40.55, fax 03.88.92.62.54, e-mail kirschner@reperes.com ev. day except Sun. 8am–12 noon 1pm–7pm

MICHEL NARTZ Muscat 1998

□ 0.16 ha 1,200 50-69 F

Michel Nartz runs his business in a 17th-century house, which he has fitted out for visitors with a tasting cellar and guest rooms. Clearly the product of a granite soil, his Muscat Grand Cru is very intense in the nose, where in addition to the grape aroma there are scents of white flowers and mint. Its power and presence on the palate are reinforced by a slight touch of carbon dioxide which shows that it is still young. (Residual sugar: 10.5 g/l.)
Michel Nartz, 12, pl. du Marché, 67650 Dambach-la-Ville, tel. 03.88.92.41.11, fax 03.88.92.63.01 by appt.

Alsace Grand Cru Froehn

SCHEIDECKER Muscat 1998★

□ 0.15 ha 1,200 30-49 F

Zellenberg is a picturesque little village perched high on a rocky spur and overlooking the slopes of the Froehn *grand cru*. This Muscat is very thoroughbred in the nose, with fresh aromas of spices and ripe fruits which show that it comes from a marly chalk soil. Slightly round on the palate, it turns out to have very good length. A real treat with asparagus in a sauce mousseline! (Residual sugar: 13 g/l.)
Philippe Scheidecker, 13, rue des Merles, 68630 Mittelwihr, tel. 03.89.49.01.29, fax 03.89.49.06.63 ev. day 9am–12.30pm 2pm–8pm

Alsace Grand Cru Furstentum

DOM. PAUL BLANCK

Riesling Sélection de grains nobles 1995★★

□ 1.65 ha 900 300-499 F

The other Blancks in Kientzheim are also resolutely orientated towards international markets, since they sell 55% of their produce abroad. With this Riesling they have pulled off a little masterpiece. Its colour is a deep yellow verging on gold, and it shows its intensity right from the start with a distinctive nose which mingles honey with citrus and dried fruits. It has the same power on the palate, where it is combined with a beautiful suppleness. Here again there is honey (acacia), along with notes of apricot and a touch of crystallised lemon. Freshness and good length complete the picture of a wine to be treasured. (37.5 cl. bottles.)
Dom. Paul Blanck anc. Comtes de Lupfen, 32, Grand-Rue, 68240 Kientzheim, tel. 03.89.78.23.56, fax 03.89.47.16.45, e-mail info@claude-alsace.com ev. day except Sun. 9am–12 noon 1.30pm–6pm

ANDRE BLANCK ET SES FILS

Ancienne Cour des Chevaliers de Malte

Gewurztraminer VT 1997★

□ 0.6 ha 2,000 70-99 F

This business is established at Kientzheim, next to the Château de Schwendi which is now the headquarters of the Confrérie Saint-Etienne. It exports half of its produce. Straw-yellow with amber glints, its late-harvest Gewurztraminer has complex aromas in a nose which ends on a slight note of menthol, and is expressive in the mouth, where the dominant flavours are of quince and other crystallised fruits. (Half-litre bottles)
EARL André Blanck et Fils, Ancienne Cour des Chevaliers de Malte, 68240 Kientzheim, tel. 03.89.78.24.72, fax 03.89.47.17.07 ev. day except Sun. 8am–12 noon 2pm–7pm

DOM. BOTT-GEYL

Gewurztraminer 1998★★

□ 0.5 ha 3,000 100-149 F

Since 1993 Jean-Christophe Bott has been running the family estate, where he works a

large variety of Crus. He has reaped several *coups de coeur* over the last few years, and his new vintages are closely watched. Wine-lovers will find that this 1998 matches all their expectations. Golden yellow in colour, it offers aromas of citrus fruits qualified by mineral notes of great finesse. On the palate it is fleshy, fruity, elegant and superbly balanced. Why not try it with some Munster cheese? (Residual sugar: 27 g/l.)
Dom. Bott-Geyl, 1, rue du Petit-Château, 68980 Beblenheim, tel. 03.89.47.90.04, fax 03.89.47.97.33 by appt.
Jean-Christophe Bott

RENE FLEITH-ESCHARD

Tokay-pinot gris 1998★★★
☐ 0.33 ha 1,800 70–99 F

René Fleith and his son Vincent keep an estate of 9 ha (22 acres). They say that they use the most natural wine-making method they can, in order to make their wines as rich and distinctive as possible. With this 1998 Pinot Gris they have certainly achieved that aim! It creates a striking impression from the outset with a powerfully aromatic nose dominated by exotic fruits (mango and passionfruit). These reappear and linger in a palate that is round, luscious and well-strucured. 'A Tokay liqueur' which deserves to be tasted for its own sake but could also be served with foie gras or dessert. (Residual sugar: 45 g/l.)
René Fleith-Eschard, lieu-dit Lange Matten, 68040 Ingersheim, tel. 03.89.27.24.19, fax 03.89.27.56.79 by appt.

DOM. ALBERT MANN

Tokay-pinot gris 1998★★
☐ 0.38 ha 3,000 70–99 F

With its marly chalk soil mingled with Vosges sandstone, its south-south-east aspect and gradients as steep as 1 in 2.5, the Furstentum Grand Cru is an exceptional terrain. It has nothing but advantages, and the wine producers who work on it vie successfully with one another to make the most of them! This is another admirable Tokay, with a rich nose combining crystallised fruits and dried apricots with notes of smokiness and toast which are a mark of the grape variety. It has a fine presence on the palate, becoming rich, well-structured, round and long. A wine of character, to be enjoyed as an aperitif or with foie gras. (Residual sugar: 31 g/l.)
Dom. Albert Mann, 13, rue du Château, 68920 Wettolsheim, tel. 03.89.80.62.00, fax 03.89.80.34.23, e-mail vins@mann-albert.com by appt.
Barthelmé

ALBERT MANN

Gewurztraminer 1998★★
☐ 0.54 ha 3,500 70–99 F

Located near Kaysersberg at the entrance to the Weiss valley, the slopes of the Furstentum are characterised by a brown, chalky soil with an extremely thin, stony structure which drains well. Because of its rather sharp gradient it attracts a great deal of sunshine. Thanks to the efforts of the Barthelmés it has yielded a great Gewurztraminer. Pale yellow with golden glints, this 1998 has an appealingly clean nose which releases aromas of very ripe fruits mingled with hints of flowers. Fruity and spicy in the mouth, it combines richness, fullness and good length. (Residual sugar: 36 g/l.)
Dom. Albert Mann, 13, rue du Château, 68920 Wettolsheim, tel. 03.89.80.62.00, fax 03.89.80.34.23, e-mail vins@mann-albert.com by appt.

Alsace Grand Cru Geisberg

KIENTZLER

Riesling Vendanges tardives 1997★
☐ 0.5 ha 1,200 150–199 F

The Geisberg has been a highly regarded vineyard since the 14th century, thanks to its southern aspect and its stony, chalky-clay soil which produces wines for longer maturing. Brilliant golden yellow in colour, this 1997 has a discreet nose with some hints of butter. At the same time it shows a great deal of potential; complex and rich in the mouth, it has a slightly mineral flavour with a touch of crystallised pear, is already very agreeable to drink and, according to the jury, 'gives much pleasure'.
André Kientzler, 50, rte de Bergheim, 68150 Ribeauvillé, tel. 03.89.73.67.10, fax 03.89.73.35.81 by appt.

KIENTZLER Riesling 1998

☐ 1.3 ha 6,800 100–149 F

This Ribeauvillé concern has also received a mention for a Riesling with intense notes of fresh flowers which make tasting it hard to resist. It has an enjoyable balance in the mouth, and displays the characteristics of the grape variety, with the first hints of a mineral flavour. (Residual sugar: 4 g/l.)

🗝 André Kientzler, 50, rte de Bergheim, 68150 Ribeauvillé, tel. 03.89.73.67.10, fax 03.89.73.35.81 ☑ 🍷 by appt.

Alsace Grand Cru Gloeckelberg

KOEBERLE KREYER

Tokay-pinot gris 1998★

☐ 0.13 ha 900 50–69 F

Grapes have been grown since the Middle Ages on this locality of just 23 ha, which is characterised by sandy soils on a granite substratum. It has yielded a Pinot Gris whose nose is centred on ripe fruits, with a hint of honey. Rich, round and supple in the mouth, it is clearly still a young wine which will need to remain in the cellar for three or four years in order to achieve its full harmony. (Residual sugar: 10 g/l.)

🗝 Koeberlé Kreyer, 28, rue du Pinot-Noir, 68590 Rodern, tel. 03.89.73.00.55, fax 03.89.73.00.55 ☑ 🍷 by appt.

CHARLES NOLL

Tokay-pinot gris 1998

☐ 0.1 ha 980 50–69 F

Wine-growers since 1864, the Nolls keep an estate of 6 ha (15 acres). They have some vines in the Gloeckelberg, where they mainly grow Gewurztraminer and Pinot Gris. Coming from the latter variety, this wine has fine aromas of fruit and acacia honey, and is characterised by elegance and lightness. A very good wine, which should acquire more character with age. (Residual sugar: 18.5 g/l.)

🗝 EARL Charles Noll, 2, rue de l'Ecole, 68630 Mittelwihr, tel. 03.89.47.93.21, fax 03.89.47.86.23 ☑ 🍷 ev. day 9am–9pm

Alsace Grand Cru Goldert

LUCIEN GANTZER Riesling 1998★

☐ 0.26 ha 2,000 30–49 F

Lucien Gantzer left the co-operative to found his own cellar in 1970. The business, which was taken over by his daughter Jeannine in 1995, has produced an excellent Goldert Riesling, as it did last year. The 1998 has a rich, intense, fruity nose, in which citrus fruits are especially in evidence. A clean attack on the palate is followed by a noticeable richness and a powerful finish with very good length. The qualities of the terrain will come through better in the course of the months to come. (Residual sugar: 8 g/l.)

🗝 SCEA Lucien Gantzer, 9, rue du Nord, 68420 Gueberschwihr, tel. 03.89.49.31.81, fax 03.89.49.23.34 ☑ 🍷 by appt.

CLAUDE ET GEORGES HUMBRECHT Gewurztraminer 1998

☐ 0.25 ha 1,800 50–69 F

The Goldert is located on mountainous terrain, the highest part of which slopes very steeply. With its east-south-east aspect, the vineyard catches the sun's rays for most of the day, and its chalky soils are highly advantageous for growing well-ripened grapes. This Gewurztraminer has straw-yellow glints which give it a beautiful appearance. Aromas of lychee break through in a nose which is still immature. The palate is already developed and rich, revealing good early content, but needs a little time to achieve complete balance.

🗝 EARL Claude et Georges Humbrecht, 31, rue de Pfaffenheim, 68420 Gueberschwihr, tel. 03.89.49.31.51 ☑ 🍷 by appt.

MAURICE SCHUELLER

Gewurztraminer 1998★

☐ 0.3 ha n.c. 70–99 F

Gueberschwir holds a Wine Festival every August, and also has one of the best Grands Crus for growing Gewurztraminer grapes. The Goldert's soils are a mixture of chalk, tertiary conglomerates and quaternary deposits, and these give its wines a beautiful complexity. This one sparkles with golden glints in the glass. The nose is as yet immature, but nevertheless shows interesting potential. The palate already has almost perfect balance: all this wine needs is a little more time to gain in expression. (Residual sugar: 18 g/l.)

🗝 EARL Maurice Schueller, 17, rue Basse, 68420 Gueberschwihr, tel. 03.89.49.31.80, fax 03.89.49.26.60 ☑ 🍷 by appt.

🗝 Marc Schueller

Alsace Grand Cru Hatschbourg

DOM. JOSEPH CATTIN

Gewurztraminer 1998★

☐ 1.67 ha 11,000 50–69 F

Founded in 1850, this vineyard has more than 30 ha (74 acres), which makes it quite large by the region's standards. It has just installed a winery in order to produce wine according to soil type and plot of land. Coming from a Grand Cru with a gravelly, marly chalk soil, this yellow Gewurztraminer with gold glints has a striking intensity in the nose, which is marked both by the soil type and by

overripening. In the mouth it is fruity and concentrated, but dominated for the moment by a sweetness which masks the finesse of the flavours. This 1998 will reach its peak in a year or two. (Residual sugar: 30 g/l.)
🔑 Joseph Cattin, 18, rue Roger-Frémeaux, 68420 Voegtlinshoffen, tel. 03.89.49.30.21, fax 03.89.49.26.02 ☒ Y ev. day 8am–12 noon 2pm–6pm; Sun. by appt.
🔑 Jacques et Jean-Marie Cattin

ANDRE HARTMANN

Tokay-pinot gris Armoirie Hartmann 1998★

☐ 0.3 ha n.c. 50–69 F

The Hartmann family has been working its vineyard since the 17th century. It has the good fortune to own vines in the Hatschbourg, a locality which was famous long before it was consecrated as a Grand Cru. It has now produced this 1998 Tokay, which has a fine, fruity nose with a note of mandarin orange, which reappears on the palate. Lightish, well-balanced and persistent, it will be a welcome accompaniment to any meal. (Residual sugar: 20 g/l.)
🔑 André Hartmann, 11, rue Roger-Frémeaux, 68420 Voegtlinshoffen, tel. 03.89.49.38.34, fax 03.89.49.26.18 ☒ Y ev. day except Sun. 9am–12 noon 1.30pm–6pm

GERARD ET SERGE HARTMANN

Tokay-pinot gris Vendanges tardives 1996★

☐ 0.2 ha 1,500 100–149 F

This is another Hartmann family, this time in the village of Voegtlinshoffen, where they too have been established since the 17th century. They offer a gold-yellow Pinot Gris with a nose bordering on crystallised fruits, with hints of undergrowth. Fairly floral in the mouth, it has medium length sustained by good acidity. A late-harvest wine which is ready to drink now.
🔑 Gérard et Serge Hartmann, 13, rue Roger-Frémeaux, 68420 Voegtlinshoffen, tel. 03.89.49.30.27, fax 03.89.49.29.78 ☒ Y by appt.

LES VIGNERONS DE PFAFFENHEIM ET GUEBERSCHWIHR Riesling 1998★★

☐ 0.62 ha 5,000 70–99 F

This 1998 Riesling originates from the village of Hattstat, which is overlooked by the Hatschbourg Grand Cru, famous since the 16th century for its grapes grown on gravelly, marly chalk soils. Its beautiful green-gold colour heralds a complex array of aromas, ranging from flowers, peaches and citrus fruits to citronella. After a clean, refreshing attack on the palate, it achieves its balance with richness, a full structure, power and good length. A promising wine, which will go well with fish and white meats. (Residual sugar: 8.2 g/l.)
🔑 Cave vinicole de Pfaffenheim, 5, rue du Chai, B.P. 33, 68250 Pfaffenheim, tel. 03.89.78.08.08, fax 03.89.49.71.65, e-mail cave@pfaffenheim ☒ Y ev. day 8am–12 noon 2pm–6pm

Alsace Grand Cru Hengst

BUECHER-FIX

Tokay-pinot gris 1998★★★

☐ 0.42 ha 5,400 50–69 F

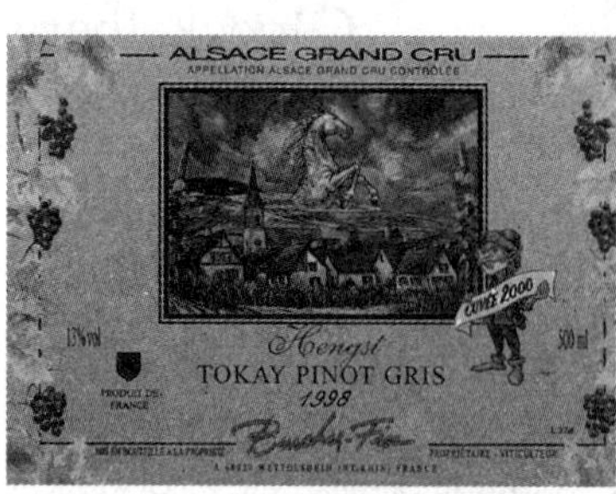

The label, painted in the naive style, shows a stallion (Hengst) looking down over the village of Wettolsheim. These wine-makers have 'tamed' him in their cellar, where traditional practices are used with discernment to guarantee the excellence of the wines. This one is a subtle shade of pale yellow, and releases a delightful aroma which is fine and typical of the grape variety. With a rich, fleshy balance and no excessive roundness, it lingers on in an enchantingly silky finish. 'I'd love to have some in my cellar!' concluded one taster. (Residual sugar: 20 g/l.) (Half-litre bottles)
🔑 Buecher-Fix, 21, rue Sainte-Gertrude, 68920 Wettolsheim, tel. 03.89.80.64.93, fax 03.89.79.61.56 ☒ Y by appt.

BUECHER-FIX Gewurztraminer 1998★

☐ 0.71 ha 6,000 70–99 F

Located to the west of Colmar, in the Wintzenheim and Wettolsheim area, the Hengst Grand Cru has the reputation of yielding wines whose full richness takes some time to become apparent. In the case of this Gewurztraminer, however, wine-lovers will be delighted to hear that there is no need to wait. Gold-yellow in colour, it has an intense nose of roses which reflects the grape variety perfectly. On the palate it is harmoniously balanced between sugar and acidity, and shows good length. Despite its concentration it is easy to enjoy, even as an aperitif. (Residual sugar: 15 g/l.)
🔑 Buecher-Fix, 21, rue Sainte-Gertrude, 68920 Wettolsheim, tel. 03.89.80.64.93, fax 03.89.79.61.56 ☒ Y by appt.

J.-V. HEBINGER ET FILS

Tokay-pinot gris 1998

☐ 0.25 ha 2,000 30–49 F

The wines that come from this marly chalk Grand Cru have a slightly wild character, with a fieriness reminiscent of the animal which is the mascot of the locality. That cannot really be said of this wine, which is easy to drink and ready to be served with food. It is a Tokay which is lacking in complexity but has no faults either, offering the characteristic aromas of the grape variety. Fairly dry, it has a fine attack and good balance. A classic. (Residual sugar: 14 g/l.)

🔑 Jean-Victor Hebinger et Fils, 14, Grand-Rue, 68420 Eguisheim, tel. 03.89.41.19.90, fax 03.89.41.15.61 ☑ 🍷 ev. day except Sun. 8am–12 noon 2pm–6pm

BERNARD STAEHLE

Gewurztraminer 1998

☐ 0.25 ha n.c. 50–69 F

The south-south-east facing Hengst Grand Cru rises in terraces at an altitude of between 170 and 360 m (557–1,180 ft). Its steep gradient gives maximum exposure to the sun's rays. Straw-yellow in appearance, this wine releases aromas of very ripe fruit with slight mineral notes. Full, rich and balanced in the mouth, it is already showing a fine degree of depth, but will gain from being kept. (Residual sugar: 24 g/l.)

🔑 Bernard Staehlé, 15, rue Clemenceau, 68920 Wintzenheim, tel. 03.89.27.39.02, fax 03.89.27.59.37 ☑ 🍷 ev. day except Sun. 9am–12 noon 1.30pm–7.30pm

Alsace Grand Cru Kastelberg

ANDRE ET REMY GRESSER

Riesling Vieilles vignes 1998★★

☐ 0.84 ha 1,500 100–149 F

The reputation of this 5.82 ha (15-acre) vineyard goes back a very long way. It is characterised by shaly, Silurian soils which are very well suited to Riesling. This wine is like a basket of flowers and fruit, rich in overripe, exotic smells. This beautiful fruitiness continues in a palate which is full of roundness and richness, lingering on into a delightful finish. (Residual sugar: 15.6 g/l.)

🔑 Dom. André et Rémy Gresser, 2, rue de l'Ecole, 67140 Andlau, tel. 03.88.08.95.88, fax 03.88.08.55.99, e-mail remy.gresser@wanadoo.fr ☑ 🍷 by appt.

GUY WACH

Riesling Vendanges tardives 1997★★

☐ 0.22 ha 650 100–149 F

The Kastelberg is the only vineyard in Alsace located on shale, which produces very stony, perfectly drained soils. The wines that come from it are highly unusual. This one has an intense yellow colour in the glass, and draws attention to itself straight away by the finesse of its nose of passionfruit and citrus fruits. The palate follows on perfectly with a complex range of aromas and beautiful harmony. 'A wine which is difficult to describe . . . As you taste it, it's as if you were going on a journey . . . and what a wonderful journey!', wrote one member of the jury who had fallen under its spell.

🔑 Guy Wach, Dom. des Marronniers, 67140 Andlau, tel. 03.88.08.93.20, fax 03.88.08.45.59 ☑ 🍷 by appt.

GUY WACH

Riesling Cuvée Vieilles vignes 1998★★

☐ 0.6 ha 3,800 70–99 F

Guy Wach has certainly got the best out of this Grand Cru. Grapes harvested on 9 November from 45-year-old vines have yielded this remarkable Riesling, whose aromatic range varies from white flowers and honey to citrus fruits, with a slight mineral note. Overripening asserts itself on the palate, with a rich, full structure and a beautiful fruitiness. At the finish the flavours return to the floral and mineral hints of the nose. (Residual sugar: 22 g/l.)

🔑 Guy Wach, Dom. des Marronniers, 67140 Andlau, tel. 03.88.08.93.20, fax 03.88.08.45.59 ☑ 🍷 by appt.

Alsace Grand Cru Kirchberg de Barr

DOM. HERING

Gewurztraminer Clos Gaensbroennel Cuvée des Frimas 1998

☐ 0.5 ha 3,000 70–99 F

Founded in 1652, this estate in Barr consistently aims for quality. Great-grandfather Hering used hybridisation to create a grafting stock especially suited to the vineyard. This Cuvée des Frimas ('Wintry Weather') may owe its name to the late date of the grape harvest (10 November 1998). Although the nose has powerful aromas of great finesse, the residual sugar is still too much in evidence on the palate. Seems sure to do well in the future. (Residual sugar: 20 g/l.)

🔑 Pierre et Jean-Daniel Hering, 6, rue Sultzer, 67140 Barr, tel. 03.88.08.90.07, fax 03.88.08.08.54, e-mail jdh@infonie.fr ☑ 🍷 ev. day except Sun. 8.30am–12 noon 1.30pm–6.30pm

ANDRE KLEINKNECHT

Riesling 1998

☐ 0.3 ha 1,500 30–49 F

Wine-growers since 1621, the Kleinknechts keep 8 ha (20 acres) of vines. The marly chalk Kirchberg Grand Cru yields wines which are slow to mature: this Riesling, for instance, which the tasters do in fact recommend should be kept. In the nose it mingles keen notes of citrus fruits with a touch of honey. After a fine attack on the palate it is quite

well-balanced, showing good length and a slight hint of bitterness at the finish. (Residual sugar: 6 g/l.)
André Kleinknecht, 45, rue Principale, 67140 Mittelbergheim, tel. 03.88.08.49.46, fax 03.88.08.49.46 ☑ Y ev. day 10am–11.30am 1pm–7pm

KLIPFEL

Clos Zisser Gewurztraminer Vendanges tardives 1997*

☐ 3 ha 4,000 100–149 F

This wine-merchant, who owns 40 ha (98 acres) of vines on his own account, has played a pioneering role in the promotion of Alsatian wines. Straw-yellow and beautifully clear, this 1997 gives off aromas of vanilla, crystallised fruits and candy sugar. There is a fleshy, rich attack on the palate, which combines freshness and concentration. A wine which is still evolving.
Klipfel, 6, av. de la Gare, 67140 Barr, tel. 03.88.58.59.00, fax 03.88.08.53.18 ☑ Y by appt.
A. Lorentz

LUCAS ET ANDRE RIEFFEL

Tokay-Pinot Gris 1998*

☐ 0.48 ha 2,900 50–69 F

This Pinot Gris still has the typical aromas of the grape variety: hints of smokiness and toast, with some mineral notes. It hits the palate cleanly, then becomes powerful, rich and elegant. Its excellent length inspired one taster to describe it as follows: 'Just the sort of Tokay I love!'. (Residual sugar: 26.3 g/l.)
André et Lucas Rieffel, 11, rue Principale, 67140 Mittelbergheim, tel. 03.88.08.95.48, fax 03.88.08.28.94 ☑ Y ev. day except Sun. 8am–12 noon 1pm–6pm

WILLM Tokay-pinot gris 1998*

☐ n.c. 2,000 70–99 F

On a marly chalk soil with chalky stones, the south-east-facing Kirchberg overlooks the town of Barr. It has yielded a 1998 with fruity aromas accompanied by hints of menthol. This wine has an impressively luscious, rich body, and above all conveys a sense of overripening. (Residual sugar: 25 g/l.)
Alsace Willm SA, 32, rue du Dr-Sultzer, 67140 Barr, tel. 03.88.08.19.11, fax 03.88.08.56.21 ☑ Y by appt.

Alsace Grand Cru Mambourg

DOM. JEAN-MARC BERNHARD

Gewurztraminer Vendanges tardives 1997*

☐ 0.28 ha 1,500 100–149 F

The Bernhard family has been in the wine-growing business since 1802. The new generation is represented by Frédéric, a wine-specialist who has just joined the vineyard after several periods of training which have taken his as far as South Africa. With its golden-yellow colour, this late-harvest Gewurztraminer promises great things from the start. The first impression is confirmed by a complex nose of blond tobacco and flowers. These reappear on the palate, which has already acquired good length and a beautiful balance.
Domaine Jean-Marc Bernhard, 21, Grand-Rue, 68230 Katzenthal, tel. 03.89.27.05.34, fax 03.89.27.58.72 ☑ Y ev. day except Sun. 9am–12 noon 1.30pm–7pm

DOM. PIERRE SCHILLE

Gewurztraminer 1998

☐ 0.35 ha 3,000 70–99 F

The Mambourg is characterised by soils consisting of marly chalk conglomerates. Its southern aspect gives this vineyard maximum exposure to the sun's rays. This Grand Cru has yielded a Gewurztraminer with an intense yellow colour and aromas of roses. In the mouth the wine seems very rich, but is dominated by residual sugar. It is best kept until it achieves better balance. (Residual sugar: 52 g/l.)
Pierre Schillé et Fils, 14, rue du Stade, 68240 Sigolsheim, tel. 03.89.47.10.67, fax 03.89.47.39.12 ☑ Y by appt.

MARC TEMPE

Riesling Vendanges tardives 1997

☐ 0.21 ha 1,200 200–249 F

Coming from a family of wine producers in Sigolsheim, Marc Tempé moved to Zellenberg in 1995 after several years with the INAO. From the south-facing locality of Mambourg he has produced a straw-yellow wine with a discreet nose of citrus fruits. Quite well balanced in the mouth, it is still dominated by residual sugar. Its power and good structure augur well for its future development. Best kept for a while.
Marc Tempé, 16, rue du Schlossberg, 68340 Zellenberg, tel. 03.89.47.85.22, fax 03.89.47.85.22 ☑ Y by appt.

Alsace Grand Cru Mandelberg

DOM. DU BOUXHOF

Gewurztraminer 1998*

☐ 0.2 ha 1,500 50–69 F

Founded some 800 years ago, the Mandelberg, or 'Almond-tree Mountain', is an elite vineyard, which is famous for its early-maturing grapes. Rising in terraces on the southern side of the hill, the vines grow on marly chalk soils which are good for producing distinctively aromatic wines. Pale yellow and very young to look at, this one already has an expressive nose, in which notes of candied fruits are combined with an aroma of honey. It has the same intensity in the mouth, where it is fruity, balanced and fresh. The sort of Gewurztraminer everyone likes. (Residual sugar: 43.3 g/l.)

🗝 EARL François Edel et Fils, Dom. du Bouxhof, 68630 Mittelwihr, tel. 03.89.47.90.34, fax 03.89.47.84.82 ☑ Y ev. day 9am–7pm

DOM. BURGHART-SPETTEL

Riesling 1998

☐ 0.4 ha 3,000 50–69 F

This Grand Cru takes its name from the almond trees which blossom here as early as February. With a discreet but clearly-defined nose, this Riesling has fairly good balance and a certain finesse. It is also rich and shows good length. (Residual sugar: 5 g/l.)

🗝 Dom. Burghart-Spettel, 9, rte du Vin, 68630 Mittelwihr, tel. 03.89.47.93.19, fax 03.89.49.07.62 ☑ Y by appt.

Alsace Grand Cru Marckrain

BESTHEIM

Gewurztraminer 1998★

☐ 9.37 ha n.c. 50–69 F

The winemakers of Bennwihr have joined with those of Westhalten to form one large unit known as Bestheim. They work the best soils of their respective communes. The east-south-east-facing Marckrain is characterised by marly chalk soils and yields beautifully distinctive Gewurztraminers. This one has golden glints and a very fine nose in which pineapple is particularly evident. Powerful, fruity and long in the mouth, it retains its balance despite a certain unctuous quality which dominates. Given a little time it should gain in harmony. (Residual sugar: 18 g/l.)

🗝 Cave de Bestheim-Bennwihr, 3, rue du Gal-de-Gaulle, 68630 Bennwihr, tel. 03.89.49.09.29, fax 03.89.49.09.20 ☑ Y ev. day 9am–12 noon 2pm–6pm

Alsace Grand Cru Muenchberg

RENE KOCH ET FILS Riesling 1998★

☐ 0.57 ha 4,000 30–49 F

These stony, sandy, sandstone soils were cultivated by the Cistercians as early as the 12th century: hence the name 'Muenchberg' or 'Monks' Mountain'. This a good terrain for Rieslings. This one releases intense aromas of white flowers, with some mineral and lemony notes. On the palate the fruity flavours develop agreeably, and there is a beautiful lingering freshness at the finish. This is a wine which will go well with grilled fish, and will improve as it develops over the next four or five years. (Residual sugar: 8 g/l.)

🗝 GAEC René et Michel Koch, 5, rue de la Fontaine, 67680 Nothalten, tel. 03.88.92.41.03, fax 03.88.92.63.99 ☑ Y by appt.

Alsace Grand Cru Ollwiller

VIEIL ARMAND

Tokay-pinot gris 1998★

☐ n.c. 5,000 70–99 F

Located to the south of Guebwiller, Wuenheim is overlooked by the Château d'Ollwiller, which has given its name to this Grand Cru in the southernmost part of the Alsatian vineyards. The castle itself was almost completely destroyed during the First World War, but the vineyard has carried on. Although it is generally regarded as being particularly suited to Riesling and Gewurztraminer, it has done very well with this Pinot Gris, whose nose is clean and fruity with a mineral note. The palate has medium length and shows a fine balance, which relies more on elegance than on body. (Residual sugar: 15 g/l.)

🗝 Cave vinicole du Vieil-Armand, 3, rte de Cernay, 68360 Soultz-Wuenheim, tel. 03.89.76.73.75, fax 03.89.76.70.75 ☑ Y by appt.

Alsace Grand Cru Pfersigberg

PAUL GINGLINGER Riesling 1998★★

☐ 0.48 ha 3,500 50–69 F

This family was already devoted to wine-making in 1636... and in the same cellar! The generation in charge today cultivates 12 ha (30 acres) of vines, and sells 40% of its wines abroad. This year its Pfersigberg Riesling returns to the fore with a remarkable 1998 vintage. The nose evokes ripe fruits, with a note of muscat and a strong mineral emphasis. There is a fairly supple attack on the palate, which is balanced and has great fullness and richness, especially at the finish. (Residual sugar: 5 g/l.)

Paul Ginglinger, 8, pl. Charles-de-Gaulle, 68420 Eguisheim,
tel. 03.89.41.44.25, fax 03.89.24.94.88 Y by appt.

ROGER HEYBERGER Riesling 1998★

☐ 0.15 ha 850 50–69 F

The Pfersigberg is a marly chalk vineyard located on the heights of Eguisheim. Its name was mentioned as early as the 16th century, and it was brought back to the fore in 1927, when the first Colmar Wine Fair took place. It has yielded a Riesling with an aromatic nose which is a harmonious combination of flowery notes and a slight mineral touch. The balance is rich but not without freshness. A wine which needs to be kept patiently until it more fully reflects the qualities of the terrain. (Residual sugar: 3.7 g/l.)

Roger Heyberger et Fils, 5, rue Principale, 68420 Obermorschwihr,
tel. 03.89.49.30.01, fax 03.89.49.22.28 Y ev. day except Sun. 8am–11.45am 2pm–6.30pm

ROGER HEYBERGER

Tokay-pinot gris 1998

☐ 0.25 ha 1,400 50–69 F

The name Pfersigberg (Alsatian for 'Peach-tree Mountain') suggests a certain climatic mildness. The mountain is said to owe its name to the peach trees which used to grow on its slopes. Its marly chalk soils promote the richness and elegance of the wines that come from it. This one is intensely fruity with notes of toast, and has very good balance. It has average structure and good length, and finishes on a slightly bitter note. (Residual sugar: 10.5 g/l.)

Roger Heyberger et Fils, 5, rue Principale, 68420 Obermorschwihr,
tel. 03.89.49.30.01, fax 03.89.49.22.28 Y ev. day except Sun. 8am–11.45 2pm–6.30pm

JEAN-LOUIS ET FABIENNE MANN

Riesling 1998★★★

☐ 0.38 ha 2,300 50–69 F

This golden yellow Riesling has an attractive nose, with fruity aromas which are subtle, distinctive and true to type. After a clean attack on the palate, citrus fruit flavours return, developing from lemon to grapefruit. With its balance and finesse this is a most elegant wine, which lingers for a long time in the mouth. (Residual sugar: 12 g/l.)

EARL Jean-Louis Mann, 6 A, rue de Colmar, 68420 Eguisheim,
tel. 03.89.24.26.47, fax 03.89.24.09.41 Y by appt.

FERNAND STENTZ Riesling 1998

☐ 0.28 ha 2,400 50–69 F

This wine has a discreet nose, with a few hints of citrus fruits breaking through. In the mouth, the fruity flavours are dominated by a note of grapefruit. Its freshness gives it length and is pleasantly noticeable at the finish. A Riesling that has not yet taken on the characteristics of the terrain: best kept for a while. (Residual sugar: 4 g/l.)

Fernand Stentz, 40, rte du Vin, 68420 Husseren-les-Châteaux, tel. 03.89.49.30.04, fax 03.89.49.32.88 Y by appt.

Alsace Grand Cru Pfingstberg

FRANCOIS SCHMITT Riesling 1998

☐ 0.23 ha 2,000 30–49 F

This 1998 comes from the upper part of the Pfingstberg Grand Cru, where the sandstone soils produce Rieslings with floral aromas. This one makes no attempt to conceal its origins, with its distinctive nose of white flowers. A clean attack on the palate leads on to a freshness in the mouth, which is quite lively and pleasant. Very good length. (Residual sugar: 7 g/l.)

Cave François Schmitt, 19, rte de Soultzmatt, 68500 Orschwihr,
tel. 03.89.76.08.45, fax 03.89.76.44.02 Y by appt.

Alsace Grand Cru Praelatenberg

DOM. ENGEL Riesling 1998

□ 1.5 ha 10,000 50-69 F

The brothers Christian and Hubert Engel represent the third generation of their family on this estate of 18 ha (44 acres), three-quarters of which is located in the Praelatenberg. Yellow with green glints, their Grand Cru Riesling has a nose of fine intensity which combines fruits, a note of candying and a mineral impression. The fruitiness returns on the palate, within a balanced, smooth structure, slightly dominated by residual sugar, which will need to fade. Best kept for two or three years. (Residual sugar: 14.7 g/l.)

Dom. Christian et Hubert Engel, 1, rue des Vignes, 67600 Orschwiller, tel. 03.88.92.01.83, fax 03.88.82.25.09 ev. day 9am–11.30am 2pm–6pm

CAVE D'ORSCHWILLER-KINTZHEIM Riesling 1998★

□ 0.7 ha 5,000 30-49 F

The Praelatenberg (18.70 ha/45 acres) is located on gneiss. The flinty soils are heavy and shallow. This locality has been recognised and coveted for more than a millennium! It has yielded a Riesling which is complex, powerful and also fine in the nose. Balanced between freshness and roundness, in the mouth it is pleasant and has a very elegant finish. Even so this wine will gain from spending two or three years in the cellar. (Residual sugar: 4 g/l.)

Cave vinicole d'Orschwiller-Kintzheim, rte du Vin, BP 2, 67600 Orschwiller, tel. 03.88.92.09.87, fax 03.88.82.30.92 ev. day 10am–12 noon 2pm–5pm

SIFFERT Gewurztraminer 1998★

□ 0.52 ha 4,010 70-99 F

Founded over 200 years ago at the foot of the Haut-Koenigsbourg, this estate has made a good name for itself within the profession by its rigorous policy of maintaining high quality. Part of its produce comes from the Praelatenberg, a vineyard whose flinty soils are well-suited to Gewurztraminer. The first impression of this one is a yellow colour with brilliant golden lights and a nose of intense rose fragrances. These fine aromas linger for a long time on the palate, whose chief assets are its freshness, balance, maturity and good length. A promising overall impression. (Residual sugar: 26 g/l.)

SCEA Dom. Siffert, 16, rte du Vin, 67600 Orschwiller, tel. 03.88.92.02.77, fax 03.88.82.70.02, e-mail siffert@rmcnet.fr ev. day 9am–12 noon 1.30pm–7pm; Sun. by appt.; cl. 15 Jan.–15 Feb.

Alsace Grand Cru Rangen de Thann

CLOS SAINT-THEOBALD

Tokay-pinot gris Sélection de grains nobles 1996★★

□ 0.5 ha 1000 150-299 F

Truly quintessential, this Sélection de Grains Nobles represents a pinnacle of achievement. It is a Pinot Gris, which is golden yellow in the glass, has a powerful nose of candying and overripeness, and in the mouth is balanced, full, rich, and sustained by good acidity. The finish is characterised by flavours of crystallised fruits and honey. A wine to be treasured that and one which will become even better with time. (Half-litre bottles.)

Dom. Schoffit, 66 Nonnenholz-Weg (par la rue des Aubépines), 68000 Colmar, tel. 03.89.24.41.14, fax 03.89.41.40.52 by appt.

CLOS SAINT-THEOBALD

Tokay-pinot gris Vendanges tardives 1996★★★

□ 1.5 ha 5,000 200-249 F

The Schoffit estate is one of the few which keep vines in the Rangen, a Grand Cru made up of shaly rocks. From grapes grown there it produces wines which stand out from the crowd in the Guide, such as this late-harvest Tokay, which has a straw-yellow colour and a delightful nose of crystallised fruits, mandarin zest and orange peel. With a structure that is both substantial and pleasant, the balance is perfect. An exceptional wine.

Dom. Schoffit , 66 Nonnenholz-Weg (par la rue des Aubépines), 68000 Colmar, tel. 03.89.24.41.14, fax 03.89.41.40.52 by appt..

Alsace Grand Cru Rosacker

DAVID ERMEL Riesling 1998★

□ 0.3 ha 3,600 30-49 F

This very distinctive Riesling is based on the white flowers range, with some hints of overripening. It is beginning to develop that slight mineral aroma which is characteristic of marly chalk soils. The attack on the palate has a pleasant, lemony freshness. This lingers on the palate in a manner that is balanced, rich and full. (Residual sugar: 7 g/l.)

Jean-David Ermel, 30, rte de Ribeauvillé, 68150 Hunawihr, tel. 03.89.73.61.71, fax 03.89.73.32.56, e-mail ermeldavid.com ev. day 8am–12 noon 1.30pm–7pm; groups by appt.

CAVE VINICOLE DE HUNAWIHR

Riesling 1998

☐ 4 ha 28,000 30–49 F

Founded in 1954, the Hunawihr cellar produces wines from grapes grown on 200 ha (495 acres) of vines. This year we look again at its Riesling from the Rosacker, a 26-ha (65 acres) chalky clay vineyard, half of which is planted with this grape variety, and whose reputation goes back a 1,000 years. The 1998 vintage makes an impact with a powerful nose of citrus fruits. The same aromas dominate on the palate right from the attack, which is clean and fresh. More mineral savours should appear with time. (Residual sugar: 5 g/l.)

Cave vinicole de Hunawihr, 48, rte de Ribeauvillé, 68150 Hunawihr, tel. 03.89.73.61.67, fax 03.89.73.33.95 ev. day 8am–12 noon 2pm–6pm

MADER Riesling 1998

☐ 0.5 ha 3,500 50–69 F

Fine and typical in the nose, this 1998 still needs to mature. The attack is a little sweet, but afterwards it has a pleasant freshness. Its fruit aromas become a little assertive on the palate. An attractive wine, which will gain from being kept until it more fully conveys the qualities of the terrain. (Residual sugar: 11; g/l.)

EARL Jean-Luc Mader, 13, Grand-Rue, 68150 Hunawihr, tel. 03.89.73.80.32, fax 03.89.73.31.22 by appt.

FREDERIC MALLO ET FILS

Riesling Vieilles vignes 1998*

☐ 0.35 ha 1,800 50–69 F

Coming from 45-year-old vines, this Riesling has an attractively powerful nose. The aromas are mainly fruity, with a slight touch of overripening. The intensity and richness of this wine become fully apparent in the mouth, where the flavours include notes of maturity (honey), grape variety (citrus fruits) and soil (smokiness and toast). The tasting ends with a long, rich, full finish. (Residual sugar: 7 g/l.)

EARL Frédéric Mallo et Fils, 2, rue Saint-Jacques, 68150 Hunawihr, tel. 03.89.73.61.41, fax 03.89.73.68.46 by appt.

Dominique Mallo

FRANCOIS SCHWACH ET FILS

Riesling 1998*

☐ 0.2 ha 1,600 50–69 F

This 20-ha (49 acre) vineyard has developed a great deal over the last 15 years. Its key principles are the selection of soils and the search for quality. Still a little immature, its Rosacker Riesling releases restrained hints of a fruitiness which comes through more distinctly on the palate. Its dry character, fullness and richness give it excellent balance. With its power, aromatic diversity and slight touch of freshness, it is a pleasant wine. (Residual sugar: 7 g/l.)

Dom. François Schwach et Fils, 28, rte de Ribeauvillé, 68150 Hunawihr, tel. 03.89.73.62.15, fax 03.89.73.37.84, e-mail schwach@rmcnet.fr by appt.

Alsace Grand Cru Saering

DIRLER Riesling 1998

☐ 0.14 ha 1,230 70–99 F

The sandy marl soil of the Saering is especially well-suited to Rieslings. This one conforms well to type, with a very fine floral bouquet and some added notes of citrus fruits and toast. Overripening gives it roundness and power in the mouth, where along with the fruity flavour there is a delicate freshness. It will need to be kept until it gains more harmony. (Residual sugar: 11 g/l.)

EARL Dirler, 13, rue d'Issenheim, 68500 Bergholtz, tel. 03.89.76.91.00, fax 03.89.76.85.97, e-mail jpdirler@terre-net.fr by appt.

Alsace Grand Cru Schlossberg

ANDRE BLANCK

Riesling Vendanges tardives Cuvée Pierre Louis 1997**

☐ 2 ha 1,200 70–99 F

André Blanck runs his business in the old Court of the Knights of Malta in Kientzheim, next to the castle where the Confrérie Saint-Etienne has its headquarters and which used to belong to the Baron de Schwendi who was responsible for the spread of Pinot Gris in Alsace. Blanck won enthusiastic support from the jury for a 1997 Riesling from the same *grand cru*. This late-harvest wine is of the same lineage. It is a bright, strong, golden yellow in colour, and has a fresh nose which releases aromas of flowers and lemon. In the mouth these develop agreeably into notes of passion-fruit. There is a fine attack on the palate, followed by almost perfect harmony. A distinguished wine, which one taster suggests should be served with fish en croûte. (Half-litre bottles.)

🔑 EARL André Blanck et Fils, Ancienne Cour des Chevaliers de Malte, 68240 Kientzheim, tel. 03.89.78.24.72, fax 03.89.47.17.07 ☑ 🍷 ev. day except Sun. 8am–12 noon 2pm–7pm

SALZMANN Tokay-pinot gris 1998★

☐ 0.17 ha 1,500 70–99 F

Of monastic origin – it belonged to the abbey at Pairis – this vineyard has been in the Salzmann-Thomann family since the French Revolution. The cellar is an old tithe court. Thus Grand Cru Tokay has distinctive notes of dried fruit and aromas of overripening. After an impressively luscious attack on the palate, it achieves its full impact on some notes of quince. (Residual sugar: 30 g/l.)

🔑 Salzmann-Thomann, Dom. de l'Oberhof, 3, rue de l'Oberhof, 68240 Kaysersberg, tel. 03.89.47.10.26, fax 03.89.78.13.08 ☑ 🍷 by appt.

SALZMANN

Gewurztraminer 1998★

☐ 0.39 ha 2,000 70–99 F

Albert Schweitzer came from Kaysersberg, which is one of the best-known villages in Alsace. Its Grand Cru vineyard, the Schlossberg, is located on a granite substratum which leaves its mark on the wines. Golden in colour and with a deep aroma of roses in the nose, this one is rich and very complex. In the mouth it is round and has some of the features of overripening. Full-bodied and persistent. (Residual sugar: 50 g/l.)

🔑 Salzmann-Thomann, Dom. de l'Oberhof, 3, rue de l'Oberhof, 68240 Kaysersberg, tel. 03.89.47.10.26, fax 03.89.78.13.08 ☑ 🍷 by appt.

SALZMANN

Gewurztraminer Vendanges tardives 1997★★

☐ 0.25 ha 800 70–99 F

This is a remarkable late-harvest Gewurztraminer: its colour is a beautiful yellow with golden glints of great brilliance, and it has a powerful nose dominated by white flowers. On the palate the first impression is especially agreeable, and the balance is already very good. The aromas are mainly fruity, and it has a long finish with a great deal of freshness. One taster described it as 'bordering on quintessential.' (Half-litre bottles)

🔑 Salzmann-Thomann, Dom. de l'Oberhof, 3, rue de l'Oberhof, 68240 Kaysersberg, tel. 03.89.47.10.26, fax 03.89.78.13.08 ☑ 🍷 by appt.

DOM. WEINBACH

Riesling Clos des Capucins 1998★★

☐ 1 ha 6,400 70–99 F

The Schlossberg is a highly-reputed Grand Cru, not only because of its size – almost 82 ha (202 acres) – but also thanks to the rigorous standards of production which have been in force there since 1928. It yields great Rieslings. This 1998 has been produced by Colette Faller and her daughters, on an estate which is renowned far beyond the borders of France. It has a nose which at first is intensely floral, then mineral. After a fresh attack on the palate, it becomes rich, balanced and persistent in the mouth, with a return of the mineral aroma. (Residual sugar: 3.8 g/l.)

🔑 Colette Faller et ses Filles, Dom. Weinbach, Clos des Capucins, 68240 Kaysersberg, tel. 03.89.47.13.21, fax 03.89.47.38.18 ☑ 🍷 by appt.

Alsace Grand Cru Schoenenbourg

DOPFF ET IRION Riesling 1998★

☐ 2.16 ha 12,000 100–149 F

The Château de Riquewihr used to belong to the Dukes of Wurtemberg. In 1752, Voltaire lent them some 540,000 *livres*, and in return was given a mortgage on the vines which they owned in the Schoenenbourg! In 1998, this Grand Cru has yielded a Riesling with an attractive nose of white flowers and linden flowers. The same aromas reappear, along with a touch of honey, in a palate which is thoroughbred, fresh and very harmonious, with good length at the finish. A wine with distinctive personality and great promise for the future. (Residual sugar: 9.4 g/l.)

🔑 Dopff et Irion, Dom. du château de Riquewihr, 68340 Riquewihr, tel. 03.89.47.92.51, fax 03.89.47.98.90, e-mail post@dopff-irion.com ☑ 🍷 by appt.

ANTOINE ZIMMER Riesling 1998★

☐ 0.95 ha 7,300 70–99 F

In 1644, Merian mentioned the Schoenenbourg in his *Topographia Alsatiae*, saying that it was the vineyard where 'the noblest wine in the region grows'. These days Riesling takes pride of place there. This one is a brilliant golden yellow in colour, and opens with fresh aromas of peach and apricot, with an added hint of flowers. After a good attack on the palate it achieves its full richness, filling the mouth and displaying fleshiness and vigour. A lemony note contributes to its good length at the finish. Best kept so that it can gain in harmony. (Residual sugar: 8 g/l.)

🔑 Antoine Zimmer, 44, rue du Gal-de-Gaulle, 68340 Riquewihr, tel. 03.89.47.85.01, fax 03.89.47.99.39 ☑ 🍷 by appt.

Alsace Grand Cru Sommerberg

ALBERT BOXLER Riesling 1998★★

☐ n.c. 2,800 🛢 70–99 F

From a slope facing due south, above the village of Niedermorschwir, come very typical Rieslings which bear the stamp of a granite, mica-schist soil. Well-known to the jury, Albert Boxler knows how to get the best out of the Sommerberg. His memorable 1992 vintage was awarded a *coup de coeur*. The 1998 has fine, distinctive aromas. The mineral note is slight, however. On the palate, fullness is balanced with freshness. This Grand Cru already has good length and also great promise. It will achieve full maturity in two to three years. (Residual sugar: 7 to 8 g/l.)

🔑 Albert Boxler, 78, rue des Trois-Epis, 68230 Niedermorschwihr, tel. 03.89.27.11.32, fax 03.89.27.70.14 ☑ 🍷 by appt.

KUEHN Riesling 1998

☐ 2 ha 14,800 🛢 50–69 F

This light yellow Riesling combines slight mineral touches with a musky note. A pleasant attack in the mouth is followed by a fruitiness of great finesse. Despite its average length, it has an interesting harmony. (Residual sugar: 8 g/l.)

🔑 Kuehn Vins d'Alsace, 3, Grand-Rue, 68770 Ammerschwihr, tel. 03.89.78.23.16, fax 03.89.47.18.32 ☑ 🍷 ev. day 8am–12 noon 1.30pm–6pm

GERARD WEINZORN

Tokay-pinot gris 1998

☐ 0.64 ha 1,400 🍾 50–69 F

Claude Weinzorn took over the family vineyard in 1992. The estate was founded four centuries ago, and as a sign of its great old age, the house on it is listed as a historic monument. The Sommerberg is well known for its Rieslings, but here it has yielded a Pinot Gris that is not without interest. It has a very ripe, fine fruitiness in the nose, and a clean attack on the palate, which is followed by a somewhat surprising freshness. The richness and balance of this wine bode well for its future development. (Residual sugar: 22 g/l.)

🔑 EARL Gérard Weinzorn et Fils, 133, rue des Trois-Epis, 68230 Niedermorschwihr, tel. 03.89.27.40.55, fax 03.89.27.04.23, e-mail weinzorn@free.fr ☑ 🍷 ev. day 8am–12 noon 2pm–6pm

GERARD WEINZORN

Riesling Vieilles vignes 1998★

☐ 0.15 ha 600 🍾 70–99 F

This Riesling, harvested in mid-November, has a golden colour which is in keeping with its aromas of flowers and overripening fruits. In the mouth it is a little heavy and somewhat lacking in sinew, but the content is delightful. (Residual sugar: 13 g/l.)

🔑 EARL Gérard Weinzorn et Fils, 133, rue des Trois-Epis, 68230 Niedermorschwihr, tel. 03.89.27.40.55, fax 03.89.27.04.23, e-mail weinzorn@free.fr ☑ 🍷 ev. day 8am–12 noon 2pm–6pm

Alsace Grand Cru Sonnenglanz

DOM. BOTT-GEYL

Tokay-pinot gris 1998★

☐ 1 ha 5,600 🍾 🌡 100–149 F

The Sonnenglanz is located on marly chalk soils wich are particularly well-suited to Gewurztraminer and Pinot Gris. The latter variety yielded a superb 1996 vintage on this same Grand Cru. The main features of the1998 are those of a young wine: its beautiful, intense aromas come from the grape variety. A sweet attack on the palate is followed by a rich structure. The finish is dominated by residual sugar. (Residual sugar: 37 g/l.)

🔑 Dom. Bott-Geyl, 1, rue du Petit-Château, 68980 Beblenheim, tel. 03.89.47.90.04, fax 03.89.47.97.33 ☑ 🍷 by appt.

🔑 Jean-Christophe Bott

HEIMBERGER Gewurztraminer 1998★

☐ 3 ha 18,000 🍾 🌡 50–69 F

The Sonnenglanz is one of the oldest vineyards in Alsace mentioned by name on labels. This south-east-facing Grand Cru has a heavy chalk and marl soil which is aerated by gravel. It has yielded a Gewurztraminer with an intense yellow colour and a nose that, although as yet discreet, has some detectable hints of peach and apricot. There are more fruity notes, accompanied by pepper, in a palate which is pleasantly full and rich. A harmonious overall impression. (Residual sugar: 30 g/l.)

🔑 Cave vinicole de Beblenheim, 14, rue de Hoen, 68980 Beblenheim, tel. 03.89.47.90.02, fax 03.89.47.86.85 ☑ 🍷 by appt.

HEIMBERGER Riesling 1998★★

☐ 1 ha 8,000 🍾 🌡 50–69 F

Already famous in the 19th century, the Sonnenglanz is mainly known for its Pinot Gris and Gewurztraminer grapes, which occupy most of the vineyard's 38 ha (94 acres). All the same, the Cave de Beblenheim has produced a very attractive Riesling from grapes grown there. It has a white-gold colour with green glints, and a very distinctive nose combining notes of citrus fruits, white flowers and overripening. The same fruity, fine, clean aromas continue in a palate which is rich and full. The finish is agreeably round, with a fruitiness which conforms delightfully to type. An elegant, engaging wine. (Residual sugar: 15 g/l.)

⊶ Cave vinicole de Beblenheim, 14, rue de Hoen, 68980 Beblenheim,
tel. 03.89.47.90.02, fax 03.89.47.86.85 ☑ 𝐘 by appt.

Alsace Grand Cru Spiegel

LOBERGER

Riesling Vendanges tardives 1997★

☐ 0.45 ha 1,500 100–149 F

This 6-ha (15 acre) vineyard dating back to 1617 owns plots of vines in both the Saering and the Spiegel *grands crus*. This golden Riesling with green glints comes from the latter. In the nose it combines honey with spicy notes which dominate the palate. Very expressive and elegant, it has excellent potential for further development. One taster thinks it would be good to serve with fish en croûte, or a pike soufflé.

⊶ Dom. Joseph Loberger, 10, rue de Bergholtz-Zell, 68500 Bergholtz,
tel. 03.89.76.88.03, fax 03.89.74.16.89 ☑ 𝐘 ev. day except Sun. 8am–12 noon 2pm–6pm

LOBERGER Gewurztraminer 1998★

☐ 0.2 ha 1,500 50–69 F

The soils of the east-facing Spiegel are made up of sandstone congomerates and marls mingled with scree. Its relatively gentle gradient makes it quite easy to work. Pale gold in colour, this Gewurztraminer offers fine, slightly liquoricy aromas which are typical of wines produced from this terrain. It is harmonious in the mouth, revealing notes of crystallised fruits qualified by hints of flowers. A delightful wine, which is rich, full and complex. (Residual sugar: 22 g/l.)

⊶ Dom. Joseph Loberger, 10, rue de Bergholtz-Zell, 68500 Bergholtz,
tel. 03.89.76.88.03, fax 03.89.74.16.89 ☑ 𝐘 ev. day except Sun. 8am–12 noon 2pm–6pm

DOM. SCHLUMBERGER

Pinot gris 1998★

☐ 2.6 ha 10,000 ▮ ⦀ 100–149 F

This vast property exports almost two-thirds of its produce. Founded in 1810, it was developed first and foremost by Ernest Schlumberger. Today it has some 70 ha (173 acres) which are classed in the Grand Cru category. The Spiegel, with its clay and sandstone soil, has enjoyed a high reputation for over 50 years. This Pinot Gris releases notes of fruitiness and overripening. Very supple, fine and expressive, it has an agreeable balance. The finish is marked by notes of candied fruits and spices. (Residual sugar: 25 g/l.)

⊶ Domaines Schlumberger, 100, rue Théodore-Deck, 68501 Guebwiller Cedex,
tel. 03.89.74.27.00, fax 03.89.74.85.75,
e-mail jvschlum@aol.com ☑ 𝐘 by appt.

Alsace Grand Cru Sporen

ROGER JUNG ET FILS

Gewurztraminer 1998★★

☐ 0.25 ha 1,500 ▮ 🌡 70–99 F

Owing to its mineralogical make-up, the Sporen has a reputation for producing very early-maturing grapes and wines of beautiful complexity. The know-how of Rémy and Jacques Jung has done the rest. Their Gewurztraminer, with its very clear, yellow colour, is remarkable. Its discreet but very fine aromas are of roses and crystallised fruits. These reappear in the mouth, which is powerful, harmonious and very long. (Residual sugar: 27 g/l.)

⊶ SARL Roger Jung et Fils, 23, rue de la 1re-Armée, 68340 Riquewihr,
tel. 03.89.47.92.17, fax 03.89.47.87.63,
e-mail rjung@terre-net.fr ☑ 𝐘 ev. day 10am–12 noon 2pm–7pm

DOM. DE LA VIEILLE FORGE

Gewurztraminer 1998

☐ 0.2 ha 600 70–99 F

The Sporen is a natural amphitheatre with a gentle, south-east-facing slope. It has a clay and marl soil, very rich in phosphoric acid, on which grapes ripen particularly early. Wine specialist Denis Wurtz has used them to produce this Gewurztraminer, which is in its first vintage. It is a very young wine, judging by its pale yellow colour and the restraint and lack of complexity of its crystallised fruit aromas. The fact that it is full, rich and harmonious in the mouth gives cause for hope. Needs to be kept. (Residual sugar: 16 g/l.)

⊶ Dom. de La Vieille Forge, 5, rue de Hoen, 68980 Beblenheim,
tel. 03.89.86.01.58, fax 03.89.86.01.58 ☑ 𝐘 ev. day except Sun. 10am–12.30pm 1pm–7.30pm

⊶ Denis Wurtz

ANTOINE ZIMMER

Gewurztraminer 1998★

☐ 0.58 ha 3,700 ⦀ 100–149 F

Antoine Zimmer is at the head of a 10-ha (25 acre) vineyard founded in 1848. His Sporen Gewurztraminer has a superb golden colour. The nose is dominated by aromas of crystallised fruits, with an added hint of exotic fruits. The palate has good continuity and length, and is rich and full with the same flavour of crystallised fruits as in the nose. An elegant wine, which can be enjoyed straight away. One member of the jury suggests serving it at four in the afternoon with some dry petits fours. (Residual sugar: 20 g/l.)

⊶ Antoine Zimmer, 44, rue du Gal-de-Gaulle, 68340 Riquewihr,
tel. 03.89.47.85.01, fax 03.89.47.99.39 ☑ 𝐘 by appt.

Alsace Grand Cru Steinert

ANTOINE MOLTES ET FILS

Tokay-pinot gris Vendanges tardives 1997★

☐ 0.31 ha 1,600 ▮ 70–99 F

With its stony chalk soil structure, the Steinert gives the wines produced from its grapes the structure and richness that make for great vintages. This one has a brilliant golden-yellow colour, and releases scents of flowers (heather) and fruit (peaches). After a delicate attack, it has a liquorice flavour in the mouth which is not yet mature; it does have good length, however. A promising overall impression.

🗝 GAEC Dom. Antoine Moltès et Fils, 8–10, rue du Fossé, 68250 Pfaffenheim, tel. 03.89.49.60.85, fax 03.89.49.50.43, e-mail gmoltes@terre-net.fr ☑ 𝐘 ev. day 8am–12 noon 2pm–7pm

RIEFLE Gewurztraminer 1998★

☐ 0.68 ha 6,000 ▮ ⦀ ⫰ 70–99 F

Nowadays the Rieflé estate is regarded as a point of reference. M. Rieflé has also ruled over the destiny of the Conseil Interprofessionnel du Vin d'Alsace. Straw-yellow in colour, his Steinert Gewurztraminer has pronounced aromas of crystallised fruits, with hints of flowers. This is a 'wine for pleasure'. Elegant, balanced, rich in the mouth and as spicy as one could wish, it is ready to drink straight away, and will delight even the most difficult palates. (Residual sugar: 23 g/l.)

🗝 Dom. Rieflé, 11, pl. de la Mairie, 68250 Pfaffenheim, tel. 03.89.78.52.21, fax 03.89.49.50.98, e-mail riefle@riefle.com ☑ 𝐘 by appt.

RIEFLE Riesling 1998★

☐ 0.4 ha 3,200 ▮ ⦀ ⫰ 70–99 F

For more than 40 years, quality and soil selection have been the constant preoccupation of this vineyard, which has been showered with praise in recent times (the 1996 was awarded a *coup de coeur*). This Riesling is discreet at first, then develops more powerful notes of citrus fruits, with a hint of exotic fruits. The attack on the palate is sweet, after which it recovers its freshness and achieves a fine balance. There is a delicate roundness at the finish, which is sustained and pleasant. (Residual sugar: 13.7 g/l.)

🗝 Dom. Rieflé, 11, pl. de la Mairie, 68250 Pfaffenheim, tel. 03.89.78.52.21, fax 03.89.49.50.98, e-mail riefle@riefle.com ☑ 𝐘 by appt.

PIERRE-PAUL ZINK

Gewurztraminer 1998★

☐ 0.15 ha 1,000 ⦀ 50–69 F

The east-facing Steinert has a largely chalky soil, aerated by a very large gravel component which has given its name to the locality (the word 'Steinert' refers to the stones in the soil). It has yielded a light yellow wine with golden glints and a 'vivid' nose. Complex and intense, its range of aromas, from mineral notes to fruits, flowers and spices, lingers on in the mouth. A great wine of remarkable finesse. (Residual sugar: 16 g/l.)

🗝 Pierre-Paul Zink, 27, rue de la Lauch, 68250 Pfaffenheim, tel. 03.89.49.60.87, fax 03.89.49.73.05 ☑ 𝐘 by appt.

PIERRE-PAUL ZINK Riesling 1998

☐ 0.14 ha 800 ⦀ 50–69 F

Located on chalky clay soil with a particularly high gravel content, the Steinert has been recognised since the Middle Ages. Many abbeys kept vines there. This 1998 has a markedly golden colour and is intense in the nose, with notes of ripe or slightly crystallised fruits and hints of toast. In the mouth it is very rich and full, but at the same time retains its balance. It will need to be kept until it acquires more finesse. (Residual sugar: 3 g/l.)

🗝 Pierre-Paul Zink, 27, rue de la Lauch, 68250 Pfaffenheim, tel. 03.89.49.60.87, fax 03.89.49.73.05 ☑ 𝐘 by appt.

Alsace Grand Cru Steingrübler

STENTZ-BUECHER Riesling 1998

☐ 0.38 ha 1,600 ▮ 70–99 F

The Steingrübler has been known since the 15th century. The fairly sandy soil on its higher slopes produces excellent Rieslings. This one has a discreet but elegant nose which opens gradually, releasing delicate, pleasant, floral notes. After a rather sweet attack on the palate, it becomes clean, fresh and slightly fruity, with an impression of power. A young, promising wine. (Residual sugar: 11 g/l.)

🗝 Dom. Stentz-Buecher, 21, rue Kleb, 68920 Wettolsheim, tel. 03.89.80.68.09, fax 03.89.79.60.53 ☑ 𝐘 by appt.

Alsace Grand Cru Vorbourg

DOM. DE L'ECOLE

Tokay-pinot gris 1998★★

☐ 0.8 ha 2,100 ▮ ⫰ 50–69 F

The Domaine de L'Ecole (School Estate) belongs to the school of wine-growing in Rouffach. For more than 50 years the estate's production has been closely linked with the training of young wine-growers and technicians. The combination of the terrain's qualities and good, well thought-out practices produces remarkable wines such as this 1998 Tokay-Pinot Gris. Pale gold in colour, it brings together a complex array of aromas: crystallised fruits and notes of toast, with a slight touch of overripening. It is very well-balanced in the mouth, where its rich array of flavours lingers on to the finish. A harmonious wine which conforms well to type. (Residual sugar: 22 g/l.)

🗝 Dom. de L'Ecole, Lycée viticole, 8, Aux Remparts, 68250 Rouffach, tel. 03.89.78.73.16, fax 03.89.78.73.01, e-mail legta.rouffach@educagri.fr ☒ Y ev. day except Sat. Sun. 9am–12 noon 1.15–5.15; Aug. by appt.

Alsace Grand Cru Wineck-Schlossberg

JEAN-MARC BERNHARD

Riesling 1998★★

☐ 0.35 ha 2,000 ▮ 50–69 F

The Bernhard family has been in the wine trade for two centuries. Frédéric, the son, has just come back to the vineyard after numerous periods of training both in France and abroad. His Wineck-Schlossberg Riesling is floral in the nose, with a hint of lime and a slight mineral touch. In the mouth it has an appealing mixture of finesse and intensity, richness and power. A wine which cannot fail to please. (Residual sugar: 16 g/l.)

🗝 Domaine Jean-Marc Bernhard, 21, Grand-Rue, 68230 Katzenthal, tel. 03.89.27.05.34, fax 03.89.27.58.72 ☒ Y ev. day except Sun. 9am–12 noon 1.30pm–7pm

JEAN-PAUL ECKLE Riesling 1998★

☐ 0.21 ha 1,500 ◖▮◗ 50–69 F

This Grand Cru takes its name from the Château du Wineck, which overlooks it. The granite, mica-schist soils contribute to the aromatic character and structure of the wines they yield. This one has a light yellow colour with golden glints, and is rich and fat. Its aromas are complex, with a spicy touch and a hint of minerals. Forthcoming and harmonious. The 1996 was awarded a *coup de coeur.* (Residual sugar: 5 g/l.)

🗝 Jean-Paul Ecklé, 29, Grand-Rue, 68230 Katzenthal, tel. 03.89.27.09.41, fax 03.89.80.86.18 ☒ Y ev. day 8am–12 noon 2pm–7pm

VINCENT SPANNAGEL

Riesling Vendanges tardives 1997★★

☐ 0.3 ha 1,500 ◖▮◗ 70–99 F

Nestling at the far end of a valley which is closed in on three sides and sheltered from the prevailing winds, the village of Katzenthal enjoys a very favourable microclimate. Vincent Spannagel's father bought the first plots of land there in 1958, and since then has patiently built up the family vineyard. Today the estate has 9 ha (22 acres). The first impressions of his late-harvest Riesling are a strong, golden yellow colour and a nose of great

Alsace Grand Cru Wiebelsberg

BOECKEL Riesling 1998

☐ 2.5 ha 11,000 ◖▮◗ 50–69 F

With a reputation going back to 1852, the slopes of the Wiebelsberg are characterised by a sandy, sandstone soil, which produces top-class Rieslings. This one has appealing aromas of exotic fruits which permeate its excellent content. The attack on the palate has less vigour and freshness than one might expect, but because of its honeyed quality the wine has a satisfying persistence. (Residual sugar: 6 g/l.)

🗝 Emile Boeckel, 2, rue de la Montagne, 67140 Mittelbergheim, tel. 03.88.08.91.91, fax 03.88.08.91.88 ☒ Y by appt.

ANDRE ET REMY GRESSER

Riesling Vendanges tardives 1997★★

☐ 0.82 ha 2,000 ▮ ◖▮◗ 🌡 150–199 F

A document signed in 1520 by Thiebaut Gresser, winemaker and Provost of Andlau, testifies to the long history of wine-growing in this family. There is as much know-how here as ever, witness this remarkably promising 1997 late-harvest Riesling. Pale gold in the glass, it releases complex aromas of citrus fruits and crystallised fruits. The palate is quite magnificent: full, well balanced and rich in aromas of great finesse.

🗝 Dom. André et Rémy Gresser, 2, rue de l'Ecole, 67140 Andlau, tel. 03.88.08.95.88, fax 03.88.08.55.99, e-mail remy.gresser@wanadoo.fr ☒ Y by appt.

finesse, combining crystallised fruits and honey. The same flavours reappear in a palate which is powerful, balanced, rich and fleshy.
Vincent Spannagel, 82, rue du Vignoble, 68230 Katzenthal, tel. 03.89.27.52.13, fax 03.89.27.56.48 by appt.

DOM. MICHELE ET JEAN-LUC STOECKLE Gewurztraminer 1998

□ 0.45 ha 3,000 50–69 F

This 6-ha (15 acre) vineyard belonged to the old Klur-Stoecklé firm, a partnership between two families which ended in 1999. With his passionate love of the mountains, Jean-Luc Stoecklé is proud of his Wineck-Schlossberg hillside vineyard and the complex wines it yields from granite, mica-schist soils, which compared with some are quite heavily eroded. This one has a brilliant golden-yellow colour and a very floral nose with hints of dried fruits. It could have been fresher on the palate, but it is not without charm. (Residual sugar: 43 g/l.)
Michèle et Jean-Luc Stoecklé, 9, Grand-Rue, 68230 Katzenthal, tel. 03.89.27.05.08, fax 03.89.27.33.61 ev. day except Sun. afternoon 8am–12 noon 1pm–7pm

Alsace Grand Cru Winzenberg

RENE KIENTZ FILS Riesling 1998*

□ 0.2 ha 1,500 30–49 F

The name of the Blienschwiller vineyard appears as early as the ninth century. This Grand Cru of only 19.20 ha (48 acres) is located on a granitic, mica-schist soil which is particularly suited to Rieslings. This one's nose is not yet mature, but it has good balance and fresh flavours with hints of lemon. Its good length indicates that it is a promising wine, which should open up by the end of 2000. (Residual sugar: 6 g/l.)
René Kientz Fils, 49, rte du Vin, 67650 Blienschwiller, tel. 03.88.92.49.06, fax 03.88.92.45.87 by appt.

HUBERT METZ Riesling 1998*

□ 0.33 ha 2,500 50–69 F

This business has its headquarters in an old tithe cellar built in 1728. Even today its vault shelters beautiful, ornate casks, in which great wines such as this 1998 Riesling still mature. In the nose it combines fruit, honey and mineral notes derived from the soil. Balanced and harmonious, its fine, lemony acidity blends well with the beautiful exotic fruit flavours which accompany a long finish. (Residual sugar: 7 g/l.)
Hubert Metz, 3, rue du Winzenberg, 67650 Blienschwiller, tel. 03.88.92.43.06, fax 03.88.92.62.08, e-mail hubertmetz@aol.com ev. day except Sun. 8am–7pm

Alsace Grand Cru Zinnkoepflé

LEON BOESCH ET FILS Gewurztraminer Vendanges tardives 1997*

□ 0.5 ha 3,000 100–149 F

The Zinnkoepflé overlooks the picturesque valley of the Ohmbach, known as the Noble Valley. Its southern aspect makes it a good environment for growing Mediterranean-type flora. This estate, which has been established here since 1832, nowadays keeps more than 10 ha (25 acres) of vines. As last year, the tasters went for a late-harvest Gewurztraminer. Golden yellow in colour, this 1997 offers an intense nose which combines honey, crystallised apricots and exotic fruits. Powerful, full-bodied and rich in aromas, the palate makes it a very promising wine.
Léon Boesch et Fils, 6, rue Saint-Blaise, 68250 Westhalten, tel. 03.89.47.01.83, fax 03.89.47.64.95 ev. day except Sun. 9.30am–11.30am 2pm–6pm
Gérard Boesch

DIRINGER Gewurztraminer 1998*

□ 0.7 ha 5,000 50–69 F

Since 1982, Sébastien and Thomas Diringer have been running this 13-ha (32-acre) vineyard, which was founded in 1740. This year they offer a very interesting Gewurztraminer. This light yellow, almost transparent wine develops aromas of exotic fruits with some added spicy notes. It is powerful but not at all heavy in the mouth, where it is dominated by intense flavours of roses. A wine to be drunk with fine food, it will go well with Asian specialities. (Residual sugar: 31 g/l.)
Dom. Diringer, 18, rue de Rouffach, 68250 Westhalten, tel. 03.89.47.01.06, fax 03.89.47.62.64, e-mail diringer.westhalten@wanadoo.fr ev. day except Sun. 9am–12 noon 2pm–7pm

DIRINGER Riesling 1998*

□ 0.5 ha 4,000 50–69 F

Anyone climbing up the Zinnkoepflé, the 'roof' of the Alsatian vineyard, will come upon the arid slopes and chalky, conchiferous soils which have yielded this Riesling. It has a beautiful, intense nose of flowers, after which its more lemony character in the mouth is surprising. It has a full, rich attack on the palate, and is well-balanced, with a slight hint of bitterness and a good finish. The 1995 was awarded the *coup de coeur* by the jury. (Residual sugar: 10 g/l.)
Dom. Diringer, 18, rue de Rouffach, 68250 Westhalten, tel. 03.89.47.01.06, fax 03.89.47.62.64, e-mail diringer.westhalten@wanadoo.fr ev. day except Sun. 9am–12 noon 2pm–7pm

JEAN-MARIE HAAG

Tokay-pinot gris Cuvée Théo 1998★

☐ 0.38 ha 1,200 100–149 F

This wine has fine, fruity aromas and some added mineral notes. On the palate it develops a beautiful, distinctive flavour of ripe fruits, against a supple, round background. Good length combined with freshness give it elegance at the finish. A wine marked by overripening – perhaps too much so – but which should appeal to lovers of late-harvest wines. (Residual sugar: 60 g/l.)

Jean-Marie Haag, 17, rue des Chèvres, 68570 Soultzmatt, tel. 03.89.47.02.38, fax 03.89.47.64.79 ev. day 9am–12 noon 2pm–6pm; Sun. and groups by appt.

RAYMOND ET MARTIN KLEIN

Gewurztraminer Vendanges tardives 1997★

☐ 0.92 ha 3,000 70–99 F

Established at Soultzmatt, a charming village at the entrance to the Noble Valley and overlooked by the Zinnkoepflé, this firm offers a golden-yellow, late-harvest Gewurztraminer. Its nose is still closed, but even so it lets out some spicy notes and fragrances of roses and candying. A full, delicate palate is the sign of a captivating wine which will only reach its peak in a few years' time. The 1993 was awarded a *coup de coeur* by the jury.

Raymond et Martin Klein, 61, rue de la Vallée, 68570 Soultzmatt, tel. 03.89.47.01.76, fax 03.89.47.64.53 ev. day 9am–12 noon 2pm–6pm

FRANCIS MURE

Gewurztraminer 1998★

☐ 0.2 ha 1,600 50–69 F

The Zinnkoepflé is probably the highest vineyard in the Alsatian wine-country. It is protected from damp sea air by the tallest peaks of the Vosges. Its chalky sandstone soil yields great wines, such as this Gewurztraminer, which has an intense yellow colour with golden glints and a very candied nose of quince and roses, and is full, structured and long in the mouth. A wine in the late-harvest style, which can be drunk straight away as an aperitif or with foie gras. (Residual sugar: 30 g/l.)

Francis Muré, 30, rue de Rouffach, 68250 Westhalten, tel. 03.89.47.64.20, fax 03.89.47.09.39 by appt.

ERIC ROMINGER

Gewurztraminer Les Sinneles 1998★★★

☐ 0.8 ha 2,300 70–99 F

No doubt about it, Eric Rominger (*Grappe d'Argent*-winner in 1998) seems to have made *coups de coeur* his speciality. His Les Sinneles Gewurztraminer a well-deserved reputation, and this year it lands the highest distinction. A very strong golden yellow in colour, it has an intense nose which reflects both the grape variety and the soil. Well balanced and delicate in the mouth, it develops fruity aromas with the emphasis on crystallised quince. Its fullness, richness and length command the

greatest respect. It will make a memorable aperitif, or it could be drunk with the foie gras at a very special meal. (Residual sugar: 45 g/l.)

SCEA Eric Rominger, 16, rue Saint-Blaise, 68250 Westhalten, tel. 03.89.76.14.71, fax 03.89.74.81.44 by appt.

ERIC ROMINGER Riesling 1998★★

☐ 0.6 ha 2,000 50–69 F

This Eric Rominger Riesling is remarkable. Its fruity aroma of citrus fruits with shades of exotic fruits continues on the palate. Full and rich, this wine fills the mouth pleasantly. The distinctive features of the terrain should become apparent with time. The 1996 was awarded a *coup de coeur* by the jury. (Residual sugar: 13 g/l.)

SCEA Eric Rominger, 16, rue Saint-Blaise, 68250 Westhalten, tel. 03.89.76.14.71, fax 03.89.74.81.44 by appt.

SCHLEGEL-BOEGLIN Riesling 1998★

☐ 0.6 ha 3,000 30–49 F

Jean-Luc Schlegel, who took over the 11.5 ha (28-acre) family vineyard in 1991, distinguished himself last year with a Riesling which was awarded a *coup de coeur*. The 1998 is not yet mature. On the palate it is powerful and full of fire, while at the same time retaining a delightful acidity. The aromas are as yet unforthcoming: a wine to be kept for three or four years so that it can reach its full potential. (Residual sugar: 13 g/l.)

Dom. Schlegel-Boeglin, 22, rue d'Orschwihr, 68250 Westhalten, tel. 03.89.47.00.93, fax 03.89.47.65.32 ev. day except Sun. 8am–12 noon 2pm–6pm

FRANCOIS WISCHLEN

Tokay-pinot gris 1997★

☐ 0.4 ha 2,600 100–149 F

Since 1981, François Wischlen has been working the 5 ha (12-acre) family estate which was founded by his grandfather at Westhalten. His Grand Cru Tokay can also be found in this edition. The warmth of his golden-yellow 1997 reflects the sunny position of the Zinnkoepflé, which faces due south. In the nose it has a fine fruitiness with hints of candying, and the palate has excellent balance, good presence and an agreeable freshness which guarantees that this wine will keep well. (Residual sugar: 32 g/l.)

🔑 François Wischlen, 4, rue de Soultzmatt, 68250 Westhalten, tel. 03.89.47.01.24, fax 03.89.47.62.90 ☒ Y by appt.

Alsace Grand Cru Zotzenberg

PIERRE ET JEAN-PIERRE RIETSCH

Riesling 1998★★

□ 0.3 ha 2,600 50–69 F

This old estate stands out for the originality of its labels and the quality of its wines. Painted in the style of Magritte, the label on this 1998 shows two grapes falling from the sky, or the Zotzenberg, and being watched with interest by men who look like Lilliputians. Are we really as insignificant as that compared with a Riesling? Perhaps in this case, because it is a very great one. Its nose is expressive, complex and true to type, combining notes of lemon and toast with fragrances of white flowers which linger on in the mouth. There is a full attack on the palate, where it achieves a fine balance between sweetness and freshness. A long, elegant finish leaves behind a memory of real harmony. (Residual sugar: 7.5 g/l.)

🔑 Pierre et Jean-Pierre Rietsch, 32, rue Principale, 67140 Mittelbergheim, tel. 03.88.08.00.64, fax 03.88.08.40.91 ☒ Y by appt.

FERNAND SELTZ ET FILS

Riesling 1998

□ n.c. 2,700 50–69 F

The marly chalk soil of the Zotzenberg was once known mainly for its Sylvaner. Nowadays other Alsatian grape varieties, such as this Riesling, contribute to its renown. A beautiful gold in colour, this 1998 starts by releasing aromas of overripening, which leave floral and fruity nuances somewhat in the background. Similarly in the mouth, the lusciousness and fleshiness of the wine have the upper hand, masking its freshness and the distinctive qualities of the terrain. Needs to be kept. (Residual sugar: 29.5 g/l.)

🔑 EARL Fernand Seltz et Fils, 42, rue Principale, 67140 Mittelbergheim, tel. 03.88.08.93.92, fax 03.88.08.93.92 ☒ Y ev. day except Sun. 8.30am–7pm

ALFRED WANTZ Riesling 1998★

□ 0.25 ha 2,000 30–49 F

This family has been making wine since the 13th century, and its cellars date back to 1618. As for the vineyard, it was mentioned by name as early as the 14th century. It has yielded a Riesling with a delicate nose which combines exotic fruits and notes of toast. A clean attack on the palate gives way to a superb acidity. Its power, fullness and richness show that it has good content, while the flavours linger on in a long finish. A wine of character. (Residual sugar: 6 g/l.)

🔑 Jean-Marc et Liliane Wantz, 3, rue des Vosges, 67140 Mittelbergheim, tel. 03.88.08.91.43, fax 03.88.08.58.74 ☒ Y by appt.

Crémant d'Alsace

When this appellation was created in 1976, there was an immediate increase in production of sparkling wines made by the *méthode traditionelle*, or Champagne method. They had always been produced, but on a smaller scale. Crémant d'Alsace is made from a blend of various grape varieties: Pinot Blanc, Auxerrois, Pinot Gris, Pinot Noir, Riesling and Chardonnay. The production of this sparkling wine, steadily gaining in reputation, increased to 163,000 hl (4,303,200 gal) in 1999.

AMBERG 1997★

○ 1 ha 10,000 50–69 F

Yves Amberg has been running the vineyard since 1987, and now has 10 ha (25 acres) of vines at Epfig. No stranger to the jury, he too has started to produce Alsatian Crémants. This one is of 1997 vintage, and is a blend of Pinot Gris and Auxerrois. It has already developed somewhat, as is indicated by the notes of honey which are present in the nose. With excellent fullness in the palate, it is a balanced and distinctive wine.

🔑 Yves Amberg, 19, rue Fronholz, 67680 Epfig, tel. 03.88.85.51.28, fax 03.88.85.52.71 ☒ Y by appt.

BARON KIRMANN 1998★

○ 0.68 ha 7,500 30–49 F

With their 10 ha (25 acres) of vines, the Kirmanns occupy an enviable position in Rosheim. The picture on the label of the Empire Baron Kirmann was tailor-made for this Crémant. With its intensity and hints of honey, the nose succeeds very well in conveying a blend of Pinot Gris and Auxerrois. The palate has a beautiful freshness, and is well-balanced and elegant. Best drunk as an aperitif.

🔑 Philippe Kirmann, 2, rue du Gal-de-Gaulle, 67560 Rosheim, tel. 03.88.50.43.01, fax 03.88.50.22.72 ☒ Y by appt.

RENE BARTH 1998★

○ 0.65 ha 7,000 30-49 F

After training as an oenologist, Michel Fonné took over the vineyard from his uncle René Barth in 1989. Its modest size (5 ha/12acres) does not prevent it from producing wines of quality, witness this Crémant with a full and floral nose and a *mousse* of very high quality. Well-structured in the mouth, it is a wine whose good length and presence are in keeping with the blend of grape varieties – Pinot, Auxerrois and Riesling – from which it is made.

Dom. René Barth succ. Michel Fonné, 24, rue du Gal-de-Gaulle, 68630 Bennwihr, tel. 03.89.47.92.69, fax 03.89.49.04.86 by appt.

FREY-SOHLER

Cuvée de l'An 2000 1997★

○ n.c. 3,000 50-69 F

Passed on from generation to generation, the Frey-Sohler firm is established in Schwerwiller, to the north-east of Sélestat and halfway between the castles on the Haut-Koenigsbourg and the Ortenbourg. This special cuvée, which comes from the 1997 vintage and is made 100% from Riesling, has an intense, complex nose combining floral and mineral aromas. With a noticeably fresh attack on the palate, it is a very powerful wine with good length. Delightfully harmonious!

Frey-Sohler, 72, rue de l'Ortenbourg, 67750 Scherwiller, tel. 03.88.92.10.13, fax 03.88.82.57.11 ev. day 8am–12 noon 1.15–7pm; Sun. by appt.

Sohler

JOSEPH GRUSS ET FILS Brut 1998★

○ 1.41 ha 16,000 30-49 F

Since 1997, André Gruss, who is a trained oenologist, has been helping his father Bernard. There is no shortage of work for both of them on this 13-ha (32-acre) vineyard in the beautiful village of Eguisheim. Coming from a chalky clay soil, this Crémant is a blend of 80% Pinot Blanc and 20% Riesling, which gives it a remarkable nose of flowers and honey. Well balanced on the palate, fresh and well structured, this wine will be suitable to drink both as an aperitif and with food.

Joseph Gruss et Fils, 25, Grand-Rue, 68420 Eguisheim, tel. 03.89.41.28.78, fax 03.89.41.76.66, e-mail gruss@hotmail.com ev. day 8am–12 noon 1.30pm–6pm

DOM. HERING

Blanc de noirs Cuvée du troisième millénaire 1997★

○ 0.15 ha 1,500 70-99 F

For five generations the Hering family has been producing highly distinctive wines of the dry type favoured in a region with a great concern for gastronomy. Pierre and his son Jean-Daniel are carrying on this tradition. Their Blanc de Noirs has a very full nose dominated by notes of fruitiness and toast. After a clean attack on the palate, this is a long, structured wine which has the necessary fleshiness to go well with food.

Pierre et Jean-Daniel Hering, 6, rue Sultzer, 67140 Barr, tel. 03.88.08.90.07, fax 03.88.08.08.54, e-mail jdh@infonie.fr ev. day except Sun. 8.30am–12 noon 1.30pm–6.30pm

KIEFFER Blanc de noirs 1998★

○ 0.6 ha 6,000 30-49 F

Jean-Charles Kieffer is descended from a line of wine-makers going back to 1737. Since 1985 he has been at the head of the estate, which he has chosen to run from a house with a remarkable half-timbered façade. Elegant and complex in the nose, his Blanc de Noirs has already developed well. It has a clean, fresh attack on the palate, which is marked by long aromas of ripe fruits, and by a certain suppleness at the finish.

Jean-Charles Kieffer, 7, rte des Vins, 67140 Itterswiller, tel. 03.88.85.59.80, fax 03.88.57.81.44 by appt.

DOM. KIEFFER 1997★

○ 0.31 ha 3,600 30-49 F

The village of Itterswiller is famous for its beauty and for the warm welcome it offers to visitors. François and Vincent Kieffer keep seven hectares (17 acres) of vines there. The Crémant they offer is rather unusual, since it is made from pure Chardonnay. The grape variety comes through clearly in the nose, which has very intense notes of toast. With a beautifully fine, light *mousse* which adds to the freshness of its attack on the palate, it is an elegant, well-balanced wine.

François Kieffer, 76, rte du Vin, 67140 Itterswiller, tel. 03.88.85.50.22, fax 03.88.57.80.91, e-mail kiefferfrançois@minitel.net ev. day except Sun. 8am–12 noon 1pm–6pm

KOBUS 1997

○ n.c. 80,000 30-49 F

The Cave Vinicole d'Obernai, which, along with the Divinal group, is of top-ranking importance in Alsace, has chosen to label this Crémant with the emblematic figure of Fritz Kobus (Fritz the Friend). Still very young for a 1997, it makes a very elegant impression with its aromas of fresh bread which give a lovely smell of fermentation in bottles. With good presence and length on the palate, it finishes on a slight note of roundness.

Cave vinicole d'Obernai, 30, rue du Gal-Leclerc, 67210 Obernai, tel. 03.88.47.60.20, fax 03.88.47.60.22 by appt.

DOM. DE LA TOUR

Cuvée Jean-Sébastien 1997

○ 0.6 ha 6,000 30-49 F

Jean-François Straub's ancestors have been wine-makers or coopers since the beginning of the 16th century, and the cellar still has its original cob walls and sandstone pillars. Bearing the stamp of the 1997 vintage and a schistose soil, this Crémant is very intense in the nose. Its relative suppleness on the palate

is the sign that it comes from Auxerrois grapes.
🔑 Jean-François Straub, Dom. de la Tour, 35 rte du Vin, 67650 Blienschwiller, tel. 03.88.92.48.72, fax 03.88.92.62.90 ☑ Y ev. day 8am–12 noon 2pm–6pm; Sat. Sun. by appt.

ARTHUR METZ Blanc de noirs 1997*

○ n.c. n.c. 30-49 F

A merger between two firms, Arthur Metz and Léon Laugel, has created the Metz-Laugel company, which is now in a leading position, especially where Alsatian Crémant is concerned. This Blanc de Noirs, produced from a blend of different grape varieties, is already well developed in the nose, and has very intense aromas of fruit and brioche. It has quite a lively attack on the palate, and is characterised by the excellent quality of its *mousse*, and by a delightful freshness.
🔑 Sté vins et crémants d'Alsace Metz-Laugel, 102, rue du Gal-de-Gaulle, 67520 Marlenheim, tel. 03.88.59.28.60, fax 03.88.87.67.58 ☑ Y ev. day 10am–7pm; groups by appt.

RENE MURE Cuvée Prestige*

○ 10 ha 80,000 50-69 F

Descended from Michel Muré who came here from Switzerland in 1648, the Muré family acquired the walled vineyard at Saint-Landelin in 1935, and now finds itself running one of the most beautiful estates in the region. It offers a Crémant that comes from a skilful blend of Riesling, Pinot and Chardonnay. This very clear wine has a powerful nose combining floral, herbaceous and delicately mineral touches. With a well-sustained quality of *mousse*, it makes a supple impression and has an especially pleasant finish.
🔑 René Muré, Clos Saint-Landelin, rte du Vin, 68250 Rouffach, tel. 03.89.78.58.00, fax 03.89.78.58.01, e-mail rene@mure.com.fr ☑ Y by appt.

SCHIRMER 1998

○ 0.6 ha 6,000 30-49 F

Heir to an estate founded in 1865 in the picturesque village of Soultzmatt, Lucien Schirmer keeps 7 ha (17 acres) of vines. His Crémant, which is a blend of true Pinot Blanc and Auxerrois, is developing a very typical nose of flowers and brioche. Beautifully fresh in the attack, it has good presence and expressiveness on the palate. Ideal as an aperitif.
🔑 Dom. Lucien Schirmer et Fils, 22, rue de la Vallée, 68570 Soultzmatt, tel. 03.89.47.03.82, fax 03.89.47.02.33 ☑ Y ev. day 8am–12 noon 1pm–7pm

SPERRY Cuvée 2000 1997

○ 0.43 ha 4,000 50-69 F

This very well-known Blienschwiller vineyard with 10 ha (25 acres) of vines offers a Crémant whose nose of toast and brioche is characteristic of the Chardonnay grape variety. This wine has a fairly clean attack on the palate and a very harmonious *mousse*.
🔑 EARL Pierre Sperry Fils, 3, rte du Vin, 67650 Blienschwiller, tel. 03.88.92.41.29, fax 03.88.92.62.38, e-mail sperry@reperes.com ☑ Y ev. day 8am–12 noon 1pm–7pm

DOM. SPERRY-KOBLOTH Le Burgrave 1997

○ 0.23 ha 2,500 150-199 F

Belonging to a family which has been connected with the wine trade for a long time, not only as growers but also as wine-brokers, the Sperry-Kobloths run a vineyard of almost 7 ha (17 acres). In keeping with its granitic origins, this Burgrave already has a very rich nose of complex, smoky aromas. It has a fine attack on the palate, and develops long, lingering, fruity aromas in the mouth.
🔑 Sperry-Kobloth, 50, rue du Winzenberg, 67650 Blienschwiller, tel. 03.88.92.40.66, fax 03.88.92.63.95 ☑ Y by appt.
🔑 Jean Sperry

A. WITTMANN FILS 1997*

○ 0.66 ha 4,800 30-49 F

The Wittmanns have been in the wine trade since 1785. Today they produce the complete range of Alsatian Appellations on 8 ha (20 acres) of vines. Their Crémant is characterised in the nose by aromas of overripening and exotic fruits, and has all the fullness of the 1997 vintage. Coming from a blend of Pinot Blanc, Pinot Gris and Riesling, it has good balance and length on the palate.
🔑 EARL André et Nicolas Wittmann, 7–9, rue Principale, 67140 Mittelbergheim, tel. 03.88.08.95.79, fax 03.88.08.53.81 ☑ Y ev. day 9am–12 noon 6pm–8pm; Sun. 9am–12 noon

The Wines of the East

The Côtes de Toul and the Moselle are the last remaining vineyards of the once flourishing wine-growing area of Lorraine. In their heyday, Lorraine wines were held in high esteem, and in 1890 the vineyards covered more than 30,000 ha (74,100 acres). The reputation of these two areas was at its height in the late 19th century. After that, various disasters contributed to its decline: the vines were destroyed by phylloxera, and the hybrid stock planted to replace them was of inferior quality; there was a slump in the wine industry in 1907; the battlefields of the First World War covered much of this part of eastern France; and the industrialisation of the region led to a massive exodus of workers from the country to the town to work in the factories. The local authorities ultimately acknowledged the originality of the wines produced in these vineyards, but it was not until 1951 that the Côtes de Toul and the Moselle wines were officially recognised, finally regaining their place among the old-established wines of France.

Côtes de Toul

Located just west of Toul and the elbow-bend of the Moselle, the Côtes de Toul vineyards cover eight communes along the hillside. Sedimentary layers from the eastern part of the Paris Basin have been eroded away to expose geological structures from the Jurassic period, mainly Oxford clay with significant deposits of calcareous scree, which gives good drainage. The slopes face south or south-east, and the semi-continental climate means high summer temperatures, which help to ripen the grapes. However, there are often frosts in spring.

The majority of the vineyards are planted with Gamay, although much is being replaced by Pinot Noir. The blending of these two varieties makes characteristic Vin Gris, which is obtained by direct pressing. To qualify as Vin Gris, the decree stipulates that at least 10% of Pinot Noir grapes must be blended with Gamay, which gives the wine greater roundness. Some Pinot Noir is made into single-variety red wines which are pleasant and full-bodied, while the locally grown Auxerrois makes light white wines.

The vineyards cover some 100 ha (247 acres), sometimes producing more than 6,000 hl (158,400 gal) of wine, of which only 4,460 hl (117,744 gal) were recognised.

As you leave Toul, there is a well signposted Route du Vin et de la Mirabelle, which takes you through the vineyard.

On 31 March 1998, the vineyard was officially recognised as an AOC.

VINCENT GORNY Pinot noir 1999★★

■ 1.5 ha 7,200 ▮ 20–29 F

In 1991 Vincent Gorny took over the family vineyard, a modest estate of 6.5 ha (16 acres). He has shown his commitment to producing wines of quality by planting new vines and then, in 2000, by renovating the winemaking cellar. His efforts and investments will be rewarded by the *coup de coeur* he has received for his Pinot Noir, a wine with a very strong red colour, and a discreet but pleasant nose. It won the day by its very fine structure, good balance and fruity aromas. The **Vin Gris Collection 2000** from the same estate has been awarded a star. It is a wine which has a fresh, aromatic nose and is balanced and long in the mouth.

Vincent Gorny, 86, rue des Triboulottes, 54200 Bruley, tel. 03.83.63.80.41, fax 03.83.63.80.41 ☑ Y by appt.

DOM. DE LA LINOTTE
Pinot noir 1999

■ 0.34 ha 2,400 ▮ 20–29 F

This new estate created in 1997 by Marc Laroppe offers a Pinot Noir with a beautifully clear, raspberry red colour. It owes its charm not to the power of its structure, which is somewhat tannic, but to its attractive nose centred on soft fruits, and its pleasant, smooth quality.

Marc Laroppe, 90, rue Victor-Hugo, 54200 Bruley, tel. 03.83.63.29.02 by appt.

MARCEL ET MICHEL LAROPPE

Auxerrois 1999★

□ 2.5 ha 12,000 30–49 F

The Laroppes have been established at Bruley since 1722. Marcel and Michel Laroppe, who run this charming 18-ha (44-acre) vineyard, are pillars of the Appellation. They were joined in 1988 by Marcel's son Vincent, who has a diploma in oenology. Their Auxerrois has immediate appeal owing to its beautiful colour and brilliant glints. The nose is discreet but pleasantly subtle, and it has a very fruity palate of equal finesse.

Marcel et Michel Laroppe, 253, rue de la République, 54200 Bruley, tel. 03.83.43.11.04, fax 03.83.43.36.92 ev. day except Sun. 8am–12 noon 1.30pm–7pm

ANDRE ET ROLAND LELIEVRE

Auxerrois 1999

□ 2.6 ha 17,060 30–49 F

Founded in 1970, this vineyard now has 15 ha (37 acres), and has contributed to the renown of the Appellation by producing wines which often win much praise. This year it received two mentions: one for this Auxerrois, a pale wine with brilliant glints which has a discreet but pleasant nose of citrus fruits, a slight acidity under the tongue and a hint of bitterness at the finish: the other for a **1998 Pinot Noir** which has been matured in barrels and as a result has a strong colour, a powerful oaky nose and a structured palate with well-dosed tannins.

André et Roland Lelièvre, 3, rue de la Gare, 54200 Lucey, tel. 03.83.63.81.36, fax 03.83.63.84.45 by appt.

LES VIGNERONS DU TOULOIS

Pinot noir 1999

■ 1.15 ha 8,200 20–29 F

This cellar, which took over from a wine-merchant in 1990, declares itself to be the smallest co-operative in France. It offers a pale red Pinot Noir which is discreet in the nose but fruity in the mouth and, although it is somewhat lacking in structure, is pleasant.

Les Vignerons du Toulois, 43, pl. de la Mairie, 54113 Mont-le-Vignoble, tel. 03.83.62.59.93, fax 03.83.62.59.93 ev. day except Mon.2pm–6pm

Moselle AOVDQS

The vineyards are planted on the hillsides of the Moselle valley, which were originally layers of sedimentary rock at the eastern limit of the Paris Basin. The vineyards are clustered in three main centres: the first is south and west of Metz; the second in the region of Sierck-les-Bains, and the third along the Seille valley, around Vic-sur-Seille. Wine-making in this AOVDQS is influenced by that in neighbouring Luxembourg; the vines grow tall and wide producing dry, fruity white wines. In terms of quantity, the AOVDQS is still modest producing 1,214 hl (32,050 gal) in 1999, but the wine-growing area cannot expand because the land is broken up into very small plots.

GAUTHIER

Cuvée Georges de La Tour 1999★

■ 0.8 ha 2,000 30–49 F

Given that Claude Gauthier's ancestors worked this vineyard for the lord of the manor before the French Revolution, it is hardly surprising that he has not resigned himself to seeing it disappear from Vic-sur-Seille. He develops several types of wine from grapes grown on his 2-ha(5-acre) estate. The Cuvée Georges de la Tour, which is a clear cherry red in colour, comes from a combination of Pinot Noir (70%) and Gamay. The presence of the Pinot comes through in pleasant, very fruity aromas which reappear in a supple, round palate. A beautiful, well-balanced wine. For his **1999 Muller-Thurgau Réserve de la Porte des Evêques**, Claude Gauthier receives a star (20–29F).

Claude Gauthier, 4, pl. du Palais, 57630 Vic-sur-Seille, tel. 03.87.01.11.55, fax 03.87.05.41.91 by appt.

LA VACQUINIERE Pinot gris 1999★

□ 0.45 ha 3,500 30–49 F

The La Vacquinière vineyard (1.60 ha/4 acres) was founded in 1988 by a Thionville lawyer who was a lover of nature and wine. Some years on it has yielded a Pinot Gris with a pale colour, a very aromatic nose of pear drops, and a palate which is fine and not over-fresh. A balanced overall impression.

Jean-Philippe Bertrand, La Vacquinière, 57570 Berg-sur-Moselle, tel. 03.82.54.82.60, fax 03.82.53.11.15 by appt.

MICHEL MAURICE

Vignobles d'Ancy 1999★

◪ 0.46 ha 7,200 ▮ ♁ 20–29 F

Combining Pinot and Gamay in equal parts, this wine catches the eye with its delicate, salmon colour with pinkish glints. It has a pleasantly fruity nose, followed by a palate which is both supple and slightly acid, well-balanced and refreshing. Michel Maurice has also received a mention for a white **Auxerrois du même millésime**, which has the aromatic nose that is characteristic of the grape variety, and a supple, rich palate.

🔑 Michel Maurice, 1–3, pl. Foch, 57130 Ancy-sur-Moselle, tel. 03.87.30.90.07, fax 03.87.30.90.07 ☑ Y by appt.

OURY-SCHREIBER

Cuvée du Maréchal Fabert 1999★★

☐ 0.6 ha 3,900 ▮ ♁ 30–49 F

In the hierarchy of the Hachette Guide, a

Marshal of France can have two stars and it is considered an eminent distinction! Why the name Fabert? Because Abraham de Fabert, a marshal of Louis XIV, kept a vineyard on the same plots of land on which Pascal Oury cultivates the young vines which have yielded this wine. Coming from a combination of wines in which the dominant Pinot Gris (80%) is complemented by an equal mixture of Auxerrois and Gewurztraminer, this 1999 is pale in colour but very aromatic in the nose, with fragrances of mango and pear drops. Very balanced, it fills the mouth well and has freshness and good length.

🔑 Pascal Oury, 29, rue des Côtes, 57420 Marieulles-Vezon, tel. 03.87.52.09.02, fax 03.87.52.09.17, e-mail oury-pascal-viticulteur@wanadoo.fr ☑ Y by appt.

OURY-SCHREIBER Auxerrois 1999★★

☐ 0.4 ha 3,500 ▮ ♁ 20–29 F

Barely five years since his vineyard was founded, Pascal Oury has already harvested a fine crop of stars! Very pale in the glass, his Auxerrois is remarkable for the intensity of its nose of exotic and citrus fruits, and the excellent balance of its palate, which is round and has great length. As for the **1999 Pinot Noir** mentioned by the jury, it is a promising wine which has been partially matured in barrels. It has a deep colour with purplish glints, a nose of oak and vanilla with a hint of toast, and a balanced palate with the same empyreumatic notes as in the nose.

🔑 Pascal Oury, 29, rue des Côtes, 57420 Marieulles-Vezon, tel. 03.87.52.09.02, fax 03.87.52.09.17, e-mail oury-pascal-viticulteur@wanadoo.fr ☑ Y by appt.

JEANNE SIMON-HOLLERICH

Pinot blanc 1999★

☐ 0.44 ha 4,000 ▮ 20–29 F

This wine-grower has made a great success of her Pinot Blanc. Pale in colour, it has an appealing, characteristic nose of fine intensity. The palate is well-balanced, rich with just the right amount of freshness, and full of beautiful floral aromas. The same estate has received a mention for a **1999 Muller-Thurgau** *petite cuvée*, which is a clear wine with a nose of citrus fruits and a light, fresh palate.

🔑 Jeanne Simon-Hollerich, 16, rue du Pressoir, 57480 Contz-les-Bains, tel. 03.82.83.74.81, fax 03.82.83.69.70 ☑ Y by appt.

BEAUJOLAIS AND THE LYONS REGION

Beaujolais

Officially, Beaujolais is part of the Burgundy wine-growing region, although it has become separately identified and through skilful promotion and marketing has become famous in its own right through the whole world. Who can be unaware of the much-trumpeted arrival of the Beaujolais Nouveau on the third Thursday of November? The soil and the topography of the Beaujolais differ significantly from the countryside of its celebrated neighbour, where the vineyard slopes form an almost straight north-south line. The steeper hills and deeper valleys of the Beaujolais mean many vineyards are frequently bathed in sunshine. The houses are different, too; rather than the roofs being covered by the flatter tiles of Burgundy, they are covered with bowed, Roman tiles which convey a Mediterranean flavour.

The Beaujolais region lies south of Burgundy, and is a gateway to southern France. There are 96 communes covering 23,000 ha (56,810 acres), stretching 50 km (31 miles) from north to south, through two departments, the Saône-et-Loire and the Rhône, and average 15 km (9 miles) wide, though narrower in the south. In the north, the Arlois is the border with the Mâconnais. In the east, on the other hand, the Saône plain, where the sparkling river meanders her slow majestic way south, makes a natural barrier. Julius Caesar remarked that the river moved so slowly that it was virtually impossible to judge in which direction it was flowing. To the west, the Beaujolais hills form the foothills of the Massif Central. The highest point, Mont Saint-Rigaux, 1,012 m (3319 ft), is a gigantic milestone marking the junction of the lands of the Saône and Loire rivers. In the south, the Lyon wine country takes over as far as the city of Lyon itself, irrigated, as the saying goes, by three great 'rivers': the Rhône, the Saône and . . . the Beaujolais.

The great renown of Beaujolais wines owes a massive debt to Lyon. The wines are still sold in the city's famous small wine bars or *bouchons*, where they had a ready market after the highly successful expansion of the vineyards in the 18th century. Two hundred years previously, Villefranche-sur-Saône had become the region's capital, in place of Beaujeu, which had given the area its name. The lords of Beaujeu were skilful and wise; they carefully planned the expansion of their wealth and their domains, stimulated not least by their concern to protect themselves from their powerful neighbours, the Counts of Mâcon and Forez, the Abbots of Cluny and the Bishops of Lyon. The rapid development of the vineyard came about when Beaujolais was added to the ranks of the five Royal 'farms', areas which were exempted from certain taxes normally levied for transporting goods to Paris. For many years, Beaujolais produce was carried via the Briare canal.

Beaujolais

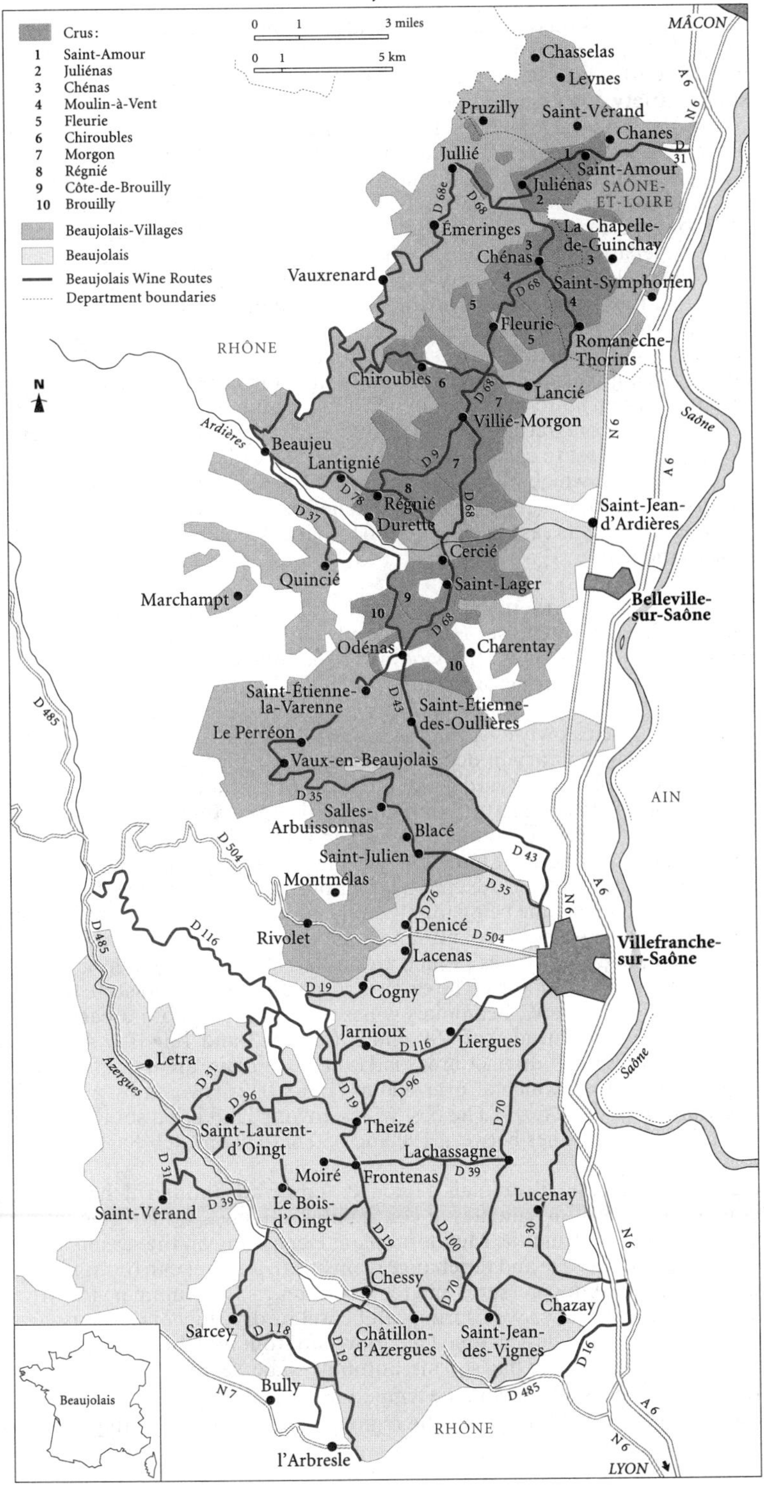

Crus:

1 Saint-Amour
2 Juliénas
3 Chénas
4 Moulin-à-Vent
5 Fleurie
6 Chiroubles
7 Morgon
8 Régnié
9 Côte-de-Brouilly
10 Brouilly

Beaujolais-Villages
Beaujolais
Beaujolais Wine Routes
Department boundaries

0 1 3 miles
0 1 5 km

MÂCON
Chasselas
Leynes
Pruzilly
Saint-Vérand
Chanes
Jullié
Saint-Amour
Juliénas
SAÔNE-ET-LOIRE
Émeringes
La Chapelle-de-Guinchay
Chénas
Vauxrenard
Saint-Symphorien
Fleurie
Romanèche-Thorins
RHÔNE
Chiroubles
Lancié
Villié-Morgon
Ardières
Beaujeu
Lantignié
Régnié
Durette
Saint-Jean-d'Ardières
Cercié
Quincié
Saint-Lager
Marchampt
Belleville-sur-Saône
Odénas
Charentay
Saint-Étienne-la-Varenne
Saint-Étienne-des-Oullières
Le Perréon
Vaux-en-Beaujolais
AIN
Salles-Arbuissonnas
Blacé
Saint-Julien
Montmélas
Rivolet
Denicé
Villefranche-sur-Saône
Lacenas
Cogny
Jarnioux
Liergues
Letra
Azergues
Saint-Laurent-d'Oingt
Theizé
Lachassagne
Moiré
Frontenas
Lucenay
Saint-Vérand
Le Bois-d'Oingt
Chessy
Chazay
Sarcey
Châtillon-d'Azergues
Saint-Jean-des-Vignes
Bully
RHÔNE
l'Arbresle
LYON
Saône

Beaujolais

Today, Beaujolais produces an average of 1,400,000 hl (36,960,000) of red wines of a distinctive character (there is virtually no white). With only the rare exception, Beaujolais reds are made from a single variety, the Gamay, a black-skinned grape with white flesh. This is one of the fundamental differences with Burgundy, where several varieties are grown. The wines produced fall into three appellations: Beaujolais, Beaujolais Supérieur and Beaujolais Villages, and there are also ten recognised Crus: Brouilly, Côte de Brouilly, Chénas, Chiroubles, Fleurie, Morgon, Juliénas, Moulin à Vent, Saint-Amour and Régnié. The first three appellations may apply to reds, whites or rosés, while the ten others are exclusively reds which qualify legally as AOC Bourgogne. Geologically speaking, the Beaujolais was affected by the folding of the earth's crust in the Hercynian period of the Primary era and again in the Tertiary era when the Alps were formed. This was the era that created the relief of the present-day Beaujolais; the sedimentary deposits from the Secondary era were fractured when outcrops of rocks formed in the Primary period were pushed up. More recently, in the Quaternary era, glaciers and rivers flowing from west to east gouged out numerous valleys and fashioned the landscape from which outcrops of hard rock that are resistant to erosion stand out like islands. This is when the relief of the present-day Beaujolais was created with its eastern-facing slopes that descend like a gigantic staircase to the Saône.

Northern and southern Beaujolais have distinctive features and Villefranche-sur-Saône stands on an invisible dividing line between the two parts of the vineyard. The hills in the north are softly rounded and the bottoms of the valleys are filled with sand. It is a region of ancient rocks such as granite, porphyry, shale and diorite. As the granite has decomposed slowly over time, it has left siliceous sands, known locally as *gore*, which can vary in depth from a few tens of centimetres (inches) down to several metres (yards) and are areas of clay and sand. This poor, acid soil lacks organic matter and retains neither moisture nor nutrients, so it is prone to drying out though it is easy to work. This terrain, with other areas of shale, is where the local appellations and Beaujolais Villages wines are grown. The southern area has a larger proportion of sedimentary soil, with clay and limestone being found on the more steeply sloping hills. The soils are richer in limestone and sandstone than in the north. This area is known for its'golden stones', which are coloured by ferrous oxide, giving a warm look to the buildings. The earth is richer and retains moisture better. This is where the AOC Beaujolais wines are grown. In both areas, vines prosper between altitudes of 190 and 550 m (623 and 1804 ft). A background to these two distinct areas is Haut Beaujolais, an area of harder metamorphic rock which at over 600 m (1,968 ft) is covered by pine and chestnut forests and ferns. The best wine-growing land has a south-south-easterly aspect and lies between 190 and 350 m (623 and 1,148 ft).

The Beaujolais region is temperate though it has three competing prevailing climates: a continental influence, a maritime influence and another from the Mediterranean. Depending on the season, each of them can dominate and the change from one to another can be rapid and unexpected, making pressures and temperatures rise or plummet violently. Winters can be cold or wet; spring can be wet or dry; July and August are scorching when the desiccating wind blows up from the Midi, or drenched when there are rain and hail storms; autumn can be wet or hot. The average rainfall is 7.5 cm (2.95 in) and the temperature ranges from -20°C to +38°C (-4°F to +100°F). Throughout the region, however, there are tiny microclimates which do not follow the general rule and vines can flourish in situations which, on the face of it, should not be propitious. Generally speaking, the vineyards have good sunshine and enjoy good conditions for the grapes to ripen.

To describe the grape varieties planted in Beaujolais is particularly simple: 99% of the vineyards are planted with Gamay, often called 'Gamay Beaujolais' locally. In 1395, Philip the Brave banished Gamay from the Côte d'Or, considering it a 'disloyal plant', which it was, when compared with Pinot Noir. However, it is a very adaptable variety which can prosper in many different climates – some 33,000 ha (81,510 acres) are planted with Gamay in France and it is remarkably well suited to the soils of the Beaujolais. It has a trailing habit so has to be staked and supported for the first ten years of its life; in the north of the region you will see fields of vine props holding up the plants. It is susceptible to spring frosts and to the main parasites and vine diseases. The vines can bud early, at the end of March, but more usually in the second week of April. As the Beaujolais saying goes, 'When the vines shine in Saint George's tide, they are not late'. The flowering season is the first fortnight in June and the harvest starts in mid-September.

Varieties other than Gamay are also entitled to the appellation: Pinot Noir and Pinot Gris for red and rosé wines and Chardonnay and Aligoté for white wines. Until the year 2015, the expansion of Pinot Noir planting has been restricted to a total of 15% of the Beaujolais vineyard (currently very much less than that is planted); blends of red or rosé wines using up to a maximum of 15% of Pinot Noir or Pinot Gris, Chardonnay, Melon or Aligoté are also permitted. Vines are pruned in one of two ways: a hard prune, training the plant into the shape of a goblet or fan is used for all appellations, while for the Beaujolais appellation vines are pruned to one stem, known as a 'baguette' (the French word for the typical Fench loaf shape). Vines can also be pruned as cordons in the AOC Beaujolais vineyards.

All the red Beaujolais wines are made according to the same precepts: the bunches are kept whole and there is a short maceration period of three to seven days, depending on the type of wine. The technique used is classic fermentation for the 10–20% of juice produced when the grape skins are broken as the clusters are loaded into the vat; meanwhile intracellular fermentation ensures a quite considerable breaking down of malic acid which releases particular aromas. This is what gives Beaujolais wines their structure and their aromatic characteristics which are both enhanced and individually defined by the soil on which the vines are grown. Because so much of this technique depends on letting the grapes work by themselves, it is very difficult for the wine-maker to control the wine's development reliably in this early stage, given the unpredictablility of the reactions between the volume of must released in relation to the entire content of the vat. On the whole, Beaujolais wines are dry but not tannic, supple, fruity and very aromatic; they are usually 12-13% volume, with a total acidity of 3.5 g/l in terms of H_2SO_4.

One of the common peculiarities in the Beaujolais vineyards is *métayage*, a system from the past but one that has persisted and still lives on. This means that the harvest and certain costs are shared between the grower and the owner, who provides the vineyard, lodgings, a vat room equipped with all that is required to make the grapes into wine, any products required during wine-making as well as the plantations of vines. The grower, or *métayer*, provides all the machinery required for cultivation, engages any workers, pays the pickers at harvest-time and ensures that the vines are kept in perfect condition. These management contracts start on St Martin's Day, 11 November, and many growers find it attractive to use them; 46% of Beaujolais vineyards are managed in this way compared with 45% which are managed by the owner. The remaining 9% of vineyards are run by tenant farmers. It is not unusual for growers to be owners of certain parcels of vineyards and *métayers* as well. A typical Beaujolais vineyard covers 7–10 ha (17–25 acres), and they tend to be smaller in the area of the recognised Crus, where the system of *métayage* dominates, while in the south, where mixed farming is more common, the vineyards are larger. Nineteen co-operatives vinify 30% of the grapes produced, while 85% of the wine is sold by growers and local shippers. AOC Beaujolais is sold by the 216-litre barrel, and AOC Beaujolais Villages and the Crus are sold by the 215-litre barrel. The wine is sold throughout the year but local incomes rise most appreciably when the Vins de Primeur, or new season's wines, are released onto the market. Some 50% of the wine is exported to Switzerland, Germany, Belgium, Luxembourg, Britain, the United States, the Netherlands, Denmark, Canada, Japan, Sweden and Italy.

Beaujolais Nouveau is red or rosé wine that comes only from the non-Cru appellations, usually from the Beaujolais or Beaujolais Villages appelattions. The wines, grown on sandy granite soil in certain parts of Beaujolais Villages, are vinified after a short maceration which lasts only four days, creating soft, light wines with a mouthful of flavour. The colour is not particularly intense and the fruity perfumes sometimes have a hint of ripe banana. There are strict regulations which lay down the criteria the wine must meet and how it can be marketed. By mid-November, the Vins de Primeur are ready to be drunk around the world. In 1956 only 13,000 hl (343,200 gal) of this wine was sold; by 1970 the figure was 100,000 hl (2,640,000 gal), 200,000 hl (5,280,000 gal) in 1976, 400,000 hl (10,560,000 gal) in 1982, 500,000 hl (13,200,000 gal) in 1985, rising to 600,000 hl (15,840,000 gal) in 1990 and 655,000 hl (17,292,000 gal) in 1996. From 15 December, the Crus are tasted and judged, then marketed. The majority of sales of these are made after Easter. Beaujolais wines are not for keeping and most are consumed within two years. However, some particularly good bottles can be kept up to ten years and drink very well. The appeal of these wines lies in their freshness and the delicacy of their nose, reminiscent of flowers — peony, rose, violet, iris — and also certain fruits, including apricot, cherry, peach and summer fruits (berries).

Beaujolais and Beaujolais Supérieur

Nearly half of the wine produced is Appellation Beaujolais. Some 10,320 ha (25,490 acres), mainly south of Villefranche, provide an average of 669,000 hl (17,661,600 gal). Of this, 8,758 hl (231,211 gal) are white wines made from Chardonnay, 20% of the Chardonnay grapes being harvested in the small canton of La Chappelle-de-Guinchay, where the flinty soil of the Crus changes to the limestone terrain of the Mâconnais. In the area of the 'golden stones', east of Bois-d'Oingt and south of Villefranche, the red wines are aromatic with scents that are more fruity than flowery with even some traces of vegetation. These colourful wines are well-structured, if sometimes a little rustic, and keep quite well. In the upper part of the

Azergues valley, in the west of the region, the crystalline rocks give the wine a more flinty flavour which improves with age. The vineyards at the top of the slopes produce more sharply flavoured wines that are lighter in colour but also less heavy in hot years. The nine Caves Coopératives in this area have put a great deal of effort into developing their techniques and have significantly improved the economy of the area which produces about 75% of the 'Vins Primeurs'.

The Appellation Beaujolais Supérieur does not come from a specifically defined area. To qualify for this appellation, the wines must be identified each year and are required to meet certain criteria: the must, at harvest, should have an alcoholic content 0.5° higher than the Appellation Beaujolais wines. Altogether, 4,000 hl (105,600 gal) are declared as Appellation Beaujolais Supérieur each year, principally from the area of AOC Beaujolais.

Villages are scattered and the architecture of the wine-growers' houses is attractive; traditionally they have the cellar at ground level and an exterior staircase leads to a canopied balcony and the living quarters. At the end of the 19th century, large vat rooms were built separately from the proprietor's house. The one at Lacenas, 6 km (4 miles) from Villefranche, which is on the domain of the Château de Montauzan, is the headquarters of the Confrérie des Compagnons du Beaujolais, established in 1947 to regulate and promote Beaujolais wines. Today, it is recognised internationally. The Confrérie des Grappilleurs des Pierres Dorées was set up in 1968 with the task of organising a whole range of festivals and fairs in the region. When it comes to downing a *pot* of Beaujolais, the heavy-bottomed bottle containing 46 cl of wine that is plonked on every bistro table, it goes perfectly with pork scratchings, tripe, black pudding, saucisson and charcuterie of all kinds and also with quenelles topped with cheese. The fresh young wines are a good accompaniment for dishes such as cardoons with bone marrow or gratiné potatoes and onions.

Beaujolais

MICHEL BARROT 1999

◪ 0.27 ha 2,500 ■ 20–29 F

This wine is produced from 3,000 square metres (0.75 acre) of very young vines planted in marl soils. A salmon-coloured rosé, it has a characteristic peardrop aroma. Fresh, aromatic and well-balanced, this 99 is ready to drink now. It would suit being served with grilled meats.

Michel Jean Barrot, Chantemerle, 69380 Charnay, tel. 04.78.43.96.45, fax 04.78.47.98.45 ☑ Y by appt.

CAVE DU BEAU VALLON

Au pays des pierres dorées 1998★

☐ 7 ha 30,000 ■ ♁ 30–49 F

Beaujolais is a multi-faceted region. Its houses are the colour of well-baked bread. This is also the hue of the marl soils, which produce a bright young wine with scents of white fruits and flowers. The wine is very fresh and has the fleshy character of a Chardonnay, qualities that will make it enjoyable to drink throughout the coming year.

Cave du Beau Vallon, Le Beau Vallon, 69620 Theizé, tel. 04.74.71.48.00, fax 04.74.71.84.46, e-mail info@cave-beauvallon.com ☑ Y by appt.

DOM. DE BELLEVUE 1999

■ 5.5 ha 60,000 ■ ♁ 20–29 F

The Saint-Cyr family, one of whom was named 'Vigneron of the Year 1999', produces this wine, as well as the **Beaujolais Blanc 99** cited by the jury. The wine has a rich red colour flecked with purple. Fairly strong berry fruit and floral scents precede a predominantly tannic palate.

EARL Saint-Cyr, Les Perrelles, 69480 Anse, tel. 04.74.60.23.69, fax 04.74.60.23.26 ☑ Y ev. day except Sun. 10am–12 noon 4pm–7pm

BELVEDERE DES PIERRES DOREES 1999

■ 3.5 ha 30,000 20–29 F

The tasting cellars of this co-operative have a panoramic view over the Pierres Dorées. The **Beaujolais Banc 98** cited by the jury is as enjoyable as this brilliant and clear pale red wine. The nose is dominated by the scent of bananas, but raspberries and cherries are also discernible. This well-balanced and fruity 99 is reminiscent of a Nouveau wine. It is ready to drink now.

Cave coop. Beaujolaise de Saint-Laurent-d'Oingt, Le Gonnet, 69620 Saint-Laurent-d'Oingt, tel. 04.74.71.20.51, fax 04.74.71.23.46 Y by appt.

XAVIER BENIER Cuvée Réserve 1998★

□ n.c. 5,000 30–49 F

The product of a wine-making firm established in 1995, this Cuvée Réserve has been matured half in tanks and half in barrels. The resulting 98 has a brilliant and limpid colour with, initially, a marked woody and dried fruit aroma. Fresher floral notes develop later, giving the wine its elegance. A strong, well-balanced wine with character, it will be ready to drink in two years.

Xavier Benier, av. Germain, 69640 Saint-Julien, tel. 04.74.60.51.41, fax 04.74.67.52.58 Y by appt.

CLAUDE BERNARDIN 1999

■ 3 ha 10,000 30–49 F

A family estate which exports nearly 60% of its production. This limpid light red with a sharp, fine, red-berry nose has the style of a Nouveau wine. Well-balanced and easy to drink, it has been made for immediate consumption.

Claude Bernardin, Le Genetay, 69480 Lucenay, tel. 04.74.67.02.59, fax 04.74.62.00.19 Y by appt.

CH. DE BLACERET-ROY

Cuvée de l'Artiste 1998

□ 1.5 ha 8,000 20–29 F

Dedicated to the Beaujolais sculptor, Pierre Fouesnant, this bright, full-bodied wine is still a little young. However, it is well-balanced with pleasant liveliness on the palate. It is probably best to wait a year before drinking it, when it will be enjoyable with either fish dishes or desserts.

Thierry Canard, Ch. de Blaceret-Roy, 69460 Saint-Etienne-des-Oullières, tel. 04.74.03.45.42, fax 04.74.03.52.10 Y by appt.

CAVE DU BOIS DE LA SALLE

Cuvée des Amis 1999

◪ n.c. 8,000 20–29 F

An orange-tinged pink in colour, the Cuvée des Amis of the Juliénas co-operative is bursting with redcurrant aromas. The wine's liveliness and well-balanced body will make it pleasant drinking as of now.

Cave coop. du Ch. du Bois de La Salle, Ch. du Bois de La Salle, 69840 Juliénas, tel. 04.74.04.42.61, fax 04.74.04.47.47 Y by appt.

DOM. DU BOIS DU JOUR 1998

□ 0.25 ha 2,400 20–29 F

At first, the nose of this pale yellow wine with green reflections is reminiscent of a Muscat. The scent of white flowers with overtones of toast develops later. Round and well-balanced, this quaffable 98 should be drunk this year.

Gilles Carreau, Lachanal, 69640 Cogny, tel. 04.74.67.41.40, fax 04.74.67.46.24 Y by appt.

MICHEL CARRON

Coteaux de Terre Noire 1998★

□ 0.5 ha 3,000 20–29 F

Under the same label, Michel Carron has produced both a **Beaujolais Rouge 99**, also cited by the jury, and this yellow-green white wine. The wine has a floral aroma, with developing notes of gingerbread and honey. This full-bodied 98 is persistent and well-balanced. It is ready to drink now, but could also be kept for up to two years.

Michel Carron, Terre-Noire, 69620 Moiré, tel. 04.74.71.62.02, fax 04.74.71.62.02 Y ev. day 8am–8pm

CH. DE CHANZE 1998

□ 0.65 ha 2,000 20–29 F

A *cave coopérative* turns the Chardonnay grapes grown on land surrounding a beautiful 19th-century château into a pale straw-coloured wine. It has a gently floral and citric nose. In the mouth, its initial freshness becomes gradually more unctuous. Well-balanced, pleasant but a little thin, this 98 should be drunk this year.

Cave Beaujolaise de Saint-Vérand, Le Bady, 69620 Saint-Vérand, tel. 04.74.71.73.19, fax 04.74.71.83.45, e-mail C.B.S.V.@wanadoo.fr Y by appt.

LUCIEN ET JEAN-MARC CHARMET

Cuvée la Ronze 1999

■ 4 ha 20,000 30–49 F

Fans of smooth, easy-to-drink wines will enjoy this light red 99. Limpid and bright, it gives off the strong tangy aroma of peardrops.

Lucien et Jean-Marc Charmet, La Ronze, 69620 Le Breuil, tel. 04.78.43.92.69, fax 04.78.43.90.31 Y by appt.

DOM. CHASSELAY

Cuvée des Quatre Saisons 1999★

■ 3 ha 4,000 20–29 F

This vineyard has been owned by the same family for over 300 years. Vines planted on marl soils have produced a rich and limpid ruby wine with pleasant notes of redcurrant and peach. The wine's full-bodied attack has slightly acidic overtones that rapidly blend

with the aromas, resulting in a balanced palate. The Cuvée des Quatre Saisons may be drunk all year round, as the name suggests.
Jean-Gilles Chasselay, La Roche, 69380 Châtillon-d'Azergues, tel. 04.78.47.93. 73, fax 04.78.43.94.41 ev. day except Sun. 9am–12 noon 2pm–6pm

CH. DU CHATELARD

Vieilles vignes 1998

☐ 1.3 ha 8,000 30–49 F

This wine is the product of vines that are almost a century old. It has a green-gold colour, and a gingerbread and dried-fruit nose with hints of menthol. The measured liveliness of this 98 persists satisfyingly in the mouth. A distinctive wine, it is ready to drink now but could wait another year or two. It would complement goat's cheese or white fish.
Robert Grossot, Ch. du Châtelard, 69220 Lancié, tel. 04.74.04.12.99, fax 04.74.69.86.17 by appt.

DOM. CHATELUS DE LA ROCHE

1999★

■ 19 ha 140,000 20–29 F

Saint-Laurent-d'Oignt is on the D 96, near Oignt. This very pleasant rich ruby wine is fragrant with the scents of blackcurrants and mulberries. The powerful, rounded, vinous, well-balanced and long flavour in the mouth dictates that it should be kept for several months. This 99 should be drunk in a year's time.
Pascal Chatelus, La Roche, 69620 Saint-Laurent-d'Oingt, tel. 04.74.71.24.78, fax 04.74.71.28.36 by appt.

MICHEL CHATOUX Vieille vigne 1999

■ 1.5 ha 5,000 20–29 F

With one of the few Beaujolais labels still printed on parchment, this dark red wine has a soft scent of raspberries. Its full body compensates for a shy nose, but a few months' keeping will allow it to develop more character. It will be ready for drinking some time between Christmas and the New Year.
Michel Chatoux, Le Favrot, 69620 Sainte-Paule, tel. 04.74.71.20.50 by appt.

DOMINIQUE CHERMETTE

Cuvée Vieilles vignes 1999

■ 2 ha 15,000 30–49 F

The old vines that produce this ruby wine grow close to the picturesque medieval village of Oingt. With an exotic fruit nose and the aroma of violets on the palate, this is an elegant and fine wine. It is ready to drink now.
Dominique Chermette, Le Barnigat, 69620 Saint-Laurent-d'Oingt, tel. 04.74.71.20.05, fax 04.74.71.20.05 by appt.

DOM. CHEVALIER-METRAT 1999

■ 0.6 ha 5,000 20–29 F

This vineyard, established in 1956, was acquired by Sylvain Métrat 13 years ago. A dark red wine with complex fruity aromas of mulberry, peach and cherry, it lingers nicely on the palate. Its well-balanced and lively character suggests it should be kept for a few months, after which it will complement an informal dinner.
Sylvain Métrat, Le Roux, 69460 Odenas, tel. 04.74.03.50.33, fax 04.74.03.50.33 ev. day 8am–8pm

CLOS DU MUZARD

Cuvée Alain Gardon 1999

■ 1.5 ha 5,000 30–49 F

The wine-making tradition in this family stretches back more than three centuries. This rich, limpid red 99 is redolent of cherries and strawberries. Reasonably full-bodied with a lengthy finish, it is for drinking within the year.
EARL Jean-Claude et Maryse Arnaud, chem. des Oncins, 69210 Saint-Germain-sur-l'Arbresl e, tel. 04.78.47.91.28, fax 04.78.47.91.57 by appt.

OLIVIER COQUARD

Réserve particulière 1999

■ 0.65 ha 1000 30–49 F

This wine-grower has been implementing environmentally friendly practices since taking charge of the vineyard three years ago. The wine has a good purple-red colour and a pleasantly assertive woody nose. It should be kept for a while in order to realise the promise indicated by its upfront attack and rounded, structured tannins.
Olivier Coquard, Chalier, rte de Saint-Fonds, 69480 Pommiers, tel. 04.74.03.92.91, e-mail olivier.coquard@mageos.com by appt.

CH. DE CORCELLES 1998

☐ 1.5 ha 12,000 30–49 F

For 15 years, the Richard family have been the proprietors of this 15th-century château, a listed historical building. The château's splendid cellars produce this bright and limpid pale yellow wine. Intense acacia and hazelnut smells enliven an otherwise light wine that is for drinking within the year.
SA Ch. de Corcelles, 69220 Corcelles, tel. 04.74.66.00.24, fax 04.74.69.60.94 ev. day except Sun. 10am–12 noon 2pm–6.30pm

DOM. DES CRETES

Cuvée des Varennes 1999★★

■ 2.1 ha 15,000 30–49 F

A complex dark red Beaujolais which will reward those willing to wait until late 2001, or perhaps even longer. This promising 99 is a rich wine with a blackcurrant and berry nose, young tannins and good acidity.
GAEC Brondel Père et Fils, rte des Crêtes, 69480 Graves-sur-Anse,

tel. 04.74.67.11.62, fax 04.74.60.24.30, e-mail domaine.descretes@wanadoo.fr ☑ Y by appt.

DOM. DE CRUIX 1999*

■ 11.71 ha 20,000 ▮ 20–29 F

Made from 40-year old vines and sold in serial-numbered bottles, this wine is a fine example of its appellation. It has a light colour and is distinguished by an insistent smell of redcurrants and blackcurrant leaves. A fairly complex flavour on the palate is in harmony with the nose and appears to be at its peak. This 99 should be drunk within the year.

🔑 Jean-Claude Brossette, Dom. de Cruix, 69620 Theizé, tel. 04.74.71.24.74, fax 04.74.72.29.16 ☑ Y by appt.

BERNARD DUMAS 1999

■ 1 ha 2,000 ▮ 30–49 F

Four generations of wine-makers have tended this estate, located 3 km (1¾ miles) from the medieval village of Ternand. It has produced a ruby-coloured wine with lively, pleasant scents dominated by almond over-tones. A well-balanced wine with good structure and length, this 99 will be at its best next spring.

🔑 Bernard Dumas, Ronzières, 69620 Ternand, tel. 04.74.71.38.57 ☑ Y by appt.

VINCENT FONTAINE

Vieilles vignes 1999

■ 1 ha 2,500 ▮ 🌡 20–29 F

Located 1.5 km (1 mile) from a scenic spot with unique views over the Saône valley and the hills of Beaujolais, this vineyard has produced a ruby wine with purple reflections. The wine's rounded attack, accompanied by subtle scents of blackberries and red fruits, does not obscure its youthful tannins. This already appealing 99 will improve if kept for a few months.

🔑 Vincent Fontaine, Les Gondoins, 69480 Pommiers, tel. 04.74.02.59.15, fax 04.74.65.97.68 ☑ Y by appt.

DOM. DES FORETS FULLY 1998

□ 0.8 ha 3,000 🛢 30–49 F

Martine Vermorel has created a bright green-gold wine with a powerful and complex nose from vines grown on marl soils in the shadow of an 18th-century signalling tower. A bold and pleasant attack, followed by hints of honey, contributes to a heady taste. A pleasant wine that should be drunk this year.

🔑 Martine Vermorel, Les Forests, 69480 Marcy, tel. 04.74.67.56.37, fax 04.74.67.51.08 ☑ Y by appt.

DOM. DES FORTIERES 1999

■ 3 ha 6,000 ▮ 🌡 30–49 F

This estate was founded in the 20th century by the grandfather of the current owner. It has produced a lively red vintage with powerful fruit and peardrop smells. A wine whose fruitiness lingers on the palate, it is ready for drinking now. (The Roman cloister of Salles-Arbuissonnas, 2 km [1¼ miles] from the estate, is worth a visit.)

🔑 Daniel Texier, Les Fortières, 69460 Blacé, tel. 04.74.67.58.57, fax 04.74.67.58.57, e-mail dtexier@vins-du-beaujolais.com ☑ Y by appt.

JEAN-FRANCOIS GARLON

Cuvée Vieilles vignes 1999*

■ n.c. 20,000 ▮ 30–49 F

The estate that has made this bright, deep red wine is located near a oenological centre. Unusual, intense flavours of morello cherries, almonds and anise linger on the palate. This full-bodied, fruity wine is well-balanced and distinctive, and has a long finish. It should be drunk within the year.

🔑 Jean-François Garlon, Le Bourg, 69620 Theizé, tel. 04.74.71.11.97, fax 04.74.71.23.30 ☑ Y by appt.

CH. DU GRAND TALANCE 1999

■ 14 ha 123,200 ▮ 🛢 🌡 20–29 F

This estate, which dates back to 1842, has created a very bright and lively wine. Floral aromas mingle with more mineral notes. Fruity, fresh and supple, this 99 is not for keeping but is pleasantly drinkable now.

🔑 Jean-Marc Truchot, GFA du Grand Talancé, Ch. du Grand Talancé, 69640 Denicé, tel. 04.74.67.55.04 ☑ Y by appt.

VIGNOBLE GRANGE-NEUVE 1999

■ 5 ha 20,000 🛢 20–29 F

Housed in a renovated old winery, this estate will soon be able to accept holiday-makers. Its 99 has the sharp but unobtrusive smell of red berries commonly found in such ruby-coloured wines. A pleasant balance of banana notes and supple tannins in the mouth suggests that it should be drunk within the year.

🔑 Denis Carron, chem. des Brosses, 69620 Frontenas, tel. 04.74.71.70.31, fax 04.74.71.86.30 ☑ Y by appt.

DOM. LA CRUISILLE 1999***

■ 0.5 ha 2,500 🛢 20–29 F

In 1986, brothers Hubert and Vincent Laverrière returned to run the family estate in the heart of Theizé, a picturesque village whose buildings are constructed of the local golden stone. Unanimously picked as a *coup de coeur* by the Beaujolais grand jury, their 99 is the product of 40-year old vines planted on marl soils. With a firm, clear ruby colour, it

smells subtly of berries with a hint of cherry. A fairly firm attack reveals strength, body and very ripe fruit flavours. With a long and harmonious finish, this rich and distinguished 99 is a very good example of Beaujolais. It may be enjoyed over the next two to three years.
🗝 Hubert et Vincent Laverrière, GAEC de La Cruisille, rue de la Treille, 69620 Theizé, tel. 04.74.71.22.10, fax 04.74.71.22.90, e-mail gcruisil@terrenet.fr ☑ Y by appt.

DOM. LAFOND 1999*

■ 12.5 ha 20,000 20–29 F

Vines growing on clay soils have produced this very attractive bright garnet-coloured wine fragrant with the fresh scents of raspberries, blackberries and violets. At the moment, the tannins of this powerful 99 are still a little strong, but it will make delightful drinking in one or two years' time.
🗝 EARL Dom. Lafond, Bel Air, 69220 Saint-Lager, tel. 04.74.66.04.46, fax 04.74.66.37.91 ☑
Y ev. day 7h–12 noon 1pm–8pm

DOM. DE LA LOGERE 1999

■ 11.9 ha 10,000 20–29 F

The proprietor has set up a museum of tools used by wine-makers and coopers in this erstwhile hunter's lodge. The estate's 99 vintage is light purple with soft scents of strawberry and lemon. A fine, fresh and smooth Beaujolais with redcurrant flavours, it should be drunk before Christmas.
🗝 Pascal Gayot, La Logère, 69480 Anse, tel. 04.74.67.00.34, fax 04.74.67.20.37
Y by appt.

VIGNOBLE LA MANTELLIERE 1999

■ 2.5 ha 20,000 30–49 F

The Braymand family have been wine-makers since 1895. This fine ruby-coloured wine, which smells of red berries and flowers, is gently spritzy, intriguing the palate without shocking it. Round, tender and smooth, it is certainly enjoyable at the moment, but it is difficult to predict how it will develop.
🗝 Christophe Braymand, Le Bourg, 69620 Le Breuil, tel. 04.74.71.85.77, fax 04.74.71.85.72 ☑ Y by appt.

L'AME DU TERROIR 1999

■ n.c. 120,000 20–29 F

This wine is made by Maison Thorin in Quincié as an own-label brand for the Cora supermarket chain in Belgium. Suffused with the scent of raspberries and mulberries, this limpid ruby wine is very easy to drink. Long and smooth, its light structure dictates that it should be drunk now. Readers should note that the labelling only mentions the wine-maker, Thorin, and not the distributors.
🗝 Cora, Dom. de Beaubourg, B.P. 81, Croissy-Beaubourg, 77423 Marne-la-Vallée Cedex, tel. 04.74.69.09.10, fax 04.74.69.09.28

DOM. DE LA REVOL 1999

■ 1 ha 5,000 20–29 F

The property where this wine was made is located several kilometres from Arbresle, the home of the Thimmonier Museum, dedicated to the inventor of the sewing-machine. It a deep red wine that opens on notes of almonds, ripe fruits and spices. Long in the mouth, full but firm, this wine is still in its infancy and should be kept for a couple of years.
🗝 Bruno Debourg, La Croix, 69490 Dareizé, tel. 04.74.05.78.01, fax 04.74.05.66.40 ☑ Y by appt.

CH. DE LAVERNETTE 1998*

□ 2.5 ha 18,000 30–49 F

An intense yellow wine with green reflections, this vintage is the product of a vineyard known as the 'Vignoble de la Roche'. The wine has a distinctive character with honeysuckle and honey scents accented with hints of menthol. The round and well-balanced palate echoes these notes, and adds a touch of pepper. This 98 has good length, and will be drinkable for the next two years.
🗝 Bertrand and Anke de Boissieu, Ch. de Lavernette, 71570 Leynes, tel. 03.85.35.63.21, fax 03.85.35.67.32, e-mail ba.de-boissieu@wanadoo.fr ☑
Y by appt.

CH. DE L'ECLAIR 1999**

■ 7.8 ha 15,000 30–49 F

This estate was founded by Victor Vermorel, inventor of the shoulder-mounted vine-sprayer, the 'Éclair', and part of the property is dedicated to experiments in all aspects of wine production. The **Beaujolais Blanc 99** cited by the jury joins this lively and persistent red wine on the honours list. Awarded a *coup de coeur* by the Beaujolais grand jury, it is pleasantly intense with a blend of raspberry, strawberry and blackcurrant notes. Fleshy, well-structured and balanced, this 99 is a fine, hefty wine, and may be drunk over the next two years.
🗝 SICAREX Beaujolais, Ch. de l'Eclair, 69400 Liergues, tel. 04.74.68.76.27, fax 04.74.68.76.27 ☑ Y by appt.

CH. DE LEYNES 1998*

□ 2 ha 10,000 30–49 F

The château, whose vineyards used to belong to the monks of Tournus, has a

Maconnais-style arcade, a characteristic feature of the local architecture. The estate's 98 is a bright, limpid straw-coloured wine with amber reflections. A fairly intense hazelnut nose is followed by a fresh and floral flavour in the mouth. The wine's bouquet appears to be at its peak. Well-balanced and rather fine, this wine is for drinking within the year.

Jean Bernard, Les Correaux, 71570 Leynes, tel. 03.85.35.11.59, fax 03.85.35.13.94, e-mail jean.bernard@wanadoo.fr
by appt.

LA CAVE DES VIGNERONS DE LIERGUES 1999

5 ha 20,000 20-29 F

This wine has been made by the oldest cooperative in Beaujolais. It is a brilliant pink wine with pleasant scents of grapes and strawberries. It pleasantly fills the mouth with its fleshiness and floral flavours, and is for drinking straight away.

Cave des Vignerons de Liergues, 69400 Liergues, tel. 04.74.65.86.00, fax 04.74.62.81.20 ev. day except Sun. 8am–12 noon 2pm–6pm

CH. DE LONGSARD 1998

0.5 ha 2,000 30-49 F

The Château de Longsard is an 18th-century château with formal French-style gardens. A gleaming, dark gold wine that has been matured in oak casks is made here. Complex scents of lime, linden and acacia blossoms are given off by this 98, which is vigorous in the mouth, with pronounced mineral notes.

SCI Ch. de Longsard, Ch. de Longsard, 69400 Arnas, tel. 04.74.65.55.12, fax 04.74.65.03.17, e-mail longsard@wanadoo.fr
ev. day 2pm–5.30pm
Du Mesnil

DOM. DU LOUP 1999★★

5 ha 42,000 20-29 F

A rich red wine with dark reflections smells of peonies and spices (cloves). It is elegant and harmonious in the mouth with a rounded, vinous and aromatic palate. This distinctive Beaujolais will make pleasant drinking over the next two years, and will be an enjoyable accompaniment to chicken.

Jean Bosse-Platière, Les Places, 69480 Lucenay, tel. 04.74.09.60.00, fax 04.74.67.67.40

DOM. MANOIR DU CARRA 1999

1.5 ha 3,000 20-29 F

A deep red colour, this wine has strong scents of bananas, raspberries and blackcurrants. Very aromatic but also very young, this still rough-and-ready wine needs time to mature.

Jean-Noël Sambardier, Dom. Manoir du Carra, 69640 Denicé, tel. 04.74.67.38.24, fax 04.74.67.40.61 by appt.

DOM. DE MILHOMME 1999★

n.c. n.c. 30-49 F

The Perrin family have been making wine for over four centuries on their estate near the hilltop village of Ternand. The purple-red 99 is a strongly constituted wine with banana notes and berry fruit scents. A very good example of the AOC, complex, young and well-built, this wine has been made for keeping, and should be allowed to mature for another year or two.

Robert and Bernard Perrin, Dom. de Milhomme, 69620 Ternand, tel. 04.74.71.33.13, fax 04.74.71.30.87
by appt.

PIERRE MONTESSUY 1999

0.75 ha 5,000 30-49 F

Located in an ancient village dominated by a 12th-century château, this cellar has a museum of gemstones and old-fashioned tools. While visiting, one can take the opportunity to taste this light red 99. With characteristic notes of bananas and raspberries and a well-balanced structure, it should be drunk within the year.

Pierre Montessuy, La Chanal, 69640 Jarnioux, tel. 04.74.03.83.13 by appt.

DOM. DU MOULIN BLANC 1999

1.5 ha 13,000 20-29 F

This rich red wine is the product of vines grown on marl soils. It boasts intense smells of bananas, red berries and blackcurrants. Although the full and acidic palate is somewhat rustic, this aromatic wine should be drunk within the year. The estate also presented the jury with a **Beaujolais Blanc**, which received the same mark (30–49 F).

Alain and Danièle Germain, Dom. du Moulin Blanc, Crière, 69380 Charnay, tel. 04.78.43.98.60, fax 04.78.43.98.60
ev. day 8am–8pm

DOM. DES PAMPRES D'OR

Cuvée Vieilles vignes 1999

2 ha 10,000 30-49 F

This estate has been selling directly to the public for over a decade. A limpid red, the Cuveé Vieilles Vignes smells of bananas with a fairly assertive note of blackcurrant, which continues on the palate. Such a lightly structured wine, with characteristic Nouveau aromas, should be drunk within the year.

Paul and Nicole Perras, Dom. des Pampres d'Or, Le Guérin, 69210 Nuelles, tel. 04.74.01.42.85, fax 04.74.01.31.15
by appt.

DOM. PEROL 1999

1.5 ha 5,000 20-29 F

Situated near an enigmatic medieval château that looks down on the city, this property has produced a purple-red wine with pleasing peardrop smells. Well-balanced, despite some residual fizz, this rather light yet fruity wine is for drinking within the year.

🔑 Frédéric Pérol, La Colletière, 69380 Châtillon-d'Azergues, tel. 04.78.43.99.84, fax 04.78.43.90.06 ☑ 𝐓 by appt.

DOM. DE PIERRE FOLLE 1998

☐ 1.5 ha 5,000 30–49 F

This estate is near the Pierre Folles Museum, which is dedicated to the subject of vineyard soils. Chardonnay grapes have produced a golden wine with butter and vanilla scents. Blessed with a well-structured and fruity attack, this 98 is for drinking over the next two years.

🔑 Bouteille Frères, Rotaval, 69380 Saint-Jean-des-Vignes, tel. 04.78.43.73.27, fax 04.78.43.08.94 ☑ 𝐓 ev. day except Sun. 8am–12 noon 1.30pm–7pm

RESERVE DU MAITRE DE CHAIS DE PIZAY 1999★

■ 7 ha 50,000 20–29 F

Château Pizay's tenant farm has produced a clear but dark red wine with intense aromas of red fruits and blackcurrants that continue on to the palate. A wine made in the modern style, this 99 is long and well-balanced with a pleasant tannic structure. It is for drinking within the year.

🔑 Gilles Perez, Pizay, 69220 Saint-Jean-d'Ardières, tel. 04.74.66.26.10, fax 04.74.69.60.66

🔑 Ch. de Pizay

CAVE DE PONCHON 1999★

■ n.c. n.c. 30–49 F

Grown in sandy soils, this brilliant and limpid ruby 99 has a red berry and liquorice nose. A lively attack and delicate tannins contribute to its appeal. Full-bodied and fleshy, it will benefit from being kept for a year, when it will be the perfect accompaniment to sausages.

🔑 EARL cave de Ponchon, Ponchon, 69430 Régnié, tel. 04.74.04.35.46, fax 04.74.69.03.89 ☑ 𝐓 by appt.

DOM. DE POUILLY-LE-CHATEL 1999★★

☐ 0.8 ha 4,000 30–49 F

Bruno Chevalier has been overseeing his family estate for 20 years. He has made a very attractive white Beaujolais. This green-gold wine has a complex array of scents: an initial impression of white peaches is joined by floral and almondy notes, which continue in the mouth. The vigorous attack is followed by a hefty, mouth-filling, yet lively palate. A distinctive wine with good length, it may be enjoyed over the next two years, either as an apéritif or with grilled fish.

🔑 Sylvaine and Bruno Chevalier, Pouilly-le-Chatel, 69640 Denicé, tel. 04.74.67.41.01, fax 04.74.67.37.86, e-mail br.chevalier@free.fr 𝐓 by appt.

DOM. DE ROCHEBONNE 1998★

☐ 0.7 ha 3,000 20–29 F

This family-owned estate, which dates back to the 17th century, only started making white wine 11 years ago. The rich yellow colour of this 98 reflects its concentrated style. Generous apple, linden and spice aromas hit the nose. The wine's strong attack and the complexity of its rounded and lively flavours all contribute to its appeal.

🔑 Jean-François Pein, La Roche, 69620 Theizé, tel. 04.74.71.21.47, fax 04.74.71.21.47 ☑ 𝐓 ev. day 8am–8pm

DOM. DE ROTISSON

Cuvée Tradition 1999

■ 1.66 ha 14,000 20–29 F

This estate changed hands in 1998. The new owner, a wine connoisseur and wine-grower himself, has made this limpid ruby wine with quite intense fruity and spicy aromas. Youthful tannins are still discernible on the aromatic and well-balanced palate. We suggest waiting a few months before drinking this 99.

🔑 Dom. de Rotisson, rte de Conzy, 69210 Saint-Germain-sur-L'Arbresle, tel. 04.74.01.23.08, fax 04.74.01.55.41, e-mail domaine-de-rotisson@wanadoo.fr ☑ 𝐓 ev. day except Sun. 9am–1pm 2pm–7pm

🔑 Didier Pouget

DOM. DES SABLES D'OR 1999★

■ 10 ha n.c. 30–49 F

Grown on sandy volcanic soils and matured in casks, the Sables d'Or has a garnet colour with purple reflections. It has a complex and gently powerful nose where blackcurrant, peach and wild strawberry scents can be detected. Fruity, well-balanced and long, this well-made wine finishes on a tannic note, which suggests that it should be kept a year before drinking.

🔑 EARL Olivier Ravier, Dom. des Sables d'Or, Les Descours, 69220 Belleville-sur-Saône, tel. 04.74.66.12.66, fax 04.74.66.57.50, e-mail olivier.ravier@wanadoo. fr ☑ 𝐓 by appt.

DOM. DES SOURCES 1999

■ 6 ha 8,000 20–29 F

Opening with fresh notes of red berries, this violet-red coloured wine is limpid, fresh and lively. Well-balanced and pleasant, it is for drinking within the year.

🔑 Stéphane Lacondemine, Dom. des Sources, 69460 Le Perréon, tel. 04.74.02.14.20, fax 04.74.02.14.21 ☑ 𝐓 by appt.

DOM. DE TANTE ALICE 1999★★★

☐ 0.4 ha 3,000 30–49 F

This 99 vintage, grown at the foot of the hill of Brouilly in the heart of Beaujolais, by the Tante Alice estate, was awarded a *coup de coeur* by the white Beaujolais grand jury. An elegant, pale yellow wine with almost blue reflections, it is powerful and full-bodied. Pleasing floral and buttery aromas are joined by a note of vanilla. Fresh, long and distinctive, this wine may be enjoyed over the next two years as a worthy companion for the finest food.

SCEA Dom. de Tante Alice, La Pilonnière, 69220 Saint-Lager, tel. 04.74.66.89.33, fax 04.74.66.86.20 by appt.

DOM. DES TERRASSES DE SAINT-PRE 1999

5 ha 40,000 20–29 F

The product of 40-year-old vines growing on south-facing slopes, this is a dark ruby-coloured wine. The red berry nose has a great deal of finesse. Well-balanced, supple and smooth, this 99 has more of the style of a Nouveau wine than one meant for keeping. It should be drunk now.

Jean-Michel Coquard, Chem. du Neyra, 69480 Pommiers, tel. 04.74.62.20.73 by appt.

DOM. DES TREILLES 1999

4.5 ha 12,000 20–29 F

A combination of 80% traditional carbonic maceration with wine that has been given a hot pre-ferment maceration produces this agreeable, limpid cherry-red cuvée. Scents of ripe berry fruits and violets and a satisfying mouth-feel contribute to a well-balanced wine that is for drinking within the year.

Dominique Romy, 1020, rte de Saint-Pierre, 69480 Morancé, tel. 04.78.43 .65.06, fax 04.78.43.65.06 by appt.

JEAN-MARC TRONCY 1999

1 ha n.c. 20–29 F

This distinctive rich ruby wine shows true to type right away with its intense blackcurrant flavours, which linger in the mouth. Well-balanced and reasonably fleshy, this vintage is for drinking within the year.

Jean-Marc Troncy, Le Brêt, 69640 Cogny, tel. 04.74.67.41. 19, fax 04.74.67.41. 19 by appt.

Beaujolais supérieur

ALAIN CHATOUX

Cuvée Vieilles vignes 1999★★

2.5 ha 10,000 20–29 F

A garnet-coloured, brilliant and limpid wine that is the product of 60-year-old vines. Liquorice, pepper and iris scents herald a structured wine with good balance. Harmonious and full-bodied, it has an attractive finish, and should be drunk within the year.

Alain Chatoux, Le Bourg, 69620 Sainte-Paule, tel. 04.74.71.24.02 by appt.

CUVIER DE LA MARTINIERE

1999★

17.27 ha 60,000 30–49 F

The vines that contributed to this cuvée were selected before the grapes were harvested. A rich, limpid and brilliant red wine, it has clean floral (peony) scents that linger in the mouth. Fresh, well-balanced and smooth, this is a quaffing wine that should be drunk within the year. The **Beaujolais Blanc 99** (39–40 F) made by this producer was judged of equal merit by the jury.

Cave beaujolaise de Bully, 69210 Bully, tel. 04.74.01.27.77, fax 04.74.01.14.53 by appt.

Beaujolais Villages

The term 'Villages' was adopted to replace a multitude of commune names that used to be attached to the Beaujolais appellation to identify wines that were considered superior. Nearly all the producers opted for the name Beaujolais Villages.

Thirty-eight communes, including eight in the canton of La Chappelle-de-Guinchay, qualify for the appellation Beaujolais Villages, but only 30 are entitled to add the name of the commune after it. Identifying wines as Beaujolais Villages has been helpful in marketing them since 1950. In 1999, the 6,017 ha (14,862 acres), located mostly between the Beaujolais and the Crus vineyards, produced 356,250 hl (9,405,000 gal) of red wine and 3,188 hl (84,163 gal) of whites.

The wines of the appellation grown nearest the Crus are cultivated under the same terms (pruned either in a goblet or fan shape; the alcoholic content of the must should be 0.5(higher than that required for Beaujolais). Grown on sandy granite soil, they are fruity, smooth wines with a beautiful, rich red colour, typical of the first pressings for the Vins Primeurs. The wines from granite soils on some upper slopes have enough character to develop, and drink well into the following year. Between these two extremes there is every shade of difference; some wines have finesse, a good nose and sufficient body to accompany dishes of all kinds, and gratify every taste; both pike with cream sauce and grilled Charolais steak will be well complemented by a good Beaujolais Villages.

DOM. DES AMPHORES 1999

■ 6 ha 10,000 ▮ 20–29 F

This large estate, which encompasses nine communes, has made a limpid ruby Beaujolais-Villages with an intense raspberry, strawberry and blackcurrant nose. Supple, fresh, long and very flavourful, this wine has been made for drinking in the spring of 2001.

Pascal Gonnachon, La Ville, 71570 Saint-Amour-Bellevue, tel. 03.85.37.42.44, fax 03.85.37.43.01 ☑ Y by appt.

ANTOINE BARRIER 1999

■ 26 ha 200,000 ▮ 20–29 F

That this wine-merchant closely monitors the composition and provenance of his wines is evident in the quality of this selection. Subtle notes of preserved fruits and red berries are discernible on the nose. A vigorous and complex attack heralds a substantial wine that is both lively and rich. The aromas will become more balanced and the tannins softer if the wine is allowed to age a little. In a few months, this 99 will be ready to serve with grilled meats or perhaps a St-Marcellin cheese.

SCAMARK, rue Camille-Desmoulins, 92135 Issy-les-Moulineaux, tel. 01.46.62.76.37, fax 01.46.44.38.32

DOM. DE BEL AIR 1999

■ 6 ha 18,000 ▮ ♁ 30–49 F

This estate has produced a lively and brilliant red wine with pleasant red berry smells. A bold and supple attack is followed by an elegant, full-bodied palate. A slight bitterness on the finish reflects the youth of this 99. It is for drinking within the year.

EARL Jean-Marc Lafont, Bel-Air, 69430 Lantignié, tel. 04.74.04.82.08, fax 04.74.04.89.33 ☑ Y by appt.

DOM. FRANCOIS BEROUJON 1999★★

■ 6 ha 47,000 ▮ ♁ 20–29 F

The cellars which produced this wine have hosted many actors and singers. Garnet-coloured with purple reflections, this splendid wine has a light and harmonious fruity scent of great purity. Its powerful structure is balanced by firm and elegant tannins. A hint of undergrowth on the finish completes the aromatic range of this remarkable 99.

François Beroujon, La Laveuse, 69460 Salles-Arbuissonnas, tel. 04.74.67.52.47, fax 04.74.67.52.47 ☑ Y by appt.

DOM. DU BOIS DE LA BOSSE

Cuvée Prestige 1999★

■ 6 ha 10,000 ▮ 20–29 F

Georges Desprès has been managing the family estate since 1980. He has made a very bright ruby wine with purple highlights. Notes of undergrowth and clay that should develop towards peony combine with a chewy, extremely well-structured and lengthy palate. This 99, which could be served throughout a meal, is ready to drink but could withstand keeping for another year or two.

Georges Desprès, Le Vernay, 69460 Saint-Etienne-des-Oullières, tel. 04.74.03.48.98, fax 04.74.03.31.55 ☑ Y by appt.

GERARD BRISSON 1999

■ 1 ha n.c. ▮ ♁ 30–49 F

Villié-Morgon's town-hall is in a 17th-century château whose wine-tasting cellars host a celebration of Beaujolais Nouveau every year on 11 November. Heading out along the Roman road, you will arrive at Gérard Brisson's estate where vines have been cultivated since 1431. He has made a purple-red wine with a subtle nose. The palate, although well-structured and balanced, is slightly tannic, which suggests that the wine would benefit from being kept for a few months.

Gérard Brisson, chem. des Romains, 69910 Villié-Morgon, tel. 04.74.04.21.60, e-mail gérard.brisson@wanadoo.fr ☑ Y ev. day except Sun. 9am–12 noon 1.30pm–7pm; cl. 2 weeks in Aug., 25–31 Dec.

DOM. DES CHARMEUSES 1999

■ 1.2 ha 6,000 ▮ ⦀ 20–29 F

The label of this old-vine cuvée is adorned with the picture of a rather seductive female grape-picker. A bright and limpid ruby colour, the wine has an attractive redcurrant and cassis nose with a touch of muskiness. Silky tannins follow a pleasing attack. Agreeable from start to finish, this wine should be drunk within the year.

Bruno Jambon, Le Charnay, 69430 Lantignié, tel. 04.74.69.53.93, fax 04.74.69.53.95 ☑ Y by appt.

DOM. CHASSAGNE

Lantignié 1999★

■ 8.96 ha 10,000 ▮ ♁ 30–49 F

The **Beaujolais-Villages Bouquet Rosé 99,** which was judged a very fine wine, was rated equal to this bright purple-red cuvée with a red berry and peach preserve nose. Fleshy, aromatic and harmonious, this wine has a pleasant finish. It should be drunk within the year.

🔑 SCEA Chassagne-Bertoldo, Les Bruyères, 69430 Lantignié, tel. 04.74.04.82.11, fax 04.74.69.25.53 ☑

CORINNE ET ANDRE CHAVEL

Le Perréon 1999

■ 1 ha 7,000 🍷 20–29 F

This estate which is situated at the start of the 'Cadolles' trail, has made a dark red wine with scents of red berries and plums. Supple and well-balanced, this frank and unpretentious 99 is for drinking now.

🔑 André and Corinne Chavel, Le Glabat, 69460 Le Perréon, tel. 04.74.03.24.17 ☑
🍸 by appt.

CH. DU CHAYLARD 1999

■ 5.33 ha 4 500 🛢 20–29 F

Château d'Emeringes and its vineyard have been owned by the Chaylard family since 1636. Forty years ago, when they were obliged to change the estate's designation, they gave it the family name. This is a fruity wine with a brilliant garnet colour. Distinctive and fresh, with fine tannins, this 99 will be ready to drink in a year's time.

🔑 GFA du Ch. du Chaylard, Les Chavannes, 69840 Emeringes-en-Beaujolais, tel. 04.74.04.44.95 ☑ 🍸 by appt.
🔑 J. du Chaylard

CH. DU CHAYLARD Emeringes 1999

■ 5.5 ha 7,000 🍷 20–29 F

Château du Chaylard's tenant grower has made this cuvée. A light ruby wine, it has a seductively fruity nose. Firm tannins give the wine structure and make it suitable for keeping. One to wait for.

🔑 Bernard and Josiane Canard, Les Grandes Vignes, 69840 Emeringes, tel. 04.74.04.44.49, fax 04.74.04.45.16, e-mail bernard.canard@wanadoo.fr ☑
🍸 by appt.

RECOLTE CHERMIEUX 1999★

■ 3 ha 5,000 🍷🌡 30–49 F

This rich ruby 99 is distinguished by wonderfully intense aromas of raspberries, blackcurrants and wild strawberries, which bloom in the mouth, giving it an elegant flavour. A silky wine of such finesse and balance, it will be hard not to drink it within the year!

🔑 Gérard Genty, Vaugervan, 69430 Lantignié, tel. 04.74.69.23.56, fax 04.74.69.23.56 ☑ 🍸 ev. day 8am–8pm

DOM. DES COMBIERS 1999

■ 5 ha 4,000 🍷 30–49 F

The same family has been making wine on this estate, which is located on the Vauxrenard wine trail, for several generations. This deep ruby vintage has powerful scents of raspberries and redcurrants with overtones of more exotic fruits. The attack is both aromatic and lively. The palate is reminiscent of a Nouveau in its lightness. A wine to drink now.

🔑 Yves Savoye, Les Combiers, 69820 Vauxrenard, tel. 04.74.69.92.69, fax 04.74.69.92.69 ☑ 🍸 by appt.

DOM. COTES DE MONTJOLY 1999

■ 6.76 ha 34,000 🍷🌡 30–49 F

This estate, 2 km (1¼ miles) from the Claude Bernard de Saint-Julien Museum has made a purple wine with violet highlights. It has a fresh red berry nose with banana overtones. Fleshy and well-balanced, this 99 is ready to drink.

🔑 Yves Mathieu, Mont-Joli, 69460 Blacé, tel. 04.74.67.51.13, fax 04.74.67.51.96 ☑
🍸 by appt.

DOM. CROIX-CHARNAY

Cuvée Vieilles vignes 1999★★

■ 1 ha 5,500 🍷🌡 30–49 F

A special selection of the Beaujolais grand jury, this cuvée has been made from the harvest of 80-year-old vines. Intense aromas of redcurrant are joined by bilberry flavours in the mouth. An attractive attack and rich, well-structured body make this a delicious wine that will be drinkable over the next two years.

🔑 Jérôme Lacondemine, Dom. Croix-Charnay, 69430 Beaujeu, tel. 04.74.69.29.80, fax 04.74.69.29.80, e-mail domcharnay@aol.com ☑ 🍸 by appt.
🔑 Maillot

F. DESCOMBES 1999

■ 5.4 ha 6,000 🍷 20–29 F

Carefully tended 45-year-old vines produced this deep garnet wine that is redolent of blackcurrants and fresh butter. In the mouth, the wine is structured, flavourful and well-balanced. A 99 that is ready to drink now.

🔑 François Descombes, 69430 Lantignié, tel. 04.74.69.20.33 ☑ 🍸 by appt.

DOM. DES ESSERVIES 1999★

■ 1.7 ha 9,330 🍷🌡 30–49 F

A bright, lively and limpid red wine that is the product of vines planted on arid gravelly soil. Subtle scents of cherries, blackcurrants and raspberries announce a supple and well-balanced wine with harmonious tannins. This wine is ready to drink now, but may be kept for a year.

🔑 Jean-Luc Tissier, 71570 Leynes, tel. 04.74.06.10.10, fax 04.74.66.13.77 ☑
🍸 by appt.

EMMANUEL FELLOT

Cuvée Tradition 1999★

■ 1.5 ha 2,300 20–29 F

This 99, which has a very classic style, is the product of vines planted on steep slopes. It is a richly coloured red wine with elegant notes of red berries, violets and spices. Its flavourful palate has plenty of flesh, and is well-structured and balanced. This distinctive and concentrated wine will be drinkable for the next two or three years.

Emmanuel Fellot, Dom. de Pierre-Filant, 69640 Rivolet, tel. 04.74.67.37.75, fax 04.74.67.39.06 by appt.

DOM. DES FOUDRES 1999★

■ 1 ha 6,000 20–29 F

Gabriel Chevallier, author of the 1934 novel, *Clochemerle*, set in a fictionalised version of Vaux-en-Beaujolais, would have enjoyed this vivid red wine with violet highlights and exuberant fruity scents. The wine's aromas persist on to the fresh and remarkably well-balanced palate. Cheerful and seductive, this wine is for drinking within the year.

Roger and Jean-Philippe Sanlaville, Le Plageret, 69460 Vaux-en-Beaujolais, tel. 04.74.03.24.03, fax 04.74.03.21.77 ev. day 8am–7pm

DOM. DES GAROCHES 1999

■ 0.4 ha 3,000 30–49 F

The Dufaitre family have been wine-makers since 1750. Their garnet-coloured Beaujolais-Villages has charred notes with hints of raspberries and stone fruits. The tannins have character, but this 99 should be kept for a year. It will then be a good partner for coq au vin.

Pierre-Louis Dufaitre, Garanches, 69460 Odenas, tel. 04.74.03.40.16, fax 04.74.03.40.16 ev. day 9am–6pm

GERARD ET JEAN-PAUL GAUTHIER 1999

■ 16 ha 40,000 30–49 F

Brothers Gérard and Jean-Paul Gauthier joined together to create the La Merlatière farm syndicate. They have made a garnet-coloured wine with a redcurrant and cherry nose. It has a full-bodied, fruity and fresh palate, and is for drinking within the year. The estate's **Moulin-à-Vent 99** was also cited by the jury.

GAEC de La Merlatière, M. Gérard Gauthier, 69220 Lancié, tel. 04.74.04.13.29, fax 04.74.69.86.84 by appt.

DOM. DE GIMELANDE 1999

■ 1.2 ha 8,000 30–49 F

The château at Montmelas was remodelled in the Gothic revival style by the 19th-century architect Louis Dupasquier. Domaine de Gimeland has made a dark red Beaujolais-Villages with a fairly intense fruity nose. This powerfully tannic 99 is an excellent wine for keeping.

Armand Large, Dom. de Gimelande, Le Clerjon, 69640 Montmelas, tel. 04.74.67.30.95, fax 04.74.67.47.34 by appt.

DAVID GOBET 1999

■ 1.5 ha n.c. 30–49 F

One half of David Gobet's three-hectare (7½ acre) holding in the commune of Régnié-Durette is devoted to the production of this bright red wine. The wine displays strong banana and floral scents. A pleasing, light wine that is supple and aromatic, it is for drinking now.

David Gobet, L'Hermitage, 69430 Régnié-Durette, tel. 04.74.69.22.10, fax 04.74.69.22.10, e-mail dgobetaol.fr by appt.

DOM. DU GRAND CHENE 1999★

■ 6.5 ha 13,330 30–49 F

There is a century-old tradition of viticulture on this domaine. Some of the vines are 80 years old! Distributed by the Éventail des Vignerons Producteurs at Corcelles, this brilliant light red wine is fruity and fresh. Supple, fleshy and aromatic, it may be enjoyed throughout the coming year.

André Jaffre, 69220 Charentay, tel. 04.74.06.10.10, fax 04.74.66.13.77 by appt.

DOM. DU GUELET 1999

■ 0.8 ha 6,000 30–49 F

The commune of Rivolet is surrounded by a picturesque patchwork landscape of woods, vineyards and pasture. It also contains the quarries that supplied porphyry for the construction of TGV tracks. This is a fairly bright red wine with a delicate raspberry and redcurrant nose. In the mouth, it turns out to be light-bodied, despite the presence of some youthful tannin. Like its stablemate, the **Beaujolais 99** (20–29 F), which was also cited by the jury, it should be drunk this year.

Didier Puillat, Le Fournel, 69640 Rivolet, tel. 04.74.67.34.05, fax 04.74.67.34.05 by appt.

Branciard

DOM. DES HAYES 1999

■ 10 ha 30,000 30–49 F

The renovation of this estate's wine-cellars in 1993 has contributed to the success of this limpid garnet wine with red berry and peach tones. Well-balanced with pleasant tannins, the wine is ready for drinking now.

Pierre Deshayes, Les Grandes-Vignes, 69460 Le Perréon, tel. 04.74.03.25.47, fax 04.74.03.23.90 by appt.

DOM. DE LA BEAUCARNE

Quintessence 1999

■ 2 ha 10,000 30–49 F

This cuvée has been named after a Belgian poet and singer. It is a bright ruby wine with a fragrant nose of redcurrants, blackcurrants and spices. The supple and rounded attack heralds a light wine suitable for immediate consumption.

Michel Nesme, La Combe de Chavanne, 69430 Beaujeu, tel. 04.74.04.86.23, fax 04.74.04.83.41 by appt.

DOM. DE LA BOURDISSONNE

Cuvée Vieilles vignes 1999

■ 1 ha 4,000 ▮ 30–49 F

A limpid garnet wine smelling of cherries, this is the product of 80-year-old vines. Distinguished by promising, but still youthful, tannins, this generously proportioned wine should be kept for a year before drinking.

Nicole and Robert Santiquet-Loup, Dom. de La Bourdissonne, 69460 Vaux-en-Beaujolais, tel. 04.74.03.22.18, fax 04.74.03.28.80 ▣
ev. day 9am–7pm; groups by appt.

DOM. DE LA CHAPELLE DE VATRE Cuvée Allys 1999

■ 2 ha n.c. ▮ 30–49 F

Planted at an altitude of 450 m (1,475 ft), this vineyard surrounds a Norman chapel dating from the 12th century. It has produced a deep ruby wine that smells of preserved red fruits, blackcurrants and cherries. The firm and long palate needs at least a year to develop finesse. Wasn't it said, at the beginning of the 20th century, that Vâtre wines stood up for themselves?

Dom. de La Chapelle de Vâtre, Le Bourbon, 69840 Jullié, tel. 04.74.04.43.57, fax 04.74.04.40.27 ▣ by appt.
Dominique Capart

DOM. DE LA COMBE DES FEES 1999*

■ 1 ha 6,000 ▮ 30–49 F

This estate, established in 1862, was also cited for its **Beaujolais Blanc 98**, but it is this *Villages* that excels. A ruby wine with violet highlights, it develops slowly on the nose, gradually revealing burnt aromas. It fills the mouth with its fleshy, long and well-balanced character. A robust wine that is ready for drinking now, but will remain enjoyable for another year.

Jean-Charles Perrin, La Maison Jaune, 69460 Vaux-en-Beaujolais, tel. 04.74.03.24.55, fax 04.74.03.24.55 ▣
by appt.

DOM. DE LA CROIX SAUNIER

Sélection Vieilles vignes 1999

■ 3 ha 10,000 ▮ 30–49 F

This bright ruby wine with its scents of cherries and hyacinths is the product of extremely old vines. The palate is lively but only just long enough. A wine to be drunk within the year alongside a plate of good charcuterie.

GAEC dom. de La Croix Saunier, Jean Dulac et Fils, 69460 Vaux-en-Beaujolais, tel. 04.74.03. 22.46, fax 04.74.03.28.97 ▣
by appt.

DOM. DE LA FLEUR DE BRUYERE 1999*

■ 2 ha 4,000 ▮ 30–49 F

This richly-coloured red wine, named after a plot of land known as the 'Great Heath', has a pleasing nose of blackcurrants, wild cherries and crushed strawberries. Well-balanced and fleshy, with no assertive tannins, this elegant 99 will be enjoyed over the next two years.

Mireille and Jean-Michel Sauzon, Nety, 69460 Saint-Etienne-des-Oullières, tel. 04.74.03.42.84, fax 04.74.03.42.84 ▣
ev. day 8am–8pm

GERARD ET JEANNINE LAGNEAU 1999**

■ 4,61 ha 7,000 ▮ 20–29 F

As well as making this *coup de coeur* of the Beaujolais-Villages grand jury, Gérard and Jannine Lagneau run a charming four-room *chambre d'hôte*. This purple 99 with violet highlights has the subtle scent of red berries. The palate is characterised by very ripe, almost jammy, fruitiness and mellow tannins. Distinctive, persistent and full-bodied, this exceptional wine will be enjoyable for another two or three years. It will suit being served with red meats, game birds or cheese.

Gérard and Jeannine Lagneau, Huire, 69430 Quincié-en-Beaujolais, tel. 04.74.69.20.70, fax 04.74.04.89.44 ▣
by appt.

DOM. DE LA JOUBETTE 1999*

■ 0.5 ha 1,000 ▮ 20–29 F

The quality of this first vintage produced by Chantal Guigner shows that she is a wine-grower to watch. This clear, bright, garnet wine is fragrant with red berries and undergrowth. In the mouth, it is rounded and well-structured with a subtle fruity aroma. An attractive, concentrated wine, it should be kept for one or two years before drinking.

Chantal Guignier, Le Bourg, 69820 Vauxrenard, tel. 04.74.69.90.65, fax 04.74.69.90.65 ▣ by appt.

DOM. DE LA MADONE

Le Perréon 1999

■ 15 ha 120,000 ▮ 30–49 F

Near the Croix-Rosier pass, Le Perréon is a stop on the wine-lovers' route through the hills of Beaujolais. A dark ruby colour with garnet highlights, this is gently flowery and fruity. A thirst-quenching Beaujolais-Villages with good length, it is ready for drinking now.

Jean Bérerd et Fils, SCEA de La Madone, 69460 Le Perréon, tel. 04.74.03.21.85, fax 04.74.03.27.19 ▣
ev. day except Sun. 9am–12 noon 2pm–7pm

DOM. DE LA MILLERANCHE 1999

■ 4 ha 7,000 20–29 F

The product of granite terraces, this clear, fairly light red wine has a fresh redcurrant and red berry nose. A good attack and a robust and reasonably full-bodied palate indicate that this wine is probably best drunk within the year.

Fernand Corsin, Le Bourg, 69840 Jullié, tel. 04.74.04.40.64, fax 04.74.04.49.36 ☑
Ү by appt.

CUVEE DE LA MOUTONNIERE 1999

■ n.c. n.c. 30–49 F

The Société des Vins de Pizay is a company that markets the wines of several producers. This dark red wine is fragrant with the scent of blackcurrants, raspberries and violets. Persistent and well-rounded in the mouth, it is an unusual and very aromatic wine that should be drunk soon.

NDLR: The attractive label reads: Cuvée de La Moutonnière, *mise en bouteilles à la propriété à Saint-Jean-d'Ardières 69220 pour François de Nanton 69910*.

Sté des vins de Pizay, 69910 Villié-Morgon, tel. 04.74.66.26.10, fax 04.74.69.60.66 Ү by appt.

DOM. DE LA PLAIGNE 1999★★

■ 2 ha 16,000 30–49 F

The estate has produced both this dark ruby Beaujolais-Villages and a **Régnié 99**, which was also cited by the jury. The Beaujolais-Villages is redolent of red berries and blackcurrants. Redcurrant notes are apparent on the palate, which is fat, harmonious and well-balanced. A youthful wine, full of promise, which will be enjoyable for the next three years.

Gilles and Cécile Roux, La Plaigne, 69430 Régnié-Durette, tel. 04.74.04.80.86, fax 04.74.04.83.72 ☑ Ү by appt.

DOM. DE LA ROCHE 1999

■ 6.94 ha 6,000 20–29 F

This light ruby-coloured wine has been made from vines planted on rocky soil. It has an elegant nose of flowers and red berries, and a lively palate. This attractive 99 could accompany most types of food and is probably best drunk within the year.

Alain Démule, La Roche, 69430 Quincié-en-Beaujolais, tel. 04.74.04.31 .37 ☑ Ү by appt.

DOM. DE LA TONNELLE 1999★★

■ n.c. 4,000 20–29 F

La Tonnelle means 'arbour' in French, evoking images of reclining in the shade sipping this youthful, rich ruby-coloured wine. It has a strong scent of raspberries and blackcurrants and a well-balanced and lengthy palate. A concentrated and promising wine that will drink well over the next two years.

Gilles and Nathalie Nesme, Appagnié, 69430 Lantignié, tel. 04.74.04.88.40, fax 04.74.04.88.40 ☑ Ү by appt.

DOM. DE LA TREILLE 1999

■ 2 ha 2,500 30–49 F

The Gauthiers receive visitors in their tasting cellar by appointment. There, you may sample this bright red Beaujolais with its strong, forthright aroma – a 'true' Villages. A classically fruity and well-structured wine, it should be ready for drinking in a few months' time.

EARL Jean-Paul and Hervé Gauthier, Les Frébouches, 69220 Lancié, tel. 04.74.04.11.03, fax 04.74.69.84.13 ☑
Ү by appt.

PATRICK LE BOURLAY 1999

■ 4 ha 10,000 20–29 F

Here is a light-coloured wine with 'nouveau' scents of raspberries and redcurrants. These features, along with a vivid attack and an aromatic and well-balanced palate, all contribute to the jaunty character of this wine. It is best drunk within the year.

EARL Patrick et Odile Le Bourlay, Forétal, 69820 Vauxrenard, tel. 04.74.69.90.44, fax 04.74.69.90.44 ☑
Ү by appt.

DOM. LES MARGOTS 1999★

■ 1 ha 4,000 20–29 F

This wine, made by a family concern, is a bright and clear ruby colour. Redolent of cherries and redcurrants, it has a beguilingly fruity, fresh and well-balanced palate. An easy-drinking wine, it may be opened now, but could equally be kept for one or two years.

André Longin, Les Laforest, Andilleys, 69430 Beaujeu, tel. 04.74.04.83.25, fax 04.74.04.83.25 ☑ Ү by appt.

DOM. LES VILLIERS 1999

■ 5 ha 6,000 20–29 F

The estate received a mention from the jury both for this red wine and its similarly labelled **Blanc 99** (30–49 F). This is a bright ruby-coloured red with a subtle aroma of blackcurrants and ripe berries. Rich and quite well-structured, this Villages is for drinking now.

Lucien Chemarin, Les Villiers, 69430 Marchampt, tel. 04.74.04.37.11 ☑
Ү ev. day 8am–8pm

CH. DES LOGES 1999★

■ n.c. 25,000 30–49 F

The Perréon co-operative holds its tastings in the beautiful vaulted cellars of the Château des Loges. The co-operative's **Brouilly 99**, also marketed under the Château des Loges label, received a citation from the jury. This Beaujolais-Villages is a very dark red wine with aromas of wild cherries and liquorice. Rich, complex and heady, it may be drunk now but could also be kept for one or two years.

Cave Beaujolaise du Perréon, 69460 Le Perréon, tel. 04.74.03.22.83, fax 04.74.03.27.60 ☑ Ү by appt.

DOM. DES MAISONS NEUVES 1999★★★

■ n.c. 5,000 20–29 F

The grower here has particularly distinguished herself with the success of this vintage, her first as the head of the estate. A rich red wine with violet highlights, it has an excellent berry nose with a nuance of undergrowth. Possessing a powerful and fruity structure, this harmonious wine of great finesse is ready to drink now but it could also be stored for a year – perhaps even longer.

Emmanuel Jambon, Le Gonnu, 69460 Blacé, tel. 04.74.60.56.36, fax 04.74.66.70.00 ev. day 8am–6pm

DOM. DU MARRONNIER ROSE 1999

■ 4 ha 5,000 20–29 F

Made from wines grown on sandy granite soils, this light red 99 has the aroma of peardrops characteristic of young wines. Aromatic and smooth, this nouveau-style wine is for drinking now.

Sylvain and Nathalie Dory, Le Bourg, 69820 Vauxrenard, tel. 04.74.69.90.80, fax 04.74.69.90.80 by appt.

DOM. CHRISTIAN MIOLANE 1999★

■ 10 ha 15,000 20–29 F

The village of Salles-Arbuissonas is renowned for the cloister of its 12th-century priory and the chapter of Benedictine canonesses who lived there from 1300 until the French Revolution. This clear ruby wine has an elegant nose of blackcurrants and grapes. Well-structured and full-bodied, it is fresh and lively on the palate. A fruity and well-balanced 99, which will be enjoyable for the next two years.

EARL Dom. Christian Miolane, La Folie, 69460 Salles-Arbuissonnas, tel. 04.74.67.52.67, fax 04.74.67.59.95 by appt.

CH. DE MONTMELAS 1999★★

■ 2.5 ha 5,000 30–49 F

Rebuilt in the 19th century on the ruins of a tenth-century fortress, the so-called 'Sleeping Beauty' château has been in the d'Harcourt family since 1566. This well-made vintage has been matured in the cellars of the château. It is a dark red Villages redolent of raspberries and cherries. An attractive attack, fine tannins and exceptional aromas all combine to create an elegant and lengthy wine.

SARL d'Harcourt, Ch. de Montmelas, 69640 Montmelas, tel. 04.74.67.32.94, fax 04.74.67.30.54, e-mail chateau.de.montmelas@wanadoo.fr by appt.

DOM. PERRIER 1999

■ 9 ha 18,000 30–49 F

The Perrier family has tended this vineyard since 1864. Their light ruby-coloured wine glints in the light. It has a well-developed nose of ripe bananas and red berries. A smooth and well-structured wine, it should be drunk within the year, preferably in the company of good friends.

Marlyse and Gérard Perrier, Le Saule, 69430 Lantignié, tel. 04.74.04.88.93, fax 04.74.04.88.93 by appt.

DOM. DES QUARANTE ECUS 1999

■ 1.5 ha 10,000 30–49 F

This estate is also a Gîte de France. It has produced a ruby wine with complex flowery and fruity scents. On the palate, it is aromatic and light with soft tannins. A wine that would accompany chicken well, it should be drunk within the year.

Bernard Nesme, Les Vergers, 69430 Lantignié, tel. 04.74.04.85.80, fax 04.74.69.27.79 by appt.

CAVE BEAUJOLAISE DE QUINCIE 1999★

■ 5 ha 30,000 20–29 F

This is a bright, but deeply coloured red wine with a very pleasant red fruit nose. Robust and distinctive, if a little harsh with young tannins for now, this lively 99 will develop into a fine wine in a year or two. The **Brouilly** (30–49 F) of the same vintage was also awarded a star by the jury.

Cave coopérative de Quincié-en-Beaujolais, 69430 Quincié-en-Beaujolais, tel. 04.74.04.32.54, fax 04.74.69.01.30 by appt.

DOM. DE ROCHEBRUNE 1999

■ 6 ha 2,000 20–29 F

To get to the estate which has made this Villages 99, one must descend from Le Perréon through the beautiful vineyards of Saint-Etienne-des-Oullières. With its very bright and clear ruby colour, this wine is redolent of black pepper and red berries. Not for immediate consumption, it is a fruity and well-structured wine that will need time for its tannins to soften.

EARL dom. de Rochebrune, Le Pont-Mathivet, 69460 Saint-Etienne-des-Oullières, tel. 04.74.03.46.41 by appt.

Xavier Dumont

JOEL ROCHETTE 1999★

■ 1.98 ha 15,000 20–29 F

Matured in the estate's new *chai*, this is a rich ruby-coloured wine with a rather shy nose. On the palate, however, it is attractively balanced with silky tannins. A well-made, lengthy 99, it may be drunk over the next two years.

Joël Rochette, Le Chalet, 69430 Régnié-Durette, tel. 04.74.04.35.78, fax 04.74.04.31.62 by appt.

CH. SAINT-VINCENT 1999

■ 5.5 ha 42,000 20–29 F

The château, which dates from 1880, has produced a wine the colour of black cherries. It has a powerful nose of bananas and

blackcurrant leaves. Lively, with well-modulated tannins, this is a 99 that is ready for drinking.
Philippe de Vaublanc, Le Saint-Vincent, 69430 Quincié, tel. 04.74.04.39.59

DOM. DE SERMEZY 1999★★

■ 5 ha 12,000 20–29 F

This wine is the product of just part of the extensive 12 ha (30 acre) vineyard. Bright red in colour, it has a powerful flowery and fruity nose. Young tannins combine with a fresh attack and persistent fruit aromas to make for a very satisfying wine that should be drunk within the year.
Patrice Chevrier, Dom. de Sermezy, 69220 Charentay, tel. 04.74.66.86.55, fax 04.74.66.86.55, e-mail pchevrier@free.fr
by appt.

DOM. DU TRACOT

Cuvée Côte d'Appagnié et des Pins 1999

■ 9 ha 90,000 30–49 F

Pebbly granitic soils have given a very dark, almost opaque, wine with an aroma of very ripe red berries softened with a hint of vanilla. At the moment, this otherwise well-structured wine is too tannic. It needs to mature for a year or two.
Henri and Jean-Paul Dubost, Le Tracot, 69430 Lantignié, tel. 04.74.04.87.51, fax 04.74.69.27.33, e-mail dubost@francebeaujolais.com ☑
by appt.

TROPHEE DIRIET 1999★

■ 8 ha 3,000 30–49 F

Every year, the Beaujeu Wine Championship awards the Diriet Trophy to the best Beaujolais-Villages. This year the Saint-Julien cellar won it for the first time. Their dark red wine has a well-developed red-fruit nose dominated by the scent of raspberries. In the mouth, elegant fruit, good body and well-balanced structure all combine to make this a wine that will continue to be enjoyed over the next two years. The **Beaujolais de la Cave de Saint-Julien 99** also received a citation.
Cave beaujolaise de Saint-Julien, Les Fournelles, 69640 Saint-Julien, tel. 04.74.67.57.46, fax 04.74.67.51.93, e-mail stjulien@vins-du-beaujolais.com ☑
by appt.

CH. DE VAUX

Cuvée traditionnelle 1999

■ 3 ha 20,000 30–49 F

This wine is the product of a small château, parts of which date back to the 12th century. The château's cellars are located in the centre of Vaux-en-Beaujolais, where Chevallier set his celebrated novel *Clochemerle*. The clear ruby-coloured wine has red berry aromas accented with a subtle note of undergrowth. Raspberry and strawberry flavours are apparent on the supple palate. A wine for immediate consumption.
EARL Jacques de Vermont, Le Bourg, 69460 Vaux-en-Beaujolais, tel. 04.74.03.20.03, fax 04.74.03.24.10 ☑
by appt.

CH. DES VERGERS

Cuvée Tradition 1999

■ 18 ha 35,000 30–49 F

The roof of this château is shaped like the upside down hull of a ship. Its cellars have produced a garnet-coloured Villages with powerful aromas of morello cherries and blackcurrants. Fairly alcoholic and tannic on the palate, this distinctive and persistent young wine should be allowed to mature for a few months before drinking.
GFA Les Vergers du Chayla, Les Vergers, 69430 Lantignié, tel. 04.74.04.85.63, fax 04.74.04.83.50 ☑ by appt.
Robert du Chayla

HENRI DE VILLAMONT

Les Trois Grâces 1999★★

■ n.c. 18,000 30–49 F

This Beaune merchant's **Chambellan en Moulin-à-Vent 98** (50–69 F) was awarded one star by the jury. His Beaujolais-Villages has a complex nose of ripe berries with vinous overtones, which complement its rich and lively ruby colour. It has an agreeable well-structured palate with a concentrated flavour. A generous wine in the style of a *petit cru*, it will be enjoyable for the next two to three years.
Henri de Villamont, rue du Dr-Guyot, 21420 Savigny-lès-Beaune, tel. 03.80.24.70.07, fax 03.80.22.54.31, e-mail hdv@planetb.fr
ev. day except Tue. 10am–6.30pm; Thu. 2pm–6.30pm; cl. 15 Nov.–Easter

Brouilly and Côte de Brouilly

On the last Saturday in August, the vineyards ring with song and music. Even though the harvest has not begun, crowds of walkers carrying baskets clamber 484 m (1,588 ft) up Mont Brouilly to the top where, near the chapel, bread, wine and salt are given away. From the summit there is a panoramic view over the Beaujolais, the Mâconnais, the Dombes and the Mont d'Or. There are two sister appellations next to each other, Brouilly and Côte de Brouilly, which have had many disputes about the precise limits of their territories.

Côte de Brouilly is an AOC, on the slopes of the mount which is hard granite and greenish-blue shale, nick-named 'green horn', or diorite. The mount is the remains of ancient volcanic activity or, according to legend, where the giant who dug out the Saône emptied his hod. Production, 18,800 hl (496,320 gal) from 325 ha (650 acres), covers four communes: Odenas, Saint-Lager, Cercié and Quincié. The Brouilly appellation runs around the foot of the mount, covering 1,300 ha (3,211 acres) and producing 75,000 hl (1,980,000 gal). Other neighbouring communes are Saint-Étienne-la-Varenne and Charentay while the famous 'Pisse Vieille' vineyard is in the Cercié commune.

Brouilly

CH. DE BAGNOLS 1998★

■ 9 ha 10,000 30–49 F

The Château de Bagnols, which dates from the 18th century, is located 700 m (half a mile) from a Norman church. The château and its estate are exclusively engaged in wine production. This bright, deep ruby-coloured cuvée is redolent of red berries. The pleasantly generous palate is aromatic and supple with good tannins. A wine that would nicely complement roast red meats, it should be drunk within the next two years.

EARL Alain Ravier, Bagnols, 69460 Saint-Etienne-la-Varenne, tel. 04.74.03.42.77, fax 04.74.03.42.77
ev. day 10am–12 noon 2pm–6pm

DOM. DE BERGIRON 1999

■ 5.75 ha 3,000 30–49 F

In 1995, this family-run estate refurbished its cellars. It has produced a fairly deeply coloured wine with a subtle nose of red berries. The supple, light and elegant palate ends on a mineral note. This highly typical, distinctly graceful wine, is ready for drinking now.

Jean-Luc Laplace, Bergiron, 69220 Saint-Lager, tel. 04.74.66.88.42 by appt.

DOM. BERTRAND 1998★★

■ 2.5 ha 8,000 30–49 F

The Bertrand estate at the foot of the Brouilly hill has made a rich ruby wine with both the fragrance and the flavour of ripe berries. It has an excellent attack and well-structured tannins. The understated power of this full and round 98 is leavened with a touch of spiciness. It will keep well for two or three years.

Jean-Pierre and Maryse Bertrand, Bonnège, 69220 Charentay, tel. 04.74.66.85.96, fax 04.74.66.72.46
by appt.

DOM. LIONEL BERTRAND Bonnège 1999★

■ 1.7 ha 13,330 30–49 F

This wine is the product of Bonnège, a tenant farm managed by young winemaker Lionel Bertrand. It is marketed by the Eventail des Vignerons à Corcelles group. A deep purple colour, the wine gives off a subtle scent of verbena and new-mown hay. A fresh attack is followed by a supple and harmonious palate with soft tannins. A wine with character and finesse, this Brouilly 99 is for drinking now.

Lionel Bertrand, 69220 Charentay, tel. 04.74.06.10.10, fax 04.74.66.13.77
by appt.

CH. DU BLUIZARD 1998★

■ 8 ha 60,000 50–69 F

Jean de Saint-Charles owns 43 ha (106 acres) of vineyards in Beaujolais. He submitted both an accomplished **Beaujolais-Villages blanc 99** (30–49 F) and this lively red Brouilly to the selectors. The latter is bright red with a powerful cherry nose. On the palate, it tastes of wild cherries with hints of hazelnuts, spices and wood. Full, attractive and gently tannic, the wine is ready to drink now, and would go well with poultry.

SCE des Dom. Saint-Charles, Le Bluizard, 69460 Saint-Etienne-la-Varenne, tel. 04.74.03.3 0.90, fax 04.74.03.30.90
by appt.
Jean de Saint-Charles

PIERRE CHANAU 1999

■ n.c. 150,000 30–49 F

A bright, rich and lively red wine with a slightly closed nose of red-berry preserves mixed with a hint of peach-skin. On the palate, it has a lively attack, aromatic body and mellow tannins. This well-made wine will be enjoyable over the next two years.

Chanut Frères, Les Chers, 69840 Juliénas, tel. 04.74.06.78.00, fax 04.74.06.78.71, e-mail auf@free.fr by appt.

DOM. CRET DES GARANCHES 1999★★

■ 8 ha n.c. 30–49 F

A clear garnet-coloured wine distinguished by a powerful blackcurrant nose, this elegant cuvée is fat, well-rounded and long. It will be enjoyable for another one or two years, and is best served with red meat or game birds.

Yvonne Dufaitre, Dom. Crêt des Garanches, 69460 Odenas, tel. 04.74.03.41.46, fax 04.74.03.51.65
by appt.

DOM. DIT BARRON 1998★

■ 9 ha 10,000 ▮ 30–49 F

This 14 ha (35-acre) estate was established in 1983. It has produced a deeply coloured red wine with a delicate and harmonious nose of ripe berries. On the palate, its forthright, aromatic and well-structured character indicates that the wine is at its peak. It will remain there for another two years.

🔑 Gilles Aujogues, Les Bruyères, 69220 Cercié-en-Beaujolais, tel. 04.74.66.87.59, fax 04.74.66.72.55 ☑ Y by appt.

HENRY FESSY Cuvée Pur Sang 1998★

■ n.c. 4,000 ▮ 🌡 50–69 F

A bright red wine with well-developed aromas of wild cherries and other stone fruits. Fine, fresh and aromatic, this elegant wine should be kept for a year before drinking.

🔑 SCI Vignoble de Bel-Air, Bel-Air, 69220 Saint-Jean-d'Ardières, tel. 04.74.66.00.16, fax 04.74.69.61.67, e-mail vins-fessy@wanadoo.fr ☑ Y by appt.

🔑 Henry Fessy

JEAN-FRANCOIS GAGET 1998★

■ 6.3 ha 10,000 ▮ 30–49 F

As well as this Brouilly 98, Jean-François Gaget has made a **Beaujolais-Villages 99** that was also cited by the jury. The Brouilly has fine powerful scents of preserved fruit and a supple, full-bodied palate with soft tannins. It will be enjoyable over the next two years as a pleasant accompaniment to red meats in sauces.

🔑 Jean-François Gaget, La Roche, 69460 Odenas, tel. 04.74.03.46.23, fax 04.74.03.51.40 ☑ Y by appt.

GRAND CLOS DE BRIANTE 1999

■ 15 ha 60,000 ▮ 🌡 30–49 F

This bright, rather pale ruby Brouilly has a good aroma of almonds and roses. The lively, almost vigorous attack leads on to a palate that is still very youthful. This wine should be kept for one or two years to allow it to achieve its balance.

🔑 GFA des Beillard, Briante, 69220 Saint-Lager, tel. 04.74.09.60.00, fax 04.74.67.67.40

DANIEL GUILLET 1999★

■ 1.5 ha 10,000 ◖▮◗ 30–49 F

A clear ruby wine made from vines growing on sandy soil, this Brouilly has an attractively forthcoming nose of raspberries and other red fruits. A rich and very well-balanced impression develops on the palate. Fruity and vinous with round tannins, this elegant wine should be drunk within the next two years. The **Beaujolais-Villages Vieilles Vignes 99** by the same maker was also awarded a star; it is a very good wine for the price (20–29 F).

🔑 Daniel Guillet, Les Lions, 69460 Odenas, tel. 04.74.03.48.06, fax 04.74.03.48.06 ☑ Y by appt.

CH. DE LA CHAIZE 1998

■ 95.7 ha 432,000 ▮ ◖▮◗ 30–49 F

Built in 1676, the château was designed by Mansart, Louis XIV's architect, and its gardens by Lenôtre, who planned the gardens at Versailles. In 1996 the château and its cellars, which are listed, hosted the wives of the heads of state who were attending the G7 summit in Lyons. The 98 vintage is a bright, deep cherry-red colour. Its nose is a pleasing combination of cherries, blackcurrants and mulberries with floral overtones. The palate, however, needs time to mature. Keep for one to two years.

🔑 Marquise de Roussy de Sales, Ch. de La Chaize, 69460 Odenas, tel. 04.74.03.41.05, fax 04.74.03.52.73, e-mail chateaudelachaize@wanadoo.fr ☑ Y by appt.

DOM. DE LA MAISON ROSE 1999★★

■ n.c. n.c. ▮ 30–49 F

This négociant's **Moulin-à-Vent, Champ de Cour 99** was as highly rated by the jury as this dark red Brouilly. It begins with quite powerful and complex aromas of ripe red berries. On the palate, the wine is supple with rich, soft tannins. Well-balanced, pleasing and distinctive, it may be enjoyed over the next three years.

🔑 Jacques Charlet, 71570 La Chapelle-de-Guinchay, tel. 03.85.36.82.41, fax 03.85.33.83.19

DOM. DE LA PISSEVIEILLE 1999

■ n.c. 27,000 ▮ 🌡 30–49 F

This wine comes from the *climat* of La Pissevieille, whose name it carries. A rich red colour, it has a nose of ripe berries. Although quite generous and full-bodied, the wine has not yet reached its full potential and will need further maturation in the bottle.

🔑 Mme Gaillard, 435, rte du Beaujolais, 69220 Cercié-en-Beaujolais, tel. 04.74.09.60.00, fax 04.74.67.67.40

DOM. M. LARGE 1999

■ 1.2 ha 5, 330 ◖▮◗ 30–49 F

M. Large's vineyards are on the steep granite and schist slopes of Mont Brouilly. He has made a **Côte de Brouilly 99**, cited by the jury, together with this bright garnet-coloured wine. A nose of blackcurrants and cherries is accented by a hint of peonies. The powerful attack, which echoes the style of the nose, is dazzling. On the palate, it is relatively lean, indicating that it should be drunk in 2001.

🔑 Michel Large, 69460 Odenas, tel. 04.74.06.10.10, fax 04.74.66.13.77 ☑ Y by appt.

DOM. DE LA ROCHE SAINT MARTIN

■ 6.3 ha 20,000 ▮ 🌡 30–49 F

From his premises near the Croix Briante crossroads, Jean-François Béréziat offers two accomplished wines. Their labels show a gold *taste-vin*, with the chapel of Brouilly in the

background. The **Côte de Brouilly** received the same mark as this lively red Brouilly. The wine has a subtle aromatic nose with banana overtones. Rounded and fairly substantial with good fruit tannins, this appetising 99 is ready to drink now.
Jean-Jacques Béréziat, Briante, 69220 Saint-Lager, tel. 04.74.66.85.39, fax 04.74.66.70.54 by appt.

DOM. DE LA SAIGNE 1999

0.5 ha 3,500 30–49 F

The estate, established in 1957, has matured this garnet-coloured wine in oak barrels. Soft aromas of red fruits (cherries) develop slowly. The palate develops fascinatingly, the supple attack followed by a harmonious balance of tannins and vinosity.
Lenoir Fils, Cimes de Cherves, 69430 Quincié-en-Beaujolais, tel. 04.74.69.02.03, fax 04.74.69.01.45 by appt.

JEAN LATHUILIERE

Pisse-Vieille 1999★

10 ha 50,000 30–49 F

The old story that gave its name to this renowned *climat*, or plot, originated on these south-facing slopes. This wine's colour, ruby with garnet highlights, and clean red fruit and spice scent are wholly characteristic of its locality. The palate is fleshy with mellow tannins and fresh aromas. Harmonious and elegant, it will be drinkable for the next two years.
Jean Lathuilière, La Pisse-Vieille, 69220 Cercié-en-Beaujolais, tel. 04.74.66.81.80, fax 04.74.66.70.55 by appt.

DOM. DU CH. DE LA VALETTE 1999

2.74 ha 14,000 30–49 F

Jean-Pierre Crespin purchased this vineyard in 1983. His vines, growing on the soft soil of Mont Brouilly, are now 45 years old. The 99 vintage produced a violet-ruby wine that has a red-berry nose with overtones of red stone fruits and spices. Its rich tannic structure is highly promising, but will need at least a year to show at its best. One to try.
Jean-Pierre Crespin, Le Bourg, 69220 Charentay, tel. 04.74.66.81.96, fax 04.74.66.71.72 by appt.

LA VANDAME 1999★

n.c. n.c. 30–49 F

This Villefranche négociant has made a **Beaujolais-Villages Château de Vauxonne 99**, which was awarded a star, and a **Juliénas Domaine Grand Croix 99**, also cited by the jury, as well as this lively and bright ruby wine. It has a good red-berry nose and a rounded palate with pleasant aromas and soft tannins. Well-balanced and long, this wine will still be enjoyable in two years' time.
Dupond d'Halluin, B.P.·79, 69653 Villefranche-en-Beaujolais, tel. 04.74.60.34.74, fax 04.74.68.04.14

LE JARDIN DES RAVATYS 1999★★

7 ha 10,000 30–49 F

This estate was bequeathed to the Insititut Pasteur by Mathilde Courbe in 1937. It has produced a brightly coloured red wine with potent aromas of raspberry, blackcurrant and violet that are also very evident on the palate. An initial roundness is balanced by underlying tannic and acid notes. It would be worth letting this wine age for three or four years before serving it with game. An enjoyable way to support the Institute's research.
Institut Pasteur, Ch. des Ravatys, 69220 Saint-Lager, tel. 04.74.66.47.81 by appt

DOM. DE MONTBRIAND 1999

3 ha 18,000 100–149 F

Pierre André of Aloxe-Corton, one of the important merchants of Burgundy's Côte d'Or, also produces Beaujolais. The estate's **Juliénas, Domaine des Poiriers 98** (70–99 F), was cited by the jury. This ruby-coloured Brouilly with violet highlights has a nose of very ripe red berries, preserves and a hint of undergrowth. The palate is fruity, supple, charming and persistent, making for a very likeable wine that is best drunk within the year.
Pierre André, Dom. de Montbriand, Ch. de Corton André, 21420 Aloxe-Corton, tel. 03.80.26.44.25, fax 03.80.26.43.57, e-mail pandre@axnet.fr

PARDON ET FILS Les Quartelets 1998

n.c. 4,000 30–49 F

This Beaujeu négociant house was established in 1820. Its Brouilly 98 is an intensely ruby-colured wine with violet highlights. The wine's fruity and flowery aroma nicely balances its slightly tannic finish. Aromatic and well-structured, this is a bottle for drinking now.
Pardon et Fils, 39, rue du Gal-Leclerc, 69430 Beaujeu, tel. 04.74.04.86.97, fax 04.74.69.24.08, e-mail pardon-fils.vins@wanadoo.fr by appt.

DOM. ROLLAND 1999

n.c. 80,000 50–69 F

The fifth generation is now running the family wine business that has produced this clear, dark garnet wine. There is a hint of muskiness in the predominantly red-berry nose. The same lively and elegant aromas are more subtly perceptible on the palate and reassert themselves at the finish.
Pierre Ferraud et Fils, 31, rue du Mal-Foch, 69220 Belleville, tel. 04.74.06.47.60, fax 04.74.66.05.50, e-mail ferraud@asi.fr by appt.

DOM. ROLLAND-SIGAUX 1998★

17 ha 1,500 30–49 F

This estate uses the traditional wine-making technique known as *pied de cuve*, in which a starter culture of must from an earlier harvest is used to kick-start the fermentation.

The result is a clear ruby wine with a fruity nose. Powerful and structured, it nevertheless maintains a certain roundness, and is a good example of its *cru*. It should be drunk within the next two years.
🔑 Dom. Rolland-Sigaux, Les Sigaux, 69460 Odenas, tel. 04.74.03.42.23, fax 04.74.03.48.41 ☑
🍷 ev. day except Sun. 8am–7pm
🔑 Rolland

DOM. RUET 1999★★

■ 3 ha 22,000 🍾 🌡 30–49 F

Another successful wine from the estate whose 98 was declared a *coup de coeur* last year by the jury. Jean-Paul Ruet, in Voujon, is worth a visit. His vines grow on south-facing granitic slopes, an advantageous location that has contributed to the character of this dark garnet wine with elegant notes of overripe fruit, mulberries and cherries. The very full and round palate – ample with well-structured, lengthy tannins – is a triumph. You will love this wine now, and it will continue to please for the next three or four years.
🔑 Dom. Jean-Paul Ruet, Voujon, 69220 Cercié-en-Beaujolais, tel. 04.74.66.85.00, fax 04.74.66.89.64, e-mail ruet.beaujolais@wanadoo.fr ☑
🍷 by appt.

DOM. DE SAINT-ENNEMOND 1999

■ 5.5 ha 30,000 🍾 🌡 30–49 F

The 15 ha (37-acre) estate makes two wines and also offers bed and breakfast for visitors. Its Brouilly 99 has bright ruby colour and a pleasant fresh berry nose. Structured tannins indicate that the wine should be stored for a year or two. From the same vintage, the estate has made a **Beaujolais-Villages** that was also cited by the jury, and noted for being good value (20–29 F).
🔑 Christian Béréziat, Saint-Ennemond, 69220 Cercié-en-Beaujolais, tel. 04.74.69.67.17, fax 04.74.69.67.29, e-mail christian.bereziat@wanadoo.fr ☑
🍷 ev. day 8am–8pm

CH. DE SAINT-LAGER 1999

■ 8.5 ha 55,000 🍾 🌡 30–49 F

The estate, which dates back to the 14th century, is owned by the Château de Pizay. It has produced a wine with an attractive rich red colour and a good red-berry nose. Light and well-balanced, this very rounded 99 should be drunk within the year.
🔑 Denis Geoffray, Ch. de Saint-Lager, 69220 Saint-Lager, tel. 04.74.66.26.10, fax 04.74.69.60.66 ☑ 🍷 by appt.
🔑 Ch. de Pizay

DOM. JEANNE TATOUX

Garanche 1999

■ 3 ha 9,790 🛢 30–49 F

Vines grown on poor hillside soils have produced a rich red wine that is marketed by the Eventail des Producteurs à Corcelles. A raspberry and blackcurrant nose and a supple, rounded palate declare that this wine should be drunk now, preferably with a *terrine*.
🔑 Jeanne Tatoux, 69220 Charentay, tel. 04.74.06.10 .10, fax 04.74.66.13.77 ☑
🍷 by appt.

DOM. BENOIT TRICHARD 1999★★

■ n.c. 25,000 🍾 🌡 30–49 F

As well as a **Moulin-à-Vent 98** (50–69 F) cited by the jury, this highly regarded estate has made a very attractive deep garnet Brouilly with powerful scents of both black and red-berry fruits. A fleshy, well-rounded attack is supported by fruity and spicy aromas. Harmoniously structured and lengthy, this wine will dazzle palates for the next two years.
🔑 Dom. Benoît Trichard, Le Vieux-Bourg, 69460 Odenas, tel. 04.74.03.40.87, fax 04.74.03.52.02, e-mail dbtricha@club-internet.fr ☑
🍷 by appt.

FREDERIC TRICHARD 1998★

■ 1.47 ha 10,000 🍾 🛢 🌡 30–49 F

The estate, 1 km (2/3 mile) from Château de Saint-Lager, has produced a clear purple wine with a delicate nose of red berries. After a supple and round attack, it has a pleasing impression on the palate. Well-balanced and harmonious, this attractive 98 is at its peak; it should be drunk within the year.
🔑 Frédéric Trichard, Polanche, 69220 Saint-Lager, tel. 04.74.66.07.16, fax 04.74.66.81.60 ☑ 🍷 ev. day 7.30am–12 noon 1.30pm–7pm

GEORGES VIORNERY 1999★★

■ 5.15 ha 10,000 🍾 30–49 F

Traditional Beaujolais wine-making methods have created a very dark garnet wine with a fine, complex, banana and red-berry nose. A generous wine, it is ample and well-balanced on the palate, with mellow tannins and remarkable body. It has a very long finish. This wonderful 99, which is faultless from start to finish, should last several years. We suggest serving it with white meats.
🔑 Georges Viornery, Brouilly, 69460 Odenas, tel. 04.74.03.41.44, fax 04.74.03.41.44 ☑ 🍷 ev. day 8am–8pm

DOM. DE VURIL 1998★

■ 10 ha 35,000 30–49 F

A rich purple wine made from vines growing on marl soils. Its aroma of berries and undergrowth has mineral overtones. A supple attack introduces a generous, full-bodied palate. This Brouilly has charm and character, and will continue to be enjoyable for another two years.

EARL M.-France and Gabriel Jambon, Chapoly, 69220 Charentay, tel. 04.74.66.84.98, fax 04.74.66.80.58 Y by appt.

Côte de Brouilly

DOM. DU BARVY 1999

■ 0.39 ha n.c. 30–49 F

On the other side of the D 43 from their vineyard, Pascal and Dominique Bouillard run a rural gîte conveniently located near the Odenas fishing lake. They have made a light ruby-coloured 99 with elegant scents of flowers, red berries and leather. The wine has a good attack, very fine tannins and a strong finish. This Côte de Brouilly is ready for drinking now.

Dom. du Barvy, La Commune, 69460 Odenas, tel. 04.74.03.40.30, fax 04.74.03.49.27 Y by appt.

Pascal Bouillard

DOM. DES BUSSIERES 1999

■ 5.2 ha 2,500 30–49 F

This wine is made by a vineyard in Saint-Lager, 'International City of Vines and Wine'. Aromas of cherries, peaches and toast waft from a garnet-coloured, almost purple wine. The powerful, tannic and fresh palate has a slightly sharp red-berry finish. The wine is still young, but could be served in a couple of years' time with red meats.

Colette Deverchère, Dom. des Bussières, 144, av. de la Libération, 69400 Villefranche-sur-Saône, tel. 04.74.65.13.51, fax 04.74.65.47.00 Y by appt.

PAUL CHAMPIER 1998

■ 3 ha n.c. 30–49 F

Rolland-Sigaux's *métairie* markets this cuvée itself. A rich ruby colour with violet highlights, it has intense aromas of preserved fruit, blackcurrant, mulberry and raspberry. Its well-structured tannins are balanced by fruity flavours. While this elegant 98 is ready to be drunk now, perhaps as an accompaniment to red meat with a sauce, it could be kept for up to two years.

GAEC Paul Champier, Les Sigaux, 69460 Odenas, tel. 04.74.03.42.23, fax 04.74.03.48.41, e-mail champier@vins.du.beaujolais Y ev. day except Sun. 8am–7pm

Dom. Rolland

DOM. DE CHARDIGNON 1998★★

■ 9 ha 9,000 30–49 F

This exceptional 98 was allowed to ferment for over ten days, resulting in a garnet-coloured wine with gentle highlights and toasty red-berry aromas. The palate is well-developed: harmonious and balanced, it has soft tannins and good length. This Côte de Brouilly will keep for two or three years, and will drink well with game birds.

Roger Manigand, Les Maisons-Neuves, 69220 Saint-Lager, tel. 04.74.66.84.97, fax 04.74.66.84.97 Y by appt.

DOM. DU CHEMIN DE RONDE 1999

■ n.c. 8,000 30–49 F

A garnet wine with purple highlights made by a family-run estate. It has a mulberry and blackcurrant nose and a smooth, fruity and fresh palate. This supple, seductive wine would be enjoyable with quiche lorraine.

Gérard Monteil, 70, Grande-Rue, 69220 Cercié, tel. 04.74.66.80.50, fax 04.74.66.70.31 Y by appt.

DOM. CHEVALIER-METRAT 1998

■ 1.6 ha 10,000 30–49 F

Although Sylvain Métrat has managed this 6 ha (15-acre) estate since 1956, it was only purchased in 1987. A clear deep garnet colour, this wine has a subtle scent of undergrowth with liquorice overtones. The attack is sound and the palate is full-bodied and quite structured, if a little austere. Like all self-respecting quality *crus*, this well-balanced wine needs to mature.

Sylvain Métrat, Le Roux, 69460 Odenas, tel. 04.74.03.50.33, fax 04.74.03.50.33 Y ev. day 8am–8pm

DOM. DES FOURNELLES 1999

■ 8 ha 25,000 30–49 F

Alain Bernillon has matured this bright purple wine in cellars made out of the blue granite of Mont Brouilly. It has a pleasant nose of spicy ripe black fruits with a hint of peonies. Quite long, but still a little youthful, it will be ready in a year or two. It would then go well with a fillet steak.

Alain Bernillon, Godefroy, 69220 Saint-Lager, tel. 04.74.66.81.68, fax 04.74.66.70.76 Y by appt.

DOM. DE LA FEUILLEE

Cuvée des Pêchers 1999

■ 1.1 ha 11,000 30–49 F

This estate on the slopes of Mont Brouilly, 1.5km (1 mile) from the chapel, has made a rich, mauve wine with a very subtle nose. The wine is well-structured, but its young tannins need to soften for a few months. We were told that it would go well with duck with baby turnips!

Gilbert Thivend, La Côte de Brouilly, 69460 Odenas, tel. 04.74.03.45.13, fax 04.74.03.31.02 Y by appt.

BENOIT LAFONT 1999

■ n.c. 18,000 ▮ 50–69 F

Together, Benoît Lafont's grandsons and the house of Paquet form an important group within the Beaujolais wine industry. This deep purple wine with ruby highlights has a complex aroma that includes notes of liquorice, flowers, cloves and toast. The fresh, lively and well-structured palate may be a little lean, but is still attractive. To be drunk within the next two years.

Benoît Lafont, Le Treve, B.P. 1, 69460 Le Perréon, tel. 04.74.02.10.00, fax 04.74.03.26.99 ☑ Y by appt.

DOM. DE LA MERLETTE

Cuvée Tradition 1999★★

■ 0.77 ha 5,500 30–49 F

The La Merlette estate owns over 16 ha (40 acres) of vineyards. It makes its wines in Vaux, the village made famous in Gabriel Chevallier's Beaujolais saga, *Clochemerle.* The estate's **Beaujolais-Villages 99** was awarded one star, but this bright ruby Côte de Brouilly with garnet highlights was awarded a *coup de coeur.* A vivid nose of violet and peony scents has mineral overtones derived from the local blue granite. Those aromas linger on the palate, which is fresh and supple. Well-balanced and lengthy, this fine 99 will continue to please for another two or three years. It could be served with beef bourguignon.

René and Marie-Claire Tachon, Le Sottizon, 69460 Vaux-en-Beaujolais, tel. 04.74.03.24.80, fax 04.74.03.24.80, e-mail wine.tachon@wanadoo.fr

Y by appt.

CH. DE LA PERRIERE 1998

■ 2 ha 12,000 30–49 F

This wine, made by a négociant from Nuits-Saint-Georges, has a light ruby colour with soft highlights. The moderately powerful nose is enhanced with notes of undergrowth. A hint of liquorice can be tasted on the palate, which is straightforward and quite long. Should be drunk within the year.

Moillard SA, 2, rue François-Mignotte, 21701 Nuits-Saint-Georges, tel. 03.80.62.42.22, fax 03.80.61.28.13 ☑

Y ev. day 10am–6pm, cl. Jan.

RENE MONTERNIER 1999★

■ 0.9 ha 4,000 30–49 F

This 2 ha (5-acre) estate has belonged to the Monternier family since 1840. Thirty-five-year-old, so-called 'paradise' vines have produced a clear ruby wine with pink highlights. It is fragrant with the scent of strawberries, blackcurrants and mulberries. The palate has a good balance of acidity, tannins and alcohol. This well-made 99 is aromatic and rounded; it should be drunk within the next two years.

René Monternier, Pierreux, 69460 Odenas, tel. 04.74.00.40.11 ☑ Y by appt.

DOM. DU PETIT PRESSOIR 1999

■ 3 ha 4,400 30–49 F

A bright garnet wine made from vines growing on east-facing slopes has a moderately intense nose of redcurrants with hints of muskiness. The fruity attack is followed by a warmer, rounder character. This wine should be drunk this year, preferably to accompany roast chicken.

J. Mathon, 69220 Saint-Lager, tel. 04.74.06. 10.10, fax 04.74.66.13.77 ☑

Y by appt.

JEAN-CHARLES PIVOT 1998★

■ 3 ha n.c. 30–49 F

Part of the commune of Quincé is classed as Côte de Brouilly. This vineyard is overlooked by the Brouilly chapel, dedicated to the Virgin of the Grapes. Jean-Charles Pivot has harvested top-quality fruit to produce a youthful ruby wine with mauve highlights. It has a delicate nose of preserved red berries with a hint of liquorice. Structured tannins and attractive aromas follow a gentle attack, and the wine has good length. This well-balanced 98 may be drunk over the next two years. It could accompany coq au vin or charcuterie.

SARL des domaines Jean-Charles Pivot, Montmay, 69430 Quincié-en-Beaujolais, tel. 04.74.04.30.32, fax 04.74.69.00.70 ☑

Y by appt.

DOM. DU SANCILLON 1998

■ 1.33 ha n.c. 30–49 F

Grapes grown on diorite soils have produced a clear ruby wine with a powerful, complex nose of leather, liquorice, spice and undergrowth scents with mineral overtones. A fairly harmonious attack is followed by a robust palate. This well-structured wine has begun to mature, and should accompany red meats.

Charles Champier, Le Moulin Favre, 69460 Odenas, tel. 04.74.03.42.18, fax 04.74.03.30.62 ☑ Y by appt.

Mme Braillon

CH. THIVIN 1999

■ 8.3 ha 60,000 30–49 F

This estate has played an important part in the history of Beaujolais wine. Cited by the jury alongside the **Brouilly 99**, the dark purple-red Côte de Brouilly is fragrant with the scents of red and black fruits, especially ripe cherries. The powerful, well-structured palate has subtle woody and spicy aromas. This bottle will be enjoyable for another two to three years.

🔑 Claude Geoffray, Ch. Thivin, 69460 Odenas, tel. 04.74.03.47.53, fax 04.74.03.52.87 ☑ Y by appt.

GILLES VINCENT 1999★

■ 1.6 ha 7,000 ⅢⅠ 30–49 F

The Vincent estate has been expanding its holdings since it was founded in 1942; it now covers 10 ha (25 acres). Bernadette and Gilles Vincent's son is studying viticulture, so its future is secure! This garnet wine has a complex, powerful nose of red and black fruits. The hefty palate has fresh fruity aromas. Well-balanced and long, it will continue to be enjoyable for another three years, and may be served with red meats.

🔑 Gilles Vincent, Les Grands Croix, 69220 Saint-Lager, tel. 04.74.66.82.05, fax 04.74.66.82.05 ☑ Y ev. day 9am–7pm

Chénas

According to legend, a vast oak forest once covered this land. A woodcutter noticed that a wild vine had grown from a grape pip, apparently dropped by a bird. Convinced of divine intervention, the man set about making a clearing in the forest to cultivate the plant – which proved to be none other than the great Gamay, the black-skinned grape with white flesh.

Chénas is one of the smallest appellations in the Beaujolais, covering only 285 ha (704 acres) on the borders of the departments of Rhône and Saône-et-Loire. It produces 16,450 hl (434,280 gal) harvested from the communes of Chénas and La Chapelle-de-Guinchay. The wines produced on the steep granite slopes to the west are intensely coloured, strongly flavoured but not aggressively so, and release scents of rose and violet; they are not dissimilar to the perfumes of the wines from Moulin à Vent, which occupies most of the land in the commune. Chénas, which is produced on the boggier and less hilly eastern part of the vineyard, is usually less full-bodied. This wine tends to be regarded as the poor relation of the Crus and, because of the size of the vineyard, is also limited to producing small quantities. The 17th-century cellar of the Coopérative du Château vinifies 45% of the appellation and is an impressive sight when it is full of large oak barrels, or *foudres*, filled with wine.

CH. DES BOCCARDS 1999

■ n.c. 10,000 Ⅰ 30–49 F

The Boccards estate dates back to 1800. These days it is run on organic principles. The dark ruby 99 has intense red-berry and spice aromas that improve if the wine is allowed to breathe. Soft, rounded tannins give the wine a good structure. Aromatic, full, and reasonably lengthy, this is an excellent wine for drinking now. Be sure to decant it.

🔑 GFA du ch. des Boccards, Ch. des Boccards, 71570 La Chapelle-de-Guinchay, tel. 03.85.36.81.70 ☑
Y ev. day 9am–12 noon 2pm–6pm
🔑 Pelloux

BERNARD BROYER 1999★★

■ 3.5 ha 6,500 ⅢⅠ 30–49 F

This estate used to belong to Bernard Boyer's grandfather-in-law. A deep red Chénas made from 85-year-old vines growing on marl soils, it has a powerful nose of very ripe berry fruits, undergrowth and flowers. The rounded attack is followed by a fresh palate with raspberry, peardrop and vanilla flavours, nicely balanced by evident tannins. A distinctive wine that, though pleasant now, will improve if kept for a year or two. The estate's **Juliénas** is also cited.

🔑 Bernard Broyer, Les Bucherats, 69840 Juliénas, tel. 04.74.04.46.75, fax 04.74.04.45.18 ☑ Y by appt.

DOM. DE CHENEPIERRE

Sélection Vieilles vignes 1998

■ 2.8 ha 7,000 Ⅰ ⅢⅠ 30–49 F

A garnet-red wine with orange highlights, it has a fairly intense, vinous, woody nose with overtones of morello cherries. These aromas are repeated on the palate, where they are joined by vanilla and a hint of menthol. Although the wood character is a little too pronounced, this 98 may be drunk now with roast chicken or veal. The **Moulin-à-Vent 98**, another cask-aged wine, was also cited by the jury.

🔑 Gérard Lapierre, Les Deschamps, 69840 Chénas, tel. 03.85.36.70.74, fax 03.85.33.85.73 ☑ Y by appt.

DOM. DES DARROUX 1999

■ 3 ha 15,000 ▮ 30–49 F

The **Moulin-à-Vent** of the same vintage is equally as good as this bright garnet wine. The intense red fruit-and spice-scented nose develops subtly. A firm and lively attack and powerful tannins mark this as a wine for keeping. Fruity aromas soften the tannic impression. This ripe 99 should be stored for two to three years to allow it to round out.

Pascal Colvray, Dom. des Darroux, 71570 La Chapelle-de-Guinchay, tel. 03.85.36.73.97, fax 03.85.36.79.37 ☑
Y ev. day 8.30am–7pm

CH. DESVIGNES

■ 13 ha 80,000 ▮ 30–49 F

This négociant's **Beaujolais Domaine Romy 99** (20–29 F) and **Fleurie Domaine Vert-Pré 99** (50–69 F) were both cited by the jury, but only the Chénas, made from its own family vineyard, received a star. A bright ruby colour, the wine is redolent of red berries and undergrowth with warm, musky overtones. It has a lively attack and good structure, with tannins that meld harmoniously with the fruity aromas, boding well for the future. A full wine, alcoholic and distinctive, which should be kept for two to three years before drinking.

Paul Beaudet, rue Paul-Beaudet, 71570 Pontanevaux, tel. 03.85.36.72.76, fax 03.85.36.72.02 ☑ Y ev. day except Sat. Sun. 8am–12 noon 1.30pm–5pm; cl. Aug.

JEAN GEORGES ET FILS 1998

■ 2.7 ha 4,300 ▮ ⦀ ♁ 30–49 F

This family-owned estate has also received a citation for its **Moulin-à-Vent** of the same vintage. The garnet-coloured Chénas has a pleasant nose of macerated red berries, almonds, peonies and spices. A fleshy and fruity attack is followed by aromatic tannins and a hint of undergrowth. This harmonious wine is for drinking now.

GAEC Jean Georges et Fils, Le Bourg, 69840 Chénas, tel. 04.74.04.48.21, fax 04.74.04.42.77 ☑ Y by appt.

DOM. DU GREFFEUR 1998★★

■ 2 ha 2,500 ▮ 30–49 F

The estate, established in 1977, has matured this bright, deep garnet wine in large barrels. This has resulted in complex scents of red fruits and spices. The superb palate is rich and full, with supple tannins. Notes of leather and vanilla are evident on the lengthy finish. A fine example of Chénas, it is ready to drink now, but could also be kept for up to three years. A wine to drink with game.

Jean-Claude Lespinasse, 71570 La Chapelle-de-Guinchay, tel. 03.85.36.70.42, fax 03.85.33.85.49 ☑ by appt.

HUBERT LAPIERRE 1999

■ 4.2 ha 25,000 ▮ ♁ 30–49 F

In 1997, this estate made important advances in temperature-controlled fermentation. Clear and bright red, the wine gives off blackcurrant and wild cherry scents. The fine, aromatic palate is well-rounded, encouraging you to drink it within the year.

Hubert Lapierre, Les Gandelins, 71570 La Chapelle-de-Guinchay, tel. 03.85.36.74.89, fax 03.85.36.79.69 ☑
Y by appt.

DOM. DU MATINAL 1999★★

■ 0.8 ha 5,500 ▮ 30–49 F

A dark red Chénas with a nose of red fruits and undergrowth. The attack is round and aromatic, with notes of redcurrants and cherries, and the overall palate is fat and powerful, producing a crescendo in the mouth. A wine with character, well-balanced, long and distinctive, this structured 99 should keep anywhere from one to three years.

EARL Simone and Guy Braillon, Le Bourg, 69840 Chénas, tel. 04.74.04.48.31, fax 04.74.04.47.64 ☑ Y ev. day 9am–8pm; groups by appt.; cl. mid-Aug.

DANIEL PASSOT 1999★

■ 2.02 ha 15,000 ▮ 30–49 F

Passot took over this estate upon finishing his military service in 1968. His Chénas has an attractive dark red colour and intense, complex aromas of red berries, liquorice, flowers and spices. A good structure and perfectly balanced tannins suggest that it will age well. This ample, supple and fruity 99 is beginning to drink, but could also be kept for two or three years.

Daniel Passot, Les Journets, 71570 La Chapelle-de-Guinchay, tel. 03.85.36.75.35, fax 03.85.33.83.72 ☑
Y ev. day 8am–12 noon 2pm–7pm

DOM. GILBERT PICOLET

Cuvée Vieilles vignes Vieilli en fût de chêne 1998

■ 0.7 ha 2,000 ⦀ 30–49 F

This rich red Chénas with blue highlights has delicate aromas of raspberries, cherries and blackberries with floral notes. On the palate, the wine is forthright, rounded and supple. It is a little on the light side, but nonetheless harmonious, and should be drunk within the year. The same estate's **Moulin-à-Vent 98**, made from old vines and matured in oak, was judged equal to the Chénas.

Gilbert Picolet, Les Seignaux, 69840 Chénas, tel. 04.74.04.48.65, fax 04.74.04.40.94 ☑ Y by appt.

DOM. DES PINS 1998

■ 4.5 ha 4,000 ▮ ♁ 30–49 F

Vines planted on sandy soils have produced a dark red wine with a bouquet of ripe stone fruits, heather, undergrowth and violets. The powerful but somewhat austere palate tastes of morello cherries and vanilla. This Chénas needs another year's ageing.

Pascal Aufranc, En Rémont, 69840 Chénas, tel. 04.74.04.47.95, fax 04.74.04.47.95 ☑ Y by appt.

DOM. DES ROSIERS 1999**

■ 2 ha 12,000 30-49 F

Gérard Charvet's **Moulin-à-Vent 97** was awarded a *coup de coeur* by the jury. This year, the Chénas has taken that honour. Only 500 m (600 yards) to the west of Chénas village, the estate is worth visiting. The wine is a rich ruby colour with a strong aroma of kirsch, fresh cherries and peonies. The palate is elegant, fleshy and round. Thoroughbred aromatic tannins complete a well-balanced structure. A wine that displays all the characteristics of good Chénas, this elegant cuvée will continue to be enjoyable for another two or three years. Best served with red meats, either plain-grilled or in a sauce.

Gérard Charvet, Les Rosiers, 69840 Chénas, tel. 04.74.04.48.62, fax 04.74.04.49.80 ev. day 8am–8pm

GEORGES ROSSI
Vignoble en Guinchay 1999

■ 2.5 ha 9 330 30-49 F

This estate, a member of the Eventail des Vignerons à Corcelles, was bought in 1962. It has produced a dark red wine with notes of red berries, flowers and spices, and forthright but elegant tannins. This ample and fruity 99 should be kept for a year before drinking.

Georges Rossi, 71570 La Chapelle-de-Guinchay, tel. 04.74.06.10.10, fax 04.74.66.13.77 by appt.

Chiroubles

Perched at 400 m (1,312 ft), Chiroubles is the highest of the Cru vineyards in Beaujolais. It covers 378 ha (934 acres) of light, impoverished granite sand, in a single commune, and produces 21,700 hl (572,880 gal) of red wine from the Gamay grape. Chiroubles is an elegant, delicate, charming and smooth wine, containing little tannin and with traces of violet perfumes. The Confrérie des Demoiselles de Chiroubles, supported by their Chevaliers, was created in 1996 to assist in the marketing of this wine which is sometimes referred to as 'the ladies' Beaujolais'. It is a wine for early drinking and is sometimes reminiscent of Fleurie or Morgon, which are neighbouring vineyards. Chiroubles is the perfect wine to drink with charcuterie. On the route to Fût d'Avenas, which leads out of the village towards the top of the mount, there is a *chalet de dégustation* where the wine can be tasted.

Every April, Chiroubles holds a festival to celebrate the memory of Victor Pulliat, born there in 1827. His considerable research into the pace of growth of different vine varieties and their comparative grafting qualities is world-famous. He made his observations in his domain at Tempéré and gathered a collection of over 2,000 vine varieties. Chiroubles has a cooperative cellar which vinifies 3,000 hl (79,200 gal) of the cru.

DOM. BERLIOZ SAINT-ROCH 1999

■ 7 ha 49,000 30-49 F

This purple-red 99 is a little shy on the nose. The vinous, tannic, full-bodied palate suggests that it needs to mature in order to fulfil its potential. One or two years will be enough.

Louis Chedeville, 435, rte du Beaujolais, 69830 Saint-Georges-de-Reneins, tel. 04.74.09.60.00, fax 04.74.67.67.40

Michel Rotival

ARMAND CHARVET Bel Air 1998

■ n.c. n.c. 30-49 F

Fermented on wild yeasts, this clear garnet wine has a complex, intense aroma of raspberries and strawberries with a hint of peonies, as well as buttery notes. The ample attack is followed by firm tannins, so this wine will keep for a couple of years.

Armand Charvet, Bel Air, 69115 Chiroubles, tel. 04.74.69.13.08, fax 04.74.69.13.13 ev. day 8.30am–1pm 1.30pm–8pm

DOM. DU CLOCHER 1999

■ 5 ha 6,000 30-49 F

This estate, located 50 m (55 yards) from a church with a steeple in the oriental style, has produced a ruby wine with violet highlights and a delicate scent of red fruits and peonies. Generous raspberry aromas are evident on

the palate. Fruity and extremely fresh, this harmonious 99 should be drunk over the next two years. It could be served with rabbit in a cream sauce.
🗝 Jean-Noël Mélinand, Le Bourg, 69115 Chiroubles, tel. 04.74.69.11.96, fax 04.74.69.16.89 ☒
Y ev. day 9am–12 noon 2pm–6pm

DOM. DU CLOS VERDY 1998★★

■ n.c. 30,000 ▮ ⦶ 🌡 30–49 F

An estate which has been steadily enlarging its holdings since 1970, Clos Verdy has made a bright garnet wine with a complex, intense nose of peonies and strawberries. The powerful and rich palate has sinuous tannins and fruity aromas with mineral notes: a very nicely balanced mouthful. This excellent Chiroubles should be drunk within the next two years.
🗝 Georges Boulon, Le Bourg, 69115 Chiroubles, tel. 04.74.04.27.27, fax 04.74.69.13.16 ☒ Y ev. day 8am–12 noon 2pm–6pm; Sat. Sun. by appt.

DOM. DU CRET DES BRUYERES 1999

■ 1.9 ha 6,000 ▮ 🌡 30–49 F

Purchased in 1983, this little property has been a pitstop in the past for racing drivers such as Pescarolo and Beltoise. A deep red-purple, the 99 cuvée, with its nose of rose-petals, crystallised fruits and pineapple, is still very young. Its powerful, though not aggressive, tannins nonetheless leave a touch of bitterness on the finish. A wine of great substance, it should be allowed to age for at least a year.
🗝 GFA Desplace Frères, Aux Bruyères, 69430 Régnié-Durette, tel. 04.74.04.30.21, fax 04.74.04.30.55 ☒ Y by appt.

ANNE-MARIE ET ARMAND DESMURES 1998

■ 6.3 ha 15,000 ▮ 30–49 F

Forty-year-old vines have produced this light red wine with subtle highlights. A raspberry-scented nose with quince overtones is followed by a well-rounded, fruity palate with raspberry and strawberry aromas. This harmonious 98 is not intended for keeping, but is very attractive now.
🗝 Anne-Marie and Armand Desmures, Le Bourg, 69115 Chiroubles, tel. 04.74.69.10.61, fax 04.74.69.15.12 ☒
Y by appt.

DOM. GOBET 1999

■ 1.2 ha 5,500 ▮ 30–49 F

When he was appointed the estate's manager in 1998, the son-in-law became the sixth generation of this family to succeed to the post. This brilliant ruby wine has an aroma of irises and peonies. The palate is generous and powerful, but held back for the time being by its still youthful tannins. It needs another couple of years to mature.
🗝 Christophe Jeannet, Le Bourg, 69115 Chiroubles, tel. 04.74.04.21.04, fax 04.74.04.23.58, e-mail christophe.jeannet@wanadoo.fr ☒
Y ev. day except Sun. 8am–12 noon 2pm–7pm

DOM. DE GUISE 1998

■ 3.8 ha 11,000 ▮ 30–49 F

The estate takes its name from the locality. Its light red Chiroubles 98 has a lively nose of raspberries and cherries with spicy notes. The stimulating and aromatic attack enlivens a rounded, well-balanced and slightly tannic wine. A good example of its AOC, it should be served with white meat dishes.
🗝 Michel and Claire Mélinand, Dom. de Guise, 69115 Chiroubles, tel. 04.74.04.24.22 ☒ Y ev. day 8am–12.30pm 1.30pm–7pm

DOM. DE LA COMBE AU LOUP 1998★★

■ 5 ha 35,000 ▮ 🌡 

A **Régnié 98**, sold under the same label, was cited by the jury. Garnet-coloured with tawny highlights, the Chiroubles has a wonderfully intense nose of lilacs, irises, raspberries and redcurrants. The full, heady palate, tasting of fruits and violets, has structured tannins. Silky and persistent, this is a 98 for drinking over the next two years.
🗝 Méziat Père et Fils, Dom. de la Combe au Loup, Le Bourg, 69115 Chiroubles, tel. 04.74.04.24.02, fax 04.74.69.14.07 ☒
Y ev. day except Sun. 8.30am–12 noon 2pm–6.30pm

DOM. DE LA COUR PROFONDE 1999

■ 2.8 ha 5,000 ▮ 30–49 F

This house, established at the beginning of the last century, is housed in seven vaulted cellars. Its cherry-red wine has an intense nose with a hint of undergrowth. Still slightly pétillant, the 99 vintage is hefty on the palate. Aromatic and attractive, despite its youthful tannins, it needs another year or two to mature.
🗝 EARL Revollat, La Cour Profonde, 69115 Chiroubles, tel. 04.74.69.13.72, fax 04.74.04.22.84 ☒ Y ev. day 9am–8pm
🗝 Méziat

VIGNOBLE LA FONTENELLE 1999

■ 5 ha 10,400 30–49 F

This deep ruby wine is redolent of bananas with hints of redcurrants and mint. It has a flawless palate that is fruity and well-balanced, with fine tannins. An easy-drinking Chiroubles, it should be consumed within the year.

Gobet-Jeannet, 69115 Chiroubles, tel. 04.74.06.10.10, fax 04.74.66.13.77
by appt.

DOM. DE LA GROSSE PIERRE 1999

■ 9 ha 50,000 30–49 F

A wine made from grapes grown on the eastern slopes of Chiroubles, this is pale red in colour, with a vinous, forthcoming nose marked by hints of red berries. A tender, velvety palate indicates that this wine should be drunk within the year.

Alain Passot, La Grosse Pierre, 69115 Chiroubles, tel. 04.74.69.12.17, fax 04.74.69.13.52 ev. day 9am–7pm

DOM. DE LA ROCASSIERE 1998

■ 6 ha 8,000 30–49 F

This is a bright red wine with orange highlights, and a pure floral nose composed of peony, rose and violet scents. The palate is fresh with well-structured tannins, and persistent fruity and flowery aromas. Quite well-balanced already, it should be drunk within the next two years.

Yves Laplace, Javernand, 69115 Chiroubles, tel. 04.74.69.12.23, fax 04.74.69.16.49 by appt.

DOM. BERNARD PAUL MELINAND 1998*

■ 2 ha 8,000 30–49 F

The Mélinand 98 has a youthful, clear, bright red colour. Its complex nose is fruity, flowery and spicy with vegetal notes. Fresh, lively tannins and velvety, persistent fruit flavours with hints of violet blend to create a wine with great potential, but it needs to mature for a year or two.

Bernard Mélinand, Le Verdy, 69115 Chiroubles, tel. 04.74.04.23.15
by appt.

DOM. MORIN 1999**

■ 2.7 ha 21,000 30–49 F

An estate located in the heart of the village has made this remarkable dark red wine with beautiful violet highlights. The attractive nose draws you into the wine; very intense yet fine scents of peonies and blackcurrant leaves are accented with a touch of smokiness. Despite some lingering spritziness, this is a powerful 99. Solid, pleasant tannins and aromatic flavours contribute to the velvety palate. A fine example of this AOC that, though very enjoyable now, will improve if kept for a year or two.

Sté Nouvelle J. Pellerin, 435, rte du Beaujolais, 69830 Saint-Georges-de-Reneins, tel. 04.74.09.60.08, fax 04.74.67.60.17
Guy Morin

DOM. DU MOULIN 1999

■ n.c. 5,000 30–49 F

In 1984 this oenological consultancy established a négociant company dealing in the wines of several estates. The Dom. du Moulin is a dark red wine with violet highlights and a mineral and fruity aroma. Its palate, which starts off reasonably round, has quite a tannic finish. Although it doesn't have quite the exuberance of a Gamay made in the classic Beaujolais style, it is nonetheless a fine wine, and should be aged for two or three years.

Janny, La Condemine, 71260 Péronne, tel. 03.85.36.97.03, fax 03.85.36.96.58
by appt.

DOM. DU MOULIN-FAVRE

Cuvée Vieilles vignes 1999

■ 1.5 ha 8,000 30–49 F

A clear, deep red wine with bright highlights, this is redolent of very ripe fruits: raspberries, redcurrants and morello cherries. Hefty and a little austere, its promising tannins will need to soften over the next two years.

Armand Vernus, Le Vieux-Bourg, 69460 Odenas, tel. 04.74.03.40.63, fax 04.74.03.40.76 by appt.

DOM. DE PRE-NESME 1998

■ 6.68 ha 8,148 30–49 F

In 1998, the estate's cellars were renovated and extended to provide a vaulted tasting-room for visitors. This dark red wine with violet highlights is still very young. It has a complex nose of strawberries, morello cherries and peonies. A powerful attack and rounded tannic structure make for a robust wine. It may be drunk now, but should also improve if kept for a year.

André Dépré, Le Moulin, 69115 Chiroubles, tel. 04.74.69.11.18, fax 04.74.69.12.84
ev. day 8.30am–7pm

DOM. RENE SAVOYE 1999*

■ 3.4 ha 5,330 30–49 F

The vineyard dates back to 1870, but the vines that have produced this wine are only 20 years old. A pellucid deep ruby colour, it has a pleasant aroma of raspberries and cherries. The rounded, fruity palate is well-structured. A harmonious wine made the more elegant by a mildly spicy finish.

René Savoye, Le Bourg, 69115 Chiroubles, tel. 04.74.06.10.10, fax 04.74.66.13.77 by appt.

CHRISTOPHE SAVOYE 1999**

■ 5 ha 8,000 30–49 F

This choice wine with a clear, dark purple colour and violet highlights may be tasted in Christophe Savoye's vaulted cellars in the centre of town. It has a pleasant, complex

nose of raspberries and redcurrants, leading to a nicely structured wine with flowery and fruity aromas. Elegant and fine, this distinctive 99 is for drinking within the next two to three years, preferably with red meat.
Christophe Savoye, Le Bourg, 69115 Chiroubles, tel. 04.74.69.11.24, fax 04.74.04.22.11
ev. day except Sun. 8am–7pm

Fleurie

A chapel surmounts the rounded hillock of the Fleurie and appears to keep a watchful eye over the vineyard that is planted entirely with Gamay. This is the Madonna of Fleurie and it marks the physical location of the third most important Cru after Brouilly and Morgon. The 860 ha (2,124 acres) of the vineyard are inside the commune boundaries and produce 49,000 hl (1,293,600 gal). The terrain is similar throughout the vineyard and made up of crystalline granite which contributes to the wine's finesse and charm. The wine can be drunk cool or at room temperature and, either way, it is the perfect accompaniment for *andouillette beaujolaise* made with Fleurie. It has the promise of the countryside in spring: light, bright and with a bouquet of iris and violets.

There are two wine-tasting cellars in the centre of the village, one near the town hall and the other in the Cave Coopérative which vinifies 30% of the cru. They offer a full range of local wines with evocative names: La Rochette, La Chappelle-des-Bois, Les Roches, Grille-Midi and la Joie-du-Palais.

FABIEN BAILLAIS

Cuvée spéciale Climat des Garants Elevé en fût de chêne 1998★

0.6 ha 2,000 30–49 F

This bright ruby wine is made from grapes crushed in a 200-year-old wooden wine-press. Although it has quite evidently been matured in barrels, the oakiness does not overwhelm the palate's freshness or the crystallised fruit and acacia flavours. An excellent, distinctive 98 that is well-balanced and persistent, it may be kept for three or four years.
Fabien Baillais, Les Garants, 69820 Fleurie, tel. 04.74.04.13.28, fax 04.74.04.13.28
ev. day 8am–12 noon 2pm–8pm; cl. Aug.

CH. DU BOURG 1999

6 ha 25,000 30–49 F

The estate's vineyards, wine-making premises and equipment were all renovated in 1992. This purple-ruby 98, with its delicate aroma of irises and smoke, is fresh and fruity rather than powerful. Well-balanced, but still closed, this wine should be kept for a year before drinking.
Bruno and Patrick Matray, Le Bourg, 69820 Fleurie, tel. 04.74.69.81.15, fax 04.74.69.86.80, e-mail matraybruno@minitel.net
by appt.

CUVEE DU CARDINAL BIENFAITEUR 1998★★

1 ha 7,000 30–49 F

The 98, made in honour of the Cardinal of Fleury, is a clear, deep ruby colour. It has a complex nose dominated by the scent of cherries and redcurrants with additional peony, blackcurrant and mulberry notes. A balanced, fleshy, distinctive and harmonious wine that is ready to drink now, it has supple tannins and pleasant aromas. An attractive wine that could accompany a veal escalope with morels.
Cave Prod. des Grands Vins de Fleurie, B.P. 2, 69820 Fleurie, tel. 04.74.04.11.70, fax 04.74.69.84.73 by appt.

DOM. DES CHAFFANGEONS

Cuvée Michel et Martine 1999

6 ha 12,000 30–49 F

This is a deep ruby-coloured wine with red fruit and flower aromas more tentatively echoed on the palate. Supple and long, this fairly harmonious 99 should be drunk within two years.
Michel Perrier, La Chapelle-des-Bois, 69820 Fleurie, tel. 04.74.69.83.05
by appt.
Robert Depardon

DOM. DU COTEAU DE BEL-AIR

Cuvée Tradition 1998

1 ha 4,000 30–49 F

The Cuvée Tradition has a bright purple-ruby colour, deriving its aromas of undergrowth and clay, mixed with red-berry fruits, from the vineyard's red soils. The full-bodied palate is cherry-scented, well-balanced and reasonably long. A wine for drinking within the next two years.
Jean-Marie Appert, Bel-Air, 69115 Chiroubles, tel. 04.74.04.23.77, fax 04.74.69.17.13 by appt.

LA MAISON DES VIGNERONS

1999★

■ 1.05 ha 8,000 ▮ 30-49 F

With this wine, the smallest co-operative in Beaujolais, cited for its **Morgon Cuvée de la Chenevière 98**, shows that it can play in the big league. A crystal-clear, rich ruby wine, it has fine complex aromas of peony and violet mixed with wild cherries and spices. The palate is ample, fat and charming; fruit and tannins are nicely balanced in this distinctive wine. Easy-drinking and harmonious, it will keep for two or three years.

🗝 La Maison des Vignerons de Chiroubles, Le Bourg, 69115 Chiroubles, tel. 04.74.69.14.94, fax 04.74.69.10.59 ☑
Y ev. day 10am–12 noon 2pm–6pm

DOM. LARDY

Vieilles Vignes 1998★

■ 1.5 ha 10,000 ▮ ⦀ 50-69 F

This is a light red wine with pale highlights, made from 60-year-old vines. An aroma of plums with flowery overtones carries through from the nose to the palate. It has a strong attack with good tannins. Perhaps a little austere just now, the 98 should still drink within the year. The estate's **Beaujolais-Villages 99** was awarded a star.

🗝 Lucien Lardy, Le Vivier, 69820 Fleurie, tel. 04.74.69.81.74, fax 04.74.04.12.30 ☑
Y by appt.

DOM. LES ROCHES DES GARANTS

Les Moriers 1999

■ 4 ha 13,000 ▮ 🌡 30-49 F

Over the last 50 years, this estate has tripled the extent of its vineyard plantings. A deep garnet colour, the powerful 99 shows intense aromas of blackcurrants, almonds and peonies. A rounded attack is followed by a more evidently tannic finish. Distinctive, full-bodied and aromatic, it needs to mature for another year or so yet.

🗝 Jean-Paul Champagnon, La Treille, 69820 Fleurie, tel. 04.74.04.15.62, fax 04.74.69.82.60 ☑ Y ev. day 8am–8pm

DOM. MATHRAY 1998★

■ 2.5 ha 3,000 ▮ 30-49 F

This is a deep ruby wine redolent of red berries mixed with iris, acacia and undergrowth. The palate is fruity with rich tannins and a floral aroma. The fine, well-balanced palate promises two to four years' cellaring potential.

🗝 Jean-Paul Mathray, Montgenas, 69820 Fleurie, tel. 04.74.04.13.84, fax 04.74.69.85.69 ☑ Y by appt.

DOM. METRAT ET FILS

La Roilette 1998★★

■ 2 ha 10,000 30-49 F

This wine, made from 55-year-old vines, was awarded a *coup de coeur* by the Fleurie grand jury. A glittering deep garnet colour, it has a powerful nose of violets, peonies and

irises complete with spices and crystallised fruit. The palate is unctuous, with elegant, though dense tannins. Well-balanced and long, it should continue to be enjoyable for another three to five years.

🗝 Bernard Métrat, Le Brie, 69820 Fleurie, tel. 04.74.69.84.26, fax 04.74.69.84.49 ☑ Y by appt.

CLOS DES MORIERS Moriers 1999★

■ 5 ha 20,000 ▮ 30-49 F

The Clos des Moriers is a dark red wine with a subtle and complex nose of undergrowth, anise and flowers, but its vigorous palate needs time to soften. Full-bodied and well-structured, it will be very enjoyable in three years' time.

🗝 GFA Clos des Moriers, Les Moriers, 69820 Fleurie, tel. 04.74.09.60.00, fax 04.74.67.67.40

DOM. PARDON 1999

■ 1.2 ha 9,000 ▮ 30-49 F

A ruby-coloured wine with violet highlights, this light-bodied 99 with its assertively aromatic palate is ready to drink now.

🗝 GFA Pardon des Labourons, 39, rue du Gal-Leclerc, 69430 Beaujeu, tel. 04.74.04.86.97, fax 04.74.69.24.08, e-mail pardon-fils.vins@wanadoo.fr ☑
Y by appt.

DOM. DU PRESSOIR FLEURI

1998★

■ 1 ha 5,000 ▮ 50-69 F

The estate's **Morgon 99** (30–49 F) was awarded a star. While the Morgon is very good value, this Fleurie is just that bit more beguiling. A clear ruby colour, it has an intense nose of blackcurrants and strawberries, with topnotes of peonies and spice. Dried-fruit flavours are evident on the supple, round and well-structured palate. A very harmonious wine that should be drunk within the next two years.

🗝 André and Monique Méziat, Le Bourg, 69115 Chiroubles, tel. 04.74.04.23.12, fax 04.74.69.12.65 ☑ Y ev. day 8am–12 noon 1pm–6pm; Sun. and groups by appt.

DOM. DE ROCHE-GUILLON 1999★

■ 3 ha 8,000 ▮ 30-49 F

This wine-grower also runs two *chambres d'hôtes*. The estate presented two wines to the jury: a **Beaujolais-Villages 99** (20–29 F),

which received a citation, and this attractive Fleurie. A dark red wine, it has a clean aroma of apricots, plums and spices. The full-bodied, well-balanced and concentrated palate will become more aromatic in a few months' time.
Bruno Coperet, Roche-Guillon, 69820 Fleurie, tel. 04.74.69.85.34, fax 04.74.04.10.25 by appt.

Juliénas

A wine with an imperial heritage, Juliénas, with Moulin à Vent the leading wine of Beaujolais, does indeed owe its name to Julius Caesar, as does Jullié, another of the four communes which make up the vineyard (the others are Emeringes and Pruzilly, which is just over the border in Saône-et-Loire). The soil in the western part of the vineyard is granite while in the east the soil is sedimentary with ancient alluvial deposits. Its 605 ha (1,494 acres) are planted exclusively with Gamay, and produce 34,900 hl (921,360 gal) of well-structured wine. The richly-coloured wines drink well in the spring, after being kept only a few months. They are as vigorous and spirited as the characters on the frescoes in the Caveau de l'Église, the wine-tasting cellar in the centre of the town where, in November of each year, the Victor Peyrat prize ceremony is held. The prize is awarded to the artist, painter, writer or journalist who has celebrated the Crus with the most distinction. The actual prize consists of 104 bottles of wine, two for each weekend in the year. The Cave Coopérative, situated in the old priory of the Château du Bois de la Salle, vinifies 30% of the appellation.

JEAN ET BENOIT AUJAS 1998*

9 ha 3,000 30–49 F

An old-vine cuvée made by an estate located 200 m (220 yards) from the Maison de la Dîme. Purple with garnet highlights, it has an inviting nose of peonies and cherries. The full palate is well-balanced, with fresh aromas and chewy tannins. A robust and distinctive 98 that, while ready to drink now (perhaps with veal), will also keep for two or three years.
GAEC Jean and Benoît Aujas, La Ville, 69840 Juliénas, tel. 04.74.04.41.35 by appt.

CH. BONNET Vieilles vignes 1999

1.8 ha 12,000 30–49 F

This estate dates back to 1630. It has produced a pale garnet wine with fascinating aromas of violets, peonies, black pepper and menthol. A rounded palate reveals elegant tannins. Well-suited to ageing, this fairly firm wine should be stored for one or two years.
Pierre-Yves Perrachon, Ch. Bonnet, Les Paquelets, 71570 La Chapelle-de-Guinchay, tel. 03.85.36.77.47, fax 03.85.36.77.27 by appt.

DOM. CHATAIGNIER DURAND 1999

2 ha n.c. 30–49 F

A ruby wine with a scent of berries and black pepper. Well-balanced and delicately aromatic, it should be drunk within the next two years.
Jean-Marc Monnet, 69840 Juliénas, tel. 04.74.04.45.46, fax 04.74.04.44.24 by appt.

DOM. DU CLOS DU FIEF 1999

7 ha 35,000 30–49 F

The estate's **Beaujolais-Villages 99** (20–29 F) was also cited by the jury. This rich ruby Juliénas has a clean, fruity nose. Round and well-balanced, with a lean structure, it doesn't require long ageing, and may be enjoyed now.
Michel Tête, Les Gonnards, 69840 Juliénas, tel. 04.74.04.41.62, fax 04.74.04.47.09 ev. day except Sun. 8am–12 noon 2pm–6pm; cl. 12–25 Aug.

THIERRY DESCOMBES Coteau des vignes 1999

2.5 ha 10,000 30–49 F

In charge since 1978, Thierry Descombes is the fourth generation of his family to run this estate. He has made a garnet wine fragrant with spice and vanilla aromas, with hints of peonies and undergrowth. The powerful, tannic palate is still rather closed, though. It will reach its full potential in a year or two.
Thierry Descombes, Les Vignes, 69840 Jullié, tel. 04.74.04.42.03 by appt.

J. GONARD ET FILS 1998

2 ha 10,000 30–49 F

This négociant, based in Juliénas, received the same marks for its **Morgon 98** as it did for this bright ruby wine redolent of red berries. The velvety palate has rounded, soft tannins. Long and well-balanced, the wine is ready to drink now, but it will keep for another year or two.

⊶ J. Gonard et Fils, Les Gonnards, 69840 Juliénas, tel. 04.74.04.45.20, fax 04.74.04.45.69 ☑
Y ev. day 9am–12 noon 2pm–7pm

P. GRANGER

Cuvée spéciale 1999

■ 2 ha 10,000 30–49 F

The jury's opinion of this wine was divided. While it had much to recommend it, it suffered from being very young when tasted. A purple wine, it has a fruity nose with iris and elderberry notes. The aromatic palate is rather hard with youthful tannins that still need time to settle down. With a little more maturity, it will surely win over any sceptics.

⊶ Pascal Granger, Les Poupets, 69840 Juliénas, tel. 04.74.04.44.79, fax 04.74.04.41.24 ☑
Y ev. day 8am–7pm; cl. 15–30 Aug.

DOM. DU GRANIT DORE

1999

■ 3.5 ha 15,000 30–49 F

A portion of Georges Rollet's estate is tenanted out, but the vines that produced this wine have been in the property since 1924. The clear, bright red wine has a powerful and vinous fruit nose. A positive attack is followed by warming sensations developing on the palate. It may be drunk now alongside meat dishes with sauces.

⊶ Georges Rollet, La Pouge, 69840 Jullié, tel. 04.74.04.44.81, fax 04.74.04.49.12 ☑
Y by appt.

FRANCK JUILLARD

Vieilles vignes 1999★★

■ 5 ha 19,400 30–49 F

This garnet wine with purple highlights, made from very old vines, has been matured in the estate's beautiful vaulted cellars. Pleasant black fruit, nutmeg and gingerbread aromas continue on to the palate. Well-balanced, with supple tannins, this long, distinctive 99 will keep for three or four years. It may be served with red meats, game or cheese.

⊶ Franck and Nicole Juillard, Les Poupets, 69840 Juliénas, tel. 04.74.04.42.56, fax 04.74.04.43.82, e-mail fjuillard@waika9.com Y by appt.

DOM. JUILLARD 1999★★

■ 2 ha 15,000 30–49 F

This company, established in 1821, also offers a **Moulin-à-Vent, Domaine Bourisset 99** (50–69 F), cited by the jury, and a **Régnié, Domaine de la Charrière 99** (30–49 F), which was awarded a star. The dark purple Juliénas has beautiful ripe black- and red-berry scents with spicy overtones. Its tannins, flavours and vinosity are nicely balanced. Ample and long on the palate, this distinctive, powerful and rich wine could keep for two or three years, perhaps even longer.

⊶ Coll in-Bourisset Vins Fins, av. de la Gare, 71680 Crèches-sur-Saône, tel. 03.85.36.57.25, fax 03.85.37.15.38, e-mail cbourisset@compuserve.com
Y by appt.

CH. DE JULIENAS

Vieilli en fût de chêne 1998

■ 33 ha 35,000 30–49 F

Parts of this château date from 1852. In its cellars was matured this clear, ruby-coloured Juliénas with a fine fruity and flowery nose complete with mineral overtones. The palate is hefty and well-structured. This is a wine for drinking within the next two years.

⊶ F. and T. Condemine, Ch. de Juliénas, 69840 Juliénas, tel. 04.74.04.41.43, fax 04.74.04.42.38 ☑

DOM. DE LA COMBE-DARROUX

1999

■ 4 ha 10,000 30–49 F

This estate, which dates back to 1818, has produced a fairly dark ruby wine with a redcurrant and black pepper nose. The palate is light, but quite aromatic and gently acid. A wine with character, it should keep for one or two years.

⊶ EARL Anne and Pascal Guignet, Dom. de La Combe-Darroux, 71570 La Chapelle-de-Guinchay, tel. 04.74.06.70.90, fax 04.74.04.45.08 ☑

DOM. DE LA COTE DE CHEVENAL 1999

■ 1.2 ha 5,000 30–49 F

This bright ruby wine with its strong nose of red berries, flowers and spices, has been made in the estate's new winery, constructed in 1998. The positive attack is followed by an explosion of fruit on the palate and a lively finish: the sins of youth! The wine should be ready to drink in two years' time.

⊶ GAEC Jean-François and Pierre Bergeron, Les Rougelons, 69840 Emeringes, tel. 04.74.04.41.19, fax 04.74.04.40.72 ☑
Y by appt.

DOM. DE LA MAISON DE LA DIME 1999★

■ 5 ha 37,000 30–49 F

Roland Bouchacourt's **Fleurie, La Chapelle des Bois 99** was cited by the jury, but this Juliénas was awarded a star. A bright ruby colour, it has a pleasant fruity nose of cocoa-beans and spices. The powerful palate displays firm tannins, as well as redcurrant and strawberry flavours. A robust, serious 99 that will definitely improve with age. It should be kept for two to three years. The Roland Bouchacourt brand also markets a **Juliénas, Domaine de La Bottière-Pavillon 99**, which was also judged worthy of a star: 'a fine expression of the grape,' was the jury's consensus.

⊶ Vins et Vignobles, 435, rte du Beaujolais, 69830 Saint-Georges-de-Reneins, tel. 04.74.09.60.00, fax 04.74.67.67.40, e-mail info@vinsetvignobles.com

DOM. DE L'ANCIEN RELAIS

Vieille vigne 1998★

■ 0.75 ha 2,800 30–49 F

This estate, with its beautiful vaulted cellars, is located on the site of an old inn. It has made a clear, deep garnet wine with a pretty powerful fruity and floral nose. The frank and generous attack is allied to a full-bodied palate and supple, harmoniously structured tannins. A promising wine that needs to age for a year or two.

EARL André Poitevin, Les Chamonards, 71570 Saint-Amour-Bellevue, tel. 03.85.37.16.05, fax 03.85.37.40.87 by appt.

DOM. DE LA VIEILLE EGLISE

1999

■ n.c. n.c. 30–49 F

The négociant's family property has produced a lively red wine with violet highlights. The subtle nose is promising, with spicy aromas. A powerful attack is followed by supple but slightly aggressive tannins on the palate. This fairly rich, lengthy 99 should be allowed to mature for a few months.

Ets Loron et Fils, Pontanevaux, 71570 La Chapelle-de-Guinchay, tel. 03.85.36.81.20, fax 03.85.33.83.19, e-mail vinloron@wanadoo.fr

LE CLOS DU FIEF 1998

■ 0.5 ha 2,500 30–49 F

A small-production wine made from old vines. It is dark red and has a suggestion of undergrowth on the nose. The attractive palate lacks neither roundness nor tannin. A wine that could be served now, and would be very good with grilled sausages.

Gabriel Gauthier, Les Chanoriers, 69840 Jullié, tel. 04.74.04.43.31 ev. day 8am–12 noon 1pm–8pm

DOM. JEAN-PIERRE MARGERAND 1999★

■ 6.1 ha 10,000 30–49 F

The estate can be traced back all the way to 1760. This year it has presented the jury with two very nice wines: a small production of **Beaujolais-Villages 99** and this Juliénas. It has a crystal-clear deep ruby colour and fruity redcurrant nose. The subtly aromatic and well-structured palate is full of character. In another year or two, it would grace any table.

Jean-Pierre Margerand, Les Crots, 69840 Juliénas, tel. 04.74.04.40.86, fax 04.74.04.46.54 by appt.

DOM. DES MOUILLES 1999★★

■ 4.4 ha 10,000 30–49 F

Records place the Perrachon family in Juliénas as long ago as 1601. Four centuries later, Laurent Perrachon has made a **Morgon Les Versands 98**, cited by the jury, and this *coup de coeur* Juliénas. It has a beautiful deep ruby colour with a well-developed floral scent and good vinosity. A harmonious and well-balanced wine, the 99 is full and aromatic on

the palate with a slightly acid, but long finish. A distinguished wine that will keep for three or four years.

Laurent Perrachon, Dom. des Mouilles, 69840 Juliénas, tel. 04.74.04.40.44, fax 04.74.04.40.44 by appt.

DOM. DU MOULIN BERGER

Vayolette 1999

■ 2.7 ha 8,000 30–49 F

Although the Laplace family has been managing this estate for many years, they have only owned it since 1985. This beautiful deep garnet wine is a little shy on the nose: black fruit aromas develop very slowly. The powerful palate echoes the nose and has a gently warming finish. A wine to keep.

Michel and Pascale Laplace, Le Moulin Berger, 71570 Saint-Amour-Bellevue, tel. 03.85.37.41.57, fax 03.85.37.44.75 by appt.

JEAN-FRANCOIS PERRAUD 1999

■ 6.8 ha 8,000 30–49 F

Jean-François Perraud owns 10 ha (25 acres) of vineyards. He presented two wines to the jury, both of which were selected: a **Beaujolais-Villages 99** with a beautiful label, and this lively, bright red Juliénas. The nose is spicy, with musky overtones. The fruity palate is delicious and quite supple. A well-made, if not all that concentrated, 99 for drinking within the year.

Jean-François Perraud, Les Chanoriers, 69840 Jullié, tel. 04.74.04.49.09, fax 04.74.04.49.09 by appt.

DOM. PLACE DES VIGNES 1998

■ n.c. 300 30–49 F

The third generation of this family of winemakers took charge of the estate in 1995. They have made a small vintage of this intense red wine with pale highlights. Complex aromas of stewed fruits are present on the nose and palate. Structured tannins give the wine distinction.

Agnès and Thierry Roussot, Les Darroux, 71570 La Chapelle-de-Guinchay, tel. 03.85.33.85.51, fax 03.85.33.85.51 by appt.

ESPRIT THORIN TERRES DE GALENE 1999

■ n.c. 60,000 30–49 F

The Thorin brand of Groupe Boisset was cited for both its **Fleurie Esprit Thorin Terres**

de Granit Rose and this Juliénas. Soils rich in sulphur and lead are the source of a dark garnet wine with complex scents of macerated fruits. A round and forthright wine, it has youthful, yet light tannins. An aroma of the *garrigue*, the rough southern French terrain, completes the palate. A young wine for drinking over the next two years.
🔑 Maison Thorin, Le Pont des Samsons, 69430 Quincié-en-Beaujolais, tel. 04.74.69.09.10, fax 04.74.69.09.28, e-mail information@maisonthorin.com
Y by appt.

RAYMOND TRICHARD 1999

■ 1 ha 4,000 ▮ 30–49 F

Made from venerable, 50-year-old vines, this clear, deep red wine slowly develops powerful aromas of concentrated ripe fruit. The pleasing attack is followed by well-structured tannins. This Juliénas needs to mature; it will be ready to drink in a year's time.
🔑 Raymond Trichard, Les Blémonts, 71570 La Chapelle-de-Guinchay, tel. 03.85.36.79.41, fax 03.85.36.79.41 ☑
Y ev. day 8am–12 noon 2pm–8pm

Morgon

Morgon is the second largest Cru after Brouilly, its vineyards located in a single commune. The 1,115 ha (2,754 acres) of AOC produce an average of 64,500 hl (1,702,800 gal) of robust, generous, fruity wine with flavours of cherry, bitter cherry and apricot. It is often the most robust of the Crus and many of its characteristics come from the soil which is made from weathered, mainly alkaline shale with deposits of ferrous oxide and manganese, described by the local wine-makers as *terre pourrie* or rotten land. It is said of the Morgon wines that they *morgonne*, ie that they develop in their own unique way. The situation of the vineyard is particularly propitious for Gamay and makes a wine that is for keeping and which, with age, can take on some of the qualities of a red Burgundy. It is a robust enough wine to drink with *coq au vin*. The soil of the Py hill, which rises 300 m (984 ft) in a perfectly shaped rump near the old Roman road between Lyon and Autun, is typical of the area.

The commune of Villié-Morgon is justifiably proud to have been the first to promote their wines, encouraging wine-drinkers who appreciate Beaujolais to visit the wine-tasting cellars in the Château de Fontcrenne which can cater for several hundred visitors. The cellar has a welcoming atmosphere which is very popular with the visitors and associations who visit.

DOM. AUCŒUR

Cuvée Prestige 1998

■ 1 ha 6,000 ▮ 30–49 F

The first vintage made by the eighth generation! A clear, deep-coloured wine, it has a moderately intense nose of wild berries with a hint of vanilla. After a very youthful attack, it softens up on the palate, with a pleasant finish tasting of fruit and menthol. Rounded and attractive, this wine is for drinking within two years.
🔑 Dom. Aucœur, Le Rochaud, 69910 Villié-Morgon, tel. 04.74.04.22.10, fax 04.74.69.16.82, e-mail AACOEUR@aol.com ☑ Y by appt.

CAVE DES VIGNERONS DE BEL-AIR 1999*

■ 16 ha 30,000 ▮ 🌡 30–49 F

This co-operative farms 400 ha (1,000 acres). It has produced a **Beaujolais-Villages 99**, cited by the jury, a **Brouilly 99** which was awarded one star, and this Morgon. Initial aromas of very ripe fruits develop and linger on the palate. A well-structured and ample wine that will continue to please for two years.
🔑 Cave des Vignerons de Bel-Air, rte de Beaujeu, 69220 Saint-Jean-d'Ardières, tel. 04.74.06.16.05, fax 04.74.06.16.09, e-mail cvba@wanadoo.fr ☑ ev. day except Sun. 9am–12 noon 2pm–6pm

DOM. DES BOIS 1998*

■ 1.1 ha 7,700 ⏸ 30–49 F

The estate is also a gîte with rooms for visitors. It has matured this clear, bright red wine in oak. The nose is redolent of fruits, peonies, elderflowers and spices, with a hint of green pepper. The tannins are just strong enough to balance the palate. Fresh and easy to drink, this wine should be kept for a few months. It would be perfect with roast white meats.
🔑 Roger and Marie-Hélène Labruyère, Les Bois, 69430 Règnié-Durette, tel. 04.74.04.24.09, fax 04.74.69.15.16, e-mail roger-labruyere@wanadoo.fr ☑
Y by appt.

ROLAND BOUCHACOURT 1999

■ 10 ha 75,000 30–49 F

This wine is an *assemblage*, or blend, of grapes harvested from 10 ha (25 acres) of vineyards. A garnet colour with violet highlights, its pleasant, complex primary and secondary aromas of black fruits, raspberries, spices and flowers continue on to the palate. A fragrant, fresh and reasonably concentrated wine for drinking within the next two years.

Roland Bouchacourt, 435, rte du Beaujolais, 69830 Saint-Georges-de-Reneins, tel. 04.74.09.60.00, fax 04.74.67.67.40

DANIEL BOULAND

Vieilles vignes Vieilli en fût de chêne 1998

■ 1 ha 6,000 30–49 F

Seventy-two-year-old vines produce this bright, clear dark garnet wine. A powerful nose of red berries and leather is followed by a fleshy and lively palate with spicy flavours of macerated fruit. This is a good 98 that is ready to drink now, but could be kept for a year.

Daniel Bouland, Corcelette, 69910 Villié-Morgon, tel. 04.74.69.14.71, fax 04.74.69.14.71 ☑
ev. day 9am–12 noon 2pm–6pm

DOM. JEAN-PAUL BOULAND 1998

■ 5 ha 20,000 30–49 F

This dark ruby wine with violet highlights is crystal-clear. It has a fresh and subtle liquorice nose that, while pleasant, is quite short-lived. With an aromatic and light-bodied palate, this easy, agreeable 98 is for drinking within the year.

Dom. Jean-Paul Bouland, Fond-Long, 69910 Villié-Morgon, tel. 04.74.04.25.23, fax 04.74.04.21.06 ☑ by appt.

NOEL BULLIAT

Cuvée Vieilles vignes 1998

■ 0.7 ha 4,000 30–49 F

This clear, dark garnet wine with orange highlights is the product of 70-year-old vines. Its clean, fairly powerful, nose has hints of toast, cherries and spices. The rounded, aromatic and forthright palate finishes on a tannic note. An attractive wine that should be cellared for a year to give the tannins a chance to soften.

Noël Bulliat, Le Colombier, 69910 Villié-Morgon, tel. 04.74.69.13.51, fax 04.74.69.14.09 ☑ by appt.

DOM. DU CALVAIRE DE ROCHE GRES Les Charmes 1999★★

■ 0.9 ha 7,000 30–49 F

Thirteen monumental representations of the Stations of the Cross and a replica of the grotto of Lourdes, all built in 1934, sit in the middle of this vineyard. As well as a **Fleurie 99**, cited by the jury, the estate has made this Morgon, our Pick of the Bunch for the best of the appellation. A very attractive deep purple wine with garnet highlights, it has a powerful aroma of roses, peonies, irises and elderflowers. The palate is particularly charming; a

berry bouquet is sustained by dense, elegant tannins. Ample and well-balanced, this remarkably harmonious 99 could be served now with roast beef, but is likely to improve over the next five years.

EARL Didier Desvignes, Saint-Joseph, 69910 Villié-Morgon, tel. 04.74.69.92.29, fax 04.74.69.91.23 ☑ by appt.

ARMAND ET RICHARD CHATELET 1998★

■ 3.2 ha 25,000 30–49 F

The Chatelets have taken advantage of the qualities of old vine grapes growing on schist soils.

Their clear, bright garnet wine has orange highlights and a powerful, vinous nose of cherries, redcurrants, blackcurrants and leather. The fruity and spicy palate is nicely rounded. Harmoniously structured and long, it is for drinking within the next two years.

EARL Armand et Richard Chatelet, Les Marcellins, 69910 Villié-Morgon, tel. 04.74.04.21.08, fax 04.74.69.16.48 ☑
ev. day 9am–12 noon 2pm–6pm

CYRILLE CHAVY 1999

■ 2.5 ha 8,000 30–49 F

This estate used to belong to the inventor of the Marmonier or vertical "basket" press. Its 99 is very dark with violet highlights. It has a gentle scent of red berries and alcohol. A frank attack is followed by blackcurrant aromas on the palate. Reasonably powerful and long, the wine needs to mature for a year or two so that its finish can soften.

Cyrille Chavy, Les Versauds, 69910 Villié-Morgon, tel. 04.74.04.20.47, fax 04.74.69.20.00 ☑

DOM. DU COTEAU DES LYS 1998

■ 4 ha 15,000 30–49 F

The Passot family distributes 20% of its production in Germany, Holland and Great Britain. A rich bright red, their 98 has a red berry and spice nose. Powerfully structured with a complex, fruity palate, this wine is for medium-term drinking.

Maurice Passot, Corcelette, 69910 Villié-Morgon, tel. 04.74.04.20.27, fax 04.74.69.15.57, e-mail maurice.passot@wanadoo.fr ☑
by appt.

CAVE JEAN ERNEST DESCOMBES 1999

■ 1 ha 7,500 ▮ 🌡 30–49 F

Many famous restaurateurs have visited this estate, which has been in the same family for several generations. A nose of clay minerals, faded roses and fruits distinguishes this very dark red wine. It is well-structured, but needs the civilising influence of time. In one to three years' time, it will be ready to serve with either a rib of beef or a strong cheese.

Nicole Descombes-Savoye, Les Micouds, 69910 Villié-Morgon, tel. 04.74.04.20.11, fax 04.74.04.26.04 ☑ Y by appt.

DOM. DONZEL Cuvée An 2000 1998

■ 1.5 ha 9,000 ▮ 🌡 30–49 F

A garnet wine with purple highlights, this 98 with its nose of blackcurrant, cherry, peony and leather, has been dressed up to celebrate the end of the century. A fine, elegant attack is followed by a pleasant and well-balanced palate. It is ready to drink, but will keep for up to two years and would suit being served alongside charcuterie.

Bernard Donzel, Fondlong, 69910 Villié-Morgon, tel. 04.74.04.20.56, fax 04.74.69.14.52 ☑ Y by appt.

GERARD DUCROUX 1999

■ 1.08 ha 8,100 ▮ 30–49 F

A bright, clear, ruby 98 with complex flowery and fruity aromas, this is ample and powerful on the palate with spicy flavours and a slightly austere finish. A well-made wine that will fully develop its character over the next few months.

Gérard Ducroux, Saint-Joseph-en-Beaujolais, 69910 Villié-Morgon, tel. 04.74.69.90.14, fax 04.74.69.90.14 Y by appt.

DOM. DE FONTRIANTE 1999

■ 4.6 ha 10,000 ▮ 🌡 30–49 F

Grown on the characteristic schist soil of the region, this ruby wine with beautiful violet highlights has abundant aromas of blackcurrants and some vinosity. A rounded attack gives way to warmer notes on the palate. A fairly structured and balanced 99 that is for drinking within two years.

Jacky Passot, Fontriante, 69910 Villié-Morgon, tel. 04.74.69.10.03, fax 04.74.69.14.29, e-mail jacky.passot@wanadoo.fr ☑ Y ev. day 8am–8pm

DOM. GOUILLON 1998

■ 0.6 ha 4,500 30–49 F

Clay soils have produced a ruby wine with golden highlights. A pleasant redcurrant/blackcurrant nose is sustained by good vinosity. This well-structured wine is still quite fresh, and is for drinking within the year. The **Beaujolais-Villages 99** was also cited.

Danielle Gouillon, Les Grandes Granges, 69430 Quincié-en-Beaujolais, tel. 04.74.04.30.41, fax 04.74.69.00.67 ☑ Y ev. day 8am–12 noon 2pm–7pm

DOM. DE GRY-SABLON 1999★★

■ 2.4 ha 10,000 ▮ ⦀ 🌡 30–49 F

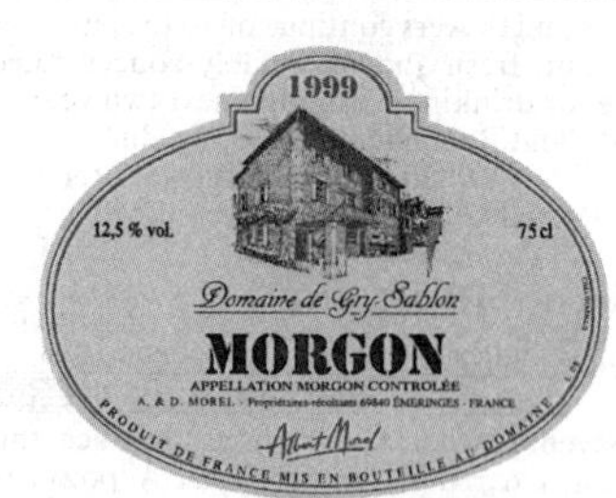

Temperature control and pre-fermentation maceration have resulted in a wine that is our *coup de coeur* as the second most successful Morgon we have tasted. A bright violet-red colour, it has a nose evocative of ripe fruits and violets. Concentrated, fat and well-structured, this fruity 99 should be drunk within the next year or two.

Dominique Morel, Les Chavannes, 69840 Emeringes, tel. 04.74.04.45.35, fax 04.74.04.42.66 ☑ Y by appt.

DOM. DOMINIQUE JAMBON 1999

■ 2 ha 5,000 ▮ 30–49 F

In 1995 Dominique Jambon returned to the family vineyard after having run other estates as a *métayer* (tenant grower). He has made a rich red wine whose cherry-scented nose has hints of spiciness. While the palate is certainly well-rounded, the tannic structure seems a little light. It is ready to drink now.

Dominique Jambon, Arnas, 69430 Lantignié, tel. 04.74.04.80.59, fax 04.74.04.80.59 ☑ Y by appt.

JEAN DE MOULINSART 1998★

■ n.c. 30,000 ▮ 🌡 30–49 F

The Tresch company has bought Maurice Chenu Wines and now sells its products under several labels. The **Beaujolais, Charles Aîné** received a citation (20–29 F). The Jean de Moulinsart Morgon is a very youthful deep red wine with violet highlights. While the nose is somewhat shy, the distinctive palate has a good balance of strong tannins, acidity and spiced fruit and vanilla flavours. This wine could be served now, with red meat or game, but it will also keep for up to two years.

Jean de Moulinsart, chem. de la Pierre-qui-Vire, 21200 Montagny-lès-Beaune, tel. 03.80.26.37.37, fax 03.80.24.14.81

DOM. DE LA CHANAISE Côte du Py 1998★

■ 4 ha 25,000 ▮ 50–69 F

The estate, which dates from the 16th century, was also cited for its **Régnié 99** (30–49 F).

The Morgon has a bright, deep purple colour and a subtle scent of peonies and spices with overtones of ripe berries and a hint of game. The appealing attack is followed by a fruity, full-bodied palate with quite powerful tannins. A complex and persistent 98 that will keep for up to three years.

Dominique Piron, Morgon, 69910 Villié-Morgon, tel. 04.74.69.10.20, fax 04.74.69.16.65, e-mail dominique-piron@domaines-piron.fr ev. day except Sun. 9am–6pm; Sat. by appt.

DOM. DE LA CHAPONNE 1999★

6 ha n.c. 30–49 F

Twelve days' fermentation with its cap of grapeskins punched down, maximising the extraction of colour and flavour from the grapes, has resulted in a warm red wine with violet highlights. Powerful aromas of macerated red berries, blackcurrants, raspberries and violets are echoed on the palate. Well-balanced, with chewy tannins, rich body and good length, it should be drunk within two years. It would be a satisfying accompaniment to red meat, braised wild boar or cheese.

Laurent Guillet, Morgon, 69910 Villié-Morgon, tel. 04.74.69.15.73, fax 04.74.69.11.43 ev. day 9am–12 noon 2pm–6pm

DOM. DE LA COTE DES CHARMES

Les Charmes 1999★

6.3 ha 12,000 30–49 F

A purple-red wine redolent of cherries, strawberries and blackcurrants with hints of spices. Well-balanced and aromatic, the hefty palate displays a fine balance of fruit and tannins. This well-made 99 is a very distinctive wine with good length. It is ready to serve now, with game, but could also be kept for three or four years.

Jacques Trichard, Les Charmes, 69910 Villié-Morgon, tel. 04.74.04.20.35, fax 04.74.69.13.49 ev. day 9am–12 noon 2pm–6pm

DOM. DE LA CROIX MULINS 1999

6 ha 44,000 30–49 F

A translucent, ruby wine with powerful aromas of blackcurrants, peonies and red berries. The full-bodied palate has a lively finish. You will need to age it for a few months.

Pierre Depardon, Les Raisses, 69910 Villié-Morgon, tel. 04.74.03.45.75

JEAN-MARC LAFONT

Les Versauds 1998★★

3.5 ha n.c. 30–49 F

Jean-Marc Lafont has been a négociant for several years now. His **Juliénas vieilles vignes 98** was cited by the jury, and his **Brouilly, Domaine de Bel-Air, cuvée Briante 99** was awarded a star. As for this rich red Morgon, it has a powerful nose of wild cherries and mulberries with hints of musk and leather. Fleshy, well-structured tannins combine with an aromatic palate to create a balanced and harmonious wine. Ready to drink now, it will continue to please for another two years.

EARL Jean-Marc Lafont, Bel-Air, 69430 Lantignié, tel. 04.74.04.82.08, fax 04.74.04.89.33 by appt.

DOM. DE LA FOUDRIERE 1999

1.8 ha 10,000 30–49 F

This Beaujeu négociant offers a clear, deep ruby wine with grape, raspberry, peach and blackcurrant aromas. The subtle but sinewy palate tastes of raspberries with a hint of pine-resin. Balanced but light, the wine should be drunk over the course of the next two years.

Les Vins Gabriel Aligne, La Chevalière, 69430 Beaujeu, tel. 04.74.04.84.36, fax 04.74.69.29.87 ev. day except Sat. Sun. 8am–12 noon 2pm–6pm

DOM. DE LA LEVRATIERE 1998

7 ha 20,000 30–49 F

The vineyard is one of many which belong to the Marmonier family. André Meyran has made a dark red wine with lively purple highlights. It has a subtle, clear scent of forest fruits. Fresh, with good structure and vanilla-strawberry aromas on the palate, this pleasant, easy-going 98 is for drinking within the year.

André et Marylenn Meyran, Dom. de La Levratière, Les Presles, 69910 Villié-Morgon, tel. 04.74.69.11.80, fax 04.74.69.16.51 by appt.

DOM. DE LA MERLATIERE 1998

2.2 ha 16,000 30–49 F

You arrive at Lancié by driving east along the D 9 from Villié-Morgon. This is a purple wine with orange highlights. It has a potent, attractive nose of blackcurrants, roses, wild cherries and spices. With a light and vivacious palate, this wine is not for keeping. It should be enjoyed now, perhaps with charcuterie or small game birds.

Paul Pariaud, La Merlatière, 69220 Lancié, tel. 04.74.04.10.16, fax 04.74.69.83.64 by appt.

DOM. DE LA TOUR DES BANS 1998★

2 ha 10,000 20–29 F

A *métairie* (tenant estate) of the Château de Pizay, this domaine has produced a clear ruby wine with pink highlights. An initially flowery aroma develops fruity blackcurrant and red berry notes.

On the palate it is fat, smooth and quite fresh. A charming wine that tastes of morello cherries, it is for drinking now. The estate's **Beaujolais 99** has also been cited by the jury.

Raphaël Blanco, Pizay, 69220 Saint-Jean-d'Ardières, tel. 04.74.66.20.10, fax 04.74.69.60.66 by appt.

Château de Pizay

DOM. DE L'HERMINETTE

Cuvée Prestige 1998

■ 0.4 ha 2,500 30–49 F

An *herminette* is an adze used by barrel-makers. Located 1 km (2/3 mile) from the Château de Pizay, this family-owned estate has made a bright, deep brick-red Morgon whose oakiness suits its name. Toasty aromas of new oak predominate over hints of blackcurrant. The woody, toasty palate is well-balanced. The wine should last for at least two years.

EARL Laurent and Marinette Gauthier, Morgon-le-Bas, 69910 Villié-Morgon, tel. 04.74.04.26.57, fax 04.74.69.12.08 Y by appt.

DOM. MARIE-ANTOINETTE

Climat Douby 1999

■ 3.15 ha 20,000 30–49 F

Some of the grapes used to make this wine are harvested from vine rootstock which dates back to the 19th century. It is a clear, garnet Morgon with an aroma of wildflowers, and banana and liquorice overtones. The attractive palate is lively and quite long. This relatively light 99 is for drinking within the year.

Marie-Antoinette Cimetière, Dom. de Font Chatonne, rte de Fleurie, 69910 Villié-Morgon, tel. 04.74.69.15.10, fax 04.74.69.14.86 Y ev. day 8am–8pm

CAVEAU DE MORGON 1998★★

■ 2.8 ha 18,600 30–49 F

Established in 1953, this was the first tasting cellar to be run by producers of its own wine. The dark red Morgon has a very lively and elegant bouquet of ripe berries and leather. A rounded attack is followed by complex aromas, which develop well on the palate. An exceptional combination of mature and youthful characteristics, the wine is perfect now, but should also keep for another two years.

Caveau de Morgon, rue du Château de Fontcrenne, 69910 Villié-Morgon, tel. 04.74.04.20.99, fax 04.74.04.20.25 Y ev. day 9am–12 noon 2pm–7pm; cl. 2 weeks in Jan.

Assoc. Producteurs Cru Morgon

DOM. DES MULINS 1999

■ 8 ha n.c. 30–49 F

Made from grapes grown on sandy soils, this very dark ruby wine has an iris and peony nose. A round attack is balanced by a firm palate. Well-structured and distinctive, it needs ageing for at least a year. It will then be a fine accompaniment to red meat.

Alain Aufranc, Les Mulins, 69910 Villié-Morgon, tel. 04.74.69.13.02 Y by appt.

DOM. DES NUGUES 1999★

■ 0.45 ha n.c. 30–49 F

This 20 ha (50-acre) estate has made a bright, crystal-clear purple Morgon with an intense, yet delicate, fruity and spicy nose. Strong tannins keep the palate in balance. Fruity, elegant, and quite long, this wine will improve if kept for two years.

EARL Gelin, Les Pasquiers, 69220 Lancié, tel. 04.74.04.14.00, fax 04.74.04.16.73 Y by appt.

CH. DE PIZAY 1999★

■ 19 ha 150,000 30–49 F

Parts of this château date from AD 970. A complex of several buildings, today it is a renowned hotel-restaurant. As well as a starred **Beaujolais blanc 99**, the estate has made a ruby Morgon with dark highlights. A very aromatic wine, it has scents of the forest, together with peonies and elderflowers, on the nose, and a predominant flavour of cherries. The palate is quite full-bodied, with firm tannins and a vigorous finish. A promising 99 for serving with red meat.

SCEA Dom. Château de Pizay, 69220 Saint-Jean-d'Ardières, tel. 04.74.66.26.10, fax 04.74.69.60.66 Y by appt.

DANIEL RAMPON 1998★★

■ 2 ha 15,000 30–49 F

A dark red colour with some orange highlights, the Rampon 98 has fine, sustained scents of leather, toast and liquorice with vinous notes. The powerful, intensely aromatic palate tastes of coffee and spices. An exceptional wine whose substantial character and very structured finish suggest that it will keep well for up to two years.

Daniel Rampon, Les Marcellins, 69910 Villié-Morgon, tel. 04.74.69.11.02, fax 04.74.69.15.88 Y ev. day except Sun. 9am–12 noon 2pm–6pm

DOM. SAVOYE Côte du Py 1999★

■ 1.2 ha 8,500 30–49 F

This dark red wine is the product of vines planted on the Côte du Py in the heart of the appellation. A forthcoming nose of overripe fruits hints at black cherries, blackcurrants and mulberries. Powerful and aromatic, the palate is structured with chewy tannins that re-emerge on the finish. This rich, distinguished 99 will develop further as it ages, and is worth keeping for three to five years.

Pierre Savoye, Les Micouds, 69910 Villié-Morgon, tel. 04.74.04.21.92, fax 04.74.04.26.04 Y ev. day 8.30am–11.30am 1.30pm–6.30pm; Sat. Sun. by appt.

DOM. DES SORNAY

Les Versauds 1999

■ 17 ha 60,000 30–49 F

Here is another estate owned by the family of the man who invented the Marmonier press. This is a clear, dark garnet wine with a well-developed and vinous red-berry nose. An extremely pleasing palate is generous and well-structured. The wine should be cellared for two or three years to give the tannins time to soften.

Jacques Dépagneux, Les Chers, 69840 Juliénas, tel. 04.74.06.78.00, fax 04.74.06.78.71, e-mail avr@free.fr by appt.

DOM. DES SOUCHONS 1998★★

■ 10 ha 60,000 30–49 F

This family, which has been making wine since 1752, declares its dedication to viticulture with a motto on its label: *Notre vin est notre vie* (Our wine is our life). Their Morgon captivated the jury: a clear, dark red wine with a fragrant nose of grapes, mulberries and leather. The palate has good vinosity. Structured, full-bodied and tasting of wild cherries, this weighty wine has the beautiful balance worthy of a *cru* wine. A harmonious and rich 98 that will keep for two to three years.

Serge Condemine-Pillet, Morgon-le-Bas, 69910 Villié-Morgon, tel. 04.74.69.14.45, fax 04.74.69.15.43 ✉ Y ev. day 8.30am–12 noon 2pm–6pm; cl. 25 Dec.–2 Jan.

DOM. DU THIZY Cave Collonge 1998

■ 1.5 ha 10,000 30–49 F

Vines grown on alluvial sand have produced a clear, ruby wine with an attractive, but youthful, nose of fresh red berries. The appealing, lively palate, with its hints of liquorice, seems ready. Drink now.

GAEC du Dom. du Thizy, Le Thizy, 69430 Lantignié, tel. 04.74.04.84.29, fax 04.74.04.84.29 ✉

Y ev. day 8am–12 noon 2pm–6pm

Collonge Frères

THOMAS FRERES 1998

■ 8 ha 40,000 50–69 F

The **Beaujolais-Villages 99** (30–49 F) offered by this négociant was also cited by the jury. Their Morgon has a rich red colour with some yellow highlights. The reasonably intense nose evokes wild cherries. Powerful and alcoholic on the palate, this wine is for drinking now.

Thomas Frères, 2, rue François-Mignotte, 21700 Nuits-Saint-Georges, tel. 03.80.62.42.10, fax 03.80.61.28.13 ✉

Y ev. day except Sun. 10am–6pm; cl. Jan.

Moulin à Vent

The domain of the 'lord' of the Beaujolais Crus is 660 ha (1,630 acres) of vineyard stretching over the communes of Chénas in the Rhône and Romanèche-Thorins in Saône-et-Loire. The emblem of the appellation is an ancient windmill at Les Thorins, standing proudly on the top of a gently rounded hillock, 240 m (787 ft) high, consisting of pure granite sand. The vineyard produces 38,000 hl (1,003,200 gal) of wine made from Gamay grapes. The thin topsoil is rich in manganese and other minerals which give the wines their strong, deep colour and scent of iris. These are full-bodied wines, sometimes reminiscent of their sturdier Burgundy cousins in the Côte-d'Or. Each year, in a traditional rite, the vintage is carried to the baptismal fonts in the local villages, starting at Romanèche-Thorins at the end of October and finishing at the 'capital' in early December.

Moulin à Vent can readily be drunk young, in its first few months, but also keeps well for a number of years. This 'prince' of wines was one of the first Crus recognised as an Appellation d'Origine Contrôlée in 1936, after its borders were legally defined by the Civil Tribunal in Mâcon. There are two wine-cellars where you can taste the wine: one at the foot of the windmill and the other at the edge of the main road. Moulin à Vent will accompany any dish and hold its own against many other reds.

DOM. JEAN BRIDAY 1999

■ 1 ha 7,700 30–49 F

The third generation of this family returned to the estate in 1986. Through the Eventail de Vignerons à Corcelles, they market this purple-red wine with rich aromas of flowers and spices and hints of blackcurrant. The palate is fat, with good tannins and an acidic finish. It should be cellared for two to three years before being served with red meat dishes.

Jean Briday, 69820 Fleurie, tel. 04.74.06.10.10, fax 04.74.66.13.77 ✉

Y by appt.

DOM. MICHEL BRUGNE

Le Vivier 1999★

■ 1.2 ha 9,000 30–49 F

A black cherry-coloured vintage made from young vines. It has an extremely concentrated nose of very ripe black fruits. A supple and round attack is followed by warm, firm tannins. Balanced, rich, but perhaps a little rustic, this wine needs to be aged for a year. It will then make a good accompaniment for tournedos with shallots.

Michel Brugne, 69820 Fleurie, tel. 04.74.06.10.10, fax 04.74.66.13.77 ✉

Y by appt.

DOM. DES CAVES Cuvée Etalon 1998

■ 2 ha 8,000 30–49 F

Vaulted cellars dating from 1620 have matured this garnet wine with scents of undergrowth, spices and oak. Spicy and woody aromas echo on the long, fruity palate. Still a little austere, it should be kept for a year or two before drinking.

Laurent Gauthier, Les Caves, 69840 Chénas, tel. 04.74.69.86.59, fax 04.74.69.83.15 Y by appt.

DOM. DE CHAMP DE COUR Réserve 1998★

■ n.c. n.c. 30–49 F

Marketed by Maison Mommessin of the Boisset company, this very dark, garnet-coloured wine slowly develops scents of liquorice, leather and vanilla. A lively attack introduces a powerful palate with very young tannins that enliven the ripe red berry flavours and give the wine ageing potential. It should be put away in your cellar and forgotten for three or four years while it matures.

GFA Champ de cour, 71570 Romanèche-Thorins, tel. 04.74.69.09.30, fax 04.74.69.09.28

DOM. A. DEGRANGE 1998★

■ 2 ha 12,000 30–49 F

This vineyard, which dates from 1933, has produced a clear ruby wine with orange highlights. Its fragrant nose has a complex scent of cherries and spices. The tannins are in balance with the overall structure of the wine. Ample, round and vigorous, it is attractive now, but it will improve over the next two years.

Amédée Degrange, Les Vérillats, 69840 Chénas, tel. 04.74.04.48.48, fax 04.74.04.46.35 Y by appt.

GEORGES DUBŒUF 1998★★

■ n.c. 30,000 30–49 F

The '*Hameau en Beaujolais*', a wine-centre and museum, is the brain-child of this négociant. Its **Fleurie 99** was cited by the jury, but this Moulin-à-Vent was the jury's choice as the best example of its appellation. A crystal-clear, deep garnet colour, it has a charred nose redolent of toast and vanilla. A forthright attack is followed by a riot of coffee and vanilla flavours. The wine's roundness is nicely counterbalanced by structured tannins, creating a perfectly weighted and harmonious palate. A very well-made wine, matured in oak, it will be a welcome addition to your table for the next four or five years, alongside grilled meats and chicken.

Les Vins Georges Dubœuf SA, quartier de la Gare, B.P. 12, 71570 Romanèche-Thorins, tel. 03.85.35.34.20, fax 03.85.35.34.25, e-mail mcvgd@csi.com Y ev. day 9am–6pm until Hameau in Beaujolais; cl. 1–15 Jan.

DOM. CHRISTIAN FLAMY Les Amandilliers 1999

■ 0.85 ha 6,660 30–49 F

A clear, ruby-coloured wine that has subtle aromas of raspberries, cherries and overripe fruits with hints of toast. The aromas continue on the palate. A well-balanced, ample wine with good tannins. We suggest waiting a year to allow the flavours to develop.

Christian Flamy, 71570 Romanèche-Thorins, tel. 04.74.06.10.10, fax 04.74.66.13.77 Y by appt.

CH. DES GIMARETS 1999

■ 1 ha 5,000 30–49 F

The 9 ha (22-acre) estate dates from 1850. A deep garnet colour with purple highlights, this vintage is fragrant of wild peaches, plums and vanilla. Rich and full-bodied, the palate is dominated by woody aromas and tannins. A distinctive wine that will develop its full character after it is aged for at least two years.

SCEA ch. des Gimarets, Les Maisons-Neuves, 71570 Romanèche-Thorins, tel. 04.74.66.47.81, fax 04.74.69.61.38 Y by appt.

Jacquemont

DOM. DU GRANIT Cuvée Vieilles vignes Elevé en fût de chêne 1998

■ 1.4 ha 4,500 50–69 F

This clear dark ruby wine has been matured in oak barrels. The nose is a mixture of redcurrant and leather scents. A lengthy palate is dominated by tannins that are still a little on the austere side. Needs to mature.

Dom. du Granit, La Rochelle, 69840 Chénas, tel. 04.74.04.48.40, fax 04.74.04.47.66 Y by appt.

Alfred-Gino Bertolla

DOM. DU HAUT-PONCIE 1998

■ 3.2 ha 6,800 50–69 F

A youthful-looking 98 with a rather powerful woody and anise nose. The palate, while quite well-structured, is not overly aromatic. Still, the overall effect is distinctive.

GAEC Tranchand, Dom. du Haut-Poncié, 69820 Fleurie, tel. 04.74.04.16.06, fax 04.74.69.89.97 Y ev. day 8am–8pm; Sun. by appt.

DOM. DE LA ROCHELLE 1998★★

■ 8 ha 8,000 30–49 F

The estate belongs to a family whose Swedish ancestors moved to France in the 17th century. It has produced a deep garnet wine with purple highlights that offers up fine scents of bilberries, mulberries and liquorice. Flowery and fruity aromas predominate on a rounded palate. A well-balanced wine with a complex bouquet and good length, the 98 is ready to drink now but could keep for three or four years.

GFA des domaines Sparre, La Tour du Bief, 69840 Chénas, tel. 04.74.66.47.81, fax 04.74.69.61.38 by appt.

DOM. LES FINES GRAVES 1998

■ 2,5 ha 16,000 30-49 F

This estate, which is named after its locale, has produced a garnet wine with some tawny highlights. It has an array of attractive red and black berry scents. Supple and well-structured, it is for drinking within two years.

Jacky Janodet, Les Garniers, 71570 Romanèche-Thorins, tel. 03.85.35.57.17, fax 03.85.35.21.69 by appt.

LE VIEUX DOMAINE 1998*

■ 9 ha 6,000 30-49 F

This highly regarded estate makes only two wines: the **Chénas 98** cited by the jury, and this Moulin-à-Vent. The bright, rich purple Moulin-à-Vent releases elegant scents of raspberries, blackcurrants and spices. Ample, round and supple, the concentrated palate is structured with chewy tannins. It is highly aromatic, and has a long finish. This delicious and charming 98 will be enjoyable for the next three years.

EARL M.-C. et D. Joseph, Le Vieux Bourg, 69840 Chénas, tel. 04.74.04.48.08, fax 04.74.04.47.36, e-mail le.vieux.domaine@wanadoo.fr by appt.

DOM. JACQUES ET ANNIE LORON 1999*

■ 1.3 ha 6,000 30-49 F

A wine made from 60-year-old vines planted in granitic soils on slopes facing south-east. It has a deep, purple colour and a complex aroma of very ripe stone fruits and spices. Initially quite young, firm tannins are apparent on the palate, but are balanced by savoury, elegant fruit. In a year's time, it will have matured and be a fine complement to meats in rich sauces.

EARL Jacques et Annie Loron, Les Blancs, 69840 Chénas, tel. 04.74.04.48.76, fax 04.74.04.42.14 by appt.

CH. DES MICHAUDS 1999*

■ 4 ha 6,400 30-49 F

The château has a beautiful elliptically vaulted cellar. It offers a garnet wine with bluish highlights and a concentrated nose of very ripe berries. The attractive attack introduces a well-structured palate. This ample, promising and generous 99 is ready to drink now but could be kept for a while.

Ch. de Chénas, 69840 Chénas, tel. 04.74.06.10.10, fax 04.74.66.13.77 by appt.

DOM. DU MOULIN D'EOLE

Les Thorins Réserve 1998**

■ 1.72 ha 13,000 50-69 F

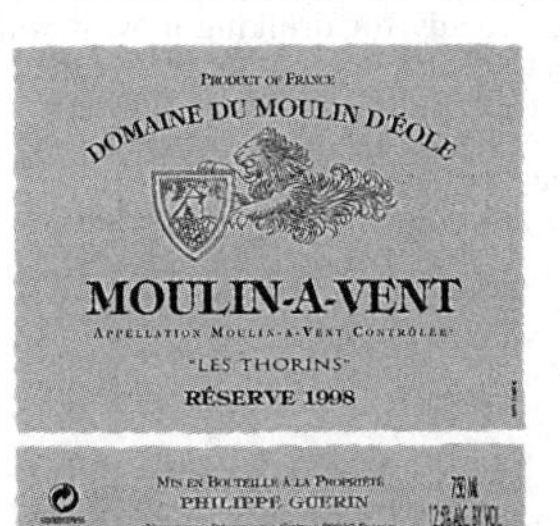

Vines growing in decomposed granite soils are the source of this wine, our *coup de coeur* of the Moulin-à-Vent appellation. A rich, purple colour with garnet highlights, this wine has an elegant, spicy and woody nose that shows the effects of being matured in oak for ten months. On the palate, it is lively and well-balanced, with chewy tannins. The long finish has only a discreet hint of oakiness. The wine should keep for three to five years.

Philippe Guérin, Le Bourg, 69840 Chénas, tel. 04.74.04.46.88, fax 04.74.04.47.29 ev. day except Sun. 9am–12 noon 2pm–7pm

DOM. DES PERELLES

Cuvée spéciale Elevé en fût de chêne 1998*

■ 2 ha 10,000 30-49 F

The estate, established in 1877, has aged this dark garnet wine in oak for a year. Intense, attractive woody notes of vanilla and macerated fruits are apparent on the nose. The ever-present oakiness re-emerges on the palate alongside the tannins. Thanks to masterful vinification, this well-structured 98 will drink well over the next two years, perhaps with roast beef. The estate's **Juliénas, Château de la Bottière 98** was also cited by the jury.

Jacques Perrachon, La Bottière, 69840 Juliénas, tel. 03.85.36.75.42, fax 03.85.33.86.36 by appt.

DOM. DU POURPRE 1999*

■ 10 ha 20,000 30-49 F

An attractive purple wine made in newly renovated cellars. It has a fairly intense nose of roses and peonies with hints of red berries. The rich, concentrated palate has very ripe berry flavours. This flavoursome, powerful 99 is ready to drink now, but could be stored for a year or two.

EARL Dom. du Pourpre, Les Pinchons, 69840 Chénas, tel. 04.74.04.48.81, fax 04.74.04.49.22 ev. day 9am–11.30am 2pm–7pm Méziat

DOM. DE ROCHE NOIRE 1999*

■ 2 ha 5,000 30-49 F

Both the grapes used to make the **Chénas 99** cited by the jury, and those used in this crystal-clear dark garnet wine were grown on

sandy soils. Concentrated red-berry and pepper scents accompany a fleshy, ample and aromatic palate. The wine's fruit and structure are well-balanced, and it has a lengthy finish. Ready for drinking now, it will continue to please for another two years.
🔑 Patrick Balvay, Le Vieux Bourg, 69840 Chénas, tel. 04.74.04.49.08, fax 04.74.04.49.81 ☑
🍷 ev. day 8am–12 noon 2pm–7pm

Régnié

Régnié was officially recognised in 1988. This recent Cru closes the breech between Morgon to the north and Brouilly to the south, extending the limits of the ten Beaujolais appellations.

Apart from a tiny parcel of 5.93 ha (15 acres) on the neighbouring commune of Lantignié, the 746 ha (1,843 acres) of the appellation are all in the area of Régnié-Durette. As is the case with Morgon, its older sibling, the single village name Régnié designates the wine. Only 577 ha (1,425 acres) were declared as AOC Régnié in 1999.

The aspect of the commune is north-west and south-east, so the vineyards get sun most of the day, and they may be planted on the hillsides from 300 m (984 ft) to as high as 500 m (1,640 ft) up.

The hillsides are part of the granite Fleurie range, and the mainly sandy and stony soil is exclusively planted to Gamay, There are, however, some areas which also contain some clay.

The vines are cultivated like all the other local appellations and the wines are made in the same way. However, an exception in the local regulations means that the wine-makers of Régnié are unable to request an AOC Bourgogne for their wines.

In the Caveau des Deux Clochers – the church it is next to has unusual architecture, symbolising wine – you can taste examples of the local wines, of which 33,880 hl (894,432 gal) were produced in 1999. They are fruitily aromatic with scents of redcurrant, strawberries and flowers. Overall, they are fleshy and supple, well balanced and elegant, sometimes described as 'frivolous', 'fun' or 'feminine' wines.

DOM. DU CHAZELAY 1999

■ 2 ha 10,000 ▮ 🌡 30–49 F

The **Morgon 99** also made by this grower was given the same mark by the jury as this rich red Régnié with violet highlights. It has a complex, fruity and flowery nose. An aromatic and rather elegant 99, this is a very attractive wine that is ready for drinking now.
🔑 Henri Chavy, Le Chazelet, 69430 Régnié-Durette, tel. 04.74.69.24.34, fax 04.74.69.20.00 ☑ 🍷 by appt.

CLAUDINE ET CLAUDE CINQUIN 1999★

■ 1.2 ha 8,000 ▮ 🌡 30–49 F

Although he has run this estate since 1973, Claude Cinquin has only been selling his own wines since 1990. A clear, deep ruby wine, it floods the palate with clean, fresh aromas of red berries. The palate is well-balanced and supple with silky tannins. This bottle is beginning to drink.
🔑 Claudine and Claude Cinquin, Les Forchets, 69430 Régnié-Durette, tel. 04.74.69.01.28, fax 04.74.69.01.28 ☑
🍷 by appt.

DOM. DE COLETTE Sélection Vieilles vignes 1999★

■ 7.5 ha 15,000 ▮ 🌡 30–49 F

Jacky Gaulthier uses organic farming methods. In order to produce the best possible wines, he carefully selects all his grapes before crushing. This fruity wine, made from old vines, is a dark garnet colour. The nose gives off scents of blackcurrants, peardrops, red berries and pears. The palate is forthright and intense, with a pleasant red-berry aroma. Well-made, round and harmonious, this wine should be drunk within the year. It would complement white meat dishes. The **Beaujolais-Villages 99** made by the same estate, and also cited by the jury, could be served with charcuterie.
🔑 Jacky Gauthier, Colette, 69430 Lantignié, tel. 04.74.69.25.73, fax 04.74.69.25.14 ☑
🍷 by appt.

DOM. DE COLONAT

Cuvée Vieilles vignes 1998

■ 0.76 ha 5,000 ▮ 30–49 F

Bernard Collonge has twice had a wine selected as a *coup de coeur* by the jury, a Morgon 90 and a Régnié 95. A sixth-generation wine-grower, he has managed this vineyard since 1970. This rich ruby vintage has an attractive nose of very ripe red berries. A fruity and well-balanced wine with a slightly austere finish.

🗝 Bernard Collonge, Dom. de Colonat, Saint-Joseph, 69910 Villié-Morgon, tel. 04.74.69.91.43, fax 04.74.69.92.47 ☒ Y by appt.

DOM. DU COTEAU DE VALLIERES 1999*

■ 4.9 ha 8,000 ▮ ♁ 30–49 F

This 12 ha (29-acre) estate has produced both a **Beaujolais-Villages 99** (20–29 F) cited by the jury, and this excellent Régnié. A dark garnet wine with violet highlights, it has pleasant scents of pinks and red berries. The wine's richness becomes more evident on the palate. A good structure and promising tannins support delicate and persistent floral aromas. This distinctive 99 would benefit from being cellared for two to three years.

🗝 Lucien and Lydie Grandjean, Vallières, 69430 Régnié, tel. 04.74.69.24.92, fax 04.74.69.23.36 ☒ Y by appt.

DOM. DU CRET D'ŒILLAT 1999

■ 9.4 ha 6,000 ▮ 20–29 F

Forty-year-old vines have produced a dark purple wine with a forthcoming berry nose. The palate is fine and fresh with some slight spritziness still in evidence.

🗝 EARL du Crêt d'Œillat, Le Bourg, 69430 Régnié-Durette, tel. 04.74.04.38.75, fax 04.74.04.38.75 ☒ Y by appt.

🗝 J.-F. Matray

DOM. CROIX DE CHEVRE 1999

■ 3 ha 3,000 ▮ ⦀ ♁ 30–49 F

Bernard Striffling exports nearly 30% of his production as far as the United States. Judging by the quality of this clear, dark red wine with its subtle blackcurrant aroma, he is a good ambassador for Régnié. The well-structured palate indicates that this is a wine that needs to be kept for two years in order to reach its full potential.

🗝 Bernard Striffling, La Ronze, 69430 Régnié-Durette, tel. 04.74.69.20.16, fax 04.74.04.84.79 ☒ Y by appt.

REMY CROZIER 1999

■ 2 ha 3,500 ▮ 20–29 F

A bright garnet wine with a subtle nose of blackcurrants and redcurrants. Its forthright and fresh attack is followed a rounded and well-balanced palate, and a finish that still shows plenty of liveliness.

🗝 Rémy Crozier, Les Maisons Neuves, 69430 Régnié-Durette, tel. 04.74.04.39.59, fax 04.74.04.39.59 ☒ Y by appt.

FRANCOIS ET MONIQUE DESIGAUD 1998

■ 4 ha 4,000 ▮ 30–49 F

This estate is equidistant from Villié-Morgon and Régnié-Durette, near the village of Saint-Joseph, famous for its church with two belfrys. It has produced a glittering garnet wine redolent of red berries with spicy overtones. A wine of considerable finesse, this balanced and fairly long 98 is for drinking now.

🗝 François et Monique Désigaud, Les Fûts, 69430 Régnié-Durette, tel. 04.74.69.92.68, fax 04.74.69.92.68 ☒ Y by appt.

CAVEAU DES DEUX CLOCHERS 1999**

■ n.c. n.c. ▮ 30–49 F

Every year 200 cycle-racers gather on the premises of this cellar. It offers a crystal-clear, dark ruby 99 that the jury has chosen as a *coup de coeur*. The nose has a very delicate scent of peonies, cloves, liquorice and spices. The velvety attack leads on to dense, elegant tannins that give structure to this harmonious, thoroughbred, full-bodied and distinctive wine. It is ready to drink now but could be kept for a year or two.

🗝 Caveau des Deux Clochers, Le Bourg, 69430 Régnié-Durette, tel. 04.74.04.38.33 Y ev. day except Wed. mat. 10am–12 noon 2.30pm–7pm; cl. 23 Dec.–15 Jan.

DOM. DU LABOUREUR 1999*

■ 5 ha 8,530 ▮ ♁ 30–49 F

Jean-Charles Braillon, an oenologist, has been managing his family's estate since 1983. He had matured a bright and clear deep ruby wine with a nose of cherries, redcurrants and flowers. This supple and smooth 99 envelops the palate with delicious strawberry and cherry aromas. An elegant and thoroughbred wine for drinking within two years. It could be served with a shoulder of lamb.

🗝 Jean-Charles Braillon, 69430 Régnié-Durette, tel. 04.74.06.10.10, fax 04.74.66.13.77 ☒ Y by appt.

JEAN-MARC LAFOREST 1999*

■ 7.75 ha 45,000 ▮ ♁ 30–49 F

Stainless-steel vats and a vaulted tasting cellar will attract wine-lovers, who will not be disappointed by the two vintages offered this year. A deep purple colour with violet

highlights, the Régnié has reasonably powerful, fresh and complex aromas of ripe fruits. Round, well-structured and long, it will continue to be enjoyable for another year or two. Jean-Marc Laforest's **Brouilly 99** also received a star.
Jean-Marc Laforest, Chez le Bois, 69430 Régnié-Durette, tel. 04.74.04.35.03, fax 04.74.04.69.01 ☒ Y ev. day 8am–8pm

STEPHANE LAPUTE 1999★★

■ 7.6 ha 2,500 30–49 F

This property dates back to the 18th century. Five successive generations of the same family have managed it. One of Stéphane's wines was selected as our *coup de coeur* last year. A maker of consistently fine wines, he has made an exceptional wine this year. Its plum-red colour suits the aromas of blackcurrants, mulberries and bilberries. These impressions linger on the palate, which is attractively balanced. Well-made and distinctive, it should be enjoyed over the next few months.
Stéphane Lapute, Les Braves, 69430 Régnié-Durette, tel. 04.74.04.36.65, fax 04.74.04.36.65 ☒ Y by appt.
Clément

DOM. DE LA ROCHE ROSE 1999★

■ 7 ha 5,000 30–49 F

In 1976, the fourth generation started managing this family estate that was created in 1911. They have produced a dark violet wine with fresh young scents of blackcurrants and peonies. An elegant structure and fruity aromas that persist on the palate make this an enjoyable wine for drinking now, but it will also keep for another two years and continue to be a fine accompaniment to grilled meats.
Georges Demont, Les Braves, 69430 Régnié-Durette, tel. 04.74.04.38.98, fax 04.74.04.33.28 ☒ Y by appt.

DOM. DE LA ROCHE THULON 1999★★

■ 7 ha 10,000 30–49 F

Pascal Nigay has been running this estate since 1990. He has used grapes from 35-year-old vines to make an exceptional Régnié 99. Elegant and intense scents of redcurrants and mulberries mixed with caramel notes emanate from this beautiful rich purple wine. An ample mouthful, very concentrated and dense, it will be sought out for its fruitiness and persistence, which should help to keep it for up to three years. The jury loved it . . .
Pascal and Chantal Nigay, Dom. de la Roche Thulon, 69430 Lantignié, tel. 04.74.69.23.14, fax 04.74.69.26.85 ☒ Y by appt.

DOM. DE LA RONZE

Grande sélection Cuvée vieillie en fût de chêne 1998

■ 1 ha 6,000 30–49 F

A family estate of long standing. This clear, deep red wine with its toasted almond, coffee and vanilla nose has been aged in oak barrels for nine months. Despite the oakiness, which pervades the palate, it manages to remain fresh. It should be drunk now with a red meat dish.
Séraphin Bernardo, La Haute-Ronze, 69430 Régnié-Durette, tel. 04.74.6 9.20.06, fax 04.74.69.21.69 ☒ Y by appt.

DENIS ET VALERIE MATRAY 1998★

■ 0.5 ha 3,000 30–49 F

Owned by the Hospices de Beaujeu, this *métairie* has produced a lively and brilliant red vintage that is still developing. Subtle, fresh aromas of red berries and blackcurrant leaves re-assert themselves more forcefully on the palate. A harmonious and balanced wine with good length.
Denis Matray, La Plaigne, 69430 Régnié, tel. 04.74.69.22.54, fax 04.74.69.22.54 ☒ Y by appt.

DOM. PASSOT LES RAMPAUX

Les Côtes 1998

■ 1.8 ha 7,000 30–49 F

Although it is located in Chiroubles, this estate also makes a dark red Régnié with fairly strong scents of blackcurrants and red fruits. Well-balanced, despite having strong tannins and a slightly astringent finish, this youthful, substantial 98 needs to mature for a year or two before being served with white meats.
EARL Dominique and Rémy Passot, Les Prés, 69115 Chiroubles, tel. 04.74.69.16.19, fax 04.74.04.21.93 ☒ Y by appt.

DOM. PASSOT LES RAMPAUX

La Ronze 1998★

■ 1 ha 4,000 30–49 F

These fourth-generation wine-makers have produced a lively red wine with rich and potent scents of red berries, wild cherries and blackcurrants. Although it is full, rounded and long on the palate, its finish is still a little firm; it needs to continue developing. It will be ready in about a year's time, and will be a fine food wine.
Bernard and Monique Passot, Le Colombier, rte de Fleurie, 69910 Villié-Morgon, tel. 04.74.69.10.77, fax 04.74.69.13.59 ☒ Y by appt.

CH. DE PIZAY 1999★

■ n.c. n.c. 30–49 F

The Château de Pizay is an attractive hotel-restaurant that also markets wines made by a group of producers. Its bright, deep ruby Régnié 99 has complex aromas of wild cherries, strawberries, mulberries and redcurrants. Fine tannins elegantly fill the palate. A thoroughbred, seductive, wine that could benefit from keeping for a year or two before being served with cold meats.
Sté des vins de Pizay, 69910 Villié-Morgon, tel. 04.74.66.26.10, fax 04.74.69.60.66 ☒ Y by appt.

BEAUJOLAIS

DOM. DE PONCHON 1999★

■ 10 ha 4,000 30–49 F

Since 1984, when Yves Durand became manager, the cellar here has been continually updated. It has produced a clear, bright ruby vintage with an expressive, ripe red-berry nose. The palate has an attractive balance of fresh and tannic notes. Lively and fruity, with a satisfying finish, this wine is for drinking within the next two years.

Yves Durand, Ponchon, 69430 Régnié-Durette, tel. 04.74.04.34.78, fax 04.74.04.34.78 by appt.

DOM. DE PONCHON 1999

■ 1.7 ha 10,000 30–49 F

Jean Durand has been managing this estate since 1961. His **Brouilly 99** was also cited by the jury. This glittering red Régnié has a pronounced scent of peardrops and black-currants. While the palate is smooth and fresh, and full of cherry aromas, the tannins are a little slight for a *cru* wine. A good quaffing wine.

Jean Durand, Ponchon, 69430 Régnié-Durette, tel. 04.74.04.30.97 ev. day 8am–8pm

JEAN-LUC ET MURIELLE PROLANGE 1999

■ 6.3 ha 8,000 30–49 F

This wine-grower began his career as cellar master at the Hospices de Beaujeu. He now manages the family estate. His dark red Régnié has an intensely fruity aroma with a hint of blackcurrant leaves. The fresh attack is followed by a lively, youthful palate, but the tannins need time to ripen. This rich and robust 99 should be kept for one to two years.

Jean-Luc Prolange, Les Vergers, 69430 Régnié-Durette, tel. 04.74.69.0 0.22, fax 04.74.69.00.22 by appt.

Yemeniz

JEAN-PAUL RAMPON 1998

■ 6 ha 15,000 30–49 F

For six generations, the same families have jointly owned and cultivated this estate. Its 98 has a dark red colour with tawny highlights and a subtle red-berry nose. The wine is full and supple on the palate, which is enlivened with fruity and spicy aromas. At the moment, the tannins are still a little aggressive, but they should soften over the next few months.

EARL Jean-Paul Rampon, Les Rampeaux, 69430 Régnié-Durette, tel. 04.74.04.36.32, fax 04.74.69.00.04 by appt.

MICHEL RAMPON ET FILS 1999

■ 6.7 ha 15,000 30–49 F

Last year this producer submitted a fine Morgon 97. This year, he has come up with a Régnié 99 that has been made for keeping. It has a lively, attractive purple colour and complex aromas of red berries, blackcurrants and bananas. The vigorous attack lingers on the palate long enough to suggest that it will be worth waiting for this wine to mature.

GAEC Michel Rampon et Fils, La Tour Bourdon, 69430 Régnié-Durette, tel. 04.74.04.32.15, fax 04.74.69.00.81 by appt.

DOM. THIERRY ROBIN 1998

■ 5.6 ha 7,000 30–49 F

Thierry Robin cultivates 3.5 ha (8.5 acres) of his own vines. He also manages vineyards belonging to the Comtesse de Flamericourt's niece. The combined harvests produce this youthful, bright 98 with its fresh, fruity nose. Well-balanced and lively, the palate shows nicely developing fruit flavours.

Thierry Robin, Le Bourg, 69430 Régnié-Durette, tel. 04.74.04.37.71, fax 04.74.04.37.71 by appt.

DOM. TANO PECHARD 1999

■ 6 ha 18,000 30–49 F

A few of the buildings on this estate date back to Napoleonic times. The owner, Patrick Péchard, welcomes wine professionals and amateurs. He has made a violet Régnié with a subtle nose of ripe red berries and black-currants. Aromatic and powerful, the 99 will age well, and will make an ideal accompaniment to coq au vin. The **Beaujolais-Villages** (20–29 F) that was also cited by the jury could accompany charcuterie.

Patrick Péchard, Aux Bruyères, 69430 Régnié-Durette, tel. 04.74.04.38.89, fax 04.74.04.33.35 by appt.

DOM. DE THULON 1999★

■ 4 ha 25,000 30–49 F

The estate is a *métairie* of the 15th-century Château de Thulon. It has already been cited for its **Morgon-Charmes 98**. This dark garnet Régnié has an attractive fragrance of fresh and crystallised berries. The fresh palate echoes the aromatic complexity of the nose. Harmonious and well-made, this is a wine to drink within the year with a stuffed shoulder of veal.

Annie and René Jambon, hameau Thulon, 69430 Lantignié, tel. 04.74.04.80.29, fax 04.74.69.29.50 by appt.

Saint-Amour

All 317 ha (783 acres) of the Appellation Saint-Amour are in the department of Saône-et-Loire, producing some 18,400 hl (485,760 gal) of wine. The soil is decalcified sandstone and clay and granite pebbles, and forms the boundary between the primary rock of the south and the limestone soils of neighbouring Mâcon and

Saint-Véran in the north. Two different approaches are taken to bringing out the qualities of the Gamay grape: the first, using grapes grown on the granite rocks, favours the traditional method of long fermentation in vats, creating wines with body and strong colour that are made to keep; the second is better adapted to Primeur wines which can be drunk early and so assuage the curiosity of wine-lovers. Saint-Amour goes well with snails, fried fish, frogs' legs, mushrooms and chicken with cream sauces.

The appellation has become a great favourite with wine-drinkers outside France and a large proportion of the wine is exported. Visitors to Plâtre-Durant can taste Saint-Amour in a cellar which was established in 1965, before continuing to the church and the town hall which, standing on a hill 309 m (1,014 ft) high, dominates the region. On the corner by the church there is a statue commemorating the conversion of the Roman soldier after whom the commune is named.

MICHEL BENON ET FILS 1999

■ 1.1 ha 8,600 30–49 F

This vermilion wine has a complex, fruity aroma with singed, earthy overtones. Fresh and gentle on the palate, it is an attractive wine for drinking now.

Michel and Rémy Benon, Les Blémonts, 71570 La Chapelle-de-Guinchay, tel. 03.85.33.84.22, fax 03.85.33.89.54 Y by appt.

DOM. DU CARJOT 1999

■ 3 ha 20,000 30–49 F

This clear, light red wine from the Carjot estate is sold by a négociant based in Juliénas.

It has a distinctive, complex aroma of crystallised fruits, flowers and peardrops, with a hint of new-mown hay. The palate is full-bodied. It is ready to drink now, but will keep. Jean-Marc Aujoux also offers a **Morgon Côte-de-Py, Domaine Charles Jenny 98**: a highly distinguished wine aged in vats and barrels, which was also cited by the jury.

Jean-Marc Aujoux, Les Chers, 69840 Juliénas, tel. 04.74.06.78.00, fax 04.74.06.78.01, e-mail avf@free.fr Y by appt.

DOM. DES DUC 1999

■ 9.5 ha 55,500 30–49 F

This estate keeps expanding; it currently owns 27 ha (67 acres) of vineyards. At the moment, vanilla scents obscure any fruity aromas that may be present in this purple wine. Robust, with a rich and firm structure, it needs to age for two to four years.

GAEC des Duc, La Piat, 71570 Saint-Amour-Bellevue, tel. 03.85.37.10.08, fax 03.85.36.55.75 Y by appt.

PASCAL DURAND 1999

■ 2.5 ha 15,000 30–49 F

These vineyards date back to 1864. To dwell in 'Paradise' making Saint-Amour wines, what a life! Pleasing, fresh and complex aromas of citrus fruits, raspberries and flowers are combined with a supple, rounded palate. A purple-ruby 99 for immediate consumption.

Pascal Durand, En Paradis, 71570 Saint-Amour-Bellevue, tel. 03.85.36.52.97, fax 03.85.36.52.50 Y by appt.

DOM. DE LA CERISAIE 1998*

■ 2.5 ha 10,000 30–49 F

This bright red 98 with dark reflections has a nose of very ripe red berries with hints of wild cherries and plums. The strong stone fruit flavours that balance some good tannins are promising. A very interesting wine that could benefit from being cellared for three years, perhaps even longer.

Gérard Besson, En Bossu, 71570 Chânes, tel. 03.85.33.83.27, fax 03.85.33.86.87 Y by appt.

FRANCOIS LAUNAY

Vieilles Vignes 1999

■ 0.5 ha 2,500 50–69 F

A pretty label depicts a young lover singing a courtly love song appropriate to this appellation. The rich ruby wine is redolent of ripe stone fruits with a hint of menthol. On the palate, it is initially supple, but concentrated tannins emerge later. We suggest waiting until the autumn of 2001 to drink this wine.

François Launay, Les Bruyères, 71570 Chânes, tel. 03.85.36.52.11, fax 03.85.37.46.62 Y by appt.

DOM. LE COTOYON 1999**

■ 2 ha 5,000 30–49 F

Frédéric Bénat, a regular on our pages, also runs a rural gîte. While visiting, one can sample this exceptional Saint-Amour. Subtle aromas of peonies, redcurrants and spices rise from this dark garnet wine. Youthful fruit and body balance forceful tannins on the elegant palate. This wine will achieve its full potential after two or three St Valentine's Days have passed. Then, it could be served with a piece of grilled beef.

Frédéric Bénat, Les Ravinets, 71570 Pruzilly, tel. 03.85.35.12.90, fax 03.85.35.12.90 Y by appt.

DOM. DES PIERRES 1999

■ 6 ha 40,000 ▮ 30–49 F

Georges Trichard was awarded a *coup de coeur* for his 97 vintage by the jury. Some of the best sommeliers in the world have tasted this estate's wines. The dark ruby 99 has subtle aromas of peaches, flowers and liquorice. A fruity and frank attack is followed by a powerful, even severe palate. This is a distinctive *Cru* that should be allowed to mature for another two or three years.

Georges Trichard, rte de Juliénas, 71570 La Chapelle-de-Guinchay, tel. 03.85.36.70.70, fax 03.85.33.82.31 ☒ Y by appt.

DOM. DES PINS 1999

■ 3 ha 22,800 ▮▮ 30–49 F

This 8 ha (20-acre) estate, which is surrounded by pine trees, matures its wines in oak barrels. The purple-red colour of the 99 is reminiscent of peonies, but they are not evident on the nose! Reasonably strong floral and fruity aromas linger on the palate. This is an appetising, full-bodied wine that should be drunk within the next two years, perhaps with grilled white meats.

Jean-François Echallier, La Piat, 71570 Saint-Amour-Bellevue, tel. 03.85.37.15.76, fax 03.85.37.19.17 ☒ Y by appt.

Le Lyonnais

The vineyards that produce wines under the Coteaux du Lyonnais appellation are situated on the eastern slopes of the Massif Central. In the east they are bordered by the Rhône and the Saône, in the west by the Monts du Lyonnais. Their northern limit is the Beaujolais vineyards, and they go south as far as the Rhône valley. The historic vineyards of Lyon have been cultivated since Roman times and wine-growing reached its zenith at the end of the 16th century when religious institutions and wealthy merchants favoured and protected the cultivation of the vine. A land survey dating from 1836 identified 13,500 ha (33,345 acres) of vineyards. Phylloxera decimated them and the city of Lyon expanded significantly, thus reducing the area under vines. Nowadays it is down to only 346 ha (855 acres), divided among 49 communes which form a semi-circle to the west of the city, from Mont d'Or in the north to the Gier valley in the south.

The area is 40 km (25 miles) long and 30 km (19 miles) wide and is marked by a succession of valleys at about 250 m (820 ft) high, running south-west to north-east with hills reaching some 500 m (1,640 ft). The ground is varied, being made from granite, metamorphic and sedimentary rocks with alluvial or loess deposits. The soil is light with good drainage and is very shallow, as is common in wine-growing areas where the underlying geological structure is ancient rock.

Coteaux du Lyonnais

The three prevailing climates of Beaujolais are also found in this region, though there is a greater influence from Mediterranean weather. However, the topology of the area is particularly susceptible to the influences of the oceanic and continental climates which means the vines can be planted only up to 500 m (1,640 ft) and not on exposed, north-facing slopes. The best areas are on the plateau. The vine varieties planted are essentially Gamay, vinified according to the Beaujolais method to give appealing red wines which are the favourites of the local Lyonnais clientele. Chardonnay and Aligoté also qualify under the appellation and are used for making white wines. Vineyards must be planted at a density of 6,000 plants per hectare and are pruned either in the shape of a goblet, as in the Beaujolais, cordoned or reduced to a single stem. Production bases start at 60 hl/ha (648 gal per acre). Red wine has a minimum strength of 10° and a maximum strength of 13° while white wine goes from 9.5° to 12.5°. In 1999 19,763 hl (521,743 gal) of red and 2,057 hl (54,305 gal) of white were produced. The Cave Coopérative de Saint-Bel vinifies three- quarters of the harvest and is a significant force in the region where there is a good deal of mixed farming with large tracts of land being given over to cultivating fruit trees.

The Coteaux du Lyonnais became an AOC in 1984. They are fruity, fresh, well-scented wines which go perfectly with all sorts of Lyonnais pork dishes, including sausages, saveloys, pig's tails, salted pork, pigs' trotters, knuckles of ham, together with goats' cheeses of the region.

MICHEL DESCOTES 1999★

□ 1 ha 7,000 20–29 F

The wine's vibrant golden colour with violet highlights is not indicative of its nose; it has a very delicate aroma of lilies-of-the-valley, honey and violets. Earthiness and acid are nicely balanced on the palate. This wine will continue to be enjoyable for another year or two.

Michel Descotes, 12, rue de la Tourtière, 69390 Millery, tel. 04.78.46.31.03, fax 04.72.30.16.65 ☑ Y by appt.

REGIS DESCOTES 1999

■ 1.57 ha 12,000 20–29 F

Twenty-five-year-old Gamay vines have produced a bright, not too deeply coloured wine. It has a subtle, but pleasing, nose of red berries and bananas. Balanced and light-bodied, this is a wine made for drinking within the year. It would suit pot-roasted beef.

Régis Descotes, 16, av. du Sentier, 69390 Millery, tel. 04.78.46.18.77, fax 04.78.46.16.22 ☑ Y by appt.

ETIENNE DESCOTES ET FILS

Vieilles vignes 1999

■ 1.2 ha 10,000 30–49 F

A single harvest of 60-year-old vines, half carbonically macerated, then aged in oak barrels, has resulted in a violet wine with an open, complex, red-berry nose. It has a harmonious, fruity and fairly light-bodied palate with silky tannins. A wine for drinking within the year.

GAEC Etienne Descotes et Fils, 12, rue des Grès, 69390 Millery, tel. 04.78.46.18.38, fax 04.72.30.70.68 ☑ Y ev. day except Sun. 8am–12 noon 2pm–7pm

DOM. DE LA PETITE GALLEE

1998

□ 2 ha 10,000 20–29 F

A blend of Aligoté and Chardonnay grapes results in an aromatic, flowery 98 that is very lively. This fresh and harmonious pale yellow wine with green highlights is for drinking within the year.

Robert and Patrice Thollet, La Petite Gallée, 69390 Millery, tel. 04.78.46.24.30, fax 04.72.30.73.48, e-mail www.domainethollet.free.fr ☑ Y by appt.

ANNE MAZILLE 1999

■ 1.5 ha 9,000 20–29 F

Anne Mazille has run this 5 ha (12-acre) estate since 1995. The wine's fairly light purple-red colour, and banana and red-berry aromas, suggest that it has not been made for keeping. A supple and smooth palate confirms its nouveau style. A well-balanced, long 99, it could be served with charcuterie or light cheeses.

Anne Mazille, 10, rue du 8-Mai, 69390 Millery, tel. 04.72.30.14.91, fax 04.72.30.16.65 ☑ Y by appt.

DOM. DE PETIT FROMENTIN

Vieilles vignes 1999★★

■ 2 ha 15,000 ▮ 🌡 20–29 F

The Monts d'Or region to the north of Lyons, known in Celtic as the Spring Mountains, has several tourist attractions. This superb deep red vintage with a pleasantly powerful scent of grapes and berries is made from 70-year-old vines. Its harmonious palate is a balance of fruity aromas and structured tannins. This hefty 99 with its unusual mineral overtones would benefit from being aged for two or three years. The estate's **Coteaux du Lyonnais blanc** was also cited by the jury.

🔑 André et Franck Decrenisse,
Petit Fromentin, 69380 Chasselay,
tel. 04.78.47.35.11, fax 04.78.47.35.11 ☑
🍷 by appt.

DOM. DE PRAPIN 1999

■ 5 ha 40,000 ▮ 🌡 20–29 F

A light-coloured wine with a pleasant and powerful aroma of grapes that continues on the palate, this 99 has been made for drinking within the year. The well-structured palate has reasonably persistent aromas, making for a congenial wine that could be served with grilled meats or goat's cheese.

🔑 Henri and François Jullian, Prapin,
69440 Taluyers, tel. 04.78.48.24.84 ☑ 🍷 ev. day 9am–7pm

CAVE DE SAIN-BEL L'Hommée 1999★

■ 8 ha 60,000 ▮ 🌡 30–49 F

This wine takes its name from the 19th-century term for the area one man could harvest in a day, *une hommée*. Thus, more than 125 *hommées* contributed to the making of this clear wine with its fresh aroma of strawberries and redcurrants. Those aromas continue on to the palate where they are supported by youthful tannins. This lively, elegant and distinctive wine is for drinking within the year. The estate's secondary production, made into a **Beaujolais 99, Domaine du Soly**, was also cited by the jury.

🔑 Cave de Vignerons réunis de Sain-Bel,
RN 89, 69210 Sain-Bel, tel. 04.74.01.11.33,
fax 04.74.01.10.27 ☑ 🍷 ev. day 8.30am–12 noon 2pm–6pm; groups by appt.

BORDEAUX

Bordeaux is the ultimate symbol of wine, everywhere in the world, but visitors seeking an old wine town with beautiful rows of hogsheads stretching along the port near the inviting wine stores of the shippers will be disappointed: the shippers have long since relocated to the industrial zones on the outskirts of the town, and the small cellar bars, where you could down a glass of sweet wine in the early morning, have practically disappeared. Echoes of another time, another way of life.

The history of wine in Bordeaux stretches back to ancient times. A wine trade was recorded in the area even before vines were cultivated there. In the first half of the 1st century BC, some years before Roman legions invaded Aquitaine, merchants from Campania in Italy came to sell their wine to the Bordelais. Thus, in some ways, wine was the medium through which the people of Aquitaine first experienced Roman life. Vine-growing was under way during the 1st century AD, but it seems that more serious cultivation began in the 12th century. The marriage of Eleanor of Aquitaine to Henry Plantagenet, the future King Henry II of England, encouraged the export of 'clarets' (as the English called them) to Britain. The wines of the year were shipped to England before Christmas. In those days no one knew how to preserve wine, and it would deteriorate after a year as a result of natural chemical changes.

At the end of the 17th century claret encountered stiff competition from the introduction of new beverages – tea, coffee and chocolate – and also from other, more robust wines from the Iberian peninsula. In addition, the foreign wars waged by Louis XIV led importing countries to levy punitive taxes on French wines. In spite of this, high society in England remained devoted to the flavour of claret. In the early 18th century some London shippers sought to create a new style of more refined wines, 'the new French clarets', which they bought young to lay down. In an inspired marketing initiative, shippers started to sell the wine in bottles that were corked and sealed to guarantee their origin, and could thus be sold at a premium. Almost imperceptibly, the connection between the *terroir*, the château and Grands Vins (fine wines) evolved, bringing about wines of a more reliable standard. Wines began to be judged, appreciated and priced according to their quality. As a consequence, wine-growers began to select land for cultivating the vines more carefully, limiting the amount of wine produced and improving the conditions for maturing the wines in casks. At the same time, they introduced new methods, protecting their wines during ageing through the use of sulphur dioxide and clarifying wine by fining or racking. The first ranking of the Bordeaux Crus was established at the end of the 18th century. In spite of the French Revolution and the Napoleonic Wars, which closed the English market for a period, the prestige of the Grands Vins of Bordeaux increased through the 19th century, as illustrated by the classification of the Crus du Médoc in 1855. This system, although not without its critics, is still in use today.

Following this period of growth, the Bordeaux vineyards were devastated by two major vine diseases, phylloxera and mildew, and suffered further from economic slumps and two world wars. Between 1960 and the end of the 1980s, however, Bordeaux recovered its prosperity by virtue of a remarkable improvement in the quality of its wines and a significantly increased world-wide demand for fine wines in general. The hierarchy of Bordeaux's *terroirs* and crus regained some international respect, although the red wines benefited more than the whites. At the beginning of the 1990s the market suffered from a variety of economic factors affecting the structure of all the Bordeaux vineyards.

The Bordeaux vineyards are situated along three major waterways: the Garonne, the Dordogne and the estuary they both feed into, the Gironde. The environment they create – sunny, sheltered slopes and steady temperatures – is ideal for growing vines. These waterways have historically also played an important economic role as the means for transporting the wines to market. The climate in the Bordelais region is temperate, with average annual temperatures of 7.5°C (45.5°F) minimum and 17°C (62.6°F) maximum, and the vineyards are sheltered from ocean storms by pine forests. Winter frosts are rare (1956, 1958, 1985), but if the temperature drops to –2°C (28.4°F) or below in April and May the young shoots can be severely damaged or destroyed. The vines flower in June, and cool, rainy weather during this period can wash away the pollen: as a result the flowers do not pollinate and the grapes do not form. Spring frosts and summer rains alike can have a critical impact on the amount of grapes harvested and thus explain the great year-to-year variations in the quantity of wine produced. The final quality of the harvest depends on having hot, dry weather from July to October, particularly in the four weeks just before picking begins (in all, grapes need 2,008 hours of sun each year to ripen properly). The local climate is in fact fairly wet, 900 mm (35.5 in) of rain per year falling mainly in the spring, when the weather can be very poor. Autumns, on the other hand, are famously warm, and exceptional late-season weather has often saved many vintages. The reputation of the Grands Vins de Bordeaux depends entirely on this fortuitous combination of location and climate.

Along the Gironde the vine is cultivated on a variety of different soils; and no particular soil type determines the quality of the wine. Most of the Grands Crus red wines are from alluvial, sandy and gravelly soils, other reputable wines come from clay on limy subsoil, sandstone or even sedimentary clay. The vines for dry white wines grow equally well on soil with layers of sand or gravel, chalky soils, on alluvium or sandstone. Vines for sweet wines are usually grown on gravelly sand or clay. In every case, natural or mechanical methods of drainage and control over how much water the vines receive are essential factors in the production of good-quality wines, to the extent that fine wines with the same high reputation can be grown on soils of entirely different geological types. However, the distinctive aromatic flavours of the wines are influenced by the structure of the soils: the Médoc and Saint-Émilion wines are good examples. Here and elsewhere, the same soil type may well produce red wines, dry white wines and sweet white wines.

The Bordeaux vineyards cover more than 115,000 ha (284,050 acres). At the end of the 19th century they extended over more than 150,000 ha (370,500 acres), but wine-growing was discontinued in some areas where the soil was inadequate. With the improvement of cultivating techniques, the total production has remained about the same, currently approaching 7 million hl (184,800,600 gal). While the average size of a vineyard is still about 7 ha (17 acres), changes in ownership have resulted in a progressive reduction in the number of producers (from 22,200 in 1983 to 16,000 in 1992, then from 13,358 in 1993 down to 12,852 in 1996).

The Bordeaux appellations

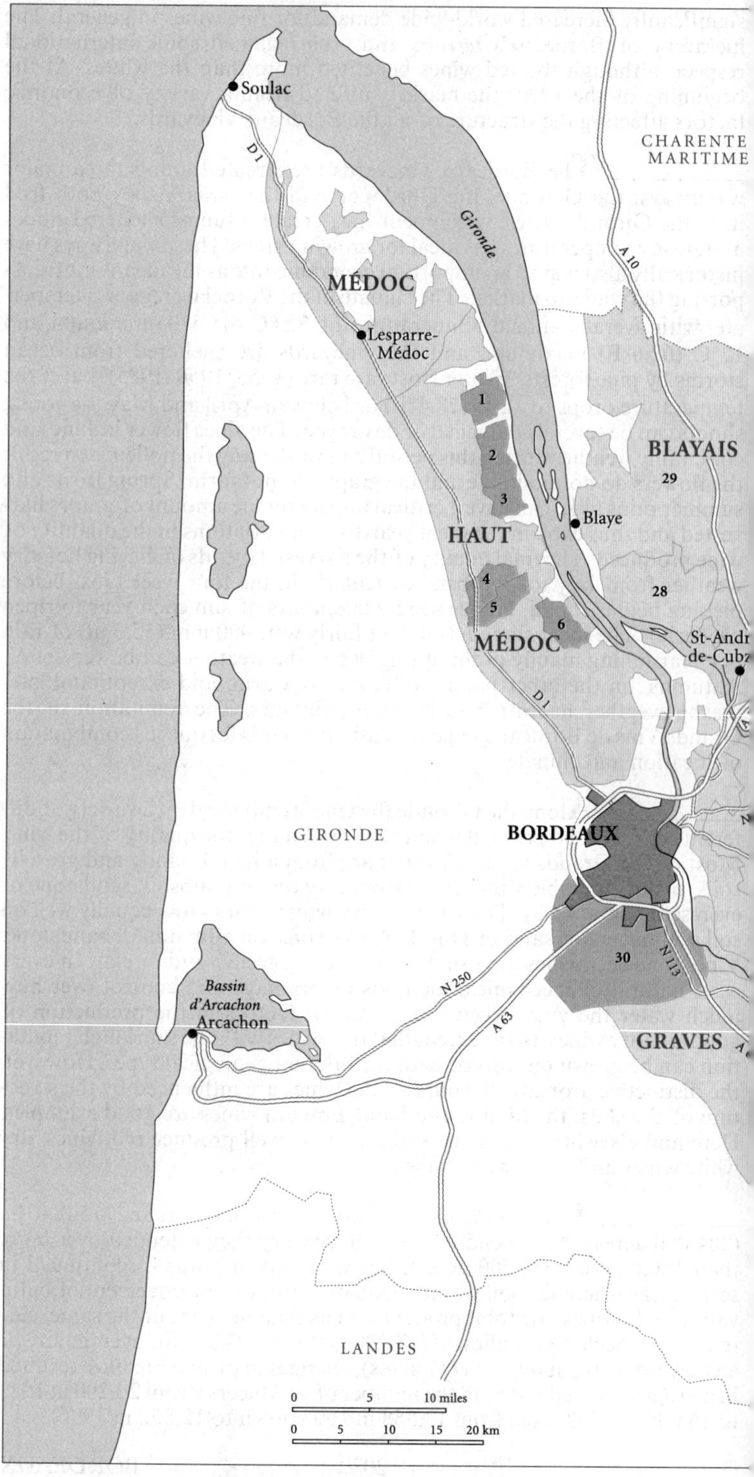

Soulac
CHARENTE MARITIME
D 1
Gironde
A 10
MÉDOC
Lesparre-Médoc
1
2
3
BLAYAIS
29
Blaye
HAUT
4
5
6
28
MÉDOC
St-Andr
de-Cubz
D 1
GIRONDE
BORDEAUX
30
N 113
Bassin d'Arcachon
N 250
Arcachon
A 63
GRAVES
LANDES
0 5 10 miles
0 5 10 15 20 km

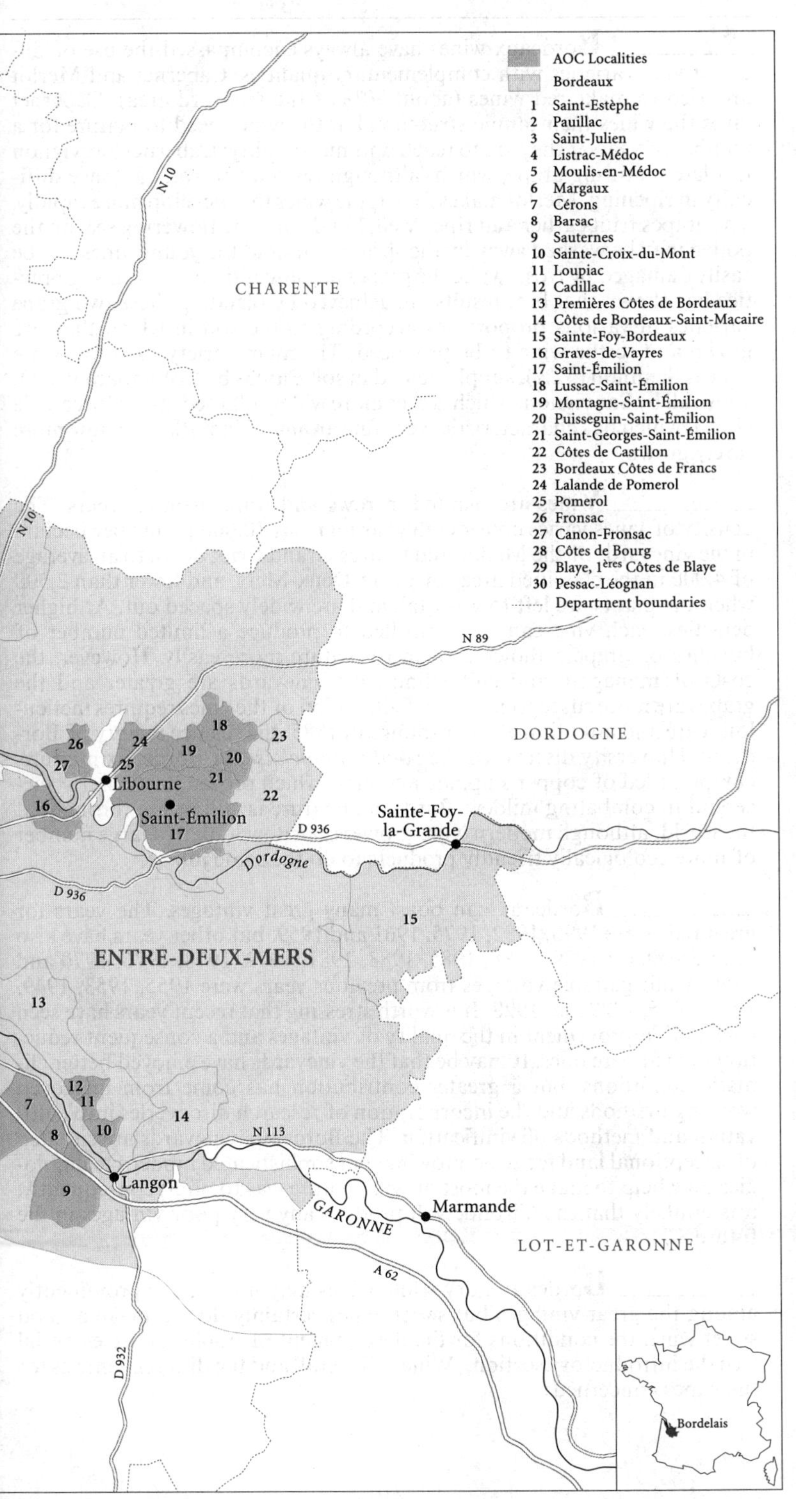

AOC Localities
Bordeaux
1 Saint-Estèphe
2 Pauillac
3 Saint-Julien
4 Listrac-Médoc
5 Moulis-en-Médoc
6 Margaux
7 Cérons
8 Barsac
9 Sauternes
10 Sainte-Croix-du-Mont
11 Loupiac
12 Cadillac
13 Premières Côtes de Bordeaux
14 Côtes de Bordeaux-Saint-Macaire
15 Sainte-Foy-Bordeaux
16 Graves-de-Vayres
17 Saint-Émilion
18 Lussac-Saint-Émilion
19 Montagne-Saint-Émilion
20 Puisseguin-Saint-Émilion
21 Saint-Georges-Saint-Émilion
22 Côtes de Castillon
23 Bordeaux Côtes de Francs
24 Lalande de Pomerol
25 Pomerol
26 Fronsac
27 Canon-Fronsac
28 Côtes de Bourg
29 Blaye, 1ères Côtes de Blaye
30 Pessac-Léognan
Department boundaries
CHARENTE
N 10
N 89
DORDOGNE
Libourne
Saint-Émilion
Sainte-Foy-la-Grande
D 936
Dordogne
ENTRE-DEUX-MERS
N 113
Langon
Marmande
GARONNE
LOT-ET-GARONNE
A 62
D 932
Bordelais

Bordeaux wines have always encompassed the use of different vine varieties with complementary qualities. Cabernet and Merlot are used to make red wines (about 90% of the vineyard area). Cabernet gives the wines their tannic structure, but the wines need to mature for a number of years if they are to reach optimum quality; Cabernet Sauvignon is a late-maturing grape, which, although resistant to rot, can have difficulty in ripening. Merlot makes for supple wines that develop more rapidly. The grapes fruit earlier and ripen well, but during the flowering season the pollen may be washed away by the spring rains and the young vines can be easily damaged by frost, while the grapes are susceptible to rot. Long practice has shown that best results are achieved by blending these two grape varieties in various proportions according to the soil in which they are grown and to the wine to be produced. The main variety used for white wine is Sémillon (52%), supplemented in some areas by Colombard (11%), above all by Sauvignon, which is ever more widely planted, and Muscadelle (15%), which has characteristic, very fine aromas. Ugni Blanc is now more rarely grown.

Vines are planted in rows and trained on espaliers. The density of vines varies considerably: as many as 10,000 plants per hectare in the vineyards of the Médoc and Graves Grand Crus, down to an average of 4,000 in the classified areas of Entre-Deux-Mers, and fewer than 2,500 when the plants are left to grow tall and are widely spaced out. At higher densities, each vine can be controlled to produce a limited number of bunches of grapes, allowing them to mature more easily. However, the costs of managing and cultivating such vineyards are greater and the grapes are more susceptible to rot. Cultivation of the vines requires meticulous care and attention all year round. In 1885, the science faculty of Bordeaux University discovered the *bouillie bordelaise*, or Bordeaux mixture, compounded of copper sulphate and lime, which proved particularly successful in combating mildew. Bordeaux mixture is still in use throughout the world, although modern wine-growers can now look to a large number of more ecologically friendly products to do the same job.

Bordeaux can boast many great vintages. The years for great reds were 1990, 1982, 1975, 1961 and 1959, but other years have also been excellent: 1989, 1988, 1985, 1983, 1981, 1979, 1978, 1976, 1970 and 1966. Unforgettable vintages from previous years were 1955, 1953, 1949, 1947, 1945, 1929 and 1928. It is worth stressing that recent years have seen a general improvement in the quality of vintages and a consequent reduction in mediocre ones. It may be that the vineyards have enjoyed better climatic conditions, but a greater contribution has come from improved working methods and the incorporation of research discoveries into cultivation and methods of vinification. The Bordeaux vineyards are situated on exceptional land for wine-growing, but sophisticated modern technologies now help to make the most of what nature was to offer; consequently, it is unlikely that the Gironde will produce any very poor vintages in the future.

Bordeaux's dry white wines may not feature prominently among the great vintages but sweet wines certainly do. To make a good sweet wine, the conditions for the development of noble rot are essential (see the introductory section, 'Wine – General' and the different entries for the wines concerned).

Médoc – Graves – Saint-Émilion – Pomerol – Fronsac

vintages	to drink	to keep	to drink or keep
exceptional	**45 47 61 70 75**		**82 85**
very good	**49 53 55 59 62 64 66 67 71* 76 78 79**	**88 89 90 95 96**	**81 83 86 89 93 94**
good	**50 73 74 77 80 84 87 92**	**97**	**91**

***** For Pomerol this vintage is exceptional.

– Appellation Bordeaux wines and the red Vins de Côte should be drunk in 5 or 6 years. Some can be kept for as long as 10 years.

Dry white Graves

vintages	to drink	to keep	to drink or keep
exceptional	**78 81 82 83**		
very good	**76 85 87 88 92**	**95 96 98**	**93 94**
good	**79 80 84 86**		**89 90 97**

– It is preferable to drink the other dry white Bordeaux wines very young, within 2 years.

Sweet white wines

vintages	to drink	to keep	to drink or keep
exceptional	**47 67 70 71 75 76**	**90 95 97**	**83 88 89**
very good	**49 59 62**	**96 98**	**81 82 86**
good	**50 55 77 78 79 80 91**		**84 85 87 94**

– Sweet wines can be drunk young (as an aperitif their fruitiness can be particularly enjoyed), but they acquire their classic qualities only after long ageing.

Bordeaux Grands Crus wines have long been bottled at the property, but it is only in the last ten or fifteen years that the whole task, from vinification to bottling, has been carried out there. For other wines (generic appellations or regional wines), the wine-grower was traditionally primarily responsible for cultivating the vines and making the grapes into wine. In this system, *négociants* (local wholesale wine-buyers and shippers) not only undertook the sales of the wines but also oversaw their production right up to the time of bottling in order to ensure their quality. The situation is gradually changing, and nowadays, on the whole, the great majority of AOC wines are grown, aged and warehoused by the producers. Progress in wine technology makes it possible to produce reliable wines on a regular basis and, naturally enough, the wine-makers wish to make the most profit by bottling the wine themselves. The Caves Coopératives have played a significant role in this change by creating organisations that take care of the ageing and marketing of the wines on behalf of their members. The *négociant* still has an important role in distributing the wines, particularly for export, exploiting long-established sales networks. On the other hand, it is possible to envisage a time in the future when it will be more profitable for producers to sell their wines directly to the consumer.

Marketing the significant quantities of wine produced in Bordeaux is subject to the vagaries of economic conditions as well as to the volume and quality of the harvest. In recent years, the Conseil Interprofessionel des Vins de Bordeaux has played an important role in sales and marketing by establishing benchmark levels of stockholding and production, by stipulating certain conditions of quality and by implementing financial measures relating to the organisation of the market.

The regional *syndicats* or wine unions also protect the different Appellations d'Origine Contrôlées by defining criteria for quality. Under the management and control of INAO, they organise tastings at which all the wines produced each year are judged; they have the power to take away the appellation rights of a wine if its quality is deemed inadequate.

The various wine Confréries (Jurade in Saint-Émilion, Commanderie du Bontemps in Médoc and Graves, Connétablie in Guyenne and so on) organise regular festivals and popular events to promote Bordeaux wines. Their activities are co-ordinated by the Grand Conseil du Vin de Bordeaux.

All these promotional and marketing activities and production controls demonstrate that Bordeaux wines make up a major industry that is rigorously managed. The AOC wines produced in Bordeaux represent 26.54% of the all wines produced in France, with a volume of 6,879,693 hl (181,623,897 gal) in 1999, worth thousands of million francs in total, of which FF3,000 million is earned through exports. The industry plays an important role in the life of the region, since it is estimated that one Girondin in six is directly or indirectly dependent on the activities of the wine industry. But for Gascony, the region of the Bordeaux wines, wine is more than simply a product of the economy. It is also, and above all, part of the culture. Behind the labels may lie châteaux with stunning architecture or simple peasant houses, but always also the vineyards and the wine cellars where people work, applying their know-how and contributing their traditions and their memories to the production of great wine.

Bordeaux: the regional appellations

While it is relatively straightforward to identify the Appellation Communale wines, it is not so easy to understand what the Appellation Bordeaux means. In fact, the definition is quite simple: it applies to all good-quality wines produced within the boundaries of the department of the Gironde, excluding any that come from the sandy area to the west and south (namely La Lande, which has been set aside as a pine forest since the 19th century). Put more simply, the appellation applies to all wines from the designated wine-growing areas of the Gironde. All the wines produced there have the right to use it subject to meeting the fairly strict regulations concerning the selection of grape varieties, limits on quantities produced and so on. However, this simple provision conceals great variations. Indeed, rather than talking about a single Bordeaux appellation, it is more correct to talk about the Bordeaux appellations, which include red wine, rosé, clairets, both dry and sweet white wines, and white or rosé sparkling wines. The variety of geographical origins for Bordeaux appellation wines gives rise to several types of wines that can claim the appellation. In some cases it means wines that are produced in parts of the Gironde that have the right to use only the Bordeaux appellation, such as the marshy districts (made up of alluvial soils) near the rivers or in parts of the Libournais (communes such as Saint-André-de-Cubzac, Guîtres, Coutras, for example). In other cases, the wines come from regions that also have the right to a specific appellation (Médoc, Saint-Émilion, Pomerol, and so on). Alternatively, a regional appellation can be used by a local appellation that may be less well known commercially (such as the Bordeaux Côtes-de-Francs, Bordeaux Haut-Benauge, Bordeaux Sainte-Foy or Bordeaux Saint-Macaire); the specific appellation is, in real terms, no more than an adjunct to the Appellation Régionale and, in fact, adds nothing to the intrinsic value of the product. In such cases, wine-makers are happier to rely on the image of the Bordeaux 'brand name'. Occasionally, Bordeaux wines may come from a property located in the production area of a particular, sometimes prestigious, appellation, an occurrence that can provoke a good deal of curiosity among inquisitive wine-lovers. But here, too, the explanation is not difficult to find: traditionally, many properties in the Gironde produced several types of wine (more usually both reds and whites); now, in numerous cases (Médoc, Saint-Émilion, Entre-Deux-Mers and Sauternes), the specific appellation applies to only one type. Consequently, the other wines produced are marketed as Bordeaux or Bordeaux Supérieur.

Though these wines may be less celebrated than the Grands Crus, in a quantitative sense all these Bordeaux constitute the largest appellation of the Gironde with, in 1999 3,267,768 hl (86,269,075 gal) of red, 568,180 hl (14,999,952 gal) of white and 12,715 hl (335,676 gal) of sparkling Crémant de Bordeaux.

Taken at face value, the quantity of wine produced and the impressive area of the vineyards (58,000 ha/143,260 acres) could lead one to suppose that there are few similarities among Bordeaux wines. The wines do indeed have distinctions in character, but they, also have qualities in common that give an overall identity to the Appellations Régionales. Thus Bordeaux red wines are well-balanced, and delicate; generally they should be fruity but not too full-bodied, so they can be drunk young. The Bordeaux Supérieur reds tend to be more complete; they are made from the best grapes and vinified by a method that will ensure they can keep for some time. They form a select group among Bordeaux wines.

Bordeaux clairets and rosés are made by allowing red-grape varieties to macerate for a short time; the clairets have a slightly more intense colour. They are fresh, fruity wines, but only a limited quantity is produced.

White Bordeaux are dry, lively, fruity wines. In recent years their quality has been improved by new techniques of vinification, but it should be said that this appellation does not yet enjoy the popularity it deserves. Some of these wines are 'demoted' to table wines, not least because the difference in profit is slight and it is sometimes easier to sell it as table wine than as Bordeaux Blanc. As a group, white Bordeaux Supérieur wines are luscious and rich; production, though, is small.

There is also an Appellation Crémant de Bordeaux. To qualify, all the grapes used must come from the designated Bordeaux appellation region. The second fermentation (the *prise de mousse*), must occur in bottle at wine cellars in the Bordeaux region.

CH. ARNEAU-BOUCHER 1998

■ 20.6 ha 12,000 ▮ 30-49 F

Aromas of blackcurrant and raspberry enhanced by lychee feature in this wine's somewhat discreet nose, becoming a more obvious feature of the firm, elegant though vinous palate. A Merlot in its prime, a dependable accompaniment to grilled red meat.

EARL Jacques Sartron et ses Enfants, 8, le Bourg, 33240 Saint-Genès-de-Fronsac, tel. 05.57.43.11.12, fax 05.57.43.56.34 ☒

CH. D'AUGAN 1998★

■ 5 ha 40,000 30–49 F

This co-operative's wines are often praised, for example its 1995 Château Langel-Mauriac. This Château d'Augan is a great success. The jury liked its round, rich body, perfumes of red fruits and tannins for good keeping. Over the next two to five years it will be a superb accompaniment to entrecôte steak with mushrooms, for instance. The cask-matured **1998 Château Langel Mauriac** is recommended. It is a wine of vanilla-flavoured roundness, with intense, subtle perfumes of small red fruits in alcohol. The tannins will not hold out as long as the nose might suggest. Worth visiting in the vicinity is a fine abbey with a remarkable doorway.

Vignerons de Guyenne, Union des producteurs de Blasimon, 33540 Blasimon, tel. 05.56.71.55.28, fax 05.56.71.59.32 by appt.

CH. BASTIAN 1998★★

■ 7 ha 53,000 20–29 F

The vineyard on this former Rivet Abbey smallholding is still young, dating only from 1988. It is already a success. Grown on silty sand, the Merlot component in this wine is balanced by Cabernets. It fills the mouth well, with a roundness set off by aromas of black fruits. The tannins are silky, yet have a presence which bodes well for ageing. 'Well above par for the appellation,' observed one of the jury.

Stéphane Savigneux, Ch. Bastian, 33124 Auros, tel. 05.56.65.51.59, fax 05.56.65.43.78, e-mail stéphane.savigneux@wanadoo.fr by appt.

BEAU MAYNE 1998★

■ n.c. n.c. 20–29 F

A classic construction by Dourthe using 50% Merlot and 35% Cabernet-Sauvignon grapes, this elegant wine is an attractive purple with orangey lights and has a complex range of aromas, comprising crystallised fruits, almonds and flowers. Its round body has excellent length, accompanied by spicy notes. Ready for drinking now throughout a meal, preferably with meats in sauce and tomme cheeses (from Savoie).

Dourthe, 35, rte de Bordeaux, B.P. 49, 33290 Parempuyre, tel. 05.56.35.53.00, fax 05.56.35.53.29, e-mail contact@cvbg.com by appt.

BEAU RIVAGE 1998★

■ 100 ha 350,000 20 F+

This blend by the large Bordeaux firm comprises 45% Merlot, 45% Cabernet-Sauvignon and 10% Cabernet Franc. The lovely red-purple colour is superb and appetising. The body, evocative of ripe blackberries and raspberries, benefits from a balanced tannic structure. The finish is full, indicating that the wine may be enjoyed straight away, though it could improve still further, cellar permitting. A classic Bordeaux that may be found in any of 65 countries outside France.

Borie Manoux, 86, cours Balguerie-Stuttenberg, 33082 Bordeaux Cedex, tel. 05.56.00.00.70, fax 05.57.87.48.61

CH. BEL AIR Perponcher 1998★★

■ n.c. n.c. 30–49 F

The Despagne family share with their wine-manager and oenologist an enthusiasm for vines and wines that every year attracts star-ratings. This is their 'standard' Bordeaux. Grown on extremely favourable limestone-clay soils and comprising three-quarters Merlot to one-quarter Cabernet-Sauvignon, it has a deep, dense colour whose promise is amply fulfilled. The nose is characterised by aromas of red fruits, whilst the powerful palate is rich in fruity, slightly smoky flavours. The wine's body is sustained by tannins that are not just sturdy, but subtle and long. This 1998 wine needs to age. Lovers of a good cellar will not be disappointed.

GFA de Perponcher, Ch. Bel Air, 33420 Naujan-et-Postiac, tel. 05.57.84.55.08, fax 05.57.84.57.31, e-mail despagne@vignobles-despagne.com by appt.

J. Despagne

CH. BELLE-GARDE

Cuvée élevée en fût de chêne 1998★

■ 6 ha 40,000 30–49 F

Made from 30-year-old vines of Merlot (70%), Cabernet-Sauvignon (20%) and Cabernet Franc (10%), this wine is accustomed to star-ratings. The nose is richly redolent of raspberry and blackcurrant, roasted oaky notes and spices. The fruity palate is not overwhelmed by the oak. A wine to sample now, but also to journey with as it ages. High hopes are in order.

Eric Duffau, Ch. Belle-Garde, Monplaisir, 33420 Génissac, tel. 05.57.24.49.12, fax 05.57.24.41.28 ev. day except Sun. 8am–12 noon 2pm–7pm; cl. 15–31 Aug.

CH. DE BERTIN 1998★

■ 4 ha 20,000 30–49 F

Four hectares (ten acres) of vines on limestone clay have yielded a wine moderately dominated by Cabernets (60%). It has a velvety richness with a tantalising slight hint of undergrowth. Could well be a charming accompaniment to salty dishes.

EARL Bertin, lieu-dit Bertin, 33760 Cantois, tel. 05.56.23.61.02, fax 05.56.23.94.77, e-mail bertin@caves-particulieres.com by appt.

Mano

CH. BONNET

Réserve Elevé en fût de chêne 1998★★

■ 57 ha n.c. 30–49 F

André Lurton is a happy owner, being not just a producer of great wines but also one of those Bordeaux wine-growers whose views command most respect. Bonnet is the headquarters of his operation. In the recent past, his 1996 wine was highly praised, and this 1998 version, like its 1997 predecessor, comes close to it. An informed taster may feel that fullness gets the upper hand over subtlety, but at this level of quality the complex opulence of the wine's mature fleshiness, assisted by grape and oak tannins, will delight any wine-lover. The **1998 Château Guibon** is awarded one star: its elegant, concentrated harmony of ripe fruits and slight touch of mint is something to savour unhurriedly with grilled red meat or game-birds.

Vignobles André Lurton, Ch. Bonnet, 33420 Grézillac, tel. 05.57.25.58.58, fax 05.57.74.98.59, e-mail andre.lurton@wanadoo.fr ☑ Y by appt.

CELLIER DE BORDES 1998

■ n.c. 100,000 20–29 F

Cellier de Bordes is a Cheval-Quencard trademark. It is a very round, supple wine, neither excessively soft nor over-dominated by tannins. The nose is redolent of wild strawberries. It is a pleasant, direct, typical Bordeaux, like its fellow, the **1998 Chai de Bordes**. Also recommended is the **1998 Grande Tradition Gourmet**, which is distributed by the Monoprix-Prisunic chain and is a simple, straightforward, easy-drinking wine suitable for everyday dishes.

Cheval Quancard, La Mouline, 33560 Carbon-Blanc, tel. 05.57.77.88.88, fax 05.57.77.88.99 Y by appt.

CH. BRION DE LALANDE 1998★

■ 3 ha 12,000 30–49 F

This wine's aromas are dominated by oak, though with enriching delicacy. The long, fleshy body readily responds with fruity, vanilla tones. Made exclusively from Merlot grapes, this is an enjoyable wine that is ready to drink – though there is no hurry – alongside roast poultry or a duck steak.

Roux, Brion, 33750 Baron, tel. 05.57.88.78.52 ☑ Y by appt.

CH. CHANTELOISEAU 1998★★

■ 25.03 ha 65,000 30–49 F

The basilica and calvary at Verdelais overlook the landscape of the Garonne's northern slopes. Merlot and Cabernets occupy about one half each of this 30-year-old vineyard. The vines' ideal age is reflected in the wine, which has a ruby colour and an intense, complex nose of ripe, crystallised fruits. An initial impression of fullness is followed by sensations of fleshiness and richness provided by the wine's extremely well-balanced palate with hints of fruits of the forest. 'A wonderful accompaniment to leg of lamb,' was one expert opinion.

SCEA Dulac et Séraphon, 2, Pantoc, 33490 Verdelais, tel. 05.56.62.02.08, fax 05.56.76.71.49 ☑ Y by appt.

CHAPELLE DE BRIVAZAC 1998★

■ 13.64 ha 110,000 30–49 F

Between the small port of Bourg and the citadel of Blaye, the Château de Barbe overlooks the Gironde. The chapel, in the midst of the vineyard, has long been a landmark to mariners. The product of a long vatting process and well-judged proportions (55% Merlot, 20% Cabernet Franc), this dark-coloured wine has a full, robust, already rich body perfumed with notes of liquorice, smokiness and spices. Though the tannins still seem astringent, this actually bodes well for ageing in a wine that will suit lovers of traditional wines.

Société viticole du Ch. de Barbe, 33710 Villeneuve-de-Blaye, tel. 05.57.42.64.00, fax 05.57.64.94.10 ☑ Y by appt.

Famille Richard

CH. CHAUBINET 1998

■ 12 ha 93,000 20 F+

This powerful concern led by co-operatives is represented here by its Château Chaubinet, which has a seductive, highly subtle nose of fruits, spices and green coffee; it would go well with cold dishes. Also recommended is the **1998 Château de Laborde**, cask-matured for nine months and possessing the respectful oakiness befitting a fine, subtle, mouth-filling wine. The tannins are a trifle rough and need watching over time.

Producta SA, 21, cours Xavier-Arnozan, 33082 Bordeaux Cedex, tel. 05.57.81.18.18, fax 05.56.81.22.12, e-mail producta@producta.com Y by appt.

CLOS DE PELIGON 1998★

■ 7 ha 40,000 20–29 F

At this vineyard, established nearly 40 years ago on the gravel and clay of the southern bank of the Dordogne downstream of Liborne, they work the soil in the old manner and harvest the grapes by hand. The wine is 70% Merlot, with a round, supple body that virtually slides down the throat. The aromas are of flowers and fruits finely tinged with vanilla, all well set off by the oak. A pleasure to sample unhurriedly with roast meat.

EARL Vignobles Reynaud, 13, rte de Libourne, 33450 Saint-Loubès, tel. 05.56.20.47.52, fax 05.56.20.47.52 ☑ Y by appt.

CH. DUCLA Permanence IV 1998★★

■ 2 ha 8,000 30–49 F

Château Ducla is an 85-ha (210-acre) property belonging to the Mau family. This is the fourth of its Permanence wines, a selection of 64% Merlot to 36% Cabernet-Sauvignon, which undergoes its malolactic fermentation in new, exclusively French, oak barrels, where it matures for 12 months. The complex fruitiness and well-judged oakiness result in great harmony. The wine has length, and indeed it lasted through to a grand jury finish. The main vintage, the **1998 Ducla**, is not oak-matured, and has a production of 266,000 bottles. A round-tasting wine, with a concentration of crystallised fruit aromas, it is awarded one star.

SA Yvon Mau, B.P. 1, 33193 Gironde-sur-Dropt Cedex, tel. 05.56.61.54.54, fax 05.56.61.54.61 ☑ Y by appt.

FONT-DESTIAC 1998★

■ 10 ha 66,000 20–29 F

A trademark of the Univitis group of co-operatives, this wine makes no secret of its intentions, namely to be drunk right away. An exclusively Merlot product, the vatting lasted one week. The intense colour, the aromatic freshness (blackcurrant) and supple, firm roundness of the body are a source of undeniable pleasure.

Closerie d'Estiac, Les Lèves, 33320 Sainte-Foy-la-Grande, tel. 05.57.56.02.02, fax 05.57.56.02.22 ev. day except Sun. Mon. 9am–12 noon 3pm–7pm

CH. DE FONTENILLE 1998

■ 30 ha 185,000 30–49 F

The vineyard is only 15 years old and is located on sandy, clay, or gravelly soils. The proportions of Merlot (50%), Cabernet Franc (35%) and Cabernet-Sauvignon (15%) make themselves felt in a delicate, round wine with very unobtrusive tannins. The complexity of aromas is interesting: notes of undergrowth and autumn leaves mingle with spicy fruits. A nice accompaniment to white meats, but must be drunk now.

SC Ch. de Fontenille, 33670 La Sauve, tel. 05.56.23.03.26, fax 05.56.23.30.03, e-mail defraine@chateau-fontenille.com by appt.

CH. GILLET 1998★

■ 68 ha 48,000 20–29 F

Midway between Branne and Targon, the château is located in the heart of the Entre-Deux-Mers district. This 1998 wine, made from a majority of Merlot grapes set off by Cabernet-Sauvignon, seems reticent at first and proffers a nose of fruits with undertones of leather, even musk. The body is simple but elegant and has good persistence. The oak-matured **1997 Réserve Elevée en Fût** is a full wine with notes of stone fruits (Morello cherry) and vanilla. Both wines are ready for drinking and will provide a charming accompaniment to white meats.

EARL Nadau, La Gourdine, 33760 Faleyras, tel. 05.56.23.94.58, fax 05.57.34.40.21 by appt.

CH. GIRUNDIA 1998★

■ 3 ha 25,000 30–49 F

Grown close to the citadel of Blaye, which guards the Gironde downstream of Bordeaux, this wine has the originality of being composed of half Merlot and half Malbec varieties. It has a deep-purple, ruby-red colour and blackcurrant aromas which strengthen and open out throughout the tasting. The round palate, free of tannic aggression, makes this a welcome companion to family meals.

SCEA Ch. Segonzac, 39, Segonzac, 33390 Saint-Genès-de-Blaye, tel. 05.57.42.18.16, fax 05.57.42.24.80, e-mail segonzac@chateau-segonzac.com by appt.

CH. GRAND CLAUSET 1998★

■ 5 ha 33,000 30–49 F

Patrick Carteyron is one of the truly excellent wine-growers of the Bordeaux region; he started out in 1982. Worthy of its star-rating, this wine is 20% Cabernets on a base of Merlot, harvested at optimum maturity. It has a dense, round fleshiness, with a concentration of fruit and a well-judged amount of tannins. Beautiful structure, elegance and length. A real pleasure to drink with a meal.

SCEA Patrick Carteyron, Ch.Penin, 33420 Génissac, tel. 05.57.24.46.98, fax 05.57.24.41.99 by appt.

CH. DE GRANDE-FONT 1998

■ 1.5 ha 12,000 20–29 F

This young vineyard is located on gravelly and silty soils. The wine is made from half Merlot, half Cabernets grapes. Its fruity roundness delighted one member of the jury and worried another. People must judge for themselves according to their personal preferences, but this 1998 wine needs to be drunk soon. Its structure was intended for early drinking.

SCEA du Bru, 33220 Saint-Avit-Saint-Nazaire, tel. 05.57.46.12.71, fax 05.57.46.10.64 by appt.

Guy Duchant

CH. DU GRAND FERRAND 1998

■ 30.2 ha 38,000 30–49 F

This vineyard, which belongs to the Rocher-Cap de Rive group, is a classic. Its gorgeous appearance is complemented by aromas of red fruits. A gulpable wine whose round, well-balanced texture can already be enjoyed as an accompaniment to grills.

SCEA Ch. Grand Ferrand, 33540 Sauveterre-de-Guyenne, tel. 05.56.71.51.34

CH. GROSSOMBRE

Elevé en fût de chêne 1998★★

■ 7 ha n.c. 30–49 F

The charterhouse buildings are austere, elegant and beautiful, like the wine they house. The 60% Cabernet-Sauvignon, grown on limy, silty clay, lends power and structure to what is a very fruity wine. The perfectly judged oakiness also helps. This Bordeaux is for keeping. Drink with red meats and game – the wine has its own musky notes. Wait for it to yield its best: it is full of promise.

Béatrice Lurton, B.P. 10, 33420 Grézillac, tel. 05.57.25.58.58, fax 05.57.74.98.59, e-mail andre.lurton@wanadoo.fr by appt.

CH. HAUT-GRAVEYRON 1998★

■ 4 ha 32,000 30–49 F

Jean-Louis Roumage tends a huge property which also produces AOC Bordeaux Supérieur wines. This dark-red, nearly black wine has an intense nose in which musk (from the 90% Merlot) emphasises the fullness of the fruits it evokes (bilberry and currants). On the palate it has a well-structured, fleshy, persistent roundness. An ideal companion to red

meats, but deserves to be kept a little longer before drinking.
Jean-Louis Roumage, Lestrille, 33750 Saint-Germain-du-Puch, tel. 05.57.24.51.02, fax 05.57.24.04.58 by appt.

CH. HAUT-MAZIERES 1998★★

■ n.c. 154,133 30–49 F

Several hundred yards from a feudal château, the wineries of this Union de Producteurs deserve a visit. This Château Haut-Mazières (60% Merlot), with its good vinification and perfectly ordered 12 months of oak-maturing, is the product of an expert, enthusiastic and demanding team. Awarded a *coup de cœur* by the grand jury, the wine has a very authentic Bordeaux clarity. The body is elegant, with a superb fruity presence, well-behaved oak tannins, and aromatic complexity – all the palate requires, in fact.
Union de producteurs de Rauzan, 33420 Rauzan, tel. 05.57.84.13.22, fax 05.57.84.12.67 by appt.

CH. HAUT-PIGEONNIER 1998★★

■ 2.35 ha 16,000 20–29 F

This wine is grown on the gravelly clay common to the Libourne vineyards along the Isle valley. The proprietor-grower uses minimal chemical treatments in order to produce a 'natural' wine. This requires a mastery which we here applaud. His 1998 wine exhales aromas of very ripe, even crystallised fruit (prune, cherry), and caresses the palate with its full, well-structured, complex and persistent roundness. A wine to accompany red meats which can be drunk now, though there is no hurry.
Philippe Junquas, Ch. Haut-Pigeonnier, 72, chem. des Treilles, 33910 Saint-Denis-de-Pile, tel. 05.57.24.30.96, fax 05.57.24.30.96 by appt.

CH. DE JABASTAS 1998★

■ 1 ha 6,600 20–29 F

Visitors to the château can sometimes see the tidal bore that surges up the Dordogne at very high tides and the surfers who ride on it. This wine's charm is more accessible. It exhales a range of aromas from woodland flowers in summer to cherry, nutmeg, pepper and spices. The same complexity is found on the palate, adorning a round fleshiness sustained by silky tannins, and leaving a memory that is slow to fade. A lovely wine that can be drunk without haste (during the next two to four years), with lamprey for instance.
Jean-Marie Nadau, Ch. de Jabastas, 35, av. des Prades, 33450 Izon, tel. 05.57.84.97.13, fax 05.57.84.97.14 by appt.

KRESSMANN Grande Réserve 1998★

■ n.c. n.c. 20–29 F

Selected and matured by Kressmann, a Bordeaux wine-merchant for more than a century and part of the CVBG group, this wine is made mainly from Merlot, with a fiery garnet colour and a nose of stewed fruits and smokiness. The well-structured palate is enlivened by hints of spices and menthol. As one expert ventured, 'A wine for lovers of strong aromas.'
Kressmann, 35, rte de Bordeaux, 33290 Parempuyre, tel. 05.56.35.53.00, fax 05.56.35.53.29, e-mail contact@cvbg.com by appt.

DOM. DE LA FONTANILLE 1998

■ 5 ha 40,000 20–29 F

The extreme subtlety of the aromas, which are floral and fruity (grenadine mixed with raspberry and blackcurrant), plus a touch of flower-buds, give this wine real charm.
Vignobles Arnaud et Marcuzzi, Le Vic n° 13, 33410 Cardan, tel. 05.56.62.60.91, fax 05.56.62.67.05 by appt.

CH. LA GRAVE 1998★★

■ 6.8 ha 6,500 30–49 F

This wine has a superb purple colour and a powerful nose which first reveals violets, then ripe fruit tinged with vanilla, toast and coffee, each contributing to the complex and subtle harmony of the whole. Its round, rich, meaty body is sustained by oak tannins which are evident yet well-mannered, silky and respectful of the grape. This wine narrowly missed a *coup de cœur*. The main vintage, the **1998 Sentiers d'Automne**, which is not oak-matured, is an adjudged success. It has complex aromas (cherry, redcurrant, blackcurrant, undergrowth) and a supple, honest, perhaps somewhat slender body which makes it suitable for white meats and soft cheeses. Visitors to Sainte-Croix-du-Mont will find a medieval town in a district known for very sweet white wines.
Jean-Marie Tinon, Ch. La Grave, 33410 Sainte-Croix-du-Mont, tel. 05.56.62.01.65, fax 05.56.62.00.04, e-mail tinon@terre-net.fr by appt.

CH. LALANDE-LABATUT

Cuvée Prestige Vieilli en fût de chêne 1998★

■ 10 ha 72,000 30–49 F

This 45-ha (114-acre) château devotes a large share of its vines to its Cuvée Prestige. This is a marriage of 70% Merlot and Cabernets (including 25% Sauvignon), whose youth is a source of joy. The deep garnet colour and range of overripe fruit aromas with hints of vanilla and a light touch of menthol are extremely appetising. The meaty, rich body is sustained by well-blended tannins whose remarkable persistence indicates that the wine will age well. A good accompaniment to fillet of duck or goose or grilled red meat.

🔑 SCEA Vignobles Falxa, 38, Labatut, 33370 Sallebœuf, tel. 05.56.21.23.18, fax 05.56.21.20.98, e-mail chateau.lalande-labatut@wanadoo.fr ☒ 𝐘 by appt.

CH. DE LA MINGERIE 1998

■ 4 ha 13,000 ▮ 🌡 20–29 F

Dominated by Merlot (75%), this wine has gained smoothness from Cabernet Franc (20%) and sweet-pepper spiciness from Cabernet-Sauvignon (5%). It forms a harmonious whole and is pleasantly perfumed with red fruits. A wine for uncomplicated drinking, which would suit roast poultry. The oak-matured **1997 Cuvée Prestige** is richer in Cabernet-Sauvignon (20%) at the expense of Merlot. The marriage between oak and wine has resulted in a silky charm and a delicate, not to say discreet, bouquet. The latter wine should be drunk straight away with white meats or soft cheeses (30–49F).

🔑 GAEC Jean-Jean Père et Fils, Girolatte, 33420 Naujan-et-Postiac, tel. 05.57.84.60.51, fax 05.57.74.98.03 ☒

CH. LA MIRANDELLE 1998★

■ 8.66 ha 50,000 ▮ 🌡 20–29 F

This large co-operative is located just outside the historic fortifications of Sauveterre-de-Guyenne. Its modern techniques yield red and white wines of recognised quality. One such is this Château La Mirandelle (approximately 60% Merlot), produced from 25-year-old vines growing on limy-clay soil. Round and expressive, with a touch of menthol and spices and a strong finish, this is a wine for meals of plain but good-quality food.

🔑 Cellier de La Bastide, Cave coop. vinicole, 33540 Sauveterre-de-Guyenne, tel. 05.56.61.55.21, fax 05.56.71.60.11 ☒ 𝐘 ev. day except Sun. 9am–12.15 1.30pm–6.15; groups by appt.

🔑 Yves Moncontier

CH. LA MOTHE DU BARRY

Cuvée Design 1998★

■ 3 ha 24,000 ⏸ 30–49 F

Following its successful 1996 and 1997 predecessors, this 1998 Cuvée Design gains one star. This Merlot selection has aged 12 months in the barrel. The first impression made by the nose is of violets, followed by ripe red fruits with strong undertones of toast, even coffee. The palate confirms the full character of this round, harmonious, long-lasting wine, designed for unhurried drinking alongside red meats. The **1998 Le Barry** (50–69F) contains 25% Cabernet-Sauvignon. It too is oak-matured and receives one star for its young, dense body and concentrated aromas of blackcurrant and redcurrant with undertones of meat, grilling and spices. The tannins already have elegance and silkiness, but time will only diversify and enrich the pleasure of this wine. Two vintages particularly recommended to wine-lovers.

🔑 Joël Duffau, Les Arromans n°2, 33420 Moulon, tel. 05.57.74.93.98, fax 05.57.84.66.10 ☒ 𝐘 ev. day except Sun. 8am–12 noon 2pm–7pm

CH. LANGRAGNAT 1998★

■ 6 ha 36,000 ▮ 🌡 20–29 F

Prodiffu is a large concern run by the winegrowers of the rather jagged landscape close to Lot-et-Garonne. It is represented here by the purplish garnet Château Langragnat, which has a round, full and rich palate full of fresh fruits (cherry, strawberry, redcurrant). A scrumptious wine, ready now for drinking right through a meal.

🔑 Union Prodiffu, 17–19, rte des Vignerons, 33790 Landerrouat, tel. 05.56.61.33.73, fax 05.56.61.40.57, e-mail prodiffu@prodiffu.com

CH. DE L'AUBRADE 1998

■ 22.41 ha n.c. 30–49 F

This estate is located not far from Castelmoron-d'Albret, reputed to be the smallest commune in France, enclosed within its fortifications. The jury were won over by the wine's aromatic freshness (raspberry), set off by charred nuances of walnut, leather, and grilling. The tannic structure, though present, holds back. Its excellent persistence at the finish suggests it should be kept in a cellar for a year or two.

🔑 EARL Jean-Pierre et Paulette Lobre, 33580 Rimons, tel. 05.56.71.55.10, fax 05.56.71.61.94 ☒ 𝐘 by appt.

LA VIEILLE EGLISE 1998★★

■ 20 ha 133,000 ▮ 🌡 20 F+

This wine, selected by Jean-Marie Portier, the oenologist in the Univitis team, is superb. Its powerful scents evolve from wild flowers, through small fruits of the forest to burnt earth. They set off a body which is supple yet sustained by good-quality tannins. The finish is lengthy, well-blended and generous. It would only have needed one more vote from the grand jury to gain the *coup de cœur.* The **1998 Mayne Sansac** (20–29F) also gained good marks and is a short-vatted (seven days) pure Merlot. Its complex nose of crystallised fruits enriched with spices and chocolate, together with its well-crafted, structured palate, whose silky tannins support a dense, perfumed meatiness, delighted the jury.

🔑 Domainie de Sansac, Les Lèves, 33220 Sainte-Foy-la-Grande, tel. 05.57.56.02.02, fax 05.57.56.02.22 𝐘 by appt.

CH. L'EGLISE DE SAGET 1998★

■ 12 ha 36,000 ▮ 🌡 30–49 F

The Quai des Chartrons in Bordeaux tells the story in stone of the historic wine-trade and of the wines of Aquitaine that have passed through there. Schröder et Schÿler is one of its famous names. This deep-red 1998 wine is their own. Notes of musk and spices add to the aromatic complexity. The body is concentrated, round and rich, structured by tannins which are still evident but ripe. A classic wine. Drink in the next two years, perhaps with a stew.

🔑 Maison Schröder et Schÿler, 55, quai des Chartrons, 33027 Bordeaux Cedex, tel. 05.57.87.64.55, fax 05.57.87.57.20 Y by appt.

🔑 Bouffard

CH. LE NOBLE 1998★

■ n.c. 21,000 30–49 F

Pierre Coste, a man of wine but also of letters, left his strong stamp on the family wine-merchants currently managed by Sichel. The balance between Cabernets (55%) and Merlot (45%) is what characterises this wine, which has lightly spiced aromas of cherry and mint. Its round body continues through a well-covered, aromatic finish, yielding a pleasure that may be sampled either now or later. The same merchants' very round and delightfully perfumed **1998 Château Tuilerie Rivière** is an easy-drinking wine which our tasters have similarly awarded one star. Also cited are the **1998 Cave Bel Air** and **1998 Château Mondeau**, which are supple and well-structured wines, ready for drinking now.

🔑 Maison Sichel-Coste, 8, rue de la Poste, 33210 Langon, tel. 05.56.63.50.52, fax 05.56.63.42.28

CH. LES BRUGES 1998★★

■ 32 ha 175,000 20–29 F

This highly reputable Bordeaux wine-merchants was established in 1873 and has remained in the same family. A number of their wines impressed the jury. This one has a round attack and dense body. The nose is redolent of ripe cooked fruit (prunes, Morello cherry tart). It has youthful power, traceable to its 70% Cabernets, the residue being of Merlot. Proposed for a *coup de cœur*, this 1998 wine came high up the grand jury's list. Expert opinion was that the wine's true worth, already estimable, would show itself fully in time. Other wines applauded were: the fleshy and concentrated **1998 Château Hermitage des Bruges**, recommended; the fresh and lively **1998 Château Carayon-la-Rose**, awarded one star (an attractive label and excellent value for money like the Bruges); in similar vein, the strongly walnut-scented **1998 Château Cailloux du Haut**, ready to drink now and awarded one star;the round-tasting **1998 Château des Deux Rives**, redolent of stewed fruit and liquorice and recommended.

🔑 Dulong Frères et Fils, 29, rue Jules-Guesde, 33270 Floirac, tel. 05.56.86.51.15, fax 05.56.40.66.41, e-mail dulong@mmkm.com Y by appt.

🔑 Faure

LES DERNIERS MILLESIMES DU SIECLE 1998★

■ n.c. 500,000 20–29 F

Ginestet is a large Bordeaux wine-merchants which offered several wines from its huge range. This 1998 version of the specially created end-of-century label, the Derniers Millésimes du Siècle, is a distinguished classic: perfumed (crushed red fruits), spicy, well-structured, assured and reassuring, and ready to drink now. The **1998 Château La Jalgue** is also a large-volume wine (266,000 bottles) with attractive potential: it has a complex nose and a somewhat closed yet fruity, peppery palate with harmonious length. This one-star wine is, as one taster remarked, 'an attractive wine that will delight the consumer.' The **1998 Bordeaux Selectionné par Bernard Taillan pour Carrefour** achieved a citation; at less than 20F this silky, easy-drinking wine will be a welcome accompaniment to everyday meals. The **1998 Terres Douces** receives one star. Its 231,000 bottles will be good ambassadors for the appellation.

🔑 SA Maison Ginestet, 19, av. de Fontenille, 33360 Carignan-de-Bordeaux, tel. 05.56.68.81.82, fax 05.56.20.96.99, e-mail contact@ginestet.fr Y by appt.

CH. LES FAURES

Vieilli en fût de chêne 1998★

■ 2.5 ha 19,000 30–49 F

The valley of the Dropt lies below this property, which is located on alluvial soil. Cabernets (60% Sauvignon, 15% Franc) predominate. One-fifth of the harvest has been cask-matured. Over-ripened fruit and an elegant, discreet oakiness have created a rich, lightly vanilla-flavoured wine which has subtlety and length. It will go well with roasts.

🔑 Jacky Certain, 9, Les Faures-Est, 33190 Camiran, tel. 05.56.71.41.86, fax 05.56.71.32.76 Y by appt.

CH. LES VERGNES 1998

■ 20 ha 133,000 20–29 F

The strong technical team of the co-operative group Univitis here offer their Château Les Vergnes, whose harvest (75% Merlot) was vinified over ten days. Aromatic complexity, in which notes of liquorice and smokiness mingle with those of fruits, enhance a round body with silky tannins. A wine to drink without further ado, with grills and cheeses.

🔑 Univitis, Closerie d'Estiac, 33220 Sainte-Foy-la-Grande, tel. 05.57.56.02.02, fax 05.57.56.02.22 Y ev. day except Sun. Mon. 9am–12.30pm 3pm–7pm

CH. LION BEAULIEU 1998★

■ n.c. n.c. 30–49 F

This property belongs to the oenologist of the Despagnė vineyards. The deep, almost black appearance is instantly attractive. The intense nose is redolent of beautifully mature grapes (80% Merlot, 20% Cabernet-Sauvignon). The frank, chewy palate reveals structured tannins which will need more than two years of ageing to mature. So be patient.

🔑 GFA de Lyon, 33420 Naujan-et-Postiac, tel. 05.57.84.55.08, fax 05.57.84.57.31, e-mail despagne@vignobles-despagne.com Y by appt.

🔑 J. Elissalde

CH. DE LYNE 1998★

■ 9 ha 54,000 30–49 F

The Châteaux de Lyne and **La Cour d'Argent** continue their shining career. Both these 1998 versions merit a star. They are essentially Merlot-based (90%). Cabernet-Sauvignon (5%) distinguishes the Cour d'Argent from the Lyne. Their regulated ageing in the cask adds vanilla touches to the complexity of ripe fruits. The body is round and sturdy; the grape and oak tannins need still to calm down, like the spicy finish. The Cour d'Argent's aromas of narcissus distinguish it from the Cour de Lyne with its perfumes of cedar and honey. Compare the two, but take your time.

SCEA des Vignobles Denis Barraud, Ch. Haut-Renaissance, 33330 Saint-Sulpice-de-Faleyrens, tel. 05.57.84.54.73, fax 05.57.84.52.07, e-mail denis.barraud@wanadoo.fr Y by appt.

HENRY BARON DE MONTESQUIEU

Le Secondat 1998

■ n.c. n.c. 30–49 F

Charles de Secondat, baron of La Brède and Montesquieu, was one of the 18th century's great philosophers. He too was a winegrower, like H. de Montesquieu, the La Brède wine-merchant. This is a classic wine which marries ripe grapes to tannins acquired from barrels of differing ages (a quarter of them new). The goal has been elegantly achieved. Serve this Bordeaux now without further ado.

Vins et Dom. Henry de Montesquieu, Aux Fougères, 33650 La Brède, tel. 05.56.78.45.45, fax 05.56.20.25.07, e-mail montesquieu@bordeaux-montesquieu.com

CH. MOTTE MAUCOURT 1998★

■ 8 ha 30,000 20–29 F

The château vineyard (near a 12th-century church adorned with frescoes) surrounds a feudal mound. It has acquired much more ground and this is planted with more or less young vines. Merlot dominates the main 1998 vintage, which is vat-matured. This wine offers lovely fruit aromas (blackcurrant and cherry) mixed with discreet notes of musk, plus a well-constructed body with good persistence – a joyous wine. The exclusively Merlot **Sélection 98 Vieillie en Fût** (30–49F), oak-matured for 12 months, is recommended. The finish is marked by oak, and notes of toast and liquorice enrich the fruity nose and palate, which recommend this as a wine to accompany marinated meats.

GAEC Villeneuve et Fils, Ch. Motte Maucourt, 33760 Saint-Genis-du-Bois, tel. 05.56.71.54.77, fax 05.56.71.64.23 Y ev. day except Sun. 9am–12 noon 2pm–7pm

CH. MOUSSEYRON 1998

■ 16 ha 40,000 30–49 F

For the past 25 years, Jacques Larriaut has been in charge of this family estate near Saint-Macaire on the northern bank of the Garonne. Excellent limy-clay soil and 60% Cabernet-Sauvignon blended with Merlot have yielded a wine with a very strong colour and nose of small red fruits. The palate is well structured, but the tannins are still young. A classic wine to accompany stews.

Jacques Larriaut, 33490 Saint-Pierre-d'Aurillac, tel. 05.56.76.44.53, fax 05.56.76.44.04 Y by appt.

NAPOLEON 1998★

■ n.c. n.c. 30–49 F

Stone fruits (prune, cherry) aromatically inform the entire tasting with an intensity that is assured and elegant. The balance between meatiness and tannins never fails the palate, and the finish is open and long. This is the essential definition of a wine that needs a few more months at least.

Ets E. Parrot et Cie, Dom. de Fleurenne, B.P. 61, 33292 Blanquefort Cedex, tel. 05.56.95.55.20, fax 05.56.95.55.29, e-mail e.parrot@parrot-et-cie.fr

CH. NARDIQUE LA GRAVIERE 1998★

■ 11.35 ha 40,000 30–49 F

Grown on a gravelly soil, Cabernets (Sauvignon 30%, Franc 20%) balance the Merlot, and the outcome is the product of taste-led vatting. The result is convincing: a ruby appearance still with hints of purple, and intense aromas of fruits (blackcurrant, bilberry and blackberry) enriched with spices. The stout body is well-crafted, concentrated, subtle, and beautifully persistent. Drink throughout any meal or with red meats. Don't hurry to open.

Vignobles Thérèse, Ch. Nardique La Gravière, 33670 Saint-Genès-de-Lombaud, tel. 05.56.23.01.37, fax 05.56.23.25.89 Y ev. day except Sun. 9am–12 noon 3pm–6pm; cl. 15–31 Aug.

CH. DE PERRE 1998

■ 22 ha 23,000 20–29 F

Several miles from the medieval town of Saint-Macaire, this 20-year-old vineyard lies on soils of silt and sand mixed with clay. The wine is dominated by Cabernet-Sauvignon, a presence appreciated by a juror from the Médoc who inferred it would age well. Another said the aromas should be enjoyed straight away. Sample it and see.

Claude Mayle, 15, rue de Gaussen, 33490 Caudrot, tel. 05.56.62.83.31, fax 05.56.62.75.30 Y by appt.

CH. PICHAUD SOLIGNAC 1998★

■ 2.8 ha 20,000 30–49 F

This property dating from the early 19th century changed hands in 1998. This 1998 wine is promising: 25% Cabernets and a touch (5%) of Malbec accompany the Merlot in this well-sourced wine. The colour is deep purple, the body round and meaty with tannins that are still young but of good quality. The rich, complex aromas elegantly evoke black fruits (blackberry, cherry, prune). 'Good with a thick entrecôte steak,' suggested one of the jury.

🔑 EARL Delbeuf Pichaud Solignac, La Niocaise, 33790 Pellegrue, tel. 05.56.61.43.55, fax 05.56.61.43.55, e-mail ch-pic-sol@terre-net.fr ☒ 🍷 ev. day 9am–7pm

PREMIUS Elevé en fût de chêne 1998★★★

■ n.c. n.c. 30–49 F

Yvon Mau presents two wines with special labels. Unfortunately, we do not know how many bottles there are. The *coup de cœur Premius and* **Millénium** are made from scheduled selections of grapes made according to the plots they come from and developed by a team of in-house oenologists. Perfectly chosen casks enhance wine that is produced from ripe grapes through well-regulated vatting. One of the jury ended his tasting of Millénium with the words, 'What lovely harmony this oak-matured wine has – superb nose, full palate, good balance between the fruit and the oak.' Two non-oak-matured wines were also singled out: the **1998 Yvecourt**, an easy-drinking wine recommended for its classicism, and the **1998 Château La Forêt**, which gains a star for its elegant body and silky tannins. These two wines sell in the range 20–29F.

🔑 SA Yvon Mau, B.P. 1, 33193 Gironde-sur-Dropt Cedex, tel. 05.56.61.54.54, fax 05.56.61.54.61 🍷 by appt.

CH. PREVOST 1998★

■ 30 ha 225,000 20–29 F

Basically a Merlot wine, this Prévost has all that variety's generous character. The round, rich palate is flavoured with blackberry, and the finish elegantly shows good potential for ageing. A definite success. Elisabeth Garzaro presents other attractive 1998 wines: the **Château Les Murailles** with its structured tannins; the **Château Bel Air Moulard** (30–49F), redolent of raspberry with a slight hint of sweet pepper and of good body with red fruit flavours.

🔑 Elisabeth Garzaro, Ch. Le Prieur, 33750 Baron, tel. 05.56.30.16.16, fax 05.56.30.12.63, e-mail garzaro@vingarzaro.com 🍷 by appt.

CH. PRIEURE GUILLAUME

Elevé en fût de chêne 1998★

■ 13.7 ha 110,000 20–29 F

This priory spreads its vines over steep hillsides several miles from the fortifications of Sainte-Foy-la-Grande, a one-time martial town on the banks of the Dordogne. The wine (35% Merlot to 65% Cabernets) has spent six months in the barrel. It has acquired a vanilla bouquet with toasted nuances which are well matched to the slightly liquorice fruitiness of the grapes. 'Interesting complexity, mouth-filling character and balance,' wrote one of the tasters, predicting a bright future for this wine.

🔑 SCEA Ch. Guillaume, lieu-dit Guillaume-Blanc, 33220 Saint-Philippe-du-Seignal, tel. 05.57.41.91.50, fax 05.57.46.42.76 ☒ 🍷 by appt.

CH. RAUZAN DESPAGNE 1998★

■ n.c. n.c. 30–49 F

No need to introduce the wine-team of the Vignobles Despagne. Their various Bordeaux region AOC wines, in different colours, are frequent candidates for stars and awards. Both the 1998 wines share the same rating: one star. The 30% Cabernet-Sauvignon **Cuvée Passion** (70–99F) has spent 12 months in the barrel. It is powerful and mouth-filling, besides possessing an aromatic complexity that is already remarkable – red fruits hinting at vanilla, notes of cooking and good-quality oak. The structure is still very noticeable, but it can be taken for granted that the tannins will calm down in a few months, when this wine will go well with mushrooms and roasts, such as leg of lamb or duck. As for the main entry here (20% Cabernet-Sauvignon), this is a round, rich wine with aromas of spiced fruits. The tannins are firm but so constituted as to sustain the wine for years to come without overpowering it in its youth. So try it now.

🔑 GFA de Landeron, 33420 Naujan-et-Postiac, tel. 05.57.84.55.08, fax 05.57.84.57.31, e-mail despagne@vignobles-despagne.com 🍷 by appt.

🔑 Despagne

CH. ROC DE LEVRAUT 1998

■ 19 ha 30,000 20–29 F

To create this vineyard some 15 years ago huge rocks had to be moved. Cabernet-Sauvignon (60%) and Cabernet Franc (10%) are dominant with floral notes (violets) tinged with sweet pepper. Dense, spicy tannins emphasise the body's power. A wine for jugged hare or rabbit chasseur, commented the jury – though at the time they did not know that the name of the wine referred to a young hare or leveret.

🔑 Roger Ballarin, 33540 Sauveterre-de-Guyenne, tel. 05.56.71.53.65, fax 05.56.71.53.65 ☒ 🍷 by appt.

CH. SAINT-ANTOINE

Réserve du Château 1998★

■ 70 ha 490,000 ▮ 🌡 30–49 F

Proprietors of La Couspaude at Saint-Emilion, the Vignobles Aubert also have vines in the Entre-Deux-Mers district. Réserve du Château Saint-Antoine is made from 35% Cabernet Franc. Its ripe fruit aromas are set off by notes of musk. The fleshy body reveals silky tannins and has seductive length. The wine will increase in charm in a few months' time for those who can wait a little. The **1998 Château Haut-Mérigot** will not disappoint. It is meaty and elegant; its fresh tannins will settle down like those of the Château Saint-Antoine.

🔑 Vignobles Aubert, Ch. La Couspaude, 33330 Saint-Emilion, tel. 05.57.40.15.76, fax 05.57.40.10.14 ☒ Y by appt.

CH. SEGONZAC LA FORET 1998

■ 18 ha 76,000 ▮ 🌡 30–49 F

A 35-year-old vineyard and a wine in which Merlot (44%) balances Cabernet-Sauvignon (38%), with Cabernet Franc completing the blend. Hence the sensation of peaceful, pleasantly flavoured and fruity roundness enlivened by a lightly spiced finish. A wine to accompany white meat, better drunk sooner rather than later. The **1998 Baron de Luze Elevé en Fût de Chêne**, oak-matured for 12 months, has a reliably charming body, in which notes of raspberry mix with those of vanilla toast and summer undergrowth. This round, supple, flavoursome wine is an ideal accompaniment to white meats and cold poultry.

🔑 A. de Luze et Fils, Dom. du Ribet, 33450 Saint-Loubès, tel. 05.57.97.07.20, fax 05.57.97.07.27 Y by appt.

🔑 Jeanine Segonzac

CH. TIRE PE La Côte 1998★★

■ 1 ha 6,000 ⦀ 30–49 F

La Côte is grown on rocky limy clay. Merlot (20%) and Cabernet-Sauvignon conspire to form a silky body finely flavoured with very ripe fruits and an elegant oakiness. Oak and grape tannins are in evidence, though they are already well-blended and complex. A harmonious composition, with a richness that will continue to develop for several more years. 'Remarkable: worthy of AOC Bordeaux Supérieur,' was one judge's note. The wholly vat-matured **1998 Cuvée Principale** is an imposing wine with a meaty, ripe, well-structured complexity. It too is worth two stars.

🔑 David Barrault, Ch. Tire Pé, 33190 Gironde-sur-Dropt, tel. 05.56.71.10.09, fax 05.56.71.10.09, e-mail tirepe@aol.com ☒ Y by appt.

CH. TOUR DE BIOT 1998★

■ 12 ha 95,000 ▮ 🌡 20–29 F

This château was much praised last year for a 1997 oak-matured wine grown on old vines. Its 1996 Cuvée Principale attracted similar praise. This 1998 wine has a very lovely strong purple colour and an intense nose of ripe fruits. Round-tasting from the moment it arrives on the palate, it fills the mouth well and testifies to the excellence of its raw material.

🔑 Gilles Gremen, EARL La Tour Rouge, 33220 La Roquille, tel. 05.57.41.26.49, fax 05.57.41.29.84 ☒ Y by appt.

CH. TOUR DE MIRAMBEAU 1998★

■ n.c. n.c. ▮ 🌡 30–49 F

Made from 80% Merlot and 20% Cabernet-Sauvignon – classic proportions for the period when they were planted, 30 or 35 years ago – this is a concentrated wine with aromas of red fruits, spices, and musk. The tannins are still somewhat rough, though the body is of good quality. In time this robust wine will have plenty of takers. For the moment, drink only with sauces and spicy dishes.

🔑 SCEA Vignobles Despagne, 33420 Naujan-et-Postiac, tel. 05.57.84.55.08, fax 05.57.84.57.31, e-mail despagne@vignobles-despagne.com ☒ Y by appt.

CH. TURCAUD 1998

■ 20 ha 146,000 ▮ ⦀ 🌡 30–49 F

Grown on La Sauve's siliceous gravels, this wine blends the three Bordeaux varieties. The nose and first impressions on the palate are full of promise: fruits with spicy hints enhance a roundness that is evident from the outset. The tannins then make their presence felt through to the finish. This wine is best left in a cellar for two years to realise its full potential.

🔑 EARL Vignobles Robert, Ch. Turcaud, 33670 La Sauve, tel. 05.56.23.04.41, fax 05.56.23.35.85 ☒ Y by appt.

TUTIAC 1998★★

■ 15 ha 100,000 ▮ 20–29 F

This co-operative cellar located north of the citadel of Blaye offers a wide range of products. Tutiac is based on rigorous selection. Made from 80% Merlot and 20% Cabernet-Sauvignon, it is short-vatted in order to maintain a fruity freshness and avoid too stout a structure. It is fleshy, round, and vinous, yet cannot be accused of weakness, for there is a definite tannic presence. The aromas of red-fruit jam and hint of tobacco subtly release their burgeoning richness. A

Bordeaux to drink now, while keeping some back to follow its evolution, for this 1998 wine will doubtless age well.

🔑 Cave des Hauts de Gironde, La Cafourche, 33860 Marcillac, tel. 05.57.32.48.33, fax 05.57.32.49.63, e-mail contact@tutiac.com ☑ Y by appt.

CH. DE VAURE 1998★

■ 21 ha 100,000 ▮ ♁ 20-29 F

Vinified by members of the Ruch co-operative, whose winery overlooks a pretty valley, this wine breathes scents of violets, then ripe and lightly blanched cherries, raspberries and strawberries. The palate is open, meaty and round, with a very slightly acid finish. The same team are responsible for the **1998 Château de Blaignac**. The nose is freshly redolent of blackcurrants and meadow flowers; the palate is supple and mouth-filling, though characterised by rustic, spicy tannins. A wine to accompany hot charcuterie and picnics.

🔑 Producteurs réunis Chais de Vaure, 33350 Ruch, tel. 05.57.40.54.09, fax 05.57.40.70.22 ☑ Y ev. day except Sun. 8.30am–12.30pm 2pm–6pm

CH. DE VERTHEUIL

Elevé en fût de chêne 1998★

■ 2 ha 7,000 ⦀ 30-49 F

The communes of Sainte-Croix-du-Mont and Saint-Macaire are both near the château and worth a visit. The wine, made from 60% Cabernets, has spent ten months in the barrel, which has endowed its range of ripe black fruit aromas with fine oaky vanilla notes that are readily perceived when the wine is left to breathe. This aromatic harmony informs the well-balanced body, in which velvety tannins persist without arrogance. The **1998 Château Grand Picque-Caillou** is not oak-matured. Its slightly plant-like berry flavours combine with a powerful body to produce a spirited style that will have its devotees. Best for salty or spicy dishes (20–29F).

🔑 SCEA des Vignobles Ricard, Ch. de Vertheuil, 33410 Sainte-Croix-du-Mont, tel. 05.56.62.02.70, fax 05.56.76.73.23 ☑ Y by appt.

🔑 Geneviève Ricard

DOM. DU VIEIL ORME 1998★

■ 3 ha 16,000 ▮ ♁ 20-29 F

The high proportion of Cabernets (80% Sauvignon, 5% Franc) contributes a very fruity aromatic elegance (strawberry and raspberry). The round body of this wine heightens its charm; it also benefits from some slightly acid touches. 'A Bordeaux simply to enjoy!' concluded one taster. A worthy successor to last year's 1996 wine: one star.

🔑 Jean-Pierre et Michèle Peyrondet, 33760 Saint-Pierre-de-Bat, tel. 05.56.23.93.96, fax 05.57.34.40.17 ☑ Y by appt.

Bordeaux clairet

BENJAMIN DU PREVOST 1999★★

◪ 8 ha 60,000 ▮ ♁ 20-29 F

This Benjamin wine from a very reputable château marries 40% Cabernets (Franc and Sauvignon in equal proportions) with Merlot. The colour is a pretty pink-mauve verging on crimson, suggesting a freshness that is confirmed by the nose. There is an unrestrained bouquet of flowers (seringa and orange blossom) and fruits (peach, raspberry, redcurrant, strawberry), modulated by hints of flower buds. The body begins grapey and chewy, then becomes a round, mouth-filling fruit-drop with a slight fizz at the finish. This charmer of a wine was almost a *coup de cœur.* But should a clairet have such insolent freshness? The specialists may talk about this for a long time, but this will not prevent the wine from giving pleasure while they make up their minds.

🔑 Elisabeth Garzaro, Ch. Le Prieur, 33750 Baron, tel. 05.56.30.16.16, fax 05.56.30.12.63, e-mail garzaro@vingarzaro.com Y by appt.

CH. FAYAU 1999★★

◪ 5 ha 20,000 ▮ ♁ 20-29 F

The Classical, Renaissance architecture of the Duke of Epernon's château imposes its majesty on the town of Cadillac. This clairet too obeys classic rules: made from Merlot (60%) and Cabernet-Sauvignon, it has been made in part using the *saignée* method, in part by direct pressing of the grapes. Malolactic fermentation was interrupted so that the body could retain a certain freshness. The plan was successful. Take your time to smell the flowers and stone fruits in its perfume and appreciate the body's rich, firm life. The finish is enlivened by a slight effervescence. 'Bright and seductive,' was one jury member's comment.

🔑 SCEA Jean Médeville et Fils, Ch. Fayau, 33410 Cadillac, tel. 05.57.98.08.08, fax 05.56.62.18.22 ☑ Y ev. day except Sat. Sun. 8.30am–12 noon 2pm–6pm

CH. HAUT MAURIN 1999★★

◪ 2 ha 15,000 ▮ 20-29 F

This wine was made in a winery close to the Château of Benauge, a feudal citadel dominating the landscape several miles from Cadillac, the township of the Duke of Epernon, Henry III's favourite, who built an imposing château there. Merlot and Cabernet-Sauvignon have together wrought this very fruity, complex wine, with its full-flavoured harmony and hints of musk. Its structure, like its pale ruby colour, brings it close to a rosé. A fresh, light clairet, which will suit cold white meats or a paëlla.

🔑 Jean-Louis Sanfourche, Grand Village Nord, 33410 Donzac, tel. 05.56.62.97.43, fax 05.56.62.16.87 ☑ Y by appt.

CH. HAUT-MONGEAT 1999★

◢ 2 ha 8,000 ▮ 🌡 20–29 F

An independent producer since 1988, Bernard Bouchon has been joined by his daughter since 1996. Following Gilles Pauquet's advice, they have succeeded in making a really nice clairet. The colour shines like a ruby lit up with amber. The nose of this pure Merlot is evocative of stone fruits. The round, supple, fresh meatiness of this wine and its well-covered finish make it suitable for barbecues and exotic dishes.

🔑 Bernard Bouchon, Le Mongeat, 33420 Génissac, tel. 05.57.24.47.55, fax 05.57.24.41.21, e-mail mongeat@aol.com ☒ Y by appt.

CH. DE HAUX 1999★

◢ 2 ha 15,000 ▮ 🌡 30–49 F

Here is a clairet that confirms the expertise of the wine-grower and his oenological team. Cabernets (70%) and Merlot make up a light, intensely floral creation with a very rounded, rich body and fruity persistence (lychee). An attractive wine to go with smoked salmon and barbecue grills.

🔑 Peter et Plenning Jorgensen, SCA Ch. de Haux, 33550 Haux, tel. 05.57.34.51.12, fax 05.57.34.51.15 ☒ Y by appt.

CH. LA BRETONNIERE 1999

◢ 2 ha 15,000 ▮ 🌡 20–29 F

The château is north-east of the beautiful citadel of Blaye. The wine is exclusively Merlot. It exhales raspberry and sloe, and its very round palate is heavy with more complex crystallised notes which include a hint of liquorice.

🔑 Stéphane Heurlier, EARL La Bretonnière, 33390 Mazion, tel. 05.57.64.59.23, fax 05.57.64.59.23 ☒ Y ev. day except Sun. 9am–12.30pm 2pm–7pm

CH. LA SALARGUE 1999★★

◢ 2.8 ha 24,000 ▮ 🌡 20–29 F

The River Dordogne divides this region from that of Saint-Emilion; the grape varieties here are essentially Merlot followed by Cabernet Franc. These two (71% and 14% respectively) have provided the meat of this remarkable wine, which came close to winning a *coup de cœur.* The colour is an honest, thoroughly clairet-type ruby. The intense nose breathes notes of flowers (rose and seringa) and stone fruits (peach and cherry) with an elegance which similarly informs the supple and round, yet firm palate. The finish adds the delights of crystallised fruits. Crisp and crunchy.

🔑 SCEA Vignoble Bruno Le Roy, La Salargue, 33420 Moulon, tel. 05.57.24.48.44, fax 05.57.24.49.93, e-mail vignoble-bruno-le-roy@wanadoo.fr ☒ Y by appt.

CH. LESTRILLE CAPMARTIN Cuvée Tradition 1999★

◢ 0.75 ha 6,000 ▮ 🌡 30–49 F

The range of products presented by this esteemed proprietor includes this 1999 clairet, which is an ideal companion to entrées and desserts. A well-constructed wine, it has a rich roundness which approaches that of a light red, together with a fresh aromatic richness of ripe fruits. A very authentic clairet. Recommended.

🔑 Jean-Louis Roumage, Lestrille, 33750 Saint-Germain-du-Puch, tel. 05.57.24.51.02, fax 05.57.24.04.58 ☒ Y by appt.

CH. DE LISENNES 1999★

◢ 10 ha 80,000 ▮ 🌡 20–29 F

This château, located a few miles from Bordeaux, has an estate of 50 ha (124 acres). Its clairet has tradition behind it: successive proprietors have exported to England since the 18th century. The Merlot is balanced by two Cabernets (30% Sauvignon, 20% Franc). The highlights of the raspberry-like colour and the quality of the aromas are a definite invitation. Though the attack on the palate is discreet, the rich body and aromatic finish make this quite simply a real fun wine.

🔑 Jean-Pierre Soubie, Ch. de Lisennes, 33370 Tresses, tel. 05.57.34.13.03, fax 05.57.34.05.36 ☒ Y by appt.

CH. DE MONS 1999

◢ 2 ha 16,000 ▮ 🌡 30–49 F

Daniel Mouty has several properties and numerous reasons to figure in this Guide. His clairet (70% Cabernet Franc, 30% Sauvignon) was grown on the gravel soils of the Saint-Emilion district. The two varieties make their presence felt in small-fruit aromas which are somewhat discreet yet subtle. The fresh, elegant body and more energetic finish require attentiveness to reveal their delicate richness. A wine to drink with starters.

🔑 SCEA Daniel Mouty, Ch. du Barry, B.P. 5, 33350 Sainte-Terre, tel. 05.57.84.55.88, fax 05.57.74.92.99, e-mail daniel-mouty@wanadoo.fr ☒ Y by appt.

CH. PENIN 1999★★

◢ 4.7 ha 40,000 ▮ 🌡 30–49 F

Few estates are more regularly written about than this château. Essentially made from Merlot grown on gravel soils with a 10% component of Cabernet-Sauvignon, this clairet was kept three months on the fermenting lees. Its elegant, very persistent aromas evoke blackcurrant buds and roses. The body is supple and fresh despite its power; the wine is harmonious, fruity and well-blended without being oversoft, and has length. A wine to accompany charcuterie and mixed salads.

🔑 SCEA Patrick Carteyron, Ch. Penin, 33420 Génissac, tel. 05.57.24.46.98, fax 05.57.24.41.99 ☒ Y by appt.

ĿES VIGNERONS DE SAINT-ĿARTIN 1999★

■ 1.27 ha 10,800 ▮ 🌡 20-29 F

Made by the co-operative at Génissac, this is a pure Merlot which typifies that variety: an honest ruby colour and a nose of fruit aromas with more complex touches of fruit stones and liquorice. The first impressions on the palate are of a mellow, round, supple body, which develops to a fresh, perfumed finish with a slight hint of bitterness. Good for mixed salads and certain fromages frais.

🔑 Cave coop. vinicole de Génissac, 54, le Bourg, 33420 Génissac, tel. 05.57.55.55.65, fax 05.57.24.40.87 ☒ Y ev. day except Sun. 9am–12 noon 2pm–6pm; Sat. 9am–12 noon

CH. THIEULEY 1999★

■ 13 ha 120,000 ▮ 🌡 30-49 F

The Abbey of La Sauve-Majeure lies hard by this equally famous property. This garnet-red wine is dominated by the Cabernet Franc variety (50%). The nose is somewhat discreet, but the aromas become more evident on the palate: those of blackcurrant buds and fruit stones are conveyed through a fresh-tasting attack, while the palate and finish are characterised by roundness. A classic wine that will be a good accompaniment for exotic dishes or cold poultry.

🔑 Sté des Vignobles Francis Courselle, Ch. Thieuley, 33670 La Sauve, tel. 05.56.23.00.01, fax 05.56.23.34.37 ☒ Y by appt.

Bordeaux sec

BARON DE GRAVELINES

Vieilli en fût de chêne 1999★

□ n.c. n.c. ⏸ 20 F+

A trademark wine, this Baron is the outcome of good wine-merchanting. The colour is a brilliant pale-greenish- yellow and the nose intense, subtle and delicate, revealing fruits (lychee and citrus) and discreet, elegant notes of oak. The palate is round and supple; the lively finish evolves on a base of oak, caramel and honey. Appreciate this wine unhurriedly with starters or baked or grilled fish.

🔑 SA Yvon Mau, B.P. 1, 33193 Gironde-sur-Dropt Cedex, tel. 05.56.61.54.54, fax 05.56.61.54.61 Y by appt.

CH. BAUDUC 1999

□ 6.88 ha 53,000 ▮ 🌡 30-49 F

The bright translucent colour is barely yellow. Sauvignon (63%) and Sémillon (37%) give this wine a joyful aromatic complexity which mixes peach, strawberry and mango. The body is delicately round and elegant, with rather greater liveliness when arriving on the palate and at the finish. It has a beautifully appetising structure.

🔑 SCEA Vignobles Quinney, Ch. Bauduc, 33670 Créon, tel. 05.56.23.23.58, fax 05.56.23.06.05 ☒ Y by appt.

CAVE BEL-AIR 1999★

□ n.c. 30,000 ▮ 🌡 20-29 F

This pure Sauvignon was vinified by the merchants, Sichel. Selected grapes, well-timed partial maceration in the grape-skins, three months on the lees: these measures have created an attractive and successful wine. The variety's well-extracted aromas are joyous companions throughout the tasting. The round, full flesh sits easy on the palate, and the finish leaves one wanting more.

🔑 Maison Sichel-Coste, 8, rue de la Poste, 33210 Langon, tel. 05.56.63.50.52, fax 05.56.63.42.28

CH. BELLE-GARDE 1999★★

□ 4 ha 30,000 ▮ 🌡 20-29 F

Selective, partial maceration in the grape-skins and three months on the lees have achieved the desired result. This marriage of Sauvignon (60%) and Sémillon (40%) is aromatic enchantment. To the classic aromas of these varieties, the complex, delicate nose adds evolved notes of coconut and brioche with nuances of smokiness and toast. A mineral touch enlivens the body, which is rich in flavour, full and lively at the finish. This wine calls for grilled bass or shad.

🔑 Eric Duffau, Ch. Belle-Garde, Monplaisir, 33420 Génissac, tel. 05.57.24.49.12, fax 05.57.24.41.28 ☒ Y ev. day except Sun. 8am–12 noon 2pm–7pm; cl. 15–31 Aug.

CH. BOIS-MALOT Tradition 1999★

□ 0.5 ha 4,000 ⏸ 30-49 F

This particular blend of Sémillon (50%) and Sauvignon (40%) includes 10% Sauvignon Gris, a variety known for its aromatic richness and perfect maturity. Here it is married to oak. After six months in the cask, a slight effervescence appears, revealing a silky, round harmony which is rich, not to say powerful (too powerful, perhaps?). The aromas open out, developing from white flowers (acacia blossom) to acid-drop with touches of honey and oak enlivened with hints of clove. This 1999 wine 'makes you want to sit down and eat,' enthused one of the jury.

🔑 F. Meynard et Fils, 133, rte des Valentons, 33450 Saint-Loubès, tel. 05.56.38.94.18, fax 05.56.38.92.47 ☒ Y ev. day except Sat. Sun. 8am–12 noon 2pm–6.30pm

CH. DE BONHOSTE 1999★

□ 8 ha 20,000 ▮ 🌡 30-49 F

The Château de Bonhoste invites us to a blend of Sauvignon (40%), Sémillon (50%) and Muscadelle (10%). When it is served, a stream of minuscule bubbles animates this wine's pale appearance with its golden and green highlights. Abundant aromas of acacia, citrus, apple and pineapple all dance on the trim flesh of this wine. Fresh, charming and elegant, this companion of fish, seafood and

cheeses awaits you. This château introduced us to some very attractive wines.
🗝 SCEA des Vignobles Fournier, Ch. de Bonhoste, 33420 Saint-Jean-de-Blaignac, tel. 05.57.84.12.18, fax 05.57.84.15.36 ☑ Y by appt.
🗝 Bernard Fournier

CH. BOURDICOTTE

Haut de gamme 1999★

☐	5.04 ha	40,000	20–29 F

In the Gascon dialect, Cazaugitat means 'a thrown-down garden', in reference to the crocuses, narcissi and other bulb flowers that naturally bloom among the vines in early spring, a tradition the region's wine-growers are keen to maintain. The musts of this wine, obtained from Sémillon and Sauvignon grapes, are macerated for 18 hours with the skins, decanted after seven days of cold storage, and fermented in new barrels; they remain six months on the lees. Such sophisticated techniques call for a combination of modern technical means and perfect mastery of traditional expertise. The aromas here are delicate but timid. They are borne upon the subtle, fresh, well-balanced flesh by a slight effervescence. A pleasure to drink.
🗝 SCEA Rolet Jarbin, Dom. de Bourdicotte, 33790 Cazaugitat, tel. 05.56.61.32.55, fax 05.56.61.38.26

CH. DE BRANDEY

Vieilli en fût de chêne 1999

☐	1 ha	4,200	30–49 F

This wine is made from selected Sauvignon grapes fermented and kept in new barrels. Several touches of mint enliven a well-blended nose from which proceed notes of citrus, smokiness and wax. The palate, in contrast, is floral and lively; lychee and grapefruit appear against an insistent semi-sparkling background. A wine for shellfish. It ought to wait several months, keeping its freshness.
🗝 GAEC Vignobles Chevillard, Ch. de Brandey, 33350 Ruch, tel. 05.57.40.54.18, fax 05.57.40.54.18 ☑ Y by appt.

CH. CARSIN 1998★

☐	15 ha	54,000	30–49 F

In 1990, a Finnish lover of the Garonne bought a few acres near the little medieval town of Rions to live in a country house there. Since then, a love of Bordeaux wines has enlarged the property into a 56-ha (139-acre) vineyard. A blend of Sémillon (70%) and Sauvignon (30%) has spent ten months on the lees. The wine's aromatic complexity is revealed in a bouquet that marries notes of Muscat and brioche to those of fruits and acacia honey. The body's harmony and the fullness of the finish suggest accompanying the wine with cheeses. The recommended **1999 La Gabarre** is partly (15%) oak-matured, and is a Bordeaux Sec fermented on the lees. There is an attractive range of aromas: gunflint with ripe, crystallised grapes, continuing through bitter orange peel and citrus. The flesh is round and fresh. A wine of contrasts suitable for seafood.
🗝 Berglund, GFA Ch. Carsin, 33410 Rions, tel. 05.56.76.93.06, fax 05.56.62.64.80 ☑ Y by appt.

CORDIER

Collection privée Désiré Cordier 1999★

☐	n.c.	n.c.	20–29 F

The famous wine-merchants, Cordier, are recommended here for two wines made from the same Sauvignon grapes. The intense and distinguished perfumes of the Collection Privée wine are those of a widely-sold product. Peach, apricot and mandarin combine in a well-matched complexity, and the body is elegant, rich, well-balanced and very persistent. One of the jury suggested it as an accompaniment to pike. The recommended **1999 Labottière** comes from the name of a listed 18th-century Bordeaux mansion. The wine is delicate, slender, and long. It would nicely suit shellfish or cold starters.
🗝 Ets D. Cordier, 53, rue du Dehez, 33290 Blanquefort, tel. 05.56.95.53.00, fax 05.56.95.53.01

CH. DE CUGAT

Cuvée Fleur Elevé en barrique de chêne 1998

☐	2.4 ha	5,000	30–49 F

Alongside some very attractive reds, this property, which is close to the Abbey of Blasimon and a fortified water-mill, offers a white wine vinified and matured in oak. Sauvignon dominates (70%) with floral and mineral touches, and the oak makes its presence felt in notes of toast, grilling and vanilla, which today somewhat overburden the body, but which will be excellent with white meats.
🗝 Benoît Meyer, Ch. de Cugat, 33540 Blasimon, tel. 05.56.71.52.08, fax 05.56.71.60.29 ☑ Y by appt.

CHARLES DELATOUR

Cuvée Callypso 1999★

☐	n.c.	n.c.	50–69 F

The wine-merchants Charles Delatour is associated with Château Citran in the Haut-Médoc. This blend of three varieties (only 5% of which is Muscadelle) needs care in order to be properly tasted and assessed. The nose has a beautiful harmony of white flowers enhanced by notes of fresh bread and brioche. The palate has a delicate, well-made body, with good balance and persistence. A wine of elegance and distinction.
🗝 Charles Delatour, Ch. Citran, 33480 Avensan, tel. 05.56.58.21.01 ☑

CH. DOISY-DAENE 1998★

☐	7 ha	26,000	70–99 F

This is a dry-white Cru Classé Sauternes. Needless to say, the region is known worldwide for its great sweet wines, but this pure Sauvignon is highly successful and charmed our tasters. Fermented and kept for ten months on the lees, the typically Sauvignon aromas of citronella, grapefruit and broom are here enhanced by well-regulated nuances of oak and vanilla which emphasise the legance of the vigorous, well-balanced, fresh ody. Take time to follow its development ver several months.

🔑 EARL Vignobles Pierre et Denis Dubourdieu, Ch. Doisy-Daëne, quartier Gravas, 33720 Barsac, tel. 05.56.27.15.84, ax 05.56.27.18.99 ☑ 𝕐 ev. day except Sat. Sun. 9am–12.30pm 1.30pm–6pm

CH. FONREAUD Le Cygne 1999

☐ 1.9 ha 12,000 ⬛ 50–69 F

Listrac is esteemed above all for its AOC ed Médoc, but there have always been some white-grape vines grown there. This vineyard was reconstituted in 1988–9 around the classic varieties: Sauvignon (60%), Sémillon 20%), and Muscadelle (20%). This wine stayed on the lees in the barrels in which its fermentation took place. Its aromatic harmony – lemon, vanilla, *pain d'épice* and kouglof (respectively, a spice loaf and a kind of bun) – make a cheery accompaniment for the round, rich, agreeably spirited body, whose attack and finish both have a touch of liveliness. Good for starters, fish and platters of shellfish.

🔑 Ch. Fonréaud, 33480 Listrac-Médoc, tel. 05.56.58.02.43, fax 05.56.58.04.33 ☑ 𝕐 ev. day except Sat. Sun. 9am–12 noon 2pm–6pm

🔑 Héritiers Chanfreau

CH. FRANC-PERAT 1998★

☐ 6 ha 30,000 ⬛ 50–69 F

This wine has great freshness, marrying Sémillon (70%) and Sauvignon (30%) in an aromatic union of great finesse (white flowers and green citrus). Slender yet very elegant, long and joyously redolent of grapefruit, it will be a good accompaniment to seafood, if not already served as an aperitif.

🔑 SCEA de Mont-Pérat, 33550 Capian, tel. 05.57.84.55.08, fax 05.57.84.57.31, e-mail despagne@vignobles-despagne.com 𝕐 by appt.

🔑 J.-L. Despagne

GINESTET

Vinifié et élevé en fût de chêne 1999★

☐ n.c. 95,000 ⬛ 20–29 F

This Genestet dry Bordeaux exhaled scents of orange-blossom, pineapple and oak alongside soft, silky caramel when it was tasted on 21 April 2000. Its rich, creamy palate, enlivened at the finish by a slightly sparkling freshness, is the mark of an attractive wine.

🔑 SA Maison Ginestet, 19, av. de Fontenille, 33360 Carignan-de-Bordeaux, tel. 05.56.68.81.82, fax 05.56.20.96.99, e-mail contact@ginestet.fr 𝕐 by appt.

CH. GREYSAC 1999

☐ n.c. 11,000 ⬛ 30–49 F

About 15 years ago, the wine-growers of Médoc planted Sauvignon and Muscadelle vines on the last few hills of limy clay gravel in the Gironde, just before it meets the Atlantic. They recall, perhaps, the time half a century before, when whites played a classic role among the varieties of the region. After fermentation in the barrel, this wine was kept on its lees, as is shown by the round attack, fleshy, well-blended body, long finish and the captivating harmony of the aromas: acacia, white flowers, lemon and vanilla with well-behaved notes of oak and grilling. A wine for white meats and cheese.

🔑 SA Domaines Codem, Ch. Greysac, 33340 Bégadan, tel. 05.56.73.26.56, fax 05.56.73.26.58 ☑ 𝕐 by appt.

CH. GUILLAUME BLANC

Vinifié et élevé en fût de chêne 1999

☐ 2.31 ha 9,000 ⬛ 30–49 F

The man who gave this château its name was the 13th-century magistrate of the fortified town of Sainte-Foy-la-Grande several miles away. Grown on gravelly soil, the wine is made from 66% Sémillon and 34% Sauvignon. It has been fermented and matured in oak. The golden yellow colour signals a maturity that is confirmed by the aromas: floral notes derived from the Sauvignon slide around in an intense silkiness of honey and vanilla. 'Virtually a liqueur nose,' was one taster's comment. The body is well made, round, fresh and appetising. Try with a half-ripe Camembert.

🔑 SCEA Ch. Guillaume, lieu-dit Guillaume-Blanc, 33220 Saint-Philippe-du-Seignal, tel. 05.57.41.91.50, fax 05.57.46.42.76 ☑ 𝕐 by appt.

CH. HAUT-CHARDON 1999

☐ 3 ha 15,000 ⬛ 20–29 F

The Vignobles Louis Marinier AOC reds are often recommended. But here is a white, made from 40% Muscadelle, 40% Sauvignon and 20% Sémillon. It has great aromatic finesse and a body which, though apparently somewhat fragile, has an interesting smoothness.

🔑 Vignobles Louis Marinier, Dom. Florimond-La Brède, 33390 Berson, tel. 05.57.64.39.07, fax 05.57.64.23.27 ☑ 𝕐 ev. day 8am–12 noon 2pm–6pm; Sat. Sun. by appt.; cl. Aug.

CH. HAUT-GUILLEBOT 1999

☐ n.c. n.c. ⬛ 20–29 F

This business has passed from mother to daughter for seven generations. Known and sold over three continents, its attractive wines include this dry Bordeaux whose aromatic harmony is based on 60% Sauvignon. The aromas and structure of the palate reflect its being kept on fine lees; the flesh is rich, set off by nuances of crystallised fruits and brioche, and the finish is lively. A partner for shellfish (crustaceans), after an aperitif.

🔑 Evelyne Rénier, Lugaignac, 33420 Branne, tel. 05.57.84.53.92, fax 05.57.84.62.73 ☑ 𝕐 by appt.

CH. HAUT RIAN

Cuvée Excellence 1998

☐ 2 ha 12,000 ⬛ 30–49 F

This vast vineyard, built up gradually by

the current owner, is not far from Rions, a town which has been able to retain its gates and fortified walls. The pure Sémillon offered here is made from selected grapes vinified and kept on fine lees in new oak for nine months. The delicate aromas mix vanilla and coconut with citrus. Time will allow the oak to blend in with the lively, fresh, flavoursome, floral, honeyed body. A wine that can be enjoyed without haste as an accompaniment to white meats and fish in sauce.

Michel Dietrich, La Bastide, 33410 Rions, tel. 05.56.76.95.01, fax 05.56.76.93.51 ev. day except Sun. 9am–12 noon 2pm–6pm

CH. LA CHEZE

Elevé en fût de chêne 1998★

0.6 ha 3,000 30–49 F

Grown on excellent gravelly-clay soil, this pure Sauvignon has been vinified in new oak and kept ten months on its lees. The nose is both intense and remarkably complex. There are nuances of orange- and lemon-blossom, fruits (grapefruit, citrus peel), and an attractive oakiness (vanilla, coconut). The body has freshness, vigour, flavour and length. This is a wine of exquisite charm, to drink unhurriedly with white meats or cheese, or perhaps by itself.

SCEA Ch. La Chèze, 33550 Capian, tel. 05.56.72.11.77, fax 05.56.25.96.82 by appt.

Rontein et Priou

DOM. DE LA CROIX 1999

5 ha 6,000 20 F+

The wine-lover will find this estate at Gabarnac, a walk of several miles from the Château d'Epernon at Cadillac. The wine is a good classic, appreciated and assessed as such by the tasters (besides being so intended by its creator). The body fills the mouth well and has good balance. It is redolent of white flowers and citrus.

Jean-Yves Arnaud, La Croix, 33410 Gabarnac, tel. 05.56.20.23.52, fax 05.56.20.23.52 by appt.

CH. LA FREYNELLE 1999★

6 ha 50,000 30–49 F

The Vignobles Barthe offer two wines of interest to wine-lovers made from different proportions of the same grape varieties. The 1999 La Freynelle comprises 40% Muscadelle, 30% Sémillon and 30% Sauvignon and has been kept on the lees. Its intense perfumes are of orange, linden-flowers and kouglof (a kind of bun). The body is harmonious and rich, and aromatically informed by dried fruits, figs, apricots, liquorice and honey. The spirited yet silky finish denotes a well-behaved wine suitable for white meats and baked fish. The Sauvignon (40%) with 30% each of Sémillon and Muscadelle, makes its presence felt in the **1999 Moulin de Poncet**. The floral intensity of broom and seringa, the round, fresh body and energetic, lemony finish are evidence of a wine that is true to type, which will suit oysters, shellfish or cold fish.

Vignobles Ph. Barthe, Peyrefus, 33420 Daignac, tel. 05.57.84.55.90, fax 05.57.74.96.57, e-mail vbarthe@club-internet.fr by appt.

DOM. DE LA GRAVE

Cuvée Tradition 1999★

0.5 ha 4,000 20–29 F

The master's house is an 18th-century charterhouse about half a kilometre (one-third of a mile) from the Maison des Bordeaux et Bordeaux Supérieurs. The vineyard has belonged to the Roche family for five generations. Cuvée Tradition is made from 80% Sémillon and 20% Sauvignon kept on the lees in a vat. The intense and subtle nose, with undertones of broom and citronella, yields to a palate where perfumes of lychee and citrus lengthen a fleshy, rich body which has a lively, persistent finish. A classic wine. The **1999 Cuvée Prestige** (30–49F) is a selection of grapes from 45-year-old vines, including 70% Sémillon, matured over eight months in a new barrel. Its elegant perfumes evoke apricot, beeswax and good-quality oak. The full palate is enriched by discreet notes of roasting. A wine to go with baked fish or roasted legs of poulty. One star.

SCEA Roche, Perriche, 33750 Beychac-et-Caillau, tel. 05.56.72.41.28, fax 05.56.72.41.28 ev. day 8am–7pm

CH. LA MOTHE DU BARRY 1999

1 ha 6,000 20–29 F

Alongside his attractive red Bordeaux wines, Joël Duffau offers this composition of Sauvignon (70%) and Sémillon (30%), strongly evocative of white flowers and fruits (mandarin) with discreet oaky undertones. The liveliness of the citric finish contrasts with the perfumed suppleness of the body. This is an ideal wine for platters of seafood.

Joël Duffau, Les Arromans n°2, 33420 Moulon, tel. 05.57.74.93.98, fax 05.57.84.66.10 ev. day except Sun. 8am–12 noon 2pm–7pm

CH. LANGEL MAURIAC

Elevé en fût de chêne 1999

5 ha 32,000 20 F+

Producta's **1999 Bordeaux Sec** intended for Carrefour comprises 50% Sémillon, 40% Sauvignon and 10% Muscadelle, each variety supplying individual characters which the tasters noted. They liked the fairly heavy roundness of the orange-zest and mandarin-perfumed flesh and the fullness and harmony of the finish. A wine for starters and cold fish. Château Langel Mauriac (40% Sauvignon, 10% Muscadelle) was vinified and matured in oak by one of the shareholders. The nose's discreet character is compensated for by the subtlety and elegance of its white-flower and crystallised-fruit perfumes. A light fizziness emphasises the body's freshness, in contrast to the oakiness that unobtrusively prolongs the finish.

🔑 Producta SA, 21, cours Xavier-Arnozan, 33082 Bordeaux Cedex, tel. 05.57.81.18.18, fax 05.56.81.22.12, e-mail producta@producta.com Y by appt.

DOM. DE LAUBERTRIE 1999

☐ n.c. 6,000 20-29 F

This 14-ha (35-acre) estate has belonged to the Pontallier family since the 16th century. Such continuity is rare indeed. Grown on limy clay, the wine blends 60% Sauvignon, 30% Muscadelle, and 10% Sémillon. Beautifully clear with a lovely green glint, this is a very subtle wine. It is well-balanced, fresh, and fruity, and leaves the mouth with a lemony feel. Excellent for seafood.

🔑 Bernard Pontallier, Laubertrie, 33240 Salignac, tel. 05.57.43.24.73, fax 05.57.43.24.73 ☑ Y by appt.

CH. LE BOUSCAT 1999★

☐ n.c. n.c. 20-29 F

Offered by the powerful Union des Producteurs at Rauzan, this wine is a charmer. It has aromas of acid-drops and citronella, a slightly effervescent body with tiny floral bubbles, and a finish skirted by bitter orange peel.

This is a good accompaniment to a seafood platter or a fry-up of small freshwater fish.

🔑 Union de producteurs de Rauzan, 33420 Rauzan, tel. 05.57.84.13.22, fax 05.57.84.12.67 Y by appt.

CH. LES FAURES 1999

☐ 6 ha 3,500 20-29 F

The cold maceration in the grape-skins prior to fermentation doubtless accounts for the bitter hint in the finish, which divided the tasters. However, they all acknowledged the authenticity of this trio of varieties where Sauvignon (60%) contributes a nose of peach and grapefruit, Sémillon (25%) provides suppleness, and Muscadelle (15%) affords a subtle aromatic counterbalance of apricot and honey in the flesh and finish. A 1999 classic.

🔑 Jacky Certain, 9, Les Faures-Est, 33190 Camiran, tel. 05.56.71.41.86, fax 05.56.71.32.76 ☑ Y by appt.

CH. LES VIEILLES TUILERIES 1999★

☐ n.c. n.c. 20-29 F

This château is not far from the Château du Haut-Benauge, whose ramparts are visible in the distance. The pure Sauvignon grapes here express their perfect maturity: delicate peach perfumes, a tender, fresh body, a tantalising effervescence, and a complex and persistent return of aromas. Pure mastery from vine to bottle. This is an excellent wine to accompany a platter of seafood.

🔑 SCEA des Vignobles Menguin, 194, Gouas, 33760 Arbis, tel. 05.56.23.61.70, fax 05.56.23.49.79 ☑ Y by appt.

CH. DE L'ORANGERIE 1999★

☐ 16 ha 106,000 20-29 F

The vineyard was established in 1789. This pure Sauvignon wine was made according to modern principles, including keeping on the lees, which has given it a nose of smoky, toasted complexity and a body of rich, well-blended fullness. Its attractive persistence is very slightly accentuated by tantalising mineral notes. A successful single-variety Bordeaux.

🔑 Jean-Christophe Icard, Ch. de l'Orangerie, 33540 Saint-Félix-de-Foncaude, tel. 05.56.71.53.67, fax 05.56.71.59.11, e-mail orangerie@quaternet.fr ☑ Y by appt.

CH. DE LOS 1999

☐ 2.5 ha 15,000 20-29 F

There is a water-mill on the boundary of this very old family property, whose vineyard was established in 1713. The white wine is lively and long-lasting, with a slightly acid finish. From start to finish, it exhales scents of seringa, acacia and blackcurrant buds, to which the palate adds peach, mandarin and honey. This is a gulpable Bordeaux made of 60% Sémillon, 30% Muscadelle, and 10% Sauvignon, which has evidently benefited from being kept on the lees. It would have merited a star had it been a little less sharp. It will suit shellfish (crustaceans), charcuterie and mixed salads.

🔑 SCEA Vignobles Signé, 505, Petit Moulin Sud, 33760 Arbis, tel. 05.56.23.93.22, fax 05.56.23.45.75, e-mail signevignobles@wanadoo.fr ☑ Y by appt.

CH. MALAGAR 1999★

☐ 7.5 ha 49,000 30-49 F

One cannot mention Malagar without thinking of François Mauriac, winner of the Nobel Prize for literature. The author's house has become a museum of the Aquitaine Regional Council, and the Domaines Cordier have cultivated the vineyard since 1989. The wine is grown on sandy gravelly soils planted with Sémillon (60%) and Sauvignon (40%). It has been fermented in barrels, half of which are new, remaining on the lees for four months. The fine, well-regulated oakiness enhances the round body, which has hints of citrus and pineapple refreshed by slight effervescence. Its harmonious character may take time to develop further.

The pale golden-yellow **1999 Château Tanesse**, grown on a mound in the Langoiran hills and oak-matured for three months, is recommended. Its nose is dominated by the Sauvignon (60%), but its bite is tempered on the palate by the Sémillon (40%) and the oak, which comes though especially at the finish. A pleasing classic.

🔑 Domaines Cordier, 160, cours du Médoc, 33300 Bordeaux, tel. 05.57.19.57.77, fax 05.57.19.57.87 Y by appt.

CH. MEMOIRES 1999

☐ 2.5 ha 16,000 🍾 🌡 20–29 F

Very near Malagar, the house where François Mauriac, the author of *Thérèse Desqueyroux*, lived, Château Mémoires offers a charming, well-constructed Sauvignon with nuances of flowers and brioche. A refreshing wine to drink after a walk.

🔑 SCEA Vignobles Ménard, Ch. Mémoires, 33490 Saint-Maixant, tel. 05.56.62.06.43, fax 05.56.62.04.32, e-mail memoires@aol.com ☑ Y by appt.

CH. MEZAIN 1999★

☐ 5 ha 40,000 🍾 🌡 20 F+

Two one-star wines offered by the reputed wine-merchants at Floirac. First, this Château Mezain, a rather rare example of a half-Sauvignon, half-Muscadelle blend. It is characterised by fullness and subtle aromas. White flowers and lychee are fundamental, but its richness is susceptible to various interpretations. The trademark **1999 Marquis d'Alban** is a pure Sauvignon, with a reassuringly round, mouth-filling, long-lasting palate, impressive aromas of honey and ripe fruits, and a very calm finish. Two styles of wine, the first suitable for seafood, the second for white meats. The price of the second is 20–29F.

🔑 Dulong Frères et Fils, 29, rue Jules-Guesde, 33270 Floirac, tel. 05.56.86.51.15, fax 05.56.40.66.41, e-mail dulong@mmkm.com Y by appt.

CH. MONIER-LA FRAISSE 1999★★

☐ 8 ha 10,000 🍾 🌡 20–29 F

The wineries of this Union, one of the most important units of production in the Gironde, are located at the gates of the well-ordered fortified town of Sauveterre-de-Guyenne in the heart of the Entre-Deux-Mers district. Château Monier-La-Fraisse is made from 70% Sauvignon, 20% Sémillon and 10% Muscadelle. Specialists will want to praise the master's expertise in adapting the duration of grape-skin contact to the maturity of each particular variety. The nose is not as strong as one would like, but the reward is in the exquisite subtlety and complexity of the floral and fruit aromas. The body's balance and aromatic persistence are everything a top Bordeaux should be – this was nearly a *coup de cœur*! The **1999 Cellier de La Bastide** is a pure Sauvignon. The very floral nose (lemon and orange blossom) with the merest hint of broom, the richness of the flesh, the citrus-perfumed length, all delighted the jurors, who gave it one star.

🔑 Cellier de La Bastide, Cave coop. vinicole, 33540 Sauveterre-de-Guyenne, tel. 05.56.61.55.21, fax 05.56.71.60.11 ☑ Y ev. day except Sun. 9am–12.15 1.30pm–6.15; groups by appt.

🔑 Claude Laveix

CH. MONTAUNOIR 1999★

☐ 3 ha 12,500 ⏸ 20–29 F

Sainte-Croix-du-Mont – better known for its wines than for its beds of fossilised oysters – and the fortified village of Saint-Macaire are several miles away. Five per cent Muscadelle complete the Sémillon-Sauvignon blend, which remained on the lees for more than a month. Box and lychee are the basic aromatic elements which reveal themselves more on the palate than in the nose, subtly ensuring that this fresh-tasting wine will give pleasure with its round, fruity flesh and long-lasting character.

🔑 SCEA des Vignobles Ricard, Ch. de Vertheuil, 33410 Sainte-Croix-du-Mont, tel. 05.56.62.02.70, fax 05.56.76.73.23 ☑ Y by appt.

HENRY BARON DE MONTESQUIEU

Réserve le Secondat 1999★

☐ n.c. n.c. 🍾 🌡 20–29 F

Needless to say, the château that belonged to the famous wine-growing baron and author of the *Esprit des lois* is not far away. The marriage between Sauvignon and Sémillon is here emphasised by a small amount (5%) of Muscadelle. The palate is round and rich, informed by aromas of exotic fruits (mango and lychee) accompanied by citrus, which slowly fade into concentrated fine touches. A very successful wine well-suited to starters or smoked salmon.

🔑 Vins et Dom. Henry de Montesquieu, Aux Fougères, 33650 La Brède, tel. 05.56.78.45.45, fax 05.56.20.25.07, e-mail montesquieu@bordeaux-montesquieu.com ☑

CH. MYLORD 1999★

☐ 1.5 ha 15,000 🍾 🌡 20–29 F

There are some charming walks around Grézillac, between the little churches, the châteaux of varying ages and the views over the Saint-Emilion district. As for the wine, the various elements in this perfectly balanced blend have been selected and vinified using appropriate techniques, the wine staying on the lees in the vat until it was bottled. The three Bordeaux varieties used are in equal proportions. The wine's floral and fruity aromas ranges from acacia through peach and apricot to lime, supplying the dense, round palate with pleasurable sensations, and persisting with lightness. This is good for well-prepared cooked dishes and small round cheeses (*crottins*).

🔑 Michel et Alain Large, Ch. Mylord, 33420 Grézillac, tel. 05.57.84.52.19, fax 05.57.74.93.95 ☑ Y by appt.

PAVILLON BLANC DU CHATEAU MARGAUX 1998★★

☐ n.c. n.c. ⏸ 200–249 F

Like many white Bordeaux made in Médoc vineyards, this wine comes from a gravelly source particularly favourable to the production of high-quality wine. This year's wine proves the point by the elegance with which its lovely rich, full palate marries the expressive bouquet of white flowers, white-flesh fruits and menthol. Fresh, crisp, full and long.

SC du Ch. Margaux, 33460 Margaux, tel. 05.57.88.83.83, fax 05.57.88.83.32

CH. RAUZAN DESPAGNE

Cuvée Passion 1998★

☐ 7 ha 10,000 50–69 F

Forty-year-old vines, regulated yields, a 70:30 ratio of Sauvignon to Sémillon, fermentation and vinification in new barrels – all figure in the work of the Despagne team! This wine breathes white flowers and lightly vanilla-tinged exotic fruits. The palate is like a basket of fruits sitting on good quality oak. A lovely companion to fish in sauce and white meats. The **1999 Cuvée Principale** (30–49F) is not oak-matured. It gets a citation for its liveliness, nose of peach and apricot, and palate of white flowers. This is a wine to gulp down with shellfish (crustaceans). The same producer's two **1999 Cuvée Principale** wines in this AOC are given the same rating.

GFA de Landeron, 33420 Naujan-et-Postiac, tel. 05.57.84.55.08, fax 05.57.84.57.31, e-mail despagne@vignobles-despagne.com by appt.

J.-L. Despagne

CH. REYNON Vieilles vignes 1998★

☐ 12 ha 73,000 50–69 F

Château Reynon, established in 1850, is owned by Denis Dubourdieu, a university oenologist with an international reputation. This wine is grown on gravel and limy clay. It is 90% Sauvignon with a residue of Sémillon and is vinified with grape-skin contact. The contribution of the oak has been perfectly judged in this beautiful pale-yellow 1999 wine with green highlights. The nose is true to the main variety used, with notes of flowers and citronella. The palate is fresh, full of flavour and vigorous.

Denis et Florence Dubourdieu, Ch. Reynon, 33410 Béguey, tel. 05.56.62.96.51, fax 05.56.62.14.89, e-mail reynon@gofornet.com by appt.

CH. DE RICAUD 1999★

☐ 1.5 ha 10,000 30–49 F

The marriage between Sauvignon and Sémillon represents a mere 1.5 ha (3.70 acres) out of the 120 ha (297 acres) on this estate, which, being near Loupiac, concentrates mainly on rich, sweet whites. The château received a Neo-Gothic makeover in the 19th century. Though the balance of this 1999 wine is somewhat discreet, both nose and palate are harmonious. Notes of cocoa and honey mingle with those of lychee and orange blossom in a flavoursome, elegant, persistent complexity. A delight for the subtle and attentive wine-lover.

Ch. de Ricaud, 33410 Loupiac, tel. 05.56.62.66.16, fax 05.56.76.93.30 by appt.

Alain Thiénot

DOM. DE RICAUD 1999★

☐ 4.3 ha 35,000 30–49 F

This wine is the product of technical stringency. It is made from two-thirds Sémillon to one-third Sauvignon, with a cold maceration of the grapes in the skin, followed by fermentation after clarification at 16–18°C (60.8–64.4°F); it is then kept on the lees. The intense straw-yellow colour is attractive. The Sauvignon makes its presence felt in the aromas, while the Sémillon plays its part in establishing the rich roundness of the flesh. The finish recalls what has been extracted in the maceration. This wine will go well with poultry in sauce and dry cheeses.

Vignobles Chaigne et Fils, Ch. Ballan-Larquette, 33540 Saint-Laurent-du-Bois, tel. 05.56.76.46.02, fax 05.56.76.40.90, e-mail rchaigne@vins-bordeaux.fr by appt.

R DE RIEUSSEC 1999★★

☐ n.c. n.c. 50–69 F

Grown in a vineyard belonging to one of the most prestigious of the Sauternes crus, this dry Bordeaux lives up to its noble origins. Made of 40% Sauvignon and 60% Sémillon delicately supported by a well-judged dose of oak, this pale golden wine with green lights has a charming and subtle bouquet with floral notes (honeysuckle) and fruit aromas (citrus). On the palate it begins full of flavour and goes on to delight with its freshness and tenderness, which highlight the elegance of its aromatic expression.

Ch. Rieussec, 33210 Fargues-de-Langon, tel. 01.53.89.78.00, fax 01.53.89.78.01 by appt.

CH. ROQUEFORT 1999★

☐ n.c. n.c. 30–49 F

A huge estate which Jean Bellanger tends with expertise, as is proved yet again by this successful wine. Citrus fruits (grapefruit and orange) are its soul, but they share the nose and palate with a ripe, concentrated, vigorous grapeyness. The fresh, rich, complex harmony of this wine delighted the jurors.

SCE du Ch. Roquefort, 33760 Lugasson, tel. 05.56.23.97.48, fax 05.56.23.51.44 by appt.

J. Bellanger

CH. DE SEGUIN Cuvée Prestige 1999

☐ 2.5 ha 20,000 50–69 F

Visitors to the Château de Seguin, 15 km (9 miles) east of Bordeaux, will see the elegant sobriety of its towers, the vastness of its vineyard (127 ha/314 acres) and the modern beauty of its wineries. This wine is the outcome of a careful selection of varieties and plots prior to fermentation of the must and time spent in new barrels. There are delightful ripe fruit aromas from the Sémillon (60%), the Sauvignons Blanc (30%) and Gris (5%) and a similar small proportion of Muscadelle. There is some oakiness too. The body is full and the liveliness of the finish has an attractive freshness. A wine to drink with fish.

Michael Carl, Ch. de Seguin, 33360

Lignan-de-Bordeaux, tel. 05.57.97.19.75, fax 05.57.97.19.72, e-mail cwi@chris-wine.dk ☒ Y by appt.

CH. THIEULEY 1999

□ 24 ha 200,000 30-49 F

Francis Courselle has perfectly tempered the Sauvignon by combining it with 50% Sémillon. Broom is the first aroma one senses, followed quickly by acacia flowers and exotic fruits, plus notes of toast and brioche. The palate and finish are round, fleshy and honeyed. Suitable for an aperitif or with a poultry salad.

Sté des Vignobles Francis Courselle, Ch. Thieuley, 33670 La Sauve, tel. 05.56.23.00.01, fax 05.56.23.34.37 ☒ Y by appt.

LE BLANC DE JEAN-LOUIS TROCARD 1999★

□ 3.33 ha 20,000 20-29 F

Jean-Louis Trocard is better known for his red wines (and professional activities in the wine world), but this white wine (half Sémillon, half Sauvignon) impressed the tasters with its very definite features of green fruits, box, and white flowers which enliven the flesh and finish. This is a style of wine that some devotees will have no reservations about serving with oysters.

Cellier des Charmettes, 2, Les Petits Jays Ouest, 33570 Les Artigues-de-Lussac, tel. 05.57.55.57.99, fax 05.57.55.57.98, e-mail trocard@wanadoo.fr ☒ Y by appt.

Bordeaux rosé

CELLIER DE BORDES 1999★

n.c. 50,000 20-29 F

A fun wine well put together by the merchants, Cheval-Quancard. It has expressive aromas of blackcurrant and a pleasantly fresh, not to say lively body and finish. A rosé to be drunk as an aperitif.

Cheval Quancard, La Mouline, 33560 Carbon-Blanc, tel. 05.57.77.88.88, fax 05.57.77.88.99 Y by appt.

COUP DE SOLEIL 1999★

1 ha 5,000 20-29 F

Old vines (40 years old) have produced this rosé made from 60% Merlot and 25% Cabernet Franc supported by 15% Cabernet Sauvignon. The great subtlety and well-judged intensity of the aromas endow the wine's body with a complexity of concentrated ripe fruits. There are hints of blackcurrant or redcurrant jam and raspberry on a bed of caramel. It has beguiling length.

Arnaud Pauchet, Le Pin, 33420 Saint-Vincent-de-Pertignas, tel. 05.57.84.02.56, fax 05.57.84.02.56, e-mail arno.pauchet@wanadoo.fr ☒ Y by appt.

CH. CRABITAN-BELLEVUE 1999★

0.5 ha 4,500 20-29 F

Single-variety – especially Merlot – rosés are a frequent subject for debate among wine experts. One juror feared that the wine evolved too fast into a well-blended roundness with complex aromas, whilst others expressed their pleasure and confidence in the citrus aromas (orange peel and grapefruit) and intense fruitiness of the flesh. Make up your own mind. But don't leave it too long. For this château's good reputation can be relied on.

GFA Bernard Solane et Fils, 33410 Sainte-Croix-du-Mont, tel. 05.56.62.01.53, fax 05.56.76.72.09 ☒ Y ev. day except Sun. 8am–12 noon 2pm–6pm

CH. GABARON 1999★

11.36 ha 100,000 20-29 F

This large property and its ultra-modern wineries are dominated by the ruined bell-tower of the former Abbey of La Sauve – making two interesting visits in one. Two Cabernets each account for 30% of this blend, with Merlot making up the other 40%. The colour is a bright, slightly salmon-pink ruby, and the aromas are evocative of strawberry and raspberry. The body is round and expressive of these same berry-fruit flavours. The finish makes this a convincing meal-time wine, suited to first-courses and cold poultry.

GAEC des vignobles Latorse, 33670 La Sauve, tel. 05.56.23.92.76, fax 05.56.23.61.65 ☒ Y by appt.

ROSE DE GENIBON 1999

0.23 ha 2,000 20-29 F

It is relatively rare in the Bordeaux region to come across a pure Cabernet Franc. So this rosé is worthy of note. It has pleasant, fresh, merging aromas, a fruity palate whose roundness is set off by a teasing fizziness, and an elegant finish. An attractive wine.

Jean-Claude et Christine Sudre, Genibon, 33710 Bourg-sur-Gironde, tel. 05.57.68.25.34, fax 05.57.68.25.34 ☒ Y by appt.

GRANDES VERSANNES 1999★

4 ha 35,000 20-29 F

The cellar-master of this powerful Union de Producteurs is known for his expertise and technical rigour. Made from 70% Merlot and 30% Cabernet-Sauvignon grapes treated by the *saignée* method and fermented after clarification, this rosé has a distinctly raspberry nose. The well-blended body is enlivened by a spirited touch of effervescence, which sets off its long persistence. A great pleasure to drink as an aperitif or with goat's cheese.

Union de producteurs de Lugon, 6, rue Louis-Pasteur, 33240 Lugon, tel. 05.57.55.00.88, fax 05.57.84.83.16 ☒ Y by appt.

CH. GROSSOMBRE 1999★

n.c. n.c. 30–49 F

Within the range of attractive wines produced here, this very pale rosé is distinguished by its aromatic freshness based on the fruitiness of Merlot (blackcurrant and strawberry) and the floral character of Cabernet-Sauvignon, each variety contributing 50%. The body is slender and supple, and the finish has a cheery liveliness.

Béatrice Lurton, B.P. 10, 33420 Grézillac, tel. 05.57.25.58.58, fax 05.57.74.98.59, e-mail andre.lurton@wanadoo.fr by appt.

CH. HAUT-GARRIGA 1999★

6 ha 35,000 20–29 F

This is a pure Merlot with salmon-pink highlights. The strong, elegant nose exhales aromas of peach, white flowers, then plum and grenadine. Its round flesh and finish of blending fruits give it a particular character. A very nice, sunny rosé.

EARL Vignobles Claude Barreau et Fils, Ch. Haut-Garriga, 33420 Grézillac, tel. 05.57.74.90.06, fax 05.57.74.96.63 ev. day except Sun. 9am–12 noon 2pm–6pm

Claude Barreau

CH. DE JABASTAS 1999★

0.5 ha 4,000 20–29 F

When Cabernet-Sauvignon is really ripe, the wine made from it loses its peppery aggressiveness. This wine is a case in point. The body gains in roundness, and the aromas, which are of more than merely fruity, are closer to those of a mature wine. It has an elegance which the slight effervescence sets off. An attractive wine.

Jean-Marie Nadau, Ch. de Jabastas, 35, av. des Prades, 33450 Izon, tel. 05.57.84.97.13, fax 05.57.84.97.14 by appt.

CH. LA COMMANDERIE DE QUEYRET 1999★

n.c. 14,000 30–49 F

In the 13th century, the Knights of Saint John of Jerusalem established a commander's residence here. Vines have been grown ever since. Cabernet-Sauvignon and Merlot have together produced a cherry-coloured rosé that is fruity (raspberry and banana), fresh and spicy. The good-natured roundness of the flesh and its long-lasting aromas make this a successful wine which will be enjoyed with charcuterie.

Claude Comin, La Commanderie, 33790 Saint-Antoine-du-Queyret, tel. 05.56.61.31.98, fax 05.56.61.34.22 by appt.

CH. LAGNET 1999★

2.85 ha 22,000 20 F+

Since 1976, Hélène Levieux has managed her father Edouard Leclerc's three Bordeaux properties. Merlot (60%) and Cabernet Franc (40%) here join to produce a pale, very slightly salmon-pink wine with a delicate nose of small red fruits (strawberry and raspberry) and a hint of acid-drops. A welcome semi-sparkling character enlivens the supple, fleshy body, and the long, perfumed, buttery finish. A very successful wine to drink as an aperitif.

GFA Leclerc, Ch. Lagnet, 33350 Doulezon, tel. 05.57.40.51.84, fax 05.57.40.55.48 by appt.

LA ROSE CASTENET 1999★

4 ha 34,000 20–29 F

Five kilometres (three miles) from the Abbey of Saint-Ferme, which is austere yet full of charm, the wine-lover will find a lime and a chestnut tree that are just a hundred years old. The property on which they stand has been in the same family for four generations. This classically conceived rosé has the art of good balance. Everything is as it should be: the aromatic quality of the contrasting fruits (sweet and sour), the tender body and attack, and also the finish with its lively fresh flavours. A wine for an aperitif or to drink with starters.

EARL François Greffier, Castenet, 33790 Auriolles, tel. 05.56.61.40.67, fax 05.56.61.38.82, e-mail ch.castenet@wanadoo.fr by appt.

CH. DE LA VIEILLE TOUR 1999

3 ha 20,000 30–49 F

This is a rosé for the garden, to drink on ice in the late afternoon at the end of a hard-working or hot day. It has a lovely clear cherry colour. Budding flowers and redcurrants inform the nose, and the body has the slightly acid freshness typical of just-ripe Cabernet grapes (these two varieties comprising 60% of the wine). Pretzels or small pizzas would show it off at its best.

Vignobles Boissonneau, Cathelicq, 33190 Saint-Michel-de-Lapujade, tel. 05.56.61.72.14, fax 05.56.61.71.01, e-mail vignobles.boissonneau@wanadoo.fr by appt.

CH. LESTRILLE 1999★

2.38 ha 20,000 30–49 F

The proprietor and château have acquired great fame. This very attractive rosé has a seductive luminous raspberry colour and intense aromas of rose and fruits with exotic notes of lychee. They persist through to the finish, accompanying a fresh, round flesh which is enlivened by an energy that adds to its charm.

Jean-Louis Roumage, Lestrille, 33750 Saint-Germain-du-Puch, tel. 05.57.24.51.02, fax 05.57.24.04.58 by appt.

CH. LE TREBUCHET 1999★

2 ha 12,000 20–29 F

The trebuchet was a large sling-type war-machine in the Middle Ages, but it was also used to catch small birds – which is something that this trim, fresh, elegantly raspberry-scented rosé also does, in a manner of speaking, being a classic wine to go with cold poultry salads or charcuterie.

Bernard Berger, Ch. Le Trébuchet, 33190 Les Esseintes, tel. 05.56.71.42.28, fax 05.56.71.30.16 ev. day except Sun. 8am–12 noon 2pm–6pm

CH. MARAC 1999★

1.1 ha 9,600 30–49 F

The small town of Pujols dominates the Dordogne south of Castillon-la-Bataille. From the terrace of the château (where there are 12th-century ruins), there is a beautiful panoramic view over to the Saint-Emilion district. This wine betrays the roundness and generosity of its 55% Merlot, obtained by the *saignée* method after a short period of maceration in the skins. The aromatic subtlety comes from the 45% Cabernet Franc, obtained by direct pressing of the grapes. The wine is delicately redolent of strawberry, raspberry and fresh fruit. A slight effervescence enlivens the well-balanced body and agreeable finish. A clean-tasting, successful wine suitable for starters or cheeses.

SA Bonville Fils, Ch. Marac, 33350 Pujols, tel. 05.57.40.53.21, fax 05.57.40.71.36 by appt.

MAYNE SANSAC 1999★

5 ha 33,000 20–29 F

This is an attractive bright raspberry-coloured wine made from half Merlot, half Cabernet grapes. The tasting is informed by aromas of red fruits, redcurrant jam and bananas, along with an invigorating slight fizziness. The harmonious, rather tender flesh is highly classic to the appellation. A fresh and pleasant wine.

Domaine de Sansac, Les Lèves, 33220 Sainte-Foy-la-Grande, tel. 05.57.56.02.02, fax 05.57.56.02.22 by appt.

MISSION SAINT-VINCENT

Vieilli en fût de chêne 1999★

40 ha 290,000 20 F+

From the Producta group, three wines vinified by its members and blended according to the group's directions attracted the jurors' attention. The first two shared the same composition: 50% Merlot, 30% Cabernet-Sauvignon and 20% Cabernet Franc. The blend is very successful in this Mission Saint-Vincent, which is a very typical, classic, dependable wine. **Etalon**, which is similarly rated, has a delightful intense aromatic freshness. A citation goes to the **Maine-Brilland**, which is a blend of 55% Merlot, 30% Cabernet-Sauvignon and 15% Cabernet Franc. Its aromas come through very strongly on the palate, and the richness of the body is pleasurably set off by sparks of acidity. A touch of bitter almond spices the finish. Drink from this autumn on.

Producta SA, 21, cours Xavier-Arnozan, 33082 Bordeaux Cedex, tel. 05.57.81.18.18, fax 05.56.81.22.12, e-mail producta@producta.com by appt.

CH. MOUSSEYRON 1999★★

1 ha 9,000 20–29 F

The art of of making rosé wines is not a simple one. The grapes have to be harvested at their aromatic optimum, while the effects of the yeasts and the proportions of the varieties have to be carefully considered. Here 50% Cabernet-Sauvignon, 35% Merlot and 15% Cabernet Franc have resulted in this pale wine, whose delights result from the artful complexity of relationships between floral aspects, fruits and yeasts revealed in the discreet elegance of the nose and the flesh's supple acidity. A remarkable wine to be drunk straight away.

Jacques Larriaut, 33490 Saint-Pierre-d'Aurillac, tel. 05.56.76.44.53, fax 05.56.76.44.04 by appt.

CH. NAUDONNET PLAISANCE

Perle Rose d'Apr. 1999

1 ha 5,000 30–49 F

This 90% Merlot wine was fermented in new oak and kept on the lees for eight months, an ancient technique readopted a few years ago especially for white wines. Hence the rich complexity of the aromas and flavours, evoking raspberry and strawberry inside a buttered brioche. Not just a curiosity, but an original pleasure.

Danièle Mallard, Ch. Naudonnet-Plaisance, 33760 Escoussans, tel. 05.56.23.93.04, fax 05.57.34.40.78, e-mail mallard@caves-particulieres.com by appt.

CH. PENIN 1999★

3 ha 26,000 30–49 F

This well-respected wine-grower offers a 75% Merlot rosé with a round, tender body. The palate is more floral than fruity, and the floral character provides a calm finish. A wine to enjoy and savour for its own sake.

SCEA Patrick Carteyron, Ch. Penin, 33420 Génissac, tel. 05.57.24.46.98, fax 05.57.24.41.99 by appt.

CH. DE RICAUD 1999★

1.5 ha 11,000 30–49 F

The Château de Ricaud is close to Loupiac, an area well-known for its white wines. There is room for rosé too, however. This laudable marriage of Merlot and Cabernet allies power, aromatic subtlety, roundness and freshness. The lively notes of the finish suggest that this attractive, very slightly salmon-pink rosé will best suit starters or salty dishes.

Ch. de Ricaud, 33410 Loupiac, tel. 05.56.62.66.16, fax 05.56.76.93.30 by appt.

Alain Thiénot

CH. DE SOURS 1999★★

12 ha 80,000 30–49 F

A well-known rosé specialist is here rewarded with stars, and narrowly missed a *coup de cœur* for this wine. Mostly ripe Merlot (90%), with contributions from the two Cabernets, it was fermented at a low

temperature (10–14°C/50–57.2°F) and kept in a vat at 8°C (46.4°F) until bottling. Hence the intense and complex aromas that characterise this wine: flowers and fresh fruits (roses, linden-flowers, raspberry and strawberry) in a well-blended, well-balanced and long-lasting harmony. This wine will give intense pleasure until summer 2001.
SCEA Ch. de Sours, 33750 Saint-Quentin-de-Baron, tel. 05.57.24.10.81, fax 05.57.24.10.83 Y by appt.
E. Johnstone

TERRES DOUCES 1999★

n.c. 300,000 20–29 F

This half-Merlot, half-Cabernets classic wine comes from the 'sweet lands' of the Maison Ginestet. There is a hint of fire in the rosé colour, while the nose is elegant in its expression rather than intense. The palate is fruity, mouth-filling, and persistent. A wine to drink with friends, nicely appetising when accompanying a starter.
SA Maison Ginestet, 19, av. de Fontenille, 33360 Carignan-de-Bordeaux, tel. 05.56.68.81.82, fax 05.56.20.96.99, e-mail contact@ginestet.fr Y by appt.

VILLOTTE 1999★

n.c. n.c. 30–49 F

There are three sites to visit in Rauzan: a charming Romanesque church with two naves; the feudal château's imposing ruins, and the wineries of the large, ultra-modern Union des Producteurs. This Villotte rosé is highly successful. The colour is a luminous redcurrant-red, and the nose is intensely perfumed with blackcurrant and acid-drops. The wine fills the mouth well, is welcoming, comforting and fresh, with a slightly acid finish which makes one want more. A wine to drink with salads. The **1999 Comte de Ruel Rosé** (20–29F) is similarly rated.
Union de producteurs de Rauzan, 33420 Rauzan, tel. 05.57.84.13.22, fax 05.57.84.12.67 Y by appt.

Bordeaux supérieur

CH. BARDOS 1998★★

16.89 ha 136,800 30–49 F

A feudal château proudly guards one of the entrances to the small town of Rauzan. The Union des Producteurs' imposing wineries are on the other side and no less worth visiting. Château Bardos has been vinified and outstandingly well matured for 12 months in oak. It nearly achieved three stars. This attractively lustrous deep purple wine has a heady, open nose mixing scents of vanilla, spices and grilling with those of cooked fruits (plum or cherry tart). The palate reveals a dense, succulent, rich, long-lasting flesh with fine, roasted flavours which are accompanied by strong yet well-blended oaky tannins (too much for one expert, who then tempered his enthusiasm). The more austere **1998 Château Balan** receives a citation; its elegant flavours (oak and small fruits) and well-balanced body make it attractive for game.
Union de producteurs de Rauzan, 33420 Rauzan, tel. 05.57.84.13.22, fax 05.57.84.12.67 Y by appt.

BARON D'ESPIET 1998★★

4.69 ha 40,000 30–49 F

It may seem somewhat lost among the vineyards, but this co-operative, the first to be established in the Gironde, in 1932, is actually on a tourist route that takes in a prehistoric grotto, an abbey, churches and Roman remains. Baron d'Espiet is a remarkable wine, a sagacious blend of ageing in the vat and in oak (30%). Its rich aromatic range brings together aromas of ripe fruits, spicy prune, vanilla and lightly toasted bread. Although for the moment the palate and finish are dominated by oak and the round, velvety flesh is masked by young tannins, time must be allowed to do its work, and then the beauty of its personality will come through. The **1998 Seigneur des Ormes, Cuvée Réservée**, which receives a citation, is wholly matured in oak, which has left an intense mark (too much for some palates). Time also should be allowed to hone this wine, which favours lovers of oakiness.
Union de producteurs Baron d'Espiet, Lieu-dit Fourcade, 33420 Espiet, tel. 05.57.24.24.08, fax 05.57.24.18.91, e-mail baron-espiet@dial.oleane.com Y by appt.

CH. BARREYRE 1998★

7 ha 45,000 30–49 F

Petit Verdot (10%) and Cabernet-Sauvignon (40%) join Merlot in this Médoc Bordeaux from near the small port of Macau – allow time to admire the unity of sky and sea here. The oak discreetly highlights the youthful aromas of raspberry, blackcurrant and a hint of green pepper. This wine is well-balanced, round and liquorice-like, and will improve with age. It would go well with leg of lamb, a regional speciality.
SC Ch. Barreyre, Beau-Rivage, 33460 Macau, tel. 05.57.88.07.64, fax 05.57.88.07.00 Y by appt.
Giron

BEAURILEGE

Elevé en fût de chêne 1997★★

10 ha 66,000 30–49 F

This wine has spent 12 months in oak. Its explosive perfumes show it has been well kept in the barrel, with notes of roasting and coffee on a deep base of very ripe, cooked or crystallised fruits in which blackcurrant and prune predominate. The supple, generous flesh and the liquorice-like finish are admirably served by the distinguished silky tannins. It is already a rewarding drink, and it will be interesting to sample over several years to come. *Awarded a coup de coeur, regrettably at the time of going to press the label was not available to reproduce here*. The same co-operative's **1998 Château Bellevue** (20–29F), made from Merlot and equal proportions of the two Cabernets, gains one star.

🔑 Domainie de Sansac, Les Lèves, 33220 Sainte-Foy-la-Grande, tel. 05.57.56.02.02, fax 05.57.56.02.22 Y by appt.

CH. BEAU RIVAGE

Elevé en fût de chêne 1998★

■ 4.5 ha 32,000 30–49 F

This winery has wooden vats and is on the marshlands of Macau, where the vines were flooded by the storm of 27 December 1999. The vineyard includes Malbec, a rare variety in the Gironde, and Petit Verdot, which survives in the Médoc district. Another original feature of the vineyard is its use of cold maceration prior to fermentation. This main vintage has a beautifully intense nose characterised by Morello cherry and fruits in alcohol. The body's powerful tannic structure is balanced by the perfumed richness of ripe grapes. The **1998 Cuvée Prestige** (70–99F), which is cited, has spent 16 months in the barrel: its aromas are rich in notes of vanilla, toast and roasting which pay due respect to the grape. The body is powerful and heady, the finish an invitation to open another bottle. However, this wine should really be kept, so that its youthful ardour can acquire greater harmony.

🔑 SCEA Ch. Beau Rivage, 7, chem. du Bord-de-l'eau, 33460 Macau-en-Médoc, tel. 05.57.10.02.03, fax 05.57.10.02.00 ☑ Y ev. day 8am–12 noon 1pm–5pm; Sat. Sun. by appt.

🔑 Christine Nadalié

CH. BEL AIR PERPONCHER

Grande Cuvée 1998★★

■ n.c. n.c. 70–99 F

The vines and techniques resulting in this wine are under the supervision of the same brilliant team who produced Château Tour de Mirambeau (see below). Without the oakiness that some tasters judged still somewhat overpowering, it would have gained a *coup de cœur*. The product of first-class fruit, the concentrated meaty texture and associated aromas appeared to some to be overpowered by the still too imposing wood. This will be a talking point for lovers of very good wine, who will nevertheless rejoice in the richness and complexity of this work of art.

🔑 GFA de Perponcher, Ch. Bel Air, 33420 Naujan-et-Postiac, tel. 05.57.84.55.08, fax 05.57.84.57.31, e-mail despagne@vignobles-despagne.com ☑ Y by appt.

🔑 J.-L. Despagne

CH. BELLEVUE LA MONGIE

Cuvée vieillie en fût de chêne 1998★

■ 2.3 ha 15,000 30–49 F

The Génissac region on the south bank of the Dordogne near Libourne adheres to a particular Saint-Emilion tradition. This wine is a case in point, made from 90% Merlot and 10% Cabernet Franc, the result of long vatting and keeping for 12 months in the barrel. Its supple attack, full body with perfumes and aromas of crystallised fruits, orange-blossom, orange zest and vanilla, are good reasons to try it with red meats and with lamprey when the tannins have calmed down in a few months.

🔑 Michel Boyer, Ch. Bellevue La Mongie, 33420 Génissac, tel. 05.57.24.48.43, fax 05.57.24.48.43 ☑ Y by appt.

CH. BELLEVUE PEYCHARNEAU

Vieilli en fût de chêne 1998★

■ n.c. 72,000 20–29 F

This wine is made from Merlot (60%) and Cabernet-Sauvignon (40%) planted on undulating slopes of limy clay. The colour is purple with redcurrant-red highlights. The structure is good, with a lovely balance between grape and oak with aromas of slightly acid red fruits and notes of roasting and vanilla softened with beeswax. The finish is marked by a hint of astringency, which will fade. Serve with grilled meat.

🔑 Louis Eschenauer, rte de Balizac, 33720 Landiras, tel. 05.57.98.07.33, fax 05.56.62.49.14

CH. BOIS NOIR

Elevé en fût de chêne 1998★

■ 22.09 ha 40,000 30–49 F

This 1998 wine comes from a vineyard that is still young (about 15 years old), planted on the alluvial soils of the district of Guîtres, where there is a cathedral worth visiting. One taster complained of woodiness (12 months in the barrel). Others appreciated its complex aromas of citrus and crystallised fruits, which inform a powerful flesh possessed of rather sturdy tannins. Time will calm the tannic austerity of this traditional wine. The vat-matured **1998 Château Vieux Dominique** (20–29F) receives a citation. It mixes crushed strawberry and fruits of the forest with hints of musk. It has a round body, dense texture, and a long finish. Now and for some months to come it will go well with braised meats and lamprey.

🔑 SARL Ch. Bois Noir, 33230 Maransin, tel. 05.57.49.41.09, fax 05.57.49.49.43 ☑ Y by appt.

DOM. DE BOUILLEROT 1998★

■ 1.8 ha 8,000 30–49 F

Made from 80% Merlot and 20% Cabernet Franc grapes grown on 25-year-old vines, this wine is the outcome of strong extraction and long maceration. Its tannins are young. The spicy perfumes, the flesh that is firm and dense yet agreeably textured, and its length are very good points. Doubtless it will gain from being allowed to age before being served with game and marinated red meats.

🔑 Thierry Bos, Lacombe, 33190 Gironde-sur-Dropt, tel. 05.56.71.46.04, fax 05.56.71.46.04 ☑ Y by appt.

CH. DE CAMARSAC

Sélection élevée en barrique 1998★

■ 8 ha 50,600 30-49 F

The Château de Camarsac is a former 11th/13th-century fortress modified in 1857. It overlooks a vast landscape from the Garonne to the Saint-Emilion district. The vineyard's soils vary from more or less deep lime to beds of gravel, and the selection of grapes takes account of these differences. This 61% Merlot and 31% Cabernet-Sauvignon wine is a lovely ruby colour which reflects its youth. Red fruit and blackcurrant aromas are accompanied by a light oakiness. The developing palate is sustained by quite subtle tannins which will blend in further.

Bérénice Lurton, Sté Fermière Ch. de Camarsac, 33750 Camarsac, tel. 05.56.30.11.02, fax 05.56.30.12.92 by appt.

CH. CANTELON LA SABLIERE

1998

■ 3 ha n.c. 30-49 F

This wine blends Merlot (60%) and Cabernet (40%) and is the product of long vatting followed by 14 months in oak. The pleasing nose has intense aromas of Morello cherry and crystallised fruits accompanied by notes of spices and vanilla. First impressions on the palate are of roundness and fullness. The powerful tannins are respectful of the dense flesh, but come in strongly at the finish, which evokes cherry-stones. A classic.

EARL Bertin, lieu-dit Bertin, 33760 Cantois, tel. 05.56.23.61.02, fax 05.56.23.94.77, e-mail bertin@caves-particulieres.com by appt.

Mans

CH. CANTELOUP 1997

■ n.c. 20,000 20-29 F

Near the Maison des Bordeaux, which also deserves a visit, this château, located on gravelly clay soils, offers a round, full-bodied 1997 wine redolent of red stewed fruits and endowed with well-behaved tannins. Intended to accompany simple meals, this is a pleasing wine that does credit to its year.

EARL Landreau, l'Hermette, 33750 Beychac-et-Caillau, tel. 05.56.72.97.72, fax 05.56.72.49.48

DOM. DE CANTEMERLE

Cuvée Prestige Vieilli en fût de chêne 1998

■ 33 ha 10,000 50-69 F

In 1998, two young brothers took over this property in Saint-Gervais, whose Romanesque church dominates the Dordogne plain north of Bordeaux. Overwhelmingly a Merlot wine (90%), their Cuvée Prestige has an attractive nose of fruits of the forest (raspberry and strawberry) and *pain d'épice* (a kind of spice loaf). The well-structured body's well-blended tannins and moderate oaky perfumes reveal time spent in the barrel. This 1998 wine can accompany red meats and lamprey straight away.

Vignobles Mabille, 9, Cantemerle, 33240 Saint Gervais, tel. 05.57.43.11.39, fax 05.57.43.11.39, e-mail cantemerle@wanadoo.fr by appt.

CH. DE CAZENOVE 1998

■ 4.67 ha 27,300 30-49 F

Here is a vineyard of young vines, half Merlot and half Cabernet-Sauvignon, planted on the Macau marshlands. It has produced some nice Bordeaux wines from land adjoining the Aire du Margaux. This one has spent eight months in the barrel, and exhales delicate fragrances of vanilla-scented blackcurrant. The palate's fleshy charm finishes on a tannic note which no doubt will soften with time. This wine will then be suitable for serving with red meats or game accompanied by a wine sauce.

Mme de Cazenove, Ch. de Cazenove, 33460 Macau, tel. 05.57.88.79.98, fax 05.57.88.79.98, e-mail cazessen@club-internet.fr by appt.

CH. CHAMP DE FLEURET 1998

■ 24 ha 120,000 20-29 F

This wine from the Libourne area, grown according to the principles of sustainable agriculture, was elaborated by the Puisseguin co-operative. Though the colour is modest and the nose subdued, the palate is round, supple and warm, with welcome persistence. Serve for months to come with poultry and grills. A wine to drink with friends.

Cave coop. de Puisseguin-Lussac-Saint-Emilion, Durand, 33570 Puisseguin, tel. 05.57.55.50.40, fax 05.57.74.57.43 by appt.

Lacroix

CHAPELLE DE BARBE 1998

■ 12.85 ha 102,000 30-49 F

The Château de Barbe overlooks the Gironde and the pretty road from Bourg to Blaye, near Roque-de-Thau. The chapel stands among the vines. This is a blend of 55% Merlot, 25% Cabernet-Sauvignon and 20% Cabernet Franc. The 18 months spent in oak subtly bring out complex aromas of red fruits which are enhanced by the body's roundness. The very evident tannins are nonetheless restrained and provide a violet-flavoured finish.

SCV villeneuvoise, Ch. de Barbe, 33710 Villeneuve, tel. 05.57.42.64.00, fax 05.57.64.94.10 by appt.

Famille Richard

CH. DE CORNEMPS 1998★★

■ 27 ha 150,000 20-29 F

Dominating the southern slopes of the Isle, between the high-point of Puynormand and the church perched in the hollow of Petit-Palais, stand the ruins of Cornemps Abbey. The property's wineries are under the cliff. This vineyard is well known, and this year provides a wine of remarkable general harmony. The nose is an elegant complexity of ripe grapes with smoky, toasted notes. The body is round and silky, with a structure of restrained tannins and a perfumed, persistent

finish which is subtly oaky. It has a definite charm, destined to endure some years.
🔑 Henri-Louis Fagard, Cornemps, 33570 Petit-Palais, tel. 05.57.69.73.19, fax 05.57.69.73.75, e-mail vignobles.fagard@wanadoo.fr ☑ Y by appt.

CH. COTES DE CASSAGNE 1998

■ n.c. 7,500 ▮ 30–49 F

This tiny property (1.8 ha/4.4 acres), bought in March 1998, is well tended. Its wine is a classic Libourne blend (70% Merlot, 30% Cabernet-Sauvignon) redolent of ripe grapes grown on rocky terrain. The balance between the smooth flesh and unobtrusive tannins is emphasised by the flavours of stone fruits (Morello cherry), spices and toast.
🔑 Cyril Chancelier, Ch. Côtes de Cassagne, 33350 Castillon-la-Bataille, tel. 05.57.40.53.13 ☑

CH. COTTE DES RAMBAUX

Cuvée Jean-Claude Jambon 1998★

■ n.c. 30,000 ▮ 🌡 20–29 F

This wine reflects a traditional approach within the appellation. Essentially a Merlot vintage (70%), complemented by Cabernet-Sauvignon (20%) and Cabernet Franc (10%), it is unreserved in communicating its clean aromas of ripe grapes and very slightly spiced grilling, together with a well-structured body and a persistent finish. The same firm's **1998 Château Poncharac**, in which the Cabernet varieties (25% each) balance the Merlot, receives a citation. The structure of this wine has a tannic note alongside the fresh aromas of wild fruits (woodland strawberries) and prunes. It will be nicely mature in a few months' time.
🔑 SA Yvon Mau, B.P. 1, 33193 Gironde-sur-Dropt Cedex, tel. 05.56.61.54.54, fax 05.56.61.54.61 Y by appt.

CH. COURONNEAU

Cuvée Pierre de Cartier Elevé en barrique 1998★

■ 4 ha 12,000 ⦀ 50–69 F

Ligueux is on the very edge of the department, several miles south of Sainte-Foy-la-Grande. The opulent, if austere-looking, 15th-century château is worth a visit. Sights also include a vathouse and a fine-quality winery. This pure Merlot is made from a selection of 4 ha (10 acres) of grapes. Its complex aromas mix fruits, a toasted oakiness, coffee and musk. The round, rich, vinous body has a harmony that some tasters judged remarkable. Though this wine really ought to be kept in order to develop further, the impatient might well enjoy it now with game or roast beef.
🔑 Piat, Ch. Couronneau, 33220 Ligueux, tel. 05.57.41.26.55, fax 05.57.41.27.58 ☑ Y by appt.

DOM. DE COURTEILLAC 1998★

■ 8 ha 90,000 ⦀ 50–69 F

This 1998 wine comes from the wine-growing plateau of Ruch, which overlooks the small valley of the Gamage. It is a harmonious wine whose aromas evoke ripe fruits in alcohol, elderflower and vanilla. Its charm lies in round flesh and well-blended tannins, which support a long-lasting finish still marked by oak. Before long it will be a good accompaniment to cheese.
🔑 SCEA Dom. de Courteillac, 33350 Ruch, tel. 05.57.40.79.48, fax 05.57.40.57.05

CH. DE CRAIN 1998

■ 22 ha 20,000 ▮ 🌡 20–29 F

This property goes back to the 19th century, and 13th-century remains of buildings have been found. The 90% Merlot intrigued the tasters with its musky and mineral notes which enhance its spicy fruitiness. The attack is round and supple, the body powerful and the finish spirited. It will go well with white meats and salty dishes.
🔑 SCA de Crain, Ch. de Crain, 33750 Baron, tel. 05.57.24.50.66, fax 05.45.25.03.73 ☑ Y by appt.
🔑 Fougère

CH. CROIX DE CALENS 1998★

■ 8 ha 40,000 ▮ 🌡 30–49 F

Not far from the Château de La Brède, which once belonged to Montesquieu, the vineyard was completely reconstructed after 1965 on the alluvial clay soils of the Garonne's southern bank. The wine is a balance of Merlot and Cabernet-Sauvignon, the result of lengthy vatting in a winery with very modern techniques. Its structure is sturdy yet subtle, with a nose of very ripe fresh fruits (Morello cherry) and a finish slightly marked by a hint of fruit-stone. A very representative Bordeaux Supérieur.
🔑 EARL Vignobles Albert Yung, Ch. Haut-Calens, 33640 Beautiran, tel. 05.56.67.05.25, fax 05.56.67.24.91 ☑ Y by appt.

CH. DE CUGAT

Cuvée Francis Meyer 1998★★

■ 2.5 ha 9,000 ⦀ 50–69 F

The Château de Cugat dominates the charming valley of the Gamage, where Blasimon lies with its well-known 13th-century abbey – it has a beautiful doorway – and fortified water-mill. Benoît Meyer has produced a pure Merlot there which is harvested in trays and undergoes malolactic fermentation in oak for 14 months. The care taken is reflected in the elegant and intense aromas, the complex marriage of grape, vanilla, eucalyptus, tobacco and toasted notes. The supple body's harmony is sustained by flavoursome tannins. 'Nice work, good balance between wood and grape,' wrote one taster. This authentic Bordeaux Supérieur will already suit braised red meats (in mushroom sauce, for example).
🔑 Benoît Meyer, Ch. de Cugat, 33540 Blasimon, tel. 05.56.71.52.08, fax 05.56.71.60.29 ☑ Y by appt.

CH. DALLAU 1998

■ 30 ha n.c. 30–49 F

This 1998 wine comes from vines growing on the siliceous clay of the Isle valley north of Libourne. A 70% Merlot, it has a deep purple colour and an impressive complexity of perfumes (menthol-scented blackcurrant, liquorice, and spices). The palate betrays a supple, long-lasting opulence, though the rough-mannered tannins still have a rusticity in the finish. Time will smooth them out.

SCEA Bertin et Fils, Dallau, 8, rte de Lamarche, 33910 Saint-Denis-de-Pile, tel. 05.57.84.21.17, fax 05.57.84.29.44 Y by appt.

CH. DAMASE 1998★

■ 10 ha 80,000 30–49 F

Savignac, perched on the hills of the Isle's right bank, commands beautiful views over Pomerol and the Saint-Emilion district. Sober, elegant buildings house the barrels in which this pure Merlot was made. Scents of tuberoses (narcissi), red fruits, vanilla and cocoa accompany the tasting. The body, though it seems to have some rough aspects, nevertheless has compensations. A wine for passing the time among friends.

Xavier Milhade, Ch. Damase, 33910 Savignac-de-l'Isle, tel. 05.57.55.48.90, fax 05.57.84.31.27, e-mail milhadeg@aol.com Y by appt.

CH. FONCHEREAU 1997★

■ 20.05 ha n.c. 20–29 F

The four traditional varieties are present in this 1997 wine grown on gravel and limy clay: 60% Merlot, 20% Cabernet-Sauvignon, 17% Cabernet Franc, 3% Malbec. The blend expresses itself in a nose first of fruits and then of jam, mixed with hints of moss and humus. The palate is robust, structured by well-mannered tannins whose increasingly firm presence bodes well for keeping. Serve with charcuterie and canned foods.

SCA Ch. Fonchereau, BP 9, 33450 Montussan, tel. 05.56.72.96.12, fax 05.56.72.44.91 Y by appt.

Madar

CH. FON DE SERGAY 1998

■ n.c. 36,000 20–29 F

This 1998 vintage is from a roughly 5-ha (12-acre) selection of Cabernet-Sauvignon (70%) and Merlot (30%). Notes of undergrowth and leather add complexity to the other aromas. The palate reveals good harmony rather than power. 'A friendly wine,' was one juror's comment. The vineyard has obtained a further recommendation for its **1997 wine**, similarly dominated by Cabernet-Sauvignon (70%), Cabernet Franc (10%) and Merlot (20%). A year in the barrel completed the education of this supple, round wine endowed with aromas of small fruits (blackcurrant and redcurrant) and subtle oakiness. Drink now (30–49F).

Pierre Aroldi, Ch. Fon de Sergay, 33540 Saint-Hilaire-du-Bois, tel. 05.56.71.53.77, fax 05.56.71.61.78 Y by appt.

CH. FREYNEAU 1997★★

■ 9 ha 40,000 20–29 F

Halfway between Bordeaux and the imposing Château de Vayres, near the Maison des Bordeaux et Bordeaux Supérieurs at Beychac, that elegant shop-window of the Union for these appellations, the vineyard is at least 80% Merlot blended with Cabernets grown on gravel and limy clay. This main vintage includes 5% Cabernet Franc: its easy-drinking suppleness enriched by silky tannins, its elaborate bouquet with notes of undergrowth, mushrooms and spicy red fruits delighted the jurors, who thought it remarkable for its year. The **1997 Cuvée Traditionnelle** (30–49F), in which Cabernet-Sauvignon (10%) replaces the Cabernet Franc, has aged 12 months in the barrel. Its full and supple palate, spicy and toasted aromas of ripe fruits, tannic structure and agreeably oaky finish constitute a successful wine.

GAEC Maulin et Fils, Ch. Freyneau, 33450 Montussan, tel. 05.56.72.95.46, fax 05.56.72.84.29, e-mail chateau-freyneau@wanadoo.fr Y by appt.

CH. DE FUSSIGNAC 1998★

■ 14 ha 80,000 30–49 F

The front of the church at Petit-Palais is renowned for its purity of line and its sculptures. It is dominated by vine-covered hillsides. This 1998 wine is a blend of Cabernet-Sauvignon (30%) and Merlot (70%), a small proportion (15%) of which was aged in the barrel. This has subtly informed its fruit and liquorice aromas with an oaky vanilla. The supple harmony of the flesh and its persistence constitute a wine of lovely finesse, to drink from now on with white meats or cheese.

Jean-François Carrille, pl. du Marcadieu, 33330 Saint-Emilion, tel. 05.57.24.74.46, fax 05.57.24.64.40 Y by appt.

CH. GAILLARTEAU 1998

■ 0.92 ha 8,000 30–49 F

This selection of Merlot (65%) and Cabernet-Sauvignon (35%) from vines over 40 years old has aged 18 months in the barrel. The oak shows its power in accents of toast, but is nonetheless respectful of the wine's fruitiness, though it both accompanies and highlights the grape tannins' own astringency. The style is robust, good for grilled, spicy meat dishes. A wine that will need to age to suit delicate palates, but which will already please lovers of tradition.

GFA Ch. Gaillarteau, 5, Ch. Gaillarteau, 33410 Mourens, tel. 05.56.61.98.21, fax 05.56.61.99.06 Y by appt.

CH. GAMAGE

Elevé en barrique 1998★

■ 31 ha n.c. 50–69 F

A lovely view over the Dordogne valley awaits the visitor who climbs up to the Templar church dominating the small town

BORDEAUX

of Saint-Pey. This wine fulfills a classic Bordeaux formula (70% Merlot, 20% Cabernet-Sauvignon and 10% Cabernet Franc) and method of vinification. The maturing uses one-third new barrels, which strongly mark the aromas. The nose retains its fruity, somewhat roasted accents, while the palate is dominated by interesting oak tannins which should become less obtrusive in the months to come. A wine of character, for red meats and conserves. The same proprietor's **1998 Château Dartigues** (30–49F) uses 80% Merlot and 20% Cabernet. There is less oakiness, and the round, supple palate makes room for lightly spiced, vanilla-flavoured, fondant red fruits to appear. The finish is still austere, however. Do not rush to open.

SARL Ch. Gamage, 33350 Saint-Pey-de-Castets, tel. 05.57.40.52.02, fax 05.57.40.53.77 by appt.

Lavie-Spurrier

CH. GRAND-JEAN

Elevé en fût de chêne 1998★

7 ha 57,000 30–49 F

Cabernet-Sauvignon (70%) dominates the Merlot (30%) in this 1998 wine matured 12 months in oak. Its deep, almost black colour with violet lights proclaims a dense wine with an oaky nose in which notes of toasted bread mingle with those of wild black fruits. The flavoursome palate develops on a tannic support that should become velvety after two or three years of keeping.

Michel Dulon, Ch. Grand-Jean, 33760 Soulignac, tel. 05.56.23.69.16, fax 05.57.34.41.29 by appt.

CH. HAUT MALLET 1998★

5 ha 29,000 30–49 F

This is an organic wine grown five kilometres (three miles) from the Château de Benauge and the austere church at Targon. A subtle nose mixes flowers (violets), fruits (blackberry, raspberry) and a discreet vanilla caramel. The palate is no less pleasure-giving, with its pleasant union of tannins and grape flesh. A successful, agreeably aromatic wine, which will suit slightly spicy dishes.

SCA Vignoble Boudon, Le Bourdieu, 33760 Soulignac, tel. 05.56.23.65.60, fax 05.56.23.45.58 ev. day 9am–12 noon 2pm–6pm; Sat. Sun. by appt.; cl. end Aug.

CH. HAUT NADEAU 1998★★

6 ha 45,000 30–49 F

Hard by the huge church at Targon and the tower of La Sauve Abbey, this estate offers a wine matured in barrels of which a third are renewed each year. The colour is deep garnet and the nose redolent of truffles and roasted meat with hints of prune. The attack on the palate is fresh, but the wine's ripe flesh and well-covered tannins quickly fill the mouth. A subtle, discreet oakiness prolongs the finish. 'Beautifully complex, very elegant,' was one comment. This specialist wine-grower is to be congratulated.

SCEA Ch. Haut Nadeau, 3, chem. d'Estévenadeau, 33760 Targon, tel. 05.56.20.44.07, fax 05.56.20.44.07

Audouit

CH. HAUT NIVELLE 1998★

18 ha n.c. 30–49 F

This young, 15-year-old vineyard is on the slopes of the Isle near the church at Petit-Palais and Cornemps Abbey. The two Cabernets (10% Franc) balance the Merlot in this 1998 wine produced by lengthy vatting and malolactic fermentation under the marc, vatting with controlled aeration over several months and, finally, twelve months in the barrel. Visits to the vineyard's modern installations are welcomed. The delicate nose exhales grape, prune, vanilla and liquorice aromas. First impressions on the palate are of suppleness, followed by the tannins which strengthen to become somewhat invasive at the finish. However, this well-designed and aromatic wine will soon reveal its assets. A wine for unpretentious drinking among friends.

SCEA Les Ducs d'Aquitaine, Favereau, 33660 Saint-Sauveur-de-Puynormand, tel. 05.57.69.69.69, fax 05.57.69.62.84, e-mail scealesducsdaquitaine@wanadoo.fr by appt.

Le Pottier

CH. HAUT-PEYREDOULLE 1997★

5 ha 15,000 50–69 F

This 1997 selection of Merlot (60%), Cabernet (30%) and Malbec (10%) fits the Bordeaux tradition. It has a bouquet of very slightly meaty stewed prunes mingled with fresh, plant-like notes and a concentrated body with robust tannins. An interesting, long-living wine, which will evoke the memory of this uneven year for some time to come.

Vignobles Louis Marinier, Dom. Florimond-La Brède, 33390 Berson, tel. 05.57.64.39.07, fax 05.57.64.23.27 ev. day 8am–12 noon 2pm–6pm; Sat. Sun. by appt.; cl. Aug.

CH. HAUT SORILLON Prestige 1998★

3 ha 24,000 50–69 F

This pure Merlot comes from the terraces of the Isle, in the extreme north-east of the Libourne district. It has been oak-matured with malolactic fermentation for 14 months. Opinions were divided. Some tasters did not care much for the 'animal' notes (leather) included in the complex range of perfumes: fruits, cocoa, spices and toast. The oak still dominates the palate, though without overdrying it; it has a harmonious body and a pleasantly liquorice-flavoured finish. A wine for braised meats and, in a few months' time, cheese.

Jean-Marie Rousseau, Petit-Sorillon, 33230 Abzac, tel. 05.57.49.06.10, fax 05.57.49.38.96 by appt.

CH. JALOUSIE-BEAULIEU 1997★

90 ha 60,000 20–29 F

This 1997 wine, grown on the slopes north of the Fronsadais, was appreciated for its nose of cooked cherries and more complex, surprising nuances. Also for the somewhat wild character of a well-structured body containing jammy flesh and still-austere tannins. An original wine to serve with spiced dishes or grills. La Guyennoise, a wine-merchants at Sauveterre-de-Guyenne, also offers a **1998 Château Gandoy-Perrinat** grown in the heart of the Entre-Deux-Mers district and in which Merlot counterbalances the two Cabernets. The charm of this wine cited by the jury lies in its floral, fruity nose and crisp body.

La Guyennoise, B.P. 17, 33540 Sauveterre-de-Guyenne, tel. 05.56.71.50.76, fax 05.56.71.87.70

CH. DES JOUALLES 1998★

30 ha 200,000 30–49 F

This château at Ruch belongs to the owners of Château Lassègue. Made from 65% Merlot, 25% Cabernet Franc and 10% Cabernet-Sauvignon grown on limy clay, this wine has a dense structure with perfumes of small red fruits. Though wine of this sort deserves to mature, its evolution may be sampled along the way by drinking it as an accompaniment to poultry in sauce or pastry.

SC des Vignobles Freylon, 33330 Saint-Hippolyte, tel. 05.57.24.72.83, fax 05.57.74.48.88 by appt.

Bruno Freylon

DOM. DES JUSTICES 1998★

6 ha 22,000 30–49 F

Everyone knows Christian Médeville, whose nickname is 'the Sauternes antique-dealer' in view of his star Cru, Château Gilette, which he only markets when it is old. But he also takes time to make red wine, as is shown by this Bordeaux Supérieur, made from almost equal parts of Merlot and Cabernet-Sauvignon grown on modern sandy and alluvial soils. Oak-matured for 12 months, this 1998 wine has a bright colour and a nose of intense perfumes more typical of Cabernet than Merlot. It has scarcely begun to open. The palate, too, is still reticent: well-balanced, powerful and long, it denotes a well-crafted wine.

Christian Médeville, Ch. Gilette, 33210 Preignac, tel. 05.56.76.28.44, fax 05.56.76.28.43, e-mail christian.medeville@wanadoo.fr by appt.

CH. LA BASTIDE MONGIRON

Cuvée noire 1998

1 ha 6,000 30–49 F

Made from Merlot and 10% Malbec fermented after cold fermentation and kept on the lees in oak, this wine divided the jury. Its suppleness, easy-drinking flesh and subdued tannins either worried or enchanted. Yet all the jury admired the deep carmine colour and the subtle, powerful aromas of raspberry tart, chocolate and caramel with hints of fur or leather. Sample with cheese.

Jean-Michel Queron, Mongiron, 33750 Nerigean, tel. 05.57.24.53.16, fax 05.57.24.06.36 by appt.

CH. LABATUT Cuvée Prestige 1998

n.c. n.c. 30–49 F

This 13th-century château, which once belonged to the lords of Duras, dominates the nearby slopes of the small town of Pujols. The vineyards are run according to the rules of organic agriculture. The attractive, typical Bordeaux colour of this wine matches its fruity aromas. The youthful, fresh, supple and long harmony of the palate would appear to be due to the beautifully ripe Cabernet Franc grapes used (40%). It should be tried now and sampled again in the future, as it evolves. The same producer's **1998 Château Lagnet**, also cited, has a similar structure. Its attractively perfumed graciousness will charm lovers of slender yet intense wines.

GFA Leclerc, Ch. Lagnet, 33350 Doulezon, tel. 05.57.40.51.84, fax 05.57.40.55.48 by appt.

CH. LA CADERIE

Elevé en fût de chêne 1997

6 ha n.c. 30–49 F

The vineyard is hidden among a world of austere little Romanesque churches near the abbey-church of Guîtres, which is both huge and even lovelier inside than out. The vinification of this 1997 wine, made mainly with Merlot (90%), was preceded by several days of cold maceration, and the temperature at the beginning of fermentation was kept relatively low to favour the appearance of aromas of freshness in the wine. Oak-ageing extended over 18 months. Experts remarked that, besides the grapey fruitiness, the wine has notes of linden-flowers and dried flowers in the delicate perfumes accompanying the tasting of its supple, well-blended flesh. Though this wine perhaps lacks power, it nonetheless has charm and a delightful oakiness.

François Landais, Ch. La Caderie, 33910 Saint-Martin-du-Bois, tel. 05.57.49.41.32, fax 05.57.49.41.32 by appt.

CH. LA COMMANDERIE DE QUEYRET 1998★★

13 ha 40,000 30–49 F

This estate is well known and nearly gained a *coup de cœur* with this classic 60% Merlot, 40% Cabernet-Sauvignon wine. Its charm and remarkable success are due to the grower's wine-making expertise. The intense, complex nose mixes aromas of red and black fruits (especially blackcurrant) with discreet touches of musk and plants (hay). Fleshy, dense, with adequate, friendly, persistent tannins, the palate leaves an impression of peaceful balance. A very fine wine, which may be drunk young, but may equally be kept for ten years. The tasters suggest serving it with leg of lamb. The **1998 Cuvée Elevée en Fût de Chêne** is given a one-star rating. It is a buxom, well-made wine.

Claude Comin, La Commanderie, 33790 Saint-Antoine-du-Queyret, tel. 05.56.61.31.98, fax 05.56.61.34.22 by appt.

BORDEAUX

CH. LA FAVIERE 1998

■ 15.88 ha 100,000 20–29 F

This vineyard extends over Isle river-terraces several miles from the lovely Romanesque church of Petit-Palais. The vineyard and its wine-making are handled with the same seriousness. Pruning, thinning, harvesting according to date and plot, length of vatting – nothing is left to chance. This traditional Bordeaux has a fine nose of ripe grapes with notes of roasting, though the round palate is still somewhat closed. It has definite potential, which will strengthen with time. It may be drunk and enjoyed for some years to come.

SCEA Dom. de La Cabanne, 32, rue Antoine-de-Saint-Exupéry, 33660 Saint-Seurin-sur-l'Isle, tel. 05.57.49.72.02, fax 05.57.49.64.89 by appt.

Grawitz

CH. LA FRANCE

Cuvée barriques 1997*

■ 66 ha 53,000 30–49 F

The vineyard of this ancient (1689), huge (77-ha/190-acre) and lovely property comprises Cabernets (20% each) and Merlot (60%). The plant is extremely modern, but the vinification and maturation (15 months in oak) are pure tradition. Notes of green pepper and mint accompany aromas of crystallised fruits and vanilla. Such aromatic complexity goes well with the well-blended and powerful tannins of an atypical, yet really delightful wine.

SCEA de Foncaude, Ch. La France, 33750 Beychac-et-Caillau, tel. 05.57.55.24.10, fax 05.57.55.24.19 by appt.

DOM. DE LA GRAVE

Cuvée Prestige 1998**

■ 3 ha 10,000 30–49 F

Five hundred metres (550 yd) from the Maison des Bordeaux et Bordeaux Supérieurs, five generations of the Roch family have cultivated vines on gravelly soils. A rigorous selection from old vines (90% Merlot), long vinification and maturation in new oak have resulted in this remarkable wine, which was very nearly a *coup de cœur*. Its oakiness is firm, elegant, vanilla-flavoured, roasted, intense, yet respectful of the ripe grapes that have yielded a fleshy, well-constructed body which progresses well from the initial fruity impression to a complex finish. This 1998 wine needs storing for three years, even longer to reach its very best.

SCEA Roche, Perriche, 33750 Beychac-et-Caillau, tel. 05.56.72.41.28, fax 05.56.72.41.28 ev. day 8am–7pm

CH. LA GRAVETTE DES LUCQUES 1998*

■ 4 ha 32,000 30–49 F

In 1991, Patrice Haverlan took over the family estate in the Graves. The winery contains a curiosity: a vine stock that resembles a crucifix. This wine, a 90% Merlot, is the result of long maceration. Although the nose seems a touch closed, the ripeness of the grape and the palate's structure already reveal true richness.

Vignobles Patrice Haverlan, 11, rue de l'Hospital, 33640 Portets, tel. 05.56.67.11.32, fax 05.56.67.11.32, e-mail patrice.haverlan@worldonline.fr by appt.

CH. LAMARCHE Lutet 1998*

■ 5 ha 30,000 30–49 F

This wine from old vines (over 60 years old) has been matured in 400-l barrels, following a custom that no doubt owes much to the proximity of the coopers of Cognac. Blackcurrant, strawberry and liquorice join with the oak to create a slightly grilled harmony well suited to the round, elegant body of ripe grapes. Tannins, which in time will soften, declare their presence in the finish.

Vignobles Germain et Associés, Ch. Peyredoulle, 33390 Berson, tel. 05.57.42.66.66, fax 05.57.64.36.20, e-mail bordeaux@vgas.com by appt.

L. Julien

CH. LANDEREAU

Cuvée Prestige Elevé en fût neuf 1998*

■ 5 ha 30,000 70–99 F

From the owner of Château L'Hoste Blanc, Château Landereau is also distinguished by the regular quality of its production. This Cuvée Prestige has been aged for 18 months in new oak. Its elegant, fleshy body, enlivened at the finish by the presence of well-controlled tannins, is redolent of blackcurrant and smooth red fruits with undertones of oaky vanilla. The vat-matured **1998 Cuvée Principale** (30–49F) is equally successful: well-structured and sturdy without roughness, it evokes fresh ripe fruits and may be drunk straight away with roast meats.

Vignobles Michel Baylet, Ch. Landereau, 33670 Sadirac, tel. 05.56.30.64.28, fax 05.56.30.63.90 ev. day except Sat. Sun. 8am–12 noon 1.30pm–5pm

CH. DE LA TOUR

Réserve du Château 1997*

■ 98.28 ha 220,500 50–69 F

This vineyard is named after the tower remaining from the château built by Bertrand de Got, later Pope Clement V. It commands a vast panorama of the Entre-Deux-Mers region. The winery and equipment date from 1990, and can accommodate all manner of selections of plots or wines. This 1997 wine was oak-matured over 12 months. Its concentration of perfumes and flesh took the jury by surprise. The well-blended tannins emphasise its depths of ripe fruit taste accompanied by accents of prune and walnut and a well-mannered oakiness. The finish is still powerful and bodes well for the wine's evolution, which will occur over the next two or three years.

SC du Ch. de La Tour, 23, chem. de Cougnot, 33270 Sallebœuf,

tel. 05.56.35.53.00, fax 05.56.35.53.29, e-mail contact@cvbg.com Y by appt.
Dourthe

CH. LATOUR-LAGUENS 1998*

■ n.c. n.c. 30–49 F

The firm of Louis Eschenauer offers two wines labelled Château Latour-Laguens. The tank-matured Cuvée Principale was preferred by the jury: a classic with charming spicy red-fruit aromas hinting at blackcurrant and cinnamon. The round, firm flesh is sustained by ripe, liquorice-flavoured tannins, which confer a harmonious structure and signal good ageing. 'Well worth watching as it evolves,' noted one taster. The oakiness of the oak-matured **1998 Elevé en Barrique** (recommended) introduces notes of walnut and dried fig, but these were not yet well-blended at the time of the tasting.

Louis Eschenauer, rte de Balizac, 33720 Landiras, tel. 05.57.98.07.33, fax 05.56.62.49.14

CH. LAUDUC

Cuvée Prestige Elevé en fût de chêne 1998**

■ 3.5 ha 25,000 30–49 F

A rigorous selection from old vines more than 40 years old and vinified by modern techniques that respect tradition, 12 months' maturing in oak, skill in pumping over, and accurate judging of maceration times have all resulted in this remarkable wine. The judicious blend of varieties (60% Merlot, 30% Cabernets, and 10% Malbec) releases pleasant notes of cherry and prune, with an oakiness hinting at vanilla and toast. Concentrated, supple harmony of ripe grapes and respectful oak lead to a palate whose roundness fans out like a peacock's tail. Drink with fillet of duck, game and entrecôte steaks.

GAEC Grandeau et Fils, Ch. Lauduc, 33370 Tresses, tel. 05.57.34.11.82, fax 05.57.34.08.19, e-mail maison.grandeau.lauduc@wanadoo.fr Y by appt.

CH. LA VERRIERE 1998*

■ 25 ha 80,000 30–49 F

Located in the east of the Bordeaux region, Château Verrière exports more than half its production. This classic 1998 wine, grown on clay hillsides close to the Lot-et-Garonne department and several miles from the fortified town of Sainte-Foy-la-Grande, is redolent of ripe grapes and crystallised fruit. Its well-balanced, honeyed body may favour subtlety over power, but this is not a fault.

GAEC La Verrière-Bessette, La Verrière, 33790 Landerrouat, tel. 05.56.61.36.91, fax 05.56.61.41.12 Y by appt.
André et Jean-Paul Bessette

CH. LE COMTE 1998*

■ 3.12 ha 26,700 30–49 F

Vinified by the Union de Producteurs Baron d'Espiet, this 1998 wine comes from a vineyard located at Blessignac, near the Abbey of La Sauve-Majeure. A well-balanced marriage of 80% Merlot and 20% Cabernet-Sauvignon, this pleasantly oaky, vinous wine has a marked fruitiness of wild strawberries and restrained tannins. Very well made, and may mature further.

Union de producteurs Baron d'Espiet, Lieu-dit Fourcade, 33420 Espiet, tel. 05.57.24.24.08, fax 05.57.24.18.91, e-mail baron-espiet@dial.oleane.com Y by appt.
Jean-Louis Maigné

CH. LE GARDERA 1998*

■ 23 ha 120,000 30–49 F

Grown on gravel and alluvial soils at Langoiran, a place dominated by the ruins of a feudal château clinging to the sleep hillsides above the Garonne, this 1998 wine blends 60% Merlot with 40% Cabernet-Sauvignon. Its attractive colour, subtle nose and round flesh, a cooked note and marked yet well-blended tannins reveal a concentrated wine with aromas of crystallised fruits. The finish is long and liquorice-flavoured. Ready to drink, but there is no rush.

Domaines Cordier, 160, cours du Médoc, 33300 Bordeaux, tel. 05.57.19.57.77, fax 05.57.19.57.87 Y by appt.

CH. LE GRAND VERDUS

Cuvée Tradition 1998**

■ 77.5 ha 450,000 30–49 F

A wine that regularly wins awards, this 1998 Grand Verdus may just have missed a *coup de cœur*, but is nonetheless a top-of-the-range Bordeaux Supérieur. It reveals a powerful harmony of round, supple fruit, well-blended tannins, aromatic complexity due to the blend of 50% Merlot, 30% Cabernets and 20% Franc, notes of ripe grapes and touches of mentholated chocolate, all contained in a dark, velvety wine with purple tints. The **1998 Cuvée Réservée** (50–69F) spent ten months maturing in new oak. A real concentration of crystallised fruits with notes of mint, fennel, pepper and grilling, the body has a firm, warm, liquorice-flavoured roundness married to long-lasting tannins. Two remarkable wines to have in the cellar.

SCEA Ph. et A. Legrix de La Salle, Le Grand Verdus, 33670 Sadirac, tel. 05.56.30.50.90, fax 05.56.30.50.98, email le.grand.verdus.legris.de.la.salle@wanadoo.fr Y by appt.

CH. LE MUGRON Cuvée 2000 1998

■ n.c. 14,000 30–49 F

Pair-non-Pair grotto is nearby, and the gorgeous panoramic site of Bourg-sur-Gironde is several kilometres away. Some readers may know the property without realising it, as a number of films have been shot there. Merlot and Cabernets form equal parts of this wine, which has a curiously smoky nose with musky hints and a very supple palate with a well-balanced tannic structure and a 'burnt' finish. A wine for lamprey and grills. Start drinking it now.

SCEA Ch. Grand-Jour, 87, av. des Côtes-de-Bourg, 33710 Prignac-et-Marcamps, tel. 05.57.68.44.06, fax 05.57.68.37.59

CH. LE PIN BEAUSOLEIL 1998★★

■ 4.7 ha 10,000 50–69 F

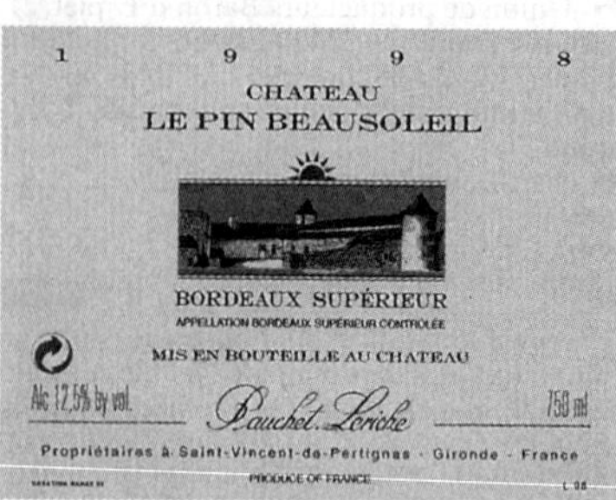

The church at Saint-Vincent-de-Pertignas, a village overlooking the Gamage valley, is a must for the visitor. This *coup de coeur* wine was lovingly produced and matured on a small 15th-century property taken over in 1994. The perfectly chosen oak is still dominant, with spicy, grilled tones, but the elegant complexity of vanilla-tinged crystallised fruits is already clear. The dense, creamy flesh has a velvety power, with ripe tannins which are discernible yet friendly. The finish is so long, it almost seems to renew itself over and over. 'It's so, so good!' exclaimed one enraptured juror.

Arnaud Pauchet, Le Pin, 33420 Saint-Vincent-de-Pertignas, tel. 05.57.84.02.56, fax 05.57.84.02.56, e-mail arno.pauchet@wanadoo.fr by appt.

CH. LE PRIEUR 1998★

■ 4 ha 25,000 30–49 F

This estate had two hectares (five acres) of vines when it was acquired by Elisabeth Garzaro's family at the start of the 20th century. Now there are 80 ha (198 acres). The 1998 Château Le Prieur is a sturdy wine with young, still overpowering tannins. Its bilberry-flavoured strength pleased the tasters. Made with traditional long-vatting, it spent six months in the barrel, there completing its malolactic fermentation. This form of vinification and maturation doubtless explains why this 1998 wine needs ageing. Its future course might be tracked by drinking it first with red meats, then with spicy dishes.

Elisabeth Garzaro, Ch. Le Prieur, 33750 Baron, tel. 05.56.30.16.16, fax 05.56.30.12.63, e-mail garzaro@vingarzaro.com by appt.

CH. L'ESCART

Cuvée Omar Khayyam Vieilli en fût de chêne 1998★★

■ 1.4 ha 4,800 70–99 F

The method practised here comprises cold maceration followed by fermentation at 28°C (82.4°F), lengthy maceration with slight pumping over and maturation in oak for 12 months. Successful use of these techniques requires a good knowledge of the grapes and a sure touch. All due homage to this 'Persian poet' of a wine, made of equal parts of the three Bordeaux varieties and remarkable for its perfumes and mouth-filling fruit – oakiness, crystallised fruits, vanilla, wax, pepper and spices, and Indian ink. It has a youthful complexity that age will enrich further. The **1998 Cuvée Prestige Julien** (50–69F) is chiefly Merlot-based (62%) with 34% Cabernet-Sauvignon and 4% Cabernet Franc. The large aromatic range mixes crystallised fruits, prune and liquorice, and the full, rich body along with the rich tannins make a successful product that lovers of pronounced oakiness will really go for. Time will quieten its oaky ardour and give it a broader appeal.

Ch. L'Escart, 70, chem. Couvertaire, B.P. 8, 33450 Saint-Loubès, tel. 05.56.77.53.19, fax 05.56.77.68.59 by appt.

Gérard Laurent

CH. LES GRANDS JAYS 1998★

■ 10 ha 70,000 30–49 F

This estate of this family, whose archives go back to the 17th century, is located 4 km (2.5 miles) from the menhir at Lussac and the windmills at Calon, offering a magnificent view over the Libourne district. The wine is 95% Merlot; the nose is developing intense balsamic scents, which lead to the round but sturdy, mature and complex palate. The **1998 Grand Lavergne** has more fruity notes owing to the use of Cabernet grapes (70%); the body is well-structured with obvious tannins. Those who like such wines might try it with grilled meat.

EARL Vignobles Boireau, Les Grands Jays, B.P. 2, 33570 Les Artigues-de-Lussac, tel. 05.57.24.32.08, fax 05.57.24.33.24 by appt.

CH. LESTRILLE CAPMARTIN

Cuvée Tradition Elevé en fût de chêne 1998★

■ 9 ha 70,000 30–49 F

This vineyard has a long-established reputation. The Cuvée Tradition delighted the jury. A long-vatted Merlot, which has spent 12 months in oak, this wine has evolving aromas of very ripe grapes, well-matured tannins and a flavoursome, slightly liquorice flesh which is highlighted by an effective yet respectful oakiness. The lovely finish suggests

it may be drunk with roasts and cows' milk cheeses. The **Cuvée Prestige**, which has spent 12 months in new oak, continues to suffer from too much wood. This very provisional handicap is compensated for by an aromatic complexity (fruit, toast, spices and coffee) which enhances the already flavoursome, elegant, velvety flesh. Drink in three or four years' time with leg of lamb or magret de canard with haricots verts and mushrooms.
Jean-Louis Roumage, Lestrille, 33750 Saint-Germain-du-Puch, tel. 05.57.24.51.02, fax 05.57.24.04.58 Y by appt.

CH. L'HOSTE-BLANC
Elevé en fût de chêne 1998★★

■ 5 ha 30,000 30–49 F

This vineyard, taken over by the present owner in 1980, has retained its old vines on varying terrains. This half-Merlot, half-Cabernet Sauvignon wine was put into barrel as soon as it ceased fermentation, and stayed there 12 months. It has an attractive dark-garnet colour and a complex range of aromas sustained by ripe fruits, floral touches (rose), and notes of spices, toast, liquorice and roasting. Such richness enhances the body, which is vigorous and charming with fleeting tannins at the finish. This suggests that the wine's life-span will be on the short side, and that it should be drunk straight away with game or red meat. A great mature wine.
Vignobles Michel Baylet, Ch. Landereau, 33670 Sadirac, tel. 05.56.30.64.28, fax 05.56.30.63.90 Y ev. day except Sat. Sun. 8am–12 noon 1.30pm–5pm

CH. DE LISENNES 1998

■ 10 ha 65,000 30–49 F

This huge estate on the edge of Bordeaux gets its name from the limestone-clay soils which Rabelais referred to as *lize*. Cabernets (35% each) dominate this wine with its nose hinting at green pepper and its round and concentrated body. The tannins from the oak, like those from the grapes, seem discreet and are enhanced by a vanilla flavour which opens at the finish. A wine to drink straight away with mild sauces, and perhaps with cheese.
Jean-Pierre Soubie, Ch. de Lisennes, 33370 Tresses, tel. 05.57.34.13.03, fax 05.57.34.05.36 Y by appt.

CH. DE LUGAGNAC 1997

■ 49 ha 105,000 30–49 F

Located between the small fortified town of Pellegrue and the tiny fortified town of Castelmoron, the Château de Lugagnac is a sober yet beautiful stronghold. All three varieties are present in the vineyard which grows 50% Merlot. This 1997 wine was enjoyed for its aromatic freshness and the spirited roundness of the flesh; the tannins are somewhat austere but pleasant. A wine for family celebrations.
Mylène et Maurice Bon, SCEA du Ch. de Lugagnac, 33790 Pellegrue, tel. 05.56.61.30.60, fax 05.56.61.38.48, e-mail lugagnac@caves-particulieres.com Y ev. day 9am–7pm

CH. MAJUREAU-SERCILLAN 1998

■ n.c. 58,000 30–49 F

This estate, which was already exporting its wines in the 18th century, continues to send them in equal measure to Europe and the USA. This is a very nice classic wine, made from 15-year-old vines. Its cheery expression includes a ruby colour and round body structured by unobtrusive tannins and perfumed with red fruits, prunes and a subtle vanilla oakiness. Ready to drink now, with meat or cheese (Cantal and Laguiole, for example).
Alain Vironneau, Le Majureau, 33240 Salignac, tel. 05.57.43.00.25, fax 05.57.43.91.34, e-mail alainvironneau@wanadoo.fr Y by appt.

CH. MALEDAN 1998

■ 11 ha 35,000 30–49 F

This former 18th-century hunting-lodge has a vineyard on gravel soils. Its 1998 blend of Merlot (75%) and Cabernet Franc (25%) is redolent of blackcurrant with hints of musk and spices. The flesh has strong flavours of ripe fruits and is pleasantly long-lasting. Can be drunk straight away, with lamprey, for example.
SCEA J.B. Brunot et Fils, 60, rte de l'Eglise, 33370 Loupes, tel. 05.57.55.09.99, fax 05.57.55.09.95, e-mail vignobles.brunot@wanadoo.fr Y by appt.

CH. MALROME
Cuvée Comtesse Adèle 1998

■ n.c. 80,000 50–69 F

The château's labels depict works by Toulouse-Lautrec, who died in this family property and was buried at Verdelais. The Cuvée Comtesse Adèle (named after the artist's mother) is a blend of Merlot (50%), Cabernet-Sauvignon (30%) and Cabernet Franc (20%), matured for 14 months in new oak. The round body is still marked by the oak: its interesting fruit flavours (grape and blackcurrant) are underlined by oaky vanilla and musky notes. The tannins should be well blended in a year or two.
Ch. Malromé, 33490 Saint-André-du-Bois, tel. 05.56.76.44.92, fax 05.56.76.46.18, e-mail p.decroix@malrome.com Y by appt.
Ph. Decroix

CH. MARAC 1998★

■ 7.26 ha 60,000 30–49 F

The church and terrace of the former Château of Pujols, the present-day town-hall, afford lovely panoramas of the Dordogne Valley and the Saint-Emilion district. This wine is 80% Merlot. The intense red-fruit aromas are enlivened by spicy, peppery notes. The concentrated, fleshy palate contains harmonious tannins, reflecting good judgment and a respectful skill in the handling of mature, well cared-for grapes. 'A good wine to leave to age' and 'I really love it,' were two jurors' conclusions.

Alain Bonville, Ch. Marac, 33350 Pujols, tel. 05.57.40.53.21, fax 05.57.40.71.36 Y by appt.

MARQUIS D'ABEYLIE 1997★★

■ 10 ha 66,000 30–49 F

The colour of this 'Marquess' is, as one juror exclaimed, 'the intense purple worn by cardinals'. It is a pure Merlot with hints of grilling and roasting due to a year spent in oak – *French* oak, as the grower says firmly. The fruit has gained from such complexity. Nose and palate both evoke grapes, blackcurrants, redcurrants and blackberries. Powerful yet well-absorbed tannins emphasise the supple denseness of the slightly heady flesh. Superb! The same co-operative offers a **1998 Château de la Beauze**, which is recommended. An enjoyable wine to drink straight away.

Closerie d'Estiac, Les Lèves, 33320 Sainte-Foy-la-Grande, tel. 05.57.56.02.02, fax 05.57.56.02.22 Y ev. day except Sun. Mon. 9am–12 noon 3pm–7pm

CH. MARTOURET

Vieilli en barrique 1998★

■ 20 ha n.c. 30–49 F

Dominique Lurton runs this attractive 37-ha (91-acre) estate with a passion shared by many other members of this large Bordeaux family. Martouret is made from 66% Merlot, the residue coming from the two Cabernet varieties, all grown on a limestone-clay soil. Twelve months maturing in the barrel have yielded a deep colour with garnet highlights. Oak is discernible throughout, yet never overwhelms. The wine's fruitiness hints at crystallised cherry; the oak contributes vanilla and liquorice. Wait a year or two before drinking.

Dominique Lurton, Ch. Martouret, 33750 Nérigean, tel. 05.57.24.50.02, fax 05.57.24.03.30, e-mail d.lurton@martouret.com Y by appt.

CH. MEILLAC Elevé en barrique 1997★

■ 6.5 ha 19,000 30–49 F

The tower of a former windmill, 55 m (180 ft) tall, dominates the Dordogne Valley here. The vineyard is close to the Eiffel bridges (take a look at the undersides of the arches). This wine is 85% Merlot, with a suspicion of Cabernet Sauvignon (3%) and a stronger contribution from Cabernet Franc (12%). The creamy roundness of the flesh is perfumed with spicy, oaky orange peel. The oak, resulting from 12 months' ageing (some of the wine in new barrels), is a fitting partner for the grapes. A lovely wine that can be drunk now or kept a while longer.

Claude Bertrand, Ch. Meillac, 33240 Saint-André-de-Cubzac, tel. 05.57.58.20.58, fax 05.57.58.21.73 Y by appt.

CH. MESTE JEAN

Elevé en fût de chêne 1998

■ 2.5 ha 17,000 30–49 F

Not far from this vineyard, an undulating road takes the visitor to the fortified town of Rions or to the impressive château of the Dukes of Epernon at Cadillac. This wine was partly matured in American oak, the aromatic influence of which is always considerable; in this half-Merlot, half-Cabernet Sauvignon blend, it brings the typical green pepper-like quality of Sauvignon closer to prune and dried fig. It also reinforces a tannic character which will appeal to certain wine-lovers. A wine of style and originality.

EARL Vignobles Cailleux, La Pereyre, 33760 Escoussans, tel. 05.56.23.63.23, fax 05.56.23.64.21 Y by appt.

DOM. DE MONREPOS 1998

■ 5 ha 40,000 30–49 F

Much has been written about the versatile owners of this estate. This 1998 wine has aromas of stone fruits (Morello cherry and prune) and toast. The body indicates good keeping potential. The **1998 Château de Faise**, grown on the wine estate of the former Cistercian Abbey of Faise, is a more discreet and classic wine, which will be suitable for grills and roasts, especially at informal meals with friends.

EARL Vignobles D. et C. Devaud, Faise, 33570 Les Artigues-de-Lussac, tel. 05.57.24.31.39, fax 05.57.24.34.17 Y by appt.

CH. MONTLAU

Vieilli en fût de chêne 1997

■ 15 ha 100,000 30–49 F

Planted with two-thirds Merlot and one-third Cabernet Franc, this vineyard is located on the slopes of Moulon, on the southern bank of the Dordogne, opposite the bell-tower of Saint-Emilion. Visitors will admire the beauty all around and the sober elegance of the château's towers. The harvesting of the grapes, the vinification and maturing (seven months in oak, one-fifth of the barrels replaced each year with new ones) all reflect the rigour and skill dictated by tradition. This 1997 wine has a cherry-red colour and astonishing aromas of Morello cherry, blackcurrant, menthol and liquorice. Its balanced and harmonious body reveals mellow fruit, well-behaved tannins and a fresh, sweet, long finish. Ready for drinking now, it will go well with red meat or lamprey.

Armand Schuster de Ballwil, Ch. Montlau, 33420 Moulon, tel. 05.57.84.50.71, fax 05.57.84.64.65 Y by appt.

CH. MORTON 1998

■ n.c. 80,000 30–49 F

Grown on the Garonne gravels and silty clay, this wine is 90% Merlot from old vines. Morello cherry aromas mingle with powerful aromas of grilling and vanilla endowed by the oak. The first impressions are supple, and the

tannins make a strong show at the finish. A wine for grills and underdone roasts.
🔑 EARL Dom. de La Mette, Ch. Morton, 33640 Portets, tel. 05.56.67.18.18, fax 05.56.67.53.66 ☑ 🍷 by appt.
🔑 Solorzano

CH. MOULIN DE FERRAND 1998★

■ 7 ha 55,000 🍾 🌡 30–49 F

Saint-Michel-de-Lapujade nestles in the hills about ten kilometres (six miles) from the fortified town of La Réole. This product is intended for export. Half-Merlot, half-Cabernets (30% Sauvignon, 20% Franc), it has a delightful palate of toasted roundness evoking prune and lightly spiced blackcurrant. An enjoyable wine to drink within two years, with grilled poultry. The **1998 Château de la Vieille Tour** marries 35% Cabernet-Sauvignon and 25% Cabernet Franc to 40% Merlot. A well-rounded body is dominated by blackcurrant; the tannins are well-balanced and the finish silky. A fresh-tasting accompaniment to white meats and poultry.
🔑 Vignobles Boissonneau, Cathelicq, 33190 Saint-Michel-de-Lapujade, tel. 05.56.61.72.14, fax 05.56.61.71.01, e-mail vignobles.boissonneau@wanadoo.fr
🍷 by appt.

CH. MOUTON 1998★★

■ 9 ha n.c. 🛢 70–99 F

A welcome second harvest for J.-Ph. Janoueix, who took over the château in 1997. 'Mouton' comes from 'motte', which means 'on top'. The presence of 5% Petit Verdot in this 42-year-old vineyard is a curiosity. Merlot (70%) and Cabernet Franc (25%) are more traditional to the region. The nose really explodes with aromas of wild black fruits, orange peel, cinnamon, vanilla and cardamom against a background of roast coffee. The flesh is mouth-filling and smooth, strongly structured with well-blended, mature, elegant tannins. The impressive oakiness calls for two to five years' ageing, when it will give pleasure to the majority of enthusiasts. There was talk of drinking it alongside a confit of eel with truffle-juice.
🔑 Jean-Philippe Janoueix, 83, cours des Girondins, 33500 Libourne, tel. 05.57.25.91.19, fax 05.57.48.00.04 ☑ 🍷 by appt.

CH. MOUTTE BLANC 1998★

■ 2.4 ha 14,000 🛢 30–49 F

This Bordeaux Supérieur hails from Macau in the Médoc. It includes 30% Petit Verdot, which has given it an originality heightened by malolactic fermentation and ageing in 20% new oak barrels. Since it has been vinified plot by plot, allowing for individual differences, one imagines the master's pleasure in finally blending the whole. The generosity of the tannins delighted one taster. Others wondered how these would evolve, but readily appreciated the aromatic complexity which marries blackcurrant, wild strawberry, sloe and musk. The palate is full and comforting. A curiosity that needs ageing, suitable for entrecôte steaks.
🔑 Dejean-de Bortoli, 33, av. de la Coste, 33460 Macau, tel. 05.57.88.42.36, fax 05.57.88.42.36 ☑ 🍷 by appt.

CH. NARDIQUE LA GRAVIERE

Elevé en fût de chêne 1998

■ 6.08 ha 25,000 🛢 30–49 F

Regular sampling determined how long this half-Merlot, half-Cabernets (20% Franc) was vinified. It was then aged for 15 months in oak, which has left a strong trace. Some jurors deemed it over-powerful, despite its high quality. It will take three years to establish whether the flesh, which promises to be dense and full, will develop along with notes of ripe fruits that are already discernible. Some, however, will not wait that long.
🔑 Vignobles Thérèse, Ch. Nardique La Gravière, 33670 Saint-Genès-de-Lombaud, tel. 05.56.23.01.37, fax 05.56.23.25.89 ☑ 🍷 ev. day except Sun. 9am–12 noon 3pm–6pm; cl. 15–31 Aug.

CH. NAUDONNET-PLAISANCE

Vieilli en fût de chêne 1998★

■ 25 ha 180,000 🛢 30–49 F

A wine grown on gravelly soil, half-Merlot, half-Cabernets. Oak-lovers will enjoy this one: it has spent 18 months in oak, which has left an imposing presence, blending oak and fruit that were made for each other. The colour is light, but the nose powerful, evocative of ripe fruits and fruit-cake. The fleshy palate has absorbed its tannins well. This wine will accompany dishes with sauces and game, but needs three years to age.
🔑 Danièle Mallard, Ch. Naudonnet-Plaisance, 33760 Escoussans, tel. 05.56.23.93.04, fax 05.57.34.40.78, e-mail mallard@caves-particulieres.com ☑
🍷 by appt.

CH. PANCHILLE 1998★

■ 8 ha 50,000 🍾 🌡 20–29 F

This 30-year-old vineyard is located on the mixed soils of the Dordogne's river-terraces downstream of Libourne. Merlot predominates (70%), then Cabernet Franc (20%) and Cabernet Sauvignon (10%). Though the attack is somewhat rough, the dense palate is very aromatic (blackcurrant, Morello cherry with a hint of burnt earth); the long, complex, slightly meaty finish suggests it will keep well. The **1998 Cuvée Alix** (30–49F) is a selection of this wine, 70% matured in barrels of varying ages. A quality oaky wine, with hints of vanilla and grilling which bring to the grapes a complexity to delight enthusiasts. This too is a one-star wine. They make an interesting comparison.
🔑 Pascal Sirat, Ch. Panchille, 33500 Arveyres, tel. 05.57.51.57.39, fax 05.57.51.57.39 ☑ 🍷 by appt.

CH. DE PARENCHERE

Cuvée Raphaël Gazaniol 1998★★

■ n.c. 60,000 50–69 F

Ligueux is shyly tucked away some ten kilometres (six miles) south of the fortified town of Sainte-Foy-la-Grande, on the department's edge. The qualities of Château de Parenchère have nonetheless been clear for some years. The red-black colour and the intense aromas of stewed fruits with a hint of menthol, which are subtle yet still very marked by the oak (grilling, spices and cedar), delighted the jury. The dense, full fruit and well-structured body with its distinguished tannins, and the long finish with its perfumes of vanilla and liquorice reveal a good potential for ageing. The **1998 Cuvée Principale** (30–49F), which is recommended, brings out the power and richness of its ripe grapes. A good wine to have in the cellar.

Jean Gazaniol, Ch. de Parenchère, 33220 Ligueux, tel. 05.57.46.04.17, fax 05.57.46.42.80 Y by appt.

CH. PASCAUD

Vieilli en fût de chêne 1998

■ 3 ha 20,000 30–49 F

This wine is made from a selection of old vines (90% Merlot, 10% Cabernet Franc), and matured for 12 months in oak (25% new). The vineyard's efforts to upgrade quality have paid off in the aromas of ripe grapes, prune and vanilla which accompany a palate needing some more time to blend fully.

SCEA Vignobles Avril, B.P. 12, 33133 Galgon, tel. 05.57.84.32.11, fax 05.57.74.38.62, e-mail ch.pascaud@aol.com Y by appt.

CH. PENIN Tradition 1998★

■ 15 ha 95,000 30–49 F

Patrick Carteyron has been much praised in the last few years. This deep-purple 85% Merlot was grown on gravelly soil. The body has a round, fleshy attack, which contrasts with the energetic yet rich finish. Spicy, toasted, ripe-fruit aromas are a feature of both nose and palate. Their distinguished nature was a source of delight. The **1998 Cuvée Sélection**, which is also awarded one star, includes 10% Cabernet Franc and has spent a full year in oak. The marriage with quality oak has yielded a subtle nose. The wine is crisp and charming. Drink this attractive classic without delay (50–69F).

SCEA Patrick Carteyron, Ch. Penin, 33420 Génissac, tel. 05.57.24.46.98, fax 05.57.24.41.99 Y by appt.

CH. PEUY-SAINCRIT Montalon 1998

■ 4 ha 20,000 30–49 F

Château Peuy-Sainscrit lies exactly 45°N. A windmill perched on the Butte de Montalon, above Saint-André-de-Cubzac, offers a panoramic view over the Gironde section of the River Dordogne. The vineyard includes some very old vines growing on south-facing limestone-clay slopes. After 12 months in barrel, this wine has an attractive concentration of tannins, possibly slightly at the expense of the fruit. The nose is discreet and finely oaky. It will need patience and careful future sampling, as the bouquet develops, to assess how its currently severe character will evolve.

Vignobles Germain et Associés, Ch. Peyredoulle, 33390 Berson, tel. 05.57.42.66.66, fax 05.57.64.36.20, e-mail bordeaux@vgas.com Y by appt.

CH. PEYNAUD 1998★

■ 9 ha 40,000 30–49 F

A few miles from the property, visitors can see the church at Castelviel, then travel on to Verdelais. This wine is almost one-half Cabernet-Sauvignon; Merlot accounts for more than one-third. The maturity of the grapes is reflected in the rounded fruit and the aromas, which result from long fermentation and maceration. Good-quality tannins show their presence and indicate good keeping potential. A great companion for roast red meats or game.

Vignobles Chaigne et Fils, Ch. Ballan-Larquette, 33540 Saint-Laurent-du-Bois, tel. 05.56.76.46.02, fax 05.56.76.40.90, e-mail rchaigne@vins-bordeaux.fr Y by appt.

LES GRAVES DE CH. PICON 1997★

■ 10 ha 40,000 30–49 F

This château is located on gravelly soils several kilometres from the fortified town of Sainte-Foy-la-Grande. The two Cabernets are responsible for 50% of the wine, but the 50% Merlot dominates. The colour of this 1997 wine is dense ruby with hints of black. The creamy, mouth-filling palate, whose tannins are still marked, is enlivened by notes of exotic fruits, wild berries and slightly vegetal touches. The nose is young and discreet, and the finish needs to calm down. Enthusiasts of well-structured wines will enjoy sampling this one's evolution over the next few years.

SCEA Ch. Picon, 33220 Eynesse, tel. 05.57.41.01.91, fax 05.57.41.01.02 Y by appt.

CH. POLIN

Elevé en barrique de chêne 1998

■ 12 ha 30,000 30–49 F

This wine comes from Beychac-et-Caillau, where it is worth visiting the Maison des Bordeaux et Bordeaux Supérieurs run by the Union for the AOC. This 30-year-old vineyard is located on gravelly clay. The time spent in oak has been good for this wine, whose round flesh and joyous, fresh-tasting perfumes of raspberry, blackcurrant and oak make it a suitable companion for meals with friends. A good wine for *bons vivants*.

GAEC La Lande de Taleyran, Ch. Polin, 33750 Beychac-et-Caillau, tel. 05.56.72.98.93, fax 05.56.72.81.94 Y by appt.

J. Burliga

CH. PUY-LABORDE 1998

■ n.c. n.c. ▮ 20–29 F

The vineyard is 20 years old, but the property itself, which is located on a rocky spur, has belonged to the same family for a number of generations. Blended evenly from the three AOC varieties, this wine is wholly representative of its year, having a tendency to roundness and fruitiness and being ready to drink now. Would suit family Sunday lunches. Distributed by the firm of Cordier de Blanquefort.

EARL Trabut-Cussac, 32, le Bourg, 33580 Taillecavat, tel. 05.56.61.62.66

CH. RECOUGNE 1998★

■ 55 ha 200,000 ▮ 30–49 F

'Recougne' means 'recognised' (of acknowledged quality). In recent years, this wine's quality has been widely recognised. The 1998 version breathes forth perfumes of spices and pepper against a background of ripe fruits. The same complexity informs the palate, whose roundness is accompanied by well-blended tannins. This wine makes the best use of ripe grapes and can be drunk for some time to come as an accompaniment to red meats. The **1998 Château Montcabrier**, a half-Merlot, half-Cabernets blend, is the second Recougne vintage. Its body is more lean and peppery (at the expense of fruitiness), and is recommended.

SCEV Jean Milhade, Ch. Recougne, 33133 Galgon, tel. 05.57.55.48.90, fax 05.57.84.31.27 Y by appt.

CH. DE REIGNAC

Cuvée Prestige 1998★★

■ 45 ha 307,000 30–49 F

The Malbec variety (5%) says its piece in this classic construction of 60% Merlot and 35% Cabernets. The vinification uses micro-oxygenation under the marc, and new barrels are used (with 12 months of maturing). These techniques have resulted in a remarkable deep-purple wine with raspberry lights. The intense aromas open with the scent of violets, which evolves towards pears and intensely toasted or grilled red fruits. A supple attack gives way to mouth-filling fruit. The palate's tannic exaggerations will calm down in time. A rich, well-balanced wine with a magnificent potential that is well worth waiting for.

SCI Ch. de Reignac, 33450 Saint-Loubès, tel. 05.56.20.41.05, fax 05.56.68.63.31 Y by appt.

Yves Vatelot

ROC DU BEL AIR 1998★

■ n.c. 550,000 ▮ 20–29 F

This blend of Merlot (50%), Cabernet-Sauvignon (40%) and Cabernet Franc (10%) is very aromatic, charming and complex, with musky notes enlivening the red-fruit aromas. The round, rich body has much appeal, making it hard to resist. The large Producta group also offers the trademarked **Roque Bel Air**, which resembles its fellow in its conception and is almost as well rated. One juror voiced the opinion of the absolute majority in noting, 'Enjoyable now because of its nice fruitiness, but good keeping potential.' The labels illustrate listed buildings in Bordeaux.

Producta SA, 21, cours Xavier-Arnozan, 33082 Bordeaux Cedex, tel. 05.57.81.18.18, fax 05.56.81.22.12, e-mail producta@producta.com Y by appt.

CH. ROC MEYNARD 1998★

■ 12 ha 60,000 ▮ 30–49 F

The château vineyard, close to the hills of Fronsac, is coming of age. The vines grown on its limestone-clay soils are mainly Merlot (90% of this wine). The black colour, dense, round yet well-structured fruit, and young aromas of forest fruits (blackberry, raspberry, bilberry) all indicate good ageing potential, which will reveal itself when the wine is drunk with grills and roasts in another year or two.

Philippe Hermouet, Clos du Roy, 33141 Saillans, tel. 05.57.55.07.41, fax 05.57.55.07.45, e-mail hermouetclosduroy@wanadoo.fr Y by appt.

CH. ROQUES MAURIAC 1998

■ n.c. n.c. ▮ 30–49 F

This estate, which follows organic principles, offers a wine marked by the Cabernet varieties. As one taster noted, 'Nice nose, notes of Cabernet, subtle.' Cabernet Franc (40%) and Sauvignon (10%) have produced a slender yet well-balanced structure with a hint of spiced pepper. Drink unhurriedly with white meats, and compare it with the **1998 Cuvée Hélène**, to which 18 months in the barrel have added a delicate vanilla complexity.

GFA Leclerc, Ch. Lagnet, 33350 Doulezon, tel. 05.57.40.51.84, fax 05.57.40.55.48 Y by appt.

CH. SAINT-GERMAIN 1998★

■ 85 ha 660,000 ▮ 20–29 F

The famous wine-merchants, Calvet, offer two wines exclusive to them. They handle the vinification and maturing of the wines of Château Saint-Germain, an historic monument whose façade visitors will admire. On the palate, this 80% Merlot makes a supple beginning, then becomes more robust and powerful. The tannins are still obtrusive, but promising in tone. The wine's mouth-filling quality is informed by aromas of ripe fruits and musky tones. Also recommended is the **1998 Château La Croix de Nauze** (85% Merlot), which has a nose of wild strawberries and crystallised fruits, plus a supple, charming body with light, subtle tannins. A wine to serve now, slightly chilled, with white meats or mild cheeses.

Calvet, 75, cours du Médoc, B.P. 11, 33028 Bordeaux Cedex, tel. 05.56.43.59.00, fax 05.56.43.17.78

Weber

CH. SAINT-PIERRE 1997★

■ 8.11 ha 50,000 ▮ 20–29 F

No effort is spared to ensure the success of the wines made on this estate near the listed church at Haux: inspection of individual plots for signs of maturity, sifting and cleaning of the harvested grapes, controlled maceration, monitoring of the length and intensity of the oak-maturation, and so on. This 1997 wine is enticing, with its dark colour and successive yet harmoniously blended scents of Morello cherry, dried fig, *pain d'épice* (a kind of spice loaf), oaky smokiness and coffee. The palate's balance reveals the ripe fruitiness of the grapes (50% Cabernet-Sauvignon) and the strength of the oak, which time and patience will surely soften.

🔑 Peter et Plenning Jorgensen, SCA Ch. de Haux, 33550 Haux, tel. 05.57.34.51.12, fax 05.57.34.51.15 ☑ 🍷 by appt.

🔑 Denis Roumegous

CH. TAYET

Cuvée Prestige Elevé en fût de chêne neuf 1998★

■ 4.09 ha 30,000 50–69 F

A wine from the marshy terrains of Macau in the Médoc, the Cuvée Prestige has spent 11 months in the barrel. Its full, complex nose blends notes of cherry, raspberry, blackcurrant and eucalyptus-tinged oak, providing an enchanting accompaniment to the rich, supple fruit. Vigorous tannins prolong its harmony. A wine to go with a leg of lamb. The tank-matured **1998 Cuvée Principale**, though less complex, is undeniably charming, with red-fruit aromas and silky tannins. A wine to enjoy straight away, with poultry or lamprey (30–49F).

🔑 SCEA Ch. Haut Breton Larigaudière, 33460 Soussans, tel. 05.57.88.94.17, fax 05.57.88.39.14 ☑ 🍷 by appt.

CH. TERTRE CABARON 1997★

■ 12.12 ha 16,435 30–49 F

This estate in the heart of the Entre-Deux-Mers district offers an attractive 1997 wine, its garnet colour fringed with orange lights. The nose and palate both evoke stewed fruit. The rounded palate has gamey accents, and the nice long finish fades on notes of liquorice. A wine to go with grilled meat or goats' cheese. Drink it now, while waiting for the 1998 version.

🔑 GAEC Dom. de Bastorre, 33540 Saint-Brice, tel. 05.56.71.54.19, fax 05.56.71.50.29 ☑ 🍷 by appt.

🔑 Dugrand

CH. THIEULEY

Réserve Francis Courselle 1998★★

■ 8 ha 48,000 70–99 F

La Saulve, in the Entre-Deux-Mers district, is dominated by its famous abbey. Château Thieuley is a well-known grower, and this Réserve de Francis Courselle is a pure Merlot, grown on clay-gravel. The intense nose mixes prune, cocoa and spices (clove), all with notes of grilling, though not overly so. These aromas reveal their complexity immediately the wine is served, and accompany the finish. The body's mouth-filling structure inspires confidence in its keeping quality. A wine for mushrooms and fillets of goose or duck.

🔑 Sté des Vignobles Francis Courselle, Ch. Thieuley, 33670 La Sauve, tel. 05.56.23.00.01, fax 05.56.23.34.37 ☑ 🍷 by appt.

CH. TOUR D'ALBRET 1998★

■ n.c. n.c. 20–29 F

They say that King Henri IV spent a night at the château when he visited his mother, Jeanne d'Albret, at Castelmoron, the tiny fortified town nearby. The 20-year-old vineyard combines Merlot (60%) and Cabernet-Sauvignon (40%). This strong-coloured wine has a similar balance, and is fleshy, robust and very fruity. The subtle tannic structure means that it is ready to drink now, but there is no hurry. Exclusive to the merchants, Cordier de Blanquefort.

🔑 GAEC Lopez et Frères, Saint-Martin-du-Puy, 33540 Sauveterre-de-Guyenne, tel. 05.56.71.57.58

CH. TOUR DE MIRAMBEAU

Cuvée Passion 1998★★★

■ n.c. n.c. 70–99 F

In this its second year in the Bordeaux Supérieur AOC, Tour de Mirambeau receives a *coup de coeur.* It is a very classic blend of 70% Merlot and 30% Cabernet-Sauvignon, but the vines are 40 years old, their vigour and yield have been finely regulated, and the oenological team are pastmasters of technique – wines of such quality are the fruit of practice in the art of wine and wood! This is a most excellent example of the harmony between grape and oak: an inky black colour with purple lights; elegant, persistent aromas of red fruits (blackcurrant), marmalade, dried fruits, vanilla, toast done just right and buttered, wax, cedar, and roasted hazelnut – in all, an enchanting assortment. The body is dense and supple with vigorous yet rich and discreet tannins (some of them from the oak).A gorgeous wine, to be drunk long and often.

🔑 SCEA Vignobles Despagne, 33420 Naujan-et-Postiac, tel. 05.57.84.55.08, fax 05.57.84.57.31, e-mail despagne@vignobles-despagne.com ☑ 🍷 by appt.

🔑 J.-L. Despagne

CH. TROCARD 1998★

■ 35 ha 220,000 🍷 🌡 20–29 F

Close to an airfield known to microlight enthusiasts is this essentially Merlot vineyard. Vinification and maturing follow traditional methods overseen by Jean-Louis Trocard, who plays an important role in organisations of wine-makers and growers both regionally and nationally. Some wines are oak-matured; this one has been kept in the vat. Notes of undergrowth enhance the fruity charm (blackcurrant) of the aromas. The palate is round and fleshy; the grape tannins reveal themselves with a well-blended elegance which lengthens the pleasure. A wine to go with red meat at meals with friends, though its personality will develop further if it is kept.

🔑 SCEA des Vignobles Jean-Louis Trocard, 2, Les Petits Jays ouest, 33570 Les Artigues-de-Lussac, tel. 05.57.55.57.90, fax 05.57.55.57.98, e-mail trocard@wanadoo.fr ✉ 🍸 by appt.

CH. VERTHAMON 1998

■ n.c. 45,000 🍷 🌡 30–49 F

This wine has a luminous peony-red colour and a young nose showing aromas of blackcurrant, cherry and raspberry. The attack is one of frank, ripe fruitiness, with an attractive balance. The finish is extended by notes of liquorice. A fleshy, fruity wine, which is good to drink now and has good keeping potential.

🔑 Christian Quancard, Dom. Auberive, 33360 Latresne, tel. 05.56.20.71.03, fax 05.56.20.11.30 ✉ 🍸 by appt.

CH. VIALLET NOUHANT 1998

■ 4.6 ha 12,000 🍷 20–29 F

This blend of 70% Cabernet-Sauvignon and 30% Merlot was grown in the Médoc on the banks of the Gironde. The colour is violet-purple, and the aromas of ripe black fruits are accompanied by supple yet sustaining tannins. An enjoyable wine that may last for some time.

🔑 Alain Nouhant, 5, rue Jeanne-d'Arc, 33460 Cussac-Fort-Médoc, tel. 05.57.88.51.43, fax 05.57.88.51.43, e-mail alain.nouhant@libertysurf.fr ✉ 🍸 by appt.

CH. VIEUX BOMALE 1998★

■ 5 ha 15,000 🍷 🌡 20–29 F

This is a good place to visit, both for its position on the Dordogne and also for the underground tunnels quarried in the limestone, under the vineyard. This wine is 80% Merlot. The nose has a pleasant complexity of fresh red-fruit aromas evocative of flower-buds. The palate, which hints at prune, has a subtle, well-balanced flesh accompanied by discreet tannins. The finish is long and flavoursome. A wine for mushrooms and grills.

🔑 SCEA Jean-Pierre Chaudet, Caneveau, 33240 Lugon, tel. 05.57.84.49.10, fax 05.57.84.42.07, e-mail sceachaudet-j.p.@wanadoo.fr ✉ 🍸 ev. day 9am–12 noon 2pm–5.30pm; Sat. Sun. by appt.

CH. VIEUX CARREFOUR 1998

■ 10.5 ha 45,000 🍷 20–29 F

The property is old; documents dating from 1745 contain the current owner's family name. The winery, on the other hand, like the vineyard, is modern (12 years old). Merlot accounts for 75% of this wine, and Cabernet Franc for 10%. The subtle, floral nose is still reticent. The body is characterised by suppleness, but the tannins make their presence felt in the finish. A wine that can be opened now, for drinking with meats in wine sauces.

🔑 EARL François Gabard, Le Carrefour, 33133 Galgon, tel. 05.57.74.30.77, fax 05.57.84.35.73 ✉ 🍸 by appt.

Crémant de Bordeaux

The sparkling Crémant de Bordeaux was created in 1990. It is made according to the same strict fermentation and ageing rules as all other Appellations Crémants, using traditional Bordelais grape varieties. Generally speaking, Crémants are white but they can also be rosé. Production figures for 1999 were 12,715 hl (335,676 gal).

REMY BREQUE Cuvée Prestige★★

○ n.c. 6,500 30–49 F

The small Romanesque church of Saint-Gervais overlooks the wide valley of the Dordogne's lower reaches several miles from Eiffel's bridges. The voluptuous union of Sémillon and Muscadelle (50% each) has yielded a bright, pale-yellow wine with a continuous, fine, stable fizziness. The body is pleasantly mouth-filling and long-lasting with a mint freshness sustained by a background of pear, quince jelly, linden-flowers and honey. The liveliness of the finish enhances the pleasure. A wine for celebrations.

🔑 Maison Rémy Brèque, 8, rue du Cdt-Cousteau, 33240 Saint-Gervais, tel. 05.57.43.10.42, fax 05.57.43.91.61 ✉ 🍸 by appt.

BROUETTE PETIT-FILS Grande Cuvée★

○ n.c. 25,000 30–49 F

The premises of Brouette Petit-Fils are in the *galeries* of the 'Pain de Sucre' on the outskirts of Bourg-sur-Gironde, perched up high and overlooking the confluence of the Garonne and Dordogne rivers. Its Crément range is based on some very diverse blends.

The jurors singled out this Grande Cuvée, in which Ugni Blanc (20%) unites with Sémillon to yield a yellow wine with green highlights and a discreet, fine *mousse* pleasantly redolent of apricots, citrus and sharp apples. The rich palate evokes hazelnuts and pepper. Such aromatic complexity gives added life and length to the finish. Also recommended are the pure Sémillon **Tradition**, which has an intense nose of orange-flowers and lime, plus a lively body, and the **Cuvée de l'Abbaye** (60% Sémillon, 30% Muscadelle and 10% Sauvignon), with its fresh and complex harmony.

🔑 SA Brouette Petit-Fils, Le Pain de Sucre, 33710 Bourg-sur-Gironde, tel. 05.57.68.42.09, fax 05.57.68.26.48 Y ev. day except Sun. Mon. 9am–12 noon 2pm–6pm

GRANGENEUVE 1998

○ 5 ha 6,000 ▮ 🌡 50–69 F

This Crémant is a pure Sémillon from the co-operative at Romagne. A regular stream of bubbles, a persistent *mousse*, and a pale-yellow hue introduce a fresh, round body, which is well-balanced and lively, perfumed with fruits and flowers. A wine to be drunk as an aperitif.

🔑 Cave coop. de Grangeneuve, 33760 Romagne, tel. 05.57.97.09.40, fax 05.57.97.09.41 ☒ Y ev. day except Sun. Mon. 8am–12 noon 2pm–5pm

BRUT DE LANDEREAU

Blanc de blancs 1998★

○ 1 ha 4,000 ▮ 🌡 50–69 F

This pure Sémillon comes from grapes chosen from plots of siliceous-clay-gravel soils. Its persistent effervescence is redolent of dried fruit, lemon and vanilla. The body is rich and fills the mouth well, and the attack and finish have a liveliness which beautifully shapes the whole experience. Drink as an aperitif.

🔑 Vignobles Michel Baylet, Ch. Landereau, 33670 Sadirac, tel. 05.56.30.64.28, fax 05.56.30.63.90 ☒ Y ev. day except Sat. Sun. 8am–12 noon 1.30pm–5pm

LATEYRON 1998★

◐ n.c. 7,000 ▮ 30–49 F

This pure 1998 Rosé is made from Cabernet grapes (80% Franc, the rest Sauvignon). It spent 15 months in a cellar near the windmills of Calon, whence there are wide and gorgeous views over the Libourne district and beyond! The wine is bright salmon-pink and produces a fine, copious *mousse*. The palate is fine and round, perfumed with red fruits, and finishes expansively with a cheery freshness. A successful dessert wine. There was disagreement about the recommended **1998 Blanc Brut** (75% Sémillon, 25% Sauvignon). Its rich body with flavours of dried fruit and grilling detracted from the freshness. It needs to accompany cakes and pastries or cooked cheeses.

🔑 SA Lateyron, Ch. Tour Calon, B.P. 1, 33570 Montagne, tel. 05.57.74.62.05, fax 05.57.74.58.58, e-mail lateyron@wanadoo.fr ☒ Y by appt.

LE TREBUCHET 1998★

○ 0.5 ha 5,000 30–49 F

No longer a contraption of warfare threatening La Réole, the trebuchet is now part of the wine-grower's stock-in-trade. This Crémant marries Sémillon (70%) and Sauvignon in a ring of very aromatic bubbles redolent of ripe fruits. The well-blended, long-lasting body is well balanced between freshness and suppleness. Ready for drinking and good as an aperitif.

🔑 Bernard Berger, Ch. Le Trébuchet, 33190 Les Esseintes, tel. 05.56.71.42.28, fax 05.56.71.30.16 ☒ Y ev. day except Sun. 8am–12 noon 2pm–6pm

LISENNES★★

○ n.c. 5,000 30–49 F

The vast Château de Lisennes, with its gigantic entrance-gate, is famous. In this Crémant, the Sémillon is touched by Muscadelle (10%). The aromatic complexity, borne aloft on a well-formed stream of bubbles, is remarkable: orange-flowers and grapefruit give voice against a no less persistent background of fresh bread and brioche. The body is round, and the whole experience has charm, unity and length. Drink with a meal rather than as an aperitif.

🔑 Jean-Pierre Soubie, Ch. de Lisennes, 33370 Tresses, tel. 05.57.34.13.03, fax 05.57.34.05.36 ☒ Y by appt.

PAUL RIBES 1998★

○ n.c. 30,000 ▮ 🌡 30–49 F

This union of wine-growers has been involved in developing Crémants since the appellation began in 1990. It has invested much in facilities for dealing with the harvested grapes and in wineries for selecting grapes and processing them according to the AOC's rules. The Paul Ribes vintage is 70% Sémillon, 30% Muscadelle. The attractions of its fine bubbles and pale straw-yellow colour herald a nose of finesse and intense aromas. The finish pleasantly extends the pleasure afforded by the flesh, which has the roundness and freshness of well-ripened grapes.

🔑 Union Vignerons d'Aquitaine, ZI de Barbet, 33350 Castillon-la-Bataille, tel. 05.57.40.04.31, fax 05.57.40.17.60 Y by appt.

DU PREVOST★

◐ n.c. n.c. ▮ 🌡 30–49 F

Merlot accounts for 60% of this Crémant, a fact which is somewhat unusual. Equal proportions of the two Cabernets make up the difference. The colour is an honest, lively pink, the nose elegant, fruity and buttery. These aromas also inform the fresh, vibrant flesh. The finish is very lively. The vineyard's **Crémant du Prieur Blanc** is recommended: its fruit and quince-jelly perfumes accompany and prolong the experience of a well-balanced, fresh, lively, harmonious wine.

🔑 EARL Vignobles Garzaro, Ch. Le

Prieur, 33750 Baron, tel. 05.56.30.16.16, fax 05.56.30.12.63, e-mail garzaro@vingarzaro.com ☑ Y by appt.

PRINCESSE LEA★★

○ n.c. 30,000 30–49 F

J.-L. Ballarin, a Crémant grower and merchant, has premises near the small Romanesque church in Haux, halfway between the pleasant fortified town of Créon and the feudal remains of Langoiran. He has a rich product range, essentially based on balancing Sémillon and Muscadelle, of which this Princesse Léa is a good example. The wine's very pale-yellow colour and green lights are enlivened by a persistent stream of fine, abundant bubbles. The nose develops lemony notes against a background of crystallised fruits and dried fig. The supple flesh has a flavoursome character which continues right through the fresh, long finish. A remarkable Crémant which one juror suggested should accompany seafood. Two other wines were selected (one star each): **Etiquette Bleue**, an aperitif wine, and **Marquis de Haux**, which will go well with shellfish.

⊶ Jean-Louis Ballarin, Haux, 33550 Langoiran, tel. 05.56.67.11.30, fax 05.56.67.54.60 ☑ Y by appt.

PERLE DE SEGUIN Cuvée Prestige★

○ 1.3 ha 13,000 50–69 F

This marriage between Sémillon (70%) and Sauvignon was grown about ten kilometres (six miles) from Bordeaux and matured in cellars at Saint-Emilion. The body is slender and fresh. The slightly acid finish amplifies the somewhat discreet aromas of the nose and attack, expanding the floral character and evoking roses and carnations. An enjoyable aperitif wine.

⊶ Michael Carl, Ch. de Seguin, 33360 Lignan-de-Bordeaux, tel. 05.57.97.19.75, fax 05.57.97.19.72, e-mail cwi@chris-wine.dk ☑ Y by appt.

Blayais and Bourgeais

Blayais and Bourgeais are two small villages on the border between the Charente department and the Gironde. They are delightful to come upon for the first time, since both contain historic sites: the prehistoric paintings in the Pair-Non-Pair caves are almost as splendid as the ones at Lascaux. Both Blaye and Bourg are fortified towns, and there are several small châteaux and old hunting lodges. The landscape of hills and valleys creates an intimate atmosphere, which is in sharp contrast to the almost maritime horizons of the banks of the estuary. This is the only place outside Russia and Iran where sturgeon have been caught; it has also been wine country since Gallo-Roman times, which gives this historic landscape a special charm. Up to the beginning of the 20th century there was a considerable production of white wines, used in the distillation of Cognac. This old custom was revived by the more recent creation of Fine de Bordeaux, an eau-de-vie or brandy made by distilling wine in a Charentais still. Nowadays, white wine production has significantly declined against the much more economically viable reds.

Blaye, Premières Côtes de Blaye, Côtes de Blaye, Bourg, Bourgeais, Côtes de Bourg, reds and whites ... there are so many slight differences in the names that it is not always easy to be clear about the different appellations of the region. Nonetheless, it is possible to identify two main groups: the wines from Blaye, where the soil types are varied, and the ones from Bourg, which is geologically more uniform.

Côtes de Blaye and Premières Côtes de Blaye

The fortress of Blaye was built by the great military engineer Vauban and is still completely intact. Today, the vineyards cover about 4,600 ha (11,362 acres) and are planted with both red and white grape varieties. The appellations Blaye and Blayais are used less and less frequently because the wine-growers prefer to produce wines using more noble vine varieties, which are entitled to the appellations Côtes de Blaye and Premières Côtes de Blaye. Nevertheless, 6,688 hl (176,563 gal) of Blaye was produced in 1999. The red wines of Premières Côtes de Blaye – 316,683 hl (8,360,431 gal) in 1999 – are intensely coloured and have an authentic simplicity, and are strong and fruity. The whites – 12,138 hl (320,443 gal) in 1999 are aromatic. The Côtes de Blaye whites – 2,854 hl (75,346 gal) in 1999 – are mainly light-coloured dry wines that are best served at the beginning of a meal, while the red Premières Côtes go better with meat dishes and cheeses.

Premières Côtes de Blaye

CH. ANGLADE-BELLEVUE

Cuvée Prestige 1998★

■ 5 ha n.c. 30–49 F

Known for its utter reliability, this vineyard keeps faith with its tradition of quality by offering this attractive Cuvée Prestige. Resolutely classic in conception, it marries tannins of good potential to a sober, elegant bouquet of spices, prunes and ripe fruits. Another product of this vineyard, distributed by the local merchants, is the vat-matured **1998 Château Moulin d'Anglade**, which is recommended.

SCEA Mège Frères, Aux Lamberts, 33920 Générac, tel. 05.57.64.73.28, fax 05.57.64.53.90 by appt.

CH. BERTHENON

Cuvée spéciale du Père Henri Elevé en fut de chêne 1998

■Cru bourg. 4 ha 24,000 30–49 F

Simple yet well made, this wine has a somewhat austere finish which nevertheless retains the savours of a round and supple palate in sympathy with its accompanying fruity and floral bouquet.

GFA Henri Ponz, Berthenon, 33390 Saint-Paul-de-Blaye, tel. 05.57.42.52.24, fax 05.57.42.52.24, e-mail chateau-berthenon@epicuria.com ev. day 8am–12 noon 2pm–7pm; Sat. Sun. by appt.

CH. CANTELOUP 1998★

■ 9 ha 15,000 30–49 F

This vineyard has produced an attractive and successful wine. Though already pleasing, with an expressive bouquet, this 1998 wine has good keeping potential thanks to a good-quality tannic structure balancing grape and oak tannins (it spent 13 months in the barrel).

Eric Vezain, Canteloup, 33390 Fours, tel. 05.57.42.13.16, fax 05.57.42.26.28 by appt.

CH. CAP SAINT-MARTIN 1998★

■ 10 ha 36,000 30–49 F

A name that would suit some freighter setting off to seek adventure on the high seas. This wine, too, evokes distant horizons with its bouquet of spice and vanilla. Well put together, as its intense ruby colour suggests, it is supported by fine yet powerful tannins which promise to develop favourably in the future and suggest that the bottle be kept for two years before opening. A second wine from this producer is the recommended **1998 Château Les Rousseaux, Rouge**; vat-matured, it also needs time before it is drunk.

Vignobles Ardoin, 13, rte de Mazerolles, 33390 Saint-Martin-Lacaussade, tel. 05.57.42.91.73, fax 05.57.42.91.73 by appt.

CH. CHANTE ALOUETTE

Elevé en fût de chêne 1998★

■ 21 ha 100,000 50–69 F

A charming name for a wine with an attractive appearance, a deep-garnet colour and a bouquet revealing a good balance between fruit and vanilla. Its well-blended tannins guarantee a keeping potential of two to three years.

SCEA Lorteaud et Filles, Ch. Chante Alouette, 33390 Plassac, tel. 05.57.42.16.38, fax 05.57.42.85.66 by appt.

CH. CHARRON Les Gruppes 1998

■ 6 ha 40,000 50–69 F

Despite specialising in whites, this vineyard produces some interesting reds, like this 1998 wine. It has a bouquet of ripe fruits and a concentrated structure whose tannins will require two or three years to mature.

SCEA Ch. Charron, Vignobles Germain et Associés, 33390 Berson, tel. 05.57.42.66.66, fax 05.57.64.36.20, e-mail bordeaux@vgas.com by appt.

CH. CORPS DE LOUP 1998

■Cru bourg. 7 ha 20,000 30–49 F

Legend has it that in 1589, a wolf hunted and wounded by the military captain de Buch and Henri IV in Médoc managed to escape (at Trompeloup, Pauillac), cross the Gironde and die here. Imbued with tannins and good

aromatic expression (ripe black fruits and spices), this beautiful deep-garnet wine also has stamina and needs to be kept some three years for it to attain harmony.
🔑 Françoise Vidal-Leguénédal, Ch. Corps de Loup, 33390 Anglade, tel. 05.57.64.45.10, fax 05.57.64.45.05 ☒ Y ev. day 10am–12 noon 3pm–6.30pm; Sat. Sun. by appt.

CH. CRUSQUET DE LAGARCIE

1998★★

■Cru bourg.	20 ha	70,000	30–49 F

Made in a two-storey *chai-cuvier* unique in the Blayes district, this wine has a strong personality. It shows itself, first, in its bouquet, where it reveals elegant notes of roasting, and then on the palate, where excellent tannins demonstrate a tangible capacity for good ageing. This rich and subtle 1998 wine keeps all the promises announced by the intense colour, and is a worthy exponent of the family traditions of this venerable vineyard. It has received much praise in the past, and was nominated for a *coup de coeur* before the grand jury this year. A one-star rating is given to another product of the same enterprise, the **1998 Château Le Cone de Taillasson de Lagarcie, Rouge** (30–49F).
🔑 GFA des vignobles Ph. de Lagarcie, Le Crusquet, 33390 Cars, tel. 05.57.42.15.21, fax 05.57.42.90.87 ☒ Y ev. day except Sat. Sun. 9am–12 noon 2pm–6pm

CH. CRUSQUET SABOURIN

Elevé en barrique de chêne 1997

■Cru bourg.	20 ha	120,000	30–49 F

This oak-matured wine bears the imprint of its year, yet nevertheless has good balance and pleasant fruity aromas which make it very likeable. Ready for drinking now.
🔑 Sabourin Frères, 49, Le Bourg, 33390 Cars, tel. 05.57.42.15.27, fax 05.57.42.05.47 ☒ Y by appt.

CH. GAUTHIER

Elevé en fût de chêne 1998

■	9.88 ha	50,000	30–49 F

This property is located at Civrac-de-Blaye with vinification in the co-operative cellar at Pugnac. Oak-aged for six months, the wine has backbone, with robust, ripe tannins which give it good presence on the palate.

The Blayais and Bourgeais appellations

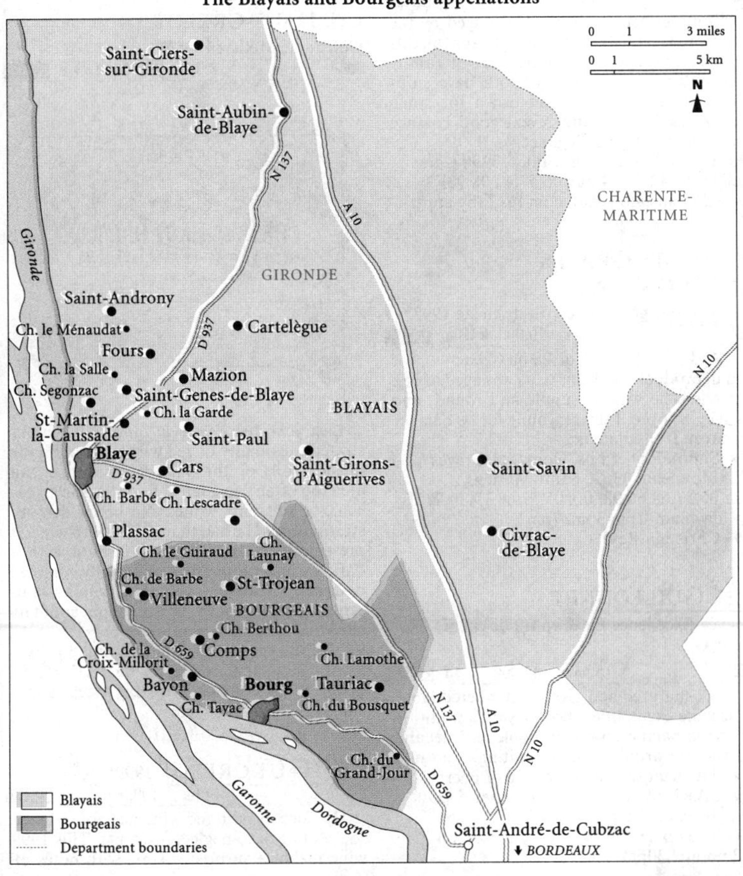

Union de producteurs de Pugnac, Bellevue, 33710 Pugnac, tel. 05.57.68.81.01, fax 05.57.68.83.17, e-mail udep.pugnac@wanadoo.fr by appt.
Michel Massé

CH. DU GRAND BARRAIL

Cuvée Prestige Elevée en fût de chêne neuf 1998★★

n.c. 5,000 50–69 F

The Lafon vineyards make consistently good wine, remaining true to their traditions and reputation with the small production of this wine, which spent 12 months in oak and reached the *coups de coeur* finals before the grand jury. Youthful in appearance, it asserts its personality with a robust structure whose virtues are maximised by well-regulated maturation. A nice wine to keep in the cellar for a while.

Denis Lafon, 1, Bracaille, 33390 Cars, tel. 05.57.42.33.04, fax 05.57.42.08.92, e-mail denislafon@aol.com by appt.

CH. GRAULET Cuvée Prestige 1998★★

n.c. 5,000 50–69 F

Coming from a vineyard managed by the Château Grand-Barrail team (see above), this special vintage bears more than a family resemblance to its cousin. Both have sufficient structure to be laid down for some considerable time, and reveal good balance between power and elegance.

Denis Lafon, 1, Bracaille, 33390 Cars, tel. 05.57.42.33.04, fax 05.57.42.08.92, e-mail denislafon@aol.com by appt.

DOM. DES GRAVES D'ARDONNEAU

Cuvée Prestige Vieilli en fût de chêne 1998★

2.9 ha 20,000 30–49 F

Made on an estate of 28 ha (69 acres), the small production of this wine was aged in oak barrels. The wine is supple and round, and will be enjoyed if drunk young for its balance between fruit and oak.

Simon Rey et Fils, Dom. des Graves d'Ardonneau, 33620 Saint-Mariens, tel. 05.57.68.66.98, fax 05.57.68.19.30 ev. day 8am–1pm 3pm–7pm
Christian Rey

CH. GUILLONNET

Cuvée Excellence Elevé en fût de chêne 1998★

4 ha 45,000 30–49 F

Oak-matured and given a numbered label, this wine exemplifies the vineyard's tradition of good balance. Simple, supple and elegant, it may be drunk without waiting. The jury liked its fruity finish, evocative of cherry.

EARL Menanteau, Guillonnet, 33390 Anglade, tel. 05.57.64.62.97, fax 05.57.64.52.54 ev. day 8.30am–12 noon 2.30pm–7pm

CH. HAUT CANTELOUP 1999

1.5 ha 9,000 20–29 F

This family concern of 33 ha (82 acres) offers an attractive, pale yet lively wine. Besides its simplicity, freshness, richness and good aromatic expression, the wine bears the mark of the Sauvignon variety in its notes of broom and blackcurrant bud. A pleasant aperitif wine.

Sylvain Bordenave, La Palanque, 33390 Fours, tel. 05.57.42.87.12, fax 05.57.42.36.69 ev. day except Sun. 9am–12 noon 2pm–6pm

CH. HAUT DU PEYRAT 1998

8 ha 40,000 20–29 F

This property was substantially restructured after 1985. Today it has 33 ha (82 acres). Although the tannins in this wine are somewhat austere, they will ensure good keeping in the coming two years. Also recommended is the **1998 Clos Lascombes Cuvée Prestige, Rouge** from the same producer (30–49F). Wait a while for the oak to blend in further.

Muriel et Patrick Revaire, 33390 Cars, tel. 05.57.42.20.35, fax 05.57.42.12.84 by appt.

CH. HAUT-GRELOT

Coteau de Methez 1998★★

3.3 ha 20,000 30–49 F

Last year, the *Esprit du Bordeaux* demonstrated the quality of red wines grown on the hillside soils of the Saint-Ciers district, an area too often considered, for viticultural reasons, to suit only whites. No better demonstration could be had than this superb wine. It presents itself in exemplary fashion with a dark-garnet colour and wonderfully complex bouquet. As for the palate, its tannins, concentration and length leave no doubt about its class and keeping potential.

Joël Bonneau, Ch. Haut-Grelot, 33820 Saint-Ciers-sur-Gironde, tel. 05.57.32.65.98, fax 05.57.32.71.81 ev. day except Sun. 8am–12.30pm 2pm–7pm

CH. HAUT GRELOT 1999★

14 ha 100,000 20–29 F

His success with red wine has not induced Joël Bonneau to neglect his white. This 1999 wine makes a surprising start with notes of blackcurrant bud, then goes on to reveal its harmonious character with lovely perfumes of white peaches and a structure of real finesse.

🗝 Joël Bonneau, Ch. Haut-Grelot, 33820 Saint-Ciers-sur-Gironde, tel. 05.57.32.65.98, fax 05.57.32.71.81 ☑ Y ev. day except Sun. 9am–12.30pm 2pm–7pm

HOMMAGE A SAINT VINCENT 1998★★

■ n.c. 20,000 ⏸ 70–99 F

This deep-ruby wine is the first vintage produced, and comes from a selection of the best grapes. It is made by the totally committed Marcillac wine-making team, and is all that might be hoped for. The bouquet marries fruits and oak, and the palate has soft, voluptuous tannins which bear the imprint of Merlot.

🗝 Cave des Hauts de Gironde, La Cafourche, 33860 Marcillac, tel. 05.57.32.48.33, fax 05.57.32.49.63, e-mail contact@tutiac.com ☑ Y by appt.

CH. LA BRAULTERIE DE PEYRAUD

Cuvée Prestige Vieilli en fût de chêne neuf 1998★

■ 2 ha 12,000 ⏸ 30–49 F

Of the property's 36 ha (89 acres), only two are devoted to this Cuvée Prestige. The maturing in oak has been well judged, as is demonstrated by the way in which the vanilla has enriched the grape aromas and by the beautifully blended tannins. The **1999 Blanc** (20–29F) also receives a one-star rating.

🗝 SCA La Braulterie-Morisset, Les Graves, 33390 Berson, tel. 05.57.64.39.51, fax 05.57.64.23.60 ☑ Y ev. day except Sat. Sun. 9am–6pm

CH. LA BRETONNIERE 1998

■ 8 ha 35,000 ▮ 🌡 30–49 F

This vineyard offers a red wine with pleasant, round, supple tannins; these unite with the aromas of ripe grapes to signal the influence of the 70% Merlot variety (30% Cabernet-Sauvignon). The well-balanced and successful **1999 Blanc** is also recommended.

🗝 Stéphane Heurlier, EARL La Bretonnière, 33390 Mazion, tel. 05.57.64.59.23, fax 05.57.64.59.23 ☑ Y ev. day except Sun. 9am–12.30pm 2pm–7pm

CH. LA CROIX DE ROUSSET

Fût de chêne 1998★

■ 0.9 ha 6,000 ⏸ 30–49 F

An estate of about 30 ha (74 acres) here offers an oak-matured wine which reveals its history in a bouquet of spicy notes and hints of grilling. Its intense, purplish colour heralds a well-structured, harmoniously balanced palate complete with a pleasant finish. Keep in the cellar for two to three years.

🗝 EARL La Croix de Rousset, 30, av. du Bourg, 33390 Berson, tel. 05.57.64.32.77, fax 05.57.64.24.29 ☑ Y ev. day except Sun. 9am–12 noon 2pm–6pm

🗝 Alins Frères

CH. LAFON LAMARTINE

Elevé en fût de chêne 1998★★

■ 8.28 ha 8,000 ⏸ 50–69 F

This wine comes from a pure Merlot vineyard, and reveals its origins in the roundness of its tannins, which give it real charm. The bouquet still bears the imprint of its wood ageing, but the oak influence has been well judged and respects the richness and maturity of the fruit. A recommendation goes to the **1998 Cuvée Principale**, 15,000 bottles, which was not kept in oak (30–49F).

🗝 Bruno Lafon, 7, pl. de La Libération, 33710 Cars, tel. 05.57.68.36.84, fax 05.57.68.36.84 ☑ Y ev. day 8am–12 noon 2pm–7pm; cl. 1–15 Aug.

CH. DE LA SALLE 1999★

□ n.c. n.c. ▮ 🌡 30–49 F

This 16th-century château has guest-rooms for wine-lovers, offering a way not only to explore the region, but also to sample a wine which seizes the attention with the intensity and complexity of its aromatic expression and notes of fruits (citrus and white peach). Well-balanced, fresh and harmonious, this 1999 wine will go well with a Pyrenean ewes' cheese.

🗝 SCEA Ch. de La Salle, 33390 Saint-Genès-de-Blaye, tel. 05.57.42.12.15, fax 05.57.42.87.11 ☑ Y by appt.

🗝 Bonnin

CH. LE MENAUDAT

Elevé en fût de chêne 1998★

■ 0.5 ha 4,800 ⏸ 30–49 F

This wine, which comes from a tiny part of this 15-ha (37 acre) cru, is still somewhat restrained. This does not stop it from being an authentic Côtes wine, full of colour and well worth keeping. To these qualities it adds a complex bouquet of ripe fruits and vanilla.

🗝 SCEA F.J.D.N. Cruse, Le Menaudat, 33390 Saint-Androny, tel. 05.56.65.20.08, fax 05.57.65.21.37 ☑ Y ev. day except Sat. Sun. 8am–12 noon 2pm–6pm

CH. LE QUEYROUX 1997★

■ 1.3 ha 7,000 ▮ ⏸ 🌡 70–99 F

A small traditional vineyard where equal portions of Merlot and Cabernet-Sauvignon have yielded a wine harvested on 5 October. Its strong personality, due to robust tannins and a powerful bouquet, promises to evolve very well over time.

🗝 Léandre-Chevalier, 6, Coulon, 33390 Anglade, tel. 05.57.64.46.54, fax 05.57.64.42.41 ☑ Y by appt.

CH. LES BERTRANDS

Cuvée Prestige Elevé en fût de chêne 1999★★

□ 2.5 ha 10,000 30–49 F

This cru, which is a sizeable property of 75 ha (185 acres), has achieved great success with this oak-matured Cuvée Prestige, which has also undergone maceration on the skins. The Sauvignon from which it is made joins its aromas to those of the oak to produce a quality bouquet. The palate is similarly round, fleshy and fresh. Though already pleasant, the wine's bouquet will reach its full potential if left for a couple of years. The **1998 Cuvée Prestige, Rouge** is awarded one star. Keep it for two or three years.

EARL Vignobles Dubois et Fils, Les Bertrands, 33860 Reignac, tel. 05.57.32.40.27, fax 05.57.32.41.36, e-mail chateau.les.bertrands@wanadoo.fr Y by appt.

CH. L'ESCADRE Grande Réserve 1998

■ 2.5 ha 16,000 30–49 F

This vineyard, a fair-sized property of about 30 ha (74 acres), owes its name to a long-distance sea-captain who owned the estate in the 19th century. Simple, supple and round, this Cuvée Prestige is sufficiently well balanced to permit the aromas to express their delicacy without constraint.

Carreau et Fils, Ch. Les Petits Arnauds, 33390 Cars, tel. 05.57.42.36.57, fax 05.57.42.14.02, e-mail scevcarreau@wanadoo.fr Y by appt.

CH. LES GRAVES

Elevé en fût de chêne 1998★★

■ 4 ha 25,000 30–49 F

This very reliable vineyard again offers a superb oak-matured wine whose youthfulness is clear in its ruby colour and mauvish highlights. Although oak is still significantly present on the nose, it does not overwhelm the perfumes of red fruits but forms a coherent whole with them. The same richness can be felt in the structure, which is sustained by harmonious tannins. Be patient before opening this lovely wine, which is crowned by a flavoursome finish somewhere between vanilla and chocolate.

SCEA Pauvif, 33920 Saint-Vivien-de-Blaye, tel. 05.57.42.47.37, fax 05.57.42.55.89 Y by appt.

CH. LES HAUTS DE FONTARABIE

1998

■ 15 ha 110,000 30–49 F

The Vignobles Faure, which also produce Côtes de Bourg, offer a wine with robust tannins which should reach their full potential in one or two years' time.

Vignobles Alain Faure, 33710 Saint-Ciers-de-Canesse, tel. 05.57.42.68.80, fax 05.57.42.68.81, e-mail belair-coubet@wanadoo.fr Y by appt.

CH. LES JONQUEYRES 1997

■ 5.5 ha 30,000 70–99 F

This wine, whose structure is characteristic of the year, has pleasing roundness and finesse. It is made from 90% Merlot, 5% Cabernet Franc and 5% Malbec, grown on blue and grey clay containing fossils. Twelve months in the barrel have given it an elegant note of oak which does not mask the fruit.

Isabelle et Pascal Montaut, Courgeau, 33390 Saint-Paul-de-Blaye, tel. 05.57.42.34.88, fax 05.57.42.93.80 Y by appt.

CH. LES RICARDS 1998

■ 5 ha 30,000 50–69 F

Grown in a vineyard containing a sizeable portion of Malbec (25%), this wine has good tannic presence and a very pleasing general balance.

EARL Chevrier-Loriaud, Les Ricards, 33390 Cars, tel. 05.57.42.91.34, fax 05.57.42.32.87 Y by appt.

CH. LE VIROU

Les Vieilles Vignes 1998★

■ 7 ha 45,500 30–49 F

This large vineyard (about 100 ha/247 acres) has exploited its plots of 30-year-old vines to make an oak-matured wine with rich, concentrated tannins. It is a well-balanced and promising product, and will gain from being kept a while.

Ch. Le Virou, Le Virou, 33920 Saint-Girons-d'Aiguevives, tel. 05.57.42.44.40, fax 05.57.42.44.40

Bessede

CH. DES MATARDS

Cuvée Nathan Elevé en fût de chêne 1998

■ 4 ha 30,000 30–49 F

This oak-matured wine is very true to type and expresses its personality through a structure of round, supple tannins which are in sympathy with the bouquet. The oak supports the aromatic potential of the fruit.

GAEC Terrigeol, 27, av. du Pont-de-la-Grâce, 33820 Saint-Ciers-sur-Gironde, tel. 05.57.32.61.96, fax 05.57.32.79.21 Y by appt.

CH. MONTFOLLET

Vieilles vignes 1998★★

■ 8 ha 35,000 30–49 F

Made from the oldest vines on the estate by the Cave Coopérative du Blayais, this wine has benefited from maturing in barrel. The oak's aromatic contribution (vanilla, coconut, toast) marries perfectly with the mellow, well-blended tannins, which plunge the palate into sweet harmony from start to finish.

Cave coop. du Blayais, 9, Le Piquet, 33390 Cars, tel. 05.57.42.13.15, fax 05.57.42.84.92 Y by appt.

SCEA Raimond

CH. PETIT-BOYER 1998

3 ha 5,300 30–49 F

The bottles are numbered, and the oak-matured wine in them comes from 30-year-old vines. Despite its somewhat discreet aromatic expression, the wine will be appreciated for its balance and roundness. Wait two years and it will go well with jugged hare.

EARL Vignobles Bideau, 5, les Bonnets, 33390 Cars, tel. 05.57.42.19.40, fax 05.57.42.19.40 Y ev. day 10am–12 noon 2pm–6pm

CH. PEYBONHOMME LES TOURS 1998★

■ Cru bourg. 55 ha 300,000 30–49 F

This fair-sized vineyard offers a wine that is anything but discreet. No-one will complain when they discover its bouquet of ripe fruits and structure of round, well-blended tannins that make it a very tasty treat. A one-star rating also goes to the 1998 Cuvée de Prestige (6,000 bottles), entitled **Quintessence de Peybonhomme**, made from older vines (70–99F).

Vignobles Bossuet-Hubert, Ch. Peybonhomme-les-Tours, 33390 Cars, tel. 05.57.42.11.95, fax 05.57.42.38.15, e-mail peybonhomme@terre-net.fr Y by appt.

CH. PEYREDOULLE

Maine Criquau Vieilles vignes 1998★★

■ 4 ha 25,000 50–69 F

This selection of 90% Merlot, grown on limestone, is a credit to its producer. Not only does it have a lovely colour, it remains satisfying throughout the tasting. Well-served by its bouquet, which hints at fresh and dried fruits, it is developing a sturdy tannic structure which needs time to soften but which will eventually be good with strong dishes like game.

Vignobles Bernard Germain, 33390 Berson, tel. 05.57.42.66.66, . fax 05.57.64.36.20 Y by appt.

CH. RICAUD

Elevé en fût de chêne 1998★

■ 15 ha 100,000 30–49 F

Faithful to Blaye traditions with its 10% of Malbec vines, this vineyard offers a well-constructed wine with a lovely dark colour, a bouquet with elegant notes of coffee and a real presence on the palate supported by well-blended tannins.

Vignobles Michel Baudet, Ch. Monconseil Gazin, 33390 Plassac, tel. 05.57.42.16.63, fax 05.57.42.31.22 Y by appt.

CH. ROLAND LA GARDE 1998★★★

■ 6 ha 18,000 100–149 F

Bruno Martin is a brilliant and amiable representative of the rising generation. This wine is proof that the Bordeaux wine-making region has far from exhausted its capacity for steady evolution. The garnet colour, which is almost black with mauvish highlights, suggests the intensity and complexity of the bouquet, in which notes of grilling accompany those of blackcurrant, leather, and spices. The rich tannins, the fleshy and silky body, the fruity aromas of the palate and the long-lasting finish all appealed to the jury. It should be laid down in the cellar for at least five years.

Ch. Roland La Garde, 8, La Garde, 33390 Saint-Seurin-de-Cursac, tel. 05.57.42.32.29, fax 05.57.42.01.86 Y ev. day except Sun. 8am–12 noon 2pm–7pm

Bruno Martin

CH. ROLAND LA GARDE

Prestige 1998★★

■ 10 ha 60,000 50–69 F

Even though it is not the equal of the château's Grand Vin, this Prestige vintage is also very good. Less expressive and complex in its aromas, it still has a rich, fleshy, well-structured palate, guaranteeing good potential for ageing (three to four years).

Ch. Roland La Garde, 8, La Garde, 33390 Saint-Seurin-de-Cursac, tel. 05.57.42.32.29, fax 05.57.42.01.86 Y ev. day except Sun. 8am–12 noon 2pm–7pm

CH. SEGONZAC

Les Vieilles vignes 1997★

■ Cru bourg. 7 ha 50,000 50–69 F

Established by Jean Dupuy, Minister of Agriculture under the Third Republic, this vineyard has taken advantage of some of its vines (41 years old) to offer an old vines (*Vieilles Vignes*) vintage. The delicate bouquet has attractive notes of red fruits and an

excellent palate thanks to a round, full structure. This 1997 wine is a successful alliance of mouth-filling qualities and elegance. It only goes to show that a year which is too roundly decried can come up with pleasant surprises.
SCEA Ch. Segonzac, 39, Segonzac, 33390 Saint-Genès-de-Blaye, tel. 05.57.42.18.16, fax 05.57.42.24.80, e-mail segonzac@chateau-segonzac.com by appt.

CH. TERRE-BLANQUE

Cuvée Noémie 1998*

■ 2 ha 5,000 50–69 F

This year marks the start of the vineyard's new policy on quality, which includes limiting yields, leaf-stripping, green harvests and longer maceration. This wine proves the sense behind the changes. It has very good tannic structure, a fruity bouquet and excellent support from the oak, all of which creates a well-balanced and charming whole. It will gain from being laid down for about two years.
Paul-Emmanuel Boulmé, Ch. Terre-Blanque, 33990 Saint-Genès-de-Blaye, tel. 05.57.42.18.48 by appt.

CH. DES TOURTES

Cuvée Prestige Vinifié en fût de chêne 1999*

□ 4 ha 26,000 50–69 F

A nice family concern of about 50 ha (124 acres), which has a long tradition, this vineyard offers a Cuvée Prestige, a powerful aromatic wine which is at once fresh and round. Wait a year to allow the tannins to blend in.
EARL Raguenot-Lallez, Ch. des Tourtes, 33820 Saint-Caprais-de-Blaye, tel. 05.57.32.65.15, fax 05.57.32.99.38 ev. day 9am–12.30pm 1.30pm–7pm; Sun. by appt.

CH. VOLLAND 1998

■ 1.5 ha 12,000 30–49 F

This wine, distributed by a *négoce*, is simple but friendly and dependable. It has a good tannic constitution and pleasant aromas of red fruits.
Germe, rue de la Cabeyre, 33240 Saint-André-de-Cubzac, tel. 05.57.33.42.42, fax 05.57.43.22.22
GAEC Baillou

Côtes de Bourg

The AOC covers about 3,600 ha (8,892 acres). The Merlot grape variety dominates and the reds – 230,000 hl (6,072,000 gal) in 1999 – often have a distinctively beautiful colour and a marked aroma of soft fruits. They are quite tannic when young so in many cases may need to be kept. There are only a few whites – 1,331 ha (35,138 gal) in 1999 – which are generally dry and have a distinctive nose.

CLOS ALPHONSE DUBREUIL

1997*

■ n.c. 3,500 70–99 F

Though better known for their Blaye wines the Montauts also take good care of this small Bourg estate. This wine proves it with its powerful structure, successfully integrating the oak, which comes through in the toasty aromas. Already pleasant, this wine will improve further if kept.
Isabelle et Pascal Montaut, Courgeau, 33390 Saint-Paul-de-Blaye, tel. 05.57.42.34.88, fax 05.57.42.93.90 by appt.

BAILLI DE BOURG 1998

■ 4.4 ha 35,000 20–29 F

This wine, a brand of the co-operative at Bourg and Tauriac, links an expressive bouquet of ripe fruits to a structure which is good enough to allow the tannins to blend in.
Cave de Bourg-Tauriac, 3, av. des Côtes-de-Bourg, 33710 Tauriac, tel. 05.57.94.07.07, fax 05.57.94.07.00, e-mail cave.bourg-tauriac@wanadoo.fr ev. day except Sun. 8am–12 noon 2pm–6pm

CH. BEGOT 1998

■ n.c. 20,000 30–49 F

This 16-ha (39-acre) family estate offers a 1998 wine with a very intense, almost black colour. Though the finish is a trifle short-lived, the wine leaves the taster with an interesting overall impression, especially the aromas of notes of ripe or stewed fruits and the very concentrated tannins.
Alain Gracia, Ch. Bégot, 33710 Lansac, tel. 05.57.68.42.14, fax 05.57.68.29.90 ev. day 9am–12 noon 2pm–6pm; Sat. Sun. by appt.

CH. DU BOIS DE TAU 1998**

■ 14 ha 100,000 30–49 F

The Faure family are well known for their Côtes de Bourg as well as their Côtes de Blaye and Bordeaux. This year their ambassador is the two-star Bois de Tau. It hides nothing of its richness and complexity, having a bouquet which marries notes as diverse as red fruits, tobacco, clove and other spices to a structure which is full, round, tannic and rich. A lovely wine worth waiting three to five years for.
Vignobles Alain Faure, 33710 Saint-Ciers-de-Canesse, tel. 05.57.42.68.80, fax 05.57.42.68.81, e-mail belair-coubet@wanadoo.fr by appt.

CH. BRULESECAILLE 1998**

■ 20 ha 120,000 50–69 F

This fair-sized estate on limestone-clay and gravelly-clay hillsides is one of the most eliable and reputable vineyards in the appellation. Their 1998 wine's powerful tannic tructure, length and intense bouquet, in which ripe fruit blends happily with toasty notes, show how well-founded their reputaion is.

Jacques Rodet, Brulesécaille, 33710 Tauriac, tel. 05.57.68.40.31, ax 05.57.68.21.27, e-mail brulesecaille@cavesparticulieres.com by appt.

CH. BUJAN 1998*

8.3 ha 60,800 50–69 F

Château Bujan (16.3 ha/40 acres) was taken over by Pascal Méli in 1987. Having come from an entirely different sphere of life, he has taken to his new calling with passion. This 1998 wine is true to the AOC, with its top-quality, rich, velvety tannins working in harmony with the bouquet of ripe fruits and deep colour. Well balanced overall, it will keep well.

Pascal Méli, Ch. Bujan, 33710 Gauriac, tel. 05.57.64.86.56, fax 05.57.64.93.96, e-mail pmeli@alienor.fr ev. day 9am–12 noon 2pm–7pm; Sun. by appt.

CH. CANA-BEAUBOURG 1998*

1.5 ha 10,000 30–49 F

Distributed by the wine trade, this wine is a half-Merlot, half-Cabernet. It is balanced and well put together, with powerful yet well-blended tannins. The pleasant bouquet shows elegant, rounded ripe red fruits.

André Quancard-André, rue de la Cabeyre, 33240 Saint-André-de-Cubzac, tel. 05.57.33.42.42, fax 05.57.43.01.71

GFA Château Cana

CH. COLBERT

Cuvée Prestige Elevé en fût de chêne 1998*

2 ha 10,000 30–49 F

Nothing to do with the Sun King's minister, this wine is named after a ship, the *Colbert*, which ran aground in the estuary and was refloated using a procedure devised by the estate's owner. The château was built in an eclectic style with the reward money. Though still somewhat severe, this 1998 Cuvée Prestige has all the tannic structure, aromatic assets (red fruits) and necessary length to produce a very attractive wine in two or three years' time.

Duwer, Ch. Colbert, 33710 Comps, tel. 05.57.64.95.04, fax 05.57.64.88.41 ev. day 9am–6pm

SCA Château Colbert

CH. CONILH HAUTE-LIBARDE

Vieilli en fût de chêne 1998

vineyard bourg. 5.5 ha 25,000 30–49 F

Grown on a vineyard surrounding an 18th-century charterhouse, this wine has high-quality aromas and is full, round and tannic. It will evolve favourably in the next two to three years.

Dom. Bernier, 33710 Lansac, tel. 05.57.68.46.46, fax 05.57.68.36.09, e-mail maximebernier@berniervins.fr by appt.

CH. CROUTE-CHARLUS 1998*

6 ha 40,000 20–29 F

This is a blend of 45% Merlot, 45% Cabernet-Sauvignon, and 10% Malbec, this last planted on its favourite soil: limestone-clay. The wine has a distinctive aromatic complexity (ripe fruits with chocolate). Still a little severe, it has power and good tannins, both of which suggest waiting two to three years before opening.

Cédric Baudouin, Ch. Croûte-Charlus, 5, rte de Croûte, 33710 Bourg-sur-Gironde, tel. 05.57.68.25.67, fax 05.57.68.25.77 by appt.

CH. ESCALETTE 1998

8 ha 64,000 20–29 F

The vineyard is relatively modest in size, but belongs to a vast family estate. The bouquet of this 1998 wine is delicate, with floral notes, but is sustained by a good structure which allies fruits and tannins. The same producer's **1998 Château Tour Bidou** is also recommended.

SCV villeneuvoise, Ch. de Barbe, 33710 Villeneuve, tel. 05.57.42.64.00, fax 05.57.64.94.10 by appt.

Famille Richard

CH. FALFAS

Elevé en fût de chêne 1998*

22 ha 120,000 50–69 F

This Louis XIII gentleman's residence is one of the loveliest houses in the canton of Bourg. Its very expressive wine has character and robust tannins, and will require laying down for three or four years.

John et Véronique Cochran, Ch. Falfas, 33710 Bayon, tel. 05.57.64.80.41, fax 05.57.64.93.24 by appt.

CH. FOUGAS Maldoror 1998**

5 ha 30,000 70–99 F

A Cuvée Spéciale established in 1993 to express the terroir's originality (sandy colluvium), which it does brilliantly. The colour is a bright and intense ruby-red, which shows the wine's serious ambitions. The bouquet contains a fine touch of oak, which supports the lovely notes of ripe fruits. The structure is superb, long, fleshy and complex, sustained by well-blended, well-covered tannins which provide the best guarantee one can have that this wine will keep in a cellar for four to nine years. Also given a two-star rating is their **1998 Cuvée Prestige du Château Fougas** (30–49F).

🔑 Jean-Yves Béchet, Ch. Fougas, 33710 Lansac, tel. 05.57.68.42.15, fax 05.57.68.28.59, e-mail jean-yves.bechet@wanadoo.fr ☑ Y ev. day except Sat. Sun. 9am–6pm
🔑 GFA Fougas

CH. GALAU 1998★★

■ 6.5 ha 40,000 30–49 F

This wine cares little if it is less well-known than the Château Nodoz from the same producer. The elegant bouquet, with notes of clove and grilled toast, combines with a dense, full and complex structure to form a harmonious whole which will gain in quality from being laid down for several years.

🔑 Magdeleine, Ch. Nodoz, 33710 Tauriac, tel. 05.57.68.41.03, fax 05.57.68.37.34 ☑ Y by appt.

CH. GRAND LAUNAY 1998★

■ 9 ha 47,700 30–49 F

Are good wines necessarily matured in oak? This very successful 1998 wine suggests it is not always so. The presentation is excellent: an intense colour and a pleasant fruity and floral bouquet. The palate is developing a good structure, which is already harmonious but will improve further. Equally well balanced and structured is the one-star **1998 Cuvée Réserve Lion Noir** (50–69F), whose oakiness means it should be kept for four or five years.

🔑 Michel Cosyns, Ch. Grand Launay, 33710 Teuillac, tel. 05.57.64.39.03, fax 05.57.64.39.03 ☑ Y by appt.

CH. GRAVETTES-SAMONAC

Sélection Vieilli en fût de chêne 1998★

■ 7 ha 20,000 50–69 F

A selection of the best *cuvées*, matured in oak and presented in numbered bottles, this wine has excellent ageing potential, judging by its tannic power and length. It needs to be left in the bottle for a further two or three years to allow the oak, which is still very evident, to blend in. The **1998 Cuvée Principale** (yellow label, 30–49F), not oak-matured, is recommended.

🔑 Gérard Giresse, Le Bourg, 33710 Samonac, tel. 05.57.68.21.16, fax 05.57.68.36.43 ☑ Y by appt.

CH. GUERRY

Elevé en fût de chêne 1998★

■ 22 ha 140,000 30–49 F

The personal estate of the *négociant* Bertrand de Rivoyre, this vineyard offers a wine which is still somewhat austere. However, the intense garnet colour, bouquet of ripe fruits and tannic structure indicate that it will be a delightful wine in about three years' time.

🔑 SC du Ch. Guerry, 33710 Tauriac, tel. 05.57.68.20.78, fax 05.57.68.41.31 ☑ Y by appt.
🔑 B. de Rivoyre

CH. GUIRAUD

Vieilli en fût de chêne 1997★

■ 3 ha 20,000 30–49 F

A ten-hectare (24-acre) estate with three hectares (seven acres) devoted to this Cuvée Prestige. There is no need to drink this 1997 wine in a hurry. Long and complex, it has a bouquet showing elegant red fruits, plus a well-constructed palate with a rich, round structure.

🔑 Jacky Bernard, 3, Guiraud, 33710 Saint-Ciers-de-Canesse, tel. 05.57.64.91.02, fax 05.57.64.91.46 ☑ Y by appt.

CH. HAUT-GUIRAUD

Péché du Roy 1998★★

■ 10 ha n.c. 30–49 F

Legend tells that as a child Louis XIV loved the peaches on this estate. Hence the name of this wine, which has spent 12 months in oak. Its temptations are easy to fall for. Behind the good-quality oakiness, lovely aromas of red fruits and spices break through. In time these will get the upper hand, profiting from the robust tannins that will enable this wine to age well.

🔑 EARL Bonnet et Fils, Ch. Haut-Guiraud, 33710 Saint-Ciers-de-Canesse, tel. 05.57.64.91.39, fax 05.57.64.90.95 ☑ Y by appt.

CH. HAUT-LAUNAY

Vieilli en fût de chêne 1997★

■ 9 ha 12,000 30–49 F

An oak-aged wine whose tannic power is typical Côtes de Bourg. Its aromas are pleasantly marked by the Merlot with notes of red fruits, and it has good keeping potential.

🔑 François Noailles, 7, Ch. Haut-Launay, 33710 Teuillac, tel. 05.57.64.34.26, fax 05.57.64.23.16 ☑ Y by appt.

HAUT-MEVRET 1998★★

■ 15 ha 100,000 30–49 F

This wine is a brand of the Pugnac co-operative and makes an excellent contribution to their image. It is as pleasing to the eye as to the nose, where it shows a bouquet of fine red-fruit notes. The palate is powerful, round and well balanced.

🔑 Union de producteurs de Pugnac, Bellevue, 33710 Pugnac, tel. 05.57.68.81.01, fax 05.57.68.83.17, e-mail udep.pugnac@wanadoo.fr ☑ Y by appt.

CH. HAUT-MOUSSEAU 1998★

■ 30 ha 10,000 30–49 F

This wine will not keep its would-be consumers waiting too long. In a year or two it will reveal all its elegance and harmony, with a bouquet of delightful red-fruit notes and a good structure due to well-blended tannins.

ᵒ Dominique Briolais, 1, Ch. Haut-
Mousseau, 33710 Teuillac,
tel. 05.57.64.34.38, fax 05.57.64.31.73 ☑ Y
by appt.

CH. JANSENANT 1998★★

13 ha 85,000 ▮ 🌡 30-49 F

This concern, which both produces and deals in wine, offers a deep garnet wine with an intense bouquet dominated by perfumes of ripe fruits and a full, well-blended and perfectly balanced palate. This is a really enjoyable wine, which will be ready to drink in three or four years' time. A one-star rating goes to **Château Tour Neuve**.

ᵒ Belair Sélection, Coubet, 33710
Villeneuve, tel. 05.57.42.68.80,
fax 05.57.42.68.81 Y by appt.

CH. LABADIE

Vieilli en fût de chêne 1998★★

10.5 ha 84,000 ⓘ 30-49 F

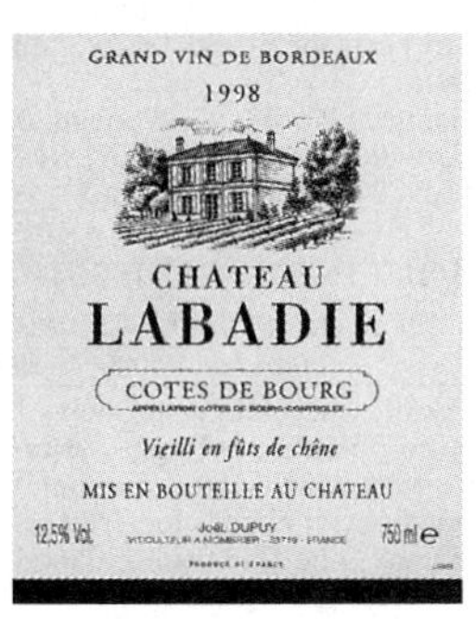

This highly successful 1998 oak-matured wine is a good example of elegance combined with good structure. Its refined character is expressed as much in the delicacy of the fresh fruit and vanilla notes as in the tannins. These do, however, provide a powerful structure guaranteeing that the wine will age well. The tank-matured **1998 Château Laroche Joubert** is a sterling classic of a wine: one star.

ᵒ Joël Dupuy, 1, Cagna, 33710 Mombrier,
tel. 05.57.64.23.84, fax 05.57.64.23.85 ☑ Y
ev. day except Sat. Sun. 9am–12 noon 2pm–
6pm

CH. LA COULEE DE BAYON 1998★

■ 0.36 ha 1,200 ⓘ 30-49 F

Although this recently-established property is tiny, it has vines of a respectable age and diversity (65% Merlot, 20% Malbec and 15% Cabernet-Sauvignon). The interesting result is a wine somewhat marked by oak yet well put together and enhanced by lovely fruit and spice aromas. Wait three or four years before serving with a baron of lamb.

ᵒ Jean-Marc Delhaye, 2, Le Bourg, 33710
Bayon, tel. 05.57.64.81.74 ☑ Y by appt.

CH. LA CROIX-DAVIDS

Prestige 1998★

■ 4.5 ha n.c. ⓘ 30-49 F

This estate of 38 ha (94 acres) has produced a small *cuvée* of 1998 Prestige wine with a fine bouquet and sturdy tannic support. It fulfills the promise of its lovely deep, bright colour. The tannins should blend in with time.

ᵒ SCE Birot Meneuvrier, 57, rue Valentin-
Bernard, 33710 Bourg-sur-Gironde,
tel. 05.57.94.03.94, fax 05.57.94.03.90 ☑ Y
by appt.

CH. LA CROIX DE ROUSSET

Cuvée Séduction 1998★

■ 0.7 ha 4,000 ⓘ 50-69 F

Made from rigorously selected grapes on a property of 30 ha (74 acres), this wine well deserves its name. Though somewhat monopolised by the wood at present, it nonetheless has the youth and necessary structure to form a harmonious blend in three to four years, given the right conditions.

ᵒ EARL La Croix de Rousset, 30, av. du
Bourg, 33390 Berson, tel. 05.57.64.32.77,
fax 05.57.64.24.29 ☑ Y ev. day except Sun.
9am–12 noon 2pm–6pm
ᵒ Alins Frères

LA PETITE CHARDONNE

Elevé en fût de chêne 1998★

■ 5 ha 32,000 ⓘ 30-49 F

This wonderfully successful 1998 oak-aged wine from Louis Marinier's heirs is eloquently elegant, both in the bouquet, where the oak respects the fruits, and on the palate, where the structure is full of freshness and youth.

ᵒ Vignobles Louis Marinier, Dom.
Florimond-La Brède, 33390 Berson,
tel. 05.57.64.39.07, fax 05.57.64.23.27 ☑ Y
ev. day 8am–12 noon 2pm–6pm; Sat. Sun.
by appt.; cl. Aug.

CH. LA TUILIERE 1998★

■ 12.5 ha n.c. ⓘ 30-49 F

How wonderfully adventurous of Philippe Estournet to abandon all else in 1991 in order to buy this vineyard and pursue his enthusiasm for wine. This characterful vintage has a bouquet of fruits, coffee and toastiness, and a dense, promising structure. Ample recompense for his efforts, and a real pleasure for the patient wine-lover who, in four or five years, will be richly rewarded.

ᵒ Les Vignobles Philippe Estournet, Ch.
La Tuilière, 33710 Saint-Ciers-de-Canesse,
tel. 05.57.64.80.90, fax 05.57.64.89.97 ☑ Y
by appt.

CH. LE BREUIL

Cuvée du Dragon Elevé en fût de chêne
1997

■ 1 ha 7,640 ⓘ 30-49 F

A family property of about 20 ha (49 acres), Le Breuil offers this small-scale prestige wine, which is oak-matured and well made, with a good tannic structure and

sympathetic aromas of red fruits and oak. Store in the cellar for three years.
GAEC Doyen et Fils, Ch. Le Breuil, 33710 Bayon-sur-Gironde, tel. 05.57.64.80.10, fax 05.57.64.93.75, e-mail chateau.le.breuil@wanadoo.fr ev. day except Sat. Sun. 9am–12 noon 3pm–7pm

CH. LE CLOS DU NOTAIRE 1998★★

15 ha 90,000 50–69 F

This reliable vineyard is located where the Dordogne and Garonne rivers meet, and contains a small oratory built among the vines. Here it offers a lovely brilliant ruby-coloured wine with an intense, complex bouquet. Its harmony, good balance and length suggest that it will give equal pleasure whether drunk young or kept in a cellar for three or four years.
Roland Charbonnier, SCEA du Ch. Le Clos du Notaire, 33710 Bourg-sur-Gironde, tel. 05.57.68.44.36, fax 05.57.68.32.87, e-mail closnot@club-internet.fr by appt.

LES MOULINS DU HAUT-LANSAC

Séduction Vieilli en fût de chêne 1998★

n.c. 12,000 30–49 F

This small-scale prestige wine has a beautiful deep-red colour. Matured in oak, it is developing an elegant fruity bouquet and good structure, and shows that it will evolve favourably in time.
Les Vignerons de la Cave de Lansac, La Croix, 33710 Lansac, tel. 05.57.68.41.01, fax 05.57.68.21.29 ev. day except Sat. Sun. Mon. 8am–12 noon 2pm–6pm

CH. LES ROCQUES

Cuvée Elégance Elevé en fût de chêne 1998★

1 ha 6,000 50–69 F

This small-scale wine in numbered bottles was matured in new oak and still bears its imprint. In time the fruit will show itself and gain the upper hand thanks to the reserves of tannin and good length.
Feillon Frères et Fils, Ch. Les Rocques, 33710 Saint-Seurin-de-Bourg, tel. 05.57.68.42.82, fax 05.57.68.36.25 ev. day except Sun. 9am–12 noon 2pm–6pm

CH. MACAY Original 1998★

2 ha 12,000 70–99 F

This special wine is certainly original, being made of 70% Cabernet Franc. The grape variety is surely what explains the elegant bouquet of ripe-fruit notes. The well-balanced, round, long palate reveals a good tannic presence, which bodes well for the wine's development. Ready in about three years.
Eric et Bernard Latouche, Ch. Macay, 33710 Samonac, tel. 05.57.68.41.50, fax 05.57.68.35.23 ev. day except Sun. 8am–12 noon 2pm–6pm; Sat. by appt.

CH. MERCIER

Cuvée Prestige 1998★★

11 ha 72,000 30–49 F

A pioneer of sustainable agriculture Philippe Chéty gives masterly proof of his effectiveness with this very successful 1998 wine. A beautiful garnet colour, it achieves real harmony between the fruitiness of the grape and the toastiness derived from well regulated maturation in oak. Patience will be needed, but the result will be of interest.
Philippe et Christophe Chéty, Ch. Mercier, 33710 Saint-Trojan, tel. 05.57.42.66.99, fax 05.57.42.66.96 by appt.

CH. MONTAIGUT

Vieilli et élevé en fût de chêne 1998★★

2.5 ha 17,000 30–49 F

A small property of 12 ha (29 acres), when François de Pardieu bought it in 1975, this vineyard is now a fair-sized 33 ha (82 acres). His 1998 wine has plenty of character, with a fleshy, full, round palate. The bouquet is complex, with notes of fruits, vanilla and roasting. A wine to keep for a year or two, and then serve often.
François de Pardieu, 2, Nodeau, 33710 Saint-Ciers-de-Canesse, tel. 05.57.64.92.49, fax 05.57.64.94.20 by appt.

CH. MOULIN DU GUIET

Vieilli en fût de chêne 1998★★

9.01 ha 50,000 30–49 F

This small wine-making property belonging to the co-operative at Pugnac offers a very attractive 1998 wine. Matured in oak but not excessively oaky, it exudes red-fruit and ripe-grape aromas. The fine, well-balanced, harmonious palate is sustained by fresh, supple tannins to yield a quality wine. Wait two or three years.
Union de producteurs de Pugnac, Bellevue, 33710 Pugnac, tel. 05.57.68.81.01, fax 05.57.68.83.17, e-mail udep.pugnac@wanadoo.fr by appt.
Philippe Blanchard

CH. NODOZ 1998★★

10 ha 60,000 30–49 F

Last year, Nodoz was much praised for its 1997 wine, which was a difficult year, thereby proving his expertise and the quality of his terroir. The 1998 wine only confirms its reputation. The colour is a beautiful garnet, and the bouquet is generous (ripe fruits with notes of grilling and toast). The rich structure makes clear that this wine will need some time in the cellar.
Magdeleine, Ch. Nodoz, 33710 Tauriac, tel. 05.57.68.41.03, fax 05.57.68.37.34 by appt.

CH. PEYCHAUD

Maisonneuve Vieilles vignes 1998★

6 ha 40,000 50–69 F

Matured in the barrel and still rather firm, this wine will need to be laid down. Its tannic

structure gives it excellent potential for evolution, and the bouquet is beginning to come through the oak.
🗝 Vignobles Germain et Associés, Ch. Peyredoulle, 33390 Berson, tel. 05.57.42.66.66, fax 05.57.64.36.20, e-mail bordeaux@vgas.com ☑ Y by appt.

CH. SAUMAN

Cuvée particulière Elevé en fût de chêne 1998

■ 2 ha 12,000 50–69 F

This family property of 24 ha (59 acres) offers a small-quantity Cuvée Particulière of excellent structure. Its concentrated and tannic character means that it should evolve well and be ready in two or three years' time.
🗝 SCEA des Vignobles Braud, Ch. Sauman, 33710 Villeneuve, tel. 05.57.42.16.64, fax 05.57.42.93.00, e-mail chateau.sauman@libertysurf.fr ☑ Y ev. day 10am–1pm 3pm–7pm

CH. VIEUX PLANTIER

Cuvée Collection 1998

■ 0.5 ha 3,000 50–69 F

This small-production prestige wine still bears the imprint of new oak, which makes it a little austere. However, the excellent tannic structure and the intense bouquet mean that it should with time become harmonious and attractive.
🗝 SCEA Ch. Vieux Plantier, La Loge, 33710 Teuillac, tel. 05.57.64.34.60, fax 05.57.64.25.54 ☑ Y ev. day except Sun. 10am–12 noon 2pm–7pm
🗝 Pauvif

Le Libournais

Although there is no 'Appellation Libourne', the Libournais district exists in its own right. While Bordeaux is the major town and the Dordogne is the major waterway, Libourne has a distinct individuality in the Gironde and is not as dependent as other areas on the regional metropolis. It is not unusual for the Libournais to be distinguished from the Bordelais itself, with its less ostentatious architecture, its wine châteaux and wine-merchant quarter. But what sets the Libournais apart most of all is undoubtedly the concentration of the vineyards, which start right on the edge of the town and cover nearly the whole countryside in several communes, producing famous appellations, such as Fronsac, Pomerol and Saint-Émilion, on land that is parcelled up into small or medium-sized properties. Large properties, like those of the Médoc, or the wide expanses characteristic of Aquitaine, are practically unknown here.

The vineyard's individuality also comes from the varieties of grape grown: Merlot predominates, giving fruitiness and finesse to the wines, which are able to age well, even if they keep for less time than the appellations made mainly from Cabernet-Sauvignon. On the other hand, they can be drunk a little sooner and accompany a variety of foods (red and white meat, cheeses and even certain fish, such as lamprey).

Canon-Fronsac and Fronsac

The Fronsadais is bounded by the Dordogne and Isle rivers. The beautiful countryside is very divided up and has two hills, which offer magnificent views over the area. The region is a strategic point and under Charlemagne a sturdy fortress was built there; during the following centuries the area continued to play an important role in the history of France. Nowadays there is no trace of the original fortress, but the Fronsadais has some beautiful churches and numerous châteaux. Wine-growing is an ancient activity, and the vineyards, which cover six communes, produce individual wines that are balanced and full-bodied, while also being fine and distinguished. All the communes are entitled to use the Appellation Fronsac – 46,670 hl (1,232,088 gal) in 1999 – but of the wines produced on the limestone and clay slopes on a footing of opaline lime, only Fronsac and Saint-Michel-de-Fronsac are entitled to use the Appellation Canon-Fronsac – 16,607 hl (438,425 gal) in 1999.

Canon-Fronsac

CH. BARRABAQUE Prestige 1997★★

■ 4 ha 25,000 70-99 F

88 |89| |90| 91 92 |94|(95)(96) **97**

This vineyard surely leads the appellation. Its 1997 wine is a dense and brilliant ruby colour. The bouquet is intense and complex, evocative of ripe fruit, vanilla and roasted coffee. But it is the palate that shows all the wine's potential, with its powerful, ripe, well-balanced tannins, which are developing with great length. A bottle to open in two years' time and keep till 2005. You can depend on this wine: a *coup de coeur.*

SCEA Noël Père et Fils, Ch. Barrabaque, 33126 Fronsac, tel. 05.57.55.09.09, fax 05.57.55.09.00, e-mail chateaubarrabaque@yahoo.fr by appt.

CH. CAPET BEGAUD 1997

■ 4 ha 15,000 50-69 F

This 1997 wine, with its deep colour and ruby highlights, has a complex bouquet of caramel and ripe fruits and a fresh, mellow tannic structure with a highly aromatic finish. Drink over the next three years.

GFA Vignobles Alain Roux, Ch. Coustolle, 33126 Fronsac, tel. 05.57.51.31.25, fax 05.57.74.00.32 by appt.

CH. CASSAGNE HAUT-CANON La Truffière 1997★

■ 13 ha 36,000 70-99 F

86 88 |89| 90 91 **|93|** 94 96 97

This wine is called 'La Truffière' after the presence of a productive truffle-ground in the heart of the vineyard. A very reputable wine, its 1997 version is highly successful. The deep garnet colour, the intense aromas of spices, red fruits and vanilla delighted the jury. The first impressions of the supple, flavoursome tannins are powerful and elegant. Two to three years' storage should enable the finish to lose its youthful austerity.

Jean-Jacques Dubois, Ch. Cassagne Haut-Canon, 33126 Saint-Michel-de-Fronsac, tel. 05.57.51.63.98, fax 05.57.51.62.20 by appt.

CLOS SAINT-MICHEL 1997

■ 0.46 ha 2,500 50-69 F

Grown in a tiny vineyard (46 ares/1 acre), this 1997 wine deserves to be recommended for its aromatic freshness (cherry and spices) and its good tannic balance. A nice wine to drink now, but may be kept for two or three years.

Marie-Christine Aguerre, 1, Lariveau, 33126 Saint-Michel-de-Fronsac, tel. 05.57.24.95.81 ev. day 5pm–8pm

CH. COUSTOLLE 1997★

■ 20 ha 60,000 50-69 F

|90| 93 94 |95| 96 |97|

This 1997 Canon-Fronsac contains, in addition to the basic Merlot, 30% Cabernet and 5% Malbec, which have given it a particular character: aromas of crystallised fruits, hazelnut and grilling predominate. The palate is velvety, silky and well-balanced. Although this wine is capable of giving much pleasure now, it should be opened in two to five years' time.

GFA Vignobles Alain Roux, Ch. Coustolle, 33126 Fronsac, tel. 05.57.51.31.25, fax 05.57.74.00.32 by appt.

CH. HAUT BALLET 1997

■ 3 ha 16,000 50-69 F

This wine is almost exclusively a Merlot (95%). Its distinctiveness is essentially a matter of the palate, where the elegant, velvety tannins harmonise with a discreet vanilla oakiness. A pleasant wine to drink in one to three years' time.

Fournial, Ch. Haut Ballet, 33126 Saint-Michel-de-Fronsac, tel. 05.57.68.00.56, fax 05.57.68.03.22 by appt.

CH. HAUT-MAZERIS 1997

■ 5.97 ha 44,000 50-69 F

This 1997 wine is ruby in colour with bright highlights. It has intense fruity aromas and powerful tannins, which are a little harsh in the finish. Good balance should be achieved in one to three years' time.

SCEA de Haut-Mazeris, Ch. Haut-Mazeris, 33126 Saint-Michel-de-Fronsac, tel. 05.57.24.98.14, fax 05.57.24.91.07 by appt.

LA FLEUR CAILLEAU 43 1997★

■ n.c. 1,200 200-249 F

This special *cuvée* is a limited edition of only 1,200 bottles and the product of organic

viticulture. It spent 18 months in the barrel and has a deep colour. The intense aromas evoke very ripe grapes and coffee. Clear and persistent tannins continue to predominate, and it will be another two to six years before the bottle will be ready. On the other hand, the classic **1997 Château La Fleur Cailleau** (70–99F), recommended for its suppleness, can be enjoyed straight away.
Paul et Pascale Barre, La Grave, 33126 Fronsac, tel. 05.57.51.31.11, fax 05.57.25.08.61, e-mail p.p.barre@wanadoo.fr by appt.

CH. LAMARCHE CANON

Candelaire 1997

3 ha 20,000 50–69 F

|94| 95 |96| |97|

Located on the eastern slope of Canon, this château matures its wines in 400-l casks. This wine deserves a recommendation for the quality of its red-fruit aromas and vanilla oakiness. The suppleness and harmony of the palate make it a pleasant wine to drink now and for the next two to three years.
Eric Julien, Ch. Lamarche, 33126 Fronsac, tel. 05.57.51.28.13, fax 05.57.51.28.13, e-mail bordeaux@vgas.com ev. day except Sun. 8am–12 noon 2pm–6pm

CH. LARCHEVESQUE 1997

3.62 ha 14,000 50–69 F

The distinguishing feature of this 1997 wine is the quality of its fruit aromas (crystallised cherry) and the tannic freshness of the palate. The round finish indicates that the wine should be drunk straight away.
SARL Cave de Larchevesque, 1, rue Guadet, 33330 Saint-Emilion, tel. 05.57.24.67.78, fax 05.57.24.71.31 ev. day 10am–12.30pm 1.30pm–7pm
Viaud

CH. MAZERIS 1997★

13 ha 60,000 50–69 F

92 94 95 |96| 97

This château, located on limestone-clay sandstone, has been tended by the same family since 1769. Their long experience has enabled them to produce a very fruity 1997 wine, whose round, supple tannins are now perfectly harmonious. The special *cuvée* **1997 La Part des Anges** is recommended. It will delight lovers of oaky, spicy wines. These wines are to be drunk in two to five years' time.
EARL de Cournuaud, Ch. Mazeris, 33126 Saint-Michel-de-Fronsac, tel. 05.57.24.96.93, fax 05.57.24.98.25 by appt.

CH. MAZERIS-BELLEVUE 1997

10 ha 60,000 50–69 F

This vineyard has been in the same family for more than a hundred years. It offers a 1997 wine with a deep garnet colour, complex aromas of spices and jam, and tannins which are obvious yet quite subtle. A wine to enjoy over the next three years.
Jacques Bussier, Ch. Mazeris Bellevue, 33126 Saint-Michel-de-Fronsac, tel. 05.57.24.98.19, fax 05.57.24.98.19, e-mail ch-mageris-bellevue@wanadoo.fr ev. day except Sun. 8am–12 noon 2pm–6pm

CH. MOULIN PEY-LABRIE 1997★

6.5 ha 30,000 70–99 F

88 **|89|** |90|91 92 93 **|94| 95 96** 97

This château takes its name from a very old mill on the top of a hill which overlooks the entire appellation. This is a good-quality wine with a deep, almost black colour and a bouquet evoking grilled oak, black fruits and pepper. The rich, full tannins are evolving well and strongly, though the oak predominates. A bottle to open in two to five years.

The Libournais appellations

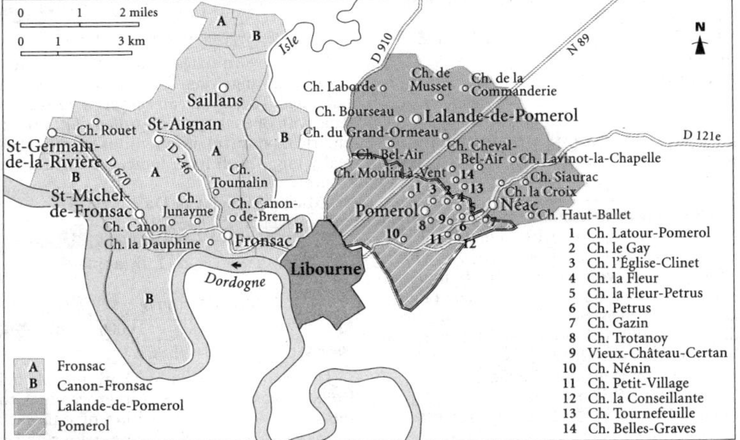

🔑 B. et G. Hubau, Ch. Moulin Pey-Labrie, 33126 Fronsac, tel. 05.57.51.14.37, fax 05.57.51.53.45 ☑ 🍷 by appt.

CH. ROC DE CANON 1997

■ 4 ha 18,000 50–69 F

This 1997 wine will appeal to lovers of powerful wines typical of the region. It has a developed bouquet of game, leather and menthol, together with a full, well-balanced structure. Open before 2002.

🔑 Françoise Roux, Bordeaux Rive droite, 33500 Libourne, tel. 05.57.55.00.50, fax 05.57.55.00.56 ☑

CH. ROULLET 1997*

■ 2.61 ha 7,500 50–69 F

This small vineyard of scarcely more than two hectares (five acres) has gone from father to son through four generations. The 1997 wine is purple in colour with ruby highlights, and has a developing bouquet of smoke, coffee and leather. Its tannins are rich, fleshy and complex. The very oaky finish indicates that keeping for two to four years will make it more harmonious. The **1997 Haut-Gros Bonnet**, named after a property in the commune of Saint-Michel-de-Fronsac leased and run by the Dorneau family for the past 23 years, is similarly given a one-star rating.

🔑 SCEA Dorneau, Ch. La Croix, 33126 Fronsac, tel. 05.57.51.31.28, fax 05.57.74.08.88, e-mail sceadorneau@wanadoo.fr ☑ 🍷 by appt.

CH. SAINT-BERNARD 1997*

■ 0.26 ha 2,500 30–49 F

This 100% Merlot from a family-run château is a successful 1997 wine. Dense and deep in colour, it has delicate, fruity aromas which, though still dominated by strong oakiness, herald a palate with supple, generous and fairly persistent tannins. A wine to drink for its aromatic quality and freshness.

🔑 Jean Gaucher, La Matheline, 33126 Saint-Michel-de-Fronsac, tel. 05.57.24.90.24, fax 05.57.24.90.24 ☑ 🍷 by appt.

🔑 Indivision Gaucher

CH. VRAI CANON BOUCHE 1997*

■ 8 ha 40,000 70–99 F

|90| 91 |94| 95 96 97

This vineyard is located on the hill at Canon, above quarries which hid members of the Resistance in the last war. Today's wine is a 90% Merlot, with a burgeoning bouquet of ripe fruits, roasting and pepper. The tannins are strong when they hit the palate, then develop subtly with good persistence. It will be ready in one to three years.

🔑 Françoise Roux, Ch. Lagüe, 33126 Fronsac, tel. 05.57.51.24.68, fax 05.57.25.98.67 ☑ 🍷 ev. day except Sat. Sun. 9am–12.15 2pm–6pm

Fronsac

CH. BARRAIL CHEVROL 1997

■ 6 ha 46,000 30–49 F

A selection proposed by the merchants Yvon Mau and chosen by Jean-Claude Jambon, the 1998 world champion wine-waiter. This 1997 wine has a fruity bouquet with musky notes and a fresh, well-balanced tannic structure, though the finish is rather thin. A wine to be drunk in its youth, within the next two years.

🔑 SA Yvon Mau, B.P. 1, 33193 Gironde-sur-Dropt Cedex, tel. 05.56.61.54.54, fax 05.56.61.54.61 🍷 by appt.

🔑 Dorneau

CH. BEAU SITE DE LA TOUR 1997

■ 10.5 ha 70,000 30–49 F

This 1997 wine's aromatic elegance, round palate and concentrated, harmonious tannic structure will appeal to many consumers. It is a no-nonsense, authentic product respectful of its terroir. It will be at its best in two to three years' time.

🔑 De La Tour du Fayet Frères, Ch. Gueyrot, 33330 Saint-Emilion, tel. 05.57.24.72.08, fax 05.57.24.67.51 ☑ 🍷 by appt.

CLOS DU ROY Cuvée Arthur 1997*

■ 5 ha 30,000 50–69 F

This dark-coloured Cuvée Arthur comes from old vines: Merlot (90%) and Cabernet Franc (10%). The nose of red fruits melts into oaky notes and supple, spicy tannins which provide a sufficiently powerful finish to recall the spicy aromas. A wine to drink over the next five years.

🔑 Philippe Hermouet, Clos du Roy, 33141 Saillans, tel. 05.57.55.07.41, fax 05.57.55.07.45, e-mail hermouetclosduroy@wanadoo.fr ☑ 🍷 by appt.

CH. DALEM 1997*

■ 10 ha 58,000 100–149 F

82 (85) 86 |88| |89| |90| 91 92 |93| 94 95 96 97

This vineyard dates from 1610. The present-day tasting room is part of the period buildings. There you can sample a very good wine with open aromas of grilled oak, vanilla and rich, powerful, harmonious tannins. The really long finish is an indication of a great future.

🔑 Michel Rullier, Ch. Dalem, 33141 Saillans, tel. 05.57.84.34.18, fax 05.57.74.39.85, e-mail château-dalem@wanadoo.fr ☑ 🍷 by appt.

CH. FONTENIL 1997*

■ 9 ha 55,000 70–99 F

|88| |89| |90| 92 |93| |94| **95** 96 |97|

This château, owned by Dany and Michel Rolland, has recently seen improvements to the winery and the acquisition of oak vats. This 1997 wine has an intense colour and a

burgeoning bouquet of prune, fig and flowers. The palate is firm, well-balanced and structured. A wine to enjoy over the next three years.
🔑 Michel et Dany Rolland, Catusseau, 33500 Pomerol, tel. 05.57.51.23.05, fax 05.57.51.66.08 ☑

HAUT-CARLES 1997★★★

■ 5 ha 25,000 ⏸ 100–149 F

GRAND VIN DE BORDEAUX
FRONSAC
HAUT-CARLES
1997
Mis en bouteille à la propriété
APPELLATION FRONSAC CONTRÔLÉE
G.F.A. Château de Carles, 33141 Saillans, Gironde, France - A. Chastenet, S. Droulers, gérants

Five hectares (12 acres) of the Château de Carles have been rigorously selected for this top-of-the-range 1997 vintage, which is a 99% Merlot. The superb colour is a brilliant deep purple. The jury was attracted by its intense and complex aromas, comprising fruits of the forest, coffee, liquorice and vanilla. The palate is intensely pleasurable; the mature, fresh tannins are in perfect balance due to well-judged maturation in oak. A velvet texture, red fruits and great persistence characterise the finish. This wine will definitely need two to eight years of keeping. The principal wine, the **1997 Château de Carles** is recommended (30–49F). It will help us to be patient while we wait for its more prestigious fellow.
🔑 SCEV du Ch. de Carles, Ch. de Carles, 33141 Saillans, tel. 05.57.84.32.03, fax 05.57.84.31.91, e-mail droulers.cs@aol.fr ☑ Y by appt.

CH. HAUT LARIVEAU 1997

■ 7.9 ha 30,000 ⏸ 70–99 F

89 |90| 91 92 |**93**| |94| 95 96 |97|

This wine comes exclusively from old Merlot vines planted on gravelly clay. It has plentiful aromas of grilled oak, coconut and spices. Its supple, well-balanced tannic structure evolves through a firm finish of silky persistence. A wine to drink within the next three years.
🔑 B. et G. Hubau, Ch. Haut Lariveau, 33126 Saint-Michel-de-Fronsac, tel. 05.57.51.14.37, fax 05.57.51.53.45 ☑ Y by appt.

CH. HAUT-MAZERIS 1997

■ 4.94 ha 38,000 ▮ ⏸ 50–69 F

This 1997 wine has a brilliant garnet colour, a burgeoning bouquet of spices, a creamy, well-balanced tannic structure, and a somewhat uncomplicated finish. Ready to drink now or keep for two to three years.
🔑 SCEA de Haut-Mazeris, Ch. Haut-Mazeris, 33126 Saint-Michel-de-Fronsac, tel. 05.57.24.98.14, fax 05.57.24.91.07 Y by appt.

CH. JEANDEMAN 1997

■ 6 ha 35,000 ▮ 🌡 30–49 F

Located at the furthest point of the Coteaux de Fronsac, this château offers a wine with aromas that are still discreet but which has an attractive, supple and fruity tannic structure. A wine to drink over the next three years.
🔑 SCEV Roy-Trocard, Ch. Jeandeman, 33126 Fronsac, tel. 05.57.74.30.52, fax 05.57.74.39.96 ☑ Y by appt.

CH. JEANROUSSE

Elevé en fût de chêne 1997

■ 14.25 ha 59,800 ▮ ⏸ 🌡 30–49 F

This 1997 wine comes from the co-operative at Lugon, which has proved itself before. The very fruity aromas (cherry and strawberry) inform both nose and palate, where they balance the delicately oaky flavours. A friendly wine that can be drunk now.
🔑 Union de producteurs de Lugon, 6, rue Louis-Pasteur, 33240 Lugon, tel. 05.57.55.00.88, fax 05.57.84.83.16 ☑ Y by appt.

CH. LA BRANDE 1997★★

■ 5 ha 30,000 ▮ ⏸ 🌡 50–69 F

This large property of 22 ha (54 acres), whose history goes back to the 18th century, offers a 1997 wine with a dense, almost black colour. The bouquet of prunes, ripe fruits and leather is highly expressive. The supple, authentic tannins evolve with great maturity and much charm. The particularly well-balanced finish bodes well for good ageing (three to five years minimum).
🔑 Vignobles Béraud, La Brande, 33141 Saillans, tel. 05.57.74.36.38, fax 05.57.74.38.46 ☑ Y ev. day 9am–12.30pm 2pm–7pm; groups by appt.
🔑 Pierre Béraud

CH. LA GARDE

Elevé en fût de chêne 1997

■ 2.71 ha 4,800 ⏸ 30–49 F

This 1997 wine is evidence of the first year under new owners. It has a deep-garnet colour, an intense bouquet of fruits and spices, and supple, uncomplicated yet harmonious tannins. Drink over the next three years.
🔑 M. et Mme Ronald Wilmot, La Fontenelle, 33240 Lugon, tel. 05.57.84.82.13, fax 05.57.84.84.17 ☑ Y by appt.

CH. DE LA HUSTE 1997★

■ 5 ha 30,000 ▮ ⏸ 🌡 70–99 F

This property has belonged to the same family since the middle of the 19th century, and its 95% Merlot vineyard produces excellent wines. This 1997 version is black in colour, with a nose of ripe fruits melting into oaky, vanilla notes. The tannic structure is

honest and strong, demonstrating an evolution of some firmness. Wait at least two to three years before opening.
🔑 Michel Rullier, Ch. de la Huste, 33141 Saillans, tel. 05.57.84.34.18, fax 05.57.74.39.85, e-mail chateau-dalem@wanadoo.fr ☑ Y by appt.

CH. DE LA RIVIERE 1997★

■ 56 ha 215,000 70–99 F

The splendid, much rebuilt château is one of the most interesting estates in the Fronsac district. All the efforts of the last few years to upgrade quality are now beginning to bear fruit, as can be seen in this 1997 wine, with its expressive nose (leather and red fruits). The creamy, well-balanced tannins are still very young. It is imperative that this wine be kept two to three years before drinking.
🔑 SA Ch. de La Rivière, B.P. 50, 33126 Fronsac, tel. 05.57.55.56.56, fax 05.57.24.94.39 ☑ Y by appt.
🔑 Jean Leprince

CH. LAROCHE PIPEAU

Elevé en fût de chêne 1997

■ 3.88 ha 25,000 70–99 F

This wine has been aged in oak in quarries occupying 10,000 m^2 (12,000 sq yd). The subtlety of its fruity aromas are well balanced with the supple, round, delicately oaky tannins. An enjoyable wine, ready to drink now.
🔑 Jean Grima, Ch. Laroche Pipeau, 33126 La Rivière, tel. 05.57.24.90.69, fax 05.57.24.90.61, e-mail jean.grima@wanadoo.fr ☑ Y by appt.

CH. LA ROUSSELLE 1997

■ 3.06 ha 14,500 70–99 F

|88| |89| |90| 91 92 |93| 94 95 96 97

This estate was saved from dereliction in 1972. The winery has been restored, the vines replanted (they are now 24 years old). The Davaus offer a round, fruity 1997 wine, needing to be drunk within the next three years.
🔑 Jacques et Viviane Davau, Ch. La Rousselle, 33126 La Rivière, tel. 05.57.24.96.73, fax 05.57.24.91.05 ☑ Y by appt.

CH. LA VIEILLE CROIX

Cuvée DM 1997★

■ 5 ha 30,000 50–69 F

This château has seen eight successive generations of single daughters, and today another young woman has taken over direction of the vineyard. The wine is very successful: a deep-garnet colour; a bouquet of red fruits, leather and vanilla; mellow, tender tannins still dominated by toasted oak notes, and attractive length. A wine to drink now or keep for three to five years.
🔑 SCEA de La Vieille Croix, La Croix, 33141 Saillans, tel. 05.57.74.30.50, fax 05.57.84.30.96 ☑ Y by appt.
🔑 Isabelle Dupuy

CH. LA VIEILLE CURE 1997★★

■ 20 ha 60,000 70–99 F

|88| |89| |90| 91 92 **|93| |94| 95** 96 **97**

This château is ideally placed on limestone-clay slopes Every year it produces excellent wines, as this deep garnet-coloured 1997 wine proves. It has perfumes of roasted oak, game and tobacco. The palate has obvious structure, equipped with powerful, rich, very elegant tannins. The wine-maker has got the best out of the grapes. An excellent wine that will be perfect in two to six years.
🔑 SNC Ch. La Vieille Cure, 1, Coutreau, 33141 Saillans, tel. 05.57.84.32.05, fax 05.57.74.39.83, e-mail vieillecur@aol.com Y by appt.
🔑 Ferenbach

CH. LES ROCHES DE FERRAND

Elevé en fût de chêne 1997★

■ 5 ha 30,000 50–69 F

Located on classic limestone-clay, this estate has the sort of modern equipment required to produce good-quality wines. This 1997 vintage, with its superb dark-garnet colour has fruity (blackberry) and spicy aromas accompanying a powerful, well-balanced and structured palate, which will need two to three years in the cellar to attain harmony. A second wine, the **1997 Château Vray Houchat**, is recommended for its suppleness and freshness. It is ready to drink now (30–49F)
🔑 Rémy Rousselot, Ch. Les Roches de Ferrand, Hulmat, 33126 Saint-Aignan, tel. 05.57.24.95.16, fax 05.57.24.91.44 ☑ Y by appt.

CH. LES TROIS CROIX 1997★★

■ 12.2 ha 80,000 100–149 F

This château, bought by Patrick Léon in 1995, continues its excellent progress with a magnificent 1997 wine. The purple colour shines and glistens. The intense, complex bouquet evokes crystallised fruits, coffee, liquorice and vanilla. The tannins open on the palate with fullness and develop with great maturity, harmony and good length. This wine is a credit to its appellation and will be best appreciated in two to eight years' time.
🔑 Famille Patrick Léon, Ch. Les Trois Croix, 33126 Fronsac, tel. 05.57.84.32.09, fax 05.57.84.34.03 ☑ Y by appt.

CH. MAGONDEAU Beausite 1997

■ n.c. 35,000 50–69 F

This château offers a garnet-coloured 1997 wine with a developing bouquet of ripe fruits and toasted oak. The tannins on the palate are round and well-blended with a very pleasant finish. A wine that can be drunk immediately.

SCEV Ch. Magondeau, 1, le Port-de-Saillans, 33141 Saillans, tel. 05.57.84.32.02, fax 05.57.84.39.51 by appt.

CH. MAYNE-VIEIL

Cuvée Aliénor 1997

■ 3 ha 18,500 50–69 F

This Cuvée Aliénor, a selection from three hectares (seven acres) of grapes out of the 45 ha (111 acres) forming the estate, is a pure Merlot. The colour is a quite vivid ruby, the nose has fruit and spice aromas, and the palate has round, delicately oaky tannins providing a decent degree of persistence. Keep for one to two years.

SCEA du Mayne-Vieil, 33133 Galgon, tel. 05.57.74.30.06, fax 05.57.84.39.33, e-mail maynevieil@aol.com by appt.

Famille Seze

CH. MEYNEY 1997★★

■ 7.58 ha 53,300 50–69 F

Made from 100% Merlot, this lovely wine greatly appealed to the jury as much for its intense purple colour and cherry highlights as for its aromas of black fruits, pepper, vanilla and toast. The fullness and generosity of the well-extracted tannins with their delightful oakiness are no less important. Already a harmonious wine, it will reach its full potential if left to age for two to three years.

Vignobles Olivier Devigne, Ch. La Cabanelle, 33220 Port-Sainte-Foy, tel. 05.53.61.63.41, fax 05.53.22.45.59 by appt.

CH. MOULIN HAUT-LAROQUE 1997★★

■ 13 ha n.c. 70–99 F

86 |**88**|(89)|**90**| **91 92** |93| |94| 95 **96 97**

This château has been in the same family since the 16th century, which is a great rarity in Bordeaux, and its owners have built upon many years of expertise both in the vineyard and in the cellar. Yet again its wine is one of the best in the appellation. The intense colour has black highlights. The nose has powerful aromas of vanilla, smoke, kirsch and ripe fruits. The palate is equipped with well-blended, full tannins sustained by a well-judged amount of oak. The finish is very subtle and has good length, boding well for the future. Open in three to eight years' time.

Jean-Noël Hervé, Ch. Cardeneau, 33141 Saillans, tel. 05.57.84.32.07, fax 05.57.84.31.84, e-mail hervejnoel@aol.com by appt.

CH. PETRARQUE 1997★★

■ 1.5 ha n.c. 50–69 F

This tiny vineyard, established on a gravel-clay soil and named after the 14th-century Italian poet who celebrated Laura, has a reputation for quality. This sumptuous purple, almost black 1997 wine has a developing bouquet of liquorice, ripe fruits, vanilla and roasted coffee, which informs the entire experience. The tannic structure starts on a mellow note, then evolves with good balance, subtlety and fruity aromas. The wine will be at its best when it has been cellared for two or three years.

GFA Chabiran, 1, av. de la Mairie, 33500 Néac, tel. 05.57.25.93.79, fax 05.57.25.93.44 by appt.

CH. PUY GUILHEM 1997★★

■ 4 ha 20,000 50–69 F

This vineyard dates from the 18th century and last changed hands in 1995. The new policy is beginning to bear fruit, as this deep, almost black 1997 wine testifies. The nose is powerfully perfumed with prune, cocoa, spices and vanilla. The palate contains full-bodied, ripe, powerful tannins, which evolve harmoniously and highly aromatically through the finish. A wine at the top of the appellation in what was a difficult year. Drink in two to five or six years' time. The same producer's **1997 Château Puy-Saint-Vincent**, oak-matured for four months, is recommended and may be drunk now.

SCEA Ch. Puy Guilhem, 33141 Saillans, tel. 05.57.84.32.08, fax 05.57.74.36.45 by appt.

M. et Mme J.-F. Enixon

CH. RENARD MONDESIR 1997★

■ 7 ha 21,000 70–99 F

|**93**| |94| |95| 96 |97|

This château is distinguished for the great diversity of its soils: fox-coloured sands (hence probably the name of the vineyard) and limestone-clay. The 1997 wine is a brilliant purple, and has an expressive bouquet of red fruits, spices and roasted coffee. The palate has perfect balance, with powerful, rich tannins which develop lightly at the finish. Ready to drink, but could equally be kept for two to five years.

Xavier Chassagnoux, Ch. Renard-Mondésir, 33126 La Rivière, tel. 05.57.24.96.37, fax 05.57.24.90.18, e-mail chassag@quaternet.fr by appt.

CH. REYNAUD 1997

■ 1.86 ha 6,500 50–69 F

This small-scale vineyard was established in 1990. Marie-Christine Aguerre offers guest-house accommodation as well as this bright, dense 1997 wine, with its delicate, fresh and fruity perfumes. On the palate, this Fronsac opens out with honesty and power and finishes with persistence and authenticity. A very genuine wine, best enjoyed in two to five years' time.

Marie-Christine Aguerre, 1, Lariveau, 33126 Saint-Michel-de-Fronsac, tel. 05.57.24.95.81 ev. day 5pm–8pm

CH. RICHELIEU
Vieilli en fût de chêne 1997★

■ n.c. 25,000 50–69 F

This charterhouse was built in 1630 and belonged to Maréchal de Richelieu, nephew to the cardinal and known at court as 'Fronsac'. It was bought in 1996 by a couple of Parisian industrialists, who have done everything to produce wines of quality. They offer a 1997 wine with an intense garnet colour and a bouquet of black fruits, roasted coffee and prune. The supple and generous tannic structure are in perfect accord with the well-judged maturation in oak. Wait two or three years to drink this excellent wine.

EARL Ch. Richelieu, 1, chem. du Tertre, 33126 Fronsac, tel. 05.57.51.13.94, fax 05.57.51.13.94 Y ev. day 9.30am–12.30pm 2pm–6pm

CH. ROUMAGNAC LA MARECHALE 1997

■ n.c. 23,000 30–49 F

93 |94| 95 96 97

This château, which commands a magnificent view over the Dordogne, offers a delicate, fruity 1997 wine with spicy, musky notes. The palate is fleshy and on the powerful side, but the finish is still austere and calls for a year or two more in the cellar.

SCEA Pierre Dumeynieu, Roumagnac, 33126 La Rivière, tel. 05.57.24.98.48, fax 05.57.24.90.44 Y by appt.

CH. TOUR DU MOULIN 1997★

■ 7 ha 25,000 50–69 F

This family château offers wines of quality every year. This year is no exception with a most promising bright, garnet-coloured 1997 wine. It has a complex bouquet of blackcurrant, blackberry and vanilla, and a rich, fleshy structure. Drink in the next three years with casseroled venison.

SCEA Ch. Tour du Moulin, 22, av. de l'Europe, 33290 Blanquefort, tel. 05.56.35.10.23, fax 05.56.35.10.23 Y by appt.

Mme Dupuch

Pomerol

Pomerol covers only about 800 ha (1,976 acres). It is one of the smallest appellations in the Gironde and one of the least interesting from an architectural point of view.

The 19th-century fashion for building wine châteaux in an eclectic architectural style appears not to have impressed the Pomerolais, who were happier with their rural or bourgeois houses. All the same, the appellation does boast the Château de Sales, built in the 17th century, which is undoubtedly the model for many of the charterhouses in the Gironde, and the Château Beauregard, which is one of the most beautiful houses built in the 18th century. A copy was built by the Guggenheims on their Long Island estate in New York.

The simplicity of the architecture is in harmony with this AOC, whose originality is staunchly defended by each individual, and where each inhabitant has his or her own vision, while seeking to maintain the harmony and cohesion of the community. This may explain why the wine-producers have been more than reticent in defining the guidelines for classifying the Crus.

The quality and specific nature of the *terroirs* alone should justify official recognition of the merit of the wines in this appellation. As with all the great *terroirs*, Pomerol is the result of the action of a river, in this case the Isle, which began by breaking down the limestone substratum and strewing it with layers of stones that assisted further erosion. The result is a complicated muddle of gravel and smoothed stones which originated in the Massif Central. The soils are particularly complex and hard to identify separately. However, four general types can be identified: in the south, towards Libourne there is a sandy area; near Saint-Émilion gravel lies on sand or clay (the soil is similar to that found on the Plateau de Figeac); in the middle of the AOC the soil is gravel, sometimes on top of clay and sometimes underneath it (Pétrus); finally, in the north-east and north-west the gravel is finer and more sandy.

This variety of soils does not prevent Pomerol wines

from having a basically common structure. They are very fragrant, round and supple with a real strength which allows them to keep for a long time although they can be drunk quite young. Their character means they go well with a range of different dishes and are just as good with sophisticated dishes as they are with simpler ones. In 1999, the appellation produced 39,944 hl (1,054,522 gal).

CH. BEAUCHENE 1997★★

■ 3.2 ha 18,000 150–199 F

(95) 96 **97**

This vineyard has enjoyed much critical success in recent years, and this 1997 wine is another remarkable achievement. Like its predecessors, it comes from the fruit of old Merlot vines planted on ancient sand and gravel soils. The colour is a dark, dense garnet, with deep black highlights. The expressive bouquet evokes wood fires, stewed fruit, vanilla and caramel. The fleshy, rich, creamy tannins develop on the palate around an elegant, well-bred structure, which ends in a flavoursome, persistent finish.

Charles Leymarie et Fils, SCEA Clos Mazeyres, B.P. 132, 33502 Libourne Cedex, tel. 05.57.51.07.83, fax 05.57.51.99.94, e-mail leymarie@ch-leymarie.com Y by appt.

CH. BEAUREGARD 1997★★

■ 12 ha 53,000 200–249 F

75 78 81 (82) **83 84 85 86** |88| 89 |90| |92| **|93| |94| 95 96 97**

Beauregard, a beautiful 18th-century charterhouse, receives a unanimous *coup de cœur* for its 1997 wine. Difficult years like 1997 really sort out the good wine-makers. The excellent gravel-clay terroir also possibly had something to do with it. This wine is remarkable for its lovely dark Bordeaux colour and for the powerful complexity of the nose, which marries grape to toasted oak and vanilla. The warm, harmonious, flavoursome palate finishes on some superb tannins. A very fine wine for keeping, one of the best 'investments' in the Guide. Not to be opened until 2005.

SCEA Ch. Beauregard, 33500 Pomerol, tel. 05.57.51.13.36, fax 05.57.25.09.55, e-mail beauregard@dial.oleane.com Y by appt.

LE BENJAMIN DE BEAUREGARD 1997

■ 5 ha 30,000 70–99 F

Beauregard's second wine, Benjamin, comes from the youngest vines and less favourable soils. Its shorter maturing process means that it can be enjoyed sooner. The colour is an honest ruby of average intensity. The nose is fruity, sustained by a slightly spiced oakiness. After a supple attack, the wine develops with the aid of tannins which are somewhat austere but should evolve quickly. Drink as an accompaniment to grilled red meats.

SCEA Ch. Beauregard, 33500 Pomerol, tel. 05.57.51.13.36, fax 05.57.25.09.55, e-mail beauregard@dial.oleane.com Y by appt.

CH. BELLEGRAVE 1997★★

■ 7 ha 39,000 100–149 F

88 89 91 **92** |93| |94| |95| |96| **97**

As its name suggests, this seven-hectare (17-acre) vineyard is grown on a fine terroir of fine gravels. It is 75% Merlot and 25% Cabernet Franc. The dark, youthful garnet colour is superb, and the elegant bouquet contains aromas of red fruits and wood fires which blend harmoniously, delicately refreshed by notes of liquorice and mint. The palate is just as fine, with silky, velvety tannins wrapped in a robust, vinous, fleshy covering. The long, flavoursome, persistent finish provides a beautiful note on which to end the tasting.

Jean-Marie Bouldy, 'René', 33500 Pomerol, tel. 05.57.51.20.47, fax 05.57.51.23.14 Y by appt.

CH. BONALGUE 1997★

■ 5.5 ha 26,000 100–149 F

|85| |86| |88| |89| |90| |93| 94 **95** 96 97

This vineyard, much favoured by the experts, is shared between 85% Merlot and 15% Cabernet Franc, planted on soils which mix sand, gravel and clay. The colour of this 1997 wine is a dark, deep garnet, and the bouquet is very mature, with aromas of plums in alcohol, notes of *rancio* and well-blended oak, plus a light touch of vanilla. The palate is no disappointment, being robust, vinous and generous; it has great structure and excellent length with agreeably persistent flavours of stewed fruits.

SA Pierre Bourotte, 62, quai du Priourat, 33500 Libourne, tel. 05.57.51.62.17, fax 05.57.51.28.28, e-mail jeanbaptiste.audy@wanadoo.fr Y by appt.

BORDEAUX

CH. BOURGNEUF-VAYRON 1997★

■ 9 ha 40,000 ⊕ 150–199 F

|89| |90| 91 93 94 **95** 96 97

A lovely uninterrupted vineyard on clay and clay-gravel soils planted with 90% Merlot vines. The wine has good colour and black-currant aromas. Fleshy and structured by good oak and grape tannins, it moved one taster to note that it revealed 'excellent ripeness grown on a clay soil'. Not bad for a blind tasting.

⊶ Xavier Vayron, Ch. Bourgneuf-Vayron, 1, le Bourg-Neuf, 33500 Pomerol, tel. 05.57.51.42.03, fax 05.57.25.01.40 ☑ Y by appt.

CH. CERTAN DE MAY DE CERTAN 1997★

■ 5 ha 24,000 ⊕ 300–499 F

85 86 88 |89| |(90)| 94 95 96 97

This clay-gravel terroir, classic to the AOC, contains old vines in a proportion of 70% Merlot to 30% Cabernets. Its wines are regularly singled out by the experts, as indeed is this successful 1997 vintage. Its colour is still evolving, and the nose has fruity, blackberry and raspberry aromas. The palate is very pleasant, with fruity, meaty, delightfully oaky notes, and finishes with persistent tannins. It would go well with a good barbecued entrcôte steak.

⊶ Mme Barreau-Badar, Ch. Certan de May de Certan, 33500 Pomerol, tel. 05.57.51.41.53, fax 05.57.51.88.51 ☑ Y by appt.

CLOS DES AMANDIERS

Vieilli en fût de chêne 1997

■ 1 ha 6,000 ∎ ⊕ ♨ 70–99 F

This wine comes from a one-hectare (2.5-acre) plot out of the four that the Garzaro family has in Pomerol (they also own a large estate in the Entre-Deux-Mers district). Only Merlot vines are grown on these sandy soils. The wine is purple in colour with amber highlights. The finely oaked bouquet includes notes of spices and vanilla. The attack is subtle, supported by elegant tannins, and this 1997 wine may be drunk fairly soon, with white meats in sauce, for instance.

⊶ EARL Vignobles Garzaro, Ch. Le Prieur, 33750 Baron, tel. 05.56.30.16.16, fax 05.56.30.12.63, e-mail garzaro@vingarzaro.com ☑ Y by appt.

CLOS DU CLOCHER 1997

■ 5 ha 21,800 ⊕ 150–199 F

82 83 |**85**|(86)|**88**| |**89**| |90| 92 |93| 94 95 96 97

This 1997 wine (80% Merlot with Cabernet Franc) was grown on gravelly clay and has spent 12 months in the barrel. It is very true to type; its clear, dark-ruby colour is very attractive. The subtle, fruity bouquet contains well-blended oaky notes. The palate is pleasant and has good structural balance. Ready to drink soon, but may be kept for three to five years.

⊶ SC Clos du Clocher, 41, rue des Quatre-Frères-Robert, 33500 Libourne, tel. 05.57.51.62.17, fax 05.57.51.28.28, e-mail jeanbaptiste.audy@wanadoo.fr Y by appt.

CLOS DU PELERIN 1997

■ 3.2 ha 10,000 ∎ ⊕ 70–99 F

|93| |95| 96 |97|

This small three-hectare (7.5-acre) vineyard with sandy soils produces an authentic Pomerol which is simple, delicate and affordable. Merlot predominates, supported by 10% Cabernet Franc and 10% Cabernet-Sauvignon. The colour is a very intense garnet. The bouquet is sweet, with aromas of ripe fruits and very subtle woody scents. The robust, subtle, round palate makes up for any slight lack of power. It has charming silky, soft tannins, which leave a very pleasing impression at the finish.

⊶ Norbert Egreteau, Clos du Pèlerin, 3, chem. de Sales, 33500 Pomerol, tel. 05.57.74.03.66, fax 05.57.25.06.17 ☑ Y by appt.

CH. ELISEE Vieilli en fût de chêne 1997★

■ 1.5 ha 10,000 ∎ ⊕ ♨ 100–149 F

This Merlot wine, made from selected grapes, is complemented by 10% Cabernet Franc. The moderate garnet colour is starting to fade. Already complex, the bouquet sends out woody notes, mixed with humus, cinnamon and clove. The palate is both supple and rich, supported by elegant, liquorice-flavoured tannins. May be drunk soon, for example with grilled red meats.

⊶ EARL Vignobles Garzaro, Ch. Le Prieur, 33750 Baron, tel. 05.56.30.16.16, fax 05.56.30.12.63, e-mail garzaro@vingarzaro.com Y by appt.

CH. FERRAND 1997

■ 12.17 ha n.c. ⊕ 70–99 F

This lovely estate of a dozen hectares (29 acres) has soils of sand and gravel, where Cabernet Franc accounts for 60% of the vines, which is not common in the Libourne district. This delicate 1997 wine can be drunk quite soon. Its colour has already evolved, and the bouquet is subtle and elegant. A supple, easy-drinking Pomerol.

⊶ SCE du Ch. Ferrand, 33500 Pomerol, tel. 05.57.51.21.67, fax 05.57.25.01.41 ☑ Y by appt.

⊶ H. Gasparoux

CH. FONTMARTY 1997★

■ 11.5 ha 21,100 ⊕ 100–149 F

Like Château Taillefer, this vineyard of 11.5 ha (27 acres) belongs to the Libourne merchants, Bernard Moueix. Here the soil is sand and gravel; the varieties grown are 75% Merlot and 25% Cabernet Franc. These have yielded a well-balanced, agreeable 1997 wine, with a deep, clear colour. The nose is still very fruity, though spices and vanilla are also evident. The palate is well-structured; it is still somewhat closed, but of sufficient quality to

envisage keeping for three to five years.
SC Bernard Moueix, Ch. Taillefer, 33500 Libourne, tel. 05.57.25.50.45, fax 05.57.25.50.45

CH. FRANC MAILLET

Cuvée Jean-Baptiste 1997★

■ 5.65 ha 38,400 100–149 F

Located on gravel soils with 90% Merlot vines and a complement of Cabernet Franc, this vineyard offers an attractive 1997 wine. The dark-red colour still looks young. The fine, subtle bouquet exhales aromas of red fruits, vanilla and cocoa. The palate is well-balanced, with silky, round tannins that have presence. A harmonious wine that is already very pleasant.
Vignobles G. Arpin, Maillet, 33500 Pomerol, tel. 06.16.97.53.09, fax 06.57.51.96.75, e-mail gaelarpin@excite.com by appt.

CH. GAZIN 1997

■ 23 ha 56,000 300–499 F

70 75 76 78 79 80 81 82 83 84 85 86 87 88 89 90 91 92 93 94 95 96 97

Nicolas de Bailliencourt is the heir to an old family, one of whose ancesters was decorated for feats of arms by King Philip Augustus of France in 1214. Although Gazin is one of the best vineyards in the Pomerol AOC, this particular version, which is an 85% Merlot, is difficult to assess because while the colour is superb (ruby with black highlights) and the nose complex and remarkable (ripe fruits, clove and pepper mixed with notes of oak), the palate begins well, only to be utterly swamped by the oak. It will take another two or three years for it to be absorbed.
GFA Ch. Gazin, 33500 Pomerol, tel. 05.57.51.07.05, fax 05.57.51.69.96, e-mail chateau.gazin@wanadoo.fr by appt.

CH. GRAND MOULINET 1997

■ 1 ha 7,000 70–99 F

|94| |96| |97|

Despite the 'Grand' in the title, this vineyard covers only one hectare (2.5 acres) of sandy soil on top of iron slag, planted with 90% Merlot. The discreet bouquet is supported by notes that are still fruity. The equally fresh and fruity palate marks it out for drinking soon.
Ollet-Fourreau, Ch. Haut-Surget, 33500 Néac, tel. 05.57.51.28.68, fax 05.57.51.91.79 by appt.

CH. GRANDS SILLONS GABACHOT 1997

■ 4 ha 18,000 100–149 F

The Janoueix family came from the Corrèze in the 19th century to set up business as wine-merchants in the Libourne district. They have several vineyards. This one is planted with very old vines on clay-gravel or siliceous gravel soils. The wine has an honest ruby colour. The nose is still discreet, but is beginning to open with notes of ripe grapes. The palate is supple and pleasant, clean and well-balanced. Good for its year.
François Janoueix, 20, quai du Priourat, B.P. 135, 33500 Libourne, tel. 05.57.55.55.44, fax 05.57.51.83.70 by appt.

CH. GUILLOT 1997

■ 4.7 ha 30,000 100–149 F

82 83 |85| 86 |88| **|89|** |93| 94 95 96 97

This vineyard of almost five hectares (12 acres) has belonged to the Luquot family since 1937. The soils are siliceous gravel, the varieties two-thirds Merlot, one- third Cabernet Franc. The colour is clear and shimmering, mixing shades of garnet, ruby and carmine. The bourgeoning bouquet is still somewhat closed, but exudes fresh notes of undergrowth with undertones of musky leather. Fresh, energetic and robust on the palate, this 1997 wine should develop well in the next two to three years.
SCEA Vignobles Luquot, 152, av. de l'Epinette, 33500 Libourne, tel. 05.57.51.18.95, fax 05.57.25.10.59 by appt.

CH. HAUT-MAILLET 1997

■ 5 ha 28,000 100–149 F

86 88 90 92 |94| |95| 96 97

This vineyard of five hectares (12 acres), comprising 60% Merlot and 40% Cabernet Franc, is located on ancient sandy gravel on the very edge of the Saint-Emilion AOC. A deep garnet colour with carmine lights, the wine has a subtle, elegant bouquet which allies scents of leather and spices to aromas of stewed prune and caramel. The palate is robust and energetic. The structure is good; though somewhat firm and austere at present, it guarantees excellent future development.
Jean-Pierre Estager, 33–41, rue de Montaudon, 33500 Libourne, tel. 05.57.51.04.09, fax 05.57.25.13.38, e-mail estager@estager.com by appt.
Delteil

CH. HAUT-TROPCHAUD 1997★★

■ 2.1 ha 12,000 100–149 F

88 |90| |93| 94 95 96 **|97|**

This vineyard represents two hectares (five acres) out of the 58 ha (143 acres) cultivated by Michel Coudroy on the highest clay-gravel portion of Pomerol. The vines are exclusively Merlot and very old. They have produced a remarkable 1997 wine with a lovely Bordeaux colour verging on black. The bouquet is beginning to express aromas of red fruits and a well-regulated oakiness. The palate, too, is brilliantly balanced, its harmony due to the presence of ripe grapes and fine tannins. The classic style of a good Pomerol.
Michel Coudroy, Maison-Neuve, 33570 Montagne, tel. 05.57.74.62.23, fax 05.57.74.64.18 ev. day except Sat. Sun. 8am–12 noon 2pm–5pm

CH. LA BASSONNERIE 1997*

■ 3.07 ha 15,000 100–149 F

Composed of two-thirds Merlot and one-third Cabernets grown on sand, gravel and clay, this vineyard takes its name from the fact that the former owner, M. Faisandier, was a well-known basoonist. Since 1995, it has belonged to Dominique Leymarie. Garnet in colour with ruby highlights, this 1997 wine releases an elegant and complex bouquet which mixes lively, fruity aromas, spicy notes and hints of musky leather. The palate is smooth and generous, supported by fleshy, velvety tannins which provide a long, persistent finish.

SCEA La Bassonnerie, 'René', 33500 Pomerol, tel. 06.09.73.12.78, fax 06.57.51.99.94, e-mail leymarie@ch-leymarie.com by appt.

CH. LA CONSEILLANTE 1997

■ 12 ha n.c. 500 F+

82 85 88 |89| |90| 91 **|92| |93|** 95 96 97

Catherine Conseillante gave her name to this vineyard in the 17th century. It is in great demand; some 65% of its production goes abroad to three continents. After 21 months in the barrel, this wine is somewhat closed. The colour is a lovely intense, clear garnet, which still looks very young – it lacks the signs of development that many of its fellow-1997s possess. The structure is firm and tannic, and it is difficult to assess this wine because of the immediacy of the oak.

SC Héritiers L. Nicolas, Ch. La Conseillante, 33500 Pomerol, tel. 05.57.51.15.32, fax 05.57.51.42.39 by appt.

CH. LA CROIX 1997

■ n.c. 53,000 150–199 F

86 **|89|** |90| 92 |94| |95| |(96)| 97

This vineyard is located on ten hectares (25 acres) of sandy, gravelly soils in the heart of Pomerol and comprises 60% Merlot, 20% Cabernet Franc and 20% Cabernet-Sauvignon. This is an attractive 1997 wine with a lovely dark and intense garnet colour and shimmering orangey highlights. The bouquet evokes red fruits, with a spicy note of green pepper and good oaky vanilla. The well-balanced palate contains a tannic presence which is still somewhat over-firm, requiring several years of further ageing.

SC Joseph Janoueix, 37, rue Pline-Parmentier, B.P. 192, 33506 Libourne Cedex, tel. 05.57.51.41.86, fax 05.57.51.53.16, e-mail info@j-janoueix-bordeaux.com by appt.

CH. LA CROIX SAINT GEORGES 1997

■ 3.5 ha 20,000 150–199 F

(82) 83 85 86 **|88| |89|** |90| 92 **|93|** |94| **|96|** |97|

The château, now restored, once belonged to the Hospitallers of Saint John of Jerusalem. Inside its 18th-century gates, the winery reveals a sculpted St George on horseback. Evidently, the wine's restorative virtues were known even then to the crusaders and pilgrims to Compostela. This 1997 wine has a nose of black-fruit aromas and an expressive touch of toasted, buttery oakiness. The structure is well balanced, with a pleasing fruitiness and good roundness, which makes the wine ready to drink now.

SC Joseph Janoueix, 37, rue Pline-Parmentier, B.P. 192, 33506 Libourne Cedex, tel. 05.57.51.41.86, fax 05.57.51.53.16, e-mail info@j-janoueix-bordeaux.com by appt.

CH. LA CROIX-TOULIFAUT 1997**

■ 1.62 ha 8,500 150–199 F

75 78 79 81 82 83 **85** 86 88 |89| |90| 92 93 |94| |95| |(96)| **97**

This small-scale vineyard is exclusively planted with Merlot on sand and gravel over a ferruginous substructure. After an exceptional 1996, the old-French word 'Toulifaut' ('All succumb to it') is an apt name for this remarkable 1997 wine. The jury were enchanted by its lovely dark, dense purple colour and its intense, complex bouquet, which elegantly marries aromas of ripe black fruits (blackcurrant and bilberry) and scents of spices. The palate, too, is pleasurably harmonious owing to its fullness, density and round, fleshy tannic structure, which makes for a persistent finish. Bravo!

Jean-François Janoueix, 37, rue Pline-Parmentier, B.P. 192, 33506 Libourne Cedex, tel. 05.57.51.41.86, fax 05.57.51.53.16, e-mail info@j-janoueix-bordeaux.com by appt.

CH. LAFLEUR 1997*

■ 3.15 ha 12,000 500 F+

|85| |86| |88| 89 |90| |92| |(93)| **94** 95 96 97

A Pomerol with an original make-up: half-Merlot, half-Cabernet Franc, grown on a terroir that mixes sands, clays and gravels. The proportion of Cabernet implies a rather long period of maturing in the bottle in order for the wine to attain full expression. Such is certainly true of this intense ruby, very young-looking 1997 wine. It has a developing nose of fresh red, slightly acid fruits, spices and leather. The palate begins smoothly and sweetly, revealing an excellent tannic structure which is still a little marked by the oak, but which promises much for the future.

🗝 Sylvie et Jacques Guinaudeau, Grand Village, 33240 Mouillac, tel. 05.57.84.44.03, fax 05.57.84.83.31 Y by appt.
🗝 Marie Robin

PENSEES DE LAFLEUR 1997

■ 1.35 ha 4,800 ⬛ 250–299 F

This is the second wine of Château Lafleur, owned by Mademoiselle Robin, grown by Sylvie and Jacques Guinaudeau, and marketed by Jean-Pierre Moueix – a very local arrangement, typical of the Libourne. The wine is an intense ruby colour, and the nose is still somewhat closed. When the wine is twirled slightly, it exhales notes of ripe fruits and blackcurrants. The fruity, well-balanced palate is already pleasant.

🗝 Sylvie et Jacques Guinaudeau, Grand Village, 33240 Mouillac, tel. 05.57.84.44.03, fax 05.57.84.83.31 Y by appt.

CH. LAFLEUR-GAZIN 1997

■ 8.6 ha 40,000 ⬛ 200–249 F

The vineyard is planted mainly with Merlot vines (92%) growing on clay and sand. This 1997 wine is full of freshness and has a Bordeaux colour which is still very vivid. The developing bouquet evokes red, acid fruits with perfumes of undergrowth and spices. After an agreeably supple attack, the palate goes on to reveal a well-balanced structure comprising firm tannins which will need a further three to five years' maturing.

🗝 Ets Jean-Pierre Moueix, 54, quai du Priourat, 33500 Libourne
🗝 Mme Delfour-Borderie

CH. LAFLEUR GRANGENEUVE 1997

■ 1.66 ha 11,000 ⬛ 70–99 F

93 95 96 97

A small wine estate owned by the Estager family, who also own vines producing Lalande de Pomerol and Montagne Saint-Emilion wines. This moderately intense garnet wine is an 80% Merlot grown on sand and gravel soils. The nose is beginning to express musky notes alongside the red fruits and slight oakiness. The palate is supple and fresh, and likely to develop fairly fast. But it already makes enjoyable drinking.

🗝 Claude Estager et Fils, Ch. Fougeailles, 33500 Néac, tel. 05.57.51.35.09, fax 05.57.25.95.20 ☑ Y by appt.

CH. LA FLEUR-PETRUS 1997★

■ 10.41 ha n.c. ⬛ 250–299 F

82 83 **85** 86 |**88**| |(89)| **90** 92 |**94**| 95 **96** 97

Only a road separates La Fleur Pétrus from Pétrus, and although the same men are in charge of both properties, they do not share the same terroir (here gravel over a clay subsoil) or mix of varieties (75% Merlot and 25% Cabernet Franc). This 1997 wine has a lovely intense and vivid ruby colour. The nose is still somewhat marked by the oak, with notes of roasting and toast. The well-balanced palate has a good weave of tannins and pleasant vinosity. The finish is long and aromatic, though still a little closed. Several years of ageing are still required for it to reach its best.

🗝 SC du Ch. La Fleur-Pétrus, 33500 Pomerol

CH. LA GANNE 1997

■ 3.8 ha n.c. ⬛ 70–99 F

86 88 |90| |93| 94 96 97

This small family property located on ferruginous sands and planted with 80% Merlot and 20% Cabernet Franc vines produces a well-made Pomerol. The colour of this 1997 wine is still a very young-looking, honest, quite intense garnet. The nose has extremely attractive aromas of stewed prune and vanilla mixed with fresher notes of leather and stone-fruit kernels. The palate is well-balanced. The tannins are still rather firm and energetic, but promising.

🗝 Michel Dubois, 224, av. Foch, 33500 Libourne, tel. 05.57.51.18.24, fax 05.57.51.62.20, e-mail laganne@aol.com ☑ Y by appt.

LA GRAVETTE DE CERTAN 1997

■ 14 ha 20,000 ⬛ 150–199 F

Vieux Château Certan, owned by the Thienpont family, is well-known in the Libourne district. This is their second wine, grown on gravelly clay, where Cabernets hold equal place with Merlots. Though not as good as their 1995 wine, this 1997 vintage has an interesting character. The garnet colour is still somewhat thick. The emerging bouquet is buttery and musky, with a floral evolution. The palate is charming and agreeably fresh. Keep it a little longer.

🗝 SC du Vieux Château Certan, 33500 Pomerol, tel. 05.57.51.17.33, fax 05.57.25.35.08, e-mail vieuxchateaucertan@wanadoo.fr

CH. LA POINTE 1997

■ 22 ha 120,000 ⬛ 100–149 F

82 83 85 86 88 |**89**| |**93**| |**94**| **95**(**96**)|**97**|

A beautiful Directoire-style residence reigns over this important estate of 25 ha (60 acres) between Libourne and Pomerol. Its complex terroir mixes sands and gravels with ferruginous and marly components. This 1997 wine, made from 75% Merlot and 25% Cabernet, is sufficiently developed to be drunk straight away. The clear garnet colour has a good intensity with amber highlights. Elegant oaky and balsamic hints strongly inform the nose. The palate is supple, delicate, and subtle, the tannins smooth and silky.

🗝 SCE Ch. La Pointe-Pomerol, 33500 Pomerol, tel. 05.57.51.02.11, fax 05.57.51.02.11 ☑ Y by appt.
🗝 d'Arfeuille

CH. LA ROSE FIGEAC 1997★★

■ 2.5 ha 12,000 ⬛ 150–199 F

82(85)**86** |**88**| |**89**| |90| 92 **93** 94 95 96 **97**

The Despagne-Rapin family, who have been proprietors in the Saint-Emilion district since 1812, own several estates whose wines are regularly singled out by tasters. This wine

comes from old vines in the Figeac sector. It is especially remarkable in view of its year and is worth a *coup de coeur*. The colour is a lovely dark Bordeaux. The nose is a harmonious mix of strong aromas from the fruit and vanilla tannins bequeathed by the oak. Warm and concentrated on the palate, with a chewy texture and good length, it would be very enjoyable with chicken with morels, but will improve if left a little longer.

🔑 SCEA Despagne-Rapin, Ch. Maison Blanche, 33570 Montagne, tel. 05.57.74.62.18, fax 05.57.74.58.98 ☑ 🍷 by appt.

CH. LATOUR A POMEROL 1997

■ 7.93 ha n.c. 🛢 250–299 F

61 64 66 67 70 71 75 (76) 80 81 82 83 85 86 **87 88 89 90** 92 (93) **94** 95 96 97

Madame Lily Lacoste-Loubat has entrusted Latour-à-Pomerol to the team of Christian Moueix. This 1997 wine is less dense than its predecessors. It has a fine colour and elegant, subtle perfumes. Their floral character is accompanied by red fruits and a hint of oaky menthol. The palate is similar, being well-balanced and fairly marked by its maturing in oak. The delicate structure of this 1997 wine suggests it should be laid down for two to five years.

🔑 Ets Jean-Pierre Moueix, 54, quai du Priourat, 33500 Libourne

🔑 Lily Lacoste

CH. LE BON PASTEUR 1997★★

■ 7 ha 35,000 🛢 250–299 F

78 79 81 |(82)|83 **|85| |86| |88|** |89| **90 92 93 94** (95) 96 97

This vineyard, on assorted clay, gravel and sandy soils in the Maillet locality, belongs to the Libourne oenologist Michel Rolland. His wines are always well-received, and this 1997 version is remarkably powerful and well balanced despite its difficult year of origin. The dark and dense garnet colour, the complex bouquet of crystallised fruits, vanilla and toasted notes, are at one with the palate's superb concentration, in which fleshy, rich, ripe tannins are strong, full and vinous. The impressive finish extends the effect of the savours of fruit and oak. A great wine which will be all the more appreciated if kept a little longer.

🔑 SCEA Fermières des domaines Rolland, 'Maillet', 33500 Pomerol, tel. 05.57.51.23.05, fax 05.57.51.66.08 ☑ 🍷 by appt.

CH. DU DOM. DE L'EGLISE 1997

■ 7 ha 38,000 🛢 150–199 F

This pretty cherry-coloured wine comes from a seven-hectare (17-acre) vineyard where Merlot (75%) and Cabernets grow on a gravelly soil. Still somewhat closed, the nose has scents of stone-fruit kernels. The palate is well-balanced and finishes on pleasant tannins. A good accompaniment to poultry with cream. Exclusive to Borie-Manoux.

🔑 Indivision Castéja-Preben-Hansen, 33500 Pomerol, tel. 05.56.00.00.70, fax 05.57.87.48.61 🍷 by appt.

CLOS L'EGLISE 1997★

■ 5 ha 13,146 🛢 500 F+

The current owner of this five-hectare (12-acre) vineyard on the famous plateau of Pomerol took over in 1997; the soils are gravel-clay mixed with iron slag. This 1997 wine is made from 80% Merlot and 20% Cabernet Franc, and has a superb dark, clear garnet colour. It is developing a powerful bouquet, in which notes of grilling and toasting mingle agreeably with aromas of ripe fruits and vanilla. The palate reveals a firm tannic structure harmoniously balanced by good vinosity. A wine with promise.

🔑 Sylviane Garcin-Cathiard, Clos L'Eglise, 33500 Pomerol, tel. 05.57.51.70.25, fax 05.57.51.70.25, e-mail h-bergey@worldnet.fr ☑ 🍷 by appt.

ESPRIT DE L'EGLISE 1997

■ 1 ha 2,358 🛢 250–299 F

A tiny *cuvée* made from Cabernet Franc with only 25% Merlot – a real curiosity for the appellation. The colour is strong, an intense, dark ruby. The nose is frank and honest, expressive of vanilla and cocoa, with spicy notes and nuances of musky leather. The firm, attractive tannic structure gives the palate an excellent harmony which should develop fully in two to three years' time.

🔑 Sylviane Garcin-Cathiard, Clos L'Eglise, 33500 Pomerol, tel. 05.57.51.70.25, fax 05.57.51.70.25, e-mail h-bergey@worldnet.fr ☑ 🍷 by appt.

CLOS DES LITANIES 1997

■ 0.74 ha 3,200 🛢 150–199 F

This wine is a pure Merlot from vines nearly 50 years old; the soils are sands with a highly ferruginous foundation. The garnet colour of this very pleasant 1997 wine possesses the faded tones of evolution, and the bouquet is elegant and fruity with spicy and subtly oaky hints. The palate is well-balanced, with good roundness and an excellent tannic presence which provides a somewhat firm finish.

🔑 SC Joseph Janoueix, 37, rue Pline-Parmentier, B.P. 192, 33506 Libourne Cedex, tel. 05.57.51.41.86, fax 05.57.51.53.16, e-mail info@j-janoueix-bordeaux.com ☑ 🍷 by appt.

CH. MAZEYRES 1997

■ 19.6 ha 77,000 100–149 F

92 |93| **|94|** **|95|** 96 97

A large wine estate on siliceous or clayey gravels. In order to get a better understanding of this complex terroir, 80 trenches have been dug in the vineyard this year. The aim is to adapt their growing methods to specific plots. This wine is dark-garnet in colour with a nose of very oaky, toasted aromas, together with a little fruitiness. The palate is still oak-dominated and somewhat austere. It needs time to evolve.

SC Ch. Mazeyres, 56, av. Georges-Pompidou, 33500 Libourne, tel. 05.57.51.00.48, fax 05.57.25.22.56, e-mail mazeyres@wanadoo.fr by appt.

CH. MONTVIEL 1997

■ 5.16 ha 16,500 150–199 F

88 |89| **|90|** 91 **|93|** |94| |95| 96 97

The Péré-Vergés came here ten years ago. This is their second wine, created in order to improve selection for their main vintage. Grown on a terroir which mixes sand, gravel and clay, this 1997 wine (80% Merlot and 20% Cabernet Franc) passes the test. The colour is a gorgeous dark garnet, and although it remains slightly closed, the subtle aromas show there is more to come. The palate is well balanced, with good tannic presence; the tannins are on the firm side, but should soften in three to five years' time.

SCA Ch. Montviel, 1, rue du Grand-Moulinet, 33500 Pomerol, tel. 05.57.51.87.92, fax 05.21.93.21.03 by appt.

Yves et Catherine Péré-Vergé

CH. MOULINET-LASSERRE 1997★★

■ 5 ha 25,000 100–149 F

|89| |90| 91 92 93 **94** 95 96 **97**

This very ancient property on the edge of the Clos René has been run by the same family for several generations. The soils are sandy gravel over iron slag, and the varieties are two-thirds Merlot, with 20% Cabernet Franc and 10% Malbec. The very intense garnet colour is dark and beautiful. The nose evokes ripe fruits, stewed prune, coffee and vanilla with a slight hint of musk. The palate is powerful and dense, and the structure remarkably full and robust with a firm finish. This marvellous wine enchanted our tasters with its high class and elegance. Proposed for a *coup de coeur*, it yielded to the Clos René.

SCEA Garde-Lasserre, Clos René, 33500 Pomerol, tel. 05.57.51.10.41, fax 05.57.51.16.28 by appt.

CH. PETIT VILLAGE 1997★

■ 10 ha 48,000 250–299 F

85 86 88 **|89|** **90** **|92|** **93** |94| **95** 96 |97|

Petit Village is one of those châteaux which confirm Bordeaux's reputation for fine wines. It belongs to the galaxy of Grands Crus belonging to the insurance group AXA. Grown on gravelly clay, this 1997 wine is 65% Merlot, 18% Cabernet-Sauvignon, and 17% Cabernet Franc, and has spent 18 months in the barrel. Dark, deep garnet in colour, its appeal is instant. The powerful, mature bouquet exhales elegant and subtle oaky notes. The palate is dense and harmonious; the tannins are fleshy and extremely long-lasting. A wine worth waiting for. But why wait when it is already so pleasant?

Jean-Michel Cazes, Ch. Petit Village, 33500 Pomerol, tel. 05.57.51.21.08, fax 05.57.51.87.31, e-mail infochato@petit-village.com by appt.

AXA Millésimes

PETRUS 1997★★

■ 11.42 ha n.c. 500 F+

61 **67** **71** 74 **75** **|76|** |77| 78 **|79|** |81| (82) **|83|** **|85|** **|86|** **|87|** | (88) | **|89|** **90** **|92|** **93** **|94|** (95) (96) **97**

Pétrus, the most famous yet also the most mythical of the Pomerols, has a special place in the world of wine. Its great fame goes back to the wedding of Princess Elizabeth, now Queen Elizabeth II. The label shows an engraving of Saint Peter and the key to paradise: happy the mortals that have the pleasure of tasting thereof! The appearance of this 1997 wine is admirably dark and deep, with black highlights. The bouquet is already very expressive: fruity and vinous with hints of vanilla and toast. The flavoursome, fleshy palate reveals an excellent structure composed of mature tannins, though they remain firm in the finish. A wine of great promise for the next ten years.

SC du Ch. Petrus, 33500 Pomerol

CH. PONT-CLOQUET 1997★

■ 0.53 ha 3,600 150–199 F

A very limited-edition production from a tiny vineyard of less than a hectare (2.5 acres), created in 1996 by the Vignobles Rousseau. If the success of this 1997 wine is typical, its fame will doubtless grow. A bright, honest ruby in colour, the wine is developing a bouquet which is complex and somewhat empyreumatic, with aromas of stewed fruits, vanilla, toast and a waft of tobacco. The palate is well balanced and is enriched with mature, well-behaved tannins, which provide a long, spicy finish.

Stéphanie Rousseau, Petit Sorillon, 33230 Abzac, tel. 05.57.49.06.10, fax 05.57.49.38.96 by appt.

CH. PRIEURS DE LA COMMANDERIE 1997★★

■ 3.5 ha 10,800 150–199 F

86 **88** **|89|** |90| 91 |(93)| |94| 96 **97**

Purchased by Clément Fayat in 1984, this small vineyard is run by the same team as Château La Dominique, a nearby Saint-Emilion Grand Cru with the same owner. Dark and deep garnet in colour, this 1997 wine already has an intense nose of elegant oaky and vanilla aromas. The full, smooth palate is very aromatic, sustained by a remarkable structure which affords great persistence through a long cinnamon finish. A

BORDEAUX

most interesting wine which will give of its best in three to five years' time.
Clément Fayat, Ch. La Dominique, 33330 Saint-Emilion, tel. 05.57.51.31.36, fax 05.57.51.63.04, e-mail info@vignobles.fayat-group.com

CLOS RENE 1997★★

■ 12 ha 65,000 100–149 F

|86| |88| |89| |90| 91 92 93 95 96 **97**

This very old wine-growing property already had the name 'Reney' on a 1764 map by the geographical engineer, Pierre de Belleyme. It has been in the present owners' family for several generations. Generous, vinous and powerful, this 1997 wine charmed our jury with its dense, dark-garnet colour, its intense bouquet of stewed fruits and vanilla with a hint of *rancio*, and its exceptional palate. Robust, fleshy, rich, and remarkably well-structured, it evolves through to a finish in which there are hints of plums in alcohol harmoniously mingled with an oaky elegance.
SCEA Garde-Lasserre, Clos René, 33500 Pomerol, tel. 05.57.51.10.41, fax 05.57.51.16.28 by appt.

CH. ROCHER-BONREGARD 1997

■ 2.5 ha 15,000 50–69 F

A small vineyard of 2.5 ha (six acres) in the Tailhas sector, planted with 85% Merlot and 15% Cabernet Franc. The colour, moderate in intensity, contains highlights indicative of development, although the nose is still somewhat closed and offers a note of blackcurrant leaf. The palate is somewhat light and finishes on agreeable, subtly oaky tannins. Ready for drinking now.
Jean-Pierre Tournier, Tailhas, 194, rte de Saint-Emilion, 33500 Libourne, tel. 05.57.51.36.49, fax 05.57.51.98.70 by appt.

CH. ROUGET 1997★

■ 18.5 ha 30,000 150–199 F

|**94**| 95 |96| 97

This lovely 18th-century building overlooks an 18.5-ha (44-acre) vineyard close to the town and the ancient church. The soils are gravelly clay on a gradual slope. This intense ruby 1997 wine has authenticity. The bouquet evokes crystallised red fruits harmoniously mingling with aromas of grilling, spices, and attractive, well-blended oakiness.The palate begins with suppleness, and evolves agreeably on a quality tannic structure until it comes to a fruity, persistent finish which will enable the wine to be kept for three to five years.
SARL SGVP, Ch. Rouget, 33500 Pomerol, tel. 05.57.51.05.85, fax 05.57.55.22.45 by appt.
Labruyère

CH. DE SALES 1997★

■ 47.5 ha 150,000 100–149 F

86 |88| |89| |90| |92| |94| |97|

A splendid late 16th-century château dominates the largest wine estate in Pomerol. It is also one of the oldest, having belonged to Bruno de Lambert's family since 1464. Almost 50 ha (123 acres) of vines (70% Merlot, 15% Cabernet Franc and 15% Cabernet-Sauvignon) planted on fine gravel and sand have produced only 150,000 bottles of the 'first wine' in this successful and elegant 1997 vintage. This lovely bright ruby wine is developing a nose with a complex bouquet in which aromas of fruits mix with musky, empyreumatic notes. It is well-balanced and flavoursome, supple and delicate, and ready for drinking now.
Bruno de Lambert, Ch. de Sales, 33500 Pomerol, tel. 05.57.51.04.92, fax 05.57.25.23.91 by appt.

CH. DU TAILHAS 1997

■ 10.5 ha 60,000 100–149 F

The name of this wine goes back to a letter patent of 7 June 1289 from King Edward I of England and Aquitaine, fixing the boundary between the communes of Pomerol and Saint-Emilion at the Tailhayhat stream. Seven hundred years later, the wine has a light colour and a charming nose of red fruits. The palate is more austere but typical.
Nebout et Fils, SC Ch. du Tailhas, 33500 Pomerol, tel. 05.57.51.26.02, fax 05.57.25.17.70 by appt.

CH. TAILLEFER 1997★

■ 11.5 ha 55,000 150–199 F

93 94 95 96 97

This lovely wine estate surrounds a 19th-century château, easily visible from Libourne's eastern by-pass. It was the first property acquired by Antoine Moueix in 1923. The soils are sandy gravel, planted with 75% Merlot and 25% Cabernet Franc. The wines are always successful, even in 1997. This one has a deep colour and aromas that are already complex, mixing red fruits, brioche, coffee and toast. The concentrated palate has a tannic structure of well-toasted oak. A wine that will gain from being kept a little while.
SC Bernard Moueix, Ch. Taillefer, 33500 Libourne, tel. 05.57.25.50.45, fax 05.57.25.50.45

CH. THIBEAUD-MAILLET 1997★

■ 1 ha 6,300 100–149 F

88 |89| |90| 92 |93| |94| 95 |96| 97

This small estate of 1.4 ha (3.46 acres) in the locality of Maillet owes its name to the

Thibeaud family who established it at the start of the 19th century. This is an attractive 1997 wine made from 85% Merlot and 15% Cabernet Franc grapes grown on gravelly clay. The colour is a dark, deep garnet, and the nose finely oaky, with developing aromas of well-ripened fruit, stewed prune, vanilla and fresher nuances of undergrowth and leather. The palate is charming, supple, round and delicate, informed by silky, velvety, persistent tannins. An elegant wine for fine dishes.

Roger et Andrée Duroux, Ch. Thibeaud-Maillet, 33500 Pomerol, tel. 05.57.51.82.68, fax 05.57.51.58.43 ev. day 9am–12 noon 2pm–8pm; cl. March

CH. TOUR ROBERT 1997*

1.2 ha 6,000 100–149 F

|93| 94 95 97

Essentially made of Merlot planted on sandy gravel, this vineyard is advised by Michel Rolland, like La Bassonnerie. The deep and dark colour of this 1997 wine is indicative of good concentration, confirmed by the nose's intense aromas of well-ripened black fruits and spicy, grilled notes deriving from the delightfully well-blended oak. The experience is a harmonious one due to the smooth, rich, dense tannins, which persist through the finish. This most agreeable wine needs to be laid down for two or three years to reach its best.

Dominique Leymarie, Ch. Tour-Robert, B.P. 132, 33502 Libourne Cedex, tel. 05.57.51.07.83, fax 05.57.51.99.94, e-mail leymarie@ch-leymarie.com by appt.

CH. TROTANOY 1997

7.16 ha n.c. 300–499 F

79 80 (82) |85| |86| 87 |88| |89| |(90)| |92| 94 (95) (96) 97

This seven-hectare (17-acre) vineyard, which consists essentially of Merlot with a 7% contribution of Cabernet Franc, is one of the jewels in the crown of the Libourne merchants Jean-Pierre Moueix. The gravelly-clay soils yield wines that are powerful and tannic, like this 1997 vintage, which, though somewhat austere, has really good ageing potential. Its dark and deep appearance has carmine highlights. The bouquet is elegant and delicate, diffuses a subtle, fine, attractive oakiness, and needs to open further. The palate has an intensity and firmness of structure which is currently somewhat austere, but has great promise.

Ets Jean-Pierre Moueix, 54, quai du Priourat, 33500 Libourne

VIEUX CHATEAU CERTAN 1997

14 ha 43,000 300–499 F

81 82 83 85 86 |(88)| |89| |90| 92 **93** |94| **95 96** 97

The beautiful architecture of Vieux Château Certan is a good example of a charterhouse. This wine is a classic, from a terroir close to Pétrus. The soils are less individual than the latter, however, being a thin layer of gravels over clay. The colour is a very youthful cherry-red. The nose is full of notes of roasting. The palate begins both mellow and tannic, and continues with tannins that prevail over the fruit. The sturdy structure has promise. A traditional Pomerol.

SC du Vieux Château Certan, 33500 Pomerol, tel. 05.57.51.17.33, fax 05.57.25.35.08, e-mail vieuxchateaucertan@wanadoo.fr

VIEUX CHATEAU FERRON 1997*

1.5 ha 10,000 150–199 F

|89| |90| 93 |95| |96| 97

Another plot of vines acquired in 1987 by the Garzaro family. The variety and terroir are similar to those of the Cuvée Elisée. Like the latter, this wine has been adjudged highly successful, but has better keeping qualities and a deeper colour. The wine needs time to breathe in order to release its developing bouquet of fruity, oaky, mineral notes. The excellent tannic structure of this 1997 wine makes it a Pomerol for keeping (four or five years), and it will go well with dishes of character: entrecôte bordelaise, mushrooms or game.

Elisabeth Garzaro, Ch. Le Prieur, 33750 Baron, tel. 05.56.30.16.16, fax 05.56.30.12.63, e-mail garzaro@vingarzaro.com by appt.

CH. VIEUX MAILLET 1997

2.62 ha 11,000 100–149 F

Isabelle Motte set up here in 1994. This very young-looking, vivid and intense ruby wine is made from 80% Merlot and 20% Cabernet Franc grapes grown on sand and clay; it has spent 12 months in the barrel. When twirled in the glass, it releases a fine, fruity nose with subtle oaky notes. The palate is currently somewhat austere, containing tannins which have a firm presence but are not aggressive. They bode well for future ageing.

Isabelle Motte, Ch. Vieux Maillet, 33500 Pomerol, tel. 05.57.51.04.67, fax 05.57.51.04.67, e-mail chateau.vieux.maillet@wanadoo.fr by appt.

CH. VRAY CROIX DE GAY 1997*

3.66 ha 22,500 100–149 F

85 86 88 **|89| |90|** |93| |94| 95 97

This vineyard is linked to Château Siaurac, and similarly belongs to the family of General de Gaulle's former minister, Olivier Guichard. The vineyard comprises 80% Merlot and 20% Cabernets grown on a gravelly-clay soil. Our tasters judged this 1997 wine a great success with its lovely colour and ruby highlights; the nose is subtle and elegant, and remains floral and fruity (Morello cherry). The attack is supple, and the palate is supported by a dense weave of tannins which will enable it to go on developing.

SCE Baronne Guichard, Ch. Siaurac, 33500 Néac, tel. 05.57.51.64.58, fax 05.57.51.41.56 by appt.

Olivier Guichard

Lalande de Pomerol

The Hospitallers of the Knights of Saint John created this vineyard and its neighbour Pomerol; indeed, they also built the beautiful church in Lalande that dates from the 12th century. The vineyard covers about 1,100 ha (2,717 acres), growing classic Bordeaux grape varieties to make well-coloured red wines, which are powerful and have a good bouquet. They enjoy a good reputation and the best wines can rival Pomerols and Saint-Émilions. In 1999, 59,335 hl (1,566,444 gal) were declared.

CH. DES ANNEREAUX 1997

■ 22 ha 100,000 50–69 F

This 1997 wine has distinctive aromas of acid red fruits (redcurrant), pepper and smokiness, as well as a supple and well-balanced – if slightly bland – palatal structure. An enjoyable wine to drink now and over the next two years.

SCE du Ch. des Annereaux, 33500 Lalande-de-Pomerol, tel. 05.57.55.48.90, fax 05.57.84.31.27

Milhade-Hessel

CH. BECHEREAU 1997

■ n.c. 10,000 50–69 F

This clear cherry-red 1997 wine is a classic blend of the AOC: 80% Merlot to 20% Cabernet Franc. The bouquet has scents of red fruits and rather intense notes of undergrowth. The palate is equipped with subtle, supple, elegant tannins. Ready to drink now, but will go on for several years yet.

SCE J.-M. Bertrand, Béchereau, 33570 Les Artigues-de-Lussac, tel. 05.57.24.31.22, fax 05.57.24.34.69 ev. day 8am–12 noon 2pm–6pm

CH. DE BEL-AIR 1997

■ 16 ha n.c. 100–149 F

Grown on excellent gravel soils, this cherry-red 1997 wine already has pale brick-red lights. The bouquet has scents of leather and red fruits, and the tannins are supple and fleshy, though somewhat marked by the oak-maturing. Keep in the cellar for a year or two to help it blend in better.

Vignobles Jean-Pierre Musset, Ch. de Bel-Air, 33500 Lalande-de-Pomerol, tel. 05.57.51.40.07, fax 05.57.74.17.43 by appt.

CH. BELLES-GRAVES 1997★

■ 14.1 ha 80,000 50–69 F

This gorgeous 18th-century charterhouse commands an exceptional view over the vineyard, which comprises 80% Merlot and 20% Cabernet Franc. This 1997 wine is a great success. The colour is dark-cherry; the powerful perfumes evoke red fruits (strawberry), vanilla and coffee. The tannins are velvety, ripe and full. They give attractive length to a wine which is already enjoyable but will improve during the next three to five years.

GFA Theallet-Piton, SC Ch. Belles-Graves, 33500 Néac, tel. 05.57.51.09.61, fax 05.57.51.01.41 by appt.

CH. BOIS DE LABORDE 1997

■ n.c. n.c. 100–149 F

The colour of this 1997 wine is garnet with developing brick-red lights. It has a bouquet of sweet spices, caramel and toasted fruits. The intense, vivid palate has a powerful finish. It will reach harmony in one to three years, when it go well with grilled red meats.

Bruno Vedelago, Bois de Laborde, 33500 Lalande de Pomerol, tel. 06.07.13.95.49

CH. BOURSEAU 1997

■ 10.35 ha 150,000 50–69 F

This château is a short walk from the 12th-century church, one of the oldest in the AOC district. The gravelly clay soils have produced a wine with delicate, though still somewhat closed, aromas. The tannins are powerful and well-balanced. The finish is dominated by the oak-maturing, and will require two or three years' keeping to soften.

SARL Vignobles V. Gaboriaud-Bernard, Ch. Bourseau, 33500 Lalande-de-Pomerol, tel. 05.57.51.52.39, fax 05.57.51.70.19, e-mail matras@cavesparticulieres.com ev. day 9am–12 noon 2pm–5pm

CH. CANON CHAIGNEAU 1997

■ n.c. 18,000 70–99 F

This 20-ha (44-acre) estate is located on sandy clay. Its 1997 is well-balanced between Merlot (60%) and Cabernet (40%), with a bouquet of crystallised fruits and toasted oak. The tannins are harmonious on the palate, but somewhat dominate the finish. Wait a year or two.

SCEA Marin Audra, 3 bis, rue Porte-Brunet, 33330 Saint-Emilion, tel. 05.57.24.69.13, fax 05.57.24.69.11, e-mail louismarin@wanadoo.fr by appt.

CH. DE CHAMBRUN 1997

■ 1.42 ha 7,200 250–299 F

While the vineyard is innovative in its oak-maturing methods, this 1997 wine was not to everyone's taste: some praised its aromatic strength and general oakiness; others deplored the method used (18 months in oak for a year with little structure). One thing is sure, however. It is a wine that will give pleasure once time has softened its tannins.

🔑 Jean-Philippe Janoueix, 83, cours des Girondins, 33500 Libourne, tel. 05.57.25.91.19, fax 05.57.48.00.04 ☑ 🍷 by appt.

DOM. GALVESSES GRAND MOINE 1997

■ 1.65 ha 10,000 ▮ ⦀ ♨ 50–69 F

This 1997 wine is a pure Merlot, grown on a siliceous clay soil. It is recommended for its good balance and supple, fruity tannins, which are already well-blended. A light plant-like note informs the finish, but this should fade in a year or two.

🔑 SCEA Chanet et Fils, n° 1 A Jacques, 33570 Puisseguin, tel. 05.57.74.60.85, fax 05.57.74.59.90 ☑ 🍷 ev. day 8am–12 noon 2pm–6pm

CH. DE GARDOUR 1997

■ 19 ha 30,000 ⦀ 50–69 F

This two-thirds Merlot, one-third Cabernet is well worth trying. The jury suggests that its elegant aromas of flowers and ripe fruits, with round, attractive tannins maturing in sweet harmony, would go well with a farmyard chicken served with small vegetables and the odd *pleurote* mushroom. An easy-drinking wine to be enjoyed while it is young.

🔑 A. de Luze et Fils, Dom. du Ribet, 33450 Saint-Loubès, tel. 05.57.97.07.20, fax 05.57.97.07.27 🍷 by appt.
🔑 SCEA de Jerphanion

CH. GARRAUD 1997★★

■ 20 ha 75,000 ⦀ 70–99 F

The Count of Kermartin founded Château Garraud in the 19th century. The vineyard has modernised itself down the years and today practises techniques to enhance quality both in the vineyard and the winery, as revealed in this dense, dark 1997 wine. The nose exhales powerful, elegant aromas of very ripe red fruits (raspberry, blackcurrant), tobacco and vanilla. The subtle, fleshy tannins evolve with smoothness, harmony and persistence. An exemplary wine for its year and delightful to drink over the next three to eight years.

🔑 Vignobles Léon Nony, Ch. Garraud, 33500 Néac, tel. 05.57.55.58.58, fax 05.57.25.13.43 ☑ 🍷 ev. day except Sat. Sun. 9am–12 noon 2pm–5pm

CH. DU GRAND CHAMBELLAN 1997

■ 7 ha 40,000 ⦀ 70–99 F

This property, which has excellent gravel soils, was already in existence in the 18th century. This 1997 wine has a nose of cherry and undergrowth, and a palate whose hints of oak blend well with the pleasing, well-balanced tannins. An enjoyable wine to drink straight away.

🔑 SCEA Ch. de Viaud, 33500 Lalande-de-Pomerol, tel. 05.57.51.17.86, fax 05.57.51.79.77 🍷 by appt.

CH. GRAND ORMEAU 1997

■ 7 ha 47,000 ⦀ 100–149 F

This estate is on silty gravel. Its intensely red 1997 wine has an emerging but discreet nose of stewed fruits, with a palate informed by round, slightly oaky tannins (after 13 months in the barrel). A wine to drink in the next three years.

🔑 Ch. Grand Ormeau, 33500 Lalande-de-Pomerol, tel. 05.57.25.30.20, fax 05.57.25.22.80 ☑ 🍷 by appt.
🔑 Beton

CH. HAUT-CHAIGNEAU

Cuvée Prestige Elevé en fût de chêne 1997★

■ 8 ha 48,000 ⦀ 100–149 F

This château has received much praise in recent years, and has invested heavily in both the wineries and the residence. Its 1997 wine exemplifies its consistent quality. The ruby colour is intense and the bouquet expressive, combining blackcurrant, mint and an attractive vanilla and chocolatey oakiness. The tannins are round and charming on the palate, developing with remarkable fullness and subtlety. This is already a pleasant wine, but will keep for two to five years. Note also the **1997 Château Tour Saint-André**, a second wine, recommended for its complex bouquet of leather, flowers and fruits, though the palate is less complex. Should be drunk young (70–99F).

🔑 André Chatonnet, Haut-Chaigneau, 33500 Néac, tel. 05.57.51.31.31, fax 05.57.25.08.93 ☑ 🍷 by appt.

CH. HAUT-GOUJON 1997★

■ 8.5 ha 19,000 ▮ ⦀ ♨ 50–69 F

Grown on sandy clay, this bright, dark-ruby wine has a developed bouquet of leather, crystallised fruits (prune) and oak. It has an elegant, fleshy palate, with delicate notes of vanilla and a well-balanced finish. May be enjoyed now and for two to four years to come.

🔑 SCEA Garde et Fils, Goujon, 33570 Montagne, tel. 05.57.51.50.05, fax 05.57.25.33.93 ☑ 🍷 by appt.

CH. HAUT-SURGET 1997★

■ 36 ha 100,000 ▮ ⦀ ♨ 70–99 F

This large family property has ministered to the tastes of wine-lovers for five generations. This dark, garnet-coloured 1997 wine is powerfully redolent of vanilla, leather and black fruits. Its open, well-balanced tannins have excellent potential for future development, and it should mature completely after two years' keeping. A really lovely wine.

🔑 Ollet-Fourreau, Ch. Haut-Surget, 33500 Néac, tel. 05.57.51.28.68, fax 05.57.51.91.79 ☑ 🍷 by appt.

CH. JEAN DE GUE

Cuvée Prestige 1997★★★

■ 10 ha n.c. ⦀ 50–69 F

This Cuvée Prestige from Château Jean de Gué is awarded three stars – a rare achievement for a 1997 wine – and a *coup de coeur.*

BORDEAUX

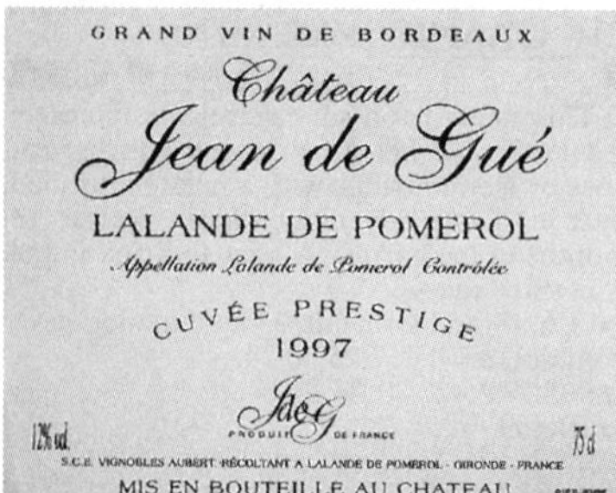

GRAND VIN DE BORDEAUX
Château
Jean de Gué
LALANDE DE POMEROL
Appellation Lalande de Pomerol Contrôlée
CUVÉE PRESTIGE
1997
MIS EN BOUTEILLE AU CHATEAU

Grown on gravelly clay, this is a wine rich in colour (purple with garnet highlights) and with intense and complex aromas (black fruits, toast, spices and vanilla). The tannins are superb and full when they hit the palate; they then evolve with great elegance and aromatic persistence (blackcurrant and cedar). A magnificent wine which should be appreciated in three to six years or so.

🔑 Vignobles Aubert, Ch. La Couspaude, 33330 Saint-Emilion, tel. 05.57.40.15.76, fax 05.57.40.10.14 Y by appt.

CH. LABORDE

Mil six cent vingt-huit 1997

■ 4 ha 12,000 70–99 F

This special *cuvée* from Château Laborde is made from selected grapes (90% Merlot) matured for 12 months in oak. Redolent of fruit and delicately oaky, this wine has real potential. The finish reveals that the firm, elegant tannins are still dominated by the oak, but should settle down in the next two to three years.

🔑 SCEV J.M. Trocard, Laborde, 33500 Lalande-de-Pomerol, tel. 05.57.74.30.52, fax 05.57.74.39.96 ☑ Y by appt.

CH. LA BORDERIE-MONDESIR

1997★★

■ 2.19 ha n.c. 70–99 F

This small family property is located on a terroir of gravels and clinker. A 60 : 40 blend of Merlot and Cabernet-Sauvignon, this 1997 wine is a bright deep-garnet colour. The intense aromas evoke leather, ripe fruits, toasting and vanilla. The tannins are forceful and generous on the palate, where they show their richness and class. The palate evolves with elegance and persistence, and there is an extremely pleasant return of the aromas. Congratulations are in order. This wine will reach its best in two to three years' time.

🔑 Jean-Marie Rousseau, Petit-Sorillon, 33230 Abzac, tel. 05.57.49.06.10, fax 05.57.49.38.96 ☑ Y by appt.

CH. LA CROIX BELLEVUE 1997

■ 8 ha n.c. 70–99 F

This 1997 wine is a 70% Cabernet-Sauvignon, something of a rarity in the Libourne district. It has lively aromas, which inform the nose and palate alike. The structure is lively and on the powerful side, and still has a woody finish, but the tannins should be blended in several months' time. Drink from January 2001 on and keep for a maximum of three years.

🔑 SC Dom. viticoles Armand Moueix, Ch. Fonplégade, 33330 Saint-Emilion, tel. 05.57.74.43.11, fax 05.57.74.44.67 ☑ Y by appt.

🔑 GFA du Dom. de Moulinet

CH. LA CROIX DES MOINES

1997

■ 8 ha 50,000 70–99 F

This bright-looking 1997 wine comes from a magnificent terroir of gravels on a ferruginous subsoil. It has very fruity aromas (raspberry and plum) and crystallised notes. The elegant, supple tannins blend with hints of slightly burnt wood. A wine to drink over the next three years.

🔑 SCEA des Vignobles Jean-Louis Trocard, 2, Les Petits Jays ouest, 33570 Les Artigues-de-Lussac, tel. 05.57.55.57.90, fax 05.57.55.57.98, e-mail trocard@wanadoo.fr ☑ Y by appt.

CH. LA CROIX SAINT-JEAN 1997

■ 1.34 ha 8,000 70–99 F

The Vignobles Tapon are well dug in in the Libourne district. Their 1997 Lalande has pleasant aromas (red fruits) and a supple tannic structure with a somewhat rustic finish. The jury recommends waiting a year or two until it has become fully harmonious.

🔑 Vignobles Raymond Tapon, Lafleur Vachon, 33330 Saint-Emilion, tel. 05.57.74.61.20, fax 05.57.74.61.19, e-mail vinstapon@aol.com ☑ Y by appt.

CH. LA FAURIE MAISON NEUVE

1997

■ 3.8 ha 25,000 50–69 F

This 1997 wine has an intense garnet colour and elegant, complex aromas of cherry, leather and toasted oak. The structure is harmonious and well-balanced, although the wood does dominate the finish. Nevertheless it is a fruity wine and very drinkable. It can equally be left in the cellar for two or three years to become more supple.

🔑 Michel Coudroy, Maison-Neuve, 33570 Montagne, tel. 05.57.74.62.23, fax 05.57.74.64.18 ☑ Y ev. day except Sat. Sun. 8am–12 noon 2pm–5pm

CH. LA FLEUR SAINT-GEORGES

1997

■ 17 ha 110,000 70–99 F

Bought on 1 July 1998 by Hubert de Bouard and his wife, co-owners of Château Angelus at Saint-Emilion, this very lovely property, with its excellent sandy clay and gravel terroir, ought to bring us some really good wines in the future. The 1997 wine comes from the outgoing team. The bouquet contains toasty notes, together with mineral touches. The tannins are a bit rustic. Don't leave it too long.

🔑 Hubert de Bouard de Laforest, SC Ch.

La Fleur Saint-Georges, B.P. 7, 33500 Pomerol, tel. 05.57.25.25.13, fax 05.57.51.65.14 ☒ Y by appt.

CH. LA ROSE HAUT MUSSET 1997★

■ 1 ha n.c. 100–149 F

This minute property of one hectare (2.5 acres) practises organic cultivation on clayey sand and gravel. Its 1997 wine is distinguished by its delicate perfumes of slightly toasted fruits, flowers and vanilla-tinged oak, and for its subtlety and balance on the palate. The long, aromatic finish implies good keeping over the next three years.

Jean-Baptiste Abbadie, 3, Grands Jays, 33570 Les Artigues-de-Lussac, tel. 05.57.24.34.71, fax 05.57.24.30.59 ☒ Y by appt.

CH. LA SERGUE 1997★

■ 5 ha 15,000 150–199 F

This wine was made by Pascal Chatonnet, the son of the oenologist, André. Here at this small château they use similar techniques to those of the region's Grands Crus both in the vineyard and the winery. Vinified in an oak vat and matured in new barrels, this 1997 wine does not mask its very oaky side, but the dense, elegant tannins support the structure well. The palate's length is remarkable for its year, and should become harmonious and long-lived (three to ten years).

André Chatonnet, Haut-Chaigneau, 33500 Néac, tel. 05.57.51.31.31, fax 05.57.25.08.93 Y by appt.

CH. LA VALLIERE 1997

■ 1 ha 5,000 50–69 F

The label reproduces a watercolour of Lalande-de-Pomerol's lovely church, built by the Order of Hospitallers. This 1997 wine has a pleasing bouquet of flowers and smokiness, plus a supple, fondant structure with a slightly musky finish. A charming wine that should be drunk while young.

SARL L. Dubost, Catusseau, 33500 Pomerol, tel. 05.57.51.74.57, fax 05.57.25.99.95 ☒ Y by appt.

CH. LES HAUTS-CONSEILLANTS 1997★★

■ 9 ha 38,200 70–99 F

This château, located on sandy-silty soils at Néac, is one of the appellation's stalwarts, as is shown by this remarkable 1997 wine. The colour is a bright and intense garnet, the bouquet a complex mix of ripe red fruits, flowers, caramel and vanilla. The attack is fleshy and vigorous, followed by a sensation of firmness and length. A well-structured wine that may be a little austere, but whose breeding can be glimpsed beneath the surface. It will reach its best within two years. Bravo.

SA Pierre Bourotte, 62, quai du Priourat, 33500 Libourne, tel. 05.57.51.62.17, fax 05.57.51.28.28, e-mail jeanbaptiste.audy@wanadoo.fr Y by appt.

CH. L'ETOILE DE SALLES 1997

■ n.c. 20,000 30–49 F

Gravel soils over iron waste and a classic blend (80% Merlot) have provided this 1997 wine with an impeccable appearance for its year: a bright cherry-red colour with mauvish highlights and elegant aromas of small red fruits with a light floral touch. The palate is very round and supple. Ready to drink now, but may be kept for two to three years.

Dubois et Fils, Pont de Guitres, 33500 Lalande-de-Pomerol, tel. 05.57.51.13.53, fax 05.57.25.91.81 ☒ Y by appt.

CH. PAVILLON BEL AIR 1997

■ 7 ha 37,000 70–99 F

This property, acquired in 1994, offers a pleasant wine with a discreet bouquet of leather, spices and fruits. The mellow tannins are developing subtly and lightly on the palate. A wine to drink while young.

J.-F. et D. Quenin, Ch. Pavillon Bel Air, 33500 Néac, tel. 05.57.40.18.02, fax 05.57.40.10.07 ☒ Y by appt.

CH. PERRON La Fleur 1997★

■ n.c. 2,400 100–149 F

This prestige wine, made from selected Merlot vines, comes from Château Perron, one of the oldest estates in the appellation. The garnet colour is intense. The bouquet has spicy, oaky notes which mingle with the fruity nuances. The ripe, generous tannins are developing with some power through the finish. A nice, well-balanced wine with definite ageing potential (two to three years).

Michel-Pierre Massonie, Ch. Perron, B.P. 88, 33503 Libourne Cedex, tel. 05.57.51.40.29, fax 05.57.51.13.37 ☒ Y by appt.

DOM. PONT DE GUESTRES 1997★

■ 2 ha 12,000 70–99 F

An exclusive Merlot which has matured 12 months in oak, this cherry-red 1997 wine with mauvish highlights has an intense bouquet which is spicy, oaky and slightly heady. Its tannic structure is round and complex. It will fulfill all its potential in two to three years' time.

Rémy Rousselot, Ch. Les Roches de Ferrand, Huchat, 33126 Saint-Aignan, tel. 05.57.24.95.16, fax 05.57.24.91.44 ☒ Y by appt.

CH. AU PONT DE GUITRES 1997★★

■ 1.5 ha 10,000 50–69 F

This *coup de coeur* is surprising for a second wine, but it is not at all the same blend as its fellow (here 30% Cabernet Franc, complementing the Merlot), and it has spent only nine months in oak. The jury were drawn to its delicacy and aromatic complexity (ripe red fruits, spices and vanilla) and the general balance of the palate. The tannins are full and mellow, and provide a very persistent finish, while retaining a great deal of freshness. Subtlety, authenticity and elegance were words which recurred often in the tasters' notes. A

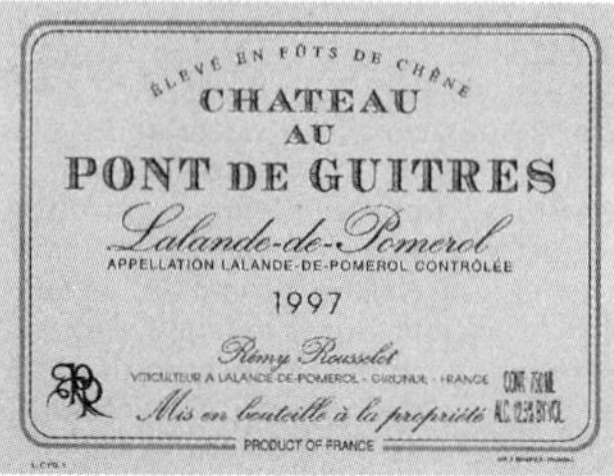

wine to leave for two years in the cellar, then drink over the next eight years.
🔑 Rémy Rousselot, Ch. Les Roches de Ferrand, Huchat, 33126 Saint-Aignan, tel. 05.57.24.95.16, fax 05.57.24.91.44 ✉ 🍷 by appt.

CH. REAL-CAILLOU
Elevé en fût de chêne 1997

■ 4.5 ha 26,694 70-99 F

This vineyard is the property of the Lycée Viticultural at Montagne, which trains large numbers of the region's wine-making staff as well as the sons and daughters of wine-growers from all over France. As in all viticultural lycées, the teaching is not restricted to theory: practical vine-growing and wine-making work are undertaken under the careful supervision of the teachers. This 1997 wine has a ruby colour with mauvish highlights, aromas dominated by delicate notes of oak, and a fruity, energetic tannic structure. An interesting wine, which needs to be drunk fairly soon.
🔑 Lycée viticole de Libourne-Montagne, Goujon, 33570 Montagne, tel. 05.57.55.21.22, fax 05.57.51.66.13, e-mail legta.libourne@educagri.fr ✉ 🍷 ev. day 8.30am–12 noon 1.30pm–5.30pm

CH. SERGANT 1997

■ 18 ha 80,000 50-69 F

This château offers a lovely ruby-red 1997 wine with fruity (cherry and redcurrant) and vanilla aromas. The palate is very fresh, though still firm, and needs keeping for one or two years to reach its best.
🔑 SCEV Jean Milhade, Ch. Recougne, 33133 Galgon, tel. 05.57.55.48.90, fax 05.57.84.31.27 🍷 by appt.

CH. TOUR DE MARCHESSEAU 1997

■ 5 ha 35,000 50-69 F

This vineyard belongs to Jean-Louis Trocard, the current president of the Bordeaux wine-growers' association. The wine offered is a 1997 with perfumes still dominated by toasted, chocolatey oak, dried fruit and vanilla. Balanced and supple, but without great power, this wine should be drunk within the next three years.
🔑 SCEA des Vignobles Jean-Louis Trocard, 2, Les Petits Jays ouest, 33570 Les Artigues-de-Lussac, tel. 05.57.55.57.90, fax 05.57.55.57.98, e-mail trocard@wanadoo.fr 🍷 by appt.

VIEUX CLOS CHAMBRUN 1997

■ n.c. 1,800 150-199 F

This limited-edition vintage comes from selected grapes grown in a 2.7-ha (6.6-acre) vineyard near Néac. The cherry-red colour has brickish lights. Intense aromas of spices, coffee and vanilla accompany an energetic, very oaky tannic structure. Wait two or three years for everything to harmonise.
🔑 Jean-Jacques Chollet, La Chapelle, 50210 Camprond, tel. 02.33.45.19.61, fax 02.33.45.35.54 ✉ 🍷 by appt.

Saint-Émilion and Saint-Émilion Grand Cru

Covering the slopes of a hill that looks down on the valley of the Dordogne, Saint-Émilion (3,300 inhabitants) is a peaceful and charming little wine village. But it is also a place full of history. It was once a stopping point on the pilgrims' route to Santiago de Compostela, a fortified town in the Hundred Years' War and the refuge of the Girondin deputies who were banished from Paris during the Revolution, and there are a good number of historic ruins to see. Local legend has it that the vineyard was originally planted by Roman legionaries. It is more likely that its beginnings, at least part of them, were in the 13th century. However that may be, Saint-Émilion today is the centre of one of the most famous vineyards in the world. It extends over nine communes and is planted on a rich range of soils. A number of classic growths come from the lime plateau and clay on the limey subsoil around the village. They make wines of good colour, which are well-structured and full-bodied. The vineyards bordering Pomerol have a more gravelly soil and produce wines noted for their great finesse (this region also produces many Grands Crus). But the majority of the Saint-Émilion appellation is on sandy alluvial soil, sloping down to the Dordogne, which produces very pleasant wines. With regard to the vine varieties, Merlot predominates but there is also Cabernet Franc, called 'Bouchet' in the region, and, in much lesser quantities, Cabernet-Sauvignon.

One of the original things in the Saint-Émilion is the classification of the wines. It was only established recently, in 1955, and it is regularly and systematically reviewed (the first revision took place in 1958 and the most recent in 1996). The Saint-Émilion appellation can be used by all the wines produced in the commune itself and in the eight other communes surrounding it. The second appellation, Saint-Émilion Grand Cru, does not correspond to a defined *terroir*, but to particular wines that must satisfy the most rigorous criteria of quality and that are selected by expert tastings. The wines must be submitted to a second tasting before they are bottled. The châteaux are selected from the Saint-Émilion Grands Crus and the wines are then classified. In 1986 74 were classified, of which 11 were Premiers Grands Crus. In the 1996 classification 68 were classified and 13 were Premiers Grands Crus. They divide into two groups: A for two of them (Ausone and Cheval Blanc) and B for the other eleven. It is worth pointing out that the Union des Producteurs de Saint-Émilion is without question the largest Cave Coopérative in France to be located in a top AOC. In 1999 Saint-Émilion produced in 118,428 hl (3,126,500 gal) and Saint-Émilion Grand Cru produced 156,506 hl (4,131,758).

The Hachette tasting was not complete in the Appellation Saint-Émilion Grand Cru. One team tasted the Saint-Émilion Grands Crus Classés (without separating out the Premiers Crus); a different team tasted the Saint-Émilion Grands Crus. The stars printed correspond to these two sets of criteria.

Saint-Émilion

CH. BARBEROUSSE 1997

■ 7 ha 40,000 30–49 F

This vineyard, which regularly receives good notices, is on siliceous gravel soils planted with 70% Merlot and 30% Cabernets. Made from well-ripened grapes, carefully vinified and matured, this is a pleasing 1997 wine.The cherry-red colour is clean and dark. The bouquet releases fresh, fruity, spicy aromas. The round, supple and well-balanced palate finishes well with aromas of *pain d'épice* (a kind of spice loaf). May be drunk now or kept for two to three years.

GAEC Jean Puyol et Fils, 33330 Saint-Emilion, tel. 05.57.24.74.24, fax 05.57.24.62.77 by appt.

CLOS CANON 1997★

■ 14 ha 33,000 70–99 F

The second wine of Château Canon, a Saint-Emilion Premier Cru Classé, is made from 70% Merlot and 30% Cabernet Franc grapes grown on the prestigious limestone-clay soils of the Coteau Saint-Emilionnais. This dense, dark, deep ruby-red 1997 wine has a powerful, complex bouquet which mixes aromas of ripe fruits, hints of oak, grilling, toast and vanilla, and a range of spices (cinnamon and pepper). The wine fills the mouth well, with palatal tannins that are round at the beginning and still firm at the end. Keep in the cellar for three to five years.

SC Ch. Canon, B.P. 22, 33330 Saint-Emilion, tel. 05.57.55.23.45, fax 05.57.24.68.00 by appt.

CH. CHEVALIER BLANC 1997

■ 1.3 ha 8,000 30–49 F

The light, shining ruby appearance shows signs of maturing with its shimmering carmine lights. The bouquet is dominated by rather restrained musky scents, but releases aromas of small red and black fruits and fruits of the forest when the wine is swirled in the glass. The fresh, supple palate is agreeably round and fruit-based. An easy-drinking, pleasurable wine that is ready to drink now.

SARL SOVIFA, 36 A, rue de la Dordogne, 33330 Saint-Sulpice-de-Faleyrens, tel. 05.57.24.68.83, fax 05.57.24.68.83 by appt.

CH. CLOS SAINT-EMILION PHILIPPE Cuvée du Père 1997★

■ 2 ha 12,000 50–69 F

The producers of this vineyard are descended from Léon Galhaud, the agronomist and nurseryman. This Cuvée du Père is grown on sand, clinker and clay near Libourne. The colour is a dense ruby with a complex bouquet. The supple palate is structured by tannins which, though obvious, are already appealing.

🔑 SEA Philippe, 101, av. Gallieni, 33500 Libourne, tel. 05.57.51.05.93, fax 05.57.25.96.39 ☑ 🍷 by appt.

CH. CROIX DE FIGEAC 1997

■ 1.3 ha 8,000 30–49 F

The vineyard is old, but the brand is recent (1997). This is the second wine of the Vieux Château Croix de Figeac and is made from Merlot grapes grown on sandy soils. The colour has bright, attractive garnet highlights, and the bouquet is already harmonious, releasing fine notes of forest fruits. The palate is well-balanced with a pleasant roundness and elegant tannins.

🔑 SCEA Meunier et Fils, Vieux Château Croix de Figeac, 33330 Saint-Emilion, tel. 05.57.24.72.54, fax 05.57.24.72.54 ☑ 🍷 by appt.

LE D DE DASSAULT 1997

■ 10.45 ha n.c. 70–99 F

Since 1997, Château Dassault's second wine has been known as 'Le D de Dassault'.The vineyard was bought in 1955 by Marcel Dassault, and used to be called Château Merissac. This is a good-quality wine, even though the year was difficult. The colour is purple, with good intensity. The nose has scents of undergrowth and spices, and the palate is warm and sufficiently firm-structured to need keeping for two years before drinking.

🔑 SARL Ch. Dassault, 33330 Saint-Emilion, tel. 05.57.24.71.30, fax 05.57.74.40.33 ☑ 🍷 by appt.

The Saint-Émilion region

FORTIN PLAISANCE 1997

■ n.c. n.c. 30–49 F

This brand belongs to a well-known Bordeaux merchants whose 1995 wine was singled out for its excellence. The 1997 version is also attractive: it has a dark-garnet colour and a burgeoning bouquet which is still fruity but fairly complex. The wine's fullness on the palate and tannic structure are in good balance.

🔑 Cheval Quancard, La Mouline, 33560 Carbon-Blanc, tel. 05.57.77.88.88, fax 05.57.77.88.99 🍷 by appt.

CH. FRANC LE MAINE 1997

■ 12.66 ha 98,266 30–49 F

A substantial viticultural property of almost 13 ha (32 acres) on the sandy soils of Saint-Laurent-des-Combes, in the south-east of the appellation, planted with two-thirds Merlot and one-third Cabernets. The colour of this 1997 wine has already seen changes, and is cherry-red with brickish highlights. It is redolent of fruits in alcohol and blackcurrant buds. The palate is supple, with evolving velvety tannins which will allow it to be drunk fairly soon.

🔑 Union de producteurs de Saint-Emilion, Haut-Gravet, B.P. 27, 33330 Saint-Emilion, tel. 05.57.24.70.71, fax 05.57.24.65.18, e-mail udp-vins.saint-emilion@gofornet.com 🍷 ev. day except Sun. 8am–12 noon 2pm–6pm

🔑 Vignobles Beaubatit

CH. GRAND BERT 1997★

■ 5 ha 37,000 30–49 F

The Lavigne family owns several vineyards in the Saint-Emilion and Castillon districts. This wine comes from an 11-ha (27-acre) property on sandy and gravel soils at Saint-Sulpice-de-Faleyrens, in the south of the appellation. This 85% Merlot with 15% Bouchet is an attractive vivid ruby colour. The nose has a delightful oaky vanilla scent with touches of roasting and black fruits. The palate is supple and round, supported by elegant tannins. Wait a little while.

🔑 SCEA Lavigne, 33350 Saint-Philippe-d'Aiguilhe, tel. 05.57.40.60.09, fax 05.57.40.66.67, e-mail scealavigne@wanadoo.fr ☑ 🍷 by appt.

CH. GUERIN BELLEVUE 1997

■ 4.81 ha 6,000 30–49 F

This wine estate is now tended by the sixth generation of a family which took over in 1869. The wine comes from 70% Merlot and 30% Cabernets grown on sandy clay and gravel soils in the south of the appellation. The pretty ruby colour has orangey lights. The bouquet is subtle, with notes of spices and stewed fruits. This charmer of a palate finishes on silky tannins which imply that the wine will soon be ready for drinking.

🔑 Bernard Augereau, La Croix, 33330 Saint-Pey-d'Armens, tel. 05.57.47.15.58, fax 05.57.47.15.58 ☑ 🍷 by appt.

CH. HAUT-BRISSON 1997

n.c. n.c. 50–69 F

This is the first year for the new owners of his wine-estate located in the south of the ppellation. Their 1997 wine is made from 0% Merlot and 40% Cabernets vines planted n sandy and gravelly soil over iron slag. It as a lovely ruby colour with developing highights. The nose and palate are dominated by aky notes which still mask the fruit, but n several years' time this wine will appeal to overs of oak.

SCEA Ch. Haut-Brisson, 33330 Vignonet, tel. 05.57.84.69.57, ax 05.57.74.93.11 ☑ Y by appt.

CH. HAUTES VERGNES 1997

6.92 ha 8,000 30–49 F

An estate in the south-west of the commune, near the River Dordogne. The varieties nclude 40% Cabernets grown on sandy gravel oils. The vineyard is tended like a garden, which is natural enough for a marketgardener. The colour is a fairly intense ruby. The complex bouquet allies aromas of stewed ruits with a very marked note of tobacco. The dense palate also has a note of tobacco nixed with leather; the tannins make their presence felt and provide good structure.

Michel Nicoulaud, 33330 Saint-Emilion, el. 05.57.74.03.04, fax 05.57.74.03.04 ☑

CH. HAUT POURRET 1997*

2.75 ha 15,000 50–69 F

A small family estate on limestone-clay barely one kilometre (half a mile) west of Saint-Emilion, planted with two-thirds Merlot vines to one-third Cabernets. This vivid garnet wine has an expressive bouquet, which is still fruity (cherry and raspberry), with evolving notes of vanilla. The round palate has a fleshiness and a texture reinforced by well-bred tannins. Already a good wine for drinking, it will keep for several years.

Mourgout-Lepoutre, Ch. Haut-Pourret, 33330 Saint-Emilion, tel. 05.57.74.46.76, fax 05.57.74.46.76 ☑ Y by appt.

CH. HAUT-RENAISSANCE 1997**

2.5 ha 16,000 50–69 F

This is the fourth excellent wine in a row from this remarkable vineyard run by Denis Barraud. Selected grapes are from old Merlot vines, and lots of careful vine-tending and skill in the winery account for this superb result. The dense, deep-ruby colour has purple highlights. The bouquet is concentrated and expressive, exhaling aromas of cherry and crystallised red fruits harmoniously linked to a superb toasted and vanilla oakiness. The exquisite palate is sustained by ripe, round, silky tannins. This admirable wine has much finesse and elegance. Let it mature for one or two years in the cellar.

SCEA des Vignobles Denis Barraud, Ch. Haut-Renaissance, 33330 Saint-Sulpice-de-Faleyrens, tel. 05.57.84.54.73, fax 05.57.84.52.07, e-mail denis.barraud@wanadoo.fr ☑ Y by appt.

SAINT-ÉMILION
Château
Haut-Renaissance
APPELLATION SAINT-ÉMILION CONTRÔLÉE
1997
S.C.E.A. des Vignobles Denis Barraud
St Sulpice de Faleyrens - Gironde - France
ALC. 12% BY VOL.
750ML
MIS EN BOUTEILLE AU CHÂTEAU
PRODUCE OF FRANCE

CH. DE LA COUR 1997

3 ha 23,000 50–69 F

Ever since he purchased this Vignonet property in 1995, Hugues Delacour's Saint-Emilion has been recommended by wine-writers. The same goes for his 1997 vintage, despite it having been a difficult year. It has an attractive colour of bigaroon cherries. The bouquet is already complex and marries notes of minerals, cherry-stone kernels and musk. After a supple attack, the palate reveals excellent extraction, with obvious but velvety tannins that finish on an oaky note. A wine to enjoy.

EARL du Châtel-Delacour, Ch. de La Cour, 33330 Vignonet, tel. 05.57.84.64.95, fax 05.57.84.65.00, e-mail delacour@caves-particulieres.com ☑ Y by appt.

CH. LA CROIX BONNELLE 1997

6 ha 30,000 30–49 F

This vineyard (90% Merlot, 10% Cabernet Franc) is located on siliceous clay. Its brilliant light-ruby 1997 wine is pleasant and ready for drinking now. When the wine is swirled in the glass, the bouquet releases musky leather notes and fresh aromas of undergrowth and liquorice. The subtle, silky palate makes up for the slight lack of concentration with its excellent harmony and agreeable aromas of fresh red fruits.

SCEA des Vignobles Sulzer, La Bonnelle, 33330 Saint-Pey-d'Armens, tel. 05.57.47.15.12, fax 05.57.47.16.83 ☑ Y by appt.

CH. LA FLEUR GARDEROSE 1997

1.86 ha 14,400 50–69 F

A small vineyard located at Libourne in the former Sables Saint-Emilion AOC, planted with two-thirds Merlot vines and one-third Bouchet (the Saint-Emilion name for Cabernet Franc). The ruby colour still has a youthful appearance. The developing bouquet, too, is young and aromatic. The robust palate fills the mouth well and is supported by good-quality tannins.

GAEC Pueyo Frères, 15, av. de Gourinat, 33500 Libourne, tel. 05.57.51.71.12, fax 05.57.51.82.88, e-mail contact@belregard-figeac ☑ Y by appt.

LA GRANDE CUVEE DE DOURTHE 1997★★

■ n.c. n.c. 50–69 F

This Grande Cuvée is a remarkably successful wine matured and bottled by the merchants Dourthe Frères, directed by Jean-Marie Chadronnier. The strong ruby colour remains quite vivid. The intense and complex bouquet links aromas of red fruits and spices with nuances of tobacco and pepper. The supple, round, full palate has excellent structure and great harmony, with a long, well-mannered finish evoking fresh fruits. May be drunk now or kept for three or four years.

Dourthe, 35, rte de Bordeaux, B.P. 49, 33290 Parempuyre, tel. 05.56.35.53.00, fax 05.56.35.53.29, e-mail contact@cvbg.com ☒ Y by appt.

CH. LE SABLE 1997

■ 4.18 ha 9,900 50–69 F

This four-hectare (ten-acre) vineyard comprises 80% Merlot and 20% Cabernet vines more than 40 years old, grown on the sandy and limestone-clay soils of Saint-Laurent-des-Combes, south-east of Saint-Emilion. The colour of this 1997 wine is a deep ruby. The aromas are rather complex, including fruits and menthol. The fresh, supple palate finishes on silky tannins which should develop well.

SARL Cave de Larchevesque, 1, rue Guadet, 33330 Saint-Emilion, tel. 05.57.24.67.78, fax 05.57.24.71.31 ☒ Y ev. day 10am–12.30pm 1.30pm–7pm

Viaud

CH. LES VIEUX MAURINS 1997

■ 8 ha 20,000 30–49 F

This vineyard is regularly recommended and improves as the vines get older. They are now more than 40 years old. This 1997 wine is everything it should be. The colour is an attractive, garnet-fringed ruby. The nose has character (pepper, spices and meatiness), and the supple, flavoursome palate moves to a finish supported by delicate tannins.

Michel et Jocelyne Goudal, Les Vieux-Maurins, 33330 Saint-Sulpice-de-Faleyrens, tel. 05.57.24.62.96, fax 05.57.24.65.03 ☒ Y by appt.

CH. MONTREMBLANT 1997★

■ 1 ha 5,000 30–49 F

This tiny vineyard of one hectare (2.5 acres) represents one-twentieth of the Puyol family's vineyard. Located on siliceous gravel soils and planted with 70% Merlot, 15% Cabernet Franc and 15% Cabernet-Sauvignon, it has produced this medium-intensity ruby-coloured 1997 wine whose highlights indicate it is developing. When swirled in the glass, the wine is still discreet but sends out aromas of flowers, spices and oak mingling with musky notes of leather. The well-balanced palate has round, mellow tannins supporting a long finish on notes of fresh fruits. A pleasant wine that should be drunk in the next two years.

GAEC Jean Puyol et Fils, 33330 Saint-Emilion, tel. 05.57.24.74.24, fax 05.57.24.62.77 ☒ Y by appt.

CH. MOULIN DE LAGNET 1997★

■ 6 ha 18,000 30–49 F

This small family property on the sandy-clay soils of Saint-Christophe-des-Bardes contains 80% Merlot and 20% Cabernet vines. The brilliantly-clear red colour contains developing glints. The bouquet exhales aromas of dried fruits (prune and apricot) which mix with subtly attractive notes of oak. The supple palate contains good-quality tannins, making up for its slight lack of power with good fruity persistence. A nice, easy-drinking 1997 wine, ready to drink now.

A.-L. Goujon et P. Chatenet, Moulin de Lagnet, 33330 Saint-Christophe-des-Bardes, tel. 05.57.74.40.06, fax 05.57.24.62.80 ☒ Y by appt.

GFA Héritiers Olivet

CH. MOULIN DES GRAVES 1997★

■ 9.87 ha 75,000 50–69 F

This family vineyard is located on gravelly and ferruginous sandy soils. It is planted with 80% Merlot, 10% Cabernet Franc and 10% Cabernet-Sauvignon vines. This 1997 wine has a bright, attractive colour with orangey highlights. The nose mixes aromas of red fruits with subtle notes of vanilla oakiness. The palate has a fine tannic structure which is round and silky with a persistent, harmonious, discreetly liquorice finish. May be drunk now or over the next three or four years.

EARL des Vignobles J.-F. Musset, Ch. Hautes Graves d'Arthus, 33330 Vignonet, tel. 05.57.84.53.15, fax 05.57.84.53.15 ☒ Y by appt.

CH. PATARABET Vieilli en fût 1997

■ 8.29 ha 60,100 70–99 F

This vineyard, established in 1912 and tended by Eric Bordas since 1959, is regularly praised. The soils are sand, gravel and iron slag, planted with 70% Merlot and 30% Cabernet Franc. This dark-garnet 1997 wine has attractive brick-red highlights. The subtle and expressive nose evokes red fruits (cherries), with floral notes (peony) and nuances of vanilla and spices. The round, supple palate is supported by a reliable, well-mannered structure. An elegant wine that is ready for drinking.

SCE du Ch. Patarabet, 33330 Saint-Emilion, tel. 05.57.24.74.73, fax 05.57.24.78.62 ☒ Y ev. day 8am–12 noon 2pm–7pm

Eric Bordas

PAVILLON DU HAUT ROCHER 1997

■ 2 ha 14,400 50–69 F

This lovely property of 18 ha (45 acres) faces due south on a limestone-clay hillside east of Saint-Etienne-de-Lisse. This vineyard, which is half barrel-matured, accounts for two of the nine hectares (five of the 22 acres)

which Jean de Monteil devotes to AOC Saint-Émilion wine. The brilliant light-ruby colour of this 1997 wine has some carmine highlights. Its bouquet is fine and subtle, composed of red stone-fruits, floral notes and oaky nuances. The palate has good balance, crisp, fresh tannins and great suppleness. A simple, pleasant wine that is ready to drink now.

⊶ Jean de Monteil, Ch. Haut Rocher, 33330 Saint-Etienne-de-Lisse, tel. 05.57.40.18.09, fax 05.57.40.08.23, e-mail hautrocher@caves-particulieres.com ☑ Ⲧ by appt.

CH. PEREY-GROULEY 1997

■ 4.5 ha 30,000 ■ ♁ 30–49 F

This wine is produced from one-third of the vineyard (almost exclusively Merlot) cultivated by Florence and Alain Xans on sandy-gravel soils in the south of the appellation. Their intense purple wine is still musky in the nose, with a round attack and a palate which is moving towards silky tannins and an interesting renewal of aromas.

⊶ Vignobles F. et A. Xans, Perey, 33330 Saint-Sulpice-de-Faleyrens, tel. 06.80.72.84.87, fax 06.57.24.63.61 ☑ Ⲧ by appt.

CH. RASTOUILLET LESCURE 1997

■ 8.01 ha 61,152 ■ ♁ 30–49 F

Grown on the siliceous-clay and sandy soils of Saint-Hippolyte, this wine is made from 75% Merlot and 25% Cabernet. It is simple and pleasant, with a brilliant, vivid ruby colour and amber lights on the surface. The attractive bouquet releases notes of crystallised fruits mixed with musky notes and nuances of grilling and smokiness. The palate is easy and supple, with fresh, fruity aromas. A friendly wine, which will go well with roast poultry over the coming two years.

⊶ Union de producteurs de Saint-Emilion, Haut-Gravet, B.P. 27, 33330 Saint-Emilion, tel. 05.57.24.70.71, fax 05.57.24.65.18, e-mail udp-vins.saint-emilion@gofornet.com Ⲧ ev. day except Sun. 8am–12 noon 2pm–6pm

⊶ Geneviève Dumery

CH. DE SARPE 1997

■ 2.1 ha 13,600 ⦀ 70–99 F

One of the many Libourne-district wine-estates belonging to the vineyards of J.-F. Janoueix. Before its acquisition by this Corrèze family, it belonged to Count Amédée de Carles, King Louis XV's lieutenant-general. The wine is a pretty, fairly intense garnet colour. The aromas are still fruity (blackcurrant) with spicy notes. The palate is well-balanced, with a mouth-filling structure of silky, velvety tannins indicating that it may be drunk fairly soon.

⊶ Jean-François Janoueix, 37, rue Pline-Parmentier, B.P. 192, 33506 Libourne Cedex, tel. 05.57.51.41.86, fax 05.57.51.53.16, e-mail info@j-janoueix-bordeaux.com ☑ Ⲧ by appt.

CH. TOINET-FOMBRAUGE 1997

■ 6.55 ha 6,000 ■ ⦀ 50–69 F

Owned by the same family since the beginning of the 20th century, this vineyard is located on the limestone-clay soils of Saint-Christophe-des-Bardes and comprises 60% Merlot, 25% Cabernet Franc and 15% Cabernet-Sauvignon vines. It also produces a Saint-Emilion Grand Cru. This 1997 Saint-Emilion is a deep, intense ruby colour. The subtly oaky bouquet is developing aromas of ripe red fruits with several spicy notes. The attack is supple, followed by a tannic presence which is well-balanced, if somewhat firm at the finish. Ready for drinking from the end of 2000.

⊶ Bernard Sierra, Toinet-Fombrauge, 33330 Saint-Christophe-des-Bardes, tel. 05.57.24.77.70, fax 05.57.24.76.49 ☑ Ⲧ ev. day 10am–12 noon 3pm–7pm

CH. TONNERET 1997★★

■ 3.2 ha 7,000 ■ ⦀ 50–69 F

This small family vineyard is located on the limestone-clay and siliceous soils of Saint-Christophe-des-Bardes and is planted with 70% Merlot and 30% Cabernets vines. It offers a remarkable 1997 wine with a striking ruby colour and carmine lights. The bouquet is intense and extremely expressive, mixing aromas of ripe red fruits with oaky notes of vanilla and liquorice spiced with pepper. The palate has an excellent tannic structure, ideal for keeping, with fruitiness, richness and length. A wine to wait three or four years for.

⊶ Jacky Gresta, Tonneret, 33330 Saint-Christophe-des-Bardes, tel. 05.57.24.60.01 ☑ Ⲧ ev. day except Sun. 9am–12 noon 2pm–6pm

Saint-Émilion Grand Cru

CH. ARNAUD DE JACQUEMEAU 1997★

■ 3.71 ha 11,000 ■ ⦀ ♁ 70–99 F

A small family property bearing the founder's name (Arnaud) and the name of its locality (Jacquemeau). Its limestone-clay soil is planted with two-thirds Merlot and one-third Cabernet. Our tasters really liked this wine, which is very successful given its year. The colour is deep garnet, and the bouquet fine and complex with scents of oak and spices. The palate is well-structured and finishes on a well-ripened cherry note. Wait three years before drinking.

⊶ Dominique Dupuy, Jacquemeau, 33330 Saint-Emilion, tel. 05.57.24.73.09, fax 05.57.24.79.50 ☑ Ⲧ ev. day 9am–12 noon 2pm–6pm

CH. AUSONE 1997★★

■ 1er gd cru A 7 ha 22,000 500 F+

61 64 75 76 78 79 80 81 |82| 83 |85| 86 |87| |88| 89 90 |92| 93 |94| 96 97

These seven hectares (17 acres) are a standard-bearer for the appellation, located high in the Saint-Emilion hierarchy. This gem has been in Alain Vauthier's family for 250 years. Though a difficult year, this half-Merlot, half-Cabernet 1997 wine is remarkable. The tasters loved its attractive Bordeaux colour and the characterful, complex nose of oak, leather, roasted almonds, blackcurrant, humus and *pain d'épice* (a kind of spice loaf). The palate is fresh and dense, with a structure of excellent tannins. A great wine for keeping.

Famille Vauthier, Ch. Ausone, 33330 Saint-Emilion, tel. 05.57.24.70.26, fax 05.57.74.47.39

CH. BALESTARD LA TONNELLE 1997★

■ Gd Cru clas. 10.35 ha 57,000 150–199 F

83 85 86 |88| |89| |90| 92 |94| 95 96 97

This vineyard is named after a canon of the chapter of Saint-Emilion, and has been famous for centuries. The 15th-century poet François Villon sang of it in verse quoted on the label. Today, senior jurat Jacques Capdemourlin ensures its smooth running. His expertise is confirmed by this 1997 wine, which is very successful despite the difficulties of this vintage. The dark-garnet colour still looks young. The nose is empyreumatic, spicy and oaky. The elegant, flavoursome palate has a silky tannic structure, and in a few years it should be a pleasant accompaniment to game and casseroles.

SCEA Capdemourlin, Ch. Roudier, 33570 Montagne, tel. 05.57.74.62.06, fax 05.57.74.59.34 Y by appt.

CH. BARDE-HAUT 1997★

■ 17 ha 37,000 150–199 F

This lovely vineyard of 17 ha (42 acres) on the limestone-clay soil of Saint-Christophe-des-Bardes consists of 85% Merlot and 15% Cabernet Franc vines. Its dark, concentrated, very deep-purple 1997 wine has a powerful bouquet showing aromas of well-ripened grapes and red and black fruits that go well with the vanilla scents of good oak. After a smooth attack, the palate reveals a lovely well-blended tannic structure with lots of richness, mouth-filling qualities and density. Already a pleasing wine, it should be at its best in four to five years.

SCEA Barde-Haut, 33330 Saint-Christophe-des-Bardes, tel. 05.57.24.78.21, fax 05.57.24.61.15 Y by appt.

Philippe

CH. BEAUSEJOUR 1997

■ 1er gd cru B 5.75 ha 20,000 300–499 F

75 78 79 81 82 83 85 86 88 89 90 91 92 93 94 95 96 97

This seven-hectare (17-acre) Premier Grand Cru Classé has been tended by the same family for more than 150 years. Its south-western aspect, calcareous soil and well-balanced varieties of vine account for its reputation and consistent quality. Although this 1997 wine is not as good as previous versions such as the excellent 1995 vintage, it is recommended for its typical nature. The ruby colour has good intensity, and the deep bouquet shows black fruits and notes of oak and tobacco accompanied by a hint of menthol. The well-balanced palate is structured by tannins which are somewhat austere, but have an attractive flavour.

Héritiers Duffau-Lagarrosse, SC Ch. Beauséjour, 33330 Saint-Emilion, tel. 05.57.24.71.61, fax 05.57.74.48.40 Y by appt.

CH. BEAU-SEJOUR BECOT 1997

■ 1er gd cru B 16.5 ha 72,000 300–499 F

75 78 79 81 82 83 85 86 87 88 89 90 91 92 93 94 95 96 97

The owners of this beautiful wine estate have made great efforts over the last decade to see their château rejoin the Saint-Emilion Premiers Grands Crus. The goal was achieved with their 1996 wine, and now they have produced a perfectly honourable wine with a classic Bordeaux colour. The nose is somewhat reticent, but when the wine is left to breathe, it releases aromas of peat, venison and tobacco. The palate is simultaneously fresh and warm, which is surprising but contributes to its personality. The oak tannins are pleasant enough for this wine to be opened within the next two to three years.

G. et D. Bécot, SCEA Beau-Séjour Bécot, 33330 Saint-Emilion, tel. 05.57.74.46.87, fax 05.57.24.66.88 Y by appt.

CH. BELLEFONT-BELCIER 1997

■ 10.8 ha 46,000 100–149 F

95 96 |97|

This beautiful wine estate of ten hectares (25 acres) faces due south at the foot of the limestone-clay hillside at Saint-Laurent-des-Combes. Its name ('beautiful fountain') alludes to the numerous springs near the château and to its founder, the Marquess of Belcier. The orange highlights of this ruby-red 1997 wine show that it has started developing. The fine, expressive nose links aromas of small red fruits and spices to an attractive oakiness with nuances of toast and coconut. The supple, elegant palate is still somewhat marked by the oak-maturing, but is well-balanced and delicate. An agreeable wine which will soon be ready to drink.

SCI Bellefont-Belcier, 33330 Saint-Laurent-des-Combes, tel. 05.57.24.72.16, fax 05.57.74.45.06 Y by appt.

CH. BELLEVUE-FIGEAC 1997

■ 5.5 ha 40,000 70–99 F

This small vineyard of 5.5 ha (13.5 acres), formerly attached to Château Figeac, is on ancient wind-driven sands bordering the road between Saint-Emilion and Libourne. The brilliant garnet colour contains orangey lights. The bouquet is still discreet and subtly

1996 CLASSIFICATION OF SAINT-ÉMILION GRANDS CRUS

SAINT-ÉMILION, PREMIERS GRANDS CRUS CLASSÉS

A Château Ausone
Château Cheval-Blanc

B Château Angelus
Château Beau-Séjour (Bécot)
Château Beauséjour (Duffau-Lagarrosse)
Château Belair
Château Canon
Clos Fourtet
Château Figeac
Château La Gaffelière
Château Magdelaine
Château Pavie
Château Trottevieille

SAINT-ÉMILION, GRANDS CRUS CLASSÉS

Château Balestard La Tonnelle
Château Bellevue
Château Bergat
Château Berliquet
Château Cadet-Bon
Château Cadet-Piola
Château Canon-La Gaffelière
Château Cap de Mourlin
Château Chauvin
Clos des Jacobins
Clos de L'Oratoire
Clos Saint-Martin
Château Corbin
Château Corbin-Michotte
Château Couvent des Jacobins
Château Curé Bon La Madeleine
Château Dassault
Château Faurie de Souchard
Château Fonplégade
Château Fonroque
Château Franc-Mayne
Château Grandes Murailles
Château Grand Mayne
Château Grand Pontet
Château Guadet Saint-Julien
Château Haut Corbin
Château Haut Sarpe
Château La Clotte
Château La Clusière
Château La Couspaude
Château La Dominique
Château La Marzelle
Château Laniote
Château Larcis-Ducasse
Château Larmande
Château Laroque
Château Laroze
Château L'Arrosée
Château La Serre
Château La Tour du Pin-Figeac (Giraud-Belivier)
Château La Tour du Pin-Figeac (Moueix)
Château La Tour-Figeac
Château Le Prieuré
Château Matras
Château Moulin du Cadet
Château Pavie-Decesse
Château Pavie-Macquin
Château Petit-Faurie-de-Soutard
Château Ripeau
Château Saint-Georges Côte Pavie
Château Soutard
Château Tertre Daugay
Château Troplong-Mondot
Château Villemaurine
Château Yon-Figeac

oaky. The palate is supple, round and well balanced despite a slight lack of concentration. A simple, easy-drinking wine, ready to drink now.

🔑 Successeur J. de Coninck, Ch. Bellevue-Figeac, 33300 Saint-Emilion, tel. 05.57.55.58.00, fax 05.57.74.18.47

CH. BELLISLE MONDOTTE

1997★★

■ 4.5 ha 19,000 100–149 F

The vineyard is planted with 80% Merlot and 20% Cabernet Franc; the soils are limestone-clay and gravel. Half the maturing takes place in new barrels and half in barrels which have matured one wine. The result is a Saint-Emilion with an intense, dark-ruby colour and a bouquet evoking crystallised fruits and stewed prunes enhanced by very subtle notes of oak, grilling and liquorice. The palate is a harmonious mix of roundness, richness and fullness, thanks to the ripe, fleshy, velvety tannins. An astonishing wine given its year. Keep for three to four years.

🔑 GFA Héritiers Escure, Ch. Bellisle Mondotte, 33330 Saint-Laurent-des-Combes, tel. 05.57.74.41.17 ☒ Y by appt.

CH. BERGAT 1997

■ Gd cru clas. 4 ha 18,500 150–199 F

92 93 95 |96| 97

A small wine estate of four hectares (ten acres) on limestone-clay soil. The 35-year-old vines are 45% Cabernets. This gives a special character to the wine. The garnet colour has carmine highlights. When left to breathe, the wine reveals a bouquet of spices, menthol and meatiness, marked by a subtle floral touch. The palate is well-structured, but the tannins are still somewhat austere and need two or three years to soften.

🔑 Indivision Castéja-Preben-Hansen, Ch. Trottevieille, 33330 Saint-Emilion, tel. 05.56.00.00.70, fax 05.57.87.48.61 ☒ Y by appt.

CH. BERLIQUET 1997★

■ Gd cru clas. n.c. 21,000 150–199 F

88 89 91 92 |93| 94 95 |96| 97

This vineyard occupies a remarkable site on the limestone-clay plateau of Saint-Emilion. The vines are 35 years old, and this 1997 wine is an 85% Merlot (with the remainder Cabernet Franc). The colour is a dark and deep purple. The nose is very oaky to begin with, but when the wine is moved about in the glass, it releases floral and fruity notes. The palate too is dominated by good-quality oak, but is still somewhat severe. It should express its full potential within two to three years.

🔑 Vte Patrick de Lesquen, SCEA Ch. Berliquet, Ch. Berliquet, 33330 Saint-Emilion, tel. 05.57.24.70.48, fax 05.57.24.70.24 Y by appt.

AILES DE BERLIQUET 1997

■ n.c. 12,700 70–99 F

This second wine of Château Berliquet, created in 1993, has spent a year in oak. It is an intense ruby colour. The nose is still discreet, and the bouquet evokes floral and spicy perfumes. The palate opens on a supple and round note; it has a lovely tannic structure which is still firm and will enable it to be kept for two to three years.

🔑 Vte Patrick de Lesquen, SCEA Ch. Berliquet, Ch. Berliquet, 33330 Saint-Emilion, tel. 05.57.24.70.48, fax 05.57.24.70.24 Y by appt.

CH. BERNATEAU

Elevé en fût de chêne 1997

■ 10 ha 60,000 50–69 F

This wine-estate, which has been in the same family for three generations, is on limestone-clay soil planted with 85% Merlot and 15% Cabernet vines. The colour is a vivid and arresting ruby, and this 1997 wine is elegantly redolent of red fruits married to an oakiness that is subtle, toasted and spicy. The palate is well-balanced, with supple, delicious tannins. A simple wine, but nonetheless pleasing and ready to drink.

🔑 Régis Lavau, Ch. Bernateau, 33330 Saint-Etienne-de-Lisse, tel. 05.57.40.18.19, fax 05.57.40.27.31 ☒ Y by appt.

CH. BOUTISSE 1997

■ 20 ha 60,000 70–99 F

Bought in 1996 by the Milhades, wine-growers and merchants from Galgon in the north of the Libourne district, this vineyard has a limestone-clay terroir planted with 80% Merlot and 20% Cabernets. This is a satisfactory result for a first harvest in a difficult year. The wine is a pretty dark-ruby colour with garnet highlights. The bouquet is already expressive, with a play on notes of red fruits and toasted oak. The palate is supported by a pleasant vanilla-flavoured oakiness.

🔑 SCEA du Ch. Boutisse, 33330 Saint-Christophe-des-Bardes, tel. 05.57.55.48.90, fax 05.57.84.31.27 ☒ Y by appt.

🔑 Milhade

CH. CADET-BON 1997

■ Gd cru clas. 4.48 ha 21,000 150–199 F

90 92 93 **94** 95 (96) |97|

After losing its classification in 1986, this vineyard regained it in 1996. The 1997 harvests were more difficult, but they have still made a successful wine. Its highlights indicate its development. The expressive nose releases a succession of notes of violet, stewed fruits, leather and oaky vanilla. The supple and well-balanced palate is supported by already well-blended tannins. This wine can be drunk soon.

🔑 Loriene SA, 1, Le Cadet, 33330 Saint-Emilion, tel. 05.57.74.43.20, fax 05.57.24.66.41, e-mail loriene@cadet-bon.com ☒ Y by appt.

CH. CANON 1997★

■ 1er gd cru B 14 ha 32,000 250–299 F

|89| |90| |94| 96 97

This prestigious wine-estate has belonged to the Wertheimer family, owners of the firm of Chanel, since 1996. Substantial works have been undertaken in the wineries. Of the 18 ha (44 acres) of vines on the limestone-clay southern slope, 14 ha (35 acres) have been selected for this first wine. It is very successful despite the difficulties of 1997, with an attractive carmine-fringed ruby colour and an already complex bouquet dominated by toasted oak, coffee and liquorice. When left to breathe, it releases notes of menthol and nuances of truffles. The palate is also under the influence of heated oak, but the chalky flavour testifies to its origin. A wine of character.

SC Ch. Canon, B.P. 22, 33330 Saint-Emilion, tel. 05.57.55.23.45, fax 05.57.24.68.00 by appt.

Wertheimer

CH. CANON-LA-GAFFELIERE 1997★

Gd cru clas. 19.5 ha 55,000 250–299 F

A substantial wine-growing estate of about 20 ha (49 acres) of 30-year-old vines (half Cabernets and half Merlot) growing on a limestone-clay soil. The result is a very interesting 1997 wine, with a lovely dark, dense ruby colour. The bouquet, which is already complex and powerful, mixes cherry, leather, toasted oak and prune. The structure is astonishing, being both full and well-structured with good-quality tannins which will enable it to age well.

SCEV des Comtes de Neipperg, Ch. Canon-La-Gaffelière, 33330 Saint-Emilion, tel. 05.57.24.71.33, fax 05.57.24.67.95, e-mail vignobles.von.neipperg@wanadoo.fr by appt.

Comtes Neipperg

CH. CARDINAL-VILLEMAURINE 1997

6.5 ha 36,000 70–99 F

A vineyard whose name evokes both the memory of Cardinal de Gaillard de Lamothe, nephew to Pope Clement V, and a Moorish observation camp established when the Arabs invaded in the eighth century. This 1997 wine is very true to type, with a deep, dark-mauve colour and surface highlights of deep purple. The bouquet is fruity and elegant, recalling crystallised cherry, violets and liquorice. The palate has excellent concentration and dense tannins which are still a little energetic and rough, but which will soften with a few years' patience.

Jean-François Carrille, pl. du Marcadieu, 33330 Saint-Emilion, tel. 05.57.24.74.46, fax 05.57.24.64.40 by appt.

CH. CARTEAU COTES DAUGAY 1997★★

12.3 ha 70,000 70–99 F

82 83 86 |88| |**89**| |90| |**92**| |93| |94| |95| 96 **97**

This pretty 12-ha (30-acre) vineyard, located on the first slopes of Saint-Emilion on the Libourne side, is brilliantly consistent, and its deep-ruby 1997 wine is remarkable. The bouquet is vinous and complex, expressive of red fruits cooked in alcohol and subtle oaky nuances. The palate is full and powerful, with a rich, round tannic structure, offering superb length at the finish with a harmonious reappearance of the wine's aromas. Astounding potential.

SCEA Vignobles Jacques Bertrand, Carteau, 33330 Saint-Emilion, tel. 05.57.24.73.94, fax 05.57.24.69.07 by appt.

CH. DU CAUZE 1997

20 ha 120,000 70–99 F

85 88 89 |90| |92| |**93**| |94| 95 97

This lovely wine-estate of 20 ha (49 acres) is located on limestone-clay soils and planted with 40-year-old Merlot vines and 10% Cabernets. Its beautiful brilliant ruby 1997 wine is developing a nose of toast and vanilla derived from good oak, married to aromas of ripe red fruits and prune. The palate is fairly full and powerful, revealing tannins which need several more years' ageing to blend in.

Bruno Laporte-Bayard, SC du Ch. du Cauze, 33330 Saint-Emilion, tel. 05.57.74.62.47, fax 05.57.74.59.12 by appt.

CH. CHANTE ALOUETTE 1997

5 ha 28,000 70–99 F

Guy d'Arfeuille has been in charge of this vineyard since 1995. Twelve months in the barrel have produced this pleasant 1997 wine with a brilliant, clear, ruby colour. The burgeoning bouquet recalls crystallised red fruits with fine oaky aromas. The palate is lovely and well-balanced. The firm tannins should soften in two or three years' time.

Guy d'Arfeuille, Ch. Chante Alouette, 33330 Saint-Emilion, tel. 05.57.24.71.81, fax 05.57.24.71.81 ev. day 9am–12 noon 2pm–7pm

CH. CHEVAL BLANC 1997★★

1er gd cru A 35 ha n.c. 500 F+

61 64 66 69 70 71 72 73 74 |**75**| 76 77 |**78**| |**79**| 80 |**81**| |**82**| **83 85 86** 87 **88 89** **(90)** |**92**| |**93**| **94 95 96 97**

One of the two most prestigious vineyards in Saint-Emilion. Despite all the learned research, it remains a mystery for the specialists. Everything about it is remarkable: the situation, the Médoc range of grape types, and especially the pleasure it gives to the happy mortals who get the chance to taste it. This year it has overcome all the difficulties of 1997. The colour is a sumptuous dark, deep Bordeaux, with a promising bouquet in which the grape is present behind a vanilla, liquorice oakiness. The palate is both fleshy and elegant, strengthened by extremely subtle tannins. This is wine-making as great art.

SC du Cheval Blanc, 33330 Saint-Emilion, tel. 05.57.55.55.55, fax 05.57.55.55.50 by appt.

CLOS DE LA CURE 1997

■ 6.87 ha 24,000 50–69 F

|93| 95 96 97

Formerly attached to the living of the church of Saint-Christophe-des-Bardes (which accounts for the name), this estate has been cultivated by the Bouyer-Arteau family for the past seven generations. This elegant 1997 wine has a pretty ruby colour which is beginning to develop. The nose releases red fruits and prunes behind an oakiness that is currently rather marked. After a supple, round and fairly rich attack, the palate reveals its somewhat firm, severe tannins, which will require two or three years of patience.

Christian Bouyer, Ch. Milon, 33330 Saint-Christophe-des-Bardes, tel. 05.57.24.77.18, fax 05.57.24.64.20 Y by appt.

CLOS DE L'ORATOIRE 1997★

■Gd cru clas. 10.32 ha 50,000 150–199 F

82 |85| |88| |89| **|90| 92** |93| 97

A lovely ten-hectare (25-acre) vineyard at the foot of a sandy sloping bank planted mainly with Merlot and a supplementary 5% of Cabernet Franc. It has belonged to Count Stephan von Neipperg since 1991, and now offers an intense and strikingly young-looking red. The bouquet is powerful and complex, marrying aromas of well-ripened Morello cherry and strawberry to notes of vanilla and roasting derived from elegant oak. After a supple, round attack, the wine reveals its well-balanced, well-assembled structure. The round, ripe tannins provide a persistent finish. Wait two years, then drink this wine over the following five or six years.

SC du Ch. Peyreau, Ch. Peyreau, 33330 Saint-Emilion, tel. 05.57.24.71.33, fax 05.57.24.67.95, e-mail vignobles.von.neipperg@wanadoo.fr Y by appt.

Comtes de Neipperg

CH. CLOS DE SARPE 1997

■ 3.68 ha 8,000 70–99 F

A family property of four hectares (ten acres) located on the limestone-clay plateau between Saint-Emilion and Saint-Christophe-des-Bardes. This vineyard is planted with old Merlot vines with a 15% supplement of Cabernet Franc. The fresh, vivid ruby wine still looks very young and needs to breathe in the glass before it will release its aromas of stewed fruits, toast and spices. The palate confirms this young impression through its very obvious firm tannins and great energy. A wine to be appreciated after keeping in the cellar for four or five years.

SCA Beyney, Ch. Clos de Sarpe, 33330 Saint-Christophe-des-Bardes, tel. 05.57.24.72.39, fax 05.57.74.47.54 Y by appt.

CLOS FOURTET 1997★★★

■1er gd cru B n.c. 60,000 250–299 F

71 73 74 75 76 78 79 81 82 83 |85| 86 87 |88| **|89| |90| |91|** 92 |93| **|94| (95) 96 97**

It is the tough years that show up the good wine-makers. So, congratulations to this vineyard. Our tasters are not a particularly indulgent band, but they could not refuse this exceptional wine a *coup de coeur*. It is the work of two brothers, who are no less exceptional, namely André and Lucien Lurton, strong personalities in the Bordeaux wine world, plus their manager, Tony Ballu, and the head of the winery, Daniel Alard. The conclusions of the tasting were unanimous: a sumptuous colour; an astonishingly concentrated nose, in which good oak respects the ripe grape; an amazingly rich palate, which is fleshy, dense, structured, well-bred, very Saint-Emilion . . . In our enthusiasm, we forget to say that this magnificent wine is an 85% Merlot, grown on remarkable limestone-clay soil, that the 18th-century residence is elegant, and that we love tasting wine at Clos Fourtet.

SC Clos Fourtet, 33330 Saint-Emilion, tel. 05.57.24.70.90, fax 05.57.74.46.52

Lurton Frères

CLOS SAINT-MARTIN 1997

■Gd cru clas. 1.26 ha 7,000 150–199 F

81 85 86 88 89 |90| 92 93 |95| 96 97

This little vineyard, which once belonged to the presbytery of the church of Saint-Martin and comprises 70% Merlot and 30% Cabernets vines growing on limestone-clay, is the smallest of the Grands Crus Classés. The tasters liked its lovely ruby colour and already expressive bouquet, in which red fruits and spices accompany notes of oak. Though still dominated by the wood, the palate's tannins are very long-lasting. Wait a year or two.

GFA Les Grandes Murailles, Ch. Côte de Baleau, 33330 Saint-Emilion, tel. 05.57.24.71.09, fax 05.57.24.69.72 Y by appt.

Famille Reiffers

CLOS SAINT-VINCENT 1997

■ 4.64 ha 35,000 50–69 F

The elegant, carefully designed label lures wine-lovers to discover this vineyard of slightly less than five hectares (12 acres) located on sandy gravel at Saint-Sulpice-de-Faleyrens. It belongs to the Latorse family, who are well known in the Entre-Deux-Mers district. The wine has pretty ruby highlights, and the bouquet is slightly mineral, with musky, liquorice and oaky notes which emerge when the wine is left to breathe. The supple, silky palate is supported by liquorice tannins, which imply that this 1997 wine can be drunk fairly soon.

SC du Clos Saint Vincent, 33330 Saint-Sulpice-de-Faleyrens, tel. 05.56.23.92.76 ☑ Y by appt.

CLOS TRIMOULET 1997

■ 7 ha 38,000 50–69 F

An attractive, family property on the northern side of the commune, located on sandy-clay soils and planted with 80% Merlot and 20% Cabernets. The rather light ruby colour heralds a wine of subtlety with perfumes of red fruits. The palate is well-balanced and fruity on a support of discreet tannins. The long finish is also sustained by the fruit.

EARL Appollot, Clos Trimoulet, 33330 Saint-Emilion, tel. 05.57.24.71.96, fax 05.57.74.45.88 ☑ Y by appt.

CLOS VILLEMAURINE 1997*

■ 2 ha 8,000 100–149 F

This vineyard, created in 1966, returns to eminence with this 1997 wine, thanks to good plot selection from its two hectares (five acres), extreme care in vinification and successful maturing in new oak, all competently executed by Jean-François Carrille. The result is a wine with a dense, dark-purple colour and a powerful, complex bouquet, mixing aromas of ripe red fruits with an attractive toasted, spicy oakiness. The very concentrated palate has a rich and fruity structure with high-quality tannins which provide a long and persistent finish. They will also help it to keep well.

Jean-François Carrille, pl. du Marcadieu, 33330 Saint-Emilion, tel. 05.57.24.74.46, fax 05.57.24.64.40 Y by appt.

CH. COTES DE ROL 1997*

■ 3 ha 21,000 70–99 F

Robert Giraud is an important Bordeaux wine-merchant-cum-grower. His Côtes de Rol is made from 75% Merlot (40-year-old vines) and 25% Cabernets, planted on wind-deposited sands. The result is a very successful 1997 wine, with a fine ruby colour and traces of vermilion. The powerful bouquet mixes spices, black fruits and fine, lightly toasted notes of oak. The round, supple palate reveals rich, mellow tannins, well-blended into a dense, sturdy structure. A wine that will reach its full potential in two to three years.

SCA Vignobles Robert Giraud, B.P. 31, 33240 Saint-André-de-Cubzac, tel. 05.57.43.01.44, fax 05.57.43.08.75, e-mail direction@robertgiraud.com ☑

CH. COUDERT-PELLETAN 1997*

■ 4 ha 24,600 70–99 F

86 **88** 92 |93| |94| **95** 96 97

Made from grapes selected from the vineyard's oldest plots, this oak-matured wine is a 60% Merlot, 20% Cabernet Franc and 20% Cabernet-Sauvignon blend, grown on the limestone-clay soils of Saint-Christophe-des-Bardes. This very successful 1997 wine has a strikingly vivid ruby-red colour and an attractive, elegant bouquet with aromas of fruit and toast. The palate reveals a good tannic structure which, though currently rather firm, should become smoother in two or three years' time.

Pierre et Philippe Lavau, Ch. Coudert-Pelletan, 33330 Saint-Christophe-des-Bardes, tel. 05.57.24.77.30, fax 05.57.24.66.24 ☑ Y ev. day 9am–6pm; Sat. Sun. by appt.

CH. CROIX DE LABRIE 1997*

■ 0.37 ha 1,200 500 F+

|91| **|92|** **|93|** 95 **96** 97

This microscopic vineyard, established in 1991, has recently had considerable success. Made up exclusively of old Merlot vines planted on gravel, its small size means it can be tended very intensively. The wine is a lovely dark and intense ruby. The nose is still somewhat closed, but very promising, with aromas of good-quality oak, toast and vanilla on top of scents of well-ripened red fruits. The balanced, robust palate is supple and round, sustained by silky, well-blended tannins. It will be ready in two to three years, when it should reach its full potential.

SCEA Puzio-Lesage, B.P. 41, 33330 Saint-Emilion, tel. 05.57.24.64.60, fax 05.57.24.64.60 Y by appt.

CH. DESTIEUX 1997*

■ 8 ha 35,000 70–99 F

81 82 83 85 86 |(88)| |89| |90| 92 93 **94** 95 96 97

Eight hectares (20 acres) of vines facing due south (two-thirds Merlot, one-third Cabernets), have again yielded a wine worthy of note. Our tasters were impressed by its good keeping qualities. Deep ruby in colour, it has an intense nose with a basis in black fruits and toasted oak. The palate is warm and powerful, stuctured by sturdy tannins which will mature fully in several (three to five) years.

Dauriac, Ch. Destieux, 33330 Saint-Hippolyte, tel. 05.57.24.77.44, fax 05.57.40.37.42 ☑ Y by appt.

CH. FAUGERES 1997*

■ 25.6 ha 110,000 100–149 F

|93| **|94|** **95 96** 97

Corinne Guisez's vineyard has an excellent reputation. Her 1997 wine is another notable success. The colour is a dark, deep ruby, with deep-purple highlights on the surface, heralding a wine still full of youthful vim. The developing bouquet released when the wine is swirled in the glass contains aromas of red fruits and spices linked to pleasant oaky perfumes. The palate reveals a structure whose firmness, power and good balance guarantee a happy future.

🗝 Corinne Guisez, Ch. Faugères, 33330 Saint-Etienne-de-Lisse, tel. 05.57.40.34.99, fax 05.57.40.36.14, e-mail faugeres@club-internet.fr ☑ Y by appt.

CH. FERRAND LARTIGUE 1997★★

■ 6 ha 24,000 ⅡⅠ 150–199 F

|94| 95 |96| 97

Old Merlot vines (90%) planted on limestone-clay and sand, careful vinification and good maturation in oak have produced this remarkable 1997 wine. The ruby colour is dense and deep with purple highlights. The complex, balanced palate marvellously marries aromas of ripe fruits and toasty nuances derived from a superb oakiness. The palate is full and powerful, with a rich, intense, firm structure making this a good wine to keep for the next four to six years.

🗝 Michelle-Pierre Ferrand, 33330 Saint-Emilion, tel. 05.57.74.46.19, fax 05.57.74.46.19 ☑ Y by appt.

CH. FIGEAC 1997

■ 1er gd cru B 40 ha 95,000 ⅡⅠ 300–499 F

62 **64 66** (70) **71** 74 **75 76** 77 **78** 79 80 |**81**| |**82**| |**83**| |**85**| |**86**| 87 **88 89** 90 92 |**93**| **94** (95) 96 |97|

Figeac, on the gravels of Saint-Emilion, is the site of a Gallo-Roman villa named Figeacus (history is often just beneath the surface in the great vineyards). Since 1892, the château has been in the same family, and Thierry Manoncourt celebrated his 50th wine-year with a memorable 1995 vintage. The vineyard is today administered by his son-in-law, Eric D'Aramon, and contains 70% Cabernets, something of a rarity in the AOC. This 1997 wine has a ruby colour of good intensity and is garnet-edged with orangey lights. The nose has aromas of ripe fruits and good-quality vanilla oak, and the palate is supported on fine, elegant tannins – 'well-made lace', as one taster put it. Good to drink while we wait for the remarkable wines of the preceeding years.

🗝 Thierry Manoncourt, Ch. Figeac, 33330 Saint-Emilion, tel. 05.57.24.72.26, fax 05.57.74.45.74, e-mail chateau-figeac@chateau-figeac.com Y by appt.

CH. FLEUR CARDINALE 1997★

■ 10 ha n.c. ⅡⅠ 70–99 F

82 83 85 86 |88| |89| |(90)| 91 92 |**93**| |**94**| 95 **96** 97

This lovely vineyard of ten hectares (25 acres) belongs to the Asséo family, who left the textile industry to come here in the early 1980s. Thanks to the balance of varieties (70% Merlot, 15% Cabernet Franc and 15% Cabernet-Sauvignon), the superb terroir of limestone-clay over rocks, and the owners' skill, this vineyard consistently provides wines of high quality. This very successful dense-garnet 1997 vintage has an intense bouquet rich in aromas of prune, crystallised fruits, coffee and toast, mixed with spicy scents. The palate reveals an excellent structure, with tannins which begin round, rich and fleshy, and move on to a rather firm finish. They will need another two or three years to become better assimilated.

🗝 Alain et Claude Asséo, Ch. Fleur Cardinale, 33330 Saint-Etienne-de-Lisse, tel. 05.57.40.14.05, fax 05.57.40.28.62 ☑ Y by appt.

CH. FOMBRAUGE 1997★★

■ 43 ha 285,000 ⅡⅠ 70–99 F

86 |88| |90| 91 92 93 (95)(96) |**97**|

This very important wine-estate of 75 ha (185 acres), of which 43 ha (106 acres) are devoted to this wine, was established in 1679. It recently belonged to a Danish group and has just been purchased by the Bordeaux merchant, Bernard Magrez. This 1997 wine has a dark Bordeaux colour. When it is swirled in the glass, the rather closed nose releases complex scents of black fruits, spices and toasty notes. The full, fleshy palate is enriched with subtly oaky, persistent tannins. A really lovely wine.

🗝 SA Ch. Fombrauge, 33330 Saint-Christophe-des-Bardes, tel. 05.57.24.77.12, fax 05.57.24.66.95 Y by appt.

🗝 M. Magrez

CH. FONPLEGADE 1997

■ Gd cru clas. 14.6 ha 80,000 ⅡⅠ 150–199 F

82 83 85 86 **88** |90| 92 |93| |94| 95 96 |97|

The name Fonplégade comes from a spring on the property which is still active. Furrows made by the Romans are still visible here. The vineyard is located on limestone-clay and siliceous lime soils, with a good balance of varieties: 60% Merlot and 40% Cabernet Franc. The 1997 wine shows signs of evolution with its shimmering light-carmine colour. The bouquet is subtle and rather fruity, with its delicately oaky aromas of cherry (including Morello cherry) and hints of vanilla and spices. A touch of menthol contributes a note of freshness. The palate's very pleasing elegant, silky tannins make up for the very slight lack of concentration.

🗝 SC Dom. viticoles Armand Moueix, Ch. Fonplégade, 33330 Saint-Emilion, tel. 05.57.74.43.11, fax 05.57.74.44.67 ☑ Y by appt.

CH. FONROQUE 1997★

■ Gd cru clas. 19.26 ha 52,800 ⅡⅠ 100–149 F

81 82 83 85 86 88 |89| |**90**| |92| |93| **95** |97|

Grown on limestone-clay soils and made from 90% Merlot and 10% Cabernet Franc grapes, Château Fonroque is carefully and traditionally vinified and attentively matured in oak casks. The result is this elegant, well-balanced 1997 wine, which has a beautiful dark and shiny, slightly faded garnet colour. The fine and complex bouquet is expressive of stewed red fruits, Morello cherry, vanilla and toast, with a floral nuance of violets. The attack on the palate is supple and round, unveiling the silky charm of well-blended tannins. 'Matured with tact,' noted one taster.

🗝 Ets Jean-Pierre Moueix, 54, quai du Priourat, 33500 Libourne

🗝 GFA Fonroque

CH. FORTIN 1997

■ 6 ha 36,000 70–99 F

This vineyard is located on gravel in the Fortin sector of the AOC. The wine is a medium-intensity ruby with amber lights, and needs to be left to breathe in order to release its fruity, meaty notes and hint of damp leather. The palate is light but well balanced, the flavour still fruity. A wine to drink quite soon. Distributed by wine-merchants Kressmann.

Laubie et Fils, Ch. Fortin, 33330 Saint-Emilion, tel. 05.56.35.53.00, fax 05.56.35.53.29, e-mail contact@cvgb.com

CH. FRANC LARTIGUE 1997

■ 7 ha 40,000 70–99 F

This vineyard of 60% Merlot and 40% Cabernet Franc vines is located on sands and gravel at Vignonet, in the south of the appellation. It is a pleasing, uncomplicated wine which is ready to drink now. The light, agreeable and subtle bouquet releases ripe red-fruit aromas with notes of vanilla and toast. The pleasant harmony of the supple, round, tender and silky palate compensates for a certain lack of structure. This 1997 wine should not be kept for longer than two years.

Vignobles Marcel Petit, 6, chem. de Pillebois, 33350 Saint-Magne-de-Castillon, tel. 05.57.40.33.03, fax 05.57.40.06.05 by appt.

Toxé

CH. FRANC-MAYNE 1997★★

■ Gd cru clas. 4 ha 22,000 150–199 F

85 86 **|88| |89|** |90| **|92|** 95 **96 97**

This seven-hectare (17-acre) vineyard is located on limestone-clay and molasses along the Gallo-Roman road between Libourne and Saint-Emilion. Purchased from the AXA group in 1996 by the Belgian wine-dealer Georgy Fourcroy, it has been the subject of huge investment to maximise the benefits of its exceptional terroir. This 1997 wine proves its excellence, with its superb dark, dense ruby colour and bouquet of ripe fruits mixing harmoniously with the vanilla notes of elegant, well-blended oak. The palate reveals a powerful, well-balanced wine which is rich and concentrated. Still a little reticent, but full of promise.

Georgy Fourcroy, SCEA Ch. Franc-Mayne, 33330 Saint-Emilion, tel. 05.57.24.62.61, fax 05.57.24.68.25 by appt.

CH. FRANC PATARABET 1997★

■ 6 ha 25,000 50–69 F

This vineyard, in the heart of the medieval town, has a fine monolithic cellar in which the bottles slowly age. The vineyard comprises 60% Merlot and 40% Cabernets, planted on siliceous clay. This 1997 wine, with its bright, clear ruby colour, still seems to have a somewhat closed nose with hints of stewed strawberries and pleasant oak. The palate is very well balanced, subtle and elegant with well-blended, silky tannins. The finish is beautifully long-lasting with aromas of vanilla and liquorice. The wine could be drunk now or any time in the next five years.

GFA Faure-Barraud, rue Guadet, B.P. 72, 33330 Saint-Emilion, tel. 05.57.24.65.93, fax 05.57.24.69.05, e-mail franc-patarabet@wanadoo.fr by appt.

CH. FRANC PIPEAU Descombes 1997

■ 5.38 ha 30,000 50–69 F

86 88 89 (90) 91 92 93 94 95 97

This former Saint-Emilion property became exclusively a vineyard in 1880. It now comprises 5.4 ha (13.2 acres) on sand and limestone-clay (70% Merlot and 30% Cabernets), and has produced this very pleasing 1997 wine with a typical, lively Bordeaux colour. The bouquet is pleasantly oaky, with a touch of vanilla over the beautiful red fruit aromas. The well-balanced and harmonious palate slightly lacks structure, but this is made up for by the subtle tannins and flavours. A pleasant wine which will be ready to drink within two or three years.

SCEA Vignobles Jacques Bertrand, Carteau, 33330 Saint-Emilion, tel. 05.57.24.73.94, fax 05.57.24.69.07 by appt.

CH. GRAND BARRAIL LAMARZELLE FIGEAC 1997★

■ 15.12 ha 105,000 100–149 F

This 1997 wine represents the first year under the new owner of an estate located between Libourne and Saint-Emilion, close to the hôtel of the same name. Vines (75% Merlot and 25% Cabernet Franc) planted on iron-rich siliceous gravel have yielded a dark, dense garnet-coloured wine which still looks very young. The developing bouquet releases crystallised cherry and other red fruits, plus notes of menthol and spices mixed with tar derived from very burnt wood. The structure is powerful and firm. Good extraction and maturing are evident, but the wine needs a few years to blend and open.

Ch. Grand Barrail Lamarzelle Figeac, 33330 Saint-Emilion, tel. 05.57.24.71.43, fax 05.57.24.63.44, e-mail grandbarrail@wanadoo.fr

MM. Parent

CH. GRAND CORBIN 1997

■ 13.27 ha 77,866 70–99 F

An attractive family property on siliceous clay. This wine, made from 68% Merlot, 5% Cabernet-Sauvignon and 27% Cabernet Franc, is light in colour and, when left to breathe, releases aromas of fruit and pepper. Its well-balanced palate has flavours of clove and oak. The obvious presence of silky tannins bodes well for ageing.

Sté Familiale Alain Giraud, 5, Grand Corbin, 33330 Saint-Emilion, tel. 05.57.24.70.62, fax 05.57.74.47.18 by appt.

CH. GRAND-CORBIN-DESPAGNE 1997★

■ 17 ha 85,000 ▮▮ 70–99 F

|89| **90** |93| 94 95 96 97

The Despagne family is widely established in the Bordeaux wine region, especially in Libourne, where they go back to the 17th century. In the north, towards Pomerol, this vineyard blends 80% Merlot with 20% Cabernet Franc, grown on sandy clay and ancient sands. The wine is an attractive cherry colour and, when left to breathe, reveals a nose that is still fruity with a fine oakiness and notes of menthol. The flavour is charmingly velvety, with a still somewhat oaky finish, but this should mature in the next three or four years.
🔑 SCEV Consorts Despagne, Ch. Grand-Corbin-Despagne, 33330 Saint-Emilion, tel. 05.57.51.08.38, fax 05.57.51.29.18, e-mail cl.despagne@grand-corbin-despagne.com ☑ Y by appt.

CH. GRAND MAYNE 1997★

■Gd cru clas. 17 ha 58,000 ▮▮ 200–249 F

75 78 81 82 83 85 86 87 88 |89| **|90|** 91 92 |93| 94 95 **96** 97

A fine estate surrounding a manor built under Henri IV, this vineyard offers a very successful 1997 wine grown on 17 ha (42 acres) out of a total of 21 ha (52 acres). The colour is a lovely deep garnet. The burgeoning bouquet exhales scents of black fruits and oaky liquorice. The palate is warm, still dominated by the oak, which needs to soften. The extraction has evidently been good and will enable the wine to evolve well.
🔑 Jean-Pierre Nony, 1, Le Grand-Mayne, 33330 Saint-Emilion, tel. 05.57.74.42.50, fax 05.57.24.68.34, e-mail grand-mayne@grand-mayne.com ☑ Y by appt.

CH. GRAND-PONTET 1997★

■Gd cru clas. 14 ha 70,000 ▮▮ 150–199 F

81 82 83 85 86 |88| |89| **|90|** 91 |93| 94 **95** 96 97

Five hundred metres (546 yd) from the ancient church of Saint-Martin-de-Mazerat, on a limestone plateau to the west of Saint-Emilion, Grand-Pontet makes attractive wines blended from 75% Merlot, 15% Cabernet Franc and 10% Cabernet-Sauvignon. This strong, lively 1997 wine reflects both the roundness of the Merlot variety and the strength of the terroir. Dark, deep ruby in colour, it has a bouquet which mixes aromas of ripe red fruits and spices with subtle, well-blended notes of oak. The palate is robust, fleshy and full, with a good, well-balanced structure which provides a very persistent finish. A nice wine to keep and to drink in four years' time with red meats and game.
🔑 Ch. Grand-Pontet, 33330 Saint-Emilion, tel. 05.57.74.46.88, fax 05.57.24.66.88 Y by appt.
🔑 Bécot-Pourquet

CH. GROS CAILLOU 1997

■ 6 ha 30,000 ▮▮ 50–69 F

A wine-estate of 20 ha (49 acres), six (15 acres) of which have yielded this 1997 wine composed of 60% Merlot and 20% each of the two Cabernets. Ruby in colour with vermilion lights, it is developing an intense bouquet of ripe fruits, leather and spices. The palate is well balanced, with supple, round tannins, good flesh and a very pleasant, long-lasting finish. A Saint-Emilion of quality, a classic, which will soon be ready to drink.
🔑 SCEA des Vignobles Jacques Dupuy, Ch. Gros Caillou, 33330 Saint-Sulpice-de-Faleyrens, tel. 05.57.24.74.91, fax 05.57.74.40.98 ☑ Y by appt.

CH. GUEYROSSE 1997★

■ 4.6 ha 18,000 ▮▮▮ 70–99 F

86 |90| 92 |93| |94| 96 97

Near the gates of Libourne, this vineyard is planted with two-thirds Merlot and one-third Cabernets. The wine, which is fined in the barrel with egg-white, is not filtered when it is bottled. The colour, ruby with vermilion lights, is clear. The forceful bouquet is marked by gamey scents and notes of spicy ripe fruits. The robust and supple palate has a dense yet soft structure, good mouth-filling qualities, and an easy, pleasant finish. Wait two years.
🔑 EARL Vignobles Yves Delol, Ch. Gueyrosse, 33500 Libourne, tel. 05.57.51.02.63, fax 05.57.51.93.39 ☑ Y by appt.

CH. HAUT-CADET

Elevé en barrique de chêne 1997

■ 1.32 ha 8,933 ▮▮▮ 70–99 F

|(89)| |90| |92| |93| |94| 95 97

This small vineyard of 1.5 ha (3.7 acres) belongs to the Belgian Roger Geens's Vignobles Rocher Cap de Rive. Planted on limestone-clay, it comprises 80% Merlot and 20% Cabernet-Sauvignon. The garnet colour of this 1997 wine betrays signs of evolution, and the nose is a little closed, though some red fruits and spicy aromas do come through together with a hint of menthol. After a supple attack, the palate continues with a tannic structure which is dense and firm. Though the palate is currently somewhat severe, it should become friendlier with ageing.
🔑 Vignobles Rocher Cap de Rive 1, Ch. Haut-Cadet, 33330 Saint-Emilion, tel. 05.57.40.08.88, fax 05.57.40.19.93, e-mail vignoblesrochercaprive@wanadoo.fr

CH. HAUT-CORBIN 1997★★

■Gd cru clas. 6.01 ha 40,300 ▮▮ 150–199 F

81 (82) **83 85 86** |88| |90| |91| |92| **|93|** 94 (97)

Located to the north of Saint-Emilion not far from Pomerol, this vineyard on sandy soils over limestone-clay is planted with well-balanced varieties: 65% Merlot, 25% Cabernet-Sauvignon and 10% Cabernet Franc. This 1997 wine defies its difficult year, charming the jury with the superb quality of its remarkable structure, vinification and maturation. The dense, deep-ruby colour has no highlights as yet. The bouquet is complex and elegant, a harmonious marriage of burnt good-quality oak, toasting, vanilla and caramel with aromas of ripe grapes, crystallised red

fruits and prunes. The palate is just as good: a robust, fleshy, vinous, flavoursome whole, possessing a magnificent tannic structure suited to long keeping. Well done!

SC Ch. Haut-Corbin, 33330 Saint-Emilion, tel. 05.57.51.95.54, fax 05.57.51.90.93 by appt.

CH. HAUT LAVALLADE 1997*

■ 5 ha 40,000 70–99 F

94 95 96 97

Established in the middle of the 19th century and regularly noticed by wine-writers, the vineyard made this wine from a severe and rigorous selection of 5 ha (12 acres) of grapes out of its total of 12 ha (30 acres). Grown on siliceous clay and the limestone-clay of the northern part of the AOC, this 1997 vintage has an intense colour. The bouquet still contains woody notes, but the palate is mouth-filling and intense with great potential. It leaves an excellent impression.

SARL J.P.M.D. Chagneau, Ch. Haut-Lavallade, 33330 Saint-Christophe-des-Bardes, tel. 05.57.24.77.47, fax 05.57.74.43.25 by appt.

CH. HAUT-PONTET 1997

■ 4.78 ha n.c. 70–99 F

93 |94| 96 97

The essentially Merlot vines of this vineyard, close to the town of Saint-Emilion, are rooted in the wind-driven sands of the Mindel, deposited more than 600,000 years ago over calcareous formations. It has produced a dark-red 1997 wine with orangey highlights which is ready to drink now. The nose is marked by the oak, with scents of tobacco, tar, coffee and toast. The palate is feminine and subtle, thanks to its supple tannins and the elegance of its aromas.

Jean Daspet, GFA Ch. Haut-Pontet, 33330 Saint-Emilion, tel. 05.57.43.17.82, fax 05.57.43.22.74 by appt.

CH. HAUT ROCHER 1997

■ 6 ha 40,000 70–99 F

This purple wine is a selection from six hectares (15 acres) of limestone-clay planted with two-thirds Merlot and one-third Cabernet. The nose is still fruity, with notes of raspberry, redcurrant and crystallised fruit. The attack is supple, the palate fruity. The tannins still make for a somewhat firm finish and need time to soften (two to three years).

Jean de Monteil, Ch. Haut Rocher, 33330 Saint-Etienne-de-Lisse, tel. 05.57.40.18.09, fax 05.57.40.08.23, e-mail hautrocher@caves-particulieres.com by appt.

CH. HAUT-VEYRAC 1997*

■ 6 ha 40,000 50–69 F

This vineyard, composed of 75% Merlot and 25% Cabernet Franc, is on limestone-clay soil. The colour of its 1997 wine is a lovely bright and vivid ruby. The bouquet is subtle and agreeable, mixing aromas of red fruits with an elegant oakiness. The structure is well-balanced: the tannins are obvious, but already velvety and well-blended, and provide excellent length. A nice bottle at an affordable price. Drink in three to five years' time.

SCA Ch. Haut-Veyrac, 33330 Saint-Etienne-de-Lisse, tel. 06.13.78.87.45, fax 06.57.74.05.98 by appt.

Claverie

CH. JEAN VOISIN

Cuvée Amédée 1997*

■ 14 ha 30,000 100–149 F

The wine is named after Amédée Chassagnoux, who acquired the vineyard in 1955. It is regularly singled out by wine-writers, and this 1997 wine is a good achievement in a not particularly easy year. It has a lovely colour with garnet highlights and a nose which, when the wine is left to breathe, exhales aromas of red fruits and caramelised oak. The dense, spicy palate has a structure of good oak tannins which are already velvety.

SCEA du Ch. Jean Voisin, 33330 Saint-Emilion, tel. 05.57.24.70.40, fax 05.57.24.79.57, e-mail chassag@quaternet.fr by appt.

Chassagnoux

CH. LA BONNELLE 1997

■ 6 ha 30,000 70–99 F

93 |94| |95| 96 97

La Bonnelle, a château dating from the start of the 19th century, overlooks a beautiful garden which is open to visitors. The vineyard is mainly Merlot vines with 10% Cabernet Franc, growing on siliceous clay to the east of the appellation. This 1997 wine is a bright and vivid ruby-red. The bouquet is still discreet, diffusing fresh aromas of red fruits mingling with musky scents. The tannic structure is well-balanced, if a little firm at the moment. Such firmness nevertheless bodes well for keeping.

SCEA des Vignobles Sulzer, La Bonnelle, 33330 Saint-Pey-d'Armens, tel. 05.57.47.15.12, fax 05.57.47.16.83 by appt.

F. Sulzer

CH. LA CHAPELLE-LESCOURS 1997

■ 4.18 ha n.c. 50–69 F

Formerly a chapel belonging to the Château of Lescours, this property has grown vines since the 14th century. Located not far

from Libourne on a hill of sandy gravel, it is planted with 80% Merlot and 20% Cabernet Franc, vinified and matured with respect for Saint-Emilion tradition. The colour is a bright, clear ruby-red. The nose is still restrained, mixing mineral aromas with fresh nuances lightly redolent of menthol. The palate is supple and well-balanced, the tannins pleasant. It will soon be ready for drinking.
🔑 François Quentin, Ch. La Chapelle-Lescours, 33330 Saint-Emilion, tel. 05.57.74.41.22, fax 05.57.74.41.22, e-mail Vitis33@Libertysurf.fr ☑
Y by appt.

CH. DE LA COUR 1997

■ 3.3 ha 22,000 70-99 F

This 1997 wine represents Hugues Delacour's third year at Saint-Emilion. The young wine-grower from Champagne has settled at Vignonet on a nine-hectare (22-acre) property. The wine is dark garnet with lovely carmine highlights. The bouquet is marked by the 95% Merlot grapes; aromas of well-ripened red and black fruits are spiced by a subtle oakiness. The palate is forceful and well-balanced, with good structure.
🔑 EARL du Châtel-Delacour, Ch. de La Cour, 33330 Vignonet, tel. 05.57.84.64.95, fax 05.57.84.65.00, e-mail delacour@caves-particulieres.com ☑ Y by appt.

CH. LA COUSPAUDE 1997

■ Gd cru clas. 7.01 ha 36,000 250-299 F

82 83 85 86 88 |(89)| |90| 91 |92| **|93|** |94| **95** 96 |97|

This seven-hectare (17-acre) family property belongs to the tight circle of Grands Vineyards classified in 1996. It is located at the gates of Saint-Emilion on the road from Saint-Christophe-des-Bardes. Every summer it hosts cultural activities. The colour of this 1997 wine reveals signs of evolution. The nose has scents of prune, liquorice and caramelised oak. The palate is already harmonious, with a supple attack and velvety tannins. A charming wine that may be drunk quite soon.
🔑 Vignobles Aubert, Ch. La Couspaude, 33330 Saint-Emilion, tel. 05.57.40.15.76, fax 05.57.40.10.14 ☑ Y by appt.

CH. LA DOMINIQUE 1997★

■ Gd cru clas. 22 ha 86,000 300-499 F

82 83 85 **86 87** |88| **|89|** |90| 91 92 **|93|** |94| 95 **96** 97

This property, located very close to Pomerol and purchased by Clément Fayat in 1969, is named after the West Indian island of Dominica, where a former, 18th-century owner made his fortune. Grown on sandy gravel and made from 80% Merlot, 15% Cabernet Franc and 5% Cabernet-Sauvignon, this very successful 1997 wine is an attractive dark-red colour with carmine highlights. Though currently dominated by rather burnt notes of oak, vanilla and toast, it has a flavoursome attack. The rich, fleshy tannins slowly evolve on the palate towards a finish which is still a little firm. Wait three to five years for it to reach its full potential.
🔑 Clément Fayat, Ch. La Dominique, 33330 Saint-Emilion, tel. 05.57.51.31.36, fax 05.57.51.63.04, e-mail info@vignobles.fayat-group.com ☑

CH. LA FLEUR CRAVIGNAC 1997

■ 7.75 ha 51,000 70-99 F

This vineyard, established in the 18th century, is on limestone-clay and siliceous clay with iron waste. The wine is a pretty garnet colour of good intensity. When left to breathe, the wine exhales notes of flowers, red fruits and oak. The palate is well-structured, with excellent tannins which should in time become more subtle. Wait two or three years.
🔑 SCEA Ch. Cravignac, Cravignac, 33330 Saint-Emilion, tel. 05.57.74.44.01, fax 05.57.84.56.70 ☑ Y by appt.
🔑 L. et A. Beaupertuis

CH. LA FLEUR DE JAUGUE 1997★

■ n.c. 18,000 70-99 F

This vineyard is a family property located at the eastern gates of Libourne in what used to be the AOC 'Sables Saint-Emilion'. In fact it is located on a small hill of clay on gravel planted with 80% Merlot and 20% Cabernet. The wine is a great success for its year. It is an attractive dark-garnet colour. The nose, which is already intense, exhales aromas of oak, toast and spices, with a touch of leather. The palate is fleshy and honest; the tannins are obvious but pleasant. A well matured wine. Wait two to three years.
🔑 Georges Bigaud, 150, av. du Gal-de-Gaulle, 33500 Libourne, tel. 05.57.51.51.29, fax 05.57.51.29.70 ☑ Y by appt.

CH. LA FLEUR PEREY

Cuvée Prestige Vieillie en fût de chêne 1997

■ 3.5 ha 24,000 50-69 F

93 94 |95| |96| |97|

Florence and Alain Xans select 3.5 ha (8.6 acres) from their total of 13 ha (32 acres) to produce this Cuvée Prestige. The wines are about 50 years old, 80% Merlot and 20% Cabernets growing on sandy gravel. The colour of this 1997 wine has developing highlights. The nose starts with flowers, then moves on to small berry-fruits such as blackcurrant. This easy-drinking wine has a supple attack and fills the mouth well before finishing on easy tannins. Good with white meats.
🔑 Vignobles F. et A. Xans, Perey, 33330 Saint-Sulpice-de-Faleyrens, tel. 06.80.72.84.87, fax 06.57.24.63.61 ☑ Y by appt.

CH. LA FLEUR PICON 1997★

■ 5.6 ha 25,000 50-69 F

94 95 97

Christian Lassègues runs this family property on siliceous clay soils planted with 70% Merlot and 30% Bouchet. The 1997 wine has a deep-red colour and a nose which, after the wine has been left to breathe, releases aromas of black fruits, spices, warm oak and pepper. The palate is well-structured with both grape

and oak tannins, and should go on developing well.
🔑 Christian Lassègues, La Fleur Picon, 33330 Saint-Emilion, tel. 05.57.24.70.60, fax 05.57.24.68.67 ☑ 🍷 by appt.

CH. LA GAFFELIERE 1997★

■ 1er gd cru B 20 ha 80,000 250-299 F

75 78 79 80 81 (82) 83 84 85 |86| 87 88 89 |90| 91 92 |93| |94| 95 96 |97|

This lovely wine-estate of more than 20 ha (49 acres) is located several hundred yards from the south gate of the medieval town, between Ausone and Pavie. The same family have been in charge for almost four centuries. But in fact the vines have been here since Gallo-Roman times, as is proved by a mosaic with a vine-stock motif. This wine is purple with carmine highlights. The nose is subtle: dried fig, vanilla and oakiness with a note of tobacco. The elegant palate has tannins which are already silky and bear flavours of vanilla and cocoa, which make it a wine to drink fairly soon.
🔑 Léo de Malet Roquefort, Ch. La Gaffelière, B.P. 65, 33330 Saint-Emilion, tel. 05.57.24.72.15, fax 05.57.24.69.06 ☑ 🍷 by appt.

CH. LA GARELLE 1997★

■ 8.35 ha 30,000 70-99 F

This 1997 wine, Jean-Luc Marette's fourth year at the vineyard, is a good piece of work. The colour is intense ruby and the nose already has complexity, mixing red fruits with scents of oak and vanilla. The structure shows excellent extraction, shaped by sturdy tannins which will guarantee good ageing for this wine.
🔑 Jean-Luc Marette, Ch. La Garelle, 33330 Saint-Emilion, tel. 05.57.24.61.98, fax 05.57.24.75.22 ☑ 🍷 by appt.

CH. LA GOMERIE 1997

■ 2.52 ha 9,600 500 F+

The manor of La Gomerie belonged to Faise Abbey for more than four centuries. The current modest vineyard of 2.5 ha (6.1 acres) corresponds to the enclosure in which the former priory buildings stood. Taken over in 1995 by the Becot family, this exclusively Merlot vineyard is well-tended and offers an attractive 1997 wine. It is a deep shade of ruby, with an intense and complex nose which mixes scents of fruits with the notes of toast and vanilla which come from good new oak. The palate is robust, round and well-balanced, with a degree of firmness at the finish which should soon fade.
🔑 G. et D. Bécot, GFA La Gomerie, 33330 Saint-Emilion, tel. 05.57.74.46.87, fax 05.57.24.66.88 🍷 by appt.

CH. LA GRACE-DIEU-LES-MENUTS 1997★

■ 13.05 ha 72,500 70-99 F

86 88 |89| 91 93 |94| 95 96 97

This is a wine-estate of more than 13 ha (32 acres), cultivated by the same family for several generations. In 1999, Odile Audier took over from her parents. The success of this 1997 wine is all the more commendable as it represents the estate's sole crop. The jury appreciated its lovely garnet colour and subtle bouquet, which needs a little airing to bring out its notes of fruits and spices. The palate is elegant, structured by subtle oaky tannins. This is a very pleasant wine, well worth keeping for three to four years.
🔑 EARL Vignobles Pilotte-Audier, La Grâce-Dieu, 33330 Saint-Emilion, tel. 05.57.24.73.10, fax 05.57.74.40.44 ☑ 🍷 by appt.

CH. LA GRANGERE 1997★

■ 6.88 ha 30,000 100-149 F

This vineyard, founded in 1995, is marketed by the wine-trade. Its 1997 wine is well made, with a pretty ruby colour and a nose dominated by aromas of stewed ripe red fruits reminiscent of crystallised cherries, with subtle notes of oak, toast and vanilla. The palate reveals an excellent tannic structure, which is powerful and robust. The rich, fleshy tannins provide a very long finish. A wine to keep.
🔑 SCEA Ch. La Grangère, 33330 Saint-Laurent-des-Combes, tel. 05.57.24.71.43, fax 05.57.24.63.44, e-mail grandburrail@wanadoo.fr
🔑 Louis et Jean Parent

CH. LAMARZELLE CORMEY 1997

■ 5 ha 24,000 50-69 F

This vineyard, exclusively planted with Merlot, occupies a surface vein of clay over ancient sands. The 1997 wine is garnet in hue with brick-red highlights caused by evolution. The nose exhales aromas of stewed red fruits mixed with spicy notes. The palate is supple and round, pepped up by a degree of energy and freshness, and the finish is spicy. A simple, pleasant wine, ready for drinking now.
🔑 SCEA Cormeil-Figeac, B.P. 49, 33330 Saint-Emilion, tel. 05.57.24.70.53, fax 05.57.24.68.20, e-mail moreaud@cormeil-figeac.com ☑ 🍷 by appt.
🔑 Richard Moreaud

CH. DES LANDES 1997

■ 5 ha 15,000 100-149 F

This vineyard, located on the sandy soils of Vignonet, blends 60% Merlot, 30% Cabernet Franc and 10% Cabernet-Sauvignon for its first year's wine. The garnet colour is clear and intense. The bouquet, though still somewhat marked by the oak-maturing, is dominated by aromas of vanilla and toast, with hints of leather and coffee. When the wine is twirled in the glass, fresh notes of liquorice appear. The palatal structure is pleasant, supple, round and full. An elegant wine, ready to be enjoyed now.
🔑 GFA du Haut-Saint-Georges, Arvouet, 33330 Vignonet, tel. 05.57.55.38.00, fax 05.57.55.38.01 ☑ 🍷 by appt.

CH. LAPELLETRIE 1997

■ 12 ha 80,000 70–99 F

An important property of 20 ha (49 acres), of which 12 ha (29 acres) are devoted to producing this wine marketed by Yvon Mau. Merlot vines, planted on slopes of limestone-clay, account for 90% of the grapes. The colour is a very young-looking ruby, and the nose is still fruity, with a touch of oak. The palate has good balance and is supported by the tannins, which are still fresh.

SA Yvon Mau, B.P. 1, 33193 Gironde-sur-Dropt Cedex, tel. 05.56.61.54.54, fax 05.56.61.54.61 Y by appt.

CH. LAPLAGNOTTE-BELLEVUE 1997*

■ 5.54 ha 31,000 70–99 F

A fine property cultivated by the descendants of the Fourcaud-Laussac family, former owners of Cheval Blanc. It is located on the siliceous clay of Saint-Christophe-des-Bardes in the north of the appellation and planted with two-thirds Merlot to one-third Cabernets. The wine's fine purple colour contains highlights due to evolution. The discreet but elegant bouquet exhales notes of red fruits and well-adjudged oakiness, with a touch of spices. The palate is both subtle and well-bred. The finish, on a note of crystallised fruits, is extremely pleasant.

Claude de Labarre, Ch. Laplagnotte-Bellevue, 33330 Saint-Christophe-des-Bardes, tel. 05.57.24.78.67, fax 05.57.24.63.62, e-mail arnauddl@aol.com V Y by appt.

CH. L'APOLLINE 1997

■ 2.8 ha 15,000 70–99 F

This 1997 wine is the first Saint-Emilion Grand Cru to be presented by this property, which is planted with two-thirds Merlot and one-third Cabernet-Sauvignon growing on sandy clay over gravel. The wine is true to type and a successful start to the new classification. The dark-garnet colour still displays youthful ruby highlights. The intense, powerful bouquet mixes well-ripened red fruits with the spicy, smoky, toasty notes of good oak. The palate has a robust and supple attack, leading to a lovely fullness, richness and fleshiness. As the finish shows, the tannins are still a little severe and require two to three years ageing.

EARL Ch. L'Apolline, Le Brégnet, 33330 Saint-Sulpice-de-Faleyrens, tel. 05.57.51.26.80, fax 05.57.51.26.80 V

Genevey

CLOS LARCIS 1997*

■ 1 ha 6,000 100–149 F

|89| |90| 91 92 |93| |94| |97|

This small-scale production comes from a little one-hectare (2.5-acre) vineyard, hemmed in on the side of a hillside between Pavie and Larcis-Ducasse. The vines are exclusively Merlot and about 30 years old. They yield a 1997 wine with a lively, clear ruby colour. The nose mixes aromas of ripe red fruits with the grilled notes of good oak. The palate is very pleasant, with supple, delicate tannins and excellent harmony between the savours of ripe grapes and those of well-adjudged oakiness.

SCA Vignobles Robert Giraud, B.P. 31, 33240 Saint-André-de-Cubzac, tel. 05.57.43.01.44, fax 05.57.43.08.75, e-mail direction@robertgiraud.com V

CH. LARMANDE 1997*

■ Gd cru clas. 25 ha 150,000 150–199 F

81 82 83 85 86 | (88) | |89| |90| 92 |93| **94 96** 97

Larmande is a fine wine-estate of 25 ha (62 acres) located one kilometre (1100 yd) north of Saint-Emilion on a limestone-clay and sandy plateau. Since 1990 it has belonged to the La Mondiale company. This 1997 wine is a blend of 65% Merlot, 30% Cabernet Franc and 5% Cabernet-Sauvignon. The colour is an attractive dark ruby. The bouquet mixes aromas of red fruits with elegant aromas of toast, burnt oak and vanilla. The supple, round attack introduces a palate with a well-formed, powerful structure which, though still firm, guarantees a good future.

SCE du Ch. Larmande, Lieu-dit Larmande, 33000 Bordeaux, tel. 05.57.24.71.41, fax 05.57.74.42.80, e-mail chateau-larmande@wanadoo.fr Y by appt.

La Mondiale

CH. LA ROSE COTES ROL 1997*

■ 5 ha 31,000 50–69 F

|94| 95 96 97

This vineyard, which regularly attracts good notices, is located on a sandy glacis planted with 65% Merlot and 35% Cabernets vines. The wine is a pretty Bordeaux colour. It has a fairly concentrated bouquet with interesting notes of chalk and leather. The robust, well-shaped palate contains long, flavoursome tannins, which make this wine good for keeping. Good with game and red meats.

SCEA Vignobles Mirande, Ch. La Rose Côtes Rol, 33330 Saint-Emilion, tel. 05.57.24.71.28, fax 05.57.74.40.42, e-mail mpmirande@aol.com V Y by appt.

CH. LA ROSE-POURRET 1997*

■ 8 ha 38,000 70–99 F

|94| |95| 96 97

This eight-hectare (20-acre) vineyard has been a family property for five generations. It comprises 70% Merlot, 20% Cabernet Franc and 10% Cabernet-Sauvignon vines growing on siliceous clay mixed with iron slag, one kilometre (1100 yd) west of the medieval town. This 1997 wine has a fine Bordeaux colour and a nose which blends aromas of ripe fruits with the grilled notes of good oak. The palate is round and vinous; the tannins are rich and silky and support a long, persistent finish of aromatic harmony.

Warion, SCEA Ch. La Rose Pourret, 33330 Saint-Emilion, tel. 05.57.24.71.13, fax 05.57.74.43.93 V Y by appt.

CH. LA ROSE PRESSAC 1997

■ 5 ha n.c. 30–49 F

This small wine-estate belongs to the Lafaye family but its wine is exclusively marketed by Cordier. It is located on the southern limestone-clay slope at Saint-Etienne-de-Lisse in the east of the AOC. This clean-cut 1997 wine has a light colour and a supple, direct palate. When the wine is twirled in the glass, the discreet nose releases pleasant fruity notes. The well-blended tannins mean it can be drunk soon.

Vignobles Lafaye Père et Fils, Saint-Etienne-de-Lisse, 33330 Saint-Emilion, tel. 05.57.40.18.28, fax 05.57.40.02.70

CH. LAROZE 1997

■ Gd cru clas. 27 ha 80,000 100–149 F

85 86 88 89 |90| 91 92 |93| |94| 95 96 97

Guy Meslin runs this family estate established in 1882. The 1997 wine is typical of its year and has spent 12 months in the barrel. The colour is a beautiful carmine, and the nose has hints of caramel and leather, plus a musky touch. The palate has mouth-filling qualities and is supported by well-formed tannins which are quite silky. Wait a little.

Guy Meslin, SCE Ch. Laroze, 33330 Saint-Emilion, tel. 05.57.24.79.79, fax 05.57.24.79.80, e-mail ch.laroze@wanadoo.fr by appt.

CH. LASSEGUE 1997

■ 25 ha n.c. 70–99 F

A fine wine-estate surrounding an 18th-century charterhouse on the south of the hillside at Saint-Hippolyte, east of Saint-Emilion. The vineyard is planted on siliceous clay and limestone-clay. The colour of this 1997 wine has clear ruby highlights. The nose is fruity, but also has a touch of musk and menthol. The palate has a supple, liquorice attack fortified by good-quality tannins. A wine that can be drunk fairly soon.

SC des Vignobles Freylon, 33330 Saint-Hippolyte, tel. 05.57.24.72.83, fax 05.57.74.48.88 by appt.

CH. LA TOUR FIGEAC 1997

■ Gd cru clas. 8 ha 32,000 150–199 F

82 83 85 86 |89| |**90**| 93 |94| 95 **96** 97

La Tour Figeac is a former branch of Château Figeac, from which it was detached in 1879. Its name comes from a tower which stood there around 1800. This first wine is a selection of eight hectares (20 acres) out of the 15 ha (37 acres) making up this property on sand and gravel soils close to Pomerol. The colour has pretty garnet highlights. The bouquet is still a little closed. Given time to breathe, the wine moves from floral scents (violets and wild rose) through venison to mineral notes (gunflint). After a supple attack, the palate evolves with tannic support which is still slightly bitter and needs time to soften a little more.

SC Ch. La Tour Figeac, B.P. 007, 33330 Saint-Emilion, tel. 05.57.51.77.62, fax 05.57.25.36.92 by appt.

Rettenmaier

CH. LA VOUTE 1997

■ 1.19 ha 7,200 70–99 F

|94| |95| |96| 97

This small-scale vineyard established by the Moreau family in 1993 is located on the brown clay of the plateau of Saint-Etienne-de-Lisse and is planted exclusively with Merlot. The 1997 wine offered is very pleasant. The colour is a superb deep ruby with purple highlights, and the bouquet is subtle and elegant, evocative of fresh small red fruits and good oak. The palate has great charm; it is supple, round and well-balanced. an enjoyable wine to serve straight away with poultry and grills.

EARL Moreau, Ch. d'Arvouet, 33570 Montagne, tel. 05.57.74.56.60, fax 05.57.74.58.33, e-mail moreaulavoute@aol.com by appt.

CH. LE PRIEURE 1997

■ Gd cru clas. 6.02 ha 36,000 100–149 F

This business came into being when the famous vineyard of the Cordeliers was broken up; it was acquired by the current owner's grandfather, Olivier Guichard, former minister of state to General de Gaulle. Made from 60% Merlot and 40% Cabernets planted on limestone-clay soil, this 1997 vintage is a fine wine, whose lack of concentration is shrewdly balanced by its subtlety and elegance. Though it appears to be developing in the glass, its aromas are still somewhat restrained (a mixture of red fruits, floral scents of violet, fresh notes of undergrowth and hints of vanilla). The round, well-blended, silky tannins leave an impression of harmony and make it suitable for drinking straight away.

SCE Baronne Guichard, Ch. Siaurac, 33500 Néac, tel. 05.57.51.64.58, fax 05.57.51.41.56 by appt.

Olivier Guichard

CH. LES GRANDES MURAILLES 1997★

■ Gd cru clas. 2 ha 2,500 150–199 F

88 |(89)| 94 |95| 96 97

This tiny vineyard of two hectares (five acres) is located beneath the ruins of a 12th-century Jacobin convent, one of Saint-Emilion's most remarkable monuments. It has been in the same family since 1643, and is today run by one of the owners, Sophie Fourcade. This 1997 wine is an intense garnet colour, and the nose is extremely expressive, with notes of spices, black fruits, toast, vanilla and liquorice. The palate is warm and well-balanced, with a structure of oak tannins which should mature well. A wine to keep.

BORDEAUX

🔑 GFA Les Grandes Murailles, Ch. Côte de Baleau, 33330 Saint-Emilion, tel. 05.57.24.71.09, fax 05.57.24.69.72 ☑ Y by appt.
🔑 Famille Reiffers

CH. LES GRAVIERES

Cuvée Prestige Vieilli en fût de chêne 1997★

■ 3.5 ha 18,000 70–99 F

89 90 **91 92 |93| |94|** (95) **96** 97

The winery and offices installed in the old buildings on the banks of the Dordogne appeared in the recent television series 'La Rivière Espérance' with Jean-Claude Drouet. The wine is well known and comes from a 10% selection of the vines grown. Though it has not scaled the heights in this difficult year, it is still judged a success: a lovely dark-garnet colour, a fruity, oaky bouquet and a palate of great potential. A wine to keep.
🔑 SCEA des Vignobles Denis Barraud, Ch. Haut-Renaissance, 33330 Saint-Sulpice-de-Faleyrens, tel. 05.57.84.54.73, fax 05.57.84.52.07, e-mail denis.barraud@wanadoo.fr ☑ Y by appt.

LES PLANTES DU MAYNE 1997★

■ n.c. 15,000 100–149 F

Château Grand Mayne's second wine has benefited from a year of excellent maturing in oak. The colour is a lovely bright, clear ruby. The bouquet is harmonious and powerful, subtly mixing aromas of well-ripened grapes with those of elegant oak. The palate is well-balanced and pleasant, with silky tannins and a flavoursome finish; it evokes fresh red and black crystallised fruits mixed with vanilla.
🔑 Jean-Pierre Nony, 1, Le Grand-Mayne, 33330 Saint-Emilion, tel. 05.57.74.42.50, fax 05.57.24.68.34, e-mail grand-mayne@grand-mayne.com ☑ Y by appt.

CH. LUCIE 1997

■ 3 ha 12,000 70–99 F

This small property was acquired in 1995 by Michel Bortolussi. It grows almost all Merlot (90%), but the soils are varied (clay, gravel and sand). The wine has a colour of good intensity. The nose begins on a musky note, then evolves on caramelised oak. The attack is supple and fresh, and the palate continues with the warm notes of a well-regulated oakiness. This well-made 1997 wine is ready now, but may be kept another three or four years.
🔑 Michel Bortolussi, 316, Grands-Champs, 33330 Saint-Sulpice-de-Faleyrens, tel. 05.57.74.44.42, fax 05.57.24.73.00 ☑ Y by appt.

CH. MAGDELAINE 1997★

■ 1er gd cru B 10.36 ha 28,800 200–249 F

70 75 78 79 80 82 (83) 85 **|86| |87| |88| |89| 90 |92| |93| |94| 95** |96| |97|

This is a vineyard that regularly proves its worth, even in difficult years – proof of good vinification skills. Environment too plays a part: this exceptional terroir lies in the heart of the Saint-Emilion Premiers Grands Crus Classés of which it is one. The pretty colour of this 1997 wine has ruby and purple highlights. The nose releases notes of stewed fruits, prune, tobacco and fine oak. On the palate, the balance between grape and oak is perfect. There is a very persistent flavour of prune, and the finish is supported by subtle tannins and has an attractive harmony.
🔑 Ets Jean-Pierre Moueix, 54, quai du Priourat, 33500 Libourne

CH. MAGNAN 1997

■ 10 ha 50,000 70–99 F

82 85 86 88 |(89)| 91 92 |94| |96| 97

This vineyard is located on ancient sands planted with 70% Merlot and 30% Cabernet Franc. It already figured among the foremost Crus of Saint-Emilion in the Cocks et Féret guide of 1861. Bought by the Moreaud family in 1979, it has since been totally reorganised. The 1997 wine is very true to type. The garnet colour contains brick-red highlights. The expressive nose mixes notes of red fruits in alcohol and crystallised fruits with nuances of toast. The palate is supple and strong, balanced by well-blended tannins, and the well-structured finish indicates that the wine can be kept for several years.
🔑 SCEA Cormeil-Figeac, B.P. 49, 33330 Saint-Emilion, tel. 05.57.24.70.53, fax 05.57.24.68.20, e-mail moreaud@cormeil-figeac.com ☑ Y by appt.
🔑 Richard Moreaud

CH. MANGOT 1997

■ 30.5 ha n.c. 70–99 F

Château Mangot is a large wine-estate of nearly 30 ha (74 acres) in the east of the appellation, standing on fossil-bearing calcareous deposits. The wine is a pretty, moderately intense ruby colour, with a subtle bouquet dominated by oak, vanilla, spices and toast with a touch of cherry. The supple palate is supported by rather charming oak tannins. An easy-drinking wine that should be drunk soon. The **1997 Cuvée Quintessence** is a developing wine, also recommended (100–149F).
🔑 Vignobles Jean Petit, Ch. Mangot, 33330 Saint-Etienne-de-Lisse, tel. 05.57.40.18.23, fax 05.57.40.15.97, e-mail chmangot@terre-net.fr ☑ Y ev. day 8am–12 noon 2pm–6pm; Sat. Sun. by appt.

DOM. DE MARTIALIS 1997★

■ n.c. 23,000 100–149 F

This is the second wine of Clos Fourtet, a Premier Grand vineyard Classé located at Saint-Emilion on a fine limestone-clay terroir. Cabernet Franc accounts for almost 40% of the blend. This is a characterful wine, ruby in colour with garnet lights. It is redolent of toast and oak with notes of clove. The subtle, elegant palate reveals that it may be served from this winter on, but it can wait some months more.
🔑 SC Clos Fourtet, 33330 Saint-Emilion, tel. 05.57.24.70.90, fax 05.57.74.46.52
🔑 Lurton Frères

CH. MATRAS 1997★

■Gd cru clas. 9 ha 30,000 100–149 F

82 **83 85** 86 |**90**| 92 |93| 94 97

Located on the southern side of the Saint-Emilion slopes, whose limestone-clay soils are mixed with iron slag, Matras has a somewhat unusual spread of varieties for Saint-Emilion: 40% Merlot, 30% Cabernet Franc, 20% Cabernet-Sauvignon and 10% Malbec. The colour of this 1997 wine is a well-presented dark, deep garnet. The nose is intensely expressive of scents of red fruits mixed with spices and notes of grilling, all refreshed by aromas of liquorice and undergrowth. The palate is supple, round, balanced and elegant, with good ripe, fleshy tannins and a long fruity finish.

Vignobles Bernard et Véronique Gaboriaud, Ch. Matras, 33330 Saint-Emilion, tel. 05.57.51.52.39, fax 05.57.51.70.19 by appt.

CH. MAUVEZIN 1997

■ 3.5 ha 15,000 100–149 F

|90| |94| |95| 96 97

Purchased in 1968 and composed of 55% Merlot and 45% Cabernets (40 years old) growing in fossil-bearing calacareous soils, this estate belongs to the Cassat family which has patented an air-conditioned grape-selecting table. This 1997 wine is a bright ruby colour. The bouquet's grilled, vanilla notes merge with the aromas of ripe red fruits. The palatal structure is still somewhat severe, being marked by the high proportion of Cabernet. It should soften in the next three to five years.

GFA P. Cassat et Fils, B.P. 44, 33330 Saint-Emilion, tel. 05.57.24.72.36, fax 05.57.74.48.54 by appt.

CH. MONBOUSQUET 1997★★

■ 33 ha 80,000 250–299 F

|93| |**94**| |**95**| 96 **97**

This 33-ha (82-acre) vineyard is one of the estates acquired by the Perse family at Saint-Emilion (Pavie, Pavie-Decesse and La Clusière). Its consistent progress since its purchase in 1993 has led to this astounding 1997 wine with its very intense, dark and deep-purple colour. The intense, harmonious palate mixes aromas of crystallised red fruits with the elegant roasted, toasty and spicy perfumes bequeathed by good oak. The palate's richness and density are due to the powerful fleshiness of the grapes, and it reveals its well-bred, rich, long-lasting tannins. A fine, very promising wine.

SA Ch. Monbousquet, 33330 Saint-Sulpice-de-Faleyrens, tel. 05.57.55.43.43, fax 05.57.24.63.99 by appt.

Gérard Perse

MONDOT 1997★

■ 3.6 ha 11,000 100–149 F

Mondot is the highest point of the commune of Saint-Emilion (106 m/348 ft). It is also the second wine of Troplong Mondot (Grand Cru Classé) grown on this limestone-clay hillock and blended from 40% Merlot and 60% Cabernets. This 1997 wine has a superbly intense, vivid garnet colour with purple highlights. The bouquet is already expressive, evocative of Morello cherry and blackcurrant buds, with very pleasant oak perfumes. The firm, dense palate reveals tannins which are still somewhat severe, but ensure good keeping.

Christine Valette, Ch. Troplong-Mondot, 33330 Saint-Emilion, tel. 05.57.55.32.05, fax 05.57.55.32.07 by appt.

CH. MONLOT CAPET 1997

■ 7 ha 45,000 100–149 F

|90| 92 **93 94** |95| |96| 97

This light-coloured 1997 wine, brick-red at the edges, was aged for 18 months in 50% new oak casks. When left to breathe, the wine is redolent of musky leather. The palate begins pleasantly, almost smoothly, then evolves on tannins which are fairly persistent, but need a little more softening.

Bernard Rivals, Ch. Monlot-Capet, 33330 Saint-Hippolyte, tel. 05.57.74.49.47, fax 05.57.24.62.33, e-mail musset-rivals@belair-monlot.com ev. day except Sat. Sun. 9am–12 noon 2pm–6pm

CH. MOULIN GALHAUD 1997

■ 2 ha 6,000 100–149 F

This vineyard is a newcomer, consisting of two hectares (five acres) out of the 5.6 ha (13.8 acres) cultivated by Martine Galhaud at Vignonet. The title links her maiden name (Moulin) with her husband's surname (Galhaud); he is a well-known wine-merchant. The pretty garnet colour of this 1997 wine has highlights caused by evolution. The nose reveals complex notes of prune with hints of pepper and roasting. The palate is supple and fresh, with an evolving structure of well-blended tannins. A successful wine for its year, like the similarly recommended **1997 Château La Rose Brisson** (50–69F).

SCEA Martine Galhaud, 33330 Vignonet, tel. 05.57.97.39.73, fax 05.57.74.96.64 by appt.

CH. MOULIN SAINT-GEORGES 1997★★

■ 7 ha 32,000 200–249 F

86 89 |(90)| 91 |**93**| |94| |95| **96 97**

This attractive vineyard was much praised last year. Located on limestone-clay soils at the southern entrance to Saint-Emilion, it has been cultivated for the last hundred years by the Vauthier family, owners of Château Ausone. This blend of 70% Merlot, (20%) Cabernet Franc and 10% Cabernet Sauvignon is highly successful. The dark and intense ruby colour reveals purple highlights. The nose evokes ripe, crystallised fruits, harmoniously joined to notes of toast and vanilla derived from good oak. The rich, powerful, full palate is sustained by firm, fleshy tannins and an excellent vinosity. The finish is long and flavoursome, with a delightful

reappearance of the earlier fruity and oaky aromas. Will keep for three to four years.
🔑 Famille Vauthier, Ch. Moulin Saint-Georges, 33330 Saint-Emilion, tel. 05.57.24.70.26, fax 05.57.74.47.39 ☒ 𝐘 by appt.

CH. MUSSET-CHEVALIER 1997

■ 12 ha 91,000 30–49 F

This 12-ha (29-acre) vineyard of 50% Merlot, 50% Cabernets is located on sands and limestone-clay at Saint-Pey-d'Armens in the east of the appellation. The property also produces the Langranne, which is very similar to this wine. It has a good, intense colour and a nose of fruity perfumes. The palate is still fresh, with flavours of fruits and fine oak. A 1997 wine to be drunk quite soon.
🔑 SC du Ch. Musset-Chevalier, Saint-Pey-d'Armens, 33240 Saint-Gervais, tel. 05.57.94.00.20, fax 05.57.43.45.72 𝐘 by appt.
🔑 Raivico SA

CH. DU PARC 1997*

■ 2.1 ha 11,000 70–99 F

This is the first harvest for the new owners of this small two-hectare (five-acre) vineyard of 75% Merlot and 25% Cabernets vines planted on gravelly and sandy soils in the south of the appellation. It is all the more successful as a first effort, given the difficulties of 1997. The colour is deep purple and the bouquet, which is already complex, provides a succession of notes of flowers, crystallised fruits and spices. The attack is generous, sustained by tannins which are obvious yet velvety enough to allow for fairly early drinking.
🔑 Philippe Lavau, Ch. du Parc, 33330 Saint-Emilion, tel. 05.57.24.77.30, fax 05.57.24.66.24 ☒ 𝐘 by appt.

CH. PATRIS 1997*

■ 6 ha 24,000 150–199 F

88 **90** 92 |(93)| 95 96 97

Forty-year-old vine stocks planted at the bottom of the hillside on sand, silt and clay between Libourne and Saint-Emilion have yielded this nice dark, deep Bordeaux-coloured 1997 wine. The powerful bouquet has scents of red and black fruits mixed with aromas of roasting, toast and chocolate. The palate is well balanced, with supple, silky tannins of good quality and a persistent finish. Wait two or three years for it to reach its best.
🔑 Michel Querre, Ch. Patris, B.P. 51, 33330 Saint-Emilion, tel. 05.57.55.51.60, fax 05.57.55.51.61 𝐘 by appt.

CH. PAVIE-DECESSE 1997**

■Gd cru clas. 10 ha 33,000 300–499 F

81 82 83 85 86 |88| |**(89)**| **|90|** 92 **|93|** |94| 96 **97**

Gérard Perse acquired this ten-hectare (25-acre) Grand Cru Classé in 1997. For his first year's effort he obtains a *coup de coeur*, which is all the more commendable as 1997 was not an easy year. 'Well done,' 'Nice work' – our tasters were impressed by this wine's particularly concentrated traits. The Bordeaux

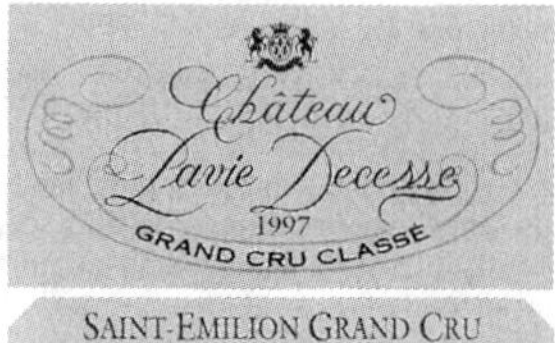

colour is so dark it is almost black. The bouquet is complex and powerful: red fruits, spices and toasted oak. The palate is remarkably mouth-filling, with a gorgeous roundness. Shaped by its evident yet fine tannins, this is a great wine for keeping.
🔑 SCA Pavie-Decesse, 33330 Saint-Emilion, tel. 05.57.55.43.43, fax 05.57.24.63.99
🔑 Gérard Perse

CH. PAVIE MACQUIN 1997

■Gd cru clas. n.c. n.c. 300–499 F

83 85 86 |88| |89| |90| 91 92 |93| 94 96(97)

This vineyard near Saint-Emilion dominates the Pavie hillside from its limestone-clay plateau. It owes its name to Albert Macquin, who saved the vineyard from phylloxera by introducing grafted vines. The concentration, fullness and power of this 1997 wine are remarkable. The garnet colour is dark and dense, with vivid highlights. The bouquet is a mixture of red and black fruits, burnt oak from the maturing, liquorice and fresh mint. The structure is remarkable: the tannins are superbly fleshy and firm; there is an impressive aromatic presence and a long, harmonious finish. Well done.
🔑 SCEA Ch. Pavie Macquin, 33330 Saint-Emilion, tel. 05.57.24.74.23, fax 05.57.24.63.78 ☒ 𝐘 by appt.
🔑 Corre-Macquin

CH. PETIT-FAURIE-DE-SOUTARD 1997

■Gd vineyard clas. 7.61 ha 46,000 100–149 F

82 83 85 86 88 |89| |90| 91 92 |93| |94| 96 |97|

Château Petit-Faurie-de-Soutard is located at the gates of the medieval town of

Saint-Emilion on a high point of the northern plateau. Jacques Capdemourlin manages this property, which belongs to his wife. The wine is light in colour with ruby highlights. The bouquet is still discreet, with hints of oaky vanilla and liquorice. The palate is supple and harmonious; its rather light structure means it can be drunk quite soon.

SCE Vignobles Aberlen, Ch. Petit-Faurie-de-Soutard, 33330 Saint-Emilion, tel. 05.57.74.62.06, fax 05.57.74.59.34 Y by appt.

Mme Capdemourlin

CH. PETIT-FIGEAC 1997

■ n.c. 14,000 100–149 F

88 **|89|** |93| |94| **95** |96| 97

This small vineyard of three hectares (seven acres) has belonged to the AXA Millésime group since 1989. The varieties are 60% Merlot, 30% Cabernet Franc and 10% Cabernet-Sauvignon. The bright, clear ruby colour has garnet lights. The bouquet contains oaky aromas with spicy, musky connotations still dominating the notes of red fruits. The structure is well-balanced, with a supple, round attack. The development is firm, which implies keeping for three to four years.

Jean-Michel Cazes, Ch. Petit-Figeac, 33330 Saint-Emilion, tel. 05.57.51.21.08, fax 05.57.51.87.31, e-mail infochato@chateauxassociés.com

Axa Millésime

CH. PETIT FOMBRAUGE 1997★

■ 2.5 ha 12,000 100–149 F

Pierre Lavau's second harvest confirms his promise. It is produced in a small vineyard with 90% Merlot vines planted on limestone-clay in the north of the appellation. The wine's ruby colour contains a few brick-red highlights. Although the nose is marked by the oak, the ripe fruit still makes its presence felt. The well-balanced, flavoursome palate is very successful, even if the rather tannic finish still needs time to blend. This wine has stunning potential.

Pierre Lavau, Ch. Petit Fombrauge, 33330 Saint-Christophe-des-Bardes, tel. 05.57.24.77.30, fax 05.57.24.66.24 Y by appt.

CH. PIGANEAU 1997

■ 5 ha 25,000 50–69 F

Piganeau was a director of the Ecole des Beaux Arts in Bordeaux in the 19th century and once owned this vineyard. Today the wine that bears his name has a light colour with ruby nuances. It is already expressive, evocative of Morello cherry, oaky liquorice, coffee and venison. The palate is supple, with a structure of fine oak tannins which will enable it to be drunk quite soon.

SCEA J.-B. Brunot et Fils, 1, Jean-Melin, 33330 Saint-Emilion, tel. 05.57.55.09.99, fax 05.57.55.09.95, e-mail vignobles.brunot@wanadoo.fr Y by appt.

CH. PIPEAU 1997★

■ 35 ha 180,000 70–99 F

86 88 |89| 92 93 |94| 95 96 97

This 35-ha (86-acre) vineyard at Saint-Laurent-des-Combes offers a well-made 1997 wine. The dark, deep ruby colour has garnet highlights. The subtle, elegant bouquet harmoniously mixes aromas of ripe red fruits with attractive notes of roasting and toast derived from good oak. The palate has supple, round, well-balanced tannins and an excellent structure making it possible to keep for three to five years.

GAEC Mestreguilhem, Ch. Pipeau, 33330 Saint-Laurent-des-Combes, tel. 05.57.24.72.95, fax 05.57.24.71.25, e-mail chateau.pipeau@wanadoo.fr Y by appt.

CH. PONTET-FUMET 1997

■ 11 ha 70,000 50–69 F

86 88 |89| 92 |93| 94 95 96 97

This vineyard is one of a number of properties cultivated by the Bardet family in the Saint-Emilion and Castillon districts, and the soils are sandy gravel. The wine is a blend of 72% Merlot and 28% Cabernets. The colour is an honest ruby and the bouquet is already intense, being marked both by the fruit and the vanilla oakiness. The promising palate is shaped by the oak tannins, which are still severe but should evolve well.

SCEA des Vignobles Bardet, 17, la Cale, 33330 Vignonet, tel. 05.57.84.53.16, fax 05.57.74.93.47, e-mail vignobles@vignobles-bardet.fr Y by appt.

CH. DE PRESSAC 1997★

■ 9 ha 56,000 100–149 F

On 20 July 1453, at the Château of Pressac, after the battle of Castillon, the English signed the surrender which put an end to the Hundred Years' War. It was here, too, that from 1737 to 1747 Vassal de Monteil introduced the Auxerrois or Cot variety, which in this region took on the name Pressac. There is just one per cent of it here now. Today's wine is a lovely clear ruby colour. The bouquet is already powerful, chocolate in character with notes of toasted oak. The palate is elegant and robust, structured by flavoursome tannins and has an interesting personality.

GFA Ch. de Pressac, 33330 Saint-Etienne-de-Lisse, tel. 05.57.40.18.02, fax 05.57.40.10.07 Y by appt.

J.-F. et D. Quenin

CH. ROC DE BOISSEAUX 1997

■ 5.4 ha 35,000 50–69 F

|92| |93| |94| |97|

Located on the sandy gravels of Saint-Sulpice-de-Faleyrens, this vineyard has been the property of the Clowez family since 1989. A blend of 80% Merlot and 20% Cabernet Franc, this 1997 wine is very true to type, with its developing ruby colour. The nose evokes red fruits (especially cherry), with fine oaky nuances redolent of vanilla and liquorice. The palate is pleasant and well balanced. Its

BORDEAUX

elegance makes up for a certain lack of power. A very pleasant wine which is ready to drink now.
🔑 SCEA du Ch. Roc de Boisseaux, Trapeau, 33330 Saint-Sulpice-de-Faleyrens, tel. 05.57.88.07.64, fax 05.57.88.07.00 ☑ Y by appt.
🔑 GFA Clowez

CH. ROCHEBELLE 1997★

■ 2.8 ha 17,000 70–99 F

This is a small but reputable wine-growing property on the limestone-clay hillside of Saint-Laurent-des-Combes, which can be reached directly by the picturesque little railway line from Saint-Emilion. It offers a very successful 1997 wine with an intense ruby colour. When it is swirled in the glass, the nose exhales very oaky notes with glimpses of fruity touches. The palate, too, is marked by the oak, but the mouth-filling quality and structure are excellent and should develop well in the next year or two.
🔑 Philippe Faniest, Ch. Rochebelle, 33330 Saint-Laurent-des-Combes, tel. 05.57.25.15.44, fax 05.57.51.01.99, e-mail faniest@archimedia.com ☑ Y by appt.

CH. ROCHER BELLEVUE FIGEAC 1997

■ 10.62 ha n.c. 500 F+

86 |(88)| **|89|** 91 92 94 95 96 97

This wine is regularly praised, and the 1997 version deserves as much, despite it having been a somewhat thankless year. It was produced on ancient sands over gravel in the west of the appellation. The ruby colour is dense. The bouquet mixes red fruit and delicately vanilla-tinged oak. The palate is full, warm and fresh. The oakiness of the finish needs time to blend further.
🔑 SC Rocher Bellevue Figeac, 14, rue d'Aviau, 33000 Bordeaux, tel. 05.57.24.71.41
🔑 M. Dutruilh

CH. ROLLAND-MAILLET 1997★

■ 3.35 ha 15,000 70–99 F

|**(82)**| 85 **|86| |89| |90|** |93| 94 95 97

This 3.5-hectare (8.6-acre) vineyard on siliceous clay and siliceous gravel in the Corbin area forms part of the family property of the Libourne oenologist Michel Rolland. This nicely matured blend of 75% Merlot to 25% Cabernet Franc has a dense, deep-ruby colour with deep-purple lights. The intense and smooth bouquet mixes scents of ripe red fruits with the grilled, vanilla aromas derived from good oak. The palate is full, with firm, obvious tannins and a finish of excellent length. A classic wine. Wait three to five years to enjoy it at its best.
🔑 SCEA Fermières des domaines Rolland, 'Maillet', 33500 Pomerol, tel. 05.57.51.23.05, fax 05.57.51.66.08 ☑ Y by appt.

ROYAL 1997

■ 10 ha 63,000 50–69 F

This is one of the oldest brands of the important Union de Producteurs cooperative located at the foot of the town's southern slope. The Union collects grapes from all over the AOC, but this wine comes from about ten hectares (25 acres) of sand and gravel planted with 60% Merlot and 40% Cabernets. The wine is quite singular, with a moderately intense garnet colour. When it is swirled in the glass, the somewhat closed nose releases scents of fruit and liquorice. The palate is supple and well-balanced. This 1997 wine can be drunk quite soon.
🔑 Union de producteurs de Saint-Emilion, Haut-Gravet, B.P. 27, 33330 Saint-Emilion, tel. 05.57.24.70.71, fax 05.57.24.65.18, e-mail udp-vins.saint-emilion@gofornet.com ☑ Y ev. day except Sun. 8am–12 noon 2pm–6pm

CH. ROZIER 1997

■ 18 ha 90,000 70–99 F

86 88 |89| |90| **|93| |94|** 96 97

The first plot was bought by the Saby family in 1796. Since then, nine generations have followed on this estate, which now runs to 18 ha (44 acres) of vines planted on limestone-clay and deep sands. This 1997 wine is a reasonably intense, still very vivid ruby colour. The fresh bouquet mixes aromas of leather, liquorice and mint, then subtle, harmonious notes of oak. The elegant palate makes up for a slight lack of power by the great quality of its velvety, silky tannins, which will enable it to be drunk fairly soon.
🔑 Vignobles Jean-Bernard Saby et Fils, Ch. Rozier, 33330 Saint-Laurent-des-Combes, tel. 05.57.24.73.03, fax 05.57.24.67.77, e-mail vignobles.saby@wanadoo.fr ☑ Y by appt.

CH. SAINT GEORGES COTE PAVIE 1997

■ Gd cru clas. n.c. 26,000 100–149 F

82 83 (85) 86 88 |89| |90| |92| 95 97

This very ancient Saint-Emilion family property faces Ausone on a fine limestone-clay hillside. It is planted with 80% Merlot and 20% Cabernet Franc vines. The intense garnet colour of this 1997 wine has carmine highlights. The nose mixes red fruits and plum jam with elegant oaky nuances of coffee and vanilla, then the fresher notes of liquorice and mint. On the palate, the slight lack of power typical of this year is agreeably made up for by the quality of the ripe, round, silky, velvety tannins, which give the wine its well-balanced, subtle character. Already pleasant to drink.
🔑 Jacques et Marie-Gabrielle Masson, Ch. Saint-Georges Côte Pavie, 33330 Saint-Emilion, tel. 05.57.74.44.23 ☑ Y by appt.

CH. TAUZINAT L'HERMITAGE 1997

■ 9.5 ha 60,000 100–149 F

88 89 |93| **|94| 95 96** 97

This limestone-clay hillside is planted with 75% Merlot and 25% Cabernets vines. The estate has a very good past record, and its 1997 wine has a good colour of medium intensity. The nose is a little closed, and needs to be allowed to breathe to express its fruity notes. The fresh palate requires time to age, but not too much in view of the year.

SC Bernard Moueix, Ch. Taillefer, 33500 Libourne, tel. 05.57.25.50.45, fax 05.57.25.50.45

Héritiers B. Moueix

CH. TOINET FOMBRAUGE 1997*

■ 0.75 ha 5,300 50–69 F

|93| |94| 95 96 97

This family property of 7.25 ha (17.9 acres) devotes only three-quarters of a hectare (1.85 acres) of its oldest vines to producing this wine; the rest goes to producing an AOC Saint-Emilion. This 1997 wine is very successful, with a good dark and intense ruby colour and strong aromas of crystallised fruits, Morello cherry and stewed prune. The palate is harmonious, round, elegant and fleshy, thanks to the smooth, creamy, finely oaky tannins. The finish is dense. A little more time is needed to reach full harmony.

Bernard Sierra, Toinet-Fombrauge, 33330 Saint-Christophe-des-Bardes, tel. 05.57.24.77.70, fax 05.57.24.76.49 ev. day 10am–12 noon 3pm–7pm

CH. TOURANS 1997*

■ 6.34 ha 43,100 70–99 F

This is one of the Bordeaux vineyards belonging to the Rocher Cap de Rive company directed by Roger Geens, a Belgian. Tourans blends 80% Merlot with 20% Cabernet-Sauvignon, all grown on limestone-clay. This vigorous 1997 wine is true to type, with an attractive dark, dense garnet colour. The intense, complex bouquet mixes aromas of red-fruit jam, stewed prune, caramel and spices. The palate marries roundness and robustness with full, velvety tannins which give a firm, well-mannered finish. Drink in three to four years' time to accompany lamprey or game.

Vignobles Rocher Cap de Rive, Ch. Tourans, 33330 Saint-Etienne-de-Lisse, tel. 05.57.40.08.88, fax 05.57.40.19.93, e-mail vignoblesrochercaprive@wanadoo.fr

CH. TOUR BALADOZ 1997

■ n.c. 57,000 70–99 F

|93| |94| 95 96 97

This is an attractive property of nearly nine hectares (22 acres) in the east of the AOC on limestone-clay. Merlot vines account for more than 80% of the total. The wine is regularly singled out by wine-experts. The 1997 vintage has a ruby colour of medium intensity, with fresh, fruity aromas and a supple, fresh palate. We recommend laying down for two years.

SCEA Ch. Tour Baladoz, 33330 Saint-Laurent-des-Combes, tel. 05.57.88.94.17, fax 05.57.88.39.14

CH. TOUR GESSAN 1997**

■ n.c. 20,000 70–99 F

This wine is a blend of 80% Merlot to 20% Cabernet-Sauvignon, belonging to Daniel Mouty and distributed by the merchants Sichel-Coste. This is a remarkable 1997 vintage, with a fine, intense, dark-garnet colour. The forceful bouquet, with strong notes of roasting and toast, gives glimpses of pleasant aromas of red and black crystallised fruits. The elegant, supple, round, velvety palate has a well-balanced structure with ripe tannins that guarantee it will keep well.

Maison Sichel-Coste, 8, rue de la Poste, 33210 Langon, tel. 05.56.63.50.52, fax 05.56.63.42.28

Daniel Mouty

CH. TOUR GRAND FAURIE 1997

■ 3.6 ha 29,000 70–99 F

88 |90| |94| |95| |96| |97|

This wine is made mainly from old Merlot vines growing on limestone-clay (90% of the stocks, the rest being Cabernet Franc). This result is a charming and agreeable 1997 vintage, with a bright ruby colour and a nose of small acid fruits accompanied by the odd musky note. The palate is well-balanced, supple, round and fleshy, with good aromatic persistence. Though already pleasant to drink, it could be kept for four or five years.

Georgette Feytit, Ch. Tour Grand-Faurie, B.P. 3, 33330 Saint-Emilion, tel. 05.57.24.73.75, fax 05.57.74.46.94 ev. day 9am–8pm

CH. TOUR RENAISSANCE 1997

■ 4 ha 24,000 50–69 F

89 |90| 92 93 94 |96| |97|

This vineyard is often praised. Located on a four-hectare (10-acre) gravel hilltop at Saint-Sulpice-de-Falyrens, it offers consistent quality, even in a difficult year like 1997. The pleasant colour of this wine reveals a few signs of evolution, but the nose is still fruity, sustained by a delicate oakiness. The well-balanced palate has fruity, oaky flavours which are supported by well-blended tannins. It can be drunk quite soon.

SCEA Daniel Mouty, Ch. du Barry, B.P. 5, 33350 Sainte-Terre, tel. 05.57.84.55.88, fax 05.57.74.92.99, e-mail daniel-mouty@wanadoo.fr by appt.

CH. TRIMOULET 1997

■ 7 ha 52,000 70–99 F

|94| 95 96 97

This substantial property in the north of the appellation has belonged to the same family for 200 years. It is named after Jean Trimoulet, the town's jurat at the start of the 18th century. This vivid ruby wine contains a sizeable proportion (40%) of Cabernet Franc, grown on siliceous clay mixed with iron slag. The nose is still marked by the oak and the

BORDEAUX

Cabernet, as is the very robust palate. It needs ageing.

🔑 Michel Jean, Ch. Trimoulet, 33330 Saint-Emilion, tel. 05.57.24.70.56, fax 05.57.74.41.69 Y by appt.

EMILIUS DE TRIMOULET 1997

■ 6 ha 42,000 50–69 F

Château Trimoulet's second wine is produced from the youngest vines on the estate, grown on the siliceous clay mixed with the iron slag of Saint-Emilion's northern plateau. This vivid ruby 1997 wine has a nose which is still discreet but mixes fruity notes with a very pleasing oakiness. After a good attack, the tannic structure affords a somewhat firm finish. It needs to be kept for several years.

🔑 Michel Jean, Ch. Trimoulet, 33330 Saint-Emilion, tel. 05.57.24.70.56, fax 05.57.74.41.69 Y by appt.

CH. TROPLONG MONDOT 1997

■ Gd cru clas. 21 ha 67,200 250–299 F

82 83 85 86 88 |89| (90) 92 |93| 95 96 |97|

This Grand vineyard Classé of more than 30 ha (74 acres) was established in 1745 by the Sèze family; its present arrangement goes back to Raymond Troplong (1850–70), whose name it bears. Since 1936, it has been in the Valette family. The wine is a youthful dark purple. The discreet note expresses scents of dried flowers, tobacco and cherry-stones. After a supple attack, the flavour evokes tobacco and dead leaves. The tannins have already matured, and this 1997 wine will be ready to drink very soon.

🔑 Christine Valette, Ch. Troplong-Mondot, 33330 Saint-Emilion, tel. 05.57.55.32.05, fax 05.57.55.32.07 V Y by appt.

CH. TROTTEVIEILLE 1997

■ 1er gd cru B 10 ha 42,000 200–249 F

75 76 82 85 86 |88| |90| 91 93 |94| 95 96 |97|

This fine wine-estate of ten hectares (25 acres) on limestone-clay, planted with equal quantities of Cabernets and Merlot vines, is several hundred yards north-east of Saint-Emilion. The name comes from an old lady who used to 'trot' to get the news when the stagecoach passed. The wine, too, goes its own sweet way, even in this unreliable year. The colour is a carmine-fringed garnet. When swirled in the glass, the wine reveals aromas of Virginia tobacco, cedar, honey and dried flowers. The delicate palatal structure will allow this wine to be drunk fairly soon – for example, with soft cheeses.

🔑 Indivision Castéja-Preben-Hansen, Ch. Trottevieille, 33330 Saint-Emilion, tel. 05.56.00.00.70, fax 05.57.87.48.61 V Y by appt.

CH. DU VAL D'OR 1997

■ n.c. n.c. 70–99 F

This vineyard run by the Barbet family is located at Vignonet in the south of the appellation. Its wine is marketed by Yvon Mau, the large Gironde merchants. The colour of this 1997 vintage is ruby with garnet highlights. The bouquet is already expressive, and releases nuances of oak, leather and tar. Well-balanced and robust owing to tannins which are still somewhat firm, this is a well-crafted representative of its year.

🔑 SA Yvon Mau, B.P. 1, 33193 Gironde-sur-Dropt Cedex, tel. 05.56.61.54.54, fax 05.56.61.54.61 Y by appt.

CH. VIEILLE TOUR LA ROSE 1997★★

■ 4.06 ha 23,000 50–69 F

This is a family property of about ten hectares (25 acres) on the ferruginous sands of the La Rose sector north of Saint-Emilion. This 80% Merlot is a pretty Bordeaux colour. The intense and complex bouquet sends out a succession of notes of red fruits, flowers, clove and cocoa. The palate fulfills the bouquet's promise, finishing on strong tannins. A remarkable wine of character.

🔑 SCEA Vignobles Daniel Ybert, La Rose, 33330 Saint-Emilion, tel. 05.57.24.73.41, fax 05.57.74.44.83 V Y by appt.

VIEUX CHATEAU L'ABBAYE

Cuvée Claude Ladères 1997

■ 1.73 ha 11,400 70–99 F

The old vines (85% Merlot, 15% Bouchet) growing on the limestone-clay of this small vineyard close to the church of Saint-Christophe-des-Bardes in the north of the appellation have yielded a wine with an intense Bordeaux colour. The nose strikes an excellent balance between grape and oak, and the palate is warm and robust, with tannins which are still firm but promising.

🔑 Françoise Lladères, Le Bourg, B.P 69, 33330 Saint-Christophe-des-Bardes, tel. 05.57.47.98.76, fax 05.57.47.93.03 V Y by appt.

CH. VIEUX FORTIN 1997★

■ 5.39 ha 30,000 200–249 F

This vineyard has been successful even in the difficult year of 1997. Its gravelly clay is planted with 60% Merlot and 40% Cabernets. The wine has a pronounced character, even if the ruby colour is but moderate in intensity. The bouquet is complex, evoking red fruits, liquorice and a variety of spices. The palate, too, is fruity, having a tannic structure which is still a little closed, but it ought to evolve harmoniously over the next two to three years.

🔑 Claude Sellan, Ch. Vieux Fortin, 6, Fortin, 33330 Saint-Emilion, tel. 05.57.24.69.97, fax 05.57.24.69.97 V Y by appt.

CH. VIEUX POURRET 1997★

■ 4.24 ha 24,000 70–99 F

86 88 |89| |90| |93| |94| 95 96 |97|

Close to the town, this small four-hectare (ten-acre) vineyard at the foot of the hillside on a sandy bank is planted with 80% Merlot and 20% Cabernet Franc vines. It is one of Michel Boutet's three Saint-Emilion properties. The brick highlights in this wine's bright-ruby colour are signs that evolution has begun. The subtle, discreet nose releases aromas of small red acid fruits and pleasing scents of flowers. The palate is fresh, toothsome and fruity, with good balance. A straightforward, pleasant wine to drink over the next three years.

🔑 SCEA des Vignobles Michel Boutet, Ch. Vieux Pourret, B.P. 70, 33330 Saint-Emilion, tel. 05.57.24.70.86, fax 05.57.24.68.30 ☑ 𝐈 by appt.

CH. VILLEMAURINE 1997

■ Gd cru clas. 7 ha 45,000 ⏸ 100–149 F

82 **83 85 86 |88| |89|** |90| 92 |93| |94| |97|

On the limestone-clay plateau by the gates of Saint-Emilion, this vineyard of 70% Merlot and 30% Cabernet-Sauvignon extends above a huge network of caves which once served as a refuge for the Moors. This 1997 wine is a vivid and intense ruby colour, with a nose of excellent freshness, which exhales aromas of small red acid fruits and Morello cherries in alcohol married to a subtle and discreet oakiness. The round and supple palate is sustained throughout by fine, well-balanced tannins. A wine that will reach full its expression in three to four years.

🔑 SCA Vignobles Robert Giraud, B.P. 31, 33240 Saint-André-de-Cubzac, tel. 05.57.43.01.44, fax 05.57.43.08.75, e-mail direction@robertgiraud.com ☑

CH. VIRAMIERE 1997★

■ 12.94 ha 18,000 50–69 F

This vineyard of almost 13 ha (32 acres) on the siliceous clay of Saint-Etienne de Lisse belongs to the Dumen family. Vinification and marketing are provided by the Union de Producteurs de Saint-Emilion. This 1997 wine's colour is light but attractive. The pleasant bouquet exhales scents of flowers, fruits and undergrowth. The pleasing, supple palate finishes on silky tannins, which will allow this wine to be drunk quite soon.

🔑 Union de producteurs de Saint-Emilion, Haut-Gravet, B.P. 27, 33330 Saint-Emilion, tel. 05.57.24.70.71, fax 05.57.24.65.18, e-mail udp-vins.saint-emilion@gofornet.com 𝐈 ev. day except Sun. 8am–12 noon 2pm–6pm

🔑 Vignobles Dumon

Other appellations in the Saint-Émilion region

Several communes bordering Saint-Émilion and that used to be under its jurisdiction are permitted to put their name on their wine labels along with that of their famous neighbour. These are the Appellatios Lussac Saint-Émilion, 1,400 ha (3,458 acres), producing 83,960 hl (2,216,544 gal), Montagne Saint-Émilion 1,540 ha (3,804 acres), producing 91,720 hl (2,421,408 gal), Puisseguin Saint-Émilion, 740 ha (1,828acres) producing 43,436 hl (1,146,710 gal) and Saint-Georges Saint-Émilion, 168 ha (415 acres) producing 9,649 hl (254,734 gal). In fact, the last two correspond to two communes that have now joined Montagne. They are all located north-east of the small town, in a charming, topographically mixed region where a number of grand historic houses top the hills. The soils are very varied and the vine varieties are the same as Saint-Émilion; consequently, the quality of the wines is also much the same.

Lussac Saint-Émilion

CH. DE BARBE-BLANCHE

Cuvée Henri IV 1997★

■ n.c. 8,200 ⏸ 50–69 F

The Château de Barbe-Blanche's Cuvée Henri IV is a selection from old vines and has spent a year in oak. The colour is garnet and the bouquet intense. The oak still somewhat dominates the fruity notes, and the supple, well-blended tannins have considerable power for a 1997 wine. The finish is persistent. A wine to drink now or leave two or three years to age.

🔑 SCE Ch. de Barbe-Blanche, 33570 Lussac, tel. 05.57.74.56.52, fax 05.57.74.52.68 ☑ 𝐈 ev. day except Sat. Sun. 8am–12 noon 2pm–6pm

🔑 André Magnon

CH. BEL-AIR 1997

■ 21 ha 150,000 ⏸ 30–49 F

This wine has an intense garnet colour and an interesting, typical aromatic complexity (blackcurrant, coffee and leather). The supple tannins are well-blended. A wine to drink now and over the next two to three years.

🔑 Jean-Noël Roi, EARL Ch. Bel-Air, 33570 Lussac, tel. 05.57.74.60.40, fax 05.57.74.52.11, e-mail jean.roi@wanadoo.fr ☑ 𝐈 by appt.

CH. DE BELLEVUE 1997*

■ 8 ha 64,000 50–69 F

In 1997, the château chose to make this wine exclusively out of Merlot grapes. It is a success. The wine is a fine bright colour, with intense aromas of stewed fruit and a welcome note of freshness. The palatal tannins are well-covered and full, releasing most agreeable aromas of fruits and roasted coffee. It will be at its best in about a year.

Ch. Chatenoud et Fils, Ch. de Bellevue, 33570 Lussac, tel. 05.57.74.60.25, fax 05.57.74.53.69 by appt.

CH. BONNIN 1997*

■ 1 ha 4,500 50–69 F

This wine, the first vintage made by the new owner of this small vineyard, is awarded one star and nearly won a second. This deep ruby-coloured wine has an expressive bouquet of ripe fruit, liquorice and sweet pepper. The well-extracted tannins are rich and intense; they fill the mouth well and are persistent. A pleasant wine to drink now or keep for two or three years.

Philippe Bonnin, Pichon, 33570 Lussac-Saint-Emilion, tel. 05.57.74.53.12, fax 05.57.74.58.26 by appt.

CH. DE BORDES 1997

■ 0.25 ha 2,100 50–69 F

This small special growth with numbered bottles is deservedly recommended for its colour with black highlights and bouquet of ripe cherry and intense oakiness. The tannins make a strong showing, marked by long maturation in oak. Wait for two or three years.

Vignobles Paul Bordes, Faize, 33570 Les Artigues-de-Lussac, tel. 05.57.24.33.66, fax 05.57.24.30.42 by appt.

CH. CAILLOU LES MARTINS 1997**

■ 8 ha 45,000 30–49 F

This vineyard offers a remarkably well-crafted 1997 wine, grown on clay soil. The deep colour has lovely mauvish highlights. The intense bouquet evokes blackcurrant, cherry and spices. The tannins provide a well-balanced attack, then evolve with much roundness and harmony. A great success, particularly for a difficult year. Congratulations are due to Paul Carrille, the head of the winery, and to Gilles Pauquet, the oenologist.

Jean-François Carrille, pl. du Marcadieu, 33330 Saint-Emilion, tel. 05.57.24.74.46, fax 05.57.24.64.40 by appt.

CH. CHEREAU 1997

■ 22 ha 50,000 30–49 F

This 1997 wine has bright ruby highlights and a developed bouquet of black fruits (blackberry) and liquorice. The tannic structure is supple, well-balanced and straightforward. A pleasant wine that can be drunk straight away.

SCEA Vignoble Silvestrini, Chéreau, 33570 Lussac, tel. 05.57.74.50.76, fax 05.57.74.53.22 ev. day 9am–12 noon 2pm–7pm

CH. CLAYMORE 1997*

■ 12 ha 80,000 50–69 F

The allusion to the Highlanders' famous broadsword, 'Claymore', recalls the Scots' occupation of this place during the Hundred Years' War. Today, military arms have yielded to vines, and this 1997 worth noting for its intense colour, expressive bouquet marked by good oak, and tannins which are both forceful and harmonious. A wine to drink soon (in two or three years). The second wine, **Cadet du château Claymore**, is recommended for its subtlety and good balance, and is ready to drink now (30–49F).

SCEA vignobles Dubard, Ch. Claymore, 33500 Lussac, tel. 05.53.82.48.31, fax 05.53.82.47.64

CH. COURRIERE-RONGIERAS 1997

■ 1.5 ha 10,000 50–69 F

Lots bought at Lussac and vinified at Château-Rosier, Saint-Emilion, have yielded this 1997 wine, with its bright- ruby colour, delicate perfumes of raspberry and strong but fruity structure. Given greater persistence, it would have been awarded one star.

Vignobles Jean-Bernard Saby et Fils, Ch. Rozier, 33330 Saint-Laurent-des-Combes, tel. 05.57.24.73.03, fax 05.57.24.67.77, e-mail vignobles.saby@wanadoo.fr by appt.

CH. CROIX DE CHOUTEAU 1997

■ 12 ha 25,000 30–49 F

The Coudroy family have been established in the wine-growing district of Lussac since the 16th century. This 1997 wine has a floral and authentic character, with notes of blackcurrant and a well-formed, persistent tannic structure. The finish is marked by the oak, but this should soften after a year or two of ageing.

Serge Coudroy, Chouteau, 33570 Lussac, tel. 05.57.74.67.73, fax 05.57.74.56.05 by appt.

CH. GONNAT 1997

■ 11 ha 78,000 30–49 F

A wine owned by Jean Boireau and marketed by André Quancard. The colour of this 1997 vintage is limpid and almost black, the bouquet floral and fruity. It will be of enormous appeal to lovers of supple wines. The palate is well-balanced, but does not have much keeping potential. Drink within the next two years.

André Quancard-André, rue de la Cabeyre, 33240 Saint-André-de-Cubzac, tel. 05.57.33.42.42, fax 05.57.43.01.71

J. Boireau

CH. HAUT-PIQUAT 1997★

22 ha 150,000 50–69 F

Many modern methods have gone into producing the high-quality grapes for this vintage. The result is a brilliant purple colour and a fine nose of redcurrant, bilberry and vanilla. The tannins are both velvety and powerful, with a superbly balanced finish. A very typical wine, ready for drinking now.

Jean-Pierre Rivière, Ch. Haut-Piquat, 33570 Lussac, tel. 05.57.55.59.59, fax 05.57.55.59.51 ev. day 9am–12 noon 2pm–6pm

CH. DE LA GRENIERE

Cuvée de la Chartreuse Elevé en fût de chêne 1997★

2 ha 11,000 50–69 F

Château de la Grenière's Cuvée de la Chartreuse is a selection from old Merlot (55%) and Cabernets (45%) vines. This 1997 is rich, well-coloured and very aromatic (spices, red fruits, vanilla). The palate's silky, full structure evolves with subtlety and harmony; the contribution of the oak is particularly well judged and successful. A wine that will reach its full potential over the next two or three years.

EARL Vignobles Dubreuil, La Grenière n° 14, 33570 Lussac, tel. 05.57.74.64.96, fax 05.57.74.56.28 by appt.

CH. LA HAUTE CLAYMORE 1997★★

2 ha 13,000 30–49 F

The vineyard belonged to the former Cistercian Abbey of Faise and takes its name from the Hundred Years' War. The bright, deep colour of this 1997 wine heralds intense aromas of undergrowth. The powerful, well-balanced structure has been well absorbed by high-quality maturing. The long, aromatic finish signals a wine that will age well (at least two to five years).

EARL Vignobles D. et C. Devaud, Faise, 33570 Les Artigues-de-Lussac, tel. 05.57.24.31.39, fax 05.57.24.34.17 by appt.

CH. LA JORINE 1997

3.5 ha 26,000 30–49 F

This small vineyard of slightly more than three hectares (seven acres) offers a pleasant 1997 wine with a developing bouquet of fruit (raspberry) and coffee. The palatal structure is supple and well-balanced, though it lacks fullness. Drink now.

Henri-Louis Fagard, Cornemps, 33570 Petit-Palais, tel. 05.57.69.73.19, fax 05.57.69.73.75, e-mail vignobles.fagard@wanadoo.fr by appt.

CH. LA TUILERIE 1997

3.5 ha 24,000 30–49 F

This 1997 wine has attractive subtle aromas (cherry, raspberry, redcurrant) and a supple, well-balanced tannic structure of medium length. This is an easy-drinking, fruity wine, ready for drinking straight away. A select, tank-matured selection from the *négociant* André Quancard.

André Quancard-André, rue de la Cabeyre, 33240 Saint-André-de-Cubzac, tel. 05.57.33.42.42, fax 05.57.43.01.71

H. Le Grelle

CH. LE GRAND BOIS 1997

0.8 ha 6,500 50–69 F

This château has splendid monolithic cellars where it keeps its wines, like this 1997 vintage with its deep colour and oaky, fruity bouquet (raspberry). The tannins attack robustly, then evolve with a subtlety and persistence which are respectable for a 1997 wine. Drink within the next two or three years.

SARL Roc de Boissac, Pleniers de Boissac, 33570 Puisseguin, tel. 05.57.74.61.22, fax 05.57.74.59.54 by appt.

CLOS LES HAUTS MARTINS 1997

3.2 ha 15,000 30–49 F

There is only 50% Merlot in this wine, with 34% Cabernet Franc and 16% Cabernet-Sauvignon. This ruby 1997 vintage already has brick-red highlights. The fresh bouquet evokes redcurrant and cashew. The tannins are supple and velvety. A wine to drink young and appreciate for its freshness.

EARL Les Hauts Martins, 33570 Lussac, tel. 05.57.74.56.67, fax 05.57.74.56.67 by appt.

CH. LION PERRUCHON 1997

10.08 han.c. 50–69 F

This 1997 wine, with its developed bouquet of cystallised prunes, has a fruity, powerful structure and a somewhat severe finish. A wine to drink in two or three years' time.

Jean-Pierre Thézard, Ch. Lion Perruchon, 33570 Lussac, tel. 05.57.74.58.21, fax 05.57.74.58.39 by appt.

CH. LYONNAT 1997★

45 ha 240,000 50–69 F

This large-scale vineyard and former supplier to the Vatican cellars belongs to the Milhade family, who are well known in the Libourne district. The bouquet of this still somewhat closed 1997 wine is vinous and oaky. The palate reveals the strong presence of fruity, remarkably well-balanced tannins. A wine of character, which can be enjoyed today, it will age harmoniously in another two to five years.

SCEV Jean Milhade, Ch. Recougne, 33133 Galgon, tel. 05.57.55.48.90, fax 05.57.84.31.27 by appt.

CH. MAYNE BLANC

Cuvée Tradition 1997★★

11 ha 45,000 50–69 F

This family estate has a very welcoming atmosphere where you can sample other wines. The cherry colour of this 1997 wine has a nose of red and black fruits. The tannins

begin velvety and evolve with power and harmony to a very aromatic finish. A wine to drink over the next five years. The oak-matured **1997 Château Mayne-Blanc, Cuvée Saint-Vincent** (70–99F) was less appreciated, owing to its intense oakiness; it is nevertheless recommended.
🗝 EARL Jean Boncheau, Ch. Mayne-Blanc, 33570 Lussac, tel. 05.57.74.60.56, fax 05.57.74.51.77 ☑ Ῑ ev. day 8am–12 noon 2pm–7pm; cl. Jan.–Feb.

CH. MICHEL DE VERT 1997

■ n.c. 62,600 30–49 F

This 1997 wine is a pretty colour with carmine highlights. It has a vinous, intense bouquet and a full, generous tannic structure. The finish is slightly austere. The balance will improve in two or three years.
🗝 SA Maison Ginestet, 19, av. de Fontenille, 33360 Carignan-de-Bordeaux, tel. 05.56.68.81.82, fax 05.56.20.96.99, e-mail contact@ginestet.fr Ῑ by appt.
🗝 Laubie

CH. MOULIN DE GRENET 1997

■ 5 ha 35,000 50–69 F

The mill, built in 1711, overlooks the entire appellation, especially the vines of this property. The bouquet of this 1997 vintage is still closed, but the wine has well-balanced and fruity (blackcurrant) tannins of medium length. A wine to drink over the next three years.
🗝 Nicole Roskam-Brunot, SCEA Ch. Cantenac, 33330 Saint-Emilion, tel. 05.57.51.35.22, fax 05.57.25.19.15, e-mail roskam@club-internet.fr ☑ Ῑ by appt.

CH. DU MOULIN NOIR 1997*

■ 5.45 ha 41,000 50–69 F

Located close to the ruins of the Moulin Noir, this vineyard has for some years been very up-to-date in its techniques in both vineyard and winery. Its wines are often well thought of, as is this 1997 vintage, with its brilliant cherry colour and intense aromas of red fruits and undergrowth. The tannins are full and generous. They guarantee a promising future over the next three years.
🗝 SC Ch. du Moulin Noir, Lescalle, 33460 Macau, tel. 05.57.88.07.64, fax 05.57.88.07.00 ☑ Ῑ by appt.

CH. DE TABUTEAU 1997

■ 18.83 ha 150,000 30–49 F

This château offers a wine with a rich colour and a complex nose, with notes of leather and red fruits. It has a well-balanced palate, although the full and quite long-lasting tannins are still a little hard at the finish. Drink in a year or two.
🗝 Vignobles Bessou, Ch. Durand-Laplagne, 33570 Puisseguin, tel. 05.57.74.63.07, fax 05.57.74.59.58 ☑ Ῑ by appt.

CH. VERDU 1997

■ 20.97 ha 20,000 50–69 F

This 1997 wine is recommended for the quality of its supple, oaky tannic structure. It will need a year or two of ageing in the bottle to become fully harmonious.
🗝 SCEA Gaury-Dubos, Tripoteau, 33230 Abzac, tel. 05.57.74.51.16, fax 05.57.74.61.24 ☑ Ῑ by appt.

VIEUX CHATEAU CHAMBEAU 1997*

■ 32 ha 79,000 50–69 F

This wine has a good reputation, and its 1997 version is also a success. The colour is a brilliant garnet, and the nose evokes red fruits, prune, vanilla and toast. The tannic structure is supple and mature, having blended particularly well with the good quality oak. Drink now or keep for two or three years.
🗝 SC Ch. du Branda, Roques, 33570 Puisseguin, tel. 05.57.74.62.55, fax 05.57.74.57.33 ☑ Ῑ by appt.

Montagne Saint-Émilion

CH. D'ARVOUET 1997**

■ 3.76 ha 6,100 50–69 F

This small château in the south-east of the appellation proves the worth of its wines year after year. Two stars go to this 1997 wine for its deep colour and garnet highlights, its perfumes of toast and menthol and hint of elegant musk, plus the very evident tannic structure, which is full, generous and well-balanced, the result of well-adjudged maturing in oak. A technically faultless wine with four to eight years' ageing potential.
🗝 EARL Moreau, Ch. d'Arvouet, 33570 Montagne, tel. 05.57.74.56.60, fax 05.57.74.58.33, e-mail moreaulavoute@aol.com ☑ Ῑ by appt.

CH. BEAUSEJOUR Clos l'Eglise 1997*

■ 5 ha 30,000 50–69 F

This 11-ha (27-acre) vineyard was taken over by B. Germain in 1995. The special Clos l'Eglise was made from very old vines, some of which date from 1903. The result is a 1997 vintage with complex aromas of liquorice, menthol, tobacco and cinnamon. The smooth, well-blended tannic structure and velvety finish reveal excellent balance. A fine wine. Open within the next two to five years.
🗝 Vignobles Germain et Associés, Ch. Peyredoulle, 33390 Berson, tel. 05.57.42.66.66, fax 05.57.64.36.20 ☑ Ῑ by appt.

CH. CAZELON 1997★

■ 4 ha 15,000 30–49 F

Grown on a classic limestone-clay soil, this wine has a clear garnet colour and a developing bouquet of leather, red fruits and oak. The palate has evident, flavoursome tannins, which harmonise with the well-adjudged oak-maturing. This 1997 wine will be particularly good over the next two to five years.

Denis Fourloubey, Cazelon, 33570 Montagne, tel. 05.57.74.58.78, fax 05.57.74.57.74 by appt.

CH. CORBIN 1997

■ 20 ha 60,000 30–49 F

A pleasant wine marked by its year. There is a developing palate of leather and black fruits. The supple, well-balanced tannins are already agreeable. Drink within three years.

François Rambeaud, Ch. Corbin, 33570 Montagne, tel. 05.57.74.62.41, fax 05.57.74.55.91 by appt.

CH. COUCY 1997★★

■ 20 ha 100,000 50–69 F

Château Coucy is located on a fine terroir of limestone-clay whose full potential is revealed in this 1997 wine. The purple colour is bright and intense. There are complex and powerful aromas of red fruits, spices and leather. The tannic structure provides a velvety attack, then evolves with good breeding, elegance and maturity. But the essential character of this wine is revealed in the finish, which is well-balanced and extremely persistent. A top wine for its year and appellation. Drink within two to three years.

SCEA du Ch. Coucy, 33570 Montagne, tel. 05.57.74.62.14, fax 05.57.74.56.07 by appt.

Maurèze

CH. FAIZEAU

Sélection Vieilles vignes 1997★★★

■ 10 ha n.c. 50–69 F

This château has provided the best wine in the appellation, winning three stars and a unanimous *coup de coeur.* This pure Merlot has a magnificent purple colour and a complex, expressive nose of bigaroon cherry, almond paste and toasted oak. The tannins begin supple and fruity, then subtly evolve with equal good balance and power. The oak-maturing has contributed remarkable harmony and persistence. An exceptional wine for its year. Drink within two to ten years. The 1995 version was similarly distinguished.

SCE du Ch. Faizeau, 33570 Montagne, tel. 05.57.24.68.94, fax 05.57.24.60.37 by appt.

CH. GARDEROSE 1997

■ 2 ha 18,000 30–49 F

This selection is offered by Yvon Mau and comes from vinification and maturing in the vat. It is noteworthy for the evolved bouquet of flowers and leather, and for the ripe, supple tannic structure, even if the finish is somewhat fleeting. Already pleasant to drink.

SA Yvon Mau, B.P. 1, 33193 Gironde-sur-Dropt Cedex, tel. 05.56.61.54.54, fax 05.56.61.54.61 by appt.

Garde et Fils

CH. GRAND BARAIL 1997★★

■ 7 ha 50,000 50–69 F

This château offers a deep garnet-red 1997 wine which has defied the difficulties of its year. It comes from old stocks of Merlot (80%) and Cabernet Franc (20%). The intense bouquet evokes red fruit, vanilla, toast and smokiness. The tannins attack with both power and smoothness, then evolve with delicacy, good balance and persistence. A superb wine, typical of the appellation. Drink after two to five years' ageing.

EARL Vignobles D. et C. Devaud, Faise, 33570 Les Artigues-de-Lussac, tel. 05.57.24.31.39, fax 05.57.24.34.17 by appt.

CH. GRAND BARIL 1997★★

■ 28 ha 90,000 30–49 F

The Lycée Viticole de Montagne was founded in 1969 to train the region's youth in vine-growing and wine-making. Its 1997 wine is remarkable, with its stunningly attractive black colour and complex nose of spices and flowers. The first impressions given by the tannic structure are of elegance. It evolves with good presence, maturity and a final balance which is marked by notes of pepper. A nice wine to drink now but which will improve over the next three to four years.

Lycée viticole de Montagne-Libourne, Goujon, 33570 Montagne, tel. 05.57.55.21.22, fax 05.57.51.66.13, e-mail legta-libourne@edueagri.fr by appt.

CH. HAUT-BERTIN 1997★

■ 7.1 ha 56,000 30–49 F

This 1997 classic blend of Merlot (70%) and Cabernets (30%) has a supple and authentic palatal structure and an elegant finish. It has everything to appeal to lovers of aromatic wines (menthol and small ripe fruits). Very characteristic of its year. Drink within three to four years.

Fortin et Fils, Ch. Haut-Bertin, Laumure, 33570 Montagne, tel. 05.57.74.64.99, fax 05.57.74.53.97, e-mail afortin@fr.packardbell.org by appt.

GFA Fortin-Belot

CH. HAUT-GOUJON 1997

■ 7.5 ha 10,000 30–49 F

This charming 1997 wine comes from 70% Merlot and 30% Cabernets grown on a sandy-clay soil. It has a ruby colour, a burgeoning bouquet of leather and small red fruits, supple and elegant tannins, and a promising, well-balanced finish. Drink in the next few years.

SCEA Garde et Fils, Goujon, 33570 Montagne, tel. 05.57.51.50.05, fax 05.57.25.33.93 Y by appt.

CH. HAUT PLATEAU 1997*

■ n.c. 6,000 20–29 F

This wine, bottled by the *négociant* Cheval Quancard, is notable for its deep-garnet colour, its aromas of black fruits and smokiness, and its powerful, velvety, well-balanced tannins. The persistent finish indicates that it will keep for two to three years.

Cheval Quancard, La Mouline, 33560 Carbon-Blanc, tel. 05.57.77.88.88, fax 05.57.77.88.99 Y by appt.

CH. JURA PLAISANCE 1997

■ n.c. 10,000 30–49 F

This eight-hectare (20-acre) estate, owned since 1938 by the Delol family, offers a 1997 wine with an intense bouquet of spices, smokiness and small red fruits. The supple and well-balanced tannic structure provides a fresh, if somewhat fleeting, finish. A wine to drink while young.

SCEV B. Delol, Ch. Jura-Plaisance, 33570 Montagne, tel. 05.57.51.91.44, fax 05.57.51.88.92 Y by appt.

CH. LA CHAPELLE

Elevé en fût de chêne 1997*

■ 11.5 ha 75,000 30–49 F

This small family property is on the southern and eastern slopes of the commune of Parsac, from which one can see a lovely Romanesque church. This 1997 wine has expressive aromas of leather, menthol and liquorice. The structure has power, richness and an oakiness which is still marked. It will reveal its potential in two to four years.

SCEA du Ch. La Chapelle, Berlière, Parsac, 33570 Montagne, tel. 05.57.24.78.33, fax 05.57.24.78.33 Y by appt.

G. H. et Th. Demur

CH. LA COURONNE 1997

■ 11 ha 24,000 50–69 F

This 1997 pure Merlot has an intense purple colour and a pleasant developing bouquet of ripe fruits and spices which also informs the palate. The round, well-blended tannins provide harmony. A fairly supple wine. Drink over the next two to three years.

Thomas Thiou, Ch. La Couronne, B.P. 10, 33570 Montagne, tel. 05.57.74.66.62, fax 05.57.74.51.65, e-mail Lacouronne@aol.com Y by appt.

CLOS LA CROIX D'ARRIAILH 1997**

■ 0.8 ha 4,200 50–69 F

This 1997 vintage is the first wine produced by this small *clos*, which is advised by Michel Rolland. It is a selection from old vines of Merlot (70%) and Cabernets (30%). It has an intense colour, a complex bouquet of fruits, vanilla and flowers, and its honest, powerful tannins which evolve with much charm and harmony. The very long finish is sustained by a fruity balance (blackcurrant). This wine should age very well for its year (at least three to six years).

Olivier Laporte, Ch. Croix-Beauséjour, Arriailh, 33570 Montagne, tel. 05.57.74.69.62, fax 05.57.74.59.21 Y by appt.

CH. LA CROIX DE MOUCHET

Cuvée sélectionnée vieillie en fût 1997

■ 12 ha 25,000 30–49 F

This is an attractive wine, with a bright colour and brick-red highlights and a bouquet of spices, menthol and smokiness. The palate is supple and well-balanced, though it has no great power. Ready to drink now.

SCEA Ch. La Croix de Mouchet, 33570 Montagne, tel. 05.57.74.62.83, fax 05.57.74.59.61 Y by appt.

Grando

CH. LA FAUCONNERIE 1997

■ 1 ha 7,000 30–49 F

This 1997 wine is notable for its aromatic complexity (fruity and delicately oaky notes) and well-balanced tannic structure. The finish is somewhat alcohol-dominated and harsh, though this should improve with time.

Bernadette Paret, Ch. Tricot, 33570 Montagne, tel. 05.57.74.65.47, fax 05.57.74.65.47 Y by appt.

CH. LA FLEUR MUSSET 1997

■ 10.5 ha n.c. 20–29 F

An exclusive label of the firm of Cordier de Blanquefort, produced by a Montagne vineyard. Grown on limestone-clay, this 1997 wine has a developing bouquet of liquorice with smoky notes and a supple, well-balanced if somewhat simple structure. Drink in the next two to three years.

Ets D. Cordier, 53, rue du Dehez, 33290 Blanquefort, tel. 05.56.95.53.00, fax 05.56.95.53.01

Dominique Nicoletti

CH. LA PAPETERIE 1997

■ 10 ha 55,000 50–69 F

Located on the site of a former pulp mill, this château offers a 1997 wine which, while the nose is still closed, has firm, fruity and persistent tannins that reveal potential. This wine will reach its best over the next two years.

Jean-Pierre Estager, 33–41, rue de Montaudon, 33500 Libourne, tel. 05.57.51.04.09, fax 05.57.25.13.38, e-mail estager@estager.com Y by appt.

CH. LA TOUR CALON

Premier des Tours 1997★★

■ 3 ha 25,000 50–69 F

This Premier des Tours comes from selected grapes from 50-year-old vines. The result is impressive. The colour is intense purple and the generous perfumes are of ripe fruits and vanilla. The tannins are both round and powerful, as well as long and well-balanced. This wine is nearly ready, but will reach full maturity after two to five years' ageing. The same owner's **Château Tour Calon** is recommended for its pleasing fruitiness and its supple, well-balanced palate. Ready for drinking straight away.

Claude Lateyron, B.P. 1, 33570 Montagne, tel. 05.57.74.50.00, fax 05.57.74.58.58 by appt.

CH. DES MOINES 1997

■ 19 ha 50,000 50–69 F

This château's name stems from its foundation by the Cistercian monks of Faize Abbey in the 16th century. The wine is pleasant and well-balanced, with a nose of floral notes and a palate of supple, fruity tannins. Drink over the next three or four years.

Vignobles Raymond Tapon, Mirande, 33570 Montagne, tel. 05.57.74.61.20, fax 05.57.74.61.19, e-mail vinstapon@aol.com by appt.

CH. MONTAIGUILLON 1997

■ 28 ha 100,000 50–69 F

About 75% of Montaiguillon's annual production goes for export, and about one-third of its barrels are replaced every year. Its 1997 wine is notable for the subtlety and elegance of its aromas and for its smooth, generous palate. The finish is marked by the oak. It needs to be kept for a year or two to lose its rough edges.

Amart, Ch. Montaiguillon, 33570 Montagne, tel. 05.57.74.62.34, fax 05.57.74.59.07 by appt.

CH. DU MOULIN NOIR 1997

■ 6.8 ha 52,000 50–69 F

This 1997 wine has an excellent appearance: a vivid red colour and pleasantly subtle aromas (leather, spices, floral and fruity notes). The palate has a balanced structure and medium persistence. Drink within the next two to three years.

SC Ch. du Moulin Noir, Lescalle, 33460 Macau, tel. 05.57.88.07.64, fax 05.57.88.07.00 by appt.

CH. NEGRIT 1997

■ 15.5 ha 60,000 30–49 F

This 1997 wine has excellent aromatic intensity (red fruits and spices), and is recommended for its structure of round, very fresh, almost acid tannins. These evolve on the palate to a simple finish. Drink soon.

SCEV Lagardère, Ch. Négrit, 33570 Montagne, tel. 05.57.74.61.63, fax 05.57.74.59.62 by appt.

CH. PETIT CLOS DU ROY 1997

■ 20 ha 85,000 50–69 F

An 18th-century charterhouse sits amidst 20 ha (49 acres) of vines that every year produce good wines. This 1997 vintage is spicy and oaky with a slightly musky character and supple, harmonious tannins which have already matured. A wine to drink straight away.

François Janoueix, 20, quai du Priourat, B.P. 135, 33500 Libourne, tel. 05.57.55.55.44, fax 05.57.51.83.70 by appt.

CH. ROCHER CORBIN 1997★★

■ 10 ha 60,000 50–69 F

This château, once a part of the lordship of Corbin, has a superb terroir on the western side of the knoll of Calon. It makes the most of its soils, as the intense nose of this 1997 wine shows, with its aromas of prune, crystallised fruit and jam. The tannins initially make a velvety impression on the palate, then evolve with power and good balance. They need time, however, to become better blended. A remarkable wine for its year, it needs two to five years' keeping to reach its best.

SCE du Ch. Rocher Corbin, 33570 Montagne, tel. 05.57.74.55.92, fax 05.57.74.53.15 by appt.

Ph. Durand

CH. ROSE D'ORION 1997★★

■ 3 ha 20,000 30–49 F

With its remarkable 1997 wine, this small vineyard of three hectares (seven acres) has done remarkably well. The purple colour is deep and bright. The pleasant aromas marry red fruits (strawberry) to a high-quality oakiness. The tannins provide a ripe and powerful attack, then subtly blend in with good balance and persistence. Everything is in place to make this a most agreeable wine after two to six years' ageing. Congratulations to Messieurs Hénot and Péquignot, the oenologist and winery master.

EARL Vignobles D. et C. Devaud, Faise, 33570 Les Artigues-de-Lussac, tel. 05.57.24.31.39, fax 05.57.24.34.17 by appt.

L'AS DE ROUDIER

Elevé en fût de chêne 1997★

■ 29.73 ha 9,000 70–99 F

Grown on limestone-clay and siliceous soils, this 1997 wine was made from a meticulous selection of grapes from certain Château Roudier plots. The ruby colour shines with multiple glints, and the burgeoning bouquet mixes the ripeness of fruit with the elegance of oak. The rich, well-blended tannins are sufficiently powerful and long-lasting to be worth keeping for two to five years.

SCEA Capdemourlin, Ch. Roudier, 33570 Montagne, tel. 05.57.74.62.06, fax 05.57.74.59.34 by appt.

DOM. DU ROUDIER 1997★

■ n.c. n.c. 50–69 F

This 1997 wine is a good blend of Merlot (60%), Cabernet Franc (20%) and Cabernet-Sauvignon (10%). The appearance is excellent. So too are the perfumes of fruits and toast. The palate reveals the wine's tannic potential, with a rather dominating oaky presence. A wine to drink now or keep for two to four years.

Vignobles Aubert, Ch. La Couspaude, 33330 Saint-Emilion, tel. 05.57.40.15.76, fax 05.57.40.10.14 by appt.

CH. SAMION

Elevé en barrique de chêne 1997★

■ 0.55 ha 4,250 30–49 F

This interesting 1997 wine is developing a discreet and sincere bouquet. The tannins are ripe and robust, though still a little lively in the finish. The wine will develop good balance after two to four years of ageing.

Vignobles Rocher-Cap-de-Rive 1, Ch. Cap d'Or, 33570 Montagne, tel. 05.57.40.08.88, fax 05.57.40.19.93, e-mail vignobles.rochercaprive@wanadoo.fr

CH. TEYSSIER 1997★

■ 19.2 ha 66,000 50–69 F

This vineyard is managed by the firm of Dourthe, who market this wine. The nose of this almost pure Merlot vintage is expressive and vinous, with notes of ripe fruits. The tannic structure is dense and rich, with a finish which is powerful yet still a little austere. The wine should age well (for at least three to five years).

Ch. Teyssier, 1, rue Teyssier, 33570 Lussac-Saint-Emilion, tel. 05.56.35.53.00, fax 05.56.35.53.29, e-mail contact@cvbg.com by appt.

Famille Durand-Teyssier

CH. VIEUX BONNEAU 1997★★

■ 14 ha 50,000 30–49 F

This château belongs to the Despagne family, who have produced a remarkable 1997 wine that marries subtlety to power. The colour contains lovely purple highlights. The intense perfumes evoke blackcurrant, vanilla and brandy. The tannins attack with richness and warmth, then develop with great density and good balance between fruit and oak. The finish is particularly long and harmonious. It implies good keeping quality, for at least four to six years. A fine success for its year.

SCEV Despagne et Fils, Bonneau, 33570 Montagne, tel. 05.57.74.60.72, fax 05.57.74.58.22 ev. day except Sun. 8am–12 noon 2pm–6pm

VIEUX CHATEAU BIROT 1997★

■ 4 ha 20,000 30–49 F

This small château of only four hectares (ten acres) has produced a very attractive 1997 wine. The colour is intense purple and the bouquet expressive of blackcurrant, spices and green pepper. The tannins are rich, supple and fruity, the finish fresh and delightful. An elegant wine. Drink over the next one to three years.

Jean-Loup Robin, Ch. Gontet, 33570 Puisseguin, tel. 05.57.84.26.16, fax 05.57.84.29.13 by appt.

CH. VIEUX MOULINS DE CHEREAU 1997★

■ 5.5 ha 30,000 30–49 F

Vinified and matured with enthusiasm by a former chemical engineer, this 1997 wine has a garnet colour, a very fruity range of aromas and a supple structure which is already harmonious. Ready to drink now, but will keep two to four years.

SCEA Vignoble Silvestrini, Chéreau, 33570 Lussac, tel. 05.57.74.50.76, fax 05.57.74.53.22 ev. day 9am–12 noon 2pm–7pm

Puisseguin Saint-Émilion

CH. BEL-AIR

Bacchus Vieilli en fût de chêne 1997

■ n.c. n.c. 30–49 F

This special wine was matured six months in a cement vat, then 12 months in a barrel. Its appearance is perfect: an attractive ruby colour, a burgeoning bouquet of flowers, liquorice and cinnamon. On the palate, the tannins are very obvious. They will need to be aged for two to three years in order to soften.

SCEA Adoue Bel-Air, Bel-Air, 33570 Puisseguin, tel. 05.57.74.51.82, fax 05.57.74.59.94 by appt.

Adoue Frères

CH. BRANDA 1997★

■ 5.5 ha 40,000 50–69 F

This reputable château grows a sizeable percentage of Cabernet Franc (40%). The 1997 wine is very successful. The bouquet releases well-blended fruits and vanilla. On the palate, the tannins attack well, then evolve with good persistence. Wait two or three years before drinking this wine.

SC Ch. du Branda, Roques, 33570 Puisseguin, tel. 05.57.74.62.55, fax 05.57.74.57.33 by appt.

CH. DURAND-LAPLAGNE

Cuvée Sélection 1997

■ 3.5 ha 9,000 50–69 F

Château Durand-Laplagne has two labels which are both recommended this year. The Cuvée Sélection is made from a selection by plot which is matured in oak. The oaky notes are well balanced with leather and violets. The tannins are supple, and the wine is ready to drink now. The vat-matured **Cuvée Classique** blends the same percentages of varieties

Merlot 70%). It offers a bouquet of small red erries and flowers. The very obvious tannins ieed one to two years' ageing in the bottle 30–49F), after which it will go well with ›igeon and peas.

Vignobles Bessou, Ch. Durand-aplagne, 33570 Puisseguin, el. 05.57.74.63.07, fax 05.57.74.59.58 Y y appt.
Sylvie et Bertrand Bessou

:H. FONGABAN 1997

7.5 ha 40,000 30-49 F

Located on excellent limestone-clay, this hâteau offers an excellent 1997 wine with a trong colour and a good nose of ripe fruits nd vanilla. The palate of this Puisseguin volves with firmness but has excellent length. t can wait two to three years.

SARL de Fongaban, Monbadon, 33570 Puisseguin, tel. 05.57.74.54.07, ax 05.57.74.50.97 Y by appt.

:H. GONTET-ROBIN 1997★★

9 ha 50,000 30-49 F

This blend of 70% Merlot and 30% Caber-iet is wholly vat-matured, which is rare in this egion but particularly advantageous for this lifficult year. It has opulence and spark. Notes of spices and flowers inform both nose nd palate alike. The tannins are ripe, round nd forceful. They are maturing with good alance and elegant aromatic persistence. A ery genuine, well-bred wine, ready in two or hree years.

Jean-Loup Robin, Ch. Gontet, 33570 Puisseguin, tel. 05.57.84.26.16, ax 05.57.84.29.13 Y by appt.

CH. GRAND RIGAUD 1997

6 ha 40,000 30-49 F

Bright in its appearance, this wine has a io less attractive bouquet of red fruits and oasted oak. On the palate, the tannins are obvious and round, but they do not guarantee ong keeping. Drink straight away.

Guy Desplat, 33570 Puisseguin, el. 05.57.74.61.10, fax 05.57.74.58.30 Y y appt.

:H. HAUT-BERNAT

Vieilli en fût de chêne 1997★★

5.65 ha 32,000 50-69 F

Over the last ten years, the new owner has gone all out for technical progress in both vineyard and winery. This 1997 wine is

brilliant – for a 1997. A pure Merlot, it is rich in colour and in aromas (crystallised cherry, spices and liquorice). The palate is especially well-balanced. The tannins are velvety, fleshy and well-blended in an elegant, charming oakiness. They evolve with power and have very pleasant aromatic persistence. A wine at the top of its appellation, which will reach perfection in three to six years' time.

SA Vignobles Bessineau, 8, Brousse, B.P. 42, 33350 Belvès-de-Castillon, tel. 05.57.56.05.55, fax 05.57.56.05.56, e-mail bessineau@cote-montpezat.com Y ev. day except Sat. Sun. 9am–12 noon 2pm–6pm; cl. Aug.

CH. HAUT-FAYAN 1997★

n.c. 13,000 30-49 F

A rigorous selection of grapes is behind this wine grown in an eight-hectare (20-acre) vineyard. It has an attractive purple colour and is intensely redolent of fruits with a round, well-balanced tannic structure. A charming, well-made wine. Drink over the next five years.

Guy Poitou, Ch. Haut-Fayan, 33570 Puisseguin, tel. 05.57.74.67.38, fax 05.57.74.54.82 Y by appt.

CH. LACABANNE-DUVIGNEAU 1997★

6 ha 20,000 30-49 F

This château also has a *gîte rural*. So you can stay there and sample their excellent wines. This one has a bright ruby colour, a complex bouquet of delicately oaky black fruits, and fleshy, ripe tannins maturing with great aromatic persistence. Leave the bottle to age for one to three years.

EARL Vignobles J.-P. et M. Celerier, Moulin Courrech, 33570 Puisseguin, tel. 05.57.74.61.75, fax 05.57.74.52.79 Y ev. day 8am–12 noon 2pm–8pm
Vignobles Paul Bordes, Faize, 33570 Les Artigues-de-Lussac, tel. 05.57.24.33.66, fax 05.57.24.30.42 Y by appt.

CH. LAFAURIE 1997

5 ha 30,000 30-49 F

This 1997 wine has been matured in new oak barrels. It has a brilliant colour with crimson glints, and a delicate nose combining stewed fruits and liquorice. Fresh tannins (menthol) on the palate are supported by a fairly dense framework which is a little dry at the finish. It should become more balanced once it has been kept for two or three years.

Vignobles Paul Bordes, Faize, 33570 Les Artigues-de-Lussac, tel. 05.57.24.33.66, fax 05.57.24.30.42 Y by appt.

LA MAURIANE 1997★★

n.c. 12,000 70-99 F

La Mauriane comes from a selection of three hectares (seven acres) of vines, essentially Merlot (90%) grown at the Chateau Rigaud. This 1997 wine is remarkable for the vintage: it has a dark, almost black colour, intense aromas of ripe dark berries, roasted

coffee and toast, tannins which are both powerful and velvety, and long, lingering flavours. All of these will ensure that this wine opens up completely in three to six years' time.
Josette Taïx, Rigaud, 33570 Puisseguin, tel. 05.57.74.54.07, fax 05.57.74.50.97 by appt.

CH. DE MOLE 1997

■ 9.35 ha 60,000 30–49 F

This 1997 wine is worth recommending for its bouquet of Morello cherries, flowers and spices, and for its structure, which is supple and well balanced at the finish. A wine which is ready to drink now.
Ginette Lenier, Ch. de Môle, B.P. 15, 33570 Puisseguin, tel. 05.57.74.60.86, fax 05.57.74.60.86 by appt.

CH. MOUCHET

Vieilli en fût de chêne 1997★

■ 6 ha 12,000 30–49 F

With 90% of Merlot in the blend, this château has produced a really delightful wine. It has a shimmering colour, and complex aromas of ripe fruits, liquorice and discreet notes of oak. The tannins are impressively mouthfilling, and still so firm that it will be essential for the wine to age for two or three years in the bottle.
SCEA Ch. La Croix de Mouchet, 33570 Montagne, tel. 05.57.74.62.83, fax 05.57.74.59.61 by appt.
Grando

CH. DU MOULIN 1997

■ 8 ha 50,000 50–69 F

As its name indicates, this château has a mill, which sits on top of a hill. The good-quality limestone-clay terroir has yielded this very aromatic wine (soft fruits, flowers and spices), with a full, balanced structure. The finish is pleasant and marked by blackcurrants. A wine which will be good to drink over the next two years.
SCEA Chanet et Fils, n° 1 A Jacques, 33570 Puisseguin, tel. 05.57.74.60.85, fax 05.57.74.59.90 ev. day 8am–12 noon 2pm–6pm

CH. MOULIN DE CURAT 1997

■ n.c. 139,000 30–49 F

This 1997 wine is the little brother of the Château de Puisseguin-Curat, but has been developed and distributed by Ginestet. It has a ruby colour with slightly orangey glints, and elegant aromas of violets, flowers and crystallised fruits. Its tannic structure is simple and silky, and it is already balanced at the finish. Should be drunk over the next two or three years.
SA Maison Ginestet, 19, av. de Fontenille, 33360 Carignan-de-Bordeaux, tel. 05.56.68.81.82, fax 05.56.20.96.99, e-mail contact@ginestet.fr by appt.
Robin

CH. DE PUISSEGUIN-CURAT

1997★

■ 2 ha 6,000 30–49 F

It is said that this château was run by th author Montaigne, and its other claim t fame is that it belonged to Jeanne d'Albre Queen of Navarre and mother of Henri IV The grape range here includes 75% Merlot This 1997 wine has complex aromas of leathe and game, and reveals full, elegant tannin which develop with great harmony and bal ance. A wine which can be drunk straigh away.
GAEC Ch. de Puisseguin-Curat, 33570 Puisseguin, tel. 05.57.74.51.06, fax 05.57.74.54.29 by appt.
Robin

CH. RIGAUD 1997★

■ n.c. 2,000 30–49 F

This vineyard is located on a limestone pla teau, and grows a range of grapes dominate by Merlot (80%). The 1997 wine has a dee colour with crimson glints and an elegan bouquet which is full of fruit aromas, along with notes of pepper and toast. On the palat it has powerful, rich, very fruity tannins which develop with finesse. A wine which wil need to be kept for two years before being drunk.
Josette Taïx, Rigaud, 33570 Puisseguin, tel. 05.57.74.54.07, fax 05.57.74.50.97 by appt.

CH. ROC DE BERNON 1997★★

■ 14.08 ha 85,000 30–49 F

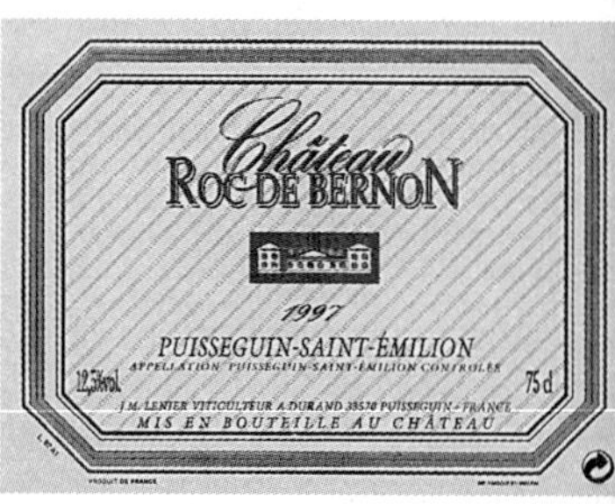

A *coup de coeur* is awarded unanimously to this 1997 wine, which is made from grapes rigorously selected by plot, and has been matured solely in vats. It has great concentration both in the colour (purplish glints) and the nose (game, leather and pepper), then reveals all its noble pedigree on the palate, where the tannins are full and powerful, with an especially lingering, fruity quality. One of our tasters described it as 'an intelligent wine, which will make a deep impression on anyone who drinks it'. Should be kept for two years, then drunk over the next three.
Jean-Marie Lenier, Ch. Roc de Bernon,, 33570 Puisseguin, tel. 05.57.74.53.42, fax 05.57.74.53.42, e-mail roc.de.bernon@wanadoo.fr by appt.

CH. ROC DE BOISSAC

Elevé en fût de chêne 1997

■ 32 ha 50,000 50-69 F

With its unbroken 40 ha (99 acres) of vines facing due south, this château is one of the jewels of the appellation. The 1997 wine has aromas of red berries which are still strongly marked by oak. Its tannic structure is supple and delightful in the attack, then develops with sufficient power to suggest that this wine has excellent prospects for at least two to three years.

SARL Roc de Boissac, Pleniers de Boissac, 33570 Puisseguin, tel. 05.57.74.61.22, fax 05.57.74.59.54 Y by appt.

Saint-Georges Saint-Émilion

CH. CALON 1997★★

■ 6 ha 30,000 70-99 F

This vineyard has been in existence for over two centuries. Located on the southern slopes of the limestone plateau facing Saint-Emilion, it receives a remarkable amount of sunshine and the natural drainage of the soil is perfect. This 1997 wine, matured 50% in barrels and 50% in vats, has a strong ruby colour and concentrated, mature aromas of soft fruits, leather and delicate oaky vanilla. The tannins on the palate are full-bodied, powerful and especially flavoursome and lingering. A wine which has excellent general balance, and will open up fully within two to five years.

Jean-Noël Boidron, Ch. Calon, 33570 Montagne, tel. 05.57.51.64.88, fax 05.57.51.56.30 Y ev. day except Sat. Sun. 8am–12 noon 2pm–6pm

CH. CAP D'OR

Elevé en barrique de chêne 1997★

■ 5.39 ha 42,400 30-49 F

This vineyard is planted on a limestone-clay soil with starfish, and grows a range of grapes dominated by Merlot (80%). Its 1997 wine has an intense bouquet of ripe fruits and coffee. After a supple attack on the palate, it develops richly, with fruit flavours and good concentration at the finish. A wine which will be ready to drink in one or two years' time.

Vignobles Rocher-Cap-de-Rive 1, Ch. Cap d'Or, 33570 Montagne, tel. 05.57.40.08.88, fax 05.57.40.19.93, e-mail vignobles.rochercaprive@wanadoo.fr

CH. HAUT SAINT-GEORGES 1997★

■ 3 ha 18,000 50-69 F

There are only three hectares (seven acres) of vines on this small vineyard, which has just renovated its vat-house using the most modern techniques. In 1997, grape selection has yielded a full-bodied, harmonious wine with aromas of undergrowth and ripe fruits, and an elegant note of oak. Even so, it will need to be kept for three years until the finish becomes less aggressive and more balanced.

SCE du ch. La Grande-Barde, 33570 Montagne, tel. 05.57.74.64.98, fax 05.57.74.64.98 Y by appt.

CH. LA CROIX DE SAINT-GEORGES 1997★

■ 6.58 ha 48,000 30-49 F

The balanced range of grapes grown on this property (51% Merlot and 49% Cabernets) has yielded good results in this 1997 wine. It has a very fruity bouquet and a structure which although still austere is promising, with powerful tannins at the finish. A wine which will open up more fully in two years' time.

Jean de bConinck/b[/i3[CON], Ch. du Pintey, 33500 Libourne, tel. 05.57.51.03.04, fax 05.57.51.59.61 Y by appt.

CH. LE ROC DE TROQUARD 1997

■ 3.05 ha 5,200 30-49 F

This fairly typical 1997 wine has a beautiful, brilliant Bordeaux colour and a nose of leather which is just beginning to open. The tannins on the palate are full-bodied and have quite good length, but need to open out and gain more balance. A two- or three-year keeping period is recommended.

SCEA des Vignobles Visage, Jupille, 33330 Saint-Sulpice-de-Faleyrens, tel. 05.57.24.62.92, fax 05.57.24.69.40 Y by appt.

CH. MACQUIN 1997★

■ 2 ha 10,000 50-69 F

Located on a good limestone-clay terroir, this château has succeeded in producing a 1997 wine which is well worth trying. It has an intense ruby colour and a bouquet of spices, crystallised fruits and raspberries which is beginning to open. The tannic structure is well balanced and elegant, and will grow rounder as the wine ages in the cellar for two to three years.

Denis Corre-Macquin, Saint-Georges, 33570 Montagne, tel. 05.57.74.64.66, fax 05.57.74.55.47 Y by appt.

CH. SAINT-ANDRE CORBIN 1997★

■ 17.5 ha n.c. 50-69 F

This 22.5-ha (56.5-acre) property is run by Jean-Claude Berrouet and Alain Moueix, two strong personalities from the Libournais who share the same passion for trying to produce great wines which reflect the qualities of their terroir. This 1997 wine is the perfect proof of their endeavours, with its strong ruby colour and elegant, complex aromas of soft fruits and spices. Its well-marked tannic structure is very typical of the appellation. A wine which is still somewhat firm, but will open out once it has aged for two to three years in the bottle.

SCEA du Priourat, 10, quai du Priourat, 33500 Libourne, tel. 05.57.55.00.50, fax 05.57.25.22.56

CH. SAINT-GEORGES 1997★★

■ 45 ha 300,000 100–149 F

This very beautiful 18th-century château overlooking all the hills of Saint-Georges-Saint-Emilion is well accustomed to winning honours. Every year it produces excellent wines, as can be seen from this 1997 vintage, to which the jury has awarded a unanimous *coup de coeur.* Its dark colour gleams with garnet glints, and it has intense, expressive aromas of cocoa, spices, ripe fruits and oaky toast. The tannins on the palate are rich and powerful, and develop with great roundness, harmony and balance. A wine to be drunk with game two to six years from now.

Famille Desbois, 33570 Montagne, tel. 05.57.74.62.11, fax 05.57.74.58.62, e-mail g.desbois@chateau-saint-georges.com Y by appt.

Côtes de Castillon

In 1989 a new appellation was created: Côtes de Castillon. It applies to an area of 2,855 ha (7,052 acres), which was extracted from the Appellation Bordeaux Côtes de Castillon, that is, the nine communes of Belvès-de-Castillon, Castillon-la-Bataille, Saint-Magne-de-Castillon, Gardegan-et-Tourtirac, Sainte-Colombe, Saint-Genès-de-Castillon, Saint-Philippe-d'Aiguilhe, Les Salles-de-Castillon and Monbadon. Nonetheless, to leave the 'Bordeaux' group, the wine-growers are obliged to follow particularly strict rules of production, especially those that apply to density of plantation, which is limited to 5,000 plants per ha (2000 per acre). Compliance has been set for the year 2010 to take account of the vines that are already planted. In 1999 180,764 hl (4,772,170 gal) of wine were produced.

ARTHUS 1997★

■ 3 ha 14,500 50–69 F

This wine is the result of a rigorous selection of vines located on the hillsides of Sainte-Colombe, which yield excellent grapes. Not surprisingly the 1997 vintage is good, with an intense, brilliant colour which heralds powerful aromas of cherries, redcurrants and strawberries. The tannins show real know-how: full-bodied, finely extracted and not overdone. A wine of character, which is already pleasant but will keep for two to five years.

Danielle et Richard Dubois, Ch. Bertinat Lartigue, 33330 Saint-Sulpice-de-Faleyrens, tel. 05.57.24.72.75, fax 05.57.74.45.43, e-mail dubricru@aol.com Y by appt.

CH. BEL-AIR

Elevé en fût de chêne 1997★

■ 15 ha 120,000 50–69 F

This estate was re-established in 1994, and is now producing attractive wines such as this 1997 vintage, which is rich in colour and has complex aromas of ripe fruits and oaky vanilla. The balance of flavours on the palate is excellent, with a finish which is still marked by maturation in oak. The harmony will be perfect two or three years from now.

SCEA du Dom. de Bellair, 33350 Belvès-de-Castillon, tel. 05.56.08.15.25, fax 05.56.42.44.47 Y by appt.

David

CH. DE BELCIER

Vieilli en barrique de chêne 1997★★

■ 52 ha 120,000 50–69 F

This very large estate of about 50 ha (124 acres) belongs to MACIF and regularly offers good wines. The 1997 vintage is awarded two stars for its dark-red colour with violet glints, and its expressive bouquet of ripe berries and vanilla, with a note of smoke and toast. After a mouth-filling attack, the tannins are well blended into an elegant oakiness, leaving an impression of character and balance at the finish. A wine which is at the peak of its appellation in this vintage, and will be ready in two to five years' time.

SCA du Ch. de Belcier, 2, Ch. de Belcier, 33350 Les Salles-de-Castillon, tel. 05.57.40.67.58, fax 05.57.40.67.58 Y by appt.

MACIF

CH. BELLEVUE

Cuvée Vieilles vignes Vieilli en fût de chêne 1998★

■ 5.5 ha 15,000 30–49 F

For the 1998 vintage, the Château Bellevue has produced two wines in more or less equal quantities. This Cuvée Vieilles Vignes is awarded one star for the agreeable character of its nose of fruit, spices and toast. The tannins on the palate are supple, rich, very mouth-filling and elegant. A wine which can be drunk now or kept for three to five years. The **1998 Cuvée Traditionelle** is not oak-matured, and is recommended for its fresh aromas of fruits in brandy and pleasant character. Best drunk within the next three years.

Michel Lydoire, Ch. Bellevue, 33350 Belvès-de-Castillon, tel. 05.57.47.94.29, fax 05.57.47.94.29 by appt.

CH. BEYNAT Cuvée Léonard 1997

■ 15.01 ha 3,150 30–49 F

Although produced with great rigour, this Cuvée Léonard met with varied reactions from the jury. Some loved its aromas of oaky vanilla and smoke and its powerful tannins, while others were bothered by the oakiness. This suggests that it will need to be kept for two or three years until it becomes more balanced.

Xavier Borliachon, 27, rte de Beynat, 33350 Saint-Magne-de-Castillon, tel. 05.57.40.01.14, fax 05.57.40.18.51 ev. day except Sun. 9am–12 noon 2pm–7pm

CH. BLANZAC

Cuvée Prestige 1997

■ 7 ha 25,000 50–69 F

This Cuvée Prestige deserves to be recommended for its intense aromas of red berries and the quality of its balanced tannins, which are brought out well in an elegant, unobtrusive oaky flavour. An attractive wine which will be ready to drink in a year or two.

Bernard Depons, Ch. Blanzac, 33350 Saint-Magne-de-Castillon, tel. 05.57.40.11.89, fax 05.57.40.49.69 ev. day 8.30am–7pm

CH. BRANDEAU 1997

■ 9.42 ha 13,000 30–49 F

This wine has been produced by organic methods, and is notable for its heady, fruity aromas accompanied by a spicy note, and its supple, smooth structure. An enjoyable wine which, like many in the 1997 vintage, should be drunk while young.

Antony King et Andréa Gray, Brandeau, 33350 Les Salles-de-Castillon, tel. 05.57.40.65.48, fax 05.57.40.65.65 by appt.

CH. CANTEGRIVE 1997

■ 16.78 ha 60,000 30–49 F

This very old estate, which used to belong to Barton et Guestier, has now produced a 1997 wine with a very powerful, complex nose containing notes of ripe fruits and undergrowth. The tannins on the palate are very round, giving way to a certain austerity at the finish which will fade after two or three years of ageing.

SC Ch. Cantegrive, Monbadon-Terrasson, 33570 Puisseguin, tel. 03.26.52.14.74, fax 03.26.52.24.02 by appt.

CH. CAP DE FAUGERES 1997★★

■ 23.25 ha 87,000 50–69 F

In 1987 this property was taken over by the cinema producer Péby Guisez and his wife Corinne, who is now carrying on the revival of this vineyard on her own. Ten years on, its achievement in a difficult vintage is rewarded with a *coup de coeur* for a wine with a brilliant cherry-red colour which is just as delightful as its complex aromas of ripe soft fruits (jam), vanilla, toast and mint. On the palate it is supple and rich, developing with great presence and good length. The note of prunes at the finish is extremely pleasant. A remarkable wine, which will be ready to drink in two to six years' time.

Corinne Guisez, Ch. Cap de Faugeres, 33350 Sainte-Colombe, tel. 05.57.40.34.99, fax 05.57.40.36.14, e-mail faugères@club-internet.fr by appt.

CH. DE CLOTTE 1997★

■ 14 ha 50,000 30–49 F

This château is located at the heart of the appellation, and grows 35% Merlot, 55% Cabernets and 10% Malbec. This 1997 wine has a dark-red colour with brick-red glints, and a rich, complex bouquet combining dark berries with some slightly oaky notes. The first impression on the palate is supple, after which the tannins develop powerfully and richly, and with very good, elegant length. A wine to be drunk in two to five years' time.

SCEA Ch. de Clotte, 33350 Les Salles-de-Castillon, tel. 05.57.40.60.15, e-mail declotte@club-internet.fr by appt.

Guerret-Denies

CH. DE COLOMBE 1998

■ 7 ha 38,000 30–49 F

This wine is still somewhat closed, but distinguishes itself by its mature, round, very fruity tannins. Its simplicity at the finish does not suggest that it has any great ageing potential: two or three years at most.

SARL Vignobles Lenne-Mourgues, Ch. du Bois, 8, rte de Sainte-Colombe, 33350 Saint-Magne-de-Castillon,
tel. 05.57.40.07.87, fax 05.57.40.30.59 by appt.

CH. COTE MONTPEZAT 1998*

n.c. 130,000 30–49 F

This vineyard is one of the pillars of the appellation. The 1998 vintage is not quite as good as the previous one, but is still a very creditable achievement. It is closed as yet, with a fruity, spicy bouquet, but oak is still dominant on the palate, where the tannins are austere. Even so, two to three years of ageing should enable this wine to attain a better balance.

SA Vignobles Bessineau, 8, Brousse, B.P. 42, 33350 Belvès-de-Castillon,
tel. 05.57.56.05.55, fax 05.57.56.05.56,
e-mail bessineau@cote-montpezat.com
ev. day except Sat. Sun. 9am–12 noon 2pm–6pm; cl. Aug.

CH. FONGABAN 1997

34 ha 30,000 30–49 F

This wine is recommended for its intense nose dominated by spices and notes of smoke and menthol. It fills the mouth very decently, and has richness and a herbaceous hint at the finish which should disappear once it has been kept for two or three years.

SARL de Fongaban, Monbadon, 33570 Puisseguin, tel. 05.57.74.54.07,
fax 05.57.74.50.97 by appt.

CH. FONTBAUDE

Vieilles vignes Elevé en fût de chêne 1998*

3 ha 15,000 50–69 F

This oak-matured 1998 wine has a cherry-red colour with black glints, and a bouquet which is still young with aromas of dark berries (blackberries) and flowers, along with a mineral note. The supple, clean tannic structure is still dominated by a somewhat immature note of oak. A wine which will need to be kept for a year or two, until the finish becomes as delightful as the nose.

GAEC Sabaté-Zavan, 34, rue de l'Eglise, 33350 Saint-Magne-de-Castillon,
tel. 05.57.40.06.58, fax 05.57.40.26.54,
e-mail chateau.fontbaude@wanadoo.fr
ev. day except Sun. 9am–12 noon 2pm–6pm

CH. HAUT-TUQUET 1998

n.c. 200,000 30–49 F

This Château Haut-Tuquet has an intense purple colour, and distinguishes itself by the finesse of its fruit and toast aromas, and by its powerful tannic structure which is unfortunately somewhat dense on the palate at the finish. Should be drunk within two or three years.

Vignobles Lafaye Père et Fils, Ch. Viramon, 33330 Saint-Etienne-de-Lisse,
tel. 05.57.40.18.28, fax 05.57.40.02.70 by appt.

CH. LABESSE 1998

n.c. n.c. 30–49 F

This 1998 wine has qualities which will delight lovers of exotic fragrances: it is very much marked in the nose by notes of coconut, mango and vanilla, which reappear on the palate with supple and quite persistent tannins, leading to a somewhat buttery finish.

Vignobles Aubert, Ch. La Couspaude, 33330 Saint-Emilion, tel. 05.57.40.15.76,
fax 05.57.40.10.14 by appt.

CH. LA BOURREE 1998*

n.c. 30,000 20–29 F

Much praised for its 1997 vintage, this château has now produced a very fine 1998. It has a purple colour with black glints, and complex aromas of very ripe dark berries, accompanied by oaky notes of toast and cocoa. On the palate the soft, rich tannins develop with finesse and balance right up to a delicately oaky finish which is quite beautiful. Should be drunk in two or three years' time. From the same producer, the oak-matured **1998 Château Roque Le Mayne** receives the same rating ((30–49F).

GAEC des Vignobles Meynard et Fils, 101, rte de La Bourrée, 33350 Saint-Magne-de-Castillon, tel. 05.57.40.17.32,
fax 05.57.40.17.32 by appt.

CH. LA CLARIERE LAITHWAITE 1997

4.6 ha 25,600 50–69 F

This 1997 wine has a bouquet which is just opening and offers aromas of almonds, cocoa, marsh flowers, irises and undergrowth. Its tannic structure is full in the attack, then develops firmly. A pleasant wine which will open out in one to three years' time. It is distributed in Britain through the 'Confrères de La Clarière' wine club.

SARL Direct Wines (Castillon) La Clarière Laithwaite, Les Confrères de La Clarière, 33350 Sainte-Colombe,
tel. 05.57.47.95.14, fax 05.57.47.94.47 by appt.

CH. LA FONT DU JEU 1997*

5 ha 20,000 50–69 F

This 1997 wine is produced by the owner of the Château Lapeyronie, and is singled out for its very spicy character (cashew nuts) and its roundness on the palate. It will be ready to drink a year or two from now.

Jean-Frédéric Lapeyronie, 4, Castelmerle, 33350 Sainte-Colombe,
tel. 05.57.40.19.27, fax 05.57.40.14.38 by appt.

CH. LA GRANDE MAYE

Elevé et vieilli en barrique de chêne 1997*

15 ha 50,000 50–69 F

This vineyard has an established reputation, and is sometimes at the very top of its appellation. The dark colour of the 1997 vintage has beautiful crimson glints, and its bouquet, which is now opening, has aromas of toast, fruit and musk. On the palate the supple, rich tannins are well structured and finish on a very agreeable floral note. A wine with good future prospects, which should be drunk in two to six years' time.

EARL P.L. Valade, Rouye, 33350 Belvès-de-Castillon, tel. 05.57.47.93.92, fax 05.57.47.93.92, e-mail paul.valade@wanadoo.fr by appt.

CH. LA ROCHE BEAULIEU

Elevé en fût de chêne 1998

1 ha 5,000 30–49 F

This oak-matured wine represents the produce of just one hectare (2.5 acres) of the 8.5 ha (21 acres) owned by this property. The expressive but as yet discreet bouquet opens out on the palate in harmony with supple, rich tannins which for the moment are dominated by oak. A wine which should be drunk over the next three years.

EARL du Vignoble Rousset, Ch. La Roche Beaulieu, 33350 Les Salles-de-Castillon, tel. 05.57.40.64.37, fax 05.57.40.65.05, e-mail olivier.rousset@waika9.com ev. day except Sun. 9.30am–12 noon 2pm–6pm

CH. LA SENTINELLE

Elevé un an en fût de chêne 1998

3 ha 15,300 30–49 F

This 1998 wine is the first vintage produced by the château's new owner. It has an elegant bouquet of red berries and heather. The tannins are very evident and quite harmonious, but there is a hint of bitterness at the finish which should fade once the wine has aged for two or three years.

Sté viticole du Dom. de Lezin, 11, Giraud-Arnaud, 33750 Saint-Germain-du-Puch, tel. 05.57.24.00.00, fax 05.57.24.00.98 by appt.

Muriel Huillier

CH. LA TREILLE DES GIRONDINS

Cuvée Cronos Top 2000 Elevé en fût de chêne 1998★★

1 ha 6,000 30–49 F

This Cuvée Cronos is made from selected grapes grown on 40-year-old vines planted on a siliceous clay soil. It has been oak-matured, and has a clear purple colour and powerful, fruity aromas which are still dominated by elegant oaky notes of cocoa and vanilla. On the palate, the tannins are superb, dense, mature and very rich, while the finish is marked by a lingering return to fruity flavours. A remarkable piece of wine-making and maturing, which can be enjoyed straight away, but can also be left to age for two to five years.

Alain Goumaud, Mézières, 33350 Saint-Magne-de-Castillon, tel. 05.57.40.05.38, fax 05.57.40.26.60 ev. day except Sat. Sun. 9am–12 noon 2pm–6pm

DOM. LA TUQUE BEL-AIR

Vieilli en fût de chêne neuf 1998

20 ha 45,000 30–49 F

This 1998 wine makes a good first impression with its dark-red colour and aromas of violets which are dominated by exotic notes of oak (coconut). On the palate, the tannins are evident but still flattened by the oak, which gives a slight note of bitterness at the finish. Best kept for two to three years until it achieves greater balance.

GAEC Jean Lavau et Fils, B.P. 13, 33330 Saint-Emilion, tel. 05.57.24.77.30, fax 05.57.24.66.24 ev. day 9am–12.30pm 2pm–6pm; Sat. Sun. by appt.

CH. DE L'ESTANG 1998★

6 ha 40,000 30–49 F

This château grows its vines on a limestone-clay soil, and produces a wine based exclusively on Merlot. This 1998 wine has an elegant, floral bouquet which develops on notes of crystallised fruits and prunes. The tannins are supple and silky, and show good harmony and balance. A delightful wine, which will be ready to be enjoyed in two to five years' time.

Bocquillon de l'Estang SA, Ch. de L'Estang, 33350 Saint-Genès-de-Castillon, tel. 05.57.47.91.81, fax 05.57.47.92.13 by appt.

CH. MONBADON

Cuvée Jeanne de l'Isle 1998★

25 ha n.c. 30–49 F

The Cuvée Jeanne de l'Isle was created for the 1998 vintage, and is a selection from the barrels at the Château Monbadon. It has a deep-cherry colour, and a bouquet of ripe fruit and oaky toast aromas which harmonises with its clean, silky, fairly powerful tannins to make this a wine for longer maturing (three to eight years).

J. Lebègue, 33330 Saint-Emilion, tel. 05.57.51.31.05, fax 05.57.74.18.47, e-mail lebegue@lebegue

Montfort

CH. MOULIN COURRECH 1997

10 ha 20,000 30–49 F

This property has been handed down from generation to generation since 1880. It offers a 1997 wine which is very fruity (blackberries and blackcurrants), with a touch of leather and spices. A round, pleasant wine, which should be drunk within the next two years as an accompaniment to red meat.

EARL Vignobles J.-P. et M. Celerier, Moulin Courrech, 33570 Puisseguin, tel. 05.57.74.61.75, fax 05.57.74.52.79 ev. day 8am–12 noon 2pm–8pm

CH. MOULIN DE CLOTTE 1998★

7.2 ha 55,000 30–49 F

This château has a classic grape range of 60% Merlot and 40% Cabernets. Its 1998 wine has a brilliant purple colour, and a bouquet which develops notes of prunes. The palate is where it really opens out, thanks to a tannic presence which is sweet and at the same time powerful and harmonious. A wine which will reach its full potential in two to three years' time. The oak-matured **1998 Cuvée Dominique** is a selection of 2,000 bottles which is also awarded one star. It is characterised by oaky aromas which are well integrated with an attractive fruitiness (bilberries and blackcurrants). Should be drunk in a year or two.

Vignobles Chupin, Ch. Moulin de Clotte, 33350 Les Salles-de-Castillon, tel. 05.57.40.60.94, fax 05.57.40.66.68 by appt.

CH. PERVENCHE PUY-ARNAUD 1998

8 ha 16,000 30–49 F

This vineyard is frequented by barn owls, which you may be able to see during your visit. You can also enjoy this 1998 wine, which is very aromatic (prunes, cherries and vanilla), and has a supple, harmonious tannic presence, but is very strongly marked by oak at the finish. Best kept for three to six years.

André Loretz, 7, Puy Arnaud, 33350 Belvès-de-Castillon, tel. 05.57.47.90.33, fax 05.57.47.90.33 by appt.

CH. PEYROU 1997

5 ha 25,000 30–49 F

Established on a beautiful clay terroir at the foot of the Saint-Emilion hills, this château belongs to a young wine-specialist who runs his vineyard with extreme care. This 1998 wine offers a bouquet marked by very ripe red berries and an elegant note of vanilla. With a supple, smooth attack on the palate, this is already a harmonious wine which should be drunk over the next three years.

Catherine Papon-Nouvel, Peyrou, 33350 Saint-Magne-de-Castillon, tel. 05.57.24.72.05, fax 05.57.74.40.03 ev. day except Sun. 8am–7pm

CH. PITRAY 1997★★

30 ha 225,000 50–69 F

This magnificent château is located at the heart of the appellation, and is worth a visit in its own right. While you are there you will also be able to discover this 1997 wine – under a wide label in two parts – which has been matured in oak for 12 months, and wins two stars. It has a deep, dark-red colour, and a rich and complex bouquet based on fruity notes and elegant touches of oak. The supple, rich tannins are very mature and well integrated into an oaky flavour acquired from well-controlled maturation in barrels. A wine which should keep for two to five years, but can also be enjoyed while young. The **Cuvée Traditionnelle** is not oak-matured and has a yellow label. It is recommended for its tannic composition, which is elegant, fruity, and not particularly complex. Can be drunk immediately.

SC de La Frérie, Ch. de Pitray, 33350 Gardegan, tel. 05.57.40.63.38, fax 05.57.40.66.24 by appt.
Comtesse de Boigne

CH. ROBIN 1997★

12 ha 59,000 50–69 F

This vineyard is one of the most reliable in the appellation, and is ideally located on the south-east slopes of Belvès. Its 1997 wine is another excellent vintage. It has a dark-red colour which sparkles brilliantly, and its intense aromas of red berries are blended with scents of oaky vanilla and toast. The silky, dense tannic structure develops delightfully towards a finish which is completely round and balanced. This will be a real pleasure to drink in two to five years.

SCEA Ch. Robin, 33350 Belvès-de-Castillon, tel. 05.57.47.92.47, fax 05.57.47.94.45 ev. day except Sat. Sun. 10am–12 noon 2pm–6pm
Sté Lurckroft

CH. ROQUEVIEILLE

Vieilli en fût de chêne 1997

11.41 ha 70,000 30–49 F

This 1997 wine has a dark-red and amber colour, and an expressive, complex bouquet of liquorice and spices. Its structure is based on supple, mature, well-balanced tannins; the smoky finish is still a little austere, but should become more balanced in the months to come. Probably best served as an accompaniment to white meats.

SCEA Ch. Roquevieille, 33350 Saint-Philippe-d'Aiguilhe, tel. 05.57.74.47.11, fax 05,57.24.69.08 by appt.
Palatin

CH. TARREYRO 1997★

n.c. 7,200 30–49 F

This oak-matured wine is a selection from wine-merchants Robert Giraud. It has a dark, brilliant colour, a bouquet of musk (leather), spices (pepper) and toast. The tannins on the palate are supple and well blended, but develop with sufficient power and harmony to allow for an ageing period of at least three years.

SCA Vignobles Robert Giraud, B.P. 31, 33240 Saint-André-de-Cubzac, tel. 05.57.43.01.44, fax 05.57.43.08.75, e-mail direction@robertgiraud.com
Francis Bonneaud

CH. TERRASSON

Cuvée Prévenche 1997★

1.3 ha 12,000 30–49 F

The Cuvée Prévenche from the Château Terrasson is a selection from old vines. The 1997 vintage is dominated by aromas of raspberries and blackcurrants. It is supple and balanced on the palate, with a well-blended note of oaky vanilla at the finish. A very successful wine which will be ready to drink in one or two years' time. The **1997 Cuvée Principale** is recommended, and can be enjoyed immediately.

EARL Christophe et Marie-Jo Lavau, Ch. Terrasson, B.P. 9, 33570 Puisseguin, tel. 05.57.56.06.65, fax 05.57.56.06.76, e-mail clavau@terre-net.fr by appt.

CH. TIFAYNE 1998★

■ 1.3 ha 12,000 ▮ 30–49 F

This 1998 vintage is the first for the new owners of this vineyard, which is located at Monbadon and stretches over several AOCs. With its beautiful, clear, dark-red colour and bouquet of crushed red berries, this wine appeals from the start, then finds its full expression on the palate, where it has a structure based on mature, powerful, aromatic tannins. It will be a great pleasure to drink in two to four years' time.

SCEA des Vignobles Limbosch-Zavagli, Tifayne, 33570 Puisseguin, tel. 05.57.40.61.29, fax 05.57.40.60.98, e-mail info@tifayne.com ☑ Y by appt.

CH. TUILIERE DE LA BORDE 1998★

■ 4.7 ha 21,000 ▮ 🌡 30–49 F

This traditionally-run family château has produced a brilliant purple 1998 wine made exclusively from Merlot. Its fruity, spicy aromas are very well blended. On the palate this supple, rich, very mature wine develops elegantly and with good length, and is a credit to the terroir. Best drunk three to six years from now.

SCEA Grelaud, Ch. Tenein, 33660 Gours, tel. 05.56.71.11.64, fax 05.56.71.11.61 ☑ Y by appt.

VALMY DUBOURDIEU-LANGE 1998★★

■ 5 ha 20,000 ⬮ 100–149 F

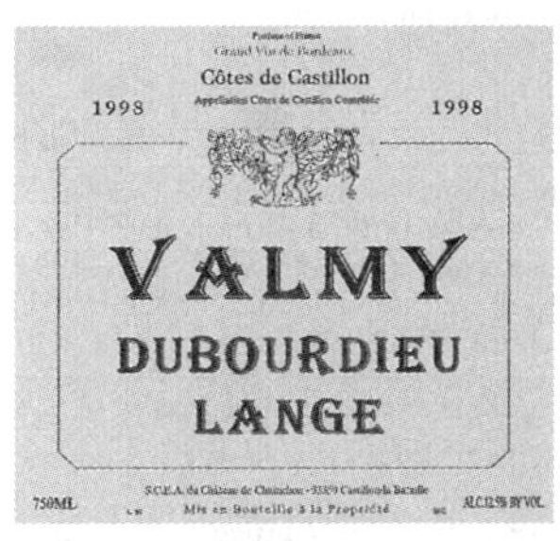

Every care has been devoted to this Cuvée Spéciale, which is perfectly produced from 70% Merlot along with Cabernet Sauvignon. This year it carries off the highest distinction, unanimously awarded and well deserved. Its intense, deep colour is almost black, and the powerful aromas of ripe fruits and candy are in harmony with an elegant oakiness with notes of caramel and vanilla. After a frank attack on the palate, this 1998 wine has dense, balanced tannins which develop in a truly delightful manner. An excellent wine, which can be drunk in two to five years' time with grilled red meat. Congratulations on coming top of the class.

Patrick Erésué, Ch. de Chainchon, 33350 Castillon-la-Bataille, tel. 05.57.40.14.78, fax 05.57.40.25.45 ☑ Y by appt.

VIEUX CHATEAU DE NOAILLES

Vieilli en fût de chêne 1998

■ 14.6 ha 13,000 ⬮ 30–49 F

This 1998 wine has agreeable aromas of hazelnuts, crystallised cherries and game, and a characteristic and powerful tannic structure which is somewhat warm at the finish. It will need to age for two to three years in order to find its balance.

Roland Mas, Ch. des Faures, 33570 Puisseguin, tel. 05.57.40.61.07, fax 05.57.40.64.87, e-mail cdesfaures@aol.com ☑ Y by appt.

Bordeaux Côtes de Francs

The vineyard of Bordeaux Côtes de Francs is 12 km (7 miles) east of Saint-Émilion and covers 487 ha (1,203 acres) in the communes of Francs, Saint-Cibard and Tayac. The vines are planted on an excellent site, on the lime, clay and marly slopes of some of the highest hills in the Gironde. They almost all produce red wines, except for about 20 ha (50 acres), and are cultivated by some dynamic winegrowers and a Cave Coopérative. Between them, they produce some very attractive wines, which are rich, with a good bouquet.

VIGNOBLE D'ALFRED 1997

■ 1.5 ha 5,000 ⬮ 50–69 F

Made with four weeks of maceration and 18 months in barrels without fining or filtration, this 1997 wine is dominated by its Cabernet Sauvignon content, which releases flavours of acidic soft fruits (redcurrants), and tannins which are still slightly biting. A promising wine, which should open out once it has aged for a year or two.

Jean-Frédéric Lapeyronie, 4, Castelmerle, 33350 Sainte-Colombe, tel. 05.57.40.19.27, fax 05.57.40.14.38 ☑ Y by appt.

A. Charrier

CH. DU BOIS MENEY 1998

■ 5 ha 48,000 ▮ 🌡 30–49 F

This 1998 wine is the first vintage produced by the new owner. It is recommended for its elegant bouquet of fruit and flowers, and for its palate, where suppleness and sweetness go hand in hand to a finish of great charm. A well-made wine. From the same owner, the **1998 Château Nardou en Rouge** (matured in oak for 12 months) also deserves praise for its pleasant qualities.

🔑 EARL Vignobles Dubard, Nardou, 33570 Tayac, tel. 05.57.40.69.60, fax 05.57.40.69.20 ☑ Y by appt.
🔑 Florent Dubard

CH. DE FRANCS

Les Cerisiers Vieilli en fût de chêne 1997★

■ 5 ha 5,000 50–69 F

This new Les Cerisiers wine was created for the 1997 vintage, and the result is already encouraging: an intense purple colour, and an expressive bouquet of fruits, spices and notes of oaky toast. The rich, full palate has a certain charm and good length, despite a slightly austere note at the finish. Best drunk in one or two years' time. The property's **1998 Vin Blanc** is commended; it has aromas of citrus fruits, honey and vanilla, and is round and powerful on the palate, where it is somewhat dominated by oak.

🔑 SCEA Ch. de Francs, 33570 Francs, tel. 05.57.40.65.91, fax 05.57.40.63.04 ☑ Y by appt.
🔑 Hébrard et de Bouard

CH. HAUT PELAN

Cuvée La Rocheline 1997

■ 3.22 ha 2,949 30–49 F

This special vintage of barely 3,000 bottles makes a good impression with its ruby colour already turning brick-red, and its aromas of red berries with a delicate note of vanilla, and evident, full-bodied tannins. There is a delightful touch of oak at the finish. A wine which is ready to drink now as an accompaniment to white meats.

🔑 Pascal Pallaro, 14, Le Pin, 33350 Les Salles-de-Castillon, tel. 05.57.40.61.00, fax 05.57.40.61.00 ☑ Y by appt.

CH. LALANDE DE TAYAC 1998

■ 12 ha 45,000 30–49 F

This 1998 wine has a deep, ruby red colour, aromas of ripe fruits or jam, and a structure based on round, elegant tannins which develop with harmony and persistence. With a little more power, this wine would have won a star. Best kept for three years.

🔑 Vignobles Lafaye Père et Fils, Ch. Viramon, 33330 Saint-Etienne-de-Lisse, tel. 05.57.40.18.28, fax 05.57.40.02.70 ☑ Y by appt.

CH. LALANDE DE TIFAYNE 1998

■ 0.75 ha 6,000 30–49 F

A first harvest for this young pair of agronomists who have recently moved to this beautiful appellation. The result is encouraging: a strong purple colour and aromas of red berries, sloes and liquorice which reappear on the palate, in harmony with supple, very fresh tannins. A wine which should be drunk within the next three years.

🔑 SCEA des Vignobles Limbosch-Zavagli, Tifayne, 33570 Puisseguin, tel. 05.57.40.61.29, fax 05.57.40.60.98, e-mail info@tifayne.com ☑ Y by appt.

CH. LAULAN 1998

■ 7 ha 45,000 30–49 F

This 1998 wine is characterised by a strong purple colour, a bouquet of very ripe fruit (jam) with spicy notes, and tannins which are well marked in the attack, powerful and then austere at the finish. It will need to be kept for a year or two until it is more balanced.

🔑 Bruno Citerne, Seignade, 33570 Francs, tel. 05.57.40.63.37, fax 05.57.40.68.05 ☑ Y by appt.

CH. LES CHARMES-GODARD 1998★

□ 1.65 ha 10,700 50–69 F

This little vineyard is frequently singled out for praise, and this year offers a highly accomplished dry white wine. It has a clear colour with golden glints, and floral aromas which are still somewhat dominated by oaky notes. On the palate it is mouth-filling and round with an interesting balance between the fruitiness of the grape and maturation in oak. A charming wine to be enjoyed straight away with friends. Also owned by Nicolas Thienpont, the **1997 Château La Claverie Rouge** has an attractive nose (soft fruits and spices), and is recommended.

🔑 GFA Les Charmes-Godard, Lauriol, 33570 Saint-Cibard, tel. 05.57.56.07.47, fax 05.57.56.07.48 ☑ Y by appt.
🔑 Nicolas Thienpont

CH. MARSAU 1997★

■ 6 ha 28,000 50–69 F

The avowed ambition of this vineyard, which grows 100% Merlot on clay, is to rise to the peak of its appellation. Since 1994, the results have shown that there is real know-how here. This 1997 wine has a brilliant purple colour, aromas of ripe fruits, cocoa, prunes and leather, and tannins which are well marked and soft, with plenty of sweetness and harmony at the finish. A wine which will achieve a perfect balance in two or three years' time.

🔑 Ch. Marsau, Ch. Marsau Bernarderie, 33570 Francs, tel. 05.56.02.26.41, fax 05.56.02.26.41 Y by appt.
🔑 S. et J.-M. Chadronnier

PELAN 1997★★

■ 4 ha 15,000 100–149 F

This *coup de coeur* is the reward for a wine with an untypical blend: 80% Cabernet Sauvignon and 20% Merlot grown on limestone with starfish. The colour is deep and brilliant, and there are complex, powerful aromas of soft fruit, pepper, vanilla and leather. The full, rich palate gains in power, while at the same time retaining a remarkable balance of mature, oaky tannins. A wine which should be left to age for two to five years. From the same owner, the **1997 Château Pelan Bellevue** is

recommended for its fruity richness and maturity on the palate (30–49F).
🗝 Régis Moro, Champs-de-Mars, 33350 Saint-Philippe-d'Aiguilhe,
tel. 05.57.40.63.49, fax 05.57.40.61.41 ☑ 🍷 by appt.

CH. PUYANCHE Moelleux 1997★★

☐ 2 ha 1,800 50–69 F

The Château Puyanche is the only one in the appellation to produce a sweet white wine, but what a success it is. Hurry along there, because production is limited, and those who are lucky enough to buy this 1997 wine will not be disappointed. The golden-yellow colour is brilliant, and there are powerful, complex aromas of apricots, raisins, caramel and crystallised fruits. The power and richness on the palate are in perfect balance with a delicate oakiness, and there is a delightfully fresh and remarkably long finish.
🗝 EARL Arbo, Godard, 33570 Francs,
tel. 05.57.40.65.77, fax 05.57.40.68.48 ☑ 🍷 by appt.

CH. PUYGUERAUD 1997★★

■ n.c. 66,000 50–69 F

Year after year, this very beautiful 16th-century château with a 32-ha (79-acre) vineyard confirms its reputation as one of the stars of the appellation. It wins two stars for its 1997 wine, which has a deep, almost black colour and evocative, complex aromas of red berries, spices, vanilla and toast. The palate is full, rich and mouth-filling, and has a very elegant finish enhanced by fruity notes. A wine which is a real achievement for the vintage, and can be enjoyed straight away or kept for two to four years.
🗝 Ch. Puygueraud, 33570 Saint-Cibard,
tel. 05.57.56.07.47, fax 05.57.56.07.48,
e-mail ch.puygueraud@wanadoo.fr ☑ 🍷 by appt.

CH. TERRASSON 1997

■ 1.4 ha 11,000 30–49 F

A very aromatic 1997 wine (fruits, flowers and notes of game), with a round, elegant tannin structure that is a little austere at the finish. A wine to drink over the next three years.
🗝 EARL Christophe et Marie-Jo Lavau, Ch. Terrasson, B.P. 9, 33570 Puisseguin,
tel. 05.57.56.06.65, fax 05.57.56.06.76,
e-mail clavau@terre-net.fr ☑ 🍷 by appt.

Between the Garonne and the Dordogne

The geographical region of Entre-Deux-Mers is the large triangular area bounded by the Garonne and Dordogne rivers and the south-east border of the department of the Gironde. Here, in one of the sunniest and most pleasant parts of Bordeaux, the vines occupy 23,000 ha (56,810 acres), about a quarter of the region's vineyard. The hilly terrain offers sweeping views as well as quiet corners adorned with fine examples of the traditional regional architecture (fortified manor-houses, small châteaux in green estates and larger numbers of fortified mills). Entre-Deux-Mers also lies at the heart of the Gironde's mythical past, with a rich heritage of beliefs and traditions dating from time immemorial.

Entre-Deux-Mers

The appellation Entre-Deux-Mers does not correspond exactly to the geographical area of Entre-Deux-Mers, excluding as it does some communes with their own appellations. It applies specifically to dry white wines produced under a set of regulations almost as rigorous as those for

Appellation Bordeaux. As a matter of practice, the wine-growers try to keep their best white wines for this appellation. As a result, production is voluntarily limited to 2,394 ha (5,913 acres) planted, producing 94,328 hl (2,490,260 gal) in 1999, and the annual tastings approving the wines are particularly demanding. The major grape variety is Sauvignon, giving the Entre-Deux-Mers whites their singular bouquet, to be appreciated particularly when the wine is young.

CH. D'AUGAN 1999

☐ n.c. 9,000 ▮ 30–49 F

Made of 75% Sauvignon and 25% Sémillon, this wine has great finesse, elegant aromas (rose petals, ripe exotic fruits and lychees), and a body which is fresh, light and slender but well made. Best drunk for its own sake as an aperitif. The **1999 Château Langel-Mauriac** (55% Sauvignon, 30% Sémillon, 15% Muscadelle) has aromas of pear drops, fresh bread and acacia. The first impression on the palate is supple, after which it develops freshly towards a vigorous finish carried along by an exquisite note of lifting acidity. A wine which will be a delicious accompaniment to entrées or cold poultry dishes.

🔑 Vignerons de Guyenne, Union des producteurs de Blasimon, 33540 Blasimon, tel. 05.56.71.55.28, fax 05.56.71.59.32 ☑ Y by appt.

BARON D'ESPIET 1999

☐ 1.1 ha 10,000 ▮ 🌡 20–29 F

The Grotte du Luc, the Roman galleries at Bonnefond, the abbey at La Sauve and the modern co-operative . . . The area offers a wealth of interesting places to visit. This Sauvignon has spent four months in vat on its lees, and in the process has lost its aggressive boxwood quality and taken on aromas of fresh bread which complement its range of floral aromas. A fresh, lively, light yet full-bodied wine, which finishes on an upbeat, slightly mineral note, and will be good to drink with seafood.

🔑 Union de Producteurs Baron d'Espiet, La Fourcade, 33420 Espiet, tel. 05.57.24.24.08, fax 05.57.24.18.91, e-mail baron-espiet@dial.oleane.com ☑ Y by appt.

CH. BONNET 1999★

☐ n.c. n.c. ▮ 🌡 30–49 F

Bonnet is a charming 18th-century château, and also the preserve of André Lurton's vineyards. This 1999 wine is beginning to release aromas of honey, acacia blossom and linden flowers, and it will not be long before these lend fuller fragrance to the flesh of a wine destined to be drunk as an elegant aperitif or with fish.

🔑 Vignobles André Lurton, Ch. Bonnet, 33420 Grézillac, tel. 05.57.25.58.58, fax 05.57.74.98.59, e-mail andre.lurton@wanadoo.fr ☑ Y by appt.

Between the Garonne and the Dordogne

CH. BOURDICOTTE 1999

☐ 6.45 ha 53,000 30–49 F

Some wine-growers in the region have planted bulbs in the vineyards to produce a fine show of indigenous flowers in springtime. Although made from three grape varieties, this 1999 wine is strongly marked by Sauvignon. It has a robust, lively, almost raw body which will appeal to some. A wine which should calm down with time, but could be drunk now with moules marinières.

SCEA Rolet Jarbin, Dom. de Bourdicotte, 33790 Cazaugitat, tel. 05.56.61.32.55, fax 05.56.61.38.26

CH. DE CASTELNEAU 1999★

☐ 8 ha 35,000 20–29 F

The château is located on the site of a little 15th-century fortified town flanked by four towers. The main wine here is built on the three grape varieties, with Muscadelle counting for only 10%. Its supple, full, lively balance in the mouth brings out all the harmonious complexity of a range of floral and fruity aromas which are elegantly marked right to the finish by a note of hazelnuts. A good accompaniment to white meats and goat's cheese. One-hundred-year-old Sémillon vine-stocks were selected for the **1998 Cuvée Barrique Réserve du Château** (30–49F), which also receives a high rating. After ten months of maturing in barrels and weekly stirring of the lees, they have produced a wine dominated by an oakiness which, although of high quality, will need to fade with time. A good accompaniment to roast poultry.

Vicomte Loïc de Roquefeuil, Ch. de Castelneau, 33670 Saint-Léon, tel. 05.56.23.47.01, fax 05.56.23.46.31, e-mail castelneau-roquefeuil@wanadoo.fr by appt.

CH. CASTENET-GREFFIER 1999

☐ 6 ha 44,000 20–29 F

This wine is made of 70% Sauvignon, with Sémillon and Muscadelle completing the blend. Partial maturation on fine lees has produced a characteristic Entre-Deux-Mers wine which is fresh, fruity and ready to drink with grilled fish.

EARL François Greffier, Castenet, 33790 Auriolles, tel. 05.56.61.40.67, fax 05.56.61.38.82, e-mail ch.castenet@wanadoo.fr by appt.

CH. DE CRAIN 1999★

☐ 12 ha 20,000 20 F+

Sauvignon Gris is a highly aromatic mutant form of Sauvignon Blanc, and both of these contribute to the composition of this wine, along with Muscadelle (30%) and Sémillon (30%). After four months of maturation on lees, it is round, fat, persistent and rich, and releases a harmony of aromas, opening out from acacia blossom to brioche, then lingering on citronella, and orange and grapefruit peel. Best drunk as an aperitif or with shellfish. A similar wine is the **1999 Château Noulet**, which is constructed in the same way.

SCA de Crain, Ch. de Crain, 33750 Baron, tel. 05.57.24.50.66, fax 05.45.25.03.73 by appt.

CH. FONDARZAC 1999★

☐ 10 ha 120,000 30–49 F

Sauvignon is tempered here by 20% Muscadelle and 20% Sémillon. The result is a very mineral nose of gunflint, with accents of bay leaves and dried fruit, and a fresh, balanced structure of excellent quality. A wine which conforms to type: ideal for fishermen!

SCA Vignobles Claude Barthe, 22, rte de Bordeaux, 33420 Naujean-et-Postiac, tel. 05.57.84.55.04, fax 05.57.84.60.23 by appt.

CH. DE FONTENILLE 1999★

☐ 6 ha 48,000 30–49 F

At La Sauve, the church tower of the abbey overlooks the building that houses the Syndicat de l'Entre-Deux-Mers: a must for every visitor. Ninety per cent of the wine is made in equal parts from the terroir's three main grape varieties, with the important addition of 10% Sauvignon Gris, which is a grape of great character. The 1999 wine has aromas of orange blossom and kugelhopf (a kind of Alsatian sponge cake), with appetising hints of honey and hazelnuts . . . After a round, rich attack on the palate, it develops towards a fresher finish (which one taster found off-putting), still permeated by complex, fine, lively aromas . . . A wine which seems to be made for white meats and smoked fish.

SC Ch. de Fontenille, 33670 La Sauve, tel. 05.56.23.03.26, fax 05.56.23.30.03, e-mail defraine@chateau-fontenille.com by appt.

CH. GAMAGE 1999

☐ 3 ha 6,000 30–49 F

One taster wrote: 'It has something of the Graves appellation about it.' This wine is both fresh and full-bodied, with aromas which play on a register of bread, wax and dried fruit. It should age well, and will be a good accompaniment to fish.

SARL Ch. Gamage, 33350 Saint-Pey-de-Castets, tel. 05.57.40.52.02, fax 05.57.40.53.77 by appt.

CH. GRAND FERRAND 1999

☐ 5.38 ha 43,000 20–29 F

This pure Sauvignon plays on the fine elegance of its aromas: discreet but skilful, they are harmoniously arranged in a bouquet of spring flowers which lends fragrance throughout the tasting. The supple, round flesh of the wine ends on a truly lively note, leaving behind a memory of acacia blossom.

SCEA Vignobles Rocher Cap Rive 2, Ch. Grand-Ferrand, 33540 Sauveterre-de-Guyenne, tel. 05.56.61.32.55

CH. GRAND-JEAN 1999★

☐ 6 ha 40,000 20–29 F

This is a classic, delightful wine which gives off a fragrance of lemony orange peel with a

touch of honey. Its body is mouth-filling but elegant, with a tantalising, slightly sparkling note at the finish. Best drunk as an aperitif and with cold meats, it was produced on lees and is made from Sémillon (50%), Muscadelle (10%) and 30-year-old Sauvignon. The **1998 Cuvée Elevée en Fût de Chêne** (30–49F) is commended; it will need to wait a little longer for the oakiness to fade.
Michel Dulon, Ch. Grand-Jean, 33760 Soulignac, tel. 05.56.23.69.16, fax 05.57.34.41.29 ▣ ‌Y by appt.

CH. GROSSOMBRE 1999★

☐ n.c. n.c. 30–49 F

Béatrice Lurton has produced this gleamingly transparent Grossombre with just a touch of straw colour, which gives off aromas of seringa and orange blossom against a background of gunflint. Boxwood is more apparent in the concentration of flavours in the mouth, where the wine is svelte and fresh, with a lingering fruitiness and a long, refined mineral finish . . . A wine to drink with oysters.
Béatrice Lurton, B.P. 10, 33420 Grézillac, tel. 05.57.25.58.58, fax 05.57.74.98.59, e-mail andre.lurton@wanadoo.fr ▣ Y by appt.

CH. HAUT-GUILLEBOT 1999

☐ 15 ha 80,000 20–29 F

This property has been handed down from mother to daughter for many years. The know-how here (selection of harvests, maceration of grapes in their skins, maturation for six months on lees) has produced an aromatic wine (ripe and exotic fruits) with round, comfortable flesh (citrus fruits and brioche bread), and a fresh, spirited finish. A classic, agreeable wine.
Evelyne Rénier, Lugaignac, 33420 Branne, tel. 05.57.84.53.92, fax 05.57.84.62.73 ▣ Y by appt.

CH. HAUT NADEAU 1999★

☐ 2 ha 17,000 30–49 F

The village of Targon clings tightly to a hill, around a sturdy church 5 km (3 miles) from the Abbey of La Sauve-Majeure. The fieriness of Sauvignon has been tempered by Muscadelle (15%), Sémillon (21%) and maturation entirely on lees. This has also added to the complexity of the aromas (peaches, passionfruit, citrus fruits and fresh brioche), and the roundness of the body. The long, fresh finish is a reminder that this is an Entre-Deux-Mers . . . and a good one.
SCEA Ch. Haut-Nadeau, 3, chem. d'Estévenadeau, 33760 Targon, tel. 05.56.20.44.07, fax 05.56.20.44.07 ▣
Audouit

CH. HAUT RIAN 1999★

☐ 13.7 ha 120,000 20–29 F

Made from two-thirds Sémillon and one-third Sauvignon grapes gathered when fully ripe and vinified 30% by maceration in their skins, this wine is an elegant example of Entre-Deux-Mers. It has an aroma of white flowers, power and freshness in the mouth, and a cheerful touch of sparkle.
Michel Dietrich, La Bastide, 33410 Rions, tel. 05.56.76.95.01, fax 05.56.76.93.51 ▣ Y ev. day except Sun. 9am–12 noon 2pm–6pm

CH. JANDILLE 1999★

☐ 3.93 ha 20,000 20–29 F

This wine is offered by the Ruch co-operative. It is frank and well constructed on the basis of 80% Sauvignon and 20% Sémillon, and has lovely aromas of lemony grapefruit, lychees and blackcurrant buds. On the palate it is as if you were chewing the grapes between your teeth until the finish, when fragrances of acacia appear. A pleasure to be enjoyed with goat's cheese.
Producteurs réunis Chais de Vaure, 33350 Ruch, tel. 05.57.40.54.09, fax 05.57.40.70.22 ▣ Y ev. day except Sun. 8.30am–12 noon 2pm–6pm

LA COQUILLE 1999

☐ n.c. n.c. 30–49 F

This 1999 wine is recommended as an accompaniment to oysters or salmon on toast; everything about it is lemony, from its appearance to its nose to its flavours. The tasting also reveals a note of white flowers, however. A lively wine which is ready to drink now.
Mähler-Besse, 49, rue Camille-Godard, B.P. 23, 33026 Bordeaux, tel. 05.56.56.04.35, fax 05.56.56.04.59, e-mail france.mahler-besse@wanadoo.fr Y by appt.

CH. LA FORET SAINT-HILAIRE 1999★

☐ 7 ha n.c. 20–29 F

Yvon Mau is a consistently sound wine-merchant. Here he is offering two closely-related wines both of which are made with Sauvignon (50%) and Sémillon, with an additional 10% of Muscadelle. The Château La Forêt Saint-Hilaire is very much marked by barely ripe Sauvignon; it has a powerful, lively nose of oak and peach stones, and a flavoursome palate with good length and a pleasantly fresh quality. It will go well with oysters and shellfish. The **1999 Château Girème** is commended for its elegance. It has very fine aromas tinged with citrus fruits, and a fresh, sharp, almost iodised body which is more spiritual than material. An ideal accompaniment to seafood.
SA Yvon Mau, B.P. 1, 33193 Gironde-sur-Dropt Cedex, tel. 05.56.61.54.54, fax 05.56.61.54.61 Y by appt.

CH. LA JALGUE 1999★★

☐ 4 ha 32,000 20 F+

This Sauvignon (75%) with a padding of Sémillon literally fills the air with fragrance; its delicate bouquet of spring flowers, white peaches and slightly smoky lychees gives it a mischievous elegance. The range of flavours increases to include notes of pepper in a body which is fresh and long. A wonderful aperitif,

and a fine achievement for the oenological team at Ginestet's wine-merchants.
SA Maison Ginestet, 19, av. de Fontenille, 33360 Carignan-de-Bordeaux, tel. 05.56.68.81.82, fax 05.56.20.96.99, e-mail contact@ginestet.fr by appt.

CH. LA ROSE DU PIN 1999

☐ 7 ha n.c. 30–49 F

Two château wines produced by the same team are commended: this one is made up of 65% Sauvignon, 12% Sémillon and 23% various grape varieties (including Muscadelle). The nose offers an open harmony of flowers and musky fruit with a crust of fresh bread. The body is carried along agreeably by a touch of sparkle, then ends with a slight note of unripeness which is very becoming. The **1999 Château de Beauregard-Ducourt**, based on 63% Sémillon, 34% Sauvignon and a hint of Muscadelle (3%), has a complex nose of white flowers, very ripe pears and well-done toast, and a rich, meaty quality within a fresh, vigorous body which is enlivened at the finish by a small amount of sparkle. Two approaches to the appellation which are interesting to compare.
SCEA Vignobles Ducourt, 18, rte de Montignac, 33760 Ladaux, tel. 05.57.34.54.00, fax 05.56.23.48.78, e-mail vignobles-ducourt@wanadoo.fr by appt.

CH. DE LAUNAY 1999

☐ 14 ha 100,000 20–29 F

This château has just changed hands: welcome to the new wine-making team. Forty per cent Muscadelle and 30% Sémillon give this wine a round, rich substance. In addition to citrus fruits and white peaches, the nose has discreet notes of candy and musk. There is no doubt that as a result the freshness one would expect from an Entre-Deux-Mers has been toned down, and this posed a problem for some tasters. Many people like this type of wine, however, and will enjoy it with oven-baked fish and cheese. The **1999 Château de Bridoire** is constructed in exactly the same way, and presents the same profile.
SCEA du Ch. de Launay, 33790 Soussac, tel. 05.56.61.31.44, fax 05.56.61.39.76 by appt.

CH. LE PRIEUR 1999★

☐ n.c. n.c. 30–49 F

In four generations the family properties have gone from four to 80 hectares (10 to 198 acres), producing various appellations which are often praised. Le Prieur's blend of 60% Sauvignon and 40% Sémillon has an appealing personality, with a lemon colour, a vigorous, slender body and aromas of exotic fruits and boxwood: a characteristic and successful approach to the appellation. The **1999 Château Prevost** also received a high rating, but was more hotly debated; behind its clear, golden-yellow colour it has a round, rich, fleshy body and aromas of very ripe fruits (lychees and pineapple) or even concentrated fruits (dried apricots), which disconcerted some and delighted others. A wine to accompany fish (20–29F).
EARL Vignobles Garzaro, Ch. Le Prieur, 33750 Baron, tel. 05.56.30.16.16, fax 05.56.30.12.63, e-mail garzaro@vingarzaro.com by appt.

CH. LESTRILLE 1999

☐ 2.22 ha 15,000 30–49 F

'Good presentation,' noted one taster. 'Well made,' wrote another. A lively, balanced wine which is both rich and fresh, and is ready to drink straight away.
Jean-Louis Roumage, Lestrille, 33750 Saint-Germain-du-Puch, tel. 05.57.24.51.02, fax 05.57.24.04.58 by appt.

CH. MONTLAU 1999

☐ 3 ha 11,330 20–29 F

Visitors are received in two very old, sombre buildings. Eighty per cent of this wine is made from Muscadelle and Sémillon (with 20% Sauvignon): a modern decision, no doubt, since the vineyard is ten years old. With a fragrant palate (white flowers, citrus fruits and pears) which prolongs the pleasure experienced in the nose, this Entre-Deux-Mers will be an excellent accompaniment to roast poultry.
Armand Schuster de Ballwil, Ch. Montlau, 33420 Moulon, tel. 05.57.84.50.71, fax 05.57.84.64.65 by appt.

CH. MYLORD 1999★

☐ 18 ha 150,000 20–29 F

This wine is an equal blend of three grape varieties, and has been matured on lees for six months. It makes an elegant start with a golden-yellow colour and a fringe of light sparkle, then explodes into aromas of Sauvignon, boxwood and citrus fruits, and lingers enjoyably to reveal a supple, meaty quality accentuated by aromas of brioche, and a vigorous finish. A wine which will go well with fish and shellfish.
Michel et Alain Large, Ch. Mylord, 33420 Grézillac, tel. 05.57.84.52.19, fax 05.57.74.93.95 by appt.

CH. POUCHAUD-LARQUEY 1999

☐ 6 ha 30,000 20–29 F

The Pivas are masters of organic growing techniques, and speak very knowledgeably about them. This wine is made from 60% Sauvignon, but the grape keeps a low profile among the chorus of very floral aromas (spring flowers and linden blossom) that make it so rich and spirited. It is ready to drink now, and will go particularly well with oven-baked fish.
Piva Père et Fils, Ch. Pouchaud-Larquey, 33190 Morizès, tel. 05.56.71.44.97, fax 05.56.71.65.16 by appt.

CH. RAUZAN DESPAGNE 1999★★

☐ n.c. n.c. 30–49 F

There's no getting away from them. The J.-L. Despagne team, led by oenologist

Elissalde, appear in many AOCs and on several properties, producing wines which always attract a lot of attention . . . This one is a silky, shimmering symphony, made from equal shares of three grape varieties. It has an intense bouquet of spring flowers, against a background of orange and lemon blossom. The flesh is complex and full, rounded and fresh, and there is a long finish ranging over a whole dish of fruits. Quite remarkable.
🔑 GFA de Landeron, 33420 Naujan-et-Postiac, tel. 05.57.84.55.08, fax 05.57.84.57.31, e-mail despagne@vignobles-despagne.com Y by appt.

CH. REYNIER 1998

☐ 2 ha n.c. 30–49 F

Marc Lurton has produced an oaky wine (six months of maturation in barrels) which is beautiful to look at (the most delightful greeny yellow), has lovely aromas (citrus fruits, vanilla and notes of toast with a slight floral hint), and is light to drink. There is still a fine touch of bitterness at the finish, which suggests that it would be advisable to keep it for a few months until the oakiness fades.
🔑 Marc Lurton, Ch. Reynier, 33420 Grézillac, tel. 05.57.84.52.02, fax 05.57.84.56.93 ☑ Y by appt.

CH. SAINTE-MARIE

Cuvée Madlys Elevé en fût de chêne 1999

☐ 1.1 ha 4,200 30–49 F

Last year this wine's 1998 vintage was highly praised. It was matured for six months in barrels, and comes from a vast property which pilgrims to Santiago de Compostela used to cross in order to drink the water from a spring which was said to be miraculous. The 1999 vintage is not quite so forthcoming, but even so the wine-maker has produced a very good wine. It has a beautiful colour with green glints, and a nose of crystallised fruits and oaky notes punctuated by touches of honey. Needs to be kept for a while.
🔑 Gilles et Stéphane Dupuch, 51, rte de Bordeaux, 33760 Targon, tel. 05.56.23.64.30, fax 05.56.23.66.80, e-mail ch.ste.marie@wanadoo.fr ☑ Y by appt.

CH. SEGONZAC LA FORET 1999★

☐ 4.5 ha 29,000 30–49 F

This Entre-Deux-Mers from near the broad expanse of the Dordogne at Saint-Loubès is based on equal shares of the AOC's three grape varieties. It has a very fruity balance, albeit strongly marked by Sauvignon, and is entirely without aggression or acidity. Its round body and fragrant finish are enlivened by a touch of sparkle. A wine to drink with fish.
🔑 A. de Luze et Fils, Dom. du Ribet, 33450 Saint-Loubès, tel. 05.57.97.07.20, fax 05.57.97.07.27 Y by appt.
🔑 Jeanine Segonzac

CH. TOUR DE MIRAMBEAU 1999★

☐ n.c. 135,000 30–49 F

A Despagne property, run on the same lines as the Château Rauzan-Despagne. The three grape varieties are blended here in equal parts. The wine has a powerful Sauvignon fragrance, along with broom-grapefruit and white flowers. These aromas permeate the round, fresh palate, and mark the finish with an agreeable touch of insolence. Time should add pleasant nuances to this very characteristic, exuberant Entre-Deux-Mers.
🔑 SCEA Vignobles Despagne, 33420 Naujan-et-Postiac, tel. 05.57.84.55.08, fax 05.57.84.57.31, e-mail despagne@vignobles-despagne.com ☑ Y by appt.

CH. TURCAUD 1999★

☐ 10.45 ha 85,500 30–49 F

This 1999 wine contains almost 60% Sauvignon and a touch of Muscadelle (4%), and has been matured on lees. It has a discreet, lemony nose, accentuated by mineral notes then soft fresh bread. The rich, full palate has flavours of dried fruit and brioche. This wine will be an excellent acompaniment to oven-baked fish and cooked cheese.
🔑 EARL Vignobles Robert, Ch. Turcaud, 33670 La Sauve, tel. 05.56.23.04.41, fax 05.56.23.35.85 ☑ Y by appt.

CH. VIGNOL 1999★

☐ 5.69 ha 40,000 30–49 F

Keen cyclists will be able to ride along the 'Entre-Deux-Mers cycle track' which runs close by. The wine is made of 50% Sauvignon, which gives it powerful aromas of broom and boxwood. The first impression in the mouth is supple, after which the body is rich and full, with a long, fresh finish. A wine which conforms comfortably to type.
🔑 B. et D. Doublet, Ch. Vignol, 33750 Saint-Quentin-de-Baron, tel. 05.57.24.12.93, fax 05.57.24.12.83 ☑ Y by appt.

Entre-Deux-Mers Haut-Benauge

CH. NICOT 1998

☐ 20 ha 25,000 30–49 F

Eighty per cent Sémillon and 20% Sauvignon go to make up this Haut-Benauge, which has spent five months in barrels maturing on fine lees. It has a straw colour and a fruity, oaky nose. Full and balanced in the mouth, it will be good to drink while it is still young and fruity.
🔑 Vignobles Dubourg, Ch. Nicot, 33760 Escoussans, tel. 05.56.23.93.08, fax 05.56.23.65.77 ☑ Y by appt.

BORDEAUX

Graves de Vayres

Despite the similarity of the name, this wine-growing district on the left bank of the Dordogne, not far from Libourne, is not be confused with the Graves wine-growing area. Graves de Vayres is a relatively small, well-defined enclave of gravelly soil of a different type to that of Entre-Deux-Mers. The appellation has been used since the 19th century, though it was not officially recognised until 1931. Initially, it was used for dry or medium white wines, but currently there is an increase in the proportion of red wines which qualify for the appellation.

The total area of the vineyards is divided into 360 ha (889 acres) of red grape varieties and 165 ha (408 acres) of whites. A significant quantity of the reds is also sold as Appellation Régionale Bordeaux. In 1999 the production of AOC Graves de Vayres reached some 36,970 hl (976,008 gal), of which 8,374 hl (221,074 gal) were white wines.

CH. BARRE GENTILLOT 1998★

■ 10.87 ha 50,000 30–49 F

With 95% Merlot in its blend, this 1998 wine has a brilliant ruby colour followed by intense aromas of cherries and redcurrants, then a supple, balanced tannic structure which develops powerfully towards a long, very aromatic finish. Best kept for two to three years.

SCEA Yvette Cazenave-Mahé, Ch. de Barre, 33500 Arveyres, tel. 05.57.24.80.26, fax 05.57.24.84.54 by appt.

CH. CANTELAUDETTE 1999

□ 12.22 ha 95,000 20–29 F

This white wine has a golden-yellow colour with green glints and highly evident floral and fruity aromas. After a rich attack on the palate it develops a very harmonious freshness and elegance. A wine which is ready to drink now with seafood.

Jean-Michel Chatelier, Cantelaudette, 33500 Arveyres, tel. 05.57.24.84.71, fax 05.57.24.83.41 by appt.

CH. CANTELOUP 1999★

□ 1.5 ha 6,000 20–29 F

Based on Sauvignon (70%) and Sémillon (30%), this 1999 wine offers attractive golden glints and a nose of floral fragrances (broom and boxwood) combined with a delicately fruity aroma of peaches. It also has a great deal of freshness in the mouth. A very elegant, classy dry white wine which should be enjoyed straightaway.

EARL Landreau, L'Hermette, 33750 Beychac-et-Caillau, tel. 05.56.72.97.72, fax 05.56.72.49.48

CH. FAGE Elevé en fût de chêne 1998★

■ 12 ha 26,000 30–49 F

Jointly owned by a Bordeaux wine-merchant, Joël Quancard, and a Languedoc producer, Maz Cazottes, this château offers a 1998 wine with a rich colour and very intense fruit aromas (redcurrants and blackcurrants), with a touch of liquorice. Its tannins are dense but well blended and very fresh, albeit with a hint of austerity at the finish. Best kept for two or three years until it achieves greater balance.

SA Ch. Fage, 33500 Arveyres, tel. 04.67.39.10.51, fax 04.67.39.15.33

CH. HAUT-GAYAT 1998★★

■ 12 ha 90,000 30–49 F

This very old property (eight generations) is located on a gravelly terroir; it has the distinctive feature of growing 50% Cabernet Sauvignon grapes, along with 50% Merlot. In this 1998 wine the result is impressive thanks to excellent maturity. The ruby colour is strong, while the bouquet is expressive and powerful, with aromas of blackcurrants, bilberries, vanilla and coffee. The tannins in the mouth are rich, velvety and vinous, developing with finesse and an excellent balance between fruitiness and oak. An attractive wine which should be left in the cellar for three to eight years.

Marie-José Degas, La Souloire, 33750 Saint-Germain-du-Puch, tel. 05.57.24.52.32, fax 05.57.24.03.72 by appt.

CH. HAUT-MONGEAT

Vieilli en fût de chêne 1998★

■ 2.5 ha 13,000 30–49 F

This wine comes from a 27-ha (67-acre) property, and is the result of the careful efforts of a father and son team advised by Gilles Paquet. It has everything it takes to delight the lover of wines with a wealth of

aromas (blackcurrants, Morello cherries, prunes, oak and vanilla) and powerful tannins that are delicately balanced with well-controlled maturation in barrels. It will be a real pleasure in two to three years' time.
Bernard Bouchon, Le Mongeat, 33420 Génissac, tel. 05.57.24.47.55, fax 05.57.24.41.21, e-mail mongeat@aol.com Y by appt.

CH. LA CAUSSADE

Vieilli en fût de chêne 1998

10 ha 7,000 30–49 F

This 1998 wine has a nose of leather and coffee which is now beginning to open. On the palate it develops a spicy, balanced flavour, albeit with a slightly hard note at the finish. A relatively complex wine which will gain from ageing for one to two years.
GFA Jean-Claude et Nathalie Ballet, Ch. La Caussade, 33870 Vayres, tel. 05.57.74.83.17, fax 05.57.84.94.53 Y by appt.

CH. LA CHAPELLE BELLEVUE

Prestige Elevé en barrique 1997

3.6 ha 5,500 30–49 F

This Prestige wine which runs to something over 5,000 bottles is already brick-red in colour. It has an intense bouquet of toast and musk (leather) with notes of undergrowth and round, delightful tannins. In short, a pleasant wine which will be enjoyable to drink.
Lisette Labeille, Ch. La Chapelle Bellevue, chem. du Pin, 33870 Vayres, tel. 05.57.84.90.39, fax 05.57.74.82.40 Y by appt.

CH. LESPARRE

Vieilli en fût de chêne 1999★

5.93 ha 52,766 30–49 F

This huge property (180 ha/445 acres) belongs to the family of Michel Gonet from Champagne. It produces a **1998 Rouge** and a 1999 Blanc, both of which receive one star in our Guide. The red wine, although still very much marked by a noticeable aroma of oak and toast acquired from new barrels with a variety of origins, has mature, fruity tannins which as yet remain firm; it will need to be kept for three to five years until it becomes more harmonious. The white wine has been fermented in barrels, and is developing a delicate nose of acacia, vanilla and ripe fruits. The palate is rich, powerful and aromatic (oak and citrus fruits), then finishes on an elegant note of acidity.
SCEV Michel Gonet et Fils, Ch. Lesparre, 33750 Beychac-et-Caillau, tel. 05.57.24.51.23, fax 05.57.24.03.99, e-mail gonet@imaginet.fr Y by appt.

CH. LES TUILERIES DU DEROC

1998

8 ha 44,000 50–69 F

Located on the site of a former tile factory on the banks of the Dordogne, this vineyard has succeeded in producing a very pleasant 1998 wine. There is a good harmony between its intense red-berry aromas and supple, very evident tannins. This is a wine to be drunk within the next three or four years.
SCEA Colombier, Montifaut, V.C. 101, 33870 Vayres, tel. 05.57.74.71.59, fax 05.26.52.97.45, e-mail vignobles-colombier@wanadoo.fr Y by appt.

CH. L'HOSANNE

Elevé en barrique de chêne 1998

1 ha 5,000 30–49 F

This wine is made from a balanced blend of Sauvignon and Sémillon, and has been fermented and matured in new barrels, which gives it a very strong oaky character. Fortunately some aromatic notes of fruit and flowers remain. A wine which should be drunk within the next year.
SCEA Chastel-Labat, 124, av. de Libourne, 33870 Vayres, tel. 05.57.74.70.55, fax 05.57.74.70.36 Y by appt.

CH. PICHON BELLEVUE 1998

26 ha 140,000 30–49 F

Located very close to the Château de Vayres, Pichon Bellevue offers a 1998 wine with a strong purplish colour, aromas of blackcurrants and bananas, and clearly evident, balanced tannins in the mouth. A pleasant wine of an almost Nouveau type, which should be drunk while young.
EARL Ch. Pichon Bellevue, 33870 Vayres, tel. 05.57.74.84.08, fax 05.57.84.95.04 Y by appt.
Reclus

Sainte-Foy-Bordeaux

CH. CAPELLE 1998

2.6 ha 18,000 20–29 F

This 1998 wine is produced by the Univitis co-operative union, and has a complex aromatic range of violets, pepper, red berries and vanilla. Although the impression in the nose is promising, the palate is quickly marked by a warm, tannic sensation which strongly suggests that the wine needs to be kept for two years.
Univitis, Closerie d'Estiac, 33220 Sainte-Foy-la-Grande, tel. 05.57.56.02.02, fax 05.57.56.02.22 Y ev. day except Sun. Mon. 9am–12.30pm 3pm–7pm

CH. CARBONNEAU-FERRIERE

Vieilli en fût de chêne 1998

6 ha 8,000 30–49 F

This château in the Napoleon III style offers a 1998 wine which is fruity and slightly musky (leather) in the nose, then develops a structure in the mouth based on powerful

tannins which as yet are very austere. Its balance should improve after two years of ageing.
🔑 Wilfrid Franc de Ferrière, Ch. de Carbonneau, 33890 Pessac-sur-Dordogne, tel. 05.57.47.46.46, fax 05.57.47.46.46, e-mail carbonneau@wanadoo.fr ☑ 🍷 ev. day 8am–6pm; cl. Dec.–Feb.

CH. DU CHAMP DES TREILLES

Moelleux Vieilles vignes 1998

☐ 0.95 ha 2,300 50–69 F

Jean-Michel Comme is reviving the tradition of sweet wines, and this limited-production wine is the result of his first grape harvest. It has a golden colour with green glints and aromas of flowers and crystallised fruits (apricots and quince). The palate is both rich and at the same time refreshingly acidic. A wine which should be drunk in a year's time.
🔑 Corinne et Jean-Michel Comme, La Bouchère, 33220 Margueron, tel. 05.56.59.15.88 ☑ 🍷 by appt.

CH. DES CHAPELAINS

Elevé en fût de chêne 1998★

■ 5.5 ha 40,000 30–49 F

Like the château where it is made, this 1998 wine is a pillar of the appellation. The ruby colour has attractive purple glints, while the intense bouquet combines notes of tobacco and ripe fruits with spices (cloves) and quite a strong oaky aroma. The fat, rich tannins have a great deal of power at the finish. A wine which will be delightful in two or three years' time. The **1998 Cuvée de la Découverte** is a dry white wine which deserves to be commended for its aromas of melon, vanilla and spices, and for its pleasant balance in the mouth.
🔑 Pierre Charlot, Les Chapelains, 33220 Saint-André-et-Appelles, tel. 05.57.41.21.74, fax 05.57.41.27.42 ☑ 🍷 ev. day 8am–12 noon 2pm–6pm; Sat. Sun. by appt.

CH. CLAIRE ABBAYE

Elevé en fût de chêne 1998★★

■ n.c. 9,700 30–49 F

It is interesting to go on a tour of the château, where you will be told about the recent discovery of a Neolithic structure dating back to 3000 BC. You will also taste this remarkable 1998 wine, which has a ruby colour with purplish glints and a very mature nose which offers notes of fruit (jam), oak (vanilla), and also spices. The pleasure on the palate is immediate, because the tannins are both powerful and harmonious, as well as rich and highly characteristic. The balance will be perfect in two to three years' time.
🔑 Sellier de Brugière, Ch. Claire Abbaye, 33890 Gensac, tel. 05.57.47.42.04, fax 05.57.47.48.16, e-mail bruno.sellier@free.fr ☑ 🍷 by appt.

CH. HOSTENS-PICANT

Cuvée Lucullus 1998★★

■ 2 ha 8,800 150–199 F

This Cuvée Lucullus from the Château Hostens-Picant is an exceptional wine made from a selection of Merlot grapes grown on a gravelly, flinty terroir and matured for 18 months in new barrels. The deep colour gleams with purple glints, and the intense oaky bouquet releases notes of dark berries (blackberries). The tannins make a particularly soft, rich attack on the palate, then develop with great freshness and harmony. A wine whose good length suggests that it will keep long into the future, for at least three to six years.
🔑 Ch. Hostens-Picant, Grangeneuve Nord, 33220 Les Lèves-et-Thoumeyragues, tel. 05.57.46.38.11, fax 05.57.46.26.23, e-mail chateauhp@aol.com ☑ 🍷 ev. day except Sun. 9am–12 noon 2pm–6pm

CH. HOSTENS-PICANT 1998★★

■ 17 ha n.c. 50–69 F

This château started the revival of the appellation, and every year it produces excellent wines, both red and white. The 1998 red is remarkable, with an almost black colour and deep aromas of crystallised fruits, liquorice and oaky vanilla. The first impression of its tannic structure is clean and dense, after which it develops with much power and nobility, thanks to highly-skilled barrel maturation. A wine with very interesting potential, which should be drunk in three to six years' time. The **1999 Cuvée des Demoiselles** is a white wine which has been vinified in barrels and is awarded one star for its aromatic complexity (a harmony of flowers, fruit and oak) and its good quality in the mouth (70–99F).
🔑 Ch. Hostens-Picant, Grangeneuve Nord, 33220 Les Lèves-et-Thoumeyragues, tel. 05.57.46.38.11, fax 05.57.46.26.23, e-mail chateauhp@aol.com ☑ 🍷 ev. day except Sun. 9am–12 noon 2pm–6pm

CH. LA VERRIERE 1998★

☐ 1 ha 4,600 30–49 F

Highly praised last year for its 1997 vintage, this château is now offering a 1998 wine which is very much in the tradition of good sweet wines. It has a golden colour shining with attractive lights, and a nose in which aromas of honey, candy and crystallised fruit are very much in evidence. On the palate it reveals a great deal of richness and balance, albeit with a certain heaviness at the finish. It should come closer to achieving complete harmony in two to five years' time.
🔑 GAEC La Verrière-Bessette, La Verrière, 33790 Landerrouat, tel. 05.56.61.36.91, fax 05.56.61.41.12 ☑ 🍷 by appt.

CH. LE MANSE DU VINAYROL

Vieilli en fût de chêne 1998★

■ 0.6 ha 5,000 30–49 F

This special wine from the Château des Thibeaud is made from a selection of grapes grown on Cabernet (70%) and Merlot (30%) vines. The 1998 vintage has a clear, ruby colour and complex aromas of pepper, carnations and very ripe red berries. After a powerful attack on the palate, it develops in a fresh and highly characteristic fashion, releasing a

delicate note of oaky vanilla at the finish which adds great balance to the overall impression. It will be ready to drink two years from now.
🔑 EARL Dom. Le Canton, 33220 Caplong, tel. 05.57.41.25.65, fax 05.57.41.27.84 ☑ 🍷 by appt.
🔑 Delaplace

CH. L'ENCLOS 1998★

■ 5 ha 13,000 🍷 30–49 F

This château belongs to Armelle de Pianelli, the dynamic President of the Sainte-Foy-Bordeaux appellation. Its 1998 has a dense colour with purplish glints, and an explosive bouquet of red and dark berries, leather, and oaky vanilla. It is full in the mouth, where it develops on the basis of balanced tannins. A wine for longer maturing, which should be drunk in two to three years' time.
🔑 SCEA Ch. L'Enclos, 33220 Pineuilh, tel. 05.57.46.55.97, fax 05.57.46.55.97, e-mail sceachateaulenclos@wanadoo.fr ☑ 🍷 by appt.
🔑 Armelle de Pianelli

CH. MARTET

Réserve de Famille Vieilles vignes Elevé en barrique 1998★★

■ 6.5 ha 30,000 🍷 100–149 F

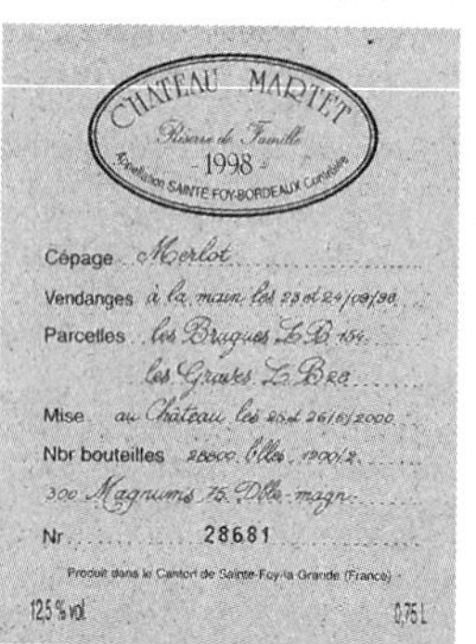

The Château Martet's 1997 Réserve de Famille was highly praised, and this year's 1998 vintage lands the *coup de coeur* for the appellation. Made exclusively from Merlot, it is a wine with a deep black colour and powerful aromas of strawberries, liquorice and toasty vanilla. The tannins make a highly elegant attack on the palate, then become powerful, full-bodied, and very much in keeping with high-quality maturation in oak. A thoroughbred wine for longer maturing (a minimum of three to eight years). Although the **1998 Cuvée Les Hauts de Martet** (30–49F) does not win a star, it is commended for its balance of both aromas and flavours, despite a certain acidity. Should be drunk one or two years from now.
🔑 SCEA Ch. Martet, 33220 Eynesse, tel. 05.57.41.00.49, fax 05.57.41.00.49 ☑ 🍷 by appt.

CH. DE VACQUES 1998★

■ 4 ha 12,000 🍷 30–49 F

Founded in the 16th century, this château dominates the whole region. Its 1998 has a purple colour and aromas of ripe fruits and spices, set off by a mineral note. The supple, rich tannins develop freshly through very pleasant floral notes which have good length. A wine which should be drunk within the next three or four years.
🔑 Christian Birac, 6 Vacques, 33220 Pineuilh, tel. 05.57.46.15.01, fax 05.57.46.16.12 ☑ 🍷 ev. day 10am–12 noon 4pm–6pm

Premières Côtes de Bordeaux

The region of the Premières Côtes de Bordeaux stretches some sixty km (37 miles) along the right bank of the Garonne, from the gates of the city of Bordeaux to Cadillac. The vines are grown on slopes facing the river, which offer magnificent views. Soils here are very varied: along the Garonne it is a recent alluvial soil, producing some excellent red wines. On the slopes, gravelly and limey soils predominate, the amount of clay in the soil increasing further away from the river. The vines, the conditions of cultivation and methods of vinification are all in the classic Bordeaux mould. In all, this appellation consists of 2,868 ha (7,084 acres) planted for reds, with 470 ha (1,161 acres) planted for sweet whites; a significant proportion of the wines, mainly whites, are also sold under the Appellation Régionale Bordeaux. The red wines, of which 185,644 hl (4,901,000 gal) were produced in 1999, have a long-established reputation for their colour, body and strength, while those produced on the slopes above add a certain finesse to these qualities. The white wines, of which 15,756 hl (415,958 gal) were produced in 1999, are soft and increasingly tend towards the sweet.

The Appellation Côtes de Bordeaux Saint-Macaire is a south-easterly extension of the Premières Côtes de Bordeaux. The area makes supple, sweet white wines, producing 2,354 hl (62,146 gal) of wine in 1998. The Appellation Sainte-Foy Bordeaux is an extension of Entre-Deux-Mers along the left bank of the Dordogne; production in 1998 totalled 12,293 hl (324,535 gal), of which 2,032 hl (53,645 gal) were white wines.

CH. BALOT
Tradition d'Excellence 1997★

■ n.c. n.c. 30–49 F

Like many Premières Côtes, this wine resolutely plays the oak card; the barrel is clearly in evidence both in the nose and on the palate. Even so its fruit aromas are not masked, and the full-bodied character of its structure should enable the oakiness to fade.

SCEA Yvan Réglat, Ch. Balot, 33410 Monprimblanc, tel. 05.56.62.98.96, fax 05.56.62.19.48 Y by appt.

DOM. DU BARRAIL
La Charmille 1998★★

■ 2.5 ha 13,000 30–49 F

This wine comes from the same producer as the Château la Rame (Sainte-Croix). It does not enjoy the same renown, but even so it distinguishes itself by a harmonious, well-blended tannin structure, supported by good maturation. A very attractive wine, which should be kept for about three years.

Yves Armand, Ch. La Rame, 33410 Sainte-Croix-du-Mont, tel. 05.56.62.01.50, fax 05.56.62.01.94, e-mail chateau.larame@wanadoo.fr Y ev. day 8.30am–12 noon 1.30pm–7pm; Sat. Sun. by appt.

CH. BAUDUC Les Faures 1998

■ 5.12 ha 40,000 30–49 F

David Thomas is the owner of this wine, which is not a frontrunner but does have a sound constitution and an agreeable nose. Its freshness suggests that it should be drunk while young.

SCEA Vignobles Quinney, Ch. Bauduc, 33670 Créon, tel. 05.56.23.23.58, fax 05.56.23.06.05 Y by appt.

CH. DU BIAC Elevé en barrique 1997★

■ 6.25 ha 8,000 30–49 F

This 1997 oak-matured wine was interesting throughout the tasting. Its palate is both supple and tannic, in keeping with the beautiful spicy notes in the nose. It will benefit from being kept for three to four years.

SCEA Ch. du Biac, 19, rte de Ruasse, 33550 Langoiran, tel. 05.56.67.19.98, fax 05.56.67.32.63 Y by appt.

Patrick Rossini

CH. DE BIROT 1997★

■ 7.8 ha 52,300 30–49 F

Not only does this château have a beautiful house of the type much loved on the slopes of the Garonne, it also has a great deal of know-how, as can be seen from this 1997 wine with its highly characteristic spicy bouquet and supple, round, full-bodied palate. A wine to be drunk within the next three to four years.

Fournier-Castéja, Ch. de Birot, Béguey, 33410 Cadillac, tel. 05.56.62.68.16, fax 05.56.62.68.16, e-mail efcdur@hotmail.com Y by appt.

CH. DU BROUSTARET
Elevé en fût de chêne 1997

■ n.c. 6,300 30–49 F

This Cuvée Spéciale bears the mark of its vintage. It remains discreet as it develops on the palate, but has a balanced structure which will enable it to become more expressive in two or three years' time.

SCEA Guillot de Suduiraut, Ch. du Broustaret, 33410 Rions, tel. 05.56.76.93.15, fax 05.56.76.93.73 Y by appt.

J.-C. Brunet

CH. DE CAILLAVET
Cuvée Prestige Elevée en fût de chêne 1998★★

■ 4.14 ha 32,500 30–49 F

Given that this wine comes from the best vines that grow on these steep, sunny hillsides, it may come as a surprise that it has been so noticeably marked by barrel maturation. Nevertheless the raw material is there, and this should enable the oak to fade and the nose to open out fully before too long.

SA Ch. de Caillavet, Morin, 33550 Capian, tel. 05.57.97.75.75, fax 05.56.72.13.23 Y by appt.

MAAF Assurances

CH. CARIGNAN 1998★★

■ n.c. 60,000 100–149 F

In every respect – buildings, acreage and so on – this *cru* is one of the most impressive producers in the appellation. In this vintage, the wine is second to none; right from the start its deep colour with purple glints shows that it is a true wine for longer maturing. This first impression is fully confirmed by a complex nose which is just beginning to open, a rich, powerful structure, very mature, strong, balanced tannins, and good length at the finish. Clearly the product of excellently controlled vinification and maturation. One star was awarded to the **1997 Cuvée Prima** (50–69F).

GFA Philippe Pieraerts, Ch. Carignan, 33360 Carignan-de-Bordeaux, tel. 05.56.21.21.30, fax 05.56.78.36.65, e-mail tt@chateau-carignan.com by appt.

CH. CARSIN Cuvée noire 1998★

■ 5 ha 20,000 70–99 F

Mr Berglund is a Finnish citizen and the son of a famous conductor. For about ten years his passion has been his 59-ha (146-acre) vineyard, which produces this Cuvée Prestige, a wine with a magnificent colour and a nose full of red berries and notes of oak. It focuses on finesse and suppleness, while at the same time revealing a good tannic structure and a long finish.

Berglund, GFA Ch. Carsin, 33410 Rions, tel. 05.56.76.93.06, fax 05.56.62.64.80 by appt.

CH. DES CEDRES 1997★

□ 1 ha 4,000 30–49 F

This vineyard is essentially given over to red wines, but it also has one little plot devoted to *liquoreux* (sweet) whites. This has yielded excellent results in the 1997 vintage. In this wine, botrytis is very much in evidence within a supple, aromatic structure. It has crystallised fruits, honey, peaches, and the whole sense of 'roasting' that one expects from a *liquoreux*.

SCEA Vignobles Larroque, Ch. des Cèdres, 33550 Paillet, tel. 05.56.72.16.02, fax 05.56.72.34.44 by appt.

CH. DE CHASTELET 1998★★

■ 6.35 ha 32,000 30–49 F

Gravelly and gravel-clay soils, a varied range of grape types (Cabernets, 40% Merlot and 10% Petit Verdot), and a great deal of dedication to both vine-growing and vinification: all of these have come together here to produce a very fine wine. It has both a deep colour and an intense nose, and offers a harmonious combination of suppleness and good length, richness and elegance. A thoroughbred which is suitable for longer maturing.

SA Dom. de Chastelet, 33360 Quinsac, tel. 05.56.44.45.10, fax 05.56.44.49.11, e-mail chateauchastelet@aol.com by appt.

Vincens

CH. DE CHELIVETTE 1997★

■ 2.4 ha 16,000 30–49 F

Jean-Louis Boulière is a passionate and wholly dedicated wine-grower who develops the wine he loves. He does not shrink from using new barrels, and they have left their mark on the nose of this 1997 wine with its attractive notes of toast. The palate still needs to gain in harmony, but the body is structured and well made, and the grape flavour is sufficiently in evidence to enable the wine to improve as it matures.

Jean-Louis Boulière, Ch. de Chelivette, B.P. 6, 33560 Sainte-Eulalie, tel. 05.56.06.11.79, fax 05.56.38.01.97 by appt.

CLOS BOURBON

Vieilli en fût de chêne 1998

■ 6 ha 26,000 30–49 F

This wine has a beautiful ruby colour, and opens with a nose of attractive fruity notes which is just as delightful as its young, fresh palate.

Catherine D'Halluin, SCEA Clos Bourbon, 33550 Paillet, tel. 05.56.72.11.58, fax 05.56.72.13.76 by appt.

CH. CLOS CHAUMONT 1997★

■ 2.71 ha 11,000 50–69 F

This vineyard offers a wine which is still a little severe but has the potential to keep well. From its dark colour to its lovely return in the nose, everything about it shows its possibilities, notably the intensity of the bouquet and the balance of the structure.

EARL Ch. Clos Chaumont, 33550 Haux, tel. 06.07.17.18.40, fax 06.56.23.30.54 by appt.

CLOS SAINTE ANNE 1998★

■ 3 ha 24,000 50–69 F

Francis Courselle is an outstanding personality in wine-growing circles between the Garonne and the Dordogne, and here once again he has shown that his fame is well deserved. Everything speaks for this attractive wine: an intense colour, an expressive bouquet (ripe soft fruits with fine notes of oak), and good substance on the palate.

Sté des Vignobles Francis Courselle, Ch. Thieuley, 33670 La Sauve, tel. 05.56.23.00.01, fax 05.56.23.34.37 by appt.

CH. CRABITAN-BELLEVUE 1998★

□ 5 ha 9,000 30–49 F

From his vineyard at Sainte-Croix-du-Mont, Bernard Solane offers an authentic *liquoreux* wine, which is powerful and concentrated. Full, rich and aromatic (toast and apricot), this 1998 vintage is already pleasant but will gain from being kept for four or five years.

GFA Bernard Solane et Fils, 33410 Sainte-Croix-du-Mont, tel. 05.56.62.01.53, fax 05.56.76.72.09 ev. day except Sun. 8am–12 noon 2pm–6pm

CH. DUDON

Cuvée Jean-Baptiste Dudon 1997★

■ 2 ha 14,600 30–49 F

The Merlauts own a fine collection of Grands Crus, but Dudon is undoubtedly one of those which have the most sentimental

value for them, as is proved by the quality of this Cuvée Spéciale. Richly aromatic, with notes of oak (toast, spices, truffles, and, of course, fruit), it has good presence on the palate before opening out into a long, fresh finish.
SARL Dudon, Ch. Dudon, 33880 Baurech, tel. 05.57.97.77.35, fax 05.57.97.77.39, e-mail jmdudon@alienor.fr ☑ Y by appt.
Jean Merlaut

CH. FAYAU Cuvée Jean Médeville 1998★

■ n.c. 15,000 30–49 F

This vineyard is the headquarters of the Médeville firm, a Cadillac wine-merchant. Once again it offers us a fine illustration of its know-how with this wine, which has a pleasantly supple, balanced palate and an equally agreeable nose of powerful yet subtle aromas. Quite close to this is the **1998 Cuvée Principale**, which has not been oak-matured and is also awarded a star: a supple, round wine, which is there to be drunk.
SCEA Jean Médeville et Fils, Ch. Fayau, 33410 Cadillac, tel. 05.57.98.08.08, fax 05.56.62.18.22 ☑ Y ev. day except Sat. Sun. 8.30am–12 noon 2pm–5.30pm

CH. DU GRAND MOUEYS 1997★★

■ 15 ha 80,000 50–69 F

Since 1989 the Bömers, who are wine-merchants in Bremen, have been running this 76-ha (188-acre) Bordelais wine-growing estate. Their 1997 wine is a highly successful version of the vintage; the whole tasting is pleasant, starting with an intense colour, then moving on to delicate fruity fragrances and a supple, concentrated palate whose mouth-filling quality and good length show that it will keep well (four to six years).
SCA Les Trois Collines, Ch. du Grand Mouëys, 33550 Capian, tel. 05.57.97.04.66, fax 05.57.97.04.60 ☑ Y by appt.

CH. GRIMONT Prestige 1998★

■ 8 ha 55,000 30–49 F

This barrel-matured wine is very modern in that it is very much dominated by oak. Even so the structure is sufficient to enable the oakiness to fade, and the complexity and elegance of the nose suggest that it will be worth waiting for (three or four years). Another wine with very good presence on the palate is the **1998 Château Sissan Grande Réserve** (30–49F), which has been awarded one star.
SCEA Pierre Yung et Fils, Ch. Grimont, 33360 Quinsac, tel. 05.56.20.86.18, fax 05.56.20.82.50 ☑ Y by appt.

CH. JONCHET

Cuvée Prestige Elevé en fût de chêne 1997★

■ 6.5 ha n.c. 30–49 F

This wine is just like its colour, light but shimmering. It is also supple and aromatic, and develops very pleasantly, notably because the oak is well integrated.
Philippe Rullaud, Ch. Jonchet, La Roberie, 33880 Cambes, tel. 05.56.21.34.16, fax 05.56.78.75.32, e-mail jonchet@caves-particulieres.com ☑ Y by appt.

CH. JORDY-D'ORIENT

Vieilli en fût de chêne 1998★★

■ 5 ha 33,000 30–49 F

This vineyard seems to have found its cruising speed. Its 1998 wine, made from 90% Merlot grown on limestone-clay soils, is more than able to meet the demands of the tasting, which leads through from a lovely dark-red colour to a long finish. It is well served by oak, showing elegance and balance. An attractive wine, which should be drunk within two to three years.
Laurent Descorps, Ch. Haut-Liloie, 33760 Escoussans, tel. 05.56.23.94.23, fax 05.57.34.40.09 ☑ Y by appt.

CH. DU JUGE Cru Quinette 1998★★

■ 2 ha 12,000 30–49 F

The Château du Juge is much respected; here it offers its Cuvée Quinette, which is barrel-matured. Although still marked by oak, it has a fruity nose and good substance on the palate, both of which show that it has the potential to develop well.
Pierre Dupleich, Ch. du Juge, rte de Branne, 33410 Cadillac, tel. 05.56.62.17.77, fax 05.56.62.17.59, e-mail pierre.dupleich@wanadoo.fr ☑ Y by appt.

CH. LABATUT-BOUCHARD 1998★

■ n.c. n.c. 30–49 F

Located in a beautiful setting above Saint-Macaire, this vineyard is now offering a well-made wine whose roundness and silky tannins make it a pleasure to drink. A highly successful piece of wine production.
Ch. Labatut-Bouchard, 2, des Arnauds, 33490 Saint-Maixant, tel. 05.56.62.02.44, fax 05.56.62.09.46 ☑ Y by appt.
F. Mehaye

CH. LA BERTRANDE

Elevé en fût de chêne 1998★★

■ 2.5 ha 15,000 50–69 F

This numbered, oak-matured 1998 wine from La Bertrande, a beautiful estate of 20 ha (49 acres), is a fine achievement: it has a lovely dark colour, and reveals a highly expressive nose (ripe soft fruits and prunes) which is beginning to open. The palate combines roundness and substance to give an overall impression of balance and elegance.
Vignobles Anne-Marie Gillet, Ch. La Bertrande, 33410 Omet, tel. 05.56.62.19.64, fax 05.56.76.90.55 ☑ Y by appt.

CH. LA CHEZE

Elevé en fût de chêne 1998★

■ 7 ha 45,000 30–49 F

In the first vintage for which the two young wine-specialists who have taken over the property are fully responsible, this 1998 wine promises great things for the future of the vineyard. The nose is still young, with oak blending into the fruit aromas, and the palate is well structured with rounded tannins; both of these indicate a perfect mastery of wine-making.

SCEA Ch. La Chèze, 33550 Capian, tel. 05.56.72.11.77, fax 05.56.25.96.82 by appt.

Priou et Rontein

CH. LA FORET

Elevé en fût de chêne 1998★★

■ 2 ha 5,600 30–49 F

This vineyard believes in ecological solutions, and aims to combine conservation of nature with improvements in quality. This very attractive 1998 Cuvée Spéciale shows that it is on the right track: both the colour and the nose are equally intense, while the palate is rich, fleshy, full and balanced, with the necessary substance to benefit from a long maturing period (five to seven years).

Ch. La Forêt, 33880 Cambes, tel. 05.56.21.31.25, fax 05.56.78.71.80 by appt.

Raba-Camus

CH. LAGAROSSE 1998★

■ 10 ha 40,000 30–49 F

This château was originally built in the 16th century, then reconstructed in 1848 after a fire. The vineyard offers a 1998 wine whose suppleness and roundness reflect the particular qualities of the grape range, which includes 80% Merlot. The nose is complex but still marked by oak, which suggests that it would be best to wait a while before opening this wine.

SCA des Vignobles du Ch. Lagarosse, B.P. 18, 33550 Tabanac, tel. 05.56.67.00.05, fax 05.56.67.12.64 by appt.

CH. LAROCHE Cuvée Eugénie 1998★

■ 1.3 ha 7,200 50–69 F

Martine Palau may have acquired a vineyard in the Libournais, but that does not mean that she is neglecting Laroche. Her Cuvée Eugénie, 'which is doing its time in the barrel', bears witness to her dedication, both by its nose of red berries and by its good structure, which is both supple and round. A well-balanced combination which deserves to be kept for two or three years. A wine with a more limited volume of production (30,000 bottles) is the **1998 Château Laroche-Bel Air** (30–49F), which has received a commendation.

Martine Palau, Ch. Laroche, 33880 Baurech, tel. 05.56.21.31.03, fax 05.56.21.36.58 by appt.

CH. LENORMAND Cuvée Prestige 1998★★

■ n.c. 12,000 30–49 F

This wine comes from an oak-matured Cuvée Spéciale, and still bears the stamp of the barrel. This has been well dosed, however, and does not stifle the nose, whose complexity was clearly apparent to the jury. Full, rich and supple, the palate has good balance and substance, which indicate that it has the potential to keep well.

SCEA des Vignobles Menguin, 194, Gouas, 33760 Arbis, tel. 05.56.23.61.70, fax 05.56.23.49.79 by appt.

CH. LES CONSEILLANS 1998★★

■ 3.4 ha n.c. 70–99 F

A tiny vineyard, but one which has had the privilege of belonging to Jean Ribéreau-Gayon. The famous oenologist would not have been ashamed to produce a wine like this one. Its intense, complex nose of toasted, spicy and vanilla notes shows that it has been matured in oak. After a supple attack on the palate, the tannins make their presence felt, but they are well balanced. A characteristic wine, which should be kept for two to three years.

GFA Dom. des Conseillans, 33880 Saint-Caprais-de-Bordeaux, tel. 05.56.68.55.88, fax 05.56.30.18.42

CH. LESCURE 1998

■ 7.01 ha 32,500 20–29 F

This wine (offered by an Occupational Therapy Centre) has an attractive nose but is still marked by tannins and oak, and needs to grow more supple within the next year or two. It should not be kept any longer than that, however, since its structure does not have broad shoulders.

C.A.T. Ch. Lescure, 33490 Verdelais, tel. 05.57.98.04.68, fax 05.57.98.04.64 by appt.

CH. DE LESTIAC Cuvée Prestige 1998★★

■ 55.7 ha 80,000 30–49 F

Once again this Cuvée Prestige is of a quality which fully justifies its name. Successfully combining complexity and elegance, it has an expressive nose (mocha, vanilla and toast) and is not only supple but round, rich and very substantial. A most attractive wine which will give of its best in three or four years' time.

SCEA Gonfrier Frères, Ch. de Marsan, 33550 Lestiac-sur-Garonne, tel. 05.56.72.14.38, fax 05.56.72.10.38, e-mail gonfrier@terre-net.fr by appt.

CH. LEZONGARS 1998★

■ 10 ha 73,000 30–49 F

In 1998, the vineyard at Lezongars was purchased by British owners, and it turns out to have been a good vintage for the wines there. This one presents itself well, with delicate aromas of red berries and toast; on the palate it reveals a well-constructed, balanced structure.

SC du Ch. Lezongars, 324, Roques-Nord, 33550 Villenave-de-Rions, tel. 05.56.72.18.06, fax 05.56.72.31.44, e-mail lezongars@free.fr by appt.

CH. MELIN Elevé en fût de chêne 1998★★

■ 5.5 ha 34,000 30–49 F

While many châteaux in the Premières Côtes area have changed hands regularly, the Modets have been running their vineyard for five generations. Their attachment to the terroir is clear from the quality of this 1998 wine, which deserves to stay in the cellar for four or five years. In addition to a superb colour, it has an equally good nose and structure. The bouquet releases elegant notes of spices, cocoa, toast and crystallised ripe fruits, and the palate is delightfully substantial, tannic, long and balanced. A less imposing wine, but one which has also been developed with care during its maturation in vats, is the **1998 Château Constantin** (30–49F); it is awarded one star.

🔑 EARL Vignobles Claude Modet, Constantin, 33880 Baurech, tel. 05.56.21.34.71, fax 05.56.21.37.72 ☑ 𝐘 by appt.

CH. MEMOIRES 1998★

■ n.c. n.c. 30–49 F

This vineyard is known primarily for its sweet *liquoreux* white wines, but it also offers a very attractive red. It is pleasant to look at, and although the nose is still discreet, its complexity is beginning to become apparent in notes of soft fruits, liquorice, blackcurrants and spices. With its long, tannic structure, it needs to be kept for two or three years.

🔑 SCEA Vignobles Ménard, Ch. Mémoires, 33490 Saint-Maixant, tel. 05.56.62.06.43, fax 05.56.62.04.32, e-mail memoires@aol.com ☑ 𝐘 by appt.

CH. MESTREPEYROT 1998★★

□ 4 ha 12,000 30–49 F

As it often does, this vineyard has chosen a powerful register to express the personality of its wine. Its intensity is already apparent in a nose which is marked by notes of toast and candy, and successfully combines power and complexity. The palate is still oaky but also velvety, thus confirming the first impression of the wine while at the same time suggesting that it should be kept for some time (four or five years).

🔑 GAEC Vignobles Chassagnol, Bern, 33410 Gabarnac, tel. 05.56.62.98.00, fax 05.56.62.93.23 ☑ 𝐘 by appt.

CH. DES MILLE ANGES 1998

■ 15.3 ha 66,000 50–69 F

Having lived in England, Africa and the United States, Heather Van Ekris moved to a French vineyard in 1994. This wine has not only an attractive name, but also a pleasant character and good structure. Fruity, supple and balanced by a fine, oaky quality, it will be ready to drink while still young, between 2002 and 2004.

🔑 Heather Van Ekris, 33490 Saint-Germain-de-Graves, tel. 05.56.76.41.04, fax 05.56.76.46.72

CH. MONT-PERAT 1998★★

■ 4 ha 18,000 70–99 F

Founded in 1998, this brand-new vineyard now makes a spectacular appearance in the Guide. It might even seem astonishing if this wine were not produced by the Despagne family, which goes from one success to the next. The colour is intense and concentrated, the nose is both complex and refined (vanilla, mocha, cocoa, toast . . .), and there is a rich, full structure, leading to a long finish. A simpler wine which nevertheless is well made and has an expressive bouquet and a well-balanced structure is the vat-matured **1998 Château Franc-Perat** (50–69F); it receives one star.

🔑 SCEA de Mont-Pérat, 33550 Capian, tel. 05.57.84.55.08, fax 05.57.84.57.31, e-mail despagne@vignobles-despagne.com 𝐘 by appt.

DOM. DU MOULIN 1998★

■ 8 ha 30,000 30–49 F

Despite being made from a range of grapes in which Merlot is dominant (80%), the green-pepper aromas of this wine are more reminiscent of a Cabernet. Even so, the soft fruit flavour and roundness of the palate are there to restore the logical order of things. Best drunk in two years' time.

🔑 M. Gillet et B. Queyrens, Ch. Peyruchet, 33410 Loupiac, tel. 05.56.62.62.71, fax 05.56.76.92.09 ☑ 𝐘 by appt.

CH. NENINE 1998★

■ 12 ha 55,000 50–69 F

Stéphane Fouquet is a wine-broker and a fine connoisseur of Bordeaux wines. With a rich, concentrated nose of mocha and toast notes, his 1998 wine has a style which is very much in the Bordelais spirit; it manages to keep the balance between a fine structure which bodes well for its ageing potential, and the suppleness which will give it charm in three or four years' time.

🔑 SCEA des coteaux de Nénine, Ch. Nénine, 33880 Baurech, tel. 05.56.78.70.78 𝐘 by appt.

CH. OGIER DE GOURGUE 1998★

■ 4.5 ha 36,000 50–69 F

The maturation here has been well-controlled and well-suited to the grape

varieties, with Merlot predominant. The result is a very successful wine whose balance and complexity are apparent both in its silky, glinting colour and in its harmonious tannin structure. The nose of fruity, spicy aromas is typical of Premières Côtes.
Josette Fourès, 41, av. de Gourgues, 33880 Saint-Caprais-de-Bordeaux, tel. 05.56.78.70.99, fax 05.56.76.46.18, e-mail p.decroix@wanadoo.fr by appt.

CH. PASCOT

Cuvée Prestige Vieilli en fût de chêne 1997★

2.1 ha 14,000 30–49 F

This barrel-matured wine is still marked by oak in the nose, then reveals a well-structured character. It will find its full balance once it has been kept for two or three years.
Nicole et Frédéric Doermann, Ch. Pascot, 33360 Latresne, tel. 05.56.20.78.19, fax 05.56.20.78.19 by appt.

CH. PEYBRUN 1998★

4 ha 12,000 30–49 F

For four centuries this vineyard has been kept by the same family. This very good 1998 wine has a clear, strong colour and a nose of powerful spicy notes. It then develops very agreeably on the palate, starting with a supple attack and then becoming full, robust and tannic. A wine which has the necessary qualities to benefit from being kept for about three years.
Catherine de Loze, Ch. Peybrun, 33410 Gabarnac, tel. 05.56.96.10.84, fax 05.56.96.10.84

CH. DE PIC 1998★

28 ha 200,000 30–49 F

This vineyard is a fine centre of production, and with its 1998 vintage it offers a wine which is clean and pleasant, very much like its strong, dark-red colour. It is beginning to release a nose of interesting soft fruit and spicy notes, and is developing a warm, well-balanced palate.
François Masson-Regnault, Ch. de Pic, 33550 Le Tourne, tel. 05.56.67.07.51, fax 05.56.67.21.22 by appt.

CH. DE PLASSAN

Elevé en fût de chêne 1997

17 ha 50,000 30–49 F

This château is a real Palladian villa built by the Clauzel family. There is no doubt at all about its charm, and the same can be said of this supple, delicate 1997 wine, which is resolutely elegant.
Jean Brianceau, Ch. de Plassan, 33550 Langoiran, tel. 05.56.67.53.16, fax 05.56.67.26.28, e-mail chateauplassan@netclic.fr by appt.

CH. PRIEURE CANTELOUP

Cuvée Faustine Elevé en fût de chêne 1997★

10 ha 10,000 30–49 F

This wine has had the benefit of well-controlled barrel maturation. The result is an overall impression which lives up to the promise of its beautiful purple colour. A fragrant, structured wine which has the necessary intensity and complexity to keep for four to five years.
Xavier et Valérie Germe, 63, chem. du Loup, 33370 Yvrac, tel. 05.56.31.58.61 by appt.

CH. PUY BARDENS

Cuvée Prestige 1998

n.c. 50,000 30–49 F

This wine comes from the barrel-matured Cuvée Prestige, and is still marked by oak. Nevertheless its structure should enable it to become rounder in two to three years' time.
Yves Lamiable, Ch. Puy Bardens, 33880 Cambes, tel. 05.56.21.31.14, fax 05.56.21.86.40 by appt.

CH. REYNON 1998★★

16 ha 66,000 50–69 F

This is a very typical 'Côtes', made from grapes grown on beautiful limestone-clay south-facing hillsides. It has a superb, strong colour, and a delightful nose of good oak, roasting, toast, and also fruit aromas. A mouth-filling, full-bodied, well-structured wine, which deserves to be kept for two to three years.
Denis et Florence Dubourdieu, Ch. Reynon, 33410 Béguey, tel. 05.56.62.96.51, fax 05.56.62.14.89, e-mail reynon@gofornet.com by appt.

CH. ROQUEBERT

Cuvée spéciale Elevée en barrique 1998★

3.4 ha 25,000 30–49 F

This barrel-matured 1998 wine is still strongly marked by oak. It will therefore appeal to lovers of very oaky wines, but others will like it too, provided that they are prepared to wait until the oak has faded and they can get the full benefit of its aromatic richness.
Christian et Philippe Neys, Ch. Roquebert, 33360 Quinsac, tel. 05.56.20.84.14, fax 05.56.20.84.14 ev. day sf Sun. 9am–12 noon 2.30pm–6pm

CH. SUAU Elevé en fût de chêne 1998★

14.15 ha 100,000 30–49 F

Run from a charming little 17th-century hunting-lodge, this château now commands a fine production unit of 82 ha (203 acres), including 60 ha (148 acres) of vines. With a beautiful, strong colour and a nose which is beginning to open, this wine makes a supple, substantial attack on the palate, then develops towards tannins which as yet are austere. Needs to be kept for three years until they become more harmonious.
Monique Bonnet, Ch. Suau, 33550 Capian, tel. 05.56.72.19.06, fax 05.56.72.12.43, e-mail bonnet-suau@wanadoo.fr by appt.

CH. DE TESTE 1998★★

☐ 4 ha 12,000 30–49 F

In this vintage, Laurent Réglat has produced a remarkably successful wine. Its intense, brilliant golden colour heralds the richness of its nose and structure. The aromas of quince, crystallised fruits and notes of toast are as complex as one could wish for; even so it comes as a surprise to find the palate so full, balanced and well-supported by oak.

EARL Vignobles Laurent Réglat, Ch. de Teste, 33410 Monprimblanc,
tel. 05.56.62.10.65, fax 05.56.62.98.80 by appt.

Côtes de Bordeaux Saint-Macaire

CH. FAYARD 1998

☐ n.c. n.c. 70–99 F

The Château Fayard is the only dry white wine in a sweet *moelleux* white appellation. It has a golden-yellow colour and aromas of citrus fruits, orange peel and oak. Fruity and rich in the mouth, it develops with a slight touch of acidity which makes for a very refreshing finish. A pleasant wine which should be drunk as an aperitif within the next two years.

Jacques-Charles de Musset, Ch. Fayard, 33490 Le Pian-sur-Garonne,
tel. 05.56.63.33.81, fax 05.56.63.60.20 by appt.
Saint-Michel SA

The Graves Region

Bordeaux wines *par excellence*, those of the Graves have nothing to prove; from Roman times, the plantations, with their rows of vines, began to encircle the capital of Aquitaine and, according to Calomel, the agronomist, to produce 'a wine that keeps for a long time and which improves after several years'. The name 'Graves' was first recorded in the Middle Ages. At that time it designated all the countryside upstream from Bordeaux that lay between the left bank of the Garonne and the Landes plateau. Later, Sauternes was individually defined as a separate area within the Graves region that was devoted to producing sweet white wines.

Graves and Graves Supérieures

The Graves vineyards extend for some fifty km (31 miles) and owe their name to the structure of the soil, principally made up of terraces deposited by the Garonne or its predecessors, which left behind a great variety of stony débris (pebbles and gravels originating in the Pyrenees and the Massif Central).

Since 1987 not all the wines produced there are sold as Graves. Pessac-Léognan is now identified by a specific appellation, even though 'Vin de Graves', 'Grand Vin de Graves' or 'Cru Classé de Graves' may be printed on its labels. In precise terms, the description Appellation Graves applies to qualifying vineyards from the south of the region.

One of the peculiarities of Graves is the balance established between the areas devoted to red wines – nearly 2,128 ha (5,256 acres), excluding Pessac-Léognan – and those growing dry whites wines – more than 809 ha (1,998 acres). The red Graves, of which 128,342 hl (3,388,288 gal) were produced in 1999, have a fine, delicately smoky bouquet and an elegant, full-bodied structure which allows them to keep well. The dry white wines, 66,770 hl (1,762,728 gal) in 1999, are elegant and plump, and ranked amongst the best in the Gironde. The finest of them, many of which are now vinified and matured in barrels, develop in richness and complexity after several years. There are also some softer wines sold under the appellation Graves Supérieures which still claim their admirers.

Graves

CH. D'ARCHAMBEAU 1997

■ 20 ha 100,000 30–49 F

The grape content here is an equal blend of Merlot and Cabernet Sauvignon, which are well suited to the gravelly-clay soil. For a 1997 wine, it is well formed, bearing the stamp of both grape varieties, apparent in the richness of the nose and the clear presence of tannins on the palate. Also recommended is the **1998 Blanc**, which is simple but pleasant.

GFA Jean-Philippe Dubourdieu, Archambeau, 33720 Illats, tel. 05.56.62.51.46, fax 05.56.62.47.98 by appt.

CH. D'ARDENNES 1998★

■ 20 ha 70,000 50–69 F

88 |89| 90 92 93 **|94| 96** 97 98

This wine is made from a variety of grape types (Cabernets, Merlot and Petit Verdot) grown on a gravel and limestone soil, and the fact that it comes from such a good background is clearly apparent to the taster. It is very well balanced, and does not succumb to the 'pure oak' temptation; the oak shows respect both for the supple, tannic grape content and for the nose of fine fruity notes, and the overall impression is one of real elegance.

SCEA Ch. d'Ardennes, Ardennes, 33720 Illats, tel. 05.56.62.53.66, fax 05.56.62.43.67 by appt.

François Dubrey

CH. D'ARRICAUD 1998

□ 5 ha 30,000 30–49 F

This is a wine of consistently good quality in which 70% Sémillon is blended with 25% Sauvignon and 5% Muscadelle. This 1998 vintage is a fresh, lively wine which asserts its personality with a nose of menthol notes and almost wild aromas.

EARL Bouyx, Ch. d'Arricaud, 33720 Landiras, tel. 05.56.62.51.29, fax 05.56.62.41.47 by appt.

BARON PHILIPPE 1998

□ n.c. n.c. 50–69 F

This *négociant*'s 1998 wine combines substance and elegance to create an overall impression of good complexity, in which Sauvignon (40% of the blend) succeeds in making its mark.

Baron Philippe de Rothschild SA, B.P. 117, 33250 Pauillac, tel. 05.56.73.20.20, fax 05.56.73.20.44

The Graves region

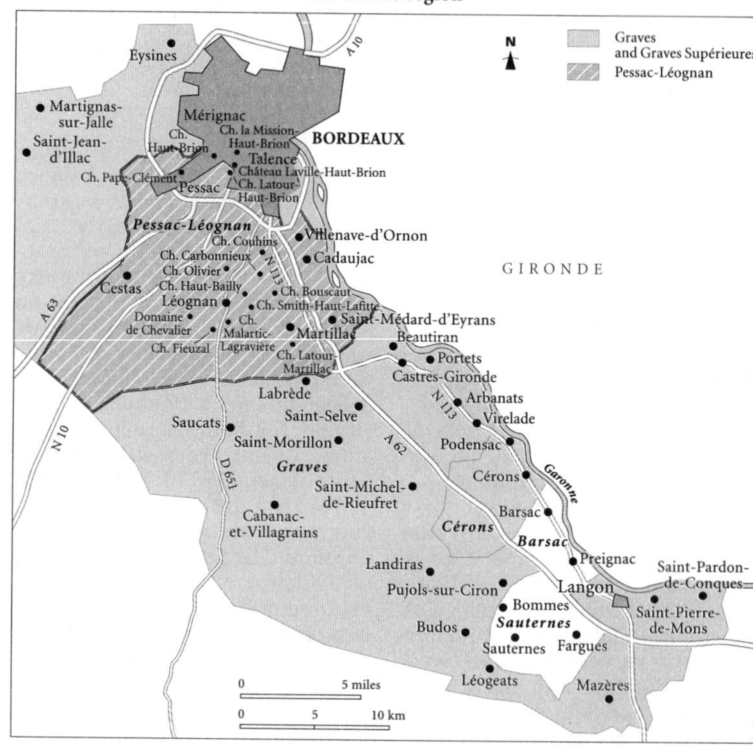

CH. BEAUREGARD-DUCASSE

Albert Duran 1997★

■ 5 ha n.c. 🍷 70–99 F

|93| |94| 95 96 |97|

Coming from the highest vineyard in the appellation, this wine has benefited from being matured in oak. This has been well controlled, and has not masked either the complexity of the nose or the personality of the palate. The long, full, rich structure will ensure good ageing potential. The pleasantly aromatic **1999 Cuvée Albertine Peyri Blanc** (50–69F) is awarded one star for its elegance. The **1997 Cuvée Principale Rouge** (30–49F) is recommended.

Jacques Perromat, Ducasse, 33210 Mazères, tel. 05.56.76.18.97, fax 05.56.76.17.73 ☑ Y by appt.

GFA de Gaillote

CH. DE BEAU-SITE 1998★★

□ 0.21 ha 1,500 🍷 30–49 F

Coming from a vineyard which likes to use traditional methods, this wine has had the benefit of being made from hand-picked grapes. The results speak for themselves; the tasters were delighted by the complexity of the nose, in which ripe fruit aromas mingle with oak. The oak is of high quality, and shows respect for the substance and flavours on the palate, which develop in a lively manner before opening out into a long finish. One star is awarded to a **1997 red, the Château Beau-Site**, which is a balanced and very interesting wine.

SA Ch. Beau-Site, Beau-Site, 33640 Portets, tel. 05.56.67.18.15, fax 05.56.67.38.12 ☑ Y by appt.

Mme Dumergue

CH. BERGER 1998

□ 4.22 ha 8,100 🍷 50–69 F

This wine comes from an estate of over 7 ha (17 acres), whose owner is an oenologist. Matured on lees that are stirred regularly for eight months, its attractions centre on its very pronounced nose of floral, buttery and oaky nuances, and its roundness on the palate.

SCA Ch. Berger, 6, chem. La Girafe, 33640 Portets, tel. 05.56.67.58.98, fax 05.56.67.04.88 ☑ Y by appt.

CH. BICHON CASSIGNOLS 1998

□ 2 ha 6,600 ▮ 🍷 50–69 F

This wine starts with a pale-yellow colour with green glints, then relies on a supple structure to bring out its pleasant, fruity aromas mingled with notes of toast acquired from five months of maturing in barrels, one-third of which are new. 'This characteristic wine is a pleasure to drink,' remarked one taster.

Lespinasse, 50, av. Edouard-Capdeville, 33650 La Brède, tel. 05.56.20.28.20, fax 05.56.20.20.08 ☑ Y by appt.

CAPRICE DE BOURGELAT 1999★

□ 2.3 ha 3,500 🍷 50–69 F

Produced by the Clos Bourgelat in Cérons, this wine has benefited from being matured in oak. In addition to the attractions of a complex bouquet (broom, acacia, chestnut, pineapple and mango), it also has a rich structure. A wine to be enjoyed.

Dominique Lafosse, Clos Bourgelat, 33720 Cérons, tel. 05.56.27.01.73, fax 05.56.27.13.72 ☑ Y by appt.

CH. BRONDELLE 1998★★

■ n.c. 70,000 🍷 50–69 F

Located in the south of the appellation on a gravel and clay soil, this property produces attractive wines. This 1998 vintage has a lovely ruby colour, then develops a concentrated nose (chocolate, vanilla and spices) before revealing a structure which is substantial, full, round, and supported by high-quality oak. One star is awarded to an oak-matured **white, the 1999 Cuvée Anaïs** (70–99F); a **1998 red, the Château la Rose Sarron**, is recommended.

Vignobles Belloc-Rochet, Ch. Brondelle, 33210 Langon, tel. 05.56.62.38.14, fax 05.56.62.23.14, e-mail chateau.brondelle@wanadoo.fr ☑ Y by appt.

CH. CABANNIEUX

Réserve du Château Elevé en barrique 1997

■ 13 ha 99,000 🍷 50–69 F

This wine is a blend of 50% Merlot, 45% Cabernet Sauvignon and 5% Cabernet Franc. It has a beautiful dark-red colour. The nose offers a range of spices, prunes, caramel and a suggestion of Cabernet Sauvignon, while the interest of the palate lies in its roundness and sweetness. Best kept for one to two years until the finish becomes more subdued.

SCEA du Ch. Cabannieux, 44, rte du Courneau, 33640 Portets, tel. 05.56.67.22.01, fax 05.56.67.32.54 ☑ Y by appt.

Mme Dudignac

CH. CALENS 1997

■ 4 ha 6,600 ▮ 🍷 30–49 F

Since 1995, the estate has expanded a great deal, from six to 15 ha (15 to 37 acres). This wine shows a good structure which is balanced and tannic. Both this and the nose suggest that it will be good to drink over the next two years.

🗝 Vignobles Artaud et Fils, 6, rue des Mages, 33640 Beautiran, tel. 05.56.67.05.48, fax 05.56.67.04.72 ☑ 🍷 by appt.

CH. DE CALLAC 1998★

■ 18 ha 120,000 50–69 F

This wine comes from a decent-sized property of 25 ha (62 acres), and is aimed at a wide market. That makes its qualities all the more agreeable: a complex, refined nose which mingles various spices (mainly cinnamon), and a structure which is balanced by substantial tannic content. A fine osmosis is taking place between the raw material and the oak. An elegant finish.

🗝 Philippe Rivière, Ch. de Callac, 33720 Illats, tel. 05.57.55.59.59, fax 05.57.55.59.51, e-mail riviere@riviere-stemilion.com ☑ 🍷 by appt.

CH. CAMARSET 1998

□ 1.3 ha 5,000 30–49 F

This wine benefits from the fact that it is made from a varied blend of grape varieties – Sauvignon, Sémillon and Muscadelle – grown on a gravel and limestone-clay soil. The result is that, in addition to being fresh, supple and light, it has good aromatic complexity: citronella, mandarins and lilac form an overall impression of finesse and delicacy.

🗝 SCEA Ch. Camarset, Ch. Camarset, 33650 Saint-Morillon, tel. 05.56.20.31.94, fax 05.56.20.31.94 ☑

🗝 M. et Mme Lagardère

CH. CARBON D'ARTIGUES

Elevé en fût de chêne 1998★

■ 10 ha 60,000 50–69 F

The quality at this vineyard is consistent; here it offers a wine which expresses itself with the greatest finesse and a real sense of subtlety. With a delicate nose of ripe fruit notes, it has the substance it needs to integrate the oak and develop favourably over the next three or four years. Sharing its soft fruit notes and subtlety is the **1998 Château La Fleur Clémence Rouge**, which is also awarded one star. The tannins are balanced and delicate, remaining elegant right through to a long, complex finish.

🗝 SC Ch. Carbon d'Artigues, 33720 Landiras, tel. 05.56.62.53.24, fax 05.56.62.53.24 ☑ 🍷 by appt.

CH. DE CASTRES 1998

■ 10 ha 43,000 50–69 F

This vineyard is in the course of being renovated; this year it offers a fine, delicate wine with a lovely ruby colour, of the type which Graves produces really well. It has an outstandingly original nose of citrus-fruit notes. The **1999 Blanc** (70–99F) is also recommended.

🗝 Rodrigues-Lalande, Ch. de Castres, 33640 Castres-sur-Gironde, tel. 05.56.67.51.51, fax 05.56.67.52.22 ☑ 🍷 by appt.

CH. CAZEBONNE 1998

□ 5 ha 30,000 30–49 F

This well-known vineyard has produced a white wine which inspires confidence from the start with its lovely green glints and delicate floral fragrances. The lively, round palate is also very successful, with fine fruit flavours.

🗝 Jean-Marc Bridet, Vignobles de Bordeaux, 33210 Saint-Pierre-de-Mons, tel. 05.56.63.19.34, fax 05.56.63.21.60, e-mail lvb.sica@libertysurf.fr 🍷 by appt.

CH. DE CHANTEGRIVE 1998★★

■ 30 ha 100,000 50–69 F

Henri Lévêque is an outstanding personality in the Bordeaux wine area. He continues to watch over his vineyard with as much care as ever, as can be seen from the success of this lovely 1998 wine, which has a superb dark bigaroon-cherry colour and a promising nose. The palate shows a good tannic presence and even real power, but without the slightest aggression. There is a lingering, peppery finish which suggests that this wine should be laid down in the cellar for five to eight years. The **1998 Cuvée Caroline Blanche** (70–99F) has a very aromatic nose combining flavoursome notes of white-fleshed fruits, citrus fruits, vanilla and honey with floral fragrances. It receives one star.

🗝 Françoise et Henri Lévêque, Ch. de Chantegrive, 33720 Podensac, tel. 05.56.27.17.38, fax 05.56.27.29.42, e-mail courrier@chateau.chantegrive.com ☑ 🍷 ev. day except Sun. 8am–12 noon 2pm–6pm

CH. CHERET-PITRES 1997

■ 1.2 ha 9,160 30–49 F

This wine from the medieval château at Langoiran is a blend of 60% Merlot and 40% Cabernet Sauvignon. It is still a little severe in its tannic development, and needs to be kept; the overall impression, however, is of a well-made wine which is improving with age.

🗝 Pascal et Caroline Dulugat, Ch. Cheret-Pitres, 33640 Portets, tel. 05.56.67.27.76, fax 05.56.67.27.76 ☑ 🍷 by appt.

🗝 Boulanger

CLOS FLORIDENE 1998★★

■ 5 ha 32,000 70–99 F

This vineyard is a well-known pillar of the appellation, and once again it passed the blind-tasting test with distinction. The wine has a beautiful colour, and shows its personality by releasing smoky and mineral (flint) notes, before opening up into aromas of dark berries and cedar. Oak is still in evidence on the palate, but not so much as to mask a supple, round overall impression which is already pleasant and elegant, while at the same time suggesting that the wine deserves to be kept for three to four years. One star was awarded to the **1998 Blanc**, a wine with very floral aromas accompanied by an elegant note of oaky toast.

🔑 Denis et Florence Dubourdieu, Ch. Reynon, 33410 Béguey, tel. 05.56.62.96.51, fax 05.56.62.14.89, e-mail reynon@gofornet.com ☑ 🍷 by appt.

CLOS LA BERNEDE 1998

■ 0.35 ha 2,000 30–49 F

This beautiful, ruby wine comes from a tiny vineyard of 0.6 ha (1.5 acres). Its production is rather limited, but it is of interest because of its nose of overripened grapes and toast. An impressively mouth-filling wine which promises to keep well (three to five years).

🔑 Thierry Dumas, La Bernède, 33210 Léogeats, tel. 05.56.76.62.54 ☑ 🍷 by appt.

CLOS LA MAURASSE 1998★

□ 2 ha 5,000 30–49 F

Despite its modest size, this vineyard offers a wine which is not ashamed to assert its personality by means of attractive, musky flavours of very ripe Sauvignon, and a nose of powerful, warm aromas of flowers and crystallised orange.

🔑 Rémy Sessacq, Clos La Maurasse, B.P. 78, 33210 Langon, tel. 05.56.63.39.27, fax 05.56.63.11.82 ☑ 🍷 ev. day 9am–7pm

CH. DOMS 1998★

■ 6.5 ha 48,000 30–49 F

This estate has been growing vines for a long time now, but it was once a religious institution. This 1998 wine shows itself worthy of such a past, both by its presentation and structure. The first of these inspires confidence, offering a deep-purple colour and a nose of ripe fruit. The structure is full and warm, relying on fine tannins which will make this wine ready to drink within the next two or three years.

🔑 SCE Vignobles Parage, Ch. Doms, 33640 Portets, tel. 05.56.67.20.12, fax 05.56.67.31.89 ☑ 🍷 by appt.

LA GRANDE CUVEE DE DOURTHE 1998★★

□ n.c. n.c. 50–69 F

For a long time now, the Dourthe firm has produced white wines of high quality. No-one will be sorry to see that tradition continue with excellent wines like this 1998 vintage. The elegance of its pale-gold colour and nose of grapefruit and acacia carries through to the palate, where harmonious fruity and floral flavours open out around a perfectly balanced framework. The **1998 Rouge** receives a recommendation, as do the **1998 Grande Réserve Rouge** and the **1999 Blanc** (both at 30–49F), produced by the sister firm of Kressmann.

🔑 Dourthe, 35, rte de Bordeaux, B.P. 49, 33290 Parempuyre, tel. 05.56.35.53.00, fax 05.56.35.53.29, e-mail contact@cvbg.com ☑ 🍷 by appt.

CH. DUC D'ARNAUTON 1998★★

□ 8 ha 6,000 30–49 F

Well known for the warm welcome they give to visitors, the Bernards also enjoy a substantial reputation for their wines. It will not be spoiled by this 1998 vintage. It has an elegant pale-yellow colour with gold glints, followed by an equally elegant nose in which notes of white flowers and crystallised orange are accentuated by well-controlled oak. The powerful, rich, balanced, expressive palate is second to none. A true Graves white. The **1998 Rouge** received a recommendation.

🔑 SCEA Domaines Bernard, Ch. Gravas, 33720 Barsac, tel. 05.56.27.06.91, fax 05.56.27.29.83 ☑ 🍷 by appt.

CH. FERNON Dumez 1998★

■ 8.09 ha 64,300 20–29 F

Presented in numbered bottles by the wine-merchants Ginestet, this wine makes a very pleasant impression, both by its attractive substance and excellent balance and by its nose, in which green peppers combine with various fruits and some muskier notes. The **1998 Château Fernon Blanc** was also awarded one star.

🔑 SA Maison Ginestet, 19, av. de Fontenille, 33360 Carignan-de-Bordeaux, tel. 05.56.68.81.82, fax 05.56.20.96.99, e-mail contact@ginestet.fr 🍷 by appt.

🔑 M. et Mme de Langlade

CH. DES FOUGERES

Clos Montesquieu 1998★★

□ 8.2 ha 30,000 50–69 F

The Château des Fougères has a beautiful park, and still belongs to the family of the philosopher/wine-maker. 'Good blood will out,' and the Montesquieus of today are still excellent wine-growers, as can be seen from this delightful 1998 vintage. It has a charming nose of hazelnut and boxwood, then delights the palate with its freshness, suppleness and balance, before opening out into a promising finish.

🔑 Vins et Dom. Henry de Montesquieu, Aux Fougères, 33650 La Brède, tel. 05.56.78.45.45, fax 05.56.20.25.07, e-mail montesquieu@bordeaux-montesquieu.com ☑

CH. DE GAILLAT

Courrèges Seguès 1997★★

■ 3.5 ha 15,000 70–99 F

The Courrèges Seguès is the Cuvée Prestige of the Coste family property. Despite 1997's reputation as a difficult vintage, this wine offers a fine lesson in oenology. Its dark-red colour is full of promise, and what follows does not disappoint. The nose goes with delightful finesse and complexity from black-currants to game. After a clean attack, the palate develops velvety tannins which both confirm the first impressions of the wine and suggest that it should be kept for four to five years until it reaches its peak. Although not so harmonious, the **1997 Cuvée Principale Rouge** (50–69F) also reveals good substance which earns it one star.

🔑 SCEA Ch. de Gaillat, 33210 Langon, tel. 05.56.63.50.77, fax 05.56.62.20.96 🍷 by appt.

🔑 Hélène Coste

CH. DU GRAND ABORD 1998★

☐ 3.4 ha 6,000 30–49 F

This 1998 wine is made from Sémillon along with 20% Sauvignon; its production is rather limited, but that does not prevent the taster from experiencing real pleasure. The nose is expressive and the palate fine, delicate and flavoursome. A wine which deserves to accompany the best fish dishes.

EARL Vignobles M.-C. Dugoua, Ch. du Grand Abord, 33640 Portets, tel. 05.56.67.22.79, fax 05.56.67.22.23 Y by appt.

CH. DU GRAND BOS 1998★

☐ 0.8 ha 2,600 50–69 F

This 1998 wine comes from a small vineyard which is part of a vast production unit of 40 ha (99 acres). It displays its ambitions by having a numbered label, and shows every sign of fulfilling them. The process of fermentation and barrel maturation with stirring of the lees took eight months. The wine presents itself very well. Along with a well-dosed oakiness, its qualities on the nose (richness and complexity) and on the palate (suppleness and fleshiness) show great elegance. The **1997 Rouge** is also numbered, and is recommended. Its very supple tannins suggest that it will be a good accompaniment to white meat over the next year or two.

SCEA du Ch. du Grand Bos, 33640 Castres, tel. 05.56.67.39.20, fax 05.56.67.16.77 Y by appt.

Vincent

CH. GRAND MOUTA

Elevé en fût de chêne 1997

■ 1 ha 6,000 30–49 F

One of the range of wines offered by the Latrille-Bonnin vineyards, this oak-matured wine makes a very agreeable impression with its powerful nose of attractive notes of soft, warm bread. Its empyreumatic quality in the mouth means that it needs to be kept for one to two years.

SCEA Dom. Latrille-Bonnin, Ch. Petit-Mouta, 33210 Mazères, tel. 05.56.63.41.70, fax 05.56.76.83.25 Y ev. day 9am–12 noon 2pm–7pm

GFA Brion

CH. DES GRAVIERES

Collection Prestige Elevé en fût 1998★

■ 7.8 ha 60,000 30–49 F

This wine is made from a rather unusual blend of grapes (containing 90% Merlot). It comes from the barrel-matured Cuvée Prestige, and still bears the stamp of oak; this in no way spoils the harmony of the overall impression, however. Supple and well composed, it has the benefit of a powerful, complex nose of notes ranging from dark berries to undergrowth.

Labuzan, Ch. des Gravières, Le Mirail, 33640 Portets, tel. 05.56.67.15.70, fax 05.56.67.07.50 Y by appt.

CH. HAUT-GRAVIER 1999★

☐ 5 ha 17,000 20–29 F

At this vineyard, where the grapes are hand-picked and sorted, no effort is spared to promote quality. The reward is this 1999 wine, which displays a beautiful yellow-green colour before developing a nose of citrus fruits and musk. The balanced, complex palate offers warm, exotic notes, along with a clearly evident but elegant oaky flavour.

Jean-Claude Labat, Téouley, 33720 Illats, tel. 05.56.62.54.17, fax 05.56.62.54.17 Y by appt.

CH. HAUT SELVE 1997★

■ 50 ha 150,000 70–99 F

This wine is a fine achievement for the vintage, and shows the progress that has been made in recent times by the vineyards of the Saint-Selve area. It has a lovely dark-red colour, and confirms its potential with an attractive bouquet of red berries and leather. The palate is supported by a good tannic structure, and continues along the same lines as the colour with its notes of red berries. The **1998 Blanc** is a truly enjoyable wine, with a harmonious structure supporting pleasant aromas of butter and dried fruit. It was also awarded one star (50–69F).

SCA Branda et de Cadillac, Ch. Haut Selve, 33650 Saint-Selve, tel. 05.56.20.29.25, fax 05.56.78.47.63 Y by appt.

Lesgourgues

CH. HURADIN 1999★

☐ 5.5 ha 4,000 30–49 F

This attractive, straightforward wine is made from Sauvignon along with 40% Sémillon. It has a light, straw colour and aromas of grapefruit, lemon, pineapple and boxwood which reappear on the palate, where it is lively, fresh and agreeable.

SCEA Vignobles Y. Ricaud-Lafosse, Ch. Huradin, 33720 Cérons, tel. 05.56.27.09.97, fax 05.56.27.09.97 Y by appt.

Catherine Lafosse

CH. JOUVENTE

Elevé en fût de chêne 1998★

■ 5.5 ha 23,000 30–49 F

This vineyard was purchased at the end of the 1980s by a native of Champagne, René Gruet. Since then he has expanded it, and it now seems to have found its cruising speed. This 1998 wine makes a pleasant first impression; the colour has dark, purple glints, and the nose contains jam and caramel notes. What follows does not disappoint. Round and elegant, it is supported by well-extracted tannins which will ensure that it develops well within three to four years.

SEV René Gruet, Le Bourg, 33720 Illats, tel. 05.56.62.49.69, fax 05.56.27.16.76 Y by appt.

CH. LA BLANCHERIE 1998

☐ 12.54 ha 60,000 30–49 F

This wine was made 2 kilometres (1.25 miles) from the Château de Montesquieu, and s a blend of 45% Sauvignon, 50% Sémillon nd 5% Muscadelle. After a gold colour with reen glints, the first impression on the palate nay seem surprisingly rich or even heavy; the inish and the bouquet are so fresh, however, hat this is quickly forgotten.

Françoise Coussié, La Blancherie, 33650 La Brède, tel. 05.56.20.20.39, ax 05.56.20.35.01 ☑ Y by appt.

CH. DE LA GRAVELIERE 1999

☐ 6 ha 7,000 30–49 F

This wine is a blend of 70% Sauvignon and 30% Sémillon grapes, grown on a gravelly soil with a subsoil of limestone and developed by maceration in their skins. It has a well-constructed palate and pleasant aromas of broom, acacia, citrus and passionfruit.

Bernard Réglat, Ch. de La Mazerolle, 33410 Monprimblanc, tel. 05.56.62.98.63, fax 05.56.62.17.98, e-mail reglat.bernard@wanadoo.fr ☑ Y by appt.

CH. DE LA MOTTE

Elevé en fût de chêne 1998★

☐ 1.07 ha 7,500 50–69 F

This vineyard can be proud of the 18th-century charterhouse from which it is run, and its 1998 wine is nothing to be ashamed of either; it not only has a nose of fresh notes of lychees and other exotic fruit against a dried-fruit background, but also a substantially constructed palate with good aromatic expression (flowers and exotic fruits).

SCEA Marie-Christine Moulin, Ch. de La Motte, 33640 Ayguemorte-les-Graves, tel. 05.56.67.18.55, fax 05.56.86.69.65 ☑ Y by appt.

CH. DE LANDIRAS 1997★★

■ 2 ha 8,000 70–99 F

This vineyard is located on a vast estate of 75 ha (185 acres), including 26 ha (64 acres) of vines, where there is a medieval fortress with one barbican still standing. This oak-matured wine is a fine example of a highly successful 1997 vintage. The intense, complex nose develops from blackcurrant and cinnamon to jam and roses. The palate is full, and supported by a substantial tannic presence, but it is clear that the wine is still young, and will need to be kept for four to five years.

SCA Dom. La Grave, Ch. de Landiras, 33720 Landiras, tel. 05.56.62.44.70, fax 05.56.62.43.78, e-mail mail@chateau-de-landiras ☑ Y by appt.

Vanquickelberghe

CH. LASSALLE 1998

■ 4.12 ha 24,000 30–49 F

The vineyard is a family property, located at La Brède. It offers a 1998 wine whose personality is noticeably marked by a touch of spice, both in the nose and on the palate, where the tannins are already supple in the attack, but more austere at the finish. Needs to be kept for a year or two.

Louis Michel Labbé, 7, allée Lassalle, 33650 La Brède, tel. 05.56.20.20.19, fax 05.56.78.42.75 ☑ Y ev. day except Sun. 9am–12 noon 2pm–6pm

CH. LA TUILERIE PEYROUX 1998

☐ 1.5 ha 1,800 30–49 F

An equal blend of Sauvignon and Sémillon, this wine has a lovely appearance and a delicate nose. On the palate, it shows all the freshness and elegance of its personality.

Eric Lavie, Peyrous, 33210 Mazères, tel. 05.56.76.26.64, fax 05.56.76.27.64 ☑ Y ev. day except Sat. Sun. 8am–12.30pm 2pm–7pm

CH. LA VIEILLE FRANCE

Cuvée Marie 1998★★

☐ 1 ha 6,000 70–99 F

Maceration of the grapes in their skins, fermentation in barrels, maturation on the lees, weekly stirring . . . No effort has been spared in the development of this vintage. The result is a wine which lives up to expectations, with an expressive nose (butter, exotic fruits and citrus), and a rich, full, harmonious palate. Other wines produced here are the **1997 Château La Vieille France Rouge** (50–69F), which is supple and ready to drink, and the **1998 Château Cadet La Vieille France Rouge** (30–49F), whose concentration makes it a very typical Graves. Both of these are awarded one star.

Michel Dugoua, Ch. La Vieille France, 1, chem. du Malbec, 33640 Portets, tel. 05.56.67.19.11, fax 05.56.67.17.54, e-mail vieille.france.dugoua@wanadoo.fr ☑ Y by appt.

TENTATION DU CH. LE BOURDILLOT 1998★★

■ 2 ha 12,000 50–69 F

Coming from a vineyard which grows half Cabernet Sauvignon and half Merlot, this wine has a substance whose power and complexity will guarantee that it develops well. Right from the start its dark, deep colour shows that it has real potential, as does the nose with its refined notes of wild berries and crystallised dark berries. A period of three or four years in the cellar is recommended. The **1998 Cuvée Prestige Rouge** is also oak-matured, and receives one star.

Vignobles Patrice Haverlan, 11, rue de l'Hospital, 33640 Portets, tel. 05.56.67.11.32, fax 05.56.67.11.32, e-mail patrice.haverlan@worldonline.fr Y by appt.

CH. LE CHEC 1998★★

☐ 2.5 ha 9,000 30–49 F

Since 1987, this vineyard's serious-minded approach to methods of wine-growing has borne fruit. This wine has a brilliant colour and presents itself skilfully with a nose whose complex aromas range from lychees to roses, with musk and roasted almond in between. The palate is supple, fleshy, long and powerful, showing a great sense of balance and fine

aromatic richness (figs and exotic fruits). A very typical Graves, which can be drunk while young or kept for several years.
🔑 Christian et Sylvie Auney, La Girotte, 33650 La Brède, tel. 05.56.20.31.94, fax 05.56.20.31.94 ☑ Ῑ by appt.

CH. LEHOUL 1999★

□ 1 ha 4,000 30–49 F

This vineyard of about ten hectares (25 acres) offers a dry Graves made exclusively from Sauvignon. This is a wine of high quality; with an elegant nose tinged by citrus fruits and a fresh palate with notes of acacia and boxwood, it is already a pleasure to drink.
🔑 EARL Fonta et Fils, rte d'Auros, 33210 Langon, tel. 05.56.63.17.74, fax 05.56.63.06.06 ☑ Ῑ by appt.

CH. DE L'EMIGRE 1998

□ 2.6 ha 7,200 30–49 F

Coming from Cérons in the very sweet *liquoreux* appellation, this is a dry Graves which has a very appealing, brilliant colour with green glints. The nose is striking, fruity, rather exotic and a little wild. It is lively in the mouth with the Sauvignon foremost, which will make it a good accompaniment to seafood.
🔑 Pierrette Despujols, Ch. de l'Emigré, 33720 Cérons, tel. 05.56.27.01.64, fax 05.56.27.13.70 ☑ Ῑ by appt.

CH. LE PAVILLON DE BOYREIN 1998

■ 13 ha 100,000 30–49 F

The vineyard has a beautiful view over the Garonne Valley, and is located on land which belonged to Clément V, the Bordeaux Pope (1305–1314). This wine shows real aromatic finesse, combining fruity notes (red berries) and spices both in the nose and on the palate. With its very well-balanced tannins, it is ready to drink straight away. The **1999 Blanc** (20–29F) has attractive aromas (including hyacinth and mango) and plenty of character; it receives a recommendation.
🔑 SCEA Vignobles Pierre Bonnet, Le Pavillon de Boyrein, 33210 Roaillan, tel. 05.56.63.24.24, fax 05.56.62.31.59 ☑ Ῑ by appt.

CH. LES CLAUZOTS 1998★

■ 14 ha 60,000 30–49 F

This vineyard's Cuvée Maxime is often praised by wine-writers. This wine, its principal production, has a colour which shows its youth, and is a good ambassador for the estate. The nose holds the promise of future complexity, and has a good, rich structure. An appealing wine, which should be kept for three to four years.
🔑 Frédéric Tach, Vignobles de Bordeaux, B.P. 114, 33210 Saint-Pierre-de-Mons, tel. 05.56.63.19.34, fax 05.56.63.21.60, e-mail lvb.sica.@libertysurf.fr ☑ Ῑ by appt.

CH. LE TUQUET 1997★

■ 35 ha 100,000 30–49

This château is an authentic 18th-centur charterhouse, with a long driveway leading u to it through the vines, and forms a fine pro duction unit whose wines are of consistentl high quality. This highly successful 1997 win bears witness to the know-how of Pau Ragon's team. It has good complexity in th nose, then develops a substantial structur before leaving the taster with the memory o an elegant finish. The **1998 Elevé en Fût d Chêne Blanc** (50–69F) is also awarded on star.
🔑 GFA du Ch. Le Tuquet, Ch. Le Tuquet, 33640 Beautiran, tel. 05.56.20.21.23, fax 05.56.20.21.83 ☑ Ῑ by appt.
🔑 Paul Ragon

CH. DE L'HOSPITAL 1997★★

■ 10 ha 45,000 70–99 F

True to its reputation, this vineyard offer an astonishing 1997 wine with a highly distin guished nose of coffee, violets, prunes, smoke toast and game. The structure is very we composed, relying on tannins which show that it has excellent ageing potential. A splen did achievement, especially for this vintage and a wine which deserves to be kept for fou to five years.
🔑 SCS Vignobles Lafragette, Darrouban, 33640 Portets, tel. 05.56.67.54.73, fax 05.56.67.09.93 ☑ Ῑ by appt.

CH. DE L'HOSPITAL 1998★★

□ 3 ha 10,000 70–99 F

The first impression of this wine is an attractive, pale-yellow colour with golden glints, which already suggests that it will deserve pride of place in the cellar. It then reveals a promising bouquet, with notes of toast giving way to fruit aromas. The palate is fresh, supple and full-bodied, and takes the taster by surprise as its qualities re-emerge in a lovely vanilla finish.
🔑 SCS Vignobles Lafragette, Darrouban, 33640 Portets, tel. 05.56.67.54.73, fax 05.56.67.09.93 ☑ Ῑ by appt.

DOM. DES LUCQUES 1998★★

□ 2.5 ha n.c. 50–69 F

Coming from the same producer as the Château Le Bourdillot, this wine is also well made. Frank and fresh, it develops a complex nose, before revealing roundness and a great deal of richness on the palate. An attractive wine which will go well with shellfish or dishes cooked in sauce. One star goes to the **1998 Rouge**, which is made from 90% Merlot and matured in oak. It has a nose of great elegance, combining crystallised fruits, musk and leather, and a charming palate which promises much for the future.
🔑 Vignobles Patrice Haverlan, 11, rue de l'Hospital, 33640 Portets, tel. 05.56.67.11.32, fax 05.56.67.11.32, e-mail patrice.haverlan@worldonline.fr ☑ Ῑ by appt.

CH. LUDEMAN LA COTE

Alix de Ludeman Elevé en fût de chêne 1998★

■ 2.5 ha 15,000 50–69 F

Coming from the south of the appellation, this wine has been matured in new barrels and needs to be kept for about three years so that the oakiness can fade. Nevertheless the oak does show respect for the basic material, and its structure has good potential. The finish and the nose of spicy, smoky notes are both noticeably young. From the same producer, the tank-matured **1998 Le Clos Les Majureaux Rouge** (30–49F) receives a recommendation.

SCEA Chaloupin-Lambrot, Ludeman, 33210 Langon, tel. 05.56.63.07.15, fax 05.56.63.48.17, e-mail mbelloc-ludeman@wanadoo.fr by appt.

CH. MAGENCE

Elevé en fût de chêne 1997

■ n.c. 4,000 50–69 F

Magence is a huge estate of 55 ha (136 acres), which already had a large vineyard in the 18th century. This 1997 wine has been matured in oak for ten months. It remains balanced, and is marked by rather wild aromas. Needs to be kept for a year or two.

Ch. Magence, 33210 Saint-Pierre-de-Mons, tel. 05.56.63.07.05, fax 05.56.63.41.42, e-mail magence@magence.com

CH. MAGNEAU

Cuvée Julien Elevé en fût de chêne 1998★★

□ 5 ha 7,000 50–69 F

This is a fine vineyard, with a terroir of high quality which the Ardurats, a family of genuine Girondin wine-makers, are determined to use to best advantage. Their Cuvée Julien is the product of selection by plot, blending 60% Sémillon with Sauvignon. This is a 1998 white of extremely high quality. The jury loved its bouquet, which is a successful combination of flowers, citrus fruits and slight notes of oak, and also its structure, which is not at all harsh and offers elegant support to agreeable flavours of exotic fruits and white peaches. Also very well constructed are the **1998 Château Magneau Rouge** (50–69F) and the **1999 Château Magneau Blanc** (30–49F), which come from the same producer and each receive one star.

Henri Ardurats et Fils, GAEC des Cabanasses,12, chem. Maxime-Ardurats, 33650 La Brède, tel. 05.56.20.20.57, fax 05.56.20.39.95, e-mail ardurats@chateau-magneau.com ev. day 9am–12 noon 2pm–6pm; Sat. Sun. by appt.

M. DE MALLE 1998★

□ 3 ha n.c. 50–69 F

This 1998 wine comes from the Graves vineyards of the prestigious 17th-century Sauternes château. Made from 70% Sauvignon blended with Sémillon, it certainly lives up to its noble origins. There is a lovely nose combining notes of oak with toast and citrus fruits, and a rich, powerful structure of equal complexity.

Comtesse de Bournazel, Ch. de Malle, 33210 Preignac, tel. 05.56.62.36.86, fax 05.56.76.82.40, e-mail chateaudemalle@wanadoo.fr by appt.

CH. DU MAYNE 1998

□ 5 ha 29,000 30–49 F

This vineyard is run from a little château which was built in the Empire style in 1849. Here it has blended 4% Muscadelle with 66% Sauvignon and 30% Sémillon. The wine releases attractive aromas of citrus and exotic fruits which combine with the roundness of its structure to form an interesting overall impression. A wine which needs to be allowed to breathe for quite a while before it is drunk.

Jean-Xavier Perromat, Ch. de Cérons, 33720 Cérons, tel. 05.56.27.01.13, fax 05.56.27.22.17 by appt.

CH. MAYNE DU CROS 1998★

□ 4 ha 9,670 50–69 F

Owned by an oenologist, the vineyard remains true to its tradition with this attractive wine. It is already pleasant to drink, but can be kept for a year or two; its good, complex range of aromas (crystallised apricots, dried figs and toast), and rich, lively palate combine with a long finish to leave the taster with a most favourable impression.

SA Vignobles M. Boyer, Ch. du Cros, 33410 Loupiac, tel. 05.56.62.99.31, fax 05.56.62.12.59, e-mail contact@chateauducros.com ev. day except Sat. Sun. 8am–12 noon 2pm–6pm

CH. MAYNE-LEVEQUE 1998★★

□ 15 ha 100,000 30–49 F

Coming from the same producer as the Château de Chantegrive, this wine is generous on the nose with beautiful notes of white peaches. It is on the palate, however, that it finds its full expression. After a very sweet *moelleux* attack, it grows livelier as the Sauvignon (boxwood) flavours develop: a faultless progression, ending on a happy note with a long finish. A wine which will go well with shellfish, but also with fine fish dishes such as turbot à la crème.

Françoise et Henri Lévêque, Ch. de Chantegrive, 33720 Podensac, tel. 05.56.27.17.38, fax 05.56.27.29.42, e-mail courrier@chateau.chantegrive.com ev. day except Sun. 8am–12 noon 2pm–6pm

CH. MOUTIN 1997★★

■ 3 ha 10,000 70–99 F

This wine's unusual grape content, containing 80% Merlot, comes through in its nose, where the soft fruit aromas make a victorious stand against the oak. The oak quality is still evident on the palate, but the substantial tannic structure and long finish will guarantee an ageing potential of five to ten years, which will be amply sufficient for the oak to fade. A wine with very attractive prospects.

🔑 SC Jean Darriet, Ch. Dauphiné-Rondillon, 33410 Loupiac, tel. 05.56.62.61.75, fax 05.56.62.63.73, e-mail vignoblesdarriet@wanadoo.fr ☒ Y ev. day 8am–12 noon 2pm–6pm; Sat. Sun. by appt.

CH. PERIN DE NAUDINE 1997*

■ 6.25 ha 27,000 30–49 F

This is the first vintage produced entirely by Olivier Colas, a former international banker who bought this beautiful charterhouse in 1996. This wine promises much for the future of the vineyard. After a delicate bouquet, it develops a good, round, full-bodied structure with well-blended tannins. A well-balanced wine which should be kept for three or four years. The **1998 Blanc** is recommended.

🔑 Ch. Périn de Naudine, 8, imp. des Domaines, 33640 Castres, tel. 05.56.67.06.65, fax 05.56.67.59.68, e-mail chateauperin@wanadoo.fr ☒ Y by appt.

🔑 Olivier Colas

CH. PEYREBLANQUE 1998**

■ 1.5 ha 7,000 50–69 F

This is a small vineyard given over entirely to Cabernet Sauvignon. It belongs to a wine-merchant from 'across the Garonne', and has the benefit of a good terroir, as is indicated by its name (' white stone ' in Gascon). The wine presents itself delightfully, with a black-currant colour and a bouquet of warm, spicy aromas. Its structure and complexity show that it deserves to be kept for four to five years.

🔑 SCEA Jean Médeville et Fils, Ch. Fayau, 33410 Cadillac, tel. 05.57.98.08.08, fax 05.56.62.18.22 ☒ Y ev. day except Sat. Sun. 8.30am–12 noon 2pm–5.30pm

CH. PINSAN 1998*

■ n.c. 17,000 30–49 F

This wine is offered by a large Bordeaux *négociant* which is well established in the Graves area. It combines delicate, fruity aromas with a substantial structure based on harmonious tannins. It may be kept for some time, but can also be drunk within the next two years.

🔑 Maison Sichel-Coste, 8, rue de la Poste, 33210 Langon, tel. 05.56.63.50.52, fax 05.56.63.42.28

CH. PONT DE BRION 1998**

■ 7 ha 35,000 50–69 F

Founded in 1987, this label brings together all the oldest vines in the vineyard. The wine has a beautiful, dark colour which is in no way deceptive. It has good length and is supported by good tannins, and should definitely be laid down for further maturing. This will bring out its complexity and elegant aromas, the fruits of careful vinification, for a long time to come. The **1998 Blanc** is recommended.

🔑 SCEA Molinari et Fils, Ludeman, 33210 Langon, tel. 05.56.63.09.52, fax 05.56.63.13.47, e-mail vignobles.molinari@wanadoo.fr ☒ Y by appt.

CH. DE PORTETS 1998*

□ 3.13 ha 21,000 50–69 F

The Château de Portets is a magnificent 18th-century residence with a remarkable wrought-iron gate at the entrance, both of which are featured on the label. Anyone familiar with this vineyard will find that this wine has the characteristics to be expected from it: a great deal of suppleness and delicate aromas of flowers and hazelnuts. An agreeable tasting, which ends delightfully with a long finish.

🔑 SCEA Théron-Portets, Ch. de Portets, 33640 Portets, tel. 05.56.67.12.30, fax 05.56.67.33.47, e-mail vignobles.theron@wanadoo.fr ☒ Y by appt.

🔑 Jean-Pierre Théron

CH. PRIEURE LES TOURS 1998*

■ 12 ha 96,000 50–69 F

Coming from a vast estate which comprises several vineyards, this wine has a beautiful colour, then develops well-extracted tannins to create an elegant, dense overall impression whose balance reappears in a long finish. The **1998 Blanc** (30–49F) is supple, rich and fine, and also receives one star.

🔑 Domaines de La Mette, 33640 Portets, tel. 05.56.67.18.18, fax 05.56.67.53.66 Y by appt.

CH. RAHOUL 1998**

□ 2 ha 11,300 70–99 F

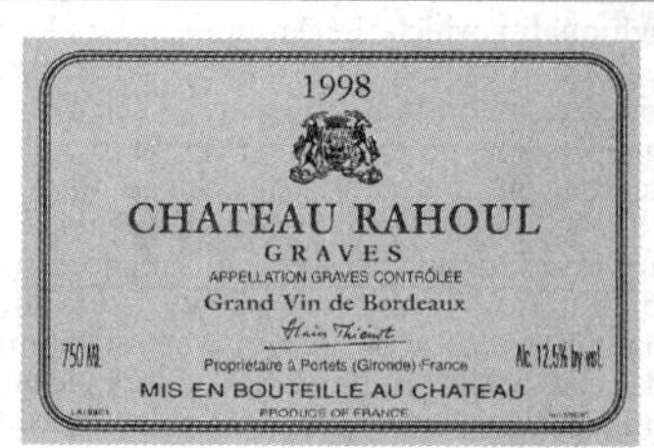

This very reliable vineyard has proved to be as consistent as ever with this superb vintage. Its personality does not come through at the start, but afterwards becomes particularly captivating; it has a pleasant colour between white and pale green, then remains discreet in the nose before revealing attractive fruity notes against an oaky background. Fresh, balanced and well structured, the palate promises very sound ageing potential (four years or more): a great wine in the making. The **1998 Château Constantin Blanc** is a highly typical Graves, and is awarded one star. It is not oak-matured and is already opening up elegantly.

🔑 Alain Thienot, Ch. Rahoul, rte du Courneau, 33640 Portets, tel. 05.56.67.01.12, fax 05.56.67.02.88 ☒ Y by appt.

:H. RESPIDE-MEDEVILLE 1998★

] 5.4 ha 18,000 70–99 F

Here we have a vineyard on a beautiful ravel-clay hillside, a house with literary asso- iations (it appears in a novel by François Aauriac), and a family with a passion for the orld of wine. With their Sémillon, Sauvi- non and Muscadelle vines, they are a far cry om the fashion for growing a single grape ariety. It is no surprise to see wines being roduced here such as this lovely 1998 vin- age, which has fresh aromas and a flavour- ome finish. 'An interesting style,' notes one f our stern experts. The **1997 Rouge** is ecommended.

Christian Médeville, Ch. Gilette, 33210 'reignac, tel. 05.56.76.28.44, ax 05.56.76.28.43, e-mail hristian.medeville@wanadoo.fr ☑ Y by ppt.

)OM. DU REYS 1997

5.87 ha 7,000 30–49 F

This wine has an interesting personality: its eautiful, dark-red colour, complex bouquet, ood substance and pleasant finish show that t has the potential to develop well.

Pouey International, chem. de Gaillardas, Jeansotte, 33650 Saint-Selve, el. 05.56.78.49.10, fax 05.56.78.49.11, -mail pouey.international.fr ☑ Y by appt.

:H. DE ROLLAND

Elevé en fût de chêne 1998★

] 4 ha 6,000 30–49 F

Coming from a small vineyard belonging o the Château de Rolland, this wine bears the tamp of very ripe Sémillon (70%) with pride. Round, lively and full-bodied, the overall mpression is of a highly characteristic and ery pleasant wine. 'It would go well with an scalope of trout with morels,' we are told.

Vignobles de Bordeaux, Saint-Pierre-de- Mons, 33212 Langon Cedex, el. 05.56.63.19.34, fax 05.56.63.21.60, :-mail lvb.sica@libertysurf.fr ☑ Y by appt.

:H. FORT DE ROQUETAILLADE 1998★

] 10 ha n.c. 30–49 F

The privilege of coming from a genuine eudal castle imposes certain duties. This eautifully made 1998 wine carries them out rilliantly; it has a pleasing yellow colour vith green glints, then opens up into a com- lex bouquet and a lively, supple, rich palate. A mouthwatering wine, which has kept its outhful bloom.

VBC SA Ch. de Roquetaillade, 33210 Mazères, tel. 05.56.76.14.16, ax 05.56.76.14.61 ☑ Y by appt.

CH. ROQUETAILLADE LA GRANGE 1999★

] 12 ha 80,000 30–49 F

This was once the vineyard of the medieval castle, but in 1962 it became independent. It is a fine piece of land, located at one of the highest points in the appellation. The vine- yard remains true to its tradition of high quality with this 1999 wine, which starts with aromas of exotic fruits, then develops on the palate on slightly more acidic notes, before fully revealing its round, balanced character.

GAEC Guignard Frères, Ch. Roquetaillade La Grange, 33210 Mazères, tel. 05.56.76.14.23, fax 05.56.62.30.62, e-mail contact@roquetaillade.com ☑ Y by appt.

CH. ROUGEMONT 1998★★

☐ n.c. n.c. 20–29 F

The year 1998 was a milestone for this vine- yard, which has made a spectacular leap for- ward. This fresh, elegant wine is dynamic and well structured, and has a particularly agree- able, complex nose of fine fruity, floral and buttery notes. The **1997 Rouge** (30–49F) is recommended; although its tannins are still austere, it has quite subtle flavours of soft fruits.

Dominique Turtaut, Rougemont, 33210 Toulenne, tel. 05.56.76.22.77, fax 05.56.76.22.74 ☑ Y by appt.

CH. SAINT-JEAN-DES-GRAVES 1998★★

■ 10 ha n.c. 50–69 F

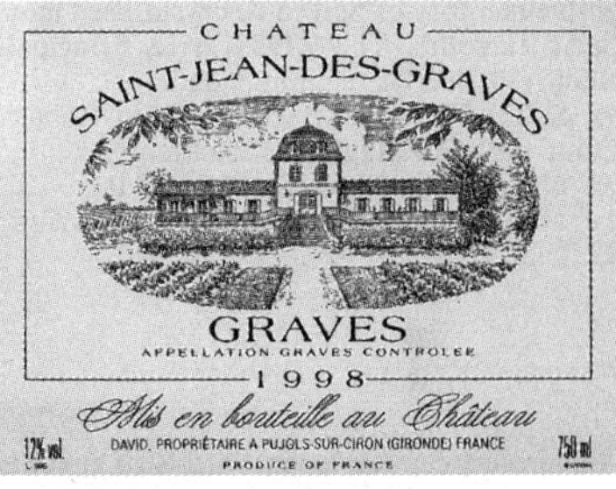

This vineyard belongs to an estate in the Sauternes, and offers a genuine wine for age- ing. It has a powerful nose, a supple attack in which its 70% Merlot content is clearly evi- dent, complex aromas with lovely notes of toast, high-quality tannins and a balanced palate, all of which contributes to the overall impression of a rich, spirited wine which deserves to be kept for four to five years, if not more.

SCEA J. David, Ch. Liot, 33720 Barsac, tel. 05.56.27.15.31, fax 05.56.27.14.42 ☑ Y by appt.

CH. SAINT-ROBERT

Cuvée Poncet-Deville 1998★★

■ 4 ha 25,000 70–99 F

89(90) 92|**93**||**94**| **95 96 97 98**

This wine is a blend of 70% Merlot and 30% Cabernet Sauvignon, and has had 13 months of careful maturation in the barrel. It is very much in the Bordeaux spirit, in that the search for power and potential is not emphasised to the detriment of harmony. Oak is certainly still in evidence, but it does not prevent either the fruit from making its presence felt in the nose, or the palate with its well-blended tannins from showing clearly that this wine will have a special place in the cellar. Once it has been kept for two to five years, it will be a good accompaniment to game or magret de canard. A wine with a fine nose but less power is the **1998 Cuvée Principale Rouge** (50–69F), which receives one star.

🔑 SCEA Vignobles Bastor et Saint-Robert, Dom. de Lamontagne, 33210 Preignac, tel. 05.56.63.27.66, fax 05.56.76.87.03, e-mail bastor.lamontagne@dial.oleane.com 🅥 🍷 by appt.

🔑 Foncier-Vignobles

CH. SAINT-ROBERT

Cuvée Poncet-Deville 1998★★

☐ 2 ha 12,000 50–69 F

Could it be that this wine has been influenced by its proximity to the very sweet Grands Liquoreux area? Whatever the case may be, its intense, elegant nose of attractive notes of roasted almonds and hazelnuts is rather reminiscent of these wines. The fleshy, full and aromatically very rich palate and finish are second to none, and leave the taster with a memory of agreeable crystallised mandarin flavours. The **1998 Cuvée Principale Blanc** (30–49F) is recommended.

🔑 SCEA Vignobles Bastor et Saint-Robert, Dom. de Lamontagne, 33210 Preignac, tel. 05.56.63.27.66, fax 05.56.76.87.03, e-mail bastor.lamontagne@dial.oleane.com 🅥 🍷 by appt.

CH. DU SEUIL 1999★★

☐ 6 ha 30,000 50–69 F

This very reputable vineyard is singled out for its Graves Blanc. Fresh and harmonious from beginning to end of the tasting, the 1998 wine shows great aromatic richness, with notes of toast, elder, acacia and pink grapefruit. This fine performance takes a lingering pause on a finish which is as long as it is fresh and lively. The **1997 Rouge** is also recommended: a wine to be drunk while still young.

🔑 Ch. du Seuil, 33720 Cérons, tel. 05.56.27.11.56, fax 05.56.27.28.79, e-mail chateau-du-seuil@wanadoo.fr 🅥 🍷 by appt.

🔑 T.-R. Watts

CH. SIMON 1997

■ 5 ha 24,000 50–69 F

This wine bears the stamp of its vintage, and although not ambitious it is pleasant and charming, with an attractive little structure which gives good support to its interesting aromas featuring notes of game.

🔑 EARL Dufour, Ch. Simon, 33720 Barsac, tel. 05.56.27.15.35, fax 05.56.27.24.79 🅥 🍷 by appt.

CH. TOUR DE CALENS

Elevé en fût de chêne 1999★

☐ 1.1 ha 8,600 30–49

Production of this wine will no doub[t] remain limited, but nonetheless it shows char[]acter, with a fine structure, richness and del[i]cate aromas of citrus fruits and pineapple.

🔑 Bernard et Dominique Doublet, Ch. Tour de Calens, 33640 Beautirant, tel. 05.57.24.12.93, fax 05.57.24.12.83 🅥 🍷 by appt.

CH. TOUR DE CLUCHON 1998★

■ 5 ha 36,000 30–49

This wine comes from a vineyard which i[s] of modest size, but is part of a vast propert[y] of 63 ha (156 acres). It has supple, well[-]balanced tannins, and continues right to th[e] finish to show a certain richness in its aro[]matic expression based on soft-fruit notes.

🔑 SCEA Counilh et Fils, 51–53, rte des Graves, 33640 Portets, tel. 05.56.67.18.61, fax 05.56.67.32.43, e-mail gervais@caves-particulières.com 🅥 🍷 ev. day 9am–12 noon 2pm–6pm, Sat. Sun. and groups by appt.

CH. TREBIAC 1998★

■ 3.5 ha 25,000 50–69

Belonging to an estate which comes from [a] former priory, this is a serious-minded vine[]yard. Its 1998 wine has a good tannic struc[]ture, and retains the pleasant quality in th[e] nose that is particular to Graves – under[]growth, red berries and warm earth. The **199[8] Château Crabitey Rouge Cuvée Spécial[e] Elevée en Fût de Chêne** is also recommended. It is marked by oak, and offers empyreumati[c] notes of toast. Best kept for three years.

🔑 Ass. Les Amis de la Chartreuse de Seillon, 63, rte du Courneau, 33640 Portets, tel. 05.56.67.18.64, fax 05.56.67.14.73

VIEUX CHATEAU GAUBERT

1998★★

■ 25 ha 60,000 70–99 F

83 85 86 87 |88| |**89**| |90| 91 |**93**| **94 95 97 98**

Once again this vineyard has distinguished itself by the quality of its wine with this superb 1998 wine whose colour shows its age[]ing potential from the start. This first impres[]sion is confirmed by the nose, which develops notes of toast and roasting with touches of pepper. Right from the attack the palate is full, revealing a substantial tannic content and a good substance which gives support while at the same time showing respect for a well-dosed oakiness. A very harmonious wine, which should be kept for three to five years. Less complex but also for longer maturing is the vineyard's second wine, the **1998 Benjamin de Vieux Château Gaubert Rouge** (50–69F), which receives one star.

🔑 Dominique Haverlan, Vieux Château Gaubert, 33640 Portets, tel. 05.56.67.52.76, fax 05.56.67.52.76 ☑ Y by appt.

VIEUX CHATEAU GAUBERT 1999★★

□ 6 ha 25,000 70–99 F

(89) 90 91 |92| 93 |94| |95| |96| |98| 99

This 1999 wine, made from 55% Sémillon and 45% Sauvignon, has a lovely pale-yellow colour, and is full and round with a sound constitution which brings out its aromatic expression to perfection. It is very elegant both in the nose and on the palate, with a complex cocktail of aromas in which white fruits accompany vanilla.

🔑 Dominique Haverlan, Vieux Château Gaubert, 33640 Portets, tel. 05.56.67.52.76, fax 05.56.67.52.76 ☑ Y by appt.

CH. VILLA BEL-AIR 1998★★

■ 24 ha 180,000 50–69 F

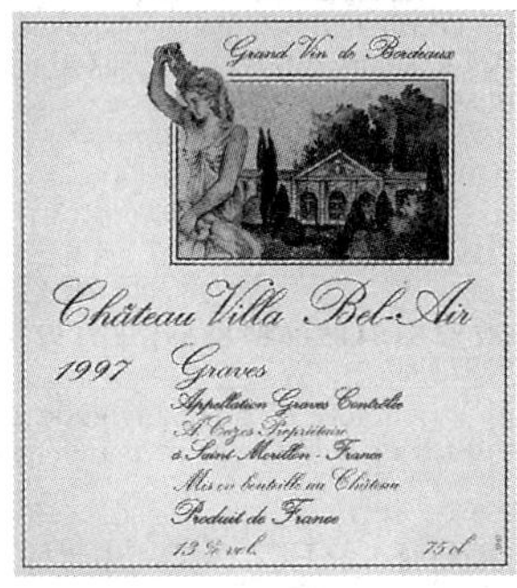

This château is an elegant 18th-century charterhouse, where they try to make wines that are true standard-bearers for the appellation. That is indeed the case with this 1998 wine, which has the support of a fresh, concentrated bouquet and combines the richness of its substance with the finesse of its flavours. It is both delightful and promising, and can be drunk immediately or kept for four or five years. The **1999 Blanc** has good balance and a fine aromatic complexity, and is awarded one star.

🔑 Jean-Michel Cazes, Ch. Villa Bel-Air, 33650 Saint-Morillon, tel. 05.56.20.29.35, fax 05.56.78.44.80 Y by appt.

CH. VILLEFRANCHE 1997★

■ 5 ha 15,000 30–49 F

This vineyard continues its good recent performance with a 1997 wine which is a fine achievement for the vintage. It starts with an intense colour, then develops a nose of the greatest subtlety, in which notes of toast mingle with undergrowth. Fine, fruity flavours emerge on a palate which is round, supple and balanced.

🔑 Benoît Guinabert, Ch. Villefranche, 33720 Barsac, tel. 05.56.27.05.77, fax 05.56.27.33.02 ☑ Y by appt.

Graves Supérieures

CH. LEHOUL 1998★

□ 1.5 ha 4,000 50–69 F

Château Lehoul is reliable and well known for its Vins Liquoreux. Once again the vineyard confirms that its reputation is well founded with a 1998 wine which fully lives up to the promise of its strong colour. Its very agreeable nose releases rich crystallised notes, delightfully combined with aromas of honey, hawthorn blossom and acacia. The palate is just as complex, with touches of wax and smoke supporting a structure whose mouth-filling quality, richness, texture and flavours of overripening make a strong overall impression.

🔑 EARL Fonta et Fils, rte d'Auros, 33210 Langon, tel. 05.56.63.17.74, fax 05.56.63.06.06 ☑ Y by appt.

CH. DE ROCHEFORT 1998★

□ 1.76 ha 2,000 30–49 F

As a producer in Preignac in the Sauternes region, Jean-Christophe Barbe is steeped in an environment where the *liquoreux* is king. This will be clear to anyone tasting this lovely Graves Supérieures, with its highly expressive nose of fresh, lemony notes, and its rich, balanced and flavoursome palate, which has beautiful crystallised notes.

🔑 Jean-Christophe Barbe, Ch. Laville, 33210 Preignac, tel. 05.56.63.28.14, fax 05.56.63.16.28 ☑ Y by appt.

Pessac-Léognan

Situated at the northern end of the Graves (and previously known as Hautes-Graves), the region of Pessac and Léognan is now an *appellation communale*, like that of the Médoc. Its new status could have been justified on historic grounds (this old vineyard on the outskirts of Bordeaux produced clarets in medieval times) but Pessac-Léognan is now identified separately because of its distinctive soil. The terraces that are found further south give way to a more hilly terrain. The sector between Martillac and Mérignac consists of a broken series of gravelly ridges: the combination of pebbly soils and steep slopes offers excellent drainage, perfect for the vine. As a result, the Pessac-Léognan wines have great originality, something specialists realised long before a separate appellation was created. At the time of the Imperial Classification in 1855, Haut-Brion in Graves was the only château outside the Médoc to be classified as a Premier Cru. When a further 16 Crus from Graves were classified in 1959, all came from the area now covered by the Appellation Communale Pessac-Léognan.

The red wines, of which 54,477 hl (1,438,193 gal) were produced in 1999, have all the Graves characteristics but are distinctive for their bouquet, their velvety quality and their structure. On the other hand, the dry white wines, with 14,280 hl (376, 992 gal) in 1999, age well in barrel, developing a richly aromatic bouquet with fine notes of broom and linden flowers as they mature.

CH. BOIS MARTIN 1997

■ 5 ha 30,000 50–69 F

Acquired in 1997 by the Perrins (of the Châteaux at Carbonnieux and Le Sartre), this vineyard will certainly undergo major changes in the years to come. This vintage already shows that they have made a good start. The wine is fresh and supple with a delicate nose of attractive fruity notes, and will be pleasant to drink while young.

GFA des Ch. Le Sartre et Bois Martin, 33850 Léognan, tel. 05.57.96.56.20, fax 05.57.96.59.19, e-mail chateau.carbonnieux@wanadoo.fr by appt.

Perrin

CH. BOUSCAUT 1997*

■ Cru clas. 39 ha 110,000 100–149 F

76 79 80 **|81|** 82 83 84 **85** (86) 87 |88| **|89| |90|** 91 92 |93| **|94|** 95 96 97

The beautiful 18th-century house was restored during the 1970s, and reminds us of the important role that Parliament played in the development of the Pessac-Léognan vineyards. The property is run by Lucien Lurton's daughter, and is now offering a wine with excellent ageing potential for the vintage (three to five years), whose structure is not quite true to the estate's tradition, though the finesse of its nose and its good length are more in keeping.

SA Ch. Bouscaut, RN 113, 33140 Cadaujac, tel. 05.57.83.12.20, fax 05.57.83.12.21 by appt.

Sophie Cogombles

CH. BOUSCAUT 1998

□ Cru clas. 8 ha 26,000 100–149 F

79 80 81 82 83 84 85 86 87 88 89 |90| **91 92** |93| 94 |95| |96| 97 |98|

With a rich nose of ripe Sauvignon and a slight touch of oak, this wine is full, round,

CRUS CLASSÉS OF THE GRAVES REGION

NAME OF CRU CLASSÉ	TYPE OF WINE	NAME OF CRU CLASSÉ	TYPE OF WINE
Château Bouscaut	red and white	Château La Mission-Haut-Brion	red
Château Carbonnieux	red and white	Château Latour-Haut-Brion	red
Domaine de Chevalier	red and white	Château La Tour-Martillac	red and white
Château Couhins	white	Château Laville-Haut-Brion	white
Château Couhins-Lurton	white	Château Malartic-Lagravière	red and white
Château de Fieuzal	red	Château Olivier	red and white
Château Haut-Bailly	red	Château Pape-Clément	red
Château Haut-Brion	red	Château Smith-Haut-Lafitte	red

balanced, and just as flavoursome on the palate. The overall impression is elegant and agreeable.
SA Ch. Bouscaut, RN 113, 33140 Cadaujac, tel. 05.57.83.12.20, fax 05.57.83.12.21 ☑ Y by appt.

CH. BROWN 1998★

☐ 3.34 ha 20,500 100–149 F

This wine comes from a vineyard with a high proportion of Sauvignon vines (70%), and has been fermented and matured in oak. It makes an exceedingly pleasant impression, not only in its elegant nose of floral and toast notes, but also through its liveliness and balance. One member of the jury wrote: 'Tasting it is a real pleasure.' The second wine here is the **1998 Le Colombier de Château Brown Blanc**, which is also supple and fresh, and is recommended.
SA Ch. Brown, allée John-Lewis-Brown, 33850 Léognan, tel. 05.56.87.08.10, fax 05.56.87.87.34 ☑
Bernard Barthe

CH. CANTELYS 1997★

■ 15 ha 30,000 70–99 F

Located on a gravelly hillock facing the research centre at Martillac, the vineyard here enjoys the benefit of a fine terroir, as is clearly apparent throughout the tasting of this 1997 wine. It has an appealing colour with purple glints, then develops an elegant nose in which red-berry aromas are accentuated by a discreet note of oak. The palate is tannic, balanced and harmonious, with well-dosed extraction and maturation, and should age well over four or five years.
Ch. Cantelys, 33650 Martillac, tel. 05.57.83.11.22, fax 05.57.83.11.21 ☑ Y by appt.
Daniel Cathiard

CH. CANTELYS 1998★★

☐ 10 ha 10,000 70–99 F

Although less extensive than the area devoted to red wine, the white wine vineyards of Cantelys are by no means neglected. This equal blend of Sémillon and Sauvignon makes for a perfectly balanced whole which is rich, supple and also very expressive, with an elegant oaky quality complemented by lovely fruity notes (peaches and dried apricots). A wine with plenty of character.
Ch. Cantelys, 33650 Martillac, tel. 05.57.83.11.22, fax 05.57.83.11.21 ☑ Y by appt.

CH. CARBONNIEUX 1997★

■Cru clas. 45 ha 200,000 100–149 F

75 81 82 83 85 (86) **87 |88|** |89| **|90|** |91| |92| |93| **94** 95 **96** |97|

Founded at the end of the 14th century, this vineyard is one of the great, classic producers of Graves wines; Thomas Jefferson visited it on his journey through the vineyards before the Revolution. The variety of different grapes grown here (Merlot, Cabernets, Malbec and Petit Verdot) is very much in keeping with Bordeaux thinking. This vintage is supple, round and supported by silky tannins. It has no great ageing ambitions, but will be just right to serve young with white meat, which will enable its bouquet to express itself fully and give free rein to its notes of fruit, flowers, chocolate and toast.
SC des Grandes Graves, Ch. Carbonnieux, 33850 Léognan, tel. 05.57.96.56.20, fax 05.57.96.59.19, e-mail chateau.carbonnieux@wanadoo.fr ☑ Y by appt.
Perrin

CH. CARBONNIEUX 1998★

☐Cru clas. 45 ha 180,000 100–149 F

81 82 83 85 86 87 **|88| |89|** |90| **|91|** 92 |93| **|94|** 95 **96 97** |98|

In the 18th century, the white wine from Carbonnieux was sold to the Sultan of Turkey under the name of 'Carbonnieux Mineral Water'. As usual, the Carbonnieux Blanc's appearance has a great deal of class – a beautiful colour with straw glints. Its complex, mouthwatering bouquet goes merrily from buttery aromas to floral fragrances, with some notes of dried fruits in between. This is a fresh, mature wine which still has some ageing potential, but the temptation to try it now is irresistible.
SC des Grandes Graves, Ch. Carbonnieux, 33850 Léognan, tel. 05.57.96.56.20, fax 05.57.96.59.19, e-mail chateau.carbonnieux@wanadoo.fr ☑ Y by appt.

DOM. DE CHEVALIER 1997★★

■Cru clas. 33 ha 68,000 200–249 F

64 66 70 73 |75| 78 79 **|83|** 84 **|85| |86|** 87 **|88|** |(89)| **|90| 91 92 |93| |94| 96 97**

Deep in the pine forest, Chevalier may have remained an 'estate' and held on to the almost ritual use of the term 'château', but it has certainly become one of the beacons of Bordeaux wine-making. It maintains its rank with wines such as this 1997 vintage. It has a perfect colour with purple and ruby glints, and an expressive and harmonious nose (ripe fruits and scents of oak). Arriving on the palate, its round, full contours combine with high-quality tannins to create the overall impression of a wine which is already flavoursome, but will gain from being kept for three to four years.
Dom. de Chevalier, 33850 Léognan, tel. 05.56.64.16.16, fax 05.56.64.18.18, e-mail domainedechevalier@domainedechevalier.co Y by appt.
Famille Bernard

DOM. DE CHEVALIER 1997★

☐Cru clas. 5 ha n.c. 300–499 F

82 83 85 86 |89| |(90)| **91 92 |93| |94|** 96 |97|

Although it does not rival certain previous vintages which were real oenological legends, this wine has much to be said in its favour, both in the intensity of its bouquet of lovely citrus fruits and honey notes, and in its development on the palate. This is full with plenty of character, and extends to a well-balanced fruity and oaky finish.

🗝 Dom. de Chevalier, 33850 Léognan, tel. 05.56.64.16.16, fax 05.56.64.18.18, e-mail domainedechevalier@domainedechevalier.co 🍷 by appt.

CH. COUHINS-LURTON 1998★

☐ Cru clas. 5.5 ha n.c. 150–199 F

82 83 85 86 87 88 89 |90| 91 **|92|** 93 **|94| 95 |(96)| 97** 98

The Couhins estate was divided up in 1968 between INRA and André Lurton, who in 1990 acquired the château itself. The fact that this wine comes from a vineyard which grows only Sauvignon grapes shows in its aromas. Nevertheless there is more to the nose than this one feature; various other notes give it richness and a great deal of charm.

🗝 Vignobles André Lurton, Ch. Bonnet, 33420 Grézillac, tel. 05.57.25.58.58, fax 05.57.74.98.59, e-mail andre.lurton@wanadoo.fr ☑ 🍷 by appt.

CH. DE CRUZEAU 1997★

■ n.c. n.c. 50–69 F

81 82 83 85 86 88 89 90 92 |93| |94| 95 96 97

This vineyard was already highly reputed in the 19th century, if one is to believe the newspapers of the time, and it maintains its position today. Its 1997 wine has a deep-red colour, and bears the stamp of maturation in its bouquet, where notes of tar then toast are mingled with liquorice. After a sweet attack, the palate develops dense tannins then opens out into a flavourful finish. Best drunk in one or two years' time.

🗝 Vignobles André Lurton, Ch. Bonnet, 33420 Grézillac, tel. 05.57.25.58.58, fax 05.57.74.98.59, e-mail andre.lurton@wanadoo.fr ☑ 🍷 by appt.

CH. DE CRUZEAU 1998★★

☐ 12 ha n.c. 50–69 F

88 89 90 92 93 94 95 |96| **|97| |98|**

Once again this vineyard has distinguished itself by the quality of its white wine. It has an attractive green colour with pale gold glints, then holds the taster's attention with the intensity and complexity of a bouquet which harmoniously combines smokiness, citrus fruits and exotic fruits with white flowers. Both the dense, rich, aromatic palate and the long, sweet finish are very elegant. A truly enjoyable wine which is already pleasant but deserves to be kept for two or three years.

🗝 Vignobles André Lurton, Ch. Bonnet, 33420 Grézillac, tel. 05.57.25.58.58, fax 05.57.74.98.59, e-mail andre.lurton@wanadoo.fr ☑ 🍷 by appt.

CH. D'EYRAN 1997

■ 12 ha 40,000 50–69 F

In 1348, the English court granted the Lord of Budos the right to build a castle here . . . After many vicissitudes, the land became the property of the de Sèze family in 1796, and still belongs to them today. This vineyard now offers a supple, light 1997 wine whose maturation marks it out clearly as suitable for lovers of oaky wines.

🗝 SCEA Ch. d'Eyran, 33650 Saint-Médard-d'Eyrans, tel. 05.56.65.51.59, fax 05.56.65.43.78 ☑ 🍷 by appt.

🗝 de Sèze

CH. FERRAN Cuvée réservée 1997★

■ 10 ha 60,000 50–69 F

83 85 88 89 |90| 94 |95| 97

Coming from a vineyard which used to belong partly to the Montesquieu estates, this wine bears the stamp of Merlot (55%) in a bouquet of great charm. The palate has plenty of stuffing and good balance, and shows by its expressive tannins and highly characteristic aromas that it comes from good stock.

🗝 Ch. Ferran, 33650 Martillac, tel. 06.07.41.86.00 ☑ 🍷 by appt.

🗝 Hervé Béraud-Sudreau

CH. FERRAN Cuvée réservée 1998★

☐ 4 ha 27,000 50–69 F

94 **|95| |97|** |98|

Although it does not rival the 1997 vintage, this wine is both charming and reliable. It opens with a fresh, fine bouquet (fruits, flowers and linden blossom), then shows the same qualities in an attack which is supple and delicate, before becoming richer as it opens out into a long finish.

🗝 Ch. Ferran, 33650 Martillac, tel. 06.07.41.86.00 ☑ 🍷 by appt.

CH. DE FIEUZAL 1997★★

■ Cru clas. 60 ha 100,000 200–249 F

70 75 76 77 78 79 80 81 82 83 84 |85| |86| |88| |89| |(90)| 91 **|92| 93 94 (95) (96) 97**

This vineyard is a fine production unit which frequently wins praise. The qualities of its white gravel terroir are well conveyed in this wine, which presents itself with a beautiful purple and dark-red colour, and a fruity bouquet of great finesse. There is a full, rich, fleshy, crisp palate which is sustained by a fine tannic presence and fully lives up to the promise of the colour. This wine will be worth keeping for four or five years.

🗝 Ch. de Fieuzal, 124, av. de Mont-de-Marsan, 33850 Léognan, tel. 05.56.64.77.86, fax 05.56.64.18.88 ☑ 🍷 by appt.

CH. DE FIEUZAL 1998★★

☐ 18 ha 45,000 250–299 F

83 84 85 86 87 |88| |89| |(90)| 91 92 |93| |94| |95| |96| 97 98

Coming from a vineyard which grows equal shares of Sauvignon and Sémillon, this wine is developing appealing aromas of peaches and apricots although the oakiness is till fairly evident. The palate is fresh in the attack, lively, rich and long, and has a fine, elegant, young structure. This is characteristic of Fieuzal wines, which rank among the best of the Bordeaux whites.

🗝 Ch. de Fieuzal, 124, av. de Mont-de-Marsan, 33850 Léognan, tel. 05.56.64.77.86, fax 05.56.64.18.88 ☑ 🍷 by appt.

CH. DE FRANCE 1997★★

■ 29 ha 50,000 🍷 100–149 F

81 82 83 85 86 88 |89| |(90)| 92 93 94 95 96 97

This vineyard was reorganised in 1971 by its new owner, and has the benefit of a very fine terroir. It is much respected for its reliability, and this wine is no exception. It is pleasant to look at, with a colour which is both deep and fresh, expressive in the nose (soft fruits and spices along with a musky note), and well composed. The structure is rich, long and full-bodied, and supported by an elegant note of oak. The very well-balanced overall impression together with the tannic finish suggests that it needs to age for four to five years.

🔑 SA Bernard Thomassin, Ch. de France, 98, rte de Mont-de-Marsan, 33850 Léognan, tel. 05.56.64.75.39, fax 05.56.64.72.13, e-mail chateau-de-france@chateau-de-france.com ☑ 𝐈 by appt.

CH. GAZIN ROCQUENCOURT 1997

■ 6.5 ha 35,000 🍷 70–99 F

In no way handicapped by its fairly modest size for the appellation, this vineyard is offering a well-constructed 1997 wine with a good tannic presence and an expressive bouquet (redcurrants, blackcurrants, fruit stones, crushed walnut leaves and smokiness, with a slight note of resin). It will need to be kept for one to two years until the finish becomes more balanced.

🔑 SCEA Ch. Gazin Rocquencourt, 74, av. de Cestas, 33850 Léognan, tel. 05.56.64.77.89, fax 05.56.64.77.89 ☑

🔑 Michotte

DOM. DE GRANDMAISON 1998

□ 3 ha 17,000 🍷 50–69 F

85 86 88 89 90 93 94 |96| 97 98

In keeping with the vineyard's tradition, this wine is a blend of Sauvignon and 30% Sémillon. It has been matured one-third in new barrels and two-thirds in stainless-steel vats, and is simple but well made, with a developing bouquet of attractive aromas (citrus fruits, dried fruits and breadcrusts) and a good palate which is lively and slightly lemony. The finish is pleasant.

🔑 Jean Bouquier, Dom. de Grandmaison, 33850 Léognan, tel. 05.56.64.75.37, fax 05.56.64.55.24 ☑ 𝐈 by appt.

CH. HAUT-BAILLY 1997★★

■ Cru clas. 26 ha 75,000 🍷 200–249 F

78 79 80 81 82 83 85 86 87 88 89 90 92 93 94 (95) 96 97

This vineyard has existed at least since the beginning of the 16th century, and has an interesting, unbroken terroir of sand and gravel on a subsoil of fossil stones. In addition, the production method shows respect for tradition. The 1997 wine is superb. Its strong colour and already expressive bouquet (cherries, fruit stones and smokiness) are more than promising. Equally rich and powerful, but without aggression thanks to its

silky tannins, the palate is going in the same direction and this, together with the finish, suggests it needs ageing for at least four or five years.

🔑 SCA du Ch. Haut-Bailly, rte de Cadaujac, 33850 Léognan, tel. 05.56.64.75.11, fax 05.56.64.53.60, e-mail mail@chateau-haut-bailly.com 𝐈 by appt.

🔑 Robert G. Wilmers

LA PARDE DE HAUT-BAILLY 1997★

■ 26 ha 35,000 🍷 70–99 F

Under a second Haut-Bailly label, this wine confirms the achievement of its predecessor by its good qualities and expressive nose (hazelnuts and leather), fruity flavours on the palate, which bear witness to a very sound harvest, round tannins and well-dosed oak. A quality wine.

🔑 SCA du Ch. Haut-Bailly, rte de Cadaujac, 33850 Léognan, tel. 05.56.64.75.11, fax 05.56.64.53.60, e-mail mail@chateau-haut-bailly.com ☑ 𝐈 by appt.

CH. HAUT-BERGEY 1997★

■ 14 ha 48,058 🍷 100–149 F

91 92 93 |94| 96 97

Located at the heart of the Léognan commune near the village, this vineyard has drawn out the quintessence of the terroir with this very accomplished 1997 wine. Its elegant bouquet shows great complexity (spices, leather, smokiness and toast, with some empyreumatic notes). The palate is rich, balanced and expressive, and has the necessary substance to grow rounder in four to five years' time.

🔑 Sylviane Garcin-Cathiard, Ch. Haut-Bergey, 33850 Léognan, tel. 05.56.64.05.22, fax 05.56.64.06.98, e-mail h-bergey@worldnet.fr ☑ 𝐈 by appt.

CH. HAUT-BERGEY 1998★

□ 1.5 ha n.c. 🍷 150–199 F

93 94 95 96 |98|

Coming from a vineyard mostly given over to Sauvignon (60%), this wine bears its stamp in a bouquet of intense boxwood aromas. Supple, full and well balanced, it develops pleasantly on the palate, which is supported by a well-dosed amount of oakiness.

Sylviane Garcin-Cathiard, Ch. Haut-Bergey, 33850 Léognan, tel. 05.56.64.05.22, fax 05.56.64.06.98, e-mail h-bergey@worldnet.fr ☑ Y by appt.

CH. HAUT-BRION 1997★★

■ 1er cru clas. 43.2 ha n.c. 500 F+

73 74 |75| 76 77 |78| |79| |81| |82| |83| 84 |85| |86| |87| 88 89 (90) |91| |92| |93| 94 (95) (96) 97

How could one fail to be amazed by this vineyard and its beautiful manor house, which today are enclosed within the town? The most surprising thing, however, is the age of the vineyard, and the role it played in the development of modern Bordeaux wines, which came into being here thanks to the Pontacs in the 16th century, and the wine-making revolution in the 18th century. Recognised as one of the greatest of the Bordeaux vineyards, it was the only one outside the Médoc to be classed as *Premier* in 1855. Once again it has produced a remarkable wine which fully lives up to its beautiful deep colour with black glints. Its bouquet of leather, raisins, fruits in brandy and precious wood is complex and expressive, without being in any way aggressive. After an exceptional attack, the same qualities reappear on the palate, which is voluptuous and has an elegant structure with velvety tannins, playing on notes of spices, cocoa and cinnamon before opening out into a full, long finish which calls for long ageing.

SA Dom. Clarence Dillon, B.P. 24, 33602 Pessac Cedex, tel. 05.56.00.29.30, fax 05.56.98.75.14, e-mail info@haut-brion.com

CH. HAUT-BRION 1998★★★

□ 2.7 ha n.c. 500 F+

79 80 81 (82) 83 84 85 87 |88| |89| |90| |93| |94| 95 96 97 98

Although unclassed and of modest size, Haut-Brion's white wine vineyard makes very reputable wine. From its beautiful lemon-yellow colour to its long, rich finish, the tasting of this 1998 wine offers one pleasure after another: powerful fragrances of white flowers and fresh hazelnuts, a fat, voluptuous attack on the palate, a rich, powerful structure and some final notes of citrus fruits which do not come in half-measures. The overall impression is remarkably balanced and characteristic. A true wine for longer maturing, which should be kept for three to ten years.

SA Dom. Clarence Dillon, B.P. 24, 33602 Pessac Cedex, tel. 05.56.00.29.30, fax 05.56.98.75.14, e-mail info@haut-brion.com

LE BAHANS DE HAUT-BRION 1997★

■ n.c. n.c. 200–249 F

Under a second Haut-Brion label, this wine makes an appealing impression, both with its mouthwatering bouquet offering a delicate combination of oak and fresh, fruity notes, and a structure featuring moderate tannins. There is a lovely finish on notes of ripe fruits (blackcurrants and blackberries), and the wine is sufficiently well structured overall to benefit from being kept for three to five years.

SA Dom. Clarence Dillon, B.P. 24, 33602 Pessac Cedex, tel. 05.56.00.29.30, fax 05.56.98.75.14, e-mail info@haut-brion.com

CH. HAUT LAGRANGE 1998★

□ 1.7 ha 12,000 50–69 F

92 94 95 |96| 97 |98|

Although mainly given over to red wines, this vineyard has a limited production of whites. Sauvignon Gris (5%) is added to 45% Sauvignon Blanc and 50% Sémillon in this 1998 wine, 20% of which has been matured in new oak for six months. It is a fragrant wine, with notes of almost roasted exotic fruits (passionfruit and pineapple) which show beyond doubt that it is the result of a very ripe harvest. Supple, round, well balanced and silky, it retains and reinforces its aromatic character on the palate.

Francis Boutemy, SA Ch. Haut Lagrange, 31, rte de Loustalade, 33850 Léognan, tel. 05.56.64.09.93, fax 05.56.64.10.08, e-mail chateau-haut-lagrange@wanadoo.fr ☑ Y by appt.

CH. HAUT-NOUCHET 1997

■ 28 ha 89,613 50–69 F

Louis Lurton has gone over to organic growing methods. This wine is a blend of 40% Merlot and Cabernet Sauvignon, and has been matured for 12 months in barrels. It is balanced and delicate, and shows its personality in a developing bouquet of undergrowth, humus and fruit.

Louis Lurton, Ch. Haut-Nouchet, 33650 Martillac, tel. 05.56.72.69.74, fax 05.56.72.56.11, e-mail info@louis-lurton.fr ☑ Y by appt.

CH. HAUT-PLANTADE 1998

□ 1.33 ha 5,000 70–99 F

Many Pessac-Léognan plots belong to the historic Bordeaux vineyards, but this one was founded in 1975 by the Plantades. The 1997 wine has a very expressive bouquet with notes of citrus-fruit peel, and although it is more discreet on the palate, the overall impression is of high quality, with a toast flavour at the finish. A wine which should be kept for a year.

GAEC Plantade Père et Fils, Ch. Haut-Plantade, 33850 Léognan, tel. 05.56.64.07.09, fax 05.56.64.02.24 ☑ Y by appt.

CH. HAUT VIGNEAU 1997

■ 15 ha 80,000 30–49 F

This vineyard is run by the Perrins and their team, and although it does not rival Carbonnieux, it has plenty of money behind it. With its rather charming fruity and smoky bouquet and its tannic composition, it should be kept for three or four years to become fully open.

GFA du Ch. Haut-Vigneau, 20, rue Jules-Guesde, 33850 Léognan, tel. 05.57.96.56.20, fax 05.57.96.59.19, e-mail chateau.carbonnieux@wanadoo.fr ☑ Y by appt.
Perrin

CH. LAFARGUE Cuvée Alexandre 1998

☐ 1.76 ha 10,000 70–99 F

As is often the case with this vineyard, this wine – 70% Sauvignon Blanc and 30% Sauvignon Gris – is recommended mainly to lovers of oaky wine, who will find that overall it is a rather imposing product with rich aromas (butter, exotic and candied fruits, liquorice, etc).

Jean-Pierre Leymarie, 5, imp. de Domy, 33650 Martillac, tel. 05.56.72.72.30, fax 05.56.72.64.61, e-mail lafargue@caves particulieres.com ☑ Y by appt.

CH. LAFONT MENAUT 1997

■ 9 ha 35,000 30–49 F

Coming from a vineyard set up at the beginning of the 1990s, this wine offers a mouthwatering bouquet of red berries combined with a harmonious smoky quality. It is substantially constructed, and has a good, robust, full-bodied palate, which will enable it to be drunk in two or three years' time.

SCEA Philibert Perrin, Ch. Lafont Menaut, 33850 Léognan, tel. 05.57.96.56.20, fax 05.57.96.59.19, e-mail chateau.carbonnieux@wanadoo.fr ☑

CH. LA GARDE 1997★

■ 40.8 ha 173,300 100–149 F

|(90)| 91 93 94 (95) 96 97

With a real charterhouse, huge barrel-stores which were built in 1882, and a beautiful gravel hilltop vineyard, La Garde is a typical vineyard in this appellation. Its wine in this delicate vintage does not disappoint: it has a Bordeaux colour, and reveals a bouquet which is just opening with a very pleasant combination of well-dosed oak, elegant fruit and notes of game. On the palate the attack is very round, and there is fine concentration, a sound body and a long finish. 'There's real wine in the glass', exclaimed one delighted taster. Keep for three to ten years.

Dourthe, 35, rte de Bordeaux, B.P. 49, 33290 Parempuyre, tel. 05.56.35.53.00, fax 05.56.35.53.29, e-mail contact@cvbg.com ☑ Y by appt.

CH. LA GARDE 1998

☐ 5.5 ha 20,000 70–99 F

Made exclusively from Sauvignon, and oak-matured with stirring on the lees for 11 months, this 1998 white wine creates a pleasant impression with a bouquet of musk accompanied by aromas of orange and grapefruit. Despite some dominant oaky notes at the finish, the palate is agreeable and well balanced. It will need to be kept for a year before being served with fish in a cream sauce.

Dourthe, 35, rte de Bordeaux, B.P. 49, 33290 Parempuyre, tel. 05.56.35.53.00, fax 05.56.35.53.29, e-mail contact@cvbg.com ☑ Y by appt.

CH. LA LOUVIERE 1997★★

■ 35 ha n.c. 150–199 F

75 80 81 82 83 85 86 |88| |89| (90) 91 92 **93 94** 95 96 **97**

Coming from one of the few vineyards to have a château classed as an historic monument (it is an elegantly Neo-Classical structure), this wine fully lives up to its noble origins. It has spent 12 months in the barrel; its strong Bordeaux colour is followed by a frank, complex bouquet of red, slightly crystallised berries, undergrowth and notes of well-dosed oak. With a fine structure which shows its ageing potential (about five years), the palate is supported by tannins which are both dense and tender, and make this a typical wine of the appellation. The second wine from this vineyard is the **1997 L de La Louvière Rouge** (50–69F). It comes from young vines, and is recommended by the jury.

Vignobles André Lurton, Ch. Bonnet, 33420 Grézillac, tel. 05.57.25.58.58, fax 05.57.74.98.59, e-mail andre.lurton@wanadoo.fr ☑ Y by appt.

CH. LA LOUVIERE 1998★★

☐ 15 ha n.c. 150–199 F

82 85 86 88 89 (90) 91 92 93 |94| |95| |96| |97| **98**

The Sauvignon component is evident in the bouquet of this wine. It is intense, complex and accentuated by an oaky aroma whose discreet presence highlights the mineral notes of gunflint. The palate is rich, full, balanced, well structured, aromatic and very thoroughbred, and calls for a good period of ageing (up to four or five years).

Vignobles André Lurton, Ch. Bonnet, 33420 Grézillac, tel. 05.57.25.58.58, fax 05.57.74.98.59, e-mail andre.lurton@wanadoo.fr ☑ Y by appt.

L. DE LA LOUVIERE 1998★

☐ n.c. n.c. 50–69 F

Fresh, round, rich, aromatic (grapefruit and passionfruit under a dominant mineral note) and well composed, this second white wine from La Louvrière will be pleasant to drink while waiting for the other one to age; it will be ready to drink in one or two years' time.

Vignobles André Lurton, Ch. Bonnet, 33420 Grézillac, tel. 05.57.25.58.58, fax 05.57.74.98.59, e-mail andre.lurton@wanadoo.fr ☑ Y by appt.

CH. LA MISSION HAUT-BRION 1997★★

■ Cru clas. 20.9 ha n.c. 500 F+

77 78 80 **|81| |82| |83| 84 |85| |86| |87| |88| 89 (90) |92| 93 94 95 (96) 97**

It was the preacher-monks of the Congrégation de Saint-Vincent-de-Paul who gave this estate its name, and also its reputation for wine-making, which goes back

BORDEAUX

several centuries. Today just one street, which is part of the road to Arcachon, separates La Mission from Haut-Brion, yet each vineyard has its own personality. Likewise the wines. This one has a lovely red colour with Bordeaux glints, and shows its originality in its notes of liquorice and fruits in brandy. Although its tannins are still very young, it is silky, full and rich, and has a warm, spicy finish. It will need to age for four to five years, and has the necessary concentration and aromatic potential to do so. The second wine here is the **1997 La Chapelle de la Mission**, which is recommended for its notes of cocoa, wax, blackcurrant buds and prunes.

🗝 SA Dom. Clarence Dillon, B.P. 24, 33602 Pessac Cedex, tel. 05.56.00.29.30, fax 05.56.98.75.14, e-mail info@haut-brion.com

CH. LARRIVET HAUT-BRION 1997★

■ 42 ha 125,000 🛢 150–199 F

82 83 86 88 |89| |90| 92 |93| |94| 95 96 97

This estate is a charming property, the park and vineyard surrounded by meadows and woods. It is also a serious-minded vineyard, as this wine shows. It has a pleasant ruby-red colour, and an equally agreeable bouquet of red berries along with toast. On the palate, the toasty flavours reappear and join the fairly powerful tannins to form an overall impression whose harmony relies on lengthy maturation in oak. Best kept for two or three years.

🗝 SNC du Ch. Larrivet Haut-Brion, 33850 Léognan, tel. 05.56.64.75.51, fax 05.56.64.53.47 ☑ Y by appt.

🗝 Andros

CH. LARRIVET HAUT-BRION 1998★

□ 9 ha 25,000 🛢 150–199 F

88 89 90 96 |97| |98|

This 1998 white wine is in a resolutely classical style, despite a very noticeable touch of toast acquired from maturation both in the bouquet and on the palate. Note (as one of our tasters did) that the Sémillon comes through perfectly in this wine, which will be good to drink with cooked fish dishes.

🗝 SNC du Ch. Larrivet Haut-Brion, 33850 Léognan, tel. 05.56.64.75.51, fax 05.56.64.53.47 ☑ Y by appt.

CH. LATOUR HAUT-BRION 1997★

■ Cru clas. 4.9 ha n.c. 🛢 200–249 F

78 79 80 81 |(82)| |83| 84 |85| |86| 87 |88| 89 90 92 |93| |94| 95 96 97

Latour Haut-Brion is a neighbour of La Mission. Originally classified in 1855, it was taken over by the Woltners in 1953 before it joined Haut-Brion at the beginning of the 1980s. There is a fine terroir here, as this 1997 wine shows. Although its bouquet is as yet somewhat closed, it has enough ageing potential to open out. The palate, which is full and supported by substantial tannins, will ensure that it has a good future.

🗝 SA Dom. Clarence Dillon, B.P. 24, 33602 Pessac Cedex, tel. 05.56.00.29.30, fax 05.56.98.75.14, e-mail info@haut-brion.com

CH. LA TOUR LEOGNAN 1997

■ 5 ha 32,000 🛢

This vineyard is closely linked to the Château Carbonnieux, and with this vintage offers a delicately fragrant wine with many shades of fruit enhanced by a note of leather It develops pleasantly on a meaty, full-bodied palate. A wine which will be ideal to drink with coq au vin in two to three years.

🗝 SC des Grandes Graves, Ch. Carbonnieux, 33850 Léognan, tel. 05.57.96.56.20, fax 05.57.96.59.19, e-mail chateau.carbonnieux@wanadoo.fr ☑ Y by appt.

🗝 Perrin

CH. LATOUR-MARTILLAC 1997★★

■ Cru clas. 30 ha 102,000 🛢 150–199 F

79 81 (82) 83 84 85 86 87 88 |89| 90 91 92 93 94 95 96 97

With its Cabernet, Merlot and Petit Verdot vines, this vineyard, which has belonged to the Kressmann family since 1929, remains true to the Bordeaux traditions. So does its wine. Behind the velvety colour is a bouquet with exploding smoky notes and more gentle fruity aromas. The palate is full-bodied, elegant and substantial, and there is a sense of well-controlled wine-making and great respect for the terroir. The second wine from this vineyard is the **1997 Lagrave-Martillac Rouge** (70–99F), which is recommended.

🗝 Dom. Kressmann, Ch. Latour-Martillac, 33650 Martillac, tel. 05.57.97.71.11, fax 05.57.97.71.17, e-mail latour-martillac@latour-martillac.com Y by appt.

CH. LATOUR-MARTILLAC 1998★★

□ Cru clas. 10 ha 42,000 🛢 150–199 F

81 82 83 84 85 86 87 (88) 89 90 91 92 93 |94| |95| 96 97 |98|

The Kressmanns have been wine-merchants since 1858, and are past-masters in the art of white wine. Coming from a vineyard planted with Sémillons (one plot dating back to 1884), Sauvignons and Muscadelles, this wine shows fine aromatic complexity with notes of oak and fruit. The palate is supple, rich, fat, elegant and full-bodied, and leaves behind a memory of a remarkable wine which it would be a pity not to drink while it is young.

🗝 Dom. Kressmann, Ch. Latour-Martillac, 33650 Martillac, tel. 05.57.97.71.11, fax 05.57.97.71.17, e-mail latour-martillac@latour-martillac.com Y by appt.

CH. LAVILLE HAUT-BRION 1998★★★

□ Cru clas. 3.7 ha n.c. 🛢 250–299 F

81 82 83 84 |85| 87 |88| |(89)| |90| |93| |94| 95 96 |97| |(98)|

Located next to La Mission and Latour Haut-Brion, Laville is supervised by the

people from Haut-Brion and enjoys a similar degree of care and attention. This wine is fully in the spirit of the great Graves wines. It has many assets: a classy pale-yellow colour with gold glints, and a correspondingly complex bouquet combining citrus fruits (mandarins and lemons) and wax with pine sap, and ending on notes of Sauvignon. The rich, fat, perfectly balanced palate is as fine as the bouquet. Fresh and harmonious, this superb wine poses only one problem: the tasters could not decide when it will give the greatest pleasure – now, or in three or four years, or even longer.
🔑 SA Dom. Clarence Dillon, B.P. 24, 33602 Pessac Cedex, tel. 05.56.00.29.30, fax 05.56.98.75.14, e-mail info@haut-brion.com

CH. LE SARTRE 1998★

☐ 7 ha 50,000 🛢 50–69 F

92 93 94 95 |96| 97 |98|

This wine has been developed by the Carbonnieux team, and there can be no doubt that it has benefited from their know-how. It is lively, young, fresh, balanced and harmonious, and makes the most of its aromas of fruit, citrus fruit and vanilla.
🔑 GFA des Ch. Le Sartre et Bois Martin, 33850 Léognan, tel. 05.57.96.56.20, fax 05.57.96.59.19, e-mail chateau.carbonnieux@wanadoo.fr ☑ 🍷 by appt.
🔑 Perrin

CH. LES CARMES HAUT-BRION 1997★

■ 4.5 ha 25,000 🛢 150–199 F

80 82 83 85 |**88**| |89| |**90**| **91** 92 93 94 |95| **96** 97

Located at the heart of the Pessac commune, this little vineyard is still resisting urbanisation and protecting its lovely terroir, whose virtues are illustrated by this wine. It has an appealing dark-red colour, a finely developing bouquet (notes of leather and smokiness from very evident oak) before revealing the richness and complexity of its structure. An attractive wine which deserves to be kept for two or three years before being served with stewed duck.
🔑 Ch. Les Carmes Haut-Brion, 197, av. Jean-Cordier, 33600 Pessac, tel. 05.56.51.49.43, fax 05.56.93.10.71, e-mail chateau@les-carmes-haut-brion.com 🍷 by appt.
🔑 Didier Furt

CH. LESPAULT 1998★

☐ 1 ha 3,000 🛢 70–99 F

This little vineyard is next to Latour-Martillac. It can be proud of its 1998 wine, which has a pale-yellow colour with golden glints, and develops attractive aromas ranging from peaches to notes of toast. The palate is rich, intense, homogeneous and well-structured, and opens out into a long, fresh finish.
🔑 Dom. Kressmann, Ch. Latour-Martillac, 33650 Martillac, tel. 05.57.97.71.11, fax 05.57.97.71.17, e-mail latour-martillac@latour-martillac.com 🍷 by appt.
🔑 SC Bolleau

CH. MALARTIC-LAGRAVIERE 1997★

■ Cru clas. 14.23 ha 44,400 🛢 150–199 F

64 66 (70) 71 75 76 79 81 82 83 |85| |86| |88| |89| 90 **|91|** 92 **|93| 95** 96 97

Founded by a family of shipowners and naval officers, this vineyard still harks back to its origins with the famous three-masted ship on its label. The estate was bought into the Laurent-Perrier group by a Belgian industrialist, Alfred Bonnie, and is undergoing a reorganisation which the 1999 vintage will be the first to benefit from. Here we have the 1997 wine, which is still marked by oak, and combines suppleness and body thanks to high-quality tannins which will guarantee its development for three or four years.
🔑 SC du Ch. Malartic-Lagravière, 43, av. de Mont-de-Marsan, 33850 Léognan, tel. 05.56.64.75.08, fax 05.56.64.99.66, e-mail malartic-lagravière@malartic-lagravière. 🍷 by appt.
🔑 A.-A. Bonnie

CH. MALARTIC-LAGRAVIERE 1998★★

☐ Cru clas. n.c. 14,215 🛢 150–199 F

Although more modest in size than the red vine plots here, the white ones at Malartic are in no way a secondary vineyard. The very strong personality of this wine, made from 100% Sauvignon, proves the point. It is high in colour, and reveals a bouquet which is both intense and complex (flowers, peaches, blackcurrants, lychees and vanilla). The rich, balanced, harmonious palate is supported by a substantial structure which, together with a full, sappy finish, heralds a true wine for longer maturing which should be kept for at least two years.
🔑 SC du Ch. Malartic-Lagravière, 43, av. de Mont-de-Marsan, 33850 Léognan, tel. 05.56.64.75.08, fax 05.56.64.99.66, e-mail malartic-lagravière@malartic-lagravière. 🍷 by appt.

CLOS MARSALETTE 1998

☐ 0.7 ha 1,500 🛢 50–69 F

What a fine venture this little vineyard is. It is made up of well-chosen plots selected by three great enthusiasts: the Comte de Neipperg, who owns Canon-La Gaffelière, Monsieur Boutemy, the owner of Haut-

Lagrange, and Monsieur Sarpoulet, a chartered surveyor. The quality of the terroir (two gravelly hilltops) is apparent in its wines, such as this 1998 white. It is supple, fresh, and then becomes richer, with excellent substance and a complex bouquet (lychees, white peaches and exotic fruits).

SCEA Marsalette, 31, rte de Loustalade, 33850 Léognan, tel. 05.56.64.09.93, fax 05.56.64.10.08 by appt.
Boutemy-von Neipperg-Sarpoulet

CH. MIREBEAU 1997

■ 4.28 ha 16,000 100–149 F

Linked to the Château d'Ardennes (Graves), this is a strongly individual wine with a grape blend containing a high proportion of Cabernet Franc (45%). It is fine and elegant both in the nose and on the delicately structured palate, and its personality is noticeably marked by the grape variety. Just for the record, we are told that this vineyard once belonged to Alexandre Dumas's daughter.

Cyril Dubrey, 35, rte de Mirebeau, 33650 Martillac, tel. 05.56.72.61.76, fax 05.56.62.43.67 by appt.

CH. OLIVIER 1997

■Cru clas. 36 ha 160,000 100–149 F

82 83 |85| |86| 87 |88| |89| |90| 91 92 93 94 95 96 97

This medieval manor house is a stern feudal fortress which has taken on all the finery of a pleasant country seat. It is here that, in 1382, the military leader Bertrand du Guesclin is said to have been held prisoner on the orders of the Black Prince. Today it is the very symbol of the historic role played by the Pessac and Léognan region in the development of the Bordeaux vineyards. The wine here has always proved equal to its prestigious past. Starting with a deep, delightfully subtle colour, this vintage expresses its strong personality in its truffle aromas. Supported by fruit, it reveals silky, very rich tannins, leading to an elegant, concentrated finish which augurs well for an ageing potential of three to five years.

Jean-Jacques de Bethmann, Ch. Olivier, 33850 Léognan, tel. 05.56.64.73.31, fax 05.56.64.54.23, e-mail chateau-olivier@wanadoo.fr by appt.

CH. OLIVIER 1998

□Cru clas. 12 ha 57,000 70–99 F

82 83 85 86 88 89 90 91 94 95 |96| |97| |98|

Made from grapes grown on limestone-clay soils below the red vineyard, this wine is a blend of Sémillon (48%), Sauvignon (44%) and Muscadelle (8%). It has been matured on its lees in barrels with weekly stirring, and despite one slightly heavy moment is extremely pleasant owing to its suppleness, roundness and richness, which combine with the complexity and delicacy of the bouquet (exotic fruits, citrus fruits and butter) to create an interesting overall impression.

Jean-Jacques de Bethmann, Ch. Olivier, 33850 Léognan, tel. 05.56.64.73.31, fax 05.56.64.54.23, e-mail chateau-olivier@wanadoo.fr by appt.

CH. PAPE CLEMENT 1997**

■Cru clas. 30 ha n.c. 250–299 F

75 78 79 80 (81) 82 83 85 |86| 87 |88| 89 90 91 92 |93| |94| 95 96 97

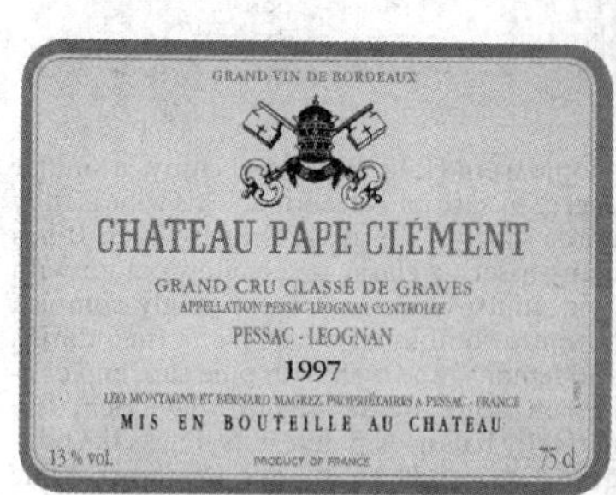

This vineyard, now enclosed within the town, is one of the last of the Bordeaux vineyards located around the outskirts in the Middle Ages, when it belonged to the Archbishops of Bordeaux. Once again it lives up to its past and its reputation with a full, complex wine whose bouquet does not merely delight with its fruity character, but also has other fine aromas to offer (very ripe grapes, spices, toast and even a note of honey). The palate is full-bodied, concentrated and round, and has the same elegance and power as the nose thanks to its silky tannins. A very harmonious finish confirms that the taster really is in the presence of a great wine, which should be kept for at least five years.

Ch. Pape Clément, 33600 Pessac, tel. 05.57.26.38.38, fax 05.57.26.38.39 by appt.
L. Montagne, B. Magrez

CH. PAPE CLEMENT 1998**

□ 2.5 ha n.c. 300–499 F

92 (93) 94 |96| |97| 98

Although it owes its fame to its red wine, Pape Clément is just as renowned for its white. Despite the fact that it is still somewhat reserved and has not yet found its definitive expression, the 1998 wine here reveals great aromatic richness: fruits, honey and caramel, all of which are enhanced by an attractive note of toast. With equally good structure and balance, this is a good wine for longer maturing.

Ch. Pape Clément, 33600 Pessac, tel. 05.57.26.38.38, fax 05.57.26.38.39 by appt.

CH. PONTAC MONPLAISIR 1997*

■ 10 ha 50,000 50–69 F

91 |92| 94 95 (96) 97

Far from limiting themselves to Haut-Brion alone, the Pontacs left their mark on the history of many vineyards, including this one.

The quality here is reliable, and this attractive 1997 wine is no exception. It is as powerful and complex on the palate as in the nose, and its full, long finish augurs well for an ageing potential of three or four years.
Jean et Alain Maufras, Ch. Pontac Monplaisir, 33140 Villenave-d'Ornon, tel. 05.56.87.08.21, fax 05.56.87.35.10 by appt.

CH. DE ROCHEMORIN 1997

■ n.c. n.c. 50–69 F

85 86 88 89 90 91 92 |93| |94| 95 96 97

Located on the highest hilltop in Martillac, this vineyard was once a fortified farm belonging to the Montesquieu estates. Here it offers a well-constructed wine with well-dosed oak which respects the personality of the bouquet. This has notes of toast and roasting which enhance the red-berry aromas without stifling them.
Vignobles André Lurton, Ch. Bonnet, 33420 Grézillac, tel. 05.57.25.58.58, fax 05.57.74.98.59, e-mail andre.lurton@wanadoo.fr by appt.

CH. DE ROUILLAC 1997

■ 7.5 ha 15,000 100–149 F

Once the property of Baron Haussmann, who created the great boulevards of Paris, this vineyard offers a 1997 wine with a light ruby colour. Its aromas are very much marked by the burnt quality of the barrel. Nevertheless, behind these empyreumatic notes the jury noticed a certain maturity in the tannins, which gives hope for what in other respects is a highly classical wine.
SCS Vignobles Lafragette, Ch. de Rouillac, 33610 Canéjan, tel. 05.56.89.41.68, fax 05.56.89.41.68 by appt.

CH. SEGUIN 1997

■ 3.75 ha 25,000 50–69 F

Coming from a little vineyard which was abandoned after 1945 and re-established in 1987, growing equal shares of Merlot and Cabernet Sauvignon, this wine is still somewhat closed, but its full-bodied, structured character will ensure that it develops well within three or four years.
SC Dom. de Seguin, chem. du Petit-Bordeaux, 33610 Canéjan, tel. 05.56.75.02.43, fax 05.56.89.35.41 by appt.

LES HAUTS DE SMITH 1998★★

□ 11 ha 15,000 70–99 F

Could this second label be out to rival the estate's Grand Vin? It is a remarkable achievement: a delightful 1998 wine with a pale, clear, brilliant colour, a harmonious bouquet of boxwood, citrus fruits and peaches, and a palate which is rich, fat and full of flavour, along with a controlled note of oak. 'It comes from good stock,' noted one juror, who recommended serving it over the next three or four years to your best friends.
SARL D. Cathiard, 33650 Martillac, tel. 05.57.83.11.22, fax 05.57.83.11.20, e-mail smithhautlafitte@smithhautlafitte.com by appt.

CH. SMITH HAUT LAFITTE 1998★★★

□ 11 ha n.c. 250–299 F

88 89 90 91 92 93 94 95 96 97 98

The reputation of Smith Haut Lafitte for white wines is already secure, and can only be consolidated by this 1998 vintage. The team, run by Daniel Cathiard and his oenologist Gabriel Vialard, have taken perfect advantage of the excellent climatic conditions of an exceptionally hot, dry month of August, and the result is a wine of great class. It has a powerful bouquet in which ripe Sauvignon blends in with an elegant oakiness, then develops an impressive structure with beautiful notes of overripening and crystallised oranges. A superb wine for longer maturing, which has complexity, good balance and length.
SARL D. Cathiard, 33650 Martillac, tel. 05.57.83.11.22, fax 05.57.83.11.20, e-mail smithhautlafitte@smithhautlafitte.com by appt.

CH. SMITH HAUT LAFITTE 1997★

■ Cru clas. 44 ha 110,000 250–299 F

61 62 70 71 72 73 (75) 80 82 83 85 86 87 |88| |89| |90| |91| 92 **|93| 94 |95|** 96 97

What with the return to hand-picked harvests in 1991 and the new vat-house (this year), the introduction of barrel maturation and the creation of a cooperage in the meantime, there has not been a single year without innovation at this vineyard. The investment has been worthwhile, as is shown by this wine, which has a lovely colour with dark purple glints. In addition to a fine, complex bouquet (ripe fruits, musk, hazelnuts and roasted almonds), it has a palate which is powerful from the beginning. Its well-extracted, harmonious tannins give it elegance and good ageing potential (four to five years). Another wine with good power and balance is the **1997 wine Les Hauts de Smith Rouge**, which is recommended. It will need to be kept for a year or two until the tannins fade.
SARL D. Cathiard, 33650 Martillac, tel. 05.57.83.11.22, fax 05.57.83.11.20, e-mail smithhautlafitte@smithhautlafitte.com by appt.

Médoc

Médoc occupies a place apart from the rest of the Gironde region, being virtually contained within the peninsula from which it gazes across the waters of the deep Gironde estuary. The Médoc and the Médocains may thus be seen as perfect illustrations of the Aquitaine temperament: they are both self-contained yet outward-looking. It is not unusual to find small family-run vineyards alongside grand, prestigious domains belonging to powerful French or foreign companies.

The Médoc vineyards (which represent only a part of the historically- and geographically-defined Médoc) occupy a strip more than 80 km (50 miles) long and 10 km (6 miles) wide. As a result, visitors can admire the great wine châteaux of the 19th century with their splendid, monumental wine stores and also make discoveries deep in the surrounding countryside. The terrain is very varied, offering flat, uniform landscapes around Margaux, hilly ridges towards Pauillac, and the entirely original world of the Bas Médoc, an unusual combination of terrestrial and maritime features. The area of the Médoc AOC covers about 14,890 ha (36,778 acres).

For those who enjoy investigating places off the beaten track, the Médoc is full of unexpected surprises. But its real riches lie in the gravelly terrain that slopes gently down towards the Gironde estuary. The soil is thin and poor in natural fertilisers, an excellent medium for the production of fine wines. In addition, the topography allows perfect drainage.

It has become usual to divide the Médoc into the Haut Médoc, from Blanquefort to Saint-Seurin-de-Cadourne, and the Bas Médoc, from Saint-Germain-d'Esteuil to Saint-Vivien. In the first area, six *appellations communales* produce the most famous wines. Virtually all of the 60 Crus Classés are from these appellations; however, five of them are labelled only as Appellation Haut-Médoc. The Crus Classés represent approximately 25% of the vineyard area, producing 20% of the wines and more than 40% of the income. In addition to the Crus Classés, the Médoc also produces a number of château-bottled Crus Bourgeois, which enjoy an excellent reputation. There are many Caves Coopératives in the Appellation Médoc and Appellation Haut-Médoc and also in three of the appellations communales.

A significant proportion of wines from the Médoc and Haut Médoc appellations is sold in bulk to shippers, who are responsible for selling and marketing the wines, which are sold under brand names.

Cabernet Sauvignon was the traditional Médoc grape but is now grown less than it was formerly; even so, it is still accounts for 52% of the whole vineyard area. At 34%, Merlot is the second most important grape; its supple wines are of excellent quality and develop quickly so they can be drunk when still young. Cabernet Franc, which gives wine finesse, is planted on 10% of the area. The Petit Verdot and Malbec varieties are also planted, although they do not play a big role.

Médoc wines enjoy an exceptional reputation; they are among the most prestigious red wines produced either in France or in the rest of the world. They are noted for their beautiful ruby colour that, takes on a tile-red hue with age, and by their fruity aromas blending the spicy notes of Cabernet with hints of vanilla from the new oak barrels. Their tannic structure is dense and full, although the wines remain elegant and soft, and their perfect balance means they age remarkably well, softening without becoming thin and gaining in bouquet and flavour.

Médoc

The whole of the Médoc vineyard, 4,740 ha (11,708 acres) has the right to the Appellation Médoc, although in practice it is used only in Bas Médoc (the northern sector of the peninsula, around Lesparre); the communes located between Blanquefort and Saint-Seurin-de-Cadourne may apply for the Appellation Haut-Médoc. In spite of this, production is significant, at 291,274 hl (7,689,637 gal) in 1999.

The Médoc and the Haut-Médoc appellations

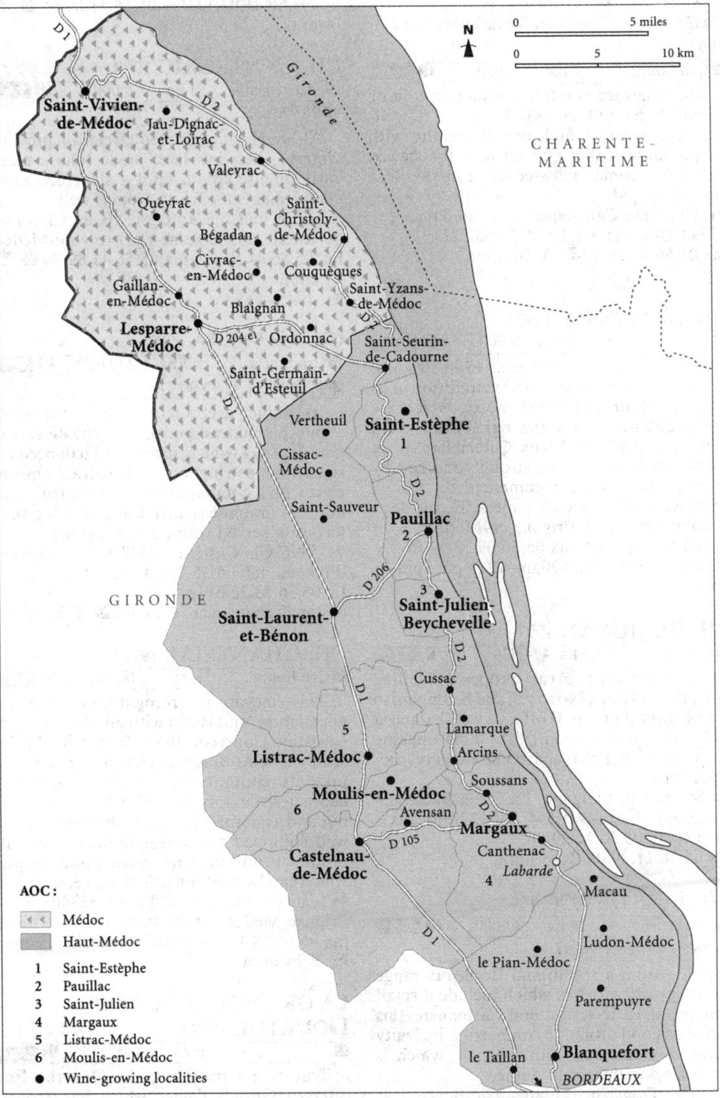

AOC:
- Médoc
- Haut-Médoc

1 Saint-Estèphe
2 Pauillac
3 Saint-Julien
4 Margaux
5 Listrac-Médoc
6 Moulis-en-Médoc
● Wine-growing localities

Noted for their intense colour, Médoc wines are made using a higher percentage of Merlot than those of Haut-Médoc and the Appellations Communales. The Merlot character makes itself felt in the fruity nose and round, mouth-filling flavour of these wines, some of which, grown on isolated, gravelly ridges, can develop great finesse and tannic depth.

CH. BELLEGRAVE

Cuvée spéciale Vieilli en fût de chêne neuf 1997

■Cru bourg. 2 ha 3,000 70–99 F

This vineyard is a fine production unit of some 18 ha (44 acres). It offers a well-balanced wine of high overall quality with supple tannins that go well with the stewed red-berry aromas released both in the nose and on the palate.

Christian Caussèque, 8, rue de Janton, 33340 Valeyrac, tel. 05.56.41.53.82, fax 05.56.41.50.10 Y by appt.

CH. DE BENSSE 1997*

■ 7.9 ha 6,600 30–49 F

Produced by the co-operative in Prignac, this wine adheres to the Médoc tradition in its intense colour and tannic notes, which are finely balanced with the oak. Their main label, the **1997 Les Vieux Colombiers**, is an equally well-made wine strongly marked by green peppers, and is recommended.

Cave Les Vieux Colombiers, 23, rue des Colombiers, 33340 Prignac-en-Médoc, tel. 05.56.09.01.02, fax 05.56.09.03.67 Y ev. day except Sun. 8.30am–12.30pm 2pm–6pm

CH. BLAIGNAN 1997

■Cru bourg. 85.66 ha 474,930 70–99 F

This vineyard is a vast property totalling more than 140 ha (346 acres) and belonging to the Mestrezat group. It offers a well-balanced 1997 wine with flavourful tannins opening onto a finish which is sharp but has good aromatic length.

SC du Ch. Blaignan, La Croix-Bacalan, 109, rue Achard, B.P. 154, 33042 Bordeaux Cedex, tel. 05.56.11.29.00, fax 05.56.11.29.01 Y by appt.

CH. BOIS DE ROC 1997

■Cru artisan 14 ha 90,000 50–69 F

85 **86** 89 90 **92** (93) |96| 97

Made from a traditional Bordeaux range of five grape varieties which include a small amount of Petit Verdot and Carmanère, this wine has good aromatic complexity. Its fruity notes combine well with the oak, which is perfectly dosed for this vintage.

GAF Dom. du Taillanet, Ch. Bois de Roc, 2, rue des Sarments, 33340 Saint-Yzans-de-Médoc, tel. 05.56.09.09.79, fax 05.56.09.06.29, e-mail boisderoc@aol.com Y ev. day except Sat. Sun. 9am–12 noon 2pm–6pm; cl. Jan. Feb.

Cazenave

BOIS GALANT 1997

■ n.c. 28,000 30–49 F

Produced under the brand name of the Union des Coopératives du Médoc, this oak-matured wine compensates for the slightly alcoholic quality of the finish by its fullness and suppleness.

Union des caves coop. Uni-Médoc, 14, rte de Soulac, 33340 Gaillan, tel. 05.56.41.03.12, fax 05.56.41.00.66 Y by appt.

CH. CANTEGRIC 1997

■Cru artisan 1 ha 6,000 30–49 F

95 96 97

Although it does not equal certain previous vintages, this wine is well made. It has a pleasantly intense colour, and a structure which complements the fruity aromas well.

GFA du Ch. Cantegric, 10, av. Charles-de-Gaulle, 33340 Saint-Christoly-de-Médoc, tel. 05.56.41.57.00, fax 05.56.41.89.36 Y by appt.

Joany Feugas

CH. CASTERA 1997

■Cru bourg. 63 ha 230,000 50–69 F

|88| |89| 90 91 92 95 96 97

Its name, architecture, and everything about this château underline its medieval origins. Its 1997 wine is supple and balanced but somewhat astringent, and has an unusual nose with a combination of spices, fruits and notes of graphite (pencil lead). It will give of its best if served young and decanted.

SNC Ch. Castéra, 33340 Saint-Germain-d'Esteuil, tel. 05.56.73.20.60, fax05.56.73.20.61, e-mail castera@chateaucastera.com Y by appt.

CH. CHANTELYS 1997*

■Cru bourg. 8 ha 48,000 50–69 F

This vineyard is a recognised pillar of the appellation, and is run with great panache by Christine Courrian, the wife of wine-broker Jean-François Braquessac. Once again it lives up to its reputation with a 1997 wine of very characteristic appearance. It has a dark colour and a complex bouquet, showing that it is well equipped for longer maturing. A full, tannic, aromatic wine with good length, which can be kept for five or six years.

Christine Courrian, Lafon, 33340 Prignac-Médoc, tel. 06.10.02.12.92, fax 06.56.58.17.20, e-mail jfbraq@aol.com Y by appt.

LA GRANDE CUVEE DE DOURTHE 1997*

■ n.c. n.c. 50–69 F

True to its tradition, the Dourthe firm offers a Grande Cuvée which has a dark-

urple colour and excellent vinosity, and eserves to be laid down (three or four years or this vintage). Its long finish needs to ecome rounder, but its mouth-filling, fruity, ull palate ensures that it will.
Dourthe, 35, rte de Bordeaux, B.P. 49, 3290 Parempuyre, tel. 05.56.35.53.00, ax 05.56.35.53.29, e-mail ontact@cvbg.com by appt.

CH. FONGIRAS

Cuvée élevée en fût de chêne 1997★

7 ha 40,000 50–69 F

This very reliable oaked wine from Producta lives up to expectations with its 1997 vintage. It has an attractive garnet colour and a bouquet of ripe-fruit notes, and onfirms its initial impression with a delightful combination of oak and fruit. It will be pleasant to drink in two to three years' time.
Producta SA, 21, cours Xavier-Arnozan, 3082 Bordeaux Cedex, tel. 05.57.81.18.18, ax 05.56.81.22.12, e-mail producta@producta.com by appt.

CH. FONTIS 1997

Cru bourg. 8.5 ha 35,000 70–99 F

This property was bought in 1995 by the on of the owner of Les Ormes Sorbet. It is ocated on a hill, and is in the course of being eorganised. The wine has a full, dark colour, a bouquet which harmoniously mingles oak and fruit, and a supple, round structure supported by well-blended tannins, all of which combine to leave an impression of good balance.
Vincent Boivert, Ch. Fontis, 33340 Ordonnac, tel. 05.56.73.30.30, fax 05.56.73.30.31 by appt.

CH. GAUTHIER

Pavillon Saint-James 1997★

3 ha 15,000 30–49 F

Made from a blend in Médoc style with 60% Cabernet Sauvignon, this is another characteristic wine. Both its structure, based on substantial tannins, and its long finish suggest that it should be kept for four to six years. Its fine, concentrated bouquet and structure augur well for a truly classical wine.
Pierre Jean, 33330 Saint-Christophe-des-Bardes, tel. 05.56.61.51.80, fax 05.56.61.51.90 by appt.
Christine Courrian

GRAND SAINT-BRICE 1997★

104.85 ha 76,666 50–69 F

After winning much praise last year, the co-operative in Saint-Yzans now offers a 1997 wine which will certainly need to be drunk while younger than its predecessor (two to three years from now), but will be extremely pleasant. It has a slightly developed ruby colour, is round but built on good tannins, and is long and aromatic, with delightful balance and elegance. The main wine here is the tenderly feminine **1997 Saint-Brice**, which is not oak-matured (30–49F), and is recommended for its fruitiness.
Cave Saint-Brice, 33340 Saint-Yzans-de-Médoc, tel. 05.56.09.05.05, fax 05.56.09.01.92 ev. day except Sun. 8am–12 noon 2pm–6pm

CH. GREYSAC 1997★

Cru bourg. 60 ha 480,000 50–69 F

82 85 **|86|** 87 **88** |89| **|91|** |93| |94| 95 96 97

This wine comes from a vast property of over 90 ha (222 acres), and the fact that its production is unlimited only adds to its interesting qualities – the elegance of its red colour with violet glints, its complex range of aromas combining red berries and toast, and its full, round, well-balanced structure.
SA Domaines Codem, Ch. Greysac, 33340 Bégadan, tel. 05.56.73.26.56, fax 05.56.73.26.58 by appt.

CH. GRIVIERE 1997

Cru bourg. 18 ha n.c. 70–99 F

92 93 **|94| 95** 96 |97|

This wine comes from a limestone-clay soil and is made from a blend of grapes using only 40% Cabernet Sauvignon to 55% Merlot, the remainder being Cabernet Franc. It has a classic dark-red Bordeaux colour, and a somewhat caramelised nose which is quite fruity and slightly crystallised. Well-balanced on the palate, it has a fresh, fragrant finish.
Les Domaines CGR, rte de la Cardonne, 33340 Blaignan, tel. 05.56.73.31.51, fax 05.56.73.31.52, e-mail cgr@vins-medoc.com ev. day except Sat. Sun. 8.30am–11.30am 1.30pm–5pm; groups by appt.

CH. HAUT-BALIRAC

Vieilli en fût de chêne 1997★

1.8 ha 7,000 30–49 F

In 1994, this co-operative producer chose to make wine from part of his 8.66-ha (21.2-acre) estate on his own account. The result is astonishing. Made from selected vines, it has been oak-matured, and although it is still very tannic, its complexity, aromas of green peppers, red berries, vanilla and toast, and also its structure ensure that it will keep for three to five years, enabling the whole combination to blend. It is also worth noting that it has that rare thing, a parchment label in the old style.
Cédric Chamaison, 2, rue du Maquis-des-Vignes, Oudides, 33340 Valeyrac, tel. 05.56.41.55.93 by appt.

CH. HAUT BRISEY 1997

Cru bourg. 9 ha 70,000 30–49 F

(86) 87 **88 89** 90 91 93 94 **95** 96 97

This is quite a new estate, founded in 1983 – a rare event in the Médoc. The wine comes from a rich, gravelly terroir and 14-year-old vines. Its extremely pleasant qualities include a lovely dark-red colour and a bouquet with powerful notes of leather, crystallised figs and spices. The palate is balanced and highly suitable for the vintage. Best drunk in a year's time.

SCEA Ch. Haut Brisey, Sestignan, 33590 Jau-Dignac-Loirac, tel. 05.56.09.56.77, fax 05.56.73.98.36 by appt.
Christian Denis

CH. HAUT-CANTELOUP
Collection 1997★

■Cru bourg. 6.25 ha 50,000 50–69 F

|94| 95 96 97

This wine comes from a property with more than 40 ha (99 acres) of vines, and is at present strongly marked by Merlot in its range of aromas. Nevertheless it is far from reaching its final state, which should become clear in two to three years' time. Note its beautiful ruby colour with mauvish-purple glints, which immediately delighted the jury.
SARL du ch. Haut-Canteloup, 33340 Saint-Christoly-Médoc, tel. 05.56.41.58.98, fax 05.56.41.36.08 by appt.

CH. HAUTERIVE 1997

■Cru bourg. n.c. 360,000 50–69 F

This wine was still very young at the time of the tasting, and the jury was not able to reach any definite conclusions. However, its silky, thick tannins, blood-red colour and good, complex finish augur well for its future.
Vignobles Rocher Cap de Rive, SCEA 3, Ch. Hauterive, 33340 Saint-Germain-d'Esteuil, tel. 05.56.73.05.49, fax 05.56.73.07.56

CH. HAUT-GARIN 1997

■Cru bourg. 6.8 ha 7,500 30–49 F

93 94 96 97

This vineyard adheres to the traditional diversity of the Médoc by growing Cabernet Sauvignon, Merlot, Cabernet Franc and Petit Verdot. As a result, the qualities of this 1997 wine are hardly surprising: delicate aromas of crystallised fruits and sweet spices, rich, full-bodied, pleasant tannins, and a supple structure.
Gilles Hue, Lafon, 33340 Prignac-Médoc, tel. 05.56.09.00.02 ev. day 9am–12 noon 2pm–7pm; Sun. by appt.

CH. LABADIE 1997★★

■Cru bourg. 9 ha 70,000 30–49 F

|(90)| 92 93 94 95 |96| **97**

For a vineyard which was on the list of Crus Bourgeois as early as 1932, this is a particularly distinguished vintage. Very typically Médoc with its ruby-red colour, this 199[7] wine has been matured in oak, but the woo[d] shows respect for the other aromas to give [a] powerful, complex bouquet. The palate [is] full, well-structured and enhanced by notes [of] chocolate, and confirms by its compositio[n] that it is a good wine for longer maturing, we[ll] worth a prominent place in the cellar, and wi[ll] be ready in six to eight years' time.
GFA Bibey, 1, rte de Chasse, Ch. Labadie, 33340 Bégadan, tel. 05.56.41.55.58, fax 05.56.41.39.47 by appt.
Yves Bibey

CH. LA CARDONNE 1997★

■Cru bourg. 75 ha n.c. 70–99 F

88 89 90 **91 92 93 94 95 96** 97

Established on gently sloping, sandy-grave[l] soils which face towards the estuary, this hug[e] property has numerous advantages, includin[g] a very high density of vines to the hectare. Like many others before, this vintage ha[s] qualities which can be traced to its fine situa-tion. It has all the classic features of the appel-lation: a strong colour, high-quality oak, and a substantial tannic stucture.
Les Domaines CGR, rte de la Cardonne, 33340 Blaignan, tel. 05.56.73.31.51, fax 05.56.73.31.52, e-mail cgr@vins-medoc.com ev. day except Sat. Sun. 8.30am–11.30am 1.30pm–5pm; groups by appt.

CH. LA CAUSSADE 1997

■ 8.84 ha 33,000 30–49 F

This wine is produced at the co-operative in Saint-Jean (Bégadan), and will give much food for discussion. Although some wine lovers may find the extraction a little over done, many will appreciate its bouquet of fruit and chocolate notes, its balance and very mature tannins which open out into a long finish.
Cave Saint-Jean, 2, rte de Canissac, 33340 Bégadan, tel. 05.56.41.50.13, fax 05.56.41.50.78 ev. day except Sun. 8.30am–12.30pm 2pm–6pm (Fri. 5pm); Sat. 8.30am–12 noon
Jean-Jacques Billa

CH. LA CLARE 1997

■Cru bourg. 20 ha 150,000 30–49 F

90 92 |94| 95 96 |97|

As ever, Paul de Rozières has sought to achieve balance with this wine, whose round-ness, simplicity and fine aromas of soft fruits make it most agreeable. 'A pleasant wine for such a difficult vintage,' noted one expert.
Paul de Rozières, Ch. La Clare, 33340 Bégadan, tel. 05.56.41.50.61, fax 05.56.41.50.69 ev. day 8am–6pm

CH. LACOMBE NOAILLAC 1997

■Cru bourg. 15 ha 100,000 50–69 F

This vineyard has a new, modern label, which is more in keeping with Jean-Michel Lapalu's character than the rather severe old one. Similarly pleasant is this 1997 wine, which is round and agreeably aromatic, with notes of blackcurrants, raspberry liqueur and flowers. It should be drunk now. If you visit the Médoc, you can find it at 1, rue du 19-Mars in Bégadan.

SC Ch. Lacombe Noaillac, Le Broustera, 33590 Jau-Dignac-Loirac, tel. 05.56.41.50.18, fax 05.56.41.54.65, e-mail info@les.trois.chateaux.com

CUVEE DE LA COMMANDERIE DU BONTEMPS 1997★

■ n.c. n.c. 30–49 F

This firm of *négociants*, run by John Kolasa, has produced good results with a difficult vintage. The wine has an opening bouquet which shows originality in its fruity notes accompanied (according to one of our tasters) by a slight hint of whisky. It is a truly classic wine with well-marked, very harmonious tannins, and is already pleasant to drink.

Ulysse Cazabonne, rte de Rauzan, 33460 Margaux, tel. 05.57.88.79.94, fax 05.57.88.36.54, e-mail ulys.c@wanadoo.fr

CH. DE LA CROIX 1997

■Cru bourg. n.c. 90,000 30–49 F

93 94 95 96 |97|

This wine is produced in considerable quantity. Made from 54% Cabernets, 45% Merlot and 1% Petit Verdot, it is supple, simple and pleasant with a roundness and delicate fruity aromas which give way at the finish to further notes of ripeness. From the same producer, but distributed by Sichel Coste de Langon, the **1997 Château Terre Rouge** (50–69F) is also recommended. Merlot is the dominant variety in this wine, which was matured in stainless-steel vats.

SCF Dom. de La Croix, 6, ch. de la Croix, Plautignan, 33340 Ordonnac, tel. 05.56.09.04.14, fax 05.56.09.01.32 by appt.

J. Francisco

CH. LAFON 1997★★

■Cru bourg. 7 ha 40,000 70–99 F

93 (95) 96 **97**

Once again Rémy Fauchey's dedication has produced good results. The bouquet of this wine combines notes of vanilla, toast and fruit, while on the palate the oak component blends harmoniously into the substantial tannic structure. Together they form an overall impression of fine quality and good ageing prospects. It should be kept for at least two or three years, and will be particularly enjoyed by lovers of empyreumatic flavours.

SCEA Lafon-Fauchey, 33340 Prignac-en-Médoc, tel. 05.56.09.02.17, fax 05.56.09.04.96 ev. day 9.30am–7pm

Fauchey

CH. LA HOURCADE

Vieilli en fût de chêne 1997★

■ 14 ha 110,000 30–49 F

With its hand-picked harvests and maturation in oak, this vineyard has travelled far from its cautious beginnings a few decades ago, when it was founded by the village postman. Starting with a lovely dark-red colour, this 1997 wine has a lot going for it: a good structure and agreeable aromas of red berries, green peppers and prunes. Very typical of the Médoc.

Gino et Florent Cecchini, 7, rue de Noaillac, Ch. La Hourcade, 33590 Jau-Dignac-Loirac, tel. 05.56.09.53.61, fax 05.56.09.57.53 by appt.

CH. LALANDE D'AUVION 1997★

■Cru bourg. 20 ha n.c. 30–49 F

The blend here of 60% Cabernet Sauvignon and 40% Merlot is well suited to the nature of the limestone terroir, and to the vintage. Once again the result is convincing. This 1997 wine has a beautiful colour with purple glints, then seems to hesitate between musky scents and notes of ripe grapes before revealing a substantial tannic structure on the palate which will enable the oak to fade. It has an ageing potential of six to eight years.

Christian Benillan, 3, rue de Verdun, 33340 Blaignan, tel. 05.56.09.05.52, fax 05.56.09.08.54 by appt.

CH. LALANDE VILLENEUVE 1997

■Cru artisan 8.21 ha 10,000 30–49 F

This wine has a limited production, and may disconcert some enthusiasts by its musky aromas. Many others will be delighted by its combination of a supple structure and a bouquet with a strong personality which will enable it to be kept for four or five years or drunk in the near future.

SCEA Lalande de Gravelongue, 19, rte de Troussas, 33340 Valeyrac, tel. 05.56.41.59.68 by appt.

CH. LA PIROUETTE 1997★

■Cru bourg. 4 ha 30,000 30–49 F

Yvan Roux, whose vineyard is located three kilometres (nearly two miles) from the Girard lighthouse which indicates the banks of the Gironde, has matured this 1997 wine in oak for 18 months. Despite a rather surprising finish on notes of menthol and eucalyptus, the wine developed well throughout the tasting. It has a brick-red colour, a bouquet of notes of green pepper, juniper berries and spices, and a balanced palate with light, well-blended tannins. Drink it now.

SCEA Yvan Roux, Semensan, 33590 Jau-Dignac-Loirac, tel. 05.56.09.42.02, fax 05.56.09.42.02 by appt.

CH. LA TILLE CAMELON

Elevé en fût de chêne 1997★

■ 14.38 ha24,000 30–49 F

This wine was developed at the Cave Saint-Brice, and bears the stamp of its dominant grape variety (Merlot) in the soft-fruit quality of its finish. A full-bodied, fragrant wine with plenty of body, it is already pleasant but will mature well over the next four to five years.

Cave Saint-Brice, 33340 Saint-Yzans-de-Médoc, tel. 05.56.09.05.05,

fax 05.56.09.01.92 ☑ 🍷 ev. day except Sun. 8am–12 noon 2pm–6pm
🔑 G. Courrian

CH. LA TOUR DE BY 1997★

■Cru bourg. 60 ha 500,000 70–99 F

82 83 85 86 |88| |89| **|90|** **|91|** |93| 94 95 **96** |97|

Famous for its beacon, an old lighthouse which overlooks the estuary, this vineyard offers a wine which could have done with a little more richness, but is nonetheless extremely well constructed and balanced. A pleasant note of originality comes out both in the nose, with its discreet aromas of roasted almonds accompanied by young fresh fruit, and on the palate, where the peppery tannins are quite firm but not immature. A good, classic, well-produced wine.

🔑 Marc Pagès, La Tour de By, 33340 Bégadan, tel. 05.56.41.50.03, fax 05.56.41.36.10 ☑ 🍷 ev. day except Sat. Sun. 8am–12 noon 1.30pm–4.30pm; groups by appt.

CH. LAULAN DUCOS 1997

■ 20 ha 6,000 30–49 F

88 |89| 90 91 92 |93| **96** 97

This wine has quite a limited volume of production. Dark and slightly developed in colour, it is marked by oak and reveals pleasant aromas of toast and red berries. It should soon become more supple, and is best drunk while fairly young.

🔑 SCEA Ch. Laulan Ducos, 4, rte de Vertamont, 33590 Jau-Dignac-Loirac, tel. 05.56.09.42.37, fax 05.56.09.48.40 ☑ 🍷 by appt.
🔑 Brigitte Ducos

CH. LE BERNARDOT 1997

■ 12.27 ha 30,000 30–49 F

This is the only Girondin vineyard operating under the twin flags of Japan and Scotland. Here it offers a wine with a very young cardinal-purple colour, and a nose of smoke, truffles and venison, which has real possibilities for development. The attack is tannic on a high-quality palate, with a very young finish on a liquorice note.

🔑 Fujiko and John Robertson, Ch. Gaudin, 33590 Vensac, tel. 05.56.09.57.94, fax 05.56.73.98.87 ☑ 🍷 by appt.

CH. LE BERNET 1997★

■ 8 ha 73,600 50–69 F

Coming from a gravel hilltop facing the estuary, this wine is not destined for longer maturing. Even so, its fruity bouquet and balance on the palate will make it very interesting to drink over the next two or three years.

🔑 La Guyennoise, B.P. 17, 33540 Sauveterre-de-Guyenne, tel. 05.56.71.50.76, fax 05.56.71.87.70
🔑 SARL Decas

CH. LE BOURDIEU 1997

■Cru bourg. 23 ha 180,000 50–69 F

88 89 |90| 91 92 93 |94| |95| 96 97

This is a fine property of almost 49 ha (121 acres). Here is a wine with an agreeable, full-bodied, well-balanced structure very much in the spirit of its predecessors. The oak-matured **1997 Château Bois Cardon** is also recommended – a second wine from Le Bourdieu which is distributed by the wine-merchants André-Quancard André.

🔑 Guy Bailly, Ch. Le Bourdieu, 1, rte de Troussas, 33340 Valeyrac, tel. 05.56.41.58.52, fax 05.56.41.36.09 ☑ 🍷 ev. day except Sat. Sun. 9am–12 noon 2pm–6pm

CH. LE GRAND SIGOGNAC 1997★

■ 5 ha 32,666 30–49 F

Although the storm on 27 December 1997 had little direct effect on the vines here, it did not entirely spare the vineyard, whose winery was blown away. The owner, Philippe Olivier, did not deserve such a misfortune, as is shown by the quality of this 1997 wine, which has an intense, aristocratic bouquet (crystallised fruits and venison), and right from the attack develops supple, persistent tannins which perfectly support a substantial, concentrated palate. It is distributed by the Etablissements Audy in Libourne.

🔑 Philippe Olivier, Ch. Le Grand Sigognac, 33340 Saint-Yzans-de-Médoc, tel. 05.56.09.06.38, fax 05.56.09.06.38

CH. LE REYSSE

Elevé en fût de chêne 1997★

■ 5 ha 32,000 30–49 F

|93| |94| |95| |96| 97

Patrick Chaumont created his brand in 1992, after spending several years in a co-operative. He has built a vat-store and a winery, and keeps a close eye on the state of his vines. This wine comes from a lovely gravel terroir and reflects the vintage. Its tannins and bouquet of mouthwatering notes of dried fruits, hazelnuts, vanilla and liquorice form an overall impression of suppleness and elegance. From the same producer, the **1997 Château Lassus** (30–49F) is recommended. This is a carefully made wine with something of 'the Médoc of yesteryear' about it.

🔑 SCEA Vignobles Chaumont, 7, rte du Port-de-By, 33340 Bégadan, tel. 05.56.41.50.79, fax 05.56.41.51.36 ☑ 🍷 ev. day except Sun. 9am–7pm

CH. LES GRANDS CHENES

Cuvée Prestige 1997★★

■Cru bourg. 7.16 ha 56,000 70–99 F

86 88 89 |90| 91 92 93 **|94| |95|** 96 **97**

This vineyard is a very reliable member of the appellation, and has been owned by Bernard Magrez since 1998. Here it offers its Cuvée Prestige, which has a beautiful, deep, fresh colour, a complex bouquet (vanilla, toast and fruits), a palate of high quality which is rich, thoroughbred and balanced, and good ageing potential (three to five years). All these qualities bear the mark of good stock and well-controlled wine-making.

🔑 Bernard Magrez, rte de Lesparre, 33340 Saint-Christoly-de-Médoc,

tel. 05.56.41.53.12, fax 05.56.41.35.69 Y by appt.

LES GRANGES DE CIVRAC 1997*

■ 16.92 ha 24,000 30–49 F

This Civracais vineyard, the property of the President of the co-operative in Saint-Yzans, has done well in a year with a reputation for being tricky. It has an agreeable bouquet (ripe fruit stone), and is well balanced, with unaggressive tannins and an elegant finish. A 1997 wine which promises to be enjoyable to drink for the next three years.

Cave Saint-Brice, 33340 Saint-Yzans-de-Médoc, tel. 05.56.09.05.05, fax 05.56.09.01.92 Y ev. day except Sun. 8am–12 noon 2pm–6pm

Jean-Paul Roland

CH. LES MOINES Prestige 1997**

■Cru bourg. 20 ha 150,000 50–69 F

86 88 89 90 91 92 |93| |94| (95) 96 97

Ever true to its tradition, this château offers a highly accomplished wine with a rich, substantial composition which is perfectly in keeping with the spirit of the vineyard. Right from the attack it shows a range of qualities which will make it a suitable accompaniment to many dishes, including red meats and also many types of game. Its full-bodied character will appeal to lovers of young wines, but it also has good keeping potential (four to five years).

SCEA Vignobles Pourreau, 9, rue Château-Plumeau, 33340 Couquèques, tel. 05.56.41.38.06, fax 05.56.41.37.81 Y by appt.

CH. LES ORMES SORBET 1997**

■Cru bourg. 19 ha 110,000 70–99 F

78 81 83 85 86 88 89 | (90) | 91 92 93 94 95 96 97

It may not claim to rival many previous vintages, but this 1997 wine is not short of assets and has a good future. The raw material is used to full advantage: starting cheerfully with a lovely red colour, it develops a thoroughbred bouquet (crystallised fruits, leather, undergrowth and a hint of stewed fruits), before showing by its fullness and concentration that it has a substantial body with delightful tannins. Best kept for four or five years.

Jean Boivert, Ch. Les Ormes-Sorbet, 33340 Couquèques, tel. 05.56.73.30.31, fax 05.56.73.30.31 Y by appt.

CH. LE TEMPLE Cuvée Tradition 1997

■Cru bourg. 15 ha 100,000 50–69 F

This wine is certainly not destined for longer maturing, but its structure, with good power at the finish, will make it extremely pleasant in a year or two when the fresh notes of red berries mature.

Denis Bergey, Ch. Le Temple, 33340 Valeyrac, tel. 05.56.41.53.62, fax 05.56.41.57.35 Y ev. day 8.30am–12.30pm 1.30pm–7.30pm

CH. LISTRAN 1997

■Cru bourg. 12 ha 40,000 30–49 F

Run from a lovely little charterhouse, this vineyard shows originality with a wine dominated by passionfruit in a bouquet which also reveals aromas of red berries and game.

Arnaud Crété, Ch. Listran, 33590 Jau-Dignac-Loirac, tel. 05.56.09.48.59, fax 05.56.09.58.70, e-mail arncrete@aol.com Y ev. day except Sun. 9am–12 noon 2pm–7pm

CH. LOUDENNE 1997**

■Cru bourg. 45 ha 233,900 70–99 F

(82) 83 85 86 88 89 90 91 93 94 95 (96) 97

The Union Jack ceased to fly in 1999, after a British presence dating back to the Victorian era. This 1997 wine retains a definite 'English' feel with its its substantial tannic structure ensuring good ageing potential. When the oak fades, the bouquet will reveal its finesse and complexity in full.

Ch. Loudenne, 33340 Saint-Yzans-de-Médoc, tel. 05.56.73.17.80, fax 05.56.09.02.87, e-mail brunot.bernet@udv.com Y by appt.

Jean-Paul Lafragette

CH. LOUSTEAUNEUF

Cuvée Art et Tradition 1997*

■Cru bourg. 8 ha 50,000 50–69 F

93 |94| (95) 96 97

This vineyard can be relied upon for quality, and emerges most honourably from the trials of the 1997 vintage with a wine made from a selection of old vines. Although the finish is simpler than in most years, it has a lovely colour, between purple and ruby, a complex bouquet combining notes of musk, undergrowth and red berries, a supple attack and good development on the palate.

Segond, Ch. Lousteauneuf, 33340 Valeyrac, tel. 05.56.41.52.11, fax 05.56.41.52.11, e-mail chateau.lousteauneuf@wanadoo.fr Y by appt.

MERRAIN ROUGE

Vieilli en fût de chêne 1997

■ 18 ha 100,000 50–69 F

As its name indicates, this wine has been matured in oak for 12 months. It has assimilated the oak component well, while at the same time remaining round and supple, which means it can be drunk while still young (in a year's time), when its fruity and wild aromas will be at their best.

Producta SA, 21, cours Xavier-Arnozan, 33082 Bordeaux Cedex, tel. 05.57.81.18.18, fax 05.56.81.22.12, e-mail producta@producta.com Y by appt.

CH. NOAILLAC 1997*

■Cru bourg. 43 ha 160,000 50–69 F

86 88 91 92 93 94 |95| 96 97

This vineyard is well served by an attractive gravel terroir, and is a recognised pillar of the appellation. It confirms its position with

this meticulously made wine, which has an intense, complex bouquet (red berries, toast and game). The body is lighter, characteristic of the vintage, and already round.
🗝 Ch. Noaillac, 33590 Jau-Dignac-et-Loirac, tel. 05.56.09.52.20, fax 05.56.09.58.75 ☒ Y ev. day except Sat. Sun. 8am–12 noon 1.30pm–5.30pm
🗝 Xavier Pagès

CH. PATACHE D'AUX 1997★

■Cru bourg. 43 ha 300,000 70–99 F

82 83 85 86 88 89 |90| 91 92 93 |94| 95 96 97

Belonging to a family which is firmly established in the Médoc and Haut-Médoc AOCs, this vast vineyard produces a large volume of high-quality wine. Starting with a lovely red colour, its 1997 vintage is pleasant in the nose, which has notes of vanilla and fruit, and on the palate, where the structure is round and tannic. An agreeable wine which should be kept for about three years.
🗝 SA Ch. Patache d'Aux, 1, rue du 19-Mars, 33340 Bégadan, tel. 05.56.41.50.18, fax 05.56.41.54.65, e-mail info@les-trois-chateaux.com ☒ Y by appt.

CH. DU PERIER 1997★

■Cru bourg. 7 ha 30,000 70–99 F

|89| |90| 91 92 |93| 94 95 96 97

Made from 50% Cabernet Sauvignon and 50% Merlot, this deep-red wine with crimson glints and straightforward tannins has an appealing nose marked by soft fruits and dark berries (blackcurrants and blackberries).
🗝 Bruno Saintout, EARL Ch. du Perier, 33340 Saint-Christoly-Médoc, tel. 05.56.41.58.32, fax 05.56.59.46.13 ☒

CH. PEY DE PONT

Vieilli en fût de chêne 1997★

■Cru bourg. 13 ha 8,000 30–49 F

Making the most of its varied range of limestone-clay and sandy-gravel terroirs, this vineyard offers a wine with a thoroughbred, complex bouquet pleasantly combining oak and fruits, and fine, structured tannins which suggest an ageing potential of four to five years.
🗝 EARL Henri Reich et Fils, 3, rte du Port-de-Goulée, Trembleaux, 33340 Civrac-Médoc, tel. 05.56.41.52.80, fax 05.56.41.52.80 ☒ Y ev. day 9am–12 noon 2pm–7pm

PIERRE CHANAU 1997

■ n.c. 180,000 30–49 F

Developed by the Dulong firm for Auchan, this is a typical wine with supple, round tannins which go well with a charming bouquet (red berries and almonds). An attractive wine which should be drunk while young.
🗝 Dulong Frères et Fils, 29, rue Jules-Guesde, 33270 Floirac, tel. 05.56.86.51.15, fax 05.56.40.66.41, e-mail dulong@mmkm.com ☒ Y by appt.

CH. PLAGNAC 1997

■Cru bourg. 30 ha 215,000 50–69 F

Offered by the Cordier group, this wine strikes a slightly unfortunate herbaceous note in the bouquet. However, that does not eclipse the fruity and spicy aromas, which combine with its tannins and chewiness to make a wine that will go well with an entrecôte à la bordelaise.
🗝 Domaines Cordier, 160, cours du Médoc, 33300 Bordeaux, tel. 05.57.19.57.77, fax 05.57.19.57.87 Y by appt.

CH. PONTAC GADET 1997

■ 10 ha 29,000 50–69 F

Although mainly producers in Bourg, the Briolais also keep this vineyard in Jau. Their 1997 wine is still somewhat dominated by oak, but is balanced and pleasant, and will be ready while still young, perhaps to be drunk with a vacherin cheese.
🗝 Vignobles Briolais, Ch. Pontac-Gadet, 33590 Jau-Dignac-Loirac, tel. 05.57.64.34.38 ☒ Y by appt.

CH. PREUILLAC 1997

■Cru bourg. 28.5 ha 7,000 50–69 F

Recently bought by the Mau family, this property enjoys a good reputation which this 1997 wine will certainly do nothing to harm. Although not a frontrunner destined for longer maturing, it has a good structure and an attractive bouquet which make it very representative of the vintage.
🗝 SCF Ch. Preuillac, 33340 Lesparre, tel. 05.56.09.00.29, fax 05.56.09.00.34 Y by appt.
🗝 J.-F. Mau

CH. RAMAFORT 1997

■Cru bourg. n.c. n.c. 70–99 F

From the same producer as the Château La Cardonne, this is a full wine which is still dominated by oak and will need to be kept for two to three years before its achieves its definitive expression.
🗝 Les Domaines CGR, rte de la Cardonne, 33340 Blaignan, tel. 05.56.73.31.51, fax 05.56.73.31.52, e-mail cgr@vins-medoc.com ☒ Y ev. day except Sat. Sun. 8.30am–11.30am 1.30pm–5pm; groups by appt.

CH. ROLLAN DE BY 1997★★

■Cru bourg. 14.23 ha 97,000 100–149 F

|89| 91 92 93 94 (96) 97

This vineyard employs an unusual grape blend with 70% Merlot dominant against a background of 20% Cabernet Sauvignon and a touch of Petit Verdot. This year it offers another highly attractive wine. Supported by a bouquet of fine complexity (vanilla and fruits – strawberries and raspberries), and high-quality tannins, it shows good ageing potential, and finishes on a note of great elegance. Once again, let us rejoice in the fact that Jean Guyon, a Parisian antique dealer, has succumbed to the charm of the Médoc.

🔑 SARL DGM Jean Guyon, 7, rte Rollan-de-By, 33340 Bégadan, tel. 05.56.41.58.59, fax 05.56.41.37.82 ☒ Y by appt.

CH. ROSE DU PONT 1997*

■ 1.19 ha n.c. 30–49 F

This wine has an appealing bouquet of spicy notes. Its palate suggests that it will be still more attractive when the tannins and the finish have become rounder.

🔑 Pierre Lambert, Courbian, 33340 Lesparre, tel. 05.56.41.36.04 ☒ Y ev. day 9am–7pm

CH. SAINT-HILAIRE

Vieilli en fût de chêne 1997*

■ 8 ha 60,000 30–49 F

This wine has a beautiful red colour, and develops pleasant aromatic notes of vanilla and menthol in keeping with its light structure. The tannins go into a long finish with a hint of tobacco. Although it is already pleasant to drink, this attractive wine will repay keeping in the cellar for five years.

🔑 EARL Adrien et Fabienne Uijttewaal, 13, chem. de la Rivière, 33340 Queyrac, tel. 05.56.59.80.88, fax 05.56.59.80.88 ☒ Y ev. day except Sat. Sun. 9am–12 noon 2pm–6pm

CAVE SAINT-JEAN

Le Grand Art 1997*

■ 10 ha 40,000 30–49 F

This brand is the star label at the Bégadan cellar, and has an firmly established reputation which will not suffer from this vintage. The wine makes a powerful, elegant first impression, both with its colour and bouquet of spicy and toast notes. It keeps its balance throughout, while at the same time allowing the tannins to assert their presence and complexity.

🔑 Cave Saint-Jean, 2, rte de Canissac, 33340 Bégadan, tel. 05.56.41.50.13, fax 05.56.41.50.78 ☒ Y ev. day except Sun. 8.30am–12.30pm 2pm–6pm (Fri. 5pm); Sat. 8.30am–12 noon

CH. SEGUE LONGUE 1997*

■ 12 ha 96,000 50–69 F

Coming from a grape blend consisting mainly of Merlot, this wine has a pleasant character. Its suppleness and roundness give free rein to its aromas, which are unusual and complex, developing from musky notes to exotic fruits.

🔑 SCV Segue Longue, 13, chem. de Lamale, 33590 Jau-Dignac-Loirac, tel. 05.56.09.57.28, fax 05.56.09.57.28 ☒

🔑 Monnier

CH. TOUR BLANCHE 1997

■Cru bourg. 27 ha 150,000 50–69 F

This Château Tour Blanche is distributed by the *négociant* Ed. Kressmann (CVBG). It blends equal shares of Merlot and Cabernet Sauvignon with 20% Cabernet Franc. The colour is fairly intense, and there is a nose of toast and fruit along with notes of musk. A supple wine with a fairly light palate, which is already pleasant to drink.

🔑 Ch. Tour Blanche, 33340 Saint-Christoly-de-Médoc, tel. 05.56.35.53.00, fax 05.56.35.53.29, e-mail contact@cvbg.com

🔑 Dominique Hessel

CH. TOUR CASTILLON 1997

■Cru bourg. 12 ha 12,000 30–49 F

The name of this wine conjures up an old castle which guards access to the Gironde. It has a very fresh colour, but will not need to be kept for long, despite its quality on the palate. A delicate wine, accompanied by toast notes of fine complexity.

🔑 EARL Vignobles Pierre Peyruse, 3, rte du Fort-Castillon, 33340 Saint-Christoly-Médoc, tel. 05.56.41.54.98, fax 05.56.41.39.19 ☒ Y by appt.

CH. TOUR HAUT-CAUSSAN 1997**

■Cru bourg. 17 ha 107,600 70–99 F

82 83 85 86 |**89**|(90)91 92 93 94 **95**(96)**97**

Here we have a terroir of high quality, a grower who both knows and loves his job, and a real family tradition. The success of this vineyard owes nothing to chance, and this wine is both typical of a good Médoc and remarkable for a 1997 wine. This is evident from its colour, a lovely purple with mauvish glints, and its bouquet, in which the oak does not overcome the fruit. The palate is tannic and promising without ever losing its finesse. The second label from this vineyard is the **1997 Château La Landotte** (30–49F), which is recommended.

🔑 Philippe Courrian, 33340 Blaignan, tel. 05.56.09.00.77, fax 05.56.09.06.24 ☒ Y by appt.

VIEUX CHATEAU LANDON

Sélection Les Meilleurs Cépages 1997*

■Cru bourg. 32 ha 160,000 50–69 F

This wine is the vineyard's selection vintage, and remains true to the label's tradition for quality. Following a lovely, deep, brilliant colour and a complex bouquet, the attack has a roundness which shows the character of the ripe, full, silky tannins.

🔑 EARL Philippe Gillet et Fils, 6, rte du Château-Landon, 33340 Bégadan, tel. 05.56.41.50.42, fax 05.56.41.57.10 ☒ Y by appt.

CH. VIEUX GADET

Elevé en fût de chêne 1997

■ 1 ha 6,600 30–49 F

This wine has quite a limited volume of production, but has a pleasant nose of red berries and a delicate palate, and may nonetheless have good ageing potential.

🔑 Thierry Trento, 1, chem. des Chambres, 33340 Gaillan-Médoc, tel. 05.56.41.21.98, fax 05.56.41.21.98 ☒ Y by appt.

CH. VIEUX ROBIN

Bois de Lunier 1997★

■Cru bourg. 14.25 ha 50,000 70–99 F

|82| 83|**85**| |86| 87|**88| 89 90 |91|** 93 **94 95 96** 97

Although it does not rival other vintages of this Cuvée Prestige, which undergoes malolactic fermentation in barrels (40% of which are new oak), this 1997 wine has a notably original bouquet of fine notes of white flowers, and a rich palate, which will make it delightful to drink straight away with game birds.

SCE Ch. Vieux Robin, 33340 Bégadan, tel. 05.56.41.50.60, fax 05.56.41.37.85, e-mail contact@chateau-vieux-robin.com Y by appt.

Maryse et Didier Roba

Haut-Médoc

Producing almost as much as the Appellation Médoc, with 246,819 hl (6,516,022 gal) in 1999 from 4,269 ha (10,544 acres), the Haut-Médoc wines have the edge on reputation, due in part to the presence of five Crus Classés grown within the AOC boundaries. Others are found in the six *appellations communales* contained within the Haut-Médoc area.

The first truly authoritative classification of Bordeaux wines was that of the Médoc in 1855 – that is, nearly a century before the other regions. This recognition arose directly from advances made in wine-growing in the Médoc area from the 18th century onwards. It was here in particular that the concept of quality came into being, along with new thinking about *terroirs* and crus, and an understanding that there was a relationship between the *terroir*, or specific vineyard, and the quality of a wine. Haut-Médoc wines are generous in character, although not excessively powerful, with real finesse on the nose and, in general, good ageing qualities. They are best drunk at cool room temperature, and go as well with white meat and poultry as with the lighter sorts of game. Drunk young and served chilled, they can also accompany some fish dishes.

CH. D'AGASSAC 1997★

■Cru bourg. 20 ha 128,000 70–99 F

In the first vintage carried out entirely under the banner of the current producer, this 1997 wine blends 50% Merlot with the Cabernets. Its round, clean, balanced structure brings out tannins which are blended into very good oak, and a fine aromatic expression with notes of blackcurrants, cherries and blackberries. Very representative of its appellation, it will keep for four or five years.

SCA du Ch. d'Agassac, 15, rue du Château, 33290 Ludon-Médoc, tel. 05.57.88.15.47, fax 05.57.88.17.61 Y by appt.

Groupama

CH. D'ARCHE 1997★★

■Cru bourg. 9 ha n.c. 100–149 F

90 91 92 9394 95 **96 97**

This vineyard, consisting of nine unbroken hectares (22 acres) on a beautiful gravel hilltop, confirms the progress it has made in recent years. This 1997 vintage has plenty of character with a lovely dark colour and the support of powerful tannins, and shows good ageing potential. At the same time its aromas are round and rich (game, cinnamon, cloves and jam, with a little note of camphor at the finish).

Mähler-Besse, 49, rue Camille-Godard, B.P. 23, 33026 Bordeaux, tel. 05.56.56.04.35, fax 05.56.56.04.59, e-mail france.mahler-besse@wanadoo.fr Y by appt.

CH. ARNAULD 1997★

■Cru bourg. 24.82 ha 150,000 70–99 F

82 83 85 (86)**88|** |89| 91 92|93| 95 96 97

This vineyard was once a priory, and is located opposite one of the best restaurants in the Médoc. Does that explain why its 1997 has such a mouthwatering character? Be that as it may, the concentrated, full-bodied richness of the palate, together with the aromas in the bouquet (ripe fruits, liquorice and spices) are sure to whet the appetite. Even so it will be best to keep this attractive wine for two or three years until the oak has had time to fade.

SCEA Theil-Roggy, Ch. Arnauld, 33460 Arcins, tel. 05.57.88.89.10, fax 05.57.88.89.20 Y ev. day except Sun. 9am–12 noon 2pm–6pm; Sat. by appt.

CH. D'AURILHAC 1997★★

■Cru bourg. 11 ha 90,000 50–69 F

This vineyard once again lives up to its reputation. Its 1997 wine blends Petit Verdot with 38% Merlot and 59% Cabernet Sauvignon and Cabernet Franc. It is almost black and richly fragrant, with notes of prunes, Morello cherries, juniper berries, liquorice and vanilla, and a palate which develops in the same spirit: concentrated, complex and

erfectly balanced, it shows by its power and ngth that it belongs to the tradition of very reat wines. Lay it down in the cellar and atch its progress for about ten years.
SCEA Ch. d'Aurilhac et La Fagotte, énilhac, 33180 Saint-Seurin-de-Cadourne, l. 05.56.59.35.32, fax 05.56.59.35.32 ☑ Y y appt.

CH. BALAC Cuvée Prestige 1997

■Cru bourg. 5 ha 40,000 50–69 F

2 83 85 86 88 89 90 91 92 93 94 95 96 97

This 17-ha (42-acre) vineyard was built in he 18th century, and now offers a wine which as been matured in new barrels. It bears the amp of oak in its burnt aromatic notes, but hey show respect for the other components, which go from cherries to spices and find their ull expression on the palate.

Luc Touchais, Ch. Balac, 33112 Saint-Laurent-Médoc, tel. 05.56.59.41.76, ax 05.56.59.93.90 ☑ Y ev. day 10am–7pm

CH. BARATEAU 1997★★

■Cru bourg. 15 ha 90,000 50–69 F

35 86|88| |89| |90| 91 92|93| |94| 95 96 **|97|**

This vineyard is always very reliable, and merges with honours from the trials of this ery tricky vintage. The wine has a lovely ark-red colour, then develops an interesting ouquet before showing itself fully on the palate, which is rich, silky, balanced and concentrated. A 1997 wine which is already very leasant to drink, but can also be kept for four r five years.

Sté Fermière Ch. Barateau, 33112 Saint-Laurent-Médoc, tel. 05.56.59.42.07, ax 05.56.59.49.91 ☑ Y ev. day except Sat. Sun. 9am–12 noon 2pm–6pm; cl. 25 Dec.– Jan.

Famille Leroy

CH. BEAUMONT 1997★

■Cru bourg. n.c. 450,000 70–99 F

86 88 89 90|93| |94| |95| 96 |97|

This vineyard is a vast property run from a beautiful château which combines the style of Napoleon III with the character of the Gironde. The quality here is very reliable, and so it comes as no surprise to see an attractive wine like this 1997 vintage, in which the soft and very evident tannins combine with the complexity of the bouquet to create an overall impression of good balance.

SCE Ch. Beaumont, 33460 Cussac-Fort-Médoc, tel. 05.56.58.92.29, fax 05.56.58.90.94, e-mail chateau.beaumont@wanadoo.fr ☑ Y by appt.

Grands Millésimes de France

CH. BEL AIR 1997★

■Cru bourg. 37 ha 249,000 50–69 F

|88| |89| |90| 92|93| 95 96 97

Coming from a Cussacais vineyard, this wine has great assets which will enable it to develop well as it ages. It has real intensity both in the colour and in the nose, and is supported by tannins which are still rather austere. It asserts itself in the substantial nature of its structure, and also in the charm of its finish.

Domaines Martin, Ch. Gloria, 33250 Saint-Julien-Beychevelle, tel. 05.56.59.08.18, fax 05.56.59.16.18 ☑ Y by appt.

Françoise Triaud

CH. BELGRAVE 1997★★

■5ème cru clas. 55 ha 260,000 100–149 F

82 **83 84 85 86** 87 88 **89** (90) **91** 92**|93| |94|** 95 **96 97**

This vineyard is a fine, large property whose reputation owes much to the quality of its terroir, which is always brought out to perfection in its wines. If proof were needed, taste this 1997 wine. It is well balanced, with a note of oak which remains discreet, and develops well-blended tannins which harmonise with the fine toast and spice notes of the bouquet and the rich flavours on the palate (coffee and cocoa) to form a complex, homogeneous overall impression. Crowned by a beautiful finish, this wine should be kept for three or four years. The second wine here is the **1997 Diane de Belgrave**. It is simpler, but fine and supple, and is recommended.

Dourthe, Ch. Belgrave, 35, rue de Bordeaux, 33290 Parempuyre, tel. 05.56.35.53.00, fax 05.56.35.53.29, e-mail contact@cvbg.com ☑ Y by appt.

CH. BELLE-VUE 1997

■Cru bourg. 7.1 ha 15,000 70–99 F

Petit Merlot represents 24% of the grape blend here, complementing Merlot (34%) and Cabernet. The wine has an intense dark-red colour and a powerful nose of fruit, musk and toast notes. It is quite concentrated on the palate, which is founded on a good structure and well-dosed oak. A uncomplicated finish suggests that it should be kept for two or three years.

SC de La Gironville, 69, rte de Louens, 33460 Macau, tel. 05.57.88.19.79, fax 05.57.88.41.79 Y by appt.

CH. BEL ORME

Tronquoy de Lalande 1997

■Cru bourg. 26 ha 150,000 70–99 F

Run from a château which is very much in keeping with the spirit of Girondin architecture, this vineyard offers a pleasant 1997 wine. It has agreeable little tannins which create an overall impression of good balance, with aromas of violets accompanied by a slight note of toast.

Jean-Michel Quié, Ch. Bel Orme, 33180 Saint-Seurin-de-Cadourne, tel. 05.56.59.38.29, fax 05.56.59.72.83 ☑ Y by appt.

CH. BERNADOTTE 1997

■Cru bourg. 30 ha 200,000 70–99 F

This vineyard owes its name to an ancestor of the Swedish royal family, and was owned by a Swedish industrialist until 1997, when it was purchased by the Château Pichon-Longueville Comtesse de Lalande. This wine

has spent 18 months in barrels, and is therefore still a little austere, since the tannins are very pronounced. Its colour and nose are appropriate and show good ageing potential.
🔑 SC Ch. Le Fournas, Le Fournas Nord, 33250 Saint-Sauveur, tel. 05.56.59.57.04, fax 05.56.59.54.84 Y by appt.
🔑 May-Eliane de Lencquesaing

BRULIERES DE BEYCHEVELLE 1997

■ 19 ha 110,000 🍷 70–99 F

Its status as the architectural jewel of the Medulian peninsula and as a Saint-Julien Cru Classé vineyard does not prevent Beychevelle from offering this Haut-Médoc, which has fresh, complex aromas and is supple and well composed on the palate.
🔑 SC Ch. Beychevelle, 33250 Saint-Julien-Beychevelle, tel. 05.56.73.20.70, fax 05.56.73.20.71, e-mail beychevelle@beychevelle.com ☑ Y ev. day except Sat. Sun. 9.30am–12 noon 2pm–5pm; groups by appt.

CH. CAMBON LA PELOUSE 1997*

■Cru bourg. 28 ha 180,000 🍷 50–69 F

Could this wine, which comes from Macau, have been influenced by the 'Margaux style'? It would be easy to think so, given the feminine character which is apparent both in its supple and round tannic structure and in the finesse of the finish. With a mouthwatering nose of notes of brioche, ripe fruits, fresh bread and vanilla, the overall impression is balanced and sufficiently well constructed to suggest that it will develop favourably for three to four years.
🔑 Jean-Pierre Marie, SCEA Cambon La Pelouse, 5, chem. de Canteloup, 33460 Macau, tel. 05.57.88.40.32, fax 05.57.88.19.12 ☑ Y by appt.

CH. CAMENSAC 1997**

■5ème cru clas. 75 ha 370,000 🍷 200–249 F

84 |85| |86| 87 |88| 92 |94| 95 (96) (97)

Camensac here proves it can take the more difficult years in its stride. The colour and bouquet clearly show that this is a powerful, complex wine. While the palate tells the same story, it does not merely confirm the initial impression but goes further and develops the elegant aromas with their notes of sweet spices, which are in keeping with the silky quality of the tannins. A round, well-structured wine, which is already pleasant to drink but also has good ageing potential (four years or more). The second wine here is the **1997 La Closerie de Camensac** (170,000 bottles, 100–149F). It is simpler and also supple, and is recommended.
🔑 Ch. Camensac, rte de Saint-Julien, B.P. 9, 33112 Saint-Laurent-Médoc, tel. 05.56.59.41.69, fax 05.56.59.41.73 ☑ Y by appt.

CH. CANTEMERLE 1997**

■5ème cru clas. 87 ha 300,000 🍷 100–149 F

81 82 83 (85) 86 87 |88| |(89)| |90| |91| 92 |93| |94| 9
96 97

This vineyard was once a powerful lord's domain, and the ruins of the first château are hidden among the vines. It lives up to its past and its classification with attractive wines such as this 1997 vintage. In the nose there are intense notes of smoke and toast which show the influence of oak. Nevertheless the palate is sufficiently substantial to assimilate the oak and give an overall impression of balance, harmony and aromatic richness (crystallised fruits). It promises to keep very well. A second wine, the **1997 Les Allées de Cantemerle** (70–99F), is recommended. 'This is a traditional Médoc,' noted the jury.
🔑 SC Ch. Cantemerle, 33460 Macau, tel. 05.57.97.02.82, fax 05.57.97.02.84, e-mail cantemerle@cantemerle.com ☑ Y by appt.

DOM. DE CARTUJAC 1997

■Cru paysan n.c. 30,000 🍷 50–69 F

This wine bears the name of Cru Paysan with modesty and pride, and shows genuine rusticity. Its structure indicates a high level of extraction, and its intense Cabernet bouquet (green peppers, ripe fruits, prunes and birthwort) needs a few more years of ageing to become fully open.
🔑 Bruno Saintout, SCEA de Cartujac, 20, Cartujac, 33112 Saint-Laurent-Médoc, tel. 05.56.59.91.70, fax 05.56.59.46.13 ☑ Y by appt.

CH. CHARMAIL 1997***

■Cru bourg. 22 ha 110,000 🍷 70–99 F

88 89 90 91 **92** 93 **94** 95 (96) **97**

This vineyard once again bears witness to the excellence of the Cadournais terroirs, notably those overlooking the Gironde. Its 1997 wine reveals ambitions for longevity

THE 1855 CLASSIFICATION REVIEWED IN 1973

PREMIERS CRUS (FIRST GROWTHS)
Château Lafite-Rothschild (Pauillac)
Château Latour (Pauillac)
Château Margaux (Margaux)
Château Mouton-Rothschild (Pauillac)
Château Haut-Brion (Pessac-Léognan)

SECONDS CRUS (SECOND GROWTHS)
Château Brane-Cantenac (Margaux)
Château Cos-d'Estournel (Saint-Estèphe)
Château Ducru-Beaucaillou (Saint-Julien)
Château Durfort-Vivens (Margaux)
Château Gruaud-Larose (Saint-Julien)
Château Lascombes (Margaux)
Château Léoville-Barton (Saint-Julien)
Château Léoville-Las-Cases (Saint-Julien)
Château Léoville-Poyferré (Saint-Julien)
Château Montrose (Saint-Estèphe)
Château Pichon-Longueville-Baron (Pauillac)
Château Pichon-Longueville Comtesse-de-Lalande (Pauillac)
Château Rauzan-Ségla (Margaux)
Château Rauzan-Gassies (Margaux)

TROISIÈMES CRUS (THIRD GROWTHS)
Château Boyd-Cantenac (Margaux)
Château Cantenac-Brown (Margaux)
Château Calon-Ségur (Saint-Estèphe)
Château Desmirail (Margaux)
Château Ferrière (Margaux)
Château Giscours (Margaux)
Château d'Issan (Margaux)
Château Kirwan (Margaux)
Château Lagrange (Saint-Julien)
Château La Lagune (Haut-Médoc)
Château Langoa (Saint-Julien)
Château Malescot-Saint-Exupéry (Margaux)
Château Marquis d'Alesme-Becker (Margaux)
Château Palmer (Margaux)

QUATRIÈMES CRUS (FOURTH GROWTHS)
Château Beychevelle (Saint-Julien)
Château Branaire-Ducru (Saint-Julien)
Château Duhart-Milon-Rothschild (Pauillac)
Château Lafon-Rochet (Saint-Estèphe)
Château Marquis-de-Terme (Margaux)
Château Pouget (Margaux)
Château Prieuré-Lichine (Margaux)
Château Saint-Pierre (Saint-Julien)
Château Talbot (Saint-Julien)
Château La Tour-Carnet (Haut-Médoc)

CINQUIÉMES CRUS (FIFTH GROWTHS)
Château d'Armailhac (Pauillac)
Château Batailley (Pauillac)
Château Belgrave (Haut-Médoc)
Château Camensac (Haut-Médoc)
Château Cantemerle (Haut-Médoc)
Château Clerc-Milon (Pauillac)
Château Cos-Labory (Saint-Estèphe)
Château Croizet-Bages (Pauillac)
Château Dauzac (Margaux)
Château Grand-Puy-Ducasse (Pauillac)
Château Grand-Puy-Lacoste (Pauillac)
Château Haut-Bages-Libéral (Pauillac)
Château Haut-Batailley (Pauillac)
Château Lynch-Bages (Pauillac)
Château Lynch-Moussas (Pauillac)
Château Pédesclaux (Pauillac)
Château Pontet-Canet (Pauillac)
Château du Tertre (Margaux)

THE SAUTERNES CRUS CLASSÉS OF 1855

PREMIER CRU SUPÉRIEUR (SUPERIOR FIRST GROWTH)
Château d'Yquem

PREMIERS CRUS (FIRST GROWTHS)
Château Climens
Château Coutet
Château Guiraud
Château Lafaurie-Peyraguey
Château La Tour-Blanche
Clos Haut-Peyraguey
Château Rabaud-Promis
Château Rayne-Vigneau
Château Rieussec
Château Sigalas-Rabaud
Château Suduiraut

SECONDS CRUS (SECOND GROWTHS)
Château d'Arche
Château Broustet
Château Caillou
Château Doisy-Daëne
Château Doisy-Dubroca
Château Doisy-Védrines
Château Filhot
Château Lamothe (Despujols)
Château Lamothe (Guignard)
Château de Malle
Château Myrat
Château Nairac
Château Romer
Château Romer-Du-Hayot
Château Suau

with an impressively deep colour, and has clearly spent 12 months in the barrel. The oak is of high quality, and blends in with a fine balance between its roundness and the tannins to produce a magnificent palate whose aromatic character (leather and tobacco accompanied by the presence of grapes) is prolonged by a lengthy, powerful finish. A great wine perfectly in the spirit of Bordeaux, which should be kept carefully in the cellar for seven or eight years, if not longer.
🔑 Ch. Charmail, 33180 Saint-Seurin-de-Cadourne, tel. 05.56.59.70.63, fax 05.56.59.39.20 ☑ 🍷 by appt.
🔑 Sèze

L'ERMITAGE DE CHASSE-SPLEEN 1997★

■ 22 ha n.c. 50–69 F

This wine belongs to the Château Chasse-Spleen, and comes from young, Grand Cru vines and others planted in the Haut-Médoc area. Not only does it develop a delightful, triumphantly fruity bouquet, it also shows good presence on the palate, whose balanced character helps to bring out very harmonious tannins which continue into a long finish. Best drunk in the next four years.
🔑 C. Villars, Ch. Chasse-Spleen, 33480 Moulis-en-Médoc, tel. 05.56.58.02.37, fax 05.57.88.84.40, e-mail chasse-spleen@vins-bordeaux.fr 🍷 by appt.

CH. CISSAC 1997★

■ Cru bourg. 82 ha 240,000 100–149 F

This wine is heir to a family tradition which goes back 130 years. It shows its personality not only in its beautiful colour, but also in a delightful bouquet in which ripe fruits combine with vanilla, after which it develops round, silky tannins enhanced by well-dosed oak. A second wine, the *1997 Reflets de Cissac* (50–69F), is recommended.
🔑 Domaines Vialard, Ch. Cissac, 33250 Cissac-Médoc, tel. 05.56.59.58.13, fax 05.56.59.55.67 ☑ 🍷 ev. day except Sat. Sun. 9am–12 noon 2pm–5pm

CH. CITRAN 1997★★

■ Cru bourg. 79 ha n.c. 70–99 F

87 **|88| |89|** (90) 91 92 **|93| 94** (95) **96 97**

Citran owes a great deal to a Puerto Rican planter called Clauzel, who founded the estate in the 19th century. Even so, without the important recent contribution of the Japanese group Touko Haus, and now that of Merlaut Villars, it would not be possible to enjoy fine wines such as this 1997 vintage, which fully lives up to the promise of its very beautiful colour. It has a very elegant bouquet with notes of toast, then reveals a concentration, substance and balance which leave one in no doubt about its potential to become a great wine in five to six years' time. Although it does not have the same meatiness as its big brother, the **1997 Moulins de Citran** is recommended (the price shown is a wine-merchant's price).
🔑 SA Ch. Citran, 33480 Avensan, tel. 05.56.58.21.01, fax 05.57.88.84.60, e-mail chasse-spleen@vins-bordeaux.fr 🍷 by appt.

CH. CLEMENT-PICHON 1997

■ Cru bourg. 25 ha 120,000 70–99 F

Despite coming from a vineyard famous for its château, built in the Renaissance style in 1881, this wine is more reminiscent of a solid medieval building thanks to its structure, which as yet is austere. Its substance and bouquet have good complexity (musky and toast notes), and suggest that it should be kept for a while.
🔑 Clément Fayat, 50, av. du Château-Pichon, 33290 Parempuyre, tel. 05.56.35.23.79, fax 05.56.35.85.23, e-mail info@vignobles.fayat-group.com ☑ 🍷 ev. day except Sat. Sun. 8am–12 noon 2pm–6pm

CH. COLOMBE PEYLANDE 1997

■ 3 ha 23,000 30–49 F

This little Cussacais property is always reliable, and now offers a wine with a still somewhat timid bouquet, with notes of dark, ripe berries, but a promisingly substantial tannic structure. The Cuvée Spéciale in honour of the estate's founder is the **1997 Aïeul Léontin** (70–99F), which is also recommended.
🔑 EARL Dedieu-Benoit, 6, chem. des Vignes, 33460 Cussac-Fort-Médoc, tel. 05.56.58.93.08, fax 05.57.88.50.81 ☑ 🍷 by appt.

CH. CONSTANT LESQUIREAU 1997

■ Cru bourg. n.c. 35,466 30–49 F

Distributed by Sichel-Coste, this wine has a lovely, fairly intense dark-red colour, but is still somewhat severe; nonetheless its rich bouquet of fruit and truffle notes, as well as its balanced tannins, will mean that it is ready to drink in one to two years' time as an accompaniment to roast red meats.
🔑 Maison Sichel-Coste, 8, rue de la Poste, 33210 Langon, tel. 05.56.63.50.52, fax 05.56.63.42.28

CH. CORCONNAC 1997

■ Cru bourg. 7.5 ha 17,000 50–69 F

As well as producing wine at Saint-Julien, the Pairaults also keep vines at Saint-Laurent which have yielded this wine blending 35% Merlot with Cabernet Sauvignon. Its ruby

colour with shades of purple heralds a nose in which stewed fruits mingle with green peppers and notes of vanilla. The tannins are still somewhat arid, which means that the wine will need to be kept for two or three years.
Ch. Corconnac, 33112 Saint-Laurent-Médoc, tel. 05.56.59.93.04,
fax 05.56.59.46.12 Y by appt.
F. et Ph. Pairault

CH. COUFRAN 1997*

Cru bourg. 76 ha 500,000 70-99 F

82 83 85 86 88 89 90 91 92 93 94 |95| 96 97

This château is the Miailhe family's main Cadournais vineyard, and also its standard bearer: a role carried off with style by this 1997 wine, whose not very typically Médoc blend combines 85% Merlot with Cabernet. Its bouquet of fine silky notes gives a discreet amount of room to oak. From the beginning the palate is powerful, with a substantial structure which shows its firmness, although not to excess, and a flavourful finish. An attractive wine which should be kept for three or four years.
SCA Ch. Coufran, 33180 Saint-Seurin-de-Cadourne, tel. 05.56.59.31.02,
fax 05.56.81.32.35 Y by appt.

CH. DILLON 1997

Cru bourg. 33.6 ha 200,000 50-69 F

82 83 85 (86) 87 88 89 |90| 91 92 93 |94| 95 96 |97|

Located just outside Bordeaux, this vineyard now houses a large school of wine-making whose buildings were severely affected by the storm of December 1999. Although the structure of its 1997 wine does not rival that of other vintages, it has pleasant tannic support which combines delightfully with the fruity aromas in the nose to give a wine which will be agreeable to drink over the next two or three years.
Lycée agricole de Blanquefort, Ch. Dillon, 33290 Blanquefort,
tel. 05.56.95.39.94, fax 05.56.95.36.75 Y by appt.
Ministère de l'Agriculture

FORT DU ROY Le Grand Art 1997**

5 ha 20,000 50-69 F

This co-operative is run by a group of 18 Cussacais wine-makers, and enjoys a solid reputation for quality which will not be damaged by this 1997 wine. It is fruity, round, supple, full-bodied and supported by silky tannins, and will give of its best in two to three years' time.
SCA les Viticulteurs du Fort-Médoc, 105, av. du Haut-Médoc, 33460 Cussac-Fort-Médoc, tel. 05.56.58.92.85,
fax 05.56.58.92.86 Y ev. day except Sun. 9.30am–12.30pm 2pm–6pm

CH. DE GIRONVILLE 1997*

Cru bourg. 9.2 ha 70,000 50-69 F

This vineyard was probably a Gallo-Roman villa and then a fortified castle. In the past it was a vast estate of over 150 ha (371 acres), and although it is of more modest size today, it nonetheless develops attractive wines such as this 1997 vintage. It has plenty of elegance, both in the first impression created by its brilliant, strong colour, and in its development on a well-structured palate. From the same vineyard, the **Belle Vue** (70–99F) is recommended.
SC de La Gironville, 69, rte de Louens, 33460 Macau, tel. 05.57.88.19.79,
fax 05.57.88.41.79 Y by appt.

CH. GRANDIS 1997*

Cru bourg. 9.6 ha 40,000 50-69 F

88 89 90 91 92 93 95 96 97

This vineyard takes its name from Dutch people who came to the Médoc to set up polders. This 1997 vintage is a very classic, well-constructed wine which suggests, both in the nose and on the palate, that the grapes were harvested very ripe. It is supple and round, with a fruity finish, and should be drunk over the next three to four years.
F. J. Vergez, Ch. Grandis, 33180 Saint-Seurin-de-Cadourne, tel. 05.56.59.31.16,
fax 05.56.59.39.85 Y by appt.

DOM. GRAND LAFONT 1997*

Cru artisan 4 ha 15,000 50-69 F

82 85 86 88 89 90 91 |93| |94| 95 96 |97|

The hand-picked harvests here are carried out by the students at the school in Blanquefort who are preparing to take their vocational certificate in wine-making. Great attention is paid to the quality of the grapes. The label carries the name of the estate, which has become more and more rare in the Médoc, and the wine itself is extremely pleasant, not only in its bouquet of fruity notes alongside vanilla, but also on the palate, which is full, aromatic, supple and well-equipped for an ageing period of three to four years.
Lavanceau, Dom. Grand Lafont, 33290 Ludon-Médoc, tel. 05.57.88.44.31,
fax 05.57.88.44.31 Y by appt.

CH. GUGES 1997*

0.76 ha 3,200 70-99 F

Coming from a tiny vineyard of 1.5 ha (3.7 acres), this wine successfully combines oak with the raw material to create a highly pleasant overall impression due also to its fine tannins and bouquet of fruity and spicy notes.
Georges-Claude Gugès et Fils, Ch. Gugès, 29, rue de la Croix-des-Gunes, 33250 Cissac-Médoc, tel. 05.56.59.58.04,
fax 05.56.59.56.19 Y by appt.

CH. GUITTOT-FELLONNEAU 1997*

Cru artisan 3.8 ha 16,000 30-49 F

Despite its modest size, this vineyard enjoys the rare luxury of an enormous park, which shows that they know how to live well in this rural spot. They also know how to work on their vineyard, as is clear from the qualities of this 1997 wine: a dark colour, a thoroughbred bouquet (leather and oak), a rich, full-bodied and tannic palate, and a substantial finish. A fine achievement, which should be kept in the cellar for two to four years.

Guy Constantin, Ch. Guittot-Fellonneau, 33460 Macau, tel. 05.57.88.47.81, fax 05.57.88.09.94 by appt.

CH. HAUT-BELLEVUE 1997*

Cru artisan 7 ha 38,000 30–49 F

Although it does not pretend to the status of a Cru Artisan, this property offers a substantial wine with a lovely ruby colour and a bouquet of redcurrant and spice notes. Its mouth-filling quality on the palate, where the structure is based on fine, well-blended tannins, will make it a good accompaniment to roast duck.

Alain Roses, EARL Haut-Bellevue, 10, chem. des Calinottes, 33460 Lamarque, tel. 05.56.58.91.64, fax 05.57.88.50.64 by appt.

CH. HAUT-BREGA

Vieilli en fût de chêne 1997

Cru artisan 8 ha 48,000 30–49 F

Although it may disconcert some wine-lovers by its strong, musky aromas, this full, rich wine deserves to be kept for a while, since its powerful tannic structure will enable it to improve as it develops. 'I like it, but it is unusual,' wrote one taster (who is himself often criticised). This is a wine for the informed wine-lover.

Joseph Ambach, 16, rue des Frères-Razeau, 33180 Saint-Seurin-de-Cadourne, tel. 05.56.59.70.77, fax 05.56.59.62.50 ev. day 10am–6pm

CH. LACOUR JACQUET 1997*

5 ha 35,000 30–49 F

89 |90| 91 92 93 94 |95| 96 97

How people take to this wine will depend largely on their wine background, and on current fashions and tastes. Its powerful oak content ensures that it will not be unanimously praised by wine-lovers any more than it was by the jury. Nevertheless, the density of the structure and the quality of the bouquet should inspire enough confidence to let it develop for two or three years.

GAEC Lartigue, 70, av. du Haut-Médoc, 33460 Cussac-Fort-Médoc, tel. 05.56.58.91.55, fax 05.56.58.94.82 by appt.

CH. LA CROIX MARGAUTOT 1997

n.c. 38,000 30–49 F

Marcel and Christian Quancard are wine-merchants at Carbon-Blanc, and also owners at Cissac, where this wine comes from. It needs to become rounder, but is already showing a character which will assert itself in two years' time. At present it has a good nose of spices and ripe fruits, and the tannins are well balanced.

Cheval Quancard, La Mouline, 33560 Carbon-Blanc, tel. 05.57.77.88.88, fax 05.57.77.88.99 by appt.

CH. LA FAGOTTE 1997*

Cru bourg. 5.1 ha 40,000 50–69

This wine comes from the same producer a the Château d'Aurilhac, and is an equal blen of Cabernet Sauvignon and Merlot. It cuts fine figure, both in its bouquet of elega notes of liquorice and dark berries, and on th palate, where its substantial tannic structu suggests that it should be kept for three c four years.

SCEA Ch. d'Aurilhac et La Fagotte, Sénilhac, 33180 Saint-Seurin-de-Cadourne, tel. 05.56.59.35.32, fax 05.56.59.35.32 by appt.

CH. LA HOURINGUE 1997

Cru bourg. 28 ha 110,000 50–69

This vineyard is established on two grav hilltops at Macau, and is worked by the sam team. The 1997 wine is simple but pleasant i its nose of leather and spice notes. An agre able, well-composed wine with evident bu unaggressive tannins.

SAE Ch. Giscours, 10, rte de Giscours, Labarde, 33460 Margaux, tel. 05.57.97.09.09, fax 05.57.97.09.00, e-mail giscours@château-giscours.fr by appt.

CH. LA LAGUNE 1997

3ème cru clas. n.c. n.c. 100–149

75 78 |81| |82| |83| |85| |86| 87 **88** **(89)** **90** |91| |92| 9 **94 95 96** 97

This vineyard is run from a beautiful 18th century charterhouse which sits elegantly a the start of the road leading through th châteaux of the Médoc, the famous CD2 This vintage, however, has a much mor down-to-earth character. It is still marked b oak, with a bouquet of toast notes and ver evident tannins on the palate, and needs to b kept for a while.

Ch. La Lagune, 81, av. de l'Europe, 33290 Ludon-Médoc, tel. 05.57.88.82.77, fax 05.57.88.82.70 by appt.

Jean-Michel Ducellier

CH. DE LAMARQUE 1997

Cru bourg. 34 ha 190,000

83 86 88 89 90 91 92 93 |94| 95 96 97

This château has a keep, a postern, battle ments, and associations with Henry V of Eng land, the Duc d'Epernon and the Comtes d Fumel. What with its architecture and famou visitors and owners, it seems that everythin here is made to delight the lover of history This simple, supple 1997 wine is fine and well balanced, and although it has no great agein potential, it will be a very pleasant wine t drink while young.

Gromand d'Evry, Ch. de Lamarque, 33460 Lamarque, tel. 05.56.58.90.03, fax 05.56.58.93.43, e-mail chdelamarque@aol.com ev. day excep Sat. Sun. 9.30am–12 noon 2pm–5pm

CH. LAMOTHE BERGERON 1997

Cru bourg. 66.04 ha 296,600 70–99 F

2 83 85 86 87 88 89 90 91 92 93 94 |95| 96 97

Although the château is in typical Napoleon III style, its origins are very much medieval, as its name suggests. Today it is part of the Mestrezat group, and with this vintage it offers a supple, full-bodied wine supported by substantial tannins which will enable it to be kept for two or three years.

SC du Ch. Grand-Puy Ducasse, La Croix Bacalan, 109, rue Achard, B.P. 154, 33042 Bordeaux Cedex, tel. 05.56.11.29.00, fax 05.56.11.29.01 Y by appt.

CH. LANESSAN 1997

Cru bourg. 40 ha 280,000 100–149 F

6 |88| |90|91 |92| |93| 94 95 96 97

In an area where the Grands Crus, both Bourgeois and Classés, frequently change hands, Lanessan is exceptional in that it has belonged to the Bouteiller family and their forebears since 1793. Despite a slight tannic note at the finish, this wine shows that it comes from good stock with its bouquet of deep-red and black berry notes. It has a round, supple structure, and needs to be kept for another year.

SCEA Delbos-Bouteiller, Ch. Lanessan, 33460 Cussac-Fort-Médoc, tel. 05.56.58.94.80, fax 05.56.58.93.10 Y by appt.

Bouteiller

CH. LA PEYRE 1997*

1.5 ha 9,000 50–69 F

Coming from a Cissac vineyard belonging to a producer from Saint-Etienne, this wine shows clearly that it was made from good stock. It asserts its youth at the start with a brilliant, dark colour, then confirms its power in the nose, where toast and menthol notes combine with eucalyptus and strawberries. Finally, the structure and long finish express the excellent character of a wine which is for longer maturing.

EARL Vignobles Rabiller, Leyssac, 33180 Saint-Estèphe, tel. 05.56.59.32.51, fax 05.56.59.70.09 Y ev. day 10am–12.30pm 3pm–7pm

CH. LAROSE-TRINTAUDON 1997**

Cru bourg. 119 ha 1,138,000 50–69 F

81 82 83 85 86 87 88 89 |90|91 92 93 |94| 95 96 **97**

This 180-ha (445-acre) vineyard has benefited from a major programme of investments. These have not been in vain, as can be seen from the qualities of this 1997 wine. It has a ruby colour with dark-red glints, and a nose revealing a perfect combination of oak and grape. This is confirmed on the palate, whose tannins are well extracted. A rich, silky wine which opens out into a long finish. The **1997 Château Larose Perganson** (153,000 bottles, 70–99F), is awarded one star. It is an enjoyable wine which can be drunk for the next three or four years.

SA Ch. Larose-Trintaudon, rte de Pauillac, 33112 Saint-Laurent-Médoc, tel. 05.56.59.41.72, fax 05.56.59.93.22, e-mail larosetrintaudon@wanadoo.fr Y by appt.

AGF

CH. LA TOUR CARNET 1997**

4ème cru clas. 43 ha n.c. 200–249 F

79 81 82 83 85 |86|87 |(88)| |89| |90|91 92 |93|94 (96) **97**

This is a Cru Classé of 126 ha (311 acres), 48 of which (119 acres) are planted with vines. It used to belong to Madame Pelegrin, and has just been taken over by Bernard Magrez, a major Bordeaux wine-merchant who already owns Pape Clément and Fombrauge. Very much like the château, which is a delightful mixture of ages and styles, this wine asserts its power by its youthful, almost black colour, its structure and the strength of its bouquet, in which there is an aroma of cloves alongside green peppers, cinnamon and intense notes of oak. An attractive wine for longer maturing.

SCEA Ch. La Tour Carnet, 33112 Saint-Laurent-Médoc, tel. 05.56.73.30.90, fax 05.56.59.48.54 Y by appt.

CH. LE BOURDIEU VERTHEUIL 1997*

Cru bourg. 57 ha 130,000 50–69 F

This vineyard is a vast property, and is able to offer a wine whose volume of production is in no way limited. It is well served by a concentrated bouquet in which fruits are prominent, and also by its fullness and balance on the palate. A wine which is developing harmoniously.

SC Ch. Le Bourdieu-Vertheuil, 33180 Vertheuil, tel. 05.56.41.98.01, fax 05.56.41.99.32 Y by appt.

Richard

CH. LE SOULEY-SAINTE CROIX 1997

22 ha 160,000 50–69 F

Coming from a vineyard located 500 m (a quarter of a mile) from the beautiful Abbey of Vertheuil, this wine no doubt lacks the power of the Romanesque building but does share something of its elegance in a complex bouquet of fruit aromas along with musk and undergrowth.

Jean et Marie-José Riffaud, 32, rue des Martyrs de la Résistance, 33180 Vertheuil, tel. 05.56.41.98.54, fax 05.56.41.95.36 Y ev. day except Sun. 9am–12 noon 2pm–6pm; Sat. 9am–12 noon

CH. MAGNOL 1997

Cru bourg. 13.73 ha 86,000 70–99 F

Coming from a property belonging to the wine-merchants Barton et Guestier, this wine does not have the substance of previous vintages. Nevertheless, it has an appealing nose of delicate notes of fruit (peaches and lychees), smoke and vanilla.

Barton et Guestier, Ch. Magnol, B.P. 30, 33290 Blanquefort Cedex, tel. 05.56.95.48.00, fax 05.56.95.48.01

CH. MALESCASSE 1997

■Cru bourg. 37 ha 180,000 70-99 F

82 83 84 87 |88| |89| |90| 91 92 93 |94| 95 96 97

Malescasse was built in 1824, and in 1992 joined Alcatel, which undertook major renovations (the barrel- and vat-stores have been completely rebuilt). This wine has a very sturdy character which will appeal to wine-lovers. Its powerful, full tannins will enable it to be kept for four or five years, and to be served with game or casseroles.

Ch. Malescasse, 6, rte du Moulin-Rose, 33460 Lamarque, tel. 05.56.73.15.20, fax 05.56.59.64.72 Y by appt.

Alcatel

CH. DE MALLERET 1997

■Cru bourg. 32 ha 100,000 50-69 F

86 87 **88 89** (90) 91 92 |94| **95 96** |97|

Although less aristocratic than the château, this 1997 wine shows that it has a genuine sense of values: there is a brilliant, intense colour, a rich, fine bouquet (notes of soft fruits and toast), and a good, harmonious, fine tannic structure.

SCEA Ch. de Malleret, Dom. du Ribet, 33450 Saint-Loubès, tel. 05.57.97.07.20, fax 05.57.97.07.27 Y by appt.

CH. MAUCAILLOU-FELLETIN 1997

■Cru bourg. 6.64 ha n.c. 50-69 F

Coming from a vineyard belonging to the Château Maucaillou estate at Lamarque, this wine shows its character in its light but pleasant colour. There is charm, too, in the roundness of its tannins and its aromas of red berries.

Magali Dourthe, 33480 Moulis-en-Médoc, tel. 05.56.58.01.23

CH. MAUCAMPS 1997

■Cru bourg. 18 ha 100,000 70-99 F

82 83 85 (86) 88 |89| |90| 91 92 |93| |94| 95 96 |97|

This vast 70-ha (173-acre) property is located on a superb hilltop site with a Garonne gravel soil, which obviously contributes to the quality of the wines made here. With this vintage the growers have gone for suppleness and balance. It is supported by tannins which are still young, and expresses its personality in very agreeable aromas of fruit, spices and oak. A well-composed wine which will be ready to drink in three to five years' time. A round, fruity, but more simple wine is the **1997 Château Dasvin-Bel-Air** (30–49F), which is recommended.

Ch. Maucamps, B.P. 11, 33460 Macau, tel. 05.57.88.07.64, fax 05.57.88.07.00 Y by appt.

Tessandier

CH. MAURAC 1997

■Cru bourg. 6 ha 40,000 50-69 F

This wine comes from the excellent terroir at Saint-Seurin, and has an attractive fruity bouquet and a rounded tannic structure. The combination of these two characteristics means that this wine can either be drunk now or kept for two to three years.

SCEA Ch. Maurac, 33180 Saint-Seurin-de-Cadourne, tel. 05.57.88.07.64, fax 05.57.88.07.00 Y by appt.

CH. MAURIAN DE PRADE

Cuvée élevée en barrique 1997★

■Cru bourg. 6 ha 42,000 50-69 F

This vineyard was replanted in 1981, and now offers an oak-matured wine which will need to be kept for at least three years. This vintage has originality, and is outstandingly well balanced. Its bouquet is unusual, with notes of *rancio* and chocolate combining with more classic aromas of blackcurrant and prune. The palate is balanced, and has a full substance which opens out into a beautiful finish on a note of liquorice.

Vignoble Cantelaube, chem. des Vignes, Le Poujeau, 33290 Le Pian-Médoc, tel. 05.56.79.36.20, fax 05.56.39.22.98 Y by appt.

CH. MEYRE Cuvée Colette 1997★

■Cru bourg. 15.5 ha 6,000 50-69

88 89 90 91 |93| |94| 95 96 97

Located between Avensan and Castelnau, this vineyard offers a wine of reliable quality, pleasantly fragrant with notes of ripe fruit accompanied by hints of toast. A fleshy, rich 1997 wine with interesting and complex tannins.

Ch. Meyre SA, 16, rte de Castelnau, 33480 Avensan, tel. 05.56.58.10.77, fax 05.56.58.13.20, e-mail chateau.meyre@wanadoo.fr Y ev. day except Sat. Sun. 2pm–5pm; 1 Nov.–30 Mar. by appt.

CH. MICALET

Elevé en fût de chêne 1997★

■Cru artisan 4 ha 27,000 30-49 F

82 83 85 86 88 89 **90** 91 92 93 **94 95 96** 97

With its hand-picked harvests and maturation in oak, this little Cussacais vineyard spares no effort to make high-quality wines. Once again it has achieved its aim with this delicately fragrant 1997 Haut-Médoc whose structure makes it pleasant and harmonious. More elegant than powerful, it should be kept for two or three years.

EARL Denis Fédieu, 10, rue Jeanne-d'Arc, 33460 Cussac-Fort-Médoc, tel. 05.56.58.95.48, fax 05.56.58.96.85 Y ev. day except Sun. 9am–1pm 3pm–7pm; groups by appt.

CH. MILOUCA 1997

■ 1 ha 6,000 30-49 F

This is a small jointly-owned vineyard. This wine is certainly not a frontrunner, but its good structure supported by intelligently dosed oak makes it interesting, as does its bouquet of stewed-fruit notes. Best kept for a year or two.

Ind. Lartigue-Coulary, 33460 Cussac-Fort-Médoc, tel. 05.56.58.91.55 Y by appt.

CH. MOULIN DE BLANCHON 1997

6 ha 40,000 30–49 F

True to the vineyard's tradition, this 1997 wine refuses to be merely enjoyable. It is discreetly oaky, and develops a concentrated empyreumatic bouquet before revealing a structure which guarantees its ageing potential. The finish is pleasant and warm.

Henri Negrier, Ch. Moulin de Blanchon, 33180 Saint-Seurin-de-Cadourne, tel. 05.56.59.38.66, fax 05.56.59.32.31 Y ev. day 8.30am–12.30pm 2pm–8pm

CH. MURET 1997*

Cru bourg. 7.1 ha 57,000 50–69 F

91 93 94 |95| 96 97

This vineyard has an attractive, unbroken vineyard located on a limestone-clay plateau. Its 1997 wine is very well turned-out. After an unaggressive attack on the palate, it reveals very ripe tannins and good balance, then goes into a long finish which suggests that it should be kept for two or three years.

SCA de Muret, Ch. Muret, 33180 Saint-Seurin-de-Cadourne, tel. 05.56.59.38.11, fax 05.56.59.37.03 Y by appt.

Boufflerd

CH. D'OSMOND 1997

Cru artisan 7.25 ha 20,000 30–49 F

This vineyard has been entirely reorganised over the last 12 years. Here they know how to combine simplicity and pleasantness, two features apparent in this 1997 wine with its supple tannins and an agreeable nose of fruits and undergrowth.

Philippe Tressol, EARL Les Gûnes, 36, rte des Gûnes, 33250 Cissac-Médoc, tel. 05.56.59.59.17, fax 05.56.59.59.17 Y by appt.

CH. PEYRABON 1997

Cru bourg. 40.69 ha 71,160 70–99 F

86 88 |89| |90| 91 92 93 |94| 96 |97|

In this last vintage produced before the change of owner (1998), this simple, supple wine relies on the finesse of the tannins and the pleasantness of its red-berry aromas to form an agreeable overall impression.

SARL Ch. Peyrabon, 33250 Saint-Sauveur, tel. 05.56.59.57.10, fax 05.56.59.59.45 Y by appt.

Bernard

CH. PONTOISE-CABARRUS 1997

Cru bourg. 24 ha 180,000 50–69 F

75 76 81 82 83 85 (86) 88 89 **90** |92| |93| |94| 95 96 97

The fact that this property is located at Saint-Seurin is enough to indicate that it has a good terroir. This has helped to give this wine good structure, making it worth keeping for one to two more years.

François Tereygeol, Ch. Pontoise-Cabarrus, 33180 Saint-Seurin-de-Cadourne, tel. 05.56.59.34.92, fax 05.56.59.72.42, e-mail françoistereygeol@wanadoo.fr Y by appt.

CH. PUY CASTERA 1997

Cru bourg. 17.5 ha 150,000 50–69 F

With a grape blend including not only Cabernet Sauvignon, Cabernet Franc and Merlot, but also Petit Verdot and Malbec, this 1997 wine respects the old Bordeaux rule of variety. It comes as no surprise to find that it has excellent diversity in a nose ranging from ripe fruits to notes of aniseed and menthol, with a very evident but already elegant oakiness. It should be ready to drink in 2001 and can be kept for two or three years, perhaps longer.

SCE Ch. Puy Castéra, 8, rte du Castéra, 33250 Cissac-Médoc, tel. 05.56.59.58.80, fax 05.56.59.54.57 Y by appt.

Marès

CH. RAMAGE LA BATISSE 1997**

Cru bourg. 33 ha 264,000 70–99 F

85 86 88 89 |**90**| 91 92 94 95 96 **97**

1997
CHATEAU
RAMAGE LA BATISSE
CRU BOURGEOIS
HAUT MEDOC
APPELLATION HAUT MEDOC CONTROLEE
MIS EN BOUTEILLES AU CHATEAU
PRODUCE OF FRANCE

This vineyard is a vast property – the estate comprises more than 60 ha (148 acres) in all – and is very well equipped. It has been particularly successful in what is known to have been a difficult vintage. The wine has a purple colour and a mature, complex and concentrated bouquet of attractive floral notes. It develops a very well-constructed palate which is supple in the attack and supported by tannins of character. Very much in the Médoc tradition, it should be kept for two or three years.

SCI Ramage La Batisse, 33250 Saint-Sauveur, tel. 05.56.59.57.24, fax 05.56.59.54.14 Y by appt.

MACIF

CH. DU RETOUT 1997**

Cru bourg. 28.11 ha 70,000 50–69 F

It has taken only three years for this vineyard to rise to the highest level. It will take longer (four or five years) for this 1997 wine to reach its peak, as is clearly indicated by its intense red colour, complex bouquet, mouth-filling palate and tannic structure. Combining power and harmony, this wine is an astonishing achievement.

Gérard Kopp, Ch. du Retout, 33460 Cussac-Fort-Médoc, tel. 05.56.58.91.08, fax 05.56.58.91.08, e-mail chateau-du-retout.com Y by appt.

CH. REYSSON Réserve 1997

■Cru bourg. 67 ha 61,400 70-99 F

Located near Vertheuil in an area which sums up the history of the whole region, Reysson is run by the Mestrezat company. Although it does not equal the 1996 vintage, this Réserve has a great deal of charm due to its suppleness and roundness and also to the elegance of its tannins. The finesse of its bouquet of fruity aromas enhanced by a spicy note is second to none. It is ready to drink now, but will also keep for two or three years.

SARL du Ch. Reysson, La Croix Bacalan, 109, rue Achard, B.P. 154, 33027 Bordeaux Cedex, tel. 05.56.11.29.00, fax 05.56.11.29.01 by appt.

CH. SAINT-PAUL 1997★★

■Cru bourg. 20 ha 95,000 50-69 F

Like many vineyards in Saint-Seurin-de-Cadourne, this estate has done very well indeed in this vintage. The wine's deep colour with dark-purple glints gives way to a powerful, complex bouquet (cocoa, liquorice, prunes, jam and toast) which creates a splendid initial impression. This is followed by a palate which is full, substantially structured and harmonious. Successfully combining oak and fruit, this wine has a beautiful liquorice finish and is very much in the Médoc spirit with good balance and ageing potential (six to ten years).

Ch. Saint-Paul, 33180 Saint-Seurin-de-Cadourne, tel. 05.56.59.34.72 by appt.

CH. SENEJAC 1997★

■Cru bourg. 27.6 ha 60,000 70-99 F

89 90 91 **|93|** |94| 95 **96** 97

The property was sold at the end of 1999 to the owner of the Château Talbot (Saint-Julien), and this wine is one of the last produced by the Comte de Guigné. Starting with a deep colour and a lovely bouquet of ripe fruit and toast notes, it is full of flavour on the palate by virtue of its meatiness and silky tannins, which suggest that it should be kept for two or three years.

SAS Ch. Sénéjac, 33290 Le Pian-Médoc, tel. 05.56.70.20.11, fax 05.56.70.23.91 by appt.

Rustmann

CH. LA BASTIDE DE SIRAN 1997

■ 1 ha 5,000 50-69 F

Coming from a Labarde vineyard mainly known for its Margaux, this wine has a very pronounced tannic character and is not unlike an old-style Haut-Médoc.

SC du Ch. Siran, Ch. Siran, 33460 Labarde, tel. 05.57.88.34.04, fax 05.57.88.70.05, e-mail chateau.siran@wanadoo.fr ev. day 10am–12.30pm 1.30pm–6pm; groups by appt.

CH. SOCIANDO-MALLET 1997★★

■ 46 ha 244,700 250-299

75 76 78 80 81 |(82)|83 84 85 86 87 **|88| |89| |90|** 9 **|92| |93| 94(95)(96)97**

With a gravel soil facing the estuary and varied range of grapes (the Cabernets, Merlo and Petit Verdot), this Cadournais vineyard not lacking in assets, as is underlined by th many vintages which have been highly praise in previous years. This 1997 wine has a ver fashionable tannic and oaky quality, but st retains the elegant, thoroughbred characte which befits a Haut-Médoc. Given this com bination of features, it should be kept fo three or four years.

SCEA Jean Gautreau, Ch. Sociando-Mallet, 33180 Saint-Seurin-de-Cadourne, tel. 05.56.73.38.80, fax 05.56.73.38.88 by appt.

LA DEMOISELLE DE SOCIANDO MALLET 1997★

■ 13 ha 135,000 70-99

The colour of this little sister of Sociando Mallet is so deep that it looks like a great win Its aromas are based on an oaky, vanilla, tho oughbred note which reappears in the mouth where it is concentrated, full-bodied, and sup ported by balanced, powerful tannins. Bes kept for a few years.

SCEA Jean Gautreau, Ch. Sociando-Mallet, 33180 Saint-Seurin-de-Cadourne, tel. 05.56.73.38.80, fax 05.56.73.38.88 by appt.

CH. SOUDARS 1997★

■Cru bourg. 22 ha 170,000 70-99 F

82 83 85 86 |89| **|90|** 91 92 93 94 |95| **96** 97

From the same producer as the Coufra but produced on a separate property, thi wine's delicate bouquet is close to that of it cousin. Its palate is more round, however. A pleasantly serene wine which will be ready t drink in three or four years' time.

Vignobles E.-F. Miailhe, 33180 Saint-Seurin-de-Cadourne, tel. 05.56.59.31.02, fax 05.56.59.72.39 by appt.

CH. TOUR DU HAUT-MOULIN 1997★

■Cru bourg. 32 ha 160,000 70-99 F

78 79 81 82(83)84 85 **|86|** 87 **|88| |89| |90|** 91 92 |93 |94| 95 96 97

Several generations of wine-making in th Médoc have taught the Poitous how equall important it is to manage both the vineyar and the work in the winery. This wine clearl comes from an excellent harvest and has bee carefully vinified. It has a lovely purple col our, a complex bouquet in which fruits and spices combine pleasantly with oak, and a balanced palate which is supported b smooth, flavourful tannins. Best drunk between 2002 and 2005, or perhaps later.

SCEA Ch. Tour du Haut-Moulin, 7, rue des Aubarèdes, 33460 Cussac-Fort-Médoc, tel. 05.56.58.91.10, fax 05.56.58.99.30 by appt.

Family Poitou

CH. TOUR-DU-ROC 1997

11.04 ha 70,000 50-69 F

Run from a beautiful house just beside the church in Arcins, this vineyard offers a wine which is still somewhat austere at the finish, but has a truly classical palate with the necessary structure to improve as it develops.
EARL Tour-du-Roc, Ch. Tour-du-Roc, 33460 Arcins, tel. 05.56.58.90.25, fax 05.56.58.94.41 by appt.
Philippe Robert

CH. DE VILLAMBIS 1997

Cru bourg. 38 ha n.c. 50-69 F

The château has an appealing history and is now an occupational therapy centre. The wine, which is distributed by the CVBG, also has attractive balance, suppleness and fruity aromas.
Ch. de Villambis, 33250 Cissac-Médoc, tel. 05.56.35.53.00, fax 05.56.35.52.29, e-mail contact@cvbg.com
CAT Cissac-Médoc

CH. DE VILLEGEORGE 1997★

Cru bourg. 15 ha 41,400 100-149 F

83 85 **|86|** 87 **|89| |90|** |93| 94 95 **96** |97|

This vineyard has a pretty charterhouse between Avensan and Margaux. It departs somewhat from its traditional line with this vintage, which has resolutely straightforward tannins. Even so they do not disturb the harmony of the overall impression. A wine which is already pleasant, but nonetheless shows good ageing potential (about three or four years), both in its structure and its aromas of gamey and spicy notes.
SC Les Grands Crus réunis, 33480 Moulis-en-Médoc, tel. 05.56.58.22.01, fax 05.56.58.15.10 by appt.
M.-L. Lurton-Roux

Listrac-Médoc

This appellation corresponds exactly to the boundaries of the Listrac commune itself. The *appellation communale* is the furthest away from the Gironde estuary, and one of the few on the tourist routes to Soulac or from the Pointe-de-Grave. The *terroir* is most original, best described in geological terms as a hollowed-out dome in an anticlinal valley where erosion has created an inverse relief. To the west, along the edge of the forest, three ridges of Pyrenean gravel rise, their limestone slopes and subsoil giving good natural drainage. The centre of the AOC, the hollowed dome, is occupied by the Peyrelebade plain, which is composed of clay and lime soils. Finally, the ridges of the Graves by the Garonne rise to the east.

Listrac is a vigorous, robust wine, which has outgrown its former reputation for a somewhat crude quality. While some Listracs may be a little hard when young, the majority balance tannic strength with roundness. They all have a good capacity for keeping – 7 to 18 years, depending on the vintage. In 1999, the 646 ha (1,596 acres) produced 37,828 hl (998,659 gal).

CH. BAUDAN

Elevé en fût de chêne 1997★

2.65 ha 17,000 100-149 F

Continuing to develop and progress, this vineyard emerges with honours from the trials of 1997. This wine has a delicate, elegant bouquet, and the additional attraction of an attack of great finesse, followed by a fine surge of power on the palate.
Sylvie et Alain Blasquez, Ch. Baudan, 33480 Listrac-Médoc, tel. 05.56.58.07.40, fax 05.56.58.04.72, e-mail chateau.baudan@wanadoo.fr ev. day 9am–7.30pm

CH. CAP LEON VEYRIN 1997

Cru bourg. 17 ha 90,000 50-69 F

|90| 91 92 93 94 **95 96 97**

The Merlot component (75%) is unusual in this wine, which develops a delicate, elegant bouquet before revealing a balanced tannic structure which opens out into a pleasantly round finish.

Moulis and Listrac

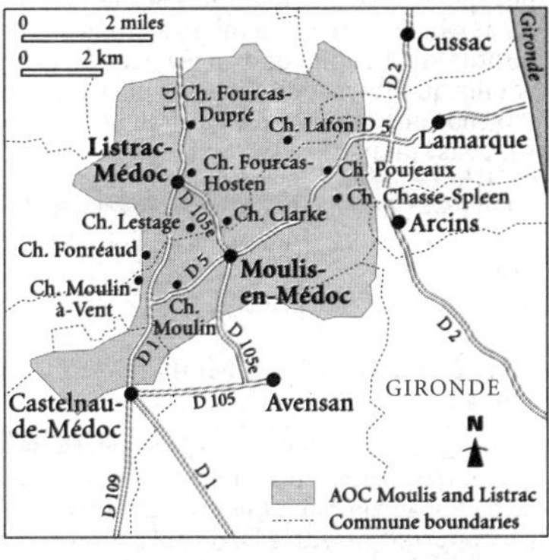

🔑 Alain Meyre, Ch. Cap Léon Veyrin, 33480 Listrac-Médoc, tel. 05.56.58.07.28, fax 05.56.58.07.50 ☒ Y ev. day 9am–12 noon 2pm–6pm; Sat. Sun. groups by appt.

CH. CLARKE 1997*

■Cru bourg. n.c. 326,000 🍾 100-149 F

81 82 83 85 (86) **88** |89| |**90**| 91 92 93 **94 95 96** 97

Although it no longer has an actual château, this vineyard's acreage and buildings make it one of the finest production units in the appellation, founded in 1973 on the basis of a very old estate by Baron Edmond de Rothschild. Its 1997 wine is richly fragrant, with notes of vanilla, toast and ripe fruits, and with the support of a supple, well-balanced structure will give of its best in two to three years' time.

🔑 Cie vin. barons Ed. et B. de Rothschild, 33480 Listrac-Médoc, tel. 05.56.58.38.00, fax 05.56.58.26.46, e-mail chateau.clarke@wanadoo.fr ☒ Y by appt.

🔑 Benjamin de Rothschild

CH. DUCLUZEAU 1997*

■Cru bourg. 4.5 ha 38,000 🍾 50-69 F

81 (82) 83 85 |**86**| |88| |89| |90| 91 92 |94| **96** |97|

Coming from a vineyard belonging to the Borie de Ducru-Beaucaillou family, this wine shows character both in its bouquet of smoky and meaty notes along with floral aromas, and on a palate whose elegance and softness are not impaired by the round, well-blended tannins. Crowned by a finish on a note of jam, the overall impression is already agreeable, but this should improve as it develops over the next three or four years.

🔑 Mme J.-E. Borie, Ch. Ducluzeau, 33480 Listrac-Médoc, tel. 05.56.73.16.73, fax 05.56.59.27.37

CH. FONREAUD 1997*

■Cru bourg. 30 ha 180,000 🍾 70-99 F

81 82 83 85 86 88 |89| |90| 91 92 |93| 95 96 97

This château is located along the road from Bordeaux to Soulac, and gives the impression that everything about it can be taken in at first glance. Round at the back, however, it becomes clear how complex its organisation is. This wine is not particularly sophisticated, but shows diversity and intensity in its bouquet, where there is a mouthwatering combination of vanilla and strawberries. This vanilla quality reappears on the palate, where it blends into a full-bodied overall impression which is still marked by oak.

🔑 Ch. Fonréaud, 33480 Listrac-Médoc, tel. 05.56.58.02.43, fax 05.56.58.04.33 ☒ Y ev. day except Sat. Sun. 9am–12 noon 2pm–5pm

🔑 Héritiers Chanfreau

CH. FOURCAS-DUMONT 1997*

■ n.c. 35,000 🍾 100-149 F

Coming from a production unit of about 30 ha (74 acres), this wine creates a delightful first impression with a beautiful colour and a bouquet of crystallised red berries enhance[d] by a note of tar. It finds its full expression o[n] the palate with a fruity quality which [is] almost exceptional for the vintage.

🔑 SCA Ch. Fourcas-Dumont, 12, rue Odilon-Redon, 33480 Listrac-Médoc, tel. 05.56.58.03.84, fax 05.56.58.01.20, e-mail infochateau-fourcas-dumont.com ☒ Y ev. day 9am–12 noon 2pm–5pm; Sat. Sun. by appt.

CH. FOURCAS DUPRE 1997

■Cru bourg. 44 ha 241,000 🍾 70-99

(78) 79 81 82 83 |**85**| |**86**| |**88**| |**89**| |90| 91 92 |93| |94| **9**[5] **96** |97|

This château has existed since 1843, and i[s] located on the Pyrenean gravel soils o[f] Listrac. Without claiming to rival certain pre[vious] vintages from the same vineyard, th[is] 1997 wine, which has been matured in oak fo[r] 12 months and contains 2% Petit Verdot, ha[s] great appeal with its elegant and fresh bou[quet] of oaky notes. Its structure is almos[t] reminiscent of fine lace, and means that it wi[ll] be ready to drink quite soon.

🔑 Ch. Fourcas Dupré, 33480 Listrac-Médoc, tel. 05.56.58.01.07, fax 05.56.58.02.27 ☒ Y ev. day except Sat. Sun. 8am–12 noon 2pm–5.30pm

CH. FOURCAS HOSTEN 1997**

■Cru bourg. 47 ha 260,000 🍾 70-99 F

75 78 81 |(**82**)| |**83**| |**85**| |**86**| |88| |89| |90| 91 92 93 9[4] **95 96 97**

This vineyard is run from an elegant, typi[cally] Girondin house, and has a fine reputa[tion] for quality which this difficult vintag[e] has not impaired. The bouquet is supporte[d] by a well-dosed oak component, and com[bines] red and dark berries and spices to form a complex, intense overall impression. Th[e] round, supple, velvety palate is alread[y] becoming pleasant, while at the same time it[s] attractive tannins show that it should be kep[t] for four or five years.

🔑 SC du Ch. Fourcas-Hosten, rue de l'Eglise, 33480 Listrac-Médoc, tel. 05.56.58.01.15, fax 05.56.58.06.73 ☒ Y ev. day except Sat. Sun. 9am–11.30am 2pm–4.30pm

GRAND LISTRAC

La Caravelle Elevé en fût de chêne 1997*

■ 4 ha 25,000 🍾 50-69 F

This wine is the co-operative's Cuvée Pres[tige]. It has a lovely blood-red colour an[d] succeeds in forming a complex, fine bouque[t] which mingles fruits and spices. The palate i[s] nicely rounded, full, mouth-filling and sup[ported] by a good tannic presence which wil[l] allow it to be kept for a few years.

🔑 Cave de vinification de Listrac-Médoc, 21, av. de Soulac, 33480 Listrac-Médoc, tel. 05.56.58.03.19, fax 05.56.58.07.22, e-mail grandlistrac@cave-listrac-médoc.com ☒ Y by appt.

CH. LALANDE Cuvée spéciale 1997

■Cru bourg. n.c. 25,000 50–69 F

Coming from the vineyard's Cuvée Spéciale, this wine is of a thoroughly high standard. It is pleasant to look at, and releases rich aromas with powerful spicy and fruity notes well accompanied by oak. Its development on the palate is still somewhat severe, but it is not weak, and leaves the taster with the memory of a well-made wine.

EARL Darriet-Lescoutra, Ch. Lalande, 33480 Listrac-Médoc, tel. 05.56.58.19.45, fax 05.56.58.15.62 ev. day 9am–12 noon 2pm–6pm; Sun. by appt.

CH. LA LAUZETTE-DECLERCQ 1997

■Cru bourg. 13 ha 80,000 50–69 F

Although still somewhat astringent in its tannic development, this wine, which will go well with an entrecôte, is not in the old Listrac style. It has a roundness which softens its character, and an unusual bouquet in which notes of caramel mingle with red-berry aromas.

SC Vignobles Declercq, Couhenne nord 1229, 33480 Listrac-Médoc, tel. 32.51.30.40.81, fax 32.51.31.90.54 by appt.

CH. LAROSEY 1997

■Cru bourg. n.c. 17,700 50–69 F

From the same producer as the Château Lalande, but distributed by the wine-trade, this wine is more rustic. Be that as it may, its flavours have been well extracted to form a pleasant overall impression.

EARL Darriet-Lescoutra, 33480 Listrac-Médoc, tel. 05.57.43.01.44, fax 05.57.43.08.75, e-mail direction@robertgiraud.com

CH. LESTAGE 1997

■Cru bourg. 42 ha 200,000 70–99 F

81 82 83 **85** |86| |**89**| |90| 91 92 **94 95 96** 97

This vineyard belongs to the same producer as Château Fonréaud, and its château is a fine example of Second Empire style. It offers a simple, supple wine with a spicy bouquet and a balanced palate.

Ch. Lestage, 33480 Listrac-Médoc, tel. 05.56.58.02.43, fax 05.56.58.04.33 ev. day except Sat. Sun. 9am–12 noon 2pm–5pm

Héritiers Chanfreau

CH. MAYNE LALANDE 1997★★

■Cru bourg. 15 ha 50,000 70–99 F

85 86 88 89 90 91 92 |94| |95| 96 **97**

This vineyard is a recognised pillar of the appellation, and once again it lives up to its reputation with a wine which has a beautiful, dark colour and a bouquet of the complexity that makes for a great wine: red berries, blackcurrants, vanilla, dark chocolate and spices. It is full, round and powerful, with rich tannins, and is a good wine for longer maturing (five years).

Bernard Lartigue, Ch. Mayne Lalande, 33480 Listrac-Médoc, tel. 05.56.58.27.63, fax 05.56.58.22.41 by appt.

CH. PEYREDON LAGRAVETTE 1997★★

■Cru bourg. 6.5 ha 42,000 50–69 F

81 (82) 83 85 86 |88| |**89**| |90| 91 92 |93| **94 95 96 97**

This vineyard has a fine Günz gravel terroir which continues in the extended part of the Poujeaux hilltop site, but this asset would be nothing without the great competence of Paul Hostein. Everything about this wine bears his stamp, starting with the bouquet, which is intense and concentrated, and ranges from very ripe red berries to floral and creamy notes. On the palate it is substantial, supple and round in the attack, then rich, long and tannic, with a structure which leads naturally to a fresh, elegant finish.

Paul Hostein, 2062 Médrac Est, Ch. Peyredon-Lagravette, 33480 Listrac-Médoc, tel. 05.56.58.05.55, fax 05.56.58.05.50 ev. day except Sun. 9am–12.30pm 2pm–7pm; cl. 20 Sep.–10 Oct.

CH. ROSE SAINTE-CROIX 1997★

■ 9.01 ha 72,000 50–69 F

The rose and the cross, the two symbols which make up this vineyard's name, could well refer to the activities of one of the many Rosicrucian societies which flourished under the French Revolution and the First Empire. Fortunately no such mystery surrounds this 1997 wine, which has a very evident range of floral aromas in its bouquet (hyacinth, narcissus and tuberose), and develops unaggressive tannins. The overall impression is one of balance and harmony.

SARL des Grands Crus, Lieu-dit Le Lieulet, 33480 Moulis-en-Médoc, tel. 05.56.58.35.77, fax 05.56.58.14.24 Mon. Tue. Thu. Fri. 8.30am–12 noon 1.30pm–5pm; cl. Aug.

Porcheron

CH. SARANSOT-DUPRE 1997

■Cru bourg. 13 ha 75,000 70–99 F

70 71 75 78 81 82 83 85 |**86**| 88 |**89**| |**90**| 91 |93| |94| **95** 96 |97|

This wine comes from a vast estate which includes vines and woods, and where the wineries are in the course of being reorganised.

BORDEAUX

Its round and pleasant character bears the stamp of Merlot (70% of the grape blend), and it has an agreeable appearance. It is ready to drink now while you wait for the remarkable 1995 vintage.

🔑 Yves Raymond, Ch. Saransot-Dupré, 33480 Listrac-Médoc, tel. 05.56.58.03.02, fax 05.56.58.07.64 ☑ 🍷 by appt.

CH. SEMEILLAN MAZEAU

Cuvée Jander 1997★

■Cru bourg. 8 ha 60,000 🛢 70–99 F

|94| 95 **96** |97|

This wine comes from a plateau called Pey-de-Minjon (one of the high points in the Médoc), and its elegance and finesse show that it comes from good stock. These qualities are present in the bouquet, whose aromas of ripe fruits are delicately enhanced by a note of oak, before reappearing on the palate, where the stamp of maturation is more noticeable.

🔑 SCE Les Vignobles Jander, 41, av. de Soulac, 33480 Listrac-Médoc, tel. 05.56.58.01.12, fax 05.56.58.01.57 ☑ 🍷 ev. day 9am–12 noon 2pm–7pm

Margaux

Margaux is the only appellation name that is also a female first name. This is unlikely to have happened by chance. You have only to taste a glass of Margaux to savour the subtle relationship between wine and *terroir*.

Margaux wines are famous for keeping well, but they are equally distinguished for their suppleness and delicacy and for the elegance of their wonderfully fruity perfumes. They are the finest examples of generously tannic, soft wines to be proudly registered in the cellar book as wines for the long term.

The originality of Margaux comes from several different factors. Human input should not be underestimated. For example, Margaux growers have historically given less predominance to Cabernet-Sauvignon than have the other great Médoc communes. Here, while still the minority variety, Merlot plays a more significant part. In addition, although the appellation stretches through five communes, namely Margaux and Cantenac, Soussans, Labarde and Arsac, only the soils that are best suited to growing vines for wine-making have been retained for the

Margaux

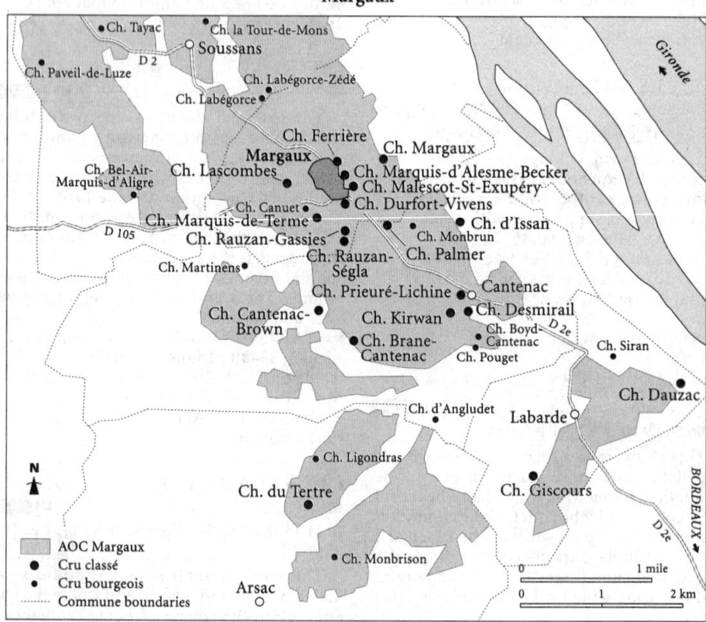

AOC. The result is a strikingly homogenous *terroir*, featuring a series of gravel ridges.

The ridges fall into two groups: on the periphery is a string of 'islands' separated by valleys, streams and boggy marsh; at the heart of the appellation, in the Margaux and Cantenac communes, what was formerly a plateau of white gravel measuring some 6 km (4 miles) by 2 km (1 mile) is now worn away into ridges by erosion. This is where the eighteen Grand Crus Classés of the appellation are grown.

The Margaux wines are remarkably elegant and should be drunk only with the finest-quality dishes such as Chateaubriand, duck, partridge or, in the local tradition, steak à la Bordelaise. In 1999 74,199 hl (1,958,854 gal) were produced.

CH. D'ANGLUDET 1997

■ Cru bourg. 32 ha 140,000 150–199 F

85 86 88 89 90 91 92 93 94 95 96 97

Angludet symbolises the dual origin of the Bordeaux vineyards; it is a genuine Médoc house, but has a lawn going down to a little river which gives it a somewhat British air. Although still marked by oak, its 1997 wine has a beautiful, deep colour and a nose of fruity notes. It has substantial potential, and will develop favourably in the next three years.

Maison Sichel-Coste, 8, rue de la Poste, 33210 Langon, tel. 05.56.63.50.52, fax 05.56.63.42.28

CH. BOYD-CANTENAC 1997★

■ 3ème cru clas. 17 ha 68,000 100–149 F

70 75 79 80 **|81|**(82)83 **|85|**86 **|88|** |89| **|90|** **|91|** |92| 94 **95** 96 |97|

Lucien Guillemet is one of those wine-growers for whom the wine must bring out the personality of the terroir. That is the case with this wine, which comes from the northern rim of the excellent Cantenac plateau. It contains 60% Cabernet Sauvignon, and starts with a deep colour, before developing a bouquet of warm notes of red berries, toast and spices. The palate is supple, with good concentration and dense, mature tannins, and the finish is marked by liquorice. A true Margaux, which is full of charm and will be ready to drink by 2007.

SCE Ch. Boyd-Cantenac et Pouget, 33460 Cantenac, tel. 05.57.88.90.82, fax 05.57.88.33.27, e-mail lucien.guillemet@wanadoo.fr by appt.

CH. BRANE-CANTENAC 1997★★

■ 2ème cru clas. 84 ha 120,000 200–249 F

70 71 75 76 78 79 **|81|**82 **|83|**84 **|85|**(86)87 **|88|** **|89|** **|90|**91 92 93 **94 95**(96)**97**

This vineyard is a fine production unit, located on the southern flank of the Cantenac-Margaux plateau, where it has a beautiful terroir. These favourable natural conditions have been well exploited by Henri Lurton to produce a typical Margaux wine with fine, elegant tannins complemented by a sweet attack on the palate, a long finish and a complex bouquet (smoke, liquorice and vanilla with some empyreumatic notes). Its appearance is second to none, with a deep, dark colour which bears witness to the overall quality of a wine which should be kept for two years, and can then be drunk over at least the next four.

SCEA du Ch. Brane-Cantenac, 33460 Cantenac, tel. 05.57.88.83.33, fax 05.57.88.72.51 by appt.

Henri Lurton

LE BARON DE BRANE 1997★

■ n.c. 90,000 100–149 F

This second label from Brane-Cantenac does not have the personality of the previous wine, but has outstanding aromatic complexity, soft, full, supple tannins, and good length.

SCEA du Ch. Brane-Cantenac, 33460 Cantenac, tel. 05.57.88.83.33, fax 05.57.88.72.51 by appt.

CH. CANTENAC-BROWN 1997★

■ 3ème cru clas. 42 ha 180,000 150–199 F

75 76 79 80 81 82 **|83|**85 **|86|** |87| **|88|** **|89|** |(90)| **|91|** **|92| 93 94 95 96** 97

Built in 1867 by John Louis Brown, the English animal painter and friend of Toulouse-Lautrec, this château bears a resemblance to certain British houses. Since being taken over by AXA Millésime and run by Jean-Michel Cazes's team, this vineyard has proved highly reliable in terms of quality, and this vintage is no exception. The initial impression is of a very young wine, with a beautiful, dark ruby colour shimmering with purple, and a bouquet which is also delightfully subtle (toast, cocoa, spices and red berries). Tha palate is supple and well structured with fine tannins, and has a good balance which means that this attractive wine is already pleasant to drink, but should be kept for three or four years before being opened.

Jean-Michel Cazes, Ch. Cantenac-Brown, 33460 Margaux, tel. 05.57.88.81.81, fax 05.57.88.81.90, e-mail infochato@cantenacbrown.com by appt.

Axa Millésime

CH. CANUET 1997

■ n.c. 60,000 100–149 F

This label used to belong to a small, independent property, but now represents the second wine from Cantenac-Brown. It is more linear than the first, and is well composed, with a substantial structure which will enable it to be kept for one or two years. Its full-bodied palate and bouquet of fruity and musky notes have great appeal.

🔑 Jean-Michel Cazes, Ch. Cantenac-Brown, 33460 Margaux, tel. 05.57.88.81.81, fax 05.57.88.81.90, e-mail infochato@cantenacbrown.com ☑ Y by appt.

CH. DAUZAC 1997★★

■5ème cru clas. 25 ha 130,000 ⬛ 200–249 F

78 79 80 81 82 83 84 85|**86**| 87|**88**| |**89**| |(**90**)| 91 92 |93| **95 96 97**

This vineyard made history in 1880 with the discovery by Millardet and Gayon of Bordeaux mixture as a remedy for attacks of oidium and mildew. It is still a wine-making Mecca today by virtue of the quality of its wines. André Lurton has made light of the difficulties of the vintage and produced a true wine for longer maturing. With its intense colour, rich bouquet of vanilla against a background of blackcurrants, toast and chocolate, a concentrated structure based on flavourful tannins, and a powerful, distinguished finish, everything about it is already pleasant, but it will gain from being kept for at least five years.

🔑 Sté d'exploitation du Ch. Dauzac, 33460 Labarde-Margaux, tel. 05.57.88.32.10, fax 05.57.88.96.00 ☑ Y by appt.

🔑 MAIF

CH. DESMIRAIL 1997★

■3ème cru clas. 30 ha n.c. ⬛ 150–199 F

81 |**82**| (83)|**85**| |**86**| 87|88| |**89**| **90** |91| |92| |93| 94 95 96 |97|

Coming from a vineyard founded at the end of the 17th century on a plot of land at Rauzan, classified in 1855, then re-established from nothing by Lucien Lurton, this wine focuses resolutely on roundness and harmony. It is supported by delicate tannins and successfully blends the oak component into the very fine bouquet of dark berries, forming an overall impression of a wine without any harshness which opens with an attractive dark-red colour with violet glints, and ends with a beautiful finish. Can be drunk while quite young and will need time to breathe.

🔑 SCEA du Ch. Desmirail, 33460 Cantenac, tel. 05.57.88.83.33, fax 05.57.88.72.51 Y by appt.

🔑 Lucien Lurton

CH. DEYREM VALENTIN 1997★

■Cru bourg. 7 ha 45,000 ⬛ 70–99 F

75 76 81 82 83 85|86| |88| |89| |90| 91 92|93| |94| 95 97

While many Margaux growers favour finesse and elegance, this Soussanais vineyard traditionally prefers to focus on the strength of the tannic structure. The palate is perfectly in keeping with the intensity of the bouquet (ripe fruits, cherry stones, smoke and toast), and will fade once the wine has been kept for a little while.

🔑 EARL des Vignobles Jean Sorge, Ch. Deyrem-Valentin, 33460 Soussans, tel. 05.57.88.35.70, fax 05.57.88.36.84 ☑ Y by appt.

CH. DURFORT-VIVENS 1997★★

■2ème cru clas. 30 ha 65,000 ⬛ 150–199 F

75 (76) 81 82 83 85|(86)| |88| |89| |90| 91 92|93| |94| 95(96)97

Like his father Lucien, Gonzague Lurton is an ardent defender of the Margaux tradition, refusing to follow fashion and preferring to seek balance and harmony. That goal has been perfectly achieved with this 1997 wine, which is a blend of 80% Cabernet Sauvignon and 20% Merlot. It has a lovely cherry colour and reveals a complex bouquet (tobacco, liquorice and almonds), before developing a supple, fine, elegant palate. With good support from soft, well-extracted tannins, the overall impression is characteristic of the Margaux spirit, and bodes well for an excellent wine in two to three years' time. Let us not forget, by the way, their celebrated 1996 vintage, which is a great wine for longer maturing.

🔑 SCEA Ch. Durfort, Ch. Durfort-Vivens, 33460 Margaux, tel. 05.57.88.31.02, fax 05.57.88.60.60 Y by appt.

🔑 Gonzague Lurton

CH. FERRIERE 1997★

■3ème cru clas. 10 ha n.c. ⬛ 200–249 F

70 75 78 81 83 84|(**85**)| |**86**| 87|88| 89 92**93 94 95 96** 97

Although rather more austere than some previous vintages, this 1997 wine is nonetheless a fine achievement, with a bouquet supported by an elegant, distinguished note of oak, and a full, long, well-composed structure with tannins which are rich and round, though more austere at the finish. Best kept for two or three years until they fade. The second wine here is the **1997 Les Remparts de Ferrière**, which is recommended (70–99F).

🔑 Claire Villars-Lurton, Ch. La Ferrière, 33460 Margaux, tel. 05.56.58.02.37, fax 05.57.88.84.40, e-mail chasse-spleen@vins.bordeaux.fr Y by appt.

CH. GISCOURS 1997★

■3ème cru clas. 78 ha 215,000 ⬛ 200–249 F

75 78 81 82 83 85|(**86**)| |**88**| **89** 90 |91| **93** 94 97

This is a vast property with a château which was built between 1825 and 1845, and is as monumental as the buildings where the wine is produced. The property was taken over in 1995 by Eric Albada-Jelgersma, and is also a modern estate where the computer is king. This modern approach has been put at the service of tradition, as is clear from this 1997 wine, whose bouquet is classically Bordeaux. The palate is frank, well marked and full-bodied, and opens out into a long finish which is supported by high-quality oak. The overall impression is of a wine which is still a little austere, and will gain from being kept for four to five years. The second wine here is the **1997 Sirène de Giscours**, which is recommended (100–149F).

🔑 SAE Ch. Giscours, 10, rte de Giscours, Labarde, 33460 Margaux, tel. 05.57.97.09.09, fax 05.57.97.09.00, e-mail giscours@château-giscours.fr ☒ Y by appt.

CH. HAUT BRETON LARIGAUDIERE 1997★

■Cru bourg. 12.46 ha 63,000 100–149 F

|90| |91| 92 |93| 94 95 96 97

This vineyard has produced wines of reliable quality over recent years, and has not failed to do so in the 1997 vintage, which has an interesting and complex range of fine vanilla and toast notes. Its beautiful dark-berry flavours blended in with the oak mean that the palate is very harmonious, as is the rich, powerful, elegant finish.

🔑 SCEA Ch. Haut Breton Larigaudière, 33460 Soussans, tel. 05.57.88.94.17, fax 05.57.88.39.14 ☒ Y by appt.

CH. D'ISSAN 1997★

■3ème cru clas. 28 ha 180,000 250–299 F

82 **83 85 86** 87 **88** |89| |90| 92 93 **94** 95 96 97

With its beautiful 17th-century manor house surrounded by remains from the feudal era, Issan is one of the most appealing châteaux in the Médoc. Its wine is not without attractive features either; its brilliant colour, lit up by cherry glints, and delightfully intense, fruity bouquet provide a feeling of elegance which reappears on the palate with a subtle balance between suppleness and fullness.

🔑 Sté Fermière Viticole de Cantenac, Ch. d'Issan, 33460 Cantenac, tel. 05.57.88.35.91, fax 05.57.88.74.24 ☒ Y by appt.

🔑 Cruse

CH. KIRWAN 1997★

■3ème cru clas. 35 ha 90,000 300–499 F

75 79 81 82 83 |**85**| |(86)| |88| **89 91 92** |**93**| 94 **95 96** 97

It was an Irish owner who gave his name in the 18th century to this estate, of which Thomas Jefferson said in 1787 that it was one of the best Margaux vineyards. Two centuries later, the qualities of this wine have won unanimous recognition, notably its beautiful dark-purple colour, its powerful attack on the palate and its structure based on dense tannins which should fade in five to six years' time to make this an excellent wine.

🔑 Jean-Henri Schÿler, Ch. Kirwan, 33460 Cantenac, tel. 05.57.88.71.00 ☒ Y ev. day 9am–5pm; Sat. Sun. by appt.; cl. Jan.

🔑 Schröder et Schÿler SA

KRESSMANN Grande réserve 1997

■ n.c. n.c. 70–99 F

This wine appears under the brand name of one of the most famous Bordeaux *négociants*. Its tannins are firm, and it has a very full bouquet, with chocolate cutting across spices, menthol and pepper, and a slight floral note into the bargain. Best kept for three or four years. The **1997 Grande Cuvée de Dourthe** (100–149F) is from the sister firm, and is also recommended.

🔑 Kressmann, 35, rte de Bordeaux, 33290 Parempuyre, tel. 05.56.35.53.00, fax 05.56.35.53.29, e-mail contact@cvbg.com ☒ Y by appt.

CH. LABEGORCE 1997

■Cru bourg. 34 ha 200,000 100–149 F

78 82 83 85 86 87 |90| 91 92 |93| 95 96 97

The château here is a superb Neo-Classical creation of majestic and severe appearance; the wine, on the other hand, is a delicate, almost timid 1997 vintage which expresses its personality in fine aromas of red berries, coconut, blackcurrants and leather. It has a very flavourful palate on which the oak is still dominant.

🔑 Ch. Labégorce, 33460 Margaux, tel. 05.57.88.71.32, fax 05.57.88.35.01, e-mail labegorce@chateau-labegorce.fr ☒ Y by appt.

🔑 Hubert Perrodo

CH. LABEGORCE ZEDE 1997★★

■Cru bourg. n.c. 90,000 100–149 F

82 (83) |**85**| |**86**| 87 |**88**| 89 90 91 **92** |**93**| |94| **95 96 97**

Under the firm rule of Luc Thienpont, who has been running the property since 1979, Labégorce Zédé has become one of the pillars of the appellation. If any further proof were needed, this vintage will provide it. Its dark-red colour and bouquet with notes of spices, leather, black cherries and blackcurrants express all the richness of this 1997 wine. The palate is full, flavourful, round, rich and long, and has a balanced structure which will enable it to reach its peak in three to four years' time.

🔑 GFA Labégorce-Zédé, 33460 Soussans, tel. 05.57.88.71.31, fax 05.57.88.72.54, e-mail Labegorce.zede@wanadoo.fr ☒ Y ev. day 8.30am–12 noon 2pm–6pm; cl. 20–31 Dec.

🔑 L. Thienpont

LA BERLANDE 1997

■ 4 ha 25,000 50–69 F

94 95 96 |97|

Henri Duboscq, the owner of Haut-Marbuzet, created this La Berlande *cuvée* for his wine-merchants' business. Although it does not claim to rival some previous vintages, this wine has a beautiful, very young, dark-red colour, and adheres to the spirit of the vineyard by virtue of its aromatic character, which offers a delightful combination of red berry, vanilla and toast fragrances.

🔑 Brusina-Brandler, 3, quai de Bacalan, 33300 Bordeaux, tel. 05.56.39.26.77, fax 05.56.69.16.84 ☒ Y by appt.

CH. LA BESSANE 1997★

■ 3 ha 12,000 200–249 F

Unusually for this area, the grape range in this wine not only includes Petit Verdot but is dominated by it (60%). Even so, the fruity aromas need to blend in with the toast notes acquired from oak. This is still very evident, and together with the raw material will ensure an ageing potential of three to four years.

🔑 SA Ch. Paloumey, 50, rue Pouge-de-Beau, 33290 Ludon-Médoc, tel. 05.57.88.00.66, fax 05.57.88.00.67, e-mail châteaupaloumey@wanadoo.fr ☑ 🍷 by appt.

CH. LA GURGUE 1997★

■Cru bourg. 10 ha n.c. 70–99 F

82 83 85 86 88 89 |90| 91 92 93 94 95 96 |97|

From the same producer as Château Ferrière, this wine has its own personality, expressed in its beautiful colour, between ruby and dark-red, a bouquet of musky notes, and very agreeable, mature, silky tannins. It is delicious now, but will also gain from further development.

🔑 Claire Villars-Lurton, Ch. La Gurgue, 33460 Margaux, tel. 05.56.58.02.37, fax 05.57.88.84.40, e-mail chasse-spleen@vins-bordeaux.fr 🍷 by appt.

CH. LARRUAU 1997

■Cru bourg. 11 ha 60,000 70–99 F

80 81 82 83 84 85 |86| 87 |88| |89| 90 91 |93| |94| 95 96 97

With this wine made from 55% Cabernet Sauvignon blended with Merlot and matured for 18 months in the barrel, 30% of which are new, Larruau has shown the qualities of its fine terroir to good advantage. True to form, this wine favours suppleness and finesse, evident in its pleasant fruity quality and well-dosed oak.

🔑 Bernard Château, 4, rue de La Trémoille, 33460 Margaux, tel. 05.57.88.35.50, fax 05.57.88.76.69 ☑ 🍷 by appt.

CH. LASCOMBES 1997★

■2ème cru clas. 50 ha 200,000 200–249 F

70 76 79 81 82 83 84 85 (86) |88| |89| 90 91 92 93 95 96 97

This strange château, half winery and half Gothic palace surrounded by a vast vineyard, is located at the heart of the little Médoc town of Margaux, and helps to shape the personality of the place by turning each district into a separate village. Although in the spirit of the vineyard and the appellation, this 1997 wine achieves a fine balance between tannic power and roundness, and also between aromas of fruit and oak. Best drunk within three or four years, while waiting for the 1995 and 1996 vintages, which are wines for longer maturing. The second wine here is the **1997 Chevalier de Lascombes**, which is recommended for its round, balanced structure (100–149F).

🔑 Ch. Lascombes, 33460 Margaux, tel. 05.57.88.70.66, fax 05.57.88.72.17 ☑ 🍷 by appt.

🔑 Bass

L'ENCLOS MAUCAILLOU 1997

■ 1.58 ha 7,500 70–99 F

|93| |94| 95 96 97

From the same producer as the Château Meyre (Haut-Médoc), this wine has particular appeal owing to its bouquet of elegant notes of vanilla and toast. The palate is still somewhat austere because of oak maturation, but it has the necessary structure to become more round in one to two years' time.

🔑 Ch. Meyre SA, 16, rte de Castelnau, 33480 Avensan, tel. 05.56.58.10.77, fax 05.56.58.13.20, e-mail chateau.meyre@wanadoo.fr ☑ 🍷 ev. day except Sat. Sun. 2pm–5pm; 1 Nov.–30 Mar. by appt.

CH. MARGAUX 1997★★★

■1er cru clas. 78 ha n.c. 500 F+

59 |61| 66 70 71 |75| 77 78 |79| 80 |81| (82) |83| ... |85| |86| |87| 88 89 90 91 |92| 93 94 (95) (96) 97

In addition to its remarkable Neo-Classical architecture, Château Margaux has a superb gravel terroir divided into three large plots, which only increases its potential for quality. All of these assets enable it to offer a 1997 wine whose ruby colour with black glints has an intensity which belies the reputation of the vintage. The fine, elegant bouquet goes cheerfully from notes of mocha to touches of spices and cloves against an elegant fruity background. The palate is rich, full and supple in the attack, then reveals a tannic substance which is noble, velvety, fresh and well-structured, guaranteeing a very good ageing potential. A wine with remarkable balance, great length, and a charming, young finish.

🔑 SC du Ch. Margaux, 33460 Margaux, tel. 05.57.88.83.83, fax 05.57.88.83.32

CH. MARQUIS D'ALESME BECKER 1997

■3ème cru clas. 13 ha 97,000 100–149 F

Although it is situated in the town's main street, this château of 17th-century inspiration is one of the most discreet Crus Classés in the appellation. That does not prevent its 1997 wine from being extremely pleasant with its dark-red colour, its agreeable complex bouquet (menthol, spices, apricots and citrus fruits), and its structure, supported by fairly dense tannins. A wine which should be kept for one or two years, then drunk over the next five years.

🔑 Jean-Claude Zuger, Ch. Marquis d'Alesme Becker, 33460 Margaux, tel. 05.57.88.70.27, fax 05.57.88.73.78 ☑ 🍷 ev. day except Sat. Sun. 8am–12 noon 2pm–6pm

CH. MARQUIS DE TERME 1997

■4ème cru clas. 40 ha 140,000 150–199 F

75 81 82 (83) 85 **86** 87 **89** 90 91 92 93 **94 95** 96 97

In 1762, the Marquis de Terme, a Gascon gentleman, received his wife's dowry in the form of plots of vines to which he gave his name. Falling well inside the lines of the AOC with a large percentage of Merlot (35%), a main component of Cabernets (58%) and a touch of Petit Verdot (7%), this vineyard offers a 1997 wine with a good balance between its suppleness, roundness and meatiness and its tannic structure. The bouquet ranges from floral aromas to mineral, spicy and liquorice notes, and also shows good complexity.

SCA Ch. Marquis de Terme, 3, rte de Rauzan, 33460 Margaux, tel. 05.57.88.31.60, fax 05.57.88.32.51 Y ev. day except Sat. Sun. 9am–11.30am 2pm–5pm

Séneclauze

CH. MARSAC SEGUINEAU 1997*

■Cru bourg. 10.22 ha 56,600 100–149 F

85 86 88 89 90 91 92 93 94 |95| 96 |97|

In 1770, a Bordeaux citizen, Pierre Séguineau, bought this vineyard which had been established on the Marsac plateau by a lawyer at the Bordeaux Parliament. Today the vineyard belongs to the Mestrezat estates, and now offers a 1997 vintage which clearly echoes the wine-makers' preferences. In the bouquet, they sought finesse and elegance, with aromas of roasted almonds enhanced by a slight hint of spices, and in the palate they went for fullness, (at least for the vintage), with very harmonious tannins and flavours of leather and game.

SC du Ch. Marsac-Séguineau, La Croix Bacalan, 109, rue Achard, B.P. 154, 33042 Bordeaux Cedex, tel. 05.56.11.29.00, fax 05.56.11.29.01 Y by appt.

CH. MONBRISON 1997**

■Cru bourg. 13.2 ha 37,000 200–249 F

82 83 84 **|85|(86)|** 87 **|88| |89| |90|** 91 92 93 94 95 96 **97**

Monbrison is not only a charming property on the edge of the Landais forest, it is also one of the most serious and reliable of the Crus Bourgeois. Its 1997 wine has a dark-red colour with a lively fringe, and makes a fine overall impression. The bouquet has oaky notes of toast blending well with red-berry aromas, and the structure is supple, full-bodied and balanced. An attractive wine still marked by oak, it will need to be kept for four or five years.

E.M. Davis et Fils, Ch. Monbrison, 33460 Arsac, tel. 05.56.58.80.04, fax 05.56.58.85.33 Y by appt.

CH. MONGRAVEY

Cuvée Prestige 1997*

■ 9 ha 36,000 70–99 F

This wine, a blend of Cabernet Sauvignon and 45% Merlot, has been matured in oak for 12 months and is a fine ambassador for the vineyard. The bouquet prolongs the favourable impression created by the colour (ruby with purple and violet glints), combining red berries, blackcurrants and prunes. The structure is supported by delicately dosed oak, and proves by its concentration and round tannins that this wine will be able to stand the test of time.

Régis Bernaleau, Ch. Mongravey, 33460 Arsac, tel. 05.56.58.84.51, fax 05.56.58.83.39, e-mail chateau.mongravey@wanadoo.fr Y by appt.

CH. MOULIN DE TRICOT 1997

■ 2 ha 15,000 70–99 F

This small vineyard was taken over by Bruno Rey in 1997, and is in the course of being reorganised. With this vintage the property offers a wine with a bouquet of good complexity (red berries and violets), a round attack on the palate, and tannins which are still very evident and call for a period of ageing.

Bruno Rey, 15, allée de Chappaz, 33460 Arsac, tel. 05.56.58.89.94, fax 05.56.58.89.94, e-mail brey@fr.packardbell.org Y by appt.

CH. PALMER 1997**

■3ème cru clas. 50 ha 140,000 500 F+

78 79 80 **|81| |82| |83|** 84 **|85| |(86)| |88| |89| 90 |91| |92| 93 94 95 96 97**

Located right at the centre of the hamlet of Issan, at the heart of the Cantenac and Margaux plateau, Palmer enjoys a well-favoured position and terroir, and bears the name of the English general who was the owner here under the Restoration. The château was built by the Pereire brothers in 1856. From its deep-purple colour to its long finish, the wine remains delightful throughout. The bouquet reveals all its finesse in notes of toast, then fruit; there is a clean, sweet attack, opening onto a mouth-filling, chewy palate which, together with the tannins, forms an overall impression of balance, complexity and harmony. It promises to age well.

Ch. Palmer, 33460 Margaux, tel. 05.57.88.72.72 Y by appt.

PAVILLON ROUGE 1997**

■ n.c. n.c. 150–199 F

78 |81| **|82| |83| |84| |85| |86| 88 89 90** |92| **93 94 95 96 97**

Like the main label here (the Château Margaux), the Pavillon Rouge is unaffected by the constraints of the vintage. We are looking here at a truly great achievement. The elegant bouquet develops delicate aromas of toast against a background of soft fruits. The supple tannins blend into a homogeneous, well-made wine which lingers on an agreeable impression of spices. It deserves to be laid down in the cellar for four or five years.

SC du Ch. Margaux, 33460 Margaux, tel. 05.57.88.83.83, fax 05.57.88.83.32

BORDEAUX

CH. POUGET 1997

■4ème cru clas. 10 ha 47,000 100–149 F

75 78 81 |83| 85 86 88 |89| |90| 92 94 95 96 |97|

Pouget is named after the family which founded it then sold it in 1906 to the Guillemets, who kept the coat of arms which had been granted by the Duc de Richelieu. Like the Boyd Cantenac, this wine has been produced by Lucien Guillemet, but the two are very different. This one has a much less complex style, although it does have a good structure.

SCE Ch. Boyd-Cantenac et Pouget, 33460 Cantenac, tel. 05.57.88.90.82, fax 05.57.88.33.27, e-mail lucien.guillemet@wanadoo.fr by appt.

CH. PRIEURE-LICHINE 1997*

■4ème cru clas. 40 ha 305,000 150–199 F

82 83 86 |88| |89| 90 91 |92| |93| 96 97

Once a monastery known as the Cantenac Priory, this vineyard owes its fame to Alexis Lichine, who ran it for half a century. It changed hands in 1999, and is surrounded by a huge vineyard on a high-quality terroir growing 53% Petit Verdot and 42% Merlot. The 1997 wine has a beautiful colour, then develops a concentrated, complex bouquet, before revealing a substantial structure and a chewy persistence. The whole combination makes it a very good wine for longer maturing (five years or more), in which the oak component has been assimilated without problems.

Ch. Prieuré-Lichine, 34, av. de la Ve-République, 33460 Cantenac, tel. 05.57.88.36.28, fax 05.57.88.78.93, e-mail prieuré.lichine@wanadoo.fr by appt.

Ballande

CH. RAUZAN-GASSIES 1997**

■2ème cru clas. 28 ha 130,000 150–199 F

|93| |94| 96 97

For years the Quiés have worked with patient dedication to improve their vineyards, including Rauzan-Gassies. Their patience has its just reward in this wine, despite the difficulty of the vintage. The intensity of its colour is astonishing, as are the freshness of the bouquet of raspberries along with blackberries, the suppleness and elegance of the tannins, and the perfectly dosed support from oak. All of this is true to the terroir and makes it a typical, genuine wine which should be kept for between three and seven years.

SCA du Ch. Rauzan-Gassies, 33460 Margaux, tel. 05.57.88.71.88, fax 05.57.88.37.49 ev. day 8am–12 noon 2pm–6pm

J.-M. Quié

CH. RAUZAN-SEGLA 1997**

■2ème cru clas. 51 ha 87,000 250–299 F

81 |83| |85| |88| |89| 90 91 92 93 94 95 (96) 97

Run from a pleasant manor house dating from the 17th and 18th centuries, this huge vineyard offers a 1997 wine, the result of rigorous grape selection, which is powerful with good maturing potential. Its bouquet plays skilfully on the contrast between the freshness of the menthol notes and the almost wild quality of the leather, musk and toast aromas. On the palate it develops a full, fleshy structure which opens out into a long vanilla finish.

Ch. Rauzan-Ségla, B.P. 56, 33460 Margaux, tel. 05.57.88.82.10, fax 05.57.88.34.54 by appt.

Wertheimer

SEGLA 1997*

■ n.c. 100,000 70–99 F

A second label from the Château Rauzan-Ségla, this wine does not have the fullness of its elder brother. Nevertheless it has a supple round structure, supported by well-extracted tannins, and a bouquet of fine notes of blackcurrant and spices, both of which make it an attractive wine. It is already pleasant to drink, but should reach its peak in two or three years time.

Ch. Rauzan-Ségla, B.P. 56, 33460 Margaux, tel. 05.57.88.82.10, fax 05.57.88.34.54 by appt.

CH. SAINT-MARC 1997

■ 8 ha 21,600 30–49 F

This wine comes from a small Soussans property, and proudly bears the stamp of Cabernet Sauvignon (70% of the grape blend) in its bouquet. The palate reveals mature tannins of elegant simplicity.

La Guyennoise, B.P. 17, 33540 Sauveterre-de-Guyenne, tel. 05.56.71.50.76, fax 05.56.71.87.70

Marc Faure

CH. SIRAN 1997*

■Cru bourg. 24 ha 900,000 100–149 F

64 66 78 79 80 81 82 83 84 |85| 86 87 88 |89| |90| 91 92 |93| 94 95 96 97

This is a beautiful, vast property of the type that is dear to the Margaux appellation. The 1997 wine is also in keeping with the spirit of the appellation by virtue of its character, which is both supple and structured, and is supported by fine tannins. Add to that a young, clean colour followed by an expressive bouquet (fruits, cocoa and burning), and the result is an appealing wine which should be kept in the cellar for three or four years.

SC du Ch. Siran, Ch. Siran, 33460 Labarde, tel. 05.57.88.34.04, fax 05.57.88.70.05, e-mail chateau.siran@wanadoo.fr ev. day 10am–12.30pm 1.30pm–6pm; groups by appt.

Alain Miailhe

CH. TAYAC 1997

■Cru bourg. 18 ha 130,000 70–99 F

Coming from an excellent property which has many other brands, this fine, pleasant wine will be best drunk while young in order to take advantage of the roundness of its tannins. The **1997 Château Labory de Tayac** is distributed by the wine-trade, and is also recommended.

SC Ch. Tayac, Tayac, 33460 Soussans, tel. 05.57.88.33.06, fax 05.57.88.36.06 ✉ Y ev. day except Sat. Sun. 9am–12.30pm 2pm–6pm

CH. TAYAC-PLAISANCE 1997★

■Cru artisan 2.24 ha 15,000 70–99 F

This is one of the few small Margaux Crus Artisans which have been able to resist being taken over by the large estates. Its 1997 wine has excellent potential, and is a blend of 5% Petit Verdot, 50% Merlot and 45% of the two Cabernets. It has real assets that will enable it to withstand the ageing period (four to five years) that it needs in order to become more supple. Its colour is dense and deep, and its thoroughbred aromas run through floral and spicy notes which are not dominated by the oak. 'Nice work,' commented one taster.

Paul Bajeux, 1, imp. Valmy-Tayac, 33460 Soussans, tel. 05.57.88.36.83, fax 05.57.88.36.83 ✉ Y by appt.

CH. DES TROIS CHARDONS 1997

■ n.c. 15,000 70–99 F

78 79 82 83 85 86 |88| |89| |90| 91 92 |94| 95 96 97

This small Cantenacais establishment is a true winemakers' vineyard. With this vintage it offers a wine in the old style, which has fine substance and still bears the stamp of oak maturation, both of which mean that it should be kept for quite a while.

Claude et Yves Chardon, Issan, 33460 Cantenac, tel. 05.57.88.39.13, fax 05.57.88.33.94 ✉ Y by appt.

CH. VINCENT 1997★★

■ n.c. 8,000 100–149 F

This vineyard was founded by the Jadouins, one of the outstanding families in the history of Margaux wine-making, and is still in the hands of their descendants today. It has the benefit of a fine terroir and the expertise of the Palmer team to carry out its production. This very accomplished 1997 wine has a characteristically deep colour and a complex bouquet of blackcurrant and pepper notes. The palate is full, dense and perfectly supported by elegant tannins, and illustrates the spirit of Margaux by demonstrating in magisterial fashion that it is possible to produce a rich, concentrated wine with excellent ageing potential without falling into the trap of over-enthusiastic extraction.

Marthe Domec, Ch. Vincent, Issan, 33460 Cantenac, tel. 02.43.29.35.57, fax 02.57.88.30.12 ✉

Moulis-en-Médoc

An area consisting of a narrow ribbon 12 km (7 miles) long and only 300 or 400 m wide (300–400 yds), Moulis is the least extensive of the *appellations communales* in the Médoc. However, it offers a range of different *terroirs*.

As with Listrac, it falls into three main areas. The Bouqueyran area, to the west near the road from Bordeaux to Soulac, has a varied topography with limestone crests and a slope of ancient, Pyrenean gravel. In the centre, a plain of clay and limestone forms an extension of the Peyrelebade plain (see Listrac-Médoc). Finally, to the east and north-east, near the railway line, there rises a series of fine ridges of Garonne gravel forming a first-class *terroir* within which the famous hillocks of Grand-Poujeaux, Maucaillou and Médrac are clustered.

Moulis wines are soft and full, with a supple, delicate character. Even though they can be kept for some time (seven or eight years), they can develop more rapidly than wines from other communes in the area. The 1999 vintage produced 31,524 hl (832,234 gal).

CH. ANTHONIC 1997★

■Cru bourg. 20.53 ha 146,000 70–99 F

82 83 **85** (86) 88 **89** |90| 91 92 |93| **94 95** 96 97

Wine-growing was established here in 1789. It did not take on its present name until 1924, and has only belonged to the Cordonniers since 1977. This solid, safe, reliable vineyard will do no damage to its reputation with a 1997 wine of great style. It has a very pleasant bouquet combining ripe fruits and oaky toast, is complex and delightfully fine, and has a charming structure. Its silky tannins will enable it to be drunk in two or three years' time.

🗝 SCEA Pierre Cordonnier, Ch. Anthonic, 33480 Moulis-en-Médoc, tel. 05.56.58.34.60, fax 05.56.58.72.76 ☒ Y ev. day except Sat. Sun. 8.30am–12.30pm 2pm–5.30pm

CH. BEL-AIR LAGRAVE

Grand vin 1997

■Cru bourg. 9 ha 50,000 100–149 F

Coming from the same producer as La Closerie du Grand-Poujeaux, this wine starts with a beautiful, dark-red colour. It has a deep nose of musky and black berry notes, while the palate has more of a vanilla quality and is marked by oak. This is a wine well equipped to face an ageing period of some years.

🗝 GFA Le Grand-Poujeaux, 33480 Moulis-en-Médoc, tel. 05.56.58.01.89, fax 05.56.58.05.21 ☒ Y by appt.
🗝 J. Bacquey

CH. BISTON-BRILLETTE 1997★

■Cru bourg. 21 ha 110,000 70–99 F

86 |88| |89| |(90)| 91 92 |93| 94 95 **96** 97

This vineyard has belonged to the Barbarins since 1930. Their blend contains equal shares of Merlot and Cabernet Sauvignon. In 1997, wisdom demanded that the vinification here be adapted to the potential of the vintage. Clearly this was a sensible decision, as is shown by the intensity of the wine's colour, its lovely bouquet of cinnamon and gamey notes, and its substantial yet silky tannins. An attractive wine, which should be kept for about four years.

🗝 EARL Ch. Biston-Brillette, Petit-Poujeaux, 33480 Moulis-en-Médoc, tel. 05.56.58.22.86, fax 05.56.58.13.16, e-mail contact@châteaubistonbrillette.com ☒ Y ev. day except Sun. 10am–12 noon 2pm–6pm; Sat. 10am–12 noon
🗝 Michel Barbarin

CH. BOUQUEYRAN 1997★

■Cru bourg. 10.72 ha 86,000 70–99 F

This wine takes its character from a grape blend in which the major component is Merlot (57%), and careful, well-dosed maturation in oak. There is a noticeable elegance in its bouquet of crystallised fruit and spice notes, and this is apparent again in the delicate sensations at the finish. The overall impression is extremely pleasant.

🗝 Philippe Porcheron, SARL des Grands Crus, Le Lieulet, 33480 Moulis-en-Médoc, tel. 05.56.58.35.77, fax 05.56.58.14.24 ☒ Y Mon. Tue. Thu. Fri. 8.30am–12 noon 1.30pm–5pm; cl. Aug.

CH. CHASSE-SPLEEN 1997★★

■ 52 ha 275,370 150–199 F

75 76 **78 79** 80 **81 82** |(83)| **|85| |86| |88|** |89| **90** |91| |92| **|93| |94| 95 96 97**

As early as 1560, a man by name of Gressier was making wine here. In about 1820, the château was divided up between two heirs, and it was then that Chasse-Spleen took on its name. Its grape range includes 73% Cabernet Sauvignon, 20% Merlot and 7% Petit Verdot. The 1997 wine starts with a lovely purple colour with violet glints, then shows its aristocratic character in a bouquet in which attractive notes of toast and ripe fruits come through the high-quality oak. The structure is full, tannic, concentrated, harmonious, balanced and persistent, and fully lives up to the initial impression. Keep for three to four years.

🗝 C. Villars, Ch. Chasse-Spleen, 33480 Moulis-en-Médoc, tel. 05.56.58.02.37, fax 05.57.88.84.40, e-mail chasse-spleen@vins-bordeaux.fr Y by appt.

L'ORATOIRE DE CHASSE-SPLEEN 1997

■ 9 ha 106,600 150–199 F

The second wine from Chasse-Spleen is made from young vines (80% Cabernet Sauvignon and 20% Merlot). Twelve months of maturation in barrels have produced a 1997 wine with an intense, deep, beautiful cherry-red colour. The nose is marked by musky notes, and is followed by a frank, balanced palate.

🗝 C. Villars, Ch. Chasse-Spleen, 33480 Moulis-en-Médoc, tel. 05.56.58.02.37, fax 05.57.88.84.40, e-mail chasse-spleen@vins-bordeaux.fr Y by appt.

CH. DUTRUCH GRAND-POUJEAUX 1997★

■Cru bourg. 24 ha 150,000 70–99 F

81 82(83)85 **|86|** |88| 89 |90| 91 |93| |94| 95 **96** |97|

François Cordonnier is now being helped by his nephew Jean-Baptiste Cordonnier, who has been building new wineries since 1999. This wine is a blend of 50% Merlot, Cabernet Sauvignon and 5% Petit Verdot, and although it does not rival some previous vintages, it has an attractive bouquet which is now opening (flowers and toast), and shows good presence on the palate, where it is supported by a delicate but well-balanced structure. This wine's attraction lies in its aromatic richness.

🗝 EARL François Cordonnier, Ch. Dutruch Grand-Poujeaux, 33480 Moulis-en-Médoc, tel. 05.56.58.02.55, fax 05.56.58.06.22 ☒ Y by appt.

CH. GRANINS GRAND-POUJEAUX 1997★

■Cru bourg. 8.08 ha 22,000 70–99 F

|95| 96 |97|

With its fine Günz gravel soil in the Poujeaux area, and a diverse range of grapes – Merlot (50%), Cabernet Sauvignon (40%), Petit Verdot (10%) and Malbec (5%) – everything is in place here to produce an attractive wine like this 1997 vintage, whose appeal is not limited to its beautiful colour with crimson glints. It also has an intense fruity bouquet (cherries) set off by notes of vanilla and liquorice, and a full-bodied aromatic structure, which together form an overall impression of quality.

SCEA Batailley, Ch. Granins Grand-Poujeaux, 33480 Moulis-en-Médoc, tel. 05.56.58.05.82, fax 05.56.58.05.26, e-mail sceabatailley@wanadoo.fr by appt.

CH. HAUT-FRANQUET 1997

Cru bourg. 5 ha n.c. 100-149 F

This vineyard belongs to the same group as Bel-Air Lagrave, and now offers a wine for longer maturing. It has a rather original bouquet of caramel and brandy notes mingled with brioche, and will need to be kept for three to five years until its tannins are rounder.

GFA Le Grand-Poujeaux, 33480 Moulis-en-Médoc, tel. 05.56.58.01.89, fax 05.56.58.05.21 by appt.

CH. LA CLOSERIE DU GRAND-POUJEAUX 1997★

Cru bourg. 7 ha 35,000 100-149 F

This wine clearly has high ambitions. It has good ageing potential, and asserts its youth without the slightest trace of rusticity. There is a very delicate nose of floral notes (roses and hyacinths), toast, spices and leather, after which it develops a sweet, full-bodied and flavourful palate.

GFA Le Grand-Poujeaux, 33480 Moulis-en-Médoc, tel. 05.56.58.01.89, fax 05.56.58.05.21 by appt.

J. Bacquey

CH. LA GARRICQ 1997★

3 ha 16,000 100-149 F

93 94 |95| 96 97

The quality at this vineyard continues to rise, and with this vintage it is offering a very accomplished wine indeed. It has a dense framework with full-bodied, elegant tannins, and a bouquet of fine complexity, which together form a harmonious, promising overall impression. A wine which deserves to stay in the cellar for four or five years.

SA Ch. Paloumey, 50, rue Pouge-de-Beau, 33290 Ludon-Médoc, tel. 05.57.88.00.66, fax 05.57.88.00.67, e-mail châteaupaloumey@wanadoo.fr by appt.

CH. MALMAISON 1997★

Cru bourg. 24.13 ha 145,000 70-99 F

88 89 90 **91** 92 93 |94| 95 96 97

Coming from a huge 134-ha (331-acre) vineyard which belongs to Benjamin de Rothschild, this wine is a blend of Cabernet Sauvignon and 64% Merlot. Its high-quality tannins have an elegance which indicates that the oak is beginning to fade. Even so it will need to be kept for some time. A well-made, balanced wine, which will be a good accompaniment to partridge.

Cie vin. barons Ed. et B. de Rothschild, 33480 Listrac-Médoc, tel. 05.56.58.38.00, fax 05.56.58.26.46, e-mail chateau.clarke@wanadoo.fr by appt.

Benjamin de Rothschild

CH. MAUCAILLOU 1997★

69 ha 530,000 150-199 F

81 **82 83 85 86** 87 **|88| |89| |90|91 92 |93| |94|** 95 96 97

This vast property was built in 1875 by Monsieur Petit-Laroche as a wedding gift for his young wife. It has belonged to the Dourthe family since 1929. Although this vintage does not claim to rival the splendid 1996 vintage, it is nonetheless of a high standard, as can be seen from its intense, brilliant colour. The bouquet is still marked by oak, with delicate notes of vanilla and cinnamon, and developing fruit aromas are beginning to break through. On the palate it finds its full expression, revealing a good substance which opens out into an aromatic finish. Keep for three to four years.

Ch. Maucaillou, quartier de la Gare, 33480 Moulis-en-Médoc, tel. 05.56.58.01.23, fax 05.56.58.00.88 ev. day 10am–12.30pm 2pm–7pm

Philippe Dourthe

CH. MOULIN A VENT 1997

Cru bourg. 25 ha 170,000 70-99 F

81 **82 83** 85 86 88 |89| |90|91 92 95 |96| |97|

This wine comes from the highest hilltop vineyard in Moulis, in the west of the appellation. It is simple but well made, with a balanced structure and a pleasant fruity bouquet.

Dominique Hessel, Ch. Moulin à Vent, Bouqueyran, 33480 Moulis-en-Médoc, tel. 05.56.58.15.79, fax 05.56.58.39.89, e-mail hessel@moulin-a-vent.com ev. day except Sat. Sun. 9am–12 noon 2pm–6pm

CH. MYON DE L'ENCLOS 1997

4 ha 20,000 50-69 F

Although not of the same standard as its Mayne Lalande cousin in Listrac, this wine is very well made. It has a delightful bouquet (ripe fruits and leather), then develops a full, tannic structure which will require a short ageing period of two or three years.

Bernard Lartigue, Ch. Mayne Lalande, 33480 Listrac-Médoc, tel. 05.56.58.27.63, fax 05.56.58.22.41 by appt.

CH. PEY BERLAND 1997

0.9 ha n.c. 100-149 F

Made entirely from Merlot grapes grown on less than one hectare (2.5 acres), this wine is not unaffected by fashion. It will be no surprise to find that it has a pronounced oaky quality which does not yet leave enough room for fruit, but which will appeal to wine-lovers with its notes of liquorice, mocha and toast, accompanied by a slight hint of exotic fruits. Good ageing potential.

Jean Charpentier, Ch. Pey Berland, 33480 Moulis-en-Médoc, tel. 05.56.58.38.84, fax 05.56.58.38.84 by appt.

CH. POUJEAUX 1997★★

■Cru bourg. 53 ha 300,000 150–199 F

81 82 83 84 |85| |86| 87 |88| |89| 90 |91| |92| 93 94 95 96 97

The Theil family, who this year are celebrating the 80th anniversary of their arrival at this vineyard, set a fine example for reliability. Just like its very intense colour, the powerful bouquet and palate of this wine show clearly that it comes from noble stock. The complexity of the first and the richness of the second perfectly express the personality of a great gravel terroir. A great wine which deserves to be kept for six to eight years.

Jean Theil SA, Ch. Poujeaux, 33480 Moulis-en-Médoc, tel. 05.56.58.02.96, fax 05.56.58.01.25, e-mail châteaupoujeaux@wanadoo.fr ev. day except Sat. Sun. 9am–12 noon 2pm–5pm

Pauillac

With a population hardly greater than that of a large market town, Pauillac has a real urban feel, enhanced by a pleasure-boat harbour on the route of the Canal du Midi. The café terraces on the quay are the place to enjoy a plate of freshly caught shrimps from the estuary. But Pauillac is also, and above all, the capital of the Médoc wine-growing region, both by virtue of its geographical location in the middle of the vineyard and by the presence of three of the Premiers Crus Classés (Lafite, Latour and Mouton), which complete a really impressive tally of 18 Crus Classés. The co-operative produces a large quantity of wines. The appellation as a whole produced 63,585 hl (1,678,644 gal) in 1999.

The appellation is cut in two by the Chenal du Gahet, a small stream running through the middle of the two plateaux where the vines are grown. The area to the north, which takes its name from the hamlet of Pouyalet, is slightly higher, by about 30 m (98 ft) and has steeper slopes. It is the home of two of the Premiers Crus Classés (Lafite and Mouton) and enjoys an outstandingly fine balance between soil and subsoil, an attribute shared by the plateau of Saint-Lambert to the south. This second area stretches south from the Gahet to the Juillac Valley, where a small stream runs along the southern border of the commune and gives excellent drainage. The area's gravels, which are formed from large stones, are particularly distinctive on the *terroir* of its Premier Cru, Château Latour.

Pauillacs from pure gravel ridges are very full-bodied wines, powerful and well-structured, but also fine and elegant, with a delicate bouquet. They develop very well as they age, and are worth waiting for. When mature, they can be served with confidence to accompany strongly flavoured dishes prepared with mushrooms, for instance, or to complement red meat, dark game meat or foie gras.

CH. D'ARMAILHAC 1997★

■5ème cru clas. 50 ha n.c. 100–149 F

72 73 74 75 78 79 80 81 |82| |83| 84 |85| |86| 87 |88| |89| 90 92 93 |94| 95 96 97

Armailhac, which took on its original name again at the beginning of the 1990s, has an excellent terroir in the middle of which there is a huge park – something which is becoming more and more rare in the Médoc. This wine has a very intense, deep-red colour. It is full and well structured, and will need three or four years to become harmonious. The palate is substantial, and there is a toasty, spicy bouquet of good intensity (juniper berries, cloves, and a menthol flavour at the end) which will give it good ageing potential.

Ch. d'Armailhac, 33250 Pauillac, tel. 05.56.73.20.20, fax 05.56.73.20.44

Baronne Ph. de Rothschild GFA

BARON NATHANIEL 1997★

■ n.c. n.c. 70–99 F

This wine is a prestige brand belonging to the Baron Philippe de Rothschild wine-merchants company, and is named after the founder, who bought Mouton in 1863. It fully lives up to its developer's hopes for it. With a blend of 80% Cabernet Sauvignon, 10% Merlot, Cabernet Franc, Malbec and Petit Verdot, this is a genuine Pauillac for longer maturing. The ageing process will enable it to grow rounder and find its perfect aromatic expression, based on a bouquet which is harmoniously balanced between fruit and oak.

Baron Philippe de Rothschild SA, B.P. 117, 33250 Pauillac, tel. 05.56.73.20.20, fax 05.56.73.20.44

CH. BATAILLEY 1997★★

■5ème cru clas. 55 ha 420,000 150–199 F

70 75 76 78 79 80 81|82| **|83| |85| |86| |88|** |89| |90| 91 92**93 95 96 97**

From the Guestiers to the Castéjas, this vast property has been linked to some of the greatest names in the Bordeaux wine business. That accounts to some extent for its fame, but it also owes much to its gravel terroir. This combination of nature and man has produced many attractive wines such as this 1997 vintage. It has a strong bouquet of *pain d'épices* (a kind of spice loaf), coffee, toast, prunes and blackcurrants, and a structure based on rich, imposing, well-extracted tannins. The harmonious finish of cherry in brandy confirms its good ageing potential.

Héritiers Castéja, 33250 Pauillac, tel. 05.56.00.00.70, fax 05.57.87.48.61 by appt.

Emile Castéja

CH. BEHERE 1997

■Cru artisan 1.8 ha 10,000 100–149 F

Coming from a very small vineyard of less than two hectares (five acres) which has been purchased plot by plot, this wine has to rely on relatively young vines. Even so, it has a substantial structure which will enable it to grow rounder once it has been kept for three or four years. It drew the jury's attention with its attractive, dark colour, a nose combining tuberose and notes of toast, and a palate marked by an oak flavour which is powerful but does not mask the fruit.

Anne-Marie et Jean-Gabriel Camou, 13, rue Paul-Doumer, 33250 Pauillac, tel. 05.56.59.11.19, fax 05.56.59.11.19 ev. day except Sun. 8am–12 noon 2pm–6pm

CH. BELLEGRAVE 1997

■ 6 ha 45,000 100–149 F

This young, tannic wine shows a certain elegance in its subtle, smoky bouquet, and good balance on the palate. Its ruby colour edged with orange seems to suggest an ageing period of less than five years.

EARL Ch. Bellegrave, 33250 Pauillac, tel. 05.56.59.06.47, fax 05.56.59.06.47 by appt.

CH. CLERC MILON 1997★★

■5ème cru clas. 30 ha n.c. 150–199 F

|75| 76 78 79**|82| |83| |85| 86** 87**88 89 90 |92| 93** |94| 95**96 97**

Most of Philippine de Rothschild's labels show the works of art that can be seen in the museum at the Château Mouton-Rothschild: in this case, two 17th-century figurines in enamel, gold and pearls. This vineyard has two fine hilltop gravel vineyards (Milon and Mousset). It has made good use of them for this wine, despite the difficulty of the vintage. It is expressive both on the palate and in the nose (smoke, spices, toast, coffee, juniper berries with notes of green pepper, prunes, redcurrant jam and even menthol). The structure, which is supported by substantial tannins, is equally rich and gives it a certain amount of ageing potential.

Ch. Clerc Milon, 33250 Pauillac, tel. 05.56.73.20.20, fax 05.56.73.20.44

Baronne Ph. de Rothschild GFA

CH. COLOMBIER-MONPELOU 1997★

■Cru bourg. 15 ha 115,000 70–99 F

|94| 95 **96** 97

This vineyard, which has been owned by Bernard Jugla since 1979 and is located on the central plateau of the commune, has a classic Médoc grape range. This wine not only has an attractive bouquet of crystallised cherry notes, but also a very well-balanced palate which develops beautiful, complex, thoroughbred flavours then goes into a rich finish on notes of chocolate. A very expressive wine which has clearly been carefully produced.

SC Vignobles Jugla, Ch. Colombier-Monpelou, 33250 Pauillac, tel. 05.56.59.01.48, fax 05.56.59.12.01 by appt.

CH. CORDEILLAN-BAGES 1997★★

■Cru bourg. 2 ha 12,000 200–249 F

|89| |91| 93 **94** 95 96 **97**

This property is famous for the four-star hotel at the château, and is also a vineyard well respected for the quality of its produce, as revealed by this wine in a vintage known to be difficult. Its red and dark-purple colour is a good sign from the start. It then develops from green peppers towards blackcurrants and leather, with shades of toast, roasting and jam. With its substantial structure and full-bodied tannins, the palate is already very

Pauillac

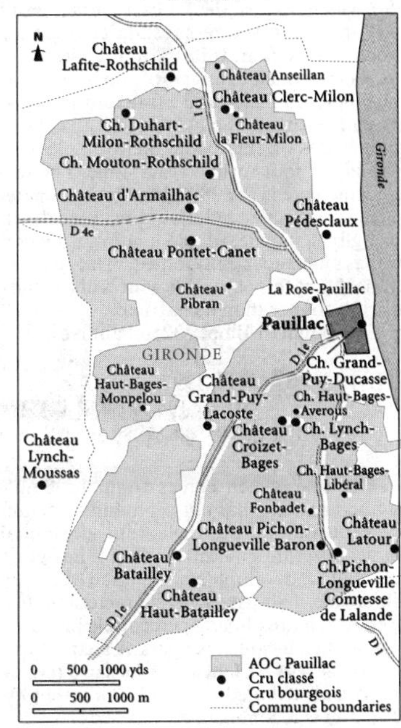

harmonious, but at the same time suggests an ageing period of six or seven years, if not more.

Jean-Michel Cazes, Ch. Cordeillan-Bages, 33250 Pauillac, tel. 05.56.73.24.00, fax 05.56.59.26.42, e-mail infochato@cordeillanbages.com

CH. CROIZET-BAGES 1997

5ème cru clas. 28 ha 160,000 100–149 F

|93| |94| 95 96 |97|

This is a château without a château, but it does have a well-located vineyard with a gently sloping terroir in the Bages district. The old estate dates back to the 16th century, and was owned by the Croizet family, from which it took its name in the 18th century. It was taken over in 1942 by Paul Quié. This wine is quite unusual for a Pauillac. It focuses on suppleness, and has an agreeable roundness and lovely, fruity aromas which suggest that it should be drunk within the next two to three years. A pleasant wine.

Jean-Michel Quié, Ch. Croizet-Bages, 33250 Pauillac, tel. 05.56.59.01.62, fax 05.56.59.23.39 ev. day except Sun. Mon. 9am–1pm 2pm–6pm

CH. DUHART-MILON 1997★★

4ème cru clas. 66 ha 270,000 300–499 F

61 70 75 76 79 80 81 **|82| |83| |85| |86|**87 **88 89 90 |91| |92|** 93 94 **95 96 97**

Located partly on the Carruades plateau and partly near the village of Milon and on the boundary of the Lafite vines, this vineyard has belonged for a little under 40 years to the Barons de Rothschild. Its gravel soil is lighter than that of its great neighbour, but nevertheless it has yielded an astonishing 1997 which, like all the Duhart vintages, will need time for its severe, substantial, balanced structure to soften. It has a young, deep colour, a nose which opens slowly on to notes of toast then soft fruits, and a frank, rather massive palate with perfectly extracted, flavourful tannins. All of this bodes well for pleasant drinking in four or five years' time. The second wine here is the **1997 Moulin de Duhard**, which is recommended. Its colour, with developed glints, its fine, supple tannins, Cabernet aromas and tender, full-bodied, meaty quality all show that this enjoyable wine will be ready to drink sooner than its partner.

Ch. Duhart-Milon, 33250 Pauillac

CH. FONBADET 1997

Cru bourg. 20 ha 100,000 100–149 F

75 76 78 79 81 **|82|**83 85 **|86|**87 88 89 9091 **|92|** 93 **|94|** 95 96 97

This wine, which comes from the Saint-Lambert plateau, has not yet found its definitive expression. Nevertheless its substantial tannic structure guarantees that it has good potential for development. A period of ageing will enable it to assert its characteristic features, which are already perceptible in a bouquet marked by green peppers. A second wine here is the **1997 Château Padarnac Elevé en Fût**. It is distributed by La Guyennoise (30–49F), and is recommended.

SCEA domaines Peyronie, Ch. Fonbadet, 33250 Pauillac, tel. 05.56.59.02.11, fax 05.56.59.22.61, e-mail pascale@chateaufonbadet.com by appt.

CH. GAUDIN 1997

10 ha n.c. 70–99 F

Coming from a vineyard managed by Linette Capdevielle, this is a simple wine which appeals by virtue of its fruit bouquet and the delicacy of its tannic presence. More of a Médoc than a Pauillac.

Linette Capdevielle, SCI du Ch. Gaudin, B.P. 12, 33250 Pauillac, tel. 05.56.59.24.39, fax 05.56.59.25.26

CH. GRAND-PUY DUCASSE 1997★

5ème cru clas. 38.16 ha 163,300 150–199 F

82 **83** 84 **85** 86 87 **88** 89 **|90|**91 **|92| |93|**94 **|95| 96** 97

This vineyard is more of a city and harbour château than any other in Pauillac, owing to its location on the river bank, where it has come into possession of a little house by the water which belonged to Jacques de Ségur until the mid–17th century. It is nonetheless representative of the appellation in that its vineyard is divided into three parts spread over all the terroirs in the commune. Its 1997 wine is a blend of 62% Cabernet Sauvignon and Merlot. It is full and well constructed on a rich, harmonious palate, and has an elegant, powerful bouquet of toast, cocoa and black berry notes which give way to an attractive menthol note at the finish. A well produced wine.

SC du Ch. Grand-Puy Ducasse, La Croix Bacalan, 109, rue Achard, B.P. 154, 33042 Bordeaux Cedex, tel. 05.56.11.29.00, fax 05.56.11.29.01 by appt.

CH. GRAND-PUY-LACOSTE 1997★

5ème cru clas. 50 ha 160,000 200–249 F

61 66 70 71 75 76 78 81 82 **|83| |85| |86|**87 **88 89 90** |91| |92| |93| |94| **95 96** |97|

Grand-Puy-Lacoste is a fine, unbroken estate with buildings for wine production, and is a good example of the substantial wine properties which give the Médoc its personality. This vintage is already pleasant to drink, but is sufficiently well made to be kept for four or five years. It has a complex bouquet of cocoa, plums, Morello cherries and ripe fruits, and a good structure based on rich, soft tannins which lead into a long finish.

Ch. Grand-Puy-Lacoste, 33250 Pauillac, tel. 05.56.59.06.66, fax 05.56.59.22.22 by appt.

CH. HAUT-BAGES AVEROUS 1997

n.c. 120,000 150–199 F

This supple, simple 1997 vintage is a second wine from Lynch-Bages. It gives priority to aromas of spices and menthol, producing a wine which is pleasant to drink straight away.

Jean-Michel Cazes, Ch. Lynch-Bages, 33250 Pauillac, tel. 05.56.73.24.00, fax 05.56.59.26.42, e-mail infochato@lynchbages.com by appt.

CH. HAUT-BAGES LIBERAL 1997★

■ 5ème cru clas. 28 ha 117,600 🍷 150–199 F

75 76 78 79 80 81 |(82)| |83| 84 |85| |86| 87 88 89 **90** |91| |92| 93 94 **95 96** 97

The Libéral family owned this vineyard from the 1750s to the end of the 19th century. Since 1983 the estate has belonged to the Merlaut empire; it is managed by the top-ranking Claire Villars-Lurton. This is a wine whose tannin extraction and maturation have been well dosed and adapted to the vintage. The result is a full-bodied, flavourful, balanced wine which releases complex aromas with attractive notes of ripe grapes, resin and liquorice, and lingers on into a vanilla finish.

🔑 Claire Villars-Lurton, Ch. Haut-Bages Libéral, 33250 Pauillac, tel. 05.56.58.02.37, fax 05.57.88.84.40, e-mail infos@haut-bages-liberal.com 🍸 by appt.

CH. HAUT-BATAILLEY 1997★

■ 5ème cru clas. 25 ha 110,000 🍷 150–199 F

66 71 75 76 78 81 82 83 84 |85| |86| |87| 88 89 90 91 |92| |93| **94 95 96** 97

After running this vineyard for a long time, Jean-Eugène Borie has given up his position and handed over to his son, François-Xavier. This 1997 'has a Saint-Julien quality,' noted one member of the jury who was tasting blind and could not have known that the wine came from the same producer as Ducru-Beaucaillou. Its well-softened tannins and the elegance of its bouquet of prune, musk and vanilla notes lend great charm to a wine which is well made and will keep for a short period.

🔑 SA Jean-Eugène Borie, 33250 Saint-Julien-Beychevelle, tel. 05.56.73.16.73, fax 05.56.59.27.37

🔑 Mme des Brest-Borie

CH. HAUT-MILON 1997

■ 2 ha 12,884 🍷 100–149 F

This Pauillac is offered by the wine-merchant Robert Giraud. It has a powerful tannic structure which is in keeping with tradition, and a very mature nose of marc, tobacco, cinnamon and Morello cherries.

🔑 SCA Vignobles Robert Giraud, B.P. 31, 33240 Saint-André-de-Cubzac, tel. 05.57.43.01.44, fax 05.57.43.08.75, e-mail direction@robertgiraud.com

CH. LA BECASSE 1997

■ 4.21 ha 30,000 🍷 100–149 F

91 92 93 |94| 95 96 |97|

Although not quite up to the standard of previous vintages, this wine has an interesting structure, which is supple in the attack but marked by a good tannic presence, and a bouquet in which the fruit blends in well with the oak. It will be ready to drink from 2001 onwards.

🔑 Roland Fonteneau, 21, rue Edouard-de-Pontet, 33250 Pauillac, tel. 05.56.59.07.14, fax 05.56.59.18.44 ☑

LA CHAPELLE DE BAGES 1997★

■ 7 ha 60,400 🍷 70–99 F

It is impossible to be indifferent to this wine, which comes under a second Haut-Bages Libéral label. Its bouquet mingles prunes and redcurrants, along with shades of caramelised jam, prunes, roses and cinnamon. With its good structure and combination of well-dosed oak and fruit, it is full of charm.

🔑 Claire Villars-Lurton, Ch. Haut-Bages Libéral, 33250 Pauillac, tel. 05.56.58.02.37, fax 05.57.88.84.40, e-mail infos@haut-bages-liberal.com 🍸 by appt.

CARRUADES DE LAFITE 1997★★

■ n.c. 220,000 🍷 200–249 F

87 88 89 90 91 92 93 94 95 96 97

This wine comes under a second Lafite label, but in no sense is it a pale imitation of the first. It announces its ambitions from the start with a very young, dark-ruby colour. The harmonious, complex bouquet of soft fruits with a slight note of oak prepares the way for an increase in power on the palate, which slowly reveals a fine, full, complex texture based on supple tannins. The finish commands admiration in a difficult vintage. Keep this wine for at least four or five years.

🔑 Ch. Lafite-Rothschild, 33250 Pauillac, tel. 01.53.89.78.00, fax 01.53.89.78.01 🍸 by appt.

CH. LAFITE-ROTHSCHILD 1997★★

■ 1er cru clas. 100 ha 185,000 🍷 500 F+

59 (61) **64** |66| 69 |70| |73| |**75**| 77 |**78**| |79| |80| |**81**| |**82**| |**83**| |84| **85** |**87**| **88 89 90 92 93 94 (95) (96) 97**

This is one of the most elegant vineyards in the Médoc. It was bought by James de Rothschild in 1868, and its circular wineries were designed by Ricardo Bofill. Just for the record, this vintage marks the bicentenary of the oldest-known bottle of château-bottled wine that has been kept, a 1797 Lafite. Its descendant will no doubt not require to stay in the cellar for 200 years, but even so an ageing period of eight to ten years can be envisaged; its substance leaves no shadow of doubt that it is a wine for longer maturing. It is expressive, however, especially at the finish, but not in such a way as to spoil the overall impression. A wine whose harmony is noticeable right from its bouquet of attractive, developing fragrances of red berries against

an oaky background, and continues to grow afterwards, leaving behind an abiding memory of a great classic.
🗝 Ch. Lafite-Rothschild, 33250 Pauillac, tel. 01.53.89.78.00, fax 01.53.89.78.01 Y by appt.

CH. LA FLEUR MILON 1997*

■Cru bourg. 12.5 ha 80,000 100–149 F
|94|(95)96 97

Located 500 m (a quarter of a mile) from Mouton and Lafite, this vineyard is undeniably well placed to benefit from a high-quality terroir. The 1997 wine does not rival the splendid 1995 vintage, but it has plenty of assets which will enable it to be kept for three or four years: a complex bouquet (smoke, liquorice and vanilla), a well-balanced, flavourful palate, and soft, silky tannins.
🗝 SCE Ch. La Fleur Milon, Le Pouyalet, 33250 Pauillac, tel. 05.56.59.29.01, fax 05.56.59.23.22 ☒ Y ev. day except Sat. Sun. 8.30am–12 noon 2pm–5pm; cl. last week Aug.–Sep.

CH. LA FLEUR PEYRABON 1997**

■Cru bourg. 4.86 ha 36,800 100–149 F

Like the Château Peyrabon (Haut-Médoc) to which it belongs, this little vineyard has undergone a major investment programme since 1998, financed by the Bernard group. This 1997 wine is a pleasant surprise. Starting with an almost black colour, it develops a bouquet which is both strong and complex (strawberries, spices, cocoa and leather). The palate is full, rich, powerful and charming, and has a substance which is as rich as its aromatic expression with accents of fruit, vanilla and roasting. The finish ends the tasting on a harmonious note, which is the sure sign of good ageing potential.
🗝 SARL Ch. Peyrabon, 33250 Saint-Sauveur, tel. 05.56.59.57.10, fax 05.56.59.59.45 ☒ Y by appt.
🗝 Bernard

CH. LATOUR 1997**

■1er cru clas. 43 ha n.c. 500 F+
|(61)| 67 71 73 74 75 |76| 77 |78| 79 |80| 81 |82| |83| |84| **85 86** |**87**| **88 89 90 91 92 93 94**(**95**)**96 97**

While there are many wine châteaux which have no history, this is not true of Latour, which was a fortified castle and lord's domain before becoming one of the most famous vineyards in the Médoc. For a long time it was under British ownership, but since 1993 it has belonged to François Pinault, who in the year 2000 has been undertaking major improvements to the wineries, thus adhering to the great tradition of Latour as a 'laboratory of innovation'. The 1997 wine is rather astonishing for the vintage. It has an imposing character which opens up interesting prospects for its ageing potential. It is still somewhat closed, and is not yet giving of its best. Nevertheless it is full, round, balanced and elegant, and is developing a bouquet in which fruit and toast notes mingle with spices.
🗝 SCV de Ch. Latour, Saint-Lambert, 33250 Pauillac, tel. 05.56.73.19.80, fax 05.56.73.19.81 Y by appt.
🗝 François Pinault

LES FORTS DE LATOUR 1997*

■ n.c. n.c. 300–499 F
80 **81 82 83 85 86 87** |**88**| **89 90** |**92**| |**94**| **95 96** 97

The second Latour wine is made from grapes harvested from the young vines in the Latour enclosure or on the plots outside it. It is very characteristic in terms of its structure, which is based on dense tannins, and also its bouquet of green pepper and gamey notes. This wine will be ready to drink sooner than the main label, but even so it will need to be kept for three to five years.
🗝 SCV de Ch. Latour, Saint-Lambert, 33250 Pauillac, tel. 05.56.73.19.80, fax 05.56.73.19.81 Y by appt.

CH. LA TOURETTE 1997*

■ 3 ha 24,300 70–99 F

This wine comes from a plot of land belonging to the Château Larose-Trintaudon, which has 175 ha (432 acres) in the Haut-Médoc, and benefits from a favourable terroir (gravel on clay). Although it is still dominated by oak, it has used this maturation period to acquire a substantial tannic structure, a sure sign of good ageing potential.
🗝 SA Ch. Larose-Trintaudon, rte de Pauillac, 33112 Saint-Laurent-Médoc, tel. 05.56.59.41.72, fax 05.56.59.93.22, e-mail larosetrintaudon@wanadoo.fr ☒ Y by appt.
🗝 AGF

CH. LYNCH-BAGES 1997*

■5ème cru clas. 90 ha 420,000 300–499 F
70 71 |**75**| 76 78 |**79**| 80 |**81**| |(**82**)| |**83**| 84 |**85**| |**86**| |**87**| |**88**| |**89**| **90** |91| 92 |93| **94** 95 **96** 97

In terms of its size, buildings, its past and present owners and its fame, this property is particularly representative of the Médoc Grand Cru, with a grape range of 73% Cabernet Sauvignon, 10% Cabernet Franc, 15% Merlot and 2% Petit Verdot, all grown on a splendid Garonnais gravel terroir. True to form, Jean-Michel Cazes is offering a balanced, elegant 1997 wine, which is perfectly well-matured and shows its tannic structure without being in any way aggressive. A complex aromatic expression playing on notes of liquorice makes this a particularly interesting wine.
🗝 Jean-Michel Cazes, Ch. Lynch-Bages, 33250 Pauillac, tel. 05.56.73.24.00, fax 05.56.59.26.42, e-mail infochato@lynchbages.com ☒ Y by appt.
🗝 Famille Cazes

CH. LYNCH MOUSSAS 1997*

■5ème cru clas. n.c. n.c. 150–199 F
81 82 83 85 86 88 |89| **90** 91 92 |93| 95 96 97

This vineyard belonged to the Lynch family from Ireland, some of whom became men of note in the Médoc, and one of whom was the mayor of Bordeaux under Napoleon

I. It is located near Batailley, and is another Castéja property. The family resemblance shows in this wine, in its substantial tannic structure and serious ageing potential, both of which are very much in the tradition of both *crus*. It also reveals a personality of its own, however, in an aromatic expression which is equally complex but different, with empyreumatic and chocolate notes, and a delicate fullness which makes for a flavourful, elegant overall impression.
Emile Castéja, 33250 Pauillac,
tel. 05.56.00.00.70, fax 05.57.87.48.61 by appt.

CH. MOUTON ROTHSCHILD 1997★★

1er cru clas. 75 ha n.c. 500 F+

71 72 73 74 |75| 76 77 |78| 79 80 81 **82 83** |**84**| **85 86** |**87**| **88 89 90 91 92 93 94 95 96 97**

At Mouton it is difficult to ignore the museum of objects linked to wine, the works of art that have been produced by illustrations of each vintage by the great painters, from Picasso to Francis Bacon, and in 1997 by Niki de Saint Phalle. Nor can one forget the great winery with its rows of new casks. The influence of the barrel is also very evident in this wine, giving it a toast aroma which serves as a constant theme throughout the tasting. Fortunately, thanks to a terroir and a grape range which are indisputably characteristic, the mark of oak (dark tobacco, smoke and precious, very roasted wood) does not stifle the raw material and the aromatic expression, both of which are concentrated and of high quality. There is a bouquet of raspberries and blackcurrants which is still opening, and a long finish of ripe fruits. The fine, silky tannins have been well extracted, and bode well for an ageing potential of ten years.
Baron Philippe de Rothschild SA, rue de Grassi, B.P. 117, 33250 Pauillac,
tel. 05.56.73.34.01, fax 05.56.59.07.82

CH. PIBRAN 1997★

Cru bourg. 10 ha 54,000 150-199 F

87 |88| |89| |**90**| 91 93 94 95 96 97

Coming from a vineyard close to Pichon-Longueville and vinified by the same team, this wine has a bouquet and a personality which combine a certain roundness with good tannic substance. The result is an attractive wine, which is pleasant and will also age well.
Jean-Michel Cazes, Ch. Pichon-Longueville, 33250 Pauillac,
tel. 05.56.73.17.17, fax 05.56.73.17.28,
e-mail infochato@chateaûassocies.com
by appt.
Axa Millésime

CH. PICHON-LONGUEVILLE BARON 1997★★

2ème cru clas. 68 ha 300,000 300-499 F

78 81 **82 83** 84 **85 86** 87 **88 89 90 91 92 93 94 95 96 97**

Pichon is a Mecca for tourists in the Médoc, combining the styles of the Napoleon III era and those of the present day. It is also a vineyard with a highly favourable terroir of excellent gravel which benefits from the proximity of the estuary. Its 1997 wine is both supple and rich, and has undoubtedly taken the best possible advantage of this environment. The aromatic development is imposing, with notes of fruit, leather, wax and caramelised strawberry jam, as well as chocolate and toast. It is already flavourful and tempting, but would be best kept for five to eight years. The second wine is the **1997 Les Tourelles de Longueville** (150–199F). It is recommended for its fine, elegant bouquet and 'well-established' tannins. It is already pleasant, and can be drunk while waiting for the Grand Vin.
Jean-Michel Cazes, Ch. Pichon-Longueville, 33250 Pauillac,
tel. 05.56.73.17.17, fax 05.56.73.17.28,
e-mail infochato@chateauassocies.com
by appt.
Axa Millésime

CH. PICHON-LONGUEVILLE COMTESSE DE LALANDE 1997★★

2ème cru clas, 75 ha n.c. 300-499 F

66 70 71 75 76 78 79 80 81 82 83 84 |**85**| |86| 87 |**88**| **89** |90| |91| 92 |93| |94| |95| 96 97|

In the 17th century this vineyard belonged to the Pichon-Longuevilles, who were members of the Bordeaux Parliament, and was divided up in 1850. A long succession of great ladies of wine have made this château one of the beacons of the AOC. True to its tradition, this fine unit, located near Saint-Julien, now offers a wine full of character. There is a sweet attack on the palate, which prolongs an equally sweet bouquet of complex notes: old honey, leather, caramelised prunes and toast. In the mouth the substance gives a feeling of roundness and harmony, while at the same time showing its fullness and ageing potential. These are confirmed by a flavourful finish of very high class.
SCI Ch. Pichon-Longueville Comtesse de Lalande, 33250 Pauillac,
tel. 05.56.59.19.40, fax 05.56.59.26.56,
e-mail pichon@pichon-lalande.com by appt.
May-Eliane de Lencquesaing

CH. PONTET-CANET 1997★★

■ 5ème cru clas. 80 ha 200,000 300–499 F

(61) 70 75 76 77 78 79 81 82 |**83**| 84 |**85**| 86 87 |**88**| |**89**| |**90**| 91 92 93 |**94**| **95 96 97**

This beautiful 18th-century château is an unmissable venue for anyone visiting either the Médoc or Pauillac. The quality of its produce also makes it a good ambassador for the appellation. With its 1997 wine it refutes the reputation of the vintage by offering a great, classic Pauillac, supported by raw materials combining elegance and richness. Its well-made tannins guarantee its ageing potential, and its aromatic complexity gives it a charm and class which are increased even more by a long finish on notes of menthol and eucalyptus.

Famille Tesseron, Ch. Pontet-Canet, 33250 Pauillac, tel. 05.56.59.04.04, fax 05.56.59.26.63, e-mail pontet@pontet-canet.com Y by appt.

Saint-Estèphe

Not very far up the Garonne from Pauillac and its port lies Saint-Estèphe. Its charming rustic hamlets fittingly suggest a locale closely bound to the soil. Apart from a few acres that are part of the Appellation Pauillac, the Appellation Saint-Estèphe, which covers 1,245 ha (3,075 acres) producing 68,842 hl (1,817,429 gal) encompasses the whole commune. As the most northerly of the six Médoc Appellations Communales, it has a fairly well-identified character, lying as it does at an average altitude of 40 m (130 ft) on gravelly soils that have a little more clay than the more southerly appellations. The Saint-Estèphe appellation includes five Crus Classés and the wines produced there have a noticeable tang of the *terroir*. Compared with other Médocs, the Saint-Estèphe wines have a higher degree of acidity in the grapes, a greater depth of colour and a more significant richness of tannin. They are very robust, and are excellent wines for laying down.

CH. ANDRON BLANQUET 1997

■ Cru bourg. 16 ha 80,000 50–69 F

75 76 79 81 82 83 85 86 87 |**88**| |**89**| |**90**| 91 92 |**93**| |**94**| 95 96 97

Andron Blanquet blends 65% Cabernet Sauvignon, 5% Cabernet Franc and 30% Merlot. Although this wine does not have the richness and complexity of the superb Cos Labory from the same producer, it has a fruity, slightly oaky nose, and deserves a mention. It is somewhat monolithic in the mouth, and still firm at the finish. Best kept for a year or two until the tannins grow rounder.

SCE Dom. Audoy, Ch. Andron Blanquet, 33180 Saint-Estèphe, tel. 05.56.59.30.22, fax 05.56.59.73.52

CH. BEAU-SITE 1997

■ Cru bourg. n.c. n.c. 70–99 F

This vineyard is owned by the Castéja family, and distributed by the wine-merchants Borie-Manoux. Although the 1997 vintage has a very 'trendy' oak quality, the oak does not crush the attractive strawberry, quince and game aromas which give this elegantly round wine its charm. The **1997 Contreforts de Beau-Site** (50–69F) is recommended. Whereas its big brother was matured in oak for 18 months, this second wine has spent only six months in the barrel, and its flavours are not masked by the oak. Both wines are unlikely to keep for long.

Héritiers Castéja, 33250 Pauillac, tel. 05.56.00.00.70, fax 05.57.87.48.61 Y by appt.

CH. BEL-AIR 1997★

■ 4.92 ha 25,000 70–99 F

This is a blend of 82% Cabernet Sauvignon, 15% Merlot and 3% Cabernet Franc. Sixteen months of maturation in one-year-old oak has produced a wine with a very characteristic tannic structure, which nevertheless

Saint-Estèphe

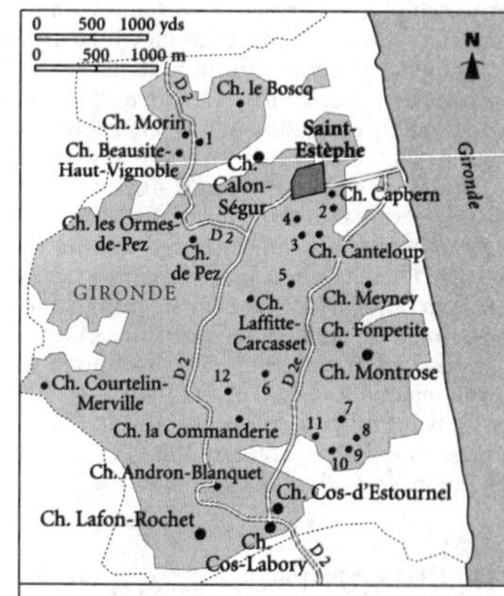

does not yield to fashion. Its mature, supple, rich body suggests that it has good ageing potential (six to seven years), but does not impair the charm of its very complex aromas (cedar, liquorice, red berries and spices).
SCEA du Ch. Bel Air, B.P. 2, 33480 Avensan-Médoc, tel. 05.56.58.21.03, fax 05.56.58.17.20, e-mail jfbraq@aol.com by appt.
Braquessac

CH. BEL-AIR ORTET 1997

n.c. 3,600 50-69 F

This well-balanced wine will need to be kept for a short while until the oak fades from the overall impression, and the subtle aromas of fruit, almonds and liquorice find their definitive expression.
Cheval Quancard, La Mouline, 33560 Carbon-Blanc, tel. 05.57.77.88.88, fax 05.57.77.88.99 by appt.

CH. CHAMBERT-MARBUZET 1997*

Cru bourg. 8 ha 50,000 100-149 F

66 76 79 81 82 |83| **85** |86| |**88**| |89| |90| 91 |92| **93 94 95** 96 97

This wine is produced by Henri Duboscq, one of the most endearing personalities in the world of Médoc wine production. It is perfectly in keeping with the Bordeaux spirit in its balance and good composition. Starting with a brilliant colour lit up by beautiful violet glints, it goes from cinnamon to fruit aromas before developing a supple, fleshy, rich, substantial structure which is supported by silky tannins. A harmonious wine which should be kept for four or five years.
Henri Duboscq et Fils, Ch. Haut-Marbuzet, 33180 Saint-Estèphe, tel. 05.56.59.30.54, fax 05.56.59.70.87 ev. day except Sun. 10am–12 noon 2pm–6pm

CH. CLAUZET 1997*

Cru bourg. 12 ha 80,000 70-99 F

In 1997 this 20-ha (49-acre) vineyard changed hands, at the same time producing a wine which fully lives up to the promise of its beautiful, dark-red colour. It has a powerful, delicate, complex bouquet, which paves the way for its full, supple, rich structure. A long, aromatic finish brings the tasting to a happy conclusion.
SA Maurice Velge, Leyssac, 33180 Saint-Estèphe, tel. 05.56.59.34.16, fax 05.56.59.37.11, e-mail chateauclauzet@wanadoo.fr ev. day except Sat. Sun. 8.30am–12 noon 2pm–6pm

COS D'ESTOURNEL 1997**

2ème cru clas. 64 ha 280,000 300-499 F

75 76 78 79 80 81 |**82**|83 |**85**| |**86**|87 **88** |**89**| |**(90)**| |**91**| |**92**| |**93**| **94 95 96 97**

This vineyard brings together every architectural style, with Oriental decoration brightening up the rigours of Western classicism. No doubt it is one of the oddest sights in the Bordeaux region, but that does not prevent its wine from adhering to the canons of the Gironde. Its 1997 wine has a lovely dark colour, and reveals an attractive bouquet of red berries, then on the palate shows the fullness of its structure and its aromatic complexity. This wine will have less ageing potential (five to eight years) than previous vintages, but it is highly acceptable for this one.
SA Domaines Prats, Cos d'Estournel, 33180 Saint-Estèphe, tel. 05.56.73.15.50, fax 05.56.59.72.59, e-mail estournel@estournel.com by appt.

LES PAGODES DE COS 1997

n.c. 118,000 250-299 F

This wine appears under a second Cis d'Estournel label, and is attractively fragrant (ripe fruits, bread crusts and toast). The attack on the palate is clean, and it has a good, substantial structure supported by fairly silky tannins. It should be ready to drink between 2001 and 2004.
SA Domaines Prats, Cos d'Estournel, 33180 Saint-Estèphe, tel. 05.56.73.15.50, fax 05.56.59.72.59, e-mail estournel@estournel.com by appt.

CH. COS LABORY 1997**

5ème cru clas. 18 ha 69,000 150-199 F

64 70 75 78 79 80 81 82 83 84 85 |**86**|87 88 |89| |(90)|91 92 |93| 94 95 **96 97**

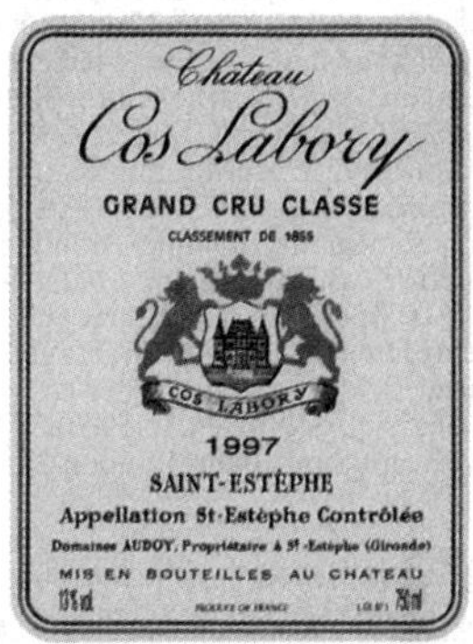

Just like the property, Bernard Audoy's team is solid and unostentatious, and seeks to achieve good but careful extraction. They have done this to perfection with their 1997 wine, which combines equal shares of Merlot and Cabernet Sauvignon. It asserts its power by the depth of its almost black colour, then reveals a bouquet which is both expressive and fresh, with lovely notes of flowers and menthol. The rich, full, velvety body is supported by well-blended tannins. The jury was most enthusiastic about the elegance and persistence of the finish. A wine which should be kept for six to eight years.
SCE Domaines Audoy, Ch. Cos Labory, 33180 Saint-Estèphe, tel. 05.56.59.30.22, fax 05.56.59.73.52 by appt.

CH. DOMEYNE 1997

■Cru bourg. 7.21 ha 40,000 70–99 F

82 83 85 86|88| |89| 90 91 92|93| 95 **96** 97

Although the severity of its tannic framework prevents it from rivalling some previous vintages, this 1997 wine is well constructed and has good aromatic complexity.

SARL d'Exploitation du Ch. Domeyne, 7, rue du Maquis-de-Vignes, Oudides, 33180 Saint-Estèphe, tel. 05.56.59.72.29, fax 05.56.59.72.21 Y ev. day 8am–12 noon 1pm–5pm; Fri. 4pm; groups by appt.

CH. FAGET 1997*

■Cru bourg. n.c. 19,130 50–69 F

This vineyard, like the Château Bel-Air Ortet, is run by Marcel and Christian Quancard, although in this case they are tenants. This 1997 vintage is a supple, round, rich wine, whose harmonious, mouth-filling palate and good length suggest that it should be kept for three to five years.

Cheval Quancard, La Mouline, 33560 Carbon-Blanc, tel. 05.57.77.88.88, fax 05.57.77.88.99 Y by appt.

CH. HAUT-MARBUZET 1997*

■Cru bourg. 55 ha 350,000 150–199 F

|61| 62 64 66 **67** 70 71 73**|75|** **|76|** 77 78 79 **80 81** (82) 83 85 86**88 89 90 |92| |93| 94 95 96** 97

This vineyard, which came into being in 1848 and now covers 58 ha (143 acres), grows a mixture of Cabernet Sauvignon (50%), Merlot (40%) and Cabernet Franc (10%). The quality of the Haut-Marbuzet terroir, which is located on a superb gravel hilltop, is beyond question. Although this wine is still marked by 18 months of maturation in oak, it shows that it comes from good stock by its brilliant colour, its elegantly complex bouquet, and its structure, which is already balanced and round. Best opened in two to three years' time.

Henri Duboscq et Fils, Ch. Haut-Marbuzet, 33180 Saint-Estèphe, tel. 05.56.59.30.54, fax 05.56.59.70.87 Y ev. day except Sun. 10am–12 noon 2pm–6pm

CH. LAFON-ROCHET 1997**

■4ème cru clas. 40 ha n.c. 200–249 F

(64) 75 76 77 78 79 81|82| **|83|** 85 86|88| |89| |90| 91 92 9394**(95)96 97**

With its superb '18th-century' folly (dating back to the 1960s), and a little Baroque chapel less than 300 m (328 yd) from the wineries, this vineyard has a lot to offer lovers of architecture. Should they also be wine-lovers, they will be equally delighted to discover wines like this 1997 vintage. Its appealing red colour creates an excellent first impression. The subtle complexity of the bouquet, combining notes of smoke, oak, spices and game, whets the appetite for what is to come. The full, rich, concentrated, well-balanced palate is in the same vein, as is the fine, flavourful finish (leather and oak). A true Saint-Estèphe, which should be kept for six or seven years. The **1997 No. 2 du Château Lafon-Rochet** (70–99F) is less complex but well made, and is recommended. Although its tannins are still firm, it can be drunk over the next four years.

SCF Ch. Lafon-Rochet, 33180 Saint-Estèphe, tel. 05.56.59.32.06, fax 05.56.59.72.43, e-mail lafon@lafon-rochet.com Y by appt.

CH. LA HAYE 1997*

■Cru bourg. 11 ha 51,165 70–99 F

89|90| 91 92 93|94| |95| 97

It is said this château was the love-nest of Henri IV and Diane de Poitiers. Although that seems rather unlikely, it is nonetheless true that the estate has existed since 1557. The vineyard now offers a wine whose extraction and maturation have been well controlled. The result is an extremely harmonious overall impression. The balance established in the bouquet between oak (tobacco and spices) and fruit reappears on the palate, whose full-bodied, rich structure is not unlike that of the 1996 vintage.

Georges Lecallier, Leyssac, 33180 Saint-Estèphe, tel. 05.56.59.32.18 Y by appt.

CH. LAMY

Vieilles vignes Elevé en fût de chêne 1997

■ 0.9 ha n.c. 70–99 F

This wine comes from a small vineyard, and is simple in its composition but round, well balanced and agreeably fragrant, with fine spicy notes. From the same producer, the **1997 Château Moulin de Blanquet** is also recommended.

EARL vignoble Lamy et Fils, G. de Mour, 3, rue des Anciens-Combattants, 33460 Soussans, tel. 05.57.88.94.17, fax 05.57.88.39.17

CH. LA PEYRE 1997

■Cru artisan 6.5 ha 50,000 70–99 F

Although it does not rival the 1996 wine, this 1997 vintage reveals a very powerful structure on the palate and a bouquet of very strong fragrances. It will need to be kept until the tannins fade.

EARL Vignobles Rabiller, Leyssac, 33180 Saint-Estèphe, tel. 05.56.59.32.51, fax 05.56.59.70.09 Y ev. day 10am–12.30pm 3pm–7pm

CH. L'ARGILUS DU ROI 1997

■Cru artisan 2 ha 15,000 70–99 F

This 1997 wine confirms the impression made last year by the first vintage from this vineyard, whose name refers to one of the oddities of the terroir, a large ball of clay that lies in the middle of the vineyard. The wine is powerful, with oak strongly in evidence both in the bouquet and on the palate. Best kept for two to three years.

José Bueno, 6, rue du Luc, 33250 Cissac, tel. 05.56.59.53.74, fax 05.56.59.53.74 Y by appt.

CH. LAVILLOTTE 1997

■Cru bourg. n.c. 50,000 70-99 F

Coming from a fine producer, this wine is something of a surprise. Its strong personality expresses itself in a bouquet of garrigue with musky notes and by tannins which are supple in the attack and austere at the finish. Even so it should not be kept for too long (two to three years).

SCEA des Dom. Pedro, 33180 Saint-Estèphe, tel. 05.56.41.98.17, fax 05.56.41.98.89 Y ev. day except Sat. Sun. 9am–12 noon 2pm–6pm; groups by appt.; cl. from 7–16 Aug.

CH. LE BOSCQ 1997*

■Cru bourg. 16.62 ha 62,000 100-149 F

82 83 |85| (86) |88| 89 90 95 96 |97|

This vineyard is managed by the Propriété de l'Union Française, and worked on a tenant basis by the Dourthe company. Starting with an attractive colour and a bouquet of delicate toast and spice notes, its 1997 vintage develops a round, elegant palate. The finish is supported by tannins which are discreet but pleasant.

Ch. Le Boscq, 33180 Saint-Estèphe, tel. 05.56.35.53.00, fax 05.56.35.53.29, e-mail contact@cvbg.com Y by appt.

LE CHARME LABORY 1997*

■ 18 ha 64,000 50-69 F

Under a second Cos Labory label, this wine is more modest than its elder brother, but also adheres to the best Saint-Estèphe tradition with its aromatic elegance and substantial composition, and needs to age for a while until it becomes rounder.

SCE Domaines Audoy, Ch. Cos Labory, 33180 Saint-Estèphe, tel. 05.56.59.30.22, fax 05.56.59.73.52 Y by appt.

CH. LE CROCK 1997*

■Cru bourg. n.c. n.c. 70-99 F

90 |95| 96 97

This vineyard belongs to the owner of Château Léoville Poyferré (Saint-Julien), and now offers a substantially made wine. There is an elegant bouquet of fruit combined with vanilla, followed by a supple attack and a palate which reveals a very good structure, substance and chewiness. The tannins express themselves but at the same time show respect for the general balance.

Domaines Cuvelier, Ch. Le Crock, 33180 Saint-Estèphe, tel. 05.56.59.30.33 Y by appt.

CH. LES ORMES DE PEZ 1997*

■Cru bourg. 33 ha 204,000 150-199 F

81 |82| |83| 84 |85| |86| 87 |88| **89 90 91** |92| 93 94 95 96 97

As is its wont, this vineyard adheres to the Saint-Estèphe tradition by offering a wine with high-quality tannins. The concentration and density of the structure will enable them to open out fully, as will the richness of a bouquet which combines fruit and oak aromas. A very attractive wine, which should be kept in the cellar for about ten years (on sale at the Château Lynch-Bages).

Jean-Michel Cazes, Ch. Les Ormes de Pez, 33180 Saint-Estèphe, tel. 05.56.73.24.00, fax 05.56.59.26.42, e-mail infochato@ormesdepez.com

Famille Cazes

CH. LILIAN LADOUYS 1997*

■Cru bourg. 30 ha 172,000 100-149 F

89 |(90)| 91 92 |93| |94| **95 96** 97

This wine's 1996 vintage was much praised, and its successor has brilliant red colour and an equally agreeable bouquet which opens out into elegant notes when swirled around in the glass. The full, well-constructed palate has real potential and suggests that this 1997 wine should be kept for three or four years.

Ch. Lilian Ladouys, Blanquet, 33180 Saint-Estèphe, tel. 05.56.59.71.96, fax 05.56.59.35.97 Y by appt.

Natexis

MARQUIS DE SAINT-ESTEPHE 1997

■ 34 ha 270,000 50-69 F

This wine is the main label sold by the Saint-Estèphe co-operative. It is well developed, and combines a fine, elegant bouquet with round, well-blended tannins.

Marquis de Saint-Estèphe, 2, rte du Médoc, 33180 Saint-Estèphe, tel. 05.56.73.35.30, fax 05.56.59.70.89, e-mail marquis.st.estephe@wanadoo.fr Y ev. day except Sat. Sun. 8.30am–12.15 2pm–6pm; cl. from 15 Sep.–15 Oct.

CH. MEYNEY 1997

■Cru bourg. 50 ha 250,000 100-149 F

80 81 |82| |83| 84 |85| (86) 87 |88| |89| 90 |91| |92| |93| |94| **95 96** |97|

With a siliceous gravel terroir on a limestone subsoil, and a very typically Médoc grape range of 70% Cabernet Sauvignon, 4% Cabernet Franc, 24% Merlot and 2% Petit Verdot, Meyney is one of the most interesting vineyards in the Saint-Estèphe area. Although the 1997 vintage does not have the richness and power associated with this wine, only someone very difficult to please would fail to appreciate the quality of its aromas, which unfold throughout, from the bouquet to the finish.

Domaines Cordier, 160, cours du Médoc, 33300 Bordeaux, tel. 05.57.19.57.77, fax 05.57.19.57.87 Y by appt.

CH. MONTROSE 1997**

■2ème cru clas. 68.39 ha 159,830 300-499 F

64 66 67 |70| |75| 76 78 |79| 81 |(82)| 83 **85 86** 87 **88 89 90 91 92 93 94 95 96 97**

This vineyard is a fine producer based on a coarse gravel terroir overlooking the estuary. Once again it has made the most of this great asset. The 1997 wine starts well with a fresh, red colour and an appealing bouquet of toast aromas and soft fruits. The palate shows the same elegance with its silky tannins, fine substance and full finish.

🔑 Jean-Louis Charmolüe, SCEA du Ch. Montrose, 33180 Saint-Estèphe, tel. 05.56.59.30.12, fax 05.56.59.38.48 ☑ Y by appt.

GRAND VIN D'OSSIAN 1997*

■ 1.6 ha 10,000 ⏸ 100–149 F

This wine takes its name from the legendary warrior-poet invented in the 18th century by James Macpherson. This is the inaugural vintage, and was created by Jean and Christophe Anney. It fully lives up to their hopes, both in its bouquet of penetrating notes of coffee, and its structure, which has suppleness, balance, elegance and good power.

🔑 Vignoble Jean Anney, Ch. Tour des Termes, 33180 Saint-Estèphe, tel. 05.56.59.32.89, fax 05.56.59.73.74 ☑ Y by appt.

CH. PETIT BOCQ 1997**

■ 8 ha 55,000 ⏸ 70–99 F

94 95 96 **97**

This little vineyard was founded in 1971, and is now run by Gaston Lagneaux, a doctor. Although this 1997 vintage has often been disparaged, it has produced some fine achievements. In this case, there is plenty of power in the colour and in the bouquet of wild dark-berry notes and toast. The palate is powerful too, and adheres to the character of the appellation by revealing substantial tannins which suggest that this attractive wine should be kept for three or four years.

🔑 SCEA Lagneaux-Blaton, 3Ch. petit Bocq, B.P. 33, 33180 Saint-Estèphe, tel. 05.56.59.35.69, fax 05.56.59.32.11 ☑ Y by appt.

CH. PHELAN SEGUR 1997*

■ Cru bourg. 64 ha 180,000 ⏸ 200–249 F

81 82 |86|87 **|88|** 89 **90 |91| |92| 93 94 95 96** 97

This wine comes from a terroir of great quality (a gravel clay hilltop overlooking the estuary), where the standard of vine-growing and maturing entirely lives up to the natural resources. It is fully open both in the nose, which shows that its maturation has been perfectly controlled, and on the palate, where it is clear from its concentration and structure, based on silky tannins, that the extraction has been carried out intelligently. A well-made wine which will need to be kept for five to six years.

🔑 Ch. Phélan Ségur, 33180 Saint-Estèphe, tel. 05.56.59.74.00, fax 05.56.59.74.10, e-mail phelan.segur@wanadoo.fr Y by appt.

🔑 X. Gardinier

FRANCK PHELAN 1997

■ 64 ha 120,000 ⏸ 100–149 F

Under a second label from Phélan Ségur, this is a truly classical wine which is extremely well composed and has a good tannic presence. It will gain from being kept for three to four years.

🔑 Ch. Phélan Ségur, 33180 Saint-Estèphe, tel. 05.56.59.74.00, fax 05.56.59.74.10, e-mail phelan.segur@wanadoo.fr Y by appt.

CH. SEGUR DE CABANAC 1997**

■ Cru bourg. 4.95 ha 30,000 ⏸ 100–149 F

|86|88 **89** 9091 92 **|93| |94|** 95 96 **97**

This astonishing 1997 wine is a tribute to the 'Prince of Vines', Joseph-Marie Ségur de Cabanac, after whom some plot boundaries are still named. It does honour to the great wine-grower with a beautiful dark colour, an attractive bouquet with notes of vanilla, cedar, mint and liquorice, a round attack on the palate, and velvety tannins, all of which bear witness to the Delons' know-how.

🔑 SCEA Guy Delon et Fils, Ch. Ségur de Cabanac, 33180 Saint-Estèphe, tel. 05.56.59.70.10, fax 05.56.59.73.94 ☑ Y by appt.

CH. TOUR COUTELIN 1997

■ 7 ha 50,000 ▮⏸🌡 70–99 F

This simple but well-made wine is distributed by the wine-trade. The delicate musky and fruity notes in its bouquet are as pleasant as the roundness and freshness of the palate. Best drunk over the next four or five years.

🔑 SA Yvon Mau, B.P. 1, 33193 Gironde-sur-Dropt Cedex, tel. 05.56.61.54.54, fax 05.56.61.54.61 Y by appt.

🔑 Arnaud

CH. TOUR DE PEZ 1997*

■ Cru bourg. 14 ha 80,000 ⏸ 100–149 F

|91| |93| |94|(95)**96** 97

This vineyard is particularly reliable in terms of quality, and this 1997 wine is no exception. Although its strong notes of oak may take some wine-lovers by surprise, the overall impression is nonetheless very accomplished. It starts irreproachably with a deep colour and a bouquet of appetising notes of toast, fruit and spices, then develops harmoniously on the palate. A rich, thoroughbred wine. The **1997 Château Les Hauts de Pez** (30–49F) is distributed through the wine-trade, and is recommended.

🔑 SA Ch. Tour de Pez, L'Hereteyre, 33180 Saint-Estèphe, tel. 05.56.59.31.60, fax 05.56.59.71.12 ☑ Y ev. day except Sat. Sun. 9.30am–12 noon 2pm–5pm; groups by appt.

CH. TOUR DES TERMES 1997

■ Cru bourg. 15 ha n.c. ⏸ 70–99 F

81 82 83 84 85 86 88 89 92 |93| |94| 95 96 97

This vineyard takes its name from a medieval tower which stands in the middle of the vines. Its 1997 wine has an appealing dark-red colour, a nose of musky, oaky notes, after which the attack on the palate is quite fresh, and the development is based on a good tannic presence which needs to fade.

🔑 Vignoble Jean Anney, Ch. Tour des Termes, 33180 Saint-Estèphe, tel. 05.56.59.32.89, fax 05.56.59.73.74 ☑ Y by appt.

CH. TOUR SAINT FORT 1997

■Cru bourg. 4.7 ha 36,791 70–99 F

This is a small vineyard, but one where no effort is spared. The reward can be seen in this wine, with its powerful, elegant bouquet which lingers on a full, supple, flavourful and well-balanced palate.

SCA ch. Tour Saint Fort, 1, rte de La Villotte, 33180 Saint-Estèphe, tel. 05.56.34.16.16, fax 05.56.13.05.54 ev. day 10am–12 noon 2pm–6pm; Sat. Sun. by appt.

Jean-Louis Laffort

Saint-Julien

The wine is Saint-Julien but the town is Saint-Julien-Beychevelle, making Saint-Julien the only Appellation Communale in the Haut-Médoc not to follow the standard practice of using the same name for both. The second name, it is true, has the drawback of being rather long. Both commune and appellation cover the same area, straddling two plateaux of pebbly and gravelly soil.

The vineyard of Saint-Julien is fairly small at 900 ha (2,223 acres) and producing 49,434 hl (1,305,058 gal) in 1999, and is located in the exact centre of the Haut-Médoc. Its wine can be thought of as a harmonious synthesis of Margaux and Pauillac, and so it is hardly surprising that Saint-Julien produces 11 Crus Classés (five of which are second growths). The wines reflect their *terroir*, offering a good balance between the qualities of Margaux (particularly their finesse) and the body of Pauillac wines. Generally speaking, Saint-Julien wines have a good colour, a fine, characteristic bouquet, good body, great richness and a beautifully aromatic flavour. It goes without saying that the wines in the 6.6 million bottles produced on average each year in Saint-Julien are far from all alike. Tasters with fine palates will distinguish between the Crus from the south (nearer to Margaux) and those from the north (which are closer to Pauillac), as well as between wines that come from nearer the estuary and those from further inland (near Saint-Laurent).

CH. BEYCHEVELLE 1997★★

■4ème cru clas. 56 ha 260,000 200–249 F

|70| 76 78 79 81 **|82|** 83 84 **|85|** **|86|** 87 **88** **(89)** 90 91 92 93 **94** **95** 96 **97**

Beychevelle is without a shadow of doubt the most beautiful château in the Médoc, and the one which best reflects the spirit of the golden age of Bordeaux, the 18th century. Perhaps it is the gracious surroundings here which have inspired this resolutely elegant 1997 wine. It is poles apart from some fashionable wines in that it focuses not so much on power and extraction as on harmony. Its good structure will enable it to be kept, while at the same time bringing out the balance between its very well-blended tannins and crisp fruitiness. There is a highly distinguished bouquet which achieves a perfect harmony between spices and fruit. A remarkable achievement. One taster suggests serving it as an accompaniment to a fricassee of pigeon in wine with wild mushrooms.

SC Ch. Beychevelle, 33250 Saint-Julien-Beychevelle, tel. 05.56.73.20.70, fax 05.56.73.20.71, e-mail beychevelle@beychevelle.com ev. day except Sat. Sun. 9.30am–12 noon 2pm–5pm; groups by appt.

Grands Millésimes de France

Saint-Julien

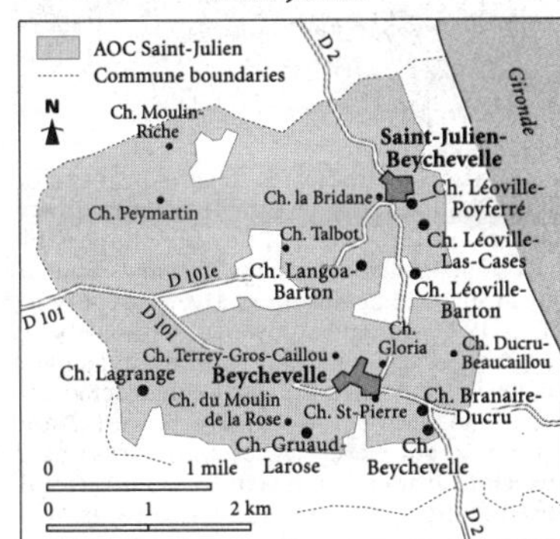

AMIRAL DE BEYCHEVELLE 1997

■ 19 ha 245,000 ⅠⅠ 100–149 F

This wine comes under a second Château Beychevelle label. It is simpler than its elder brother, but is also well made and has a very pleasant nose in which powerful fruit aromas mingle with fresh menthol notes.

SC Ch. Beychevelle, 33250 Saint-Julien-Beychevelle, tel. 05.56.73.20.70, fax 05.56.73.20.71, e-mail beychevelle@beychevelle.com ✉ Y ev. day except Sat. Sun. 9.30am–12 noon 2pm–5pm; groups by appt.

CH. BRANAIRE Duluc-Ducru 1997*

■4ème cru clas. 48 ha n.c. ⅠⅠ 150–199 F

81 82 83 84 85 86 87 **|88| 89** 90 91 92 93 **94 95** 96 97

Located on the other side of the D 2 from Beychevelle, this Directoire property uses the most modern methods, such as a vat-store using gravity-feed. Although it adheres to the tradition of the vineyard with its lovely dark-red colour and substantial tannic structure, this 1997 wine has impressively good length and an unusual bouquet which reveals notes of vanilla, toast and pencil lead. A second wine from Branaire, the **1997 Château Duluc** (70–99F), is recommended. It is a pleasant, interesting wine, with tannins which are somewhat severe in the attack but then become rounder, and a simple, fine bouquet with some acid notes.

SAE du Ch. Branaire-Ducru, 33250 Saint-Julien, tel. 05.56.59.25.86, fax 05.56.59.16.26 ✉ Y by appt.

CH. DUCRU-BEAUCAILLOU 1997***

■2ème cru clas. 50 ha 200,000 ⅠⅠ 300–499 F

|61| 64 66 **|70|** 71 **|75|** 76 77 **|78|** 79 **81 |(82)|** 83 84 **|85| |86|** 87 **88 89 90** 91 92 **93 94 (95)(96) 97**

1997
CHATEAU DUCRU-BEAUCAILLOU
GRAND CRU CLASSÉ DE MÉDOC EN 1855
SAINT-JULIEN
APPELLATION SAINT-JULIEN CONTRÔLÉE
JEAN-EUGÈNE BORIE, PROPRIÉTAIRE A SAINT-JULIEN-BEYCHEVELLE (GIRONDE)
750 ml

As its name indicates, Ducru-Beaucaillou has a high-quality terroir. It is located on a gravel hilltop overlooking the 'impassible river', in other words the estuary. True to form, it once again offers a very great wine. This 1997 vintage is powerful without being aggressive, using its silky tannins and superb materials to form a full, well-constructed palate. The bouquet is equally powerful and complex but never lapses into excess as it develops from fine notes of toast and crystallised fruits to cherries and redcurrants, with prunes in between. An exceptional achievement for the vintage, which deserves a place of honour in the cellar for about ten years to come.

SA Jean-Eugène Borie, Ch. Ducru-Beaucaillou, 33250 Saint-Julien-Beychevelle, tel. 05.56.73.16.73, fax 05.56.59.27.37 Y by appt.

CH. DU GLANA 1997

■Cru bourg. n.c. 159,000 ⅠⅠ 100–149 F

|94| |95| |96| |97|

This wine belongs exclusively to the Dourthe company, but is also sold by the owner. It has an elegant bouquet (stewed fruits and toast), and can be drunk while young or left to improve as it develops over the next three or four years. Its mouth-filling quality, harmonious tannins and long finish bode well for the future.

Ch. du Glana, 33250 Saint-Julien-Beychevelle, tel. 05.56.35.53.00, fax 05.56.35.53.29, e-mail contact@cvbg.com ✉ Y by appt.

Vignobles Meffre

CH. GLORIA 1997*

■ 48 ha 220,000 ⅠⅠ 150–199 F

64 66 70 71 75 76 78 |79| 81 82 83 84 |85| |86| 87 **|88| |89|** |90| 91 92 |93| |94| **95** 96 97

This property is made up of several plots of land located on the best terroirs in the appellation and brought together under the same banner by Henri Martin, one of the great figures in the Médoc. It is now run by his daughter. This wine has a rich, dark colour, and makes a high-class start with a dense, complex bouquet (meat, spices, truffles and game). The palate is supported by powerful, well-softened tannins, and adheres to the Saint-Julien spirit with its elegant aromatic expression.

Domaines Martin, Ch. Gloria, 33250 Saint-Julien-Beychevelle, tel. 05.56.59.08.18, fax 05.56.59.16.18 ✉ Y by appt.

Françoise Triaud

CH. GRUAUD-LAROSE 1997*

■2ème cru clas. 82 ha 197,000 ⅠⅠ 250–299 F

70 71 75 76 77 78 79 80 (81) 82 83 84 **|85|** | **(86)**| 87 **|88|** |89| **90** |91| 92 **93 94 (95) 96** 97

This vineyard was founded in 1757, and now belongs to the Bernard Taillan group. It grows an unusually diverse range of grapes, including Petit Verdot and Malbec, and their richness has clearly contributed to the complexity of this wine's bouquet, which goes from ripe fruits to toast with stewed fruits and cinnamon in between. The palate is equally rich and thoroughbred: round, fleshy, full-bodied and supported by mature, harmonious tannins.

Ch. Gruaud-Larose, B.P. 6, 33250 Saint-Julien-Beychevelle, tel. 05.56.73.15.20, fax 05.56.59.64.72, e-mail contact@chateau-gruaud-larose.com Y by appt.

Bernard Taillan Vins

H. LA BRIDANE 1997

Cru bourg. 15 ha 50,000 70–99 F

82 83 85 86 88|89| 90 91 92 93 94 |95| 96 97

This is a relatively small vineyard, at least r the appellation, but nonetheless it enjoys good reputation. Its substantial, well-mposed 1997 vintage still bears the stamp oak, giving it a 'fashionable' quality which reinforced by the intensive extraction of the nnins. A wine which will need to be kept hile it becomes more balanced.

Bruno Saintout, SCEA de Cartujac, 20, artujac, 33112 Saint-Laurent-Médoc, l. 05.56.59.91.70, fax 05.56.59.46.13 y appt.

A CROIX DE BEAUCAILLOU 997★

50 ha 60,000 150–199 F

Rather unusually for the 1997 vintage, the rand Vin at Ducru-Beaucaillou did not hog e show completely, the second label taking uch more than just a subsidiary role. The nesse and elegance of its ruby-red colour are lso apparent in the bouquet (incense, prunes, aramel, cloves and cinnamon), and on the alate, which is sweet in the attack and very romatic in its development. Best drunk ithin four to five years while waiting for the rand Vin.

SA Jean-Eugène Borie, 33250 Saint-ulien-Beychevelle, tel. 05.56.73.16.73, ax 05.56.59.27.37

H. LAGRANGE 1997★★

3ème cru clas. 109 ha n.c. 200–249 F

9 81 82 83 |85| |86| 87 88 89 (90) |91| 92 93 94 95 6 97

This is a very fine vineyard of almost 160 a (395 acres) in all, and has carved out a elect place for itself among the top names in ine-growing. Even more remarkably, it has chieved this without yielding in any way to ashion, as this 1997 wine shows. It is per-ectly suited to the character of the vintage, avouring elegance over extraction. The result s a very fine wine which is fresh, balanced and istinguished. It is already pleasant to drink, vith good aromatic complexity, but its qual-ty will improve further over the next two or hree years.

Ch. Lagrange, 33250 Saint-Julien-Beychevelle, tel. 05.56.73.38.38, ax 05.56.59.26.09, e-mail chateau-agrange@chateau-lagrange.com by appt.

Suntory Ltd

ES FIEFS DE LAGRANGE 1997★

109 ha n.c. 100–149 F

At Lagrange their sensible, considered vorking methods have brought real success. As well as an excellent Grand Vin, they have nade a fine second wine with an expressive ouquet, tannins with plenty of power, a bal-nced structure and an elegant finish. This vine will be ready to drink in two or three ears' time.

Ch. Lagrange, 33250 Saint-Julien-Beychevelle, tel. 05.56.73.38.38, fax 05.56.59.26.09, e-mail chateau-lagrange@chateau-lagrange.com by appt.

CH. LANGOA BARTON 1997★

3ème cru clas. 18 ha 90,000 200–249 F

70 75 76 |78| 80 81 |82| 83 |85| 86 87 88 (89) 90 |92| 93 94 95 96 97

Since 1821, six generations of Bartons have followed one another at this château, whose interior decoration still has a family atmosphere. The delicacy of the architecture and furniture is reflected in the beauty of this wine's classic, dark-red colour, and in the finesse and elegance of its bouquet of delicate pepper, liquorice and menthol notes. With a fine, substantial structure which is still somewhat firm, this wine fully lives up to its classification. It will need to be kept for two or three years before being served as an accompaniment to game.

Anthony Barton, Ch. Langoa Barton, 33250 Saint-Julien-Beychevelle, tel. 05.56.59.06.05, fax 05.56.59.14.29 by appt.

CH. LEOVILLE-BARTON 1997★★

2ème cru clas. 46 ha 250,000 250–299 F

64 67 70 71 75 76 |78| 79 80 81 |82| |83| |85| 86 87 88 89 (90) |91| |92| 93 94 95 96 97

This vineyard came into being after the old Léoville estate was divided up, and has been in the hands of the Barton family since 1826. Once again it lives up to this exceptional family tradition with the quality of its 1997 wine. It has a beautiful, deep-red colour, and a charming bouquet of vanilla along with ripe fruits, spices and undergrowth. After this good initial impression, the palate is rich and powerful, supported by very mature tannins, and clearly shows it has good ageing potential. The finish is long and full.

Anthony Barton, Ch. Léoville Barton, 33250 Saint-Julien-Beychevelle, tel. 05.56.59.06.05, fax 05.56.59.14.29 by appt.

CH. LEOVILLE POYFERRE 1997★★★

2ème cru clas. n.c. n.c. 200–249 F

76 78 79 80 81 |82| |(83)| 84 85 86 87 88 89 90 |91| |92| |93| 94 95 96 97

Located at the heart of the old Léoville estate, this vineyard is owned by D Duvelier,

and has a high-quality terroir which is at the heart of this exceptional 1997 wine. The deep-red colour with ruby glints inspires confidence, and there is a more than promising bouquet, successfully combining red berries, vanilla and toast. The rich, powerful structure has the necessary substance to keep for a long time, while the wine develops its rich and chewy personality still further. A truly great wine which will go well with lamb fillet.
SC Ch. Léoville Poyferré, 33250 Saint-Julien, tel. 05.56.59.08.30, fax 05.56.59.60.09 by appt.

CH. MOULIN DE LA ROSE 1997*

Cru bourg. 4.65 ha 28,000 100–149 F

|93| |94| 95 **96** 97

Although Saint-Julien is an appellation with many great aristocratic châteaux, it also has some Crus Bourgeois. Despite its modest size, this one is clearly capable of producing a high-quality wine. It comes from superb Garonne gravel soils, and combines 5% Petit Verdot with a very typically Médoc grape blend. It has had 20 months' maturation in barrel (one-third new), and the result is a very appealing wine with great aromatic elegance and a round, rich structure whose tannins will grow rounder in about three years' time.
SCEA Guy Delon et Fils, Ch. Moulin de la Rose, 33250 Saint-Julien-Beychevelle, tel. 05.56.59.08.45, fax 05.56.59.73.94 by appt.

CH. MOULIN RICHE 1997*

n.c. n.c. 70–99 F

|93| |94| 95 96 97

This second wine is produced by the Léoville-Poyferré team. Its intense ruby colour and very fine bouquet show that it comes from good stock. The palate is supported by powerful yet velvety tannins, indicating that this wine is well worth keeping.
SC Ch. Léoville Poyferré, 33250 Saint-Julien, tel. 05.56.59.08.30, fax 05.56.59.60.09 by appt.

CH. SAINT-PIERRE 1997*

4ème cru clas. 17 ha 60,000 250–299 F

82 **83** 84 **|85|** |(86)| 87 **|88|** **|89|** 90 91 92 **|93|** |94| (95) **96** 97

This vineyard has an excellent terroir (gravel and sandy gravel), and they adapt their maceration technique to suit the vintage. The result is a wine very much in keeping with the spirit of the Médoc: it has a fine structure, which is rich and powerful and supported by mature, harmonious tannins and an attractive bouquet of toast and floral notes. An elegant wine, which needs to be kept for two to four years until the oak has blended in completely.
Domaines Martin, Ch. Saint-Pierre, 33250 Saint-Julien-Beychevelle, tel. 05.56.59.08.18, fax 05.56.59.16.18 by appt.
Françoise Triaud

CH. TALBOT 1997*

4ème cru clas. 102 ha 330,000 200–249

78 79 80 81 **|82|** 83 84 |(85)| |**86**| 87 **|88|** 89 90 91 9
93 94 **95** 96 97

This wine comes from a vast productic unit located at the heart of the appellatic and near the estuary. The terroir here is exce lent, as is clearly apparent from the expre sive, complex character of this wine's bouqu of menthol notes alongside others includir cloves and pepper. The palate is supported b expansive tannins acquired from high-quali oak – this 1997 wine spent 12 months in tl barrel (40% new). They are still somewh severe, however, and call for an ageing peric of four to five years.
Ch. Talbot, 33250 Saint-Julien-Beychevelle, tel. 05.56.73.21.50, fax 05.56.73.21.51, e-mail chateau-talbot@chateau-talbot.com by appt.
Mmes Rustmann et Bignon

CONNETABLE DE TALBOT 1997

102 ha 260,000 100–149

This wine comes under a second Châtea Talbot label, and will be ready to drink befor the Grand Vin (in one or two years' time). I tannins are less powerful and already plea ant, and its full finish has the same pepper notes as the nose.
Ch. Talbot, 33250 Saint-Julien-Beychevelle, tel. 05.56.73.21.50, fax 05.56.73.21.51, e-mail chateau-talbot@chateau-talbot.com by appt.

CH. TERREY GROS CAILLOUX 1997*

Cru bourg. n.c. 100,000 100–149

This is already an extremely pleasant win and although it is certainly not first and fore most a wine for longer maturing, it does sho good potential for development over the nex two or three years. At present its charm come from its bouquet, in which ripe fruits ar enhanced by a note of fruit stones. Its tannins however, need time to mature.
Annie Fort et Henri Pradère, Ch. Terrey Gros-Cailloux, 33250 Saint-Julien-Beychevelle, tel. 05.56.59.06.27, fax 05.56.59.29.32 ev. day except Sat. Sun. 9am–12 noon 2pm–5pm; cl. Aug.
Henri Pradère

CH. TEYNAC 1997*

11.5 ha 50,000 100–149 F

92 |93| |94| 95 96 97

Coming from a vineyard with a typicall Médoc range of grapes – (Cabernets (68%) Merlot (30%) and Petit Verdot – this wine' elegance owes much to their diversity. It has fine and mouthwatering bouquet (ripe sof fruits and vanilla) and a supple, balanced an gracious structure.
Ch. Teynac, Grand-rue, Beychevelle, 33250 Saint-Julien-Beychevelle, tel. 05.56.59.12.91, fax 05.56.59.46.12 by appt.
F. et Ph. Pairault

Sweet White Wines

When you consult a wine map of the Gironde, you immediately notice that the appellations for the sweet wines (Vins Liquoreux) are clustered in a small region that straddles the Garonne, around its confluence with the River Ciron. Is this just a coincidence? Certainly not: the chill waters of this little river, whose entire course is shaded by leafy trees, contribute to a very particular micro-climate, encouraging *Botrytis cinerea*, the fungus that causes noble rot. In autumn, damp mornings and warm, sunny afternoons create ideal conditions for the fungus to develop on the perfectly ripe grapes, but without causing them to burst; the pips behave exactly like a sponge and, as the grapes shrivel, the juice evaporates and becomes concentrated. This makes for musts that are very rich in sugar.

Many problems have to be overcome to achieve this sweet must. The development of noble rot varies from grape to grape, so the vines must be picked several times, each time harvesting only individual grapes that are in their optimum state. The quantities produced per hectare are tiny, with a maximum amount permitted in Sauternes and Barsac of 25 hl per ha (270 gal per acre). The way the grapes reach over-ripeness is very unpredictable and depends entirely on climatic conditions, so it is an extremely risky time for the growers.

Cadillac

This village with its fine 17th-century chateau, known as the Fontainebleau of the Gironde, is often thought of as the capital of the Premières Côtes. But, since 1980, it is also an appellation for sweet wines and produced 6,501 hl (171,626 gal) in 1999.

CH. CARSIN 1998★★

□ 4 ha 15,000 70–99 F

Juha Berglund, who comes from Finland and is the son of a famous conductor, bought this vineyard in 1990. He is also a Premières Côtes producer. This Cadillac is supple, full and well balanced, and brings out to perfection its beautiful aromas combining honey and acacia.

Berglund, GFA Ch. Carsin, 33410 Rions, tel. 05.56.76.93.06, fax 05.56.62.64.80 by appt.

CLOS BOURBON 1997★

□ 2 ha 9,000 30–49

Muscadelle accounts for 15% of the grape range here, and emerges well in a floral bouquet completed by a touch of musk. The overall impression is of a supple, round, velvety wine which is pleasant and very accomplished.

SCEA Clos Bourbon, 33550 Paillet, tel. 05.56.72.11.58, fax 05.56.62.12.59 by appt.

d'Halluin

CH. COUSTEAU 1997★★

□ 6 ha 25,000 30–49 F

Guillaume Réglat, who also keeps a vineyard in the Sauternes, has a fine understanding of Vins Liquoreux. The richness and elegance of his 1997 wine are a credit to his powers. The bouquet is marvellously complex with its notes of crystallised fruits, vanilla and acacia, and the structure is round, long and perfectly balanced. A wine to serve with roast white meats or as an aperitif.

Guillaume Réglat, Ch. Cousteau, 33410 Monprimblanc, tel. 05.56.62.98.63, fax 05.56.62.17.98 ev. day except Sat. Sun. 8am–12 noon 2pm–5.30pm. cl. Aug.

Sweet White Wines

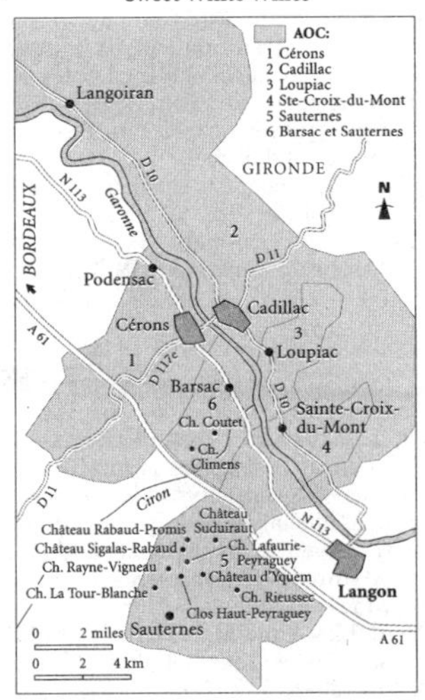

CH. FAYAU 1997

☐ 10 ha 30,000 30–49 F

Château Fayau is the Cadillac vineyard of the Médeville family, who are large Girondin wine-merchants. When this 1997 wine was tasted on 5 April 2000, it was not on its best form and did not rival some previous vintages. Nevertheless its freshness and richness made it pleasant to drink.

SCEA Jean Médeville et Fils, Ch. Fayau, 33410 Cadillac, tel. 05.57.98.08.08, fax 05.56.62.18.22 Y ev. day except Sat. Sun. 8.30am–12 noon 2pm–5.30pm

CH. FRAPPE-PEYROT 1998★★

☐ 8 ha 15,000 30–49 F

This vineyard is planted on alluvial and limestone-clay soils, and produces a blend consisting mainly of Sémillon, along with Muscadelle and Sauvignon. Although it is still marked by oak, the 1998 wine is already showing the power of its bouquet in notes of crystallised fruits. It is supported by fine substance, and promises to be an elegant wine in four to five years' time.

Jean-Yves Arnaud, La Croix, 33410 Gabarnac, tel. 05.56.20.23.52, fax 05.56.20.23.52 Y by appt.

CH. JEAN DU ROY 1998★

☐ 9 ha n.c. 50–69 F

Once again this vineyard confirms its reliability with a 1998 wine which not only has a pleasant bouquet of fresh, floral notes (acacia and honeysuckle), but also a supple, well-balanced structure.

SCEA Yvan Réglat, Ch. Balot, 33410 Monprimblanc, tel. 05.56.62.98.96, fax 05.56.62.19.48 Y by appt.

CH. DU JUGE 1998★

☐ 2.5 ha 8,000 50–69 F

Coming from a small vineyard belonging to a fine producer near Cadillac, this wine adheres to local tradition with its bouquet of elegant honeyed and crystallised notes. These recur on the palate in a rich, fleshy substance containing crystallised-fruit notes which give it a slightly nostalgic feel.

Pierre Dupleich, Ch. du Juge, rte de Branne, 33410 Cadillac, tel. 05.56.62.17.77, fax 05.56.62.17.59, e-mail pierre.dupleich@wanadoo.fr Y by appt.

CH. LA BERTRANDE 1998★★

☐ 6.5 ha 25,000 50–69 F

This vineyard, owned by the Vignobles Gillet, has done very well this vintage. The wine is delicately fragrant (white fruits and mandarins with some crystallised notes), and develops a full, harmonious palate. Its liqueur quality, aromatic persistence and ageing potential (three to five years) make it an interesting wine.

Vignobles Anne-Marie Gillet, Ch. La Bertrande, 33410 Omet, tel. 05.56.62.19.64, fax 05.56.76.90.55 Y by appt.

CH. LA CLYDE

Elevé en fût de chêne 1998

☐ 0.5 ha 2,000 50–69

Located on a 17-ha (42-acre) estate, this wine is made in very small quantities from grapes exposed to botrytis and known as *grains nobles*, as they are in Alsace. It has been matured in oak for 12 months, and is somewhat marked by oak, but remains supple, balanced and pleasantly fragrant.

EARL Philippe Cathala, Ch. La Clyde, 33550 Tabanac, tel. 05.56.67.56.84, fax 05.56.67.12.06 Y by appt.

CH. LAGAROSSE

Vieilli en fût de chêne 1997

☐ 1.2 ha 6,000 50–69 F

This vineyard also produces Première Côtes, and here offers a wine with a nose of roasting, citrus fruits and grilled almonds. A supple, round 1997 vintage which is pleasant to drink.

SCA des Vignobles du Ch. Lagarosse, B.P. 18, 33550 Tabanac, tel. 05.56.67.00.05, fax 05.56.67.12.64 Y by appt.

CH. DE L'ORANGERIE 1998★

☐ 4.3 ha 20,000 30–49 F

This wine comes from a small vineyard belonging to a large property. It is made from 100% Sémillon, and is still somewhat austere. It does have sufficient structure to improve with age, however. Its aromas of honey, roasting and dried fruits will express themselves fully in two to three years' time.

Jean-Christophe Icard, Ch. de l'Orangerie, 33540 Saint-Félix-de-Foncaude, tel. 05.56.71.53.67, fax 05.56.71.59.11, e-mail orangerie@quaternet.fr Y by appt.

CH. MEMOIRES Grains d'Or 1998★★

☐ 5 ha 20,000 50–69 F

This vineyard was hit hard by the storm of 27 December 1999, in which it lost most of its wineries and wines. Not only was this a trauma for Jean-François Ménard and his family, it will also be regretted by many wine-lovers, who have been deprived of attractive products such as this wine which survived the disaster. Its rich aromas of vanilla, toast and crystallised fruits fully live up to the power and balance of the structure to give a wine with good potential for development.

SCEA Vignobles Ménard, Ch. Mémoires, 33490 Saint-Maixant, tel. 05.56.62.06.43, fax 05.56.62.04.32, e-mail memoires@aol.com Y by appt.

CH. PEYBRUN 1997★★

☐ 5 ha 12,000 50–69 F

This vineyard is equally well represented in Premières Côtes de Bordeaux, and here distinguishes itself by the quality of its 1997 Cadillac. It needs to be allowed to breathe for quite a while before tasting, but has lovely surprises in store, such as a bouquet of great complexity including orange peel, mint tea, toast notes and honey.

⚷ Catherine de Loze, Ch. Peybrun, 33410 Gabarnac, tel. 05.56.96.10.84, fax 05.56.96.10.84 ☒

CH. RENON 1998

☐ 3 ha 6,400 ▮ 50–69 F

Coing from a vineyard with wineries dating back to the Ancien Régime and built over beautiful, vaulted cellars, this wine has good substance and an agreeable bouquet with attractive notes of crystallised lemons. It will need to be kept for three years until the palate is ready.

⚷ Claudine Boucherie, Ch. Renon, 33550 Tabanac, tel. 05.56.67.13.59, fax 05.56.67.14.90 ☒ Y ev. day except Sun. 8.15–12 noon 2.15–7pm

CH. REYNON 1998★★

☐ 5.42 ha 16,800 ⦀ 100–149 F

Although less well-known than the Premières Côtes Rouge or the Clos Floridène (Graves), this Vin Liquoreux also bears witness to Denis Dubourdieu's know-how. It has a lovely, clear, brilliant colour, and a nose dominated by honey aromas along with a fine note of oak. These combine with very ripe fruits on the palate. A powerful wine which overall is balanced and harmonious and suitable for long maturing.

⚷ Denis et Florence Dubourdieu, Ch. Reynon, 33410 Béguey, tel. 05.56.62.96.51, fax 05.56.62.14.89, e-mail reynon@gofornet.com ☒ Y by appt.

DOM. DU ROC Cuvée Quentin 1997★

☐ 2.48 ha 9,000 ▮ 🌡 50–69 F

This vineyard mainly produces regional AOCs, but also offers an attractive Cadillac wine. It starts with a lovely colour (strong yellow), then develops an intense, complex bouquet dominated by floral aromas. The palate is fruitier, and has a pleasant roundness and suppleness which suggest that it should be served as an accompaniment to roast white meat or Fourme d'Ambert cheese.

⚷ Gérard Opérie, EARL Dom. du Roc, 33410 Rions, tel. 05.56.62.61.69, fax 05.56.62.17.78 ☒ Y by appt.

LES LARMES DE SAINTE-CATHERINE

Vinifié et élevé en fût de chêne 1998

☐ 5 ha 20,000 ⦀ 50–69 F

The harvest here began on 7 October. This wine, made exclusively from Sémillon and vinified and matured in oak, is very much in keeping with the vineyard's tradition. Although not very intense in its aromatic expression, it has a pleasant suppleness and balance, which bring out the honey aromas.

⚷ SCEA du Ch. Sainte-Catherine, chem. de la Chapelle, 33550 Paillet, tel. 05.56.72.11.64, fax 05.56.72.13.62, e-mail mickel03@wanadoo.fr ☒ Y by appt.

⚷ Decoster

CH. SUAU 1998★★

☐ 1 ha 4,000 ⦀ 50–69 F

This vineyard mainly makes Premières Côtes de Bordeaux, and also devotes one small area to Cadillac. It confirms its understanding of Vins Liquoreux with this 1997 wine, whose character is clearly announced by its yellow-gold colour and bouquet of pronounced notes of honey, crystallised fruits and toast. The round, long, well-balanced and composed palate has an impressive harmony.

⚷ Monique Bonnet, Ch. Suau, 33550 Capian, tel. 05.56.72.19.06, fax 05.56.72.12.43, e-mail bonnet-suau@wanadoo.fr ☒ Y by appt.

Loupiac

The Loupiac vineyard, which declared 15,204 hl (401,386 gal) in 1999, is very ancient, its existence first recorded in the 13th century. In aspect, *terroirs* and the vines grown there, this appellation is very similar to the Appellation Sainte-Croix-du-Mont (see below). Yet, as one travels north, one can detect a subtle development in the flavour of the sweet wines, which become rounder, more in the style of the left bank.

DOM. DU CHAY 1998

☐ 10 ha n.c. 50–69 F

This vineyard has won much praise for its wines. This fresh, elegant 1998 vintage is pleasant and has expressive fruity aromas.

⚷ SCEA Tourré-Delmas, Le Chay, 33410 Loupiac, tel. 05.56.62.99.45, fax 05.56.62.19.44

CH. DU CROS 1997★

☐ 37 ha 35,000 ⦀ 70–99 F

This vineyard is a recognised pillar of the appellation. It owes its fame not only to the old stones of its 13th-century castle, but also to wines such as this one. It is fresh in the nose (vanilla with crystallised oranges and lemons) and full in its development on the palate, where it is agreeably spicy, with a good balance between its freshness and the liqueur flavour.

⚷ SA Vignobles M. Boyer, Ch. du Cros, 33410 Loupiac, tel. 05.56.62.99.31, fax 05.56.62.12.59, e-mail contact@chateauducros.com ☒ Y ev. day except Sat. Sun. 8am–12 noon 2pm–6pm

CH. GRAND PEYRUCHET 1998★★

□ 9 ha 30,000 50–69 F

This 35-ha (86-acre) vineyard also produces red Premières Côtes de Bordeaux (Domaine du Moulin). It has achieved a fine vintage with this 1998 wine. Its bouquet is both complex and intense, playing on notes of peaches, apricots and figs, while the palate proves to be imposingly mouth-filling, with fine concentration and a typical finish for the appellation with great richness and good length. A wine with solid ageing potential.

M. Gillet et B. Queyrens, Ch. Peyruchet, 33410 Loupiac, tel. 05.56.62.62.71, fax 05.56.76.92.09 Y by appt.

CH. DU GRAND PLANTIER

Elevé en fût de chêne 1997★

□ n.c. 4,000 50–69 F

Since 1991 this family vineyard has been run by two young wine-growers. Their wine has had 18 months of maturation in oak, and is presented in numbered bottles. It offers a complex bouquet (quince, honey, oranges, apricots and crystallised lemons). The structure is full, supple and elegant.

GAEC des Vignobles Albucher, Ch. du Grand Plantier, 33410 Monprimblanc, tel. 05.56.62.99.03, fax 05.56.76.91.35 Y by appt.

CH. LES ROQUES

Cuvée Frantz Elevé en fût de chêne 1998★

□ 3.5 ha 2,000 100–149 F

From the same producer as the Château du Pavillon (Sainte-Croix-du-Mont), this wine is also very successful. In addition to its promising golden-yellow colour, it has an attractive high-quality bouquet of lovely crystallised notes. The substance on the palate is just what is needed to form a rich, full overall impression.

SCEA Ch. du Pavillon, 33410 Sainte-Croix-du-Mont, tel. 05.56.62.01.04, fax 05.56.62.00.92, e-mail a.v.fertal@wanadoo.fr Y by appt.

CH. LOUPIAC-GAUDIET 1998

□ 24 ha 85,000 50–69 F

A short walk from this château there is a 12th-century Romanesque church. Although its noble rot is not very pronounced, this wine is well made with fine touches of fruity and floral aromas (lemons, apricots and broom), and will be a good accompaniment to white meats and poultry. The oak-matured **1998 Château de Loupiac** (100–149F) is also recommended.

Daniel Sanfourche, Ch. Loupiac-Gaudiet, 33410 Loupiac, tel. 05.56.62.99.88, fax 05.56.62.60.13, e-mail loupiac-gaudiet@atlantic-line.fr Y by appt.

Marc Ducau

CH. MAZARIN 1998★

□ 10 ha 15,000 30–49 F

This very successful wine remains true to the vineyard's tradition of quality. It is very supple, and delighted the jury by resolutely focusing on elegance, with beautiful, long aromas of coconut and vanilla notes.

Jean-Yves Arnaud, La Croix, 33410 Gabarnac, tel. 05.56.20.23.52, fax 05.56.20.23.52 Y by appt.

CH. PEYROT-MARGES 1998★

□ 2 ha 6,000 30–49 F

The Chassagnols own a vast 35-ha (86-acre) vineyard, and produce a **1998 Sainte-Croix-du Mont** under the **Peyrot-Marges** label. It received the same rating as this delightful Loupiac, whose personality emerges in a fresh, delicate, quite complex bouquet which leads on to a full, round, well-balanced palate.

GAEC Vignobles Chassagnol, Bern, 33410 Gabarnac, tel. 05.56.62.98.00, fax 05.56.62.93.23 Y by appt.

CH. DE RICAUD 1998

□ 22 ha 50,000 70–99 F

The Neo-Gothic architecture of this château is astonishing. This Ricaud is a wine of fairly modern conception, which has a supple, soft, well-balanced substance. This combines with the fresh, fruity bouquet to form a pleasant overall impression.

Ch. de Ricaud, 33410 Loupiac, tel. 05.56.62.66.16, fax 05.56.76.93.30 Y by appt.

Alain Thiénot

CH. RONDILLON 1998★

□ 9 ha 20,000 70–99 F

This vineyard has put its lovely limestone-clay terroir to good use with this vintage, which was harvested in four successive grape selections. It creates an excellent initial impression with its golden-yellow colour, and has a simple, pleasant bouquet of agreeable fruity notes, then develops a well-concentrated structure on the palate. The finish brings the whole experience to a happy conclusion with an unusual touch of liquorice. The **1998 Clos Jean** (50–69F) has been matured for 18 months in oak, and is also recommended.

Vignobles Bord, Ch. Rondillon, 33410 Loupiac, tel. 05.56.62.99.84, fax 05.56.62.93.55, e-mail lbord@club-internet.fr Y by appt.

Sainte-Croix-du-Mont

This area of steep hills overlooking the Garonne is comparatively little known, despite its considerable charm. The wines have long suffered from a reputation of being favourites at weddings and banquets, as have other Vins Liquoreux appellations from the right bank.

However, this appellation, which faces the Sauternes vineyards and which produced 16,726 hl (441,566 gal) in 1999, deserves better. The soil is good, mainly limestone with deposits of gravel, the micro-climate favouring the growth of noble rot. The grape varieties are similar to those grown in Sauternes, as are the methods of vinification. The wines are more rounded and soft rather than intensely sweet, with a pleasantly fruity taste. They can be served with the same dishes as their grander neighbours from the left bank, but their prices are more affordable, sufficiently so as to serve them as a sumptuous extra at drinks parties.

CH. DES ARROUCATS 1998

□ 22 ha 30,000 30–49 F

Some scenes from *La Bicyclette Bleue*, a television adaptation of Régine Deforges's novel, were shot among the vines here. For this vintage they have yielded a simple but well-made wine which develops agreeably, both in its bouquet enriched by spices and noble rot, and on the palate, where there is good substance.

EARL des Vignobles Labat-Lapouge, Ch. des Arroucats, 33410 Sainte-Croix-du-Mont, tel. 05.56.62.07.37, fax 05.57.98.06.29 ev. day except Sun. 9am–12 noon 2pm–6pm

Annie Lapouge

CH. BEL AIR Cuvée Prestige 1997★

□ 16 ha 12,000 70–99 F

This wine comes from a hillside vineyard, and is only produced in the great vintages. For Vins Liquoreux, 1997 was a very good year because the harvesters waited for the noble rot to appear. This fragrant wine, in which botrytis is noticeably present, develops a full, frank palate which must give it good ageing potential. The **1998 Cuvée Vieilles Vignes** (50–69F) is recommended.

Jean-Guy Méric, Ch. Bel Air, 33410 Sainte-Croix-du-Mont, tel. 05.56.62.01.19, fax 05.56.62.09.33 by appt.

CH. DE CRABITAN 1998

□ 6.36 ha 32,000 50–69 F

There is 2% Muscadelle in this wine, which is dominated by Sémillon. It is a very accomplished vintage, which relies on a simple but balanced structure to unfold attractive aromas of *pain d'épices* (a kind of spice loaf), roasted almonds, honey and musk.

Vincent Labouille, Ch. de Crabitan, 33410 Sainte-Croix-du-Mont, tel. 05.56.62.01.47, fax 05.56.76.71.17 ev. day except Sat. Sun. 8am–12 noon 2pm–6pm; cl. Aug.

CRU DE GRAVERE

Vieilles vignes 1998★★

□ 0.67 ha 3,000 50–69 F

Coming from a vineyard the size of a curate's garden, this wine is like a little jewel that has been carved with great care. Its bouquet is subtle and fine, and at the same time rich and concentrated, playing on notes of vanilla, dried fruits, marmalade and, of course, roasting, to create a wine with a real Vin Liquoreux feel. The structure is rich, fleshy and elegant, and has an excellent presence, its charm equalled only by the wine's ageing potential.

EARL Vignobles Laurent Réglat, Ch. de Teste, 33410 Monprimblanc, tel. 05.56.62.10.65, fax 05.56.62.98.80 by appt.

CH. LAMARQUE Cuvée Prestige 1997★

□ 2 ha 5,000 70–99 F

This oak-matured wine (80% Sémillon and 20% Sauvignon) has a rather limited volume of production. Despite that, it distinguishes itself with an elegant bouquet, well-dosed oak, a good substance and a long finish.

Bernard Darroman, Ch. Lamarque, 33410 Sainte-Croix-du-Mont, tel. 05.56.62.01.21, fax 05.56.76.72.10 by appt.

CH. LA RAME

Réserve du Château 1998★★

□ 20 ha n.c. 100–149 F

This vineyard, which is one of the powerhouses of the appellation, underwent major renovation in 1999. This 1998 did not benefit from this, but nevertheless, as in previous vintages which have always received a high rating, this wine fully lives up to the vineyard's reputation. Its rich, complex bouquet prepares the way for an equally rich, fleshy palate whose balance reappears in a long finish. A very good wine, which should be left in the cellar for a while until it finds its harmony.

Yves Armand, Ch. La Rame, 33410 Sainte-Croix-du-Mont, tel. 05.56.62.01.50, fax 05.56.62.01.94, e-mail chateau.larame@wanadoo.fr ev. day 8.30am–12 noon 1.30pm–7pm; Sat. Sun. by appt.

CH. LESCURE 1997★

□ n.c. 10,900 30–49 F

This wine was produced in beautiful 1930s wineries, and has a pleasant, interesting bouquet of great finesse and delicacy. The well-balanced, well-composed palate shows good ageing potential.

C.A.T. Ch. Lescure, 33490 Verdelais, tel. 05.57.98.04.68, fax 05.57.98.04.64 by appt.

CH. LES MARCOTTES 1998*

35 ha 186,000 30–49 F

This is no microscopic garage wine-maker, but a vineyard of respectable size. That makes the present wine all the more interesting with its brilliant golden-yellow colour and bouquet of roasting and toast notes. The palate has fine aromatic expression, and is supported by a structure which is full-bodied, rich, fleshy, long and balanced.

Gérard et Sylvie Cigana, Ch. Les Marcottes, 33410 Sainte-Croix-du-Mont, tel. 05.56.62.05.44, fax 05.56.62.06.70 Mon. Tue. Thu. Fri. 8am–12 noon 1.30pm–5.30pm

CH. DES MAILLES 1998*

17 ha 80,000 50–69 F

This wine is still reserved in the nose, which is beginning to reveal some notes of roasting, honey and toasted almonds. It asserts its personality on the palate, however, where it is supple, balanced and well concentrated.

Daniel Larrieu, Ch. des Mailles, 33410 Sainte-Croix-du-Mont, tel. 05.56.62.01.20, fax 05.56.76.71.99 by appt.

CH. DU MONT

Réserve du Château 1998**

14 ha 10,000 70–99 F

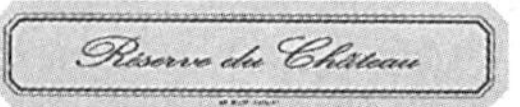

Once again this vineyard's Cuvée Prestige lives up to the renown of the Chouvac vineyards. Its superb, clear, brilliant colour shows from the start that it is a real success. This first impression is confirmed by the bouquet of crystallised notes supported by vanilla. The rich, full, fleshy palate has a fine liqueur quality and good ageing potential.

Hervé Chouvac, Ch. du Mont, 33410 Sainte-Croix-du-Mont, tel. 05.56.62.03.10, fax 05.56.62.07.58 ev. day except Sun. 9am–12 noon 2pm–7pm

CH. DU PAVILLON 1997*

4.5 ha 15,000 70–99 F

This vineyard has a beautiful house in the 18th-century Bordeaux style, and a hillside terroir which faces south-west. Its rich, fleshy, well-balanced wine is both attractive and full of potential. Its very pleasant bouquet of fresh, fruity, slightly crystallised notes suggests that it should be enjoyed while still young.

SCEA Ch. du Pavillon, 33410 Sainte-Croix-du-Mont, tel. 05.56.62.01.04, fax 05.56.62.00.92, e-mail a.v.fertal@wanadoo.fr by appt.

DOM. ROUSTIT 1997

3.49 ha 16,000 30–49 F

Like many Sainte-Croix vineyards, this estate is also a producer in other appellations. Although this wine's palate is less expressive than its delicately grapey bouquet, it has good balance.

SCEA Dulac et Séraphon, 2, Pantoc, 33490 Verdelais, tel. 05.56.62.02.08, fax 05.56.76.71.49 by appt.

Cérons

Enclosed by the Graves region (an appellation that they can also claim, unlike the Sauternes and Barsac), the wines of Cérons offer a link between Barsac and the sweet Graves Supérieurs. Production was 2,084 hl (55,018 gal) in 1999. These are, nonetheless, original wines, with a characteristic vigour and great finesse.

CH. DU CAILLOU 1997*

1 ha 3,000 50–69 F

The small size of this vineyard in no way impairs its standards of production. This wine is delicately fragrant, with notes of honey and lemon against a background of crystallised citrus fruits, and retains its finesse on the palate, where it develops without heaviness and reveals a good general balance.

SA Ch. du Caillou, rte de Saint-Cricq, 33720 Cérons, tel. 05.56.27.17.60, fax 05.56.27.00.31 by appt.

Latorse

CH. HURADIN 1997**

3.1 ha 6,500 50–69 F

This very reliable vineyard has taken advantage of the favourable conditions of the vintage to develop a Vin Liquoreux with length, richness and power, combined with intensity and aromatic complexity (honey, stewed and crystallised fruits and toast). All in all, a very good wine.

SCEA Vignobles Y. Ricaud-Lafosse, Ch. Huradin, 33720 Cérons, tel. 05.56.27.09.97, fax 05.56.27.09.97 by appt.

Catherine Lafosse

CH. DE L'EMIGRE 1998

☐ 2 ha 6,600 50–69 F

This pleasantly simple Vin Liquoreux will be a good accompaniment to many dishes thanks to the fruity character (ripe fruits) of its bouquet.

Pierrette Despujols, Ch. de l'Emigré, 33720 Cérons, tel. 05.56.27.01.64, fax 05.56.27.13.70 by appt.

LE MOULIN DE VALERIEN 1998

☐ 3.02 ha n.c. 70–99 F

The mill here no longer has its top or its sails, but bears witness to the cereal-growing and milling activity that used to go on in the Cérons and Podensac region. This supple, full-bodied, well-supported wine has a pleasant balance which prevents it from being at all heavy.

SCEA Vignobles Ducau, Clos Graouères, 33720 Podensac, tel. 05.56.27.16.80, fax 05.56.27.18.92 by appt.

CH. DE ROCHEFORT 1998★

☐ n.c. n.c. 50–69 F

This producer has made best use of his location (at Preignac) to develop this Cérons, which has a genuine Vin Liquoreux character. The bouquet offers notes of roasting and citrus fruits, while the palate develops a powerful, elegant, rich, concentrated and balanced structure.

Jean-Christophe Barbe, Ch. Laville, 33210 Preignac, tel. 05.56.63.28.14, fax 05.56.63.16.28 by appt.

Barsac

All the wines carrying the Appellation Barsac can also be Appellation Sauternes. Barsac, which covers 620 ha (1,531 acres) and produced 12,830 hl (338,712 gal) in 1999, differs from the communes of the Sauternais proper by virtue of a less hilly terrain and by the stone walls that enclose many of the vineyards. The wines themselves differ from those of Sauternes, being slightly sweeter in character. However, like Sauternes, they may be served with desserts or, as is more and more popular, to accompany a starter of foie gras or strongly flavoured cheeses, such as Roquefort.

CH. COUTET 1997

☐ 1er cru clas. 38.5 ha 48,000 200–249 F

73 75 76 78 **81** 83 85 **86 89 90** 91 93 **94 95 96 97**

This vineyard is a vast property of 50 ha (124 acres), which belonged to the Lur-Saluces until the beginning of the 20th century. A 14th-century tower and a chapel lend character to the more recent château. This is a wine which appeals to the eye with its golden-yellow colour with green glints. What follows does not disappoint, although its bouquet is still discreet, combining a delicate, supple structure with pronounced notes of noble rot and a long finish which needs time to become rounder.

SC Ch. Coutet, 33720 Barsac, tel. 05.56.27.15.46, fax 05.56.27.02.20 by appt.

CH. FARLURET 1998★

☐ 9.3 ha 28,000 100–149 F

75 81 82 83 85 **|88|(89)|90| |91|** 94 |95| **|96| 97** 98

The Lamothes also produce a Sauternes, the Haut-Bergeron. Here they offer a highly interesting wine which is round and rich, and has aromas of honey, acacia and citrus fruits accompanied by a slight musky quality.

R. Lamothe et ses Fils, Haut-Bergeron, 33210 Preignac, tel. 05.56.63.24.76, fax 05.56.63.23.31 by appt.

CH. GRAVAS 1997★

☐ 10 ha 30,000 70–99 F

75 76 81 83 85 86|88| |89| |90| 91 93 94 **95 |96| 97**

This vineyard is well-known for the warmth of its welcome, and has just invested in major improvements. The 1997 wine did not benefit from these, but nonetheless cuts a fine figure with its amber-gold colour and clear glints. The bouquet is delicately discreet at first, then develops when the wine is swirled in the glass, releasing notes of crystallised citrus fruits. It hits the palate with citronella flavours, before returning to round, rich sensations which open out into notes of quinine and stewed oranges at the finish. A wine which should be kept for four to five years.

SCEA Domaines Bernard, Ch. Gravas, 33720 Barsac, tel. 05.56.27.06.91, fax 05.56.27.29.83 by appt.

CH. GRILLON 1998

☐ 11 ha 26,000 70–99 F

Like many Barsac properties, this is a medium-sized vineyard. Its fresh, balanced 1998 wine has an expressive bouquet (white fruits, toast and overripe grapes) that develops in fullness. A wine which has opened out well.

Odile Roumazeilles-Cameleyre, Ch. Grillon, 33720 Barsac, tel. 05.56.27.16.45, fax 05.56.27.12.18 ev. day 9am–12.30pm 2pm–7pm

CH. NAIRAC 1996★★

☐2ème cru clas. 15 ha 15,000 200–249 F

73 74 **75 76** 79 **80 81 82** |(83)| 85 **|86| 88 89 90** |91| **|92|** |93| 94 (95) **96**

The 1997 vintage had not yet been bottled when we carried out our tasting on 4 May 2000, and as a result the 1996 wine was offered for a second time. Congratulations to the wine-maker and to the Guide's tasters who, one year on – and still tasting blind – have awarded a second *coup de coeur* to this wine. It has confirmed its ageing potential (ten years or more), without losing any of its charm. The very intense bouquet releases a successful combination of fruity and floral aromas, with exotic and crystallised notes reinforced by a touch of honey. The palate establishes a good balance between body and sweetness, then opens out into a flavourful finish which is fresh, fruity and promising.

🔑 Ch. Nairac, 33720 Barsac, tel. 05.56.27.16.16, fax 05.56.27.26.50 Y by appt.

🔑 Nicole Tari

CH. PIADA 1998★

☐ 9.67 ha n.c. 100–149 F

67 70 71 |75| |77| |79| |81| 82 **|83|** 85 **|86| |88| |89|** **|(90)| |91|** 95 96 97 |98|

This vineyard is rich in anecdotes, and is well-known for adapting the style of its wine to the character of the vintage. The 1998 wine has a lovely yellow colour with copper glints, and focuses resolutely on finesse both in its very floral bouquet of broom and acacia flower notes, and on its palate, which reveals a fruity quality and good balance. A pleasant wine which should be drunk over the next five years.

🔑 EARL Lalande et Fils, Ch. Piada, 33720 Barsac, tel. 05.56.27.16.13, fax 05.56.27.26.30 ☑ Y ev. day 8am–12 noon 1.30pm–7pm; Sat. Sun. by appt.

CH. ROUMIEU-LACOSTE 1998★★

☐ n.c. 14,350 100–149 F

|90| |95| |(96)| |97| **98**

Located in the Haut Barsac, this vineyard has the benefit of a high-quality terroir. Hervé Dubourdieu has turned this vintage to excellent account. The wine has a strong yellow colour and an appealing bouquet which is fine, thoroughbred and complex (dried apricots, smoke, rhubarb and acacia). Th[e] full, fleshy, rich, well-structured palate show[s] good ageing potential.

🔑 Hervé Dubourdieu, Ch. Roûmieu-Lacoste, 33720 Barsac, tel. 05.56.27.16.29, fax 05.56.27.02.65 ☑ Y by appt.

CH. SUAU 1998

☐2ème cru clas. 8 ha 19,000 70–99 F

This wine comes from a vineyard which [is] representative of Barsac in terms of terroir (fine layer of clay and stony earth on a bed of limestone with fossilised starfish). It is also typical of the appellation in its overall character, which is pleasant with a certain aromati[c] complexity.

🔑 Nicole Biarnès, Ch. de Navarro, 33720 Illats, tel. 05.56.27.20.27, fax 05.56.27.26.53 ☑ Y ev. day 8.30am–12.30pm 1.30pm–6.30pm

Sauternes

If you visit any of the châteaux in Sauternes, you will hear the story of the grower who one day had the brilliant, but perverse, idea of bringing in his harvest late, even though the grapes were over-ripe. However, if you go to five châteaux you will find that each grower has his own version of the story, which, naturally enough took place on his property. The truth is, no one knows who 'invented' Sauternes, nor when it was invented, nor where.

While history in the Sauternais insists on hiding behind legend, there is no confusion about the geography of the area. The AOC covered an area of 1,637 ha (4,043 acres) in 1996. In 1999, 33,224 hl (877,114 gal) of wine were produced. Every pebble in the five communes making up the appellation (including Barsac, which has its own appellation) is counted and every constituent recorded. The variety of soils and subsoils (limestone or chalk and clay under gravel) give a special character to each cru, with the most famous vineyards being planted on gravelly hillocks. The Sauternes wines are made from three grape varieties – Sémillon (70–80%), Sauvignon (20–30%) and Muscadelle; these are golden and luscious but also fine and delicate. Their 'toasted' bouquet develops very well with age, becoming rich and complex with notes of honey, hazelnut and crystallised orange. It is worth noting that Sauternes and Barsac were the only white wines to be classified in 1855.

CH. ANDOYSE DU HAYOT 1997★

□ 20 ha 48,000 70–99 F

90| 91 |93| |94| 95 **96** |97|

Coming from the same producer as the Château Romer du Hayot, this wine has an oustandingly complex bouquet, which ranges from notes of grapefruit to touches of wax. The round, rich palate reveals notes of crystallised fruits and apricot jam.

SCE Vignobles du Hayot, Ch. Andoyse, 33720 Barsac, tel. 05.56.27.15.37, fax 05.56.27.04.24, e-mail duhayot@usa.net by appt.

CH. D'ARMAJAN DES ORMES 1997

□ 8 ha n.c. 100–149 F

95| |96| 97

Very much like the château, which is a beautiful Girondin house, this wine focuses on finesse, with pleasant floral aromas that take over quite quickly from the earlier, more mineral notes in the bouquet.

EARL Jacques et Guillaume Perromat, Ch. d'Armajan, 33210 Preignac, tel. 05.56.63.22.17, fax 05.56.63.21.55 by appt.

Michel Perromat

CH. BARBIER Cuvée M 1998★

□ 2 ha 3,000 100–149 F

This wine comes from the same producer as the Château Fayau (Cadillac), and manages to be very *liquoreux* and at the same time fine and elegant. There is good balance between oak and fruit, then it opens out into a long finish with a lingering return of flesh and richness. A wine which deserves a place of honour in the cellar.

SCEA Jean Médeville et Fils, Ch. Fayau, 33410 Cadillac, tel. 05.57.98.08.08, fax 05.56.62.18.22 ev. day except Sat. Sun. 8.30am–12 noon 2pm–5.30pm

CRU BARREJATS Insoumis 1996★

□ 2.62 ha 1000 200–249 F

This is a wine of limited production, whose richness and power will for some people give it a sweet perfume of nostalgia. It has a beautiful amber colour, then develops an expressive, almost aggressive bouquet of polish and beeswax (the sweet smells of our grandmothers' houses). Its palate is warm, and opens out into a long, finish with notes of crystallised fruits which is in keeping with the rest of the tasting. It may be kept for five years or more. (Half-litre bottles)

SCEA Barréjats, Clos de Gensac, Mareuil, 33210 Pujols-sur-Ciron, tel. 05.56.76.69.06, fax 05.56.76.69.06, e-mail barrejats@aol.com by appt.

Mireille Daret et Ph. Andurand

CH. BASTOR-LAMONTAGNE 1997★★

□ 56 ha 70,000 150–199 F

82 83 84 85 86 87 |88| |89| |(90)| 94 95 **96 97**

Like many 1997 Vins Liquoreux, this one is the result of careful harvesting and vinification, and has taken the best possible advantage of 30 days of summer heat in the month of September. At the expense of a limited volume of production, the Foncier-Vignobles team has produced a fine, distinguished wine, whose charm is reinforced by the complexity of its aromas (vanilla, citrus fruits, butter, spices and dried fruits). Although it is already pleasant to drink, it will gain from being kept. A good accompaniment to white meat à la crème and morels. A wine which can be drunk sooner is **Les Remparts de Bastor** (70–99F), which is recommended by the jury for its delicate citrus-fruit bouquet (crystallised mandarins).

SCEA Vignobles Bastor et Saint-Robert, Dom. de Lamontagne, 33210 Preignac, tel. 05.56.63.27.66, fax 05.56.76.87.03, e-mail bastor.lamontagne@dial.oleane.com by appt.

Foncier-Vignobles

CH. BECHEREAU 1997★

□ 10.63 ha 16,000 100–149 F

Unusually for the Sauternes region, this vineyard has underground cellars. This 1997 wine has a beautiful, copper-yellow colour which resolutely indicates its classicism with a bouquet of wax, broom and acacia-flower notes. It has the same complexity on the palate, which is enriched by aromas of dried figs and a touch of noble rot. A full, fleshy, rich wine, which seems well-equipped for a good ageing period (five to ten years).

Les Vignobles Dumon, Ch. Bechereau de Ruat, 33210 Bommes, tel. 05.56.76.61.73, fax 05.56.76.67.84 ev. day except Sat. Sun. 9am–12 noon 2pm–5.30pm; groups by appt.

CH. CANTEGRIL 1996★

□ 17 ha n.c. 100–149 F

This wine comes from the same producer as the Château Doisy-Daëne. It does not rival it, but with its golden colour, its bouquet of ripe grapes well supported by a fine note of oak, and its balanced palate with long, crystallised flavours, it bears witness to the Dubourdieus' know-how.

EARL Vignobles Pierre et Denis Dubourdieu, Ch. Doisy-Daëne, quartier Gravas, 33720 Barsac, tel. 05.56.27.15.84, fax 05.56.27.18.99 ev. day except Sat. Sun. 9am–12.30pm 1.30pm–6pm

BORDEAUX

CH. DE CARLES 1998★

☐ 14 ha 40,000 70–99 F

Coming from the upper Barsac plateau, this medium-bodied wine is well served by its aromas: fragrances of white flowers and white-fleshed and crystallised fruits accentuated by a lovely note of oak. A lively, balanced wine which has real elegance.

Michel Pascaud, Ch. de Carles, 33720 Barsac, tel. 05.56.27.07.19, fax 05.56.27.13.18 by appt.

CLOS DU ROY 1998★

☐ n.c. n.c. 70–99 F

This wine produced by the Piada team (Barsac) is a fine achievement. It has a beautiful pale-gold colour, then develops a full, complex bouquet of notes of exotic and crystallised fruits, orange peel and acacia. The supple, elegant, refined stucture will ensure that this wine has good ageing potential.

EARL Lalande et Fils, Ch. Piada, 33720 Barsac, tel. 05.56.27.16.13, fax 05.56.27.26.30 ev. day 8am–12 noon 1.30pm–7pm; Sat. Sun. by appt.

CH. CLOS HAUT-PEYRAGUEY 1997★★

☐ 1er cru clas. 12 ha 24,380 200–249 F

75 76 79 81 82 83 85 |86| |88| 89 |90| 91 93 94 **95 96 97**

This wine comes from a beautiful property with buildings typical of a Girondin estate and a very fine terroir. It confirms qualities noted earlier, when its maturation was not complete (it has spent 22 months in the barrel). Since then it has developed favourably, forming a delicate, complex bouquet in which crystallised notes are released within an attractive, toasty oakiness, and a supple, rich, lively, elegant and powerful palate. It will make a good acompaniment to small game birds.

SC J. et J. Pauly, Ch. Haut-Bommes, 33210 Bommes, tel. 05.56.76.61.53, fax 05.56.76.69.65, e-mail haut-peyraguey@caves-particulieres.com ev. day 9am–12 noon 2pm–6pm; groups by appt.

GFA Clos Haut-Peyraguey

CH. DU COY 1998

☐ 7 ha 18,000 70–99 F

Nicole Biarnès is also a Barsac producer (Château Suau). Here she offers a pleasantly fragrant Sauternes with oaky and crystallised notes – citrus fruits, peaches and apricots. The wine is supported by a sweet, frank structure, and can be drunk until 2005.

Nicole Biarnès, Ch. de Navarro, 33720 Illats, tel. 05.56.27.20.27, fax 05.56.27.26.53 ev. day 8.30am–12.30pm 1.30pm–6.30pm

CH. DOISY DAENE 1997★★

☐ 2ème cru clas. 15 ha n.c. 250–299 F

50 71 |75| |76| |78| |79| |80| **|81| |82|** |(83)| 84 |85| **|86|** |88| |89| **|90| |91| |94| 95 96 97**

Produced on a select terroir in the Doisy

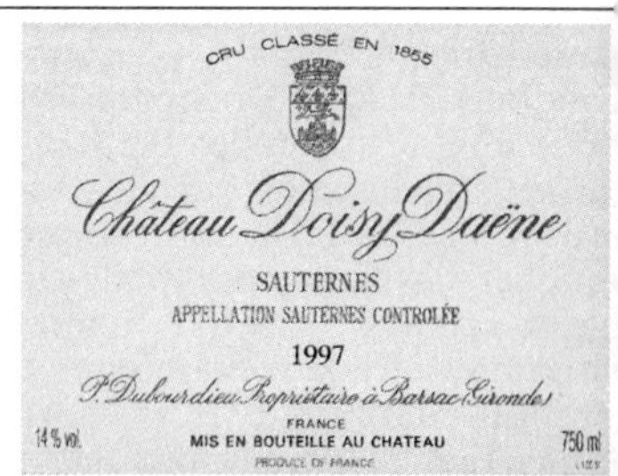

area of Barsac, and by well-known personalities like the Dubourdieus, this wine certainly comes from good stock. As if to show it, it starts with a very beautiful, brilliant golden yellow colour. Its bouquet goes from crystallised notes to honey and dried fruits (roasted almonds and raisins), and has all the necessary complexity to make a great wine. As for the palate, it shows clearly right from the attack what its character will be: full, rich aromatic and elegant. Its particularly complex finish is remarkable.

CRU CLASSÉ EN 1855
Château Doisy Daëne
SAUTERNES
APPELLATION SAUTERNES CONTROLÉE
1997
P. Dubourdieu Propriétaire à Barsac Gironde
14% vol.
FRANCE
MIS EN BOUTEILLE AU CHATEAU
750 ml

EARL Vignobles Pierre et Denis Dubourdieu, Ch. Doisy-Daëne, quartier Gravas, 33720 Barsac, tel. 05.56.27.15.84, fax 05.56.27.18.99 ev. day except Sat. Sun. 9am–12.30pm 1.30pm–6pm

CH. DOISY-VEDRINES 1998★

☐ 2ème cru clas. 27 ha 30,000 200–249 F

|70| 71 75 76 81 82 |(83)| |85| **|86| |88|** |90| 92 |94| **95** 97 98

From the Chevaliers de Védrines, whose descendants now live in Louisiana, to the current owners, whose forebears acquired the estate in 1844, this fine production unit has belonged to only two families. The jury tasted the 1997 wine here for the second time, and found that it has confirmed not only its balance and elegance, but also its power and aromatic richness. This 1998 wine has a clear colour and complex aromas of crystallised lemons and dried apricots. The round, rich, well-composed palate is very mouth-filling and has notes of fruits and honey along with a good touch of grapiness. Good length is a particularly interesting feature of this wine, which should be kept for at least two or three years before being served with roast wood pigeon or a red berry soup.

SC Doisy-Védrines, 33720 Barsac, tel. 05.56.27.15.13, fax 05.56.78.37.08 by appt.

P. Castéja

CH. DE FARGUES 1994★★

☐ 13 ha 10,000 300–499 F

|47| |49| |53| 59 62 |(67)| 71 **|75| |76| |83|** 84 **85 |86|** 87 **88 89 90 |91| |94|**

Although it is not Cru Classé, this vineyard, with its genuine fortified castle, is one of the top names of the appellation. Since 1472 it has been owned by the Lur-Saluces, an illustrious family to which Sauternes owes its fame. The 1994 wine was harvested at just the right time, and lives up to its rank. It has a beautiful, coppery-yellow colour, and a fine,

expressive bouquet of acacia, broom, pine forests in spring and noble-rot grapes with notes of crystallised mandarins and toast. The palate is balanced, and has the power and elegance to ensure that it keeps for 20 years or more.
Comte Alexandre de Lur-Saluces, Ch. de Fargues, 33210 Fargues-de-Langon, tel. 05.57.98.04.20, fax 05.57.98.04.21, e-mail fargues@chateau-de-fargues.com by appt.

CH. FILHOT 1997

2ème cru clas. 60 ha 90,000 150–199 F

81 82 83 85 86 88 89 91 92 95 97

This château is a Mecca of the Bordeaux aristocracy, with a beautiful, imposing house which was rebuilt in 1845 at the same time as the English-style park was laid out. It now offers a wine which tends towards floral aromas but was still closed at the time of the tasting. It will need to be allowed to breathe for some time before being served.
SCEA du Ch. Filhot, 33210 Sauternes, tel. 05.56.76.61.09, fax 05.56.76.67.91, e-mail filhot@filhot.com ev. day except Sun. 9am–12 noon 2pm–6pm
Famille de Vaucelles

CH. DU GRAND CARRETEY 1998*

9 ha 20,000 70–99 F

Vincent Labouille is also a producer on the right bank, but here in Barsac he owns family vines which have yielded this agreeably fragrant wine with notes of flowers (boxwood and broom) and spices. A well-balanced wine which can be drunk while young or after three or four years of ageing.
Vincent Labouille, Ch. de Crabitan, 33410 Sainte-Croix-du-Mont, tel. 05.56.62.01.47, fax 05.56.76.71.17 ev. day except Sat. Sun. 8am–12 noon 2pm–6pm; cl. Aug.

CH. GUIRAUD 1998**

1er cru clas. 85 ha n.c. 250–299 F

83 85 86 |88| |89| (90) 92 |95| 96 (97) 98

This a very fine production unit both in terms of size and terroir. Once again it has hit the right note with the quality of this 1997 wine, which makes an irreproachable first impression with a golden-yellow colour and a fine, powerful bouquet (acacia honey and citrus fruits). With its richness, fullness and sweetness, it has undeniable ageing potential. Best kept for four or five years, then served as an accompaniment to turbot à la crème.
SCA du Ch. Guiraud, 33210 Sauternes, tel. 05.56.76.61.01, fax 05.56.76.67.52, e-mail xplanty@club-internet.fr by appt.

CH. HAUT-BERGERON 1998*

15.78 ha 38,000 100–149 F

|(75)| 76 78 81 82 83 |85| 86 |88| |89| |90| 91 94 |95| 96 97 98

Representing the Preignac properties, this vineyard has scored a hit with its 1998 wine. It has an especially expressive bouquet of vanilla along with exotic and crystallised fruits. The rich, long, powerful palate has a long finish, which one of the tasters described as 'bewitching'. It should have an ageing potential of ten years. Also awarded one star by the jury, the **1996 Cuvée 100 du Millésime** celebrates the centenary of a plot of Sémillon vines. 'This is a real old-style Sauternes,' noted one taster. 200 g/l. of residual sugar, 36 months of maturation in new oak, 6,000 bottles at more than 500F.
R. Lamothe et ses Fils, Haut-Bergeron, 33210 Preignac, tel. 05.56.63.24.76, fax 05.56.63.23.31 by appt.

CH. HAUT BOMMES 1997*

5 ha 10,000 70–99 F

This high-quality wine has developed well since last year's tasting. It has a strong yellow colour, and is now opening up an appealing bouquet of white flowers which is developing towards aromas of dried fruits, then caramel and crystallised fruits at the retro-olfactive stage. One sommelière suggested drinking it with smoked eel rillettes cooked with pears.
SC J. et J. Pauly, Ch. Haut-Bommes, 33210 Bommes, tel. 05.56.76.61.53, fax 05.56.76.69.65, e-mail haut-peyraguey@caves-particulieres.com by appt.
GFA Clos Haut-Peyraguey

CH. HAUT-MAYNE 1997*

5.01 ha 8,500 70–99 F

Fifty-year-old vines have yielded this 1997 wine, which has a very expressive bouquet combining broom and acacia with beeswax. It also shows its power on the palate, where an attractive crystallised quality supports a return to acacia flavours that remain very evident right up to the long finish.
EARL Roumazeilles, Ch. Haut-Mayne, 33210 Preignac, tel. 05.56.76.88.41, fax 05.56.27.12.18 by appt.

CH. LAFAURIE-PEYRAGUEY 1998**

1er cru clas. 40 ha 75,000 200–249 F

75 |76| 77 78 79 80 |81| 82 83 84 |85| 86 |87| |(88)| |89| |90| |91| |92| |93| 94 |95| 96 97 98

Lafaurie-Peyraguey is famous for its Hispanic-Moorish style of architecture, and is also one of the recognised pillars of Sauternes. This 1998 lives up to the vineyard's reputation with its suppleness, richness, good flesh and slightly nostalgic touch of liqueur. With its very expressive aromas of roasting and crystallised fruits, this is a characteristic wine which will keep for a long time and promises to develop well as it ages.
Domaines Cordier, 160, cours du Médoc, 33300 Bordeaux, tel. 05.57.19.57.77, fax 05.57.19.57.87 by appt.

DOM. DE LA FORET 1998

11 ha 28,000 100–149 F

89 |90| 93 94 |95| 96 97 98

This wine's name refers to the forest, which is never far away in the Sauternes region. Its

pale-gold colour and light structure leave the taster with the memory of a complex range of attractive aromas of citrus fruits, broom, acacia, then crystallised or dried fruits.
🔑 Pierre Vaurabourg, Dom. de La Forêt, 33210 Preignac, tel. 05.56.76.88.46 ▣ Y by appt.

CH. LAMOTHE GUIGNARD 1997*

☐2ème cru clas. 18 ha 34,000 ▥ 100–149 F

|81| 82 |(83)| 84 |**85**| |86| 87 |**88**| 89 **90** 92 93 |**94**| |**95**| **96** 97

Coming from one of the highest points in the Sauternes commune, overlooking the Ciron, this full, warm, vinous wine reveals a slight hint of bitterness on the palate; this is far from unpleasant, however, and takes nothing away from the noble rot in the bouquet or the delightful quality of the returning flavour on the palate, which is as *liquoreux* as one could wish for.
🔑 GAEC Philippe et Jacques Guignard, Ch. Lamothe Guignard, 33210 Sauternes, tel. 05.56.76.60.28, fax 05.56.76.69.05 ▣ Y ev. day 8am–12 noon 2pm–6pm; Sat. Sun. by appt.

CH. LAMOURETTE 1997*

☐ 8.5 ha 7,000 ▮ 100–149 F

90 |**91**| 92 95 96 97

A lovely name for an agreeable wine. Has it been influenced by the fact that the property has been handed down from mother to daughter, and that it is produced by a woman? Be that as it may, this wine has chosen to express itself in terms of finesse, the delicacy of its structure in keeping with the elegance of its bouquet of beautiful citrus-fruit notes.
🔑 Anne-Marie Léglise, Ch. Lamourette, 33210 Bommes, tel. 05.56.76.63.58, fax 05.56.76.60.85 ▣ Y by appt.

CH. LANGE-REGLAT

Cuvée spéciale 1998*

☐ 12 ha n.c. ▥ 100–149 F

This Cuvée Prestige has an interesting aromatic expression which shows its personality discreetly in the nose (flowers and citrus fruits), before becoming fuller on the palate.
🔑 Bernard Réglat, Ch. de La Mazerolle, 33410 Monprimblanc, tel. 05.56.62.98.63, fax 05.56.62.17.98, e-mail reglat.bernard@wanadoo.fr ▣ Y by appt.

CH. LA RIVIERE 1998*

☐ 3.8 ha n.c. ▥ 100–149 F

Guillaume Réglat is also a producer on the right bank, at Monprimblanc. Here on his Bommes vineyard he has produced a 1998 wine which is a fine achievement. It is highly characteristic, marked by noble rot and has an appealing colour followed by a bouquet combining oak (toast) with aromas of undergrowth, dried fruits, acacia, peaches and honey. The round, full, balanced palate is well-equipped for an ageing period of about four years.
🔑 Guillaume Réglat, Ch. Cousteau, 33410 Monprimblanc, tel. 05.56.62.98.63, fax 05.56.62.17.98 ▣ Y ev. day except Sat. Sun. 8am–12 noon 2pm–5.30pm. cl. Aug.

CH. LA TOUR BLANCHE 1997**

☐1er cru clas. 34 ha 25,000 ▥ 200–249 F

(61) 62 75 79 80 |**81**| 82 |**83**| 84 |**85**| |**86**| |**88**| 89 **90** |91| |94| **95 97**

This fine production unit was bequeathed to the state in 1907 by a Bordeaux philanthropist so that it could house an agricultural college. Once again it lives up to its status with a beautiful yellow wine with a bouquet of delightful quality, in which delicate notes of honey, dried fruits (figs) and flowers are accentuated by oak. A rich, powerful, long wine, which will be good to serve with very fine dishes (asparagus in a sauce mousseline or fish cooked in sauce), but will also be perfect to drink purely for pleasure as a special aperitif.
🔑 Ch. La Tour Blanche, 33210 Bommes, tel. 05.57.98.02.73, fax 05.57.98.02.78 ▣ Y ev. day except Sat. Sun. 9am–11.30am 2pm–5pm
🔑 Ministère de l'Agriculture

CH. LATREZOTTE 1997

☐ 7 ha 13,200 ▥ 70–99 F

Located on the limestone-clay plateau on the heights of Barsac, the Château Latrezotte offers a 1997 wine which has been matured for 18 months in the barrel (50% new). It has a clear colour, and asserts its aromatic expression with notes of citrus fruits, flowers and honey. A wine which retains a pleasant freshness.
🔑 Jan de Kok, Ch. Latrezotte, 33720 Barsac, tel. 05.56.27.16.50, fax 05.56.27.08.89 ▣

CH. LAVILLE 1998**

☐ 13 ha 15,000 ▥ 70–99 F

|**92**| |94| |95| **96** 97 **98**

The year 1998 was a particularly good one for this vineyard, which is located at Preignac. The wine has an old-gold colour and a bouquet of oak or even coconut, and shows a development which is certainly unusually advanced and also extremely pleasant. With roasting and dried, crystallised and citrus fruits, the aromatic expression is very much like the structure: powerful, rich and highly characteristic. A wine which needs nothing but time to age. The tank-matured **1998 Château Delmond** (50–69F) is recommended.
🔑 EARL du Ch. Laville, 33210 Preignac, tel. 05.56.63.28.14, fax 05.56.63.16.28 ▣ Y ev. day except Sat. Sun. 8.30am–12.30pm 1.30pm–6.30pm
🔑 Y. et C. Barbe

CH. L'ERMITAGE 1997

☐ 11.71 ha 15,000 ▥ 70–99 F

This wine is made from 100% Sémillon and was matured in oak for 27 months. The colour is pale gold, while the nose is strongly marked by oak and reveals floral notes, a slight touch of roasting and some shades of crystallised fruits. The round, supple palate seems light but spruce.

SCEA Ch. L'Ermitage, 9, V.C., M. Lacoste, 33210 Preignac, tel. 05.56.76.24.13, fax 05.56.76.12.75, e-mail chateaulermitage@free.fr ev. day 8am–7pm

CH. LES JUSTICES 1998★

☐ 8.5 ha 25,000 100–149 F

(83) 85 86 88 89 90 |91| |93| |94| **95** 96 (97) 98

Christian Médeville owns the Château Gilette, where he has been producing the wines for 20 years – which has earned him the nickname of the Sauternes antique dealer. He devotes every care to his Château Les Justices, which is matured in oak for a year. This 1998 wine does not claim to rival the power of the 1997 vintage, but is very good in terms of finesse. Its bouquet is a real basket of oranges, qualified by notes of peel and spices. All of this is accompanied by a lovely little liqueur note and some crystallised touches in the background, creating an extremely pleasant overall impression. Best left to develop for three or four years.

Christian Médeville, Ch. Gilette, 33210 Preignac, tel. 05.56.76.28.44, fax 05.56.76.28.43, e-mail christian.medeville@wanadoo.fr by appt.

CH. LIOT 1998

☐ 20 ha n.c. 100–149 F

89 90 91 93 95 96 97 98

This vineyard is a fine production unit located on the Haut Barsac plateau. It remains true to its style with this wine, whose regular buyers will find a supple, pleasant overall impression, with attractive crystallised-fruit flavours and aromas of acacia flowers.

SCEA J. David, Ch. Liot, 33720 Barsac, tel. 05..27.15.31, fax 05.56.27.14.42 by appt.

CH. DE MALLE 1998★★

☐2ème cru clas. 27 ha 49,000 200–249 F

71 75 76 81 83 **|85|**86 87 **|88| |89| |90|**91 **|94| 95 96** 97 **98**

This château is exceptional not only for its eleganct 18th-century architecture and gracious gardens, it is also a Mecca of the Sauternes region because of the reliability and quality of its wine. The 1998 vintage has the richness and balance of a genuine Vin Liquoreux, and will in no way disgrace the vineyard's collection. Its aromas of roasting and botrytis bear witness to excellent grape selection. It has a very wide range of aromas, starting with notes of linden-flower tea and moving on to dried fruits (apricots and figs), before finishing on delightful almond fragrances. A highly accomplished wine, which is already pleasant to drink, but also has good ageing potential.

Comtesse de Bournazel, Ch. de Malle, 33210 Preignac, tel. 05.56.62.36.86, fax 05.56.76.82.40, e-mail chateaudemalle@wanadoo.fr by appt.

DOM. DE MONTEILS

Cuvée Sélection 1997★

☐ 8 ha 4,000 100–149 F

This 10.75-ha (26-acre) estate has been a family concern since 1867. This Cuvée Sélection has a beautiful colour and a menthol quality in the nose which comes as a surprise. There are some notes of crystallised fruits, however. All in all the wine creates a pleasant, well-balanced impression, with a lovely finish on a note of roasting.

SCEA dom. de Monteils, 3, rte de Fargues, 33210 Preignac, tel. 05.56.62.24.05, fax 05.56.62.22.30, e-mail vins.sauternes@wanadoo.fr by appt.
Fourcaud

CH. PEBAYLE DU HAYOT 1997★

☐ 10 ha 23,600 70–99 F

This very accomplished 1997 wine comes from Romer du Hayot and is distributed by the Dulong company. Six months of intelligent oak maturation have not erased the exotic- and crystallised-fruit aromas which give it a certain charm. A wine which is ready to drink now.

Dulong Frères et Fils, 29, rue Jules-Guesde, 33270 Floirac, tel. 05.56.86.51.15, fax 05.56.40.66.41, e-mail dulong@mmkm.com by appt.

CH. CRU PEYRAGUEY 1997★★

☐ 6.5 ha 18,000 100–149 F

75 76 79 82 83 **|85|** |86| |88| |89| **|90|** 91 |94| |95| |96| **97**

Although this vineyard's buildings are located in Preignac, its vineyard is at Bommes in the Haut Sauternes. That tells us that this wine comes from good stock, which is clear beyond doubt from its elegant, complex bouquet of crystallised mandarins, *pain d'épices* (a kind of spice loaf) and acacia. The palate combines spices with a superb impression of crystallised fruits, and has great power and finesse which are very much in keeping with the bouquet.

Vignobles Mussotte, 10, Miselle, 33210 Preignac, tel. 05.56.44.43.48, fax 05.56.01.71.29 by appt.

CH. RAYMOND-LAFON 1996★

☐ 17.9 ha 22,000 250–299 F

Take a high-quality terroir, add to it to the know-how of a former steward from Yquem, and you will get wines like this 1996 vintage, which has been fermented and matured for three years in new barrels. It is well balanced with a rich finish, and has an intense aromatic expression in which dried fruits are combined with honey and flowers. One serving suggestion is a filet mignon of pork with mangoes and ginger.

🔑 Famille Meslier, Ch. Raymond-Lafon, 4, Au Puits, 33210 Sauternes, tel. 05.56.63.21.02, fax 05.56.63.19.58, e-mail famille.meslier@chateau-raymond-lafon.fr ☑ Y by appt.

CH. DE RAYNE VIGNEAU 1997*

☐1er cru clas. 78.28 ha 94,600 ⓘ 250-299 F

85 **86|88|** |89| |90| **|91|** 92**|94| |95| |96|** 97

This vineyard is a fine property famous for the agates, amethysts and onyxes which have been found in its soil. Its most precious asset, however, is its gravel terroir, which has yielded this wine. It is pleasant to look at, and holds the attention with a complex bouquet. This aromatic diversity is further reinforced on the palate, where there are notes of dried apricots and noble rot in addition to floral aromas. A powerful, massive wine, which will need to be kept for four or five years.

🔑 SC du Ch. de Rayne Vigneau, La Croix Bacalan, 109, rue Achard B.P. 154, 33042 Bordeaux Cedex, tel. 05.56.11.29.00, fax 05.56.11.29.01 Y by appt.

CH. REINE CARBONNIEU 1998*

☐ 1.06 ha 2,700 ⓘ 70-99 F

This wine comes from a tiny vineyard belonging to the Château Lezongars (Premières Côtes de Bordeaux). It is of a high standard, having a golden colour with green glints and a bouquet which elegantly combines aromas of spring blossom with notes of honey and linden flowers. The palate is harmonious and thoroughbred, and this and the crystallised-fruit quality of the finish indicate that the wine has good ageing potential.

🔑 SC du Ch. Lezongars, 324, Roques-Nord, 33550 Villenave-de-Rions, tel. 05.56.72.18.06, fax 05.56.72.31.44, e-mail lezongars@free.fr ☑ Y by appt.

CH. RIEUSSEC 1997***

☐1er cru clas. 75 ha 94,000 ⓘ 300-499 F

62 67 70 71|75| |76| |78| |79| |80| |81| 82 **83 84 85|86|** 87**88 89 |(90)|** **92|94| 95(96)(97)**

Rieussec belongs to the vineyards of the Barons de Rothschild (Lafite), and comes from a sandy gravel hilltop to the west of Fargues. This wine fully lives up to its noble origins, with a high-class, dark-gold colour followed by fresh, elegant, thoroughbred notes of peaches, citrus fruits and mixed white-fleshed fruits. Its aromatic complexity on the palate is enriched by many suggestions of flowers and fruits, which, like the structure, form an overall impression that is both

powerful and light. Ending with a superb finish in which spices harmonise with fresh grapes, this is an exceptional wine which deserves a long, peaceful period of ageing in the cellar. It should be said, however, that one of the tasters noted that it could be enjoyed for 150 years, or from 2001 onwards.

🔑 Ch. Rieussec, 33210 Fargues-de-Langon, tel. 01.53.89.78.00, fax 01.53.89.78.01 ☑ Y by appt.

CH. DE ROCHEFORT 1998*

☐ 1.3 ha 2,000 ⓘ 70-99 F

This is pure Sémillon which comes from various plots. In addition to a powerful bouquet (crystallised lemons and spices with good support from oak), it has a full, rich palate which reveals a fine acidity from the noble rot which lends complexity to the flavours.

🔑 Jean-Christophe Barbe, Ch. Laville, 33210 Preignac, tel. 05.56.63.28.14, fax 05.56.63.16.28 ☑ Y by appt.

CH. ROMER DU HAYOT 1997*

☐2ème cru clas. 16 ha 31,000 ▮ⓘ↓ 100-149 F

75 76 79|81| 82|83| |85| **|86| 88 89**|90| 91 93 |95| 96 |97|

This vineyard was broken up as a result of land divisions, then deprived of its château and wineries for the sake of the Deux-Mers motorway. Although it has paid a heavy price to history, it has remained a 'true wine château', as is shown by the elegance and finesse of this wine. It is already pleasant to drink, and will reveal all its charm now if it is allowed to breathe for quite a while before it is drunk. Keep it for two or three years if you prefer.

🔑 SCE Vignobles du Hayot, Ch. Andoyse, 33720 Barsac, tel. 05.56.27.15.37, fax 05.56.27.04.24, e-mail duhayot@usa.net ☑ Y by appt.

CH. ROUMIEU 1997*

☐ 17 ha 45,000 ⓘ 100-149 F

This vineyard bears out the quality of the Haut Barsac's limestone-clay plateau as a wine-growing area. The 1997 wine is very aromatic, with notes of linden flowers and other roasting and floral aromas which are evident from the bouquet to the finish. A well-composed, balanced wine which will keep for three or four years.

🔑 Catherine Craveia-Goyaud, Ch. Roumieu, 33720 Barsac, tel. 05.56.27.21.01, fax 05.56.27.01.55 ☑ Y by appt.

CH. SAINT-AMAND 1996*

☐ 20 ha 50,000 ⓘ 100-149 F

83 85 86|88| |89| |90| 91|94| |95| 96

This vineyard is a fine property located at Preignac and once attracted many pilgrims who came to sample its water, a miraculous spring which flowed beside the château. This 1996 wine may have no great medicinal value, but its bouquet, strong in noble rot, and its rich, fleshy, balanced structure will satisfy even the most demanding wine-lover.

↑ SCEA du Ch. Saint-Amand, 33210 Preignac, tel. 05.56.76.84.89, fax 05.56.76.24.87 ☑ Y by appt.
🔑 Facchetti-Ricard

CH. SIGALAS RABAUD 1998**

☐ 1er cru clas. 13.37 ha n.c. 🍾 150–199 F

66 75 76 81 82 83 85 |86| 87 |88| |89| |90| |91| |92| 94 (95) 96 **97 98**

Although the vineyard still belongs to the descendants of Henri Drouilhet de Sigalas, who bought it in 1863 and gave it part of his name, it is run by Cordier and the Lafaurie-Peyraguey team. Once again this collaboration has borne fruit. The wine has a buttercup colour, and achieves a fine aromatic expresion throughout the tasting, with notes of citrus fruits complemented by shades of honey and vanilla. The palate is full, fleshy, rich, balanced and long, and its structure ensures good ageing potential.

🔑 Ch. Sigalas-Rabaud, Bommes-Sauternes, 33210 Langon, tel. 05.56.95.53.00, fax 05.56.95.53.01

LE CADET DE SIGALAS RABAUD 1998*

☐ 13.37 han.c. 🍾 100–149 F

This second wine from Sigalas Rabaud is also of a high standard, both in its bouquet of attractive crystallised-fruit notes and on the palate, where its substance is supple, balanced and concentrated.

🔑 Ch. Sigalas-Rabaud, Bommes-Sauternes, 33210 Langon, tel. 05.56.95.53.00, fax 05.56.95.53.01

CH. SUDUIRAUT 1997**

☐ 1er cru clas. 90 ha n.c. 🍾 200–249 F

(67) 75 76 78 82 |83| 85 86 88 |89| |(90)| 96 **97**

This vineyard has a fine, classic château surrounded by a park designed by Le Nôtre, and is also one the main reference points in the Sauternes. It maintains its status with this 1997 wine, which adheres to the perfect traditions of the vineyard with its power and elegance. Its strength is apparent from the first encounter with the bouquet, which has roasting and crystallised-fruit qualities in addition to floral aromas and a sweet scent of honey which continues throughout the tasting. The palate is equally expressive aromatically, and manages to be imposing without ever lapsing into heaviness. With a long finish, a fine return of flavour on notes of *pain d'épices* (a kind of spice loaf), and also a perfect harmony between sucrosity and acidity, the result is a wine with solid ageing potential, which should be served at a special meal with foie gras or Roquefort cheese.

🔑 Jean-Michel Cazes, Ch. Suduiraut, 33210 Preignac, tel. 05.56.63.61.92, fax 05.56.63.61.93, e-mail infochato@suduiraut.com ☑ Y by appt.
🔑 Axa Millésime

CH. D'YQUEM 1995***

☐ 1er cru sup. 104 ha n.c. 🍾 500 F+

21 29 37 42 |45| 53 55 59 (67) 70 71 |75| |76| 79 80 |81| |82| |83| |84| |85| |86| |87| **88 89 90 91** 93 94 (95)

The time to see Yquem is in the bluish dawn of the Sauternes, when the crenellations of the manor house seem like an extension of the hill. That is when one can clearly see all the strength of an exceptional terroir which yields wines like this 1995 vintage. It has a sumptuous, strong gold colour, and a bouquet whose complexity befits a great Vin Liquoreux, ranging from crystallised-fruit notes to ripe grapes and citrus fruits, not to mention honey, wax and currants. The aromatic expression on the palate is equally rich, as is the impressively mouth-filling structure, which is long, full, rich and at the same time very elegant, and heralds a cycle of development over several decades. A very great wine, which should be kept for ten or 15 years, if not much longer. The **1994 Yquem** has less ageing potential (five to 15 years) but is also extremely well composed, with a very fresh bouquet of roasted notes and crystallised lemons and a fine presence at the finish. It is awarded two stars.

🔑 Comte de Lur-Saluces, Ch. d'Yquem, 33210 Sauternes, tel. 05.57.98.07.07, fax 05.57.98.05.08, e-mail info@chateau.yquem.fr Y by appt.
🔑 LVMH

BURGUNDY

'Amiable and vinous Burgundy,' wrote the historian Michelet, and no wine-lover could fail to subscribe to his view. Around the world, Bordeaux, Champagne and Burgundy epitomise everything that's best in French fine wine, just as all are associated with the best in French gastronomy. The sheer variety of the wines from these three regions can satisfy every taste and complement the finest food.

In Burgundy the world of wine is more intricately involved with daily life than in any other wine-growing region: the culture and character of Burgundy and the Burgundians have been forged by the unchanging rhythms of the wine-making year. From the edge of the Auxerrois to the hills of Beaujolais, throughout the length and breadth of a province that connects the two great cities of Paris and Lyon, vines and wines have been a way of life, and a good life at that, since antiquity. Gaston Roupnel was a Burgundian author who wrote a history of the French countryside. He was also a wine-maker in Gevrey-Chambertin and, according to him, the vine was introduced into Gaul in the 6th century BC 'through Switzerland and the mountain passes of the Jura', ultimately being successfully cultivated on the slopes of the Saône and Rhône valleys. Other writers believe that Greek colonists in the Midi were responsible for introducing the cultivation of grapes to southern Gaul and thereafter bringing the knowledge north with trade. However, no-one can challenge the fact that vine cultivation quickly became very important in the Burgundy region, as some of the early reliefs exhibited in the archaeological museum in Dijon bear witness. And when, in the 4th century AD, the orator Eumenus addressed the Emperor Constantine at Autun, he eulogised the vines cultivated around Beaune as already 'admirable and ancient'.

In the Middle Ages the now long-established Burgundy wine trade was further re-shaped by a revolution in agricultural methods, in which the monks and the monastic movements of Cluny and Citeaux played a vital role. Burgundy's vineyards gradually developed their mosaic of *climats*, or plots of ground, and their crus, while growers constantly aimed to improve the quality and individuality of their incomparable wines. During the reigns of the four dukes of Burgundy (1342–1477), rules were laid down to ensure that the high quality of the wines was maintained. Throughout the turbulent centuries that followed, Burgundian wines consistently remained at the forefront of reputation and quality, a position continued into modern times.

It is worth noting that not all wines produced today in the administrative region of Burgundy are, in fact, Burgundies. In the Nièvre department (administratively part of Burgundy, as are the departments of the Côte-d'Or, the Yonne and the Saône-et-Loire) the vineyards of Pouilly-sur-Loire belong to the vineyards of central France and the Loire valley. In addition, the Rhône department, which in terms of judicial and administrative authority belongs to Burgundy, is home to the Beaujolais area. The Beaujolais wine region is usually treated as an autonomous entity – except in commercial terms – because it grows a specific grape variety, the Gamay (see below). This is the approach followed by this guide (see the section on Beaujolais). So Burgundy is understood to mean the vineyards of the Yonne (lower Burgundy), the Côte-d'Or and the Saône-et-Loire, even though some wines produced in Beaujolais can also be sold under the Appellation Régionale Bourgogne.

Disregarding Beaujolais, which is planted with Gamay, a variety with black skin and white flesh, Burgundy's character as a wine-growing area is dominated by two grape varieties: Chardonnay, which produces white wines, and Pinot Noir, which produces red wines. In addition there are some other minor varieties, either throwbacks to earlier wine-making practices or specific varieties to suit particular *terroirs*: Aligoté, for example, is a white grape producing the famous Bourgogne Aligoté, which is frequently used to make kir, a mixture of white wine and cassis (black-currant liqueur). The best quality Aligoté wines are produced in the small village of Bouzeron, very close to Chagny (Saône-et-Loire). The César, a red variety cultivated mainly in the region of Auxerre, is gradually falling from use. The Sacy produces Bourgogne Grand Ordinaire in the Yonne but is increasingly being replaced by Chardonnay. Gamay is used in Bourgogne Grand Ordinaire and is also mixed with Pinot Noir to make Bourgogne Passetoutgrain. Finally, Sauvignon, the famous aromatic grape variety planted in the vineyards of Sancerre and Pouilly-sur-Loire, is also grown in the region of Saint-Bris-le-Vineux in the Yonne. Currently bottled as AOVDQS Sauvignon de Saint-Bris, this wine is likely to become a recognised AOC in the near future.

Burgundy has a relatively uniform climate. It is mainly semi-continental (hot summers, cold winters) but is also affected by the Atlantic maritime climate, which reaches as far east as the edge of the Paris Basin. Thus it is the soil rather than climatic variations that gives the large number of wines grown in Burgundy their individual characteristics. As a rule, the vineyards are small plots of land mainly sited on a variety of outcrops of quite different geological origins, which can occur virtually side by side; these are the source of the rich palette of scents and flavours of the Burgundy crus. According to the specific chemical structure of the rock formation in each *climat*, or individual part of a vineyard, different wines with highly individual characteristics may be produced within a single appellation, thus complicating the overall classification and presentation of the Grands Vins de Bourgogne . . . These *climats*, which often have particularly evocative names (La Renarde, Les Cailles, Genevrières, Clos de la Maréchale, Clos des Ormes, Montrecul), have existed since at least the 18th century. They are only a few hectares in size, and sometimes only several *ouvrées* (1 ouvrée = 400 m^2/436 yds^2) and correspond to a 'natural entity which can be identified because of the specific character of the wine it produces' (A. Vedel). You can, in fact, see that there is sometimes less difference between two vines several hundred metres apart but in the same *climat* than there is between two neighbouring vines in two different *climats*.

There are four levels of appellation in the hierarchy of Burgundy wines: Appellation Régionale (56% of the production), Villages (or Appellation Communale) de Bourgogne, Premier Cru (12%) and Grand Cru (2%, consisting of 33 Grand Crus listed in the Côte-d'Or and Chablis). The number of legally defined *terroirs* or *climats* is very high; for example, 27 different denominations for the Premiers Crus are harvested in the commune of Nuits-Saint-Georges, all from barely a hundred hectares!

Recent scientific studies have confirmed earlier empirical observations about the relationship between the soils and the *lieux-dits* (names in common usage that identify a place) that gave rise to the appellations, the crus and the *climats*. Thus, for example, 59 different soil types can be identified by their external structure and physical chemistry (slope, stoniness, amount of clay and so on), all of which happen to match up with the boundaries between Grand Cru, Premier Cru, Villages and Régionale appellations.

Put more simply, and taking a more general geographical approach, it is usual to divide Burgundy's wine-growing area into four distinct zones: going from north to south these are the vineyards of the Yonne (or Basse Bourgogne), the Côte-d'Or (Côte de Nuits and Côte de Beaune), the Côte Chalonnaise and the Mâconnais.

The Chablis vineyards are the best known vineyards of the Yonne. Chablis wines were held in high esteem by the Parisian court in medieval times, when river transport made it easy to sell the wines in the capital. Indeed, for a long time the wines of the Yonne were thought of as *the* wines of Burgundy. Nestling in the charming valley of the River Serein, the town of Noyers its medieval jewel, the Chablis vineyard is like a remote satellite 100 km (62 miles) north-west of the heart of the main Burgundy vineyard. The Chablis AOC area is quite spread out, covering more than 4,000 ha (9,880 acres) of hilly slopes of varied aspect, where a 'constellation of hamlets and a scattering of farms share the harvest of this dry, light, lively, delicately perfumed wine whose astonishing limpidity, lightly flecked with gold and green, delights the eye' (P. Poupon). Ten communes stretch south from Auxerre in the Auxerrois; in the vineyards of Irancy there are still a few hectares (some acres) planted with César, a variety that gives very tannic wines. Along with Coulanges-la-Vineuse, Irancy is undergoing rapid expansion. Saint-Bris-les-Vineux is Sauvignon country and shares the production of white wines with Chitry.

Three other vineyards in the Yonne were almost completely destroyed by phylloxera, although efforts are currently being made to revive them. Joigny, in the extreme north-west of Burgundy, covers an area of barely ten hectares (25 acres), but the vineyards are laid out on the hills surrounding the town and overlooking the River Yonne. A Vin Gris, which is an Appellation Bourgogne, is produced mainly for local consumption in addition to red and white wines. The vineyard of Tonnerre, on the approach to Épineuil, was once as famous as that of Auxerre; custom allows an Appellation Bourgogne-Épineuil. Finally, a small vineyard on the slopes of the celebrated hill at Vézelay, where the grand dukes of Burgundy themselves once owned a vineyard, has been back in production since 1979. These wines, sold as Appellation Bourgogne, should continue to benefit from the crowds of visitors to Vézelay's famous Romanesque basilica, which was once a place of pilgrimage.

The arid eroded limestone of the Langres plateau is the traditional invasion route from the north-east, both in the past and for today's tourists. It separates the Chablisien, the Auxerrois and the Tonnerrois from the Côte-d'Or, the so-called 'hillside of purple and gold', more simply referred to as 'La Côte', which is the product of complex geological events in the remote past. During the Tertiary era, following the formation of the Alps, the Bresse Sea covered the region, pounding the ancient Hercynian mountains of the Morvan. This ancient sea drained away over the millennia, depositing a variety of sedimentary limestone soils. There are also numerous parallel north-south faults dating from the birth of the Alps; the great Tertiary glaciations flowed from north to south, while, combes were

Burgundy

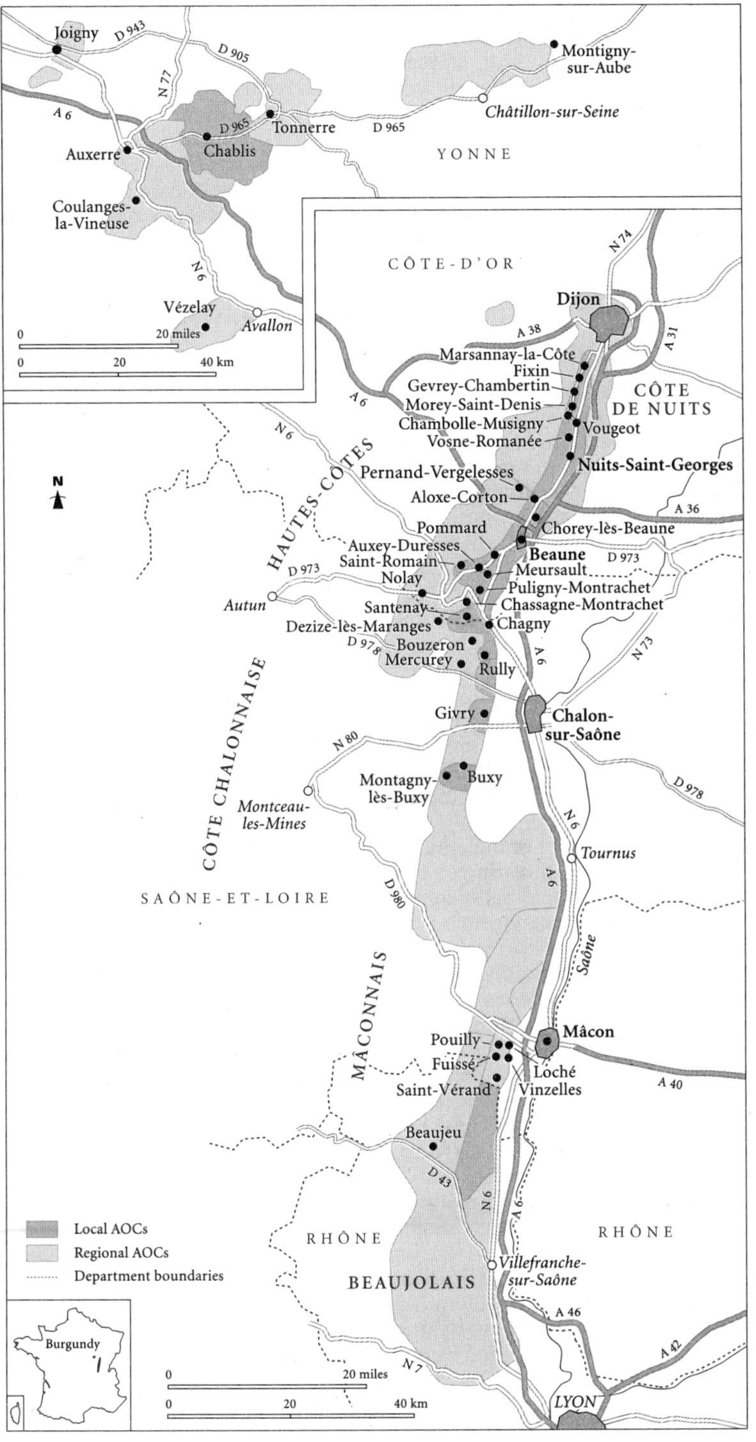
Joigny
D 943
D 905
N 77
A 6
D 965
Tonnerre
Chablis
Auxerre
D 965
Montigny-sur-Aube
Châtillon-sur-Seine
YONNE
Coulanges-la-Vineuse
N 6
Vézelay
Avallon
0
20 miles
0
20
40 km
CÔTE-D'OR
Dijon
N 74
A 38
A 31
Marsannay-la-Côte
Fixin
Gevrey-Chambertin
Morey-Saint-Denis
Chambolle-Musigny
Vosne-Romanée
Vougeot
CÔTE DE NUITS
Nuits-Saint-Georges
A 6
N 6
HAUTES-CÔTES
Pernand-Vergelesses
Aloxe-Corton
A 36
Pommard
Chorey-lès-Beaune
Auxey-Duresses
Beaune
Saint-Romain
D 973
D 973
Meursault
Nolay
Puligny-Montrachet
Autun
Santenay
Chassagne-Montrachet
Dezize-lès-Maranges
Chagny
D 978
Bouzeron
Mercurey
Rully
A 6
N 73
N
CÔTE CHALONNAISE
Givry
Chalon-sur-Saône
N 80
Montagny-lès-Buxy
Buxy
D 978
Montceau-les-Mines
N 6
Tournus
A 6
SAÔNE-ET-LOIRE
D 980
Saône
MÂCONNAIS
Mâcon
Pouilly
Fuissé
Loché
Saint-Vérand
Vinzelles
A 40
Beaujeu
D 43
N 6
A 6
Local AOCs
Regional AOCs
Department boundaries
RHÔNE
RHÔNE
Villefranche-sur-Saône
BEAUJOLAIS
A 46
A 42
Burgundy
N 7
0
20 miles
0
20
40 km
LYON

later hollowed out by powerful torrents. The result has given us an extraordinary variety of quite different subsoils lying cheek by jowl beneath a shallow uniform layer of arable topsoil. From this underlying geology flows the abundance of appellations, which are largely determined by their soils, and the even larger number of *climats*, which define the mosaic more minutely.

From the geographical point of view, the Côte runs for about fifty km (30 miles) from Dijon to Dezize-lès-Maranges in the north of the Saône-et-Loire. For the most part, the hillside faces the rising sun, essential for Grands Crus in a semi-continental climate, then slopes down from the higher plateau, indented by the vineyards of the Hautes-Côtes, and continues as far as the agricultural land of the Saône plain.

The Côte is a long, narrow feature with an excellent east-south-easterly aspect. It is traditionally divided into several sectors. The first, in the north, has been overwhelmed by the encroaching suburbs of Dijon (this is the Chenôve commune). Ever faithful to tradition, the town council of Dijon has replanted a parcel of land in the very heart of town. The next sector, the Côte de Nuits, starts at Marsannay and goes down to Clos des Langres in the commune of Corgoloin. It is a narrow hill, only a matter of a few hundred yards wide, interrupted by alpine woods and outcrops of rock weathered by cold, dry winds. This hillside produces 29 appellations, each with its own place in the hierarchy of crus, and the village names form a roll of honour: Gevrey-Chambertin, Chambolle-Musigny, Vosne-Romanée, Nuits-Saint-Georges and so on. The Premiers Crus and the Grands Crus (the highest class) include Chambertin, Clos de la Roche, Musigny and Clos de Vougeot; these are to be found higher up the hillside, between 240 and 320 m (787 and 1050 ft). The largest number of outcrops of marly limestone are to be found here among the various different types of scree, producing the best structured of the red Burgundies, which can be kept for a long time.

Next comes the more temperate Côte de Beaune, which broadens to a depth of one or two kms (1 mile). It receives moist winds, which encourage the grapes to mature more quickly. The Côte de Beaune is geologically more homogeneous than the Côte de Nuits; the lower part of the plateau is nearly horizontal, formed from layers of soft limestone, clay or shale covered by vividly coloured earth. These are the fairly deep soils in which the great red wines are grown (Beaune Grèves, Pommard Épenots and so forth). To the south of the Côte de Beaune, banks of oolitic limestone under hard limestone marl, covered with débris and scree and overlaid with limestone, give pebbly, gravelly soils, which produce the most prestigious Burgundy whites, the Premiers and Grands Crus from the communes of Meursault, Puligny-Montrachet and Chassagne-Montrachet. If people here talk of a 'côte des rouges' (red wine area) and a 'côte des blancs' (white wine area), between the two is the Volnay vineyard, which must be given special mention. It is planted on stony, clay and limestone soils that produce red wines of great finesse.

In the Côte de Beaune the vines are planted higher up than in the Côte de Nuits, to 400 m (436 yds) and sometimes higher still. The hillside is sliced through by wide combes, particularly at Pernand-Vergelesse, where the combe seems to cut the famous Corton mountain off from the rest of the Côte.

In the last thirty years sections of the Hautes-Côtes have been gradually replanted to produce Appellations Régionales Bourgognes Hautes-Côtes-de-Nuits and Bourgogne Hautes-Côtes de Beaune. The Aligoté grows at its best here, and the *terroir* shows off the wine's freshness to advantage. Other *terroirs* make excellent red wines from Pinot Noir, and these are characterised by scents of soft fruits such as raspberry and blackcurrant, which are also locally grown Burgundy specialities.

The countryside opens out somewhat in the Côte Chalonnaise, which covers 4,500 ha (11,115 acres). The linear structure of the basic relief softens into low-rising hills, which extend further to the west of the Saône valley. The geological structure differs again from the vineyards of the Côte d'Or; the soil rests on Jurassic limestone, on marl from the same period or even earlier or on sedimentary terrain made up of sandstone, limestone and marl. Red wines are produced from Pinot Noir in Mercurey, Givry and Rully, but the same communes also make white wines from Chardonnay, as does Montagny. Bouzeron, home of a highly reputable Aligoté, is also to be found here. There is a noteworthy vineyard on the way to Couches, which is dominated by its medieval château. The Romanesque churches and ancient estates of the region are worth a visit and any tourist itinerary can easily be combined with a route through the vineyards.

The range of hills in the Mâconnais, with 5,700 ha (14,079 acres) of vineyards, opens up wide horizons where white Charolais cattle speckle the green meadows. The countryside was dear to the poet Lamartine – he came from Milly, a wine-producing village where he owned vineyards – and it is geologically simpler than the Chalonnais. The sedimentary soils from the Triassic and Jurassic periods are scored by east-west faults. Some twenty per cent of the wines are *Appellations Communales* and 80% are *Appellations Régionales* (Mâcon white and Mâcon red). The highest quality white wines are made from Chardonnay grapes, planted on dark lime-rich soil on the slopes at Pouilly, Solutré and Vergisson, which have a particularly good, sunny aspect; the wines are remarkable for their appearance and their capacity to keep a long time. Appellation Bourgogne reds and rosés are made from Pinot Noir, while the black-skinned Gamay with white juice produces the Mâcons that are harvested lower down the hills or on less well-exposed, flinty, alluvial soils with good drainage.

No matter how essential the local geology and climatic conditions may be, no picture of wine-growing in Burgundy would be complete without recognising the contribution that human effort makes to the vineyards and wines. The wine-makers have a deep attachment to their land, and in some villages the family names of many owners can be traced back for five hundred years. By the same token, some of the shipping companies were founded as long ago as the 18th century.

The Burgundy vineyard is divided into family-owned plots (domains), which cover very small areas. So a domain of four or five ha (12 acres) in, say, Nuits-Saint-Georges, can provide an adequate living for a worker and his family. It is rare to find producers who own and cultivate more than about ten ha (25 acres); for example, the illustrious Clos-Vougeot covers 50 ha (124 acres) and is divided among 70 owners. This parcelling up of the ownership of *climats* results in a greater diversity of wines and leads to a healthy rivalry among producers. In Burgundy a tasting will often consist of comparing two wines made from the same grape variety and from the same appellation but coming from different *climats*, or two wines made from the same grape and the same *climat* but from different years. Thus, in Burgundy, two basic elements must constantly be kept in mind when tasting the wines: the cru, or *climat*, and the year of the vintage; you must also allow for the personal touch of the wine-grower who makes them. From the technical point of view, Burgundian wine-makers are keen to maintain traditional methods, although this does not mean they are resistant to modernisation. As a result, the mechanisation of viticulture has developed, and many wine-makers have benefited greatly from new equipment and techniques. However, some traditions remain unchallenged by wine-growers and shippers alike, and one of the best examples is the maturing of wines in oak barrels.

In 1997, 3,500 domains were registered as dedicated solely to vines. They represent two-thirds of the 24,000 ha (59,280 acres) making Appellation d'Origine wines. Nineteen co-operatives are listed: the co-operative movement is very active in Chablis and the Côte Chalonnaise, and particularly so in the Mâconnais (13 cellars). They produce about 25% of the wines. Since the 18th century an important role has been played by the *négociants-éleveurs*, the merchants who buy wine from the grower and bring it on to bottling age in their own cellars. They sell more than 60% of the wine produced and own 35% of the total area of the Grands Crus of the Côte de Beaune. On their domains the merchants produce 8% of all the wine produced in Burgundy. This represents an average of 180 million bottles (105 million white and 75 million red) and generates a turnover of 5 thousand million francs, of which 2.6 thousand million are earned from exports. In 1999 total exports were 3,000,000 hl (79,200,000 gal).

The importance of bringing on a wine (how it develops from its early youth to its optimum quality before it is bottled) demonstrates the significance of the *négociant-éleveur* to the system; in addition to being responsible for the sale of the wine, he also takes on a technical role. This technical and marketing knowledge lies at the heart of the harmonious professional relationship that has developed between wine-growers and merchants.

The Bureau Interprofessionnel des Vins de Bourgogne (BIVB), which initiates developments in the technical, economic and promotional fields, has three 'listening posts' at Mâcon, Beaune and Chablis. In 1934 the University of Burgundy was the first establishment in France, at least at university level, to set up and run courses in oenology and to offer a technical diploma. At the same time, the Confrérie des Chevaliers du Tastevin was founded to promote the reputation of Burgundy wines around the world. Its headquarters are at the Château du Clos-Vougeot and, with other local *confréries*, it makes a great contribution to keeping regional traditions alive. Without question, one of the most brilliant events is the auction sales in the Hospices de Beaune, first held in 1851. This is the meeting place of the international wine élite and the exchange for establishing the value of the Grands Crus. Together with the assembly of the Confrérie and the 'Paulée' in Meursault, the sale is one of the 'three glorious days of wine'. But the whole of Burgundy knows how to celebrate wine joyously, be it from a 228-litre hogshead or from a bottle. It does not take much to love Burgundy and its wines; it is simply a 'region that you can take away in your glass'.

Appellations Régionales Bourgogne

The Appellation [R]égionale Bourgogne and the [A]ppellation Bourgogne Grand [O]rdinaire, together with their [r]elated off-shoots or equivalents, [a]ccount for the largest area of Burgundy's vineyards. They can be pro[d]uced in the traditional wine [c]ommunes of the department of the [Y]onne, the Côte-d'Or, the Saône-et-[L]oire and the canton of [V]illefranche-sur-Saône in the [R]hône. In 1999, they produced a [t]otal of 591,677 hl (15,620,272 gal).

The registration of [l]and use and, more specifically, the [d]efinition of the *terroirs* by estab[l]ishing the borders of the parcels [o]f land within the vineyards, [c]reated a hierarchy of *appellations [r]égionales*. The Appellation [B]ourgogne Grand Ordinaire is the [m]ost common and the most pro[d]uctive in the areas defined. Using [s]pecified vines, Bourgogne Aligoté, [B]ourgogne Passetoutgrain and [C]rémant de Bourgogne are also [p]roduced in the same areas.

Bourgogne

The production [a]rea of this appellation is vast if you [t]ake into account the names of the [d]ifferent sub-regions (Hautes-[C]ôtes, Côte Chalonnaise) or of the [v]illages (Irancy, Chitry and [E]pineuil) that can be added, each of [w]hich is a separate entity and is [l]isted here as such. Given the extent [o]f this appellation, it is not surpris[i]ng that producers should have [s]ought to personalise their wines [a]nd to persuade the regulator that the area of origin should be individually identified. In the Châtillon area, whihc is in the Côte-d'Or, the name of Massingy has been used in this way, even though the original vineyard has practically disappeared. More recently (and now as a matter of course) the wine-makers on the banks of the Yonne use the name of the village and add it after the words 'Appellation Bourgogne'. This is the case in Saint-Bris, the Côtes d'Auxerre on the right bank of the river and in Coulanges-la-Vineuse on the left bank.

The average volume of wine produced by the Appellation Bourgogne is about 155,000 hl (4,092,000 gal) a year. In 1999 the white-wine producers made 78,726 hl (2,078,366 gal) of wine from Chardonnay vines, which are still known as Beaunois in the Yonne region. The Pinot Blanc, although referred to in the official texts and formerly grown more widely in the Hautes Côtes de Bourgogne, has now practically disappeared. In the past it was often confused with Chardonnay

Production of red and rosé wines from Pinot Noir is on average between 125,000 and 130,000 hl (3,300,000 and 3,432,000 gal) a year. Unfortunately, the Pinot Beurot grape has largely fallen from favour because it contained insufficient colour; it used to add remarkable finesse to red wines. In some years the volumes of wine declared can be augmented by wines that are downgraded from the Beaujolais Appellations Communales: Brouilly, Côte-de-Brouilly, Chénas, Chiroubles, Fleurie, Juliénas, Morgon, Moulin à Vent and Saint-Amour. These wines are made from the black Gamay grape only and have different characteristics. The production of rosé wines can increase in cool years when the grapes do not ripen well or when there is a great deal of grey rot, and they can be declared as Appellation

Bourgogne Rosé or Bourgogne Clairet.

To make things more difficult, some labels have the name of the *lieu-dit* (a name in common usage that identifies a place) where the wine was produced, in addition to the Appellation Bourgogne. Some old and reputable vineyards are examples justifing this practice: Chapitre à Chenôve and Des Montreculs keep alive names from the Dijon vineyards that are now smothered by the growth of the suburbs; another example is La Chapelle-Notre-Dame in Serrigny. As for the rest, some may be too easily confused with the Premiers Crus and may not always deserve the comparison.

BERTRAND AMBROISE 1998★

□ 0.77 ha 8,000 50–69 F

The **98 Rouge** is still dominated by tannins, but it has a richness that promises better things to come (30–49F). The white, on the other hand, with its lemon-gold colour and hawthorn and vanilla nose, is a lively, almost sinewy wine, full and with good length. A mountain stream that could one day become a long, peaceful river.

Maison Bertrand Ambroise, rue de l'Eglise, 21700 Premeaux-Prissey, tel. 03.80.62.30.19, fax 03.80.62.38.69, e-mail bertrand.ambroise@wanadoo.fr by appt.

PIERRE ANDRE

Réserve Vieilles vignes 1998★

■ 1 ha 7,000 70–99 F

Pierre André bought the château at Corton André back in 1927. The wine labels of this long-established *négociant* firm are illustrated with this beautiful château and its glazed-tiled roof. 'If it's not too expensive, I'll buy it', writes one taster. It may not be the cheapest, but it is a jolly good wine all the same: a little light in colour, perhaps, but with a nose that opens out immediately and seduces you with its rich, ripe fruit – almost liqueur – aromas. Intense, oaky, and with well-balanced tannins, it has enough body to develop.

Pierre André, Ch. de Corton-André, 21420 Aloxe-Corton, tel. 03.80.26.44.25, fax 03.80.26.43.57, e-mail pandre@axnet.fr ev. day 10am–6pm

CHRISTOPHE AUGUSTE

Coulanges-la-Vineuse 1999★

□ 1.8 ha 12,000 30–49 F

The **98 Rouge** is not yet showing at its best, so we suggest you wait a while for that one. Alternatively, the style of the 99 is light, and not recommended for laying down. Be drunk now to enjoy its two best qualities: i freshness and its mineral character.

Christophe Auguste, 55, rue André-Vildieu, 89580 Coulanges-la-Vineuse, tel. 03.86.42.35.04, fax 03.86.42.51.81 by appt.

L'OR D'AZENAY

Cuvée Prestige Fût de chêne 1996★

□ 2 ha 10,000 30–49

There have been many Michelin-starre chefs keen to trade their chef's hat for a win grower's cap as soon as they got the chance. I 1986 Georges Blanc trained his *coq de Bress* on the hills of Azé, in Mâconnais, and now h has this 96 (note the vintage) to show for i bright with pale lemon tints, with a freshnes that lingers on the palate. A well-balance wine best served with *quenelle* in Nantu sauce, calf sweetbreads, or even a Bress chicken.

Georges Blanc, Dom. d'Azenay, Rizerolles, 71260 Azé, tel. 03.85.33.37.93, fax 03.74.50.21.00, e-mail blanc@relaischateaux.fr by appt.

DOM. GUY BOCARD 1997★★

■ 0.35 ha 2,500 30–49 F

The richness of Burgundy . . . This super 97 vintage has everything you could ask fror this appellation: elegance and finesse, fullnes and balance, well-integrated, velvety-smoot tannins. A wine worth drinking in two c three years. Just ready in time for the Saint Vincent wine festival, which is being held i Meursault in 2001.

Guy Bocard, 4, rue de Mazeray, 21190 Meursault, tel. 03.80.21.26.06, fax 03.80.21.64.92 by appt.

DOM. DU BOIS GUILLAUME 1998★

■ 1 ha 3,000 30–49 F

There is finesse and distinction in the wa the Pinot Noir in this wine has developed bringing out an interesting medley of fla vours: undergrowth, raspberry and cherry mingled with oaky vanilla. Already soft an round, this wine will drink well over the nex year or two.

Jean-Yves Devevey, Dom. du Bois Guillaume, rue de Breuil, 71150 Demigny, tel. 03.85.49.91.11, fax 03.85.49.91.59 ev. day except Sun. 8am–7pm

JEAN-CLAUDE BOISSET 1997★

■ n.c. 90,000 50–69 F

Jean-Claude Boisset founded his own wine company, which has continued to expanc steadily, making him a pretty important fig- ure in Burgundy these days. Here are two of his flagship wines. Firstly, a Pinot Noir matured 17 months in barrel, ready to drink in another two years; try it with eggs *en meurette*. Toast and vanilla aromas dominate but red berry fruit also comes through on the nose. The palate is well-balanced: peppery tannic, and both full and fresh. They've done ell with this vintage. Also produced by oisset is a **Charles de France Bourgogne 98 lanc**. Matured 12 months in barrel, it manages to express an exceptional richness along ith the finesse of a toasty Chardonnay. One ar.

J.-C. Boisset, 5, quai Dumorey, B.P. 102, 1700 Nuits-Saint-Georges, l. 03.80.62.62.61, fax 03.80.62.37.38

OM. BORGNAT

oulanges-la-Vineuse Tête de cuvée 1997★★

3 ha 15,000 30–49 F

We thought the **Bourgogne 98 Blanc** from is estate was really excellent (one star). The d 97, meanwhile, is one of the best Pinot oirs in northern Burgundy. Deep purple ith garnet hues, this wine has firm, but not ggressive, tannins. Supple, with hints of lorello cherry, it's an ideal wine to serve with ast beef *en croûte*. Good for laying down.

Dom. Borgnat, 1, rue de l'Eglise, 89290 scolives-Sainte-Camille, tel. 03.86.53.35.28, x 03.86.53.65.00 ev. day 8am–7pm; roups by appt.

EAN BOUCHARD 1998★

n.c. 340,000 50–69 F

A lovely seductive nose, but you will need wait another 18 months to see if the wellructured tannins mellow as they should. It as the colour of a very young wine, with hades of violet and Morello cherry. This owerful and full Pinot Noir has a good two three years ahead of it.

Jean Bouchard, B.P. 47, 21202 Beaune edex, tel. 03.80.24.37.27, ax 03.80.24.37.38

OM. REGIS BOUVIER 1998★

0.32 ha 2,500 30–49 F

At first glance, not a lot of intensity in the olour, but the nose really scores a goal. Citus fruits, toast, hawthorn: it's a pleasant ocktail of aromas. Full and fresh, slightly leshy, the aromatic flavours explode on the alate.

Dom. Régis Bouvier, 52, rue de Mazy, 1160 Marsannay-la-Côte, el. 03.80.51.33.93, fax 03.80.58.75.07 y appt.

ENE BOUVIER Montre-Cul 1998★★

0.36 ha 3,000 50–69 F

You don't say no to a Montre-Cul. Between Dijon and Chenôve, this old *climat*, on one of he last hillsides planted with vines in the rea, manages to hold out against the evernreasing urban sprawl. This is a great 98. The colour? Dense and deep. The nose? Cherry stone and oak. Everything you'd xpect from a Burgundy? All of these qualiies are found on the palate.

René Bouvier, 2, rue Neuve, 21160 Marsannay-la-Côte, tel. 03.80.52.21.37, ax 03.80.59.95.96 by appt.

DOM. JEAN-MARC BROCARD

Jurassique 1999

n.c. n.c. 30–49 F

Jean-Marc Brocard has had the imaginative idea of christening his Burgundies Portlandian, Kimmeridgian, etc. This is the Jurassic, and its nose alone is a good illustration of the theory of evolution: very young and oaky, and as long as a dinosaur. An anatomical curiosity. The **Portlandian 99** is less fascinating.

Jean-Marc Brocard, 3, rte de Chablis, 89800 Préhy, tel. 03.86.41.49.00, fax 03.86.41.49.09, e-mail brocard@brocard.fr ev. day except Sun. Mon. 9.30am–12.30pm 3pm–7pm; groups by appt.

LES PRODUCTEURS DE BUXY

Grande Réserve Fût de chêne 1998

30 ha 200,000 30–49 F

When you own 850 ha (2,100 acres) of vines, as this co-operative does, the 30 ha (74 acres) given over to red Burgundy ought to be good, and this is. A ruby red wine, very ripe fruit, chewy and with plenty of body. With its firm tannins it's good for laying down for a while.

Cave des vignerons de Buxy, Les Vignes de la Croix, 71390 Buxy, tel. 03.85.92.03.03, fax 03.85.92.08.06 ev. day except Sun. 9am–12 noon 2pm–6pm

DOM. CACHAT-OCQUIDANT ET FILS Les Commeys 1998★

0.25 ha 1,800 30–49 F

This estate is situated at the foot of the Corton hills. They've come up with a distinguished wine that would go down well with fish in a creamy sauce. A pleasant wine: clean, with enough structure to age well, typical Chardonnay aromas (honey, ripe fruit, apples and pears) with a hint of oakiness.

Dom. Cachat-Ocquidant et Fils, pl. du Souvenir, 21550 Ladoix-Serrigny, tel. 03.80.26.45.30, fax 03.80.26.48.16 by appt.

MARIE-THERESE CANARD ET JEAN-MICHEL AUBINEL 1998★★

0.16 ha 1,500 30–49 F

Pale gold, with a light, fresh citrus fruit nose, this Chardonnay gives a lovely sensation of fresh grapes on the palate. The well-balanced acidity uplifts this wine and gives it presence in the glass. The perfumes linger on within a remarkable eruption of flavours. Very South Burgundy.

Marie-Thérèse Canard et Jean-Michel Aubinel, Mouhy, 71960 Prissé, tel. 03.85.20.21.43, fax 03.85.20.21.43 by appt.

DOM. CAPUANO-FERRERI ET FILS

Les Perrières 1998★★

■ n.c. n.c. 30–49 F

The first thing worth mentioning about this Côte d'Or Bugundy is that it is great value for money. It has been barrel-matured and should ideally be drunk in two to three years' time. At the moment, it needs to breathe a little. This deep-purple wine opens out to give herbaceous aromas that change rapidly to redcurrant and violets. These follow through with significant spicyness on the palate, indicating a sign of longevity.

Capuano-Ferreri et Fils, 1, rue de la Croix-Sorine, 21590 Santenay, tel. 03.80.20.64.12, fax 03.80.20.65.75 by appt.

FRANCK CHALMEAU 1999

n.c. 5,000 20–29 F

Like many in the Yonne, this 6-ha (15-acre) estate once had several different crops growing on it, but it is now entirely dedicated to growing vines. Candy pink with orange tints, this very young 99 has fruity flavours and fresh lively acidity. Reminiscent of wild strawberries and exotic fruit.

Franck Chalmeau, 20, rue du Ruisseau, 89530 Chitry-le-Fort, tel. 03.86.41.42.09, fax 03.86.41.46.84 by appt.

PATRICK ET CHRISTINE CHALMEAU Chitry 1998★

□ 1.6 ha 9,000 30–49 F

This Chardonnay would tempt a snail from its shell. It is pale gold with a nose that has developed a little, revealing its complexity, and has a flowery palate with plenty of richness. Lovely.

Patrick et Christine Chalmeau, 76, rue du Ruisseau, 89530 Chitry-le-Fort, tel. 03.86.41.43.71, fax 03.86.41.47.51 by appt.

JEAN-PIERRE CHARTON 1998★★

■ 3.3 ha 9,000 30–49 F

'A gladiator is made in the arena', says Seneca. And a wine is made in the glass. This wine has talent. Deep cherry, raspberry and cinnamon. Hiding underneath the roundness and richness, there is a fighting spirit that's rare in this appellation. Produced in the traditional way – so they say.

Jean-Pierre Charton, 29, Grande-Rue, 71640 Mercurey, tel. 03.85.45.22.39, fax 03.85.45.22.39 by appt.

DOM. DU CHATEAU DE MEURSAULT Clos du Château 1998★

□ 8 ha 40,000 70–99 F

This Clos du Château is partly surrounded by the Meursault area. The Chardonnay gives us a very clear white Burgundy with hints of green, the nose reveals a short period in barrel: elegant honey and floral notes with a touch of vanilla. The palate is lemony but does not completely mask a floral qualit[y]. Very typical.

Ch. de Meursault, 21190 Meursault, tel. 03.80.26.22.75, fax 03.80.26.22.76 by appt.

DOM. DU CHATEAU DE PULIGNY-MONTRACHET

Clos du Château 1998★

□ 4.5 ha 35,000 70–99

The masterpiece of the Crédit Foncier. produces remarkable results from its vin[e]yards, in Burgundy as well as Bordeaux. Yo[u] might be tempted to call it a 'simple Bu[r]gundy', but it is not simple at all. The terro[ir] has as much to say as the Chardonnay, and th[e] barrel-ageing is subtle indeed. Aromas of ci[t]rus and crystallised fruits follows through [to] the finish. Rich, lively, balanced.

SCEA Dom. du Château de Puligny-Montrachet, 21190 Puligny-Montrachet, tel. 03.80.21.39.14, fax 03.80.21.39.07, e-mail chateaupul@aol.com by appt.

DOM. HENRI CLERC ET FILS

Les Bergeries 1997★

■ 1.07 ha 5,333 30–49

There has been a vineyard on this esta[te] since the 16th century. Today, it consists of 2[2] ha (54 acres), most of which are given ove[r] to white grapes. This is a superbly-coloure[d] Pinot, with bilberry flavours on the pala[te] indicating strong extraction. The tannins ar[e] still present but softening out. Open it in [a] year's time, just to see.

EARL Dom. Henri Clerc et Fils, pl. des Marronniers, 21190 Puligny-Montrachet, tel. 03.80.21.32.74, fax 03.80.21.39.60 ev. day 8.30am–11.45am 2pm–5.45pm

Bernard Clerc

DOM. DU CLOS DU ROI

Coulanges-la-Vineuse 1998★

■ 10 ha 60,000 30–49 F

From Vin de Table to AOC, that's how fa[r] this estate has come in the space of a fe[w] decades. Purple, bright, this smart 98 has a[n] aroma of red berry fruit. Cherry adds dimen[-]sion to a concentrated and tannic palate. W[e] wouldn't recommend opening this bottle fo[r] two years at least.

SCEA du Clos du Roi, 17, rue André-Vildieu, 89580 Coulanges-la-Vineuse, tel. 03.86.42.25.72, fax 03.86.42.38.20 by appt.

Michel Bernard

DOM. FRANCOIS COLLIN

Epineuil 1998★

■ 1.2 ha 7,200 30–49 F

Elegant, full, very oaky, **Les Bas Fauconniers Epineuil 97 Rouge** is worth a recommendation (50–69F). This excellent 98 however, seems a cut above the rest: ripe fruit, a supple attack, rich middle and a warm finish. We have to tell you about its powerful tannins that are just waiting to mellow, its wonderful aftertaste of Morello cherry, and

how its maturity is amazing for so young a wine. Our gourmet wine-tasters recommend serving the first wine with roasted calves liver, the second with calf sweetbreads in puff pastry.
🗝 François Collin, Les Mulots, 89700 Tonnerre, tel. 03.86.75.93.84, fax 03.86.75.94.00, e-mail françois.collin@wanadoo.fr ☑ Y by appt.

EMMANUEL DAMPT

Cuvée Prestige 1998★

□	2 ha	10,000		30–49 F

Very fresh, very floral, this is a springtime wine with a characteristic texture. 'Full and explosive, it hits all the right spots', notes one taster. Make sure to buy two bottles, because the first won't last long!
🗝 Emmanuel Dampt, 3, rte. de Tonnerre, 89700 Collan, tel. 03.86.54.49.52, fax 03.86.54.49.89 ☑ Y by appt.

JOCELYNE ET PHILIPPE DEFRANCE 1998★

◪	n.c.	2,800		30–49 F

Right in the heart of the pretty village of Saint-Bris-le-Vineux, under the house once lived in by Soufflot, the local man-made-good who built the Panthéon in Paris, is the wine cellar of this old family estate. This *Rosé de Saignée* is very attractive. Particularly noteworthy is its deep colour, its polished aromas, its fullness and length (both rare in this appellation), and the redcurrant finish.
🗝 Philippe Defrance, 5, rue du Four, 89530 Saint-Bris-le-Vineux, tel. 03.86.53.39.04, fax 03.86.53.66.46 ☑ Y by appt.

DOM. DOUDET

Le Clos en Village 1998★

□	0.2 ha	1,500		50–69 F

Côte-de-Beaune, Savigny-style, this *Clos en Village* is the most beautiful gold colour. The nose is expressive: vanilla, toast, flowers (acacia). The palate has plenty of character and a good length. Round, rich yet lively, it's a good Burgundy worth waiting a year for.
🗝 Dom. Doudet, 50, rue de Bourgogne, 21420 Savigny-lès-Beaune, tel. 03.80.21.51.74, fax 03.80.21.50.69 ☑ Y by appt.

H. DE DRACY 1997★

■	12 ha	83,600		70–99 F

La Bruyère was right when he said: 'Use the simplest of language whenever you can'. This fine 97 follows his advice to the letter. Deep red, with a nose of strawberry jam that turns floral when you return to it, a fresh attack, with fruit bursting out of it. This wine is the product of a joint venture between two estates: the family estate of the barons of Charette on the Côte Chalonnaise and the firm of Bichot, which boasts Benoît de Charette as one of its directors.
🗝 SCA Ch. de Dracy, 71490 Dracy-lès-Couches, tel. 03.85.49.62.13 Y by appt.
🗝 Benoît de Charette

SYLVAIN DUSSORT

Cuvée des Ormes 1997★

□	1.5 ha	3,000		50–69 F

Sylvain Dussort's white Burgundy is a Chardonnay that comes from 30-year-old vines, planted in Meursault. It is a wine that won't go unnoticed. Intense and deep in colour, quite lively, a good example of both the vintage and the appellation. Would go well with a light dish of fish in cream sauce.
🗝 Sylvain Dussort, 12, rue Charles-Giraud, 21190 Meursault, tel. 03.80.21.27.50, fax 03.80.21.65.91, e-mail dussvins@aol.fr ☑ Y by appt.

DOM. FELIX Côtes d'Auxerre 1998★

◪	0.35 ha	2,600		30–49 F

A former employee of l'Eqiupment (a well-known Paris clothes boutique), Hervé Félix took over the family estate in 1987 and is maintaining its traditions. This explains why this wine – salmon pink in colour, with a full, aromatic nose and a titillating palate – is the best of the Yonne rosés that we have tasted. Delicate and fruity, it has a little exotic touch (mango) which gives it a piquant edge.
🗝 Dom. Félix, 17, rue de Paris, 89530 Saint-Bris-le-Vineux, tel. 03.86.53.33.87, fax 03.86.53.61.64, e-mail felix@caves-particulieres.com ☑ Y ev. day except Sun. 9am–11.30am 2pm–6.30pm

DOM. FRANCIS FICHET ET FILS

Le Vignot 1998★★

■	2 ha	12,000		30–49 F

This wine is produced by a family estate where the children share the work between them. They have paid a lot of attention to the Pinot Noir's finer subtleties (coulis of red berry fruits, mushroom, humus). A wine that is very much 'of the soil', it is definitely one to lay down, and can be counted among the best. The **99 rouge**, with its parchment-style label, spends only four months in barrel. We award it one star. As for the **La Crépillionne 98 Blanc** (20–29F), it gets two stars for its wonderful aromas of exotic and citrus fruits, for clean, pure fruit flavours, and its length.
🗝 Dom. Francis Fichet et Fils, Le Martoret, 71960 Igé, tel. 03.85.33.30.46, fax 03.85.33.44.45, e-mail olivierfichet@wanadoo.fr ☑ Y by appt.

GUY FONTAINE ET JACKY VION 1997★★

□	1.5 ha	3,500		30–49 F

The present generation is worthy of the previous two: it is rare to find a Burgundy with a regional appellation that is as golden, intense, and well-balanced as this one is. All the more so because it is still far from being at its peak and has yet more to offer. The jury was overflowing with compliments for its suppleness and freshness, slight toasty flavour, and aftertaste of nuts.
🗝 GAEC des Vignerons, Le Bourg, 71150 Remigny, tel. 03.85.87.03.35, fax 03.85.87.03.35 ☑ Y by appt.
🗝 Fontaine/Vion

CAVEAU DES FONTENILLES

1998★★

■ 10 ha 35,000 30–49 F

Initially, this was the cooperative winery for all the vineyards in Tonnerre. Today, the group of just six wine-growers work their 25 ha (62 acres) together. We've already recommended the **Bourgogne 98 Blanc**, we've given a star to the **Bourgogne 98 Rouge Marguerite des Fontenilles** and paid our compliments to this expressive, yet subtle, fruity *cuvée*. A wine full of fruit that is a great accompaniment to roast pigeon.

Caveau des Fontenilles, pl. Marguerite-de-Bourgogne, 89700 Tonnerre, tel. 03.86.55.06.33, fax 03.86.55.10.43, e-mail cavefont@aoc.com ev. day 9am–12 noon 2pm–7pm; Sun. Mon. by appt.

DOM. FOUGERAY DE BEAUCLAIR

L'Ormichal 1998★

■ n.c. n.c. 50–69 F

Roast veal *bonne femme* tonight? Here's a wine with soft tannins that doesn't lack liveliness to get the conversation going. An uncomplicated wine.

Dom. Fougeray de Beauclair, 44, rue de Mazy, B.P. 36, 21160 Marsannay-la-Côte, tel. 03.80.52.21.12, fax 03.80.58.73.83, e-mail fougeraydebeauclair@wanadoo.fr by appt.

CAVES DES VIGNERONS DE GENOUILLY

Les Champs de Perdrix 1998★

□ 1 ha 10,000 20–29 F

Grape variety and terroir combine together successfully to defend the interests of this 98 with its spring perfumes of honeysuckle and hints of hazelnut. It's an attractive, complex, well-balanced wine; fruity and robust. The co-operative at Genouilly in Saône-et-Loire doesn't produce much of this wine – 1 ha (2.5 acres) out of 60 ha (148 acres). As for the **98 Rouge**, it seems a full-bodied, robust, very promising wine. Same marks.

Cave des Vignerons de Genouilly, 71460 Genouilly, tel. 03.85.49.23.72, fax 03.85.49.23.58 ev. day except Sun. 8am–12 noon 2pm–6pm

DOM. ANNE ET ARNAUD GOISOT

Côtes d'Auxerre 1998

■ 6 ha 30,000 30–49 F

Not quite the great rolling plains, but then it's in keeping with the gentle hills of the AOC. With a light purple colour and underlying animal aromas, it's easy to see how it draws you in. Wild strawberry flavours add to the length. The **98 Blanc** gets the same mark. Both are already very drinkable.

Dom. Anne et Arnaud Goisot, 4 bis, rte. de Champs, 89530 Saint-Bris-le-Vineux, tel. 03.86.53.32.15, fax 03.86.53.64.22 ev. day except Sun. 8am–12 noon 1.30pm–7.30pm

GHISLAINE ET JEAN-HUGUES GOISOT

Côtes d'Auxerre 1998★

□ 4 ha 29,000 30–49 F

They make their wine here in cellars dating from the 11th and 12th centuries. Bright gold in colour, this wine is all spring blossom and ripe fruit. Rich, full, and delightfully long, it is very well-made, and should ideally be kept for three years, but is already drinking well. The famous **Cuvée du Corps de Garde Blanc 98**, still an AOC Bourgogne Côtes d'Auxerre, if a little on the oaky side, is nevertheless a pleasant wine. The principle *cuvée* (18,000 bottles) is the **98 Rouge** and gets a mention. An elegant wine with subtle Pinot flavours.

Ghislaine et Jean-Hugues Goisot, 30, rue Bienvenu-Martin, 89530 Saint-Bris-le-Vineux, tel. 03.86.53.35.15, fax 03.86.53.62.03 by appt.

DOM. GRAND ROCHE

Irancy 1998★

■ 0.5 ha 3,000 50–69 F

At the time of tasting this was still an AOC Bourgogne Irancy and not an AOC Irancy. Only wild boar seems capable of taking up the challenge of this dark-coloured wine with its fiendishly strong aromas. Maturation in barrel has been conducted by a master's hand. It has tannins like tigers – a circus under the eye of its tamer. Acidity, length – this is a real Burgundy.

Eric et Laurence Lavallée, Dom. Grand Roche, 6, rte. de Chitry, 89530 Saint-Bris-le-Vineux, tel. 03.86.53.84.07, fax 03.86.53.88.36 by appt.

DOM. GREUZARD

Les Fines Pierres 1998★

□ n.c. 24,000 30–49 F

A wine to enjoy with friends, they say. Shades of gold with linden flowers and peony on the nose, and a little touch of lemon on the palate, which is very attractive. Plenty of character.

Cie des Vins d'Autrefois, abbaye Saint-Martin, 53, av. de l'Aigue, 21200 Beaune, tel. 03.80.26.33.00, fax 03.80.24.14.84, e-mail mallet.b@cva-beaune.fr by appt.

GRIFFE Chitry 1999★★

□ 0.81 ha 4,000 30–49 F

This is a catalogue of seduction: the clarity of pure gold, the citrusy aromas mingling with spring blossom, mouthfilling, and a fresh lively finish with hints of acacia. . . . David Griffe took over from his father some years ago on this 13-ha (32-acre) estate, where the grapes are hand-picked.

Joël et David Griffe, 15, rue du Beugnon, 89530 Chitry-le-Fort, tel. 03.86.41.41.06, fax 03.86.41.47.36 by appt.

DOM. ROBERT GROFFIER PERE ET FILS 1998★★

■ 1.4 ha 10,000 50–69 F

This 98 is in a class above its appellation. Great? No, it's really great. Which explains the exclamations of surprise around the table. The freshness of fruit (blueberry, blackberry) is accompanied by a fantastic fullness, a dense structure, concentrated, extremely mellow. We hesitated, ready to give it the *coup de cœur.* If you like young wines, taste this one today, but it will get even better over the next three years.

SARL Robert Groffier et Fils, 3–5, rte. des Grands-Crus, 21220 Morey-Saint-Denis, tel. 03.80.34.31.53 by appt.

CHRISTIAN GROS 1998★

■ n.c. n.c. 30–49 F

The colour is ruby-red velvet, the nose shows some depth (bilberry, spices, a touch of oak). The wine shows some richness. After the upfront freshness, a certain austerity lingers, but it doesn't cancel out altogether the impression of balance and amplitude. Best drunk in two to three years' time.

Christian Gros, rue de la Chaume, 21700 Premeaux-Prissey, tel. 03.80.61.29.74, fax 03.80.61.39.77 by appt.

DOM. GUEUGNON-REMOND 1998★★

■ 73.1 ha 2,900 30–49 F

This estate, founded in 1980, was taken over from the founders by their daughter and son-in-law in 1997. And so from the Mâconnais comes this marvellous Pinot Noir born in Gamay country. It's a little rustic, but we like the bright colour and fruity, toasty aromas. Full-bodied, with hints of liquorice from the barrel, it blends well with the firm

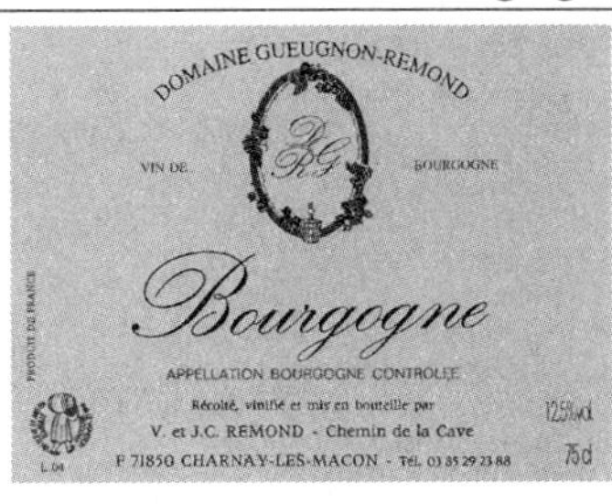

tannins. Good potential for laying down.

Dom. Gueugnon-Remond, chem. de la Cave, 71850 Charnay-lès-Mâcon, tel. 03.85.29.23.88, fax 03.85.20.20.72 by appt.

Remond

CAVES DES HAUTES-COTES Cuvée de prestige Elevée en fût 1998★

■ 3.2 ha 17,300 30–49 F

This Cuvée de Prestige comes from the co-operative winery of the Hautes-Côtes, and prestige is certainly something it has in abundance. In fact, it has everything you could wish for in a good Burgundy: enough complexity, flavour, and staying power. Perhaps there's a little hint of fragility? That's to give it feeling . . . Supple and fruity, a wine which will repay you for laying down and drinking in a couple of years' time.

Les Caves des Hautes-Côtes, rte. de Pommard, 21200 Beaune, tel. 03.80.25.01.00, fax 03.80.22.87.05 by appt.

CUVEE HENRY DE VEZELAY 1998★

□ 21.93 ha 180,000 30–49 F

This is the star *cuvée* of this co-operative (22 ha (54 acres) out of 46.3 ha (114 acres) and is a high quality wine. Bourgogne Vézelay only recently (1997) became an AOC. A classic greenish-yellow in colour, this Chardonnay has a lively freshness and a light oakiness with some mineral tones. Why not eat it with a leek pie? The red Burgundy 98 also deserves a mention. It is still closed and needs at least a year before pairing it up with a red meat dish.

Cave Henry de Vézelay, 89450 Saint-Père, tel. 03.86.33.29.62, fax 03.86.33.35.03 ev. day 10am–12 noon 2.30pm–6pm

HENRY FRERES 1998

■ 1.64 ha 10,000 30–49 F

Pascal and Didier Henry could not be accused of not knowing what they want. On their 11 ha (27 acres), they are aiming for happiness in its purest form, in the shape of this wine. Their Yonne Pinot Noir is a luminous shade of ruby red, with a convincing little hint of red berry fruit. Not with great depth. However, due to its lightness, it is pleasant to drink now.

GAEC Henry Frères, 89800 Saint-Cyr-les-Colons, tel. 03.86.41.44.87, fax 03.86.41.41.48 by appt.

LES VIGNERONS D'IGE
Elevé en fût de chêne 1998

☐ 1 ha 10,000 30–49 F

An attractive colour. Even if not yet fully open, this wine shows finesse and elegance. Well-balanced by its freshness.

Cave coop. des Vignerons d'Igé, 71960 Igé, tel. 03.85.33.33.56, fax 03.85.33.41.85, e-mail lesvigneronsdige@lesvigneronsdige.com ev. day except Sun. 8am–12 noon 2pm–6pm

DOM. GUY-PIERRE JEAN ET FILS
Les Champs Pourras 1998★

■ 1.5 ha 3,000 30–49 F

These two brothers took over the family vineyard in 1991. Under the coat of arms, showing hunting horn and boar's head, they present to us a deep ruby Burgundy with an aroma of blackcurrant buds that expands in the glass. The crystallised-fruit flavours are marked by firm, but not aggressive tannins. Best to wait a year for the fullness and finesse to develop.

Dom. Guy-Pierre Jean et Fils, rue des Cras, 21420 Aloxe-Corton, tel. 03.80.26.44.72, fax 03.80.26.45.36 by appt.

DOM. REMI JOBARD 1998★

☐ 1 ha 4,500 50–69 F

Lemon yellow, clear and brilliant, this wine comes from Meursault. The nose opens with hints of acacia mixed with apple. Round and fleshy, it is characteristic; no more and no less.

Dom. Rémi Jobard, 12, rue Sudot, 21190 Meursault, tel. 03.80.21.20.23, fax 03.80.21.67.69, e-mail rémi.jobard@libertysurf.fr by appt.

PHILIPPE ET FRANCOISE JOUBY
Côte d'Auxerre 1997★

☐ n.c. n.c. 30–49 F

This old estate (its origins go back to the 17th century), presents this wine of character, with a parchment-style label. Mushroomy like a Chablis and well-developed, but it retains that mineral characteristic that belongs to the terroir. Interesting.

Philippe Jouby, 8, rue Dorée, 89530 Saint-Bris-Le-Vineux, tel. 03.86.53.30.58 by appt.

XAVIER JULIEN Côtes d'Auxerre 1999

☐ 0.3 ha n.c. 30–49 F

Xavier Julien is an enthusiast who planted his first vines in Auxerre in 1996. He should definitely be encouraged to continue. This fine 99 is true to the appellation: peppery, buttery, not very long but with some interesting mineral character.

Xavier Julien, 6, rue Lebeuf, 89000 Auxerre, tel. 03.86.51.69.71, fax 03.86.51.69.71 by appt.

DOM. DE L'ABBAYE DU PETIT QUINCY Epineuil 1999★

☐ 3 ha 25,000 30–49 F

Dominique Gruhier is artisan, industrialist, and wine-producer, a man of boundless energy and imagination. Here he presents us with a clear, bright Burgundy, with a pronounced linden flower nose, fresh, with an attractive mellowness. Although it is still closed at the time of writing, this wine will doubtless be open by the time you read these lines.

Dominique Gruhier, Dom. de l'Abbaye, Clos de Quincy, 89700 Epineuil, tel. 03.86.55.32.51, fax 03.86.55.32.50 ev. day 9am–6pm; Sun. by appt.

CH. DE LA BRUYERE
Elevé en fût de chêne 1997

☐ 0.3 ha 2,200 30–49 F

A Mâconnais Chardonnay with warm tones, and a marked brightness, oaky but not excessively so, with lemony touches coming through on the finish. In short, charming. Drink up and enjoy this year.

Paul-Henry Borie, Ch. de La Bruyère, 71960 Igé, tel. 03.85.33.30.72, fax 03.85.33.40.65, e-mail mph.borie@wanadoo.fr ev. day 8.30am–12 noon 2pm–7pm

LA CHABLISIENNE 1998★

☐ 14 ha 100,000 30–49 F

La Chablisienne was founded in 1923. Today, they export 70% of their considerable production. This is a Chablis-style Chardonnay that follows all the rules: pale yellow with slightly darker tints. It has notes of mineral and lemon, and is fresh rather than full-bodied. Best to wait to allow its finesse to show.

La Chablisienne, 8, bd Pasteur, B.P. 14, 89800 Chablis, tel. 03.86.42.89.89, fax 03.86.42.89.90, e-mail chab@chablisienne.com by appt.

DOM. DE LA CRAS 1997

■ 4 ha 15,000 30–49 F

Jean Dubois has unfortunately left us to join the vineyards in the sky, but his nephew has taken over at Plombières, Dijon and Talant. La Cras was due to become a new district with 4,000 homes built on it, but fortunately, this plateau above Lake Kir in Dijon has been saved for better things. It's a curiosity, this Burgundy from Dijon – a brilliant deep red colour and straightforward nose, with aromas of forest-floor and crystallised cherry, round but well-structured, still tannic. Best to wait a year. The **97 Blanc**, fresh and balanced, can be drunk now.

EARL Jean Dubois, Dom. de La Cras, 21370 Plombières-lès-Dijon, tel. 03.80.41.70.95, fax 03.80.59.13.96 by appt.

·OM. DE LA GARENNE 1999

3 ha 10,000 30–49 F

In just two generations, the change over ·om cereal crops to vines has been made. The ·ne does have a long-established history in ·nnerois. Fleshy and full-bodied despite its ·uth, this distinctive golden-yellow Char- ·nnay bursts open with lavender and violet. ·lready very full, taste it now with some ·ired ham. The **Bourgogne 99 Rosé** is enjoy- ·le and would go well with a seasonal salad.

· Philippe Clément, Dom. de la Garenne, ·700 Tonnerre, tel. 03.86.55.16.30, ·x 03.86.55.02.66 ☑ Y ev. day except Sun. ·m–12.30pm 2pm–7pm

·OM. DE LA GARENNE 1998*

2 ha 18,000 30–49 F

Marcel Périnet was voted 'Best Sommelier · France' in 1978. Together with M. Renoud- ·rappin (both were managers at Georges ·lanc's restaurant) he created this estate in ·87 by clearing part of a hill (4.3 ha (11 ·res) over the last 13 years). The pair already ·ow a genuine talent for wine-making. This ·ry good wine spends eight months in barrel. ·he colour is typical for a wine made using ·e Chardonnay grape, and its perfumes ·flect the southern origin of the wine (the ·âconnais). On the palate it is fresh and ·ely, and is perfectly suited to drink with ·ellfish.

· Périnet et Renoud-Grappin, rte. de ·éronne, 71260 Azé, tel. 04.74.55.06.08, ·x 04.74.55.10.08 ☑ Y by appt.

·A GRANGE AUBERT 1999

1.4 ha 6,000 30–49 F

This is a small 4-h (10 acre) concern pro- ·ucing a Kimmeridgian Pinot Noir, a geologi- ·l influence that we usually associate with ·hardonnay. This honest little 99 deserves ·ore than a cursory inspection: intense pur- ·le, lightly perfumed, full and round, it has ·ood structure with well-defined tannins. A ·ttle hint of astringency is no great shock.

· Jean-Michel Moreau, EARL Grange ·ubert, 89700 Tonnerre, tel. 03.86.55.23.37, ·x 03.86.55.23.37 ☑ Y ev. day 6pm–9pm

·OM. LAMY-PILLOT 1998**

2 ha 10,000 30–49 F

A very elegant Pinot Noir: purple with ·eep red glints showing richness and depth. ·enerously fruity (blackcurrant, cherry), and ·pening out superbly on the palate. Dense ·nd soft with a long finish and will be at its ·est in three to five years' time.

· Dom. Lamy-Pillot, 31, rte de Santenay, ·1190 Chassagne-Montrachet, ·l. 03.80.21.30.52, fax 03.80.21.30.02, ·mail lamy.pillot@wanadoo.fr ☑ Y by ·ppt.

· René Lamy

DOM. LAROCHE

Tête de Cuvée 1999**

☐ 365 ha 150,000 30–49 F

The Laroche estate is a very busy one. It also operates in Languedoc-Roussillon, but here remains one of the crown jewels of Burgundy. This*cuvée* is deservedly named: *Tête de Cuvée*. It carries the banner for Burgundy whites, and its flinty nose, not without charms, is just as remarkable. The elegant citrus flavours combine well in this perfectly balanced wine. Its future is assured. Since they want to introduce wine onto the stock exchange in France, why not put this on offer?

⊶ Dom. Laroche, 22, rue Louis-Bro, 89800 Chablis, tel. 03.86.42.89.29, fax 03.86.42.89.00, e-mail info@domainelaroche.fr ☑ Y by appt.

DOM. DE LA TOUR 1997

☐ 0.93 ha 4,000 30–49 F

A small family estate, whose white Burgundy shows promise with a decent colour and a buttery nose. Medium acidity, a robust wine full of character.

⊶ SCEA Dom. de La Tour, 8 bis, rue Jules-Philippe, 89800 Chablis, tel. 03.86.47.55.68, fax 03.86.47.55.86, e-mail dtour@clubinternet.fr ☑ Y by appt.

DOM. DE LA TOUR BAJOLE

Vieilles vignes 1997**

■ 6 ha 15,000 30–49 F

It gives us a great deal of pleasure to salute the talents of these wine-producers from Cochois, a courageous and sadly underestimated vineyard. People used to call the Dessendres 'the pinocchios' because they planted Pinot and not hybrids. However, their 97 has all the right qualities: colour, smell, fullness. Soft-fruit jam and plenty of body make this a good option for laying down.

⊶ EARL M.-A. et J.-C. Dessendre, Dom. de La Tour-Bajole, Les Ombrots, 71490 Saint-Maurice-lès-Couches, tel. 03.85.45.52.90, fax 03.85.45.52.90 ☑ Y by appt.

OLIVIER LEFLAIVE

Les Setilles 1998*

☐ n.c. 60,000 30–49 F

Apple, lemon, quince, jasmine, with a lovely toasty, buttery background. This is a round, full-bodied Chardonnay from Burgundy, with well-balanced richness and acidity. It has the patience to wait, for two to three years, for the right occasion. Burgundy snails would go well with it, or a fish terrine with chives, or maybe even veal marengo . . .

⊶ Olivier Leflaive, pl. du Monument, 21190 Puligny-Montrachet, tel. 03.80.21.37.65, fax 03.80.21.33.94, e-mail leflaive-olivier@dial.oleane.com ☑ Y by appt.

DOM. DES LEGERES 1999★

□ n.c. n.c. 30–49 F

This wine seems destined for great things. It is pleasing on both the eye and nose. Acacia, linden flowers, exotic fruits: it's never at a loss for words, and has a softness that is very attractive on the palate. A real Burgundy.

Véronique et Pierre Janny, La Condemine, 71260 Péronne, tel. 03.85.36.97.03, fax 03.85.36.96.58 by appt.

DOM. LEJEUNE 1998★★★

■ 0.9 ha 10,000 30–49 F

Well, done, Professor! François de Pommerol has long been a teacher at the *Viti* (wine school) in Beaune, and now he is rewarded with the prize of excellence. This is an intense, cherry stone, almost creamy wine that rolls smoothly round the mouth, with a well-defined structure. A shade oaky, but not beyond the capabilities of the Pinot Noir grape which shows itself superbly here.

Dom. Lejeune, La Confrérie, pl. de l'Eglise, 21630 Pommard, tel. 03.80.22.90.88, fax 03.80.22.90.88 by appt.

Famille Jullien de Pommerol

JACQUES LEMAIGRE 1998★

■ 0.3 ha 1,379 30–49 F

Dark red, this wine is still closed, but has some fine days ahead of it. Tannic at the moment, but knows its Pinot Noir by heart. And with a structure like this, it would do justice to a jugged hare.

Jacques Lemaigre, 89700 Dannemoine, tel. 03.86.55.54.84 by appt.

DOM. CHANTAL LESCURE

Les Sorbins 1998★

■ 0.4 ha 1,700 30–49 F

Increasingly, Burgundy wine-producers have a tendency to include the name of a *climat* on their wine labels, but without explaining its importance. This is perhaps the case with this Les Sorbins? But it made a good impression on us anyway. A beautiful clear colour, cherry and spice, classic, and well-made. You should find the **98 Blanc**, one star, equally agreeable. A lovely rich wine with an exotic touch.

Dom. Chantal Lescure, 34 A, rue Thurot, 21700 Nuits-Saint-Georges, tel. 03.80.61.16.79, fax 03.80.61.36.64, e-mail domaine-lescure.com by appt.

MICHEL LORAIN

Côte Saint-Jacques 1998★

◪ 0.5 ha 3,000 30–49

When you are in command of the kitche at the famous *Côte Saint-Jacques* restauran you deserve the right to revive the vineya of the same name at Joigny. Former preside of 'Etats-Généraux de la Gastronom française', Michel Lorain presents his wo derfully coloured Pinot with a sweet litt nose and a light, supple palate. The gra variety is expressed in a simple and since way. So what does the great chef recommen we eat with it? A salad of warm mullet wi herbs.

SCEV Michel Lorain, 43, fg de Paris, 89300 Joigny, tel. 03.86.62.06.70, fax 03.86.94.49.70 by appt.

CAVE DE LUGNY 1999★

□ n.c. 100,000 30–49

This co-operative was founded in 1926 ar today boasts 1,470 ha (3,632 acres) of win production. This white Burgundy, pale go in colour, has a typical Chardonnay fr grance. 'Well-balanced', as one of our taste wrote. Following through on the palate w find citrus fruits, spring blossom and hone all lingering right to the finish. A wonderf balanced wine which you will be able to enj in three years' time.

SCV Cave de Lugny, rue des Charmes, 71260 Lugny, tel. 03.85.33.22.85, fax 03.85.33.26.46, e-mail commercial@cave-lugny.com by appt.

DOM. DE MAISON ROUGE 1998

■ 2.45 ha 4,700

'The knight of the Maison Rouge' is famous figure from French cloak and dagg literature. Did he decide to retire here in h old age? We know at least that this win graced the table of the Duke of Orleans i times past. A roast leg of lamb will go we with this light purple, elegant and fresh Pin Noir, with its remarkably delicate black currant nose.

Liebert et Fils, Dom. de Maison Rouge, rte. de Saint-Martin, 89700 Tonnerre, tel. 03.86.54.46.39, fax 03.86.54.46.39 ev. day 10am–7pm

MALTOFF

Coulanges-la-Vineuse Cuvée Prestige 1998★

■ 0.7 ha 7,600 50–69

This is a wine that doesn't laze aroun From the very first glance, you can see that is awake! It knows how to make the best of light red berry fruit that has some stayin power. A few hints of blackcurrant, wel mastered tannins everything holds togethe You could happily lay it down for two or thre years.

Dom. Maltoff, 20, rue d'Aguesseau, 89580 Coulanges-la-Vineuse, tel. 03.86.42.32.48, fax 03.86.42.24.92 by appt.

CAVE DES VIGNERONS DE MANCEY 1998★

n.c. 12,000 30–49 F

There is structure and substance behind this very attractive, dark red wine with its ruby hints. The nose is beginning to open with soft fruit, making this a wine that is ready to drink now, but which could easily wait three or four years. A bargain. A Pinot Noir that comes from Saône-et-Loire.

Cave des Vignerons de Mancey, R.N. 6, En Velnoux, 71700 Tournus, tel. 03.85.51.00.83, fax 03.85.51.71.20 Y by appt.

DOM. MARCHAND FRERES

Les Poisots 1998★★

0.22 ha 1,400 20–29 F

A vertical label on a Burgundy, that's an original idea. Violet purple in colour, this 98 is complex from the very first whiff of the nose. Still a little closed, but it has all the qualities of a wine that is going to blossom in the cellar. The tannins are good, and there are hopes for a decent future. The estate at Gevrey also offers guest rooms.

Dom. Marchand Frères, 1, pl. du Monument, B.P. 38, 21220 Gevrey-Chambertin, tel. 03.80.62.10.97, fax 03.80.62.11.01, e-mail dmarc2000@aol.com Y by appt.

CATHERINE ET CLAUDE MARECHAL Cuvée Gravel 1998★

3 ha 9,000 30–49 F

'I just love it', said one of our more sophisticated tasters: purple with hints of violet, a fruity nose (blackcurrant bud), oaky, with a touch of mineral content in the mouth, surrounded by dark fruits. A wine of substance. Well-balanced. Best drunk at least two years from now.

EARL Catherine et Claude Maréchal, 6, rte. de Chalon, 21200 Bligny-lès-Beaune, tel. 03.80.21.44.37, fax 03.80.26.85.01 Y by appt.

DOM. DES MARRONNIERS 1999

1.1 ha 10,000 30–49 F

This is a pleasant, straightforward wine: slightly *perlant*, fine and flinty. It has an elegant mineral touch on the nose and a characteristic palate. Would go well with an *andouillette de Chablis.*

Bernard Légland, 1 et 3, Grande-Rue de Chablis, 89800 Préhy, tel. 03.86.41.42.70, fax 03.86.41.45.82 Y ev. day 8am–12 noon 2pm–8pm; cl. 15 Aug.–5 Sep.

DOM. MATHIAS Epineuil 1998★★

0.56 ha 4,500 30–49 F

This is an estate that was founded in the early 1980s, when the Epineuil vineyard was going through a revival period. This fine 98, with its tantalising little hint of youth, is a perfect example of its style. Green glints? It has them. Spring blossom? That too. The follow through on the palate has all the

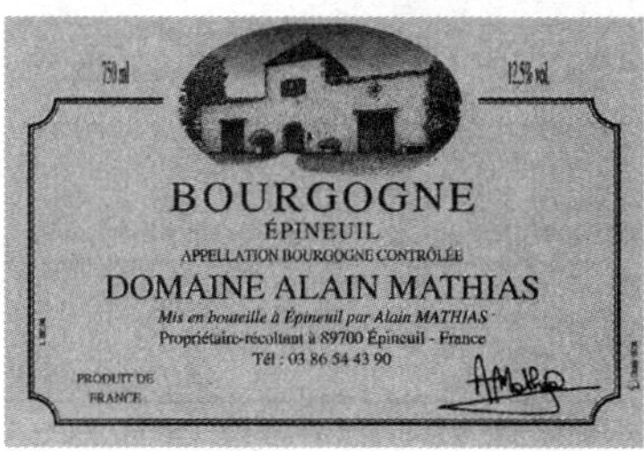

necessary qualities. A hint of mineral content. Trout *au bleu* would seem an ideal partner.

Alain Mathias, rte. de Troyes, 89700 Epineuil, tel. 03.86.54.43.90, fax 03.86.54.47.75 Y by appt.

PROSPER MAUFOUX 1997★★

n.c. n.c. 50–69 F

A lovely wine, mellow with plenty of stuffing – a very appealing Chardonnay. The 'drop of gold' colour, a slightly acrid nose, and very fine balance almost merits an appellation *village.* Best drunk over the next two or three years.

Prosper Maufoux, pl. du Jet-d'Eau, 21590 Santenay, tel. 03.80.20.60.40, fax 03.80.20.63.26 Y by appt.

DOM. MARC MENEAU

Vézelay Les Chaumonts 1998★★

2 ha 12,000 30–49 F

Georges Blanc expresses his passion for wine-growing in Azé-en-Mâconnais, and here Marc Meneau is the apostle of wine in Vézelay. He has planted 16 ha (40 acres) at the foot of the basilica. This reclamation began in 1986 and, now, 15 years later, we are seeing the results. This is a Vézelay Burgundy from a superb Chardonnay, with intense colour. A light hint of oak combines well with its complex nose. Full and rich, the flavours follow through on the palate. The woody flavours harmonise well with the slight mineral content, and that adds to its charm.

Marc Meneau, rue du Moulin-à-Vent, 89450 Vézelay, tel. 03.86.33.39.11, fax 03.86.33.26.15, e-mail marcmeneau@wanadoo.fr Y by appt.

DOM. DU MERLE 1997★

2 ha 3,000 30–49 F

This clear gold 97 with green glints has a very concentrated nose (lemon, acacia flowers, vanilla, forest-floor). It is well-balanced and long, and over the next two years will develop into a beautifully harmonious wine.

🔑 Michel Morin, Sens, 71240 Sennecey-le-Grand, tel. 03.85.44.75.38, fax 03.85.44.73.63 ☒ 🍷 ev. day 9.30am–7.30pm

DOM. MICHELOT 1998★

☐ 4 ha 30,000 ⦀ 50–69 F

With four generations of wine-growers in the family, they know what they're talking about here. So, you won't be surprised by the superb colour of this white Burgundy, nor the balance of its flavours (lightly toasted oak and an expansive fruitiness). This will be a great wine in a year's time, best drunk over the next three.

🔑 Dom. Michelot, 31, rue de la Velle, 21190 Meursault, tel. 03.80.21.23.17, fax 03.80.21.63.62 ☒ 🍷 by appt.

DOM. DE MONTPIERREUX 1999

☐ 3 ha 20,000 🍾 🌡 30–49 F

Straw gold with a touch of oxidation, this is a rustic Chardonnay which seems to come from a terroir as profound as it is austere. This is a parcel of land that was reclassified as AOC Bourgogne in 1988, situated just near the motorway services at Auxerre. No doubt it provided an excellent incentive to take to the country, especially as truffles are found on this estate. An agreeable little wine.

🔑 François Choné, Dom. de Montpierreux, 89290 Venoy, tel. 03.86.40.20.91, fax 03.86.40.28.00 ☒ 🍷 ev. day 9am–7pm

DOM. MICHEL MOREY-COFFINET 1998★★

■ 1.2 ha 4,500 ⦀ 30–49 F

Peony red, the nose is still closed but shows concentrated dark fruit (blackcurrant, blackberry, bilberry) which is supported by oak. This is delicious on the palate. A thoroughbred, solid and elegant; there is a feeling of detail and character. It will blossom further during the coming years. If you can, keep it for a while.

🔑 Dom. Michel Morey-Coffinet, 6, pl. du Grand-Four, 21190 Chassagne-Montrachet, tel. 03.80.21.31.71, fax 03.80.21.90.81 ☒ 🍷 by appt.

CHRISTIAN MORIN Chitry 1998★

☐ 4 ha n.c. 🍾 30–49 F

This is a 9-ha (22-acre) family concern that is developing the export side to the business. This still-youthful, medium gold 98 with green tints at first appears a little closed, but opens up bit by bit, revealing its lemony character. It is more fresh than rich, but that's the style of the area. There is a good length of fruit.

🔑 Christian Morin, 17, rue du Ruisseau, 89530 Chitry-le-Fort, tel. 03.86.41.44.10, fax 03.86.41.48.21 ☒ 🍷 by appt.

OLIVIER MORIN Chitry 1998★★

☐ 3 ha 20,000 🍾 ⦀ 🌡 30–49 F

This shows good wine-making methods with well-handled six month barrel ageing. The colour has been extracted, exactly as it should be, with taste and skill. There is some development perceptible on the nose, with some mature aromas. Reasonable attack leading to fruity, mineral flavours. The finish has a nice little touch of vanilla. We also recommend the **98 Rouge** for its typical Chitry style: redcurrant nose with good tannic structure. It earns one star.

🔑 Olivier Morin, 2, chem. de Vaudu, 89530 Chitry-le-Fort, tel. 03.86.41.47.20, fax 03.86.41.47.20 ☒ 🍷 by appt.

DOM. THIERRY MORTET 1998★★

■ 1 ha 6,000 ⦀ 50–69 F

Sometimes a jury cannot agree on a verdict and this is the case here. Some people liked this Pinot Noir so much thay wanted to give it the highest mark. The wine in question comes from Gevrey-Chambertin. Still closed but showing perfect extraction, it is wonderfully unctuous with excellent balance. It may not be terribly elegant just now, but has all the fine characteristics of this AOC; it will come together in two or three years' time.

🔑 Dom. Thierry Mortet, 16, pl. des Marronniers, 21220 Gevrey-Chambertin, tel. 03.80.51.85.07, fax 03.80.34.16.80 ☒ 🍷 by appt.

DOM. JEAN ET GENO MUSSO 1998★

■ 4 ha 20,000 ⦀ 30–49 F

The vineyards of Jean and Geno Musso have long been run using organic methods, and have increased considerably in size to reach their present 56 ha (138 acres). Their Burgundy is showing a good characteristic style although still very young. The pleasant subtle nose has hints of fruit – cherry and prune. The palate is round and rich, mellow and with fine well-structered tannins. There is an elegant authentic character here which should be taken advantage of right away.

🔑 Jean et Geno Musso, 71490 Dracy-lès-Couches, tel. 03.85.96.18.61, fax 03.85.96.18.62 ☒ 🍷 by appt.

ANDRE ET JEAN-RENE NUDANT La Chapelle-Notre-Dame 1997★

■ 0.4 ha 2,500 ⦀ 30–49 F

Do you have a friend who thinks he knows everything there is to know about Burgundy? Serve him this wine and ask him what's 'special' about it. You can bet that it is unlikely (unless he has read this book) that he will know that this Chapelle Notre-Dame du-Chemin à Ladoix-Serrigny is one of the very rare *climats* of the regional appellation, to officially have been granted the right to feature on the label. This 97 looks good, and explodes with lovely spicy aromas. Fresh and full of character. Keep it a year before serving it with a sauté of veal.

Dom. Nudant, 11, R.N. 74, 21550 Ladoix-Serrigny, tel. 03.80.26.40.48, fax 03.80.26.47.13, e-mail domaine.nudant@wanadoo.fr ☑ Y by appt.

DOM. NOEL PERRIN

Clos de Chenôves 1998

■ 3 ha 5,000 30–49 F

Do not confuse Chenôve near Dijon (AOC Marsannay) with Chenôves on the Côte Chalonnaise. Nor should one forget that once upon a time the parish priest of Chenôves became famous for inventing a new strawberry variety. This wine is heading towards cocoa beans, or game. It is very well-structured, tannic, and solid as a *paissiau*, the stakes that used to hold up pre-Phylloxera vines. Wait a year or two before drinking it.

Dom. Noël Perrin, 71460 Culles-les-Roches, tel. 03.85.44.04.25, fax 03.85.44.04.25 ☑ Y ev. day 8am–12 noon 1.30pm–7pm

de Faure

DENIS PHILIBERT 1998★★

■ n.c. 20,000 30–49 F

Pleasant to the eye. Interesting on the nose. Attractive on the palate. Well-structured, tannic, this is a wine that knows how to balance oak with a touch of cherry, with a big fanfare at the finish. Possessing plenty of muscle and richness, this is situated at the top of the AOC.

Maison Denis Philibert, 1, rue Ziem, 21200 Beaune, tel. 03.80.24.05.88, fax 03.80.22.37.08 Y ev. day 9am–7pm

JEAN-MICHEL ET LAURENT PILLOT 1998★

■ 4.03 ha 6,000 50–69 F

This is a precocious wine. Fresh, fruity and thirst-quenching, it should be drunk young. It sticks simply and effectively to the spirit of its appellation and the Côte Chalonnaise. Under the light brick-red colour (its only mark of development), there's a 'nouveau' feel to the character of this wine.

Dom. Jean-Michel et Laurent Pillot, rue des Vendangeurs, 71640 Mellecey, tel. 03.85.45.21.39, fax 03.85.45.20.48 ☑ Y by appt.

DOM. DU PUITS FLEURI 1998

■ 4 ha 6,000 20–29 F

An attractive, unpretentious wine, typical of the Côte Chalonnaise. Alongside an onion-skin colour which shows some signs of development, there is kirsch, preserved fruit in *eau-de-vie*, game, and a fine structure of tannins. Best drunk now with something simple like *andouille* and green beans.

GAEC du Puits Fleuri, Picard Père et Fils, 71490 Saint-Maurice-les-Couches, tel. 03.85.49.68.44, fax 03.85.45.55.61 ☑ Y by appt.

MICHEL REBOURGEON 1998★

■ 1.16 ha 7,450 30–49 F

This estate, founded in 1920, has more than 3 ha (7 acres) devoted to *villages* and Premiers Crus, but AOC Bourgogne has not been forgotten. A six-month barrel-ageing period hasn't spoilt the lovely expressive flavours of Pinot from the Côte d'Or. Though still tannic, the balance is as harmonious as you could wish. A wine that you can drink throughout its development over the next four to five years.

Michel Rebourgeon, pl. de l'Europe, 21630 Pommard, tel. 03.80.22.22.83, fax 03.80.22.90.64 ☑ Y by appt.

DOM. DES REMPARTS

Côtes d'Auxerre 1998★

□ 4 ha 15,000 30–49 F

A technically perfect, very clear lemon Burgundy, with a subtle hint of honey and a note of spring blossom, followed by a mineral finish. A wine that presses all the right buttons and makes it all look so easy, when in reality we know it isn't.

Dom. des Remparts, 6, rte. de Champs, 89530 Saint-Bris-le-Vineux, tel. 03.86.53.33.59, fax 03.86.53.62.12 ☑ Y by appt.

Sorin

DOM. RIGOUTAT

Coulanges-la-Vineuse 1998

■ 3 ha 1,830 30–49 F

An interesting, serious-minded wine. A closed nose that hides behind the attractive colour of this wine. There is plenty of character, but it is masked for the moment by the acidity and tannins, and especially the influence of the wood. So if you choose this wine, leave it for a year or two to age.

Dom. Pascale et Alain Rigoutat, 2, rue du Midi, 89290 Jussy, tel. 03.86.53.33.79, fax 03.86.53.66.89 ☑ Y by appt.

DOM. MICHELE ET PATRICE RION

Les Bons Bâtons 1998★★★

■ 0.62 ha n.c. 30–49 F

Where and indeed what are these Bons Bâtons? Who knows. Having said that, this is superb. Violet-purple with bluish hues, aromas of game and undergrowth, deliciously fresh. Finishes with an attractive hint of blackcurrant. There's scarcely a wine that can

better it. The estate is based in the former hospice of Saint-Bernard de Premeaux.
🔑 SCE Michèle et Patrice Rion, 1, rue de la Maladière, 21700 Premeaux, tel. 03.80.62.32.63, fax 03.80.62.49.63, e-mail patrice.rion@wanadoo.fr ☑ 🍷 by appt.

CAVE PRIVEE ANTONIN RODET

Les Vignes rouges 1997★

■ n.c. 10,000 🛢 70–99 F

This great Mercurey firm offers a Burgundy which one taster described as being 'not an easy wine, but it ought to grow into something big enough to go with a leg of lamb flavoured with thyme'. Good acidity, well-structured tannins, a very deep colour with a nose that holds promise – when it comes of age, it might be worth decanting.
🔑 Antonin Rodet, 71640 Mercurey, tel. 03.85.98.12.12, fax 03.85.45.25.49, e-mail rodet@rodet.com ☑ 🍷 ev. day except Sat. Sun. 9am–12 noon 1.30pm–6pm

DOM. REGIS ROSSIGNOL-CHANGARNIER 1998★

■ 1.3 ha 5,400 🛢 30–49 F

Eighty per cent of the harvest here is destemmed, which without a doubt explains the delicacy of expression of the Pinot Noir. Brilliant crimson, with a very attractive nose and light toasty flavours on the palate, it leaves a feeling of lingering subtlety.
🔑 Régis Rossignol, rue d'Amour, 21190 Volnay, tel. 03.80.21.61.59, fax 03.80.21.61.59 ☑ 🍷 by appt.

DOM. DE RUERE 1998★

■ 0.17 ha 1,500 🛢 20–29 F

Sometimes a Burgundy can be a very complex affair, labyrinthine even. You need patience with this wine, following the thread through the maze. This is a Pinot from good stock, grown in the Gamay region. Dense ruby red with a violet aureole, it has a very attractive nose of blackcurrant buds. It is still tannic, and this, along with its strong acidity, indicates that it will keep for some time in the cellar.
🔑 Mme. Thérèse Eloy, Ruère, 71960 Pierreclos, tel. 03.85.35.70.19, fax 03.85.35.70.19 ☑ 🍷 by appt.

DOM. SAINT-PRIX

Côtes d'Auxerre 1998★★

□ n.c. n.c. 30–49 F

This estate was very successful last year and this year has achieved the *coup de cœur* with a wine that has all the charms of a Chardonnay grown in Burgundy. A fine terroir and a true savoir-faire result in a wonderful structure and balance. Spring blossom and mineral notes received the jury's unanimous approval. The same mark goes to the **Bourgogne 98 Rouge**, all soft or dark fruits and spices, and with superb length.
🔑 Dom. Bersan et Fils, 20, rue du Dr Tardieux, 89530 Saint-Bris-le-Vineux, tel. 03.86.53.33.73, fax 03.86.53.38.45 ☑ 🍷 ev. day 8am–12.30pm 1.30pm–6pm; Sun. 8am–12.30pm; groups by appt.

CLAUDE ET THOMAS SEGUIN

Côtes d'Auxerre 1998★★

□ 2.8 ha 3,500 🍾 🌡 20–29 F

It is difficult to imagine a wine that is more redolent of its terroir, with a mushroom nose, followed by an anticipated fullness and richness. Maturation in tank has preserved its origins; what you might call a very fine Burgundy that is true to character.
🔑 EARL Claude et Thomas Seguin, 3 bis, rue Haute, 89530 Saint-Bris-le-Vineux, tel. 03.86.53.37.39, fax 03.86.53.61.12 ☑ 🍷 ev. day 8am–8pm

SIMONNET-FEBVRE

Coulanges-la-Vineuse 1998★

■ 0.6 ha 4,000 🍾 🌡 30–49 F

Attractive, bright purple in colour. The nose is more discreet, very true to the Pinot grape, which expresses itself on the palate. Here it is supple, light, and balanced.
🔑 Simonnet-Febvre, 9, av. d'Oberwesel, 89800 Chablis, tel. 03.86.98.99.00, fax 03.86.98.99.01 ☑ 🍷 by appt.

MARYLENE ET PHILIPPE SORIN

Julius Caesar Cuvée du Maître de Poste 1997★

■ 0.5 ha 3,000 🛢 50–69 F

A Cuvée Julius Caesar. As Vincenot used to say: 'We're not too fond of Jules round here, seeing what he did to Vercingetorix.' But to make up for his misdeeds, Caesar has left us a grape variety (the César) which makes up 100% of this wine. Unfortunately for Caesar, the César has become very rare, and we recommend this 97, with its imperial, sombre colour and nose bursting with blackberries, just to taste the grape variety. For connaisseurs. Drink with quails.
🔑 Marylène et Philippe Sorin, 12, rue de Paris, 89530 Saint-Bris-le-Vineux, tel. 03.86.53.60.76, fax 03.86.53.62.60, e-mail philippe.sorin@libertysurf.fr ☑ 🍷 by appt.

DOM. SORIN DEFRANCE

Côtes d'Auxerre 1999

□ 2.8 ha 25,000 🍾 🌡 30–49 F

Eighteen-year-old vines have produced this golden, mineral, overt wine. Full of energy.
🔑 Dom. Sorin-Defrance, 11 bis, rue de

Paris, 89530 Saint-Bris-le-Vineux, tel. 03.86.53.32.99, fax 03.86.53.34.44 ☒ Y ev. day except Sun. 8am–12 noon 1.30pm–6.30pm

HUBERT ET JEAN-PAUL TABIT

Côtes d'Auxerre 1997

☐ 4 ha 10,000 30–49 F

The 13th-century cellars and museum that boast 400 wine-growing and wine-making tools are two very good reasons to pay a visit to the Tabit family. Another is to discover a Burgundy that is rather untypical for its vintage, despite the fact that it was grown on Kimmeridgian soil. This is a honey-filled flower, but a developed one. Well-balanced, quite long – in short, a pleasant wine.

Hubert et Jean-Paul Tabit, 2, rue Dorée, 89530 Saint-Bris-le-Vineux, tel. 03.86.53.33.83, fax 03.86.53.67.97 ☒ Y ev. day 8am–12 noon 2pm–8pm; Sun. by appt.

OLIVIER TRICON 1998*

☐ n.c. 30,000 30–49 F

Classic colour and a nose full promises. Already floral – a good sign. Freshness on the palate and its liveliness point to a good structure and a long life to come.

Olivier Tricon, rte. d'Avallon, ferme de Vauroux, 89800 Chablis, tel. 03.86.42.10.37, fax 03.86.42.49.13, e-mail maison.tricon@wanadoo.fr ☒ Y by appt.

DOM. DES TROIS MONTS 1998**

■ 0.8 ha 6,400 30–49 F

If you're passing through Saint-Sernin-du-Plain on the Côte Chalonnaise, pay a visit to the butcher: his *andouillettes* are a real attraction for tourists and gourmets alike. Then visit this estate's wine cellar, where you will find two remarkable 98 Burgundies. The first is black as ink, exploding with blackcurrant. A round attack followed by a silkiness . . . This wine is all tenderness and emotion. It knows what it's doing. **Elevée en Fût de Chêne** (matured in oak barrels) for 12 months, this other *cuvée* gets the same mark for its excellent craftsmanship. The Pichards have been producing wine for 200 years. Long may they continue to do so.

Dom. des Trois Monts, En Crainchet, 71510 Saint-Sernin-du-Plain, tel. 03.85.45.58.10, fax 03.85.49.50.17, e-mail troismonts@caves-particulieres.com ☒ Y by appt.

Daniel et Claude Pichard

CLOS DE VAULICHERES 1998*

☐ 0.5 ha 1,000 70–99 F

Vaulichères formerly belonged to the Clermont-Tonnerre family (who came from these parts and were for a long time owners of the château at Ancy-le-Franc). Here we have a deep yellow wine, with aromas of dried fruit and hazelnut. A little too short on freshness to really take off, but its richness would go well with some *soumaintrain*, the local cheese.

Olivier Refait, Ch. Clos de Vaulichères, Vaulichères, 89700 Tonnerre, tel. 03.86.55.02.74, fax 03.86.55.37.57, e-mail info@vaulicheres.com Y ev. day 8am–12.30pm 1.30pm–7pm; Sun. by appt.

ALAIN VIGNOT

Côte Saint-Jacques 1998**

■ 4.16 ha n.c. 30–49 F

This wine-maker is one of the most dynamic players in the renaissance of this wine region. Here he offers us a **94 Rosé** that is almost entirely 'gris' (90% Pinot Gris, the remainder Pinot Noir), with a light vegetal nose and a little touch of exoticism. It is destined for people who like to break their routine and experience new adventures. The jury gave it a mention. The red 98 (Pinot Noir) is interesting and original; a decent wine. Deep purple, blackcurrant on the nose, with remarkable balance and a lovely velvety texture, it can be drunk now, though its overall balance and structure means that it is possible to lay it down for a few years.

Alain Vignot, 16, rue des Prés, 89300 Paroy-sur-Tholon, tel. 03.86.91.03.06, fax 03.86.91.09.37 ☒ Y by appt.

DOM. FABRICE VIGOT

Les Lutenières 1998**

■ 0.85 ha 3,000 50–69 F

RECOLTE 1998
BOURGOGNE
APPELLATION BOURGOGNE CONTRÔLEE
LES LUTENIERES
Mis en bouteille à la propriété par
DOMAINE VIGOT FABRICE
VITICULTEUR A VOSNE ROMANEE (CÔTE D'OR) FRANCE
PRODUIT DE FRANCE
12,5 % vol.
75 cl

Fabrice Vigot, born in Vosne in 1966, is the grandson of an Italian immigrant who came to live in Morey-Saint-Denis many years ago. In 1990, he very courageously took over the family estate, and his reward is the *coup de cœur* for this ambitious, deep dark-red Burgundy with its mixture of aromas of kirsch and forest-floor. Full, warm and powerful, this is a wine that you will rediscover with pleasure in two or three years' time.

Dom. Fabrice Vigot, 16, rue de la Fontaine, 21700 Vosne-Romanée, tel. 03.80.61.13.01, fax 03.80.61.13.01 ☒ Y by appt.

DOM. ELISE VILLIERS

La Chevalière 1998

☐ 2.5 ha 7,000 30–49 F

Clear, with a dry, flinty nose, lively enough on the palate. Its acidity will stand it in good stead if you want to keep it for one or two years.

Elise Villiers, Précy-le-Moult, Pierre-Perthuis, 89450 Vézelay, tel. 03.86.33.27.62, fax 03.86.33.27.62 ☒ Y by appt.

Bourgogne Grand Ordinaire

In real terms, the Appellations Bourgogne Ordinaire and Bourgogne Grand Ordinaire are used very rarely. When they are, the one that is less frequently used is Bourgogne Grand Ordinaire. This name may appear a little dull, but some *terroirs* on the margins of great vineyards can, nonetheless, produce some excellent wines that sold at very affordable prices. Almost all the Burgundy vine varieties can be used to produce white, red, rosé or clairet wines for this appellation.

The grapes used for white wine are Chardonnay or Melon. Although only a very few Melon vines remain, this variety reaches the heights of quality further west in France, where it is used to produce a reputable Muscadet in the Nantes region. The Aligoté is almost always declared as Appellation Bourgogne Aligoté. The Sacy grape, now grown exclusively in the Yonne, was once grown in the whole Chablis area and in the Yonne river valley to produce sparkling wines for export; it is now used for Crémant de Bourgogne.

The principal varieties for red and rosé, are the traditional Burgundy grapes, Gamay Noir and Pinot Noir. In the Yonne the César variety, reserved exclusively for Burgundy wines, can still be used, particularly in Irancy, while the Tressot makes an appearance in the annals but never in the vineyards. The best wines made from Gamay are found in the Yonne, especially in Coulanges-la-Vineuse, where they are bottled under that appellation. The production of wines from this AOC was 12,000 hl (316,800 gal) in 1999.

DOM. BOUZERAND-DUJARDIN 1998

■ 0.28 ha 1,400 ▮ 30–49 F

Here is a very respectable citizen, all dressed up in dark red. Two thirds Gamay, one third Monthélie Pinot. There are worse things in life! It has a pleasant nose, with hints of leather and violets. Characteristic, well-made wine.

🗝 Dom. Bouzerand-Dujardin, pl. de l'Eglise, 21190 Monthélie, tel. 03.80.21.20.08, fax 03.80.21.28.16 ☑ Y by appt.

FRANCK CHALMEAU Sacy 1998★

□ 1.03 ha 9,000 ▮ 🌡 20–29 F

This is a wine for enlightened wine-lovers and people who love curiosities, because it revives the Sacy, a once-flourishing grape that has almost disappeared today. Not only is this a cause worth supporting in itself, the results are pretty good as well. This is an almost unique wine, with perfumes of wild rose and lychees, and a lingering, lively, fruity freshness. It costs almost nothing, and is a true adventure. Well done to this courageous wine-producer for preserving this grape.

🗝 Franck Chalmeau, 20, rue du Ruisseau, 89530 Chitry-le-Fort, tel. 03.86.41.42.09, fax 03.86.41.46.84 ☑ Y by appt.

DOM. DE CHAUDE ECUELLE Chardonnay 1998

□ 1.1 ha 10,000 ▮ 🌡 30–49 F

Fresh and fruity are the words that come to mind as you put down your glass. This pale gold wine is lively and generous with ripe fruit on both the nose and palate.

🗝 Dom. de Chaude Ecuelle, 35, Grande-Rue, 89800 Chemilly-sur-Serein, tel. 03.86.42.40.44, fax 03.86.42.85.13 ☑ Y by appt.

🗝 Gabriel et Gérald Vilain

CAVE DES VIGNERONS DE GENOUILLY 1998★

■ 5 ha 10,000 ▮ 🌡 20–29 F

People hardly ever use the expression 'vin de grand ordinaire' to mean 'the Sunday wine' anymore. That's as may be, but this wine is capable of good things. There is colour here, aromas (herbaceous, strawberry) and a certain degree of structure. Rough? Of course it's rough, but that's a compliment because a Bourgogne Grand Ordinaire should be just that. Good depth of fruit.

🗝 Cave des Vignerons de Genouilly, 71460 Genouilly, tel. 03.85.49.23.72, fax 03.85.49.23.58 ☑ Y ev. day except Sun. 8am–12 noon 2pm–6pm

DOM. GUYON Les Glapignys Réserve du domaine 1998★

□ 0.15 ha 1,400 ▮ 🌡 50–69 F

In April 2000 this wine is a bit short of breath at the finish, but will open up very soon if it hasn't already. A clear colour, with flowers and citrus fruits on the nose, it comes

from the Côte de Nuits, and blends Chardonnay (75%) with Pinot Blanc (for the remainder). An interesting combination.
🗝 EARL Dom. Guyon, 11–16, R.N. 74, 21700 Vosne-Romanée, tel. 03.80.61.02.46, fax 03.80.62.36.56 ☒ Y by appt.

DOM. FABRICE VIGOT 1998

■ 0.43 ha 1,000 ▮ 20–29 F

Here, the bottles of Echezeaux sit side by side in the wine cellar with the Bourgogne Grand Ordinaire. So, it is no surprise to discover a wine with a deep colour and a decent nose, heavy on the tannins, with a lot of potential. All it needs is to smooth itself out a little. And at this price, it would be a shame to deprive yourself.
🗝 Dom. Fabrice Vigot, 16, rue de la Fontaine, 21700 Vosne-Romanée, tel. 03.80.61.13.01, fax 03.80.61.13.01 ☒ Y by appt.

Bourgogne Aligoté

This has been described as the 'Muscadet of the Burgundy'. It is an excellent carafe wine to be drunk young, when it shows off the aromas of the variety at their best. Burgundians drink it for its freshness while they wait for the Chardonnay to mature. On the Côte Aligoté has been replaced by Chardonnay and has rather 'gone downhill', literally, in terms of the areas allotted to it; it was grown previously on the slopes. But the soils influence it just as much as any other variety and there are as many types of Aligoté as there are regions producing it. The Aligotés of Pernand were renowned for their suppleness and their fruity nose (before the vines were replaced with Chardonnay); the Aligotés of the Hautes-Côtes are sought after for their freshness and liveliness; those from Saint-Bris in the Yonne are light and pleasant to drink and seem to have borrowed traces of the elderflower scents found in Sauvignon; finally, the Aligotés from Bouzeron, which have recently earned a certain recognition because of their distinct appellation, seem more like Chardonnays, and this identifies them as coming from the Côte Chalonnaise. In 1999 102,390 hl (2,703,096 gal) of Bourgogne Aligoté were produced, 3,841 hl (101,402 gal) of which were from Bouzeron.

STEPHANE ALADAME 1998

□ 0.3 ha 2,335 ▮ 30–49 F

Stéphane Aladame was only 18 when in 1992 he set up his estate at Montagny-lès-Buxy (where the Saint-Vincent wine festival will be held in 2002). His Côte Chalonnaise Aligoté has only the merest hint of gold in the colour, but there's nothing unusual about that. A little hint of mineral mixed with pippin apple. Good clean attack. Character and balance.
🗝 Stéphane Aladame, rue du Lavoir, 71390 Montagny-lès-Buxy, tel. 03.85.92.06.01, fax 03.85.92.04.97, e-mail stephane.aladame@wanadoo.fr ☒ Y by appt.

JEAN-NOEL BAZIN 1998★

□ 2 ha n.c. ▮ 30–49 F

There are a lot of Bazins in Burgundy. Before they were involved in wine they sold cloth, canvas and dimity fabric. This La Rochepot Bazin (no relation to the author of books on the wines of Burgundy) knows that experience counts. This is an Aligoté in the tradition of the region: acidic, quite mineral and attractive, with a fruity nose.
🗝 Jean-Noël Bazin, Les Petits Vergers, 21340 La Rochepot, tel. 03.80.21.75.49, fax 03.80.21.83.71 ☒ Y by appt.

JEAN BOUCHARD 1998★

□ n.c. 250,000 ▮ 🌡 50–69 F

Jean Bouchard: remember the first name, because there are hundreds of Bouchards in Beaune. A dozen snails would happily quit their shells to accompany this lightly-bronzed, golden 98 with its flinty, honeysuckle aromas. It's quite a lively wine, and certainly won't give you cause for complaint.
🗝 Jean Bouchard, B.P. 47, 21202 Beaune Cedex, tel. 03.80.24.37.27, fax 03.80.24.37.38

RENE BOUVIER 1998

□ 1.42 ha 10,000 ▮ 🌡 30–49 F

Fairly yellow colour, with an open and convivial nose, this 98 is very typical of this former hill-side Dijon vineyard that now forms the northern part of the Côte-de-Nuits. It is round, fresh and charming, with a distinctive note of the terroir. Long and smooth on the palate, it shows just one of the subtle qualities of this grape variety, which is used throughout the region, yet presents itself differently according to where it is grown.
🗝 René Bouvier, 2, rue Neuve, 21160 Marsannay-la-Côte, tel. 03.80.52.21.37, fax 03.80.59.95.96 ☒ Y by appt.

BURGUNDY

DOM. JEAN-MARIE BOUZEREAU 1998★

☐ 1 ha 7,000 30–49 F

Clear and golden, with part fruity, part floral aromas that suggest complexity. This is a good, reliable 98 that is very fresh. Don't let its timidity deceive you.

Jean-Marie Bouzereau, 7, rue Labbé, 21190 Meursault, tel. 03.80.21.62.41, fax 03.80.21.65.97 by appt.

MICHEL BOUZEREAU ET FILS 1998★

☐ 1.25 ha n.c. 30–49 F

This is an Aligoté from Meursault, so don't be surprised if, with its talent for mimicry, it has a little bit of Chardonnay about it. This is a charming wine, but it will need a bit of explanation when you serve it to your guests. Well, that's what a guide is for. Beware, this is not a typical Aligoté. An agreeable wine with buttery, dried apricot aromas; smooth and sophisticated. Matured in oak and on the lees, it undergoes the process of *bâtonnage*. So that explains that!

Michel Bouzereau et Fils, 3, rue de la Planche-Meunière, 21190 Meursault, tel. 03.80.21.20.74, fax 03.80.21.66.41 by appt.

CHRISTOPHE BUISSON 1998★

☐ 0.3 ha 2,800 30–49 F

It happens sometimes. You are disappointed by the first mouthful, then overwhelmed by the second. That's what counts. Christophe Buisson is a wine-broker who turned to wine-producing in 1996, buying a winery in Beaune. His wine is pleasant. Does it it recall the rosy-tinted dawn, as one of our jury-members put it so poetically? That's up to you to find out.

Christophe Buisson, 21190 Saint-Romain, tel. 03.80.21.63.92, fax 03.80.21.67.03 by appt.

DOM. CAPUANO-FERRERI ET FILS 1998★

☐ n.c. n.c. 30–49 F

This is not very typical, but it certainly scores top marks. Why is that? It has been barrel-matured, which is rare for this appellation, but then that is hardly a crime. Rich, golden yellow, with a hint of vanilla, superb on the palate. Yes, really, the cry from the table is unanimous. Bravo for the wine-producer.

Capuano-Ferreri et Fils, 1, rue de la Croix-Sorine, 21590 Santenay, tel. 03.80.20.64.12, fax 03.80.20.65.75 by appt.

PATRICK ET CHRISTINE CHALMEAU 1998

☐ 4.5 ha 10,000 30–49 F

You don't expect an Aligoté to be an expert on Freudian philosophy. This wine makes more of a reference to French philospher Gaston Blanchard, who had an amazing knack of finding the truth of the soul. In short, this wine is clear as a mountain spring, a little toasty, rich and unctuous, well behaved and careful not to sway too much in the direction of Chardonnay. For connoisseurs who like a lively debate.

Patrick et Christine Chalmeau, 76, rue du Ruisseau, 89530 Chitry-le-Fort, tel. 03.86.41.43.71, fax 03.86.41.47.51 by appt.

MICHEL CHAMPION 1998

☐ 0.86 ha 6,000

Gluggable, there is no other word for it. It is showing a little development and should be drunk without much delay. This supple and balanced straw-gold 98, with its floral and lemony aromas, is a perfect example of the appellation.

Michel Champion, Cercot, 71390 Moroges, tel. 03.85.47.90.94, fax 03.85.47.99.53 ev. day 8am–12 noon 2pm–7pm

DOM. JEAN CHARTRON

Clos de la Combe 1998★

☐ 0.5 ha 4,800 30–49 F

The masterpiece of the President of the BIVB. This is a very representative Aligoté which ought to win a majority at the next general assembly. Clear, with a floral and fruity intensity, it has an acidic kick that gives the wine a fresh character. Shades of Granny Smith apples.

Dom. Jean Chartron, 13, Grande-Rue, 21190 Puligny-Montrachet, tel. 03.80.21.32.85, fax 03.80.21.36.35 ev. day 10am–12.30pm 2pm–6pm

DOM. CHEVROT

Cuvée des Quatre Terroirs 1998★

☐ 1 ha 5,000 30–49 F

We turn now to Maranges, which boasts no fewer than four terroirs. This very pale yellow 98 has a slight fennel quality with a mainly acacia and verbena nose. Green apple on the palate, fine and vigorous, very pleasant. This was clearly harvested at full maturity, and it has been matured with expertise and care.

Catherine et Fernand Chevrot, Dom. Chevrot, 19, rte. de Couches, 71150 Cheilly-lès-Maranges, tel. 03.85.91.10.55, fax 03.85.91.13.24, e-mail domaine.chevrot@wanadoo.fr ev. day 9am–12 noon 2pm–6pm; Sun. 9am–12 noon

BERNARD COLIN ET FILS 1997★★

☐ 0.91 ha n.c. 30–49 F

Heil Gott! Good Lord! Is that where the word Aligoté comes from? A question that seems irrelevant when looking at this wine, which receives the *coup de cœur*. In short, we love this wine: pale gold, mineral then floral, retaining freshness from start to finish, both lively and fruity. Bernard Colin, who comes from Chassagne-Montrachet, is going to have problems in his cellar with this one, because his Chardonnays are going to be jealous . . .

🔑 Bernard Colin et Fils, 22, rue Charles-Paquelin, 21190 Chassagne-Montrachet, tel. 03.80.21.32.78, fax 03.80.21.93.23 ☒ Y ev. day 8am–7pm; Sun. by appt.

DOM. DE CORBETON 1998★

☐ 8 ha 66,600 ▮ ♁ 50–69 F

It would be hard to tell that this wine comes from Bichot. Well-made and well-balanced, an honest, straightforward wine, neither complex or intricate.This is the wine that some Burgundians brush their teeth with in the morning instead of toothpaste. Great! A wine that wakes you up and sets you on your feet for the day. Corbeton, by the way, is a medieval estate, with noble connections, on the hilltops of Beaune.

🔑 Vieilles Caves de Bourgogne et de Bordeaux, 6 bis, bd Jacques-Copeau, 21200 Beaune, tel. 03.80.24.37.47, fax 03.80.24.37.38

JOCELYNE ET PHILIPPE DEFRANCE 1998★

☐ 5.38 ha 8,000 ▮ ♁ 30–49 F

What is the connection between this wine and the Panthéon in Paris? This wine comes from the place where Germain Soufflot, the architect of Sainte-Geneviève, which later became the Panthéon, lived as a child. We should drink to his health with this very fine example of an Aligoté! Supple and lively as an Aligoté should be, with a delicious floral freshness. Best drunk now without burying it in the 'Panthéon' of your wine cellar.

🔑 Philippe Defrance, 5, rue du Four, 89530 Saint-Bris-le-Vineux, tel. 03.86.53.39.04, fax 03.86.53.66.46 ☒ Y by appt.

DOM. DENIS PERE ET FILS 1998

☐ 0.8 ha 3,000 ▮ ♁ 30–49 F

Very light on its feet, this one. Fresh and spirited with delicate shades of greenish-gold. It doesn't linger long on the palate, but then we can hardly expect an Aligoté to run the 10,000 m. Rustic, in the best sense of the word.

🔑 Dom. Denis Père et Fils, chem. des Vignes-Blanches, 21420 Pernand-Vergelesses, tel. 03.80.21.50.91, fax 03.80.26.10.32 ☒ Y by appt.

DOM. GUY DIDIER

Vieilles vignes 1998★

☐ 2.5 ha 20,000 ▮ ♁ 30–49 F

This is the Aligoté of Canon Kir, the former deputy mayor of Dijon after whom Kir is named. And it is certainly the wine one would wish him to have by his side in paradise. It has a lovely brightness, a very fine mineral and floral nose, pleasantly herbaceous at the (very long) finish. You can just imagine yourself taking the Canon by his cassock and whispering in his ear that it would be a terrible crime to put crème de cassis in this lovely 98.

🔑 Dom. Guy Didier, chem. rural no 29, 21700 Nuits-Saint-Georges, tel. 03.80.62.42.00, fax 03.80.61.28.13, e-mail nuicave@wanadoo.fr Y by appt.

DOM. YVAN DUFOULEUR 1998★★

☐ 1.05 ha 7,000 ▮ ♁ 30–49 F

It's very simple: the wine gives you a come-hither smile, you are dazzled by its brilliance. The approach is relaxed because the fruit is so open. You tell yourself this will be an easy conquest. A fresh, lively palate full of charm puts this wine among the best we have tasted.

🔑 Dom. des Belles Chaumes, 18, rue Thurot, 21700 Nuits-Saint-Georges, tel. 03.80.62.31.00, fax 03.80.62.31.00 ☒ Y by appt.

DOM. C. ET J.-M. DURAND 1998★

☐ 0.4 ha 3,500 ▮ ♁ 30–49 F

If you are familiar with old Burgundy songs, you will know that the *Bique de Bouze* (the nanny-goat of Bouze) used to butt passers-by with her horns. Well! With this Aligoté from Bouze-lès-Beaune, it's just the same. The grape variety emerges from this wine fresh and ready to lock horns with anyone. A spontaneous, full and round wine in the traditional style.

🔑 Dom. Christine et Jean-Marc Durand, 1, rue de l'Eglise, 21200 Bouze-lès-Beaune, tel. 03.80.22.75.31, fax 03.80.26.02.57 ☒ Y by appt.

SYLVAIN DUSSORT 1998

☐ 0.8 ha 5,000 ▮ 30–49 F

This rather spicy Aligoté has been matured on the lees in tank. It comes from a vineyard parcel close to Meursault, where the vines are some 60 years old. The mineral aromas give way to all of Meursault's richness. It is hard to escape your origins.

🔑 Sylvain Dussort, 12, rue Charles-Giraud, 21190 Meursault, tel. 03.80.21.27.50, fax 03.80.21.65.91, e-mail dussvins@aol.fr ☒ Y by appt.

DOM. FICHET 1999★

☐ 1 ha 4,000 ▮ ♁ 20–29 F

This is a Mâconnais Aligoté at the height of success. White gold, with a hint of toast, with each whiff there is a different aroma: it skips skilfully between lemon, grapefruit and honey. There is richness and fullness aplenty in this characteristic southern (South Burgundy) grape. The racing cyclist Jean-François Bernard came to this wine cellar to prepare for his races.

🔑 Dom. Francis Fichet et Fils, Le Martoret, 71960 Igé, tel. 03.85.33.30.46, fax 03.85.33.44.45, e-mail olivierfichet@wanadoo.fr ☒ Y by appt.

DIDIER FORNEROL 1998★★

☐ 0.2 ha 1,800 🍷 20–29 F

This smooth Aligoté curls up in the mouth and refuses to leave until a dozen snails turn up to join in, taking the tongue hostage with it. Very straightforward, produced in tank, bright in colour and well-structured.

🗝 Didier Fornerol, 15, pl. de la Mairie, 21700 Corgoloin, tel. 03.80.62.93.09, fax 03.80.62.93.09 ☑ 🍷 by appt.

DOM. MARCEL ET BERNARD FRIBOURG 1998

☐ 3 ha 6,160 🍷 20–29 F

A wine you want to flirt a little with. White gold in colour, with discreet, complex perfumes of vegetation and fruit. There's a not unpleasant touch of greenness. It doesn't have amazing length. Characteristic style – and in the Hautes-Côtes de Nuits, they know how it's done.

🗝 SCE Dom. Marcel et Bernard Fribourg, 8, rue de l'Ancienne-Cure, 21700 Villers-la-Faye, tel. 03.80.62.91.74, fax 03.80.62.71.17 ☑ 🍷 by appt.

CAVE DE GENOUILLY 1998★

☐ 12 ha 20,000 🍷 20–29 F

Not a great deal of body, but it makes its presence felt – marks out its territory, as it were. A wine that doesn't lack originality either. Its vegetal, almost Muscat-like aromas are interesting and expressive, but not aggressive. The fruity palate benefits from this and is straightforward and fresh. It comes from a co-operative on the Côte Chalonnaise which also produces a **Clos de la Massière 98** of a similarly decent quality.

🗝 Cave des Vignerons de Genouilly, 71460 Genouilly, tel. 03.85.49.23.72, fax 03.85.49.23.58 ☑ 🍷 ev. day except Sun. 8am–12 noon 2pm–6pm

DOM. GOUFFIER

Clos de Butte Soleil 1998★

☐ 3 ha 7,000 🍷 30–49 F

A name like Clos de Butte Soleil (which means, roughly, 'sunny hill-garden') is guaranteed to provoke daydreams. This is a *perlant* wine, fresh and rich, a little on the austere side perhaps, but a true product of its terroir on the Côte Chalonnaise. 'Easy to drink', is the general impression. Will it go with shellfish? Definitely. 'Those little beasts need waking up.'

🗝 Dom. Gouffier, 11, Grande-Rue, 71150 Fontaines, tel. 03.85.91.49.66, fax 03.85.91.46.98 ☑ 🍷 by appt.

DOM. OLIVIER GUYOT 1998★★

☐ 2.4 ha 6,000 🍷 30–49 F

Olivier Guyot does not go unnoticed in Marsannay, at least when the roadworks make it possible to go anywhere . . . He does his ploughing the old-fashioned way, using a draught horse. Let's be honest, the result is maybe not due to this noble feat, but the quality is impressive nonetheless. A little exotic and over-ripe, not the best example of its kind perhaps, but very good.

🗝 EARL Olivier Guyot, 39, rue de Mazy, 21160 Marsannay-la-Côte, tel. 03.80.52.39.71, fax 03.80.51.17.58 ☑ 🍷 by appt.

HONORE LAVIGNE Cuvée spéciale★

☐ n.c. 240,000 🍷 30–49 F

This wine runs through the whole gamut of tastes like a wild horse: its aromas, its fiery, flinty taste, its floral charm, the little hint of apricot, the warmth, the incredible vitality, the love of life – it is all there in this bottle. An 18th century flask. Honoré Lavigne is a brand name of the Jean-Claude Boisset estate.

🗝 Honoré Lavigne, 5, quai Dumorey, 21700 Nuits-Saint-Georges, tel. 03.80.62.61.61, fax 03.80.62.61.57

🗝 Boisset

DOM. HUGUENOT PERE ET FILS 1998★

☐ 1.1 ha 9,000 🍷 30–49 F

This wine has a way of placing a friendly hand on your shoulder and stunning you into silence. There is a hint of Chardonnay, which is enough to say it all. Just try resisting. Quince and honey confirm the first impression. Astonishing freshness and roundness in a style that is specific to the northern part of the Côte de Nuits.

🗝 Huguenot Père et Fils, 7, ruelle du Carron, 21160 Marsannay-la-Côte, tel. 03.80.52.11.56, fax 03.80.52.60.47, e-mail domaine.huguenot@wanadoo.fr ☑ 🍷 by appt.

DOM. LUCIEN JACOB 1998★

☐ 1 ha 4,300 🍷 20–29 F

This estate produces everything you need to make a kir: as well as wine, they make an excellent *crème de cassis*. But the Aligoté on its own has some merits as an apéritif, maybe served with a few *gougères*. This wine is bursting with citrus fruits. Its lively acidity – a prerequisite of the appellation – wakes the taste buds up.

🗝 Dom. Lucien Jacob, 21420 Echevronne, tel. 03.80.21.52.15, fax 03.80.21.55.65 ☑ 🍷 by appt.

DOM. ANDRE ET BERNARD LABRY 1998★★

☐ 1.5 ha 2,500 🍷 30–49 F

A glass of Aligoté is not exactly *Last Year at Marienbad*, as they say. However, this attractively-coloured wine has a fruity, floral (rose) nose that is full of thoughtfulness. If you are looking for a decent, reasonably-priced wine that is true to type, this one, with its balance, interesting length and a supple, fruity after-taste, make it a very good choice.

🗝 Dom. André et Bernard Labry, Melin, 21190 Auxey-Duresses, tel. 03.80.21.21.60, fax 03.80.21.64.15 ☑ 🍷 ev. day 9am–12 noon 2pm–6pm; Sat. Sun. by appt.

LA BUXYNOISE 1999

☐ 153.5 ha 62,000 30–49 F

The Ministers of Agriculture for the entire European Union once drank in these cellars. Let us hope they understood what they were experiencing. If they had been served this 99 Aligoté, they would have found it, as we did, a pleasant clear yellow colour, with aromas of lime and a hint of Sauvignon. Medium-bodied with an attractive, fresh acidity.

Cave des vignerons de Buxy, Les Vignes de la Croix, 71390 Buxy, tel. 03.85.92.03.03, fax 03.85.92.08.06 ev. day except Sun. 9am–12 noon 2pm–6pm

DOM. DE LA GALOPIERE 1998

☐ 1.5 ha 5,000 30–49 F

Medium gold colour, this wine has a firm, fruity background, a little severe perhaps, but rich and well-made. An *andouillette vigneronne* would cheer it up no end. It comes from a family estate in the Côte de Beaune which has – laudably – made an effort to design a label inspired by the local scenery.

Claire et Gabriel Fournier, Dom. de la Galopière, 6, rue de l'Eglise, 21200 Bligny-lès-Beaune, tel. 03.80.21.46.50, fax 03.80.21.49.93, e-mail c.g.fournier@wanadoo.fr by appt.

DANIEL LARGEOT

☐ 0.4 ha 3,000 30–49 F

People in the Chorey area really know how to bring out the best in Aligoté. On this estate, Marie-France Largeot is following in her parents' footsteps, adding to the ever-increasing numbers of women entering into wine-producing in Burgundy. To judge by this Aligoté, the great revolution of the 21st century has started well. This bright, intense, fresh wine is the very incarnation of what an Aligoté ought to be.

Daniel Largeot, 5, rue des Brenôts, 21200 Chorey-lès-Beaune, tel. 03.80.22.15.10, fax 03.80.22.60.62 by appt.

DOM. DE LA TOUR 1997

☐ 1.33 ha 6,000 30–49 F

This estate is a recent addition to the region, and its Aligoté is an unusual one, which offers interesting depths. Golden yellow with notes of very ripe apricot, it follows with generous and powerful flavours that one of the tasters describes as 'late harvest'. A wine for people who like asking questions and to enliven dinner-table conversation.

SCEA Dom. de la Tour, 8 bis, rue Jules-Philippe, 89800 Chablis, tel. 03.86.47.55.68, fax 03.86.47.55.86, e-mail dtour@clubinternet.fr by appt.

LA TOUR DU PRIEURE 1999★

☐ 1 ha 6,000 30–49 F

Back in 1560, when the priory tower was built, the monks of Cluny who lived there were already enthusiastic wine-growers. In short, this wine has a good pedigree. It has a simple, clear colour, and evokes ripe fruit with a hint of lemon that works well in this wine. Slight Muscat-like notes.

Bernard Dorry, La Tour du Prieuré, 71960 Bussières, tel. 03.85.37.75.43, fax 03.85.37.75.43 by appt.

DOM. LEJEUNE 1997★

☐ 0.4 ha 3,000 30–49 F

When you have taught at the *lycée viticole* (wine college) in Beaune, as François Jullien de Pommerol has, you owe it to yourself to set a good example. And it is not so easy to be put to the test like this, with all your students watching you, especially since creating a successful Aligoté is not something that everyone can do. This one is characterised by flinty, verbena aromas, and is well-structured.

Dom. Lejeune, La Confrérie, pl. de l'Eglise, 21630 Pommard, tel. 03.80.22.90.88, fax 03.80.22.90.88 by appt.

Famille Jullien de Pommerol

CAVE DES VIGNERONS DE MANCEY 1999

☐ n.c. 10,000 30–49 F

In the 19th century, the vineyards at Mancey were the first in Burgundy to confront Phylloxera. Underneath its grey gold colour, their Aligoté is invigorating. Aromas of violet and acacia with a lemon and hazelnut palate, which is just as it should be, give it all its charm.

Cave des Vignerons de Mancey, R.N. 6, En Velnoux, 71700 Tournus, tel. 03.85.51.00.83, fax 03.85.51.71.20 by appt.

RAYMOND MASSE 1998

☐ 0.7 ha 6,000 30–49 F

People who collect wine labels will jump at this 1930s-style example which features an old-fashioned oval photograph brought up-to-date with colour. So is this a retro 98? It seems mature, but not developed. Very dense in colour, mineral and vegetal. A decent, average wine.

Raymond Masse, Barizey, 71640 Givry, tel. 03.85.44.36.73 ev. day 8am–6pm

PASCAL MELLENOTTE 1998★★

☐ 1 ha 2,000 20–29 F

Lively, fresh, fruity, good-natured, a tad impertinent. Bright yellow in colour, with a sweet-smelling nose. Full-bodied, this overrides the acidity, yet retains some freshness. An attractive style that comes to us from the Côte Chalonnaise.

Pascal Mellenotte, Le Martray, 71640 Mellecey, tel. 03.85.45.15.64, fax 03.85.45.15.64 ev. day except Sun. 10am–7pm

ARMELLE ET JEAN-MICHEL MOLIN 1998★

☐ 0.3 ha 2,600 20–29 F

You could almost envy the carp or pike that is going to accompany this very golden and particularly aromatic (basket of ripe fruit) 98.

BURGUNDY

Round and rich on the attack, with an underlying acidity to lighten it, it will surely inspire a verse from the family's own poet-winegrower, who is well-known in the Côte.
🔑 EARL Armelle et Jean-Michel Molin, 54, rte. des Grands-Crus, 21220 Fixin, tel. 03.80.52.21.28, fax 03.80.59.96.99 ☒ 🍷 by appt.

OLIVIER MORIN 1999

□ 1.94 ha 15,000 30–49 F

Two hundred m (218 yds) from the fortified church of Saint-Valérion, you will find this estate and this Aligoté. The terroir has given it a good mineral quality, as well as an unctuous but firm character. The jury has great confidence in this lively wine, which is already offers a balanced, mouthfilling after-taste.
🔑 Olivier Morin, 2, chem. de Vaudu, 89530 Chitry-le-Fort, tel. 03.86.41.47.20, fax 03.86.41.47.20 ☒ 🍷 by appt.

CHRISTIAN MORIN 1999

□ 2.1 ha 12,000 20–29 F

This subtly-coloured Aligoté is made in Chitry, a wine-growing village with tiny picturesque streets, and it needs help. You need to swirl the wine round in the glass, at room temperature, to let it breathe and open up. Firm, dry and clean, it doesn't beat around the bush.
🔑 Christian Morin, 17, rue du Ruisseau, 89530 Chitry-le-Fort, tel. 03.86.41.44.10, fax 03.86.41.48.21 ☒ 🍷 by appt.

DENIS MUGNERET ET FILS 1998

□ 0.3 ha 1,500 30–49 F

This Aligoté has no pretensions about being a Chardonnay, but claims its rightful place loud and clear. It certainly has all the freshness of a morning breeze and positively makes your ears stand up. A good-looking wine, an almost perfect example of its type – nearly a Photofit.
🔑 Denis et Dominique Mugneret, 9, rue de la Fontaine, 21700 Vosne-Romanée, tel. 03.80.61.00.97, fax 03.80.61.24.54 ☒ 🍷 by appt.

DOM. HENRI NAUDIN-FERRAND 1998★

□ 2.51 ha 21,477 20–29 F

'Goodness, my heart is moved by all this tenderness', says one of Molière's characters, whom we imagine placing his glass of Aligoté on the table. This very light yellow 98, with aromas of lemon and green apples, is a saucy conversationalist, full of refreshing humour. The jury recommends serving it with an *andouillette vigneronne*. It is produced by Anne and Claire Naudin, who in 1997 took over from their retired parents. They make Aligoté as if it was second nature to them.
🔑 Dom. Henri Naudin-Ferrand, rue du Meix-Grenot, 21700 Magny-lès-Villers, tel. 03.80.62.91.50, fax 03.80.62.91.77, e-mail dom.hnf.@wanadoo.fr ☒ 🍷 by appt.

DOM. CLAUDE NOUVEAU 1998★★

□ 0.8 ha 6,000 30–49 F

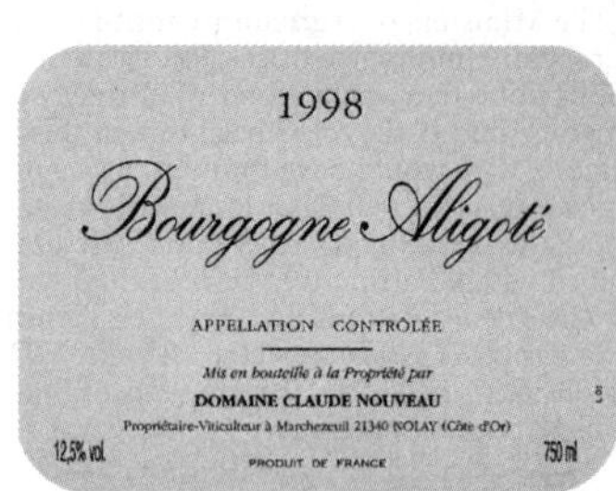

Aligoté generally does well in the Hautes-Côtes, as is proved here. *Coup de cœur* for this 98 that is simply bursting with personality. The colour of fine straw, with subtle but distinct aromas of acacia and hawthorn. It is soft, smooth, elegant and light, a model of its kind which makes you want to sit down to eat immediately.
🔑 EARL Dom. Claude Nouveau, Marchezeuil, 21340 Change, tel. 03.85.91.13.34, fax 03.85.91.10.39 ☒ 🍷 by appt.

OLIVIER-GARD 1998

□ 0.5 ha 3,600 30–49 F

Discreetly brilliant, pale straw in colour, this 98 has a fine and rather long nose. Its freshness doesn't overpower its well-structured roundness. With its hint of peardrops, it is a typical Nuits-Saint-Georges that would go perfectly with some Easter ham in aspic and parsley. Since 1990, this estate has been cultivating fruit as well as vines.
🔑 Dom. Olivier-Gard, Concœur-et-Corboin, 21700 Nuits-Saint-Georges, tel. 03.80.61.00.43, fax 03.80.61.38.45 ☒ 🍷 by appt.
🔑 Manuel Olivier

DOM. POULLEAU PERE ET FILS 1998★★

□ 0.29 ha 2,700 30–49 F

This wine has everyone around the table in agreement, and it deserves its *coup de cœur*. A very fine wine, expressive, with lots of class – these are just some of the appreciative comments found on the tasting slips. It has an intense straw colour, with a distinctive nose (broom, peach . . .) and a perfect palate.
🔑 Dom. Poulleau Père et Fils, rue du Pied-de-la-Vallée, 21190 Volnay, tel. 03.80.21.62.61, fax 03.80.26.45.90 ☒ 🍷 by appt.

DOM. VINCENT PRUNIER 1998

□ 3.5 ha 4,000 20–29 F

It is inevitable that an Aligoté from Auxey might think it has something in common with a Chardonnay. This is certainly the case with this wine. A nice-looking wine, an attractive gold colour, very agreeable on the palate, it finishes with a peach kernel flavour that does it no disservice. Definitely ready to drink now,

and pleasant at that. A typical example of the Côte's specific character.
🔑 Vincent Prunier, rte. de Beaune, 21190 Auxey-Duresses, tel. 03.80.21.27.77, fax 03.80.21.68.87 ☑ 🍷 by appt.

DOM. DES REMPARTS 1999★★

☐ 12.6 ha 30,000 ■ 🌡 30–49 F

Saint-Bris-le-Vineux boasts a 13th century church and a 16th century château, making it one of the most charming villages in France. There is plenty of history here, but also some wonderful wine-producers like the Sorin family, that has been producing wine here for 17 generations. This Aligoté is no sloth. It is fresh, mischievous, charming, a complex wine with menthol and floral aromas. Very good.
🔑 Dom. des Remparts, 6, rte. de Champs, 89530 Saint-Bris-le-Vineux, tel. 03.86.53.33.59, fax 03.86.53.62.12 ☑ 🍷 by appt.
🔑 Sorin

CH. DE ROUGEON 1998★

☐ n.c. n.c. ■ 30–49 F

A light perfume of apples and pears hovers round the glass, though the main character of this wine is wax and honey. Having said that, it doesn't have too much of the Chardonnay about it, and perks up in the mouth to do a pleasantly sharp pirouette.
🔑 Bouchard Père et Fils, Ch. de Beaune, 21200 Beaune, tel. 03.80.24.80.24, fax 03.80.22.55.88, e-mail france@bouchard.pereetfils.com 🍷 by appt.

DOM. ROUX PERE ET FILS 1998

☐ 5 ha 24,000 ■ 🌡 30–49 F

The Roux brothers went to a good school, and here they have cooked up for us an Aligoté 98 with shifting mineral-floral aromas. Fruity, it fills the mouth and tantallises the taste buds. Quite engaging.
🔑 Dom. Roux Père et Fils, 21190 Saint-Aubin, tel. 03.80.21.32.92, fax 03.80.21.35.00 ☑ 🍷 by appt.

CAVE DE SAINTE-MARIE-LA-BLANCHE 1998

☐ 4 ha 10,000 ■ 🌡 20–29 F

Essential investment is being made in refurbishing and updating this co-operative. Their crystalline-coloured Aligoté is just as an Aligoté should be: a pleasant nose, a palate that is like biting into a crisp green apple. Very agreeable and good to drink now.
🔑 Cave de Sainte-Marie-la-Blanche, rte. de Verdun, 21200 Bligny-lès-Beaune, tel. 03.80.26.60.60, fax 03.80.26.54.47 ☑ 🍷 ev. day except Sun. 8am–12 noon 2pm–7pm

DOM. SAINT-PRIX 1998★★

☐ 2.5 ha 12,000 ■ 30–49 F

This 98 Aligoté has fullness and character aplenty. Pale gold with shades of gilt, it is fruity, generous, with good body and style. A real find. Produced by an estate with an excellent reputation.
🔑 Dom. Bersan et Fils, 20, rue du Dr Tardieux, 89530 Saint-Bris-le-Vineux, tel. 03.86.53.33.73, fax 03.86.53.38.45 ☑ 🍷 ev. day 8am–12.30pm 1.30pm–6pm; Sun. 8am–12.30pm; groups by appt.

MICHEL SARRAZIN ET FILS 1998

☐ 1.5 ha 12,000 ■ 🌡 30–49 F

Light straw in colour, some depth on the nose, fruity (apple). A fullness that follows through to the finish and a rich, tender character, neither too flabby nor too tart. Approachable and full. An easy-drinking 98 that is true to the spirit of the Côte Chalonnaise.
🔑 Michel Sarrazin et Fils, Charnailles, 71640 Jambles, tel. 03.85.44.30.57, fax 03.85.44.31.22 ☑ 🍷 ev. day except Sun. 9am–12 noon 2pm–7pm

CLAUDE ET THOMAS SEGUIN 1998★★

☐ 5 ha 3,000 ■ 🌡 20–29 F

Good Aligotés from the Yonne are rare in 1998. You need to search in the best wine-cellars to find them. This is one of them. Very characteristic, from its colour to the hint of bitterness at the finish. F.F.F., which does not (despite local team AJ Auxerre) mean the French Federation of Football, but frank, fresh and fruity.
🔑 EARL Claude et Thomas Seguin, 3 bis, rue Haute, 89530 Saint-Bris-le-Vineux, tel. 03.86.53.37.39, fax 03.86.53.61.12 ☑ 🍷 ev. day 8am–8pm

HUBERT ET JEAN-PAUL TABIT 1998★

☐ 7 ha 20,000 ■ 🌡 30–49 F

This bottle's parchment label, with rolled-up edges showing a background of barrels and ancient vaults, heralds a really pleasurable wine. This is a refined 98, discreetly-coloured, a little on the wild side, but attractive. Mature, yet still retaining its freshness. Best enjoyed on the spot, combined with a visit to the estate's well-presented museum of wine-making tools.
🔑 Hubert et Jean-Paul Tabit, 2, rue Dorée, 89530 Saint-Bris-le-Vineux, tel. 03.86.53.33.83, fax 03.86.53.67.97 ☑ 🍷 ev. day 8am–12 noon 2pm–8pm; Sun. by appt.

TERROIRS ET SECRETS DE BOURGOGNE 1999

☐ n.c. 50,000 ■ 20–29 F

Terroirs and Secrets of Burgundy, a big name from Patriarche in Beaune for this very young 99, which may prickle the tongue a little now, but already shows signs of stardom. The fruit is fresh and will doubtless remain so. An agreeable wine, and not too acidic for this grape variety.
🔑 Patriarche Père et Fils, 5, rue du Collège, 21200 Beaune, tel. 03.80.24.53.01, fax 03.80.24.53.03 ☑ 🍷 ev. day 9am–12 noon 2pm–6pm

DOM. VERRET 1999★

☐ 12.75 ha n.c. 30–49 F

One of the most typical of all the Yonne Aligotés, this wine is pale yellow with hints of gold. It successfully balances mineral qualities with fruit along with a lively character. A nice snail feuilleté would go well with it.

Dom. Verret, 7, rte. de Champs, B.P. 4, 89530 Saint-Bris-le-Vineux, tel. 03.86.53.31.81, fax 03.86.53.89.61, e-mail bruno.verret@wanadoo.fr by appt.

VEUVE HENRI MORONI 1998

☐ 2 ha 16,000 30–49 F

Is this wine light yellow or pale gold? It is the kind of question our jury loves to debate. They are all in agreement, however, in their judgement of its frank, fresh, lively attack, in noticing a hint of herbaceousness round the edges and remarking a certain bitterness at the finish. A classic Aligoté that can be drunk immediately.

Veuve Henri Moroni, 1, rue de l'Abreuvoir, 21190 Puligny-Montrachet, tel. 03.80.21.30.48, fax 03.80.21.33.08, e-mail veuve.moroni@wanadoo.fr by appt.

DOM. DES VIGNES DES DEMOISELLES 1998★

☐ 0.5 ha 3,600 30–49 F

This menthol, lemony wine has no need of the Town Hall or parish priest to enjoy a great romance with the person who drinks it. Its acidity shows at the finish. Altogether a fresh and fruity wine, characteristic of the Hautes-Côtes de Beaune near the Maranges.

SCEA du dom. Gabriel Demangeot et Fils, rue de Berfey, 21340 Change, tel. 03.85.91.11.10, fax 03.85.91.16.83 by appt.

Bourgogne Passetoutgrain

This appellation applies exclusively to red and rosé wines produced in the inner part of the Bourgogne Grand Ordinaire area, and it requires the wines to be made from a blend of Pinot Noir and Gamay Noir grapes. The blend must contain a minimum of one-third of Pinot Noir. Current thinking holds that the best wines are made of roughly equal quantities of grapes from the two varieties, with a slight preponderance of Pinot Noir.

The rosé wines are obtained by the *saignée* method, a technical process distinct from the Vins Gris, which are obtained by the direct pressing of black grapes and vinifying them like white wines. In the *saignée* process the grapes are left to macerate, and the juice is extracted (or 'bled') only when the wine-maker has obtained the desired colour – which can very well occur in the middle of the night! Very little Passetoutgrain Rosé is made, and in general this appellation is regarded as a red wine. It is produced mainly in the Saône-et-Loire (about two-thirds), the remainder being made in the Côte d'Or or the Yonne valley. Between 65,000 and 75,000 hl (1,716,000 and 1,980,000 gal) are made annually, with 71,708 hl (1,893,091 gal) being produced in 1999. The wines are light, deliciously flavoured and should be drunk young.

JEAN BROCARD-GRIVOT 1998★

■ 25.86 ha n.c. 20–29 F

The *Lord of Vergy* is one of the rare minor productions of the 20th century to have had a future, having been revived at the Bouffes-Parisiens in 2000 with Jean Richard, Roger Pierre and Jean-Marc Thibault. So this Vergy Passetoutgrain probably deserves a little doff of the hat. A good purple colour, a Pinot-style nose and a little roughness that does it no harm at all.

Jean Brocard-Grivot, rue Basse, 21220 Reulle-Vergy, tel. 03.80.61.42.14, fax 03.80.61.42.14 by appt.

MICHEL CHAMPION 1998

■ 0.6 ha 4,000 20–29 F

There is 25% Pinot noir, 75% Gamay in this wine, which manages to successfully combine these two sometimes contradictory grape varieties. Pinkish ruby-red, with a good nose and a lively mouth, it is not bad at all. Elegant even for the Côte Chalonnaise.

Michel Champion, Cercot, 71390 Moroges, tel. 03.85.47.90.94, fax 03.85.47.99.53 ev. day 8am–12 noon 2pm–7pm

MAURICE CHENU 1999★

■ n.c. 30,000 30–49 F

Intense purple, quite spicy, with a fruitiness that comes to life on the palate and manages to keep the tannins in check to achieve a supple, attractive wine. A good example of the appellation. Although the Chenu business has been taken over by a native of Alsace

Tresch), the new owner plainly has Burgundy in his bones.
🔑 Bourgognes Chenu-Tresch SA, chem. de la Pierre-qui-Vire, 21200 Montagny-lès-Beaune, tel. 03.80.26.37.37, fax 03.80.24.14.81

DOM. CORNU 1998★

■ 2.26 ha n.c. 30–49 F

When you buy a Passetoutgrain at Magny-lès-Villers, you know what you are dealing with, and this good 98 represents the appellation well. Bright ruby-red with aromas of red berry fruits, it is a wine to drink on a Sunday when the children come to visit. Well-rounded it has a *je-ne-sais-quoi* of freshness. There is an interesting hint of almonds on the finish.
🔑 Dom. Cornu, rue du Meix-Grenot, 21700 Magny-lès-Villers, tel. 03.80.62.92.05, fax 03.80.62.72.22 ☒ Y by appt.

CAVE DES VIGNERONS DE GENOUILLY 1998

■ 8 ha 8,000 20–29 F

This Saône-et-Loire co-operative cultivates 60 ha (148 acres) of vineyards. Their Passetoutgrain doesn't try to boast about itself, and doesn't change the subject: it is wine pure and simple. It has presence and plenty of red berry fruit. Lots of potential.
🔑 Cave des vignerons de Genouilly, 71460 Genouilly, tel. 03.85.49.23.72, fax 03.85.49.23.58 ☒ Y ev. day except Sun. 8am–12 noon 2pm–6pm

DOM. GUEUGNON-REMOND 1999★

■ 26.54 ha 1,800 30–49 F

The spelling on the label leaves something to be desired: it is not 'passe-tout-grains'. 'Tout-grain', maybe, but this is a typical Burgundy niggle. The wine itself is well-balanced, harmonious, rich and fruity. A touch too much alcohol on the finish, but we forgive it! A decent wine (35% Gamay, 65% Pinot), rare in Mâconnais, and a well-made one.
🔑 Dom. Gueugnon-Remond, chem. de la Cave, 71850 Charnay-lès-Mâcon, tel. 03.85.29.23.88, fax 03.85.20.20.72 ☒ Y by appt.
🔑 Remond

DOM. DE LA TOUR BAJOLE Les Lyres 1998★

■ 2.3 ha 2,000 20–29 F

Pinot Noir and Gamay are mixed in equal quantaties in this well-coloured, vegetal, Morello cherry 98. *En lyre* means that the vines are trained to resemble a lyre, an unusual system pioneered by this estate. The Gamay gets the best of it, but then if Gamay is here at all it is not just to play a walk-on part.
🔑 EARL M.-A. et J.-C. Dessendre, Dom. de La Tour-Bajole, Les Ombrots, 71490 Saint-Maurice-lès-Couches, tel. 03.85.45.52.90, fax 03.85.45.52.90 ☒ Y by appt.

LA TOUR DU PRIEURE 1999★★

■ 1 ha 3,000 30–49 F

This nicely textured Passetoutgrain comes from the very heart of South Burgundy, the wine region of the monks of Cluny, and consists of 30% Pinot and 70% Gamay. It is light violet in colour, with a wonderful fruitiness that explodes on the palate, the tannins acting to break the fall. Very good, and would go perfectly with eggs *en meurette*.
🔑 Bernard Dorry, La Tour du Prieuré, 71960 Bussières, tel. 03.85.37.75.43, fax 03.85.37.75.43 ☒ Y by appt.

DOM. LEJEUNE 1998★

■ 0.35 ha 3,000 30–49 F

With its black cherry colour, this wine is one to keep for a barbecue (though not necessarily for next summer). It is not very developed for a 98, and still has a way to go. Mellow, yet well-structured with the usual hint of greenness. Well-made and with plenty of character.
🔑 Dom. Lejeune, La Confrérie, pl. de l'Eglise, 21630 Pommard, tel. 03.80.22.90.88, fax 03.80.22.90.88 ☒ Y by appt.
🔑 Famille Jullien de Pommerol

LES CHAMPS DE L'ABBAYE 1998★★

■ 0.6 ha 2,500 30–49 F

Isabelle and Alain Hasard bought their first vines in 1996 and set themselves up in business the following year. Using biodynamic methods, they produce a 50/50 Passetoutgrain which is a fine example of the style: blackcurrant leaves, round and full of vigour. It emerges from its shell little by little, like a trusting snail.
🔑 Alain Hasard, Les Champs de l'Abbaye, Le Bourg, 71510 Saint-Sernin-du-Plain, tel. 03.85.45.59.32, fax 03.85.45.59.32 ☒ Y by appt.

DOM. CHANTAL LESCURE 1998

■ 0.6 ha 1,500 30–49 F

Apparently, this wine from Nuits-Saint-Georges is 30% Gamay, 70% Pinot Noir, an unusual but not unacceptable blend, though generally the proportions are the other way round. It has a medium but solid colour, a mixture of raspberry and redcurrant aromas, and an overwhelmingly tasty palate. You could happily quaff it with just *boeuf bourguignon*.
🔑 Dom. Chantal Lescure, 34 A, rue Thurot, 21700 Nuits-Saint-Georges, tel. 03.80.61.16.79, fax 03.80.61.36.64, e-mail domaine-lescure.com ☒ Y by appt.

ARMELLE ET JEAN-MICHEL MOLIN 1998★

■ 1.2 ha 730 20–29 F

This wine certainly doesn't stint on colour, nor is it stingy on the nose. It is tenacious on the palate. Here's a wine for you! A good example of the appellation; they make it in Côtes-de-Nuits. The hint of austerity at the

BURGUNDY

finish does nothing to change our general impression.
EARL Armelle et Jean-Michel Molin, 54, rte des Grands-Crus, 21220 Fixin, tel. 03.80.52.21.28, fax 03.80.59.96.99 by appt.

MORIN PERE ET FILS 1998★

■ n.c. 120,000 30–49 F

This elegant and fine Passetoutgrain seems determined to break out of the mould and move in higher circles. Its herbaceous, forest-floor flavours are discreet and delicate from start to finish. What style. General de Gaulle, who used to serve wines from Morin (which now belongs to J.-Cl. Boisset) at the Elysée, would have kept this one for a *pot-au-feu à la Boisserie.*
Morin Père et Fils, 9, quai Fleury, 21700 Nuits-Saint-Georges, tel. 03.80.62.61.42, fax 03.80.62.37.38 ev. day 9am–12 noon 2pm–6pm; summer 8am–7pm

DOM. THIERRY MORTET 1998★★

■ 0.15 ha 1,800 30–49 F

This is superb for the appellation. 66% Gamay, the rest Pinot – and we're in business. The colour is a little unstable, but the very first whiff of the nose brings a peppery-raspberry aroma that is incredibly distinctive. The palate is stately, well-balanced and sure of its charms. A sommelier suggests this wine should go with a goulash, but it would suit other dishes too, like *pot-au-feu* or *oeuf en meurette.*
Dom. Thierry Mortet, 16, pl. des Marronniers, 21220 Gevrey-Chambertin, tel. 03.80.51.85.07, fax 03.80.34.16.80 by appt.

DOM. JEAN ET GENO MUSSO 1998★

■ 2.09 ha 17,000 20–29 F

One of our tasters suggests pairing this wine with *tourte forestière*, which seems a good choice. Light colour, discreet nose, nice roundness. In contrast to many examples of this appellation, the alcohol stays behind the scenes, which is good. Jean and Geno Musso revived this formerly neglected estate in 1981 and now practice organic agriculture.
Jean et Geno Musso, 71490 Dracy-lès-Couches, tel. 03.85.96.18.61, fax 03.85.96.18.62 by appt.

MICHEL PICARD 1998★

■ n.c. 45,000 30–49 F

The colour is dark ruby-red, the character is light but not lacking body, the structure is built on ripe fruit, and the nose makes you want to come back to it – even if only to check on the cherry aromas that are just starting to emerge. On the right track, but best to leave it for a while.
Michel Picard, rte. de Saint-Loup-de-la-Salle, 71150 Chagny, tel. 03.85.87.51.00, fax 03.85.87.51.11

DOM. JEAN-PIERRE TRUCHETET 1998★

■ 0.63 ha 5,400 20–29 F

The Passetoutgrain is not a snobbish wine. It needs to keep its spontaneity, which this wine manages to do well. The colour is rich, almost velvety. Fresh, with fruit that expands on the palate, pleasing tannins and lively acidity. Once this has all blended in it will make a very good Côtes-de-Nuits-style 98.
Jean-Pierre Truchetet, R.N. 74, 21700 Premeaux-Prissey, tel. 03.80.61.07.22, fax 03.80.61.34.35 ev. day except Sat. Sun. 9am–12 noon 2pm–7pm; cl. 15–31 Aug.

HENRI DE VILLAMONT

Les Hobereaux 1998

■ n.c. 20,000 30–49 F

This pleasant, elegant wine is a lovely purple colour. Although lightly structured, it also has plenty of fruit and likeable aromas.
Henri de Villamont, rue du Dr-Guyot, 21420 Savigny-lès-Beaune, tel. 03.80.24.70.07, fax 03.80.22.54.31, e-mail hdv@planetb.fr ev. day except Tue. 9.30am–6.30pm; Thu. 9.30am–12 noon; cl. 15 Nov.–15 Mar.

Bourgogne Hautes-Côtes de Nuit

The appellation Bourgogne Hautes-Côtes de Nuits is most often used for red, rosé and white wines produced in the 16 communes that lie in the hinterland of the Côte, together with parts of the communes above the *appellations communales* and the crus of the Côte de Nuit. In 1999 these vineyards produced 32,738 hl (864,283 gal), of which 6,451 hl (170,306 gal) were white. The amount produced has increased significantly since 1970 when the vineyards used to produce more regional wines, essentially Bourgogne Aligoté. Extensive replanting has taken place since that time, and plants infected with phylloxera have been replanted.

In some years, the best exposed slopes produce wines that can rival some of the vineyards on the Côte; the best of them tend to be white, and it is a pity that more of the vineyards have not been planted with Chardonnay, which would undoubtedly give more reliable results more often. Along with the commitment to recreating the vineyard an equal effort has been put into encouraging tourism. In particular, a Maison des Hautes-Côtes gives visitors the chance to learn about the area and to taste the wines along with good local cuisine.

JEAN-LUC AEGERTER 1997

□ n.c. 4,000 50–69 F

There are days when everything goes right. The day we tasted this 97 was exactly one of those. The pure pale gold colour was a hit. The aromas of peach and hazelnut, enlivened by a little hint of exotic fruit, were appreciated and we were delighted with its supple, rich palate with old-fashioned charm.

Jean-Luc Aegerter, 49, rue Henri-Challand, 21700 Nuits-Saint-Georges, tel. 03.80.61.02.88, fax 03.80.62.37.99 by appt.

BERTRAND AMBROISE 1998★

□ 1.42 ha 6,000 70–99 F

This fine 98, clear yet vibrant, is developing well. This wine has promising, rustic aromas; fresh grapes followed by spring blossom. Its acidity provides backbone for the fruit without overpowering it. Take your time to enjoy its depth and richness.

Maison Bertrand Ambroise, rue de l'Eglise, 21700 Premeaux-Prissey, tel. 03.80.62.30.19, fax 03.80.62.38.69, e-mail bertrand.ambroise@wanadoo.fr by appt.

JEAN-BAPTISTE BEJOT 1998

■ n.c. 10,000 30–49 F

Deep violet with, at first, red berry fruit which after a while opens out to give some musk and forest-floor aromas. It is not a very full wine, but there is a suppleness, almost a richness, which pushes the balance in the right direction. Not to be drunk immediately.

SA Jean-Baptiste Béjot, 21190 Meursault, tel. 03.80.21.22.45, fax 03.80.21.28.05

DOM. DU BOIS GUILLAUME 1998

□ 0.58 ha 4,000 30–49 F

This is a distinctive, delicate amber-gold wine with a subtle touch of oak. It retains both freshness and fruitiness, which assures us of its ageing potential. Still tannic, it should improve with a year or two in the cellar.

Jean-Yves Devevey, Dom. du Bois Guillaume, rue de Breuil, 71150 Demigny, tel. 03.85.49.91.11, fax 03.85.49.91.59 ev. day except Sun. 8am–7pm

PIERRE CORNU-CAMUS 1998★

■ 0.51 ha 3,900 30–49 F

This wine is a saver: every day it adds to its piggy bank a deep purple-red colour, a raspberry nose with a hint of hawthorn, freshness, and still-present tannins. All with an eye on the day when, in two years' time, it is going to reap the rewards of its prudent investment and accompany a dish of eggs *en meurette*.

Pierre Cornu-Camus, 2, rue Varlot, 21420 Echevronne, tel. 03.80.21.57.23, fax 03.80.26.11.94 by appt.

YVAN DUFOULEUR

Les Dames Huguette 1997★★

□ 0.3 ha 2,000 50–69 F

Yvan Dufouleur presents this superb Dames Huguette (a *climat* on the Nuits hilltops), which is a princely Chardonnay that nearly earns a *coup de cœur*. Deep yellow, very open, at first a little toasty but soon followed by rich fruit, almond and green apple. Then, with a change of scenery, we move onto citrus fruits. It certainly pulls out all the stops, and the light touch of greenness at the finish is an attractive high point. The **98 Rouge** is a decent wine that will open up. It receives one star. **Les Dames Huguette 97 Rouge** is delightful, and receives two stars. You can drink it now or wait if you prefer.

Yvan Dufouleur, Dom. des Belles Chaumes, 18, rue Thurot, 21700 Nuits-Saint-Georges, tel. 03.80.62.31.00, fax 03.80.62.31.00 ev. day 9am–7pm

DOM. FRANCOIS GERBET 1997

■ 6 ha 30,000 50–69 F

This part of the estate at Concœur, in the upper parts of Nuits, was originally fallow land. However, François Gerbet, father of the two daughters who are the current owners, decided to clear this land and plant vines. It produces a deeply fruity 97, strongly influenced by its terroir. As intense and straightforward on the eye as on the palate.

Marie-Andrée et Chantal Gerbet, Maison des Vins, 2, pl. de l'Eglise, 21700 Vosne-Romanée, tel. 03.80.62.32.99, fax 03.80.62.32.99 ev. day 10am–12 noon 2pm–6pm; cl. 1st–20 Jan.

EMMANUEL GIBOULOT 1998★

■ 0.5 ha 2,600 50–69 F

Lacking a little fruit on the nose because of its strong gamey character – and there is a lot of hunting in the Hautes-Côtes – this Pinot nonetheless has a good pedigree. It is powerful without being heavy, slightly chewy at the end, deep dark red in colour, and certainly not lacking in youth or energy. A wine which the Burgundians might describe as 'light and solid'.

Emmanuel Giboulot, Combertault, 21200 Beaune, tel. 03.80.26.52.85, fax 03.80.26.53.67 by appt.

DOM. GLANTENET

Elevé en fût de chêne 1998★

■ 9.44 ha 5,000 30–49 F

The Glantenets have lived in Burgundy since the 15th century and have been wine-producers since the 18th century. Today, they have 25 ha (62 acres) of vines. This pleasant wine does not hide the fact that it has been matured in barrel, but the flavours are well-integrated. It has strong tannins and presents also an original combination of aromas, with toasted almond making a pleasant pairing with cherry. Its colour is very deep and vibrant. A youthful wine that you should keep a year or two before drinking. This estate has only been selling direct since 1999.

⊶ Dom. Glantenet Père et Fils, rue de l'Aye, 21700 Magny-lès-Villers, tel. 03.80.62.91.61, fax 03.80.62.74.79, e-mail domaine.glantenet@wanadoo.fr ☑ Y ev. day except Sun. 8am–12 noon 1.30pm–7pm

BLANCHE ET HENRI GROS

Vieilles vignes 1998★★

■ 2.5 ha 3,500 50–69 F

It is very easy to understand why all those handsome knights were once in love with the Lady of Vergy. She probably kept a wonderful cellar, if this wine is anything to go by. It is almost too big for its AOC and gains a *coup de cœur* for its magnificent qualities. A dark red colour, with a hint of blackcurrant: they certainly know what they are doing in the Hautes-Côtes-de-Nuits. Full, complete and irreproachable, with an elegant oakiness that further enhances the wine. The **98 Blanc** (30–49F), also very well-made and balanced, receives one star.

⊶ Henri Gros, 21220 Chambœuf, tel. 03.80.51.81.20, fax 03.80.49.71.75 ☑ Y by appt.

DOM. GROS FRERE ET SŒUR

1998

□ 2.5 ha 8,845 70–99 F

Allegro vivace: the pale yellow colour with hints of emerald. *Andante*: a small nose that gradually grows bigger and toastier. *Allegro assai*: a third movement, round and fresh and fruity, with an excellent fresh backbone. The vines are situated on Nuits-Saint-Georges, near Concœur.

⊶ SCE Gros Frère et Sœur, 6, rue des Grands-Crus, 21700 Vosne-Romanée, tel. 03.80.61.12.43, fax 03.80.61.34.05 ☑ Y by appt.

⊶ Bernard Gros

DOM. DOMINIQUE GUYON

Cuvée des Dames de Vergy 1997

■ 21.8 ha 60,000 50–69 F

Twenty-five years ago, Dominique Guyon 'sewed together' hundreds of patches of land on the hillside at Meuilley that faces Vergy and the rising sun. The result is an interesting wine, matured 12 months in barrel. A violet aureole is visible beneath the brilliant red colour, perfumed with strawberries (Meuilley strawberries were once famous) just as it ought to be, and it has well-balanced fruit, tannin and acidity. An exemplary wine.

⊶ Dom. Dominique Guyon, 21420 Savigny-lès-Beaune, tel. 03.80.67.13.24, fax 03.80.66.85.87, e-mail vins@guyon-bourgogne.com ☑ Y by appt.

MONGEARD-MUGNERET 1998★

□ 0.3 ha 2,500 50–69 F

The Mongeard-Mugneret family are not afraid of hard work, as they proved in 1991, with the establishment of the estate of Mas Crémat, close to Rivesaltes. Their large range of *Grands Crus* is very profitable, along with this vineyard that is situated, we think, in the commune of Arcenat. It produces a Burgundy, with pretty shades of colour, and an upfront aroma of linden flowers. Supple and with plenty of stuffing; this wine should be put aside to rest a while before drinking.

⊶ Dom. Mongeard-Mugneret, 14, rue de la Fontaine, 21700 Vosne-Romanée, tel. 03.80.61.11.95, fax 03.80.62.35.75, e-mail mongeard@axnet.fr Y by appt.

DOM. DE MONTMAIN

Le Rouard 1997★

□ 7 ha 35,000 100–149 F

This wine has already been very successful in the past, notably with the 91 vintage, and it has become a great classic of the appellation, carried onward and upward by its 'inventor', Bernard Hudelot. A lovely colour with flinty, hawthorne aromas presenting a Chardonnay that is enlivened by an after-taste of pear. A complex wine with an great finish. Already very attractive it would improve with a little ageing. The modern buildings on the estate, reminiscent of Californian wineries, are worth a visit.

⊶ Dom. de Montmain, 21700 Villars-Fontaine, tel. 03.80.62.31.94, fax 03.80.61.02.31 ☑ Y ev. day except Sun. 8.30am–12 noon 1.30pm–6pm; Sat. by appt.

⊶ Bernard Hudelot

DOM. HENRI NAUDIN-FERRAND 1998★

□ 1.17 ha 7,323 30–49 F

We would be surprised not to see them in such company: Anne and Claire Naudin. This wine has a light yellow colour and noticeable barrel-ageing with its toasty perfumes. Lively, smooth, elegant attack.

⊶ Dom. Henri Naudin-Ferrand, rue du Meix-Grenot, 21700 Magny-lès-Villers, tel. 03.80.62.91.50, fax 03.80.62.91.77, e-mail dom.hnf.@wanadoo.fr ☑ Y by appt.

OLIVIER-GARD 1998

■ 1 ha 4,750 30–49 F

Concœur-et-Corboin is a hamlet, attached to Nuits-Saint-Georges, on the edge of the Hautes-Côtes. This family concern, following the spirit of the region, grows red berry fruit to make into liqueurs, syrups and jams. The Cot arrived in 1993, and has done well, producing this wine with Pinot Noir and black cherry flavours, a tiny bit gamey, tannic and sturdy. It has enough body to answer, in time, for its character.

Dom. Olivier-Gard, Concœur-et-Corboin, 21700 Nuits-Saint-Georges, tel. 03.80.61.00.43, fax 03.80.61.38.45 Y by appt.
Manuel Olivier

DOM. DENIS PHILIBERT

Elevé en fût de chêne 1998★

■ n.c. 20,000 50–69 F

Here we are presented with an elegant 98 with a black cherry colour of medium intensity and a nose hinting of raspberry. Well-balanced acidity and sweetness of fruit on the palate with a good finish. Clean, fresh and robust. Was Burgundy not converted to Christianity by Saint Philibert?

Dom. Denis Philibert, 1, rue Ziem, 21200 Beaune, tel. 03.80.24.05.88, fax 03.80.22.37.08 Y ev. day 9am–7pm

CH. DE PREMEAUX 1998★

■ 2.1 ha 7,000 50–69 F

Hautes-Côtes-de-Nuits from the hills of Premeaux. These are two excellent wines that stand shoulder to shoulder when it comes to quality. The **98 Blanc**, a good example of its kind, needs a while before the flavour of the oak blends in. We confess to a preference for its red brother, which gets the popular vote. Mauvey-purple in colour, overflowing with pleasing aromas, with blackcurrant turning up to do a lap of honour on the palate. All in beautiful harmony.

Dom. du Ch. de Premeaux, 21700 Premeaux-Prissey, tel. 03.80.62.30.64, fax 03.80.62.39.28 Y by appt.
Pelletier

ROPITEAU 1998★

□ n.c. 50,000 50–69 F

It was on the 4 August in 1961 that the wine producers of the Hautes-Côtes received their AOC. It was a richly-deserved honour, as is plain to see when you taste this typical Chardonnay, with its flowery and citrusy aromas, and right, sharp colour. Robust, yet lively and fresh, and with staying power and good length.

Ropiteau Frères, 13, rue du 11-Novembre, 21190 Meursault, tel. 03.80.21.69.20, fax 03.80.21.69.29 Y ev. day 9am–7pm; cl. mid-Nov. until Easter

GUY SIMON ET FILS

Les Dames Huguette Vieilli en fût de chêne 1998★

■ 0.5 ha 3,000 50–69 F

Guy Simon and his wife have played a very active role in the comeback of the Hautes-Côtes. Here, they present several *cuvées* for tasting. The AOC **98 Rouge Sans Dénomination Élevée en Fût** (one star), is worth a recommendation. It is a perfect Sunday wine to go with a roast, as is the **Cuvée des Dames Huguette Rouge 98 Élevée en Cuve**, also recommended. But most of all it was the barrel-matured Dames Huguette 98 that really attracted us. 'Only too delighted to drink it', noted one taster. Intense ruby in colour, with a fresh, almost floral nose and a hint of liquorice, it is an extremely well-balanced wine: solid, rich and attractive.

Guy Simon et Fils, 21700 Marey-lès-Fussey, tel. 03.80.62.91.85, fax 03.80.62.71.82 Y by appt.

DOM. THEVENOT-LE BRUN ET FILS

Clos du Vignon 1997★

■ 5.1 ha 11,000 50–69 F

Like Jean-Marc Roulot in Meursault, Thévenot-Le Brun senior has an unusual hobby for a wine-producer: he is a keen actor. He has even performed in a Shakespeare play at the Avignon festival. His Clos de Vignon 97 is very representative of the Hautes-Côtes towards Marey-lès-Fussey. It has a touch of brick red in the colour, powerful with a good level of acidity, and intense red berry fruit flavours. The wine-producer knows his mise en scène and does it well. The **98 Blanc** does not go unnoticed, and receives a commendation.

Dom. Thévenot-Le Brun et Fils, 21700 Marey-lès-Fussey, tel. 03.80.62.91.64, fax 03.80.62.99.81, e-mail thevenot-le-brun@wanadoo.fr Y by appt.

JEAN-PIERRE TRUCHETET 1997

□ 0.66 ha 5,700 30–49 F

Not terribly lively and bright, but still a pleasing light gold colour. There is something over-ripe about the mineral nose. Lemony on the palate, it has a decent character and is ready to drink.

Jean-Pierre Truchetet, R.N. 74, 21700 Premeaux-Prissey, tel. 03.80.61.07.22, fax 03.80.61.34.35 Y ev. day except Sat. Sun. 9am–12 noon 2pm–7pm; cl. 15–31 Aug.

DOM. ALAIN VERDET

Vieilles vignes 1997★

□ 2 ha 5,000 70–99 F

This wine-producer from Arcenant (a village known for fruit-growing) also makes excellent liqueurs, as well as *marc* and Fine de Bourgogne. Being a traditionalist, he has added some of the rare Beurot grape to his Chardonnay, 20% (so they tell us). Light gold in colour, its brioche nose is very much

influenced by its terroir. Only just beginning to develop. A curiosity for connaisseurs.
Alain Verdet, rue des Berthières, 21700 Arcenant, tel. 03.80.61.08.10, fax 03.80.61.08.10 by appt.

HENRI DE VILLAMONT

Aux Dames Huguette 1998★

n.c. 10,000 50–69 F

Here are two lovely wines from this wine-merchant. A respectable **98 Blanc**, which is given a commendation for its fruitiness, and this powerful yet elegant red, whose fruity bouquet with strong floral notes make it a very agreeable prospect. A wine with character, it will benefit from laying down for a short while.

Henri de Villamont, rue du Dr-Guyot, 21420 Savigny-lès-Beaune, tel. 03.80.24.70.07, fax 03.80.22.54.31, e-mail hdv@planetb.fr ev. day except Tue. 9.30am–6.30pm; Thu. 9.30am–12 noon; cl. 15 Nov.–15 Mar.

CH. DE VILLERS-LA-FAYE 1998

2 ha 8,000 30–49 F

This wine comes from Serge Valot, a wine-grower from Hospices-de-Beaune, who has now put his son Samuel in charge of the business. Pale but gleaming gold colour, with a well-developed, clean and straightforward nose. A citrus attack leads on to reveal suppleness and vigour. It doesn't have great length but there is plenty of time to get something out of it. Jacques Rivette filmed some scenes for his film about Joan of Arc here.

SCEA Ch. de Villers-la-Faye, rue du Château, 21700 Villers-la-Faye, tel. 03.80.62.91.57, fax 03.80.62.71.32 by appt.

Valot Père et Fils

Bourgogne Hautes-Côtes de Beaune

The Appellation Bourgogne Hautes-Côtes de Beaune applies to about twenty communes, extending in the north into the Saône-et-Loire. In 1999 the quantity of wines produced under the appellation totalled 43,476 hl (1,147,766 gal), including 8,223 hl (217,087 gal) of white, rather more than the Hautes-Côtes de Nuits production. In situation, the two areas are quite similar, and a considerable area is given over to growing Aligoté and Gamay.

The Coopérative des Hautes-Côtes, which started life in Orches, a hamlet near Baubigny is now based under the 'banner' of Pommard, at the intersection of the D973 and the main RN74, just south of Beaune. A significant amount of Bourgogne Hautes-Côtes de Beaune is vinified there. The vineyards have greatly developed since the years 1970–75, as in the north.

The countryside is more picturesque than that of the Hautes-Côtes de Nuits, and there are many places to visit, including Orches, La Rochepot and its château and Nolay, a little Burgundian town. It is worth adding that the Hautes-Côtes formerly grew a variety of crops and is still an area where soft fruits are grown to supply the liqueur-makers of Nuits-Saint-Georges and Dijon. The fruit liqueurs and brandies made from these blackcurrants and raspberries are of excellent quality. There is a single appellation for the pear brandy of Monts-de-Côte-d'Or, which is also made here.

ARNOUX PERE ET FILS 1998★

1.3 ha 6,000 30–49 F

A soft, round and light wine. Crimson in colour, the fruit is forward and has a pleasant blackcurrant nose. The palate shows a roundness balanced well by the lively acidity and delicate tannins. A wine that you don't need to keep 'for the next time'.

Arnoux Père et Fils, rue des Brenots, 21200 Chorey-lès-Beaune, tel. 03.80.22.57.98, fax 03.80.22.16.85 by appt.

JEAN-NOEL BAZIN 1998★

2.5 ha 3,000 30–49 F

This wine knows its stuff. Young and already mellow, very floral, subtle and consistant, it performs like an expert. Bright in colour with a nose that sticks to the subject, a convincing palate, and a finish with the longest *caudalies*. Will keep. The **98 Blanc**, which gets a commendation but no star, is well-made and would be a useful addition to your cellar.

Jean-Noël Bazin, Les Petits Vergers, 21340 La Rochepot, tel. 03.80.21.75.49, fax 03.80.21.83.71 by appt.

DOM. DU BOIS GUILLAUME

Les Champs Perdrix 1998★

□ 2.1 ha 13,000 30–49 F

Does the ancient oak tree that is displayed so prominently on the label mean that this is going to be a very oaky wine? Well, no, thank goodness. This greenish-gold 98 has concentrated aromas of acacia and hawthorn. The fruit flavours (grape) add intensity to the palate and give it an exotic touch. It needs a little time to open out completely.

Jean-Yves Devevey, Dom. du Bois Guillaume, rue de Breuil, 71150 Demigny, tel. 03.85.49.91.11, fax 03.85.49.91.59 ev. day except Sun. 8am–7pm

DOM. JEAN-MARC BOULEY 1997★

■ 1.2 ha 8,000 30–49 F

This year Jean-Marc Bouley presents a lovely, smooth 97 with plenty of red berry fruit, an astonishing personality, and totally faithful to the vintage. 'Easy to let yourself be sweet-talked by this one', noted one taster. No regrets, either, with its soft, warm, consistently fruity approach and elegance. An attractive rather than a powerful wine with a subtle bitter finish. We would recommend laying it down for two or three years, but some people will already find it enjoyable to drink now.

Jean-Marc Bouley, chem. de la Cave, 21190 Volnay, tel. 03.80.21.62.33, fax 03.80.21.64.78 by appt.

DOM. J.-FRANCOIS BOUTHENET

Au Paradis Elevé en fût de chêne 1998★

■ 2.7 ha 1000 30–49 F

A well-made wine that ought to be allowed to age. Cherry red, it shifts between hints of liquorice, oak and ever-present fruit, then all this steps aside for the freshness to come through. Well-structured, with firm tannins and a good finish. It has a long life ahead of it.

Jean-François Bouthenet, Mercey, 71150 Cheilly-lès-Maranges, tel. 03.85.91.14.29, fax 03.85.91.18.24 by appt.

CHRISTOPHE BUISSON

Les Pierres Percées 1998

■ 0.26 ha n.c. 30–49 F

The Burgundians adore the *'pierres percées'* that adorn their parks and gardens, but do they make a good wine? The answer is yes. This former wine-broker brings us a light red-brick Pinot Noir with a sweet and pleasant fruitiness, supple and round.

Christophe Buisson, 21190 Saint-Romain, tel. 03.80.21.63.92, fax 03.80.21.67.03 by appt.

DENIS CARRE 1998★

□ n.c. n.c. 30–49 F

A pleasant toasty nose embellished with spring blossom and citrus fruit with a background of oak. Full, sweet, long, with well-balanced acidity that adds structure. The influence of the wood still needs some time to mellow and integrate.

Denis Carré, rue du Puits-Bouret, 21190 Meloisey, tel. 03.80.26.02.21, fax 03.80.26.04.64 ev. day 8am–6pm

RENE CHARACHE-BERGERET

1999★

□ 1 ha 2,300 30–49 F

This elegant and soft Chardonnay dozes off a bit on the finish, but banishes all incongruous woodiness. Well done! An approachable, easy-to-drink wine.

René Charache-Bergeret, 21200 Bouze-lès-Beaune, tel. 03.80.26.00.86, fax 03.80.26.00.86 by appt.

DOM. FRANCOIS CHARLES ET FILS 1998★

□ 2 ha 12,000 30–49 F

An excellent Burgundian Chardonnay. Both classic and modern, it combines grapefruit, lemon, and orange peel flavours with a light mineral quality. A good moment to remember that the estate produced a very good 94 red.

Dom. François Charles et Fils, 21190 Nantoux, tel. 03.80.26.01.20, fax 03.80.26.04.84 by appt.

DOM. CHEVROT 1998★

□ 0.7 ha 3,500 30–49 F

An 11.60-ha (29-acre) family estate situated in Maranges. Pale, luminous gold and flowery, with some citrus fruit bitterness. Full and generous, this is a well-balanced wine with an interesting length. It should be left for a while to allow to develop. The **98 Rouge** smells of roses and, though still closed, already seems promising. The jury gave it a commendation.

Catherine et Fernand Chevrot, Dom. Chevrot, 19, rte. de Couches, 71150 Cheilly-lès-Maranges, tel. 03.85.91.10.55, fax 03.85.91.13.24, e-mail domaine.chevrot@wanadoo.fr ev. day 9am–12 noon 2pm–6pm; Sun. 9am–12 noon

HENRI DELAGRANGE ET FILS

1998★

□ 3 ha 25,000 30–49 F

This wine takes to the glass like a fish to water! It just loves it. Light gold in colour, with aromas of toast and hawthorn followed by a supple then fresh palate. A tasty wine that just needs a trout dish to make it complete. Will be equally pleasurable when tasted in two to three years' time.

Dom. Henri Delagrange et Fils, rue de la Cure, 21190 Volnay, tel. 03.80.21.61.88, fax 03.80.21.67.09 by appt.

RODOLPHE DEMOUGEOT

Vieilles vignes 1998★

■ n.c. 7,000 30–49 F

Too-green grapes is a familiar enough problem, but green though it may be, this wine is not made for philistines – far from it. A deep ruby red with pretty glints, and a mixture of game and pronounced fruit. Tannic, full and

powerful with quite a punch. It will be a pleasure to wait for it for two or three years.
🗝 Dom. Rodolphe Demougeot, 2, rue du Clos-de-Mazeray, 21190 Meursault, tel. 03.80.21.28.99, fax 03.80.21.29.18 ☑ Y by appt.

DOM. CHRISTINE ET JEAN-MARC DURAND 1998

☐ 0.5 ha 3,500 30–49 F

This pleasant and expressive wine goes well with monkfish *à l'armoricaine*. Deep gold in colour, with equally deep and lingering perfumes of spring blossom, fresh butter and toast. The delicate acidity gives it at least two to three years of life to look forward to.
🗝 Dom. Christine et Jean-Marc Durand, 1, rue de l'Eglise, 21200 Bouze-lès-Beaune, tel. 03.80.22.75.31, fax 03.80.26.02.57 ☑ Y by appt.

DENIS FOUQUERAND ET FILS 1998★

■ 4 ha 5,000 30–49 F

This wine from La Rochepot sports an heraldic red colour. Prettily perfumed with the taste of the region (bitter cherry and raspberry). Its attack is already lively, very spirited, full of energy. And nothing gets past its armour.
🗝 Denis Fouquerand et Fils, rue de l'Orme, 21340 La Rochepot, tel. 03.80.21.71.59, fax 03.80.21.85.58 ☑ Y ev. day 9am–12 noon 2pm–7pm

DOM. GLANTENET 1997★

☐ 3.17 ha 3,000 30–49 F

This medium gold 97 opens with powerful aromas of hazelnut, apples and pears. The fruitiness lingers on the palate together with an invigorating richness. It has a touch of bitterness that will soften out soon enough: a good wine to open and enjoy now.
🗝 Dom. Glantenet Père et Fils, rue de l'Aye, 21700 Magny-lès-Villers, tel. 03.80.62.91.61, fax 03.80.62.74.79, e-mail domaine.glantenet@wanadoo.fr ☑ Y ev. day except Sun. 8am–12 noon 1.30pm–7pm

LES CAVES DES HAUTES-COTES

La Perrière 1998★

■ 4.2 ha 18,000 50–69 F

This wine, which is already very mature for a 98, is testimony to the consistency of this co-operative, which has played such an important role in keeping wine-production at the heart of the Hautes-Côtes. Medium depth of colour, aromas of mushroom and game, integrated tannins and just the right degree of acidity. The **Mont Battois 98 Rouge** deserves both respect and its star (30–49F).
🗝 Les Caves des Hautes-Côtes, rte de Pommard, 21200 Beaune, tel. 03.80.25.01.00, fax 03.80.22.87.05 ☑ Y by appt.

HOSPICES DE DIJON

Chenovre Ermitage 1998

☐ 10 ha 51,000 70–99 F

The label alone is worth the detour. Without setting itself up as a rival to Nuits, Beaune or Beaujeu, the regional and university hospital centre at Dijon has been very intelligent in converting its meadows and fields into vineyards. The Château de Meursault (Boisseaux) is in charge here, with the help of a community aid centre that finds the workers for them. Chenovre-Ermitage is situated on the hills at Savigny-Pernand. Here we have a clear, fresh, young and mineral Hautes-Côtes de Beaune.
🗝 Hospices de Dijon, 5, rue du Collège, 21200 Beaune, tel. 03.80.24.53.01, fax 03.80.24.53.03 Y by appt.

DOM. LUCIEN JACOB

Les Larrets blancs 1998★

☐ 1.2 ha 3,000 30–49 F

When Lucien Jacob, the former member of parliament for Beaunois, entered the Palais Bourbon for the first time, he left some marks on the carpet. Jacques Chirac cried out: 'We need members of parliament with earth on their shoes!' This 98 Burgundy is similarly earthy. Pale yellow, with aromas of lime and dried fruit, it is a lively, affectionate wine. Good work. Superb at the start of a meal.
🗝 Dom. Lucien Jacob, 21420 Echevronne, tel. 03.80.21.52.15, fax 03.80.21.55.65 ☑ Y by appt.

DOM. DE LA CONFRERIE 1998

☐ 0.55 ha 2,200 30–49 F

If you pass by Cirey-lès-Nolay, visit this new winery, which was built in 1997. Their deep golden-yellow 98, with hints of apple, will go perfectly with a pike served with mayonnaise. Its prickly acidity stimulates the taste buds. We predict a long future, which is not usual with the whites of this appellation.
🗝 Dom. de La Confrérie, 21340 Cirey-lès-Nolay, tel. 03.80.21.89.23, fax 03.80.21.70.27 ☑ Y ev. day 8am–12 noon 1.30pm–7pm; Sun. by appt.
🗝 Christophe Pauchard

HENRI LATOUR ET FILS 1998★

■ 4.48 ha 15,000 30–49 F

A quality wine. Along with its cherry colour there is an excellent and subtle middle palate where sweet spice takes over from fresh fruit. A good attack and a liquorice finish.
🗝 Henri Latour et Fils, rte. de Beaune, 21190 Auxey-Duresses, tel. 03.80.21.22.24, fax 03.80.21.63.08 ☑ Y by appt.

MANOIR DE MERCEY

Au Paradis 1998★

■ 3 ha 3,000 30–49 F

Doubtless the product of young vines, the floral (acacia) **98 Blanc au Clou** has something to teach old age. The red wine is somewhere between purple and violet in colour, with vanilla and blackcurrant on the nose and the palate, and the structure is balanced by delicate tannins. Best to lay it down for two or three years. It is worth noting how tall and widely spaced the vines are here. The vintage called **Vignes en Lyres 97** receives the same mark (50–69F).

Dom. Gérard Berger-Rive et Fils, Manoir de Mercey, 71150 Cheilly-lès-Maranges, tel. 03.85.91.13.81, fax 03.85.91.17.06 Y by appt.

MOILLARD Les Alouettes 1998★

n.c. 20,000 70–99 F

The Thomas (Moillard) family have interests in the Hautes-Côtes. This parcel of vineyard is situated on the hills of Savigny-lès-Beaune. Their deep cherry-red 98 offers the taster a spectrum of flavours of spice, game and stone fruits. Well-structured with a richness on the palate. Already a good wine and has another two to four years ahead of it.

Moillard-Grivot, 2, rue François-Mignotte, 21700 Nuits-Saint-Georges, tel. 03.80.62.42.22, fax 03.80.61.28.13, e-mail nuicave@wanadoo.fr Y by appt.

MOROT-GAUDRY 1997★

3.5 ha 1,500 30–49 F

With its old-style parchment label, this clear purple wine, with a hint of prune on the nose, has a straightforward attack that does not beat about the bush. A good balance of length and fruit. We should mention that one taster was quite bowled over by this wine, and thought it was the height of sensuality.

Chantal Morot-Gaudry, Moulin Pignot, 71150 Paris-l'Hôpital, tel. 03.85.91.11.09, fax 03.85.91.11.09 Y by appt.

DOM. HENRI NAUDIN-FERRAND 1998★

1.9 ha 7,900 30–49 F

Magny-lès-Villers seems to have one foot in Hautes-Côtes-de-Nuits and the other in the Hautes-Côtes-de-Beaunes. They are not putting all their bottles in the same basket! This estate produces a bright, straw-coloured wine with aromas of butter and hazelnut, and a lively, fresh and fruity character that is typical of the appellation. Good length.

Dom. Henri Naudin-Ferrand, rue du Meix-Grenot, 21700 Magny-lès-Villers, tel. 03.80.62.91.50, fax 03.80.62.91.77, e-mail dom.hnf.@wanadoo.fr Y by appt.

DOM. CLAUDE NOUVEAU 1998★

0.5 ha 3,000 30–49 F

Here is a wine that follows wholeheartedly in the tradition of quality from this estate. With hints of green under pale gold, and light floral aromas, it is a lively 98 that needs to soften out a little more, but its freshness and elegance are undeniable. The **98 Rouge** is so well-structured it is almost as good as a *village* wine: awarded a star.

EARL Dom. Claude Nouveau, Marchezeuil, 21340 Change, tel. 03.85.91.13.34, fax 03.85.91.10.39 Y by appt.

DOM. PARIGOT PERE ET FILS

Vieilles vignes 1998★★

2 ha 10,600 50–69 F

The estate presents one of its best red wines. It is remarkable, indeed, as much for its colour and charming little red berry fruit nose, as for its liquorice-flavoured, perfectly balanced palate. Lots of character with very fine length.

Dom. Parigot Père et Fils, rte. de Pommard, 21190 Meloisey, tel. 03.80.26.01.70, fax 03.80.26.04.32 Y by appt.

CH. PHILIPPE-LE-HARDI

Clos de La Chaise Dieu 1998★

10.77 ha 75,800 30–49 F

This Clos de la Chaise Deu is excellent. Intense gold in colour, aromas of apple and quince, smoky, it manages to create an elegant balance between green vegetative flavours and opulence. Will be even better next year.

Ch. de Santenay, B.P. 18, 21590 Santenay, tel. 03.80.20.61.87, fax 03.80.20.63.66 Y by appt.

LUCIEN RATEAU 1998★

0.5 ha 2,000 30–49 F

Lucien Rateau has long been a pillar of professional organisations, but here he pleads his own cause. This strawberry-flavoured Pinot Noir is as purple as you can get, with a palate that is first warm and open, then tightens up towards the finish. All the right elements are there for a decent future.

Lucien Rateau, 21340 La Rochepot, tel. 03.80.21.80.64 Y by appt.

CAVE DE SAINTE-MARIE-LA-BLANCHE 1998

0.7 ha 3,000 30–49 F

Sainte-Marie-la-Blanche is not the 'white' Virgin here, but a red one, and with a wonderfully discreet red choir habit and a marked devotion to blackcurrant at that. This wine has richness and depth. It is charming and mouthfilling. Not so much a low mass as a full-blown service, with plenty of the faithful in attendance.

Cave de Sainte-Marie-la-Blanche, rte. de Verdun, 21200 Bligny-lès-Beaune, tel. 03.80.26.60.60, fax 03.80.26.54.47 Y ev. day except Sun. 8am–12 noon 2pm–7pm

MICHEL SERVEAU 1998★

3.2 ha 7,000 30–49 F

We suggest loin of lamb to go with this ruby red 98 with its deep vermillion tones and spring-fresh nose. The palate is both soft and reserved, causing us to wonder if it has already reached its best or whether we should wait for a while. The wine's real potential becomes apparent in the attractive fruity finish.

Michel Serveau, 21340 La Rochepot, tel. 03.80.21.70.24, fax 03.80.21.71.87 Y ev. day 8am–7pm

Crémant de Bourgogne

Like nearly all other French wine regions, Burgundy had its own appellation, the Bourgogne Mousseux, for the sparkling wines produced and made throughout the whole of the vineyard. Without being unnecessarily critical of the wine produced, it must be said that the quality was not consistent and nor, for the most part, did it compare with the reputation of the other wines of the region, undoubtedly because the base wines used were too heavy. A working group, established in 1974, laid down the rules for Crémant, setting out conditions for its production that were as strict as the ones in the Champagne region on which they were based.

A decree instituted in 1975 gave official approval to the enterprise, and eventually all the makers supported it, whether they really wanted to or not, because the Appellation Bourgogne Mousseux was terminated in 1984. After difficult beginnings, the Crémant de Bourgogne appellation is developing well and produced 74,224 hl (1,959,513, gal) in 1999.

EXCELLENCE PAR MARIE AMBAL★★

○ 115 ha 55,000 30–49 F

Made up of 60% Chardonnay and 40% Pinot Noir, it plays skilfully on the two canvasses. The nose is Pinot, the palate Chardonnay. The fruitiness adds sensitivity and character to this wine and the refreshing bitter finish is attractive. Note also the unusual *cuvée* **Saint-Charles**, which is predominately made up of Chardonnay (90%).

🔑 Veuve Ambal, B.P. 1, 71150 Rully, tel. 03.85.87.15.05, fax 03.85.87.30.15, e-mail vveambal@aol.com ☑ 🍷 by appt.

CAVE D'AZE Blanc de blancs★

○ 1 ha 7,000 ▮ 🌡 30–49 F

This Mâconnais Crémant, made from Chardonnay, is just a small part of the production of this co-operative. It is very sparkling, pale eggshell, with a honeyed perfume mixed with hints of crystallised fruit. Agreeable on the palate, with a fullness on the finish. Very suitable as a dessert wine. To be drunk over the next two years. This co-operative also produces an excellent **Blanc de Noirs** (Pinot) with a very evocative vinosity. Same mark.

🔑 Cave coop. d'Azé, 71260 Azé, tel. 03.85.33.30.92, fax 03.85.33.37.21 ☑ 🍷 ev. day 9am–12 noon 2pm–6.30pm

BRUT D'AZENAY Blanc de blancs★★

○ 6 ha 40,000 30–49 F

Georges Blanc 'discovered' Azé in 1986 and was bowled over by it. So he decided to stay, plant a vineyard and become a wine-producer. Colette Morel is the cellarmaster. This crémant may have a very light *mousse* and rather dicreet bubbles, but the nose is overflowing with passion: honeysuckle, moss, forest-floor. All in harmony with the round, supple palate. Hits all the right spots, with Chardonnay ruling the roost. It came close to acheiving a *coup de cœur.*

🔑 Georges Blanc, Dom. d'Azenay, Rizerolles, 71260 Azé, tel. 03.85.33.37.93, fax 03.74.50.21.00, e-mail blanc@relaischateaux.fr ☑ 🍷 by appt.

DOM. DU BICHERON Blanc de blancs 1996

○ 1 ha 10,000 ▮ 30–49 F

This is a real Chardonnay, with a superbly bright, pale yellow colour and delicate bubbles. This interesting 96 vintage has a mineral background, and an unusual and surprising personality that certainly grabs your attention. Worth considering if only for its vintage.

🔑 Daniel Rousset, Dom. du Bicheron, Saint-Pierre-de-Lanques, 71260 Péronne, tel. 03.85.36.94.53, fax 03.85.36.99.80 ☑ 🍷 by appt.

DOM. ALBERT BOILLOT Blanc de noirs 1997★

○ n.c. 1,050 30–49 F

A classic way to use Pinot Noir. The *mousse* glints with hues of gold. The nose shows some development of the wine with aromas of beeswax and ripe fruit. Could one expect anything else from Volnay? The finish is fresh, as expected with this style of wine. Is it more mature than its age? It is quite simply ready, in its own very particular way.

🔑 SCE du Dom. Albert Boillot, ruelle Saint-Etienne, 21190 Volnay, tel. 03.80.21.61.21, fax 03.80.21.61.21, e-mail dom.albert.boillot@wanadoo.fr ☑ 🍷 by appt.

DOM. BOUCHEZ-CRETAL 1996★

○ 0.2 ha 2,000 50–69 F

This wine has a very attractive stream of light greenish-gold bubbles: an elegant wine, still fresh and fruity, showing a little maturity in its character. Note that it is a 96 vintage.

🔑 SCEA Dom. Bouchez-Crétal, 21190 Monthélie, tel. 03.85.87.17.40, fax 03.48.05.19.32 ☑ 🍷 by appt.

LOUIS BOUILLOT
Grande Réserve Perle de Vigne★★

○	n.c.	250,000	30–49 F

This venerable Nuits-Saint-Georges business has been making sparkling wine for over a century. They know everything there is to know about bubbles, and although the business is now owned by J.-Cl. Boisset, it has continued to retain its traditional way of thinking. It walks away with the *coup de cœur.* This is a remarkably delicate, superbly structured Crémant. With a fresh green fruit nose and perfect structure, it is a delight. Bouillot is also, by the way, doing research into the comparative effervescence of different grape varieties.

🔑 Louis Bouillot, 5, quai Dumorey, 21700 Nuits-Saint-Georges, tel. 03.80.62.61.61, fax 03.80.62.37.38 ☑

CARPI-GOBET 1997

○	1 ha	6,000	▮ 30–49 F

This is a lovely little Crémant: brilliant gold, with a fresh and floral nose, quite vigorous, agreeable and pleasant. A good average: but to reach the highest standard, it would need to be perfect on just about all scores, so have no worries.

🔑 Carpi-Gobet, Dom. des Roches, Le Martoret, 71960 Igé, tel. 03.85.33.32.47, fax 03.85.33.43.60 ☑ Y by appt.

ANDRE DELORME★★

◐	n.c.	n.c.	30–49 F

We like the **Blanc de Blancs** and have given it a star. A fine wine with a brioche-like aroma, very elegant. However, the dry rosé is our favourite among the wines we tasted. Not too fizzy, with an appetising raspberry rosé colour, young and with plenty of flavour. It is a charming 'vin de saison', an apéritif wine of the best sort. You need exceptional skill to create a Burgundy rosé Crémant capable of reaching these heights of success.

🔑 Maison André Delorme, 2, rue de la République, 71150 Rully, tel. 03.85.87.10.12, fax 03.85.87.04.60 ☑ Y by appt.

DOM. DENIZOT★

○	2.1 ha	12,000	▮ 🌡 30–49 F

A constant stream of bubbles; a clear, bright colour with a very delicate, fine bouquet; and a palate, not only refreshing, but also with serious wine flavours: the Pinot Noir is the dominant partner in the blends for the 97 and 98 vintages. Yes, first and foremost this is wine.

🔑 Dom. Christian et Bruno Denizot, 71390 Bissey-sous-Cruchaud, tel. 03.85.92.13.34, fax 03.85.92.12.87, e-mail denizot@caves-particulières.com ☑ Y ev. day 8am–7pm; Sun. 8am–12 noon

BERNARD DURY Blanc de noirs★

○	0.6 ha	3,000	30–49 F

You have to like this style of wine, and this one holds its own very nicely. The Blanc de Noirs, as expected, is both tenacious and very ripe, with an exciting lift at the finish. It has lots of body and an astonishing stature. An interesting wine.

🔑 Bernard Dury, rue du Château, Cissey-Merceuil, 21190 Meursault, tel. 03.80.21.48.44, fax 03.80.21.48.44 ☑ Y by appt.

DOM. FICHET 1997

○	2 ha	1,800	50–69 F

Pierre-Yves and Olivier Fichet followed their father Francis and moved here, in 1988 and 1990, respectively. This family present us with a 97 that is 100% Chardonnay: pale yellow with an average *mousse*, and a good fresh nose. A lively wine which retains its sparkle on the palate, and the terroir is evident, which is what makes it worthy of being in this book.

🔑 Dom. Francis Fichet et Fils, Le Martoret, 71960 Igé, tel. 03.85.33.30.46, fax 03.85.33.44.45, e-mail olivierfichet@wanadoo.fr ☑ Y by appt.

DOM. GIROUX
Blanc de blancs 1997★★

○	0.5 ha	3,500	30–49 F

This Chardonnay-based wine can rub shoulders with the best of them. Unusual and attractive, with a surprising yellow-green colour. Its mineral notes are not unpleasant. The *dosage* is noticeably high in this wine, and should be drunk now. An example of a particular way of doing things.

🔑 Yves Giroux, Les Molards, 71960 Fuissé, tel. 03.85.35.63.64, fax 03.85.32.90.08 ☑ Y by appt.

LES CAVES DES HAUTES-COTES★★★

○	16 ha	100,000	▮ 🌡 30–49 F

La Cave des Haute-Côtes will be able to announce this as *coup de cœur* at its next general meeting. This wine got more than just a full discharge from the jury. They gave it their warmest congratulations for its pale gold

colour and attractive strings of bubbles, its peachy perfumes with a hint of muscat, and the fresh, fruity palate with a hint of Chardonnay. Very typical, very drinkable, but you need to like Crémants with a fairly high *dosage*. The *maillot jaune* of our *coups de cœur*, the *Guide's* equivalent of the yellow jersey in the Tour de France.
🔑 Les Caves des Hautes-Côtes, rte. de Pommard, 21200 Beaune, tel. 03.80.25.01.00, fax 03.80.22.87.05 ☑ Y by appt.

LES VIGNERONS D'IGE★

○ 15 ha 150,000 ▮ 🌡 30–49 F

Chardonnay and Pinot sit side by side in this Mâconnais Crémant that is as Mâconnais as they come: it has a real southern Burgundy accent. The nose and the highly floral palate veer towards Chardonnay. Out of a total 280 ha (692 acres), this co-operative devotes around 15 ha (37 acres) to sparkling wines.
🔑 Cave coop. des vignerons d'Igé, 71960 Igé, tel. 03.85.33.33.56, fax 03.85.33.41.85, e-mail lesvigneronsdige@lesvigneronsdige.com ☑ Y ev. day except Sun. 8am–12 noon 2pm–6pm

DOM. DE LA BOFFELINE 1998

○ 1 ha 6,500 ▮ 30–49 F

Loron has developed this characterful Crémant with its fine *mousse*. The nose is pure Chardonnay: brioche and linden flowers. The *dosage* is alittle on the high side, but the overall balance and its fruitiness are agreeable. Good but not great.
🔑 Frédéric Lenormand, En Fourgeau, 71260 Azé, tel. 03.85.33.33.82, fax 03.85.33.33.82 ☑ Y ev. day 9am–12.30pm 2pm–7.30pm

ANDRE ET BERNARD LABRY 1993★

○ 2 ha 4,000 30–49 F

This is unusual: a 93 vintage. The colour is fairly clear. The nose is plum and ratafia. The palate is well-preserved, rich and powerful. Not far off the mark.
🔑 Dom. André et Bernard Labry, Melin, 21190 Auxey-Duresses, tel. 03.80.21.21.60, fax 03.80.21.64.15 ☑ Y ev. day 9am–12 noon 2pm–6pm; Sat. Sun. by appt.

LA CHABLISIENNE 1994★

○ 2 ha 20,000 ▮ 🌡 50–69 F

Lightly beaded, with shades of yellow and gold. The nose has a subtle scent of liqueur and a hint of butter. But its real character shows on the palate: pleasant and winey with good length.
🔑 La Chablisienne, 8, bd Pasteur, B.P. 14, 89800 Chablis, tel. 03.86.42.89.89, fax 03.86.42.89.90, e-mail chab@chablisienne.com ☑ Y by appt.

MADAME MASSON

Blanc de noirs 1998★★

○ n.c. 5,000 30–49 F

Mme Masson is not an imaginary person as is often the case on the labels of sparkling wines. Following the death of her husband, an agricultural engineer, Nadine Masson took over the estate, from 1980 to 1998, and now it is Jerome's turn. A combination of Pinot Noir (80%), Chardonnay and Aligoté proves very successful. Light yellow in colour, aromas of hazelnut and flowers, full-bodied, lots of fizz and a solid finish of lemon. 'Apéritif Crémant' created by J.F. Delorme.
🔑 Jérôme Masson, rue Haute, 21340 La Rochepot, tel. 03.80.21.72.42, fax 03.80.21.72.42 ☑ Y by appt.

MEURGIS Blanc de blancs 1998

○ n.c. 150,000 ▮ 🌡 30–49F

The wine cellars are one of the undisputed specialists in making Crémant, which they produce by the millions of bottles in the most spectacular surroundings: 4 ha (10 acres) of underground quarries. It is worth a detour to visit them. Among the wines presented, we were particularly impressed by this Meurgis Blanc de Blancs. This gives you the opportunity to discover the Sacy grape (a rare variety in the Yonne), which makes up 10% of the blend, along with Aligoté and Chardonnay. A powerful and expressive character.
🔑 SICA du Vignoble Auxerrois, Caves de Bailly, 89530 Saint-Bris-le-Vineux, tel. 03.86.53.77.77, fax 03.86.53.80.94 ☑ Y ev. day 10am–12 noon 2pm–6pm

DOM. HENRI NAUDIN-FERRAND★

○ 0.7 ha 7,269 ▮ 🌡 30–49 F

They are very precise here: 20% Chardonnay, 42% Aligoté and 38% Pinot Noir. A fortunate alchemy since it results in an excellent blend of grape varieties and vintages (from 94 to 98). This wine has shades of a Hautes-de-Nuits because of the Aligoté. An intense Crémant, with a fruity roundness, suggesting hawthorne and peony but without considerable length. This wine would go well with a ham *au crémant*.
🔑 Dom. Henri Naudin-Ferrand, rue du Meix-Grenot, 21700 Magny-lès-Villers, tel. 03.80.62.91.50, fax 03.80.62.91.77, e-mail dom.hnf.@wanadoo.fr ☑ Y by appt.

CAVE DE PRISSE-SOLOGNY-VERZE★

○ 35.54 ha 120,000 ▮ 🌡 30–49 F

This Mâconnais Chardonnay is supple and even subtle, with plenty of vigorous bubbles, vanilla and toast. It is just as it should be, without being too long on the finish. Best served with *vacherin au cassis*.
🔑 Cave de Prissé-Sologny-Verzé, 71960 Prissé, tel. 03.85.37.88.06, fax 03.85.37.61.76 ☑ Y by appt.

CAVE DE SAINTE-MARIE-LA-BLANCHE★

○ 0.75 ha 6,000 30–49 F

This blend (Chardonnay 60%, Aligoté 10%, and Pinot Noir for the rest) certainly won't make you gloomy: it is full of freshness and gaiety, and as sparkling as you could wish. The *dosage* is just right. A one-act play that is over in the blink of an eye, but those are the rules of the game with this style of wine.

Cave de Sainte-Marie-la-Blanche, rte. de Verdun, 21200 Bligny-lès-Beaune, tel. 03.80.26.60.60, fax 03.80.26.54.47 ev. day except Sun. 8am–12 noon 2pm–7pm

SIMONNET-FEBVRE 1996★

○ 2.1 ha 16,000 30–49 F

Simonnet-Febvre is one of the most experienced wine-producers in the region. The estate was once famous for its sparkling Chablis and was purveyor to the Tsar in Saint Petersburg. Richard Nixon visited the cellar. This is a Crémant in which Pinot Noir dominates (the rest being Chardonnay). It sparkles with gusto. Vivacious but not very full-bodied. Goes straight to the point with no messing about.

Simonnet-Febvre, 9, av. d'Oberwesel, 89800 Chablis, tel. 03.86.98.99.00, fax 03.86.98.99.01 by appt.

ALBERT SOUNIT Blanc de blancs★★

○ n.c. 13,000 30–49 F

This business already has an ancient history. Founded in 1852 by Flavien Jeunet, it was then taken over by Albert Sounit, and finally bought in 1993 by Knud Kjellerup, his Danish importer. Kjellerup can congratulate himself on the team that he has set up here. His Chardonnay has fine bubbles. Top quality aromas, with notes of spring blossom. As to the palate, it is silky, caressing, with pronounced varietal flavours (a touch of hazelnut).

Albert Sounit, 5, pl. du Champ-de-Foire, 71150 Rully, tel. 03.85.87.20.71, fax 03.85.87.09.71 by appt.

TRIPOZ 1997

○ 1 ha 7,600 30–49 F

Céline and Laurent Tripoz are young, very motivated producers who are trying their best. And their best gets better and better. Their Crémant is made with Chardonnay, and you can tell. A 97 vintage, showing the qualities of a good harvest, and with a certain elegance

Céline et Laurent Tripoz, pl. de la Mairie, 71000 Mâcon, tel. 03.85.35.66.09, fax 03.85.35.66.09 by appt.

DOM. VERRET★★

○ 2 ha 12,000 30–49 F

The best Crémant in the Yonne, containing equal measures of Chardonnay, Aligoté, Sacy, Gamay and Pinot. Although the bubbles don't hang around long, its golden colour shines brilliantly. Fine aromas and an elegant palate. A wine that holds our attention with its maturity and strength of character. A thoroughbred, in other words. Note that this bottle has a black label. The **white label**, made only with Chardonnay, receives a recommendation.

Dom. Verret, 7, rte. de Champs, B.P. 4, 89530 Saint-Bris-le-Vineux, tel. 03.86.53.31.81, fax 03.86.53.89.61, e-mail bruno.verret@wanadoo.fr by appt.

CAVE DE VIRE★★

○ 50 ha 50,000 30–49 F

One hundred per cent Chardonnay, that's the sparkling side of the new AOC Viré-Clessé. Really not bad at all. In fact, better than not bad! Golden-yellow in colour, buttery, and rich in citrus fruits, the wine, once uncorked, offers a lovely view of the countryside. An attractive wine with a full palate and so very much a Chardonnay.

Cave de Viré, En Vercheron, 71260 Viré, tel. 03.85.32.25.50, fax 03.85.32.25.55, e-mail cavedevin@wanadoo.fr ev. day 8am–12 noon 2pm–6pm

L. VITTEAUT-ALBERTI

Blanc de blancs 1998★

○ 4 ha 30,000 30–49 F

You have a choice between the **Blanc Brut 98**, with a (dark) yellow label, which blends 40% Pinot with Chardonnay and Aligoté and receives a recommendation, or the wine mentioned above (80% Chardonnay and 20% Aligoté). Lovely *mousse* and lasting, circling beads of bubbles which rise to form a crown. This is a party wine. It makes your taste buds tingle with its honeyed flavours. You could probably keep it for a year or two.This estate, founded in 1951, keeps the flag flying for sparkling wines in its home town of Rully.

Gérard Vitteaut-Alberti, 20, rue du Pont-d'Arrot, 71150 Rully, tel. 03.85.87.23.97, fax 03.85.87.16.24 by appt.

Gérard Vitteaut

Chablis

Despite having a reputation that has seen it imitated to a fantastic degree all around the world, the Chablis vineyard once nearly disappeared altogether. Catastrophic late frosts in 1957 and 1961 added to the difficulties of cultivating the vines on very steep hills with stony soils led to vine-growing being progressively abandoned; the value of land in the Grands Crus fell to laughably low prices and the

BURGUNDY

people who bought then were very well advised.

The appellation covers an area of 6,834 ha (16,880 acres), a proportion of which lies in the commune of Chablis itself while the rest is distributed among 19 of its neighbours; 4,000 ha (9,880 acres) are presently planted with vines. Production was 269,938 hl (7,126,363 gal) in 1999. The vines cover the steeply sloping hills on both sides of the Serein, a small tributary flowing into the Yonne. At this latitude, a south-south-easterly aspect is best for the grapes to ripen well, but in some of the more favoured locations vines may be planted on slopes facing away from the sun as well as towards it. The soil is made up of Jurassic marl or Kimmeridge clay (the other end of the rim of this geological basin is in Dorset, England, which is why it has this name) or Portland stone, which is limestone. These are the perfect soils for growing white wines, and in the 12th century the Cistercian monks of the Abbey of Pontigny realised this, most likely planting Chardonnay, known locally as Beaunois. Here, more than anywhere else, Chardonnay shows off the finesse and elegance which make it a superlative accompaniment to seafood, snails or charcuterie. The Premiers and Grands Crus will complement the choicest foods: chicken, fine charcuterie, fowl or white meat dishes, especially those prepared with wine.

Petit Chablis

This appellation is at the bottom of the hierarchy of wines in the Chablis area. In 1999 34,582 hl (912,965 gal) of wine were produced. The Petit Chablis is less aromatically complex than Chablis, with a greater degree of acidity which gives its flavour a quality of greenness. It used to be served by the carafe, in the year of harvest, but it is now bottled. Held back by its name, it initially had great difficulty in getting established in its own right, but today the consumer seems to take less and less account of the diminutive adjective 'Petit'.

DOM. BACHELIER 1998★

☐ n.c. 3,200 30–49 F

This wine can stay put on the table for the next four to five years. Lively and vigorous, with touches of citrus fruit and gun flint. A fairly rich wine for this appellation, it still has some reserves. Lovely finesse.

EARL Dom. Bachelier, 13, rue Saint-Etienne, 89800 Villy, tel. 03.86.47.49.56, fax 03.86.47.57.96 Y by appt.

DOM. DU CHARDONNAY 1998

☐ 9.1 ha 50,000 30–49 F

Three associates, Etienne Boileau, Christian Simon and William Nahan (with 32 ha (79 acres) to their credit), have together created a fine 98 vintage. This wine has a pale colour, a nose with a hint of beeswax and flowers, and a fresh and very dry palate. Best to drink now.

Dom. du Chardonnay, Moulin du Pâtis, 89800 Chablis, tel. 03.86.42.48.03, fax 03.86.42.16.49, e-mail domaine.chardonnay@free.fr Y by appt.

DOM. J. CHATELAIN 1999★

☐ 6.95 ha 35,000 30–49 F

Buttercup yellow. A reasonably mature and spicy 99: fresh, aromatic and long. It has a decent structure and would go well with a *jambon chablisien*.

GAEC de Oliveira Lecestre, 11, Grand-Rue, 89800 Fontenay-près-Chablis, tel. 03.86.42.40.78, fax 03.86.42.83.72 Y ev. day except Sun. 10am–12.30pm 2pm–7pm

DOM. DU COLOMBIER 1998

☐ 1.2 ha 8,000 30–49 F

Silvery-gold, with a perky lemon nose scented with acacia and a very persuasive palate, this wine is classic in style, an Identikit version of the appellation.

Dom. du Colombier, 42, Grand-Rue, 89800 Fontenay-près-Chablis, tel. 03.86.42.15.04, fax 03.86.42.49.67 Y by appt.

Mothe frères

DOM. HERVE DAMPT
Vieilles vignes 1998★

☐ 0.6 ha 4,500 30–49 F

We would love to know how old these vines are. They make a wine that is very ripe, but not oxidised, which opens on contact with the air with a mineral element. A medium pale

yellow colour, it lingers a little too long on the middle palate, but finishes well. A bottle to open now.
🔑 EARL Hervé Dampt, rue de Fleys, 89700 Collan, tel. 03.86.55.29.55, fax 03.86.54.49.89 ☑ 𝐈 by appt.

RENE ET VINCENT DAUVISSAT 1998★

☐ n.c. 3,000 30–49 F

The Dauvissats are famous not only in Chablis but also all over the world, and their Petit Chablis is not so little as all that: light yellow, soft gold, the spitting image of a Chablis with its ripe aromas. It has a heady mixture of spring blossom and dried fruit. Too rich for oysters, perfect for fish.
🔑 GAEC René et Vincent Dauvissat, 8, rue Emile-Zola, 89800 Chablis, tel. 03.86.42.11.58, fax 03.86.42.85.32

JEAN-PAUL DROIN 1998★

☐ 1.3 ha 10,000 50–69 F

It seems that this successful 98 vintage has the protection of Saint Vincent. 1998 was the year when preparations for the Saint Vincent festival were taking place here, and Jean-Paul Droin was in charge of the operation. His Petit Chablis, with its light straw colour and aroma of hawthorn, is as discreet as anything until it gets on the palate. There, it bursts out, lively and dynamic, choosing exactly the right moment to play the mineral card. It should, without doubt, be drunk with seafood.
🔑 Jean-Paul Droin, 14 bis, rue Jean-Jaurès, 89800 Chablis, tel. 03.86.42.16.78, fax 03.86.42.42.09 ☑ 𝐈 by appt.

DOM. D'ELISE 1998★

☐ 7.02 ha 18,000 30–49 F

This estate was created from scratch in 1972 by a high-flying Parisian, then taken over in 1983 by Frédéric Prain, a Chablis wine-producer who lives in Paris. His wine has the charm of the famous piano piece *Für Elise* with its clear notes, mineral tones and and exotic harmonies. The attack is full of spirit, and this well-known piece is given new life in the hands of this artist. He renews its expression by adding a touch of richness and beeswax.
🔑 Frédéric Prain, Côte de Léchet, 89800 Milly, tel. 03.86.42.40.82, fax 03.86.42.44.76 ☑ 𝐈 by appt.

DOM. FILLON 1999

☐ 3 ha 3,000 30–49 F

This Petit Chablis is still a little on the green side, given the vintage. Fresh, floral and light: it plays the flute rather than the saxophone. You can drink it, without a qualm, as soon as the occasion arises.
🔑 Dom. Fillon, 53, rue Bienvenu-Martin, 89530 Saint-Bris-le-Vineux, tel. 03.86.53.30.26, fax 03.86.53.63.88 ☑ 𝐈 ev. day 9am–12.30pm 2pm–7pm

DOM. FOURREY ET FILS 1999★

☐ 0.5 ha 3,800 30–49 F

The label leads us straight to the mysteries of the cellar. Pale straw-yellow in colour, this very youthful wine is, as expected, a little acidic, but also has a welcome touch of flintiness. Good structure. Good aftertaste. The harmony of flavours is well-balanced.
🔑 Dom. Fourrey et Fils, 9, rue du Château, Milly, 89800 Chablis, tel. 03.86.42.44.04, fax 03.86.42.84.78 ☑ 𝐈 by appt.

DOM. DES ILES 1998★

☐ 5.5 ha 45,000 30–49 F

'Hurry slowly', is Boileau's advice. This wine can either be drunk now or laid down, because it has some lovely qualities now but also shows signs that it could mature into something better. Fresh on both nose and palate, well-balanced with an attractive mineral quality. No beating about the bush. Characteristic.
🔑 Gérard Tremblay, 12, rue de Poinchy, 89800 Chablis, tel. 03.86.42.40.98, fax 03.86.42.40.41 ☑ 𝐈 ev. day except Sat. Sun. 8am–12 noon 1.30pm–6pm; cl. Aug.

LA CHABLISIENNE 1999★

☐ 166 ha 500,000 50–69 F

The achievements of this co-operative are many. It manages to deal with a large volume of wine at a very competitive level of quality. The nose of this one doesn't quite offer the full panorama, but the palate is just as one would expect. Structure, fullness, elegance, there is enough to beat the Burgundy drum. Under the shared name of a group of co-operatives, including La Chablisienne, the Petit Chablis made by the **Blason de Bourgogne** collective (30–49F) receives the same mark.
🔑 La Chablisienne, 8, bd Pasteur, B.P. 14, 89800 Chablis, tel. 03.86.42.89.89, fax 03.86.42.89.90, e-mail chab@chablisienne.com ☑ 𝐈 by appt.

LAMBLIN ET FILS 1998★★

☐ 2.5 ha 15,000 30–49 F

Nothing less than a dozen fat oysters will go with this wine, which was the best at this tasting. Fresh and fruity, it opens out very quickly. This wine's structure and balance are 'the work of a worthy wine-producer', writes one jury member. Not surprising when one considers that the Lamblin family has been in Chablis since 1690.

🗝 Lamblin et Fils, Maligny, 89800 Chablis, tel. 03.86.98.22.00, fax 03.86.47.50.12, e-mail infovin@lamblin.com ☒ 𝐘 Mon.–Fri. 8am–12 .30pm 2pm–5pm; Sat. 8am–12.30pm

DOM. DE LA MOTTE 1999★

☐ 2 ha 16,000 ▮ 🌡 30–49 F

This is the family property of the three Michaut brothers and of Claude Robin, former members of the *La Chablisienne* co-operative who are now working under their own steam. A very convivial 99 with barbeque and vegetal aromas, and a persuasive mineral after-taste. Marie Noël, the Christian poetess of the *cru*, would surely have given in to a little gluttony for a taste of this wine between verses.

🗝 SCEA Dom. de la Motte, 35, Grande-Rue, 89800 Beines, tel. 03.86.42.43.71, fax 03.86.42.49.63 𝐘 by appt.
🗝 Michaut et Robin

DOM. LAROCHE 1999★

☐ 434 ha 190,000 ▮ 🌡 50–69 F

The Laroche estate is the only one in Burgundy to give us technical notes with information on the total acidity, volatile acidity, pH and everything else to do with this wine. A good idea. On tasting, this discretely coloured Petit Chablis opens up with floral scents and hints of flint. A straightforward wine, clean, with good length. Very typical.

🗝 Dom. Laroche, 22, rue Louis-Bro, 89800 Chablis, tel. 03.86.42.89.29, fax 03.86.42.89.00, e-mail info@domainelaroche.fr ☒ 𝐘 by appt.

DOM. DE LA TOUR 1998★

☐ 0.26 ha 1,975 ▮ 🌡 30–49 F

Silver-gold in colour, this mineral and floral 98 is very agreeable on the middle palate where it reaches its optimum balance. A fairly representative example of its AOC, offering a 'lively and dynamic harmony'.

🗝 SCEA Dom. de la Tour, 8 bis, rue Jules-Philippe, 89800 Chablis, tel. 03.86.47.55.68, fax 03.86.47.55.86, e-mail dtour@clubinternet.fr ☒ 𝐘 by appt.
🗝 Fabrici-Renato

ROLAND LAVANTUREUX 1998

☐ 4.5 ha 20,000 ▮ 🌡 30–49 F

Pale yellow in colour, this is a wine that first appears impulsive, but it stays the pace. The mineral note that dominates is very characteristic of the AOC.

🗝 Roland Lavantureux, 4, rue Saint-Martin, 89800 Lignorelles, tel. 03.86.47.53.75, fax 03.86.47.56.43 ☒ 𝐘 ev. day 8.30am–8pm; Sun. by appt.

DOM. DES MARRONNIERS 1999

☐ 1.4 ha 12,000 ▮ 🌡 30–49 F

This estate was founded in 1976, the year of the great drought. It produced an excellent 96 vintage, and since 1997, they have installed new equipment. This uncomplicated 99, clear and transparent, with an expressive nose, flows over the tongue like a trout in the Serein, the local river. A straightforward wine that would go perfectly with an *andouillette de Chablis*.

🗝 Bernard Légland, 1 et 3, Grande-Rue de Chablis, 89800 Préhy, tel. 03.86.41.42.70, fax 03.86.41.45.82 ☒ 𝐘 ev. day 8am–12 noon 2pm–8pm; cl. 15 Aug.–5 Sep.

J. MOREAU ET FILS 1998

☐ 7.58 ha 60,660 ▮ 🌡 30–49 F

This well-established Chablis business, that has interests also in Loire wines, has been taken over by Jean-Claude Boisset. Here they present a Petit Chablis that hints at citrus fruits and flint, a little on the hard side for the moment, but well-made.

🗝 J. Moreau et Fils, rte. d'Auxerre, La Croix Saint-Joseph, 89800 Chablis, tel. 03.86.42.88.00, fax 03.86.42.88.08

DOM. DES ORMES 1998★

☐ 7.7 ha 2,800 ▮ 30–49 F

This is a young vineyard, run by Daniel, Philippe and Jean-Pierre Patrice. Their Petit Chablis has a few traces of mineral, but leans more in the direction of quince and butter. It is well-balanced and round, and has a wonderful freshness to it like a Chablis.

🗝 Dom. des Ormes, 4, rte. de Lignorelles, 89800 Beines, tel. 03.86.42.40.91, fax 03.86.42.48.58 ☒ 𝐘 ev. day 8am–9pm

DOM. DE PISSE-LOUP 1998

☐ 1.93 ha 8,000 ▮ 🌡 30–49 F

Classic pale-straw colour. The nose is a still a little closed, but is frank, fine and mineral. A wine with a touch of iodine and influenced strongly by its terroir. An ideal match for seafood.

🗝 SCEA Jacques Hugot et Jean Michaut, 1, rue de la Poterne, 89800 Beines, tel. 03.80.97.04.67, fax 03.80.97.04.67 ☒ 𝐘 by appt.

DOM. YVON VOCORET 1998★

☐ n.c. n.c. ▮ 30–49 F

This has been a family business for four generations and is also popular with world leaders, who like to stop for a visit. This Petit Chablis could easily be offered to them on their arrival: it has all the freshness and liveliness of its appellation.

🗝 Yvon Vocoret, 9, chem. de Beaune, 89800 Maligny, tel. 03.86.47.51.60, fax 03.86.47.57.47 ☒ 𝐘 ev. day 8am–7pm; Sun. by appt.

Chablis

In 1999 181,520 hl (4,792,128 gal) of Chablis were produced. This wine owes its inimitable

ualities of freshness and lightness
the soils from which it springs.
l-suited to cold and rainy years,
hen it acquires too much acidity,
warm years it gains a refreshing
uality lacking in the Côte d'Or
hardonnays. It should be drunk
oung (in one to three years) but
an be left to age for up to ten years
r more, when it gains in complex-
y and in the richness of its
ouquet.

OM. DES AIRELLES 1999

10 ha 7,710 50–69 F

The two Robin sons have taken over the usiness here, producing a wine so suggestive f hazelnut that a squirrel could drink it. The alate is lively and mineral. The note of dryess at the finish indicates a good future. Vorth keeping a while. Drink it with a plate f seafood.

Thierry et Didier Robin, 40, Grande-ue, 89800 Chichée, tel. 03.86.42.80.49, ax 03.86.42.85.40 ☑ Y by appt.

Jean Robin

DOM. BILLAUD-SIMON

Tête d'Or 1998★

☐ 3 ha 23,000 50–69 F

The unoaked **Chablis 98** receives a recommendation. But the prize goes to this Tête d'Or, which recalls to mind, that Ysée from writer Paul Claudel's *Partage de Midi* lies in the cemetery at Vézelay, and that Claudel loved Burgundy wine. Although this Chablis needs to open up a little, it is a high quality wine which will become excellent in two or three years' time.

Dom. Billaud-Simon, 1, quai de Reugny, B.P. 46, 89800 Chablis, tel. 03.86.42.10.33, fax 03.86.42.48.77 ☑ Y ev. day except Sat. Sun. 9am–6pm; cl. 15 Aug.–1st Sep.

CALVET 1999

☐ n.c. 290,000 30–49 F

The Calvet business, originally from Bordeaux, has been active in Beaune for a long time with the writer Pierre Poupon competently managing the affair. This tank-produced wine (they make nearly 300,000 bottles) has a subtle nose and is fresh on the palate. Very young at the time of tasting, but seems well-made and to have a good start in life.

Calvet, 75, cours du Médoc, B.P. 11, 33028 Bordeaux Cedex, tel. 05.56.43.59.00, fax 05.56.43.17.78

Chablis

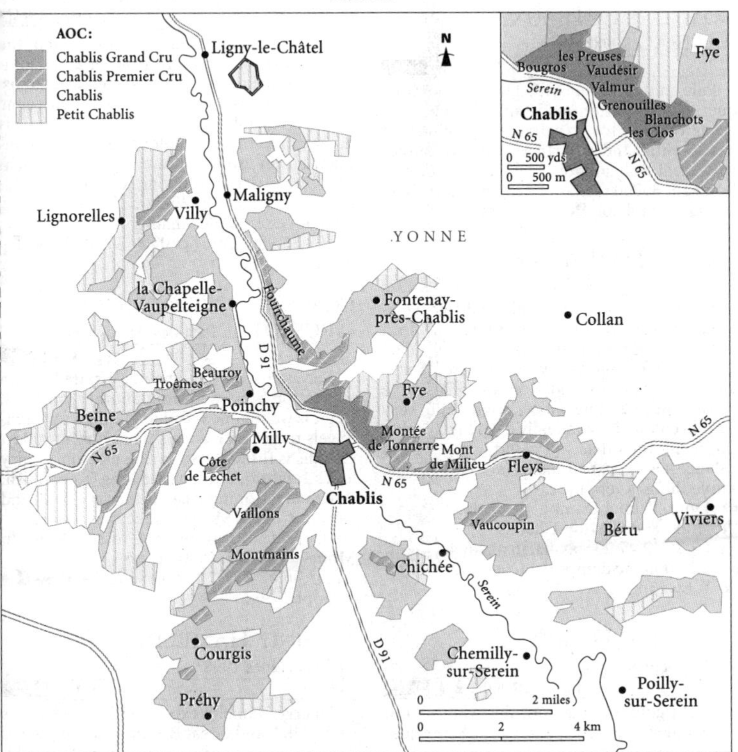

DOM. DU CEDRE DORE 1998★

☐ 5 ha 21,400 [50–69 F]

This estate was founded in Viviers, in the early 90s, by Louis Moreau, so that he could continue with the work started by his parents. With a mere 5 ha (12 acres) that he works with great dedication, under the shade of a golden cedar tree, he produces a very fine bright yellow wine of remarkable frankness and yet, with a rare complexity. Best to wait a couple of years, as it has a great future ahead of it.

Louis Moreau, 10, Grande-Rue, 89800 Beines, tel. 03.86.42.87.20, fax 03.86.42.45.59, e-mail domaine.louismoreau@wanadoo.fr ev. day 8am–12 noon 1.30pm–6pm; Sat. Sun. by appt.

PATRICK ET CHRISTINE CHALMEAU 1999★

☐ 2.2 ha 5,000 [30–49 F]

This 99 seems to have been visited by a few good fairies at its birth. Its nutty aroma is charming. The palate is light and still closed, but it is clear that this child, without being troublesome, is not going to lack 'get up and go'.

Patrick et Christine Chalmeau, 76, rue du Ruisseau, 89530 Chitry-le-Fort, tel. 03.86.41.43.71, fax 03.86.41.47.51 by appt.

DOM. DES COTEAUX DE RAMEAU 1998★

☐ 6 ha 10,000 [30–49 F]

Pale gold in colour with a herbaceous bouquet, a little bitterness is still showing that needs a year or two to soften up completely. It has potential and is worth awaiting patiently.

Pascal Boban, Dom. des Coteaux de Rameau, 89700 Collan, tel. 03.86.55.16.54, fax 03.86.54.48.08 by appt.

DANIEL DAMPT 1998★

☐ 12 ha 60,000 [50–69 F]

The estates of Jean Defaix and this wine-producer were founded at the same time. Jean Defax, who is his father-in-law, has now taken over. *Cueillez, cueillez votre jeunesse* ('Seize, seize your youth') said Ronsard. This wine doesn't need telling twice. Light and very clear in colour, it has a really deep earthy nose, and is as mineral as you could wish. A good balance between fruitiness and acidity. The whole thing is very pure.

Dom. Daniel Dampt, 1, rue des Violettes, 89800 Milly-Chablis, tel. 03.86.42.47.23, fax 03.86.42.46.41, e-mail domaine.dampt.defaix@wanadoo.fr by appt.

DOM. ERIC DAMPT

Vieilles vignes 1998

☐ 4 ha 28,000 [30–49 F]

Light gold and mineral, this wine is both fresh and supple. The palate follows the nose as if it were a guru.

Eric Dampt, 16, rue de l'Ancien-Presbytère, 89700 Collan, tel. 03.86.55.36.28, fax 03.86.54.49.89, e-mail eric.dampt@libertysurf.fr by appt.

JEAN DAUVISSAT Saint-Pierre 1998

☐ 1.8 ha 13,000 [50–69 F]

This wine, dedicated to Saint Peter, opens heaven's gates to us without having to ring three times. A lovely, bright yellow colour, well-balanced, with aromas of fern and flint. Carefully looked after during maturation in tank.

Caves Jean Dauvissat, 3, rue de Chichée 89800 Chablis, tel. 03.86.42.14.62, fax 03.86.42.45.54 by appt.

DOM. BERNARD DEFAIX 1998★★

☐ 12 ha 50,000 [50–69 F]

Bright pale yellow in colour, with powerful aromas of flowers and fruit, a pleasant mineral flavour, and a touch of acidity balanced with an elegant richness. Sylvain and Didier Defaix took over this 25-ha (62-acre) family concern in 1994.

Dom. Bernard Defaix, 17, rue du Château, Milly, 89800 Chablis, tel. 03.86.42.40.75, fax 03.86.42.40.28, e-mail didier.defaix@wanadoo.fr by appt.

DOM. WILLIAM FEVRE 1998★

☐ 15.8 ha 118,500 [50–69 F]

William Fèvre, distinguished student of the École National d'Administration and a militant enthusiast of Kimmeridgian Chablis, handed this estate over to the Champagne family Henriot. This 98 does justice to his name. It has the right colour, the desired bouquet, a lively attack followed by a note of richness. And all that from one so young.

Sté du Vignoble William Fèvre, 21, av. d'Oberwesel, 89800 Chablis, tel. 03.86.98.98.98, fax 03.86.98.98.99 by appt.

CORINNE ET JEAN-PIERRE GROSSOT La Part des Anges 1998★★

☐ 0.7 ha 3,800 [50–69 F]

The name of this wine is inspired by an expression borrowed from another vineyard, but it is well-named. You might even say archangels rather than angels. This vibrant yellow Chablis is floral (fresh spring blossom), spicy and straightforward, with a long fruity finish. Worth mentioning, also, is the very oaky and elegant **Chablis 98**, which receives a star.

Corinne et Jean-Pierre Grossot, 4, rte. de Mont-de-Milieu, 89800 Fleys, tel. 03.86.42.44.64, fax 03.86.42.13.31 by appt.

THIERRY HAMELIN

Vieilles vignes 1998★

☐ 0.5 ha 2,500 [50–69 F]

Thierry Hamelin exports 60% of his wines to the USA and Great Britain, and with wines like these, he is ready to conquer the world.

his 98 comes from half a hectare (1 acre) of d vines (a very respectable 55 years of age), ıd is the perfect wine to drink with friends. It ay be naturally greenish-gold and floral cacia), but it also has virtues of both finesse nd fullness. Very successful for this vintage. Iouthfilling.

Thierry Hamelin, 1, imp. de la Grappe, 9800 Lignorelles, tel. 03.86.47.52.79, ıx 03.86.47.53.41 ☑ Ƴ ev. day except Sun. ım–12 noon 2pm–6pm; cl. 15 days in Aug.

HEIMBOURGER PERE ET FILS

998★

☐ 3 ha 10,000 ▮ 🌡 30–49 F

Since 1994 it is Pierre Heimbourger's son ather than Pierre himself who has been running this estate. If you happen to be cooking omething exotic, try this wine: it would go erfectly with something hot and spicy. To the ye: a brilliant yellow. On the nose: citrus and hite-fleshed fruits. On the palate: deep and ull, yet with a certain delicacy.

Dom. Heimbourger Père et Fils, 5, rue e la Porte-de-Cravant, 89800 Saint-Cyr-les-Colons, tel. 03.86.41.40.88, ax 03.86.41.48.33, e-mail alotte@wanadoo.fr ☑ Ƴ by appt.

DOM. DES ILES 1998

☐ 16 ha 120,000 ▮ 🌡 30–49 F

Gérard Tremblay exports 75% of what e produces to Chile, the USA, England, and Germany. Palate and nose work in harmony ogether. This wine, gold in colour, gives an mpression of richness which aims at roundess and fullness rather than freshness. A vine that should be opened this year.

🗝 Gérard Tremblay, 12, rue de Poinchy, 89800 Chablis, tel. 03.86.42.40.98, ax 03.86.42.40.41 ☑ Ƴ ev. day except Sat. Sun. 8am–12 noon 1.30pm–6pm; cl. Aug.

DOM. LA BRETAUCHE 1998★★

☐ 5.34 ha 6,000 ▮ 🌡 50–69 F

It may not be exemplary, but this wine sticks its heels in with such boldness that one forgives it everything. Upfront, almost wild, it could almost come from a novel by the local writer, Rétif de la Bretonne. It is a rich wine for laying down.

🗝 Louis Bellot, Dom. la Bretauche, rue de la Bretauche, 89800 Chablis, tel. 03.86.42.40.90, fax 03.86.42.49.81 ☑ Ƴ by appt.

LA CAVE DU CONNAISSEUR

Prestige Vieilles vignes 1998★

☐ 0.8 ha 3,000 ▮ 🌡 50–69 F

This wine is more honey than mushroomy, and you want to take a gulp straight away. Still fresh, its soft attack follows through with firm acidity, like prose after verse. True to its appellation and vintage.

🗝 La Cave du Connaisseur, rue des Moulins, B.P. 78, 89800 Chablis, tel. 03.86.42.87.15, fax 03.86.42.49.84, e-mail connaisseur@chablis.net ☑ Ƴ ev. day 10am–6.30pm

LA CHABLISIENNE

Cuvée L. C. 1998★

☐ 100 ha 500,000 ▮ 🌡 50–69 F

Abbot Balitran can reckon on having fulfilled his mission on earth by founding this winery all those years ago. France had some pretty incredible priests in those days. It was a certain Abbot Deschamps who founded the A. J. Auxerre football team! This, 98 with its pale colour tinged with green, has added a hint of honey to the classic flinty aromas. The palate is floral, but also ripe and full. It has a fine life ahead of it.

🗝 La Chablisienne, 8, bd Pasteur, B.P. 14, 89800 Chablis, tel. 03.86.42.89.89, fax 03.86.42.89.90, e-mail chab@chablisienne.com ☑ Ƴ by appt.

BURGUNDY

DOM. DE LA CONCIERGERIE

Vieilles vignes 1998★★

☐ 1.25 ha 7,000 ▮ 🌡 50–69 F

Christian Adine lives in the former caretaker's office (conciergerie) of the château of Courgis, which is where the name of the estate comes from. The concierge, here, is lord and master, presenting a wine that does perfect justice (as if it needed to) to the 98 vintage. The jury enthused over it, one taster noting: 'This wine is so good, you don't want to spit it out!'. Which he didn't.

🗝 EARL Christian Adine, 2, allée du Château, 89800 Courgis, tel. 03.86.41.40.28, fax 03.86.41.45.75 ☑ Ƴ by appt.

DOM. LAROCHE Saint-Martin 1999

☐ 61.57 ha 400,000 ▮ 🌡 70–99 F

This wine, named after Saint Martin, whose relics were once housed in this venerable cellar, comes from 61.5 ha (152 acres) of Domaine Laroche, which consists of around 100 ha (247 acres) in total. A very young wine, it doesn't have a lot to say on the nose, but the attack is dry and clean. Our tasters found a slight sweetness on the finish. When this was checked, it was found that there was indeed 5 g/l of residual sugar, which explains the lack of aggression.

🗝 Dom. Laroche, 22, rue Louis-Bro, 89800 Chablis, tel. 03.86.42.89.29, fax 03.86.42.89.00, e-mail info@domainelaroche.fr ☑ Ƴ by appt.

ROLAND LAVANTUREUX 1998

☐ 14 ha 40,000 ▮ 🌡 30–49 F

Light straw-yellow in colour, with a floral nose which opens out when the wine is swirled in the glass, to give an aroma of freshly cut hay. Sraightforward and mineral on the palate, balanced but light. True to character. A wine that should be drunk immediately even though it could last longer.

🗝 Roland Lavantureux, 4, rue Saint-Martin, 89800 Lignorelles, tel. 03.86.47.53.75, fax 03.86.47.56.43 ☑ Ƴ ev. day 8.30am–8pm; Sun. by appt.

LE PETIT QUINCY 1999★★

☐ 0.5 ha 3,300 50–69 F

Dominique Gruhier is the daughter of Jean Delaunay (who owned the famous Hautes-Côtes business at L'Etang-Vergy), and she can congratulate herself on her decision in joining together Tonnerre and Chablis. They produced a remarkable 96 vintage and have once again produced a stunning wine. Butter and hazelnut on the palate, it is a wine with good depth and length and an unusual but interesting roundness.

Dominique Gruhier, Dom. de l'Abbaye, Clos de Quincy, 89700 Epineuil, tel. 03.86.55.32.51, fax 03.86.55.32.50 ev. day 9am–6pm; Sun. by appt.

DOM. LE VERGER

Cuvée Vieilles vignes 1998

☐ 2.5 ha 15,000 50–69 F

Although we also liked the **Chablis 98**, we prefer this *cuvée* that has been made from old vines and is presented by Alain Geoffroy under his newly-named Domaine le Verger. It has a mineral, dried fruit flavour with a hint of woodiness, and is more rich than long. A pleasant wine that should be drunk now (we noted a tendency to oxidation).

Dom. Alain Geoffroy, 4, rue de l'Equerre, 89800 Beines, tel. 03.86.42.43.76, fax 03.86.42.13.30 by appt.

DOM. LONG-DEPAQUIT 1998

☐ 22 ha 150,000 50–69 F

The Bichot family from Beaune bought the Long-Depaquit estate at the end of the 1960s. The estate lies exactly where the vineyards of the Cistercian abbey at Pontigny used to be. This white-gold Chardonnay has a nose of toasted almonds, and on the palate develops a taste of green apple, lemon, and other similar fresh fruit aromas. A young, lively wine.

Dom. Long-Depaquit, 45, rue Auxerroise, 89800 Chablis, tel. 03.86.42.11.13, fax 03.86.42.81.89 ev. day except Sun. 9am–12.30pm 1.30pm–6pm

Albert Bichot

DOM. DES MALANDES

Vieilles vignes 1998★★★

☐1er cru 14.5 ha 116,000 30–49 F

Raymond Dumay tells us that when talking about a great Chablis, 'one says that it is full of love'. Here we are presented with such a wine: a Chablis of truly exceptional quality. Its balance is superb, enlivened by a slight wild and spicy fragrance of cinnamon. A floral palate that achieves a subtle link between its acidity and richness, which is the secret of this terroir.

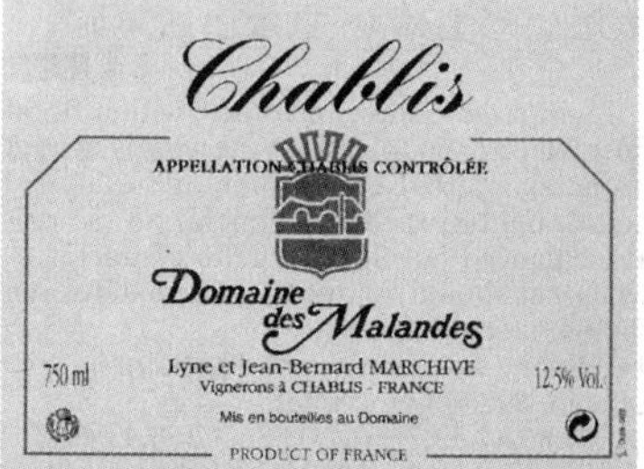

Dom. des Malandes, 63, rue Auxerroise, 89800 Chablis, tel. 03.86.42.41.37, fax 03.86.42.41.97, e-mail domaine.malandes.chablis@wanadoo.fr by appt.

Marchive

DOM. DES MARRONNIERS 1999★

☐ 11 ha 70,000 30–49 F

This estate was founded in 1976 and is now 18 ha (45 acres) in size. For enthusiasts, Bernard Légland offers a tour of the vineyard. The **Chablis 98**, which receives a recommendation, is a wine to wait for, while conversely the 99 Chablis should be drunk now. That isn't unusual. Pale yellow in colour, it opens with hazelnut aromas. There is a touch of something lively in its otherwise round palate which also offers a certain complexity. A good example of its AOC, and would go very well with an *andouillette de Chablis*.

Bernard Légland, 1 et 3, Grande-Rue de Chablis, 89800 Préhy, tel. 03.86.41.42.70, fax 03.86.41.45.82 ev. day 8am–12 noon 2pm–8pm; cl. 15 Aug.–5 Sep.

LOUIS MICHEL ET FILS 1998★

☐ 6 ha 40,000 50–69 F

The Michel family has been here since 1850 and owns 20 ha (49 acres). This interesting 98 is as yellow as a chick and already has a well-defined nose, with a good balance between lemon and mineral aromas. Its acidity on the palate suggests a good future development, which has already partially taken place. A good example of a Chablis and just perfect for the snail festival which takes place not far from Chablis, in Bassou.

Louis Michel et Fils, 9, bd de Ferrières, 89800 Chablis, tel. 03.86.42.88.55, fax 03.86.42.88.56 by appt.

SYLVAIN MOSNIER

Cuvée Vieilles vignes 1998★

☐ 12 ha n.c. 50–69 F

This wine has three good points: a clear colour with silvery glints, a well-constructed, intensely mineral and floral nose, and a rather more subdued palate.

Sylvain Mosnier, 4, rue Derrière-les-Murs, 89800 Beines, tel. 03.86.42.43.96, fax 03.86.42.42.88 by appt.

DOM. JEAN-MARIE NAULIN 1998

☐ 9 ha 6,000 30–49 F

This is an intense, exotic wine with a pleasant, slightly fruity palate and a mineral quality that gives it a bit of character.

Dom. Jean-Marie Naulin, 30, rue de la Voie-Neuve, 89800 Beines, tel. 03.86.42.46.71, fax 03.86.42.12.74 by appt.

DE OLIVEIRA LECESTRE 1998★

☐ 25.75 ha 42,000 30–49 F

This 98 is dark in colour, with a few peppery notes and a hint of gun flint on the nose. Its light attack develops and it becomes fuller on the palate. An interesting wine that still has more to offer.

GAEC de Oliveira Lecestre, 11, Grand-Rue, 89800 Fontenay-près-Chablis, tel. 03.86.42.40.78, fax 03.86.42.83.72 ev. day except Sun. 10am–12.30pm 2pm–7pm

Jacky Chatelain

DOM. DE PERDRYCOURT

Cuvée Prestige 1998

☐ 1 ha 8,000 50–69 F

This estate was founded in 1986 by Arlette Courty and had its first harvest three years later. Virginie, her daughter, has now joined the family business. They have produced a 98 that does not like to be hurried, as it is still fairly closed. Supple and tender, but lacking complexity.

EARL Arlette et Virginie Courty, Dom. de Perdrycourt, 9, voie Romaine, 89230 Montigny-la-Resle, tel. 03.86.41.82.07, fax 03.86.41.87.89 ev. day 8am–8pm

DOM. DE PISSE-LOUP 1998★★

☐ 3.94 ha 10,000 30–49 F

This is a lovely, beautifully balanced wine which received plenty of praise from our jury. 'Shining gold' in colour, and as mineral and floral as you could wish, well-rounded and rich while at the same time very fresh. This is a true Chablis that will age well and will provide the perfect accompaniment to a fine fish dish.

SCEA Jacques Hugot et Jean Michaut, 1, rue de la Poterne, 89800 Beines, tel. 03.80.97.04.67, fax 03.80.97.04.67 by appt.

DOM. DE PISSE-LOUP 1998★★

☐ 2.1 ha 2,300 30–49 F

Romual Hugot is Jacques Hugot's son, and he has produced this remarkable Chablis. Powerful, balanced and long; a perfect match with a fine fish dish.

Romuald Hugot, 30, rte. Nationale, 89800 Beines, tel. 03.86.42.85.11, fax 03.86.42.85.11 by appt.

DENIS POMMIER 1998

☐ 2.86 ha 16,848 50–69 F

The jury has absolute confidence that this wine has all the right qualities to age for a while. It is straight down the line, and achieves a good balance between the bursts of flint and the fruitiness. Deep yellow, intense and agreeable. A little touched by the faults of youth, but it will go far.

Denis Pommier, 31, rue de Poinchy, 89800 Chablis, tel. 03.86.42.83.04, fax 03.86.42.17.80 ev. day 9am–12 noon 2pm–8pm; Sun. by appt.

REGNARD 1997★★

☐ 30 ha 120,000 70–99 F

Patrick de Ladoucette, who took over this well-established Chablis business in 1984, has put aside a very fine 97 *cuvée* for the jury. On the palate it is not the charge of the light brigade. On the contrary, this is a wine with perfect mouthfilling richness and a deeply aromatic character. The colour is still fresh and the nose is linden flowers.

Régnard, 28, bd Tacussel, 89800 Chablis, tel. 03.86.42.10.45, fax 03.86.42.48.67 by appt.

DOM. JACKY RENARD 1999★★

☐ 2.05 ha 17,000 30–49 F

This wines evokes citrus fruits along with a fresh, mineral character. Very refreshing, it is ideal as an apéritif.

Dom. Jacky Renard, La Côte-de-Chaussan, 89530 Saint-Bris-le-Vineux, tel. 03.86.53.38.58, fax 03.86.53.33.50 by appt.

DOM. DE VAUROUX 1998★★

☐ 24 ha 26,000 30–49 F

This estate was set up in 1960 by the Tricon family, and they produce this attention-grabbing **Cuvée Vieilles Vignes 98** as well as a truly stunning *village*. The effect is very simple: when you put your glass down you can imagine that you are spending a weekend in the middle of Chablis! Round, long, full, and also powerful, rich, and fresh. One of the best, and will make many people very happy.

SCEA Dom. de Vauroux, rte d'Avallon, B.P. 56, 89800 Chablis, tel. 03.86.42.10.37, fax 03.86.42.49.13

Chablis Premier Cru

Chablis Premier Cru comes from around thirty locations selected for the quality of wines. They produced 48,332 hl (1,275,965 gal) in 1999. The comparison with Chablis lies chiefly in the Premier Cru's complex and lingering bouquet, the aromas offering a mixture of acacia honey, a touch of iodine and hints of vegetation. The amount produced per hectare is limited to 50 hl (540 gal per acre). All the winemakers agree that Chablis Premier Cru reaches a peak in its fifth year when it takes on a distinctive 'hazelnut' note. The most substantial examples are produced by the *climats* of La Montée de Tonnerre, Fourchaume, Mont de Milieu, Forêt, Butteaux and Léchet.

DOM. DES AIRELLES

Vosgros 1998★★

☐ 3 ha 1,370 50–69 F

This cru, which comes from Chichée, is one for the connoisseurs. It may not be very well-known, but is often remarkable, and this is a very good example. The aroma of spring blossom suggests good quality grapes. There is an astonishing continuity from end to end, and it has a subtlety that you only find with highly skilled wine-makers. With its touch of the exotic, it is truly regal. A recommendation should also go to **Vaugiraut 98**, which is a decent wine, representative of its type. Fish for the first, white meat for the second.

Thierry et Didier Robin, 40, Grande-Rue, 89800 Chichée, tel. 03.86.42.80.49, fax 03.86.42.85.40 by appt.

Jean Robin

DOM. BARAT Les Fourneaux 1998★

☐ 2 ha 5,000 50–69 F

Five generations all mad about wine-growing and wine have worked on this estate, where there are 17 ha (42 acres) to indulge themselves in their passion. This Les Fourneaux 98 is really a Premier Cru, according to the jury. It has all the elements: the hints of green that you like to see in the glass, the dominant spring blossom aromas on the nose, the freshness and length of the palate. To be drunk over the next three years. The **Vaillons 98** is equally well-made, with an added hint of citrus fruit. The jury recommends drinking it with pike *quenelles*.

EARL Dom. Barat, 6, rue de Léchet, Milly, 89800 Chablis, tel. 03.86.42.40.07, fax 03.86.42.47.88 by appt.

JEAN-CLAUDE BESSIN

Montmains 1998★★

☐ 2.8 ha n.c. 50–69 F

This Premier Cru is well-known on the Left Bank: they say that Jean Cocteau wrote the whole of *La Voix Humaine* in one night in a hotel in Chablis. This bottle could have been left on his bedside table for him. Its charm is in its sincerity: simply a very straightforward wine, honest from every point of view. A perfect example. 'We love it,', 'I'd recommend it to my best friends' – this wine won over the tasters completely.

Jean-Claude Bessin, 3, rue de la Planchotte, 89800 Chablis, tel. 03.86.42.46.77, fax 03.86.42.85.30 by appt.

DOM. BILLAUD-SIMON

Les Vaillons 1998

☐ 3.6 ha 27,000 70–99 F

This 20 ha (49 acre) estate was founded in the 19th century and has been in the same family since 1815. This Vaillons 98 opens up rapidly. Spontaneous with liveliness, a citrus nose and a light mineral quality. Charming enough if drunk this year.

Dom. Billaud-Simon, 1, quai de Reugny, B.P. 46, 89800 Chablis, tel. 03.86.42.10.33, fax 03.86.42.48.77 ev. day except Sat. Sun. 9am–6pm; cl. 15 Aug.–1 Sep.

PASCAL BOUCHARD

Fourchaume Vieilles vignes Grande réserve du Domaine 1998★★

☐ 1.3 ha 10,000 70–99 F

Fourchaume is situated just outside the Grand Cru, but it is not overshadowed by its princely neighbours. Produced from old vines, this 98 has been very skilfully matured both in tank and barrel. Its colour, light buttery fruit, pleasant attack, liveliness and well-handled oak, together paint a remarkable portrait of its origins.

Pascal Bouchard, 5 bis, rue Porte-Noël, 89800 Chablis, tel. 03.86.42.18.64, fax 03.86.42.48.11, e-mail pascal.bouchard@wanadoo.fr ev. day 10am–12.30pm 2pm–7pm; cl. Jan.

DOM. DE CHANTEMERLE

Fourchaume 1998★★★

☐ 4.8 ha 35,000 50–69 F

The Premier Cru **l'Homme Mort** is what made Francis Boudin's father's reputation. Their **98** receives a well-deserved two stars for the elegance that it demonstrated during the tasting (70–99F). As for this Fourchaume, it blew away the jury. This is a truly high-class wine, colour Chablis, nose Chablis, mouth Chablis. The very essence of Chablis Premier Cru and its mineral finish is one of the greatest. A turbot or a capon will measure up

nicely to it, but it would go equally well with almost anything, except spicy food.
Dom. de Chantemerle, 27, rue du Serein-La-Chapelle, 89800 Chablis,
tel. 03.86.42.18.95, fax 03.86.42.81.60 ☑ Y by appt.
Francis Boudin

DOM. DU CHARDONNAY

Mont de Milieu 1998★

☐ 0.41 ha 1,800 70–99 F

These three wine enthusiasts first got together in 1987. Today they own 32 ha (79 acres). Although the **Montée de Tonnerre 98** seemed austere (it receives a recommendation), the **Montmains 98** was awarded a star for its fine character. This Mont de Milieu is also very successful. Light-gold in colour with aromas of acacia flowers and toasted almonds. Spices, mineral notes and crystallised fruit reflect both the terroir they come from, and a well-handled maturation in vat.
Dom. du Chardonnay, Moulin du Pâtis, 89800 Chablis, tel. 03.86.42.48.03,
fax 03.86.42.16.49, e-mail
domaine.chardonnay@free.fr ☑ Y by appt.
Boileau-Nahan-Simon

DOM. CHEVALLIER

Montmains 1998★

☐ 0.31 ha 2,000 50–69 F

This attractive 98 is matured on the lees for six months in barrel, and expresses all the mineral elements of the cru: the maturation has been very well-handled. A well-balanced wine, pale yellow with green hues, and wonderfully fresh. The picture would be incomplete without mentioning the citrus aromas.
Dom. Chevallier, 6, rue de l'Ecole, 89290 Montallery, tel. 03.86.40.27.04,
fax 03.86.40.27.05 ☑ Y by appt.

DOM. DU COLOMBIER

Fourchaume 1998★★

☐ 2.5 ha 15,000 50–69 F

Although the very characteristic **Vaucoupin 98** ought to develop well and deserves our compliments, the Fourchaume merits something more. Deep gold colour with a delicate mushroom nose. What a lovely aroma. Rich and fruity, with a solid structure, an interesting wine, good for laying down.
Dom. du Colombier, 42, Grand-Rue, 89800 Fontenay-près-Chablis,
tel. 03.86.42.15.04, fax 03.86.42.49.67 ☑ Y by appt.
Guy Mothe et Fils

DANIEL DAMPT Vaillons 1998★★

☐ 5 ha 20,000 70–99 F

This wine producer produces four superb **98s**: **Fourchaume, Beauroy** and **Côte de Léchet**, each of which receives a star, while the Vaillons, so seductive, so intense, so complex, receives two. So many good things in one bottle! A real character. Best drunk soon, as it is already at its best.
Dom. Daniel Dampt, 1, rue des Violettes, 89800 Milly-Chablis, tel. 03.86.42.47.23, fax 03.86.42.46.41, e-mail domaine.dampt.defaix@wanadoo.fr ☑ Y by appt.

RENE ET VINCENT DAUVISSAT

La Forest 1998★

☐ n.c. 35,000 70–99 F

This is Dauvissat's Forêt 98, written Forest. Although famous, this wine doesn't have much colour and its character is still austere. With a name like this, it would be no surprise to find that the wine is oaky, which it is, and the maturation seems to have been well-executed. Already well-rounded, it needs a little time for the oak to blend in. Similarly with the **Vaillons 98**, which receives a recommendation and which should be laid down for a while for the same reason.
GAEC René et Vincent Dauvissat, 8, rue Emile-Zola, 89800 Chablis,
tel. 03.86.42.11.58, fax 03.86.42.85.32

DOM. BERNARD DEFAIX

Les Vaillons 1998

☐ 2 ha 12,000 70–99 F

Here's to Hélène and Didier Defaix, who got married in May 1999. This Vaillons, with its flinty, mushroom nose, doesn't lack body, but the finish is a little too lively, suggesting that it might be better to lay it down a while. Best opened in two or three years' time at the maximum. A dish of *noix de Saint-Jacques* is a must.
Dom. Bernard Defaix, 17, rue du Château, Milly, 89800 Chablis,
tel. 03.86.42.40.75, fax 03.86.42.40.28,
e-mail didier.defaix@wanadoo.fr ☑ Y by appt.

DOM. DANIEL-ETIENNE DEFAIX

Les Lys 1996★

☐ 3.6 ha 27,000 100–149 F

This is a historic Premier Cru, once part of the royal vines which were situated south of Milly, very close to Chablis. Light yellow, with a good brioche nose, floral, mineral, supple and round. Pleasant and ready to drink now, though it can easily age some more. The **Côte de Léchet 96** is another pleasant wine, powerful and well-balanced. Upfront floral and mineral aromas, but also lots of ripe fruit.
Daniel-Etienne Defaix, Ch. Defaix,14, rue Auxerroise, B.P. 50, 89800 Chablis,
tel. 03.86.42.42.05, fax 03.86.42.48.56,
e-mail chablis.defaix@wanadoo.fr ☑ Y ev. day 9am–12 noon 2pm–6pm; cl. 31 Dec.–5 Feb.

JEAN-PAUL DROIN Vaucoupin 1998★

☐ 0.14 ha 1,100 70–99 F

Jean-Paul Droin, whose family settled here in the 17th century, owns 20 ha (49 acres), several Grands Crus and several Premiers Crus. Here, he presents us with three Premiers Crus, all of which receive a star. **Vosgros** and **Fourchaume**, both **98**, are well-matured and have a nice light touch. They are equipped to face the future. At the other extreme is the

BURGUNDY

Vaucoupin, with an elegant well-presented colour, which is already ready for drinking. With aromas of ripe fruit and a subtle oaky touch, it is soft and supple as well as rich, complex, and very long. Can be drunk until 2003 at least.
🗝 Jean-Paul Droin, 14 bis, rue Jean-Jaurès, 89800 Chablis, tel. 03.86.42.16.78, fax 03.86.42.42.09 ☑ 𝐘 by appt.

DOM. WILLIAM FEVRE

Vaillons 1998★★

☐ 2.86 ha 13,586 100–149 F

The William Fèvre business, which has been bought by Joseph Henriot, is one of the most respected names in the Chablis region. The balance of wine with oak is a delicate exercise. When it succeeds, it is wonderful. Here, the harmony of the Chablis has been perfectly respected: the oakiness gives quality both to the body and to the aromas, leaving a pleasant aftertaste of lime.
🗝 Sté du Vignoble William Fèvre, 21, av. d'Oberwesel, 89800 Chablis, tel. 03.86.98.98.98, fax 03.86.98.98.99 ☑ 𝐘 by appt.

DOM. FOURREY ET FILS

Côte de Léchet 1999★

☐ 3 ha 4,000 50–69 F

This is a coast with its own geographical identity that justifies its recognition as a *climat* in its own right. Here the accent is on richness and suppleness, along with a toastiness and a good potential.
🗝 Dom. Fourrey et Fils, 9, rue du Château, Milly, 89800 Chablis, tel. 03.86.42.44.04, fax 03.86.42.84.78 ☑ 𝐘 by appt.

ALAIN GAUTHERON

Vaucoupin 1998★

☐ 1.41 ha 11,000 50–69 F

This particular *climat* is on the right bank of the Serien river, yet Chichée runs alongside the left bank, and although very well-situated, it has had difficulty establishing a reputation. This wine ought to help it. Fresh, mineral, and reasonably light, it has a rare straightforwardness. It should be left to mature until the moment arrives to drink it with a capon. The **Mont de Milieu 98**, which is also quite light and very attractive, receives the same mark.
🗝 Alain Gautheron, 18, rue des Prégirots, 89800 Fleys, tel. 03.86.42.44.34, fax 03.86.42.44.50 ☑ 𝐘 by appt.

DOM. ALAIN GEOFFROY

Vau-Ligneau 1998★

☐ 2.75 ha 22,000 70–99 F

The **Fourchaume 98** and this Vau-Ligneau are neck and neck in terms of quality. The Vau-Ligneau is one of the most recent of the Premiers Crus, and here, shows its justifiable ambitions. Its mineral character is very much in the Chablis style. The texture, it's true, is a little too humble, but it brings a note of simplicity to the landscape.
🗝 Dom. Alain Geoffroy, 4, rue de l'Equerre, 89800 Beines, tel. 03.86.42.43.76, fax 03.86.42.13.30 ☑ 𝐘 by appt.

DOM. JEAN GOULLEY ET FILS

Mont de Milieu 1998★

☐ 1 ha 8,000 50–69 F

Until 1985, this estate was run by Jean Goulley's niece. Then he took over the business himself, joined by his son Philippe in 1987, who has been holding the reins ever since. This Mont de Milieu is already very open, and it glistens like gold in the glass. The mineral character, which comes from the kimmeridgian soil, is balanced by the spring blossom aromas. An interesting wine, with an attractive and subtle liveliness.
🗝 Dom. Jean Goulley et Fils, 11 bis, Vallée des Rosiers, 89800 La Chapelle-Vaulpelteigne, tel. 03.86.42.40.85, fax 03.86.42.81.06 ☑ 𝐘 by appt.

DOM. HAMELIN Beauroy 1998★★

☐ 3.8 ha 29,000 50–69 F

This *climat* at Poinchy, now part of Chablis, used to be very well-known and appreciated but has perhaps lost a little of its fame in comparison with the Fourchaumes and other Vaillons. However, this wine restores it to its rightful place. A radiant colour with a floral nose, where almond also has its say. The palate is perfect, and packed so full of iodine and mineral flavours that you can almost taste the shellfish. Well done.
🗝 EARL Dom. Hamelin, 1, rue des Carillons, 89800 Lignorelles, tel. 03.86.47.54.60, fax 03.86.47.53.34 ☑ 𝐘 ev. day except Sun. 9am–12 noon 2pm–6pm

DOM. DES ILES Beauroy 1998

☐ 0.5 ha 3,500 50–69 F

The estate name suggests travel, and indeed the characteristics of the wine are exotic: a deep yellow colour, a mineral attack that develops into spring blossom, lemon, smoke and toasted almonds. Sweet and soft, the palate is generous. The **Côte de Léchet 98** is also included in our tasting panel's very rigorous selection.
🗝 Gérard Tremblay, 12, rue de Poinchy, 89800 Chablis, tel. 03.86.42.40.98, fax 03.86.42.40.41 ☑ 𝐘 ev. day except Sat. Sun. 8am–12 noon 1.30pm–6pm; cl. Aug.

LES DOMAINES LA CHABLISIENNE Les Lys 1998★★

☐ 1.9 ha 12,000 100–149 F

This Les Lys is delicious. The production of such wonderful wines has enabled La Chablisienne to become one of the best wine co-operatives in France. Very attractive dashes of colour in the glass. The palate echoes the nose's fruitiness and oakiness. It will be two or three years yet before all these elements have come together in this interesting wine. Also, the attractive label from the Domaines de la Chablisienne collection decorates a **Fourchaumes-Les Vaulorents 98**, which receives one star.

🔑 La Chablisienne, 8, bd Pasteur, B.P. 14, 89800 Chablis, tel. 03.86.42.89.89, fax 03.86.42.89.90, e-mail chab@chablisienne.com ☑ Y by appt.

DOM. DE LA CONCIERGERIE

Montmain 1999★

☐ 3.3 ha 20,000 50–69 F

The Adine family home was once the caretaker's office (conciergerie) of the château at Courgis, which explains the name of the estate. It was very successful with a 95 Montmain and returns here with a 99 that has a youthful bouquet of hyacinths and violets. It still has an impulsive feel to it, but under its air of green apple there is a nice buttery richness on the palate. Best to wait another year.

🔑 EARL Christian Adine, 2, allée du Château, 89800 Courgis, tel. 03.86.41.40.28, fax 03.86.41.45.75 ☑ Y by appt.

LAMBLIN ET FILS Fourchaume 1998★

☐ 3.5 ha 24,000 70–99 F

This estate produced a wonderful Mont de Milieu 83. This year, we liked the **Vaillon 98** (50–69F), which receives a recommendation, along with this Fourchaume from the same year. A wine that doesn't go overboard: the grape variety and the terroir are expressed by its directness and finesse. Not to be drunk too soon.

🔑 Lamblin et Fils, Maligny, 89800 Chablis, tel. 03.86.98.22.00, fax 03.86.47.50.12, e-mail infovin@lamblin.com ☑ Y Mon. until Fri. 8am–12.30pm 2pm–5pm; Sat. 8am–12.30pm

DOM. DE LA MEULIERE

Monts de Milieu 1998★

☐ 2.64 ha 15,000 50–69 F

Here, the Meulière estate brings us a light golden yellow Premier Cru, with a warm, even passionate temperament. Ample and complex, with a pleasant and discreet mushroom flavour, it takes us on a journey whose end is not yet clear to us. It has a good script, in any case.

🔑 Claude Laroche, 18, rte. de Mont-de-Milieu, B.P. 25, 89800 Fleys, tel. 03.86.42.13.56, fax 03.86.42.19.32 ☑ Y by appt.

DOM. LAROCHE

Vaillons Vieilles vignes 1998★★

☐ 6.95 ha 50,000 100–149 F

If the **Fourchaumes 98** (150–199F) is absolutely up to standard, then this Vaillons is of exceptional class. The nose and palate share between them: honey, nuts and a well-blended oakiness. 'Lovely!' wrote a British taster who had been invited to judge the Chablis. Excellent vinification, respecting all the balance of this wine, which is ideal for laying down. Note also the **Vaudevey 98**, one star, which the jury says will get even better.

🔑 Dom. Laroche, 22, rue Louis-Bro, 89800 Chablis, tel. 03.86.42.89.29, fax 03.86.42.89.00, e-mail info@domainelaroche.fr ☑ Y by appt.

DOM. LONG-DEPAQUIT

Les Lys 1998★★

☐ 1.69 ha 12,000 70–99 F

The château Long-Depaquit, one of Albert Bichot's enterprises, exports 75% of its production all over the world. The **Les Beugnons 98** would go very well with a sausage in brioche. The 25,000 bottles of the **Vaucoupins 98**, very grapey and full-bodied, would go down well with pan-fried scallops. These two crus receive a star. The Les Lys has perfect acidity and an attractive freshness as well as great richness. It would be an excellent match for the local cheese *époisses*. All of these wines deserve a place in your cellar. They are ready to drink now but are also good for laying down.

🔑 Dom. Long-Depaquit, 45, rue Auxerroise, 89800 Chablis, tel. 03.86.42.11.13, fax 03.86.42.81.89 ☑ Y ev. day except Sun. 9am–12.30pm 1.30pm–6pm

🔑 Bichot

DOM. DE L'ORME Beauroy 1998

☐ n.c. 5,000 50–69 F

Pascal Mercier, since 1994, has been employing sustainable agricultural methods in his vineyards. This practice helps preserve the balance of the ecosystem. His 98 is all finesse and discretion, but the jury has confidence in it: 'This wine will keep because the finish gives us a glimpse of a certain depth.'

🔑 Dom. de l'Orme, 16–18, rue de Chablis, 89800 Lignorelles, tel. 03.86.47.41.60, fax 03.86.47.56.66 ☑ Y by appt.

DOM. DES MALANDES

Fourchaume Vieilles vignes 1998★★

☐ 1.25 ha 10,000 70–99 F

This estate's Fourchaume manages to capture our attention. A powerful wine with a

deep yellow colour, long, fleshy and rich. Keep it for your cellar, because it will certainly last. The **Beauroy 98** is very smooth and needs less time.
Dom. des Malandes, 63, rue Auxerroise, 89800 Chablis, tel. 03.86.42.41.37, fax 03.86.42.41.97, e-mail domaine.malandes.chablis@wanadoo.fr ☑ Y by appt.
Marchive

CH. DE MALIGNY

L'Homme Mort 1998

☐ 5 ha 32,000 70–99 F

Jean Durup is one of the big personalities of the Chablis region. He has chosen this name for his prestigious terroirs of superior Jurassic bed-rock. This *climat* at Maligny is fragrant with spring in full blossom. The hint of bitterness on the palate calls for seafood, in a year or two from now.
SA Jean Durup Père et Fils, 4, Grande-Rue, 89800 Maligny, tel. 03.86.47.44.49, fax 03.86.47.55.49, e-mail durup@clubinternet.fr ☑ Y by appt.

DOM. DES MARRONNIERS

Côte de Jouan 1999

☐ 0.26 ha 2,000 70–99 F

This *climat* has gradually been making a name for itself, and gives a good standard of quality. This wine has a pale but brilliant gold colour, and a nose that goes straight to the point: hawthorn and flint. Very characteristic of the region. Refreshing on the palate, lively, with good fruit.
Bernard Légland, 1 et 3, Grande-Rue de Chablis, 89800 Préhy, tel. 03.86.41.42.70, fax 03.86.41.45.82 ☑ Y ev. day 8am–12 noon 2pm–8pm; cl. 15 Aug.–5 Sep.

LOUIS MICHEL ET FILS

Montmain 1998★

☐ 6 ha 30,000 70–99 F

This Montmain, with its characteristic colour, has a discreet and elegant nose. Flinty, as is should be, and with a decent structure. Round-bodied but never heavy, it is the kind of bottle of wine that one likes to admire a while before opening.
Louis Michel et Fils, 9, bd de Ferrières, 89800 Chablis, tel. 03.86.42.88.55, fax 03.86.42.88.56 ☑ Y by appt.

J. MOREAU ET FILS Vaillon 1998★

☐ 7.06 ha 53,300 50–69 F

Salmon with a butter sauce seems the perfect match for this classic Vaillon. Greenish-gold in colour, the nose suggests a basket full of pears and peaches. Its character asserts itself on the palate with a welcome mineral touch. The estate was taken over several years ago by Jean-Claude Boisset.
J. Moreau et Fils, rte. d'Auxerre, La Croix Saint-Joseph, 89800 Chablis, tel. 03.86.42.88.00, fax 03.86.42.88.08

MOREAU-NAUDET ET FILS

La Forêt 1998★

☐ n.c. n.c. 70–99 F

This is a very pleasant, modern Chablis, with some exotic aromas. The colour is attractive, the nose bang-on for the year, and the body has some shape to it. The whole thing has everything that a Premier Cru ought to have.
GAEC Moreau-Naudet et Fils, 5, rue des Fossés, 89800 Chablis, tel. 03.86.42.14.83, fax 03.86.42.85.04 ☑ Y ev. day 10am–12 noon 2pm–8pm

SYLVAIN MOSNIER Beauroy 1998★

☐ 0.96 ha 3,500 70–99 F

The nose and palate express a fruity, floral softness with a characteristic hint of bitterness. The balance is perfect. Clear, pale yellow in colour, the palate is stimulated by touches of flint and iodine. A good example of its type. Ready to drink, preferably with seafood.
Sylvain Mosnier, 4, rue Derrière-les-Murs, 89800 Beines, tel. 03.86.42.43.96, fax 03.86.42.42.88 ☑ Y by appt.

DOM. PINSON

Mont de Milieu 1998★★★

☐ 4.75 ha 20,000 70–99 F

This wine comes from an old Chablis family: Louis Pinson (a real character), founder of the present estate, has chosen as successors his grandsons Laurent and Christophe Pinson. They deserve our praise, as this Premier Cru is a truly great 98, showing the hand of an expert, from the colour through to the palate. This is a wine that should be saved for a special occasion and should be laid down for around five years. A true Mont de Milieu. The terroir says it all.
SCEA Dom. Pinson, 5, quai Voltaire, 89800 Chablis, tel. 03.86.42.10.26, fax 03.86.42.49.94 ☑ Y ev. day except Sun. 8am–12 noon 1.30pm–6pm

DENIS POMMIER

Côte de Léchet 1998★★

☐ 0.78 ha 3,750 70–99 F

As in Paris, in the Chablis region there is a left and a right bank. Here, in Milly, is one of the best Premiers Crus of the left bank. Pale light yellow, a nose of over-ripe fruit, quite rich, with a touch of vanilla that adds necessary richness to the palate. It has everything

that a great Chablis needs, as do the **Fourchaume** and the **Beauroy 98** likewise. This latter is a prince, if not an emperor, among wines.
🔑 Denis Pommier, 31, rue de Poinchy, 89800 Chablis, tel. 03.86.42.83.04, fax 03.86.42.17.80 ☑ Y ev. day 9am–12 noon 2pm–8pm; Sun. by appt.

DENIS RACE Mont de Milieu 1998★★

☐ 0.53 ha 2,700 ▮ ♁ 50–69 F

This estate gets a warm welcome for a Mont de Milieu that is deliciously iodised and saves us the expense of a trip to a spa. Sea air and dry stone: it is a delight. There is nothing excessive in the acidity or the character of the 98s. One could equally choose the **Vaillon 98**, which is very fruity and, in its different way, has a good future (one star).
🔑 Denis Race, 5 A, rue de Chichée, 89800 Chablis, tel. 03.86.42.45.87, fax 03.86.42.81.23, e-mail laurence.denis.race@wanadoo.fr ☑ Y by appt.

REGNARD Mont de Milieu 1998★★

☐ 2 ha 20,000 ▮ ♁ 100–149 F

This business was taken over by Patrick de Ladoucette in 1984. The morphology of Mont de Milieu makes this *climat* almost the twin brother of the Grand Cru. Without a doubt, it is one of the best Premiers Crus around. Confirmed here by a brilliant, golden yellow colour, a fine, subtle palate and, finally, the mushroom flavour that was once inseparable from the image of Chablis. **Montmains 98**, which receives one star, is a good example of its type, fine and pleasant.
🔑 Régnard, 28, bd Tacussel, 89800 Chablis, tel. 03.86.42.10.45, fax 03.86.42.48.67 ☑ Y by appt.

DOM. SAINTE CLAIRE
Côte de Jouan 1998★

☐ n.c. n.c. ▮ ♁ 50–69 F

Jean-Marc Brocard settled here in 1974. This year, with the 98 vintage, he obtains three recommendations: for the **Beauregard, Vaucoupin**, and for this *climat* (in the Les Landes and Verjuts area, near Courgis) which is one of the most recent Premiers Crus. This is a wine of great aromatic finesse and on the whole well-balanced. Although the Vaucoupins need to wait one to three years, the two other crus are ready to drink now.
🔑 Jean-Marc Brocard, 3, rte. de Chablis, 89800 Préhy, tel. 03.86.41.49.00, fax 03.86.41.49.09, e-mail brocard@brocard.fr ☑ Y ev. day except Sun. Mon. 9.30am–12.30pm 3pm–7pm; groups by appt.

DOM. VINCENT SAUVESTRE
Beauroy 1998★

☐ 4 ha 25,000 ▮ ♁ 70–99 F

A native of Meursault in Chablis might be something of a surprise, but then, the 2001 Saint-Vincent wine festival takes place at Meursault. As for this Beauroy, it has plenty of substance and is a very expressive wine in all aspects. It has all the right qualities for the appellation and is developing as it should. A pleasant almond finish.
🔑 Dom. Vincent Sauvestre, rte. de Monthélie, B.P. 3, 21190 Meursault, tel. 03.80.21.22.45, fax 03.80.21.28.05 Y by appt.

DANIEL SEGUINOT
Fourchaume 1998★★

☐ 3.8 ha 4,000 ▮ ♁ 50–69 F

This wine could take on a Grand Cru on equal terms. Youth and freshness dominate a palate that has a hint of liveliness to perk it up. Full of charming, lingering aromas. Well-balanced with perfect elegance. Good for laying down. Could scale even greater heights.
🔑 SCEA Daniel Seguinot, rte. de Tonnerre, 89800 Maligny, tel. 03.86.47.51.40, fax 03.86.47.43.37 ☑ Y by appt.

DOM. SERVIN Les Forêts 1998

☐ 0.37 ha 2,400 ▮ 50–69 F

How many Premiers Crus are there in Chablis? Seventy-nine, to be precise – gathered behind 11 different standard bearers, granted. This one enrolled in the Vau-Ligneau camp, but, thanks above all to René Dauvissat, it manages to have its own personality. This is a golden-coloured wine with a hawthorn aroma and a finely balanced richness and acidity. Plenty of length.
🔑 SCE Dom. Servin, 20, av. d'Oberwesel, 89800 Chablis, tel. 03.86.18.90.00, fax 03.86.18.90.01, e-mail servin@domaine-servin.fr ☑ Y by appt.

SIMONNET-FEBVRE Vaillons 1998★

☐ 1.75 ha 13,000 ▮ ♁ 70–99 F

'I like this very Chablis-like wine', writes one taster. You could stop there, because he has said it all: the shades of green in its gold colour, the aromas of spring blossom, citrus fruits and mineral, the freshness and length on the palate. Its future? We give it at least two years.
🔑 Simonnet-Febvre, 9, av. d'Oberwesel, 89800 Chablis, tel. 03.86.98.99.00, fax 03.86.98.99.01 ☑ Y by appt.

DOM. DE VAUROUX Forêt 1998★★

☐ n.c. n.c. ▮ ♁ 70–99 F

This is a lovely wine-maker's wine. Gold discreetly tinted with emerald, a typical vintage 98 nose, with a little exotic something to liven it up. All our judges thought it was delicious. A 'wine for drinking with friends'. A Premier Cru that has been excellently vinified.
🔑 SCEA Dom. de Vauroux, rte. d'Avallon, B.P. 56, 89800 Chablis, tel. 03.86.42.10.37, fax 03.86.42.49.13 ☑
🔑 Olivier Tricon

DOM. VERRET Beauroy 1998★

☐ 6.24 ha 20,000 ▮ ♁ 50–69 F

This Beauroy lives up to its name (which means 'handsome king'): heraldic gold in colour, with a nose of toast, acacia flowers and honey, and an upfront expressive palate.

Round but not flabby, tender and velvety. A gourmand of a wine.

🔑 Dom. Verret, 7, rte. de Champs, B.P. 4, 89530 Saint-Bris-le-Vineux, tel. 03.86.53.31.81, fax 03.86.53.89.61, e-mail bruno.verret@wanadoo.fr ☑ 🍷 by appt.

DOM. VOCORET ET FILS

La Forêt 1998*

☐ n.c. n.c. 50–69 F

This estate, founded at the turn of the 20th century, presents a very pleasant 98, well-made, with charming notes of hawthorn and oak. Still a little closed, but with acidity that augurs well. Our jury promises that it will be showing great subtlety in three or four years' time.

🔑 Dom. Vocoret et Fils, 40, rte. d'Auxerre, 89800 Chablis, tel. 03.86.42.12.53, fax 03.86.42.10.39 ☑ 🍷 by appt.

Chablis Grand Cru

Grown on the best exposed hills on the right bank of the Yonne and divided into seven *lieux-dits* (Blanchot, Bougros, les Clos, Grenouilles, Preuses, Valmur and Vaudésir), Chablis Grand Cru is a clear cut above its juniors. Chablis Grand Cru is, at its peak, a most complete wine with a lingering aroma and a certain bite from the terroir (a sedimentary layer of stones and clay) that distinguishes it from its rivals further to the south. It has an astonishing capacity for ageing, requiring between eight and 15 years to develop harmoniously and to acquire its unforgettable gunflint bouquet (in the best Clos, it even has traces of gunpowder!).

JEAN-CLAUDE BESSIN

Valmur 1998

☐ 1.8 ha n.c. 100–149 F

A Grand Cru that is golden like a crusty loaf, buttery and creamy, rich and long on the palate. Best left in the cellar for two or three years.

🔑 Jean-Claude Bessin, 3, rue de la Planchotte, 89800 Chablis, tel. 03.86.42.46.77, fax 03.86.42.85.30 ☑ 🍷 by appt.

DOM. BILLAUD-SIMON

Vaudésir 1998**

☐ 0.7 ha 4,000 150–199 F

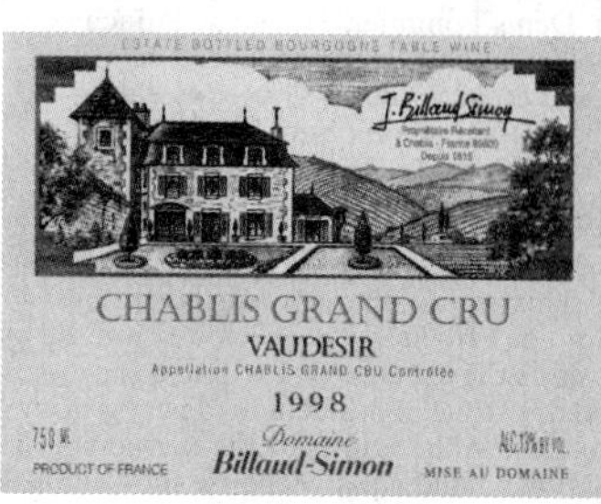

We tasted the **Blanchots Vieilles Vignes**, which gets a recommendation, and the **Preuses 98**, which gets one star, in the cellar here. Vaudésir, which is a notch above the rest, should be in your cellar. So mineral it is almost chalky, and then a moment later it feels as if you are biting into fresh fruit. Very ripe, switching between peach and apricot, and a great all-rounder. Obviously, it should be left to age.

🔑 Dom. Billaud-Simon, 1, quai de Reugny, B.P. 46, 89800 Chablis, tel. 03.86.42.10.33, fax 03.86.42.48.77 ☑ 🍷 ev. day except Sat. Sun. 9am–6pm; cl. 15 Aug.–1 Sep.

BLASONS DE BOURGOGNE

Les Preuses 1998**

☐ 3.4 ha 22,000 150–199 F

This patch of vineyard, which runs along Bougros towards the top of the coast, achieved its AOC status in 1938. They say this wine is easy to get to grips with: the most spontaneous of the family. This one is pale green, a colour that has not matured much, but its perfume of roses hints at distinction, and although not very oaky, because it is only partially-matured in barrel, this is a true Grand Cru wine. The label is from the co-operative La Chablisienne.

🔑 Blasons de Bourgogne, rue du Serein, 89800 Chablis, tel. 03.86.42.88.34, fax 03.86.42.83.75

JEAN-MARC BROCARD

Bougros 1998

☐ n.c. n.c. 100–149 F

Jean-Marc Brocard is the Guy Roux of the Chablis vineyards. He arrived in the Côte-d'Or with only his courage in his pocket and became a builder and a creator. His Bougros has a serene colour and a nose of Olympian calm. Very lively for a Grand Cru, but it is a 98, and that is the way the vintage is.

🔑 Jean-Marc Brocard, 3, rte. de Chablis, 89800 Préhy, tel. 03.86.41.49.00, fax 03.86.41.49.09, e-mail brocard@brocard.fr ☑ 🍷 ev. day except Sun. Mon. 9.30am–12.30pm 3pm–7pm; groups by appt.

DOM. CHRISTOPHE CAMU

Les Clos 1998

☐ 0.04 ha 300 100–149 F

This is the first harvest of a little vineyard parcel acquired by Christophe Camu. The result is a 98 with a coppery tint and an expressive nose of green apples. Well-made, it respects its terroir. Rich in alcohol, soft and almost mellow, giving an impression of age, but it lacks the vigour of a true Chablis.

Christophe Camu, av. de la Liberté, 89800 Maligny, tel. 03.86.42.12.50, fax 03.86.42.14.40 ev. day 9.30am–7pm

DOM. JEAN COLLET ET FILS

Valmur 1998★★

☐ 0.51 ha 3,400 100–149 F

Jean Collet is one of the great pillars of Chablis society, and he has been an important influence in this vineyard. Three parcels of land, on a half a hectare (just over an acre) in Valmur, yield this pleasantly oaky, golden sun-yellow 98 that has a little touch of the exotic but also a really noble character. 'Excellent – the work of a real pro', is the jury's verdict on a wine that is already attractive and which will keep well in the cellar.

SCEA du Dom. Jean Collet et Fils, 15, av. de la Liberté, 89800 Chablis, tel. 03.86.42.11.93, fax 03.86.42.47.43, e-mail collet.chablis@wanadoo.fr ev. day except Sun. 9am–12 noon 1.30pm–6pm

RENE ET VINCENT DAUVISSAT

Les Preuses 1998★★

☐ n.c. 5,000 100–149 F

The climat of Les Preuses extends beyond Bougros, towards the top of the coast on a long gently sloping hill. It yields a wine whose maturation in wood has been perfectly handled. Brimming with gold, it has a good character with well-balanced, subtle oaky notes and a fresh acidity on the finish that adds length. 'We were waiting for it, and here it is', concludes one delighted taster.

GAEC René et Vincent Dauvissat, 8, rue Emile-Zola, 89800 Chablis, tel. 03.86.42.11.58, fax 03.86.42.85.32

JEAN DAUVISSAT Les Preuses 1997

☐ 0.28 ha n.c. 150–199 F

A 97 is not on an equal footing with a 98, at least not during the same tasting, but this one is not at all bad. It has very pronounced aromas of cooked fruit. Not too round, but it has something nice about it, and has a fellow feeling for its vintage.

Caves Jean Dauvissat, 3, rue de Chichée, 89800 Chablis, tel. 03.86.42.14.62, fax 03.86.42.45.54 by appt.

JEAN-PAUL DROIN Vaudésir 1998★★

☐ 1.03 ha 7,000 100–149 F

Count your steps, because we are going to seventh heaven. Firstly, a very successful **Grenouille 98** (one star), and ditto the **Les Clos 98**. Two stars for the **Valmur 98** which

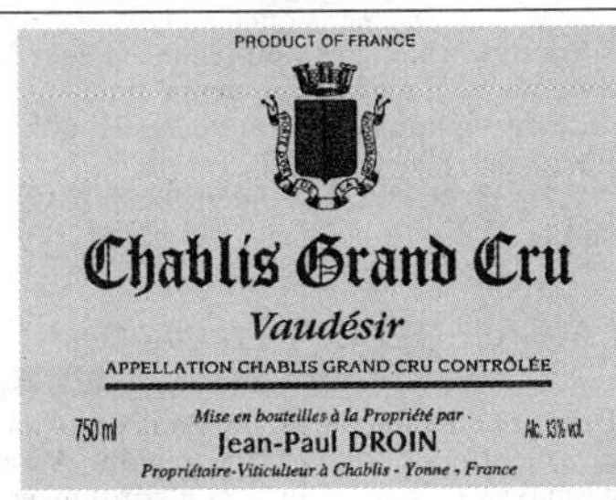

balances richness and acidity in a remarkable way. Jean-Paul Droin, who has won a few prizes in his time, now manages the feat again with this exuberant, vanilla Vaudésir, with its flinty, fresh fruit nose (grapefruit and lemon). Rich and powerful yet subtle, on the palate it brings together nutty notes resulting in something very elegant. Long life guaranteed.

Jean-Paul Droin, 14 bis, rue Jean-Jaurès, 89800 Chablis, tel. 03.86.42.16.78, fax 03.86.42.42.09 by appt.

JOSEPH DROUHIN Les Clos 1998★★

☐ n.c. n.c. 200–249 F

The vineyards of the Drouhin estate cover around 65 ha (160 acres) in Burgundy alone. They also own a vineyard in the USA. Robert Drouhin is the grandson of the founder of the estate, which began in 1880, and is very well-respected. His Les Clos is a deep yellow, with a nose of iris and orange-peel underlying a subtle but noticeable oakiness. It is rich, unpretentious, full, well-balanced and long, and still has time to spread its wings over the next three or four years and remain a very good wine.

Joseph Drouhin, 7, rue d'Enfer, 21200 Beaune, tel. 03.80.24.68.88, fax 03.80.22.43.14, e-mail drouhin@calva.net by appt.

DOM. WILLIAM FEVRE

Les Preuses 1998★★★

☐ 2.09 ha 9,240 200–249 F

William Fèvre has been taken over, like Bouchard Père et Fils, by Henriot, from Champagne. It remains one of the great estates, as this **Les Clos 98** testifies (250–299F, one star). An interesting wine, but the oak needs to blend in further to soften it. Another two wines from the estate are worthy of *coups de cœur*. There is a **Valmur 98** and, equally impressive, this greenish-gold, adorably soft

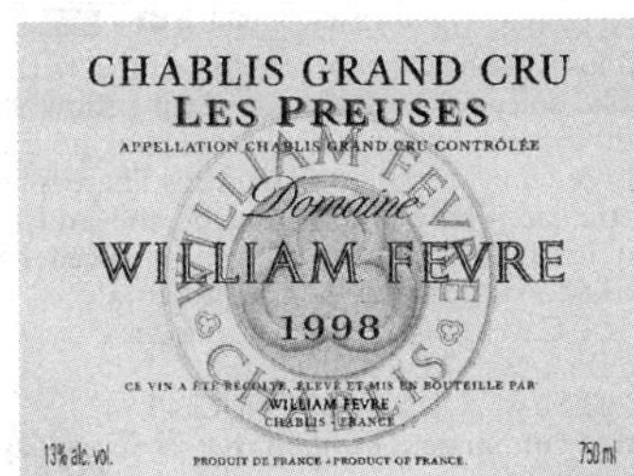

Les Preuses, which has well-balanced oak. It will be magnificent in a few years' time.
🗝 Sté du Vignoble William Fèvre, 21, av. d'Oberwesel, 89800 Chablis, tel. 03.86.98.98.98, fax 03.86.98.98.99 🅈 🍷 by appt.

ALAIN GEOFFROY Les Clos 1998★

☐ n.c. n.c. 150–199 F

Being elected mayor of Beines is proof of Alain Geoffroy's love of the region. As a wine-maker, he passes for a modern thinker, giving us inspirational wines that are easy to drink. This light yellow 98, with a very green, ferny nose, takes a while to open out, but its character comes to the fore on the palate. A subtle oakiness, strong acidity. A wine to keep for two or three years.
🗝 Dom. Alain Geoffroy, 4, rue de l'Equerre, 89800 Beines, tel. 03.86.42.43.76, fax 03.86.42.13.30 🅈 🍷 by appt.

CH. GRENOUILLE Grenouille 1998★

☐ 2 ha 12,000 🛢 150–199 F

Château Grenouille: this estate is the former property of the Testut family. Their 2 ha (5 acres) of land, which have often produced fascinating results, are now run by a group, at the head of which is La Chablisienne. This promising 98 is pale in colour and has a certain toastiness about the nose. There are still strong oak flavours on the palate, but in two or three years' time they will have blended in, as the wine itself shows decent balance.
🗝 La Chablisienne, 8, bd Pasteur, B.P. 14, 89800 Chablis, tel. 03.86.42.89.89, fax 03.86.42.89.90, e-mail chab@chablisienne.com 🅈 🍷 by appt.

DOM. MICHEL GUITTON

Les Clos 1997

☐ 0.16 ha 1,200 🛢 100–149 F

Les Clos is the biggest of all the *climats* of the Grand Cru. Very clear, golden-yellow in colour, forest-floor on the nose; the acidity is in just the right place to back up the fruit. A subtle oakiness accompanies this fine, well-matured wine.
🗝 Dom. Guitton-Michel, 2, rue de Poinchy, 89800 Chablis, tel. 03.86.42.43.14, fax 03.86.42.17.64 🅈 🍷 by appt.

LA CAVE DU CONNAISSEUR

Les Clos 1998★

☐ 0.18 ha 1,000 🛢 100–149 F

This Cave has only been selling direct to the public since 1989. Here is a deep yellow 98 with coppery tones and a nose that hovers between hawthorn and mandarin. There is an exotic, decidedly citrus note on the attack, and its slight oakiness is well-balanced by vitality. Fruity, this wine has potential.
🗝 La Cave du Connaisseur, rue des Moulins, B.P. 78, 89800 Chablis, tel. 03.86.42.87.15, fax 03.86.42.49.84, e-mail connaisseur@chablis.net 🅈 🍷 ev. day 10am–6.30pm

DOM. LAROCHE

Les Blanchots 1998★★

☐ 4.5 ha 30,000 🛢 200–249 F

Les Blanchots has made the reputation of *Obédiencerie*, and with good reason. This example is perfectly-made and of exemplary quality. Gold shines in the glass. You can smell stone and flint: an accomplished mineral quality. The palate explodes with a mixture of both fresh and crystallised fruit and finishes with a remarkable freshness. The cru is respected to perfection. Leave it in peace for four or five years, otherwise you would be insulting it.
🗝 Dom. Laroche, 22, rue Louis-Bro, 89800 Chablis, tel. 03.86.42.89.29, fax 03.86.42.89.00, e-mail info@domainelaroche.fr 🅈 🍷 by appt.

DOM. LONG-DEPAQUIT

Moutonne Monopole 1997★

☐ 2.35 ha 15,000 🛢 🌡 150–199 F

Albert Bichot managed to carve a space for himself in Chablis by taking over the Long-Depaquit estate. This Grand Cru, La Moutonne, is mineral and floral, just as it should be. The nose, however, is still a little closed, while the palate is growing in strength, and has a good freshness to it. A very agreeable wine.
🗝 Dom. de la Moutonne, 45, rue Auxerroise, 89800 Chablis, tel. 03.86.42.11.13, fax 03.86.42.81.89 🅈 🍷 ev. day except Sun. 9am–12.30pm 1.30pm–6pm
🗝 Albert Bichot

DOM. DES MALANDES

Les Clos 1996

☐ 0.53 ha 3,700 🛢 🌡 100–149 F

Which to choose? The **Vaudésir 97**? It is a wine in its prime that should be drunk now. Or this Les Clos? A lemon-green 96 with impressive length. Still very fresh, it could develop into something special late in life: it certainly hasn't said its last word.
🗝 Dom. des Malandes, 63, rue Auxerroise, 89800 Chablis, tel. 03.86.42.41.37, fax 03.86.42.41.97, e-mail domaine.malandes.chablis@wanadoo.fr 🅈 🍷 by appt.

LOUIS MICHEL ET FILS

Grenouilles 1998

☐ 0.5 ha 1000 🛢 🌡 100–149 F

After the 'Château', the Michels are the biggest producers of Grenouilles, with half a

hectare (just over an acre) devoted to it. There is a little hint of bitterness in this 98, but it has a distinctive nose of ripe, almost crystallised fruit, a soft, golden yellow colour, and a lot of character. We should also mention the very expressive **Les Clos 98**. This is a wine that grabs your attention, fills your nose and your entire mouth. A thoroughbred that has an astonishing amount of get-up-and-go for its vintage.
🔑 Louis Michel et Fils, 9, bd de Ferrières, 89800 Chablis, tel. 03.86.42.88.55, fax 03.86.42.88.56 ☑ Y by appt.

J. MOREAU ET FILS Valmur 1998★

□ 1.98 ha 12,094 100–149 F

A Valmur with a remarkably delicate colour. Its straightforward but slightly heavy, buttery nose heralds a mature palate with a lot of character. It is very true to the appellation.
🔑 J. Moreau et Fils, rte. d'Auxerre, La Croix Saint-Joseph, 89800 Chablis, tel. 03.86.42.88.00, fax 03.86.42.88.08

DENIS RACE Blanchot 1998★

□ 0.3 ha 1,900 100–149 F

The first impression is fresh fruit and flint. Then there is a short attack, followed by a solid, powerful intensity of flavours. That's a Blanchot for you.
🔑 Denis Race, 5 A, rue de Chichée, 89800 Chablis, tel. 03.86.42.45.87, fax 03.86.42.81.23, e-mail laurence.denis.race@wanadoo.fr ☑ Y by appt.

REGNARD Grenouilles 1998★

□ 0.35 ha 3,000 200–249 F

This Grenouilles could use another two or three years in the cellar. A lovely gold colour, good and rich, it has a pleasant freshness; but it is still very closed, although it shows plenty of promise. It acheives the correct standard for its appellation, no more nor less. The **Valmur 98** also gets a star but can be drunk sooner. As for the **Clos 98**, which receives a recommendation, it is well vinified, but needs another two to three years before drinking. This well-established Chablis estate has been acquired by Patrick de Ladoucette, who is well-known in the Loire Valley.
🔑 Régnard, 28, bd Tacussel, 89800 Chablis, tel. 03.86.42.10.45, fax 03.86.42.48.67 ☑ Y by appt.

DOM. SERVIN Les Preuses 1998

□ 0.69 ha 4,500 100–149 F

Here are three different versions of the Grand Cru, and every one of them has been selected. The **Les Clos 98** and **Blanchot 98** need to be left to age a while, of course. As for this winey and lemony Les Preuses, it has a bit of everything. The roundness only just arrives to hit the spot, but it reaches the right standard.
🔑 SCE Dom. Servin, 20, av. d'Oberwesel, 89800 Chablis, tel. 03.86.18.90.00, fax 03.86.18.90.01, e-mail servin@domaine-servin.fr ☑ Y by appt.

Bourgogne Irancy

The fame of this small vineyard, located about 15 km (9 miles) south of Auxerre, was acknowledged when it became an AOC commune.

The red wines of Irancy have acquired something of a reputation thanks to the César or Romain, a local grape variety which may go back as far as Gallic times. It is a rather temperamental variety, capable of giving the best and the worst of results. When production is low to average, it stamps a particularly tannic character on the wine that makes for very long-term keeping. On the other hand, when the volume of production is high, the César does not easily lend itself to good wine-making, and this is why it is not a compulsory ingredient for the appellation.

The Pinot Noir variety is the main one used, and on the slopes of Irancy it makes a high-quality, very fruity and ruddy-coloured wine. The terroir takes its character mainly from the topographical situation of the vineyard, essentially laid out on slopes forming a bowl with the village standing in the hollow. This terroir also borders on the two neighbouring communes of Vincelotte and Cravant, whose Côte de Palotte wines were once very highly thought of. Production was 6,419 hl (169,462 gal) in 1999.

BENOIT CANTIN
Cuvée Emeline 1998★

■ 2.2 ha 8,000 50–69 F

This is a 98 that that takes its role seriously. The grape variety harmonises perfectly with this chalky-limestone terroir. The wine is a deep violet-purple, with a nose of undergrowth, wild strawberries, and just a suggestion of a certain gamey quality. On the palate, it has both suppleness and length, a likeable wine with some character (of Pinot Noir).
🔑 Benoît Cantin, 35, chem. des Fossés, 89290 Irancy, tel. 03.86.42.21.96, fax 03.86.42.24.96 ☑ Y by appt.

ANITA ET JEAN-PIERRE COLINOT 1998★

■ 7 ha n.c. 50–69 F

This dynamic estate is well-known to readers of the *Guide*. The Colinots, proud of their new AOC, produce a 100% Pinot Noir Irancy **Les Mazelots 98** (one star), which has a volcanic (flinty) nose and which will give free rein to all its qualities over the next year or so. Then there is this wine, which contains 5% César, a rare and wonderful grape variety of this region, that can also draw out the best from the Pinot. It is a very purple Irancy with an intense musky, fruity nose. The palate has depth, personality, and a good length. Would go well with either hare or rabbit, depending which is available.

Anita et Jean-Pierre Colinot, 1, rue des Chariats, 89290 Irancy, tel. 03.86.42.33.25, fax 03.86.42.33.25 by appt.

ROGER DELALOGE 1998

■ 4 ha 25,000 30–49 F

Here it is, this new vintage that can simply be called Irancy, nothing more. There is just a hint of César (0.5%) in this wine: in reality it's a Pinot. A pronounced shade of red with a fruity, round and soft nose, without excessive acidity.

Roger Delaloge, 1, ruelle du Milieu, 89290 Irancy, tel. 03.86.42.20.94, fax 03.86.42.33.40 by appt.

FRANCK GIVAUDIN 1998★

■ 2 ha 15,000 50–69 F

It is easy to understand why they are so proud to be finally able to write 'Irancy' on the label and not 'Bourgogne Irancy' . . . This wine, made in a straightforward fashion, blends 5% César with Pinot. Dark in colour, quite spicy, with blackcurrant dominating as soon as it hits the palate, and with sufficient structure to age well.

Franck Givaudin, Sentier de la Bergère, 89290 Irancy, tel. 03.86.42.20.67, fax 03.86.42.54.33 by appt.

THIERRY RICHOUX 1998

■ 11 ha 45,000 30–49 F

This very old family business is proud to present its first Irancy AOC. They do things the old-fashioned way here: hand-picked grapes, hand-sorted and de-stemmed, a year in barrel. All of which combine to give this lovely wine its deep colour. Soft fruit on the nose and a round, pleasant palate.

Thierry Richoux, 73, rue Soufflot, 89290 Irancy, tel. 03.86.42.21.60, fax 03.86.42.34.35 ev. day 8am–7pm

DOM. SAINT-GERMAIN 1998

■ 7 ha 31,000 30–49 F

Christophe Ferrari became a wine-producer in 1987. His Irancy takes on two forms: this one, and *lieu-dit* **Paradis 98**, which is of similar quality. Cherry red in colour it has a good, chewy fruitiness. Well-presented example of the AOC.

Christophe Ferrari, 7, chem. des Fossés, 89290 Irancy, tel. 03.86.42.33.43, fax 03.86.42.39.30 by appt.

HUBERT ET JEAN-PAUL TABIT

Haut Champreux 1998★★

■ 2 ha 5,000 30–49 F

This stunning 98 could have won the Palme d'Or at Cannes. Best colour, best nose and what an intense, mellow, dramatic *mise en scène*. There is nothing more to say, all the qualities are there.

Hubert et Jean-Paul Tabit, 2, rue Dorée, 89530 Saint-Bris-le-Vineux, tel. 03.86.53.33.83, fax 03.86.53.67.97 ev. day 8am–12 noon 2pm–8pm; Sun. by appt.

DOM. VERRET

Elevé en fût de chêne 1998

■ 12 ha 15,000 50–69 F

This Saint-Bris estate has not been afraid to expand, most notably in the Chablis region. Its light red Irancy is lacking a little on the nose. However, it has a good palate that is fruity and well-balanced, despite a hint of alcohol – but then wine without alcohol isn't wine, is it?

Dom. Verret, 7, rte. de Champs, B.P. 4, 89530 Saint-Bris-le-Vineux, tel. 03.86.53.31.81, fax 03.86.53.89.61, e-mail bruno.verret@wanadoo.fr by appt.

Sauvignon de Saint-Bris AOVDQS

This wine used to be a more modest affair, but it is now of superior quality and, as the appellation suggests, is made from the Sauvignon grape in the communes of Saint-Bris-le-Vineux, Chitry, Irancy and parts of the communes of Quenne, Saint-Cyr-les-

[C]olons and Cravant. It is grown [m]ainly on areas of limestone pla[te]aux from which it draws a certain [a]romatic intensity. In contrast to [w]ines made from the same grape [v]ariety in the Loire Valley and the [S]ancerre, the Sauvignon de Saint-[B]ris generally goes through a [m]alolactic fermentation, though [t]his does not affect its perfumed, [s]upple character. These qualities [a]re shown to best advantage when [i]ts alcoholic content reaches [a]round 12°. Saint-Bris is due to [b]ecome an AOC.

[G]HISLAINE ET JEAN-HUGUES [G]OISOT Corps de garde gourmand 1998★

☐ 1.5 ha 10,000 50–69 F

Deep gold, with a modest floral nose and a [s]trong flavour of pear drops, soft with a good [f]inish. It lasts well on the palate, which is what [o]ne expects.

Ghislaine et Jean-Hugues Goisot, 30, [r]ue Bienvenu-Martin, 89530 Saint-Bris-le-[V]ineux, tel. 03.86.53.35.15, [f]ax 03.86.53.62.03 by appt.

[D]OM. GERARD PERSENOT 1999

☐ 2.5 ha 15,000 20–29 F

The colour is of finest, shiny gold. The nose [i]s fruity with elements of undergrowth, very [t]ypical. The attack is vigorous and warm, [t]hen the palate evolves step by step. A year in [t]he cellar will do it a world of good.

Gérard Persenot, 20, rue de Gouaix, [8]9530 Saint-Bris-le-Vineux, [t]el. 03.86.53.61.46, fax 03.86.53.61.52 [b]y appt.

[D]OM. DES REMPARTS 1999★★

☐ 4 ha 10,000 30–49 F

This is very much a Sauvignon, with its pale [s]traw colour and greyish tints. The nose is all [w]hite-fleshed fruits and exoticism. The palate [i]s a good example of this style. A wine that is [r]eady to drink but that realistically should [w]ait a while.

Dom. des Remparts, 6, rte. de Champs, [8]9530 Saint-Bris-le-Vineux, [t]el. 03.86.53.33.59, fax 03.86.53.62.12 [b]y appt.

Sorin

[P]HILIPPE SORIN 1998

☐ 4.5 ha 40,000 30–49 F

This Sauvignon is the colour of old gold with hints of silver. The nose is closed. The attack is supple and subtle and, at the same time, has firm acidity that would go well with shellfish.

Marylène et Philippe Sorin, 12, rue de Paris, 89530 Saint-Bris-le-Vineux, tel. 03.86.53.60.76, fax 03.86.53.62.60, e-mail philippe.sorin@libertysurf.fr by appt.

DOM. VERRET 1999★

☐ 5.33 ha 40,000 30–49 F

The Sauvignon de Saint-Bris is an appellation that is in the process of changing. Here, the colour is pale yellow with some silver, the nose grassy green and powerful, the attack lively. The balance is just right and it ought to go well with warm oysters in a butter sauce.

Dom. Verret, 7, rte de Champs, B.P. 4, 89530 Saint-Bris-le-Vineux, tel. 03.86.53.31.81, fax 03.86.53.89.61, e-mail bruno.verret@wanadoo.fr by appt.

BURGUNDY

La Côte de Nuits

Marsannay

Geographers are still discussing where the northern limits of the Côte de Nuits should be drawn. During the 19th century, flourishing vineyards in communes around Dijon made up the Côte Dijonnaise. Today, apart from a few remaining vines like Marcs d'Or and Montreculs, Dijon's urban sprawl has forced the vineyards to the south of the city, and even Chenôve has difficulty in keeping its pretty hillside planted with vines.

At one time, Marsannay, then Couchey, supplied the town with Grands Ordinaires, but failed to obtain recognition as AOC Communales in 1935. Little by little, the wine-growers replanted the terroirs with Pinot, starting the tradition of making rosé which is identified as a local appellation: 'Bourgogne Rosé de Marsannay'. Then red and white wines of the pre-phylloxera era were rediscovered and, after more than twenty-five years of effort and research, the AOC Marsannay was registered in 1987 for all three colours. There is also a local Burgundy peculiarity, the 'Marsannay Rosé', which is produced on the lower slopes on gravelly soil. This vineyard occupies a larger area than those given to the red and white wines, which can be grown only on the slopes of the three communes of Chenôve, Marsannay-la-Côte and Couchey.

These sturdy red wines are a little harsh in their youth and must wait a few years to mature. It is most unusual to find white wines in the Côte de Nuits, but the Chardonnay and the Pinot Blanc find the marly soils particularly well adapted to their needs and these whites are particularly sought after for their finesse and solid body.

The vineyards produced 7,908 hl (208,771 gal) of red and rosé wine and 1,667 hl (440,008 gal) of white in 1999. The hillsides are currently being replanted.

DOM. BART 1998★

2 ha 12,000 30–49 F

Marsannay is known as the 'tricolour' wine because the AOC covers red, white, and rosé wines. The rosé is what we have here, in the form of this smooth, light salmon-pink wine with its notes of hawthorn and freshly-picked fruit. Note also the **Les Champs-Salomon 97 Rouge** (one star, 50–69F): a fresh and fruity Marsannay.

GAEC Bart, 23, rue Moreau, 21160 Marsannay-la-Côte, tel. 03.80.51.49.76, fax 03.80.51.23.43 by appt.

DOM. REGIS BOUVIER Les Longeroies Vieilles vignes 1998★

1.65 ha 10,000 50–69 F

Firstly, we should turn to the pleasantly lively **Rosé 98** (30–49F), which is given a recommendation by the jury. Light, yet with plenty of character. This deep ruby-red Longeroies has its perfumes of leather and cooked fruit, plus a good structure with gentle tannins and crystallised soft fruit. A fine example.

Dom. Régis Bouvier, 52, rue de Mazy, 21160 Marsannay-la-Côte, tel. 03.80.51.33.93, fax 03.80.58.75.07 by appt.

RENE BOUVIER Clos du Roy 1998★

1.84 ha 5,000 70–99 F

René Bouvier, the father of Régis Bouvier, presents four wines for us to choose from here, and not one of them is a dud. The **98 Le Clos (Monopole)**, and **Blanc, Champ-Salomon – Longeroies Rouges** mean each receives a recommendation from the jury while, the ambitious and robust Clos du Roy is a cut above the rest. Both its colour and its vanilla an fruit aromas are intense. Well-structured wi strong, well-balanced tannins: this wine ha good depth.

René Bouvier, 2, rue Neuve, 21160 Marsannay-la-Côte, tel. 03.80.52.21.37, fax 03.80.59.95.96 by appt.

MARC BROCOT Les Echézeaux 1998

0.75 ha 4,026 50–69

Echézeaux is a name that crops up fre quently in the Côte, and it is again present i Marsannay wines. Here we have a fresh, ruby red 98 with a strawberry nose and a soft, sup ple palate with the same strawberry tender cies. It is still a little aloof and should be hel back a short while, but this is not a wine fo laying down.

Marc Brocot, 34, rue du Carré, 21160 Marsannay-la-Côte, tel. 03.80.52.19.99, fax 03.80.59.84.39 ev. day 8am–8pm

DOM. BRUNO CLAIR Les Grasses Têtes 1997★

1 ha 4,000 70–99 F

Bruno Clair had been thinking abou sheep-raising, but when your father is wine producer Bernard Clair, you have wine growing in your blood. This wine is ruby-re with shades of violet – a nice, deep colou Bigarreau cherry on the nose, followed b blackcurrant with hints of vanilla pod. It is soft, fruity wine, playing the flute rather tha the trumpet, but at least it knows th difference

Bruno Clair, 5, rue du Vieux-Collège, 21160 Marsannay-la-Côte, tel. 03.80.52.28.95, fax 03.80.52.18.14 by appt.

CLOS SAINT-LOUIS 1998

0.5 ha 2,000

Clear and with a medium depth of colour This wine has a slightly sharp nose, though just at the end of it there are little hints of raspberry and redcurrant filtering through which makes its sharpness forgiveable. Altogether, this is a light, pleasant wine that has been well-made.

Dom. du Clos Saint-Louis, 4, rue des Rosiers, 21220 Fixin, tel. 03.80.52.45.51, fax 03.80.58.88.76 ev. day except Sun. 9am–12 noon 1.30pm–6pm; cl. 20 Dec.– 3 Jan., 15–30 Aug.

BERNARD COILLOT PERE ET FILS Les Boivins 1998

0.77 ha 4,000 50–69 F

This is one of the terroirs that is situated just above the village of the same name. Find a better one if you can. The colour of this 98 is still young, yet with deep tones. The nose is heading in the direction of fruitiness, but is not clear yet if it will be red berry or bilberry fruit. The palate, meanwhile, is more along the lines of dried fruit (figs). The tannins are still pretty powerful, and this is a wine that should really be left to mature in the cellar.

Bernard Coillot Père et Fils, 31, rue du [C]hâteau, 21160 Marsannay-la-Côte, [te]l. 03.80.52.17.59, fax 03.80.52.12.75, [e-]mail domcoil@aol.com ☑ Y by appt.

[D]OM. COLLOTTE

[L]es Clos de Jeu 1998★

0.59 ha 30,000 50–69 F

This estate was very successful with a red [9]8, which is an excellent reason to explore this [lit]tle-known *climat*, hidden away high up on [M]arsannay-la-Côte, in the direction of [C]ouchey. This is a simple wine, in the best [se]nse of the word. It is straightforward and [i]mpulsive, it doesn't try to show off, but is [co]ntent to give a good impression of its [te]rroir and its characteristic style. The oddly-[sp]elled **Champsalomon 98** (which also receives [a] recommendation for the red), is also worth a [se]cond look. A wine to drink within the next [ye]ar.

Dom. Collotte, 44, rue de Mazy, 21160 [M]arsannay-la-Côte, tel. 03.80.52.24.34, [fa]x 03.80.58.74.40 ☑ Y by appt.

Philippe Collotte

[D]EREY FRERES 1998★★

1.7 ha 6,000 50–69 F

The Derey estate farms land rented from [th]e City of Dijon, at the Clos des Marcs. Here [th]ey present us with a very subtle Chardon-[n]ay with touches of mineral elements. It has [fi]nesse, with some real texture: it undoubtedly [c]omes from a good white wine terroir. A wine [th]at is not very rich and would be better [se]rved as an apértif together with a few [g]*ougères*.

EARL Derey Frères, 1, rue Jules-Ferry, [2]1160 Couchey, tel. 03.80.51.19.41, [f]ax 03.80.58.76.70 ☑ Y by appt.

[D]OM. FOUGERAY DE [B]EAUCLAIR

[L]e Dessus des Longeroies 1997★

n.c. n.c. 70–99 F

Jean-Louis Fougeray presents two wines of [s]imilar quality: the **Les Saint-Jacques 98** [(]which should not be kept for too long) and [t]his deep red Dessus des Longeroies 97, which [i]s complex from the very first sniff of the [n]ose, that opens with an aroma of cloves. The [s]pice reappears on the palate, mixed with [b]lackcurrant. Already supple and rounded. [D]rink it now or lay it down for a few years.

Dom. Fougeray de Beauclair, 44, rue de [M]azy, B.P. 36, 21160 Marsannay-la-Côte, [te]l. 03.80.52.21.12, fax 03.80.58.73.83, [e]-mail fougeraydebeauclair@wanadoo.fr ☑ Y by appt.

Jean-Louis Fougeray

[J]EAN FOURNIER Clos du Roy 1998★

1.6 ha 10,000 70–99 F

Clos du Roy is the flagship *climat* of the [A]OC, at least historically speaking. This 98 is [p]resented by the former president of the wine-[p]roducers' union, a man who has made an [e]normous contribution to the revival of [M]arsannay as an appellation. The tannins are still a little overpowering and the wine needs to soften considerably. It has a nice deep colour and quite a complex palate, with toasty, herbaceous, gamey and cooked fruit flavours. A full, long, vinous wine that is ready to drink.

Jean Fournier, 29–34, rue du Château, 21160 Marsannay-la-Côte, tel. 03.80.52.24.38, fax 03.80.52.77.40 ☑ Y by appt.

GOILLOT-BERNOLLIN

Clos du Roy 1998★

■ 0.3 ha 2,500 70–99 F

This *climat*, one of the oldest in Burgundy, situated high up on Chenôve, has been lucky to escape the ever-encroaching concrete. This very regal Clos du Roy is wearing full court dress of darkest red, with a scent of the hunt about: blackcurrant, prunes, game. Austere and still a little closed, it expresses itself rigorously. The extraction is impressive, there is a fair amount of potential here.

SCE Goillot-Bernollin, 29, rte. de Dijon, 21220 Gevrey-Chambertin, tel. 03.80.34.36.12, fax 03.80.34.16.00 ☑ Y by appt.

ALAIN GUYARD Les Etales 1997★

□ 1 ha 5,000 30–49 F

To really appreciate this very attractive wine, you have to like its beautiful pale gold colour, and enjoy its menthol notes mixed with the sweet vanilla flavours of the cask, and you don't have to place too much importance on the trace of acidity that will stand it in good stead in later years. Lively and fresh with a certain toastiness, it has good length.

Alain Guyard, 10, rue du Puits-de-Têt, 21160 Marsannay-la-Côte, tel. 03.80.52.14.46, fax 03.80.52.67.36 ☑ Y by appt.

DOM. OLIVIER GUYOT

La Montagne Vieilles vignes 1998★★

■ 0.7 ha 3,000 70–99 F

As the name suggests, this Montagne is situated high up on the hills, above Les Longeroies. Its violet-ruby colour shines brilliantly. The ripe soft fruits fill the nose with elegant aromas. It is well-structured and well-balanced, still a little young on the finish, where the tannins indicate that it is a good bet for laying down. It is a rich and remarkably successful 98.

EARL Olivier Guyot, 39, rue de Mazy, 21160 Marsannay-la-Côte, tel. 03.80.52.39.71, fax 03.80.51.17.58 ☑ Y by appt.

DOM. HUGUENOT PERE ET FILS

1998★

□ 2.5 ha 14,000 50–69 F

This wine-producer offers us the chance to share in the pleasures of his cellar with a **Rouge La Montagne 97** (a very fine wine, good for laying down, and which receives a star), and this white 98, which is already ready to drink. Very yellow in colour, it has a sunny

and attractive (gingerbread) nose, a supple and smooth palate. In brief, very pleasant.
🔑 Huguenot Père et Fils, 7, ruelle du Carron, 21160 Marsannay-la-Côte, tel. 03.80.52.11.56, fax 03.80.52.60.47, e-mail domaine.huguenot@wanadoo.fr ☑ 🍷 by appt.

CH. DE MARSANNAY 1998★★

◪ 7 ha 30,000 ▮ 🌡 30–49 F

CHATEAU DE MARSANNAY
Mise du Château
MARSANNAY
APPELLATION MARSANNAY CONTRÔLÉE
S.C. DOMAINE DU CHATEAU DE MARSANNAY
PROPRIÉTAIRE À MARSANNAY, CÔTE D'OR - FRANCE
D. DE L'ARGILLIÈRE
13% vol FRANCE 75 cl

The 95 vintage, of this rosé was excellent, and so is this 1998. Its colour is light with youthful hues. The aromas are Pinot from start to finish, and on the palate this vinosity is coupled with a combination of well-balanced richness and acidity. This is a wine of character, a million miles away from your standard rosés. The renovation of the château at Marsannay is one of André Boisseaux's latest ventures. In red, the **Echézeaux 97,** which receives one star (70–99F), is a reliable choice.
🔑 Ch. de Marsannay, rte des Grands-Crus, B.P. 78, 21160 Marsannay-la-Côte, tel. 03.80.51.71.11, fax 03.80.51.71.12 ☑ 🍷 ev. day 10am–12 noon 2pm–6.30pm; cl. 23 Dec.–3 Jan.

FRANCOIS MARTENOT 1998

■ n.c. 6,500 ▮ ⏸ 50–69 F

Although this wine shows some signs of development (most notably in its light red-brick colour), it is still worthy of inclusion in the *Guide*. It is a little short, but is supple and generally pretty pleasant. Like Henri de Villamont, François Martenot is a Burgundy label belonging to the Swiss group Schenk, which has been based here for several decades.
🔑 H.D.V. Distribution, rue du Dr-Barolet, ZI Beaune-Vignolles, 21200 Beaune, tel. 03.80.24.70.07, fax 03.80.22.54.31 🍷 by appt.

DOM. TRAPET PERE ET FILS 1998★

□ n.c. n.c. ⏸ 50–69 F

Jean Trapet did not betray Gevrey when he replanted his vineyard at Marsannay some years ago. This is still the Côte-de-Nuits, and Chardonnay does well here. Ripe, golden colour, elegantly smoky, this is a wine to lay down for a while. Well-balanced with good fullness and richness. A fine length that augurs well for the future.
🔑 Dom. Trapet Père et Fils, 53, rte. de Beaune, 21220 Gevrey-Chambertin, tel. 03.80.34.30.40, fax 03.80.51.86.34, e-mail message@domaine-trapet.com ☑ 🍷 by appt.

DOM. DU VIEUX COLLEGE 1998★

◪ 3 ha 15,000 ▮ 🌡 30–4

While most rosé wines just slip straig down leaving nothing on the palate, this o manages to leave its mark. It is bright, almo salmon-pink, with a fresh, subtle no (Morello cherry, bitter almonds), and with not unpleasant hint of greenness. Also show some depth. A good-looking wine.
🔑 Jean-Pierre et Eric Guyard-Dom. du Vieux Collège, 4, rue du Vieux-Collège, 21160 Marsannay-la-Côte, tel. 03.80.52.12.43, fax 03.80.52.95.85 ☑ 🍷 by appt.

Fixi

After visiting th wine presses of the Dukes of Bu gundy in Chenôve and tasting som Marsannay, the wine tourist arrive at Fixin, the first in a series of com munes that give their names t various Appellations d'Origin Contrôlée. Here growers produc mainly red wines – 5,320 hl (140,44 gal) of red wine and 171 hl (4,51 gal) of white – which are sturd well-structured, often tannic, an keep well. They can also reques the Appellation Côte-de-Nuits Villages when the harvest is picked.

The *climat* Hervelets, Arvelets, Clos d Chapitre and Clos Napoléon, a classed as Premiers Crus, are amon the best known, though the bes of all is Clos de la Perrière, whic has been described by eminen Burgundian writers as a 'Cuvé Hors Classe' (a wine beyond class and has been compared t Chambertin; the vineyard extends little into the commune of Brocho and neighbouring Miex-Bas.

DOM. BART Hervelets 1997★★

■ 1er cru 1.4 ha 4,000 ⏸ 70–99 F

A wine that is not far from the quality of *coup de cœur.* This *climat* is known for its soft fresh and fruity character, and that i ertainly what this superb, dark red 97 has. It s supple and crisp, with a nose showing uperb extraction (blackcurrant and blackerries). The flavour of the wood is in evience, but is not overwhelming. Then we each the second stage. Rounded and ppetising at first, it is followed by the charmng flavours of Morello cherry.

GAEC Bart, 23, rue Moreau, 21160 Marsannay-la-Côte, tel. 03.80.51.49.76, ax 03.80.51.23.43 ☒ Y by appt.

VINCENT ET DENIS BERTHAUT

Les Arvelets 1998★

1er cru	1 ha	3,000		100–149 F

The Berthaut brothers generally have a ucky touch when it comes to making their Les Arvelets. This is proved true once again in his very balanced wine. It is brilliant to look at and has a well-balanced nose. The fruit opens out with a lovely roundness and length. It is now ready to drink, but will continue to bloom for a while.

Vincent et Denis Berthaut, 9, rue Noisot, 21220 Fixin, tel. 03.80.52.45.48, fax 03.80.51.31.05 ☒ Y by appt.

DOM. REGIS BOUVIER 1998

■	0.3 ha	1,800		70–99 F

This is a rustic wine, with a leathery, damp fur, gamey perfume. Fixin is a winter wine to be drunk with game. This is a good example of its type, with persistent tannins and flavours of blackberry and undergrowth. It is a little on the solid side but is straightforward. It should be left to age a while to soften out.

Dom. Régis Bouvier, 52, rue de Mazy, 21160 Marsannay-la-Côte, tel. 03.80.51.33.93, fax 03.80.58.75.07 ☒ Y by appt.

BURGUNDY

Côte de Nuits (North 1)

RENE BOUVIER

Les Crais de chêne 1998★

■ 1.09 ha 4,000 70–99 F

Bernard Bouvier has been running this 17-ha (42-acre) family business since 1992. His Fixin is deep ruby-red, with rich, complex aromas of blackcurrant, spice and vanilla. On the palate you can feel its roundness and its strong foundations. The barrel-ageing has produced rather harsh tannins, but there is good extraction and the Pinot Noir has been respected. A thoroughbred wine with a taste of liquorice. Worth waiting for.

⊶ René Bouvier, 2, rue Neuve, 21160 Marsannay-la-Côte, tel. 03.80.52.21.37, fax 03.80.59.95.96 ☑ Y by appt.

LOUIS CHAVY 1997

■ n.c. 12,000 70–99 F

To go into detail, this wine is deep purple with shades of garnet and crimson, or more concisely, pure velvet. The nose is both generous and reserved. Well-handled extraction and lovely wood flavours. The attack is subtle, almost silenced by the tenacity of the tannins. Whether it will open up remains to be seen.

⊶ Louis Chavy, Caveau la Vierge Romaine, pl. des Marronniers, 21190 Puligny-Montrachet, tel. 03.80.26.33.00, fax 03.80.24.14.84, e-mail mallet.b@cva-beaune.fr ☑ Y ev. day 10am–6pm; cl. Nov.– Mar.

DOM. DU CLOS SAINT-LOUIS 1998

■ 4 ha 18,000 70–99 F

Situated opposite the uninspiring Fixey furnace, the Clos Saint-Louis used to be called the 'Clos Bizoutte', because lovers used to come here (bisou meaning kiss). It has been rechristened by the Bernard family, who are vinegar manufacturers turned wine-producers, amongst many other things. Their 98 is a pale cherry-red, with aromas of bilberry. It is a little woody and needs time for the various different components to integrate, which is why it should be laid down for a while.

⊶ Dom. du Clos Saint-Louis, 4, rue des Rosiers, 21220 Fixin, tel. 03.80.52.45.51, fax 03.80.58.88.76 ☑ Y ev. day except Sun. 9am–12 noon 1.30pm–6pm; cl. 20 Dec.–3 Jan., 15–30 Aug.

⊶ Philippe Bernard

MICHEL DEFRANCE 1998

■ 2 ha 4,200 30–49 F

This family's local archives go way back to 1610. Their deep ruby-red *village* appears tannic and closed, and yet it is a delight. What one can see, in fact, is its future complexity. In two or three years' time, this will be a perfect accompaniment to a meal of game.

⊶ Michel Defrance, 38–50, rte. des Grands-Crus, 21220 Fixin, tel. 03.80.52.84.67, fax 03.80.52.84.67 ☑ Y ev. day except Sun. 8.30am–12 noon 2pm–6pm

DOM. GUY DUFOULEUR

Clos du Chapitre 1997★★★

■ 1er cru 4.78 ha 5,000 150–199

This Clos de Chapitre is enough to wake u the statue of Napoleon that is found up on th hills of Fixin. This is a truly imperial wine and receives our *coup de cœur.* Dark violet i colour, the nose is blackcurrant mixed with delicate oakiness. Handled with skill, it start gently, not too decisive, then moves on t become fruity and firm. A generous win that uses its tannins wisely. A truly grea Burgundy.

⊶ Dom. Guy Dufouleur, 18, rue Thurot, 21700 Nuits-Saint-Georges, tel. 03.80.62.31.00, fax 03.80.62.31.00 ☑ Y by appt.

⊶ Xavier et Guy Dufouleur

DOM. FOUGERAY DE BEAUCLAIR

Clos Marion 1997★★

■ n.c. n.c. 150–199 F

Not the most mouthfilling of wines, bu the body is decently structured and well-balanced. The tannins are still present, with flavours of soft fruits steeped in alcohol. It seems to have very good prospects whichever way you look, whether you drink it now or keep it for a special occasion. A really pleasurable wine. Clos Marion recalls to mind the name of the great family of doctors and wine-producers from Clos de Bèze and the Academy of Medicine.

⊶ Dom. Fougeray de Beauclair, 44, rue de Mazy, B.P. 36, 21160 Marsannay-la-Côte, tel. 03.80.52.21.12, fax 03.80.58.73.83, e-mail fougeraydebeauclair@wanadoo.fr ☑ Y by appt.

DOM. PIERRE GELIN

Clos Napoléon 1997

■ 1er cru 1.8 ha 9,500 100–149 F

In the 1950s, the Gelin family bought the vines that formerly belonged to Claude Noisot, a member of Napoleon's Guard who persuaded Fixin to support the Emperor. This ruby-red Clos Napoléon has a vegetal touch on the nose and a toasty flavour on the palate. The fruit is treated with delicacy. Balanced and well-exploited depth. Not, unfortunately, destined for Napoleon's Guard: the vintage has its limits.

Dom. Pierre Gelin, 2, rue du Chapitre, 1220 Fixin, tel. 03.80.52.45.24, ax 03.80.51.47.80 ☑ Y by appt.
Stéphen Gelin

ALAIN GUYARD
Les Chenevières 1997

	1.5 ha	4,000	50–69 F

A pale ruby-red 97 with equal fruit and oak flavours, with firm strong tannins. It will be pleasant enough in a while, but will not have a long life.

Alain Guyard, 10, rue du Puits-de-Têt, 1160 Marsannay-la-Côte, tel. 03.80.52.14.46, fax 03.80.52.67.36 ☑ Y by appt.

DOM. HUGUENOT PERE ET FILS
1997★

	6 ha	30,000	50–69 F

This attractive satiny-red wine is a good example of its vintage and the Fixin style. The nose is intense but not showy, with the little touch of Morello cherry that is usual in this appellation. From the first impression, it is a very focused wine. There is a hint of heat, perhaps, but it is already pleasantly balanced

Huguenot Père et Fils, 7, ruelle du Carron, 21160 Marsannay-la-Côte, tel. 03.80.52.11.56, fax 03.80.52.60.47, e-mail domaine.huguenot@wanadoo.fr ☑ Y by appt.

JOLIET PERE ET FILS
Clos de La Perrière 1998★

1er cru	0.5 ha	3,000		100–149 F

Le Clos de la Perrière is run by the Joliet family, and although it is given over almost exclusively to Pinot Noir, they have 0.5 ha (1 acre) of Chardonnay. This is a light-coloured 98. A straightforward wine, characterised by a little note of blackcurrant buds then a hint of violet. We find it fine and agreeable. As for the **97 Rouge** from the same *clos*, it needs to develop: at the moment it is locked in by its tannins, which, though not harsh, are preventing the other elements from breaking through. Leave it for seven years until it reaches the age of reason (70–99F).

EARL Joliet, La Perrière, 21220 Fixin, tel. 03.80.52.47.85, fax 03.80.51.99.90, e-mail joliet@webiwine.com ☑ Y ev. day 8am–6pm

MOILLARD 1997★

	n.c.	10,000	70–99 F

A Bresse chicken with cream and mushrooms would seem the perfect match for this wine. We like the elegance of its brilliant ruby-red colour and its fruitiness, which obviously exists but is still searching for an identity, and the delicacy of its tannins. Leave it for a year or two so that it can really express itself.

Moillard, 2, rue François-Mignotte, 21700 Nuits-Saint-Georges, tel. 03.80.62.42.22, fax 03.80.61.28.13 ☑ Y ev. day 10am–6pm; cl. Jan.

ARMELLE ET JEAN-MICHEL MOLIN Les Hervelets 1998★

1er cru	0.57 ha	1,400	70–99 F

A **Fixin Blanc 98**, which comes from a small parcel, is commended by the jury (50–69F). It is very rich in colour, has an exotic nose with a slight hint of Muscat – which is quite often the case with Chardonnay wines grown on the Côte-de-Nuits – and the palate is very forward, so forward in fact that this wine should be drunk immediately. However, it was the Les Hervelets that really caught our attention. This cherry-red 98 has a lovely fruity nose (blackcurrants and blackberries), mingled with spice and oak. Its fine structure and rich and well-balanced tannins make it an elegant wine that needs laying down (two to three years).

EARL Armelle et Jean-Michel Molin, 54, rte. des Grands-Crus, 21220 Fixin, tel. 03.80.52.21.28, fax 03.80.59.96.99 ☑ Y by appt.

CHARLES VIENOT
Cuvée de l'Empereur 1997

	n.c.	10,000	70–99 F

Claude Noisot married into the Viénot family, which gives this Cuvée de l'Empereur from Charles Viénot a certain historical consistency. Its bright red colour has a lot of presence, whilst its nose, on the other hand, lacks eloquence. This is a fairly solid wine, and the tannins are moderate and straightforward without being aggressive. It seems to have potential.

Charles Viénot, 5, quai Dumorey, 21700 Nuits-Saint-Georges, tel. 03.80.62.61.41, fax 03.80.62.37.38

Gevrey-Chambertin

North of Gevrey, three *appellations communales* are produced in the commune of Brochon: Fixin on a small part of the Clos de la Perrière, Côtes de Nuits-Villages on the northern part (at Préau and Queue-de-Hareng) and Gevrey-Chambertin in the south.

Of these, the Appellation Communale Gevrey-Chambertin is not only the biggest producer by volume – 17,173 hl (453,367 gal) in 1999 but also the home of a number of world-famous Grands Crus producing in total less than 4,260 hl (112,464 gal) in 1999. The combe of Lavaux divides the commune in two. To the north we find, among other *climats*, Les Evocelles (which borders on Brochon), Les Champeaux, La Combe Aux Moines (once the walk of Cluny Abbey, where the monks were the first important growers of Gevrey), Les Cazetiers, Le Clos Saint-Jacques, Les Varoiles, etc. South of the village, the crus are less numerous because nearly the whole of the slope produces Grand Cru wines, for example the *climats* of Fonteny, Petite-Chapelle, Clos-Prieur, etc.

The wines of this appellation are robust and powerful when grown on the hillside, elegant and subtle when grown at the foot of the hill. With regard to the lower vineyard, some have taken the inaccurate view that the part running down to the Dijon-Beaune railway line should not qualify as Appellation Gevrey-Chambertin. This view makes a mockery of what Gevrey's wine-makers know as fact, but it gives us the opportunity to explain the background. At various times in the past, the hill has been the site of a great deal of different geological activity, some of which was the result of glacial action in the Quaternary era; a base of Bajocian limestone is overlaid by different layers of chalky soil with clay particles and pebbles. The combe of Lavaux was a sort of channel down which deposits ran, causing a huge plug of waste to be deposited at its foot, made of identical or similar minerals to those found at the top of the hillside. In some places, the soils are simply deeper, so further away from the substratum. But they form essentially the same base, with its layers of limestone pebbles, giving rise to the elegant, subtle wines mentioned above.

PIERRE ANDRE

Les Vignes d'Isabelle 1998★★

■ 0.8 ha 3,500 ⅡⅠ 250-299

The business bears the name of Pierr André who, in 1927, bought what was the called the 'Château Jaune' and renamed it th 'Château de Corton-André'. As for thi Vignes d'Isabelle, it is named after the granc daughter of the founder. This bright purp 98, with its flavours of blackberries an blackcurrants, has been skilfully handle during maturation. You can taste the oak, bu it is well-blended with the fruit. Structure and long, already very pleasant. Ver characteristic.

🔑 Pierre André, Ch. de Corton-André, 21420 Aloxe-Corton, tel. 03.80.26.44.25, fax 03.80.26.43.57, e-mail pandre@axnet.fr

Y ev. day 10am–6pm

PIERRE BOUREE FILS

Les Champeaux 1997

■ 1er cru 0.4 ha 1,500 ⅡⅠ 150-199

This business, founded in the 19th centur is today the doyen of all the *négociant-éleveu* businesses in Gevrey. This particular *climat* i halfway between the château of Grevey an that of Brochon. Between ruby and garnet i colour, this 97 has a delicate nose that is nevertheless quite open. This maturity, very characteristic of its vintage, will appeal to peopl who want to take immediate advantage of it rounded tannins.

🔑 Pierre Bourée Fils, 13, rte. de Beaune, 21220 Gevrey-Chambertin, tel. 03.80.34.30.25, fax 03.80.51.85.64 ☑ Y by appt.

🔑 Louis Vallet

DOM. REGIS BOUVIER 1998★

■ 15.5 ha 1,000 ⅡⅠ 70-99 F

In the year 2000, Régis Bouvier celebratec 20 years of wine-producing. Althougł Marsannay is where the estate began, it has been extended and now covers Fixin, Gevrey and Morey. Here we have a Pinot Noir tha stands its ground. It has roughly the right amount of acidity, and its tannins are present but not excessive. It is well-balanced, showing off its fruity perfumes with a hint of tobacco. Best drunk in two to three years' time.

🔑 Dom. Régis Bouvier, 52, rue de Mazy, 21160 Marsannay-la-Côte, tel. 03.80.51.33.93, fax 03.80.58.75.07 ☑ Y by appt.

F. CHAUVENET 1997

■ n.c. 12,000 ⅡⅠ 150-199 F

'Madam is a better wine-taster than a man', Françoise Chauvenet was told back in the 19th century, when she was the heart and soul of this business, which is now run by Jean-Claude Boisset. I wonder what she would have thought of this 97? Round and pleasing, it has a typical Côte-de-Nuits nose, but is still a little astringent, and has the structure of a 97. In short, it can join the family.

⊶ F. Chauvenet, 9, quai Fleury, 21700 Nuits-Saint-Georges, tel. 03.80.62.61.43, fax 03.80.62.37.38

DOM. BRUNO CLAIR

Clos du Fonteny Monopole 1997★

1er cru	0.68 ha	2,500	200–249 F

A cru that is situated opposite Les Ruchottes and on the other side of the ascent to Curley – this old, picturesque house has been abandoned for years and is much loved by photographers. It is owned by Bruno Clair, who has produced a deep ruby-red 97 with an elegant cherry nose which shows us tenderness, friendliness and balance, all with a softness that is anything but bland. Articulate but reserved. A pleasure that should not be put off forever.

⊶ Bruno Clair, 5, rue du Vieux-Collège, 21160 Marsannay-la-Côte, tel. 03.80.52.28.95, fax 03.80.52.18.14 ☑ Y by appt.

DOM. DUJAC Aux Combottes 1997

1er cru	1.15 ha	n.c.	250–299 F

This Premier Cru is situated between Latricières-Chambertin and Clos de la Roche. It could have been a Grand Cru, were it not for the little valley which opens into it, causing a slight change to the microclimate. This brilliantly coloured 97, with its mixed floral, redcurrant and wild berry nose, expresses both the grape variety and the terroir in the spirit of its vintage. It is a great classic.

⊶ SA Dom. Dujac, 7, rue de la Bussière, 21220 Morey-Saint-Denis, tel. 03.80.34.01.00, fax 03.80.34.01.09 ☑ Y by appt.

⊶ Seysses

FAIVELEY La Combe aux Moines 1997★

1er cru	n.c.	7,600	200–249 F

Faiveley has been in Gevrey for a very long time. Their Combe aux Moines 97 has fine origins, and the result is a wine that is still young, with a light cherry nose. Behind the clean, straightforward attack lies a body that is gradually fleshing itself out and taking form. It needs three or four years in the cellar for the oakiness to blend in.

⊶ Bourgognes Faiveley, 8, rue du Tribourg, B.P. 9, 21701 Nuits-Saint-Georges Cedex, tel. 03.80.61.04.55, fax 03.80.62.33.37, e-mail bourgognesfaiveley@wanadoo.fr ☑ Y by appt.

CAVEAU DES FLEURIERES

Vieilles vignes 1997

■	n.c.	n.c.	100–149 F

A simple colour, light and clear with good fruit and a few notes of alcohol. No actual faults, but lacking in depth. It is lively, almost firm, yet not lacking in delicacy and making no secret of its vintage.

⊶ Caveau des Fleurières, 50, rue du Gal-de-Gaulle, 21700 Nuits-Saint-Georges, B.P. 63, tel. 03.80.61.10.30, fax 03.80.61.35.76 Y by appt.

JEAN FOURNIER 1998★

■	0.55 ha	3,500	100–149 F

This very dark red wine has taken its time (14 months in barrel) to develop its aromas of cherries in alcohol, nuts, leather, even ink, all with a touch of vanilla. Then, it follows through with a lovely character. Still very closed, but with significant potential. It inspires great hopes.

⊶ Jean Fournier, 29–34, rue du Château, 21160 Marsannay-la-Côte, tel. 03.80.52.24.38, fax 03.80.52.77.40 ☑ Y by appt.

DOM. DOMINIQUE GALLOIS 1998★★

■ 1er cru	0.38 ha	1,100	100–149 F

This is the family estate of the Burgundy writer Gaston Roupnel, who would surely have appreciated this very fine example of the appellation. To the eye, it is dark, almost violet. On the nose, there are notes of very concentrated stone fruit. On the palate is a silky fullness. In short, one of the best samples we have tasted. A lovely wine, closed now but with great potential.

⊶ Dominique Gallois, 9, rue Mal-de-Lattre-de-Tassigny, 21220 Gevrey-Chambertin, tel. 03.80.34.11.99, fax 03.80.34.38.62 ☑ Y by appt.

DOM. GANDREY Les Roncevies 1997★

■	0.27 ha	1,200	150–199 F

Produced on the outskirts of Morey to the south-east of the village, this 97, which comes from a Nuits-Saint-Georges estate, is showy in colour, and has cherry aromas. It is clearly not very typical of the vintage, but has an attractive structure with power and richness. It needs to age and has the resources to do so.

⊶ Jean-François Gandrey, 18, rue Jean-Jaurès, 21700 Nuits-Saint-Georges, tel. 03.80.61.27.63, fax 03.80.61.27.63 ☑ Y by appt.

ANDRE GOICHOT 1997

■	n.c.	4,100	100–149 F

Redcurrant colour, brilliant in tone, interesting as it opens out. The richness of the fruit balances the tannic structure that follows. Should be drunk within the next two years.

⊶ SA A. Goichot et Fils, av. Charles-de-Gaulle, 21200 Beaune, tel. 03.80.26.88.70, fax 03.80.26.80.69, e-mail goichot@goichotsa.com ☑ Y by appt.

GOILLOT-BERNOLLIN

Les Billards 1998★

■	0.8 ha	3,000	100–149 F

The *climat* is right next to the property, between Brochon and Gevrey to the west of the RN 74. This wine is a good option for laying down and knows how to spread its assets. It is deep violet in colour, and hints at blackberries and raspberries. Balanced and well-made, it will go well with some game towards 2003.

🗝 SCE Goillot-Bernollin, 29, rte. de Dijon, 21220 Gevrey-Chambertin, tel. 03.80.34.36.12, fax 03.80.34.16.00 ☒ Y by appt.

DOM. ROBERT GROFFIER PERE ET FILS 1998★

■ 0.85 ha 3,600 🛢 100–149 F

When your grandfather (Jules) has competed in the Tour de France and all the other major cycle races, it is easy to understand why one might be happy just to stay in the pack. But rest assured, this 98 will not be outdistanced. It is deep violet in colour, and opens softly with a certain jammy quality along with hints of bilberry and spice. Body and structure are both well-established. Three to five years will see its fine balanced perfected.

🗝 SARL Robert Groffier et Fils, 3–5, rte. des Grands-Crus, 21220 Morey-Saint-Denis, tel. 03.80.34.31.53 ☒ Y by appt.

S.C. GUILLARD Les Corbeaux 1997★★

■ 1er cru 0.48 ha 2,250 🛢 100–149 F

This is a small wine-producing estate of 4.7 ha (12 acres), where Michel Guillard manages a group success with his three *cuvées*; **Lavaux Saint-Jacques, Corvées**, and this Corbeaux, which comes from very old vines (70 years old) and which we particularly liked. It is silky-smooth, with a promising aroma of wild fruit, and a palate that earns only praise. It may be oaky, but its lovely fullness arouses much enthusiasm. One taster wrote 'marvellous finish'.

🗝 SC Guillard, 3, rue des Halles, 21220 Gevrey-Chambertin, tel. 03.80.34.32.44 ☒ Y by appt.

JEAN-MICHEL GUILLON Les Champonnets 1998

■ 1er cru 0.83 ha 4,760 🛢 70–99 F

This Premier Cru is situated in the corner of the hill where the Grands Crus are produced, and the Lavaux Valley. Jean-Michel Guillon, who came from Paris many years ago, applies the principles of a famous previous inhabitant of Gevrey, Père Lesprit, to a 98 that is gleaming, and more than rich in colour. Red berry fruit jam, a little hint of oak, a warm fruity body. Its present development suggests that it will be at its best in three to four years' time.

🗝 Dom. Jean-Michel Guillon, 33, rte. de Beaune, 21220 Gevrey-Chambertin, tel. 03.80.51.83.98, fax 03.80.51.85.59, e-mail eurlguillon@com ☒ Y by appt.

ALAIN GUYARD 1997★

■ 0.7 ha 3,000 🛢 70–99 F

The finish is perhaps not the most pronounced, but the wine seems very agreeable, round and delicate, with aromas of toast and soft fruits. Its youthfulness is promising. It is fresh, and well-balanced, and caused one taster to comment: 'This is a pleasure'. We recommend laying it down at the right temperature until autumn 2002.

🗝 Alain Guyard, 10, rue du Puits-de-Têt, 21160 Marsannay-la-Côte, tel. 03.80.52.14.46, fax 03.80.52.67.36 ☒ Y by appt.

DOM. GUYON 1998★

■ 0.4 ha 2,500 🛢 100–149 F

Until 1993, this family from Vosne were producing both wine and barley for breweries. Then, they left the farm at Quincey and decided to concentrate on their principal subject, and have done well. This deep red 98 has delightful aromas (first cocoa, then cherry) and a charming palate. Will keep a while.

🗝 EARL Dom. Guyon, 11–16, R.N. 74, 21700 Vosne-Romanée, tel. 03.80.61.02.46, fax 03.80.62.36.56 ☒ Y by appt.

DOM. ANTONIN GUYON 1997★★

■ 2.4 ha 15,000 🛢 100–149 F

This estate extends all the way along the coast, and what a wine they have produced. Two of our jury members thought this wine worthy of the *coup de cœur.* The colour is irreproachable, the complexity of the aromas is impressive. It is staggeringly well-balanced, and will be a truly great wine in three or four years' time.

🗝 Dom. Antonin Guyon, 21420 Savigny-lès-Beaune, tel. 03.80.67.13.24, fax 03.80.66.85.87, e-mail vins@guyon-bourgogne.com ☒ Y by appt.

DOM. OLIVIER GUYOT Les Champs 1998★

■ 0.6 ha 3,000 🛢 70–99 F

This estate was founded in the 16th century and today covers 13 ha (32 acres). A horse works the vineyard here: that of Jean Lamadon, the last in Gevrey, ceased his work in the 1960s. Although Olivier Guyot's **Champeaux 98** is popular with the jury, they preferred this remarkably expressive *village.* It is an attractive wine: dark purple with blackcurrant aromas. The first impression is straightforward, and then it goes on to display a good structure. Best tasted in three or four years' time.

🗝 EARL Olivier Guyot, 39, rue de Mazy, 21160 Marsannay-la-Côte, tel. 03.80.52.39.71, fax 03.80.51.17.58 ☒ Y by appt.

DOM. HARMAND-GEOFFROY Clos Prieur 1998

■ 0.42 ha 2,400 🛢 100–149 F

This Clos Prieur has shades of brilliant purple. Its aromas are floral with developing fruit. It has a fine, supple structure followed by a very commendable length. Best left a while, of course.

🗝 Dom. Harmand-Geoffroy, 1, pl. des Lois, 21220 Gevrey-Chambertin, tel. 03.80.34.10.65, fax 03.80.34.13.72, e-mail harmand-geoffroy@wanadoo.fr ☒ Y by appt.

🗝 Gérard Harmand

DOM. HERESZTYN

es Corbeaux 1998★

1er cru 0.2 ha 1,100 100–149 F

This estate was founded by a former Polish ineyard worker of Louis Trapet, and it as successfully carved a niche for itself in ievrey. The Corbeaux 98 is like an exotic ird: wonderful plumage and wonderful song. will go beautifully with an *époisses* cheese. ery ripe nose of Morello cherry and fruit ones hinting at leather. Plenty of energy and inosity, good concentration. Its charms will irface later, as promised by its long finish of one fruit.

Dom. Heresztyn, 27, rue Richebourg, 1220 Gevrey-Chambertin, el. 03.80.34.30.86, fax 03.80.34.13.99, -mail domaine.heresztyn@wanadoo.fr ev. day 9am–12 noon 2pm–6pm; Sun. by ppt.

DOM. HUGUENOT PERE ET FILS

1997★

1er cru 0.45 ha 2,500 150–199 F

This wine is red – almost garnet – in colour, and very soothing to the eye. On the nose, the mixture of fruitiness and oak works well, managing to bring out the blackcurrant. Supple and fairly full-bodied with good balance, it is graceful and holds a potential for complexity that could show through in a few years' time. We have confidence in it.

Huguenot Père et Fils, 7, ruelle du Carron, 21160 Marsannay-la-Côte, tel. 03.80.52.11.56, fax 03.80.52.60.47, e-mail domaine.huguenot@wanadoo.fr
by appt.

DOM. HUMBERT FRERES

Craipillot 1998★

1er cru n.c. 1,050 100–149 F

This is a young wine with a gamey nose, but not lacking fruit. Powerful, round, and oaky, the tannins give it a good length. Best laid

Côte de Nuits (North 2)

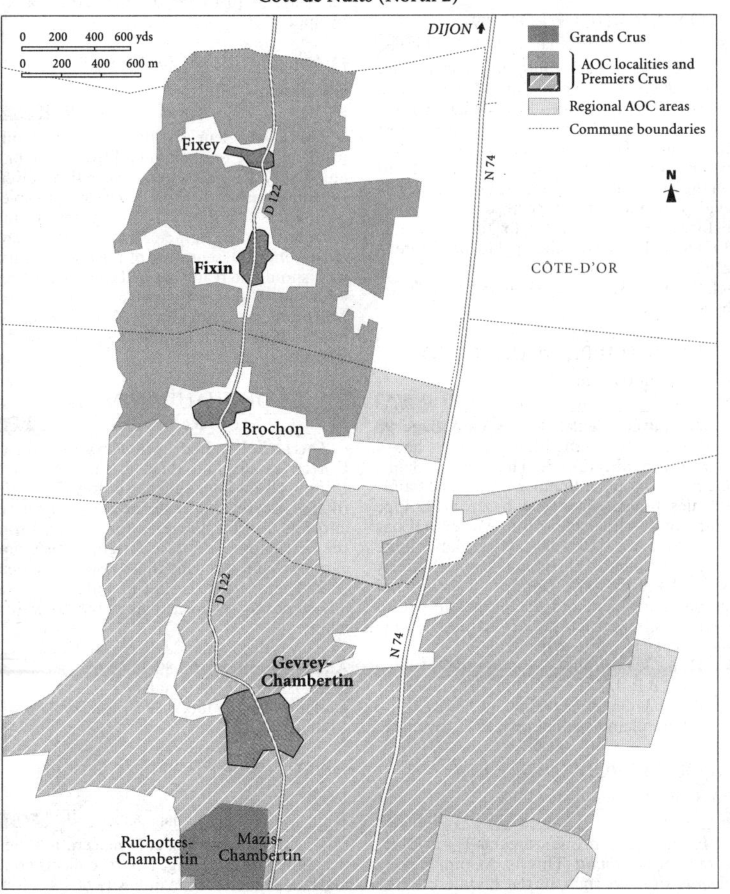

BURGUNDY

down for four to five years. This *climat* is situated opposite Clos Saint-Jacques, on the hill facing it. Also worth mentioning is the **Estournelles Saint-Jacques** of the same vintage, which receives the same mark.
Dom. Humbert Frères, rue de Planteligone, 21220 Gevrey-Chambertin, tel. 03.80.51.80.14, fax 03.80.51.80.14 by appt.

JACQUES DE VERTEUIL 1997

■ n.c. 4,000 150–199 F

Part of the Patriarche business, this *négociant-éleveur* label gives a personal touch to a wine that is refined more than tannic, with a decent colour and a nose that is dominated by prune. The body is well-structured, the palate soft and very, very long. Everything suggests that it is worth waiting for. The wine tasted came from a bottle that was numbered, reference 277, lot M.V. 0023, bottled by Jacques de Verteuil.
Marché aux vins, rue Nicolas-Rolin, 21200 Beaune, tel. 03.80.25.08.20, fax 03.80.25.08.21 ev. day 9.30am–12 noon 2pm–6pm

LIGNIER-MICHELOT 1997

■ 0.5 ha 2,500 70–99 F

Virgil has been running this family estate since 1996, and Gevrey-Morey-Chambolle is his Holy Trinity of vines. Here we have a ruby-red 97 with a good depth of colour and a nose that remains fairly closed and discreet. A well-balanced palate with a flavour of stone fruits on the finish. The fact that the tannins are still evident would make it worth waiting a while before drinking it, but not for too long.
Dom. Lignier-Michelot, 11, rue Haute, 21220 Morey-Saint-Denis, tel. 03.80.34.31.13, fax 03.80.58.52.16 by appt.

JEAN-PHILIPPE MARCHAND

Lavaux Saint-Jacques 1998

■ 1er cru n.c. n.c. 100–149 F

The **Cuvée Vieilles Vignes en Village 98** deserves a recommendation, as it has a great future ahead of it. This Lavaux Saint-Jacques honours a Premier Cru of the Saint-Jacques family. Produced by Jean-Philippe Marchand, who was born in Morey but has lived in Gevrey since 1984, at first glance it is a decent red, almost the colour of brick, deep, with a leathery, dark fruit nose. It is full and supple, and opens out on the palate with a mellow, silky structure. An attractive wine that is easy to get to grips with.
Dom. Jean-Philippe Marchand, 4, rue Souvert, B.P. 41, 21220 Gevrey-Chambertin, tel. 03.80.34.33.60, fax 03.80.34.12.77, e-mail marchand@axnet.com by appt.

DOM. MARCHAND FRERES

En Songe Vieilles vignes 1998

■ 0.2 ha 1,200 70–99 F

'En Songe' ('in one's dreams') – a lovely name for a *climat*! This is an old Gevrey *climat*, situated right in the middle of the district, amongst the houses. This 98 wit[h] powerful red berry fruit, has a lively, youn[g] palate. It needs to breathe and will open u[p] considerably in the decanter after the yea[r] 2002. It has a clean and clear black-cherr[y] colour.
Dom. Marchand Frères, 1, pl. du Monument, B.P. 38, 21220 Gevrey-Chambertin, tel. 03.80.62.10.97, fax 03.80.62.11.01, e-mail dmarc2000@aol.com by appt.

DOM. MARCHAND-GRILLOT

Perrières 1997★★

■ 1er cru n.c. 1,200 100–149 F

This attractive 97 is just right for someon[e] who likes to savour the anticipation of wait[-]ing, because it is a long way off showing it[s] full potential. We like its reserve, eleganc[e,] balance and power. Besides, you only have t[o] read the label to know that it is a mere ste[p] across the Route des Grands Crus fro[m] Perrières to Mazis. We also recommend th[e] **Vieilles Vignes 97**.
Marchand-Grillot, 13, rue du Gaizot, 21220 Gevrey-Chambertin, tel. 03.80.34.10.18, fax 03.80.58.50.87 by appt.

DOM. THIERRY MORTET

Clos Prieur 1998★

■ 0.3 ha 1,500 100–149 F

This Clos Prieur is still closed, and is onl[y] just beginning to open out a little on the pal[-]ate. A very deep-coloured wine with a power[-]ful combination of Morello cherry and spic[e] on the nose. It shows a more generous an[d] straightforward character on the palate leav[-]ing a wonderful sensation of freshness behin[d] it. It should be ready in five to ten years.
Dom. Thierry Mortet, 16, pl. des Marronniers, 21220 Gevrey-Chambertin, tel. 03.80.51.85.07, fax 03.80.34.16.80 by appt.

CAVES DES PAULANDS 1998

■ n.c. n.c. 100–149 F

This is the hundredth vintage of this Aloxe-Corton estate, and there are lots of good things about this garnet-coloured, non-filtered Gevrey. Its fresh fruit nose of blackcurrants and blackberries, for a start. From the first impression to its lengthy finish, you can see that it is a wine that knows its subject well. There is a little hint of bitterness. Our advice is not to open it now, but to wait a while.
Caves des Paulands, R.N. 74, 21550 Aloxe-Corton, tel. 03.80.26.41.05, fax 03.80.26.47.56, e-mail paulands@wanadoo.fr ev. day 8am–12 noon 2pm–6pm

DOM. HENRI PERROT-MINOT

1997★

■ 1.5 ha 6,000 100–149 F

Selective harvesting, cold maceration, neither fining nor filtering. This 97 collects good marks, as much for the intensity of its colour as the impression it makes on the nose (when swirled, we get gingerbread). Plenty of stuffing and well-structured, it is perhaps a little on the warm side while keeping all its distinction.

🔑 Henri Perrot-Minot, 54, rte. des Grands-Crus, 21220 Morey-Saint-Denis, tel. 03.80.34.32.51, fax 03.80.34.13.57 ☒ Y by appt.

ALBERT PONNELLE 1998★

■ n.c. n.c. 200-249 F

This is a good-looking young wine. Its winey nose is fruity. Its powerful acidity and strong tannins make it a vintage for laying down, as its woody flavours should soften over time. We like its upfront fleshiness, its chewiness, and its body. There is really something to this wine.

🔑 Albert Ponnelle, Clos Saint-Nicolas, 38, fg Saint-Nicolas, 21200 Beaune, tel. 03.80.22.00.05, fax 03.80.24.19.73 ☒ Y by appt.

DOM. HENRI REBOURSEAU 1998★

■ 7.02 ha 15,000 ⦀ 100-149 F

Jean de Surrel has a good role model in his grandfather, who played an important part in wine-producing in this region, and this estate is one of the oldest in Gevrey. Here, we have a positive result. This deep purpley-red 98 has a very attractive perfume of Morello cherry. It is straightforward on the attack, revealing tannins that are present but not overpowering and which will soften nicely after three to four years in the cellar. Interesting fullness, and with long fruity aromas that indicate quality.

🔑 NSE Dom. Henri Rebourseau, 10, pl. du Monument, 21220 Gevrey-Chambertin, tel. 03.80.51.88.94, fax 03.80.34.12.82, e-mail Reboursea1@aol.com ☒ Y by appt.

DOM. ROSSIGNOL-TRAPET

Clos Prieur 1997★

■ 1er cru n.c. n.c. ⦀ 500 F+

The colour of this wine is a dark and captivating black cherry. Its nose of forest-floor and soft fruit is so delightful you could inhale its perfumes forever. The palate is overwhelmed with fruity flavours. This is a sincere, warm vintage, with a lot of class. Its oakiness will soften out, and it has a good four to five years of life ahead of it. The estate was formed when the Trapet family divided up its vineyard, and the vines are situated on the Route des Grand Crus near Morey.

🔑 Dom. Rossignol-Trapet, 3, rue de la Petite-Issue, 21220 Gevrey-Chambertin, tel. 03.80.51.87.26, fax 03.80.34.31.63, e-mail info@rossignol-trapet.com ☒ Y by appt.

REMI SEGUIN Les Seuvrées 1997★

■ 1.1 ha n.c. ⦀ 70-99 F

Rémi Seguin was born in Le Clos de Tart, where his parents and grandparents were estate stewards, and you could say he fell into the magic potion as a baby. He has been running this 6.31 ha (16 acre) estate since 1989. He de-stems 100%, which explains the fine, delicate style of this wine. It is a deep ruby-red 97, more long than full, an attractive palate with notes of kirsch. This *climat* is next to Les Mazoyères and Charmes-Chambertin, near Morey.

🔑 Rémi Seguin, rue de Cîteaux, 21640 Gilly-lès-Cîteaux, tel. 03.80.62.89.61, fax 03.80.62.80.92 ☒ Y by appt.

DOM. TAUPENOT-MERME

Bel Air 1997★

■ 1er cru n.c. 2,700 ⦀ 150-199 F

This estate has an excellent view of the region, since Bel Air is the highest *climat* on the hills, situated above the Clos de Bèze. This solid and sturdy ruby-red Premier Cru that opens with a touch of redcurrant and is given a little lift on the palate by a hint of pepper. It clearly comes from fairly old vines. Best to wait two or three years before opening it.

🔑 Jean Taupenot-Merme, 33, rte. des Grands-Crus, 21220 Morey-Saint-Denis, tel. 03.80.34.35.24, fax 03.80.51.83.41 ☒ Y by appt.

DOM. TORTOCHOT

Lavaux Saint-Jacques 1997★

■ 1er cru 0.61 ha 3,000 ⦀ 150-199 F

Chantal Tortochot took over from her father, Gaby, in 1997, so it seems fitting that she should present us a 97 to taste. You can't hide good breeding: this is a Pinot Noir. In the glass we note regular, lively legs. Notes of kirsch and prune on the nose come as no surprise. The attack is supple, the acidity good. It doesn't have a huge structure– that's this vintage for you – but reveals great elegance.

🔑 Dom. Tortochot, 12, rue de l'Eglise, 21220 Gevrey-Chambertin, tel. 03.80.34.30.68, fax 03.80.34.18.80 ☒ Y by appt.

🔑 Chantal et Michel Tortochot

DOM. TRAPET 1998★

■ n.c. n.c. ⦀ 100-149 F

Pierre-Arthur Trapet planted his first vine in Gevrey in 1919. Today the estate covers 13 ha (32 acres) and his wines have brought him international renown. This wine is not called Trapet for nothing: it is rich in every respect. It has a distinctive colour. Initially a nose with gamey characteristics, which then moves on to a more subtle nose of flowers (honeysuckle) mingled with toast. Then a body that for the time being is still hiding some of its best qualities. Things will become clear, but not for at least five years.

🔑 Dom. Trapet Père et Fils, 53, rte. de Beaune, 21220 Gevrey-Chambertin, tel. 03.80.34.30.40, fax 03.80.51.86.34, e-mail message@domaine-trapet.com ☒ Y by appt.

DOM. DES VAROILLES

La Romanée 1997★

■ 1er cru n.c. n.c. ⦀ 150-199 F

There is also a Romanée at Gevrey-Chambertin. 'The sister of the other one', as

BURGUNDY

they might say here. This wine is ruby-red with an elegant nose where soft fruit and oak blend together beautifully. The palate, however, is still getting itself into shape. The jury was undecided as to how long it should be laid down for; opinions differed but no-one suggested leaving it longer than three years. The Naigeon-Chauveau business, which now has a Swiss owner, owns the Les Varoilles estate.
Dom. des Varoilles, rue de l'Ancien-Hôpital, 21220 Gevrey-Chambertin, tel. 03.80.34.30.30, fax 03.80.51.88.99 by appt.
Naigeon-Chauveau

HENRI DE VILLAMONT 1997

■ n.c. 8,000 100–149 F

This is the French branch of the Swiss group Schenk. Henri de Villamont here gives us something akin to a young marquis showing off at a Versailles ball just before the Revolution. His wine is light, fruity, and quite oaky on the palate, true to both the qualities and the limits of the vintage. For those who like to enjoy something without waiting too long for it.
Henri de Villamont, rue du Dr-Guyot, 21420 Savigny-lès-Beaune, tel. 03.80.24.70.07, fax 03.80.22.54.31, e-mail hdv@planetb.fr ev. day except Tue. 9.30am–6:30pm; Thu. 9.30am–12 noon; cl. 15 Nov.–15 Mar.

ALAIN VOEGELI 1998*

■ 2.3 ha 4,200 70–99 F

This is a wine that takes a while to get going, but once it does, it grows in fullness and richness. It shouldn't be judged too hastily. The nose is fresh, showing some red berry fruit, the colour light and brilliant: it certainly knows how to speak up for itself. This is a tiny estate (2.3 ha/5.7 acres) with an excellent reputation. The great-great-grandson of Etienne Grey's widow, who founded the estate at the turn of the 20th century, is now at the helm.
Alain Voegeli, 5, rte. de Dijon, 21220 Gevrey-Chambertin, tel. 03.80.34.37.13, fax 03.80.34.37.13 by appt.

Chambertin

Bertin, who was a wine-maker in Gevrey, owned a parcel of vineyard neighbouring the Clos de Bèze and, noting the quality of the wines the monks made there, planted the same vines and produced a similar wine. This was the 'Champ de Bertin', or Bertin's field, from which evolved the name Chambertin. In 1999 the AOC produced 506 hl (13,358 gal).

DOM. HUBERT CAMUS 1997

■Gd cru 1.69 ha 4,000 200–249 F

Hubert Camus is an important figure in the Burgundy wine-producing world, and at one time or another he has held just about every position of responsibility within it. His 1.69 ha (4.2 acres) of Chambertin (approximately 10% of the Grand Cru) has produced a light brick-red 97 with an expressive nose of soft fruit, forest-floor and mushrooms, mixed with a touch of oak. It is fresh on the palate, well-structured but not overly so, and long. It should be opened in two years' time – and make sure you decant it.
Dom. Camus Père et Fils, 21, rue du Mal-de-Lattre-de-Tassigny, 21220 Gevrey-Chambertin, tel. 03.80.34.30.64, fax 03.80.51.87.93 by appt.
Hubert Camus

COUVENT DES CORDELIERS 1997

■Gd cru n.c. 900 300–499 F

This is a wine from the house of Patriarche. This Chambertin is an attractive deep red, with herbaceous aromas on the nose and crushed strawberry on the palate. It has a subtle but agreeable presence, and should be drunk within two years at the maximum.
Caves du Couvent des Cordeliers, rue de l'Hôtel-Dieu, 21200 Beaune, tel. 03.80.25.08.85, fax 03.80.25.08.21 ev. day 9.30am–12 noon 2pm–6pm

DOM. PIERRE DAMOY 1998**

■ 0.48 ha 2,100 300–499 F

Hats off to this Chambertin. It is truly fit for an emperor, and you can just see Napoleon I giving this bottle an affectionate little pat as he pinned the cross of the Légion d'Honneur on its neck. This purple, almost black 98, with its flavours of macerated soft fruit and pleasantly toasted oak, is a rich and powerful wine of remarkable substance and great length. A lovely wine. The Damoy estate devotes 47 a 59 ca (1.2 acres) to this Grand Cru, and does marvels with it. Good news for Gevrey.
Dom. Pierre Damoy, 11, rue du Mal-de-Lattre-de-Tassigny, 21220 Gevrey-Chambertin, tel. 03.80.34.30.47, fax 03.80.58.54.79

DOM. LOUIS REMY 1998*

■Gd cru 0.35 ha 900 300–499 F

|93| 96 97 98

This great wine-producing family has been well-represented by its women: first Marie-Louise ran the estate, then Chantal. The Morey business once belonged to the Rodiers. Camille, who was the founder of Tastevin, once described Chambertin (two parcels, 32 a 6 ca/0.8 acres) as 'everything a great Burgundy can be'. This superbly-coloured 98, which is dark with violet hues, flies the flag high for the region. The nose has concentrated soft fruit with a slight hint of oakiness. At the moment the tannins dominate, but they will soften out. Full, dense and vinous, it has real stature and is a good option for laying down.

🔑 Dom. Louis Remy, 1, pl. du Monument, 21220 Morey-Saint-Denis, tel. 03.80.34.32.59, fax 03.80.34.32.59 ☑ 🍷 by appt.

DOM. ROSSIGNOL-TRAPET 1997

■Gd cru 1.6 ha 6,500 🛢 250–299 F

If Robert-J. Courtine invented *coq au Riesling* for Georges Simenon, then who thought up *coq au Chambertin*? Nobody knows the origins of this recipe, but it first appeared sometime between 1930 and 1950. Here is a wine that would go perfectly with this delicate dish, which requires a virgin cockerel (Brillat-Savarin variety) or an old hen. The colour of this wine is deep and dark, just as it should be. The nose hides aromas of soft fruit behind an initial toasty note. The palate is classic, very much the product of its vintage (it is a 97).

🔑 Dom. Rossignol-Trapet, 3, rue de la Petite-Issue, 21220 Gevrey-Chambertin, tel. 03.80.51.87.26, fax 03.80.34.31.63, e-mail info@rossignol-trapet.com ☑ 🍷 by appt.

DOM. ARMAND ROUSSEAU PERE ET FILS 1997★

■Gd cru 2.15 ha 7,300 🛢 300–499 F

This is a famous Burgundy estate whose Crus can be found all over the world, from Brazil to Japan, and from Australia to the USA. This Chambertin comes from 40-year old vines. We all know that a wine should be judged according to its vintage, and this one steps right into character. The attack is lively. The grape has been well-respected and shows in the wine's finesse and fruitiness. A very interesting exercise in style which puts the emphasis on elegance more than fullness.

🔑 Dom. Armand Rousseau, 1, rue de l'Aumônerie, 21220 Gevrey-Chambertin, tel. 03.80.34.30.55, fax 03.80.58.50.25

DOM. TORTOCHOT 1997★

■Gd cru 0.39 ha 900 🛢 250–299 F

76 87 |(88)| |89| **91** 93 **96** 97

This is a great wine for the vintage. It has been well-produced, matured *sur lie* (on the lees), and nicely bottled. It looks attractive. The nose is a little closed, but some touches of tobacco, even leather, and ripe fruit are beginning to appear. This is a velvety, distinguished 97 that has an appealing fullness, and is a wine you will have to wait for. Chantal has taken over from Gabriel, and she seems to be doing a very good job at the helm of this estate a vineyard of 39 a 83 ca/1 acre.

🔑 Dom. Tortochot, 12, rue de l'Eglise, 21220 Gevrey-Chambertin, tel. 03.80.34.30.68, fax 03.80.34.18.80 ☑ 🍷 by appt.

🔑 Chantal et Michel Tortochot

DOM. TRAPET 1998★★

■Gd cru n.c. n.c. 🛢 300–499 F

96 **98**

'The red wine of the red wines' said Matt Kramer. It is a hard reputation to live up to. However, there is no denying the fact that Chambertin is the cornerstone of Burgundy wine-making, and with this wine we are getting close to perfection. Remarkable to look at, incredible on the nose (game, spices, red berry fruits and a well-tempered oakiness), it is uncompromising on the palate. A very promising wine, with a superb character that gives it structure. An extremely complex Chambertin that can be laid down for a long time.

🔑 Dom. Trapet Père et Fils, 53, rte. de Beaune, 21220 Gevrey-Chambertin, tel. 03.80.34.30.40, fax 03.80.51.86.34, e-mail message@domaine-trapet.com ☑ 🍷 by appt.

Chambertin-Clos de Bèze

In 630 the monks from the Abbey at Bèze planted a vineyard on a small parcel of land which produced a particularly highly rated wine; today the appellation bearing the abbey's name covers about 15 ha (37 acres); the wines can also be called Chambertin. In 1999, 522 hl (13,780 gal) of wine were produced.

DOM. PIERRE DAMOY 1998★★

■Gd cru 5.36 ha 7,500 🛢 300–499 F

The Damoy family have a highly successful grocery business in Paris and now produce wine in Romanèche-Thorins and Gevrey-Chambertin. They may not have any roots here, but the graft is taking. Having gone through many difficult times, this courageous estate has now returned to the top ranks, as this Clos de Bèze demonstrates (5.35 ha and 95 ca/13.2 acres, a third of the Grand Cru). A clear, triumphant ruby-red, with an attractive nose (toast followed by roses), full and fine at the same time, long and durable, it has great potential which will burst out in five to six years' time.

🔑 Dom. Pierre Damoy, 11, rue du Mal-de-Lattre-de-Tassigny, 21220 Gevrey-Chambertin, tel. 03.80.34.30.47, fax 03.80.58.54.79

FAIVELEY 1997★

■Gd cru 1.29 ha 3,670 🛢 500 F+

89 |(90)| 92 |**93**| 94 **95** 96 97

'Peaceful and triumphant' is how Evelyn Waugh described this wine. The same subtle touch is found here in the confident colour and soft, deep attack of this 97 vintage. Vanilla, bitter liquorice and violet mixed with fruit on the nose. The wood influence creates a sensation of harmony, still punctuated by a trace of tannins. A concentrated wine, but still a little closed. Faiveley owns 1.29 ha and 42 ca (3.2 acres) of Grand Cru, which is around 10%.

Bourgognes Faiveley, 8, rue du Tribourg, B.P. 9, 21701 Nuits-Saint-Georges Cedex, tel. 03.80.61.04.55, fax 03.80.62.33.37, e-mail bourgognesfaiveley@wanadoo.fr by appt.

DOM. PIERRE GELIN 1997

Gd cru 0.6 ha 2,500 300–499 F

Under a rather timid exterior lies a crystallised soft-fruit palate. Well-handled vinification has managed to get the absolute best from this 97. It is lively, tannic and of course should be put aside for the future. This vineyard of 60 a 25 ca (1.48 acres) which was replanted in 1965, comes from the former Marion estate.

Dom. Pierre Gelin, 2, rue du Chapitre, 21220 Fixin, tel. 03.80.52.45.24, fax 03.80.51.47.80 by appt.

DOM. GROFFIER PERE ET FILS 1998★★★

Gd cru 0.41 ha 1,500 300–499 F

93 95 96 97 (98)

This is the oldest and most illustrious working vineyard in history, first mentioned in the year 640. If punctuality is the politeness of kings, the king of wines knows how to make people wait. This wine is already open, offering up notes of Morello cherry and raspberry, but it has the kind of Adonis-like body that presents infinite possibilities. For the moment, its principal quality is one of strength. Later, it will be elegance. A Clos de Bèze only really comes into its own after 15 years. An exceptional 98.

SARL Robert Groffier et Fils, 3–5, rte. des Grands-Crus, 21220 Morey-Saint-Denis, tel. 03.80.34.31.53 by appt.

DOM. ARMAND ROUSSEAU 1998★★

Gd cru 1.42 ha 3,800 300–499 F

Armand Rousseau, who died in 1959, was the most important person in Gevrey during the first half of the 20th century. His son Charles was going to study political science but could not resist the lure of the vines. 'The most generous of all Burgundians', writes Serena Sutcliffe. This Clos de Bèze 98 comes largely from old Marion vines. A brilliant wine in all respects, with a voluptuous body embracing some rather closed-up tannins. Mellow, liquorice-flavoured and fruity (blackcurrants and blackberries), it will be popular with people who like young wines, but will also age well.

Dom. Armand Rousseau, 1, rue de l'Aumônerie, 21220 Gevrey-Chambertin, tel. 03.80.34.30.55, fax 03.80.58.50.25

Other Grands Crus from Gevrey-Chambertin

Surrounding the two previous vineyards is a huddle of others which, while not quite their equal, nonetheless bear a family resemblance. The regulations for producing these wines are slightly less demanding, but the wines share the sturdiness, strength and fullness, with a hint of liquorice, that generally distinguish Gevrey wines. These are Les Latricières (about 7ha/17 acres); Les Charmes (31 ha/77 acres); Les Mazoyères, which can also be called Charmes (the reverse is not allowed); Les Mazis, including Les Mazis-Haut (about 8 ha/20 acres) and Les Mazis-Bas (4 ha/10 acres); Les Ruchottes, which comes from the word *roichot* meaning a rocky place, and which covers a tiny area comprising Les Ruchottes-du-Dessus (1.92 ha/4.7 acres) and Les Ruchottes-du-Bas (1.27 ha/3.1 acres); Les Griottes, where wild cherries are supposed to have grown (5.48 ha/13.5 acres); and finally, Les Chappelles (5.39 ha/13.3 acres), its name deriving from the chapel built in 1155 by monks from the Abbey at Bèze, but destroyed during the French Revolution.

Latricières-Chambertin

DOM. DROUHIN-LAROZE 1998

■Gd cru 0.7 ha 2,500 ◖◗ 200–249 F

This estate was founded exactly 150 years ago, and owns 67 a 45 ca (1.7 acres) of Latricières on a vineyard formerly belonging to Gillot. This wine is showing a hint of maturity. Warm, round and balanced, it hovers between strawberries and prunes. It has just the right amount of acidity.

🔑 Drouhin-Laroze, 20, rue du Gaizot, 21220 Gevrey-Chambertin, tel. 03.80.34.31.49, fax 03.80.51.83.70 ☑ 🍷 by appt.

FAIVELEY 1997★★

■Gd cru 1.2 ha 3,810 ◖◗ 300–499 F

A lion digging his spade into the ground is the company crest, and it is a good indicator of the nature of this wine (1.2 ha and 67 ca/0.3 acres in the Grand Cru). A wine of great character, it is resolute, decisive and with a frankness that is impressive, and destined for a long stretch in the wine cellar. The grapes have been handled with rare prudence and intelligence. One of our most experienced tasters wrote in his notes: 'A very great wine, fleshy, full and rich. Congratulations to the winemaker'.

🔑 Bourgognes Faiveley, 8, rue du Tribourg, B.P. 9, 21701 Nuits-Saint-Georges Cedex, tel. 03.80.61.04.55, fax 03.80.62.33.37, e-mail bourgognesfaiveley@wanadoo.fr ☑ 🍷 by appt.

DOM. LOUIS REMY 1998★

■Gd cru 0.6 ha 2,000 ▮◖◗ 250–299 F

The pretty gate at Latricières which one sees so often in photographs is actually the gate to this vineyard, erected at a time when you couldn't just wander into a vineyard as if it were a field. This is a 98 that is similar in style to the Chambertin that we also tasted. The colours are those of pure Pinot, the nose has a fine vegetal note and a delicate oakiness. It is tannic and closed, but is undeniably a good-quality wine and promises a fine future.

🔑 Dom. Louis Remy, 1, pl. du Monument, 21220 Morey-Saint-Denis, tel. 03.80.34.32.59, fax 03.80.34.32.59 ☑ 🍷 by appt.

DOM. ROSSIGNOL-TRAPET 1997

■Gd cru 0.75 ha 2,500 ◖◗ 200–249 F

Latricières – not much soil and a siliceous subsoil. Its name derives from 'land of little value' – how times have changed. This brightly-coloured 97 is a classic. Its aromas are those of the hunt: forest-floor, moss, mushrooms. On the palate it remains within the limits of the vintage, with rather more freshness than fullness. This estate owns around 10% of the Grand Cru.

🔑 Dom. Rossignol-Trapet, 3, rue de la Petite-Issue, 21220 Gevrey-Chambertin, tel. 03.80.51.87.26, fax 03.80.34.31.63, e-mail info@rossignol-trapet.com ☑ 🍷 by appt.

DOM. TRAPET 1998★

■Gd cru n.c. n.c. ◖◗ 250–299 F

This is a solid and powerful wine in the Trapet tradition. The estate, which covers around 10% of the Grand Cru, has created a *cuvée* showing fullness and power. This 98 is the kind of dark red that could have fallen from the palette of a Fauvist painter, and it really sits well in the glass. It is robust and unusually concentrated. To be laid down for a long time.

🔑 Dom. Trapet Père et Fils, 53, rte. de Beaune, 21220 Gevrey-Chambertin, tel. 03.80.34.30.40, fax 03.80.51.86.34, e-mail message@domaine-trapet.com ☑ 🍷 by appt.

BURGUNDY

Chapelle-Chambertin

DOM. PIERRE DAMOY 1998★

■Gd cru 2.22 ha 3,900 ◖◗ 300–499 F

This is just adorable. The colour is a clear, deep garnet. The aromas are divided between soft fruit and a vegetative note that you can detect if you really study it. The attack seems very straightforward, the structure is clean, with powerful, slightly sharp tannins. Which is all one can say objectively, as it should really be left in peace for eight to ten years. But of course, what did you expect?

🔑 Dom. Pierre Damoy, 11, rue du Mal-de-Lattre-de-Tassigny, 21220 Gevrey-Chambertin, tel. 03.80.34.30.47, fax 03.80.58.54.79

DOM. DROUHIN-LAROZE 1998

■Gd cru 0.52 ha 2,500 ◖◗ 200–249 F

The chapel of Notre-Dame-de-Bèze disappeared around 1830. It had stood just where the Route des Grands Crus is now. It was originally built in 1155, rebuilt in 1547, and consecrated by the bishop of Bethlehem who was at Morvan at the time. This Chapelle-Chambertin *climat* keeps a small souvenir of it. This is a fairly pale wine, with a nose of raspberries and cinnamon, and a velvety body that has been made the old-fashioned way. This estate owns nearly 10% of the Chapelle land.

🔑 Drouhin-Laroze, 20, rue du Gaizot, 21220 Gevrey-Chambertin, tel. 03.80.34.31.49, fax 03.80.51.83.70 ☑ 🍷 by appt.

DOM. MICHEL NOELLAT ET FILS 1998★

■Gd cru 0.36 ha 900 200–249 F

This Chapelle is lively and slender, but also very pure and interesting. It is a wine you should come back to in two to three years' time. A heavy dark red colour with dark purple shades, it emits spicy, toasty, then raspberry aromas when you swirl the wine in the glass. Good tannins, and a powerful, long palate that will have its say later.

SCEA Dom. Michel Noëllat et Fils, 5, rue de la Fontaine, 21700 Vosne-Romanée, tel. 03.80.61.36.87, fax 03.80.61.18.10 by appt.

DOM. TRAPET PERE ET FILS 1998★★

■Gd cru n.c. n.c. 250–299 F

91 |94| 95 96 **98**

There is no need for a prayer stool to get in touch with this Chapelle. It seems delicate, fresh, meditative; oaky, certainly, but not overly so, excellently balanced and with a finish that we expect to grow. Likely to have some 15–20 years of life. Just a little over half a hectare (one acre) for this Grand Cru, and the wine is in the Trapet style, a reference point in Gevrey.

Dom. Trapet Père et Fils, 53, rte. de Beaune, 21220 Gevrey-Chambertin, tel. 03.80.34.30.40, fax 03.80.51.86.34, e-mail message@domaine-trapet.com by appt.

Charmes-Chambertin

DOM. DES BEAUMONT 1997★

■Gd cru 0.56 ha 1,800 250–299 F

It is always a great source of regret to the jury that they can never appreciate these Grands Crus when they are really ready for drinking. A year of maturation has gained this wine a star: its colour is Pinot-red, its nose fine and subtle, with for the moment a hint of alcohol subtly mixed with the scent of old rose. The palate is straightforward, with a touch of redcurrant, full and fleshy, quite concentrated, true to the vintage. It was matured in new oak, a flavour which will blend well in the wine in four or five years' time. 'A good wine which I would like to encounter again', notes one taster.

Dom. des Beaumont, 9, rue Ribordot, 21220 Morey-Saint-Denis, tel. 03.80.51.87.89, fax 03.80.51.87.89 by appt.

ALBERT BICHOT 1997★★

■Gd cru 0.9 ha 4,200 300–499 F

It will reach a crescendo. A wine that charms us with the brilliance and brightness of its colour. The nose, on the other hand, is still closed, giving out only a hint of stewed prunes. On the palate one begins to get a taste of its complexity. Rich and concentrated with all the verve of a Grand Cru. In short, it is starting to mature already. It should be drunk in about five years, perhaps with some venison or the doe that apprears on the label with the company crest.

Maison Albert Bichot, 6 bis, bd Jacques-Copeau, 21200 Beaune, tel. 03.80.24.37.37, fax 03.80.24.37.38

DOM. CAMUS PERE ET FILS 1996

■Gd cru 6.9 ha 18,000 250–299 F

The Camus family have lived in Gevrey-Chambertin for 200 years. They own 18 ha (45 acres), two-thirds being Grands Crus. A pretty, young, lively colour brings a spring feel to a wine with classic aromas: fur, moss, forest-floor, game and ripe soft fruit. A certain amount of acidity is not surprising, considering it is a 96. Untamed on the nose, fine and elegant on the palate, it doesn't have great structure, but the tannins are already well-integrated. We recommend three years in the cellar.

Dom. Camus Père et Fils, 21, rue du Mal-de-Lattre-de-Tassigny, 21220 Gevrey-Chambertin, tel. 03.80.34.30.64, fax 03.80.51.87.93 by appt.

COUVENT DES CORDELIERS 1998

■Gd cru n.c. 750 300–499 F

This wine should be decanted. Not a typical thing to do with Burgundies, but sometimes it is useful. Rose, spice, prunes, cherry – our tasters can scarcely sort it all out, but they are agreed on one thing: this wine needs to breathe. It doesn't have much body, but there is an underlying fruit just waiting to get out. A wine that is more typical of the appellation than of the vintage. Produced by Patriarche under another name.

Caves du Couvent des Cordeliers, rue de l'Hôtel-Dieu, 21200 Beaune, tel. 03.80.25.08.85, fax 03.80.25.08.21 ev. day 9.30am–12 noon 2pm–6pm

DOM. DUPONT-TISSERANDOT 1998★

■Gd cru 0.8 ha 4,000 150–199 F

The Charmes-Chambertin has been called the crown prince of Chambertin, and indeed the two wines are closely related. This example is ruby-red with a violet rim. A light toastiness enhances the stone fruit on the nose. On the palate we have a wine with little in the way of tannins, warm and so supple and fruity it is almost unctuous. It will be a pleasure to drink. This estate was founded in 1960, and with 24.2 ha (60 acres) it is the most widely spread in Gevrey. Here, 67 a (1.7 acres) are divided into two, with one half for Charmes and the other for Mazoyères.

🗝 GAEC Dupont-Tisserandot, 2, pl. des Marronniers, 21220 Gevrey-Chambertin, tel. 03.80.34.10.50, fax 03.80.58.50.71 ☑ 𝐈 by appt.

DOM. DOMINIQUE GALLOIS 1998★

■Gd cru 0.3 ha 1,500 ⏸ 200–249 F

This estate has connections with the writer Gaston Roupnel (he was related to the family and his archives are kept here). They share with us the pleasures of a violet-tinted 98 which mixes a little hint of Morello cherry with a little hint of liquorice. There is a touch of youthful aggression, but it has a well-placed richness on the middle palate and a subtle tannic finish, making it an agreeable wine to taste. Three to five years in the cellar before drinking this wine with poultry and truffles, is the advice of one of our tasters.

🗝 Dominique Gallois, 9, rue Mal-de-Lattre-de-Tassigny, 21220 Gevrey-Chambertin, tel. 03.80.34.11.99, fax 03.80.34.38.62 ☑ 𝐈 by appt.

HUMBERT FRERES 1998

■Gd cru 0.2 ha 1,050 ⏸ 200–249 F

This Charmes (19 a 79 ca/0.5 acres) comes from vineyards that have been handed down through the family, and which were replanted in 1960. Violet-tinted, it has a nose that is a mixture of fruit and new oak flavours, that get stronger as the wine breathes. There is a certain freshness and fruitiness to this lively wine. It is peppery, fairly robust, and liquorice-flavoured. There is not much structure in evidence. Very difficult to judge at the moment.

🗝 Dom. Humbert Frères, rue de Planteligone, 21220 Gevrey-Chambertin, tel. 03.80.51.80.14, fax 03.80.51.80.14 ☑ 𝐈 by appt.

JEAN-PAUL MAGNIEN 1998★

■Gd cru 0.2 ha 950 ⏸ 150–199 F

Jean-Paul Magnien, who farms 19 a 92 ca (0.5 acre) in the Mazoyères part of Charmes, takes his calling very seriously, and his wine is very promising. As far as colour and nose are concerned, there is plenty in store. On the palate, it is dynamic, tannic, and well-structured, with a fresh astringency suggesting a long, happy life ahead of it.

🗝 Jean-Paul Magnien, 5, ruelle de l'Eglise, 21220 Morey-Saint-Denis, tel. 03.80.51.83.10, fax 03.80.58.53.27 ☑ 𝐈 by appt.

DOM. MARCHAND FRERES 1998

■Gd cru 0.14 ha 700 ⏸ 200–249 F

This is a light, ruby-red Charmes in the 1970s style. Aromatic and fruity, almost jammy. Sylphlike and as sprightly as a microlight, skimming over everything, with a certain grace. If you want to find out more, take a guest room at the estate and talk to the wine-producer about it. He is full of ideas.

🗝 Dom. Marchand Frères, 1, pl. du Monument, B.P. 38, 21220 Gevrey-Chambertin, tel. 03.80.62.10.97, fax 03.80.62.11.01, e-mail dmarc2000@aol.com ☑ 𝐈 by appt.

MARCHE AUX VINS 1997

■Gd cru n.c. 750 ⏸ 300–499 F

This is from a house owned by Patriarche. Its aromas are complex and interesting, combining liquorice with gingerbread and a little note of menthol. The colour is almost brick-red, which is about right for its age. It doesn't have much in the way of body, but does manage to avoid harshness or bitterness on the palate. It should not be laid down for longer than three years.

🗝 Marché aux Vins, rue Nicolas-Rolin, 21200 Beaune, tel. 03.80.25.08.20, fax 03.80.25.08.21 ☑ 𝐈 ev. day 9.30am–12 noon 2pm–6pm

MOILLARD-GRIVOT 1997

■Gd cru n.c. 4,000 ⏸ 250–299 F

They say that there is enough to both eat and drink in a Charmes. There is no doubt about it, this wine has a stewed nose: that is, jammy and a little over-cooked. This wine, with its hot character, is satisfyingly rich, the tannins have mellowed and it has developing leathery flavours. A wild, manly, strong wine that would be ideal paired with wild boar.

🗝 Moillard-Grivot, 2, rue François-Mignotte, 21700 Nuits-Saint-Georges, tel. 03.80.62.42.00, fax 03.80.61.28.13, e-mail nuicave@wanadoo.fr ☑ 𝐈 by appt.

DOM. PIERRE PONNELLE

Les Mazoyères 1996

■ 1 ha n.c. ⏸ 200–249 F

Championing the oft-neglected Mazoyères, the Pierre Ponnelle estate, which has been taken over by Jean-Claude Boisset, has produced a fine 96. It is somewhere between cherry and raspberry and has many virtues in its favour (acidity, balance, fruitiness). A very dense wine that is already drinking well though definitely worth laying down. It should express all the subtlety of the Cru when fully mature.

🗝 Dom. Pierre Ponnelle, 2, rue Paradis, 21200 Beaune, tel. 03.80.22.19.12, fax 03.80.24.91.87

POULET PERE ET FILS 1997★

■Gd cru n.c. 3,500 ⏸ 500 F+

Laurent Max and his masterpieces. This very well-established business of Poulet Père et Fils has seen some ups and downs. First based in Beaune, then in Nuits-Saint-George, they have produced a very fine wine that is difficult to read, but which will age well. Its balsamic vinegar and fruity nose is followed by a straightforward and lively attack, which is followed in turn by a moment of concentrated ripeness. Tannins hit the high note.

🗝 Poulet Père et Fils, 6, rue de Chaux, 21700 Nuits-Saint-Georges, tel. 03.80.62.43.02, fax 03.80.61.28.08

BURGUNDY

DOM. HENRI REBOURSEAU 1997★★

■Gd cru 1.31 ha 2,130 250–299 F

Jean de Surrel is the grandson of Pierre Rebourseau, who was a very important figure in Chambertin, and Clos de Vougeot. It was no easy task to follow in Rebourseau's footsteps, but de Surrel has proved himself a worthy successor. This clear, dark-red 97, with its powerful aromatic charm, is a model of balance and virtue. The richness and ripe tannins are in perfect harmony, and it is deliciously smooth. It has been excellently made, and comes very close to a *coup de cœur*. It has a great future in the cellar.

NSE Dom. Henri Rebourseau, 10, pl. du Monument, 21220 Gevrey-Chambertin, tel. 03.80.51.88.94, fax 03.80.34.12.82, e-mail Rebourseal@aol.com ☑ Y by appt.

DOM. HENRI RICHARD 1998★★

■Gd cru 1.11 ha 4,000 200–249 F

This is a historic vineyard of 1.11 ha 4 ca (0.27 acres) vineyard in Mazoyères which once belonged to the writer Gaston Roupnel. It was sold in 1938 to Jean Richard, father of Henri and a former cooper. The wine lives up to its position, with a shimmering red colour and a very attractive nose (blackcurrant and vanilla). Full and robust, with tannins that are still rather young, but it has a lot of class. Leave in the cellar for four or five years.

Dom. Henri Richard, 75, rte. de Beaune, 21220 Gevrey-Chambertin, tel. 03.80.34.35.81, fax 03.80.34.35.81 ☑ Y ev. day 9am–12 noon 2pm–6pm

DOM. TAUPENOT-MERME 1997

■Gd cru n.c. 8,400 200–249 F

This is a parcel of 1.44 ha 07 ca (3.56 acres) at Mazoyères or Charmes-du-Dessous which comes from the former Merme estate at Morey. This rather dark 97 is lacking a little on the nose. It is quite lively, remains faithful to the vintage and is trying, honestly and without any pretence, to express itself as best it can.

Jean Taupenot-Merme, 33, rte. des Grands-Crus, 21220 Morey-Saint-Denis, tel. 03.80.34.35.24, fax 03.80.51.83.41 ☑ Y by appt.

Griottes-Chambertin

DOM. MARCHAND FRERES 1998

■Gd cru 0.12 ha 700 200–249 F

A languorous wine, there is no other way to describe it. It uncurls itself in the mouth, light, floating, ephemeral. It is not the best of the Griottes, but represents its vintage with real sincerity. It may lack tannins and strength but is certainly pleasant to drink. It is a question of vintage: you have to make do with what you've got.

Dom. Marchand Frères, 1, pl. du Monument, B.P. 38, 21220 Gevrey-Chambertin, tel. 03.80.62.10.97, fax 03.80.62.11.01, e-mail dmarc2000@aol.com ☑ Y by appt.

DOM. PONSOT 1997★

■Gd cru 1 ha 2,666 300–499 F

The Ponsot Griotte is something of the Chanel N°5 of wines: a cult-wine. Does it smell of cherries? Yes, but the kind of cherries that make jam. A gleaming colour, liquorice flavours and a long and tannic body. Virility personified. It should be laid down for five years or even more. A curious thing to note is that the label goes all the way round the bottle. No filtration, no fining. It comes from 1 ha (2.5 acres) of land.

Dom. Ponsot, 21, rue de la Montagne, 21220 Morey-Saint-Denis, tel. 03.80.34.32.46, fax 03.80.58.51.70, e-mail info@domaine-ponsot.com

Mazis-Chambertin

DOM. DUPONT-TISSERANDOT 1998★

■Gd cru 0.35 ha 1,800 150–199 F

The few tastings we have had of the Mazis-Chambertin are enough to inspire confidence. The red, here, is deep ruby, with a bright rim. The nose is somewhere between herbaceous and raspberry. Excellent attack, with the right amount of suppleness and fruit, a big aftertaste and a structure with fine tannins that should soften and mellow.

GAEC Dupont-Tisserandot, 2, pl. des Marronniers, 21220 Gevrey-Chambertin, tel. 03.80.34.10.50, fax 03.80.58.50.71 ☑ Y by appt.

JEAN-MICHEL GUILLON 1998★★

■Gd cru n.c. 912 200–249 F

As Jean Cocteau once said, 'He runs faster than beauty'. This wine is lively, but controlled. The colour is very dark and solid, the aromas of blackcurrant, bilberry and spice are attractive, and the palate has a well-structured character. This is a full, deep Pinot Noir, soft and round. This Paris-born wine-producer, who came here out of the blue in 1979, has acquired many fans. He makes wine the way he wants and uses traditional methods that prove themselves again and again.

Dom. Jean-Michel Guillon, 33, rte. de Beaune, 21220 Gevrey-Chambertin, tel. 03.80.51.83.98, fax 03.80.51.85.59, e-mail eurlguillon@aol.com ☑ Y by appt.

DOM. HARMAND-GEOFFROY 1997

■Gd cru 0.7 ha 3,400 200–249 F

The Mazis lies between the Clos de Bèze, Les Ruchottes and the Route des Grands Crus. Mazis, 'masures', means 'hovels', perhaps a hamlet in medieval times. The soil is not deep here, just a few dozen centimetres in the top parts. This wine has not aged at all since last year. Densely-coloured, with a powerful smell of leather, it is long and expressive, all the while maintaining this unusual aroma. Gérard Harmand has taken over from his step-father, at Place des Lois in Gevrey.

Dom. Harmand-Geoffroy, 1, pl. des Lois, 21220 Gevrey-Chambertin, tel. 03.80.34.10.65, fax 03.80.34.13.72, e-mail harmand-geoffroy@wanadoo.fr by appt.

Harmand

ARMELLE ET JEAN-MICHEL MOLIN 1998

■Gd cru 0.37 ha 900 200–249 F

This is the first wine from the Côte-de-Nuits to be included in the Hospices de Beaune wine auction (donated by Thomas-Collignon in 1976). So the Mazis can look the Clos de Bèze straight in the eyes. This wine has an attractive lively colour. The liquorice and blackcurrant is not surprising. It is fairly tannic, and still rather closed on the palate. However, it is elegant. Destined for at least three good years in the cellar.

EARL Armelle et Jean-Michel Molin, 54, rte des Grands-Crus, 21220 Fixin, tel. 03.80.52.21.28, fax 03.80.59.96.99 by appt.

DOM. HENRI REBOURSEAU 1997*

■Gd cru 0.96 ha 2,410 250–299 F

We could almost give this wine another star: the colour is light, the nose is one of stewed or preserved fruits with a sprinkling of vegetation. The attack is fruity, followed by a palate: hot, full and rich, right up to a very stylish finish. It would go well with a jugged hare in a few years' time, but don't wait too long . . . The little château, dating from 1800, which was bought by Rebourseau in 1923, is one of the most beautiful buildings in Gevrey. The label on the bottle rightfully gives it pride of place.

NSE Dom. Henri Rebourseau, 10, pl. du Monument, 21220 Gevrey-Chambertin, tel. 03.80.51.88.94, fax 03.80.34.12.82, e-mail Rebourseal@aol.com by appt.

DOM. TORTOCHOT 1997**

■Gd cru 0.42 ha 2,000 200–249 F

This Grand Cru often features on some very prestigious menus, and this particular wine would certainly not be out of place on one. Strong, mellow, opulent, it fits the Grand Cru image very well. The colour has developed just a little. The nose is of crystallised cherries, which is often a characteristic of this vintage. This wine is classic with its charmingly full, fruity palate. This estate has almost half a hectare (just over an acre) of the Grand Cru.

Dom. Tortochot, 12, rue de l'Eglise, 21220 Gevrey-Chambertin, tel. 03.80.34.30.68, fax 03.80.34.18.80 by appt.

Ruchottes-Chambertin

CH. DE MARSANNAY 1997

■Gd cru 0.1 ha 450 300–499 F

Ruchottes is situated in the part of Chambertin that is still a little wild, with its crumbling walls, piles of stones and bushes. The name has nothing to do with bees (a 'rucher' is an apiary), but comes from *roichots*, small rocks that lie just on the surface of the ground. Its wines have vigour and bite. This bright ruby-red 97, with lots of different hues, has a nose that suggests a fairly ripe palate, but is still a little closed. Both tannins and acidity are evident but pleasant.

Ch. de Marsannay, rte. des Grands-Crus, B.P. 78, 21160 Marsannay-la-Côte, tel. 03.80.51.71.11, fax 03.80.51.71.12 ev. day 10am–12 noon 2pm–6.30pm; cl. 23 Dec.–3 Jan.

Morey-Saint-Denis

Covering a little more than 100 ha (247 acres), Morey-Saint-Denis is one of the smallest appellations communales in the Côte de Nuits. You can find some excellent Premier Crus and five Grands Crus which qualify for the Appellation d'Origine Contrôlée: Clos de Tart, Clos Saint-Denis, Bonnes-Mares (only a part), Clos de la Roche and Clos des Lambrays.

The appellation, which produced 4,685 hl (123,684 gal) in 1999, of which 195 hl (5,148 gal) were white, is squeezed between Gevrey and Chambolle and could be said to be halfway between the strength of the first and the finesse of the second. On the

Friday before the sale at the Hospices de Nuits (which takes place in the third week in March) the winemakers put Morey-Saint-Denis, and only this wine, on sale to the public at the festival of the 'Carrefour de Dyonisos', held in the village hall.

DOM. DES BEAUMONT 1997★

■ 1er cru 0.35 ha 1,500 ⏸ 100–149 F

This is a wine made in the image of the villagers: chatty, full of life, sociable. A very dark purple colour, with blackberries on the nose, a decent structure, a youthful spontaneity, and a certain roughness. A pleasant wine that might do better competing in the *village* category.

🔑 Dom. des Beaumont, 9, rue Ribordot, 21220 Morey-Saint-Denis, tel. 03.80.51.87.89, fax 03.80.51.87.89 ☑ 🍷 by appt.

DOM. REGIS BOUVIER

En la rue de Vergy 1998★

■ 0.5 ha 3,000 ⏸ 70–99 F

This is a wine that looks as if it has come straight out of a paintbox. The extraction has been conducted perfectly, though the nose keeps fairly quiet about it, giving us just a hint of spice. The palate is also reticent, but the finish is ample reward for all our patience. Its freshness and frankness have wonderful energy. A wine that should doubtless be discovered after leaving it to age for two or three years in the cellar.

🔑 Dom. Régis Bouvier, 52, rue de Mazy, 21160 Marsannay-la-Côte, tel. 03.80.51.33.93, fax 03.80.58.75.07 ☑ 🍷 by appt.

JEAN-MICHEL GUILLON

La Riotte 1998★

■ 1er cru 0.25 ha 1,750 ⏸ 70–99 F

Renting just 2.5 ha (6 acres) in 1980, today this fine estate covers 9 ha (22 hacres): it is not a fairy tale, but the story of an imaginative and enthusiastic Parisian wine-producer who has really mananged to create his own wine universe. He has produced a Morey from the centre of the region. Very clear, with aromas of vanilla and soft fruit, quite round and rich, and in short attractive. There is a slight hint of marc on the finish. Best drunk in two to three years' time.

🔑 Dom. Jean-Michel Guillon, 33, rte. de Beaune, 21220 Gevrey-Chambertin, tel. 03.80.51.83.98, fax 03.80.51.85.59, e-mail eurlguillon@aol.com ☑ 🍷 by appt.

DOM. LEYMARIE-CECI 1997★

■ 0.4 ha n.c. ⏸ 70–99 F

'They lack nothing', says Dr Jules Lavalle in his chapter on the wines of Morey. And indeed, this brightly-coloured *village* is characterful and ample. Its untamed nose of game and forest-floor comes straight from the Hautes-Côtes. The tannins are already mellow, and there is some acidity to ensure the wine's future. This is a wine to wait for, and we recommend letting it breathe on opening.

🔑 Dom. Leymarie-CECI, Clos du Village, 24, rue du Vieux-Château, 21640 Vougeot, tel. 03.80.62.86.06, fax 03.80.62.88.53 ☑ 🍷 by appt.

LIGNIER-MICHELOT

En la Rue de Vergy 1998★

■ 1.9 ha 4,000 ⏸ 70–99 F

This deep ruby wine is somewhat original with its roasted, liquorice aromas. After a firm and straightforward attack, its strength is confirmed by strong tannins, and the character of the terroir has been respected by skilful maturation in barrel. Overall, it lacks neither roundness nor balance. Virgile Lignier took over the family estate in 1996: in his own way, he emulates the great Roman poet for whom he is named.

🔑 Dom. Lignier-Michelot, 11, rue Haute, 21220 Morey-Saint-Denis, tel. 03.80.34.31.13, fax 03.80.58.52.16 ☑ 🍷 by appt.

JEAN-PAUL MAGNIEN

Les Faconnières 1998

■ 1er cru 0.57 ha 2,200 ⏸ 100–149 F

This wine has a heady nose of violets, and its perfume just lingers and lingers. This 98 may not be the most robust of wines, but it is a delight to taste. There is a little vegetal touch, but it doesn't bring any bitterness with it. In short, this is an attractive wine that still needs to mature. The entire harvest of this estate is de-stemmed.

🔑 Jean-Paul Magnien, 5, ruelle de l'Eglise, 21220 Morey-Saint-Denis, tel. 03.80.51.83.10, fax 03.80.58.53.27 ☑ 🍷 by appt.

DOM. MARCHAND FRERES

Les Herbuottes 1998★

■ 0.48 ha 1,800 ⏸ 70–99 F

This is a fine family estate of 7 ha (17 acres). Their Morey-Saint-Denis is cardinal purple in colour, and is very impressive. Its complex aromas of spice and fruit combine with a well-tempered oakiness. On the palate it is full and tannic, really robust but without being harsh, and should be kept at least four years in the cellar.

🔑 Dom. Marchand Frères, 1, pl. du Monument, B.P. 38, 21220 Gevrey-Chambertin, tel. 03.80.62.10.97, fax 03.80.62.11.01, e-mail dmarc2000@aol.com ☑ 🍷 by appt.

MOILLARD-GRIVOT

Monts Luisants 1998

■ 1er cru 0.8 ha 3,000 ⏸ 100–149 F

The Monts Luisants is the hill where the leaves on the trees are supposed to glow even at night. It is to the right as you leave Gevrey, near a pretty little tearoom (where we have aken tea). 'Young wine, rich Burgundy', so he proverb goes, and here is a good example of it. This brightly-coloured 98 is still finding its way. Good extraction, still woody, but it should develop well if you lay it down for three to five years.

⊶ Moillard-Grivot, 2, rue François-Mignotte, 21700 Nuits-Saint-Georges, tel. 03.80.62.42.00, fax 03.80.61.28.13, e-mail nuicave@wanadoo.fr ☑ Y by appt.

DOM. HENRI PERROT-MINOT

En la Rue de Vergy 1997★★

■ 1 ha 3,600 ⏸ 100–149 F

This estate practises a very rigorous selection, with no fining or filtration. The result is a bright, deep red wine with a hint of oakiness on the fruit then a long, tenacious body. The palate is superb, mouthfilling and well-structured: velvet touched with blackberries. A very smooth wine. Note also the **La Riotte 97 Premier Cru**, which receives a recommendation (150–199F).

⊶ Henri Perrot-Minot, 54, rte des Grands-Crus, 21220 Morey-Saint-Denis, tel. 03.80.34.32.51, fax 03.80.34.13.57 ☑ Y by appt.

DOM. LOUIS REMY

Aux Chéseaux 1997★

■ 0.25 ha 1,200 ▮⏸ 100–149 F

This is a *climat* at the very edge of Gevrey-Chambertin, just under the Clos de la Roche. It produces a deep cherry-red wine with a nose that is still wavering between bilberries and wood. On the palate, the texture appears fine and strong. A wine that is still closed (acidity and tannins need to soften), but it is worth waiting for.

⊶ Dom. Louis Remy, 1, pl. du Monument, 21220 Morey-Saint-Denis, tel. 03.80.34.32.59, fax 03.80.34.32.59 ☑ Y by appt.

REMI SEGUIN 1997★★

■ 0.51 ha n.c. ⏸ 50–69 F

Someone who is born at Clos de Tart, to a father who was one of the stewards of the estate, is bound to have Morey in his blood. Rémi Seguin brings us an excellent 97. Its brilliance is expressive, its raspberry nose a little wild and already showing some maturity. Though there are strong wood flavours, the fruit shines through in all its freshness. It fills the mouth and lingers just as it should. The final impression is one of elegance and purity. The **Premier Cru 97** is also remarkable, all finesse and soft fruits, with well-blended tannins (70–99F). Excellent value for money.

⊶ Rémi Seguin, rue de Cîteaux, 21640 Gilly-lès-Cîteaux, tel. 03.80.62.89.61, fax 03.80.62.80.92 ☑ Y by appt.

Clos de la Roche, de Tart, de Saint-Denis, des Lambrays

The Clos de la Roche – which despite its name is not a walled vineyard – covers the biggest surface area (about 16 ha/40 acres), and includes various *lieux-dits* or named locations; it produced 486 hl (12,830 gal) in 1998 and 700 hl (18,480 gal) in 1999. Clos Saint-Denis, about 6.5 ha (16 acres), is also unwalled, and it too incorporates a group of *lieux-dits* – 270 hl (7,128 gal). These two Crus are parcelled into small plots and cultivated by numerous growers. The Clos de Tart is entirely enclosed by stone walls and cultivated by one grower. It is about 7 ha (17 acres) and the wines are vinified and matured on the property – 307 hl (8,105 gal) in 1999 the cellar on two levels is well worth a visit. The Clos de Lambrays has one main grower, but it is a group of several plots and *lieux-dits*: Les Bouchots, Les Larrêts or Clos de Lambrays and Le Meix-Rentier. It covers just under 9 ha (22 acres), 8.5 (21 acres) of which are cultivated by the same grower. It produced 383 hl (10,111 gal) in 1999.

Clos de la Roche

DOM. ARLAUD PERE ET FILS

1997★

■ Gd cru n.c. n.c. ⏸ 150–199 F

This Clos de la Rocher (43.9 a/1.08 acres) is situated in Les Mochamps, and, for those who know their Morey really well, just touching the borders the original *climat*, which was decidedly smaller than the current one. This is a wine with an elegant fruitiness that can be drunk relatively soon (in three or four years' time). A pleasant colour with a rather savage and toasty nose, mingled with aromas of ripe

Côte de Nuits (Centre)

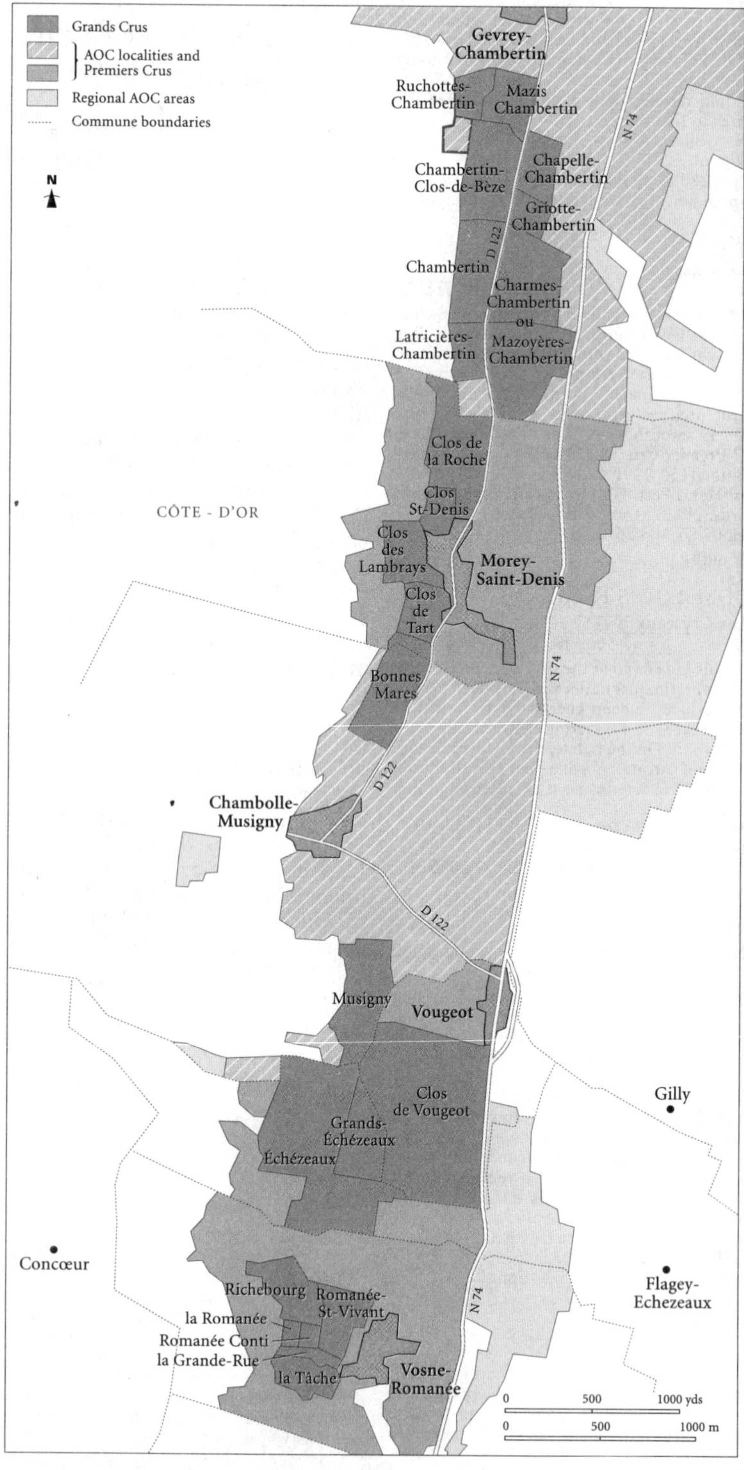

Grands Crus
AOC localities and Premiers Crus
Regional AOC areas
Commune boundaries
N
Gevrey-Chambertin
Ruchottes-Chambertin
Mazis Chambertin
N 74
Chapelle-Chambertin
Chambertin-Clos-de-Bèze
Griotte-Chambertin
D 122
Chambertin
Charmes-Chambertin ou
Latricières-Chambertin
Mazoyères-Chambertin
Clos de la Roche
Clos St-Denis
CÔTE - D'OR
Clos des Lambrays
Morey-Saint-Denis
Clos de Tart
Bonnes Mares
Chambolle-Musigny
Musigny
Vougeot
Gilly
Clos de Vougeot
Grands-Échézeaux
Échézeaux
Concœur
Flagey-Echezeaux
Richebourg
Romanée-St-Vivant
la Romanée
Romanée Conti
la Grande-Rue
la Tâche
Vosne-Romanée
0 500 1000 yds
0 500 1000 m

soft fruit. It is elegant, refined, and well-balanced.
SCEA Dom. Arlaud Père et Fils, 43, rte. des Grands-Crus, 21220 Morey-Saint-Denis, tel. 03.80.34.32.65, fax 03.80.58.52.09 by appt.

CAVES DU COUVENT DES CORDELIERS 1998

Gd cru n.c. 300 300–499 F

This is a very soft wine. It is light ruby in colour, with a gentle nose with chocolate and ripe fruit. It fills the mouth well, has a considerable length, and is reasonably well-balanced. A wine with more suppleness than concentration, it has what they call here 'good fat'. Produced by an offshoot of the Patriarche-Boisseaux business.
Caves du Couvent des Cordeliers, rue de l'Hôtel-Dieu, 21200 Beaune, tel. 03.80.25.08.85, fax 03.80.25.08.21 ev. day 9.30am–12 noon 2pm–6pm

DOM. MARCHAND FRERES 1998★★

Gd cru 0.06 ha 300 200–249 F

The Clos de la Roche is the benchmark of Morey: it is the best-constructed of these wines. This attractive Pinot-red 98 comes from a tiny little vineyard that has managed to produce something truly exceptional. Its aromas of cherry and kirsch give it real vitality. A pure and authentic, well-constructed wine that should be stowed away in the corner of your cellar because it needs time to reach its full potential.
Dom. Marchand Frères, 1, pl. du Monument, B.P. 38, 21220 Gevrey-Chambertin, tel. 03.80.62.10.97, fax 03.80.62.11.01, e-mail dmarc2000@aol.com by appt.

DOM. PONSOT

Cuvée Vieilles vignes 1997★

Gd cru 3.4 ha 8,880 500 F+

This very fine family estate, which was founded in 1872, takes great care over the quality of its grapes, and only produces small yields. The Ponsot family fine-tune their wines with aplomb, and have produced 8,880 bottles of the Cuvée Vieilles Vignes. There is a subdued brilliance about the colour of this wine, which has a spicy raspberry nose. The tannins do not overwhelm the fruit, the balance is impressive, and it has plenty of character.
Dom. Ponsot, 21, rue de la Montagne, 21220 Morey-Saint-Denis, tel. 03.80.34.32.46, fax 03.80.58.51.70, e-mail info@domaine-ponsot.com

DOM. LOUIS REMY 1998★★

Gd cru 0.65 ha 2,600 250–299 F

92 |(93)| 95 96 97 **98**

This is a handsome monster of a wine, something of a wolf in sheep's clothing perhaps. Smooth and soft on the outside, but inside the vanilla nose is veering towards blackcurrant and spice, and from the attack onwards the palate is substantial and very, very long. A very well-made wine, true to the terroir and not at all the kind of thing that will appeal to a commercial market. Time will tell, but it has impressive energy and absolute sincerity. It should be laid down for a long time and certainly not opened before 2005.
Dom. Louis Remy, 1, pl. du Monument, 21220 Morey-Saint-Denis, tel. 03.80.34.32.59, fax 03.80.34.32.59 by appt.

Clos Saint-Denis

DOM. HERESZTYN 1998★

Gd cru 0.23 ha 1,500 250–299 F

Following an excellent 97 vintage, this 98 is dark in colour, with violet hues. The nose is still closed, and it may be three to five years before it opens up. After a well-rounded and already smooth first impression, the powerful palate reveals a hint of oak. It is a well-constructed wine, thoroughbred and long. A wine that will reward anyone willing to wait for it.
Dom. Heresztyn, 27, rue Richebourg, 21220 Gevrey-Chambertin, tel. 03.80.34.30.86, fax 03.80.34.13.99, e-mail domaine.heresztyn@wanadoo.fr ev. day 9am–12 noon 2pm–6pm; Sun. by appt.

JEAN-PAUL MAGNIEN 1998

Gd cru 0.31 ha 1,500 150–199 F

These 31 a (0.76 acres) of vines have produced a lyrical ruby-red 98 with crimson glints and aromas, that skilfully follow with notes of bilberry and pepper. A complex, balanced wine that remains in this vein on the palate. It expresses the terroir digging into corners and bringing forth hidden savage, gamey flavours – but then they do call the people of Morey 'wolves'.
Jean-Paul Magnien, 5, ruelle de l'Eglise, 21220 Morey-Saint-Denis, tel. 03.80.51.83.10, fax 03.80.58.53.27 by appt.

Clos de Tart

MOMMESSIN 1998★★

Gd cru 7.53 ha 20,000 300–499 F

64 69 76 **78 82 83** 84 **|85|86 |88|** |89| |90| |93|(95)96 97 **98**

This estate is 850 years old, but has only changed hands three times, resulting in great stability for the business. This 98 is presented by Sylvain Pitiot (son-in-law of Pierre

Poupon and a specialist in the cartography of the Burgundy terroirs). Abundant red in colour, it hints at venison and leather, and has flavours of new oak. It is most certainly a Grand Cru, produced using contemporary methods, but an excellent prospect for laying down. The Mommessin family business no longer exists, but it has kept this prestigious monopoly.

🔑 Mommessin, Dom. du Clos de Tart, 7, rte. des Grands-Crus, 21220 Morey-Saint-Denis, tel. 03.80.34.30.91, fax 03.80.24.60.01 ☑ 🍷 by appt.

Clos des Lambrays

DOM. DES LAMBRAYS 1997★

■Gd cru 8.6 ha 30,000 🍾 250–299 F

79 81 **82** 83 **85** 88 **89** |**90**| 92 |93| 94 **95** 96 97

This deep ruby-red wine is the colour of blood, with an untamed nose that leaps out at you with aromas of leather, stewed fruit, game, and dead leaves on the forest floor. All the signs of a youthful wine that has yet to shape itself. Fruit and spice emerge timidly on a palate that is still closed but which one taster – not knowing that he was tasting a Côte-de-Nuits Grand Cru – said belonged to a wine that was really true to its basic terroir. This vineyard has been bought by the Freund family of Koblenz, leaving Thierry Brouin at the helm.

🔑 Sté Nlle du Dom. des Lambrays, 31, rue Basse, 21220 Morey-Saint-Denis, tel. 03.80.51.84.33, fax 03.80.51.81.97 ☑ 🍷 by appt.

🔑 Freund

Chambolle Musigny

The Musigny name alone sets the pitch in the orchestral sweep of wines in this region. This is a commune of enormous reputation despite its tiny area, founded on the quality of its wines and the fame of its Premiers Crus, the most celebrated of which is the *climat* of Les Amoureuses. But Chambolle also has Charmes, Chabiots, Cras, Fousselottes, Groseilles and Lavrottes as well. The small village, with its narrow streets shaded by trees, has magnificent cellars (Domaine des Musigny). In 1999, the vineyard produced 7,906 hl (208,718 gal).

The Chambolle wines are elegant, subtle and soft, combining the strength of Bonne-Mares and the finesse of Musigny; within the Côte de Nuits this area represents a transition from one type of terroir to another.

ALBERT BICHOT 1997

■ n.c. 11,200 🍾 150–199 F

This 97 lacks neither flesh nor roundness. Light ruby-red in colour, it expresses very ripe fruit, a little wood and a touch of vegetation. It still needs to find the right balance between tannins and alcohol, but is well-made and should be opened in two years' time.

🔑 Maison Albert Bichot, 6 bis, bd Jacques-Copeau, 21200 Beaune, tel. 03.80.24.37.37, fax 03.80.24.37.38

SYLVAIN CATHIARD

Les Clos de l'Orme 1998★★

■ 0.43 ha 2,400 🍾 100–149 F

Sylvain Cathiard works with his father André, who created this estate by sheer tenacity. He started first as a salaried vineyard worker, and then a tenant farmer. The result is here for all to see: a 98 that could be held up as an example at every stage of tasting. It has the delicacy of a traditional Chambolle, supple, round and fruity. A very good, full, round wine that stays true to the terroir. Good for laying down.

🔑 Sylvain Cathiard, 20, rue de la Goillotte, 21700 Vosne-Romanée, tel. 03.80.62.36.01, fax 03.80.61.18.21 ☑ 🍷 by appt.

CHANSON PERE ET FILS 1997★

■ n.c. 4,000 🍾 150–199 F

This really is a wine of silk and lace, as described with such admiration by the writer Gaston Roupnel. Although the colour is bright and well-defined, the nose is a little more discreet (hints of menthol and soft fruit). Like many of the 97 vintages, this Chambolle is light on structure, only just beginning to acquire some complexity, and a little abrupt on the finish. Can be kept for several years.

🔑 Chanson Père et Fils, 10, rue Paul-Chanson, 21200 Beaune, tel. 03.80.22.33.00, fax 03.80.24.17.42, e-mail tmarion@vins-chanson.com 🍷 by appt.

F. CHAUVENET Les Baudes 1997

■1er cru n.c. 3,600 🍾 150–199 F

There is nothing between Baudes and Bonnes Mares except the Route des Grands Crus, sheer heaven for wine lovers.This wine does its best to rise to the challenge, in a rather severe style. Brilliant ruby-red in colour, the aromas are of ripe fruit. A wine to be enjoyed for the pleasure of the moment and which should be drunk within a year. Chavenet is part of the Boisset group.

F. Chauvenet, 9, quai Fleury, 21700 Nuits-Saint-Georges, tel. 03.80.62.61.43, fax 03.80.62.37.38

ROBERT GROFFIER PERE ET FILS Les Hauts-Doix 1998★★

1er cru 1 ha 4,000 200–249 F

'An engaging and very personal wine', notes one taster. It may be a little woody now, but the texture is promising: it has body, chewiness, and is developing well, as it proves on the nose, which has a rich and complex fruitiness. Once the toasty notes have blended in, it will be a great wine.

SARL Robert Groffier et Fils, 3–5, rte. des Grands-Crus, 21220 Morey-Saint-Denis, tel. 03.80.34.31.53 by appt.

DOM. A.-F. GROS 1998★★

0.41 ha 2,200 150–199 F

Anne-Françoise Parent, née Gros (of Vosne), has produced a remarkable and attention-grabbing wine which possesses, in the words of Alexis Lichine, 'a charm that is both fragile and determined, precisely what people would call a feminine charm'. A deep, dark ruby-red wine scented with wild strawberries. It has both vinosity and persistence, density and finesse, and plenty of flavour. In short, a fine example of a Chambolle 98.

Dom. A.-F. Gros, La Garelle, rte. d'Ivry, 21630 Pommard, tel. 03.80.22.61.85, fax 03.80.24.03.16 by appt.

MICHEL GROS 1998★

0.69 ha 3,500 100–149 F

There has been a lot of emphasis put on the extraction during the vinification of this wine, resulting in a vivid colour and concentrated aromas of bilberry. It is more approachable on the palate, and not without elegance, but it certainly has a very special character, an unusual personality reminiscent of the 'Accadian' style which was so successful in the Côte and with critics some years ago.

Dom. Michel Gros, 7, rue des Communes, 21700 Vosne-Romanée, tel. 03.80.61.04.69, fax 03.80.61.22.29 by appt.

DOM. ANTONIN GUYON 1997

3.32 ha 14,000 150–199 F

This 97, with its flavour of steeped cherries, is not very fleshy, but its uncomplicated attack, its finesse, and its fruitiness encourage one to give it a chance. However, the vintage is what it is. With nearly 50 ha (124 acres), this is one of the biggest family estates on the Côte.

Dom. Antonin Guyon, 21420 Savigny-lès-Beaune, tel. 03.80.67.13.24, fax 03.80.66.85.87, e-mail vins@guyon-bourgogne.com by appt.

DOM. HERESZTYN 1998

0.37 ha 1,800 70–99 F

With its brilliant purple Pinot colour and promising though still woody nose, this is a full and rich wine. It is attractive and even distinctive. However, we still recommend waiting four or five years until all the flavours have blended and it has reached its best.

Dom. Heresztyn, 27, rue Richebourg, 21220 Gevrey-Chambertin, tel. 03.80.34.30.86, fax 03.80.34.13.99, e-mail domaine.heresztyn@wanadoo.fr ev. day 9am–12 noon 2pm–6pm; Sun. by appt.

LIGNIER-MICHELOT 1998★

0.7 ha 2,000 70–99 F

'The Volnay of the Côte-de-Nuits', is how André Jullien described Chambolle-Musigny at the beginning of the 19th century. Chambolle isn't called Musigny for nothing. It is always a pleasure to find confirmation of the good qualities of an appellation, as one does in this black cherry wine with its radiant nose of fresh fruits, attractive smooth richness, frank suppleness, and consummate femininity. It should be laid down, but not for too long – a year or two at the most.

Dom. Lignier-Michelot, 11, rue Haute, 21220 Morey-Saint-Denis, tel. 03.80.34.31.13, fax 03.80.58.52.16 by appt.

DOM. THIERRY MORTET Les Beaux Bruns 1998★

1er cru 0.22 ha 1,200 150–199 F

The colour is dark and dense with violet hues. The nose is closed, giving out just a hint of strawberry jam and stewed prunes, signs of an early maturity. The palate, in contrast, is fresh and young, with a growing chewiness in the middle, and satisfyingly true to character.

Dom. Thierry Mortet, 16, pl. des Marronniers, 21220 Gevrey-Chambertin, tel. 03.80.51.85.07, fax 03.80.34.16.80 by appt.

JACQUES-FREDERIC MUGNIER Les Amoureuses 1997

1er cru 0.55 ha 3,450 250–299 F

Les Amoureuses is situated a little apart in the middle of the Côte-de-Nuits. The 97 vintage is probably not the best point of reference, and this wine is certainly rather light in all aspects. A little hint of acidity, however, suggests that it does have some kind of inner life. The 90 vintage was very good.

Jacques-Frédéric Mugnier, Ch. de Chambolle-Musigny, 21220 Chambolle-Musigny, tel. 03.80.62.85.39, fax 03.80.62.87.36 by appt.

DOM. MICHEL NOELLAT ET FILS Les Feusselottes 1998★

1er cru 0.45 ha 1,200 100–149 F

This excellent, deep-red 98 has been made from grapes harvested at full maturity. It is a clean, straightforward wine with aromas of

BURGUNDY

bilberry and mushrooms. The palate follows the same path as the nose, moving towards a flavour of prunes. Good body and not far off a *coup de cœur*. Equally satisfying is the **village 98**, which receives one star.
SCEA Dom. Michel Noëllat et Fils, 5, rue de la Fontaine, 21700 Vosne-Romanée, tel. 03.80.61.36.87, fax 03.80.61.18.10 Y by appt.

DOM. HENRI PERROT-MINOT

La Combe d'Orveau 1997*

1er cru 0.47 ha 1,500 150–199 F

This Premier Cru nestles in a wonderful spot just above the Clos de Vougeot, between Echézeaux and Musigny. Deep, dark red in colour, abundant in strawberry and raspberry aromas, it is very attractive on the palate. Still a little on the hard side, but it will become more balanced. It has the means to do so.
Henri Perrot-Minot, 54, rte. des Grands-Crus, 21220 DenisMorey-Saint-Denis, tel. 03.80.34.32.51, fax 03.80.34.13.57 Y by appt.

DOM. ROBERT SIRUGUE

Les Mombies 1998*

0.27 ha 1,600 70–99 F

A saddle of hare would go very well with this *village*, which is named after a little-known *climat* situated south-east of Chambolle. Ruby-red with hints of light pink, it has a ripe nose with a light but subtle woody note. It is a little on the severe side, but the blackcurrant enhances the (very apparent) tannins to create a solid and successful 98 that needs two years before being ready to open.
Dom. Robert Sirugue, 3, av. du Monument, 21700 Vosne-Romanée, tel. 03.80.61.00.64, fax 03.80.61.27.57 Y by appt.

DOM. TAUPENOT-MERME 1997*

n.c. 5,000 100–149 F

Jean Taupenot came from Saint-Romain, married at Morey, and then took over part of the former Merme estate. He has a little less than 10 ha (25 acres) of well-placed land, with parcels in Charmes-Chambertin and even some vines at Clos des Lambrays. Virginie and Romain now represent the younger generation. This is an attractive-looking wine, with a untamed nose (forest-floor, game, and wood); it is mouthfilling, with shades of crushed fruit. Ready to drink.
Jean Taupenot-Merme, 33, rte. des Grands-Crus, 21220 Morey-Saint-Denis, tel. 03.80.34.35.24, fax 03.80.51.83.41 Y by appt.

Bonnes-Mares

This appellation, which produced 613 hl (16,183 gal) in 1999, spreads into the commune of Morey along the wall of the Clos de Tart, but most of it is located in Chambolle. This is a Grand Cru par excellence. The wines of Bonnes-Mares are full, vinous and rich and have the capacity to keep for a long time. After a few years of ageing, they make excellent accompaniments to rich stews or game birds.

DOM. ARLAUD PERE ET FILS

1997**

Gd cru 0.2 ha n.c. 200–249 F

|91| |92| |(93)| 95 96 |97|

During the second world war, a soldier named Joseph Arlaud was passing through Morey and fell in love with Renée Amiotà, which is how this estate, and their son Hervé, came into being. These 20 a 81 ca (0.5 acres) are exactly in the middle of the Grand Cru and act as a kind of junction or dividing point. They have produced a remarkable wine. Deep, dark red in colour, it comes to life with blackcurrant. Its well-integrated tannins form a velvety structure with characteristic finesse.
SCEA Dom. Arlaud Père et Fils, 43, rte. des Grands-Crus, 21220 Morey-Saint-Denis, tel. 03.80.34.32.65, fax 03.80.58.52.09 Y by appt.

DOM. DROUHIN-LAROZE

1998*

Gd cru 1.5 ha 4,000 200–249 F

95 96 98

This estate owns 11.5% of Bonnes-Mares, or 1.73 ha (4.3 acres), and there are vines here that date from 1928. This bright ruby-red 98 already shows signs of considerable maturity, with notes of blackcurrant, prunes, and forest-floor. Its noticeable but fine tannins and lingering aromas give it a convincing future. It should be laid down for at least five years.
Drouhin-Laroze, 20, rue du Gaizot, 21220 Gevrey-Chambertin, tel. 03.80.34.31.49, fax 03.80.51.83.70 Y by appt.

XAVIER DUCLERT 1997

Gd cru n.c. n.c. 250–299 F

It is not always easy for a ***négociant-éleveur*** to procure a piece of land in Bonnes-Mares. This is one who has succeeded, and he offers us a wine with violet and quince aromas. There is a fair amount of richness on the attack, and a pronounced acidity that is well supported by the fruit (crystallised cherries). This wine should become more round with

time. At the moment its youth makes it rather coarse.
🔑 Xavier Duclert, 2 bis, pl. Carnot, 21200 Beaune, tel. 03.80.22.74.77, fax 03.80.22.74.77, e-mail xavier.duclert@fnac.net ☑ Y ev. day except Mon. 10am–7pm

DOM. FOUGERAY DE BEAUCLAIR 1998*

■Gd cru 1.6 ha n.c. 300–499 F

|88| |89| |90| |92| |93| 94 **95** |96| **97** 98

This is a Bonnes-Mares from Morey-Saint-Denis, for those with an interest in details. Their 98 is like Liz Taylor in a 'B' movie: dark red, deep and brilliant, a vanilla nose with notes of blackcurrant and forest-floor, a soft attack with well-integrated tannins. On the palate, there is a tiny hint of redcurrant, but oak dominates. Ample and full. A structure that suggests it will age well.
🔑 Dom. Fougeray de Beauclair, 44, rue de Mazy, B.P. 36, 21160 Marsannay-la-Côte, tel. 03.80.52.21.12, fax 03.80.58.73.83, e-mail fougeraydebeauclair@wanadoo.fr ☑ Y by appt.

ROBERT GROFFIER PERE ET FILS 1998**

■Gd cru 0.98 ha 3,900 300–499 F

|(93)| |94| 96 **97 98**

This is a full, fine wine, a typical example. Robust rather than floral, and still very closed, though it shows some wonderful concentration. Garnet to purple in colour, with a subtle nose that reveals an aroma of cherry with little toasty touches, it possesses a fine, silky-smooth structure of dazzling velvetiness, like a red carpet unrolling on the tongue. This parcel of 98 a 48 ca (2.43 acres) was bought in 1933, from the Peloux business, and replanted little by little from 1960 to 1982.
🔑 SARL Robert Groffier et Fils, 3–5, rte. des Grands-Crus, 21220 Morey-Saint-Denis, tel. 03.80.34.31.53 ☑ Y by appt.

LOUIS JADOT 1997*

■Gd cru 1 ha 4,500 300–499 F

Jadot owns a vineyard of 33 a 45 ca (1.83 acres) that was replanted in 1987, and which once belonged to the widow of the famous Colonel Trinquier.This deep violet 97 has an oaky and very blackcurrant nose. The palate is all silk and lace, with a lovely, fruity length where warmth wins out over tight tannins.
🔑 Maison Louis Jadot, 21, rue Eugène-Spuller, 21200 Beaune, tel. 03.80.22.10.57, fax 03.80.22.56.03, e-mail contact@louisjadot.com ☑ Y by appt.

DOM. PIERRE PONNELLE 1995

■Gd cru 1 ha 500 150–199 F

This wine is the colour of imperial violets, its nose is full of raspberries, though with a hint of vegetation. An acidity that is on the retreat and with a tasty tannic finish. It can be laid down for a moderate length of time. The Pierre Ponnelle estate has been taken over by Jean-Claude Boisset, one of the main owners of the Grand Cru.
🔑 Dom. Pierre Ponnelle, 2, rue Paradis, 21200 Beaune, tel. 03.80.22.19.12, fax 03.80.24.91.87

HERVE ROUMIER 1997

■Gd cru 0.26 ha 600 200–249 F

Hervé Roumier used to work on the Vogüé estate, which has clearly proved an excellent training ground. He has produced a 97 which confirms André Maurois's maxim: 'Sincerity is in the glass, but discretion in the diamond'. This is still a young wine, but it will last well. It has a good brilliance with a fruity nose combining eau-de-vie and violets. A very respectable standard, but obviously not to be opened for some time.
🔑 Hervé Roumier, rue de Vergy, 21220 Chambolle-Musigny, tel. 03.80.62.80.38, fax 03.80.62.86.71 ☑ Y by appt.

Musigny

DOM. JACQUES PRIEUR 1997***

■Gd cru 0.76 ha 2,600 500 F+

The rocky limestone terrace occupied by Musigny is one of the most coveted positions in the area, producing 'the winiest wine'. This is a fabulous 97 (the 82 and the 89 were successful in past years) with a deep colour and a nose that is both subtle and sumptuous (leather, cloves, Morello cherry). Its mellowness and superb long tannins are deliciously exotic. But one must also admire the skilful handling that has resulted in a wonderful fullness, richness and complexity. A really classy wine.
🔑 Dom. Jacques Prieur, 6, rue des Santenots, 21190 Meursault, tel. 03.80.21.23.85, fax 03.80.21.29.19 ☑ Y by appt.

Vougeot

This is the smallest commune of the Côte, only 80 ha (198 acres) in area. Of these, the famous Clos occupies 50 ha (124 acres). Here you can find several Premiers Crus, the best-known being the Clos Blanc (white wines) and the Clos de la Perrière. Production rose to 792 hl (20,909 gal) in 1999, of which 183 hl (4,831 gal) were white

CHRISTIAN CLERGET

Les Petits Vougeot 1997★★

■ 1er cru 0.46 ha 2,570 ⏸ 100–149 F

Christian Clerget exports 75% of his wines, mainly to the USA and Great Britain. His Petits Vougeot is anything but small. A dark, concentrated red, with a nose that is full to the brim with aromas of blackcurrant and leather. It has an explosive kind of softness. The attack is supple, persistent with very fine tannins. This is a remarkable wine, full and round, an authentic Premier Cru which has no need to feel inferior next to the Grands Crus that are grown nearby. It is also excellent value for money, which should be the final point in its favour for anyone who still has doubts (but how could they?).

🔑 Christian Clerget, ancienne R.N. 74, 21640 Vougeot, tel. 03.80.62.87.37, fax 03.80.62.84.37 ☑ Y by appt.

DOM. L'HERITIER-GUYOT

Les Cras 1997

■ 1er cru 1.5 ha n.c. ⏸ 200–249 F

An unashamedly oaky wine of an attractive dark ruby-red colour. A toasty nose packed with bilberry aromas. The palate balances the two main components of this Cras, its maturation period and body. Very characteristic.

🔑 Dom. l'Héritier-Guyot, rue de l'Eglise, 21700 Premeaux-Prissey, tel. 03.80.61.25.44, fax 03.80.61.25.44

DOM. PIERRE PONNELLE

Clos du Prieuré 1998★

□ 1 ha 5,000 ⏸ 100–149 F

This is a wine that opens out gradually, offering successive pictures of its character, most of them positive. A pleasing youthful colour with hints of green. Aromas of honey and honeysuckle with a fresh charm about them. On the palate, it opens out with a mixture of richness and freshness. People are always surprised to see a white wine from Vougeot, but it was the communion wine of the monks of Cîteaux, and they had good taste.

🔑 Dom. Pierre Ponnelle, 2, rue Paradis, 21200 Beaune, tel. 03.80.22.19.12, fax 03.80.24.91.87

DOM. ROUX PERE ET FILS

Les Petits Vougeot 1997★★

■ 1er cru 1.2 ha 5,000 ⏸ 150–199 F

Marcel Roux owned 5 ha (12 acres) in 1960. Today, the estate covers over 40 ha (99 acres) of which 1.2 ha (3 acres) are given over to this appellation. This is a wine with lots of colour, with aromas of blackberries and vanilla, and a palate that follows suit but with an additional touch of blueberries. The tannins are still quite young, and the light bitterness in the finish will eventually blend in. It is a wine worth waiting for, but for two or three years at the most, given the vintage.

🔑 Dom. Roux Père et Fils, 21190 Saint-Aubin, tel. 03.80.21.32.92, fax 03.80.21.35.00 ☑ Y by appt.

Clos de Vougeot

Much has already been written about the Clos de Vougeot and the seventy plus growers who share its 50 ha (124 acres) and production of 2,100 hl (55,440 gal) as registered in 1999. Its great appeal is not just a matter of chance, but because it is good and consequently everyone in the world wants some. Of course, distinctions must be made between the wines at the top of the vineyard, those in the middle and those in the lower part, but nevertheless, when the monks of the medieval Abbey of Citeaux built their high enclosing wall, they had chosen their site very well.

Founded at the beginning of the 12th century, the Clos rapidly grew to its present size; the surrounding wall predates the 15th century. The real appeal of the Clos itself can be tasted in the quality of the wines a few years after they have been bottled. In addition, the château itself, built in the 12th century and extended in the 16th century, is worth taking time to visit. The oldest parts are the cellar, nowadays used for meetings of the Confrérie du Tastevin, its present owners, and the vat room, with its four magnificent 12th-century wine presses, one in each corner.

BERTRAND AMBROISE 1997★★

■Gd cru 0.17 ha n.c. 200–249 F

Class of 97: in every group photo there is always one face that people are automatically drawn to. Not necessarily the best-looking one, but one that looks healthy and friendly. This wine is one of those. Its nose is 'explosive', rich and complex, with touches of mocha and ripe fruits. On the palate, you realise that this is not just a wine that is full and rich, but one that is a model of originality and class. It has a great future ahead of it, though a short one.

Maison Bertrand Ambroise, rue de l'Eglise, 21700 Premeaux-Prissey, tel. 03.80.62.30.19, fax 03.80.62.38.69, e-mail bertrand.ambroise@wanadoo.fr by appt.

PIERRE ANDRE 1997★

■Gd cru 1.09 ha 3,000 500 F+

This parcel of land was acquired in 1933 by Pierre André, the founder of La Reine Pédauque, and is situated on the highest part of the *clos*. This 97 is light purple in colour with a classic nose (liquorice, spice) and a particularly solid structure. A veritable coliseum! For this style of wine, it is very successful. We will doubtless have the opportunity to talk about it again, as this is a wine for laying down.

Pierre André, Ch. de Corton-André, 21420 Aloxe-Corton, tel. 03.80.26.44.25, fax 03.80.26.43.57, e-mail pandre@axnet.fr ev. day 10am–6pm

ALBERT BICHOT 1997

■Gd cru 0.4 ha 1,800 300–499 F

From some 40 a (0.98 acres) in the southern part of the *clos*, acquired in 1964, previously owned by Grivelet, this wine has a pinkish tone, and opens on strong but not overpowering notes of cherry. It has a wild, gamey side to it that will make things easy for the cook. It is pretty clear what this wine will go with: two classic partners, either wild boar or Morvan ham *en croute*.

Maison Albert Bichot, 6 bis, bd Jacques-Copeau, 21200 Beaune, tel. 03.80.24.37.37, fax 03.80.24.37.38

JOSEPH DROUHIN 1998★

■Gd cru 1 ha n.c. 300–499 F

There are two parcels of land here (62a/1.54 acres and 29 a/0.72 acres), one in the south and the other in the centre, and they have produced a wine that is anything but shy. In fact, it welcomes you with open arms. It has an attractive depth, an expressive nose of cherry, chocolate and liquorice, and a reasonably full and well-balanced body. The finish is still on the austere side, but that is not surprising in a wine of this age.

Joseph Drouhin, 7, rue d'Enfer, 21200 Beaune, tel. 03.80.24.68.88, fax 03.80.22.43.14, e-mail drouhin@calva.net by appt.

DOM. DROUHIN-LAROZE 1998★

■Gd cru 1 ha 3,000 200–249 F

(83) 86 |88| 89 91 93 94 **95 96 97** 98

This estate, which has a little over 1 ha (2.5 acres) of the *clos*, in the top part near the château, has been highly acclaimed for a lovely 97 vintage and a very successful 83. Here is a wine that has been produced for the 900 years (as at 1998) that Cîteaux Abbey has existed. A wine of a truly Cistercian severity and austerity. Only the colour is reminiscent of a cardinal. Its aromas need to breathe before they go to confession, but then, can blackcurrant and coffee be counted as sins? This is still a very young wine, and in order to be granted grace, it needs to go on a long retreat. It has the resources to do so.

Drouhin-Laroze, 20, rue du Gaizot, 21220 Gevrey-Chambertin, tel. 03.80.34.31.49, fax 03.80.51.83.70 by appt.

R. DUBOIS ET FILS 1997★

■Gd cru 0.33 ha 1,700 200–249 F

This is a true wine-maker's estate which has managed to get a foothold (33 a/0.82 acres) in the Grand Cru, a feat similar to acquiring an apartment in the château of Versailles, This is certainly a well-constructed wine: a floral and cherry nose with an oaky structure, tender, very 'lacy'. Best tasted in two to three years' time.

R. Dubois et Fils, rte. de Nuits-Saint-Georges, 21700 Premeaux-Prissey, tel. 03.80.62.30.61, fax 03.80.61.24.07, e-mail rdubois@wanadoo.fr ev. day 8am–11.30am 2pm–6pm; Sat. Sun. by appt.

FAIVELEY 1997★

■Gd cru 1.28 ha 3,960 300–499 F

This estate owns three parcels of land situated in four different parts of the *clos*, allowing them to create a kind of synthesis of the different *climats* in their wine. This example is light, the nose is very closed, but its strict, severe body is not without character. It may not be the greatest wine in the world, but shows itself in its best light on the attack. The palate is what you might expect from this vintage, some fullness and fairly well-balanced. The association of the Chevaliers du Tastevin was founded by the grandfather of the present owner of the business and the estate.

Bourgognes Faiveley, 8, rue du Tribourg, 21700 Nuits-Saint-Georges, tel. 03.80.61.04.55, fax 03.80.62.33.37, e-mail bourgognes.faiveley@wanadoo.fr ev. day 9am–12 noon 2pm–6pm; cl. 21 Jul.–21 Aug.

CH. GENOT-BOULANGER 1997★★

■Gd cru 0.42 ha 1,680 250–299 F

'Here is something with real presence!' you might find yourself saying, along with Hugh

Johnson, about the Clos de Vougeot. In terms of the way it has been produced, this wine is one of the best we have tasted. A deep, dark red colour with a nose that is both extremely complex and at the same time very much in keeping with the character of the cru: blackcurrant and violets combine with the wood flavours of the barrel. The palate is full, with a silky texture, a good tannic structure and a liquorice finish. The lesson has not just been learned: it has been understood.

Ch. Génot-Boulanger, 25, rue de Cîteaux, 21190 Meursault, tel. 03.80.21.49.20, fax 03.80.21.49.21, e-mail genot-boulanger@wanadoo.fr by appt.

Mme Delaby

DOM. GROS FRERE ET SŒUR

Musigni 1997★

Gd cru	0.75 ha	3,826		200–249 F

This is an old repeated question: are you allowed to put the name of a *climat* that lies within the *clos* on the label of a bottle? It is what they have done here with Musigni, which is at the top, near the château. It is a question to debate, but the fact is that these *climats* exist and historically there is no reason why they shouldn't be mentioned. This *climat* was replanted in 1987 and has produced, here, a deep red wine with gamey, musky flavours and aromas, mixed with blueberry. Its make-up is at the same time both strict and balanced, warm at the finish and in general rather closed. A good-quality wine that and should be left to age and then decanted if possible.

SCE Gros Frère et Sœur, 6, rue des Grands-Crus, 21700 Vosne-Romanée, tel. 03.80.61.12.43, fax 03.80.61.34.05 by appt.

Bernard Gros

ALAIN HUDELOT-NOELLAT

1998★

Gd cru	0.68 ha	3,300		200–249 F

This 98 can be ranked among the best Clos de Vougeot we have tasted for this edition of the *Guide*. It is already very attractive, intense with wonderful aromas of blackcurrants and raspberries. A fruity, supple, well-integrated, well-balanced wine with great length. It absolutely needs to be left to mature, because it is far from having reached its best.

Alain Hudelot-Noëllat, 21640 Chambolle-Musigny, tel. 03.80.62.85.17, fax 03.80.62.83.13 by appt.

DOM. FRANCOIS LAMARCHE

1998★

Gd cru	n.c.	n.c.		250–299 F

|91| 94 95 |97| 98

This family-run estate owns 1.35 ha 89 ca (3.34 acres) of vines divided between several parcels of land situated mostly in the top part of the *clos*. Brilliant and deep in colour, this 98 smells of the harvest. It has already opened out a little, presenting flavours of violet and well-grilled toast. It is neither too heavy nor too hard and has both body and finesse, and should age well.

Dom. François Lamarche, 9, rue des Communes, 21700 Vosne-Romanée, tel. 03.80.61.07.94, fax 03.80.61.24.31 by appt.

CH. DE LA TOUR 1997★★

Gd cru	5.4 ha	n.c.		300–499 F

85 86 **87** **88** **89** 90 91 93 94 95 96 **97**

This château was founded in 1870 by Pierre Labet's ancestors, and is emblematic of the appellation. Their elegant 97 has been made with whole, uncrushed grapes using cold maceration, and has spent only 18 months in barrel, 50 per cent new oak. It is more full-bodied than well-structured, with an excellent concentration, fruity and warm. An attractive wine, full of finesse, and will be best enjoyed in five to eight years' time.

Ch. de la Tour, Clos de Vougeot, 21640 Vougeot, tel. 03.80.62.86.13, fax 03.80.62.82.72, e-mail labet@axnet.fr ev. day except Mon. 10.30am–6.30pm; cl. 30 Nov.–15 Apr.

François Labet

DOM. MONGEARD-MUGNERET

1997★

Gd cru	0.62 ha	2,300		250–299 F

These parcels of land are situated on the top part of the *clos*, where they once produced the 'Cuvée du Pape'. This wine is ready to drink but also has real potential and sufficient spirit to age well. A very ripe, spicy, vanilla nose that is attractive, as is its length. It would go well with a flambéed woodcock.

Dom. Mongeard-Mugneret, 14, rue de la Fontaine, 21700 Vosne-Romanée, tel. 03.80.61.11.95, fax 03.80.62.35.75, e-mail mongeard@axnet.fr by appt.

MORIN PERE ET FILS 1997

Gd cru	n.c.	6,000		300–499 F

For many years, Morin Père et Fils owned the Château de la Tour which was built within the *clos*. Whilst the château and its vines remain the property of the family, the *négociant-éleveur* business has been taken over by J.-Cl. Boisset, who owns .5 ha 20 ca (12.4 acres) of land in the middle part of the *clos* (L'Héritier-Guyot). The first thing you notice about this 98 is its colour: a very clear Pinot Noir, vivid red. Its aromas of pepper and musk introduce a vigorous, very clean flavour. Still young, but will open fully in four or five years' time.

Morin Père et Fils, 9, quai Fleury, 21700 Nuits-Saint-Georges, tel. 03.80.62.61.42, fax 03.80.62.37.38 ev. day 9am–12 noon 2pm–6pm; summer 8am–7pm

DENIS MUGNERET ET FILS 1998★

Gd cru	0.72 ha	1,500		200–249 F

90 93 |94| 95 97 98

This parcel of land in the very south of the *clos* (72 a/1.79 acres) belongs to the Liger-Belair family, but since 1969 it has been worked by the Mugneret family, tenant farmers from Vosne. This is a wine with a colour as vivid as that of a Fauvist painter. Its nose gives little away, just a little forest-floor and liquorice. Full-bodied and robust, this is a Pinot Noir that really fills the mouth. It should be left to age for five to ten years.

🔑 Denis et Dominique Mugneret, 9, rue de la Fontaine, 21700 Vosne-Romanée, tel. 03.80.61.00.97, fax 03.80.61.24.54 ☑ 🍷 by appt.

🔑 Liger-Belair

DOM. MICHEL NOELLAT ET FILS 1998*

■Gd cru 0.46 ha 1,200 ⓘ 200–249 F

Some people claim that wines from the Clos Vougeot are 'so full they are almost solid', and it is true that they can sometimes have such a full nose, such concentration and richness that you might start to doubt whether it is liquid after all. This particular example has a pretty nose of bitter liquorice and Morello cherry. Its power and length don't overwhelm its very real elegance: a fist of iron under a silk glove. The present austerity indicates that it needs three to four years before serving it.

🔑 SCEA Dom. Michel Noëllat et Fils, 5, rue de la Fontaine, 21700 Vosne-Romanée, tel. 03.80.61.36.87, fax 03.80.61.18.10 ☑ 🍷 by appt.

DOM. HENRI REBOURSEAU 1997

■Gd cru 2.2 ha 6,750 ⓘ 300–499 F

89 90 92 93 |94| **95** 96 97

Situated in the centre of the *clos*, these 2.2 ha (5.5 acres) have produced a wine that should be opened in five or six years' time. Although the colour is a deep, brilliant red, the nose is still closed – it offers us just the merest hint of wilted flowers – the influence of the wood is strong, and the level of extraction is perceptible on the palate. So you'll have to wait until it decides to open up.

🔑 NSE Dom. Henri Rebourseau, 10, pl. du Monument, 21220 Gevrey-Chambertin, tel. 03.80.51.88.94, fax 03.80.34.12.82, e-mail Rebourseal@aol.com ☑ 🍷 by appt.

DOM. ARMELLE ET BERNARD RION 1998

■Gd cru 0.91 ha 2,400 ⓘ 200–249 F

|90| 95 96 98

Truffles are part of the 'elite guard' of the Clos de Vougeot, and this wine-producing couple have been at the forefront of the Burgundy truffle revival. So it is no surprise to discover that beneath the dark exterior of this wine lie complex and lengthy aromas of forest-floor, game and spice. A wine that is a little dry at present, but possesses all the right qualities to improve with age.

🔑 Dom. Armelle et Bernard Rion, 8, rte. Nationale, 21700 Vosne-Romanée, tel. 03.80.61.05.31, fax 03.80.61.24.60, e-mail rion@webiwine.com ☑ 🍷 by appt.

DOM. THOMAS-MOILLARD 1998

■Gd cru 0.6 ha 3,000 ⓘ 300–499 F

There are few wines that are able to put you off the scent quite so effectively and then take you by the hand and show you the key to their complexities. This is such a wine. A very bright ruby-red with a nose that concentrates on forest-floor, humus and autumn leaves. On the palate it is a labyrinth: a maze from which you will not emerge much before 2010.

🔑 Dom. Thomas-Moillard, chem. rural n° 29, 21700 Nuits-Saint-Georges, tel. 03.80.62.42.00, fax 03.80.61.28.13, e-mail nuicave@wanadoo.fr 🍷 by appt.

🔑 SCI du clos de Thorey

Échézeaux and Grands-Échézeaux

To the south of Clos de Vougeot lies the commune of Flagey-Échézeaux, with its village to the east on the flatter land, like Gilly-lès-Citeaux (see map). Its border runs along the wall of the Clos de Vougeot, to the top of the upper slopes, taking in some of the vineyard. The vineyard on the lower slopes falls under the Appellation Vosne-Romanée. On the hills there are two Grands Crus next to each other: Le Grands-Échézeaux and L'Échézeaux. The first covers about 9 ha (22 acres) on several *lieux-dits* and produced only 444 hl (11,722 gal) in 1999, while the second covers more than 30 ha (74 acres), producing 1,304 hl (34,426 gal).

The wines of these two Crus, the most prestigious of which is the Grands-Échézeaux, are very 'Burgundian': sturdy, well-structured, intensely aromatic and very expensive. They are mostly cultivated by wine-growers from Vosne and Flagey.

Échézeaux

DOM. FRANCOIS CAPITAIN ET FILS 1998

■Gd cru 0.3 ha 1,500 ▮▮ 250–299 F

The Capitain-Gagnerot estate today covers over 16 ha (40 acres). All the best wine-writers agree that this is a very sensual Grand Cru that is easy to get to grips with. It is not a wine that hides its virtues but likes to share them. This particular 98 is brilliant purple in colour with a youthful fruitiness and hints of blackcurrant and leather. On the palate there is a touch of austerity attributed to the young tannins which will doubtless round themselves out over the next three years.

Capitain-Gagnerot, 38, rte. de Dijon, 21550 Ladoix-Serrigny, tel. 03.80.26.41.36, fax 03.80.26.46.29 ☒ Y by appt.

CHRISTIAN CLERGET 1997

■Gd cru 1 ha 4,000 ▮▮ 150–199 F

87 |89| |(90)| 91 92 93 |94| 95 97

The Clerget family has been in Vougeot for 120 years and work with 6 ha (15 acres) of vines. Their Echézeaux is a deep ruby-red with shades of cherry. The nose, open and straightforward, has a Pinot quality with a fruitiness that has a home-cooked, stewed flavour to it. On the palate, the vintage begins to tell, in the lack of structure and depth, but it is a more than respectable wine and would benefit from two to three years in the cellar.

Christian Clerget, ancienne R.N. 74, 21640 Vougeot, tel. 03.80.62.87.37, fax 03.80.62.84.37 ☒ Y by appt.

FRANCOIS CONFURON-GINDRE 1998

■Gd cru n.c. 1,350 ▮▮ 150–199 F

Its aroma of black cherry gives cause for hope that this wine will open out well. The fact that it is still unripe is hardly suprising given its age. Light red in colour, with a full, warm nose and a slight hint of oak, it is just at the beginning of a complex and well-structured journey. Best to put it at the back of your cellar and wait five years.

François Confuron-Gindre, 21700 Vosne-Romanée, tel. 03.80.61.20.84, fax 03.80.62.31.29 ☒ Y by appt.

JOSEPH DROUHIN 1998★

■Gd cru 0.5 ha n.c. ▮▮ 300–499 F

This 52-a (1.3-acre) vineyard is situated in Orveaux, one of the best *climats* of the Grand Cru, known formerly, according to the deeds, as Grand Musigny. Despite its youth, this is a very respectable 98. Its colour is deep and brilliant and has a Pinot nose mingled with notes of oak, smoke, and game. The palate follows along the same lines, balanced and long. In three to five years, it will be perfect.

Joseph Drouhin, 7, rue d'Enfer, 21200 Beaune, tel. 03.80.24.68.88, fax 03.80.22.43.14, e-mail drouhin@calva.net Y by appt.

FAIVELEY 1997★★

■Gd cru 0.86 ha 2,940 ▮▮ 300–499 F

This is a good wine of great quality for the vintage. Produced from an estate of 86 a (2.15 acres) of vines that were planted in the 1940s and 1950s in Orveaux, the noblest and formerly Cistercian part of the Grand Cru, right at the top. Its perfumes of forest-floor, mushrooms, dead leaves and a hint of game are all what one would expect from this appellation. Deep cherry in colour, full-bodied, vinous, and with length that has just the right degree of concentration. 'A very skilled wine-maker', writes one of the tasters. All our tasters suggested that it should be laid down for four to five years and then served with game.

Bourgognes Faiveley, 8, rue du Tribourg, 21700 Nuits-Saint-Georges, tel. 03.80.61.04.55, fax 03.80.62.33.37, e-mail bourgognes.faiveley@wanadoo.fr ☒ Y ev. day 9am–12 noon 2pm–6pm; cl. 21 Jul.–21 Aug.

DOM. A.-F. GROS 1998★

■Gd cru 0.26 ha 1,400 ▮▮ 250–299 F

89 **90** 94 96 97 98

Five parcels of land in the Champs Traversins (a *climat* nestling in the historical sector of the Grand Cru) make up these 26 a (0.66 acres). It is work on a fine and detailed scale. This densely-coloured wine is still closed. It has a lot of texture and is very chewy, but it needs time and patience. Soft fruit, juniper and a touch of oak on the nose. A little liquorice at the finish keeps one's hopes up for the future. Leave it three to five years.

Dom. A.-F. Gros, La Garelle, rte d'Ivry, 21630 Pommard, tel. 03.80.22.61.85, fax 03.80.24.03.16 ☒ Y by appt.

Anne-Françoise Parent

DENIS MUGNERET ET FILS 1998

■Gd cru 0.42 ha 1,800 ▮▮ 200–249 F

This full, long wine stakes out its territory immediately. Clear cherry in colour, vegetal and spicy on the nose, it gets straight to the point on the palate, where its chewiness and ripe fruit are just what one would expect from the appellation. There is perhaps a little hint of dryness, but in five or ten years' time it will be a thoroughly respectable wine.

Denis et Dominique Mugneret, 9, rue de la Fontaine, 21700 Vosne-Romanée, tel. 03.80.61.00.97, fax 03.80.61.24.54 ☒ Y by appt.

DOM. MICHEL NOELLAT ET FILS 1998★

■Gd cru 0.46 ha 1,500 ▮▮ 150–199 F

94 96 97 98

This estate owns two parcels covering nearly half a hectare (just over one acre) in Les Treux and Echézeaux du Dessus. What a happy medium. *In medio stat virtus* (virtue lies in the middle), as they say. This deep-red 98 draws attention to itself immediately with a gamey, liquorice nose, followed by a deep, full chewiness. Powerful, robust and well-

balanced, it can be laid down for a moderate period of time (four to five years) and will age well.
🔑 SCEA Dom. Michel Noëllat et Fils, 5, rue de la Fontaine, 21700 Vosne-Romanée, tel. 03.80.61.36.87, fax 03.80.61.18.10 ☑ 🍷 by appt.

REINE PEDAUQUE 1998

Gd cru n.c. n.c. 250–299 F

One should never give in to what La Rochfoucauld called 'too great a tendency to hurry', because this 98 still has a few years yet before it opens up entirely. An attractive red colour with a subtle, lively nose of forest-floor and vanilla spice, and a fine structure that is obviously still a little crude at this stage of its life. It will be two years before we will see anything more.
🔑 Reine Pédauque, Le Village, 21420 Aloxe-Corton, tel. 03.80.25.00.00, fax 03.80.26.42.00, e-mail rpedauque@axnet.fr 🍷 by appt.

DOM. FABRICE VIGOT 1997*

Gd cru 0.59 ha 900 250–299 F

90 91 92 93 **|94|** 96 97

This 97 comes from 59 a (1.47 acres) of tenant-farmed land in Mugneret-Gibourg and the Rouges du Bas (a very well-situated *climat* and the southernmost in the *clos*), and it has more than its fair share of goodness to offer. The wine is an attractive black cherry colour, with a raspberry and kirsch nose that has a few hints of tobacco, and an open, cherry-flavoured palate. Well-blended, good-quality tannins give it a good four to five years' life in the cellar.
🔑 Dom. Fabrice Vigot, 16, rue de la Fontaine, 21700 Vosne-Romanée, tel. 03.80.61.13.01, fax 03.80.61.13.01 ☑ 🍷 by appt.

Grands-Échézeaux

DOM. GROS FRERE ET SŒUR 1997**

Gd cru 0.37 ha 1,519 300–499 F

This is first and foremost a great wine rather than a great Echézeaux. It was the favourite wine of the Burgundy writer Henri Vincenot, who liked to drink it with his famous wild boar dish. This 97 is really solid. There is not a great deal of brightness in the colour, as is appropriate for Pinot, and its complexity only really begins to show when in the glass. It is (of course, at this age) rather closed. Fleshy and full-bodied, well-made, this is a wine to keep carefully in the cellar, where it will lose some of its rather austere character to shine out onto the world in four or five years' time.
🔑 SCE Gros Frère et Sœur, 6, rue des Grands-Crus, 21700 Vosne-Romanée, tel. 03.80.61.12.43, fax 03.80.61.34.05 ☑ 🍷 by appt.

DOM. FRANCOIS LAMARCHE 1998

Gd cru n.c. n.c. 300–499 F

This vintage has its limitations and this wine, which we tasted on 6 April 2000, is still very young, fresh from its maturation in barrel. However, it does call to mind René Engel's little saying about this Grand Cru: 'There is nothing but song in it!' A fine black cherry colour with a nose that combines just the right amount of wood with pepper and soft fruit. A wine that manages to remain fresh and fruity with an acidity that bodes well for the future, and tannins that bode even better.
🔑 Dom. François Lamarche, 9, rue des Communes, 21700 Vosne-Romanée, tel. 03.80.61.07.94, fax 03.80.61.24.31 🍷 by appt.

DOM. DE LA ROMANEE-CONTI 1997**

Gd cru 3.52 ha 8,076 500 F+

If the 98 vintage tends to appear rather severe in its early years, giving a hint of its character only when allowed to breathe gradually revealing its purity, the 97 firmly maintains its right to be different. With its aromas of the deep forest and its furtive hint of game, there is something about it that calls to mind the poet Lamartine, out on his horse in the Hautes-Côtes near the Château de Montculot, taking a break between verses. On the palate, however, with its raspberry fruit, the tone is different: here it is thoughtful, almost sophisticated, round and balanced.
🔑 SC du Dom. de la Romanée-Conti, 21700 Vosne-Romanée, tel. 03.80.62.48.80, fax 03.80.61.05.72

MAISON FRANCOIS MARTENOT 1997*

Gd cru n.c. 900 200–249 F

Like Henri de Villamont, François Martenot belongs to the Swiss group Schenk. This Grand Echézeaux is already very silky, allowing the nicely rounded tannins to show through. There is a classic note of bitterness which is compensated for by the fruitiness, making this a very fine wine in consequence. A clear, clean colour and an initially subtle nose which on exposure to the air bursts out with aromas of soft fruit, bilberries and oak.
🔑 HDV Distribution, rue du Dr-Barolet, Z.I. Beaune Vignolles, 21200 Beaune Cedex, tel. 03.80.24.70.07, fax 03.80.22.54.31 🍷 by appt.

Vosne-Romanée

Here again, the Burgundian customs are well respected; the name of the vineyard is better known than that of the village. Like Gevrey-Chambertin, this commune is the site of many Grands Crus and next to them are a number of famous *climats* such as Les Suchots, Les Beaux-Monts and many others. The Appellation Vosne-Romanée produced 7,325 hl (193,380 gal) in 1996, 5,939 hl (156,790 gal) in 1997, 6,268 hl (165,475 gal) in 1998 and 5,030 hl (132,792 gal) in 1999.

SYLVAIN CATHIARD

En Orveaux 1998★

■ 1er cru 0.3 ha 1,500 150–199 F

This is a family who have worked hard to get where they are. They have done everything themselves, even down to digging their own cellar. Sylvain Cathiard has been running the business since 1994, and he has a natural talent for it. His Orveaux, with its oaky nose that reveals fruitiness balanced, on going back to it for a second look, is very round, harmonious and sincere. A long finish with complex cherry flavours.

Sylvain Cathiard, 20, rue de la Goillotte, 21700 Vosne-Romanée, tel. 03.80.62.36.01, fax 03.80.61.18.21 Y by appt.

CHANSON PERE ET FILS

Suchots 1997★

■ 1er cru n.c. 1,800 200–249 F

This well-established business, which was founded in 1750 and is now owned by the Champenois Jacques Bollinger, presents a Vosne that promises well for the future. An attractive bright ruby-red colour with hints of violet and ample structure. The nose is still closed, however, there is a complexity that at the moment is overpowered by a touch of warmth.

Chanson Père et Fils, 10, rue Paul-Chanson, 21200 Beaune, tel. 03.80.22.33.00, fax 03.80.24.17.42, e-mail tmarion@vins-chanson.com Y by appt.

DOM. BRUNO CLAVELIER

Les Hautes Maizières Vieilles vignes 1997

■ 0.5 ha 2,200 100–149 F

This *climat* is next to Les Suchots and has produced a wine that is attractive to drink now but will not last long. It is both light in colour and taste, and is true to its appellation without being an exceptional example.

Dom. Bruno Clavelier, 6, R.N. 74, 21700 Vosne-Romanée, tel. 03.80.61.10.81, fax 03.80.61.04.25 Y by appt.

Clavelier-Brosson

FRANCOIS CONFURON

Les Chaumes Vieilles vignes 1998

■ 1er cru 0.37 ha 900 100–149 F

'Still needs to develop its good points, but can be included in the *Guide*', is the general comment in the tasting notes for this fine, vividly-coloured, liquorice-flavoured wine that is, however, short on length. Good overall, and very true to the Les Chaumes terroir.

François Confuron, Les Chaumes, 21700 Vosne-Romanée, tel. 03.80.61.03.23, fax 03.80.62.31.29 Y by appt.

JEAN GAGNEROT Les Suchots 1998★

■ 1er cru n.c. 2,500 100–149 F

This is a Les Suchots that is worth a detour. Blood-red in colour, it is still closed on the nose but has a wonderful palate. Age will refine all of this, and the 98, in the opinion of our experts who are notoriously hard to please (they tasted 54 wines just for this one prestigious AOC), will last a good eight to ten years. This is a merchant who knows where to get his supplies.

Jean Gagnerot, 21420 Aloxe-Corton, tel. 03.80.25.00.00, fax 03.80.26.42.00, e-mail vinibeaune@bourgogne.net Y by appt.

DOM. FRANCOIS GERBET

Aux Réas 1998★

■ 2 ha 10,000 100–149 F

This estate is run by Marie-Andrée and Chantal Gerbet. Here we tasted a deep purple Réas, which is about as Pinot as they come, and manages to keep its oakiness in check. It is showing some concentratoin of fruit. As fine as a Vosne (which says everything), tannic and complex, and showing a lot of promise. A top-of-the-range *village*, nearly getting top marks. We also tasted the **Premier Cru Les Petits Monts 98** (150–199F), which receives one star: a good-looking, well-made wine.

Dom. François Gerbet, Caveau la Maison des Vins, pl. de l'Eglise, 21700 Vosne-Romanée, tel. 03.80.61.07.85, fax 03.80.61.01.65 Y by appt.

ANDRE GOICHOT ET FILS 1997

■ n.c. 1,800 100–149 F

'We'll have to wait for this one, but that's fine', writes one jury-member in his tasting notes, summing up the overall feeling about this wine. This clean ruby-red 97, with its powerful nose of leather and bilberry, has sufficient acidity to look to the future with confidence. Good wood influence that presents itself well on the palate; despite a little hint of dryness, it is definitely on the right track.

SA A. Goichot et Fils, av. Charles-de-Gaulle, 21200 Beaune, tel. 03.80.26.88.70, fax 03.80.26.80.69, e-mail goichot@goichotsa.com Y by appt.

DOM. A.-F. GROS Aux Réas 1998★★

■ 1.65 ha 8,000 ⫼ 100–149 F

This wine is the family's pet obsession. Here is a Réas that is produced from perfectly-ripened grapes that have been perfectly-pressed. After the powerful aroma of raspberry, there is remarkable balance on the palate. A very elegant wine that should be kept with great care.

🗝 Dom. A.-F. Gros, La Garelle, rte d'Ivry, 21630 Pommard, tel. 03.80.22.61.85, fax 03.80.24.03.16 ☑ Y by appt.

MICHEL GROS Aux Brûlées 1998★

■ 1er cru 0.63 ha 3,500 ⫼ 200–249 F

Michel is founder of the fifth Gros estate in the region, created from what used to be the Jean Gros estate. This is still a young wine and shows a lot of potential without yet revealing all of its talents. Its freshness works in its favour, as does the fact that all the elements are clearly in the right place. Behind the aroma of soft fruit, there is a little hint of mushroom. The palate is calm and patient. It needs to be laid down for six to eight years.

🗝 Dom. Michel Gros, 7, rue des Communes, 21700 Vosne-Romanée, tel. 03.80.61.04.69, fax 03.80.61.22.29 ☑ Y by appt.

DOM. GROS FRERE ET SŒUR 1997

■ 3.72 ha 22,768 ⫼ 100–149 F

Jean Gros' son Bernard has taken over this estate from his uncle and aunt, neither of whom ever married, which is why it is called Gros Frère et Sœur, though you could now call it Gros Uncle and Aunt. As for the wine, it is fine and attractive, with a bright colour and aromas of game and stewed prunes.

🗝 SCE Gros Frère et Sœur, 6, rue des Grands-Crus, 21700 Vosne-Romanée, tel. 03.80.61.12.43, fax 03.80.61.34.05 ☑ Y by appt.

🗝 Bernard Gros

DOM. GUYON En Orveaux 1998★★★

■ 1er cru 0.35 ha 1,200 ⫼ 150–199 F

This estate, which is definitely on the up-and-up, produced an exceptional wine last year for the 97 vintage, and once again it has played the winning card. What can one say except that this 98 is superb and will age beautifully. It is 'primus inter pares' (first among equals). An intense wine, keeping a tight hold on its nose but offering a magnificent palate where the wine and the oak balance out perfectly right up to a very fine finish. The **Village 98** (100–149F) is still a little woody, though rich and well-balanced. It receives a star. This small estate has really reached the top.

🗝 EARL Dom. Guyon, 11–16, R.N. 74, 21700 Vosne-Romanée, tel. 03.80.61.02.46, fax 03.80.62.36.56 ☑ Y by appt.

LABOURE-ROI 1998★

■ n.c. n.c. ⫼ 100–149 F

The Cottin brothers have created a Vosne that ought to increase the value of their shares on the stock exchange. Its colour will please investors, and the oaky nose will reassure Wall Street. Having said that, it is still as soft as fresh bread and is an asset that should only be realised in two or three years to benefit from the added value on the palate.

🗝 Labouré-Roi, rue Lavoisier, 21700 Nuits-Saint-Georges, tel. 03.80.62.64.00, fax 03.80.62.64.10, e-mail laboure@axnet.fr Y by appt.

DOM DU CH. DE MARSANNAY En Orveaux 1997★

■ 1er cru 0.28 ha 760 ⫼ 150–199 F

The 95 vintage was very successful, and whilst this example doesn't quite reach the same heights, it is not without its attractions. A deep red colour, with a fairly closed nose, well-balanced but with a little too much wood. It is strong on acidity and will certainly improve with time as there is a good structure. Château de Marsannay is André Boisseaux's latest acquisition (he is also the man behind Patriarche, Kriter and Château de Meursault).

🗝 Ch. de Marsannay, rte. des Grands-Crus, B.P. 78, 21160 Marsannay-la-Côte, tel. 03.80.51.71.11, fax 03.80.51.71.12 ☑ Y ev. day 10am–12 noon 2pm–6.30pm; cl. 23 Dec.–3 Jan.

JEAN-PIERRE MUGNERET 1997★

■ 0.95 ha 5,600 ⫼ 100–149 F

There is some maturity visible in the colour of this wine. The nose tends towards game and stewed fruit. The palate is pleasantly fiery with oaky notes, and undertones of leather and sweat give this Vosne its rather wild character. Jean-Pierre Mugneret is one of a long line of Mugnerets from Vosne. A former photographer, he has a great imagination (he invented and actually constructed a new type of barrel) and has certainly found his own means of expression.

🗝 EARL Jean-Pierre Mugneret, Concœur-et-Corboin, 21700 Nuits-Saint-Georges, tel. 03.80.61.00.20, fax 03.80.62.33.04 ☑

DENIS MUGNERET ET FILS 1998★

■ 1.4 ha 6,000 ⫼ 100–149 F

This brightly-coloured Vosne is well-made and typical of the 98 vintage. Although still a little austere on the finish and with aromas that give out the barest hint of cherry, it can

hold its head up high amongst its peers. It comes from their wholly-owned and tenant-farmed estate, and unites skill with passion.
🔑 Denis et Dominique Mugneret, 9, rue de la Fontaine, 21700 Vosne-Romanée, tel. 03.80.61.00.97, fax 03.80.61.24.54 ☑ Y by appt.

DOM. MICHEL NOELLAT ET FILS 1998

■ 1.3 ha 3,000 ⬛ 100–149 F

Here we have a purple, liquorice-flavoured 98 with a subtle oaky note and a lovely rush of fruit on the attack. A very fine, elegant, charming wine which should be opened in two to five years. This vast 21-ha (52-acre) estate is owned by one of the most influential names in the region.
🔑 SCEA Dom. Michel Noëllat et Fils, 5, rue de la Fontaine, 21700 Vosne-Romanée, tel. 03.80.61.36.87, fax 03.80.61.18.10 ☑ Y by appt.

RION ET FILS Les Beaux-Monts 1997★

■ 1er cru 1.07 ha 6,000 ⬛ 150–199 F

Our jury spent a long time debating about this wine, and in general the comments were positive. The colour is intense, there is no doubt about that. The nose hovers between game and spice, but the palate is decisive: fine and full. As always with a wine that has such a strong personality, there are arguments for and against, but in the end the pros outweigh the cons. A good-quality wine that should be laid down for four years in the cellar.
🔑 Dom. Daniel Rion et Fils, R.N. 74, 21700 Premeaux, tel. 03.80.62.31.28, fax 03.80.61.13.41, e-mail patrice.rion@wanadoo.fr ☑ Y by appt.

REMI SEGUIN 1997★

■ 0.34 ha n.c. ⬛ 70–99 F

This is a well-balanced, well-presented wine with flavours and aromas of vanilla, fruit and spice. It is solid and firm, with an overall impression of a powerful wine. From what we can see, the wine-producer has skill-fully-handled this harvest to get the best from it.
🔑 Rémi Seguin, rue de Cîteaux, 21640 Gilly-lès-Cîteaux, tel. 03.80.62.89.61, fax 03.80.62.80.92 ☑ Y by appt.

DOM. ROBERT SIRUGUE 1998★

■ 4.5 ha 14,000 ⬛ 70–99 F

This sturdy, well-built 98 has an intense colour and liquorice-flavoured fruit, with a richness that is agreeable and convivial on the palate. It is a little on the tannic side and certainly needs to be laid down for a while, but in five years' time all the components will be in place. Excellent wine-making from an estate that covers 11 ha (27 acres), almost half of which are *villages*.
🔑 Dom. Robert Sirugue, 3, av. du Monument, 21700 Vosne-Romanée, tel. 03.80.61.00.64, fax 03.80.61.27.57 ☑ Y by appt.

DOM. FABRICE VIGOT 1998★

■ 1.7 ha 3,000 ⬛ 100–149 F

Fabric Vigot took over this estate ten year ago. His 98 *village* has plenty of colour. It nose is dominated by forest-floor aromas After a good first impression, the palate turn out to be rich and long. A full and round wine with a great deal of character which, as it mel lows out, ought to age well.
🔑 Dom. Fabrice Vigot, 16, rue de la Fontaine, 21700 Vosne-Romanée, tel. 03.80.61.13.01, fax 03.80.61.13.01 ☑ Y by appt.

MADAME ROLAND VIGOT Les Petits Monts 1998★

■ 1er cru 0.16 ha 900 ⬛ 200–249 F

This Les Petits Monts is produced by Fabrice Vigot's mother, and once again gains warm praise from our jury. A pleasant wine true to its vintage and well-balanced with nicely-integrated tannins. It should be kept for around ten years before opening.
🔑 Mme Roland Vigot, 16, rue de la Fontaine, 21700 Vosne-Romanée, tel. 03.80.61.17.70, fax 03.80.61.13.01 ☑ Y by appt.

Richebourg, Romanée, Romanée-Conti, Romanée-Saint-Vivant, Grande Rue, Tâche

These Crus are all equally prestigious and it would be difficult to pick out the greatest. Romanée-Conti undoubtedly enjoys the greatest fame, and through history there have been numerous references to the 'exquisite quality' of the wine. The famous vineyard of Romanée was eyed covetously by the great and the good of the ancien régime, though Madame de Pompadour failed to win it when she was pitted against the Prince of Conti who acquired it in 1760. Until the Second World War, the vines were not grafted and were treated with sulphur carbonate to protect them against phylloxera. These had later to be grubbed up and the first harvest of the new vines took place in 1952. Romanée-Conti, cultivated by a single grower on 1.8 ha (4.5 acres), is one of the most famous and expensive wines in the world.

The Romanée vineyards cover 0.83 ha (2 acres), Richebourg 8 ha (20 acres), Romanée-Saint-Vivant 9.5 ha (23.5 acres) and the Tâche covers a little more than 6 ha (15 acres). As with all the Grands Crus, the volumes produced are in the region of 20 to 30 hl per ha (216 to 324 gal per acre), depending on the year. Together, these Grands Crus produced 1,021 hl (26,954 gal) in 1999, of which 321 hl (8,474 gal) were Richebourg and 362 hl (9,557 gal) Romanée-Saint-Vivant. Grande Rue became an accredited Grand Cru on 2 July 1992.

Richebourg

DOM. A.-F. GROS 1998★★

■Gd cru 0.6 ha 3,000 500 F+

89 90 **91** 92 |93| |94| (96) 97 **98**

The monks of Cîteaux were not only responsible for the creation of Clos de Vougeot; they also 'launched' Richebourg, a wine whose noble name alone is enough to fill the glass. Having already received a lot of admiration for the 96 vintage, Anne-Françoise Gros (not to be confused with Anne and François Gros) has succeeded again by producing this exuberantly youthful 98, which undoubtedly has a long life ahead of it. Exquisite fruit, flowers and oak set the tone for its elegance. The texture is fine and firm, hinting at its future complexity. With 60 ha (148 acres), this estate is one of the main producers of the Grand Cru.

Dom. A.-F. Gros, La Garelle, rte d'Ivry, 21630 Pommard, tel. 03.80.22.61.85, fax 03.80.24.03.16 Y by appt.

Anne-Françoise Parent

DOM. GROS FRERE ET SŒUR 1997

■Gd cru 0.69 ha 2,985 500 F+

This deep, dark red 97 has aromas of ripe black grapes, or more precisely bilberries. The first impression is severe, but although the wine softens a little, it basically stays along those lines. It is, of course, not ready to drink now. This estate was created from a larger estate that was split up in 1963. The present owners are Colette and Gustave Gros, two well-known local figures whose Parisian-style house in the middle of Vosne is quite a landmark. The furniture from Stephen Liégeard's dining room at the Château de Brochon can be found here. Their nephew Bernard, son of Jean, is at the helm.

SCE Gros Frère et Sœur, 6, rue des Grands-Crus, 21700 Vosne-Romanée, tel. 03.80.61.12.43, fax 03.80.61.34.05 Y by appt.

Bernard Gros

ALAIN HUDELOT-NOELLAT 1998

■ Gd cru 0.28 ha 1,200 500 F+

This estate has exactly 28.17 a (0.7 acres) devoted to Richebourg. It is situated next to the Marey-Monge estate, which is now given over to Romanée-Conti. This wine is a brilliant, eye-catching peony colour with an aroma of stewed prunes. The palate is still a little unsure of itself, but suggests real potential, and deserves all our attention. With its deep tone of crushed black cherry, so unique to this wine, this is a worthy partner to a really special dish such a tasty seasonal hare.

Alain Hudelot-Noëllat, 21640 Chambolle-Musigny, tel. 03.80.62.85.17, fax 03.80.62.83.13 Y by appt.

DOM. DE LA ROMANEE-CONTI 1998★★★

■Gd cru 3.51 ha 12,350 500 F+

|91| 97 (98)

This estate owns almost half of the Richebourg Grand Cru which, like the Clos de Vougeot, once belonged to Cîteaux Abbey. Their wine radiates good health: it was born under a lucky star. It fills the glass with the greatest of ease, is full of fruitiness and also has a controlled strength and a serene balance. A classic Richebourg with an aroma of Morello cherry that is its only sharp point.

SC du Dom. de La Romanée-Conti, 21700 Vosne-Romanée, tel. 03.80.62.48.80, fax 03.80.61.05.72

DENIS MUGNERET ET FILS 1998

■Gd cru 0.52 ha 1,200 500 F+

|(93)|94 95 96 97 98

These are very old vines which have gradually been replanted but still have vine stock that are 'as plump as pigeons'. The property belongs to Xavier Liger-Belair, and has for many years been run as a tenant farmer enterprise by Vosne wine-producers Denis and Dominique Mugneret (52.5 a/1.3 acres). This 98 has the classic hardness of a young Grand Cru that has a long life ahead of it. It will open out with time and achieve incredible richness and smoothness. The colour shows some maturity; the aromas are direct.

Denis et Dominique Mugneret, 9, rue de la Fontaine, 21700 Vosne-Romanée, tel. 03.80.61.00.97, fax 03.80.61.24.54 by appt.

Liger-Belair

Romanée-Conti

DOM. DE LA ROMANEE-CONTI 1998★★★

■Gd cru 1.8 ha 5,055 500 F+

84 |88| 89 90 |91| 94 95(96)(97)98

This estate is a symbol of Burgundy's winemaking past. Until 1584, it belonged to the church; then it became a valuable piece of land, paid for in gold in 1760 by the discerning and elegant Louis-François de Bourbon, Prince of Conti, who gave it its name.

During the Revolution it became the property of the state, purchased by a new generation of powerbrokers. The Villaine and Leroy families are the present owners. The wine is matured in barrels made from Tronçais oak. 'Taste it! Drink it! But never try to describe it! You cannot describe something as delicious as this in words!' wrote Roald Dahl. But we can at least try. The fruitiness of this 98 is reminiscent of the 95 vintage, though its initial hint of austerity is more like the 88. It is a beautiful deep red colour, with a nose of violets and an elegant, intense and yet delicate palate. Its fullness and richness do not in any way detract from the fruitiness. This piece of land makes history once again with a 98 that seems as precociously mature as the task of trying to describe it is impossible.

SC du Dom. de La Romanée-Conti, 21700 Vosne-Romanée, tel. 03.80.62.48.80, fax 03.80.61.05.72

Romanée-Saint-Vivant

ALAIN HUDELOT-NOELLAT 1998

■Gd cru 0.47 ha 2,100 500 F+

From the very first glance at this dark almost black Romanée-Saint-Vivant, one i lost in its depths. It is produced by one of th oldest and most prestigious families in thi region. They have more Grands Crus thar you can shake a stick at, with nearly half hectare (just over one acre) for this one alone The result is a full, demonstrative, alread ripe wine that will have its say and won't b interrupted.

Alain Hudelot-Noëllat, 21640 Chambolle-Musigny, tel. 03.80.62.85.17, fax 03.80.62.83.13 by appt.

DOM. DE LA ROMANEE-CONTI 1998★★★

■Gd cru 5.28 ha 13,265 500 F+

67 72 **73 75 76 78 |(79)|80 81 |82| |87| |89| |91| |92| 95 97 98**

Of all the wines produced by this estate, this Romanée-Saint-Vivant is the one most in need of laying down. It absolutely must be left to age. Although the vinification process is the same for all the wines here, this 98 has an extraordinary concentration of fruit. With its chewiness and great presence, there are some connoisseurs who even compare it to the 52 vintage. That is how history is made, after all, by not forgetting things. The Romanée-Conti estate has just acquired the ruins of the of Saint-Vivant-de-Vergy monastery, where the Cru was first grown, and during the summer of 2000 organized a group of young volunteers to help in its restoration. It is good to know that this hitherto endangered monument is now in such good hands.

SC du Dom. Romanée-Conti, 21700 Vosne-Romanée, tel. 03.80.61.04.57

DOM. LOUIS LATOUR

Les Quatre Journaux 1997★

■ 0.76 ha 2,000 500 F+

Les Quatre Journaux is one of the most historical *clos* of the monastery of Saint-Vivant in Vosne. There have been only three owners over the last eight centuries. The Marey-Monge family sold the vineyard to the Latours in 1898, and nothing much has changed on these 76.3 a (1.89 acres) since then. This is a Grand Cru, as stated on the label illustrated with the insignia of Vergy. It is a liquoricey, silky wine, not so much Chartres Cathedral in its structure as a romanesque church, built on balanced, elegant lines. It has a moderately long future ahead of it.

Maison Louis Latour, 18, rue des Tonneliers, 21200 Beaune, tel. 03.80.24.81.00, fax 03.80.22.36.21, e-mail louislatour@louislatour.com by appt.

La Grande Rue

DOM. FRANCOIS LAMARCHE
1998
■ Gd cru 1.65 ha n.c. 500 F+
89| |90| |91| |92| |93| |94| 95 98

This Grand Cru is grown exclusively by the Lamarche estate, and this wine is the most classic colour you could imagine: a lovely deep, dark red. The aromas are true to type: there is that little hint of game as expected, then the untamed notes of smokiness and berries picked from the forest floor. The attack is clean, the balance beginning to settle down, the density what you would expect from the vintage.

Dom. François Lamarche, 9, rue des Communes, 21700 Vosne-Romanée, tel. 03.80.61.07.94, fax 03.80.61.24.31 Y by appt.

La Tâche

DOM. DE LA ROMANEE-CONTI
1998★★
■ Gd cru 6.06 ha 17,215 500 F+
72 73 75 78 79 |80| |81| |82| |87| |89| 91 92 97 98

This is a wine that is sowing seeds for its future. Members of our jury suggest not to open it for the next 15 years. The nose is liquorice, the fine, glorious palate is still taking shape. It calls to mind Saint-Simon's portrait of Fénelon: 'His features had a little of everything in them, and yet there was no conflict between opposing traits. There was gravity and gallantry, seriousness and gaiety. It required an effort actually to stop looking at it.' And indeed, you need to contemplate this wine for a long time.

SC du Dom. de La Romanée-Conti, 21700 Vosne-Romanée, tel. 03.80.62.48.80, fax 03.80.61.05.72

Nuits-Saint-Georges

Nuits-Saint-Georges, a little town of 5,000 inhabitants, does not produce the Grands Crus of its northerly neighbour; the appellation spreads into the commune of Premeaux which borders it to the south. However, the many Premiers Crus to be found here have a deserved reputation and in this, the most northerly Appellation Communale of the Côte de Nuits, we find a very different type of wine being made in the *climats*. The wines here generally have a higher tannin content, which means they can keep a long time.

The best-known Premier Cru vineyards are: Nuits-Saint-Georges, which is reputed to have been a vineyard as early as the year 1000; Les Vaucrains which produces robust wines; Les Cailles, or 'quails', which is in a spot where these birds would love to live; Les Champs-Perdrix (the 'partridge fields'); Les Porets, in the commune of Nuits, the name of which comes from *poirets* or little pears, and indeed produces a pronounced flavour of wild pears; the various clos named la Maréchale: des Argillières, des Forêts-Saint-Georges, des Corvées, de l'Arlot and sur Prémeaux. The vineyards produced 15,843 hl (418,255 gal) in 1999, of which 277 hl (7,313 gal) were white wines.

Nuits-Saint-Georges is the little wine capital of Burgundy. It also has a Hospices vineyard, which holds the annual wine auction on the Sunday before Palm Sunday. Many of the wine-shippers have their head offices in the town as do the liqueur-makers who produce Cassis de Bourgogne, and the makers of sparkling wines which have evolved today as Crémant de Bourgogne. The administrative headquarters of the Confrérie des Chevaliers du Tastevin is also to be found here.

DOM. BOUCHARD PERE ET FILS
Les Cailles 1997★
■ 1er cru 1.07 ha n.c. 200–249 F

It is hard to resist Les Cailles, whose name, by the way, does not mean 'quails' but comes from *crais*, meaning 'stones'. This light wine with its wilted rose fragrances is a wonderful example of the appellation. The colour is superb, the nose true to type but with an added touch of wild strawberries. It shows no hardness on the palate, which can be summed up in three words: full, rich and winey. Nevertheless, it still needs to age a little. From the same wine merchant comes a **Tour Blondeau, Le Nuits Village 97** (100–149F), which is commended by the jury.

🗝 Bouchard Père et Fils, Ch. de Beaune, 21200 Beaune, tel. 03.80.24.80.24, fax 03.80.22.55.88, e-mail france@bouchard.pereetfils.com 🍸 by appt.

SYLVAIN CATHIARD

Les Murgers 1998★

■ 1er cru 0.48 ha 2,400 ⏸ 150–199 F

If Graham Greene is to be believed, the best taste is that of salt. He obviously hadn't tasted this Les Murgers. Its colour is wonderfully dense. The aromas of blackcurrant are delicious, tempered with a hint of vanilla. The palate has not integrated fully yet, but it seems very fine, with good-structured tannins. A refined finish.

🗝 Sylvain Cathiard, 20, rue de la Goillotte, 21700 Vosne-Romanée, tel. 03.80.62.36.01, fax 03.80.61.18.21 ☑ 🍸 by appt.

DOM. JEAN CHAUVENET

Les Vaucrains 1998★

■ 1er cru 0.41 ha 2,400 ⏸ 150–199 F

This estate was created at the turn of the 20th century by the founding president of the wine-making co-operative of Nuits. His son Claudius left the business in around 1935 to work for himself, and his grandson Jean now carries on the family tradition. It is thanks to him and to Jean Collardot, for example, that the Premiers Crus have been signposted with raised stone markers. As to this violet-black 98, it is beginning to open up, showing simple, tasteful characteristics and a tannic style that is typical of this region.

🗝 SCE Dom. Jean Chauvenet, 3, rue de Gilly, 21700 Nuits-Saint-Georges, tel. 03.80.61.00.72, fax 03.80.61.12.87 ☑ 🍸 by appt.

DOM. JEAN CHAUVENET

Les Perrières 1998★

■ 1er cru 0.23 ha 1,200 ⏸ 150–199 F

Les Perrières covers, in total, 2.5 ha (6 acres) on the site of a former quarry, near the limestone cliff at Premeaux. This produces an elegant, well-balanced wine, vivid red with garnet hues. Its aromas and flavours are on the wild side – bilberries and raspberries. For the moment it lacks subtlety and is very concentrated, but looks a promising bet for the future. The **Damodes 98** receives the same mark.

🗝 SCE Dom. Jean Chauvenet, 3, rue de Gilly, 21700 Nuits-Saint-Georges, tel. 03.80.61.00.72, fax 03.80.61.12.87 ☑ 🍸 by appt.

CHAUVENET-CHOPIN

Charmottes 1998★★

■ 0.71 ha 3,500 ⏸ 70–99 F

The jury has unanimously awarded the *coup de cœur* to this estate. So you can do all your shopping here, though preferably not with your eyes closed, as it would be a shame to miss the morello cherry colour of this wine. The nose is toasty with touches of leather and preserved soft fruit. On the palate there is a marvellous fullness and a fruity chewiness with black cherry. It is also worth mentioning that, among all the other candidates, the **Village 98** was also judged worthy of the same distinction.

🗝 Chauvenet-Chopin, 97, rue Félix-Tisserand, 21700 Nuits-Saint-Georges, tel. 03.80.61.28.11, fax 03.80.61.20.02 ☑ 🍸 by appt.

GEORGES CHICOTOT

Les Vaucrains 1997

■ 1er cru 0.24 ha 1,280 ⏸ 100–149 F

This is a *climat* where you can find 'sheeps heads' – blocks of limestone that have been sculpted by erosion. It is well-known both to geologists and wine-lovers as the very best of the Nuits Crus are to be found here. This 97 is developing, so we would recommend drinking it immediately. The colour is average, the crystallised-fruit nose very fine, and the texture good.

🗝 Georges Chicotot, 15, rue Gal-de-Gaulle, 21700 Nuits-Saint-Georges, tel. 03.80.61.19.33, fax 03.80.61.38.94 ☑ 🍸 by appt.

A. CHOPIN ET FILS

Aux Damodes 1997★

■ 1er cru 0.13 ha 900 ⏸ 70–99 F

Although we liked **Les Murgers 98** (big personality), we have a weakness for this Damodes 97 which leaves us with a fresh, delicious sensation in the mouth. Warmth and roundness are backed up with liquorice and violets. It has a lovely bright colour and will look very nice on the dinner table.

🗝 Dom. A. Chopin et Fils, R.N. 74, 21700 Comblanchien, tel. 03.80.62.92.60, fax 03.80.62.70.78 ☑ 🍸 by appt.

DOM. DU CLOS FRANTIN 1997★

■ 0.84 ha 4,200 ⏸ 200–249 F

You must try this 97 with its vivid, deep colour and superb nose of spices and cinnamon. It fills the palate, charming and seducing it. Really excellent. The Clos Frantin belongs to Albert Bichot.

🗝 Dom. du Clos Frantin, 6 bis, bd Jacques-Copeau, 21200 Beaune, tel. 03.80.24.37.37, fax 03.80.24.37.38

🗝 A. Bichot

XAVIER DUCLERT

Les Damodes 1997★

1er cru	n.c.	n.c.		100–149 F

This bottle of wine has an art deco label. The wine is not entirely open yet, but a young Nuits is always tannic and astringent. This one will be worth waiting for. Its warmth and flavour of crystallised fruit make it an interesting proposition. A ruby-red colour that has an attractive brightness; the nose, a little macerated, is already concentrated.

Xavier Duclert, 2 bis, pl. Carnot, 21200 Beaune, tel. 03.80.22.74.77, fax 03.80.22.74.77, e-mail xavier.duclert@fnac.net ev. day except Mon. 10am–7pm

DUFOULEUR PERE ET FILS

1997★

	n.c.	1,400		150–199 F

This is a wine that could put itself forward at the local elections and not fear the result of the second round, although a second ballot would do it good as it needs time to develop. However, underneath the cherry-red robe of office, its policies as well as its balance sheet make a good impression: a nose of blackcurrant and fur that is true to the terroir and a very decent structure with a hint of vivacity. You will surely have realized by now that the wine we're talking about is the Nuits of the Mayor of Nuits . . .

Dufouleur Père et Fils, 15, rue Thurot, 21700 Nuits-Saint-Georges, tel. 03.80.61.21.21, fax 03.80.61.11.23 by appt.

FAIVELEY Les Vignerondes 1997★

1er cru	0.46 ha	2,900		200–249 F

This *climat* is supposed to produce amazingly fruity wines, a fact which was borne out at the tasting. This wine gives us the complete fruity range, from fresh right down to crystallised fruit, and if you believe what they say, it ought then to develop in the direction of sloe and leather. Light-bodied, supple and attractive, making it a wine that should stay clear of spicy foods.

Bourgognes Faiveley, 8, rue du Tribourg, B.P. 9, 21701 Nuits-Saint-Georges Cedex, tel. 03.80.61.04.55, fax 03.80.62.33.37, e-mail bourgognesfaiveley@wanadoo.fr by appt.

MAISON ALEX GAMBAL

Les Murgers 1997

1er cru	n.c.	600		250–299 F

This *négociant-éleveur* business was set up in 1997 by Alex Gambal, a Burgundy enthusiast of American origin. The Laronze and Montille team help him to run it. The nose on this wine, with its aromas of forest-floor and musk, is an attribute of the terroir. The palate is round enough but the tannins are a little on the austere side. In principle, a good wine, but saving its best for a future date. A classic Nuits.

EURL maison Alex Gambal, 4, rue Jacques-Vincent, 21200 Beaune, tel. 03.80.22.75.81, fax 03.80.22.21.66, e-mail agbeaune@aol.com by appt.

PHILIPPE GAVIGNET

Les Chaboeufs 1998★

1er cru	1 ha	6,300		100–149 F

This *climat*, right in the middle of the thalweg at Les Vallerots, is well-served by the extremely attractive wine-making style of this estate. The wine has a charming, supple, soft fullness and a pleasant subtle oakiness. It is a good clean red colour, with a little spring-like perfume of cherries, making it an attractive wine that is almost ready to drink. The similarly composed **Bousselots 98** (70–99F) is equally highly recommended, as is the **Argillats 98**.

Dom. Philippe Gavignet, 36, rue Dr-Louis-Legrand, 21700 Nuits-Saint-Georges, tel. 03.80.61.09.41, fax 03.80.61.03.56 ev. day 8am–12 noon 2pm–6pm; Sat. Sun. by appt.; cl. 25 Dec.-1 Jan.

GEISWEILER ET FILS 1997

	n.c.	4,000		150–199 F

The Geisweiler business, which has been taken over by Picard (Chagny), was for two hundred years one of the best names in Nuits-Saint-Georges. This wine has a light brick-red colour, with blackcurrant and blackberry aromas. A supple style with a hint of vegetation.

Geisweiler, 4, rte. de Dijon, 21700 Nuits-Saint-Georges, tel. 03.85.87.51.21, fax 03.85.87.51.11

Michel Picard

DOM. ANNE-MARIE GILLE

Aux Bousselots 1997★

1er cru	0.21 ha	1,100		100–149 F

The Gilles family have been in Burgundy since before the Revolution, and today own 6.5 ha (16 ha). Their vineyard at Les Bousselots in Vosne has a soil that is rich in active lime and a terrain that is full of bumps (*bosses*), as its name suggests. It would be a shame to make this 97 wait. We were pleased because it is a little out of the ordinary. A warm, oaky wine, well-formed and well-structured. The Pinot Noir comes out strongly without having to make a song and dance.

Dom. Anne-Marie Gille, 34, R.N. 74, 21700 Comblanchien, tel. 03.80.62.94.13, fax 03.80.62.99.88, e-mail gille@burgundywines.net by appt.

DOM. HENRI GOUGES

Clos des Porrets-saint-georges 1997★★

1er cru	3.57 ha	12,000		100–149 F

The Henri Gouges estate is named after one of the founders of the AOC in the Côte-d'Or. He was one of those (along with the Marquis of Angerville) who refused the honour of a Grand Cru so that people wouldn't think that they were awarding them to themselves. A true gentleman. This Porrets-Saint-Georges does him justice. It is brightly

BURGUNDY

coloured, full of ripe bilberry fruit, spicy and toasty: it is not lacking in resources. An incredibly concentrated, truly excellent wine. One of the tasters, not knowing what he was tasting, wrote: 'Why is there no Grand Cru in Nuits?' The **Les Pruliers Premier Cru** receives one star. It needs a while for the wood to blend in.

🔑 Dom. Henri Gouges, 7, rue du Moulin, 21700 Nuits-Saint-Georges, tel. 03.80.61.04.40, fax 03.80.61.32.84

DOM. DU GRAND CONTOUR

Clos des Grandes Vignes 1997★★

■ 1er cru 2.12 ha 13,500 200–249 F

This Domaine du Grand Contour does not beat about the bush. It is a deep red, dark as ink. The aromas, true to type, are of venison. On the palate there is richness, substance, structure and complexity. On the aftertaste, wild berries. This *clos* was established by the Viénot family and now belongs to the Thomas family. It is situated by the main road, but it is none the worse for it.

🔑 Dom. du Grand Contour, chem. rural 29, 21700 Nuits-Saint-Georges, tel. 03.80.61.08.92, fax 03.80.61.30.26

DOM. GUYON 1998

■ 0.22 ha 1,400 100–149 F

Fresh and yet tannic, tender and yet astringent: this wine argues the case for and against itself like a good lawyer, and although it has not achieved a balance as yet, it has potential. A deep violet colour heralds a complex and varied nose of coffee, liquorice, bilberry fruit and mineral notes.

🔑 EARL Dom. Guyon, 11–16, R.N. 74, 21700 Vosne-Romanée, tel. 03.80.61.02.46, fax 03.80.62.36.56 Y by appt.

ALAIN HUDELOT-NOELLAT

Les Murgers 1998★

■ 1er cru 0.68 ha 2,100 150–199 F

This is a pleasant wine that should be opened immediately. At least, that is the first impression it gives. Later, you realise that it merits rather higher praise. This full-bodied, tannic, very well-structured 98 is one of those wines that needs to wait at least ten years before being opened. A very attractive colour, bright with a violet rim. You can sense the complexity behind its rather closed nose.

🔑 Alain Hudelot-Noëllat, 21640 Chambolle-Musigny, tel. 03.80.62.85.17, fax 03.80.62.83.13 Y by appt.

DOM. JAVOUHEY

Vieilles vignes 1997★

■ 0.44 ha 1,500 100–149 F

This wine needs no encouragement to reveal its secrets. Deep ruby-red in colour, its nose opens on a complex note of liquorice and stewed fruit. It is well-balanced, firm on the attack, and fresh and fruity from start to finish, suggesting such elevated qualities as sincerity and uprightness.

🔑 SCEA Javouhey, 50, rue Gal-de-Gaulle, B.P. 63, 21700 Nuits-Saint-Georges, tel. 03.80.61.10.30, fax 03.80.61.35.76 Y by appt.

DOM. DE LA POULETTE

Les Poulettes 1997

■ 1er cru 1.08 ha 5,000 100–149 F

What on earth is a farmyard doing 290 m (948 feet) above sea-level, right underneath a cliff? You may well ask. This purple-shaded Les Poulettes 97, in any case, is rich in aromas of bilberry fruit, with just a hint of venison and has powerful tannins that are not unpleasant. It is quite a hard wine, but if you read the right books you will know that this is typical of this Premier Cru.

🔑 Dom. de la Poulette, 21700 Corgoloin, tel. 03.80.62.98.02, fax 03.45.25.43.23 Y by appt.

🔑 Mme Michaut-Audidier

BERTRAND MACHARD DE GRAMONT Les Vallerots 1997★

■ 0.5 ha 2,700 100–149 F

This 97 comes from the thalweg at Les Vallerots (a *climat* situated above Les Vaucrains and Saint-Georges). It is a brilliant crimson-purple, already open with fruity aromas of raspberry and blackcurrant combined with a hint of oak. The first impression given by the nose follows through to the palate, which is well-structured. Ready to drink in a year, but will last another four.

🔑 Bertrand Machard de Gramont, 13, rue de Vergy et 32, rue Thurot, 21700 Nuits-Saint-Georges, tel. 03.80.61.16.96, fax 03.80.61.16.96 Y by appt.

MAISON MALLARD-GAULIN

1998★

■ 0.25 ha 1,400 250–299 F

'There is no wine as earthly as this', wrote Curzio Malaparte about Nuits wine in his famous novel *Kaput*. In the episode in question, the wine was being served with a Karelia wild boar that was just emerging from the oven wrapped in pine branches. This 98 will doubtless never experience anything so exotic, but deserves to. There are some signs of development in the colour, and it has an already very open nose. Its rich, supple body, with a little touch of crushed strawberry, makes it possible to drink now but could last a lot longer.

🔑 Maison Mallard-Gaulin, 21420 Aloxe-Corton, tel. 03.80.26.46.10, fax 03.80.26.43.57

MARSON ET NATIER 1997

■ n.c. 8,000 100–149 F

This is Chanson Père et Fils under another name, Marson et Natier! Their cherry-coloured Nuits is exactly what one would expect of this appellation. The aromas are reminiscent of that novel by La Varende, *Nose of Leather*. Nose of blackcurrant, too. It is rich in tannins, balancing richness and acidity

with success, and has a true Pinot flavour. A good option for laying down.
Marson et Natier, 10, rue du Collège, 21200 Beaune, tel. 03.80.25.97.96, fax 03.80.24.17.42

DOM. MARTIN-DUFOUR

Aux Argillats 1997

1er cru	0.14 ha	797	100–149 F

Les Argillats is on the Vosne-Romanée side of Nuits, a clay terroir whose wine, which is said to be austere, supposedly opens up later in life. This wine shows no such reluctance. It is not a complex wine, but is supple and flavoursome, giving an impression of warmth and of forest-picked berries.
Dom. Martin-Dufour, 4a, rue des Moutots, 21200 Chorey-lès-Beaune, tel. 03.80.22.18.39, fax 03.80.22.18.39 by appt.

P. MISSEREY

Les Pruliers 1997★

1er cru	n.c.	3,000	150–199 F

This *climat*, which is situated on the Premeaux side of Nuits, takes its name from wild plum trees. Although it has not developed a great deal; all agree that this wine is rich and full, clean and fresh – a combination of qualities that is no easy task. To the eye, the wine is brilliant and clear. On the nose, it is full and ripe, with a light hint of game. From the same producer, **Les Cailles 97** (200–249F) is commended by the jury, while under the name **Coron Père et Fils** is the **Les Vaucrains 97** (200–49F), which can be served now.
Maison P. Misserey, 3, rue des Seuillets, B.P. 10, 21701 Nuits-Saint-Georges Cedex, tel. 03.80.61.07.74, fax 03.80.61.31.40 by appt.

MONGEARD-MUGNERET

Les Plateaux 1997★

	0.69 ha	2,900	100–149 F

Mongeard-Mugneret's achievements are many and great. This little-known *climat* is situated above the town of Nuits on the Premeaux side. This wine has plenty of character and is very true to its terroir: it is open, with aromas and flavours of cherries and spices and a deep ruby-red colour that is in full evolution. Already a very attractive wine, but it will benefit from some time in the cellar.
Dom. Mongeard-Mugneret, 14, rue de la Fontaine, 21700 Vosne-Romanée, tel. 03.80.61.11.95, fax 03.80.62.35.75, e-mail mongeard@axnet.fr by appt.

JEAN-PIERRE MUGNERET 1997

	0.74 ha	4,300	100–149 F

Dark red without being too dark, the colour of this wine is classic. The nose has plenty of verve to it, with aromas of forest-floor and a hovering smell of wild animals. The same gamey notes follow through on the palate, where they mix with soft fruits with a background of still-young tannins that will mellow with time.
EARL Jean-Pierre Mugneret, Concœur-et-Corboin, 21700 Nuits-Saint-Georges, tel. 03.80.61.00.20, fax 03.80.62.33.04

DOM. DES PERDRIX

Aux Perdrix Monopole 1997★★

1er cru	3.49 ha	17,000	200–249 F

The Domaine des Perdrix (which means 'partridges') is run by Antonin Rodet, who here presents us with a red-legged partridge that should not escape your gun! Its plumage? Like red ink. Its song? Seductive and attractive, with tones of macerated soft fruit, complex and very closed. The palate, despite a little hint of alcohol, is full and well-built, with a long finish. The **Village 97** has character and is a good option for laying down. It receives one star.
B. et C. Devillard, Dom. des Perdrix, Ch. de Champ Renard, 71640 Mercurey, tel. 03.85.45.13.89, fax 03.85.45.21.61

CH. DE PREMEAUX 1998

	2 ha	10,000	70–99 F

The grandfather of this family acquired the Château de Premeaux in 1933. The communes of Premeaux and Nuits share their Crus, producing a 98 that is vigorous, rigorous, very rich, and very robust in its approach. Not to be drunk for the next two to three years.
Dom. du Ch. de Premeaux, 21700 Premeaux-Prissey, tel. 03.80.62.30.64, fax 03.80.62.39.28 by appt.
Pelletier

REINE PEDAUQUE 1998★

	n.c.	10,000	100–149 F

This 98 is maturing rapidly and should be drunk without much delay. Brilliantly coloured, its nose of cherries in brandy compliment a pronounced oakiness. An attractive palate, rich and with plenty of stuffing. It is very supple and round, and not overly acidic.
Reine Pédauque, Le Village, 21420 Aloxe-Corton, tel. 03.80.25.00.00, fax 03.80.26.42.00, e-mail rpedauque@axnet.fr by appt.

HENRI ET GILLES REMORIQUET

Les Damodes 1998★

1er cru	0.4 ha	n.c.	100–149 F

The 98 vintage will not disappoint 'new age' Burgundy lovers. This is a Pinot Noir that is so dark it is almost opaque, with touches of wild fruit, extremely well-structured, and requiring a very long wait before it will get going. The **Allots 97** (70–99F) is in the same style, but the wood is so pronounced that it receives only a commendation.
Dom. Henri et Gilles Remoriquet, 25, rue de Charmois, 21700 Nuits-Saint-Georges, tel. 03.80.61.24.84, fax 03.80.61.36.63, e-mail domaine.remoriquet@wanadoo.fr by appt.

DOM. JEAN-PIERRE TRUCHET

1997

■ 1.63 ha 2,600 ▮▮ 100–149 F

Reasonably bright in colour and relatively open on the nose, this wine opens out fully on the palate. Fresh with a certain discreteness, accompanied by tannins which will soften and a fruitiness that is getting stronger and stronger.

🔑 Jean-Pierre Truchet, R.N. 74, 21700 Premeaux-Prissey, tel. 03.80.61.07.22, fax 03.80.61.34.35 ☑ Ỵ ev. day except Sat. Sun. 9am–12 noon 2pm–7pm; cl. 15–31 Aug.

CHARLES VIENOT

Clos des Corvées Paget 1997★

■ 1er cru n.c. 600 ▮▮ 150–199 F

Charles Viénot is a historical figure in the Burgundy region. Rotund and expansive, 'Gros Charles' has hands large enough to toast the health of his successors, the team led by Jean-Claude Boisset. The colour is attractive. The nose? It is a Côte-de-Nuits nose, which is all you need to say. The tannins? As they should be. Good length, finesse and subtlety, ready to drink in a couple of years' time.

🔑 Charles Viénot, 5, quai Dumorey, 21700 Nuits-Saint-Georges, tel. 03.80.62.61.41, fax 03.80.62.37.38

DOM. FABRICE VIGOT 1998★

■ 0.58 ha 2,700 ▮▮ 150–199 F

This 98 is rich in alcohol and very expansive in character. Its flavours are straightforward, it is pleasant to look at, and has a slight, characterful, oaky nose (with herbaceous and spicy aromas). This is a Nuits that will develop well.

🔑 Dom. Fabrice Vigot, 16, rue de la Fontaine, 21700 Vosne-Romanée, tel. 03.80.61.13.01, fax 03.80.61.13.01 ☑ Ỵ by appt.

Côte de Nuits-Villages

After the village of Prémeaux, the vineyard narrows to only about 200 m (218 yd) at Corgoloin, the narrowest point on the Côte. Here, the 'mountain' is not so high and the administrative jurisdiction of the Appellation Côte de Nuits-Villages, once known as 'Vins Fins de la Côte de Nuits', stops at the Clos des Langres in the village of Corgoloin. Between them are two communes: Prissey, associated with Prémeaux, and Comblanchien, famous for a particular kind of limestone (incorrectly called marble) which is extracted from the quarries in the hills. They both have terroirs that are entitled to be called Appellation Communale. But the areas of these three communes are too limited to have their own appellation, so Brochon and Fixin became associated with them to share the unique Appellation Côte de Nuits-Villages, which in 1999 produced 8,681 hl (229,178 gal) of wine, of which 305 hl (8,052 gal) were whites. You can find excellent wines at affordable prices here.

BERTRAND AMBROISE 1998★★

■ 0.28 ha 8,000 ▮▮ 70–99 F

Bertrand Ambroise wanted to be a shepherd, but life decided otherwise. Instead, he watches over the family vines, and in addition has created a *negoçiant* business that specialises in Côte-de-Nuits wines. His prizewinner this year is remarkable. This garnet-red wine, with its perfume of morello cherries, seems straightforward and well-made. It is full-bodied, in keeping with the appellation, and is ready to drink now, although it seems an equally viable option to lay down.

🔑 Maison Bertrand Ambroise, rue de l'Eglise, 21700 Premeaux-Prissey, tel. 03.80.62.30.19, fax 03.80.62.38.69, e-mail bertrand.ambroise@wanadoo.fr ☑ Ỵ by appt.

RENE BOUVIER 1998★

■ 0.49 ha 2,500 ▮▮ 70–99 F

We should not forget that the AOC covers the southern part of the Côte-de-Nuits as well, which is where this highly-coloured, strongly aromatic, vigorously-pressed wine comes from. It is very chewy. This is a wine that has been well-made for its particular style, and has been well-matured. It will last.

🔑 René Bouvier, 2, rue Neuve, 21160 Marsannay-la-Côte, tel. 03.80.52.21.37, fax 03.80.59.95.96 ☑ Ỵ by appt.

LOUIS CHAVY 1997★

■ n.c. 12,000 ▮ 🌡 70–99 F

This wine has means. It has an agreeable, deep colour, and gives a hint of interesting complex aromas (raspberry, leather, liquorice). All this giving an idea of what its palate holds. Looks promising: true to type and rather reserved.

🔑 Louis Chavy, Caveau la Vierge Romaine, pl. des Marronniers, 21190 MontrachetPuligny-Montrachet, tel. 03.80.26.33.00, fax 03.80.24.14.84, e-mail mallet.b@cva-beaune.fr ☑ Ỵ ev. day 10am–6pm; cl. Nov.–Mar.

DESERTAUX-FERRAND

Les Perrières 1997★

■ 2.6 ha 13,000 50–69 F

This purple-toned Les Perrières should be drunk immediately in order to profit from its vigour. With its nose of blackcurrant buds (they use them as the base of some very prestigious perfumes in Grasse). This is a fine, well-balanced 97 that is fresh and is reasonably long.

Dom. Désertaux-Ferrand, 135, Grande-Rue, 21700 Corgoloin, tel. 03.80.62.98.40, fax 03.80.62.70.32, e-mail desertaux@erb.com ☑ Ꮖ by appt.

R. DUBOIS ET FILS 1998★

□ 0.8 ha 1,500 50–69 F

When you have made it as far as being elected President of the 'Viti' in Beaune, you owe it to yourself to set a good example, even if the younger generation are already taking charge. This appellation opens up gradually with Chardonnay when the terroir permits, and it has a convincing advocate here. The wine is a shimmering gold, the aromas are of fresh almond and lemon, and the attack is good, followed by fullness and length in the same aromatic register.

R. Dubois et Fils, rte. de Nuits-Saint-Georges, 21700 Premeaux-Prissey, tel. 03.80.62.30.61, fax 03.80.61.24.07, e-mail rdubois@wanadoo.fr ☑ Ꮖ ev. day 8am–11.30am 2pm–6pm; Sat. Sun. by appt.

DOM. GACHOT-MONOT 1997★★

■ 4 ha 12,000 50–69 F

This appellation is in good form and has made great progress. The l'Eté des Côtes de Nuits-Villages contributed to this in no small measure last summer. This estate produced a lovely 96. This 97 does it justice yet again. It is brilliant, intense, with a lovely nose of blackberries and black cherries, and a very elegant palate. This is an attractive young wine, supple with a hint of liveliness, healthy, and with a great future.

Dom. Gachot-Monot, 13, rue Humbert-de-Gillens, 21700 Gerland, tel. 03.80.62.50.95, fax 03.80.62.53.85 ☑ Ꮖ by appt.

DOM. ANNE-MARIE GILLE 1998

■ 2.95 ha 9,000 50–69 F

Ah! These old-style labels with their curling edges ... one day someone will put them in a museum. As for the wine, it is full of good intentions, but needs laying down for a little while to allow its tannins to mellow. Its richness and freshness argue in its favour. This is one of the oldest estates in the village.

Dom. Anne-Marie Gille, 34, R.N. 74, 21700 Comblanchien, tel. 03.80.62.94.13, fax 03.80.62.99.88, e-mail gille@burgundywines.net ☑ Ꮖ by appt.

DOM. LALEURE-PIOT

Les Bellevues 1998★

■ 0.9 ha 4,800 50–69 F

This *climat* is situated on the top of Comblanchien, just near the Clos de la Maréchale. Distinct ruby-red in colour, this is a fruity, tranquil and chewy 98. It is simple and tasteful, in the spirit of the appellation.

Dom. Laleure-Piot, rue de Pralot, 21420 Pernand-Vergelesses, tel. 03.80.21.52.37, fax 03.80.21.59.48, e-mail laleure.piot@wanadoo.fr ☑ Ꮖ ev. day 8am–12 noon 2pm–6.30pm; Sat. Sun. by appt.

Frédéric Laleure

CLOS DES LANGRES 1997★

■ 2.74 ha 6,000 70–99 F

The Clos des Langres is a family monopoly (Gabriel Liogier d'Ardhuy and his children are also owners of La Reine Pédauque and Corton-André) and is situated in the extreme south of the Côte-de-Nuits. This is a wine that the canons of Langres used to put in their cruets for communion. It is supple, appealing, attractive, a little woody, easy and commercial in the best sense of the word.

Dom. d'Ardhuy, Clos des Langres, 21700 Corgoloin, tel. 03.80.62.98.73, fax 03.80.62.95.15 ☑ Ꮖ ev. day except Sun. 10am–12 noon 2pm–6pm

DOM. DE LA POULETTE 1998★★

□ 0.5 ha 1,800 70–99 F

The AOC owes a lot to Lucien Audidier (1903–1992), whose estate is now run by his daughter. This is an astonishing young vineyard planted on an unused piece of land overlooking the Corgoloin quarry, whose soil is now showing its capacity to produce great white wines. This delicate, sculpted, lightly oaky, yellow-gold wine, elaborated with notes of citrus fruits and fresh almonds, has a rare finesse.

Dom. de la Poulette, 21700 Corgoloin, tel. 03.80.62.98.02, fax 03.45.25.43.23 ☑ Ꮖ by appt.

Mme F. Michaut-Audidier

DOM. MICHEL MALLARD ET FILS 1997★

■ 1.34 ha 6,000 70–99 F

This wine is still a little on the closed side now, but will develop in the right direction. It is very concentrated, rich with touches of liquorice. A very dark colour, its nose is of spiced leather. It will turn out to be a very approachable wine.

Dom. Michel Mallard et Fils, 43, rte. de Dijon, 21550 Ladoix-Serrigny, tel. 03.80.26.40.64, fax 03.80.26.47.49 Y by appt.

DOM. HENRI NAUDIN-FERRAND Vieilles vignes 1997★★

■ n.c. 8,556 50–69 F

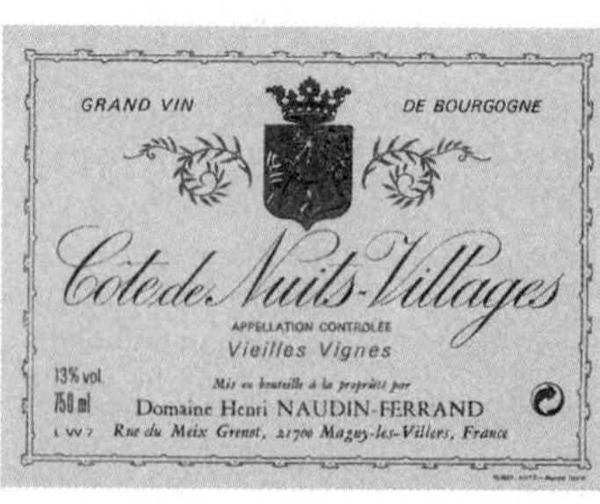

Henri Naudin can be proud of his daughters. Anne and Claire Naudin have managed to acheive a *coup de cœur* with this Vieilles Vignes 97. The colour is elegant, the nose as fruity as you could wish and pleasantly spicy. It may be a showing a little warmth, but has a wonderful richness. With its fullness, structure and concentration, this is a wine that Henri IV could have recommended to go with Sunday chicken.

Dom. Henri Naudin-Ferrand, rue du Meix-Grenot, 21700 Magny-lès-Villers, tel. 03.80.62.91.50, fax 03.80.62.91.77, e-mail dom.hnf.@wanadoo.fr
Y by appt.

DOM. ERIC PANSIOT Les Perrières 1998

■ 0.4 ha 2,400 50–69 F

There are several *climats* in this appellation. The label usually mentions if they have been separately vinified, as is the case with this Les Perrières, which comes from Corgoloin in the direction of Magny-lès-Villers. This cherry-red 98, with its fresh, yet still closed, nose is worth waiting for: it has texture and plenty of fruit, despite the strong tannins.

Eric Pansiot, 21700 Corgoloin, tel. 03.80.62.94.32, fax 03.80.62.73.14 Y by appt.

H. PROTOT 1997★

■ 2.3 ha 5,600 30–49 F

This brilliantly-coloured wine gives only the merest hint of a toasty nose which could open out in quite a different direction. It is winey, tannic though also rich, and needs to find its balance. All the elements are there for a wonderful end product.

Henriette Protot, 21700 Premeaux-Prissey, tel. 03.80.62.35.13

DOM. VINCENT SAUVESTRE 1998★★

■ 2.25 ha 15,000 50–69 F

This wine is a fine ruby-red, with an open and generous nose. Warm and fruity on the attack, while its tannins are meek as lambs. A very agreeable wine that is easy to get to grips with, it has good balance and can be laid down for three to four years.

Dom. Vincent Sauvestre, rte de Monthélie, B.P. 3, 21190 Meursault, tel. 03.80.21.22.45, fax 03.80.21.28.05 Y by appt.

La Côte de Beaune

Ladoix

Three small villages, Serrigny near the railway line, Ladoix on the RN74, and Buisson at the end of the Côte de Nuits make up the commune of Ladoix-Serrigny. The Appellation Communale is Ladoix. The hamlet of Buisson is located exactly at the geographical conjunction of the Côtes de Nuits and the Côtes de Beaune. The administrative border stops at the commune of Corgoloin, but the hill itself continues further on as do the vineyards and the wine. The Corton 'mountain' rises beyond the combe of Magny which marks the physical separation. The steep inclines made up of layers of marl have many south- and west-facing slopes, making this one of the best wine-growing areas on the Côte.

The various aspects give the Appellation Ladoix a variety of different types of wine, added to which its white wines are exceptionally well adapted to rowing on the Argovian marlstone oils. This is the case with Les réchons, for example, which is rown on the same geological soils s Corton-Charlemagne further outh, though it has a less favourable aspect. The wines from this ocation have distinctive characteristics. Having produced 4,411 hl 16,450 gal) of red wine and 847 hl 22,361 gal) of white in 1999, the ppellation Ladoix is little known, ut deserves better.

Another oddity: even though Ladoix was given a favourable classification by the Comité de Viticulture de Beaune in 1860, it was not awarded any Premiers Crus. This was put right by the INAO in 1978. The main Premiers Crus are La Macaude, La Corvée and Le Clou d'Orge, which produce wines with the same characteristics as wines from the Côte de Nuits; Les Mourottes (Basses and Hautes) which have a wild appeal, and the Bois-Roussot, planted on 'lava'.

Côte de Nuits (South)

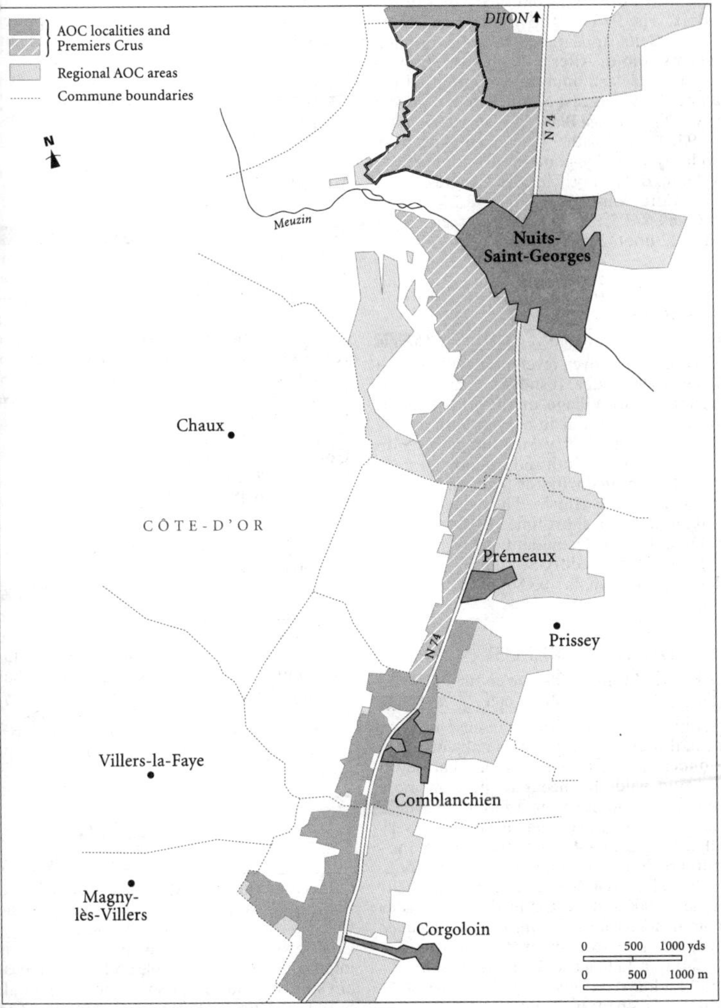

BERTRAND AMBROISE

Les Gréchons 1998★

☐ 1er cru 0.6 ha 3,000 70–99 F

An attractive colour, just as it should be. A clean, deep nose with wood and fruit that combine attractively. A well-structured palate. Could you ask for more? Only the chicken in cream sauce to go with it.

Maison Bertrand Ambroise, rue de l'Eglise, 21700 Premeaux-Prissey, tel. 03.80.62.30.19, fax 03.80.62.38.69, e-mail bertrand.ambroise@wanadoo.fr by appt.

DOM. D'ARDHUY 1997★

■ 5.35 ha 15,150 50–69 F

A family-run domaine belonging to the Liogier d'Ardhuy family (La Reine Pédauque). They live at the Clos des Langres, only a short distance from their vineyards at Ladoix. The 97 is slightly jammy and fairly oaky, and its appearance shows a brilliant flame of colour. After a distinctive, straightforward attack, tannins are pronounced but balanced and suggest another look in a year or two. The **Village Blanc 97** also gets one star (70–99F). Gold with a pale green glint, fresh and lively yet oaky, good for drinking now.

Dom. d'Ardhuy, Clos des Langres, 21700 Corgoloin, tel. 03.80.62.98.73, fax 03.80.62.95.15 ev. day except Sun. 10am–12 noon 2pm–6pm

DOM. CACHAT-OCQUIDANT ET FILS 1998★

■ 2 ha 3,600 50–69 F

No need to be over-reverential with the **Les Madonnes 98 Rouge**. It should be drunk now. The appellation **Village**, on the other hand, is worth keeping. Light in colour, with a nose that starts with bilberry fruit and moves onto gameyness. The smooth and balanced tannins are well-integrated with the fruit, and it has a sufficiently long finish. The wine will be drinking well in a short time.

Dom. Cachat-Ocquidant et Fils, pl. du Souvenir, 21550 Ladoix-Serrigny, tel. 03.80.26.45.30, fax 03.80.26.48.16 by appt.

CAPITAIN-GAGNEROT

Les Hautes Mourottes Elevé en fût 1998★

☐ 1er cru 0.42 ha 3,000 70–99 F

Golden, buttery, with an intense nose of spring flowers and honey, this oaky wine has an underlying tone that is somewhat developed and wild. It needs to develop more before we can advise when it should be drunk. One taster suggested that 'it could go very well with grilled lobster with peppercorns'. Another white, one star, is also worth a look, the **Premier Cru Les Gréchons 98**. Well-balanced oak and fruit, and the same taster recommended a *noix de veau aux champignons et à la crème* to accompany it.

Capitain-Gagnerot, 38, rte de Dijon, 21550 Ladoix-Serrigny, tel. 03.80.26.41.36, fax 03.80.26.46.29 by appt.

CHEVALIER PERE ET FILS

Les Gréchons 1998★

☐ 0.47 ha 2,500 100–14

This domaine was founded in 1885 by Dubois. Georges and Claude Chevalier a building on the wisdom of four generatior Here we have a Chardonnay of an inten golden-green, with a nose of acacia hon and a very smooth palate (lovely tones of bi ter almond). Salmon and firm-fleshed fis should go well with this wine.

SCE Chevalier Père et Fils, Buisson, 21550 Ladoix-Serrigny, tel. 03.80.26.46.30, fax 03.80.26.41.47 by appt.

DOM. CORNU 1997★

■ 0.96 ha 6,000 50–69

The look and the nose compliment eac other. Strawberry jam and an intense red co our make a very promising pairing. Hints c oak, a certain tannic vigour; the palate power ful yet well-balanced and with convincin length. The comments range from 'decent' t 'lovely wine'!

Dom. Cornu, rue du Meix-Grenot, 21700 Magny-lès-Villers, tel. 03.80.62.92.05, fax 03.80.62.72.22 by appt.

EDMOND CORNU ET FILS

Les Carrières 1997★

■ 0.62 ha 3,600 70–99

The grapes for this very characteristic win are de-stalked. It comes from around Le Mourottes, Le Rognet and Corton. Not quit heaven, but close. Highly-coloured, with nose that is closed at first, but opens out t reveal vegetal and slightly toasted-wood aro mas. The tannins are very evident, but no harsh. A good wine for keeping (three to fiv years) it will fulfill its promise.

EARL Edmond Cornu et Fils, Le Meix Gobillon, rue du Bief, 21550 Ladoix-Serrigny, tel. 03.80.26.40.79, fax 03.80.26.48.34 by appt.

CAVEAU DES FLEURIERES

Les Gréchons 1997★

☐ 1er cru n.c. n.c. 100–149 F

Monsieur Javouhey is a wine-grower and *négociant-éleveur* at Nuits. He invited us to taste a well-structured Ladoix Blanc 97. This wine, with its fairly intense yellow colour, has a strong character, and a good long finish.

Caveau des Fleurières, 50, rue du Gal-de-Gaulle, 21700 Nuits-Saint-Georges, B.P. 63, tel. 03.80.61.10.30, fax 03.80.61.35.76 by appt.

Javouhey

FRANCOIS GAY 1997★

■ 0.48 ha 2,200 50–69 F

It is noticeable that this wine-grower, based in Chorey, is very skilled with all that he touches with his secateurs: Beaune, Savigny, Corton and Ladoix. As for the 97, the red is intense and brilliant, supple and round, pleasant and without surprises. Good potential, but it has not yet reached its peak. The

omas suggest moss, undergrowth and spberry.
François Gay, 9, rue des Fiètres, 21200 horey-lès-Beaune, tel. 03.80.22.69.58, x 03.80.24.71.42 ☑ Ɪ by appt.

HRISTIAN GROS

ôte-de-Beaune 1998★

n.c. n.c. 50–69 F

Brilliant ruby-red, with well-set tannins; is appellation seems more at ease in a family mosphere. Both aromas and flavours reveal orello cherry. Best to leave this wine over the ext two or three years until it develops some alance.

Christian Gros, rue de la Chaume, 21700 remeaux-Prissey, tel. 03.80.61.29.74, x 03.80.61.39.77 ☑ Ɪ by appt.

OM. JEAN GUITON La Corvée 1998

1er cru 0.79 ha 3,000 70–99 F

The 96 vintage was very successful and it is ever a hardship to drink this wine. Leap-ogging the 97, here is the 98 that has just een bottled. Pale ruby, it presents strawberry avours that have an appealing finesse. While ot having the body or mouthfilling qualities f a great Premier Cru, it is nonetheless sup-le, not to say subtle and quite elegant.

Jean Guiton, 4, rte. de Pommard, 21200 ligny-lès-Beaune, tel. 03.80.26.82.88, ax 03.80.26.85.05 ☑ Ɪ ev. day 9am–2 noon 2pm–7pm

OM. ROBERT ET RAYMOND ACOB 1998★

1 ha 4,500 50–69 F

Pale gold with glints of green giving the oveliest effect. The nose is first honeyed, then erbena becomes evident, with notes of fruit nd scorched wood. We found the same on the alate, where there is also a lot of freshness.

Dom. Robert et Raymond Jacob, Hameau de Buisson, 21550 Ladoix-Serrigny, el. 03.80.26.40.42, fax 03.80.26.49.34 ☑ Ɪ y appt.

DOM. DE LA GALOPIERE

Les Clous 1998★

■ 0.46 ha 2,000 50–69 F

A perfect 'deep-Pinot' colour, intense on the nose with aromas of soft fruit jam, a generous, balanced palate with delicate tannins. The fruit returns at the finish: an interesting wine. The domaine was established, at the beginning of the 20th century, in an attractive building in Bligny-lès-Beaune.

laire et Gabriel Fournier, Dom. de la Galopière, 6, rue de l'Eglise, 21200 Bligny-lès-Beaune, tel. 03.80.21.46.50, fax 03.80.21.49.93, e-mail c.g.fournier@wanadoo.fr ☑ Ɪ by appt.

DOM. MAILLARD PERE ET FILS

Les Chaillots 1998★

■ 0.5 ha n.c. 70–99 F

A *climat*, or parcel of vineyard, near Corton, the illustrious Grand Cru. Daniel Maillard created his domaine in 1952, almost fifty years ago. He started with a few vines and now has 18 ha (45 acres). The light fruit in the 98 is the result of a meticulous extraction process. Made for keeping, its cards are still close to its chest. What does it smell of? Coffee, red fruit compote and preserved fruit in alcohol.

Dom. Maillard Père et Fils, 2, rue Joseph-Bard, 21200 Chorey-lès-Beaune, tel. 03.80.22.10.67, fax 03.80.24.00.42 ☑ Ɪ by appt.

DOM. MICHEL MALLARD ET FILS

Le Clos Royer 1997★★

■ 1.2 ha 4,000 70–99 F

This *climat* is very close to the village of Ladoix, and has produced a wine of great panache for the tasting. It will undoubtedly keep a long time. A deep, brilliant red colour with a lovely cocktail of soft fruit on the nose, packed with redcurrant and raspberry aromas. They follow through on the palate, which has well-balanced tannins. You can rely on the **Gréchons Village 98 Blanc**, one star, which will become more complex in three to five years.

Dom. Michel Mallard et Fils, 43, rte. de Dijon, 21550 Ladoix-Serrigny, tel. 03.80.26.40.64, fax 03.80.26.47.49 ☑ Ɪ by appt.

CATHERINE ET CLAUDE MARECHAL Les Chaillots 1998★

■ 0.63 ha 3,000 50–69 F

Brilliant purple, with undergrowth and gamey aromas, the body and texture do not disappoint. This is not a wine with strong acidity, so it can be drunk immediatley, to accompany a good roast Bresse chicken, for example.

EARL Catherine et Claude Maréchal, 6, rte. de Chalon, 21200 Bligny-lès-Beaune, tel. 03.80.21.44.37, fax 03.80.26.85.01 ☑ Ɪ by appt.

DOM. HENRI NAUDIN-FERRAND

La Corvée 1997★★

■ 1er cru 0.56 ha 3,343 70–99 F

Congratulations to the ladies once again. Anne and Claire Naudin produce a Ladoix of great class which has even picked up a *coup de*

BURGUNDY

cœur to pin to their grape hod. Perfect to the eye and the nose, with a good concentration of fruit with well-judged oak. While its roundess may well have immediate appeal on the palate, its structure means it will develop in the future. The half-hectare (just over one acre) at Corvée produces all the qualities you would expect to find in a Premier Cru. The comment on the tasting sheets of our jury was 'This is a great Burgundy'.
Dom. Henri Naudin-Ferrand, rue du Meix-Grenot, 21700 Magny-lès-Villers, tel. 03.80.62.91.50, fax 03.80.62.91.77, e-mail dom.hnf.@wanadoo.fr ☒ Y by appt.

DOM. NUDANT La Corvée 1997★

■ 1er cru 0.8 ha 5,600 70–99 F

A domaine of nearly 13 ha (32 acres) has produced a very translucent 97 with a fruity nose opening on a gamey note and a hit of kirsch. On the palate, it is fresh and well-made given the vintage. Wait two to three years to drink it. Also worth mentioning is the **Premier Cru Les Gréchons 98 Blanc**, strong gunflint aromas and fairly oaky, toasty and long; we awarded it one star.
Dom. Nudant, 11, R.N. 74, 21550 Ladoix-Serrigny, tel. 03.80.26.40.48, fax 03.80.26.47.13, e-mail domaine.nudant@wanadoo.fr ☒ Y by appt.

DOM. PARENT La Corvée 1997★

■ 1er cru 0.39 ha 2,400 70–99 F

This Premier Cru matures for eighteen months in oak casks. Cherry-red in colour, cherry and strawberry on the nose, well-balanced with delicate tannins. Very good, very elegant, and while it is already agreeable it should develop in three to five years.
SAE Dom. Parent, pl. de l'Eglise, 21630 Pommard, tel. 03.80.22.15.08, fax 03.80.24.19.33, e-mail parent-pommard@axnet.fr ☒ Y by appt.

LA MAISON PAULANDS
Les Briquottes 1998★

■ n.c. n.c. 50–69 F

This *négociant* (who also owns a well-known hotel and restaurant) is well-established in the village. Also worth mentioning is his **Champs Pussuet a Côte de Beaune Village Rouge 98**. Of their wines, we prefer Les Briquottes (on the hillside on the road going up to Magny-lès-Villers) which is a clear, straightforward red. The gamey notes blend with brandied fruits. It is fairly robust, and the fullness of body is strengthened by good tannins. It also has good acidity and should confirm our hopes as it ages.
Caves des Paulands, R.N. 74, 21550 Aloxe-Corton, tel. 03.80.26.41.05, fax 03.80.26.47.56, e-mail paulands@wanadoo.fr ☒ Y ev. day 8am–12 noon 2pm–6pm

DOM. PRIN 1997★

■ 1.19 ha 6,100 50–69 F

The parchment label does not come from the same era as the new commander who took over the tiller in 1994. This is an interesti Ladoix: cherry-red in colour, with aromas liquorice that are also evocative of peony. C the palate, Morello cherry comes to the fo within a structure enlivened by good acidit This well-balanced wine will open out aft keeping a year or two.
Dom. Prin, 12, rue de Serrigny, Cidex 10, 21550 Ladoix-Serrigny, tel. 03.80.26.40.63, fax 03.80.26.46.16 ☒ Y by appt.

Aloxe-Corto

Of the total classi fied as Corton and Corton Charlemagne, the Appellatio Aloxe-Corton applies only to a ver small part of the smallest commun of the Côte de Beaune; it produce 6,937 hl (181,137 gal) of red win and 36 hl (950 gal) of white wine i 1999. The Premiers Crus from her have a fine reputation: Le Maréchaudes, Les Valozières an Les Lolières (Grandes and Petites are the best-known.

The commune is ar important shipping centre an there are several châteaux, resplen dent with magnificent glazed tiles that are worth a visit. The Latou family owns a magnificent domair where the 19th-century vat room is a model of its type for making Burgundy wines.

ARNOUX PERE ET FILS 1998★

■ n.c. n.c. 70–99 F

A *Côte de Beaune Village* with a measure of delicacy: violet-purple, oaky and fruity at the same time, supple on the attack, well-balanced, and with liquorice flavours. It also has very fine tannins. Keep for two to three years.
Arnoux Père et Fils, rue des Brenots, 21200 Chorey-lès-Beaune, tel. 03.80.22.57.98, fax 03.80.22.16.85 ☒ Y by appt.

DENIS BOUSSEY Les Valozières 1998

■ 0.33 ha 2,400 70–99 F

Still not fully developed but, as it matures, could yet be awarded accolades. A wine with genuine potential. Its balance, but also its body guarantee that it will improve in the future. The *climat*, near to Les Bressandes produces both Premier Cru and *Côte de*

Beaune Village. And the nose? Leather, nut kernels, cherries.
🗝 Dom. Denis Boussey, rue du Pied-de-la-Vallée, 21190 Monthélie, tel. 03.80.21.21.23, fax 03.80.21.62.46 ☑ Y by appt.

DOM. CACHAT-OCQUIDANT ET FILS Les Maréchaudes 1998★

■ 1er cru 0.16 ha 1,100 ⏸ 100–149 F

This domaine is represented impressively this year. The *climat* is mainly in a Grand Cru area so it starts with a few bonus points. This is a 98 boasting cherry on the colour and the nose, lightly toasted, straightforward and quite a charmer.
🗝 Dom. Cachat-Ocquidant et Fils, pl. du Souvenir, 21550 Ladoix-Serrigny, tel. 03.80.26.45.30, fax 03.80.26.48.16 ☑ Y by appt.

CAPITAIN-GAGNEROT Les Moutottes 1997★★

■ 1er cru 1.04 ha 6,000 ⏸ 100–149 F

Moutottes and Mourottes are not to be confused. There are a few copper glints that suggest a little maturity, but on the magnificent nose there are raspberry and gamey notes. It has a good, rich body that is delicious, moderately tannic and without astringency. This 97 will be a pleasure to drink in two or three years.
🗝 Capitain-Gagnerot, 38, rte. de Dijon, 21550 Ladoix-Serrigny, tel. 03.80.26.41.36, fax 03.80.26.46.29 ☑ Y by appt.

PATRICK CLEMENCET La Coutière 1998★

■ 1er cru 0.77 ha 2,000 ⏸ 70–99 F

Heady, substantial and almost chewy, as unctuous and flashy as a Rubens, and as warming as a volcano. This isn't called Corton for nothing. Lord and master; somewhere between toastiness and blackberries, and purple edging towards black in colour. However, being a little more objective, it will need to age a year or so before it is served with *les œufs en meurette*.
🗝 Patrick Clémencet, pl. de l'Europe, 21630 Pommard, tel. 03.80.22.59.11, fax 03.80.24.17.32 ☑ Y by appt.

Côte de Beaune (North)

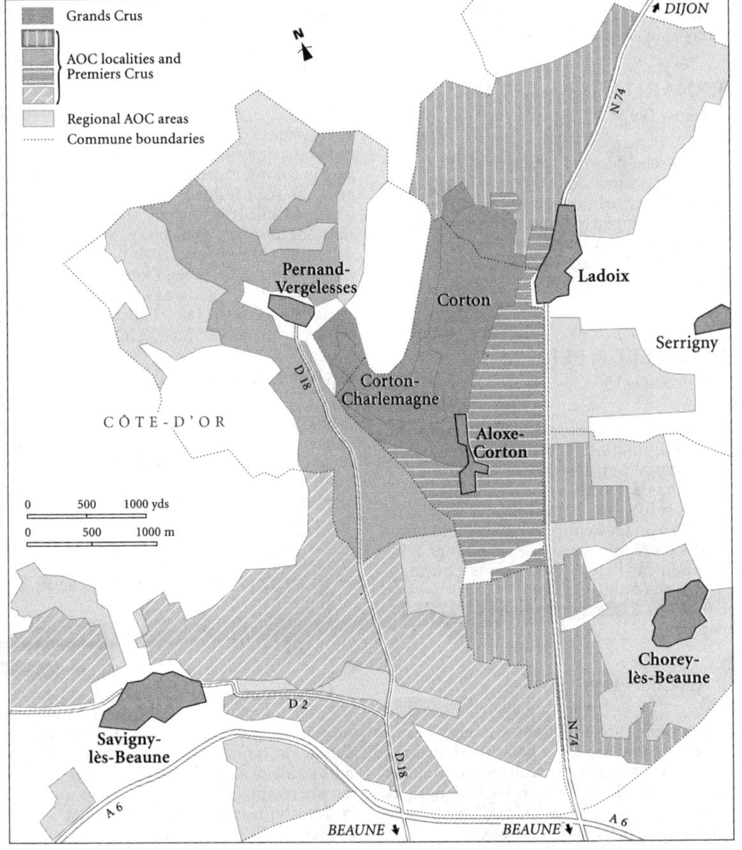

EDMOND CORNU ET FILS

Vieille vigne 1997★

■	1.98 ha	8,000	70–99 F

Fairly plump and rich, well-blended and silky as if it springs fully-formed out of the earth. There is just the right amount of acidity, and lots of mature fruit. It is slightly spicy with a strawberry jam nose and a good-looking mauvish-ruby colour. There is a note of optimism, but it is still very young. Do not uncork it too quickly.

EARL Edmond Cornu et Fils, Le Meix Gobillon, rue du Bief, 21550 Ladoix-Serrigny, tel. 03.80.26.40.79, fax 03.80.26.48.34 by appt.

JEAN-PIERRE DUBOIS-CACHAT

1998★

■	0.32 ha	1,500	70–99 F

This 98 is a real classic; purple with shades of violet in colour, and flavours of blackcurrant with a touch of vegetation. The tannins are still harsh, but they have character. The oak is well-mastered, and the wine will develop well as time passes, so the cockerel you should eat it with has time to grow.

Jean-Pierre Dubois, 2, Grande Rue, 21200 Chorey-lès-Beaune, tel. 03.80.22.27.83, fax 03.80.22.27.83 ev. day 8am–7pm

BERNARD DUBOIS ET FILS Les Brunettes 1997★

■	1.2 ha	6,000	70–99 F

A very classic wine with a brilliant garnet colour and a winey, foxy nose not unlike some Cortons. It is fairly savage, but has good acidity and is equipped to improve as time passes.

Dom. Bernard Dubois et Fils, 8, rue des Chobins, 21200 Chorey-lès-Beaune, tel. 03.80.22.13.56, fax 03.80.24.61.43 by appt.

DUFOULEUR PERE ET FILS

Les Valozières 1997

■ 1er cru	n.c.	1,200	200–249 F

This *climat* lies below Les Bressandes and can be scintillating. This wine has a superb soft cherry colour. The nose is young yet complex. It has a velvety attack then presents a tannic profile that is complete. Full-bodied and with average acidity, yet you should wait to drink it because it promises to mature well.

Dufouleur Père et Fils, 15, rue Thurot, 21700 Nuits-Saint-Georges, tel. 03.80.61.21.21, fax 03.80.61.11.23 by appt.

FRANCOIS GAY 1997

■	n.c.	4,500	100–149 F

The aromas are as equally straightforward on the nose and as on the palate with distinctive flavours of red berry fruit. But the colour did not provoke comment. The length is everything it should be. Good, well-made wine that is a little lively and oaky.

François Gay, 9, rue des Fiètres, 21200 Chorey-lès-Beaune, tel. 03.80.22.69.58, fax 03.80.24.71.42 by appt.

MICHEL GAY 1997★

■	1.23 ha	7,500	70–99 F

Here, we tasted a 97 dominated by its terroir. The name Corton makes certain demands on a wine, and this one meets them all. This is for you if like your wines young – but it will also keep a little while. Balsamic vinegar and liquoricey tints, with a deep cherry colour. A forceful, robust wine.

Michel Gay, 1B, rue des Brenôts, 21200 Chorey-lès-Beaune, tel. 03.80.22.22.73, fax 03.80.22.95.78 by appt.

CHRISTIAN GROS

Les Petites Lolières 1997

■ 1er cru	n.c.	n.c.	70–99 F

Les Petites Lolières vines are, naturally enough, next to the Grandes Lolières at Ladoix and not far from Le Rognet and Corton. A garnet-coloured wine showing a little maturity and a light nose: undergrowth, green pepper. It is not very fleshy, but holds its own and is not untypical of the vintage.

Christian Gros, rue de la Chaume, 21700 Premeaux-Prissey, tel. 03.80.61.29.74, fax 03.80.61.39.77 by appt.

DOM. DES HAUTES-CORNIERES

1997★

■	2 ha	11,000	70–99 F

Huysmans, who knew all about wine for the Mass, described this as a 'fruity' wine. It is pale in colour, vegetal and gamey on the nose, and the fruit follows through to the palate, which is full. It is sturdily structured with a smouldering, striking body. This marriage will last.

Ph. Chapelle et Fils, Dom. des Hautes-Cornières, 21590 Santenay, tel. 03.80.20.60.09, fax 03.80.20.61.01 ev. day except Sun. 9am–12 noon 2pm–6pm

DANIEL LARGEOT 1998★

■	0.6 ha	3,500	70–99 F

Balanced if a little tannic and with good length, it will improve in the next two years and will become a noticeable wine. The pretty colour has depth and the nose has breeding (the oakiness is well-judged). On the palate these are cherry stone flavours.

Daniel Largeot, 5, rue des Brenôts, 21200 Chorey-lès-Beaune, tel. 03.80.22.15.10, fax 03.80.22.60.62 by appt.

DOM. LOUIS LATOUR 1997★

■	5 ha	20,000	100–149 F

Already complex, red verging on black, rich and full, plump. Angelica and kirsch waft through on the nose. They say that the monumental vat house at Corton-Grancey will be in its stride in a few years, or in your cellar if you are tempted.

Maison Louis Latour, 18, rue des Tonneliers, 21200 Beaune,

.l. 03.80.24.81.00, fax 03.80.22.36.21, ·mail louislatour@louislatour.com Y by ppt.

DOM. MICHEL MALLARD ET FILS 1997★★

0.8 ha 4,500 100–149 F

A wine for great occasions. Ruby with bluh shades. It has clear intentions and legitiıate ambition. The nose is complex and elicate and blends sweet spices and freshlyathered blackcurrant. This 97 is robust, conentrated and marvellously eloquent. It hould age a little and will then be amongst he best.

Dom. Michel Mallard et Fils, 43, rte. de Dijon, 21550 Ladoix-Serrigny, el. 03.80.26.40.64, fax 03.80.26.47.49 Y y appt.

D. MEUNEVEAUX 1998★

1er cru 1 ha 3,000 100–149 F

Crushed morello cherry on the nose: you vant more and it gives it. A powerful palate. The acidity and tannins are very complimenary and accentuate the length of fruit. It vould readily accompany a game bird with a epper sauce. A Premier Cru worthy of its ıame.

Didier Meuneveaux, 21420 Aloxe-Corton, tel. 03.80.26.42.33 Y by appt.

DOM. NUDANT La Coutière 1997

1er cru 0.7 ha 4,500 100–149 F

A garnet-red Coutière with a fresh nose vith strong aromas of blackcurrant buds and vild rose. The body is well-structured with fullness and depth, and has length.

Dom. Nudant, 11, R.N. 74, 21550 Ladoix-Serrigny, tel. 03.80.26.40.48, fax 03.80.26.47.13, e-mail domaine.nudant@wanadoo.fr Y by appt.

DOM. CHRISTIAN PERRIN Les Boutières 1998★

n.c. 2,500 70–99 F

Christian Perrin takes a rational approach to wine-making: this is a better way of describing it than 'integrated'. But this is not the main issue. His Boutières 98 is perfectly straightforward, both in colour and on the nose, where soft fruit dominates the oak. Well-made, fairly concentrated and with good length. This is a very successful wine.

Christian Perrin, 14, av. de Corton, 21550 Ladoix-Serrigny, tel. 03.80.26.40.93, fax 03.80.26.48.40 Y ev. day except Sun. 8am–12 noon 2pm–6pm

DOM. POULLEAU PERE ET FILS 1998★

0.26 ha 1,600 70–99 F

Full and sturdy and with something in reserve. The colour is deep, the nose is Morello cherry and it seems to have a well-structured palate. It will keep for three or four years: stewed hare will be a good dish to accompany this wine. It has a bright future.

Dom. Poulleau Père et Fils, rue du Pied-de-la-Vallée, 21190 Volnay, tel. 03.80.21.62.61, fax 03.80.26.45.90 Y by appt.

DOM. RAPET PERE ET FILS 1997★

n.c. n.c. 70–99 F

Voltaire was a great admirer of the Corton growths, but his legendary impatience would have met its match here, because this is a wine for keeping. He would have appreciated its elegant fruit, complexity, balance and length and its brilliant ruby colour.

Dom. Rapet Père et Fils, 21420 Pernand-Vergelesses, tel. 03.80.21.59.94, fax 03.80.21.54.01 Y by appt.

DOM. GEORGES ROY ET FILS 1998

0.5 ha 3,000 70–99 F

A wine at a difficult moment in its development which needs to be kept for a few months. It has a pretty, intense colour, a delicate, fruity nose and a powerful body: good depth.

Dom. Georges Roy et Fils, 20, rue des Moutots, 21200 Chorey-lès-Beaune, tel. 03.80.22.16.28, fax 03.80.24.76.38 Y by appt.

DOM. DU COMTE SENARD 1997★★

3 ha 9,000 100–149 F

Philippe Sénard has produced a 97 with a distinctive flavour of the terroir, yet it comes from off the beaten track. The nose has minerals and fruit. On the palate it is full, pleasant and balanced. One taster exclaimed, 'At last, a wine with character'. Mature for its vintage, it will not be a wine to keep. It is a pleasure to drink immediately but could wait for a year or two.

SCE du Dom. Comte Sénard, 7, rempart Saint-Jean, 21200 Beaune, tel. 03.80.24.21.65, fax 03.80.24.21.44 Y ev. day except Sun. 10am–7pm

Pernand-Vergelesses

The village of Pernand is situated where two valleys meet, facing due south, and it is, beyond the slightest doubt, the most typical wine village on the Côte. Narrow streets, deep cellars, vine-clothed hillsides, enthusiastic growers and subtle wines have built the village a solid reputation, and of course the old Burgundian families have made a significant contribution, too. In 1999, 4,635 hl (122,364 gal) of red wines were produced; the most famous Premier Cru here is L'Ile des Vergelesses which has great finesse and fully deserves its reputation. Some excellent white wines are also made – 2,318 hl (61,195) in 1999.

ARNOUX PERE ET FILS 1998

□ 0.4 ha 1,900 70–99 F

Bleached-straw in colour with a nose of mirabelle plum and bergamot, or even resin. It is fresh on the palate and has traces of the garrigue and distinct acidity. None of these flavours and aromas clash. A wine better drunk in a year or two. The domaine has around 25 ha (62 acres).

Arnoux Père et Fils, rue des Brenots, 21200 Chorey-lès-Beaune, tel. 03.80.22.57.98, fax 03.80.22.16.85 by appt.

DOM. DES BALIVAUX 1998*

■ 0.8 ha 2,800 70–99 F

Garnet with bluish hues, this is a self-confident and powerful 98. It is a little oaky, definitely tannic, very well-structured, and has good depth. It has yet to open, but should do so in due course.

Dom. des Balivaux, chem. rural n° 29, 21700 Nuits-Saint-Georges, tel. 03.80.62.42.00, fax 03.80.61.28.13, e-mail nuicave@wanadoo.fr

BOUDIER PERE ET FILS

Les Fichots 1997*

■ 1er cru 1.1 ha 2,000 50–69 F

'Qui voit Pernand n'est pas dedans', a proverb meaning 'if you can see Pernand you are not in it'. You have to climb up to this village. Fleshy, strong, fruity, jammy and while this 97 is not firmly structured, it has undoubted appeal. Generally it is a good mouthful and has typical fruit for this grape variety. To enjoy in a year or two.

Pascal Boudier, rue de Pralot, 21420 Pernand-Vergelesses, tel. 03.80.21.56.43, fax 03.80.21.56.43 by appt.

DOM. CACHAT-OCQUIDANT ET FILS 1998*

□ 0.22 ha 1,100 70–99 F

The two wines produced here make a halt at this estate worth while. The Village Blanc is golden-grey and does not yet express itself fully. But behind the vanilla flavours from the cask, you can detect apricot and hazelnut. To begin with there are floral flavours; it is interesting and pleasant. The tasting jury was at pains to emphasise that there is a balance throughout the stages of tasting which reveals a consistency of character. The **Village Rouge 98** has a good constitution and should be left in the cellar for three years (50–69F).

Dom. Cachat-Ocquidant et Fils, pl. du Souvenir, 21550 Ladoix-Serrigny, tel. 03.80.26.45.30, fax 03.80.26.48.16 by appt.

DOM. CHANDON DE BRIAILLES

Ile des Vergelesses 1997**

□ 1er cru 1 ha 4,000 100–149

Here is nobility. There is a remarkable marriage between the nose and the palate worthy of the most perfect ceremony at Saint-Honoré-d'Eylau. With spring blossoms and lime, it is slightly buttery with glints of gold. On the palate, the flavours are so complex as to be almost labyrinthine. The wine is still developing and, if kept in the best cellar conditions will open over the next ten years, if you can bear to keep it that long. On the other hand, the **Vergelesses 97 Rouge** is ready for drinking (70–99F). You should order your wine now.

Dom. Chandon de Briailles, 1, rue Sœur Goby, 21420 Savigny-lès-Beaune, tel. 03.80.21.52.31, fax 03.80.21.59.15 by appt.

de Nicolay

DOM. CORNU 1997*

■ 0.39 ha 2,000 50–69 F

You will not find a wine here that is denser, darker or more intensley garnet. Flavours fall in the same range, coffee, leather and prune. This promising 97 has a charming first impression: it has plenty of stuffing and is not lacking in warmth . . .

Dom. Cornu, rue du Meix-Grenot, 21700 Magny-lès-Villers, tel. 03.80.62.92.05, fax 03.80.62.72.22 by appt.

DOM. DENIS PERE ET FILS

Ile des Vergelesses 1998*

■ 1er cru 0.35 ha 1,500 70–99 F

The **Village Rouge 98** is soft, full-bodied and well-structured. Clean with a discreet character. It receives one star (50–69F). This one has the exuberance of youth, as you can see from its vibrant colour with its touches of violet, and in its classic nose of spiced summer fruit. It is also full-bodied and well-structured; what we call a 'vin riche', (a rich wine), and needs to be left in the cellar for three or four years.

Dom. Denis Père et Fils, chem. des Vignes-Blanches, 21420 Pernand-Vergelesses, tel. 03.80.21.50.91, fax 03.80.26.10.32 by appt.

DOM. DOUDET Les Fichots 1998

■ 1er cru 0.6 ha n.c. 100–149 F

This is a fairly clear, deep purple 98. The strong tannins currently make it harsh. This is odd because the grapes are completely de-stalked in this winery, which was renovated in 1997. The vines are old, so perhaps this is where the tannins come from, because it has excellent structure. The wine should soften.

Dom. Doudet, 50, rue de Bourgogne, 21420 Savigny-lès-Beaune, tel. 03.80.21.51.74, fax 03.80.21.50.69 ☑ Y by appt.
⊶ Yves Doudet

DOM. JEAN FERY ET FILS 1997★★

■ 1er cru 0.39 ha 2,400 ◗ 70–99 F

We discussed in detail before we decided to award a *coup de cœur.* This wine is undoubtedly at the top of the range. Remarkable brilliance and the fruit (raspberry) is sincere. Its aromas are fine and exquisite, and it has a rare complexity with evident breeding. Holds its own in this vintage: but you should certainly not wait more than three years to drink it.
⊶ Dom. Jean Féry et Fils, 21420 Echevronne, tel. 03.80.21.59.60, fax 03.80.21.59.59 ☑ Y by appt.

DOM. JEAN-JACQUES GIRARD

Les Belles Filles 1998★

□ 0.35 ha 2,400 ◗ 70–99 F

The Copiaus family are young actors brought together in Perhand by Jacques Copeau (Marie-Hélène and Jean Dasté, etc.). They might well have put on a show for this wine. It is supple and round, attractively golden with a pretty nose and an appealing attack. Promises to have a good run over the next couple of years.
⊶ Dom. Girard, 16, rue de Cîteaux, 21420 Savigny-lès-Beaune, tel. 03.80.21.56.15, fax 03.80.26.10.08 ☑ Y by appt.

DOM. GIRARD-VOLLOT ET FILS 1997★★

□ 1er cru 0.42 ha 1,100 ◗ 70–99 F

A Premier Cru that knows its subject. Intense ruby colour, a forward or even opulent nose with touches of blackberry, game and tar. It is luscious without showing the least lack of structure or the slightest flabbiness. As a result of a sensitive but intelligent extraction process, it is rich, densely flavoured and well-supported by the tannins.
⊶ Dom. Girard, 16, rue de Cîteaux, 21420 Savigny-lès-Beaune, tel. 03.80.21.56.15, fax 03.80.26.10.08 ☑ Y by appt.

DOM. DOMINIQUE GUYON

Les Vergelesses 1997★

■ 1er cru 0.58 ha 3,600 ◗ 100–149 F

The **Village Blanc 98** is commended by the jury and is as elegant as it should be, with acacia flowers and peach in the background. The red Vergelesses is showered with compliments: intense and subtle, fleshy and round although still a little tannic, it unfolds its qualities with smoothness. Very true to type and definitely worth keeping.
⊶ Dom. Dominique Guyon, 21420 Savigny-lès-Beaune, tel. 03.80.67.13.24, fax 03.80.66.85.87, e-mail vins@guyon-bourgogne.com ☑ Y by appt.

DOM. ROGER JAFFELIN ET FILS

Creux de la Net 1997

■ 1er cru 0.58 ha 2,950 ◗ 70–99 F

With an average intensity, this 97 has ripe flavours (prune, quince). It is attractive, round and fleshy on the middle palate and has a long aromatic finish. It can wait a little longer but is almost ready to drink.
⊶ Roger Jaffelin et Fils, 21420 Pernand-Vergelesses, tel. 03.80.21.52.43, fax 03.80.26.10.39 ☑ Y ev. day 10am–12 noon 2pm–7pm; Sun. 10am–12 noon

DOM. LALEURE-PIOT 1998★

□ 1er cru 0.84 ha 5,000 ◗ 70–99 F

The domaine covers 10.5 ha (26 acres) and has made great strides in Pernand-Vergelesses. The **Village 98 Blanc** is recommended and has delicate flavours of green apple on its lengthy palate. The Premier Cru made by the fifth generation of this family of winemakers is something else. The colour has an inimitable green glint. The nose is fruit and minerals combined with a slight oakiness. Remarkably delicate and enlivened with a touch of curry spice. It has length and subtlety, so why wait, you might ask.? The **Village 98 Rouge** is awarded one star and has good potential as does the **Les Vergelesses Rouge 99**. They all come in the same price range.
⊶ Dom. Laleure-Piot, rue de Pralot, 21420 Pernand-Vergelesses, tel. 03.80.21.52.37, fax 03.80.21.59.48, e-mail laleure.piot@wanadoo.fr ☑ Y ev. day 8am–12 noon 2pm–6.30pm; Sat. Sun. by appt.
⊶ Frédéric Laleure

LE MANOIR MURISALTIEN

Sous le Bois de Noël et Belles Filles 1998★★

□ n.c. 2,000 ◗ 100–149 F

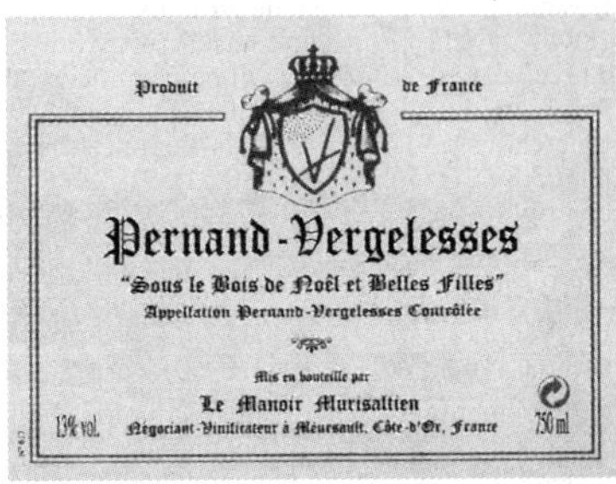

Sous le Bois de Noël et Belles Filles . . . The name is authentic. It owes nothing to the 'communications' industry, and is highly deserving of its *coup de cœur.* It has texture and complexity, and is very open with hints of hazelnut and hawthorn. This classy wine is 22-carat-gold in colour and has real character.
⊶ Le Manoir murisaltien, 4, rue du Clos-de-Mazeray, 21190 Meursault, tel. 03.80.21.21.83, fax 03.80.21.66.48, e-mail vin@demessey.com ☑ Y by appt.
⊶ Marc Dumont

BURGUNDY

JEAN-PHILIPPE MARCHAND 1998

■ n.c. n.c. 70–99 F

Jean-Philippe Marchand is a wine-grower and a *négociant-éleveur* in Gevrey-Chambertin who markets the Alfred Salbreux, Jean Virely and Jean-Philippe Marchand brands. He has sought out a Pernand with a straightforward red colour which has a gamey character on first impression and then develops a softness and a liquorice quality. There are a few hints of development that indicate its maturity. To be drunk now.

Dom. Jean-Philippe Marchand, 4, rue Souvert, B.P. 41, 21220 Gevrey-Chambertin, tel. 03.80.34.33.60, fax 03.80.34.12.77, e-mail marchand@axnet.com by appt.

PIERRE MAREY ET FILS 1998★

□ 2.45 ha 11,000 50–69 F

Finding a combination of freshness, greenness and fruit is not common. However, this wine has managed to do just that. It is rich with good structure while showing elegance and freshness. It has a golden-green colour that is classic, and while eucalyptus dominates the nose, there is a hint of apricot. The **Belles Filles 98 Rouge** is given the same mark, but this wine should wait for some time before being drunk.

Pierre Marey et Fils, rue Jacques-Copeau, 21420 Pernand-Vergelesses, tel. 03.80.21.51.71, fax 03.80.26.10.48 by appt.

JEAN-MARC PAVELOT

Les Vergelesses 1997★

■ 1er cru 0.61 ha 2,200 70–99 F

We are placing bets on this wine, which is showing its colours; it has a cherry hue and a nose of real breeding (raspberry with spring flowers). Vinous and virile with good length. It will stay the course and has a sturdy finish. Three years from now it will be a winner.

Jean-Marc Pavelot, 1, chem. des Guettottes, 21420 Savigny-lès-Beaune, tel. 03.80.21.55.21, fax 03.80.21.59.73 by appt.

ALBERT PONNELLE

Les Vergelesses 1997★

■ 1er cru n.c. n.c. 150–199 F

'Rarement mon verre je laisse quand je bois du vergelesses . . .' – a little rhyme meaning, 'when I drink Vergelesses, I rarely leave a drop in my glass'. And this wine is attractive enough to fix your gaze. It is quite 'dry' in style and this camouflages the soft, balanced notes of fruit. Cherry follows on from aromas of leather and quince. It benefits from being exposed to the air. One of our tasting team wrote that 'given due consideration, this is typical of wines from the foot of the Côte'.

Albert Ponnelle, Clos Saint-Nicolas, 38, fg Saint-Nicolas, 21200 Beaune, tel. 03.80.22.00.05, fax 03.80.24.19.73 by appt.

DOM. RAPET PERE ET FILS

Ile des Vergelesses 1998

■ 1er cru 0.65 ha 3,000 100–149 F

An Ile des Vergelesses that is hard to grasp at present. To look at, it is deep purple at the edge. It is bursting with scents of musk and black cherry. The personality of this wine is still being moulded, though you can detect some of its character. However, it is still rugged and harsh and will require a number of years to mature. The domaine is as old as the town: they still have a *tastevin* made by Rapet in 1792. The **Premier Cru Vergelesses 98 Blanc** is also interesting.

Dom. Rapet Père et Fils, 21420 Pernand-Vergelesses, tel. 03.80.21.59.94, fax 03.80.21.54.01 by appt.

DOM. ROLLIN PERE ET FILS 1998★

□ 1.5 ha 8,200 70–99 F

We tasted the white in the 98 vintage. Pale straw, and with a nose that meanders amongst new-mown hay, peony, lemon and apricot, it is well-balanced with a slightly acidic finish, something like citrus fruits, with just the slightest hint of rose. It will be long-lived.

Rollin Père et Fils, rte. des Vergelesses, 21420 Pernand-Vergelesses, tel. 03.80.21.57.31, fax 03.80.26.10.38 by appt.

NICOLAS ROSSIGNOL 1998

□ 0.12 ha 600 50–69 F

The colour is crystal clear and the aromas are citrus with bush peach. It is still somewhat closed but will open in time. Nicolas has been in charge since 1997. The younger generation inspires confidence.

Nicolas Rossignol, rue de Mont, 21190 Volnay, tel. 03.80.21.62.43, fax 03.80.21.27.61 by appt.

CH. ROSSIGNOL-JEANNIARD

Les Fichots 1997

■ 1er cru 0.9 ha 1,500 70–99 F

Grown on the hillside of Vergelesses and less well-known, this wine has the qualities of the famous Premier Cru. The 97 is dark cherry and has a very typical Pinot nose which opens with crystallised fruit, as it breathes. It is robust and well-structured and typical of wines produced by current vinification methods. Very concentrated with strong tannins, suggesting that it should keep a long time.

Ch. Rossignol-Jeanniard, rue de Mont, 21190 Volnay, tel. 03.80.21.62.43, fax 03.80.21.27.61 by appt.

Corton

The 'Corton Mountain' is made up of different types of soil and produces different wines at different levels of the slope. Topped with woods that grow on hard limestone from the Rauracian period (Superior Oxfordian), the Argovian marlstone emerges as white soil for several score metres, and is particularly good for white wines. These soils also cover shelves of pearly limestone incorporating numerous large oyster shells, overlaid by brown soil favourable for producing red wines.

The names of the *lieux-dits* appear under the Appellation Corton, and can be used for white wines but are mainly known for reds. Les Bressandes is produced on the red soils, which give the wine power and finesse. On the other hand, on the higher slopes of Les Renards, Les Languettes and the Clos du Roy, the white soils produce well-structured red wines which, as they age, take on the gamey, 'sauvage' scents that can be found in the Mourottes de Ladoix. Corton is the biggest producer of the Grand Crus – 3,692 hl (97,469 gal) of reds and 130 hl (3,432 gal) of whites.

BERTRAND AMBROISE

Le Rognet 1997★

■Gd cru 0.66 ha n.c. 200–249 F

In the past, when a wine showed the hardness that is typical of this growth when it is young, it was said to 'corton'. This lively, big wine is indeed 'cortonning' and is built to age. There is no doubt that it will give free rein to its potential in due course. It is highly concentrated and as yet has hardly opened, but its aromas are already distinct (blackcurrant and bilberry). We look forward to trying it again when it has opened fully.

Maison Bertrand Ambroise, rue de l'Eglise, 21700 Premeaux-Prissey, tel. 03.80.62.30.19, fax 03.80.62.38.69, e-mail bertrand.ambroise@wanadoo.fr ▼ Y by appt.

DOM. D'ARDHUY Renardes 1997

■Gd cru 2.06 ha 2,262 150–199 F

There are many literary allusions to Corton, not least M. Lampre, a character of Huysmans', who said: 'There is certain beauty and unquestionable art in the flavour, the colour and the bouquet of a Corton.' And this wine is a perfect illustration. Ruby-red with shades of blue, this 97 hints at redcurrant with underlying musky notes. There is an acrid hint from the oak on the palate which is fresh enough and lengthy, mouth-filling with a lively finish. The Domaine d'Ardhuy is part of the family that owns La Reine Pédauque.

Dom. d'Ardhuy, Clos des Langres, 21700 Corgoloin, tel. 03.80.62.98.73, fax 03.80.62.95.15 ▼ Y ev. day except Sun. 10am–12 noon 2pm–6pm

ARNOUX PERE ET FILS

Rognet 1998★

■Gd cru 0.33 ha 1,500 150–199 F

82 83 89 90 **|91|** |92| **97** 98

In 1984, the domaine grew to 33 ha (82 acres) when some of Charles Viénot's vineyards were acquired. Being the owner of a Grand Cru is like having an aristocrat's coat of arms. The 98 is very robust and is a fine red colour. It is open and complex with aromas of blackberry and a hint of vanilla, and has well-balanced, mellow tannins. Perfect with a good rib of beef, but you will have to wait three years minimum.

Arnoux Père et Fils, rue des Brenots, 21200 Chorey-lès-Beaune, tel. 03.80.22.57.98, fax 03.80.22.16.85 ▼ Y by appt.

JEAN-CLAUDE BELLAND

Clos de la Vigne au Saint 1998★

■Gd cru 0.48 ha 2,600 150–199 F

We tasted **Les Grèves** and **Les Perrières 98**: two good wines, commended by the jury. The colour of the Clos de la Vigne au Saint is full and its nose is opening little by little (cherry). It is soft and silky, perfectly balanced and a real Grand Cru with elegance and distinction. This *climat*, indeed, has a reputation for its finesse and capacity for ageing (the soils are quite clayey).

Jean-Claude Belland, 45, Grande-Rue, 21590 Santenay, tel. 03.80.20.61.90, fax 03.80.20.65.60 ▼ Y by appt.

BONNEAU DU MARTRAY 1997★

■Gd cru 1.6 ha 4,000 200–249 F

(80) 86 87 88 |89| |90| 91 92 |93| **94** 95 **96** 97

Any descendent of the Marquise de Sévigné, the great letter writer, could be expected to have style. This is the case here but it will be a little time before the signature of this wine will be recognisably formed. This should not be surprising because successful 97s are often like this. This one has a freshness and spontaneity with a mixture of aromas (musk and summer fruit) which make it tempting to swallow the wine down in one go. However, our advice is that it should be put to one side for three or four years.

Dom. Bonneau du Martray, 21420 Pernand-Vergelesses, tel. 03.80.21.50.64, fax 03.80.21.57.19 ▼

de la Morinière

DOM. CACHAT-OCQUIDANT ET FILS Clos des Vergennes 1998★

■Gd cru 1.42 ha 3,500 150–199 F

86 **87** 88 |**90**| 91 95 96 97 98

The estate bought this vineyard almost by chance in 1937. Since he missed out on the chance to buy the house he had his eye on at auction, Maurice Cachat's father-in-law had to make do with this small parcel of 1.42 ha (3.5 acres). The family are grateful that he did. The nose of this intensely coloured wine is slightly fiery and aggressive but, on the palate, the flavours overflow. It is fleshy, at first, then tannic and will undoubtedly mature well in the cellar. You should be able to enjoy it two to three years.

Dom. Cachat-Ocquidant et Fils, pl. du Souvenir, 21550 Ladoix-Serrigny, tel. 03.80.26.45.30, fax 03.80.26.48.16 Y by appt.

CAPITAIN-GAGNEROT

Les Renardes 1997

■Gd cru 0.33 ha 1,500 250–299 F

82 83 85 86 88 (89) **90** 91 92 96 97

In Burgundy 'nothing goes to waste'. A few years ago, the stones from the old prison at Beaune were used build the cellar at this domaine, and the feeling of liberation that can be tasted in this 97 must be down to them. It is ready to take flight. Light ruby in colour, but within the normal range, and with harsh tannins that need to soften. There is such an upfront aroma of cherry preserved in eau-de-vie that we could almost put it on a conditional discharge right away and say it is nearly ready to drink.

Capitain-Gagnerot, 38, rte. de Dijon, 21550 Ladoix-Serrigny, tel. 03.80.26.41.36, fax 03.80.26.46.29 Y by appt.

CHAMPY PERE ET CIE

Bressandes 1997★★

■Gd cru n.c. 800 250–299 F

There are the Cortons from Aloxe and others from Ladoix. This is one of the former, coming from right in the middle of the hillside. The *climat* has the reputation for being very approachable, and it is true of this wine. The colour is very intense and generous with a whiff of blackcurrant buds and cherry in eau-de-vie, and it is surprisingly powerful on the palate.

Maison Champy, 5, rue du Grenier-à-Sel, 21200 Beaune, tel. 03.80.25.09.99, fax 03.80.25.09.95 Y by appt.

Pierre Meurgey

DOM. DES HERITIERS PAUL CHANSON PERE ET FILS

Vergennes 1997

□Gd cru n.c. 500 300–499 F

Here's a riddle: can a white Corton also include the name of its *climat*, as with this Vergennes? It can indeed, though it is very rare. If you collect wine labels, this is one to add to your collection, though the colour of the wine is not mentioned on it. In short, this is a successful wine in all aspects, with a lingering honeyed nose and a fairly full body. It is still a little restrained and has a quiet nature, but is developing one step at a time.

Dom. des Héritiers Paul Chanson Père et Fils, 10, rue Paul-Chanson, 21200 Beaune, tel. 03.80.22.33.00, fax 03.80.24.17.42, e-mail tmarion@vins-chanson.com Y by appt.

MAURICE CHAPUIS Perrières 1997★

■Gd cru n.c. 4,000 100–149 F

|91| |92| 96 97

Maurice Chapuis, the man running this vineyard, studied English literature before coming here in 1985 when he became hooked on wine. His brother Claude has written several books about the vineyard. This Perrières has a good-looking, deep ruby colour. The main aromas are spices and stewed fruit. The 97 is powerful and warming but with a tiny dry note that is a sin of its youth, which will more than likely disappear after two or three years. It already has a lovely balance.

Maurice Chapuis, 21420 Aloxe-Corton, tel. 03.80.26.40.89, fax 03.80.26.40.99 Y by appt.

PATRICK CLEMENCET

Les Grandes Lolières 1998★

■Gd cru 0.92 ha 2,000 100–149 F

This *climat* in Grandes Lolières covers nearly a hectare (almost 2.5 acres) and is brusque and rustic like Ladoix. A deep garnet colour, this 98 opens up gradually with blackcurrant aromas. It is quite hard and has harsh tannins, but indicates its terroir by a trace of mushroom. Lovers of this Grand Cru know the wine is like that when young and that it needs a good four or five years to open and ready itself for beauty parades.

Patrick Clémencet, pl. de l'Europe, 21630 Pommard, tel. 03.80.22.59.11, fax 03.80.24.17.32 Y by appt.

DOM. CORNU 1997

■Gd cru 0.61 ha 2,600 150–199 F

The singer Maurice Chevalier used to claim that drinking Corton was good for the voice. True or not, he was a faithful client. Light ruby in colour and with very ripe aromas (cooked prune, leather, undergrowth), and a lightness that is often the case with this vintage.

Dom. Cornu, rue du Meix-Grenot, 21700 Magny-lès-Villers, tel. 03.80.62.92.05, fax 03.80.62.72.22 Y by appt.

EDMOND CORNU ET FILS

Bressandes 1997★★★

■Gd cru 0.56 ha 1,800 150–199 F

This is not the first time that this domaine's Corton has been highly praised. The Bressandes 90 was very successful. So lightning strikes again. Barely half a hectare (about one acre) of vines has produced one of those wines that literally blew the jury away. A fistful of keys to unlock a Corton, with its

violet-shaded garnet colour and awash with flavours of black cherry and blackcurrant buds, very soft yet subtle. What grace and ease. It matures with great finesse. Superb.

🗝 EARL Edmond Cornu et Fils, Le Meix Gobillon, rue du Bief, 21550 Ladoix-Serrigny, tel. 03.80.26.40.79, fax 03.80.26.48.34 ☑ 🍷 by appt.

DOM. DUPONT-TISSERANDOT

Le Rognet 1998★

■Gd cru 0.32 ha 1,600 ⏸ 150–199 F

The northernmost of the Cortons located at Ladoix-Serrigny, this wine has a fairly light colour. In contrast, its nose has great strength of conviction with hints of violet and blackcurrant leaves. It has certainly not yet filled out, but is an authentic Pinot Noir with its fruit and roundness. A lovely mouthful that can be drunk immediately.

🗝 GAEC Dupont-Tisserandot, 2, pl. des Marronniers, 21220 Gevrey-Chambertin, tel. 03.80.34.10.50, fax 03.80.58.50.71 ☑ 🍷 by appt.

DOM. ESCOFFIER Clos du Roi 1997★

■Gd cru 0.57 ha 3,090 ⏸ 100–149 F

The Clos du Roi is the most representative of the Corton wines. Red soils and marls meet here and complement each other. This wine is bottled at the Clos des Langes (La Juvinière) and has a subtle colour. A delicate nose of kirsch. If it lacks body, it has plenty of finesse. All in very good taste, just like its attractive label.

🗝 Franck Escoffier, 16, rue du Parc, 71350 Géanges, tel. 03.85.49.98.22, fax 03.85.49.98.22, e-mail domaine.escoffier@wanadoo.fr ☑ 🍷 by appt.

CLOS DES CORTONS FAIVELEY

1997★★★

■Gd cru 2.97 ha 8,730 ⏸ 300–499 F

85 86 **88** 89 |90| |91| 92 94 (95) **96 97**

A decision of the Court (1930) gave the J. Faiveley house the right to name its wines Clos des Cortons according to old traditions, and from that time the family name itself was also permitted to be mentioned. This is why this vineyard of only 2.97 ha (7.3 acres) is practically the only one in Burgundy to carry the name of a living person. This year's wine came very close to a *coup de cœur*. Good intensity and maturity at all stages of tasting. Bilberry, blackberry, toasted flavours with a touch of vanilla. A structure rich in fine tannins that are also very elegant. In a few words: a wonderful wine.

🗝 Bourgognes Faiveley, 8, rue du Tribourg, 21700 Nuits-Saint-Georges, tel. 03.80.61.04.55, fax 03.80.62.33.37, e-mail bourgognes.faiveley@wanadoo.fr ☑ 🍷 ev. day 9am–12 noon 2pm–6pm; cl. 21 Jul.–21 Aug.

DOM. FOLLIN-ARBELET

Bressandes 1997★

■Gd cru 0.5 ha 1,000 ⏸ 150–199 F

The colour is pale, but what followed in no way displeased the panel. It had attractive aromas of fresh cherry with spice and evident oak. On the palate it is vanilla, but there is good balance and it is well-structured with velvety tannins. It leaves a balanced impression which encourages you to taste more. As for the 'straight' **Corton 98**, it is powerful, oaky and will be good to drink with game in three to eight years' time.

🗝 Dom. Follin-Arbelet, Les Vercots, 21420 Aloxe-Corton, tel. 03.80.26.46.73, fax 03.80.26.43.32 ☑ 🍷 by appt.

MICHEL GAY Les Renardes 1998

■Gd cru 0.21 ha 900 ⏸ 150–199 F

96 **97** 98

This wine has good character and agreeable fruit: when we tasted it in April 2000, there was morello cherry supported by strong oak, but within an acceptable range. Its mellow character does not suggest great concentration, but the wine is bright, carmine-red which compliments the delicacy of the citrus fruit flavours. Buy it to drink in the next two years but not to keep.

🗝 Michel Gay, 1B, rue des Brenôts, 21200 Chorey-lès-Beaune, tel. 03.80.22.22.73, fax 03.80.22.95.78 ☑ 🍷 by appt.

DOM. ANNE-MARIE GILLE

Les Renardes 1998★

■Gd cru 0.16 ha 800 ⏸ 150–199 F

These two wines from Les Renardes stand apart from most of the Cortons, drifting away from the usual floral or fruity aromas. They are more in the wild game range. Tradition is well-respected in the essentials. This vermilion-coloured wine improves on opening, and is slightly liquorice in flavour, edging towards bilberry. This 98 is well-developed already and should be drunk now. The domaine is based at Comblanchien and the Grand Cru (16 a/0.4 acres) is their pride and joy – and not without reason.

🗝 Dom. Anne-Marie Gille, 34, R.N. 74, 21700 Comblanchien, tel. 03.80.62.94.13, fax 03.80.62.99.88, e-mail gille@burgundywines.net ☑ 🍷 by appt.

DOM. ANTONIN GUYON

Clos du Roy 1997★

■Gd cru 0.55 ha 3,000 ⏸ 200–249 F

Corton has a preferential place in *Bel-Ami* in which Guy de Maupassant remarks, 'Complete contentment, contentment of life and thought, of body and spirit' are to be found in a great Corton. This is a fine example, deep ruby in colour, with an inviting nose and a fleshy, round and flattering palate. Recently the Antonin Guyon business took over a significant part of the Thévenot-Bussière domaine. The panel also tasted a **Bressandes 97**: a big Corton with a burly body that is an all-conquering king of the Bon-Vivants. Same level of quality.

🔑 Dom. Antonin Guyon, 21420 Savigny-lès-Beaune, tel. 03.80.67.13.24, fax 03.80.66.85.87, e-mail vins@guyon-bourgogne.com ☑ 🍷 by appt.

DOM. LALEURE-PIOT

Le Rognet 1998★★★

■Gd cru 0.35 ha 1,200 🛢 150–199 F

By reputation, the Florentine painters are more interested in line and form: the Venetian painters, on the other hand, more taken by colour. This Rognet excels in both. It is a *coup de cœur* from a tiny parcel. A deep garnet colour with violet touches, the nose has a great depth of bilberry fruit which has been lightly grilled. Its composition (dense fruit; tightly woven, magnificent structure) took it to the top in this closely-fought tasting. Also worth noting, the **Bressandes 98**, with two stars, which is classic and full-bodied with some delicately lacey attributes.

🔑 Dom. Laleure-Piot, rue de Pralot, 21420 Pernand-Vergelesses, tel. 03.80.21.52.37, fax 03.80.21.59.48, e-mail laleure.piot@wanadoo.fr ☑ 🍷 ev. day 8am–12 noon 2pm–6.30pm; Sat. Sun. by appt.

DOM. MAILLARD PERE ET FILS

Renardes 1998★★

■Gd cru 0.34 ha n.c. 🛢 150–199 F

The Corton 95 was outstanding, while the Corton-Renardes, 93 and 90 vintages from this estate were also excellent: this Renardes has staying power. It is developing hesitantly, which is appealingly touching. Every wine is affected in different ways. Some toastiness accompanies the Pinot on the nose. It is massive on the palate, with blackcurrant and liquorice, and has good oak, which suggests it will keep four or five years. It is worth bearing in mind that the pillars of the cellar at Clos de Vougeot are equally massive. This 34 a (0.8 acre) parcel of the vineyard is well-managed by the wine-producer.

🔑 Dom. Maillard Père et Fils, 2, rue Joseph-Bard, 21200 Chorey-lès-Beaune, tel. 03.80.22.10.67, fax 03.80.24.00.42 ☑ 🍷 by appt.

DOM. MAILLARD PERE ET FILS

1998★★

□Gd cru 1.1 ha n.c. 🛢 150–199 F

White Corton wines were originally regarded with some mistrust. Generally speaking, Chardonnay has been planted in place of Pinot Noir. And there you have it: this has produced a white Corton *coup de cœur,* though it does not measure up to Corton Charlemagne. A very pure wine that is admirably balanced with perfect unison between the eye, the nose and the palate. It will be a great 98 in the future.

🔑 Dom. Maillard Père et Fils, 2, rue Joseph-Bard, 21200 Chorey-lès-Beaune, tel. 03.80.22.10.67, fax 03.80.24.00.42 ☑ 🍷 by appt.

DOM. MICHEL MALLARD ET FILS Les Renardes 1997★

■Gd cru 0.32 ha 1,500 🛢 200–249 F

This is an old family from Ladoix-Serrigny. Deep garnet yet brilliant, with a straightforward nose. A trace of blackcurrant can be detected behind the spicy flavours of the cask. On the palate it is powerful, yet there is more to come, and it has good length. We also tasted the **Rognet 97** (150–199F) which is commended by the panel.

🔑 Dom. Michel Mallard et Fils, 43, rte. de Dijon, 21550 Ladoix-Serrigny, tel. 03.80.26.40.64, fax 03.80.26.47.49 ☑ 🍷 by appt.

MALLARD-GAULIN

Renardes 1997★★

■Gd cru 0.6 ha 1,900 🛢 300–499 F

You can confidently choose **Les Hautes-Mourottes 97** which is highly-coloured and well-built. It is commended by the jury but needs time to develop. A better alternative is this wine. Built like *La Grande Pyramide*, it is vinous and its complexity has yet to be discovered. A deep purple with aromas of leather and undergrowth, it is full-bodied, solid and well-structured and unmistakably a Renardes. Its acidity bodes well for a good future.

🔑 Maison Mallard-Gaulin, 21420 Aloxe-Corton, tel. 03.80.26.46.10, fax 03.80.26.43.57

DOM. MARATRAY-DUBREUIL

Bressandes 1998

■Gd cru 0.71 ha 2,500 100–149 F

This is a Bressandes that conforms exactly to Claude Chapuis' description of the wine in his book on Corton. Its silky colour is crimson-purple and it has a subtle blend of vanilla and black cherry. Supple, and very drinkable. There is no harshness: it is round and plump and will keep between five and ten years.

Dom. Maratray-Dubreuil, 5, pl. du Souvenir, 21550 Ladoix-Serrigny, tel. 03.80.26.41.09, fax 03.80.26.49.07 by appt.

DOM. NUDANT Bressandes 1998*

■Gd cru n.c. 3,000 150–199 F

This has a few trumps. The nose is certainly one that helps to win the hand: it is velvety-blackcurrant with delicate overtones of roasted coffee. The palate starts with suppleness and slightly spicy fruit. The hand does not have much depth, and most of its tricks are played in the flavours. It could even pick up enough to make a small slam. The tannins are well-balanced and the liquorice flavours most appealing. Rather than drinking it with beef 'Maître de Chai', it would go better with small game birds or good poultry.

Dom. Nudant, 11, R.N. 74, 21550 Ladoix-Serrigny, tel. 03.80.26.40.48, fax 03.80.26.47.13, e-mail domaine.nudant@wanadoo.fr by appt.

DOM. PARENT Les Renardes 1997

■Gd cru 0.3 ha 800 150–199 F

Voltaire experimented with wine-growing at Ferney, taking the Corton hill as his model. He was not successful, so instead he became a regular customer for Burgundy wines supplied by the Chatelain of Aloxe. At that time, the Parent family was already cultivating its garden, or rather vineyard. Their Renardes 97 has kept a bright youthful colour. The nose is just opening out, showing pepper and cherry. A supple first impression, interesting body and an attractive finish.

SAE Dom. Parent, pl. de l'Eglise, 21630 Pommard, tel. 03.80.22.15.08, fax 03.80.24.19.33, e-mail parent-pommard@axnet.fr by appt.

PAULANDS Rognet 1998

■Gd cru n.c. n.c. 150–199 F

Madam Coulot started up business here a good century ago. The activity now includes a hotel-restaurant on the edge of the RN 74, a *negoçiant* business ,and a estate growing vines and producing wine. This garnet-coloured Rognet puts its back into it right from the nose. Freshness and liveliness with a hint of bitterness and good oak: a wine to keep. Later we will do it greater honour.

Caves des Paulands, R.N. 74, 21550 Aloxe-Corton, tel. 03.80.26.41.05, fax 03.80.26.47.56, e-mail paulands@wanadoo.fr ev. day 8am–12 noon 2pm–6pm

C. Fasquel

DOM. DU PAVILLON

Le Clos des Maréchaudes 1997*

■Gd cru 0.54 ha 3,000 300–499 F

This *climat* is squeezed between Vergennes and Paulands and is on the border of the village of Ladoix and the Bressandes vineyard. These 54 a (1.33 acres) produce a wine that is very representative of this vintage, or will be when it has opened out more. Its colour is not only usual, but even quite good for the year, with a nose somewhere between vegetal and fruity. It is well-balanced with finesse and liveliness. Fairly elegant, it will keep for an average length of time. The domaine belongs to the firm of Albert Bichot.

Dom. du Pavillon, 6 bis, bd Jacques-Copeau, 21200 Beaune, tel. 03.80.24.37.37, fax 03.80.24.37.38

DOM. JACQUES PRIEUR

Bressandes 1997*

■Gd cru 0.76 ha 1,750 300–499 F

This estate was put under the watchful management of the Antonin-Rodet team. It has produced a 97 with good colour for the year. Kirsch flavours follow through, and it has good body, which means the wine can be confident of a good future.

Dom. Jacques Prieur, 6, rue des Santenots, 21190 Meursault, tel. 03.80.21.23.85, fax 03.80.21.29.19 by appt.

DOM. PRIN Bressandes 1997**

■Gd cru 0.65 ha 2,600 150–199 F

'This year, next year' . . . Better to forget this wine for a few years, but certainly not 'sometime never'. This quality wine needs time to reach perfection. The Corton is dark purple and has a nose that has hints of game and meat with underlying aromas of clove and nutmeg. On the palate it is full body, with a toasty finish that is 'very pretty'.

Dom. Prin, 12, rue de Serrigny, Cidex 10, 21550 Ladoix-Serrigny, tel. 03.80.26.40.63, fax 03.80.26.46.16 by appt.

DOM. RAPET PERE ET FILS

1998**

■Gd cru 1 ha 3,000 150–199 F

Like the **Pougets 98** it has been very well-made indeed, and has all the necessary attributes to be assertive. This 'straight' Corton found unanimous approval. Strong but not overpowering, and it is so superb and fine that it could have been chiselled out of marble. It is a little austere, but has a very strong personality and the right qualities for keeping. It should be allowed to breathe, or even decanted.

Dom. Rapet Père et Fils, 21420 Pernand-Vergelesses, tel. 03.80.21.59.94, fax 03.80.21.54.01 by appt.

COMTE SENARD Clos du Roi 1998*

■Gd cru 1 ha 1,500 ⏸ 200–249 F

This estate was established around 1865 and belonged to an important Burgundy family that provided France with an Ambassador and a Grand Master of the Confrérie des Chevaliers du Tastevin, etc. Philippe is continuing the good work started by Daniel, his father. The colour is bright, and while this 98 is already quite elegant, it is not yet ready to come out. Its tannins are too immature at this stage and need to develop in the right way. However, the wine is well-structured and well bred.

⊶ SCE du Dom. Comte Sénard, 7, rempart Saint-Jean, 21200 Beaune, tel. 03.80.24.21.65, fax 03.80.24.21.44 ☑ Y ev. day except Sun. 10am–7pm

DOM. THOMAS Clos du Roi 1997*

■Gd cru 0.84 ha 4,500 ⏸ 200–249 F

The intense, consistent colour deserves compliments. The nose seems delicate, its approach is reticent but could well be more complex than it appears at first. This 97 is unctuous, fleshy and rich, and would certainly hold its own in the presence of any king. It is a very generous wine and it would be wiser to enjoy its generosity now because it is unlikely to last. Here we are talking about the vines owned by the Thomas family (who also own Moillard, Grivot at Nuits).

⊶ Dom. Thomas, chem. rural n° 29, 21700 Nuits-Saint-Georges, tel. 03.80.62.42.00, fax 03.80.61.28.13, e-mail nuicave@wanadoo.fr Y by appt.

⊶ SCI du Clos de Thorey

THOMAS-BASSOT 1996*

■Gd cru n.c. n.c. ⏸ 200–249 F

This wine is crying out to be drunk with very splendid dishes such as flambéed woodcock, haunch of wild boar, thrush, partridge and all those dishes you do not eat every day. The 96 (please note the year) with its aromas of cherry stones and a suppleness but lightness makes a very good impression. It should be drunk now. Thomas-Bassot is a house that has been taken over by Jean-Claude Boisset.

⊶ Thomas-Bassot, 5, quai Dumorey, 21700 Nuits-Saint-Georges, tel. 03.80.62.61.61, fax 03.80.62.37.38

DOM. MICHEL VOARICK
Clos du Roi 1998

■Gd cru 0.5 ha 1,800 ⏸ 150–199 F

The domaine was established by Pierre Voarick, Jean-Marc's grandfather, who was the wine-maker for the Hospices de Beaune in the 1920s. For a long time he was in charge of the famous Docteur Peste *cuvée*. It is strong and velvety like all Clos du Roi wines should be. The colour of this 98 is maturing slightly, but its aromas are persistent (toasty flavours with hints of blackcurrant followed by kirsch). A fairly tannic and bold wine.

⊶ Jean-Marc Voarick, 2, pl. du Chapitre, 21420 Aloxe-Corton, tel. 03.80.26.40.44, fax 03.80.26.41.22, e-mail Voarick.Michel@aol.com ☑ Y by appt.

Corton-Charlemagne

There was an Appellation Charlemagne, which until 1948 could have Aligoté grapes added to it, but this is no longer used. In 1999, Appellation Corton-Charlemagne produced 2,562 hl (67,637 gal), most of it grown in the communes of Pernand-Vergelesses and Aloxe-Corton. The wines of this appellation — which owe their name to the Emperor Charles the Great who apparently ordered white grapes to be planted so the wines would not stain his beard — are a lovely greenish-gold and reach their peak after five or ten years.

BERTRAND AMBROISE 1998**

□Gd cru 0.22 ha n.c. ⏸ 200–249 F

A *coup de cœur* with a winner's laurels. This *négociant-éleveur* does not lose a single mark for his wine in this edition of our *Guide*. His 98 is concentrated, soft and it has good complexity and so has everything going for it. Without taking back on any of these compliments we need to mention the evident – and very good – oakiness. The character and structure of the wine alone is fantastic.

⊶ Maison Bertrand Ambroise, rue de l'Eglise, 21700 Premeaux-Prissey, tel. 03.80.62.30.19, fax 03.80.62.38.69, e-mail bertrand.ambroise@wanadoo.fr ☑ Y by appt.

DOM. BERTAGNA 1997★

□Gd cru 0.25 ha 1,050 300–499 F

The cellar-master here has just become a director of the Hospices de Beaune. This is an indication of where we are in the Burgundy hierarchy. The 97 is still his work. A pale yellow Charlemagne, nestling in the finesse of its fruit. A bit crude at the moment, but it is noble and will keep for some time to come.

Dom. Bertagna, rue du Vieux-Château, 21640 Vougeot, tel. 03.80.62.86.04, fax 03.80.62.82.58, e-mail bertagna@wanadoo.fr by appt.

DOM. BONNEAU DU MARTRAY 1997

□Gd cru 9.5 ha 43,000 300–499 F

79 83 |90| |91| |92| 93 95 96 97

Sainte Jeanne de Chantal appears on the genealogical tree of this family. The wine has a golden halo and a citrus fruit nose that is still cloistered. It has breeding with more length than depth. A wine with a long future.

Dom. Bonneau du Martray, 21420 Pernand-Vergelesses, tel. 03.80.21.50.64, fax 03.80.21.57.19

de la Morinière

DOM. BOUCHARD PERE ET FILS 1997★

□Gd cru 3.25 ha n.c. 300–499 F

In 1909, Bouchard bought a single parcel of nearly 7 ha (17 acres) of the Corton and Corton-Charlemagne vineyards. It provides an elegant wine that has a pale straw colour with an open floral nose in a sophisticated, heady style.

Bouchard Père et Fils, Ch. de Beaune, 21200 Beaune, tel. 03.80.24.80.24, fax 03.80.22.55.88, e-mail france@bouchard.pereetfils.com by appt.

CHAMPY PERE ET CIE 1997

□Gd cru n.c. n.c. 300–499 F

The Meurgey couple have had great success in relaunching the venerable Champy house. Their Corton-Charlemagne has the delicate colour of old gold. There is a hint of walnut, leather and toasty flavours. The cask influence is over-prominent on the palate, overwhelming the flavours the wine seeks to show. It is technically perfect, but it is essential to leave it to mature in the cellar so the balance of flavours can find the right equilibrium.

Maison Champy, 5, rue du Grenier-à-Sel, 21200 Beaune, tel. 03.80.25.09.99, fax 03.80.25.09.95 by appt.

Pierre Meurgey

CHARTRON ET TREBUCHET 1998

□Gd cru n.c. 2,400 500 F+

'Bold, clean, white-gold in colour with pretty glints of green' according to the jury. The nose is rich, and smells of spiced bread and honey with attractive freshness and mineral notes. It has a strong attack and then becomes gourmand, delicate vanilla, allowing the white-fleshed fruit flavours to show. Not to be drunk for the next two years at least.

Chartron et Trébuchet, 13, Grande-Rue, 21190 Puligny-Montrachet, tel. 03.80.21.32.85, fax 03.80.21.36.35, e-mail jmchartron@chartron-trebuchet.com ev. day 10am–12.30pm 2pm–6pm; cl. Nov.–Mar.

CHEVALIER PERE ET FILS 1997★★

□Gd cru 0.22 ha 1,200 250–299 F

Historically, the Emperor Charlemagne is supposed to have invented schools. Corton-Charlemagne could certainly give lessons in wine-tasting. This one is a model teacher. It has a glorious golden colour and is naturally expressive. The body is not obscured by too much oak, and speaks out clearly and honestly. A wine that is endowed with great virtues (spring blossoms, toasted bread, hazelnut) and a frank flavour of the terroir. It still needs time. Best served with rich fish dishes with sauce or hard cheese.

SCE Chevalier Père et Fils, Buisson, 21550 Ladoix-Serrigny, tel. 03.80.26.46.30, fax 03.80.26.41.47 by appt.

DUFOULEUR PERE ET FILS 1997

□Gd cru n.c. 1,300 300–499 F

Flecks of gold as you might find in the bed of a gold-rush river in California. It is oaky, but there are distinctive lemon aromas followed through with notes of balsalmic vinegar. Full-bodied and firm, fleshy, round and unctuous, easy-drinking and opulent. Hard to believe it is a 97.

Dufouleur Père et Fils, 15, rue Thurot, 21700 Nuits-Saint-Georges, tel. 03.80.61.21.21, fax 03.80.61.11.23 by appt.

CH. GENOT-BOULANGER 1997★★

□Gd cru 0.29 ha 1,010 250–299 F

The jury sentenced this wine to be locked up for ten years. But you can always ask for early release and liberate it much sooner. However, this would mean foregoing long-term pleasure. This Charlemagne is worthy of an emperor. It is chewy and well-structured with aromas of walnut and traces of gunflint, and the finish has a flourish of richness. Congratulations to the jury – their suggestion was to serve it with grilled fish or skate.

Ch. Génot-Boulanger, 25, rue de Cîteaux, 21190 Meursault, tel. 03.80.21.49.20, fax 03.80.21.49.21, e-mail genot-boulanger@wanadoo.fr by appt.

DOM. ANTONIN GUYON 1998★

□Gd cru 0.55 ha 3,000 300–499 F

|92| |93| |94| 95 **96** 97 98

Charlemagne gave (or rather, returned) this vineyard to the monks of Saulieu, though he did not show such sympathy to the Burgundians when he brought them to heel. Now it does not matter so much since it is all far in the past. A lovely greenish-gold with a nose that has a slight note of gunflint, flintiness and toastiness. This is a very serious *Igrand vin*, which is a little ungiving despite its

BURGUNDY

appealing fleshiness. It will gain subtlety after five years in the cellar.
🗝 Dom. Antonin Guyon, 21420 Savigny-lès-Beaune, tel. 03.80.67.13.24, fax 03.80.66.85.87, e-mail vins@guyon-bourgogne.com ☑ Y by appt.

DOM. LOUIS LATOUR 1997*

□Gd cru 9.65 ha n.c. 300–499 F

(83) **85 89** 91 92 |93| |94| **|95| 96** 97

This is a great wine from the famous winery of Corton-Grancey, one of the significant places in the area. But it is not yet ready to fly the nest. It is pale gold and packed with aromas that prove its origins, but it is very stern and has a great many secrets to reveal in due course because it is heady and complex. It will not show any promise for the next four or five years' and then it will be superlative.
🗝 Maison Louis Latour, 18, rue des Tonneliers, 21200 Beaune, tel. 03.80.24.81.00, fax 03.80.22.36.21, e-mail louislatour@louislatour.com Y by appt.

OLIVIER LEFLAIVE 1998*

□Gd cru n.c. n.c. 300–499 F

Very pale gold with a hint of green is what we see in this wine. Beeswax with a stamp of flint is what we smell in this wine. The attack is somewhat energetic. A hint of fresh, distinctive saltiness, firmness and depth on the palate is what we taste in it. Does it have a future? Without a doubt.
🗝 Olivier Leflaive, pl. du Monument, 21190 Puligny-Montrachet, tel. 03.80.21.37.65, fax 03.80.21.33.94, e-mail leflaive-olivier@dial.oleane.com ☑ Y by appt.

LOUIS LEQUIN 1998**

□Gd cru 0.8 ha 570 250–299 F

This estate dates back to the 17th century. Two *ouvrées*, or 8 ares (2 acres), of vineyard have produced a 98 which is a splendid golden-green. The nose is like a game of hop-scotch, skipping from aroma to aroma: passion fruit, warm croissant, mango. The wine is full-bodied and rich and has a tendency towards softness, though well-constructed with firm tannins. Is it too young? Yes, indeed. In three or four years we will be able to expore its depths more throughly.
🗝 Louis Lequin, 1, rue du Pasquier-du-Pont, 21590 Santenay, tel. 03.80.20.63.82, fax 03.80.20.67.14, e-mail louis.lequin@wanadoo.fr ☑ Y by appt.

REINE PEDAUQUE 1998

□Gd cru 1.48 ha 1,200 200–249 F

This wine has reached a delightful maturity. It is warm, almost velvety, and has distinct Charlemagne character; it is fruity (peach and pear) and has a lively finish. Some might consider it 'modern' but it has been vinified according to the strict rules of the art of winemaking. Worth waiting four or five years before it delivers all that it should.
🗝 Reine Pédauque, Le Village, 21420 Aloxe-Corton, tel. 03.80.25.00.00, fax 03.80.26.42.00, e-mail rpedauque@axnet.fr Y by appt.

ROUX PERE ET FILS 1998**

□Gd cru n.c. n.c. 250–299 F

This wine has a lot of everything and is faithful to its style; a good golden colour, with mineral flavours subtly enhanced with cinnamon and nutmeg. It is as elegant as a fine meal at Lameloise's restaurant. Generous and full with rich flavours, as yet it does not have many nuances since the oak needs to integrate. Leave it to rest a while.
🗝 Dom. Roux Père et Fils, 21190 Saint-Aubin, tel. 03.80.21.32.92, fax 03.80.21.35.00 ☑ Y by appt.

Savigny-Lès-Beaune

Savigny is another typical wine village. The spirit of the terroir is well in evidence here, and the Confrérie de la Cousinerie de Bourgogne is the symbol of Burgundian hospitality. The 'Cousins' swear to welcome their guests 'with bottles on the table and their hands on their heart'.

Savigny wines are reputedly 'nourishing, prove the existence of God and stave off death'; they are fruity, supple and elegant, and are pleasant to drink young though they also age well. In 1999, the AOC produced 16,598 hl (438,187 gal) of red wine and 2,037 hl (53,777 gal) of white.

DOM. ARNOUX PERE ET FILS
Les Guettes 1998**

■1er cru 0.38 ha 1,800 70–99 F

A very beautiful estate of 24 ha (59 acres). The jury was enthusiastic about Les Guettes 98. It has a fresh and clear intensity of colour and the nose of a Spanish inn. You can detect flowers, fruit and gamey flavours when tasting it. It has a delicate palate that is long and supple with underlying, full-bodied tannins where the oak does not dominate. Should be kept in the cellar for a couple of years. We awarded the **Village Rouge** one star. A fleshy wine with length.

Arnoux Père et Fils, rue des Brenots, 1200 Chorey-lès-Beaune, el. 03.80.22.57.98, fax 03.80.22.16.85 ▣ Y by appt.

DOM. CAMUS-BRUCHON

Aux Grands Liards Vieilles vignes 1998

■ 0.52 ha 2,400 50–69 F

We could not decide between the **Narbantons 98**, which is not very full, though it is attractive and tasty (70–99F), and this wine. We hope this Grands Liards will be long-lived. It has an unusual name: 'liard' means a black poplar. Here again, it is lightly structured but has an acceptable balance with hints of red berry fruit which give it a lovely centre. The tannins are not overwhelming. There is the merest hint of spicy bitterness at the finish which suggests we should wait a little.

Lucien Camus-Bruchon, Les Cruottes, 16, rue de Chorey, 21420 Savigny-lès-Beaune, tel. 03.80.21.51.08, fax 03.80.26.10.21 ▣ Y by appt.

NICOLE ET JEAN-MARIE CAPRON-CHARCOUSSET

Les Pimentiers 1997

■ 0.33 ha 1,850 50–69 F

The estate is only 400 m (436 yards) from the 12th century church and has 7.5 ha (17 acres) of vines. The Pimentiers shows a colour that is in full development. It has a pretty nose of peaches and well-ripened and deliciously-perfumed bush peach, a rare experience these days. On the palate this aromatic tone is repeated and enhanced by well-made tannins. It has a certain elegance.

Nicole et Jean-Marie Capron-Charcousset, 3, rue Couturie, 21420 Savigny-lès-Beaune, tel. 03.80.21.55.37, fax 03.80.21.55.37 ▣ Y by appt.

CHAMPY PERE ET CIE 1998

□ n.c. 1,800 100–149 F

A wine with luminosity and a fresh, acid-drop nose that is only just beginning to open. Very appealing on its first impression on the palate, it continues with a fruitiness that is enhanced with a mineral touch. A good point in its favour is that it is not overpowered with oakiness. It is clear that Pierre Meurgey knows the good cellars in Savigny.

Maison Champy, 5, rue du Grenier-à-Sel, 21200 Beaune, tel. 03.80.25.09.99, fax 03.80.25.09.95 ▣ Y by appt.
Pierre Meurgey

DOM. CHANDON DE BRIAILLES

1997★★

■ 1 ha 2,300 70–99 F

Jean-Claude Bouveret is in charge of the cultivation of the vines and of the cellar. The gardens of the estate are classified as a historic monument and, for the record, the Queen Mother has visited here. A Savigny in a class of its own. It is ruby-garnet, with a strong vanilla nose that gives way to aromas of the terroir. On the palate, it is warm and opens with morello cherry flavours as it makes contact with the air. A wine of great class that can be enjoyed for many a long year.

Dom. Chandon de Briailles, 1, rue Sœur-Goby, 21420 Savigny-lès-Beaune, tel. 03.80.21.52.31, fax 03.80.21.59.15 ▣ Y by appt.
Nicolay

DOM. BRUNO CLAIR

La Dominode 1997★★

■ 1er cru 1.4 ha 5,000 100–149 F

A great classic. A glance at the colour is enough to know the wine has a future. The subtle nose reinforces the first impression. The attack is direct and pleasant and the underlying tannins are well-defined. It is complex, sturdy and has staying power. La Dominode can't be found on every vineyard map because it is in the middle of Les Jarrons.

Bruno Clair, 5, rue du Vieux-Collège, 21160 Marsannay-la-Côte, tel. 03.80.52.28.95, fax 03.80.52.18.14 ▣ Y by appt.

PIERRE CORNU-CAMUS 1997★

■ 1.17 ha 2,100 50–69 F

A wine that is so richly perfumed that it would prompt many a flight of fancy. It is simply brilliant. A full nose with a little red fruit. The aromas (principally blackcurrant) stay on the palate and interlace with the soft tannins. The wine is rich and complex and would be ideal with a good slice of Charolais steak.

Pierre Cornu-Camus, 2, rue Varlot, 21420 Echevronne, tel. 03.80.21.57.23, fax 03.80.26.11.94 ▣ Y by appt.

RODOLPHE DEMOUGEOT

Les Bourgeots 1998★

■ 0.75 ha 3,000 50–69 F

For wine-lovers who prefer a long extraction process. This wine has serious aromas with some maturity – bilberry jam. It is rich and concentrated on the palate. This *climat* is very close to Les Narbantons. The estate was established in 1992 and has recently grown, in the direction of Meursault.

Dom. Rodolphe Demougeot, 2, rue du Clos-de-Mazeray, 21190 Meursault, tel. 03.80.21.28.99, fax 03.80.21.29.18 ▣ Y by appt.

DOUDET-NAUDIN

Les Marconnets 1998★★

■ 1er cru 1.5 ha 2,690 100–149 F

It was here, or here abouts, that Georges Pompidou opened the A6 motorway in 1970. Les Marconnets vineyard is exactly half-way between Lille and Marseille. Very toasty, at the moment, but with a well-balanced character with substance and structure. It is very deep red and will certainly keep for a few years. For a **Blanc 98**, look at Les Vermots which is discreet, with subtle notes of white blossom and dried apricot, and has good length. Recommended.

🔑 Doudet-Naudin, 3, rue Henri-Cyrot, 21420 Savigny-lès-Beaune, tel. 03.80.21.51.74, fax 03.80.21.50.69 ☑ Y by appt.
🔑 Yves Doudet

DOM. DUBOIS D'ORGEVAL

Les Marconnets 1997

■ 1er cru 0.61 ha 1,800 ⏸ 70–99 F

Though it does not have immense body, this 97 has character nonetheless. There are shades of terracotta detectable in the deep colour. The nose is intense with aromas of nut kernels, kirsch and spices. The tannins are soft and pleasant and leave a lasting flavour. Above all it is supple.

🔑 Dom. Dubois d'Orgeval, 3, rue Joseph-Bard, 21200 Chorey-lès-Beaune, tel. 03.80.24.70.89, fax 03.80.22.45.02 ☑ Y by appt.

R. DUBOIS ET FILS

Les Narbantons 1997★

■ 1er cru 0.25 ha 1,600 ⏸ 70–99 F

Béatrice Dubois is an oenologist, and she has returned to the family property. She and Raphaël, the cellar-master, have produced a 97 that is bold. Its deep ruby colour gives the first clue. Fruit aromas dominate as the wine opens. On the palate it has a good deal of depth, vigour and length: still a little closed, but we believe that it will throw itself wide open in time.

🔑 R. Dubois et Fils, rte. de Nuits-Saint-Georges, 21700 Premeaux-Prissey, tel. 03.80.62.30.61, fax 03.80.61.24.07, e-mail rdubois@wanadoo.fr ☑ Y ev. day 8am–11.30am 2pm–6pm; Sat. Sun. by appt.
🔑 Régis Dubois

BERNARD DUBOIS ET FILS

Les Ratausses 1997★★

■ 1 ha 5,000 ⏸ 70–99 F

This 97 is produced on the part of the appellation that is closest to Chorey and it was very close to being awarded a *coup de cœur*. It is still a bit young to be in full bloom but has three Burgundy traits: very red with hues of blue, very perfumed, and it has admirable staying power. It is complete with charm, body and length. A high-class wine. You can also take great pleasure in the **Clos des Guettes Rouge 97** which is awarded a star.

🔑 Dom. Bernard Dubois et Fils, 8, rue des Chobins, 21200 Chorey-lès-Beaune, tel. 03.80.22.13.56, fax 03.80.24.61.43 ☑ Y by appt.

DOM. LOIS DUFOULEUR

Les Planchots 1997★★

■ 0.33 ha 1,700 ⏸ 50–69 F

You need to know Savigny wines well to identify Les Planchots correctly, and we failed. The vineyard was acquired by SAFER de Bourgogne, in 1997, and this is their first wine. An impressive baptism of fire! Its colour and glinting shades are very seductive. Toasted aromas and the flavour of cherries that are still on the tree. It has the same silky quality on the palate. This 'vin plaisir', [a]n easy-drinking wine, was one of the contend[ers] for a *coup de cœur*.

🔑 Dom. Loïs Dufouleur, chem. des Bressandes, La Montagne, 21200 Beaune, tel. 03.80.22.70.34, fax 03.80.24.04.28 ☑ Y by appt.

DUFOULEUR PERE ET FILS

1997★★

■ n.c. 2,500 ⏸ 100–149 F

A wine in perfect balance. The year, th[e] terroir and the grape variety are all shown of[f] to their best advantage by the hand of a master. It has earned a *coup de cœur* for being such a typical example. But the wine should be lef[t] to age a little: open in two years and serve fo[r] five or six years after. It has an admirable purple colour, and the nose is rich in ripe frui[t] with elegant, toasted oak. The suppleness and roundness of the 97s are characterised b[y] well-blended tannins.

🔑 Dufouleur Père et Fils, 15, rue Thurot, 21700 Nuits-Saint-Georges, tel. 03.80.61.21.21, fax 03.80.61.11.23 ☑ Y by appt.

DOM. LIONEL DUFOUR

Les Goudelettes 1998★

□ 0.46 ha 3,200 ⏸ 150–199 F

This *climat* is on the hilltop on the road to Bouilland. Here, it is shown off to great advantage. It is yellow-gold and quite intense in colour. It is both full and round. White flowers, sweet chestnut, sweets and fruit. Its freshness makes it good to drink young, but it could also wait a year or two.

🔑 SCI Lionel Dufour, 7, rte. de Monthélie, 21190 Meursault, tel. 03.80.21.67.02, fax 03.87.69.71.13

DOM. DUPONT-TISSERANDOT

Les Gollardes 1998★

■ 0.49 ha 2,300 ⏸ 50–69 F

A clear, fresh peony colour, this 98 has aromas of strawberry and cherry. It is soft to begin with and takes a little time to express itself. It has a wonderland of after-taste. It has been well brought up and should be drunk quite young because it is probably not for long keeping.

🔑 GAEC Dupont-Tisserandot, 2, pl. des Marronniers, 21220 Gevrey-Chambertin, tel. 03.80.34.10.50, fax 03.80.58.50.71 ☑ Y by appt.

FRANCOIS GAY 1997★

■ 0.69 ha 4,300 70-99 F

This wine can be drunk immediately, but it also has good potential for the next few years. It has a deep colour that shows no signs of development, and the nose is vegetal, with crystallised fruits. It has been well-vinified with flavours that are precise and well-developed. And, what's more, it has body. It could also be described as 'rustic', but that is not to its detriment.

François Gay, 9, rue des Fiètres, 21200 Chorey-lès-Beaune, tel. 03.80.22.69.58, fax 03.80.24.71.42 by appt.

MICHEL GAY Vergelesses 1998

■ 0.39 ha 2,300 70-99 F

A **Les Serpentières Rouges 98 Premier Cru** which is commended, and a Vergelesses which is also in the picture. We appreciated its oakiness, which was well-blended and not agressive, and its persistant fruit. The tannins do not overwhelm but, nonetheless, are sufficiently in evidence to suggest the wine should be kept for two years. It goes through the first stages effortlessly and then settles down very well on the palate.

Michel Gay, 1B, rue des Brenôts, 21200 Chorey-lès-Beaune, tel. 03.80.22.22.73, fax 03.80.22.95.78 by appt.

CH. GENOT-BOULANGER 1997★

□ 0.73 ha 3,700 100-149 F

There is an old tasting manual on the subject of tasting Burgundy: 'The taster's eye must be seduced and caressed.' This attractive and gleaming 97 is succulent and well-representative of the year. It also has an intense, rich nose. An interesting wine.

Ch. Génot-Boulanger, 25, rue de Cîteaux, 21190 Meursault, tel. 03.80.21.49.20, fax 03.80.21.49.21, e-mail genot-boulanger@wanadoo.fr by appt.

DOM. PHILIPPE GIRARD

Les Narbantons 1998★

■ 1er cru 0.64 ha 3,600 70-99 F

This domaine has a history going back five hundred years: nowadays it covers nearly 9 ha (22 acres). The jury recommended the red **Les Peuillets 98**, which should be left in the cellar for two years. Also the jury was unanimous about Les Narbantons, admiring the deep violet colour with glints of black. The nose is a combination of fruit and oak, but the fruit is more evident and expressive on the palate. It is very well-balanced. A real Premier Cru.

Dom. Philippe Girard, 37, rue Gal-Leclerc, 21420 Savigny-lès-Beaune, tel. 03.80.21.57.97, fax 03.80.26.14.84 by appt.

JEAN-JACQUES GIRARD 1998★

□ 0.86 ha 3,300 70-99 F

Savigny does not produce very much white wine. Only about 200,000 bottles compared to two million bottles of red. Occasionally you come across a rare member of the species. This is one and it would be a splendid partner for a fish terrine. It is lively, fine, very fruity and there is a good balance between ripeness and power. Already agreeable to drink but could also be kept for a while.

Dom. Girard, 16, rue de Cîteaux, 21420 Savigny-lès-Beaune, tel. 03.80.21.56.15, fax 03.80.26.10.08 by appt.

DOM. PIERRE GUILLEMOT

Dessus des Golardes 1998★

□ 1.4 ha 3,000 70-99 F

A *coup de cœur* for this lovely 97. This estate regularly produces a good performance with this AOC. Pierre Guillemot is well known for talking fascinatingly about wine (particularly his own). The jury enjoyed **Les Narbantons 98**, which has a fetching colour, a fruity nose with its slighty scorched aromas, and a delicate structure. It is recommended. **Les Jarrons 98 Rouges** has attained a good level of quality and is attractively and generously proportioned, so the jury awarded one star. The white particularly attracted the jury's attention. One taster wrote: 'I would be happy to put it in my cellar'. It is nicely oaked with lots of almond and hawthorn within a good structure. A wine to drink with pleasure straight away. Also worth mentioning is the red **Les Serpentières 98**, which has good potential. One star.

SCE du Dom. Pierre Guillemot, 1, rue Boulanger-et-Vallée, 21420 Savigny-lès-Beaune, tel. 03.80.21.50.40, fax 03.80.21.59.98 by appt.

DANIEL LARGEOT 1998★★

■ 0.68 ha 3,500 50-69 F

Marie-France is already working here and in due course will take over from her parents. If this wine is anything to go by, she has been taught well. This is a Savigny to keep on one side. We should be able to watch how it evolves over the next ten years. It has plenty of stuffing and is robust. Excellent breeding with aromas reminiscent of cherry jam bubbling away. Splendid for a wine that is so young.

Daniel Largeot, 5, rue des Brenôts, 21200 Chorey-lès-Beaune, tel. 03.80.22.15.10, fax 03.80.22.60.62 by appt.

DOM. MAILLARD PERE ET FILS 1998★

■ 1.8 ha n.c. 70-99 F

This domaine was created in 1952 by Daniel Maillard and covers vineyards in seven villages. As for the Savigny, it is silky and caressing and is easy to get on with. A very approachable wine, but with an oakiness that is quite evident which contributes to its attractive flavour. The vinification is not very long and produces a fresh wine that is easy to drink. It is a really typical Savigny.

Dom. Maillard Père et Fils, 2, rue Joseph-Bard, 21200 Chorey-lès-Beaune, tel. 03.80.22.10.67, fax 03.80.24.00.42 by appt.

CATHERINE ET CLAUDE MARECHAL 1998★

■ 1.2 ha 6,400 70–99 F

These *village* wines are reputedly divine. Nourishing? Undoubtedly. This is the way they are traditionally described. The deep garnet 98 has a slightly locked-in nose (cherry). It is four-square, sturdy, well-structured but has yet to mature. A Savigny to its finger tips.

EARL Catherine et Claude Maréchal, 6, rte de Chalon, 21200 Bligny-lès-Beaune, tel. 03.80.21.44.37, fax 03.80.26.85.01 by appt.

GHISLAINE ET BERNARD MARECHAL-CAILLOT 1998

■ 2.22 ha 2,700 70–99 F

The first names of both Madam and Monsieur appear on the label: they did not wait for parliament to sanction the emancipation of women here. Ghislaine and Bernard are the pair in question. Their Savigny is a very direct wine, carmine in colour with aromas of pepper and blackcurrant. There is sufficient acidity, and it has an overall balance but only an average length. Good with sautéed pork in a light gravy.

Ghislaine et Bernard Maréchal-Caillot, 10, rte. de Chalon, 21200 Bligny-lès-Beaune, tel. 03.80.21.44.55, fax 03.80.26.88.21 by appt.

DOM. MARTIN-DUFOUR

Narbantons 1997

■ 1er cru 0.24 ha 1,489 70–99 F

There is a choice here, since our juries registered approval for the red **Village 97** (50–69F), but they did comment that the Premier Cru is obviously the more promising. It is highly-coloured and aromatic (cherry stones and mushroom) with a direct attack, but needs to open out with a stay in the cellar. In due course it will be delicious with a veal casserole.

Dom. Martin-Dufour, 4A, rue des Moutots, 21200 Chorey-lès-Beaune, tel. 03.80.22.18.39, fax 03.80.22.18.39 by appt.

DOM. PARIGOT PERE ET FILS

Les Peuillets 1998★

■ 0.8 ha 4,800 70–99 F

Altough this wine has enough to make a good marriage, the relationship is not yet entirely harmonious. It is vivid purple with a violet edge, the liquorice nose is already open and fairly complex. The 98 has plenty of stuffing and a good deal yet to show: it has finesse, richness, even some distinction and a certain warmth.

Dom. Parigot Père et Fils, rte. de Pommard, 21190 Meloisey, tel. 03.80.26.01.70, fax 03.80.26.04.32 by appt.

JEAN-MARC PAVELOT 1997★

■ 5.36 ha 14,000 50–69 F

This estate was very successful with the 85 and 93 vintages. So we are in known territory when tasting the **Dominode Premier Cru 97 Rouge**, which is a very successful wine (70–99F). The *village* also pleased us. It is purple and young with raspberry flavours that lean towards blackcurrant on the palate where it also shows good balance. The mellow tannins have good length. It would be appealing to drink with a good chicken dish.

Jean-Marc Pavelot, 1, chem. des Guettottes, 21420 Savigny-lès-Beaune, tel. 03.80.21.55.21, fax 03.80.21.59.73 by appt.

ALBERT PONNELLE

Les Dentellières 1997★

■ 1er cru n.c. n.c. 100–149 F

It is hard to find Les Dentellières. The actual name of this excellent Savigny *climat* is Connardises, but its vulgar associations would not be appealing on a wine label (*connard* is rather a strong word for fool). However, this wine has prominent but integrated tannins and its fruitiness is just breaking out. The toastiness does not impress us as much as the aromas of preserved cherries.

Albert Ponnelle, Clos Saint-Nicolas, 38, fg Saint-Nicolas, 21200 Beaune, tel. 03.80.22.00.05, fax 03.80.24.19.73 by appt.

DOM. DU PRIEURE

Les Lavières 1998★★

■ 1er cru 1 ha 4,500 70–99 F

This was another serious candidate for a *coup de cœur* this year. The Lavières is deep garnet and opens with bilberry aromas. It follows with strength and breeding and a liquorice warmth but has a direct, gluggable quality we particularly enjoyed. This Premier Cru should shine out in the next year or two which is a very reasonable period. The white **Village 98** completes the range: it obtained one star. This wine should be left to slumber for two or three years and then it will be superb (50–69F).

Jean-Michel Maurice, Dom. du Prieuré, 23, rte. de Beaune, 21420 Savigny-lès-Beaune, tel. 03.80.21.54.27, fax 03.80.21.59.77, e-mail maurice.jean-michel@wanadoo.fr by appt.

DOM. PRIN 1997

■ 0.84 ha 4,500 50–69 F

Pale purple but already developing. The 97 opens its account interestingly: blackcurrant leaves. Tannic by nature but with a pleasant fruity finish. Not a 97 for nothing.

Dom. Prin, 12, rue de Serrigny, Cidex 10, 21550 Ladoix-Serrigny, tel. 03.80.26.40.63, fax 03.80.26.46.16 by appt.

REINE PEDAUQUE 1998*

■ n.c. 16,000 70–99 F

This wine, with its shades of peony, is an honorable emissary of the Reine Pédauque domaine. There is freshness in the fruit as it opens out and has some distinction. A little lively now, but in due course it will become a good wine. A fine example of good work and careful vinification: a wine that would go wonderfully with duck. Didn't the Reine Pédauque have webbed feet?

Reine Pédauque, Le Village, 21420 Aloxe-Corton, tel. 03.80.25.00.00, fax 03.80.26.42.00, e-mail rpedauque@axnet.fr by appt.

ROGER ET JOEL REMY

Les Fourneaux 1998**

■ 1 ha 5,000 50–69 F

When a Savigny is as good as this one is, it is said that 'even after you have licked your lips three times you can still say good things about the wine'. The *climat* is a neighbour of Pernand. A brilliant colour and already complex, holding the promise of a great future. It is well-structured, a little tannic now – only a question of its youth – and liquoricey. It is one of those Crus that is built to last and there are fewer and fewer of them, especially ones that are of real quality.

SCEA Roger et Joël Rémy, 4, rue du Paradis, 21200 Sainte-Marie-la-Blanche, tel. 03.80.26.60.80, fax 03.80.26.53.03 by appt.

DOM. GEORGES ROY ET FILS

Les Picotins 1998

■ 1.86 ha 3,000 50–69 F

Vincent took over from his father in 1998. This is therefore his debut. Fine Pinot colour with a bright tint. Redcurrant and dried fruit next. It is firm and vigorous on the palate and, as yet, the wine is not very accessible but undoubtedly has the qualities for keeping. The Picotins are near Chorey.

Dom. Georges Roy et Fils, 20, rue des Moutots, 21200 Chorey-lès-Beaune, tel. 03.80.22.16.28, fax 03.80.24.76.38 by appt.

DOM. SERRIGNY Petit Vallon 1997*

■ n.c. 9,000 100–149 F

This merchant quotes where his wines come from, which is exceptional in the trade. Here is the Domaine Serrigny. However, we have not heard of the Petit Vallon *climat*. That said, it has pretty colour with many hues and confidently opens out with blackberry that quickly follows onto gamey tones. It is quite warm and, with its touch of raspberry flavour, is representative of the style.

Cie des Vins d'Autrefois, abbaye Saint-Martin, 53, av. de l'Aigue, 21200 Beaune, tel. 03.80.26.33.00, fax 03.80.24.14.84, e-mail mallet.b@cva-beaune.fr by appt.

Jean-Pierre Nié

Chorey-Lès-Beaune

Chorey-Lès-Beaune is situated on flat land, opposite the pile of scree at the foot of the Combe de Bouilland , and some of the village's *lieux-dits* are neighbours to Savigny. In 1999, the Appellation Communale produced 7,172 hl (189,341 gal) of red wine and 193 hl (5,095 gal) of white.

BOISSEAUX-ESTIVANT 1997*

■ n.c. n.c. 100–149 F

A wine to drink for pleasure and to quench your thirst. Uncomplicated and with a charm that is immediate. Flavours of raspberry and redcurrant dominate. The tannins have already softened, so it would be better to drink the wine now.

Boisseaux-Estivant, Clos Saint-Nicolas, 38, fg Saint-Nicolas, 21200 Beaune, tel. 03.80.22.00.05, fax 03.80.24.19.73 by appt.

DOM. DUBOIS D'ORGEVAL 1997

■ 2.15 ha 4,600 50–69 F

A neat, fresh, yet light wine which is a treat for the palate. It is not going to become a big wine, more likely a friendly, intimate one. The purple colour and cocktail of fruit aromas suggest the 97 is good, though it should be drunk quite soon.

Dom. Dubois d'Orgeval, 3, rue Joseph-Bard, 21200 Chorey-lès-Beaune, tel. 03.80.24.70.89, fax 03.80.22.45.02 by appt.

XAVIER DUCLERT

Les Beaumonts 1997**

■ n.c. n.c. 50–69 F

This wine has a place on the winners' podium. Les Beaumonts is a *climat* in Chorey on the border with Savigny. It is well-structured and tannic, and rich even to the eye. Cherry, almost preserved cherry, with cinnamon in the background. A straightforward wine that will keep with no problem through the current decade.

Xavier Duclert, 2 bis, pl. Carnot, 21200 Beaune, tel. 03.80.22.74.77, fax 03.80.22.74.77, e-mail xavier.duclert@fnac.net ev. day except Mon. 10am–7pm

FRANCOIS GAY 1997

■ 2.75 ha 12,000 50–69 F

A dense, velvety and tightly woven wine. The colour leads on to a nose that is deep and generous in fruit and roasted coffee aromas. The palate is very approachable, which suggests that it should be drunk this year.

🔑 François Gay, 9, rue des Fiètres, 21200 Chorey-lès-Beaune, tel. 03.80.22.69.58, fax 03.80.24.71.42 ☑ 🍷 by appt.

DOM. GUYON Les Bons Ores 1998

■ 0.87 ha 5,400 🛢 50-69 F

This *climat* belongs to Chorey and is across the RN 74 from Aloxe-Corton. The Guyon family have made a successful choice. They gave up cultivating barley for the brewing trade to concentrate on vines and wine. Their lovely 98 is robust, powerful and well-built with tight tannins. Best not to try it before 2002 when it is likely to show off all its qualities.

🔑 EARL Dom. Guyon, 11–16, R.N. 74, 21700 Vosne-Romanée, tel. 03.80.61.02.46, fax 03.80.62.36.56 ☑ 🍷 by appt.

LA P'TIOTE CAVE

Les Beaumonts 1997*

■ 0.26 ha 5,000 🍾 🛢 50-69 F

One of the few Chorey *climats* to the west of the *route nationale*, near Savigny. A lovely carmine-purple colour with a well-presented aroma of raspberry jelly, it is light and slightly oaky. On the palate it is clean and shows more structure than flesh, and the fruit is still confined. A wine that is still developing and will show to the full in 2002.

🔑 La P'tiote Cave, 71150 Chassey-le-Camp, tel. 03.85.87.15.21, fax 03.85.87.28.08 ☑ 🍷 by appt.

DANIEL LARGEOT

Les Beaumonts 1998*

■ 1.5 ha 8,000 🛢 50-69 F

This attractive 98 has a straightforward colour with a nose that is restrained at present (bilberry, liquorice). A classic structure which would be excellent with roast pork. Best to be drunk in three years' time.

🔑 Daniel Largeot, 5, rue des Brenôts, 21200 Chorey-lès-Beaune, tel. 03.80.22.15.10, fax 03.80.22.60.62 ☑ 🍷 by appt.

DOM. MAILLARD PERE ET FILS

1998*

■ n.c. n.c. 🛢 50-69 F

This Chorey has a lovely, gleaming ruby colour and profits from a powerful, attractive nose (leather, game and roasted coffee). It is supple and mellow and very correct, and would go well with a rabbit stew.

🔑 Dom. Maillard Père et Fils, 2, rue Joseph-Bard, 21200 Chorey-lès-Beaune, tel. 03.80.22.10.67, fax 03.80.24.00.42 ☑ 🍷 by appt.

DOM. MARATRAY-DUBREUIL

Les Bons Ores 1998

■ 2 ha n.c. 🛢 50-69 F

All living things evolve. This light wine, with shades of terracotta, combines aromas of leaf mould, damp undergrowth and brandied fruit. It is fully mature. Fresh and lively on the palate although a little harsh. It needs to settle down and has the capacity to do so.

🔑 Dom. Maratray-Dubreuil, 5, pl. du Souvenir, 21550 Ladoix-Serrigny, tel. 03.80.26.41.09, fax 03.80.26.49.07 ☑ 🍷 by appt.

CLAUDE MARECHAL 1998**

■ 0.78 ha 3,700 🛢 50-69 F

A serious candidate for a *coup de cœur* – it only missed out by one vote. A clear garnet coloured 98 with toasty notes and blackcurrant bud aromas. Mouth-filling with delicate, well-balanced tannins. Congratulations from the jury.

🔑 EARL Catherine et Claude Maréchal, 6, rte. de Chalon, 21200 Bligny-lès-Beaune, tel. 03.80.21.44.37, fax 03.80.26.85.01 ☑ 🍷 by appt.

DOM. MARTIN-DUFOUR

Les Beaumonts 1997*

■ 4.55 ha 4,896 🍾 🛢 🌡 50-69 F

Freshly coloured, expressive and complex. This wine has a good concentrated attack and has the gourmand character necessary for a successful wine of the vintage. Its tannins present themselves on the finish and ensure that it will continue to develop well. This appealing, pleasant 97 will age well (two or three years with no problem).

🔑 Dom. Martin-Dufour, 4A, rue des Moutots, 21200 Chorey-lès-Beaune, tel. 03.80.22.18.39, fax 03.80.22.18.39 ☑ 🍷 by appt.

DOM. POULLEAU PERE ET FILS

1998*

■ 0.45 ha 2,700 🛢 50-69 F

Ruby and blackcurrant combine together on a good quality tannic base. It already has an attractive character and a pronounced roundness. As a result of attentive vinification this wine will improve with time. The perfect escort for duck with olives.

🔑 Dom. Poulleau Père et Fils, rue du Pied-de-la-Vallée, 21190 Volnay, tel. 03.80.21.62.61, fax 03.80.26.45.90 ☑ 🍷 by appt.

DOM. LOUIS VIOLLAND 1998

■ 2.36 ha 12,000 🛢 70-99 F

This typical 98 lacks any faults, it is light and convivial, fulfilling its commitments. A brilliant colour, a fruity nose and a nicely balanced palate which gives immediate pleasure.

🔑 Dom. Louis Violland, Abbaye Saint-Martin, 53, av. de l'Aigue, 21200 Beaune, tel. 03.80.26.33.00, fax 03.80.24.14.84 🍷 by appt.

Beaune

The Appellation Beaune is one of the biggest on the Côte in terms of area. But Beaune, a town of some 20,000 inhabitants, is also and above all the wine capital of Burgundy, the headquarters of many wine shippers, and one of the most attractive tourist towns in France. The Hospices de Beaune wine sales have become an event with a world-wide reputation and are certainly one of the most celebrated of all the Burgundy charity sales. Situated at the hub of a motorway network, Beaune will undoubtedly continue to develop its appeal as a tourist destination.

Beaune is best known for its powerful and distinctive red wines. Its geographical advantages mean that a large part of the vineyard has been classified as Premiers Crus: amongst the most prestigious we should list Les Bressandes, Le Clos du Roi, Les Grèves, Les Turons and Les Champimonts. In 1999, the AOC produced 20,035 hl (528,924 gal) of red wine and 2,062 hl (54,437 gal) of white.

LYCEE VITICOLE DE BEAUNE

Les Perrières 1997★★

■ 1er cru 0.77 ha 3,579 70–99 F

The Lycée Viticole does not qualify for the first prize yet, but it has passed its advanced exams with flying colours. This is indeed a lovely wine which shows the expertise of the younger generation and their teachers. A wine with good colour and powerful aromas. On the palate it is word-perfect and has a heart. Everything is perfectly incorporated and both strength and distinction are there. Also worth trying are the **Les Bressandes 97** and **La Montée Rouge 97**, both of which have a star.

Dom. du Lycée Viticole de Beaune, 16, av. Charles-Jaffelin, 21200 Beaune, tel. 03.80.26.35.81, fax 03.80.22.76.69 ☑ Y ev. day except Sun. 8am–11.30am 2pm–5pm; Sat. 8am–11.30am

BITOUZET-PRIEUR

Cent Vignes 1998★

■ 1er cru n.c. 3,000 100–149 F

Let the wine breathe a little in the glass and it will improve. Age will also do it good. That said, it is deep-coloured with dominant violet tones that match perfectly with its intense nose with concentrated fruit and touches of roasting coffee. It follows through on the palate with the same flavours, but there is slight bitterness from the tannins at this stage of its maturity. To keep for three to five years.

Vincent Bitouzet-Prieur, rue de la Combe, 21190 Volnay, tel. 03.80.21.62.13, fax 03.80.21.63.39 ☑ Y by appt.

DOM. BOUCHARD PERE ET FILS

Les Sizies 1998★

□ 1er cru 1.56 ha n.c. 150–199 F

This *climat* half-way up the slope is a Premier Cru admired by the connoisseurs. This clear yellow-gold 98 is settling down or indeed, settling in. A concentrated, perfumed, fleshy and generous wine that reveals its quality long before it is tasted. Then it presents a suppleness with a certain oakiness that some found very prominent and over-exaggerated. Best with grilled fish.

Bouchard Père et Fils, Ch. de Beaune, 21200 Beaune, tel. 03.80.24.80.24, fax 03.80.22.55.88, e-mail france@bouchard.pereetfils.com Y by appt.

DOM. BOUCHEZ-CRETAL

Les Chouacheux 1997★

■ 1er cru 0.49 ha 3,200 70–99 F

It is almost like biting into a bunch of grapes. The *climat* has an odd name, but produces a wine of breeding which is deep, intense garnet in colour. It is well-blended and has class with aromas that indicate a fully-ripe harvest, and it has a jamminess that recalls the smell of fruit cooking on the stove. A wine with a confident style and a good expansive length.

SCEA Dom. Bouchez-Crétal, 21190 Monthélie, tel. 03.85.87.17.40, fax 03.48.05.19.32 ☑ Y by appt.

REYANE ET PASCAL BOULEY

1998★

■ 0.65 ha 3,600 50–69 F

This *village* is smooth, neither harsh or aggressive. A little neutral perhaps, but we think it is simply resting. Violet-red with an adequate intensity of colour, it is beginning to release its aromas.

Pascal Bouley, pl. de l'Eglise, 21190 Volnay, tel. 03.80.21.61.69, fax 03.80.21.66.44 ☑ Y by appt.

PIERRE BOUREE FILS

Les Epenottes 1997★

■ 1er cru 1.2 ha 6,500 100–149 F

The Vallet family are responsible for maintaining the tradition of this respected estate at Gevrey. The Premier Cru is a Beaune from near Pommard. This wine has an expressive colour, and the nose is a marriage of spice and undergrowth with interesting character. The attack is fruity and its structure is acceptable, with soft tannins on the finish.

⊶ Pierre Bourée Fils, 13, rte. de Beaune, 21220 Gevrey-Chambertin, tel. 03.80.34.30.25, fax 03.80.51.85.64 ☑ Y by appt.
⊶ Louis Vallet

MICHEL BOUZEREAU ET FILS

Les Vignes Franches 1998★

■ 1er cru 0.5 ha n.c. ⦀ 100–149 F

Les Vignes Franches is the neighbouring vineyard to the Clos des Mouches. The wines have a reputation for their panache. They are rich and deep, they have fullness and texture and present all the merits of a true Premier Cru, as our tasting of this wine confirms. It is direct, fresh and clean, packed with flesh and ripe fruit. The colour adds a touch of elegance while its nose of leather and gamey notes already indicate maturity.
⊶ Michel Bouzereau et Fils, 3, rue de la Planche-Meunière, 21190 Meursault, tel. 03.80.21.20.74, fax 03.80.21.66.41 ☑ Y by appt.

CHANSON PERE ET FILS

Clos des Mouches 1997★

■ 1er cru 2.5 ha 7,000 ⦀ 150–199 F

This business celebrated its two hundred and fiftieth anniversary in the year 2000. Its **Clos des Mouches 97** is deep ruby in colour, well-structured, authentic and vigorous. The tannins do not grab all your attention but allow the fruit to show. There are straightforward aromas of undergrowth and strawberries. The **Clos des Fèves 97**, recommended, is equal to the reputation of the 'Chanson Père et Fils' monopoly. Turning finally to the anniversary wine, the **Clos des Marches Blanc 97 Cuvée 250th Anniversary** (200–249F) is awarded a star for the subtlety of its aromas and its well-balanced palate.
⊶ Chanson Père et Fils, 10, rue Paul-Chanson, 21200 Beaune, tel. 03.80.22.33.00, fax 03.80.24.17.42, e-mail tmarion@vins-chanson.com Y by appt.

RENE CHARACHE-BERGERET

1998★

■ 1er cru 0.27 ha 750 ⦀ 70–99 F

Beyond our wildest dreams. This estate is in the Hautes-Côtes de Beaune and is quite large (20 ha/49 acres), but this parcel covers only about six *ouvrées*, or 24 a (0.6 acre). This balanced, complex 98 does not overwhelm you with anything but its intense purple colour. The rest is skilfully suggested with tannins that are, as yet, well-hidden. An attractive after-taste of prunes.
⊶ René Charache-Bergeret, 21200 Bouze-lès-Beaune, tel. 03.80.26.00.86, fax 03.80.26.00.86 ☑ Y by appt.

C. CHARTON FILS 1997★

■ 1er cru n.c. n.c. ⦀ 300–499 F

This wine is comes from a Beaune estate where the Ponnelle family live. This blended Premier Cru is extremely satisfying. It frankness is evident from its colour, appearing again on the nose which has spices and raspberry. Fine, round, supple, and it is already mellow. This 97 can be served from 2001 on.
⊶ C. Charton Fils, Clos Saint-Nicolas, 38, fg Saint-Nicolas, 21200 Beaune, tel. 03.80.22.00.05, fax 03.80.24.19.73 ☑ Y by appt.

CH. DE CITEAUX Teurons 1997★

■ 1er cru n.c. 2,500 ⦀ 70–99 F

Dark and deep in colour, yet it does not have an impressive nose. On the palate it is rich, powerful, concentrated and burly. Being so highly concentrated, it will inevitably keep, but at present is still somewhat crude. A typical vinification for this wine that has been matured with love and care. The first vineyard of the monks of Citeaux was at Meursault.
⊶ Philippe Bouzereau, Ch. de Cîteaux, 18–20, rue de Cîteaux, B.P.25, 21190 Meursault, tel. 03.80.21.20.32, fax 03.80.21.64.34, e-mail domaine.bouzereau@wanadoo.fr ☑ Y by appt.

DOM. HENRI CLERC ET FILS

Chaume Gaufriot 1997

■ 0.3 ha 1,882 ⦀ 70–99 F

The *climat* is perched at the top of the appellation and, when presenting well, can develop complex aromas where you can detect spiced bread and roasted notes against a background of liquorice. On the palate, the tannins need to mellow. This 97 probably has a future and is likely to develop body.
⊶ EARL Dom. Henri Clerc et Fils, pl. des Marronniers, 21190 Puligny-Montrachet, tel. 03.80.21.32.74, fax 03.80.21.39.60 ☑ Y ev. day 8.30am–11.45am 2pm–5.45pm
⊶ Bernard Clerc

DOM. DOUDET Clos du Roy 1998★★★

■ 1er cru 0.41 ha 1,800 ⦀ 100–149 F

This wine was close to being awarded a *coup de cœur*. The colour is brilliant cherry-red and the nose leans towards blackcurrant. It has everything the vintage has to offer in richness, roundness and stuffing – a wine of character. Needs to be left to age for two or three years, which is not long to wait, and it will undoubtedly improve. The **Cent-Vignes 98** is also superb and is of the same quality – it was also a finalist in our tasting.
⊶ Dom. Doudet, 50, rue de Bourgogne, 21420 Savigny-lès-Beaune, tel. 03.80.21.51.74, fax 03.80.21.50.69 ☑ Y by appt.
⊶ Yves Doudet

DOM. DUBOIS D'ORGEVAL

Les Marconnets 1997★

■ 1er cru 0.68 ha 1,700 ⦀ 70–99 F

A wine sufficiently well-structured to accommodate the oakiness and to calm the tannins. It is persistent and relatively supple and fruity, so the prognosis is favourable. However, it should not be left longer than two years. The colour is faultless. Liquorice nose, straightforward and classic style.

⊶ Dom. Dubois d'Orgeval, 3, rue Joseph-Bard, 21200 Chorey-lès-Beaune, tel. 03.80.24.70.89, fax 03.80.22.45.02 ☑ Y by appt.

BERNARD DUBOIS ET FILS

Les Aigrots 1997*

■ 1er cru 0.34 ha 2,000 ⏸ 70–99 F

It is strong purple with glints of carmine and has an oaky nose, but the attack is delicate and elegant. Added to that, the structure is good, and there is a pleasant return to fruit at the finish. In short, this is a great success and very typical for the style. Make the most of this now or in a few years.

⊶ Dom. Bernard Dubois et Fils, 8, rue des Chobins, 21200 Chorey-lès-Beaune, tel. 03.80.22.13.56, fax 03.80.24.61.43 ☑ Y by appt.

R. DUBOIS ET FILS

Blanche Fleur 1997*

■ 0.3 ha 1,500 ▮⏸♁ 50–69 F

The Blanche Fleur vineyard overlooking the A6 on the hills up to Savigny, on the Beaune side, is dedicated not to white wines but reds from Pinot Noir. The younger generation have taken over from Régis and a grandfather who was honoured by a famous Cuvée Familiale. Their 97 is cherry-coloured with garnet hues and has a pleasing look. It is balanced, vinified carefully, and supported by good tannins. The wood has been well-handled and used to good advantage.

⊶ R. Dubois et Fils, rte. de Nuits-Saint-Georges, 21700 Premeaux-Prissey, tel. 03.80.62.30.61, fax 03.80.61.24.07, e-mail rdubois@wanadoo.fr ☑ Y ev. day 8am–11.30am 2pm–6pm; Sat. Sun. by appt.

DOM. LOIS DUFOULEUR

Clos du Dessus des Marconnets 1998**

■ 0.4 ha 2,000 ⏸ 50–69 F

This vineyard is at the top, near Savigny-lès-Beaune. The wine is such a deep garnet colour that it is almost black. Dark-skinned fruit such as blackcurrant and bilberry on the nose, but this wine is certainly not in mourning. On the contrary, it is dense and ripe but durable and could possibly be remarkable when the wood has integrated a good deal more (four to five years).

⊶ Dom. Loïs Dufouleur, chem. des Bressandes, La Montagne, 21200 Beaune, tel. 03.80.22.70.34, fax 03.80.24.04.28 ☑ Y by appt.

DUFOULEUR PERE ET FILS

Les Cent Vignes 1997**

■ 1er cru n.c. 3,800 ⏸ 150–199 F

Two wines which received positive comments and pleased the jury a good deal: **Les Grèves 97** and, from the same year, the Cent Vignes with its supple attack, opening out with flavours of red berry fruit which coat the palate. Length and persistence enhance the fleshiness of the Pinot Noir very well. Besides that, it is lovely to look at and attractive to smell. The tiny note of toasted aromas will quiet down.

⊶ Dufouleur Père et Fils, 15, rue Thurot, 21700 Nuits-Saint-Georges, tel. 03.80.61.21.21, fax 03.80.61.11.23 ☑ Y by appt.

MAISON ALEX GAMBAL

Grèves 1997

■ 1er cru n.c. 1,200 ⏸ 100–149 F

Alex Gambal is originally from America. He set up his *négociant-éleveur* firm in 1997. His Grèves is purplish-ruby, with fine aromas, and the oakiness combines well with the fruit. Good, lasting fruit on the palate. It is more supple than powerful and should be drunk in the next year. The imprint of the vintage is evident.

⊶ EURL maison Alex Gambal, 4, rue Jacques-Vincent, 21200 Beaune, tel. 03.80.22.75.81, fax 03.80.22.21.66, e-mail agbeaune@aol.com ☑ Y by appt.

MICHEL GAY Les Toussaints 1998**

■ 1er cru 0.43 ha 2,600 ⏸ 70–99 F

This Toussaints will be around for some time to come. It is partly red and partly garnet in colour, lightly oaked but with flavours of kirsch and eau-de-vie. It is full of life, freshness and vivacity. Full-bodied and soft in the mouth, it should be at its peak quite soon, then leave us with sweet memories.

⊶ Michel Gay, 1B, rue des Brenôts, 21200 Chorey-lès-Beaune, tel. 03.80.22.22.73, fax 03.80.22.95.78 ☑ Y by appt.

DOM. LUCIEN JACOB

Les Toussaints 1998*

■ 1er cru 0.3 ha 1,800 ⏸ 70–99 F

We were told this was Bordeaux red. But we do not plan to make a song and dance about it. The nose of cooked prunes is already mature. It has a dense, tannic texture on the palate which should soften – it already lacks aggression. Following on from the nose, it is showing some sophistication. Jean-Michel Jacob took over from Lucien, his father, who used to be a Deputy for Beaune and was a great defender of the Burgundy vineyards.

⊶ Dom. Lucien Jacob, 21420 Echevronne, tel. 03.80.21.52.15, fax 03.80.21.55.65 ☑ Y by appt.

DOM. PIERRE LABET

Clos du Dessus des Marconnets 1998*

■ 1 ha n.c. ⏸ 70–99 F

One end of the vineyard is close to the Château de la Tour (Clos de Vougeot), and the other is in Beaune. This Dessus des Marconnets is on good form. Its nose is currently infused with blackcurrant buds, smoke and leather. This 98 is well-structured and suggests it has the qualities to age with dignity. There is a slight note of bitterness at the finish which is classic with a wine of this age but always a little unwelcome. Keep for five or six years. To accompany a dish of fish with sauce, the reader should select a **Clos des Monsnières Blanc 98** (100–149F), which was

recommended by the jury: strong oak at the moment, but the wine will blossom in a year or two.
🔑 Dom. Pierre Labet, Clos de Vougeot, 21640 Vougeot, tel. 03.80.62.86.13, fax 03.80.62.82.72, e-mail labet@axnet.fr ☑ 🍸 ev. day except Mon. 10.30am–6.30pm; cl. Nov.–1 Apr.
🔑 François Labet

MICHEL LAHAYE

Les Bons Feuvres 1997★★

■ 0.44 ha 1,200 70–99 F

Much praise for this *climat*, which is on the way towards Pommard. Mauvish-red in colour, it has a charming reluctance to show itself at the moment. A graceful palate with fruit and liquorice, it has some warmth, a touch of liveliness, and is preparing itself for the future.
🔑 Michel Lahaye, pl. de l'Eglise, 21630 Pommard, tel. 03.80.22.52.22, fax 03.00.00.00.00 ☑ 🍸 by appt.

LA JOLIVODE 1998★★★

■ 0.86 ha 4,200 50–69 F

The hand of God seems to have descended on Les Grèves, because this wine has won a *coup de cœur* for the wine-grower. It has a lovely nose with strong toast and vanilla aromas from the barrel that do not obscure the aromas of blackcurrant and blackberry. Clear and clean with subtle liquorice and velvet on the palate suggesting maturity and excellence.
🔑 Christian Menaut, rue Chaude, 21190 Nantoux, tel. 03.80.26.01.53, fax 03.80.26.01.53 ☑ 🍸 by appt.

DANIEL LARGEOT Les Grèves 1998★

■ 1er cru 0.61 ha 3,000 100–149 F

In one of his books, Marcel Proust describes the pleasure to be gained when wandering round a town like Beaune and the even greater pleasure in enjoying its Crus. This Grèves was outstanding for the 95 and 96 vintages. The wine-grower is in the process of handing over to his daughter, Marie-France but the 98 is still his wine. It has a velvety colour and a nose of crushed fruit (blackcurrant, blackberry) infused with touches of undergrowth. This wine should be left to mature because its acidity and tannins need time to learn to live together.
🔑 Daniel Largeot, 5, rue des Brenôts, 21200 Chorey-lès-Beaune, tel. 03.80.22.15.10, fax 03.80.22.60.62 ☑ 🍸 by appt.

DOM. DE LA SALLE

Champimonts 1997★

■ 1er cru 2 ha 7,300 150–199 F

This wine was presented by an offshoot of the Albert Bichot firm. This Champimonts gets straight to the point. It has a lovely, brilliant intensity of colour, and the nose is a composition of spices and red berry fruit with a vegetal tone. A lively finish, and on the palate it is attractive and well-made with an emphasis on suppleness. Ready for drinking.
🔑 Vieilles Caves de Bourgogneetde Bordeaux, 6 bis, bd Jacques-Copeau, 21200 Beaune, tel. 03.80.24.37.47, fax 03.80.24.37.38

LOUIS LATOUR 1997

□ n.c. 22,000 100–149 F

The name of Latour in Beaune and the Hôtel-Dieu are mentioned virtually in the same breath and indeed, the family has long played a role in the foundation. The jury commended a **Beaune Village Rouge 97** (70–99F) which has good balance on the whole but has more definition on the nose, which is soft, measured Pinot. The white Village 97 is not very full, but the quality of its golden-green colour appealed to the jury as did the gentle toastiness on the nose and its promising palate.
🔑 Maison Louis Latour, 18, rue des Tonneliers, 21200 Beaune, tel. 03.80.24.81.00, fax 03.80.22.36.21, e-mail louislatour@louislatour.com 🍸 by appt.

CH. DE LA VELLE Marconnets 1997

■ 1er cru 0.8 ha 1,800 100–149 F

Purplish-garnet with delicate shades of blackcurrant in colour, this wine is clean and lively on the attack. Its body lacks concentration but is fresh and supple. Recommended for early drinking. If you can, drink it on the spot. The 13th century château is a *gîte rural* and a *gîte d'étape* and an excellent place to stay in the heart of the terroir.
🔑 Bertrand Darviot, Ch. de la Velle, 17, rue de la Velle, 21190 Meursault, tel. 03.80.21.22.83, fax 03.80.21.65.60, e-mail chateaudelavelle@infonie.fr ☑ 🍸 by appt.

DOM. MAILLARD PERE ET FILS

1998★

■ 1.3 ha n.c. 70–99 F

A wonderful 95 vintage, this time the producer is emphasising the youthfulness of his wine. Between 1952 and now, the vineyard has grown from only a few vines to 18 ha (45 acres) with 1.3 ha (0.3 acre) in this appellation. Ripe white-heart cherry in colour with blackcurrant buds on the nose. The fruit is accompanied by well-integrated oak and it is quite long. The wine could easily wait for two or three years, when it would be fine with roast lamb.

⊶ Dom. Maillard Père et Fils, 2, rue Joseph-Bard, 21200 Chorey-lès-Beaune, tel. 03.80.22.10.67, fax 03.80.24.00.42 ☑ Y by appt.

DOM. MAZILLY PERE ET FILS

Vignes Franches 1998★

■ 1er cru	0.3 ha	2,200	⏸ 70–99 F

While it is firmly rooted in the soil, (showing excellent balance between tannins, alcohol and acidity) this 98 retains a youthful nose where cherry and nut kernels can be detected along with traces of oak. It has been made with care using cold maceration. A delicate wine that will keep for an average length of time. The domaine covers 14 ha (35 acres) and is in the Hautes-Côtes de Beaune.

⊶ Dom. Mazilly Père et Fils, rte. de Pommard, 21190 Meloisey, tel. 03.80.26.02.00, fax 03.80.26.03.67 ☑ Y by appt.

DOM. RENE MONNIER

Toussaints 1998★★

■ 1er cru	0.81 ha	4,000	⏸ 70–99 F

There is a Van der Weyden retable depicting the Archangel Michael weighing souls. This Toussaints (All Saints) wine is on the side of the angels; it has a colour with great honesty and a frank nose (prominent young fruit), clean body and a smooth character. Its fine tannins, straightforwardness, elegance on the palate and long finish all deserve a golden future. The **Cent Vignes 98** was given a star and has a good fruitiness.

⊶ Dom. René Monnier, 6, rue du Dr-Rolland, 21190 Meursault, tel. 03.80.21.29.32, fax 03.80.21.61.79 ☑ Y ev. day 8am–12 noon 2pm–6pm

⊶ M. et Mme Bouillot

DOM. PARIGOT PERE ET FILS

Les Aigrots 1998★

■ 1er cru	0.8 ha	5,000	⏸ 70–99 F

A wine that is neither too thin nor too heady: this sensual and fruity wine is typical of the appellation. The violet-red colour recalls clouds at sunset over the Montagne de Beaune. It has notes of humus, undergrowth and damp earth with a lively body, a good tannic structure and strong acidity. Substantial wine with potential.

⊶ Dom. Parigot Père et Fils, rte. de Pommard, 21190 Meloisey, tel. 03.80.26.01.70, fax 03.80.26.04.32 ☑ Y by appt.

CH. PHILIPPE-LE-HARDI

Clos du Roi 1998★★

■ 1er cru	0.83 ha	5,100	⏸ 70–99 F

We should wait for this Clos du Roi for two or three years, because it needs more muscle under the armour of the tannins. It has sufficient acidity to develop well. A princely red colour with a vanilla and raspberry nose. This huge estate covers about 90 ha (222 acres) notably at Mercurey, and it was Paul Pidault's old business that he sold to a Swiss group.

⊶ Ch. de Santenay, B.P. 18, 21590 Santenay, tel. 03.80.20.61.87, fax 03.80.20.63.66 ☑ Y by appt.

DOM. JACQUES PRIEUR

Grèves 1997★★

■ 1er cru	1.7 ha	6,300	⏸ 100–149 F

This Grèves is an intense, deep red and has a nose hinting at bilberries. This full-bodied 97 is homogenous and concentrated and has good potential. However, its astringency suggests that we set it aside. The Antonin Rodet firm manages the estate. The **Champs Pimont 97** also deserves a mention for the red (solid and robust) and their white (a wine to drink young): each is awarded a star.

⊶ Dom. Jacques Prieur, 6, rue des Santenots, 21190 Meursault, tel. 03.80.21.23.85, fax 03.80.21.29.19 ☑ Y by appt.

DOM. PRIEUR-BRUNET

Clos du Roy 1997★

■ 1er cru	0.4 ha	2,300	⏸ 100–149 F

A wine of nobility that is a credit to the Clos du Roi name. It is powerful and fine, and likely to be worth drinking for a number of years. The oakiness does not overpower the wine. The 97 has pedigree and is rich. It lacks harshness or dryness and the taninns play a good supporting role.

⊶ Dom. Prieur-Brunet, rue de Narosse, 21590 Santenay, tel. 03.80.20.60.56, fax 03.80.20.64.31, e-mail uny-prieur@prieursantenay.com ☑ Y by appt.

DOM. RAPET PERE ET FILS

Clos du Roi 1998★

■ 1er cru	0.5 ha	2,500	⏸ 70–99 F

'Rapet 1792' is engraved on an old tasting cup belonging to the estate. They own half a hectare (just over one acre) of Clos du Roi. We tried the 98 with pleasure and it hits the right note: silky, round and fleshy with aromas of game and toastiness and with a decisive colour. Good finesse.

⊶ Dom. Rapet Père et Fils, 21420 Pernand-Vergelesses, tel. 03.80.21.59.94, fax 03.80.21.54.01 ☑ Y by appt.

CAVE PRIVEE ANTONIN RODET

1997★

■	0.5 ha	2,000	⏸ 200–249 F

'Cave Privée' is a range of Antonin Rodet wines. Bertrand Devillard manages the business. This wine could be left to mature for a number of years in any wine-lover's cellar, but will already appeal to anyone who likes strong tannins in a wine that has complex aromas of ripe fruit. Best to drink with roast meat.

⊶ Antonin Rodet, 71640 Mercurey, tel. 03.85.98.12.12, fax 03.85.45.25.49, e-mail rodet@rodet.com ☑ Y ev. day except Sat. Sun. 9am–12 noon 1.30pm–6pm

BURGUNDY

REGIS ROSSIGNOL-CHANGARNIER Les Theurons 1997★

■ 1er cru 0.6 ha 1,800 70–99 F

Les Theurons (or Teurons) falls on the dividing line between two administrative districts. It has a good balance between the influences of Savigny and Pommard. We tasted this concentrated 97, which is somewhat dark with strong bilberry fruit aromas. It is very clean and still young, and has yet to open completely and show off its body to the full. Partially de-stemmed and de-stalked and a short time in tank, according to good old traditions.

Régis Rossignol, rue d'Amour, 21190 Volnay, tel. 03.80.21.61.59, fax 03.80.21.61.59 by appt.

DOM. LOUIS VIOLLAND

Montée Rouge 1998★

■ 5.25 ha 18,000 100–149 F

This business was taken over by Jean-Claude Boisset and re-located in the Abbaye Saint-Martin. It has its own vineyards including the famous Montée Rouge which overlooks the whole hillside. The wine we tasted here is a fairly intense peony red which opens with concentrated red fruit (a little air does it good). Structure and complexity make this a powerful, tannic wine which should wait a little.

Dom. Louis Violland, Abbaye Saint-Martin, 53, av. de l'Aigue, 21200 Beaune, tel. 03.80.26.33.00, fax 03.80.24.14.84 by appt.

Côte de Beaune

The Appellation Côte de Beaune is not to be confused with Côte de Beaune-Villages, and can be produced only on a few specified places on the Beaune slopes. The appellation declared 942 hl (24,869 gal) of red wine and 595 hl (15,708 gal) of white in 1999.

DOM. DUBOIS D'ORGEVAL 1997★

□ 0.47 ha 3,000 50–69 F

The structure of this wine is balanced and it could be drunk from now. Intense colour and nose; floral, buttery and toasted bread. The 97 has good body and the oakiness does not overwhelm it. It is characteristic of the appellation and though it can be drunk now, it could also be kept for six months or a year.

Dom. Dubois d'Orgeval, 3, rue Joseph-Bard, 21200 Chorey-lès-Beaune, tel. 03.80.24.70.89, fax 03.80.22.45.02 by appt.

DOM. LOIS DUFOULEUR

Les Longes 1998

■ 0.75 ha n.c. 50–69 F

A wine that pleases with its simplicity. Purple-garnet, blackcurrant, supple and easy to drink despite a touch of astringency. There is no need to worry about its evolution: should be drunk in the next two years. The *climat* is located at the top of the Montagne de Beaune.

Dom. Loïs Dufouleur, chem. des Bressandes, La Montagne, 21200 Beaune, tel. 03.80.22.70.34, fax 03.80.24.04.28 by appt.

EMMANUEL GIBOULOT

La Grande Châtelaine 1998

□ 2.3 ha 5,200 50–69 F

This wine is produced from grapes grown according to the regulations of organic farming. It is developed on the lees and stays in the barrel for eleven months (18% new barrels each year). This 98 is delicately oaked with well-mingled flavours and is rich in mineral and honeyed aromas, with a ripe golden colour.

Emmanuel Giboulot, Combertault, 21200 Beaune, tel. 03.80.26.52.85, fax 03.80.26.53.67 by appt.

DOM. CHANTAL LESCURE

Le Clos des Topes Bizot Vieilles vignes 1998★

■ 4.28 ha 4,500 50–69 F

The *clos* is in good company, just above Les Bressandes and the Clos de l'Ecu. A fairly deep ruby colour with notes of liquorice and raspberry, this is a supple 98, but its tannins are still strong. Patience is undoubtely needed to see it develop its potential, but it will be worth the wait.

Dom. Chantal Lescure, 34A, rue Thurot, 21700 Nuits-Saint-Georges, tel. 03.80.61.16.79, fax 03.80.61.36.64, e-mail domaine-lescure.com by appt.

DOM. POULLEAU PERE ET FILS

Les Mondes Rondes 1998

■ 3.2 ha 9,000 30–49 F

This *climat* above Les Grèves is well-named. It is a real 'fortress', overlooking Beaune, in the middle of the countryside. A black cherry-red with humus and blackcurrant aromas. The wine is well-structured but the harsh tannins are vying with the fruit. Its balance is promising. The **98 Blanc La Grande Châtelaine** is opening gradually and developing well: it gained the same marks.

Dom. Poulleau Père et Fils, rue du Pied-de-la-Vallée, 21190 Volnay, tel. 03.80.21.62.61, fax 03.80.26.45.90 by appt.

Pommard

This appellation is the best-known Burgundy outside France. The vineyard produced 16,472 hl (434,861 gal) in 1999. Argovian marlstone is here replaced by soft limestone, and the vines it produces are sturdy, tannic and good for keeping. The best *climats* are classified as Premier Crus, of which the most celebrated are Les Rugiens and Les Épenots.

ROGER BELLAND Les Cras 1998★

■ 0.98 ha 5,200 100–149 F

Perfect to go with a traditional roast chicken. The colour of this Pommard is not particularly eloquent. On the nose it has strong barrel influences and aromas hovering between wood and undergrowth. However, on the palate, it is soft, silky and haloed with red berry fruit flavours. The oakiness is well-integrated, giving an attractive character.

Dom. Roger Belland, 3, rue de la Chapelle, B.P. 13, 21590 Santenay, tel. 03.80.20.60.95, fax 03.80.20.63.93, e-mail belland.roger@wanadoo.fr Y by appt.

DOM. GABRIEL BILLARD

Vaumuriens 1997★★

■ 0.78 ha 3,000 70–99 F

Laurence Jobard is an associate of Mireille Desmonet and an eminent oenologist. She makes her own family's wines and has produced a *village* which is a sumptuous shining gold as brilliant as the sun's rays illuminating a Romanesque stained glass window. The nose is well-composed with a good balance between oak and fruit. Liquorice and cinnamon meet on the palate, which is soft, well-structured, very complex, long and balanced. It impressed the jury. The Premier Cru Les Charmots 97 (100–149F) was awarded a star and a half.

Dom. Gabriel Billard, imp. de la Commaraine, 21630 Pommard, tel. 03.80.22.27.82, fax 03.85.49.49.02 Y by appt.

Jobard-Desmonet

DOM. BILLARD-GONNET

Chaponnières 1997★

■ 1er cru 1 ha 3,271 100–149 F

From the various wines the jury tried here, this was the one that appealed most. A strong peony colour with very expressive toasted aromas. The wine has a number of aces: the oakiness is well-blended, a distinctive and convincing suppleness which is characteristic of the Cru. To drink now or later if preferred. The **Rugiens 97** and Premier Cru received the same compliments.

Dom. Billard-Gonnet, rte d'Ivry, 21630 Pommard, tel. 03.80.22.17.33, fax 03.80.22.68.92 Y by appt.

CH. DE BLIGNY 1998

■ n.c. 5,200 100–149 F

GMP and the Japanese Suntory company sold the property to SAFER, who sold it on to the Cave de Sainte-Marie-la-Blanche. The Château de Bligny is where we find the Co-operative's headquarters. Their Pommard is a ochre-red with tones of cloves and cinnamon. The lightness of the 98 suggests it will be ready for drinking in three or four years.

Ch. de Bligny, Caves de la Vervelle, 21200 Bligny-lès-Beaune, tel. 03.80.21.47.38, fax 03.80.21.40.27 Y ev. day except Sun. Mon. 10am–12 noon 2pm–6pm

ERIC BOIGELOT 1997

■ 0.35 ha 2,000 100–149 F

This wine spends a dozen months first in tank, then in barrel, and produces a fairly fresh red wine. Gamey, leathery, musky aromas with cherry to add the touch of fruit. On the palate it is quite direct and has character and finesse, and is not overly powerful. It has a little acidity on the finish, but this will soften in a year or two.

Eric Boigelot, rue de Beaune, 21190 Monthelie, tel. 03.80.21.65.85, fax 03.80.21.66.01 Y by appt.

BOISSEAUX-ESTIVANT 1998★

■ n.c. n.c. 250–299 F

Nothing to say that has not been said before. This Ponnelle (there are several in Beaune) is a very good Pommard and opens out progressively, starting with morello cherry. It is light on the palate initially, but gradually firms up as the fruit develops. It is round and seductive. For keeping, of course.

Boisseaux-Estivant, Clos Saint-Nicolas, 38, fg Saint-Nicolas, 21200 Beaune, tel. 03.80.22.00.05, fax 03.80.24.19.73 Y by appt.

DOM. BOUCHARD PERE ET FILS

Rugiens 1997★★

■ 1er cru 0.41 ha n.c. 200–249 F

A Rugiens that is light carmine, and with a scent of wild strawberries that invites you to breathe more deeply. Good cherry is detected on the middle of a very youthful palate. Its oakiness and tannins mean it will keep for five to ten years with ease. This is a wine for the future, and patience will be well rewarded.

🔑 Bouchard Père et Fils, Ch. de Beaune, 21200 Beaune, tel. 03.80.24.80.24, fax 03.80.22.55.88, e-mail france@bouchard.pereetfils.com 🍷 by appt.

REYANE ET PASCAL BOULEY
1998

■ 0.39 ha 1,200 🛢 70–99 F

A fine example of good extraction. This is a wine that is open and bright. A violet colour with a fruity nose, and a palate that opens out gradually. For the moment, it is not very round, but the capacity is there, you can rely on it. Best not to open this for three years or even more.

🔑 Pascal Bouley, pl. de l'Eglise, 21190 Volnay, tel. 03.80.21.61.69, fax 03.80.21.66.44 ☑ 🍷 by appt.

DOM. DENIS BOUSSEY 1998★

■ 0.56 ha 3,000 🛢 100–149 F

Perfect balance between acidity, alcohol and tannin. Blueish-purple with aromas of fruit preserves, it is supple and delicately fine. Well-ripened black cherry with complexity and an agreeable ampleness. It has been commercially made, but no matter, because it is so good.

🔑 Dom. Denis Boussey, rue du Pied-de-la-Vallée, 21190 Monthélie, tel. 03.80.21.21.23, fax 03.80.21.62.46 ☑ 🍷 by appt.

DENIS CARRE Les Noizons 1998★★

■ n.c. n.c. 🛢 70–99 F

A wine that runs the gamut with kirsch, undergrowth and toasted aromas. It is round and supple, yet has a good tannic structure with a touch of leanness. However, it has great charm and would be excellent with beef and morel mushrooms.

🔑 Denis Carré, rue du Puits-Bouret, 21190 Meloisey, tel. 03.80.26.02.21, fax 03.80.26.04.64 ☑ 🍷 ev. day 8am–6pm

CHANSON PERE ET FILS
Clos Blanc 1997★

■ 1er cru n.c. 2,700 🛢 150–199 F

A very well-made wine that should have a good future. A ruby and peony colour with honeyed notes on the nose, which are a little surprising in a red. The attack is supple, the structure well-founded, and there are fairly delicate tannins and good acidity. The finish is a little hard and should soften as it ages. Aromatically unusual but absolutely orthodox on the palate.

🔑 Chanson Père et Fils, 10, rue Paul-Chanson, 21200 Beaune, tel. 03.80.22.33.00, fax 03.80.24.17.42, e-mail tmarion@vins-chanson.com 🍷 by appt.

DOM. DU CHATEAU DE MEURSAULT Clos des Epenots 1997★★

■ 1er cru 3.5 ha 16,000 🛢 150–199 F

The Château de Meursault belongs to the Boisseaux empire. **Les Petits Noizons 97** is grown on the stony soils at the top of the hill; this is worth mentioning because it shows in the tannins and the astringency. The general harshness on the palate is not at all surprising in a 97 (100–149F). But this Clos des Epenots, which is a magnificent ruby colour, has a richness, a suppleness and a balance that enchanted the jury. Blackcurrant and raspberry combine on the nose. Good in two years or perhaps even in twenty.

🔑 Ch. de Meursault, 21190 Meursault, tel. 03.80.26.22.75, fax 03.80.26.22.76 ☑ 🍷 by appt.

PATRICK CLEMENCET
Clos des Charmots 1998★

■ 1er cru 0.2 ha 700 🛢 100–149 F

This is another family-owned estate which has produced a robust, full-bodied Premier Cru where the tannins are prominent but well-integrated. The nose is open and appetising: well-ripened bilberry fruit, hints of resin and spices. Advisable to wait four or five years to enjoy its quality to the full.

🔑 Patrick Clémencet, pl. de l'Europe, 21630 Pommard, tel. 03.80.22.59.11, fax 03.80.24.17.32 ☑ 🍷 by appt.

HENRI DELAGRANGE ET FILS
Les Bertins 1997★

■ 1er cru 0.44 ha 2,500 🛢 100–149 F

Odd to think that the founding father of Le Chambertin had vineyards in the Côte-de-Beaune. This vintage of Les Bertins is an ardent red and has a very straightforward nose. One of the tasters noted 'this wine has something' – which we felt was somewhat understated. Morello cherry and undergrowth confirm that it is a Pommard, and its aromas burst out in the mouth. Very pleasant straight away or for keeping.

🔑 Dom. Henri Delagrange et Fils, rue de la Cure, 21190 Volnay, tel. 03.80.21.61.88, fax 03.80.21.67.09 ☑ 🍷 by appt.

RODOLPHE DEMOUGEOT
Les Vignots 1998★★

■ n.c. n.c. 🛢 100–149 F

Two very high quality 98s: the **Village** perfectly representative, and this Les Vignots. The whole harvest is de-stemmed, and the wine spends fourteen months in wood and there is no filtration. This is meticulous work which allows the Pommard to show off all its best qualities. It is so dense in colour that you cannot see the bottom of the glass. It has a nose with aromatic herbs: thyme and bay leaf. Perfect passage on the palate, straightforward and without the slightest harshness. It holds great promise for the future. Two stars twice.

🔑 Dom. Rodolphe Demougeot, 2, rue du Clos-de-Mazeray, 21190 Meursault, tel. 03.80.21.28.99, fax 03.80.21.29.18 ☑ 🍷 by appt.

CH. DE DRACY 1997

■ 0.4 ha 2,000 🛢 200–249 F

This is deep red rather than vivid red. The first aroma is vanilla, the second more attenuated with hints of cherry. Light, delicate flavours in the same spirit which some describe feminine. Certainly a wine to investigate, st like the 13th century château which is an pressive fortress in the Côte Chalonnaise. enoît de Charette is the lord of this manor, d he divides his time between this wine and e Albert Bichot business.

SCA Ch. de Dracy, 71490 Dracy-lès-ouches, tel. 03.85.49.62.13 by appt.

Benoît de Charette

H. GENOT-BOULANGER

es Sazenay 1997*

1er cru	1.8 ha	8,200	70–99 F

A deep ruby colour. The wine is delicate d subtle with tannins that will need five ars to soften. The palate is direct, quite ele-nt and promising. The **Village 97** is deep rnet. It opens its account with a touch of erry opening out to aromas of violets. The st must wait, but it deserves a commenda-on. François Delaby has just taken over om Guillaume de Castelnau as head of the tate that was bought by his grandfather in 975.

Ch. Génot-Boulanger, 25, rue de Cîteaux, 21190 Meursault, tel. 03.80.21.49.20, fax 03.80.21.49.21, e-mail genot-boulanger@wanadoo.fr by appt.

GILBERT ET PHILIPPE GERMAIN 1997

■	1 ha	2,000	70–99 F

This wine will give pleasure while young, but will also be good after a time in the cellar. This vineyard was taken over from the parents in 1995, and has since been enlarged and developed. Nuances of black cherry in this 97 which also has aromas of undergrowth and nut kernels. It is of average intensity but full of flavour, and has silky tannins against a liquorice background.

Philippe Germain, 21190 Nantoux, tel. 03.80.26.05.63, fax 03.80.26.05.12 by appt.

BURGUNDY

Côte de Beaune (North Central region)

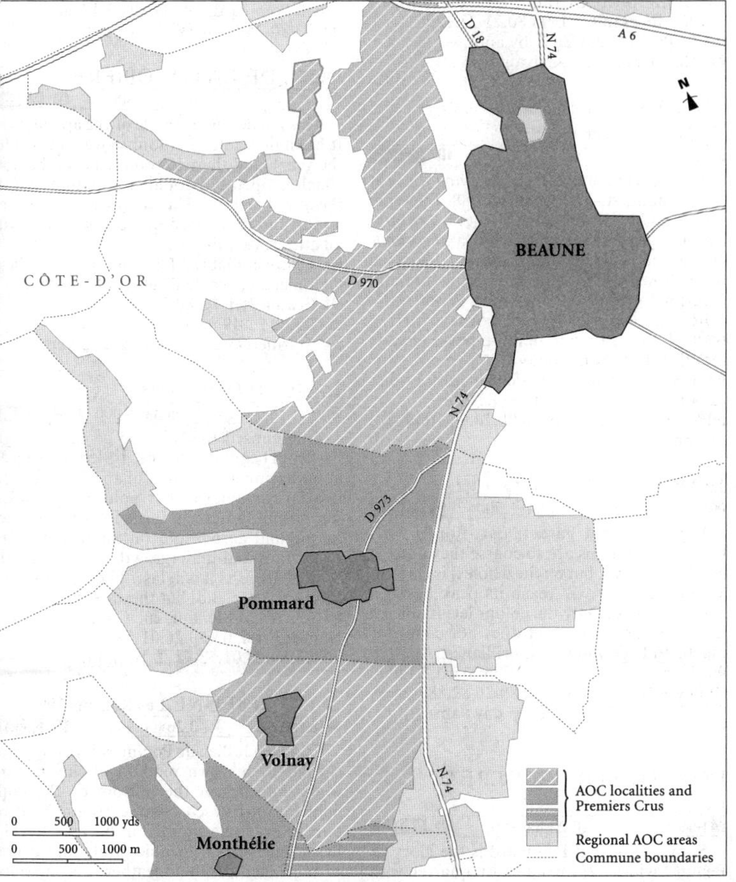

DOM. GEORGES GLANTENAY

Les Rugiens 1997*

■ 1er cru 0.22 ha n.c. 100–149 F

The bunches of grapes are de-stalked, then a medium-length fermentation of about ten days takes place. This Pommard is not very powerful, but is awarded points throughout the tasting. Delicate ruby and pleasant to look at, it has a very direct nose which is open, floral and inevitably vanilla. It is round, supple and balanced on the palate and very seductive.

Dom. Georges Glantenay et Fils, chem. de la Cave, 21190 Volnay, tel. 03.80.21.61.82, fax 03.80.21.68.66 ev. day 10am–6pm

ALBERT GRIVAULT Clos Blanc 1998*

■ 1er cru 0.89 ha 3,800 100–149 F

Le Clos Blanc in Pommard produces red, not white, wine. But the wine has no identity crisis. It is a pretty cherry colour with charming oakiness. A lively, tannic palate that is powerful with good characteristics. It is easy to understand why the Carmélite sisters in Beaune used to venerate this vineyard! Well up to the standard of a Premier Cru.

Dom. Albert Grivault, 7, pl. du Murger, 21190 Meursault, tel. 03.80.21.23.12, fax 03.00.00.00.00 by appt.

Héritiers Bardet-Grivault

CH. DES GUETTES

Le Clos de Verger 1998*

■ 1er cru n.c. 1,200 150–199 F

François Parent has been vinifying wines at the Domaine A.-F. Gros since 1988. Ten years on, he feels totally at home. Sometimes a family wine-grower and sometimes a *négociant-éleveur*, he is an imaginative man. The wine label shows a Burgundy truffle: picture and description. His wine, however, is not *truffé* (idiotic), but green peppercorns with red fruits. It needs time to develop but is already mouth-filling. Fairly oaky.

François Parent, Ch. des Guettes, 14 bis, rue Pierre-Joigneaux, 21200 Beaune, tel. 03.80.22.61.85, fax 03.80.24.03.16 by appt.

JEAN GUITON 1997*

■ 0.64 ha 1,500 100–149 F

Light-coloured garnet; part-floral, part-fruity. The tannins are so coarse they need to be planed down, but on the whole it is elegant. We anticipate it will reach its peak between 2005 and 2010. Only the colour lets it down a little. On the palate that does not count for much, and age will give it brilliance.

Jean Guiton, 4, rte. de Pommard, 21200 Bligny-lès-Beaune, tel. 03.80.26.82.88, fax 03.80.26.85.05 ev. day 9am–12 noon 2pm–7pm

DOM. HUBER-VERDEREAU

Bertins 1998**

■ 1er cru 0.22 ha 900 100–149 F

Some claim that Pommard is the glory of Beaune wines. We would not quarrel with that, and the Bretins confirms the view. Sele tive harvesting of the grapes and cold mace tion contribute to a high level of extraction colour. It has a spicy nose (with woody ton and a vinification that has been carefully ha dled to bring to the fore the qualities of t vintage. It needs to open more, and promis a bright future.

Dom. Huber-Verdereau, rue Moulin-Mareau, 21630 Pommard, tel. 03.80.22.51.50, fax 03.80.22.48.32 by appt.

JEAN-LUC JOILLOT

Les Rugiens 1998**

■ 1er cru 0.25 ha 1,500 150–199

Within a whisker of a *coup de cœur*, this is dramatic Rugiens which should keep for long time. Alfred Hitchcock placed Pomma at the centre of a riddle in one of his films a like a Hitchcock film, the wine keeps you suspense to the end. Deep garnet in colo with perfumes of truffle and undergrow and game; it is very mature, supple, long ar well-made, so it will keep you on tenterhoo for a long time to come.

Jean-Luc Joillot, rue Marey-Monge, 21630 Pommard, tel. 03.80.22.47.60, fax 03.80.24.67.54 by appt.

DOM. DE LA GALOPIERE 1998

■ n.c. 900 100–149

This is a decent example of the appellatio It has a light amber colour (a little brown fc the year), and there is good fruit on the nos which is open but could still mature. A fu flavoured palate. The tannins are not to strong and it has medium length, fruity wi an attractive finish.

Claire et Gabriel Fournier, Dom. de la Galopière, 6, rue de l'Eglise, 21200 Bligny-lès-Beaune, tel. 03.80.21.46.50, fax 03.80.21.49.93, e-mail c.g.fournier@wanadoo.fr by appt.

LA JOLIVODE 1998*

■ 1.06 ha 5,000 70–99

A Pommard that likes to go in a straigh line from beginning to end. Its lengthy mace ation has made it powerful and long (twent two days in tank which is 'going some' as the say in Burgundy, meaning 'a lot'. It is betwee purple and garnet and on the nose we fin redcurrant and undergrowth. Promising: th acidity suggests it will last. The tannins com through at the end, but they are quite soft.

Christian Menaut, rue Chaude, 21190 Nantoux, tel. 03.80.26.01.53, fax 03.80.26.01.53 by appt.

DOM. LEJEUNE Les Rugiens 1997

■ 1er cru 0.26 ha 900 200–249

François Jullien de Pommerol was very pre cise about his own method of vinification whole bunches at the bottom of the tank lightly foot-pressed, semi-carbonic macera tion, twenty two months in barrel, etc. Thi Les Rugiens has carmine glints and a nos with blackcurrant and leather. The ensembl ems a little over-developed, but it shows me youth still on the palate. It will keep for average length of time (two to five years) hile the **Les Poutures 97** (100–149F), which as given the same grade, should not be unk for at least five years.

Dom. Lejeune, La Confrérie, pl. de Eglise, 21630 Pommard, . 03.80.22.90.88, fax 03.80.22.90.88 ☑ Y appt.

Famille Jullien de Pommerol

OM. CHANTAL LESCURE

es Vignots 1998

1.01 ha 2,000 100–149 F

Intense purple colour and a really woody ste. Coffee, smoky and toasty aromas com- ine together on the nose. On further consid- ation, we detected a handsome jammy avour, a fresh attack that was straightfor- ard and well-structured. It is a wine to wait r. Chantal Lescure, who is no longer with s, was the inventor of a famous French pres- re cooker. Her children are continuing the eat work.

Dom. Chantal Lescure, 34A, rue Thurot, 1700 Nuits-Saint-Georges, l. 03.80.61.16.79, fax 03.80.61.36.64, -mail domaine-lescure.com ☑ Y by appt.

OM. MAILLARD PERE ET FILS

a Chanières 1998★

0.78 ha n.c. 100–149 F

Back in 1952, Daniel Maillard started his omaine with just a few vines, but it now cov- rs 18 ha (45 acres) and seven *villages*, includ- ng this one. It is deep red and evocative of amey undergrowth and well-ripened fruit. he oak is very evident. It is a lively thorough- red with good tannins that have yet to be amed.

Dom. Maillard, 2, rue Joseph-Bard, 1200 Chorey-lès-Beaune, el. 03.80.24.00.42, fax 03.80.24.00.42 ☑ Y y appt.

ATHERINE ET CLAUDE MARECHAL La Chanière 1998★

0.87 ha 4,400 100–149 F

This wine is full and fairly round on the pal- te, and has concentrated aromas of black- urrant and bilberry. It is making steady rogress. It does not have the sturdiest of tructures but has drive, attack and cleanness. The tannins are calming down. Very dark in olour with hints of violet. Oak on the nose, eering towards raspberry.

EARL Catherine et Claude Maréchal, 6, te. de Chalon, 21200 Bligny-lès-Beaune, el. 03.80.21.44.37, fax 03.80.26.85.01 ☑ Y y appt.

MOILLARD 1997

■ n.c. n.c. 150–199 F

'Le Rouge et le Noir' could be the name of his wine, from what you see in the glass. Its ose is a mixture of vanilla (the first scent) nd then animal fur and raspberry. It is an archetypal Pommard, which is sturdy, stern and in control.

Moillard, 2, rue François-Mignotte, 21700 Nuits-Saint-Georges, tel. 03.80.62.42.22, fax 03.80.61.28.13 ☑ Y ev. day 10am–6pm; cl. Jan.

DOM. MOISSENET-BONNARD

Les Charmots 1998★★

■ 1er cru 0.22 ha 1,000 100–149 F

A quartet of trumps. We tried four wines which all received good marks and were warmly commended. If one had to be selected, then it would be the Charmots 98 Premier Cru. Notes of kirsch play deliciously with the velvety tannins. Great panache! It should be allowed to age, of course. The **Epenots Premier Cru 98** has great qualities (two stars) and the simple **Village**, is admira- ble (70–99F). The silky tannins in this one won over the team. Finally, the **Pézerolles Premier Cru 98** (100–149F) is awarded one star. All the wines will keep well. A estate to remember.

Dom. Moissenet-Bonnard, rte d'Autun, 21630 Pommard, tel. 03.80.24.62.34, fax 03.80.22.30.04 ☑ Y by appt.

DOM. RENE MONNIER

Les Vignots 1998★

■ 0.77 ha 4,000 70–99 F

The bunches of grapes for this wine are 100% de-stalked, and come from a vineyard which– it is claimed – escaped the phylloxera beetle in the 15th century. Its colour is more like a Bordeaux wine, and the aroma is faintly like lightly fried mushrooms. Its body is still a little young, but has breeding, well-structured in a virile style. A warm and inviting wine. Good to accompany saddle of rabbit with onion purée, for example.

Dom. René Monnier, 6, rue du Dr-Rolland, 21190 Meursault, tel. 03.80.21.29.32, fax 03.80.21.61.79 ☑ Y ev. day 8am–12 noon 2pm–6pm

M. et Mme Bouillot

DOM. MUSSY Epenots 1998★

■ 1er cru 0.57 ha 2,000 100–149 F

This Epenots 98 has all the class of a tradi- tional Pommard. Its colour is cloaked in cherry, and while the nose is austere, with care, it has the potential to produce great things. Pleasantly fresh with good structure and staying power in its length, the method of extraction produces more body than fruit, but, it will be a good wine in five years' time.

Dom. Mussy, anc. rte. d'Autun, 21630 Pommard, tel. 03.80.22.89.11, fax 03.80.24.79.79 ☑ Y by appt.

DOM. DES OBIERS Rugiens 1998★

■ 1er cru 0.45 ha 1,800 200–249 F

The producer claims this is made in a revolving tank. A Rugiens with colour of great depth. The nose is reminiscent of jam being made on the stove, cooked fruit, bil- berry and spices. It has silky tannins and con- centrates on bilberry fruit with persistent

jammy flavours, but its intensity, length and structure suggest a very successful wine.
Dom. des Obiers, chem. rural n° 29, 21700 Nuits-Saint-Georges, tel. 03.80.62.42.00, fax 03.80.61.28.13, e-mail nuicave@wanadoo.fr by appt.

DOM. PARENT Les Epenots 1997★★

■ 1er cru n.c. 3,600 150–199 F

The estate had the honour of having Thomas Jefferson as one of its customers. It has produced this very great Epenots. A deep purple colour, it releases on the nose spiced, peppery notes with overtones of bilberry and blackberry. Fleshy and seductively round: the fleshiness is more than agreeable, and it will probably last. Besides this, in their **Village** wines, the **Croix Blanche 97** (100–149F), one star, as well as **Les Chaponnières 97** (150–199F), which is very well-made and has well-integrated tannins.
SAE Dom. Parent, pl. de l'Eglise, 21630 Pommard, tel. 03.80.22.15.08, fax 03.80.24.19.33, e-mail parent-pommard@axnet.fr by appt.

DOM. ANNICK PARENT Les Rugiens 1997★

■ 1er cru 0.5 ha 3,000 100–149 F

Annick Parent is not curt about anything, especially her vineyard and her grapes. Her wine is her reward. The Clos Gauthey domaine has been passed down from mother to daughter, and it has 18th century charm. Her Rugiens 97 is on the pale side. With aromas of wild strawberries, it is lively and light and not at all unpleasant, though it would improve from spending time in the cellar.
Dom. Annick Parent, rue du Château-Gaillard, 21190 Monthélie, tel. 03.80.21.21.98, fax 03.80.21.21.98, e-mail annick.parent@wanadoo.fr by appt.
Jean Parent

DOM. PARIGOT PERE ET FILS Charmots 1998★

■ 1er cru 0.55 ha 3,300 100–149 F

A good Pommard should be deep garnet in colour. This one is. It should have a good nose. This one has. It should be well-made, full and well-structured. This lacks none of those. It should show off its fruit. As it does. The tannins should be under control. As they are. Though it still has the greenness of youth, we are sure it has time ahead of it.
Dom. Parigot Père et Fils, rte. de Pommard, 21190 Meloisey, tel. 03.80.26.01.70, fax 03.80.26.04.32 by appt.

DOM. DU PAVILLON Clos du Pavillon Monopole 1997★

■ 3.86 ha 22,000 200–249 F

A soft, smooth fruity wine, dark ruby in colour with hues of blue. It has a vinous nose in the good sense of the term, and traces of mushroom. It is not very expansive on the palate but it is undoubtedly a Pommard. A *climat* which should merit being better known for delicate wines.
Dom. du Pavillon, 6 bis, bd Jacques-Copeau, 21200 Beaune, tel. 03.80.24.37.37, fax 03.80.24.37.38

MICHEL PICARD 1997

■ n.c. 10,000

E solo robur – it has an appropriate mott but we could add *quercus*, or oak. The red lightly tinged with brown, and it has smo aromas with leather and game in the blend. lively, tannic wine that needs to matu because its strength and length have not se tled down yet.
Michel Picard, rte. de Saint-Loup-de-la Salle, 71150 Chagny, tel. 03.85.87.51.00, fax 03.85.87.51.11

GEORGES ET THIERRY PINTE 1997★

■ 0.69 ha 1,200 70–99

The bottle has a traditional label of parchment with curling edges. The grapes ar de-stalked, left in the tank for ten days, an matured both in the tank and the cask. Da ruby. Ripe fruit and sweet mignonette. background of forest and undergrowth aro mas. Solidly structured and full-bodie Complexity. Delicacy. Should be tasted agai in a few years. It is already balanced.
GAEC Georges et Thierry Pinte, 11, ru du Jarron, 21420 Savigny-lès-Beaune, tel. 03.80.21.51.59, fax 03.80.21.51.59 ev. day 9.30am–11.30am 2pm–7pm; Sun. by appt.

DOM. PRIEUR-BRUNET Les Platières 1997

■ 1er cru 0.12 ha 700 150–199

Fairly lively ruby colour with touches c blackcurrant, though this is not yet very pro nounced. An honest approach which show off the fruit but also includes the right quan tity of tannin. It has length and promise, bu is still a little closed and is waiting to be dis covered. Wooden fermenting vats deliver th goods.
Dom. Prieur-Brunet, rue de Narosse, 21590 Santenay, tel. 03.80.20.60.56, fax 03.80.20.64.31, e-mail uny-prieur@prieursantenay.com by appt.

MICHEL REBOURGEON Rugiens 1997★★

■ 1er cru 0.17 ha 980 100–149

It is a magnificent peony red. The nose ha depth and is perfumed with lilac, pepper an blackcurrant. It is full and rich on the palat with a unctuous body that is well-structured This is a genuine Rugiens which should be pu in the cellar and forgotten for two or thre years.
Michel Rebourgeon, pl. de l'Europe, 21630 Pommard, tel. 03.80.22.22.83, fax 03.80.22.90.64 by appt.

REBOURGEON-MURE 1997★

■ 1.52 ha 3,600 70–99 F

An elegant wine which is not too powerful and has character. It is exactly what to expect from a *village* of this vintage. The **Clos des Arvelets 98** and the **Grands Epenots 97** (this one priced 100–149F) should also find a place in your cellar. The first should be kept for a long time, the second should be drunk earlier, in three or four years.

Daniel Rebourgeon-Mure, Grande-Rue, 21630 Pommard, tel. 03.80.22.75.39, fax 03.80.22.71.00 by appt.

REINE PEDAUQUE 1998★

■ n.c. 6,000 100–149 F

A legendary Pommard with well-balanced tannins (good maceration) and an intense, brilliant colour. It has a cherry nose and a tannic structure which is very solid with has a perfumed after-taste. A wine that holds much in reserve yet it is generous. No fears for the future.

Reine Pédauque, Le Village, 21420 Aloxe-Corton, tel. 03.80.25.00.00, fax 03.80.26.42.00, e-mail rpedauque@axnet.fr by appt.

REGIS ROSSIGNOL-CHANGARNIER 1997★

■ 0.51 ha 2,000 100–149 F

This wine provoked an intense discussion. They do not strip the grapes from the stalks here. Short fermentation period: only eleven days. An attractive 97 of an average ruby colour with light, though delicate, perfumes and strong oakiness, but you are aware of the fruit the second time. One taster remarked on the good concentration. Another said it was tannic and quite austere. In many cases this means the same thing. It is nonetheless atypical, but should certainly be opened sometime in 2003 for another look.

Régis Rossignol, rue d'Amour, 21190 Volnay, tel. 03.80.21.61.59, fax 03.80.21.61.59 by appt.

DOM. VINCENT SAUVESTRE

Clos de La Platière 1998★★

■ 2 ha 14,000 150–199 F

'Vin vert, riche Bourgogne', a local saying meaning 'green wine, rich Burgundy'. This Pommard is a little green, indeed, but it is not a wine for you if you prefer something facile. Ruby and blackcurrant to the eye, opening with kirsch and cherry in brandy on the nose. It has genuine distinctive elegance and hints of liquorice and fresh grapes. We had great confidence in this wine because it is complete and confident.

Dom. Vincent Sauvestre, rte. de Monthélie, B.P. 3, 21190 Meursault, tel. 03.80.21.22.45, fax 03.80.21.28.05 by appt.

VEUVE DE MALVAUX

Cuvée Prestige 1997★★

■ n.c. 4,500 100–149 F

A Philibert wine from the SEDVPD brand. White-heart cherry and cinnamon. Remarkably toned-up for a *village*! A very pleasing body. Well-structured, mature, long with soft liquorice flavours. Please forgive us if that is all we have to say about this wine: it is perfect, full-stop. It is practically at its peak and would be a worthy partner for some good red meat.

Veuve de Malvaux, 1, rue Ziem, 21200 Beaune, tel. 03.80.24.05.88, fax 03.80.22.37.08 ev. day 9am–7pm

CHRISTOPHE VIOLOT-GUILLEMARD

Clos Orgelot 1998★

■ 1er cru 1.1 ha 3,800 100–149 F

The jury agreed that this wine is homogenious. Clear colour and delicate oak, fruity, strong tannins and full-flavour. It is far from open. In three or four years we would be inclined to have another look! A star also for the **Rugiens 97** which is still bursting with youth (150–199F).

Christophe Violot-Guillemard, rue de la Refene, 21630 Pommard, tel. 03.80.22.03.49, fax 03.80.22.03.49 by appt.

Volnay

Snuggling in the hollow of the hill, the village of Volnay is as pretty as a postcard. Though less well known than Pommard to the north, the appellation yields nothing to its neighbour and the wines have all the finesse you could hope for. They vary from the lightness of Les Santenots, situated on the neighbouring commune of Meursault, to the robustness and vigour of the Clos des Chênes or the Clos des Champans. We shall not list all of them here for fear of omitting some. Le Clos des Soixante Ouvrées is another very well-known wine, and provides the opportunity to explain the origin of the word: an *ouvrée* dates from the Middle Ages and measures four ares and twenty-eight centiares, representing a basic unit of vineyard soil that a worker could break up in a day, using a

BURGUNDY

pick. This area corresponds to 100 m^2 (109 yds^2).

Many 19th-century writers have referred to Volnay wines. When the Viscount de Vergnette addressed the Congrès des Vignerons Français in 1845, he finished his erudite report with the following words: 'The wines of Volnay will continue for a long time into the future to be the best wines in the world, as they were in the 16th century under our Dukes who owned the de Caille-du-Roy vineyards there.' 'Caille-du-Roy' became 'Cailleray' then 'Caillerets'. In 1999, 11,362 hl (299,957 gal) of Volnay were produced.

BITOUZET-PRIEUR Caillerets 1997★

■ 1er cru 0.15 ha 900 100–149 F

There was an old saying that if a wine-producer had no vines in Les Caillerets then he had no notion of Volnay's worth. This particular 97 has elegance and finesse, made in a style that appeals to today's tastes. It is graceful and firm. The wine is clear red, with strong cherry flavours combined with assertive tannins. A good example of what can be done with this vintage. Small parcel, small production.

Vincent Bitouzet-Prieur, rue de la Combe, 21190 Volnay, tel. 03.80.21.62.13, fax 03.80.21.63.39 by appt.

DOM. JEAN-MARC BOULEY

Clos des Chênes 1997★★

■ 1er cru 0.4 ha 2,000 100–149 F

This was amongst the best wines in the tasting. The Clos des Chênes was highly praised by the jury. It can be drunk now with pleasure, though it is wiser to wait. It does not stint with anything, not even the colour which is very characteristic for a 97. There are aromas of undergrowth, mushroom, a hint of violets, red berry and bilberry fruit and roasting coffee; it is rich. The **Caillerets 97 Premier Cru** is awarded a star for its elegance and the **Village 97** (70–99F), not quite so good but still not at all bad.

Jean-Marc Bouley, chem. de la Cave, 21190 Volnay, tel. 03.80.21.62.33, fax 03.80.21.64.78 by appt.

REYANE ET PASCAL BOULEY

1998★★

■ 1er cru 0.52 ha 2,000 100–149 F

We award one star to the **Champans 98**, it is still a chewy mouthful but very representative of its terroir. This, naturally, needs to age. The Premier Cru is more agreeable already and is intense from start to finish. Supple but spicy with underlying blackcurrant. A well-made wine with good oak that harmonises well without overwhelming the fruit. This *cuvée* comes from the Robardelle and Roncere *climats* near to Les Caillerets.

Pascal Bouley, pl. de l'Eglise, 21190 Volnay, tel. 03.80.21.61.69, fax 03.80.21.66.44 by appt.

DOM. JEAN-MARIE BOUZEREAU

1997★★

■ 0.4 ha 1,000 70–99 F

This Volnay comes from good stock. It is garnet with lovely violet glints and has an attractive spicy and fruity nose. On the palate it is very tightly woven, precise, well structured and, inevitably, a little oaky. Its capacity to age adds to the pleasure that we experience right from the beginning. In addition, the **Champans 97 Premier Cru** also looks good and is commended by the jury. (100–149F).

Jean-Marie Bouzereau, 7, rue Labbé, 21190 Meursault, tel. 03.80.21.62.41, fax 03.80.21.65.97 by appt.

DOM. VINCENT BOUZEREAU

Les Champans 1998★

■ 1er cru 0.25 ha 600 100–149 F

The **Village 98** (70–99F) lacks neither body or fruit or richness. It should be put aside for two years. The Champans, on the other hand is full-bodied, warm and virile as a Champans should be. It is very typical of the vintage and the terroir. Court circular: Princess Mathilde of the Belgians recently honoured this cellar with a visit.

Vincent Bouzereau, 7, rue Labbé, 21190 Meursault, tel. 03.80.21.61.08, fax 03.80.21.65.97 by appt.

DOM. FRANCOIS BUFFET

Clos de la Rougeotte Monopole 1997★

■ 1er cru n.c. 2,000 100–149 F

The **Clos des Chênes** was stunning for a 94 vintage, and the 97 from the same *climat* is awarded a star. This wine continues to improve. It is concentrated, powerful and for keeping. It has not developed a great deal, and is still closed, long, and will benefit from two or three years in the cellar. The Clos de la Rougeotte is a Premier Cru from a 'monopole' (Frémiets, near Pommard).

Dom. François Buffet, petite place de l'Eglise, 21190 Volnay, tel. 03.80.21.62.74, fax 03.80.21.65.82, e-mail dfbuffet@aol.com by appt.

Jacques Buffet

DOM. CAILLOT

Clos des Chênes 1997★★

■ 1er cru 0.13 ha 700 100–149 F

Bossuet loved Volnay wines, and on the eve of his death he ordered some to be delivered to the Bishopric of Meaux, for his funeral. He could have chosen this superb Clos des Chênes. It is dark, heavy velvet with a nose of damp animal fur, with well-ripened blackberry and a touch toasty. A well-bred wine with silk and spice, and the oak is well-

ıtegrated. Not to be opened for three or four ears.
Dom. Caillot, 14, rue du Cromin, 21190 Meursault, tel. 03.80.21.21.70, ax 03.80.21.69.58 ☑ Y by appt.

F. CHAUVENET 1997

■ n.c. 6,000 ⅢⅠ 100–149 F

'There is only one Volnay in France' the Abbé Courtépée quite rightly observed, over 200 years ago. It has a wonderful colour with a perfume of fruit steeped in brandy. Most obviously, raspberries. On the palate, it is more blackberry, cooked plums and good firm tannins. Colette wrote an enthusiastic report about this firm at Nuit, which has been taken over by Jean-Claude Boisset.
F. Chauvenet, 9, quai Fleury, 21700 Nuits-Saint-Georges, tel. 03.80.62.61.43, fax 03.80.62.37.38

LOUIS CHAVY 1997*

■ n.c. 6,000 ⅢⅠ 100–149 F

In the past, some writers believed Volnay was the crater of an extinct volcano. This wine does indeed have a warm core. It is purple-garnet with a nose that has presence, subtle with mixed fruit aromas. Good attack without any harshness. Well-structured, but the oak does not dominate the Pinot Noir. To drink in three to five years.
Louis Chavy, Caveau la Vierge Romaine, pl. des Marronniers, 21190 Puligny-Montrachet, tel. 03.80.26.33.00, fax 03.80.24.14.84, e-mail mallet.b@cva-beaune.fr ☑ Y ev. day 10am–6pm; cl. Nov.–Mar.

DOM. CYROT-BUTHIAU 1998*

■ 0.45 ha 2,300 ⅢⅠ 100–149 F

This wine is not filtered. This perhaps explains its slight lack of clarity, but we should point out that we tried it when it was very young. On the nose there are tones of undergrowth and musk. It was harsh in February 2000 and was not showing in its best light, but if allowed to develop quietly, it will be excellent quality when decanted.
Dom. Cyrot-Buthiau, rte. d'Autun, 21630 Pommard, tel. 03.80.22.06.56, fax 03.80.24.00.86 ☑ Y by appt.

HENRI DELAGRANGE ET FILS 1997*

■ 1.73 ha 10,000 ⅢⅠ 70–99 F

At the moment this wine is not at its best, however, it still upholds the family honour (since 1500). It is deep purple and silky, with a combination of cherry stone and grilled aromas. However, all the different elements have not yet settled in. It is supple on the attack and has a satisfactory texture, with fine tannins and a classy finish. A true *village* from this terroir which would hold its own with a bœuf bourguignon.
Dom. Henri Delagrange et Fils, rue de la Cure, 21190 Volnay, tel. 03.80.21.61.88, fax 03.80.21.67.09 ☑ Y by appt.

JOSEPH DROUHIN Chevret 1997**

■ 1er cru n.c. n.c. ⅢⅠ 150–199 F

Burgundy does not have a reputation for being soft. However, here is a friendly example that has been well brought up. A brilliant colour, with cherry and a sweet, delicate oakiness on the nose. On the palate, it is very elegant and balanced. A very good wine. This *climat* is in a tiny corner of Le Cailleret.
Joseph Drouhin, 7, rue d'Enfer, 21200 Beaune, tel. 03.80.24.68.88, fax 03.80.22.43.14, e-mail drouhin@calva.net Y by appt.

CH. GENOT-BOULANGER Les Aussy 1997*

■ 1er cru 0.4 ha 1,800 ⅢⅠ 100–149 F

You can count on this wine. The fruit and tannins are balanced, it has good length but is a bit young and closed. However, it has promise. The colour is as deep as the ocean. There is not a lot on the nose yet. The label illustrates the front of the property and makes you want to be invited to stay.
Ch. Génot-Boulanger, 25, rue de Cîteaux, 21190 Meursault, tel. 03.80.21.49.20, fax 03.80.21.49.21, e-mail genot-boulanger@wanadoo.fr ☑ Y by appt.
Mme Delaby

DOM. GEORGES GLANTENAY ET FILS Santenots 1997

■ 1er cru 0.52 ha n.c. ⅠⅢⅠ 100–149 F

Les Santenots is an enclave in the commune of Meursault and covers only 29 ha (72 acres). This is a brilliantly-coloured 97. The nose jumps between fresh white bread and toasted bread before showing its youthful aspect. It is fresh, clean and has promising fine tannins but beware, do not uncork this bottle before two or three years' time.
Dom. Georges Glantenay et Fils, chem. de la Cave, 21190 Volnay, tel. 03.80.21.61.82, fax 03.80.21.68.66 ☑ Y ev. day 10am–6pm

GOICHOT 1997*

■ n.c. 1,800 ⅢⅠ 100–149 F

Goichot is a *négociant-éleveur* who produces a Volnay with good quality freshness and firmness. The fruit is forthcoming and the tannins scrupulously smooth. The nose is open and the wood does not obscure the fruit. The colour is bright garnet with a ruby background.
SA A. Goichot et Fils, av. Charles-de-Gaulle, 21200 Beaune, tel. 03.80.26.88.70, fax 03.80.26.80.69, e-mail goichot@goichotsa.com ☑ Y by appt.

JEAN GUITON Les Petits Poisots 1997

■ 0.34 ha 1,500 ⅢⅠ 70–99 F

This the neighbour of Les Famines (the name of a *climat* that you never see on a wine label). This Petits Poisots is between the main road and the Premier Cru vineyards. Light youthful colour hints of pink. This is an intense and spicy 97, developing towards musk, and quite oaky. Somewhat lacking in

BURGUNDY

body but it is not bad for a *village*.
Jean Guiton, 4, rte. de Pommard, 21200 Bligny-lès-Beaune, tel. 03.80.26.82.88, fax 03.80.26.85.05 ev. day 9am–12 noon 2pm–7pm

DOM. ANTONIN GUYON

Clos des Chênes 1997★

1er cru 0.87 ha 4,800 150–199 F

The Antonin Guyon estate owns nearly 1 ha (2.5 acres) of this Premier Cru that is superbly situated on the hillside just above Les Caillerets. He produces a Volnay here that matches the blueprint of the appellation in every particular. It is intense, lively, fresh, elegant and that is just the way it looks. The nose and the palate are in perfect harmony.
Dom. Antonin Guyon, 21420 Savigny-lès-Beaune, tel. 03.80.67.13.24, fax 03.80.66.85.87, e-mail vins@guyon-bourgogne.com by appt.

DOM. HUBER-VERDEREAU

Fremiets 1998★

1er cru 0.11 ha 600 100–149 F

Volnay is often described as a 'feminine' wine, meaning soft or light. Not this one. This attractive 98 has a brilliant and intense colour and a nose with bilberry fruit mixed with oak. It is tannic and well-structured at first and, to be accurate, fairly masculine. Representative of the vintage. It will keep for an average time but is characteristic of a new-style Volnay.
Dom. Huber-Verdereau, rue Moulin-Mareau, 21630 Pommard, tel. 03.80.22.51.50, fax 03.80.22.48.32 by appt.

DOM. JESSIAUME PERE ET FILS

Brouillards 1998★

1er cru 0.26 ha 1,500 150–199 F

The Jessiaume family have been cultivating these 15 ha (37 acres) for five generations and today they have an oenologist in their ranks. Their Volnay passes all the first trials with flying colours. Its brilliant colour and very aromatic nose with game and leather mark it out from the pack. On the palate, it is not quite up to par, but this 98 is a fine example of a 'vin plaisir', a wine to drink among friends. A wine with good potential which adds to its interest.
Dom. Jessiaume, 10, rue de la Gare, 21590 Santenay, tel. 03.80.20.60.03, fax 03.80.20.62.87 by appt.

DOM. LA POUSSE D'OR

Clos de la Bousse d'Or Monopole 1997

1er cru 2.13 ha 8,737 200–249 F

Clos de la Bousse d'Or. Domaine de la Pousse d'Or. Connoisseurs are aware that they have recently been taken over by an important wine-grower. The team that took over La Pousse d'Or in December 1997 presents this 97 which is deep, gleaming red. Opens wonderfully with game and leather aromas. You think you are dealing with an old trooper, but this is in fact a Volnay that is quite different. It is still closed, of course, bu has evident warmth. Produced by th Monopole du Clos.
Dom. de la Pousse d'Or, rue de la Chapelle, 21190 Volnay, tel. 03.80.21.61.33, fax 03.80.21.29.97, e-mail la-pousse-d'or.fr by appt.
Landanger

DOM. CHANTAL LESCURE 1998★

1.5 ha 2,000 100–149

This is the wine to choose for a meal after day's hunting, and it has a label for the occa sion. The tannins are untamed and auster and far from soft. But the colour is impecca ble and the cherry jam flavours combine we with the oak from barrel ageing. It has char acter and spirit. To be opened for a futur celebration, And not too soon.
Dom. Chantal Lescure, 34A, rue Thurot 21700 Nuits-Saint-Georges, tel. 03.80.61.16.79, fax 03.80.61.36.64, e-mail domaine-lescure.com by appt.

LOUIS MAX Clos des Chênes 1997★

1er cru n.c. n.c. 500 F+

Light ruby in colour. A Volnay with a nos of red berry fruit and vanilla (with a sligh smokiness from the wooden cask). Althoug powerful, it does not lack elegance.
Louis Max, 6, rue de Chaux, 21700 Nuits-Saint-Georges, tel. 03.80.62.43.01, fax 03.80.62.43.16

DOM. DES OBIERS

Clos des Chênes 1998★

1er cru 0.4 ha 3,000 100–149 F

Sometimes good things are worth waiting for. This wine needs time because its finish is somewhat harsh, but it has some good qualities: violet-ruby in colour, opening with blackcurrant and a supple vinosity that is pronounced. It is typically characteristic. Should be allowed to mature for three or four years.
Dom. des Obiers, chem. rural n° 29, 21700 Nuits-Saint-Georges, tel. 03.80.62.42.00, fax 03.80.61.28.13, e-mail nuicave@wanadoo.fr by appt.

DOM. ANNICK PARENT

Fremiets 1997★

1er cru 0.64 ha 2,700 100–149 F

This *climat* borders Pommard. The Parent family is knowledgeable about this area. Annick has produced a very masculine, direct wine. It has a ripe blackcurrant and leather nose with absolute staying power. On the palate, it lacks totally in softness but has fruit and richness, structure and length. Characteristic and very promising for a 97. It will be a good wine in four or five years.
Dom. Annick Parent, rue du Château-Gaillard, 21190 Monthélie, tel. 03.80.21.21.98, fax 03.80.21.21.98, e-mail annick.parent@wanadoo.fr by appt.

DOM. JEAN PARENT

Clos des Chênes 1997

1er cru 0.24 ha 450 100–149 F

This wine is soft and light. 'A good wine', so the saying goes in Burgundy, 'is one that likes its neighbour'. It has a straightforward colour which is a hint of good things to come. A few vegetal aromas enliven the nose. The 97 is more open than you would expect for the year as it finishes with a tiny touch of austerity.

Dom. Jean Parent, rue du Château-Gaillard, 21190 Monthélie, tel. 03.80.21.21.98, fax 03.80.21.21.98, e-mail annick.parent@wanadoo.fr by appt.

DOM. PARIGOT PERE ET FILS

Les Echards 1998

■ 0.72 ha 4,500 70–99 F

On the map, Les Echards is next to Le Ronceret, that is to say it borders a Premier Cru. The dark red colour is seductive. The nose is dominated by blackcurrant from the start to the finish. It has the combined qualities of finesse and staying power. The estate has one part in the Côte and the other in the Hautes-Côtes covering a total of 17 ha (42 acres).

Dom. Parigot Père et Fils, rte. de Pommard, 21190 Meloisey, tel. 03.80.26.01.70, fax 03.80.26.04.32 by appt.

DENIS PHILIBERT

Les Brouillards 1997

■ n.c. 1,500 100–149 F

Les Brouillards is one of the group of *climats* that are next to Pommard, near Les Angles. This Volnay is a winner. An interesting nose with bay leaf and very ripe fruit, along with oaky and peppery aromas, it is quite astringent and tannic at this stage in its development and should be allowed to mature and soften.

Maison Denis Philibert, 1, rue Ziem, 21200 Beaune, tel. 03.80.24.05.88, fax 03.80.22.37.08 ev. day 9am–7pm

MICHEL PICARD 1997

■ n.c. 12,400 100–149 F

A round wine which is light, undoubtedly, but has great finesse. A wine in part measures that is not intensely coloured, but this reminds us that a Volnay usually has shades of violet. It is best to drink quite young and its grace should be enjoyed before it wanes.

Michel Picard, rte. de Saint-Loup-de-la-Salle, 71150 Chagny, tel. 03.85.87.51.00, fax 03.85.87.51.11

MAX ET ANNE-MARYE PIGUET-CHOUET

Les Grands Champs 1998

■ 0.28 ha 1,200 70–99 F

A Volnay from an old estate, which has been run by Max and Anne-Marye since 1999, and likely to be taken over by their three sons. It is light red with glints of redcurrant. The nose of this 98 remains furtive. It is fresh and lively on the palate with red berry fruit and sweet spice. There is a touch of bitterness which is not at all surprising. An honest wine that needs a little time.

Max et Anne-Marye Piguet-Chouet, rte. de Beaune, 21190 Auxey-Duresses, tel. 03.80.21.25.78, fax 03.80.21.68.31 by appt.

THIERRY PINQUIER-BROVELLI

1997

■ 0.5 ha 3,300 70–99 F

Maurice Pinquier is an *ouvrier-vigneron* who established his domaine in 1955. His son is following in his footsteps. In the good old days, you could acquire 5 ha (12 acres) through hard work. This wine has aggressive tannins which will soften with time. The nose gradually distinguishes itself from the oak. The palate is good and honest.

Thierry Pinquier, 5, rue Pierre-Mouchoux, 21190 Meursault, tel. 03.80.21.24.87, fax 03.80.21.61.09 ev. day 8am–7pm

DOM. POULLEAU PERE ET FILS

1998★

■ 1.22 ha 4,100 70–99 F

Three wines selected from this estate of 8 ha (20 acres), which has been run by the younger generation since 1996. The **Village 98 en Vieilles Vignes** and the **Premier Cru 98** (several *climats* together, more than likely), were both commended. The straightforward *village* from the same year is awarded a star. It is raspberry red and has aromas of cherry and undergrowth and has the right amount of richness with fruit on the finish. They create a very good impression.

Dom. Poulleau Père et Fils, rue du Pied-de-la-Vallée, 21190 Volnay, tel. 03.80.21.62.61, fax 03.80.26.45.90 by appt.

DOM. JACQUES PRIEUR

Clos des Santenots 1997★★

■ 1er cru 1.2 ha 890 150–199 F

This is one of the best Volnay wines. It has a perfect balance between good acidity and mellow tannins. A wine with a nose of discreet red berry fruit and strong oakiness. Jacques Prieur's estate has largely been taken in hand by Antonin Rodet and this is proving successful. Nadine Gublin is one of the best oenologists in Burgundy.

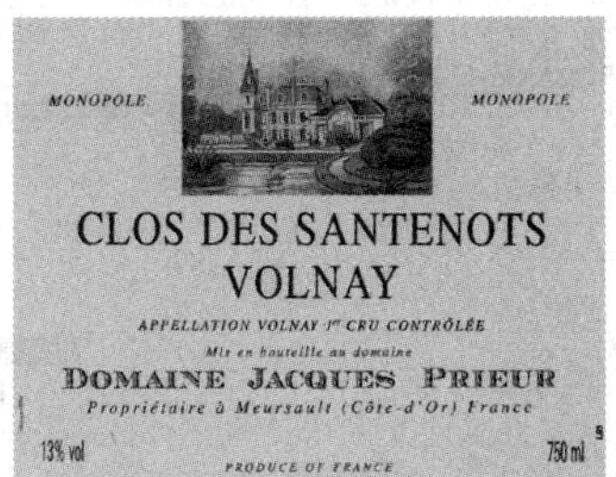

🔑 Dom. Jacques Prieur, 6, rue des Santenots, 21190 Meursault, tel. 03.80.21.23.85, fax 03.80.21.29.19 ☑ Y by appt.

DOM. REBOURGEON-MURE

Caillerets 1997★

■ 1er cru 0.32 ha 1,500 🍷 70-99 F

This year we tried a Caillerets with a velvety colour and a nose which has the scent of animal fur. It opens well, and morello cherry can already be detected. On the palate, freshness and fruit give maximum pleasure.

🔑 Rebourgeon-Mure, Grande-Rue, 21630 Pommard, tel. 03.80.22.75.39, fax 03.80.22.71.00 ☑ Y by appt.

NICOLAS ROSSIGNOL

Ronceret 1997★

■ 1er cru 0.24 ha 600 🍷 100-149 F

This *climat* is cradled just below Le Champans. This young wine-grower is presenting the first offspring from his labours. Pronounced purple in colour, at first the nose on this 97 presents liquorice and vanilla. Powerful for a Volnay, it is a wine with good staying power whose elegance is almost refined, and with a touch of astringency at the finish. 'In general and in detail, the wine satisfied us.'

🔑 Nicolas Rossignol, rue de Mont, 21190 Volnay, tel. 03.80.21.62.43, fax 03.80.21.27.61 ☑ Y by appt.

REGIS ROSSIGNOL-CHANGARNIER 1997

■ 1.7 ha 5,000 🍷 70-99 F

With 80% of the harvest being de-stalked this has produced a 97 that is deep and clear. The colour leads on to a nose which is half fruit and half oak. It is still a little hard but the wine has the structure of a good *village*. It will not take offense at the time needed to soften the taninns.

🔑 3 Régis Rossignol, rue d'Amour, 21190 Volnay, tel. 03.80.21.61.59, fax 03.80.21.61.59 ☑ Y by appt.

ROSSIGNOL-FEVRIER PERE ET FILS 1997★★

■ n.c. 4,000 🍷 50-69 F

Notre-Dame des Vignes that is depicted on the label was built on the hill after the 1870 war. This wine is blessed with a deep garnet colour and a blackcurrant nose. On tasting it has substance, structure, finesse and length. For the time being it is quite closed but is a very attractive Volnay that will improve in time. Very good value for money.

🔑 GAEC Rossignol-Février, rue du Mont, 21190 Volnay, tel. 03.80.21.64.83, fax 03.80.21.67.74 ☑ Y by appt.

CH. ROSSIGNOL-JEANNIARD

Santenots 1997★★

■ 1er cru 2 ha 1,500 🍷 100-149 F

This wine should be drunk with well-seasoned meat dishes and will not disappoint. It is powerful to the very end with great depth, but is elegant nonetheless. A wine with grea length. It is obviously rather young, but wi open out more (keep for three to five years)

🔑 Ch. Rossignol-Jeanniard, rue de Mont, 21190 Volnay, tel. 03.80.21.62.43, fax 03.80.21.27.61 ☑ Y by appt.

CHRISTOPHE VAUDOISEY 1998★

■ 4 ha n.c. 🍷 70-99

Christophe Vaudoisey is the current repre sentative of a family that has been in the win business for eight generations. His well-bre **Clos des Chênes 98** is commended by the jur It presents a basket of red berry and bilberr fruit with aromas of roasted coffee (100 149F). The **Village** should also be given time Its attractive colour invites you to taste th wine. The nose is all cherry and raspberry an does not disappoint. The oakiness is agree able on the palate and does not spoil th balance. It will be pleasant in two or thre years.

🔑 Christophe Vaudoisey, pl. de l'Eglise, 21190 Volnay, tel. 03.80.21.20.14, fax 03.80.21.27.80 ☑ Y by appt.

JOSEPH VOILLOT Les Champans 199

■ 1er cru 1.07 ha 3,000 🍷 100-149 F

A 10 ha (25 acre) – family-run estate. Thi Les Champans has a colour that is very typi cal of the vintage. It is straightforward witl no frills. The nose is quite sweet and the per fumes of raspberry and undergrowth mi with the vanilla from the cask. Good, light easy-going flavours on the palate which i direct rather than thought-provoking. It ca be drunk straight away and would go wel with roast guineafowl.

🔑 Joseph Voillot, pl. de l'Eglise, 21190 Volnay, tel. 03.80.21.62.27, fax 03.80.21.66.63 ☑ Y by appt.

Monthélie

The combe of Saint-Romain separates the terroirs producing red wines from those producing whites. Monthélie is on the south-facing slope of the combe. This little village is somewhat overshadowed by its more famous neighbours but produces wines of excellent quality. In 1999 production totalled 5,723 hl (151,087 gal) of red wine and 501 hl (13,226 gal) of white.

ERIC BOIGELOT Sur la Velle 1997

■ 1er cru 0.26 ha 1,400 🍷 70-99 F

A precocious, engaging wine that is good to look at and to taste. The tannins do not make it too dry. The fruit aromas on the nose follow through to the finish and end with a slight akiness. Eric Boigelot cultivates his 8 ha (20 cres) with care and he has a few *ouvrées* (4 a / .98 acres each) of highly-reputed Premier 'ru. This is an interesting 97 that is doing the est it can and its youthful charm makes up or the depth lacking in the vintage.

Eric Boigelot, rue de Beaune, 21190 Monthelie, tel. 03.80.21.65.85, ax 03.80.21.66.01 by appt.

ACQUES BOIGELOT 1997

0.2 ha 1,300 70–99 F

There is a choice between red and white in his estate. We had a slight preference for the white. It is shiny gold and says everything an loquent Chardonnay can. Crystallised fruit, oasted almond and honey on a lively palate with good staying power.

Jacques Boigelot, 21190 Monthélie, el. 03.80.21.22.81, fax 03.80.21.66.01 by appt.

DOM. BOUCHEZ-CRETAL 1997

0.28 ha 1,400 50–69 F

Its deep colour is worthy of a painting. The wine is intense and certainly not made for mpatient people. Its nose is still wrapped in cellophane, but becomes more complex as the wine breathes. Improvement will take time. We were tasting a 97 which will keep well. It seems to be quite a light wine but has undoubtedly greater ambitions.

SCEA Dom. Bouchez-Crétal, 21190 Monthélie, tel. 03.85.87.17.40, fax 03.48.05.19.32 by appt.

DENIS BOUSSEY

Les Champs Fulliots 1998★

1er cru 0.58 ha 3,000 70–99 F

Here we have a red of high extraction. It already has a good garnet colour and the nose has a partiality for blackcurrant and vanilla. The wood dominates. It needs time to balance out, so it should not be drunk in the immediate future.

Dom. Denis Boussey, rue du Pied-de-la-Vallée, 21190 Monthélie, tel. 03.80.21.21.23, fax 03.80.21.62.46 by appt.

DOM. BOUZERAND-DUJARDIN 1998★

☐ 0.8 ha 2,400 50–69 F

We greatly appreciated the lemony freshness of this white Monthélie that has fresh acidity. A welcome change from the forceful wines that are so pretentious. It has lovely glints of green and lots of floral aromas on the nose. It is not too rich but is true to its type. In the 1950s, Bernard Bouzerand and his son Xavier put the domaine back on its feet. Xavier is passionate about wood carving.

Dom. Bouzerand-Dujardin, pl. de l'Eglise, 21190 Monthélie, tel. 03.80.21.20.08, fax 03.80.21.28.16 by appt.

RODOLPHE DEMOUGEOT

La Combe Danay 1998★★

0.3 ha 1,800 50–69 F

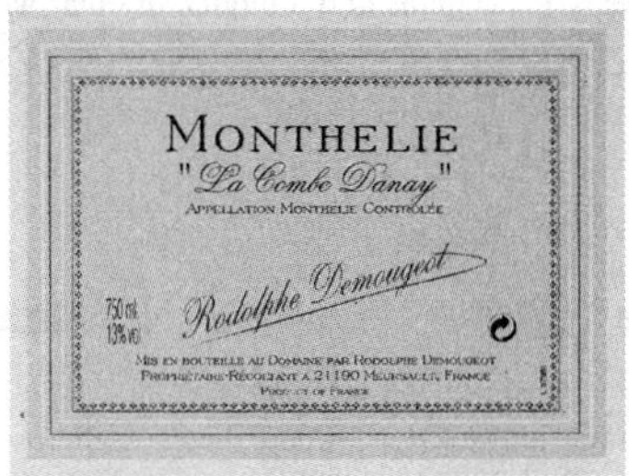

An attractively well-made 98 which has been awarded a *coup de cœur.* A deep carmine red and a wine that has been particularly successfully vinified. The wide-ranging aromatic palette goes from rose to nutmeg via peony and pepper. It is so warm and velvety, with nuances of cherry and cocoa, that it is practically ready. This wine-maker has had a foothold in Monthélie for near ten years, and now has one in Meursault.

Dom. Rodolphe Demougeot, 2, rue du Clos-de-Mazeray, 21190 Meursault, tel. 03.80.21.28.99, fax 03.80.21.29.18 by appt.

MICHEL DESCHAMPS 1998★

☐ 0.76 ha 3,000 50–69 F

A pair of wines that run neck and neck: the **Village 98 Rouge** has good concentration and strong tannins so it will undoubtedly keep well, and the other is a good introduction to the whites of the appellation. The nose rests with citrus and exotic fruits followed by floral fragrances (hyacinth). It is a lively wine that is full of verve and will go well with a *tourte bourguignonne.*

Michel Deschamps, rue du Château-Gaillard, 21190 Monthélie, tel. 03.80.21.28.60, fax 03.80.21.65.77 by appt.

GUY DUBUET 1998

0.4 ha 2,500 50–69 F

This is a small estate of less than 5 ha (12 acres). We tasted a young wine that was bright ruby. Its nose sets out with good aromas that are specific to the terroir. On the palate it takes time to open but is an attractive wine that develops well. The supporting tannins suggest it will age happily. To keep an eye on.

Guy Dubuet, rue Bonne-Femme, 21190 Monthélie, tel. 03.80.21.26.22, fax 03.80.21.29.79 by appt.

PAUL GARAUDET

Le Clos Gauthey 1998

1er cru 1.1 ha 4,300 70–99 F

The colour is dark but it still shines. The nose is only just beginning to show: toasted aromas, roasted coffee as well, but it is likely to develop more complexity with game and

red berry fruit. The 98 takes a long time to open on the palate but is not too oaky at this stage (a good mark). Anyone discarding this wine will regret it later, because it has character, good tannins and a hidden life that will develop in due course.
🔑 Paul Garaudet, imp. de l'Eglise, 21190 Monthélie, tel. 03.80.21.28.78, fax 03.80.21.66.04 ☑ 𝐘 by appt.

GILBERT ET PHILIPPE GERMAIN 1998★

■ 2.2 ha 5,000 ⏸ 30–49 F

Like a good student, this wine is serious, hard-working, quite austere but true. An ample and sturdy 98 where there are glimpses of good potential. Garnet red, finely oaked and a generous nose. Aromas of plums with jammy notes; as well as sweet chestnut and cooked chestnut. Philippe Germain took over the family estate six years ago.
🔑 Philippe Germain, 21190 Nantoux, tel. 03.80.26.05.63, fax 03.80.26.05.12 ☑ 𝐘 by appt.

DOM. REMI JOBARD

Les Vignes-Rondes 1998★

■ 1er cru n.c. 2,000 ⏸ 70–99 F

Ruby colour with fine oaky perfumes with fruity notes. A well-made wine that is supple on the palate and quite full, with a pleasant floral side. Wait for two or three years for the oak to soften. The red Premier Cru, **Les Champs-Fulliot 98**, receives a commendation; the oak influence, from its maturation period in barrel, is very strong, so it needs to wait some time for the fruit to express itself more clearly.
🔑 Dom. Rémi Jobard, 12, rue Sudot, 21190 Meursault, tel. 03.80.21.20.23, fax 03.80.21.67.69, e-mail rémi.jobard@libertysurf.fr ☑ 𝐘 by appt.

OLIVIER LEFLAIVE 1997

■ 1er cru n.c. 6,000 70–99 F

This will accompany a roast very well. But there is no time to be lost. We are dealing with a slight wine, though the colour is bright and attractive. The nose shows some maturity; part-vegetal and part-fruit. On the palate, the touch of elegance puts it into a different bracket. To be drunk now. Olivier Leflaive comes from the famous Leflaive line but he has set up as a *négociant-éleveur* in Puligny.
🔑 Olivier Leflaive, pl. du Monument, 21190 Puligny-Montrachet, tel. 03.80.21.37.65, fax 03.80.21.33.94, e-mail leflaive-olivier@dial.oleane.com ☑ 𝐘 by appt.

MANOIR MURISALTIEN

Les Champs-Fulliots 1997★

■ 1er cru n.c. 3,900 ⏸ 100–149 F

A *négociant-éleveur* business that also trades under the name of Château de Demessey, (which is near Tournus). The 97 is vermilion and presents a good quality nose. It is delicate, balanced and has good length. Sound body with touches of tannic astringence. To be judged in the context of th year.
🔑 Marc Dumont, Manoir Murisaltien, 4, rue du Clos-de-Mazeray, 21190 Meursault, tel. 03.80.21.21.83, fax 03.80.21.66.48 ☑ 𝐘 by appt.

DOM. RENE MONNIER 1998★

■ 0.87 ha 2,000 ⏸ 50–69

A dish of sautéd veal kidneys with a goo wine sauce would be the perfect dish fc this ruby-coloured 98 . . . How should it b described? Burgundy-ruby for a start. Th nose is full of gamey aromas: musk an leather, spices and red fruit. Only of mediur length, but it has structure without an aggres sive finish.
🔑 Dom. René Monnier, 6, rue du Dr-Rolland, 21190 Meursault, tel. 03.80.21.29.32, fax 03.80.21.61.79 ☑ 𝐘 ev. day 8am–12 noon 2pm–6pm
🔑 M. et Mme Bouillot

CH. DE MONTHELIE

Sur la Velle 1997★

■ 1er cru 3 ha 8,700 ⏸ 70–99

The Sur la Velle *climat* is the workhorse o the estate. We are always interested to se what this wine has to say early on in its life. I is wearing the same baptismal robe as man wines the château has produced in previou generations. Deep ruby, silky and soft, i already has charm. However, the little devil i complex and has promise. It falls pleasantl between blackcurrant and spice. The **Villag Rouge 97** is awarded one star. Its nose is full o fruit, the tannins have softened nicely and i has good length with definite oaky tones.
🔑 EARL de Suremain, Ch. de Monthélie, 21190 Monthélie, tel. 03.80.21.23.32, fax 03.80.21.66.37 ☑ 𝐘 by appt.

DOM. J. PARENT Sur la Velle 1998★

■ 1er cru n.c. 1,000 ⏸ 70–99 F

An old Beaune family with three centuries of wine-makers and coopers. Here they say 'mon–tlee' (not 'mon–té–lee') but this garnet-coloured Premier Cru speaks with a different accent: the nose is an exotic experience marked with a light note of cinnamon. It is very chewy and opens out on the palate and follows through to the finish. It matures in barrel, which does it great service, and it is rich and intense with Pinot Noir flavours that are stronger than the oak. Also worth looking at, the **Clos Gauthey 97 Rouge**, which is where the family home is. The jury commended the **Premier Cru**.
🔑 Dom. Jean Parent, rue du Château-Gaillard, 21190 Monthélie, tel. 03.80.21.21.98, fax 03.80.21.21.98, e-mail annick.parent@wanadoo.fr ☑ 𝐘 by appt.

ALBERT PONNELLE

En Percherottes 1997

■ n.c. n.c. 100–149 F

There is an old saying that 'a chicken in Monthélie dies of hunger during the grape

harvest'. There are so many vines around the village. This Monthélie is shown by one of the Ponnelle houses of Beaune but, as yet, the nose is not very eloquent; it has genuine simplicity on the palate and an appealing directness. A 'good lad'. Notes of kirsch.
Albert Ponnelle, Clos Saint-Nicolas, 38, fg Saint-Nicolas, 21200 Beaune, tel. 03.80.22.00.05, fax 03.80.24.19.73 by appt.

PASCAL PRUNIER 1998

■ 0.38 ha 1,400 50–69 F

Bright cherry. This wine does not hide its light under a bushel. It has a communicative nose (game, undergrowth, a hint of rubber), that is helped by the stylish tannins that fade delicately into the background. A robust, vigorous wine. The **Premier Cru Les Vignes Rondes 98 Rouge** (70–99F) could also find a place in your cellar but should not be kept for long. For your information, this estate has changed address from Auxey-Duresses to Meursault.
Pascal Prunier, 23, rue des Plantes, 21190 Meursault, tel. 03.80.21.66.56, fax 03.80.21.67.33 by appt.

PRUNIER-DAMY 1998

■ 1.48 ha 4,000 50–69 F

This estate produces a red **Village 98** which is very supple on the palate, and the nose veers towards cherries in brandy. It is likely to keep for some time – at least for three years.
Philippe Prunier-Damy, rue du Pont-Boillot, 21190 Auxey-Duresses, tel. 03.80.21.60.38, fax 03.80.21.26.64 ev. day except Sun. 9am–11.30am 2pm–6pm

Auxey-Duresses

Two wine slopes are to be found at Auxey-Duresses. The Premier Crus of Duresses and Le Val are highly regarded. The 'Meursault' slope produces excellent white wines which, although they lack the reputation of the great appellations, are very affordable. This appellation produced 2,145 hl (56,628 gal) of white wine in 1999, and 4,927 hl (130,073 gal) of red.

CORINNE ET PASCAL ARNAUD-PONT Le Reugne 1998

□ 1er cru 0.43 ha 1,200 70–99 F

Vincent Pont is a tenant-farmer at Auxey-Duresses, and he has vinified and bottled this wine. It is already golden, and the subtle nose has notes of apricot and minerals, and almost iodised aromas. It is fruity and soft and should be kept a little longer.
Pascal et Corinne Arnaud-Pont, 36, av. Théophile-Gautier, 75016 Paris, tel. 01.42.24.74.80, fax 01.40.78.24.78

DOM. BILLARD ET FILS

Les Jonchères 1998

■ 0.32 ha 1,500 50–69 F

This house has a lovely tradition: Grandma (93 at the last harvest) cuts the last bunch of grapes. This estate is in the Hautes-Côtes and has gradually extended towards Beaune, Saint-Romain and as far as Jonchères. This is a lively, brilliant red with aromas of flowers and fresh fruit. It has a clean taste but takes time to express itself, though it is likely to fulfill its promise in a year or two.
Dom. Billard et Fils, rte. de Beaune, 21340 La Rochepot, tel. 03.80.21.87.94, fax 03.80.21.72.17 by appt.

BOUCHARD PERE ET FILS

Les Duresses 1997★

■ 1er cru n.c. n.c. 70–99 F

Auxey has recently added its name to this Premier Cru, but not by chance. It is a reddish Duresses with a voluptuous nose (leather, tobacco, game) which progresses through to firm tannins, and has a certain chewiness which is in no way unpleasant.
Bouchard Père et Fils, Ch. de Beaune, 21200 Beaune, tel. 03.80.24.80.24, fax 03.80.22.55.88, e-mail france@bouchard.pereetfils.com by appt.

DENIS CARRE Bas des Duresses 1998★

■ 1er cru n.c. n.c. 50–69 F

Two wines with practically equal good marks. We slightly preferred the Premier Cru, though the **Village 98 Rouge** was given the same score. On the palate, Les Bas des Duresses is spicy on the finish, densely woven, robust with a good deal of flesh and spirit. The oak is discreet: the fruity notes (blackberry) and pronounced tannins suggest it will keep well. Deep, dark colour.
Denis Carré, rue du Puits-Bouret, 21190 Meloisey, tel. 03.80.26.02.21, fax 03.80.26.04.64 ev. day 8am–6pm

LOUIS CHAVY 1997★

■ n.c. 6,000 70–99 F

The nose ranges from blackcurrant to peony. An intense garnet-red that is in tune with what should be expected. It is fruity, and the richness strikes a resonant chord. Full on the palate and long with a lively finish. It can stay in the cellar for several years.
Louis Chavy, Caveau la Vierge Romaine, pl. des Marronniers, 21190 Puligny-Montrachet, tel. 03.80.26.33.00, fax 03.80.24.14.84, e-mail mallet.b@cva-beaune.fr ev. day 10am–6pm; cl. Nov.–Mar.

CHRISTIAN CHOLET-PELLETIER

1998★

□ 0.25 ha 600 50–69 F

This wine has been made with care, as is evident from its structure and concentration. It has light acidity but is more friendly and soft by nature, and is wrapped up with the sweet flavours of honey. The nose is somewhere between roasted almonds and lemon. It is the lovely golden-yellow shade that you will find in the vineyards in autumn. The winemaker is installed on La Plaine de Meursault, and he already produced an exceptional 97 vintage.

Christian Cholet, 21190 Corcelles-les-Arts, tel. 03.80.21.47.76, fax 03.80.21.47.76 ev. day 8am–12 noon 2pm–6pm

CH. DE CITEAUX Les Duresses 1997★

■ 1er cru n.c. 3,000 70–99 F

The violet-red is similar to the colour of vine leaves in the autumn. The nose has mineral and blackcurrant notes. It is powerful, solid and very rich on the palate, almost monolithic. The extraction was undoubtedly significant, but this is a wine that will only wake up in four or five years.

Philippe Bouzereau, Ch. de Cîteaux, 18–20, rue de Cîteaux, B.P. 25, 21190 Meursault, tel. 03.80.21.20.32, fax 03.80.21.64.34,
e-mail domaine.bouzereau@wanadoo.fr by appt.

CLOS DU MOULIN AUX MOINES

Monopole Elevé en fût de chêne 1998★

■ 3 ha 15,000 50–69 F

These vines once belonged to Cluny, and the monks used to vinify the grapes grown in this *clos*. Later it became the estate of Roland Thévenin, the wine-producer and poet. It is now the turn of Muriel and Emile Hanique, who have been here since 1995. Their very young 98 shows signs of being firm and vigorous (gamey nose). Good-looking, and it has a frank, balanced body which is still tannic and has length. Not to be opened before 2002.

Emile Hanique, Dom. du Moulin aux Moines, 21190 Auxey-Duresses, tel. 03.80.21.60.79, fax 03.80.21.60.79 ev. day 9am–12 noon 2pm–7pm

DOM. JEAN-PIERRE DICONNE

1998★

■ 1.4 ha 3,500 50–69 F

There is a lovely view over the countryside, and the hilltops of the *Côte*, from this estate. This Auxey has well-built tannins with the attributes of its terroir, clear and beginning to open out with some red berry fruit. However, its richness suggests it will be sumptuous – without doubt it will soften. A wine that would stand up to a cheese made from *lait cru*.

Jean-Pierre Diconne, rue de la Velle, 21190 Auxey-Duresses, tel. 03.80.21.25.60, fax 03.80.21.26.80 by appt.

LES VILLAGES DE JAFFELIN

1998★★

□ n.c. 9,000 70–99 F

A fine example from 'Villages de Jaffelin'. Jean-Claude Boisset took over this enterprise but retains the Côte-de-Beaune spirit. A light greyish-gold colour with aromas of gunflint and lemon maintaining a touch of mineral throughout. The handling of the wood is exemplary. Perfect as an partner for a good Saône pike.

Jaffelin, 2, rue Paradis, 21200 Beaune, tel. 03.80.22.12.49, fax 03.80.24.91.87 by appt.

DOM. JESSIAUME PERE ET FILS

Les Ecusseaux 1998★

□ 1er cru 0.31 ha 2,100 100–149 F

One of our tasting team noted 'this is good work'! A wine that is brilliant, though pale in colour, with a floral nose touched with apple. Its rich opulence even made an impression in the *tastevin*. It is round but has enough nerve, sinew and acidity to age and will be formidable when it reaches its peak in a year or two.

Dom. Jessiaume Père et Fils, 10, rue de la Gare, 21590 Santenay, tel. 03.80.20.60.03, fax 03.80.20.62.87 by appt.

DOM. DE LA ROCHE AIGUE 1998★

□ 1.5 ha 3,800 50–69 F

A pallid gold wine with a nose of hawthorn and hazelnut. It is balanced, supple and flowery with a touch of oak. A fullness on the palate that makes its presence felt.

Eric et Florence Guillemard, EARL La Roche Aiguë, rue du Glacis, 21190 Meloisey, tel. 03.80.26.02.04, fax 03.80.26.06.14 by appt.

HENRI LATOUR ET FILS 1998★★

□ 0.56 ha 3,180 70–99 F

Both the **Rouges Village** (50–69F) and the **Premier Cru 98** (70–99F) are awarded one star, but this wine is also remarkable. Fine lees and *bâtonnage*, we're at the right school here. This wine would go marvellously with chicken in cream sauce. It has perfect looks and a nose of grapefruit and apricot set off by a mineral touch. An elegant, clean wine that thrills the palate.

Henri Latour et Fils, rte. de Beaune, 21190 Auxey-Duresses, tel. 03.80.21.22.24, fax 03.80.21.63.08 by appt.

MALLARD-GAULIN 1998★

□ 0.2 ha 1,000 100–149 F

Pale straw with glints of green – this looks like a classic. The nose is spicy, vanilla, flowery, in the modern style. So a modern classic. After a lively attack, it starts discreetly to open with soft flavours of sweet almond and honey. An elegant, clean wine.

Maison Mallard-Gaulin, 21420 Aloxe-Corton, tel. 03.80.26.46.10, fax 03.80.26.43.57

CATHERINE ET CLAUDE MARECHAL 1998★

■ 2.24 ha 4,000 70–99 F

A typical 98 which has a long story to tell; a clean, frank first impression and a remarkable persistence that evolves through the tasting. The colour is still young. The second time around, the nose is better than the first, showing some fruit. In 2001, Catherine and Claude Maréchall will have been running this place for twenty years.

EARL Catherine et Claude Maréchal, 6, rte. de Chalon, 21200 Bligny-lès-Beaune, tel. 03.80.21.44.37, fax 03.80.26.85.01 Y by appt.

CHRISTOPHE MARY 1998★

■ 0.15 ha 450 50–69 F

Deep red enhanced by first vegetal then fruity aromas. It was a little harsh when we tasted it, but has a lot in reserve and the length is promising. Do not open before 2003.

Christophe Mary, 21190 Corcelles-les-Arts, tel. 03.80.21.48.98, fax 03.80.21.48.98 Y by appt.

PIGUET-GIRARDIN

Les Grands Champs 1997★

■ 1er cru 0.18 ha 1,200 50–69 F

A *climat* on the lower Premier Cru slopes. Les Grands Champs is cherry in colour and blackcurrant on the nose. Good attack, rich and full, good balance between body and tannins, attractively aromatic. We did not tire of this wine, which is easy to drink. Two estates merged in 1985 to ensure that this one, 12 ha (30 acres), had a future.

Dom. Piguet-Girardin, rue du Meix, 21190 Auxey-Duresses, tel. 03.80.21.60.26, fax 03.80.21.66.61 Y by appt.

VINCENT PONT 1998★

■ 1.32 ha 2,000 50–69 F

He has only just turned twenty and is just starting out, though his name is well-known in the region. His bright purple, slightly terracotta-red wine presents raspberry and linden flower at first then it is severe, even austere because of its tannins, not unusual at this age. It should not be opened up too early, because it must wait its turn (two or three years).

Vincent Pont, rue des Etoiles, 21190 Auxey-Duresses, tel. 03.80.21.27.00, fax 03.80.21.24.49 Y by appt.

DOM. JEAN-PIERRE ET LAURENT PRUNIER 1998★

□ 1.2 ha 3,000 50–69 F

When you ask for the way to the Prunier cellar at Auxey, you have to remember a first name. Pruniers fill the whole telephone book of this village. Here we are talking about Jean-Pierre and Laurent, who have produced a well-attired Chardonnay. It has a mineral, iodine nose which suits it perfectly. The next stage shows a good balance between its acidity and richness, some power and hints of beeswax.

Dom. Jean-Pierre et Laurent Prunier, rue Traversière, 21190 Auxey-Duresses, tel. 03.80.21.27.51, fax 03.80.21.27.51 Y by appt.

MICHEL PRUNIER 1998★★

■ 1er cru n.c. 4,600 70–99 F

Auxey is often hard and virile when young. Don't throw your eyes heavenwards when you come across it, because the structure of this 98 is exactly what a concentrated Premier Cru should be at this stage and it has great potential. You can taste that they do not de-stalk the grapes. The initial vegetal aromas open out into redcurrant.and, though it is still mute on the palate, it will have a lot to say when the time comes.

Dom. Michel Prunier, rte. de Beaune, 21190 Auxey-Duresses, tel. 03.80.21.21.05, fax 03.80.21.64.73 Y by appt.

PASCAL PRUNIER 1998★★

□ 1.16 ha 5,000 50–69 F

Pascal Prunier produced a very successful Les Duresses 89. Here, we recommend his pleasing **Village Rouge 98**. The white version has one of the most attractive colours of the region. On the palate, honeysuckle flavours feature in its complexity and it has just enough acidity to stand the test of time. The wine is the fruit of excellent work in the vineyard and barrel. Pascal Prunier has recently moved to Meursault.

Pascal Prunier, 23, rue des Plantes, 21190 Meursault, tel. 03.80.21.66.56, fax 03.80.21.67.33 Y by appt.

DOM. VINCENT PRUNIER

Les Grands Champs 1998★★

■ 1er cru 0.35 ha 1,600 70–99 F

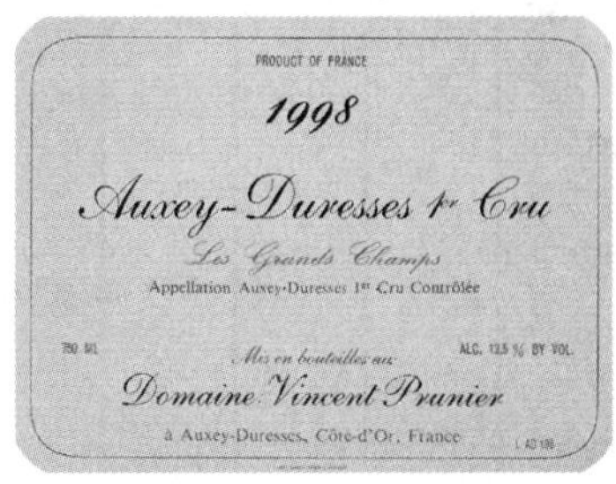

Vincent Prunier was not born a wine-producer, but he became one when he established his estate in 1988. This is his tenth vintage. There is a school of 'line drawing' in cartoons, and this wine is similarly marvellously uncluttered. So, we voted it a *coup de cœur*. Its colour is worthy of a painting, and the red berry fruit aromas have been enhanced by the wood but remain distinct. It has splendid concentration and an after-taste of morello cherry. The tannins are softened by its richness.

Vincent Prunier, rte. de Beaune, 21190 Auxey-Duresses, tel. 03.80.21.27.77, fax 03.80.21.68.87 by appt.

JEAN-MARC VINCENT

Les Hautes 1998★

☐ 0.9 ha 1,000 70–99 F

This is an original label: it shows the bottle you are looking at with the same label on the bottle with the label on the bottle . . . disappearing into infinity, but this wine will not make you see double. Jean-Mark Vincent took over his grandfather's vineyards five years ago. His 98 is deep gold, a flint and citrus fruit style with carefully judged oak. It is solidly built and there is enough acidity to ensure it will age well.

Jean-Marc Vincent, 3, rue Sainte-Agathe, 21590 Santenay, tel. 03.80.20.67.37, fax 03.80.20.67.37 by appt.

Saint-Romain

This vineyard is situated midway between the Côte and the Hautes Côtes. The wines of Saint-Romain – 4,992 hl (131,789 gal) – are mainly whites – 2,690 hl (71,016 gal) in 1999, fruity, fresh-flavoured and, according to the wine-makers, always ready to give more than they promise when young. In 1996 production was 1,922 hl (50,741 gal) of red wines, rising to 2,302 hl (60, 773 gal) in 1999. The location itself is magnificent and very much worth a special trip to see.

FRANCOIS D'ALLAINES 1997★

☐ n.c. 3,300 70–99 F

A Chardonnay with a virtual presence at 'dallaines.com', a site that is worth a visit, but the wine is anything but virtual. So far, it is intense and still evolving but is nicely honeyed with minerals and vegetal hints. The richness and acidity are equaly present. Although the wine is still a little green, it is complete and should be left to rest for a few more months.

François d'Allaines, La Corvée du Paquier, 71150 Demigny, tel. 03.85.49.90.16, fax 03.85.49.90.19, e-mail francois@dallaines.com by appt.

BERTRAND AMBROISE 1998★

☐ 2.47 ha 8,000 70–99 F

Saint Romain was a hermit in the Jura and a brother of the order of Saint Lupicin. This wine would have drawn him out of his cave. Clear, light yellow, an apricot nose, warm and slightly honeyed. Characteristic, in a word. In two years' time it will be perfect.

Maison Bertrand Ambroise, rue de l'Eglise, 21700 Premeaux-Prissey, tel. 03.80.62.30.19, fax 03.80.62.38.69, e-mail bertrand.ambroise@wanadoo.fr by appt.

DOM. BILLARD ET FILS

La Perrière 1998★

■ 0.85 ha 3,500 50–69 F

This is what you would call a good wine-producer's wine. Blackberry in colour and a wide open nose; red berry fruit, of course, but there is complexity too. It develops smoothly after being a little savage to begin with. We are not far from the Hautes-Côtes, which is where the wine-grower comes from. Good raw materials, satisfactory balance. This 98 could age a little.

Dom. Billard et Fils, rte. de Beaune, 21340 La Rochepot, tel. 03.80.21.87.94, fax 03.80.21.72.17 by appt.

BOUCHARD PERE ET FILS 1997★

■ n.c. n.c. 70–99 F

All the qualities you would expect from this *négociant-éleveur* are found in this appellation. This is a 'very honest' wine, as they say around here. A typical garnet-red. Pure and simple raspberry and blackcurrant on the nose. It has freshness on the palate, and the tannins are as ethereal as angels. To drink in the next two years.

Bouchard Père et Fils, Ch. de Beaune, 21200 Beaune, tel. 03.80.24.80.24, fax 03.80.22.55.88, e-mail france@bouchard.pereetfils.com by appt.

CHRISTOPHE BUISSON

Sous le Château 1998★

■ 0.5 ha n.c. 50–69 F

This wine has an underlying mineral note with good acidity, tannins, and a touch of bitterness. There is a flavour of redcurrants and some warmth from the alcohol. To put to one side for two to four years.

Christophe Buisson, 21190 Saint-Romain, tel. 03.80.21.63.92, fax 03.80.21.67.03 by appt.

Gilles Buisson

DENIS CARRE Le Jarron 1998★

■ n.c. n.c. 50–69 F

In the village this *climat* is highly regarded for producing a very red red. It opens with a little blackcurrant and its acidity ensures both freshness and length. This is not a wine you would keep for seven years, but it could easily be kept for four.

Denis Carré, rue du Puits-Bouret, 21190 Meloisey, tel. 03.80.26.02.21, fax 03.80.26.04.64 ev. day 8am–6pm

CHARTRON ET TREBUCHET

Vieilli en fût de chêne 1998★★

☐ n.c. 9,500 100–149 F

Sometimes the Ecole Polytechnique leads to Burgundy wine. It did in the case of Louis Trébuchet, an old boy from the Ecole Polytechnique – who made a career change after his association with Jean Chartron, the former mayor of Puligny and local wine-grower. This 98 appears well-structured, round and pleasant with strong vanilla tones. It needs time to mature.

Chartron et Trébuchet, 13, Grande-Rue, 21190 Puligny-Montrachet, tel. 03.80.21.32.85, fax 03.80.21.36.35, e-mail jmchartron@chartron-trebuchet.com ev. day 10am–12.30pm 2pm–6pm; cl. Nov.–Mar.

DOM. DU CHATEAU DE PULIGNY-MONTRACHET 1997

☐ 0.46 ha 3,000 70–99 F

This Saint-Romain is true to the domaine's motto: 'Vérité contre tout', or 'Truth above all'. The golden-grey is typical of the terroir and the grape variety. It awakens the senses first with its expressive aromas, with a good mineral finesse, also tending towards hazelnut and quince. The oak is very subtle. It has an average length and, on the palate, finishes with a touch of honey.

SCEA Dom. du Château de Puligny-Montrachet, 21190 Puligny-Montrachet, tel. 03.80.21.39.14, fax 03.80.21.39.07, e-mail chateaupul@aol.com by appt.

F. CHAUVENET 1998

☐ n.c. 9,000 70–99 F

Chauvenet was founded at Nuits-Saint-Georges in 1853 and has always been run by women. Colette brought enthusiasm to the place, Françoise Chauvenet took it through its first hesitant steps while Nathalie, Jean-Claude Boisset's daughter, watches over its development. Greenish-gold with greyish glints, this is a wine that would be excellent with a mushroom *tourte*: it is direct, clean and lively. The fruit is still hiding.

F. Chauvenet, 9, quai Fleury, 21700 Nuits-Saint-Georges, tel. 03.80.62.61.43, fax 03.80.62.37.38

JOSEPH DROUHIN 1998★

☐ n.c. n.c. 100–149 F

The attractive nose of this Saint-Romain presents white-fleshed fruit and flowery notes, embellished with citronella. It is a lightly structured but very accommodating 98 that has a fairly fruity finish. It is ready for drinking and would make a good opener to a dinner.

Joseph Drouhin, 7, rue d'Enfer, 21200 Beaune, tel. 03.80.24.68.88, fax 03.80.22.43.14, e-mail drouhin@calva.net by appt.

Robert Drouhin

GERMAIN PERE ET FILS

Côte de Beaune 1998★

■ 3.23 ha 6,500 50–69 F

'Côte-de-Beaune' next to the name of the *village* is permitted. A superb 98 that is as spectacular as the cliffs at Saint-Romain. It is still closed but gives a hint of prunes. Very dark and immediately seductive on the palate. Fleshy with some muscle and a hint of morello cherry. A wine that does not have great depth, but provides great plesaure.The **Sous le Château 97 Rouge** is very impressive and is a wine to be kept. It was given the same marks.

EARL Dom. Germain Père et Fils, rue de la Pierre-Ronde, 21190 Saint-Romain, tel. 03.80.21.60.15, fax 03.80.21.67.87 ev. day 8am–8pm; Sun. by appt.

DOM. GUY-PIERRE JEAN ET FILS 1998

■ 0.35 ha 1,000 50–69 F

An unusual nose for this bright, deep red 98. It does not have much astringency but holds together on the palate and has balance and concentration. Morello cherry aftertaste.

Dom. Guy-Pierre Jean et Fils, rue des Cras, 21420 Aloxe-Corton, tel. 03.80.26.44.72, fax 03.80.26.45.36 by appt.

MICHEL PICARD 1997

■ n.c. 5,800 70–99 F

This 97 is purple with flecks of brown, so it is changing anchorage, but what a nose. It has a delicate cherry stone aroma that is a little gamey. Clean attack; supple, fruity body; but the alcohol is a little fierce. It is not a wine that has a long voyage to make, but is fresh and has a good wind in its sails.

Michel Picard, rte. de Saint-Loup-de-la-Salle, 71150 Chagny, tel. 03.85.87.51.00, fax 03.85.87.51.11

PRUNIER-DAMY Sous le château 1998

■ 0.19 ha 900 50–69 F

This is cherry-coloured from start to finish. The oak is still evident, but will have softened in two to three years: it has scorched, charred aromas of good quality that contribute to the general balance.

Philippe Prunier-Damy, rue du Pont-Boillot, 21190 Auxey-Duresses, tel. 03.80.21.60.38, fax 03.80.21.26.64 ev. day except Sun. 9am–11.30am 2pm–6pm

FRANCOIS RAPET ET FILS

Côte de Beaune 1998★

■ 4.5 ha 2,000 50–69 F

This Saint-Romain has the right to be labelled 'Côte-de-Beaune'. It is very pale and uncomplicated. It opens with notes of strawberry, gingerbread and has a good hand to play the rest of the game. The tannins are soft, the acidity just so, genuine length and undeniable Sant-Romain character. An attractive wine that should be enjoyed now.

🗝 EARL François Rapet et Fils, rue Sous-le-Château, 21190 Saint-Romain, tel. 03.80.21.22.08, fax 03.80.21.60.19 ☒ Ɪ ev. day 9.30am–12 noon 2pm–6pm

HENRI DE VILLAMONT 1998*

□ n.c. 15,000 ⏸ 100–149 F

This is the Burgundy branch of Shenk, the Swiss group. Henri de Villamont occupies the three lovely buildings and cellars of the late Léonce Bocquet in Savigny. His Saint-Romain white is pleasant with aromas of hawthorn and mandarin: a lovely nose. Good balance. A delicate and interesting character.

🗝 Henri de Villamont, rue du Dr-Guyot, 21420 Savigny-lès-Beaune, tel. 03.80.24.70.07, fax 03.80.22.54.31, e-mail hdv@planetb.fr ☒ Ɪ ev. day except Tue. 9.30am–6.30pm; Thu. 9.30am–12 noon; cl. 15 Nov.–15 Mar.

Meursault

The area producing great white Burgundies really begins at Meursault. In 1999, 19,563 hl (516,463 gal) were produced, and the Premiers Crus are famous world-wide: Les Perrières, Les Charmes, Les Poruzots, Les Genevrières, Les Gouttes d'Or, etc. They combine subtlety and strength, flavours of bracken and grilled almond, the appeal to be drunk young and the quality to keep. Meursault is undoubtedly the 'capital of white Burgundy wines'. A small amount of red wine – 938 hl (24,763 gal) – is also produced.

The 'little châteaux' which still exist in Meursault are relics of a former opulence, and bear witness to a long tradition of famous wines from the area. The festival known as La Paulée began here as a communal banquet that everyone enjoyed at the end of the harvest. It became a traditional event marking the third of the 'Trois Glorieuses', the annual three-day Burgundy wine festival.

CH. DE BLAGNY 1997

□ 1er cru n.c. 30,000 ⏸ 150–199 F

A Meursault-Blagny, and the appellation deserves to be mentioned. It is not very common and commemorates the Château de Blagny, the venerated estate run by Latour. The 97 is fresh and light, golden-straw in colour with glints of green. The nose is white-fleshed with notes of citrus fruits rounded off with a touch of menthol. It has a mineral edge that weighted the balance in its favour.

🗝 Maison Louis Latour, 18, rue des Tonneliers, 21200 Beaune, tel. 03.80.24.81.00, fax 03.80.22.36.21, e-mail louislatour@louislatour.com Ɪ by appt.

CH. DE BLIGNY 1998

□ 0.5 ha 1,900 ⏸ 100–149 F

A wine like a darting fish: it is delicate and fleeting but leaves its mark on your taste buds. Attractive to look at, it is doing its best on the nose. This is a wine from the Château de Bligny which was sold on 1 September 1999 to the Cave de Sainte-Marie-la-Blanche on the intervention of the SAFER (owned by GMF and Suntory).

🗝 Ch. de Bligny, Caves de la Vervelle, 21200 Bligny-lès-Beaune, tel. 03.80.21.47.38, fax 03.80.21.40.27 ☒ Ɪ ev. day except Sun. Mon. 10am–12 noon 2pm–6pm

DOM. GUY BOCARD

Charmes 1998**

□ 1er cru 0.67 ha 4,000 ▮⏸🌡 150–199 F

Albert Camus's central character in his novel *L'Etranger* was called Meursault. Odd, given that the wine is so supple and round. This wine is pale-coloured and has a nose overflowing with hawthorn and hazelnut. It is round on the palate and a real treat. Rich, buttery and well-developed, it conjures up flavours of dried fruit. This 8.5-ha (21-acre) estate has been very successful in the past with its 92 and 94 vintages) and this wine is on the same track. Also think about trying the **Narvaux 97** (100–149F) when you go to the cellars. They are awarded one star.

🗝 Guy Bocard, 4, rue de Mazeray, 21190 Meursault, tel. 03.80.21.26.06, fax 03.80.21.64.92 ☒ Ɪ by appt.

BOUCHARD PERE ET FILS

Clos des Corvées de Cîteaux 1997*

□ n.c. n.c. ⏸ 200–249 F

The Abbey at Citeaux had its first vineyards at Meursault well before those at Clos de Vougeot. This is why this wine has the right to commemorate the monks or rather their wine-producers, who, like serfs, worked for tithes. Would this 97 grace the Abbot's table? In colour, nose and character, it is respectful of the sparceness that the Cistercians demanded, however it is a typical Chardonnay and likely to become more opulent than they would have liked. The balanced **Meursault Village 97** (150–199F), is also awarded one star.

🗝 Bouchard Père et Fils, Ch. de Beaune, 21200 Beaune, tel. 03.80.24.80.24, fax 03.80.22.55.88, e-mail france@bouchard.pereetfils.com Ɪ by appt.

DOM. JEAN-MARIE BOUZEREAU
1998★

☐ 1.2 ha 5,000 70–99 F

Brilliant gold. The nose starts with honey immediately followed by spices and as it opens it becomes more complex, finishing with the voluptuousness of the Orient. On the palate it is lively and fruity and slightly mineral and has interesting prospects for the medium term. The jury imagined it with 'grilled king-prawns'. Pay attention to the first name: Bouzereau is a common family name.

Jean-Marie Bouzereau, 7, rue Labbé, 21190 Meursault, tel. 03.80.21.62.41, fax 03.80.21.65.97 by appt.

DOM. VINCENT BOUZEREAU
Les Charmes 1998★

☐ 1er cru 0.25 ha 600 150–199 F

Vincent Bouzereau is, here, presenting two good wines for the 98 vintage. The **Village 98** will certainly not disappoint you (70–99F) but if you can stretch to it, opt for the Premier Cru. This wine is a dream to accompany fish in sauce. In truth, it lacks aroma, but has finesse on the palate which is a change from Mersaults that are sometimes too heavy. Les Charmes is aptly-named.

Vincent Bouzereau, 7, rue Labbé, 21190 Meursault, tel. 03.80.21.61.08, fax 03.80.21.65.97 by appt.

MICHEL BOUZEREAU ET FILS
Les Tessons 1998★★★

☐ 1er cru 0.5 ha n.c. 100–149 F

Encore! The estate was awarded a *coup de cœur* this year. A brilliant golden wine with a fruity nose, and the oak is well-handled. It is warm in temperament and would suit a dish with a cream sauce, such as pike-perch. It has remarkable staying power on the palate. If you felt like it, take a look at **Les Grands Charrons 98** (one star), the image of finesse and suppleness with notes of citrus fruit. Excellent with fillet of sea bream with olives. The *coup de cœur* would be ideal with fish in a cream sauce.

Michel Bouzereau et Fils, 3, rue de la Planche-Meunière, 21190 Meursault, tel. 03.80.21.20.74, fax 03.80.21.66.41 by appt.

MICHEL BOUZEREAU ET FILS
Les Charmes Dessus 1998★★

☐ 1er cru 0.3 ha n.c. 150–199 F

Four wines on offer from this AOC, all with good grades. The Bouzereaus, who own 11 ha (27 acres), handle the maturing of their wines to perfection. Take a look at these Premiers Crus: they have charm and elegance in colour, nose and structure. They are very complex with toasty oak which does not camouflage the fruit. **Les Genevrières 98** is awarded one star for its lovely nose of wax, honey, spring blossom and toasted bread.

Michel Bouzereau et Fils, 3, rue de la Planche-Meunière, 21190 Meursault, tel. 03.80.21.20.74, fax 03.80.21.66.41 by appt.

DOM. HUBERT BOUZEREAU-GRUERE
Charmes 1998★

☐ 1er cru 0.65 ha 2,000 150–199 F

Hubert comes from an old wine-growing family in Meursault. He has worked on his parents' estate since he was fourteen. Two of his sisters now help him with the business that also has a cellar at Chassagne, and a guest house. Now, for the Charmes; it has the clearest straw colour, and the nose is perfectly balanced between ripe fruit and toasted almond. It is full and has strength and a good deal of liveliness on the palate.

Hubert Bouzereau, 22A, rue de la Velle, 21190 Meursault, tel. 03.80.21.20.05, fax 03.80.21.68.16 by appt.

DOM. CAILLOT
Le Limozin 1997★★★

☐ 0.41 ha 2,500 100–149 F

The reward of a *coup de cœur* for this 97 that knows its classics by heart. A beautiful colour. The nose is fresh fruit to begin with but it hints at its terroir. It is dry and sweet at the same time, fresh and mouth-filling, pleasant but with a promising future. In 1995, Michel Caillot took over his in-laws' vineyards which are mainly Villages in the Côte-de-Beaune. You can put the **La Barre Dessus – Clos Marguerite 97** on one side: it is an excellent *village* and has one star.

Dom. Caillot, 14, rue du Cromin, 21190 Meursault, tel. 03.80.21.21.70, fax 03.80.21.69.58 by appt.

DOM. DU CERBERON
Clos des Cras 1998

☐ 1er cru 0.6 ha 1,900 100–149 F

A nose with almost hidden aromas of bees wax,but it is also oaky and tinted with spring blossom. The same delicacy is found on the palate but with both richness and fullness. A

wine to drink in the near future. This *climat* is near Volnay, next to Les Santenots.
🗝 Dom. du Cerberon, 18, rue de Lattre-de-Tassigny, 21190 Meursault, tel. 03.80.21.22.95, fax 03.80.21.65.00, e-mail domaine-cerberon@wanadoo.fr ☑ 🍷 by appt.
🗝 GFA des Belles Côtes

DOM. DU CHATEAU DE PULIGNY-MONTRACHET 1998★

□ 0.73 ha 3,200 🛢 100–149 F

'Vérité contre tout' ('Truth above all') is printed on the label. The Château de Puligny passed through many hands before becoming the property of the Crédit Foncier de France, and one of its directors who was smitten by a passion for this estate in 1989. A Meursault with powerful and round aromas of good ripe fruit and crystallised apricot. Lamartine is said to have been a visitor. As was Sempé, the cartoonist who apparently is not particularly familiar with local habits: not long ago he made a memorable visit to the cellars.
🗝 SCEA Dom. du Château de Puligny-Montrachet, 21190 Puligny-Montrachet, tel. 03.80.21.39.14, fax 03.80.21.39.07, e-mail chateaupul@aol.com ☑ 🍷 by appt.

VINCENT DANCER Perrières 1998★

□ 1er cru 0.29 ha 900 🛢 150–199 F

This wine is not extravagant but soft, just as it should be. It is rich and strong on the palate that also has elegance and a little warmth. The colour is pale gold and the nose has slight menthol aromas. This is the third vintage for this young wine-producer who lacks no inspiration with his Perrières.
🗝 Vincent Dancer, 23, rte. de Santenay, 21190 Chassagne-Montrachet, tel. 03.80.21.94.48, fax 03.80.21.94.48, e-mail vincentdancer@aol.com ☑ 🍷 by appt.

DOM. DARNAT 1998★

□ 1.5 ha 7,000 🛢 100–149 F

Golden yellow. A bottle to open a little beforehand. Toasty flavours, notes of fig, nuts and citrus fruit right throughout the palate. Here, they say that 'he who drinks Meursault will neither live or die in ignorance' – have a try! All you need is a terrine of monk fish.
🗝 Dom. Darnat, 20, rue des Forges, 21190 Meursault, tel. 03.80.21.23.30, fax 03.80.21.64.62 ☑ 🍷 by appt.
🗝 Henri Darnat

JOSEPH DROUHIN 1997★★

□ n.c. n.c. 🛢 150–199 F

When Joseph Drouhin sent out New Year's greetings for 2000, the firm had the charming idea to comment on all the Burgundian vintages of the 20th century. However, the 97 he is showing here suggests he judged too swiftly. This is a *village* worthy of a Premier Cru. It is a magnificent golden-green. The nose finishes with splendid buttery aromas. It is balanced and long on the palate, very characteristic and full of breeding. A very great wine.
🗝 Joseph Drouhin, 7, rue d'Enfer, 21200 Beaune, tel. 03.80.24.68.88, fax 03.80.22.43.14, e-mail drouhin@calva.net 🍷 by appt.

DUFOULEUR PERE ET FILS 1997★

□ n.c. 1,200 🛢 250–[illegible]

It doesn't ask for pity nor beg for charity This is a golden-coloured Meursault with a very rich nose (vanilla, almond and buttered brioche). There is nothing mean or poor about it. It is fairly intense and its body has richness with a tiny note of bitterness on the finish. It will age well.
🗝 Dufouleur Père et Fils, 15, rue Thurot, 21700 Nuits-Saint-Georges, tel. 03.80.61.21.21, fax 03.80.61.11.23 ☑ 🍷 by appt.

LIONEL DUFOUR Les Cras 1997

■ 1er cru n.c. 3,000 300–499 F

We did not mention anywhere else that the Premier Cru Les Cras which is near Volnay is somewhat unusual. It produces a red as well as a white wine. Logical given its location. This is garnet red with a firm attack of blackcurrant buds with softened tannins. The fruit is attractive with a structure that is characteristic of a 97 wine.
🗝 SCI Lionel Dufour, 7, rte. de Monthélie, 21190 Meursault, tel. 03.80.21.67.02, fax 03.87.69.71.13

DOM. BERNARD DURY 1998

■ 0.26 ha 1,000 🛢 50–69 F

Brilliant ruby-red, without overstating it, and an attractive 98 that starts with raspberry, and follows on with morello cherry. On the palate it is more a wine to drink to quench your thirst than one to while away the time in conversation. It has a little acidity: good balance between freshness and fruit.
🗝 Bernard Dury, rue du Château, Cissey-Merceuil, 21190 Meursault, tel. 03.80.21.48.44, fax 03.80.21.48.44 ☑ 🍷 by appt.

PAUL GARAUDET Vieilles vignes 1998★

□ 2 ha 7,500 🛢 100–149 F

After a luscious approach, the wine shows some sinew; there is the right amount of mineral and an oakiness that will require time to develop. This is a 'macho wine'. It certainly has muscle and something to say or, perhaps, to ram home. Lemon and grapefruit on the nose and with length on the palate that you do not encounter every day.
🗝 Paul Garaudet, imp. de l'Eglise, 21190 Monthélie, tel. 03.80.21.28.78, fax 03.80.21.66.04 ☑ 🍷 by appt.

CH. GENOT-BOULANGER Clos du Cromin 1997★

□ 1.4 ha 7,400 🛢 100–149 F

'Donner du temps au temps', ('Give time to time'). Saint Bernard said it before François Mitterrand. This precept applies to this 97 which needs time for its lively acidity to temper. A gorgeous golden-green colour with distinguished glints. Its mineral flavours and richness could, by common consent, be described as 'feminine', and, with age, its youthful liveliness could become appealingly soft.

🔑 Ch. Génot-Boulanger, 25, rue de Cîteaux, 21190 Meursault, tel. 03.80.21.49.20, fax 03.80.21.49.21, e-mail genot-boulanger@wanadoo.fr ☑ 🍷 by appt.

🔑 Mme Delaby

ANDRE GOICHOT 1998★

☐ n.c. 8,000 🛢 150–199 F

This is an odd wine. It is hiding in the glass, and is very slow to show its qualities on the palate. However, wines are like people, and this one has a pure soul and a good structure behind its youthful shyness. It is a complex 98 with a nose full of brioche and a hint of minerals, but it is a wine that you have to work at. It is very tightly woven but in due course will open up though it is not the kind of wine to kick up its heels.

🔑 SA A. Goichot et Fils, av. Charles-de-Gaulle, 21200 Beaune, tel. 03.80.26.88.70, fax 03.80.26.80.69, e-mail goichot@goichotsa.com ☑ 🍷 by appt.

ALBERT GRIVAULT

Clos des Perrières 1998

☐ 1er cru 0.95 ha 6,100 🛢 300–499 F

This wine is up to a good standard and the reader should know that, in total, the jury tasted one hundred and twenty six different Meursaults. This has a pale colour and aromas of breadcrumbs and white-fleshed fruit. It has fine body that is balanced with attractive fruit. Le Clos des Perrières was bought by Albert Grivault in 1879. Today it belongs to his descendants, Chevignard-Bardet.

🔑 Dom. Albert Grivault, 7, pl. du Murger, 21190 Meursault, tel. 03.80.21.23.12, fax 03.00.00.00.00 ☑ 🍷 by appt.

🔑 Héritiers Bardet-Grivault

Côte de Beaune (South Central region)

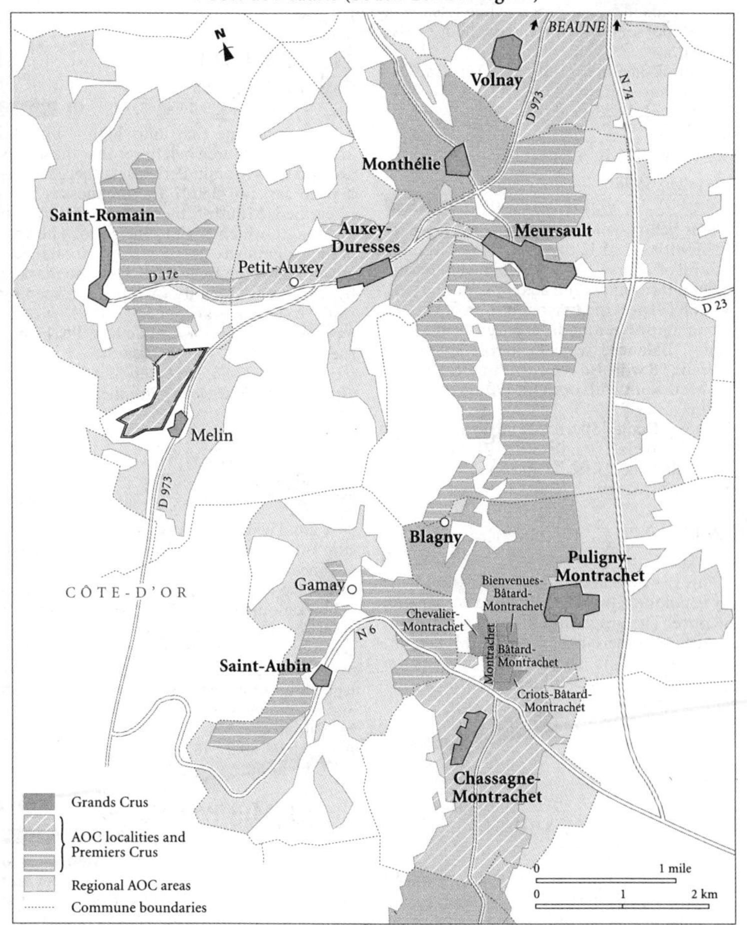

DOM. ANTONIN GUYON

Les Charmes Dessus 1998

☐ 1er cru 0.69 ha 3,000 200–249 F

This Les Charmes Dessus has attractive roundness. It is golden-green with a generous nose: pineappe, menthol and has a well-balanced attack, seasoned with the right amount of acidity. The warmth at the finish is cloaked in richness. For fish accompanied with a sauce.

Dom. Antonin Guyon, 21420 Savigny-lès-Beaune, tel. 03.80.67.13.24, fax 03.80.66.85.87, e-mail vins@guyon-bourgogne.com by appt.

PATRICK JAVILLIER Les Clous 1998

☐ 0.4 ha 1,500 100–149 F

Patrick Javillier has already impressed us with his Narvaux 85 and Tillets 86. Here we are dealing with Les Clous. It is brilliant and clear with a fruity nose. There is enough body and structure, but only average fullness. Nor should you lose sight of the **Cuvée Tête de Murger 98**: lots of energy. Excellent with veal sweetbreads in a pastry case, while Les Clous should be served with a poached Bresse chicken.

Patrick Javillier, 7, imp. des Acacias, 21190 Meursault, tel. 03.80.21.27.87, fax 03.80.21.29.39 by appt.

DOM. EMILE JOBARD

Les Tillets 1998★

☐ 0.38 ha 1,300 70–99 F

This yellow-gold wine has a striking nose laden with all sorts of good things: vanilla, almond of course, but also stinging nettle and apricot. Its richness and acidity combine well, but don't expect too much too soon of this 98. It can improve and is excellent value for money. Balanced wine in a soft style. The **Narvaux 98** will also repay waiting: an attractive Meursault with one star (70–99F). Three great classics.

Dom. Emile Jobard, 1, rue de la Barre, 21190 Meursault, tel. 03.80.21.26.43, fax 03.80.21.60.91 by appt.

Jobard-Morey

LA P'TIOTE CAVE Bouchères 1997★

☐ 1er cru 0.16 ha 900 150–199 F

This Les Bouchères is very successful. Ripe hay in colour, citronella, mint and verbena on the nose. The grapes are picked over-ripe so this is a Wagnerian version of Meursault. That said, it is long and balanced; a Meursault from olden times that brings back many good memories.

La P'tiote Cave, 71150 Chassey-le-Camp, tel. 03.85.87.15.21, fax 03.85.87.28.08 by appt.

Mugnier

JEAN LATOUR-LABILLE

Clos des Meix Chavaux 1998★

☐ 3.5 ha 6,500 70–99 F

Gold with glints of green, this wine has all the characteristics of the grape variety on the nose, with an additional touch of wood not forgetting the terroir. Very characteristic, with a good balance and softness that is already appealing but could well wait another two or three years. The **Premier Cru Les Charmes 98** is recommended (100–149F).

Dom. Jean Latour-Labille et Fils, 6, rue du 8-Mai, 21190 Meursault, tel. 03.80.21.22.49, fax 03.80.21.67.86 by appt.

JEAN LATOUR-LABILLE ET FILS

Les Cras 1998★

■ 1er cru 0.2 ha 1,100 70–99 F

This is a red Les Cras Premier Cru. It comes from just next to Volnay and is one of the rare *climats* that can produce both red and white wines. This is the purplest of purples, with a cherry nose. The oakiness has mellowed well. It has enchanting aromas which almost weave a fairy spell. On the palate it is neither over-fleshy or crude.

Dom. Jean Latour-Labille et Fils, 6, rue du 8-Mai, 21190 Meursault, tel. 03.80.21.22.49, fax 03.80.21.67.86 by appt.

CH. DE LA VELLE

Clos de la Velle 1998★

☐ 0.5 ha 3,000 100–149 F

This is a wine that aims high – like the arrow on the church bell tower that the fairies are said to have built. Perhaps it is because it is kept in casks of 350 l? The oakiness is well-integrated. Mouth-filling with concentration and length which is all to the good. The aromatic complexity is shown off to its best advantage at the finish, which is also marked by an edge of acidity. A wine for keeping (three to four years).

Bertrand Darviot, Ch. de la Velle, 17, rue de la Velle, 21190 Meursault, tel. 03.80.21.22.83, fax 03.80.21.65.60, e-mail chateaudelavelle@infonie.fr by appt.

CHRISTOPHE MARY

Les Charmes 1998★

☐ 1er cru 0.16 ha 150 100–149 F

A good wine that gives a good deal of pleasure and one that Saint Vincent has blessed in advance: it will improve in the cellar and will be on top form in four or five years. Golden-yellow colour. The vanilla is not too strong. It is very open, rich in aromas but with sufficient acidity to make it a pleasure to taste. Unlike many others, it has an easy approach. The **Village 98** is recommended (50–69F). It is fresh and should be drunk young.

Christophe Mary, 21190 Corcelles-les-Arts, tel. 03.80.21.48.98, fax 03.80.21.48.98 by appt.

CH. DE MEURSAULT 1997

☐ 1er cru 5 ha 30,000 200–249 F

The grounds of the château were due to become a residential estate and the water and telephone were already connected. Even the houses were built. Then André Boisseaux decided to buy it all and replant vines. The **Meursault du Château de Meursault**, recommended (150–199F), is produced on only 3.4 ha (8 acres). It is partly matured in wood, partly in tank. A lovely pale gold colour with a clean, straightforward, well-defined nose. As for the Premier Cru, it is greenish-gold with ripe fruit on the nose. It is fleshy, mouth-filling and generous, and the oak is well-integrated. A touch of warmth.

Ch. de Meursault, 21190 Meursault, tel. 03.80.26.22.75, fax 03.80.26.22.76 by appt.

DOM. MICHELOT

Clos Saint-Félix 1998★

□ 1 ha 5,400 100–149 F

It is well-known that Saint Félix brings good fortune and happiness. The same is true in this *clos*, wholly-owned by the estate. The vineyard is always the first to be picked because it has a micro-climate that results in an early harvest. This bright straw-coloured 98 is no exception to the Michelot tradition. It is full and silky and has all the qualities you might hope to find, though it has a heavy-handed oakiness which, over the next year or two, could soften and benefit the wine.

Dom. Michelot, 31, rue de la Velle, 21190 Meursault, tel. 03.80.21.23.17, fax 03.80.21.63.62 by appt.

MOILLARD-GRIVOT

Les Narvaux 1998★

□ n.c. 3,600 150–199 F

Decked out for the evening and ready to go and join the beautiful people. This wine has chosen to be diverse, not to say complex: vanilla, white-fleshed fruit, nuts and honey. A hard wine to define. It is not very rich, its interest lies elsewhere, but it has a certain sensitivity: dreamy, endearing. One of our team suggested it would be good with a crayfish soufflé.

Moillard-Grivot, 2, rue François-Mignotte, 21700 Nuits-Saint-Georges, tel. 03.80.62.42.22, fax 03.80.61.28.13, e-mail nuicave@wanadoo.fr by appt.

BERTRAND DE MONCENY

Bellevue 1998★★

□ n.c. 12,000 150–199 F

There is already talk of a *coup de cœur* for next year, this young man is so talented. This 98, made under the name of the Compagnie des Vins d'Autrefois, a merchant now at the Abbaye Saint-Martin in Beaune, is a great Meursault. One to open to celebrate the *Saint-Vincent Tournante* festival. It presents itself perfectly: it has a nose with brioche and truffle, with flavours of flint and citrus fruit. In a word, Meursault. It has tremendous potential and drinking it brings a moment of great pleasure.

Cie des Vins d'Autrefois, abbaye Saint-Martin, 53, av. de l'Aigue, 21200 Beaune, tel. 03.80.26.33.00, fax 03.80.24.14.84, e-mail mallet.b@cva-beaune.fr by appt.

DOM. RENE MONNIER

Le Limozin 1998★

□ 0.86 ha 5,000 70–99 F

Jean-Marie Rouart is a recent winner of the Paulée de Meursault prize, and now he is here. A wine like this cannot fail to be inspirational. It shows all the signs of careful handling, with good wood influence and smoothness of character. In brief, all its sharp corners are rounded off. We can also recommend the **Les Charmes 98, Premier Cru** (100–149F), a wine to keep a little longer than the **Les Chevaliers 98 Village**.

Dom. René Monnier, 6, rue du Dr-Rolland, 21190 Meursault, tel. 03.80.21.29.32, fax 03.80.21.61.79 ev. day 8am–12 noon 2pm–6pm

M. et Mme Bouillot

DOM. JEAN-PIERRE ET LAURENT PRUNIER 1998

□ 0.26 ha 1,200 70–99 F

This wine does not have a lots of colour, yet the nose is fairly well-developed with toasted aromas (almond in particular). It is vigorous and rich in alcohol and not lacking in sinew or bite. Advisable to keep it for one to two years.

Dom. Jean-Pierre et Laurent Prunier, rue Traversière, 21190 Auxey-Duresses, tel. 03.80.21.27.51, fax 03.80.21.27.51 by appt.

REINE PEDAUQUE 1998★

□ n.c. 12,000 100–149 F

Greenish-gold, of course. The nose is still overpowered by the wood influence, yet it is dense and sturdy. It flavour really fills the palate. There is a little hint of walnut that is not at all unpleasant. A wine to go with any fish, fresh or salt-water.

Reine Pédauque, Le Village, 21420 Aloxe-Corton, tel. 03.80.25.00.00, fax 03.80.26.42.00, e-mail rpedauque@et.fr by appt.

ROPITEAU 1997★

□ n.c. 24,000 100–149 F

Cardinal de Bernis is said to have chosen Meursault as his altar wine, so the Creator, or so he claimed, would not see him pulling a face. This wine would have done the trick. It is strong yellow-gold and 'Chardonnays' expressively – it does what you would expect a quality Chardonnay to do. Also take a look at **Les Perrières Premier Cru 97**, recommended, and though it still has detectable oaky flavours, it should improve in two years.

Ropiteau Frères, 13, rue du 11-Novembre, 21190 Meursault, tel. 03.80.21.69.20, fax 03.80.21.69.29 ev. day 9am–7pm; cl. mid-Nov.–Easter

ROPITEAU 1997

■ n.c. 3,000 70–99 F

A red Meursault is not a black sheep in a pen of white ones. It well deserves its place. Here Ropiteau (taken over by Jean-Claude Boisset) is showing a supple wine with a well-

balanced body. Fruity, medium-bodied with a delicate dash of oak.
🔑 Ropiteau Frères, 13, rue du 11-Novembre, 21190 Meursault, tel. 03.80.21.69.20, fax 03.80.21.69.29 ☑ 🍷 ev. day 9am–7pm; cl. mid-Nov.–Easter

DOM. ROUX PERE ET FILS

Clos des Poruzots 1998★

☐ 1er cru	0.22 ha	1,500	🍷 200–249 F

The 88 was a stunning wine, as we remember it. This is another Poruzot. It is elegant and full-bodied, well-structured with a attractive freshness. The barrel flavours are well-integrated. This 98 is wide open and has class without a doubt.
🔑 Dom. Roux Père et Fils, 21190 Saint-Aubin, tel. 03.80.21.32.92, fax 03.80.21.35.00 ☑ 🍷 by appt.

DOM. SAINT-FIACRE

Les Narvaux 1998★★

☐	0.36 ha	2,000	🍷 70–99 F

A domaine that has been in the same family for several generations. For their 1997, Aline and Joël Patriarche chose Saint Fiacre, the patron saint of their village, to be their protector. This wine has an appealing colour, it is perfumed and generous on the palate. It is very fleshy and tasty, and while it is not extremely complex, it is everything a classic Meursault should be. This *climat* is just above Les Genevrières.
🔑 Aline et Joël Patriarche, Dom. Saint-Fiacre, 21190 Tailly, tel. 03.80.26.84.38, fax 03.80.26.87.97 ☑ 🍷 by appt.

DE SOUSA-BOULEY

Les Millerans 1998

☐	0.51 ha	1,800	🍷 70–99 F

Half a hectare (just over one acre) has produced this wine with glints of silver. Its nose opens with linden flower. On the palate, it is almost smooth and fluid. This *climat* is below the village, one of the most eastern, and deserves to be better known.
🔑 Albert de Sousa-Bouley, 7, R.N. 74, 21190 Meursault, tel. 03.80.21.22.79 ☑ 🍷 ev. day 8am–8pm

DOM. VIRELY-ROUGEOT 1998★

☐	1.39 ha	1,228	🍷 70–99 F

When a young man coming from Pommard adopts a Meursault, he goes from red to white. He had the luck to find an excellent teacher in his father-in-law, and he was himself the grandson of the manager of Château de Meursault. So do not be surprised, when you taste this, to find a characteristic wine. A pale gold colour with a honeyed vanilla nose, vinous and classic, and it will keep.
🔑 Dom. Virely-Rougeot, pl. de l'Europe, 21630 Pommard, tel. 03.80.22.34.34, fax 03.80.22.38.07 ☑ 🍷 by appt.

Blagny

The Blagny vineyard, straddling the communes of Meursault and Puligny-Montrachet, is a self-contained vineyard that grew up around the village. Remarkable red wines are produced labelled Appellation Blagny – 366 hl (9,662 gal) in 1999 – but the majority of the area is planted with Chardonnay, producing Meursault Premier Cru or Puligny-Montrachet Premier Cru, depending on the commune.

GILLES BOUTON Sous le Puits 1998

■ 1er cru	0.4 ha	2,500	🍷 70–99 F

Fresh and soft, between purple and garnet in colour. More silky than velvet. An aroma of honest candour. Raspberry on the nose. On tasting, it is a little aggressive, still struggling with its tannins and does not yet have a classically voluptuous body. In an understatement typical of Burgundians, it is not unattractive.
🔑 Gilles Bouton, Gamay, 21190 Saint-Aubin, tel. 03.80.21.32.63, fax 03.80.21.90.74 ☑ 🍷 by appt.

DOM. HENRI CLERC ET FILS

Sous le Dos d'Ane 1997★

■ 1er cru	0.93 ha	3,906	🍷 150–199 F

94 95 **96**

You can approach this wine with sheer enjoyment. Intensely purple and lustrous. Cinnamon and blackcurrant combine well on the nose. There is a fruity oakiness on the medium-bodied palate which is tannic and sensual.
🔑 EARL Dom. Henri Clerc et Fils, pl. des Marronniers, 21190 Puligny-Montrachet, tel. 03.80.21.32.74, fax 03.80.21.39.60 ☑ 🍷 ev. day 8.30am–11.45am 2pm–5.45pm
🔑 Bernard Clerc

DOM. LARUE Sous le Puits 1998★★

■ 1er cru	0.2 ha	1,200	🍷 70–99 F

94 95 96 97 |**98**|

This Sous le Puits is a Blagny classic. It shows good colour extraction which is not excessive or overdone, and produces a velvety garnet. The oak is immediately prominent amongst the somewhat unobtrusive aromas, but they may not be non-existant in time. Quite favourable first impressions on the palate, where there is fullness and sweetness. It has structure. The nuances will develop in time; just how it will compares with its peers depends on whether you have the patience to let it develop.
🔑 Dom. Larue, Gamay, 21190 Saint-Aubin, tel. 03.80.21.30.74, fax 03.80.21.91.36 ☑ 🍷 by appt.

Puligny-Montrachet

Puligny-Montrachet is the fulcrum of the Côte d'Or white wines, situated between its two neighbours, Meursault to the north and Chassagne to the south. The vineyards of this small, peaceful commune occupy half the area of those in Meursault and are two-thirds the size of those in Chassagne, but despite their apparently modest extent they produce the greatest Grand Cru white wines in Burgundy, sharing the Montrachet name with Chassagne.

The geologists of the University of Dijon have discovered that the Grands Crus are located on an outcrop of Bathonian limestone, giving them greater finesse, harmony and aromatic subtlety than the wines harvested on the neighbouring marlstone. The AOC produced 12,453 hl (328,759 gal) of white wines and 107 hl (2,825 gal) of red in 1999.

The other *climats* and Premier Crus of the commune have a notably expressive bouquet smelling of vegetation with hints of essential oils and vegetal resins.

JEAN-CLAUDE BACHELET Sous le puits 1997*

☐ 1er cru 0.23 ha n.c. 100–149 F

In control: a serene yellow wine that compensates for its light structure with elegant and natural liveliness. It has the impertinence of youth. A flowery and mineral nose opens up with vanilla, then peach and quince.
Jean-Claude Bachelet, rue de la Fontaine, 21190 Saint-Aubin, tel. 03.80.21.31.01, fax 03.80.21.97.71, e-mail JCBachelet@aol.com by appt.

DOM. ROGER BELLAND Les Champs-Gains 1998

☐ 1er cru 0.45 ha 2,400 150–199 F

The 94 vintage of this Premier Cru was very successful for the same wine-producer. The 98 is still young and shows its paces with a pale golden colour, and then takes off with toasted aromas, the same flavours on the palate. A powerful, massive, liqourice Champs-Gains.
Dom. Roger Belland, 3, rue de la Chapelle, B.P. 13, 21590 Santenay, tel. 03.80.20.60.95, fax 03.80.20.63.93, e-mail belland.roger@wanadoo.fr by appt.

BOUCHARD PERE ET FILS 1998

☐ n.c. n.c. 150–199 F

This straw-coloured *village*, with glints of green, has spirit. Green apple, lemon, pear and grapefruit on the nose, while it is more mineral and spice on the palate where it is rich as well as fresh and long. An elegant wine.
Bouchard Père et Fils, Ch. de Beaune, 21200 Beaune, tel. 03.80.24.80.24, fax 03.80.22.55.88, e-mail france@bouchard.pereetfils.com by appt.

GILLES BOUTON Les Garennes 1998

☐ 1er cru 0.75 ha 5,200 100–149 F

This *climat* is in a corner near the hamlet of Blagny and produces red Blagny and white Puligny-Montrachet. Honey and beeswax are the dominating aromas. Good acidity accompanies its richness. The wine, produced on the lees, finishes with a hint of bitterness; its oakiness will soften in the next few months.
Gilles Bouton, Gamay, 21190 Saint-Aubin, tel. 03.80.21.32.63, fax 03.80.21.90.74 by appt.

HUBERT BOUZEREAU-GRUERE 1998*

☐ 0.49 ha 1,200 70–99 F

A wine of an intense gold with wonderful penetrating aromas (toasted bread with acacia honey). It is mouth-filling and powerful, lightly oaked, balsamic vinegar with flavours of crystallised fruits. It is very ripe and showing fine potential.
Hubert Bouzereau, 22A, rue de la Velle, 21190 Meursault, tel. 03.80.21.20.05, fax 03.80.21.68.16 by appt.

DOM. CAILLOT Les Pucelles 1997**

☐ 1er cru 0.19 ha 500 200–249 F

Being an immediate neighbour of Bâtard-Montrachet helps to explain this Premier Cru's well-deserved reputation. However, its complexity is generally restrained. The 97 is a faithful example of the characteristics of the *climat*: finesse, elegance, frankness, spontaneity . . . We also enjoyed the **Les Folatières 97** (150–199F) which has a wonderful sensuality (one star).
Dom. Caillot, 14, rue du Cromin, 21190 Meursault, tel. 03.80.21.21.70, fax 03.80.21.69.58 by appt.

EMILE CHANDESAIS 1997

☐ n.c. 1,500 200–249 F

A wine that should be drunk to the memory of Emile Chandesais, who passed away in Spring 2000. He sold his business to Picard (Chagny) a few years ago. A pale-coloured wine with a light nose of flint and white blossom. It keeps on a straight path, marked out by hazelnut and almond.

🔑 Emile Chandesais, rue Saint-Nicolas, 71150 Chagny, tel. 03.85.91.41.77, fax 03.85.91.40.26
🔑 Michel Picard

CHANSON PERE ET FILS

Hameau de Blagny 1998★

☐ 1er cru	n.c.	1,200	🛢	200–249 F

An exotic and very pleasant Puligny that practically turns the hamlet of Blagny into a West Indian island. Vanilla and coconut with a hint of aniseed: conjures up holidays under a golden sun. A wonderfully perfumed wine that is best served as an apéritif. The prestigious house of Chanson has just come under the management of Les Champenois, as did Bouchard Père et Fils, recently.

🔑 Chanson Père et Fils, 10, rue Paul-Chanson, 21200 Beaune, tel. 03.80.22.33.00, fax 03.80.24.17.42, e-mail tmarion@vins-chanson.com 🍷 by appt.

DOM. DANIEL CHANZY

Les Reuchaux 1997

☐	0.7 ha	3,800	🛢	100–149 F

Les Reuchaux, which is on the way to Meursaul, is a good *village*. The wine-grower is enterprising and active on the 45 ha (111 acres) he has on the three *Côtes*. He has produced a classic wine with a nose that bursts with toasted almond but which has still to open. It is fairly rich and spicy on the palate with high acidity: the moment to drink it should not be delayed.

🔑 Daniel Chanzy, 1, rue de la Fontaine, 71150 Bouzeron, tel. 03.85.87.23.69, fax 03.85.91.24.92, e-mail daniel.chanzy@wanadoo.fr ☑ 🍷 by appt.

DOM. JEAN CHARTRON

Clos du Cailleret 1998★★

☐ 1er cru	1.24 ha	8,500	🛢	300–499 F

The **Puligny 98 Blanc** looks good and is awarded one star (200–249F). This Premier Cru is on a completely different level. It is worth remembering that INAO recently attached a small parcel of the vineyard belonging to the same domaine to the Grand Cru Chevalier-Montrachet. This wine is so full that you immediately realise, with its hazelnut flavours, that it is something special. A few hints of grapefruit, a body of great; it has a class, complex yet silky long life ahead of it.

🔑 Dom. Jean Chartron, 13, Grande-Rue, 21190 Puligny-Montrachet, tel. 03.80.21.32.85, fax 03.80.21.36.35 ☑ 🍷 ev. day 10am–12.30pm 2pm–6pm

DOM. DU CHATEAU DE MEURSAULT 1997★

☐	0.52 ha	3,000	🛢	150–199 F

The Château de Meursault is the Côte-de-Beaune slope belonging to the Patriarche Boisseaux empire. This is a Puligny – it is golden with ochre glints – with a very aromatic nose divided between toasted hazelnuts and lemon peel. On the palate, it releases its flavours without pretention. A touch of alcohol supports the finish.

🔑 Ch. de Meursault, 21190 Meursault, tel. 03.80.26.22.75, fax 03.80.26.22.76 ☑ 🍷 by appt.

DOM. DU CHATEAU DE PULIGNY-MONTRACHET 1997★★

☐	1.49 ha	10,000	🛢	150–199 F

Acquired by the Crédit Foncier de France in 1988 and managed since by a financier who is passionate about wine, the Château de Puligny has produced a 97 that has been vinified with precision yet without frills. It is deep, brilliant gold with the most distinguished aromas. It is a perfect example of the appellation and the vintage. A balanced wine that has a finesse that is rich in personality.

🔑 SCEA Dom. du Château de Puligny-Montrachet, 21190 Puligny-Montrachet, tel. 03.80.21.39.14, fax 03.80.21.39.07, e-mail chateaupul@aol.com ☑ 🍷 by appt.

CH. DE CITEAUX

Les Champs Gains 1998★

☐ 1er cru	n.c.	2,000	🛢	150–199 F

An offspring from Cîteaux which is goodness itself. A sparkling gold colour and an engaging perfume (green apple and honeyed peach). It is lively and fresh, in good taste, and very characteristic.

🔑 Philippe Bouzereau, Ch. de Cîteaux, 18–20, rue de Cîteaux, B.P. 25, 21190 Meursault, tel. 03.80.21.20.32, fax 03.80.21.64.34, e-mail domaine.bouzereau@wanadoo.fr ☑ 🍷 by appt.

DOM. HENRI CLERC ET FILS 1998

☐	0.6 ha	8,542	🛢	150–199 F

Bernard Clerc has been here since 1965. Already very successful with his 94 Puligny, here, he presents a wine that is full and silky, very rich yet fresh and with a touch of acidity. It has mineral, buttery and Muscat-like aromas. To suit all tastes.

🔑 EARL Dom. Henri Clerc et Fils, pl. des Marronniers, 21190 Puligny-Montrachet, tel. 03.80.21.32.74, fax 03.80.21.39.60 ☑ 🍷 ev. day 8.30am–11.45am 2pm–5.45pm
🔑 Bernard Clerc

JOSEPH DROUHIN

Les Folatières 1997★★

☐ 1er cru	n.c.	n.c.	🛢	250–299 F

Les Folatières derives from a 'folle terre', or 'mad soil'. The land here is stony and the precious limestone is much sought after. This lively 97 frolics between peach and quince before settling down into the parameter of the Cru. It is like a bucking bronco, but the excellent George Saintsbury said, correctly, that a good Puligny 'strains its sinews like the lashes of a whip'. Not to be opened for a year or two.

🔑 Joseph Drouhin, 7, rue d'Enfer, 21200 Beaune, tel. 03.80.24.68.88, fax 03.80.22.43.14, e-mail drouhin@calva.net 🍷 by appt.

DOM. DUPONT-FAHN

Les Grands Champs 1998

☐ 0.16 ha n.c. 70–99 F

This *village* is right next to the Premier Cru Clavaillon. Exactly the colour to be hoped for. A simple nose releasing a hint of bitter almond. A warm, powerful, fat and buttery wine which lacks nothing. It is showing signs of development and should be drunk in the near future.

Michel Dupont-Fahn, Les Toisières, 21190 Monthélie, tel. 03.80.21.26.78, fax 03.80.21.21.22 by appt.

RAYMOND DUREUIL-JANTHIAL

Les Champs Gains 1998★

☐ 1er cru 0.19 ha 1,200 150–199 F

A *climat* half-way up the hillside going towards Blagny. The soil is principally limestone, which gives the wines the spirited finesse, and very successful firmness and texture found here. There is not too much acidity. For people who like mellow wines.

Raymond Dureuil-Janthial, rue de la Buisserolle, 71150 Rully, tel. 03.85.87.02.37, fax 03.85.87.00.24 ev. day 9am–12 noon 3pm–7pm; Sun. by appt.

DOM. HERITIERS LOUIS JADOT

Les Folatières 1997

☐ 1er cru n.c. 1,500 300–499 F

Good presentation both of the colour (pale golden-green) and the palate (light vanilla and oak, pineapple and grapefruit). The good balance between its fine tannins, oakiness and liveliness are evidence of the wine's high quality.

Maison Louis Jadot, 21, rue Eugène-Spuller, 21200 Beaune, tel. 03.80.22.10.57, fax 03.80.22.56.03, e-mail contact@louisjadot.com by appt.

DOM. DES LAMBRAYS

Les Folatières 1997

☐ 1er cru 0.3 ha 2,000 250–299 F

The Saier brothers acquired not only Clos des Lambrays but also a few vines in Puligny, but they have now been re-sold to Gunter Freund, along with the Domaine de Morey. This island of Chardonnay in an ocean of Pinot Noir presents a very golden-coloured wine with flattering characteristics (toasted, roasted aromas with hazelnut and lemon). It has good length and warmth, but should wait until 2002.

Sté Nlle du Dom. des Lambrays, 31, rue Basse, 21220 Morey-Saint-Denis, tel. 03.80.51.84.33, fax 03.80.51.81.97 by appt.

Freund

DOM. HUBERT LAMY

Les Tremblots 1998★

☐ 0.9 ha 6,000 100–149 F

This wine is so successful it deserves time to age. It comes from just below Bâtard, near to Chassagne. It is deep golden-yellow in colour and the nose suggests exotic fruits, though shouldn't such an exquisite style have a little roundness?

Dom. Hubert Lamy, Paradis, 21190 Saint-Aubin, tel. 03.80.21.32.55, fax 03.80.21.38.32 by appt.

DOM. LARUE Les Garennes 1998★

☐ 1er cru 0.59 ha 1,832 100–149 F

'You must see with your nose and drink with your eyes'... so runs the saying. Here we 'see' a white wedding: white blossom, white-fleshed fruit . . . and the colour is cloaked in white gold. It has a gentle attack, but what follows is entirely satisfactory. Good to drink with scallops.

Dom. Larue, Gamay, 21190 Saint-Aubin, tel. 03.80.21.30.74, fax 03.80.21.91.36 by appt.

BURGUNDY

A. LIGERET 1998★

☐ n.c. 10,000 200–249 F

Ligeret has belonged to the Thomas family (Moillard at Nuits) since 1952. Their 98 is pale, brilliant gold with a green glint. It is oaky but behind this you can detect green apple, lime, pineapple and honey. It is full and rich, quite smooth (honey still), balanced and persistant. It is a very attractive wine that could be drunk in three years' time.

A. Ligeret, 10, pl. du Cratère-Saint-Georges, 21700 Nuits-Saint-Georges, tel. 03.80.61.08.92, fax 03.80.61.30.26, e-mail ligeret@aol.com

ROLAND MAROSLAVAC-LEGER

Les Combettes 1997

☐ 1er cru 0.16 ha n.c. 150–199 F

Stephan came to France from Yugoslavia seventy years ago and ended up in Puligny-Montrachet by chance. The family put down roots here through hard work. His Les Combettes (usually a lovely wine) has tone and maturity. It has the right characteristics, though not a very deep colour. It has a fragrant nose and above all, on the palate, it is typical of the Cru with flavours of almond and truffle.

Dom. Maroslavac-Léger, 43, Grande-Rue, 21190 Puligny-Montrachet, tel. 03.80.21.31.23, fax 03.80.21.91.39 by appt.

DOM. RENE MONNIER

Les Folatières 1998★

☐ 1er cru 0.83 ha 5,000 100–149 F

It is a very short distance from Les Folatières to Le Montrachet. And every monarch needs a crown prince . . . This one is golden but not profligate with a fruity, yet restrained nose. It is reserved now but preparing seriously for its future responsibilities. A fairly round, powerful 98 with an interesting length and with a trace of hazelnut.

Dom. René Monnier, 6, rue du Dr-Rolland, 21190 Meursault, tel. 03.80.21.29.32, fax 03.80.21.61.79 ev. day 8am–12 noon 2pm–6pm

M. et Mme Bouillot

REINE PEDAUQUE 1998★

☐ n.c. 9,000 ◼ 100–149 F

Puligny is twinned with Johannisberg in memory of the Prince de Metternich. This is a bright and mineral wine. It is rich, unctuous, and full of noble descent. On the nose there is a mixture of white blossom and ripe fruit with mineral notes. Requires patience for a few years.

Reine Pédauque, Le Village, 21420 Aloxe-Corton, tel. 03.80.25.00.00, fax 03.80.26.42.00, e-mail rpedauque@net.fr
Y by appt.

VEUVE HENRI MORONI 1998★

☐ 1.96 ha 11,000 ◼ 100–149 F

A wine that presents three impressive stages. Visually it is unobtrusive yet deep. This Puligny is clear pale gold with green glints. Aromatically, it is redolent of fresh hawthorn. On the palate, it positively blossoms. Like Puligny wines used to be. Also worth trying is **Les Pucelles 98**, a white, of course: so buttery and honeyed that it will not keep long (150–199F). Commended by the jury.

Veuve Henri Moroni, 1, rue de l'Abreuvoir, 21190 Puligny-Montrachet, tel. 03.80.21.30.48, fax 03.80.21.33.08, e-mail veuve.moroni@wanadoo.fr ☑ Y by appt.

CHARLES VIENOT

Les Champs Gains 1998★

☐ 1er cru n.c. 3,000 ◼ 200–249 F

With its colour and nose, this wine is to Chardonnay what honey is to sugar. It is unctous and tasty but perhaps still a little closed. There is a good balance between alcohol, tannins and acidity. Well-vinified and to be drunk in four to five years.

Charles Viénot, 5, quai Dumorey, 21700 Nuits-Saint-Georges, tel. 03.80.62.61.41, fax 03.80.62.37.38

Montrachet, Chevalier, Bâtard, Bienvenus Bâtard, Criots Bâtard

In the recent past, the most astonishing characteristic of the Grands Crus was that they took quite some time before fully revealing the exceptional quality expected of them. It could mean waiting ten years for a 'great' Montrachet to reach maturity or five years for the Bâtard and its cohorts; the Chevalier-Montrachet alone seemed to be more expressive much earlier.

However, in the last few years some of the Montrachet pressings show a bouquet of exceptional power and complex flavours whose quality can be appreciated immediately, without having to guess how they may develop in the future. The amount of wine is very small: all the Montrachet Grands Crus accounted for only 1,635 hl (43,164 gal) in 1999.

Montrachet

CHARTRON ET TREBUCHET 1998★

☐ Gd cru n.c. 300 ◼ 500 F+

Canary yellow colour. Subtle and with a pleasant oakiness. This is a round, full Montrachet. Toasted almond, toasted bread, brioche, acacia honey, white blossom . . . It has good length and is sufficiently well-structured. A dish of grilled lobster with young vegetables should accompany it in a few years, when the wood flavours have melted away. It will show better in 2001/2002.

Chartron et Trébuchet, 13, Grande-Rue, 21190 Puligny-Montrachet, tel. 03.80.21.32.85, fax 03.80.21.36.35, e-mail jmchartron@chartron-trebuchet.com
☑ Y ev. day 10am–12.30pm 2pm–6pm; cl. Nov.–Mar.

DOM. DE LA ROMANEE-CONTI 1998★★★

☐ Gd cru 0.67 ha 2,670 ◼ 500 F+

|83| |86| (90) |91| 93 97 98

The grapes are harvested very late, with identifiable touches of botrytis. This wine is extremely mature and exceptionally concentrated. It is undoubtedly the richest wine this estate produces today. It gobbles up the sun and it exceeds 14°. The nose is delightful:

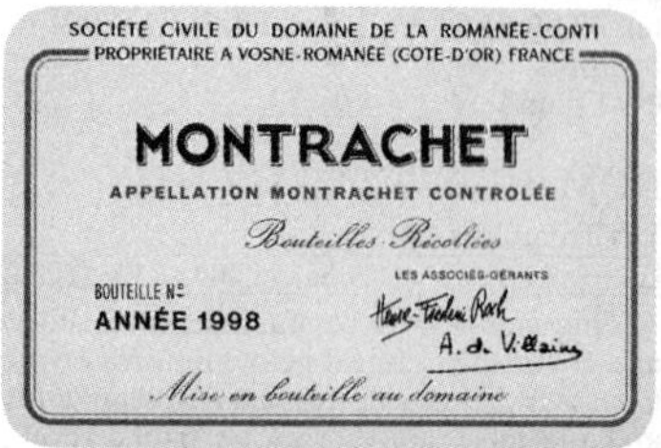

above all, notes of spice and cinnamon. Very complex flavours add to the more usual honey, and you can perhaps detect bush peach. The acidity ensures its freshness and capacity for keeping. A giant of a wine, but very approachable

⊶ SC du Dom. de la Romanée-Conti, 21700 Vosne-Romanée, tel. 03.80.62.48.80, fax 03.80.61.05.72

DOM. JACQUES PRIEUR 1997★★

☐ Gd cru 0.59 ha 2,250 500 F+

83 85 |86| 87 |**88**| |(90)| 93 **96 98**

The divine Montrachet should be drunk kneeling and with a bowed head. Many precious parcels of land make up the vineyard's 58 a (145 acres), which includes the famous Dents de Chien, which was incorporated into the Cru in a judgement made by the Tribunal de Beaune in 1921. The vines are near Chassagne, and were planted in 1957, 1979 and 1986 under the guidance of Antonin Rodet. This wine is superb. It is bronze-yellow with an exotic nose and is lingering and glorious on the palate with flavours of honey and rose petals. It is worth a *coup de cœur* for rousing such emotion. The 90 and 96 vintage were also excellent.

⊶ Dom. Jacques Prieur, 6, rue des Santenots, 21190 Meursault, tel. 03.80.21.23.85, fax 03.80.21.29.19 ◩ Y by appt.

Chevalier-Montrachet

DOM. JEAN CHARTRON

Clos des Chevaliers 1998★★

☐Gd cru 0.55 ha 2,500 ⦀ 500 F+

91 92 93 **94** |**95**| **96** 97 **98**

This wine could almost be described as glamorous. It has a sheen to its colour such as you would see in the shiny pages of high-class women's magazines. A nose with elegant hyacinth combined with fresh bread and a remarkable mineral note. It makes life worth living! On the palate it is not ready to show itself, but we predict, from its toasted (almond, hazelnut) and honey aromas, an interesting future. It has a good structure and persistent length. Worthy of lobster.

⊶ Dom. Jean Chartron, 13, Grande-Rue, 21190 Puligny-Montrachet, tel. 03.80.21.32.85, fax 03.80.21.36.35 ◩ Y ev. day 10am–12.30pm 2pm–6pm

DOM. LOUIS LATOUR

Les Demoiselles 1997

☐Gd cru 1 ha 1,500 ⦀ 500 F+

Adèle and Julie Voillot used to own what was called 'La Vigne des Demoiselles' in Le Cailleret at the beginning of the 19th century. Louis Latour and Louis Jadot, who bought it in 1913, successfully pleaded their cause, and in 1939, were given the right to this name and the recognition of Chevalier-Montrachet Cru, because it had regularly produced excellent wines. This seductive 97 is still closed on the nose. Fresh and lively but medium-bodied. This wine is light, but a sea-bass in a salt crust served with *beurre blanc* would accompany it well, as one of the team noted.

⊶ Maison Louis Latour, 18, rue des Tonneliers, 21200 Beaune, tel. 03.80.24.81.00, fax 03.80.22.36.21, e-mail louislatour@louislatour.com Y by appt.

Bâtard-Montrachet

DOM. BACHELET-RAMONET PERE ET FILS 1998★★

☐Gd cru 0.5 ha 1,700 ⦀ 300–499 F

This wine is recognisable with your eyes shut. The Bâtard has made a good start in life. Its colour, nose and palate are all perfectly in place and play their parts well, though it will not be at its best for three, five or ten years, or even longer. Ripe yellow-skinned fruit, white blossom, honey, hazelnut and marzipan are all to be found in this wine which is exceptionally concentrated for a 98. It is full, rich and firm. There are two parcels of land, one belonging to André (Beaune) of 39 a (0.98 acre) which is tenant-farmed and the other, 16 a (0.41 acre) wholly owned. The vines in the first were replanted in 1965 and in 1980 for the other.

⊶ Dom. Bachelet-Ramonet Père et Fils, 11, rue du Parterre, 21190 Chassagne-Montrachet, tel. 03.80.21.32.97, fax 03.80.21.91.41 ◩ Y by appt.

DOM. J.M. BOILLOT 1998★

☐Gd cru 0.19 ha 1,020 ⦀ 300–499 F

As the writer André Jullien used to say, you should find the qualities of a very profound wine in this Cru. A wine with body and great strength, it is concentrated and has a powerful and smooth nose: nuts, compact, and very concentrated. It has a langorous attack then

unleashes reinforcements. We certainly looked for full maturity. Not to be investigated for at least five years.
Dom. Jean-Marc Boillot, rue Mareau, 21630 Pommard, tel. 03.80.22.71.29, fax 03.80.24.98.07

OLIVIER LEFLAIVE 1998★

☐Gd cru n.c. 1,500 500 F+

This Bâtard has a lovely traditional presentation. Discreet nose with minerals and a touch of linden flower. It is still quite green, and this young wine must gather its forces rather than dissipate them. From what we can see, it needs time, as do all the Crus from this terroir.
Olivier Leflaive, pl. du Monument, 21190 Puligny-Montrachet, tel. 03.80.21.37.65, fax 03.80.21.33.94, e-mail leflaive-olivier@dial.oleane.com by appt.

LOUIS LEQUIN 1998★

☐Gd cru 0.12 ha 750 300–499 F

A golden wine with a mature nose of honeysuckle and hazelnut. Lots of panache with very favourable first impressions. The next phase, on the palate, suggests it should keep for three to five years, and then it would be ideal to serve with pike.
Louis Lequin, 1, rue du Pasquier-du-Pont, 21590 Santenay, tel. 03.80.20.63.82, fax 03.80.20.67.14, e-mail louis.lequin@wanadoo.fr by appt.

RENE LEQUIN-COLIN 1998★★★

☐Gd cru 0.12 ha 750 300–499 F

A recent estate (established in 1986) with 1.5 ha (3.7 acres) of vines. The winery was new in 1993, and is constantly being expanded. This Bâtard, picked from only three *ouvrées* (12 a/0.3 acre in total), has been awarded a *coup de cœur.* This wine is not made for drinking right away, but should be kept for a grand occasion. It has beautiful golden colour and is very aromatic, with discreet honey and mineral tones. On the palate it is very concentrated and vigorous. A whole panoply streams across the taste buds. Unanimously awarded a *coup de cœur.*
René Lequin-Colin, 10, rue de Lavau, 21590 Santenay, tel. 03.80.20.66.71, fax 03.80.20.66.70, e-mail renelequin@aol.com by appt.

VEUVE HENRI MORONI 1998

☐Gd cru 0.32 ha 1,000 300–499 F

A *négociant-éleveur* business, established in 1922 and run by the Jomain family alongside their own estate. A wine with a very pale colour but not lacking in distinction when it is allowed to breathe: sweet spices, nuts and discreet vanilla. A hint of oxidation supports this wine, which is limited because of the year.
Veuve Henri Moroni, 1, rue de l'Abreuvoir, 21190 Puligny-Montrachet, tel. 03.80.21.30.48, fax 03.80.21.33.08, e-mail veuve.moroni@wanadoo.fr by appt.

Bienvenues-Bâtard-Montrachet

JEAN-CLAUDE BACHELET 1997★★

☐Gd cru 0.09 ha n.c. 250–299 F

Here, 9 a 42 ca (2.2 acres) of vines, acquired in 1960, produce this brilliant wine that is very open and stands out from the crowd. Flowery, mineral and uncomplicated, it is content to be a good Chardonnay without forgetting its terroir. It is pure and true with a superbly balanced body. The little hint of acidity gives it a second level of interest and means it will last beyond the next five years.
Jean-Claude Bachelet, rue de la Fontaine, 21190 Saint-Aubin, tel. 03.80.21.31.01, fax 03.80.21.97.71, e-mail JCBachelet@aol.com by appt.

DOM. BACHELET-RAMONET PERE ET FILS 1998★

☐Gd cru 0.14 ha 480 300–499 F

A parcel of only 13 a 20 ca (2.5 acres). In 1971, it was replanted with vines which have produced a wine that is canary yellow with very appealing green glints. Its nose is very typical of the area: fresh butter, white truffle and very ripe grapes. On the palate it is still young and aggressive, but its fullness and richness add to its concentration. It has undoubted potential for keeping. A wine to drink with the finest food; and one taster suggested crayfish . . . in five years' time.
Dom. Bachelet-Ramonet Père et Fils, 11, rue du Parterre, 21190 Chassagne-Montrachet, tel. 03.80.21.32.97, fax 03.80.21.91.41 by appt.

CHARTRON ET TREBUCHET 1998★

☐Gd cru n.c. 300 500 F+

One member of the panel wrote, 'I wanted to pause so I could inhale it for a long time'. Truffle makes its appearance. The wine is clear and transluscent with glints of green. It is rich with acacia, citrus fruit, verbena and honey on the nose, and has elegant oak. It is firm, with flavours of linden flower and warm brioche. The yield is small, of course, so it is very concentrated. With the truffle aromas it would go well with fresh foie gras. But wait for three years and you will enjoy it for the following ten.

Chartron et Trébuchet, 13, Grande-Rue, 21190 Puligny-Montrachet, tel. 03.80.21.32.85, fax 03.80.21.36.35, e-mail jmchartron@chartron-trebuchet.com ev. day 10am–12.30pm 2pm–6pm; cl. Nov.– Mar.

DOM. HENRI CLERC ET FILS 1998★

☐Gd cru 0.46 ha 1,646 500 F+

Henri Vincenot, a local author, used to claim that Burgundians could never agree, but this wine shows he was wrong. The jury unanimously gave it a good mark. Produced from vines that were replanted in 1978, this attractive 98 has a sparkling golden yellow colour. The aromas explode with touches of Muscat-like tones deriving from its advanced maturity. The structure, the balance of acidity and roundness, and the length on the palate all contribute to make a whole. All the tasters consider this wine will be past its best in a few years. The jury's advice is to serve it with fresh foie gras and preserved citrus fruit.

EARL Dom. Henri Clerc et Fils, pl. des Marronniers, 21190 Puligny-Montrachet, tel. 03.80.21.32.74, fax 03.80.21.39.60 ev. day 8.30am–11.45am 2pm–5.45pm

Bernard Clerc

DOM. GUILLEMARD-CLERC 1998★

☐Gd cru 0.18 ha 1,143 250–299 F

Documents in the Abbaye de Maizières speak of the 'vigne bienvenue', or welcomed vine, as early as 1397, and after all this time the soil is still benevolent and generous towards it. A buttercup-yellow Chardonnay that is very aromatic, with exotic overtones on a background of spices and honey. It has the finesse found in nearly all the 98s, but should wait as all self-respecting Grand Crus should.

Franck Guillemard-Clerc, 19, rue Drouhin, 21190 Puligny-Montrachet, tel. 03.80.21.34.22, fax 03.80.21.94.84 by appt.

Criots-Bâtard-Montrachet

ROGER BELLAND 1998★★★

☐Gd cru 0.61 ha 2,000 300–499 F

89 |94| |95| 96 **98**

Les Criots fought hard to achieve their ranking as a Grand Cru which is situated on the soil of Chassagne. This parcel of land was acquired in 1982 from the Marcilly associates. The crystalline clarity reveals a classic green-gold. The aromas of peach, hawthorn, and linden flower on a background of vanilla are extremely complex, while the texture is very rich, generous, soft, clean and long. It is wonderfully elegant and complex. Totally characteristic. Why was it not given a *coup de cœur*? One taster noted: 'We must wait a long time for this . . . but not until after my death, because I should like to be there to taste it' .

Dom. Roger Belland, 3, rue de la Chapelle, B.P. 13, 21590 Santenay, tel. 03.80.20.60.95, fax 03.80.20.63.93, e-mail belland.roger@wanadoo.fr by appt.

LOUIS LATOUR 1997

☐Gd cru n.c. n.c. 300–499 F

|93| |**94**| 95 96 97

This Latour Grand Cru does not disappoint. The 97 has classic shades of white-gold and a mineral nose that is still closed. The Chardonnay emerges with freshness. We could say it is a *vin de terroir*. At the moment it is not giving too much away. It has creditable length and a light structure, great finesse and is very successful for this vintage.

Maison Louis Latour, 18, rue des Tonneliers, 21200 Beaune, tel. 03.80.24.81.00, fax 03.80.22.36.21, e-mail louislatour@louislatour.com by appt.

OLIVIER LEFLAIVE 1998

☐Gd cru n.c. n.c. 500 F+

Even though this Grand Cru is tiny, the *négociant-éleveur* usually manages to squeeze out a bottle or two. Here we are looking at a pale gold 98. Its nose presents honey, blossom and brioche. The body does not impress by its bulk but rather by its finesse. It is svelte yet elegant, and with a long finish. To open in three years' time.

Olivier Leflaive, pl. du Monument, 21190 Puligny-Montrachet, tel. 03.80.21.37.65, fax 03.80.21.33.94, e-mail leflaive-olivier@dial.oleane.com by appt.

Chassagne-Montrachet

A new combe rises at Saint-Aubin, running alongside the RN6, and more or less marks the southern limit of white wine production before red wines begin; Les Ruchottes vineyard is at the dividing line. Clos Saint-Jean and Clos Morgeot, both sturdy, vigorous wines, are the most famous of the Chassagnes. In 1999, the whites produced 10,096 hl (266,534 gal) and the reds 7,116 hl (187,862 gal).

FRANCOIS D'ALLAINES 1997*

□ n.c. 3,000 100–149 F

All the qualities of a good, honest *village* 97. Brilliant colour that is perfectly golden, a fine, complex nose with hawthorn or honeysuckle. A supple approach followed by a freshness that lasts. This youthful, delicate wine is a joy for the taste buds. Serve with crayfish or pike-perch.

François d'Allaines, La Corvée du Paquier, 71150 Demigny, tel. 03.85.49.90.16, fax 03.85.49.90.19, e-mail francois@dallaines.com Y by appt.

BERTRAND AMBROISE

La Maltroie 1998*

□ 1er cru n.c. 1,800 200–249 F

Bertrand Ambroise chose a bunch of grapes, an oak tree and a wild boar as his coat of arms, in memory of his ancestors Chenot and Reboux. His Maltroie has a strong oak influence, but the jury concluded that age would soften this trait of youthfulness and the quality of this 98 would be revealed in time. The panel was very confident about this.

Maison Bertrand Ambroise, rue de l'Eglise, 21700 Premeaux-Prissey, tel. 03.80.62.30.19, fax 03.80.62.38.69, e-mail bertrand.ambroise@wanadoo.fr ☑ Y by appt.

JEAN-CLAUDE BACHELET 1997

■ 0.5 ha n.c. 50–69 F

The **Premier Cru La Boudriotte 97 Rouge** deserves to be recommended. As for the *village*, it is fruity with traces of vegetal aromas. A deep garnet red with acidity that is not typical of the year, which will assist it to age. A balanced wine where the tannins are still pronounced. Best to leave it to mature in the cellar.

Jean-Claude Bachelet, rue de la Fontaine, 21190 Saint-Aubin, tel. 03.80.21.31.01, fax 03.80.21.97.71, e-mail JCBachelet@aol.com ☑ Y by appt.

CH. BADER-MIMEUR 1997

□ 3 ha 10,000 100–149 F

A *négociant-éleveur* established in 1919. A golden-yellow wine with aromas of toasted bitter almond. These flavours follow through on the palate. The richness is not dominant and there are underlying nutty flavours.

Ch. Bader-Mimeur, 1, chem. du Château, 21190 Chassagne-Montrachet, tel. 03.80.21.30.22, fax 03.80.21.33.29 ☑ Y by appt.

BALLOT-MILLOT ET FILS

Morgeot 1998*

□ 1er cru 0.59 ha 2,000 150–199 F

A family property that can trace its origins back to the 17th century. It extends from Beaune to Chassagne-Montrachet. Their Morgeot 98 is pale yellow. The nose opens up with notes of aniseed that are soft and sweet. Without having a great complexity, it has finesse on the palate.

Ballot-Millot et Fils, 9, rue de la Goutte-d'Or, B.P. 33, 21190 Meursault, tel. 03.80.21.21.39, fax 03.80.21.65.92 ☑ Y by appt.

JEAN-CLAUDE BELLAND

Morgeot Clos Charreau 1998*

■ 1er cru 0.48 ha 2,400 100–149 F

Le Clos Charreau is found, just after Morgeot, on the edge of Santenay. It is one of the *climats* united under the Morgeot name, but it can also use its own name if it comes from this unique *lieu-dit*. Here we have a wine with a nose that hides itself well but on the palate it is vigorous, full and complete. It is attractive, even unctuous, and should appeal to the restaurant trade since this 98 is so amenable. It would be wise to wait.

Jean-Claude Belland, 45, Grande-Rue, 21590 Santenay, tel. 03.80.20.61.90, fax 03.80.20.65.60 ☑ Y by appt.

ROGER BELLAND

Morgeot Clos Pitois Monopole 1998***

□ 1er cru 1.21 ha 6,000 150–199 F

The Bellands have been wine-producers for five generations. This *climat* is somewhat neglected nowadays, but in the past it was thought of as the best of the best. The vintage has done it proud since it was only short of one vote for a *coup de cœur* for the **98 Rouge** (70–99F) and, the jury was unanimous about the white. This minerally wine in its pure state is full of distinction. It is rare to make both red and white wines so successfully from the same *climat*.

Dom. Roger Belland, 3, rue de la Chapelle, B.P. 13, 21590 Santenay, tel. 03.80.20.60.95, fax 03.80.20.63.93, e-mail belland.roger@wanadoo.fr ☑ Y by appt.

JEAN-CLAUDE BOISSET 1998*

□ n.c. 6,000 150–199 F

The wine produced here is of good quality. We loved the *village*, which has a splendid colour with a nose of apricot and notes of butter and hazelnut that go beautifully together. It is silky and as soft as new bread. A devil of a Chassagne and one that will certainly keep.

J.-C. Boisset, 5, quai Dumorey, B.P. 102, 1700 Nuits-Saint-Georges, l. 03.80.62.62.61, fax 03.80.62.37.38

OM. BORGEOT

e Clos Saint-Jean 1998★★

1er cru 0.4 ha 2,400 100–149 F

'Qui bon vin boit, Dieu voit' ('Drink good ine and see God Divine'): this is supposed to e a maxim of the Cistercian monks which as repeated by Romain Rolland in *Colas reugnon*. This Chassagne, under the patron-ge of Saint John, takes you straight to eaven. It is a remarkable Premier Cru that is ıll, round and elegant with a reasonable mount of oak. It is certainly not very power-ıl, but this lovely 98 shows off its *terroir* ith a certain finesse. One of the joys of the ısting . . .

Dom. Borgeot, rte. de Chassagne, 71150 émigny, tel. 03.85.87.19.92, ıx 03.85.87.19.95 ☑ Y by appt.

EAN BOUCHARD 1997

n.c. 7,200 100–149 F

A Chassagne that is already garnet in col-ur and is veering towards violet. It has inter-sting aromas but is slow to show itself and is ıore mellow than tannic. We would not be urprised if it kept well.

Jean Bouchard, B.P. 47, 21202 Beaune edex, tel. 03.80.24.37.27, ıx 03.80.24.37.38

HILIPPE BOUCHARD 1998★

☐ n.c. 1,200 100–149 F

Straw-yellow, discreet and mineral, this vine then opens out with aromas of white lossom and exotic fruit. It is rich, silky and ively, and develops on the palate with touches of raisin; then its complexity emerges. It is not et at its peak but it certainly has potential.

Philippe Bouchard, 21420 Aloxe-Corton, tel. 03.80.25.00.00, ax 03.80.26.42.00, e-mail vinibeaune@bourgogne.net Y by appt.

OM. HUBERT BOUZEREAU-GRUERE

Les Blanchots dessous 1998★

☐ 0.22 ha 1,000 70–99 F

Hubert Bouzereau comes from an old wine-growing family in Meursault, and has been working on his parents' estate since he was fourteen. Today his daughters are carry-ing the torch. They have produced this wine that is true to its *terroir* where the aromas of apple and toasted almond combine with truf-fle. It is fresh, well-structured and should be drunk in three to five years' time. The *climat* is next to Les Criots-Bâtard-Montrachet, which was considered for classification as a Grand Cru in the 1930s.

Hubert Bouzereau, 22A, rue de la Velle, 21190 Meursault, tel. 03.80.21.20.05, fax 03.80.21.68.16 ☑ Y by appt.

CH. DE CHASSAGNE-MONTRACHET

En Pimont 1998★

☐ 2.66 ha 18,200 150–199 F

Michel Picard's team in Chagny is working to revive the name of the Château de Chassagne, which they took over in May. This pale gold 98 has a combination of hawthorn, lime and citrus fruit. After the highly fla-voured attack, there is a complex aromatic performance. A little richness completes the picture, and the final impression is lively and full-bodied.

Ch. de Chassagne-Montrachet, 21190 Chassagne-Montrachet, tel. 03.85.87.51.00, fax 03.85.87.51.11

Michel Picard

DOM. DU CHATEAU DE PULIGNY-MONTRACHET 1998★

☐ 0.9 ha 5,200 100–149 F

The Crédit Foncier de France recently acquired and renovated this estate that had been passed down from generation to genera-tion and lost its lustre. It is a lovely golden col-our with a floral notes which are just waiting to open out. This is a fresh, aromatic 98. It is very refined but still discreet. A wine that should flourish soon.

SCEA Dom. du Château de Puligny-Montrachet, 21190 Puligny-Montrachet, tel. 03.80.21.39.14, fax 03.80.21.39.07, e-mail chateaupul@aol.com ☑ Y by appt.

CH. DE CITEAUX 1997

■ n.c. 1,500 50–69 F

Slightly liquorice vegetal notes dominate here and the colour is imperial ruby. It is a sturdy, broad-shouldered wine, and though the tannins are very pronounced, there is no excessive harshness. This wine-maker set up at the Château de Cîteaux in Meursault in 1995. He gradually set about putting this beautiful and ancient house in order.

Philippe Bouzereau, Ch. de Cîteaux, 18–20, rue de Cîteaux, B.P. 25, 21190 Meursault, tel. 03.80.21.20.32, fax 03.80.21.64.34, e-mail domaine.bouzereau@wanadoo.fr ☑ Y by appt.

RAOUL CLERGET 1998

■ n.c. 8,000 50–69 F

The business of Raoul Clerget claims it can trace its foundations back to the 13th century. It has been taken over by Tresch, the Alsace business (like Chenu). This purple Chassagne has a good intensity of colour. It is not too oaky, which is welcome, and has good fruit and an elegant simplicity. It is a so-called commercial wine, but there is nothing wrong with that.

Bourgognes Raoul Clerget, chem. de la Pierre-qui-Vire, 21200 Montagny-lès-Beaune, tel. 03.80.26.37.37, fax 03.80.24.14.81

BERNARD COLIN ET FILS

Clos Saint Jean 1997★★

□ 1er cru 0.52 ha n.c. 100–149 F

It is a pleasure to taste at the Colins'. The Premier Cru, **Les Chenevottes 97 Blanc** (70–99F), is very perfumed and well-made and is awarded one star. This superb golden-coloured Clos Saint Jean has mushroom hints on the nose, and is mellow. Its low-level acidity and lightness could denote an insignificant wine, but this is not the case here: it will keep well.

Bernard Colin et Fils, 22, rue Charles-Paquelin, 21190 Chassagne-Montrachet, tel. 03.80.21.32.78, fax 03.80.21.93.23 ev. day 8am–7pm; Sun. by appt.

VINCENT DANCER

La Romanée 1998

□ 1er cru 0.45 ha 1,800 100–149 F

Yes, there is a Romanée at Chassagne, besides the one in Givry and the grandest one at Vosne. A fairly rich Premier Cru, as you would suspect from here, and it is only the third vintage produced by this estate, which is a new arrival in the appellation. It has a soft body with the slightest trace of rawness. All things are possible. A respectable wine, not short of keeping qualities.

Vincent Dancer, 23, rte. de Santenay, 21190 Chassagne-Montrachet, tel. 03.80.21.94.48, fax 03.80.21.94.48, e-mail vincentdancer@aol.com by appt.

DOUDET-NAUDIN 1998★

■ 0.85 ha 1,800 100–149 F

This little business belonging to an independent *négociant-éleveur* was founded a hundred and fifty years ago. It ploughs a traditional furrow and has produced here a tannic, somewhat rustic 98 that has a strong nose and raspberry fullness. A wine to await for four or five years.

Doudet-Naudin, 3, rue Henri-Cyrot, 21420 Savigny-lès-Beaune, tel. 03.80.21.51.74, fax 03.80.21.50.69 by appt.

Yves Doudet

GUY FONTAINE ET JACKY VION

Clos Saint-Jean 1998★

■ 1er cru 0.65 ha 2,000 70–99 F

The **98 Village Rouge** (one star) is at a difficult age, but could produce something good in three or four years. As for this one, it has been excellently vinified, oaked with skill, has concentrated aromas and more than adequate length. Well-structured, powerful and distinguished. The third generation is now running this estate, and produced a particularly successful 95 vintage.

GAEC des Vignerons, Le Bourg, 71150 Remigny, tel. 03.85.87.03.35, fax 03.85.87.03.35 by appt.

Fontaine-Vion

ANDRE GOICHOT 1997★

■ n.c. 11,600 70–99

'If you don't come to Chassagne, Chassagne will come to you', to paraphrase the saying. This is a Chassagne where the Pinot Noir comes right at you. The colour is beginning to develop. Strawberry and raspberry embellish the nose. It is fairly full-bodied with tannic kirsch flavours, but the freshness and fullness soften the overall impression.

SA A. Goichot et Fils, av. Charles-de-Gaulle, 21200 Beaune, tel. 03.80.26.88.70, fax 03.80.26.80.69, e-mail goichot@goichotsa.com by appt.

DOM. DES HAUTES-CORNIERES

Morgeot 1997★

■ 1er cru 2 ha 11,000 70–99 F

Full marks for the way it looks. The nose is strawberry jam and spices to begin with. There is already a firm, structured body and the concentration is good. A wine that needs keeping.

Ph. Chapelle et Fils, Dom. des Hautes-Cornières, 21590 Santenay, tel. 03.80.20.60.09, fax 03.80.20.61.01 ev. day except Sun. 9am–12 noon 2pm–6pm

LOUIS JADOT 1997★★

□ n.c. 15,000 200–249 F

Is the shortest route always the best? Not necessarily. It is worth taking time to admire the pretty green glints and explore the aromas of humus and ripe fruit – almost vanilla in flower. On the palate it needs no time, and fullness balances the freshness. It concentrates on the matter in hand. A good complete wine, almost as good as the excellent 83 vintage.

Maison Louis Jadot, 21, rue Eugène-Spuller, 21200 Beaune, tel. 03.80.22.10.57, fax 03.80.22.56.03, e-mail contact@louisjadot.com by appt.

GABRIEL JOUARD Les Baudines 1997

□ 1er cru 1.4 ha 1,800 70–99 F

The *climat* is high up on the Premiers Crus' hillside and just next to Santenay. The wine is produced by Paul Jouard who took over his parents' vineyard in 1992. The 97 is light and clear, with character and balance. It is very interesting to taste.

EARL Dom. Gabriel et Paul Jouard, 3, rue du Petit-Puits, 21190 Chassagne-Montrachet, tel. 03.80.21.30.30, fax 03.80.21.30.30 by appt.

CH. DE LA MALTROYE

Clos du Château de la Maltroye Monopole 1998

■ 1er cru 1.37 ha 8,200 100–149 F

Le Clos du Château de la Maltroye is wholly owned by the Cournut family (started by an airline pilot who landed and decided to stay). This wine is an interesting example of what, in Burgundy, is called *une vinification à l'ancienne* – an old-fashioned method of

-nification. It has a little warmth, a degree of -idity and, above all, a good deal of bitter-ss on the finish. This will soften. The **Vil-ge Rouge 98** is a very dainty wine with -omas of bilberry and liquorice, and it will -ep for several years with no problem (70-F).

SCE Ch. de la Maltroye, 16, rue de la -urée, 21190 Chassagne-Montrachet, -l. 03.80.21.32.45, fax 03.80.21.34.54 by appt.

Cournut

-ICHEL LAMANTHE

-s Vergers 1998

-ler cru	0.26 ha	1,500	100–149 F

The colour is clear, richer on the palate -an in the glass, light and fruity – a short -hme rather than an epic poem, but there is -mple, spontaneous poetry in this 98 which -as been inspired by its expressive terroir. The *-imat* is near Clos Saint-Jean. The 92 vintage -as particularly good.

Michel Lamanthe, 21190 Saint-Aubin, -l. 03.80.21.33.23, fax 03.80.21.93.96 by appt.

-OM. HUBERT LAMY

-a Goujonne 1998

	2 ha	9,000	70–99 F

The *climat* is at the foot of the hill on the -entral part of the administrative district. It -roduces this fortifying red, which has some -llness, though its unsettled tannins make it -uite harsh at present. Deep ruby in colour -ith aromas suggesting wild cherry, it has a -uperb aromatic delicacy. It is very character--tic and should be put on one side for later.

Dom. Hubert Lamy, Paradis, 21190 -aint-Aubin, tel. 03.80.21.32.55, -ax 03.80.21.38.32 by appt.

-OM. LAMY-PILLOT Boudriotte 1998

-ler cru	0.4 ha	2,800	70–99 F

A Pinot Noir that has more brilliance than -epth in the colour. It is straightforward and -as a spontaneous fineness. If you are inter--sted in corkscrews, have a look at the phe--omenal collection held at this cellar. Also -orth a mention is the **Village Blanc 98**, which -s oaky but rich and full.

Dom. Lamy-Pillot, 31, rte. de Santenay, -1190 Chassagne-Montrachet, -el. 03.80.21.30.52, fax 03.80.21.30.02, -mail lamy.pillot@wanadoo.fr by -ppt.

René Lamy

-YLVAIN LANGOUREAU

-es Voillenots Dessous 1997★

	0.73 ha	2,300	50–69 F

The recent expansion of the estate includes - vaulted cellar in attractive stone, built in -998 by a master mason. You can buy white -vine here – **Les Perclos 98 Village** (70–99F), is -ery refined. In red, we recommend this one -hat we tasted. Everything comes to he who -vaits and this 97 will age well while remaining -upple and perfumed with blackcurrant.

Sylvain Langoureau, Hameau de Gamay, 21190 Saint-Aubin, tel. 03.80.21.39.99, fax 03.80.21.39.99 by appt.

OLIVIER LEFLAIVE

Abbaye de Morgeot 1997★

☐1er cru	n.c.	8,000	200–249 F

If you feel hungry when you are hereabouts, you could try the *Table d'Olivier*, as you can visit the cellars and have lunch there. This wine will have no difficulty in settling down. It is pale-coloured, flowery and buttery with a tiny hint of bitterness. It is well balanced in all departments, and well-handled. A retreat in this Abbey would be very welcome.

Olivier Leflaive, pl. du Monument, 21190 Puligny-Montrachet, tel. 03.80.21.37.65, fax 03.80.21.33.94, e-mail leflaive-olivier@dial.oleane.com by appt.

LE MANOIR MURISALTIEN

Morgeot 1997★

☐1er cru	n.c.	1,500	200–249 F

We were like bees, buzzing around this deep golden wine, smooth as a gold bar. Its perfumes are equally intense (undergrowth). There is a note of warmth and a hint of bitterness, but they are not overwhelming. The harmony is never broken.

Le Manoir Murisaltien, 4, rue du Clos-de-Mazeray, 21190 Meursault, tel. 03.80.21.21.83, fax 03.80.21.66.48, e-mail vin@demessey.com by appt.

Marc Dumont

RENE LEQUIN-COLIN

Les Vergers 1998★

☐1er cru	0.45 ha	3,200	100–149 F

The Premier Cru **Les Caillerets 98 Blanc** is most appealing and recommended. You could also choose this Les Vergers as we did. What a tiny distance there is between this *climat* and the most illustrious Montrachet. This very fruity wine is beginning to open. We give it five to six flourishing years. Only fifteen years ago, the estate was 1.5 ha/3.7 acres, and it is now 8.75 ha/22 acres.

René Lequin-Colin, 10, rue de Lavau, 21590 Santenay, tel. 03.80.20.66.71, fax 03.80.20.66.70, e-mail renelequin@aol.com by appt.

MESTRE PERE ET FILS

Tonton Marcel Monopole 1998

☐1er cru	0.25 ha	1,800	150–199 F

Tonton Marcel is a very ancient *lieu-dit* in Chassagne: it came from the name given to a standing stone by the people who lived in the region four thousand years ago. There are no traces left of this Burgundian menhir, but it is recorded on the land registry. The Mestre family have total ownership of this *climat*, and market their wines themselves. This is an almost white 98. Resembling Asterix more than Obélix, it is densely flavoured and full of character, and there is a nice touch of softness.

🔑 Mestre Père et Fils, 12, pl. du Jet-d'Eau, B.P. 24, 21590 Santenay, tel. 03.80.20.60.11, fax 03.80.20.60.97, e-mail gilbert-mestre@wanadoo.fr ☑ 🍷 by appt.

MICHEL MOREY-COFFINET

La Romanée 1998

☐1er cru 0.8 ha 4,200 🛢 150–199 F

Handsome, good, fruity . . . This young Romanée with its princely name is just hinting at gold in the colour, but it was born with a golden spoon in its mouth. It is buttery, honeyed and dashing on the palate. Its freshness is as expected. Also worth mentioning is the **Village Blanc 98** (100–149F) with its lovely exotic nose of both fruit and elegance, and in red, if you change sides, the **Village 98** (70–99F); lots of blackcurrant bud, very approachable, still developing.

🔑 Dom. Michel Morey-Coffinet, 6, pl. du Grand-Four, 21190 Chassagne-Montrachet, tel. 03.80.21.31.71, fax 03.80.21.90.81 ☑ 🍷 by appt.

DOM. VINCENT PRUNIER 1998★

■ 0.24 ha 1,475 🛢 50–69 F

The garnet colour with its glints of ruby shows the family resemblance. When it matures it will show cocoa, red berry fruit and toasty musk. Very open on the palate with flavours of blackcurrant and cherry, it has a firm attack. It is vinous and balanced, the tannins are softened and the finish is good. It is expressive and expansive and already pleasant, though it could wait five years. It is a relatively new estate (1988). Vincent Prunier's parents were not wine-growers, and this is very unusual in this village.

🔑 Vincent Prunier, rte. de Beaune, 21190 Auxey-Duresses, tel. 03.80.21.27.77, fax 03.80.21.68.87 ☑ 🍷 by appt.

ANTONIN RODET 1997★

☐ 2 ha 10,000 🛢 150–199 F

The second impression only reinforces the first. Golden-yellow with emerald glints, the wine is perfumed with peach and white-fleshed fruit. On the palate it is round, rich and has the lemony suppleness typical of Chassagne. An worthy example of the wine that should also be complimented for its long finish.

🔑 Antonin Rodet, 71640 Mercurey, tel. 03.85.98.12.12, fax 03.85.45.25.49, e-mail rodet@rodet.com ☑ 🍷 ev. day except Sat. Sun. 9am–12 noon 1.30pm–6pm

DOM. ROUX PERE ET FILS 1998★★

☐ 0.8 ha 5,000 🛢 100–149 F

The Roux sons have already produced an excellent 95, and this white 98 is beyond reproach. The nose is very mature with aromas of walnut, hay, spices, fruit and hints of oak. On the palate the flavours unroll impressively with rich, full, mouth-filling flavours and the length of a wine that is at its peak. To be drunk rather than kept.

🔑 Dom. Roux Père et Fils, 21190 Saint-Aubin, tel. 03.80.21.32.92, fax 03.80.21.35.00 ☑ 🍷 by appt.

Saint-Aubin

Saint-Aubin is topographically the neighbour of the Hautes-Côtes, but some of the commune borders Chassagne to the south and Puligny and Blagny to the east. The Murgers des Dents de Chien, Saint-Aubin's Premier Cru, is grown only a very short distance from Chevalier-Montrachet and Les Caillerets and it must be said that the Saint-Aubin Premier Cru is fully their equal in quality. The vineyards have begun to produce a little more red wine – 2,903 hl (76,639 gal) in 1999 – but the whites – 5,683 hl (150,031 gal) – reveal St Aubin at its best.

JEAN-CLAUDE BACHELET 1997★

☐1er cru 0.44 ha n.c. 🛢 50–69

The **Champlots 97 Blanc** is recommended by the jury. Both the look and the nose are particularly nicely balanced and well pronounced: gold and honey, mint and cumin. From the first impression there is some fullness and conviction in the flavour with discreet oak. It is rich and long. A wine to be appreciated over time.

🔑 Jean-Claude Bachelet, rue de la Fontaine, 21190 Saint-Aubin, tel. 03.80.21.31.01, fax 03.80.21.97.71, e-mail JCBachelet@aol.com ☑ 🍷 by appt.

DOM. BACHELET Les Cortons 1997

■1er cru 1 ha 4,000 🛢 50–69 F

Les Cortons is situated on the edge of RN 6, and they have managed to produce this lovely wine. Bilberry on the nose, fully-flavoured on the palate, it is a wine with a touch of warmth that is already very mature.

🔑 Dom. B. Bachelet et ses Fils, rue des Maranges, 71150 Dezize-lès-Maranges, tel. 03.85.91.16.11, fax 03.85.91.16.48 ☑ 🍷 by appt.

DOM. BILLARD ET FILS

Les Castets 1998

■ 0.04 ha 2,000 🛢 50–69 F

A well-balanced wine that is vermilion in colour with a well-developed nose of crystallised cherry. The small hint of acidity is nothing out of the ordinary. Do not open for two years.

Dom. Billard et Fils, rte de Beaune, 21340 La Rochepot, tel. 03.80.21.87.94, fax 03.80.21.72.17 by appt.

GILLES BOUTON En Rémilly 1998

☐ 1er cru 0.8 ha 5,700 50–69 F

Straw-gold. A substantial, full wine. It is open and friendly and belies its age because it is ready to drink and has a good structure. The estate is in the hamlet of Gamay, across from the old fortress, which this wine-grower inherited from his grandfather in 1977. He started with just 3.7 ha (9 acres), and now the estate comprises 13 ha (32 acres) in twenty one different appellations. The choice is wide.

Gilles Bouton, Gamay, 21190 Saint-Aubin, tel. 03.80.21.32.63, fax 03.80.21.90.74 by appt.

DOM. DE BRULLY

Les Cortons 1998★★★

☐ 1er cru 0.6 ha 4,000 70–99 F

This Saint-Aubin is quite simply marvellous. It has a lovely, lively colour with aromas hovering between white blossom and fruit (hawthorn and grapefruit). The attack is sincere, the body is well-structured, and it has its sights on the future. A firm, elegant wine, a *coup de cœur* remarkably well-proportioned. It is thirst-quenching and perfumed, and will be splendid for five to six years.

Dom. de Brully, 21190 Saint-Aubin, tel. 03.80.21.32.92, fax 03.80.21.35.00 by appt.

DOM. JEAN CHARTRON

Les Murgers des Dents de Chien 1998★

☐ 1er cru 0.55 ha 4,000 150–199 F

Brilliant pale gold, more oaky than flowery; is it a 'vin de tonnelier', (a cooper's wine), as one of our jury wrote? If this is a style that appeals to you, you will be happy indeed: the oakiness is fine but not overwhelming. Its underlying richness, balance and length will become more expressive with age.

Dom. Jean Chartron, 13, Grande-Rue, 21190 Puligny-Montrachet, tel. 03.80.21.32.85, fax 03.80.21.36.35 ev. day 10am–12.30pm 2pm–6pm

CH. DE CHASSAGNE-MONTRACHET

Le Charmois 1998★

☐ 1er cru 5.68 ha 15,900 70–99 F

Le Charmois is near Chassagne. This wine is produced by the Picard de Chagny company. A very good, straw-yellow white that is full of vigour and verve. It is spirited and, when all is said and done, comparatively rich.

Ch. de Chassagne-Montrachet, 21190 Chassagne-Montrachet, tel. 03.85.87.51.00, fax 03.85.87.51.11

Michel Picard

DOM. DU CHATEAU DE PULIGNY-MONTRACHET

En Rémilly 1997★

☐ 1er cru 1.34 ha 8,000 70–99 F

This is the 97 vintage from the same *climat* that produced a wonderful 94. Old gold, very oaky with a sinewy, firm structure and an interesting array of secondary aromas: pepper, green chilli and cardamom . . . but quince and peach too, with a few mineral notes. A wine with promise.

SCEA Dom. du Château de Puligny-Montrachet, 21190 Puligny-Montrachet, tel. 03.80.21.39.14, fax 03.80.21.39.07, e-mail chateaupul@aol.com by appt.

FRANCOISE ET DENIS CLAIR

1998★★

■ 1er cru 1 ha 6,000 50–69 F

The white Premier Cru **Les Murgers des Dents de Chien** is awarded one star (70–99F). It is somewhat evocative of gentian and, beneath the distinct vanilla softness, has character. The red Premier Cru had an even more favourable reception. It is fruity and perfectly ripe, and can be served now. It will benefit from being drunk while still in the bloom of youth.

Françoise et Denis Clair, 14, rue de la Chapelle, 21590 Santenay, tel. 03.80.20.61.96, fax 03.80.20.65.19 by appt.

JOSEPH DROUHIN 1997★

☐ 1er cru n.c. n.c. 100–149 F

The Indian summer of 1997 produced an attractive wine that, while being a little thin, is not lacking in other qualities. It has a fine balance between softness and acidity. Aromas of almond, peach and cinnamon with an aftertaste of quince; an elegant wine. Ready now.

Joseph Drouhin, 7, rue d'Enfer, 21200 Beaune, tel. 03.80.24.68.88, fax 03.80.22.43.14, e-mail drouhin@calva.net by appt.

ECHANSONNERIE DU GOUT-VINAGE

Les Murgers des Dents de Chien 1998

☐ 1er cru 1 ha 4,000 200–249 F

A sumptuous gold wine with a striking label from the *Echansonnerie de l'Ordre du Goût, Vinage de France* (sic), which takes refuge in the Mosel. The wine has fairly mature perfumes (wilted flowers, apple). The flavour from the wood is not dominant. It is smooth and ample on the palate with a spicy finish.

Echansonnerie du Goût-Vinage, rte de Moince, 57420 Louvigny, tel. 03.87.69.79.69, fax 03.87.69.71.13

DOM. HUBERT LAMY

Clos de la Chatenière 1998★★★

☐1er cru 1.3 ha 8,000 100–149 F

The good Saint Aubin was abbot of Tincillac and bishop of Angers. He was very popular because he was always ready to perform a useful miracle. This 98 is endowed with such grace that its finesse and declicacy has won it a *coup de cœur.* Pale and brilliant, it has a floral nose embellished with nuts with a well-balanced oakiness. A wine of rich sensations that pleases with its princely charm. **Rémilly 98** is awarded one star.

Dom. Hubert Lamy, Paradis, 21190 Saint-Aubin, tel. 03.80.21.32.55, fax 03.80.21.38.32 by appt.

DOM. HUBERT LAMY

Les Frionnes 1998★★

☐1er cru 3 ha 2,000 70–99 F

Rarely is a producer so successful. One taster referred to the excellent Frionnes 98 as 'the wine that I love'. Clear gold with superb perfumes of white blossom and brioche, the wine takes shape from the very beginning and does not depart from its elegant line on the way to the finish. It is very young. In the same price range is the red **Les Castets 98**, also two stars. It is remarkably substantial, as is the **Derrière Chez Edouard** (oddly, the name of a Premier Cru), one star, a beautiful, very powerful wine.

Dom. Hubert Lamy, Paradis, 21190 Saint-Aubin, tel. 03.80.21.32.55, fax 03.80.21.38.32 by appt.

DOM. LAMY-PILLOT

Les Pucelles 1998★

☐ 0.82 ha 6,000 70–99 F

This *climat* is situated on the hillside on the road to La Rochepot. A wine with a lustrous-looking colour. Its nose is slightly menthol, toasted and vanilla as well. It has a rich, soft body and good length, but the wood is still very prominent. Best to wait a year.

Dom. Lamy-Pillot, 31, rte. de Santenay, 21190 Chassagne-Montrachet, tel. 03.80.21.30.52, fax 03.80.21.30.02, e-mail lamy.pillot@wanadoo.fr by appt.

René Lamy

SYLVAIN LANGOUREAU

Les Frionnes 1998★

☐1er cru 0.3 ha 1,900 50–69 F

This Les Frionnes has a very pale colour and a nose of toasted almond and crystallised fruits. Full of vigour and go, it is rich and supple. A wine that will give complete satisfaction at a reasonable price.

Sylvain Langoureau, Hameau de Gamay, 21190 Saint-Aubin, tel. 03.80.21.39.99, fax 03.80.21.39.99 by appt.

DOM. LARUE En Rémilly 1998★

☐1er cru 0.35 ha 2,120 70–99 F

Rémilly is part of the Saint-Aubin vineyards that is closest to Puligny-Montrachet; they are first cousins to the prestigious white Grands Crus. This classy 98 has linden flowers on the nose. There is little acidity, so it is advisable to drink it in the next two years. Its suppleness, richness and roundness are the indisputable qualities of a Premier Cru.

Dom. Larue, Gamay, 21190 Saint-Aubin, tel. 03.80.21.30.74, fax 03.80.21.91.36 by appt.

OLIVIER LEFLAIVE

Le Charmois 1997

☐1er cru n.c. 20,000 100–149 F

This Saint-Aubin is still very young, but is already fine, with a little green hue in its gold colour. Honey and beeswax at first, then some bitter orange and grapefruit. It is attractively consistent. Wait for a short while, then drink it over a long period.

Olivier Leflaive, pl. du Monument, 21190 Puligny-Montrachet, tel. 03.80.21.37.65, fax 03.80.21.33.94, e-mail leflaive-olivier@dial.oleane.com by appt.

MALLARD-GAULIN 1998★★

☐ 0.35 ha 2,000 150–199 F

This pale yellow wine heralds spring in the cellar with its fragrant hawthorn. It is rich and vinous and embraces the taste buds with great style and staying power! Good in company with sole *meunière.* The grand jury voted it third in the contest for the *coup de cœur.*

Maison Mallard-Gaulin, 21420 Aloxe-Corton, tel. 03.80.26.46.10, fax 03.80.26.43.57

ROLAND MAROSLAVAC-LEGER

Les Murgers des Dents de Chien 1998★

☐1er cru 0.37 ha 2,200 100–149 F

As the crow flies, this *climat* is very close to the illustrious Montrachet. Fairly pale in colour but with golden flecks, it has a heady nose (apple and almond dominate). It has good flavour, is generous and will undoubtedly keep well.

Dom. Maroslavac-Léger, 43, Grande-Rue, 21190 Puligny-Montrachet, tel. 03.80.21.31.23, fax 03.80.21.91.39 by appt.

OM. DES MEIX

es Murgers des Dents de Chien 1998★

1er cru | 1.1 ha | 4,000 | 50–69 F

This oenologist took over his grandfather's nes, which used to be cultivated by a tenant-rmer. He is a traditionalist and de-stalks alf the harvest, stirring the must with the ame vigour as ringing the angelus bell. All is attention to detail results in a good wine. he 98 has shades of copper yellow and its ready powerful nose is floral in style. It is a ttle oaky and expansive on the palate. One ster said it had a 'Meursault spirit'.

Christophe Guillo, Dom. des Meix, 1200 Combertault, tel. 03.80.26.67.05, ax 03.80.26.67.05, e-mail uillochristophe@aol.com Y by appt.

ERNARD PRUDHON

es Castets 1997★

1er cru | 0.74 ha | 1,000 | 50–69 F

Our tasters could not agree on the dish that ould go perfectly with this wine; one said œuf bourguignon another thought *magret e canard*. All agreed that the colour was dmirable and that it would last over time. s nose of spices and blackcurrant could evelop more. It is balanced and warm and robably a wine for 2002.

Bernard Prudhon, 21190 Saint-Aubin, el. 03.80.21.35.66 Y by appt.

OM. ROUX PERE ET FILS

a Pucelle 1998★★

2.5 ha | 12,000 | 70–99 F

The younger sibling of the excellent 97 vin-age. Attractively golden-green with a slightly oasty, flowery nose enhanced with a few xotic notes. A supple, round wine with a min-ral note, it has a certain personality that sug-ests it should wait two to three years. This ast estate is situated in Saint-Aubin.

Dom. Roux Père et Fils, 21190 Saint-ubin, tel. 03.80.21.32.92, ax 03.80.21.35.00 Y by appt.

IICHEL SERVEAU En l'Ebaupin 1998

0.15 ha | 1,000 | 50–69 F

An attractive, deep peony colour. The nose s chock-full of cherries and has more to give. The palate is still too young and needs time or the fruit to develop. This *climat* is on the oad to La Rochepot.

Michel Serveau, 21340 La Rochepot, el. 03.80.21.70.24, fax 03.80.21.71.87 Y v. day 8am–7pm

ERARD THOMAS

a Chatenière 1998

1er cru | 0.53 ha | 3,600 | 50–69 F

La Chatenière is in the middle of Saint-ubin. Being surrounded by all the local nfluences, it has produced a gilt-edged 98 hat is lemony and fresh, and does not isappoint.

Gérard Thomas, 21190 Saint-Aubin, el. 03.80.21.32.57, fax 03.80.21.36.51 Y y appt.

Santenay

The village of Santenay is dominated by the Trois-Croix mountain and, thanks to its salt-water spa which has the most lithium-rich waters in the whole of Europe, became a famous spa resort. The village has many attractions, among which are some excellent red wines. Les Gravières, La Comme and Beauregard are the best-known Crus. Like Chassagne, the vineyard is often awarded the Ribbon of Royat, a high tribute to its quality. The two appellations of Chassagne and Santenay edge over into the Commune de Remigny, in Saône-et-Loire, where we find the appellations of Cheilly, Sampigny and Dezize-lès-Maranges, now included under the Appellation Maranges. In 1999 the AOC Santenay produced 2,032 hl (59,645 gal) of white wine and 16,342 hl (431,429 gal) of red wine.

DOM. ALEXANDRE 1998★

■ | 2.25 ha | 4,000 | 50–69 F

This estate is at Remigny, covering 13 ha (32 acres) in all, and it shares the AOC *village* with Santenay. This 98 is not badly made. For now it certainly is sturdy, but the fruit is pronounced on the palate. There is good body with tannins that have yet to soften. The flavour of cherries in syrup is particularly prominent. The colour is a shade between carmine and mauve.

Dom. Alexandre Père et Fils, pl. de la Mairie, 71150 Remigny, tel. 03.85.87.22.61, fax 03.85.87.22.61 Y by appt.

DOM. BACHELET 1997★

■ | 2.5 ha | 10,000 | 50–69 F

The water-nymph and the god of wine . . . The wine is completely de-stalked, and the 97 has a direct, well-integrated nose with toasted aromas and wild rose. On the palate it is delicate and soft, fresh and light but with the right amount of acidity to indicate it will keep a while (two to three years).

Dom. Bernard Bachelet et Fils, rue des Maranges, 71150 Dezize-lès-Maranges, tel. 03.85.91.16.11, fax 03.85.91.16.48 Y by appt.

DOM. BART En Bievau 1997★

□ | 0.35 ha | 1,500 | 70–99 F

It is quite a stretch from Marsannay to Santenay. The white is a success. The colour is

appealing to the eye and the nose is perfumed with wood. Very supple on the attack and there is a little underlying acidity and a durable balance. This *climat* is between the village and Saint-Jean-de-Narosse, the hamlet on the hill.
GAEC Bart, 23, rue Moreau, 21160 Marsannay-la-Côte, tel. 03.80.51.49.76, fax 03.80.51.23.43 by appt.

JEAN-CLAUDE BELLAND

Clos des Gravières 1998★

1er cru 1.21 ha 6,120 70–99 F

The **Comme 98 Premier Cru Rouge** is a wine with a future. It is tightly-woven, very delicate and well-perfumed. This particular vintage is in full development. It is already showing some very deep garnet. The nose is slightly pepper, perhaps horse chestnut . . . Excellent texture, and the tannins are still firm. It lacks neither fruit nor character; its length shows promise.
Jean-Claude Belland, 45, Grande-Rue, 21590 Santenay, tel. 03.80.20.61.90, fax 03.80.20.65.60 by appt.

ROGER BELLAND Gravières 1998★★

1er cru 1.14 ha 6,000 70–99 F

This Belland has 23 ha (57 acres) with its headquarters in Les Gravières. An enterprising wine that is dark and demonstrative and is beginning to show well: dark ruby in colour and with a strong nose where there is pronounced wood. But on the palate it shows superb structure and body: the red berry fruits are not camouflaged by the oak. To keep four or five years. The **Charmes 98 Rouge Village** deserves the same comments (50–69F). It is full-bodied and powerful, and the nose has distinctive, elegant notes of roasting coffee. It has remarkable length. Good value for money.
Dom. Roger Belland, 3, rue de la Chapelle, B.P. 13, 21590 Santenay, tel. 03.80.20.60.95, fax 03.80.20.63.93, e-mail belland.roger@wanadoo.fr by appt.

ALBERT BICHOT 1997★

n.c. 3,000 100–149 F

A vigorous, developing wine that will age well. It is purple in colour, vegetal and slightly liquorice, and has a lot in reserve. But when the time comes to drink it, it will give a great deal. More hefty than rich but with a certain charm.
Maison Albert Bichot, 6 bis, bd Jacques-Copeau, 21200 Beaune, tel. 03.80.24.37.37, fax 03.80.24.37.38

DOM. CAILLOT 1997★

1 ha 6,000 50–69 F

An attractive wine that is characteristic. Light yellow colour, gunflint and white blossom nose; the Chardonnay here is full of richness and pleasing aromas (hints of apricot). It is true, when you are born and bred in Meursault you master this variety wonderfully. The estate has Crus from Beaune to Santenay, in nearly all the villages.
Dom. Caillot, 14, rue du Cromin, 21190 Meursault, tel. 03.80.21.21.70, fax 03.80.21.69.58 by appt.

DOM. CAPUANO-FERRERI ET FILS

La Comme 1998★

1er cru n.c. n.c. 70–99 F

We have always enjoyed the wines from this estate. The **Village 98 Rouge** (50–69F) is awarded a commendation and the **Passe Temps 98 Rouge Premier Cru**, which is fine and elegant, is awarded one star (50–69F). This La Comme would suit a haunch of venison. The whole of the tasting is dominated by its Santenay characteristics; harmony from beginning to end, a brilliant colour with a powerful body, rich and beautifully chewy and the lingering aromas go from red berry fruit to liquorice.
Capuano-Ferreri et Fils, 1, rue de la Croix-Sorine, 21590 Santenay, tel. 03.80.20.64.12, fax 03.80.20.65.75 by appt.

LOUIS CHAVY 1997★

n.c. 15,000 70–99 F

When a wine is good, why not say so? This one is not very attractive to look at as it is only moderately brilliant with shades of terracotta, but the nose is inexhaustible and, on the palate, it is well-built. It is inevitably a little hard, but a red Santenay stays in its shell for the first few years. Very classic, well-constructed with good breeding.
Louis Chavy, Caveau la Vierge Romaine, pl. des Marronniers, 21190 Puligny-Montrachet, tel. 03.80.26.33.00, fax 03.80.24.14.84, e-mail mallet.b@cva-beaune.fr ev. day 10am–6pm; cl. Nov.–Mar.

MAURICE CHENU 1998

n.c. 6,000 50–69 F

The business has been taken over by Tresch, the Alsatian company, but the Santenay has lost none of its local accent. The curtain goes up on a ruby colour of moderate intensity, followed by a duet of blackcurrant and cherry. This is still a tannic 98, but it will be easy to drink because it does not lack richness or body. It strives for finesse and succeeds.
Bourgognes Chenu-Tresch SA, chem. de la Pierre-qui-Vire, 21200 Montagny-lès-Beaune, tel. 03.80.26.37.37, fax 03.80.24.14.81

FRANCOISE ET DENIS CLAIR

Clos Genet 1998★★

1.2 ha 6,000 50–69 F

This estate has good links with the United States and Great Britain. It has produced a very good 98. A lovely velvety colour, the nose is slightly balsamic vinegar, over-ripe, with an emphasis of cooked prunes and follows through with a round, rich, robust and lengthy body: perfect on the palate. It is rich, strong and a typical Santenay with a lot to say. Excellent with game.

🔑 Françoise et Denis Clair, 14, rue de la Chapelle, 21590 Santenay, tel. 03.80.20.61.96, fax 03.80.20.65.19 ☑ Y by appt.

DOM. HENRI CLERC ET FILS

Les Pôtets 1997*

■ 0.69 ha 1,314 ⏸ 70–99 F

The origins of this estate go back to the 16th century. It has produced this wine in oak barrels, a fifth of which are new. This *climat* is on the east-facing slope at Santenay. The nose shows some crystallised fruit, has a decent attack, a supple palate and it all looks very good. The wine is produced by a Chardonnay specialist who makes some Pinot Noir for his own enjoyment.

🔑 EARL Dom. Henri Clerc et Fils, pl. des Marronniers, 21190 Puligny-Montrachet, tel. 03.80.21.32.74, fax 03.80.21.39.60 ☑ Y ev. day 8.30am–11.45am 2pm–5.45pm

🔑 Bernard Clerc

RAOUL CLERGET 1998

■ 1er cru n.c. 6,000 ⏸ 70–99 F

A good luscious wine with a bit of bite, vinosity and a certain amount of fruit; it has mushroom aromas and a fairly deep colour. It is not very powerful, but pleasant and marketable. This house is part of Tresch, the Alsatian group that owns vineyards in Burgundy.

🔑 Bourgognes Raoul Clerget, chem. de la Pierre-qui-Vire, 21200 Montagny-lès-Beaune, tel. 03.80.26.37.37, fax 03.80.24.14.81

CLOS DE GATSULARD MONOPOLE 1997*

■ 2.95 ha 10,000 ▮ ⏸ 70–99 F

Raymond Launay is the founder of the Assurances Agricoles Mutuelles that exists throughout the region; one of many strings to his bow. He also raises horses, grows arable crops and here, he grows vines. The Clos de Gatsulard is a monopoly.The colour looks as if it is changing, and the nose is savage ,leaning towards musk and leather. On the palate it is typical of the vintage, and is round and well-built, qualities that come from the Pinot.

🔑 Dom. Raymond Launay, rue des Charmots, 21630 Pommard, tel. 03.80.24.08.03, fax 03.80.24.12.87, e-mail raymond.launay@wanadoo.fr ☑ Y by appt.

EDOUARD DELAUNAY ET SES FILS

Clos Rousseau 1997

■ 1er cru n.c. 9,000 ⏸ 100–149 F

Vince in bono malum is the motto of this very ancient business that Jean-Claude Boisset has taken over. 'Conquer ill with good' is not a bad idea. This wine does its best. It has intense fruit with some juniper, is very mouthfilling and has some roundness. A well-made wine.

🔑 Edouard Delaunay et ses Fils, 5, rue du Moulin, 21700 Nuits-Saint-Georges, tel. 03.80.62.61.46, fax 03.80.62.37.38

DOUDET-NAUDIN La Maladière 1998

■ 1er cru 1.2 ha 3,900 ⏸ 100–149 F

La Maladière leans southward and is based on limestone marl and limestone brown soils. So, it is not surprising to find a wine with some staying power and a structure of oak. It gains some confidence from its acidity. It has a good ruby colour and flourishing blackcurrant nose. For the last century and a half, this family have been wine-producers and *négociants-éleveurs*.

🔑 Doudet-Naudin, 3, rue Henri-Cyrot, 21420 Savigny-lès-Beaune, tel. 03.80.21.51.74, fax 03.80.21.50.69 ☑ Y by appt.

🔑 Yves Doudet

BURGUNDY

GUY FONTAINE ET JACKY VION

1997**

■ 2.3 ha 4,000 ⏸ 50–69 F

By reputation, Santenay has always shone because of its vineyards. This AOC stretches into the commune of Remigny. These local wine-growers work to good standards. Their *village* is sappy and fleshy, and expressive in all departments. It is young but promising and already a pleasure to drink. Amongst the best in the tasting.

🔑 GAEC des Vignerons G. Fontaine et J. Vion, Le Bourg, 71150 Remigny, tel. 03.85.87.03.35, fax 03.85.87.03.35 ☑ Y by appt.

DOM. GADANT ET FRANCOIS

1998

■ 1 ha 3,300 50–69 F

The wine is straining at the leash, but held in check by its tannins. It clearly wishes to develop, but already has good structure. It is peppery and a lovely, brilliant light red. A wine to put away but not forever (three to five years).

🔑 Dom. Gadant et François, GAEC le Clos Voyen, 71490 Saint-Maurice-lès-Couches , tel. 03.85.49.66.54, fax 03.85.49.60.62 ☑ Y by appt.

DOM. LOUIS JADOT

Clos de Malte 1997**

□ 1.5 ha 7,000 ⏸ 100–149 F

Rich aromas of brioche escape from this Clos de Malte. Gold and emerald hues. It is perfect on the palate and expresses itself with intensity, but also with finesse and length. The aromas linger (honeysuckle, toasted bread) and promise many a happy tomorrow.

🔑 Maison Louis Jadot, 21, rue Eugène-Spuller, 21200 Beaune, tel. 03.80.22.10.57, fax 03.80.22.56.03, e-mail contact@louisjadot.com ☑ Y by appt.

DOM. JESSIAUME PERE ET FILS

Les Gravières 1998

☐ 1er cru 0.71 ha 4,500 100–149 F

A white Les Gravières with a deep golden colour. A 98 that tastes of ripe grapes and oak. At first it is rich on the palate, then it follows with a fresh finish and average length: the oakiness will take at least a year to integrate.

Dom. Jessiaume Père et Fils, 10, rue de la Gare, 21590 Santenay, tel. 03.80.20.60.03, fax 03.80.20.62.87 by appt.

GABRIEL JOUARD 1997

■ 1.3 ha 2,500 50–69 F

This wine earns very good marks for its intense purple colour. The nose is delicate, vegetal, and raspberry, with a shake of pepper. Complex, in a word. On the palate it has a lively attack but can rely on its good structure, though it does not have a very pronounced personality. Shades of oak. It may well be worth a commendation in a year or two.

EARL Dom. Gabriel et Paul Jouard, 3, rue du Petit-Puits, 21190 Chassagne-Montrachet, tel. 03.80.21.30.30, fax 03.80.21.30.30 by appt.

DOM. HUBERT LAMY

Clos des Hâtes 1998★★

■ 0.7 ha 2,100 70–99 F

This could win the jackpot in the casino at Santenay! A Clos des Hâtes (found between the two Premiers Crus of Clos Faubard and Beaurepaire) it is deep cherry in colour with slightly jammy and spiced bread aromas, once it has opened out. Awarded a *coup de cœur* because of its soft body, which is also full and ripe. The tannins are pronounced but softening. Perfect for the vintage and appealingly complex. To drink in three to five years.

Dom. Hubert Lamy, Paradis, 21190 Saint-Aubin, tel. 03.80.21.32.55, fax 03.80.21.38.32 by appt.

LOUIS LATOUR 1997★★

☐ n.c. 20,000 70–99 F

The house of Louis Latour is in the great line of *négociants-éleveurs* in Burgundy. It was founded in 1797 and comprises 50 ha (124 acres) of vineyard. This Santenay is not matured in wood. It has a superb pale gold colour with aromas of white blossom and sweet almond. On the palate it is delicate but firm. A good deal of fruit, softness and

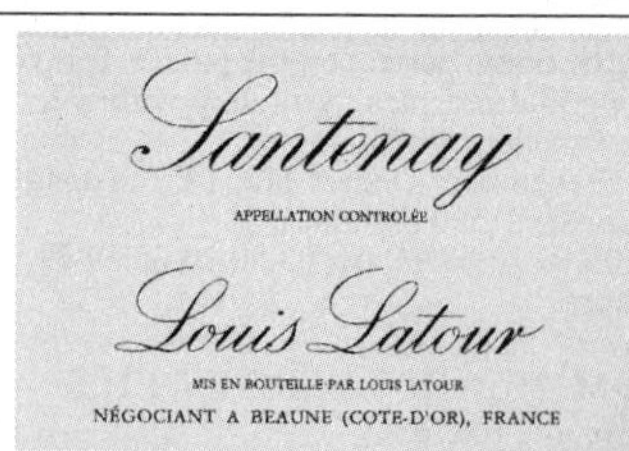

liveliness. Latour is completely satisfying. The wine is already in full bloom, and it seems unnecessary for it to mature further.

Maison Louis Latour, 18, rue des Tonneliers, 21200 Beaune, tel. 03.80.24.81.00, fax 03.80.22.36.21, e-mail louislatour@louislatour.com by appt.

RENE LEQUIN-COLIN

Les Charmes 1998★

■ 0.46 ha 2,900 50–69 F

A remarkable colour with superb glints of violet and an intense, frank nose, rather floral. It is well-structured with excellent tannins. Worth waiting two or three years.

René Lequin-Colin, 10, rue de Lavau, 21590 Santenay, tel. 03.80.20.66.71, fax 03.80.20.66.70, e-mail renelequin@aol.com by appt.

JEROME MASSON Beaurepaire 1998★

■ 1er cru n.c. 600 50–69 F

In 1998 Jérôme Masson successfully took over the family estate that his mother used to run. His first wine bowled the jury over; one taster remarked: 'This is a good expressive Pinot.' It has an intense colour and aromas of blackcurrant buds and little wild cherries. The tannins are fine and well-integrated on the palate, and everything plays together in harmony.

Jérôme Masson, rue Haute, 21340 La Rochepot, tel. 03.80.21.72.42, fax 03.80.21.72.42 by appt.

PROSPER MAUFOUX

Beauregard 1997

■ 1er cru n.c. n.c. 70–99 F

Prosper Maufoux was a notary, but he threw away his brass nameplate and became a *négociant-éleveur* in Santenay. That was back in 1860. Cyprien, Pierre, now Vincent . . . the family line continues. We were invited to taste a red Beauregard that is spicy and liquoricey, as it should be. It has good acidity and a fairly round body with a touch of austerity at the finish. The blackcurrant bud fragrance, as you take a second breath, has charm. Wait for two years.

Prosper Maufoux, pl. du Jet-d'Eau, 21590 Santenay, tel. 03.80.20.60.40, fax 03.80.20.63.26 by appt.

DOM. DU CH. DE MERCEY 1997

■ 1.3 ha 5,400 70–99 F

This Santenay produced by Antonin Rodet is perhaps a little insubstantial but it has the most glorious colour possible, and the nose is well-established: leather, prunes, terroir. A little mature, on the palate it is intense and warm and friendly. An ideal wine for Sunday lunch.

🔑 Ch. de Mercey, Mercey, 71150 Cheilly-lès-Maranges, tel. 03.85.91.13.19, fax 03.85.91.16.28 ☑ 🍷 by appt.

MESTRE-MICHELOT

Gravières 1997★

■ 1er cru 0.4 ha 2,000 70–99 F

The estate was established in 1985 and is a fine example of a marriage between Meursault and Santenay. A Gravières 97 of estimable ruby with a very fresh nose of red berry fruit. This pleasant experience follows through on the palate. The acidity, alcohol and tannins combine intelligently together. Just the wine to serve to friends without worrying about their reactions.

🔑 Mestre-Michelot, 12 bis, rue de Mazeray, 21190 Meursault, tel. 03.80.21.23.17, fax 03.80.21.63.62 ☑ 🍷 by appt.

MESTRE PERE ET FILS

Passe-Temps 1998★

□ 1er cru 0.53 ha 3,000 70–99 F

The estate is proud of the fact that its 89 Corton was served at the celebration dinner for the wedding of the Princess of Denmark. Here are two white Santenays of equal quality: a **Beaurepaire 98**, and a Premier Cru with its citrus fruit aromas. There is a good deal of youthful freshness behind the pale gold and glinting green colour. Lime, a wisp of smokiness and a rich body with an elegant hint of acid-drop. A lively wine chicken in cream sauce would be lovely with either.

🔑 Mestre Père et Fils, 12, pl. du Jet-d'Eau, B.P. 24, 21590 Santenay, tel. 03.80.20.60.11, fax 03.80.20.60.97, e-mail gilbert-mestre@wanadoo.fr ☑ 🍷 by appt.

Côte de Beaune (South)

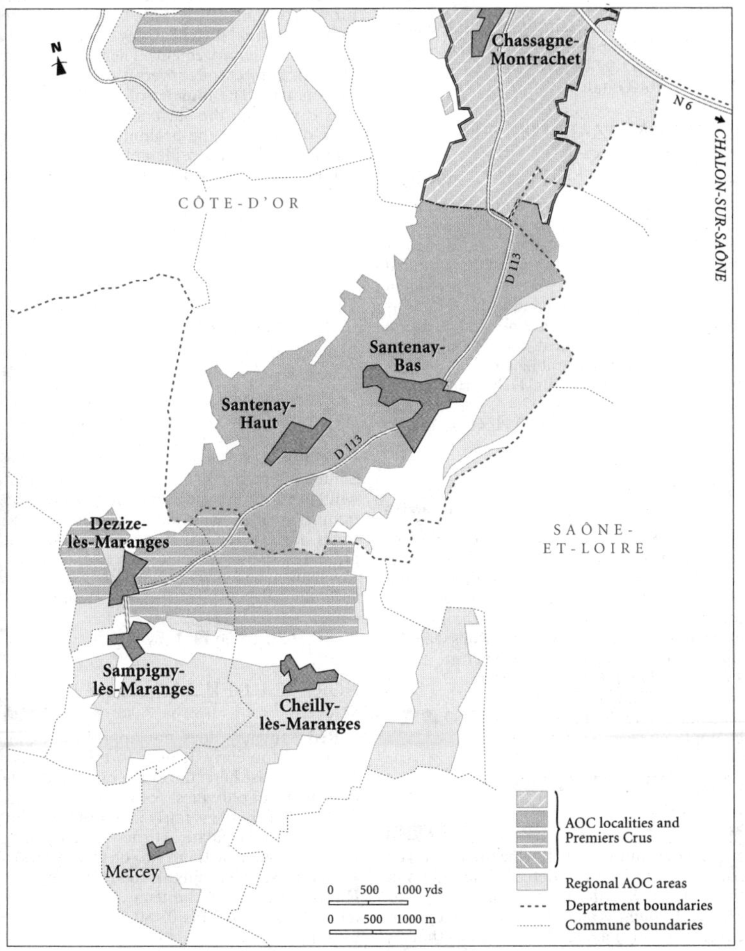

EDMOND MONNOT

Les Charmes-dessus 1998★

■ 0.56 ha n.c. 70–99 F

Whenever you come across a bottle like this, make sure you snap it up. Rich carmine with vermilion shades. Perfumed with blackberries and blackcurrant buds. A touch of warmth on the palate, with mellow tannins; it is unambiguous and sound.

Edmond Monnot, rue de Borgy, 71150 Dezize-lès-Maranges, tel. 03.85.91.16.12, fax 03.85.91.15.99 by appt.

CH. MOROT-GAUDRY 1997★

■ 0.67 ha 1,000 50–69 F

We were advised that this wine should be decanted to appreciate it better. A shade of development in the colour, vegetal traces on the nose, finesse and elegance on the palate: a good Santenay. This was formerly a mill, set in the pretty Vallée de la Cozane (Les Maranges). It closed down in 1965 and the Morot-Gaudry swapped the sacks of grain for grape hods.

Chantal Morot-Gaudry, Moulin Pignot, 71150 Paris-l'Hôpital, tel. 03.85.91.11.09, fax 03.85.91.11.09 by appt.

B. Morot-Gaudry •

LUCIEN MUZARD ET FILS

Clos Faubard 1998★

■ 1er cru 1.75 ha 8,800 70–99 F

We like to tell things as they are: we liked this **Maladière 98 Rouge, Premier Cru** a good deal. It is full of valour and style and is commended, but the other Premier Cru is ranked higher. It is violet purple with a perfumed nose (cherry and vanilla) and its hard tannins are prominent, but they are not crude. There is a hint of alcohol but it doesn't unbalance the wine. A serious, durable wine.

Lucien Muzard et Fils, 11 bis, rue Cour-Verreuil, 21590 Santenay, tel. 03.80.20.61.85, fax 03.80.20.66.02 by appt.

DOM. CLAUDE NOUVEAU 1998

□ 1.3 ha 6,000 70–99 F

Claude Nouveau enjoyed two excellent vintages with his 89 and 95 Grand Clos Rousseau. His *village* is golden with some glittering silver. The nose is quite open and gives an impression of strength and length. Equally enjoyable is the **Grand Clos Rousseau 97 Rouge** which is beginning to open out.

EARL Dom. Claude Nouveau, Marchezeuil, 21340 Change, tel. 03.85.91.13.34, fax 03.85.91.10.39 by appt.

PAUL PERNOT ET SES FILS

Bieveau 1998

■ n.c. 3,500 50–69 F

A tender, amorous little wine full of cooked fruit flavours. You can detect violet glints in the pale ruby colour and the nose is, as expected, slightly smokey, ripe, gamey and developed. It has a clean attack that is appealing. It should be ready very soon.

EARL Paul Pernot et ses Fils, 7, pl. du Monument, 21190 Puligny-Montrachet, tel. 03.80.21.32.35, fax 03.80.21.94.51 by appt.

DENIS PHILIBERT Passe-temps 1998★

□ 1er cru n.c. 900 70–99 F

We can recommend this Passe-Temps (which means 'hobby'). Light and lemony with hawthorn and hazelnut. On the palate it is rich and warm, and there is a distintive flavour from the oak that is very classy. The **Passe-Temps Rouge** has assorted kirsch tones; it is light, supple and has warmth. It is recommended.

Maison Denis Philibert, 1, rue Ziem, 21200 Beaune, tel. 03.80.24.05.88, fax 03.80.22.37.08 ev. day 9am–7pm

PAUL REITZ Clos Genêt 1997

■ n.c. 1,800 70–99 F

This wine, with its morello cherry colour, provoked contrasting views. Should it be drunk or should it wait? Enjoy it for what it is or hope for improvement? There is fruit but also oak: subjects of conversation to fascinate the amateur. The founder of the Reitz business came from the Sarre and settled in the Côte-de-Nuits at the beginning of the 19th century. He had a considerable reputation for making *foudres*, which are 1,000 litre wooden casks.

Maison Paul Reitz, 120–122, Grande-Rue, 21700 Corgoloin, tel. 03.80.62.98.24, fax 03.80.62.96.83, e-mail reitz.paul@laposte.fr

DOM. ROUX PERE ET FILS

Beauregard 1997★

■ 1er cru 1.9 ha 8,000 100–149 F

This estate had just 5 ha (12 acres) in 1960; now it has 60 ha (148 acres) on the Côte-de-Beaune as well as the Côte-de-Nuits, not to the detriment of its quality, as proved by this Santenay Premier Cru. It is a good wine that will keep for an average length of time. The tannins are mellowing and spicy, and toasted tones are developing. It is warm and, as it gradually opens, is beginning to take form. Lovely blend of wine and oak.

Dom. Roux Père et Fils, 21190 Saint-Aubin, tel. 03.80.21.32.92, fax 03.80.21.35.00 by appt.

SORINE ET FILS Beaurepaire 1998

■ 1er cru 0.89 ha 3,000 50–69 F

Red Santenay does not appreciate being disturbed too early. It likes to take its time. This is the case here: the estate prefers to bottle the wine from old vines. A light ruby colour. The nose of this 98 is fairly inaccessible but it improves on the palate. Attractive, fairly long but it needs a little time (two or three years).

Dom. Sorine et Fils, 4, rue Petit, Le Haut-Village, 21590 Santenay, tel. 03.80.20.61.65, fax 03.80.20.61.65 by appt.

DOM. DES VIGNES DES DEMOISELLES 1998★★★

■ 1.07 ha 5,700 70–99 F

If you were christened by the future Canon Kir, while he was the priest in Nolay, it really means you have wine in your veins. Gabriel is proud of the fact that not everyone can make that claim. His *coup de cœur* Santenay is blessed by heaven. It is rich, sturdy and typical of the vintage: vanilla, raspberry and liquorice . . . Its lovely deep ruby colour has hints of blue. All the tannic harshness and astringence has already disappeared, leaving lasting ripe fruit. The jury was full of congratulations. To look at again in three to five years.

SCEA du Dom. Gabriel Demangeot et Fils, rue de Berfey, 21340 Change, tel. 03.85.91.11.10, fax 03.85.91.16.83 by appt.

Maranges

The Maranges vineyard is in Saône-et-Loire (Chailly, Dezize and Sampigny). Since 1989, following a re-organisation, it has had its own AOC, which includes six Premiers Crus. Wine production here is predominantly of red, with some white; the reds may also be labelled AOC Côte de Beaune-Villages, which was how they were previously sold. The wines are fruity, full-bodied and well-structured; they can age for between five and ten years. In 1999 10,921 hl (288,314 gal) of AOC Maranges were produced, of which 256 hl (6,758 gal) were white.

DOM. BACHELET

La Fussière Vieilles vignes 1998★

□ 1er cru 0.5 ha 2,500 50–69 F

A good wine of relative complexity reminiscent of the excellent Fussière Rouge 94. A Chardonnay of a fairly intense gold with a nose of fruit and toasted bread. The oak is fairly pronounced, but the underlying fruit has strength. It is vinous and warm: an English taster asked 'is this a terroir for reds?' as he enjoyed its length. A recommendation for the **Fussière 97 Rouge** and **Les Clos Roussots 98 Rouge**, two wines for the future.

Dom. B. Bachelet et ses Fils, rue des Maranges, 71150 Dezize-lès-Maranges, tel. 03.85.91.16.11, fax 03.85.91.16.48 by appt.

ROGER BELLAND

La Fussière 1998★★

■ 1er cru 1.25 ha 6,600 50–69 F

This wine is very attractive. The vermilion colour presents its attractive, youthful freshness. It has no hard edges and it is fully-formed. It leaves behind perfumes of violet and liquorice. There is a touch of alcohol on the finish. Coming back down to earth, all the jury gave it good marks.

Dom. Roger Belland, 3, rue de la Chapelle, B.P. 13, 21590 Santenay, tel. 03.80.20.60.95, fax 03.80.20.63.93, e-mail belland.roger@wanadoo.fr by appt.

DOM. JEAN-FRANCOIS BOUTHENET

Sur le chêne Elevé en fût de chêne 1998★

□ 0.37 ha 2,000 50–69 F

This is a white wine, and that is not common. Gold with green glints. It has an honest nose of honey and bush peach. It has a fresh attack which, while not being very long, shows vigour, and some nerve in the middle just when it needs to grab your attention. The rest is rich and well-oaked.

Jean-François Bouthenet, Mercey, 71150 Cheilly-lès-Maranges, tel. 03.85.91.14.29, fax 03.85.91.18.24 by appt.

MAURICE CHARLEUX

Le Clos des Rois 1998★

■ 1er cru 0.3 ha 1,500 50–69 F

This *climat* at Sampigny is a neighbour of Les Clos Roussots. This 98 is beautifully transparent with glints of violet. The nose tends towards gamey notes lightly touched with blackcurrant. It has a soft texture and is unobtrusive but complex on the nose and smooth on the palate. The acidity and tannins are well-balanced: not too much but not too little. Not very expressive, but well-knit.

Maurice Charleux, Petite-Rue, 71150 Dezize-lès-Maranges, tel. 03.85.91.15.15, fax 03.85.91.11.81 by appt.

Y. ET C. CONTAT-GRANGE

La Fussière 1998★

■ 1er cru 0.37 ha 2,000 50–69 F

You immediately notice this producer because of his diamond-shaped labels, which are inspired by abstract art. The wine, on the other hand, is very figurative and has a deep garnet red colour. The aromas of blackberry, elderberry and fruit in eau-de-vie blend subtly with the oak. A clean first impression, full and supple. Good finish with well-structured, fine tannins.

🔑 EARL Yvon Contat-Grangé, Grande-Rue, 71150 Dezize-lès-Maranges, tel. 03.85.91.15.87, fax 03.85.91.12.54 ☑ 🍷 by appt.

ERIC DUCHEMIN 1997★

■1er cru 1 ha 3,000 30–49 F

Eric took over from his father, René, in 1991 and has restructured the estate. He de-stalks 100% of his grapes. If you visit the estate, you will see a superb 18th century wine press, and you will undoubtedly taste the **Clos Roussots 97 Rouge** that we recommend with pleasure (50–69F), and this *village* which is pale ruby with red berry fruit. An archetype of the appellation as it is so fine, clean and mouth-filling with a symphony of aromas.

🔑 Eric Duchemin, Dom. du Vieux-Pressoir, 71150 Sampigny-lès-Maranges, tel. 03.85.87.32.02, fax 03.85.91.15.76 ☑ 🍷 r.-v

HERVE GIRARD ET ISABELLE ROIZOT 1997★★

■1er cru 2 ha 1,500 30–49 F

Les Hauts de Paris is the address, so you might imagine yourself amongst the vineyards in Suresnes or Montmartre. But this is Paris-l'Hôpital, and the vines are from a Lopitau, not a Parisian. Very good wine indeed. Intense garnet, perfumed, well-structured and full-bodied with soft tannins which give some character. It is very smooth. Could be kept a little while.

🔑 EARL Les Hauts de Paris, rte de Saint-Sernin, 71150 Paris-l'Hôpital, tel. 03.85.91.11.56, fax 03.85.91.16.22 ☑ 🍷 by appt.

🔑 Hervé Girard & Isabelle Roizot

BERTRAND DE MONCENY

Clos Roussots Elevé en fût de chêne 1997★

■1er cru n.c. 10,000 70–99 F

Le Clos Roussots is often used as a yardstick for quality in Cheilly and Sampigny. Santenay is close by. This wine is deep, brilliant ruby, full of character and well-made. The nose lacks staying power but it is appealing on the palate with firm, but not harsh, tannins. Notes of kirsch. Produced by Jean-Pierre Nié (Compagnie des Vins d'Autrefois), a merchant in Beaune.

🔑 Compagnie des Vins d'Autrefois, Abbaye Saint-Martin, 53, av. de l'Aigue, 21200 Beaune, tel. 03.80.26.33.00, fax 03.80.24.14.84, e-mail mallet.b@cva-beaune.fr

🔑 Jean-Pierre Nié

DOM. RENE MONNIER

Clos de la Fussière Monopole 1998★★

■1er cru 1.2 ha 7,000 50–69 F

We considered awarding a *coup de cœur.* The cry went up: 'a Premier Cru at last'! It is a wine which has several dimensions; whether it is the balance between the fruit, the discreet nose or, indeed, the well-composed palate with real substance that manoeuvres the acidity and tannins into their proper places. A very approachable wine, though it keeps its distance. Bravo!

🔑 Dom. René Monnier, 6, rue du Dr-Rolland, 21190 Meursault, tel. 03.80.21.29.32, fax 03.80.21.61.79 ☑ 🍷 ev. day 8am–12 noon 2pm–6pm

🔑 M. et Mme Bouillot

EDMOND MONNOT

Le clos des Loyères 1998

■1er cru 1.09 ha 3,900 70–99 F

Giving equal scores, we agreed that sufficient quality-level had been achieved by the **Clos de La Boutière 98 Rouge, Cuvée Vieilles Vignes** and this Loyères which is white-heart cherry coloured. It has a nose showing pepper and undergrowth with an overall aroma of roasting coffee beans. It is a full, vinous wine and we can predict a good future in two years' time. Strong oakiness.

🔑 Edmond Monnot, rue de Borgy, 71150 Dezize-lès-Maranges, tel. 03.85.91.16.12, fax 03.85.91.15.99 ☑ 🍷 by appt.

DOM. CLAUDE NOUVEAU

La Fussière 1997★

■1er cru 0.3 ha 1,800 50–69 F

Claude Nouveau is not unknown amongst the wine-makers in Maranges. His red Fussière is very brilliant with hints of blue. We loved it! The nose opens out with fruit, mainly cherry. Lacks a little body for such a characteristic wine that is tannic and well-structured (but not too much). The **Village 97** is a lovely wine fully representative of its category. It also deserves its star.

🔑 EARL Dom. Claude Nouveau, Marchezeuil, 21340 Change, tel. 03.85.91.13.34, fax 03.85.91.10.39 ☑ 🍷 by appt.

BERNARD REGNAUDOT 1998★

■ n.c. 2,800 30–49 F

A **Clos des Rois 98 Rouge**: after its twelve day fermentation period it needs time to mature in the bottle. Good comments from the jury (50–69F). This *village* also shows well. Its ruby colour would fascinate a jeweller. Strawberry aromas, at first, on the nose. The structure is strengthened with good body, a little nervous but it has an interesting personality and some richness.

🔑 Bernard Regnaudot, rte. de Nolay, 71150 Dezize-lès-Maranges, tel. 03.85.91.14.90, fax 03.85.91.14.90 ☑ 🍷 by appt.

JEAN-CLAUDE REGNAUDOT

Les Clos Roussots 1998★

■1er cru 0.53 ha 2,900 50–69 F

The wine-grower has 6 ha 53 a (16 acres) of which 53 a (1.3 acres) are in the Clos Roussots. Clear, violet colour. After letting it breathe, this 98 presents aromas of roasted coffee and bilberry while, on the palate, it shows youthful, lively fruit. It is intense and

complex and has good keeping qualities (two to four years). It would go well with jugged hare. We also appreciated: the honest **Fussière Rouge 98** and, from the same year, the **Village Rouge**, which was awarded one star (30–49F).
Jean-Claude Regnaudot, 71150 Dezize-lès-Maranges, tel. 03.85.91.15.95, fax 03.85.91.16.45 by appt.

Côte de Beaune-Villages

Not to be confused with the Côte de Nuits-Villages appellation, which has its own special production area, the Côte de Beaune-Villages appellation is not confined to a specific place but may be used by all the red-wine appellations communales in the Côte de Beaune, with the exception of Beaune, Aloxe-Corton, Pommard and Volnay. In 1999, 625 hl (16,500 gal) were produced.

JEAN-CLAUDE BOISSET 1997

■ n.c. 30,000 70–99 F

A slightly amber-coloured 97 that is ready to serve, though there is still a little room for development. Its nose of spiced bread and crystallised fruits is in its prime. The tannins are exquisitely well-mannered. What you would call an 'easy-drinking wine'.
J.-C. Boisset, 5, quai Dumorey, B.P. 102, 21700 Nuits-Saint-Georges, tel. 03.80.62.62.61, fax 03.80.62.37.38

DOM. GUY DIDIER 1998★

■ 0.91 ha 4,800 70–99 F

Ruby with blueish gleams make an eye-catching cocktail of colour. The nose is not in a hurry, but the body is bold, liquorice and simply waiting to bloom. Ideal if you like your Pinot Noir fleshy and full. A wine sold by the Moillard firm.
Dom. Guy Didier, chem. rural n° 29, 21700 Nuits-Saint-Georges, tel. 03.80.62.42.00, fax 03.80.61.28.13, e-mail nuicave@wanadoo.fr by appt.

LA TOUR BLONDEAU 1998★

■ n.c. n.c. 50–69 F

Bouchard Père et Fils make this slightly violet 98 which is pleasing and attractive. It has a firm structure, open and fruity, supple and appealing. Perfect for the appellation.
Grands Vins Forgeot, 15, rue du Château, 21200 Beaune, tel. 03.80.24.80.50

La Côte Chalonnaise

Bourgogne Côte Chalonnaise

The new AOC Bourgogne Côte Chalonnaise was created on 27 February 1990. It comprises 44 communes, which produced 29,327 hl (774,233 gal) of red wine and 7,942 hl (209,669 gal) of white in 1999. According to the system also applied in the Hautes-Côtes, agreements about quality are reached following a second tasting to supplement the compulsory tasting that takes place everywhere else.

Located between Chagny and Saint-Gengoux-le-National (Saône et Loire), the Côte Chalonnaise has an individual identity that deserves the recognition it has received.

RENE BOURGEON

Les Pourrières 1998★

■ n.c. n.c. 30–49 F

On the palate, a 98 that is fairly rich on the finish after a vigorous, chewy first impression. It has a typical ruby and garnet colour. The nose is only partially communicative, with mainly very attractive juniper aromas. Like a cat, it almost purrs.
GAEC René Bourgeon, 2, rue du Chapitre, 71640 Jambles, tel. 03.85.44.35.85, fax 03.85.44.57.80 by appt.

CAVE DES VIGNERONS DE BUXY 1997

■ 146 ha 223,000 30–49 F

The estate has 146 ha (360 acres) and some 220,000 *bouteilles*. The Cave Coopérative de Buxy paints a big picture. It has to. This pale ruby 97 shows a little maturity in its colour. Packed with aromas of macerated berries, it has a very distinctive nose. It is soft and easy, with raspberries on the palate. A wine to drink in the coming year.
Cave des Vignerons de Buxy, Les Vignes de la Croix, 71390 Buxy, tel. 03.85.92.03.03, fax 03.85.92.08.06 ev. day except Sun. 9am–12 noon 2pm–6pm

BURGUNDY

CH. DE CARY-POTET

Vieilles vignes 1998

■ 1 ha 4,000 30–49 F

A Directoire-style château built over 17th century cellars. Matured for a year in oak, this 98 needs at least two years for the wood to integrate. Rustic, with a vanilla nose and notes of blackcurrant.

Charles du Besset, rte de Chenevelles, 71390 Buxy, tel. 03.85.92.14.48, fax 03.85.92.11.88 by appt.

CH. DE CHAMILLY 1997★

■ 7.5 ha 45,000 30–49 F

Véronique Desfontaine is in her element at Château de Chamilly, a very fine, ancient country house. Her wine is deep purple and silky to look at. Impressive on the nose, though as yet it is undefined. Enjoy drinking it with roast duck. An easy wine that has elegance and breeding but could mature for two to four years.

Véronique Desfontaine, EARL Ch. de Chamilly, 71510 Chamilly, tel. 03.85.87.22.24, fax 03.85.91.23.91 by appt.

DOM. CHAUMONT PERE ET FILS 1997★

■ 1.03 ha 4,400 30–49 F

If you plan a menu with game, this is the red wine to serve. Deep ruby in colour, it comes directly to the point. Its nose presents spices and bilberry fruit with strong oak. Proud and straightforward attack, tinged with flavours of stone fruit. The tannins are fairly soft and there is good length on the finish. All this will age for three to four years. Already an agreeable 97.

Dom. Chaumont Père et Fils, Le Clos Saint-Georges, 71640 Saint-Jean-de-Vaux, tel. 03.85.45.13.77, fax 03.85.45.27.77 by appt.

DOM. DU CRAY 1997

■ 4 ha 12,000 30–49 F

Following a very successful 92 red, this estate presents their concentrated ruby 97, with strawberry and blackcurrant and oak on the nose. It has a direct attack and pronounced tannins. Perfectly correct and ready to drink now. From father to son, generations of Narjoux have been producing wine since 1640.

Roger et Michèle Narjoux, Dom. du Cray, Cidex 712, 71640 Saint-Martin-sous-Montaigu, tel. 03.85.45.13.17, fax 03.85.45.29.10 by appt.

DANIEL DAVANTURE ET FILS 1997★

■ 8.5 ha 5,400 30–49 F

Tile-red colour. This 97 has a modest nose (a few hints of undergrowth), with some finesse. Lightly fruity with tannins that do not intrude. Everything about this approachable wine makes it easily accessible to the drinker.

Daniel Davanture et Fils, GAEC des Murgers, rue de la Montée, Cidex 1548, 71390 Saint-Désert, tel. 03.85.47.90.42, fax 03.85.47.99.88 by appt.

CAVE DES VIGNERONS DE GENOUILLY 1998

□ 10 ha 20,000 20–29 F

Even the mostly tightly closed oyster shell would open willingly when this wine is placed on the table. A white-gold wine with swirling vegetal and flowery aromas. It has the freshness needed for seafood; it even has a complimentary, slightly lemon flavour.

Cave des vignerons de Genouilly, 71460 Genouilly, tel. 03.85.49.23.72, fax 03.85.49.23.58 ev. day except Sun. 8am–12 noon 2pm–6pm

DOM. MICHEL GOUBARD ET FILS Mont-Avril 1998★

■ 9.5 ha 58,000 30–49 F

It is always a pleasure to come across this label. In his famous *Description de la Bourgogne* written in the 17th century, Abbot Courtépée praises the vineyard of the Mont Avril. We have checked, and it is indeed there – and we are always happy to try the wine as well. Brilliant ruby, opening with kirsch and undergrowth and with excellent staying power. To be drunk in two to three years. The **Blanc 98** is like a darting trout. If you fancy yourself a fisherman . . .

Dom. Michel Goubard et Fils, 71390 Saint-Désert, tel. 03.85.47.91.06, fax 03.85.47.98.12 ev. day 8am–12 noon 2pm–7pm; Sun. by appt.

DOM. GOUFFIER

Clos de Malpertuis 1997★

□ 1 ha 3,000 30–49 F

This is a good, reliable wine to try when just starting to learn about Burgundies, and it offers reasonable value for money. It is a light, straw-yellow Côte Chalonnaise that has a vegetal, fresh buttery nose. Clean, well-balanced and very full and round, there is no difficulty in taking a sip from this glass. The estate is at Fontaines near Chalon-sur-Saône where there is a famous agricultural school.

Dom. Gouffier, 11, Grande-Rue, 71150 Fontaines, tel. 03.85.91.49.66, fax 03.85.91.46.98 by appt.

MICHEL ISAIE 1997

■ 3 ha 22,000 30–49 F

Michel Isaïe is a direct descendent of a wine-producing family going back to the 18th century. Witness this Pinot Noir 97 that is deep cherry where the toasted aromas vie with raspberry tones. Good potential showing on the palate with a whole armoured regiment of tannins. It has richness, substance and depth. The battle will be won in twelve to eighteen months when peace and harmony will break out.

Michel Isaïe, chem. de l'Ouche, 71640 Saint-Jean-de-Vaux, tel. 03.85.45.23.32, fax 03.85.45.29.38 by appt.

DOM. FRANCE LECHENAULT 1998★★

□ 0.68 ha 2,880 30–49 F

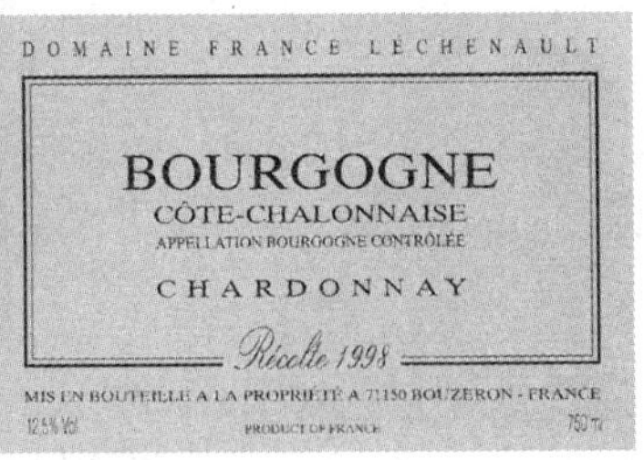

France Léchenault was recently Senator and Mayor of Bouzeron, and her daughter Claudette sits on the Economic and Social Council in Paris. This *coup de cœur* deserves promotion to the Burgundian Order of Merit! The votes were unanimous for this 98 Chardonnay: a magnificent wine and worthy to be counted among the greatest. A lovely golden-green, it is perfumed with flowers and very typical buttery aromas, and a mentholated oak touch that is very successful. It is straightforward, round and lively all at the same time and delivers on the palate all that was promised by the nose. The **Rouge 98** should also be mentioned even though it did not get a star. It is destined to age a little, then should be drunk with a family Sunday lunch.

Dom. France Léchenault, 11, rue des Dames, 71150 Bouzeron, tel. 03.85.87.17.56, fax 03.85.91.27.17 by appt.

DOM. MAZOYER Sous Saint-Germain 1997★

■ 6 ha 4,000 30–49 F

The appellation celebrated its tenth anniversary in 2000. It has proved a success because the general quality is improving appreciably. Take this good red, almost purple Pinot Noir which, on the nose, is impeccably clean. The oak does not smother the fruit. The body stays within the strict bounds of the vintage, but it has heart and spirit. Good to set aside for one or two years.

Dom. Mazoyer, imp. du Ruisseau, 71390 Saint-Désert, tel. 03.85.47.95.28, fax 03.85.47.98.91 by appt.

DOM. DES MOIROTS 1998

■ 1.5 ha 4,500 30–49 F

Denizot is a name that Henri Vincenot used for the fictitious characters in his Burgundy novels. Take a look at *La Pie Saoûle* and *Les Chevaliers du Chaudron*. This is a name that is straight from Côte Chalonnaise, from Maranges where the writer's in-laws lived. A magnificent colour, a faultless, pleasing nose, and a sturdy wine that should be tried again later, as would be expected. A wine to keep, which has become quite a rarity in the AOC.

Dom. des Moirots, 14, rue des Moirots, 71390 Bissey-sous-Cruchaud, tel. 03.85.92.16.93, fax 03.85.92.09.42 by appt.

Lucien et Christophe Denizot

ALBERT SOUNIT 1998

■ n.c. 3,000 30–49 F

The European Union is on the march. The firm of Albert Sounit has belonged to a Danish importer since 1993. He is crazy about Burgundy. This 98 is morello cherry with a violet rim. There is detectable vinosity on the nose, which is quite complex. The blackcurrant increases in strength in a fruity way against the background of the terroir.

Albert Sounit, 5, pl. du Champ-de-Foire, 71150 Rully, tel. 03.85.87.20.71, fax 03.85.87.09.71 by appt.

FLORENCE ET MARTIAL THEVENOT 1998★

■ 2.4 ha 3,600 30–49 F

A garnet-coloured 98 with iridescent glints. A nose that is nicely balanced between violet and blackcurrant. Fresh, a good average: classic, and it needs to wait a little.

Florence et Martial Thévenot, 4, rue du Champ-de-l'Orme, 71510 Aluze, tel. 03.85.45.18.43, fax 03.85.45.09.98 by appt.

LAURENT VENOT Les Pirrelées 1999

■ 7.3 ha 25,000 30–49 F

A major town in the Côte Chalonnaise. Germolles was the secret garden of Marguerite of Flanders, the wife of Philippe the Brave. She created an enclosed vineyard of 16 ha (40 acres). Today the Pinot is more violet-carmine than vermilion, as in times past. Bilberry and cooked fruit. It is lively, forthcoming, full-bodied and rustic.

Laurent Venot, imp. des Petites-Chaumes, 71640 Germolles, tel. 03.85.45.15.07 by appt.

Bouzeron

FORGEOT PERE ET FILS 1998★

□ n.c. n.c. 30–49 F

Bouchard Père et Fils have always had an eye on Bouzeron. Flint and gunflint, a wine for the archaeologists, and indeed, the vineyard is not far from the prehistoric site at Camp de Chassey. Shimmering gold with a toasted bread nose. This wine has the right amount of acidity, and notes of kiwi and mirabelle plums, to arouse the palate.

Grands Vins Forgeot, 15, rue du Château, 21200 Beaune, tel. 03.80.24.80.50

Côte Chalonnaise and the Mâconnais

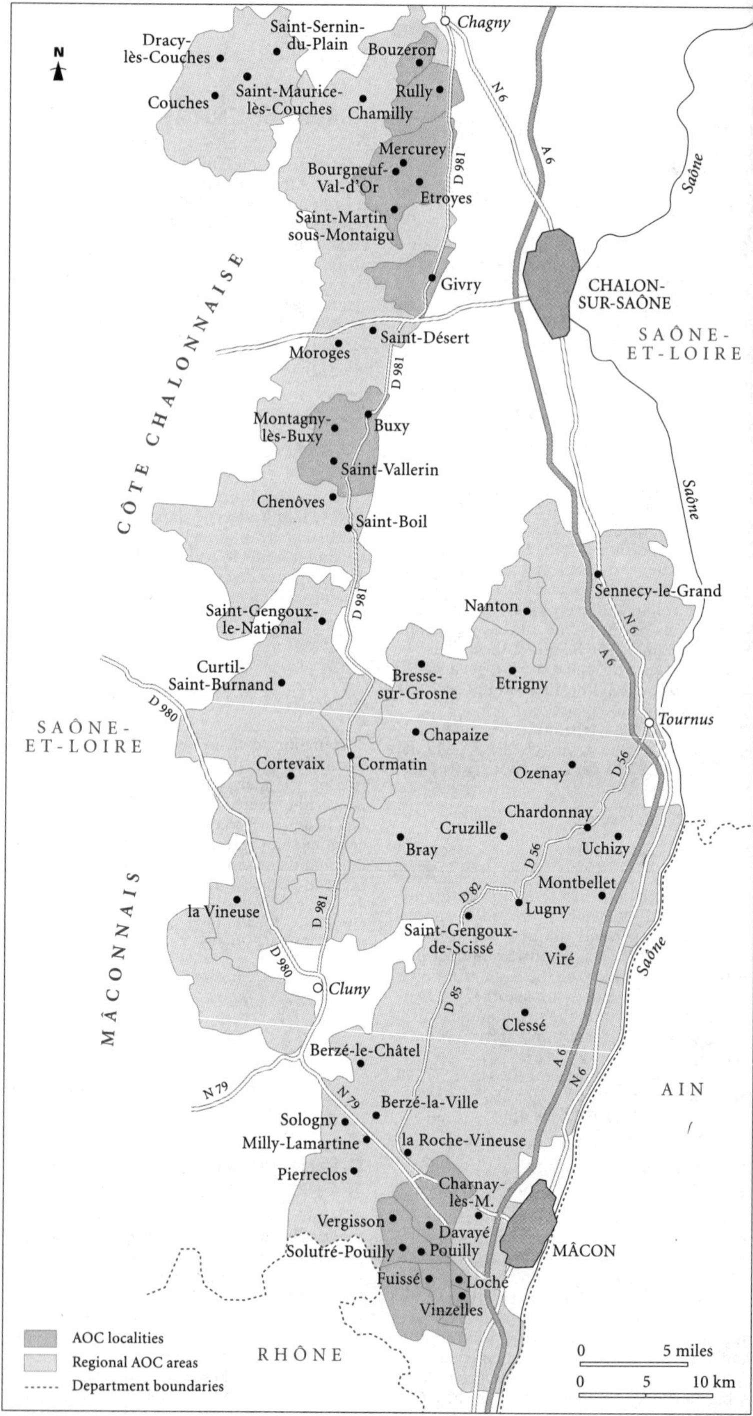
N
Chagny
Dracy-lès-Couches
Saint-Sernin-du-Plain
Bouzeron
Couches
Saint-Maurice-lès-Couches
Rully
Chamilly
N 6
A 6
Saône
Mercurey
Bourgneuf-Val-d'Or
Etroyes
D 981
Saint-Martin sous-Montaigu
CÔTE CHALONNAISE
Givry
CHALON-SUR-SAÔNE
Saint-Désert
Moroges
SAÔNE-ET-LOIRE
Montagny-lès-Buxy
Buxy
Saint-Vallerin
Chenôves
Saint-Boil
Sennecy-le-Grand
Nanton
Saint-Gengoux-le-National
Curtil-Saint-Burnand
Bresse-sur-Grosne
Etrigny
D 980
Tournus
SAÔNE-ET-LOIRE
Chapaize
Cortevaix
Cormatin
Ozenay
D 56
Chardonnay
Cruzille
Uchizy
Bray
Montbellet
D 82
Lugny
la Vineuse
MÂCONNAIS
Saint-Gengoux-de-Scissé
Viré
Cluny
D 85
Clessé
Berzé-le-Châtel
AIN
N 79
Berzé-la-Ville
Sologny
Milly-Lamartine
la Roche-Vineuse
Pierreclos
Charnay-lès-M.
Vergisson
Davayé
Solutré-Pouilly
Pouilly
MÂCON
Fuissé
Loché
Vinzelles
AOC localities
Regional AOC areas
Department boundaries
RHÔNE
0 5 miles
0 5 10 km

PATRICK GUILLOT 1998

☐ 1.52 ha n.c. 30–49 F

A lemony-looking 98 that is clear and brilliant. A nutty nose with a touch of the exotic. There is a lively attack but this wine is only cantering at the moment. It needs time, not too much, to get into its stride. It will develop staying power on the palate: this Aligoté is certainly not like any other.

Dom. Patrick Guillot, rue de Vaugeailles, 71640 Mercurey, tel. 03.85.45.27.40, fax 03.85.45.28.57 by appt.

LA P'TIOTE CAVE 1997

☐ 0.2 ha 1,700 30–49 F

At first there is bracken and fresh grass, followed by a considerably more exotic touch (passion fruit and lychee). An attractive nose though still a little sharp (lime) on the palate, but we like it. N.B.: This is its inaugural vintage, because the 97s were the first to be bottled under the colours of the new AOC Communale Bouzeron.

La P'tiote Cave, 71150 Chassey-le-Camp, tel. 03.85.87.15.21, fax 03.85.87.28.08 by appt.

Mugnier

DOM. DE LA RENARDE

Les Cordères 1998

☐ 1.7 ha 12,000 30–49 F

The word Aligoté is not scrawled in big letters on the label because here the *climat* is of greater importance. Maturation in tank produces this pale gold wine that goes from hawthorn to hazelnut, acacia to brioche on the nose. Its greenness reaches the level that makes it unmistakable as an Aligoté.

Maison André Delorme, 2, rue de la République, 71150 Rully, tel. 03.85.87.10.12, fax 03.85.87.04.60 by appt.

J.-F. Delorme

DOM. FRANCE LECHENAULT

Vieilles vignes 1998★★

☐ 1 ha 1,950 30–49 F

The village of Bouzeron owes a great deal to France Léchenault, who was the Senator and Mayor for a long time. This wine pays her hommage. It was selected at the first round because of its lovely grapefruit yellow colour, complete nose (unobtrusive and complex) and its full maturity. Mineral and vinous with a good structural balance. Matured in tank.

Dom. France Léchenault, 11, rue des Dames, 71150 Bouzeron, tel. 03.85.87.17.56, fax 03.85.91.27.17 by appt.

Rully

The Côte Chalonnaise, or Mercurey region, is the transition point between the Côte-d'Or and the Mâconnais. The Appellation Rully extends beyond its original commune into Chagny, which is a local centre of gastronomy. In 1999 more white wine was produced – 11,927 hl (314,873 gal) – than red – 6,248 hl (164,947 gal). Grown on soils originating in the Superior Jurassic era, the wines are appealing and generally keep well. Some of the locations classified as Premiers Crus have already established a good reputation.

DOM. BELLEVILLE

Les Chauchoux 1998

■ 5.57 ha 20,000 50–69 F

A textbook **Premier Cru Rouge 98** (if still available). So, you can rely on it. The colour shows a bit of maturity but still has a good tone. This Les Chaucoux has a musky, almost cooked nose. It is quite well-structured, not a great deal of length, fruity even though it has tight tannins. Wait two to three years.

Dom. Belleville, 7, rue de la Loppe, 71150 Rully, tel. 03.85.91.22.19, fax 03.85.87.05.19, e-mail dombellevi@aol.com by appt.

JEAN-CLAUDE BRELIERE

Les Préaux 1998★★

■ 1er cru 2.35 ha 12,000 50–69 F

A wine to drink with friends. The winegrower knows his subject and has a diploma in oenology from the Université de Bourgogne. Attractive colour with blackcurrant that is just beginning to come through on the nose. This 98 has some cherry initially, but it is still a little austere. It does have a future. Rabbit fricassee? Why not?

Jean-Claude Brelière, 1, pl. de l'Eglise, 71150 Rully, tel. 03.85.91.22.01, fax 03.85.87.20.64, e-mail domainejean-claudebreliere@wanadoo.fr by appt.

DOM. MICHEL BRIDAY

Champs Cloux 1998★

■ 0.62 ha 3,000 70–99 F

Two whites attracted our attention here. A young, sincere **Bergerie 98** which, in due course, will reveal its hidden riches (one star), and a **Pucelle Premier Cru 98** with a colour as brilliant as a ballgown for the Saint-Vincent festivities. It is round, supple, vinous and slightly mineral (70–99F). The red **Les Quatre Vignes 98** is awarded two stars (50–69F) for its impressive mouth filling qualities but the

Champs Cloux runs off with the top prize. This 98 is still tinged with the barrel but it is rich, concentrated and very promising. An estate not to be missed.
Dom. Michel Briday, 31, Grande-Rue, 71150 Rully, tel. 03.85.87.07.90, fax 03.85.91.25.68, e-mail stephane.briday@wanadoo.fr by appt.

EMILE CHANDESAIS 1998

■ n.c. 20,000 50–69 F

Emile Chandesais is a name that will not be forgotten along the Côte Chalonnaise, even though Picard has taken over. A delicate nose showing some liquorice followed by a hint of morello cherry on the palate. It is quite tannic, which is common in young Pinot Noir wines in Rully. Its strength and potential show that it is capable of becoming an interesting wine in the next year or two.
Emile Chandesais, rue Saint-Nicolas, 71150 Chagny, tel. 03.85.91.41.77, fax 03.85.91.40.26
Michel Picard

CHARTRON ET TREBUCHET

La Chaume 1998

□ n.c. 50,000 70–99 F

Pale gold and brilliant in colour, this wine is still closed. It was matured for nine months in oak barrels, 20% new. The nose opens with vanilla, and then ripe white-fleshed fruits take over. The palate is elegant, balanced and fresh. From this winter, the 98 will be ready to accompany poached salmon.
Chartron et Trébuchet, 13, Grande-Rue, 21190 Puligny-Montrachet, tel. 03.80.21.32.85, fax 03.80.21.36.35, e-mail jmchartron@chartron-trebuchet.com ev. day 10am–12.30pm 2pm–6pm; cl. Nov.–Mar.

LOUIS CHAVY 1998

□ n.c. 18,000 70–99 F

A fetching, lively colour touched with lemon. A discreet, gentle nose with minerals and flowers. The acidity provides backbone for the crisp fruit and the well-measured richness.
Louis Chavy, Caveau la Vierge romaine, pl. des Marronniers, 21190 Puligny-Montrachet, tel. 03.80.26.33.00, fax 03.80.24.14.84, e-mail mallet.b@cva-beaune.fr ev. day 10am–6pm; cl. Nov. until Mar.

ANNE-SOPHIE DEBAVELAERE 1997

□ 1er cru 3 ha 10,000 50–69 F

A good-looking, 97; it releases a hint of aniseed on the flowery nose. The palate revolves around nuts and beeswax with just about the right balance. To drink right away.
Anne-Sophie Debavelaere, 14, rue de Cloux, 71150 Rully, tel. 03.85.48.65.64, fax 03.85.93.13.29 by appt.

DEMESSEY 1998

■ n.c. 15,000 70–99 F

This red 98 is presented by the team from the Manoir Murisaltien in Meursault and the Château de Messey near Ozenay, not far from Tournus. Fairly vibrant red colour. A winner on the palate with spicy after-taste and approachable tannins. The nose is surprising: scorched aromas, juniper, pepper.
Ch. de Messey, Demessey, 71700 Ozenay, tel. 03.85.51.33.83, fax 03.85.51.33.82, e-mail vin@demessey.com by appt.

DUFOULEUR PERE ET FILS

Meix Cadot 1997★

□ 1er cru n.c. 5,500 100–149 F

Xavier Dufouleur is the mayor of Nuits-Saint-Georges and a senatorial substitute, but he still finds time to uncover some good wines. This Premier Cru, for example. A lovely, deep, grey-gold with a little time to breathe, it presents some menthol tones. A fairly mineral attack, the body roundish and the finish more explosive. All this gives a complete wine of some quality.
Dufouleur Père et Fils, 15, rue Thurot, 21700 Nuits-Saint-Georges, tel. 03.80.61.21.21, fax 03.80.61.11.23 by appt.

VINCENT DUREUIL-JANTHIAL 1998★★★

■ 0.91 ha 5,000 70–99 F

Vincent Dureuil-Janthial was a pupil at the Lycée Viticole in Beaune. Here he has won his first *coup de cœur* for his Rully, and he has hit the jackpot with his **Village Rouge 98**, awarded two stars. One taster noted, 'at last, a *village* that has ambition' (50–69F). This one is very richly coloured and has a nose packed with blackcurrant and sloe with a delicate toasted background. It has a magnificent palate that shows off a balanced body full of fruit and fine tannins. A perfect example, neither too harsh nor too soft, and it has great character. Barrel-fermented; 80% de-stalked.
Vincent Dureuil-Janthial, rue de la Buisserolle, 71150 Rully, tel. 03.85.87.26.32, fax 03.00.00.00.00 by appt.

RAYMOND DUREUIL-JANTHIAL 1997★

■ 1.67 ha 8,000 70–99 F

Dark ruby and shimmering with delicate copper, 97 has notes of leather and

undergrowth that give a certain finesse on the palate, also a hint of liquorice. The tannins are still tight but quite delicate. Bilberry flavours complete the picture. The Janthial family is one of the oldest in Rully.
🗝 Raymond Dureuil-Janthial, rue de la Buisserolle, 71150 Rully, tel. 03.85.87.02.37, fax 03.85.87.00.24 ☑ 🍷 ev. day 9am–12 noon 3pm–7pm; Sun. by appt.

GUY FONTAINE ET JACKY VION

La Bergerie 1998★

■ 0.5 ha 2,500 50–69 F

Today the nose is better than the flavour, but this is a 98. Its balance, powerful tannins and length promise good things. The nose has red berry fruit, spices (juniper) and well-integrated oak. It will develop into a very fine wine in three or four years.
🗝 GAEC des Vignerons, Le Bourg, 71150 Remigny, tel. 03.85.87.03.35, fax 03.85.87.03.35 ☑ 🍷 by appt.

DOM. DES FROMANGES

La Chatalienne 1998

■ 2.2 ha 12,000 70–99 F

This 97 white was highly praised. This producer (SA F. Protheau et Fils) has also produced a red 98 which is showing signs of maturity, which divided the jury a little. It has a good texture, flavours of crystallised fruit and a well-built structure.
🗝 Dom. des Fromanges, 71640 Mercurey, tel. 03.85.98.99.10, fax 03.85.98.99.00 ☑ 🍷 by appt.

DOM. DE LA FOLIE Clos La Folie 1998★

□ 1.25 ha 7,559 70–99 F

Amongst the seventy three Rullys tasted, here we have two wines that were each awarded one star: the **Clos Saint-Jacques 98 Blanc** is light but well-made, and this other white has a clear colour and a charming nose (vegetal and mineral). The story on the palate unravels like the plot of a perfect film, and you feel like going back to the beginning and seeing it all over again. Chardonnay is the star. In the 19th century, the vines belonged to E.-J. Marey, one of the fathers of the cinema. Great figures of the silver screen, from Lelouch to Polanski and including Tchernia, know this cellar well.
🗝 Dom. de la Folie, 71150 Chagny, tel. 03.85.87.18.59, fax 03.85.87.03.53 ☑ 🍷 ev. day 9am–7pm
🗝 Noël-Bouton

DOM. DE LA RENARDE

Varot 1998★

■ 10.13 ha 25,000 50–69 F

The ex-Mayor of Rully presented us with this Varot red 98. The wine shows more finesse and suppleness than structure. It is pale garnet in colour and the nose is perfumed with wild berries. Very characteristic. The **Varot Blanc 98**, is light but straightforward and would make a good apéritif wine. Get the cheese puffs heated up.
🗝 Maison André Delorme, 2, rue de la République, 71150 Rully, tel. 03.85.87.10.12, fax 03.85.87.04.60 ☑ 🍷 by appt.
🗝 J.-F. Delorme

LA TOUR BLONDEAU 1998★

□ n.c. n.c. 50–69 F

An understated, elegant wine that is pale and unadorned. It has aromas of vanilla flower tinged with gunflint with a well-rounded and spicy charm. Is it approachable? It is for you to take the first step. Produced by Bouchard Père et Fils.
🗝 Grands Vins Forgeot, 15, rue du Château, 21200 Beaune, tel. 03.80.24.80.50

DOM. DE L'ECETTE 1997★

□ 5 ha 6,000 30–49 F

A 97 with a firm step. Old gold, a very ripe nose, it opens up an engaging dialogue with the taster. There is richness and honey, and it has potential. The finish is pleasant. It has a Muscat-like quality that is part of its character. In 1983, the wine-grower left the Mâconnais where he used to be a wine-maker and came to Rully. He has been joined by his son Vincent. Today he owns 14 ha (35 acres).
🗝 Jean et Vincent Daux, Dom. de l'Ecette, 21, rue de Geley, 71150 Rully, tel. 03.85.91.21.52, fax 03.85.91.24.33 ☑ 🍷 by appt.

DOM. ANDRE LHERITIER

Clos Roch 1997

□ 0.5 ha 2,200 50–69 F

It would not be a waste of time to wait a year of two for this light gold Clos Roch with its eloquent perfumes: honey, grapefruit, broom and quince, according to our fine tasters. An upfront wine that puts everything into the first impression, yet it has a tinge of over-maturity that is the result of the method of vinification.
🗝 André Lhéritier, 4, bd de la Liberté, 71150 Chagny, tel. 03.85.87.00.09 ☑ 🍷 by appt.

MANOIR DE MERCEY

En Rosey 1998

■ 3.54 ha 8,000 50–69 F

Mercey is a 19th-century manor house. Here they mature the wine for twelve months in wood. Ruby-coloured with a nose full of strawberries and raspberries. Clean with imposing tannins that are still too harsh. Wait a year or two.
🗝 Dom. Gérard Berger-Rive et Fils, Manoir de Mercey, 71150 Cheilly-lès-Maranges, tel. 03.85.91.13.81, fax 03.85.91.17.06 ☑ 🍷 by appt.

PHILIPPE MILAN ET FILS 1998★

■ 1.65 ha 7,000 50–69 F

This wine has an attractive, soft colour. It expresses itself well: raspberry with a background of undergrowth. It has spicy flavours but, as yet, the tannins have not softened sufficiently and it lacks fullness. Even though it was matured in tank and wood, the oakiness

is prominent. To drink now or to wait for three or four years.
🗝 Philippe Milan et Fils, Valotte, 71150 Chassey-le-Camp, tel. 03.85.91.21.38, fax 03.85.87.00.85 ☑ 🍷 by appt.

CH. DE MONTHELIE Préaux 1997*

■ 1er cru | 1 ha | 3,700 | 50–69 F

One of the tasting slips read 'well-balanced richness'. Everyone made similarly flattering comments about this Préaux. Suremain is established in the Côte-de-Beaune as well as the Côte Chalonnaise, both of which they know like the back of their hand. Garnet colour with aromas of red berry fruit and leather. A firm, solid wine, maybe even a little hard, but it has remarkable presence.
🗝 EARL de Suremain, Ch. de Monthélie, 21190 Monthélie, tel. 03.80.21.23.32, fax 03.80.21.66.37 ☑ 🍷 by appt.

MUGNIER PERE ET FILS
Les Chênes 1997*

□ | 0.8 ha | 1,850 | 50–69 F

One author described white Rully as: 'all the polish and coolness of marble'. Here we have a fresh 97. Old gold in colour with a nose showing citrus fruit, honey and the merest hint of shag tobacco. The wine has a pleasant attack, it is light with toasty flavours but not overly intense.
🗝 La P'tiote Cave, 71150 Chassey-le-Camp, tel. 03.85.87.15.21, fax 03.85.87.28.08 ☑ 🍷 by appt.

ROPITEAU 1998

□ | n.c. | 40,000 | 50–69 F

This wine practically purrs in the glass and only needs a stroke to show itself off to best advantage. It is as soft as can be, green-gold and attractively clear. The aromas are equally divided between flowers and minerals. There is a hint of development. A well-structured and approachable wine, it has freshness and roundness, and also has a lively side to it. Ropiteau is one of the companies in the Vins J.-C. Boisset group.
🗝 Ropiteau Frères, 13, rue du 11-Novembre, 21190 Meursault, tel. 03.80.21.69.20, fax 03.80.21.69.29 🍷 ev. day 9am–7pm; cl. mid-Nov. until Easter

CH. DE RULLY 1997*

□ | 18 ha | 100,000 | 70–99 F

The Counts of Ternay put their vineyard into the hands of Antonin Rodet. The estate has noble antecedents. This Chardonnay is richly perfumed. The flavour of the oak is affirmative but well-integrated, giving flavours of lightly toasted bread. Attractive colour with depth. Also worth a look is the **La Bressande Premier Cru Blanc 97**, with its very aromatic nose and well-built body. Frogs' legs would go well with it in 2002.
🗝 Dom. du Ch. de Rully, 71640 Mercurey, tel. 03.85.98.12.12, fax 03.85.45.25.49 ☑ 🍷 by appt.

ROLAND SOUNIT La Bergerie 1998*

■ | 1 ha | 6,500 | 50–69 F

A deep garnet with shimmering violet hues, this is a Pinot Noir with aromas of kirsch and cooked red berry fruit. Such a great pleasure to encounter a Rully that is so characteristic. A supple, fine wine with breeding. It could do with a few more years in the cellar, but will stay soft rather than robust.
🗝 SCEA Dom. Roland Sounit, rte. de Monthélie, 21190 Meursault, tel. 03.80.21.22.45, fax 03.80.21.28.05

Mercurey

Mercurey is 12 km (7 miles) north-west of Chalon-sur-Saône, on the edge of the Chagny-Cluny road, and borders the Rully vineyard to the south. This appellation communale produces the largest volume of wine on the Côte Chalonnaise: in 1999 28,797 hl (760,241 gal), 3,956 hl (104,438 gal) of which were white wines. It extends into three communes: Mercurey, Saint-Martin-sous-Montaigu and Borgneuf-Val-d'Or.

Some locations are also classified as Premier Cru. The wines are generally light and pleasant, with some keeping qualities.

JEAN BOUCHARD 1998*

■ | n.c. | 66,000 | 100–149 F

This wine is showing lots of good qualities. It comes from Albert Bichot, who has added another Bouchard to the Beaune part of the family. The tannins add structure to its vinosity. At its peak, it will certainly show cherry flavours. To keep a while.
🗝 Jean Bouchard, B.P. 47, 21202 Beaune Cedex, tel. 03.80.24.37.27, fax 03.80.24.37.38

BOUCHARD AINE ET FILS 1997**

■ | n.c. | 24,000 | 70–99 F

Ideal for *coq au Mercurey*. It shows off all the best qualities and virtues of the appellation. Intense cherry colour and, keeping the same theme, it has a cherry nose with floral notes. On the palate it is elegant and firm and has an astonishing, delicate youthfulness. Bouchard Aîné et Fils belongs to the Boisset family who, in Beaune, welcome you in their beautiful mansion, the Hôtel du Conseiller du Roy. Also take note of the **Village Blanc 98**, commended, which is rich, fleshy and oaky.

🔑 Bouchard Aîné et Fils, Hôtel du Conseiller-du-Roy, 4, bd Mal-Foch, 21200 Beaune, tel. 03.80.24.24.00, fax 03.80.24.64.12 ☑ 🍷 ev. day 9.30am–12.30pm 2pm–6.30pm
🔑 J.-C. Boisset

DOM. MICHEL BRIDAY

Clos Marcilly 1998★

■ 1er cru	0.89 ha	1,000	🛢 70–99 F

Marcilly is one of the very first Premiers Crus delimited in Mercurey. This wine, produced by Stéphane Briday, has a glamorous colour. Fairly toasty, but there is also a liquorice element. This rests on the palate, which also has richness. The vinification has been carefully handled. It is recommended to wait a while.

🔑 Dom. Michel Briday, 31, Grande-Rue, 71150 Rully, tel. 03.85.87.07.90, fax 03.85.91.25.68, e-mail stephane.briday@wanadoo.fr ☑ 🍷 by appt.

CH. DE CHAMIREY 1998★

□	9 ha	60,000	70–99 F

This offspring is from Antonin-Rodin's estate at Mercurey, the Château de Chamirey which belongs to the Marquis of Jouennes d'Herville's daughter. A wine of quality. Straw-coloured with glints of green, it is clean and flowery, rich and complete and when presented to the world it should have the best chance of succeeding. There is a slight Muscat-like quality that could be a family trait. In any case, it comes from good stock.

🔑 Dom. du Château de Chamirey, 71640 Mercurey, tel. 03.85.98.12.12, fax 03.85.45.25.49 ☑ 🍷 ev. day except Sat. Sun. 9am–12 noon 1.30pm–6pm
🔑 Christine Devillard

DOM. CHANZY Les Carabys 1998★

□	0.46 ha	3,300	🛢 50–69 F

The *climat* this wine comes from recalls to mind an old French song that should appeal to Compère Guilleri. Its colour would thrill him. The nose opens with fruit and is embellished by the oak. The strawberry flavour, its little hint of liveliness, richness and roundness impart a delicate character. To be snapped up immediately.

🔑 Daniel Chanzy, 1, rue de la Fontaine, 71150 Bouzeron, tel. 03.85.87.23.69, fax 03.85.91.24.92, e-mail daniel.chanzy@wanadoo.fr ☑ 🍷 by appt.

JEAN-PIERRE CHARTON

Clos du Roy 1998★

■ 1er cru	1 ha	3,500	🛢 50–69 F

If all the vineyards in Burgundy called Clos du Roy are anything to go by, the King had a fine nose. This has a warm approach. At the moment, its tannic structure is closed and rustic, but this is a sincere wine with depth, and it should fulfill our hopes in two or three years. This is a fairly new property belonging to a wine family from Savigny.

🔑 Jean-Pierre Charton, 29, Grande-Rue, 71640 Mercurey, tel. 03.85.45.22.39, fax 03.85.45.22.39 ☑ 🍷 by appt.

COUVENT DES CORDELIERS

1997★

■	n.c.	6,500	🛢 70–99 F

Produced by Boisseaux (Patriarche, Château de Meursault, this wine, although light in colour, shows good spirit. From start to finish its aromas show an intensity of ripe fruit and game. It is approachable and ready to drink, but can equally wait for a time.

🔑 Caves des Cordeliers, rue de l'Hôtel-Dieu, 21200 Beaune, tel. 03.80.25.08.85, fax 03.80.25.08.21 ☑ 🍷 ev. day 9.30am–12 noon 2pm–6pm

DOUDET-NAUDIN

Les Bussières 1998★

■	2.2 ha	5,100	🛢 70–99 F

Plaudite cives! Let the citizens rejoice, because this is a good wine. The *table de tri*, where the grapes are carefully selected, temperature-controlling equipment and fittings were renovated in 1999. The 98 is still in the flush of youth and needs time. It already has a complex nose and a perfect colour. Good overall balance with roundness and length. This wine has a lot in reserve and a good future.

🔑 Doudet-Naudin, 3, rue Henri-Cyrot, 21420 Savigny-lès-Beaune, tel. 03.80.21.51.74, fax 03.80.21.50.69 ☑ 🍷 by appt.
🔑 Yves Doudet

CH. D'ETROYES Les Velley 1998★

■ 1er cru	1.39 ha	8,000	🛢 70–99 F

Slightly amber-garnet in colour, it kicks off with cherry in eau-de-vie. On the palate it is powerful, not to say massive, in temperament, and its acidity and tannins are only playing a small role at the moment. The jury banished it to the depth of the cellar for four to five years.

🔑 Dom. Maurice Protheau, Ch. d'Etroyes, 71640 Mercurey, tel. 03.85.98.99.10, fax 03.85.98.99.00 ☑ 🍷 by appt.
🔑 Famille Maurice Protheau

DOM. GOUFFIER

Champs Martin 1997★★

■ 1er cru	0.5 ha	1,500	🛢 70–99 F

A bright ruby, almost garnet colour. Blackcurrant on the nose. Shades of musk add to the picture. A superb attack that is strong and round with a faultless palate. It could wait a little in the cellar. The **Clos de la Charmée 97** also merits a recommendation. A more easy-going style of red wine (50–69F).

🔑 Dom. Gouffier, 11, Grande-Rue, 71150 Fontaines, tel. 03.85.91.49.66, fax 03.85.91.46.98 ☑ 🍷 by appt.

DOM. PATRICK GUILLOT

Clos des Montaigu 1998★

■ 1er cru 0.8 ha 3,200 50–69 F

Black cherry colour showing some signs of maturity. Reveals pleasant aromas of fruit compote. It is both round and rigid, which is often the case with young wines. The tannins do not get in the way of its balanced flavours, nor the complexity which is beginning to show. The jury advises keeping it for three to five years. There is no de-stalking in this 6.8-ha (17-acre) estate, which Patrick Guillot has been running since 1988. This is his tenth vintage.

Dom. Patrick Guillot, rue de Vaugeailles, 71640 Mercurey, tel. 03.85.45.27.40, fax 03.85.45.28.57 by appt.

JEANNIN-NALTET PERE ET FILS

Clos des Grands Voyens 1997★

■ 1er cru 4.91 ha 28,000 50–69 F

A local family who know about wine. Their Clos des Grands Voyens presents itself well. It has a light nose, but on the palate is abundantly rich. Full, warm and companionable and absolutely on the top rung of the appellation.

Jeannin-Naltet Père et Fils, 4, rue de Jamproyes, 71640 Mercurey, tel. 03.85.45.13.83, fax 03.85.45.18.24 ev. day 8am–12 noon 2pm–6pm; Sat. Sun. by appt.

JEAN-HERVE JONNIER 1997★

■ 3 ha 7,200 50–69 F

When you are in Chassey, it is hard to imagine that the Chassian civilisation influenced a substantial part of Europe four or five thousand years ago. Today, wine brings fame to the area. This 97 will be splendid with *œufs en meurette* or eggs in red wine sauce. Fine colour, with aromas of raspberry and vanilla. The wine is fresh and light and has some personality. Interesting because it is so characteristic.

Jean-Hervé Jonnier, Bercully, 71150 Chassey-le-Camp, tel. 03.85.87.21.90, fax 03.85.87.23.63 by appt.

DOM. EMILE JUILLOT

Les Combins 1998★★

■ 1er cru 0.92 ha 4,500 50–69 F

Here are two Premiers Crus reds to choose from, both of which we enjoyed: the **Champs Martins 98** (one star) or this one of the same vintage. Deep purple and matured in good quality wood, the red berry fruit is still finding its place. A pleasing wine and a perfect accompaniment for good classic dishes. While it is still young, it will benefit from decanting. The white **La Cailloute 98**, Premier Cru Monopole, receives one star for its nose that is a blend of honey, white blossom and citrus fruit, as well as, for its balance. Serve with a *tourte* or a fish dish.

EARL N. et J.-C. Theulot, Dom. Emile Juillot, Clos Laurent, 71640 Mercurey, tel. 03.85.45.13.87, fax 03.85.45.28.07 by appt.

DOM. MICHEL JUILLOT 1998★

■ 11 ha 55,000 70–99 F

A lovely ruby colour, it makes its presence felt at the first sniff that goes from musk to spice via stone fruit. On the palate it is fresh yet almost ripe, and with no aggressive tannins, just suppleness and elegance. To serve next year.

Dom. Michel Juillot, 59, Grande-Rue, B.P. 10, 71640 Mercurey, tel. 03.85.98.99.89, fax 03.85.98.99.88, e-mail infos@domaine.michel.juillot.fr ev. day except Sun. 9am–12 noon 2pm–6pm; groups by appt.

Michel et Laurent Juillot

DOM. DE LA CROIX JACQUELET

Clos du Roy 1997★

■ 1er cru 2.54 ha 6,300 70–99 F

This is the vast Faiveley estate at Mercurey (79 ha/195 acres). A powerful, spicy, well-bred Premier Cru with aromas of cooked fruit and a colour tinged with violet. The tannins are still burly. It will become a good wine in four to five years.

Dom. de la Croix Jacquelet, SBEV, 71640 Mercurey, tel. 03.85.45.14.72, fax 03.85.45.26.42 ev. day 8am–12 noon 1.30pm–6pm; Sat. Sun. by appt.

LOUIS LATOUR 1997

□ n.c. 30,000 50–69 F

Not a very intense gold colour, but it is easy on the eye. The Mercury wafts past the nose and lands firmly on the palate. An attractive wine that is pleasantly full, balanced and quite warm (with a note of alcohol). It should be drunk in the next year.

Maison Louis Latour, 18, rue des Tonneliers, 21200 Beaune, tel. 03.80.24.81.00, fax 03.80.22.36.21, e-mail louislatour@louislatour.com by appt.

DOM. DE L'EUROPE

Vignes des Chazeaux 1998★

■ 1.75 ha 5,000 50–69 F

What happens when a Burgundian winegrower meets a Belgian artist? This union, consumated in 1994, produced the Domaine de l'Europe with labels showing the European Union flag. Amongst the wines produced by this duo, we opted for this 98 which is a fair representation of the vintage. Ruby-coloured, raspberry nose, a little nervy and tannic: it should spend some time in the cellar for the fruit to develop properly.

Chantal Côte et Guy Cinquin, Dom. de l'Europe, 5 pl. du Bourgneuf, 71640 Mercurey, tel. 03.85.45.23.82, fax 03.85.45.23.82 by appt.

DOM. LEVERT-BARRAULT 1998★

■ 1er cru 0.4 ha 2,000 ⫼ 70–99 F

This young individual is still a little shy, but that is not a problem. Brilliant purple with a feather in its cap, it is robustly-structured, tannic, liquoricey and made for keeping a while. Its velvety finish suggests that it will give pleasure in the not-too-distant future. With tender red meat, it will be perfect.

🔑 Dom. Levert-Barrault, rue de Mercurey, 71640 Mercurey, tel. 03.85.87.51.00, fax 03.85.87.51.11

🔑 Michel Picard

DOM. LORENZON

Les Champs Martin Vieilles vignes 1998★★

■ 1er cru 1 ha 4,500 ⫼ 70–99 F

Bruno Lorenzon took over the family estate (4.5 ha/11 acres) in 1997. His **Village Rouge 98**, one star (50–69F) has the distinctive features of the appellation. It has a deep, intense colour and still smells of the harvest. Full and rich, the tannins are pronounced yet fine. It is still oaky and has 'le temps d'y voir' (time to sort itself out) as they say in Burgundy. The Champs Martin 98 Premier Cru Vieilles Vignes is remarkable. Do not hesitate: a hefty, concentrated wine that is characteristic of the AOC. It has a deep colour, and a nose of ripe red berry fruit that we find again on the palate despite the prominent tannins. Ideal with game in three to four years, but it will live a good deal longer than that. The **Cuvée des Champs Martin Rouge 98**, produced from young, thirty-year-old vines, is awarded one star.

🔑 Dom. Bruno Lorenzon, 14, rue du Reu, 71640 Mercurey, tel. 03.85.45.13.51, fax 03.85.45.15.52 ☑ Y by appt.

DOM. LOUIS MAX Les Vasées 1997

■ 1er cru n.c. 6,000 ⫼ 300–499 F

Its unusual label is like a theatre curtain. This wine comes in three acts. The first is the morello cherry colour that has already matured a little. The second, the fairly strong oak, is intended to be a crowd-pleaser, but it does not upstage the fruit. The third, warmth (traces of alcohol) is pleasant. As this good, commercial wine takes its bow, the critics decided it was a good show. Also worth a look, the **Village Blanc 98 Les Rochelles**: not at all bad!

🔑 Louis Max, 6, rue de Chaux, 21700 Nuits-Saint-Georges, tel. 03.80.62.43.01, fax 03.80.62.43.16

DOM. DU MEIX-FOULOT 1997★

■ 1er cru 1.5 ha 6,000 ▮ ⫼ 70–99 F

Paul de Launay was a colourful figure on the Côte chalonnaise, and in 1996, he handed over to his daughter, Agnès. Here she shows off what she can do: the aromas of this Mercurey are discreet (kirsch, marron glacé, roasting coffee) with a pretty colour and a fresh and fruity, firm and very agreeable palate. A wine that is full of promise with its touch of oak.

🔑 Dom. du Meix-Foulot, 71640 Mercurey, tel. 03.85.45.13.92, fax 03.85.45.28.10 ☑ Y by appt.

🔑 Paul de Launay

DOM. L. MENAND PERE ET FILS

Les Champs Martin 1998★★

■ 1er cru 1 ha 5,000 ⫼ 50–69 F

A 9-ha (22-acre) family estate that is already well-established in the United States, Belgium and Switzerland produces this concentrated, typical Mercurey that is well-made and will keep. It is spontaneous, interesting for its age, certainly solid and decidedly classic. The Clos des Combins is wholly-owned by the estate, but here, we are looking at the Champs Martin.

🔑 Dom. L. Menand Père et Fils, Clos des Combins, 71640 Mercurey, tel. 03.85.45.19.19, fax 03.85.45.10.23 ☑ Y by appt.

MOILLARD La Chassière 1997

■ 1er cru n.c. 3,600 ⫼ 70–99 F

Deep, brilliant red with a nose divided between vanilla and crystallised cherry. The wine is very direct, clean and fruity on the palate. The tannins are prominent and very powerful. Hard to say how they will develop. The jury was divided on whether it should be drunk as it is, or given a long time to mature.

🔑 Moillard, 2, rue François-Mignotte, 21700 Nuits-Saint-Georges, tel. 03.80.62.42.22, fax 03.80.61.28.13 ☑ Y ev. day 10am–6pm; cl. Jan.

CH. PHILIPPE-LE-HARDI 1998★

■ 1er cru 1.24 ha 7,800 ⫼ 50–69 F

The old Paul Pidault estate has planted a great deal, recently, in Mercurey. Under this name, we have a wine with a dark red colour. Its nose plays skillfully with notes of musk, roasted coffee and a little fruit. It is interestingly complex. A tight-knit palate, vinous yet balanced. Wait at least three years.

🔑 Ch. de Santenay, B.P. 18, 21590 Santenay, tel. 03.80.20.61.87, fax 03.80.20.63.66 ☑ Y by appt.

ADRIEN PIERARNAULT

Les Champs Martin 1997★

■ 1er cru n.c. 5,300 ⫼ 70–99 F

Brilliant ruby-red, in perfect harmony with the open nose that has the delicacy of raspberry and the liveliness of redcurrant – you need to go a long way before finding better. A well-made wine, ample, long, and finishes with touches of liquorice, but not very full-bodied, yet it pays its dues. A brand from Goichot et Fils.

🔑 SA A. Goichot et Fils, av. Charles-de-Gaulle, 21200 Beaune, tel. 03.80.26.88.70, fax 03.80.26.80.69, e-mail goichot@goichotsa.com ☑ Y by appt.

FRANCOIS RAQUILLET

Les Puillets 1998★

■ 1er cru 1.5 ha 8,000 50–69 F

Try the reds **Les Naugues** or **Les Vasées Premiers Crus 98**, or this one that has both fullness and texture. A velvety red with shimmering violet, the nose opens readily with aromas of liquorice, spices and blackcurrant. We would like to take a second look at this 98. It is remarkable in its classic Pinot Noir style. It needs to settle down for two years and then you can drink it over five to six years. A white Premier Cru **98** the **Les Veleys** is excellent – rich and balanced, with very good length. A good dish of fish would help it flourish in two or three years.

François Raquillet, rue de Jamproyes, 71640 Mercurey, tel. 03.85.45.14.61, fax 03.85.45.28.05 by appt.

DOM. ROLAND SOUNIT

Les Murgers Elevé et vieilli en fût de chêne 1998★

■ 0.4 ha 2,500 50–69 F

Lustrous cherry-purple with mauve glints. After breathing, it shows an elegant nose mixing fruit and vanilla from the wood. On the palate, its solid balance does not overwhelm the red berry fruit, even if the tannins are still strong and somewhat dominant. It has attractive acidity that will allow it to mature. Very characteristic. Also worth looking at for the patient wine-lover is the **Les Varennes 98**, which is very well-made.

SCEA Dom. Roland Sounit, rte. de Monthélie, 21190 Meursault, tel. 03.80.21.22.45, fax 03.80.21.28.05

Givry

Givry is 6 km (4 miles) south of Mercurey, and is a typical Burgundian village with a wealth of historic monuments. Givry is claimed to have been the favourite wine of Henri IV of France, and mainly red wines are produced – 11,088 hl (292,723 gal) in 1999). However, the whites – 2,216 hl (58,502 gal) in 1999 – are also of interest. Prices are very affordable. The appellation lies principally in the commune of Givry but spills over slightly into Jambles and Dracy-le-Fort.

GUILLEMETTE ET XAVIER BESSON Les Grands Prétans 1998★

■ 1er cru 1.5 ha 9,000 50–69 F

If you pass this way, do not miss the *Festival Musicaves:* music and tastings at the estates. The white **Petit Prétan 98** is a symphony (30–49F) of citrus fruit in a soft, gentle key. The red is still a little young. A sombre garnet colour with a rustic nose (musk) with good intensity. It has a good deal of fullness and distinction. A year in the cellar will bring it balance.

Dom. Guillemette et Xavier Besson, 9, rue des Bois-Chevaux, 71640 Givry, tel. 03.85.44.42.44, fax 03.85.44.42.44 by appt.

RENE BOURGEON

Clos de la Brûlée 1998★

□ n.c. n.c. 50–69 F

White Givry was very rare in the past (only 75,000 bottles out of a total of 850,000). Little by little it is growing in confidence. The nose touches on white blossom with an underlying aroma of nuts and toasted bread. It needs to be watched during its maturing period. At the moment it is still in hiding. The **Givry Rouge 98** bodes well: ardent, powerful and full of fruit. Excellent potential. It is awarded one star.

GAEC René Bourgeon, 2, rue du Chapitre, 71640 Jambles, tel. 03.85.44.35.85, fax 03.85.44.57.80 by appt.

LOUIS CHAVY 1997★

■ n.c. 15,000 70–99 F

Cherry with violet hues, a real *village* perfumed with morello cherry and blackberry. Its body, tannins and power would undoubtedly have gladdened the heart of good King Henry. However, at the moment, the fruit is playing hide and seek. Of course, it will keep.

Louis Chavy, Caveau la Vierge Romaine, pl. des Marronniers, 21190 Puligny-Montrachet, tel. 03.80.26.33.00, fax 03.80.24.14.84, e-mail mallet.b@cva-beaune.fr ev. day 10am–6pm; cl. Nov.–Mar.

DOM. CHOFFLET-VALDENAIRE

Clos de Choue 1998

■ 1er cru 3 ha 15,000 50–69 F

This estate has been held by the same family for two hundred and fifty years, and comprises 11 ha (27 acres). Their 98 is for drinking in the immediate future. A very deep red colour. The Pinot is showing roundness, the nose has crushed fruit with a hint of musk and a good tannic structure.

Dom. Chofflet-Valdenaire, Russilly, 71640 Givry, tel. 03.85.44.34.78, fax 03.85.44.45.25 by appt.

CLOS SALOMON 1998

■ 1er cru 6.8 ha 28,000 50–69 F

The panel did not bring the judgement of Solomon to bear on this Clos Salomon. The

brilliant vermilion colour is promising. The nose has a touch of blackcurrant. On the palate it opens slowly. A concentrated wine with some reserves, it is worth waiting a year or two for it to flourish fully.
Dom. du Clos Salomon, 16, rue du Clos-Salomon, 71640 Givry, tel. 03.85.44.32.24, fax 03.85.44.49.79 ev. day except Sun. 8am–7pm
du Gardin

PROPRIETE DESVIGNES
La Grande Berge 1997*

1er cru 1.7 ha 11,000 50–69 F

The *climat* **Clos Charlé 98 Rouge** was planted fairly recently and classified as a Premier Cru in 1988. Commended by the jury for its clean, well-made texture, and its finesse. Of the 97 reds, the Grande Berge wins. It is a wine worth keeping; it has a superb, intense colour that suggests a complex wine. It is still very oaky at the moment but well-built: its strength does not harm its finesse. Bilberry fruit on the palate. To drink with a plump capon.
Propriété Desvignes, 36, rue de Jambles, Poncey, 71640 Givry, tel. 03.85.44.37.81, fax 03.85.44.43.53 by appt.

DIDIER ERKER En Chenèvre 1998*

0.6 ha 4,200 30–49 F

The wine-producer who took over this estate five years ago has produced a golden Givry with a pearly sheen, and buttery, floral perfumes where you can also detect a touch of grapefruit. It is fresh (the acidity is pronounced but not unpleasant) and the palate follows on in the same spirit. To drink before the Saint-Vincent Tournante festival in 2002.
Didier Erker, 7 bis, bd Saint-Martin, 71640 Givry, tel. 03.85.44.39.62, fax 03.85.44.39.62, e-mail Erker@givry.net ev. day except Sun. 8am–12 noon 2pm–6pm

DOM. MICHEL GOUBARD ET FILS
La Grande Berge 1998

1er cru 2.3 ha 13,000 50–69 F

The Goubard family has had an interest in vines since the beginning of the 17th century. The windmill on the label might make you think of a Beaujolais, but not at all. This is Givry, and the windmill an emblem of the Côte Chalonnaise. This is a no-frills Pinot that is nicely balanced and with a clear colour. It is light, but pleasant.
Dom. Michel Goubard et Fils, 71390 Saint-Désert, tel. 03.85.47.91.06, fax 03.85.47.98.12 ev. day 8am–12 noon 2pm–7pm; Sun. by appt.

LES VILLAGES DE JAFFELIN 1997

n.c. 10,000 50–69 F

A medium-full depth of colour, the nose is very ripe, or even well-developed. Muskiness, leather, dead leaves: aromas you would find in the woods in autumn. The acidity and tannins get along all right. Interesting aromas on the finish, almost cooked fruit. To be drunk next year.
Jaffelin, 2, rue Paradis, 21200 Beaune, tel. 03.80.22.12.49, fax 03.80.24.91.87 by appt.

LA SAULERAIE Champ Pourrot 1998**

0.47 ha 3,500 30–49 F

This wine-producer always offers us a large selection of wines to try. We enjoyed his red **98 Les Grandes Vignes Premier Cru** and the **Champ Nalot** (50–69F). The jury commended the first and awarded one star to both of them. It is the white, pale gold with honey and hazelnut and a charming fullness, that wins the laurels: a very ripe harvest without doubt, providing balance, richness, complexity and length . . . Overall finesse.
Gérard et Laurent Parize, 18, rue des Faussillons, 71640 Givry, tel. 03.85.44.38.60, fax 03.85.44.43.54 ev. day 9am–7pm; Sun. by appt.

GERARD MOUTON Clos Jus 1997*

1er cru 2 ha 13,000 50–69 F

This Clos Jus is very balanced. It is smooth and strong and has the character of the terroir. A lovely garnet colour. It is beginning to show some complexity with a superb palate that follows right through to the finish. Round and rich, then it takes off . . . Enjoy!
SCEA Gérard Mouton, 6, rue de l'Orcène, Poncey, 71640 Givry, tel. 03.85.44.37.99, fax 03.85.44.48.19 by appt.

DOM. RAGOT Clos Jus 1998

1er cru 1 ha 6,500 50–69 F

This wine provoked varying comments. Everyone agreed that it is bright purple. Views were divided on the nose: game or fresh fruit. It does have a good structure, but not great staying power. However, all agreed that it has subtlety.
Dom. Jean-Paul Ragot, 4, rue de l'Ecole, Poncey, 71640 Givry, tel. 03.85.44.35.67, fax 03.85.44.38.84 ev. day except Sun. 8am–8pm

MICHEL SARRAZIN
Champs Lalot 1998*

n.c. 15,000 50–69 F

From among the **red 98s** we tasted, this was a respectable **Grands Prétans Premier Cru**, commended by the jury. It will not gain a great deal from waiting. This wine has a straightforward colour and a younthful nose with red berry fruit. The wine has nerve but is not very characterful, expansive with a little warmth, an attractive touch of vanilla, and it is well-structured, so should be allowed to age.
Michel Sarrazin et Fils, Charnailles, 71640 Jambles, tel. 03.85.44.30.57, fax 03.85.44.31.22 ev. day except Sun. 9am–12 noon 2pm–7pm

BURGUNDY

JEAN TATRAUX ET FILS

Les Grandes Berges 1998

■ 1er cru 0.95 ha 6,000 30–49 F

Sylvain Tatraux has run the family estate of over 5 ha (12 acres) since 1996. His Premier Cru is matured in large wooden casks. Lovely colour, with a nose presenting at first some vanilla, then fruit. On the palate it is more rustic, but the attractive, concentrated red berry fruit re-emerges. The wine is somewhat reticent but will mature well.

EARL Jean Tatraux et Fils, 20, rue de Locène, 71640 Givry, tel. 03.85.44.36.89, fax 03.85.44.59.43 by appt.

Sylvain Tatraux

DOM. BERNARD TATRAUX-JUILLET Clos Jus 1998★★

■ 1er cru 0.25 ha 2,500 30–49 F

Clos Jus is responsible for the reputation of Dracy-le-Fort. The Abbé Courtépée ranked it at the top of the Côte Chalonnaise terroirs. It was decimated by phylloxera, but has regained its position and, to judge by this high quality wine, is back at the same level. Deep purple and generously scented, the 98 has notes of musk enhanced by aromas of crushed fruit; a rich attack, a silky body and perfect architecture. Excellent with capon.

Dom. Bernard Tatraux-Juillet, 33, rue de la Planchette, Poncey, 71640 Givry, tel. 03.85.44.57.41, fax 03.85.44.57.20 by appt.

EMILE VOARICK 1998

■ 1.99 ha 12,400 50–69 F

Michel Picard bought this Voarick estate, which presented an appealing Givry with a bright red colour. The nose is heavy with oak, undergrowth and berry fruit. It is round and good-natured and for drinking today, without too much fuss.

Dom. Emile Voarick, 71640 Saint-Martin-sous-Montaigu, tel. 03.85.45.23.23, fax 03.85.45.16.37 ev. day except Sat. Sun. 8am–12 noon 2pm–6pm

Michel Picard

Montagny

Producing only white wines, Montagny, which is the southernmost village of the region, heralds the neighbouring Mâconnais. The appellation can be produced in four communes: Montagny, Buxy, Saint-Vallerin and Jully-lès-Buxy. A *climat* can only be claimed in the commune of Montagny. Production in 1999 reached 16,704 hl (440,986 gal).

STEPHANE ALADAME

Cuvée Sélection 1998

□ 1er cru 0.85 ha 5,340 50–69 F

Rather a pallid colour, but an enterprising nose; undergrowth and bracken leading to peach. It will improve when it opens out. The estate is young (established in 1992), and its wine is matured 75% in tank and and 25% in wood.

Stéphane Aladame, rue du Lavoir, 71390 Montagny-lès-Buxy, tel. 03.85.92.06.01, fax 03.85.92.04.97, e-mail stephane.aladame@wanadoo.fr by appt.

DOM. ARNOUX PERE ET FILS

Les Bonnevaux 1998

□ 1er cru 0.5 ha 3,000 30–49 F

Since this wine is matured in tank, it does not have the vanilla and nutty flavours from an oak cask. No complaints, especially since there is so much enjoyment in its radiant freshness. Pale gold, with a floral nose that is not too perfumed, more delicate than opulent, and a wine that falls in with the real spirit of the appellation.

Dom. Arnoux Père et Fils, 7, rue du Lavoir, 71390 Buxy, tel. 03.85.92.11.06, fax 03.85.92.19.28 by appt.

BOUCHARD AINE ET FILS 1998★

□ 1er cru n.c. 12,000 70–99 F

Fresh aromas and clear intentions. This 98 Montagny is straightforward and smooth, elegant and silky, and its character is typical for this grape variety: it knows what it is about.

Bouchard Aîné et Fils, Hôtel du Conseiller-du-Roy, 4, bd Mal-Foch, 21200 Beaune, tel. 03.80.24.24.00, fax 03.80.24.64.12 ev. day 9.30am–12.30pm 2pm–6.30pm

J.-C. Boisset

BOUCHARD PERE ET FILS 1998★

□ 1er cru n.c. n.c. 50–69 F

Straw-coloured with an expressive nose: almond and hazelnut with a background of hawthorn. Nicely balanced and delicate like a real Montagny. It is still very young on the palate and lightly honeyed, and will go better with trout than with crayfish.

Bouchard Père et Fils, Ch. de Beaune, 21200 Beaune, tel. 03.80.24.80.24, fax 03.80.22.55.88, e-mail france@bouchard.pereetfils.com by appt.

LES VIGNERONS DE BUXY

Cuvée spéciale 1998★

□ 1er cru 8 ha 90,000 50–69 F

The Cave de Buxy has produced this *village* (rare since nearly all the AOC is classified as Premier Cru). The **97 Domaine des Pierres Blanches** scores a good average, and is recommended by the jury, as is this Cuvée Spéciale

with it slightly golden-yellow colour and exotic fruit aromas (grapefruit). It is tender and tasty with a little butteriness. A good young wine, like the Léo Ferré song *Jolie môme . . .*
🗝 Cave des Vignerons de Buxy, Les Vignes de la Croix, 71390 Buxy, tel. 03.85.92.03.03, fax 03.85.92.08.06 ☒ Y ev. day except Sun. 9am–12 noon 2pm–6pm

CH. DE CARY POTET

Les Jardins 1998★

☐ 1er cru 0.92 ha 4,000 50–69 F

'A fresh Montagny that is absolutely delicious', commented Serena Sutcliffe, who has marvellous knowledge of the Burgundy vineyards. Lime and gunflint with youth, vivacity and discretion, but this 98 will open out a good deal more. For the past five hundred years, this family has dedicated itself to its vines in this old and beautiful château.
🗝 Charles du Besset, rte. de Chenevelles, 71390 Buxy, tel. 03.85.92.14.48, fax 03.85.92.11.88 Y by appt.

CH. DE DAVENAY Clos Chaudron 1998

☐ 1er cru 4.42 ha 28,000 50–69 F

Very lively from the start with good citrus fruit flavours. It is oaky, and so has toasty flavours of brioche and toasted bread, but the citronella and flint still shine through. Its richness is not yet very pronounced, but this is a 98 that needs to calm down. It will be a good wine in 2001–2002. The wine is produced by the house of Michel Picard.
🗝 SCEA Dom. Château de Davenay, 71390 Buxy, tel. 03.85.45.23.23, fax 03.85.45.16.37
🗝 Michel Picard

JOSEPH DROUHIN 1998★★

☐ n.c. n.c. 70–99 F

The great poet André Frénaud was an ardent admirer of Montagny. A lyrical wine, if this green-gold 98 is anything to judge by. It has a rainbow of aromas: peach and apricot on a bed of brioche. The flavours are still unobtrusive, though it has great potential. Its richness (at the beginning) and its complexity (on the finish) have started to compose good rhymes.
🗝 Joseph Drouhin, 7, rue d'Enfer, 21200 Beaune, tel. 03.80.24.68.88, fax 03.80.22.43.14, e-mail drouhin@calva.net Y by appt.

DOM. DE LA CROIX JACQUELET 1997★★

☐ 1er cru 0.19 ha 500 50–69 F

This clear gold Faivelay offspring has a good balance between alcohol and acidity. It is supple, almost unctuous, and presents an interesting complexity. The wood influences are present throughout.
🗝 Dom. de la Croix Jacquelet, SBEV, 71640 Mercurey, tel. 03.85.45.14.72, fax 03.85.45.26.42 ☒ Y ev. day 8am–12 noon 1.30pm–6pm; Sat. Sun. by appt.

CH. DE LA GUICHE 1998

☐ 0.9 ha 5,436 50–69 F

A selection from the merchant André Goichot. Gold glinting with green, as it should, delicate smokiness from the wood, grapefruit on the nose which becomes orange on the palate. Soft and powerful at the same time. A wine that needs a little time.
🗝 Dom. du Château de la Guiche, SA André Goichot, rue Paul-Masson, 21190 Merceuil, tel. 03.80.26.88.70, fax 03.80.26.80.69, e-mail goichot@goichotsa.com ☒ Y by appt.

DOM. DE LA RENARDE 1998★

☐ 1er cru 3.86 ha 12,000 50–69 F

Buxy stone is one of the glories of the area and much sought-after by architects. Given that, it is not surprising to find the wines have mineral tones combined with white blossom and lemon. Citrus flavours enliven the palate. For the time being, it appears to be well-structured and to deserve a year's keeping. Only 5% of the wine matures in cask.
🗝 Maison André Delorme, 2, rue de la République, 71150 Rully, tel. 03.85.87.10.12, fax 03.85.87.04.60 ☒ Y by appt.
🗝 J.-F. Delorme

CH. DE LA SAULE

Elevé en fût de chêne 1998★

☐ 1er cru 4 ha 25,000 50–69 F

Pale gold and vinous from the first whiff. Although it is round, it also has vivacity. The balance is enhanced by a tinge of oakiness. Montagny is a perfect partner for calves' sweetbreads. To be drunk over two to three years.
🗝 Alain Roy, La Saule, 71390 Montagny, tel. 03.85.92.11.83, fax 03.85.92.08.12 ☒ Y by appt.

DOM. DE LA TOUR

Vieilli en fût de chêne 1997

☐ 1er cru 2.5 ha 12,000 30–49 F

The estate has passed from father to son. Since 1987, the wine has been vinified here, on the old property of the Counts d'Ivernoy. This wine has a good intensity of colour, and there is a hint of mineral present on the nose and palate. We like this lively, dry style that is a little sharp. It keeps you alert.
🗝 Daniel Joblot, SCEV dom. du Hameau La Tour, 71390 Saint-Vallerin, tel. 03.85.92.13.69, fax 03.85.92.09.43 ☒ Y by appt.

LES CAVES DU CHANCELIER

Elevé en fût de chêne 1998★★

☐ 1er cru n.c. 10,000 70–99 F

Denis Philibert, the *négociant-éleveur* from Beaune, has won us over with his 98. It has a clear but intense colour and the nose is developing gradually with aromas of ripened fruit. The palate has strength and length which suggests the wine should wait, and to complete the picture, there is a trace of vanilla.

BURGUNDY

🔑 Les Caves du Chancelier, 1, rue Ziem, 21200 Beaune, tel. 03.80.24.05.88, fax 03.80.22.37.08 Y ev. day 9am–7pm

DOM. NOEL PERRIN Les Las 1998*

□ 1er cru 0.3 ha 1,000 50–69 F

This wine already has a golden colour but lacks any obvious aromas; however, it has punch. Elegant with warmth and power. Well-made. The original label is a reproduction of a painting by P. Bendine, in shades of blue.

🔑 Dom. Noël Perrin, 71460 Culles-les-Roches, tel. 03.85.44.04.25, fax 03.85.44.04.25 ☑ Y ev. day 8am–12 noon 1.30pm–7pm

ALBERT PONNELLE 1997

□ n.c. n.c. 70–99 F

Bright straw colour, immediate and long. This well-made 97 is pale, clean and precise. It has a hint of hazelnut that is well-integrated. A wine with spirit and so, something in reserve.

🔑 Albert Ponnelle, Clos Saint-Nicolas, 38, fg Saint-Nicolas, 21200 Beaune, tel. 03.80.22.00.05, fax 03.80.24.19.73 ☑ Y by appt.

Le Mâconnais

Mâcon, Mâcon Supérieur and Mâcon-Villages

The appellations Mâcon, Mâcon Supérieur and Mâcon followed by the commune of origin are used for red, white and rosé wines. The white wines can also be called Pinot-Chardonnay-Mâcon and Mâcon-Villages. The vineyard is huge and, from the region of Tournus to the suburbs of Mâcon, the great variety of situations and aspects produces an equally wide range of different wines.

The area of Virée, Clessé, Lugny and Chardonnay is well-suited to producing the light, pleasant white wines for which it is known. A large number of wine-growers have grouped together in co-operatives to vinify their harvest and market their wines, and production has developed significantly as a result. In 1999 196,358 hl (5,183,851 gal) of white wine and 48,760 hl (1,287,264 gal) of red wine were produced.

Mâcon

CAVE D'AZE Azé 1998*

■ 25 ha 8,000 30–49 F

To summarise, a complex wine that is liquoricey, reliable on the palate, and one to drink straight away or enjoy in the future. Deep red in colour with a good, powerful nose. We considered it more a good wine for the future than one for hasty drinking. It is often worth waiting. However, if you wish to try now, it is already very attracive.

🔑 Cave coop. d'Azé, 71260 Azé, tel. 03.85.33.30.92, fax 03.85.33.37.21 ☑ Y ev. day 9am–12 noon 2pm–6.30pm

CAVE DE CHARNAY Charnay 1999

■ 2.3 ha 20,000 30–49 F

Ideal for a light lunch, no question. This is a deeply-coloured 99. The unpretentious nose should open out. The wine is characteristic but not complex, though it has the imprint of the terroir. Needs to age a little.

🔑 Cave de Charnay, En Condemine, 71850 Charnay-lès-Mâcon, tel. 03.85.34.54.24, fax 03.85.34.86.84 ☑ Y by appt.

DOM. ELOY Pierreclos 1999*

■ 1 ha n.c. 20–29 F

This archetypal Gamay smells of redcurrant and has an after-taste of muskiness. It is rustic, impertinent and pale in colour but hides more than it shows. Both the nose and palate present fruit that is quite supple. A wine to drink now. This 99 will have no time to get wrinkles.

🔑 Jean-Yves Eloy, Le Plan, 71960 Fuissé, tel. 03.85.35.67.03, fax 03.85.35.67.07 ☑ Y by appt.

MARIE-ODILE FREROT ET DANIEL DYON Etrigny 1999*

■ 0.8 ha 4,600 20–29 F

Etrigny, in the Tournus area, is at the northern crossroads of Mâcon, and the village is all vines and stones. This 99 has a good intense ruby colour and a delicate nose: a slight oakiness accompanies the fruity Gamay tones. A warm, characteristic wine that is balanced by agreeable tannins. Good length with a 'primeur' spirit: to drink in the next year.

🔑 Marie-Odile Frérot et Daniel Dyon, Veneuse, 71240 Etrigny, tel. 03.85.92.24.31, fax 03.85.92.24.31 ☑ Y by appt.

LES VIGNERONS D'IGE

Igé Elevé en fût de chêne 1999★

n.c. 9,000 30–49 F

The nose has finesse with aromas of red berry fruit and the palate is round, tannic and expansive. Fullness and warmth combine on the finish and it has great length. For a steak with shallots.

Cave coop. des Vignerons d'Igé, 71960 Igé, tel. 03.85.33.33.56, fax 03.85.33.41.85, e-mail lesvigneronsdige@lesvigneronsdige.com ev. day except Sun. 8am–12 noon 2pm–6pm

DOM. DE L'ABBE DUMONT 1999

0.17 ha 1,500 30–49 F

Only two rosés are considered worthy of being included here. This wine provides the excellent opportunity of visiting a presbytery that has a place in history and that has been converted into a vineyard (they also make goat's cheese). Raspberry, light, reeking of the terroir. Honest and not lacking in interest

Benoît Dorry, Bussières, 71960 Pierreclos, tel. 03.85.37.71.60, fax 03.85.37.71.97 ev. day 8am–8pm

CH. DE LA BRUYERE Igé 1998★

2 ha 6,500 20–29 F

Immediately appealing with its intense, deep colour. The nose holds back a little but has aromas of cherry and crystallised fruit. The wine is very mouth-filling and the tannins are strong but 'have a good finish', as one of the tasters commented. It will go well with meat dishes with sauce.

Paul-Henry Borie, Ch. de la Bruyère, 71960 Igé, tel. 03.85.33.30.72, fax 03.85.33.40.65, e-mail mph.borie@wanadoo.fr ev. day 8.30am–12 noon 2pm–7pm

DOM. LACHARME ET FILS

La Roche-Vineuse Sélection de vieilles vignes 1999★★

0.7 ha 4,300 30–49 F

A Gamay in all its splendour. It has a very striking, almost purple, colour. Blackcurrant on the nose. A gentle attack that follows through with a velvety, round palate with red berry fruit flavours. Superb balance. A significant length. La Roche-Vineuse is appropriately named.

Dom. Lacharme et Fils, Le Pied du Mont, 71960 La Roche-Vineuse, tel. 03.85.36.61.80, fax 03.85.37.77.02 by appt.

DOM. DE LA CREUZE NOIRE 1999★

0.94 ha 5,000 30–49 F

Its pale, brilliant colour proclaims pure Chardonnay. A full, spring blossom nose. Youthful freshness. A wine for a picnic – but don't forget the cooler bag.

Dominique et Christine Martin, La Creuze Noire, 71570 Leynes, tel. 03.85.37.46.43, fax 03.85.37.44.17 by appt.

DOM. DE LA FEUILLARDE

Prissé 1999★

1.7 ha 15,000 30–49 F

Since 1930, there have been three generations of women wine-makers here. Deep morello cherry in colour following on with a cherry nose crossed with musk. On the palate the Gamay reaches the fullest expression that it is capable of. A wine to drink in the next three years because it has some keeping qualities, and that is not so common in this appellation.

Lucien Thomas, Dom. de la Feuillarde, 71960 Prissé, tel. 03.85.34.54.45, fax 03.85.34.31.50 ev. day 8am–12 noon 1pm–7pm

DOM. DE LA SARAZINIERE

Bussières Les Devants Vieilles vignes 1998★

0.8 ha 5,000 30–49 F

Rich in character and with tannins. Uninspiring colour and you must go beyond the nose (discreet and vegetal) to appreciate its intensity. It is frank, clean and nervy and needs time in the cellar to settle down.

Philippe Trébignaud, Dom. de la Sarazinière, 71960 Bussières, tel. 03.85.37.76.04, fax 03.85.37.76.23, e-mail philippe.trebignaud@wanadoo.fr by appt.

DOM. NICOLAS MAILLET

Verzé 1999

0.2 ha 800 20–29 F

Clear, brilliant cherry hue with a nose showing very ripe strawberry. On the palate it is fresh and fruity. The estate left the neighbouring *coopérative* in 1999 to make its own way.

Nicolas Maillet, La Cure, 71960 Verzé, tel. 03.85.33.46.76, fax 03.85.33.46.76 by appt.

CAVE DES VIGNERONS DE MANCEY 1999

n.c. 13,000 30–49 F

'je vois la vie en rose.' This wine is pearly-pink in colour. It tickles the nose and explodes joyously on the palate. Round and rich with an acid-drop finish. A wine for grilled meat.

Cave des Vignerons de Mancey, R.N. 6, En Velnoux, 71700 Tournus, tel. 03.85.51.00.83, fax 03.85.51.71.20 by appt.

DOM. MATHIAS 1998

3 ha 20,000 30–49 F

Enough richness on the palate to set you dreaming. Perfect colour. The nose is apricot, honey and well-outlined. In a word, consistent. This wine is neither round nor very long but it plays its role convincingly.

Béatrice et Gilles Mathias, Dom. Mathias, rue Saint-Vincent, 71570 Chaintré, tel. 03.85.27.00.50, fax 03.85.27.00.52 by appt.

DOM. DE MONTERRAIN

Serrières 1999

■ 9 ha 40,000 30–49 F

Light as a feather and easy to drink. A wine with *joie de vivre*. It is not highly-coloured and the nose has a streak of wildness. Made to drink with all sorts of cold meats.

EARL Patrick et Martine Ferret, Dom. de Monterrain, 71960 Serrières, tel. 03.85.35.73.47, fax 03.85.35.75.36 by appt.

ALAIN NORMAND

La Roche-Vineuse 1998★

■ 3.5 ha 3,000 20–29 F

A quality wine showing all the virtues of Gamay. Well-balanced acidity and alcohol without any aggression. Mellow and attractive. This wine-producer, who came here in 1994, knows his subject.

Alain Normand, chem. de la Grange-du-Dîme, 71960 La Roche-Vineuse, tel. 03.85.36.61.69, fax 03.85.51.60.97 by appt.

PASCAL PAUGET 1998★

□ 1.3 ha 3,000 30–49 F

Yellow with glints of grey. The nose suggests over-ripeness, almost honey. On the palate, similar flavours along with some dried fruit. The wine is warm and has great length but you can detect traces of residual sugar. Hardly possible to see it accompanying anything but foie gras.

Pascal Pauget, La Croisette, 71700 Tournus, tel. 03.85.32.53.15, fax 03.85.51.72.67 by appt.

CAVE DE PRISSE-SOLOGNY-VERZE 1999

■ n.c. 25,000 30–49 F

Ruby with glints of violet. A Mâcon bobbing about on a wave of red berry fruit. Clean, simple, balanced and characteristic.

Cave de Prissé-Sologny-Verzé, 71960 Prissé, tel. 03.85.37.88.06, fax 03.85.37.61.76 by appt.

DOM. DE RUERE

Pierreclos Cuvée Prestige 1999★

■ 0.7 ha 6,000 20–29 F

A Gamay from vineyards planted on sandy soil. Garnet with hints of raspberry in colour. Its nose is almost exotic, even complex. It has sufficient structure, balance and power, and so cannot fail to improve over the next year. A wine for a roast.

Mme Thérèse Eloy, Ruère, 71960 Pierreclos, tel. 03.85.35.70.19, fax 03.85.35.70.19 by appt.

DOM. DU TERROIR DE JOCELYN

Bussières 1999

■ n.c. 5,000 20–29 F

Le terroir de Jocelyn – this recalls Lamartine's epic poem. The writer could not have anticipated appearing on so many labels . . . after so long. He is the only poet who does: there are 'Domaines Lamartine' in the whole of France but none called Musset or Victor Hugo. A ruby-garnet wine, tasting of blackcurrant and raspberry. It is vinous, fresh and fruity, rich and a little tannic on the finish. Peppery too. Lots of character.

Daniel et Annie Martinot, Les Fuchats, 71960 Bussières, tel. 03.85.36.65.05, fax 03.85.36.65.05 by appt.

Mâcon Supérieur

DOM. DU BICHERON 1998★

■ 1 ha 4,000 20–29 F

In general, Mâcon Supérieur showed well during this tasting. Witness this 98 with its cooked fruit aromas. However, it is straightforward on the palate and well-structured. The new generation, daughter and son, now run the estate.

Daniel Rousset, Dom. du Bicheron, Saint-Pierre-de-Lanques, 71260 Péronne, tel. 03.85.36.94.53, fax 03.85.36.99.80 by appt.

LA BUXYNOISE 1998★★

■ 24 ha 140,000 30–49 F

Mâcon Supérieur is a somewhat kitsch appellation, but sometimes it provokes deep emotions. Arresting to look at. Subtle perfumes. Something engaging in the body. Superior indeed. The co-operative wine-makers in Buxy produce a great deal, and it is very good!

Cave des vignerons de Buxy, Les Vignes de la Croix, 71390 Buxy, tel. 03.85.92.03.03, fax 03.85.92.08.06 ev. day except Sun. 9am–12 noon 2pm–6pm

LORON ET FILS 1999★★★

■ n.c. n.c. 30–49 F

Superior is not adequate. This is super-superior. A perfect, exemplary wine. Deep-coloured, fruity, powerful, intense, long and complex: genuine praise. This one can make an appearance at any celebration.

Ets Loron et Fils, Pontanevaux, 71570 La Chapelle-de-Guinchay, tel. 03.85.36.81.20, fax 03.85.33.83.19, e-mail vinloron@wanadoo.fr by appt.

DOM. THEUROT

Les Champaronds 1998★

■ n.c. 36,000 30–49 F

A nose that reminds us of strawberries bubbling away on the stove. On the palate there are notes of red berry fruit. This is a Pinot oir wine. Its chewy density is complex and ccessful.

Cie des Vins d'Autrefois, abbaye Saint-artin, 53, av. de l'Aigue, 21200 Beaune, . 03.80.26.33.00, fax 03.80.24.14.84, mail mallet.b@cva-beaune.fr 🍷 by appt.

Mâcon-Villages

AVE COOPERATIVE D'AZE

zé Cuvée Jules Richard 1998★

65 ha 7,500 30–49 F

All our respects to Jules Richard, the pillar the local *Cave Coopérative*. This is a gold-ated wine. The nose has mineral notes, most kely the imprint of the terroir. It has good oneyed, well-structured balance. A real wine quality.

Cave coop. d'Azé, 71260 Azé, l. 03.85.33.30.92, fax 03.85.33.37.21 ☑ 🍷 . day 9am–12 noon 2pm–6.30pm

DOM. ANDRE BONHOMME

iré Cuvée spéciale 1998★★

5 ha 40,000 30–49 F

The new AOC Viré-Clessé was only established in 1999, so this Mâcon-Viré will be of terest to label collectors. It is a slightly veet, heady wine with a slightly exotic richess (passion fruit). The oak flavours are not ominant. Ideal with a Bresse chicken in ream sauce.

Dom. André Bonhomme, Cidex 2108, 1260 Viré, tel. 03.85.33.11.86, ax 03.85.33.93.51 ☑ 🍷 ev. day 8am–8pm; un. by appt.

CUVEE PIERRE BONTEMPS 1998★

n.c. 50,000 30–49 F

A wine made by the Maison Patriarche in eaune. A somewhat reserved Mâcon though has both minerals and richness. Good keeping qualities but not for too long.

Patriarche Père et Fils, 5, rue du Collège, 1200 Beaune, tel. 03.80.24.53.01, ax 03.80.24.53.03 ☑ 🍷 ev. day 9am–2 noon 2pm–6pm

FRANCOIS BOURDON 1998★★

0.64 ha 3,500 30–49 F

Middling-gold but it makes sparks fly, ecause this is a *village* such as you do not rink every day. Flint and honey vie with each other, creating a universe of complexities. Yet here is a good deal in reserve. With such a great wine the wine-producer will soon be exporting to Japan with great success.

François Bourdon, Pouilly, 71960 Solutré-Pouilly, tel. 03.85.35.81.44, ax 03.85.35.81.44 ☑ 🍷 by appt.

CAVE DES VIGNERONS DE BUXY

Clos de Mont-Rachet 1998★

☐ 12 ha 80,000 30–49 F

If you are having a dinner party for friends who know a bit about wine and you are not sure what to serve with the starter, choose this wine without hesitation. This is the other Mont-Rachet, an authentic *lieu-dit* at Savigny-sur-Grosne which is also known for a famous cheese. Golden-yellow and white-fleshed fruit. It can age a little and the name game is amusing.

Cave des Vignerons de Buxy, Les Vignes de la Croix, 71390 Buxy, tel. 03.85.92.03.03, fax 03.85.92.08.06 ☑ 🍷 ev. day except Sun. 9am–12 noon 2pm–6pm

CH. DU CHARNAY 1999

☐ 7 ha 3,330 30–49 F

This château at Sologny had Lamartine as a neighbour. When the poet joked 'What does the sun matter', as a wine-grower himself, he knew perfectly well that without sun the harvest was meagre. The gold is perfect in this 99, the nose has finesse and the palate has perfect manners. A fine example of a lovely, characteristic wine.

Ch. du Charnay, 71960 Sologny, tel. 04.74.06.10.10, fax 04.74.66.13.77 ☑ 🍷 by appt.

DOM. DU CLOS GANDIN 1998★★

☐ 4 ha 6,000 30–49 F

'Hand-made harvest', is written in English on the label. A 98 that is a good example of the appellation. A contrast of intensity and delicacy: medium colour, a spring nose, and voluptuousness on the palate with almond, and finishing with a hint of appetising bitterness. So it will be very good as an apéritif.

Thierry Delorme, Dom. du Clos Gandin, La Cortière, 71700 Plottes-près-Chardonnay, tel. 03.85.40.50.89, fax 03.85.40.50.89 ☑ 🍷 ev. day 8am–8pm

COTEAUX DES CHENES ET CROIX JARRIER Verzé 1998★★

☐ 6.42 ha 40,000 30–49 F

The Cave Coopérative de Prissé has 884 ha (2,183 acres) of vines. This *cuvée* is very characteristic. Nothing to change in this 98 – perfect colour, great elegance on the nose with hints of hazelnuts. The palate follows on in the same vein as the nose, but with a certain added liveliness.

Cave de Prissé-Sologny-Verzé, 71960 Prissé, tel. 03.85.37.88.06, fax 03.85.37.61.76 ☑ 🍷 by appt.

DEMESSEY

Cruzille Les Avoueries 1998★

☐ 5 ha n.c. 50–69 F

Cruzille is on the 'Circuit des Brigands' described in the *Guide Bleu*. The château suffered at their hands in 1789. There is a little aggression in this wine that comes from a tiny flavour of acid-drops, though it is not at all

unpleasant. A beautifully-golden colour with a nose full of honey and hawthorn.
Demessey, Ch. de Messey, 71700 Ozenay, tel. 03.85.51.33.83, fax 03.85.51.33.82, e-mail vin@demessey.com ☑ Y by appt.
Marc Dumont

JACQUES DEPAGNEUX 1998

☐ n.c. 100,000 ▮ 30–49 F

More muslin than lace. This *négociant-éleveur* from Juliénas has ferreted out a *village* that is as gentle as an Easter lamb. It is pale gold, not very rich, somewhat light but it is extremely delicate. It melts in the mouth. Ideal as an apéritif.
Jacques Dépagneux, Les Chers, 69840 Juliénas, tel. 04.74.06.78.00, fax 04.74.06.78.71, e-mail avf@free.fr Y by appt.

MAISON DESVIGNES 1998★★

☐ n.c. 1,200 ▮ 30–49 F

Desvignes is a name that is respected in the Mâconnais. Greyish-gold, mineral, peach kernels, elegant; this is a remarkable 98. On the palate, sublime, does not overstate it. It is open, lovely, rich, unctuous and perfumed.
Maison Desvignes, rue Guillemet-Desvignes, 71570 La Chapelle-de-Guinchay, tel. 03.85.36.72.32, fax 03.85.36.74.02 ☑ Y by appt.

DOM. DES DEUX ROCHES 1998★

☐ 10 ha n.c. ▮ ♨ 50–69 F

Spring blossom, hints of aniseed then quince jelly and almond with an underlying mineral base . . . a perfumed garden. The palate continues in the same vein, round, unctuous and is similarly very attractive.
Dom. des Deux Roches, 71960 Davayé, tel. 03.85.35.86.51, fax 03.85.35.86.12 ☑ Y by appt.

GEORGES DUBŒUF 1999

☐ n.c. 120,000 ▮ ♨ 30–49 F

Pierre Albuisson, who designs the flowery labels for Georges Dubœuf, lives near Cluny. He also designs some of the most attractive stamps in the world. It is unusual for a label to be commissioned from a great artist. The wine is the colour it should be, lively and floral fresh with a pleasing attack and light as a feather but with length.
Vins Georges Dubœuf SA, quartier de la Gare, B.P. 12, 71570 Romanèche-Thorins, tel. 03.85.35.34.20, fax 03.85.35.34.25, e-mail mcvgd@csi.com ☑ Y ev. day 9am–6pm until Hameau en Beaujolais; cl. 1–15 Jan.

MICHEL FOREST Vergisson 1998★

☐ 0.3 ha 2,500 ⏸ 30–49 F

A typical example of a white Mâcon that will keep (a few years). The flavour of the wood needs to integrate and the slightly harsh character of the wine needs to soften. It is all the consequence of an attentive, meticulous vinification. The wine has not been made for early drinking.
Michel Forest, Les Crays, 71960 Vergisson, tel. 03.85.35.84.79, fax 03.85.35.86.14 ☑ Y by appt.

FORGEOT PERE ET FILS 1998

☐ n.c. n.c. ▮ ♨ 30–49

Forgeot is also Bouchard Père et Fils. pale gold wine with mineral and toasty arc mas. It is pure and clean with flavours c white-fleshed fruit. Lively and warm. Wel constructed but still closed. On the face of i it needs time.
Grands Vins Forgeot, 15, rue du Château, 21200 Beaune, tel. 03.80.24.80.50

DOM. GAILLARD 1998

☐ n.c. 1,500 ▮ 30–49 F

The very original label suggests real taste Abstract art to honour wine. This one doe not have great ambition, but it has integrity In colour it is not out to make a splash. Th nose with thyme and mint is developing wit caution. On the palate it is full with the dry ness of a well brought-up Chardonnay.
Roger Gaillard, Les Plantes, 71960 Davayé, tel. 03.85.35.83.31, fax 03.85.35.80.81 ☑ Y by appt.

DOM. DE LA BOFFELINE Azé 1998

☐ 1 ha 2,500 ▮

A wine to charm a squirrel! It smells s strongly of hazelnuts. It is pleasant on the eye and has a flowery nose. It runs out of steam towards the finish, but is a decent representative of the appellation.
Frédéric Lenormand, En Fourgeau, 71260 Azé, tel. 03.85.33.33.82, fax 03.85.33.33.82 ☑ Y ev. day 9am–12.30pm 2pm–7.30pm

DOM. DE LA CROIX SENAILLET Davayé 1998★

☐ 1.3 ha 7,000 ▮ ♨ 50–69 F

Wild rose takes turns with flint in a diverse aromatic array with real variety. The acidity gives contours to the palate which is faintly tinged with citrus fruit. It does not have tremendous length, but it has the full complement of charm. To accompany a fresh sheep's milk cheese from the region.
GAEC Richard et Stéphane Martin, Dom. de la Croix Sénaillet, En Coland, 71960 Davayé, tel. 03.85.35.82.83, fax 03.85.35.87.22 ☑ Y by appt.

DOM. DE LA DENANTE 1999★

☐ 1.5 ha 10,000 ▮ ♨ 30–49 F

A wine of character. The gold is quite pale and the nose expressive and even powerful. A tang of Muscat-like flavour adds attractiveness and charm, even refinement. Its extreme youth would explain any shortcomings.
Robert Martin, Les Peiguins, 71960 Davayé, tel. 03.85.35.82.88, fax 03.85.35.86.71 ☑ Y by appt.

DOM. DE LALANDE Chaintré 1998★

□ 1.5 ha 6,000 30–49 F

This estate has been handed down from generation to generation of wine-growers and coopers to the present one, who has been in charge for nearly twenty years. His Mâcon-Chaintré is dazzling gold. The nose is still very young and blossomy. On the palate it is reserved, but it has a solid body and could keep for two to three years.

Dominique Cornin, chem. du Roy-de-Croix, 71570 Chaintré, tel. 03.85.37.43.58, fax 03.85.37.43.58, e-mail dominique.cornin@fnac.net by appt.

DOM. MICHEL LAPIERRE

Solutré-Pouilly 1998★

□ 0.5 ha 4,500 30–49 F

The label reads Solutré-Pouilly, so Pouilly-Fuissé cannot be far away. This rich, supple and lively 98 resembles its famous neighbour a little. But it remains true to type and is an honest, gulping wine.

Michel Lapierre, 71960 Solutré-Pouilly, tel. 03.85.35.80.45, fax 03.85.35.87.61 by appt.

DOM. LA SOUFRANDISE

Fuissé Le Ronté 1998★★

□ 1 ha 6,000 30–49 F

Awarded a *coup de cœur*, and it is not from a new company with an uncertain future, but from a serious estate that receives regular plaudits and is often among the award-winners. Their 98 is remarkable again. Dark gold in colour. A superb citrus nose with honeysuckle, iris and crystallised fruit. The palate reveals a well-structured body. It is delicious and has great length.

Françoise et Nicolas Melin, EARL Dom. la Soufrandise, 71960 Fuissé, tel. 03.85.35.64.04, fax 03.85.35.65.57 by appt.

CH. DE LA TOUR DE L'ANGE 1999

□ 14 ha 90,000 30–49 F

The first prefect of the Saône-et-Loire, nominated by Napoleon I, was lord of this estate, which was apparently previously run by Claude Brosse (who made the whole court at Versailles drink the health of Mâcon). History oozes out of each vine and the wine is worthy of the story. Greenish-gold and fruity and to drink in the coming year.

SCE Ch. de la Tour de l'Ange, chem. du Bourg, 71850 Charnay-lès-Mâcon, tel. 03.85.34.96.67, fax 03.85.34.97.98, e-mail info@latourdelange.com by appt.

CH. DE LA TOUR PENET 1998★

□ n.c. n.c. 30–49 F

There is a touch of fizz. Sheer youthfulness with a degree of petulance. By now, this will have disappeared. The colour is stunning. The nose is hazelnut and honey. It lasts from the very first impression on the palate, right through to the finish.

Jacques Charlet, 71570 La Chapelle-de-Guinchay, tel. 03.85.36.82.41, fax 03.85.33.83.19

DOM. DES LEGERES Péronne 1999★★

□ n.c. n.c. 30–49 F

This newborn is already golden and does what a Chardonnay does best. Quince on the nose, it follows through with the same notes on the palate. Not very powerful but truly evocative of the melodious Mâconnais.

Véronique et Pierre Janny, La Condemine, 71260 Péronne, tel. 03.85.36.97.03, fax 03.85.36.96.58 by appt.

LES BRUYERES 1998★

□ 4 ha 25,000 30–49 F

Greyish-gold with a nose that has not yet much to say. It is fresh and clean with a touch of lemon. This young wine should not be disturbed. It will show its true colours in the next year or two.

Maurice Lapalus, Les Bruyères, 71960 Pierreclos, tel. 03.85.35.71.90, fax 03.85.35.71.90, e-mail lapalus.maurice@wanadoo.fr by appt.

DOM. ROGER LUQUET

Clos de Condemine 1998★★

□ 4.2 ha 35,000 30–49 F

Yellow colour with ripe fruit on the nose. No point in looking for anything complicated because this 98 already has what it takes. The palate is full with underlying mineral flavours that complete the picture. It could wait two or three years.

Dom. Roger Luquet, 71960 Fuissé, tel. 03.85.35.60.91, fax 03.85.35.60.12 ev. day except Sun. 8am–7pm

MARSON ET NATIER 1998★★

□ n.c. 40,000 30–49 F

This brand was created by Chauson about fifty years ago and 80% is exported (England, Germany and Japan). These countries are lucky to have such a good wine. It is pale gold. On the palate there is virtually a limitless mineral finesse. A stunning wine.

Marson et Natier, 10, rue du Collège, 21200 Beaune, tel. 03.80.25.97.96, fax 03.80.24.17.42

P. MISSEREY 1998★

□ n.c. 30,000 50–69 F

Misserey at Nuits Saint-Georges (the Lanvin family) has close connections in the

BURGUNDY

Mâconnais and a good address book. This 98 Chardonnay with its greenness is attired like a young cavalry officer. It is a good mouthful, very characteristic and, like a warm spring breeze, it will make your heart dance.
🗝 Maison P. Misserey, 3, rue des Seuillets, B.P. 10, 21701 Nuits-Saint-Georges Cedex, tel. 03.80.61.07.74, fax 03.80.61.31.40 ☑ Y by appt.

DOM. PHILIPPE Vieilles vignes 1998*

☐ 2 ha 12,000 30–49 F

This is an unpretentious wine and should be drunk now. It has an appealing nose of honeysuckle and very ripe fruit. On the palate it is round and rich as it should be, and fairly easy-going.
🗝 Jean-Claude et Corinne Philippe, Chapotin Cidex 2163, 71260 Viré, tel. 03.85.33.90.91, fax 03.85.33.90.91 Y ev. day 9am–7.30pm

DOM. SAINT-PHILIBERT

Loché 1998

☐ 1.05 ha n.c. 30–49 F

Simple and in good taste. A grey-gold wine with a pleasurable perfume of wild rose. Freshness from start to finish. Supple attack then some bite. It is robust but still has breeding.
🗝 Philippe Bérard, Dom. Saint-Philibert, 71000 Loché, tel. 04.78.43.24.96, fax 04.78.35.90.87, e-mail berard-loche@wanadoo.fr ☑ Y by appt.

RAPHAEL ET GERARD SALLET

Chardonnay Dom. de l'Arfentière 1998*

☐ 0.54 ha 4,800 30–49 F

A 4 m (13 ft) high statue of Saint Vincent was carved out of cedar. It would be good to taste this wine with a portion of brioche. Deep yellow in colour it has freshness and liveliness. It is tasty, full of flavour yet subtle at the same time. An aperitif wine.
🗝 EARL R. et G. Sallet, rte de Chardonnay, 71700 Uchizy, tel. 03.85.40.50.45, fax 03.85.40.58.05 ☑ Y by appt.

DOM. SAUMAIZE-MICHELIN

Les Sertaux 1998*

☐ 1 ha 4,500 30–49 F

Still very, very young. It would be good to try this again in a year or two but its golden yellow entices you to try now. The nose is very ripe nectarine with an oakiness that needs taming. The acidity is still in its adolescence. We look forward to tasting it again a little later.
🗝 Roger et Christine Saumaize, Dom. Saumaize-Michelin, Le Martelet, 71960 Vergisson, tel. 03.85.35.84.05, fax 03.85.35.86.77 ☑ Y by appt.

GERALD ET PHILIBERT TALMARD

Chardonnay Cuvée Joseph Talmard 1998*

☐ 6 ha 36,000 30–49 F

Chardonnay by Chardonnay – as you would say of a perfume, Molinart by Molinart. Buttercup colour. Intense and complex on the nose. It has a superb structure which is finely woven. Ideal for dishes with cream sauces, because it has enough richness.
🗝 Dom. Gérald et Philibert Talmard, rue des Fosses, 71700 Uchizy, tel. 03.85.40.53.18, fax 03.85.40.53.52, e-mail gerald.talmard@wanadoo.fr ☑ Y by appt.

DOM. DU TERROIR DE JOCELYN

Bussières 1999*

☐ 3 ha 6,000 30–49 F

This 99 sticks to its principles, harsh but already showing signs of maturity. It is agreeable and shows a harmony with no obvious faults but should not be hurried. Needs to be allowed time to develop in the bottle.
🗝 Daniel et Annie Martinot, Les Fuchats, 71960 Bussières, tel. 03.85.36.65.05, fax 03.85.36.65.05 ☑ Y by appt.

DOM. THIBERT PERE ET FILS

Prissé En Chailloux 1999***

☐ 1.3 ha 9,000 30–49 F

After training in a winery in New Zealand, the daughter of the business came home. Her first vintage (99) is awarded a *coup de cœur*: a good start. The wine is very soft golden yellow in colour. It is particularly successful and enchants the taste buds. Blackberry buds and violet contribute to the unusual nose. A very aromatic wine with an extraordinarily fresh fruitiness on the length. A worthy accompaniment for seafood in a pastry case. In addition, the jury awarded one star to the **Mâcon-Fuissé 99**.
🗝 Dom. Thibert Père et Fils, Au Bourg, 71960 Fuissé, tel. 03.85.35.61.79, fax 03.85.35.66.21, e-mail domthibe@club-internet.fr ☑ Y by appt.

DOM. DES VALANGES

Davayé 1999*

☐ 0.5 ha 4,500 30–49 F

An exotic cruise: the aromas of mango and pomegranate come from far-away islands. A

…e yellow with an intense concentration of …omas that follow through onto the palate, …d continue right to the fiinish. It has prom… but it should wait a little before being …ved with matured goat's cheese.
… Michel Paquet, Les Valanges, 71960 …vayé, tel. 03.85.35.85.03, … 03.85.35.86.67, e-mail …mainedesvalanges@wanadoo.fr ☑ Ῑ by …pt.

…HANTAL ET DOMINIQUE …AUPRE

…lutré 1998★★

0.5 ha 4,500 30–49 F

…Thomas Wolfe wrote, 'There are people …o have had riches and joy and are able to …mmunicate them to everyone they meet'. …e same is true of some wines, such as this …e. It sparkles and has aromas hinting at …den flower and verbena. Superb, with …thentic breeding and very rich. It deserves …ea fish, particularly red mullet.
… Dominique Vaupré, Au Bourg, 71960 …lutré-Pouilly, tel. 03.85.35.85.67, … 03.85.35.86.63 ☑ Ῑ by appt.

…OM. DU VIEUX PUITS 1998★★

1.8 ha 8,000 30–49 F

A bottle you would like to open with …ends. An intensely flavoured yet subtle wine …at gives the impression that it is produced …om a small yield. Discretely-coloured and …ually lemon, mineral and flowery. A …âcon-Villages to the end.
… Corinne et Thierry Drouin, Le Grand …é, 71960 Vergisson, tel. 03.85.35.84.36, …x 03.85.35.86.84 ☑ Ῑ by appt.

Viré-Clessé

Viré-Clessé is a new …ppellation, created as recently as 4 …ovember 1998, and has solid …mbitions for its white wines. The …rea of the appellation is 552 ha …1,363 acres), 401.6 (992 acres) of …hich are currently planted with …ines. The current denominations …lâcon-Viré and Mâcon-Clessé will …isappear in 2002.

…OM. ANDRE BONHOMME

…ieilles vignes 1998

☐ 2 ha 10,000 50–69 F

The vines are more than sixty years old, …0% new oak. This is where it starts. The …ood contributes toasty, scorched, smoky fla…ours. A lovely gold colour with hints of …nden flower, this wine opens out to reveal soft exotic aromas. A wine to lull you rather than challenge you to an adventure.
Dom. André Bonhomme, Cidex 2108, 71260 Viré, tel. 03.85.33.11.86, fax 03.85.33.93.51 ☑ Ῑ ev. day 8am–8pm; Sun. by appt.

DOM. LES COMBELIERES 1998

☐ n.c. n.c. 30–49 F

Deep gold. Slightly menthol aromas with white peaches. It is pleasant to drink and with its Muscat-like note it would be a perfect apéritif.
Prosper Maufoux, pl. du Jet-d'Eau, 21590 Santenay, tel. 03.80.20.60.40, fax 03.80.20.63.26 ☑ Ῑ by appt.

DOM. LES COMBELIERES 1998★

☐ 8 ha 6,000 30–49 F

This relatively young appellation needs wines like this to give it a good start in life. A warmly-coloured wine with floral and vegetal aromas – this Chardonnay is generosity itself. Toasted almonds, a trace of bitterness, an interesting finish all add up to a good wine. To enjoy with a Mâconnais goat's cheese.
EARL Claudius Rongier et Fils, rue du Mur, 71260 Clessé, tel. 03.85.36.94.05, fax 03.85.36.94.05 ☑ Ῑ by appt.

DOM. DU MONT EPIN

Vieilles vignes 1998

☐ 3.5 ha 6,000 50–69 F

A generous wine but very mature. It is very rich and has an immense character and body where you can detect traces of cooked fruit. Dazzling gold. The nose has a few blossomy tones. A creamy fish dish would be an ideal companion.
Jean-Claude Terrier, Briconnat, 71260 Clessé, tel. 03.85.36.93.85, fax 03.85.36.98.78 ☑ Ῑ by appt.

DOM. PHILIPPE 1998★

☐ 3 ha 13,300 30–49 F

This wine-grower belonged to the Cave coopérative until 1997, when he set up independently. His 98 is more dark yellow than soft gold but it is extremely bright. Lilac and mint enhance the nose, which is certaily not lacking in personality. Lots of horsepower under the bonnet: A powerful wine with attractive fruit. It would probably go well with a pike from the Saône.
Jean-Claude et Corinne Philippe, Chapotin Cidex 2163, 71260 Viré, tel. 03.85.33.90.91, fax 03.85.33.90.91 ☑ Ῑ ev. day 9am–7.30pm

RIJCKAERT L'Epinet 1998

☐ 1.3 ha 10,500 70–99 F

A wine-grower and merchant based in Leynes. The name recalls the fact that Flanders once belonged to Burgundy. Pale gold and a distinctly oaky wine that will please fans of this style. There is honey and beeswax as well. It is unctuous and still has a lot of tricks in its hand to play as it opens out.

🔑 Rijckaert, Correaux, 71570 Leynes, tel. 03.85.35.15.09, fax 03.85.35.15.09 ☒ 𝐓 by appt.

CAVE DE VIRE Cuvée spéciale 1999★★

☐ 100 ha 70,000 ▮ 🌡 30-49 F

One star for the **Grande Réserve 99 Blanc**. It is fresh and honeyed but has yet to fully express itself. A commendation for the *cuvée* **Prestige 98 Blanc**, which is very oaky but has class, and this one, the Cuvée Spéciale 99, with a simple white label. It is a promising wine, gold in colour with an apricot nose. It is lively in its youthfulness. A well-balanced, long palate. This is undoubtedly the best.

🔑 Cave de Viré, En Vercheron, 71260 Viré, tel. 03.85.32.25.50, fax 03.85.32.25.55, e-mail cavedevin@wanadoo.fr ☒ 𝐓 ev. day 8am–12 noon 2pm–6pm

Pouilly-Fuissé

The cliffs of Solutré and Vergisson stretch proudly towards the sky like the prows of two great ships; at their feet lies the most prestigious vineyard of the Mâconnais, Pouilly-Fuissé, stretching over the communes of Fuissé, Solutré-Pouilly, Vergisson and Chaintré. Production reached a total of 44,306 hl (1,169,678 gal) in 1999.

The wines from Pouilly have achieved a very substantial reputation, particularly in the export market, and from a price point of view they have always competed with Chablis. The wines are lively, aromatically flavoured and perfumed. Matured in oak barrels, they develop the characteristic flavours of grilled almond or hazelnut as they age.

AUVIGUE-BURRIER-REVEL Vieilles vignes 1998★★

☐ n.c. 7,000 ⏸ 70-99 F

Jean-Pierre Auvigue runs this wine merchant business and presents here two superb wines. The **Chailloux 98** from Solutré gains one star. It is lemon-yellow with dried flowers and pineapple on the nose, and is direct and quite round. On the finish the same aromas return dripping with honey. This *coup de cœur* reeks of the terroir; it is exceptionally classy.

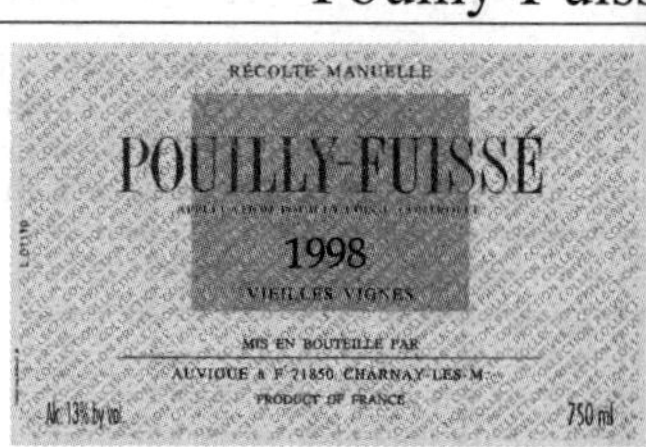

Acacia flowers, hazelnut, toasted almon a fine attack that expands on the palate ar follows through to a complex finish.

🔑 Auvigue-Burrier-Revel, Le Moulin-du-Pont, 71850 Charnay-lès-Mâcon, tel. 03.85.34.17.36, fax 03.85.34.75.88, e-mail vins-auvigue@wanadoo.fr ☒ 𝐓 by appt.

🔑 Michel Auvigue

CH. DE BEAUREGARD 1998★

☐ 10 ha n.c. ▮ ⏸ 🌡 70-99

We are in the heart of Lamartine countr so we were quite lyrical about this wine. It attractive with its shades of yellow and i vegetal and floral aromas. It also has a nc unpleasant touch of over-ripeness. Youthf but with some roundness too. Also wort mentioning, **La Maréchaude 98**, with th same mark. The estate was established in 181 and Frédéric-Marc Burrier has now take over.

🔑 Joseph Burrier, Ch. de Beauregard, 71960 Fuissé, tel. 03.85.35.60.76, fax 03.85.35.66.04, e-mail josephburrier@mageos.com ☒ 𝐓 by appt.

CLOS DE LA CHAPELLE 1998★★

☐ 0.4 ha 1,600 ⏸ 100-149

Catherine and Pascal Rollet have been her for nearly twenty years. They originally raise Charolais beef. When they came here the were determined to restore the estate to it previous fame, and they did. We enjoyed th *cuvée* **Vieilles Vignes 98** (one star – 70–89F which is very typically lightly oaked. It i pleasant and can be served for the next thre or four years. Then there is this **Clos de l Chappelle**: honey and toasted bread, rich warm, well-structured and full of promise.

🔑 Pascal Rollet, hameau de Pouilly, 71960 Solutré-Pouilly, tel. 03.85.35.81.51, fax 03.85.35.86.43 ☒ 𝐓 by appt.

CLOS DU MARTELET 1998

☐ 0.9 ha 5,000 ▮ ⏸ 🌡 70-99 F

Michelle Galley-Golliard has a foothold ir Morey and Chambolle and another here or the slopes of the Roche de Vergisson. His 98 shows deftness and skill. Pale yellow, butte and spring blossom showing on the discree nose. It gradually opens out with a mellow oakiness.

🔑 Michelle Galley-Golliard, Le Tremblay, 71250 Cluny, tel. 03.85.59.11.58, fax 03.85.59.21.46 ☒ 𝐓 by appt.

'HRISTIAN COLLOVRAY ET :AN-LUC TERRIER 1998★★

n.c. 8,000 70–99 F

This fiddle plays a very good Chardonnay ne. It is elegant, well-bred and achieves a rtain subtlety. It is delicately-coloured with pretty floral composition on the nose. The ine comes from a vineyard that is quite high ı the slopes under the Roche de Vergisson. It st missed out on a *coup de cœur.*

Collovray-Terrier, Vins des Personnets, 960 Davayé, tel. 03.85.35.86.51, x 03.85.35.86.12 by appt.

OM. CORDIER PERE ET FILS

ieilles vignes 1998★★

2.5 ha 15,000 100–149 F

Vers Cras and **Vers Pouilly 98** (150–199F) e excellent guides for discovering the quali- es of the cru. All the same, we prefered the *ivée* Vieilles Vignes. Brimming with bright old. A citrus fruit nose with some toastiness. hen a great, subtle depth of flavours (rich- ess, beeswax). Worth keeping. To try with esh foie gras or any other great dish.

Dom. Cordier Père et Fils, 71960 Fuissé, l. 03.85.35.62.89, fax 03.85.35.64.01 y appt.

)OM. MICHEL DELORMET

ır la Roche 1998★★

0.56 ha 4,000 50–69 F

A utilitarian label. It simply depicts a typi- al Mâconnais house in Vergisson where, with our guide in your pocket, you will be made ery welcome. This is a particularly well- ıade Pouilly-Fuissé with attractive intensity. rich, powerful, complex wine, both bal- nced and long. It should be left in the cellar or two years and drunk within five to six ears.

Dom. Michel Delorme, Le Bourg, 71960 'ergisson, tel. 03.85.35.84.50, ıx 03.85.35.84.50 by appt.

:ORINNE ET THIERRY DROUIN

'ieilles vignes Vinifié en fût de chêne 1998★★

0.1 ha 1,600 70–99 F

Very clean, very lively, very well- tructured, very . . . well, very everything. 'ery brilliant. Very pears and quinces. Very ich. Very softened. Very rich. Very long. It vill be at its best for one to three years. ?emarkably well-vinified.

Corinne et Thierry Drouin, Le Grand 'ré, 71960 Vergisson, tel. 03.85.35.84.36, ax 03.85.35.86.84 by appt.

;EORGES DUBŒUF 1997

n.c. 40,000 50–69 F

If Georges Dubœuf were not here, there vould be something missing. The Pope of Beaujolais is the Cardinal of Mâconnais. This vine is dressed in gold and presents vanilla on he nose. Chicken with morels will be the ideal lish for it in a year or two.

Vins Georges Dubœuf SA, quartier de la Gare, B.P. 12, 71570 Romanèche-Thorins, tel. 03.85.35.34.20, fax 03.85.35.34.25, e-mail mcvgd@csi.com ev. day 9am–6pm until Hameau en Beaujolais; cl. 1–15 Jan.

DOM. DUTRON 1998

n.c. 15,000 70–99 F

Almost impossible to find a greater classic. Bronzed gold, with aromas tending to the exotic and mango. A classic, but perhaps, more precisely, a neo-classic. It is fresh and fruity, with a touch of pear-drop on the palate, not particularly well-structured, but it is a pleasure to drink. The finish is still somewhere in the Antilles; travel broadens the mind.

Cie des Vins d'Autrefois, Abbaye Saint-Martin, 53, av. de l'Aigue, 21200 Beaune, tel. 03.80.26.33.00, fax 03.80.24.14.84, e-mail mallet.b@cva-beaune.fr by appt.

Jean-Pierre Nie

DOM. ELOY 1998★★

1 ha 1,200 50–69 F

Jean-Yves Eloy has been running this estate since 1987. His galleried house is typical of the architecture in the region. The wine is complete in all departments, as perfect as Cluny or Paray-le-Monial, but it is not under starters orders yet and should not be hurried – it has all the time in the world. Golden colour, lemon on the nose, it jumps the first hurdles with ease. On the palate it is something else; it's a winner from the attack right through to the finish. Perfect.

Jean-Yves Eloy, Le Plan, 71960 Fuissé, tel. 03.85.35.67.03, fax 03.85.35.67.07 by appt.

CH. FUISSE Les Combettes 1998★★

2 ha 3,500 100–149 F

The question is often asked whether Pouilly-Fuissé will be awarded any Premier Crus. Opinion is divided in the region but it needs to be discussed seriously. Not least because a *climat* such as this produces a wine with its own personality. A Les Combettes easily equals some of its relations on the Côte-de-Beaune. The golden colour, and honeyed aromas give the wine great charm and character, and it will keep well.

SC Ch. de Fuissé, 71960 Fuissé, tel. 03.85.35.61.44, fax 03.85.35.67.34, e-mail jean-jacques.vincent@wanadoo.fr by appt.

Jean-Jacques Vincent

ROGER GAILLARD Les Crays 1998★

n.c. 1,000 50–69 F

Pale old-gold; fresh walnut and lemon, peach and spring blossom contribute to the seductive nose. The wine isn't very rich but is very characteristic and characterful. A wine to drink with frogs' legs from the Dombes.

Roger Gaillard, Les Plantes, 71960 Davayé, tel. 03.85.35.83.31, fax 03.85.35.80.81 by appt.

DOM. DES GERBEAUX

Aux Chailloux 1998★

☐	n.c.	600	50–69 F

This is a small parcel of vineyard at Pouilly harvested using the traditional wine crates. A green-gold Chardonnay that is clean on the palate with notes of blossom and hazelnut, and finishing with a lively, inviting, spicy note. Failing that, the **Vieilles Vignes Terroir de Solutré 99** has a future, then again, there is the **Terroir Pouilly et Fuissé Vieilles Vignes 99** which has better balance and should be worth two stars next year.

Béatrice et Jean-Michel Drouin, Dom. des Gerbeaux, 71960 Solutré-Pouilly, tel. 03.85.35.80.17, fax 03.85.35.87.12 by appt.

DOM. GONON Vieilles vignes 1998

☐	0.4 ha	5,000	50–69 F

Generally, a Pouilly is expected to have more richness than this, however, this wine will be delicious in a year or two. Light lemon colour, ripe lemon on the nose and a freshness that is appealing. It slides down easily. A river trout would be ideal with it.

Dom. Gonon, 71960 Vergisson, tel. 03.85.37.78.42, fax 03.85.37.77.14 by appt.

CAVE DES GRANDS CRUS BLANCS 1998

☐	4.42 ha	30,000	50–69 F

The cave de Vinzelles vinifies grapes from 134 ha (331 acres), of which 4.4 ha (11 acres) are Pouilly-Fuissé. It is minerally and toasty, very open and mouth-filling, well-made with a delicate structure.

Cave des Grands Crus Blancs, 71680 Vinzelles, tel. 03.85.35.61.88, fax 03.85.35.60.43 by appt.

LOUIS JADOT

Le Mont de Pouilly Vieilli en fût de chêne 1998

☐	n.c.	36,000	100–149 F

Grey-gold with a very attractive nose that starts with lemon and develops towards white-fleshed fruit and toasted almonds. The quality oak and mineral notes suggest a wait of about two years, which will give it time for its uneven temperament to settle down. It will keep its best quality, freshness, without a doubt.

Maison Louis Jadot, 21, rue Eugène-Spuller, 21200 Beaune, tel. 03.80.22.10.57, fax 03.80.22.56.03, e-mail contact@louisjadot.com by appt.

DOM. DE LA CREUZE NOIRE

Le Clos de Monsieur Noly 1997

☐	2.35 ha	5,000	50–69 F

Le Clos de Monsieur Noly is a classic hereabouts. Lucky man to be commemorated by such a good wine. Almond and honey aromas, well-structured, a little upfront, quite oaky and with a hint of bitterness on the finish that is common in the majority of Chardonnays. Ready to be served. Ideal for salmon wit sorrel.

Dominique et Christine Martin, La Creuze Noire, 71570 Leynes, tel. 03.85.37.46.43, fax 03.85.37.44.17 by appt.

DOM. DE LA CROIX SENAILLET

1998★

☐	0.17 ha	1,300	70–99

Yellow gold with shade of straw, it show already the extent of its potential. It has a expressive and complex nose with dried flowers and crystallised fruit which suggest mor to come. On the palate it is first and foremos fruity. Rich, full and heavenly.

GAEC Richard et Stéphane Martin, Dom. de la Croix Sénaillet, En Coland, 71960 Davayé, tel. 03.85.35.82.83, fax 03.85.35.87.22 by appt.

DOM. DE LA FEUILLARDE

Vieilles vignes 1998★★

☐	0.5 ha	3,000	50–69 F

Not highly-coloured, but it deserves praise for its typical character. Blossom aromas follow through on the palate, which is very intense, expressive and long. It is dry as a Pouilly-Fuissé should be and a bench mark.

Lucien Thomas, Dom. de la Feuillarde, 71960 Prissé, tel. 03.85.34.54.45, fax 03.85.34.31.50 ev. day 8am–12 noon 1pm–7pm

DOM. LAPIERRE Vieilles vignes 1998

☐	0.3 ha	2,000	70–99 F

The wine has developed somewhat is but is nicely golden with honeyed and toasty aromas. It has a good balance between softness and acidity but falls away abruptly on the finish – La Roche de Solutré does not encourage you to do things in half measures.

Michel Lapierre, 71960 Solutré-Pouilly, tel. 03.85.35.80.45, fax 03.85.35.87.61 by appt.

DOM. LA SOUFRANDISE

Vieilles vignes 1998★

☐	3.5 ha	16,000	70–99 F

A former leper colony, La Soufrandise is the masterpiece of a soldier of Napoleon's Old Guard. This 98 is arrayed in a golden yellow uniform. Honey and hawthorn do the honours. There is the slightest hint of over-ripe fruit (possibly pear). It is clean, balanced and upright but very rich, even corpulent and calls for a fish dish with cream.

Françoise et Nicolas Melin, EARL Dom. la Soufrandise, 71960 Fuissé, tel. 03.85.35.64.04, fax 03.85.35.65.57 by appt.

DOM. PASCAL ET MIREILLE RENAUD Cuvée aux Chailloux 1998★

☐	0.4 ha	2,300	50–69 F

This *climat* at Solutré has a fine reputation. A lovely, brilliant, pale gold colour. The nose is curranty, and the wine has well-balanced ichness and acidity though it lacks length. Good for a dinner in Paris: indeed the vineyard used to belong to the wife of Edouard Balladur, a former Prime Minister. They were married at Saint-Amour.

Dom. Pascal Renaud, Pouilly, 71960 Solutré-Pouilly, tel. 03.85.35.84.62, fax 03.85.35.87.42 by appt.

MICHEL REY Les Crays 1998★

☐ 0.12 ha n.c. 70–99 F

Michel Rey presented a **Cuvée Vieilles Vignes Les Charmes 98** which is easy drinking now. His Les Crays should be kept for some time because it is still tannic and closed, in spite of the hints of blossom and honey and its toasty background. Its qualities are evident nonetheless. To drink in five to ten years, which is is rare for a Pouilly-Fuissé.

Michel Rey, Le Repostère, 71960 Vergisson, tel. 03.85.35.85.78, fax 03.85.35.87.91 by appt.

Burrier

DOM. DU ROURE DE PAULIN 1998★

☐ 1.1 ha 4,000 70–99 F

Impossible to resist this wine, with its golden colour and its touch of the exotic on the nose. It opens up rapidly on the palate and is lively as well as round.

Jean-Claude du Roure, 71960 Fuissé, tel. 03.85.35.65.48, fax 03.85.35.68.50 by appt.

JACQUES SAUMAIZE Vieilles vignes 1998★★

☐ 0.9 ha 4,000 70–99 F

This full, rich, perfumed wine explains why the Americans are crazy about Pouilly-Fuissé. It is a giant of a wine, velevty and full of character and it craftily hides its aces up its sleeve. The nose has honeysuckle, wild rose, vanilla and citrus fruit, and rolls found your tongue like a roulette wheel. A winner with a *coup de cœur.*

Jacques et Nathalie Saumaize, Les Bruyères, 71960 Vergisson, tel. 03.85.35.82.14, fax 03.85.35.87.00 by appt.

DOM. SAUMAIZE-MICHELIN Clos sur la Roche 1998★★

☐ 1.59 ha 9,000 70–99 F

A white-gold wine with aromas of toasted bread touched with acacia – all in moderation. It is heady, full and assertive like one of the best 98s, so much so that it was considered for a *coup de cœur*. The *climat* recalls the Roche de Vergisson, the twin sister of the Roche de Solutré. Also worth mentioning, the **Les Ronchevats 98**, as well as the **Vigne Blanche 98**, both of which strongly appealed to our tasting panel and were both awarded one star.

Dom. Roger et Christine Saumaize-Michelin, Le Martelet, 71960 Vergisson, tel. 03.85.35.84.05, fax 03.85.35.86.77 by appt.

DOM. DES TROIS TILLEULS 1999★

☐ 6 ha 36,000 50–69 F

The 99s are like an express train flashing by that you don't think you can stop. There are in fact four, not three Tilleuls, near Solutré. This minerally wine is still closed but it has vim and bounce and could well have a surprisingly good future stretching far ahead of it.

Paul Beaudet, rue Paul-Beaudet, 71570 Pontanevaux, tel. 03.85.36.72.76, fax 03.85.36.72.02, e-mail paulbeaudet@compuserve.com ev. day except Sat. Sun. 8am–12 noon 1.30pm–5.30pm; cl. Aug.

VESSIGAUD Vers Pouilly 1998★

☐ 0.4 ha 2,500 70–99 F

From its original label, you might imagine a wine of exemplary discretion. This is not the case. Its personality is not that reserved: there are strong aromas (grapefruit, pear and linden flower) and a soft, supple, pleasant mouth.

Dom. Vessigaud Père et Fils, hameau de Pouilly, 71960 Solutré-Pouilly, tel. 03.85.35.81.18, fax 03.85.35.84.29 by appt.

DOM. DES VIEILLES PIERRES La Roche Vieilles vignes 1998★★

☐ 0.36 ha 2,000 70–99 F

It is Pouilly-Fuissé through and through. The grapes are picked when fully ripe producing this supreme example of a southern Chardonnay. Perfection.

Jean-Jacques Litaud, Les Nembrets, 71960 Vergisson, tel. 03.85.35.85.69, fax 03.85.35.86.26 by appt.

Pouilly-Loché and Pouilly-Vinzelles

These small appellations in the communes of Loché and Vinzelles are much less well-known than their neighbour. They produce wines of the same style as Pouilly-Fuissé, though perhaps with a little less body. Only white wines are produced; in 1999, Loché made 1,764 hl (46,570 gal) and Vinzelles 2,830 hl (74,712 gal).

Pouilly-Loché

DOM. DU CHATEAU DE LOCHE 1998

□ n.c. 15,000 70–99 F

The Nuits-Saint-Georges firm of Misserey (Lanvin) is intimately acquainted with this estate. The pale wine doesn't reveal itself until it reaches the palate, which is lively, fruity and a little complex– somewhere between citrus fruit and quince. Ideally we would prefer it to be fuller and longer. That's the way it is.

Maison P. Misserey, 3, rue des Seuillets, B.P. 10, 21701 Nuits-Saint-Georges Cedex, tel. 03.80.61.07.74, fax 03.80.61.31.40 by appt.

DOM. CORDIER PERE ET FILS 1998★★

□ 0.45 ha 1,800 70–99 F

A famous Fuissé estate. This Pouilly-Loché, which is at its peak, says everything: yellow gold shaded with bronze, quince and caramel aromas and good grip on the palate. Well-measured tannins giving a glimpse of hidden riches, it has remarkable complexity.

Dom. Cordier Père et Fils, 71960 Fuissé, tel. 03.85.35.62.89, fax 03.85.35.64.01 by appt.

ALAIN DELAYE 1998

□ 0.98 ha 6,500 50–69 F

Alain Delaye's cellar is a convivial place. He has produced a Loché with hints of almond and blossom and a clear colour. A wine with character. Throughout the palate, the thread is light yet lively. Very much a super model.

Alain Delaye, Les Mûres, 71000 Loché, tel. 03.85.35.61.63, fax 03.85.35.61.63 by appt.

DOM. GIROUX Au Bûcher 1998★

□ 1 ha 5,000 30–49 F

The Loché appellation at Pouilly was practically non-existant for a long time. Various producers have become interested in it now, which is all to the good. This is one of them. The structure of his 98 shows blossomy aromas to begin with, then follows on with citrus fruits. A wine that is very representative of the Cru, here it is more robust than fresh.

Yves Giroux, Les Molards, 71960 Fuissé, tel. 03.85.35.63.64, fax 03.85.32.90.08 by appt.

CAVE DES GRANDS CRUS BLANCS Les Mûres 1998★★

□ 2.89 ha 15,000 50–69 F

This Loché just missed a *coup de cœur*. It is a musical promenade starting with fine, elegant chords. However, the ensemble is like a triumphal march. Good, spicy finish and a fruity encore.

Cave des Grands Crus Blancs, 71680 Vinzelles, tel. 03.85.35.61.88, fax 03.85.35.60.43 by appt.

DOM. SAINT-PHILIBERT Clos des Rocs 1997★★

□ 2.37 ha n.c. 50–69 F

This is the summit. Sovereign gold. The nose opens with hawthorn then hazelnut. Not unusual, but on the palate it makes up for lost time with interest. Attack, structure, acidity and length, it has it all. Better to drink while the freshness lasts rather than waiting too long.

Philippe Bérard, Dom. Saint-Philibert, 71000 Loché, tel. 04.78.43.24.96, fax 04.78.35.90.87, e-mail berard-loche@wanadoo.fr by appt.

Pouilly Vinzelles

DOM. DES CLOSAILLES Vieilles vignes 1997★★

□ 3.5 ha 8,000 30–49 F

This Vinzelles is mainly produced at the château. It is stunningly golden and the nose is lively with well-judged oak. It has the body of a greek god. There is a trace of bitterness on the finish. They are all like this. The next vintage, **98 Élevé en Cuve** totals bottles; it has very good staying power and is awarded the same mark.

Dom. des Closailles, 71680 Vinzelles, tel. 03.85.35.63.49, fax 03.85.35.67.40 by appt.

DOM. DE FUSSIACUS 1998

☐ 0.35 ha 2,600 50–69 F

The name of the estate might suggest origins going back to the relatives of Astérix and Obélix. This has the colour of gold cloth. Toasty on the nose but not masking the fruit. A discreet wine that is pleasant and easy to drink.

Jean-Paul Paquet, 71960 Fuissé, tel. 03.85.35.63.65, fax 03.85.35.67.50 by appt.

CH. DE LAYE 1998

☐ 11.72 ha 15,000 50–69 F

Gilbert Cornier has just succeeded Michel Moreau as president of the *Cave*. There are one hundred members with 136 ha (336 acres) including 16.5 ha (41 acres) of this Cru. This Château de Layé 98 is up to par: you can rely on it just as Thomas Jefferson once did, during his stay, when he drank the wine like a true connoisseur.

Cave des Grands Crus Blancs, 71680 Vinzelles, tel. 03.85.35.61.88, fax 03.85.35.60.43 by appt.

DOM. MATHIAS 1998*

☐ 1 ha 7,000 50–69 F

Brillant colour with hints of honey and minerals. It is very successful and complete with well-balanced roundness and freshness. We generally enjoyed it and have nothing else to say. Rabbit cooked with Pouilly-Vinzelles is the speciality to try with this very attractive wine.

Béatrice et Gilles Mathias, Dom. Mathias, rue Saint-Vincent, 71570 Chaintré, tel. 03.85.27.00.50, fax 03.85.27.00.52 by appt.

DOM. RENE PERRATON

Les Buchardières 1999

☐ 0.26 ha 2,000 30–49 F

A Vinzelle with wings. A mineral, fruity and very open wine. It is a pleasure to explore its fullness. The present lack of liveliness commits us to taste it again in two years.

René Perraton, rue du Paradis, Cidex 411, 71570 Chaintré, tel. 03.85.35.63.36, fax 03.85.35.67.45 by appt.

DOM. THIBERT PERE ET FILS 1998*

☐ 1.1 ha 8,000 50–69 F

This fresh 98 is still very closed, but promising. It is very light and exotic. Mineral and fresh butter, pleasant and supple with discreet oak, which was a point that the jury congratulated it on.

Dom. Thibert Père et Fils, Au Bourg, 71960 Fuissé, tel. 03.85.35.61.79, fax 03.85.35.66.21, e-mail domthibe@club-internet.fr by appt.

Saint-Véran

Producing only white wines in eight communes in the Saône-et-Loire, Saint-Véran is the last of the Mâcon appellations to be created (1971). In 1999, 38,774 hl (1,023,634 gal) were produced, and in quality the wines are somewhere between Pouilly and the Mâcons followed by the village name. The wines are light, elegant, fruity and accompany the first courses of meals wonderfully well.

Grown mainly on limestone soil, this appellation marks the southern limit of the Mâconnais.

DOM. ACERBIS 1998*

☐ n.c. n.c. 30–49 F

Domaine Acerbis? What an amusing name. One can read this wine like a good book. White-peach and pear on the opening pages, then a flattering, substantial body.

Véronique et Pierre Janny, La Condemine, 71260 Péronne, tel. 03.85.36.97.03, fax 03.85.36.96.58 by appt.

JEAN BARONNAT 1999*

☐ n.c. n.c. 30–49 F

This is no billet doux, but a twelve page declaration of love. It is fresh and golden with a very intense, exotic nose (lychee and guava). Stylishly expressive with length and complexity and sufficient acidity on the finish that indicates that it could wait a year or two.

Jean Baronnat, Les Bruyères, rte de Lacenas, 69400 Gleizé, tel. 04.74.68.59.20, fax 04.74.62.19.21, e-mail info.@baronnat.com by appt.

CHARTRON ET TREBUCHET

Château de Chasselas 1998*

☐ n.c. 12,000 50–69 F

It presents a pale gold colour then a citrus fruit nose, flowers and honey complemented with a degree of freshness. It is supple, rich with a vigorous structure. Good length on the finish.

Chartron et Trébuchet, 13, Grande-Rue, 21190 Puligny-Montrachet, tel. 03.80.21.32.85, fax 03.80.21.36.35, e-mail jmchartron@chartron-trebuchet.com ev. day 10am–12.30pm 2pm–6pm; cl. Nov.–Mar.

DOM. CHAVET 1998*

☐ 9 ha 20,000 50–69 F

This wine has its own very distinctive character, and an authentic one at that. It does not

cloud the senses with exotic fragrances. Here, we have a sincere, mineral nose. On the palate it starts off rich then finishes with a slight bitterness. Fine and with commendable length. One of our lucky discoveries in the 98s.
🔑 GAEC Chavet et Fils, Aux Durandys, 71960 Davayé, tel. 03.85.35.82.48, fax 03.85.35.80.32 ☑ 🍷 ev. day 7.30pm–8pm

DOM. CORDIER PERE ET FILS

Clos à la Côte 1998★★★

☐ 0.38 ha 2,000 70–99 F

A *coup de cœur* because it is so true to type. Patience will be required because it should be left to age but, meanwhile, it still gives a glimpse of the rewards to come. Stunning yellow-gold and a ravishing nose (peach, nuts), and it is already soft, unctuous and full of flavour. The finish goes on forever. Superb.
🔑 Dom. Cordier Père et Fils, 71960 Fuissé, tel. 03.85.35.62.89, fax 03.85.35.64.01 ☑ 🍷 by appt.

DOM. CORSIN 1998★★

☐ 4.7 ha 33,000 50–69 F

This beautifully-coloured 98 has rich flowery aromas. It has a clean attack and is both Chardonnay and Saint-Véran at the same time: silky, complex and balanced. The cuvée **Tirage Précoce 99** is excellent, and very successful for the vintage. It is awarded two stars. Matured five months in tank and bottled in the following February. Congratulations.
🔑 Dom. Corsin, Les Plantés, 71960 Davayé, tel. 03.85.35.83.69, fax 03.85.35.86.64 ☑ 🍷 by appt.

ANDRE DEPARDON 1999★

☐ 2.75 ha 3,380 30–49 F

The 85 vintage was exceptional. Not something to be forgotten. Trying this 99 is like cradle-snatching, but it does show promise. A very clear colour, nuts and lime on the nose, and it has well-balanced richness and acidity.
🔑 André Depardon, 71570 Leynes, tel. 04.74.06.10.10, fax 04.74.66.13.77 ☑ 🍷 by appt.

DOM. DES DEUX ROCHES 1998★★

☐ 12 ha 60,000 50–69 F

This estate is Doctor *honoris causa* of the appellation. They always provide us with a good wine bursting with very ripe fruit, like this one. A mouth-filling wine. Good for a fish dish but it could also be served chilled with a grilled Mâconnais goat's cheese and a green salad. The *cuvée* **Vieilles Vignes 98** is a good quality wine and would be better with a chicken dish with cream sauce. It has great potential (70–99F).
🔑 Dom. des Deux Roches, 71960 Davayé, tel. 03.85.35.86.51, fax 03.85.35.86.12 ☑ 🍷 by appt.

JOSEPH DROUHIN 1998★

☐ n.c. n.c. 50–69 F

An important figure from Beaune on foreign soil. He must have some good contacts because this Saint-Véran has a lovely old-gold colour and a fruity, flinty nose. Very characteristic, very pleasant and not in the least dull.
🔑 Joseph Drouhin, 7, rue d'Enfer, 21200 Beaune, tel. 03.80.24.68.88, fax 03.80.22.43.14, e-mail drouhin@calva.net 🍷 by appt.

DOM. DE FUSSIACUS 1999★★

☐ 1.1 ha 9,800 30–49 F

A *coup de cœur* for a 99? Yes, indeed. It was harvested on 16 September 2000, equally tank-matured and barrel-matured for six months. Tasted on 6 April 2000, it made the the best of this vintage which some described as diluted. The oak is well-adapted and has made a fine but powerful wine with a lovely pale gold colour with flashes of green. White truffle and raisins on the nose. Very full for a 99 and well-balanced. It was awarded a *coup de cœur* by the jury, and elected by the grand jury.
🔑 Jean-Paul Paquet, 71960 Fuissé, tel. 03.85.35.63.65, fax 03.85.35.67.50 ☑ 🍷 by appt.

DOM. GONON 1998★

☐ 0.4 ha 3,200 30–49 F

Very agreeable, slightly acidic but round. Not a lot of body but well-balanced. It has a discreet white gold colour and a delicate nose with citrus fruit and white-fleshed fruit aromas. A wine we really didn't want to spit out (apologies).
🔑 Dom. Gonon, 71960 Vergisson, tel. 03.85.37.78.42, fax 03.85.37.77.14 ☑ 🍷 by appt.

DOM. DE LA CREUZE NOIRE 1999★

☐ 0.93 ha 6,400 30–49 F

Some vines are owned by the family, others are rented and they combine to make a markably balanced Saint-Véran. The whole ry complimented it warmly. It needs couragement since it has a rare complexity r one so young.

Dominique et Christine Martin, La reuze Noire, 71570 Leynes, l. 03.85.37.46.43, fax 03.85.37.44.17 ☒ Y y appt.

DOM. DE LA CROIX SENAILLET

hardonnissime 1998★★★

	2 ha	5,000		50–69 F

Chardonnissime, one jury member wrote in heir notes. A little over the top maybe, but istified because this was number one among ne *coups de cœurs* in the appellation: a magificent wine. Hardly any point in giving etails: flowery and mineral with fruit and ints of honey. It simply blew the jury away. It as unrivalled length. That said, the **Cuvée Principale 98** is awarded one star.

GAEC Richard et Stéphane Martin, Dom. de la Croix Sénaillet, En Coland, 1960 Davayé, tel. 03.85.35.82.83, ax 03.85.35.87.22 ☒ Y by appt.

DOM. DE LA DENANTE 1999★

	6 ha	20,000		50–69 F

It is sometimes said that Saint-Véran is he younger sibling of Pouilly-Fuissé. This asy-drinking 99 has citrus aromas, is easy to pproach and is well-vinified. It is not too hin and has a good white-fleshed fruit aftertaste.

Robert Martin, Les Peiguins, 71960 Davayé, tel. 03.85.35.82.88, ax 03.85.35.86.71 ☒ Y by appt.

DOM. ROGER LUQUET

Les Grandes Bruyères 1998★

	1.4 ha	9,000		30–49 F

A super classic from a well-reputed wineproducer. Gold colour with glints of green. Flowery and mineral with honey and vanilla. Clean and sharp as the moment, so it needs more bottle age to reach its peak: two years or more.

Dom. Roger Luquet, 71960 Fuissé, tel. 03.85.35.60.91, fax 03.85.35.60.12 ☒ Y ev. day except Sun. 8am–7pm

DOM. DES MAILLETTES

La Bruyère 1998★

☐	1.3 ha	11,000		30–49 F

Davayé-Solutré-Vergisson is a estate in the holy triangle! As the poet André Chénier said, 'qu'aimable est la vertu que la grâce environne' (virtue is so pleasant when grace is near). Clear, fresh, flowery and has a lively finish. It has no time to waste. Its greenness and piquancy give it charm.

Guy Saumaize, Dom. des Maillettes, 71960 Davayé, tel. 03.85.35.82.65, fax 03.85.35.86.69 ☒ Y by appt.

CH. DE MESSEY 1998★

☐	n.c.	n.c.		70–99 F

Is there such a thing as a feminine wine? If there is, this is one of them. It is clear gold. The nose is hazelnut and honeysuckle and has elegance. It has a smooth body, with flowers and fruit. You'll be pleased with it.

Demessey, Ch. de Messey, 71700 Ozenay, tel. 03.85.51.33.83, fax 03.85.51.33.82, e-mail vin@demessey.com ☒ Y by appt.

Marc Dumont

GENEVIEVE ET BERNARD MONTEIRO Elevé en fût de chêne 1998

☐	1 ha	5,000		30–49 F

Gold through and through; it does not do things by halves. Then there is honey and brioche, spices and yellow peaches, just like a journey between Chassagne and Meursault. Vibrant attack, then round and supple with a warm finish. Well-structured, almost tannic. An unusual wine, but an appealing one.

Bernard et Geneviève Monteiro, En Durandys, 71960 Davayé, tel. 04.85.35.82.40, fax 04.85.35.81.32 ☒ Y by appt.

ALAIN NORMAND 1998★

☐	0.25 ha	1,500		30–49 F

This 98 is knocking to come in and should not be left outside. It should be in the cellar. A brilliant yellow colour, with blossom and ripe fruit aromas, skilfully-oaked. It needs to open, and when it does it will wake up with another star. Very rich with a promising acidity. A pretty label showing the landscape.

Alain Normand, chem. de la Grange-du-Dîme, 71960 La Roche-Vineuse, tel. 03.85.36.61.69, fax 03.85.51.60.97 ☒ Y by appt.

DOM. DES PERELLES 1999★

☐	0.33 ha	2,400		30–49 F

Clear gold. This Saint-Véran is lively and has hints of oak. Its lemony tones add freshness, but we also detected aromas of white truffle. Well-balanced wood and fruit on the palate. Do not wait more than two years to drink it.

Jean-Marc Thibert, Les Pérelles, 71680 Crêches-sur-Saône, tel. 03.85.37.14.56, fax 03.85.37.46.02 ☒ Y by appt.

DOM. PHILIBERT 1998★

☐	n.c.	19,700		50–69 F

Fresh salmon would be ideal with this wine. Silvery-gold with bright glints. Citrus fruit and flowers on the nose. This Saint-Véran reminds us that the town's patron saint was a

famous dragon-slayer. Well-balanced and stylish.
🔑 Cie des Vins d'Autrefois, Abbaye Saint-Martin, 53, av. de l'Aigue, 21200 Beaune, tel. 03.80.26.33.00, fax 03.80.24.14.84, e-mail mallet.b@cva-beaune.fr 🍷 by appt.
🔑 Jean-Pierre Nie

DOM. DES PONCETYS 1999

☐ 1.4 ha 10,987 30–49 F

The Lycée Viticole at Mâcon-Davayé cultivates an estate of 18 ha (45 acres) which it received as a gift in 1963. The 99 presented was matured for four months in tank. Gold with glimmering green. The nose is fine with lemon and aniseed. The palate has flavours in the same range with a hint of fruitiness and a good deal of freshness.
🔑 Lycée Viticole de Mâcon-Davayé, Les Poncetys, 71960 Davayé, tel. 03.85.33.56.20, fax 03.85.35.86.34, e-mail legta.macon@wanadoo.fr ☑ 🍷 ev. day except Sun. 9am–12 noon 2pm–5.30pm; Sat. 9am–1pm

CAVE DE PRISSE-SOLOGNY-VERZE 1998★★

☐ 174.26 ha 100,000 30–49 F

A very important *coopérative* in the Mâconnais uniting 884 ha (2,184 acres) of vines. You cannot fail to fall in love with this wine the moment you see, on its label, the hunting lodge of the Château de Monceau, where Lamartine wrote *The History of the Girondins* (it was re-built after being burned down). Apricot, pear, fruitiness, richness – enough to inspire any poet. He was a successful wine-grower, or at least an attentive owner in this Cru. This wine came fourth with the grand jury. You can count on it. The price is very reasonable indeed.
🔑 Cave de Prissé-Sologny-Verzé, 71960 Prissé, tel. 03.85.37.88.06, fax 03.85.37.61.76 ☑ 🍷 by appt.

DOM. SAUMAIZE-MICHELIN

Vieilles vignes 1998★

☐ 0.7 ha 5,000 30–49

This wine is non-conformist, according t our tasters' views. Good, pale gold colou Well-balanced nose with fruit and toasty arc mas. Very soft on the palate, light as a feathe but still very oaky.
🔑 Dom. Roger et Christine Saumaize-Michelin, Le Martelet, 71960 Vergisson, tel. 03.85.35.84.05, fax 03.85.35.86.77 ☑ 🍷 by appt.

DOM. DES VALANGES

Cuvée hors Classe 1998★

☐ 2 ha 12,000 50–69

The vintages of 88, 89, 94, 95 and 97 wer all very successful. Does any other estat equal the record in the same AOC? It belong to the very select group of our 'têtes de cuvée' This is a selection of the best *climats*: Terre Noires, Valanges, Crêches. Beautifully golde or even buttercup gold. The wine has peon and ripe fruit on the nose, and is fresh, an fruity and appealing.
🔑 Michel Paquet, Les Valanges, 71960 Davayé, tel. 03.85.35.85.03, fax 03.85.35.86.67, e-mail domainedesvalanges@wanadoo.fr ☑ 🍷 by appt.

DOM. DES VIEILLES PIERRES

Les Pommards 1998★

☐ 0.65 ha 5,200 50–69 F

This wine spends ten months in oak and undergoes regular *bâtonnage*. Its has richness but with a pronounced oakiness. But the freshness adds balance. Citrus fruits are also evident. Wait at least a year before serving it to friends who like good wines and appreciate a roasted coffee-bean oakiness.
🔑 Jean-Jacques Litaud, Les Nembrets, 71960 Vergisson, tel. 03.85.35.85.69, fax 03.85.35.86.26 ☑ 🍷 by appt.

CHAMPAGNE

The wine of kings and princes and now the wine for every celebration, Champagne is cloaked in glory and prestige and conveys to the world all that is French elegance and seductiveness. Its reputation has as much to do with its history as with its particular characteristics, which means, for many, that the only wine from Champagne is *the* Champagne; however, it is not as simple as that . . .

The Champagne region, which is situated less than 200 km (125 miles) north-east of Paris, contains three Appellations d'Origine Contrôlée, Champagne, Coteaux Champenois and Rosé des Riceys, but the last two of these produce only around 100,000 bottles. This northernmost wine-growing region in France extends chiefly over the Marne and the Aube regions, with small areas in the Aisne, Seine-et-Marne and Haute-Marne. The total vineyard area covers more than 34,000 ha (83,980 acres), of which 31,220 (77,113 acres) are planted with vines.

Between them, Reims and Épernay in the Marne share the role of capital of Champagne. The former has the additional appeal of its monuments and museums, which draw crowds of visitors who, at the same time, can discover the cellars belonging to the 'great houses', many of which are very ancient.

The whole of the wine-growing area has a similar, undulating countryside, where four main regions are traditionally identified. In La Montagne de Reims some of the vineyards face north and are on sandy soil. The Côte des Blancs, just outside Épernay, benefits from a relatively predictable climate, the valley of the Marne, extending into the vineyards in the Aisne, where 2,000 ha (4,940 acres) are planted, and where the river flows between chalky hills, the slopes of both banks are covered in vines. Here, despite what one might expect, the quality of the grapes produced rarely varies, whether the vineyards face north or south. Finally, there is the vineyard of the Aube, in the extreme south-east of the appellation, 75 km (47 miles) away from the other three areas and separated from them by a zone where no vines are grown. The Aube is higher and more susceptible to spring frosts than the other areas, yet it produces wines of no lesser quality. This is where you find the only *appellation communale*: Rosé des Riceys.

As the sea retreated some 70 million years ago upheavals caused by tellurian quakes ensued, forming a chalk base that is permeable and rich in essential minerals and brings finesse to the wines of Champagne. A shallow layer of clay and limestone covers the subsoil on nearly 60% of the land devoted to vines. In the Aube, the soil composition is marl, which is closer to that found in neighbouring Burgundy.

If frost – and at this latitude, spring frosts are frequent – makes reliable production difficult, the climatic extremes are nevertheless tempered by extensive mountain forests, which balance out the mild Atlantic maritime climate and the harsher continental one, maintaining a certain level of humidity. The lack of extreme heat is also a determining factor in the fine quality of the wines. Naturally enough, the choice of grape variety is made in the context of the wine-growing and climatic conditions. Of the 31,000 ha (76,570 acres) devoted to vine-growing, Pinot Noir takes up

Champagne

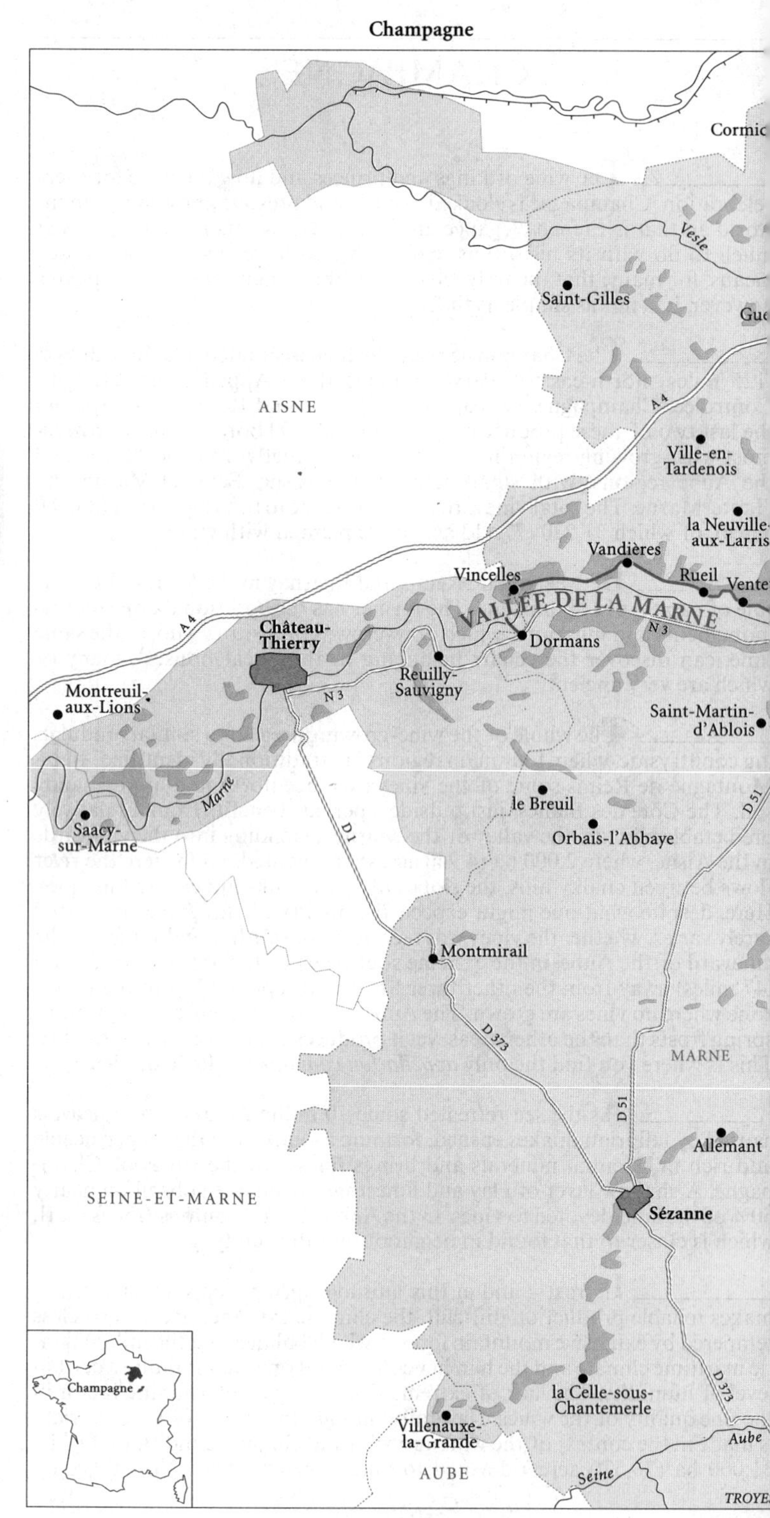

Cormic
Vesle
Saint-Gilles
Gue
AISNE
A 4
Ville-en-
Tardenois
la Neuville-
aux-Larris
Vandières
Vincelles
Rueil
Vente
VALLÉE DE LA MARNE
N 3
A 4
Château-
Thierry
Dormans
Reuilly-
Sauvigny
Montreuil-
aux-Lions
N 3
Saint-Martin-
d'Ablois
Marne
Saacy-
sur-Marne
le Breuil
Orbais-l'Abbaye
D 51
D 1
Montmirail
D 373
MARNE
D 51
Allemant
SEINE-ET-MARNE
Sézanne
Champagne
la Celle-sous-
Chantemerle
D 373
Villenauxe-
la-Grande
Aube
AUBE
Seine
TROYES

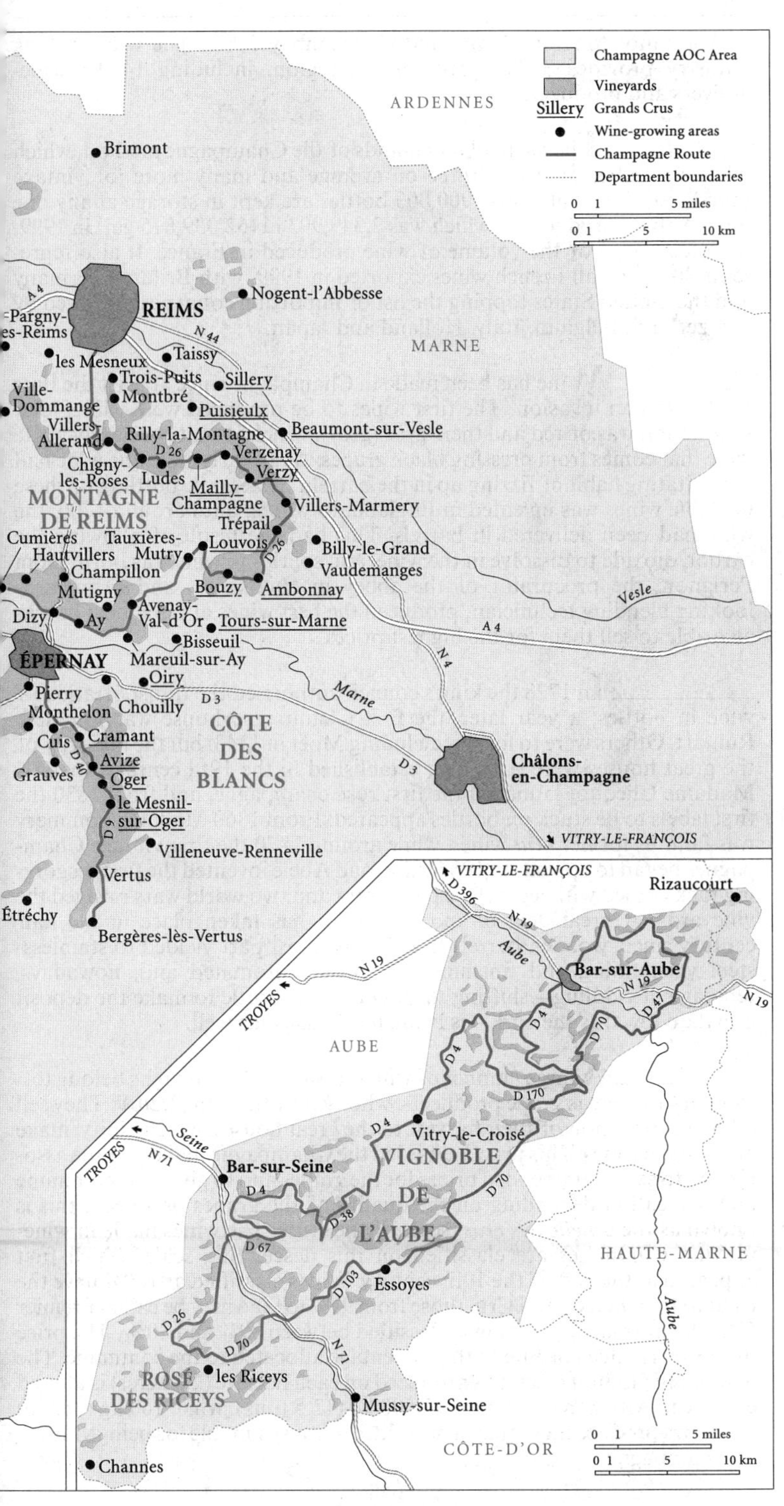

Champagne AOC Area
Vineyards
Sillery Grands Crus
Wine-growing areas
Champagne Route
Department boundaries
0 1 5 miles
0 1 5 10 km
ARDENNES
MARNE
Brimont
Nogent-l'Abbesse
REIMS
A 4
N 44
Pargny-les-Reims
les Mesneux
Taissy
Trois-Puits
Sillery
Ville-Dommange
Montbré
Puisieulx
Villers-Allerand
Rilly-la-Montagne
Beaumont-sur-Vesle
D 26
Verzenay
Chigny-les-Roses
Ludes
Verzy
Mailly-Champagne
MONTAGNE DE REIMS
Villers-Marmery
Trépail
Cumières
Tauxières-Mutry
Hautvillers
Louvois
Billy-le-Grand
Champillon
Vaudemanges
Mutigny
Bouzy
Ambonnay
Avenay-Val-d'Or
Dizy
Ay
Tours-sur-Marne
Vesle
A 4
Bisseuil
ÉPERNAY
Mareuil-sur-Ay
N 4
Pierry
Oiry
Monthelon
Chouilly
D 3
Marne
CÔTE DES BLANCS
Cuis
Cramant
Avize
Grauves
D 40
Oger
D 3
Châlons-en-Champagne
le Mesnil-sur-Oger
D 9
VITRY-LE-FRANÇOIS
Villeneuve-Renneville
Vertus
Étréchy
Bergères-lès-Vertus
VITRY-LE-FRANÇOIS
Rizaucourt
D 396
N 19
Aube
N 19
Bar-sur-Aube
N 19
TROYES
N 19
D 47
D 4
D 70
AUBE
D 4
D 170
D 4
Vitry-le-Croisé
TROYES
Seine
N 71
Bar-sur-Seine
VIGNOBLE DE L'AUBE
D 70
D 4
D 38
D 67
HAUTE-MARNE
Essoyes
D 103
D 26
Aube
D 70
N 71
ROSÉ DES RICEYS
les Riceys
Mussy-sur-Seine
CÔTE-D'OR
0 1 5 miles
0 1 5 10 km
Channes

37.5%, Pinot Meunier 35.5% and Chardonnay 27% . The wine-making industry provides 31,000 jobs for the region, including 14,695 wine-growers and producers.

The particular demands of the Champagne method, which takes a number of years (three on average and many more for vintage years), requires that nearly 900,000 bottles are kept in storage at any one time. Annual production, which was 2,349,993 hl (62,039,815 gal) in 1999, represents 11% of the volume of wine produced in France. It also represents 30.6% of all French wines exported in 1999, with Britain, Germany and the United States topping the list of importing countries, followed by Switzerland, Belgium, Italy, Holland and Japan.

Wine has been made in Champagne since at least the time of the Roman invasion. The first wines to be produced were white, later production was of red and then 'gris' (grey), which is white or nearly white wine that comes from pressing black grapes. At an early stage the wine had the irritating habit of fizzing up in the barrels. Systematic bottling of these unstable wines was invented in England, to where, until around 1700, the wine had been delivered in barrels. This had the result of allowing the carbon dioxide to dissolve in the wine, and sparkling wine was born. Dom Pérignon, the procurator of the abbey in Hautvillers and a forward-looking blending technician, produced the best wines at his abbey; he was also able to sell them for the highest prices.

In 1728 the king's council authorised the transportation of wine in bottles; a year later, the first Champagne house was founded: Ruinart. Others were to follow, including Moët in 1743, but the majority of the great houses were started or established in the 19th century. In 1804 Madame Clicquot launched the first rosé champagne, and from 1830 the first labels to be stuck on bottles appeared. From 1860 Madame Pommery was famous for her *brut* wines, while around 1870 the first vintage Champagnes began to appear. In 1884 Raymond Abelé invented the first disgorging rack cooled with ice, before phylloxera and two world wars ravaged the vineyards. A great deal of modernisation has taken place in the half century since: wooden barrels have for the most part yielded to stainless-steel vats, fining and finishing have been automated and, nowadays, remuage or riddling – shifting the angle of the bottle to make the deposit gravitate towards the cork – is being mechanised as well.

A large number of wine-growers in Champagne belong to a category known as grape producers, who 'sell by the kilo (2.2lb)'. They sell all or a proportion of their harvest to the great houses, which vinify, make and sell the wines. This practice has led the Champagne makers' trade association to set recommended prices for the grapes and to give each commune a classification depending on the quality of the grapes produced: this is known as the *échelle des crus* (scale of the crus). The wines made in wine-making communes are classified on this descending scale, which first appeared at the end of the 19th century. Wines classified as 100% have the right to be called Grand Cru, those from 99% to 90% may be called Premier Cru; the normal appellation is classified between 89% and 80% . The price of grapes is set according to the percentage allocated to the commune. The maximum amount of grapes produced on each hectare (2.5 acres) is altered each year, with a maximum of 12,500 kg (12.5 tons), while 160 kg (352 lb) of grapes produce more than a hectolitre of must suitable for being vinified as Champagne.

Champagne

The uniqueness of Champagne is apparent right from the harvest itself. No harvesting machines are permitted, and everything is picked by hand because it is essential that the grapes get to the press in perfect condition. Rather than the hods used elsewhere, pickers carry small baskets to ensure that the grapes are not too crushed. Presses are set up in the heart of the vineyards to shorten the time the grapes are transported. Why is such care taken? Because Champagne is a white wine made for the most part from a black grape, the Pinot Noir, and it is essential that the colourless juice should not be stained by contact with the grape skins.

Pressing has to take place as quickly as possible and in such a way as to collect the juice from different concentric parts of each fruit one after the other. This explains the particular shape of the traditional presses in Champagne: to avoid squashing the grapes and to facilitate the circulation of the juice, the grapes are piled over a very wide area but not very deeply. The skins of the harvested grapes must never be damaged.

The pressing itself is strictly regulated. There are 2,000 pressing centres and each must obtain official registration in order to operate. From 4,000 kg (4 ton) of grapes, only 25.5 hl (673 gal) of must, a unit known as a 'marc', may be extracted in two pressings. The pressing is done in two phases: the first is known as the *cuvée*, 20.5 hl (541 gal), and the second as the *taille*, 5 hl (132 gal). The grapes can be pressed again, but the resulting juice is of no interest and has no appellation. The *rebêche*, or new pressing of the *marc*, is destined for the distillery. The more you press, the greater the drop in quality. The must is taken from the pressing centres to the wineries by lorry and is then carefully vinified according to the classic white wine method.

At the end of winter, in early spring, the cellar-master proceeds to 'assemble' or mix the *cuvée*. To do so, he tastes all the wines available and blends them in such proportions as to make a wine that reflects the flavour and style of the house. When he makes a non-vintage wine, he may call on wines from the reserve, which was produced in previous years. It is legal in Champagne to add a little red wine to the white wine to make a rosé (although this is forbidden everywhere else). However, some rosé Champagnes are obtained by allowing the colour of the skins to 'bleed' into the must.

Once the blending is completed, the real work of making the wine begins. This is to change a still wine into a sparkling wine. A *liqueur de tirage*, made of yeasts, old wines and sugar, is added to the wine, which is then bottled: this is called *tirage*. The yeasts will turn the sugar into alcohol and produce carbon dioxide, which dissolves in the wine. This second fermentation in the bottles takes place very slowly, and at low temperatures (11°C 51°F), in the famous Champagne cellars. After long ageing on the lees (residues left by the second fermentation), which is essential for making small bubbles and producing the aromatic qualities of the wines, the bottles are subjected to *dégorgement*, a process that gradually drains away the lees.

Each bottle is placed in one of the famous *pupitres*, or disgorging racks, so that the deposits will settle in the neck of the bottle, beneath the cork. For two or three months the bottles will be periodically shaken and tilted, neck down, until the wine is perfectly clear (automated riddling in a gyropallet is on the increase). To evacuate the deposit, the neck is frozen in a refrigerating bath and the cork is removed; once the deposit is expelled, the bottle is topped up with a wine that may or may not be sweetened: this is the *dosage*. If pure wine is added, a 100% brut wine is obtained (Brut Sauvage from Piper-Heidsieck, Ultra-Brut from Laurent-Perrier, and Champagnes known as *non-dosés*, or not sweetened, and now called Brut Nature). If only a very small amount (1%) of sweetened wine is added, the Champagne is Brut; a content of 2% to 5% produces dry Champagne; 5% to 8% produces demi-sec, and 8% to 15% sweet. The bottles are then shaken to blend the wines together and set to rest again to allow the taste of the yeast to disappear. They are then labelled and released onto the market. From then on the Champagne is ready to be appreciated at the top of its form. Allowing it to age for too long can only harm it: serious houses flatter themselves that they put their wines on sale only when they have reached their peak.

Some excellent wines made from the first pressing, together with numerous 'reserve' wines (for the non-vintages), the talent of the cellar-master, with his finely judged, minimal, undetectable dosing, and the long maturing of the Champagne on the lees will combine to produce wines of the highest quality. But it is rare for a buyer to be fully informed about all these issues, and certainly there is no guarantee that the information will be accurate.

What can be read on a Champagne label? The brand and the name of the maker; the dosage (brut, sec and so on); the year or lack of a year; the phrase *blanc de blancs* when only white grapes have been used in the wine; when possible (though this is rare), the commune of origin of the grapes, and finally, sometimes, but less and less often, the qualitative classification of the grapes: Grand Cru for the 17 communes that have the right to the description or Premier Cru for 41 others. The professional standing of the producer must appear, printed in small letters: NM (*négociant-manipulant*), meaning a merchant-winemaker; RM (*récoltant-manipulant*), a grower making Champagne from his or her own grapes, with 5% bought in from other sources; CM (*Coopérative de manipulation*), a co-operative that makes and sells its own Champagne using grapes from its member growers; MA (*marque d'acheteur*), the brand of the buyer; RC (*récoltant-coopérateur*), a small grower who sends his grapes to one or several co-operatives to be made into Champagne because he does not have the equipment to do so himself, and who receives the finished Champagne to sell; or SR (*société de récoltants*), a registered firm set up by Champagne growers of the same family who pool their production resources.

What can be gleaned from all this? Simply that the Champenois have deliberately adopted a sales policy that is focused on the brand. A customer will, therefore, order Moët et Chandon, Bollinger or Taittinger because he or she prefers the flavour and style adopted by this or that brand. It is the same for the Champagnes produced by the *négociants-manipulants,* the co-operatives and related brands, but not for the *récoltants-manipulants,* who, to qualify as such, make Champagne only from their own grapes, generally grouped in a single commune. These Champagnes are the so-called Monocrus, and the name of the Cru will generally appear on the label.

Although there is only the one appellation, 'Champagne', a great many different Champagnes exist, and the range of characteristics of flavour, smell and appearance can readily satisfy the different needs and varying tastes of every drinker. So, Champagne can be blanc de blancs, blanc de noirs (from Pinot Meunier, Pinot Noir or from both) or blends of blanc de blancs and blanc de noirs in any imaginable proportion. It can be from one cru alone or from several, originating from a Grand Cru, a Premier Cru or communes of lesser prestige. It can be vintage or non-vintage (the non-vintage Champagnes can be made from young wines or be made up from wines from the reserve, and they are sometimes produced from an assemblage of vintage years). It can be non-dosed or very variably dosed and it can undergo short or long maturation on the lees. It may be disgorged for a longer or shorter time, or be white or rosé (which is obtained either by blending or by bleeding). Then again, most of these options can be combined together in different ways, so there is in fact an infinite number of Champagnes. Whatever the type, the general consensus is that the best Champagne has matured for a long time on the lees (five to ten years), and is consumed, in France at least, in the six months following disgorgement.

Given all this, it is easy to understand why the price of bottles can vary so widely and why there are wines at the top of the range or special wines, *cuvées spéciales*. It is unfortunately true that, among the better known brands, the cheapest Champagnes are the least appealing. On the other hand, the big price differences between the upper range (vintage Champagnes) and the top- price wines do not always guarantee an equivalent step in quality.

Champagne should be drunk when it is between 7° and 9°C (44.6–48.2°F), chilled for the blancs de blancs and young Champagnes, not so cold for the vintage and sweeter Champagnes. In addition to the classic 75 cl bottle, Champagne is also sold in a quarter bottle, a half, a magnum (twice a single bottle), Jeroboam (4 bottles), Methuselah (8 bottles) and Salmanazar (12 bottles). The bottle should be cooled gradually by immersing it in a Champagne bucket containing water and ice. To remove the cork, take off the wire cage and foil. If the cork is likely to be pushed out by the pressure, allow it to come out with the cage and foil. If the cork resists, hold it in one hand and turn the bottle with the other. The cork should be removed slowly and noiselessly, avoiding rapid decompression.

Champagne should not be served in goblets but in tall, slender glasses that are completely dry and free from any traces of detergent, which will kill the bubbles and the foam. It can be drunk equally well as an apéritif as with starters and non-oily fish. The richer wines, mostly blanc de noirs, and the great vintages are frequently served with meat dishes with sauce. Drink a demi-sec wine rather than a brut with dessert or sweet dishes, because the sugar in the dish will over-emphasise the palate's sensitivity to the acidity of the brut.

The most recent vintages are 1982, a great vintage everywhere; 1983, straightforward; 1984 was not a vintage, so we can ignore it; 1985, good bottles; 1986, average quality, few wines declared a vintage; 1987, a bad year; 1988, 1989 and 1990, three wonderful years to enjoy; 1991, poor, generally not declared a vintage; 1992, 1993 and 1994, average years; a few important houses declared 1992 and 1993 a vintage; 1995, the best year since 1990; 1996, a great year.

HENRI ABELE Le Sourire de Reims★★

◕ n.c. n.c. 300–499 F

This very old-established firm was set up in 1757 by Théodore van der Veken from Belgium, and taken over in 1985 by the Spanish conglomerate, Freixenet, which specialises in cava. Le Sourire de Reims rosé, their special blend, is a rosé produced from black grapes (100% Pinot Noir) that is well-structured, fruity, complex and elegant with aromas of blueberry, wild cherry, wild strawberry and other acidulated soft fruits. It is only lightly dosed, has charming freshness and goes well with food. 'Buy!', wrote one taster, under its potent spell. In addition to this, the firm received a citation for their **Sourire de Reims 86** (90% Chardonnay, 10% Pinot Noir), which was otherwise a difficult vintage rather lacking in complexity. (NM)

Champagne Henri Abelé, 50, rue de Sillery, 51100 Reims, tel. 03.26.87.79.80, fax 03.26.87.79.81 by appt.

ADAM-GARNOTEL Tradition★

○ 1er cru 9.2 ha 60,000 70–99 F

This firm in the Montagne de Reims has just clocked up its first century, as it was set up by Louis Adam in 1899. Since 1971, it has gone under the name of Adam-Garnotel, and now owns a vineyard of some 9 ha (22 acres). Their Tradition, which comes from the three champagne grape varieties harvested in 1997, is a richly textured, generous, mature champagne with a powerful palate. It will be the perfect accompaniment to a hot first course or white meat. A star also goes to their **1995 premier cru**, in which Chardonnay (80%) has the upper hand over Pinot Noir. There are suggestions here of vanilla-scented citrus fruits, pineapple and liquorice: in a word, complexity. (NM)

Champagne Adam-Garnotel, 17, rue de Chigny, 51500 Rilly-la-Montagne, tel. 03.26.03.40.22, fax 03.26.03.44.47, e-mail Garnotel@terre-net.fr ev. day except Sat. Sun. 9am–12 noon 2pm–5pm; cl. Aug.

AGRAPART ET FILS Blanc de blancs

○ Gd cru 6.5 ha n.c. 70–99 F

The Agrapart family have been working 9.5 ha (23 acres) of vines in the Côte des Blancs for four generations. It therefore comes as no surprise to find two of their Blancs de Blancs receiving a mention in the *Guide*. This Brut comes from the 1996 harvest, topped up with one-third reserve wines from 1995. Its aromas are floral and elegant; on the palate, the most dominant aromas are yellow fruits. The **Réserve**, on the other hand, derives from the 1994 (mainly) and 1993 harvests. It is notable for its harmony and length. (RM)

EARL Agrapart et Fils, 57, av. Jean-Jaurès, 51190 Avize, tel. 03.26.57.51.38, fax 03.26.57.05.06, e-mail champagne.agrapart@wanadoo.fr by appt.

GILLES ALLAIT Tradition★

○ n.c. n.c. 70–99 F

Passy-Grigny is on the banks of a small tributary of the Marne, not far from Dormans. Gilles Allait has been working 3.5 ha (9 acres) of vines since 1973. With 80% Meunier and 15% Pinot Noir, his Tradition blend is almost a blanc de noirs. Its aromas call to mind quince jelly and ripe lychees, while the palate shows generous dosage. A star also goes to the **95**, which is aged in oak casks (50% Chardonnay and equal parts of the two Pinots), and has firm, lively form and good length. (RC)

Gilles Allait, 2, rue du Château, 51700 Passy-Grigny, tel. 03.26.52.92.19, fax 03.26.52.97.22 by appt.

JEAN-ANTOINE ARISTON Carte jaune★★

○ 2 ha 20,000 70–99 F

This family operation of 6.5 ha (16 acres) is situated in the ring of Romanesque churches in the Ardre valley. Three of its wines have been particularly noted. First choice goes to the Carte jaune, which is produced from equal parts of the three champagne grapes from the 1997 harvest. Its distinguished, expressive nose presages a well-balanced and complex palate. A very polished, sophisticated champagne. The **Carte or** and **Carte blanche** are both worthy of citation. The first (80% of the two Pinots and 20% Chardonnay from the 1996 harvest) is well-balanced, forthright, rounded and harmonious, the second (60% Chardonnay, 40% Pinot Noir) is very floral, fresh and lively. (RM)

Jean-Antoine Ariston, 4, rue Haute, 51170 Brouillet, tel. 03.26.97.47.02, fax 03.26.97.49.75 ev. day 8am–12 noon 2pm–6pm

ARISTON FILS Carte blanche★★

○ 7 ha 8,000 70–99 F

The Ariston family have been wine producers since 1794 and now work a vineyard of 10 ha (25 acres). All three of the champagne grapes come together in their Carte blanche, which is floral and spicy, with a clean entry and perfect balance. Open this one as an apéritif before a celebration meal. (RM)

Rémi Ariston, 4 et 8, Grande-Rue, 51170 Brouillet, tel. 03.26.97.43.46, fax 03.26.97.49.34, e-mail champagne.ariston.fils@wanadoo.fr ev. day 9am–12 noon 1.30pm–6pm; Sun. 10am–12 noon 3pm–5pm

ARNAUD DE BEAUROY Tradition

○ 10 ha 15,000 70–99 F

Arnaud de Beauroy, which is based at Riceys in the Aube, is a brand of Gallimard Champagne. This blend is a blanc de noirs (100% Pinot Noir). Although it seems a little fleeting and transient, its high alcohol content, powerful fruit, suppleness and overall balance nonetheless earn it a place here. (RM)

🗝 Champagne Gallimard Père et Fils, 18–20, rue Gaston-Cheq, Le Magny, 10340 Les Riceys, tel. 03.25.29.32.44, fax 03.25.38.55.20 ☒ ♈ ev. day Sun. 9am–12 noon 2pm–6pm; Sat. by appt.

MICHEL ARNOULD ET FILS

Réserve★★

○Gd cru 3.5 ha 25,000 ▮ 70–99 F

Michel Arnould runs a vineyard of 12 ha (30 acres) in one of the most famous villages in the Montagne de Reims, and has been producing wine since 1961. In his Réserve, he blends 70% Pinot Noir and 30% Chardonnay harvested in 1994 and 1995. An expressive, thoroughbred champagne. One enthusiastic taster called it 'refined and elegant, with charm and good structure'. The **Tradition** is an identical blend except that it uses 1995 and 1996 wines. It is highly developed and very strongly dosed. It received a special citation. (RM)

🗝 Michel Arnould et Fils, 28, rue de Mailly, 51360 Verzenay, tel. 03.26.49.40.06, fax 03.26.49.44.61, e-mail michelarnould@wanadoo.fr ☒ ♈ by appt.

L. AUBRY FILS Tradition 1995★★

○1er cru 1.4 ha 6,000 ⫼ 100–149 F

Based in the Montagne de Reims, the Aubry family runs a vineyard of 16.5 ha (41 acres), working with great care to produce champagnes of character. This wine is the result of blending 70% Chardonnay with 30% Meunier. This *monocru* from Jouy spends nine months in wooden barrels, and is harmonious, long and slightly smoky, with complex hints of roasting and toasted bread. The **Brut classique** (70–99F) is produced from 60% Meunier, 20% Pinot Noir and 20% Chardonnay from 1996, 1997 and 1998: it is a promising wine, lively and pleasant and slightly oaked (one star). Finally there is a mention for the **Sablé Rosé** (100–149F, 60% Pinot and 40% Chardonnay), which is bottled semi-sparkling, and is well-balanced with good vinosity. (RM)

🗝 SCEV Champagne L. Aubry Fils, 4–6, Grande-Rue, 51390 Jouy-lès-Reims, tel. 03.26.49.20.07, fax 03.26.49.75.27 ☒ ♈ by appt.

AUTREAU DE CHAMPILLON

1995★★

○ 9.7 ha 10,000 ▮ 100–149 F

For three centuries the Autréau family have been wine-producers in Champillon, which is near Ay, Hautvillers and Epernay. They created their brand in 1953 and work a vineyard of 27 ha (67 acres). This 1995 wine, made half from black grapes and half from white, develops delicate, expressive aromas of white blossom and candied lemon, and is fresh and long on the palate. Also worthy of note are the **Réserve premier cru** (70–99F), which is likewise a blend of half black grapes and half white with the aromatic liveliness of grapefruit, and **Les Perles de la Dhuy 95** (100–149F, 90% Chardonnay), which is spicy, well-balanced and now at its peak. (NM)

🗝 SARL Vignobles Champenois, 15, rue René-Baudet, 51160 Champillon, tel. 03.26.59.46.00, fax 03.26.59.44.85 ☒ ♈ ev. day 9am–12 noon 2pm–6pm; Sat. Sun. by appt.; cl. 10–20 Aug.

🗝 Eric Autréau

AUTREAU-LASNOT Prestige 1995

○ 2 ha 7,500 ▮ ⫼ 70–99 F

This outfit was set up in 1932 and has a vineyard of some 10 ha (25 acres) in the Marne valley, at Venteuil and Châtillon. Bringing together Chardonnay and Pinot Noir in equal parts, their Prestige blend has spent six months in cask. It is worthy of citation both for its nose, which mingles floral notes and hazelnut, and for its flavours of cherry and pear. Also receiving a citation is the **Rosé** (Pinot Noir 40%, Pinot Meunier 20%, Chardonnay 40%, harvested in 1995, 1996 and 1997), which has a soft, gentle entry and good length. (RM)

🗝 Champagne Autréau-Lasnot, 6, rue du Château, 51480 Venteuil, tel. 03.26.58.49.35, fax 03.26.58.65.44 ☒ ♈ by appt.

🗝 Gérard Autréau

AYALA 1995

○ n.c. n.c. ▮ ♁ 150–199 F

The beginnings of this Ay firm date back to a marriage during the Second Empire between the son of a Colombian diplomat and a noblewoman from the Champagne region. Ayala received as dowry a fine vineyard that has been managed since 1979 by Jean-Michel and Alain Ducellier. The three champagne varieties – with Pinot Noir making up a substantial proportion – work side by side in this 1995 wine, which has supple texture and a very harmonious palate. Also receiving a mention is a **Blanc de Blancs 95**, which is astonishingly youthful, straightforward, vigorous, minerally and elegant. (NM)

🗝 Champagne Ayala, 2, bd du Nord, 51160 Ay, tel. 03.26.55.15.44, fax 03.26.51.09.04 ☒ ♈ by appt.

🗝 Ducellier

BAGNOST PERE ET FILS

Cuvée Prestige★★

○ 0.75 ha 6,000 ▮ ♁ 70–99 F

This family outfit of 8 ha (20 acres) was set up in 1889 in Pierry, to the south of Épernay, and proves that it is possible to produce a great champagne from grapes harvested in 1993, even though the vintage may have a poor reputation. A classic blend of Chardonnay (70%) and Pinot Noir (30%), this Cuvée Prestige has winning ways, with its clear

golden colour and delicate bubbles, its fruity, mineral nose and intense, long, delicate, full and perfectly balanced palate. It will be perfect on its own, or as an accompaniment to baked fish. The **Non-vintage Blanc de Blancs** produced from the 1992 harvest is very delicate, intense and well-balanced, and receives a star. (RM)

Champagne Bagnost Père et Fils, 30, rue du Gal-de-Gaulle, 51530 Pierry, tel. 03.26.54.04.22, fax 03.26.55.67.17 ev. day 8am–12 noon 2pm–7pm

PAUL BARA Réserve

○Gd cru 11 ha 50,000 70–99 F

This estate, which has been established in Bouzy – a Grand Cru – over 140 years, has 11 ha (27 acres) of vines. 80% Pinot Noir and 20% Chardonnay come together in this Réserve, which has aromas of quince and honey, and a rounded, balanced palate. Also receiving a citation is the **Spécial Club 96** (150–199F), which is produced from two-thirds Pinot Noir and one-third Chardonnay. A fresh, full-bodied champagne that hasn't yet reached its peak. (RM)

Champagne Paul Bara, 4, rue Yvonnet, B.P. 11, 51150 Bouzy, tel. 03.26.57.00.50, fax 03.26.57.81.24 by appt.

BARDOUX PERE ET FILS

Cuvée du 3e millénaire★★

○ 3 ha n.c. 150–199 F

Villedommange is a pretty village in the northern part of the Montagne de Reims: from the Saint-Lié chapel, visitors are treated to a fine panorama over the vineyard and the Plaine Rémoise. Here the Bardoux family works an estate of 4 ha (10 acres), which was established in 1929. This blend combines the three champagne grapes, including 58% Pinot Meunier and 20% Pinot Noir, 1996 topped up with reserve wines from 1992 to 1995. It is honeyed and lemony, full and long. A very fine champagne for accompanying food. The **An 2000** (100–149F), a blend in the same style that is highly developed and yet lively, received a special citation. (RM)

Pascal Bardoux, 5–7, rue Saint-Vincent, 51390 Villedommange, tel. 03.26.49.25.35, fax 03.26.49.23.15 by appt.

EDMOND BARNAUT Blanc de noirs

○Gd cru 2.5 ha 20,000 70–99 F

The vineyard was set up in 1874 by Edmond Barnaut; today Philippe Secondé, his fifth-generation descendant, works some 14.5 ha (36 acres). A base wine dating from 1997, backed up by reserve wines, is the heart of this rounded, harmonious and well-structured champagne, which is of honourable length. (RM)

Champagne Edmond Barnaut, 2, rue Gambetta, B.P. 19, 51150 Bouzy, tel. 03.26.57.01.54, fax 03.26.57.09.97, e-mail contact@champagne-barnaut.com by appt.

Philippe Secondé

BARON ALBERT La Préférence 1994★★

○ n.c. 12,000 70–99 F

As long ago as 1677, the Baron family was already tending the vines at Charly-sur-Marne, to the west of Château-Thierry. In 1947, Albert Baron was the first to produce champagne under his own brand. The wines spend some time in wood and do not go through a malolactic fermentation. This one is a blend of 70% Chardonnay and 30% Pinots (including 10% Pinot Meunier). It is slightly oaked, and combines finesse and power. Those that received a citation are the **Rosé**, which is well-balanced and long, and the **Tradition** Brut (90% Pinot Meunier, 10% Chardonnay), which is fresh and well-developed, and has good length. (NM)

Champagne Baron Albert, 1, rue des Chaillots, Grand-Porteron, 02310 Charly-sur-Marne, tel. 03.23.82.02.65, fax 03.23.82.02.44 by appt.

BARON-FUENTE Cuvée Prestige★★

○ 5 ha 22,000 100–149 F

The Baron family has been devoting itself to wine for three centuries, and is based in the western part of the vineyard (Aisne). The Baron-Fuenté label was first launched by Gabriel Baron in 1967 after his marriage to Dolorès Fuenté from Andalusia. The three champagne grapes contribute in equal proportions to this wine, which has a slightly smoky nose, and whose palate suggests complex flavours of red berries and hazelnuts. (NM)

Champagne Baron-Fuenté, 21, av. Fernand-Drouet, 02310 Charly-sur-Marne, tel. 03.23.82.01.97, fax 03.23.82.12.00, e-mail champagne.baron-fuente@wanadoo.fr by appt.

BAUCHET PERE ET FILS Réserve★

○1er cru n.c. 20,700 70–99 F

Two brothers work a vineyard of 36 ha (89 acres) in Bisseuil, a commune in the valley of the Marne between Tours-sous-Marne and Ay. The family launched its first champagne in 1960. Chardonnay (60%) and Pinot Noir (40%) combine to produce this wine, in which dosage is evident, and whose red berry flavours are as striking on the nose as they are in the mouth. (RM)

Sté Bauchet Frères, rue de la Crayère, 51150 Bisseuil, tel. 03.26.58.92.12, fax 03.26.58.94.74 by appt.

BAUGET-JOUETTE

Blanc de blancs 1993★

○ n.c. n.c. 150–199 F

This firm launched its brand in 1973, and owns a vineyard of some 14 ha (35 acres). Its Blanc de Blancs 1993 has now reached its peak. It is a round, harmonious champagne, which is high in alcohol, full and generous, and whose aromatic palate mingles lemony notes and nuances of crystallised fruits. (NM)

🗝 Champagne Bauget-Jouette, 1, rue Champfleury, 51200 Epernay, tel. 03.26.54.44.05, fax 03.26.55.37.99 🍷 by appt.
🗝 Bauget

ANDRE BEAUFORT 1992★★

○ 4.5 ha n.c. 100–149 F

Jacques Beaufort follows the practice of agrobiology, and also shows the disgorgement date on his labels. His 1992 (80% Pinot Noir, 20% Chardonnay) is outstanding for its bouquet of honey, butter and crystallised fruits, and for its full, well-balanced palate. The **Cuvée 2000** (150–199F), which is of the same composition, was awarded a star. There are hints of acacia honey, violets and pear drops here. (RM)

🗝 Jacques Beaufort, 1, rue de Vaudemanges, 51150 Ambonnay, tel. 03.26.57.01.50, fax 03.26.52.83.50 ☒ 🍷 by appt.

BEAUMET Blanc de blancs

○ n.c. 40,000 ▮ 🌡 100–149 F

This brand was created in 1878 and taken over in 1977 by Jacques Trouillard, who is also the owner of Jeanmaire and Oudinot. The Blanc de Blancs has a charmingly aromatic nose, opening up with hints of vanilla and white blossom, anticipating a fresh, lively palate. (NM)

🗝 Champagne Beaumet, 3, rue Malakoff, 51207 Epernay Cedex, tel. 03.26.59.50.10, fax 03.26.54.78.52
🗝 J. et M. Trouillard

BEAUMONT DES CRAYERES Grande Réserve★

○ 34 ha 220,000 ▮ 🌡 70–99 F

This group of producers was created in 1955 and produces wine from 75 ha (185 acres) of vines. It exports 80% of its production, going as far afield as the United States and Malaysia. Blending together three harvests, their Grande Réserve wine is predominantly made from black grapes (75% Pinot, including 60% Pinot Meunier). The hefty, rich aroma of the Pinot Meunier is particularly noticeable, and the wine lingers on the palate. Another star is awarded to the **Fleur de Rose 95** (140–149F), which is made from half white grapes and half black, a fruity, forthcoming, powerful and well-balanced champagne. The **Nuit d'Or 90** blend (100–149F) received a star for its intense, toasty nose (70% Chardonnay). (CM)

🗝 Champagne Beaumont des Crayères, B.P. 1030, 51318 Epernay Cedex, tel. 03.26.55.29.40, fax 03.26.54.26.30, e-mail champagne-beaumont@wanadoo.fr ☒ 🍷 ev. day 10am–12 noon 2pm–6pm; cl. Sat. Sun. from Christmas until Easter

L. BENARD-PITOIS 1995★

○ 1er cru n.c. 3,335 ▮ 100–149 F

The firm was set up in 1938. Today it numbers some 10 ha (25 acres) divided between two Grands Crus and four Premiers Crus. This 1995 wine blends 70% Chardonnay with 30% Pinot Noir. A champagne with pronounced citrus fruit flavours, its lightness marks it out as an apéritif.

🗝 Champagne L. Bénard-Pitois, 23, rue Duval, 51160 Mareuil-sur-Ay, tel. 03.26.52.60.28, fax 03.26.52.60.12 ☒ 🍷 by appt.

BERECHE ET FILS★★

○ 1er cru 2 ha n.c. ▮ 70–99 F

Jean-Pierre Berèche works the family vineyard, which was set up in the Montagne de Reims in 1847. The non-vintage Brut he presented is produced from equal quantities of the three champagne varieties, and won enthusiastic support from several members of the jury who were keenly aware of its fine complexity, its splendid balance, its beguiling length and its brioche and floral aromas. (RM)

🗝 Champagne Berèche et Fils, Le Craon-de-Ludes, B.P. 18, 51500 Ludes, tel. 03.26.61.13.28, fax 03.26.61.14.14 ☒ 🍷 by appt.

CH. BERTHELOT Blanc de blancs

○ Gd cru n.c. 5,000 ▮ 70–99 F

Christian Berthelot is a wine producer in Avize, a commune on the Côte des Blancs that is classified as a Grand Cru. His non-vintage Blanc de Blancs Grand Cru blends Chardonnay grapes harvested in 1995, 1996 and 1997. Its intense and lively aromas of lemon clearly mark this out as an apéritif. (RM)

🗝 Christian Berthelot, 32, rue E.-Valle, 51190 Avize, tel. 03.26.57.58.99, fax 03.26.51.87.26 ☒ 🍷 by appt.

PAUL BERTHELOT Blason d'Or

○ n.c. n.c. ▮ 70–99 F

This firm based in Dizy, close to Epernay, runs a vineyard of 22 ha (54 acres). Its Blason d'Or blend, which is made from half black grapes and half white, has been highly praised for its delicacy, its freshness, its aromas of hazelnut and its silky balance. One taster suggests serving it with a gougère (cheesy choux pastry) or a brioche. (NM)

🗝 SARL Paul Berthelot, 889, av. du Gal-Leclerc, 51530 Dizy, tel. 03.26.55.23.83, fax 03.26.54.36.31 ☒ 🍷 by appt.

BERTIN ET FILS Carte blanche★

○ 3 ha 18,000 ▮ 70–99 F

This grower-winemaker in the Côte des Blancs grows 3 ha (7 acres) of Chardonnay and 1 ha (2.5 acres) of Pinot Noir. He launched his champagne in 1978. The Carte Blanche is a blanc de blancs 1995. There are faint suggestions of undergrowth, fresh butter and toast discernible here; in the mouth, the dominant flavours are gingerbread and mirabelle plums. The whole impression is delicate and well-balanced, with good length. Also worthy of note, and receiving a citation from the jury, is the **Carte d'Or**, a blanc de blancs from the 1992 harvest; it is very close in style to the above, but has perceptible dosage. Serve it with lemon tart. (RM)

🔑 Bertin et Fils, 64, rue Saint-Gibrien, 51530 Cramant, tel. 03.26.57.93.38, fax 03.26.58.46.79, e-mail francis.bertin@fnac.net ☑ Y by appt.

BILLECART-SALMON

Cuvée Nicolas François Billecart 1995

○ n.c. n.c. 300–499 F

The Billecarts have been established in Mareuil-sur-Ay for more than four centuries. The firm was set up in 1818, and is well known for its up market champagnes such as those described below, which were mentioned by the jury. The Nicolas François Billecart blend is produced from 60% Pinot Noir and 40% Chardonnay taken from Grands Crus; it has a complex nose and a lingering, well-balanced palate. As for the **Elisabeth Salmon 95** (over FF 500), which is produced from half black grapes and half white, this is a rosé coloured with red wine from Mareuil-sur-Ay. Salmon-pink in colour, it is lively and well-balanced. (NM)

🔑 Champagne Billecart-Salmon, 40, rue Carnot, 51160 Mareuil-sur-Ay, tel. 03.26.52.60.22, fax 03.26.52.64.88, e-mail billecart@champagne-billecart.fr ☑ Y by appt.

BINET 1992★★

○ n.c. n.c. 150–199 F

This firm was created by Léon Binet in 1849, taken over in 1948 by Henri Germain (of Champagne Germain) and handed over in 1985 to the Frey group. Blended from Chardonnay (60%) and Pinot Noir (40%), this 1992 wine has been judged outstanding for its freshness and elegance. Its nose is lemon-scented, while the palate suggests grapefruit. The **Brut Elite** (100–149F), which was given a citation by the jury, is a blend dominated by black grapes. This is a very light champagne on the palate, with aromas of lime. (NM)

🔑 Champagne Binet, 31, rue de Reims, 51500 Rilly-la-Montagne, tel. 03.26.03.49.18, fax 03.26.03.43.11, e-mail info@champagne-binet.com ☑ Y by appt.

🔑 Daniel Prin

H. BLIN ET CIE Tradition

○ 90 ha 400,000 70–99 F

This producers' collective works 120 ha (296 acres) of vines and has its main centre in the valley of the Marne. The Tradition, in which Pinot Meunier is especially pronounced (77%), is produced from grapes harvested in 1995, 1996 and 1997. It is a flowery champagne, long on the palate and with noticeably high dosage. The **Chardonnay** blend (100–149F), which also receives a citation, is produced from the same vintages. It is full of youth and promise, with its aromas of lemon leading to peach and honey flavours. (CM)

🔑 SC Champagne H. Blin et Cie, 5, rue de Verdun, 51700 Vincelles, tel. 03.26.58.20.04, fax 03.26.58.29.67 ☑ Y by appt.

R. BLIN ET FILS★

◑ n.c. n.c. 70–99 F

The Blins have a vineyard of 11 ha (27 acres) in the Massif de Saint-Thierry, one of the cradles of champagne. This rosé is appealing for its balanced and elegant palate, which is full of fruit and redolent of cherries and blackcurrants. Also worth noting, and given a citation by the jury, is the **Millésimé 93**, a blanc de noirs, which is vinous, fleeting but pleasant on the palate, and full of red berry flavours. (RM)

🔑 R. Blin et Fils, 11, rue du Point-du-Jour, 51140 Trigny, tel. 03.26.03.10.97, fax 03.26.03.19.63, e-mail contact@champagne-blin-et-fils.fr ☑ Y by appt.

BOIZEL Joyau de France 1991★

○ n.c. 50,000 200–249 F

Auguste Boizel set up his firm in 1834. His descendants still manage it at the heart of the Boizel-Chanoine-Champagne group. The Joyau de France was first launched in 1961, is produced from 70% Pinot Noir and 30% Chardonnay and spends some time in wooden casks. There are hints of hazelnut, dried fruit and honey here. The palate is well-balanced and rounded. A special citation is also awarded to the **Grand Vintage 95** (150–199F), in which Chardonnay (48%) and Pinot are in nearly equal proportions. A supple, harmonious champagne, in which acacia honey and citrus fruits play their parts. (NM)

🔑 Champagne Boizel, 46, av. de Champagne, 51200 Epernay, tel. 03.26.55.21.51, fax 03.26.54.31.83

🔑 Groupe Boizel-Chanoine

BOLLINGER R.D. 1988★★

○ n.c. n.c. 300–499 F

This firm was established in 1829, and grew out of a marriage between the German Josef Bollinger (who became Jacques Bollinger) and an aristocratic lady whose family was deeply rooted in Champagne and owned vineyards in Ay and Cuis. Today, it exports its wines to 80 countries and has a vast vineyard, nearly 150 ha (370 acres) of the highest quality. Its upmarket wines, like the cuveé RD, are fermented and matured in wood. RD, an acronym patented by Bollinger, means 're-cently disgorged'. This technique aims to achieve complex wines that lose nothing of their freshness. The goal is attained with this 1988, a blend of 72% Pinot Noir and 28% Chardonnay. It succeeds in being highly developed without having tired, and is appealing for the infinite complexity of its aromatic palate where oakiness, spices and vanilla mingle with crystallised citrus fruits, honey, dried fruits and toast . . . And what harmony! What length! This is unanimously voted a connoisseur's champagne, 'one to get the conversation flowing around a table'. (NM)

🗝 Bollinger, 16, rue Jules-Lobet, 51160 Ay, tel. 03.26.53.33.66, fax 03.26.54.85.59

BOLLINGER Grande Année 1992★

○ n.c. n.c. 300–499 F

The Grande Année is one of the flagship vintages of the Bollinger firm. The 1990 was considered an exceptional wine in its class. The 1992, a more modest vintage, is fractionally less good, but is certainly not lacking in merit, with its mixture of vanilla and almond on a palate that has now reached its peak. The blend brings together 65% Pinot Noir with 35% Chardonnay. As for the **Spécial Cuvée** (75% produced from Pinot, including 15% Meunier, and 25% Chardonnay), it is a champagne rich in brioche and honey flavours (150–199F). It fully deserves a citation. (NM)

🗝 Bollinger, 16, rue Jules-Lobet, 51160 Ay, tel. 03.26.53.33.66, fax 03.26.54.85.59

BONNAIRE Blanc de blancs★

○Gd cru 10 ha n.c. 70–99 F

This estate was established in 1932 on the Côte des Blancs by Fernand Bouquemont, grandfather of Jean-Louis Bonnaire, the present operator. The vineyard includes 13 ha (32 acres) of Chardonnay and 9 ha (22 acres) of the two Pinots. This wine is a result of the blending of Chardonnays harvested in 1995 and 1996. A Grand Cru reminiscent of fresh butter and roasted hazelnuts, scented with lemons, it is fresh and supple: 'everything that you expect from a blanc de blancs'. The Premier Cru blanc de blancs **Gelminger** (a second brand) is worthy of citation: it is a straightforward champagne, suitable as an apéritif. (RM)

🗝 SA Bonnaire, 120, rue d'Epernay, 51530 Cramant, tel. 03.26.57.50.85, fax 03.26.57.59.17, e-mail info@champagne-bonnaire.com ☒ Y by appt.

🗝 Jean-Louis Bonnaire

ALEXANDRE BONNET

Madrigal 1993

○ 12 ha 7,000 100–149 F

This brand was launched in 1932, and has been in the lap of the BRC group since 1998. The Madrigal blend – 'a short passage in verse expressing tender feelings' – is produced from half black grapes and half white and certainly deserves its name: it is delicate, floral, strikes the palate directly and lingers in the memory. (NM)

🗝 SA Alexandre Bonnet, 138, rue du Gal-de-Gaulle, 10340 Les Riceys, tel. 03.25.29.30.93, fax 03.25.29.38.65 ☒ Y by appt.

🗝 Philippe Baijot

BONNET-PONSON 1995

○1er cru n.c. n.c. 70–99 F

The vineyard first saw the light of day in 1835 with Maxim-Isidore Bonnet. Today, it covers about 10 ha (25 acres) in Chamery, a pretty village in the Montagne de Reims. This 1995 blend is the work of Thierry Bonnet, who has married 40% Chardonnay with 60% Pinot. Well-balanced, round and harmonious, it represents the qualities of the vintage well, and will go perfectly with poultry. (RM)

🗝 Champagne Bonnet-Ponson, 20, rue du Sourd, 51500 Chamery, tel. 03.26.97.65.40, fax 03.26.97.67.11, e-mail champagne.bonnet.ponson@wanadoo.fr ☒ Y by appt.

🗝 Thierry Bonnet

BOREL-LUCAS

Blanc de blancs Cuvée Sélection

○Gd cru 1.8 ha n.c. 70–99 F

Well-known for its 17th-century château, Etoges is on the far side of the Côte des Blancs. This operation was established there in 1929. It offers a Grand Cru produced from the 1995 vintage, topped up with one-third 1994 reserve wines. The nose may be discreet, but the palate is complex with its hints of almonds. Also cited is the **Rosé** (80% Meunier, 10% Pinot Noir, 10% Chardonnay, harvested in 1996 and mainly 1997), which is fresh, well-balanced and long. (RM)

🗝 EARL Borel-Crépaux, 1, rue Richebourg, 51270 Etoges, tel. 03.26.59.30.46, fax 03.26.51.59.84 ☒ Y ev. day 9am–12 noon 2pm–6pm; Sun. 9am–12 noon; cl. 15–31 Aug.

BOUCHE PERE ET FILS

Cuvée réservée★

○ n.c. 300,000 70–99 F

Established in 1945, this firm launched its marque in 1955 and today has 35 ha (86 acres) of grapevines in 11 different Crus, including five Grands Crus. It offers a vintage produced half from black and half from white grapes (30% Pinot Noir, 20% Meunier), including 20% reserve wines. A very attractive champagne owing to its biscuity elegance and its balance, which accentuates freshness. Another star is awarded to the **An 2000** blend (50% Pinot Noir, 50% Chardonnay), which is round, harmonious and now at its peak, and to the **Grande Réserve 91** (Pinot 55%, Chardonnay 45%), which is flowery and has hints of menthol. (NM)

🗝 Champagne Bouché Père et Fils, 10, rue Charles-de-Gaulle, 51530 Pierry, tel. 03.26.54.12.44, fax 03.26.55.07.22 ☒ Y by appt.

RAYMOND BOULARD Réserve★

○ 5 ha 10,000 70–99 F

The Boulards have been wine-growers since the Revolution and merchant-winemakers since 1952. Their vineyard of 10 ha (25 acres) extends over seven different Crus. Some of the wines are matured in wood. This Réserve, blending 25% Chardonnay and 75% Pinot

CHAMPAGNE

(including 45% Meunier), is produced from the 1997 vintage and from reserve wines. It is full of fruit, richly textured, light and forthcoming. The **Rosé** (100–149F), which is fashioned from a maceration of equal parts of the two Pinots, is evocative of the rich aromas of blackcurrants, raspberries, vanilla and smoke. It receives a star. Finally there is a citation for the **Carte d'Or Blanc de Blancs** (100–149F), which is fresh and delicate. (NM)

Champagne Raymond Boulard, 1, rue du Tambour, 51480 La Neuville-aux-Larris, tel. 03.26.58.12.08, fax 03.26.61.54.92, e-mail info@champagne.boulard.fr Y by appt.

JEAN-PAUL BOULONNAIS

Blanc de blancs Réserve**

○ 5 ha 5,000 70–99 F

In five generations, the Boulonnais have developed a vineyard of 5 ha (12 acres) at Vertus, on the south side of the Côte des Blancs. Their Réserve is a characteristic blanc de blancs. Combining floral traces and aromas of honey, it is supple and perfectly balanced. It will serve equally well as an apéritif or with food. As for the Premier Cru **Tradition**, it offers a complex range of fruit, in which aromas of pear are especially striking (80% Chardonnay, 20% Pinot Noir). It receives a citation for its richness and balance. (NM)

Jean-Paul Boulonnais, 14, rue de l'Abbaye, 51130 Vertus, tel. 03.26.52.23.41, fax 03.26.52.27.55 Y by appt.

R. BOURDELOIS

Blanc de blancs Cuvée de réserve

○ n.c. n.c. 70–99 F

This grower based in Dizy, close to Epernay, offers a classic blanc de blancs. It has a discreet nose, showing hints of bread and brioche, followed successively by ripe fruit flavours, then dried fruits and finally candied fruits. (RM)

Raymond Bourdelois, 737, av. du Gal-Leclerc, 51530 Dizy, tel. 03.26.55.23.34, fax 03.26.55.29.81 Y by appt.

BOURGEOIS Cuvée de l'Ecu 1995

○ n.c. n.c. 100–149 F

The Bourgeois have been producing champagne for three generations. Michel Bourgeois offers this Cuvée de l'Ecu under a blue-starred label (could this écu perhaps be a euro?). It is a blanc de blancs that didn't complete its malolactic fermentation. Is that why it has stayed young? It is certainly lively and light. (NM)

Champagne Bourgeois, 43, Grande-Rue, 02310 Crouttes-sur-Marne, tel. 03.23.82.15.71, fax 03.23.82.55.11, e-mail bourgeois-mhb@compuserve.com Y by appt.

CH. DE BOURSAULT Tradition*

○ 10 ha 56,000 70–99 F

Madame Veuve Clicquot built this château in 1845, lived in it and died here. Since 1927, the estate has been the property of the Fringhian family. The three champagne varieties work together in roughly equal proportions in this distinguished and well-structured non-vintage Brut, which has now reached its peak. Receiving citations in the upper price bracket are the **93**, which is produced from equal parts Chardonnay and Pinot Meunier, and is spicy, vanilla-scented, toasted and harmonious, and the **Tradition Rosé**, a *saignée* rosé produced from the two Pinot varieties that is straightforward, oaky and elegant. (NM)

Champagne Ch. de Boursault, 2, rue Maurice-Gilbert, 51480 Boursault, tel. 03.26.58.42.21, fax 03.26.58.66.12 Y by appt.

BOUTILLEZ-GUER Tradition**

○ 1er cru n.c. n.c. 70–99 F

For several centuries, the Boutillez have been wine-producers in Villers-Marmery, a commune in the Montagne de Reims that is well known for the quality of its Chardonnay wines. They work 3.6 ha (9 acres). Their Tradition consists of 75% Chardonnay with 25% Pinot Noir. The dominant grape variety impregnates this champagne with aromas of Viennese pastries and white blossom, followed by flavours of lemon and grapefruit. Chardonnay also clearly leaves its mark in the **Blanc de Blancs premier cru**, which gets two stars as well for its delicacy and elegance. Two wines to be drunk on their own or with fish. (RM)

Champagne Boutillez-Guer, 38, rue Pasteur, 51380 Villers-Marmery, tel. 03.26.97.91.38, fax 03.26.97.94.95 Y by appt.

Marc Boutillez

G. BOUTILLEZ-VIGNON

Blanc de blancs

○ 1er cru 0.25 ha 2,500 70–99 F

This family has been established in Villers-Marmery since the 16th century, has been producing wine since 1976, and today owns a vineyard of some 5 ha (12 acres). They offer a blanc de blancs from the 1995 and 1997 harvests that is buttery and complex, with a straightforward attack leading to great freshness on the palate. Likewise cited is the **Cuvée Prestige premier cru**, which is produced from Pinot Noir (40%) and Chardonnay (60%) harvested in 1996, 1997 and 1998. Its rich, complex nose dominates a fresh, spicy palate. Ideal as an al fresco apéritif. (RM)

G. Boutillez-Vignon, 26, rue Pasteur, 51380 Villers-Marmery, tel. 03.26.97.95.87, fax 03.26.97.97.23 Y ev. day 10am–12 noon 2pm–6pm; Sat. Sun. by appt.; cl. 15 Aug.–5 Sep.

BRICE Ay

○Gd cru n.c. 3,500 ▮ 150–199 F

The firm itself is of recent provenance, having been founded in 1994, but the Brice family has been established in Bouzy since the 17th century. They are the owners of a vineyard of 7 ha (17 acres). This firm has the distinctive feature of producing and selling Grands Crus marketed under its own name, such as this wine from Ay (90% Pinot Noir and 10% Chardonnay), which receives a citation for its floral, fruity character, its roundness and its length on the palate. (NM)

Champagne Brice, 3, rue Yvonnet, 51150 Bouzy, tel. 03.26.52.06.60, fax 03.26.57.05.07, e-mail ebea@wanadoo.fr Y by appt.

BRICOUT Cuvée Arthur Bricout★

○Gd cru n.c. n.c. ▮ 150–199 F

The house was founded by a German, Charles Koch, in 1820, and took on the name Bricout et Koch when Arthur Bricout came into the family. Afterwards, it became German again until its recent acquisition by the Martin group. This special cuvée is a blanc de blancs. It has now reached its peak, and offers a complex nose that is very characteristic of Chardonnay. Its palate is a little slow to develop, but its length on the palate adds interest. The **Millésime 92** is worthy of a citation. This is also a blanc de blancs but, in contrast to the above, its straightforward, fresh, well-balanced palate outshines the nose, which is minerally and immature. (NM)

SA Champagne Bricout et Koch, 59, rte de Cramant, 51190 Avize, tel. 03.26.53.30.00, fax 03.26.57.59.26 Y by appt.

Groupe Delbeck

BROCHET-HERVIEUX

Cuvée An 2000 1995

○ n.c. 4,000 100–149 F

Based in Ecueil, near Reims, the Brochets have just (in May 2000) lost Henri Brochet, who was a powerful and elegant personality of the Champagne region. His children are working the 16 ha (40-acre) vineyard. The Cuvée An 2000 is made predominantly from black grapes (80% Pinot, including 5% Meunier). It is hefty, well-balanced and long, and will please all those who like highly developed champagnes. (RM)

Brochet-Hervieux, 12, rue de Villers-aux-Nœuds, 51500 Ecueil, tel. 03.26.49.77.44, fax 03.26.49.77.17 Y by appt.

ANDRE BROCHOT★

○ 1 ha n.c. ▮ 70–99 F

This grower-winemaker launched his champagne in the years immediately after the war. Two of his wines receive a star: this non-vintage Brut, which is pleasant and full of youth, and a **Grande Réserve**, a special blend with a rich aromatic palette (hints of flowers, verbena, cooked peaches and citrus fruit), a first impression of suppleness, a rounded and harmonious palate, and good length. (RM)

Francis Brochot, 50, rue Julien-Ducos, 51530 Saint-Martin-d'Ablois, tel. 03.26.59.91.39, fax 03.26.59.91.39 Y by appt.

EDOUARD BRUN ET CIE 1995

○ n.c. 25,000 ▮ 100–149 F

This house in Ay was set up more than a century ago (in 1898, to be precise) by the enterprising son of a cooper. It offers a blend of half black grapes with half white that has a lively attack and obvious freshness, despite having a substantial dosage. (NM)

Edouard Brun et Cie, 14, rue Marcel-Mailly, B.P. 11, 51160 Ay, tel. 03.26.55.20.11, fax 03.26.51.94.29 Y ev. day 8am–12 noon 2pm–6pm; Sat. Sun. by appt.

ERIC BUNEL Tradition

○Gd cru 4.5 ha 30,000 ▮ 70–99 F

The Louvois company formerly used to own a château constructed by Louis XIV's ambitious minister for war, Michel le Tellier. The palace has disappeared, but the wine-growers remain, supporting themselves with more pacific weapons. Among them is Eric Bunel, who launched his first champagne in 1970. His Tradition wine is made from a blend of Pinot Noir (70%) and Chardonnay (30%), some harvested in 1996, but mainly in 1997. It was especially noted for its nose, which mingles white blossom and hints of smoke, and for its palate, which is full of ripe fruit. Also cited is the **1992**, blended from half black and half white grapes, which is also smoky, generous, well-structured and balanced (100–149F). (RM)

Eric Bunel, 32, rue Michel-Letellier, 51150 Louvois, tel. 03.26.57.03.06, fax 03.26.52.31.66 Y ev. day 9.30am–12 noon 2pm–5.30pm

CHRISTIAN BUSIN Tradition

◐Gd cru 4 ha 40,000 ▮ 70–99 F

Famous for its old mill, Verzenay is one of the best-known communes in the Montagne de Reims, and is classified as a Grand Cru. The Busin family has been tending vines for four generations, and today owns 4 ha (10 acres). This Tradition (80% Pinot Noir, 20% Chardonnay, made from grapes harvested in 1995 and 1996) is a rosé of intense colour, with supple texture in no way diminishing its freshness. Still among the Grands Crus but now in white, the **Cuvée 2000 Vieilles vignes** (150–199F), a blend similar to the above but produced from the 1994 and 1995 harvests, is fruity, rich and supple. In itself worthy of citation, this is a champagne to accompany food. (RM)

Christian Busin, 4, rue d'Uzès, 51360 Verzenay, tel. 03.26.49.40.94, fax 03.26.49.44.19 Y by appt.

JACQUES BUSIN Cuvée 2000

○Gd cru 0.6 ha 5,000 100–149 F

Jacques Busin has the good fortune to run a vineyard situated among four Grands Crus: Verzy, Verzenay, Ambonnay and Sillery. His Cuvée 2000 is a single Cru from Verzenay, produced from 75% Pinot Noir topped up with 25% Chardonnay – from vines which are more than 40 years old, harvested in 1995. It is a fresh, minerally champagne, quite rounded and serious on the palate. (RM)

Jacques Busin, 17, rue Thiers, 51360 Verzenay, tel. 03.26.49.40.36, fax 03.26.49.81.11 by appt.

DANIEL CAILLEZ

5 ha 3,500 50–69 F

This grower-winemaker runs a vineyard of 5 ha (12 acres) at Damery in the valley of the Marne. His rosé is a rosé de noirs made from Pinot Meunier; its pleasing pink colour borders almost on red, the nose is full of Pinot, whilst the palate asserts itself with authority, freshness and length. This is a rosé to drink with food. The price is gentle, but then the wine is a well-kept secret! (RM)

Daniel Caillez, 19, rue Pierre-Curie, 51480 Damery, tel. 03.26.58.46.02, fax 03.26.52.04.24 by appt.

CAILLEZ-LEMAIRE Grande Réserve*

○ 2 ha 14,817 70–99 F

Henri Caillez runs a vineyard of 6 ha (15 acres), which was created in 1942. Blended from half white grapes and half black (with 25% Pinot Meunier), his Grande Réserve cuvée had only partial malolactic fermentation. It is a product of the 1995 and 1996 vintages. Its aromas are redolent of citrus fruits and honeyed brioche; on the palate, it is lively, round and harmonious. This is an apéritif champagne. (RM)

SARL Champagne Caillez-Lemaire, 14, rue Pierre-Curie, B.P. 11, 51480 Damery, tel. 03.26.58.41.85, fax 03.26.52.03.24 by appt.

Henri Caillez

PIERRE CALLOT Blanc de blancs

○Gd cru 4.93 ha n.c. 70–99 F

From the moment that he was born in Avize in 1784, Louis Callot was a child of the vines. Today, his descendants run a vineyard of 6 ha (15 acres) that is still in that same commune of the Côte des Blancs, now classified as a Grand Cru. They have been producing champagne since 1955. This blanc de blancs is largely a product of the 1997 harvest, topped up with reserve wines from 1995 and 1996. Full of floral scents (white blossom) and elegance, it displays fine freshness and liveliness without aggression. We must also mention the **Grande Réserve grand cru** (100–149F), a blanc de blancs from Avize drawn from the years 1991, 1992 and 1993, which is noted for its powerful florality and fruity freshness. (RM)

Champagne Pierre Callot et Fils, 100, av. Jean-Jaurès, 51190 Avize, tel. 03.26.57.51.57, fax 03.26.57.99.15 by appt.

CANARD-DUCHENE 1991*

○ n.c. n.c. 100–149 F

This brand was established in the 19th century and linked with Veuve Clicquot, so today it is in the bosom of LVMH. Produced from the three champagne grapes, this 1991 – a difficult vintage – still manages to retain its youth. The aromas of honeyed dried fruit are as striking on the nose as they are in the mouth, forming a harmonious whole that is both lively and complex. A star goes likewise to the **Grande Cuvée Charles VII** (150–199F), a blend that is very close to the above (albeit with less Pinot Meunier) and made in the same style. 'Exquisite as lace', wrote one taster. (NM)

Canard-Duchêne, 1, rue Edmond-Canard, 51500 Ludes, tel. 03.26.61.11.60, fax 03.26.40.60.17, e-mail info@canard-duchene.fr ev. day except Sun. Mon. 11am–1pm 2.30pm–5pm; cl. 15 Oct.–1st Apr.

JEAN-YVES DE CARLINI

Cuvée de réserve

○Gd cru 3.5 ha 6,500 70–99 F

The Carlinis arrived in Champagne in 1906. Carlini's R label appeared in 1955, and was followed in 1984 by Jean-Yves de Carlini's brand. The vineyard covers some 6.5 ha (16 acres) around Verzenay, a commune in the Montagne de Reims classified as a Grand Cru. And that is the category into which the three cited champagnes from this estate fall. This Cuvée de Réserve, produced from half black grapes and half white, is a blend of wines from 1995, 1996, 1997 and 1998. The hefty richness of the Verzenay Pinots can be felt in this fresh young champagne. The **Cuvée Montgolfière**, a blanc de noirs from the same four years, is well-balanced and full; the **1996** (100–149F), half black grapes, half white, is very close in style to the Cuvée de Réserve, but more rounded and harmonious. (RM)

Jean-Yves de Carlini, 13, rue de Mailly, 51360 Verzenay, tel. 03.26.49.43.91, fax 03.26.49.46.46 by appt.

CATTIER 1995

○1er cru 18 ha 40,000 100–149 F

The Cattiers have owned vines since 1763, and have been producing their own wine since 1920. Their vineyard covers some 18 ha (44 acres). This Premier Cru draws on the three champagne varieties in roughly equal quantities. It is very 'winey', well-balanced, round and harmonious.(NM)

Cattier, 6, rue Dom-Pérignon, 51500 Chigny-les-Roses, tel. 03.26.03.42.11, fax 03.26.03.43.13, e-mail jeancatt@cattier.com ev. day except Sat. Sun. 9am–11am 2pm–5pm; groups by appt.

CLAUDE CAZALS

Blanc de blancs 1995*

○Gd cru 2 ha 20,000 70–99 F

This hundred-year-old house launched its first champagne in 1950, and now works a vineyard of 9 ha (22 acres) in the Grands Crus of the Côte des Blancs. Generous, complex, fresh and long, its 1995 blanc de blancs has now reached its peak. A fine champagne and an extremely good buy. We must also mention, for those who like non-dosed wines, the **Cuvée vive**, a **Blanc de Blancs Extra Brut** from the 1994 vintage, which is clean, floral and full of spice. (RC)

Claude Cazals, 28, rue du Grand-Mont, 51190 Le Mesnil-sur-Oger, tel. 03.26.57.52.26, fax 03.26.57.78.43 by appt.

CHARLES DE CAZANOVE

Tradition Père et Fils 1995★★

○ n.c. n.c. 100–149 F

This house was founded in Avize in 1811 and has remained in the same family, although today it is based at Epernay. The 1995 is a blend of Pinot Noir (60%) and Chardonnay (40%). The jury found the expressive qualities of this champagne very appealing, with its strong suggestion of smoke (roasted hazelnuts) and its aromatic, spicy, elegant palate. Suitable for drinking as an apéritif, with white meat or with fish in a cream sauce. The same high rating goes to the **Brut Azur premier cru**, in which the white grapes are blended in inverse proportion (40% Pinot, including 10% Meunier): this is a beautifully harmonious wine, with its aromas of vanilla and fresh butter and its direct attack on the palate. (NM)

Charles de Cazanove, 1, rue des Cotelles, 51200 Epernay, tel. 03.26.59.57.40, fax 03.26.54.16.38

Lombard

CHANOINE Grande Réserve★★

○ n.c. n.c. 70–99 F

The Chanoine house was established in 1730, that is to say, one year after the most senior brand, Ruinart, and was revived by the BBC group. The Grande Réserve blend is very black (85% Pinot, including 15% Meunier). Its complex aromas are full of fruit and brioche, but show great delicacy. This thoroughbred, harmonious richness is sumptuously confirmed on the palate. The **Cuvée Tsarine 95**, which is half white grapes and half black, is generous and full-bodied and is awarded a star, while the **1991**, which is powerful and well-balanced, receives a citation (100–149F each). (NM)

Champagne Chanoine Frères, av. de Champagne, 51100 Reims, tel. 03.26.36.61.60, fax 03.26.36.66.62, e-mail chanoine-freres@wanadoo.fr

P. Baijot

JACQUES CHAPUT

Blanc de blancs 1994★

○ 2 ha 4,000 100–149 F

This outfit has a vineyard of 12 ha (30 acres) in Arrentières (a region in Bar-sur-Aube), where the hillsides enjoy fine exposure. Their Blanc de Blancs 1994, which is very far from being shy and retiring, seems to be at once powerful and well-balanced, with good length. The same verdict goes to the **Cuvée Calypso 95**, which is half white grapes and half black, and has very lively aromas of hazelnut and brioche. It will be just the thing at the apéritif hour. (RM)

EARL Champagne Jacques Chaput, La Haie-Vignée, 10200 Arrentières, tel. 03.25.27.00.14, fax 03.25.27.01.75, e-mail champagne.chaput.jacques@wanadoo.fr

CHAPUY

Blanc de blancs Réserve Carte verte★

○Gd cru 6.25 ha 12,000 100–149 F

The Chapuys are heirs to a long line of wine producers going back to the 18th century, and have been producing their champagnes since 1952. They have a vineyard of more than 6 ha (15 acres) in a Grand Cru on the Côte des Blancs. This Brut Réserve has consistently been a highly successful wine. This year, it is produced from a blend of the 1995, 1996 and 1997 harvests; it certainly proves a worthy example of the style, with its floral, vanilla-scented aromas anticipating a supple palate that is seductively fruity, round and harmonious. (NM)

SA Champagne Chapuy, 8 bis, rue de Flavigny, B.P. 14, 51190 Oger, tel. 03.26.57.51.30, fax 03.26.57.59.25, e-mail champagne.chapuy@oger.51.telepost.fr by appt.

CHARDONNET ET FILS

Cuvée brut★★

○ 2 ha 10,000 70–99 F

The vineyard is a century old, but the champagne was only launched in 1970. Michel Chardonnet cultivates 3 ha (7 acres) in the Côte des Blancs; he has blended 70% Chardonnay and 30% Pinot Noir to develop this Cuvée Brut and his **Brut Réserve**, each of which is awarded two stars. The former comes from the 1993, 1994 and 1995 harvests, the latter from 1990, 1991 and 1992. These are two very closely related champagnes, full of brioche, butter and honey, and both showing good length. As for the **Blanc de Blancs** from the 1992 harvest, it receives a citation for its lemon and grapefruit flavours. (RM)

Michel Chardonnet, 7, rue de l'Abattoir, 51190 Avize, tel. 03.26.57.91.73, fax 03.26.57.84.46 ev. day 10am–12 noon 2pm–8pm

GUY CHARLEMAGNE

Blanc de blancs Mesnillésime 1995★

○Gd cru 2 ha 12,000 100–149 F

The Charlemagnes have been wine-growers for more than a century. They first ventured into direct sales in 1950, and since then they have worked a 14 ha (35-acre) vineyard in the Côte des Blancs. This top-of-the-range wine spends six months in vats and six months in casks. The 1990 was a runaway favourite. The 1995 presents a rich, complex, vanilla-scented nose with notes of lychee. It has a well-balanced, round and harmonious palate that is complex and lightly oaky. Still among the Grands Crus, the **Charlemagne 95** blend,

which is also a **Blanc de Blancs**, receives a citation. It is very close in style to the above, although with less oak. (RM)
🔑 Champagne Guy Charlemagne, 4, rue de La Brèche-d'Oger, 51190 Le Mesnil-sur-Oger, tel. 03.26.57.52.98, fax 03.26.57.97.81 ☒ Y by appt.

ROBERT CHARLEMAGNE

Blanc de blancs Réserve

○Gd cru 4 ha 30,000 70–99 F

This champagne was first launched by Robert Charlemagne at the beginning of the 1940s. The company is sutuated in the Côte des Blancs, and owns 4.3 ha (11 acres) of vines. There is a suggestion of may blossom on the generous, fresh nose of this blanc de blancs, a freshness that comes as no surprise in a wine produced from the 1997 harvest. On the palate, the same generous richness comes through subtly. The **Rosé** (85% 1995 Chardonnay, tinted with red wine from Pinot Noir) receives a citation for its freshness and its lively, rich robustness. (RM)
🔑 Champagne Robert Charlemagne, av. Eugène-Guillaume, B. P. 25, 51190 Le Mesnil-sur-Oger, tel. 03.26.57.51.02, fax 03.26.57.58.05 ☒ Y by appt.

CHARLES COLLIN★

○ n.c. n.c. 70–99 F

This producers' collective was created in 1952, bringing together 150 wine-growers, and it processes a total harvest of 300 ha (740 acres) delivering 900,000 bottles. The centre of these vineyards is in Essoyes, in the Côte des Bars (Aube). Pierre-Auguste Renoir, who had a studio in this village and drew part of his inspiration from it, now lies in the commune cemetery. After visiting these places of interest, you might taste this very well-made non-vintage Brut. In spite of its single-varietal character, this blanc de noirs (Pinot Noir) shows complexity; its 'highly professional' dosage adds still further to its length. Two other champagnes were worthy of citation: the Brut **Tradition** (Pinot Noir, Chardonnay and reserve wines drawn from three different years), which is intense, honeyed and supple, and the **1989** (100–149F), which is full and well-developed. (CM)
🔑 Champagne Charles Collin, B.P. 1, 10360 Fontette, tel. 03.25.38.31.00, fax 03.25.29.68.64 ☒ Y by appt.

CHARLIER ET FILS 1995

○ 14 ha n.c. 100–149 F

This operation of 14 ha (35 acres) of vineyards has the distinction of maturing all its wines for one year in wooden casks. The 1995 blend is the product of equal parts of the three champagne grape varieties. It is rich and complex, with flavours of preserved or crystallised fruit and coffee, and has now reached its peak. Tasters suggested that it should be drunk with food. (RM)
🔑 Charlier et Fils, 4, rue des Pervenches, Aux Foudres de Chêne, 51700 Montigny-sous-Châtillon, tel. 03.26.58.35.18, fax 03.26.58.02.31, e-mail champagne.charlier@wanadoo.fr ☒ Y ev. day 8am–12 noon 2pm–6pm; Sun. 10am–12 noon

JEAN-MARC ET CELINE CHARPENTIER

Prestige Terre d'Emotions★★★

○ 0.5 ha 4,000 100–149 F

The Charpentiers, who were selling their wine to the boatmen of the Marne before champagne first got its bubbles, only created their brand in 1992. They cultivate a vineyard of 9 ha (22 acres) in the Aisne. This blend certainly deserves its name, for it has made a powerful impression. It is produced from 60% Pinot (including 50% Pinot Meunier) and 40% Chardonnay, harvested in 1992. Delicate bubbles rise to the surface through a pleasant golden hue. The nose mingles dried fruits and honeyed dried apricot; the palate comes through very elegantly, lemon-scented and slightly smoky. As for the **Brut Réserve** (70–99F), it receives a citation for its good balance. (RC)
🔑 Jean-Marc et Céline Charpentier, 4, rue de l'Ecole, 02310 Charly-sur-Marne, tel. 03.23.82.10.72, fax 03.23.82.31.80 ☒ Y by appt.

J. CHARPENTIER Réserve★

○ 3.5 ha 30,000 70–99 F

Jacky Charpentier works a vineyard of some 12 ha (30 acres), which he planted in 1974 on the right bank of the valley of the Marne. His Brut Réserve is a blanc de noirs in which Pinot Meunier plays the key role (80%). A mature champagne with a nose of apricot and quince jelly and a honeyed, well-balanced palate. It will go well with a first course. (RM)
🔑 Jacky Charpentier, 88, rue de Reuil, 51700 Villers-sous-Châtillon, tel. 03.26.58.05.78, fax 03.26.58.36.59 ☒ Y by appt.

CHARTOGNE-TAILLET

Cuvée Sainte-Anne 1995★

○ 11 ha n.c. 70–99 F

The Chartognes have been established since 1450 in Merfy, near to Saint-Thierry, whose monastery vineyard was famous long before the appearance of champagne. They work 11 ha (27 acres) of vines. Half white grapes and half black (with 10% Pinot Meunier), this cuvée is slightly smoky and vinous on the nose. Its palate is full of brioche and liquorice, which clearly marks it out as a food wine. (RM)
🔑 Philippe Chartogne-Taillet, 37–39, Grande-Rue, 51220 Merfy, tel. 03.26.03.10.17, fax 03.26.03.19.15 ☒ Y by appt.

CHASSENAY D'ARCE

◑ n.c. 15,000 70–99 F

This is the brand of an important group of producers created in 1956 on the Côte des Bar, and which produces wine from 310 ha (770 acres) of vines. 85% Pinot Noir and 15% Chardonnay mingle in this orange-coloured rosé, which has flavours of strawberries, raspberries and honey, and which some members of the jury would have preferred to have been less heavily dosed. Try it with a dessert of red berries. (CM)

Champagne Chassenay d'Arce, 10110 Ville-sur-Arce, tel. 03.25.38.30.70, fax 03.25.38.79.17 by appt.

GUY DE CHASSEY

Cuvée réservée Nicolas d'Olivet**

Gd cru 9.42 ha 1,500 70–99 F

The bottles labelled Nicolas d'Olivet are produced by Guy de Chassey champagne, based in Louvois. This non-vintage wine from the 1992 vintage is for drinking up now, as it is already well-developed. Developed does not, however, mean old. A nose of vanilla-scented quince jelly and plums precedes distinct aromas of crystallised fruit on the palate. What is surprising is the attack, which is lively and fresh. Serve it with woodcock or with a pear tart. (RM)

Champagne Guy de Chassey, 1, pl. de la Demi-Lune, 51150 Louvois, tel. 03.26.57.04.45, fax 03.26.57.82.08, e-mail mo.de.chassey@wanadoo.fr ev. day 9am–12.30pm 2pm–6.30pm

CHAUVET Cuvée An 2000**

n.c. n.c. 100–149 F

The Chauvet firm is more than 150 years old, its seven vineyards covering some 10 ha (25 acres). The Cuvée An 2000 brings together 30% 1990 Pinot Noir with the same proportion of 1991 Pinot Noir and 40% 1994 Chardonnay. The straightforward, powerful, buttery nose announces a well-structured palate that is intense and long, with good vinosity. This is a champagne to drink with food, one that will go particularly well with poultry and other white meats. As to the **Grand Rosé**, which received a citation but was not awarded a star (60% Chardonnay and 30% Pinot Noir, tinted with 10% red wine from Bouzy), the tasters particularly appreciated its balance and its lightness of touch. (NM)

Chauvet, 41, av. de Champagne, 51150 Tours-sur-Marne, tel. 03.26.58.92.37, fax 03.26.58.96.31 by appt.

MARC CHAUVET 1994

1er cru 1 ha 9,000 70–99 F

In the 12th-century church in Rilly, a plaque marks the tomb of Nicolas Chauvet, who died in 1529. His descendants still live in Rilly, tending some 12 ha (30 acres) of vines. They offer a classic blend (60% Pinot Noir, 40% Chardonnay) that has not undergone malolactic fermentation. Its aromas are evocative of citrus fruits (lemon and grapefruit) with a more exotic note (pineapple). Its full and intense palate makes this 1994 an excellent champagne to drink with food, and one that would go particularly well with white meat. (RM)

Champagne Marc Chauvet, 3, rue de la Liberté, 51500 Rilly-la-Montagne, tel. 03.26.03.42.71, fax 03.26.03.42.38 by appt.

HENRI CHAUVET ET FILS*

1 ha 1,500 70–99 F

Henri Chauvet was a nurseryman and wine-grower at the beginning of the 20th century. His descendants tend a vineyard of 8 ha (20 acres) in the Montagne de Reims. This Rosé gives pride of place to black grapes (80% Pinot Noir to 20% Chardonnay) from the 1995 and 1996 harvests. It is full of the scents of raspberries, blackcurrants and vanilla, while the palate is distinguished by its youthfulness. Wines receiving a citation were the **1995** (55% Chardonnay, 45% Pinot Noir), which is highly developed and full of brioche aromas, and the **Blanc de Noirs**, which has a complex nose and rounded palate. (RM)

Damien Chauvet, 6, rue de la Liberté, 51500 Rilly-la-Montagne, tel. 03.26.03.42.69, fax 03.26.03.45.14, e-mail champagnechauvet@aol.com by appt.

ANDRE CHEMIN*

1er cru 0.5 ha n.c. 70–99 F

The label bears the name of the grandfather, who launched his first champagne in 1948. His son Jean-Luc followed him in 1971, and was joined in 1997 by Sébastien, who represents the third generation. Their enterprise extends over some 6.5 ha (16 acres) in the north-western part of the Montagne de Reims. The Rosé Brut owes everything to Pinot Noir. The jury praised the delicacy of its floral aromas (roses and carnations) mixed with hints of little berries, as well as its soft, delicate fullness on the palate. As regards the **Cuvée Prestige premier cru**, which is very black (only 10% Chardonnay), though light and elegant, it will make an excellent apéritif champagne. (RM)

Champagne André Chemin, 3, rue de Châtillon, 51500 Sacy, tel. 03.26.49.22.42, fax 03.26.49.74.89 by appt.

Jean-Luc Chemin

ARNAUD DE CHEURLIN Réserve

2 ha 12,000 70–99 F

The Cheurlin family are to be found all over the Aube region. This particular enterprise has a vineyard of some 6 ha (15 acres). It was the Brut Réserve (75% Pinot, 25% Chardonnay from the 1996 and 1997 harvests) that emerged as the jury's first choice. A mature, well-balanced champagne, it is pleasantly fruity on the nose as well as on the palate, straightforward on entry and fairly long. (RM)

Arnaud de Cheurlin, 58, Grande-Rue, 10110 Celles-sur-Ource, tel. 03.25.38.53.90, fax 03.25.38.58.07 by appt.

RICHARD CHEURLIN Brut H**

1 ha 8,000 70–99 F

Richard Cheurlin inherited a mini-vineyard that he then expanded to some 8.3 ha (21 acres). He launched his champagne in 1978. The Brut H is produced from half black

CHAMPAGNE

grapes and half white of the 1996 and 1997 vintages, and has been widely praised. Elegance is the key tasting note here, with beautifully delicate aromas, freshness and structure. This is still a youthful champagne. The **Brut H Vintage 96** (70% Pinot Noir, 30% Chardonnay), which is full, rich and vinous, earns a star, as does the Brut **Carte Or** (the same blend as the above, but from the 1995, 1996 and 1997 harvests), which is honeyed and harmonious, and the **Blanc de Blancs 96**, which has all the freshness of white blossom. (RM)

⊶ Richard Cheurlin, 16, rue des Huguenots, 10110 Celles-sur-Ource, tel. 03.25.38.55.04, fax 03.25.38.58.33 ☑ Y by appt.

CHEURLIN-DANGIN

Carte Or Réserve

○ 8.3 ha 30,000 ▮ 70–99 F

The union of two families gave birth to this champagne in 1960. The vineyard extends over 18 ha (44 acres), at the heart of the Côte des Bar in the Aube. Pinot Noir is very extensively grown at Celles-sur-Ource, and has a strong influence on this Carte Or (70% from this grape variety to 30% from Chardonnay, coming from the 1996 and 1997 harvests). Supple on entry, fresh and straightforward, this is a very worthy non-vintage Brut. (RM)

⊶ Champagne Cheurlin-Dangin, 17, Grande-Rue, B.P. 2, 10110 Celles-sur-Ource, tel. 03.25.38.50.26, fax 03.25.38.58.51, e-mail cheurlin-dangin.fr ☑ Y by appt.

GASTON CHIQUET

Spéciale Club 1995★★

○ 3 ha 12,500 ▮ ♁ 100–149 F

Nicolas Chiquet was a wine-producer in 1746. The Chiquet brothers launched their first champagne in 1919, but they went their separate ways in 1935, hence this Gaston Chiquet label. Established in Dizy, to the north of Epernay on the right bank of the Marne, the enterprise presently occupies 22 ha (54 acres), notably across the Ay region, which is the neighbouring commune. Curiously, although this village is famous for its Pinot Noir, it is Chardonnay that reigns supreme in the vineyard. It dominates this top-of-the-range blend by 70%, with the balance made up of Pinot Noir. Floral, toasty, well-balanced, if still firm, this is 'a wine for tomorrow', to quote the words of one taster. (RM)

⊶ Champagne Gaston Chiquet, 912, av. du Gal-Leclerc, 51530 Dizy, tel. 03.26.55.22.02, fax 03.26.51.83.81, e-mail gaston.chiquet@wanadoo.fr ☑ Y by appt.

CLEMENT ET FILS

○ 6 ha 50,500 70–99 F

Congy is near to the marshes of Saint-Gond which were the site of a famous battle in 1914. The Clément family works a vineyard of some 6 ha (15 acres) here, which was established in 1950. One-quarter Chardonnay and three-quarters Pinot (5% Pinot Noir) make up their non-vintage Brut, produced from the 1997 harvest, backed up by reserve wine from 1996. A highly developed champagne that has already reached its peak. (RM)

⊶ GAEC Champagne Clément et Fils, 15, rue des Prés, 51270 Congy, tel. 03.26.59.31.19, fax 03.26.59.22.63 ☑ Y by appt.

CLERAMBAULT Carte noire★

○ n.c. n.c. 100–149 F

This important group of producers (600, 000 bottles) has assumed the name Seigneurs de Neuville-sur-Seine, the commune where they are based. Two of their blends have been deemed a great success. This Carte noire is dominated by Pinot grape varieties (57% Pinot Noir, 21% Meunier, 22% Chardonnay). The tasters were very eloquent about its aromatic range, which is strongly marked by dried fruit, hints of brioche and candied fruits, giving particular praise to its balance. As for the **Carte Or 91** champagne (100–149F; 50% Chardonnay), which was tasted and given a good report by an earlier jury, it puts an acceptable face on a rather thankless vintage, with its aromas of toast and its fine freshness and directness on the palate. It has now reached its peak. (CM)

⊶ Champagne Clérambault, 122, Grande-Rue, 10250 Neuville-sur-Seine, tel. 03.25.38.38.60, fax 03.25.38.24.36, e-mail champagne-clerambault@wanadoo.fr ☑

PAUL CLOUET

○Gd cru 3 ha n.c. ▮ ♁ 70–99 F

This grower-winemaker has the good fortune to be based in Bouzy, which is a commune classified as a Grand Cru and famous for its Pinot Noir. That is where the 70% of black grapes come from that go into this Brut; as for the 30% Chardonnay, it was grown in Chouilly, in the north of the Côte des Blancs. The result is a classic, though still youthful, champagne. The **Brut Rosé**, which is a similar blend except that it includes 12% Bouzy rouge, is certainly a little fleeting, but it has been cited for its forthright style. (RM)

⊶ Paul Clouet, 10, rue Jeanne-d'Arc, 51150 Bouzy, tel. 03.26.57.50.85, fax 03.26.52.64.65 ☑ Y ev. day 10am–12 noon 2pm–5pm

COLIN

Blanc de blancs Blanche de Castille★

○1er cru 5 ha 20,000 100–149 F

The Colin family were already wine-producers in 1829, at Vertus and at Bergères-lès-Vertus in the Côte des Blancs. Today, their descendants work 12 ha (30 acres) of vines. This blanc de blancs comes from the 1997 and 1996 harvest. The words 'finesse' and 'delicacy' keep recurring in the tasters' notes to evoke this very 'feminine' champagne, which is lively and ethereal with subtle aromas of citrus fruit. A refreshing wine, and good company too! (RM)

⊶ Champagne Colin, 101, av. du Gal-de-Gaulle, 51130 Vertus, tel. 03.26.58.86.32, fax 03.26.51.69.79, e-mail info@champagne-colin.com ☑ Ɪ ev. day 9am–12 noon 2pm–5pm; Sun. by appt.

COLLARD-CHARDELLE

Cuvée Prestige

○ n.c. 40,000 ▮▮ 70-99 F

This enterprise in the Marne valley handles a vineyard of more than 8 ha (20 acres). Their Prestige blend draws on the three champagne grapes (25% Chardonnay and 75% Pinot, including 50% Meunier). It comes from three years: 1995, 1996 and 1997. The tasters weren't all in agreement in praising the balance on this fat and fruity champagne. (RM)

🔑 Champagne Collard-Chardelle, 68, rue de Reuil, 51700 Villers-sous-Châtillon, tel. 03.26.58.00.50, fax 03.26.58.34.76 ☑ Ɪ by appt.

COLLARD-PICARD 1996*

○ n.c. 4,000 ▮ ▮▮ 100-149 F

This champagne has only recently been launched by Olivier Collard, who works 6.3 ha (16 acres) of vines in the Marne valley. One-quarter Chardonnay and three-quarters Pinot (including 50% Pinot Meunier) form the basis of this 1996, which exhibits strong Pinot characteristics, aspires towards length, but finds its balance. A promising combination. (RM)

🔑 Champagne Collard-Picard, 6, rue du Château, 51700 Villers-sous-Châtillon, tel. 03.26.52.36.93, fax 03.26.58.34.76, e-mail champcp51@aol.com ☑ Ɪ by appt.

DANIEL COLLIN Tradition*

○ 2 ha 22,000 ▮ 🌡 70-99 F

Baye is near the Petit Morin, a tributary on the left bank of the Marne. In 1959, Daniel Collin set up a vineyard there that today runs to some 4 ha (10 acres). His son Hervé in now in charge of the business. The Brut Tradition, a blanc de noirs (including 60% Pinot Meunier) from the 1996 and 1997 harvests, was unanimously praised for its aromatic profile with mingled hints of spices and fruit on the one hand, and for the fine structure of its full and well-built palate on the other. There is also a citation for the **Brut Rosé**, a rosé de noirs (including 60% Pinot Noir) with a discreet nose and light palate, 'a sensual and feminine wine', according to one taster. (RM)

🔑 Daniel Collin, 3, rue Caye, 51270 Baye, tel. 03.26.52.80.50, fax 03.26.52.33.62 ☑ Ɪ by appt.

COMTE DE NOIRON Cœur de Cuvée

◑ 4.5 ha 30,000 ▮ 🌡 70-99 F

This négociant house from Reims has produced its rosé by blending 1995, 1996 and 1997 wines, using 70% Pinot Noir and 30% Chardonnay. It is orangey-pink in colour, and the nose emits discreet hints of citrus fruit. After its supple entry, the palate proves to well-balanced. The **Cœur de Cuvée blanc** comes from the same base wine; this is a charming champagne for drinking in the late afternoon, for it is fresh and well-balanced. The **Charles du Roy premier cru** is a fine champagne, produced from the 1997 harvest, whose dosage compensates for its nervous youth. (NM)

🔑 Champagne Comte de Noiron, 17, rue des Créneaux, 51100 Reims, tel. 03.26.82.70.67, fax 03.26.82.19.12 ☑ Ɪ by appt.

🔑 Rapeneau

JACQUES COPINET

◑ 1 ha 7,000 70-99 F

Nearer to the Seine than to the Marne (within the département of Seine-et-Marne), Mongenost seems a little off the beaten track, but its vineyard has been favourably evaluated by several commentators. Jacques Copinet runs an estate of 7 ha (17 acres) that was established in 1975. His Brut Rosé comes from two-thirds Pinot Noir and one-third Chardonnay harvested in 1996 and 1997. There are aromas of little red berries here, discreet but with plenty of length. In the upper price bracket, the **Cuvée Marie Etienne 95 Blanc de Blancs** (a wine that was a *coup de coeur* in the 1992 vintage), has been cited for its complexity and its structure; it can only develop further with time. (RM)

🔑 Jacques Copinet, 11, rue de l'Ormeau, 51260 Montgenost, tel. 03.26.80.49.14, fax 03.26.80.44.61, e-mail champagne.copinet@wanadoo.fr ☑ Ɪ by appt.

STEPHANE COQUILLETTE

Cuvée LD**

○ 1.5 ha 10,368 ▮ 100-149 F

Based in Chouilly since 1978, Stéphane Coquillette offers a blend dominated by Pinot Noir (67%), with the rest Chardonnay. A very fine straw-gold hue, it has a very young, expressive nose full of strawberries and cooked red berries. Its impressive presence in the mouth, its fullness and its elegance particularly appealed to the jury. 'Serve it with zander with a duck stock sauce and girolles,' was the precise advice of one taster. A great non-vintage Brut. (RM)

🔑 Stéphane Coquillette, 31 bis, rue des Bergers, 51530 Chouilly, tel. 03.26.51.74.12, fax 03.26.54.96.55 ☑ Ɪ by appt.

COUCHE PERE ET FILS

○ 2.5 ha 19,794 ▮ 🌡 70-99 F

This 7 ha (17-acre) enterprise on the Côte des Bar in the Aube launched its brand in 1992. The Brut is a blend of 70% Pinot Noir and 30% Chardonnay from 1993 and 1994. It is a rich, well-balanced champagne with good length, and one that doesn't need to wait any longer. (RM)

🔑 EARL Champagne Couche, 29, Grande-Rue, 10110 Buxeuil, tel. 03.25.38.53.96, fax 03.25.38.41.69 ☑ Ɪ by appt.

ROGER COULON Grande Réserve**

○ 2 ha 20,000 ▮ ▮▮ 🌡 70-99 F

The Coulon family has been established over many years in Vrigny, to the west of Reims, and has 8.5 ha (21 acres) of vines there.

CHAMPAGNE

They mature some of their wines in cask, such as the Chardonnay that goes into this Grande Réserve blend, which is produced from equal parts of the three champagne varieties. Well-balanced, supple and high in alcohol, this wine mingles spices and ripe fruits. It is an interesting champagne of great character, which will go very well with food. The jury also cited the **Brut Tradition** and the **Brut Rosé**, which similarly blend the three grape varieties, but give pride of place to the black grapes: the first is intense and honeyed, the second is fruity, harmonious and well-balanced. (RM)

🔑 Champagne Roger Coulon, 12, rue de la Vigne-du-Roi, 51390 Vrigny, tel. 03.26.03.61.65, fax 03.26.03.43.68, e-mail champagne.coulon.roger@wanadoo.fr ☑ 🍷 by appt.

🔑 Eric Coulon

ALAIN COUVREUR

Blanc de blancs Réserve★

○ 1.5 ha 15,000 ▮ 🌡 70–99 F

Alain Couvreur works a vineyard of 5.5 ha (14 acres) in Prouilly, a commune rated at 85% on the *échelle des crus* and situated to the west of Reims. His Blanc de Blancs, produced from the 1990 and 1991 harvests and dominated by hints of butter and fresh hazelnuts, is beautifully balanced. The **Blanc de Noirs Réserve** (60% Pinot Noir to 40% Meunier, from the 1985 and 1986 harvests) also deserves a mention for its complexity, its balance and its length. (RM)

🔑 Champagne Alain Couvreur, 18, Grande-Rue, 51140 Prouilly, tel. 03.26.48.58.95, fax 03.26.48.26.29 ☑ 🍷 by appt.

REMI COUVREUR

Blanc de noirs Réserve

○ 1 ha n.c. ▮ 🌡 70–99 F

Rémi Couvreur is Alain Couvreur's son and established himself in 1997. His Blanc de Noirs Réserve gives pride of place to Pinot Noir, harvested in 1993 and 1994. It is appealing for its very fruity palate. (RM)

🔑 Rémi Couvreur, 18, Grande-Rue, 51140 Prouilly, tel. 03.26.48.58.95, fax 03.26.48.26.29 ☑ 🍷 by appt.

LYCEE AGRICOLE DE CREZANCY

Cuvée Euphrasie-Guynemer 1995

○ 0.3 ha 3,000 ▮ 70–99 F

The agricultural and viticultural school at Crézancy, in the Marne valley, has a vineyard of 3 ha (7 acres); it produces champagnes that are sold directly to the public. This one is made from Chardonnay (60%) and Pinot Meunier (40%). If it perhaps seems a little light, its buttery aromas are nonetheless very winning. (RM)

🔑 Lycée agricole et viticole de Crézancy, rue de Paris, 02650 Crézancy, tel. 03.23.71.50.70, fax 03.23.71.50.71 ☑ 🍷 by appt.

PAUL DANGIN ET FILS

Prestige 1995★

○ 3 ha 20,000 ▮ 🌡 70–99 F

Paul Dangin is the son of a wine-grower and made his first bottle of champagne in 1947. Today, his son and grandson own more than 30 ha (74 acres) in the Aube. Their 1995 gives pride of place to Chardonnay (70%). A well-balanced, full and complex champagne. (RM)

🔑 SCEV Paul Dangin et Fils, 11, rue du Pont, 10110 Celles-sur-Ource, tel. 03.25.38.50.27, fax 03.25.38.58.08, e-mail c.dangin@champagne-dangin.com ☑ 🍷 by appt.

DANTAN OUDIT★

○ 5 ha 15,000 ▮ 🌡 70–99 F

Produced from a vineyard of 5 ha (12 acres) created in 1969 in the region of Vitry-le-François, on wine-growing land that had been abandoned since the phylloxera outbreak, this wine is as white as it is red, with equal quantities of the two Pinots (from grapes harvested in 1994, 1995 and 1996). It is full of brioche and hints of grapefruit that give it liveliness and balance. An appealing champagne to be drunk as an apéritif. (RC)

🔑 Champagne Dantan Oudit, 35, rue de Vavray, 51300 Bassuet, tel. 03.26.97.72.47, fax 03.26.40.52.90, e-mail champagne.dantan@wanadoo.fr ☑ 🍷 by appt.

DEHOURS Grande Réserve★

○ n.c. n.c. ▮ 🌡 70–99 F

This house was founded by Ludevic Dehours in 1930, and is now run by his descendants. The Grande Réserve blend is a product of the three champagne grapes in equal proportions; it is minerally and floral; its powerful palate ends on an attractive note of bitterness. A classic. A star also goes to the **Cuvée confidentielle** (100–149F), which is more red than white (30% Chardonnay and 10% reserve wines). It is a well-balanced and lingering wine. (NM)

🔑 Champagne Dehours et Fils, 2, rue de la Chapelle, Cerseuil, 51700 Mareuil-le-Port, tel. 03.26.52.71.75, fax 03.26.52.73.83, e-mail champagne-dehours@wanadoo.fr ☑ 🍷 by appt.

DEHU PERE ET FILS

Cuvée Léon Lhermitte★

○ n.c. 525 ▮ 🌡 100–149 F

Here is a wine with an unusual label. It reproduces a famous painting by Léon Lhermitte, who lived and painted in the Marne valley: *Paying the Harvesters*. The background to the scene is a farm in Fossoy, which is the home village in the Aisne of the Déhu family, whose vineyard constitutes 10 ha (25 acres). This wine is produced from a blend of the three champagne grapes (including 55% Pinot Meunier, harvested in 1992). It is buttery and full of brioche aromas, its opening impression is of freshness and its finish is supple. The **Brut Tradition** (70–99F), which has even more Pinot Meunier (75%), is a powerful champagne destined for the dinner table. It receives a citation. (RC)

🔑 Déhu Père et Fils, 3, rue Saint-Georges, 02650 Fossoy, tel. 03.23.71.90.47, fax 03.23.71.88.91, e-mail varocien@aol.com ☑ Y by appt.

DELABARRE

○	2.5 ha	20,000	▮ 🌡 70–99 F

This family firm has been marketing champagne since 1956, and has a vineyard of 6 ha (15 acres) in the Marne valley. With 5% Chardonnay, their non-vintage Brut is practically a blanc de noirs (20% Pinot Noir, 75% Meunier). The grapes were harvested in 1996. Although it may not be very long on the palate, it is lively and appealing, and will drink well as an apéritif. The same verdict is pronounced on the **Cuvée Prestige** (100–149F), which is made from half white and half black grapes (30% Pinot Noir) from the 1994 harvest. It is a well-balanced and long wine, and one that shows its dosage. (RM)

🔑 Christiane Delabarre, 26, rue de Châtillon, 51700 Vandières, tel. 03.26.58.02.65, fax 03.26.57.10.94 ☑ Y by appt.

DELAHAIE Cuvée Prestige

○	n.c.	5,000	70–99 F

The Cuvée Prestige from this Epernay producer accords pride of place to Chardonnay (60%). It is smooth and easy-going, and the price is certainly right. (NM)

🔑 Brochet, 22, rue des Rocherets, 51200 Epernay, tel. 03.26.54.08.74, fax 03.26.54.34.45 ☑ Y by appt.

ANDRE DELAUNOIS

Cuvée du Fondateur*

○ 1er cru	1 ha	8,000	▮ 100–149 F

The Delaunay family has, since 1920, cultivated a vineyard of 7.7 ha (19 acres) in Rilly-la-Montagne, which is a commune in the Montagne de Reims classified as Premier Cru. Their Cuvée du Fondateur is predominantly Chardonnay (70%). The base wine is from 1996, and is topped up with 15% reserve wines from the years 1993, 1994 and 1995. The nose is floral (white blossom), and the palate lemony, harmonious and full. A champagne for the dinner table. Two wines that have been produced from all three champagne varieties, but with a predominance of Pinot (from grapes harvested in 1997, plus 20% reserve wines) are the **Cuvée Sublime** and the **Carte d'or**, both of which deserve citation for their length. The price bracket is on the low side (70–99F). (RM)

🔑 SCE André Delaunois, 17, rue Roger-Salengro, B.P. 42, 51500 Rilly-la-Montagne, tel. 03.26.03.42.87, fax 03.26.03.45.40 ☑ Y by appt.

DELAVENNE PERE ET FILS

Cuvée Tradition

○ Gd cru	4.8 ha	50,000	▮ 70–99 F

This family concern, created in 1930 and run by Jean-Louis and Christophe Delavenne, receives two mentions: first of all for the Tradition blend, which is produced from Pinot Noir (60%) and Chardonnay (40%) harvested in 1996 and 1997, and which is lemony, complex and long; secondly for the **1995 3e millénaire** (100–149F), which offers a powerful palate and noticeably high dosage. (RM)

🔑 Delavenne Père et Fils, 6, rue de Tours, 51150 Bouzy, tel. 03.26.57.02.04, fax 03.26.58.82.93 ☑ Y ev. day except Sun. 9am–12 noon 2pm–7pm

DELBECK Cramant**

○ Gd cru	n.c.	n.c.	150–199 F

This house, which was founded in 1832 and was a supplier to the French court, was famous for a while and then seemed to go to sleep. It has now been revived, and handed over to its present owners. Cru champagnes are a rarity: this one, a blanc de blancs from Cramant, is exemplary. It makes its presence felt at once and confirms it on the palate, which is full and harmonious, with a rich aromatic range mingling hints of butter, dried grass and citrus fruits. An extraordinary wine, and one for true connoisseurs. In the same cru style, two other champagnes received citations: the **Grand Cru Bouzy** (80% Pinot Noir, 20% Chardonnay), which is rich and powerfully dosed, and the **Brut Origines 95**, which is only sold by the magnum (at more than 500F). That isn't a bad idea. It allows us better to appreciate this well-balanced, round and powerful wine. (NM)

🔑 Champagne Delbeck, 39,rue du Gal-Sarrail, B.P. 77, 51053 Reims Cedex, tel. 03.26.77.58.00, fax 03.26.77.58.01, e-mail chdelbeck@aol.com ☑

🔑 Martin de La Giraudière

DELOUVIN NOWACK

Extra Sélection 1994*

○	1.2 ha	15,000	▮ 🌡 70–99 F

The Delouvin family have been wine-producers in Vandières (in the Marne valley) since 1930, with the current label dating back to 1943. Their vineyard boasts some 6.5 ha (16 acres). Made from half white grapes and half black (50% Pinot Meunier), this Extra Sélection blend, with its slightly smoky nose, its richness, fullness and length, is in every respect a champagne for the dinner table. As regards the **Carte d'Or**, a blanc de noirs made from Pinot Meunier (from the 1996 and 1997 harvests), it is well-structured and powerful, deserving of a citation. (RM)

🔑 Champagne Delouvin-Nowack, 29, rue Principale, 51700 Vandières, tel. 03.26.58.02.70, fax 03.26.57.10.11 ☑ Y by appt.

SERGE DEMIERE Réserve★

○Gd cru 2.2 ha 20,000 70–99 F

With his 6 ha (15 acres) near Ambonnay, the famous commune classified as a Grand Cru on the southern slopes of the Montagne de Reims, Serge Demière has some solid advantages when it comes to winning stars. This Réserve and the **Prestige**, which are produced from Pinot Noir and Chardonnay harvested in 1997, have each been awarded a star. While both have touches of smoke, with additional hints of toastiness, the first seems crystallised and sweet, whereas the second is fresh and lively. (RM)

Serge Demière, 7, rue de la Commanderie, 51150 Ambonnay, tel. 03.26.57.07.79, fax 03.26.57.82.15 by appt.

E. DESAUTEZ ET FILS Tradition

○Gd cru 2 ha 18,000 70–99 F

P. Deibener succeeded his father-in-law in 1975. The firm has a vineyard of nearly 4 ha (10 acres) around Verzenay, a commune with Grand Cru classification. This blend is predominantly black (Pinot 70%), and is produced from grapes harvested in 1997 and 1998. It is very supple on entry, and has a rich palate, albeit with evident dosage. (RM)

Champagne Désautez et Fils, 22, rue de Mailly, 51360 Verzenay, tel. 03.26.49.40.59, fax 03.26.49.46.88 by appt.

DESBORDES-AMIAUD

Cuvée An 2000 1989★★★

○1er cru n.c. 2,000 150–199 F

This enterprise of 9 ha (22 acres) in the Montagne de Reims has been run for more than half a century by women, currently by Marie-Christine Desbordes and her daughter Elodie. And there is certainly no doubt about their great skill and experience, judging from this excellent 1989, which is the result of some classic vinification, even though the wines have not undergone malolactic fermentation. It is a blend of Pinot Noir (80%) and Chardonnay (20%), and presents a complex, aromatic profile mingling smoky aromas (coffee and roasted dried fruits) with hints of flowers and honey on a rounded, delicate palate with great length. A subtle, but concentrated wine. (RM)

Marie-Christine Desbordes, 2, rue de Villers-aux-Nœuds, 51500 Ecueil, tel. 03.26.49.77.58, fax 03.26.49.27.34 by appt.

LAURENT DESMAZIERES

Cuvée Tradition★

◑1er cru 18 ha n.c. 70–99 F

Cattier champagne is responsible for the Laurent Desmazières brand. This Tradition rosé draws on the two Pinots, backed up by 10% Chardonnay. A few hints of toast, vanilla and caramel give unctuous richness to this dinner-table champagne, which would make the perfect accompaniment to roast veal. (NM)

Laurent Desmazières, 9, rue Dom-Pérignon, 51500 Chigny-les-Roses, tel. 03.26.03.44.46, fax 03.26.03.43.13

J. -J. Cattier

A. DESMOULINS ET CIE

Cuvée Prestige★

○ n.c. n.c. 100–149 F

This is still a family firm. It was created by Albert Desmoulins in 1908, and still to this day practises manual riddling and disgorgement. Two of its champagnes win a star: this Cuvée Prestige and the **Grande Cuvée 2000**, which is produced by blending together some 20 different Crus. The first of these is mostly Chardonnay, which gives it liveliness and freshness, while the second boasts a good attack and fine, harmonious roundness on the palate. There is also a citation for the **Brut Rosé**, which shows great power and vinosity. (NM)

Champagne A. Desmoulins et Cie, 44, av. Foch, B.P. 10, 51201 Epernay Cedex, tel. 03.26.54.24.24, fax 03.26.54.26.15 by appt.

DEUTZ 1995★★

○ n.c. n.c. 200–249 F

This house was founded in 1838 by two Germans from Aix-la-Chapelle, and has been run since 1993, though without losing its autonomy, by Louis Roederer. The 1995 blends 70% Pinot (including 10% Pinot Meunier) with 30% Chardonnay. Its nose is refined and complex, and foreshadows an exemplary palate that is full, well-balanced, fleshy but delicate. Also receiving citations are the **Rosé 96** (250–299F), a concentrated, supple rosé de noirs, and a **Blanc de Blancs** – a type of champagne that always works well for Deutz – **Vintage 95** (300–499F), which is minerally, lemon-tinged, well-balanced and long. (NM)

Champagne Deutz, 16, rue Jeanson, 51160 Ay, tel. 03.26.56.94.00, fax 03.26.56.94.10 by appt.

DOM BASLE Cuvée Première 1992★★★

○Gd cru 1 ha 8,500 70–99 F

Dom Basle is the name of a hermit who lived in Verzy during the Merovingian era. It is also the second label of Lallement-Deville, a house established in 1892 whose vineyard covers 3.5 ha (9 acres). The jury, and afterwards the grand jury, showed great enthusiasm for this wine, which is 55% Pinot Noir to 45% Chardonnay. A delicate thread of bubbles rises through its elegant pale straw

colour. The nose is highly complex, pulling together exotic, intense suggestions of fig jam, cooked fruit and prunes. The palate is also in the same league, and shows great length. A thoroughbred champagne. (RM)

🔑 Champagne Lallement-Deville, 28, rue Irénée-Gass, B.P. 29, 51380 Verzy, tel. 03.26.97.95.90, fax 03.26.97.98.25 ✉ 🍷 by appt.

🔑 Damien Lallement

PIERRE DOMI Cuvée spéciale*

○ 0.5 ha 1,800 ▮ 70–99 F

Based near Avize and Cramant, this firm was established by Pierre Domi in 1947 and is run today by his grandchildren. It receives a star for a special cuvée that is a blanc de blancs from the 1996 harvest. This is a honeyed, buttery, toasty champagne with hints of citrus fruit on the palate. The **Blanc de Blancs** (1997 harvest) is fat and rich, and deserves a citation. The same applies to the **Grande Réserve**, which is produced with grapes from the 1998 harvest (Chardonnay 60%, Pinot Meunier 40%), backed up by 25% of reserve wine from 1997. This last wine is fruity and well-balanced. (RM)

🔑 Champagne Pierre Domi, 8, Grande-Rue, 51190 Grauves, tel. 03.26.59.71.03, fax 03.26.52.86.91 ✉ 🍷 by appt.

DOQUET-JEANMAIRE

Blanc de blancs 1990*

○ 1er cru 9 ha 10,000 ▮ 🌡 100–149 F

Since 1995, Pascal Doquet has run the firm that was created by his parents in 1974. The vineyard covers 15 ha (37 acres) around Vertus and the surrounding communes on the Côte des Blancs. Consequently, the three champagnes of note are **blancs de blancs**. This 1990 has reached its peak. Thanks to the vintage, it is a generous and powerful wine, with aromas of preserves and honey. A wine to drink with a celebration dinner. A better choice for an apéritif would be the champagne sold under the label **De La Cense** (70–99F), which is a blend of 1995, 1996 and 1997 wines: it is lively, lemony, fresh and young, and has likewise been awarded a star. Last of all, there is a mention for the **Tradition premier cru Brut** (produced from the 1995 and 1996 vintages), a supple and elegant wine. (SR)

🔑 SA Champagne Doquet-Jeanmaire, 44, chem. Moulin-Cense-Bizet, 51130 Vertus, tel. 03.26.52.16.50, fax 03.26.59.36.71, e-mail doquet.jeanmaire@wanadoo.fr ✉ 🍷 ev. day 9.30am–12 noon 2pm–6pm; Sat. Sun. by appt.

DIDIER DOUE Blanc de blancs 1994

○ 3 ha n.c. ▮ 70–99 F

Didier Doué has been running a vineyard of 4 ha (10 acres) in Montgueux in the Aube since 1973. The Chardonnays in this commune are well known for their quality and character. Here, they have produced a toasty, buttery, honeyed but fresh champagne for drinking as an apéritif. (RM)

🔑 Didier Doué, chem. des Vignes, 10300 Montgueux, tel. 03.25.79.44.33, fax 03.25.79.40.04 ✉ 🍷 by appt.

ETIENNE DOUE Grande Réserve

○ 1 ha 6,000 ▮ 70–99 F

Not far from Troyes, Montgueux forms an island of wine-growing in the département of the Aube. Etienne Doué cultivates 4.5 ha (11 acres) of vines here, and has been making champagne since 1977. This Grande Réserve is a blanc de blancs produced from the 1995, 1996 and 1997 harvests. It displays aromas of honey and dried fruits and evident dosage on the palate, yet remains delicate and well-balanced. (RM)

🔑 Etienne Doué, 11, rte de Troyes, 10300 Montgueux, tel. 03.25.74.84.41, fax 03.25.79.00.47 ✉ 🍷 by appt.

DOURDON-VIEILLARD

Grande Réserve

○ n.c. 8,000 ▮ 🌡 70–99 F

This vineyard to the west of Epernay in the Marne valley extends over 9.5 ha (23 acres), and was established around a century ago. This Cuvée Grande Réserve is produced from all three champagne grapes (including 60% Chardonnay), and from a blend of 75% 1994 wines with 25% from 1993. Traces of peach lend elegance to the nose, and it has a fruity, supple finish. A very attractive combination. (RM)

🔑 Dourdon-Vieillard, 7, rue du Château, 51480 Reuil, tel. 03.26.58.06.38, fax 03.26.58.35.13 ✉ 🍷 by appt.

R. DOYARD ET FILS

Blanc de blancs Cuvée Vendémiaire

○ 1er cru 4 ha 25,000 ▮ 🛢 🌡 100–149 F

Maurice Doyard is famous in the Champagne region for having created, together with Robert Jean de Vogüé, the Comité Interprofessionnel des Vins de Champagne (CIVC), the industry's governing body. The brand was launched in 1997, and has 7 ha (17 acres) of vineyard at its disposal. This cuvée is cleverly produced: part of it is vinified in cask, and it receives only a partial malolactic fermentation. The blend is made up of wines from 1993, 1994 and 1995. The tasters detected aromas of lemon-scented hazelnut and interesting balance in the wine. (RM)

🔑 Champagne Robert Doyard et Fils, 61, av. de Bammental, 51130 Vertus, tel. 03.26.52.14.74, fax 03.26.52.24.02 ✉ Y ev. day except Sat. Sun. 9am–12 noon 1.30pm–6pm; cl. Aug.

DOYARD-MAHE

Cuvée blanc de blancs Carte d'Or

○ 1er cru n.c. n.c. 70–99 F

Philippe Doyard is a descendant of Maurice Doyard, one of the two founders of the CIVC. He manages a vineyard of 6 ha (15 acres) around Vertus on the Côte des Blancs. Three of these Premier Cru champagnes were cited. All come from the 1995 harvest, and are essentially based on Chardonnay. There are two blancs de blancs: this Carte d'Or, which is young, very delicate, vigorous and long, and the **1995** (100–145F), a subtle, lively, lemony champagne that still has room to develop further. Lastly, the **Brut Rosé** (88% Chardonnay with 12% red wine from Pinot Noir) has aromas of morello cherries and strawberries, and combines delicacy with vinosity. (RM)

Philippe Doyard, Le Moulin d'Argensole, 51130 Vertus, tel. 03.26.52.23.85, fax 03.26.59.36.69 ✉ Y ev. day 10am–12 noon 2pm–6pm; Sun. 10am–12 noon

DRIANT-VALENTIN★★

○ 1er cru 2 ha 15,000 70–99 F

Based in Grauves, near Avize, this family estate of 5.5 ha (14 acres) launched its champagne in 1972. It is the result of a classic blend of Chardonnay (60%) and Pinot Noir (40%) from the 1995 and 1996 harvests. The nose mingles floral traces with hints of toast. Its lively entry on the palate is followed by flavours of crystallised citrus fruits and honey. Its balance and harmony earn it two stars. (RM)

Jacques Driant, 4, imp. de la Ferme, 51190 Grauves, tel. 03.26.59.72.26, fax 03.26.59.76.55 ✉ Y by appt.

GERARD DUBOIS

Blanc de blancs 1992★★

○ Gd cru 3 ha 3,500 70–99 F

Here is a property created in 1920 on the Côte des Blancs, and a champagne that was launched in 1970. It sometimes happens that a blanc de blancs goes all out for delicacy, and loses by ending up too thin. Not in this case. With its aromas of honey and quince jelly, and with its strong presence on the palate, this is a dinner-table champagne that will go well with white meat. (RM)

Gérard Dubois, 67, rue Ernest-Vallé, 51190 Avize, tel. 03.26.57.58.60, fax 03.26.57.99.26 ✉ Y by appt.

HERVE DUBOIS

Blanc de blancs 1991★★

○ Gd cru 2.5 ha 3,000 100–149 F

This champagne was launched in 1980. The company is based on the Côte des Blancs and owns 4.05 ha (10 acres) of vines. Their Blanc de Blancs won the support of the jury for the richness of its aromas of peach, apricot and cinnamon, and for its elegant, lively palate. In the lower price bracket, the estate was awarded a star for its **Blanc de Blancs Réserve Grand Cru non-vintage**, which is round and supple and in the same style as the first wine, and received a citation for its **Brut** produced from the three champagne grapes, which is rounded and light on the finish (70–99F each). (RM)

Hervé Dubois, 67, rue Ernest-Vallé, 51190 Avize, tel. 03.26.57.52.45, fax 03.26.57.99.26 ✉ Y by appt.

ROBERT DUFOUR ET FILS

Chardonnay Cuvée Prestige 1989★

○ n.c. 3,000 100–149 F

This grower-winemaker runs a vineyard of 14 ha (35 acres) in the Aube. His Blanc de Blancs 1989 has already received recognition by juries of the *Guide* on two previous occasions. Here once again, we encounter its rich aromatic profile (crystallised fruits, coffee and gingerbread, with additional aromas of apricots and honey in the mouth). Two other champagnes received citations in the lower price bracket: the **Brut Rosé** from the 1995 harvest, which is intense, vanilla-scented and generous on the palate, and the **Cuvée Benjamine** (70% Pinot Noir, 30% Chardonnay), which is floral and light. (RM)

Champagne Robert Dufour, 4, rue de la Croix-Malot, 10110 Landreville, tel. 03.25.29.66.19, fax 03.25.38.56.50 ✉ Y by appt.

J. DUMANGIN FILS Grande Réserve

○ 1er cru 5.2 ha 30,000 70–99 F

This young firm, which was founded in 1968, has a vineyard of more than 5 ha (12 acres) at Chigny-les-Roses in the Montagne de Reims. Its Grande Réserve blend gives pride of place to Pinot (75%, including 50% Meunier, harvested in 1995 and 1996). The jury particularly praised its forthcoming style and the richness of its aromatic range, which has traces of bread dough, lychees and ripe apples. A citation likewise went to the **Brut Rosé premier cru** (100–149F), produced from half white grapes and half black (including 10% Meunier) from the 1996 harvest, and which has a lively attack and flavours of strawberries and redcurrants. (RM)

Champagne Jacky Dumangin Fils, 3, rue de Rilly, B.P. 23, 51500 Chigny-les-Roses, tel. 03.26.03.46.34, fax 03.26.03.45.61, e-mail info@champagne-dumangin.fr ✉ Y by appt.

DANIEL DUMONT Grande Réserve

○ 1er cru 6 ha 50,000 70–99 F

Daniel Dumont has taken over and enlarged his parents' vineyard. He now works 10 ha (25 acres) in the Montagne de Reims. His Grande Réserve includes 40% Chardonnay, 40% Pinot Noir and 20% Pinot Meunier; 70% of this constitutes grapes harvested in 1997, and the remaining 30% is 1996 reserve wine. It all adds up to a fruity, round and well-balanced champagne. (RM)

Daniel Dumont, 11, rue Gambetta, 51500 Rilly-la-Montagne, tel. 03.26.03.40.67, fax 03.26.03.44.82 by appt.

R. DUMONT ET FILS

Blanc de blancs*

○ 2 ha 1,980 70–99 F

The Dumonts have been wine-producers for two centuries, and now run an estate of 22 ha (54 acres) in the Aube. They launched their champagne in 1974. The Blanc de Blancs is a blend of wines from 1996 and 1997. White blossom and citrus fruits mingle on the nose, while a lively balance makes its presence felt on the palate. This champagne will serve very well as an apéritif. The **1996** (65% Pinot Noir, 35% Chardonnay) deserves a citation for its powerful richness and its length. (RM)

R. Dumont et Fils, 10200 Champignol-lez-Mondeville, tel. 03.25.27.45.95, fax 03.25.27.45.97 by appt.

DUVAL-LEROY Fleur de Champagne**

○ 1er cru n.c. 1,000,000 100–149 F

This great firm in Vertus on the Côte des Blancs was created in 1859 and remains a family concern, with a vast vineyard of 150 ha (370 acres). The Fleur de Champagne Brut (75% Chardonnay, 25% Pinot Noir) has superb delicacy and elegance, and is fresh and lively with aromas of citrus fruit. Two other blends received the same report: the **Fleur de Champagne Blanc de Blancs 95**, which has appealing aromas of vanilla-scented and buttered quince, and the **Fleur de Champagne 95** (65% Chardonnay, 35% Pinot Noir), which is lemony, supple and lightly dosed. (NM)

Champagne Duval-Leroy, 69, av. de Bammental, B.P. 37, 51130 Vertus, tel. 03.26.52.10.75, fax 03.26.52.37.10, e-mail champagne@duval-leroy.com by appt.
Carol Duval

ESTERLIN Sélection*

○ 120 ha n.c. 70–99 F

This is a wine from a group of producers set up in 1948, and which launched this brand in 1985. Their vines cover some 120 ha (300 acres). Blending Chardonnay (60%) and the two Pinots (40%), this champagne is elegant and very attractive. The jury particularly praised its aroma of lychees, which gives it fine complexity, as well as its liveliness and length. This is a bottle just as suitable for an apéritif as for the dinner table. (CM)

Champagne Esterlin, 25, av. de Champagne, B.P. 342, 51334 Epernay Cedex, tel. 03.26.59.71.52, fax 03.26.59.77.72 by appt.

CHRISTIAN ETIENNE

Cuvée de l'Espérance 1995**

○ 5 ha 5,000 70–99 F

With a vineyard of 9 ha (22 acres) in the Aube, this company has been producing champagne since the end of the 1970s. The 1995 vintage confirms the hopes that were

born last year of their remarkable cuvée . . . l'Espérance. Blending 70% Pinot Noir with 30% Chardonnay, it presents a soft, floral and honeyed bouquet. Following a gentle first impression that echoes the nose comes a lingering palate of great finesse, which together ended up winning the hearts of the jury. There was also a citation for the **Blanc de Noirs Cuvée de l'An 2000**, which is a blend of the 1992 and 1993 harvests, and which has a lively attack and flavours of crystallised fruit. (RM)

Christian Etienne, rue de la Fontaine, 10200 Meurville, tel. 03.25.27.46.66, fax 03.25.27.45.84 by appt.

CHAMPAGNE

JEAN-MARIE ETIENNE

◑ 1er cru 1 ha 3,000 70–99 F

This Marne estate has been established over four generations. Jean-Marie Etienne started producing champagne in 1958. Today, it is his two sons who run the operation. Their rosé is blended from the three champagne varieties, mainly harvested in 1996, 1997 and 1998. It has a pleasant, clear colour, is light, delicate and fresh, and offers up lovely raspberry aromas. (RM)

Champagne Etienne, 33, rue Louis-Dupont, 51480 Cumières, tel. 03.26.51.66.62, fax 03.26.55.04.65 by appt.

EUSTACHE DESCHAMPS

Blanc de blancs

○ 1.1 ha 9,533 70–99 F

The poet Eustache Deschamps was born in Vertus in 1346. The group of wine-producers known as La Vigneronne in this Côte des Blancs commune therefore quite naturally chose his name for their blanc de blancs. A blend of 1990 and 1991 wines, it is now reaching its peak, as can be seen from its richly textured character, its suppleness and complexity. This is a champagne for serving with food; indeed, one taster suggests drinking it with a warm apple tart with caramel ice-cream. (CM)

Champagne Eustache Deschamps, 38, av. de Bammental, 51130 Vertus, tel. 03.26.52.18.95, fax 03.26.58.39.47 by appt.

FRANCOIS FAGOT

◑ 0.7 ha 8,000 70–99 F

This family firm has 7 ha (17 acres) of vines in the Montagne de Reims, and launched its champagne in 1960. Its rosé is produced by the *saignée* method, and displays a pleasant salmon-pink colour, together with aromas of lemon and apricot. It is well-balanced and has good length. (NM)

🗝 SARL François Fagot, 26, rue Gambetta, 51500 Rilly-la-Montagne, tel. 03.26.03.42.56, fax 03.26.03.41.19 ☑ 🍷 by appt.

FALLET-DART

◐ 5 ha 13,466 ▮ 70–99 F

This vineyard already existed as far back as the beginning of the 17th century. Today, it covers 17 ha (42 acres) near Charly-sur-Marne, not far from Château-Thierry. The champagne was launched in 1966. This rosé de noirs is produced from both Pinots (80% being Pinot Meunier), harvested in 1996 and 1997. It is well-balanced and harmonious, a classic wine. (RM)

🗝 Fallet-Dart, Drachy, 2, rue des Clos-du-Mont, 02310 Charly-sur-Marne, tel. 03.23.82.01.73, fax 03.23.82.19.15 ☑ 🍷 by appt.

Made up of half white grapes and half black

FANIEL-FILAINE*

○ 3 ha 25,000 70–99 F

Faniel-Filaine is the result of a marriage between two Cru houses, and although the label itself was only recently established (1992), the Filaine family have actually been wine-producers for three centuries. The house owns a vineyard of 5.5 ha (14 acres) around Damery, in the Marne valley. This non-vintage Brut is a blanc de noirs (including 80% Pinot Meunier) from the 1996 harvest. It has hints of green apples, citrus fruits and crystallised fruit. (RM)

🗝 Faniel-Filaine, 48, quai de Verdun, 51480 Damery, tel. 03.26.58.62.67, fax 03.26.58.03.26 ☑ 🍷 by appt.

SERGE FAYE Tradition

○ 1er cru 3 ha 24,300 ▮ 70–99 F

In 1984, Serge Faÿe took over this estate from his father Robert who had created it in 1952. He manages 4 ha (10 acres) around Louvois, in the south of the Montagne de Reims. His Brut Tradition contains 80% Pinot Noir and 20% Chardonnay, harvested in 1996 and 1997. This champagne is discreet on the nose and not especially long, but its fairly pleasant palate nonetheless wins it a mention here. (RM)

🗝 Serge Faÿe, 2 bis, rue André-Le-Nôtre, 51150 Louvois, tel. 03.26.57.81.66, fax 03.26.59.45.12 ☑ 🍷 by appt.

NICOLAS FEUILLATTE

Réserve particulière**

○ 1er cru n.c. 3,000,000 ▮ 🌡 100–149 F

The Réserve Particulière will please more than a chosen few, for there is nothing very 'particular' about the scale of its production: no fewer than three million bottles have been put on the market! Which is just as well, for this champagne has been judged exceptional. It is made at the very important wine-producing centre of Chouilly, created in 1986. It is elegant and complex, and has fine freshness, owing to its aromas of grapefruit flavours of pineapple give it an exotic dimension. One taster suggests serving it with refined first courses (salmon or scallops). Two stars also go to the expensive (300–499F) **Palmes d'Or 92**: a champagne produced from half black grapes and half white, which is fresh, honeyed, buttery, vanilla-scented, long and full. (CM)

🗝 Champagne Nicolas Feuillatte, B.P. 210, Chouilly, 51206 Epernay, tel. 03.26.59.55.50, fax 03.26.59.55.82 ☑ 🍷 by appt.

BERNARD FIGUET Cuvée de réserve

○ 3 ha 25,000 ▮ 70–99 F

Based in the Marne valley, not far from Château-Thierry, the Figuet family has been producing its own champagne since 1946. Their vineyard extends over 11 ha (27 acres). Made from half white grapes and half black (including 30% Meunier) from the 1996 harvest, their Cuvée de Réserve is a very dry, straightforward, floral champagne. (RM)

🗝 Bernard Figuet, 144, rte Nationale, 02310 Saulchery, tel. 03.23.70.16.32, fax 03.23.70.17.22 ☑ 🍷 by appt.

FLEURY PERE ET FILS 1993**

○ 3 ha 25,000 ▮ 🌡 100–149 F

This estate was founded at the end of the 19th century in the Aube, and the brand launched in 1929 by Robert Fleury. Today, Jean-Pierre Fleury owns 13 ha (32 acres), which he works organically. This very black grape-based blend (only 20% Chardonnay) is an example of success in a vintage that has been judged inferior. The compliments flow thick and fast: 'outstanding, wonderful, magnificent', 'an exceptional champagne'. It has very fine effervescence in a golden-hued wine, a positive firework-display on the nose and a rich, complex palate in which dried fruit, toast, honey and white blossom all come together. It will go well with a sophisticated first course and white meats. (NM)

🗝 Champagne Fleury, 43, Grande-Rue, 10250 Courteron, tel. 03.25.38.20.28, fax 03.25.38.24.65 ☑ 🍷 by appt.

🗝 Jean-Pierre Fleury

G. FLUTEAU

Blanc de blancs Cuvée Prestige 1996

○ n.c. n.c. ▮ 🌡 70–99 F

This house, which was set up in 1935 by Georges Fluteau, the great-grandfather of he current proprietors, has a vineyard of 8 ha 20 acres) and claims to be the smallest business operation in the Champagne region! Their Blanc de Blancs Cuvée Prestige offers a discreet, delicate nose, with aromas of dried fruits and linden blossom. The palate, on the other hand, is more forthcoming and is distinguished by fruit flavours – pineapple, grapefruit and lemon. (NM)

Hérard et Fluteau, 5, rue de la Nation, 0250 Gyé-sur-Seine, tel. 03.25.38.20.02, fax 03.25.38.24.84, e-mail champagne.fluteau@wanadoo.fr ☑ Y by appt.

FORGET-CHEMIN Carte blanche★★

○ 11 ha 60,000 ▮ 70–99 F

Over the course of four generations, the Forget family have assembled a vineyard of 11 ha (27 acres) near to Ludes in the Montagne de Reims. All three grape varieties blended in equal parts, from three different vintages and 44 plots of land, form the identity card for Carte Blanche, which offers a mixture of honeyed, crystallised, floral notes, with flavours of exotic fruit compote, hazelnuts and citrus fruits, followed by flavours of brioche on the palate. This is a champagne to go with an elegant first course. We should also point out the star won by the **Brut Rosé**, which is blended from the three champagne grapes (including 50% Pinot Noir), and which has a discreet nose and powerful, harmonious palate. (RM)

Champagne Forget-Chemin, 15, rue Victor-Hugo, 51500 Ludes, tel. 03.26.61.12.17, fax 03.26.61.14.51 ☑ Y by appt.

FOURNAISE-THIBAUT 1995★

○ 1 ha 8,000 ▮ 🌡 70–99 F

Daniel Fournaise runs a vineyard at Châtillon-sur-Marne, and exports half of his production to Germany. His 1995, which is made from half black grapes and half white, offers a fresh nose with traces of menthol and hints of fern alongside toast, while on the palate it displays flavours of crystallised fruits, grapefruit and kiwi. A few tasters found the dosage a little high. Two other champagnes are cited: the **Brut Rosé**, a vigorously fruity rosé de noirs (from Pinot Meunier), and the **Cuvée Prestige**, made from equal proportions of the three grape varieties harvested in 1994, which is very close to the 1995 in style. (RM)

Daniel Fournaise, 2, rue des Boucheries, 51700 Châtillon-sur-Marne, tel. 03.26.58.06.44, fax 03.26.51.60.91 ☑ Y by appt.

PHILIPPE FOURRIER Carte d'or★★

○ 3 ha n.c. 70–99 F

The first vines to be owned by this house were acquired in 1947. Today, they cover some 8 ha (20 acres). The first champagne was launched in 1981. This Carte d'or, which is a blanc de noirs made from Pinot Noir harvested in 1997, almost achieved a *coup de coeur.* It has everything that one could desire: elegance, delicacy, freshness, complexity and length. The estate also won one star for its **Cuvée du 3ᵉ** Millénaire (100–149F), which includes 20% Chardonnay and is a lively and well-balanced wine. (SR)

Champagne Philippe Fourrier, 10200 Baroville, tel. 03.25.27.13.44, fax 03.25.27.12.49, e-mail champagne.fourrier@wanadoo.fr ☑ Y by appt.

J.C. FRANCOIS Carte d'or 1995★

○ n.c. 1,500 100–149 F

This family company in the Montagne de Reims owned 30 ha (74 acres) at the time of setting up in 1963. Today, they have regrouped with 12 ha (30 acres). Their Carte d'or 1995 cuvée releases scents of peardrops, banana and red fruits on the nose, whilst on the palate one can detect vanilla and almond, following a supple first impression. This is a champagne to drink as an apéritif, with a first course or with white meats. (NM)

J.-C. François-Delage, B.P. 40, 51500 Ludes, tel. 03.26.61.12.97, fax 03.26.61.11.91 ☑ Y by appt.

FRANCOIS-BROSSOLETTE Cuvée Prestige

○ 3 ha 3,118 ▮ 🌡 70–99 F

In the space of four generations, these growers have acquired 12 ha (30 acres) in the Aube. Their Cuvée Prestige, which is made from half black grapes and half white, offers a nose of ripe fruit and a lively attack, although it is a touch short on the palate. An honourable performance nonetheless. (RM)

François-Brossolette, 42, Grande-Rue, 10110 Polisy, tel. 03.25.38.57.17, fax 03.25.38.51.56 ☑ Y by appt.

RENE FRESNE Carte Argent★

○ 2 ha 15,000 ▮ 🌡 70–99 F

This house has a vineyard of some 8.5 ha (21 acres) in the Montagne de Reims. Produced from half black grapes and half white, their Carte Argent blend is minerally and fresh on the nose. It has a clean attack and appreciable length. The **Carte Noire** champagne is practically a blanc de noirs (5% Chardonnay, with both Pinots in roughly equal quantities). It is discreet on the nose and feels gentler on the palate than the above, making it suitable for drinking as an apéritif, and for receiving a citation. (RM)

GAEC du Monastère, 20, rue du Franc-Mousset, 51500 Sermiers, tel. 03.26.97.60.38, fax 03.26.97.67.63 by appt.

FRESNET-BAUDOT

○Gd cru 2 ha 12,000 70–99 F

Sillery, in the Montagne de Reims, contributed to the fame of the wine-growing areas of Champagne as early as the 16th century, before its wines even got their sparkle. Laurent Fresnet has managed a vineyard of 3 ha (7 acres) since 1976. He offers a Grand Cru that brings together Pinot (60%) and Chardonnay (40%) from the harvest of 1996, backed up by wines from 1994 and 1995. The nose is jammy and honeyed, and the palate, if a little brief, is well-structured. The wine will go well with white meats. (RM)

Fresnet-Baudot, 9, rte de Puisieulx, 51500 Sillery, tel. 03.26.49.11.74, fax 03.26.49.10.72, e-mail courrier@champagne-fresnet-baudot.fr by appt.

FRESNET-JUILLET

○1er cru 4 ha 35,000 70–99 F

Gérard Fresnet created his vineyard in 1954, and dug his cellar with his own hands. The house now has an estate of 9 ha (22 acres). This Brut Premier Cru comprises 75% Pinot Noir to 25% Chardonnay. Wine from 1997 is blended with 40% reserve wines of 1995 and 1996. This is a classic champagne, fleshy and rich and balanced by a touch of vigour. (NM)

Champagne Fresnet-Juillet, 10, rue de Beaumont, 51380 Verzy, tel. 03.26.97.93.40, fax 03.26.97.92.55 ev. day except Sun. 9am–6pm; cl. Aug.

G. DE BARFONTARC Extra Quality*

○ 90 ha 150,000 70–99 F

This brand was launched in 1964 by a group of wine-producers in the Aube. The grapes – mostly Pinot (50% Meunier and 35% Pinot Noir, as against 15% Chardonnay) – were harvested in 1997. This blend, which is at the same time lively and slightly crystallised, has a very fruity, full palate with great finesse. The whole effect is very appealing indeed. The cooperative also offers **Cuvée Sainte-Germaine 95**: a good vintage at a very worthwhile price. This is a champagne for the dinner table, with a powerful nose of hazelnut, apricot and crystallised mirabelle plums and a rounded, rich palate. It too receives a star. (CM)

Champagne G. de Barfontarc, rte de Bar-sur-Aube, 10200 Baroville, tel. 03.25.27.07.09, fax 03.25.27.23.00, e-mail g.de.barfontarc@wanadoo.fr ev. day except Sun. 8am–12 noon 1.30pm–4.30pm

LUC GAIDOZ Tradition

○1er cru n.c. 10,000 70–99 F

Luc Gaidoz has been running a vineyard at Ludes (Montagne de Reims) since 1983. His Tradition is a blend of 80% Pinot Meunier, accompanied by Pinot Noir and Chardonna in equal proportions, harvested in 1996 an 1997. This is a gentle wine distinguished b fullness and roundness rather than youthfu vivacity. It has aromas of preserved fruits (RM)

Luc Gaidoz, 4, rue Gambetta, 51500 Ludes, tel. 03.26.61.13.73, e-mail lgaidoz@wanadoo.fr by appt.

GAIDOZ-FORGET Carte d'or**

○1er cru n.c. n.c. 70–99 F

Ludes is a commune in the Montagne de Reims classified as a Premier Cru. Danie Gaidoz runs a vineyard of 9 ha (22 acres here. His Carte d'or, which is a predominantl black-grape blend (90% Pinot, including 80% Meunier, harvested in 1995 and 1996), wo over the tasters completely. Its nose o almonds, undergrowth, leather and carame leads on to a palate that is long and full of brioche flavours. This is a mature champagne, ready for drinking. A star also goes to the **Premier Cru Brut Rosé** (an identical blend, with Pinot Noir red wine added to it), which is blended from the 1996 and 1997 harvests. This supple, velvety, rounded wine is ready to drink and should go very well with a dessert (100–149F). (RM)

Gaidoz-Forget, 1, rue Carnot, 51500 Ludes, tel. 03.26.61.13.03, fax 03.26.61.11.65 ev. day except Sun. 9am–11.30am 2pm–6.30pm; cl.Aug.

GAILLARD-GIROT*

○ n.c. n.c. 70–99 F

The Gaillard-Girot family has been working a vineyard at Mardeuil, to the west of Epernay, for four generations. A blend of three different years, their non-vintage Brut gives pride of place to Pinot Meunier (78%, accompanied by 15% Chardonnay and 7% Pinot Noir). The maturation of the wines takes place partly in oak. This is a champagne for the dinner table, fleshy and rich, and with good length. (RM)

EARL Gaillard-Girot, 43, rue Victor-Hugo, 51530 Mardeuil, tel. 03.26.51.64.59, fax 03.26.51.70.59 by appt.

GALLIMARD PERE ET FILS

◑ 10 ha 8,700 70–99 F

The Gallimard family are growers and wine-makers based at Riceys in the Aube, and exporting 45% of their production. They have been producing champagne since 1930, and oversee a vineyard of 10 ha (25 acres). Their Rosé blend is made by a short maceration, and comes exclusively from Pinot Noir. With a pink colour bordering almost on red, it gives off floral aromas with a touch of lychee, which makes it particularly appealing as an accompaniment to spicy dishes. (RM)

Champagne Gallimard Père et Fils, 18–20, rue Gaston-Cheq, Le Magny, 10340 Les Riceys, tel. 03.25.29.32.44, fax 03.25.38.55.20 ev. day Sun. 9am–12 noon 2pm–6pm; Sat. by appt.

Didier Gallimard

GAUDINAT-BOIVIN Tradition

○ 5 ha 33,600 ▮ 70–99 F

This family operation of 5 ha (12 acres) has been in commercial operation since 1970. Majoring in black grapes (85% Pinot, including 80% Meunier), their Tradition blend attracts the attention with its aromas of coffee, chocolate and burnt notes. It is a very mature champagne, and should be drunk now. (RM)

EARL Gaudinat-Boivin, 6, rue des Vignes, Mesnil-le-Huttier, 51700 Festigny, tel. 03.26.58.01.52, fax 03.26.58.97.47 Y by appt.

Roger Gaudinat

GAUTHEROT Cuvée de réserve**

○ 7.5 ha 65,880 ▮ 70–99 F

François Gautherot is based in the Aude and comes from a long line of wine-producers going back to 1695. It was his two grandfathers who first went into champagne production in 1935. The estate became the supplier to the *Royale* (the French navy) in the 1950s. Today, it extends over 12 ha (30 acres). Produced from the 1996 and 1997 vintages and consisting of 75% Pinot Noir with 25% Chardonnay, his Cuvée de Réserve is a non-vintage Brut that is already exceptionally promising. On the nose, aromas of lemon-scented apricot develop into white blossom, while on the palate, honey, supported by a touch of grapefruit, contributes to the roundness. The **Sélection 95**, which is an almost identical blend, also earned a citation. It is lively and vinous, and will go well with grilled fish. (RM)

François Gautherot, 29, Grande-Rue, 10110 Celles-sur-Ource, tel. 03.25.38.50.03, fax 03.25.38.58.14 Y by appt.

MICHEL GENET

Blanc de blancs Brut Esprit*

○ Gd cru 4 ha 40,000 ▮ 70–99 F

This operation was founded by Michel Genet in 1960, and owns a vineyard of 7 ha (17 acres) on the Côte des Blancs. Esprit is a Grand Cru blanc de blancs, a delicate, long, well-structured champagne with an attractive nose of may blossom and white flowers. Another blanc de blancs Grand Cru, the **Grande Réserve 95**, is still too young but does nonetheless merit citation. (RM)

Michel Genet, 22, rue des Partelaines, 51530 Chouilly, tel. 03.26.55.40.51, fax 03.26.59.16.92, e-mail champagne.genet.michel@wanadoo.fr Y by appt.

RENE GEOFFROY

Cuvée Prestige 1996*

○ 1er cru 1 ha 9,000 100–149 F

The Geoffroys have been wine-producers for four centuries in Cumières, whose hillsides dominate the Marne valley. They cultivate 13 ha (32 acres). Their Cuvée Prestige (75% Chardonnay, 25% Pinot Noir) spends six months in barrel, and is not given malolactic fermentation. The tasters praised its straightforward attack, its roundness and its long finish. They also gave a citation to the **Cuvée de réserve Premier Cru** (70–99F), which is produced from the three champagne varieties, harvested in 1996 and 1997. This is a promising champagne, which is supple, delicate and long. (RM)

René Geoffroy, 150, rue du Bois-des-Jots, 51480 Cumières, tel. 03.26.55.32.31, fax 03.26.54.66.50, e-mail info@champagne-geoffroy.com Y by appt.

PIERRE GERBAIS Prestige***

○ 1 ha 4,000 ▮ 70–99 F

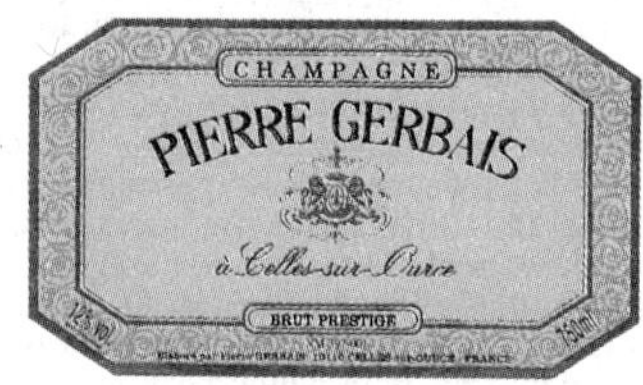

This vineyard in the Aube was established in 1906. Pierre Gerbais launched his first champagne in 1960, and the house possesses nearly 14 ha (35 acres). His Prestige blend comes from the 1996 harvest and is almost a blanc de blancs (only 10% Pinot Noir). Its Chardonnay is very evident in its green highlights. This is an outstanding wine, according to the tasters, who admired its balance, freshness, delicacy, intensity and elegance. Its aromatic profile mingles mineral notes with white blossom and lychees. As regards the **Cuvée 2000** (150–199F), which received a citation, this is 'a good champagne to celebrate with', according to one member of the jury. (NM)

Pierre Gerbais, 13, rue du Pont, B.P. 17, 10110 Celles-sur-Ource, tel. 03.25.38.51.29, fax 03.25.38.55.17 Y by appt.

GIMONNET-GONET Tradition

○ 4 ha 20,000 ▮ 70–99 F

This champagne, launched in 1988, comes from a vineyard of some 8.5 ha (21 acres) mainly situated on the Côte des Blancs. The Tradition blend is made from half black grapes and half white from the 1995 and 1996 harvests, and is vanilla-scented, spicy and has a hint of mirabelle plum. On the palate, it presents a lively and light character. (RM)

Gimonnet-Gonet, 166, rue du Gal-de-Gaulle, 51530 Cramant, tel. 03.26.57.51.44, fax 03.26.58.00.03 Y by appt.

BERNARD GIRARDIN

Cuvée de réserve

○ 1.2 ha 4,000 70–99 F

This operation was established in 1970 by Bernard Girardin, and taken over by his daughter Sandrine Britès-Girardin in 1991. All three champagne varieties from the 1992 harvest are present (including 60% Chardonnay) in this Cuvée de Réserve, which has aromas of brioche, butter and toast on the nose,

CHAMPAGNE

together with the acidity of lime. It would go very well with turbot in a sauce. There is a citation also for the **Cuvée Vibrato**, a blanc de blancs from the 1995 harvest, which has a supple first impression and is full of vigour (100–149F). (RM)

🔑 Sandrine Britès-Girardin, Champagne Bernard-Girardin, 14, Grande-Rue, 51530 Mancy, tel. 03.26.59.70.78, fax 03.26.51.55.45 ☑ Y by appt.

PAUL GOBILLARD Cuvée Régence*

○ n.c. n.c. 150–199 F

This house was founded in 1858, and also owns the Château de Pierry (the tasting, for which there is a charge, includes a visit to the 18th-century château). Cuvée Régence is a blend of wines exclusively from years that are considered to be of vintage quality; its average age is ten years. Seventy per cent Chardonnay and 30% Pinot (including 10% Meunier) contribute to its floral and vanilla aromas and its well-structured, fresh, lengthy palate. Serve it at any time, but particularly at the dinner table, with white meat accompanied by mushrooms in cream. (NM)

🔑 Paul Gobillard, Ch. de Pierry, B.P. 1, 51530 Pierry, tel. 03.26.54.05.11, fax 03.26.54.46.03 ☑ Y ev. day except Sun. 4.30pm; groups by appt.

J.-M. GOBILLARD ET FILS

Grande Réserve**

○ 1er cru 10 ha 90,000 70–99 F

It was at the Benedictine Abbey of Hautvillers, the commune where this house is based, that Dom Pérignon was the cellar-master from 1668 to 1715. The monk was not, as is usually said, the inventor of the bubbles, but he nonetheless played a key role in the advent of champagne through his research into the quality of grapes and the refinement of blending techniques. Indeed, it is the success of the blending of equal parts of Pinot (25% each) and Chardonnay, harvested in 1996 and 1997 that ensures the excellence of this Grande Réserve cuvée: a delicately raspberry-scented nose, freshness, fine balance and length. In short, everything that one could wish for. The **Privilège des moines** cuvée (100–149F), made from 70% Chardonnay and 30% Pinot Noir from 1995 and 1996, was clearly produced with great care. It was matured for a year in oak, with periodic stirring of the lees, and wins a star. It displays delicate, elegant aromas of crystallised citrus fruits, with a very lightly oaky note. On the palate, lingering flavours of lemon, mandarin, vanilla and cocoa come through. (NM)

🔑 J.-M. Gobillard et Fils, 38, rue de l'Eglise, B.P. 8, 51160 Hautvillers, tel. 03.26.51.00.24, fax 03.26.51.00.18 ☑ Y by appt.

GODME PERE ET FILS*

◑ Gd cru 1 ha 6,000 70–99 F

It took five generations to build up an estate of 11.5 ha (28 acres) here. It is an exceptional vineyard, for it covers three Grand Crus (Verzenay, Verzy and Beaumont-sur Vesle) and two Premiers Crus (Villers-Marmery and Villedommange). This rosé which is strongly influenced by Pinot Noir (80%, as against 20% Chardonnay), is distinguished by its aromas of orange, apricot and figs, and by its supple attack. Two other champagnes from this house were cited. In the same price bracket, the **Brut Réserve Premier Cru** is made from half white grapes and half black, and its powerful nose, according to one taster, 'will make you think of a sub-saharan oasis in the middle of the lemon harvest'. Drink it with chicken in ginger. The **95 Grand Cru** (100–149F) is aromatically rich and supple and is clearly also destined for the dinner table. (RM)

🔑 Champagne Godmé Père et Fils, 10, rue de Verzy, 51360 Verzenay, tel. 03.26.49.48.70, fax 03.26.49.45.30 ☑

PAUL GOERG Tradition

○ 1er cru n.c. 180,000 70–99 F

This group of producers from Vertus in the Côte des Blancs produces its wines from a harvest of 120 ha (296 acres). The brand has been in existence since 1985. This Tradition blend is made from Chardonnay (60%) and Pinot Noir (40%), harvested in 1994, 1995 and 1996. It is a fresh, straightforward champagne. The same verdict is given on the **Blanc de Blancs Premier Cru** (blended from the 1995, 1996 and 1997 harvests), which is also fresh, but which offers an interesting roundness of texture. (CM)

🔑 Champagne Paul Goerg, 4, pl. du Mont-Chenil, 51130 Vertus, tel. 03.26.52.15.31, fax 03.26.52.23.96, e-mail champagnegoerg@wanadoo.fr ☑ Y by appt.

FRANCOIS GONET

Blanc de blancs Cuvée de réserve**

○ 2 ha 10,000 70–99 F

François Gonet took over the family property on the Côte des Blancs in 1962, and has extended the vineyard towards the Marne

alley. He has been producing champagne ince 1972. This blanc de blancs comes from he 1993 harvest. It reveals an aromatic range t the same time rich and delicate: fresh hazel-uts, butter, orange and grapefruit. And all hese aromas are echoed on a palate replete vith finesse and balance. (RM)

François Gonet, 5, rue du Stade, 51190 e Mesnil-sur-Oger, tel. 03.26.57.53.71, ax 03.26.57.93.66 by appt.

IICHEL GONET

lanc de blancs Prestige 2000 1996*

Gd cru — 5 ha — 50,000 — 100–149 F

The Gonet family has been around on the Côte des Blancs since 1802. Michel Gonet is n charge of a substantial family vineyard of 40 ha (99 acres) in the Champagne region, and also of vast properties in Bordeaux. He exports 50% of his production, and is a spe-ialist in blanc de bancs. This Prestige 2000, nade up of 1996 wine, is outstanding for its reshness both on the nose and palate. It is ypical of its grape variety (showing floral, buttery, slightly toasty notes) and it is charac-terised by its youth. The **Non-vintage Brut Réserve** (70–90F), which is made from half black grapes and half white from the 1997 and 1998 vintages, received a citation. This is a full, rounded, well-balanced champagne. (RM)

SCEV Michel Gonet et Fils, 196, av. Jean-Jaurès, 51190 Avize, tel. 03.26.57.50.56, fax 03.26.57.91.98 by appt.

VINCENT GONET*

9 ha — 82,490 — 70–99 F

Another of the Gonet brothers from the Côte des Blancs owns a vineyard of 14.5 ha (36 acres). The jury's favourite wine of his was this blend of 60% Pinot Noir and 40% Char-donnay, praised for its aromas of under-growth, linden blossom and red berry fruits, as well as its elegant power on the palate. They also cited the **Blanc de Blancs Spécial Club 95**, labelled **Gonet-Sulcova** (100–149F), which has a lively attack and a pleasant finish. (RM)

SCEV Beauregard, 13, rue Henri-Martin, 51200 Epernay, tel. 03.26.54.34.63, fax 03.26.55.36.71, e-mail gonet-sulcova@wanadoo.fr by appt.

Vincent Gonet

GOSSET Grande Réserve**

n.c. — 400,000 — 200–249 F

Gosset champagne has been in the hands of the founding family for a long time, and the parish records bear witness to their deep roots in the village of Ay. They owned vines in the region as early as the 15th century. Today, Béatrice Cointreau watches over the fortunes of the company. The Grande Réserve is made from slightly more black grapes than white (52% Pinot as against 48% Chardonnay, from the 1996, 1997 and 1998 harvests). Its nose, which is highly complex, opens up multiple fragrances, most notably floral ones (honey-suckle, may blossom, linden, orange and verbena). The jury found the palate very appealing – well-balanced, powerful and fine, with superb length. (NM)

Champagne Gosset, 69, rue Jules-Blondeau, 51160 Ay, tel. 03.26.56.99.56, fax 03.26.51.55.88, e-mail info@champagne-gosset.com

Béatrice Cointreau

GOSSET Grand Rosé**

n.c. — 50,000 — 200–249 F

This rosé also receives a *coup de coeur*, despite the fact that the *Guide* does not normally award more than one to the same producer within a particular appellation. It is made up of 56% Chardonnay, 35% Pinot Noir and 9% red wines from Grands Crus Bouzy and Ambonnay. Its aromatic profile shows great finesse, hinting at raspberries and wild strawberries. The elegance, liveliness and balance of this champagne make it a model of its kind. Two stars are also awarded to a vintage cuvée that is often highly distinguished, the **Grand Millésime 96** (300–499 F). Produced from 62% Chardonnay and 38% Pinot, this 1996 wine is admirable for its suppleness, its finesse and its length. (NM)

Champagne Gosset, 69, rue Jules-Blondeau, 51160 Ay, tel. 03.26.56.99.56, fax 03.26.51.55.88, e-mail info@champagne-gosset.com

GOSSET-BRABANT Tradition

1er cru — 4 ha — 28,000 — 70–99 F

Based in the famous vineyard of Ay, the vineyards of this house comprise 7.5 ha (19 acres). It has been producing champagne since 1930. The Tradition blend is dominated by Pinot (70% Pinot Noir, 10% Meunier), and is made up of 1997 and 1996 wines. It is powerful on the nose, rich in scents of undergrowth, and the palate has great character too. One of the tasters said he would particularly enjoy it sitting by the fireside after a long walk in the rain. (RM)

Gosset-Brabant, 23, bd du Mal-de-Lattre-de-Tassigny, 51160 Ay, tel. 03.26.55.17.42, fax 03.26.54.31.33 by appt.

J.-M. GOULARD Tradition**

7 ha — 18,950 — 70–99 F

Jean-Marie Goulard is a son of wine-producers who has now built up his own vineyard of 70 ha (173 acres), having started out selling by the bottle in 1978. His Tradition is a blanc de noirs made from the two Pinot varieties (two-thirds Meunier), harvested in 1997. Full of the scents of undergrowth, leather and spices, it is very well-balanced and long on the palate. (RM)

🗝 Jean-Marie Goulard, 13, Grande-Rue, 51140 Prouilly, tel. 03.26.48.21.60, fax 03.26.48.23.67, e-mail goulard@club-internet.fr ✉ Y by appt.

GEORGE GOULET

Première cuvée spéciale*

○	6 ha	60,000		70–99 F

This house was created in 1834 by François Goulet. His son, George, gave his first name to the business, which has changed hands several times since the war; Lionel Chaudron handed it over in April 2000 to Jean-Louis Malard. This Première Cuvée Spéciale, which is made up of 70% Pinot Noir and 30% Chardonnay, is floral, elegant and well-balanced. (NM)

🗝 Champagne George Goulet, 65, av. de Champagne, B.P. 95, 51203 Epernay Cedex, tel. 03.26.57.77.24, fax 03.26.52.75.54, e-mail champexport@wanadoo.fr

🗝 Jean-Louis Malard

GOUSSARD ET DAUPHIN

Prestige*

○	n.c.	5,500	70–99 F

In 1989, after gaining his oenology diploma, Didier Goussard decided to produce his own champagne and went into partnership with his brother-in-law. The business has a vineyard of some 7 ha (17 acres) in the Aube. The vinification and blending of the Prestige cuvée (40% Pinot Noir and 60% Chardonnay, harvested in 1995 and 1996) are classic in style, and have resulted in a champagne with a discreet nose of white blossom and a flattering, elegant palate. (RM)

🗝 Goussard et Dauphin, GAEC du Val de Sarce, 2, chem. Saint-Vincent, 10340 Avirey-Lingey, tel. 03.25.29.30.03, fax 03.25.29.85.96, e-mail goussard.dauphin@wanadoo.fr ✉ Y by appt.

HENRI GOUTORBE

Cuvée traditionnelle*

○	n.c.	50,000		70–99 F

The Goutorbe family have been nurserymen for a long time, having created their brand of champagne in 1945. Their vineyard covers 18 ha (44 acres). Their Cuvée Traditionnelle Brut, like their **Cuvée Prestige**, wins a star. Both are made up of 75% black grapes to 25% white, and both are floral and have good intensity on the palate. Each would go well with white meat. (RM)

🗝 Champagne Goutorbe, 9 *bis*, rue Jeanson, 51160 Ay, tel. 03.26.55.21.70, fax 03.26.54.85.11 ✉ Y by appt.

ALFRED GRATIEN Cuvée Paradis*

○	n.c.	n.c.		300–499 F

This family house is very well-known for its top-of-the-range blends. It was set up in 1864, and still uses the traditional technique of wine production in small used casks. The Paradis blend wins a star for its white as well as for its **rosé**. These two champagnes combine about two-thirds white grapes to one third black. The tasters were particularly impressed by their complex, spicy elegance as well as by the crystallised fruit flavours that give the palate extra length. We should also mention the success of the **1991** vintage (250–299F) – a very difficult vintage – which has a positive attack and pleasant length. (NM)

🗝 Champagne Alfred Gratien, 30, rue Maurice-Cerveaux, B.P. 3, 51201 Epernay Cedex, tel. 03.26.54.38.20, fax 03.26.54.53.44, e-mail contact@alfredgratien.com ✉ Y by appt.

GRUET 1995**

○	n.c.	62,768		70–99 F

Claude Gruet is the heir to a long line of wine-producers going back to 1670, He created his own brand in 1975. His vineyard is on the Côte des Bar in the Aube, and covers 10 ha (25 acres). This 1995 is produced from two-thirds Pinot Noir and one-third Chardonnay. Its hints of dried fruits and toasted brioche, and its high alcohol content, lend it complexity, and it is full and fruity on the palate. Two other champagnes win a star: the **Brut Rosé**, which is dominated by black grapes (only 10% Chardonnay), rich, highly developed and perfect for the dinner table, and the **Charles I 95** (100–149F), which is a rich, peppery, menthol-scented and well-balanced blanc de blancs. (NM)

🗝 SARL Champagne Gruet, 48, Grande-Rue, 10110 Buxeuil, tel. 03.25.38.54.94, fax 03.25.38.51.84 ✉ Y ev. day 8.30am–12 noon 2pm–6pm; Sat. Sun. by appt.; cl. Aug.

G. GRUET ET FILS Blanc de blancs

○	117 ha	96,000		70–99 F

Bethon is situated between Sézanne and Nogent. This champagne bears the name of the founder of a group of producers who, between them, work 117 ha (289 acres) of vines. This blanc de blancs has a floral nose, which then opens up to a powerful and vigorous palate underlined by a sharp touch of bitterness. (CM)

🗝 Coop. Union viticole des Coteaux de Bethon, 5, rue des Pressoirs, 51260 Bethon, tel. 03.26.80.48.19, fax 03.26.80.44.57 ✉

🗝 Bruno Henrich

MAURICE GRUMIER*

◐	n.c.	5,000		70–99 F

This company has a vineyard of 7.5 ha (19 acres) at Venteuil in the Marne valley. The Brut Rosé is a blend of 40% Chardonnay and 50% Pinot Meunier, tinted with 10% red wine from Pinot Noir. A sustained pink hue and a nose of cherry and blackcurrant lead on to a supple, long and harmonious palate. This is a champagne for the dinner table. A citation has also been given to the **Sélection** blend, a blanc de noirs made from Meunier grapes from 1996 and 1997, which is straightforward and lively, and the **Cuvée de Réserve**, another blanc de noirs (80% Meunier to 20% Pinot Noir, harvested in 1995 and 1996), which has lemon-scented freshness and good length. (RM)

🔑 Guy Grumier, 13, rte d'Arty, 51480 Venteuil, tel. 03.26.58.48.10, fax 03.26.58.66.08 ☒ Y by appt.

RENE GUE Blanc de blancs

○ 3 ha 25,000 70–99 F

This estate, which was set up in 1971, runs a vineyard of 6.5 ha (16 acres) on the Côte des Blancs. The Blanc de Blancs is floral, buttery and redolent of apple on the nose, well-balanced and fresh on the palate. (RM)

🔑 Philippe Gué, 2, rue de Monthelon, 51530 Chouilly, tel. 03.26.54.50.32, fax 03.26.54.01.45 ☒ Y by appt.

GUY DE FOREZ**

○ 7 ha 26,000 ▮ 70–99 F

This vineyard of 8 ha (20 acres) in the Aube was created by M. Spagnesi. His daughter Sylvie took it over in 1987, in conjunction with her husband Francis Wenner. Their non-vintage Brut comes from the 1995 and 1997 harvests. It offers a vinous nose, composed of citrus notes and very attractive peppery hints, together with a well-structured palate of great complexity and freshness. It would go very well with fish served in beurre blanc or lobster à l'armoricaine. (RM)

🔑 Guy de Forez, rte de Tonnerre, 10340 Les Riceys, tel. 03.25.29.98.73, fax 03.25.38.23.01 ☒ Y by appt.

HAMM Sélection

○ n.c. 40,000 ▮ 70–99 F

This firm was created by Henri Hamm in 1910, and is run today by his descendants. It has a vineyard of some 4 ha (10 acres). The wines do not undergo malolactic fermentation. The Brut blend is produced from all three of the champagne varieties, including 20% Chardonnay. Its nose is floral (with a slight touch of juniper berries) and buttery, and precedes a well-balanced palate that ends on a note of citrus. (NM)

🔑 Champagne Hamm, 16, rue N.-Philipponnat, 51160 Ay, tel. 03.26.55.44.19, fax 03.26.51.98.68 ☒ Y by appt.

HARLIN Harmonie

○ n.c. n.c. ▮ 100–149 F

This house was created by Constant Harlin in 1848 at Tours-sur-Marne, and is still in the same family. The vineyard comprises 10 ha (25 acres). The Brut Harmonie blend contains twice as much Pinot Noir as Chardonnay. Suggestions of apple are very noticeable both on the nose and on the palate, and it ends with an impression of freshness that would make it suitable as an apéritif. (NM)

🔑 Harlin, 41, av. de Champagne, 51150 Tours-sur-Marne, tel. 03.26.51.88.95, fax 03.26.58.96.51 ☒ Y by appt.

🔑 Famille Paillard-Chauvet

HARLIN PERE ET FILS Prestige 1995

○ 2 ha 1,500 ▮ 70–99 F

The Harlin family have been wine producers for a century, but this brand only dates from 1975. The vineyard consists of 8 ha (20 acres). This Brut Prestige blend is produced from 60% Pinot Noir and 40% Chardonnay, harvested in 1995. Its floral nose anticipates a long, harmonious palate. The **Grand Cru 96** is well-structured and generous, gaining it a citation. (RM)

🔑 Harlin Père et Fils, 8, rue de la Fontaine, 51700 Port-à-Binson, tel. 03.26.58.34.38, fax 03.26.58.63.78 ☒ Y ev. day except Sun. 9am–12 noon 2pm–6pm

JEAN-NOEL HATON

Cuvée Prestige**

○ n.c. n.c. ▮ 🌡 100–149 F

Jean-Noël Haton has a vineyard of 13 ha (32 acres) at his disposal to make up a brand that was launched in 1928. The Prestige blend is made with half black grapes and half white; the dates of its component wines are unknown, although these are a decisive factor in determining the quality of the champagne. Its floral nose is very gratifying, and on the palate, roundness and fruit are the salient features. The cuvée that the jury tasted is exceptionally good. The **Cuvée de Réserve** (70–99F), which is based on the three champagne grapes, also earns a citation for the liveliness of its flavours of grapefruit and lemon. (NM)

🔑 Jean-Noël Haton, 5, rue Jean-Mermoz, 51480 Damery, tel. 03.26.58.40.45, fax 03.26.58.63.55 ☒ Y by appt.

HATON ET FILS Grande Réserve*

◐ 7 ha n.c. ▮ 70–99 F

This is a family firm located at Damery that has been directed by Philippe Haton since 1983. This rosé de noirs produced from the two Pinots – including 10% Pinot Noir from the 1997 harvest – is notable for its aromas of red fruits and for its delicacy. This is a rosé to drink as an apéritif. (NM)

🔑 Haton et Fils, 3, rue Jean-Mermoz, 51480 Damery, tel. 03.26.58.41.11, fax 03.26.58.45.98 ☒ Y by appt.

JEAN-PAUL HEBRART Sélection*

○ 1er cru n.c. 6,000 70–99 F

This vineyard belongs to Jean-Paul Hébrart, son of Marc, and is classified Premier Cru. The Sélection cuvée is a blend of 60% Pinot Noir and 40% Chardonnay; it is intense, well-balanced and long. Also worthy of note is the **Brut Blanc de Noirs**, which is produced solely from Pinot Noir, and is vinous, full and rich, with all the characteristic features of its type. (RM)

🔑 Jean-Paul Hébrart, 10, quai du Moulin, 51160 Mareuil-sur-Ay, tel. 03.26.52.05.57, fax 03.26.52.92.64 ☒ Y by appt.

MARC HEBRART Spécial Club 1996*

○ 1er cru n.c. n.c. 100–149 F

Mareuil-sur-Ay is a pleasing little village on a side-canal of the Marne. If you go pleasure-boating here, you only need walk 300 m (325 yards) from the canal to encounter Marc and Jean-Paul Hébrart, who created a company in 1997 by amalgamating their two enterprises. This blend of 60% Pinot and 40% Chardonnay proves to be a floral, delicate, straightforward and well-balanced wine. (RM)

Marc Hébrart, 18–20, rue du Pont, 51160 Mareuil-sur-Ay, tel. 03.26.52.60.75, fax 03.26.52.92.64 by appt.

CHARLES HEIDSIECK

Réserve Mis en cave en 1996★

○ n.c. n.c. 150–199 F

This house was founded in 1851, and has been run by the Rémy-Cointreau group since 1985. The cellarmaster, Daniel Thibault, invented the formula 'mise en cave', which allows him to show the date the bottle was cellared, in this case 1996. This bottle contains 60% wine from 1995 topped up with 40% old reserve wines, with black grapes in the majority. The nose is floral and very distinctive, while the palate is well-balanced and the finish fresh. Open it any time, but particularly to drink with a grand fish dish served with beurre blanc. (NM)

Charles Heidsieck, 4, bd Henry-Vasnier, 51100 Reims, tel. 03.26.84.43.50, fax 03.26.84.43.86 by appt.

HEIDSIECK & CO MONOPOLE

Extra dry Goût américain★

○ n.c. n.c. 100–149 F

This house was established in 1834, taken over by Seagram in 1972, and then sold off again to Paul-François Vranken in 1996. The Extra Dry draws heavily on Pinot grapes; the result is a well-structured and well-balanced wine that has good length and is only moderately dosed. (NM)

Heidsieck & Co Monopole, 17, av. de Champagne, 51200 Epernay, tel. 03.26.59.50.50, fax 03.26.52.19.65 ev. day 9.30am–4.30pm; Sun. and groups by appt.

P.-F. Vranken

D. HENRIET-BAZIN Blanc de blancs

○ 1er cru 3 ha n.c. 70–99 F

This 7.5 ha (19-acre) estate was founded in 1890 and is today directed by Marie-Noëlle Henriet-Bazin. The blanc de blancs has one distinctive feature: it comes from the Montagne de Reims. It has aromas of ripe fruit, crystallised fruits and honey. The palate is not long, but it is notably fleshy. The **Grand Cru**, which is a blanc de noirs, is cited for its rich, long, fruity roundness. It would go particularly well with sauced white meats. (RM)

D. Henriet-Bazin, 9 *bis*, rue Dom-Pérignon, 51380 Villers-Marmery, tel. 03.26.97.96.81, fax 03.26.97.97.30, e-mail henriet.bazin@wanadoo.fr by appt.

HENRIOT 1995★

○ n.c. n.c. 150–199 F

This brand was founded in 1808 by Appoline Henriot, and is currently run by Joseph Henriot. The 1995 vintage gives pride of place to Pinot Noir (53%), but it is the Chardonnay that gives this delicate, fresh, long and elegant wine its character. The **Brut Souverain** (40% Chardonnay, 60% Pinot Noir) is also awarded a star for its balance and the finesse of its floral nose (140–150F). (NM)

Champagne Henriot, 3, pl. des Droits-de-l'Homme, B.P. 457, 51066 Reims, tel. 03.26.89.53.00, fax 03.26.89.53.10 by appt.

PAUL HERARD★

◐ n.c. 5,000 70–99 F

Notre-Dame-des-Vignes dominates this vineyard in the Aube, which was created in 1925 and has remained in the same family to this day. Today, Philippe Hérard is helped by his children. This is a rosé de noirs produced from Pinot Noir harvested in 1996. It is supple, fruity and delicate. The **Cuvée Paul**, which is more expensive (100–149F), is made from 40% Pinot and 60% Chardonnay. Its structure is very fine and its balance superb. (NM)

Champagne Paul Hérard, 31, Grande-Rue, 10250 Neuville-sur-Seine, tel. 03.25.38.20.14, fax 03.25.38.25.05 by appt.

DIDIER HERBERT 1995★

○ 1er cru n.c. n.c. 100–149 F

Didier Herbert is based in the Montagne de Reims. His 1995 is a particularly accomplished wine, backed up by rich, warm, fruity aromas with a slight smokiness. His **Rosé Premier Cru** is also awarded a star. It is well-made, with good length, and certainly inspired one taster: 'I love it!' he wrote. (RM)

Didier Herbert, 32, rue de Reims, 51500 Rilly-la-Montagne, tel. 03.26.03.41.53, fax 03.26.03.44.64, e-mail champagne-herbert@terre-net.fr ev. day except Sun. 8am–6pm; cl. Aug.

HEUCQ PERE ET FILS

Cuvée Antique 1996★

○ 0.5 ha 4,000 100–149 F

This house was created after the war, and today its vineyard covers a surface of 5.5 ha (14 acres). The Cuvée Antique is made with half black grapes and half white. This young champagne is particularly appealing for its aromas and flavours of coffee, chocolate and caramel. 'A winter wine,' thought one taster. (RM)

André Heucq, 51700 Cuisles, tel. 03.26.58.10.08, fax 03.26.58.12.00 by appt.

M. HOSTOMME Blanc de blancs 1995★

○ Gd cru n.c. 20,000 100–149 F

Paul Hostomme began producing and bottling wine at the beginning of the 20th century. Since then, the vineyard has grown to

contain 10 ha (25 acres) of Chardonnay in the commune of Chouilly (a Grand Cru) and 3.5 ha (9 acres) of Pinot to the west of Epernay. The 1995 vintage has subtle scents of brioche and a lively attack; its lemon-scented aromas are sustained by its youthful structure. (NM)
M. Hostomme et Fils, 5, rue de l'Allée, 51530 Chouilly, tel. 03.26.55.40.79, fax 03.26.55.08.55 by appt.

BERNARD HUBSCHWERLIN Réserve*

○ 0.8 ha 5,000 70-99 F

Bernard Hubschwerlin, whose wines do not undergo a malolactic fermentation, runs a vineyard of 4 ha (10 acres). His Tradition champagne normally elicits rave reviews, and now this Aube producer earns a star for his Réserve blend, which has a beautiful hue of old gold, and a well-evolved, buttery and harmonious palate. (RM)
EARL Bernard Hubschwerlin, 12, Grande-Rue, 10250 Courteron, tel. 03.25.38.24.11, fax 03.25.38.47.80 ev. day 8.30am–6.30pm; Sat. Sun. by appt.

HUGUENOT-TASSIN Cuvée Tradition

○ n.c. 30,000 70-99 F

Benoît Huguenot is a wine producer at Celles-sur-Ource in the Aube. He manages a vineyard of 6 ha (15 acres), which is the source of this Tradition blend based on half Pinot Noir. Brioche and citrus aromas lead on to a long, honeyed palate. (RM)
Benoît Huguenot, 4, rue du Val-Lune, 10110 Celles-sur-Ource, tel. 03.25.38.54.49, fax 03.25.38.50.40 by appt.

HUSSON Rosé de Mme Husson

◑ Gd cru 1 ha 10,000 100-149 F

This brand was launched in 1975 and has at its disposal 4.5 ha (11 acres) of vines, in particular in the commune of Ay, a Grand Cru. This rosé comes from the 1994 harvest and is a wine for those who like their champagnes mature. It is indeed well-evolved in all respects: on the eye, with its onion-skin hue; on the nose, with its aromas of baked fruit and wax polish; and on the palate, which has supple texture and a flavour of gingerbread. (NM)
Jean-Pierre Husson, 2, rue Jules-Lobet, 51160 Ay, tel. 03.26.55.43.05, fax 03.26.55.03.02 by appt.

IVERNEL Prestige*

○ n.c. n.c. 100-149 F

This brand was created at the end of the 19th century, and was taken over in 1993 by Gosset, which is directed today by Béatrice Cointreau. All three champagne grapes (including 15% Pinot Meunier) are drawn on in this Prestige, whose strong points are balance, harmony and length. (NM)
Champagne Ivernel, B.P. 15, 51160 Ay, tel. 03.26.55.21.10, fax 03.26.51.55.88

ROBERT JACOB 1990*

○ 6 ha 6,000 70-99 F

This vineyard of 6 ha (15 acres) was created in 1960 by Robert Jacob, and taken over by his son Daniel in 1976. His champagnes do not undergo malolactic fermentation. Four times as much Chardonnay as Pinot Noir goes into this 1990 vintage, which has aromas of baked fruit, prunes, honey and quince, both on the nose and on the palate. (RM)
Champagne Jacob, 14, rue de Morres, 10110 Merrey-sur-Arce, tel. 03.25.29.83.74, fax 03.25.29.34.86 ev. day except Sun. 9am–12 noon 2pm–6pm

ANDRE JACQUART ET FILS Blanc de blancs Spécial Club 1995*

○ 0.8 ha 6,500 150-199 F

Between 1960 and the present day, this vineyard has grown from 2 ha (5 acres) to nearly 19 ha (47 acres). This blanc de blancs has already established a good reputation, and wins a star in the *Guide*. The palate shows advanced development, with flavours of crystallised fruits, figs, apricot and honey. (RM)
André Jacquart et Fils, 6, av. de la République, 51190 Le Mesnil-sur-Oger, tel. 03.26.57.52.29, fax 03.26.57.78.14 by appt.

YVES JACQUES Cuvée Gisèle 1995*

○ 0.8 ha 4,500 100-149 F

Cuvée Gisèle is produced by Gisèle Jacques. Is it her photograph that adorns the label? For this blend, she uses 70% Chardonnay and 30% Pinot Noir. The champagne is long on the palate, and is particularly striking for its high alcohol content and red berry flavours. The **Tradition** cuvée (70–99F), which is produced from all three champagne varieties (with 50% Pinot Meunier) from the 1997 harvest, lifted by reserve wines, receives a citation: it is a supple and harmonious champagne. (RM)
Champagne Yves Jacques, 1, rue de Montpertuis, 51270 Baye, tel. 03.26.52.80.77, fax 03.26.52.83.97 ev. day 9am–6.30pm; Sun. 9am–12 noon
Rémi Jacques

JACQUESSON ET FILS Perfection**

○ n.c. n.c. 150-199 F

This great champagne house was founded in 1738. It failed dramatically at one point, but recovered its fortunes thanks to the Chiquet family. The Perfection blend comprises 52% Pinot Meunier, 32% Chardonnay and 16% Pinot Noir. Part of the wine is matured in wood. It is well-balanced, intense, spicy, long and very fine. The top-of-the-range blend, **Grand Vin Signature**, earns a star: this champagne is made from half white grapes and half black, and also matures in wood. It is very powerful and meaty, but has now reached its peak (300–499F). These wines are only available from the cellar itself. (NM)
Champagne Jacquesson et Fils, 68, rue du Colonel-Fabien, 51530 Dizy,

tel. 03.26.55.68.11, fax 03.26.51.06.25 Y by appt.

JACQUINET-DUMEZ Grande Réserve

○ 1er cru 2.5 ha 22,000 70–99 F

This brand was launched in 1935, and the vineyard now covers 7 ha (17 acres). Olivier Jacquinet has produced all the wines himself since 1982. This blanc de noirs (which includes 20% Pinot Meunier) is floral, vinous on the palate and very true to type. (RM)

Jacquinet-Dumez, 26, rue de Reims, 51370 Les Mesneux, tel. 03.26.36.25.25, fax 03.26.36.58.92 Y by appt.

E. JAMART ET CIE Cuvée de réserve

○ n.c. 20,000 70–99 F

In St-Martin-d'Ablois, you can see a baroque church whose bell-tower looks like a champagne cork. This négociant house, which was created in 1934 by Emilien Jamart, the grandfather of today's proprietors, has marketed a Cuvée de Réserve containing four times more Pinot Meunier than Chardonnay. It is lively, light and youthful. It only needs to age for another year or so. (NM)

Champagne E. Jamart et Cie, 13, rue Marcel-Soyeux, 51530 Saint-Martin-d'Ablois, tel. 03.26.59.92.78, fax 03.26.59.95.23, e-mail champagne.jamart@wanadoo.fr Y ev. day 9am–12 noon 2pm–6pm; Sun. by appt., cl. 15–31 Aug.

J.-Michel Oudart

PH. JANISSON Grande Réserve

○ 1er cru 4 ha 3,000 100–149 F

This négociant brand was created in 1984, and runs a vineyard established in four Grands Crus and three Premiers Crus. The Grande Réserve brings together Pinot Noir and Chardonnay in proportions of 50/50, from grapes harvested in 1995 and 1996. It is a champagne with a fresh attack, suitable for the end of the evening or for drinking alongside pork with orange, caramel or cherries; what might be called a sweet-and-sour match. The **Rosé** (70–99F) is produced from 40% Pinot Noir and 60% Chardonnay from the 1995, 1996 and 1997 harvests, and is fruity, lemon-scented and lingering. (NM)

Philippe Janisson, 17, rue Gougelet, 51500 Chigny-les-Roses, tel. 03.26.03.46.93, fax 03.26.03.49.00, e-mail champagne.ph.janisson@wanadoo.fr Y by appt.

JANISSON-BARADON ET FILS Cuvée Prestige Georges Baradon 1990★★★

○ 1 ha 6,275 100–149 F

In 1922, the great ambition of Georges Baradon, a *remueur* or riddler, was to develop his own champagne in partnership with his son-in-law Maurice Janisson, a cooper. Its founder would have been proud of the welcome now given to this Prestige cuvée that has been named after him in homage. This vintage wine made from 70% Chardonnay and 30% Pinot Noir comes from a great year. It is undoubtedly a superb champagne. The aromas are evidence enough. They are intense, mingling hints of honey with dried and crystallised fruits. All these flavours come through on the palate after a forthright attack. The wine is a model of harmony and balance. An elegant wine for a sophisticated dinner. (RM)

Champagne Janisson-Baradon, 65, rue Chaude-Ruelle et 2, rue des Vignerons, 51200 Epernay, tel. 03.26.54.45.85, fax 03.26.54.25.54, e-mail info@champagne-janisson.com Y by appt.

R. Janisson

JANISSON-BARADON ET FILS Collection du Millénaire 1996★★

○ 1 ha 5,148 100–149 F

The firm Janisson-Baradon is based in Epernay, and owns a vineyard of 9 ha (22 acres). The bottle tasted was disgorged on 28 June 1999, information that is stated on the label. It contains a champagne made from 70% Chardonnay and 30% Pinot Noir. It is a full, suave, rich, smoky and well-balanced wine. Drink on its own for the sheer pleasure of it. Also awarded a star is the **Cuvée 95 An 2000**, a blend in the same style as the above that is very well-balanced, and would be excellent served with a dessert. (RM)

Champagne Janisson-Baradon, 65, rue Chaude-Ruelle et 2, rue des Vignerons, 51200 Epernay, tel. 03.26.54.45.85, fax 03.26.54.25.54, e-mail info@champagne-janisson.com Y by appt.

RENE JARDIN Cuvée Noir et Blanc★

○ 7 ha 70,000 70–99 F

The firm of Louis Jardin has been producing champagne since 1889. René Jardin is currently developing the brand, which is well provisioned by vineyard holdings of 20 ha (49 acres). All three champagne grapes work together in equal proportions in this blend, which is well-rounded and has good length. The **Cendre de Rose Clos Saint-Roch** is a rosé de noirs champagne, whose Pinot Noir comes from Les Riceys. It is well-balanced, lively and elegant. (RM)

Champagne René Jardin, 3, rue Charpentier-Laurain, 51190 Le Mesnil-sur-Oger, tel. 03.26.57.50.26, fax 03.26.57.98.22, e-mail champagne-jardin@bpchamp.com Y by appt.

JEANMAIRE Elysée 1989★★

○ n.c. 8,000 300–499 F

The magnificently equipped Château Malakoff in Epernay is home to this brand. It was created in 1933 by André Jeanmaire, and taken over in 1981 by the Trouillard family, who have a vineyard of 124 ha (306 acres). Although it doesn't seem immediately obvious, this champagne is a blanc de blancs. It would appear to have gained in complexity without losing any of its freshness. This is a great, powerful and well-balanced wine. The **Rosé** de noirs (which includes 30% Pinot Meunier) is delicate, well-balanced and youthful, and wins one star (100–149F). Finally, the **Blanc de Blancs** (100–149F) turns out to be powerful and long, and well worthy of a citation from the jury. (NM)

Champagne Jeanmaire, 12, rue Godart-Roger, 51200 Epernay, tel. 03.26.59.50.10, fax 03.26.54.78.52

M. et J. Trouillard

RENE JOLLY Blanc de noirs★

○ 9 ha 25,000 70–99 F

The Jolly family have been wine-producers in the Aube since 1737, and today they work a vineyard of 10 ha (25 acres). Pierre-Eric Jolly took charge of the estate in 2000. The Blanc de Noirs made from Pinot Noir, harvested in the years 1994 and 1996, is a straightforward, warm-hearted and versatile champagne. (RM)

René Jolly, 10, rue de la Gare, 10110 Landreville, tel. 03.25.38.50.91, fax 03.25.29.12.43, e-mail jollyperic@easynet.fr ev. day 9am–6pm; Sun. by appt.

Hervé Jolly

BERTRAND JOREZ Rosé

◑ 1er cru n.c. n.c. 70–99 F

The house of Bertrand Jorez manages a vineyard of nearly 5 ha (12 acres) in Ludes. There is as much Pinot as Chardonnay in this blend, which is tinted with 16% red wine. The result is convincing: the dominant flavour is cherries, the attack is lively and the sense of balance complete. (RM)

Bertrand Jorez, rue de Reims, B.P. 21, 51500 Ludes, tel. 03.26.61.14.05, fax 03.26.61.14.96 by appt.

JEAN JOSSELIN Tradition

○ 0.65 ha 6,117 70–99 F

Established 7 km (5 miles) from Les Riceys, the Josselin family have been wine-producers since 1854, but it was only in 1957 that Jean Josselin registered his brand name, which was later taken over by his son Jean-Pierre in 1980. The vineyard extends over nearly 10 ha (25 acres). Tradition suits its name since it comes from a traditional marriage of 60% Pinot Noir and 40% Chardonnay from the 1997 harvest. It is a frisky champagne, full of freshness, and would be perfect as an apéritif. (RM)

Jean-Pierre Josselin, 14, rue des Vannes, 10250 Gyé-sur-Seine, tel. 03.25.38.21.48, fax 03.25.38.25.00 by appt.

KRUG Rosé★★★

◑ n.c. 11,000 500 F+

In 1843, Johann Joseph Krug, a German from the Rhine valley, founded the firm that is still in the hands of his descendants today, although LVMH took day-to-day control of it in 1999. Krug had traditionally declined to make a rosé. Henri Krug only made the decision to produce it a few years ago. Of course, it is a top-of-the-range rosé – that goes without saying – if only because the base wine, which is coloured with Ay Rouge from the firm's own vineyards, is itself a wine in the Grande Cuvée style. As one might have expected, Krug receives a *coup de coeur* (they have earned two, in fact – see below) as a result of the complexity of the wine's aromatic range – hints of smokiness, cocoa, almonds, hazelnuts, liquorice, vanilla-pods and spices such as curry. Its richness and harmony make a powerful impact on the palate. (NM)

Krug Vins fins de Champagne, 5, rue Coquebert, B.P. 22, 51100 Reims, tel. 03.26.84.44.20, fax 03.26.84.44.49 by appt.

KRUG Collection 1979★★★

○ n.c. n.c. 500 F+

Some people think that Krug's vintage wines need 20–30 years to reach their peak. This 1979 (36% each of Pinot Noir and Chardonnay, with 28% Pinot Meunier), matured in small casks, has been widely praised elsewhere. It is now perfect in every respect, being worthy of a *coup de coeur.* The jury appreciated the intensity and complexity of its aromatic profile, which mingles a variety of smoky aromas such as chocolate and mocha with various dried fruits, as well as hints of butter and liquorice, and the elegance and harmony of its palate, which is full, rich and long and yet manages to preserve its freshness. This is a champagne to drink with a fine gastronomic dish, such as sautéed foie gras. (NM)

Krug Vins fins de Champagne, 5, rue Coquebert, B.P. 22, 51100 Reims, tel. 03.26.84.44.20, fax 03.26.84.44.49 by appt.

KRUG Clos du Mesnil 1986★★

○ n.c. 14,479 500 F+

Clos du Mesnil is a rare wine (over 1,300F), and is an exception even in the house of Krug, which specialises in top-of-the-range champagnes. As is shown on the label, this champagne actually comes from one single plot of vineyard of just 1.85 ha (4.5 acres), which has been enclosed within its walls since 1698, and is now completely surrounded by the village of Mesnil-sur-Oger. Its position helps to shelter the vines from the rigours of the Champagne climate. The 1986 charmed the tasters, one of whom wanted to award it a *coup de coeur* for its aromas, which mingle hints of honey with the oak in which it has matured, and also for its length. The jury also awarded a star to the non-vintage **Grande Cuvée**, which is noticeably oaky, and to the **1988**, which is well-structured and long, with a fairly developed nose, and which shows distinctive aromas of gingerbread and honey. All these prestige wines are priced in excess of 600F. (NM)

Krug Vins fins de Champagne, 5, rue Coquebert, B.P. 22, 51100 Reims, tel. 03.26.84.44.20, fax 03.26.84.44.49 by appt.

MICHEL LABBE ET FILS

Blanc de blancs

1er cru 1.3 ha 2,500 70–99 F

The Labbé family have been wine-producers for a century, and currently manage a vineyard of 10.5 ha (26 acres). This non-vintage Blanc de Blancs is from the 1996 harvest. It has a very rounded initial impression on the palate, and then opens up with suppleness, offering a succession of toasty notes and ripe citrus flavours, finishing smartly on a touch of spice. (RM)

Champagne Michel Labbé et Fils, 5, chem. du Hasat, 51500 Chamery, tel. 03.26.97.65.45, fax 03.26.97.67.42

Didier Labbé

LACROIX Grande Réserve

2.5 ha 20,000 70–99 F

Jean Lacroix has been running a vineyard of 11 ha (27 acres) since 1968. A proportion of each of the wines he produces is matured in large oak casks. All three of the champagne varieties (including 55% Pinot Noir) from the 1996 harvest have their place in this Grande Réserve, which is golden, lemony, rounded and young. (RM)

Champagne Jean Lacroix, 14, rue des Genêts, 51700 Montigny-sous-Châtillon, tel. 03.26.58.35.17, fax 03.26.58.36.39 ev. day 9am–12 noon 2pm–5pm; Sun. by appt.

LACROIX-TRIAULAIRE ET FILS

Tradition*

n.c. 10,000 70–99 F

François Lacroix is a wine-grower in Merrey-sur-Arce – a village where the fittings in the 16th-century church have been listed – and has managed a vineyard of 7.5 ha (19 acres) since 1972. Tradition is produced from three times as much Pinot Noir as Chardonnay. It has a delightful nose of brioche, and charming elegance. The **Prestige 95**, in which the proportions of the previous blend are reversed, shows up as slightly smoky and rather evolved, gaining a citation. (RM)

Lacroix-Triaulaire, 4, rue de La Motte, 10110 Merrey-sur-Arce, tel. 03.25.29.83.59 by appt.

CHARLES LAFITTE

Orgueil de France 1989*

n.c. n.c. 150–199 F

Charles Lafitte, which was first launched in 1983, is one of the Vranken-Monopole champagne brands. The 1989 vintage is strongly recommended to everyone who likes well-developed wines. It is produced from half black grapes and half white, and has a nose marked by tertiary aromas and a powerful palate. This is a wine to drink at the dinner table. The **Grande Cuvée** (70–99F), which is produced from all three of the champagne grapes is also worthy of note: it is simple, direct and young. (NM)

Charles Lafitte, 17, av. de Champagne, 51200 Epernay, tel. 03.26.59.50.50, fax 03.26.52.19.65 ev. day 9.30am–4.30pm; Sun. and groups by appt.

P. F. Vranken

BENOIT LAHAYE**

Gd cru 0.5 ha 1,600 70–99 F

Benoît Lahaye has been running the family vineyard of 4.5 ha (11 acres) since 1992. He has made an exhibit of the old vine-tending implements that his ancestors once used. This Rosé is obtained by briefly macerating destemmed grapes from the 1998 harvest. It is therefore a rosé de noirs that doesn't undergo malolactic fermentation. It has a dark pink colour with a lively, gay and spirited bouquet, and flavours of violets and red berries mingling on the palate. (RM)

Benoît Lahaye, 33, rue Jeanne-d'Arc, 51150 Bouzy, tel. 03.26.57.03.05, fax 03.26.52.79.94 by appt.

LAMIABLE Extra Brut*

Gd cru 5.7 ha 10,000 70–99 F

The Lamiable family was established in Tours-sur-Marne as far back as the 16th century. Their vineyard covers 6 ha (15 acres) in the village, which is classified as Grand Cru. The Extra Brut is very lightly dosed, and is produced from 70% Pinot Noir and 30% Chardonnay, with reserve wines making up one third of the blend. The smoky aromas are intense, and the lively palate is distinguished by flavours of red berries (cherries and raspberries). Like all Extra-dry champagnes, this one is for true connoisseurs of the style. (RM)

Champagne Lamiable, 8, rue de Condé, 51150 Tours-sur-Marne, tel. 03.26.58.92.69, fax 03.26.58.76.67, e-mail champagne.lamiable@wanadoo.fr by appt.

LANCELOT FILS

Blanc de blancs Cuvée spéciale Cramant 1995

Gd cru 0.65 ha 5,000 70–99 F

The vaulted cellars on this estate were built in 1823, which gives some idea how far back the family tradition goes. Claude Lancelot runs a vineyard of nearly 5 ha (12 acres) on the Côte des Blancs. This Cramant wine is very young, which is its only fault, for it will certainly be awarded stars in a year or two. It offers aromas of pear, wax (the wax polish our grandmothers used to use) and brioche, whilst on the palate supple flavours of smoked lemon and pineapple come to the fore. (RM)

🔑 Lancelot-Goussard, 30, rue Ernest-Vallé, 51190 Avize, tel. 03.26.57.94.68, fax 03.26.57.79.02 ☑ 🍷 by appt.

LANCELOT-PIENNE Sélection 1995**

○ 1.7 ha 15,000 70–99 F

Gilles Lancelot is an oenologist, and has brought together the family estate and its new Cramant firm, which has splendid views over the Côte des Blancs. The Brut Sélection, which only just missed out on a *coup de coeur*, is two-thirds Pinot (with 15% Pinot Noir) and one-third Chardonnay. This is a wine of golden hue, mingling hints of stewed fruit with yellow plums, dried fruits, honey and toasty notes. It is full, rounded, rich and fleshy, and will go very well with white meat. (RM)

🔑 Champagne Lancelot-Pienne, 1, allée de la Forêt, 51530 Cramant, tel. 03.26.57.55.74, fax 03.26.57.53.02 ☑ 🍷 by appt.

P. LANCELOT-ROYER

Blanc de blancs 1995**

○ 1 ha 4,000 70–99 F

Cramant has chosen as its emblem a huge bottle, which they have erected 50 m (55 yards) from their cellar. The 1995 Blanc de Blancs has a complex nose in which all the aromas of a Chardonnay champagne play their parts, making for a supple, mellow and harmonious palate. The **Cuvée des Chevaliers** (one star) is another blanc de blancs, and takes on the challenge that confronts all lightly dosed wines; it is labelled Extra Dry. Chardonnay from the 1995 and 1996 harvests contributes to its nose of flowers (may blossom) and Granny Smith apples, and those apples are present again on the palate, which is still youthful. The **Cuvée de Réserve RR**, a blanc de blancs from the 1996 and 1997 harvests, is still direct, supple and well-rounded, and receives a citation. (RM)

🔑 EARL P. Lancelot-Royer, 540, rue du Gal-de-Gaulle, 51530 Cramant, tel. 03.26.57.51.41, fax 03.26.57.12.25 ☑ 🍷 by appt.

LANSON Black Label 1994**

○ n.c. n.c. 150–199 F

This famous house was founded in 1760, and is now controlled by Marne et Champagne, who don't follow the practice of malolactic fermentation, although the style of the brand theoretically requires it. Three tasters gave their highest acclaim to this beautiful wine, but one gave it a numerical score, meaning that it just missed out on a *coup de coeur*. All the same, this remarkable 1994 deserves full credit. It is produced from almost as much Chardonnay as Pinot Noir, and is a clear gold in colour – a powerful, lengthy, fine wine of great character. (NM)

🔑 Lanson, 12, bd Lundy, 51100 Reims, tel. 03.26.78.50.50, fax 03.26.78.53.88 ☑ 🍷 by appt.

GUY LARMANDIER*

○ 1er cru 3.5 ha n.c. 70–99 F

Based on the Côte des Blancs, where he manages 9 ha (22 acres) with his son François, who is now the estate manager, Guy Larmandier has produced three very well-executed champagnes (each of which wins a star). It will come as no surprise that all of these are dominated by Chardonnay. Produced from the 1996 and 1997 harvests, this Premier Cru is almost a Blanc de Blancs, containing only 10% Pinot Noir. It is 'quite clearly a model white wine,' wrote one taster of this youthful cuvée. The **Blanc de Blancs Cramant Grand Cru** seems well-balanced, delicate, subtle and elegant with its aromas of white blossom, citrus fruits and Granny Smith apples. The **Blanc de Blancs 95 Grand Cru**, which is 'elegant and well-delineated', is along the same lines (100–149F). (RM)

🔑 EARL Champagne Guy Larmandier, 30, rue du Gal-Koenig, 51130 Vertus, tel. 03.26.52.12.41, fax 03.26.52.19.38 ☑ 🍷 by appt.

🔑 Guy et François Larmandier

LARMANDIER-BERNIER

Blanc de blancs Vieilles vignes de Cramant Extra brut 1995**

○ Gd cru 1.5 ha 10,000 100–149 F

When her husband died, Elisabeth Larmandier-Bernier took up the torch and handed it on to her son, Pierre. The business has 11 ha (27 acres) on the Côte des Blancs, in Cramant (a Grand Cru) and in Vertus (Premier Cru), and exports some 70% of its production. Very lightly dosed champagnes such as this Extra-Brut are the house speciality. Produced from 50-year-old vinestocks, this Vieilles Vignes blend is an exemplary wine – well-balanced, and with a finish of great persistence and purity. The fact that it is so lightly dosed contributes to its appreciable freshness. A star also goes to the **Blanc de Blancs Brut Premier Cru** (70–99F), which is at once supple and lively. (RM)

🔑 Champagne Larmandier-Bernier, 43, rue du 28-Aug., 51130 Vertus, tel. 03.26.52.13.24, fax 03.26.52.21.00, e-mail larmandier@terre-net.fr ☑ 🍷 by appt.

🔑 Famille Larmandier

LARMANDIER PERE ET FILS

Chardonnay Spécial Club 1995*

○ Gd cru n.c. 5,000 150–199 F

Françoise Gimonnet – née Larmandier – has champagne running in the family, as she is descended from Jules Larmandier who was one of the first grower-winemakers to sell his blanc de blancs champagne from the Côte des Blancs. That was in 1899. She carries on the tradition with Spécial Club 1995, which makes a typically lively first impression, with its aromas of citrus fruits and its fine length.

The **Cramant Blanc de Blancs**, produced from the 1993 harvest (100–149F) is likewise awarded a star for its impeccable typicity. (RM)

Larmandier Père et Fils, 1, rue de la République, 51530 Cuis, tel. 03.26.57.52.19, fax 03.26.59.79.84 by appt.

J. LASSALLE Cuvée Angeline 1992*

○ 1er cru n.c. n.c. 100–149 F

This enterprise in the Montagne de Reims (at Chigny-les-Roses, a Premier Cru) exports about two-thirds of its production. Their Angeline champagne is a blend of 60% Pinot Noir and 40% Chardonnay. It is very appealing for its balance and the complexity of its aromatic profile, which shows hints of quince, ripe fruits and caramel. In the lower price bracket, there is the **Préférence** cuvée, which is produced from all three of the champagne grapes (including 60% Meunier and 15% Pinot Noir). It is expressive and warm, with good length, and it was awarded a star having attained maturity: it is ready to drink. (RM)

Champagne J. Lassalle, 21, rue du Châtaignier, 51500 Chigny-les-Roses, tel. 03.26.03.42.19, fax 03.26.03.45.70 by appt.

P. LASSALLE-HANIN 1990*

○ 0.6 ha 2,700 100–149 F

This grower-winemaker launched his brand in 1953, and his vineyard runs to 9 ha (22 acres). This 1990 vintage is as white as it is black (Pinot Noir); it is rounded, richly textured and powerful, and would go well with white meats. (RM)

Champagne P. Lassalle-Hanin, 2, rue des Vignes, 51500 Chigny-les-Roses, tel. 03.26.03.40.96, fax 03.26.03.42.10 by appt.

MARIE FRANCE DE LATOUR
Cuvée Troisième Millénaire*

○ 1 ha 760 300–499 F

A watercolour by Hans Vleugels (a landscape with grape-harvest) adorns the label of this magnum of the Troisième Millénaire blend. As will already be clear, this is a bottle to open at dinner on 1 January 2001: it is well-structured, without being aggressive. Apricots, candied fruits, pineapple and flowers are evident in tasting it. (RM)

Champagne Marie-France de Latour, 48, rue Saint-Vincent, 51390 Vrigny, tel. 03.26.03.60.41, fax 03.26.03.64.25 ev. day 10am–12 noon 3pm–7pm

CH. DE L'AUCHE
Nectar de Saint-Rémi 1993*

○ n.c. 2,000 100–149 F

This group of wine-producers was set up in 1961, and embraces 125 ha (310 acres) of vines. They launched the brand in 1970. This 1993 wine is made from half white grapes and half black. There are suggestions here of floral, vanilla-scented aromas and hints of coffee. The first impression on the palate is lively, and the finish harmonious. Two other blends, which owe everything to the Pinot varieties, are worthy of mention in the 70–99F price bracket: the **Rosé**, on account of its balance, and the **Sélection**, which is lively and immediate, with a very nice floral nose. (CM)

Coop. vinicole Germigny-Janvry-Rosnay, rue de Germigny, 51390 Janvry, tel. 03.26.03.63.40, fax 03.26.03.66.93 by appt.

LAUNOIS PERE ET FILS
Blanc de blancs 1995

○ Gd cru 6 ha 40,000 70–99 F

A member of the Launois family was already selling champagne in 1872; he might have been the first grower-winemaker on the Côte des Blancs. Today the vineyard extends over 20 ha (49 acres), a far from negligible area. The 1995 is a well-balanced and fresh blanc de blancs, altogether an honourable ambassador for its category. (RM)

Champagne Launois Père et Fils, 2, av. Eugène-Guillaume, 51190 Le Mesnil-sur-Oger, tel. 03.26.57.50.15, fax 03.26.57.97.82 by appt.

LAURENT-GABRIEL 3e Millénaire

○ 1er cru 1 ha n.c. 100–149 F

There are two special mentions for this firm of 2.5 ha (5 acres), established in Avenay (to the east of Epernay and Ay), whose traditional production methods do not forgo the use of casks for a small part of the wine. They are used in this blend, which is very dominant in black grapes (80% Pinot Noir), very well-developed (perhaps it contains a good number of reserve wines), fleshy, rich and mature with a touch of oakiness, and also in the **Prestige 93** (85% Pinot Noir), which is powerful and well-rounded. (RM)

EARL Laurent-Gabriel, 2, rue des Remparts, 51160 Avenay-Val-d'Or, tel. 03.26.52.32.69, fax 03.26.59.92.08, e-mail champagne.laurent-gabriel@voila.fr by appt.

LAURENT-PERRIER
Grand Siècle Lumière du millénaire 1990**

○ n.c. n.c. 500 F+

This house, established at Tours-sur-Marne, was founded by a former cooper in 1812, and came to prominence in the 19th century. It went through a difficult time after the First World War, falling back to a more modest position until the 1950s. It then went through a spectacular expansion, which transformed it one of the most important

champagne firms, with a reputation for the reliability of its wines. Its Prestige wine, the Grand Siècle blend, is only declared a vintage if the harvest is exceptional, which was indeed the case in 1990. The blend includes Pinot Noir and Chardonnay in roughly equal proportions. The tasters were completely won over by it: 'A fresh, delicate wine, plenty of citrus fruit, discreet alcohol, very long on the palate – a pleasure'. (NM)

🔑 Champagne Laurent-Perrier, Dom. de Tours-sur-Marne, 51150 Tours-sur-Marne, tel. 03.26.58.91.22, fax 03.26.58.77.29 ☑ 🍷 by appt.

ALBERT LE BRUN Vieille France★

◑ n.c. n.c. 70-99 F

Bearing the signature of one of the two Châlons-en-Champagne companies, which were set up in 1860, this is a rosé produced from a classic blend of grape varieties (60% Pinot Noir, 30% Chardonnay and 10% red wine from Pinot Noir, which gives it its brick-like colouring). This is a well-balanced champagne, with aromas of fresh fruit, and it particularly appealed to one of the tasters who awarded it his highest accolade. (NM)

🔑 SCV Albert Le Brun, 93, av. de Paris, 51000 Châlons-en-Champagne, tel. 03.26.68.18.68, fax 03.26.21.53.31, e-mail info@champagne-lebrun.com ☑ 🍷 by appt.

🔑 Raulet

PAUL LEBRUN

Blanc de blancs Grande Réserve★★

○ 5 ha 35,000 🍾 70-99 F

This family firm was founded in 1902, and has a vineyard in the Côte des Blancs of 16.5 ha (41 acres), planted exclusively with Chardonnay. This Grande Réserve is a blanc de blancs whose distinguishing marks are roundness and fullness: it is a champagne for the dinner table. The **Prestige** blend, another blanc de blancs from the 1996 harvest (100–149F), offers aromas of stone fruits and crystallised fruits, which go hand in hand with a noticeable level of dosage. It receives a citation. (NM)

🔑 SA Champagne Vignier-Lebrun, 35, rue Nestor-Gaunel, 51530 Cramant, tel. 03.26.57.54.88, fax 03.26.57.90.02 ☑ 🍷 by appt.

🔑 M. P. Vignier

LE BRUN DE NEUVILLE

Blanc de blancs Cuvée Chardonnay★

○ n.c. 50,000 🍾 🌡 70-99 F

This modern, dynamic group of producers was created in 1963, and produces wine from 145 ha (358 acres) of vines. Their Chardonnay blend mingles floral notes and crystallised citrus fruits. The initial impression on the palate is lively; fruit and freshness harmonise together. The **Millésime 92** (100–149F) is only 5% off being a blanc de blancs and has all the buttery freshness and liquorice aromas of one. Its dosage is quite noticeable. (CM)

🔑 Champagne Le Brun de Neuville, rte de Chantemerle, 51260 Bethon, tel. 03.26.80.48.43, fax 03.26.80.43.28 ☑ 🍷 by appt.

LE BRUN-SERVENAY 1993

○Gd cru 1.3 ha 9,000 🍾 🌡 70-99 F

This family estate was established in 1947 and is based in Avize, a commune on the Côte des Blancs classified as Grand Cru. The vines are now about 60 years old. This 1993 is a supple blanc de blancs with good length on the palate. It offers cherry aromas, which is curious in a wine produced from Chardonnay. The **Spécial Club 94** (100–149F) is made up of 80% Chardonnay and the two Pinot grapes in equal proportions. The wines do not undergo malolactic fermentation, a fact that may explain the freshness of this 1994 blend. It is mineral, lemony and lively, and would go well with grilled fish. (RM)

🔑 EARL Le Brun-Servenay, 14, pl. Léon-Bourgeois, 51190 Avize, tel. 03.26.57.52.75, fax 03.26.57.02.71 ☑ 🍷 by appt.

LECLERC BRIANT

Cuvée divine 1990★

○ 1.5 ha 10,000 🍾 🌡 200-249 F

The Leclerc family were already wine-producers in Ay as long ago as the days of the Sun King. Louis Leclerc sold his first bottle in 1872. Today Pascal Leclerc-Briant owns 30 ha (74 acres) of organically farmed vineyard. Made from half black grapes and half white, the Cuvée Divine – a top-of-the-range blend – is produced from the great 1990 vintage. It presents a complex nose, mingling exotic, honeyed fragrances and dried fruits. The palate is rich, opulent indeed. (NM)

🔑 Champagne Leclerc Briant, 67, rue Chaude-Ruelle, B.P. 108, 51204 Epernay Cedex, tel. 03.26.54.45.33, fax 03.26.54.49.59 ☑ 🍷 ev. day 9am–12 noon 1.30pm–5.30pm; Sat. Sun. by appt.; cl. 5–25 Aug.

🔑 Pascal Leclerc-Briant

LECLERC-MONDET

○ 6 ha 38,000 70-99 F

The little village of Chassins around which the grandson of Henri Leclerc, who created the vineyard in 1952, manages 8 ha (20 acres), is situated in the Marne valley, near Dormans. All three of the champagne varieties (including 65% Pinot), from the 1996 and 1997 harvests, have been drawn on to put together this non-vintage Brut blend, which is well-balanced and full-bodied on the palate, and has an elegant nose with hints of wax and acacia honey, and even fern and sponge-cake. The **Grande Réserve**, which is a similar blend of all three varieties, but in this case drawn from the 1992 and 1993 harvests, has aromas of almonds and gingerbread. It was awarded the same score. (RM)

🔑 Champagne Leclerc-Mondet, 5, rue Beethoven, Chassins, 02850 Trélou-sur-Marne, tel. 03.23.70.26.40, fax 03.23.70.10.59 ☑ 🍷 by appt.

LEGOUGE-COPIN Tradition★

○ n.c. 8,000 70–99 F

This enterprise of 4.5 ha (11 acres) is in the Marne valley. The Legouge-Copin label is a reminder of the marriage, in 1992, of the eldest daughter of the founder of this vineyard, Serge Copin, to Jean-Marc Legouge. All three champagne grapes (including 70% Pinot Meunier), drawn from the harvests between 1994 and 1997, combine in this Tradition blend, which is full of raspberry and biscuit flavours, and is elegant and well-structured. The **Rosé** (66% Pinot Noir, 30% Chardonnay and a subtle hint of Meunier) also has the scent of raspberries. On the palate, raspberries again . . . and considerable dosage. (RM)

Jean-Marc Legouge, 6, rue de l'Abbé-Bernard, 51700 Verneuil, tel. 03.26.52.96.89, fax 03.26.51.85.62 by appt.

ERIC LEGRAND Cuvée Prestige★

○ 0.4 ha 4,000 70–99 F

Eric Legrand has been working 7 ha (17 acres) of vines in the Aube since 1982. He organises introductions to champagne in his cellars. His Prestige blend is dominated by Chardonnay (70%, as against 30% Pinot Noir) and comes from the 1997 and 1998 harvests. The tasters noted suggestions of white blossom and crystallised citrus fruits – a very pleasant combination. The **Cuvée Rubis** includes, notwithstanding its name, still more Chardonnay (80%). It has flavours of brioche and is delicate, elegant and lively, making it an excellent apéritif champagne. (RM)

Eric Legrand, 39, Grande-Rue, 10110 Celles-sur-Ource, tel. 03.25.38.55.07, fax 03.25.38.56.84 ev. day except Wed. Sun. 9am–12.30pm 2pm–6pm; cl. Aug.

LEGRAND-BROQUET

Cuvée 2000 1995

○Gd cru 2.2 ha n.c. 100–149 F

Jean-Yves Legrand manages a little family vineyard of 2.2 ha (5.5 acres) created in 1946 and which is situated in Chouilly, a commune classified as Grand Cru. His Cuvée 2000 is a blanc de blancs. The aromas range from honey to toast, with a herbaceous touch becoming apparent on the fleshy, rich palate. (RM)

Jean-Yves Legrand, 16, rue des Gouttes-d'Or, 51200 Epernay, tel. 03.26.55.00.30 by appt.

R. ET L. LEGRAS

Blanc de blancs Présidence 1990★★

○ 10 ha 60,000 150–199 F

This négociant house is situated in Chouilly, a commune to the east of Epernay classified as Grand Cru. It owns a vineyard of 14 ha (35 acres), which was formed as long ago as 1790. Their Présidence blend, a Blanc de Blancs 1990, retains its youth in spite of the richness of the vintage, to which it owes its fullness, its chewiness and its length. 'This is a wine to go with white meat,' wrote one taster; another would happily drink it all through the evening! The non-vintage **Blanc de Blancs** (70–99F) is perhaps lacking in complexity but with its hints of hazelnuts and spices, its freshness and especially its delicacy, it is 'not bad at all'. (NM)

Champagne R. et L. Legras, 10, rue des Partelaines, 51530 Chouilly, tel. 03.26.54.50.79, fax 03.26.54.88.74, e-mail contact@legras.fr ev. day except Sun. 8.30am–12 noon 2pm–5pm; Sat. by appt.

LEGRAS ET HAAS

Blanc de blancs Sélection du millénaire 1995★★

○Gd cru 14 ha 10,000 100–149 F

This family firm has built up a vineyard of 25 ha (62 acres) over the course of five generations, notably in Chouilly (a Grand Cru). A great vintage, a Grand Cru, a great grape variety and careful vinification: everything contributes to the quality of this harmonious, elegant, long, spicy, well-rounded champagne. In the lower price bracket (70–99F), two wines were awarded a star each: the **Non-vintage Blanc de Blancs Grand Cru** from the 1996 and 1997 harvests, which is rich and full with well-harmonised acidity, and the **Tradition**, produced from all three champagne grapes (with 60% Chardonnay) from the 1996 and 1997 harvests. 'A champagne that explodes on the palate,' wrote one taster. (NM)

Legras et Haas, 7–9, Grande-Rue, 51530 Chouilly, tel. 03.26.54.92.90, fax 03.26.55.16.78 by appt.

LELARGE-PUGEOT Réserve★

○ 0.5 ha 4,000 70–99 F

Dominique Lelarge has been producing wine in Vrigny (to the west of Reims) since 1986. His Brut Réserve is produced from all three champagne varieties, especially Pinot Meunier (60%) from the 1990 harvest. It was a fine year. The wine is rich, the nose flattering and the palate full and well-balanced, with liquorice flavours. This is a wine for the dinner table. (RM)

Dominique Lelarge, 30, rue Saint-Vincent, 51390 Vrigny, tel. 03.26.03.69.43, fax 03.26.03.68.93, e-mail champagnelelarge-pugeot@wanadoo.fr ev. day except Sun. 9am–12 noon 2pm–6pm

PATRICE LEMAIRE 1995★★

○ n.c. 2,500 70–99 F

Planted at Boursault in the Marne valley, this vineyard was created in the 1920s. In 1950, Claude Lemaire went into production and bottling. His son Patrice took over in 1988. His 1995 is a blanc de blancs with a complex nose combining white blossom and hints of menthol and honey, leading to a full, aromatic palate. Under the **Claude Lemaire** label, Patrice Lemaire has produced a rosé made from all three champagne grapes (including 40% Chardonnay), to which an additional 10% of red wine contributes colour. This champagne is cited for its good balance and its fruit flavours. (RM)

Patrice Lemaire, 9, rue Croix-Saint-Jean, 1480 Boursault, tel. 03.26.58.40.58, ax 03.26.52.30.67 ☑ Ⲩ by appt.

PHILIPPE LEMAIRE 1993★

○ 0.8 ha 2,300 ▮ ◖◗ ♁ 70–99 F

Philippe Lemaire has been producing champagne since 1992. He matures his wines n wood and stirs the lees in the barrel. The oakiness is very discreet and does not detract from the freshness of this 1993 wine, which is a pleasant, delicate blanc de blancs with characteristic aromas of toasted almonds. A citation also goes to the **Dame de Louis** blend, which is produced from all three champagne varieties (including 60% Meunier) from the 1997 harvest. This is a wine with a positive attack, slightly smoky aromas of dried fruits and a fresh finish. (RM)

🔑 Philippe Lemaire, 40, rue du 8-Mai, 51480 Œuilly, tel. 03.26.58.30.82, fax 03.26.52.92.44 ☑ Ⲩ by appt.

R.C. LEMAIRE Chardonnay 1995★★

○ 1er cru n.c. 5,000 ◖◗ 150–199 F

Gilles Tournant runs a vineyard of 10 ha (25 acres) in the Marne valley. The grapes that go to make up this 1995 wine have been picked from 28-year-old vines planted in the commune of Hautvillers, which is where Dom Pérignon worked. The wine spends seven years in wooden casks and stays on its yeasts in the bottle for five more. It is excellent. The tasters were tireless in praising its powerful, varied aromas (lime, pineapple, toast, vanilla), its freshness, its silky, fleshy richness and its finesse. The **Cuvée Trianon** (55% Pinot Noir, 45% Chardonnay) does not undergo malolactic fermentation. It is lively and vigorous with hints of menthol and receives a star (70–99F). An important point to note is the ecological awareness of this company, where they combat pests only with natural methods. (RM)

🔑 Gilles Tournant, rue de la Glacière, 51700 Villers-sous-Châtillon, tel. 03.26.58.36.79, fax 03.26.58.39.28, e-mail tournant@clubinternet.fr ☑ Ⲩ by appt.

LEMAIRE-RASSELET Tradition★

○ 9.2 ha 17,000 ▮ ♁ 70–99 F

This is an enterprise of more than 9 ha (22 acres) in the Marne valley. Their Tradition blend comes from all three of the champagne grapes, especially Meunier (75%), from the 1995 and 1996 harvests. The nose is evocative of crystallised citrus fruits and peaches, whilst on the palate hazelnut and caramel come to the fore. One taster particularly noted its 'presence'. The same verdict is awarded to the **Sélection**, which is an almost identical blend to the previous one, with slightly smoky aromas (roasting coffee, mocha and caramel) and a lingering finish. This is a champagne at its peak, to serve with poultry and white meats. (RM)

🔑 SCEV Lemaire-Rasselet, 5, rue de la Croix-Saint-Jean, 51480 Boursault, tel. 03.26.58.44.85, fax 03.26.58.09.47 ☑

MICHEL LENIQUE 1995

○ 1 ha 8,000 ▮ ♁ 100–149 F

The Lenique family have been producing wine for more than two centuries. At present the vineyard covers 9 ha (22 acres). Only 10% Pinot Meunier goes into this blend, which is chiefly composed of Chardonnay. Linden blossom, acacia and white flowers make up the aromatic profile of this lively, minerally wine, which should be drunk as an apéritif or with fish. (NM)

🔑 SA Lenique et Fils, 20, rue du Gal-de-Gaulle, 51530 Pierry, tel. 03.26.54.03.65, fax 03.26.51.57.14, e-mail champagne.michel.lenique@wanadoo.fr ☑ Ⲩ by appt.

A. R. LENOBLE Blanc de blancs★★

○ Gd cru 9 ha 40,000 ▮ 100–149 F

Armand Raphaël Graser was the son of an Alsatian who fled his native province in 1870. He served his apprenticeship in a champagne house, became a courtier and then, after the First World War, created his own firm. Today, the vineyard extends over 18 ha (44 acres), and is run by his great-great-grandchildren. The Lenoble brand was first launched in 1941. The letters AR no doubt represent the initials of the founder. This Grand Cru wins on every count. From the very outset, it appeals by the great delicacy of its aromas, which are floral, honeyed and smoky, and for its elegance and complexity. That complexity is to be found once again on the long, fresh, supple, rounded, liquorice-flavoured palate. This is a well-structured wine that will go admirably with a sauced fish dish. The **Réserve** (70–99F), which is made from all three champagne grapes, wins a star for its vinous minerality and its balance. (NM)

🔑 Champagne A. R. Lenoble, 35–37, rue Paul-Douce, 51480 Damery, tel. 03.26.58.42.60, fax 03.26.58.65.57, e-mail champagne.lenoble@wanadoo.fr ☑ Ⲩ by appt.

🔑 Malassagne

LIEBART-REGNIER Brut de brut★

○ 3 ha 4,000 ▮ ♁ 70–99 F

All the wines in this company, which owns 8 ha (20 acres) of vines, come from two Crus from the Marne valley: Baslieux and Vauciennes. Brut de Brut is a blanc de noirs made from both Pinot grapes (70% Meunier) from the years 1993 and 1994. It is highly developed and fairly vinous, developing aromas of hazelnut, almonds, rhubarb and

crystallised fruits. A star is also awarded to the **cuvée Excelia 94** (100–149F), which comes from all three grape varieties (including 70% Pinot Noir), and which is full of brioche flavours and particularly noted for its long finish, highlighted by hints of orange. (RM)
Liébart-Régnier, 6, rue Saint-Vincent, 51700 Baslieux-sous-Châtillon, tel. 03.26.58.11.60, fax 03.26.52.34.60, e-mail liebart-regnier@wanadoo.fr by appt.
Laurent Liébart

LILBERT-FILS Blanc de blancs*

○Gd cru n.c. n.c. 70–99 F

The Lilbert family were wine-producers even before 1750. Today they manage 4 ha (10 acres) in Cramant, a Côte des Blancs commune classified as Grand Cru. The estate puts up a very fine performance, with three of its champagnes winning a star. All of them are Grand Cru blanc de blancs wines. The first, which comes from the 1994, 1995 and 1996 vintages, is richly textured, honeyed and perfectly balanced. The **Brut Perlé** blend brings together the 1991, 1992 and 1994 harvests, together with 50% from the 1995; this type of champagne is bottled at 4 kg of gas pressure, and was formerly called *crémant*. It is supple, spicy and long. The **1995** (100–149F) has spent some time in wood, as is apparent from a certain oakiness on the palate, mingled with lemony quince, honey and vanilla. (RM)
Georges Lilbert , 223, rue du Moutier B.P. 14, 51530 Cramant, tel. 03.26.57.50.16, fax 03.26.58.93.86 by appt.

MICHEL LORIOT 1996***

○ 1.5 ha 10,000 100–149 F

The Loriot family are based in Festigny in the Marne valley, and began cultivating their first vines in 1931. Today they work a little more than 6 ha (15 acres). This 1996 wine is made up of a blend that has stood the test of time: 80% Pinot Meunier and 20% Chardonnay. The tasters were bowled over by it: 'a first impression of velvet, a very fine palate in perfect harmony, very great length, a forthright, natural wine with perfect lightness'. A star is also awarded to the **Loriot Extra Brut** (with its illustration of a bird on the label), which is an identical blend produced from the 1997 harvest. This is a supple, straightforward, fresh, lively and full-textured champagne. (RM)
Michel Loriot, 13, rue de Bel-Air, 51700 Festigny, tel. 03.26.58.33.44, fax 03.26.58.03.98 by appt.

JOSEPH LORIOT-PAGEL

Blanc de blancs 1995

○ 1 ha 3,000 70–99 F

This company has a vineyard of 8 ha (2 acres) spread over four Crus in the Marne valley and two Grands Crus on the Côte des Blancs. This 1995 wine, which is almost colourless, was particularly commended for its fresh nose of white blossom and for its well-constructed palate. (RM)
Joseph Loriot, 33, rue de la République, 51700 Festigny, tel. 03.26.58.33.53, fax 03.26.58.05.37 by appt.

YVES LOUVET Cuvée de réserve*

○ 1 ha 10,000 70–99 F

Yves Louvet cultivates 6.5 ha (16 acres) of vines near Tauxières (between Ay and Bouzy). His Cuvée de Réserve comes from the 1994 harvest; it is a blend of 75% Pinot Noir and 25% Chardonnay. A fresh nose of may blossom and honey is followed by an imposing palate showing plenty of richness. (RM)
Yves Louvet, 21, rue du Poncet, 51150 Tauxières, tel. 03.26.57.03.27, fax 03.26.57.67.77 by appt.

PHILIPPE DE LOZEY Prestige*

○ 12 ha 6,000 70–99 F

This brand was launched in 1990 by Daniel Cheurlin and his son Philippe. Their Prestige is made from half white grapes and half black (Pinot Noir), harvested in 1994. It wins a star for its nose of honeyed white blossom and for its freshness on the palate, which is not unbalanced by the noticeably high dosage. (NM)
Champagne Philippe de Lozey, 72, Grande-Rue, B.P. 3, 10110 Celles-sur-Ource, tel. 03.25.38.51.34, fax 03.25.38.54.80, e-mail de.lozey@wanadoo.fr by appt.
Ph. Cheurlin

M. MAILLART

Brut Cuvée de réserve 1994

○ n.c. 16,500 70–99 F

The Maillart family will soon have clocked up three centuries as wine-producers, although this brand was only created in 1965. Their vineyard covers 8.4 ha (21 acres). Chardonnay and Pinot grapes work in practically equal proportions in this Réserve, which is already evolved (it was a difficult vintage). It loses in delicacy what it gains in length. (RM)
Michel Maillart, 13, rue de Villers, 51500 Ecueil, tel. 03.26.49.77.89, fax 03.26.49.24.79 by appt.

MAILLY GRAND CRU

Blanc de noirs*

○Gd cru n.c. 40,000 100–149 F

This group – one might almost say club – of producers, founded in 1927, only admits growers whose vines are situated in the commune of Mailly, which is a Grand Cru. Consequently, there can be no Pinot Meunier in the blends. This Blanc de Noirs is full of brioche flavours; its richness does no harm to its elegance. Three other champagnes must be

mentioned, all made from three-quarters Pinot Noir and one-quarter Chardonnay: the **Extra Brut** with aromas of pear, apple, may blossom and lime blossom; the **Rosé**, which is well-balanced if a little fleeting (50–199F); and **Les Echansons 88**, which is very well-developed and extremely expensive (300–499F). A visit to the cellars, which are 1 km (0.67 miles) long and were dug by members of the group between 1930 and 1967, is highly recommended. (CM)
🔑 Champagne Mailly Grand Cru, 28, rue de la Libération, 51500 Mailly-Champagne, tel. 03.26.49.41.10, fax 03.26.49.42.27, e-mail contact@champagne-mailly.com ☑ 🍷 by appt.

JEAN-LOUIS MALARD
Sélection 2000 1991★

○ n.c. n.c. 100–149 F

This négociant firm was created in 1970 in Oiry. The label states the blending proportions: 60% Pinot Noir and 40% Chardonnay. It is a classic champagne, floral, lemony and fresh on the palate. Under the label Malard (without the first name) should also be noted the **Cuvée Excellence** (70–99F), a blanc de blancs Grand Cru cited for its hints of roasting coffee, its roundness, balance and length. (NM)
🔑 Champagne Malard, 65, av. de Champagne, B.P. 95, 51203 Epernay Cedex, tel. 03.26.57.77.24, fax 03.26.52.75.54

HENRI MANDOIS 1995★★

○ 1er cru 2 ha 15,000 70–99 F

This is a venerable old house whose 18th-century cellars were dug out beneath the church in Pierry. It possesses 35 ha (86 acres) of vines. The three champagne grapes work together in this vintage wine, which is light, delicate, mineral, smoky and lemony, with faint suggestions of may blossom. Its balance, harmony and length make it fully worthy of two stars – only just short of a *coup de coeur*. This champagne will make a perfect match for fish or poultry dishes. Its price-quality ratio is excellent. The **Cuvée de Réserve**, which is made from half black grapes and half white (with 40% Meunier), receives a citation for the lightness of its finish. (RM)
🔑 Champagne Henri Mandois, 66, rue du Gal-de-Gaulle, 51530 Pierry, tel. 03.26.54.03.18, fax 03.26.51.53.66 ☑ 🍷 by appt.

MANSARD★

○ 1er cru 15 ha 100,000 70–99 F

This Epernay négociant has an important vineyard, being well-known to the house of G H Martel. This Premier Cru blend, made from half white grapes and half black (Pinot Noir), comes from the 1995 and 1997 vintages. After a supple opening, the wine demonstrates its balance and length. Another champagne particularly noted by the jury, and receiving a citation, is the **Carte noire** blend; all three champagne varieties from the 1995, 1996 and 1997 harvests combine here to produce sharply lemony flavours, compensated by evident dosage. (NM)
🔑 Champagne Mansard, 14, rue Chaude-Ruelle, B.P. 1066, 51319 Epernay Cedex, tel. 03.26.54.18.55, fax 03.26.51.99.50 ☑ 🍷 by appt.
🔑 Rapeneau

PATRICE MARC Cuvée noir et blanc★

○ 2 ha 21,584 70–99 F

The three champagne grapes contribute equally to this blend, which is made from a mixture of wines from the 1994 and 1995 harvests. It is all fruit: peaches, stone fruits, crystallised citrus fruits, apricots and mandarins. It would, as a result, go well with duck à l'orange. (RM)
🔑 Patrice Marc, 1, rue du Creux-Chemin, 51480 Fleury-la-Rivière, tel. 03.26.58.46.88, fax 03.26.59.48.21 ☑ 🍷 by appt.

A. MARGAINE★★

○ 1er cru 5.3 ha 50,000 70–99 F

This house is directed by the great-grandson of the founder. It owns a vineyard of 6.5 ha (16 acres), including a good deal of Chardonnay, a grape variety with a reputation for excellence in Villers-Marmery. The non-vintage Brut is dominated by white grapes, including only 16% Pinot Noir. The wines from which it is blended are 1997 (57%), topped up with the 1992, 1994, 1995 and 1998 vintages. It was awarded two stars for the quality of its almond and hazelnut aromas, as well as for its supple freshness and its harmonious balance. The **Cuvée Spécial Club**, which is always a vintage wine – in this case **1995** – is sold in a distinctive bottle. Winning one star, it shows plenty of finesse, subtlety and balance (100–149F). (RM)
🔑 Champagne A. Margaine, 3, av. de Champagne, 51380 Villers-Marmery, tel. 03.26.97.92.13, fax 03.26.97.97.45 ☑ 🍷 by appt.

MARIE STUART Cuvée de la Reine★

○ n.c. 70,000 150–199 F

This house was founded in 1867, and sold off in 1927, 1954, 1972 and, most recently, in 1994 to Alain Thiénot. The Cuvée de la Reine is almost a blanc de blancs (only 10% Pinot Noir). The Chardonnay comes right to the fore, with notes of yellow fruits, honey, dried apricots and hazelnuts. It is a champagne of great finesse. The **1996** vintage was awarded a star. Its bouquet is that of Chardonnay, and the palate shows great potential (100–149F). Also receiving citations are the **Non-vintage Blanc de Blancs**, which is lively and harmonious, and the **Rosé**, which is very marked by Pinot Noir, with its discreet nose of red berries and well-balanced weight (100–149F). (NM)
🔑 Champagne Marie Stuart, 8, pl. de la République, 51100 Reims, tel. 03.26.77.50.50, fax 03.26.77.50.59, e-mail Laurent-Fedou@alian-thienot.fr ☑ 🍷 by appt.

CHAMPAGNE

MARQUIS DE SADE

Blanc de blancs Prestige 2000 1996

○Gd cru 5 ha 50,000 100–149 F

This brand belongs to Michel Gonet, an important wine-producer on the Côte des Blancs; the label says Grand Cru, for the grapes are from the communes of Oger and Mesnil-sur-Oger, which are both so classified. It is a classic blanc de blancs with aromas of toast, citrus fruits (lemon) and then soft yellow fruits. Its elegant liveliness will allow it to age. (RM)

SCEV Michel Gonet et Fils, 196, av. Jean-Jaurès, 51190 Avize, tel. 03.26.57.50.56, fax 03.26.57.91.98 by appt.

G. H. MARTEL & Co Prestige

○ 37.5 ha 250,000 70–99 F

This house was founded in 1869. It belongs to an Epernay négociant who sells under his own brand name and under various buyers' brand names. The firm has significant vineyard holdings. Prestige is a blend of 70% Pinot Noir and 30% Chardonnay, from grapes harvested in 1995, 1996 and 1997. It is reminiscent of peardrops. The initial impression on the palate is straightforward, and the wine has firm texture. (NM)

Champagne G.H. Martel, 69, av. de Champagne, B.P. 1011, 51318 Epernay Cedex, tel. 03.26.51.06.33, fax 03.26.54.41.52 by appt.

Rapeneau

PAUL LOUIS MARTIN

Cuvée Vincent Chardonnay 1995★

○Gd cru 1.8 ha 12,000 70–99 F

Produced by the same outfit as Martel and Mansard champagnes, this blanc de blancs from Bouzy is rather distinctive for its mineral nose and its aromas of white blossom. It turns out to be harmonious right through to the finish. The **Non-vintage Bouzy Grand Cru** blends 60% Pinot Noir with 40% Chardonnay from the 1994, 1995 and 1996 harvests. It shows its dosage a little conspicuously, but deserves a citation for its fruity aromas. (RM)

Champagne Paul-Louis Martin, 3, rue d'Ambonnay, 51150 Bouzy, tel. 03.26.57.01.27, fax 03.26.57.83.25 by appt.

D. MASSIN 1996★

○ 0.5 ha 5,000 100–149 F

Dominique Massin sold his first bottles in 1975. His vineyard of 11 ha (27 acres) is planted solely with the two noble grape varieties of the Champagne region, Pinot Noir and Chardonnay. The 1996 blend is classic: 60% and 40% respectively. It is fruity, bready and supple, and full of appley freshness. One taster suggested serving it with cooked first courses. The **Cuvée de Réserve en Rosé**, which is a rosé de noirs (70–99F), is dark in colour and very full on the palate. (RM)

Dominique Massin, rue Coulon, 10110 Ville-sur-Arce, tel. 03.25.38.74.97, fax 03.25.38.77.51 by appt.

THIERRY MASSIN Réserve

○ n.c. 28,000 70–99

Thierry and Dominique Massin ar brother and sister, and own a vineyard c some 10 ha (25 acres). The first bottles to bea this label appeared in 1977. This Réserv blend is almost a blanc de noirs, since onl 10% of Chardonnay is added to the Pinc Noir. It is made with Côte des Bar grape from the 1995, 1996 and 1997 harvests. It i still very young, but already pleasing to th eye on account of its golden-yellow straw co our and its fine stream of bubbles. On th nose, a few floral suggestions come through and its lively palate is full of promise. (RM)

Thierry Massin, 6, rte des Deux-Bar, 10110 Ville-sur-Arce, tel. 03.25.38.74.01, fax 03.25.38.79.10 ev. day 9am–12 noon 1.30pm–6.30pm; Sat. Sun. by appt.

LOUIS MASSING Cuvée Prestige★★★

○Gd cru 2 ha 14,000 100–149

This is a commercial brand that was launched a quarter of a century ago, with a vineyard of some 11 ha (27 acres). It is only a non-vintage Brut, to be sure, but it is a Prestige blend and a Grand Cru, according to the label – and from Avize, moreover. It was highly likely that this wine would turn out to be a blanc de blancs, and indeed it is. It is everything that this style should be, full of elegance and finesse, with harmony, complexity and length to boot. The vintage version of **Cuvée Prestige** (which is a **1992**, a worthy vintage) is faultless, for all that it has appreciably high dosage, and wins a citation. (NM)

SA Deregard-Massing, La Haie-Maria, R.D. 9, 51190 Avize, tel. 03.26.57.52.92, fax 03.26.57.78.23 by appt.

HERVE MATHELIN

◐ 0.3 ha 2,000 70–99 F

This brand was created in 1961 by a wine-producer from Troissy with a vineyard of 14 ha (35 acres). This rosé, which is produced from all three champagne grapes from the 1997 harvest, has overtones of overripe fruits, perhaps plums or apples. This is what gives it weight. (RM)

Hervé Mathelin, 2, rte de Paris, 51700 Troissy, tel. 03.26.52.74.42, fax 03.26.57.16.54 by appt.

ERGE MATHIEU★

n.c. 6,000 70–99F F

Serge Mathieu is a grower in the Aube with ‹ ha (27 acres) of vines, who practises the *itte intégrée*, allowing grass to grow natu-illy between his rows of vines. He has pro-uced three champagnes that each win a star. he first, a rosé made from Pinot Noir, is dis-nguished, full of red berries (particularly iorello cherries), well-balanced, vinous and ›ng, and clearly meant to be drunk with 'hite meats. The second, a **Vintage Brut 95** .00–149F), is made up of 70% Pinot Noir nd 30% Chardonnay: it is a full and well-ounded wine. The third, **Brut Select Tête de Cuvée** (100–149F), which has equal propor-ons of Chardonnay and Pinot Noir, is more omplex than subtle on the nose, giving a vely, refreshing first impression, and has een judiciously dosed. (RM)

Champagne Serge Mathieu, 6, rue des 'ignes, 10340 Avirey-Lingey, el. 03.25.29.32.58, fax 03.25.29.11.57, -mail champagne.mathieu@wanadoo.fr by appt.

MATHIEU-PRINCET 1995★★

1er cru 4 ha 20,000 100–149 F

Michel Mathieu is a wine-producer in Grauves (to the west of Avize), where he tends 8 ha (20 acres). He makes a sensational entry into the *Guide* with this very simple blend of half white grapes and half black (Pinot Noir) from the wonderful 1995 vintage. This champagne is a model of its kind, owing to the complexity and finesse of its aromas, with suggestions of citrus and exotic fruits (mango), backed up by the softness and suppleness of acacia. This complexity also comes through on a palate marked by lightness and freshness, and continues through to a harmonious finish. His **Blanc de Blancs 93** wins a star on account of its richness, which does not undermine its finesse (70–99F). (RM)

SARL Mathieu-Princet, 16, rue Bruyère, 51190 Grauves, tel. 03.26.59.73.72, fax 03.26.59.77.75 by appt.

MAXIM'S Cuvée an 2000 1994

4.5 ha 30,000 100–149 F

Maxim's champagne is produced by the same outfit responsible for G. H. Martel, P. Louis Martin and Mausard champagnes (see entries). Cuvée 2000 is made from half black grapes and half white, using grapes from the 1994 harvest. The style is daring: indeed, it was the subject of debate among the tasters, who could only agree on the descriptions 'light' and 'well-developed'. (MA)

Champagne Maxim's, 17, rue des Créneaux, 51100 Reims, tel. 03.26.82.70.67, fax 03.26.82.19.12 by appt.

Rapeneau

MERCIER Cuvée Eugène Mercier★

n.c. n.c. 100–149 F

This house was founded in 1858 by Eugène Mercier, the man who democratised champagne. The Mercier vineyard now extends to some 231 ha (570 acres). Visiting the cellars is a must, with their 18 km (12 miles) of tunnelled-out galleries. In the entrance hall, you will see a sculpted *foudre* (huge wooden cask) with a capacity equivalent to 213, 000 bottles. All three champagne varieties (10% Chardonnay, 55% Pinot Noir and 35% Pinot Meunier), not to mention 30% of reserve wines, contribute to this blend, created in honour of the founder. It is a beautifully made wine, clearly stamped by the forceful presence of Pinot Noir, with a well-balanced palate and good length. It has now reached its peak. One member of the jury wished very much to taste it with red meat or game. (NM)

Champagne Mercier, 75, av. de Champagne, B.P. 134, 51333 Epernay, tel. 03.26.51.22.00, fax 03.26.54.84.23 by appt.

DE MERIC

Cuvée Prestige Catherine de Médicis 1993★

Gd cru n.c. n.c. 100–149 F

This house, launched by Christian Besserat in 1960, has produced a powerful and well-developed 1993, in which the aromatic range extends as far as mushroom. A champagne for the dinner table. (NM)

SA Christian Besserat Père et Fils, Champagne de Meric, 17, rue Gambetta, 51160 Ay, tel. 03.26.55.20.72, fax 03.26.55.69.23 by appt.

J.B. MICHEL Blanc de blancs★

1 ha 7,000 70–99 F

Bruno Michel is an oenologist. He has a vineyard of 10 ha (25 acres) with vines of a respectable average age: more than 30 years old. Two blends were particularly noted. The **1993** is a blanc de blancs (100–149F). White blossom, dried apricots and dried fruits are well supported by the wine's liveliness. It receives a citation from the jury. This non-vintage Blanc de Blancs is elegant on the eye, very fruity on the nose, well-balanced, supple and harmonious. (RM)

Bruno Michel, 4, allée de la Vieille-Ferme, 51530 Pierry, tel. 03.26.55.10.54, fax 03.26.54.75.77, e-mail champagne.j.b.michel@cdr.fr by appt.

G. MICHEL Tradition 1982★★

2.5 ha 12,000 100–149 F

With 20 ha (49 acres) spread over some ten Crus, this grower is able to produce a vast range of champagnes. His 1982 is one of the

oldest champagnes in the *Guide*. Notwithstanding that, it is made largely from a grape variety that has a reputation for fragility, Pinot Meunier (80%, with 20% Chardonnay). It is incredibly fresh, delicate and lingering. The **Blanc de Blancs 90** was awarded one star. This wine has not undergone malolactic fermentation but, in spite of that, it has developed strongly. A star also goes to the **Réserve** blend made from all three champagne grapes from the 1996 and 1997 harvests: it is reminiscent of white blossom and honey, and seems full of youthfulness. These two last wines are in the 70–99F price bracket. (RM)
🗝 G. Michel, 19 bis, rte Nationale, Le Clos du Prieuré, 51530 Moussy, tel. 03.26.54.03.17, fax 03.26.58.15.84 ☑ Y by appt.

JOSE MICHEL ET FILS

Blanc de blancs 1995*

○ 1 ha 6,500 ▮ 100–149 F

Bruno Michel has been assisting his father since 1980 on the estate created by his ancestors in 1860 in Moussy, a village 4 km (2.5 miles) from Epernay. It has very appealing floral and mineral hints from the outset, and is a delicate, well-balanced and very attractive champagne. (RM)
🗝 Champagne José Michel et Fils, 14, rue Prelot, 51530 Moussy, tel. 03.26.54.04.69, fax 03.26.55.37.12 ☑ Y by appt.

CHARLES MIGNON Grande Réserve

○ 1er cru n.c. n.c. 100–149 F

This is a recently created brand of the Mignon family, négociants in Epernay. The tasters were of the opinion that this Grande Réserve was mainly distinguished by its youthfulness. It is lemony on the nose and palate, and the structure of the wine is very interesting. Serve it in a year's time with a platter of seafood. (NM)
🗝 Charles Mignon, 1, av. de Champagne, 51200 Epernay, tel. 03.26.58.33.33, fax 03.26.51.54.10, e-mail bruno-mignon@champagne-mignon.fr ☑ Y by appt.
🗝 Bruno Mignon

PIERRE MIGNON Grande Réserve*

○ 6 ha n.c. ▮ 70–99 F

Not far from the abbey church of Orbais – an example of the earliest Gothic art, and whose 13th-century stained-glass window of the Redemption alone justifies the trip – lies Le Breuil, home of Pierre Mignon champagne. The brand was created in 1970, and owns a vineyard of more than 10 ha (25 acres). A great deal of Pinot Meunier (80%), and as much Pinot Noir as Chardonnay, give this straightforward and well-balanced champagne aromas of apple and lychees, as well as considerable freshness. The **Brut Prestige** is blended from a great deal of Pinot Meunier (65%), supported by the other two varieties; it receives a citation for its initial suppleness and for its lively finish. (NM)
🗝 Pierre Mignon, 5, rue des Grappes-d'O 51210 Le Breuil, tel. 03.26.59.22.03, fax 03.26.59.26.74, e-mail p.mignon@lemel.fr ☑ Y by appt.

MIGNON ET PIERREL Cuvée floral

◑ 1er cru n.c. n.c. 100–1

This négociant firm in Epernay is we known for its strangely coloured bottle which contrast sharply with the sober style o the label. They are fond of Chardonnay Mignon et Pierrel. This rosé is a blanc blancs tinted with 10% Pinot Noir red wine. has finesse and harmony. The vintage 9 **Cuvée Florale** Premier Cru (150–199F) is blanc de blancs, even though the label doesn say so. Its aromas of wax and honey, howeve can't disguise the fact. A well-balanced, fir champagne. (NM) F
🗝 SA Pierrel et Associés, 26, rue Henri-Dunant, B.P. 295, 51200 Epernay, tel. 03.26.51.00.90, fax 03.26.51.69.40, e-mail champagne@pierrel.fr ☑ Y by appt

JEAN-CHARLES MILAN

Blanc de blancs Cuvée de réserve**

○ Gd cru n.c. n.c. 70–99

The vineyard first saw the light of day i 1864, and the marque itself a century late Henri-Pol Milan today owns 6 ha (15 acres The Blanc de Blancs is a wine of great styl rated with three stars by some tasters. It comprised of wines from the 1995 and 199 vintages that have been matured in wood This champagne has great delicacy; hone and white blossom are underscored by a sligh oakiness, with all the flavours gaining in full ness on the palate. Very promising. (NM)
🗝 Champagne Milan, 6, rue d'Avize, 5119(Oger, tel. 03.26.57.50.09, fax 03.26.57.78.47, e-mail champagne.milan@wanadoo.fr ☑ Y by appt.

MOET ET CHANDON

Brut Impérial**

○ 1er cru n.c. n.c. ▮ 150–199 F

The house was founded in 1743 by Claud Moët, a négociant descended from a famil first established in the Champagne region in the 14th century. It once numbered Mme de Pompadour among its clients, a fact that did not prevent Jean-Remy Moët from later being on excellent terms with Napoleon. From the 1960s on, the takeover of respected old firms multiple acquisitions abroad, and then the formation of the LVMH group in 1987,

elped to give it a major role in the Cham-agne region. With 771 ha (1,900 acres) of ineyards, the largest holding in the region, he firm occupies the top rank in the export ield. The Brut Impérial is a blend of all three f the champagne grapes. Its subtle nose ains in intensity, presenting harmonious, oneyed and fruity aromas. The balanced alate is well-constructed, long and full of rioche flavours. This is a well-made cham-agne, which lends itself as much to the péritif hour as to the dinner table. (NM)

🗝 Champagne Moët et Chandon, 20, av. de hampagne, B.P. 140, 51200 Epernay, el. 03.26.51.20.00, fax 03.26.54.84.23 ☑ Y v. day 9.30am–11.30am 2pm–4.30pm; roups by appt.

MOET ET CHANDON

Dom Pérignon 1990★★★

◑ n.c. n.c. ▮ 500 F+

This is by far the best rosé champagne in the *Guide*. Of course it is expensive (more than 1,000F). Everything about the produc-tion of Dom Pérignon is a secret, right down to the number of bottles produced. The com-position to which Moët most commonly admits is 40% Chardonnay and 60% Pinot Noir from three red and two white Grands Crus. To that must be added the Hautvillers Premier Cru, if only for historical reasons! This rosé, which is a coppery gold in colour, presents a slightly smoky nose of cocoa beans, roasted hazelnuts, almonds, strawber-ries and morello cherries steeped in *eau-de-vie*. These aromas come through on the palate, blending together harmoniously, fully and with sublime finesse, adding a touch of liquo-rice. The **Dom Pérignon Blanc 93** is not in the same class; to our demanding tasters, its real elegance is marred to a certain extent by the dosage. This vintage, like the 1992, only serves to remind us how superb the 1990 was. (NM)

🗝 Champagne Moët et Chandon, 20, av. de Champagne, B.P. 140, 51200 Epernay, tel. 03.26.51.20.00, fax 03.26.54.84.23 ☑ Y ev. day 9.30am–11.30am 2pm–4.30pm; groups by appt.

PIERRE MONCUIT

Blanc de blancs Vieilles vignes Cuvée Nicole Moncuit 1992

○Gd cru 0.75 ha 9,000 ▮ 100–149 F

This century-old property manages a vine-yard of some 15 ha (37 acres) on the Côte des Blancs. The fine yellow hue of this 1992 champagne is enlivened by its delicate mousse. The nose is very true to type, and is evocative of ripe and crystallised fruits as well as hazelnuts. It is already well-developed. Fla-vours of dried and crystallised fruits come through on the palate. (RM)

🗝 Champagne Pierre Moncuit, 11, rue Persault-Maheu, 51190 Le Mesnil-sur-Oger, tel. 03.26.57.52.65, fax 03.26.57.97.89 ☑ Y by appt.

🗝 Nicole Moncuit

MONMARTHE Grande Réserve

○1er cru 4 ha 30,000 ▮ 70–99 F

The Monmarthe family were already wine-producers 50 years before the French Revolu-tion. Ernest created this brand in 1930. Today, the vineyard covers 17 ha (42 acres) in the commune of Ludes, a Premier Cru. The Grande Réserve, which is made from half black grapes and half white, comes from the 1994, 1995 and 1996 harvests. It presents aro-mas of cooked prunes, toast and caramel, and achieves good balance on the palate. The **Carte Blanche** blend, which is made from wines of less than a year old and from all three champagne grapes, affirms its youthfulness with all sorts of exotic flavours. (RM)

🗝 Jean-Guy Monmarthe, 38, rue Victor-Hugo, 51500 Ludes, tel. 03.26.61.10.99, fax 03.26.61.12.67, e-mail champagne-monmarthe@wanadoo.fr ☑ Y by appt.

DE MONTESPAN Grande Cuvée★

○ n.c. n.c. ▮ 🌡 100–149 F

This is a recently created négociant brand. The Grande Cuvée, which is a non-vintage Brut, more than earns its name, for it really inspired the tasters. Its intense golden colour, enlivened by a an attractive mousse, the well-developed, fruity complexity of its aromas (dried – or very ripe – fruits, honey and bri-oche) and the fine balance on its mature but still fresh palate, make this a bottle for wine-lovers at the peak of proficiency. (NM)

🗝 Champagne de Montespan et Cie, Galerie Sacres, 18, rue Tronsson-du-Coudray, 51100 Reims, tel. 03.26.86.81.14, fax 03.26.40.54.18 ☑ Y by appt.

🗝 Desbleds

DANIEL MOREAU

Carte noire Blanc de noirs★

○ 4 ha 30,000 ▮ 70–99 F

The Moreau family have been wine-growers since 1875, and Daniel Moreau has been producing his own wine since 1978. The Carte Noire is a blanc de noirs made from Pinot Meunier harvested in 1996 (25%) and 1997. It is a simple recipe for a wine with a flo-ral nose and a light, fresh palate full of lemony aromas. The dosage is noticeably high. A citation is given to the **Blanc de Blancs Carte d'Or**, from the 1997 harvest, which astonishes and fascinates on account of the aromatic touches (flowers and linden blos-som, then menthol and lemon, honey and aromas of the bakery) that give it such char-acter. (RM)

🗝 Daniel Moreau, 5, rue du Moulin, 51700 Vandières, tel. 03.26.58.01.64, fax 03.26.58.15.64 ☑ Y by appt.

MOREL PERE ET FILS

Rosé de cuvaison 1997★

◑ 1 ha 3,700 ▮ 🌡 70–99 F

The Morel family, who are specialists in Rosé des Riceys, have only been making this champagne since 1997. It is a special form of pink champagne, since it is produced by the *saignée* method, and is therefore a rosé de

CHAMPAGNE

noirs. There are red berries on the nose, which is at the outset of its development. They are followed by good balance and a long, caramelly finish on the palate. (RM)
🔑 Pascal Morel, 93, av. du Gal-de-Gaulle, 10340 Les Riceys, tel. 03.25.29.10.88, fax 03.25.29.66.72 ☑ Y by appt.

MORIZE PERE ET FILS Réserve*

○ 11 ha 42,600 🍾 🌡 70–99 F

The Morizes have been settled in les Riceys since 1830, and own a 12th-century cellar, although they only created the brand in 1964. This Réserve blend is dominated by black grapes (only 10% Chardonnay), and is made from grapes harvested in 1995, backed up by a small quantity from 1994 and 1993. It is a light champagne with hints of grapefruit and other citrus fruits, and the honeyed finish makes the dosage very apparent. (RM)
🔑 Morize Père et Fils, 122, rue du Gal-de-Gaulle, 10340 Les Riceys, tel. 03.25.29.30.02, fax 03.25.38.20.22 ☑ Y by appt.

PIERRE MORLET Prestige 2000*

○ 1er cru 1.53 ha 13,000 🍾 🛢 🌡 70–99 F

Fifty metres (55 yards) from this winery in Avenay, the church of St-Trésain (named after a monk who came from Scotland to evangelise the region in the fifth century) is a worth a visit for its fine 13th-century remains. Pierre Morlet's Prestige 2000 is a blend of 60% Pinot Noir and 40% Chardonnay from the 1995 harvest. The wine matures in wood, and has great elegance, roundness and clarity. The **Grande Réserve Premier Cru**, produced from 30% Pinot and 70% Chardonnay, brings together wines from 1992, 1993, 1995 and 1996. It is cited for its vanilla-scented, toasty and well-developed character. (NM)
🔑 Champagne Pierre Morlet, 7, rue Paulin-Paris, 51160 Avenay-Val-d'Or, tel. 03.26.52.32.32, fax 03.26.59.77.13 ☑ Y by appt.

JEAN MOUTARDIER 1993**

○ 3 ha 30,000 🍾 🌡 70–99 F F

The Moutardier family have been wine-producers since 1650, although the marque only dates from 1920. Today, the vineyard covers 16 ha (40 acres). The 1993 vintage – a delicate year – is an unusual blend of 70% Pinot Meunier and 30% Chardonnay. It charmed the tasters on account of its fruity, smoky, spicy (cinnamon) aromas, and its length and readiness on the palate. Two stars are also awarded to the **Sélection**, which is half Pinot Noir and half Chardonnay, and is a floral, well-balanced, supple champagne with perfect colouring – a class act. (NM)
🔑 SA Champagne Jean Moutardier, 51210 Le Breuil, tel. 03.26.59.21.09, fax 03.26.59.21.25 ☑ Y by appt.

MOUTARD PERE ET FILS

Grande Réserve**

○ 3 ha 18,000 🍾 🌡 70–99

The Moutard family has been producin champagne since 1927. François Moutard who has a vineyard of 21 ha (52 acres), i enthusiastically replanting forgotten cham pagne varieties. This Grande Réserve blend i a blanc de blancs . . . from the Aube! Its ele gance, its aromas of hazelnuts, acacia hone and beeswax, its length and its harmoniou roundness: all combine in the triumph of *coup de coeur.* Half black and half whit grapes, the **Cuvée Prestige** (100–149F) i another very special wine, on account of it richness, its fullness and, above all, its individuality. It is fully worthy of two stars. (NM)
🔑 SARL Champagne Moutard-Diligent, 6, rue des Ponts, B.P. 1, 10110 Buxeuil, tel. 03.25.38.50.73, fax 03.25.38.57.72, e-mail champagne.moutard@wanadoo.fr ☑ Y by appt.

R. MOUZON-JUILLET**

○ Gd cru n.c. 2,400 🛢 100–149 F

This marque belongs to Philippe Mouzon, who acts here as vigneron. He blends two-thirds Chardonnay with one-third Pinot Noir from 1990 (30%) and 1991 (70%). The palate is rich in flavour (crystallised orange, honey, blackcurrant, mocha and spices), round and harmonious, full, fleshy and richly textured. This elegant champagne bordered on a *coup de coeur.* It only lacked a little more length to be considered outstanding. (RM)
🔑 EARL Mouzon-Leroux, 16, rue Basse-des-Carrières, 51380 Verzy, tel. 03.26.97.96.68, fax 03.26.97.97.67 ☑ Y by appt.

Y. MOUZON LECLERE Carte d'or*

○ 1er cru n.c. 1,800 70–99 F

The Mouzons were producing champagne before the First World War, but Mouzon Leclère has only been in existence since 1959. The Carte d'Or is dominated by white grapes, with 80% Chardonnay as against 20% Pinot Noir, from 1993 and 1994. Its freshness derives from the aromas of flowers and apples, while the palate is interestingly reminiscent of crystallised citrus fruits, bergamot and honey. The dosage is exactly right. (RM)
🔑 Yvon Mouzon, 1, rue Haute-des-Carrières, 51380 Verzy, tel. 03.26.97.91.19, fax 03.26.97.97.89 ☑ Y by appt.

H. MOUZON-LEROUX

Grande Réserve★

○Gd cru n.c. 80,000 70–99 F

The village of Verzy in the Montagne de Reims is famous for a forest containing a natural curiosity, *tortillards*, beech-trees grown into tortured shapes. It is also classified as Grand Cru, and the Mouzon family cultivates nearly 10 ha (25 acres) of vines here. Their Grande Réserve blend (80% Pinot Noir, 20% Chardonnay) is made up of 40% 1996 wine and 60% from the years 1992 to 1995. It is an excellent champagne, full, rounded, delicately fruity, and suitable for drinking at the end of a meal. There is also a citation for the **Rosé Premier Cru**, which is made from an identical blend to the above, coloured with 10% red wine. It is clear to the eye and easy to drink. (RM)

🔑 EARL Mouzon-Leroux, 16, rue Basse-des-Carrières, 51380 Verzy, tel. 03.26.97.96.68, fax 03.26.97.97.67 ✉ 🍷 by appt.

MUMM DE CRAMANT

Chardonnay★

○Gd cru 50 ha 80,000 200–249 F

The long and varied history of Mumm, which started in 1827, opened a new chapter in June 1999, when Seagram, who had been the owners since 1969, sold this brand (and Perrier-Jouët) to the American group Hicks, Muse, Tate and First. Two blends in particular receive a mention. The **Cordon Rouge**, made with all three champagne grapes, is classic and well-balanced, and there are six million bottles of it (100–149F). In the same price bracket, the **Cordon Rosé**, which is also made up of all three grapes but with a good deal of Pinot Noir (60%), is rounded, rich and harmonious. As for the famous label Mumm de Cramant (a blanc de blancs Grand Cru), it is a fine, well-balanced, supple, spicy champagne. (NM)

🔑 Champagne G.-H. Mumm et Cie, 29, rue du Champ-de-Mars, 51100 Reims, tel. 03.26.49.59.69, fax 03.26.77.40.69 ✉ 🍷 ev. day 10am–12 noon 2pm–6pm

LUCIEN ORBAN Carte d'or★

○ n.c. n.c. 70–99 F

This is a champagne that has now reached its peak. Its aromas of candied lychees precede a supple attack and flavours of crystallised fruits on the palate. (RM)

🔑 Lucien Orban, 8, rue du Général-de-Gaulle, 51700 Cuisles, tel. 03.26.58.10.51, fax 03.26.52.84.82 🍷 by appt.

CHARLES ORBAN

Cuvée spéciale 2000★

○ 2.25 ha 15,000 70–99 F

This brand belongs to a grower-winemaker in Troissy, who owns a vineyard of 6 ha (15 acres) and is part of the Rapeneau group. His Cuvée Spéciale 2000 is made from four times as much Chardonnay as Pinot Noir from the 1994, 1995 and 1996 harvests. On the palate, it has liveliness as well as the finesse of its principal grape variety, and well-balanced structure. There is also a citation for the **Carte Noire**, in which each of the three champagne grapes makes an equal contribution (the younger wines in it are from 1995, 1996 and 1997). The jury found its balance particularly appealing. (RM)

🔑 Champagne Charles Orban, 44, rte de Paris, 51700 Troissy, tel. 03.26.52.70.05, fax 03.26.52.74.66 ✉ 🍷 by appt.

🔑 Rapeneau

OUDINOT★

○ n.c. 700,000 100–149 F

This house was founded in 1889, and taken over by Jacques and Michel Trouillard in 1981. It now owns a vineyard of 124 ha (306 acres) on the Côte des Blancs. The Brut blend draws on the three champagne grapes in equal parts. Aromas of butter, honey and caramel come to the fore on a rich palate that nonetheless retains freshness. A star likewise goes likewise to the **Rosé**, which is a blend of the two Pinot grapes, and is fruity, supple and full. (NM)

🔑 Champagne Oudinot, 12, rue Godart-Roger, 51200 Epernay, tel. 03.26.59.50.10, fax 03.26.54.78.52

🔑 M. et J. Trouillard

BRUNO PAILLARD Première Cuvée★

○ n.c. 525,000 100–149 F

Bruno Paillard launched his marque in 1981. He blends 32 Crus and wines from five different vintages in his Première Cuvée, which draws on all three of the champagne varieties. It is a wonderfully accomplished champagne that is well-balanced and complex. Although Bruno Paillard may say that he doses the wine only very slightly, it is nonetheless very noticeable. The **Rosé Première Cuvée** is just as delicate as the white – 'a thinking person's rosé,' according to one taster. Lastly, the **Chardonnay Réserve Privée** earns a citation; it is still a fine wine, but extremely young. These two last champagnes are in the 150–199F price bracket. (NM)

🔑 Champagne Bruno Paillard, av. de Champagne, 51100 Reims, tel. 03.26.36.20.22, fax 03.26.36.57.72 ✉ 🍷 by appt.

PALMER & CO★

○ n.c. n.c. 70–99 F

This is a dynamic group of producers responsible for a vastly wide-ranging output. The non-vintage Brut (Pinot and Chardonnay) is particularly appealing for its unusual aromas of undergrowth and vanilla, with a slight hint of muskiness. Freshness and length are both very evident on the palate. Also cited is the **Blanc de Blancs 93**, which has already developed, and which comes from a difficult vintage. Fine and well-rounded, it will assuredly be ideal as an apéritif (100–149F). (CM)

🔑 Champagne Palmer et Co, 67, rue Jacquart, 51100 Reims, tel. 03.26.07.35.07, fax 03.26.07.45.24 ✉ 🍷 by appt.

PANNIER 1995★

○ n.c. n.c. 100–149 F

Château-Thierry, where you can see the house in which La Fontaine was born in 1621, is the operational centre of Pannier, a cooperative whose members' vines extend over 560 ha (1,380 acres). The 1995, which is made from all three champagne varieties, has now reached its peak. Tasters particularly noted flavours of acacia honey, candied quince, beeswax and a rich variety of very ripe fruits on the palate. One sommelier recommends serving this bottle as an accompaniment to guinea-fowl with peaches, but it will do just as well as an apéritif. Also cited is the **Cuvée Louis Eugène** (150–199F), another blend of the three grapes that places the emphasis on Pinot Noir. It is an elegant, if very youthful wine. (CM)

SCVM COVAMA, 25, rue Roger-Catillon, B.P. 55, 02403 Château-Thierry Cedex, tel. 03.23.69.51.30, fax 03.23.69.51.31, e-mail chppannier@aol.com Y by appt.

PASCAL-DELETTE Cuvée de réserve★

○ 5 ha 40,300 70–99 F F

Yves Pascal has two sons, and hopes that they will continue the task begun by his wine-producing ancestors. Today, he works a vineyard of 5 ha (12 acres), and has made a blanc de noirs from both Pinot varieties – 75% Meunier and 25% Noir, from the 1996 harvest. In spite of that simple constitution, complexity is the keynote of the wine: the fruity, buttery, exotic flavours mingle harmoniously, and with the lightest touch. (RM)

Yves Pascal-Delette, 48, rue Valentine-Régnier, 51700 Baslieux-sous-Châtillon, tel. 03.26.58.11.35, fax 03.26.57.11.93 Y by appt.

ERIC PATOUR

○ n.c. n.c. 70–99 F F

Eric Patour is a wine-producer at Celles-sur-Ource in the Aube, and has submitted a champagne that the tasters identified as deriving solely from Pinot Noir. His non-vintage Brut is indeed a blanc de noirs made from Pinot Noir from 1996. It shows fruity, toasty aromas on a well-balanced palate that also boasts good length. (RM)

Eric Patour, 11, rue du Vivier, 10110 Celles-sur-Ource, tel. 03.25.38.25.33, fax 03.25.38.22.65 Y by appt.

DENIS PATOUX 1992★★

○ n.c. n.c. 100–149 F

A huge statue of Pope Urban II, who launched the First Crusade, towers over the vines, not far from where the Patoux family have been vignerons for the past century. This very charming champagne offers a fine, elegant nose of gingerbread and citrus fruits. It is well-constructed on the palate, with flavours of almond and linden blossom. The **Vintage 95** receives a citation for its exotic fruit flavours and its richness. (RM)

Denis Patoux, 1, rue Bailly, 51700 Vandières, tel. 03.26.58.36.34, fax 03.26.59.16.10 Y by appt.

PEHU-SIMONET Cuvée Junior 1993★

○Gd cru 0.15 ha 1,150 100–149

The Péhu-Simonet family have owned the 5 ha (12 acres) of vineyard for a century. The have produced two very well-made wines. Th **Sélection Grand Cru** (70–99F) contains twic as much Pinot as Chardonnay, drawn fro the harvests of 1994 to 1997. It is an excelle champagne, fine, fresh, rich and harmoniou and with plenty of character. There is eve more character in this Junior 1993, which half black grapes and half white, produce from bunch-thinned vines and matured fc one year in cask without malolactic fermenta tion (like the above). This is a champagne fc connoisseurs: highly developed, oaky an with flavours of caramel and toast. (RM)

Pehu-Simonet, 7, rue de la Gare, B.P. 22 51360 Verzenay, tel. 03.26.49.43.20, fax 03.26.49.45.06 Y by appt.

JEAN-MICHEL PELLETIER

Cuvée Anaëlle 1995★

○ n.c. 1,300 70–99 F

When Jean-Michel Pelletier took over th Pelletier-Maillet brand, he acquired new pa cels of vineyard land. His vines now cove 4 ha (10 acres). This wine, which is made fro half white grapes and half black, is worthy o note, for only Chardonnay and Pinot Noir ar used in it. The Chardonnay spends fou months in cask after its malolactic fermenta tion. Aromas of apple and toast are comple mented by a slight hint of muskiness. Th complex palate has a note of liquorice on th finish. (RC)

Jean-Michel Pelletier, 22, rue Bruslard, 51700 Passy-Grigny, tel. 03.26.52.65.86, fax 03.26.52.65.86 Y by appt.

JOSEPH PERRIER Cuvée royale

◐ n.c. 30,000 150–199 F

This house, founded in 1825, was not tha long ago amalgamated with Laurent-Perrie and has been part of the Alain Thiénot group since 1998. The Cuvée Royale Rosée is made from three times as much Pinot Noir as Chardonnay. It is coloured with red wine from Cumières, and has a fine salmon-pink hue and a bouquet of spiced, vanilla-scented strawberries. On the palate, it has appealing suppleness and a flavour of raspberries. (NM)

SA Champagne Joseph Perrier, 69, av. de Paris, B.P. 31, 51000 Châlons-en-Champagne, tel. 03.26.68.29.51, fax 03.26.70.57.16 Y by appt.

PERRIER-JOUET Belle Epoque 1995★★

○ n.c. n.c. 300–499 F

Pierre Nicolas-Marie Perrier-Jouët founded this house in 1816. In 1959, Mumm took it over, and then in 1969, Mumm was in turn acquired by Seagram, who sold Perrier-Jouët to the American group Hicks Muse in 1999. The Belle Epoque 1995 is made from all ıree of the champagne varieties from five Grands Crus, and with Pinot Meunier from Dizy. It is a top-class wine, lively without being aggressive, delicate without being vapid, and elegant without pretentiousness. A star goes to the **Vintage Brut 92**, which is also made from the three grapes and from 30 crus. It has the richness and the delicacy of acacia honey, brioche dough and roasted hazelnuts. (NM)

🔑 Champagne Perrier-Jouët, 28, av. de Champagne, 51380 Verzy, tel. 03.26.53.38.00, fax 03.26.54.54.55 ☑ 🍸 by appt.

DANIEL PERRIN Cuvée Prestige

○ 1 ha 7,000 70-99 F

Daniel Perrin took control of the family estate in 1957. He runs a fine vineyard, producing 50,000 bottles of champagne a year. Two-thirds Pinot Noir and one-third Chardonnay make up this Cuvée Prestige, which has aromas of apple and a fine, fruity palate. (RM)

🔑 EARL Champagne Daniel Perrin, 10200 Urville, tel. 03.25.27.40.36, fax 03.25.27.74.57 ☑ 🍸 by appt.

PERSEVAL-FARGE Blanc de blancs★

○ 1er cru 1 ha 4,000 70-99 F

Using organic methods and according due consideration to the environment, the Perseval family has been established in Chamery since the 18th century. Their **Blanc de Noirs** (100–149F) received a citation. Made from equal proportions of the two Pinot varieties, it is an attractive champagne with a colour that appeals to the eye. It is powerful, richly textured and doesn't beat about the bush. The Blanc de Blancs is a blend of wines from 1994, 1995 and 1996. It is pale gold in colour with green highlights. Firstly floral on the nose, it displays flavours of citrus fruits on the palate, which is lively, fresh and very young. (RM)

🔑 Isabelle et Benoist Perseval, 12, rue du Voisin, 51500 Chamery, tel. 03.26.97.64.70, fax 03.26.97.67.67, e-mail champagne.perseval-farge@wanadoo.fr ☑ 🍸 by appt.

PIERRE PETERS

Blanc de blancs Cuvée spéciale 1996★

○ Gd cru 3 ha 20,000 100-149 F

Pierre Peters is a specialist in blanc de blancs, with a vineyard that extends over 17.5 ha (43 acres). This is a 'great wine', according to one taster. Indeed, there is little more to add concerning this fine, fresh, elegant, well-balanced, virile, rich wine, which shows perfect dosage. (RM)

🔑 Champagne Pierre Peters, 26, rue des Lombards, 51190 Le Mesnil-sur-Oger, tel. 03.26.57.50.32, fax 03.26.57.97.71 ☑ 🍸 by appt.

🔑 F. Peters

PETITJEAN-PIENNE Blanc de blancs

○ Gd cru 2.5 ha 2,000 70-99 F

There have been several Petitjean brands since the war, with various secondary names. The vineyard currently covers nearly 4 ha (10 acres). This classic Blanc de Blancs with fresh citrus aromas is lively, well-balanced and persistent on the palate. (RM)

🔑 Petitjean-Pienne, 4, allée des Bouleaux, 51530 Cramant, tel. 03.26.57.58.26, fax 03.26.59.34.09 ☑ 🍸 by appt.

PHILIPPONNAT

Clos des Goisses 1990★

○ 5.5 ha 30,000 300-499 F

The Philipponnat family has deep roots in Mareuil, going back to the 16th century. Their sloping vineyard is right by the Marne river. Clos des Goisses, which comes from the largest *clos* in the Champagne region (5.5 ha or 14 acres), is an exceptional wine, which has no malolactic fermentation and matures in large oak casks. The blend combines 70% Pinot Noir with 30% Chardonnay. The tasters particularly praised its aromas of red berries and of roasting coffee, its freshness, its structure and its length. A star was likewise awarded to the **Réserve Millésimé 91** and **le Reflet du Millénaire**, which are blended to the same style (with the Pinot varieties dominant). Both are well-balanced champagnes in the 150–199F price bracket. (NM)

🔑 SA Champagne Philipponnat, 13, rue du Pont, 51160 Mareuil-sur-Ay, tel. 03.26.56.93.00, fax 03.26.56.93.18, e-mail champagne.philipponnat@wanadoo.fr ☑ 🍸 by appt.

PIERREL Cuvée Tradition

○ 1er cru 10 ha n.c. 100-149 F

This brand is related to Mignon et Pierrel champagne, and was created in 1990. Although it is not stated on the label, the Cuvée Tradition is a blanc de blancs. It is a complex, velvety, well-balanced and attractive champagne. Likewise worthy of citation is the **Cuvée Arabesque**, which appears under the two labels: **Etiquette Or** and Blanche. The gold-label is 60% Chardonnay and the white 80%, with the balance in each case being made up of Pinot Noir. The Or is floral and buttery, with redcurrants on the palate, and is a very well-balanced wine. (NM)

🔑 SA Pierrel et Associés, 26, rue Henri-Dunant, B.P. 295, 51200 Epernay, tel. 03.26.51.00.90, fax 03.26.51.69.40, e-mail champagne@pierrel.fr ☑ 🍸 by appt.

Made up of half white grapes and half black

PIERSON-CUVELIER

Prestige Carte d'or★

○ Gd cru 2.5 ha 24,000 70-99 F

This estate was created in 1901 in the Grand Cru of Louvois and holds a vineyard of some 8 ha (20 acres). This Carte d'Or is a Pinot Noir with a nose that is quite close to that of a blanc de blancs; it is a blend of wines from 1993, 1994 and 1995. Aromas of honey,

CHAMPAGNE

crystallised fruits, mirabelle plums, brioche and butter are reinforced on the palate in flavours of roasted almonds and hot brioche. All is in perfect balance and harmony. (RM)
🔑 François Pierson-Cuvelier, 4, rue de Verzy, 51150 Louvois, tel. 03.26.57.03.72, fax 03.26.51.83.84 ☑ 🍷 by appt.

PIPER-HEIDSIECK

○ n.c. n.c. 100–149 F

Piper-Heidsieck's history is typical of that of numerous champagne houses: its beginnings are to be found in the fruitful alliance between a foreign, dynamic and much-travelled négociant and various local worthies. The alliance was sealed in 1785 by the marriage of Florens Louis Heidsieck from Westphalia to the daughter of a wool and wine merchant from Reims. Vigorous marketing directed at the royal households of Europe ensured that the business flourished, and it split up in 1835 into three companies of which Piper-Heidsieck is one of the branches. Its non-vintage Brut blend is dominated by the two Pinot varieties (65% Pinot Noir and 15% Meunier, as against 20% Chardonnay), which make their presence strongly felt on the palate. This is a champagne in perfect harmony, rich and aromatic, though still youthful. (NM)
🔑 Piper-Heidsieck, 51, bd Henry-Vasnier, 51100 Reims, tel. 03.26.84.43.00, fax 03.26.84.43.49 ☑ 🍷 by appt.

REGIS POISSINET Cuvée Prestige★★

○ n.c. 3,000 70–99 F

The Pinot Meunier grapes harvested by Régis Poissinet are from the same vineyard as the wine listed below, and they are of top quality. This producer makes a blanc de noirs from them that is floral and full of aromas of brioche and citrus fruits. Roundness and liveliness mingle together harmoniously on the palate. 'The wine-producer has done excellent work here,' writes a teacher of oenology. Régis Poissinet created his own brand in 1995. (RM)
🔑 Champagne Régis Poissinet, 10, *bis* rue de Ménicourt, 51480 Cuchery, tel. 03.26.58.16.20, fax 03.26.58.16.20 ☑ 🍷 by appt.

POISSINET ASCAS

Blanc de blancs 1994

○ n.c. n.c. 70–99 F

This family outfit of 8.6 ha (21 acres), which has been run by Jean-Pierre Poissinet since 1967, has produced a Blanc de Blancs from grapes grown on clay soils. Vintage champagnes from 1994, like those from 1991, are few and far between. These are two vintages that will develop rapidly. This champagne is enjoyable for its aromas of buttered toast and yellow fruits. The hint of caramelised walnuts on the palate is a sign of its maturity. (RM)
🔑 Jean-Pierre Poissinet, 8, rue du Pont, 51480 Cuchery, tel. 03.26.58.12.93, fax 03.26.52.03.55 ☑ 🍷 by appt.

POL ROGER Blanc de blancs 1993★★

○ n.c. n.c. 200–249

This is one of the few champagne houses t have remained family-owned. It was founde a century and a half ago in 1849, and owns 8 ha (210 acres) of vines. As early as the 19t century, it gravitated first towards the Britis market, and then the Commonwealth cour tries. Winston Churchill was one of those wh particularly enjoyed Pol Roger champagne Nobody will be surprised at this *coup de coeu* for every "champagnophile" knows that th Blanc de Blancs produced by this firm is on of the best and one of the most consistent th there is. Its aromatic profile, mingling but tered bread, fern and white and yellow fruits its complexity, its finesse and most of all it freshness receive unanimous praise. This dis tinction is to the credit of James Coffinet erstwhile Pol Roger cellarmaster (he has jus left the company) and an excellent taster. A star is awarded to the **Cuvée de Prestige 9** (300–499F), which is a blend of Chardonna and Pinot Noir. This is a long, complex cham pagne, ideal for the dinner table, and whic has now reached its peak. (NM)
🔑 SA Pol Roger, 1, rue Henri-Lelarge, 51200 Epernay, tel. 03.26.59.58.00, fax 03.26.55.25.70, e-mail polroger@abc.net ☑ 🍷 by appt.

POMMERY Apanage★

○ 40 ha 1,000,000 150–199 F

In 1856, Louis-Alexandre Pommery wen into partnership with a company from the Champagne region that had been created some 20 years before. He died in 1858. His widow, Louise Pommery, then developed the business and gave it its present-day form which makes it one of the two finest vineyards in the region. The Brut Apanage draws on al three of the champagne varieties (including 20% Pinot Meunier). It is a very floral champagne that strives for, and achieves, grea finesse. (NM)
🔑 Pommery, 5, pl. du Gal-Gouraud, B.P. 87, 51100 Reims, tel. 03.26.61.63.98, fax 03.26.61.63.98 ☑ 🍷 by appt.
🔑 LVMH

CHARLES POUGEOISE

Blanc de blancs

○ 1er cru 8 ha n.c. 70–99 F

This brand was launched in 1950 with a tiny vineyard of 0.5 ha (1.2 acres) that has grown today to 9 ha (22 acres) in the commune of Vertus. This champagne is a Blanc de Blancs, and has all the characteristics of one:

floral, lemon-scented nose and a palate in ıe same delicate, lively spirit. (RM)
SCEV Charles Pougeoise, 21, bd Paul-ɜoerg, 51130 Vertus, tel. 03.26.52.26.63, ıx 03.26.52.02.66, e-mail hpougeoise@aol.fr by appt.

ROGER POUILLON ET FILS

.e brut Vigneron

◌ 1er cru 0.7 ha 4,500 70–99 F

The Pouillon family have been wine-producers for generations at Mareuil-sur-Ay, ınd created this marque in 1947. Their vineard amounts to 6.5 ha (16 acres). The Brut Vigneron is a blend of half black grapes and ıalf white, from the 1995 and 1996 harvests. This is a classic, elegant champagne, with ıints of citrus and other ripe fruits. Although his house matures many of its champagnes in wood, that is not the case with this particular vine. (RM)
Roger Pouillon et Fils, 3, rue de la Couple, 51160 Mareuil-sur-Ay, el. 03.26.52.60.08, fax 03.26.59.49.83, e-mail champagne.pouillon@wanadoo.fr ev. day 9am–12 noon 2pm–6pm; Sat. Sun. by appt.
James Pouillon

PRESTIGE DES SACRES

Réserve spéciale★

○ n.c. 140,000 70–99 F

This group of producers was established in 1961, and has been marketing its own champagne since 1970. The members' vineyards extend over 125 ha (309 acres). This non-vintage Brut is made from the 1994 and 1997 harvests, and from equal parts of the three champagne grapes. A wine of great character, it owes its finesse to its aromas of roasted hazelnuts, on the nose as well as on the palate. (CM)
Coop. vinicole Germigny-Janvry-Rosnay, rue de Germigny, 51390 Janvry, tel. 03.26.03.63.40, fax 03.26.03.66.93 by appt.

YANNICK PREVOTEAU

Carte d'or★★

○ n.c. 50,000 70–99 F

Yannick and Eric Prévoteau are the sons of Gérald and Mireille. They run 10 ha (25 acres) of vines as a family business. Their non-vintage Brut is made from equal parts of all three champagne grapes from the 1997 and 1998 harvests. The wines do not undergo malolactic fermentation. Toasty aromas give this wine distinction, and its roundness on the palate adds to its richness and length. Also cited is the **Rosé**, likewise produced from the three grape varieties, which is tinted with red wine made from Pinot Meunier. It has aromas of kirsch and wild strawberries, and very impressive length. (RM)
EARL Prévoteau Père et Fils, 4 bis, av. de Champagne, 51480 Damery, tel. 03.26.58.41.65, fax 03.26.58.61.05 by appt.

PREVOTEAU-PERRIER

◑ n.c. 31,000 70–99 F

This brand was launched in 1946, and owns a vineyard of 13 ha (32 acres). The Rosé is produced from the Cuvée Tradition wine, into which is mixed 15% red wine from Pinot Noir. Floral and raspberry aromas enliven this well-balanced wine. The base wine, the **Cuvée Tradition**, itself receives a citation. It is produced from an equal quantity of each of the two Pinot grapes, made up with 15% Chardonnay. This champagne is light, a little exotic in flavour, and complex. (RM)
Champagne Prévoteau-Perrier, 15, rue André-Maginot, 51480 Damery, tel. 03.26.58.41.56, fax 03.26.58.65.88 by appt.

ACHILLE PRINCIER

Grande Tradition

○ n.c. n.c. 100–149 F

This firm was created in Epernay after the war. Its **Blanc de Blancs Vintage 95** (150–199F) fully exploits the characteristics of the Chardonnay grape: it makes a lively first impression with lemon-scented aromas, finesse and elegance. This wine, the Grande Tradition, which is produced from all three champagne grapes (including 20% Meunier) from the 1995 harvest mingles red berries and floral aromas. (NM)
Achille Princier, 9, rue Jean Chandon Moët, 51200 Epernay, tel. 03.26.54.04.06, fax 03.26.59.16.90 ev. day 10am–8pm

PRIN PERE ET FILS

Blanc de blancs 1995★★

○ n.c. n.c. 150–199 F

This brand is managed by oenologist Daniel Prin, and is based on the Côte des Blancs, in Avize. The Blanc de Blancs 95 is respectably priced and appealed very greatly to the tasters, who foresaw a fine career for it as an apéritif champagne. They judged it to be suave, honeyed, delicate, fresh and long. The **Tradition**, 70% Chardonnay and 30% Pinot Noir, is full of brioche flavours, richly textured, honeyed and strongly dosed, and receives a citation (100–149F). (NM)
Champagne Prin Père et Fils, 28, rue Ernest-Valle, 51190 Avize, tel. 03.26.53.54.55, fax 03.26.53.54.56 by appt.

SERGE RAFFLIN★★

○ 1er cru n.c. n.c. 70–99 F

The Rafflin family has been growing vines since 1740. In 1950, the Serge Rafflin brand name replaced the one used in the 1920s: Rafflin-Peters. All three champagne varieties (including 20% Chardonnay) work together in this excellent non-vintage Brut, which is perfectly constructed and balanced, characteristics that reappear in the **Rosé** blend, which wins a star for its fruity perfumes (blackberries and raspberries), its excellent constitution and its attractive length. (RM)

⊶ Denis Rafflin, 10, rue Nationale, B.P. 25, 51500 Ludes, tel. 03.26.61.12.84, fax 03.26.61.14.07, e-mail denis.rafflin@wanadoo.fr ☑ Y by appt.

DIDIER RAIMOND Tradition★★

○ 1 ha 7,000 ▮ 70–99 F

This newly founded family firm in Epernay has more than 5 ha (12 acres) of vines. It shows off its skills with this Tradition blend by bringing together two-thirds Chardonnay and one-third Pinot grapes (including 10% Meunier) from 1996 and 1997. The complex nose, which is very typical of this style with its citrus and crystallised fruits, and the structure and fullness on the palate of this champagne filled the tasters with enthusiasm. A star also goes to the **Cuvée Sublime**, a special non-vintage blend (in fact a 1996 blanc de blancs), a wine full of freshness and finesse. (RM)

⊶ Didier Raimond, 39, rue des Petits-Prés, 51200 Epernay, tel. 03.26.54.39.05, fax 03.26.54.51.70 ☑ Y by appt.

RASSELET PERE ET FILS Réserve★★

○ 3 ha 8,000 ▮ 70–99 F

This grower-winemaker runs a vineyard of nearly 8 ha (20 acres) with a beautiful view over the Marne valley. One-fifth Chardonnay and four-fifths Pinot (including 30% Pinot Meunier) go to make up this non-vintage Brut. Full of citrus, dried fruits, honey and apricots, this is a supple and flattering champagne. (RM)

⊶ Champagne Rasselet Père et Fils, 13, rue des Hussards, Montvoisin, 51480 Œuilly, tel. 03.26.58.30.26, fax 03.26.57.10.65 ☑ Y by appt.

CHAMPAGNE DU REDEMPTEUR Blanc de blancs★★

○ 0.5 ha n.c. ⅢⅠ 70–99 F

Edmond Dubois, who played a key role in the wine-growers' revolt of 1911, was nicknamed 'The Saviour (*Rédempteur*) of the Champagne Region'. Claude Dubois, his grandson, who works 7 ha (17 acres) in the Marne valley, pays homage to him in this blend. The wine is from the 1996 harvest, and has spent 11 months in large oak casks. It is a rounded and harmonious champagne, well-balanced and elegant, and wasn't far off a *coup de coeur*. As for the **Cuvée de l'An 2000** (100–149F), which is produced from 40% Pinot Noir and 60% Chardonnay from the 1995 and 1996 harvests, and which has spe 12 months in cask, it is complex, with brioc flavours, toasted and well-balanced. It wins star. The **Les Almanachs Grande Réserve Rosé** earns a citation; it too is produced large barrels, resulting in a very well-rounde champagne. (RM)

⊶ EARL du Rédempteur Dubois Père et Fils, rte d'Arty, 51480 Venteuil, tel. 03.26.58.48.37, fax 03.26.58.63.46 ☑ Y ev. day 8am–12 noon 2pm–5.30pm; Sat. Sun. by appt.

⊶ Claude Dubois

PASCAL REDON 1995

○ 1er cru 0.2 ha 1000 ▮ ♁ 70–99

This wine-producer from Trépail has bee cultivating his 4 ha (10-acre) vineyard sinc 1980. This champagne is practically a blan de blancs (just 5% Pinot Noir). It is fresh well-balanced, simple and straightforwar and is adorned with a fine bouquet of crysta lised citrus fruits. (RM)

⊶ Pascal Redon, 2, rue de la Mairie, 5138 Trépail, tel. 03.26.57.06.02, fax 03.26.58.66.54 ☑ Y by appt.

BERNARD REMY Carte blanche

○ n.c. 55,000 ▮ ♁ 70–99

This brand was registered in 1975, and ha 6.5 ha (16 acres) of vineyard at its disposa The Carte Blanche blend brings togethe equal quantities of Chardonnay and Pino Noir harvested in 1997, backed up by win from 1996. It is a fine, floral champagne. Th **Rosé**, which likewise receives a citation, is th coloured version of this blend; its nose i discreet and its palate well-balanced. (RM)

⊶ Françoise Rémy, 19, rue des Auges, 51120 Allemant, tel. 03.26.80.60.34, fax 03.26.80.37.18 ☑ Y by appt.

⊶ Bernard Rémy

R. RENAUDIN Grande Réserve 1995

○ n.c. 92,669 ▮ ♁ 100–149 F

With a vineyard of some 24 ha (59 acres) this estate was created in 1933 and now exports 60% of its production. This is a blend of Chardonnay and Pinot Noir, giving prid of place to the white grapes (70%), and is a great success. The first impression on the palate is forthright, the development is elegant and fruity, and the finish lively. Its youthfulness makes it a good apéritif wine. (RM)

⊶ SCEV Champagne R. Renaudin, 31, rue de la Liberté, 51530 Moussy, tel. 03.26.54.03.41, fax 03.26.54.31.12 ☑ Y by appt.

MARC RIGOLOT Blanc de blancs

○ 0.5 ha 20,518 ▮ ♁ 70–99 F

This was a splendid performance from a grower based not far from Epernay with a vineyard of 4 ha (10 acres). Two Blancs de Blancs are worthy of note: the non-vintage is supple, well-constructed and powerful, fruity and slightly honeyed, whilst the **Cuvée An 2000** is fleshy and rich, full and complex with hints of toast, flowers and yellow fruits. Try it with grilled fish (100–149F). (RM)

🔑 Champagne Marc Rigolot, Côtes d'Epernay, 54–56, rue Julien-Ducos, 51530 Saint-Martin-d'Ablois, tel. 03.26.59.95.52, fax 03.26.59.94.95, e-mail champagne.rm@wanadoo.fr ☒ Y by appt.

ANDRE ROBERT

Blanc de blancs Cuvée de réserve**

○Gd cru	n.c.	28,000	▮ 70-99 F

The Robert family have been dedicating themselves to wine production for a century, owning vines in Mesnil-sur-Oger, a village on the Côte des Blancs quite rightly classified as Grand Cru. Their Cuvée de Réserve Blanc de Blancs is exceptionally good. Some members of the jury were so impressed by the elegant finesse of its aromas (white blossom, citrus and exotic fruits), and the sustained fruit flavours on its complex, rounded and supple palate, that they were all for awarding it a *coup de coeur*. There is the reward of another star, though, for **Le Mesnil Blanc de Blancs 95** (100–149F), which is likewise a Grand Cru, and which is excellent if still a little young. In the same price bracket, the **Cuvée Séduction 95**, a champagne very similar to the above except that it contains 25% Pinot Noir from Vertus, earns a citation for its balance. (RM)

🔑 Champagne André Robert, 15, rue de l'Orme, B.P. 5, 51190 Le Mesnil-sur-Oger, tel. 03.26.57.59.41, fax 03.26.57.54.90 ☒ Y ev. day 9am–12 noon 2pm–7pm; Sat. Sun. by appt.

🔑 Bertrand Robert

ERIC RODEZ Cuvée des Crayères*

○Gd cru	6.12 ha	n.c.	▮ ▮▮ ♁ 70-99 F

Eric Rodez heads his estate of 6 ha (15 acres) in Ambonnay (a Grand Cru) and emlpoys very refined vinification techniques: with or without wood, with or without malolactic fermentation. This blend, which is made from half black grapes and half white, is fresh and intense, although its dosage is rather noticeable. It has a very fine nose (flowers, citrus fruits, menthol and mineral hints). The **1993** is of the same composition and is cited for its rounded fruitiness and its elegant development. And there is yet another success story from this wine-producer: a star is awarded to the **Cuvée des Grands Vintages**, a blend of 60% Pinot Noir with Chardonnay, a great oak-matured wine for keeping (100–149F). (RM)

🔑 Eric Rodez, 4, rue d'Isse, 51150 Ambonnay, tel. 03.26.57.04.93, fax 03.26.57.02.15, e-mail e.rodez@champagne-rodez.fr ☒ Y by appt.

LOUIS ROEDERER Brut Premier**

○	n.c.	n.c.	▮ ♁ 150-199 F

This family firm was founded in 1776 and today owns a substantial vineyard of 200 ha (494 acres). Jean-Claude Rouzaud is a descendant of the founders, and has presided over the fortunes of the business as much by the acquisition of other champagne firms (Deutz), as by the takeover of firms in Bordeaux and the port region. Brut Premier is Roederer's flagship, a top-of-the-range non-vintage Brut that is roughly half black and half white (including 10% Pinot Meunier), and which is based on reserve wines matured in large oak casks. This golden-yellow champagne has flashes of green, and is powerful, floral, well-balanced and long, with scents of flowers, juniper berries and honey. One delighted taster declares that its dosage is impeccable. Another calls it simply 'a perfect bottle'. The **1994** (250–299F) is also worthy of note. It is two-thirds Pinot Noir to one-third Chardonnay, a powerful wine. (NM)

🔑 Champagne Louis Roederer, 21, bd Lundy, 51100 Reims, tel. 03.26.40.42.11, fax 03.26.47.66.51, e-mail com@champagne-roederer.com

ROGGE CERESER Cuvée de réserve

○	2.3 ha	1,717	▮ ♁ 70-99 F

This family firm was founded in 1997 and runs a vineyard of nearly 7 ha (17 acres). Three-quarters Pinot Noir and one-quarter Meunier from the 1997 harvest are blended in this blanc de noirs, which offers an engaging, buttery, toasted nose and a well-balanced, lively palate. This is a champagne that needs a few more months' bottle-age to show at its best. (RM)

🔑 SCEV Rogge Cereser, 1, imp. des Bergeries, 51700 Passy Grigny, tel. 03.26.52.96.05, fax 03.26.52.07.73 ☒ Y by appt.

JACQUES ROUSSEAUX

Cuvée de la Montgolfière

○Gd cru	0.4 ha	3,000	70-99 F

This is a family property of 8 ha (20 acres) that launched its brand in 1968. As much Pinot Noir as Chardonnay, from the 1996 and 1997 harvests, come together here in a wine with fruity aromas that also register on a well-balanced, long and attractive palate. (RM)

🔑 Jacques Rousseaux, 5, rue de Puisieulx, 51360 Verzenay, tel. 03.26.49.42.73, fax 03.26.49.40.72 ☒ Y by appt.

ROUSSEAUX-BATTEUX*

◐	0.25 ha	2,000	▮ 70-99 F

Denis Rousseaux is the third generation of a family of grower-producers, and runs a vineyard of more than 3 ha (7 acres). His Rosé is a rosé de noirs (Pinot Noir) produced from the 1996 and 1997 harvests. Its healthy colour is attuned to the scents of red fruits on the nose (cherries and wild strawberries). Those aromas then come through vigorously on the palate. 'Drink it with strawberries for two!', wrote one member of the jury. (RM)

🔑 Rousseaux-Batteux, 17, rue de Mailly, 51360 Verzenay, tel. 03.26.49.81.81, fax 03.26.49.48.49 ☒ Y by appt.

PAUL ROYER Cuvée réservée

○	n.c.	n.c.	▮ ▮▮ 70-99 F

This brand was created in 1888, and taken over by the Edouard Brun company in 1928. The Cuvée Réservée is dominated by black grapes: 86% Pinot grapes, including 50% Pinot Meunier, harvested in 1995, 1996 and

1997. This is a lively apéritif champagne that is well-balanced and has a refreshing tinge of bitterness. (NM)
🔑 Edouard Brun et Cie, 14, rue Marcel-Mailly, B.P. 11, 51160 Ay, tel. 03.26.55.20.11, fax 03.26.51.94.29 ☑ 🍸 ev. day 8am–12 noon 2pm–6pm; Sat. Sun. by appt.
🔑 Delescot

ROYER PERE ET FILS★★

○ n.c. n.c. 70–99 F

This is a vineyard of 21 ha (52 acres) in the Aube, in the heart of the Côte des Bar. The non-vintage Brut is a flavourful wine with a nose of white blossom and very dry hay. Flavours of crystallised citrus register strongly on the palate. 'This is a very original wine that is way off the beaten track,' wrote one taster, who is also an oenologist. The house also receives a citation for its **Rosé de Noirs** harvested in 1997, which is vinous and richly textured, and another for its **Cuvée de Prestige**, a supple and well-balanced blanc de blancs, which comes from the 1996 harvest and is scented with may blossom and hazelnuts. (RM)
🔑 Champagne Royer Père et Fils, 120, Grande-Rue, 10110 Landreville, tel. 03.25.38.52.16, fax 03.25.29.92.26, e-mail champagne.royer@wanadoo.fr ☑ 🍸 by appt.

RUELLE-PERTOIS

○ 4.5 ha 30,000 70–99 F

The Pertois family manages a vineyard of 6 ha (15 acres). The non-vintage Brut, which is predominantly black grapes, devotes the greatest part to Pinot Noir (70%), with only 10% white grapes, harvested in 1996 and 1997. There are aromas of very ripe fruit and quince here, confirmed by a palate of overripe peaches and fruit jelly. One sommelier suggested drinking this champagne with tarte Tatin. (RM)
🔑 Michel Ruelle-Pertois, 11, rue de Champagne, 51530 Moussy, tel. 03.26.54.05.12, fax 03.26.52.87.58 ☑ 🍸 ev. day 8.30am–12 noon 1.30pm–7pm; Sat. Sun. by appt.; cl. 7–31 Aug.

RUFFIN ET FILS

Cuvée chardonnay d'or

○ 2 ha 20,000 70–99 F

This brand was launched in 1946 by the father of Dominique Ruffin, who today has a vineyard of 11 ha (27 acres), but who also obtains his stock from Cramant, Rilly and Ecueil. This blanc de blancs is floral, buttery and fresh, almost too fresh because it is so young, and has an elegant hue of pale gold with green highlights. (NM)
🔑 Champagne Ruffin et Fils, 20, Grande-Rue, 51270 Etoges, tel. 03.26.59.30.14, fax 03.26.59.34.96 ☑ 🍸 ev. day except Sun. 9am–12 noon 2pm–5.30pm; cl. Nov. until Mar.

RUINART "R"★

◑ n.c. n.c. 200–249 F

We know that Dom Ruinart, a contemporary of Dom Pérignon, was also an official at the abbey of Hautvillers. It was his nephew who, in 1729, set up what is today the oldest champagne house of them all, run by LVMH. This rosé is a classic champagne made from both Pinot varieties and Chardonnay (60/40) and tinted with red wine. It is rounded, rich and fleshy, elegant and well-balanced, with aromas of wild strawberries. The **Dom Ruinart Rosé 1986** also receives two stars, an extraordinary result for a 14-year-old rosé (more than 500F). Finally, a star goes to the **"R" Blanc**, made from Pinot Noir and Chardonnay (150–199F), which is particularly charming owing to its balance and finesse. (NM)
🔑 Champagne Ruinart, 4, rue des Crayères, B.P. 85, 51053 Reims Cedex, tel. 03.26.77.51.51, fax 03.26.82.88.43 ☑ 🍸 by appt.

LOUIS DE SACY★

◑Gd cru 3 ha 10,000 100–149 F

The Sacy family, who run a vineyard of some 25 ha (62 acres), have lived in the Champagne region since 1633. Their rosé de noirs, which includes 20% Pinot Meunier, has a powerful bouquet of plums and violets. It is long and compelling on the palate. This is a dinner-table rosé, and one to try with tournedos in a blueberry sauce, if you follow the jury's advice. The **Grand Soir Millenium** blend (150–199F), which received a citation, will particularly appeal to those who like well-developed champagnes; it is toasty, honeyed and caramelised, with hints of crystallised fruits – an extremely stylish wine. (NM)
🔑 Champagne Louis de Sacy, 6, rue de Verzenay, B.P. 2, 51380 Verzy, tel. 03.26.97.91.13, fax 03.26.97.94.25, e-mail contact@champagne-louis-de-sacy.fr ☑ 🍸 by appt.
🔑 Alain Sacy

SAINT-CHAMANT

Blanc de blancs 1991★

○ n.c. 14,760 100–149 F

Christian Coquillette only produces blancs de blancs, drawn from the 11.5 ha (28 acres) he holds in the commune of Chouilly (a Grand Cru). The wine lives up to expectations with its aromas of citrus fruits (lemon), and its freshness on the palate. One taster recommended pairing it classically with fish or white meat. (RM)
🔑 Christian Coquillette, Champagne Saint-Chamant, 50, av. Paul-Chandon, 51200 Epernay, tel. 03.26.54.38.09, fax 03.26.54.96.55 ☑ 🍸 by appt.

DE SAINT GALL

Blanc de blancs 1995★

○1er cru n.c. 100,000 100–149 F

St-Gall is one of the brands of Avize's substantial cooperative. It specialises in blanc de blancs, and exports 50% of its production to three different continents. Although it is five years old, this vintage wine is still youthful, a factor that doesn't prevent it making a supple first impression on the palate. It has a fine golden colour with flashes of green, and offers elegant floral and brioche scents. The **Cuvée Orpale** is a top-of-the-range champagne (Grand Cru) from the superb 1990 vintage, and is full of dried fruits and honey, tending towards candied flavours, and is so rich that it tastes almost sugary. It receives a citation (250–299F). (CM)

Union Champagne, 7, rue Pasteur, 51190 Avize, tel. 03.26.57.94.22, fax 03.26.57.57.98, e-mail info@de-saint-gall.com by appt.

DENIS SALOMON

Cuvée Prestige 1996*

○ 0.7 ha 4,005 70–99 F

Denis Salomon has been working his vines on the hillsides of the Marne valley since 1974. We tasted his **Cuvée Elégance**, a blanc de blancs produced from the 1993 and 1994 harvests, which has developed well. Flavours of cooked fruit, acacia and then honey register strongly on a full-bodied palate (100–149F). The other blend, called Prestige, is a blanc de noirs in which 30% is from old Pinot Meunier. Its fine structure supports very ripe fruitiness. A highly popular wine. (RM)

Denis Salomon, 5, rue Principale, 51700 Vandières, tel. 03.26.58.05.77, fax 03.26.58.00.25, e-mail denis.salomon@wanadoo.fr by appt.

SALON Blanc de blancs Le Mesnil 1988*

○Gd cru 7 ha 70,000 500 F+

This was the favourite champagne at Maxim's in Paris during the golden years. It is still a blanc de blancs, still a vintage and still a *monocru* (from the Grand Cru, Le Mesnil). In the course of a century, there have only been 32 Salon vintages. Some tasters are critical of its age. Its colour is of old gold, its nose is powerful and marked by a slight nutty aroma, and its palate is at once vinous and lively. This is a champagne for the dinner table that is ready to drink now. (NM)

Champagne Salon, 5, rue de la Brèche-d'Oger, 51190 Le Mesnil-sur-Oger, tel. 03.26.57.51.65, fax 03.26.57.79.29 by appt.

SANGER Blanc de blancs*

○Gd cru n.c. n.c. 70–99 F

Since 1952, the Lycée Viticole de la Champagne at Avize has been producing various champagnes under the brand name of Sanger. The Blanc de Blancs is distinguished by aromas of crystallised citrus fruits, which are echoed on the palate, together with lemon-scented spices. Two other champagnes were cited: the **Non-vintage Brut**, which is classically blended from all three champagne varieties, and the **Rosé**, which is a tinted blanc de blancs. Both are supple, rounded and well-balanced. (CM)

Coopérative des Anciens Elèves du Lycée viticole d'Avize, 51190 Avize, tel. 03.26.57.79.79, fax 03.26.57.78.58 ev. day except Sat. Sun. 8am–12 noon 2pm–6pm

CAMILLE SAVES Carte blanche**

○1er cru 9 ha 34,780 70–99 F

In 1894, Anaïs Jolicœur, the daughter of a Bouzy vigneron, married Eugène Savès, an agricultural engineer. Their descendants now run a vineyard of 9 ha (22 acres), which includes 7.5 ha (18.5 acres) of Grand Cru Bouzy. This Carte Blanche blend is made up of 80% Pinot Noir and 20% Chardonnay harvested in 1996 and 1997. It is a very young but perfectly balanced wine, an exceptional achiever in the difficult category of non-vintage Brut. (RM)

Camille Savès, 4, rue de Condé, 51150 Bouzy, tel. 03.26.57.00.33, fax 03.26.57.03.83 by appt.

Hervé Savès

JOEL SCHMIT**

○Gd cru 2.5 ha n.c. 70–99 F

Joël Schmit is a cooperative member, but he produced this remarkable blend himself, blending 85% Pinot Noir with Chardonnay from the 1993 and 1994 vintages. The mousse is as straightforward as the yellow hue of this non-vintage Brut, and just as forthright as its nose and its vinous, rounded, well-structured palate. This is a champagne for the dinner table. (RC)

Joël Schmit, 11, allée des Dames de France, 51150 Louvois, tel. 03.26.57.04.22, fax 03.26.58.46.97 by appt.

FRANCOIS SECONDE

Blanc de blancs 1995*

○Gd cru 0.7 ha 2,500 100–149 F

François Secondé oversees 5 ha (12 acres) of vines in Sillery, a commune classified as Grand Cru, and he has produced a Blanc de Blancs full of finesse and distinguished by its minerality. It has great freshness and beautiful harmony, and is a very accomplished wine. The **Non-vintage Brut**, which is 66% Pinot Noir and 34% Chardonnay (70–99F), is a rounded, well-constructed and balanced champagne for serving with food. (RM)

François Secondé, 6, rue des Galipes, 51500 Sillery, tel. 03.26.49.16.67, fax 03.26.49.11.55 by appt.

CRISTIAN SENEZ 1994*

○ 5 ha 12,780 100–149 F

The champagne firm of Cristian Senez was founded in 1973 and owns a vineyard of 30 ha (74 acres). The 1994 vintage contains three times more Chardonnay than Pinot Noir. Tasters were in full agreement about its elegance. On the other hand, is the nose only strongly perfumed, or does it show signs of over-development? On the palate, is it sticky-sweet, or is there a coffeeish flavour? We leave it to the reader to choose, and can only add that the Carte Verte blend from the same producer is highly recommended. (NM)

Champagne Cristian Senez, 6, Grande-Rue, 10360 Fontette, tel. 03.25.29.60.62, fax 03.25.29.64.63, e-mail champagne.senez@wanadoo.fr ✉ Y by appt.

SERVEAUX FILS 1996

○ 0.5 ha 3,400 ▮ 100–149 F

This vineyard was established in 1959 by the father of the current owner, and extends over 11 ha (27 acres). A good deal of Chardonnay (70%) is blended with both Pinot varieties in the **Cuvée Carte d'or** (70–99F), which is drawn from the 1996 and 1997 harvests. With a nose of white blossom and dried fruits, great freshness on the palate and a lemon-scented finish, this blend receives a citation, as also does the 1996 vintage, which is produced from 60% Chardonnay and 40% Pinot Noir. It is pale, clear and brilliant, a well-balanced champagne full of youth, which is expressed in its citrus aromas (lemon and grapefruit). (RM)

Pascal Serveaux, 2, rue de Champagne, 02850 Passy-sur-Marne, tel. 03.23.70.35.65, fax 03.23.70.15.99, e-mail serveauxp@aol.com ✉ Y by appt.

SIMART-MOREAU Grande Réserve★

○ 1er cru 3.5 ha 15,000 ▮ 70–99 F

In 1976 Pascal Simart married a Moreau; it was therefore logical to combine the two names when they created their brand on this vineyard of 4 ha (10 acres). Three-quarters Chardonnay and one-quarter Pinot animate this blend, which is made mainly from 1995 wines, backed up by some from 1994. It is a champagne for the table with its powerful, almost musky nose, whilst on the palate it is full-bodied, vinous and rich, suggesting it might go well with game. (RM)

Pascal Simart-Moreau, 9, rue du Moulin, 51530 Chouilly, tel. 03.26.55.42.06, fax 03.26.57.53.66, e-mail simart.moreau@wanadoo.fr ✉ Y by appt.

PATRICK SOUTIRAN Précieuse d'Argent 1993

○ Gd cru 0.5 ha 4,000 ▮ 🌡 100–149 F

Patrick Soutiran has been running the family firm for 25 years. He has 3 ha (7 acres) of vines. Précieuse d'Argent is a blanc de blancs, as its name might lead one to suspect, although the label doesn't say so. Its aromas of stewed pears, honey and crystallised fruits are restated on the palate. The finish lingers, and is reminiscent of dried apricots. A sommelier advises drinking it with poultry. (RM)

Patrick Soutiran, 3, rue des Crayères, 51150 Ambonnay, tel. 03.26.57.08.18, fax 03.26.57.81.87, e-mail patrick.soutiran@wanadoo.fr ✉ Y by appt.

A. SOUTIRAN-PELLETIER

○ Gd cru 7 ha 60,000 ▮ 🌡 70–99 F

The house vineyard of this brand is composed of purchases extending over more than 12 ha (30 acres). This Grand Cru blend is made up of 70% Pinot Noir from Ambonnay, 15% Chardonnay from the same commune and 15% Chardonnay from Avize, from the years 1996 and 1997. The result is a champagne with a fine attack, power and fullness. (NM)

Soutiran-Pelletier, 12, rue Saint-Vincent, 51150 Ambonnay, tel. 03.26.57.07.87, fax 03.26.57.81.74, e-mail alain.soutiran@wanadoo.fr ✉ Y by appt.

STEPHANE ET FILS Grande Réserve

○ n.c. 5,000 ▮ 70–99 F

The family firm, established in 1907 by Auguste Foin, is run today by his descendants. Apart from the odd 5%, this is a blanc de noirs made from both Pinot varieties harvested in 1995 and 1996. Its aromas are complex and dominated by hazelnuts and spices. On the palate, hazelnuts, walnuts and quince come to the fore, and are sustained through to a lingering finish. (RM)

Xavier Foin, 1, pl. Berry, 51480 Boursault, tel. 03.26.58.40.81, fax 03.26.51.03.79 ✉ Y by appt.

SUGOT-FENEUIL Blanc de blancs Spécial club 1985

○ Gd cru 1 ha 600 ▮ 🌡 200–249 F

This brand existed before the war, but its current name dates from 1970. The vineyard covers 10 ha (25 acres). This wine will be very popular with those who like an evolved style of champagne: its colour is firmly golden, and its bouquet is reminiscent of smoked hazelnuts and crystallised fruit. Crystallised and dried fruits are detectable on the palate. This is a rich wine for drinking with sautéed foie gras. (RM)

Champagne Sugot-Feneuil, 40, imp. de la Mairie, 51530 Cramant, tel. 03.26.57.53.54, fax 03.26.57.17.01 ✉ Y by appt.

TAITTINGER Réserve

○ n.c. n.c. 150–199 F

This Reims house was founded in 1734 by Jacques Fourneaux, and has gone by the name of Taittinger since 1937. It is in charge of a vineyard of some 250 ha (618 acres). Taittinger's champagnes tend to prove very popular with our tasters, who have cited the **Prestige Rosé** on account of its balance, the **Vintage 95** for its elegant development (it is ready to drink now), and finally this **Réserve**, produced from all three champagne varieties. This last is a delicate and honeyed wine with flavours of brioche, and is ready to drink now. (NM)

Taittinger, 9, pl. Saint-Nicaise, 51100 Reims, tel. 03.26.85.45.35, fax 03.26.85.17.46 Y by appt.

TAITTINGER

Blanc de blancs Comtes de Champagne 1994★★

○	n.c.	178,900	500 F+

This is the sort of stunningly wonderful blanc de blancs that everyone loves: the hint of citrus fruits is slightly crystallised, while the suggestion of vanilla and brioche blends in voluptuously with the overall softness of the palate, which is languorous and yet somehow vigorous at the same time. Such is the eternal paradox of great wines. (NM)

🔑 Taittinger, 9, pl. Saint-Nicaise, 51100 Reims, tel. 03.26.85.45.35, fax 03.26.85.17.46 Y by appt.

TARLANT Réserve★

○	n.c.	25,000	▮ ♁	70–99 F

Eleven generations of Tarlants have dedicated themselves to the grape. Jean-Mary Tarlant firmly believes in rational viticulture, and for about ten years has been producing some of his wines in new oak barrels. All three of the champagne varieties work together simply and naturally. This Réserve, which has not had any contact with wood, is well-balanced, has flavours of brioche and would be excellent as an apéritif. The **Cuvée Louis** is also extremely well-made. It is a blend of half black grapes and half white from the 1993, 1994 and 1995 harvests, and is matured in wood (150–199F). Complexity and body are here in plenty, and so too is pleasure. (RM)

🔑 Champagne Tarlant, 51480 Œuilly, tel. 03.26.58.30.60, fax 03.26.58.37.31, e-mail champagne@tarlant.com ☑ Y ev. day except Sun. 10am–12 noon 1.30pm–5.30pm; cl. 14–16 Aug.

J. DE TELMONT

Blanc de blancs Cuvée Grand Couronnement 1990★

○	n.c.	32,000	▮ ♁	100–149 F

Just 6 km (4 miles) from Epernay, Damery offers the tourist the interesting 12th-century church of St-Georges, with its richly sculpted transept. And after looking round the church, there is nothing to stop you going to explore the deep cellars of this champagne house, which belongs to the Lhopital family. Their Blanc de Blancs 1990 received high praise for its finesse, its floral freshness and its hint of citrus. It would ideally partner fish served in a beurre blanc. (NM)

🔑 Champagne J. de Telmont, 1, av. de Champagne, 51480 Damery, tel. 03.26.58.40.33, fax 03.26.58.63.93, e-mail telmont@wanadoo.fr ☑ Y by appt.
🔑 Famille Lhopital

V. TESTULAT Cuvée de réserve★

○	3 ha	40,000	▮ ♁	70–99 F

The firm of Testulat has a vineyard of 20 ha (49 acres), the first of which was acquired in 1862. This Réserve is a blanc de noirs, including three-quarters Pinot Meunier, drawn from the 1994 and 1995 harvests. It is a lively, floral champagne whose elegant fruitiness is well-balanced and has good length. Drink it with shellfish. (NM)

🔑 Champagne V. Testulat, 23, rue Léger-Bertin, B.P. 21, 51200 Epernay, tel. 03.26.54.10.65, fax 03.26.54.61.18, e-mail vtestulat@champagne-testulat.com ☑ Y by appt.

JACKY THERREY★

◕	1 ha	3,000	70–99 F

The commune of Montgueux is interesting for its quality soils. Besides the **François 95**, a fine blanc de blancs with a supple attack, great harmony and impressive length that received a citation from the jury, Jacky Therrey produces this Rosé, which is 100% Pinot Noir and which charmed and astonished everyone. It is a very fruity, spicy and powerful rosé. One taster wrote that it was a model of its kind. Those who like wines of character, take note. (RM)

🔑 Jacky Therrey, 8, rte de Montgueux, La Grange-au-Rez, 10300 Montgueux, tel. 03.25.70.30.87, fax 03.25.70.30.84 ☑ Y by appt.

THEVENET-DELOUVIN

Prestige du Millénaire★

○	0.5 ha	4,000	70–99 F

The Thévenet family manages a vineyard of 4 ha (10 acres) in Passy-Grigny, where you can see the chapel of an ancient Templar residence, now called Temple Farm. This blend was produced in celebration of the millennium. It is made from all three champagne grape varieties harvested in 1995 and 1996. Its aromas of brioche on the nose also come through strongly on the palate, which is full and fruity. A star is likewise awarded to the **Réserve** blend, which has a higher Pinot content and is drawn from the 1995 and 1996 harvests. It is as well-balanced as it is fruity, and 'would make a royal match with a dish of guinea-fowl and morels'. (RM)

🔑 Xavier Thévenet, rue Bruslard, 51700 Passy-Grigny, tel. 03.26.52.91.64, fax 03.26.52.97.63 ☑ Y by appt.

GUY THIBAUT

○Gd cru	n.c.	n.c.	70–99 F

This highly regarded property is wholly situated in the commune of Verzenay, and has produced a Grand Cru of great character. The composition of the blend does not vary, being four times more Pinot Noir than

Chardonnay, and it is distinguished by both length and freshness. (RM)
🗝 SCEV Guy Thibaut, 7, rue des Perthois, 51360 Verzenay, tel. 03.26.08.41.30, fax 03.26.49.42.16 ☑ 🍷 by appt.

ALAIN THIENOT Grande Cuvée 1995*

○ n.c. 30,000 300–499 F

The talented Alain Thiénot is a proficient wine-maker whose champagnes are reliably excellent. His **Non-vintage Brut** bears witness to this. Its composition does not vary: one-quarter Chardonnay, one-third Pinot Noir and the rest Pinot Meunier. It is always complex and long, and is awarded one star (100–149F). This Grande Cuvée 95, which is a blend of 60% Chardonnay and 40% Pinot Noir, displays a very delicate stream of bubbles, an oaky nose mingled with hints of roasting coffee and a mineral sharpness, and a palate that is still fresh but has elegant length. It has now reached its peak. (NM)
🗝 Alain Thiénot, 4, rue Joseph-Cugnot, 51500 Taissy, tel. 03.26.77.50.10, fax 03.26.77.50.19, e-mail alain-thienot@alain-thienot.fr ☑ 🍷 by appt.

DIOGENE TISSIER ET FILS

◑ 0.6 ha 6,000 70–99 F

This enterprise, which was founded in 1931, is 7 km (4.5 miles) south of Epernay, and has a vineyard of around 8 ha (20 acres). This rosé is based on the Cuvée de Réserve blend (wines from 1996 and 1997), made up with 14% red wine. It has a discreet nose and a lively attack, and would make a good apéritif champagne. (SR)
🗝 Diogène Tissier et fils, 10, rue du Gal-Leclerc, 51530 Chavot-Courcourt, tel. 03.26.54.32.47, fax 03.26.51.88.94 ☑ 🍷 by appt.

GUY TIXIER Cuvée de réserve*

○ 2.8 ha 20,000 70–99 F

This family firm, which was created in 1960 and has 5 ha (12 acres) of vines, is run by Olivier Tixier, son of the founder. All three champagne grapes work together in the Cuvée de Réserve, which was very well received by the tasters, who praised its fresh fruitiness and the elegance of its structure. Also cited by the jury was the **Sélection Grande Année**, made from Pinot Noir and Chardonnay (60/40), which makes a lively first impression leading to a lemon-scented finish, but is still a very young wine. (RC)
🗝 Olivier Tixier, 12, rue Jobert, 51500 Chigny-les-Roses, tel. 03.26.03.42.51, fax 03.26.03.43.00 ☑ 🍷 by appt.

MICHEL TIXIER Cuvée réservée

○ 3 ha 20,000 70–99 F

Michel Tixier has been running the family estate of nearly 4.5 ha (11 acres) since 1956. The Cuvée Réservée is produced from all three champagne varieties harvested in 1995, and also from reserve wines. It is full of brioche and fruit flavours, and is a full-bodied wine of good breeding. It may be drunk now. (RM)
🗝 Champagne Michel Tixier, 8, rue des Vignes, 51500 Chigny-les-Roses, tel. 03.26.03.42.61, fax 03.26.03.41.80 ☑ 🍷 by appt.

LOUIS TOLLET Cuvée Prestige**

○ 1er cru n.c. n.c. 70–99 F

This brand belongs to Charles Mignon, an Epernay négociant house that also bottles champagne under its own name. The tasters showered this non-vintage Brut with compliments, noting flavours of gingerbread, Virginia tobacco and honey, and sensations of richness, roundness and balance. This is a wine to enjoy as an apéritif and as an accompaniment to meat. (NM)
🗝 Charles Mignon, 1, av. de Champagne, 51200 Epernay, tel. 03.26.58.33.33, fax 03.26.51.54.10, e-mail bruno-mignon@champagne-mignon.fr 🍷 by appt.
🗝 Bruno Mignon

G. TRIBAUT Cuvée de réserve 1996*

○ n.c. 30,000 70–99 F

Five members of the family work among the vines and in the cellars of this house, which has holdings of 12 ha (30 acres). They have opened a little museum of viticultural tools in a cellar in the heart of Hautvillers. All three champagne varieties come together in this Cuvée de Réserve, which has an intense nose of red berries, and is lively, full-bodied and young on the palate. (RM)
🗝 Champagne G. Tribaut, 88, rue d'Eguisheim, B.P. 5, 51160 Hautvillers, tel. 03.26.59.40.57, fax 03.26.59.43.74, e-mail tribaut@epicuria.fr ☑ 🍷 ev. day 9am–12 noon 2pm–6.30pm

TRIBAUT-SCHLŒSSER 1995*

○ 10 ha 40,000 70–99 F

It was in 1929 that Léon Tribaut and René Schlœsser joined forces to create this house, which has a vineyard of some 30 ha (74 acres). The 1995 vintage is a blend of Pinot Noir and Chardonnay (60/40). It is biscuity on the nose and on the palate, and has a long finish. The **Cuvée René Schlœsser** (150–199F) contains three times as much Chardonnay as Pinot Noir, harvested in 1995, 1993 and 1992; it is complex, rich and strongly vanilla-scented, and is also awarded a star. The **Cuvée Tradition** should also be noted: all three champagne grapes are used (the years being 1996, 1997 and 1998). It is delicate and extremely young. (NM)
🗝 Tribaut-Schlœsser, 21, rue Saint-Vincent, 51480 Romery, tel. 03.26.58.64.21, fax 03.26.58.44.08, e-mail tribaut-romery@wanadoo.fr ☑ 🍷 by appt.

TRICHET-DIDIER Cuvée spéciale**

○ 1er cru 0.7 ha n.c. 70–99 F

The first vines were planted in 1951 by the grandparents of Pierre Trichet, who operates a vineyard of 2.7 ha (7 acres), at the same time as running a *négociant* business. This Cuvée Spéciale is a blanc de blancs, as is evident from the nose, which is full of the typical aromas of fern, buttered bread and mirabelle plums. On

the palate, a powerful structure gives this harmonious wine impressive length. (NM)
🗝 Trichet-Didier, 11, rue du Petit-Trois-Puits, 51500 Trois-Puits, tel. 03.26.82.64.10, fax 03.26.97.80.94 ☑ 🍷 by appt.
🗝 Pierre Trichet

ALFRED TRITANT 1995★

○Gd cru 3.37 ha 10,000 ▮ 100–149 F

All the harvest here comes from the commune of Bouzy, which is classified as Grand Cru. The 1995 wine is a blend of two-thirds Pinot Noir and one-third Chardonnay. It is a very well-crafted champagne, at once fresh, delicate, floral and powerful. The **Cuvée Prestige** (70–99F) is an identical blend to the one above, but is produced from grapes harvested in 1994 and 1995. It is close in style to the 1995, but is even more youthful. (RM)
🗝 Alfred Tritant, 23, rue de Tours, 51150 Bouzy, tel. 03.26.57.01.16, fax 03.26.58.49.56, e-mail champagne-tritant@wanadoo.fr ☑ 🍷 ev. day 9am–12 noon 2pm–6pm; Sat. Sun. by appt.

JEAN VALENTIN ET FILS

Blanc de blancs Saint-Avertin★

○ 0.3 ha 2,400 ▮ 🌡 70–99 F

This house was established in 1922 and operates a vineyard of 6 ha (15 acres) in Sacy, where the Saint-Rémy church, with its 17th-century organ loft, is well worth a visit. Gilles Valentin offers a Blanc de Blancs from the Montagne de Reims that is pale gold in hue, with aromas of Virginia tobacco, white blossom and citrus fruits, accompanied by a light touch of menthol. It is fresh, young and well-made, and it has noticeable dosage. (RM)
🗝 Champagne Jean Valentin et Fils, 9, rue Saint-Remi, 51500 Sacy, tel. 03.26.49.21.91, fax 03.26.49.27.68, e-mail givalentin@wanadoo.fr ☑ 🍷 by appt.
🗝 Gilles Valentin

JEAN-CLAUDE VALLOIS

Blanc de blancs 1993★

○ 4 ha 20,000 ▮ 🌡 70–99 F

The 12th-century church of Saint-Nicolas in Cuis adjoins the property of the Vallois family, who have built up a vineyard of 6 ha (15 acres) in the course of four generations. This champagne has the true colour of a blanc de blancs, and also the buttery aromas of this style, with a lingering palate full of brioche flavours. It would make a good apéritif wine, in the opinion of one member of the jury. A vintage wine that still has a few years ahead of it. (RM)
🗝 Jean-Claude Vallois, 4, rte des Caves, 51530 Cuis, tel. 03.26.59.78.46, fax 03.26.58.16.73 ☑ 🍷 by appt.

VAUTRAIN-PAULET 1995

○ 1 ha 5,000 100–149 F

This firm in Dizy has a vineyard of 11 ha (27 acres). This vintage is a blanc de blancs, for all that the label is silent on the matter. It has a firm golden colour, and its liveliness on the palate is reminiscent of green apples. Also cited by the jury is the **Carte Blanche** Premier Cru, which blends 60% Pinot Noir with equal parts of Pinot Meunier and Chardonnay (70–99F). Its richness makes it a suitable wine for the table. (RM)
🗝 Vautrain-Paulet, 195, rue du Colonel-Fabien, 51530 Dizy, tel. 03.26.55.24.16, fax 03.26.51.97.42 ☑ 🍷 by appt.

F. VAUVERSIN Blanc de blancs

○Gd cru 1 ha 7,000 ▮ 70–99 F

The Vauversin family have been vignerons for three-and-a-half centuries. They created their brand in 1930, and their vineyard now extends to 3 ha (7 acres). This Blanc de Blancs Grand Cru is drawn from the 1996 harvest, topped up with a little 1995; it is supple on entry, after presenting its bouquet of honey, wax, flowers and dried fruits. From then on, it develops lively flavours of citrus fruits. (RM)
🗝 Champagne F. Vauversin, 9 bis, rue de Flavigny, 51190 Oger, tel. 03.26.57.51.01, fax 03.26.51.64.44, e-mail bruno.vauversin@wanadoo.fr ☑ 🍷 by appt.

CHAMPAGNE

VAZART-COQUART ET FILS

Blanc de blancs Réserve

○Gd cru 8 ha 60,000 ▮ 🌡 70–99 F

The Vazart family established its brand in 1953, and tends a vineyard of 11 ha (27 acres). This Blanc de Blancs Grand Cru comes mainly from the 1997 harvest, backed up by 30–40% of reserve wines from the four previous years. It shines for its finesse and length. Likewise worthy of note is the **Cuvée Grand Bouquet Blanc de blancs Grand Cru 1993** (100–149F), which is scented with lemon and menthol and full of white fruit flavours. (RM)
🗝 Champagne Vazart-Coquart, 6, rue des Partelaines, 51530 Chouilly, tel. 03.26.55.40.04, fax 03.26.55.15.94, e-mail vazart@cder.fr ☑ 🍷 by appt.

JEAN VELUT Tradition

○ 6 ha 20,000 ▮ 70–99 F

Vigneron Jean Velut runs a vineyard of 7 ha (17 acres) in Montgueux, which is well-known as a good location for Chardonnay. The brand has been in existence for a quarter of a century. The non-vintage Brut blend is a mixture of 1995, 1996 and 1997 wines, composed of 85% Chardonnay and 15% Pinot Noir. It is elegant and harmonious, with inviting vinosity. Another cuvée worthy of citation is the vintage **1995** (90% Chardonnay), which is rich, fresh and lively, and will clearly go very well with seafood. (RM)
🗝 Champagne Jean Velut, 9, rue du Moulin, 10300 Montgueux, tel. 03.25.74.83.31, fax 03.25.74.17.25 ☑ 🍷 by appt.

DE VENOGE Blanc de blancs 1995★★

○ n.c. 80,000 ▮ 🌡 150–199 F

This house was founded in 1837 by Henri-Marc de Venoge, a Swiss. Today, it belongs to the BCC group, which is led by Bruno Paillard who has a vineyard of 115 ha (284 acres). The brand put up a sparkling performance, with

three of its champagnes awarded stars. Two went to this Blanc de Blancs 1995, with its nose of very great floral finesse and its roundness and length on the palate. One star was awarded to the **Grand Vin des Princes 1992** (300–499F), another well-balanced blanc de blancs in the substantial and full-bodied style. And yet another was given to the **Sélect Cordon Bleu** (100–149F), which is a blend of all three champagne varieties from 1995 and 1996, and is a long and powerful wine. (NM)
🗝 Champagne de Venoge, 46, av. de Champagne, 51200 Epernay, tel. 03.26.53.34.34, fax 03.26.53.34.35 ☒

J.-L. VERGNON Blanc de blancs

○Gd cru n.c. 36,000 🍾 70–99 F

This brand was launched in 1950, and has a vineyard of more than 5 ha (12 acres). The Blanc de Blancs Grand Cru is a lively and well-balanced wine of moderate length. The 1996 and 1997 harvests are the source here, as indeed they are in the **Blanc de Blancs Extra Brut**, which likewise receives a citation from the jury, and is very close in style to the foregoing. It is a thoroughbred champagne of great finesse, ideal for serving with oysters. (RM)
🗝 SCEV J.-L. Vergnon, 1, Grande-Rue, 51190 Le Mesnil-sur-Oger, tel. 03.26.57.53.86, fax 03.26.52.07.06 ☒ Y by appt.

GEORGES VESSELLE Juline*

○Gd cru 0.25 ha 2,000 🍾 🌡 150–199 F

Georges Vesselle, whose family has been dedicated to the vine since the 16th century, has been mayor of Bouzy for 25 consecutive years. He runs a vineyard of more than 15 ha (37 acres) in this Grand Cru commune. Juline is a blend of mature wines from 1980, 1982 and 1985. It is made predominantly from black grapes: 90% Pinot Noir. It has a superb hue of old gold, and its rounded, well-balanced palate is of very creditable length. There are flavours of crystallised fruit here, together with hints of roasting coffee. The **Grand Cru Vintage 1995** (100–149F) caught the jury's attention with its balance and its liveliness. (NM)
🗝 Georges Vesselle, 16, rue des Postes, 51150 Bouzy, tel. 03.26.57.00.15, fax 03.26.57.09.20, e-mail contact@champagne-vesselle.fr ☒ Y ev. day except Sat. Sun. 9am–12 noon 2pm–5pm

B. VESSELLE

○1er cru n.c. 50,000 🍾 🌡 100–149 F

Georges Vesselle's son created his own brand in 1994. This Premier Cru owes its character to all three champagne varieties: a classic blend of 50% Pinot Noir, 20% Pinot Meunier and 30% Chardonnay. The tasters particularly noted its smoothness of texture. Its golden-yellow colour makes a pleasing background to its fine mousse. (NM)
🗝 Georges Vesselle, 16, rue des Postes, 51150 Bouzy, tel. 03.26.57.00.15, fax 03.26.57.09.20, e-mail contact@champagne-vesselle.fr Y ev. day except Sat. Sun. 9am–12 noon 2pm–5pm

JEAN VESSELLE Prestige

○ n.c. n.c. 🍾 🌡 150–199 F

This champagne is sold in no fewer than four continents. Although the Vesselle family have been wine-producers for three centuries, the company bearing the forename 'Jean' was only created in 1972. Delphine has managed the 11 ha (27-acre) estate since her father's death. The Brut Prestige is produced from 70% Pinot Noir and 30% Chardonnay. It is green-gold in colour, a fresh and well-balanced wine with aromas of citrus fruits and a lively finish. (RM)
🗝 Champagne Jean Vesselle, 4, rue Victor-Hugo, 51150 Bouzy, tel. 03.26.57.01.55, fax 03.26.57.06.95 ☒ Y by appt.

MAURICE VESSELLE 1988*

○Gd cru 3 ha 15,000 🍾 🌡 100–149 F

This property of 8.5 ha (21 acres) was established in 1955 at Bouzy and Tours-sur-Marne, two Grands Crus that are particularly auspicious for Pinot Noir. There is 85% of it in this 1988 vintage, an excellent year. This is a harmonious, complex champagne that has stayed fresh. It has a bouquet of crystallised fruits, figs, quince and gingerbread. (RM)
🗝 Maurice Vesselle, 2, rue Yvonnet, 51150 Bouzy, tel. 03.26.57.00.81, fax 03.26.57.83.08 ☒ Y ev. day 10am–12 noon 2pm–6pm

VEUVE A. DEVAUX Grande Réserve*

○ n.c. n.c. 🍾 🌡 100–149 F

This brand was launched more than a century-and-a-half ago, and was taken over in 1967 by the Union Auboise cooperative. The Grande Réserve keeps all its promises: it is floral (violetty), and then citrus fruits and almonds come through. The **Cuvée Spéciale Blanc de Blancs** is likewise awarded a star for its smoky freshness, its forthright attack and its length. (CM)
🗝 Union Auboise des prod. de vin de Champagne, Dom. de Villeneuve, 10110 Bar-sur-Seine, tel. 03.25.38.30.65, fax 03.25.29.81.53, e-mail champagnedevaux@wanadoo.fr ☒ Y by appt.

VEUVE CLICQUOT PONSARDIN La Grande Dame 1993**

○ n.c. n.c. 🍾 🌡 500 F+

The 'Grande Dame' of the name, as everyone knows, refers to Madame Veuve Clicquot. It is a fitting tribute to pay to the woman who acquired the Grand Cru vineyards that would eventually provide the grapes for this distinguished prestige cuvée. To use an orchestral metaphor, the predominant Pinot Noir has the suppleness of the cellos and the power of the brass, whilst the agile Chardonnay plays the parts of the violins and flutes. It is a harmonious fusion, that echoes on and on. Evening dress and black ties are the order of the day! (NM)

Veuve Clicquot-Ponsardin, 12, rue du Temple, 51100 Reims, tel. 03.26.89.54.40, fax 03.26.85.23.89, e-mail marketing@veuve-clicquot.fr ☑ Y by appt.

VEUVE CLICQUOT PONSARDIN

Réserve 1995

	n.c.	n.c.	200–249 F

Madame Veuve Clicquot was the first person to market a rosé champagne. It even became a house speciality, a reputation that survives to this day. If proof were needed, it is in the Rosé 1995, which is dominated by the Pinot varieties (mixed with 28% Chardonnay), and tinted with red wine from Bouzy. Crystallised fruits, orange-peel, caramel and vanilla-scented milk are to be found here, together with a soft, gentle roundness. (NM)

Veuve Clicquot-Ponsardin, 12, rue du Temple, 51100 Reims, tel. 03.26.89.54.40, fax 03.26.85.23.89, e-mail marketing@veuve-clicquot.fr ☑ Y by appt.

VEUVE FOURNY ET FILS

Réserve★★

○ 1er cru	4 ha	40,000	70–99 F

Madame Veuve Fourny, along with her two children, manages a vineyard mainly based in Vertus (a Premier Cru commune on the Côte des Blancs). The champagne was launched in the 1950s. This Réserve is a blend of 80% Chardonnay and 20% Pinot Noir, harvested in 1993, 1995 and 1996. Full of brioche, vanilla and floral aromas (white blossom) with suggestions of green walnuts, its aromas show great finesse. The wine has length too. Two stars also go to the **Blanc de Blancs Premier Cru**, which is lively, fresh, delicate, full and well-balanced. (NM)

Champagne Veuve Fourny et Fils, 5, rue du Mesnil, 51130 Vertus, tel. 03.26.52.16.30, fax 03.26.52.20.13, e-mail info@champagne-veuve-fourny.com ☑ Y ev. day except Sun. 9am–12 noon 2pm–6pm

VEUVE MAITRE-GEOFFROY

Blanc de blancs Cuvée du Centenaire

○ 1er cru	0.6 ha	6,000	70–99 F

This house was founded in 1878 by Madame Veuve Maître-Geoffroy. Since 1984, it has been Thierry Maître who has produced the wine. This Blanc de Blancs comes from Cumières, a commune classified as Premier Cru, from grapes harvested in 1996. The champagne is pale in colour, with a bouquet reminiscent of little white fruits and Golden Delicious apples. Its fullness on the palate is very striking. (RM)

Veuve Maître-Geoffroy, 51480 Cumières, tel. 03.26.55.29.87, fax 03.26.51.85.77 ☑ Y by appt.

VEUVE MAURICE LEPITRE

Demi-sec★

○ 1er cru	1 ha	5,000	70–99 F

This family firm, created in 1905 by Maurice Lepitre, owns 7 ha (17 acres) around Rilly in the Montagne de Reims. A Demi-sec champagne with a star is quite a rare thing in the *Guide*. This one is produced from equal parts of all three champagne varieties. The base wine is of a high quality and is not smothered by the sugar, but has integrated it into a rich and harmonious whole. The **Brut Extra Réserve Premier Cru** of the same composition receives a citation for its full-bodied suppleness. (RM)

Veuve Maurice Lepitre, 26, rue de Reims, 51500 Rilly-la-Montagne, tel. 03.26.03.40.27, fax 03.26.03.45.76, e-mail lepitrem@aol.com ☑ Y by appt.

B. Rilliex

MARCEL VEZIEN

Cuvée Armand Vezien 1993

○	0.8 ha	n.c.	100–149 F

This long-established family estate in the Aube once played an important part in the fight against phylloxera. Jean-Pierre Vézien has recently taken over the business from his father. This cuvée pays homage to the founder, blending together 70% Pinot Noir and 30% Chardonnay, and offering a charming nose of crystallised fruit and peaches, followed by a full, rounded palate with flavours of quince jelly. It has very impressive length. (RM)

SCEV Champagne Marcel Vézien et Fils, 68, Grande-Rue, 10110 Celles-sur-Ource, tel. 03.25.38.50.22, fax 03.25.38.56.09 ☑ Y ev. day 8.30am–6pm; Sat. Sun. by appt.

FLORENT VIARD

Cuvée Prestige 1995★

○	0.22 ha	800	100–149 F

Florent Viard started out in 1994 with a vineyard of 2 ha (5 acres). Except for the final 5%, this rich and well-balanced champagne is a blanc de blancs, which explains its scent of acacia flowers. Wax and honey mingle on the palate. One taster suggests serving it to accompany a dish of John Dory with spinach. (RC)

Champagne Florent Viard, 3, rue du Donjon, 51130 Vertus, tel. 03.26.51.60.82 ☑ Y by appt.

VOIRIN-DESMOULINS Réserve★

○ Gd cru	n.c.	n.c.	70–99 F

Bernard Voirin and Nicole Desmoulins amalgamated their vineyards in 1960, and today cultivate 9 ha (22 acres). The Réserve blends Pinot Noir and Chardonnay in equal parts. White blossom and gingerbread make up a pleasant bouquet, which is confirmed by the full and fresh palate. (RM)

🗝 SCEV Voirin-Desmoulins, 41, rue Dom-Pérignon, 51530 Chouilly, tel. 03.26.54.50.30, fax 03.26.52.87.87 ☑ 🍷 by appt.

VOLLEREAUX 1996*

◑ 2.5 ha 20,000 ▮ 🌡 70–99 F

This family firm produces 400,000 bottles from its own vines. Pink champagnes made by maceration are rare. This one comes from Pinot Noir. It is a lively pink in colour and very fruity, as much on the nose as on the palate (strawberries and blackcurrants) – a real gourmet rosé. The **Marguerite 93** blend (100–149F) was also cited. It contains three times more Chardonnay than Pinot Noir, and is floral, smoky and light. (NM)

🗝 Champagne Vollereaux, 48, rue Léon-Bourgeois, 51530 Pierry, tel. 03.26.54.03.05, fax 03.26.54.88.36, e-mail champagne.vollereauxsa@wanadoo.fr ☑ 🍷 ev. day 9am–12 noon 2pm–6pm; Sat. Sun. by appt.

VRANKEN Demoiselle*

○ n.c. n.c. ▮ 🌡 100–149 F

Paul Vranken founded a company in 1976, and then created the Demoiselle brand in 1985. He floated the empire on the Paris Stock Exchange in 1998. This Demoiselle is produced from 60% Chardonnay and 40% Pinot Noir. It was highly praised for its floral freshness (white blossom) and for its elegant and well-balanced liveliness on the palate. It is a wine for drinking either as an apéritif, or with fish in a cream sauce. The **Demoiselle 1995**, which contains even more Chardonnay (80%), is similar in style to the non-vintage. In both cases, the production and dosage are exemplary, which is why both wines are awarded a star. (NM)

🗝 Vranken Monopole, 17, av. de Champagne, 51200 Epernay, tel. 03.26.59.50.50, fax 03.26.52.19.65 ☑ 🍷 ev. day 9.30am–4.30pm; Sun. and groups by appt.

🗝 P.-F. Vranken

WARIS-LARMANDIER

Blanc de blancs Cuvée Collection*

○Gd cru 0.5 ha 1000 ▮ 🌡 100–149 F

This young vigneron of 33 has established himself with nearly 6 ha (15 acres) on the Côte des Blancs. Drawn from the 1996 harvest, this special blend mingles white blossom, honey, citrus fruits and brioche in a fresh and full-bodied champagne. (RM)

🗝 Waris-Larmandier, 608, rempart du Nord, 51190 Avize, tel. 03.26.57.79.05, fax 03.26.52.79.52 ☑ 🍷 by appt.

Coteaux Champenois

Called Vins Nature de Champagne, or still wines, they became AOC in 1974 and took the name of Coteaux Champenois. They are white, red or, more rarely, rosé still wines. Drink the whites with respect and a degree of historical curiosity, remembering that they are a survival from ancient times, before Champagne was created. Like Champagne itself, Coteaux Champenois can be made from black grapes vinified to make white wine (blanc de noirs), from white grapes (blanc de blancs) or from mixed wines.

The best known Coteaux Champenois Rouge carries the name of the most celebrated commune of Bouzy (a Grand Cru of the Pinot Noir). In this commune you can admire one of the two strangest vineyards in the world (the other is at Ay). A huge notice proclaims 'old, pre-phylloxera French vines'; these would be virtually indistinguishable from the others were they not free-growing, following an ancient technique that has been abandoned everywhere else. All the work is done by hand using old tools. The House of Bollinger maintains this jewel, which is intended for making the rarest and most expensive Champagne of all.

The Coteaux Champenois wines are drunk young, at a temperature of 7–8°C (44.6–46.4°F) for the whites and accompanying dishes that go with very dry wines, and at 9–10°C (48.2–50°F) for the reds, to accompany light dishes (white meats and oysters). In exceptional years, they may be left to age.

PAUL BARA Bouzy 1990

■ Gd cru 2.5 ha 10,000 ▮ 🌡 100–149 F

As at Ay, the Coteaux Champenois from Bouzy are only red wines produced from Pinot Noir. This is the *pynos*, a variety of which the poet Eustache Deschamps wrote in the 14th century. At the Bara estate, the must from the 1990 harvest was fermented for ten days, with pumping over and some grape-treading, and the wine was not cask-aged. The result is a very fruity ensemble that has now reached its peak. The jury particularly praised the advanced nature of this Bouzy, with its spicy, well-balanced palate.

🔑 Champagne Paul Bara, 4, rue Yvonnet, B.P. 11, 51150 Bouzy, tel. 03.26.57.00.50, fax 03.26.57.81.24 ☒ Y by appt.

HERBERT BEAUFORT Bouzy 1994

■ 1 ha 8,000 ⦀ 100–149 F

Marcelin Beaufort produced his first bottles of champagne in 1932. His grandsons now manage a vineyard of 16.5 ha (41 acres). This Bouzy red, which is made in the Burgundian style, has been matured for two years in cask. It has a fine ruby colour and medium concentration, as befits the vintage.

🔑 Herbert Beaufort, 32, rue de Tours-sur-Marne, 51150 Bouzy, tel. 03.26.57.01.34, fax 03.26.57.09.08 ☒ Y ev. day 9am–12 noon 2pm–5pm

CAILLEZ-LEMAIRE Damery★★

■ 0.6 ha 1000 ▮ ⦀ 70–99 F

This very firmly coloured Coteaux Champenois is a beautiful deep red. It is produced from a blend of different years, from two-thirds Pinot Noir to one-third Pinot Meunier. Red berries are in evidence on the nose and on the palate, as well as on the fine, lingering finish.

🔑 SARL Champagne Caillez-Lemaire, 14, rue Pierre-Curie, B.P. 11, 51480 Damery, tel. 03.26.58.41.85, fax 03.26.52.03.24 ☒ Y by appt.

🔑 Henri Caillez

CHARLES DE CAZANOVE 1993

■ n.c. n.c. ⦀ 70–99 F

Charles de Cazanove is one of the oldest brands in the Champagne region. It was created in 1811 at Avize, but the firm is also established in Epernay. Here, it has produced a red Coteaux Champenois from Pinot Meunier, matured in champagne vats of 205 l (54 gallons). This wine has a fine deep colour, with concentrated aromas of morello cherries and red berry fruits. It would make a wonderful accompaniment to red meats.

🔑 Charles de Cazanove, 1, rue des Cotelles, 51200 Epernay, tel. 03.26.59.57.40, fax 03.26.54.16.38 ☒

🔑 Lombard

R. DUMONT ET FILS 1998

■ 1 ha 600 ⦀ 50–69 F

Pierre, Charles and Bernard Dumont took over this family estate at the beginning of the 1980s, but it has been established in Champignol for 200 years. In 1998, they produced a Coteaux Champenois from destemmed Pinot Noir that was matured for six months in cask. A purplish-red hue adorns this wine, which has slightly oaky scents mingled with flavours of blackberries and blackcurrants. (RM)

🔑 R. Dumont et Fils, 10200 Champignol-lez-Mondeville, tel. 03.25.27.45.95, fax 03.25.27.45.97 ☒ Y by appt.

FRESNET-BAUDOT Sillery★

■ Gd cru 0.5 ha 1000 ⦀ 70–99 F

The red wines of Sillery were famous in the 19th century, but they are few and far between today. This one, which has been produced by Burgundian methods and matured for nine months in oak, is therefore a rare example. It is firmly coloured, aromatically rich and complex, and displays good structure on the palate. Noble tannins and evident oakiness mark it out as a wine for laying down.

🔑 Fresnet-Baudot, 9, rte de Puisieulx, 51500 Sillery, tel. 03.26.49.11.74, fax 03.26.49.10.72, e-mail courrier@champagne-fresnet-baudot.fr ☒ Y by appt.

RENE GEOFFROY Cumières 1997

■ 0.6 ha 3,800 ⦀ 100–149 F

Thirty-five-year-old vines are the source of this Coteaux Champenois that has been matured in wood for ten months. It has a firm, attractive colour, spicy, peppery nose and well-built palate with good length.

🔑 René Geoffroy, 150, rue du Bois-des-Jots, 51480 Cumières, tel. 03.26.55.32.31, fax 03.26.54.66.50, e-mail info@champagne-geoffroy.com ☒ Y by appt.

GOSSET-BRABANT Ay 1996

■ Gd cru 0.3 ha 1,800 ⦀ 100–149 F

This red Coteaux Champenois 96, made from Pinot Noir, has benefited from a vatting of six to seven days, with regular treading and pumping over, and then a maturation of 18 months in old casks. It has an intense colour, and is redolent of red berries on both the nose and palate.

🔑 Gosset-Brabant, 23, bd du Mal-de-Lattre-de-Tassigny, 51160 Ay, tel. 03.26.55.17.42, fax 03.26.54.31.33 ☒ Y by appt.

LACROIX-TRIAULAIRE ET FILS

■ n.c. 1000 50–69 F

Against a background of deep red, there are the beginnings of evolution visible in the colour of this wine. The nose is no less delicate with its suggestions of elderflower and liquorice, and the palate leaves a pleasant impression of lightness.

🔑 Lacroix-Triaulaire, 4, rue de La Motte, 10110 Merrey-sur-Arce, tel. 03.25.29.83.59 ☒ Y by appt.

LARMANDIER-BERNIER
Vertus 1996★★
■ 1er cru 0.5 ha 1,500 🍷 100–149 F

Coups de coeur are very few and far between for Coteaux Champenois reds, because it is so difficult to produce red wines in the northern regions. This Vertus wine is therefore all the more remarkable. The grapes have been sorted and partially destemmed, and have undergone their vatting with periodic treading and pumping over. The wine was then matured for 18 months in wood. And here it is: deep red in colour, with a complex nose and a similarly complex palate sustained by harmonious tannins.
🔑 Champagne Larmandier-Bernier, 43, rue du 28-Aug., 51130 Vertus, tel. 03.26.52.13.24, fax 03.26.52.21.00, e-mail larmandier@terre-net.fr ☑ 🍸 by appt.

DIDIER RAIMOND Epernay★
■ 0.25 ha 500 🍷 50–69 F

Didier Raimond, whose family firm is established right in the centre of Epernay, cultivates his vineyard using rational viticultural methods. A red wine from Epernay has to be yet another rarity. A blend of two-thirds Pinot Meunier and one-third Pinot Noir from the 1996 harvest, it has a fine colour that is already well-developed. The nose evokes morello cherries and sweet spices, the legacy of two years' maturation in cask. Its rounded palate will invite you to drink this wine now.
🔑 Didier Raimond, 39, rue des Petits-Prés, 51200 Epernay, tel. 03.26.54.39.05, fax 03.26.54.51.70 ☑ 🍸 by appt.

FRANCOIS SECONDE Sillery 1997★
■ Gd cru 1 ha 2,500 70–99 F

This is an appealing Sillery wine from the 1997 harvest. Its colour is not lacking in charm with its purplish highlights. The flattering bouquet releases scents of red berries and spices. On the palate, noble tannins augur well for a good development, and bear eloquent witness to the ability of the master craftsman both in the vineyard and in the cellar.
🔑 François Secondé, 6, rue des Galipes, 51500 Sillery, tel. 03.26.49.16.67, fax 03.26.49.11.55 ☑ 🍸 by appt.

A. SOUTIRAN Ambonnay Les Crupots
■ n.c. 2,500 🍷 70–99 F

The Pinot Noir grapes from which this wine is made were drawn from 1988, 1989, 1990, 1994, 1996 and 1998, in an exposed locality in the south-east of the region, Les Crupots. The wine has been matured in champagne barrels for a period of six to nine months. The result is this well-bred Ambonnay, which is black cherry in colour. That same fruit appears on both the nose and the palate, crying out for a game dish to drink it with.
🔑 Soutiran-Pelletier, 12, rue Saint-Vincent, 51150 Ambonnay, tel. 03.26.57.07.87, fax 03.26.57.81.74, e-mail alain.soutiran@wanadoo.fr ☑ 🍸 by appt.

TARLANT Œuilly★
■ n.c. n.c. 🍷 70–99 F

In his vineyard of 13 ha (32 acres), Jean-Mary Tarlant has chosen a few vines from Œuilly for his red Coteaux Champenois. The wine contains 80% Pinot Noir and 20% Pinot Meunier from the 1996 harvest, for all that it is not vintage-dated. An attractive deep red colour, it offers vanilla scents and sensual fruitiness. The well-balanced palate puts the finishing touches to this appealing ensemble.
🔑 Champagne Tarlant, 51480 Œuilly, tel. 03.26.58.30.60, fax 03.26.58.37.31, e-mail champagne@tarlant.com ☑ 🍸 ev. day except Sun. 10am–12 noon 1.30pm–5.30pm; cl. 14–16 Aug.
🔑 Jean-Mary Tarlant

EMMANUEL TASSIN Les Fioles 1998
□ 0.25 ha 700 🍷 50–69 F

Emmanuel Tassin has been managing a vineyard of 5.5 ha (14 acres) since 1987. He has given this Coteaux Champenois Blanc de Blancs the most lavish treatment, with both the alcoholic and malolactic fermentations carried out in cask (with 25% new wood). This wine is therefore oaky, certainly, but it is also full of the aromas of lemon, menthol and butter. It may be enjoyed now or laid down in the cellar. Under the same label, the **Coteaux Champenois Rouge 98**, which has been matured for 15 months in cask, likewise receives a citation for its aromas of blackcurrants and redcurrants and for its highly concentrated palate (50–70F).
🔑 Emmanuel Tassin, 104, Grande-Rue, 10110 Celles-sur-Ource, tel. 03.25.38.59.44, fax 03.25.29.94.59, e-mail emmanuel.tassin@wanadoo.fr ☑ 🍸 by appt.

Rosé des Riceys

The three villages of Les Riceys (Haut, Haute-Rive and Bas) are located in the extreme south of the Aube, not far from

Bar-sur-Seine. The commune of Les Riceys consists of three appellations: Champagne, Coteaux Champenois and Rosé des Riceys. The last is a still wine of great rarity – only 819 hl (21,622 gal) were harvested in 1999 – and of great quality: it is one of the best rosés in France. The wine was already being drunk in the reign of Louis XIV and is said to have been taken to Versailles by the builders who were digging the foundations of the château and who came from Les Riceys.

The rosé is the result of vinification that includes a short maceration of Pinot Noir with a natural alcohol level that cannot be less than 10% . The maceration must be stopped – *saigner la cuve* or bleeding the vat – at the precise moment that the unique Riceys flavour appears, otherwise it vanishes. Only the rosés with this special flavour are labelled. The Rosé des Riceys is matured in vat and drunk young, at 8–9°C (46.4–48.2°F), as an apéritif or with a first course. Matured in barrels, it can develop over three to ten years and should then be served at 10–12°C (50–53.6°F) throughout the meal.

ALEXANDRE BONNET 1996**

6 ha 9,000 100–149 F

Alexandre Bonnet's brand was created in the 1930s by the grandfather of the current owners, who have become the most important producers of Rosé des Riceys. This 1996, with its firm colour, offers a bouquet of fruits, prunes, caramel and liquorice. It leaves a fresh, lingering flavour of cherries on the palate. This is a fine, typical, well-balanced wine that is perfectly suited to serving with first courses.

SA Bonnet Père et Fils, 138, rue du Gal-de-Gaulle, 10340 Les Riceys, tel. 03.25.29.30.93, fax 03.25.29.38.65 by appt.

GUY DE FOREZ 1998

1 ha 9,000 70–99 F

This is a Rosé des Riceys made by brief maceration (72 hours), exactly as it should be. It has an attractively deep, intense colour, and offers aromas of cherries and citrus fruits. Red berry flavours linger long on the rounded, harmonious palate.

Guy de Forez, rte de Tonnerre, 10340 Les Riceys, tel. 03.25.29.98.73, fax 03.25.38.23.01

MOREL PERE ET FILS 1996*

2 ha 10,000 70–99 F

Until 1995, the Morel family produced nothing but Rosé des Riceys. Today, they have expanded their range with some Brut and Rosé champagnes. Their Rosé des Riceys is matured in barrel for 12 months. The 1996 is very well-made, with the proper Riceys taste. Aromas of morello cherries and citrus fruits, as well as vanilla and spices, are registered on the nose, while the palate shows great suppleness and balance.

Pascal Morel, 93, av. du Gal-de-Gaulle, 10340 Les Riceys, tel. 03.25.29.10.88, fax 03.25.29.66.72 by appt.

JURA, SAVOY AND BUGEY

Jura

A mirror-image of the vineyards of the Haute Bourgogne, on the opposite side of the Saône valley, the Jura vineyards occupy the slopes that descend from the first plateau of the Jura mountains to the plain below. The wine-growing region runs from north to south across the whole department, from the area of Salins-les-Bains in the north to Saint-Amour in the south. Compared with the Côte-d'Or, across the valley, the Jura slopes are scattered and irregular, with many different aspects and exposures. Vines are cultivated only on the most favourably sited slopes, at an altitude of between 250 and 400 m (820–1312 ft). The vineyard covers about 1,828 ha (4,515 acres) from which about 110,758 hl (2,924,011 gal) were produced in the abundant year of 1999.

The classic continental climate is unusually exaggerated, because of both the general westward orientation of the region and the particular characteristics of its Jurassic contours, especially the boxed-off features known as 'blind alleys'. Winters are harsh, and the summer weather is unreliable, but there are often many hot days. The harvest takes place over a fairly long period, even extending into November because of the difficulties the grapes have in ripening fully. The soils are in the main sedimentary Triassic deposits, or liassic deposits of Jurassic marl, particularly in the north, and there is also a chalk overlay, mostly found in the south of the department. The local grape varieties are perfectly adapted to the clay soils and produce wines of a remarkably specific regional character. The vines need to be trained quite high to raise the grapes above damaging autumn humidity. They are pruned *en courgées* – that is, in long, arching stems such as can be found on the similar soils of the Mâconnais. If one can believe the writings of Pliny, vine cultivation in the region dates back to at least the beginning of the Christian era; and there is no doubt that the Jura vineyards, particularly appreciated by Henri IV of France, were very much in fashion from the Middle Ages.

The old, peaceful city of Arbois, the wine capital of the region, is full of charm. There are many reminders that the great 19th-century scientist Louis Pasteur, who spent his youth in Arbois, frequently returned to it. It was here, using the vines that grew at his family home, that he began his researches into fermentation that were to prove so important to the nascent science of oenology (from the Greek *oinos*, meaning wine) and that led, among other things, to the discovery that harmful micro-organisms could be killed by heat, a technique still known as pasteurisation.

Local grape varieties grow alongside later arrivals from Burgundy. One of the native varieties, the Poulsard (or Ploussard), from the lower foothills of the Jura mountains, was apparently only ever cultivated in the Revermont, a geographical area that also includes the Bugey vineyard, where it is known as the Mècle. This very pretty grape, with its large, oblong berries, is deliciously perfumed and has a thin, lightly coloured skin containing little tannin. A typical grape variety for rosé wines, it is more often used here to make red wines. The Trousseau, another local grape variety is, on the other hand, rich in both colour and tannin, and it, too, produces classic red wines that are characteristic of the Appellations d'Origine du Jura. The Pinot Noir, imported from Burgundy, is most frequently added in small quantities in the making of red wines. It also has an important future in the vinification of white wines made from black grapes intended for assembly with blanc de blancs to make high-quality sparkling wines. As in Burgundy, the Chardonnay grows perfectly successfully on the clay soils and gives the white wines their unmatched bouquet. The Savagnin, a local white grape variety, is cultivated on the poorest marly soils and, after six careful years of development on ullage in barrel, produces the magnificent Vin Jaune, or 'yellow wine', a Jura classic. Vin de Paille (straw wine) is also produced in small quantities in the Jura.

The region appears to be particularly favourable for obtaining excellent sparkling wine made, as previously mentioned, from blending blanc de noirs (Pinot Noir), white juice from black grapes, with blanc de blancs (Chardonnay), or white juice from white grapes. To achieve their high standards of quality and in order to ensure the necessary freshness, these sparkling wines have to be made from grapes selected at a particular stage of ripeness.

The white and red wines are classic in style, but, apparently because of the appeal of Vin Jaune, growers try to give them a highly developed character that is almost oxidised. Half a century ago, even some red wines were aged for more than a hundred years, but now makers have returned to more normal time frames for the wine's development.

As for the rosé, it is a lightly coloured red wine with low tannin, more frequently resembling red wine than rosés from other vineyards. Because of this, it can be kept for a time. It goes very well with fairly light dishes, the real reds – particularly those made from Trousseau grapes – being kept for more strongly flavoured dishes. The whites accompany the usual dishes, white meats and fish; the older whites partner Comté cheese very well. Vin Jaune excels with Comté and also with Roquefort and some other dishes for which it can be difficult to find an appropriate wine, such as duck with orange or dishes with sauce américaine.

Arbois

This is the best known of the Appellations d'Origine du Jura, and the name applies to all types of wines produced in the 12 communes in the Arbois region, which cover about 849 ha (2,097 acres). In 1999 production reached about 50,395 hl (1,330,428 gal), of which 26,749 hl (706,174 gal) were reds and rosé, 23,432 hl (618,605 gal) were whites and yellows and about 213 hl (5,623 gal) were sparkling. The Triassic marls of the *terroir* influence the quite particular character of the rosés made from Poulsard grapes.

FRUITIERE VINICOLE D'ARBOIS

Grande Réserve 1995

☐ 20 ha 30,000 30–49 F

The Fruitière Vinicole, a wine co-operative, has three tasting premises in Arbois. There is yet another one in Arc-et-Senans, across the way from the Royal salt-works. A blend of Chardonnay with a small but perceptible quantity of Savagnin, this wine has an aroma of apples, hazelnuts and citrus fruit. A little too lively at present, it should be kept for a while before drinking.

Fruitière vinicole d'Arbois, 2, rue des Fossés, 39600 Arbois, tel. 03.84.66.11.67, fax 03.84.37.48.80 ☑ Y by appt.

FRUITIERE VINICOLE D'ARBOIS

Vin Jaune 1993★

☐ 35 ha 400,000 150–199 F

Large institutions like the Fruitière can make excellent Vin Jaune. The proof is this 93, a worthy successor to the previous vintage which was a 'Pick of the Bunch' last year. It has a characteristic *jaune* nose with an intense aroma of walnuts and black pepper. A well-balanced wine that is ready to drink now.

Fruitière vinicole d'Arbois, 2, rue des Fossés, 39600 Arbois, tel. 03.84.66.11.67, fax 03.84.37.48.80 ☑ Y by appt.

LUCIEN AVIET

Réserve du Caveau Cuvée des Docteurs 1998★

☐ 0,4 ha 2,500 50–69 F

Bacchus senior, Lucien Aviet, joined forces with his son, Vincent, at the beginning of 1999. The father and son partnership should lead to a fruitful exchange of wine-making knowledge. Their Cuvée des Docteurs could well be a cure for all your woes. The superb nose has a lively and complex aroma of almonds and hazelnuts. The palate needs time to develop, and so this wine should be kept for a few months.

Lucien Aviet et Fils, Caveau de Bacchus, 39600 Montigny-lès-Arsures, tel. 03.84.66.11.02 ☑ Y by appt.

LUCIEN AVIET

Vin Jaune Cuvée de la Confrérie 1993★

☐ 0.3 ha 1,000 150–199 F

Before you may taste the Confrérie's wine, you must be initiated by the grand master, Bacchus. It has an aroma of Reinette apples and fresh walnuts. The palate is still very young but well-structured; this is a Vin Jaune that will age well, given time. As one juror put it, this wine will be ready to drink in the time it takes to raise the chicken to serve it with. As, presumably, he meant a poulet de Bresse, the wine should be ready in a year or two.

Lucien Aviet et Fils, Caveau de Bacchus, 39600 Montigny-lès-Arsures, tel. 03.84.66.11.02 ☑ Y by appt.

LUCIEN AVIET Réserve du caveau

Cuvée des Géologues 1998★

■ 0.6 ha 3,000 50–69 F

This Cuvée des Géologues may help you revise your idea of geology. Trousseau vines have flourished in limestone soil to create an attractive wine. The nose opens on blackcurrant notes, but develops redcurrant overtones. On the palate, it is fruity with a very slight spritz, but well-balanced all the same.

Lucien Aviet et Fils, Caveau de Bacchus, 39600 Montigny-lès-Arsures, tel. 03.84.66.11.02 ☑ Y by appt.

PAUL BENOIT

Pupillin Chardonnay 1998★★

☐ 3 ha 20,000 30–49 F

Only wines produced within the communal boundaries of Pupillin are entitled to use the name on an AOC Arbois wine. Paul Benoit is one of the few wine-growers who have this privilege. This attractive white wine has a forthcoming nose of hazelnuts, toast and apricots. It has a lively attack, and the flavours on the palate develop in harmony with the nose. Full of breeding and charm, it has all that you could wish in a wine.

Paul Benoit, La Chenevière, 39600 Pupillin, tel. 03.84.66.15.61, fax 03.84.37.40.17 ☑ Y ev. day 9am–7.30pm

COLETTE ET CLAUDE BULABOIS

Chantemerle 1996★

☐ 1.2 ha 4,000 30–49 F

Claude and Colette Bulabois have been selling directly to the public since 1996. This

Jura

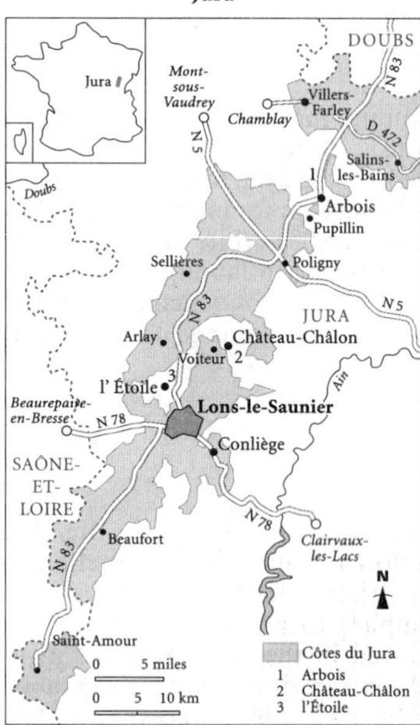

wine is a blend, at harvest, of Savagnin with a little Chardonnay (20%). It has a subtle but distinctive nose dominated by the aroma of walnuts. The wine may lack a little liveliness on the palate, but it is nicely persistent, and will repay cellaring.

Claude et Colette Bulabois, 1, Petite-Rue, 39600 Villette-lès-Arbois, tel. 03.84.66.01.93 ev. day except Sat. Sun. 2pm–7pm

MARCEL CABELIER 1997★★

n.c. 19,000 30–49 F

The Compagnie des Grands Vins du Jura is a Crançot négociant located just above the vineyards as you climb up towards the Jura plateau. A blend of 80% Pinot Noir and 20% Trousseau, it has a beautiful deep red colour and a wonderful red-berry nose. The palate is powerful, concentrated and complex. Well-structured, this wine has the potential to keep. It should be served with wild boar for a true gourmet experience.

Cie des Grands Vins du Jura, rte de Champagnole, 39570 Crançot, tel. 03.84.87.61.30, fax 03.84.48.21.36 by appt.

JOSEPH DORBON

Trousseau Vieilles vignes 1998★

0.6 ha 3,500 30–49 F

Joseph Dorbon has been involved in wine-making since 1996. He offers an **Arbois blanc 97** made from Chardonnay grapes and matured in oak barrels from the earliest stages of fermentation; its ageing potential was remarked upon by the jury. As for this Trousseau, it is very well made: 'An aristocratic nose of fruit and vanilla!' The palate is classic, with structured tannins and good body. All the characteristics of the terroir are expressed in this bottle, but it does need to age for a while. It would suit being served with a leg of lamb.

Joseph Dorbon, pl. de la Liberté, 39600 Vadans, tel. 03.84.37.47.93, fax 03.84.37.47.93 ev. day 10am–7pm

DANIEL DUGOIS

Trousseau 1998★

0.6 ha 2,800 50–69 F

Light-coloured but with a very expressive bouquet, this Trousseau is both delicate and elegant. The palate is not very structured, but it is extremely aromatic. As it is so light in character, it would be enjoyable now, but it also has the potential to last for a long time.

Daniel Dugois, 4, rue de la Mirode, 39600 Les Arsures, tel. 03.84.66.03.41, fax 03.84.37.44.59 by appt.

DOM. FORET

L'instant Flora Trousseau 1998★

2 ha 4,000 70–99 F

This Arbois, made from Trousseau grapes, has a powerful, open, fruity nose and an extremely fruity palate with good length and structure. It would be a perfect accompaniment to fish or any other main course, but don't drink it with cheese.

Dom. Foret, 13, rue de la Faïencerie, 39600 Arbois, tel. 03.84.66.23.01, fax 03.84.66.10.98 by appt.

RAPHAEL FUMEY ET ADELINE CHATELAIN

Trousseau 1997★

0.5 ha 3,000 30–49 F

The Trousseau has a powerful nose fragrant with red berries, violets and a hint of vanilla. Its full-bodied palate has some pleasant woody notes, as well as supple texture. The wine is ready for drinking now. Add a leg of lamb with flageolets and all will be well with the world.

EARL Raphaël Fumey et Adeline Chatelain, 39600 Montigny-lès-Arsures, tel. 03.84.66.27.84, fax 03.84.66.27.84 by appt.

RAPHAEL FUMEY ET ADELINE CHATELAIN

Méthode Traditionnelle★

0.8 ha 5,000 30–49 F

Tiny bubbles rise in your glass. Here is an Arbois sparkling wine made by the traditional method that has an elegant flowery, fruity, slightly yeasty nose. The bubbles may be a little feisty, but the attractive palate is aromatic and has finesse. 'Very well turned-out', was one taster's verdict.

EARL Raphaël Fumey et Adeline Chatelain, 39600 Montigny-lès-Arsures, tel. 03.84.66.27.84, fax 03.84.66.27.84 by appt.

MICHEL GAHIER

Trousseau Grands Vergers 1998★

1.2 ha 6,000 30–49 F

Michel Gahier's cellar is 20 metres (22 yards) from the church of Montigny-lès-Arsures. There you will find this Arbois made from 45-year-old Trousseau vines. Very deeply coloured, even for a Trousseau, it has a fragrant, complex nose of fruity, meaty and aniseed scents. The persistent and elegant aromas are echoed on the palate, which has substance, structure and length. A good example of the Arbois appellation that should be kept for a year or two before being served with braised beef.

Michel Gahier, pl. de l'Eglise, 39600 Montigny-lès-Arsures, tel. 03.84.66.17.63 by appt.

DOM. AMELIE GUILLOT

Chardonnay Vieilles vignes 1997

0.4 ha 2,000 50–69 F

The estate, which is run by a young oenologist, was established in 1995, but the vines are 50 years old. This Chardonnay, like the one from the previous vintage, has sustained acidity. While it is very full, it leaves an attractive, fresh impression on the palate. A harmonious, very dry wine. The **Arbois Poulsard Vieilles Vignes 97** was also cited by the jury. Round, light, fruity, balanced and fresh, it is a wine for autumn drinking.

🔑 Amélie Guillot, 37, rue de Courcelles, 39600 Arbois, tel. 03.84.66.11.78, fax 03.84.66.11.78, e-mail amelie.guillot@wanadoo.fr ☑ Y by appt.

PATRICK JOHANN

Savagnin 1996★★

☐ 1 ha 2,000 ▮▮ 70–99 F

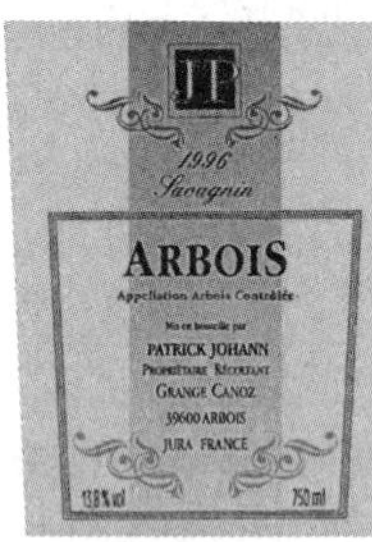

This Savagnin has clearly benefited from its four years in oak barrels. It has a very attractive gold colour with green highlights. The nose is magnificent: walnut and green apple scents compete for dominance. One taster appropriately described the palate as 'captivating'. Aromas of walnuts, oranges and apricots persist in a perfectly balanced structure. It is not a Vin Jaune, but similar in style. Definitely one to try.

🔑 Patrick et Michèle Johann, Grange Canoz, 39600 Arbois, tel. 03.84.66.13.82, fax 03.84.37.48.81 ☑ Y by appt.

LA CAVE DE LA REINE JEANNE

Chardonnay 1998★

☐ 9 ha 50,000 ▮ ▮▮ ⚲ 30–49 F

Bénédicte and Stéphane Tissot established this small cellar as part of their family estate. Their selective purchase of grapes and their particular wine-making skills have created a very successful house style. This white wine with green highlights has a leafy nose with fine, earthy notes. Supple and full-bodied, it has a seductive aroma of green apples on the palate. A masterfully made bottle of wine. The **Arbois Poulsard 98**, which has not been oaked, was cited by the jury for its agreeably light and supple character; it is a rosé for drinking now.

🔑 SARL Le Cellier des Tiercelines, 54, Grande-Rue, 39600 Arbois, tel. 03.84.66.25.79, fax 03.84.66.25.08 ☑ Y ev. day 10am–12 noon 1.30pm–7pm, cl. Oct.–May

🔑 Bénédicte et Stéphane Tissot

DOM. DE LA PINTE

Les Genevrets 1997

■ 2 ha 8,000 ▮ ▮▮ ⚲ 30–49 F

This wine has been matured in oak for 18 months. Phillipe Chatillon is the cellar-master and manager of the estate, which was created by Roger Martin in 1952. These Genevans have blended 1% Trousseau with Poulsard grapes planted on marl soils. The pure, fine nose has a hint of caramel along with the typical Poulsard fruitiness. Fruit is also perceptible on the palate. An enjoyable wine.

🔑 Dom. de La Pinte, 39600 Arbois, tel. 03.84.66.06.47, fax 03.84.66.24.58 ☑ Y ev. day 9am–12 noon 2pm–6pm; Sun. by appt.

🔑 Roger Martin

DOM. DE LA RENARDIERE

Pupillin Chardonnay 1998

☐ 2 ha 12,000 ▮▮ 30–49 F

In 1999 the estate gained an 'r' – Renadière became Renardière. This Chardonnay has been allowed to rest on its lees after fermentation. The nose is powerful and concentrated, with a strong aroma of walnuts and suggestions of overripeness. An ample and warm palate will please fans of emphatically flavoured wines.

🔑 Jean-Michel Petit, rue du Chardonnay, 39600 Pupillin, tel. 03.84.66.25.10, fax 03.84.66.25.10, e-mail renardiere@libertysurf.fr ☑ Y ev. day 10am–12 noon 1.30pm–7pm

DOM. DE LA TOURNELLE

Fleur de savagnin 1998★

☐ 1.4 ha 2,500 ▮▮ 50–69 F

After five years as an adviser to Jura winemakers, Pascal Clairet decided to go into production for himself. Several years on, this Fleur from Savagnin confirms that it was a good decision. If at first the nose is a little harsh, it is nonetheless very typical. Very elegant on the palate, this is a wine full of varietal character, and all the better for it!

🔑 Pascal Clairet, 5, Petite-Place, 39600 Arbois, tel. 03.84.66.25.76, fax 03.84.66.27.15 ☑ Y by appt.

DOM. DE LA TOURNELLE

Ploussard 1998★

■ 1.3 ha 6,500 ▮▮ 30–49 F

A beautiful onion-skin rosé. The nose is subtle, but nonetheless very attractive. This is a well-balanced and fruity 98 that will go well with a terrine.

🔑 Pascal Clairet, 5, Petite-Place, 39600 Arbois, tel. 03.84.66.25.76, fax 03.84.66.27.15 ☑ Y by appt.

DOM. LIGIER PERE ET FILS

Trousseau 1998★

■ 1 ha 4,000 ▮ ▮▮ ⚲ 30–49 F

This Trousseau is made from grapes handpicked at the end of September 1998. The nose is spicy and fruity. Well balanced on the palate, it is very refreshing, almost smooth. A highly pleasing wine, then. Ready to drink now, it could also be kept for a few years.

🔑 Ligier Père et Fils, 7, rte de Poligny, 39380 Mont-sous-Vaudrey, tel. 03.84.71.74.75, fax 03.84.81.59.82 ☑ Y by appt.

DOM. LIGIER PERE ET FILS

Savagnin Elevé en fût de chêne 1996★

□ 1 ha 5,000 70–99 F

Savagnin grapes grown on marl soils have produced a bright, clear wine with a potent nose. Walnut and orange-peel aromas are powerfully expressed. The palate is well developed and balanced, with good length. Here is a perfect example of a wine that approximates to the celebrated taste of a Vin Jaune.

Ligier Père et Fils, 7, rte de Poligny, 39380 Mont-sous-Vaudrey, tel. 03.84.71.74.75, fax 03.84.81.59.82 by appt.

FREDERIC LORNET

Trousseau des Dames 1998★★

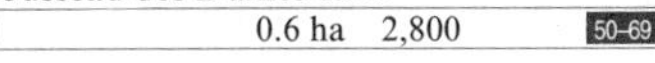

■ 0.6 ha 2,800 50–69 F

It may be called a ladies' Trousseau, but it has a decidedly masculine personality. The classy cherry nose has leather and musk overtones. On the palate, it is well-structured with round tannins. It is worth noting that this wine is the product of a region renowned for the concentration of its grapes. Fermented for 18 days, it is a good representative of its appellation, as well as the potential of this grape variety. It would hold its own alongside wild boar.

Frédéric Lornet, l'Abbaye, 39600 Montigny-lès-Arsures, tel. 03.84.37.44.95, fax 03.84.37.40.17 by appt.

FREDERIC LORNET Ploussard 1998★

◪ 1.5 ha 9,000 30–49 F

First you notice the beautiful bright colour and clarity of this wine. The nose starts off vegetal, but becomes more complex with plenty of citrus notes. The freshness of the nose continues on the palate, giving the wine a very attractive style. A good apéritif wine.

Frédéric Lornet, l'Abbaye, 39600 Montigny-lès-Arsures, tel. 03.84.37.44.95, fax 03.84.37.40.17 by appt.

DOM. MARTIN FAUDOT

Chardonnay 1998★★

□ 0.8 ha 4,000 30–49 F

A slightly forward wine, but one very much in the Jura style. The nose is intense and open, with vanilla and cocoa scents rather than fruit. Nutty and chocolate flavours compete on a perfectly structured and balanced palate. From the same AOC, the **Poulsard 98** was also cited by the jury for its young red-berry and cinnamon nose, as well as its roundness and freshness.

Dom. Martin-Faudot, 1, rue Bardenet, 39600 Mesnay, tel. 03.84.66.29.97, fax 03.84.66.29.84 by appt.

DOM. DE MONTFORT 1996★

■ n.c. 24,000 100–149 F

The de Montfort estate belongs to the house of Henri Marie, a business renowned for its large-scale direct marketing of wines. An attractive deep red blend, it is primarily composed of Pinot Noir with lesser quantities of Poulsard and Trousseau grapes. The musky nose is forthcoming and powerful, but the tannins are firm. A robust wine that will reach its full potential in two or three years.

Dom. de Montfort, Ch. Boichailles, 39600 Arbois, tel. 03.84.66.12.34, fax 03.84.66.42.42 by appt.

SCV H. Maire

DESIRE PETIT ET FILS

Pupillin Ploussard 1998★

◪ 3.5 ha 18,000 30–49 F

The Petit brothers, Gérard and Marcel, spare no expense publicising Jura wines. With 17,000 clients, they direct most of their effort at private buyers. A powerful bouquet of fruits and a note of wild undergrowth introduce this rosé. Round and warm, it feels almost like a red on the palate. Red or rosé, however, this is a very good wine.

Désiré Petit, rue du Ploussard, 39600 Pupillin, tel. 03.84.66.01.20, fax 03.84.66.26.59 ev. day 8.30am–12 noon 2pm–7pm

Gérard et Marcel Petit

JACQUES PUFFENEY Poulsard 1998★

◪ 1.5 ha 10,000 50–69 F

Montigny-lès-Arsures is one of the most appealing villages in Arbois. Have a stroll round to get a feel for the wine-maker's gentle pace of life. This wine made from Poulsard grapes has a potently fruity, fresh nose. The palate is still a little oaky, but ample and well-balanced. It should be stored for a while before drinking. The same merchant's **Arbois Jaune 92** was cited by the jury for its ample, rich palate.

Jacques Puffeney, Saint-Laurent, 39600 Montigny-lès-Arsures, tel. 03.84.66.10.89, fax 03.84.66.08.36 by appt.

JACQUES PUFFENEY

Trousseau 1998★★

■ 0.8 ha 4,000 70–99 F

This Trousseau has a distinctive spicy and musky nose. The uncomplicated fruity aroma on the palate is more appealing. Round and warm, with a hint of oak, this well-constructed 98 could be drunk now, but has enough substance to age for several years. A great wine to drink after a long autumn walk.

Jacques Puffeney, Saint-Laurent, 39600 Montigny-lès-Arsures, tel. 03.84.66.10.89, fax 03.84.66.08.36 by appt.

FRUITIERE VINICOLE DE PUPILLIN Pupillin Chardonnay 1998★★

☐ 28 ha 100,000 ■ 🌡 30–49 F

For over 90 years, the Fruitière Vinicole from Pupillin has been making wines with a deservedly good reputation. The nose of this Chardonnay has suggestions of white flowers. Quite opulent in style, it has a substantial palate with classy honey and almond flavours. It is a rich wine that could be drunk now, or stored for the future. The Fruitière also offers a **Pupillin Plousard rosé 98**, which was cited by the jury for its engaging lightness.

🔑 Fruitière vinicole de Pupillin, 39600 Pupillin, tel. 03.84.66.12.88, fax 03.84.37.47.16 ☑ Y by appt.

ROLET PERE ET FILS Vin de Paille Caveau des Capucins 1996★★

☐ 2 ha 4,000 ⦀ 100–149 F

This Vin de Paille is made from only white grape varieties: 75% Chardonnay and 25% Savagnin. A nose of quince jelly and prunes is followed by an especially vivid, rich and powerful palate, the result of a careful fermentation of exceptional grapes. Dried and crystallised fruit flavours also grab your attention. A delightful experience.

🔑 Dom. Rolet Père et Fils, rte de Dole, 39600 Arbois, tel. 03.84.66.00.05, fax 03.84.37.47.41, e-mail rolet@wanadoo.fr ☑ Y by appt.

ROLET PERE ET FILS Vin Jaune 1992★

☐ 4 ha 9,000 ⦀ 150–199 F

Domaine Rolet is the second largest estate in Jura and the producer of some of its best wines. This Vin Jaune has an undeveloped nose with just the merest hint of curry spices. The pleasant attack develops into a rich, well-rounded and harmonious palate with good persistence. The wine should be cellared for a few years so that it can achieve its full potential. The red **Mémorial en Arbois 97** (50–69F) was also cited. Powerful and fruity, it could accompany red meats.

🔑 Dom. Rolet Père et Fils, rte de Dole, 39600 Arbois, tel. 03.84.66.00.05, fax 03.84.37.47.41, e-mail rolet@wanadoo.fr ☑ Y by appt.

ANDRE ET MIREILLE TISSOT Vin de Paille 1996★

☐ 1.2 ha 4,000 ■ ⦀ 150–199 F

André and Mireille Tissot are established Jura wine-makers. In line with current trends, they have recently decided to convert their estate to organic viticulture. Poulsard, Chardonnay and Savagnin grapes harvested in September 1996 were dried, and then crushed between late January and early March 1997. This has produced a Vin de Paille with beautiful quince and apricot scents. This deliciously sweet 96 has maintained a hugely interesting aromatic profile.

🔑 André et Mireille Tissot, 39600 Montigny-lès-Arsures, tel. 03.84.66.08.27, fax 03.84.66.25.08 ☑ Y by appt.

🔑 André et Stéphane Tissot

JACQUES TISSOT Trousseau 1997★

■ 2 ha 10,500 ■ ⦀ 🌡 50–69 F

Meeting Jacques Tissot is a pleasure. He is a genial man with a likeable, straightforward manner. His Trousseau has a slightly closed nose that opens with vegetal notes, and then develops a more fruity character. On the palate, the wine is quite light but well balanced. This silky and agreeable 97 will charm you as much as its maker does.

🔑 Jacques Tissot, 39, rue de Courcelles, 39600 Arbois, tel. 03.84.66.14.27, fax 03.84.66.24.88 ☑ Y by appt.

JACQUES TISSOT Vin Jaune 1992★

☐ 3.5 ha 8,000 ■ ⦀ 🌡 150–199 F

A beautiful golden wine with a potent alcoholic nose. The very distinctive palate has fascinating length. You should try it with a piece of good Comté, the AOC cheese also made in Arbois, where there is a cheese-makers' co-operative.

🔑 Jacques Tissot, 39, rue de Courcelles, 39600 Arbois, tel. 03.84.66.14.27, fax 03.84.66.24.88 ☑ Y by appt.

JEAN-LOUIS TISSOT Vin Jaune 1992★

☐ 0.6 ha 1,000 ⦀ 100–149 F

Jean-Louis Tissot's family enjoys introducing the public to the pleasures of Jura wine, of which this Vin Jaune is a seductive example. The nose is quite discreet, yet fine; the palate is soft and attractive. Although it could keep, the wine is ready for those eager to taste it right away. Serve it as an apéritif with a piece of Comté, a wonderful combination. The **Arbois rouge** (30–49F), made from Trousseau grapes, was also cited by the jury. It has a bouquet of ripe red berries, cherries and liquorice, and a distinguished palate.

🔑 Jean-Louis Tissot, Vauxelles, 39600 Montigny-lès-Arsures, tel. 03.84.66.13.08, fax 03.84.66.08.09 ☑ Y ev. day 9am–12 noon 2pm–6pm; Sun. and groups by appt.

Château-Chalon

The most prestigious of the Jura wines is exclusively the famous Vin de Voile, produced on 45 ha (111 acres). This is a Vin Jaune, made according to strict regulations. The grape is harvested in a remarkable landscape of black liassic marl, overlooked by towering cliffs on top of which the old village is perched. Production is limited but in 1999 it reached 2,054 hl (54,226 gal). The wine is put on sale precisely six years and three months after the harvest. It is worth noting that the producers themselves, who are constantly concerned to maintain a high level of quality, refused the AOC classification for the harvests of 1974, 1980 and 1984.

BAUD 1992*

☐ 1.8 ha 2,300 150–199 F

Eight generations of wine-growers have successively enlarged this estate, which now encompasses 16 ha (40 acres). The Château-Chalon vineyards were acquired in 1986. The 92 vintage has a slightly closed, walnut-scented nose of great finesse. By contrast, the palate is fully developed with good acidity, body and length. The powerful finish has a superb toasty flavour.

Dom. Baud Père et Fils, rte de Voiteur, 39210 Le Vernois, tel. 03.84.25.31.41, fax 03.84.25.30.09 by appt.

MARCEL CABELIER 1992

☐ n.c. 7,000 150–199 F

This Crançot wine business not only specialises in sparkling wines but also offers a selection of other Juras. Its Château-Chalon has a fairly pale colour but an extremely fragrant nose: ripe nut, crystallised fruit and toasted almond scents are all present. Already well-developed, the palate is well-balanced and nicely aromatic. Ready for drinking now, it shouldn't be kept for too much longer.

Cie des Grands Vins du Jura, rte de Champagnole, 39570 Crançot, tel. 03.84.87.61.30, fax 03.84.48.21.36 by appt.

RESERVE CATHERINE DE RYE 1983**

☐ n.c. 12,000 300–499 F

The Henri Maire company has the world's largest reserves of Vin Jaune, which is why it can offer such an old vintage. In 1997, the French jury declared it to be very good. On 24 January 2000, we tasted a dark gold wine. The well-developed nose has complex aromas, still dominated by the scent of nuts. Thanks to its good acidity, this Château-Chalon continues to age well. Walnut and dried-fruit flavours of great finesse are apparent on the palate. This wine is certainly very fine now, but will easily keep for several decades more.

Henri Maire SA, Ch. Boichailles, 39600 Arbois, tel. 03.84.66.12.34, fax 03.84.66.42.42 by appt.

D. ET P. CHALANDARD 1992

☐ 1 ha 2,000 150–199 F

Daniel Chalandard, a grower who favours environmentally friendly methods of production, took over this estate in 1970. This year, his son will join him. As it is still quite young, it was difficult for the jury to decide if this pale yellow Vin Jaune with green highlights had a shy nose or one that had yet to open. On the other hand, they all agreed that it had a forthright, well-balanced and long palate where elegant aromas of ripe walnuts and toast developed in waves. In all, a little discreet, but with many assets that should express themselves after three to five years' cellaring.

GAEC du Vieux Pressoir, rte de Voiteur, 39210 Le Vernois, tel. 03.84.25.31.15, fax 03.84.25.37.62 by appt.

DESIRE PETIT ET FILS 1992*

☐ 0.3 ha 1,400 150–199 F

Only 1.5% of the estate's 20 ha (49 acres) qualify for the production of AOC Château-Chalon. The 1,400 bottles of this vintage contain a Vin Jaune de Paille that only reveals a walnut-scented nose after it has been allowed to breathe. Powerful and rich on the palate, it slowly develops soft aromas of dried fruits, almonds and hazelnuts. It should be cellared for five years.

Gérard et Marcel Petit, rue du Ploussard, 39600 Pupillin, tel. 03.84.66.01.20, fax 03.84.66.26.59 ev. day 9am–12 noon 2pm–7pm; groups by appt.

AUGUSTE PIROU 1992**

☐ n.c. 15,000 100–149 F

This wine business, run by P Menez of the Henri Maire company, also has a large stock of Vin Jaune. Once again, the jury was impressed by the skilful way this vintage had been matured. The nose has finesse rather than potency. This Château-Chalon is rich and elegant on the palate, with a subtle but persistent taste of walnuts. The acidity, vital

for all good Vin Jaune, is discreetly evident at the finish. A fine, complex wine that would be enjoyable now, but that could also keep for another ten to 15 years.
Auguste Pirou, Les Caves Royales, 39600 Arbois, tel. 03.84.66.42.70, fax 03.84.66.42.42

FRUITIERE VINICOLE DE VOITEUR 1989

□ 10 ha 60,000 150–199 F

Ten of the 70 ha (173 acres) cultivated by the members of the Fruitière Vinicole from Voiteur are classed as AOC Château-Chalon. This is a significant proportion of the appellation. Their 89 is still very youthful. Although the nose may not be very strong, it has a fresh and agreeable walnut aroma. The palate is equally subtle, but shows finesse.
Fruitière vinicole de Voiteur, 60, rue de Nevy-sur-Seille, 39210 Voiteur, tel. 03.84.85.21.29, fax 03.84.85.27.67, e-mail voiteur@fruitiere-vinicole-voiteur.fr
ev. day 9am–12 noon 1.30pm–6pm

Côtes du Jura

The appellation incorporates the whole area of the vineyard producing fine wines. In 1999 the area of plantation was 619 ha (1,529 acres) which produced 37,596 hl (992,534 gal) of all types of wine.

CH. D' ARLAY 1996★

■ 12 ha 20,000 50–69 F

The estate has not been sold since it was established in the 12th century. Alain de Laguiche followed in his father's footsteps in 1995. Unusually for a Jura estate, 40% of the vineyards are planted with Pinot Noir. The 96 Arlay has a blackcurrant-leaf nose and a fairly structured palate that will soften in time. A perfect accompaniment to a plate of strong French cheeses, such as Livarot or Munster.
Ch. d'Arlay, rte de Saint-Germain, 39140 Arlay, tel. 03.84.85.04.22, fax 03.84.48.17.96, e-mail chateau@arlay.com
ev. day except Sun. 8am–12 noon 2pm–6pm
Comte A. de Laguiche

CH. D'ARLAY 1995

□ 6 ha 25,000 70–99 F

The grapes for this blend of 70% Chardonnay and 30% Savagnin were mixed together before being pressed. The result has a fruity Muscat-like fragrance. On the palate, there is a concentrated balance of fruity and spicy flavours. It doesn't have the oxidised character of a Jura, but seems more reminiscent of an Alsace wine. Enjoyable, and slightly unusual.
Ch. d'Arlay, rte de Saint-Germain, 39140 Arlay, tel. 03.84.85.04.22, fax 03.84.48.17.96, e-mail chateau@arlay.com ev. day except Sun. 8am–12 noon 2pm–6pm

BERNARD BADOZ Vin Jaune 1992★

□ 1.25 ha 1,200 150–199 F

As Bernard Badoz recommends, Vin Jaune must be served at room, not cellar, temperature. This one has an appealing dried-fruit and tobacco nose. The attack is still a little sharp, but the green walnut aromas on the palate are interesting. The wine needs time to reach its potential. The jury suggests that you should put your faith in this bottle, and be willing to store it in your cellar for the next decade. The wait will be worthwhile for what will turn out to be a very good Vin Jaune.
Bernard Badoz, 15, rue du Collège, 39800 Poligny, tel. 03.84.37.11.85, fax 03.84.37.11.18 ev. day 8am–8pm

BERNARD BADOZ Tradition du Terroir 1996★

□ 1.5 ha 5,000 50–69 F

Powerful yet fine, the nose has vanilla, hazelnut and white flower scents. The palate is ample, with fresh almond and citronella flavours. Very well-balanced, it has an enjoyably powerful finish. The same estate's **Rosé 98** (30–49F) was also awarded a star. It has a pleasant red-berry aroma, and would be a good accompaniment to a salad of duck livers.
Bernard Badoz, 15, rue du Collège, 39800 Poligny, tel. 03.84.37.11.85, fax 03.84.37.11.18 ev. day 8am–8pm

BAUD PERE ET FILS Vin jaune 1992

□ 3.5 ha 2,500 150–199 F

The Baud estate produces Vin Jaune for both the Château-Chalon and the Côtes du Jura appellations. This Côtes has a subtle but likeable nose. Like other wines from this exceptional year, this Vin Jaune is balanced and full of appealing finesse. It could be served with a hot starter.
Dom. Baud Père et Fils, rte de Voiteur, 39210 Le Vernois, tel. 03.84.25.31.41, fax 03.84.25.30.09 by appt.

BAUD PERE ET FILS Savagnin 1996★

□ 4 ha 4,000 70–99 F

The combination of hazelnut and curry aromas, with overtones of butter and spice, is as enjoyable on the nose as it is on the palate. Lengthy and complex, this wine, made entirely from Savagnin grapes, is very typical of its AOC. The woody palate is marked by balanced structure and great finesse.
Dom. Baud Père et Fils, rte de Voiteur, 39210 Le Vernois, tel. 03.84.25.31.41, fax 03.84.25.30.09 by appt.

PHILIPPE BUTIN Vin Jaune 1993

□ 0.5 ha 1,200 150–199 F

The Butins have been wine-growers for three generations, with Philippe running the

estate since 1981. This small production of Vin Jaune has a beautiful gold colour. Robust, with a very structured palate and quite high alcohol content, this fine 93 should be allowed to age.
Philippe Butin, 21, rue de la Combe, 39210 Lavigny, tel. 03.84.25.36.26, fax 03.84.25.39.18 ev. day 8am–7pm

CAVEAU DES BYARDS

Chardonnay 1997★★

1.2 ha 8,000 30-49 F

The Caveau des Byards has made great technological improvements in its handling of grapes, and this Chardonnay bears witness to the advances. A pale gold colour, it has a bouquet of acacia flowers. The palate strikes a nice balance between alcohol and acidity and has a superb aroma. Honey, toasted dried fruit and fresh almond flavours are all present. All of these impressions linger on the palate for a very long time: proof that small producers can make great wines. A harvest of only 25 ha (62 acres) of vineyards makes it into the Byards' cellars.
Caveau des Byards, 39210 Le Vernois, tel. 03.84.25.33.52, fax 03.84.25.38.02 by appt.

CAVEAU DES BYARDS

Vin Jaune 1992★

2 ha 2,700 150-199 F

A small co-operative cellar that has all of the advantages of a large one. Using just two hectares' (five acres') production of Savagnin grapes, the cellar-master has made a beautiful Vin Jaune the colour of old gold. The well-developed nose is quite fresh with notes of gingerbread and nuts. The palate is rounded and slightly maderised. A member of the jury who had almost missed this tasting was so pleased that he had not after all missed the unique thrill of discovering a *vin jaune* so carefully crafted by a dedicated wine-maker.
Caveau des Byards, 39210 Le Vernois, tel. 03.84.25.33.52, fax 03.84.25.38.02 by appt.

MARCEL CABELIER

Chardonnay 1997

n.c. 18,000 30-49 F

A good first impression: the pale gold colour is extremely clear and bright. The nose has a scent of vanilla and hazelnuts with a hint of burnt toast. This appealing and lively 97 is ready for drinking now. The jury suggests that you serve it with frogs' legs in a cream sauce.
Cie des Grands Vins du Jura, rte de Champagnole, 39570 Crançot, tel. 03.84.87.61.30, fax 03.84.48.21.36 by appt.

DANIEL ET PASCAL CHALANDARD 1997

3 ha 9,000 30-49 F

Like several other Jura producers, Daniel and Pascal Chalandard have been convinced by the argument for organic viticulture. This father-son team, which was awarded a *coup de coeur* citation last year by the jury, has made a blended wine of Chardonnay (70%) and Savagnin (30%) grapes, of which the Savagnin component is the more perceptible. An enjoyable 97 with a fragrant, complex nose and a very aromatic palate.
GAEC du Vieux Pressoir, rte de Voiteur, 39210 Le Vernois, tel. 03.84.25.31.15, fax 03.84.25.37.62 by appt.

DENIS ET MARIE CHEVASSU

Chardonnay 1997

2 ha 2,000 30-49 F

This is one of the few estates that still maintains pastures for cows alongside its vineyards. The milk is used to make Comté, another cornerstone of the Jura's gastronomic heritage. This Côtes du Jura has a slightly closed, honey-scented nose. The supple and fleshy palate is nicely balanced by a good dose of acidity. Although fruity aromas are present now, they will improve if allowed to develop for another two or three years.
Denis Chevassu, Granges Bernard, 39210 Menétru-le-Vignoble, tel. 03.84.85.23.67, fax 03.84.85.23.67 by appt.

DOM. VICTOR CREDOZ

Chardonnay 1997★

3 ha 10,000 30-49 F

The Victor Credoz estate specialises in the production of white wines. This Chardonnay is very floral with a hint of burnt toast. The lively attack does not mask the pleasantly toasty aromas that persist on the palate. This attractively fresh 97 needs to develop further.
Dom. Victor Credoz, 39210 Menétru-le-Vignoble, tel. 06.80.43.17.44, fax 06.84.44.62.41 ev. day 8am–12 noon 1pm–7pm

DOM. VICTOR CREDOZ

Pinot Noir 1998★★

1 ha 5,000 30-49 F

Notes of blackcurrant and musk make the nose of this red wine instantly likeable. The palate is dominated by Pinot Noir flavours and an echo of blackcurrant. The tasters recognised the 98's potential greatness, for all that it didn't have the characteristic Jura style. It could be served with venison.
Dom. Victor Credoz, 39210 Menétru-le-Vignoble, tel. 06.80.43.17.44, fax 06.84.44.62.41 ev. day 8am–12 noon 1pm–7pm

RICHARD DELAY

Pinot Noir 1998★★★

1.75 ha 7,000 30-49 F

Over the years, Richard Delay's Pinot Noir has been followed with interest by our tasters. The 98 fulfils their best expectations. Its violet highlights are very attractive. The appealing, vernal nose leads on to a tannic and richly alcoholic palate tasting of cherries and blackcurrants. This wine has serious concentration. A high point for this southern

JURA

CÔTES DU JURA
1998
Richard DELAY
12,5% VOL.
75 CL

Revermont vineyard, which has been defended and promoted assiduously for many years by its owner.

🔑 Richard Delay, 37, rue du Château, 39570 Gevingey, tel. 03.84.47.46.78, fax 03.84.43.26.75 ☒ 🍷 by appt.

JACQUES ET BARBARA DURAND-PERRON 1996

☐ 2 ha 5,000 🛢 30–49 F

Maruis Perron was a renowned Château-Chalon wine-producer. Now his son-in-law has followed suit. This Côtes du Jura has an attractive pale gold colour, a toasty nose and yeasty palate. At the moment, it is still a little too lively, but the finish is long. In two or three years, it could be served with fish in a cream sauce.

🔑 Jacques et Barbara Durand-Perron, 9, rue des Roches, 39210 Voiteur, tel. 03.84.44.66.80, fax 03.84.44.62.75 ☒ 🍷 by appt.

DOM. GRAND FRERES

Chardonnay 1998★★

☐ 4 ha 25,000 🛢 30–49 F

The Grand brothers have certainly made a grand wine. Pale gold, it has a scent of honey, quinces and white flowers. The complexity and finesse of the nose continue on the palate, which is like nectar. Very well-balanced and nicely alcoholic, it has an aroma of honey that persists on the long finish. This distinctive 98 has been crafted by a master wine-maker. The jury also cited two other wines by the estate: first, a **Vin Jaune 93** (100–149F), which needs to be kept for at least five years; and second, a **Rouge 98**, a pale, supple, fruity and light Trousseau which could be served with the smoked meats produced in the Jura mountains.

🔑 Dom. Grand Frères, rue du Savagnin, 39230 Passenans, tel. 03.84.85.28.88, fax 03.84.44.67.47 ☒ 🍷 ev. day 9am–12 noon 2pm–6pm; cl. Sat. Sun. in Jan. Feb.

CH. GREA Vin de Paille 1996

☐ n.c. 500 🛢 100–149 F

Nicolas Caire is the wine-maker at Château Gréa. He has made just 500 bottles of Vin de Paille using mostly white grapes. The 96 has a honey and raisin nose and a very aromatic palate, compensating for a slight lack of acidity and the presence of significant residual sugars.

🔑 Nicolas Caire, Ch. Gréa, 39190 Rotalier, tel. 06.81.83.67.80, fax 06.84.25.05.47 ☒ 🍷 by appt.

CLOS DES GRIVES Savagnin 1996★

☐ n.c. 2,500 🛢 70–99 F

Claude Charbonnier has been managing his vineyards organically for a while. His golden Savagnin has a powerful nose of vanilla, caramel and hazelnuts. Very slightly acid, the palate is well-balanced with a pleasantly fresh walnut aroma and a spicy finish. A distinctive wine that needs to age.

🔑 Claude Charbonnier, 204, Grande-Rue, 39570 Chillé, tel. 03.84.47.23.78, fax 03.84.47.29.27 ☒ 🍷 by appt.

FRANCK GUIGNERET

Fruité 1996★★

☐ 2 ha 6,000 🍾 🌡 50–69 F

The *Guide* is always pleased to discover new wine-makers. Parisian Franck Guigneret has taken over a small vineyard in Château-Chalon. He continues to practise his other passion, flying raptors, in Arley. His fruity white wine has a very delicate, flowery nose with hints of vanilla, toast and hazelnuts. Well-balanced, it is wonderfully persistent on the palate. A real achievement for a newcomer, who has impressed the jury by producing such a harmonious wine. His **Typé 96**, matured for two years in oak, was also cited for its intense fruitiness.

🔑 Franck Guigneret, rue des Chèvres, 39210 Château-Chalon, tel. 03.84.44.67.97, fax 03.84.44.69.20, e-mail savagnin@aol.com ☒ 🍷 by appt.

CAVEAU DES JACOBINS

Savagnin 1994★

☐ n.c. 8,200 🛢 70–99 F

It's not every day that you get to taste wines in a deconsecrated church. It is quite easy to find this cellar in the centre of Poligny. While the setting alone is worth a detour, this cellar also houses some extremely good, pure Savagnin Côtes du Jura wines. With its walnut and curry nose, and a concentrated, distinctive but slightly austere palate, this wine will certainly not give you cause for repentance.

🔑 Caveau des Jacobins, rue Nicolas-Appert, 39800 Poligny, tel. 03.84.37.01.37, fax 03.84.37.30.47 ☒ 🍷 by appt.

CLAUDE JOLY Pinot Noir 1998

n.c. 4,500 30–49 F

The 97 vintage of the same wine was selected as a *coup de coeur* last year by the jury. This time, the Côtes du Jura made from pure Pinot Noir has a powerful vegetal nose. The palate is also predominantly vegetal, but has an additional hint of morello cherries, allied to supple tannins. It should be drunk fairly young, after only a short period of cellaring.

Claude Joly, chem. des Patarattes, 39190 Rotalier, tel. 03.84.25.04.14, fax 03.84.25.14.48 by appt.

ALAIN LABET

Fleur de Chardonnay 1998

□ 1.2 ha 4,550 50–69 F

Rotalier is a wine-producing village in Revermont, the southern portion of the Jura wine region. There, Alain Labet makes his Fleur de Chardonnay. The nose is flowery, with slight woody notes. This rather oaky, round and warm wine is not really in the Jura style. Nevertheless, it is very well made. It could be served with hot starters.

Alain Labet, pl. du Village, 39190 Rotalier, tel. 03.84.25.11.13, fax 03.84.25.06.75 by appt.

DOM. MOREL-THIBAUT

Vin de Paille 1996

□ 1 ha 3,000 100–149 F

Across the street from the dairy school on the southern route into Poligny, Jean-Luc Morel and Michel Thibaut make an assertive Vin de Paille. The colour of golden straw, as it should be, it has a chocolate and raisin nose. The palate is round and well-balanced. A good example of this style of wine, it may be drunk now or kept for a while.

Dom. Morel-Thibaut, 8, rue Coittier, 39800 Poligny, tel. 03.84.37.07.61, fax 03.84.37.07.61 ev. day 3pm–7pm; Sun. 10am–12 noon

DOM. MOREL-THIBAUT 1997★★

□ 3 ha 10,000 30–49 F

A blend of 95% Chardonnay grapes with just 5% Savagnin. The powerful and complex nose evokes acacias, beeswax and toast. Well-balanced and long, the palate echoes the aromas of the nose with additional hints of gingerbread and caramel. A delicate and persistent wine, it is substantial enough to serve alongside a crayfish gratin.

Dom. Morel-Thibaut, 8, rue Coittier, 39800 Poligny, tel. 03.84.37.07.61, fax 03.84.37.07.61 ev. day 3pm–7pm; Sun. 10am–12 noon

PIGNIER PERE ET FILS

Trousseau 1998★★

■ 0,6 ha 2,500 30–49 F

Marie-Florence, Antoine and Jean-Etienne Pignier believe in organic viticulture. One of the methods they use is growing grass between the rows of vines. We strongly recommend their Côtes du Jura made from hand-picked Trousseau grapes. The nose is a veritable basket of summer fruit: morello cherries, blackcurrants and raspberries. With a slight residual spritz and quite strong tannins on the palate, this 98 needs time to mature. It would be a worthy accompaniment to venison, or perhaps quail with raisins.

Dom. Pignier, Cellier des Chartreux, 39570 Montaigu, tel. 03.84.24.24.30, fax 03.84.47.46.00 ev. day 8am–12 noon 1.30pm–7pm; Sun. 8am–12 noon; groups by appt.

AUGUSTE PIROU

Rouge Chaud 1998★★★

■ n.c. 16,000 30–49 F

Auguste Pirou is a subsidiary brand of the Henri Maire company. This so-called 'hot red' blend is marked by the character of its principal grape Pinot Noir, here showing an almost blackcurranty nose. The engaging palate has overtones of red berries and wild cherries, and is full-bodied and well-balanced. A velvet-smooth wine, it is ready to drink now, but will also keep well. It should be served at around 14°C with grilled meats.

Auguste Pirou, Les Caves Royales, 39600 Arbois, tel. 03.84.66.42.70, fax 03.84.66.42.42

XAVIER REVERCHON

Les Boutasses 1998★

■ 0,5 ha 3,000 30–49 F

Xavier Reverchon uses grapes from just one locality in each of his wines. The cuvée des Boutasses is the product of Poulsard and Trousseau vines growing in Poligny. The nose develops slowly: vegetal at first, then revealing toasty notes. Gently acid, the palate is fresh. Rounded tannins create a well-structured finish. This wine could be served with ham on the bone.

Xavier Reverchon, EARL Chantemerle, 2, rue du Clos, 39800 Poligny, tel. 03.84.37.02.58, fax 03.84.37.00.58 by appt.

PIERRE RICHARD

Vin de Paille 1996★★★

□ 0.3 ha 1,00 100–149 F

A Vin de Paille made from Chardonnay, Poulsard, Savagnin and Trousseau grapes pressed on 1 March 1997, after being dried for five months. It has a seductive pale gold

JURA

colour. The nose has a breathtaking array of intense aromas; pineapples, peaches, tropical and crystallised fruits and vanilla are all present. The palate is equally impressive with a superb balance of alcohol and sweetness and a beeswax-tinged flavour at the finish – an absolute delight! On its own or served with foie gras, it is the apotheosis of a Vin de Paille.
Pierre Richard, 39210 Le Vernois, tel. 03.84.25.33.27, fax 03.84.25.36.13 by appt.

PIERRE RICHARD

Vin Jaune 1992★

□ 1 ha 1,00 150–199 F

At first, this Vin Jaune has a yeasty, cheese-rind nose, but when it is allowed to breathe, it develops a much more fruity character. Subtle aromas of walnuts and hazelnuts enrapture the taste-buds. This well-balanced wine should be decanted before serving so that its Vin Jaune flavours can develop fully. While it could be served with the traditional *coq au vin jaune*, it may be even better with morels on toast.
Pierre Richard, 39210 Le Vernois, tel. 03.84.25.33.27, fax 03.84.25.36.13 by appt.

MARIE-CLAUDE ROBELIN ET FILS

Vin Jaune 1992★★

□ 2 ha 2,000 150–199 F

Since 1999, Philippe and Didier Robelin have managed this family estate in conjunction with M. Quillot. The nose of this Vin Jaune is a little closed at first, but rapidly develops tobacco and hazelnut scents. The attack is fairly lively, but the rich, beautifully balanced palate immediately makes you forget that youthful trait. This is a fine, harmonious wine that will improve with time. A Vin Jaune that you must include in your cellar. When it has aged, it may be served with a creamy savoury tart.
Dom. Quillot-Robelin Fils, pl. de l'Eglise, 39210 Voiteur, tel. 03.84.44.69.12, fax 03.84.85.26.03 ev. day 10am–12 noon 2pm–7pm

DOM. DE SAVAGNY

Poulsard 1998★

□ 0.8 ha 4,000 30–49 F

Nearly a third of the production of this estate is used to produce a Chardonnay, the **97** of which, cited by the jury, needs to age a further three years in order to reach its full potential. More immediate pleasure can be derived from this richly coloured 98 Poulsard. The nose is musky at first, but later develops red berry aromas. The palate is ample and well-rounded with fine tannins. Attractive and well-constructed, it is a perfect example of a Jura red. It is for drinking within the next three years with a light supper.
Claude Rousselot-Pailley, 140, rue Neuve, 39210 Lavigny, tel. 03.84.25.38.38, fax 03.84.25.31.25 by appt.

JEAN TRESY ET FILS

Trousseau 1998★

■ 0.5 ha 2,800 30–49 F

Livestock farming is quite prevalent in this *département*. This estate, like many others, also had dairy cows up until 1985. Now it concentrates on wine production. Since 1998 Denis Trésy has been making wine from Trousseau grapes grown in the Mesnay commune. This is a cherry-coloured vintage, cellar-matured for ten months. The nose is fine if a little closed. Red-berry scents develop slowly. Ready for drinking now, it could accompany a roast guinea-fowl. The estate's **Cuvée Mont Royal 98**, 100% Chardonnay, was also cited for its acacia-flower nose and forthright palate. It is for drinking now.
Jean Trésy et Fils, rte des Longevernes, 39230 Passenans, tel. 03.84.85.22.40, fax 03.84.44.99.73, e-mail tresy.vin@wanadoo.fr by appt.

FRUITIERE VINICOLE DE VOITEUR

Savagnin 1995

□ 2 ha 10,000 70–99 F

Although the Fruitière Vinicole from Voiteur was created in the late 1950s, it has kept up with the times. This has been especially evident in recent vintages. The co-operative makes a range of wines from the Côtes du Jura, Crémant du Jura and the famous Château-Chalon AOCs. This year they have presented the jury with a pure Savagnin wine, made in vats and matured for three years in oak. It has a powerful nose of buttery and toasty scents with a hint of spice. The palate is equally rich with a slightly alcoholic tinge.
Fruitière vinicole de Voiteur, 60, rue de Nevy-sur-Seille, 39210 Voiteur, tel. 03.84.85.21.29, fax 03.84.85.27.67, e-mail voiteur@fruitiere-vinicole-voiteur.fr ev. day 9am–12 noon 1.30pm–6pm

Crémant du Jura

The AOC Crémant du Jura was recognised by a decree of 9 October 1995, and it applies to sweet *mousseux* wines made from grapes harvested within the production area of the AOC Côtes du Jura and vinified according to the strict rules applying to Vins Crémants. The approved red-grape varieties are the Poulsard (or Ploussard), Pinot Noir (known locally as Gros Noirien), Pinot Gris and Le Trousseau. The white varieties are the

Savagnin (known locally as Naturé), Chardonnay (known as Melon d'Arbois or Gamay Blanc). In 1999, a total of 12,873 hl (339,847 gal) was declared.

MARCEL CABELIER 1997

○ n.c. 100,320 30–49 F

The Compagnie des Grands Vins du Jura, selling under the Marcel Cabelier brand, is the main producer of Crémant du Jura. Made from Chardonnay grapes, this one is bright and clear with a fine ruff of bubbles. Relatively closed on the nose, it is lively and aromatic on the palate. A Crémant to drink as an apéritif.

Cie des Grands Vins du Jura, rte de Champagnole, 39570 Crançot, tel. 03.84.87.61.30, fax 03.84.48.21.36 Y by appt.

DOM. VICTOR CREDOZ 1998★★

○ 1.5 ha 6,000 30–49 F

Founded in 1859 by Victor Crédoz, this estate of more than 10 ha (25 acres) is currently being run by Daniel and Jean-Claude Crédoz. A fine stream of small bubbles rises to the surface of this fairly rich yellow 98. The nose has predominantly mineral scents. After an agreeable, gentle attack, the palate is ample and well-balanced with elegant aromas of citrus and berry fruits that dance on the tongue. A harmonious wine.

Dom. Victor Credoz, 39210 Menétru-le-Vignoble, tel. 06.80.43.17.44, fax 06.84.44.62.41 Y ev. day 8am–12 noon 1pm–7pm

RICHARD DELAY

Cuvée 2000 R. D. 1998★

○ n.c. 13,400 30–49 F

This is a pale straw-coloured wine with fine, persistent effervescence and an excellent nose of green apples and hazelnuts. The palate is fresh, thanks to subtly marked acidity and a touch of lemon, with an appley retronasal aroma, and good length. A fine Crémant du Jura.

Richard Delay, 37, rue du Château, 39570 Gevingey, tel. 03.84.47.46.78, fax 03.84.43.26.75 Y by appt.

MICHEL GAHIER 1998★★

○ 1 ha 3,000 30–49 F

This Crémant is the product of young vines. That could have been a handicap in the production of other types of wine, but it has not adversely affected this delightful sparkler. The bubbles are persistent, floating up in a beautiful lemon-yellow wine. Its flowery nose is very attractive. The palate, confirming the promise of the nose, is perfectly balanced with good acidity and delicate fruit. Green apples at the finish complete the aromatic fireworks of the 98. Quality and personality – an exceptional wine.

Michel Gahier, pl. de l'Eglise, 39600 Montigny-lès-Arsures, tel. 03.84.66.17.63 Y by appt.

DOM. GRAND FRERES

Brut Prestige

⊙ 7 ha 50,000 50–69 F

A Crémant with a fine mousse and an elegant, only slightly vinous, fruity nose. The harmonious palate is balanced by good fruit on the finish. This Crémant is a little timid, but would do well served as an apéritif.

Dom. Grand Frères, rue du Savagnin, 39230 Passenans, tel. 03.84.85.28.88, fax 03.84.44.67.47 Y ev. day 9am–12 noon 2pm–6pm; cl. Sat. Sun. in Jan. Feb.

CH. GREA 1998★★

○ 1 ha 4,000 30–49 F

A pretty, pale yellow wine with gently foaming little bubbles, this Crémant makes a good first impression. Lemon dominates the refreshing and lively citrus nose. Also lively on the palate, the wine finishes on a delicate, fruity note. Extremely elegant, it is a fine example of the appellation.

Nicolas Caire, Ch. Gréa, 39190 Rotalier, tel. 06.81.83.67.80, fax 06.84.25.05.47 Y by appt.

CH. DE L'ETOILE 1997

○ 2 ha 11,000 30–49 F

This négociant, whose premises are perched on Mont Muzard, has been making sparkling wines for a long time. The Vandelles diversified into making Crémant du Jura several years ago. The nose of this one shows modest vinosity, while the lively palate is dominated by the flavour of ripe apples.

Vandelle et Fils, GAEC Ch. de L'Etoile, 39570 L'Etoile, tel. 03.84.47.33.07, fax 03.84.24.93.52 Y by appt.

DOM. MARTIN-FAUDOT 1998

○ 0.8 ha 4,500 30–49 F

Jean-Pierre Martin and Michel Faudot run a family estate that distinguished itself in the fight against phylloxera in 1896. A bright yellow colour with green highlights, this Crémant has fine bubbles that rise to the top of the glass in a persistent stream. The nose is a little shy, but has finesse. Fruity aromas are apparent on the lively palate. An apéritif wine.

Dom. Martin-Faudot, 1, rue Bardenet, 39600 Mesnay, tel. 03.84.66.29.97, fax 03.84.66.29.84 Y by appt.

CH. DE PERSANGES 1997★

○ 1 ha 5,000 30–49 F

The Château from Persanges wine estate was established as recently as 1983. Only Chardonnay grapes are used in the making of their Crémant. Its bubbles are small, and the nose is a mixture of floral and green apple scents. These aromas are echoed by the palate, which has a good, lemony finish, adding an agreeably acidic note. Quite original, well-balanced, this wine would make a good springtime apéritif.

Ch. de Persanges, rte de Saint-Didier, 39570 L'Etoile, tel. 03.84.86.03.36, fax 03.84.47.46.56 ☑ Y ev. day 9.30am–12 noon 2.30pm–7pm; cl. Sun. Mon.
Lionnel-Marie d'Arc

DESIRE PETIT 1997*

◑	n.c.	4,000	30–49 F

The house motto is *petit de nom, grand de renom* ('little by name, large by fame'). This sparkling rosé has a fine, rich colour. With its raspberry nose and attractive fruity palate, the jury described it as a feminine wine. It is ready for drinking now.

Gérard et Marcel Petit, rue du Ploussard, 39600 Pupillin, tel. 03.84.66.01.20, fax 03.84.66.26.59 ☑ Y ev. day 9am–12 noon 2pm–7pm; groups by appt.

AUGUSTE PIROU 1997*

○	n.c.	10,000	30–49 F

The house of Henri Maire markets its Crémant under the Auguste Pirou label. The wine is not sold from the estate, but is widely distributed. Made only from Chardonnay grapes, it has a good colour and very fine bubbles. While most Crémants have floral or fruity scents, this one is predominantly vegetal with dried-flower notes – unusual but enjoyable. It fizzes gently on the palate and has a persistent finish of some finesse. An appealing, interesting wine.

Auguste Pirou, Les Caves Royales, 39600 Arbois, tel. 03.84.66.42.70, fax 03.84.66.42.42

ROLET PERE ET FILS 1996**

◑	1 ha	8,000	30–49 F

Last year, the jury fell in love with the estate's Cuvée 2000. This rosé, a tawny golden-pink wine with just the right degree of effervescence, also garnered an enthusiastic reception. The nose has a powerful, fruity, quince-jelly aroma – a wonderful, if slightly surprising, first impression of great finesse. The well-balanced palate, with good acidity, is quite forward in character. The quince-jelly aroma persists through to the finish. This very special vintage should be served as a dessert wine rather than as an apéritif.

Dom. Rolet Père et Fils, rte de Dole, 39600 Arbois, tel. 03.84.66.00.05, fax 03.84.37.47.41, e-mail rolet@wanadoo.fr ☑ Y by appt.

CLAUDE ROUSSELOT-PAILLEY 1998**

○	2 ha	16,000	30–49 F

This softly sparkling pale yellow wine makes a good first impression. Its nose is dominated by tropical fruit aromas but, as if to remind us that it was made in a temperate climate, it has overtones of green apples. While the palate is sufficiently acidic to lend this Crémant its liveliness, it also has hints of dried fruits. A wine to drink with friends.

Claude Rousselot-Pailley, 140, rue Neuve, 39210 Lavigny, tel. 03.84.25.38.38, fax 03.84.25.31.25 ☑ Y by appt.

ANDRE ET MIREILLE TISSOT 1998**

○	4.5 ha	25,000	30–49 F

Stéphane Tissot returned to the family estate in 1990. He and his father adopted organic viticulture in 1999. This wine was bottled in February 1999 and disgorged the following December. It sparkles with great finesse. The subtle nose has attractive floral notes but the full character of this Crémant is revealed on the palate. With just enough acidity to prove its quality, it is floral, lemony, very long and squeaky-clean. An elegant Crémant, perfect as an apéritif.

André et Mireille Tissot, 39600 Montigny-lès-Arsures, tel. 03.84.66.08.27, fax 03.84.66.25.08 ☑ Y by appt.
André et Stéphane Tissot

JACQUES TISSOT Cuvée 2000 1998

○	n.c.	20,000	30–49 F

This Crémant, made to celebrate the year 2000, will still be here well into the new millennium. Tiny bubbles flutter upwards in a pale gold wine. The nose has very subtle hints of white flowers. It is silky on the palate, revealing very enjoyable white flower and fresh fruit flavours.

Jacques Tissot, 39, rue de Courcelles, 39600 Arbois, tel. 03.84.66.14.27, fax 03.84.66.24.88 ☑ Y by appt.

L'Étoile

The village owes its name, 'The Star', to a certain type of fossilised plant found in the rocks of the area; cross-sections of the plant (a sea lily) form a five-pointed star. In 1999 the vineyards, which cover 76 ha (188 acres), produced 4,762 hl (125,717 gal) of white, yellow, straw and sparkling wine.

DOM. GENELETTI

Vin de Paille 1996★

☐ 0.5 ha 2,000 100–149 F

Michel Geneletti and his son have made a Vin de Paille from 80% Chardonnay, 10% Savagnin and 10% Poulsard grapes. A dark, leathery colour, this complex 96 has a rich and elegant nose. Aromas of dried fruits, quince jelly, citrus fruit and honey come in waves. The palate is attractive and well-balanced. A perfect match for chocolate cake.

Dom. Michel Geneletti et Fils, 373, rue de l'Eglise, 39570 L'Etoile, tel. 03.84.47.46.25, fax 03.84.47.38.18 ☒ Y by appt.

DOM. GENELETTI 1997

☐ 3 ha 12,000 30–49 F

The estate concentrates on producing white wines, primarily made from Chardonnay and Savagnin grapes. 'This is the smell of good wine,' noted one juror of this seductively coloured Etoile, before proceeding to identify honey and apple scents. Interesting floral aromas emerge on the palate. This is a wine that should age well.

Dom. Michel Geneletti et Fils, 373, rue de l'Eglise, 39570 L'Etoile, tel. 03.84.47.46.25, fax 03.84.47.38.18 ☒ Y by appt.

CH. DE L'ETOILE 1997★★

☐ 12 ha 20,000 30–49 F

Over the years this estate, which was bought by Auguste Vandell in 1883, has had many wines selected as **coups de coeur.* Here is yet another one. 'A gorgeous colour, 24-carat gold', wrote one taster. We haven't been able to confirm this, but we do know that this wine is a treasure! The complex nose of linden, white flowers and honey, with a hint of burnt toast, is followed by a very good attack and a rounded palate. Superbly sturctured, it has a rich floral aroma. Keep for at least two years. **At the time of going to press we were regrettably unable to include a picture of the label.*

Vandelle et Fils, GAEC Ch. de L'Etoile, 39570 L'Etoile, tel. 03.84.47.33.07, fax 03.84.24.93.52 ☒ Y by appt.

CH. DE L'ETOILE

Vin Jaune 1992★

☐ 5 ha 15,000 100–149 F

A deep golden colour and heavy tears, or 'legs': this Vin Jaune has substance. The nose is rich and complex, showing walnut, almond, spice and coffee scents with buttery overtones. The thoroughbred palate is structured and lengthy. We are thrilled to have tasted a wine that is the epitome of good Vin Jaune.

Vandelle et Fils, GAEC Ch. de L'Etoile, 39570 L'Etoile, tel. 03.84.47.33.07, fax 03.84.24.93.52 ☒ Y by appt.

DOM. DE MONTBOURGEAU

1997★

☐ 6 ha 40,000 30–49 F

Nicole Deriaux is carrying on in the footsteps of her father, Jean Gros. A crystal-clear pale yellow with fine vinosity, this wine has a seductive and complex nose of honey, ripe apples and dried fruit. Although the palate is a little unctuous, it is a very well-made wine overall. It should be served with white meats.

Jean Gros, Dom. de Montbourgeau, 39570 L'Etoile, tel. 03.84.47.32.96, fax 03.84.24.41.44 ☒ Y by appt.

DOM. DE MONTBOURGEAU

Vin Jaune 1993

☐ 1.5 ha 2,000 150–199 F

In February 2000, Etoile held the third Perceé du Vin Jaune, a festival held in celebration of this inimitable wine. This example, from the Montbourgeau estate, has a fairly subtle nose that promises to evolve. Like all of the Vins Jaune from this vintage, it is a little rough on the palate. It needs to age for a year or two.

Jean Gros, Dom. de Montbourgeau, 39570 L'Etoile, tel. 03.84.47.32.96, fax 03.84.24.41.44 ☒ Y by appt.

DOM. DE MONTBOURGEAU

Vin de Paille 1996★★

☐ 0.5 ha 2,000 100–149 F

This wine is a **coup de coeur.* Its glorious amber colour is an achievement in itself. Fine and subtle, the nose reveals a blend of honey, wax and dried fruits. The palate is full-bodied and perfectly balanced with prune, quince and fig flavours all present. A wine destined for drinking with foie gras. **At the time of going to press we were regrettably unable to include a picture of the label.*

Jean Gros, Dom. de Montbourgeau, 39570 L'Etoile, tel. 03.84.47.32.96, fax 03.84.24.41.44 ☒ Y by appt.

CH. DE PERSANGES

Vin de Paille 1995

☐ 0.5 ha 2,000 70–99 F

A Vin de Paille made from a blend of mostly white Chardonnay and Savagnin grapes with a small quantity of red Poulsard. Its dark apricot colour is very attractive. The nose is a subtle and fairly classic blend of dried fruit aromas. The palate is not very long, but pleasant nonetheless.

Ch. de Persanges, rte de Saint-Didier, 39570 L'Etoile, tel. 03.84.86.03.36, fax 03.84.47.46.56 ☒ Y ev. day 9.30am–12 noon 2.30pm–7pm; cl. Sun. Mon.

SAVOY

From the French shore of Lake Geneva to the Isère valley in the departments of Savoie and Haute-Savoie, the vineyards occupy favourable lower slopes of the Alps. The vineyard is constantly expanding, currently nearly 1,800 ha (4,446 acres), and year on year, produces about 130,000 hl (3,432,000 gal). The individual wine-growing areas together form a complex mosaic dictated by the shapes of the various valleys, which are planted in bigger or smaller islets of cultivation. This geographical diversity is echoed in local climatic variations, which are either exaggerated by the relief or tempered by the proximity of Lake Geneva and the Lac du Bourget.

Vin de Savoie and Roussette de Savoie are regional appellations, used nearly everywhere; they may be followed by the name of a cru, but apply exclusively to still wines which, for the Roussettes, mean whites only. Wines from Crépy and Sayssel each have a right to their own appellation.

Because of the widely dispersed vineyards, numerous grape varieties are in use but, in fact, many are planted in only limited amounts: this is particularly true of Pinot Noir and Chardonnay. The main varieties are two reds and four whites, alongside others that produce specifically local wines. Gamay, imported from neighbouring Beaujolais post-phylloxera, produces fresh, light red wines to be drunk in the year of production. Mondeuse, a local, quality variety, produces full-bodied red wines, particularly in Arbin, where it is the only variety under cultivation. Pre-phylloxera this was the most widely grown variety in Savoy, and it is to be hoped that it will one day regain its rightful place, because the wines it produces are of good quality with terrific character. Jacquère is the most widely planted white variety; it produces fresh, light white to be drunk young. Altesse, a very delicate variety, typically Savoyard, produces wines sold as Roussette de Savoie. Finally, Roussanne, locally known as Bergeron, also produces white wines of very high quality, especially in Chignin, where it is grown with the cross variety Chignin-Bergeron.

Crépy

Chasselas is the only variety planted in the 80 ha (198 acres) Crépy vineyard, as it is along both the French and Swiss shores of Lake Geneva. It produces about 4,800 hl (126,720 gal) of light white wine. This little region obtained its AOC in 1948.

DOM. DE LA GRANDE CAVE

Réserve La Goutte d'Or Crépytant 1998★

□ 33 ha 160,000 30–49 F

First, Claude Mercier's grandfather and later, his father, campaigned to get Crépy recognised as an AOC. The estate now comprises 39 ha (96 acres). Here, they take their time and mature their wine slowly; the 98 spent a year in vat, and six months in barrel. This vintage has all the characteristics of its appellation. The nose is floral at first, slowly developing fresh walnut and sweet almond scents. The rounded attack is sustained by a good level of acidity. A wine that is just beginning to develop. We have confidence in its future.

STEF Claude Mercier, Dom. de La Grande Cave de Crépy, 74140 Ballaison, tel. 04.50.94.01.23, fax 04.50.94.19.86 Y by appt.

DOM. LE CHALET 1999★

□ 2 ha 13,000 30–49 F

Jean Métral purchased the estate in 1962. Ten years later, his son Jacques took over the operation. He has made a Crépy that clearly has a richly aromatic future ahead of it, but

which, on the day of tasting, remained a little closed. A powerful, rich impression dominates the attack, which is followed by a touch of preserved fruits on the finish, lending the wine an overall roundness. It should be ready to drink by the time the *Guide* is published.
🗝 Jacques Métral, Dom. Le Chalet, 74140 Loisin, tel. 04.50.94.10.60,
fax 04.50.94.18.39 ☑ 🍷 ev. day except Sun. 9am–12 noon 2pm–7pm

Vin de Savoie

The vineyard classed as Appellation Vin de Savoie is generally to be found on the ancient glacial moraines (continuous linear deposits of rocks and gravel left by glaciers), or on scree, which because of its geographical dispersal contributes to great diversity in the wines; these are frequently identified by adding a local denomination to the regional appellation. On the French shore of Lake Geneva, in Marin, Ripaille and Marignan, Chasselas produces light, white, often slightly fizzy wines, which are best drunk young. Other areas grow different varieties and, depending on the soil types, produce white or red wines. From north to south, from Ayze to the banks of the Arve river, sparkling and fizzy whites give way (south of the Appellation Seyssel) to the red wines of the Lac du Bourget and La Chautagne, where the reds in particular have a marked character. South of Chambéry, the flanks of Mont Granier produce fresh white wines such as the Apremont and the Cru des Abymes, a vineyard established on a site where the mountain collapsed in 1248, killing thousands of

Savoie

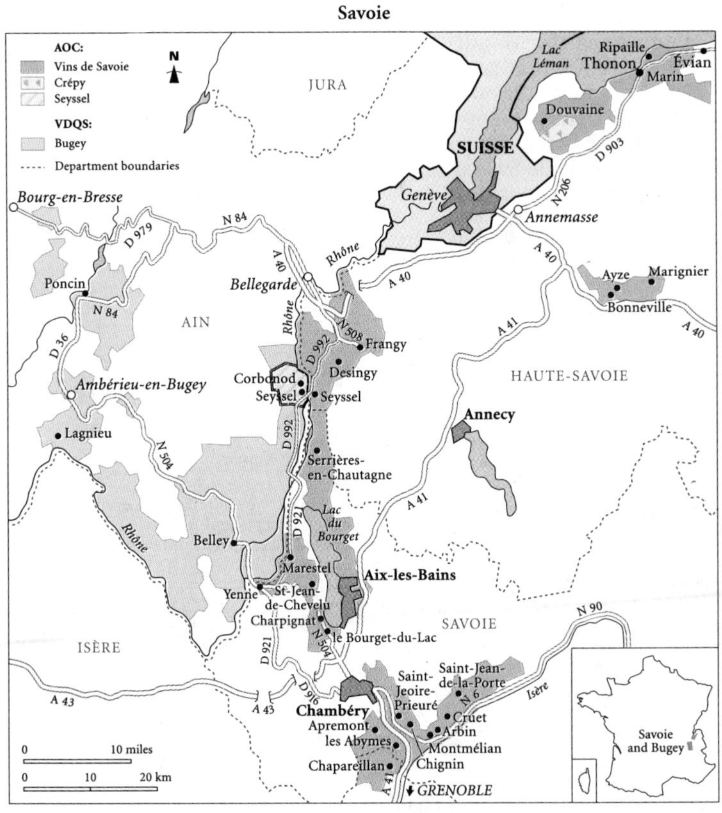

people. Facing it, Monterminod has been smothered by housing developments, but has retained a vineyard which produces remarkable wines; next to it lie the vineyards of Saint-Jeoire-Prieuré, on the far side of Challes-les-Eaux, then Chignin, where the fame of the Bergeron grape is absolutely justified. Going up the Isère on the right bank, the south-east-facing slopes are occupied by the crus of Montmélian, Arbin, Cruet and Saint-Jean-de-la-Porte.

Produced only in limited quantities, around 130,000 hl (3,432,000 gal), in a region very popular with tourists, the Savoie wines are mainly drunk young, mostly locally, and sold into a market where demand sometimes outstrips supply. The white Savoy wines go well with freshwater and sea fish, while the reds (made from Gamay) are very versatile. It is a shame to drink the Mondeuse reds too young as they need several years to develop and soften: these high-quality wines accompany strongly flavoured dishes such as game, the excellent Tomme de Savoie and the famous Reblochon cheeses.

DOM. DES ANGES Aligoté 1999

☐ 1.5 ha 13,000 20–29 F

This 99 has a powerful nose with tropical fruit aromas. The jury enjoyed its harmonious palate, sustained by a controlled liveliness that indicates it may be suited to ageing. Open, straightforward, genial, this wine would be best served alongside grilled fish or white meat.

Angelier Frères, Hameau des Murs, 73800 Les Marches, tel. 04.79.28.03.41, fax 04.79.71.52.59 ev. day 8am–8pm

DOM. BELLUARD FILS

Gringet 1998★

☐ 4 ha 18,000 30–49 F

The Belluard family farms 13 ha (32 acres) of vines in Ayze. For several years now, they have concentrated on producing still wines in a region that focuses on sparklers. This one is made from Gringet grapes, a local variety similar to the Savagnin that is rarely found outside the Arve valley. The jury was beguiled by its aniseed nose and a fine attack supported by fruity aromas. You will enjoy introducing your friends to this original and very rare wine.

Dom. Belluard, Les Chennevaz, 74130 Ayze, tel. 04.50.97.05.63 ev. day except Sun. 8am–12 noon 2pm–6pm

BLARD ET FILS

Abymes Cuvée Hubert Vieilles vignes 1999★

☐ 0.3 ha 30,000 30–49 F

A few years ago, the Blard estate invested in modern storage cellars to ensure that their wines were able to maintain their initial quality. That is the case with the 99, which has straw-coloured highlights and damson scents. A very good example of its appellation, the palate displays a good balance of fruit and acidity. A well-structured wine that will suit grilled fish or white meat dishes.

Blard et Fils, Le Darbé, 73800 Les Marches, tel. 06.11.50.30.37, fax 06.79.28.01.35 by appt.

DOM. G. ET G. BOUVET

Méthode traditionnelle Brut 1997★★

○ 1.5 ha 10,000 30–49 F

A masterfully made sparkling wine from a 22 ha (54-acre) estate in Fréterive in the Isère valley. Both the look of the wine, with its fine, plentiful bubbles, and the lemony, fruity nose with bergamot notes are seductive. An elegant bottle, ample with the requisite touch of acidity that results in a remarkably well-balanced palate. A classy apéritif.

Dom. G. et G. Bouvet, Le Villard, 73250 Fréterive, tel. 04.79.28.54.11, fax 04.79.28.51.97 ev. day except Sun. 8am–12 noon 2pm–7pm

EUGENE CARREL ET FILS

Jongieux Mondeuse 1999★★★

■ 2 ha 8,000 20–29 F

A deep colour, powerful aromas that are both fresh and spicy, and a lengthy finish combine to make this an exceptional wine. Eugène Carrel destems most of his harvest. This has resulted in superb palate where silky tannins deliver waves of harmonious flavour. Unanimously elected a *coup de coeur.*

GAEC Eugène Carrel et Fils, 73170 Jongieux, tel. 04.79.44.00.20, fax 04.79.44.03.06 ev. day except Sun. 8am–7pm

EUGENE CARREL ET FILS

Jongieux Gamay 1999★★

■ 5 ha 10,000 20–29 F

The jury declared this deep purple wine to be of exceptional quality. Its robustness on the palate equals the intensity of its aromas, a

nix of red berries, toast and liquorice. While it was a little rustic still on the day it was tasted, it had all the hallmarks of a great wine. It should be perfect by the time the *Guide* is published. A well-deserved double star!
🔑 GAEC Eugène Carrel et Fils, 73170 Jongieux, tel. 04.79.44.00.20, fax 04.79.44.03.06 ☑
Y ev. day except Sun. 8am–7pm

CAVE DE CHAUTAGNE

Chautagne 1999★

■ 40 ha 300,000 30–49 F

Newly modernised facilities enable the Cave de Chautagne successfully to vinify harvests from all parts of this diverse region in the foothills of the French Alps. The soils are principally marl on a gravel substrate, which suits both red and white grape varieties. You will be seduced by the ample palate of this Gamay. Its silky tannins and fruity bouquet will marry well with grilled meats.
🔑 Cave de Chautagne, Saumont, 73310 Ruffieux, tel. 04.79.54.27.12, fax 04.79.54.51.37 ☑ Y ev. day 9am–12 noon 2pm–7pm; cl. 30–31 Aug.

C. DELALEX

Marin Clos de Pont 1999★

□ n.c. 12,000 30–49 F

Joined in 1998 by his son Samuel, Claude Delalex, along with several other producers, has contributed to the rejuvenation of the Marin vineyard. On a terrace overlooking Lake Léman, it has its own appellation. Chasselas grapes produce a wine that was slightly closed on the day it was tasted, but showed promise. The dominant aroma is that of lychees. It is full and lively on the palate, and sustained by good acidity. This bottle should be kept for a few years.
🔑 Cave Delalex, EARL La Grappe dorée – Marinel, 74200 Marin, tel. 04.50.71.45.82, fax 04.50.71.06.74 ☑ Y by appt.

DOM. DUPASQUIER

Jacquère 1998★

□ 3 ha 18,000 30–49 F

This wine-maker prefers to harvest his grapes quite late and practises 'slow oenology'. Here he has made a white wine that has impressive ageing potential, especially considering that it is made from Jacquère grapes, normally renowned for producing short-lived wines. The 98 will certainly hold for a few years. Its empyreumatic aromas and striking palate, sustained by residual sweetness, give it quite an unusual style. One to try.
🔑 Dom. Dupasquier, Aimavigne, 73170 Jongieux, tel. 04.79.44.02.23, fax 04.79.44.03.56 ☑ Y by appt.

ANDRE GENOUX Arbin Mondeuse

Cuvée des Grands Lacs 1999★

■ 0.5 ha 2,000 50–69 F

André Genoux vinifies his half-hectare (1.2 acres) of vines with as much care as others take over far larger harvests. After all, he is descended from a line of wine-makers that dates back to 1248! This vintage comes from Arbin, a region famous for the Mondeuse grape. Its dark red colour and powerful aroma of berry fruits make this a generous and approachable wine. Only when you taste it do you realise that it also has serious ageing potential. Already well-balanced, it has extremely well-structured tannins that bode well for the future.
🔑 André Genoux, 450, chem. des Moulins, 73800 Arbin, tel. 04.79.65.24.32, fax 04.79.65.24.32 ☑ Y by appt.

CHARLES GONNET

Chignin 1999★

□ 5 ha 45,000 30–49 F

Charles Gonnet, who trained as an engineer, has made this wine from vines that are 40 years old. It is an elegant, classy 99 with a mineral nose. Slightly lemony on the palate, it gives an overall impression of great finesse and balanced structure. Typical of its appellation, it could be drunk as an apéritif or with freshwater fish.
🔑 Charles-Humbert Gonnet, Chef-lieu, 73800 Chignin, tel. 04.79.28.09.89, e-mail charles.gonnet@wanadoo.fr ☑ Y by appt.

DOM. LA COMBE DES GRAND'VIGNES Chignin 1999★

□ 5 ha 40,000 30–49 F

In 1997, Denis Berthollier took over the family estate and began concentrating on getting the best out of his Chignin grapes grown on the limestone scree of the Bauges massif. This wine, made from 40-year-old vines, has an aroma dominated by the scent of white flowers. Forthright on the palate, it finishes on a classically refreshing note. A typical Savoie white.
🔑 EARL La Combe des Grand'Vignes, Le Viviés, 73800 Chignin, tel. 04.79.28.11.75, fax 04.79.28.16.22, e-mail berthollier@chignin.com ☑
Y ev. day 8am–12 noon 2pm–7pm
🔑 Denis Berthollier

LE VIGNERON SAVOYARD

Les Abymes Les Pierrailles ensoleillées 1999

□ 8.9 ha 12,600 30–49 F

This wine was selected for the quality of its nose, which has citrus notes enlivened by floral scents. Very forthcoming, it is a credit to its makers. The palate is still lively and needs to soften, but when it does, this 99 will be a persuasive ambassador for Savoyard wines.
🔑 Le Vigneron Savoyard, rte du Crozet, 73190 Apremont, tel. 04.79.28.33.23, fax 04.79.28.26.17, e-mail vigneron-savoyard@epicuria.fr ☑ Y ev. day except Sun. Mon. 8am–12 noon 2pm–6pm; cl. 1st–20 May

MICHEL MAGNE Abymes 1999

□ 2.84 ha 7,000 30–49 F

Michel Magne has run this 12 ha (30-acre) estate since 1998. He has made a 99 that is highly typical of its appellation. Notes of passion-fruit, with mineral overtones, can be detected on its very open nose. A lively attack and good length on the palate are let down by a touch of bitterness at the finish. An adolescent wine that should be perfect by the time the *Guide* is published.

🔑 Michel Magne, Saint-André, 38530 Chapareillan, tel. 04.79.28.07.91, fax 04.79.28.17.96 ☑ Y by appt.

MICHEL, JEAN-PAUL ET SAMUEL NEYROUD Mondeuse 1998★★★

■ 1,5 ha 8,000 30–49 F

What a revelation! The Haute-Savoie, a region better known for its white wines, has produced a stunning Mondeuse. Dazzling and opulent on the nose and palate, it delighted the jurors. This is the product of old vines growing on the slopes of Desingy and Frangy. The very complex nose has notes of musk and vanilla. A wine well-equipped for ageing.

🔑 Michel et Jean-Paul Neyroud, GAEC Les Aricoques, 74270 Desingy, tel. 04.50.32.22.73, fax 04.50.44.75.42 ☑ Y by appt.

DOM. PERRIER PERE ET FILS

Abymes Cuvée Prestige 1999★

□ 9 ha 20,000 20–29 F

A 20 ha (49-acre) estate whose vineyards grow on the scree of Mont Granier and around Lac Saint-André. It was established in 1853. The Perrier family also runs a négociant business. This vintage comes from the family holdings. It has an attractive aroma of tropical fruits intertwined with mineral notes. Although the palate is a little heavy, owing to the presence of residual sugar, it is nevertheless a very well-made wine from a high-quality harvest. It should be drunk right now.

🔑 SCEA dom. Perrier Père et Fils, Saint-André, 73800 Les Marches, tel. 04.79.28.11.45, fax 04.79.28.09.91 ☑ Y ev. day except Sun. 9am–12 noon 2pm–6pm

DOM. MARC PORTAZ

Apremont 1999

□ 0.7 ha 5,000 30–49 F

In Isère, only the commune of Chapareillan is designated a part of the Vin de Savoie appellation. Marc Portaz and his son do their best to demonstrate its merits. They have made a classic Apremont with a delightfully flowery nose. The palate is well-balanced from start to finish. A wine with all the characteristics of its appellation and its vintage.

🔑 Dom. Marc Portaz, allée du Colombier, 38530 Chapareillan, tel. 04.76.45.23.51, fax 04.76.45.57.60 ☑ Y by appt.

🔑 Jean-Marc Portaz

ANDRE ET MICHEL QUENARD

Chignin Bergeron Coteau de Torméry 1999★★

□ 6.5 ha 15,000 50–69 F

The wines of André and Michel Quénard have always been popular with the French jury. Over the years, their Chignins have several times been selected as *coups de coeur*. This year's selection is a *grand vin*, a Bergeron directly descended from the great 96. Made from grapes harvested in several pickings, it will not reach its full potential for quite some years. The nose, with a marked scent of figs, announces a richly aromatic palate that will only be fully revealed when the wine matures. Very concentrated and structured, this is a Savoie for drinking with foie gras.

🔑 André et Michel Quénard, Torméry, 73800 Chignin, tel. 04.79.28.12.75, fax 04.79.28.19.36 ☑ Y by appt.

ANDRE ET MICHEL QUENARD

Chignin Mondeuse Vieilles vignes Coteau de Torméry 1999★

■ 1.38 ha 7,000 30–49 F

André and Michel Quénard also make very good red wines. Witness this Mondeuse made from a harvest of partially destemmed whole grapes. Already very refined, the 99 has a complex nose and a well-balanced attack. It is powerful and long, and is ready to drink now with red meat or game.

🔑 André et Michel Quénard, Torméry, 73800 Chignin, tel. 04.79.28.12.75, fax 04.79.28.19.36 ☑ Y by appt.

LES FILS DE RENE QUENARD

Chignin 1999★

■ 1.15 ha 7,000 30–49 F

Very few Savoie wines are made from Pinot Noir grapes. René Quénard's son has made it a point of honour to succeed with this grape. Here is his 99, which has a scent of morello cherries. The palate is round and delicate with a slight liquorice flavour. An agreeable wine that will be perfect by the time the *Guide* is published, it should be served with game.

🔑 Les Fils de René Quénard, Le Cellier des Tours, 73800 Chignin, tel. 04.79.28.01.15, fax 04.79.28.18.98 ☑ Y by appt.

PHILIPPE RAVIER

Chignin Bergeron 1999★

☐ 3.6 ha 20,000 30–49 F

When it was tasted, the 99 was considered too youthful, but this is a wine with great promise. The rather vigorous initial impression masks a wine that is capable of ageing well. Rich, with dried-fruit scents, it fills the palate with its body, liveliness and slight bitterness. This wine can be locked away in your cellar with complete confidence and forgotten about for several years.

Philippe Ravier, Léché, 73800 Myans, tel. 04.79.28.17.75, fax 04.79.28.17.75 ☑ by appt.

PHILIPPE RAVIER

Mondeuse 1999★

■ 0.8 ha 5,000 20–29 F

A garnet wine with purple highlights, this Mondeuse has a very open fruity and spicy nose. Young, impetuous tannins attack the palate. This wine has the necessary structure and body to age well, and should fulfil its excellent potential in three or four years' time.

Philippe Ravier, Léché, 73800 Myans, tel. 04.79.28.17.75, fax 04.79.28.17.75 ☑ by appt.

BERNARD ET CHRISTOPHE RICHEL Apremont Vieilles vignes 1999★★

☐ 1.06 ha 8,000 30–49 F

The grandfather, Joseph Richel, planted the St-Baldolph slopes. The father, Bernard, focused the estate on wine-making, and Christophe, the grandson, enlarged the vineyards to cover almost 9 ha (22 acres). Made from 50-year-old vines, this Apremont is an exceptional wine. A very complex aroma is dominated by the scent of white flowers. The ampleness of the palate carries through to a persistent finish, which displays more the characteristics of the locality than of the grape variety. This bottle will be ready to drink by the time the *Guide* is published.

Bernard et Christophe Richel, rte de Fontaine-Lamée, 73190 Saint-Baldoph, tel. 04.79.28.36.55, fax 04.79.28.36.55 ☑ by appt.

DOM. DE ROUZAN

Gamay 1999★

■ n.c. 3,500 30–49 F

Denis Fortin has used semi-carbonic maceration to ferment his Gamay grapes. The resulting wine has the fragrant nose characteristic of Gamay. A harmonious and balanced wine that has reached its full potential, it could be served with charcuterie or white meat dishes.

Denis Fortin, 152, chem. de la Mairie, 73190 Saint-Baldoph, tel. 04.79.28.25.58, fax 04.79.28.21.63 ☑ by appt.

GUY TOURNOUD

Abymes 1999★★

☐ 2.5 ha n.c. 30–49 F

A wine that was judged almost good enough to be a *coup de coeur*. Despite being quite young, Guy Tournoud's 99 already has the typical style of an Abymes, the product of the Mont Granier sink-hole. A particularly fine nose has mineral notes. The attack is characteristic of the appellation, and the palate is very well-balanced with a fairly long minerally and lemony finish. Ready to drink now, the wine could equally well be kept for a few years.

Guy Tournoud, Bellecombe, 38530 Chapareillan, tel. 04.76.45.22.05, fax 04.76.45.22.05 ☑ by appt.

CHARLES TROSSET

Arbin Mondeuse Cuvée 2000 Prestige des Arpents 1999

■ 3.6 ha 30,000 30–49 F

Practitioners of 'slow œnology', the Trosset brothers have managed to make a 99 Arbin that already has quite an open nose with blackcurrant and red-berry scents. The palate is dominated by tannins that seemed a little rustic still when the wine was tasted, and the jury would have liked more substance at the finish. By the time the *Guide* is published, this Mondeuse will have matured to its full potential.

Charles Trosset, chem. des Moulins, 73800 Arbin, tel. 04.79.84.30.99, fax 04.79.84.30.99 ☑ by appt.

JOSEPH TROSSET Arbin 1999★★

■ 1 ha 5,000 30–49 F

Although this Mondeuse has been bottled under the name of Joseph Trosset, it has been made by the same establishment as the wine in the previous entry. This vintage has been made from less than fully ripe grapes, which has resulted in a more concentrated wine with a powerful palate. It is well-suited to ageing. The tannins are already ripe, though, which means that those of you who are impatient to try this remarkable wine can do so at around the time of publication.

Joseph Trosset, Les Rochettes, 73800 Arbin, tel. 04.79.84.05.22 ☑ by appt.

DOM. DE VERONNET

Chautagne 1999

■ 2.5 ha 22,000 30–49 F

The head of this 7.5 ha (19-acre) estate, Alain Bosson, bottles his own wines and sells them directly to the public. Here he has made a Chautagne de Gamay grapes. The well-structured palate of this 99 has aromas of crème brûlée with hints of raspberries. The bouquet is persistent and gives the wine a particularly rich finish. For drinking at the time of publication.

Alain Bosson, Dom. de Veronnet, 73310 Serrières-en-Chautagne, tel. 04.79.63.73.11, fax 04.79.63.73.11, e-mail alain.bosson@wanadoo.fr ☑ by appt.

SAVOY

DOM. VIALLET

Chignin Bergeron Les Bouillettes 1999★

☐ 1.2 ha 12,000 30–49 F

Established in Apremont, Pierre Viallet crossed the valley to cultivate several hectares of Roussanne grapes on his south-facing slopes around Chignin. The harvest has produced a rich, fat 99 with an aroma of crystallised fruits – a well-made wine. The slight bitterness noted on the day it was tasted should soften after a few months in the cellar. By the time the *Guide* is published, it should be ready to accompany a sophisticated dinner.

GAEC dom. Viallet, rte de Myans, 73190 Apremont, tel. 04.79.28.33.29, fax 04.79.28.20.68 by appt.

DOM. JEAN VULLIEN

Mondeuse Cuvée particulière Elevé en fût de chêne 1999★★

■ 2.4 ha 18,000 30–49 F

With his two sons, David and Olivier, who joined him in 1999, Jean Vullien cultivates 18 ha (44 acres) of vineyards. This is one of his most promising wines. A sumptuous garnet colour, it is immediately charming with a rich aroma of morello cherries and spicy overtones. The aromas are carried on to the palate, which has strong, still slightly aggressive tannins that nonetheless indicate the wine should keep well.

EARL dom. Jean Vullien, La Grande Roue, 73250 Fréterive, tel. 04.79.28.61.58, fax 04.79.28.69.37

ev. day except Sun. 8.30am–12 noon 2pm–7pm

Roussette de Savoie

Made exclusively from the Altesse grape (following a new decree dated 18 March 1998), the Roussette de Savoie is mainly found in Frangy, along the River Usses, in Monthoux and in Marestel, on the shore of the Lac du Bourget. The habit of serving the Roussettes too young is a shame since, as they open with age, they are splendid with fish and white meat dishes, and form a perfect accompaniment to the local Beaufort cheese.

DOM. G. BLANC ET FILS 1999

☐ 0.6 ha 5,300 20–29 F

Since Gilbert Blanc's son, Willy, began managing the estate in 1996, it has concentrated on marketing its wines and encouraging visitors. The product of sound wine-making knowledge and good technology, this is an attractive wine, lacy and suave. It has a fruity and floral aroma and a subtly harmonious palate – a style one might call 'soft chamber music'. A sophisticated wine that could be served as an apéritif before a sumptuous dinner.

Dom. Gilbert Blanc et Fils, 73, chem. de Revaison, 73190 Saint-Baldoph, tel. 04.79.28.36.90, fax 04.79.28.36.90, e-mail domaine.blanc@wanadoo.fr

ev. day except Tue. Sun. 9am–12 noon 3pm–7pm

GILBERT BOUCHEZ 1999★

☐ 0.95 ha n.c. 30–49 F

The product of one of the most beautiful estates in Savoie, this wine is complex on both the nose and palate. It announces itself with an aroma of gingerbread. The palate is structured, with gentle acidity. Unctuous and long, this is a wine of real class, and one that may be cellared with great confidence in its future.

Gilbert Bouchez, Saint-Laurent, 73800 Cruet, tel. 04.79.84.30.91, fax 04.79.84.30.50 by appt.

FRANCOIS CARREL ET FILS

Marestel Cuvée Prestige 1998★

☐ 0.8 ha n.c. 30–49 F

François Carrel and his son Eric, who joined him in 1993, manage this 10 ha (25-acre) estate established in 1948. Their Roussette has the complex aromas and flavours characteristic of the Marestel terroir. Its nose is moderately fragrant with a marked buttery scent. The attack leads into a first-class palate. It is a quality wine that should be kept for a while so that its body and acidity can come into balance, whereupon it could be served with the finest dishes.

François et Eric Carrel, GAEC de la Rosière, 73170 Jongieux, tel. 04.79.44.02.20, fax 04.79.44.03.73 by appt.

SYLVAIN CHEVALLIER

Marestel 1998★★

☐ 1 ha 8,500 30–49 F

Sylvain Chevallier took over the family estate in 1990. He is the fourth generation to work this land. This wine is made from Roussette grapes grown on the Marestel terroir. A sumptuous nose of peaches and pears has a subtle overtone of vanilla. Nor does the palate disappoint: a frank and fresh attack is followed by an ample, gently acidic palate. That acidity bodes well for the future. A magnificent Savoyard wine whose development will be eagerly watched.

Sylvain Chevallier, Le Haut, 73170 Jongieux, tel. 04.79.44.03.30, fax 04.79.44.03.13

ev. day 8am–7.30pm

LA CAVE DU PRIEURE

Marestel 1999★

☐ 2 ha 15,000 30–49 F

A small estate of just 2 ha (5 acres) that had very successful vintages in 1994 and 1996, both of which were selected as *coups de coeur*. The 99 has all the characteristics of a quality Roussette. The nose is a little closed, but already has fairly complex hazelnut aromas. A frank and fresh attack is followed by a palate tasting of dried fruits and walnuts. A harmonious and elegant wine, it should be ready to drink by the time the *Guide* is published.

Raymond Barlet et Fils, La Cave du Prieuré, 73170 Jongieux, tel. 04.79.44.02.22, fax 04.79.44.03.07 ev. day except Sun. 2pm–7pm

Le Bugey

Bugey AOVDQS

Located in the Ain department, the Bugey vineyard occupies the lower slopes of the Jura from Bourg-en-Bresse to Ambérieu-en-Bugey (to the extreme south of Revermont), as well as those which run down to the right bank of the Rhône, from Seyssel to Lagnieu. A large vineyard at one time, it is now smaller and more dispersed.

For the most part, it stands on fairly steep slopes of limestone scree. The grape varieties reflect the area's famous neighbours: for reds, the Jura Poulsard – restricted to blending with sparkling wines from Cerdon – is grown alongside Mondeuse from Savoie and Pinot Noir and Gamay from Burgundy. For the whites, Jacquère and Altesse compete with Chardonnay (the most widely grown variety) and Aligoté, as well as Molette, the only truly local variety.

ANGELOT

Chardonnay 1999★

☐ 2.5 ha 25,000 30–49 F

Philippe and Eric Angelot run a 20 ha (49-acre) family estate established by their parents. They have made a wine from Chardonnay grapes, a variety well adapted to the soil of Bugey. It has a fresh, open nose with hints of toast. The palate is reasonably long, with a well-managed liveliness that gives it elegance. A good wine, in the style of its appellation, it will be ready to drink by the time the *Guide* is published.

GAEC maison Angelot, 01300 Marignieu, tel. 04.79.42.18.84, fax 04.79.42.13.61 by appt.

CHRISTIAN BOLLIET

Cerdon Pétillant Méthode ancestrale Cuvée spéciale 1999★

◑ 0.44 ha 4,500 30–49 F

Christian Bollet has used all his expertise to craft this gently sparkling wine from Poulsard grapes. Regular readers will recall recommendations from previous vintages. The 99 is still a little closed, with just a hint of menthol on the nose. The palate has a good balance of liveliness and residual sugar. A perfect example of Cerdon, this wine has a nice touch of originality.

Christian Bolliet, hameau des Bôches, 01450 Saint-Alban, tel. 04.74.37.37.21, fax 04.74.37.37.69 by appt.

BONNARD FILS

Roussette du Bugey 1998★

☐ 0.36 ha 2,500 30–49 F

Montagnieu is considered a *microterroir* of this appellation. Altesse grapes fare very well on its exposed limestone slopes. The Bonnard brothers have used the fruit of vines that are more than 50 years old to make a very elegant wine with a richly fragrant nose showing notes of crystallised fruits. The palate is developing complexity, with a mixture of fruit aromas and a hint of toast at the finish. A charming wine with some residual sugar, which suggests that it should be put away for several years in order for it to mellow.

🗝 GAEC Bonnard Fils, Crept, 01470 Seillonnaz, tel. 04.74.36.73.11, fax 04.74.36.14.50 ☑ 🍷 by appt.

LE CAVEAU BUGISTE

Brut Blanc de blancs Méthode traditionnelle 1997★

○ 3 ha 20,000 50–69 F

In 1967, six wine-growers with a total of 35 ha (86 acres) of vines joined forces to create the Caveau Bugiste. This year, they offer a very elegant and mature sparkling wine. The bubbles are very fine, and the appealing nose is scented with white fruits, heightened with the aroma of brioche. The round and harmonious palate makes this an excellent apéritif wine.

🗝 Le Caveau Bugiste, 01350 Vongnes, tel. 04.79.87.92.32, fax 04.79.87.91.11 ☑ 🍷 by appt.

P. CHARLIN

Montagnieu Altesse Elevé en fût de chêne 1998★

□ 0.35 ha 1,700 30–49 F

Patrick Charlin planted his vineyard in 1976 and started making wine with his fourth harvest in 1980. From his 5 ha (12-acre) holding, he has produced three wines selected by the jury. The one considered to be the best is this Altesse. High-extract grapes are matured in oak from fermentation, giving a powerful, toasty palate that is long and lively. A distinctive Altesse, it will improve if allowed to mature for a few years. The jury also cited a sparkling **Montagnieu 97**, the product of a village that has long specialised in sparkling wines. Made from Pinot Noir (30%) and Chardonnay (70%), this flowery, lively wine should be served cold with fish. Finally, there is the **Pinot Noir 98, élevé en fût de chêne**, a cherry-coloured wine that has an aroma of macerated stone fruit and the vanilla of oak maturation. Its soft tannins make this wine suitable for drinking from the time of publication of the *Guide*. It would accompany grilled meats.

🗝 Patrick Charlin, Le Richenard, 01680 Groslée, tel. 04.74.39.73.54, fax 04.74.39.75.16 ☑ 🍷 by appt.

DUPORT ET DUMAS

Mondeuse 1999★★★

■ 1 ha 6,000 30–49 F

Jacques Duport has been managing this 7 ha (17-acre) estate since 1996. The Mondeuse 97 was a very good wine and the 99 is

phenomenal! It has a rich purple colour and a complex nose, where fruity scents compete with leather and cocoa. Extremely full-bodied, the palate has spicy, almost liquoricey aromas and dense tannins. Although this Bugey almost begs to be drunk now, it will be even more exceptional after a few years cellaring.

🗝 EARL Duport Dumas, Caveau du Pont Bancet, 01680 Groslée, tel. 04.74.39.74.21, fax 04.74.39.70.95 ☑
🍷 ev. day 10am–12 noon 2pm–7pm
🗝 Jacques Duport

MARJORIE GUINET ET BERNARD RONDEAU

Cerdon Méthode ancestrale 1999★★

◐ 1.3 ha 8,000 30–49 F

This couple carefully craft their Cerdon using old-fashioned methods. With this vintage, their efforts have been richly rewarded. While the nose is fragrant enough, it is on the palate that the full richness of this rosé becomes apparent. A panoply of red-berry flavours burst forth. A wine of finesse, it is subtly balanced and harmonious. A wonderful apéritif!

🗝 Marjorie Guinet et Bernard Rondeau, Cornelle, 01640 Boyeux-Saint-Jérôme, tel. 04.74.37.12.34, fax 04.74.37.12.34 ☑
🍷 by appt.

DOM. LAUBEZ

Chardonnay Elevé sur fine lie Réserve Tonton Marcel 1999★

□ 0.8 ha 3,600 30–49 F

René Laubez has a 4 ha (10-acre) family estate. This wine opens with a powerful scent reminscent of box, violets and dog-roses. A small quantity of residual sugar gives the palate a roundness that is balanced by its vivacity. (The jury felt that if the wine had been drier, it would have been rated even more highly.) An agreeable wine overall.

🗝 René Laubez, 01300 Andert-Condon, tel. 04.79.81.16.10, fax 04.79.81.16.10 ☑
🍷 by appt.

DOM. MONIN

Chardonnay Les Bâtardes Tête de cuvée 1999★

□ 2 ha 15,000 30–49 F

These 'bastards' were welcomed with open arms by the jury, who admired their beautiful amber hue, and their scent of honeysuckle with overtones of toast. The wine's powerful attack leads to a complex palate that finishes on a mineral note. A bottle that should be cellared for a few years so that it can become even richer and more balanced. Hubert and Philippe Monin, who manage more than 20 ha (50 acres) of vineyards, have also made two other equally successful (one-star) wines: a **Pinot Noir, Cuvée Vieilles Vignes 99**, a very 'talkative' wine with complex red-berry and bay-leaf aromas and chewy, woody tannins (it should be cellared for two to three years); and a **Mondeuse, Cuvée Vieilles Vignes 98**, a deep, clear purple wine with the spicy and fruity aromas characteristic of this variety, and a vigorous palate – another well-made wine that needs to age.

🗝 Dom. Hubert et Philippe Monin, 01350 Vongnes, tel. 04.79.87.92.33, fax 04.79.87.93.25 ☑ Y ev. day 8am–12 noon 2pm–7pm; groups by appt.

LANGUEDOC AND ROUSSILLON

From the southern edge of the Massif Central to the eastern regions of the Pyrenees, the Languedoc-Roussillon vineyards stretch over four coastal departments: the Gard, the Hérault, the Aude and the Pyrénées-Orientales. This substantial area can be visualized as a ring of hills and mountains running down to the coastal plain. Descending from the heights to sea level there are four successive types of terrain. The highest is a mountainous region, formed mostly from the ancient rocks of the Massif Central; below is a region of rocky outcrops and arid moors (the garrigue), which is the oldest wine-growing areas in the region; further down still is the rolling alluvial plain, quite sheltered, with a number of low-lying slopes (200 m/656 ft); the fourth, the coastal area itself, is a continuous strip of low-lying beaches and lagoons, recently developed into one of Europe's liveliest holiday spots. Greek traders and colonists may have planted vines near their settlements in the region as early as the eighth century BC. Under the Romans, the Languedoc vineyard developed rapidly, competing with Roman vineyards in Italy to such an extent that in 92 AD Emperor Domitian ordered half the area of the vineyards to be grubbed up! For two centuries vine cultivation was limited to the Narbonne area, but in 270 Probus annulled the decrees of 92, giving the vineyards of Languedoc-Roussillon a new start. Production was maintained under the Visigoths, but perished during the Saracen invasions of the ninth century. The beginning of the 11th century marked the rebirth of the vineyard, with monasteries and abbeys playing a significant role. At that time the vines were largely confined to the hillsides, the plains being reserved for food crops.

The wine trade grew considerably during the 14th and 15th centuries as new techniques emerged and the number of vineyards increased. Brandy-making became established in the 16th and 17th centuries.

In the 17th and 18th centuries the economic life of the region began to take off: a new port was built at Sète, the Canal des Deux Mers was opened, and the old Roman road was reconstructed. Along with the development of local weaving and silk industries, this economic revival gave a new impetus to vine-growing. A growing export trade of wines and brandies was significantly assisted by the new transport infrastructure.

New vineyards were planted in the plain, utilising the latest ideas about vine-growing *terroirs*. At that time sweet wines occupied a substantial area. The construction of the railways, between 1850 and 1880, shortened distances and guaranteed the opening of new markets whose needs were to be met by the plentiful production of vineyards that were replanted after the phylloxera crisis.

Taking advantage of propitious soils on the slopes in the Gard, the Hérault, Minervois, Corbières and Roussillon, a new vineyard, planted with traditional vine varieties, was developed in the 1950s, adjacent to vineyards that had been the glory of Languedoc-Roussillon a century before. A large number of wines were subsequently recategorised as AOVDQS and AOC, part of a general move to produce higher quality wines in the region.

Wine-growing in the Languedoc-Roussillon takes place in a range of very different conditions as regards altitude, proximity to the sea, growth on terraces or on slopes, soils and *terroirs*.

The soils and the *terroirs* include schist from the primary mountains, as at Banyuls and Maury, in Corbières, Minervois and at Saint-Chinian; sandstone from the Liassic or the Triassic periods, which often alternate with marl, as in Corbières and at Saint-Jean-de-Blanquière; gravel terraces and smoothed pebbles from the Quaternary era, an excellent *terroir* for the vine, to be found at Rivesaltes, Val-d'Orbieu, Caunes-Minervois in the Méjanelle or les Costières de Nîmes. Limestone and stony terrain, occurring as slopes or as plateaux, as in Roussillon, Corbières and Minervois contrasts with the recent alluvial soils of the Languedoc slopes, as well as with the arenas of granite and gneiss found at Les Fenouillèdes.

The Mediterranean climate, prone as it is to extremes of weather, is a unifying feature throughout Languedoc-Roussillon. It is the hottest region in France (the average annual temperature is close to 14°C/57°F, with temperatures that often exceed 30°C/86°F in July and August); rainfall is infrequent, unreliable and falls unevenly across the area. The warm season, from 15 May to 15 August, is always significantly dry. In many areas in Languedoc-Roussillon vines or olives are the only crops it is possible to grow. Only 350 mm (14 in) of rain falls on Barcarès, the driest area in France. However, the quantity of rain can vary by three depending on the place – 400 mm (16 in) on the coast, 1,200 mm (47 in) in the mountains. The winds make the climate even drier when they blow from the land (the Mistral, Cers or Tramontane); on the other hand, winds blowing from the sea temper the effects of the heat and bring a welcome humidity for the vines.

The network of watercourses is particularly dense. There are at least 20 rivers, which may swiftly become torrents after storms or dry up altogether during periods of drought. These rivers have contributed substantially to the formation of the landscape and to the *terroir* of the Rhône valley as far as Têt in the Pyrénés-Orientales.

In Languedoc-Roussillon soils and climate combine to create an environment that is exceptionally well suited to vine-growing, which explains why about 40% of France's total annual wine production comes from the area. This totals about 2,700,000 hl (71,280,000 gal) of AOC wines and 30,000 hl (792,000 gal) of AOVDQS per year.

The AOC wines include 300,000 hl (7,920,000 gal) of Vin Doux Naturel (a sweet wine, fortified with wine alcohol), mostly produced in the Pyrénées-Orientales, the balance coming from the Hérault (see page 0000); 66,000 hl (1,742,400 gal) of sparkling wine in the Aude; 2,270,000 hl (59,928,000 gal) of red wine and 150,000 hl (3,960,000 gal) of white wine.

There have been changes in the vine varieties used for table wines since 1950: a significant reduction in the Aramon, a variety making light table wines, widely planted in the 19th century, a corresponding increase in the traditional varieties of the Languedoc-Roussillon (Carignan, Cinsault, Grenache Noir, Syrah and Mourvèdre), and the adoption of other, more aromatic varieties (Cabernet-Sauvignon, Cabernet Franc, Merlot and Chardonnay).

Among the vineyards producing fine wines, the red variet ies are essentially as follows: Carignan, representing more than 50% of th vines planted because it is robust and gives the wines structure, strengtl and colour; Grenache, a variety that, although susceptible to spring rains gives the wine warmth and bouquet, even though it can oxidise easily wher kept too long; Syrah, a fine-quality variety, contributing tannins and a perfume that develops with time; Mourvèdre, which ages well and produces well-bodied wines that have good colour, are rich in tannin and resistant to oxidisation; and finally, Cinsault, which grows on poor soil and gives the wines suppleness and a pleasant fruitiness.

Languedoc

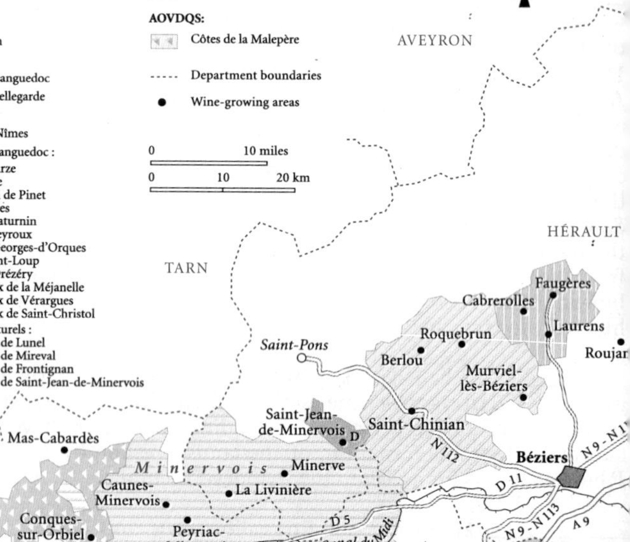

The still white wines are produced mainly from Grenache Blanc, along with Picpoul, Bourboulenc, Macabeu and Clairette – giving wines with a degree of warmth but that maderise quite quickly. In recent years Marsanne, Roussanne and Vermentino have been added to the vine varieties grown. Mauzac, Chardonnay and Chenin are used for sparkling wines.

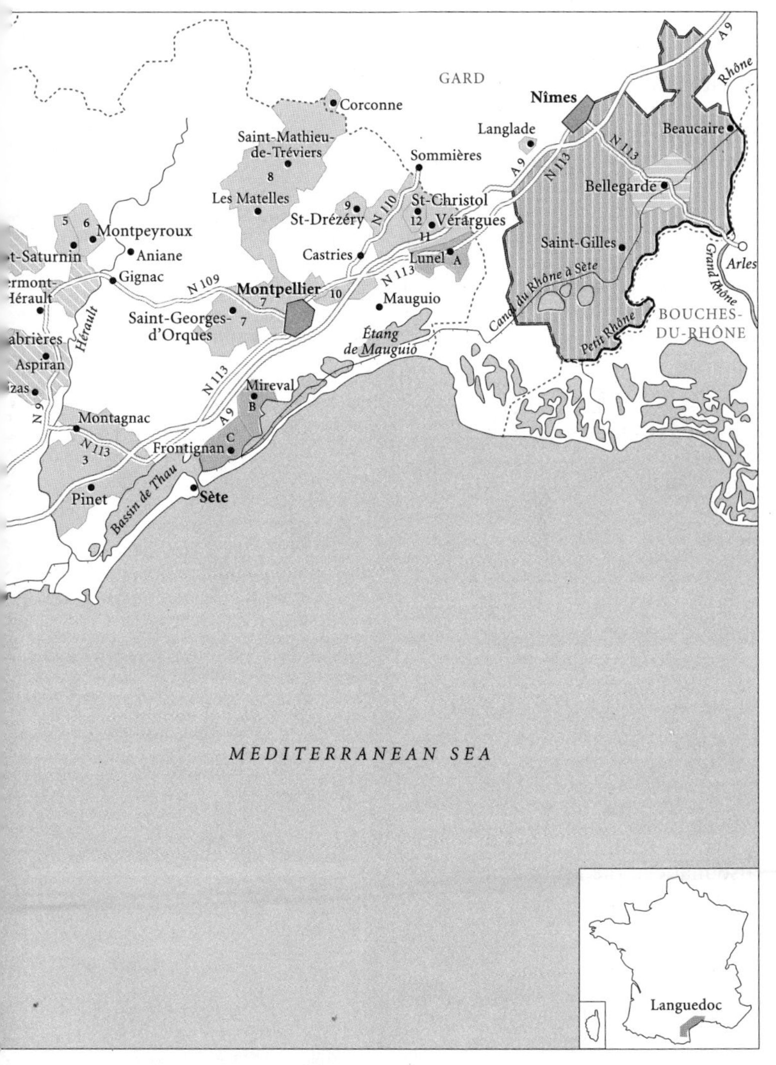

Blanquette de Limoux

The monks of Saint-Hilaire Abbey, which is near Limoux, noticed that their wines went into a second fermentation and were the first people to make Blanquette de Limoux. Three varieties are used to make the wine: Mauzac (90% minimum), Chenin and Chardonnay. The last two of these were introduced in place of Clairette, and they give Blanquette its characteristic acidity and aromatic finesse.

Blanquette de Limoux is made according to the Méthode Traditionelle (Champagne method) in three different styles as brut (dry), demi-sec (medium dry) or doux (sweet).

Blanquette Méthode Ancestrale is a separate AOC, and the method used is kept secret. The characteristic difference of its production lies in a final fermentation in the bottle. Today, modern techniques allow a low-alcohol sweet wine to be produced from 100% Mauzac.

A still, dry white AOC wine, called simply Limoux, is also made in the Limouxin.

CUVEE PRINCESSE DE AIMERY**

○ n.c. 150,000 30–49 F

Alain Gayda, the dynamic director of the Cave de Sieur d'Arques, who already has a wine named after him here, allows this to be overshadowed by the Cuvée Princess de Aimery. Pale gold and with light bubbles, this wine wavers between scents of freshly cut hay and grilled hazelnuts. The honeyed, mature palate is full-bodied and balanced. A mouth-filling wine.

Aimery-Sieur d'Arques, av. de Carcassonne, B.P. 30, 11303 Limoux Cedex, tel. 04.68.74.63.00, fax 04.68.74.63.13 Y by appt.

PIERRE CHANAU Tête de Cuvée 1998

○ n.c. 100,000 30–49 F

Françoise Antech will ensure a good future for the Limoux-based Antech company and will give it charm too. The Tête de Cuvée seems at first a nice, classic Limoux with the pale colour and green apple and toasty notes that are typical of the Mauzac variety. Then, the palate excels with a touch of red berry fruit making this wine ideal with strawberry tart.

Georges et Roger Antech, Dom. de Flassian, 11300 Limoux, tel. 04.68.31.15.88, fax 04.68.31.71.61, e-mail courriers@antech-limoux.com Y ev. day except Sat. Sun. 8am–12 noon 2pm–6pm

DOM. COLLIN

Cuvée Jean Philippe 1998***

○ 10 ha 56,000 20–29 F

After 18 years of production, the Château de Villelongue does very well with this successful wine. It has an attractive pale gold colour with a regular stream of light bubbles and is accompanied by floral scents of acacia. Very pleasant and fruity, the palate shows peach notes with a delicious kernel finish, both balanced and long. Also note a very good **Domaine Collin-Rosier 98**.

Dom. Collin-Rosier, rue Farman, 11300 Limoux, tel. 04.68.31.48.38, fax 04.68.31.34.16 V Y by appt.

DIAPHANE★★★

○ 500 ha 150,000 30–49 F

Limoux is known for its carnival, the incomparable 'fécos' (masked revellers) and the wine-producers attached to the Cave de Sieur d'Arques, who work towards making this a successful festival. The **Tête de Cuvée Aimery**, a pale-coloured Diaphane, is flowery with remarkable development on the palate. The wine is full and fruity with a touch of spice on the finish, the light grilled nut flavours marking the first impact on the mouth.

⊶ Aimery-Sieur d'Arques, av. de Carcassonne, B.P. 30, 11303 Limoux Cedex, tel. 04.68.74.63.00, fax 04.68.74.63.13 ☒ Y by appt.

G. GUINOT Cuvée Réservée★

○ 4.16 ha 30,000 ■ ♁ 30–49 F

Century-old cellars, a reputation dating back to the grand era of Russia at the time of Nicolas II, a farming family based in the Limoux since the time of François 1st, and yet, they are on the Internet . . . The golden colour indicates the way it was matured, and this is confirmed on the nose of ripe apples, toast and hazelnuts. Full and balanced, the palate is rounded and pleasing, both fruity and honeyed with a good length.

⊶ Maison Guinot, 3, av. Chemin-de-Ronde, 11304 Limoux, tel. 04.68.31.01.33, fax 04.68.31.60.05, e-mail guinot@blanquette.fr ☒ Y ev. day except Sat. Sun. 9am–12 noon 2pm–6pm

⊶ Michel Rancoule

LE PROPRIETAIRE Méthode Ancestrale★★

○ 500 ha 150,000 30–49 F

Working on behalf of the wine-producers, the cellar uses traditional methods for this special, very sweet, 100% Mauzac wine which has just 6% alcohol by volume. The golden colour is quite deep with a delicate sparkle. The appley nose is intense with very ripe fruit. The *Méthode Ancestrale* gives very sweet green apple flavours and an excellent balance of sweetness and acidity, providing the wine with a pleasant freshness.

⊶ Aimery-Sieur d'Arques, av. de Carcassonne, B.P. 30, 11303 Limoux Cedex, tel. 04.68.74.63.00, fax 04.68.74.63.13 ☒ Y by appt.

ROBERT Méthode Ancestrale★

○ 4 ha 10,000 30–49 F

With just 7% alcohol by volume and a characteristic sweetness, this rare Blanquette *Méthode Ancestrale* is hard to classify as a wine. Pale gold with a persistent sparkle, it expresses fruity and honeyed notes from the start. The typical very sweet green apple notes are almost reminiscent of cider. The whole effect is very honeyed – this really is a classic *Ancestrale*.

⊶ GFA Robert, Dom. de Fourn, 11300 Pieusse, tel. 04.68.31.15.03, fax 04.68.31.77.65 ☒ Y by appt.

TAILHAN-CAVAILLES 1998★

○ n.c. 30,000 ■ 30–49 F

This newcomer to Limoux has taken over the Tailhan vineyard in the medieval village of Magrie, the old cavalry headquarters of the *l'Ordre de Malte* (Order of Malta). From the outset he has made his mark with this fine, pale golden 98 with its light and consistent bubbles. Between honeyed flowers and peaches, the palate delights with its soft and fruity notes. Very well-balanced, this wine is ready to drink.

⊶ Alain Cavaillès, 6, chem. Furinier, 11300 Limoux, tel. 04.68.31.66.14, fax 04.68.31.11.01, e-mail cavailles.alain@wanadoo.fr Y by appt.

Crémant de Limoux

Even though the Crémant de Limoux was officially categorised only as recently as 21 August 1990, it is a tried and tested product. The strict regulations originally laid down for the production of Limoux are very close to those used for Crémant, so there is no difficulty in including the Limouxins in this elite group.

The mature wines have been appearing in wine stores for some time now, and customers are learning to appreciate the subtle blend of the personality and character of Mauzac, the elegance and roundness of Chardonnay and the youth and freshness of Chenin.

J. LAURENS Cuvée Domaine JL 1998★

○ 10 ha 25,000 ■ ♁ 30–49 F

If you head off the main road towards La Digne, you will discover a peaceful vineyard landscape with winding terraces clustered around this well-preserved old village. The pale gold colour dazzles and leads you towards a nose of green apples, acacia and hawthorn flowers. The wine is vivacious, fresh and elegant. Peaches and green apples make a lively combination, perfect for an apéritif. Note the **Clos des Demoiselles 98** that was much liked.

⊶ SARL Dervin, rte de La Digne-d'Amont, 11300 La Digne d'Aval, tel. 04.68.31.54.54, fax 04.68.31.61.61 ☒ Y by appt.

⊶ Michel Dervin

DOM. LAURENT-MAUGARD 1997

○ 2.6 ha 6,000 30–49 F

At the edge of the Limoux area, the south-facing slopes of Cépie have the most Mediterranean climate with the earliest-ripening terroir. The wine from this estate matches the sunny image with a warming appearance of tarnished gold, a nose of honeyed yellow flowers and quince. Rich and full, it has a sweet balance with a rounded, forward palate, with notes of quince and very ripe fruits. Serve with cake or dessert.

Dom. Laurent-Maugard, 33, rte du Piemont, 11300 Cépie, tel. 04.68.31.33.85, fax 04.68.31.22.14 ev. day 8am–8pm
Christian Laurent

MICHEL OLIVIER

Tête de cuvée 1998★★

○ 5 ha 28,000 30–49 F

The Blanquette won a *coup de cœur* and the Crémant is much liked too, providing real success for the Collin-Rosier estates, accustomed as they are to being in the honours lists. A very lively, pretty gold, the nose has acacia notes giving freshness with an aroma of summer fruits providing finesse. A serious wine that should evolve steadily, it is round and ripe, very fresh with a toasty finish reminiscent of *petits fours*. From the same producer, the jury mentioned a **Château de Villelongue**.

Dom. Collin-Rosier, rue Farman, 11300 Limoux, tel. 04.68.31.48.38, fax 04.68.31.34.16 by appt.

ROBERT 1996★★

○ 6 ha 30,000 50–69 F

From the Domaine de Fourn, every other mountain pass leads to foreign parts. Ambassadors for this wild yet gentle region on the borders of the beautiful Aude department, the talented Robert family are one of the region's best assets. The pale gold colour is embellished by a good stream of bubbles liberating delicate scents of orchard flowers and broom. Toasty with some mango flavours, the wine gives a rounded and full impression whilst remaining lively and balanced.

GFA Robert, Dom. de Fourn, 11300 Pieusse, tel. 04.68.31.15.03, fax 04.68.31.77.65 by appt.

SIEUR D'ARQUES 1998★★★

○ 500 ha 150,000 50–69 F

The instigators of a move towards working with the local terroir, the co-operative of Sieur d'Arques has set very strict production specifications, but are daily reaping the benefits from this serious approach. With a pale gold colour and delicate sparkle, the fine and subtle floral nose of hawthorn has a touch of nuttiness to it. Lively, full and very floral, this Brut has a remarkable balance. Some citrus fruit at the front of the palate leads to very sweet brioche notes at the end.

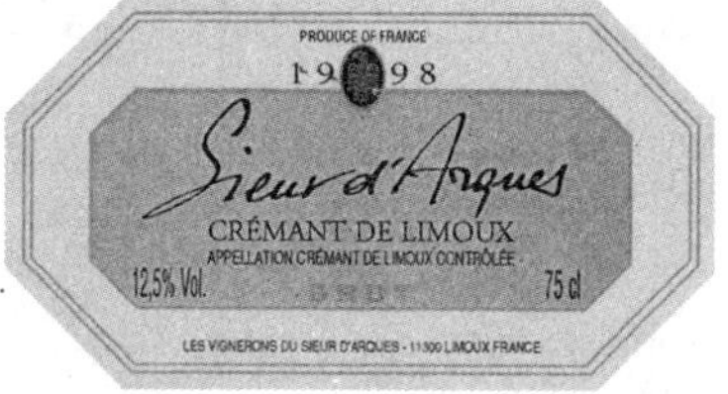

Aimery-Sieur d'Arques, av. de Carcassonne, B.P. 30, 11303 Limoux Cedex, tel. 04.68.74.63.00, fax 04.68.74.63.13
by appt.

SIEUR DE LIMOUX Extra-Brut 1999★

○ 500 ha 150,000 50–69 F

This cellar is one of the places you must visit in the Aude. It has one of the most modern installations, with part of the vat room suspended like a balcony; you can keep cool by wandering through the tunnels filled with *barriques*. This is the Extra-Brut, very clean and lively from the start, with scents of spring flowers. A touch of exotic fruit completes the pleasant sensation of freshness. Equally noted are the **Grande Cuvée 1531** and **Renaissance**.

Aimery-Sieur d'Arques, av. de Carcassonne, B.P. 30, 11303 Limoux Cedex, tel. 04.68.74.63.00, fax 04.68.74.63.13
by appt.

Limoux

The Appellation Limoux Nature, recognised in 1938, was in reality a wine used as the base in the making of Appellation Blanquette de Limoux, and all the shippers used to handle a little of it.

In 1981 this AOC regrettably saw the use of the term 'Nature' being prohibited, and it became simply Limoux. The wine is still made from 100% Mauzac but has slowly declined, while the wines now used as a base for Blanquette de Limoux are a blend of Chenin, Chardonnay and Mauzac.

This appellation has started up again and was included for the first time at the harvest of 1992. It may now be made from a mixture of Chenin and Chardonnay grapes, but Mauzac must still be present. Unusually, fermentation and development until 1 May must be carried out in oak barrels. The energetic Limouxin team is now starting to reap the benefits of all their hard work.

DOM. ASTRUC

Elevé en Fût de Chêne 1998

☐ 1 ha 6,500 50–69 F

The requirement to both ferment and mature in wood automatically limits production levels. It also puts constraints on both vine-grower and wine-maker to conduct this process faultlessly. This pale-coloured 98 has an astonishing floral nose reminiscent of the garrigue. These notes also emerge on the palate, which is rich with well-integrated oak. Already drinking well.

SARL Pierjacq Astruc, 20, av. from Chardonnay, 11300 Malras, tel. 04.68.31.13.26, fax 04.68.31.72.11 by appt.

Jacques Astruc

COLLOVRAY ET TERRIER 1998★★★

☐ n.c. 1,300 70–99 F

Here are two newcomers from the Mâconnais with every intention of being noticed. *Négociants* and owners of the Château d'Antugnac, they have brought us this wine that begins discreetly with hints of almond blossom with a background of oak, but which is excellent on the palate, elegant, fresh, harmonious and balanced. The marriage of barrel and wine is perfect: structured and lightly toasty, this really is a top-class wine to enjoy.

Collovray et Terrier, Vins des Personnets, Ch. d'Antugnac, 11190 Antugnac, tel. 03.85.35.86.51, fax 03.85.35.86.12

CH. DE FLANDRY

Elevé en Fût de Chêne★

☐ 50 ha 35,000 30–49 F

Purchased a dozen years ago by the Sieur d'Arques co-operative, the Château de Flandry, which nestles in the countryside just outside Limoux, seems to stand guard against the possible expansion of the city into the vineyards. The bright gold colour leads on to a very pleasant smell of toasted hazelnuts. Initially straightforward, a mouth-filling, distinctive wine emerges with roundness and vanilla notes behind. Serve it with fish in butter sauce. Note their good range that includes **Les Hauts Clochers** and **Les Quatre Clochers**.

Aimery-Sieur d'Arques, av. de Carcassonne, B.P. 30, 11303 Limoux Cedex, tel. 04.68.74.63.00, fax 04.68.74.63.13 by appt.

TOQUES ET CLOCHERS

Terroir Haute Vallée Elevé en Fût de Chêne★★

☐ 50 ha 35,000 30–49 F

Toques et Clochers cannot be ignored. The fight is always on between the four famous terroirs; the **Terroir d'Autan** being left behind by the brilliant golden-coloured Haute Vallée. With liquorice and fruit on the nose, the wine tastes lively, sophisticated and very crisp with a background flavour of toast. Still youthful, it will be perfect in a year or two.

Aimery-Sieur d'Arques, av. de Carcassonne, B.P. 30, 11303 Limoux Cedex, tel. 04.68.74.63.00, fax 04.68.74.63.13 by appt.

Clairette de Bellegarde

This AOC was recognised in 1949. Clairette de Bellegarde is produced on red, stony soil in the south-eastern part of the Costières de Nîmes, in a small region that is squeezed between Beaucaire and Saint-Gilles, and between Arles and Nîmes. Annual production of this wine, with its characteristic bouquet, totals 2,000 hl (52,800 gal).

DOM. DU MAS CARLOT 1999

☐ 15 ha 64,000 20–29 F

From a pebbled soil, this wine has the characteristic nose of Clairette, with citrus peel and nutty notes giving way to a balanced palate with a slight touch of bitterness on the finish, typical of this appellation.

Mas Carlot, 30127 Bellegarde, tel. 04.66.01.11.83, fax 04.66.01.62.74 ev. day 8am–12 noon 2pm–5pm; Sat. Sun. by appt.

Clairette de Languedoc

The vines are cultivated in eight communes in the Hérault valley and produced 3,663 hl (96,703 gal) in 1999. After vinification at low temperature, with a minimum of oxidation, a generous white wine is produced with an intense yellow robe. It can be dry, medium or sweet. As it ages, it acquires a rancio, toasted flavour, that finds its fans. It goes well with Bourride Sétoise, a local fish stew.

ADISSANIMUS Rancio Doux 1992★★

□ 1 ha 800 150–199 F

Both a curiosity and a tradition revived, the co-operative at Adissan has numerous wine-producers that love working with Clairette. They have conceived this rare wine, which has provoked many comments. The conclusion is simple: 'This is an enjoyable wine of great complexity' (chocolate, coffee, caramel, mocha, apricot jam). A dessert wine that deserves support, to be enjoyed amongst close friends. Bravo!

Cave coop. La Clairette d'Adissan, 34230 Adissan, tel. 04.67.25.01.07, fax 04.67.25.37.76, e-mail clairette.adissan@wanadoo.fr ev. day except Sat. Sun. 9am–12 noon 3pm–6pm

DOM. LA CROIX CHAPTAL 1999

□ 1.2 ha 5,500 30–49 F

Monsieur Pacaud used to work for a large firm known all over the world for its Vin Gris. A true wine fanatic, he has allowed himself to be seduced into becoming a wine-grower. He has done well with this bright, pale yellow coloured wine, which has a fairly intense nose, toasty, buttered, floral, with notes of peach, citrus and exotic fruits and a touch of the garrigue. The palate appeals with its lively grip, but it is also balanced by plenty of richness and roundness. Good length.

Pacaud-Chaptal, Dom. de Cambous, 34725 Saint-André-de-Sangonis, tel. 04.67.16.09.36, fax 04.67.16.09.36 by appt.

Corbières

Corbières wines, categorised VDQS from 1951, became AOC in 1985. The extent of the appellation covers 87 communes, producing 650,000 hl (17,160,000 gal) (7% of white and rosé and 93% of red). They are powerful wines, ranging between 11% and 13% alcohol, produced from vineyards planted with a maximum of 60% of Carignan vines.

Les Corbières is a typical wine-growing area in that it is hardly suitable for any other type of crop. Yet it is a difficult region to classify because, although the Mediterranean influence dominates, there is also a certain degree of maritime Atlantic influence to the west. The great diversity of soil types, the preponderance of Carignan and the partitioning of plots due to the very broken relief contribute to a sense of uniqueness. Les Corbières has its own wine Confrérie, the Illustre Cour des Seigneurs de Corbières, which has its headquarters at Lézignan-Corbières.

CH. AIGUILLOUX

Cuvée des Trois Seigneurs 1998★★

■ 6 ha 25,000 50–69 F

At the highest point of the crest of Aiguilloux, a post marks the limits of the ancient counties of Narbonne, Durban and Lézignan; so naturally the best wine could only be named 'Des Trois Seigneurs' (the three Lords). This slightly musky 98 still has some lightly oaky tones present but also some of the jammy red fruit character shown on the 96. The **99 Rosé** proves that Marthe and François Lemarié really love good wine.

Marthe et François Lemarié, Ch. Aiguilloux, 11200 Thézan-des-Corbières, tel. 04.68.43.32.71, fax 04.68.43.30.66 by appt.

DOM. DE BELLEVUE

Cuvée Grande Délicatesse Elevé en Fût de Chêne 1998★

■ 5 ha 20,000 50–69 F

This estate is known for being planted exclusively with Carignan and Grenache on the old terraces above the Orbieu River. Bright purple and with intense, wide-ranging aromas (spices, cocoa, red berry fruit, vanilla), this wine has great personality, with a well-balanced, firm and nicely integrated structure. It is rounded with good length.

Vignerons de la Méditerranée, 12, rue du Rec-de-Veyret, ZI Plaisance, 11100 Narbonne, tel. 04.68.42.75.00, fax 04.68.42.75.01, e-mail valdorbieu-didierferrier@wanadoo.fr by appt.

CH. CANOS 1999★

◪ 6 ha 13,000 30–49 F

Pierre Galinier, the top Corbières rosé practitioner, has produced this distinctive 99 with a crystal clear pale pink colour and salmon hints. It has a complex nose with notes of raspberry, violet and exotic fruits. The first ıpression is straightforward, with a full-ɔdied palate with fine flavours and a reason-ɓle length.

⊸ Pierre Galinier, Dom. de Canos, 11200 uc-sur-Orbieu, tel. 04.68.27.00.06, ɪx 04.68.27.61.08 ☒ Y by appt.

:H. DE CAPENDU

'uvée Eugénie 1998★

■ 3.5 ha 18,000 50–69 F

Christophe Barbier can be proud of this ery solid wine in which the finely crafted :ructure brings out its power. The very pleas-nt, dark-coloured 98 exudes amazingly oaky otes which lead on to the clean and straight-ɔrward palate. Generous and balanced tan-ins recall the nose. The finish indicates a ine that is still a little young, but promising.

⊸ SA Ch. de Capendu, pl. de la Mairie, 1700 Capendu, tel. 04.68.79.01.36, ax 04.68.79.01.36 ☒

CASTELMAURE

Grande Cuvée 1998★★★

■ 30 ha 57,000 50–69 F

We're in the heart of Corbières with the scents of the garrigue, the craggy rocks and of course the traditions of the wine-grower with his low-yielding vines that are nevertheless generous in their quality. Half Syrah, half Grenache; half limestone, half schist, but absolutely perfect. Liquorice and vanilla blend in with the flavours of crystallised fruits. Both powerful and mouth-filling, the wine is ready to drink now, but has the poten-tial to fill out in the months to come. A few years will allow the wine to develop fully.

⊸ SCV Castelmaure, 4, rte des Cannelles, 11360 Embres-et-Castelmaure, tel. 04.68.45.91.83, fax 04.68.45.83.56 ☒ Y ev. day except Sat. Sun. 8am–12 noon 2pm–6pm

PIERRE CHRISTMAN 1998

■ 15 ha 12,000 50–69 F

This young merchant bottles his own wines, and chooses to blend his Syrah-based wine with some Carignan, both vinified half traditionally and half with carbonic macera-tion, and then adds a touch of Grenache, Cinsault and Mourvèdre. The lack of oak ageing gives a lightly peppered, vinous nose. This straightforward 98 has a full-bodied palate with the characteristic tannins of Corbières.

⊸ Pierre Christman, rte de Cazedarnes, 34360 Pierrerue, tel. 04.67.38.18.15, fax 04.67.38.25.11 ☒ Y by appt.

⊸ Ph. de La Boisse

CH. CRUSCADES HORTALA 1998★

■ 20 ha 103,400 20–29 F

This very classic wine is made from the three main Corbières varieties and put through the most traditional vinification with no barrel maturation. However, it is excellent. On tasting, we found a rich and dense 98, expressing concentrated ripe fruit and bal-ance, both soft and long. All the wine pro-duced by the Château de Cruscades is bottled by this Mèze-based merchant.

⊸ SA Bessière, 40, rue du Port, 34140 Mèze, tel. 04.67.18.40.40, fax 04.67.43.77.03

⊸ Duquesne

CELLIER DES DEMOISELLES

Cuvée des Vignerons 1998

■ 15 ha 35,000 30–49 F

In every vintage, Le Cellier des Demoiselles succeeds in producing a memorable **Blanc de Blancs**, and the **99** follows on from its prede-cessors, receiving a mention. However, it is this red Corbières 98 with its very deep, pur-ple-tinted colour that has a good future. Still slightly herbaceous, it is full of promise, with plums and caramel notes livening up the nose. On the taste, it is rich, balanced and complete. The powerful tannic structure and its great length are signs of its undoubted potential to develop.

⊸ SCV Cellier des Demoiselles, 5, rue de la Cave, 11220 Saint-Laurent-de-la-Cabrerisse, tel. 04.68.44.02.73, fax 04.68.44.07.05 ☒ Y ev. day except Sun. 8am–12 noon 2pm–6pm

CH. ETANG DES COLOMBES

Bicentenaire Vieilles Vignes 1998★★

■ 20 ha 90,000 30–49 F

A step ahead of the other dynamic produc-ers of Corbières, Henri Gualco has never relinquished his efforts to be amongst the best; the vineyard, the vinification and ageing cellars are all perfect. This fresh wine is cherry red with glints of purple and provides a very pleasantly intense fruity aroma with slight vanilla notes. The immediate impression on the palate is superb. Round and fat, it is rich in subtle and elegant flavours, all per-fectly balanced with remarkable length. A truly enjoyable wine.

⊸ Henri Gualco, Ch. Etang des Colombes, 11200 Lézignan-Corbières, tel. 04.68.27.00.03, fax 04.68.27.24.63 ☒ Y ev. day 8am–7pm

CH. FABRE-GASPARETS

Elevé en Fût de Chêne 1998★

■ 5 ha 26,000 30–49 F

The terroir of Boutenac allied with the classic varieties of Mourvèdre (plenty), Syrah (discerningly) and Grenache (sparingly) and the dexterity of Louis Fabre combine to

produce this dark ruby 98. The nose is both fruity and floral, with a light spicy note. Revealing a very pleasant palate, despite its youthful tannins, this wine is fruit-driven with very good depth of flavour, which will guarantee it an excellent future.
Louis Fabre, Ch. de Luc, rue du Château, 11200 Luc-sur-Orbieu, tel. 04.68.27.10.80, fax 04.68.27.38.19, e-mail chateauluc@aol.com ☑ Y by appt.

CH. DU GRAND CAUMONT

Cuvée Tentation 1998★★

■ 8 ha 48,000 50–69 F

Château Grand Caumont owes much to Patrick Blanchard, the vineyard manager. This wine is just a simple combination of a small quantity of Carignan and Grenache used in a whole berry fermentation for the classic Corbières base, allied with just over 50% Syrah, picked at perfect ripeness. Yet, it manages to marry power and elegance with a range of ripe fruits, notably masses of plums. Warming and balanced, it will age well.
SARL F.L.B. Rigal, Ch. du Grand Caumont, 11200 Lézignan-Corbières, tel. 04.68.27.10.82, fax 04.68.27.54.59 ☑ Y by appt.
Françoise Rigal

DOM. DU GRAND CRES

Cuvée Majeure 1997

■ 3 ha n.c. 70–99 F

Hervé and Pascaline Leferrer prefer their wines mature, aiming to bring out all their strength of character. Amidst all the 1998s we tasted, here is a worthy 97. The blend is dominated by Syrah (75%) and balanced by Grenache (25%), grown on a high-altitude, late ripening terroir, which enabled the grapes to come to full maturity after the rains of early September. The range of flavours goes from cherries to plums; round and balanced, the wine is slightly oaky on the finish. We should point out that Hervé Lefferrer had an unusual background as manager of the famous Romanée-Conti estate in Burgundy before becoming enamoured with Corbières.
Hervé et Pascaline Leferrer, Dom. du Grand Crès, 40, av. de la Mer, 11200 Ferrals-les-Corbières, tel. 04.68.43.69.08, fax 04.68.43.58.99 ☑ Y by appt.

CH. GRAND MOULIN

Vieilles Vignes 1998

■ 13.5 ha 80,000 30–49 F

Jean-Noël Bousquet, a determined character, has had to battle to create his vineyard, and worst of all, suffered in the terrible floods of November 1999. By some miracle, this wine was already bottled. It has a fine and satisfying nose with elegant and complex notes of spice and tobacco. Structured with fine-grained tannins and a touch of acidity, this rounded and balanced wine could be drunk or kept.
Jean-Noël Bousquet, Ch. Grand Moulin, 11200 Luc-sur-Orbieu, tel. 04.68.27.40.80, fax 04.68.27.47.61 ☑ Y ev. day 8am–12 noon 2pm–7pm

CH. HAUT-GLEON

Elevé en Fût de Chêne 1998★

■ 12 ha 45,000 50–69

Enthused by Corbières and by this 16th century estate, in 1991 Monsieur Duhamel gave in to his wish to become a wine-grower and bought Château Haut-Gléon. He reorganised the vineyard, transformed and modernised the tank and storage cellars, installed an ageing area and began production, but it has taken him some years to achieve recognition. Ready to drink now, this strongly flavoured 98 has striking notes of macerated fruits and bay leaves. Rich and full, a very pleasant wine.
Ch. Haut-Gléon, Villesèque-les-Corbières, 11360 Durban, tel. 04.68.48.85.95, fax 04.68.48.46.20, e-mail châteauhautgleon@wanadoo.fr ☑ Y ev. day 8am–12 noon 1.30pm–5.30pm
Duhamel

CH. LA BARONNE

Montagne d'Alaric Vigne La Prière 1998

□ 8 ha 15,000 50–69 F

This white Corbières 98 is of another style altogether. A bright, golden colour that has not seen any oak ageing, it is a serious and poised wine with polished aromas of citrus fruits, pepper and cinnamon. The balanced palate impresses with its solid, rich style and perfect length. This very unusual wine will not leave any taster with an indifferent opinion.
Suzette Lignères, Ch. la Baronne, 11700 Fontcouverte, tel. 04.68.43.90.20, fax 04.68.43.96.73 ☑ Y by appt.

DOM. DE LA BOUYSSE

Mazerac 1998★

■ 1.58 ha 8,000 50–69 F

Martine Pages and Christophe Molinier, both oenologists, are trying to put some life back into the family estate. With a very youthful, dark purple and lively appearance, this extremely well-made 98 still has some dominant oak. Ripe and warming, it gives a good first impression on the palate and provides interesting nutty flavours with a vanilla finish.
Dom. de la Bouysse, rue des Ecoles, 11200 Saint-André-de-Roquelongue, tel. 04.68.45.15.23, fax 04.68.45.50.34 ☑ Y by appt.
Molinier

DOM. DE LA PEYROUSE

Elevé en Fût 1998★★

■ 3 ha 5,000 50–69 F

La Peyrouse has submitted an oak-aged 98 and receives a worthwhile reward for an estate that was strongly tied to the local co-operative until 1995. It has an intense colour and a classic Corbières nose. Very well-made, this is a powerful, spicy wine with light vanilla notes. Nicely balanced, the palate has good fine-grained tannins signifying the presence of

some attractive oak flavours that does not detract from the fruit on the finish.
🔑 Jean-Louis et Laurent Gili, Dom. de la Peyrouse, av. de Narbonne, 11360 Durban-Corbières, tel. 04.68.45.85.69, fax 04.68.45.85.69 ☒ Y ev. day 10am–12 noon 3pm–7pm

CH. LA VOULTE-GASPARETS

Cuvée Romain Pauc 1998★★

■ 15 ha 34,000 ⏸ 70–99 F

Should one talk about the best 'Boutenac', or the 'Château La Voulte' or 'La Romain Pauc'? Patrick Reverdy chooses his plots from the round pebbled soils, selects his Carignan from his old, faithful Carignan vines, adds some 'ancient' Grenache and a finishing touch of Syrah and Mourvèdre. He uses only whole-berry fermentation and then matures (or even nurtures) the wine in barrel. This wine reveals influences of both the terroir and the grape varieties, and shows personality, body, sensuality, power and richness. A real tribute to its producer.
🔑 Patrick Reverdy, Ch. la Voulte-Gasparets, 11200 Boutenac, tel. 04.68.27.07.86, fax 04.68.27.41.33 ☒ Y ev. day 9am–12 noon 2pm–7pm

CH. LES OLLIEUX

Elevé en Fût de Chêne 1998

■ 9 ha 60,000 ⏸ 30–49 F

The first female Cistercian order was founded on this spot in 1153. Today it is a beautiful estate of 50 ha (124 acres), which produces excellent Corbières. From the southern slopes of Boutenac, the blend is of half old Carignan vines, a quarter Grenache and a quarter Syrah, all fermented as whole berries. A dark garnet colour with a mineral touch, the wine seems slightly charred but is lifted by the carbonic maceration. The palate is full, with a tannic structure that will allow it to age well.
🔑 François-Xavier Surbezy, Ch. les Ollieux, 11200 Montséret, tel. 04.68.43.32.61, fax 04.68.43.30.78, e-mail ollieux@free.fr ☒
Y ev. day 9am–8pm; Sat. Sun. 10am–8pm

CH. LES PALAIS

Cuvée Randolin 1998★

■ 10 ha 40,000 ▮ ⏸ 50–69 F

Saint Randolin founded a monastery in the Middle Ages and lends his name to this wine. The Château les Palais has received several *coups de cœur* from French juries, and the 98 vintage is hardly different from its glorious predecessors. The attractive nose is deep with coffee and cocoa smells lifted by a touch of vanilla. Supple on the palate, the elegant taste is given structure by distinctive and elegant tannins.
🔑 Ch. Les Palais, 11220 Saint-Laurent-de-la-Cabrerisse, tel. 04.68.44.01.63, fax 04.68.44.07.42 ☒ Y ev. day 9am–12 noon 2pm–6pm; Sat. and Sun. by appt.
🔑 de Volontat

CH. DE L'ILLE 1998

■ 6 ha 30,000 ⏸ 30–49 F

This is a modern-day Corbières produced without Carignan and born somewhere between the beach and the garrigue and between the lakes and the salt marshes. The colour is deep with a nose of undergrowth, enhanced by strawberries and raspberries. An attractive taste, soft and light but with good length, the palate is mouth-filling, structured by rounded tannins.
🔑 Pol Flandroy, Ch. de l'Ille, rue de L'Etang, 11440 Peyriac-de-Mer, tel. 04.68.41.05.96, fax 04.68.42.81.73 Y by appt.

CH. MANSENOBLE

Cuvée Marie-Annick 1998★★★

■ 13.5 ha 6,000 ▮ ⏸ 🌡 70–99 F

Guido Jansegers, a Belgian wine critic and œnologist settled in Corbières in 1993. He brought all his passion for wine with him and has modified the cellar of Château Mansenoble and unerringly selected the best vineyard plots. Five years later, he is managing to get the best from his terroir: an already attractively dark ruby wine, with the aromas of spice and ripe fruit marrying superbly and coming through on the mouth. The tannins are as velvety and silky as one might wish for, with notes of cocoa, and even coffee, which provide it with a very good depth of flavour.
🔑 Guido Jansegers, Ch. Mansenoble, 11700 Moux, tel. 04.68.43.93.39, fax 04.68.43.97.21, e-mail mansenoble@wanadoo.fr ☒ Y ev. day except Sun. 10am–11.30am 2.30pm–5.30pm
🔑 Jansegers-Dewitte

CH. DE MATTES-SABRAN

Cuvée Sabran 1998★

■ 22 ha 25,000 ▮ 🌡 20–29 F

This characterful 98 shows well due to the effects of the terroir, the characteristic grape variety mix and the lack of oak ageing. We have already mentioned the specificity of this clay-limestone soil. This wine is a blend of 60% Syrah with equal amounts of Carignan and Grenache. Very approachable, it has a primary floral perfume of violets together with more developed fruity aromas and a charming and unctuous flavourful palate. Will taste best in its youth.

⊶ Brouillat-Arnould, Ch. de Mattes, B.P. 44, 11130 Sigean, tel. 04.68.48.22.77, fax 04.68.48.55.32, e-mail jlbrouillat@compuserve.com ☑ Ὺ ev. day 8.30am–12 noon 1.30pm–7.30pm

CH. MERVILLE 1998★★

■ 7.5 ha 32,400 ⅡⅠ 30–49 F

Great wine results from a combination of the authenticity of the terroir, grape varieties (Grenache and Syrah) and people. François and Jacques Lurton from Bordeaux have started their innovative *négociant* business here in Corbières. Having established an excellent reputation, they select grapes, vinify, mature and distribute wines throughout the world. This perfectly coloured 98 provides scents of the garrigue mixed with vanilla and floral notes. The taste appears graceful with a fleshy richness to support the sweet, intense tannins. The silky flavours with barbecued notes contribute to the charm of this juicy wine.

⊶ SA Jacques et François Lurton, Dom. de Poumeyrade, 33870 Vayres, tel. 05.57.74.72.74, fax 05.57.74.70.73, e-mail jflurton@jflurton.com

CH. MEUNIER SAINT-LOUIS

A Capella 1998★★

■ n.c. 32,400 ⅡⅠ 50–69 F

This estate seeks only to produce highly expressive wines. With its new label, the deeply intense A Capella 98 certainly fits the bill. The obviously fine nose is oaky and sophisticated. The palate is extremely well-balanced with elegance and harmony. The potential of the grapes has been 'delivered and not extracted', a sign of respect for the raw materials. It just needs a little time for the oak flavours to integrate. Perhaps that's why the jury described it as a feminine wine?

⊶ Ch. Meunier Saint-Louis, 11200 Boutenac, tel. 04.68.27.09.69, fax 04.68.27.53.34 ☑ Ὺ by appt.

⊶ Ph. Pasquier-Meunier

PEYRES NOBLES 1999★

◢ 24 ha 146,600 30–49 F

A cellar which works in the true sense of 'co-operation'. The members become genuine wine-producers, helping with the work in the vat room, the barrel cellar and at bottling. This liberal approach is apparent in the cherry-coloured rosé, which is floral and intense with a fresh, but rounded palate, full of flavours: a real summer rosé.

⊶ Vignerons de Camplong, 11200 Camplong-d'Aude, tel. 04.68.43.60.86, fax 04.68.43.69.21 ☑ Ὺ ev. day except Sun. 8am–12 noon 2pm–6pm

CH. PRIEURE BORDE-ROUGE

Cuvée Signature 1998

■ 5.6 ha 30,000 ⅡⅠ 30–49 F

Here are a couple of contented producers: in the space of six years, they have become as deeply embedded as the roots of the old Carignan vines of Borde-Rouge. They have shown an unfailing enthusiasm that i[s] obvious in this attractive wine. The lively sparkling aromas are delicately fruity with strawberries, cherries and some subtle oak flavours. With its major attributes being balance and softness, this wine slips down really easily, yet still finishes well.

⊶ SCEA Devillers-Quénehen, Dom. de Borde-Rouge, 11220 Lagrasse, tel. 04.68.43.12.55, fax 04.68.43.12.51, e-mail quenehen@aol.com ☑ Ὺ ev. day 9am–1pm 2pm–7.30pm

PRIEURE SAINTE-MARIE D'ALBAS

Clos de Cassis Elevé en fût de chêne 1998★★

■ 3 ha 10,000 ⅡⅠ 30–49 F

This estate has proudly submitted this wine from the 98 vintage, a successful one all over Corbières. A real gem, it has impressively pronounced and characterful flavours of menthol, pepper and some balsam. Firm on the palate with plenty of tannin, it is also perfectly oaked.

⊶ Gisèle et Jean-Louis Galibert, Prieuré Sainte-Marie-d'Albas, 11700 Moux, tel. 04.68.79.09.64, fax 04.68.79.28.39 ☑ Ὺ by appt.

CH. ROQUEFORT SAINT-MARTIN

Grande Réserve 1998★★

■ 8 ha 25,000 ⅡⅠ 70–99 F

Situated right on the edge of both the lakes and the Mediterranean, facing the sun, this vineyard really expresses its very specific terroir. This dark-coloured wine is from Roquefort, on a good stony terrace, planted with one-third each of Grenache, Mourvèdre and Syrah. Enveloped in the flavours of the garrigue, it is balanced and rich, if a touch heady.

⊶ Celliers Saint-Martin, 11540 Roquefort-des-Corbières, tel. 04.68.48.21.44, fax 04.68.48.48.76 ☑ Ὺ by appt.

ROQUE SESTIERE

Vieilles Vignes 1999★

□ 3 ha 15,000 ▮ ♁ 30–49 F

It is said that routine becomes monotonous and yet, each year the white Roque Sestière appears more than perfect: very pale, but really bright, with absolute clarity on the nose, subtle and discreet notes of hawthorn and a slight amylic note. There is freshness, balance and length in this mouth-filling wine – it really goes on and on. Note that real praise must go to the **1998 Rouge Roque Sestière Cuvée Carte Blanche**.

⊶ EARL Roland Lagarde, rue des Etangs, 11200 Luc-sur-Orbieu, tel. 04.68.27.18.00, fax 04.68.27.18.00 ☑ Ὺ by appt.

DOM. ROUIRE-SEGUR

Cuvée Tradition 1998★

■ 8 ha 15,000 ▮ ⅡⅠ 20–29 F

The producer here, Geneviève Bourdel, is often noted for her 'feminine' rosé. She has

ıade the most of an excellent vintage to submit to us her red Corbières 98. On the nose the ıany aromas have been perfectly lifted by a hort time in wood. The rich flavours and leshiness of the palate give an elegant strucure to this wine, which finishes with a touch f barbecued flavours.
Geneviève Bourdel, 11220 Ribaute, el. 04.68.27.19.76, fax 04.68.27.62.51
Y by appt.

CH. SAINT-ESTEVE

Cuvée Prestige Elevé en Fût de Chêne 1998★

■ 5 ha 15,000 30–49 F

With a location half-way up the slope in the geographic heart of Corbières, and a grape variety mix, tempered by age, dominated by Syrah and complemented by Grenache, Carignan and Mourvèdre, this wine already has excellent assets. To this one must add destemming and carbonic maceration. The jury found that this wine had crunchy notes of toast and tasted straightforward, clean, weighty and long with a touch of tannin which should make it last.
GFA Ch. Saint-Estève, 11200 Thézan-les-Corbières, tel. 04.68.79.16.04, fax 04.68.79.16.19 Y ev. day 8am–7pm
Eric Latham

DOM. SAINT-JEAN-DE-LA-GINESTE

Carte Noire 1998★★★

■ 4 ha 10,000 30–49 F

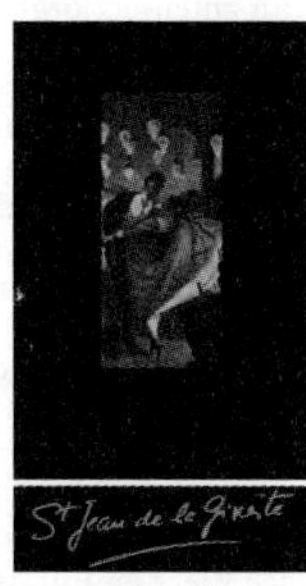

Marie-Hélène Bacave and her loyal husband have decided to put the family estate back on its feet. A real challenge: from the vineyards, to the barrel cellar, to the tasting room, everything has been reviewed, improved and perfected, and then nature has done the rest. The Carte Noir, with its deep colour and shades of purple, is a major asset to them. It has a sophisticated aroma of violets mixed with notes of jammy black fruit leading to intense oak flavours that recur on the palate. The structure shows powerful, but silky tannins giving a wine of character, depth and personality. The result is a wine in which you can really feel the passion of the wine producers.
Marie-Hélène Bacave, Dom. Saint-Jean-de-la-Gineste, 11200 Saint-André-de-Roquelongue, tel. 04.68.45.12.58, fax 04.68.45.12.58 Y by appt.

SEIGNEURS DE QUERIBUS 1999★

◪ n.c. 5,000 20–29 F

The section of the Corbières vineyards that is overlooked by the Cathar citadels and blessed by the priest of Cucugnan may not yield a Communion wine, but it certainly does give a divine rosé. Delicate and pale with purple and ivory hues, it is very perfumed and a real fruit-salad wine. Agreeable, very drinkable and long, make the most of this wine.
SCA Vignerons du château de Quéribus, 11350 Cucugnan, tel. 04.68.45.41.61, fax 04.68.45.02.25
Y ev. day 9am–12 noon 2pm–6pm

DOM. SERRES-MAZARD 1998

■ 15 ha 50,000 30–49 F

Jean-Pierre Mazard harbours a secret desire to be able produce a characterful Corbières in every vintage, with a distinct and quite outstanding personality. It is impossible not to reach for the words that describe the charm of the garrigue after a warm day accompanied by a few drops of rain: rosemary, thyme, mint, *ciste* (a Provençal shrub), bay leaf, some mineral notes . . . the descriptions are endless. There is more of the same on the supple and full-bodied palate.
Annie et Jean-Pierre Mazard, 11220 Talairan, tel. 04.68.44.02.22, fax 04.68.44.08.47 Y ev. day 9am–7pm

CH. THEZANNES

Cuvée spéciale Elevé en Fût de Chêne 1998★

■ n.c. n.c. 50–69 F

An exceptional year for this light-coloured wine, made from 60% Syrah and 40% Carignan grown close to the Mediterranean. The slightly oaky nose has touches of spices and nutmeg. Firm and straightforward, balanced, and structured mainly by tannins with a marked but not dominant, elegant oaky touch, this rounded 98 is just beginning to open up.
Caves Rocbère, 11490 Portel-des-Corbières, tel. 04.68.48.28.05, fax 04.68.48.45.92
Y ev. day 9am–12 noon 2pm–6pm

CH. DU VIEUX PARC

La Sélection 1998★

■ 10 ha 45,000 50–69 F

Château Vieux Parc produces a wine that manages to be both classic and modern. Aged in one- to three-year-old oak, it has some Carignan, made through carbonic maceration, and a predominance of Syrah with Grenache and Mourvèdre that have been destemmed. The intense nose has touches of menthol and tends towards herbaceous characters with notes of undergrowth. The rich and fleshy palate has a light, but balanced structure. Very elegant and sensual.
Louis Panis, av. des Vignerons, 11200 Conilhac-Corbières, tel. 04.68.27.47.44, fax 04.68.27.38.29, e-mail louis.panis@wanadoo.fr Y by appt.

Costières de Nîmes

Some 25,000 ha (61,750 acres) of land have been classified as AOC of which 12,000 ha (29,640 acres) are currently planted. Red, rosé or white wines are produced from sunny slopes of smoothed pebbles within a rectangular area bounded by the towns of Maynes, Vauvert, Saint-Gilles and Beaucaire, south-east of Nîmes and north of the Camargue. In 1999, 197,748 hl (5,220,547 gal) of wine were sold under the classification of Appellation Costières de Nîmes (75% of red, 22% of rosé and 3% of white), which is produced in an area covered by 24 communes. The rosés go well with the typical charcuterie of the Cévennes, the whites are a natural complement to seafood and Mediterranean fish, and the reds, which are warm and full-bodied, are especially good with grilled meats. An energetic wine society, the Ordre de la Boisson de la Stricte Observance des Costières de Nîmes, has recently revived local wine-related traditions originally established in 1703. A wine route runs through the region, starting from Nîmes.

CH. DES AVEYLANS

Vieilli en Fût de Chêne 1999★

■ 2.2 ha 6,000 30–49 F

From 85% Syrah, this wine is deep-coloured with a touch of crimson and particularly pungent vanilla and smoky notes, from its 11 months in barrel. It has a well-balanced structure of tannin, acidity and sweetness. Good use of oak. This wine needs a little patience and should be at its best in three or four years.

EARL Hubert Sendra, Dom. des Aveylans, 30127 Bellegarde, tel. 04.66.70.10.28, fax 04.66.01.02.80 ☑ Ⲧ by appt.

CH. BEAUBOIS Cuvée Tradition 1998★

■ 15 ha 100,000 30–49 F

In years gone by, this large property was part of the Cistercian abbey of Franquevaux above the lakes of La Petite Camargue. The jury enjoyed the deep red Cuvée Tradition with its initial nose of gamey notes, followed by blackcurrant juice. The palate is rounded and balanced, with slightly bitter tannins in the background and a herbaceous touch o the finish. This fine Costières de Nîme should be opened a couple of hours befoı serving and drunk with grilled meats.

SCEA Ch. Beaubois, 30640 Franquevaux, tel. 04.66.73.30.59, fax 04.66.73.33.02, e-mail fannyboyer@chateau-beaubois.com ☑ Ⲧ ev. day except Sun. 8am–12 noon 2pm–6pm

CELLIER DU BONDAVIN 1999★

■ 12.23 ha 25,000 20–29

The name of this co-operative is that of th oldest part of the village of Redessan. Th wine they have submitted is excellent, show ing a deep red colour and a range of rich aro mas of crystallised fruits, pepper and violet. I is rounded on the palate with a fairly comple: after-taste. Its youthful tannins are still a littl bitter, but indicate that it will last. Only thos who are patient will appreciate this wine at it best.

Cellier du Bondavin, 43, av. de Provence, 30129 Redessan, tel. 04.66.20.22.06, fax 04.66.20.59.41 ☑ Ⲧ by appt.

MAS DES BRESSADES

Cuvée Tradition 1999★★

□ 2 ha 13,000 20–29 F

The Cuvées Tradition from the Mas des Bressades are not oaked, and show at least as well as the Cuvées Excellence. This one has a superb light yellow colour with green hues and provides an intense floral nose with a touch of exotic fruits and white peaches. Very fresh on the palate, it has an overall good balance with a tasty finish. The **Tradition 99 Rosé** receives one star. It is a summery wine that should be enjoyed from the end of 2000 to liven up an evening with friends.

Cyril Marès, Mas des Bressades, 30129 Manduel, tel. 04.66.01.11.78, fax 04.66.01.63.63 ☑ Ⲧ ev. day except Sat. Sun. 8.30am–12 noon 2pm–5pm

MAS DES BRESSADES

Cuvée Excellence Elevé en Fût de Chêne 1999★★

□ 2 ha 8,000 50–69 F

Cyril Marès has been the satisfied owner of this estate since 1996. His special *cuvée* certainly merits its name. With an intense pretty yellow colour, it has a full and complex nose with aromas that combine pastries, vanilla, orange blossom and dried apricots. The taste shows both nice roundness and richness, with a fresh balance of acidity. The wine was given a well-judged length of time in wood. It has finesse and a good length on the palate, guaranteeing it a good future of three to four years. The **Cuvée Excellence 98 Rouge**, one star, is a powerful wine, with very southern accents of the garrigue and of thyme.

Cyril Marès, Mas des Bressades, 30129 Manduel, tel. 04.66.01.11.78, fax 04.66.01.63.63 ☑ Ⲧ ev. day except Sat. Sun. 8.30am–12 noon 2pm–5pm

CH. DE CAMPUGET

Tradition de Campuget 1999★★

☐ 7 ha 50,000 ■ ♁ 20-29 F

From a sandstone soil and made with a classic blend of Grenache Blanc (40%), Roussanne (55%) and Marsanne, the jury loved the straightforwardness of this wine and its balance. The resinous and nutty flavours lasted right through to the finish. Rich and round, this is an excellent example of Costières de Nîmes that can be simply enjoyed for what it is.

SCA Ch. de Campuget, 30129 Manduel, tel. 04.66.20.20.15, fax 04.66.20.60.57 ☒ Y ev. day except Sun. 10am–12 noon 2pm–5pm

CH. DE CAMPUGET

Tradition de Campuget 1999★★

◪ 9 ha 60,000 ■ ♁ 20-29 F

The Château de Campuget received a lot of praise for its **Sommelière de Campuget 98 Rouge, Élevé en Fût** (oak-aged) and earned a star for its complex flavours of peppery spice, black fruit and a slightly burnt touch. It is a wine to drink in four or five years' time. Enthusiasm was reserved above all for the rosé with its brilliant, ripe cherry colour. The fine and elegant nose brought out flavours of honeysuckle, exotic fruits and almost crunchy citrus fruits. Nicely balanced, fresh with vibrant acidity, this very harmonious 99 finishes with a light touch of bitterness, which is far from unpleasant.

SCA Ch. de Campuget, 30129 Manduel, tel. 04.66.20.20.15, fax 04.66.20.60.57 ☒ Y ev. day except Sun. 10am–12 noon 2pm–6pm

Famille Dalle

DOM. DES CANTARELLES

Cuvée Vieilles vignes 1999★

■ 2.8 ha 8,000 ⫼ 30-49 F

This estate has submitted a wine that has spent 11 months in barrel. The attractive, deep colour has hints of purple, and the complex nose at first smells of oak, but after aeration the scents of stewed fruits emerge, followed by a spicy, toasty note. The mouth is full and powerful, structured by firm tannins, and it finishes with a slightly bitter flavour. A wine to be laid down.

Jean-François Fayel, Dom. des Cantarelles, 30127 Bellegarde, tel. 04.66.01.16.78, fax 04.66.01.02.80 ☒ Y by appt.

JEUNES VIGNES DE CARLOT 1999★

☐ 3 ha 12,000 ■ ♁ 20-29 F

Nathalie Blanc-Marès has taken on the wine-making at Mas Carlot. Young vines of the three white grape varieties of this AOC, grown in a pebbled soil, give a very attractive, deep yellow wine. It develops fine and complex aromas with mineral notes leading to flavours of peach and apricot, with a touch of toast. The full and long palate has plenty of finesse with a note of acidity on the finish.

Mas Carlot, 30127 Bellegarde, tel. 04.66.01.11.83, fax 04.66.01.62.74 ☒ Y ev. day 8am–12 noon 2pm–5pm; Sat. Sun. by appt.

Paul Blanc

DOM. DE CESAR 1999★

■ 13.3 ha 55,000 20-29 F

The wines from this property come from two linked estates and are vinified by the co-operative Costières et Soleil. Two of the wines submitted were retained and are equally good: firstly, a **99 Rosé**, which has a pleasant nose with dominant smells of red fruits and blackcurrant, and a balanced palate with a delightful, fresh finish; secondly, this excellent red that is deeply coloured, almost black. On the nose it is powerful and complex: violets, very ripe fruits of blackcurrant and strawberry from Syrah, picked at optimum maturity and given a long maceration. The palate follows well with youthful, firm tannins and a long finish.

SCA Costières et Soleil, rue Emile-Bilhau, B.P. 25, 30510 Générac, tel. 04.66.01.31.31, fax 04.66.01.38.85, e-mail costières-et-soleil@wanadoo.fr ☒ Y ev. day except Sun. 10am–12.30pm 3.30pm–7pm

CH. CLAUSONNE 1998★

■ 3 ha 7,000 ⫼ 30-49 F

This is a very pretty, deep and bright 98 from Syrah and Grenache grown on a pebbly soil. The nose shows simple vanilla oak notes, but powerful and complex flavours emerge on the palate, with blackcurrants, forest fruits and plums that all persist through to the long, attractive finish. The structure is full-bodied and dense with tannins which will become more refined in a year or two.

SCA Grands Vins de Pazac, rte de Redessan, 30840 Meynes, tel. 04.66.57.59.95, fax 04.66.57.57.63 ☒ Y ev. day except Sun. 8am–12 noon 2pm–6pm; Sat. 8am–12 noon

DOM. DE COUVIN 1999★

■ 8 ha 20,000 ■ 30-49 F

Garrigue once covered the area where this estate now lies. The colour is a pretty garnet with purple hues. The intense, fine nose is of a typical red-berry fruit character. On the palate it appears rounded and tasty with a structure that combines richness with some soft and elegant tannins. A very pleasant wine to drink now.

Jean Senmartin, Dom. du Mas de Couvin, 30840 Meynes, tel. 04.66.57.51.52, fax 04.66.57.28.45 ☒ Y by appt.

CH. GRANDE CASSAGNE 1999★

◪ n.c. 40,000 ■ ♁ 20-29 F

This estate has stayed in the same family for five generations, and offers us a delicious rosé from a blend of three grape varieties including 30% Mourvèdre. The nose is fine and delicate and the palate is full-bodied with just the right amount of body to make this a very enjoyable wine. The jury has also given a star

LANGUEDOC

to **Château Grande Cassagne 1999 Blanc**. Grenache Blanc (60%) and Roussanne planted on a good terroir of sandstone and clay-limestone produce this pale yellow wine. On the nose there are floral aromas with a touch of white peach. The palate is rounded with a fine balance.
⊶ Dardé Fils, La Grande Cassagne, 30800 Saint-Gilles, tel. 04.66.87.32.90, fax 04.66.87.32.90 ☒ Y by appt.

CH. GUIOT 1999★

■ 46 ha 200,000 ▮ ♁ 20 F+

An equal mix of Grenache and Syrah go into this very enjoyable, purple-coloured wine, which has notes of the garrigue and of crystallised fruits on the nose. The palate is balanced and soft with some youthful, but good quality tannins that lead to an agreeable finish. This Costières should be drunk within a year.
⊶ GFA Ch. Guiot, Dom. de Guiot, 30800 Saint-Gilles, tel. 04.66.73.30.86, fax 04.66.73.32.09 ☒ Y by appt.
⊶ Cornut

DOM. DU HAUT PLATEAU 1999★★

■ 3 ha 20,000 20–29 F

A fight between the stallions of the Camargue features on the label and inspires this tasting note. The Syrah (60%) gives this thoroughbred its power and spirit. Very fruity on the palate with powerful tannins make it a favourite to win the race.
⊶ Denis Fournier, Dom. du Haut-Plateau, 30129 Manduel, tel. 04.66.20.31.78, fax 04.66.20.20.53, e-mail FDenis2501@aol.com ☒ Y by appt.

DOM. DE LA BAUME Réserve Saint-Jacques 1998★

■ 2 ha 10,000 ▮ ♁ 30–49 F

Pilgrims on the road to Saint-Jacques-de-Compostelle used to stop off around here. If only they had discovered this Réserve wine en route! The first impression on the nose is undeniably gamey, but after a little time, the clear-cut scents of young blackcurrant leaves appear. It is a full-bodied wine with lively tannins on the palate leading to an aftertaste of blackcurrants and spices. The fairly long finish indicates a good ageing potential. Uncork it two hours before drinking.
⊶ Jean-François Andreoletti, Dom. de la Baume, 30800 Saint-Gilles, tel. 04.66.87.30.77, fax 04.66.87.16.47 ☒ Y by appt.

CH. DE LA CADENETTE 1999★

◪ 10 ha 10,000 ▮ ♁ 20–29 F

This pretty and delicate pink wine charmed the jury. The nose has pronounced smells of boiled sweets and red berry fruits and the first impression on the palate is quite rounded. This rosé is of a pleasant, vigorous style with a good finish.
⊶ Pierre Dideron, Dom. de la Cadenette, 30600 Vestric-et-Candiac, tel. 04.66.88.21.76, fax 04.66.88.20.59, e-mail chbommel@club-internet.fr ☒ Y by appt.

DOM. DE LA COLOMBE D'OR 1999★

■ n.c. 60,000 20–29 F

There is not much to choose between these two, as both are good wines: the **99 Rouge Élevé en Barrique** (oak-aged) has an appealing garnet colour with an attractive blackcurrant and vanilla nose. It is full-bodied on the palate with fairly young tannins and a long finish. The wine noted here shows more of a liquorice and crystallised fruits nose with a rich palate showing sophisticated tannins and an after-taste revealing liquorice once again or even pepper. A very balanced wine and like the first, it needs some time.
⊶ Les Domaines Bernard, rte de Sérignan, 84100 Orange, tel. 04.90.11.86.86, fax 04.90.34.87.30

CH. LAMARGUE Cuvée Prestige 1999★

□ 5 ha 25,000 30–49 F

This château on the edge of the Camargue has been taken over by the Bonomi family. The exquisitely pale yellow-coloured 99 does not disappoint. It has a light nose, which reminds one of springtime, with iris flowers and a touch of lychee on the end. The palate is fine with light, but balanced acidity and freshness on the finish.
⊶ SCI du Dom. de Lamargue, rte de Vauvert, 30800 Saint-Gilles, tel. 04.66.87.31.89, fax 04.66.87.41.87, e-mail domaine.de.lamargue@wanadoo.fr ☒ Y by appt.
⊶ Bonomi

CH. DE L'AMARINE Cuvée de Bernis 1999★★

◪ 3.5 ha 25,000 ▮ ♁ 20–29 F

A very delicate and attractive pink colour leads to a powerful, yet charming nose, dominated by floral notes and attracting much praise for this excellent wine. It has the rounded and full-bodied palate typical of the best southern rosés. An attractive floral character appears once again on the after-taste with a balanced finish that gives an overall impression of perfect harmony.
⊶ SCA Ch. de L'Amarine, Ch. de Campuget, 30129 Manduel, tel. 04.66.20.20.15, fax 04.66.20.60.57, e-mail campuget@wanadoo.fr ☒ Y ev. day except Sun. 10am–12 noon 2pm–6pm
⊶ Famille Dalle

DOM. DE L'ARBRE SACRE 1999★★

□ n.c. 15,000 30–49 F

The legend relates that this is the tree beneath which the pilgrims of Saint-Jaques sheltered. Whether this is true or not, it is a fine emblem for this excellent wine, notable for both its appearance and its powerful nose. The palate is rich, round and almost fleshy with a very long smoky and nutty finish. In

all, this is a wine for those who enjoy powerful, well-made wines.
🔑 SCA Costières et Soleil, rue Emile-Bilhau, B.P. 25, 30510 Générac,
tel. 04.66.01.31.31, fax 04.66.01.38.85,
e-mail costières-et-soleil@wanadoo.fr ☑ Y
ev. day except Sun. 10am–12.30pm 3.30pm–7pm

CH. DE LA TUILERIE

Cuvée Eole 1998★

■ 7.8 ha 36,000 100–149 F

In the Middle Ages, La Tuilerie supplied communion wine and firewood to the monks of the Abbey of Saint-Gilles and also provided lodgings for the pilgrims on their way to Saint-Jacques-de-Compostelle. The estate has produced a successful 98 with a dark, almost black colour that reflects the power of this vintage. The flavours are astonishingly intense, marrying black fruit and smoke with a touch of pepper, toast and a burnt character on the end. It has a powerful structure and will not reach its peak for several years.
🔑 Chantal et Pierre-Yves Comte, SCA Ch. de la Tuilerie, rte de Saint-Gilles, 30900 Nîmes, tel. 04.66.70.07.52,
fax 04.66.70.04.36, e-mail
vins@chateautuilerie.com ☑ Y by appt.

DOM. DU MAS DE LA TOUR

1999★

■ 13.55 ha 90,000 20–29 F

The co-operative Costières et Soleil at Générac has put its name to yet another rich wine with a deep, lively red colour. The nose brings out flavours of very ripe fruits, as well as undergrowth leading towards a gamey note. The palate is full-bodied and rounded, despite the firm, yet silky high-quality tannins and it has a good finish. Uncork this wine two hours before serving.
🔑 SCA Costières et Soleil, rue Emile-Bilhau, B.P. 25, 30510 Générac,
tel. 04.66.01.31.31, fax 04.66.01.38.85,
e-mail costières-et-soleil@wanadoo.fr ☑
Y ev. day except Sun. 10am–12.30pm 3.30pm–7pm

CH. MAS NEUF

Prestige des Gibelins Elevé en Barrique 1998★★★

■ 1.5 ha 15,000 30–49 F

This wine, a good standard-bearer for the estate, is simply named after its producer. An immediately attractive deep garnet-red 98, it represents one of the finest wines of the tasting. It has an intense and complex nose, combining red berry fruits with spices (bay leaves, in particular) and distinct leather notes. The first impression on the mouth is full-bodied, but it is blessed with nice balance and liquorice-flavoured tannins and is very long on the finish. Overall, a particularly well-made, powerful wine that will be very enjoyable in two years' time.
🔑 Olivier Gibelin, Ch. Mas Neuf, 30600 Gallician, tel. 04.66.73.33.23,
fax 04.66.73.33.49, e-mail
olivier.gibelin@wanadoo.fr ☑ Y by appt.

CH. MOURGUES DU GRES

Capitelles des Mourgues 1998★★

■ 2 ha 10,000 50–69 F

With a bright, deep inky colour, this wine shows vanilla on the nose, still influenced by its time in oak, and at present the fruit is somewhat muted. However, thanks to its excellent clean and balanced structure with fine, silky tannins, it should show well in two or three years. As for the **Galets Rosés 99** (30–49 F), which received a star, this is a largely floral style, with a pleasant and balanced palate, allied with a touch of softness and elegance on the finish.
🔑 François Collard, Ch. Mourgues du Grès, rte de Bellegarde, 30300 Beaucaire,
tel. 04.66.59.46.10, fax 04.66.59.34.21 ☑ Y by appt.

CH. MOURGUES DU GRES

Terre d'Argence 1999★★

■ 5 ha 30,000 30–49 F

This estate, a former convent of the Ursulines de Beaucaire, has achieved a good result with three wines judged worthy of commendation. This Cuvée Terre d'Argence has an attractive garnet colour with a purple edge, and the wine aroused admiration for its concentrated aroma, mild spices balancing the mainly red fruit flavours. It has superb balance and a nice roundness that works well with the high tannins. A very promising wine for the future.
🔑 François Collard, Ch. Mourgues du Grès, rte de Bellegarde, 30300 Beaucaire,
tel. 04.66.59.46.10, fax 04.66.59.34.21 ☑
Y by appt.

CH. DE NAGES

Cuvée Joseph Torrès 1998★

■ 8 ha 50,000 50–69 F

With 90% Syrah in the blend, this is a deep red wine with a pleasant vanilla flavour revealing its 12 months in barrel. The palate is round, rich and complex, structured by powerful, vanilla tannins, with a long finish. For those who enjoy fleshy, concentrated wines.
🔑 EARL Roger Gassier, Ch. de Nages, 30132 Caissargues, tel. 04.66.38.44.20,
fax 04.66.38.44.21, e-mail
m.gassier@châteaudenages.com ☑
Y by appt.

CH. D'OR ET DE GUEULES

Cuvée Prestige 1998*

■ 10 ha 20,000 50–69 F

Highly coloured with tinges of purple, this Cuvée Prestige really caught the attention of the jury. The enjoyable nose is concentrated, with predominantly black fruits, blending blackcurrant, blackberry and blueberry. The structure is as good as the aromas and it shows a powerful balance. This wine needs three or four years for the tannins to soften.

Ch. d'Or et de Gueules, rte de Générac, 30800 Saint-Gilles, tel. 04.66.87.32.86, fax 04.66.87.39.11, e-mail Châteaudoretdegueules@wanadoo.fr Y by appt.

Puy Morin

PAVILLON DE L'ESCALION 1998*

■ 8.2 ha 22,000 30–49 F

This estate was consolidated in 1800 after having been in the hands of various different foreign owners. Everything about the wine submitted seems to be encapsulated in the word 'power': a powerful deep and dark red colour, a powerful nose with intense notes of leather, humus and undergrowth. The palate is powerful and structured too, with tight-knit, round tannins and a long, fruity finish. This 98 should be left for a year or two.

SCI Dom. du Grand Escalion, rte de Nîmes, 30510 Générac, tel. 04.66.01.31.72, fax 04.66.01.31.72, e-mail vinescal@wanadoo.fr Y by appt.

DOM. DE PIERREFEU 1999*

□ 1 ha 6,500 30–49 F

Olivier Gibelin submitted this excellent Domaine de Pierrefeu, from the same estate that won a *coup de cœur* for the Château du Mas Neuf. With a brilliant, pale yellow colour, it is notable for a touch of fine and elegant citrus fruit that lasts right through the tasting. It has a good balance on the palate and its long, pleasant finish endorses its quality.

Olivier Gibelin, Ch. Mas Neuf, 30600 Gallician, tel. 04.66.73.33.23, fax 04.66.73.33.49, e-mail olivier.gibelin@wanadoo.fr Y by appt.

DOM. SAINT-ANTOINE 1999**

◪ 12 ha 13,000 20–29 F

This estate submitted a very attractive bright pink rosé that does not disappoint. The nose is intense and elegant, exuding aromas of fresh strawberries and raspberries and some blackcurrant sweets. A touch of carbon dioxide livens up the balanced palate. Both rounded and fresh, it has an extremely good depth of flavour.

Jean-Louis Emmanuel, EARL Dom. Saint-Antoine, 30800 Saint-Gilles, tel. 04.66.01.87.29, fax 04.66.01.87.29

CH. SAINT-BENEZET 1999*

◪ 17 ha 55,000 20–29 F

This estate was taken over in 1999. The current owners submitted this bright and pretty, delicate pink rosé 99 that caught our attention. The reasonably intense nose is a delicate mixture of fruits and flowers. The palate, which is on the whole rounded, gives a clean, mainly floral after-taste. Overall it is both fine and balanced and a wine that will appeal to those who love southern rosés.

SCEA Saint-Bénézet, Dom. Saint-Bénézet, 30800 Saint-Gilles, tel. 06.16.57.32.02, fax 06.66.70.05.11 Y ev. day except Sun. 9am–8pm

Bosse-Platière

CH. SAINT-CYRGUES 1999**

■ 5 ha 25,000 20–29 F

Vine-grower and wine-maker, Evelyne and Guy de Mercurio from Switzerland have run this property since 1991. They submitted two wines that were much liked by the jury. Firstly, this excellent deep purple-coloured red, which has a powerful blackcurrant nose with a somewhat herbaceous feel at the back. It has fine and elegant tannins on the palate with a fleshy, full-bodied, rounded style that is very appealing. The wine has a long, slightly bitter finish and we firmly believe that it has a great future. Secondly the brilliant, deep black-coloured **Cuvée Amérique 98** (30–49 F) received a star. The wine bears the original estate name in memory of the former son of the house who has gone on to pastures new. It shows unobtrusive oaky notes from time spent in wood. The palate still shows rather obvious tannins that need some years to soften out.

Guy de Mercurio, Ch. Saint-Cyrgues, rte de Montpellier, 30800 Saint-Gilles, tel. 04.66.87.31.72, fax 04.66.87.70.76 Y by appt.

CH. SILEX 1999*

■ n.c. n.c. 30–49 F

This intensely red-coloured wine has a purple rim and is a blend of Syrah and Grenache with a touch of Mourvèdre. Straightforward to begin with, the middle palate shows a good balance of tannins, richness and acidity. This excellent wine can be enjoyed right away.

SCEA Saint-Bénézet, Dom. Saint-Bénézet, 30800 Saint-Gilles, tel. 06.16.57.32.02, fax 06.66.70.05.11 Y ev. day except Sun. 9am–8pm

CH. DES SOURCES

Elevé en Fût de Chêne 1999*

■ 10.9 ha n.c. 20 F+

A very dark-coloured red with a powerful and concentrated nose. After the first sip, one finds a structured wine with vigorous tannins. It must be left for some time to be at its best.

Jean-François Fayel, Dom. des Cantarelles, 30127 Bellegarde, tel. 04.66.01.16.78, fax 04.66.01.02.80 Y by appt.

CH. DE VALCOMBE 1999*

◪ 2 ha 5,000 20–29 F

In the hands of the same family since the 18th century, Valcome gives us an attractive

rosé 99 with a pleasantly fruity nose. The palate is rounded and shows flavours of red berry fruit, with a fairly long finish. The overall impression is one of softness and balance, which will make this wine an excellent companion for your meals beneath a parasol.
Dominique Ricome, Ch. de Valcombe, 30510 Générac, tel. 04.66.01.32.20, fax 04.66.01.92.24, e-mail valcombe@wanadoo.fr by appt.

Coteaux du Languedoc

These wines are grown in an area of moors and hills stretching from Narbonne to Nîmes. A total of 168 communes, five of which are in the Aude and 19 in the Gard, the remainder in the Hérault, contribute to the appellation, specialising in red and rosé wines. AOC Coteaux du Languedoc has been an Appellation Générale since 1985, added to which are 11 specific denominations of red and rosé wines: La Clape and Quatourze in the Aude, Cabrières, Montpeyroux, Saint-Saturnin, Pic-Saint-Loup, Saint-Georges-d'Orques, Les Coteaux de la Méjanelle, Saint-Drézéry, Saint-Christol and the Coteaux de Vérargues in the Hérault; there are also two white denominations: La Clape and Picpoul de Pinet.

All are descended from wines that have been renowned for centuries. The Coteaux du Languedoc produce 435,000 hl (11,484,000 gal) of wines.

A wine brotherhood, the Ordre des Ambassadeurs des Coteaux du Languedoc, has now been established for the Coteaux du Languedoc.

ABBAYE DES MONGES

La Clape 1999★★

1.8 ha 4,000 20–29 F

The terroir at La Clape enjoyed really good weather conditions in the 1999 vintage, with plenty of sunshine and just the right amount of summer rain when the vine needed it. Here, the Abbaye des Monges has given us an exquisite wine. Pale-coloured with a golden rim, it has an excellent nose with scents of apricot, peach, honey and flowers with a touch of toastiness. On the palate it is tasty, fresh, lively, full-bodied and long; a most congenial wine.
Paul de Chefdebien, 45, rue Parerie, 11100 Narbonne, tel. 04.68.42.36.27, fax 04.68.41.53.07 by appt.

ABBAYE DE VALMAGNE

Cuvée de Turenne 1998★★

4.27 ha 20,000 50–69 F

The Abbaye de Valmagne is certainly worth a visit to look at the expert restoration of the 12th-century Cistercian architecture, though once you have crossed the cloisters to venture into the cellars, you won't want to leave. This will certainly be true once you have tasted the white Cuvée de Turenne 98. It has an attractive pale yellow colour, with an intense, yet subtle nose of crystallised fruits, honey, acacia and toast, with a light oaky touch. The mouth-filling palate has a good balance of richness and body, with real fleshiness on the long finish.
D'Allaines, SCEA Dom. de Valmagne, Abbaye de Valmagne, 34560 Villeveyrac, tel. 04.67.78.06.09, fax 04.67.78.02.50, e-mail valmagne@aol.com by appt.

ARNAUD DE NEFFIEZ 1998★

2 ha 5,000 50–69 F

The *cuvée* Arnaud de Neffiez lives up to its illustrious predecessors. Born under a lucky star, with an intense red colour, the wine reveals a plethora of blackcurrant, coffee and spicy flavours. With a fine touch of oak, it has a direct approach on the palate, but is rounded and full-bodied with sufficiently good weight and length. The **Catherine de Saint-Juéry** was particularly successful in the 98 vintage and receives a mention (30–49 F).
Cave coop. de Neffiès, av. de la Gare, 34320 Neffiès, tel. 04.67.24.61.98, fax 04.67.24.62.12 by appt.

DOM. HONORE AUDRAN

Cuvée Terroir 1998★

3 ha 4,000 50–69 F

A consistently successful estate, Honoré Audran has submitted this very balanced 98 with a deep red colour and an intense jammy fruit nose, showing nutty characters and toast. The palate is rich and fleshy, with a nice structure of soft tannins and good length. Very well balanced.
GAEC Luc Biscarlet, 8, chem. du Moulin, 34700 Le Bosc, tel. 04.67.44.73.44, fax 04.67.44.73.44 by appt.

LANGUEDOC

DOM. D'AUPILHAC

Montpeyroux 1998★★

■ 10 ha 50,000 ◍ 50–69 F

Still showing the impetuosity of youth, but destined to become a classic, the dark red Domaine d'Aupilhac 98 has a vigorous nose of very ripe blackcurrants, notes of thyme and cumin as well as slightly burnt vanilla, and the oakiness is held well in check. It has a firm and clean attack on the palate, which opens up towards richness and fleshiness. Silky tannins are still very much in evidence as in all the good 1998s.

Sylvain Fadat, Dom. d'Aupilhac, 28, rue du Plô, 34150 Montpeyroux, tel. 04.67.96.61.19, fax 04.67.96.67.24, e-mail aupilhac@wanadoo.fr ☒ Y by appt.

DOM. DE BAUBIAC 1998★

■ 3.14 ha 13,470 ◍ 30–49 F

If you like full-bodied wines, you will love the wines of Baubiac. The blackberry-coloured 98 is a good example, with a bouquet of dried flowers, red berry fruits and undergrowth, and with good weight on the palate. The oak is not allowed to dominate, and the wine will open up more in the years to come.

SCEA Philip Frères, Dom. de Baubiac, 30260 Brouzet-lès-Quissac, tel. 04.66.77.33.45, fax 04.66.77.33.45, e-mail philip@dstu.univ-montp2.fr ☒ Y by appt.

CH. BELLES EAUX Tradition 1999★

◢ 4 ha 8,000 ■ 🌡 30–49 F

Château Belles Eaux has produced an enticing and stylish wine in 1999 with an attractively bright pale pink colour. It has intense floral aromas with red berry fruits as well as burlat cherries. The rounded and rich palate is soft and sweet with delicious balance.

Ch. Belles Eaux, 34720 Caux, tel. 04.67.09.30.95, fax 04.67.09.30.95 ☒ Y by appt.

MAS BLANCHARD

Cuvée Tradition 1998★

■ 6 ha 15,000 ■ 🌡 30–49 F

This wine is produced from a selection of old-vine Grenache and Carignan. It presents a deep purple colour with touches of violet and a pleasant nose that is full of spicy fruit. The palate has noticeable tannins, but they are sufficiently well-integrated to give a good balance and attractive length.

Dominique Chiapino, 10, rue Louis Guy, 34490 Murviel-les-Béziers, tel. 04.67.89.63.15, fax 04.67.89.65.17 ☒

BOIS D'ELEINS 1999★

■ 3.5 ha 4,000 ■ 🌡 20–29 F

The co-operative at Crespian appears with the new, garnet-coloured 1999 vintage. Initial aromas of blackcurrant and redcurrant give way to notes of liquorice and pepper. Soft and very drinkable, it will be best enjoyed in its youth. On the other hand, the **Grande Réserve 98**, which received a mention from the jury, should be kept (30–49 F).

SCA Les vignerons d'Art, R.N. 110, 30260 Crespian, tel. 04.66.77.81.87, fax 04.66.77.81.43, e-mail w.valgalier@lemel.fr ☒ Y ev. day except Sun. Mon. 9am–6pm

MAS BRUGUIERE

Pic Saint-Loup la Grenadière 1998★

■ 4 ha 18,000 ◍ 70–99 F

You will have to hurry to reserve a bottle if you want to try the Grenadière 98 from Mas Bruguière, because as well as being good, it is in limited supply. The colour is bright, but dark; the nose is fairly powerful with black fruit, roasted garrigue, and nutmeg. It opens onto a weighty palate with grainy tannins, balanced by high alcohol. The **Les Muriers 98 Blanc** was also noted by the jury (50–69 F).

Guilhem Bruguière, La Plaine, 34270 Valflaunès, tel. 04.67.55.20.97, fax 04.67.55.20.97 ☒ Y by appt.

CH. CABRIERES

Cabrières Elevé en Fût de Chêne 1998★

■ 10 ha 10,000 ◍ 50–69 F

Château Cabrières, which was well known in the time of Louis 14th, distinguishes itself again in obtaining a star for the oak-aged 98. It has a lively, deep colour; an intense, fine nose, which exudes spices, the garrigue, burnt oak and red berry fruit aromas. It is concentrated on the palate, with a silky feel and a good balance. The garnet-coloured **Fulcran de Cabanon 99** is spicy, fruity and deliciously mouth-filling. The jury also gave it a mention.

Cave des Vignerons de Cabrières, 34800 Cabrières, tel. 04.67.88.91.60, fax 04.67.88.00.15 ☒ Y ev. day except Sun. 9am–12 noon 2pm–6pm

MAS CAL DEMOURA 1998★

■ 5 ha 21,000 ■ ◍ 50–69 F

In staying rooted to the land and obstinately refusing to partake in any rural exodus, Jean-Pierre Jullien demonstrates his philosophy of good living by producing wines of the highest quality and interest. The very young red 98, still quite restrained, has a good intense colour, a closed but promising nose with ripe red berry fruits and notes of smokiness and the garrigue. The palate has much weight with youthful tannins that are still slightly coarse. This wine needs three or four years of cellar age.

Jean-Pierre Jullien, Mas Cal Demoura, 34725 Jonquières, tel. 04.67.88.61.51, fax 04.67.88.61.51 ☒ Y by appt.

CAMPLAZENS LE CHATEAU

La Clape Elevé en fût de chêne 1998

■ 14 ha 50,000 ◍ 70–99 F

Château de Camplazens is an interpretation of La Clape and the Mediterranean by producers originally from the North of France. This deep garnet-red wine has been made to give an intense nose, revealing red fruit aromas, cocoa, vanilla and burnt wood. The palate is slightly closed and rustic at

present, all it needs to smooth out the rough edges is a couple more years of ageing.
🔑 SCEA Dom. de la Jasse, La Jasse, 34980 Combaillaux, tel. 04.67.84.34.62, fax 04.67.84.30.51 🍷 by appt.

CH. DE CAPITOUL

La Clape les Rocailles 1998★★

☐ 4 ha 6,000 30–49 F

The Grand Crus of the Languedoc are on the threshold of discovery, but for the moment they are cautiously promoting themselves in the face of general disbelief. Nevertheless, one can very easily be persuaded of their existence on opening a Capitoul Rocailles 98. A bright golden yellow, the power of this wine asserts itself on the nose, which has a very rich character of apricots, citrus fruits, herbs from the garrigue, ginger, spices and honey. This is a mouth-filling wine, even voluptuous, with a superb balance, both rich and ripe. **Les Rocailles 98 Rouge** was awarded a mention.
🔑 SA du Ch. de Capitoul, rte de Gruissan, 11100 Narbonne, tel. 04.68.49.23.30, fax 04.68.49.55.71, e-mail chateau.capitoul@wanadoo.fr ☒
🍷 ev. day 8am–8pm
🔑 Charles Mock

DOM. CELINGUET 1998★

■ 7.5 ha 24,000 30–49 F

Justifiably noted amongst the highest awards in previous years, the Domaine Célinguet 98 offers an intense and bright purple colour still showing youth, and an equally intense nose with macerated fruits, cherries, prunes, spices, bay leaves and a hint of gamey aromas. The palate is still quite restrained due to the pronounced, firm tannins, with a very respectable finish.
🔑 Pierre et Myriam Rouquette, 34380 Argelliers, tel. 04.67.55.62.36, fax 04.67.55.52.11, e-mail rouquette.celinguet@wanadoo.fr ☒ 🍷 by appt.

DOM. CHARTREUSE DE MOUGERES

Clos de l'Abbaye Elevé en Fût de Chêne 1998★

■ 2 ha 10,000 30–49 F

Quite rightly, monks and nuns have been renowned for many years as specialists in making wines, liqueurs and brandies, and with the Clos 98 from the Abbaye des Chartreuse de Mougères, we are approaching paradise. Judge for yourself this intensely red-coloured wine, full of grace. It has an attractive spicy nose, showing some bay leaf, liquorice, prune and a good deal of oak, with a well-structured, rich palate that indicates several years of serenity.
🔑 Sareh Bonne Terre, Dom. Chartreuse de Mougères, 34720 Caux, tel. 04.67.98.40.01, fax 04.67.98.46.39, e-mail nicolas.lebecq@libertysurf.fr ☒ 🍷 Tue. Thu. Fri. Sat. 9am–12 noon 2pm–5pm

COMBEROUSSE Rocalhan 1998★★

☐ 3.5 ha 2,000 50–69 F

Once a sheep farmer, Alain Reder is now a specialist in white wine-making. The Rocalhan 98, from Roussanne and Rolle, is almost sublime. It has a pale yellow colour of good intensity, and a string of aromas including notes of toast, smoke, quince, fruit jelly, menthol, spices and some flowers. Richness and smoothness dominate the distinguished and powerful palate. A second glass of this extremely nice, easy-going wine will make you reach for the superlatives.
🔑 Alain Reder, SCEA du Djebel, Comberousse, rte de Gignac, 34660 Cournonterral, tel. 04.67.85.05.18, fax 04.67.85.05.18 ☒ 🍷 by appt.

DOM. COUR SAINT VINCENT 1999

☐ n.c. 5,000 30–49 F

This is the first time Francis Bouys has made wine in a private capacity. He submits a bright, pale yellow 99 with a green rim and a fine, elegant nose reminiscent of wild roses and citrus fruits. Both tangy and round on the palate, the wine is rich, with a good balance and pleasant finish.
🔑 Francis Bouys, 1, pl. Saint-Vincent, 34730 Saint-Vincent-de-Barbeyrargues, tel. 04.67.59.60.74, fax 04.67.59.60.74 ☒ 🍷 Fri. Sat. 9am–7pm; cl. 1–15 Aug.

ERMITAGE DU PIC SAINT-LOUP

Pic Saint-Loup Cuvée Sainte-Agnès 1998★

■ 4 ha 8,000 30–49 F

The coat of arms with its three fish can be found on the labels of both Ermitage du Pic Saint-Loup retained by the jury: the **Guilhem Gaucelm 97**, given a mention (100–149 F), and this bright purple-coloured Cuvée Sainte-Agnès. The nose shows fruit, spice and toast, followed by vanilla notes. Full-bodied, it has a weighty and powerful palate with just the right amount of oak.
🔑 Ravaille, GAEC Ermitage du Pic Saint-Loup, Cazevieille, 34270 Saint-Mathieu-de-Tréviers, tel. 04.67.55.20.15, fax 04.67.55.23.49 ☒ 🍷 by appt.

DOM. FERRI ARNAUD

La Clape Cuvée Romain Elevé en Fût de Chêne 1998★

■ 1.5 ha 6,500 70–99 F

Domaine Ferri Arnaud is situated at Fleury, one of the villages of La Clape, a few hundred yards from the Mediterranean. The Cuvée Romain (the Romans were there too, of course) spends 14 months in oak and is a dark red, flecked with tinges of brown. The incredible nose is roasted and peppery, with notes of menthol, liquorice and blackcurrant. The oak is still noticeable on the palate but integrates with the velvety tannins. Also worth tasting is the **Domaine 98 Rouge**, which has just nine months in oak and received a mention (50–69 F). You will not be disappointed.

EARL Ferri Arnaud, av. de l'Hérault, 11560 Fleury-d'Aude, tel. 04.68.33.62.43, fax 04.68.33.74.38 ☑ Y by appt.

Joseph Ferri

CH. DE FLAUGERGUES

La Méjanelle Cuvée Sommelière 1998★

■ 13 ha 60,000 50–69 F

The Château du Flaugergues is a superb 17th-century country house on the edge of Montpellier, Flaugergues. Its prestige is maintained with the star granted to the deep-coloured Sommelière 98, garnet with brilliant purple tinges. The wine has a distinguished nose of fruits, leather and spices, with a touch of undergrowth. This balanced 98 fills the palate with its obvious silky tannins.

Henri de Colbert, Ch. de Flaugergues,1744, av. Albert-Einstein, 34000 Montpellier, tel. 04.99.52.66.37, fax 04.99.52.66.44, e-mail colbert@flaugergues.com ☑ Y by appt.

CAVE DE FLORENSAC

Picpoul de Pinet Cuvée Ressac 1999★

□ 20 ha 40,000 20–29 F

This terroir rooted in a stony clay-limestone soil has produced a fresh and balanced 99 white. With a crystal-clear, green tinged colour, the wine shows lemon and acacia notes on the nose. The delightful palate marries roundness with acidity, characteristic of Picpoul de Pinet.

Cave coopérative de Florensac, B.P. 9, 34510 Florensac, tel. 04.67.77.00.20, fax 04.67.77.79.66 ☑ Y ev. day except Sun. 9am–12 noon 2pm–6pm

CH. FONDOUCE 1998★

■ 4 ha 6,486 50–69 F

The slopes of volcanic origin on the edge of Pézenas produce some very nice surprises, not least this charming Foundouce. A dark red 98 that gives real pleasure, it has an intensely leathery nose, with roasted and very ripe red fruit notes. Very immediate on the palate, it is round and fleshy with balanced and integrated tannins.

Jean-Claude Magnien, Dom. de Fondouce, rte de Roujan, 34120 Pézenas, tel. 04.67.98.30.32, fax 04.67.98.29.76, e-mail sicla@wanadoo.fr ☑ Y ev. day except Sat. Sun. 10am–12 noon 2pm–6pm

MAS DE FOURNEL

Pic Saint-Loup Cuvée Pierre 1998★★

■ 3 ha 2,200 50–69 F

According to him, 70-year-old Gérard Jeanjean is a 'young wine-maker'. Previously he used to transport bulk wine in his tanker, but for three years now he has managed the family estate. These three years have enabled him to perfect this magnificent, deep garnet *coup de cœur*, Cuvée Pierre 98. The nose is very complex with notes of black fruits, smoke, spice and liquorice. The oak character is present on the palate but integrates well with a superb structure, unctuous, mouth-filling and with a delightful finish. The icing on the cake is that one star is awarded to the **Mas de Fournel 98 Rouge** (30–49 F) a wine that has not even been near an oak barrel.

Gérard Jeanjean, Mas de Fournel, 34270 Valflaunes, tel. 04.67.55.22.12, fax 04.67.55.22.12 ☑
Y ev. day 9am–12 noon 2pm–7pm

CH. DE FOURQUES

Saint-Georges d'Orques Cuvée Jeanne 1999

◢ 3 ha 5,500 30–49 F

The rosés from the Château de Fourques are nearly always delicate and charming. The fresh and balanced 99 is no exception, with its pretty salmon-pink appearance, its elegant nose of raspberries and wild flowers and its mouth-filling, lively palate.

Mme Fons-Vincent, Ch. de Fourques, rte de Laverune, 34990 Juvignac, tel. 04.67.47.90.87, fax 04.67.27.48.72, e-mail fourques@caves-particulieres.com ☑
Y ev. day 8.30am–7.30pm

CUVEE DES GENTILSHOMMES VERRIERS Pic Saint-Loup 1999★

◢ 15 ha 8,000 20–29 F

To be found on the same road as the glass-works, the Vignerons du Pic offer for tasting this enchanting wine, with a pretty pink colour, both pale, bright and lively. The nose has very intense green apples, with notes of wild flowers and red berries. On the palate it is straightforward and all in all, full and balanced. The **Château d'Assas 99 Blanc** is awarded a mention for its delicious freshness and its fine balance.

🔑 Les Vignerons du Pic, 285, av. de Sainte-Croix, 34820 Assas, tel. 04.67.59.62.55, fax 04.67.59.56.39 ☑ 🍷 by appt.

MAS GRANIER Les Marnes 1998★★

□ 3 ha 5,000 ⏸ 30–49 F

A stony limestone soil, big Russian oak casks and continual care and attention have resulted in this remarkable wine, Les Marnes 98. It has a bright lemon yellow colour with the most delicious range of aromas: citrus fruits, apricots, verbena, flowers, a touch of toastiness and some vanilla. Rich, fleshy and full, the palate lingers on and on. A star is also awarded to the deep-coloured **Mas Granier 98 Rouge**, which has an intense nose, a good structured palate and a long finish. Note also the **Les Grès 98 Rouge** (50–69 F), which has a good future.

🔑 EARL Granier, Mas Montel, 30250 Aspères, tel. 04.66.80.01.21, fax 04.66.80.01.87, e-mail montel@wanadoo.fr ☑ 🍷 ev. day except Sun. 9am–7pm

DOM. DE GRANOUPIAC

Elevé en Fût 1998★

■ 5.2 ha 4,000 ⏸ 30–49 F

Claude Flavord makes a wine that expresses well the character of Syrah (60% of the blend) produced on a clay-limestone soil and matured in wood. With a deep garnet colour, the intense nose provides notes of the garrigue, red berry fruit, hints of gaminess and aromas associated with juniper tar oil and spices. The palate is full-bodied and rich with firm tannins that are sufficiently velvety to describe as elegant. The un-oaked and finely balanced **Cuvée Principale 98** also appealed to the tasters, who gave it a mention.

🔑 Claude Flavard, Dom. de Granoupiac, 34725 Saint-André-de-Sangonis, tel. 04.67.57.58.28, fax 04.67.57.95.83 ☑ 🍷 by appt.

DOM. DES GRECAUX

Montpeyroux 1999

■ 3.15 ha 11,500 ▮ 50–69 F

This new estate at Montpeyroux has already produced some very successful wines. The light ruby-coloured 99 has a fruity nose revealing some grilled meat character. It has a delicate, straightforward palate with red fruit flavours. Ready to drink now.

🔑 Isabelle Caujolle-Gazet, 4, av. du Monument, 34150 Saint-Jean-de-Fos, tel. 04.67.57.38.83, fax 04.67.57.38.83, e-mail caujolle@club-internet.fr ☑ 🍷 Sat. Sun. 5pm–7pm; cl. 25 Aug.–30 Jun.

CH. GRES SAINT-PAUL

Antonin 1998★★

■ 7 ha 28,000 ⏸ 70–99 F

This Cuvée Antonin 98 from Grès Saint-Paul, an extremely classy wine, is awarded *coup de cœur* and was classed second overall

by the grand jury. It has a dark red colour with shades of black and purple. The intense aromas have some subtle, but very ripe red fruit notes, burnt oak, spices, cocoa and liquorice that are present both on the nose and the palate. The latter has a good structure of well-integrated, velvety tannins and has the weight and length that one would expect of any wine of this class. We would also like to mention the tank-matured **Romanis 99**, which is well-made and is another wine that should be kept for a little time.

🔑 Ch. Grès Saint-Paul, rte de Restinclières, 34400 Lunel, tel. 04.67.71.27.90, fax 04.67.71.73.76 ☑ 🍷 by appt.

HAUT BLANVILLE 1998★★

■ 4 ha 13,000 ⏸ 70–99 F

Monsieur and Madame Nivollet, originally from northern France, but with a hankering for Mediterranean life, have gone into viticulture, fortuitously, as proven by this Haut Blanville 98. With an intense red colour, the nose of this wine provides a powerful expression of very ripe red berries, a roasted character, leather and spices. The palate is extremely well balanced and full, with evident, but well-integrated tannins typical of the vintage. The wine has incredible length.

🔑 Bernard et Béatrice Nivollet, dom. Rieutort de Blanville, rte de Gignac, 34230 Saint-Pargoire, tel. 04.67.98.47.66, fax 04.67.98.49.93, e-mail deblanville@wanadoo.fr ☑ 🍷 ev. day except Sun. 10am–12.30pm 4pm–6.30pm

MAS HAUT-BUIS

Terrasse du Larzac 1999★

■ 5 ha 15,000 ▮ ⏸ 50–69 F

Here is a new estate producing Appellation Contrôlée wines in the terraced region of Larzac. They have still to build their reputation. This 99 starts off well: a deep colour with a purple edge and aromas of spices, smoke and over-ripe red berry fruit. The palate is still very young, but gives a good body and structure, which will allow it to develop well in the years to come.

🔑 Olivier Jeantet, 34520 La Vacquerie, tel. 04.67.88.64.92, fax 04.67.88.64.92 ☑ 🍷 by appt.

CH. HAUT-CHRISTIN

Terres de Sommières 1998★

■ 5 ha 24,000 ▮ 30–49 F

Not far from Sommières la Romaine, towers the imposing and ancient mansion of Haut-Christin. This bright, intense red Château 98 shows notes of undergrowth, the garrigue, fruit macerated in good brandy and a sliver of leather. Fine and tightly knit, the palate is not slow in coming forward and is full-bodied, structured, mouth-filling and long. Note also the **Domaine de Christin, Cuvée Tradition 97 Rouge, Vieillie en Fût** (barrel-aged), mentioned but not given a star, it is ready to drink now (50–69 F).

André et Marie-France Mahuzies, rte d'Aubais, 30250 Junas, tel. 04.66.80.95.90, fax 04.66.80.95.90, e-mail mahuzies@aol.com ☒ Y by appt.

DOM. HAUT LIROU

Pic Saint Loup 1999★

◪ 4 ha n.c. 30–49 F

Here is a rosé that reflects the great charm of the village where it is produced, Saint-Jean-de-Cuculles. It has a pastel and salmon-pink colour with a nose of red berry fruit and flowers. The palate is full and rich, giving an impression of crunching ripe fruits.

Rambier et Fils, 34270 Saint-Jean-de-Cuculles, tel. 04.67.55.38.50, fax 04.67.55.38.49, e-mail rambier@rambier.com ☒ Y ev. day except Sun. 9am–12.30pm 2pm–6.30pm

DOM. HENRY

Saint-Georges d'Orques 1998★

■ 4 ha 15,000 ▮ 🌡 70–99 F

The vineyard that produced the grapes for this wine can be found on the broken limestone soil. This attractive 98 has a luminous garnet-red appearance and a nose that reminds one of the garrigue, of cinnamon and of cooked strawberries. The palate offers silky tannins, with a full body and a spicy finish. It might make a good partner to roast lamb with thyme.

Dom. Henry, av. d'Occitanie, 34680 Saint-Georges-d'Orques, tel. 04.67.45.57.74, fax 04.67.45.57.74, e-mail domainehenry@wanadoo.fr ☒ Y by appt.

HUGUES DE BEAUVIGNAC

Picpoul de Pinet 1999★★

□ 100 ha 400,000 ▮ 🌡 20–29 F

It is said in the Languedoc that the 1999 vintage produced some memorable white wines, and tasting this marvellous Picpoul de Pinet Hugues de Beauvignac, we would quite agree. It is made by the co-operative at Pomérol, close to the Bassin de Thau, the lake right by Sète. With an enticing light straw-yellow colour, the nose has equal amounts of intensity and elegance with notes of citrus fruits, aniseed, dill and wild flowers. The palate is lively and fresh at the start, then evolves with a smoothness that balances with lively acidity and richness, ending with a good finish. The **Domaine Saint Peyre 99** has most attractive roundness and balance and is awarded a star.

Cave les Costières de Pomérols, 34810 Pomérols, tel. 04.67.77.01.59, fax 04.67.77.77.21, e-mail pomerols@mnet.fr ☒ Y by appt.

CH. DE JONQUIERES

Comte de Lansade 1998★

□ 1 ha 4,500 ⦀ 50–69 F

The Château de Jonquières is produced in two forms. To start with, the white Comte de Lansade 98 has a bright, clear yellow colour with good legs. The nose has an attractive depth, with buttery flavours from some lees contact, as well as vanilla and smoke. On the palate it appears straightforward and fruity, developing a good balance of weight and length. Also noted is the very young and oaky **Baronnie 98 Rouge**.

François de Cabissole, Ch. de Jonquières, 34725 Jonquières, tel. 04.67.96.62.58, fax 04.67.88.61.92, e-mail chateau.de.jonquieres@wanadoo.fr ☒ Y by appt.

MAS DE LA BARBEN Tradition 1999

■ 28.1 ha 130,000 ▮ 🌡 20–29 F

The Mas de la Barben gives us this purple iris-coloured wine. It has quite an intense nose with notes of red berry fruits and a touch of leather, and the rounded palate shows decent length.

Mas de La Barben, rte de Sauve, 30900 Nîmes, tel. 04.66.81.15.88, fax 04.66.63.80.43 ☒ Y by appt.

Marcel Hermann

ELIXIR DE LA CONDAMINE BERTRAND Pézenas 1999★

■ 2 ha 4,000 ⦀ 100–149 F

Is this elixir a medicine to protect against heart disease, or perhaps the essence of a magic potion? An intense purply red colour leads to a complex and powerful nose of roasted flavours, undergrowth, cut hay, spices, ripe berries and prunes. This in turn leads to a tight palate, balanced by soft tannins.

Bernard et Charles Jany, Ch. la Condamine Bertrand, 34230 Paulhan, tel. 04.67.25.27.96, fax 04.67.25.07.55 ☒ Y ev. day 10am–12 noon 3pm–7pm

DOM. DE LA COSTE

Saint Christol 1998★

■ 15 ha 35,000 ▮ 🌡 30–49 F

In this wine from Domaine de la Coste, the characteristic bouquet of wines from the pebbled terroir is revealed, with notes of spices, stewed fruits and liquorice. Intensity is not only good on the appearance, but also on the palate, which marries a rich body with a solid and velvety structure. On the strength of its length of flavours, this should be a wine to keep.

Luc et Elisabeth Moynier, Dom. de la Coste, 34400 Saint-Christol, tel. 04.67.86.02.10, fax 04.67.86.07.71 ev. day except Sun. 9am–7pm

DOM. LA CROIX SAINTE EULALIE

Elevé en Fût 1999*

□ 1 ha 4,000 50–69 F

The vines are situated on the schistose terroir of Saint-Chinian, which yields highly expressive wines. This is noticeable on the **Saint-Chinian 99 Rosé** and a **98 Rouge** (30–49 F), both given a mention by the tasters. This particular Coteaux du Languedoc wine gives a classy nose with complex notes of nuts, brioche and flowers. The palate is direct and shows good balance. A most agreeable wine.

Michel et Aline Gleizes, Combejean, dom. la Croix Sainte-Eulalie, 34360 Pierrerue, tel. 04.67.38.08.51, fax 04.67.38.08.51, e-mail michel.gleizes@libertysurf.fr by appt.

DOM. LACROIX-VANEL

Clos Mélanie 1998

■ 3 ha 5,000 50–69 F

The story behind the Domaine Lacrois-Vanil is of a restaurateur from Sète and his companion, both lovers of good books, fine food and wine. This fine example is the result of their first production. Attractive with an intense red colour with hints of blue, it is floral, fruity, toasty and reminiscent of cut hay. Spicy on the nose, their most attractive 98 is elegant and silky with a soft and balanced palate.

Jean-Pierre Vanel, 46, bd du Puits-Allier, 34720 Caux, tel. 04.67.09.32.39, fax 04.67.09.32.39 by appt.

CH. DE LA DEVEZE MONNIER

1998*

□ 2 ha 2,000 50–69 F

A very worthy entrant in the *Guide* for this, the most northernmost vineyard in the Coteaux du Languedoc, and only classed as Appellation Contrôlée since 1997. The whites from here have great finesse: a light golden colour with green tinges, complex floral aromas, with toast and coconut notes too, and the palate is both lively and warming. The maturation in wood has been well judged.

Laurent Damais, GAEC du Dom. de la Devèze, 34190 Montoulieu, tel. 04.67.73.70.21, fax 04.67.73.32.40, e-mail damais@deveze.com by appt.

Marcel Damais

DOM. L'AIGUELIERE

Montpeyroux Côte Rousse 1998**

■ 2.5 ha 12,000 100–149 F

L'Aiguelière has submitted a marvellous 98 that has received nothing but praise. The colour is a concentrated purple and the nose is complex, intense and elegant, with notes of cherry, undergrowth, leather, smoke, spices and a touch of balsam. On the palate it is round and fleshy, full-bodied and long, with a structure of firm tannins, which will require at least five years of ageing to soften.

Commeyras, 2, pl. du square Michel-Teisserenc, 34150 Montpeyroux, tel. 04.67.96.61.43, fax 04.67.96.61.43 by appt.

CH. DE LANCYRE

Pic Saint-Loup Grande Cuvée 1998**

■ 5 ha 20,000 70–99 F

The Grand Cuvée 98 has proved to be really excellent. With an intense red colour, the aromas show currants, herbs from the garrigue, liquorice and vanilla, and these lead on to a fabulously rich palate. With powerful but ripe tannins, this wine has impressive length. A really classy wine to lay down for five years. Its alter ego is the **98 Blanc**, which is also finely oaked, and receives a star.

GAEC de Lancyre, 34270 Valflaunès, tel. 04.67.55.22.28, fax 04.67.55.23.84 by appt.

Durand et Valentin

CH. DE LA NEGLY

La Clape Cuvée la Brise Marine 1999*

□ 6 ha 19,600 30–49 F

La Négly has astounded us with its reds for some time. Now it's the turn of a white from Marsanne, Bourboulenc and Grenache Blanc, varieties that manage to reveal all their character when grown on the wild terroir of La Clape, barely one km (0.6 miles) from the sea. This very elegant-looking 99 has a golden colour and heady aromas of honey and crystallised fruit. On the palate these are balanced with richness and weight. A very ripe wine to drink at the finest tables.

SCEA Ch. de La Négly, 6, rue de l'Albigeois, 11560 Fleury-D'Aude, tel. 04.68.32.36.28, fax 04.68.32.10.69 by appt.

Jean Paux-Rosset

DOM. DE LA PROSE

Saint-Georges d'Orques 1998*

■ 3 ha 11,000 30–49 F

Established on the limestone plateau above the area around Saint-Georges-d'Orques, the young vineyard of La Prose produces really nice wines, year after year. We could not fail to be attracted by the Domaine 98. The star awarded by the jury was given for its pretty appearance of garnet, tinged with purple, for its delicate and charming nose evoking cherries, the garrigue and spices, and for its good, silky structure. A couple of words to highlight the **Grande Cuvée du Domaine, 98 Blanc** (70–99 F), which is also worthy of appearing in the *Guide*.

Bertrand de Mortillet, Dom. de la Prose, 34570 Pignan, tel. 04.67.03.08.30, fax 04.67.03.48.70 by appt.

LANGUEDOC

CH. LA ROQUE

Pic Saint-Loup Cupa Numismae 1998★

■ 20 ha n.c. 50–69 F

A very fine, concentrated wine from Château La Roque, it has a colour of intense garnet and a nose that shows fragrances of mocha, vanilla and burnt oak mixed with spicy notes. Round and powerful on the palate, the wine is dominated by plenty of tight tannins. The oaky character needs about three or four years to soften and integrate.

Jack Boutin, Ch. La Roque, 34270 Fontanès, tel. 04.67.55.34.47, fax 04.67.55.10.18 ev. day except Sun. 10am–12 noon 2pm–6pm; groups by appt.

DOM. DE LA ROSE

Picpoul de Pinet Elevé en Fût de Chêne 1998★

□ 2 ha 13,000 20–29 F

In the tasting line-up of Picpoul de Pinet white wines, this stood out, first because it was from the 98 vintage and second in that it was matured in wood. A rich golden colour leads to a very characteristic nose with vanilla, notes of toast and nuts. The palate marries fleshiness and acidity with the oak. The jury recommends that this be kept until late 2000 before drinking.

SCV de l'Ormarine, 1, av. du Picpoul, 34850 Pinet, tel. 04.67.77.03.10, fax 04.67.77.76.23

CH. LA SAUVAGEONNE

Cuvée Prestige 1999★

■ 6 ha 40,000 30–49 F

The Château La Savageonne 99 is a prestigious wine, deep red in appearance, and with barbecued notes, leather, spices and violets. It has a palate that is still showing its youth, though with soft tannins, typical of the 1999 vintage. Well-balanced.

Gaëtan Poncé et Fils, Ch. La Sauvageonne, 34700 Saint-Jean-de-la-Blaquière, tel. 04.67.44.71.74, fax 04.67.44.71.02, e-mail yvanof@aol.com ev. day 9am–12 noon 1.30pm–7pm

CH. DE LASCAUX

Pic Saint-Loup les Nobles Pierres 1998★

■ n.c. 45,000 50–69 F

Lascaux is the name of a holding on which Jean-Benoît Cavalier, newly elected president of the Appellation Contrôlée Coteaux du Languedoc, cultivates his vineyard. Les Nobles Pierres is the focus of his attention. This wine is appealing with its deep purple colour and nose of black fruits, with roasted and gamey flavours. The full-bodied palate shows very tight tannins, and the finely judged cellar techniques have produced a wine full of character. A wine for those prepared to leave it to cellar for five years.

Jean-Benoît Cavalier, 34270 Vacquières, tel. 04.67.59.00.08, fax 04.67.59.06.06, e-mail j.bcavalier@wanadoo.fr ev. day except Sun. 10am–12.30pm 2pm–7pm

CH. DE LASCOURS

Pic Saint-Loup 1999

◪ n.c. 6,500 30–49 F

This *Rosé de Saignée* has a very bright salmon-pink colour and a fruity, creamy and toasty nose. On the palate, the first impression is balanced, and both mouth-filling and appetising. The two keys to its character are finesse and length.

Claude Arlès, Ch. de Lascours, 34270 Sauteyrargues, tel. 04.67.59.00.58, fax 04.67.59.00.58 ev. day 9am–8pm

CH. LAVABRE Pic Saint-Loup 1998★★

■ 4 ha 16,000 70–99 F

Once enamoured with laboratory research, Olivier Bridel then came across the Lavabre farmhouse, which was up for sale. He was smitten instantly, as we are today when we taste his red wine. A dark red with purple hints, it has a good intensity and range of aromas including blackberry, cherry, blackcurrant, coffee and spices. It is a worthy two-star 98, both delicate and concentrated on the palate; it finishes well with a real velvety feel.

Dom. de Lavabre, Lavabre, 34270 Claret, tel. 04.67.59.02.25, fax 04.67.59.02.39 by appt.

Bridel

CH. LA VERNEDE 1998★

■ n.c. n.c. 20–29 F

The Romans, the first to cultivate the vine here, originally founded a military settlement. The estate then passed into the hands of the monks who kept up the vine-growing traditions. A beautiful purple-coloured wine with a nose of leather, red berry fruit and roasted flavours, and a full-bodied, balanced palate with evident tannins. Equally good are the **Fût de Chêne 98** (oak-aged) (50–69 F) and the **99 Blanc** also oak-aged (70–99 F). The latter has an intense bouquet of honey, toast, beeswax and peaches, all in all very elegant to serve as an apéritif.

Jean-Marc Ribet, GFA La Vernède, 34440 Nissan-lez-Ensérune, tel. 04.67.37.00.30, fax 04.67.37.60.11 ev. day 9am–12 noon 2pm–7pm

CH. DE L'ENGARRAN

Saint-Georges d'Orques Cuvée Quetton Saint-Georges 1998★★

■ 5 ha 25,000 70–99 F

At l'Engarran, the pleasure of tasting the wines increases as their quality asserts itself. A very happy experience: to start with, we have the distinguished Quetton Saint-Georges 98, with its attractive deep, garnet-red colour. The nose is certainly concentrated, fine and elegant, with complex notes of black fruits, leather, roasted flavours, coffee and spices (particularly pepper), as well as floral and liquorice touches. There is power on the palate that distinguishes itself in being full-bodied, sophisticated, balanced and with a fine-grained structure and exquisite length. The **Saint-Georges 98 Rosé**, a product of

masterful wine-making, has also had its quality acknowledged by awarding it two stars.
SCEA du Ch. de l'Engarran, Ch. de l'Engarran, 34880 Laverune, tel. 04.67.47.00.02, fax 04.67.27.87.89 ev. day 12 noon–7pm; Sat. Sun. 10am–7pm
Grill

DOM. LES FERRAGERES

Pic Saint Loup 1998★★

6 ha 40,050 20–29 F

A wine bottled by the Bessière company, the Domaine Les Ferragères from Monsieur Poncet has an intense red colour, with hints of brown and blue, and a subtle nose of leather, raspberry, the garrigue, violets and spices. This is a clean wine with a very appealing weighty body on the palate, chewy, mouth-filling and with a very good length. Don't forget to decant it.

SA Bessière, 40, rue du Port, 34140 Mèze, tel. 04.67.18.40.40, fax 04.67.43.77.03
M. Poncet

LES TERRES ROUGES

Picpoul de Pinet 1999★

n.c. n.c. 20–29 F

This most attractive Picpoul de Pinet comes from vineyards planted on red clay soil. This clear-coloured, green-tinged 99 has a pronounced nose with floral notes and exotic fruits. The palate is notably fresh and full-bodied, with lemon notes on the finish. The **Domaine du Roc 99 Blanc** (30–49 F) is awarded a star.

Cave coop. La Montagnacoise, 15, rte d'Aumes, 34530 Montagnac, tel. 04.67.24.03.74, fax 04.67.24.14.78

LE TARRAL Montpeyroux 1998★

2 ha 12,000 50–69 F

Le Tarral is the local name for the north-east wind that blows away the bad weather and brings the sunshine. The grapes for this wine appear to have been filled with sunshine. The subtle garnet colour doesn't lead one to expect such a wild nose: garrigue, juniper tar oil, musk and spices. The palate appears quite sweet and rounded, given structure and very good balance by the tannins.

Cave coop. de Montpeyroux, Les coteaux du Castellas, 5, pl. Franç-Villon, 34150 Montpeyroux, tel. 04.67.96.61.08, fax 04.67.88.60.91
ev. day 8.30am–12.30pm 2pm–6pm; cl. Sun. Jan.—Apr.

CH. L'EUZIERE

Pic Saint-Loup Cuvée les Escarboucles 1998★

6 ha 13,500 50–69 F

Escarboucles is a Languedoc name for this wine from the heart of Pic Saint-Loup. Behind the dark red colour are some beautiful aromas of grilled meat, eucalyptus, stewed fruits and undergrowth. The palate is full and round, with plenty of fine tannins and a finely judged use of oak. This is certainly worth waiting for, and in the meantime you can drink the **Tradition 98**, which was also given a mention by the jury (30–49 F).

Michel et Marcelle Causse, ancien chem. d'Anduze, 34270 Fontanès, tel. 04.67.55.21.41, fax 04.67.55.21.41 by appt.

DOM. LEYRIS-MAZIERE 1999

2 ha 6,000 20–29 F

This Gard estate charmed the jury with its first vintage, which has a light ruby colour with a red berry fruit and toasty nose. Soft and balanced on the palate, it can be drunk right away.

Yvon Leyris, rue Cantarel, 30260 Cannes-et-Clairan, tel. 04.66.77.88.17 by appt.

LUCIAN Saint-Saturnin 1999★

12.06 ha 50,000 30–49 F

Here are two very decent wines, the Lucian 99 and the **Seigneur des Deux Vierges 98**. The co-operative at Saint-Saturnin excels once again. Two wines of an intense red colour, with strawberry and blackcurrant on the 99, and cooked fruits, spice and smoke for the barrel-aged 98. The first is soft and round with the benefit of powerful tannins, and the second shows richness and a good length. Difficult to resist; shut your eyes and give in to temptation.

Les Vins de Saint-Saturnin, rte d'Arboras, 34725 Saint-Saturnin-de-Lucian, tel. 04.67.96.61.52, fax 04.67.88.60.13 by appt.

CH. MALAVIEILLE Alliance 1999★

1 ha 2,000 30–49 F

All the hills on the banks of Lake Salagou in this part of the world consist of so-called *ruffes*, deep red rocky gullies, eroded by storms. It is sometimes known as Colorado. At Malavieille, we start with the salmon-coloured 99 rosé with its distinguished nose of flowers, redcurrant, strawberry, citrus fruits and spiced cake. It has an unctuous, yet lively palate that is rich, full-bodied and velvety on the finish. The juries also retained, although without a star, the **Alliance 98 Rouge** that is still quite restrained from 16 months in barrel.

Mireille Bertrand, Malavieille, 34800 Mérifons, tel. 04.67.96.34.67, fax 04.67.96.32.21 by appt.

CH. MANDAGOT

Montpeyroux Grande Réserve 1998★

2 ha 10,000 50–69 F

The Grande Réserve 98 from Château Mandagot needs to remain in your cellar for another three or four years before it will lose ... its reserve. It has a very intense garnet colour with a nose that reveals blackcurrant, blackberry and figs with animal notes and some spices. On the powerful palate there are some pronounced tannins, together with richness, body and something quite warming. It has respectable length.

LANGUEDOC

🔑 Jean-François Vallat, Dom. les Thérons, 34150 Montpeyroux, tel. 04.67.96.64.06, fax 04.67.96.67.63 ☑ 🍷 by appt.

MAS DES CHIMERES 1998*

■ 3 ha 16,000 50–69 F

Mas des Chimères 98 is just like its producer: warming and generous. It has an intense red colour with pretty purple glints. The nose has an appealing range of aromas including ripe fruits, spices, cocoa and leather. The palate is clean, and shows weight and richness with silky tannins that coat the mouth.

🔑 Guilhem Dardé, Mas des Chimères, 34800 Octon, tel. 04.67.96.22.70, fax 04.67.88.07.00, e-mail mas.des.chimeres@free.fr ☑ 🍷 by appt.

CH. MINISTRE

Terroir de la Méjanelle Réserve 1998*

■ 8 ha 14,000 50–69 F

Who are the potential customers for the wines from Château Ministre? Any enlightened wine lover with a modest amount of money to spare, can have the privilege of pulling the cork on the deeply garnet-coloured 98 Réserve. With some brick-red notes on the rim, the nose is rich and intense with spicy garrigue flavours and some crystallised fruits. The palate is firm and sweet with smooth tannins that are, in a word, balanced. There is also a pleasant **Classique 98 Rouge** (30–49 F).

🔑 SCEA Ch. Ministre, Mas du Ministre, chem. du Ministre, 34130 Mauguio, tel. 04.67.15.03.64, fax 04.67.15.13.66, e-mail chateau@ministre.org ☑ 🍷 ev. day 10.30am–12.30pm; cl. Jan.

CH. MIRE L'ETANG La Clape 1999**

□ 6 ha 12,000 30–49 F

The estate of Mire l'Etang is east-facing, and benefits from the sea-spray off the nearby Mediterranean and from plenty of sunshine. It offers this bright, golden-coloured La Clape 99 with a fairly intense floral nose that has touches of honey, citrus fruits, quince and toast. This white wine has good acidity and an enticing freshness, which provide balance for the remarkably full-bodied palate. In all, it's a wine that gives great satisfaction.

🔑 Ch. Mire l'Etang, 11560 Fleury-d'Aude, tel. 04.68.33.62.84, fax 04.68.33.99.30 ☑ 🍷 by appt.

LES VIGNERONS DE MONTARNAUD-MURVIEL

Saint-Georges d'Orques Sélection Prestige Cuvée 2000 1998*

■ 4.7 ha 18,800 50–69 F

The co-operative at Montarnaud-Murviel-les-Montpellier has provided here a really nice dark purple wine. With a fine and rich nose producing notes of liquorice and coffee, with nuts and some red berry fruit, it has a ripe and velvety palate with plenty of body and well-integrated tannins.

🔑 Les Vignerons de Montarnaud-Murviel, 401, av. Saint-Paul, 34570 Montarnaud, tel. 04.67.55.59.45, fax 04.67.55.59.45 ☑ 🍷 ev. day except Sun. 9am–12 noon 2pm–7pm

CH. DE MONTBAZIN 1999

■ n.c. 20,000 30–49 F

The Montbazin co-operative has made a good selection of Syrah and Grenache for this 1999 wine. A fairly intense colour leads to an expressive nose, dominated by undergrowth, red berry fruit, violets and roasted flavours. The palate is certainly balanced, with softness and roundness, both warming and harmonious.

🔑 Cave coop. Les Costières, 305, av. de la Gare, 34560 Montbazin, tel. 04.67.18.63.80, fax 04.67.78.64.46, e-mail cave-coopérative-les-costières@wanadoo.fr ☑ 🍷 ev. day except Sun. 9am–12 noon 2pm–6pm

CH. DE MONTPEZAT

La Pharaonne 1998*

■ 1 ha 3,500 70–99 F

Montpezat is a notable estate situated in Pézenas that ha submitted a blend of carefully ripened Mourvèdre and Grenache. It has an intense colour with purple highlights and a still slightly closed nose, with aromas of blackcurrant, smoke and spices. The palate has well-integrated tannins that balance with the body and richness of the wine. This wine has class.

🔑 J.-Christophe Blanc, Ch. de Montpezat, 34120 Pézenas, tel. 04.67.98.10.84, fax 04.67.98.98.78, e-mail contact@chateau-montpezat.com ☑ 🍷 ev. day except Sun. 10am–7pm; winter by appt.

MORTIES Pic Saint-Loup 1998*

■ 8 ha 18,000 50–69 F

This wine provides a good insight into the range from Mortiès. This 98 is decked in a dark purple colour and has a fine nose, leaning towards red berry fruit mixed with notes of leather, passing through truffles and scents of the garrigue. Showing good length, the palate is quite deep and coated with pronounced, but fine tannins. A star is also awarded for the lightly oaked **98 Blanc**, where the dominant variety, Roussanne gives a delicately complex nose and a sophisticated balance. Also retained and given a mention is the **Mortiès Jamais Content 98 Rouge**.

🔑 Mortiès, 34270 Saint-Jean-de-Cuculles, tel. 04.67.55.11.12, fax 04.67.55.11.12 ☑ 🍷 by appt.

🔑 Jorcin-Duchemin

CH. MOUJAN

La Clape Cuvée Baronne de Rivières 1998*

■ 1.05 ha 3,200 30–49 F

At Moujan, the vineyard's reputation and traditions stretch back to Roman times. The Moujan 98 receives a star for this wine that has spent 12 months in oak. We enjoyed it for the intense colour and for the nose of spices (vanilla and cloves) and berry fruits. The well-balanced palate shows powerful but toned-down tannins. The jury were impressed by the carefully judged maturation.

SCE de la Clape, Ch. Moujan, 11100 Narbonne, tel. 04.68.65.24.71, fax 04.68.65.83.31, e-mail chateaumoujan@libertysurf.fr
by appt.
M. de Braquilanges

CH. NOTRE-DAME DU QUATOURZE 1999★

	4 ha	25,000	20-29 F

An ancient crossroad of civilisation, Narbonne has always been closely affiliated to the history of wine. The Château Notre-Dame du Quatourze is renowned for the consistent quality of its wines. Today, the white 99 has a charming, bright, pale yellow colour with an attractive nose of apples and citrus fruits as well as a floral note. Lastly, the palate seduced us with its crunchy apple flavour, full body and length.

Georges Ortola, Ch. Notre-Dame-du-Quatourze, 11100 Narbonne, tel. 04.68.41.58.92, fax 04.68.42.41.88, e-mail georges.ortola@libertysurf.fr
ev. day 8am–12 noon 2pm–7pm

CH. PECH-CELEYRAN La Clape 1998★

	38 ha	220,000	30-49 F

Château Pech-Céleyran is owned by the Saint-Exupéry family. The colour of this wine is a deep garnet, and the nose is characteristic of La Clape, with notes of the garrigue, pepper and liquorice. Nuances of fruit appear on the palate, side by side with powerful tannins. A wine that needs keeping, which will open up with time.

Jacques de Saint-Exupéry, Ch. Pech-Céleyran, 11110 Salles-d'Aude, tel. 04.68.33.50.04, fax 04.68.33.36.12, e-mail pech-celeyran@mnet.fr
ev. day except Sun. 9am–6pm

CH. PECH REDON

La Clape L'Epervier 1998★★

	15 ha	30,000	30-49 F

Tasted by the grand jury, L'Epervier 98 from Pech Redon missed the highest awards by a whisker. It has a black, concentrated colour, with a leathery nose, showing ripe red berry fruits, toast and notes of the garrigue. Good substance followed on the palate that has very evident, but relatively silky tannins. Balance and length attest to the high class of this wine. The **Cuvée Clape l'Epervier 99 Blanc** received a mention. Grenache Blanc and Malvoisie gave delicious flavours and a rounded, lively and long palate.

Christophe Bousquet, Ch. Pech Redon, rte de Gruissan, 11100 Narbonne, tel. 04.68.90.41.22, fax 04.68.65.11.48
ev. day except Sun. 9am–12 noon 2pm–7pm

CH. PERIES 1998★

	5 ha	3,300	30-49 F

Between the Oppidium of Nissan-lez-Enserune and the old city of Narbonne, much reputed by the Gallo-Romans for its wines, lie the terraces of Béziers, where, if time permits, you might be able to taste this wine from Périès. With a deep purple-red colour, it offers a luxurious basket of red fruits and a touch of linden flowers. The tannins still dominate the overall balance of this 98 wine.

J.-Jacques et Micheline Ortiz-Bernabé, Ch. Périès, 34440 Nissan-lez-Ensérune, tel. 04.67.37.01.34, fax 04.67.37.01.34
ev. day 8am–12 noon 1pm–8pm

CH. PETIT ROUBIE

Picpoul de Pinet 1999★

	9.7 ha	n.c.	20-29 F

This is an organically produced Picpoul de Pinet. The pale greenish 99 shows marked delicacy on the nose with wild flowers and citrus notes. As for the palate, the richness and acidity would make a superb match with oysters from Bouzigues.

Olivier Azan, EARL Les Dom. de Petit Roubié, B.P. 4, 34850 Pinet, tel. 04.67.77.09.28, fax 04.67.77.76.26, e-mail roubie@club-internet.fr
by appt.

CH. DE PINET Picpoul de Pinet 1999★

	n.c.	40,000	30-49 F

This elegant and fairly powerful wine comes from a clay-limestone soil, not far from the Etang de Thau. Behind its delicate, pale yellow colour the nose expresses fresh aromas of citrus and exotic fruits with some dill. Both rounded and lively, this wine shows nice intensity on the palate and good length.

Simonne Arnaud-Gaujal, Ch. de Pinet, 34850 Pinet, tel. 04.68.32.16.67 by appt.

DOM. DU POUJOL 1999★★

	5 ha	24,000	30-49 F

The *Guide* includes two magnificent starred wines from the Domaine du Poujol starting with this fairly pale rosé that reveals a very fine and elegant nose with floral and apricot notes. The wine is mouth-filling on the palate, complete with a fine balance of richness and freshness, and remarkable length. Also worth noting is the **Podio Alto 98 Rouge** which receives a star. Complex, powerful and warming, this wine will not reach its peak in less than four or five years (50–69 F).

Robert et Kim Cripps, Dom. du Poujol, 34570 Vailhauquès, tel. 04.67.84.47.57, fax 04.67.84.47.57, e-mail kcripps@aol.com
by appt.

PRIEURE SAINT-HIPPOLYTE 1999★

	10 ha	15,000	20-29 F

The co-operative of Fontès is a past master of the art of making rosés. This distinguished 99 has an intense pink and purple iris colour and a fine, intense nose with flavours dominated by red berries and exotic fruits. The palate is energetic with plenty of freshness, weight and length.

🗝 Cave coop. la Fontesole, 34320 Fontès, tel. 04.67.25.14.25, fax 04.67.25.30.66 ☑ Y ev. day except Sat. Sun. 8am–12 noon 2pm–6pm

PRIMA TERRA Montpeyroux 1998★★

■ n.c. 100,000 30–49 F

Despite being bottled at Château Canet, rather than by this merchant in its region of origin, this delightful wine from Montpeyroux is true to its terroir of origin. Following on from the magnificent garnet colour, there are complex aromas that take you into a world of mild spices, jam and the garrigue. A straightforward palate is structured with good length. This well-balanced 98 could go right through a meal and could equally be enjoyed now, or in three years' time.

🗝 Domaines du Soleil, Ch. Canet, 11800 Rustiques, tel. 04.90.12.32.41, fax 04.90.12.32.49

DOM. PUECH Cuvée Spéciale 1998★

■ 2 ha 4,700 ▮ ◖◗ 50–69 F

In the past three or four years, Christophe Puech has taken over from the family trio. He offers this extremely well-made dark garnet wine, with notes of smoke, ripe fruits and cherry, as well as some careful use of oak. With good structure, the full-bodied, rich palate has velvety tannins. Reasonable length completes the picture.

🗝 J.-Louis, Christine et Christo Puech, GAEC Dom. Puech, 34980 Saint-Clément-de-Rivière, tel. 04.67.84.12.31, fax 04.67.66.63.16, e-mail domaine.puech@libertysurf.fr ☑ Y by appt.

CH. PUECH-HAUT Saint-Drézéry Tête de Cuvée 1998

■ 18 ha 52,000 ◖◗ 100–149 F

One man, two estates and three wines, Gérard Bru, Puech-Haut and Silènes des Peyrals. Firstly, the dark garnet Puech-Haut 98 Tête de Cuvée has an intense blackcurrant nose, with vanilla and roasted flavours and a good attack on the palate. Structure and concentration combine with richness and some still rather angular tannins, as well as still obvious oak flavours. One star is awarded to the dark red **Silène des Peyrals 98 Rouge**, which has a powerful nose, also with noticeable oak together with vanilla fruits and an impressive structure on the palate (150–199 F). Finally, Marsanne and Roussanne are blended in the **Puech-Haut 99 Blanc Tête de Cuvée** (100–149 F). Vinified and matured in oak with a fairly long finish, this wine has also been awarded a mention.

🗝 SCEA Ch. Puech-Haut, 2250, rte de Teyran, 34160 Saint-Drézéry, tel. 04.67.86.93.70, fax 04.67.86.94.07 ☑ Y by appt.

🗝 Gérard Bru

CH. RICARDELLE La Clape Blason du Château Ricardelle 1998★

■ 7 ha 35,000 ◖◗ 70–99 F

The fourth Duke of Fleury made Ricardelle his home in the year 1696. We bet that he would have liked the beautiful and traditional bottles used by this estate. To prove the point, the jury tasted the Blason (coat of arms) from Château Ricardelle. It has a garnet-red colour, slightly browning from the *barriques*. The nose is rich in crystallised fruits and roasted flavours, with the palate tasting quite closed, but delicately oaked and presenting a fairly long finish. We have also awarded a star to the golden-yellow coloured **Duc de Fleury 98 Blanc**, which has marked flavours of citrus fruits and verbena with both good weight and length (30–49 F).

🗝 Ch. Ricardelle, rte de Gruissan, 11100 Narbonne, tel. 04.68.65.21.00, fax 04.68.32.58.36, e-mail ricardelle@wanadoo.fr ☑ Y ev. day 9am–8pm

🗝 Pellegrini

CH. RIVIERE LE HAUT Réserve Elevée en Fût de Chêne 1998★

■ 0.26 ha 1,200 ▮ ◖◗ 50–69 F

Almost forgotten, the once famous Château Rivière le Haut has fortunately been rediscovered by Josiane Segondy. The restoration works on the estate are already bearing fruit, as proven by tasting this Réserve. It has a deep purple appearance and delivers an intense nose of macerated fruits, vanilla and smoke. The full-bodied palate shows discreet notes of oak and is both powerful and structured. Good balance.

🗝 Josiane Segondy, Ch. Rivière le Haut, 11560 Fleury-d'Aude, tel. 04.68.33.61.33, fax 04.68.33.90.32, e-mail rivierelehaut@wanadoo.fr ☑ Y ev. day except Sat. Sun. 9am–12 noon 2pm–5pm

CH. ROUMANIERES Les Garrics Vieilli en Fût de Chêne 1998★

■ 4 ha 15,000 ◖◗ 70–99 F

Cuvée Garrics, as its name suggests, comes straight from the Mediterranean garrigue. This star-bright 98 is of a deep garnet colour with a purple rim. Its powerful nose exudes aromas of vanilla, ripe fruit and some oak, whilst the palate, rich in tannin and oaky too, will develop with time.

🗝 GFA Gravegeal, EARL Ch. Roumanières, 34160 Garrigues, tel. 04.67.86.81.71, fax 04.67.86.82.00 ☑ Y ev. day except Sun. Mon. 9am–12 noon 3pm–7pm

CH. ROUQUETTE-SUR-MER La Clape 1999★

◪ 10 ha 10,000 ▮ 🌡 30–49 F

All that remains from the old country house are scattered rocks and sections of walls, but in the new buildings there are some good wines being made, such as this intense and bright-coloured rosé Château Rouquette 99. With a nose of menthol and fruits (blackcurrants and strawberries), it is fresh and lively on the palate, revealing an extremely good balance between weight and acidity. The **98 Rouge** was given a mention by the jury, who enjoyed its deep colour, as well as its delicate nose and delicious palate.

Jacques Boscary, rte Bleue, 11100 Narbonne-Plage, tel. 04.68.49.90.41, fax 04.68.65.32.01
ev. day 10am–12 noon 3pm–7pm

DOM. DES ROUVRES 1999★

1.45 ha 8,000 30–49 F

Newcomers to the AOC club, the co-operative of Villevieille have submitted this Domaine des Rouvres 99. It has an intense garnet-red colour with an elegant purple rim, and releases equally intense flavours of prunes, juniper tar oil, spices and some baked character. As for the palate, here we find a good balance between fleshiness and richness, as well as very good length for a wine that is reaching its peak.

SCA les Vignerons de Villevieille, 67, av. de la Calmette, 30250 Villeville, tel. 04.66.80.02.90, fax 04.66.77.70.51, e-mail lesvignerons.villevieille@voila.fr
ev. day except Sat. Sun. 9am–12 noon 2pm–6pm

CUVEE SAINT-CHRISTOPHE 1999★

25 ha 20,000 20–29 F

Just a few steps from the Abbey of Fontcaude, a famous place of meditation where the pilgrims stayed before getting back on the road for Saint-Jacques-de-Compostelle, is this attractive white wine terroir. This fresh and balanced 99 has a charming, clear and bright colour with scattered golden highlights. It has an evocative nose of citrus fruits, wild flowers and hazelnut. The palate lives up to the rest with its richness and acidity nicely balanced.

Les Vignerons de Puisserguier, 29, rue Georges-Pujol, 34620 Puisserguier, tel. 04.67.93.74.03, fax 04.67.93.87.73
by appt.

CLOS SAINTE-CAMELLE 1999★

3 ha 17,000 30–49 F

Catherine Do is already well known by wine drinkers for some excellent Vin de Pays made from grapes destined for the better AOCs. Le Clos Sainte-Camelle is of course from this latter category. The bright colour shows it to be a concentrated wine, and it has a nose that inclines towards power at the same time as finesse, marrying these qualities with ripe fruits, nuts and a note of the garrigue. Very good body and smooth on the palate, it is balanced with integrated tannins. The **Clos 99 Rosé** is both unusual and elegant and for these reasons has been awarded a star (20–29 F).

Catherine Do, Dom. de Campaucels, 34530 Montagnac, tel. 04.67.24.19.16, fax 04.67.24.19.16 by appt.

CLOS SAINTE-PAULINE P 1998★★

3 ha 8,000 50–69 F

Alexandre Pagès is a young wine-producer with just what one looks for: passion and competence. Whilst remaining a member of the co-operative, he is also starting his own private venture. His first production reaps two stars, a masterstroke. With a deep ruby colour, it has a good range of flavours including leather, a touch of undergrowth, ripe red berry fruit, spices and toast. Richness with evident but silky tannins and a good length confirms the quality of this Syrah (65%) and Grenache blend. This bottle has a label with a maroon strip on the top to distinguish it from another **Clos Sainte-Paluine** (30–49 F), a blend of Carignan with two other varieties, which is commended by the jury for its pleasant fruitiness.

Alexandre Pagès, 1, rue Raspail, 34230 Paulhan, tel. 04.67.25.29.42, fax 04.67.25.29.42 ev. day except Sun. 1pm–6pm

SAINT-JACQUES 1999★

4 ha 26,000 20–29 F

The alliance of Saint-Jacques with the co-operative of Saint-Félix provides some surprises. Notably this wine with its glistening pink colour with glints of purple and an intensity of captivating flavours, which suggest a full and varied basket of fruit and a little bouquet of flowers. Rounded with delicious warming and velvety fruit on the palate, it also has a touch of richness on the structure giving it an attractive weight.

Cave des Vignerons de Saint-Félix, 21, av. Marcelin-Albert, 34725 Saint-Félix de Lodez, tel. 04.67.96.60.61, fax 04.67.88.61.77 by appt.

CH. SAINT-JEAN D'AUMIERES

Cuvée Noble de Massane 1998★

4.88 ha 13,066 30–49 F

Following on from the ruby colour, it was the attractive range of aromas that appealed to the jury: notes of honey, spiced cake, resin and liquorice. The warming and fruity palate has soft and liquorice-flavoured tannins on the finish. This wine could still improve with time.

Daniel Delclaud, Dom. Saint-Jean d'Aumières, rte de Montpellier, 34150 Gignac, tel. 04.67.57.52.57
by appt.

CH. SAINT-JEAN DE BUEGES

Elevé en Fût de Chêne 1998

1 ha 5,100 50–69 F

The Buège area is wild and unusual, almost at the end of the world. However, both vines and *barriques* have managed to reach here, as this dark-coloured wine bears witness. With a nose of vanilla and toast, the palate is complex with pronounced tannins. At present, the wine has slightly excessive oak flavours, but these will integrate with time. Very promising.

SCA des Coteaux de Buèges, rte des Graves, 34380 Saint-Jean-de-Buèges,

LANGUEDOC

tel. 04.67.73.10.07, fax 04.67.73.12.38 ☒ Y ev. day except Mon. Wed. Fri. 10am–12 noon 3pm–5pm

CAVE DE SAINT-JEAN DE LA BLAQUIERE Cuvée des Oliviers 1999★

◪ 10 ha 44,000 ▮ 20-29 F

On the steep hillsides farmed by the producers of the Saint-Jean de la Blaquière co-operative, there is a little of everything: 'ruffes' (eroded granite rocks), basalt, schist and limestone. Thanks to these well-exposed south-facing slopes, we have this pretty, bright and intense-coloured rosé. Embellished by a bouquet of fruits such as blackcurrants and strawberries, as well as some toast, the palate is fresh, rounded, smooth and rich, balanced with good length. Also given a mention is the really soft **Domaine du Relais 98 Rouge** (30–49 F).

⚿ Les vignerons de Saint-Jean-de-la-Blaquière, 34700 Saint-Jean-de-la-Blaquière, tel. 04.67.44.70.53, fax 04.67.44.75.06 ☒ Y by appt.

CUVEE SAINT-JEAN DES SOURCES

Picpoul de Pinet 1999★

□ 3 ha 15,000 ▮ 20-29 F

Some very good Picpoul de Pinet is produced at the estate of Saint-Paul-Colline. This wine has a bright straw-yellow colour with a delectable nose of acacia, honey, citrus fruit, aniseed, fennel, cleaning polish and toast. The palate is weighty with well-balanced richness and acidity.

⚿ Pascale Morin, Dom. Saint-Paul-Colline, 34140 Meze, tel. 04.67.43.58.01, fax 04.67.43.33.60 ☒ Y by appt.

CH. SAINT-MARTIN DE LA GARRIGUE 1998★

■ 3.1 ha 20,000 ⦀ 70-99 F

This terroir, with its calcareous sandstone soil, received the AOC for its red wines in 1997. This fine 98 confirms the suitability of these slopes for producing distinctive wines. The very bright, dark red colour gives way to aromas of vanilla, with notes of fruit and toast behind. The elegant palate has good structure, with some oak character that will soften with time. This château has also received a star for its **98 Blanc**.

⚿ SCEA Saint-Martin de la Garrigue, Ch. Saint-Martin de la Garrigue, 34530 Montagnac, tel. 04.67.24.00.40, fax 04.67.24.16.15 ☒ Y by appt.

⚿ Umberto Guida

CH. SAINT-MARTIN DES CHAMPS

Elevé en Fût de Chêne 1998★

■ 7.89 ha 20,000 ▮ ⦀ 🌡 30-49 F

In the time of Charlemagne, Saint-Martin-des-Champs was an abbey surrounded by vineyards. Partly thanks to those religious orders, we now have a much better understanding of the science of wine. The Briot family, who have been wine-producers since the dawn of time, have benefited much from the secular experience. Witness this deep red 98 which has had a fine maturation in oak. It gives scents of fruit, the garrigue, dried flowers, a touch of extract of rosemary, the liquorice found in good Syrah, the inevitable roasted character and finally, pronounced, but sufficiently velvety tannins, with very good length.

⚿ Pierre et Michel Birot, Ch. Saint-Martin-des-Champs, 34490 Murviel-les-Béziers, tel. 04.67.32.92.58, fax 04.67.37.84.49, e-mail domaine@saintmartindeschamps.com ☒ Y ev. day except Sun. 9am–12 noon 3pm–6pm

DOM. DE SALENTE 1999★

◪ 1.84 ha 3,500 ▮ 20-29 F

Try this tasty, deep-coloured rosé 99 from the Salente estate on the edge of the Larzac terraces. It has aromas of strawberries, raspberries and cherries, accentuated by a touch of liquorice. Soft and round, this wine is both elegant and balanced on the palate.

⚿ SCEA Dupin-Leygue, Dom. de Salente, 34150 Gignac, tel. 04.67.57.54.79, fax 04.67.57.81.84 ☒ Y by appt.

DOM. DES SAUVAIRE 1999

■ 3 ha 6,000 ▮ 20-29 F

Hervé Sauvaire is one of the most recent arrivals in the Coteaux du Languedoc club. He makes his mark with this deep red 99 that exudes cherry and other red berry fruits, spices and roasted notes. The palate is really soft and round, with integrated tannins, and the wine has good balance.

⚿ Hervé Sauvaire, Mas de Reulhe, 30260 Crespian, tel. 04.66.77.89.71, fax 04.66.77.89.71 ☒ Y by appt.

CH. DE TARAILHAN 1999★★

□ n.c. 2,000 ▮ 🌡 30-49 F

Is it the nearby pine forests in the heart of the La Clape mountains which give this yellow-gold Château de Tarailhan 99 its subtle resinous notes? It smells intensely of pine essence, juniper tar oil, beeswax, honey and has a fruity touch, too. The palate has a pleasant lively start to it, moving on to an overall rich character, with harmonious balance, and showing very great length.

⚿ Jean-Yves Duret et Marie-José Richaud, Dom. du Ch. de Tarailhan, 11560 Fleury-D'Aude, tel. 04.68.33.91.88

DOM. DE TERRE MEGERE

Les Dolomies 1998★

■ 3 ha 16,000 ▮ 🌡 30-49 F

Michel Moreau has brought out the quintessential characters from the garrigue that was cleared here 15 years ago. He regularly produces excellent wines, such as Les Dolomies 98 from Terre Mégère, a deep-coloured 98 with an intense nose showing minerals, burnt or barbecued notes, spices and gamey flavours with some prunes. Powerful and sappy, it has a nice balance with good

texture. To drink over the next three or four years.
🗝 Michel Moreau, Dom. de Terre Mégère, Cœur de Village, 34660 Cournonsec, tel. 04.67.85.42.85, fax 04.67.85.25.12 ✉ 🍷 by appt.

CH. DE VALCYRE

Pic Saint-Loup 1998★

■ 5 ha 9,000 30–49 F

This is from the first bottling by the Château de Valcyre, which has produced a very drinkable wine. A purple colour, with a nose of blackcurrant, blackberry and violets, and a round, clean palate. Drink while the wine is still showing good fruit, even if some spirited tannin remains.
🗝 Ch. de Valcyre-Benezech, 34270 Valflaunes, tel. 04.67.55.28.99, fax 04.67.55.28.99 ✉

CH. VALOUSSIERE

Elevé en Fût de Chêne 1998★

■ 12 ha 80,000 30–49 F

Le Château Valoussière and **Les Hauts de Lunes 97**, both estates owned by the Jeanjean company, have produced two successful bottles. The 98 vintage is a concentrated red with touches of blue, and the fine, powerful and complex 97 shows even more intensity of colour. Both are rich in flavours and elegant scents of spices, with red berry fruits and a touch of leather, still showing a structure of dense tannin. Good wines to keep.
🗝 Hugues Jeanjean, SARL les Hauts de Lunes, 34230 Cabrials, tel. 04.67.88.41.30, fax 04.67.88.41.33

DOM. DES VIGNES HAUTES

Pic Saint Loup 1998★

■ 2.11 ha 9,800 50–69 F

Two wines from the co-operative of Corconne receive a star: the well-known **Gravette 99 Rouge** (30–49 F) and this dense purple 98 with its characteristic, complex aromas of fruit tarts, spices and pepper. The attack on the palate is round and full, moving on to a good structure with notes of oak on the finish. Wait a while for this 98.
🗝 SCA La Gravette, 30260 Corconne, tel. 04.66.77.32.75, fax 04.66.77.13.56 ✉ 🍷 by appt.

DOM. ZUMBAUM-TOMASI

Clos Maginiai 1998★★

■ 4 ha 13,600 70–99 F

A newcomer to the Languedoc vineyards, the owner is an international lawyer from Germany. He studied law here and loved the region so much that he ended up buying an estate near Pic Saint-Loup. The result of his first production is the dark red 98. On the nose it marries confectionery, with pastries and crystallised fruit, toast, undergrowth, leather and some noble oak flavours. The powerful palate is full and rich with a good body that promises six or seven years of ageing. We have been told that this estate is converting to organic viticulture.
🗝 Dom. Zumbaum-Tomasi, rue du Cagarel, 34270 Claret, tel. 04.67.02.82.84, fax 04.67.02.82.84 ✉ 🍷 by appt.

Faugères

The wines from Faugères have been AOC since 1982, as have those of its neighbour, Saint-Chinian. The region of production covers seven communes north of Pézenas and Béziers and south of Bédarieux, and produces 60,000–70,000 hl (1,584,000–1,848,000 gal) of wine. The vineyards are planted quite high – 250 m (820 ft) – on steeply sloping hillsides situated on the lower, poorly fertile, schist outcrops of the Cévennes. Faugères is a heady wine with a good purple colour and characteristic perfumes of the moors and summer fruits.

CH. DES ADOUZES

Elevé et Vieilli en Fût de Chêne 1998★

■ 4 ha 8,000 30–49 F

The 1995 and 1996 vintages, both remarkably good, won fast acclaim for this estate. The predominantly fruity 98 is made from old Carignan vines (50%) and Syrah. It has a simple character and is round and soft, a pleasant easy-drinking wine that would work well with barbecued lamb.
🗝 Jean-Claude Estève, Tras du Castel, 34320 Roquessels, tel. 04.67.90.24.11, fax 04.67.90.12.74 ✉ 🍷 by appt.

CH. CHENAIE Les Douves 1998★★

■ 7.5 ha 26,000 70–99 F

The **Cuvée Les Douves Blanches 98 Blanc** and this Les Douves 98 did equally well in the grand jury selection for the *coup de cœur*. This estate really knows how to extract the quality from its fantastic terroir. A very well-made Faugères of nice character, marrying fine flavours with quality tannins. A classic, which does not, however, take itself too seriously.
🗝 EARL André Chabbert et Fils, Ch. Chenaie, 34600 Caussiniojouls, tel. 04.67.23.17.73, fax 04.67.95.44.98 ✉ 🍷 by appt.

CH. DES ESTANILLES 1998★

■ 5 ha 20,000 100–149 F

This estate is well known by informed wine lovers. Its name comes from the combination of Estagnols and Fontanilles. The results of

reasonably old vines and a manual, selective harvest can be seen in this purple-coloured 98, which has a closed but concentrated nose. The palate is particularly attractive, with roundness and fine balance. It is plain to see that this wine has a good future.
Michel Louison et Sophie Louison, Ch. des Estanilles, 34480 Cabrerolles, tel. 04.67.90.29.25, fax 04.67.90.10.99, e-mail earl.louison@worldonline.je by appt.

DOM. DE FRAISSE 1999*

5.35 ha 25,000 30–49 F

Autignac lies on schist in the Faugères area, on the foothills of the extreme southern end of the Massif Central. Monsieur and Madame Pons, who appreciate a nicely made wine, each year divulge to us the secrets of making their first-rate rosés. A bright, pale colour leads to a characterful, intense and refined nose of red berry fruits, flowers, and a touch of smoke. The palate is full-bodied with richness and balance.
Jacques Pons, 1 bis, rue du chem. de Ronde, 34480 Autignac, tel. 04.67.90.23.40, fax 04.67.90.10.20, e-mail jacques.pons6@wanadoo.fr by appt.

CH. DE LA LIQUIERE Cistus 1998

6 ha 19,000 70–99 F

Good terroir never lies. This wine is not very expressive at present, but its promising colour bodes well for the future. A discreet nose reveals some toasty and smoky notes. On the palate there is overall good texture, with soft and fine tannins.
Famille Vidal, Ch. de la Liquière, 34480 Cabrerolles, tel. 04.67.90.29.20, fax 04.67.90.10.00, e-mail bvidal@terre-net.fr ev. day except Sat. Sun. 9am–12 noon 2pm–6pm

DOM. DES LAURIERS

Elevé en Fût de Chêne 1997*

12 ha 70,000 30–49 F

The Cuvée des Lauriers has achieved better results than the **Domaine de Fenouillet 98**, which received a mention. The Jeanjean family make this wine at the Laurens co-operative and know how to extract the most from this nice terroir. With a dark red colour and a nose of cleaning polish and bay leaves, this venerable wine shows the potential quality of the 1997 vintage in Faugères. Now at its peak, this wine has good balance.
Vignerons et Passions, B.P. 1, 34725 Saint-Félix-de-Lodez, tel. 04.67.88.80.39, fax 04.67.96.65.67

LE MOULIN COUDERC

Elevé en Fût de Chêne 1998*

4 ha 6,000 30–49 F

Concentrated colour and a nose of stewed fruits, mixed with violets, spices and toast: all the warmth of the terroir is expressed on the very powerful, but elegant palate, which shows very good depth of flavours. This 1998 can be enjoyed right away, but it will improve more given time.
Vincent Fonteneau, chem. de l'Aire, 34320 Roquessels, tel. 04.67.90.23.25, fax 04.67.90.11.05 by appt.

DOM. DU METEORE

Réserve Elevé en Fût de Chêne 1998***

3 ha 9,500 50–69 F

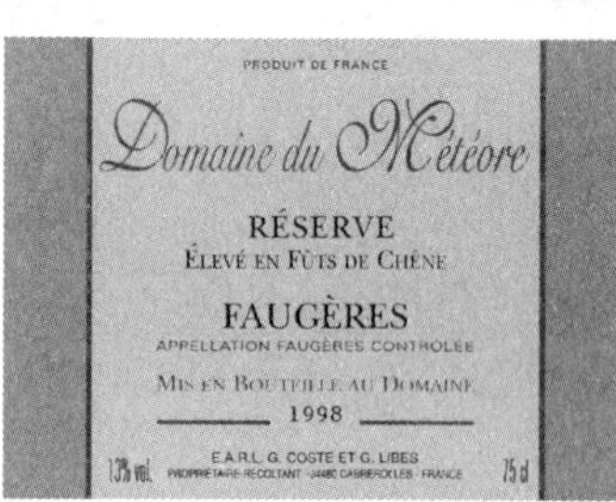

This estate owes its name to an ancient meteor, 10,000 years old, which can be seen at the base of a crater. This superb and impressive wine was unanimously awarded the *coup de cœur* by the grand jury. It has a very dark colour and a nose with distinguished flavours of toast, smoke, pepper and balsam. This wine is solid and balanced, with a firm and weighty finish. A good illustration of the schistose terroir, this Faugères is sumptuous and should be decanted.
Geneviève Libes-Coste, Dom. du Météore, 34480 Cabrerolles, tel. 04.67.90.21.12, fax 04.67.90.11.92 ev. day 10am–12.30pm 3pm–7.30pm; winter by appt.

MOULIN DE CIFFRE Eole 1998**

2 ha 7,000 70–99 F

Only recently settled in the region, the Lésineau family have not taken long to settle in, or to get to know their terroir, as proven by the stars they have received for both Faugères and for a **Saint-Chinian 98** (one star, 30–49 F). Unlike the Saint-Chinian, the Eole has been matured in barrel. A classy wine in which the power of stewed fruits and a mineral touch lie comfortably side by side with well-balanced fruit. Structured and silky, the palate is well-integrated and has a good length. An attractive *vin de terroir.*
SARL Ch. Moulin de Ciffre, Moulin de Ciffre, 34480 Autignac, tel. 04.67.90.11.45, fax 04.67.90.12.05 by appt.
B. et J. Lésineau

DOM. OLLIER TAILLEFER

Cuvée Castel Fossibus 1998**

5 ha 12,000 50–69 F

This superb schistose terroir could only produce very characterful wines. This wine fulfils most of the appellation criteria as shown by its purple colour and its mineral nose that opens up to toasty and smoky aromas. With an excellent fresh finish, the

tannins are still young, but they are not excessive. Serve in four or five years.
🔑 Dom. Ollier-Taillefer, rte de Gabian, 34320 Fos, tel. 04.67.90.24.59, fax 04.67.90.12.15 ☑ Y by appt.
🔑 Alain Ollier

CH. DES PEYREGRANDES
Prestige 1998
■ 3 ha 8,660 ⫼ 50–69 F

From schistose soils, this young and pleasant 98 is produced from old Carignan vines, with Syrah, Grenache and Mourvèdre. It has a dark colour with a nose that is still rather withdrawn but showing good concentration. The wine has good weight on the palate, which should develop given a little time.
🔑 SCEA Dom. Bénézech et Fils, Tras du Castel, 34320 Roquessels, tel. 04.67.90.15.00, fax 04.67.90.15.60 ☑ Y by appt.
🔑 Marie G. Boudal

DOM. RAYMOND ROQUE
Elevé en Fût de Chêne 1998★
■ 4 ha 6,500 ⫼ 50–69 F

We think this is a well-made, captivating and balanced wine. The nose is delicate with a subtle smoky character, typical of its schistose terroir. This is an attractive wine with elegant, integrated tannins, which could be drunk with game bird.
🔑 GAEC Raymond Roque et Fils, quartier de l'Ancien-Château, 34480 Cabrerolles, tel. 04.67.90.21.88 ☑ Y by appt.

TERRASSES DU RIEUTOR 1998★★
■ 20 ha 20,000 ⫼ 50–69 F

Two stars are awarded to the **Cuvée Terrasses du Rieutor 99 Blanc** (30–49 F), as well as for this red. Once again this year the co-operative at Faugères confirms its position amongst the best of the appellation. This oak-aged 98 has a purple colour, with notes of *ciste* (a Mediterranean shrub), smoke and tar. The complex palate is mouth-filling with plenty of class.
🔑 Les Crus Faugères, Mas Olivier, 34600 Faugères, tel. 04.67.95.08.80, fax 04.67.95.14.67 ☑ Y by appt.

Fitou

The Appellation Fitou, the oldest AOC for a red wine in Languedoc-Roussillon (1948), is to be found in the Mediterranean part of the Corbières region. It covers nine communes, which are also authorised to produced Vin Doux Naturel Rivesaltes and Muscat Rivesaltes. In 1999 103,680 hl (2,737,152 gal) were produced. The wine is a beautiful deep ruby colour and has 12% of alcohol; maturation in casks takes a minimum of nine months.

DOM. ASTRUC Cuvée Privilège 1998★
■ 3 ha 7,500 ⫼ 50–69 F

Only carefully-handled old Carignan and Grenache vines, from several selective pickings, can afford the luxury of maturation for 12 months in *demi-muids* (300-litre oak casks) and present such an intense purple colour in the glass. Vanilla, oak and toastiness come through with some *ciste* (a Mediterranean shrub). With vanilla also evident on the palate, it is powerful and virile, ideal for game in red wine.
🔑 Claudine et Eric Astruc, rue de La Gare, 11350 Tuchan, tel. 04.68.27.66.24, fax 04.68.27.66.32 ☑ Y by appt.

DOM. BERTRAND-BERGE
Tradition 1998★
■ 15 ha 60,000 ▮ 🌡 30–49 F

Having run the estate for seven years, Jérôme Bertrand has not been slow to make a name for himself in Fitou, particularly on export markets. The old Carignan needs time to express itself. Already very pleasant and ready to drink, the garnet-coloured 98 has toasty aromas along with coffee, spices and prunes. A good example of finesse and balance.
🔑 Jérôme Bertrand, av. du Roussillon, 11350 Paziols, tel. 04.68.45.41.73, fax 04.68.45.41.73 ☑ Y by appt.

LES MAITRES VIGNERONS DE CASCASTEL Cuvée Spéciale 1998★★★
■ 60 ha 150,000 ▮ 🌡 30–49 F

The floods of November 1999 have redrawn the map: no more bridges, no more roads and a devastated landscape all along the Berre river. The weakened cellars held, but will need rebuilding, and the producers have decided to look to the future. It must be said that this co-operative has plenty of aces up its sleeve and the choice was difficult between the superb **Carte Or 98**, the distinctive **Sélection** and **Château de Seigneur d'Arse 98**. The full and rich Cuvée Spéciale wins nonetheless with its attractive garnet colour and mixture

LANGUEDOC

of ripe fruit, spicy, roasted and green, leafy blackcurrant notes. The power of the tannins is softened by a velvety texture, and the wine has perfect balance. Still improving and should be fully developed in two years' time.
Les Maîtres Vignerons de Cascastel, 11360 Cascastel, tel. 04.68.45.91.74, fax 04.68.45.82.70 by appt.

DOM. DES ESTAGNELS 1998

6 ha 26,000 30–49 F

To get to know that unique landscape and to really understand Fitou, you have to be able to stop and take the time to lose yourself along the little roads leading out of the village, winding their way into the mineral hills of the Corbières. This very intense wine offers scents of spices and the delicate toasty notes of Mourvèdre. Integrated but full, balanced as well as warming, this is quintessential Fitou.
SCV Fitou, B.P. 1, 11510 Fitou, tel. 04.68.45.71.41, fax 04.68.45.60.32

DOM. DE LA ROCHELIERRE

Elevé en Fût de Chêne 1998★★

3 ha 7,000 30–49 F

Barriques have happily replaced *foudres* (big casks) here to improve the Syrah and Mourvèdre next to the more traditional Fitou varieties of Carignan and Grenache. The intense solid purple colour of this 98 does not hold back the developed scents of fruit and spices. Rounded, powerful and spicy, this Fitou is balanced, with good quality, integrated tannins.
Jean-Marie Fabre, 17, rue du Vigné, 11510 Fitou, tel. 04.68.45.70.52, fax 04.68.45.70.52
ev. day 9am–12 noon 1.30pm–7.30pm; Nov.—Apr. 1.30pm–7.30pm

DOM. LERYS Cuvée Prestige 1998★★★

n.c. 20,000 30–49 F

Badly affected by the floods of November 1999, Maguy and Alain Izard were determined not to let the elements beat them. They present a good lesson in willpower, energy and optimism. The dark ruby 98 leads on to delightfully fresh smells of ripe fruits and spices. Both soft and full-bodied, this wine has superb balance in which the fruit holds up well against the many still youthful tannins. A fine and long future can be expected.
Dom. Lerys, 11360 Villeneuve-les-Corbières, tel. 04.68.45.95.47, fax 04.68.45.86.11, e-mail domlerys@aol.fr
ev. day 10am–8pm
Izard

DOM. LES MILLE VIGNES

Cuvée les Vendangeurs de la Violette 1998★

2 ha 2,600 150–199 F

A wine-lover who, after purchasing 1,000 vines in 1979, today finds himself with 5 ha (12 acres) in production, but still he maintains the same will to do things right (such as harvesting into small boxes). This deep garnet 98 starts off solidly, with rich scents of ripe fruits, prunes and undergrowth. On the palate, the fruit is of the crystallised kind and the wine is still tough and youthful, supported by still hard tannins. Needs time.
Jacques Guérin, 24, av. Saint-Pancrace, 11480 La Palme, tel. 04.68.48.57.14, fax 04.68.48.57.14 by appt.

DOM. MAYNADIER

Cuvée de l'Ancêtre 1998★

5 ha 6,483 20–29 F

The name Fitou comes from *Fita* (frontier or border post) and not as in the humorous French play on words 'Dieu fit tout, l'homme le fitou'. This is a colourful wine right from the start with a dark colour and powerful nose that is spicy, charred and wild with a very concentrated palate and pronounced tannins. A characterful wine that needs time, as does the **98 Élevé en Fût** (oak-aged version) also mentioned by the jury.
Maynadier, R.N. 9, 11510 Fitou, tel. 04.68.45.63.11, fax 04.68.45.60.94
ev. day 9am–12 noon 2pm–7pm

MONT TAUCH Prestige 1998★★

25 ha 60,000 50–69 F

Following a good harvest, the members of the Mont Tauch co-operative were faced with a devastated land after the floods in November 1999. The Ségure area suffered, but as always here, everyone got together to heal the wounds and to get back on track. Blackberry and blackcurrant with some violet notes dominate this attractive purple-coloured Prestige. The pleasure continues on the palate, which is fruity, silky and subtly spicy. The key tasting note is balance. Also note the excellent **Seigneurie Don Neuve 98** and **Château de Ségure 98**.
Cave du Mont Tauch, 11350 Tuchan, tel. 04.68.45.41.08, fax 04.68.45.45.29 by appt.

TERRE ARDENTE 1998

n.c. 25,000 50–69 F

Leucate holds all the aces when it comes to welcoming visitors: oysters, wines, a long sandy beach and a lake known for windsurfing. All the more so, since the charismatic president of this co-operative cellar had the excellent idea of restoring the walled vineyard areas. Very dark, this intense 98 has a nose of undergrowth, civet and ripe grapes with a touch of juniper. An overall solid, warming but soft wine, the palate is powerful with a tannic finish. Suitable accompaniment for a good game dish.
Les Vignerons du Cap Leucate, 2, av. F.-Vals, 11370 Leucate, tel. 04.68.40.01.31, fax 04.68.40.08.90 by appt.

Minervois

Minervois is an AOC wine produced in 61 communes, 45 of which are in the Aude and 16 in the Hérault. This is a mainly limestone area of low hills with south-facing slopes, protected from the cold winds by the Montagne Noire. It produces white, rosé and red wines; the latter represent 95% of the production. In 1999 a total of 212,276 hl (5,603,849 gal) was produced in all three colours from an area of 5,000 ha (12,350 acres).

The Minervois vineyard is crossed by many enchanting tourist routes; the local Route des Vins is a signposted itinerary that offers numerous opportunities to visit tasting cellars along the way. The chief tourist attractions of the area include a famous historical site in the ancient city of Minerve, a host of Romanesque chapels and interesting churches in Rieux and Caune. The local wine Confrérie or brotherhood, the Compagnons du Minervois, has its headquarters at Olonzac.

ABBAYE DE THOLOMIES 1997*

■ 7 ha 36,000 30–49 F

An ultra-modern cellar hides underneath the ancient Benedictine abbey. Yet, in this devout atmosphere, it is not simply left to providence to produce such a concentrated, mouth-filling and warming wine. The fine aromas of balsam and toast exist side by side with stewed fruits. An excellent wine that is full-bodied and long.

SARL Lucien Rogé, 34210 La Livinière, tel. 04.68.78.10.21, fax 04.68.78.36.04

ABBOTTS Cumulo Nimbus 1998**

■ 10 ha 36,000 100–149 F

Of Australian origin, the Sneyd and Abbott winery is certain of the good potential of the Minervois area. The choice of name may be astonishing – cumulo-nimbus clouds bring rain – but the wine is superb. Aged for 14 months in barrel, the Syrah is sumptuous with an intense, almost scintillating colour and a plethora of flavours on both nose and palate. Vanilla, spices and coffee express themselves within a framework of high quality tannins. The long finish guarantees this wine's future. Try it with a game-bird casserole.

SARL Abbott Sneyd Anderson, 5, rue de la Friperie, 34000 Montpellier, tel. 04.67.91.31.00, fax 04.67.91.31.07, e-mail abbotts@wanadoo.fr

DOM. DE BARROUBIO 1999**

1 ha 3,500 20–29 F

From the solid limestone of Saint-Jean-de-Minervois, a terroir known for its Muscats, this tile-coloured rosé from Raymond Miquel is splendid. The subtle nose, reminiscent of springtime, combines elegance and richness; its complexity is amazing. The palate has nice notes of the garrigue, and the finish exceeds all expectations. This wine will show its best with spicy food.

Raymond Miquel, Dom. de Barroubio, 34360 Saint-Jean-de-Minervois, tel. 04.67.38.14.06, fax 04.67.38.14.06, e-mail barroubio@club-internet.fr
ev. day 9am–12 noon 3pm–7pm

CH. BELVIZE Cuvée des Oliviers 1997

■ 0.8 ha 25,000 30–49 F

Already well respected for its whites, the château has produced an excellent, intensely dark red Cuvée des Oliviers in 1997. Red berry fruit and spices cope easily with the balanced and warming structure dominated by tannins from Mourvèdre. You will have to wait a while before this wine has toned down.

Ch. Belvize, La Lecugne, 11120 Bize-Minervois, tel. 04.68.46.22.70, fax 04.68.46.35.72, e-mail belvize@terre-net.fr by appt.
Amiel

CH. DE BLOMAC
Cuvée Tradition 1998

■ 8 ha 45,000 30–49 F

Faithful to tradition in its choice of grape varieties (40% Carignan vinified using carbonic maceration), this attractive wine is evidence of a return to basics. The first impression is of a depth of black fruit that this variety shows so well once it is toned down. Full-bodied, fine and with good length, this 98 needs a little more time.

SCEA Ch. de Blomac, 11700 Blomac, tel. 04.68.79.01.54, fax 04.68.79.22.28
by appt.

CH. BONHOMME 1997

■ 7 ha 30,000 50–69 F

Old vines of Carignan and Cinsault, harvested at full ripeness, provide this wine with an easy-going fruity palate, with some cocoa. The length of finish shows both finesse and freshness. This 97 is ready to drink.

SCE Ch. Bonhomme, Dom. de Bonhomme, 11800 Aigues-Vives, tel. 04.68.79.28.47, fax 04.68.79.28.48 by appt.

DOM. BORIE DE MAUREL
Cuvée Sylla 1998***

■ 6 ha 10,000 100–149 F

A *coup de cœur* for this excellent wine destined to become world-famous and to make

heads turn. As bright as a ruby, the nose hints at undergrowth and aromas of violets, truffles, mocha and liquorice. The palate is a real revelation, with a power that opens the gateway to paradise. The flavours are alive with finesse in a harmonious balance. With an extreme sweetness, the finish is pure ecstasy. This wine is equal to the finest.
🔑 Michel Escande, Dom. Borie de Maurel, 34210 Félines-Minervois, tel. 04.68.91.68.58, fax 04.68.91.63.92 ☑ 🍷 by appt.

DOM. DES CAUSSERELS 1998★★

■ 1.8 ha n.c. ■ 30–49 F

This wine is from Syrah and Grenache vinified using carbonic maceration. With a garnet colour providing great presence, this 98 gives a range of interwoven, complex flavours of liquorice, fruits of the forest and vanilla together with good quality tannins. Full-bodied and eloquent, the palate is refined. A wine to buy.
🔑 Michel Sicart, chem. des Aires, 34210 Siran, tel. 04.68.91.54.06 ☑
🍷 ev. day 9.30am–8pm

DOM. DE CERENS 1999★

□ 0.89 ha 3,000 ■ 🌡 20–29 F

Driven by a constant concern for perfection, Christian Lauber, the cellar-master of the co-operative, submits a bright white Minervois, just starting to deepen, with floral and spicy aromas. Balanced and warming on the palate, this teasing southerner adds a delicate touch of resinous flavour to the finish.
🔑 Cellier Armand de Bezons, 11600 Villalier, tel. 04.68.77.16.69, fax 04.68.77.15.85 ☑ 🍷 by appt.

CH. COUPE ROSES

Rosé Frémillant 1999

◪ 1 ha 6,000 ■ 🌡 30–49 F

Exported to the four corners of the earth, this pale and bright rosé will please many. Demonstrating perfect technology in its production, the wine nevertheless expresses attractive fruit, body and richness. Served very cool, it would be ideal with a salad.
🔑 Frissant, Ch. Coupe Roses, rue de la Poterie, 34210 La Caunette, tel. 04.68.91.21.95, fax 04.68.91.11.73, e-mail couperoses@aol.com ☑ 🍷 by appt.

DOM. CROS Les Aspres 1998★★★

■ 1.5 ha 5,000 🛢 100–149 F

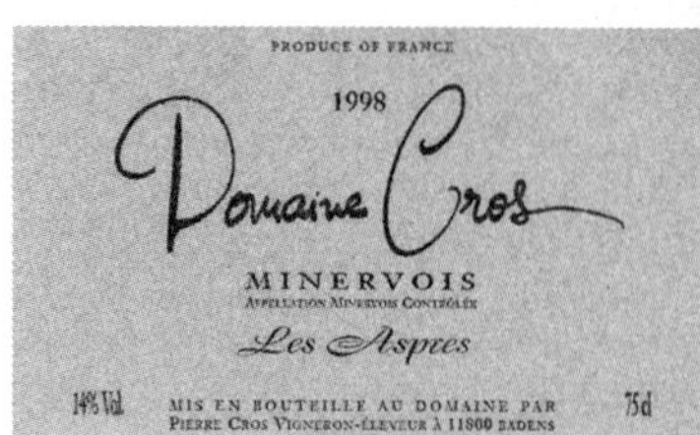

A character of tempered steel and a terroir of fire! Les Aspres: Pierre Cros, with first-class assistance from the œnologist Claude Gros, carries off the Guide's *coup de cœur* with great panache. This garnet-coloured wine impresses with its immediate power. Vanilla, liquorice and violets form a high-powered trio helped along by sturdy, but finely developed tannins. The taste buds will love the endless length of this wine. A wine to be listed amongst your cellar's finest for a long time.
🔑 Pierre Cros, 20, rue du Minervois, 11800 Badens, tel. 04.68.79.21.82, fax 04.68.79.24.03 ☑ 🍷 by appt.

CH. DU DONJON

Cuvée Prestige Elevé en Fût de Chêne 1998★★

■ 5 ha 35,000 🛢 50–69 F

The keep of the château emerges in the middle of the cellar! The descendants of this family estate, which goes back to the 15th century, are proud of this attractive 98 that is garnet-coloured with a purple hue. Full of spices, fruits of the forest and cocoa, the wine is intense from the start. Warming with a powerful body that ensures perfect balance and long ageing potential.
🔑 Jean Panis, Ch. du Donjon, 11600 Bagnoles, tel. 04.68.77.18.33, fax 04.68.72.21.17, e-mail jean.panis@wanadoo.fr ☑
🍷 ev. day 9am–6pm

PREMIER DE FONTALIERES 1998★★

■ 6.5 ha 15,000 🛢 50–69 F

This wine graduates from the co-operative first in its year. They are proud to have such a good student that excels with class in all its subjects! Given a schooling of carbonic maceration, 'raised' for a long time in wood, this is an excellent wine with spicy and oaky notes. Perfectly educated tannins and good balance are the basis for receiving one of the awards on prize-giving day. It should have a great future.
🔑 Caves des producteurs de Pouzols-Minervois, RDS Les Auberges, 11120 Pouzols-Minervois, tel. 04.68.46.13.76, fax 04.68.46.33.95 ☑
🍷 ev. day 8am–12 noon 2pm–6pm; groups by appt.; cl. Sun. 10 Oct.–30 Mar.

CH. GUERY Elevé en Fût de Chêne 1998

■ 0.8 ha 3,000 30–49 F

Eight generations of wine-producers have lived on this estate. René-Henry, the latest in the line, submits a pretty, bright cherry-red 98. A very ripe nose shows spices first, then blackcurrant and raspberry. Silky and with light barbecued flavours, this wine is ready to drink. Perfect with lamb and meat served with sauce.

GAEC L'Ermitage, 4, av. du Minervois, 11700 Azille, tel. 04.68.91.44.34, fax 04.68.91.44.34 by appt.

DOM. DES HOMS 1998

■ 2 ha 6,000 30–49 F

The estate prides itself in sorting the grapes of the whole harvest, which results in this intense and structured red. The wine reveals delicate spices and red berry fruits with a balance that indicates definite ageing ability. So, leave this one for a while in your cellar.

Bernard de Crozals, Dom. des Homs, 11160 Rieux-Minervois, tel. 04.68.78.10.51, fax 04.68.78.10.51 by appt.

CUVEE IMAGE 1998*

■ 4 ha 6,000 30–49 F

The Cuvée Image looks like a modern painting with a purple background and shades of violet. With good structure, it has elegant tannins and reveals a full range of red fruit that will still develop. A good wine to keep. For now, you can enjoy the **Vidal La Marquise 99 Rosé**.

Les crus du Haut-Minervois, Cave coop., 34210 Azillanet, tel. 04.68.91.22.61, fax 04.68.91.19.46, e-mail cavelescrusduhautminervois @wanadoo.fr by appt.

JACQUES DE LA JUGIE
Vieilli en Fût de Chêne 1998

■ 25 ha 150,000 20–29 F

A selection from a specific plot and ten months' ageing in oak for this delicate Minervois, which at first reveals full-bodied cherry flavours, and then slowly develops with the sweetness of liquorice. To drink now.

Cave coop. de la Livinière, 34210 La Livinière, tel. 04.68.91.42.67, fax 04.68.91.51.77 by appt.

CH. LA GRAVE Expression 1999*

□ n.c. 30,000 30–49 F

The sense of family is not a superficial expression here, for parents, children and in-laws all contribute towards producing this dashing white, full of exotic fruits. Pineapple, grapefruit and oranges all appear, and the lively palate has good length. The **Expression 99 Rosé** comes a good second. This estate is certainly one of the more reliable choices to make from the wines of Minervois and even of France.

Jean-Pierre et Jean-François Orosquette, SCEA Ch. la Grave, 11800 Badens, tel. 04.68.79.16.00, fax 04.68.79.22.91 ev. day 9am–12 noon 2pm–7pm; Sat. Sun. by appt.

CLOS L'ESQUIROL 1998*

■ 10 ha 35,000 30–49 F

Our Languedoc 'esquirol' (squirrel) escapes once again from its cage not alone, but in the company of 35,000 others! Obvious carbonic maceration notes of stewed fruit show on this wine. Very powerful, marrying finesse and balance, its structure is stunning. Its finish is equalled only by its complexity. This is a very classic example of the AOC.

La Siranaise, 34210 Siran, tel. 04.68.91.42.17 by appt.

CH. MALVES BOUSQUET 1999

□ 1 ha 4,000 30–49 F

'We talk little and drink well' is the château's motto. However, this is a wine that loosens tongues with its scintillating appearance and its expressive fruity aromas of apples, pears and exotic fruits. Powerful, or rather, rich, with an eloquent balance. It shows good acidity and leaves you open-mouthed at the finish.

SCEA Bousquet, Ch. de Malves, 11600 Malves, tel. 04.68.72.25.32, fax 04.68.77.18.82 by appt.

CH. D'OUPIA Les Barons 1998*

■ 6 ha 33,000 30–49 F

Château d'Oupia is a very successful and vast estate of 55 ha (136 acres). With a purple coat of arms, this distinguished 98 is very powerful with plenty of vanilla and toast flavours, side by side with clear-cut tannins. The finish is extremely good.

Famille André Iché, EARL Ch. d'Oupia, 34210 Oupia, tel. 04.68.91.20.86, fax 04.68.91.18.23 by appt.

DOM. PICCININI 1999**

□ 3 ha 5,000 30–49 F

Maurice Piccinini is the man responsible for getting La Livinière into the closed club of Appellation Contrôlée wines. Still enjoying work on his estate, he offers a pale and luminous white, full of peachy aromas. Straightforward, lively and warming on the palate, vanilla notes on the finish reveal the method of maturation. Honey and some Muscat nuances blend together, providing an incomparable sweetness.

Dom. Piccinini, rte des Meulières, 34210 La Livinière, tel. 04.68.91.44.32, fax 04.68.91.58.65

CH. PLO DU ROY
Le Balcon du Diable Elevé en Fût de Chêne 1998**

■ 7 ha 16,000 30–49 F

Franc Benazeth is not a man to give up. Extremely badly hit by the floods of November 1999, he has managed to ward off the worst in presenting the jury with this superb 98. It has an intense ruby-red colour with very appealing notes of the garrigue and vanilla. This elegant wine is as complex as it is

LANGUEDOC

warming, with powerful tannins that would make it best to drink with game dishes.
🔑 M. et Mme Benazeth, 8, chem. de Bel-Mati, 11160 Villeneuve, tel. 04.68.26.13.64, fax 04.68.26.13.64

DOM. SAINTE-LEUCHERE

Cuvée du Clos de Mathieu Vieilli en Fût de Chêne 1998

■ n.c. 2,500 30–49 F

Here are the keys to success: an estate completely replanted with Syrah and Grenache, an excellent clay-limestone soil, good wine-making. With a garnet colour, the red berry crystallised fruits dally with some teasing tannins. This wine is still young, but shows particularly good quality on the finish.
🔑 Yves Bru, Dom. Sainte-Leuchère, rue des Ecoles, 34210 Aigne, tel. 04.68.91.34.93, fax 04.68.91.82.27 ☒ Y ev. day 2pm–7pm

CH. SAINT-LEON

Cuvée Amour Elevé en Fût de Chêne 1997

■ 1.5 ha 5,000 30–49 F

The lively scene is set with shades of violet. The nose has mainly mineral notes, but on the palate, it is the red berry fruit that builds steadily as the tannins come in to play. This wine certainly has an extended finish. A characteristic wine of the AOC.
🔑 Guy et Emmanuel Giva, Dom. de Sautes, R.N. 113, 11000 Carcassonne, tel. 04.68.78.77.98, fax 04.68.78.51.66, e-mail domainesautes@infonie.fr ☒ Y ev. day except Sun. 2pm–7pm

CH. VILLERAMBERT JULIEN

1999★

◪ 15 ha 80,000 30–49 F

Four varieties are used for this unique rosé. Michel Julien, an artistic wine-producer, paints a radiant and brightly coloured canvas with a palette of complex fruits. Strawberries, grenadine and blackcurrants intertwine with freshness and power, leading to a perfectly framed finish. Ideal with exotic foods.
🔑 Michel Julien, Ch. Villerambert Julien, 11160 Caunes-Minervois, tel. 04.68.78.00.01, fax 04.68.78.05.34 ☒ Y ev. day 9am–11.30am 1pm–6.30pm; Sat. Sun. by appt.

CH. DE VILLERAMBERT MOUREAU 1999

◪ 40 ha 5,300 30–49 F

From predominantly Syrah, grown on schist, this rosé has a good appearance. A mass of red berry fruits come together to give a mouth-filling and unctuous character. Drink this fresh and balanced 99 right away with a barbecue.
🔑 Marceau Moureau et Fils, Ch. de Villerambert, 11160 Caunes-Minervois, tel. 04.68.77.16.40, fax 04.68.77.08.14 ☒ Y ev. day except Sat. Sun. 2pm–7pm

DOM. VORDY-MAYRANNE

Cuvée Louise 1998★

■ 2 ha 8,600 20–29 F

This estate is situated close to Minerve, heart of the Cathar region, where Carignan and Grenache are particularly suited to the soil type. This rugged and warming Minervois is built on a spicy structure. Full-bodied and rich, its stewed fruit and toasty aromas emerge particularly intensely on the finish.
🔑 Didier Vordy, Mayranne, 34210 Minerve, tel. 04.68.91.80.39, fax 04.68.91.80.39 ☒ Y ev. day 9am–7pm

Minervois la Livinière

DOM. BORIE DE MAUREL

Cuvée La Féline 1998★★★

■ 6 ha 21,000 50–69 F

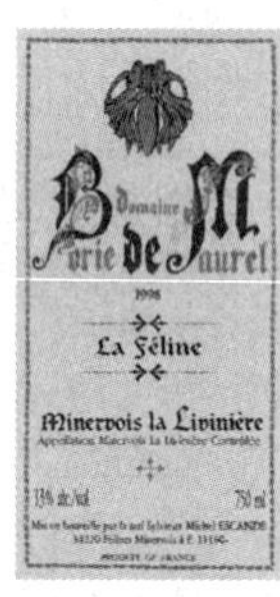

An excellent vine-grower, and president of this new appellation, Michel Escande sets an example by reaching for the moon with his Cuvée Féline. A concentrated wine that shows the terroir well, it exudes spices, strawberries and nutmeg, and develops distinction on the palate with rounded and classy tannins. Warming, full-bodied and complex, this regal wine will remain one of the joys in your cellar for a long time.
🔑 Michel Escande, Dom. Borie de Maurel, 34210 Félines-Minervois, tel. 04.68.91.68.58, fax 04.68.91.63.92 ☒ Y by appt.

DOM. CHABBERT-FAUZAN

Clos La Coquille 1998★

■ 2.8 ha 9,000 30–49 F

On this privileged site of hard limestone in the hamlet of Fazan, wines of the highest order are produced. A cherry-red colour, this wine exudes scents of strawberry, eucalyptus and sweet spices. Some violets appear on the structured palate. Although the tannins are tightly knit, the substance remains silky and there is good length.

ᵒ Gérard Chabbert, Dom. Chabbert-'auzan, 34210 Cesseras, tel. 04.68.91.23.64, ax 04.68.91.31.17 ☑ Y by appt.

:UVEE GAIA 1998*

■ 7 ha 40,000 50–69 F

They use a unique way of receiving the har-est here, in small 1,000-kg trucks. The result of this special technique is a red wine with otes of the garrigue and of cloves. Fairly aky right from the start, the well-balanced alate reveals graceful and integrated tannins. The weighty finish shows a nice hint of acidity t the end. This wine has a characteristic and ttractive style.

ᵒ Les Crus du Haut-Minervois, Cave :oop., 34210 Azillanet, tel. 04.68.91.22.61, ax 04.68.91.19.46, :-mail cavelescrusduhautminervois @wanadoo.fr ☑ Y by appt.

:H. DE GOURGAZAUD

Réserve 1998*

■ 15 ha 80,000 ⦀ 30–49 F

This château is the stronghold of the *cru*, and emphasises its terroir giving a deep, structured and concentrated wine. Well-made, the liquorice tannins are silky. The palate does not hold back and shows a range of stewed fruits and vanilla on a long finish. To drink or keep.

ᵒ SA Ch. de Gourgazaud, 34210 La Livinière, tel. 04.68.78.10.02, fax 04.68.78.30.24 ☑ Y by appt.

CLOS DE L'ESCANDIL 1998**

■ 4 ha 12,000 ⦀ 70–99 F

A classic wine from this appellation, and one that always occupies a choice position at prize-giving events. With a dark red appearance, this intensely perfumed wine is full of red berry fruit, blackcurrants and blackberries. With an elegance and fine quality from the oak, it has excellent integrated tannins that extend through the palate together with a powerful body and notes of the garrigue. It has a long ageing potential.

ᵒ Gilles Chabbert, chem. des Aires, 34210 Siran, tel. 04.68.91.54.40, fax 04.68.91.54.40 ☑ Y by appt.

Saint-Chinian

Saint-Chinian has been a VDQS from 1945 and became an AOC in 1982. The appellation covers 20 communes and produces 130,000 hl (3,432,000 gal) of red and rosé wines. Located in the Hérault, north-west of Béziers, it lies on seaward-facing hills that rise to 100 and 200 m (328–656 ft). The soils are schists, which are mainly in the north, and limestone gravel in the south. The wine has a distinguished tradition, its name having been recorded as early as 1300. A Maison des Vins has been established in Saint-Chinian itself.

DOM. DE BASTIDE ROUSSE

Haute Gastronomie 1997

■ n.c. 3,500 ⦀ 30–49 F

The attractive, clear colour announces a nose that is still quite closed. On the other hand, the palate is coated with fine tannins. This wine needs good aeration, but then could be ready to drink quite soon.

ᵒ Anne et Jean-Paul Crassus, Dom. de Bastide Rousse, 34360 Villespassans, tel. 04.67.38.18.54 ☑ Y by appt.

BERLOUP COLLECTION 1998*

■ 20 ha 10,000 ⦀ 50–69 F

You can smell the schist in the wines from this expressive terroir in the little village of Berlou at the foot of the Cévennes mountains. This Saint-Chinian is garnet with hints of blue. The nose is quite delicate at first, but opens up during tasting, mixing blackcurrant with strawberry, leather and mineral notes. Complexity is also evident on the spicy palate, which strikes a very good balance between weight and tannin. The same mark was awarded to the **Coteaux du Languedoc Cuvée Schisteil 99 Blanc**, (30–49 F).

ᵒ Les Coteaux du Rieu Berlou, av. des Vignerons, 34360 Berlou, tel. 04.67.89.58.58, fax 04.67.89.59.21, e-mail cve.berloup@wanadoo.fr ☑ Y by appt.

CANET VALETTE

Le Vin Maghani 1998**

■ 12 ha 35,000 ▮ ⦀ 70–99 F

In his new two-year-old cellar, Marc Vallette is a great exponent of daily *pigeage* (punching down of the cap) in order to get the most character from his terroir. With a sumptuous, deep and intense colour, this wine shows a classy nose, expressing charred notes, truffles and spices. A powerful, weighty and mouth-filling palate full of richness indicates a wine of great class and ageing potential. Leave for a few years.

ᵒ EARL Canet-Valette, rte de Causses-et-Veyran, 34460 Cessenon, tel. 04.67.89.37.50, fax 04.67.89.37.50 ☑ Y by appt.

ᵒ Marc Valette

CH. DE CASTIGNO Le Sabinas 1998*

■ 5 ha 11,000 ▮ ♁ 30–49 F

Based in a magnificent setting on a clay-limestone terroir, Jean-Pierre Sireyjol knows how to make wines with the scents of the garrigue. After swirling the glass, Le Sabinas also reveals fruity and tobacco notes. On the palate, the tannins are rounded and balanced,

LANGUEDOC

making this wine an ideal partner to game bird.
Jean-Pierre Sireyjol, Castigno, 34360 Villespassans, tel. 04.67.38.05.50, fax 04.67.38.05.50, e-mail castigno@caves-particulieres.com by appt.

CH. CAZAL-VIEL

Larmes des Fées 1998★★

■ 3 ha 3,000 150–199 F

No competition: Larmes des Fées remains the finest from the Château Cazal-Viel. This 98 has a powerful nose that blends fruit and spices with aromas of incense and fruits macerated in alcohol. Integrated tannins provide good balance. The un-oaked **Cuvée des Fées 99**, receives a star (50–69 F). The characteristic Saint-Chinian notes are less obvious in its youth.
Ch. Cazal-Viel, dom. Cazal-Viel, 34460 Cessenon-sur-Orb, tel. 04.67.89.63.15, fax 04.67.89.65.17 ev. day 8.30am–12.30pm 1.30pm–6pm; Sun. by appt.
Henri Miquel

CLOS BAGATELLE

Sélection du Clos 1998★

■ 7 ha 40,000 50–69 F

A well-made wine, but certain tasters found the nose was closed. Good aeration reveals scents of crystallised fruit and a palate full of powerful tannins that require some maturation. This Sélection du Clos should be able to age gracefully.
Henry Simon, Clos Bagatelle, 34360 Saint-Chinian, tel. 04.67.93.61.63, fax 04.67.93.68.84 ev. day except Sun. 8am–12 noon 1pm–6pm

DOM. DE FONTCAUDE

Elevé en Fût de Chêne 1998★★

■ 15 ha 35,000 30–49 F

This co-operative now has a young, motivated president, who is very quality-orientated. This is a pleasant and very well balanced Saint-Chinian, structured and rounded, with intense flavours of bay and liquorice on the palate. Soft, rich tannins have allowed this wine to achieve a good result in the Guide.
Les Vignerons du Pays d'Ensérune, 235, av. Jean-Jaurès, 34370 Maraussan, tel. 04.67.90.09.80, fax 04.67.90.09.55 by appt.

DOM. DE GABELAS

Cuvée Juliette Elevé en Fût de Chêne 1998

■ 4 ha 5,600 30–49 F

This simple, but elegant wine is the product of a clay-limestone soil, 85% Syrah with Grenache of an average age of 20 years, plus 12 months in oak. It is very fruity, blessed with a light tannic structure. Ready to drink.
Pierrette Cravero, Dom. de Gabelas, 34310 Cruzy, tel. 04.67.93.84.29, fax 04.67.93.84.29 by appt.

DOM. DES JOUGLA 1997★★

■ 3 ha 13,000 30–49

The Jougla family has been based here for five generations. Marrying tradition and modernity, this charming wine is full of personality. The deep colour has light shades of roof-tiles. Good intensity of red berry fruit and vanilla flavours, which lead on to pronounced tannins, providing this wine with good balance and a spicy finish.
Alain Jougla, 34360 Prades-sur-Vernazobre, tel. 04.67.38.06.02, fax 04.67.38.17.74 by appt.

CH. LA DOURNIE Elise 1998★★

■ 4 ha 7,300 70–99

This estate shines with its **99 Rosé** (one star 30–49 F) and its new wine, named Elise. The latter is characteristic of its schistose terroir. With a deep, pretty purple colour, the nose exudes perfumes of black fruit and violets. The palate has an impressive velvety texture to it with fine and promising tannins. This is elegance in a glass!
EARL Ch. la Dournie, 34360 Saint-Chinian, tel. 04.67.38.19.43, fax 04.67.38.00.37 by appt.
Etienne

DOM. DU LANDEYRAN

Cuvée Emilia 1998

■ 1.8 ha 7,000 50–69 F

From a terroir famous for its superb vineyards, this attractive 98 reveals shades of violet. The subtle nose comes alive little by little with notes of ripe fruit. The balance between tannin and richness shows that this wine will age extremely well.
EARL du Landeyran, rue de la Vernière, 34490 Saint-Nazaire-de-Ladarez, tel. 04.67.89.67.63, fax 04.67.89.67.63 by appt.

DOM. MARQUISE DES MURES

Les Sagnes 1998★

■ 14 ha 15,000 50–69 F

This small 'artisan' vineyard was planted by three generations: Carignan by the grandfather, Grenache by the father and Syrah by the son. This gives a wine of great finesse, with the nose showing bay leaves and the garrigue, and the palate, soft and silky. Drink in two or three years.
Jean-Jacques Mailhac, Dom. des Marquises, 34460 Roquebrun, tel. 04.67.89.55.63, fax 04.67.89.55.63 by appt.

MAS CHAMPART

Causse du Bousquet 1998★★

■ 4.25 ha 12,000 50–69 F

Isabelle and Mathieu Champart offer an exceptional wine, to which the jury awarded a *coup de cœur*. The colour is deep with violet hues; the powerful and complex nose combines charred notes with fruits macerated in brandy, black olives and spices. The initial impression is straightforward, but the palate

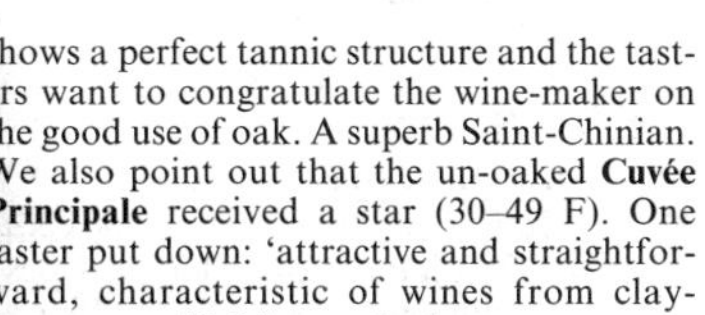

hows a perfect tannic structure and the tasters want to congratulate the wine-maker on he good use of oak. A superb Saint-Chinian. We also point out that the un-oaked **Cuvée Principale** received a star (30–49 F). One aster put down: 'attractive and straightforward, characteristic of wines from clay-imestone soil'. It's exactly that.

🔑 EARL Champart, rte de Villespassans, 34360 Saint-Chinian, tel. 04.67.38.20.09, fax 04.67.38.20.09, e-mail mas.champart@libertysurf.fr ☒ Y by appt.

CH. MAUREL FONSALADE

La Fonsalade Vieilles Vignes 1997★★

■ 1.5 ha 6,900 50–69 F

This Fonsalade Vieilles Vignes is from a rigorous selection of grapes from the best terroirs of the estate, produced in a difficult vintage. The patience and hard work of the producer has given a powerful and complex wine in which the length is that of a very fine wine. This will hold up well for some time.

🔑 Philippe et Thérèse Maurel, Ch. Maurel Fonsalade, 34490 Causses-et-Veyran, tel. 04.67.89.57.90, fax 04.67.89.72.04 ☒ Y by appt.

CH. MILHAU-LACUGUE

◢ 4 ha 23,000 30–49 F

This rosé is a blend of Cinsault, Grenache and Syrah, vinified with some skin maceration. A deep, bright pink colour leads on to a nose showing strawberries and raspberries. With good acidity and well-balanced, the palate shows the same aromas as the nose and presents a harmonious finish.

🔑 Ch. Milhau-Lacugue, Dom. de Milhau, rte de Cazedarnes, 34620 Puisserguier, tel. 04.67.93.64.79, fax 04.67.93.51.93 ☒ Y ev. day 9.30am–12 noon 1.30pm–5pm; Sat. Sun. by appt.

🔑 Lacugue

DOM. NAVARRE

Cuvée Olivier Elevé en Fût de Chêne 1999★★★

■ 6 ha 12,000 50–69 F

Thierry Navarre has been here on the exceptional terroir of Roquebrun for 12 years. He has produced a masterstroke with this Cuvée Olivier 99. Notwithstanding its youth, the jury enjoyed the intense nose, which marries notes of mocha, blueberry, figs and grey pepper. The palate is similar to the nose with rounded tannins and a very good length. A plethora of sensations and pleasures. One star is awarded for the **Le Laouzil 98** (30–49 F).

🔑 Thierry Navarre, av. de Balaussan, 34460 Roquebrun, tel. 04.67.89.53.58, fax 04.67.89.70.88 ☒ Y ev. day except Sun. 9am–12 noon 2pm–6pm

PRIEURE SAINT-ANDRE

Cuvée Angelus 1997★

■ 1.5 ha 3,000 50–69 F

Adorned with a garnet colour showing slight age, this wine takes the taster into a world of schist (on the terroir of Roquebrun) with toasty notes and flavours of dried figs and blackcurrant. The warming palate is supported by a lightly tannic structure. Will be enjoyed with small game such as partridge or rabbit.

🔑 Michel Claparède, Prieuré Saint-André, 34460 Roquebrun, tel. 04.67.89.70.82, fax 04.67.89.71.41 ☒ Y by appt.

LES VINS DE ROQUEBRUN

Prestige 1999★

■ 35 ha 140,000 50–69 F

The Roquebrun co-operative remains faithful to this terroir, where it knows how to produce some prestigious wines. The **Coteaux du Languedoc 99 Blanc** receives a star, as does the **Saint-Chinian Cuvée Roches Noires 98**. This Prestige has a garnet colour with notes of leather on the fine nose, as well as charred aromas. The palate is silky and mineral with smoky and toasty notes on the finish. Very characterful.

🔑 Cave les Vins de Roquebrun, av. des Orangers, 34460 Roquebrun, tel. 04.67.89.64.35, fax 04.67.89.57.93, e-mail info@cave.roquebrun.fr ☒ Y ev. day except Sun. 8am–12 noon 2pm–6pm

JEAN DE ROUEYRE 1999★★

◢ 15 ha 82,000 20 F+

The members of the Rouïere co-operative have worked as one producer to obtain a splendid rosé worthy of serving during a dinner party. With a clear salmon-pink colour the wine shows a dignified nose including nuances of blackcurrant, raspberry, peach, exotic fruits and a floral touch. On the palate, this bold 99 has substance and weight. Its mouth-filling style could not fail to charm us.

LANGUEDOC

🗝 Les Vignerons de Roueïre, Dom. de Roueïre, 34310 Quarante, tel. 04.67.89.40.10, fax 04.67.89.32.20 ☑ 𝐘 ev. day except Mon. 10am–6pm

DOM. DU SACRE-CŒUR

Cuvée Kevin 1998*

■ 8 ha 25,000 ▮ ⊪ 🌡 30-49 F

Marc Caberet was the owner of a chain of supermarkets before he dedicated himself to this vineyard in 1991. From a clay-limestone soil, it is the robust structure of this Cuvée Kevin that stands out most. Despite this, in a delicate vintage, the producer has managed to make a complex wine with scents of the garrigue such as thyme and bay leaf. A rich body, which simply needs time to develop fully.

🗝 GAEC du Sacré-Cœur, Dom. du Sacré-Cœur, 34360 Assignan, tel. 04.67.38.17.97, fax 04.67.38.24.52 ☑ 𝐘 by appt.

🗝 Cabaret Père et Fils

DOM. SORTEILHO 1999*

■ 25 ha 750 ▮ 20-29 F

All three colours were noted by the tasters. The wine is from schist soil and has an attractive young purple colour with notes of grey pepper on a background of *ciste* (a Mediterranean shrub) and spices. On the other hand, the palate is more restrained than the nose, though soft and integrated. Ready to drink.

🗝 Cave des Vignerons de Saint-Chinian, rte de Sorteilho, 34360 Saint-Chinian, tel. 04.67.38.28.41, fax 04.67.38.28.43 ☑ 𝐘 by appt.

CH. SOULIE DES JONCS 1998*

■ 2.66 ha 8,000 ⊪ 30-49 F

This estate has been handed down from father to son since 1610. The 1998 has an attractive, concentrated purple colour with a nose of pepper, spices, the garrigue and crushed blackberries. The power and aromatic depth on the palate is due to the clay-limestone soil. A wine that needs to be kept for several more years.

🗝 Dom. des Soulié, Carriera de la Teuliera, 34360 Assignan, tel. 04.67.38.11.78, fax 04.67.38.19.31, e-mail remysoulie@aol.com ☑ 𝐘 by appt.

DOM. DU TABATAU Albin 1999*

◪ 2 ha 4,300 ▮ 🌡 30-49 F

Formerly the expert wine representative for the Coteaux du Languedoc promotional office, Bruno Gracia, with his brother Jean-Paul, swapped jobs to become a wine-producer. Cuvée Albin has a very pale, bright pink colour with an extremely delicate nose, really flowery, with strawberries, hazelnuts and a mineral touch. The palate has balanced richness, acidity and weight.

🗝 Bruno Gracia, Le village, rue des Anciens Combattants, 04360 Assignan, tel. 04.67.38.19.60, fax 04.67.38.19.54 ☑ 𝐘 by appt.

DOM. DE TRIANON 1998***

■ 8 ha 40,000 ▮ 30-49

Vignerons et Passions has made an attractive selection from the cooperative of Saint-Chinian. The colour of this deep, intense 9 leads one to discover the complex, fine and enjoyable nose of spices, cherry and ripe red berry fruits. Notes of liquorice appear on the rich palate, well-integrated into the structure. A wine that requires some patience but promises well.

🗝 Vignerons et Passions, B.P. 1, 34725 Saint-Félix-de-Lodez, tel. 04.67.88.80.39, fax 04.67.96.65.67

CH. VEYRAN

Cuvée Henri Elevé en Fût de Chêne 1998**

■ 4.75 ha 15,000 ⊪ 50-69 F

In this 16th-century cellar, which includes a vaulted section dating back to the 12th century, Gérard Antoine has made a superb wine. Careful ageing in oak gives a tannic structure of the best quality, fine and round with a concentrated body. The tasters noted particularly the magnificent depth of colour. The wondrous nose marries flavours of the garrigue with fruits macerated in spirit, liquorice and blackcurrants. A very successful wine.

🗝 Gérard Antoine, Veyran, 34490 Causses-et-Veyran, tel. 04.67.89.65.77, fax 04.67.89.65.77 ☑ 𝐘 by appt.

CH. VILLESPASSANS

Elevé en Fût de Chêne 1998**

■ 12 ha 80,000 ▮ ⊪ 30-49 F

This co-operative cellar is one to follow closely. We chose this Château wine for its purple colour and nose of mocha with over-ripe red berry fruit. The structured palate, whose tannins are already very rounded, gives a wine to watch carefully over the next two years, but which is already ready to drink.

🗝 Cave coop. de Cruzy-Montouliers-Cebazan, 34310 Cruzy, tel. 04.67.89.41.20, fax 04.67.89.35.01 ☑

Cabardès

The wines of the Côtes de Cabardès and Obiel come from *terroirs* north of Carcassonne and west of the Minervois. The vineyard covers 2,200 ha (5,434 acres) in 18 communes. In 1999 production was 21,953 hl (579,650 gal) of both red and rosé wines, which mix vine varieties suited to both the Mediterranean and the Atlantic areas of the appellation. The Atlantic influence in this, the most vesterly appellation in the region, nake its wines substantially different from other wines in Languedoc-Roussillon.

CH. BANCALIS 1998

■ 14.78 ha 55,000 30–49 F

To get to this estate, you have to cross the very pretty and historically rich village of Aragon, where the appellation syndicate is based. Delicately spiced on the nose, this 98 has a fairly lively colour. Rounded tannins and a touch of acidity give an elegant wine that is ready to drink.

SCV les Celliers du Cabardès, 11600 Aragon, tel. 04.68.24.90.64, fax 04.68.24.87.09 by appt.

CH. BOURNONVILLE 1998★★

■ 6.7 ha 12,100 30–49 F

This estate, bought by the current proprietors in 1994, has submitted a promising wine. Showing good development, the nose reveals notes of prunes and crystallised fruit and the palate is mouth-filling and weighty with a warming finish. This 98 needs more time and would benefit from being decanted before serving.

EARL Bournonville, 11170 Moussoulens, tel. 04.68.24.86.74, fax 04.68.24.90.61 by appt.

DOM. DE CABROL

Cuvée Vent d'Ouest 1997★

■ 5 ha 15,000 30–49 F

An attractive high-altitude vineyard, the highest one reached before the Montagne Noire. The mountain's proximity encourages a slow but perfect ripening period and each year, the producer waits until exactly the right time to pick. A very expressive wine with a deep and intense colour, it has good depth of ripe fruit aromas and a powerfully tannic palate with notes of liquorice and undergrowth.

Claude et Michel Carayol, Dom. de Cabrol, 11600 Aragon, tel. 04.68.77.19.06, fax 04.68.77.54.90 ev. day 11am–7pm

DOM. DE CAUNETTES HAUTES

1999★

◪ 0.9 ha 5,000 20–29 F

This very pretty vineyard at the edge of the limestone plateau is often recommended for its rosés. Worth noting is a grape variety tour around the property, which allows you to learn about the different varieties of the appellation. A very attractive delicate pink colour with a touch of salmon leads on to a fresh nose, combining floral and fruity notes. An excellent richness is joined by balancing acidity with a very good fruity finish.

SCEA Dom. de Caunettes Hautes, 11170 Moussoulens, tel. 04.68.24.93.15, fax 04.68.24.81.77 by appt.

Gilbert Rouquet

CH. DE PENNAUTIER

Collection Privée Elevé en Fût de Chêne 1998★★★

■ 1.5 ha 5,200 100–149 F

Mention of Château de Pennautier recalls the great historical moments of the Languedoc, notably the construction of the Canal du Midi. This is one of the most beautiful 16th-century châteaux, subsequently modified in the 18th and 19th centuries when the park was created, designed by Le Nôtre. One must also remember that Molière stayed here once. Today it is the wine that keeps up the traditions, and this one is exceptional. A very deep colour with shades of dark purple reveals a complex range of aromas including very ripe blackberries with vanilla and smoky oak notes behind. Good tannins on the palate lead to a very long finish. This wine should be kept. Also note the second wine, **Esprit de Pennautier 97**, which received a mention (30–49 F).

SCEA Ch. de Pennautier, 11610 Pennautier, tel. 04.68.72.65.29, fax 04.68.72.65.84, e-mail contact@Vignobles-Lorgeril.com by appt.

N. de Lorgeril

CH. SALITIS Cuvée Premium 1998★

■ 14 ha 50,000 30–49 F

An old dependence of the Abbaye de Lagrasse, this estate was the first in Cabardès to use that perfect mix of Mediterranean and Atlantic grape varieties. A consistently successful wine characterised by elegance and youth, it gives notes of fresh fruits, with a good attack on the palate and real body. Ready to drink, one could also leave it a while.

Depaule-Marandon, Ch. Salitis, 11600 Conques-sur-Orbiel, tel. 04.68.77.16.10, fax 04.68.77.05.69 ev. day 8.30am–11.30am 1.30pm–5.30pm

CH. VENTENAC

Cuvée Les Pujols 1998★★★

■ 12 ha 40,000 20–29 F

A consistently excellent wine-producer, Alain Maurel's new cellar buildings that marry the old with the new are worth a visit. The key note to this wine is finesse, both on the nose, where fruit and oak work well together, and on the palate, where the tannins

LANGUEDOC

are powerful, yet rounded. Very elegant and rich.

Alain Maurel, 1, pl. du Château, 11610 Ventenac-Cabardès, tel. 04.68.24.93.42, fax 04.68.24.81.16, e-mail alainmaurel@wanadoo.fr ☑ Y by appt.

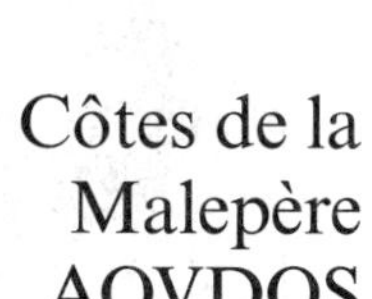

Côtes de la Malepère AOVDQS

A total of 40,000 hl (1,056,000 gal) of wine is produced in this AOVDQS, which covers 31 communes in the Aude. The *terroir* receives Atlantic influences and is situated in the north-west of the Hauts-de-Corbières, which protect it from Mediterranean aridity. The red and rosé wines, full-bodied and fruity, come not only from Carignan grapes but also from Bordeaux varieties, mainly Cabernet-Sauvignon, Cabernet Franc and Merlot, in addition to Grenache and Cot.

CH. DE COINTES 1999★

1.2 ha 10,000 20–29 F

André and Jean Cointes were the first consuls of Carcassonne in the 17th century, and gave their name to this estate. There is consistent quality both for reds and rosés here. With the colour of pink rose petals, this wine is intense and complex with aromas of iris and spices. Lively and full-bodied, it has great balance on the palate with a long finish showing redcurrant flavours. The **98 Rouge** is also very good.

Anne Gorostis, Ch. de Cointes, 11290 Roullens, tel. 04.68.26.81.05, fax 04.68.26.84.37, e-mail info@châteaudecointes.com ☑ Y by appt.

CH. DE FESTES 1998★★★

n.c. 8,000 20–29 F

The Cave de la Malepère at Arzens attains a *coup de cœur* vindicating the background work and dynamism of this young appellation. The wine is characterised by its perfect balance. A complex nose with scents of very ripe fruit and of the garrigue leads onto superb structure on the palate with rounded tannins, accompanied by good body and a very sweet finish. Already ready to drink, it can be kept too. The jury also retained the very fruity **Domaine de Foucauld 98**, which is for immediate drinking.

Cave de la Malepère, av. des Vignerons, 11290 Arzens, tel. 04.68.76.71.71, fax 04.68.76.71.72, e-mail oeno@cavelamalepere.com ☑ Y ev. day except Sat. Sun. 8am–12 noon 2pm–6pm

CH. GUIRAUD 1998★★

18 ha 20,000 30–49

Château Guiraud asserts itself as the jewe from the Cave du Razès. With a deep colour, nose of black fruit and red pepper as well a elegant oak, the wine has nice acidity on th palate with very good quality tannins. Th wine has been well-matured in oak and i seems ready to drink already, though it coul be cellared, too. Also mentioned is the ver soft **Domaine de Majou 98** (20–29 F).

Cave du Razès, 11240 Routier, tel. 04.68.69.02.71, fax 04.68.69.00.49 ☑ Y ev. day except Sat. Sun. 8am–12 noon 2pm–6pm

CH. HERAIL DE ROBERT

Cuvée Merlin 1998★★★

n.c. 10,000 50–69 F

Situated at the western end of the appellation on a gravel terrace, Château de Rober derives benefit from the slow ripening conditions and low yields that produce a wine of great concentration. This has a superb, deep ruby colour. The nose is of red fruits, redcurrants and cherries, combined with some mild spices. Very smooth on the palate which is altogether mouth-filling. Balanced and long, this is a wine with personality to drink or to keep.

Marie-Hélène Herail-Artigouha, Ch. de Robert, 11150 Villesiscle, tel. 04.68.76.11.86, fax 04.68.76.58.62 ☑ Y ev. day 9am–12 noon 2pm–6pm

CH. DE ROUTIER

Cuvée Renaissance 1997★★

8 ha 1,100 50–69 F

This very attractive château dating back to the 15th century has superb vaulted cellars, where this very young, dark garnet wine was matured. The nose is both intense and complex with very expressive notes of spices such as cloves and *badiane* (an aniseed-flavoured shrub). The palate is powerful, with tannins still noticeable and full-bodied towards the finish. A promising wine.

Michèle Lézerat, Ch. de Routier, 11240 Routier, tel. 04.68.69.06.13, fax 04.68.69.06.58 ☑ Y ev. day 10am–12 noon 1.30pm–8pm

Roussillon

Growing vines in Roussillon may date as far back as the eventh century BC, perhaps instigated by Greek traders, drawn to the atalan coast by its rich mineral deposits. The trade was well developed by edieval times, and the sweet wines of the region built a solid reputation ery early on. After their devastation by phylloxera in the early 20th entury, the vineyards were abundantly replanted to flourish once again on he hills of France's southernmost vine-growing area.

Facing the Mediterranean, the Roussillon vineyards are urrounded by three mountain ranges: the Corbières in the north, the anigou in the west and the Albères, which forms the border with Spain, in he south. The Têt, Tech and Agly rivers have shaped a landscape of gravel erraces where the washed, stony soils are ideally suited to produce wines f quality, particularly Vin Doux Naturels (see page 1140). Also found are oils from different origins made up of black or brown schists and sandy ranites as well as hills of Pliocene limestone.

The Roussillon vineyards enjoy a particularly sunny limate, with mild winters and high temperatures in summer. The rainfall – 50–650 mm (14–26 in) – is very uneven and often falls in torrential storms hat are not beneficial for the vines. Fortunately, a dry, summer period ollows, and the heat is intensified by the Tramontane wind, which helps he grapes to ripen.

The vines are trained in the traditional goblet shape and lanted 4,000 to the hectare (1620 to the acre). Tradition still plays a great art in cultivation, which is often only partly mechanised. However, the wine-making equipment in the cellars is being modernised in line with a iversification in vine varieties and vinification techniques. After being arefully checked for ripeness, the harvest is transported in trailers or small rucks without being crushed; some of the grapes are treated by carbonic maceration. Increasingly, temperature during vinification is controlled to protect the delicacy of the aromas: in Roussillon, tradition and modern echnology work side by side.

Côtes du Roussillon and Côtes du Roussillon-Villages

These two appellations are produced from the best soils in the region. In 1999 the vineyards, about 6,800 ha (16,796 acres), produced 347,382 hl (9,170,885 gal) across the whole of the appellation. The Côtes du Roussillon-Villages are clustered in the northernmost part of the Pyrénées-Orientales department; two communes have an appellation with the village name: Caramany and Latour-de-France. Gravel terraces, sandy granite and schist give the wines a richness and a qualitative difference that the winegrowers certainly know how to exploit.

The vine varieties used to produce the white wines are mainly Macabeu, Malvoisie du Roussillon and Grenache Blanc, but Marsanne, Roussanne and Rolle are also used and are mainly vinified by direct pressing. The wines themselves are green in type, light and vigorous, with a fine, floral aroma and so go well with seafood, fish and shellfish.

The rosé and red wines are produced using several varieties: Carignan Noir (a maximum of 60%), Grenache Noir, Lladonner Pelut and Cinsault are the main varieties, with Syrah, Mouvèdre and Macabeu (10% maximum in the red wines) as additional varieties; two main varieties are required with another additional variety. All the varieties (except the Syrah) are pruned short down to two buds. Often, a proportion of the harvest is vinified by carbonic maceration: Carignan in particular produces excellent results with this method. The ro wines are, of necessity, vinified l the *saignée*, or bleeding method.

The rosé wines a fruity, full-bodied and lively; the re wines are fruity, spicy and rich alcohol, about 12%. The Côtes d Roussillon-Villages are warmer an more full-bodied; some can l drunk young but others can be ke longer and these develop an intens complex bouquet. Such appeal an individuality make Roussillo wines versatile accompaniments t a wide variety of dishes.

Côtes du Roussillo

ARNAUD DE VILLENEUVE 1999*

n.c. 40,000 30–49

For a long time, rosé has been a side product here, but thanks to excellent moder wine-making equipment and a careful choic of vineyard sites, it has become a safe bu from the Roussillon. With a very lively, rasp berry-pink colour, this wine is still amylic o the nose, though scents of strawberry an *flambé* bananas do come through. Lifted by touch of carbon dioxide, it has a good balanc

Roussillon

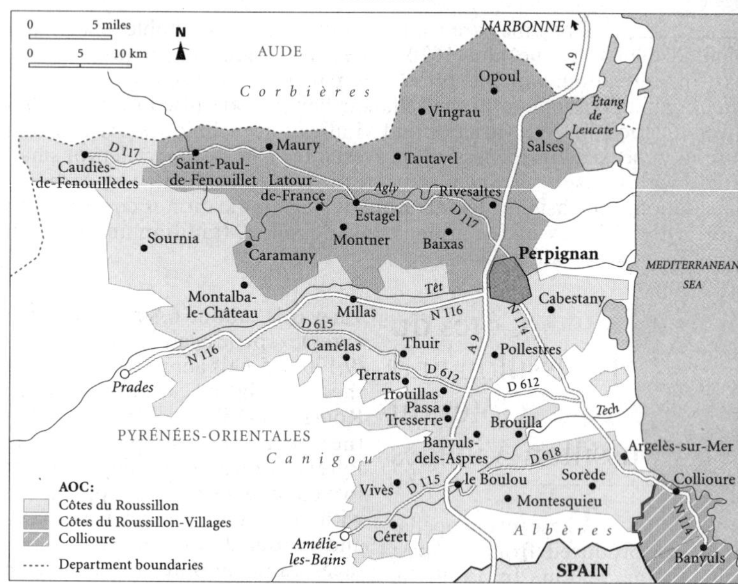

of acidity and richness, with a pleasant fruity character. One to note.

Les Vignobles du Rivesaltais, 1, rue de la Roussillonnaise, 66602 Rivesaltes-Salses, tel. 04.68.64.06.63, fax 04.68.64.64.69, e-mail vignobles.rivesaltais@wanadoo.fr by appt.

CH. DE BLANES

Elevé en Fût de Chêne 1998*

n.c. 40,000 30–49 F

Better known for its red Côtes du Roussillon and Villages, or even for its VDN, the co-operative at Pézilla has also attracted attention for the **Château de Blanes 99 Blanc** and the **99 Rosé**. This seems a subtle red at the start, though the sweetness of ripe fruit and fresh grapes comes through. The palate is spirited with an explosion of violets and forest fruits, which intercept the roasted flavours. Full-bodied, with dense tannins, it has a good life ahead.

SCV les Vignerons de Pézilla, 66370 Pézilla-la-Rivière, tel. 04.68.92.00.09, fax 04.68.92.49.91 ev. day except Sun. 8.30am–12.30pm 2pm–6.30pm

DOM. JOSEPH BORY

Elevé en Fût de Chêne 1998*

n.c. 2,500 30–49 F

Whether for dry or sweet wines, Bages likes to think of itself as a wine-producers' village: cellars and wine shop signs fight for your attention and no-one doubts that here, what gives the wine character is the determination of the men . . . and of Madame Verdeille. The deep red colour gives an impression of the fruits to come in the glass: blackcurrant, cherry and blackberry on an oaky background. Already integrated and balanced, this wine has a spicy finish and will go well with dried ham. Ready to drink.

Andrée Verdeille, 6, av. Jean-Jaurès, 66670 Bages, tel. 04.68.21.71.07, fax 04.68.21.71.07
ev. day except Mon. Sun. 3pm–7pm

DOM. CAZES 1999*

3.75 ha 10,000 30–49 F

The Cazes brothers have a vast vineyard holding of 160 ha (395 acres) and are the driving forces for the international scene. Remaining at the height of their reputation, they have managed to produce a superb white with a subtle combination of the finesse of Macabeu and the power of Vermentino. A pale gold colour leads on to an amylic nose with touches of lemon. It has a very appealing personality, weight and softness. A judicious amount of carbon dioxide lifts the palate of this easy-drinking wine, ideal to drink with fish in butter.

Sté Cazes Frères, 4, rue Francisco-Ferrer, B.P. 61, 66602 Rivesaltes, tel. 04.68.64.08.26, fax 04.68.64.69.79, e-mail info@cazes-rivesaltes.com
by appt.

DOM. DES DEMOISELLES 1999**

1.24 ha 3,700 20–29 F

This wine has a feminine scent, not surprising since it has been made and matured in a feminine way, on a family estate that has been handed down from mother to daughter over three generations. Grenadine at the start, then the intense nose mixes cherry, raspberry and blackberry with the amylic flavours. Straightforward and structured, this is a bold wine, but fine too, fruity with raspberry to the fore. Full and long, it would suit a Catalan *escalivade*.

Isabelle Raoux, Dom. des Demoiselles, Mas Mulès, 66300 Tresserre, tel. 04.68.38.87.10, fax 04.68.38.87.10 ev. day except Mon. 12 noon–2pm 4pm–8pm

FORCA 1998*

n.c. 150,000 20–29 F

The view from the chapel of Força Réal is sublime and looks over the whole of Roussillon. Nestled below, protected from the wind is the Mas de la Garrigue with its vineyards extending out into the sunshine. A very intense garnet-coloured 98, the nose is wild, with strong leather notes, mixed with undergrowth and blackcurrant. Supple to begin with, the pleasant palate is well-integrated with barbecued notes and a fresh, peppery finish.

J.-P. Henriquès, rue Pierre-Pascal-Fauvelle, 66002 Perpignan, tel. 04.68.85.06.07, fax 04.68.85.49.00, e-mail henriquès@forca-real.com

LES VIGNERONS DE FOURQUES

Cuvée 2000 1998*

5 ha 6,000 50–69 F

Away from any hubbub, and reputed for its *charcuterie*, Fourques remains linked to its vineyards, which it refuses to relinquish to the forest of the Aspres. With a bright, clear garnet colour, the wine expresses forceful notes of venison, musk, pepper and leather. It is gentler on the palate, but there are still blackberry notes and liquorice-flavoured tannins that integrate well with a nice balance.

SCV les Vignerons de Fourques, 1, rue des Taste-Vin, 66300 Fourques, tel. 04.68.38.80.51, fax 04.68.38.89.65 ev. day except Sun. 9am–12 noon 2pm–6pm

DOM. JOLIETTE

Cuvée Nicole Mercier 1999

1.37 ha 5,800 50–69 F

The name is very apt for this superb estate, very Mediterranean in style with pine trees, rosemary bushes, cicadas and a fantastic view over the Mediterranean sea. Light and bright, the wine has delightful floral notes and a touch of sweetness from some very good oak. Delicate and enveloped in honeyed flavours, it remains lively and fresh; ideal with seafood.

EARL Mercier, Dom. Joliette, rte de Vingrau, 66600 Espira-de-l'Agly, tel. 04.68.64.50.60, fax 04.68.64.18.82
by appt.

LE CELLIER DE LA BARNEDE

Cuvée du 3e Millénaire 1998★★

■ 20 ha 8,000 50–69 F

Bages owes much to Henri Vidal, a charismatic character who founded the co-operative in 1938. Today the cellar is worth knowing for its Vins Doux Naturels and dry wines such as this superb red. It is a clean-cut wine with a complex and intense nose showing very developed notes: undergrowth, leather, spices and a mixture of blackberries, blackcurrants and vanilla. On the balanced palate you will discover a full-bodied, rich and weighty wine in which the *barrique* brings a soft and toasty character. It needs time.

SCAV les Producteurs de Barnède, 5, av. du 8-Mai-1945, 66670 Bages, tel. 04.68.21.60.30, fax 04.68.37.50.13 by appt.

LA CASENOVE

Cuvée Commandant François Jaubert 1997

■ 15 ha 7,000 100–149 F

This man has a talent and obstinacy that allows him to take both his ideas and the expression of terroir to their logical conclusions. The Commandant has a severe and very intense start, full of ripe fruit and chewy cherries with spices at the back. The palate needs time for the superb extract, body, structure and weight to integrate.

Ch. la Casenove, 66300 Trouillas, tel. 04.68.21.66.33, fax 04.68.21.77.81 ev. day except Sun. 10am–12 noon 4pm–8pm

DOM. LAFAGE 1998★★★

■ 18 ha 30,000 30–49 F

After a successful trip across the New World, and with their newly gained experience, these two œnologists have returned full of technical know-how to strive for better things on their family estate in Roussillon. Just reward for excellent work both in the vineyard and the cellar, this extremely intense-coloured 98 shows very fruity aromas: cherry, blackberry and a delightful touch of apricot. The wine is full-bodied, soft and unrestrained. The cherries are chewy, the blackberries melt in the mouth with a touch of vanilla, with roasted flavours on the finish. Superb.

GAEC Dom. Lafage, Mas Llaro, 66100 Perpignan, tel. 04.68.67.12.47, fax 04.68.62.10.99, e-mail enofool@aol.com by appt.

DOM. LAPORTE Domitia 1998★★★

■ 10 ha 25,000 50–69 F

Of course the purists will say 'the Syrah overwhelms the wine'. It is also true that Lafage, Miraflors and now Laporte, all neighbours growing Syrah, are on the same terroir. A deep purple with mauve hints, there is a strong character of blackcurrant, violets, over-ripe fruit and spices. The palate is in keeping, full-bodied, again with ripe fruits and joined by powerful tannins to give it a great future.

Dom. Laporte, Château-Roussillon, 66000 Perpignan, tel. 04.68.50.06.53, fax 04.68.66.77.52, e-mail domaine-laporte@wanadoo.fr by appt.

CH. LAS COLLAS

Cuvée Classique 1996★★

■ n.c. 8,000 30–49 F

At the foot of the lower hills of the Aspres, forestry shares the land with vineyards, clustered around some superb residences, such as Château las Collas. Given a mention by the jury, but still young, the **E. Rous 98** was not enjoyed as much as this more developed wine with its rich notes of venison, leather and smoky peat. An enjoyable fruit character follows with a pleasantly soft palate, structured but integrated, and with a very fresh finish.

Jacques Bailbé, Ch. las Collas, 66300 Thuir, tel. 04.68.53.40.05, fax 04.68.53.40.05 by appt.

CH. L'ESPARROU

Elevé en Fût de Chêne 1998

■ 7.7 ha 13,000 50–69 F

Surrounded by the lakes and the coastline of Canet-Plage, this estate is much coveted by property developers, perched as it is on a terrace, like an island of green. The ripeness of the grapes and vanilla from the *barrique* join to give a really attractive wine, distinguished by warm notes of the garrigue and of old leather. In keeping, the palate shows a very Mediterranean character. A mellow wine.

J.-L. et M.-P. Rendu, Ch. l'Esparrou, 66140 Canet-en-Roussillon, tel. 04.68.73.30.93, fax 04.68.73.58.65 by appt.

DOM. MAS BECHA 1999

□ 10 ha 4,000 20–29 F

This newcomer, who bought the estate in 1997, has the firm intention of delighting us by working with a balanced blend of traditional grape varieties. A clear colour leads first to a fruity peach nose, then to acacia flowers. Subsequently, the sweetness of Grenache Blanc asserts its honeyed power, counter-balanced by fresh acidity from Macabeu, before moving on to a delicate lemon finish.

Dom. Mas Bécha, 1, av. de Pollestres, 66300 Nyls-Ponteilla, tel. 04.68.54.52.80, fax 04.68.55.31.89

Perez

DOM. DU MAS CREMAT 1998★★

■ 10 ha 35,000 30–49 F

Comparing an oaked wine to be kept for ageing and an un-oaked wine, it is the latter which is ahead today: showing power after its deep appearance, it reveals notes of lemon trees, blackcurrant and slight pepper. Full-bodied and rich, the fleshy fruit blurs the very nice tannins. The wine is already enjoyable.

Dom. du Mas Cremat, 66600 Espira-de-l'Agly, tel. 04.68.38.92.06, fax 04.68.38.92.23 ☑ Y ev. day except Sun. 10am–12 noon 3pm–6.30pm

MAS DES OLIVIERS 1998★

■ 5 ha 17,200 30–49 F

With Mas des Oliviers, Méditerroirs, who specialise in high-quality wines, are demonstrating both their good understanding of the terroirs and the consummate art of good labelling. This 98 shows a good continuity between the aromas on the nose and flavours on the palate. Crystallised fruit, cinnamon and toast come together with a structured, full wine whose tannins are still pronounced. Already enjoyable, this wine should be kept.

Méditerroirs, Ch. Cap-de-Fouste, Villeneuve-de-la-Raho, 66100 Perpignan, tel. 04.68.85.69.25, fax 04.68.85.22.26

DOM. DU MAS ROUS 1998★★★

■ 5 ha 20,000 30–49 F

The Albères hills, which shadow the Pyrenees right up to the sea, are exceptional both for their beauty and for the unrivalled finesse that they provide the wines, witness this deep purple 98. Very spicy, peppered and with scents of venison, leather and crystallised fruit, it comes into its own on the palate. Fine and velvety, the silky tannins accompany ever-present ripe fruit before a fresh and enjoyably lifted finish. From the same producer in a superb oaked version is **Mas Rous Sélection 97**.

José Pujol, Dom. du Mas Rous, 66740 Montesquieu-des-Albères, tel. 04.68.89.64.91, fax 04.68.89.80.88, e-mail joseph.pujol@.fr ☑ Y by appt.

CH. MIRAFLORS Tramuntana 1998★★

■ 5 ha 5,000 50–69 F

On the high terrace of the Têt, the estate stretches out between Perpignan and the sea. The medieval village of Villarnau was discovered very recently under the vines. The Tramuntana is a very developed wine showing warming notes of venison and undergrowth with crystallised fruit and roasted flavours in the background, also recurring on the palate. A good tannic structure contributes to the superb balance.

SA Cibaud-Ch. Miraflors et Belloch, 7, rue Béranger, 66000 Perpignan, tel. 04.68.34.03.05, fax 04.68.51.31.70, e-mail vins.cibaud@wanadoo.fr ☑ Y ev. day except Sun. 9.30am–12.30pm 3pm–7pm; cl. Jan.

MOULIN DE BREUIL 1998★

■ 17 ha 40,000 20–29 F

Joseph de Massia has successfully taken over and preserved the integrity of this beautiful estate at the foot of the Albères. Apart from its attractive colour and scents of undergrowth, blackberry and blackcurrant, it is in particular the integrated and fine qualities of the palate, especially the soft, spicy tannins that make it a pleasant wine for drinking today.

Joseph de Massia, Moulin de Breuil, 66740 Montesquieu, tel. 04.68.89.67.68, fax 04.68.89.67.68, e-mail joseph@sacedi.fr ☑ Y by appt.

DOM. PARCE

Vieilli en Fût de Chêne 1997★★

■ 3 ha 15,150 30–49 F

Little by little, with patience, serious application and competence, André Parcé has managed to transform his vineyard so successfully that this grape farmer has also become a vine-grower. This marvellous 97 has a deep and intense garnet colour with a nose combining red berry fruit and spices on an already attractive oaky wine. Very integrated and balanced with fruit, toast and spicy characters, the palate follows through with dense and fine-grained tannins. For drinking now and in the future.

EARL A. Parcé, 21 ter, rue du 14-Juillet, 66670 Bages, tel. 04.68.21.80.45, fax 04.68.21.69.40 ☑ Y ev. day except Sun. 9.30am–12.15pm 4pm–7.30pm

DOM. PIQUEMAL

Elevé en Fût de Chêne 1998

■ 20 ha 40,000 50–69 F

Sure, it takes some driving through the back streets of Espira to find the cellar, but once found, no-one regrets the journey. The welcome, the friendliness, seriousness and above all, the ability to allow the famous black earth to express itself, make it all worthwhile. A lively, deep red appearance is enhanced by scents of red berry fruit softened by vanilla. Supple, integrated and velvety, the wine has wedded the oak in a marriage made to last.

Pierre et Franck Piquemal, 1, rue Pierre-Lefranc, 66600 Espira-de-l'Agly, tel. 04.68.64.09.14, fax 04.68.38.52.94 ☑ Y by appt.

CH. PLANERES Prestige 1999★

□ 8 ha 25,000 30–49 F

With a new and extremely well laid-out cellar, Jaubert and Noury have not ceased to surprise us or to bring life to the Aspres terroir. This developed white has been extremely well-made to show scents of honey, broom and peaches. Weighty and full-bodied, this is a wine with a rich structure showing lemon touches at the end, ideal for fish cooked in butter.

ROUSSILLION

🗝 Jaubert-Noury, Ch. Planères, 66300 Saint-Jean-Lasseille, tel. 04.68.21.74.50, fax 04.68.37.51.95 ☑ Y ev. day except Sun. 8.30am–12 noon 2pm–6pm

CH. PRADAL 1998★

◢ 2 ha 6,500 ■ 🌡 20–29 F

Bordered by the town of Perpignan, a few paces away from the centre of the world (according to Dali) with its vines watching the passing trains, this estate has stamina. There is a young, fresh colour suiting the flavours of red berries and blackcurrants that characterise the wine. The fruity palate is in keeping, with a smoky and full-bodied taste before a very fresh, blackcurrant finish.

🗝 André Coll-Escluse, Ch. Pradal, 58, rue Pépinière-Robin, 66000 Perpignan, tel. 04.68.85.04.73, fax 04.68.56.80.49 ☑ Y by appt.

ROC DU GOUVERNEUR 1999

■ n.c. 30,000 ■ 🌡 20–29 F

A nice contrast between the solid and imposing fort of Salses and the delicate wines from this cellar, such as the remarkable **Roc du Gouverneur Blanc** and a rosy-pink **99 Rosé** full of fresh fruit. With its very young appearance, one is surprised to smell so much development of crystallised fruit, and to discover a wine that is so ready to drink. Soft, easy-going with a crisp finish, this is just waiting for a plate of *charcuterie*.

🗝 Les Vignobles du Rivesaltais, 1, rue de la Roussillonnaise, 66602 Rivesaltes-Salses, tel. 04.68.64.06.63, fax 04.68.64.64.69, e-mail vignobles.rivesaltais@wanadoo.fr ☑ Y by appt.

CH. ROMBEAU

Cuvée Elise Vieilles Vignes 1997★

■ 2.5 ha 12,000 🛢 50–69 F

The *Babau*, terror of the people of Rivesaltes, no longer frightens anyone. However, his figure, made of rounded pebbles, can be seen in the vaulted cellar of Pierre-Henri de la Fabrègue. From here, after 12 months in oak, the Cuvée Elise emerges with a garnet colour, full of toasty notes, ripe cherries and spices. Very fruity, and really soft, the oak mellows the wine, also giving it an excellent peppery finish.

🗝 P.-H. de la Fabrègue, SCEA Dom. de Rombeau, 66600 Rivesaltes, tel. 04.68.64.35.35, fax 04.68.64.64.66 ☑ Y ev. day 8am–11pm

DOM. DE SAINTE-BARBE 1995

■ 15 ha 13,000 ■ 🌡 30–49 F

Close to the edge of Perpignan, at the foot of the Serrat d'en Vaquer hill, famous for its fossils, you will find an impeccable vineyard. It belongs to Robert Tricoire, storyteller and philosopher and above all, a true man of the land. This excellent 95 has developed slowly, revealing a brick-red colour and warming flavours, enhanced by notes of venison, spices and leather. Soft and integrated, some tannins appear at the end. This is the ideal wine for grilled meat.

🗝 Robert Tricoire, Dom. de Sainte-Barbe, chem. de Sainte-Barbe, 66000 Perpignan, tel. 04.68.54.61.22, fax 04.68.54.61.22 ☑ Y by appt.

DOM. SAINTE-HELENE 1998

■ 6 ha 8,000 ■ 🌡 20–29 F

Nicely positioned in the foothills of the Pyrenees, Sorède is an extremely pleasant village. From an intense ruby colour emerge scents of undergrowth, leather and spices. Supple and integrated, the wine gives an expression of ripe fruit and continues onto a sustained length.

🗝 Henri Cavaillé, 10, rue Moulin-Cassanyes, 66690 Sorède, tel. 04.68.89.30.30, fax 04.68.95.42.66 ☑ Y ev. day except Sun. 9am–12 noon 5pm–7pm

DOM. SALVAT Taïchac 1999

◢ 12 ha 15,000 ■ 🌡 30–49 F

Between Fenouillèdes and Ribéral, J.-Ph. Salvat, very much a composer, enjoys playing with the complementary natures of his terroirs, backed-up by a solid technical team. The delicate pink colour emerges from scents of red berry fruits and a touch of leafy blackcurrant. The palate is lively and fresh with a balanced amylic note and more of a spicy finish. A nice 'ensemble' to drink with *charcuterie*.

🗝 Dom. Salvat, Pont-Neuf, 66610 Villeneuve-la-Rivière, tel. 04.68.92.17.96, fax 04.68.38.00.50 ☑ Y ev. day 10am–6.30pm

DOM. SARDA-MALET

Terroir Mailloles 1997★

■ 5 ha 11,000 🛢 100–149 F

The landscape is gentle and restful. Sheep graze near the bridge, dating from the time of Charlemagne and surrounded by vineyards against the backdrop of the Canigou Mountains. This estate is in Perpignan at the Mas Saint-Michel. Very dark and dense, the wine has distinct notes of glacé cherries, with undergrowth, some venison and a slight smokiness. The fruit explodes onto the palate where blackberries meet spices. Well-integrated with superb tannins, this is a wine for the future.

🗝 Dom. Sarda-Malet, Mas Saint-Michel, chem. de Sainte-Barbe, 66000 Perpignan, tel. 04.68.56.72.38, fax 04.68.56.47.60 ☑ Y by appt.

🗝 Suzy Malet

CH. DE SAU Cuvée Réservée 1996★

■ n.c. n.c. ■ 🌡 30–49 F

A prudent choice of vineyard plots and a good balance between the trilogy of Carignan, Grenache and Syrah, with carbonic maceration for the first and a traditional vinification for the others. No oak. Everything appears simple when Henri Passama and Hervé Parayre are at the controls. A purple colour leads to a nose wavering

›etween undergrowth, leather, blackcurrant ›nd redcurrant. Pleasantly fruity, it is also ›eighty and full-bodied. You just need to ›rill some meat . . . then take a siesta.

🔑 Hervé Passama, Ch. de Saü, 66300 ›huir, tel. 04.68.53.21.74, ›ax 04.68.53.29.07, ›e-mail chateaudesau@aol.com ☑ Y by ›ppt.

TERRASSOUS 1998★

■ 50 ha 40,000 ▮ ♁ 20–29 F

The co-operative cellar, established in 1932, is situated in the heart of the Aspres ›ineyards. Proud of its 110 members, it has ›uccessfully moved with the times to embrace ›ll the technological advances. After aeration, ›he venison and toasted coffee beans usher in ›ome more muted notes of green leafy black- ›urrant. Very assertive on the full-bodied, ›ich palate, this wine is still young and will ›each its peak within a year or two.

🔑 SCV les Vignerons de Terrats, B.P. 32, 66302 Terrats, tel. 04.68.53.02.50, fax 04.68.53.23.06 ☑ Y ev. day except Sun. 8am–12 noon 2pm–6pm

CELLIER TROUILLAS

Cuvée du Gouverneur Vieilli en Fût de Chêne 1995★

■ 25 ha 42,000 ⦀ 30–49 F

It was in a farmhouse, close to the village, that Arnaud de Villeneuve, a famous doctor of the 13th century, discovered the principal of *mutage* (stopping fermentation by adding alcohol), the basis for making Vins Doux Naturels. The colour of this Gourverneur is deep and intense and leads on to a scent of undergrowth, with notes of leather and prunes. The silky tannins on the palate are a pleasant surprise, and there is delicate fruit, a nice toasty character and very good balance.

🔑 SCV le Cellier de Trouillas, 1, av. du Mas-Deu, 66300 Trouillas, tel. 04.68.53.47.08, fax 04.68.53.24.56 ☑ Y by appt.

DOM. DU VIEUX CHENE 1999

■ 10 ha 6,000 ▮ ♁ 30–49 F

Overlooking the Roussillon plain, with a breathtaking view to the Pyrenees and the Canigou Mountains, plus the big blue sea in the background . . . What a place to work in! And what a pleasure it is to taste the still very dark and fruity 99: cherries, blackcurrants and fresh grapes. Rich and pronounced, the wine just needs a little time to develop.

🔑 Dom. du Vieux Chêne, Mas Kilo, 66600 Espira-de-l'Agly, tel. 04.68.38.92.01, fax 04.68.38.95.79 ☑ Y by appt.

Côtes du Roussillon-Villages

CH. AYMERICH 1998★★

■ 5 ha 24,000 ▮ ♁ 50–69 F

A high proportion of Syrah (80%) and a terroir of schist account for the superb characters found in this wine: aromas of blackcurrant with very ripe fruit, elegant tannins and a harmonious balance between weight and structure. What better to provide a tasty accompaniment to this wine than a piece of beef direct from the barbecue. Here is confirmation of this young estate's *savoir-faire*.

🔑 Jean-Pierre et Catherine Grau-Aymerich, Ch. Aymerich, 52, av. Dr-Torreilles, 66310 Estagel, tel. 04.68.29.45.45, fax 04.68.29.10.35 ☑ Y by appt.

DOM. REGIS BOUCABEILLE

Les Orris 1998

■ 1 ha 2,000 ⦀ 100–149 F

Regis Boucabeille settled in the Roussillon area in 1990. He farms 12 ha (30 acres) of vineyards and puts into practice his international commercial experience to distribute 95% of his wines on the European export markets (notably Germany, Switzerland and Holland). This has a solid tannic structure. Some oaky notes mix with flavours of very ripe grapes, which recur on the palate. Hints of honey help to enhance the depth of flavours on the finish. Needs time.

🔑 EARL Régis Boucabeille, 146, rte Nationale, 66550 Corneilla-la-Rivière, tel. 04.68.57.22.02, fax 04.68.57.11.63 ☑ Y by appt.

DOM. BOUDAU

Cuvée Henri Boudau 1998

■ 2 ha 6,000 ⦀ 30–49 F

From the stony terraces of the Crest de Rivesaltes, this balanced 98 has a pretty colour with shades of deep purple revealing aromas of very ripe berry fruits. The oak notes on the palate blend in well with the richness of the structure, and finally the tannins come into play with a touch of liquorice.

🔑 Dom. Véronique et Pierre Boudau, 6, rue Marceau, B.P. 60, 66600 Rivesaltes, tel. 04.68.64.45.37, fax 04.68.64.46.26 ☑ Y ev. day except Sun. 10am–12 noon 3pm–7pm Jun.–Sep.

CH. DE CALADROY

Les Schistes 1998★★★

■ 45 ha 38,000 ▮ ♁ 30–49 F

This vast estate is situated on the schistose hills between the valley of the Têt and the valley of Agly, very close to the village of Belesta. Its wine, Les Schistes, has a deep, bright garnet colour and shows crystallised fruit aromas lifted by spices. There is an appealing weight on the palate and a softness of delicately liquorice-flavoured tannins. Kernel notes persist towards the finish.

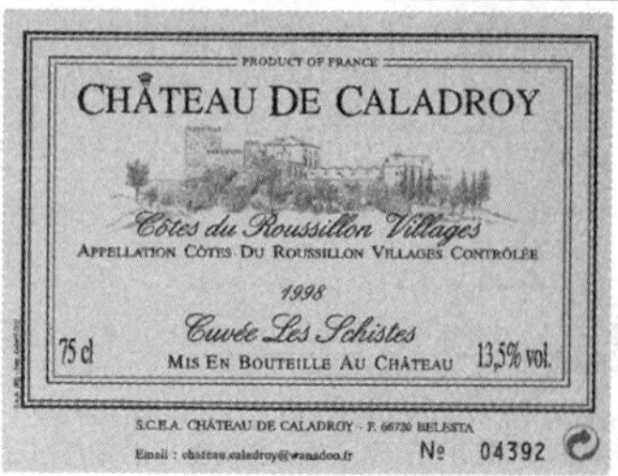

🔑 Mezerette, SCEA Ch. de Caladroy, 66720 Belesta, tel. 04.68.57.10.25, fax 04.68.57.27.76, e-mail château.caladroy@wanadoo.fr ☑
🍷 ev. day except Sat. Sun. 8am–12 noon 1.30pm–5.30pm (4.30pm le Fri.)

LES VIGNERONS DE CARAMANY

Caramany Cuvée du Presbytère 1998★

■ 50 ha 80,000 30–49 F

The wines of Caramany are known for their roundness and their spicy flavour from carbonic maceration. This is certainly the case with the Cuvée du Presbytère 98. With aromas of ripe fruits, the palate has an appealing richness and is both smooth and tasty. Note also the oak-aged **Cuvée Élevée en Fût de Chêne**, which though of a completely different style was enjoyed; a wine to keep.
🔑 SCV de Caramany, 66720 Caramany, tel. 04.68.84.51.80, fax 04.68.84.50.84 ☑
🍷 by appt.

DOM. CAZES 1996★★★

■ 7 ha 25,000 50–69 F

Pioneers for Roussillon wine, the Cazes brothers are today known on all the continents from the USA to Japan. Their vast 160-ha (395-acre) estate enables them to produce the whole range of wines from the region. Quantity goes hand in hand with quality, as confirmed by this 96, which has an attractively deep red colour with some hints of ruby. Intense and complex, the nose reveals toasted fruit, homemade jam, with some vanilla touches from the maturation period in oak. The delicate tannins, linked with flavoursome richness and a long finish, conclude this very enjoyable tasting. An exceptional wine.
🔑 Sté Cazes Frères, 4, rue Francisco-Ferrer, B.P. 61, 66602 Rivesaltes, tel. 04.68.64.08.26, fax 04.68.64.69.79, e-mail info@cazes-rivesaltes.com ☑
🍷 by appt.

DOM. DES CHENES Tautavel 1997★

■ 3 ha 13,000 50–69 F

Domaine des Chênes is already very well known for its Côtes du Roussillon Villages and its Muscat. It makes an entrance into the realms of the Tautavel appellation with a very ripe 97. A bright ruby colour with slight touches of brick, it has developed aromas reminiscent of cut hay, autumn undergrowth and oriental spices. Fairly soft tannins complement the very good depth of flavour on the palate.
🔑 Razungles, Dom. des Chênes, 7, rue Mal-Joffre, 66600 Vingrau, tel. 04.68.29.40.21, fax 04.68.29.10.91 ☑
🍷 by appt.

DOM. BRIAL

Elevé en Fût de Chêne 1997★★

■ n.c. 45,000 30–49 F

The Baixas co-operative currently offers range of wines that is both rich and varied. It submits an already quite mature 97 with aromas of musk, old leather and crystallised fruit, ruby in colour with a slightly brick coloured edge. The oak notes are completely integrated with the fine tannins on the palate. This wine is ready to partner the best game dishes of the season.
🔑 Cave des Vignerons de Baixas, 14, av. Mal-Joffre, 66390 Baixas, tel. 04.68.64.22.37, fax 04.68.64.26.70, e-mail baixas@smi-telecom.fr ☑ 🍷 by appt.

DOM. FONTANEL

Tautavel Prieuré Vieilli en Fût de Chêne 1998★★★

■ 5 ha 8,000 50–69 F

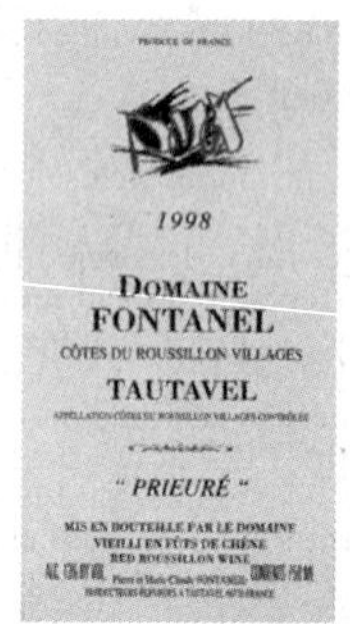

Power and elegance come together in this wine, which offers superb concentration and fruit characters, promising it a great future. Liquorice tannins, wild berry fruits and weightiness on the palate appealed to the entire tasting panel. An excellent representative of this terroir that is amongst the best of the Côtes du Roussillon Villages.
🔑 Dom. Fontanel, 25, av. Jean-Jaurès, 66720 Tautavel, tel. 04.68.29.04.71, fax 04.68.29.19.44 ☑ 🍷 by appt.
🔑 Fontaneil

DOM. FONTANEL 1998★★

■ 11 ha 18,000 30–49 F

With a garnet colour that still has a deep purple edge, this vintage 98 still shows great youth. Spicy notes dominate on the nose, and the palate shows a balance of flavours together with great class, all wrapped in tremendous richness.
🔑 Dom. Fontanel, 25, av. Jean-Jaurès, 66720 Tautavel, tel. 04.68.29.04.71, fax 04.68.29.19.44 ☑ 🍷 by appt.

DOM. FORCA REAL 1999★★★

■ 5 ha 15,000 50–69 F

Wines from this estate follow one after another with the same regularity as the characteristics shown by the terroir. The deep ruby 99 has aromas of wild red berry fruits with some nuances of violets. The richness of the tannins and notes of cherry on the finish give a delicious wine with a great future. A saddle of lamb, cooked Catalonian style, would bring the best out of it.

J.-P. Henriquès, Dom. Força Réal, Mas de la Garrigue, 66170 Millas,
tel. 04.68.85.06.07, fax 04.68.85.49.00,
e-mail domaine@força-real.com
by appt.

LES VIGNERONS DE FORCA REAL 1998

■ 30.32 ha 19,300 20–29 F

There is more elegance than power to be found in this ruby-coloured 98. A really supple palate together with notes of very ripe, fresh grapes and good length enable the wine to be enjoyed right away.

SCV les Vignerons de Força Réal, rue Léo-Lagrange, 66170 Millas,
tel. 04.68.57.35.02, fax 04.68.57.28.09
ev. day except Sun. Mon. 3pm–6.30pm

DOM. GARDIES

Tautavel la Torre 1998★★★

■ n.c. 6,000 70–99 F

A dazzling wine from this young wine-producer. A quite intense cherry-red colour appears before a nose of very ripe red berry fruits, which recur on the palate, lifted by some spicy touches. Very soft-grained tannins with a liquorice note emerge with balanced warmth. Will the exception become the norm in this estate? One to watch.

Dom. Gardiés, 66600 Vingrau,
tel. 04.68.64.61.16, fax 04.68.64.69.36
by appt.

DOM. GARDIES Les Millères 1998★★

■ n.c. 20,000 30–49 F

This Millères has had an excellent track record. Here is a superb 1998. It has aromas of wild red berries with accents of the garrigue and spicy notes accompanied by tannins on the palate that are both soft and powerful. The very long finish leaves a sense of balance. A typical local rabbit stew would seem perfect for this wine.

Dom. Gardiés, 66600 Vingrau,
tel. 04.68.64.61.16, fax 04.68.64.69.36 by appt.

CH. DE JAU 1998

■ 60 ha 250,000 30–49 F

Every year the Château de Jau organises a contemporary art exhibition at which visitors can taste the wines with food. This one reveals aromas of red berry fruits. The palate has a sense of elegance and roundness with fine tannins and an overall flavoursome balance.

Ch. de Jau, 66600 Cases-de-Pène,
tel. 04.68.38.90.10, fax 04.68.38.91.33,
e-mail jau66@aol.com
ev. day except Sat. Sun. 8am–4pm; 10am–7pm 15 Jun.–1 Oct.
Famille Dauré

JEAN D'ESTAVEL

Elevé en Fût de Chêne 1997★

■ n.c. 20,000 30–49 F

This merchant has a very attractive selection of wines. This one is fully mature with toasty notes that harmonise well with the oaked character. The palate gives an impression of softness and roundness. All told, a very good, balanced wine.

SA Destavel, 7bis, av. du Canigou, 66000 Perpignan, tel. 04.68.68.36.00,
fax 04.68.54.03.54
M.G. Baissas

DOM. JOLIETTE

Cuvée Romain Mercier 1999

■ 3 ha 12,000 50–69 F

From Domaine Joliette, you can see the Salses fort, and from there, the Leucate lake and the Mediterranean. The vineyard nestles between the pine forests at the foot of the Corbières hills. This deep garnet-coloured 99 has aromas of wild red berry fruits and of spices. The solid tannic structure still dominates the flavours on the palate, but this indicates a wine with a good future.

EARL Mercier, Dom. Joliette, rte de Vingrau, 66600 Espira-de-l'Agly,
tel. 04.68.64.50.60, fax 04.68.64.18.82
by appt.

DOM. LA PLEIADE 1998

■ 1.4 ha 6,000 30–49 F

Based in the north-west section of the appellation, this estate is known for its Maury wines. It also makes some good Côtes du Roussillon Villages like this 1998 example. There are aromas of blackberries on this garnet-coloured wine, and a richness on the palate, which leads on very quickly to the finish, still dominated by tannins.

Dom. la Pléiade, Hameau de la Roque, 66220 Lesquerde, tel. 04.68.52.21.66,
fax 04.68.52.21.66 by appt.
Delcour

LES HAUTS DE FORCA REAL 1998★

■ 5 ha 15,000 70–99 F

Kernel aromas are still overwhelmed by the powerful tannins in this 98. But, the agreeable structure and the balance between an oak-aged character and the intrinsic flavours of the wine appealed to the entire jury. Liquorice notes are gradually emerging on the palate.

J.-P. Henriquès, Dom. Força Réal, Mas de la Garrigue, 66170 Millas,
tel. 04.68.85.06.07, fax 04.68.85.49.00,
e-mail domaine@força-real.com by appt.

CH. LES PINS 1997*

■ n.c. 104,000 50–69 F

This is a wine that is barely starting to soften, with tannins that are both mild and liquorice-flavoured, as well as some fine quality oak notes. The palate reveals a rich body with honeyed notes and some touches of old leather.

Cave des Vignerons de Baixas, 14, av. Mal-Joffre, 66390 Baixas, tel. 04.68.64.22.37, fax 04.68.64.26.70, e-mail baixas@smi-telecom.fr by appt.

LESQUERDE

Lesquerde les Arènes de Granit 1997

■ 11.3 ha 40,000 30–49 F

This wine takes its name from a terroir with the reputation of yielding wines with very high quality tannins. It has produced a wine that is maturing rapidly. The ruby colour has a brick-red edge and leads on to aromas of red berry fruit *gratin*, as well as some spicy notes on the palate. The taste is characterised by the softness and elegance of the tannins.

SCV Lesquerde, 66220 Lesquerde, tel. 04.68.59.02.62, fax 04.68.59.08.17 ev. day except Sun. 8am–12 noon 2pm–6pm

CH. MONTNER

Grande Réserve 1998**

■ 40 ha 150,000 20–29 F

The schistose terroir of Montner has often been the source for some good wines. Such is the case for this 98 wine, which from the first sniff gives aromas of baked red berry fruits and some smoky notes. The wine is already starting to develop. The palate, however, shows a richness of body and a tannic structure that is both soft and virile.

Vignerons Catalans, 1870, av. Julien-Panchot, 66011 Perpignan Cedex, tel. 04.68.85.04.51, fax 04.68.55.25.62, e-mail vignerons.catalans@wanadoo.fr by appt.

DOM. DU MOULIN Romani 1998***

■ 3 ha 8,000 70–99 F

Henri Lhériter manages to make his two wines, Crest and Romani, as well as he writes the literary essays dedicated to his vineyard. Romani means rosemary in the Catalan language. With an intense garnet colour, this wine reveals aromas of ripe fruits and the garrigue. Intense, powerful tannins and good character give this wine a structure that is both robust and majestic. It will make a perfect partner to a roast of young wild boar.

Henri Lhéritier, av. Gambetta, 66600 Rivesaltes, tel. 04.68.38.56.53, fax 04.68.38.56.52, e-mail domainelheritier@wanadoo.fr ev. day except Sun. 8am–12 noon 2pm–7pm

LES VIGNERONS DE PEZILLA 1998*

■ 45 ha 13,000 20–29 F

The co-operative of Pézilla-la-Rivière makes wine from 790 ha (1,951 acres) of vineyards. Roundness and softness, as well as a full, rich body characterise this wine, which has aromas of very ripe grapes and wild red berries. A very seductive wine that can be enjoyed from now, although the 1998 vintage of many wines is still very closed.

SCV les Vignerons de Pézilla, 66370 Pézilla-la-Rivière, tel. 04.68.92.00.09, fax 04.68.92.49.91 ev. day except Sun. 8.30am–12.30pm 2pm–6.30pm

DOM. PIQUEMAL

Elevé en Fût de Chêne 1998**

■ 6 ha 40,000 50–69 F

The cellar of Domaine Piquemal lies close to the very beautiful roman church of Espira-de-l'Agly. It has made a deep garnet 98 that gradually reveals some aromas of cherry and blackcurrant. It was the richness of the tannins and the length of finish which really appealed to the tasters.

Pierre et Franck Piquemal, 1, rue Pierre-Lefranc, 66600 Espira-de-l'Agly, tel. 04.68.64.09.14, fax 04.68.38.52.94 by appt.

LES VIGNERONS DE PLANEZES-RASIGUERES

Les Gravières 1998***

■ 20 ha 25,000 30–49 F

Known for their rosés, the producers of this co-operative also offer some extremely well-made red wines such as this excellent 98. The ripe fruity nose with lightly toasty and spicy notes leads on to a structure that is starting to soften. The flavours on the palate really find expression on the finish.

Les Vignerons de Planèzes-Rasiguères, 5, rte de Caramany, 66720 Rasiguères, tel. 04.68.29.11.82, fax 04.68.29.16.45, e-mail rasigueres@little.france.com ev. day except Sun. 8am–12 noon 2pm–6pm

ROC DU GOUVERNEUR 1998

■ n.c. 30,000 30–49 F

Matured in a gallery of a château dating back to the 15th century, this ruby-coloured wine gives aromas of red fruit compote. A very fleshy character to start with then reveals a tannic structure promising a wine that can be aged for a long time.

Les Vignobles du Rivesaltais, 1, rue de la Roussillonnaise, 66602 Rivesaltes-Salses, tel. 04.68.64.06.63, fax 04.68.64.64.69, e-mail vignobles.rivesaltais@wanadoo.fr by appt.

DOM. DU ROUVRE Força Réal 1998*

■ 4 ha 6,000 30–49 F

From the schistose slopes of the Força Réal hill, this is a very youthful-looking wine with shades of deep purple. Notes of red berry fruits dominate the flavours, which develop slowly on the nose and then recur on the palate. The oaky imprint marries well with the tannic structure, and there is good balance on the finish.

🔑 GFA Domaines du Château Royal, Los Parès, 66550 Corneilla-la-Rivière, tel. 04.68.57.22.02, fax 04.68.57.11.63 ☑ 🍷 by appt.
🔑 Pouderoux

DOM. DES SCHISTES Tradition 1998★

■ 7 ha 20,000 ▮ ♁ 30–49 F

Jacques and Nadine Sire regularly make two wines: one, matured in oak, **Les Terrasses**, which needs time to age, and the other, called Tradition, ready to drink. The latter has an attractive ruby colour with hints of garnet. Very ripe red fruit shows on both the nose and the palate, with a tannic structure that is attractive in its elegance and its liquorice touch.

🔑 Jacques Sire, 1, av. Jean-Lurçat, 66310 Estagel, tel. 04.68.29.11.25, fax 04.68.29.47.17 ☑ 🍷 by appt.

LES MAITRES VIGNERONS DE TAUTAVEL

Tautavel Vieilli en fût de chêne 1998★★

■ 58 ha 24,000 🛢 30–49 F

Situated a few steps from the museum of prehistory, this co-operative has shown great consistency. With two stars, the 98 does not go against the rule. There are aromas of very ripe blackcurrant and cherry with a bright ruby colour. The tannins are noticeably elegant with an extremely good balance, showing a fleshy style with solid weight and great depth of flavour.

🔑 Les Maîtres Vignerons de Tautavel, 24, av. Jean-Badia, 66720 Tautavel, tel. 04.68.29.12.03, fax 04.68.29.41.81, e-mail vignerons.tautavel@wanadoo.fr ☑ 🍷 by appt.

Collioure

This very small appellation of 330 ha (815 acres) produces about 15,000 hl (396,000 gal). The soil is the same as that found in the Appellation Banyul. The four communes are Collioure, Port-Bendres, Banyuls-sur-Mer and Cerbère.

The vine varieties grown are principally Grenache Noir, Carignan and Mourvèdre, with Syrah and Cinsault as additional varieties. The exclusively red or rosé wines are made at the beginning of the harvest, before the grapes for Banyuls are picked. The small crop produces warm, full-bodied, highly coloured red wines, with aromas of well-ripened soft fruits. The rosés are aromatic, rich but typically lively.

CH. DES ABELLES 1998★★★

■ 24 ha 77,000 ▮ ♁ 70–99 F

Visitors to the Cellier des Templiers at Banyuls will find the new cellar tour is a model of education and aesthetics. It provides an introduction to the vineyards and wines of the appellations Banyuls and Collioure. With a deep ruby appearance, this red Collioure has a fruity character together with some oriental spices. The mouth-filling palate has a perfect tannic structure and leads on to a very meaty finish.

🔑 Cellier des Templiers, rte du Mas-Reig, 66650 Banyuls-sur-Mer, tel. 04.68.98.36.70, fax 04.68.98.36.91 ☑ 🍷 by appt.

DOM. DE BAILLAURY 1998★★

■ n.c. 8,480 ▮ ♁ 50–69 F

From the very first sniff, there are scents of well-ripened cherries and blackberries, with some spicy notes emerging from part whole-berry fermentation. The power of the tannic structure implies that this is a wine to keep.

🔑 La Cave de L'Abbé Rous, 56, av. Charles-de-Gaulle, 66650 Banyuls-sur-Mer, tel. 04.68.88.72.72, fax 04.68.88.30.57, e-mail contact@banyuls.com

DOM. CAMPI 1998★

■ n.c. 30,000 ▮ ♁ 50–69 F

This ruby-coloured 98, both deep and bright, has aromas of red fruits that have ripened for a long period in the sun. Peppered notes on the palate precede a solid structure of elegant tannins that are just starting to integrate into the overall taste of the wine.

🔑 Cellier des Templiers, rte du Mas-Reig, 66650 Banyuls-sur-Mer, tel. 04.68.98.36.70, fax 04.68.98.36.91 ☑ 🍷 by appt.

CASTELL DES HOSPICES 1997★★★

■ n.c. 10,002 🛢 100–149 F

The abbot François Rous was one of the first to make known the wines of Banyuls. Homage to him is paid today by the establishment of this cellar, which distributes a complete range of regional produce. This already mature 97 shows good development, with the

colour showing shades of roof-tiles and flavours of toast and stewed fruit, along with some old leather notes on the palate. Elegant tannins and good length complete the picture.
🔑 La Cave de L'Abbé Rous, 56, av. Charles-de-Gaulle, 66650 Banyuls-sur-Mer, tel. 04.68.88.72.72, fax 04.68.88.30.57, e-mail contact@banyuls.com

CLOS CHATART 1998

■ 2 ha 6,000 70–99 F

Owing its name to an entomologist from Banyuls, the Clos Chatart is situated just next door to the tomb of the famous sculptor Aristide Maillol who lived in the neighbourhood. The red Collioure, ruby-coloured with cherry hues, offers aromas of fruits macerated in brandy. These become particularly apparent on the full-bodied and structured palate.
🔑 Clos Chatart, 66650 Banyuls-sur-Mer, tel. 04.68.88.12.58, fax 04.68.88.51.51 ☑
Y by appt.
🔑 Laverrière

DOM. DE LA MARQUISE

Rosé de l'Arquette 1999★★

◪ 0.6 ha 2,800 30–49 F

From a vineyard looking down onto the Collioure inlet, good quality vintages of this rosé follow one after another. A pale pink colour, with salmon hues announces the aromas of red berry fruits mixed with amylic notes. Richness dominates the palate with fresh flavours on the finish.
🔑 Dom. de la Marquise, 17, rue Pasteur, 66190 Collioure, tel. 04.68.98.01.38, fax 04.68.82.51.77 ☑ Y by appt.
🔑 Jacques Py

DOM. LA TOUR VIEILLE

Puig Ambeille 1998★★★

■ 2 ha 7,971 70–99 F

The 1998 vintage confirms the excellent quality from this estate. A deep ruby, this wine develops aromas of wild red berry fruit and cherries in brandy. Very soft tannins and a delicate body complete the picture on the palate with an overall mouth-filling harmony.
🔑 Dom. La Tour Vieille, 3, av. du Mirador, 66190 Collioure, tel. 04.68.82.44.82, fax 04.68.82.38.42 ☑ Y by appt.
🔑 Cantié et Campadieu

DOM. LA TOUR VIEILLE

Rosé des Roches 1999★★

◪ 2 ha 8,712 50–69 F

Domaine de la Tour Vieille has also produced this excellent rosé. There is a lively pink colour with touches of purple and intense aromas of red fruits, lifted by spices. It offers an almost sensual taste on the palate, and will provide a perfect riposte to the local fish stew.
🔑 Dom. la Tour Vieille, 3, av. du Mirador, 66190 Collioure, tel. 04.68.82.44.82, fax 04.68.82.38.42 ☑ Y by appt.

L'ETOILE Vieilli en Montagne 1998★

■ 5 ha 13,500 50–69 F

The co-operative cellars of l'Etoile still have a collection of very old vintage Banyuls, which have kept remarkably well. This Collioure 98, *vieilli en montagne* (matured in the mountains) gives toasty and spicy notes showing the good development of this vintage. On the palate, the tannins are still evident and dominate the taste. From the same cooperative, the jury retained the **99 Rosé**. A pale pink with salmon hints, it will go well with the Mediterranean seafood.
🔑 Sté coop. l'Etoile, 26, av. du Puig-del-Mas, 66650 Banyuls-sur-Mer, tel. 04.68.88.00.10, fax 04.68.88.15.10 ☑
Y ev. day except Sat. Sun. 8am–12 noon 2pm–6pm

DOM. DU MAS BLANC

Clos du Moulin 1998

■ n.c. n.c. 100–149 F

Jean-Michel Parcé has now taken over the torch from his father, who worked all his life to promote the appellations Banyuls and Collioure. With a deep ruby colour, his Clos du Moulin is a wine that needs to be kept for a long time, judging by the power and quality of the tannins on the structure. Cherry aromas emerge little by little through the toasty notes and suggest that it will be very easy to choose a good culinary match for this Collioure.
🔑 Dom. du Mas Blanc, 66650 Banyuls-sur-Mer, tel. 04.68.88.32.12, fax 04.68.88.72.24 ☑ Y ev. day except Sat.–Sun. 9am–12 noon 3pm–6pm
🔑 Jean-Michel Parcé

MAS CORNET 1999★

◪ n.c. 5,610 50–69 F

The first impression on the nose gives notes of banana liqueur, then, gradually the flavours of strawberry and raspberry develop on the palate. This wine is fresh and enjoyable with a balanced structure.
🔑 La Cave de l'Abbé Rous, 56, av. Charles-de-Gaulle, 66650 Banyuls-sur-Mer, tel. 04.68.88.72.72, fax 04.68.88.30.57, e-mail contact@banyuls.com

LES CLOS DE PAULILLES 1998★

■ 7 ha 35,000 70–99 F

You can taste this Collioure at the estate's farm guesthouse of the estate, situated by the edge of one of the inlets in the shadow of Cap Béar, between Port-Vendres and Banyuls. Flavours of wild red berries blend into vanilla notes that result from the oak ageing. On the palate, the tannins from Mourvèdre (70% of the blend) appear through the solid structure of this wine.
🔑 Les Clos de Paulilles, Baie de Paulilles, 66660 Port-Vendres, tel. 04.68.38.90.10, fax 04.68.38.91.33, e-mail jau66@aol.com ☑ Y ev. day 11am–11pm
🔑 Famille Dauré

DOM. PIETRI-GERAUD 1999

◪ 0.7 ha 3,500 ▮ ♁ 30–49 F

Within the boundaries of Collioure itself, established on terraces of schist, Maguy Pietri-Géraud and her daughter Laetitia run their estate with great enthusiasm. They have just renovated their ageing cellar. Their Collioure rosé has a peony pink colour with aromas of fruit over-ripened in the sun, and some spicy notes. These rich flavours prevail over the acidity.

🗝 Maguy et Laetitia Piétri-Géraud, 22, rue Pasteur, 66190 Collioure, tel. 04.68.82.07.42, fax 04.68.98.02.58 ☑
Y ev. day 10am–12.30pm 3.30pm–6.30pm

CH. REIG 1996

■ n.c. 61,000 ⦀ 70–99 F

Lovers of old wines will enjoy tasting this mature 96. The colour has a brick edge to it, not dissimilar to the colour of Banyuls, and there are aromas of musk, leather and red fruit jam. Oaky notes work together with the tannic structure that dominates the palate.

🗝 Cellier des Templiers, rte du Mas-Reig, 66650 Banyuls-sur-Mer, tel. 04.68.98.36.70, fax 04.68.98.36.91 ☑ Y by appt.

DOM. DU ROUMANI 1998★★

■ 30 ha 41,160 ▮ ♁ 70–99 F

The garnet-coloured 98 vintage of the Domaine du Romani, made by the Cellier des Templiers, is well worth trying. With aromas of crushed ripe fruits, blended in with some charred notes, the tannins are dominant on the palate, but of excellent quality, with some liquorice flavours. A wine that should be left in your cellar for some time, but will you have the patience to wait for it?

🗝 Cellier des Templiers, rte du Mas-Reig, 66650 Banyuls-sur-Mer, tel. 04.68.98.36.70, fax 04.68.98.36.91 ☑ Y by appt.

DOM. DU TRAGINER 1998★★

■ 3 ha 6,500 ⦀ 70–99 F

The *traginer* led the mule that brought the grapes to the cellar . . . an idyllic image of harvest-time in Banyuls. The label of this wine also plays on nostalgia, showing an old photograph of the port of Collioure with its fishing boats and nets. This is a deep garnet-coloured red Collioure with flavours of wild red berry fruits, which develop little by little on the palate. An excellent balance of integrated and vanilla-flavoured tannins. The **Cuvée d'Octobre** from the same estate has more concentrated and over-ripe flavours and is awarded a mention.

🗝 Dom. du Traginer, 56, av. du Puig-del-Mas, 66650 Banyuls-sur-Mer, tel. 04.68.88.15.11, fax 04.68.88.31.48 ☑ Y by appt.
🗝 J.-F. Deu

DOM. VIAL-MAGNERES

Les Espérades 1998★

■ 2 ha 6,000 ▮ ⦀ ♁ 70–99 F

Based in Banyuls-sur-Mer, Bernard Sapéras produces a whole range of wines that are both unusual and of good quality. Les Espérades has a cherry-red colour with notes of red berry fruit reminiscent of Sangria. The tannins dominate on the palate and are still a little hard. Hopefully time will soften them.

🗝 Dom. Vial-Magnères, Clos Saint-André, 66650 Banyuls-sur-Mer, tel. 04.68.88.31.04, fax 04.68.55.01.06, e-mail al.tragou@wanadoo.fr ☑ Y by appt.
🗝 M. et B. Sapéras

PROVENCE AND CORSICA

Provence

Provence means holidays, a place where 'the sun always shines' and where the people, with their melodious accents, take the time to live life as it should be lived . . . For the wine-growers it is also a place where the sun shines, for three thousand hours a year! Rain is rare, but violent storms and ferocious winds batter the terrain. When the Phocaean Greeks disembarked at Marseilles around 600 BC, they found vines already growing in the region, and began to cultivate them systematically. Vine-growing continued under the Romans, followed in medieval times by the abbeys and local aristocratic landowners up to and including the wine-grower king, René of Anjou, Count of Provence.

Eleanor of Provence, wife of Henry III of England, was the first to give the wines of Provence an international cachet, just as her mother-in-law, Eleanor of Aquitaine, had done for the wines of Gascony. In the centuries which followed, Provençal wines fell out of favour with the international shippers due to difficulties in transport compared with other wine areas. However, in recent decades the development of tourism has brought the wines back to prominence, particularly the rosés, which are fun to drink – perfect companions for summer holidays and delicious Provençal dishes.

The Provençal vineyard is a patchwork of numerous small areas, which helps explain why nearly half of the wine produced is organised though co-operatives: there are no fewer than a hundred in the Var department alone. But the larger 'domaines' (which, for the most part, are also bottlers) have retained their influence, and their active presence in marketing and promoting the wines is considered invaluable throughout the region. The annual production reaches between 2 and 3 million hl (52,800,000–79,200,000 gal), of which between 700,000 and 800,000 (18,480,000 – 21,120,000 gal) come from the seven AOCs, and about one million from eight Appellations d'Origine. In the Var department, typical of the region, wine represents 45% of the total agricultural production and vineyards cover 51% of the area.

In common with other southern vineyards, quite a few vine varieties are grown: the Appellation Côtes de Provence allows a total of thirteen. And yet, sadly, the Muscats, the glory of the Provençal terroirs before the phylloxera devastation, have now vanished. The vines are for the most part pruned in the traditional low goblet shape; however, plants rained along cordons are becoming increasingly common. Rosé and white vines (the latter more rare but frequently surprisingly good), are generally lrunk young. This might change if it were possible to find conditions for ıgeing in bottles that were less extreme than those offered by the local limate. The same thought applies to many of the lighter reds. However, the uller-bodied reds from the Provençal appellations age very well.

The tiny Palette vineyard, at the gates of Aix, incorporates he old enclosure belonging to King René. Its whites, rosés and reds are vorthy of attention.

Since Provençal is still spoken in some of the domaines, it is ıseful to know some of the local terminology: *avis* is the local word for *sarment* (wine shoot), a *tine* is a *cuve* or vat, and a *crotte* is a cave or cellar. You may be told that one of the grape varieties is called *pecouitouar* or *queue tordue* (which means 'twisted tail'), while *ginou d'Agasso* means 'magpie knee', because of the peculiar shape of the stem of the bunch of grapes.

Côtes de Provence

This appellation has a substantial production (nearly 800,000 hl (21,120,000 gal) per year), and covers a good third of the department of the Var, with extensions into the Bouches-du-Rhone to the edge of Marseilles, and an enclave in the Alpes-Maritimes. In 1999 934,086 hl (24,659,870 gal) were produced. Three terroirs identify it: the crystalline rocks of the Maure mountains in the south-east, bordered to the north by a band of red sand from Toulon to Saint-Raphaël and, beyond, a sizeable massif of hills and limestone plateaux that prefigure the Alps. The charm of these wines lies in their sheer diversity: made from a number of different vine varieties in varying proportions, and grown on equally varied soils with as many different aspects, they share little but the influence of the fierce southern sun. Perhaps this was the charm that the Greek Protis, according to legend, tasted as early as 600 BC when Gyptis, the daughter of a local king, offered him a goblet of wine as a pledge of her love.

The whites from the coast are soft but lively, and are perfectly suited to very fresh seafood; those from a little further north are more 'focused' and will go very well with lobster à l'Américaine and tangy cheeses. The rosés can be either soft or lively and, depending on your mood or taste, are best combined with full flavours, such as soup with pesto, anchoïade, aïoli and bouillabaisse, as well as fish and seafood, particularly red mullet, sea urchins and shellfish. The soft reds (which should be drunk slightly chilled) go well with joints of meat, roasts and pot-au-feu and especially with cold pot-au-feu salad. Finally, some of the strong, full-bodied reds are suitable for daubes (rich, slowly cooked stews) and woodcock. And for those who are attracted by unexpected pairings, try cold rosé with mushrooms, red with stewed shellfish, or white with daube of lamb (made with white wine).

CH. D'ASTROS Cuvée Spéciale 1999★

◢ 3 ha 20,000 ▮ 🌡 30–49 F

The Château d'Astros was where Yves Robert chose to shoot his film *Le Château de ma Mère*. It certainly is a delightful setting, but visitors will find the wines just as appealing. This one is made from a selection of old Grenache vines, and has a very pale colour and exceptionally strong aromas of bananas and exotic fruits. A wine that is memorable for its quality and balance on the palate, and is ready to drink now.

SCEA du Ch. d'Astros, rte de Lorgues, 83550 Vidauban, tel. 04.94.99.73.00, fax 04.94.73.00.18 ☑ Y ev. day except Sun. 8.30am–12 noon 2pm–6pm

CH. BARBANAU

1999★

6 ha 30,000 30–49 F

This estate's produce generally receives a very high rating. Once again, the jury singled out its rosé, perhaps for its attractive, pale peony colour, but certainly for the elegance of its aromas of citrus and exotic fruits. Round, sweet and balanced, it is an attractive wine with very good length.

GAEC Ch. Barbanau, Hameau de Roquefort, 13830 Roquefort-la-Bédoule, tel. 04.42.73.14.60, fax 04.42.73.17.85, e-mail barbanau@aol.com ev. day except Sun. 10am–12 noon 3pm–6pm

Cerciello

CH. BARBEIRANNE

Cuvée Camille 1999

1.3 ha 3,500 50–69 F

The Château Barbeiranne has more tha 30 ha (74 acres) of vines at Pignans, a prett wine-growing village dating back to the 16t century. Its rosé has had the benefit of si months' well-managed maturation in barre which has given it a range of vanilla and toas aromas, pierced by a hint of fruitiness. Not a all typical of the appellation, but a very goo wine nonetheless.

Ch. Barbeiranne, La Pellegrine, 83790 Pignan, tel. 04.94.48.84.46, fax 04.94.33.27.03 ev. day 9am–6pm

Sonnpez

Provence

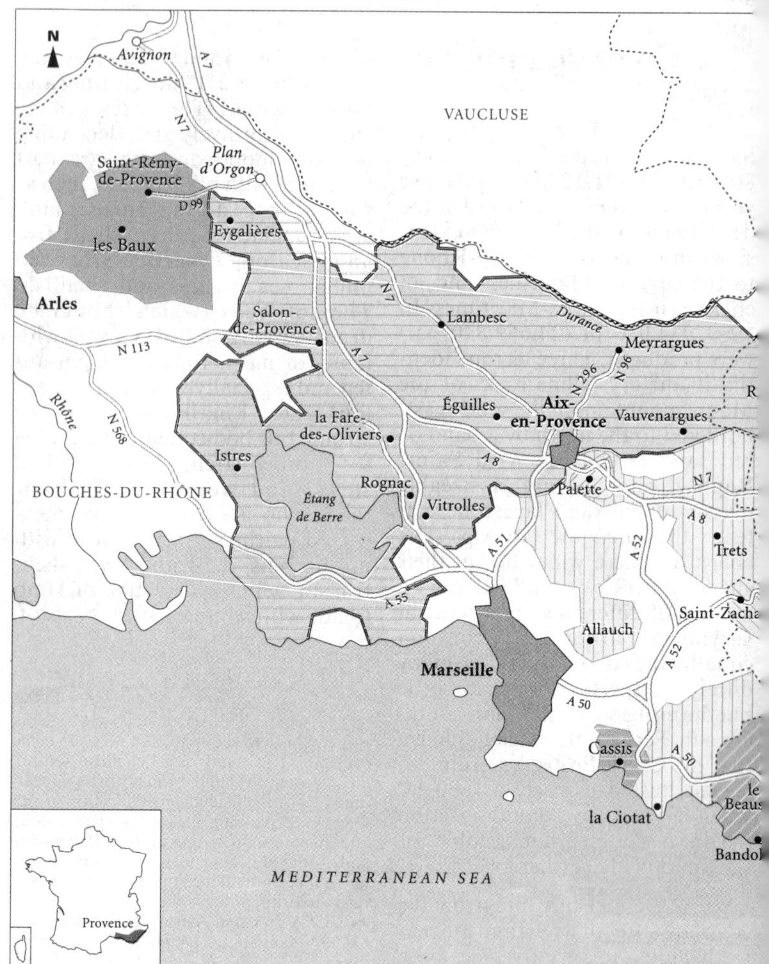

LOU BASSAQUET

Cuvée des Rascailles 1999★

■ 4 ha 19,600 🍾 🌡 30–49 F

Despite its very Provençal name, this wine is more suggestive of the Atlantic coast, with Cabernet Sauvignon dominating its rich blend of intense spicy and musky aromas. Round, fine and subtle on the palate, it is pleasant to drink now, but can also be kept.

🔑 Coopérative Vinicole Le Mont Aurélien, chem. du Loup, 13530 Trets, tel. 04.42.29.20.20, fax 04.42.29.32.03 ☑ 🍷 by appt.

DOM. DE BELEOUVE

1999★

■ 2 ha 12,000 🍾 🌡 30–49 F

This vast property is well known for its Bandols, but also produces excellent Côtes de Provence. This one has a very dark purple colour, and delightful aromas of leather and undergrowth. Both structured and balanced, it is an attractive wine that will achieve its full potential when it has been kept for a while.

🔑 Domaines Bunan, B.P. 17, 83740 La Cadière-d'Azur, tel. 04.94.98.58.98, fax 04.94.98.60.05 ☑ 🍷 by appt.

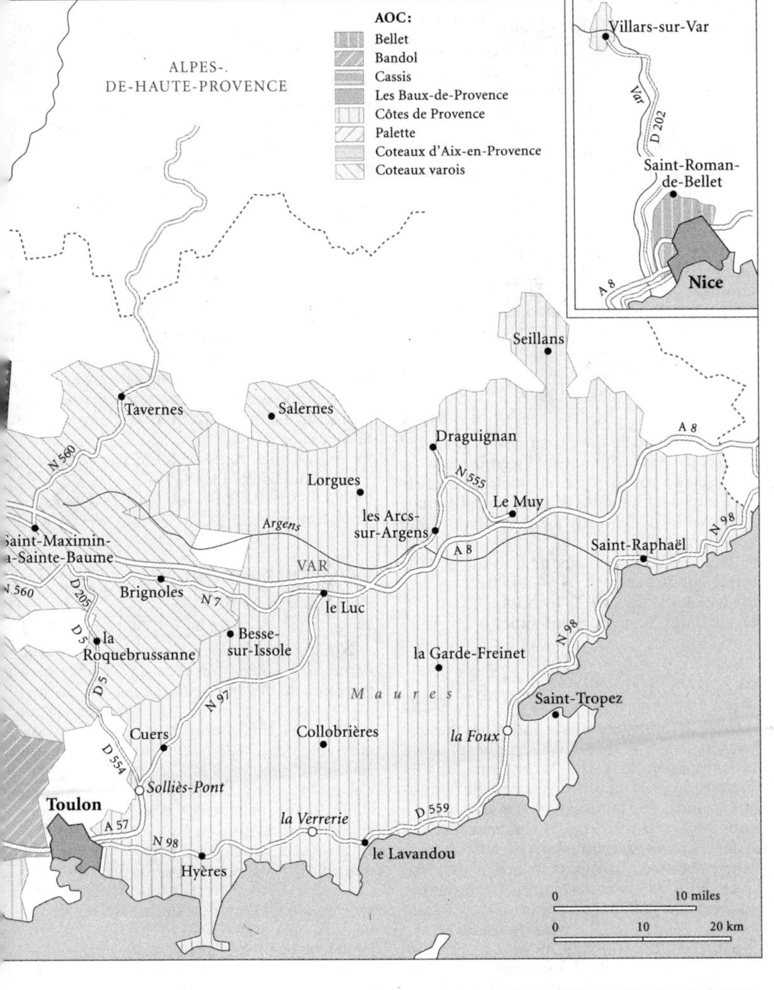

PROVENCE

CH. DE BERNE Cuvée Spéciale 1998★

■ 8 ha 50,000 50–69 F

There is always something going on at the Château de Berne: exhibitions, plays, concerts, gastronomic meetings, and also wine-tastings with a theme, at which the three Cuvées Spéciales selected by the jury deserve to feature prominently. This well-constructed red wine has a purple colour and a bouquet of vanilla and toast. The **1999 Rosé Cuvée Spéciale** (30–49F) is equally successful, and typical of the vintage. Finally, the **1999 Blanc Cuvée Spéciale** (50–69F), matured in barrel for eight months, also merits a star; it shows great potential.

Ch. de Berne, Flayosc, 83510 Lorgues, tel. 04.94.60.43.60, fax 04.94.60.43.58, e-mail info@chateau-berne.fr
ev. day 10am–6pm

CH. DE BREGANCON

Cuvée Prestige 1999★

Cru clas. 10 ha 10,000 30–49 F

This is an idyllic spot, with a wonderful view over the islands from the terrace of the château. There are pleasant wines to be tasted here, such as this rosé, which is very fruity, full, persistent and refreshing on the palate. The jury also awarded a star to the **1999 Réserve Rouge du Château**, which shows excellent potential.

Jean-François Tézenas, Ch. de Brégançon, 639, rte de Léoube, 83230 Bormes-les-Mimosas, tel. 04.94.64.80.73, fax 04.94.64.73.47, e-mail chbregancon@terre.net.fr ev. day except Sat. Sun. 9am–12 noon 2pm–6pm

CH. DE CABRAN

Cuvée du Pont Romain 1999★

3.2 ha 15,300 30–49 F

The Château de Cabran grows its 15 ha (37 acres) of vines on an unusual terroir made up of volcanic rocks. This has yielded a fairly classic rosé with shades of salmon-pink, characterised by delightfully focused flavours and good length.

Ch. de Cabran, chem. de Cabran, 83480 Puget-sur-Argens, tel. 04.94.40.80.32, fax 04.94.40.75.21 by appt.
de Saint-Seine/de Saint-Julien

MAS DE CADENET 1999★

20 ha n.c. 30–49 F

With its narrow streets and Romanesque houses, Trets still looks like a medieval town. It is located near the Montagne Sainte-Victoire, in the part of Provence made famous by Cézanne. The landscape is dense and luminous, and so is this Mas de Cadenet rosé. Its aromas create an impression of great homogeneity between fruitiness (exotic fruits) and spice, after which it develops a fresh quality on the palate, while losing none of its fullness.

Guy Négrel, EARL Mas de Cadenet, 13530 Trets, tel. 04.42.29.21.59, fax 04.42.61.32.09 by appt.

CH. CARPE DIEM Premium 1999★

□ n.c. 9,000 30–49 F

Carpe diem . . . This philosophy has proved very successful for Francis Adam. His Côtes de Provence Blanc has golden highlights, intense aromas of very ripe fruit (white-fleshed fruits, peach and quince), and makes quite an impact on the palate. Take care that you don't get hooked on it. Also cited is the **1998 Cuvée Major Rouge** (50–69F), which has a deeply gamey quality and is rich and soft in the mouth. Ready to drink now.

Francis Adam, Ch. Carpe Diem, R.D. 13, rte de Carces, 83570 Cotignac, tel. 04.94.04.76.65, fax 04.94.04.77.50
ev. day 10am–12.30pm 3pm–6.30pm

CH. DE CHAUSSE 1997★

■ 7 ha 30,000 30–49 F

This new estate, founded in 1990, has planted its 15 ha (37 acres) of vines in a hillside vineyard. A successful wine in previous years, the 1997 is wilder, releasing notes of game, leather and toast. A fine, well-delineated wine with good length, it can be drunk immediately.

Ch. de Chausse, 83420 La Croix-Valmer, tel. 04.94.79.60.57, fax 04.94.79.59.19
ev. day 10am–12 noon 3pm–6pm
Y. et R. Schelcher

COSTE BRULADE

Cuvée spéciale 1999★

20 ha 11,000 30–49 F

This wine is made from grapes selected from the oldest vines, and then given a cold maceration. It has quite a pronounced candy-pink colour, and a very fragrant nose consisting mainly of banana and strawberry aromas. A straightforward, well-composed rosé that pulls out all the stops, and has appreciable body too.

SCA Cellier Saint-Sidoine, rue de la Libération, 83390 Puget-Ville, tel. 04.98.01.80.50, fax 04.98.01.80.59
by appt.

DOM. DE CUREBEASSE

Roches noires 1998★★

■ 2.6 ha 8,500 30–49 F

Not a very safe place, if one is to believe the name *cure biasse*, that is to say 'empty beggar's pouch' in Provençal. It's just an old saying . . . What you can have confidence in, however, is this remarkable, intensely coloured red wine. With its flavour of vanilla and very good balance, it is already showing very well on the palate, but deserves to be kept for a while longer. The **1999 Blanc** is also very good, and can afford to wait another year. It is an aromatic wine, punctuated by a note of oak, and with a surge of youthful zest at the finish, thanks to its fresh, rounded character.

Paquette, Dom. de Curebeasse, rte de Bagnols-en-Forêt, 83600 Fréjus, tel. 04.94.40.87.90, fax 04.94.40.75.18, e-mail curebeasse@infonie.fr by appt.

CH. DEFFENDS Cuvée première 1999

◪ 2 ha 12,800 ▮ ♁ 30–49 F

The colour is discreet, but the nose is much more expressive, with fruity notes of banana and peardrops. A fresh, balanced rosé that has good presence on the palate, and is very true to type.

EARL Ch. Deffends, 83660 Carnoules, tel. 04.94.28.33.12, fax 04.94.28.33.12 ☒
Y by appt.
Verges

DOM. DU DRAGON

Cuvée Saint-Michel Vieillie en fût de chêne 1998★★★

■ 6 ha 22,000 30–49 F

After a change of ownership some years ago, this estate underwent thorough and beneficial renovations. This 1998 speaks of the influence of Cabernet Sauvignon and maturation in oak. Dark, powerful, full and fruity, with well-defined shades of vanilla and cloves, it wins three stars for the impression of nobility it leaves on the palate.

M. Waroquier, Dom. du Dragon, rte de Montferrat, 83300 Draguignan, tel. 04.94.68.14.46, fax 04.94.68.14.46 ☒
Y ev. day 10am–12 noon 4pm–6pm
M. Houppertz

DOM. DES FERAUD

Cuvée réservée 1999★★

◪ 7.5 ha 34,000 ▮ ♁ 30–49 F

This very pale rosé has an array of floral and fruit aromas: lilac, hawthorn blossom, peach, lime and other fragrances that give it a rather atypical character. On the palate, the flavours come together to create a velvety, harmoniously balanced overall impression, with a slight hint of freshness at the finish. An excellent wine.

Dom. des Féraud, rte de La Garde-Freinet, 83550 Vidauban, tel. 04.94.73.03.12, fax 04.94.73.08.58 ☒
Y by appt.

CH. DES FERRAGES 1999★

◪ 5 ha 30,000 30–49 F

The discreet elegance of the rose-petal colour sets the tone for the tasting. An attractive compromise between intensity and finesse, this wine has a lovely scent of citrus fruits, and stimulates the tastebuds with a silky quality on the palate that is reinforced by its youthful vigour.

José Garcia, Ch. des Ferrages, R.N. 7, 83470 Pourcieux, tel. 04.94.59.45.53, fax 04.94.59.72.49 ☒ Y ev. day 8.30am–12.30pm 2pm–6.30pm; Sun. by appt.

CH. DU GALOUPET 1999★

□ Cru clas. n.c. 30,000 30–49 F

The strong, almost lemon colour with shades of gold augurs well for a rich, complex wine. This impression is confirmed on the nose, where there are well-developed aromas of white flowers, ripe fruit, iodine and roasted hazelnuts. Rich and fleshy on the palate, this 1999 has no shortage of personality, and will make a delicious accompaniment to many types of food.

Ch. du Galoupet, Saint-Nicolas, 83250 La Londe-les-Maures, tel. 04.94.66.40.07, fax 04.94.66.42.40 ☒ Y ev. day except Sun. 9am–12 noon 2pm–6pm (7pm summer)
S. Shivdasani

LES VIGNERONS DU GARLABAN 1999★

■ 5 ha 13,000 ▮ ♁ 20–29 F

Located just outside Marseilles, at the foot of Marcel Pagnol's beloved Massif du Garbalan, this cooperative cellar offers an intense, expressive red wine with good structure. It is still a little young, and will need to be watched over the next two years. The **1999 Rosé** also wins one star. It has a strong colour, and is equally forthcoming with fruity aromas on the nose. A well-made *rosé de saignée*.

Les Vignerons du Garlaban, 8, chem. Saint-Pierre, 13390 Auriol, tel. 04.42.04.70.70, fax 04.42.72.89.49 ☒
Y by appt.

GASPERINI Dame Jardin 1999

◪ 5 ha 10,000 ▮ ♁ 30–49 F

Dame Jardin is a tribute to Joséphine Jardin, who founded this estate in 1834. The overall impression of the 1999 is one of warmth, which suggests that this rosé will be good to serve, from now, with food. The **1999 Joachim Blanc** is also cited. It exhibits good balance, showing equal fruitiness on the nose and the palate, and deserves to be drunk with food.

Vignoble Gasperini, 42, av. de la Libération, 83260 La Crau, tel. 04.94.66.70.01, fax 04.94.66.10.33 ☒
Y ev. day except Sat. Sun. 8am–12 noon 2pm–7pm

CH. GASQUI Cuvée Prestige 1996★

■ 0.8 ha 6,000 50–69 F

Long maceration and maturation in oak are the keys to this wine, which is already in an advanced stage of development. Even so, it has a delightful nose of peppery and spicy notes, with aromas of vanilla and fresh butter. With both softness and good length on the palate, this well-made wine is ready to drink now.

SCEA Ch. Gasqui, rte de Flassan, 83590 Gonfaron, tel. 04.94.78.23.14, fax 04.94.78.27.16 ☒ Y ev. day 9am–6pm
G. Fiat

DOM. GAVOTY

Cuvée Clarendon 1998★

■ 6.5 ha 30,000 50–69 F

Clarendon was the pseudonym of Bernard Gavoty, the famous music critic of *Le Figaro*. The estate carries on the artistic tradition by providing a venue for classical concerts in the summer. This wine offers a powerful, complex bouquet of toast and spices, and then fills the palate with long-lasting flavour. With two years of ageing, it will gain more refinement.

One star is also awarded to the **1999 Cuvée Clarendon Rosée**. This is a full, rich wine with good presence on the palate, and a bouquet that promises to open out fully very soon.
Pierre et Roselyne Gavoty, Le Grand Campdumy, 83340 Cabasse, tel. 04.94.69.72.39, fax 04.94.59.64.04
by appt.

CH. GRAND'BOISE 1999★

10 ha 53,000 30–49 F

This very unusual vineyard is located in the middle of the Mediterranean forest, between 300 and 600 m (325 and 650 yards) up on the north side of the Sainte-Baume. The estate has undergone a complete renaissance, the first fruit of which is this crystal-clear rosé with elegant shades of salmon-pink. Fragrant and punctuated by notes of exotic fruits and white flowers, it is both round and fresh on the palate, and has excellent concentration. A delightful wine, which clearly bears the stamp of Grenache.
SCEA La Grenobloise, Ch. Grand'Boisé, Ch. de Grisole, 13530 Trets, tel. 04.42.29.22.95, fax 04.42.61.38.71, e-mail grandboise@wanadoo.fr
by appt.
Nielsen

DOM. DU GRAND CROS

Cuvée Classique 1998

3 ha 13,300 30–49 F

There are 22 ha (54 acres) of vines and a beautiful 17th-century building at the Grand Cros, which wins two citations for its Côtes de Provence. One is this red *vin de terroir*, which needs to be kept for a while. It has a moderately intense nose of red berries and spices, and good structure on the palate, where it is still somewhat firm. The other is the **1999 Rosé Esprit de Provence**, which has great overall freshness.
EARL Dom. du Grand Cros, 83660 Carnoules, tel. 04.98.01.80.08, fax 04.98.01.80.09, e-mail info@grandcros.fr
by appt.
J.-H. Faulkner

DOM. DE GRANDPRE

Cuvée Spéciale 1998★★

3 ha 7,000 30–49 F

Under the same label, the 1997 vintage was a success story, and the 1998 came close to receiving a *coup de coeur*, since it too reached the final grand jury stage. It has the same highly characteristic notes of fruit, vanilla and liquorice, and above all the same dense yet silky tannins that give it character and complexity, and augur well for a very bright future.
Emmanuel Plauchut, Dom. de Grandpré, 83390 Puget-Ville, tel. 04.94.48.32.16, fax 04.94.33.53.49
ev. day 9am–12 noon 1.30pm–6.30pm

CH. DE JASSON Cuvée Eléonore 1999★

9.1 ha 60,000 50–69 F

It would be hard to describe Provence without mentioning this highly successful estate. Once again, the jury thought very highly this year of the rosé. It is salmon-pink, elegant and appealingly fruity, and has great presence and fullness on the palate. Under the same label, the **1999 Blanc** is a very expressive wine, and also wins a star.
Benjamin de Fresne, Ch. de Jasson, R.D. 88, 83250 La Londe-les-Maures, tel. 04.94.66.81.52, fax 04.94.05.24.84, e-mail chateau.de.jasson@wanadoo.fr
ev. day 9am–12.30pm 2.30pm–7.30pm

DOM. DE LA BASTIDE NEUVE

Cuvée d'Antan 1997★

2.6 ha 12,000 50–69 F

This wine is made from Syrah, Mourvèdre and Cabernet Sauvignon grapes, and has been matured in 600-litre (158-gallon) wooden casks known as *demi-muids*, or in Provence as *boulés*. No doubt this is what has enabled the aromas to develop notes of kirsch, liquorice and other scents indicative of good breeding. Structured and stylish on the palate, this is a wine that will need to be kept for a while.
SCEA Dom. de la Bastide Neuve, M. Paquette, 83340 Le Cannet-des-Maures, tel. 04.94.50.09.80, fax 04.94.50.09.99, e-mail dnebastideneuve@compuserve.com
by appt.
Wiestner

DOM. DE L'ABBAYE

Cuvée Pugette 1999★

6 ha 35,000 30–49 F

Although this estate adjoins the Cistercian abbey at Thoronet, its owner is first and foremost a vigneron skilled in growing the fruits of the earth here below. More grey than pink in colour, this rosé has a bouquet of exotic fruits, and light, balanced flavours. In a spicier, deeper register, the **1999 Rosé de Saignée** has also been awarded a star (50–69F).
Franc Petit, Dom. de l'Abbaye, 83340 Le Thoronet, tel. 04.94.73.87.36, fax 04.94.60.11.62 ev. day except Sun. 8am–12 noon 1pm–6pm

DOM. DE LA BOUVERIE 1999★

3 ha 15,000 30–49 F

The vines of La Bouverie grow in the magnificent setting of the Argens valley, which is dominated by the imposing mass of the red sandstone rocks of Roquebrune. A well-handled fermentation, followed by maturation in oak for six months, has given this white wine a fine nose of hazelnuts and toast. It shows plenty of stuffing on the palate, before finishing on an intriguing note.
Jean Laponche, Dom. de la Bouverie, 83520 Roquebrune-sur-Argens, tel. 04.94.44.00.81, fax 04.94.44.04.73
ev. day except Sun. 9.30am–12.30pm 2pm–5pm

CH. DE LA CASTILLE 1998

■ 12.05 ha 7,300 20–29 F

The Château de la Castille once belonged to the Comtes de Provence and is now the Bishop's palace. Out of its vaulted cellars, which were dug out in 1730 by the convicts of Marseille and La Ciotat, comes this 1998. It has great character that will require some taming. Attractive to look at and expressive on the nose, it has a substantial palate that will ensure it develops well if kept for at least two years.

Fondation la Castille, 83260 La Crau, tel. 04.94.66.23.63, fax 04.94.33.42.15 by appt.

CH. DE LA COULERETTE 1999

40 ha 200,000 30–49 F

Located at La Londe-les-Maures, at the entrance to the Massif des Maures, the Château de la Coulerette cultivates 40 ha (99 acres) of vines. It has produced a substantial, robust rosé, with a strong colour, a fresh, moderately intense nose and a well-balanced palate.

S. Brechet, SCA Ch. la Coulerette, 83250 La Londe-les-Maures, tel. 04.90.12.32.42, fax 04.90.12.32.49

LA COURTADE 1998★★

■ 9.5 ha 44,000 100–149 F

Located on the island of Porquerolles, La Courtade has the benefit of a very special environment in which the sunshine and sea atmosphere play a vital role in the ripening of the grapes. This 1998 is essentially made from Mourvèdre, and the greatest care was taken in its production with regard to yield, fermentation and maturation. The jury was impressed by its complex range of aromas, which include notes of smoke, musk, truffles and undergrowth. The wine becomes oakier in the mouth, where its structure is powerful and still robust.

Dom. de la Courtade, 83400 Ile-de-Porquerolles, tel. 04.94.58.31.44, fax 04.94.58.34.12, e-mail la-courtade@terre-net.fr by appt.

M. H. Vidal

CELLIER DE LA CRAU

Cuvée des Vieux Ceps 1998★★

■ 10 ha 10,000 20–29 F

The La Crau co-operative offers a wine with a rich colour and lustrous highlights. In keeping with the fig and jam aromas of the nose, it is already well-balanced on the palate, and the tannins are so harmonious as to give it a velvety quality. It is pleasant to drink now, but can also be kept for three to five years.

Cellier de La Crau, 85, av. de Toulon, 83260 La Crau, tel. 04.94.66.73.03, fax 04.94.66.17.63 ev. day except Sun. 8am–12 noon 2pm–5.30pm

DOM. DE LA CRESSONNIERE

Cuvée Prunelle 1999★

2 ha 12,500 30–49 F

A plane-tree more than 200 years old stands at the entrance to this estate, which was founded in 1639. Coming from limestone-clay and shale soils, the Cuvée Prunelle has a pale colour with an array of highlights, and is a wine of great elegance and finesse. The nose has aromas of red berries, which give way to notes of citrus fruits on the palate. Another very good wine is the **1999 Côtes de Provence Blanc Cuvée Bel-Avi**, which has spent several months in barrels and will improve over the course of this winter.

GFA Dom. de la Cressonnière, R.N. 97, 83790 Pignans, tel. 04.94.48.81.22, fax 04.94.48.81.25, e-mail cressoniere@wanadoo.fr by appt.

Gourdon et Depeursinge

CH. LA FONT DU BROC 1999★★

5.3 ha 20,000 50–69 F

The fact that this estate is also a breeding centre for Lusitanian horses makes its own contribution (manure to spread between the rows of vines) to its wine-making renown. The overall impression of this 1999 is delicate, but nonetheless it has plenty of presence. From the beauty of its colour to its subtle, slightly amylic aromas, this is a charming, balanced wine.

Sylvain Massa, Ch. la Font du Broc, chem. du Font-du-Broc, 83460 Les Arcs-sur-Argens, tel. 04.94.47.48.20, fax 04.94.47.50.46 by appt.

CH. L'AFRIQUE 1999★★

5 ha 35,000 30–49 F

The Château l'Afrique owes its name to the orientalist trend that developed in the 19th century, and its label accordingly shows a picture by Géricault. What an aromatically exuberant wine this salmon-pink rosé is! Grapefruit stands out clearly from the range of aromas, after which it develops great fullness on the palate. A real delicacy. The more classical **1998 Rouge** bears witness to its maturation in barrel. It will improve in the cellar for three to five years.

Famille Elie Sumeire, Ch. l'Afrique, 83390 Cuers, tel. 04.42.61.20.00, fax 04.42.61.20.01, e-mail sumeire@chateaux-elie-sumeire.fr by appt.

DOM. DE LA GARNAUDE

Cuvée Santane 1998★

■ 2 ha 5,000 30–49 F

Behind its quite classical appearance, this wine has a large and very appealing range of aromas: many fruits, as well as spices (nutmeg) and a little leather. Pleasant and supple in the mouth, it has reached its full potential and deserves to be drunk.

⊶ SCEA Martel-Lassechère, Dom. de la Garnaude, 83590 Gonfaron, tel. 04.94.78.20.42, fax 04.94.78.24.71 ☒
Ɏ by appt.
⊶ GFA Dom. de la Garnaude

DOM. DE LA GERADE 1998★

■ 1 ha 3,000 30–49 F

This mouthwatering red Côtes de Provence has an intense bouquet of soft fruit (raspberries), with a fine note of liquorice. A well-balanced, entirely unaggressive wine, it is ready to drink now, and will go well with red meat or soft cheese. The **1999 Rosé** also deserves citation for its unusual aromas.
⊶ EARL de la Gérade, 1300, chem. des Tourraches, 83260 La Crau, tel. 04.94.66.13.88, fax 04.94.66.73.52 ☒
Ɏ ev. day except Sun. 9am–11.45
⊶ B. Henry

DOM. DE LA GISCLE

Carte noire 1998★

■ 2.5 ha 5,000 30–49 F

Before being given over to wine-growing around the end of the 16th century, the La Giscle estate was first a flour mill and then a silk farm. It is located in a valley surrounded by the peaks of the Maures, and has yielded this red wine matured in barrels for seven months. Fragrant with vanilla and liquorice, it is dense and very persistent on the palate. Keep it for two to three years. A rosé that also merits a star is the **1999 Moulin de L'Isle**.
⊶ EARL Dom. de la Giscle, hameau de l'Amirauté, rte de Collobrières, 83310 Cogolin, tel. 04.94.43.21.26, fax 04.94.43.37.53 ☒ Ɏ ev. day 9am–12.30pm 2pm–7pm; Sun. 9am–12.30pm
⊶ Audemard

CH. LA GORDONNE

Les Gravières 1999

◪ 12 ha 80,000 20–29 F

The Château la Gordonne forms part of the Listel estates, which since 1995 have belonged to Val d'Orbieu, a large Languedoc conglomerate. This rosé is singled out for its texture and its forthrightness. It also has a classical range of fruity aromas (amylic notes, backed by strawberries), and a strong, almost cherry colour.
⊶ Domaines Listel, Ch. la Gordonne, 83390 Pierrefeu-du-Var, tel. 04.94.28.20.35, fax 04.94.28.20.35 ☒ Ɏ ev. day 8am–12 noon 1pm–6pm; Sat. Sun. by appt.

DOM. DE LA LAUZADE 1999★★

□ 10 ha 50,000 30–49 F

Where La Lauzade is now located was a Roman villa, around 46 BC. At that time the site was highly valued for its springs, and for the fact that it was sheltered from the Mistral by a wall of hills. Today the estate is known not only for its wines, but also for its experimental conservatory in which 60 grape varieties are cultivated. A gourmet experience awaits you: a 1999 white wine that is full of youth, and whose intensely expressive nose is reminiscent of the freshness of citrus fruits. It harmonises around an attractive balance of flavours, lingering delightfully on the palate.
⊶ Dom. de La Lauzade, rte de Toulon, 83340 Le Luc, tel. 04.94.60.72.51, fax 04.94.60.96.26, e-mail lauzade.abouvier@wanadoo.fr ☒
Ɏ by appt.

DOM. DE LA LAUZADE 1999★

■ 25 ha 140,000 30–49 F

A salad of citrus fruits with spices: both in the nose and on the palate, this wine has surprising attributes for a red wine, in addition to richness and good length. The jury describes this Côtes de Provence as atypical, but is unanimous in defining it as attractive and ready to drink. The **1999 Rosé** has a gleaming colour, captivating aromas, and flavours on the palate that will stimulate your tastebuds.
⊶ Dom. de la Lauzade, rte de Toulon, 83340 Le Luc, tel. 04.94.60.72.51, fax 04.94.60.96.26, e-mail lauzade.abouvier@wanadoo.fr ☒
Ɏ by appt.

DOM. DE LA MAYONNETTE

Cuvée Prestige 1998★★

■ 1.6 ha 5,000 50–69 F

This wine has a deep colour and all the structure one could wish for. It is supported by well-built tannins, ensuring that it lingers for a considerable time on a liquorice flavour that echoes the spicy aromas of the nose. A wine that has every chance of developing well and offering real pleasure as it does so.
⊶ Julian, Dom. de la Mayonnette, rte de Pierrefeu, 83260 La Crau, tel. 04.94.48.28.38, fax 04.94.28.26.66 ☒
Ɏ ev. day except Sun. 9am–12 noon 1.30pm–6.30pm

DOM. DE LA NAVARRE

Cuvée Les Roches 1999★

■ 1.5 ha 6,000 50–69 F

This estate, founded in the 19th century by Saint Jean Bosco, is still run by the Salesian Brothers. In the 1999 vintage, it offers a wine with a strong colour and notes of summer berries (blackcurrants and raspberries). Its tannins are still young, and it will need cellaring for two to three years.
⊶ Fondation La Navarre, Cave du domaine, 3451, chem. de la Navarre, 83260 La Crau, tel. 04.94.66.04.08, fax 04.94.35.10.66 ☒ Ɏ by appt.

CLOS LA NEUVE Prestige 1998★★

5 ha 20,000 20–29 F

Not only is the 1998 Clos La Neuve agreeable to look at, it also offers an attractive range of aromas: violets and dark berries, mingled with a slight smoky note. On the palate, it reveals noticeable roundness and vinosity. A wine that should develop further over a period of two to five years.

EARL Dom. de la Neuve, 83910 Pourrières, tel. 04.94.78.17.02, fax 04.94.59.86.42
ev. day 9am–12 noon 2pm–7pm

DOM. DE L'ANGUEIROUN 1999★

2 ha 12,000 30–49 F

A change of hands: Eric Dumon has now taken over the property, and is clearly making a success of it, if this rosé is anything to go by. It is very fruity, with aromas of pears, peaches and lemons. A fresh, balanced, full-bodied wine that becomes rich and round on the palate.

Eric Dumon, 1077, chem. de l'Angueiroun, 83230 Bormes-les-Mimosas, tel. 04.94.71.11.39, fax 04.94.71.75.51
ev. day except Sun. 8am–12 noon 2pm–7pm

LES MAITRES VIGNERONS DE LA PRESQU'ILE DE SAINT-TROPEZ

Carte noire 1999★★

40 ha 150,000 30–49 F

It would be hard to explore Provence without encountering this label belonging to a group of producers already renowned for its abilities. The wine has a very pale colour, and explodes with fruity notes on the palate: pineapple, yellow peaches, apricots and mint. Round, soft, balanced and persistent, it will more than meet your expectations.

Maîtres vignerons de la Presqu'île de Saint-Tropez, 83580 Gassin, tel. 04.94.56.32.04, fax 04.94.43.42.57 ev. day except Sun. 9am–12 noon 3pm–7pm

DOM. DE LA SANGLIERE 1999★★★

2.5 ha 10,000 30–49 F

Located on the mimosa-lined road to the Fort de Brégançon, the La Sanglière estate enjoys a beautiful position for its 42 ha (104 acres) of seaside vineyard. This exceptional 1999 came close to winning a *coup de cœur*. Its success lies in the explosion of aromas it offers both on the nose and on the palate. Citrus fruit flavours are combined with a round, rich texture. A complete, highly elegant wine. The **1999 Cuvée Spéciale Rosée** merits a star for its brilliant rose-petal colour and expressive balance.

François et Rémy Devictor, Dom. de la Sanglière, 83230 Bormes-les-Mimosas, tel. 04.94.66.68.20, fax 04.94.66.60.72
ev. day except Sun. 8am–12 noon 2pm–7pm

DOM. DE LA SAUVEUSE 1999★★

5.45 ha 27,800 20–29 F

Of the various wines on offer at this estate, the jury singled out this one, which has a great deal of character. It is aromatic, complex, rich, elegant and long: all the signs of a great rosé. Another delightful wine from the same producer is the **1999 Plan de Loube Rosé**; it merits one star.

SCEA Dom. de la Sauveuse, chem. de la Sauveuse, 83390 Puget-Ville, tel. 04.94.28.59.60, fax 04.94.28.52.48
ev. day except Sat. Sun. 8am–12 noon 1pm–5.30pm
Salinas

DOM. DE LA SEIGNEURIE 1999

9.06 ha 58,800 30–49 F

Located in the former home of the Princes de Condé, the La Seigneurie estate offers a Côtes de Provence with purplish highlights. It is still young and shy on the nose, but its structure on the palate is good enough to suggest a fascinating development to come.

SCEA Dom. de la Seigneurie, rte de Cabasse, 83340 Flassans-sur-Issole, tel. 04.94.69.72.27, fax 04.94.59.62.71
by appt.

DOM. LA TOUR DES VIDAUX 1999★★

12 ha 9,000 30–49 F

The cellar is of very recent construction, but the vineyard has already been producing for 30 years. This wine delighted the jury with its purity, and with the contrast between the elegance and finesse of its aromas and its firmness and quality on the palate. An excellent wine that undoubtedly has a bright future.

Marlena et Paul Weindel, quartier Les Vidaux, 83390 Pierrefeu-du-Var, tel. 04.94.48.24.01, fax 04.94.48.24.02
ev. day except Sun. 8.30am–12 noon 2.30pm–6.30pm

DOM. LA TOURRAQUE 1999★★

1.5 ha 6,000 50–69 F

Everyone thinks of the Pampelonne beach at Ramatuelle – not Saint-Tropez – as an exotic spot. The same exoticism is apparent in this rosé, which has a charming colour and the fruitiest, most delicate aromas. On the palate, it is characterised by elegance, balance and length. The **1998 Rouge Vieilli en Barrique** merits a citation for its openness and aromatic complexity.

GAEC Brun Craveris, Dom. la Tourraque, 83350 Ramatuelle, tel. 04.94.79.25.95, fax 04.94.79.25.95
ev. day except Sun. 8am–12 noon 2pm–6pm

CH. DE L'AUMERADE

Cuvée Sully 1999★

3 ha 20,000 30–49 F

This estate is rich in history; its oil and wines were used at court, from the time of Henri IV to Louis-Philippe. Today it offers the visitor an attractive collection of *santons*

PROVENCE

(ornamental crib figures), as well as this pale white wine, whose nose is discreet but does release some citrus fruit aromas. It is balanced and fresh on the palate. The **1999 Cuvée Marie-Christine rouge** deserves to be commended for its range of soft fruit aromas and its suppleness.
SCEA des Dom. Fabre, Ch. de l'Aumerade, 83390 Pierrefeu, tel. 04.94.28.20.31, fax 04.94.48.23.09
by appt.

CH. DES LAUNES

Cuvée Prestige 1998*

1 ha 3,400 50–69 F

This little estate at the foot of the Massif des Maures embodies all the magic of Provence. Apart from the vines its trees include cork oak, bay, umbrella pine, eucalyptus and others, all of which flourish despite the arid, shaly soils and burning sun. Sitting under age-old plane trees, you will enjoy this oaky, toasty red wine with its slight note of vanilla, its rich flavours and its very balanced tannins.
Hans-Y. et Brigitte Handtmann, Ch. des Launes, R.D. 558 vers le Luc, 83680 La Garde-Freinet, tel. 04.94.60.01.95, fax 04.94.60.01.43 by appt.

DOM. LE BERCAIL

Cuvée de l'Opale 1999*

3 ha 11,000 30–49 F

The clear colour of this Opale is embellished by crystal highlights. It has a range of citrus and apricot aromas on the nose, and then opens up in the mouth with a sweetness and harmony that have much to do with Grenache. Also commended is a red wine, the **1998 Cuvée Confidence**, which is already so well-balanced that it can be drunk straight away.
Dom. le Bercail, 864, chem. de la Plaine, 83480 Puget-sur-Argens, tel. 04.94.19.54.09, fax 04.94.19.54.09
ev. day except Sat. Sun. 8am–4.30pm

CH. LES CROSTES 1999**

20 ha 50,000 30–49 F

The 1997 Cuvée Spéciale Rosée from the Château les Crostes was a fine vintage. This year the jury salutes the estate's classic rosé. It has an irreproachably luminous pale pink colour and releases a fine, intense, fruity aroma (passion-fruit), before confirming its elegance by its harmonious structure on the palate. A perfect alchemy of good raw material and expertise.
SARL H.L. Ch. les Crostes, 83510 Lorgues, tel. 04.94.73.98.40, fax 04.94.73.97.93, e-mail chateau.les.crostes@wanadoo.fr
ev. day except Sun. 10am–6.30pm

L'ESTANDON 1999*

n.c. n.c. 30–49 F

This is a wine of great charm with a fresh colour that reminds one of springtime, and aromas that suggest summer fruits: peaches, raspberries and blackcurrants. The overall impression as it develops is of a balanced long-lasting palate, still permeated by this basket of fruit flavours.
SA Bagnis et Fils, quartier des Aubregades, 83390 Cuers, tel. 04.94.48.50.08, fax 04.94.48.50.18
by appt.

L'ESTELLO Sextant d'Or 1999**

3 ha 18,000 30–49 F

The navigator-turned-winemaker's venture is still going remarkably well. This forthcoming rosé is delightful to look at and very fragrant – even explosive – on the nose. It is a well-made wine that can be drunk throughout the coming year. The **1999 Sextant d'Or Blanc** is more floral but just as harmonious, full and round. The jury also awarded it two stars.
Dom. de l'Estello, rte de Carces, 83510 Lorgues, tel. 04.94.73.22.22, fax 04.94.73.29.29, e-mail rtordjman@aol.fr
by appt.
R. Tordjmann

CH. MAIME 1999*

7.5 ha 35,000 30–49 F

In 1999, Château Maïme made an extremely attractive rosé. Don't let its very pale colour and as yet discreet nose deter you from discovering a lovely surprise on the palate: a real balance of acidity and sweetness. The **1999 Blanc** is a little shy on the nose, but merits a star for its elegant harmony.
SCEA Ch. Maïme, quartier La Maïme, 83460 Les Arcs-sur-Argens, tel. 04.94.47.41.66, fax 04.94.47.42.08, e-mail maime@terre-net.fr
ev. day 10am–12 noon 3pm–7pm
Sibran et Garcia

CH. MARAVENNE

Collection Privée 1999*

1.5 ha 6,600 30–49 F

Located at La Londe-les-Maures, a large summer resort with unspoiled beaches of wild beauty, the estate grows 70 ha (173 acres) of vines on schist soils. This pale salmon-pink rosé has an exquisite bouquet that leaves the taster with an impression of elegance. It is lifted by a slightly lemony, mineral note on the palate, and the balance is excellent.
EARL Gourjon, rte de Valcros, 83250 La Londe-les-Maures, tel. 04.94.66.80.20, fax 04.94.66.97.79 ev. day except Sun. 9am–12 noon 2pm–6pm

DOM. DE MARCHANDISE 1999★

◢ n.c. 100,000 ▮ 🌡 30–49 F

As sober and elegant as the label on the bottle, the Marchandise estate's rosé has such a pale colour that its highlights look positively grey. There is nothing sombre about what lies behind its appearance, however: an explosion of floral aromas, a silky texture in the mouth and a balanced finish.

🗝 GAEC Chauvier Frères, Dom. de Marchandise, 83520 Roquebrune-sur-Argens, tel. 04.94.45.42.91, fax 04.94.81.62.82 ☑ 🍷 ev. day 9am–7pm

CH. DE MAUPAGUE 1998★★

■ 9 ha 40,000 🛢 30–49 F

Located at the foot of the Montagne Sainte-Victoire, this property run by the Elie Sumeire family obtains low yields from soils composed of clay and sandstone scree: hence the name Maupague (literally, 'gives little'). Its 1998 red has a strong colour and a range of aromas varying from crystallised fruits to prunes, with a note of vanilla in between acquired from a year's maturation in oak. Supported on the palate by a solid structure, it returns to fruit and vanilla at the finish. A wine that should be kept for at least two years. The château's second red wine is the **1998 Cézanne** (20–29F), which is awarded a star. It contains 10% Grenache, and is just as well-made as the first.

🗝 Famille Elie Sumeire, Ch. de Maupague, 13114 Puyloubier, tel. 04.42.61.20.00, fax 04.42.61.20.01, e-mail sumeire@chateau-elie-sumeire.fr ☑ 🍷 by appt.

DOM. DE MAUVAN 1999★

◢ 3 ha 20,000 30–49 F

The Mauvan estate is one of those Sainte-Victoire vineyards whose wines are highly rated for their personality and typicity. This rosé has a pale colour very much in the Provençal style, and a spirited, lively character that stimulates the palate. After that, its youthful vigour is tempered by roundness as it takes on flavours of fresh fruits, peardrops and small flowers.

🗝 Gaëlle Maclou, Dom. de Mauvan, R.N. 7, 13114 Puyloubier, tel. 04.42.29.38.33, fax 04.42.29.38.33 ☑ 🍷 by appt.

CH. DE MAUVANNE Cuvée 2 1999★★

■ Cru clas. 10 ha 39,000 🛢 30–49 F

In the mid-20th century, this vast estate owned by Simone Berriau was a much-prized meeting-place for personalities from the world of art and literature. A few decades later, it has just changed hands and is undergoing a viticultural and oenological revival, enabling it to aim for the top of the market. Although this wine was still very young at the time of the tasting, the jury was full of enthusiasm for its aromatic complexity, its felicitous combination of fruity and chocolate notes, and above all its promise on the palate. A forthcoming, rich and concentrated wine that is already full of elegance.

🗝 SCA Ch. de Mauvanne, 2805, rte de Nice, 83400 Hyères, tel. 04.94.66.40.25, fax 04.94.66.46.29 ☑ 🍷 ev. day 9am–12.30pm 2pm–6.30pm

CH. DES MESCLANCES

Cuvée Saint-Honorat 1998★★

■ n.c. 6,000 🛢 30–49 F

It is hard not to succumb to the charm of this old Provençal house where a Roman cellar from the first century AD was discovered in 1996. Similarly, one would be hard pushed not to respond to the fullness and complexity of this dark red, deep and very spicy 1998 that has lovely aromas of pepper, the garrigue and black olives. Still a young wine, but one that will drink well with food.

🗝 Xavier de Villeneuve Bargemon, Les Mesclances, 83260 La Crau, tel. 04.94.66.75.07, fax 04.94.35.10.03, e-mail mesclances@yahoo.fr ☑ 🍷 ev. day except Sun. 9am–12 noon 2pm–6.30pm

CH. MINUTY Prestige 1999★

◢ Cru clas. 6 ha 40,000 ▮ 🌡 70–99 F

On the sandy, shaly soils of the Golfe de Saint-Tropez, Grenache and Tibouren are inimitable features of the landscape. This Prestige has all the attributes of a wine of character: a subtle, pale colour with a discreet touch of ochre, skilfully harmonised aromas of apricot, grapefruit, peach and pineapple, and good length on the palate, where it leaves an impression of richness and freshness.

🗝 Matton-Farnet, Ch. Minuty, 83580 Gassin, tel. 04.94.56.12.09, fax 04.94.56.18.38 ☑ 🍷 ev. day except Sun. 9am–12 noon 2pm–6.30pm

🗝 Matton

CH. MONTAGNE

Réserve du Coseigneur 1998★

■ 3 ha 15,000 🛢 30–49 F

The 'Coseigneur' is none other than François de Montagne, who held this title at Pierrefeu in 1780. Syrah is dominant in this 1998 wine with its strong, dark red colour. It has plenty of stuffing but is already quite well-integrated on the palate, which is underpinned by elegant aromas of dark berries, violets and chocolate. A harmonious wine that is ready for drinking now.

🗝 Henri Guérard, Ch. Montagne, 83390 Pierrefeu-du-Var, tel. 04.94.28.68.58, fax 04.94.28.51.28, e-mail guerard@club-internet.fr ☑ 🍷 ev. day 9am–6pm

PROVENCE

DOM. DE MONT REDON

Cuvée Louis Joseph 1999★★

■ 1.5 ha 6,000 ▮ 🌡 30–49 F

This dark red 1999 offers up a concentrated bouquet, embellished by aromas of violets and warmer notes (leather, spices). It is a powerful wine with a firm, multi-layered structure that, given time, will turn out to be a remarkable achievement.

🔑 Michel Torné, SCEA Dom. de Mont Redon, 2496, rte de Pierrefeu, 83260 La Crau, tel. 04.94.66.73.86, fax 04.94.57.82.12 ☑ 🍷 by appt.

CH. MOURESSE 1999★★

□ 2 ha 9,000 ▮ 🌡 20–29 F

The new team at the Château Mouresse has made its mark by producing a white Côtes de Provence with an elegantly floral nose. A few months of maturation on fine lees have given this wine mouthwatering ripeness and richness, with very fruity notes on the palate.

🔑 Michael Horst, Ch. Mouresse, 3353, chem. de Pied-de-Banc, 83550 Vidauban, tel. 04.94.73.12.38, fax 04.94.73.57.04, e-mail info@chateau-mouresse.com ☑ 🍷 ev. day except Sun. 8am–12 noon 2pm–7pm

DOM. DES MYRTES

Cuvée spéciale 1999

□ 2 ha 4,000 ▮ 🌡 30–49 F

On the Myrtes estate, vines rub shoulders with the flowers that are cultivated there as well. The Cuvée Spéciale reflects this: just taste it to discover a combination of flower fragrances and honey right through to the long finish. A good accompaniment to grilled fish, and even fromage frais.

🔑 GAEC Barbaroux, Dom. des Myrtes, 83250 La Londe-les-Maures, tel. 04.94.66.83.00, fax 04.94.66.65.73 ☑ 🍷 by appt.

MAS NEGREL CADENET 1998★

■ 2 ha n.c. 🛢 70–99 F

To the west of the appellation, the vignerons of Sainte-Victoire work hard to assert the identity and characteristics of their terroir. Their efforts are not in vain, as is proved by this wine with its very strong aromas of spices and liquorice, tinged with Syrah. It is a good reflection of the way in which the soils and climate of this area affect the balance on the palate of its red wines, making them both elegantly structured and harmonious, neither too heavy nor too dry.

🔑 Guy Négrel, EARL Mas de Cadenet, 13530 Trets, tel. 04.42.29.21.59, fax 04.42.61.32.09 ☑ 🍷 by appt.

CUVEE NOTRE-DAME 1999★

◪ 5 ha 30,000 ▮ 🌡 20–29 F

The La Londe-les-Maures cooperative is well represented by this 1999 rosé, which is destined for great things. It has a classic colour, and great presence on the palate: a combination of substance and freshness. A delightful wine, and quite a delicacy. The **1999 Château Pansard Rouge** deserves a citation for its fresh, strawberry-scented nose and its suppleness (30–49F).

🔑 Cave des vignerons Londais, 83250 La-Londe-les-Maures, tel. 04.94.66.80.23, fax 04.94.05.20.10 ☑ 🍷 by appt.

DOM. DES PEIRECEDES

Tradition 1999★

□ 1.9 ha 8,000 ▮ 🌡 20–29 F

This pale but brilliant Tradition has a great deal of presence on the nose with its intense, slightly spicy aromas. After a good attack on the palate, it continues to develop at some length. Try it with seafood. Also cited is the **1999 Rosé Tradition** (30–49F), a charming, expressive wine full of fruity notes.

🔑 Alain Baccino, SCEA Beauvais, Dom. des Peirecèdes, 83390 Pierrefeu, tel. 04.94.48.67.15, fax 04.94.48.52.30, e-mail alain.baccino@wanadoo.fr ☑ 🍷 by appt.

CH. DE POURCIEUX 1999★

◪ 6 ha 40,000 ▮ 🌡 30–49 F

This ancient vineyard, partly in the Var and partly in Bouches-du-Rhône, has for a long time been gracing the best tables of Aix-en-Provence with its wines. A judicious blend of Syrah and Grenache, this rosé has a clean, strong colour, with shades of raspberries. It also has a raspberry aroma on the nose, becoming full, round and rich on the palate.

🔑 Michel d'Espagnet, Ch. de Pourcieux, 83470 Pourcieux, tel. 04.94.59.78.90, fax 04.94.59.32.46, e-mail pourcieux@terre-net.fr ☑ 🍷 ev. day 9am–12 noon 2pm–6pm; Sat. Sun. by appt.

CH. REAL MARTIN 1999★

◪ 10 ha 40,000 ▮ 🌡 50–69 F

Located at the bottom of the Ribeirotte valley, the little medieval village of Le Val has some lovely surprises in store for the visitor. It is barely 5 km (3 miles) away from the vines of the Château Réal Martin, whose Côtes de Provence Rosé has been judged excellent. It has a pastel colour and floral nuances, and attacks the palate roundly before finishing on a somewhat more austere note. It would be good with seafood. The **1999 Rouge** is a warm wine, but is nonetheless well-balanced and deserves its citation (70–99F).

🔑 Jacques Clotilde, Ch. Réal Martin, rte de Barjols, 83143 Le Val, tel. 04.94.86.40.90, fax 04.94.86.32.23 ☑ 🍷 ev. day 8am–12 noon 2pm–6pm (7pm in summer); Sat. Sun. by appt.

CH. REILLANNE

Grande Réserve 1999★★

◪ n.c. 250,000 ▮ 🌡 30–49 F

Of the two rosé wines that were tasted, the Grande Réserve won the preference of the jury for its complex range of floral, spicy and mineral aromas. It has plenty of stuffing on the palate, where it combines finesse, balance and presence. 'This rosé has character, and would be just right for a night out in Saint-

Tropez', said one taster. One star is also awarded to the **1999 Prestige Rosé**.
🔑 Comte G. de Chevron Villette, Ch. Reillanne, rte de Saint-Tropez, 83340 Le Cannet-des-Maures, tel. 04.94.50.11.72, fax 04.94.47.92.06 ☑ Y ev. day except Sat. Sun. 8am–12 noon 2pm–5pm

CH. REQUIER

Cuvée spéciale 1999

□ 10 ha 10,000 30–49 F

The Château Réquier is ideally located in the commune of Cabasse, in the Issole valley. This fascinating little town contains numerous traces of Gallo-Roman history, and even of prehistoric times (the dolmen at La Gastée is the finest megalith in the region). The 1999 vintage has yielded a delightful result in this Cuvée Spéciale, which is almost transparent to look at. It has a very aromatic nose ranging from citrus fruits to notes of aniseed, but then develops more simply on the palate.
🔑 Ch. Réquier, La Plaine, 83340 Cabasse, tel. 04.94.80.25.72, fax 04.94.80.21.14 ☑
Y ev. day except Sun. 8.30am–5pm

RIMAURESQ 1999★

◪ Cru clas. 17 ha 94,000 50–69 F

A very pale rosé is the wine that the jury singled out from this producer. Silky and caressing at first, then a little livelier, it tantalises the tastebuds and leaves behind a pleasant memory. The **1999 Blanc** and the **1998 Rouge** are not without merit either, and each receive a citation.
🔑 SA Dom. de Rimauresq, rte de Notre-Dame-des-Anges, 83790 Pignans, tel. 04.94.48.80.45, fax 04.94.33.22.31 ☑
Y ev. day except Sat. Sun. 8am–12 noon 1.30pm–5.30pm
🔑 Wemyss Devel

CH. ROUBINE

Cuvée Philippe Riboud 1999★★

□ Cru clas. 1 ha 4,000 50–69 F

The town of Lorgues was for a long time the largest olive-growing commune in France, and the evidence of its past wealth shows in its architecture. Owned first by the Knights Templar and then by the order of Saint-Jean-de-Jérusalem, the Château Roubine has also seen the influence of great Provençal families. Today it tends 77 ha (190 acres) of vines, and in the 1999 vintage offers a wine (70% Clairette, 30% Sémillon) with complex aromas, the forthrightness and intensity of which contribute to its mouthwatering character. Good to drink with fish or white meat.
🔑 Ch. Roubine, R.D. 562, 83510 Lorgues, tel. 04.94.85.94.94, fax 04.94.85.94.95, e-mail riboud@toulon.pacwan.net ☑
Y by appt.
🔑 Valérie et Philippe Riboud

CH. DE ROUX 1999

■ 3.74 ha 26,000 30–49 F

This wine's strong colour is a sign that it is suitable for ageing. On a base of red berries and undergrowth, the tannins make themselves firmly felt. The slight hint of acidity should fade with time (in two or three years).
🔑 Ch. de Roux, 83340 Le Cannet-des-Maures, tel. 04.94.60.73.10, fax 04.94.60.89.79 ☑
Y ev. day 9am–12 noon 2pm–5.30pm
🔑 J.-G. Cupillard

DOM. SAINT-ANDRE DE FIGUIERE

Grande Cuvée Vieilles vignes 1998★

■ 2 ha 8,000 50–69 F

The estate now has a brand new bottling room, as well as a tasting cellar where visitors can try this Cuvée Vieilles Vignes (from 35-year-old vines), based on Mourvèdre and Carignan and matured in oak. Still a young wine, it has purplish highlights and takes on accents of fresh fruit, moss and fern. It is powerful and firm, and shows interesting depth. Leave it in the cellar for a year or two to soften.
🔑 Dom. Saint-André de Figuière, B.P. 47, 83250 La Londe-les-Maures, tel. 04.94.66.92.10, fax 04.94.35.04.46 ☑
Y ev. day 9am–12 noon 2pm–6pm
🔑 Alain Combard

DOM. DE SAINTE-CROIX

Rose Sharmeur 1999

◪ 10 ha 30,000 30–49 F

It is now 30 years since the Sainte-Croix estate was founded in Carcès, a commune rich in history where the houses are joined together around a fortress. It is also not far from the Cistercian abbey at Thoronet. Its rosé has a cherry colour and a strawberry flavour on the palate. The overall impression is perhaps a little wild, but certainly a cut above the average.
🔑 SCEA Pélépol Père et Fils, Dom. de Sainte-Croix, 83570 Carcès, tel. 04.94.04.56.51, fax 04.94.04.58.10 ☑
Y by appt.

M DE CH. SAINTE-MARGUERITE

Cuvée Saint-Pons 1999★★

◪ Cru clas. 2 ha 10,000 50–69 F

This estate was founded in 1929 by Monsieur Chevillon, the concert pianist. In 1977, it was bought by the Fondation de France, and the money raised by the sale was used to fund a music prize named after the founder. This *tête de cuvée*, made from a selection of

PROVENCE

45-year-old vines (mainly Grenache, with some Cinsault and Syrah) growing on a distinctive terroir, regularly lives up to its promise. In quite a difficult vintage, Jean-Pierre Fayard has managed to create a remarkable wine. It has just the right pale colour, finesse and elegance, but in addition shows concentration and complexity on the palate that produce a multitude of sensations. A great rosé.
Jean-Pierre Fayard, Ch. Sainte-Marguerite, B.P. 1, 83250 La Londe-les-Maures, tel. 04.94.00.44.44, fax 04.94.00.44.45, e-mail christine.fayard@wanadoo.fr ev. day except Sat. Sun. 8.30am–12.30pm 2pm–6pm

CLOITRE DE SAINTE-ROSELINE 1999*

25 ha 120,000 30–49 F

A visit to the Sainte-Roseline is a must, not only for its wines but also to see the abbey's chapel, parts of which date back to the 12th century. The greatest modern artists have left their stamp there: it has a mosaic by Chagall, stained glass windows by Bazaine, and a bronze bas-relief by Giacometti. The 1999 rosé is shy to start off with, perhaps owing to an unusual nose that shows traces of gunflint. Notwithstanding that, the palate is quick to display directness and balance. A wine that is ready to open now.
SCEA Ch. Sainte-Roseline, 83460 Les Arcs, tel. 04.94.99.50.30, fax 04.94.47.53.06 ev. day 8am–12 noon 14–6.30pm
Bernard Teillaud

DOM. DU SAINT-ESPRIT

Grande Cuvée 1998*

12 ha 10,000 30–49 F

A well-run vineyard, a balanced blend and maturation in barrel are the components of this 1998, which although a little discreet in its appearance is decidedly more expressive both on the nose and on the palate. Hints of spices and oak reinforce the impression of density, fullness, balance, but also of its youthfulness. A promising wine, which as yet is a little spirited. From the same producer, the **1998 Château Clarettes, Grande Cuvée Rouge** receives the same rating.
EARL Crocé Spinelli, Dom. des Clarettes, 83460 Les Arcs-sur-Argens, tel. 04.94.47.45.05, fax 04.94.73.30.73 by appt.

CH. DE SAINT-JULIEN D'AILLE

Cuvée des Rimbauds 1997*

51 ha 6,000 30–49 F

Hiding behind a dark, almost opaque appearance is a wine of spirited temperament and pleasant aromas of oak and chocolate. It is well-balanced but still young, and needs to age for a few months yet. A rich, promising Côtes de Provence.
Ch. de Saint-Julien d'Aille, n° 5480, R.D.48, 83550 Vidauban, tel. 04.94.73.02.89, fax 04.94.73.61.31 by appt.

DOM. DE SAINT-MARC 1998*

1.2 ha 8,000 50–69 F

A small production, coming essentially from old Syrah vines, has succeeded in highlighting the characteristics of the grape variety, both by its peppery, herbaceous and floral aromas and by its palate, which is more structured than sweet. The tannins are fine and silky, as is typical of wines produced on shaly soils.
Miyamoto, Dom. de Saint-Marc Leï Crottes, 83310 Cogolin, tel. 04.94.54.69.92, fax 04.94.54.01.41 by appt.

CH. SAINT-PIERRE

Cuvée Marie 1999*

2 ha 10,000 30–49 F

The Château Saint-Pierre grows its 36 ha (89 acres) of vines on a limestone-clay soil, 1.5 km (about a mile) from the medieval village of Les Arcs. Its pale Cuvée Marie has the scents of springtime, and a harmonious, balanced palate. A joyous combination that should not be forgotten when sitting on the terrace in the still-warm days of early autumn.
Jean-Philippe Victor, Ch. Saint-Pierre, Les Quatre-Chemins, 83460 Les Arcs, tel. 04.94.47.41.47, fax 04.94.73.34.73 by appt.

DOM. DE SAINT-QUINIS 1999*

20 ha 13,000 20–29 F

The jury was delighted by this very pale, extremely pleasant rosé. It is a well-balanced wine that releases aromas of exotic fruits, peaches and apricots. Also cited is the **1999 Rouge**, which deserves to be kept through the coming winter until its structure is a little less rigid.
Les Maîtres Vignerons de Gonfaron, Cave coopérative, 83590 Gonfaron, tel. 04.94.78.30.02, fax 04.94.78.27.33 ev. day 8am–12 noon 2pm–6pm

SAINT-ROCH-LES-VIGNES 1999*

60 ha 200,000 20–29 F

The wines of the Saint-Roch cooperative in Cuers are looked after by the *Maîtres Vignerons* of the Saint-Tropez Peninsula. This well-made, attractive rosé cannot fail to attract attention. It has a delicate colour verging on rose-petal, followed by an intense nose of citrus fruits, and then a truly fresh quality on the palate that enhances a long, slightly lemony finish.
Cave Saint-Roch-les-Vignes, rte de Nice, 83390 Cuers, tel. 04.94.28.60.60 Mon. Tue. Thu. Fri. 9am–12 noon 2pm–6pm

DOM. DE SAINT-SER

Hauts de Sainte-Victoire 1998*

3 ha 4,000 70–99 F

On the south side of the Sainte-Victoire, the heat that ripens the grapes is moderated by the high altitude of the terroirs. This unusual wine is a happy blend of Syrah and Cabernet matured in oak, giving it hints of fruit, olives and vanilla. An attractive, balanced and well-integrated wine. Also cited

from this producer is the very aromatic **1999 Rosé Prestige**, which has been awarded a star.
🗝 Dom. de Saint-Ser, R.D. 17, 13114 Puyloubier, tel. 04.42.66.30.81, fax 04.42.66.37.51, e-mail saintser@europost.org ☒ Y ev. day 10am–12 noon 2pm–6pm; groups by appt.
🗝 Pierlot

CH. DES SARRINS 1998★

■ 1.5 ha 5,000 50–69 F

According to legend a Saracen chief, killed in the eighth century at the time of the Arab invasions, is buried here in his golden armour. An armour of velvet protects this 1998, whose elegance on the nose can be measured by its peppery, spicy aromas and a slight hint of undergrowth. One taster predicts that it will be a good accompaniment to poultry. Also worthy of note is the **1999 Rosé**, which is very pale with grey highlights, nicely rounded on the palate, and full of citrus fruits on the nose (30–49F).
🗝 SCEV Dom. des Sarrins, 83510 Saint-Antonin-du-Var, tel. 04.94.73.26.93, fax 04.94.73.26.93 ☒

DOM. SIOUVETTE

Cuvée Marcel Galfard 1999★

□ 2 ha 10,000 30–49 F

A stone's throw away from Saint-Tropez, this old 18th-century country house grows 20 ha (49 acres) of vines on a silty soil. This wine is made from a happy blend of Sémillon and Vermentino, and has been fermented and matured in barrel. It fills the mouth and has good balance, as well as a complex range of toast, cinnamon, plum and crystallised fruit aromas, which – it must be said – do somewhat mask the influence of the terroir.
🗝 Sylvaine Sauron, Dom. Siouvette, R.N. 98, 83310 La Mole, tel. 04.94.49.57.13, fax 04.94.49.59.12 ☒ Y by appt.

DOM. DES THERMES 1999★★

◪ 1.78 ha 13,000 20–29 F

The Domaine des Thermes this year offers only its second vintage of rosé, but one that is fully in keeping with the promise that was shown by the first. There is a luminous note in its pale, salmon-pink colour, while the nose gives off a real sense of freshness with notes of citrus fruits and red berries. That impression is turned to good advantage on the palate, where the wine has sound quality and good length. From the same producer, the **1999 Blanc** deserves a star.
🗝 EARL Robert, Dom. des Thermes, 83340 Le Cannet-des-Maures, tel. 04.94.60.73.15, fax 04.94.60.73.15 ☒ Y by appt.

CH. TOUR SAINT-HONORE

Grande Réserve 1999★

◪ 6 ha 20,000 30–49 F

This Grande Réserve has a delightful, salmon-pink colour and a beautifully intense nose with notes of grapefruit and other citrus fruits. After a lively initial impression, it reveals a harmonious, highly aromatic quality on the palate. A white wine that is sharper, but just as fragrant, is the **1999 Olivier** (50–69F); it merits a star.
🗝 Serge Portal, Ch. Tour Saint-Honoré, R.D. 559, 83250 La Londe-les-Maures, tel. 04.94.66.98.22, fax 04.94.66.52.12 ☒ Y by appt.

DOM. TURENNE

Cuvée Bastien 1999★

■ 5 ha 20,000 50–69 F

On this limestone-clay terroir between Pierrefeu and Cuers, the red wines are at their very best. Witness this cuvée, based on Mourvèdre, which has been matured in oak for ten months. It has a beautiful, deep ruby colour, and benefits from well-sculpted tannins that are surrounded by an intensely fruity structure. The overall impression is one of power: a wine that will age without mishap for four to five years.
🗝 Philippe Benezet, Dom. Turenne, 83390 Cuers, tel. 04.94.48.68.77, fax 04.94.28.57.13 ☒ Y ev. day except Sun. 8am–12 noon 2pm–6pm

CH. VANNIERES 1998★★

■ 6 ha 18,000 70–99 F

This estate, whose castle dates back to the 16th century, is well-known for its wines in the Bandol AOC, but it also produces a Côtes de Provence whose vinification in red wine vats is inspired by Bordeaux techniques. With the Mourvèdre in it making itself felt, the wine is powerful, sustained and complex, with aromas of truffles, fruit and spices. It is very tannic, and although already impressive, deserves to be kept for a little while until it asserts its richness to the full.
🗝 Ch. Vannières, 83740 La Cadière-d'Azur, tel. 04.94.90.08.08, fax 04.94.90.15.98 ☒ Y ev. day except Sun. 8am–12 noon 2pm–6pm
🗝 Boisseaux

CH. DE VAUCOULEURS 1999★

◪ 4 ha 20,000 30–49 F

This rosé made from Grenache and Syrah is both discreet and substantial. Pale in colour and floral on the nose, and imbued with finesse and elegance, it has sufficient quality and length to delight both now and in the future.
🗝 P. Le Bigot, Ch. de Vaucouleurs, R.N. 7, 83480 Puget-sur-Argens, tel. 04.94.45.20.27, fax 04.94.45.20.27 ☒ Y ev. day except Sun. 10am–12 noon 2pm–6pm; cl. Nov.

CH. VEREZ 1999★

◪ 21 ha 20,000 30–49 F

A luminous pale pink with fuchsia highlights, this rosé mingles flowers and fruit in a range of aromas both deep and intense. It is slightly sweet on entry, and then develops greater liveliness on the palate. A lovely wine to drink as an apéritif or with brochettes.

⊶ Ch. Verez, Le Grand Pré, 83550 Vidauban, tel. 04.94.73.69.90, fax 04.94.73.55.84, e-mail verez@wanadoo.fr ☑
Ｙ ev. day except Sun. 9am–7pm

VIEUX CHATEAU D'ASTROS

Cuvée du Commandeur 1999★★

◪ n.c. n.c. 30–49 F

Whether in terms of colour, aromas or flavours, some rosés are more expressive than others. This one did not fail to inspire the jury, which was particularly struck by its pastel shades and notes of flowers, citrus fruits, spices and bergamot orange. More than its many aromas, however, it was the pleasure it gave on a vigorous palate balanced between finesse, directness and character that earned it its two stars.

⊶ Christian Maurel, Vieux Château d'Astros, rte de Lorgues, 83550 Vidauban, tel. 04.94.73.02.56, fax 04.94.73.66.27 ☑
Ｙ ev. day except Sun. 8.30am–12.30pm 2pm–6pm

DOM. DES VINGTINIERES

1999★

◪ 3.5 ha 18,000 30–49 F

From the top of its rocky peak, some 127 m (415 feet) high, the Vieux Cannet affords a beautiful view of the Massif des Maures. Four km (two-and-a-half miles) away from there, the Vingtinières estate keeps its 26 ha (64 acres) of vines. Grown on limestone-clay soil, Grenache and Cinsault have contributed to the floral and fruity complexity of this rosé. A slightly sweet, but balanced wine that can be drunk straight away, perhaps with fillets of red mullet.

⊶ Patrice Moreux, Dom. des Vingtinières, rte de Saint-Tropez, 83340 Le Cannet-des-Maures, tel. 04.94.99.81.12, fax 04.94.99.81.12 ☑ Ｙ by appt.

Cassis

Accessible only over relatively high passes from Marseilles or Toulon, and tucked away at the foot of the highest cliffs in France, lies Cassis with its inlets, its anchovies and a particular fountain which, the inhabitants claim, makes their town more remarkable than Paris . . . However, there is also a vineyard over which powerful abbeys disputed ownership in the 11th century, finally calling upon the Pope to arbitrate. Nowadays, the vineyard covers about 175 ha (432 acres), of which 123 ha (304 acres) are planted with white varieties. The wines are red and rosé but white above all. Mistral said of the whites that he smelled rosemary, heather and myrtle. Don't expect to find important vintages: as soon as they are made they are mostly consumed locally with bouillabaisse, grilled fish and shellfish.

CLOS D'ALBIZZI

☐ 11 ha 40,000 30–49 F

This 13-ha (32-acre) estate has a slightly Italian feel, which is a reminder that the Albizzi family originally came from Florence, before moving to the Cassis area at the beginning of the 15th century. The jury singled out this rounded wine that is simple but openly expressive on the palate. It has an enjoyable nose of fresh fruits such as pineapple and banana, mingled with toast and brioche.

⊶ François Dumon, Clos d'Albizzi, 13260 Cassis, tel. 04.42.01.11.43 ☑ Ｙ by appt.

DOM. DU BAGNOL

Marquis de Fesques 1999

☐ 3.5 ha 20,000 30–49 F

This wine is named after the man who founded the du Bagnol estate in the second half of the 19th century. The spell is cast as soon as one looks at its pale yellow-gold colour. On the palate, it develops subtle notes of pâtisserie that are just as delicate as its appearance.

⊶ Dom. du Bagnol, 12, av. de Provence, 13260 Cassis, tel. 04.42.01.78.05, fax 04.42.01.11.22, e-mail jeanlouisgeno@aol.fr ☑ Ｙ ev. day except Sun. 10am–12.30pm 2.30pm–6.30pm
⊶ Genovesi

DOM. CAILLOL 1999★

◪ 3 ha 17,000 30–49 F

In the 1999 vintage, it is the rosé from this estate that has pride of place, winning one star. It has a pink colour with very fetching deep purple highlights, and is surrounded by notes of red berries – strawberries and raspberries – that linger on to create a delicious, well-balanced overall impression.

⊶ Caillol Frères, 11, chem. du Bérard, 13260 Cassis, tel. 04.42.01.05.35, fax 04.42.01.31.59 ☑ Ｙ ev. day except Sun. 8am–12 noon 2pm–6.30pm; groups by appt.

CH. DE FONTBLANCHE 1999

☐ 10 ha 40,000 50–69 F

There once lived a man who revived the language of the Provençal poets and the wines of Cassis: Emile Bodin, who in 1890 founded this vineyard, which now covers about 40 ha (99 acres). Here, the Château de Fontblanche offers a light yellow wine with mixed aromas of dried fruit, verbena, linden flower and mint. A round, rich wine.

SCEA Bontoux-Bodin Père et Fils, Ch. [de] Fontblanche, 13260 Cassis, [te]l. 04.42.01.00.11, fax 04.42.01.32.11 ✉ Y [e]v. day except Sun. 9am–12 noon 3pm–6pm

[C]H. DE FONTCREUSE
[C]uvée F 1998★★

□	13.99 ha	60,000	30–49 F

This 17th-century château owes its name to [a] fountain dug out from the rock. Its Cassis [B]lanc has won aclaim time and again (notably [i]n 1995 and 1996). In the 1998 vintage, its [g]old-braided colour creates a beautifully ele[g]ant effect. It has a minty quality, and a euca[l]yptus aroma that gradually gives way to [g]rilled almonds. The wine asserts itself in a [s]tructured, rich and generous style, before [t]aking on an even richer note of honey. It is [s]till fresh on the finish, which is all to the [g]ood. A wine to drink with food. The **1999 [C]uvée F Rosée** is a more discreet wine that [m]ingles fruits and flowers within a silky, bal[a]nced structure. It is awarded one star.

SA J.-F. Brando, Ch. de Fontcreuse, 13, [rou]te de La Ciotat, 13260 Cassis, [t]el. 04.42.01.71.09, fax 04.42.01.32.64 ✉ Y ev. day except Sat. Sun. 8am–12 noon [2]pm–5.30pm

[D]OM. LA FERME BLANCHE 1997

■	3 ha	9,000	50–69 F

A small production of a red wine that [m]akes for a intriguing tasting. It has a very [d]eep colour, and needs a certain amount of [a]ir contact before it reveals its aromatic range, [i]n which musky notes mingle with the sweet[n]ess of morello cherries in brandy. The struc[t]ure is balanced and supple.

Dom. de la Ferme Blanche, R.N. 559, [1]3260 Cassis, tel. 04.42.01.00.74, [f]ax 04.42.01.73.94 ✉ Y ev. day 9am–7pm

F. Paret

DOM. DU PATERNEL 1999

◢	6 ha	30,000	50–69 F

Ever since its foundation in 1951, this [e]state has aimed its produce at the restaurant [m]arket. This rosé will be ideal to drink with [P]rovençal dishes. It is marked by floral scents, [a]nd has a delightful simplicity as well as liveli[n]ess and exemplary balance throughout.

Jean-Pierre Santini, Dom. du Paternel, [1]1, rte Pierre-Imbert, 13260 Cassis, [t]el. 04.42.01.76.50, fax 04.42.01.09.54 ✉ Y ev. day except Sun. 10am–12 noon 2pm–[6]pm

DOM. DES QUATRE-VENTS 1999★

□	4 ha	20,000	30–49 F

In 1985, Alain de Montillet took over this estate, which has more than eight ha (20 acres) of limestone-clay soils. In the 1999 vintage his Cassis Blanc is delightfully floral, with a nose accentuated by slight hints of menthol and lemon. It has a pale colour with green highlights, and the overall impression is springlike and charming, despite a rather austere finish.

Alain de Montillet, Dom. des Quatre-Vents, 13260 Cassis, tel. 04.42.01.88.10 ✉ Y ev. day except Sat. Sun. 8am–12 noon 2pm–6pm

CLOS SAINTE-MAGDELEINE 1999★

□	11 ha	40,000	50–69 F

This Cassis has a straw-yellow colour, but there can be no doubt about its maturity: it is characterised by a rounded first impression, followed by plenty of substance and moderate power on the palate. The aromatic range goes from ripe fruit to toast, releasing touches of verbena and linden flowers. A wine to be enjoyed with grilled fish.

Sack-Zafiropulo, Clos Sainte-Magdeleine, av. du Revestel, 13260 Cassis, tel. 04.42.01.70.28, fax 04.42.01.15.51 ✉ Y by appt.

CLOS VAL BRUYERE 1998★

□	7 ha	25,000	50–69 F

This Cassis has retained some of its youth in its range of floral aromas. Rich and full, it expresses its maturity, however, on the palate through flavours of ripe and crystallised fruits.

GAEC Ch. Barbanau, Hameau de Roquefort, 13830 Roquefort-la-Bédoule, tel. 04.42.73.14.60, fax 04.42.73.17.85, e-mail barbanau@aol.com ✉ Y ev. day except Sun. 10am–12 noon 3pm–6pm

Cerciello

PROVENCE

Bellet

Only the privileged few know this minute vineyard, 32 ha (79 acres), on the heights above Nice, with a modest production (about 800 hl (21,120 gal)) of wines almost impossible to find anywhere other than in Nice itself. Its original, aromatic whites derive from the high-class Rolle vine variety and the Chardonnay (which is happy this far south when planted facing north and sufficiently high up). The rosés are supple and fresh, the reds sumptuous: two local varieties, the Fuella and the Braquet, give them their highly individual character. They form an entirely appropriate accompaniment to the rich, very distinctive cuisine of Nice, with dishes such as chard pie, baked vegetables, estoficada (a local stew), tripe and pissaladière, and onion tart.

CH. DE BELLET Cuvée Baron G 1998*

■ n.c. n.c. 100–149 F

The ancient towers of the Château de Bellet have regained their deep red colour, thanks to the work of master fresco painter Guy Ceppa. The same shade can also be found in this strong, dark red Bellet. Although it opens tentatively with notes of smoke and fruit in brandy, the wine displays a concentrated palate based on tannins that are firm but already attractive. Its dominant aromas of spices and oak will become gentler in five to seven years' time.

Ghislain de Charnacé, Ch. de Bellet, 440, chem. de Saquier, 06200 Nice, tel. 04.93.37.81.57, fax 04.93.37.93.83

CLOT DOU BAILE 1999**

□ 0.9 ha 3,200 70–99 F

The Clot dóu Baile used to be just a hillside lying fallow, but has now become a handsome estate growing six ha (15 acres) of vines on mixed soils. It offers a radiant young Bellet with a basket of exuberant fruit aromas (peaches and exotic fruits) that contribute to the complexity of this round, fresh wine. It is assured of a bright future, and it will be interesting to see how it has developed in three to five years' time.

SCEA Clot Dou Baile, 277, chem. de Saquier, Saint-Roman-de-Bellet, 06200 Nice, tel. 04.93.29.85.87, fax 04.93.29.85.87 by appt.

COLLET DE BOVIS 1999

□ 0.25 ha 1,000 50–69 F

As part of the 'Art et Vigne' campaign, the estate is offering a venue for the second time to painters of the Nice school. It is also a good opportunity to discover this 1999. Oak is omnipresent, but the wine manages nonetheless to carve its identity on the palate, where there is a combination of roundness and freshness, in addition to a slight hint of citrus fruits. As a result, although it is balanced and rich, it will need to be kept for at least three years until it settles down enough to be enjoyed at its best.

Jean Spizzo, Dom. du Fogolar, 370, chem. de Crémat, 06200 Nice, tel. 04.93.37.82.52, fax 04.93.37.82.52, e-mail gianni.spizzo@wanadoo.fr
ev. day 8.30am–7pm

COLLET DE ROUSTAN 1998*

□ 0.35 ha 1,300

The Collet de Roustan estate was founde in 1992. Its Rolle and Chardonnay vine grown on mixed soils, were therefore in the seventh year when they produced this pa Bellet with green highlights. Although som what lacking in concentration, it has an aro matic profile very much in keeping with t vintage: mineral and slightly floral (wallflov ers and broom blossom). It is round on t palate, with spicy flavours and good length.

Blanc-Gonnet, 30, chem. de la Pouncia, 06200 Nice, tel. 04.93.37.89.84, fax 04.93.37.89.84
ev. day 8am–12 noon 13–6pm

MAX GILLI 1998

■ 0.5 ha 2,000 50–69

After a confident entry on the palate, th deep, dark red wine develops with appreciab roundness, on a base of fine, elegant tannin Its aromas are partly of berries shadin towards jam, with toasty notes. A wine fo drinking now.

Gilli, chem. de Saint-Roman, 06200 Nice, tel. 04.93.37.82.71, fax 04.93.37.82.71 by appt.

LES COTEAUX DE BELLET 1999*

□ 1.95 ha 9,300 70–99

This pale yellow 1999 with green highlight thoroughly deserves its star. It develops pow erfully on the palate, while releasing fresh aro matic notes (citrus fruit) mingled with ver fine oak. A well-balanced wine that is repre sentative of its appellation and is assured of bright future.

SCEA Les Coteaux de Bellet, 325, chem de Saquier, 06200 Nice, tel. 04.93.29.92.99, fax 04.93.18.10.99 by appt.
Hélène Calviera

CLOS SAINT-VINCENT 1999

□ 0.5 ha 2,500 70–99

Made exclusively from Rolle, this wine ha a complex nose of citrus fruits and flora notes. A range of that sort lends a touch o gaiety to a palate still marked by the influenc of oak-ageing (12 months), and by a hottis finish. It will benefit from being kept for on or two years.

Joseph Sergi et Roland Sicardi, Collet des Fourniers, Saint-Roman-de-Bellet, 06200 Nice, tel. 04.92.15.12.69, fax 04.92.15.12.69 by appt.

Bandol

A fine wine produced, not in Bandol itself, but on the sun-scorched terraces of the urrounding villages, which cover an area of 1,300 ha (3,211 acres) and produced 53,440 hl (1,410,816 gal) in 1999. Bandol wines are white, rosé or red. The reds are very tannic and full-bodied, qualities contributed by the Mourvèdre variety, which makes up more than half the proportions of grapes used. This powerful wine, with its subtle aromas of pepper, cinnamon, vanilla and black cherry, is the perfect accompaniment to venison and red meats. It can be kept for a long time.

DOM. DES BAGUIERS 1997*

1.6 ha 6,000 50–69 F

Baguier is the Provençal name for sweet bay, an aromatic plant much prized in the region. This 25-ha (62-acre) estate located at the pretty medieval village of Le Castellet offers a substantial 1997 red, which although a little rustic has lovely aromas of berries, spices and oak. On the palate, it is forthright, expressive and firmly structured. An excellent accompaniment to autumn dishes such as civet or wild boar casseroled with Herbes de Provence.

GAEC Jourdan, Dom. des Baguiers, 83330 Le Plan-du-Castellet, tel. 04.94.90.41.87, fax 04.94.90.41.87

Y by appt.

DOM. DU CAGUELOUP 1999**

5.7 ha 24,000 50–69 F

Located at Saint-Cyr-sur-Mer, the Cagueloup estate is a pillar of the appellation. The star attraction is an elegant, eminent rosé with a soft, pale colour and a fine range of citrus fruit aromas. It is both round and full on the palate, and echoes the nose by releasing the same fruity flavours. The **1999 Bandol Blanc** is awarded one star for its fresh mineral quality and good balance.

SCEA Dom. de Cagueloup, quartier Cagueloup, 83270 Saint-Cyr-sur-Mer, tel. 04.94.26.15.70, fax 04.94.26.54.09

Y by appt.

CH. DE CASTILLON 1998**

1.5 ha 5,000 50–69 F

René de Saqui de Sannes is a direct descendant of the lords of Castellet who founded this property 500 years ago, at the time of King René. This wine harbours all the potential of the terroir and local tradition in its fragrances. It has herbaceous aromas of the garrigue, myrtle, dark berries and pepper, as well as deeper scents of leather, fur and toast. Very dense, with tannins that are true to type, this wine is a fine embodiment of a traditional Bandol for long maturing.

René de Saqui de Sannes, Dom. de Castillon, 83330 Sainte-Anne-du-Castellet, tel. 04.94.32.66.74, fax 04.94.32.67.36

Y Thu. Fri. Sat. 8am–7pm

DOM. DE FONT-VIVE 1999*

6.5 ha 26,000 50–69 F

Philippe Dray founded his vineyard right at the beginning of the 1990s in the commune of Beausset, a village that grew up on the plain in the 16th century. His Bandol Rosé is in no way extravagant, but is nonetheless well-made. Delightfully supple, it develops progressively through aromas of citrus fruits and white flowers. An equally good wine is the **1999 blanc**, which has fruity aromas, and is fresh and well-structured.

Philippe Dray, quartier Val-d'Arenc, 83330 Le Beausset, tel. 04.94.98.60.06, fax 04.94.98.65.31 Y by appt.

DOM. DE FREGATE 1998*

3.5 ha 13,000 50–69 F

The estate shares its beautiful location with a golf course that is both attractive to look at and difficult to play. In the land of the vine and the olive tree, so much green grass is an oddity . . . Much more typical of the region is this 1998 with its youthful aromas of cherries, other stone fruits, liquorice and pepper. The palate is pleasant, rich and well-structured by elegant, balanced tannins. Already an attractive wine, but with the potential to age for several years yet.

Dom. de Frégate, rte de Bandol, 83270 Saint-Cyr-sur-Mer, tel. 04.94.32.57.57, fax 04.94.32.24.22 Y by appt.

PROVENCE

CH. JEAN-PIERRE GAUSSEN 1998★

■ 3 ha 13,300 70–99 F

This Bandol has a deep, almost purple colour, and releases a fruity bouquet with notes of bilberries and morello cherries. Once exposed to air, it becomes flavourful on the palate: its tannic density asserts itself in an aromatic context where liquorice is more dominant, expressive of two years' cask maturation. A wine that will certainly keep a long time, just as its label states.

Jean-Pierre Gaussen, La Noblesse, 1585, chem. de l'Argile, B.P. 23, 83740 La Cadière-d'Azur, tel. 04.94.98.75.54, fax 04.94.98.65.34 by appt.

LA BASTIDE BLANCHE 1998★★

■ 10 ha 50,000 50–69 F

In vintage after vintage for ten years, Michel Bronzo has maintained a high level of quality with his red Bandols. This one is typical of 1998 in that it is still very reserved and a little secretive, but has the potential to develop fascinatingly over the next few years.

EARL Bronzo, 367, rte des Oratoires, 83330 Sainte-Anne-du-Castellet, tel. 04.94.32.63.20, fax 04.94.32.74.34
by appt.

DOM. DE LA BEGUDE 1999★

◪ 1.5 ha 6,000 50–69 F

The continued success of this wine shows that the Bordelais school – Guillaume Tari made his debut in the Grands Crus of Bordeaux – adapts well to Provence and to Mourvèdre, which dominates this rosé with its very herbaceous notes of the garrigue and the peel of citrus fruits. Dense and substantial on the palate, it is an excellent example of its type.

Guillaume Tari, Dom. de La Bégude, 83330 Le Camp-du-Castellet, tel. 04.42.08.92.34, fax 04.42.08.27.02, e-mail domaines.tari@wanadoo.fr
by appt.

DOM. LAFRAN-VEYROLLES 1998★

■ 3 ha 6,000 70–99 F

This estate, which dates back to the 17th century, is located on the slopes of Veyrolles. The wine it submitted is a very characteristic Bandol, taking its time to reveal its nature. The palate has a range of rich aromas, among which are black fruits, leather and a very typical note of resin. This elegant and robust wine makes for pleasant drinking now, but equally has good ageing potential.

Mme Jouve-Férec, Dom. Lafran-Veyrolles, 2115, rte de l'Argile, 83740 La Cadière-d'Azur, tel. 04.94.90.13.37, fax 04.94.90.11.18 by appt.

DOM. DE LA LAIDIERE 1998★★

■ 3 ha 14,000 70–99 F

The sandy clay soils and orientation of the La Laidière estate produce wines that are highly characteristic of the appellation and the 1998 red has been awarded two stars. Its aromatic character is of fresh, slightly oak grapes. The first impression on the palate full and concentrated, the firm, straightfo ward tannins making this a wine that already attractive, but also has good keepin quality. The **1998 Blanc** is also delightful, an has been awarded one star.

SCEA Estienne, Dom. de La Laidière, 426, chem. de Font-Vive, 83330 Sainte-Anne-d'Evenos, tel. 04.94.90.35.29, fax 04.94.90.38.05, e-mail freddy-estienne@laidiere.com
ev. day except Sun. 9.30am–12 noon 1.30pm–6pm; Sat. by appt.

LA ROQUE Les Baumes 1999★

□ 6 ha 32,000 30–49 F

La Roque undoubtedly represents the larg est group of wine-growers in the appellatior Concerned to promote awareness of thei efforts to improve quality, the cellar offer wines made from grapes grown on its bes plots. Their best white is a Clairette that ha aromas of yellow flowers and peaches, and refreshing and slightly acid palate. The **199 Rosé** was appreciated for its lovely structure for which it too gains one star.

Cave du Moulin de La Roque, quartier Vallon, B.P. 26, 83740 La Cadière-d'Azur, tel. 04.94.90.10.39, fax 04.94.90.08.11
ev. day except Sun. 8am–12 noon 1.30pm–5.30pm

MAS DE LA ROUVIERE 1998★★

■ 4 ha 15,000 70–99 F

The small farmhouse of La Rouvière form part of the Bunan family estates. This wine i made from the oldest vines on the property and is an unusual blend of grapes. The fla vours explode on the palate: full, supple, pow erful, elegant are the best words to describe the flavour. The nose is no less excellent, being particularly noteworthy for its complexity. I had members of the jury putting down thei pens to express their enthusiasm for this wine verbally.

Domaines Bunan, B.P. 17, 83740 La Cadière-d'Azur, tel. 04.94.98.58.98, fax 04.94.98.60.05 by appt.

DOM. LA SUFFRENE Cuvée Les Lauves 1998★

■ 2 ha 8,000 70–99 F

The estate's oldest vines are reserved for this vintage. Certain of them are well over 50

ears old. The wine they have yielded is con-
ntrated and deeply aromatic, with notes of
ices, pepper, sandalwood and coffee. The
nnins of this 1998 are still young, indicating
at it will be at its best in three to four years'
me.

Cédric Gravier, Dom. la Suffrene, 1066,
nem. de Cuges, 83740 La Cadière-d'Azur,
l. 04.94.90.09.23, fax 04.94.90.02.21
ev. day except Sun. 8.30am–12 noon
pm–6.30pm; Sat. 8.30am–12 noon

DOM. DE LA TOUR DU BON 1999★★

1.2 ha 4,000 50–69 F

This 1999 wine is dominated by the Clairette variety, which gives it a floral character with toasty notes. It is both fresh and well-integrated on the palate, as well as generous and elegant, fine and long. Above all, it leaves a sensation of youthful freshness and an aftertaste of divine nectar. A gorgeous Bandol.

Dom. de La Tour du Bon, Le Brûlat-du-Castellet, 83330 Le Brûlat, tel. 04.94.32.61.62, fax 04.94.32.71.69, e-mail tourdubon@aol.com by appt.

Hocquard

DOM. DE LA VIVONNE 1998★

■ n.c. n.c. 50–69 F

The intense garnet colour of this wine is enhanced by deep purple highlights. Its complex bouquet is in harmony with the flavourful palate, whose dense tannins will soften before too long. A good wine to lay down for five years.

EARL Walter Gilpin, 3345, montée du Château, 83330 Le Castellet, tel. 04.94.98.70.09, fax 04.94.90.59.98 by appt.

LE GALANTIN 1998

■ n.c. 55,000 50–69 F

This Galantin is made from 95% Mourvèdre grapes. It seems shy at first, but when left to breathe reveals a surprising nose, emphasising aromas of liquorice. The supple, powerful palate is well-balanced and leaves a long-lasting impression of sweetness.

Famille Achille Pascal, Dom. Le Galantin, 690, chem. Le Galantin, 83330 Le Plan-du-Castellet, tel. 04.94.98.75.94, fax 04.94.90.29.55, e-mail galantin@caves-particulieres.com by appt.

DOM. LES LUQUETTES 1997

■ 4 ha 2,500 50–69 F

The 1997 vintage is the first bottling Elisabeth Lafourcade made on this 12-ha (30-acre) family estate, which is also devoted to raising ewes. It is a well-structured wine that makes for pleasant tasting. The nose marries red fruits, truffles and undergrowth, while the palate finishes on more liquoricey, peppery notes. If allowed to mature for three to five years, this Bandol would go very well with *boeuf en daube*.

Dom. Les Luquettes, 20, chem. des Luquettes, 83740 La Cadière-d'Azur, tel.04.94.90.02.59, fax 04.94.98.31.95 ev. day 8am–12 noon 2pm–8pm

E. Lafourcade

DOM. DE L'HERMITAGE 1998★

■ 11.3 ha 50,000 50–69 F

This place has a short, yet already very rich history. Thirty years ago, the estate lay fallow. Since then, after much toil and effort, the personality of its wines has made its mark and established the estate in the appellation. The 1998 red found favour with the jury. The nose is full of fresh fruits, tobacco and spices. Though young, it is nevertheless very subtle and well-balanced, and will reach maturity in two to three years' time.

SCEA Gérard Duffort, Le Rouve, B.P. 41, 83330 Le Beausset, tel. 04.94.98.71.31, fax 04.94.90.44.87 ev. day except Sun. 9am–12 noon 2pm–6pm; Sat. 8am–12 noon

DOM. DE L'OLIVETTE 1998★★

■ n.c. n.c. 50–69 F

During the 1970s, the Olivette estate, which was established in 1790, underwent total restructuring, starting from scratch again with only three ha (seven acres) of vines. Thirty years later, the vinyard comprises some 55 ha (136 acres). The 1998 vintage has a garnet colour, and a still somewhat restrained nose with the emphasis upon red fruits (cherry, blackcurrant), undergrowth and liquorice. Its intensity and structure testify to the influence of the Mourvèdre variety. This is a wine with lots of personality, which will need five years' cellaring. The **1999 Rosé** is a generous, aromatic wine that gains one star; the **1999 Blanc** (70–99F) merits citation for flavours that fully reflect the ripeness of the grapes.

SCEA Dumoutier, Dom. de L'Olivette, 83330 Le Castellet, tel. 04.94.98.58.85, fax 04.94.32.68.43 ev. day except Sat. Sun. 8am–12 noon 2pm–6pm

DOM. MAZET DE CASSAN 1999★

13 ha 65,000 50–69 F

This is a very intense, fruity rosé evocative of peaches and grapefruit. It has presence on the palate and good balance. A perfect accompaniment for grilled fish.

Monique Barthès, chem. du Val-d'Arenc, 83330 Le Beausset, tel. 04.94.98.60.06, fax 04.94.98.65.31 by appt.

MOULIN DES COSTES 1998★★

■ 12 ha 50,000 70–99 F

It has been a long time since the mill here last turned. The premises are now a vast cellar, a combination of stainless steel, iron and wood. There is no shortage of quality labels here either. One such is this red Bandol, the nose of which shows complex aromas of liquorice, cocoa and black fruits. It is a dense, elegant and attractive wine, though still somewhat reticent. The **Blanc** and **1999 Rosé** have each garnered one star.

PROVENCE

🔑 Domaines Bunan, B.P. 17, 83740 La Cadière-d'Azur, tel. 04.94.98.58.98, fax 04.94.98.60.05 ☑ Y by appt.

DOM. DU PEY-NEUF 1999★★

□ 1 ha 4,000 50–69 F

Though small in size, this estate produces some remarkable wines. This pale 1999 exhibits a truly exotic array of aromas that help to soften the slightly bitter finish. A well-balanced Bandol to drink as an apéritif, with a sauced fish dish, or with goat's cheese. The **1998 Rouge**, awarded one star, is best decanted in order to release its aromas and flavours.

🔑 Guy Arnaud, Dom. du Pey-Neuf, 367, rte de Sainte-Anne, 83740 La Cadière-d'Azur, tel. 04.94.90.14.55, fax 04.94.26.13.89 ☑ Y by appt.

CH. DE PIBARNON 1998★★

■ 25 ha 80,000 100–149 F

Representing the Saint-Victor family's 20th year of wine-making, this wine amply justifies the estate's international reputation. This 1998 is a rich wine, and has complex aromas (black fruits, morello cherries, liquorice) and a particularly well-balanced palate characterised by mouth-filling intensity, length, harmony and subtlety. A Bandol to keep.

🔑 Eric de Saint-Victor, 410, chem. la Croix-des-Signaux, 83740 La Cadière-d'Azur, tel. 04.94.90.12.73, fax 04.94.90.12.98 ☑ Y by appt.

DOM. ROCHE REDONNE

Cuvée La Lyre 1999

◪ 4 ha 18,000 50–69 F

A special blend of old Cinsault and Mourvèdre has produced this very expressive wine, noteworthy for its forthcoming aromas of citrus and exotic fruits.

🔑 Henri et Geneviève Tournier, Dom. Roche Redonne, 83740 La Cadière-d'Azur, tel. 04.94.90.11.83, fax 04.94.90.00.96, e-mail roche-redonne@dial.oleane.com ☑ Y by appt.

CH. SALETTES 1998★

■ 8.86 ha 42,000 70–99 F

This is an ancient property rich in history, where both vines and olive-trees have been cultivated. Since the frost of 1956 and the present grower's takeover, the olives have all yielded their place to vines. This 1998 has a still-youthful garnet colour with the odd flash of deep purple. The tone of the vintage is set by the dense, well-structured but already silky tannins, the round generous character, and the aromas of ripe fruits, clove and other spices.

🔑 Jean-Pierre Boyer, Ch. Salettes, 83740 La Cadière-d'Azur, tel. 04.94.90.06.06, fax 04.94.90.04.29 ☑ Y by appt.

DOM. SORIN 1998★

■ 2.5 ha 11,000 70–99 F

This estate produces Bandol and Côtes-de-Provence from 12 ha (30 acres) of vines. Luc Sorin, who hails from Auxerre, took over in 1994. He has endowed this wine, which has been kept 16 months on the lees with periodic stirring, with a somewhat Burgundian character. It is expressive, chewy, and fills the mouth well. A very oaky wine, but one that is faithful to the spirit of the estate.

🔑 Dom. Sorin, 1617, rte de La Cadière-d'Azur, 83270 Saint-Cyr-sur-Mer, tel. 04.94.26.62.28, fax 04.94.26.40.06 ☑ Y by appt.

DOM. DE SOUVIOU 1999★

□ 1.5 ha 4,000 70–99 F

This estate, which dates back to the 15th century, is as well-known for its olive oil as for its wine. The jury liked this harmonious Bandol with its smooth fruitiness and sweet savours that last attractively. Undoubtedly a wine to serve with lightly spiced grilled fish.

🔑 SCEA Dom. de Souviou, R.N. 8, 83330 Le Beausset, tel. 04.94.90.57.63, fax 04.94.98.62.74 ☑ Y by appt.

🔑 Cagnolari

DOM. DE TERREBRUNE 1998★★

■ 6 ha 25,000 70–99 F

This is one of the estates in the Bandol appellation that is closest to the sea, with an impressive *vinothèque* and the opportunity to purchase old vintages. Rather more focused on youth is this 1998 Bandol, which is very true to type with its vegetal and floral fragrances. The wine's complexity and richness are well expressed and add up to a coherent, already well-balanced whole that bodes well for the next three years.

🔑 Delille, Dom. de Terrebrune, 724, chem. de la Tourelle, 83190 Ollioules, tel. 04.94.74.01.30, fax 04.94.88.47.51 ☑ Y ev. day except Sun. 9am–12.30pm 2pm–6.30pm

CH. VANNIERES 1998★★

■ 12 ha 30,000 100–149 F

The château's somewhat unusual architecture hides a much older cellar containing a number of secrets. This 1998 red is one of them. The nose has notes of black fruits, leather, musk and wax. Though it has presence and is as full, well-integrated and generous as one could wish for, it is still currently a little shy and will have more to say in due course. Patience will be rewarded.

🔑 Ch. Vannières, 83740 La Cadière-d'Azur, tel. 04.94.90.08.08, fax 04.94.90.15.98 ☑ Y ev. day except Sun. 8am–12 noon 2pm–6pm

🔑 Boisseaux

Palette

A tiny vineyard just
utside Aix, this includes the old
nclosed vineyard that originally
elonged to King René, Count of
rovence.

Whites, rosés and
eds are regularly produced. The
eds can be kept for a long time,
uring which they develop scents of
iolet and pine.

H. SIMONE 1997★

] n.c. 28,000 100–149 F

Two centuries ago, the Rougier family
cquired Château Simone, a beautiful place
hose main structure and cellars were built by
he Carmelite monks of Aix in the 16th cen-
ury. Cézanne loved the surrounding land-
capes, and set up his easel on the banks of the
Arc. The label on the bottle has not changed
or 80 years. The wine is straw-yellow with
olden highlights, displaying floral aromas
hat are still fresh (broom). It envelops the
alate, melding with roundness and balance
nto an intensity that includes a flavour of
oney, a sign of its growing maturity. Power-
ul and complex, this 1997 could be drunk
ow, but it still has something in reserve. A
rue Château Simone.

René Rougier, Ch. Simone, 13590
Meyreuil, tel. 04.42.66.92.58,
ax 04.42.66.80.77 Y by appt.

Coteaux d'Aix en Provence

The AOC Coteaux d'Aix en Provence belongs to the western part of the limestone area of Provence, situated between the Durance in the north and the Mediterranean in the south, the Rhodian plains to the west and a region of crystalline rocks from the Triassic period to the east. The relief is formed from a succession of secondary mountain chains running parallel to the sea coast and covered variously with scrub, aromatic moorland vegetation and pine woods: the Nerthe is near the Étang de Berre, and the chain of Costes in the north extends into the Alpilles.

Between these outcrops lie sedimentary basins of different sizes (the Bassin de l'Arc, the Bassin de la Touloubre, and that of the lower Durance) where vine-growing is located. Here limestone and marly structures underlie a matrix of stony, alluvial clays, alternating with structures of molasses and sandstone underlying sandy soils or stony sand and alluvium. The total area of 3,500 ha (8,645 acres) produced 195,418 hl (5,159,035 gal) in 1999. The production of rosé wines has increased recently (70%). Grenache and Cinsaut are still the mainstays, with Grenache predominant; Syrah and Cabernet-Sauvignon are on the increase and are progressively replacing the Carignan.

The rosé wines are light, fruity and pleasant, and have benefited significantly from improved vinification techniques. They should be drunk young with local Provençal dishes: ratatouille, artichokes barigoules (braised with fat bacon), fish grilled with fennel, aïoli . . .

The reds are balanced, sometimes robust, giving of their best according to terroir and micro-climate. When young, these are fruity, supple wines, excellent with grilled meat and dishes topped with grilled cheese. They reach their peak after two or three years of keeping, when they should be served with meat dishes (particularly those with sauce) and game. These interesting reds are well worth looking out for.

The production of white wines is limited. They seem to do better in the northern part of the vineyard, where they combine the roundness of Grenache Blanc with the finesse of Clairette, Rolle and Bourboulenc.

CH. BARBEBELLE Réserve 1998

■ n.c. n.c. 30–49 F

Château Barbebelle dates back to the 17th century. Its vines are planted on 37 ha (91 acres) of clay-limestone hillsides. The 1998 Réserve wine is currently dominated by its oak and carried by its closely packed tannins. In time, it will become more supple and gain in complexity.

Brice Herbeau, Ch. Barbebelle, R.D. 543, 13840 Rognes, tel. 04.42.50.22.12, fax 04.42.50.10.20 ev. day 9am–12 noon 2pm–6pm

JEAN BARONNAT 1998★

■ n.c. n.c. 20 F+

This *négociant* offers an attractive fresh red wine whose menthol aromas marry with liquorice and spicy hints to constitute a well-balanced palate. The whole experience is most attractive. A wine that can be drunk from now.

Jean Baronnat, Les Bruyères, rte de Lacenas, 69400 Gleizé, tel. 04.74.68.59.20, fax 04.74.62.19.21, e-mail info.@baronnat.com by appt.

CH. BAS Cuvée du Temple 1999★★

◪ 3 ha 2,500 50–69 F

This 1999 wine is not a classic Provence rosé but the result of care and study, a product for the enlightened wine-lover. Having been kept for six months in oak, it has a strong colour and a powerful, oaky nose with complex notes of vanilla, fruits and flowers. It is well-structured on the palate and, if allowed to mature, will undoubtedly regale the tastebuds with new sensations in the future. Congratulations to Philippe Pouchin for successfully charting new territory for rosé.

EARL Georges de Blanquet, Ch. Bas, 13116 Vernègues, tel. 04.90.59.13.16, fax 04.90.59.44.35, e-mail chateaubas@wanadoo.fr by appt.

CH. BAS Cuvée du Temple 1998★★

■ 4 ha 10,000 50–69 F

Cuvée du Temple is equally good in both red and white versions. The vivid red, though not quite achieving *coup de cœur* status, well deserves its two stars. The nose shows oaky, liquorice notes, and the well-balanced palate is sustained by integrated tannins. Length is provided by spicy and vanilla aromas derived

from eight months in oak. Meanwhile, t **1998 Cuvée du Temple Blanc** is just as no worthy for its fullness, aromas of dried frui and very subtle note of oak.

EARL Georges de Blanquet, Ch. Bas, 13116 Vernègues, tel. 04.90.59.13.16, fax 04.90.59.44.35, e-mail chateaubas@wanadoo.fr by appt.

CH. BEAUFERAN 1999

◪ 15 ha 20,000 30–4

Near the commune of Velaux, in the A valley, the pre-Roman sanctuary Roquepertuse is a must-see on the way Château Beauferan. This 72-ha (178-acr estate has produced two wines cited by th jury. The first is a delicately salmon-pink ros whose aromas of apricot compote are indic tive of late-harvested grapes. The impressio of ripeness is confirmed on the warm, full pa ate. The **1995 Rouge** is a traditional Provenç wine: black in colour, complex and long, wit the flavour emphasis on preserved red fruits

Ch. Beauferan, 870, chem. de la Degaye 13880 Velaux, tel. 04.42.74.73.94, fax 04.42.87.42.96, e-mail beauferan@cavesparticulieres.com ev. day except Sun. 9am–12 noon 2pm–4pm; Sat. 9am–12 noon

Sauvage-Veysset

CH. DE BEAUPRE
Collection du Château 1999★★

□ 1 ha 4,000 50–69 F

Beaupré is a superb 18th-centur Provençal country house set in a wine estate The Beaupré reds are consistently good, as i the 1999 white that the jury tasted. There is very evident vanilla note that comes from oa maturation, but it is above all the impressio of intensity and balance that so impresses.

Christian Double, Ch. de Beaupré, 13760 Saint-Cannat, tel. 04.42.57.33.59, fax 04.42.57.27.90, e-mail chbeaupre@aol.com ev. day 8am–12 noon 2pm–6.30pm

CH. DE CALAVON Grande Cuvée 1998

■ 10 ha 10,000 30–49 F

Built on the site of a Roman villa, the estate is at the centre of 47 ha (116 acres) of vines. The cellar is located at Lambesc, a town of note whose elegant architecture recalls that of Aix-en-Provence. This 1998 wine has a definite musky note and, if drunk now, needs a chance to breathe in order to develop its aromatic complexity. It would be better, though, to let time do its work.

Michel Audibert, Ch. de Calavon, B.P. 4, 13410 Lambesc, tel. 04.42.57.15.37, fax 04.42.57.15.37 ev. day except Sun. 9am–12 noon 3pm–6pm

CH. CALISSANNE
Clos Victoire 1998★★★

■ n.c. n.c. 70–99 F

Château Calissanne is a consistently good wine, but it is this 1998 red Coteaux d'Aix that is the apotheosis of the range, with its delicate

liquorice, smoky nose and long-lasting palate endowed with well-integrated tannins. It is the product of supreme mastery of the art. It is not the only wine to receive a citation; the **1999 Clos Victoire Rosé** (50–69F), **1999 Cuvée Prestige Blanc** and vat-matured **1999 Cuvée du Château Rouge** (both 30–49F) each receive one star.

Ch. Calissanne, R.D. 10, 13680 Lançon-de-Provence, tel. 04.90.42.63.03, fax 04.90.42.40.00, e-mail calissan@club-internet.fr

Compass et AXA

DOM. CAMAISSETTE 1999★

5.5 ha 30,000 30–49 F

White or rosé? It matters not, for 1999 was a highly successful year in both colours at the Camaïsette estate, on the ancient Roman Via Aureliana. The *saignée* rosé is extremely long-lasting. It hits the palate in a forthright and lively way, and leaves an impression of fullness. The **1999 Blanc** is also a highly successful, well-balanced wine of great subtlety.

Michelle Nasles, Dom. de Camaïssette, 13510 Eguilles, tel. 04.42.92.55.57, fax 04.42.28.21.26, e-mail michelle.nasles@wanadoo.fr

ev. day except Sun. 9.30am–12 noon 2.30pm–6.30pm

COMMANDERIE DE LA BARGEMONE Cuvée Tournebride 1997★

1 ha 5,000 30–49 F

This 13th-century *commanderie* offers a very fruity wine: raspberry-like according to some tasters, blackcurranty according to others. 'Light, but beautifully well-balanced' was the unanimous opinion of all. Ready to drink now.

Jean-Pierre Rozan, La Bargemone, R.N. 7, 13760 Saint-Cannat, tel. 04.42.57.22.44, fax 04.42.57.26.39 by appt.

DOM. DE COSTEBONNE 1996★

15 ha 40,000 20–29 F

Located on the Alpilles around Eygalières, the commune of Mollégès contains the remains of a former Cistercian abbey whose beautiful Renaissance façade can still be admired by the visitor. Here too the Costebonne estate has produced a surprisingly good wine, given the vintage conditions in 1996. Well-structured and balanced, it leaves an impression of round tannins and lightly crystallised red fruits.

SCIEV, B.P. 17, quartier de la Gare, 13940 Mollégès, tel. 04.90.95.19.06, fax 04.90.95.42.00 ev. day except Sun. 9am–12 noon 2pm–6pm

DOM. D'EOLE Cuvée Léa 1998★

4 ha 10,000 70–99 F

A blend of 55% Grenache with 45% Syrah, a yield of 23 hl/ha (1.3 tons per acre), and a rigorous selection of the harvested grapes – such are the conditions applied to production of the estate's prestige wine, which bears the founders' daughter's name. Time will need to pass before the oak integrates fully with the wine, but already the richness, the red fruit and blackcurrant notes are perceptible. This well-crafted 1998 should be kept for three years. The **1999 rosé** equally gains one star for its pleasing balance, and the **1998 Rouge** is also cited (both 30–49F).

EARL Dom. d'Eole, rte de Mouries, 13810 Eygalières, tel. 04.90.95.93.70, fax 04.90.95.99.85, e-mail domaine@domainedeole.com

ev. day except Sat. Sun. 9am–12.30pm 1.30pm–5.30pm

C. Raimont

CH. DE FONSCOLOMBE Cuvée spéciale 1999★

10 ha 30,000 30–49 F

The château of Fonscolombe is a huge estate of 160 ha (395 acres), elegant as much for its vines as for the building itself. The latter was restored in the 19th century, along with its double staircase that leads up to a terrace guarded by two sphinxes and decorated with large sculpted vases. This Coteaux d'Aix is no less charming than the place in which it was made. It is subtle, powerful and complex, and yet lively and fruity too. Although the Sauvignon variety is but one element in the blend of this Cuvée Spéciale, the palate unmistakably bears its mark.

SCA des Domaines de Fonscolombe, 13610 Le Puy-Sainte-Réparade, tel. 04.42.61.89.62, fax 04.42.61.93.95, e-mail mail@fonscolombe.com

by appt.

de Saporta

DOM. DES GLAUGES 1999

2 ha 9,000 30–49 F

The Glauges estate is currently undergoing restructuring, with investment not simply in technical equipment, but also in facilities to welcome the public. This 1999 wine is made from 90% Rolle grapes, with a balance of Ugni Blanc. A 12-hour maceration of the grape skins has left its mark on this wine with its discreet citrus aroma, but it is not yet expressive of its terroir.

Dom. des Glauges, voie d'Aureille, 13430 Eyguières, tel. 04.90.59.81.45, fax 04.90.57.83.19 ev. day except Sun. 10am–12.30pm 2.30pm–6pm

PROVENCE

CH. GRAND SEUIL 1998★★

■ 9 ha 15,000 50–69 F

The parkland and façade of the Château du Seuil figure among recognised historic monuments. It is a former summer residence of the nobility, occupying 55 ha (136 acres) on the slopes of the Trévaresse, which was for a long time shared by olive trees, almond trees and vines, but where vines alone now grow. The 1998 red is impeccably turned out, denoting its noble origins. Its 18 months in oak have given it excellent balance, with harmonious notes of tar and vanilla. The **1999 Château du Seuil Rosé** (30–49F) owes its success to its aromatic complexity (crystallised citrus fruits, bitter orange, pink grapefruit); the **1999 Château Grand Seuil Blanc** (50–69F), which has spent 11 months in barrel, also merits a citation.

Philippe et Janine Carreau-Gaschereau, Ch. du Seuil, 13540 Puyricard, tel. 04.42.92.15.99, fax 04.42.28.05.00 ☒ Y ev. day 9am–12 noon 2pm–7pm

CH. LA BOUGERELLE 1998★

■ 3 ha 3,000 20–29 F

In the 18th century, the archbishop of Aix, Monseigneur de Vintimille, lived here after having demolished the Château of Puyricard in 1709. The ecclesiastical red is commemorated today only by the red colour of the Coteaux d'Aix wine. The well-integrated tannins and aromas of morello cherry, cocoa and vanilla of this 1998 vintage seemed to the jury to indicate oak-ageing, whereas the reality is that the wine was vat-matured. The **1999 Blanc** also receives a citation.

EARL Ch. La Bougerelle, 1360, rte de Berre, Les Granettes, 13090 Aix-en-Provence, tel. 04.42.20.18.95, fax 04.42.20.18.95 ☒ Y ev. day except Sun.10am–7pm (9am–7pm summer)

Granier

CH. LA COSTE Cuvée Lisa 1999★

◪ 15 ha 10,000 30–49 F

Cuvée Lisa comes in two versions, rosé or red, both equally successful. The **1999 Rosé** is very fresh and subtle, having been made from a judicious choice of grape varieties, namely Grenache supported by Mourvèdre. Its quality is evident. The **1996 Rouge**, which also merits one star, has an extremely appealing fruity character and good balance.

GFA du Ch. La Coste, C.D. 14, 13610 Le Puy-Sainte-Réparade, tel. 04.42.61.89.98, fax 04.42.61.89.41 ☒ Y by appt.

Bordonado

DOM. DE LA REALTIERE

Cuvée Clara 1998★

■ 1.35 ha 6,000 50–69 F

Located at 400 m (1,300 feet) above sea-level on the slopes of La Vautubière, the La Réaltière estate was taken over in 1994 by the agronomist Jean-Louis Michelland on his return to France after a career in the South Pacific. The same word appeared repeatedly in the tasters' notes to describe this dark red 1998: power. Its nose is dominated by vanill aromas, while its palate will need a little mor time to demonstrate a balanced expression o its origins in the Cabernet Sauvignon grape which evokes a different great wine regio from this one. We must not forget the **199 Cuvée Spéciale Rosé**, which also gains on star (30–49F).

Jean-Louis Michelland, rte de Jouques, 83560 Rians, tel. 04.94.80.32.56, fax 04.94.80.55.70 ☒ Y by appt.

DOM. DE LA VALLONGUE 1999

□ 3 ha 5,000 50–69 F

This particular Coteaux d'Aix-en-Provence was produced from a painstaking vinification of equal parts Grenache Blanc, Rolle, Clairette and Sémillon grapes. Slow fermentation and three months' vat maturation have yielded a well-wrought wine with a rich palate and aromas of fennel and exotic fruits.

Ph. Paul-Cavallier, Dom. de La Vallongue, B.P. 4, 13810 Eygalières, tel. 04.90.95.91.70, fax 04.90.95.97.76, e-mail vallongue@caves-particulieres.com ☒ Y by appt.

DOM. DES LAVANDES 1999★

■ 5 ha 20,000 30–49 F

Not far from the old Lower Provençal market town of Salon-de-Provence lies Sénas, where the 14th-century Gothic church well deserves a visit. Here the Lavandes estate produces its deep red Coteaux d'Aix, which is strongly redolent of blackcurrant. The dense tannins guarantee the future of this wine, which at the tasting was still a little on the shy side, though it is clearly already a great success.

Cellier Saint-Augustin, quartier de la Gare, 13560 Senas, tel. 04.90.57.20.25, fax 04.90.59.22.96 ☒ Y by appt.

LE MAGISTRAL DES VIGNERONS 1998★

■ 2 ha 10,000 30–49 F

This co-operative cellar has for the first time produced a top-of-the-range wine. Each grape variety (Cabernet Sauvignon, Grenache, Syrah) was macerated for 22 days, and then matured in new oak for ten months to produce this excellent wine. It has great roundness of texture, together with aromas of gingerbread, cinnamon and vanilla.

Les Vignerons de Mistral, av. de Sylvanes, 13130 Berre l'Etang, tel. 04.42.85.40.11, fax 04.42.74.12.55 ☒ Y ev. day except Sun. 9am–12 noon 2pm–6pm

DOM. LES BASTIDES

Cuvée Valéria 1998★

■ n.c. n.c. 50–69 F

A surprisingly strong menthol note appears in this dark red wine. The still very evident tannins are accompanied by aromas of cherry, tar and dried fruits (prune and fig). They all bode well for the future.

Carole et Jean Salen, Dom. les Bastides, te de Saint-Canadet, 13610 Le Puy-Sainte-Réparade, tel. 04.42.61.97.66, ax 04.42.61.84.45

CH. MONTAURONE 1998

20 ha 50,000 20-29 F

It is already possible to enjoy the two Château Montaurone wines cited by the jury. The **1999 Blanc** is well made, and this frank, warm, simple **1998 Rouge**, which has not had any contact with wood, can be drunk without standing on ceremony. A wine to enjoy immediately.

Pierre Decamps, SCEA Berthoune, Ch. Montaurone, 13760 Saint-Cannat, tel. 04.42.57.20.04, fax 04.42.57.32.80 by appt.

DOM. DES OULLIERES

Réserve Louis Charles 1998★★

■ 15 ha 18,000 30-49 F

The first impression is one of balance. Thereafter, the sensations afforded by this musky wine are best described as fullness and generosity. The nose gives pride of place to aromas of stewed and crystallised fruits, highlighted by a touch of vanilla. Drink now, or keep for three to five years.

Les Treilles de Cézanne, R.N. 7, 13410 Lambesc, tel. 04.42.92.83.39, fax 04.42.92.70.83 by appt.

CH. PARADIS 1999★

◪ 4.5 ha n.c. 30-49 F

This rosé needs to be left to breathe for some length of time for the complexity of its fruit aromas to be appreciated. The finish is slightly sharp on the palate, though it will soften in the months to come. The **1999 Cuvée Prestige Blanc**, which has obvious Sauvignon character, is equally deserving of one star for its aromatic intensity and roundness.

Dom. de Paradis, quartier Paradis, 13610 Le Puy-Sainte-Réparade, tel. 04.42.54.09.43, fax 04.42.54.09.41 by appt.

CH. PETIT SONNAILLER 1999

◪ 20 ha 150,000 30-49 F

This former Knights Templar manor located on the salt route is today a guest house. A tower with a stone stairway that is worth a look provides evidence of its past history. The strong presence of the Carignan grape partly explains the slightly acid palate of this pale rosé. The wine's array of aromas is dominated by citrus, both upfront and in opening up on the palate.

Dominique Brulat, Ch. Petit Sonnailler, 13121 Aurons, tel. 04.90.59.34.47, fax 04.90.59.32.30 by appt.

CH. PIGOUDET 1998

■ n.c. 6,000 20-29 F

'Already well-developed', was how the tasters characterised this wine. Its slightly faded colour and the notes of cocoa on the nose are good signs of evolution. The oak influence is now well-integrated, but the tannins remain an austere presence on the finish.

SCA Ch. Pigoudet, rte de Jouques, 83560 Rians, tel. 04.94.80.31.78, fax 04.94.80.54.25 by appt.

Schmidt-Rabe

CH. PONT-ROYAL

Cuvée Gourmande 1999★

◪ n.c. 10,000 30-49 F

The vaulted stables of Château Pont-Royal, which from 1740 to 1890 housed the horses of the Royal Mail, nowadays host art exhibitions and regional product fairs. They also contain this subtle, well-balanced *saignée*-method rosé, grown on the pebbly hillside of Alleins, where Sylvette and Jacques-Alfred Jauffret are converting to organic production.

Sylvette Jauffret, Ch. Pont-Royal, 13370 Mallemort, tel. 04.90.57.40.15, fax 04.90.59.12.28, e-mail chateau-pont-royal@mnet.fr ev. day except Mon. Wed. Sun. 9am–12 noon 3pm–7pm

Jacques-Alfred Jauffret

CELLIER DES QUATRE TOURS

Cuvée Prestige 1999

◪ n.c. n.c. 20-29 F

The Cellier des Quatre Tours is located in Venelles, a high-sited village that was destroyed by an earthquake in 1909, and subsequently rebuilt. It offers a classic rosé made from 70% Grenache macerated on its skins, with the balance made up by Syrah. The wine is straightforward and dominated by notes of raspberry, its attractive balance making it ready to drink.

Cellier des Quatre Tours, R.N. 96, 13770 Venelles, tel. 04.42.54.71.11, fax 04.42.54.11.22 ev. day except Sun. 8.30am–12 noon 2pm–7pm

CH. REVELETTE 1999

□ 3 ha 13,000 30-49 F

The strong presence of the Ugni Blanc variety (50%) alongside Sauvignon, Rolle and Clairette has much to do with the wine's subtlety on the nose. Its first impression on the palate is somewhat lively, but notes of sweet almond arrive to restore balance.

Peter Fischer, Ch. Revelette, 13490 Jouques, tel. 04.42.63.75.43, fax 04.42.67.62.04 by appt.

GFA Dom. de Revelette

MAS SAINTE-BERTHE 1999★★

□ 4 ha 23,000 30-49 F

Christian Nief never leaves anything to chance. The jury greatly appreciated the structure of this wine, a combination of subtlety and power. Its nose is of delicate white flowers, while the palate offers the aromatic mix of Sauvignon, pears and fruit salad, with a remarkable balance of acidity, alcohol and richness. A *coup de cœur* wasn't far off.

PROVENCE

🔑 GFA Mas Sainte-Berthe, 13520 Les-Baux-de-Provence, tel. 04.90.54.39.01, fax 04.90.54.46.27 ☑ Y by appt.
🔑 Hélène David et Fils

DOM. SAINT-ESTEVE 1999*

■ 3 ha 12,000 ▮ 🌡 30–49 F

The red **1998 Terra d'Or** (250–299F) caught the jury's attention with its very evident tannins, and is cited on account of its future promise. It was, however, this other Coteaux d'Aix that won the day. Though the tannins need to become more refined, the fruit is already very evident and direct. The wine's impact is enlivened by its acidity. Two wines worth waiting for.

🔑 Dom. des Béates, rte de Caireval, 13410 Lambesc, tel. 04.42.57.07.58, fax 04.42.57.07.58, e-mail chapoutier@chapoutier.com ☑ Y by appt.
🔑 Chapoutier et Terrat

CH. DE VAUCLAIRE 1998

■ 8 ha 20,000 ▮ 20–29 F

In the Château de Vauclaire, owned by his family since 1774, Uldaric Sallier offers a fine Coteaux d'Aix-en-Provence that is representative of its terroir. The nose offers toasty notes with morello and dessert cherries, while the palate evokes red fruits and pepper. A fresh, rounded wine. Also cited is the **1999 Blanc**, barrel-matured for six months and worth waiting for.

🔑 Uldaric Sallier, Ch. de Vauclaire, 13650 Meyrargues, tel. 04.42.57.50.14, fax 04.42.63.47.16, e-mail chateau-de-vauclaire@libertysurf.fr ☑ Y ev. day except Sun. 9am–12 noon 2pm–6pm

CH. VIGNELAURE 1997*

■ 28 ha 67,000 ⏸ 70–99 F

Château Vignelaure was purchased five years ago by David O'Brien. The jury was full of praise for his 1997 red, and predicted a good future for it in the cellar. Powerful, tannic and yet balanced, it is supported by evident oakiness, which never leads to overdryness. The wine's aromas lie in the realms of blackberry and bilberry. Still a little young? Yes, but the more patient among us will reap their reward. The **1999 La Source de Vignelaure Rosé** (30–49F) is just as successful.

🔑 Ch. Vignelaure, rte de Jouques, 83560 Rians, tel. 04.94.37.21.10, fax 04.94.80.53.39, e-mail david.obrien@wanadoo.fr ☑
Y ev. day 9.30am–12.30pm 2pm–6pm

CH. VIRANT Tradition 1999**

☐ 3 ha 20,000 ▮ 🌡 20–29 F

What wonderful scents of Provence there are at Château Virant, with its 100 ha (247 acres) of vines and 20 ha (49 acres) of olive trees. Apart from the Château's olive oil, there is this white Coteaux d'Aix, in which the Rolle variety performs with great panache. It is a crystal-clear, brilliant wine, extremely expressive in its notes of exotic fruits. On the palate, it evolves subtly towards a long finish. The red **1997 Cuvée des Oliviers**, matured in oak, also receives a citation and may be drunk from now on (30–49F).

🔑 SCEA Ch. Virant, C.D. 10, 13680 Lançon-de-Provence, tel. 04.90.42.44.47, fax 04.90.42.54.81 ☑
Y ev. day 8am–12 noon 2pm–6.30pm
🔑 Robert Cheylan

Les Baux-de-Provence

The Alpilles, the most western secondary chain in the anticlinal mountains of Provence, is an eroded massif with a stunning landscape of crested oblique peaks made of limestone scree and Cretaceous marly limestone. This is paradise for the olive tree, and vines equally flourish on the stony deposits characteristic of the region. The terrace deposits are very thin and the fineness or otherwise of the composition is very important as the water retention ability of the soil depends on it. Here, around the fortified village of Baux-de-Provence, in the heart of the AOC Coteaux d'Aix-en-Provence, a distinctive microclimate makes for a highly productive area, 300 ha (741 acres), that is hot, sunny and rarely subject to frost or rain (650 mm (26 in)). Only reds (80%) and rosés are produced, but a detailed plan of action has been put in place to get the best out of this terroir.

More precise production regulations (lower yield, higher density of planting, harder pruning, development for a minimum of 12 months for the red wines, a minimum of 50% of 'bleeding' (*saignée*) for the rosés), more clearly defined vine varieties based on the pairing of Grenache and Syrah, sometimes augmented by Mourvèdre, are at the core of the renaissance of this sub-regional appellation nominated in 1995.

MAS DE LA DAME Stèle 1998★

35 ha 18,000 70–99 F

Vincent van Gogh was sufficiently inspired by this property to paint a picture of its eastern facade. Perhaps the richness of his colours has entered the estate's wines. The colour of this one is deep garnet, and it has a complex range of scents including very ripe red fruits and shades of musk. The nose will open further in time and acquire even greater aromatic richness, testimony to a harvest of perfectly mature grapes. The palate is warm, and sustained by tannins that will soften further. It would be worth waiting two to five years in order to enjoy this wine to the full.

Mas de la Dame, R.D. 5, 13520 Les Baux-de-Provence, tel. 04.90.54.32.24, fax 04.90.54.40.67 by appt.

A. Poniatowski et C. Missoffe

DOM. DE LA VALLONGUE Cuvée Murielle 1997★

n.c. 30,000 50–69 F

Grenache, Cabernet Sauvignon, Syrah, Cinsault, Counoise and Carignan: no fewer than six varieties went into this complex and very successful red wine. What pleases is its nose of morello cherries and spices, and then its full, rich palate. A wine of undeniable class.

Ph. Paul-Cavallier, Dom. de la Vallongue, B.P. 4, 13810 Eygalières, tel. 04.90.95.91.70, fax 04.90.95.97.76, e-mail vallongue@caves-particulieres.com by appt.

MAS SAINTE-BERTHE Cuvée Louis David 1998★

5 ha 23,000 30–49 F

Christian Nief is now in total charge of the Mas Sainte-Berthe, and his serious approach to wine-making is as evident as ever. He fashions complexity for the pleasure of the palate. This wine of quite strong hue releases pleasant aromas of spices and toast. The well-crafted palate has good balance and is sustained by dense, subtle tannins that reveal the excellent work of maturation. Discernible too are more evolved notes of cocoa and tobacco. The red **1998 Tradition** and rosé **1999 Passe Rose** also gained citations from the jury.

GFA Mas Sainte-Berthe, 13520 Les Baux-de-Provence, tel. 04.90.54.39.01, fax 04.90.54.46.17 by appt.

David

DOM. TERRES BLANCHES 1999

10 ha 35,000 30–49 F

A rosé dominated by red fruits – raspberries, blackcurrants and wild strawberries. These make their presence felt throughout the tasting and give the wine much charm. Drink with grilled white meats.

Dom. Terres Blanches, 13210 Saint-Rémy-de-Provence, tel. 04.90.95.91.66, fax 04.90.95.99.04 ev. day 9am–1pm 2.30pm–6.30pm; Sat. Sun. 11am–6.30pm; groups by appt.

Coteaux Varois

The Coteaux Varois wines are produced in the green, rolling countryside around Brignoles, in the heart of the Var. The wines, best drunk young, are fruity, fun and soft, very much in the image of this pretty little Provençal market town, once the summer residence of the counts of Provence. Coteaux Varois became an AOC on 26 March 1993, and the delimited area covers 1,700 ha (4,199 acres). In 1995 85,000 hl (2,244,000 gal) of rosé, red and white were produced.

DOM. DES CHABERTS Cuvée Prestige 1999★★

n.c. 10,000 30–49 F

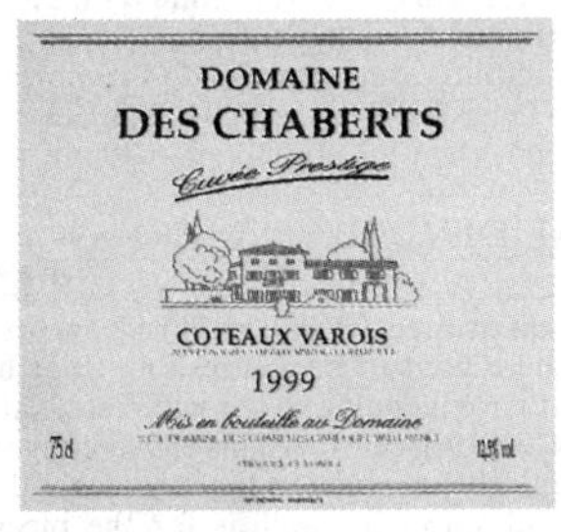

With its 30 ha (74 acres) of vines in the Issole valley, the Chaberts estate is no stranger to awards and receives a *coup de cœur* for its 1999 Prestige white wine. Its intense, complex nose exhibits aromas of exotic fruits, grapefruit and white flowers. The harmoniously balanced palate has great length sustained by a welcome touch of acidity. All in all, a delicious Coteaux Varois. In similar vein is the **1999 Cuvée Prestige Rosé**, which is expressive, not to say explosive. A sturdy, well-crafted wine well deserving of its two stars.

SCI Dom. des Chaberts, 83136 Garéoult, tel. 04.94.04.92.05, fax 04.94.04.00.97, e-mail chaberts@wanadoo.fr ev. day 9am–12 noon 2pm–7pm; Sun. by appt.

DOM. COULOMB La Cuvée du Grand-Père 1998★

3 ha 15,000 20–29 F

Seillons, a village perched on a ridge, is the source of the river Argens. It is also the home of the Coulomb family. Even if 'Grandfather's wine' doesn't have quite the stuff of which long-keeping wines are made, it is still a

PROVENCE

forthcoming, well-bred product with notes of toasted bread and fern. The subtle, integrated tannins help to make it an appetizing wine.
Patrick Apkarian, rue du Moulin, 83470 Seillons, tel. 04.94.72.16.18, fax 04.94.72.12.01 by appt.

CH. DUVIVIER Les Mûriers 1997

4.5 ha 12,900 70–99 F

In this organically produced 1997 wine, one catches glimpses of the fruit behind notes of cocoa and vanilla. The tannins are still young, but overall this is a product of well-handled oak maturation. It could afford to wait another year before being drunk.
SCEA Ch. Duvivier, rte de Draguignan, 83670 Pontevès, tel. 04.94.77.02.96, fax 04.94.77.26.66, e-mail antoine.kaufmann@delinat.com by appt.

LES BARRIQUES DE GARBELLE 1998

n.c. 2,250 30–49 F

The Garbelle estate offers a wine that has spent 12 months in oak. Deep and intense, with a gorgeous dark red colour, this Coteaux Varois has warm, inviting aromas, though the wood remains, for the time being, very pronounced.
Gambini, Vieux chemin de Brignoles, 83136 Garéoult, tel. 04.94.04.86.30 ev. day 9am–12 noon 2pm–6.30pm

DOM. DE LA BATELIERE 1997*

0.25 ha 1,500 20–29 F

Given its breezy location, it isn't surprising that there used to be a threshing-floor here, until it gave its name to the wine estate at the end of the 19th century. This 1997 vintage was particularly appreciated for its notes of beeswax and spices, as well as for the pleasing structure and oaky finish that initiates will enjoy. It may be drunk now, but will come to no harm if kept for up to five years.
Philippe Chabas, Dom. de La Batelière, 83470 Saint-Maximin, tel. 04.94.78.01.21, fax 04.94.78.01.21, e-mail philippe.chabas@wanadoo.fr by appt.

CH. LA CALISSE Cuvéee Etoiles 1999**

0.3 ha 1,500 70–99 F

Once a silk farm, this wine estate converted its vineyard to organic production in the early 1990s. Located in the Barjols region, with its

diverse agriculture, the estate also grows two ha (five acres) of lavender for its essential oils. This flaming, deep red wine with iridescent highlights deserves both the stars in its name and the stars awarded here. The expressive nose releases perfumes of ripe fruits, cocoa and tobacco. On the palate, it yields its flavours from within a powerful, rich constitution, contributing to the remarkable harmony of this *coup de cœur* wine. The **1999 Rosé** (50–69F) is complex, well-structured and smooth. Its nose and palate are perfectly well matched, and permit the wine to achieve one-star status.
Patricia Ortelli, Ch. La Calisse, 83670 Pontevès, tel. 04.93.99.11.01, fax 04.93.99.06.10 ev. day 9am–7pm

CH. LA CURNIERE 1997*

4.7 ha 18,000 50–69 F

Michèle and Jacques Pérignon arrived in 1989, and have entirely renovated this 15-ha (37-acre) property. The fine aromas of their Coteaux Varois (garrigue, blackcurrant buds, red fruits) inform both the nose and the palate, where they are sustained by firm, yet already welcoming tannins. If its structure means that this wine can be drunk now, it may equally well be kept for another two to three years. Excellent with game birds.
Michèle et Jacques Pérignon, Dom. la Curnière, 83670 Tavernes, tel. 04.94.72.39.31, fax 04.94.72.30.06 by appt.

DOM. LA ROSE DES VENTS 1999

8 ha 45,000 30–49 F

Since 1994, Jean-Louis Baude and his son Gilles have looked after this estate of over 24 ha (59 acres) at La Roquebrussanne, a small viticultural town that grew up on the Issole plain in the 14th century. Their 1999 rosé is a classic blend of Grenache and Cinsault, and is very typical of the appellation. A clear wine with salmon-pink highlights, it develops subtly and roundly with unusual notes of brioche and almonds marrying with those of stone fruits, especially peach.
EARL Baude, Dom. la Rose des Vents, rte de Toulon, 83136 La Roquebrussanne, tel. 04.94.86.99.28, fax 04.94.86.91.75, e-mail rosedesvents@infonie.fr ev. day except Mon. Sun. 9am–12 noon 2pm–6pm

CH. DE L'ESCARELLE Les Hautes Bastides 1999

15 ha 40,000 30–49 F

From the cellar built in 1920 by the then owner of the island of Porquerolle, François-Joseph Fournier, comes this 1999 rosé with its frank colour and unusually toasty aromatic character. A palate-warming, appetising wine.
Ch. de l'Escarelle, 83170 La Celle, tel. 04.94.69.09.98, fax 04.94.69.55.06 by appt.

H. MARGILLIERE 1998

	5 ha	n.c.	30–49 F

Since its acquisition by Patrick Caternet in 996, Château Margillière has undergone a reat deal of renovation, enabling it to produce some attractive wines, like this finely ructured 1998. It develops a liquorice note n the palate, together with still very evident annins. The **1999 Rosé** also deserves citation or its balance and pleasant freshness. It represents a happy marriage of flowers and fruit.

SCEA Ch. La Margillière, rte de abasse, 83170 Brignoles,
el. 04.94.69.05.34, fax 04.94.72.00.98
by appt.
Patrick Caternet

DOM. DE RAMATUELLE 1998

	5.5 ha	27,000	20–29 F

Brignolles has always been an active commercial city, lying at the crossroads between he upper Var and the Côte d'Azur. In the ast, it was renowned for its olives and plums; ow it is mainly noted for its wines. The Ramatuelle estate offers a Coteaux Varois vith notes of musk tempered by vegetal ouches (fern, mushroom). A harmonious vine with a well-rounded structure.

Bruno Latil, Dom. de Ramatuelle, Les Gaëtans, 83170 Brignoles,
el. 04.94.69.10.61, fax 04.94.69.51.41
by appt.

CH. ROUTAS Agrippa 1997★

	6 ha	24,000	50–69 F

A large part of Château Routas's production goes to the USA, so let us hope that European readers will still be able to get hold of some of this very successful Agrippa. Dark garnet in colour, it has varied aromas – vanilla, almonds, spices. The finish is evocative of fruits steeped in brandy. It is a well-structured, user-friendly wine with driving tannins. The intense **1999 Rosé** (20–29F) has good presence and merits a citation.

SARL Rouvière-Plane, 83149 Châteauvert, tel. 04.94.69.93.92,
fax 04.94.69.93.61, e-mail
rouviere.plane@wanadoo.fr by appt.
P. Bieler

LE CELLIER DE LA SAINTE-BAUME Elevé en Fût de Chêne 1998★

	n.c.	15,000	30–49 F

The Sainte-Baume cellar brings together the growers of Tourves and Saint-Maximin. Its red Coteaux Varois is a clear wine of dark garnet hue. The nose is complex, but the wine's character is more apparent on the palate, where there is a good aromatic spread: liquorice, vanilla, undergrowth. Its initial impression of softness is answered by a finish of pure silk.

Le Cellier de la Sainte-Baume, R.N. 7, 83470 Saint-Maximin-la-Sainte-Baume,
tel. 04.94.78.03.97, fax 04.94.78.07.40
by appt.

CH. SAINT-ESTEVE Prestige 1999

	1.5 ha	7,000	30–49 F

Jacques Ortet acquired this estate in September 1998. The 1999 rosé was thus produced 'under new management'. Well-crafted, it dispenses with peripheral details in order to go straight to the heart of the matter. Its sturdiness of structure fits it for grilled lamb with herbs.

Jacques Ortet, Ch. Saint-Estève, 83119 Brue-Auriac, tel. 04.94.72.14.70,
fax 04.94.72.11.89, e-mail
st.esteve@wanadoo.fr
ev. day 9am–7pm

DOM. SAINT-JEAN LE VIEUX Cuvée du Grand Clos 1998★★

	0.75 ha	3,800	30–49 F

Visitors to Provence ought not to bypass Saint-Maximin and its remarkable Gothic church dedicated to Saint Mary Magdalene. Nor should they miss the Saint-Jean-Le-Vieux estate, where a wine with a true Provençal bouquet awaits them. Garrigue, thyme, verbena: all find elegant expression, sustained by the well-integrated tannins of this wine, which has a finish to charm the senses. This Coteaux Varois went before the grand jury. The **1999 Blanc** was judged a great success. Its floral nose heralds a fresh and forthright palate with exotic accents. The **1999 Rosé** is an exuberant, well-made wine, which also achieves one star (both 20–29F).

GAEC Dom. Saint-Jean-le-Vieux, rte de Bras, 83470 Saint-Maximin,
tel. 04.94.59.77.59, fax 04.94.59.73.35
by appt.
Boyer

CH. SAINT-JULIEN 1998★★

	5 ha	15,000	20–29 F

The Garrassin family is well known in the region of Brignoles. Purchased in 1992, their estate is undergoing restructuring and renovation. It enters the *Guide* in fine style with this remarkable 1998. A dense, profound wine with a nose that is still quite reticent, it is nonetheless elegantly oaky and punctuated with notes of coconut. The first impression on the palate is of freshness, with notes reminiscent of its terroir, after which it becomes firm-textured, yet sensual and long-lasting. A wine with a bright future. Another star goes to the **1999 Rosé**, a fresh, sweet wine that proffers a peppery note.

EARL Dom. Saint-Julien, ZI Les Consacs, 83170 Brignoles,
tel. 04.94.77.52.00 by appt.
M. Garrassin

DOM. DE SAINT-MITRE Clarté 1999

	2.9 ha	18,000	20–29 F

The Saint-Mître estate was one of the earliest to leave the cooperative cellar of Saint-Maximin in 1964. For the last two years, the new owners have been moving towards a rationalised approach to their viticulture. The 1999 rosé will encourage conviviality at the dinner table. There is continuity between the

PROVENCE

aromas on the nose and those on the palate, which endures through to a long, fruity finish.
🗝 Dom. de Saint-Mître, 83470 Saint-Maximin-la-Sainte-Baume, tel. 04.94.71.07.54, fax 04.98.05.82.88, e-mail saintmitre@wanadoo.fr ☑
🍷 by appt.

CH. TRIANS 1999★★

◪ 2 ha 11,000 30–49 F

Late-harvesting of grapes in early October and the Grenache-Syrah blend have here yielded a highly attractive result. The full, generous and rounded palate of this 1999 develops in a crescendo of fruity aromas. Although the nose still seemed reticent at the tasting, it nonetheless showed promise.
🗝 Dom. de Trians, chem. des Rudelles, 83136 Néoules, tel. 04.94.04.08.22, fax 04.94.04.84.39, e-mail trians@compuserve.com ☑
🍷 ev. day 9am–12 noon 2pm–6pm
🗝 Jean-Louis Masurel

DOM. DE VALCOLOMBE 1999★

☐ 1 ha 4,200 30–49 F

Pierre and Marie Léonetti, two doctor[s,] restored an abandoned farmstead set in seve[n] ha (17 acres) of vines. Their 1999 white an[d] rosé wines each receive one star. The deligh[t]ful pale shade of the white Coteaux Varoi[s] befits the wine's fresh, exotic character. It i[s] delicate, well-balanced and persistent, an[d] would go well with a fish terrine. The **199[9] Rosé** is no less agreeably expressive, having [a] fine attack, roundness, and pleasant, authen[tic] character.
🗝 Dom. de Valcolombe, chem. des Espèces, 83690 Villecroze, tel. 04.94.67.57.16, fax 04.94.67.57.16 ☑
🍷 ev. day except Tue. Fri. 10am–12 noon 1pm–6pm
🗝 Léonetti

Corsica

'A mountain in the sea': the traditional definition of Corsica is as appropriate when applied to its wines as it is in describing its tourist attractions. The topography of the whole island is folded and buckled to an extreme degree, and even the stretch called the west coast – and which, were it on the Continent would more properly be described as a coastal area – is far from lacking in elevation and relief. The vine is to be found virtually everywhere on this multiplicity of slopes and hills, normally sun-drenched, but kept relatively damp because of the influence of the sea. Only altitude limits its planting.

The production of wine, mostly vin de pays or table wine, is determined by the island's relief and the climatic variations it causes, in association with three main types of soil. The most common soil was originally granite; it covers nearly the whole of the south and west of the island; between this area and the schists of the north-east you find a small deposit of limestone soils.

In addition to the imported vine varieties are highly individual varieties native to Corsica, particularly the Niellucio which has a dominant tannic characteristic and which excels on limestone. The Sciacarello produces fruitier wines best appreciated when they are young. For the whites, the Malvasia (Vermentino or Malvoisie) is capable of producing the best wines grown on the shores of the Mediterranean.

As a general rule, the whites are better when young and this is even more the case for the rosés. Both go well with fish and seafood and with the excellent local goats' cheeses, as well as with brocciou, another local cheese made from goat's or ewe's milk. The reds, depending on bottle age and tannic strength, will complement a variety of different meat dishes and, naturally, all of Corsica's famous sheep's milk cheeses.

Vins de Corse

The vineyards of this appellation cover an area of 1,803 ha (4,455 acres). The proportions of grape varieties used, and the different nature of the terroirs, can produce variations in tone and colour from one region to another and between local vineyards. Mostly, these are accounted for by grouping them under the name of a sub-region associated with the appellation (Coteaux du Cap Corse, Calvi, Figari, Porto-Vecchio and Sartène). These wines may be produced virtually anywhere in Corsica except for the Patrimonio region. Most of the 70,460 hl (1,860,144 gal) vinified in 1999 came from the East Coast, where there are a large number of co-operatives.

DOM. D'ALZIPRATU Calvi 1999★

n.c. 10,000 20–29 F

This 25-ha (62-acre) estate, planted mainly with traditional varieties, is in Balagne, near Calvi. Maurice and his son Pierre offer a highly successful 1999 white. Straw-yellow in colour, this expressive wine is richly supplied with aromas of fresh fruits, dried fruits and honey. The palate is well-balanced, round and fresh. A wine for drinking at any time, especially in view of its reasonable price.

Dom. d'Alzipratu, 20214 Zilia, tel. 04.95.62.75.47, fax 04.95.60.32.16
ev. day 8am–12 noon 2pm–6pm
Acquaviva

CORSICAN 1998★

50 ha 100,000 20 F+

Corsican is a very sound wine from the co-operative cellar of Marana, classically produced from 75% Nielluccio, 15% Syrah and 10% Grenache. Do not be put off by its low price. Beautifully dark red in colour, this wine has an intense nose that mixes red fruits with notes of cherries and spices. With some bottle age, its sturdy structure should gain in suppleness on the palate.

SICA Uval, Rasignani, 20290 Borgo, tel. 04.95.58.44.00, fax 04.95.38.38.10
ev. day except Sun. 9am–7pm

CLOS CULOMBU Calvi 1999★

5 ha 20,000 30–49 F

Not far from the 11th-century Chapel of San Petru is the Culombu estate on 39 ha (96 acres) of granitic clay soils. Etienne Suzzoni, who has been in charge since 1989, shows his talent as a wine-grower with two 1999 wines. The pretty pale salmon-pink rosé is very expressive, a good representative of the Sciacarello variety. On the palate, it demonstrates good balance, attractive aromas and freshness. The unblended **Vermentino Blanc** is gold in colour with greenish highlights; its attractive nose and pleasing palate will appeal to all wine-lovers. Serve with a platter of shellfish.

Etienne Suzzoni, Clos Culombu, chem. San-Petru, 20260 Lumio, tel. 04.95.60.70.68, fax 04.95.60.63.46, e-mail culombu.suzzoni@wanadoo.fr
ev. day 8.30am–12 noon 2pm–8pm

DOM. FILIPPI 1998★★

30 ha n.c. 30–49 F

The Filippi estate caused a stir when it triumphantly carried off a *coup de cœur* for this really delightful 1998. The vineyard consists of 42 ha (104 acres) of vines planted in 1972, situated near the sea at Linguizzetta. The wine is made from carefully selected grapes: 70% Nielluccio, 15% Syrah and 15% Mourvèdre. Its nose is rich in very ripe fruit scents tending towards blackcurrant, with lots of spicy complexity and notes of liquorice. On the palate, it is intense, with an ample structure built on solid foundations. A superb wine, which it would be wise to lay down for at least two years before drinking.

Toussaint Filippi, La Ruche Foncière, Arena, 20215 Venzolasca, tel. 04.95.58.40.80, fax 04.95.36.40.55
by appt.

DOM. FIUMICICOLI Sartène 1999★★

5 ha n.c. 30–49 F

Félix and Simon Andréani continue to do well. All three wines they offer have been

CORSICA

commended by the judges, two of them very highly. The 1999 Sartène white is very true to type and will, before too long, be less shy in releasing its locked-in aromas. It is beautifully balanced on the palate, possessing power, structure and intensity. What more can one say, other than urge patience to allow its full potential to be enjoyed? The **1999 Rosé**, made exclusively from Sciacarello grapes, is cited for its typicity too, as well as its lively, light character. Drink well-chilled, accompanied by a simply dressed crab.
🔑 EARL Andréani, rte de Levie, 20100 Sartène, tel. 04.95.76.14.08, fax 04.95.76.24.24 ☒ Y by appt.

DOM. FIUMICICOLI

Sartène Cuvée Vassilia Elevé en Fût de Chêne 1997★★

■ 3 ha n.c. 50–69 F

This 1997 Nielluccio wine, vat-matured for six months and oak-aged for another 14, appealed enormously to the jury, which hailed its gorgeous strong red colour and brick-red highlights. The nose has the Nielluccio spiciness, together with notes of oak and vanilla. On the palate, it abounds in rich sensations sustained by a well-rounded and balanced tannic structure. Already an extremely pleasing wine, it will benefit from being kept for another year or two.
🔑 EARL Andréani, rte de Levie, 20100 Sartène, tel. 04.95.76.14.08, fax 04.95.76.24.24 ☒ Y by appt.

DOM. MAESTRACCI

Calvi E Prove 1999★

□ 2 ha 7,000 50–69 F

Made with pre-fermentation skin contact, this 1999 pure Vermentino from grapes grown by Michel Raoust on sandy clay is a great success. Its aromas are subtle and the palate is round, well-balanced and harmonious, with a fruitiness sustained by delicate freshness. The **1999 Rosé** is energetic, and yet also well-balanced. A very pleasant wine to accompany skewered fish or spiced white meats.
🔑 Michel Raoust, Clos Reginu, 20225 Feliceto, tel. 04.95.61.72.11, fax 04.95.61.80.16, e-mail clos.reginu@wanadoo.fr ☒ Y summer ev. day except Sun. 9am–12 noon 2pm–7.30pm

DOM. MAESTRACCI

Calvi Reginu 1999★

◢ 5 ha 25,000 30–49 F

The Clos Reginu 1999 rosé is a little marvel. Very pale salmon-pink in colour, it has an array of aromas that is very characteristic of the Sciacarello variety. The flavourful, fruity, well-balanced palate would be a perfect accompaniment to baked fish (perhaps gilt-head bream). The **1999 Blanc** of the same appellation has an attractive, subtle, delicate nose. Its rather evident acidity marks it out as a suitable accompaniment to oysters.
🔑 Michel Raoust, Clos Reginu, 20225 Feliceto, tel. 04.95.61.72.11, fax 04.95.61.80.16, e-mail clos.reginu@wanadoo.fr ☒ Y summer ev. day except Sun. 9am–12 noon 2pm–7.30pm

CLOS D'ORLEA 1999

◢ n.c. n.c. 20–29 F

François Orsucci cultivates a 30 ha (74-acre) estate midway between Bastia and Porto-Vecchio, on a limestone-clay plateau in the hills above Aléria. His is a nice rosé with a luminous colour and very good balance. A perfect and appealing accompaniment to a lunch of typical Corsican charcuterie.
🔑 François Orsucci, Le Clos Léa, 20270 Aléria, tel. 04.95.57.13.60, fax 04.95.57.09.64 ☒
Y ev. day 9am–12 noon 3pm–8pm

COMTE PERALDI 1999★

□ n.c. 25,300 30–49 F

The Peraldi estate, reputed for its Ajaccio wines, also produces every year some white AOC Corse. The 1999 version is very floral, mellow and long-lasting in the mouth. Its somewhat mellow character means that it would go better with a blanquette of veal than shellfish, but thoroughly chilled, it would make a wonderful apéritif.
🔑 Guy Tyrel de Poix, Dom. Peraldi, chem. du Stiletto, 20167 Mezzavia, tel. 04.95.22.37.30, fax 04.95.20.92.91 ☒
Y by appt.

DE PERETTI DELLA ROCCA

Figari Prestige Cuvée Alexandra 1999★★

□ 3 ha 10,000 30–49 F

The Tanella estate, owned by the Peretti della Rocca family for several generations, is not far from the marvellous and mythical beach of Palombaggia south of Porto-Vecchio. The 57-ha (141-acre) vineyard has selected just three ha (seven acres) of Vermentino grapes for its Cuvée Alexandra, which is a triumph and receives a *coup de cœur*. This magnificent wine is complex and powerful. Very authentic aromas of citrus and green apples herald a superb palate that marries good balance, roundness, exuberance and length. Drink on its own as an apéritif, or as an accompaniment to fine fish dishes.
🔑 Jean-Baptiste de Peretti della Rocca, Dom. de Tanella, 20114 Figari, tel. 04.95.70.46.23, fax 04.95.70.54.40 ☒
Y by appt.

DE PERETTI DELLA ROCCA

Figari Prestige Cuvée Alexandra 1998★

■ 8 ha 32,000 50–69 F

As if their *coup de cœur* this year were not enough, the Peretti della Rocca family confirms its expertise with this 1998 red and a **1999 Rosé**, both very successful wines. The red is a well-judged blend of Nielluccio, Sciacarello and Syrah. A beautiful dark red in colour, it has a lightly oaked, musky nose and well-balanced, persistent palate defined by the Nielluccio. The **1999 Rosé**, made from half Nielluccio, half Sciacarello grapes, has a diaphanous appearance with orangey highlights. The fruity nose is unusual, with notes of Virginia tobacco and toast. A genuine, lively, well-balanced wine that would perfectly accompany spicy food.

Jean-Baptiste de Peretti della Rocca, Dom. de Tanella, 20114 Figari, tel. 04.95.70.46.23, fax 04.95.70.54.40 ☑ by appt.

DOM. PERO-LONGO Sartène 1999★★

□ 2 ha 7,000 20–29 F

Pierre Richarme restructured his vineyard in 1994 and installed a wine-making cellar. His 1999 white is the compound product of a granitic sandy hillside and the Vermentino grape variety. His vines are located between the lion of Roccapina and Sartène in an area of wild, well-preserved beauty. This still discreet young wine releases aromas that are both true and promising. Full, fat, and rich in fruits, the palate finishes on a highly attractive, slightly acid note. Small-scale production at a small-scale price.

Pierre Richarme, lieu-dit Navara, 20100 Sartène, tel. 04.95.77.10.74, fax 04.95.77.10.74 ☑ by appt.

DOM. DE PETRA BIANCA

Figari Prestige 1997★

■ 10 ha 40,000 50–69 F

Congratulations are due to this producer for all three colours of its Cuvée Prestige. The 50-ha (124-acre) estate lies at the extreme southern end of the island in a magnificent verdant setting. Its cellar was renovated in 1996, and is a former co-operative structure that has been entirely replanned for more individual production. Jean Curallucci and Joël Rossi have joined forces in a drive for quality that is beginning to bear fruit. Their 1997 red, dominated by Nielluccio grapes, is dark in colour, with a nose of discreet pepper and liquorice, elements that appear again on the rounded, supple palate. The **1999 Rosé** (30–49F), made from Sciacarello grapes, is well-constructed, fresh and lively, and also receives one star. It expresses its subtlety and complexity through floral aromas and a fruity, slightly acid, blackcurranty palate. It would go well with shellfish or grilled red mullet. The somewhat shy **1999 Blanc** (30–49F), made exclusively from Vermentino grapes, is cited for its highly typical, rounded, well-balanced character.

GAEC de Petra Bianca, 20114 Figari, tel. 04.95.71.01.62, fax 04.95.71.01.62 ☑ by appt.

DOM. DE PIANA

■ 15 ha n.c. 30–49 F

For the second year running, the Poli family is distinguished by two wines. First is their 1998 red, noteworthy for its base blend of 60% Nielluccio and 30% Syrah grapes grown in a vineyard restructured 15 years ago. Its extreme subtlety would charm the most fastidious of senses. Its complexity, aromatic richness, balanced palate and suppleness are underpinned by flavours of spicy red fruits and liquorice. The highly successful **1999 Blanc** is made exclusively from Vermentino grapes. It has excellent aromatic intensity with ever-changing, slightly buttery, crystallised notes, which on the palate take on more of a citrus character. A slight hint of bitterness on the finish, not unusual with the Vermentino grape, does nothing to disturb the wine's balance.

Ange Poli, Linguizzetta, 20230 San-Nicolao, tel. 04.95.38.86.38, fax 04.95.38.94.71 ☑ by appt.

DOM. PIERETTI

Coteaux du Cap Corse 1998★★

■ 2.12 ha 6,700 30–49 F

The estate is named after Ghjuvan (Jean), who handed it over to his daughter Lina in

Corsica

1991. A leading figure in the viticultural world of Cap Corse, he was still, ten years ago, making wines by rudimentary methods in a 17th-century cellar. Today, everything is thoroughly modern, although the old cellar may still be visited. This deep red 1998, made from 75% Nielluccio and 25% 'Elégante' grapes, has great typicity and was a grand jury finalist. Abounding in the spicy, aromatic complexity of the Nielluccio variety and endowed with sturdy tannic structure, it has excellent balance. However, it is going to need another year or two before all its qualities can be fully appreciated. The **1999 Blanc** is also extremely successful, with a very fruity nose (citrus and green apples), and lively, long-lasting palate. A good accompaniment to herb-flavoured quiche.

⊶ Lina Venturi-Pieretti, Santa-Severa, 20228 Luri, tel. 04.95.35.01.03, fax 04.95.35.01.03 ☒ Y by appt.

PRESTIGE DU PRESIDENT 1998★★

■ 6 ha 40,000 30–49 F

The name of this vintage honours the founding president of the cooperative cellar of Aléria. Made from 60% Nielluccio and 40% Syrah, and kept for ten months in oak, it has a very beautiful dark colour and a nose of ripe red fruits and liquorice, all gently borne up by vanilla. After a good entry, the wine fills the mouth impressively and continues with roundness, body and tannins full of subtlety and presence. It needs laying down for at least three years. The **1998 Blanc** is pale gold in colour, and very true to type. Though a trifle lightweight on the palate, it is nonetheless rounded and well-balanced. A perfect accompaniment to grilled sea bass with fennel.

⊶ Union de Vignerons de l'Ile de Beauté, Cave coop. d'Aléria, 20270 Aléria, tel. 04.95.57.02.48, fax 04.95.57.09.59 ☒ Y by appt.

DOM. RENUCCI Calvi 1999

□ n.c. n.c. 30–49 F

Established in 1870 by the Renucci family, this estate has submitted two delightful wines to the jury. The 1999 white is very expressive, releasing aromas of white flowers. The palate is well-balanced, fairly lively and attractive. The **1998 Rouge**, which is a blend of Nielluccio, Sciacarello and Syrah, will open out in the coming months. The extra time will enable this balanced, well-structured wine to develop fully the aromas of ripe berry fruits (such as blackcurrant) that make only a bashful appearance as yet.

⊶ Bernard Renucci, 20225 Feliceto, tel. 04.95.61.71.08, fax 04.95.61.71.08 ☒ Y ev. day except Sun. 10am–12 noon 4pm–8pm; cl. Oct. until Apr.

RESERVE DU PRESIDENT 1999★★

◪ 80 ha 500,000 20–29 F

The team at this co-operative cellar is a very dynamic one, as this 1999 rosé proves. The colour is admirably direct and clear, and the nose intensely redolent of fresh berry fruits, especially strawberry and blackcurrant. The palate is enchanting: it has a superb attack balance and fruity persistence.

⊶ Union de Vignerons de l'Ile de Beauté, Cave coop. d'Aléria, 20270 Aléria, tel. 04.95.57.02.48, fax 04.95.57.09.59 ☒ Y by appt.

DOM. SAN-ARMETTO

Sartène 1998★★

■ 15 ha 30,000 20–29 F

Founded in 1963 by Paul Seroin, this estate supplied the co-operative until 1995. In 1998, his son Gilles replanted it with essentially Corsican varieties and set up his own private cellar. His **1999 Blanc** is very discreet, round and well-balanced, with aromas of citrus and green apple. It may be drunk now with baked fish or goat's cheese. The **1999 Rosé** has an elegant rose-pink colour and a discreetly floral nose. Well-balanced, long-lasting and round in the mouth, it should be served thoroughly chilled. It is above all the 1998 red, however, that impressed the most with its intense garnet colour, and fine, complex aromas. The palate boasts high-quality, well-integrated, vanilla-softened tannins that are round in contour, with notes of pepper. An unambiguous treat of a wine, suitable for drinking now with roast leg of lamb, but that could be kept for another two years.

⊶ San-Armetto, Les Cannes, 20113 Olmeto, tel. 04.95.76.05.18, fax 04.95.76.24.47 ☒ Y by appt.

DOM. DE SAN-MICHELE

Sartène 1998★

■ 8 ha 35,000 30–49 F

Nestling at the heart of a vast property of 240 ha (593 acres), the estate benefits from a very dry climate and soils that are either clay or silico-granite. This 1998 Sartène red, based on the Nielluccio variety, is well-structured, round and balanced, with prominent musky aromas. If laid down for a year or two, it will be an excellent accompaniment to a Provence-style casserole or one of the characterful cheeses of Corsica. The **1999 Rosé**, dominated by Sciacarello grapes, is round and well-balanced, and is showing some secondary aromas and notes of blackcurrant. It finishes very attractively.

⊶ Dom. San-Michele, 24, rue Jean-Jaurès, 20100 Sartène, tel. 04.95.77.06.38, fax 04.95.77.00.60 ☒

⊶ Phelip

DOM. SANTA MARIA

Coteaux de Santa Maria-Bravone 1998★★

■ 90 ha 600,000 20–29 F

Made from 70% Nielluccio grapes, this wine, which impressed the jury, is the flagship vintage of a huge 470-ha (1,160-acre) estate. An intense, flaming red, it has a nose to match: concentrated and powerful aromas of every sort, including spices, leather, liquorice, and those of the *maquis*. The palate is princely, with a good attack and great structure. The still somewhat austere finish is a sign that the wine should be kept for at least another three years. The estate also offers wine-lovers a new vintage, **1998 Centenaire Rouge** (30–49F). This highly successful wine is dark red with black glints, and has a strong concentration of ripe fruits and spices. The palate is attractive, with evident tannins. This wine should be laid down for a year or two. What may be drunk now, though, is the **1999 Blanc** with its pale gold colour and scent of green apple.

🗝 Dom. de Santa Maria, Coteaux de Santa Maria, 20230 Bravone, tel. 04.95.38.81.91, fax 04.95.38.81.91

🗝 Famille J.-B. Casabianca

SANT'ANTONE 1998★

■ 50 ha 300,000 20F+

The Saint-Antoine cellar offers a 1998 wine made from 80% Nielluccio and 20% Syrah grapes. This is an utterly delightful vintage, with a lovely, slightly faded purple colour, a nose of small black fruits and spices, and a subtle, elegant, well-structured palate. Not to be missed!

🗝 Cave de Saint-Antoine, 20240 Ghisonaccia, tel. 04.95.56.61.00, fax 04.95.56.61.60 Y by appt.

DOM. DE TORRACCIA

Porto-Vecchio Oriu 1998

■ 10 ha 25,000 50–69 F

This Oriu wine is the combined expression of 80% Nielluccio and 20% Sciacarello grapes, and a granitic, sandy terroir close to the sea. The 1998 version is lighter than usual, but has agreeable spicy, vegetal aromas. Its rounded, aromatic palate has excellent balance.

🗝 Christian Imbert, Dom. de Torraccia, Lecci, 20137 Porto-Vecchio, tel. 04.95.71.43.50, fax 04.95.71.50.03

Y ev. day except Sun. 8am–12 noon 2pm–6pm

DOM. VICO 1999★

◪ 10 ha 70,000 20–29 F

Jean-Marc Venturi is the manager, Yves Mellerey the oenologue, and Hamed Karaz the enthusiastic cellarman who pool their talents every year. The colour of their 1999 rosé, made from Sciacarello and Nielluccio, is on the pale side. Its nose, however, is very expressive, and gives forth wave after wave of flowers and fresh fruits. The palate is forthright, well-balanced and persistent. The **1999 Blanc**, made exclusively from Vermentino grapes, is very true to type. Leaving it to breathe helps release its light, floral scents, while its balance and roundness on the palate hint at citrus. A wine fully worthy of its citation.

🗝 SCEA Dom. Vico, 20218 Ponte-Leccia, tel. 04.95.36.51.45, fax 04.95.36.50.26

Y ev. day except Sun. 9am–12 noon 2.30pm–6.30pm

Ajaccio

The vineyards of this appellation occupy 205 ha (507 acres) in a strip several dozen kilometres long running along the hills surrounding the chief town of southern Corsica and its famous gulf. The soils are mostly granitic, and Sciacarello is the main grape variety. The red wines are suitable for keeping and account for 60.5% of the 1999 production of around 6,902 hl (182,213 gal).

CUVEE ANTOINE ABBATUCCI 1999★

□ 7 ha 10,000 30–49 F

The Abbatucci estate again confirms the high quality of its wines, cited three times this year. Made exclusively from Vermentino grapes grown on granitic sand, the white Cuvée Antoine Abbatucci, with its long palate and fruity finish, is a great success, the perfect accompaniment to grilled fish. The **1999 Rosé** is no less of an accomplishment, derived from a clever blend of Barbarossa, Sciacarello and Vermentino grapes. It is very pale, fruity and harmonious, with a spritz on the tastebuds caused by slight residual carbon dioxide. The **1998 Rouge** (90% Sciacarello), with its strong red colour, is ready for drinking and also cited.

🗝 Dom. Comte Abbatucci, Lieu-dit Chiesale, 20140 Casalabriva, tel. 04.95.74.04.55, fax 04.95.74.04.55, e-mail dom-abbatucci@infonie.fr

Y by appt.

CLOS D'ALZETO 1995★

■ 10 ha 50,000 30–49 F

Pascal Albertini's detailed expertise guarantees him a place in the *Guide*. This 1995 wine bears the stamp of the Sciacarello variety, and very successful it is too. It is bright in colour, with brick-red and orangey highlights. The nose is a joy, with its rich, peppery scents, and the balanced, round, long-lasting palate is testimony to five years of evolving flavours. Drink now with jugged hare or a platter of Corsican charcuterie. The **1999 Rosé d'Alzeto** is cited for its colour and liveliness. Served well-chilled, it is the perfect wine for a picnic lunch.

🗝 Pascal Albertini, Clos d'Alzeto, 20151 Sari-d'Orcino, tel. 04.95.52.24.67, fax 04.95.52.27.27 Y by appt.

CLOS CAPITORO 1999★

◪ 10 ha 50,000 30–49 F

This 50-ha (124-acre) estate on siliceous clay, established in 1821 by Martin Bianchetti, today exports 10% of its wines to

CORSICA

England, Germany, Switzerland and Denmark. Jacques Bianchetti offers a most delightful rosé, possessed of a delicate rose-petal appearance, subtle, fine, floral perfumes, and a fruity, enlivening palate. A wine to drink with your feet in the water or your head in the stars! The **1999 Blanc** is cited for its genuineness, and the **1998 Rouge** for its intriguing aromas, in spite of tannins that remain somewhat severe.

Jacques Bianchetti, Clos Capitoro, Pisciatella, 20166 Porticcio, tel. 04.95.25.19.61, fax 04.95.25.19.33, e-mail info@clos-capitoro.com ☑
Y by appt.

DOM. ALAIN COURREGES 1998

■ 6.5 ha 6,500 50–69 F

A citation is awarded to Alain Courrèges, for his small red wine production at 'A Cantina' on the Porto Polo road. This ruby-coloured red offers a complex nose of smoky and undergrowth aromas, together with a lightly structured palate, and is ready to drink now. The **1999 Rosé** is rich and long. Drink it after a visit to the prehistoric site of Filitosa.

Alain Courrèges, A Cantina, 20123 Cognocoli, tel. 04.95.24.35.54, fax 04.95.24.38.07 ☑ Y by appt.

CLOS ORNASCA 1998★

■ 1.78 ha 10,785 30–49 F

Two highly successful wines are offered by Laeticcia Tola, the young Ajaccio vigneronne whose work confirms the quality of the Ornasca terroir. First, the **1999 Blanc**, of which only 5,300 bottles were produced, receives one star for its powerful aromas. The good balance and length on the palate suit it to grilled prawns. But to accompany a fine rib of beef, you need this 1998 deep red, which will dance on your tastebuds to the rhythms of Ajaccio.

Laetitia Tola, Clos Ornasca, Eccica Suarella, 20117 Cauro, tel. 04.95.25.09.07, fax 04.95.25.96.05 ☑ Y ev. day except Sun. 8am–6pm; groups by appt.

DOM. COMTE PERALDI 1998★★

■ n.c. 128,000 30–49 F

The Peraldi estate is one of the leading exporters of AOC Ajaccio to the USA and Japan. Its reputation needs no further bolstering here, and the consistent quality of its wines, and in particular the **1999 Rosé** and this 1998 red, earns it a place in the *Guide*. The very pale salmon-pink rosé releases subtle and lively floral perfumes; on the palate, it has length and a subtle, fruity mellowness. The 1998 red has a dark colour and aromas that are already complex, though still holding much in reserve. This impression is confirmed by the richness of the palate, which marries spices and red fruits in a sturdy, yet rounded structure. Could be drunk now, but we advise patience.

Guy Tyrel de Poix, Dom. Peraldi, chem. du Stiletto, 20167 Mezzavia, tel. 04.95.22.37.30, fax 04.95.20.92.91 ☑
Y by appt.

DOM. DE PRATAVONE 1997★★

■ 7 ha 40,000 30–49 F

Isabelle Courrèges has enchanted the jury with this 1997 red that wins a *coup de cœur.* Dark in colour with a little fading at the rim, it expresses its aromatic complexity as strongly on the nose as in the mouth. Its balance, which combines roundness and finesse, is especially remarkable. The **1999 Rosé** also won over the jury, gaining one star. Bright salmon-pink in colour, it displays discreet floral aromas. The fruit and acidity are well-balanced, and the finish is very impressive.

Jean et Isabelle Courrèges, Dom. de Pratavone, 20123 Cognocoli-Monticchi, tel. 04.95.24.34.11, fax 04.95.24.34.74 ☑
Y ev. day except Sun. 8.30am–12 noon 3.30pm–7.30pm, out of season by appt.

Patrimonio

This small enclave, occupying 388 ha (1,039 acres) in 1998, is made up of limestone terroirs extending east and mainly south from the Gulf of Saint-Florent. They are remarkably consistent from one to another and can with good management produce high-quality wines. The chief grape varieties are Nielluccio for reds and Malvasia for whites, and these look likely to become the only varieties used. They make very typical wines of excellent quality, especially the sumptuous reds which can be laid down for long maturing. Production was up to 14,000 hl (369,600 gal), of which 1,900 hl (50,160 gal) were whites.

CLOS DE BERNARDI

Crème de tête 1998★★

■ 4 ha 15,000 30–49 F

The Clos de Bernardi has been in existence since 1884. Jean Laurent's father pioneered

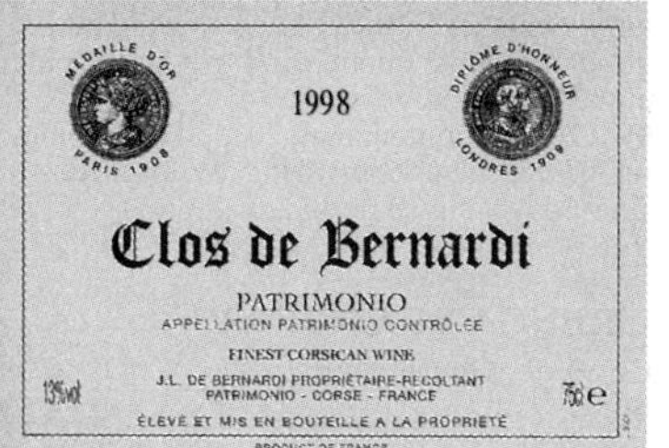

the Patrimonio appellation against much opposition just after the war. Now his son has greatly honoured him by obtaining the *coup de cœur* for a limited series of 15,000 bottles of a 1998 red. The exceptional terroir sloping gently down to the Baie de Saint-Florent, impeccable care in the vineyard, low yields of 30 hl/ha (1.7 tons per acre), and sheer expertise have come together to produce this magnificent wine. The colour is dark, punctuated by garnet and brick-red tones. On the nose, it is bewitching and complex, evocative of very ripe red fruits and prunes. The palate is intense, well-structured and voluptuous, dominated by the complex alliance of red fruits and meatiness. A beautiful wine that will be ready for drinking in two to three years. The **1999 Rosé d'une Nuit** is a highly polished, forthcoming wine ideal for accompanying meals with friends.

Jean-Laurent de Bernardi, 20253 Patrimonio, tel. 04.95.37.01.09, fax 04.95.32.07.66
ev. day 8am–12 noon 2pm–7pm

NAPOLEON BRIZI 1998*

■ 6 ha 13,000 30–49 F

Renovated in 1996, the Brizi cellar has created a fine red wine from 90% Nielluccio and 10% Grenache. The colour is dark with purplish highlights, the nose breathes fragrances of red fruits like ripe strawberries, and the heady palate is well-structured and complex – the perfect accompaniment to roast beef. The **1999 Blanc**, made exclusively from Malvoisie grapes, is well-crafted, full, round and harmonious. Its mineral and floral aromas are very attractive.

Napoléon Brizi, 20217 Saint-Florent, tel. 04.95.37.08.26 by appt.

DOM. DE CATARELLI 1999**

2.5 ha 10,000 30–49 F

This family estate offers three wines. To start with, this 1999 rosé greatly attracted the jury. A pale pink wine with purple highlights, it charms the nose with its freshness and its peardrop character. The palate is lively, round and fruity, which suggests it would go well with cooked shellfish. The **1999 Blanc**, made exclusively from Vermentino grown on clay-limestone soils, is highly typical and expressive, with a part-floral, part-citrus character. Well-chilled, it slips down like spring water, and receives one star. A citation goes also to the **1998 Rouge**, the current aloofness of which will eventually melt to reveal its true personality. Another year should do the trick.

EARL Dom. de Catarelli, Marine de Farinole, 20253 Patrimonio, tel. 04.95.37.02.84, fax 04.95.37.18.72
by appt.
Laurent Le Stunff

DOM. GIUDICELLI 1999

0.87 ha 3,920 30–49 F

Muriel Giudicelli is a young grower who made her début last year with her very first vintage. Her professional talents are confirmed with a citation for her first traditional Patrimonio rosé. The colour is very intense, and the palate fruity. Serve well-chilled.

Muriel Giudicelli, Hameau Paese Novu, 20213 Penta di Casinca, tel. 04.95.36.45.10, fax 04.95.36.45.10 by appt.

DOM. LAZZARINI 1999*

□ 4 ha 10,000 20–29 F

This bright, attractive, light golden wine is excellent value for money. Its nose is intense and fine, with scents of white flowers, the palate well-balanced with a slightly sweet finish. It would make an excellent accompaniment to a roast corn-fed chicken with garlicky potatoes. The jury also cited the charmingly authentic **1999 Rosé de Niellucciu**, made traditionally by the *saignée* method.

GAEC Lazzarini, 20253 Patrimonio, tel. 04.95.37.18.61
ev. day 8am–7.30pm; cl. Nov.–Apr.

DOM. LECCIA 1999**

□ n.c. 13,000 50–69 F

This is one of the most reliable Corsican estates for quality and faithfulness to type. Yves Leccia is a discreet, reserved man who prefers to express his character through his wines with great talent and much modesty. The grand jury considered that his is undoubtedly the best white wine this year from any of the Corsican appellations. It is a harmonious creation that has everything one could wish for. Pale yellow and sprinkled with golden highlights, it gives forth an intense fragrance whose elegant notes of white flowers and slight mintiness will charm every nose. The palate is a gift to the senses owing to its beautiful balance, aromatic power and uncommon length. Drink at the earliest opportunity with simple grilled fish, and keep some back to drink in the future with more elaborate dishes.

GAEC Dom. Leccia, 20232 Poggio-d'Oletta, tel. 04.95.37.11.35, fax 04.95.37.17.03 by appt.

DOM. LECCIA 1998**

■ 10 ha 25,000 50–69 F

No wonder the Americans and Japanese demand a fifth of this estate's production of red wine. The remarkable, deep red 1998 Patrimonio, whose very colour delights the eye, is an aromatic feast of blackberry and cherry that is both intense and complex. On the palate, it is concentrated, powerful and structured, representing a very good year for

the Nielluccio variety. It releases its pent-up flavours with gusto to the awaiting tastebuds, but let us not forget the highly successful **1999 rosé** (30–49F), with its strong colour, fruity morello-cherry nose, and balanced, seductive palate. An excellent accompaniment to a piquant Corsican cheese.

🔑 GAEC Dom. Leccia, 20232 Poggio-d'Oletta, tel. 04.95.37.11.35, fax 04.95.37.17.03 ☑ 🍷 by appt.

CLOS MARFISI Goccie di Sole 1998

■ 2.5 ha 12,000 50–69 F

The gorgeously intense red colour and odd brick-red highlight, the great aromatic subtlety with hints of musk and oxidation, and the balanced, well-structured palate make this a typical Patrimonio. Made exclusively from Nielluccio grapes by Toussaint Marfisi, it is ready to drink now with game.

🔑 Toussaint Marfisi, Clos Marfisi, 20253 Patrimonio, tel. 04.95.37.01.16, fax 04.95.37.01.16 ☑
🍷 ev. day 9am–12.30pm 2pm–7pm

CLOS MONTEMAGNI 1999★

◪ 5 ha 30,000 30–49 F

Established in 1850, the estate is today run by two of Louis Montemagni's daughters. Its 64 ha (158 acres) of vines make up a significant part of the production of Patrimonio. The **1999 Blanc** is very floral. A touch more acidity would have added to its attractiveness, but it nevertheless has good balance on the palate. Drink well-chilled. This very light-coloured rosé has agreeable estery aromas. The palate is well-balanced, with a very rounded impression and some delightful fruity notes. It would perfectly accompany a crab salad. The **1999 Cuvée Prestige du Menhir Blanc** (50–69F) also achieves a one-star rating.

🔑 GAEC Montemagni, 20253 Patrimonio, tel. 04.95.37.14.46, fax 04.95.37.17.15 ☑
🍷 ev. day 8am–12 noon 2pm–6pm

DOM. LOUIS MONTEMAGNI 1999★

◪ 5 ha 30,000 30–49 F

Entry in the *Guide* for this cellar, renovated in 1999, is assured by its highly successful rosé. Lightly orange-tinged and with a lovely, aromatically subtle nose, it is well-balanced and persistent on the palate. It would make a good accompaniment to Cap Corse spider crab.

🔑 GAEC Montemagni, 20253 Patrimonio, tel. 04.95.37.14.46, fax 04.95.37.17.15 ☑
🍷 ev. day 8am–12 noon 2pm–6pm

ORENGA DE GAFFORY

Cuvée des Gouverneurs 1998

■ 5.5 ha 18,400 50–69 F

The estate's three wines have all been awarded citations. The **1999 blanc** opens with exotic and floral notes, and goes on to develop more mineral flavours in the mouth. Drink it chilled as an apéritif. The very pale **1999 rosé** has a nose of delicate floral aromas, and a more expansive palate owing to its floral-scented roundness and liveliness (both 30–49F.) The Cuvée des Gouverneurs has a strong imprint left by barrel-ageing. It would be prudent to age it a further two to three years.

🔑 Dom. Orenga de Gaffory, Lieu-dit Morta-Majo, 20253 Patrimonio, tel. 04.95.37.45.00, fax 04.95.37.14.25 ☑
🍷 by appt.

DOM. PASTRICCIOLA 1999★★

□ 2.5 ha 7,000 30–49 F

Three men from Patrimonio with three wines. This is a great success for the Pastricciola estate, which confirms its talent for consistency. This 1999 wine, which went before the grand jury, demands to be drunk. Its bright, light appearance and subtle, floral nose herald a round, well-balanced and elegant palate. The **1998 Rouge** (one star), an unblended Nielluccio wine, was grown on limestone-clay soils. Deep red in colour, it exhibits notes of overripe fruits and spices. Great mellowness and balance on the palate give it considerable charm. Drink within two years. The **1999 Rosé** needs to breathe before sampling. Its colour is strong and slightly orangey. Made in the traditional manner from Nielluccio and Malvoisie grapes, the palate has both charm and presence.

🔑 Dom. Pastricciola, Maestracci Giovannetti Gilormini, 20253 Patrimonio, tel. 04.95.37.18.31, fax 04.95.37.08.83 ☑
🍷 ev. day 9.30am–12 noon 3pm–7pm

DOM. SAN QUILICO 1999

□ 6.28 ha n.c. 30–49 F

This 1999 white is cited for its excellent overall balance and very typical Vermentino aromas. It would go very well with *salmon en papillote*. The **1998 Rouge** has a strong colour with scents of the *maquis* and of red fruits. The slightly austere finish makes it a suitable companion for soft cheeses.

🔑 Dom. San Quilico, Lieu-dit Morta Majo, 20253 Patrimonio, tel. 04.95.37.45.00, fax 04.95.37.14.25 ☑ 🍷 by appt.

THE SOUTH-WEST

Grouping appellations as far apart as Irouléguy, on the border with Spain, Bergerac, on the Garonne, and Gaillac, on the Tarn, the wine-growing region of the south-west encompasses what the Bordelais call 'wines from the high country' and the Adour vineyard. Until the railway was laid, the vineyards of the Garonne and the Dordogne were subject to Bordeaux wine regulations. With the benefit of its strong geographical location and royal support, the port of Lune was in a position to establish laws controlling the wines of Duras, Buzet, Fronton, Cahors, Gaillac and Bergerac. These regions had to wait for the whole of the Bordeaux harvest to be sold, primarily to the English and Dutch, before their wines could be shipped, and they were routinely employed as 'dosing' wines to bolster certain clarets. The wines from the foothills of the Pyrenees were not subject to Bordeaux wine law but had to undergo a hazardous journey on the Ardour to reach Bayonne. Understandably, their reputation hardly extended beyond their immediate vicinity.

Yet these vineyards, among the oldest in France, represent a living history of the vines of ancient times. In no other area do you find such a range of varieties. The Gascon taste in wine, as in all else, has always been marked by a determined individualism and a preference for the particular. The Mansent, Tannat, Negrette, Duras, Len-de-l'el (Loin de l'œil), Mauzac, Fer Servadou, Arrufiac or Baroque (the Cot), as well as the charmingly named Raffiat de Moncade, are varieties that emerge from the mists of viticultural history and give the local wines their authentic identity, honesty and unmatchable style. Far from despising the term 'peasant' wine, these appellations embrace it with pride and give it due nobility. Wine-growing is far from the only agricultural activity in the region, and the wines have always been sold alongside other local produce that they accompany perfectly and naturally, making the south-west a region where one can still enjoy the privilege of a traditional gastronomy.

Today, all the vineyards of the region are burgeoning, driven along by the wine co-operative movement and by committed owners. The great efforts being made to raise quality standards, through improved methods of cultivation, by researching cloned varieties better suited to local soils and conditions and by modernising vinification techniques, mean that the wines are gradually becoming the best value for money in French wine.

Cahors

The Cahors vineyard, dating from Roman times, is one of the oldest in France. John XXII, the Pope of Avignon, recruited wine-makers from Quercy, in Cahors, to cultivate Châteauneuf-du-Pape. François I planted a vine variety from Cadurce in Fontainebleau that the Orthodox Church adopted as the wine for Mass, while the court of the Tsars chose it as a ceremonial wine. Yet the Cahors vineyard has had to come back from the brink. It was totally wiped out by frosts in 1956 and fell back to only 1% of its previous surface area. It was re-established in the meanders of the Lot valley and planted with traditional varieties, mainly Auxerrois, also known as Cot or Malbec, which represents 70% of the plantation along with Tannat (under 2%) and Merlot (about 20%). The terroir of Cahors has now regained the place it deserves among the areas producing wines of quality – 4,215 ha (10,411 acres) produced 244,017 hl (6,442,049 gal) in 1999. In addition, brave attempts are being made to re-establish vineyards on the limestone plateaux that were cultivated in the past.

Cahors wines are powerful and robust, with a deep colour that has given rise to the English term 'black wine'. These are undoubtedly wines to be kept, yet Cahors wine can also be drunk young: at that stage it is plump and aromatic with good fruit, to be drunk slightly chilled with grilled meat, for example. After two or three years' bottle age it becomes firm and austere, becoming harmonious again after about the same period of time, when it produces aromas of undergrowth and spices. At this stage, its round, mouthfilling qualities make it an ideal wine to accompany charcoal-grilled truffles, cep mushrooms and game of the region. Though the character of the terroir and the varieties planted tend to produce wines capable of being kept, there is also a current trend to produce lighter wines that can be drunk more quickly.

CH. ARMANDIERE

Diamant rouge Vieilli en Fût de Chêne 1998★

■ n.c. 4,222 30–49 F

Bernard Bouyssou is continuing the family estate under the new name of Château Armandière by way of homage to his grandfather Armand. His 'Red Diamond' wine has spent 14 months in the barrel. Dark and glistening, it has an engaging nose of subtly vanilla-tinged red fruits, mint and oaky power. The concentrated structure gently evolves on the palate to a warm, complex finish supported by well-integrated tannins. Pleasant spices and an oaky, toasted note are then detectable. A Cahors that can be enjoyed straight away, but will also keep.

Bernard Bouyssou, 46140 Parnac, tel. 05.65.30.72.47, fax 05.65.36.02.23 Y by appt.

CH. DE CAIX 1998★★

■ 18 ha 80,000 50–69 F

The Château of Caïx, which is run by Jean-Baptiste de Monpezat, belongs to the Prince Consort of Denmark. This 1998 wine proudly wears the colours of Cahors. Dark in hue, the aromas it releases are intense; a scent of fruit, together with a hint of mineral, joins those of oak and vanilla gained during the 12 months spent in barrel. After a forthright attack, the palate is enveloped by concentrated flavours of violet and liquorice. Elegance and balance mark the finish of this well-made wine, worth laying down for five years.

SCEA Prince Henrik, Ch. de Caïx, 46140 Luzech, tel. 05.65.20.80.80, fax 05.65.20.80.81 Y by appt.

CH. DE CALASSOU 1998★

■ 8 ha 16,000 30–49 F

A blend of Cot (75%) and Merlot, this typical Cahors from the Château of Calassou is a medium intense cherry-red. The nose is redolent of red fruits in *eau de vie* with a softening hint of oaky vanilla. The palate is warm but quite supple, the finish fruity and spicy.

Michel Souveton, Ch. de Calassou, 46700 Duravel, tel. 05.65.24.62.67, fax 05.65.36.47.22 Y ev. day 8am–9pm

DOM. DE CARREYRES 1998★

■ 0.83 ha 2,500 20–29 F

A small proportion of Tannat rounds off this 95% Cot vintage. Spicy notes accompany the delicate scents of fruit, flowers and plants. This wine is of a glistening ruby colour, and is fairly light and pleasantly fruity on the palate; the balance between structure and aromas is precisely as it should be, revealed by the fineness of the tannins and the soft finish. Real harmony, which two or three years of keeping will improve further.

Georgette Hartmann, Carreyrés, 46700 Vire-sur-Lot, tel. 05.65.36.53.61, fax 05.65.30.89.96 Y by appt.

DOM. DE CAUSE

Notre-Dame-des-Champs Elevé en Fût de Chêne 1998★★

■ 1.2 ha 8,000 50–69 F

Serge and Martine Costes took over this family estate in 1994. They offer a beautifully clear wine with shades of violet. It has an intense aromatic profile, evocative of small red fruits and spices. Perfectly judged extract from the grapes has yielded a smooth, generous palate with a long, persistent finish. A rich and attractive wine.

Serge Costes, Cavagnac, 46700 Soturac, tel. 05.65.36.41.96, fax 05.65.36.41.95, e-mail montalieu@infonie.fr Y ev. day 9.30am–12 noon 2pm–6.30pm; Sun. by appt.

DOM. DE CAUSE

La Lande Cavagnac 1998★★

■ 3.6 ha 23,000 30–49 F

Almost black as it swirls in the glass, this wine has violet reflections. A long succession of overripe black fruits – plum, fig, blackberry – with a touch of oxidation honed by slight oakiness. A fleshy, rich, vinous attack leads to an opulent impression on the tastebuds. The tannins are pronounced but soft, and the powerful aromas persist. A wine of great concentration and presence.

Serge Costes, Cavagnac, 46700 Soturac, tel. 05.65.36.41.96, fax 05.65.36.41.95, e-mail montalieu@infonie.fr ☑
Y ev. day 9.30am–12 noon 2pm–6.30pm; Sun. by appt.

CH. DU CEDRE Le Cèdre 1998★★★

■ 7 ha 35,000 150–199 F

A unanimous *coup de cœur* for this outstanding Cahors produced by the Verhaeghe brothers, a recompense for their perfect mastery of wine production and testimony to the wine's 24 months in the barrel. The colour is a sumptuous, deep purple-black. The nose is elegant and thoroughbred, revealing an elegant oakiness within a remarkably complex configuration of aromas. The palate reveals superb balance: powerful, full of body, smooth and harmonious, it boasts the ripest tannins, whose satin softness sustains a long finish. A wine with a great future ahead of it.

Le Cèdre 1998
CAHORS
MIS EN BOUTEILLE AU CHÂTEAU

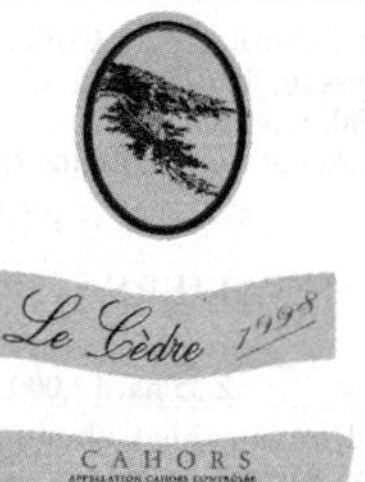

Verhaeghe et Fils, Bru, 46700 Vire-sur-Lot, tel. 05.65.36.53.87, fax 05.65.24.64.36
☑ Y ev. day except Sun. 9am–12 noon 2pm–6pm

CHEVALIER DE MALECROSTE

Cuvée Tradition Elevé en Fût de Chêne 1998★

■ 2 ha 8,500 30–49 F

A blend of Cot (80%) and Tannat (20%), the Tradition version of this Chevalier de Malecroste has not a note out of place. The colour is lively and moderate in intensity; the nose is not overplayed, being slightly musky with notes of red fruits and a hint of vanilla; the palate is aromatic, supple, and harmonious, owing to the roundness of the tannins.

The South-West

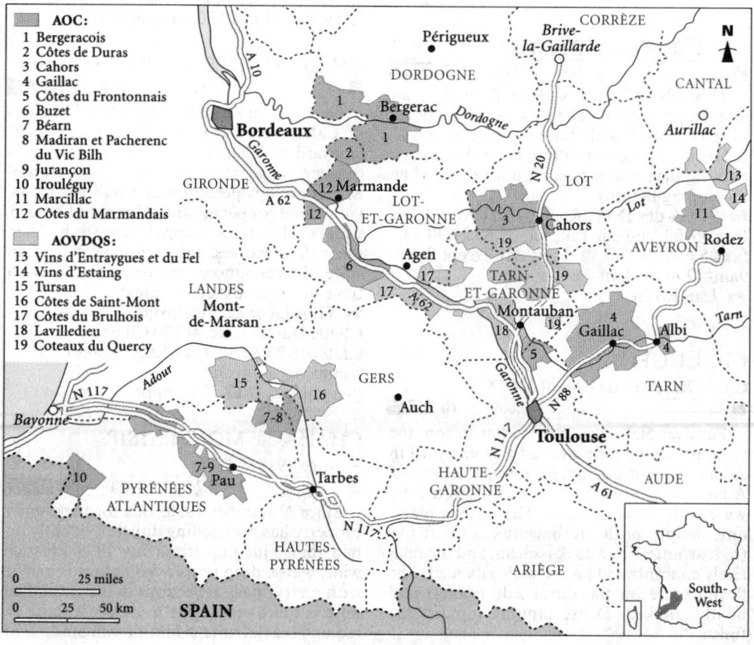

AOC:
1 Bergeracois
2 Côtes de Duras
3 Cahors
4 Gaillac
5 Côtes du Frontonnais
6 Buzet
7 Béarn
8 Madiran et Pacherenc du Vic Bilh
9 Jurançon
10 Irouléguy
11 Marcillac
12 Côtes du Marmandais
AOVDQS:
13 Vins d'Entraygues et du Fel
14 Vins d'Estaing
15 Tursan
16 Côtes de Saint-Mont
17 Côtes du Brulhois
18 Lavilledieu
19 Coteaux du Quercy
Périgueux
Brive-la-Gaillarde
CORRÈZE
N
DORDOGNE
CANTAL
Bergerac
Dordogne
Aurillac
Bordeaux
Garonne
A 10
N 20
LOT
GIRONDE
A 62
Marmande
LOT-ET-GARONNE
Lot
Cahors
Rodez
AVEYRON
Agen
TARN-ET-GARONNE
LANDES
Mont-de-Marsan
Montauban
Gaillac
Albi
Tarn
A 62
Adour
N 117
GERS
Auch
TARN
Bayonne
Toulouse
N 88
N 117
Pau
Tarbes
HAUTE-GARONNE
AUDE
A 61
PYRÉNÉES ATLANTIQUES
N 117
HAUTES-PYRÉNÉES
ARIÈGE
South-West
0 25 miles
0 25 50 km
SPAIN

🔑 Gérard Delbru, rte du Collège, 46220 Prayssac, tel. 05.65.22.42.40, fax 05.65.30.67.41 ☑
Y ev. day except Sun. 8.30am–7pm

DOM. CHEVALIERS D'HOMS 1998★★

■ 2.35 ha 12,000 30–49 F

Matured in vat, this Cahors, made exclusively from Auxerrois grapes, is one of the best of the selection. The colour is brilliant cherry with flashes of violet. The nose is fragrant with scents of ripe red fruits, spices and mint. Its powerful, warm, richly substantial palate has accents of overripeness and dense, flavoursome tannins. A remarkable piece of work.

🔑 SCEA Dom. d'Homs, Les Homs, 46800 Saux, tel. 05.65.31.92.45, fax 05.65.31.96.21 ☑ Y ev. day 8.30am–7.30pm

CROIX DU MAYNE 1998★

■ 13 ha 20,000 20–29 F

This Cahors (90% Auxerrois: 10% Merlot) is excellent value for money. The strong cherry-red colour is reflected around the sides of the glass. The nose is redolent of overripened fruits, together with an intense spicy, and more specifically roasted, oakiness. Supple and well-balanced, the wine releases its flavours in the mouth all the way through to a finish supported by essentially oaky tannins, which then begin to merge.

🔑 SCEV François Pélissié, 46140 Anglars-Juillac, tel. 05.65.21.45.37, fax 05.65.21.45.38 ☑ Y by appt.

CH. CROZE DE PYS 1998★

■ 30 ha 180,000 30–49 F

This 1998 Cahors of Jean Roche's is an intense, black wine. The nose is subtle; notes of spices mingle with those of small black and red fruits. The flavour fills the mouth, giving a rich, supple sensation that is not belied by the developing tannins.

🔑 SCEA des Dom. Roche, Ch. Croze de Pys, 46700 Vire-sur-Lot, tel. 05.65.21.30.13, fax 05.65.30.83.76 ☑ Y ev. day except Sun. 9am–12 noon 3pm–7pm
🔑 Jean Roche

CH. EUGENIE

Cuvée Réservée de l'Aïeul 1998★

■ 8 ha 40,000 30–49 F

For over 500 years, from father to son, the Couture family have worked this vineyard in Albas. Their distant ancestor was the Lord of Albas's wine-grower in 1470. This is a ruby wine with violet nuances. The nose is pleasant, being both herbaceous and fruity (redcurrant). The attack is clean, and the relatively concentrated palate well-balanced. The flavours are on the floral side (violet) and lightly smoked. Dense tannins support the finish.

🔑 Ch. Eugénie, Rivière-Haute, 46140 Albas, tel. 05.65.30.73.51, fax 05.65.20.19.81 ☑ Y ev. day 8am–12 noon 1.30pm–7pm; Sun. and groups by appt.
🔑 Couture

CH. DE GAUDOU Renaissance 1998★

■ 2.2 ha 16,000 70–99 F

The Château of Gaudou is a vineyard of 32 ha (79 acres) in the commune of Vire-sur-Lot. Its Renaissance Cahors has gained from being kept for 14 months in new oak barrels, and has acquired a deep colour with violet reflections. The nose is a successful balance of black fruits, spices and an oakiness with nuances of coffee and vanilla. On the palate, there is a good deal of richness within its ample structure. The tannins are powerful, but enveloped in vanilla. A wine with guts.

🔑 Durou et Fils, Gaudou, 46700 Vire-sur-Lot, tel. 05.65.36.52.93, fax 05.65.36.53.60 ☑ Y by appt.
🔑 René Durou

DOM. DE HAUTERIVE 1998★

■ 7 ha 50,000 30–49 F

Hauterive is a contraction of Haut de Vire, the commune in which the estate is located, climatically well-exposed and on a clay-gravel soil. This intense, brilliant 1998 is made from Malbec and Merlot grapes. The vinous nose evokes marc or kirsch; then on to the scene come spices and a pencil-like mineral note. The attack may seem soft, but the wine's development on the palate is more robust. The firm, rustic tannins provide the structure for this virile wine.

🔑 Filhol, Le Bourg, 46700 Vire-sur-Lot, tel. 05.65.36.52.84, fax 05.65.24.64.93 ☑
Y ev. day 8am–12.30pm 2pm–7pm

CH. DE HAUTE-SERRE 1998

■ 60 ha 260,000 50–69 F

Georges Vigouroux is one of the celebrities of Cahors. He has restored this magnificent vineyard, which had been in ruins for almost a century. Vivid ruby in colour, this Haute-Serre develops perfumes of small red fruits, violets and pepper around a dominant note of vanilla. The attack is supple and fresh. Then the palate evolves, maintaining its fruit in spite of pronounced oak tones that leave a trace of bitterness on the finish.

🔑 GFA Georges Vigouroux, Ch. de Haute-Serre, 46230 Cieurac, tel. 05.65.20.80.80, fax 05.65.20.80.81, e-mail vigouroux@g-vigouroux.fr ☑ Y by appt.

CH. HAUT-MONPLAISIR

Prestige 1998★

■ 2.7 ha 14,400 50–69 F

Since November 1998, this former family property has been selling direct. Evidently no bad thing, judging from this 1998 Prestige wine, whose deep purple-red colour is bright with pretty, lively reflections in the glass. The nose is quite vinous, with varied aromas of red and black fruits, a hint of cinnamon and some toasty nuances. Supple and soft as it hits the palate, the wine fills the mouth with an aromatic, rich flavour. Its balance endures to the finish, thanks to a weave of subtle tannins. The **Tradition 98** version similarly deserves a mention (30–49F).

Salinié-Fournié, Monplaisir, 49700 Lacapelle-Cabanac, tel. 05.65.24.64.78, fax 05.65.24.68.90
ev. day 3pm–7pm; Sat. 10am–12 noon 3pm–7pm; Wed. Sun. by appt.

DOM. LA BORIE

Cuvée Prestige Vieilli en fût de chêne 1998★

3 ha 15,000 30–49 F

The Cot variety does its stuff in this Cahors that has been matured in barrel for a year. The colour is dark red cherry, and the nose is of red fruits with accents of coffee and vanilla. Beneath its tannic structure and strong oaky character, this quite rich wine retains a fruity side.

Froment et Fils, GAEC des Coteaux, Dom. La Borie, 46220 Prayssac, tel. 05.65.22.42.90, fax 05.65.30.64.70
ev. day 9am–8pm

CH. LA CAMINADE

La Commandery 1998★

10 ha 35,000 50–69 F

This La Commandery wine owes its personality to the Auxerrois variety grown on limestone-clay gravel soil. This highly successful wine is deep ruby in colour. The nose has character and complexity: musk, leather, fruits and oak are in harmony here. The rounded, rich flavour is well balanced around pleasantly spicy tannins that sustain the finish.

Resses et Fils, SCEA Ch. La Caminade, 46140 Parnac, tel. 05.65.30.73.05, fax 05.65.20.17.04 ev. day except Sat. Sun. 8am–12 noon 2pm–7pm

CH. LA COUSTARELLE

Cuvée Prestige 1998

15 ha 100,000 50–69 F

Michel and Nadine Cassot have been working tirelessly in pursuit of quality since 1980. On the dark side of garnet in colour, their 1998 reveals an intense nose which has both a fruity (cherry) smell and a scent of violets. Its oakiness is mediated by notes of vanilla and smokiness. After an honest attack, the wine develops powerfully in the mouth. The closed, rather rustic tannins still need time to blend in.

SCEA Michel et Nadine Cassot, Ch. La Coustarelle, 46220 Prayssac, tel. 05.65.22.40.10, fax 05.65.30.62.46
ev. day 8.30am–12.30pm 2pm–8pm; groups by appt.; cl. 20 Aug.-8 Sep.

CLOS LA COUTALE 1998★

50 ha 280,000 30–49 F

The vast 55-hectare (136 acres) estate of Clos La Coutale has been in the hands of the Bernède family for six generations. It has yielded this clear and quite intense Cahors with glimpses of violet colour. The powerful nose is dominated by black fruits and vanilla. On the palate, it is round and full. The tannins, owing in part to a strong oakiness with charred overtones, establish themselves quickly and soon fill out, reaching their full force on the finish.

V. Bernède et Fils, Clos La Coutale, 46700 Vire-sur-Lot, tel. 05.65.36.51.47, fax 05.65.24.63.73 ev. day 8am–7pm

CH. LAMARTINE Expression 1998★

3 ha 14,000 100–149 F

The Château Lamartine has played a dynamic part in restoring the vineyards of Cahors. Located in the west of the AOC, it benefits from Atlantic influences. The colour of this 1998 is an attractive, intense ruby. Its

SOUTH-WEST

Cahors

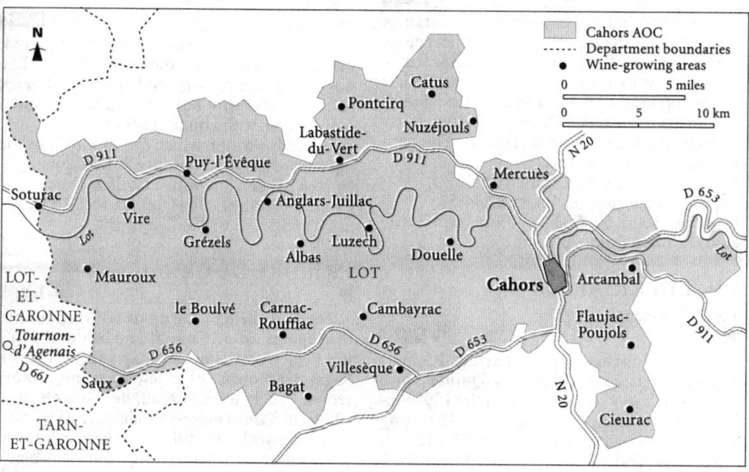

expressive, keen nose marries red fruits to a pleasant, delicate vanilla oakiness. The palate is round, full and rich, with good extract and fine tannins. The oakiness has a conspicuous presence, but slowly blends in with the rest. A well-balanced wine.
SCEA Ch. Lamartine, 46700 Soturac, tel. 05.65.36.54.14, fax 05.65.24.65.31
by appt.
Alain Gayraud

LES BOUYSSES 1998★

n.c. 105,000 50–69 F

The cellar of the Côtes d'Olt matures good wines in both vat and barrel. Both their **André de Monpezat 98** and **Beauvillain-Monpezat 98** deserve a mention (30–49F). This particular wine has a lovely distinctive dark ruby colour. The nose has a powerful, lengthy oakiness, and the scent of vanilla outruns that of the fruit. After a soft attack, the palate is quite full. The tannins, which dominate the finish, recall the presence of an oakiness which, though fading, gives the wine excellent persistence.
Côtes-d'Olt, 46140 Parnac, tel. 05.65.30.71.86, fax 05.65.30.35.28
by appt.

CH. LES GRAUZILS 1998★

17 ha 120,000 30–49 F

This is a well-balanced blend of 80% Cot, 15% Merlot and 5% Tannat. The colour, dark red, almost black, has a very concentrated appearance. The nose is similarly deep, evoking overripened fruits, macerated in spiced *eau de vie*. A generous, warm palate confirms the impression of concentration. The wine fills the mouth and is chewy, sustained by a strong framework of tannins. Wait at least five years before drinking.
Philippe Pontié, Gamot, 46220 Prayssac, tel. 05.65.30.62.44, fax 05.65.22.46.09 ev. day except Sun. 9am–12 noon 2pm–7pm

CH. LES IFS 1998★

8 ha 36,000 30–49 F

Cot (80%) and 20-year-old Merlot varieties have yielded this elegant Cahors with its deep, dark red nose of mixed red and black fruits, liquorice, spices and a hint of musk. The wine's soft attack leads on to an impression of fullness on the palate, demonstrating fairly concentrated, aromatic structure. The tannins remain very evident.
Buri et Fils, EARL La Laurière, 46220 Pescadoires, tel. 05.65.22.44.53, fax 05.65.30.68.52 ev. day except Sun. 8am–12 noon 2pm–7pm

CH. LES RIGALETS

La Quintessence 1998★★

2.5 ha 10,500 70–99 F

The local archives show that Les Rigalets vineyard existed in 1830. Its Quintessence wine, which was so successful in the 1997 vintage, thus defends a tradition. The long extraction process from 90% Cot: 10% Tannat grapes has yielded a deep purple, almost black wine. Its intense aromas are for the moment dominated by oak, but one already senses notes of crystallised black fruits and many spices. The wine is full, powerful and rich on the palate; its structure is reinforced by an oakiness that will blend in over the coming two years.
Bouloumié et Fils, Les Cambous, 46220 Prayssac, tel. 05.65.30.61.69, fax 05.65.30.60.46 ev. day 8am–12.30pm 2pm–8pm; Sun. by appt.

CH. METAIRIE-HAUTE

Vieilli en Fût de Chêne 1998

10 ha 22,000 20–29 F

Dark ruby with shades of purple, this Cahors offers a nose that is moderate in intensity but pleasing for its notes of small black fruits. A suspicion of spices and a waft of smoke are equally perceptible. After a soft attack, the palate's structure is revealed as being well-rounded but firm.
EARL Ch. des Colombiers, 46140 Anglars-Juillac, tel. 05.65.36.29.44, fax 05.65.36.21.32 by appt.

CH. PECH DE JAMMES 1998★

9 ha 60,000 30–49 F

Château Pech de Jammes is currently owned by Americans, Sherry and Stephen Schechter, with vinification by Vigouroux. They offer a perfectly clear garnet-coloured product whose intense, complex nose distils perfumes of red fruits, alongside those of plants, floral at first, followed by spices. Fresh-tasting at the outset, the palate develops a concentrated structure that is well sustained by the tannins. The vigorous finish is marked by aromas of fresh fruits that are full of youthful verve.
SCEA du Pech de Jammes, 46090 Flaujac-Poujols, tel. 05.65.20.80.80, fax 05.65.20.80.81, e-mail vigouroux@g-vigouroux.fr
Schechter

CH. DU PORT Cuvée Prestige 1998★

6 ha 35,000 30–49 F

This is a well-turned-out wine, having a red, purplish colour with dark reflections. The nose comprises overripened, macerated black fruits together with notes of vanilla-flavoured oak. The smooth attack leads to a round, full, rich, heady flavour, which finally envelops the liquorice-flavoured tannins. A lively wine.
GAEC de Circofoul-Pelvillain, Circofoul, 46140 Albas, tel. 05.65.20.13.13, fax 05.65.30.75.67 by appt.

PRIEURE DE CENAC 1998★★

n.c. 100,000 50–69 F

Formerly held by the monks of Picpus until the separation of Church and State in 1905, the Priory of Cénac is today run by Franck Rigal, who owns other jewels in the Cahors crown, such as **Château de Grézels** and **Château Saint-Didier-Parnac**, the **1998** versions of which (30–49F) have been adjudged great successes. The strong purplish-black

Prieuré de Cénac has an aristocratic nose that respects the balance between richness and elegant oakiness. The attack is forthright, and the silky palate replete with substantial body and powerful tannins. Within the wine's pleasing texture are persistent spicy and toasted aromas. A well-made wine with plenty of potential.

SCEA Ch. Saint-Didier-Parnac, 46140 Parnac, tel. 05.65.30.70.10, fax 05.65.20.16.24

ev. day 9am–12 noon 2pm–6pm

CLOS RESSEGUIER

Vieilli en Fût de Chêne 1998★

■ 13.53 ha 3,000 20–29 F

The premises contain a large paved and vaulted chamber where the barrels were formerly stored. The 1998 Clos Rességuier is a beautiful purple colour with vivid red highlights. The expressive nose mixes aromas of red fruits with those of spices and liquorice, and the wine has an oaky character. Despite the liveliness of the attack, the structure is silky and round; there is no bitterness. The palate develops well, supported by lush tannins.

EARL Clos Rességuier, 46140 Sauzet, tel. 05.65.36.90.03, fax 05.65.31.92.66

ev. day except Sun. 9am–12 noon 2pm–6pm

CH. ROUQUETTE

Cuvée d'honneur Vieilli en Fût de Chêne 1998★

■ 2 ha 10,000 30–49 F

Although there have been four generations of wine-growers at the Château Rouquette, the first bottling dates from 1994. The vintage of four years later is very dark red. Its nose emphasises prunes and other black fruits macerated in marc, supported by a gently oaky foundation. Soft and silky as it hits the palate, the wine develops its full vinosity in the mouth. The tannins and oakiness persist, but not excessively so.

GAEC Ch. Rouquette, Les Roques, 46140 Saint-Vincent-Rive-d'Olt, tel. 05.65.30.76.40, fax 05.65.30.52.99

by appt.

CH. SAINT-SERNIN

Prestige Vieilli en Fût de Chêne 1998★★

■ 12 ha 85,000 30–49 F

This family vineyard, which goes back several generations, was re-established after the frosts of 1956. The lovely dark red colour and ruby highlights of this wine have immediate appeal. The nose is uninhibited, releasing at first a gorgeous peony perfume, then aromas of red fruits and of pleasant, spicy oak. Upfront and intensely aromatic on the palate, the wine develops an impression of balance and ample concentration. It is sustained by subtle tannins that add to its elegance.

SCEA Ch. Saint-Sernin, Les Landes, 46140 Parnac, tel. 05.65.20.13.26, fax 05.65.30.79.88

ev. day except Sun. 8am–12 noon 2pm–7pm

DOM. DU THERON

Cuvée Prestige 1998★★

■ 2 ha 11,000 70–99 F

This year Vic Pauwels, the Belgian industrialist whose passion is this vineyard, offers two excellent wines: the **Tradition 1998**, whose suppleness and fruitiness are highly successful (30–49F), and this remarkable Cuvée Prestige. The colour is a magnificent dark purple of great density. Similarly concentrated is the aristocratic range of scents that make up the bouquet: ripe red and black fruits, muskiness and a strong charred aroma. The palate is in the same vein, rich and powerful, sustained by fine structure built around well-judged oakiness. A promising future.

SCEA Dom. du Théron, rte du chemin-du-Théron, 46220 Prayssac, tel. 05.65.30.64.51, fax 05.65.30.69.20, e-mail vic.pauwels@pauwels.com

ev. day 9.30am–7pm; Sun. by appt.

Vic Pauwels

CLOS TRIGUEDINA 1998★★★

■ 48 ha 150,000 50–69 F

It was in 1830 that Etienne Baldès planted his first vines in the Clos Triguedina. This wine, grown on historic terraced vineyards above the river Lot, is one of the best Cahors of all. It will need another five years before it can be best appreciated, but already this *coup de cœur* wine transports us with its deep red, almost black colour and intense, complex nose, comparable to the sort of sauce reduction that sends out harmoniously mixed aromas, concentrated and well-seasoned. The palate evolves beautifully around a core of dense richness; it is full and perfectly balanced, still full of youth but built for the future. It has a gourmet finish, very elegant, perfumed with vanilla and liquorice. Superb!

Baldès et Fils, Clos Triguedina, 46700 Puy-l'Evêque, tel. 05.65.21.30.81, fax 05.65.21.39.28, e-mail triguedina@crdi.fr

ev. day 9am–12 noon 2pm–6pm; Sun. and groups by appt.

Jean-Luc Baldès

DOM. DE VINSSOU 1998★

■ 2 ha 12,000 20–29 F

This wine has a very concentrated appearance, owing to its deep aubergine, almost black colour. The nose is restrained, but quite

SOUTH-WEST

true to type; it is full of appealing fruit and spices, with a slight hint of smokiness. The attack is soft, but its structure on the palate is both tender and rich. It fills the mouth pleasurably, despite the still-astringent tannins, which will need more time to evolve. A good typical Cahors.
⊶ Louis Delfau, dom. de Vinssou, 46090 Mercuès, tel. 05.65.30.99.91, fax 05.65.30.99.91 ☒ Y ev. day 10am–7pm

Coteaux du Quercy AOVDQS

Located between Cahors and Gaillac, the Quercy wine region is of recent date although, as is common throughout the South-West region, vines were grown there in prehistoric times. In between, wine-making suffered several setbacks. In the first century AD, an edict by the Emperor Domitian banned the planting of new vines outside Italy: in the 15th century, the supremacy of Bordeaux spoiled the region's markets, and at the beginning of the 20th century the sheer volume of production in Languedoc-Roussillon had the same effect. Research aimed at improving quality was launched in 1965; hybrid stocks were replaced, and this raised the region to Vin de Pays status in 1976.

Gradually, producers managed to sort out the best grape varieties and the best soils. These improvements in quality culminated in promotion to the AOVDQS category on 28 December 1999. The official territory extends across 33 communes in the departments of Lot and Tarn-et-Garonne.

Appellation wines are limited to reds and rosés. The red wines have a deep-purple colour and are full-bodied and hearty, with complex aromas deriving from their Cabernet Franc content, the main variety which may account for up to 60% of a particular wine, the others being Tannat, Cot, Gamay Noir and Merlot, each up to a limit of 20%. The rosé wines are fruity and lively, and made from the same varieties.

Total production amounts to about 23,000 hl (607,200 gal) from vines covering nearly 500 ha (1,236 acres), and comes from about thirty producers, three of which are co-operatives.

BESSEY DE BOISSY
Tradition 1997★

■ 6 ha 45,000 ▮ 🌡 30–49 F

Already three years old, and yet this wine still has a youthful air. The nose is minty, rich in scents of ripe fruits, leather and undergrowth. The palate is no less rich, with tannins that blend in well together alongside flavours of red fruits and blackcurrants.
⊶ Vignerons du Quercy, R.N. 20, 82270 Montpezat-de-Quercy, tel. 05.63.02.03.50, fax 05.63.02.00.60 ☒ Y by appt.

DOM. DE CERROU 1999★

■ 6 ha 53,000 ▮ 🌡 20–29 F

While it is certainly still young, this 1999 has promise, and will gain a more settled character as it ages. It is bright in colour, with scents of blackcurrant and raspberry. The well-integrated, almost silky tannins give it all the personality of a real Quercy.
⊶ Côtes-d'Olt, 46140 Parnac, tel. 05.65.30.71.86, fax 05.65.30.35.28 ☒ Y by appt.

DOM. DE LA GARDE 1998★★

■ 8 ha 14,900 ⦀ 30–49 F

This intense red, bright wine has a persistent, slightly oaky nose with aromas of red fruits (dominated by cherry) and vanilla. After a straightforward attack on the palate, the tannins, which are as powerful as they are supple and round, give the wine structure, richness and length. Even though it is ready to drink, a little ageing will undoubtedly enhance its personality.
⊶ Jean-Jacques Bousquet, Le Mazut, 46090 Labastide-Marnhac, tel. 05.65.21.06.59, fax 05.65.21.06.59 ☒ Y by appt.

DOM. DE MAZUC 1998★★

■ 4 ha 25,000 🍾 🌡 20–29 F

The Mazuc estate has held its own as one of the more important Quercy vineyards for over ten years now. A terrior that suits red grape varieties, together with consistently good vinification, gives this Quercy a character that is quite unmistakable, even when tasted blind. It has a signature all its own, written in its bouquet of blackcurrants!

🔑 Erick Carles, Mazuc, 82240 Puylaroque, tel. 05.63.64.90.91, fax 05.63.64.90.91 ☑
🍷 by appt.

Gaillac

The origins of the Gaillac vineyard date back to the Roman occupation, as the Roman amphorae (terracotta wine vessels) made in Montels bear witness. In the 13th century, Raymond VII, Count of Toulouse, awarded his domains one of the first equivalents of an Appellation Contrôlée, while the Provençal poet, Auger Gaillard, sang the praises of sparkling Gaillac wine long before champagne had been invented. The vineyard (2,500 ha/6,175 acres) is divided into the Premières Côtes (or lower slopes), the Hauts Coteaux, the higher slopes on the right bank of the Tarn, and the plain, the area around Cunac and the district of Cordais. In total the appellation produces 130,000 hl (3,432,000 gal), of which 60% are red wines.

The limestone slopes are ideal for the cultivation of traditional white vine varieties such as Mauzac, Len-de-l'En (Loin-de-l'œil), Ondenc, Sauvignon and Muscadelle. The gravel areas are reserved for red wine varieties such as Duras, Braucol or Fer Sarvadou, Syrah, Gamay, Bégrette, Cabernet and Merlot. The range of varieties gives rise to the wide palette of flavours to be found in Gaillac wines.

Among the whites are to be found fresh and aromatic dry and sparkling wines, as well as the soft wines of the lower slopes, which are rich and supple. These wines draw their particular character from the Mauzac grape, historically responsible for the reputation of Gaillac wines. Sparkling Gaillac can be made either by the traditional local method of adding natural grape sugar, producing rather fruity wines, or by the Méthode Champenoise, which European legislation has decreed shall henceforth be known as Méthode Traditionelle. The easy-drinking rosés are produced by *saignée* method, which allows the colour of the red skins to bleed into the must, while the red wines, which are said to keep well, have striking character and bouquet.

MAS D'AUREL Cuvée Alexandra 1998★

■ 3 ha 20,000 🍾 🌡 30–49 F

Strong ruby in colour, this Cuvée Alexandra is expressive and quite intense. The nose is redolent of spiced red fruit jam, pepper and liquorice. Sweet and fruity from the moment it enters the mouth, it leaves an impression not simply of roundness but also of great structure. The tannins start out supple, but firm up at the finish. This particular cuvée is made from half Braucol and half Cabernet Sauvignon grapes.

🔑 Mas d'Aurel, 81170 Donnazac, tel. 05.63.56.06.39, fax 05.63.56.09.21 ☑
🍷 ev. day 8am–12 noon 2pm–7pm
🔑 Albert Ribot

DOM. BARREAU
Doux Caprice d'Automne 1998★★

□ 5 ha 16,800 🍾 30–49 F

This Cuvée Caprice d'Automne is a triumph for the Barreau estate. It is a blend of various local varieties harvested at perfect maturity. The appearance is gold-chased, bright and beautiful. The nose is at once powerful, concentrated and refined, evoking a remarkable array of crystallised fruits. More impressive still is the palate, possessed of

great fullness and perfect balance. The wine's elegance is further heightened by its rich, persistent aromas. A divine caprice indeed!

🔑 Jean-Claude Barreau, Boissel, 81600 Gaillac, tel. 05.63.57.57.51, fax 05.63.57.66.37 ☑ 🍷 by appt.

BRUMES Doux 1998★

☐ 0.3 ha 700 ▮ 70–99 F

The Salesses estate, founded in 1959, today comprises 25 ha (62 acres) of vines. The Loin-de-l'Œil variety is late-harvested, producing a Gaillac with 95 g/l of sugar. Pale gold and beautifully clear, the Brumes vintage has an intense nose hinting at crystallised fruits and honey. The wine has warmth when it hits the palate, and develops in the mouth, borne along by the generous richness of the alcohol, taking on hints of crystallised fruit (quince), and rising to a powerful finish.

🔑 GAEC Les Salesses, Sainte-Cécile-d'Avès, 81600 Gaillac, tel. 05.63.57.26.89, fax 05.63.57.26.89 ☑
🍷 ev. day except Sun. 8am–8pm
🔑 Litre

DELIRES D'AUTOMNE

Doux 1998★★

☐ n.c. 1,200 ⏸ 50–199 F

With a lot of enthusiasm and a little madness: that is how Patrice Lescarret has managed to produce two remarkable wines, his **Gaillac Blanc Sec Zacmau 1999** – Mauzac in backslang! – (30–49F) and this Gaillac Doux containing 207 g/l of residual sugar. The colour of this 1998 is deep, with copper nuances. Its nose is powerful and complex, full of dried or crystallised fruits. The attack is smooth and sweet, heralding a voluptuous palate, very rich and concentrated. Flavours of honey, dried apricot and grape syrup linger long in the mouth. The finish is dominated by the wine's sweetness.

🔑 Patrice Lescarret, Dom. de Causse-Marines, 81140 Vieux, tel. 05.63.33.98.30, fax 05.63.33.96.23, e-mail causse-marines@infonie.fr ☑
🍷 by appt.

CH. D'ESCABES

Prestige Vieilli en Fût de Chêne 1998★

■ 15 ha 100,000 ⏸ 30–49 F

A four-quarters blend this: equal proportions of Fer Servadou (or Braucol), Duras, Syrah and Merlot have produced this bright, intense red Gaillac with shades of vermilion. The nose displays a variety of scents, floral, fruity and spicy, supported by discreet oakiness. Round and attractive when it hits the palate, the wine wraps the tastebuds in a warm, silky embrace. Like the tannins, the fruit and oak melt away together in a well-sustained finish.

🔑 SCEA Ch. d'Escabes, 33, rte d'Albi, 81800 Rabastens, tel. 05.63.33.73.80, fax 05.63.33.85.82

DOM. D'ESCAUSSES

Doux Vendanges Dorées 1998★

☐ 1 ha 8,000 ⏸ 50–69 F

Located halfway between Albi and the medieval village of Cordes, this 20 ha (49-acre) estate offers two one-star wines with poetic names: the **Gaillac Blanc Sec, La Vigne**

Gaillac

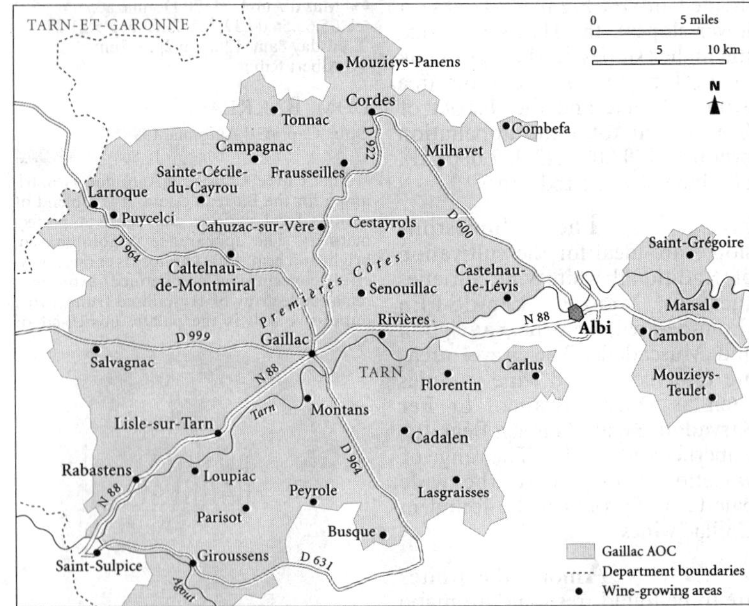

de l'Oubli 1998 (30–49F) and this Vendanges Dorées. A sweet Gaillac, it has a golden colour and an intense nose that evokes apples with honey and candied orange, accompanied by strong burnt notes. An attack that is both sweet and fresh leads on to an expressive, concentrated palate. The oak is very evident, but marries well with flavours of dried fruits. The finish is on the rich side and leaves an impression of smoothness. (50 cl bottles)
EARL Denis Balaran, Dom. d'Escausses, 81150 Sainte-Croix, tel. 05.63.56.80.52, fax 05.63.56.87.62, e-mail jean-marc.balaran@wanadoo.fr ev. day 9am–7pm; Sun. and groups by appt.

FASCINATION 1998

■ n.c. n.c. 30–49 F

The Técou cellar makes wine from 850 ha (2,100 acres) of vines and produces a range of wines with delightful names: Séduction, Passion, Fascination. This Gaillac Rouge, a bright, ruby-coloured wine, has a nose of medium intensity. The dominating spices are accompanied by a number of red fruit aromas. After a supple attack, it delivers a fruitier, quite tender feel to the palate. The structure is light but well-balanced, the tannins smooth. A wine for easy drinking.
Cave de Técou, 81600 Gaillac, tel. 05.63.33.00.80, fax 05.63.33.06.69, e-mail passion@cave-de-tecou.fr by appt.

DOM. DE GINESTE

Grande Cuvée 1998★★

■ 0.5 ha 3,000 50–69 F

The Gineste estate has produced three excellent Gaillac Rouge wines. Their **Rouge Fût 1998** (30–49F) and **Cuvée Pourpre 1998** (20–29F) are both one-star wines. The Grande Cuvée is distinguished for its intensity and depth both in sight and smell. What rises from the glass is a superb and powerful bouquet of leather, undergrowth, red and black fruits either ripe or stewed, and spices. The palate is perfectly homogeneous, broad, full and generous, supported by velvet tannins that make for a lengthy finish. Remarkable.
EARL Dom. de Gineste, 81600 Técou, tel. 05.63.33.03.18, fax 05.63.81.52.65 by appt.
Laillier-Bellevret

CH. GRADDE Doux 1998★

□ 2 ha 7,000 20–29 F

Mauzac grapes grown on the stony slopes of the Château Graddé have yielded a sweet, quite pale Gaillac with green tinges. The nose releases notes of white-fleshed fruits (apple and pear). After a supple attack, the wine develops roundness and interesting balance on the palate. Elements of dried fruits join other flavours detected earlier on the nose, leading to a sense of freshness on the finish.
SCEA Dom. de Graddé, 81140 Campagnac, tel. 05.63.33.12.61, fax 05.63.33.20.75 ev. day except Sun. 9.30am–12 noon 2pm–7pm

DOM. DE LABARTHE

Cuvée Guillaume 1998★★

■ 5.8 ha 37,300 30–49 F

Jean Albert and his son here do homage to their ancestor Guillaume Albert, a winegrower of the 16th century. Their bright, intense garnet-red wine reveals a powerful nose. A certain smokiness dominates, but aromas of very ripe, sweetly spiced black fruits jostle for attention. The first impression in the mouth is of a fleshy, full, well-structured wine. The oakiness and substantial tannins will soften after four or five years of keeping. Also very successful are the **Gaillac Rosé 1999** (20–29F) and **Gaillac Doux 1998** (30–49F), meriting one star each.
EARL Albert et Fils, Dom. de Labarthe, 81150 Castanet, tel. 05.63.56.80.14, fax 05.63.56.84.81, e-mail jean.albert@wanadoo.fr by appt.
Jean-Paul Albert

CAVE DE LABASTIDE DE LEVIS

Méthode Gaillacoise Brut 1998★★

○ 100 ha 200,000 30–49 F

The Labastide de Lévis cellar, founded in 1949, played a part in the origins of the Perlé de Gaillac style. Sparkling wines are undeniably their speciality, judging by this one. Full marks for presentation: a bright, pale yellow colour, shot through with persistent fine bubbles; a subtle and fresh nose of apple and citrus; an agreeable flavour that develops well, borne along by delicate bubbles. No less elegant is the finish, preceded and supported by the wine's aromatic liveliness. The **Gaillac Blanc Sec, Perle d'Amour 1999**, whose sugar is very perceptible, was also cited.
Cave de Labastide-de-Lévis, 81150 Marssac-sur-Tarn, tel. 05.63.53.73.73, fax 05.63.53.73.74 by appt.

DOM. DE LA CHANADE

Sec 1999★

□ 5.75 ha 40,500 30–49 F

Located on the Cordes Plateau, the La Chanade vineyard changed hands in 1997. The current owner is himself a Gaillac winegrower's grandson who has thus returned to his roots. His Gaillac Sec has pretty touches of gold, with abundant tears running down the glass. The pleasing, quite intense nose mixes more or less crystallised white-fleshed fruits with a touch of honey. The palate retains a slight sparkle that emphasises the wine's freshness and highlights the aromas, but it nevertheless has richness. A well-balanced wine with an attractive finish.
Dom. de La Chanade, 81170 Souel, tel. 05.63.56.31.10, fax 05.63.56.31.10 ev. day 9am–12 noon 2pm–7pm
Hollevoet

DOM. LA CROIX DES MARCHANDS

Cuvée Élevée en Fût de Chêne 1998★

■ 2 ha 10,000 30–49 F

This estate – in Gallo-Roman times a place where potters gathered – has long had a viticultural tradition. The 11 months that this La Croix des Marchands Gaillac spent in wood has left it with a slight brick-red tinge. The powerful nose evokes fruits macerated in *eau de vie*, but it is also intensely marked by the oak, which has produced a slight smokiness. The palate is surprisingly warm, soft and round. It is aromatic and grows in the mouth, building around an oakiness that still slightly dominates the finish. The **La Croix des Marchands Gaillac Doux 1998** was also cited for its classic character.

J.-M. and M.-J. Bezios, av. des Potiers, 81600 Montans, tel. 05.63.57.19.71, fax 05.63.57.48.56, e-mail croixdesmarchands@wanadoo.fr ✉ Y ev. day except Sun. 9am–12 noon 1.30pm–7pm

CH. DE LACROUX 1998★

■ 19 ha 130,000 30–49 F

Forty per cent Braucol, 30% Duras, 15% Syrah and 15% Merlot: such a blend is a good compromise for a Gaillac Rouge. Its deep purple colour is very inviting, and the nose is forthright, well-balanced between blackcurrant, liquorice, mint and spices. The fresh-tasting palate is supple and smooth, built upon silky tannins, tailing away pleasantly to a lightly spicy finish.

Pierre Derrieux et Fils, Ch. de Lacroux, 81150 Cestayrols, tel. 05.63.56.88.88, fax 05.63.56.86.18, e-mail chateau.de.lacroux@libertysurf.fr ✉ Y by appt.

DOM. DE LA RAMAYE

Doux La Quintessence 1998★

□ 1 ha 1,200 150–199 F

Michel Issaly feels that a wine should take after its grower. Made from one hectare (2.5 acres) of Mauzac, his La Quintessence 1998 is straw-coloured with substantial golden highlights. The expressive and complex nose conjures up crystallised fruits, honey and white truffles. Discreet oakiness is also perceptible. An impression of richness and concentration is evident on the palate. There are traces of toastiness that blend into sweetly rich flavours, and the wine finishes on a slightly bitter note.

Michel Issaly, Sainte-Cécile-d'Avès, 81600 Gaillac, tel. 05.63.57.06.64, fax 05.63.57.35.34 ✉ Y by appt.

CH. LASTOURS

Cuvée Spéciale Elevé en Fût de Chêne 1998

■ 5 ha 30,000 50–69 F

The archive record of this estate's viticultural tradition goes back to the 17th century. Run today by two brothers, Château Lastours is distinguished for two Gaillac Rouge wines cited by the jury. The vat-matured **Cuvée Classique 1998** (30–49F) is evenly matched with this Cuvée Spéciale Elevé en Fût de Chêne. It is a cherry-red wine with hints of brick, strongly redolent of ripe red fruits and spices sustained by a slight note of oak. The palate develops with suppleness, mirroring the aromas picked up on the nose. Strong oakiness on a layer of austere tannins features on the finish.

H. and P. de Faramond, Ch. Lastours, 81310 Lisle-sur-Tarn, tel. 05.63.57.07.09, fax 05.63.41.01.95 ✉ Y by appt.

CH. LECUSSE Cuvée Spéciale 1998★

■ 1.8 ha 13,000 30–49 F

Awarded a *coup de cœur* previously, this estate has belonged to M. Mogens N. Olesen, a Danish geneticist, since 1994. Made exclusively from Braucol grapes, this Cuvée Spéciale, with its dark colour, has scents of blackcurrant, delightfully sustained by hints of leather and spices. Even though the tannins come through more on the finish, this wine is nonetheless highly attractive and enjoyable.

SCA du ch. Lecusse, Broze, 81600 Gaillac, tel. 05.63.33.90.09, fax 05.63.33.94.36, e-mail lecusse@poulsenroser.dk ✉ Y by appt.

Olesen

LE PAYSSEL 1999★

◪ 0.41 ha 3,600 30–49 F

A very pale salmon-pink rosé, yet beautifully radiant, shot through with fine bubbles. The intense nose evokes fruit-drops. The palate is supple, yet still slightly sparkling, and has a good, keen aromatic quality. Very appealing.

Louis Brun et Fils, Vignoble Le Payssel, 81170 Frausseilles, tel. 05.63.56.00.47, fax 05.63.56.09.16 ✉ Y ev. day 9am–12 noon 2pm–6pm; Sun. 4pm–6pm

Eric Brun

CH. LES MERITZ Cuvée Prestige 1998★

■ n.c. 50,000 20–29 F

This Cuvée Prestige has a strong red colour of perfect clarity. Still somewhat restrained, the nose begins with scents of leather; when left to breathe, the wine emits notes of black-fruit jam and spices. The fruitiness strengthens in the mouth after a straightforward attack, and the palate reveals concentration and substantial structure. The tannins are very present throughout, and are a strong feature of the finish. Lay down for two or three years.

Les Dom. Philippe Gayrel, 81140 Cahuzac-sur-Vère, tel. 05.63.33.91.16, fax 05.63.33.95.76

DOM. DE LONG PECH Cuvée Jean-Gabriel Vieilli en Fût de Chêne 1997

■ 0.6 ha 3,600 50–69 F

The Long Pech estate has 14 ha (35 acres) of vines on a limestone-clay and gravel hillside. Its Gaillac Rouge comes from a majority of Braucol grapes with a proportion of Merlot and Cabernet. Beautifully dark in colour,

it has a nose that is still restrained, though fairly deep, with signs of liquorice and a degree of oakiness. The round, concentrated palate develops with warmth and generosity towards a long finish.
🔑 Christian Bastide, Dom. de Long-Pech, Lapeyrière, 81310 Lisle-sur-Tarn, tel. 05.63.33.37.22, fax 05.63.40.42.06 ☒ 🍷 ev. day except Sun. 9am–12.30pm 2pm–6.30pm

MANOIR DE L'EMMEILLE
Tradition 1998

■ 6 ha 40,000 🍾 30–49 F

In the cellars of the Manor l'Emmeillé, Charles and Janine Poussou will let you taste this Gaillac Rouge that drew the attention of the jury. Ruby in colour, with lively highlights, it reveals a fairly intense, forthright nose comprising spices, liquorice, blackcurrants and peppers. The same frankness characterises the palate, which leaves a bracing, fresh, spicy impression. The aromatic finish is sustained by tannins that will in time harmonise.
🔑 EARL Manoir l'Emmeillé, 81140 Campagnac, tel. 05.63.33.12.80, fax 05.63.33.20.11 ☒ 🍷 by appt.
🔑 Charles Poussou

DOM. DE MATENS
Cuvée Joseph Vieilli en Fût de Chêne 1998★

■ 1 ha 3,200 🍾 🛢 30–49 F

The Matens estate is located on the lower slopes within the Gaillac appellation zone. Its 5 ha (12 acres) of organically farmed vines produce a harvest whose small quantity is compensated by richness and concentration. The resulting wine has a rich appearance, with an intense deep purplish colour. Its appealing, expressive nose gives forth aromas of red fruits and a note of liquorice, with an underlying subtly spiced oakiness. Round and soft when the wine hits the palate, the flavour evolves towards vanilla-tinged fruit. The oak then comes to the fore, emphasising the youth of the tannins, which need another two years to soften.
🔑 Martine Lecomte, Dom. de Matens, 81600 Gaillac, tel. 05.63.57.43.96, fax 05.63.57.43.82 ☒ 🍷 by appt.

CH. MONTELS
Doux Les Trois Chênes Elevé en Fût de Chêne 1998★★

□ 4 ha 3,000 🛢 50–69 F

A 22 ha (54-acre) estate whose wines do not disappoint. Much appreciated this year for two wines in its 'Three Oaks' range, Château Montels has again demonstrated its skill. The **Gaillac Blanc Sec 1998** (30–49F) gains a star, while this Gaillac Doux was the jury's preference. One only has to see the golden colour and bright highlights, then to linger on the riches of its very natural fragrance – dried or crystallised fruits and oaky, roasted aromas – to see why. The rich attack heralds a sweet, rounded flavour in the mouth. The palate is filled with a complex structure that releases many different aromas, leading to a finish that is a harmonious conjunction of wine and oak.
🔑 Bruno Montels, Burgal, 81170 Souel, tel. 05.63.56.01.28, fax 05.63.56.15.46 ☒ 🍷 ev. day 9.30am–7pm

CH. MOUSSENS Doux 1998★

□ 1.5 ha 3,500 🍾 🌡 30–49 F

Made exclusively from the Mauzac variety, this Gaillac Doux lights up the glass with its very pure golden-yellow colour. It charms the nose with notes of well-ripened white fruits and floral nuances. The palate is harmoniously balanced between sweetness and freshness, and its ample structure is readily appreciable.
🔑 Alain Monestié, Moussens, 81150 Cestayrols, tel. 05.63.56.86.60, fax 05.63.56.86.60 ☒ 🍷 ev. day except Sun. 9am–12 noon 3pm–7pm

DOM. DES PARISES Loin de l'Œil Doux 1998★

□ 1.5 ha 4,200 🍾 🌡 30–49 F

The Loin-de-l'œil variety (Len de Lel in Occitan, meaning 'far from the eye'), gets its name from the grape's distance from the originating bud (the *œil*). It has produced this straw-yellow Gaillac with glimmering highlights, and an intense nose suggesting well-ripened fruits (quince), beeswax and hints of sweet spices. On the palate, it has good presence and balance.
🔑 SCEV Arnaud, rue de la Mairie, 81150 Lagrave, tel. 05.63.41.78.63, fax 05.63.41.78.63 ☒ 🍷 ev. day 8am–12 noon 2pm–6pm

PERLE D'AUTAN Sec Perlé 1999★

□ 100 ha 450,000 🍾 🌡 20 F+

Established more than 40 years ago, the Rabastens co-operative today makes all types of wine: red, rosé, dry white, sweet white, Méthode Gaillacoise or perlé. Perlé is so called because it is slightly sparkling. This 1999 Sec Perlé, which is pale and crystalline, offers a reliable, intensely perfumed nose in which fresh fruit aromas with the accent on the exotic. After a forthright attack, the wine leaves a refreshing sensation in the mouth owing to its semi-sparkling character, which is well maintained on the finish. A highly attractive wine.
🔑 Cave de Rabastens, 33, rte d'Albi, 81800 Rabastens, tel. 05.63.33.73.80, fax 05.63.33.85.82, e-mail rabastens@vins-du-sud-ouest.com 🍷 ev. day 9am–12.30pm 3pm–7pm

PEYRES-COMBE Doux 1998★

□ 0.6 ha 2,350 🍾 🌡 30–49 F

Victor Brureau has adopted a methodical approach towards finding the best varieties to suit particular terrains. Hence the citation by the jury of his **Gaillac Rouge 1997, Cuvée La Combe**, and this sweet wine, whose straw colour with pale green highlights is full of freshness. The intense, quite subtle nose is marked by delicate scents of fruits and flowers. After a supple attack, the wine goes on to achieve a

pleasant balance between sweetness and acidity, retaining its fruitiness right to the finish. An elegant wine.
🗝 Victor Brureau, La Combe, 81140 Andillac, tel. 05.63.33.94.67, fax 05.63.33.94.67, e-mail peyrescombe@wanadoo.fr ☒ Y by appt.
🗝 Brureau-Marty

VIN DE VOILE DE ROBERT PLAGEOLES ET FILS Sec 1992*

□ 2 ha n.c. 150–199 F

Robert and Bernard Plageoles are the bards and specialists of the ancestral varieties of Gaillac wine-making. Made from Mauzac Roux, their Vin de Voile is an off-beat product, aged for seven years without topping-up, like the *vin jaune* of the Jura. This amber-coloured 1992 reveals a powerful, oxidative nose. Quite correctly, it comprises balsamic aromas and notes of green walnut. The palate is upfront, beautifully lively and quite supple. There is perceptible alcohol, but it serves to support the aromas of macerated fruits and other more typical elements within a warm finish. Definitely worth trying.
🗝 EARL Robert Plageoles et Fils, Dom. des Très-Cantous, 81140 Cahuzac-sur-Vère, tel. 05.63.33.90.40, fax 05.63.33.95.64 ☒ Y ev. day 8am–12 noon 2pm–6pm; Sun. by appt.

DOM. RENE RIEUX

Doux Concerto Elevé en Fût de Chêne 1998*

□ 1.5 ha 2,200 70–99 F

Two well-interpreted variations on a mellow theme: a **Gaillac Doux, Harmonie 98** (30–49F) and this more prestigious Concerto wine with its beautiful golden highlights. The first aromatic tones, still reticent but complex, are composed of crystallised fruits with burnt elements. The palate is rich and concentrated, with a long finish of preserved fruits. A mellow wine to enjoy on its own.
🗝 Dom. René Rieux, hameau de Boissel, 81600 Gaillac, tel. 05.63.57.29.29, fax 05.63.57.51.71, e-mail domaine.rene.rieux@wanadoo.fr ☒ Y ev. day except Sun. 9am–12 noon 2pm–7pm
🗝 CAT Boissel

DOM. ROTIER

Doux Renaissance 1998**

□ 4.2 ha 15,000 70–99 F

Besides the very successful **Gaillac Rouge, Cuvée Renaissance 1998** (50–69F), there is this remarkably high-quality sweet version. The colour is strong gold, while the nose is highly complex and perfectly matured, subtle notes of oak mingling with aromas of preserved fruits. The palate starts out sweet and intense, then reveals its rich, generous, concentrated, fleshy, fruity character. The long, flavoursome finish makes this wine a real pleasure.
🗝 Dom. Rotier, Petit Nareye, 81600 Cadalen, tel. 05.63.41.75.14, fax 05.63.41.54.56 ☒ Y ev. day 8am–12 noon 2pm–7pm; Sun. by appt.
🗝 Alain Rotier et Francis Marre

CH. DE SALETTES

Doux L'Aoutouno 1998*

□ n.c. 12,000 30–49 F

One star was shared by the **Château de Salettes Sec 1998** and this Gaillac Doux made from Muscadelle and Loin-de-l'œil grapes. It is a wine of quite intense hue with straw-coloured nuances. Its powerful and concentrated nose strikes a good balance between aromas of ripe fruits and honey. The attack is round and, although the wine goes on to be rich and fleshy, there is no lack of freshness. Persistent and slightly oaky, the finish has a pleasant suggestion of bitterness.
🗝 SCEV Ch. de Salettes, Salettes, 81140 Cahuzac-sur-Vère, tel. 05.63.33.60.60, fax 05.63.33.60.61, e-mail chateau-de-salettes@wanadoo.fr ☒ Y by appt.
🗝 Roger Le Net

CH. DE TAUZIES Sec 1999*

□ 3 ha 9,000 20–29 F

This Gaillac derives from blending Sauvignon, an international variety, with regionally typical Loin-de-l'œil grapes. Light in colour with pale green highlights, this wine releases scents of flowers and white-fleshed fruits. It hits the palate gently, and then develops a good balance between freshness and mellowness. The fruit is well-expressed within a full palate, and positively bursts out at the finish.
🗝 Pierre and Olivier Mouly, Ch. de Tauzies, rte de Cordes, 81600 Gaillac, tel. 05.63.57.06.06, fax 05.63.41.01.92, e-mail chateau-tauzies@wanadoo.fr ☒ Y ev. day except Sun. 8am–12 noon 2pm–6pm

DOM. DES TERRISSES

Méthode Gaillacoise Cuvée Saint-Laurent*

○ 1 ha 6,000 50–69 F

Alain and Brigitte Cazottes offer a natural (undosed) Méthode Gaillacoise Brut. It has a fine sparkling golden colour, and a generous nose with scents of ripe fruits and honey. The palate is smooth and fruity, and the bubbles quickly dissolve, but the wine keeps its lively character right to the finish. The jury also singled out the **Gaillac Rouge, Cuvée Saint-Laurent 1998**.
🗝 Brigitte et Alain Cazottes, Dom. des Terrisses, 81600 Gaillac, tel. 05.63.57.16.80, fax 05.63.41.05.87, e-mail domaine.des.terrisses@wanadoo.fr Y ev. day except Sun. 9am–12 noon 2pm–6pm

DOM. DE VAYSSETTE 1998**

■ 5 ha 11,000 30–49 F

In addition to the star given to the Vayssette estate for their **Gaillac Doux 1998**, the jury expressed admiration for their Gaillac Rouge, awarding it a new *coup de cœur*. Encouragingly true to type, the 1998 version is intense cherry in colour with

pronounced violet highlights. The nose opens with fresh, floral scents, and then develops a wide range of fruity and spicy aromas. On the palate, the wine is extremely forthright and perfectly balanced. Its first-class palate is sustained by a remarkable structure composed of silky, unobtrusive tannins. Although not oak-matured, this is a great wine.

🔑 Dom. de Vayssette, Laborie, 81600 Gaillac, tel. 05.63.57.31.95, fax 05.63.81.56.84 ☒ 🍷 by appt.

CH. VIGNE-LOURAC

Doux Vieilles Vignes 1998★★

☐ n.c. 20,000 30–49 F

The Château Vigne-Lourac Gaillac Doux, Vieilles Vignes is as remarkable as ever. The 1998 version is intense gold in colour with pretty highlights in the glass. Its rich, intense nose is suggestive of ripened fruits laced with honey. A gourmet experience enjoyed to the full on the palate, this wine has voluminous, perfectly balanced flavour. Rich and highly perfumed, the aromas persist on a very gentle finish.

🔑 Vignobles Gayrel, B.P. 4, 81600 Gaillac, tel. 05.63.81.21.05, fax 05.63.81.21.09

Buzet

The Buzet vineyard, sited between Agen and Marmande, has been recognised since the Middle Ages as an integral part of the Haut-Pays Bordelais area. It was originally a monastic domain, which was then developed by the burgers of Agen. Buzet faded into a memory after the devastation of the vineyards by phylloxera but, from 1956, it became a symbol of the renaissance of the vineyards in the Haut-Pays. Two individuals, Jean Mermillod and Jean Combabessouse, presided over the vineyard's revitalisation, which also owes a great deal to the Cave Coopérative des Producteurs Réunis, where all the wines are brought on in hogsheads which are regularly renewed. The vineyard now stretches between Damazan and Sainte-Colombe on the lower slopes of the Garonne; it irrigates the tourist towns of Nérac and Barbaste.

The alternating terroirs of alluvial clay, pebbly soils and sandy limestones produce varied wines of striking character. The strong, deeply coloured, fleshy reds are velvety enough to rival some of their Girondin neighbours, and marvellous with local gastronomic dishes such as duck breast, confits (duck or goose preserved in fat), and rabbit cooked with prunes. Buzet wines are traditionally red, with 113,583 hl (2,998,591 gal) in 1999, but whites and rosés, of which 4,904 hl (129,466 gal) were produced in 1999, add to a range that is nevertheless dedicated above all to a palette of purples, garnets and vermilions.

BARON D'ALBRET 1997★★

■ 200 ha 273,040 30–49 F

The Baron d'Albret and Marquis du Grez wines represent more than a third of all Buzet produced. The nose of the former is complex, marrying aromas of fruits and vegetables. Its flavours evolve in the mouth, beginning with fruitiness, then becoming more complex, and finishing with rounded tannins. Rich, fruity and flavoursome, this wine will be at its best in 2001. The **Marquis du Grez, Sélection Vieilles Vignes Rouge 1997** has a more discreet nose. Its tannins are a little more austere, but still have a general freshness. This wine should find its proper balance in two to three years.

🔑 Les Vignerons de Buzet, B.P. 17, 47160 Buzet-sur-Baïse, tel. 05.53.84.74.30, fax 05.53.84.74.24, e-mail buzet@vignerons-buzet.fr ☒ 🍷 ev. day except Sun. 9am–12 noon 2pm–6pm

BARON D'ARDEUIL

Elevé en Fût de Chêne 1999★★

☐ 10 ha 25,000 30–49 F

The red Baron d'Ardeuil is well-known. We now need to reckon with this white version, which in its very first year gains a *coup de cœur*. The nose is elegant, abounding in aromas of flowers and toasted almonds. Its rich, structured elements make for an interesting palate, which contains plenty of ripe fruits, including peach. The distinguished and

SOUTH-WEST

complex finish is pleasantly fresh. A turbot would do justice to it.
🔑 Les Vignerons de Buzet, B.P. 17, 47160 Buzet-sur-Baïse, tel. 05.53.84.74.30, fax 05.53.84.74.24, e-mail buzet@vignerons-buzet.fr ☑ 🍷 ev. day except Sun. 9am–12 noon 2pm–6pm

LES VIGNERONS DE BUZET

Grande Réserve 1997★★

■ 32 ha 47,416 150–199 F

This upmarket wine is made from rigorously selected fruit. Its nose is largely dominated by oak, but there is room for notes of stewed fruits, including prune. The tannins express their strength with density, straightforwardness and clarity, though one senses still a certain reserve. The finish, on the other hand, is extremely gentle, which makes this 1997 a convivial wine that is ready to drink, but that may also be laid down. The **Cuvée Jean-Marie Hébrard** (70–99F) is awarded one star: it is full of muscle and character, but needs a further two to three years' ageing to be appreciated.
🔑 Les Vignerons de Buzet, B.P. 17, 47160 Buzet-sur-Baïse, tel. 05.53.84.74.30, fax 05.53.84.74.24, e-mail buzet@vignerons-buzet.fr ☑ 🍷 ev. day except Sun. 9am–12 noon 2pm–6pm

CH. DU FRANDAT

Cuvée du Majorat 1997★

■ 6 ha 34,000 30–49 F

The nose of this Cuvée du Majorat is full of ripened fruits with musky, gamey notes. Its powerful tannins nevertheless lead on to an elegant finish, adding up to a promising wine that will improve with age. The **Cuvée du Château 1998** also garnered a star. The nose is marked by oak (notes of toastiness), but fruit is very evident too. It fills the mouth in an interesting way, and finishes on a fresh note. An appealing wine.
🔑 Patrice Sterlin, Ch. du Frandat, 47600 Nérac, tel. 05.53.65.23.83, fax 05.53.97.05.77 ☑
🍷 ev. day except Sun. 10am–12 noon 3pm–6pm; cl. Jan.

CH. LARCHE 1997★★

■ 20 ha 182,148 30–49 F

The best growing areas are often those that overlook the river Garonne, and these two interesting châteaux are no exception. The Larché has a somewhat immature nose of stewed fruit and spices. Full, round and warm in the mouth, it is a flavoursome wine possessed of perfect balance. Ready for drinking now, it may also be kept for a further two to three years. Another very successful 1997 is the **Château de Bougigues** (which means 'fallow land' in Gascon). Its nose evokes bay leaves and pepper, with hints of leather, and its tannic structure is broad and well-balanced for such a meaty wine as this. From a production of 156,000 bottles, it needs to wait several more years.
🔑 Les Vignerons de Buzet, B.P. 17, 47160 Buzet-sur-Baïse, tel. 05.53.84.74.30, fax 05.53.84.74.24, e-mail buzet@vignerons-buzet.fr ☑
🍷 ev. day except Sun. 9am–12 noon 2pm–6pm
🔑 M. de Tretaigne

CH. TOURNELLES Cuvée Prestige 1999★

◢ 1.5 ha 10,000 30–49 F

Taken over in 1995 by the Vigouroux family of Cahors, this property happily went into the production of rosé in 1999. The nose is fresh, with aromas of small red fruits, strawberries and peardrops. The palate is full of flavour and has good body. There is lots of fruit there, and the wine as a whole is pretty lively. A handsome accompaniment for white meat.
🔑 EARL Bertrand Gabriel, Ch. Tournelles, 47600 Calignac, tel. 05.65.20.80.80, fax 05.65.20.80.81 ☑
🔑 B. Vigouroux

CH. TOURNEMINE 1997★

■ 30 ha 149,861 30–49 F

A fine property on gravel soil founded by M. Beaussier from Provence. The wine is good, in spite of not being cask-matured. Aromas of fruits and spices dominate the nose. The palate is rounded with well-ripened tannins. Very smooth and moreish, this is an easy-drinking, round and silky wine. The jury also liked the **Château de Piis 1998** from a vineyard more to the north, close to the Landes forest. It is a real red-fruit wine, with densely packed tannins. A wine of fine flavour and great charm.
🔑 Les Vignerons de Buzet, B.P. 17, 47160 Buzet-sur-Baïse, tel. 05.53.84.74.30, fax 05.53.84.74.24, e-mail buzet@vignerons-buzet.fr ☑ 🍷 ev. day except Sun. 9am–12 noon 2pm–6pm
🔑 Beaussier

Côtes du Frontonnais

The Côtes du Frontonnais are Toulousain wines from a very old vineyard which was once the property of the Knights of the Order of Saint John of Jerusalem. During the siege of Montauban, Louis XIII and Richelieu were said to have succumbed to comparative tastings . . . Rebuilt as a result of the establishment of the co-operative cellars of Fronton and Villaudric, the vineyard has stuck to its original varieties including the Negrette, a local variety found in Gaillac, as well as Cot, Cabernet Franc, Cabernet-Sauvignon, Syrah, Gamay and Mauzac.

The terroir of silts, clays and pebble layers covers about 2,000 ha (4,940 acres) of the terraces of the river Tarn. The red wines, with a high proportion of Cabernet, Gamay or Syrah, are light, fruity and aromatic. The wines with the greatest proportion of Negrette are stronger, tannic and have a distinctive flavour of the terroir. The rosés are clean, fresh and pleasantly fruity. Production is about 110,000 hl (2,904,000 gal).

CH. BELLEVUE LA FORET

La Cuvée Or 1998

■ 3 ha 20,000 30–49 F

This estate has gained a solid reputation thanks to the output of its 110 ha (272 acres) of vines. Dark and deep, La Cuvée Or yields intense aromas of red fruits with hints of spices. After a forthright attack, it reveals a well-crafted palate with good consistency and fruit. A well-made wine.

Ch. Bellevue la Forêt, 4500, av. de Grisolles, 31620 Fronton, tel. 05.34.27.91.91, fax 05.61.82.39.70, e-mail contact@chateaubellevuelaforet.com by appt.

Patrick Germain

CH. BOUISSEL 1998★★

■ 1.5 ha 10,000 30–49 F

The Bouissel vineyard extends over the ancient Tarn river-terrace, where there is a prehistoric stone-cutting site. Négrette, Cabernet Franc, Syrah and Cot are more obvious features of the site today, and are responsible for the best Côtes du Frontonnais. Deep and dark in colour, this 1998 has a nose strong in aromas of ripe red fruits and spices. After a good attack, the wine beautifully fills the mouth with well-structured and harmonious body. The silky tannins melt into a warm finish. Note also the highly successful **Cuvée Or 1998 Rouge**.

EARL Pierre Selle, Ch. Bouissel, 82370 Campsas, tel. 05.63.30.10.49, fax 05.63.64.01.22 ev. day except Sun. 9am–12.30pm 2pm–7.30pm; Wed. 2pm–7.30pm

CH. CAHUZAC

Fleuron de Guillaume Elevé en Fût de Chêne 1998★

■ 6.85 ha 32,000 30–49 F

In 1766, Guillaume Cahuzac acquired land within the Frontonnais wine-growing district that would become the Château Cahuzac estate. This intense ruby-coloured wine, which bears his name, smells of flowers and fruits, sustained by oak. After a forthright attack, it is aromatic and fresh on the palate, its balance deriving from a mesh of oaky tannins. Well-made and ready to drink.

EARL de Cahuzac, Les Peyronnets, 82170 Fabas, tel. 05.63.64.10.18, fax 05.63.67.36.97 by appt.

Ferran Père et Fils

CH. CAZE Villaudric 1999★

◪ 1 ha 4,000 20–29 F

Founded in 1776, this estate extends over 12 ha (30 acres) of reddish alluvial sand and pebbles, arid soils that give the vineyard its originality. The 18th-century cellar, full of vats and casks, is built underground. This 1999 rosé, with its pretty salmon colour, has a bright, lively appearance. Its *tutti frutti* nose smells distinctly of strawberries, sustained by a note of liquorice. The fresh, harmonious palate continues in this fruity vein, and the finish leaves a very striking impression. Also good is the **Villaudric Rouge 1998** cited by the jury.

Martine Hérail, Ch. Caze, 31620 Villaudric, tel. 05.61.82.92.70, fax 05.61.82.09.95, e-mail chateau.caze@libertysurf.fr ev. day except Sun. 9am–12 noon 3pm–7pm

CH. CLOS MIGNON

Villaudric Tradition Elevé en Fût de Chêne 1998★

■ 2 ha 7,000 30–49 F

After two centuries of general agriculture, Château Clos-Mignon is today exclusively a vineyard. Maybe the medal awarded to it by the Ministry of Agriculture in 1893 for its 'perfect maintenance of old vines' had something to do with the change; it was certainly well-founded, judging by this Villaudric wine. The garnet colour is of medium intensity, while the nose has scents of ripe fruits and spices on an underlay of oak. The highly aromatic palate has developed roundness and suppleness, and is marked by wood, making for an attractive wine that is ready to drink. Equally good is the **Villaudric rosé 1999** (20–29F).

GAEC du Cap de l'Homme, Ch. Clos Mignon, 31620 Villeneuve-les-Bouloc, tel. 05.61.82.10.89, fax 05.61.82.99.14, e-mail omuzart@aol.com by appt.

Muzart Frères

COMTE DE NEGRET 1998★

■ n.c. n.c. 20 F-

Comte de Négret is the top label marketed by the co-operative cellar at Fronton. No less than three versions were cited: the **Rosé 1999** with its remarkable fruitiness, the **Excellence Rouge 1998 Elevé en Fût de Chêne** (20–29F), and this 1998 red. The colour is a particularly seductive, sumptuous purple, so dark that it is almost opaque. A powerful, mature nose exhibits notes of red fruits and violets, while the freshness of the palate is accompanied by a weighty structure, with supporting tannins that persist through to the finish. A well-composed wine.

Cave de Fronton, av. des Vignerons, 31620 Fronton, tel. 05.62.79.97.79, fax 05.62.79.97.70 by appt.

CH. COUTINEL 1998

■ 27 ha 200,000 20-29 F

The firm of Arbeau, established in 1878, has diversified its activities down the years, being in turn producer, négociant, wine-maker and distiller. In 1920, the firm was attracted to Château Coutinel, which today offers this deep red wine with shades of purple. On the nose, which is quite fresh and intense, it releases fruity, discreetly oaky notes. After a pleasing attack, the wine reveals structure, suppleness and balance, retaining throughout an aromatic character with a slight touch of vanilla.

Jean-Claude Arbeau, 82370 Labastide-Saint-Pierre, tel. 05.63.64.01.80, fax 05.63.30.11.42, e-mail arbeau@wanadoo.fr by appt.

DOM. CROIX DE PEYRAT 1998★

■ 8 ha 9,000 20-29 F

Two years ago, Denis Dussère took over this estate, which dates back to 1880. This is his first vintage. Vivid cherry-red, it has a lovely bouquet offering a range of red fruits. Its roundness and balance make it a flavour-some wine, a well-balanced mélange of red fruits. An elegant, mature Côtes du Frontonnais.

Denis Dussère, Dom. Croix de Peyrat, 82370 Campsas, tel. 05.63.30.58.50, fax 05.63.30.00.67 by appt.

CH. DEVES 1999★★

1 ha 6,700 20-29 F

Owned by the same family since 1900, this 11 ha (27-acre) estate was restructured in 1975 to achieve appellation status. Since then all the wines produced by André and Michel Abart have been true to type. Take this remarkable rosé. Clear and bright, it has an intense and complex nose of red fruits, white-fleshed fruits and flowers. The harmonious palate is fresh, round, full and perfectly balanced, leading to an aromatic and very long-lasting finish.

André and Michel Abart, Ch. Devès, 31620 Castelnau-d'Estretefonds, tel. 05.61.35.14.97, fax 05.61.35.14.97 by appt.

CH. LA COLOMBIERE

Villaudric Vin gris 1999★

2.55 ha 20,133 30-49 F

This former property belonging to the Abbaye de la Daurade in Toulouse offers a 1999 salmon-pink *vin gris* made from Gamay and Négrette grapes. This bright, clear wine has scents of fruits (raspberry) and flowers. Lively when it hits the palate, it gently evolves on the palate with plenty of richness, warmth and aromatic complexity (red fruits and liquorice). A well-crafted wine with a vibrant finish.

Baron François de Driésen, Ch. La Colombière, 31620 Villaudric, tel. 05.61.82.44.05, fax 05.61.82.57.56, e-mail françois@chateaulacolombiere.com ev. day except Sun. 9am–12 noon 2pm–6pm

CH. LA PALME Privilège 1998★

■ 30 ha 180,000 20-29 F

Although Château La Palme had the distinction in 1850 of being cultivated by the then mayor of Toulouse, Henri Lignières, it has also had its share of disaster. The 100 ha (247-acre) vineyard has in its time been wiped out by phylloxera and frost. Happily, it is now fully restored and demonstrates its good health in this bright, clear wine with aubergine highlights. The aromas of sharp red fruits evoke the joys of spring. Its supple attack introduces a flavoursome palate, well-supported by acidity, and which is fruity and harmonious to the finish. An attractive and approachable wine.

Ch. La Palme, 31340 Villemur-sur-Tarn, tel. 05.61.09.02.82, fax 05.61.09.27.01 by appt.

Ethuin

CH. LAS PLACES 1998★

■ 12 ha 80,000 20-29 F

The Négrette variety, which plays a special part in this appellation, here tops the bill, as it accounts for half the blend, while Gamay and Cabernet grapes play supporting roles. The show is a success! The deep colour with purple highlights is almost entirely clear, while the forthright and appealing nose displays aromas of red fruits in *eau de vie*, as well as notes of flowers and spices. The palate is lively, supple and lithe, finishing with a warmth that brings back the aromas of red fruits over discreet tannins. An ideal accompaniment for Toulouse sausages with fried cep mushrooms.

Pierre Lescure, 82370 Labastide-Saint-Pierre, tel. 05.63.64.01.80, fax 05.63.30.11.42

CH. LE ROC Cuvée Don Quichotte 1998★

■ n.c. 7,500 30-49 F

With his established reputation, this talented young wine-grower has led us to expect characterful wines. This Cuvée, named in honour of Don Quixote, is a carefully judged blend of Négrette and Syrah. It has a gorgeous scent of violets and peonies beneath lightly spiced oak. The attack is silky, the

palate round, fresh and aromatic. The finish, which is supported by frisky tannins, presages an excellent development.
🗝 GAEC Ribes, Dom. Le Roc, 31620 Fronton, tel. 05.61.82.93.90, fax 05.61.82.72.38 ☑ Y by appt.

CH. MONTAURIOL Mons Aureolus 1998

■ n.c. n.c. 🛢 30–49 F

The Château de Montauriol has been taken over by Nicolas Gélis. Evidently, the moment has come for this indispensable Frontonnais property to renew itself. Two wines are offered: a **Rosé 1999**, and this 1998 red, the Mons Aureolus. The colour is deep garnet with a touch of maturation. The nose is quite complex, releasing first of all notes of red and black fruits, and then spices on a gently oaky base. The wine is warm on the palate, revealing density of structure over still evident tannins. A robust wine that can afford to wait a little longer.
🗝 Nicolas Gélis, Ch. Montauriol, 31340 Villematier, tel. 05.61.35.30.58, fax 05.61.35.30.59 Y by appt.

CH. PLAISANCE Thibaut de Plaisance Vieilli en Fût de Chêne 1998★★

■ 1.5 ha 8,000 🛢 30–49 F

Agronomist and confirmed wine-grower Marc Penavayre well deserves his *coup de cœur* for all the effort he has put in over the past ten years to make the family vineyard prosper. His black-cherry Thibaut de Plaisance has a nose of character; exceptionally fruity and spicy, it has acquired some lovely oak tones from its 12 months in barrel. Smooth in the mouth from the first entry, the wine has an aromatic and perfectly balanced palate that is round and full. Gentle tannins accompany the wine's persistent finish. The Côtes du Frontonnais **Château Plaisance Rouge 1998 Elevé en Cuve** and **Rosé 1999** also gain citations (20–29F).
🗝 EARL de Plaisance, pl. de la Mairie, 31340 Vacquiers, tel. 05.61.84.97.41, fax 05.61.84.11.26 ☑ Y by appt.
🗝 Penavayre

DOM. DE SAINT-GUILHEM Amadeus 1998★

■ 2 ha 600 🛢 50–69 F

Saint-Guilhem is one of the oldest estates in the Frontonnais. A century ago, it was celebrated for its fine wines and *eaux de vie*. The purple colour of this Amadeus announces the lavish scent of violets that, accompanied by aromas of preserved red fruits and pepper, fills the nose. Rich and warm in the mouth, the wine rejoices in fine oak tannins, supporting a fairly long, peppery finish. A fully rounded wine.
🗝 Philippe Laduguie, Dom. de Saint-Guilhem, 31620 Castelnau-d'Estretefonds, tel. 05.61.82.12.09, fax 05.61.82.65.59 ☑ Y by appt.

CH. SAINT-LOUIS Elevé en Fût de Chêne 1998★

■ 10 ha 60,000 🍷🛢🌡 30–49 F

Château Saint-Louis is located on the ancient river-terrace of the Tarn, where the pebbly soil is typical of the region. Since its purchase by Alain Mahmoudi in 1991, the property has undergone extensive transformation. Almost a decade on, his efforts have issued in this 1998 garnet – almost brick-coloured – wine. The generous nose evolves through notes of black fruits (blackcurrant), violet and spices, and then takes on a strong scent of mocha coffee. The palate is quite powerful but balanced, with an emphasis on toasty aromas sustained by a network of silky tannins. Ready for drinking.
🗝 Alain Mahmoudi, 82370 Labastide-Saint-Pierre, tel. 05.63.64.01.80, fax 05.63.30.11.42, e-mail saintlouis@wanadoo.fr ☑ Y by appt.

Lavilledieu AOVDQS

North of the Frontonnais, on the terraces of the Tarn and the Garonne, the little vineyard of Lavilledieu covers about 150 ha (370 acres) and produces red and rosé wines. The production, classified as AOVDQS, is still very little known. The Negrette (30%), Cabernet Franc, Gamay, Syrah and Tannat are the authorised varieties.

CUVEE DES CAPITOULS Grand Capitouls 1998★

■ 5 ha 10,000 🍷🛢🌡 20–29 F

The Cuvée des Capitouls results from a partnership between the Confrérie des Capitouls and the La Ville-Dieu-du-Temple co-operative. This 1998 wine is a fairly dense ruby, and describes a shining disc when swirled around the glass. The nose starts with

red and black fruits, and then extends into vegetal and woody notes, lightly tinged with spice. The palate is supple, smooth, round and relatively concentrated. The fruity, vanillary flavours are supported by fine tannins.
🔑 Cave de La Ville-Dieu-du-Temple, 82290 La Ville-Dieu-du-Temple, tel. 05.63.31.60.05, fax 05.63.31.69.11 V
Y by appt.

DOM. DE MAGNAC 1998*

■ n.c. 26,000 20-29 F

Another wine from the La Ville-Dieu-du-Temple co-operative, this Domaine de Magnac blends Négrette, Gamay, Syrah, Cabernet Franc and Tannat varieties. The ruby-red colour is no less deep than in the previous wine. Its nose shows intense and complex aromas of stewed red fruits, with the merest touch of liquorice and notes of undergrowth. Supple and round as it develops in the mouth, the wine restates its fruitiness with gorgeous aromatic presence, combined with sufficient freshness and well-integrated tannins.
🔑 Cave de La Ville-Dieu-du-Temple, 82290 La Ville-Dieu-du-Temple, tel. 05.63.31.60.05, fax 05.63.31.69.11 V
Y by appt.

Côtes du Brulhois AOVDQS

Since November 1984, these former Vins de Pays have been AOVDQS, and are produced on both banks of the Garonne, in the departments of Lot-et-Garonne and Tarn-et-Garonne, near the small town of Layrac. The appellation covers an area of about 200 ha (494 acres). Production is mainly of reds from Bordelais varieties and the local Tanat and Cot. The majority of the wine-making is undertaken by two co-operative cellars.

LA VOUTE SAINT-ROC
Elevé en Fût de Chêne 1998**

■ 50 ha 50,000 20-29 F

This is a wine whose dense hue well illustrates why the term 'black wine' was applied in former days to the Brulhois region's production. The nose releases concentrated aromas of black fruits (blackcurrant and cherry), followed by warm spicy notes. On the palate it is silky at first, before developing generous black-fruit flavours, sustained by elegant, discreetly oaky tannins. A balanced wine.
🔑 Vignerons du Brulhois, 82340 Dunes, tel. 05.63.39.91.92, fax 05.63.39.82.83
Y ev. day except Sun. Mon. 8am–12 noon 2pm–6pm

PARVIS DES TEMPLIERS 1998*

■ 200 ha 100,000 20-29 F

Amidst the diverse grape varieties of earlier times, the Vignerons du Brulhois have held on to Tannat, Cot and Fer-Servadou, which they have blended with Merlot and both Cabernets to produce this cherry-red wine with violet highlights. The nose is elegant, on the fruity side, and somewhat toasty. After a forthright attack, the wine is well-balanced, round and aromatic through to a finish of bitter cocoa, supported by firm tannins. The cellar's **Château Grand Chêne 1998** is also recommended.
🔑 Vignerons du Brulhois, 82340 Dunes, tel. 05.63.39.91.92, fax 05.63.39.82.83
Y ev. day except Sun. Mon. 8am–12 noon 2pm–6pm

Côtes du Marmandais

Not far from the gravels of Entre-deux-Mers and the wines of Duras and Buzet, the Côtes du Marmandais wines are mainly produced by the co-operatives in Beaupuy and Cocumont on both banks of the Garonne. The white wines, generally made from Sémillon, Sauvignon, Muscadelle and Ugni Blanc, are dry, lively and fruity. The supple, pleasingly aromatic red wines are made mainly from Bordelais varieties, along with Abouriou, Syrah, Cot and Gamay. The vineyard covers about 1,500 ha (3,705 acres) and produced 91,544 hl (2,416,762 gal) in 1999.

BARON COPESTAING
Elevé en Fût de Chêne 1998***

■ n.c. 50,000 30-49 F

There are vines to the right and vines to the left, but it is those of the left bank of the Garonne that have given us this *coup de cœur* from the Cocumont cellar. The complex nose bursts forth with aromas of ripe fruits,

punctuated by the most delicate oaky notes, and the palate reinforces these impressions. After the flavour of fruit comes that of the tannin, dense and lush, leaving an enjoyable touch of vanilla at the finish. A charming wine, amazingly rich, in which the grapes have really been allowed to express themselves. Not to be opened before 2003.
🔑 Cave coop. de Cocumont, La Vieille Eglise, 47250 Cocumont, tel. 05.53.94.50.21, fax 05.53.94.52.84 Y ev. day except Sat. Sun. 9am–12 noon 2.30pm–5pm

CH. DE BEAULIEU
Elevé en Fût de Chêne 1998★

■ 20 ha 90,000 30–49 F

Work on the renovation of the cellar and reorganisation of the vineyard is still in progress at the Château de Beaulieu, and is already producing excellent results. This wine's range of fruity aromas is still dominated by new oak, but after a very fine attack on the palate, vanilla and oak quickly give way to ripe fruit, softened by much richness. Long on the finish, this 1998 will keep for three or four years.
🔑 Robert et Agnès Schulte, Ch. de Beaulieu, 47180 Saint-Sauveur-de-Meilhan, tel. 05.53.94.30.40, fax 05.53.94.30.40 ☑ Y ev. day 9am–6pm; Sat. Sun. by appt.

BEROY Elevé en Fût de Chêne 1998★★

■ 20 ha 50,000 30–49 F

This wine was unanimously praised for its richness and sense of well-managed vinification. The nose is both subtle and powerful, and although it is still dominated by notes of spices and toast, there are some fruity aromas. Oakiness is less evident on the palate, where it appears as a background to dense, very mature tannins. There is a long finish, with a delightful resurgence of fruit flavours. A wine that promises much in the future.
🔑 Cave coop. de Cocumont, La Vieille Eglise, 47250 Cocumont, tel. 05.53.94.50.21, fax 05.53.94.52.84 ☑ Y ev. day except Sat. Sun. 9am–12 noon 2.30pm–5pm

CONFIDENTIEL
Elevé en Fût de Chêne 1998★

■ 15 ha 28,500 50–69 F

Although vanilla and toast come through very strongly in the nose, soft fruit aromas are also clearly in evidence. There is a powerful attack on the palate, then elegance in the mouth, where the wine is supported by an interesting balance between fruit and vanilla, before ending on an oaky note. A highly concentrated Côtes du Marmandais that will see its tannins come into harmony in a few years' time.
🔑 Cave de Beaupuy, Dupuy, 47200 Beaupuy, tel. 05.53.76.05.10, fax 05.53.64.63.90 ☑ Y ev. day except Sun. 8.30am–12 noon 2pm–6.30pm

DIGNITE-PRIEUR 1998★

■ 30 ha 60,000 30–49 F

The high quality of the raw material is evident throughout the tasting. The nose has aromas of ripe fruit and blackcurrant, against a fairly unobtrusive oaky background. The attack on the palate is supple and fruity. The tannins are well-softened and not at all aggressive at the finish. This harmonious Côtes du Marmandais should keep for two to three years.
🔑 Cave coop. de Cocumont, La Vieille Eglise, 47250 Cocumont, tel. 05.53.94.50.21, fax 05.53.94.52.84 Y ev. day except Sat. Sun. 9am–12 noon 2.30pm–5pm

CH. LA BASTIDE 1998★

■ 30 ha 100,000 20–29 F

In the **1998** vintage, the Cocumont cellar has produced two more highly successful wines. **Le Tap de Perbos** (30–49F) is a Côtes du Marmandais matured in barrel for 15 months. Its ripe fruit aromas are framed by elegant oak, and with its very concentrated structure, it should keep for three years. This Château de Bastide has a fine, concentrated nose of very pleasant blackcurrant and blackberry aromas. These reappear on the palate, along with supple, harmonious tannins. A soft, fruity wine that should be drunk while still young.
🔑 Cave coop. de Cocumont, La Vieille Eglise, 47250 Cocumont, tel. 05.53.94.50.21, fax 05.53.94.52.84 ☑ Y ev. day except Sat. Sun. 9am–12 noon 2.30pm–5pm

Vins d'Estaing AOVDQS

The vineyard of Aveyron is surrounded by the limestone plateaux of Aubrac, the Cantal mountains and the Lévezou plateau, so it should really be classified with the vineyards of the Massif Central. The little appellations here are very old: their original foundation by the monks of Conques goes back to the 11th century.

The Vins d'Estaing, 7 ha (17 acres), are divided between

the fresh, perfumed reds (blackcurrant and raspberry) made from Fer and Gamay and the very original whites from mixtures of Chenin, Mauzac and Rousselou. The latter are lively, flinty wines with strong terroir character.

LES VIGNERONS D'OLT

Cuvée Prestige 1999★

■ 4 ha 21,500 ▮ 20–29 F

Les Vignerons d'Olt offer two interesting wines. The first is a **1998 Estaing Blanc** produced from Mauzac and Chenin grapes, which deserves a commendation for its balance; the second, this special red Cuvée, is awarded a star. The tasters were attracted from the start by the look of its ruby halo glinting with violet, and after that their senses succumbed to its scents of green peppers and red berries, against a background of buttercream. After a vigorous attack on the palate, it continues fresh and rather light in the mouth. A pleasant, aromatic, and not at all aggressive wine.

SCA Les Vignerons d'Olt, Z.A. La Fage, 12190 Estaing, tel. 05.65.44.04.42, fax 05.65.44.04.42 ☑ Y by appt.

Vins d'Entraygues et du Fel AOVDQS

The white wines from Entraygues, 9 ha (22 acres), are cultivated on schist soils on narrow terracing cut into the steep hillsides. Made from Chenin and Mauzac, they are fresh and fruity: splendid with wild trout and the delicate Cantal cheese. The sturdy, earthy reds, made from Fel, are good paired with lamb from the Causses and *Potée Auvergnate* – a substantial soup of vegetables and meat.

JEAN-MARC VIGUIER

Cuvée Spéciale 1998★★

□ 2 ha 10,000 ▮ ♁ 30–49 F

Jean-Marc Viguier's vineyard overlooks the valleys of the Lot and the Truyère. Growing on shale and granite slopes, his Chenin vines have yielded this remarkable 1998 matured on fine lees. Luminous yellow with green glints, it gives off fresh, clean aromas, floral at first (broom, acacia, lime-blossom), then fruity (citrus) and mineral (gunflint). After a lively, slightly sparkling attack on the palate, the feel on the palate is fresh, but also full and round, with lingering flavours of citrus fruits leaving a slightly acid sensation.

Jean-Marc Viguier, Les Buis, 12140 Entraygues, tel. 05.65.44.50.45, fax 05.65.48.62.72 ☑

Y ev. day 9am–12 noon 2pm–7pm

Marcillac

Cultivated in a natural hollow, the 'valley', with a propitious micro-climate, the Mansoi variety (also known as the Fer Servadou) gives the red Marcillac wines their great originality, marked by a tannic simplicity and aromas of raspberries. In 1990, this specialist approach was acknowledged with the award of an AOC, which now covers 140 ha (346 acres) and in 1999 produced 8,097 hl (213,761 gal) of a highly individual wine that is always instantly recognisable.

FRANCIS COSTES Réserve 1998★

■ 2.3 ha 10,600 ▮▮ 20–29 F

This is an attractive cherry-red wine with violet highlights. It has a fine, complex nose with notes of blackcurrant, pepper and green peppers. The attack is clean, and it has good balance on the palate, thanks to substantial structure supported by evident tannins that are in no way aggressive, but give a ripe, liquorice flavour at the finish. In short, all the right qualities!

Francis Costes, La Baronie, 12330 Mouret, tel. 05.65.69.83.05 ☑ Y by appt.

DOM. DU CROS

Lo Sang del Païs 1998★

■ 15 ha 70,000 ▮ ▮▮ ♁ 20–29 F

'The Blood of the Region'. This is Fer Servadou's gift to Marcillac, and in particular to Philippe Teulier's estate. The wine has a brilliant, blood-red colour. It has an intense nose full of ripe red berries, with very slight hints of musk and toast. There is the same harmony of flavours in the mouth, where the fruit content is supported by well-integrated tannins right up to an attractive, slightly acid finish. This wine will be the perfect accompaniment to regional dishes, for example the famous Aveyron lamb.

Philippe Teulier, Dom. du Cros, 12390 Goutrens, tel. 05.65.72.71.77, fax 05.65.72.68.80 ☑ Y by appt.

JEAN-LUC MATHA 1998★★

■ 9 ha 60,000 ▮ 20–29 F

A producer who cultivates authenticity and offers wines of character, such as these two excellent 1998 Marcillacs. One has been **oak-matured** for 18 months (30–49F); this note is mainly concerned with the other, which has spent 12 months maturing in vats. Its deep colour reveals a brilliant halo with shades of dark purple. The nose opens with summer berry aromas (blackcurrant and raspberry), then takes on a pleasant note of the garrigue. After a lively attack on the palate, the impression that develops in the mouth is concentrated but still fresh, and based on fruit. A straightforward, well-balanced wine.

Jean-Luc Matha, Bruejouls, 12330 Clairvaux, tel. 05.65.72.63.29, fax 05.65.72.70.43 Y by appt.

LES VIGNERONS DU VALLON

Cuvée Réservée 1998

■ 25 ha 65,000 30–49 F

Made from the Mansoi, or Fer Servadou, grapes grown on a red-soiled terroir known as the 'Vallon', this 1998 has a beautiful, clear, cherry-red colour and a fairly intense nose. After some musky notes, fruit aromas become dominant and are then accompanied by pepper. The same flavours develop with admirable harmony in the mouth, supported by a framework of smooth tannins that linger agreeably at the finish.

Les Vignerons du Vallon, RN 140, 12330 Valady, tel. 05.65.72.70.21, fax 05.65.72.68.39 Y by appt.

Côtes de Millau AOVDQS

The appellation AOVDQS Côtes de Millau was officially recognised on 12 April 1994. The wines are made from Syrah and Gamay Noir and, in a very small proportion, from Cabernet-Sauvignon and Fer Servadou. Production reaches about 1,500 hl (39,600 gal).

PEYSIR 1999★

□ 1.26 ha 8,000 20–29 F

The Vignerons des Gorges du Tarn are offering two very successful wines in the 1999 vintage. One is a **rosé** called **Seigneurs de Peyreviel**, whose strawberry syrup and caramel aromas are as mouthwatering as its fresh flavours and fruity finish. The other is this white wine, which has a light yellow colour and a nose of dried fruits and vanilla. Balanced and supple in the mouth, its flavours have a nice touch of vanilla, a sign of its six-month maturation, half in vat and half in barrel. It is a good ambassador for Côtes de Millau white wine. Get there quickly; there is only a limited number of bottles.

Les Vignerons des Gorges du Tarn, rue du Colombier, 12520 Aguessac, tel. 05.65.59.84.11, fax 05.65.59.17.90 Y ev. day except Sun. 8am–12 noon 2pm–6.30pm

SEIGNEURS DE PEYREVIEL 1998★★

■ 19.9 ha n.c. 20–29 F

This red Côtes de Millau has a fairly intense colour and a nose of blackberries and raspberries. It leaves an impression of balance and roundness in the mouth, despite the presence of tannins that are still young but clearly of good quality. Retronasal flavours of wild berries linger on into a well-balanced finish. A remarkable wine, which can be kept for a year or two in the cellar.

Les Vignerons des Gorges du Tarn, rue du Colombier, 12520 Aguessac, tel. 05.65.59.84.11, fax 05.65.59.17.90 Y ev. day except Sun. 8am–12 noon 2pm–6.30pm

Béarn

Béarn wines can be produced in three different areas. The first two are the same as for Jurançon and Madiran. The other, Béarn alone, encompasses the communes around Orthez and Salies-de-Béarn, including Bellocq. This AOC covers about 160 ha (395 acres) and produced 4,100 hl (108,240 gal) of wine in 1999.

The vineyard was reconstituted after the phylloxera epidemic and occupies the gravels and pre-Pyrenean hills of the Gave valley. The red varieties include Tannat, Cabernet-Sauvignon and Cabernet Franc (Bouchy), as well as the old varieties of Manseng Noir, Courby Rouge and Fer Servadou. The wines are full-bodied and rich, and are good with 'garbure' (a local soup), and grilled squab. The rosés of Béarn, the best wines of the appellation, are lively but delicate with fine aromas from the Cabernet.

FEBUS Bellocq 1999★★

□ 10 ha 15,000 20–29 F

A name like Fébus could only refer to the jewel of the Vignerons de Bellocq cellar. This crystal-clear, raffia-coloured wine shines with green glints, and gives off a mixture of herbaceous aromas (menthol) and scents of flowers and fruits (lemon and grapefruit). It is rather fresh on the palate at first, but quickly becomes rounder thanks to a structure that is both rich and slightly acid, and lingers warmingly on notes of fruit. Those who wish to discover the wines of Béarn-Bellocq should also try the **1998 Henri de Navarre**, which is excellent (30–49F).

Les Vignerons de Bellocq,
64270 Bellocq, tel. 05.59.65.10.71,
fax 05.59.65.12.34 Y by appt.

DOM. LAPEYRE 1998★★

■ 3 ha 15,000 50–69 F

The wines of this 11-ha (27-acre) estate are always highly esteemed. Yet again, it offers this year one of the best examples of wine from the Pyrenean foothills. Consider this 1998; even its purple colour is deep and opaque. Breathe in its pronounced, complex nose, ranging from dark berries and spices to liquorice. The aromas are still wild! Taste its powerful, concentrated, substantial structure. Imagine the future of this wine as you savour its warming, spicy finish, supported as it is by very evident tannins.

Pascal Lapeyre, 52, av. des Pyrénées,
64270 Salies-de-Béarn, tel. 05.59.38.10.02,
fax 05.59.38.03.98 Y by appt.

Irouléguy

Irouléguy wines are grown on the last remnants of a big Basque vineyard (known as Chacoli on the Spanish side), founded in the 11th century by the monks of Roncevaux abbey, and today's winemakers are determined to maintain this ancient tradition. The vineyard is laid out on foothills in the communes of Saint-Etienne-de-Baïgorry, Irouléguy and Anhaux, covering some 200 ha (494 acres) and producing 7,000 hl (184,800 gal).

The older vine varieties have virtually disappeared in favour of Cabernet-Sauvignon, Cabernet Franc and Tannat for red wines, and of Courbu and Gros and Petit Manseng for the whites. Practically the whole production is vinified by the co-operative in Irouléguy but new vineyards are now beginning to appear. The Irouléguy red is fragrant and somewhat tannic, worth trying with confits (duck or goose preserved in fat). The cherry-coloured rosé is lively, fragrant and light, and goes well with pipérade (eggs with peppers) and charcuterie.

DOM. ARRETXEA Hegoxuri 1999★★

□ 1 ha 2,400 100–149 F

Located in a mountainous area, this little vineyard keeps 6 ha (15 acres) of vines. They are grown in terraces, and the methods used are organic or even biodynamic, as in the case of the plot that yielded this *coup de coeur* wine. Everything about this Hegoxuri is remarkable, from its golden straw colour with green highlights to its subtle nose, in which white flowers mingle harmoniously with extremely fresh exotic fruits. On the palate, it is a real delight. Although very rich and satisfying, it still retains plenty of freshness and balance as its aromas linger on in a ravishing finish. An exquisite wine! Also worth trying is the very successful **1998 Irouléguy Rouge** (30–49F).

Thérèse et Michel Riouspeyrous,
Dom. Arretxea, 64220 Irouléguy,
tel. 05.59.37.33.67, fax 05.59.37.33.67
Y by appt.

DOM. BRANA 1998★

■ 10 ha 30,000 50–69 F

Facing towards Haute Navarre and the Col de Roncevaux stands a tower in the typical Navarrian style of architecture, overlooking the terraced vineyard of the Brana estate, which was founded on the Arradoy mountain in 1985. It now contains an underground vat house in which this intensely purple 1998 Irouléguy was produced. Although somewhat restrained, it does release some deep aromas of crystallised dark berries, and has acquired a vanilla background from 13 months of maturation in barrel. Straightforward on the palate, it is powerfully structured by tannins that are still much in evidence, but should blend into this pleasantly soft, oaky surround. Certainly a wine for keeping.

🔑 Jean et Adrienne Brana, 3 bis, av. du Jaï-Alaï, 64220 Saint-Jean-Pied-de-Port, tel. 05.59.37.00.44, fax 05.59.37.14.28, e-mail brana-etienne@wanadoo.fr ☑
Y by appt.

DOM. ETXEGARAYA

Cuvée Lehengoa 1998

■ 2 ha 8,000 ▮ ♁ 30–49 F

The Etxegaraya estate extends over about 7 ha (17 acres) of vines, grown mainly in terraces on red sandstone or silica and clay soils. This wine comes from 80% century-old Tannat vines and 20% Cabernet Sauvignon. With its subtle shades of purple, it offers a simple but fine nose of herbaceous aromas accompanied by dark berries. After a fresh attack on the palate, it becomes rounder in the mouth, while at the same time maintaining a slightly acid streak reminiscent of boiled sweets. The structure is loose-knit, and the slightly astringent tannins leave a spicy flavour on the finish.

🔑 Joseph and Marianne Hillau, Dom. Etxegaraya, 64430 Saint-Etienne-de-Baïgorry, tel. 05.59.37.23.76, fax 05.59.37.23.76, e-mail etxegaraya@wanadoo.fr ☑
Y by appt.

GORRI D'ANSA 1998★

■ 17.5 ha 93,000 ▮ ♁ 30–49 F

It was the Vignerons du Pays Basque cellar, founded in 1952, who started the revival of the Irouléguy appellation. In 20 years it doubled the area of its vineyard and made great strides in the quality of its wines. Our first mention goes to this remarkable red, which is almost black in colour and has a deep, warming nose of dark berry jam, with a slight note of cocoa. Rich, ripe and concentrated, and built on a solid foundation of substantial tannins, this tank-matured wine should keep well. The oak-aged **1998 Comte de Leispars** can also wait patiently in your cellar for four years, but receives a citation here and now.

🔑 Les Vignerons du Pays Basque, 64430 Saint-Etienne-de-Baïgorry, tel. 05.59.37.41.33, fax 05.59.37.47.76 ☑
Y by appt.

Jurançon and Jurançon Sec

'When I was a young woman, I made the acquaintance of a dazzling, imperious prince, as treacherous as any great seducer: Jurançon.' So wrote the novelist Colette. Jurançon has been famous since it was served at the baptism of Henri IV and thereafter became the wine of occasion at all royal ceremonies of the House of Navarre. This is the first historical appearance of the notion of Appellation Protégée – since it was forbidden to import foreign wines – as well as the first steps towards Cru and classification, since all the parcels of land were recorded, according to their value, by the Parliament of Navarre. Like the Béarn wines, those of the Jurançon, then both red and white, were shipped as far as Bayonne via the sometimes hazardous waters of the Gave. Much appreciated by the Dutch and the Americans, Jurançon acquired a star quality which was only extinguished by phylloxera. Under the dynamic leadership of the Cave de Gan and a few committed vineyard owners, the vineyard (1,000 ha/2,470 acres today) was completely replanted with traditional varieties grown and trained according to the old ways.

Here more than anywhere, year of vintage is extremely important, especially for the sweet Jurançons, for which the grapes must be ripened late on the vine by the *passerillage* method. In this traditional practice, the stalks of the grapes are pinched just above the clusters shortly before they are picked in late autumn, cutting off the passage of sap between the grapes and the vine. The grapes are then allowed to ripen thoroughly in the hot sun and, since no sap can get to them, they dry out, leaving the grapes extra-rich in natural sugar. This process allows the wine to attain the legal minimum of 15% alcohol. The traditional varieties used for Jurançon are whites only, the Gros and Petit Manseng and the Courbu. In cultivation, the vines are trained high to avoid the frosts, and it is not unusual for the harvest to continue until the first snows.

The dry Jurançon, 75% of the production, is a white wine made from white grapes (Blanc de Blancs), noted for its beautiful colour with glints of green, its aromas and its honeyed flavours. It is a good accompaniment to fresh trout and salmon from the river Gave. The sweet Jurançons have a lovely golden colour, and offer complex aromas of exotic fruits (pineapple and guava) and spices (such as nutmeg and cinnamon). Their balance between acidity and sweetness makes them a perfect foil for foie gras. Sweet Jurançons can be kept for a long time to provide big wines for a whole meal from aperitif to dessert, as well as to accompany fish with sauce and ewe's milk cheeses from the Ossau valley. The best vintages are: 1970, 1971, 1975, 1981, 1982, 1983, 1987, 1989, 1990 and 1995. In 1999 production had reached 29,826 hl (787,406 gal) of sweet wines and 12,934 (341,458 gal) of dry wines.

Jurançon

DOM. BARTHELEMY 1998

□ 1 ha 5,333 30–49 F

This property of some 5 ha (12 acres) has been back in business for seven years now, thanks to the considerable investments made in it by Olivier Tessier. Reward is at hand, as this clear Jurançon with green-gold highlights proves beyond doubt. There is plenty of freshness on the nose, which has notes of exotic and especially citrus fruits. After a clean attack on the palate it is smooth, rather fresh and light in the mouth, the flavours lingering as it finishes on a strong note of acidity.

⊶ Olivier Tessier, Dom. Barthélemy, 64360 Parbayse, tel. 05.59.21.42.67, fax 05.59.71.52.03 ☑ Y by appt.

DOM. BORDENAVE Cuvée Savin 1998

□ 5 ha 10,000 70–99 F

Since the 1998 vintage, the Bordenave estate has had its labels painted by local artists, such as Alain Laborde, who is responsible for the one on the Cuvée Savin. He has used warm, golden-to-copper shades that reflect the colour of this Jurançon. The wine is still somewhat reserved, and dominated by a rich, oaky aroma. It is round, full and sweet on the palate, where the aromas are once more in evidence as one savours the wine, but there is a surprisingly obtrusive flavour of oak, which will need to fade.

⊶ Dom. Pierre and Gisèle Bordenave, quartier Ucha, 64360 Monein, tel. 05.59.21.34.83, fax 05.59.21.37.32 ☑
Y ev. day 8.30am–12 noon 2pm–6.30pm

ETIENNE BRANA

Collection Royale Premières Neiges 1999*

□ n.c. n.c. 50–69 F

This estate has been producing and selling wine for over 100 years. Its sweet white wine comes from pure Gros Manseng. It has a pale yellow colour with slight green highlights, and then a fine, elegant nose of exotic aromas. After a supple attack on the palate, it is very aromatic in the mouth, developing freshly and cleanly along the same lines as the bouquet. A real delicacy. The **1999 Jurançon Sec Collection Royale** (30–49F) also deserves a star for its pleasant, fruity character.

⊶ Etienne Brana, 3 bis, av. du Jaï-Alaï, 64220 Saint-Jean-Pied-de-Port, tel. 05.59.37.00.44, fax 05.59.37.14.28, e-mail brana-etienne@wanadoo.fr ☑
Y ev. day except Sat. Sun. 9am–12 noon 2pm–6pm

DOM. BRU-BACHE

L'Eminence 1998**

□ n.c. n.c. 200–249 F

Claude Loustalot seems to have the same Midas touch as his uncle; certainly he runs the estate with the same talent. The famous L'Eminence is one star ahead of **La Quintessence 1998**, which is also excellent (70–99F). The jury unanimously praised its magnificent colour, which is a brilliant, extremely intense gold. Its highly concentrated nose has a range of flower and fruit aromas, against a very rich background of oak. On the palate, it is succulently sweet and rich, with perfect balance. The lingering concentration is sustained by noble oak flavour that allows the exotic fruits, dried apricots, lemon, and notes of resin and ginger to express themselves. A rich Jurançon that promises great things for the future.

⊶ Dom. Bru-Baché, rue Barada, 64360 Monein, tel. 05.59.21.36.34, fax 05.59.21.32.67 ☑ Y by appt.
⊶ Claude Loustalot

DOM. DE CABARROUY

Cuvée Sainte-Catherine Elevé en fût de chêne 1998★★

☐ 2 ha 5,000 50–69 F

Patrice Limousin and Freya Skoda moved from the Muscadet region to the Cabarrouy estate in 1988. They have produced not only a very good **1999 Jurançon Sec** (30–49F), but also this Cuvée Sainte-Catherine, which shows how perfectly they have mastered the art of making sweet white wines. It colour is a brilliant yellow verging on gold, and it has a complex nose of great finesse, composed of acacia blossom and fresh then crystallised fruits, along with a slight oaky aroma. The opening impression is of roundness, which is sustained on the palate, where it develops elegantly, thanks to a good balance of sugar and acidity. Its lovely, distinctive aromas and concentration of flavours will not be easily forgotten. (50 cl bottles)

Patrice Limousin and Freya Skoda, Dom. de Cabarrouy, 64290 Lasseube, tel. 05.59.04.23.08, fax 05.59.04.21.85 Y by appt.

CANCAILLAU Gourmandise 1998★

☐ 1 ha 1,800 70–99 F

A wine for pleasure . . . A wine to make the mouth water . . . Just looking at its intense yellow colour with coppery glints is enough to feel tempted. The fairly complex nose has aromas of citrus and ripe fruits, and also a slight touch of truffle. After a round, fresh attack on the palate, it goes on to show excellent concentration of well-balanced fruit richness, and an attractive finish.

EARL Barrère, 64150 Lahourcade, tel. 05.59.60.08.15, fax 05.59.60.07.38 Y ev. day except Sun. 8am–7pm; cl. 8 Oct.-15 Nov.

CLOS CASTET

Cuvée Spéciale Vieilli en Fût de Chêne 1998

☐ 2 ha 5,000 70–99 F

Golden tears flow down the sides of the glass. In addition to its splendid appearance, this Jurançon also has a very forthcoming nose. Ripe fruits are strongly in evidence: apricots, quince and medlar against a floral background, set off by a slight hint of wax. There are crystallised fruit flavours on the palate, which is quite full and very rich, for all that the impression of freshness remains quite modest.

Alain Labourdette, 64360 Cardesse, tel. 05.59.21.33.09, fax 05.59.21.28.22 Y ev. day 8am–12 noon 2pm–7.30pm

DOM. CAUHAPE

Quintessence du Petit-Manseng 1998★★

☐ 3 ha n.c. + de 500 F

Powerful . . . Apricots, citrus fruits and passion-fruit open a festival of aromas. Impressive . . . It already has a rich and extremely concentrated attack on the palate, but is not yet displaying all its assets in the mouth; and yet the finish is already so long! This superstar will be able to go on developing for more than 20 years in the cellar . . . An ambition to which only the great *liquoreux* wines can aspire. The **1998 Noblesse du Temps** (150–199F) receives the same rating. These two wines justify Henri Ramonteu's international reputation.

Henri Ramonteu, Dom. Cauhapé, quartier Castet, 64360 Monein, tel. 05.59.21.33.02, fax 05.59.21.41.82 Y by appt.

CLOS GASSIOT Mémoire 1998★★

☐ 5 ha 5,000 70–99 F

Two Jurançons made from an equal mixture of Petit Manseng and Gros Manseng. The **1998 Moelleux Elégance** (50–69F) is very good. One taster said that it made him feel like eating strawberry bavarois. This Mémoire has a remarkable, brilliant colour with shades of gold. Its nose is delicate and still fresh, with clean, very distinct aromas of white flowers, peaches, apricots, pineapple and pepper. As soon as it hits the palate it is full, and its attractive, rich structure lingers right up until a finishing note of crystallised fruits.

Antoine Tavernier, rte de Pau, 64360 Abos, tel. 05.59.60.10.22, fax 05.59.71.58.92 Y by appt.

CLOS GUIROUILH 1998★

☐ 6 ha 20,000 50–69 F

Which Clos Guirouilh would you prefer, the classic version, or the **1998 Petit Cuyalàa** (200–249F)? Not sure? The jury could not make up its mind between these two Jurançons Liquoreux, and awarded each of them a star. Even so it was the first one that initially inspired us. It has a golden colour with green highlights, and a forthcoming nose of crystallised fruits (apricots and lemon), accentuated by a slight oaky aroma. After a round, sweet attack on the palate, it has a fine, very sweet *liqoureux* flavour in the mouth. The mouthfeel is rich and sufficiently full, with a finish that flows like honey.

Jean Guirouilh, rte de Belair, 64290 Lasseube, tel. 05.59.04.21.45, fax 05.59.04.21.45 Y by appt.

CAVE DES PRODUCTEURS DE JURANCON Prestige d'Automne 1998★★

☐ 100 ha 100,000 50–69 F

The Cave des Producteurs de Jurançon offers an interesting range of wines. This very sweet wine is not oak-matured. It impresses from the start with its straw colour and gold highlights, and a powerful nose that reveals complexity and maturity in its aromas of apricots, quince, honey and dried fruits. It is equally powerful on the palate, where there are very intense flavours, a great deal of richness and excellent balance. A combination of concentration, freshness and finesse, with a well-balanced finish.

Cave des producteurs de Jurançon, 53, av. Henri-IV, 64290 Gan, tel. 05.59.21.57.03, fax 05.59.21.72.06 Y ev. day except Sun. 8am–12.30pm 1.30pm–7pm

DOM. LARREDYA Cuvée François 1998★

☐ 1 ha 1,800 100–149 F

Jean-Marc Grussaute has been developing wines in his own private cellar for 12 years now. Sweet or dry, they are equally good; take, for instance, the **1999 Jurançon Sec** (30–49F), the **1998 Liquoreux Sélection des Terrasses** (70–99F), and this Cuvée François, all of which are awarded a star. The François has beautiful golden highlights and a powerful array of aromas. These are still dominated by a rich oaky flavour with slight hints of vanilla and resin, but scents of honey and truffles are beginning to break through. There is a sweet attack in the mouth, after which, with the fruit no longer masked by oak, the palate is full and warm.

Jean-Marc Grussaute, Chapelle-de-Rousse, 64110 Jurançon, tel. 05.59.21.74.42, fax 05.59.21.76.72 Y by appt.

DOM. LARROUDE Un Jour d'Automne 1998★★

☐ n.c. n.c. 100–149 F

What happened one day in autumn 1998 on the Larroudé estate? They harvested the white, winged bunches of Petit Manseng grapes that would be used to make this beautiful, very sweet wine. Its shades of gold or copper shine brilliantly in the glass, and it has a dense, deep nose that makes one think of slices of cinnamon gingerbread and crystallised ripe fruits. As well as fullness on the palate, it has richness and very noticeable power, but its warmth is tempered by acidity to just the right extent. A rich, forthcoming wine.

EARL du Dom. Larroudé, 64360 Lucq-de-Béarn, tel. 05.59.34.35.92, fax 05.59.34.35.92 Y by appt.

Estoueigt

DOM. DE MALARRODE Cuvée Prestige Vieilli en fût de chêne 1998★

☐ 2 ha 8,000 70–99 F

Made from Petit Manseng grapes, this Jurançon has quite a lively, golden straw colour. Its fresh, intense nose releases floral scents and notes of exotic fruits and spices against an oaky background. It is agreeably dense on the palate. Although rich and slightly honeyed, it has plenty of acidity. It also remains very fresh at the finish, where it is enriched by toasty notes.

Gaston Mansanné, dom. de Malarrode, 64360 Monein, tel. 05.59.21.44.27, fax 05.59.21.44.27 Y by appt.

DOM. DE NAYS LABASSERE 1998

☐ 4 ha 20,000 30–49 F

A classic Jurançon made from 80% Gros Manseng and 20% Petit Manseng. It has a relatively pale yellow colour with attractive green highlights, and a delicate nose of fresh fruits as well as white flowers. This rather light but well-balanced wine has great charm on the palate, where it releases some notes of oak before returning to fruit flavours at the finish.

Philippe de Nays, Chapelle-de-Rousse, 64110 Jurançon, tel. 05.59.21.70.57, fax 05.59.21.70.67

Y ev. day except Sun. 10am–7pm

CLOS THOU Suprême de Thou 1998★★

☐ 2.5 ha 7,500 70–99 F

The vineyard was already here in 1538, when it belonged to a lady called Raymonde de Thou. This wine is a tribute to her. It has a golden straw colour, and beautiful tears appear as it swirls around in the glass. Its richness becomes evident on the nose, where it releases aromas of honey, jam, and dried and roasted fruits. On the palate, it continues along the same lines: powerful, very full and also very sweet. The epitome of suppleness, and a truly traditional Jurançon.

Henri Lapouble-Laplace, chem. Larredya, 64110 Jurançon, tel. 05.59.06.08.60, fax 05.59.06.08.60

Y ev. day except Sun. 9am–12 noon 2pm–6.30pm

CLOS UROULAT 1999★

☐ 5 ha 20,000 70–99 F

Produced on magnificent silica clay soils, Charles Hours' Jurançon Petit Manseng never fails to excite. Its colour is gold, and its intense, characteristic aromas (citrus fruits and flowers, exotic fruits, apricots) are accompanied by a very discreet note of oak. It is full and concentrated, but still tempered by remarkable acidity on the palate, where it displays elegance, good length and very great finesse.

Charles Hours, Clos Uroulat, quartier Trouilh, 64360 Monein, tel. 05.59.21.46.19, fax 05.59.21.46.90

Jurançon Sec

DOM. CAUHAPE Noblesse 1998★★

☐ 3 ha 9,000 100–149 F

A Jurançon sec of exemplary quality. It has a strong, golden yellow colour, very much like honey. Its power and concentration on the nose also remind one of a sweet white wine, although here there is liveliness as well. It is already rich as it hits the palate, but its

concentration really becomes apparent as the wine is savoured. With plenty of meatiness as well as structure, it shows perfect harmony and leaves behind a delightful aromatic impression.

Henri Ramonteu, Dom. Cauhapé, quartier Castet, 64360 Monein, tel. 05.59.21.33.02, fax 05.59.21.41.82 by appt.

DOM. DU CINQUAU 1999★★

□ 1 ha 6,000 30–49 F

This estate has been in the family since 1800, and in the 1980s it returned to its wine-growing traditions. The man responsible for this revival was Pierre Saubot, and one can only congratulate him on his achievement. Made from a classic blend of 70% Gros Manseng and 30% Petit Courbu, this wine was much praised for its overall harmony. It is light yellow with green-gold lights, and has an expressive nose with a wealth of subtle floral and fruity aromas, against a background of fresh butter. The almost sweet attack is one of its attractive features on the palate, where it is well-constructed, round and rich. It is delightfully sweet but at the same time pleasantly acid, with good fruit and impressive length.

Pierre Saubot, Dom. du Cinquau, Cidex 43, 64230 Artiguelouve, tel. 05.59.83.10.41, fax 05.59.83.12.93 by appt.

CHARLES HOURS

Cuvée Marie 1998★

□ 2 ha 12,000 50–69 F

Cuvée Marie is made of 90% Gros Manseng and 10% Courbu, and has a straw colour with gold highlights and a complex, contrapuntal range of white flower notes and oaky aromas. The balance on the palate is sustained throughout, owing to a combination of richness and acidity. This Jurançon sec has excellent structure and a great deal of fruitiness. It would go well with turbot in a cream sauce.

Charles Hours, Clos Uroulat, quartier Trouilh, 64360 Monein, tel. 05.59.21.46.19, fax 05.59.21.46.90

CH. JOLYS 1999★

□ n.c. 50,000 30–49 F

Closed in by the moraines of Pyrenean glaciers, the steep slopes of Chappelle de Rousse form a striking landscape. The wine, on the other hand, is as gentle as can be, and conforms attractively to type . . . It has a clear, straw colour, and a lovely scent of vanilla and white flowers. The attack has a freshness that then combines on the palate with relatively rich extract to form a well-balanced overall impression. The palate aromas start out the same as those on the nose, but end on a note of butter.

Sté Domaines Latrille, Ch. Jolys, 64290 Gan, tel. 05.59.21.72.79, fax 05.59.21.55.61 by appt.

CLOS LAPEYRE

Cuvée Vitatge Vielh 1998★

□ n.c. 15,000 50–69 F

Once again the Vitatge Vielh, or 'Old Vine', is very appealing indeed. It has a strong, clear gold colour, and its intense nose is mainly composed of aromatic fruits: apricots, lychees and other exotic fruits, mingled with a slight touch of spice and a lovely hint of toast. It is fresh on the palate at first, then fleshy, with a rich, balanced feel centring on good structure. The oak notes blend into a spicy finish. Equally successful is the **1998 Jurançon Moelleux Cols Lapeyre Sélection**, which stands out for its very aromatic character (70–99F).

Jean-Bernard Larrieu, Chapelle-de-Rousse, 64110 Jurançon, tel. 05.59.21.50.80, fax 05.59.21.51.83 ev. day except Sun. out of season 10am–12 noon 2pm–6pm

DOM. LASSERRE 1999★

□ 10 ha 26,200 30–49 F

Made by the Jurançon co-operative from grapes grown on the so-called pudding soils of the Jurançon area (65% Gros Manseng blended with Petit Manseng), this wine is very representative of its AOC. It has a brilliant colour with shades of straw and green highlights. The nose combines apricots, citrus fruits, pears and bergamot orange. It is both firm and rich on the palate, where it has good balance and length, with notes of grapefruit, lime and white flowers (acacia). A wine to drink for pleasure, within two to three years.

Cave des producteurs de Jurançon, 53, av. Henri-IV, 64290 Gan, tel. 05.59.21.57.03, fax 05.59.21.72.06 ev. day except Sun. 8am–12.30pm 1.30pm–7pm

Lasserre

LES HAUTS DE MONTESQUIOU 1999★

□ n.c. 6,000 30–49 F

At the beginning of the 1990s, Jacques Balent was running the oenological laboratory of the Jurançon AOC. For seven years now he has been producing wine from his vineyard at Monein, one of the largest communes in the Béarn. His 1999 Jurançon sec has a pale colour lit up by shades of green, and a straightforward nose that leaves a fresh and very flowery sensation, accentuated by an attractive note of menthol. It has a lively attack, becoming sweeter as it develops on the palate. The final impression is of silkiness and aromatic fruit flavour. A forthright, attractive wine.

Jacques Balent, av. de la Résistance, 64360 Monein, tel. 05.59.21.49.44, fax 05.59.21.43.01 by appt.

DOM. NIGRI Réserve 1998★

□ 0.5 ha 1,800 30–49 F

Jean-Louis Lacoste has produced two excellent **Réserve** wines in the 1998 vintage, one **sweet** (50–69F), and the other dry. The Jurançon sec draws the attention just by the look of its golden colour in the glass. Its qualities become even more apparent in an intense, fine and complex nose that combines flowers, honey, fruit, vanilla and notes of brioche. After a supple attack on the palate it confirms its potential by filling the mouth with its richness and balance, revealing many subtle flavours that linger on into a very sweet, oaky finish.

🔑 Jean-Louis Lacoste, Dom. Nigri, Candeloup, 64360 Monein, tel. 05.59.21.42.01, fax 05.59.21.42.59 ☑
Y ev. day 8.30am–12 noon 1.30pm–7pm; Sun. by appt.

DOM. DE SOUCH 1999★

□ 1 ha 8,000 50–69 F

This estate is named after Jean de Souch, who was a member of a vine-breeders' syndicate in the 14th century. His wine has a gold colour that gives it a warming appearance. The attractive nose is balanced between slight floral notes and shades of ripe fruits. The light but expressive palate leads on to a flavoursome finish with just a hint of bitterness. A good accompaniment to smoked salmon.

🔑 Yvonne Hegoburu, Dom. de Souch, Laroin, 64110 Jurançon, tel. 05.59.06.27.22, fax 05.59.06.51.55 ☑ Y by appt.

Madiran

Madiran has its origins in Roman times and, later, was the wine of pilgrims making the long journey to Santiago de Compostela in Spain. The gastronomy of the Gers region and its popularity in Paris have also helped to promote this Pyrenean wine. Much of the 1,400 ha (3,458 acres) of the appellation is planted with Tannat, which produces a wine that is tannic in youth, vividly coloured, with preliminary scents of raspberries; it develops after long ageing. Cabernet-Sauvignon and Cabernet France (or Bouchy) and Fer Servadou (or Pinenc) are blended with it. The vines are trained to half-height. The production was 67,871 hl (1,791,794 gal) in 1999.

The Madiran is a supremely virile wine. Its vinification can be adapted so it can be drunk young when its fruitiness and suppleness can be best displayed. It goes well with goose confits (preserved in fat) and duck breasts served rare. The traditional Madiran, with its high proportion of Tannat, ages very well in wooden casks and can mature for a number of years. The mature Madirans are sensual, fleshy and full-bodied, with aromas of toasted bread, and go well with game and the ewe's milk cheeses from the high valleys.

CH. D'AYDIE Odé d'Aydie 1997★

■ 15 ha 80,000 30–49 F

The Laplace vineyards have had a high reputation for a long time, and have contributed to the fame of the appellation. This year they offer two well-made **Château d'Aydie** wines, a 1997 Madiran and a **1998 Pacherenc du Vic-Bilh Moelleux** (50–69F). The star goes to this Cuvée Odé d'Aydie. Inky-black in colour, it releases deep aromas of dark berries and spices, along with a powerful note of toast. Its balance on the palate is derived from a substantial, but nicely softened structure. The tannins are now fading, and the oaky flavour is taking on pleasant accents of vanilla. An elegant wine.

🔑 GAEC vignobles Laplace, 64330 Aydie, tel. 05.59.04.08.00, fax 05.59.04.08.08 ☑
Y ev. day 9am–1pm 2pm–8pm

DOM. BERNET 1998★

■ 1.5 ha 12,000 30–49 F

This Madiran is made from 80% Tannat and 20% Cabernet grapes, grown on a fine gravel soil. It has an inky colour with purple glints, and an already well-developed nose in which aromas of fruit preserves and prunes are overlaid by spicy oak. It is appealingly round and interestingly fruity on the palate, although the finish is still spicy and leaves a tannic impression that will soften when the wine has had two or three years to mature.

🔑 Yves Doussau, Bernet, 32400 Viella, tel. 05.62.69.71.99, fax 05.62.69.75.08
Y by appt.

DOM. BERTHOUMIEU
Cuvée Tradition 1998★★

■ n.c. 80,000 30–49 F

The jury was bowled over by this Cuvée Tradition whose colour is a very deep, dark red with shades of purple. The nose is well-developed and offers a wide range of

fragrances: strawberries, raspberries, liquorice, peppers, with an added note of leather. The tasters couldn't stop praising its qualities on the palate: a fine surge in power, a large and complex array of flavours, great fullness and a long finish in which the tannins are already harmonious and velvety. The **Cuvée Charles de Batz Elevée en Fût de Chêne** also wins a star in the **1997** vintage, having won two consecutive *coups de coeur* previously from the jury (50–69F). This estate was founded in 1850, and has been run in masterly fashion by Didier Barré since 1983.

Didier Barré, 32400 Viella, tel. 05.62.69.74.05, fax 05.62.69.80.64, e-mail barre.didier@wanadoo.fr ev. day 8am–12 noon 2pm–7pm; Sun. by appt.

DOM. CAPMARTIN

Cuvée du Couvent Elevé en fût de chêne neuf 1997★★★

■ 2 ha 11,000 50–69 F

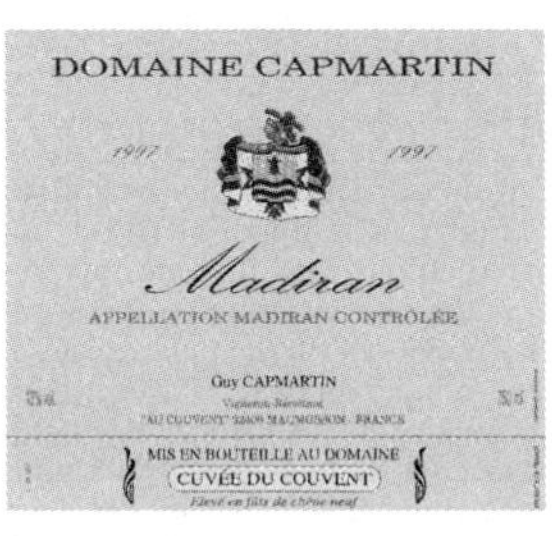

The Capmartin estate is amassing a collection of stars and *coups de coeur* from the jury. This time it is the Cuvée du Couvent that meets with unqualified approval. The taster admires its sumptuous black colour in the glass, and then breathes in its deep, powerful aromas, which give off notes of leather, dark berries and spices. On the palate, it has a substantial structure softened by noble, concentrated extract. The tannins are unobtrusive, and the oaky flavour is well-judged. A perfectly articulate overall impression. The jury also enjoyed the **1998 Pacherenc du Vic-Bilh Moelleux Cuvée du Couvent Elevée en Fût de Chêne Neuf**, and awarded it a star.

Guy Capmartin, Le Couvent, 32400 Maumusson, tel. 05.62.69.87.88, fax 05.62.69.83.07 ev. day 9am–1pm 2pm–7pm; Sun. by appt.

DOM. DAMIENS Tradition 1998★

■ 4 ha 27,000 30–49 F

Located on one of the five hillsides of Aydie, this 15 ha (37-acre) estate planted in a single bloc offers a typical Madiran made from Tannat and Cabernet Franc grapes. Its colour is a lively, very nuanced red, and it has an intense nose, somewhere between fresh and ripe fruits. On the palate, it is light and full of energy, supported by a framework of young, vigorous tannins. The **1997 Madiran Cuvée Vieillie en Fût de Chêne** (50–69F) is also very successful. Two wines to be kept for two to three years.

André and Pierre-Michel Beheity, Dom. Damiens, 64330 Aydie, tel. 05.59.04.03.13, fax 05.59.04.02.74 by appt.

DOM. DE GRABIEOU

Cuvée Prestige 1998★

■ 2 ha 14,000 30–49 F

With a colour as dark as pitch, together with strikingly distinct, forthcoming aromas of soft fruits in brandy and sweet spices, this Madiran made from Tannat grapes increases rapidly in power on the palate. Tannins are still very evident with warm, spicy flavours, and although they are already very mature, they will become even more harmonious when the wine has been kept for four or five years. The finish is marked by notes of coffee.

René and Frédéric Dessans, Dom. de Grabieou, 32400 Maumusson-Laguian, tel. 05.62.69.74.62, fax 05.62.69.73.08, e-mail dessans@wanadoo.fr by appt.

DOM. LABRANCHE LAFFONT

Vieilles vignes 1997★★

■ 1.5 ha 9,000 30–49 F

This family vineyard was taken over in 1993 by winemaker-oenologist Christine Dupuy, and regularly offers wines of high quality. Its Madiran comes from old vines, some of which predate phylloxera, and is dark cherry-red in colour. It is a sensual wine with a combination of strong spices, roasting aromas, soft fruits and vanilla on the nose, and then a delightful chewiness and freshness on the palate. In addition to flavours of soft fruits and liquorice, a rich tannic framework is in evidence, but the overall impression is one of softness.

Christine Dupuy, 32400 Maumusson, tel. 05.62.69.74.90, fax 05.62.69.76.03 by appt.

CH. LAFFITTE-TESTON

Tradition 1998★

■ 20 ha 12,000 30–49 F

Jean-Marc Laffitte has installed an underground cellar that can hold 800 casks in which to mature his wines. The **1999 Pacherenc du Vic-Bilh Sec Cuvée Erika** has spent ten whole months there, and is an excellent example of what he can produce. The art of maturing in tank is also well understood at the château, as this brilliant, clear, bright red Madiran proves. It has an open nose of soft fruits, light spices and pâtisserie, and is just as fresh and fruity in the mouth, where it develops more roundness. The tannic framework remains discreet and delicious until the finish. A real delicacy.

Jean-Marc Laffitte, 32400 Maumusson, tel. 05.62.69.74.58, fax 05.62.69.76.87 by appt.

DOM. LAFFONT Tradition 1998★

■ 1.22 ha 9,000 20–29 F

The blend is eclectic, but representative of the appellation's grape varieties: Tannat at the head of the list (40%), then Cabernet

Sauvignon (25%), Fer Servadou (20%) and Cabernet Franc (15%). The result is convincing. Look at the dark purple colour. Breathe in the fine nose of red and dark berries underpinned by a discreet oaky aroma. Taste the full, well-balanced extract, at the heart of which fruit flavours mingle with notes of vanilla. A distinguished wine, in which the tannins are mature and smooth. The **1997 Madiran Erigone** is also very well-made, but still needs to mature (30–49F).

Pierre Speyer, Dom. Laffont, 32400 Maumusson, tel. 05.62.69.75.23, fax 05.62.69.80.27 ▣ Y by appt.

LA MOTHE PEYRAN

Elevé en fût de chêne 1997★★

■ 100 ha 80,000 50–69 F

Intense . . . A deep, black colour . . . A thoroughbred, warming wine whose aromas of spices and dark berries are qualified by a slight hint of muskiness. The rich extract on the palate is reinforced by strong vinosity and substantial tannins, which will need to grow rounder with time. Also worthy of mention is the very well-made **1997 Arte Benedicte Vieilles Vignes Elevée en Fût de Chêne**.

Producteurs Plaimont, 32400 Saint-Mont, tel. 05.62.69.62.87, fax 05.62.69.61.68 ▣ Y ev. day except Sun. 9am–12 noon 2pm–6pm; group by appt.

LAPERRE COMBES

Grande Réserve Vieilles vignes Elevé en fût de chêne 1997★

■ 120 ha 80,000 30–49 F

Madiran is also produced in Saint-Mont, where the two appellations rub shoulders on the viticultural landscape. As a result we find two excellent wines vying for the limelight: the **1998 Chênaie du Tilh**, and this Grande Réserve. It has a very young ruby colour, and is initially marked by a strong oaky aroma with notes of roasted coffee, after which there are scents of jam. It comes on sweetly, and then leaves an impression of freshness and lightness. At the end, it envelops the palate with charred oak flavours. A very persuasive Madiran.

Vignoble de Gascogne, 32400 Saint-Mont, tel. 05.62.69.62.87, fax 05.62.69.61.68 ▣ Y ev. day except Sun. 9am–12 noon 2pm–6pm; groups by appt.

DOM. DE MAOURIES

Vieilli en fût de chêne 1998

■ 4 ha 27,000 30–49 F

The Maouriès estate, founded in 1909, has 23 ha (57 acres) of vines, shared between the Madiran and Côtes de Saint-Mont appellations. Its very dark purple Madiran has an intense nose of spices and overripe red berries macerated in alcohol. After a rounded first impression, it is clean and still aromatic on the palate. A true country wine, dominated on the finish by tannins.

GAEC Dufau Père et Fils, Dom. de Maouriès, 32400 Labarthète, tel. 05.62.69.63.84, fax 05.62.69.65.49 ▣ Y by appt.

CH. MONTUS Cuvée Prestige 1998★★

■ n.c. n.c. 150–199 F

Alain Brumont has succeeded in turning Tannat wine into a drama, with the Pyrenean terroir as scenery. His 1998 production is a great hit . . . It has a satiny black colour, and gives off aromas of dark berries, tobacco and spices, with a charming toasty note. Its rich extract fills the mouth powerfully, providing a soft surround for a balanced structure and pleasant-tasting tannins. The **1998 Château Bouscassé** (50–69F) is another remarkable play by the same scriptwriter.

Alain Brumont, SA Domaines et Châteaux, 32400 Maumusson-Laguian, tel. 05.62.69.74.67, fax 05.62.69.70.46 ▣ Y ev. day except Sun. 9am–12.30pm 2pm–7pm

DOM. DU MOULIE Cuvée Chiffre 1998★

■ n.c. 3,000 30–49 F

In certain respects this Cuvée Chiffre is still developing; this is apparent from both its cherry-red colour, and its notes of plums in brandy and other macerated soft fruits. Great maturity is evident on the palate, with a powerful, full-bodied quality, a flavour that seems almost sweet, and well-softened tannins. A wine that is close to achieving its potential. Another enjoyable wine is the **1998 Pacherenc du Vic-Bilh Moelleux**, which was cited by the jury (50–69F).

Michel Charrier, Dom. du Moulié, 32400 Cannet, tel. 05.62.69.77.73, fax 05.62.69.83.66 ▣ Y ev. day except Sun. 8am–7pm

CRU DU PARADIS Tradition 1997★

■ 20 ha 50,000 30–49 F

Musky at first on the nose, this crimson Madiran quickly opens out with aromas of soft fruits. Its aromatic range is further accented with notes of menthol and discreet oak. It is angular on the palate where, after a supple attack, it develops without harshness, leaving a lingering sense of freshness and spices. The discreet finish is supported by fine tannins. A pleasant wine that can be enjoyed straight away, as can the one-star **1998 Pacherenc du Vic-Bilh Moelleux Réserve Royale** (70–99F).

Jacques Maumus, Cru du Paradis, lieu-dit Le Paradis, 65700 Saint-Lanne, tel. 05.62.31.98.23, fax 05.62.31.93.23 ▣ Y by appt.

DOM. TAILLEURGUET

Elevé en fût de chêne 1997★

■ n.c. 6,000 30–49 F

A blend of 80% Tannat, 15% Cabernet Sauvignon and a touch of Cabernet Franc has undergone lengthy maceration to produce this dark Madiran with purplish highlights. It has a forthcoming nose of spices and soft fruits, accompanied by slight musky notes and a discreet oaky aroma. The impression of suppleness on the palate is followed by one of richness. Although quite loose-knit, the structure is supported by tannins that are clearly evident and have good texture. Not only that, but the oak flavour is well-judged too. Another equally successful wine is the **1998 Madiran Elevé en Cuve** (20–29F).

EARL dom. Tailleurguet, 32400 Maumusson, tel. 05.62.69.73.92, fax 05.62.69.83.69 ☑ Y ev. day except Sun. 9am–12.30pm 2pm–7pm

Bouby

CH. DE VIELLA

Vieilli en fût de chêne 1997★★

■	5 ha	30,000	30–49 F

Alain Bortolussi can be proud of this remarkable Madiran. It has a deep ruby colour and very forthcoming aromas that intensify with air contact: musky notes at first, followed by dark berries, spices and a toasty quality with accents of butter. As it develops on the palate, it becomes harmonious, rich and silky, with fine structure. Well-softened tannins sustain a long finish. The **1998 Pacherenc du Vic-Bilh Moelleux** was also awarded a star.

A. and C. Bortolussi, Ch. de Viella, rte de Maumusson, 32400 Viella, tel. 05.62.69.75.81, fax 05.62.69.79.18 ☑ Y ev. day except Sun. 8.30am–12.30pm 2pm–7pm

Pacherenc du Vic-Bilh

From the same area as Madiran, this white wine is made from local varieties (Arrufiac, Manseng, Courbu) and others from the Bordelais (Sauvignon, Sémillon); this combination creates a notably rich aromatic palette. According to the climatic conditions of the year concerned, the wines can be dry and perfumed or medium and lively. Their finesse is quite remarkable; they are fleshy and strong with a nose melding almond, hazelnut and exotic fruits. Pacherenc du Vic-Bilh make excellent aperitif wines and, when medium, are perfect with a terrine of foie gras. In 1999 2,939 hl (77,590 gal) of dry wine and 5,949 hl (157,054 gal) of sweet wine were produced.

CH. BARREJAT

Moelleux Cuvée de la Passion Elevé en fût de chêne 1998★★

□	0.8 ha	3,000	30–49 F

The tasters were indeed inspired with the passion mentioned in the name of this wine. From beneath its golden highlights, it releases a remarkable range of intense dried-fruit aromas against an oaky background with hints of vanilla and menthol. It is full and powerful on the palate where, despite a great deal of warmth, there is also real balance. Dried-fruit flavours continue alongside an oaky quality, which becomes spicier as the wine finishes on an attractive note of nougat. In the **Madiran** AOC, the **1998 Cuvée des Vieux Ceps Elevée en Fût de Chêne** was also awarded two stars, while one star went to the **1998 Tradition** (20–29F).

Denis Capmartin, Ch. Barréjat, 32400 Maumusson, tel. 05.62.69.74.92, fax 05.62.69.77.54 ☑ Y ev. day except Sun. 8am–12 noon 2pm–6pm

DOM. BERTHOUMIEU

Sec 1999★

□	1 ha	n.c.	50–69 F

Didier Barré's talents are not limited to Madiran; he also produces very good Pacherenc du Vic-Bilh, such as this dry wine with a brilliant, strong yellow colour. Its somewhat reserved, extremely delicate nose releases aromas of white flowers and exotic fruits. The first impression is almost sweet, after which, although rich and full on the palate, it is also sustained by vivaciousness. The fresh, fruity flavour lingers on into a delicious finish, which is enhanced by a slight touch of bitterness.

Didier Barré, 32400 Viella, tel. 05.62.69.74.05, fax 05.62.69.80.64, e-mail barre.didier@wanadoo.fr ☑ Y ev. day 8am–12 noon 2pm–7pm; Sun. by appt.

DOM. DU CRAMPILH

Sec 1999★★

□	2 ha	3,000	30–49 F

The wine that stands out here from a selection of Pacherenc du Vic-Bilhs is made from a blend of Gros Manseng (50%), Petit Manseng (30%), Arrufiac (10%) and Courbu (10%). It has a strong, straw-yellow colour and a very intense, complex, attractively sweet nose of acacia and crystallised citrus-fruit aromas, which rise from the glass. After a lively attack on the palate, the wine fills the mouth with its rounded structure, as all the elements blend together into a full, harmonious whole. The finish leaves behind a delightful, slightly acid sensation. A wine whose personality comes as a pleasant surprise.

Alain Oulié, 64350 Aurions-Idernes, tel. 05.59.04.00.63, fax 05.59.04.04.97, e-mail crampilh@cavesparticulieres.com ☑ Y ev. day except Sat. Sun. 9am–12 noon 2pm–7pm

CAVE DE CROUSEILLES

Moelleux Hivernal 1998★★

☐ 2 ha 700 150–199 F

The 1997 won a *coup de coeur*, and this 1998 Cuvée Hivernal, made from overripe grapes harvested in the first days of winter, is also remarkable. Its gleaming, polished gold and copper colour makes a beautiful setting for its concentrated aromas of confectionery, exotic fruits and honey. It has a supple, rich attack, and then becomes rounder on the palate, where there is perfect balance and great fullness. The original aromas grow even more distinct as one savours the wine. There is a long, harmonious finish, with an added note of quince. A very elegant wine. Another one worth discovering is the **1998 Moelleux Grains de Givre** (50–69F), which is also awarded two stars.

Cave de Crouseilles, 64350 Crouseilles, tel. 05.59.68.10.93, fax 05.59.68.14.33 ☒
by appt.

CH. DE DIUSSE Sec 1999

☐ 0.67 ha 6,200 30–49 F

The Château de Diusse is an occupational therapy centre that involves its residents in the production of its various Madiran and Pacherenc du Vic-Bilh wines. This 1999 sec stands out straight away for its fine, clear quality. The nose is forthcoming and very fresh, owing to notes of lemon or kiwi. After a clean attack on the palate, it remains lively and fruity in the mouth. A well-balanced, pleasantly simple wine.

Ch. de Diusse, 64330 Diusse, tel. 05.59.04.02.83, fax 05.59.04.05.77 ☒
by appt.

DOM. LAFFONT

Moelleux Elevé en fût de chêne neuf 1998★

☐ 0.23 ha 1,300 50–69 F

Petit Manseng and Gros Manseng have yielded a straw-yellow wine with shades of gold. Although it has strong notes of toast on the nose, there are also intense aromas of peaches, apricots, honey and orange blossom. Rich in flavour and very full as soon as it hits the palate, this Pacherenc du Vic-Bilh is carried along by its great vivacity, which makes for a very long finish with a continuing note of vanilla.

Pierre Speyer, Dom. Laffont, 32400 Maumusson, tel. 05.62.69.75.23, fax 05.62.69.80.27 ☒ by appt.

DOM. LAOUGUE Doux Vieilli en barrique 1998★

☐ 2 ha 6,000 50–69 F

This golden-yellow Pacherenc du Vic-Bilh is rich to look at, and the impression is confirmed by the nose, which has heady aromas of white flowers and honey, along with some notes of crystallised fruits. After a supple attack on the palate, it develops in the mouth towards very ripe fruits (figs and grapes), and flavours of roasting which come from the oak. The Laougué estate's **1998 Madiran Tradition** (30–49F) was also awarded a star.

Pierre Dabadie, rte de Madiran, 32400 Viella, tel. 05.62.69.90.05, fax 05.62.69.71.41 ☒
ev. day except Sun. 8am–12 noon 2pm–6pm

L'OR DU VIEUX PAYS Moelleux 1998★

☐ 15 ha 100,000 50–69 F

Three sweet Pacherenc du Vic-Bilhs from the Vignobles de Gascogne and the Union de Producteurs Plaimont have each won a star. Two of them are late-harvest (November): the **1998 Saint-Martin** and the **1998 Saint-Albert** (70–99F). Made from the same grape varieties (Manseng and Courbu) harvested at the end of October, the Or du Vieux Pays creates a delightful impression from the word go with its pale gold colour full of sparkling highlights. The thoroughly modern aromas still have the characteristics of youth: flowers, fruit and a soft aroma of oak. After a clean, sweet attack, it continues along the same lines as before on the palate, where it develops richly and harmoniously. A balanced, fairly full and pleasantly aromatic wine.

Vignoble de Gascogne, 32400 Saint-Mont, tel. 05.62.69.62.87, fax 05.62.69.61.68 ☒ ev. day except Sun. 9am–12 noon 2pm–6pm; groups by appt.

CH. MONTUS Sec 1999★★

☐ 4 ha 22,400 70–99 F

This is indeed a great wine in the making: a Pacherenc du Vic-Bilh made from Petit Courbu, with fine intensity and a colour that seems to be speckled with gold. On the nose it develops noble aromas of lemon, pineapple and medlar, bathed in honey and enlivened by a few notes of oak. There is great fullness on the palate, and a good balance of richness and freshness. The flavours are well sustained on a balanced finish where high-quality fruit combines with attractive oakiness. A wine that seems destined for a very bright future.

Alain Brumont, SA Domaines et Châteaux, 32400 Maumusson-Laguian, tel. 05.62.69.74.67, fax 05.62.69.70.46 ☒
ev. day except Sun. 9am–12.30pm 2pm–7pm

DOM. SERGENT

Doux Cuvée élevée en fût de chêne neuf 1998★

☐ 1 ha 5,000 50–69 F

Gilbert Dousseau has put forward three excellent wines, two of which are Madirans: the **1997 Domaine Sergent Vieilles Vignes Elevée en Fût de Chêne** (30–49F) and the tank-matured **Cuvée Classique du Domaine** in the **1998** vintage (20–29F). What gives the Pacherenc du Vic-Bilh star billing here is an attractive colour with amber highlights, and an intense, well-developed nose with strong notes of crystallised exotic fruits. It is just as good on the palate: balanced, quite fat and rich, and still aromatic. The finish is completed by subtle hints of oak.

⊶ Gilbert Dousseau, Dom. Sergent, 32400 Maumusson-Laguian, tel. 05.62.69.74.93, fax 05.62.69.75.85 ☒ Y ev. day except Sun. 8am–12.30pm 2pm–7.30pm

Tursan AOVDQS

This vineyard was once the property of Eleanor of Aquitaine. Nowadays the Tursan terroir covers some 460 ha (1,136 acres) and produces an average of 20,000 hl (528,000 gal) of red, rosé and white wines (35%). The most interesting are the whites made from the original vine variety, the Baroque. Dry, vigorous and inimitably perfumed, Tursan whites go very well with shad, elvers and grilled fish.

CH. DE BACHEN 1998*

□ 17 ha 36,000 50–69 F

In 1983, Michel Guérard, the 'wizard' of Eugénie-les-Bains and inventor of *nouvelle cuisine*, embarked on the restoration of the Château de Bachen, followed by the renovation of the old cellars. These were the last necessary steps towards becoming a professional winemaker, which he has now succeeded in doing: witness these two white Tursans, the **1998 Baron de Bachen**, which we highly commend (70–99F), and more especially this 1998 Château de Bachen. It is pale gold, and offers superb, delightfully toasty and buttery aromas, along with a basket of fresh fruits. After a fresh attack, the full, rich extract fills the palate with flavours of white-fleshed, citrus and dried fruits. The tasting ends with mineral notes and a fine flavour of oak.

⊶ Michel Guérard SA, Cie fermière et thermale d'Eugénie-les-Bains, 40800 Duhort-Bachen, tel. 05.58.71.76.76, fax 05.58.71.77.77 ☒ Y by appt.
⊶ SCA Ch. de Bachen

CH. BOURDA Elevé en fût de chêne 1998*

■ 15 ha 40,000 30–49 F

The 15 ha (37 acres) of vines that have yielded this Tursan are located in the commune of Classun. Cabernet Franc, Cabernet Sauvignon and Tannat rub shoulders on a very shingly, silica clay soil. What we see in the glass is a wine with an intense colour and very pretty highlights. It has a well-developed nose, dominated by red berries and spices. Even so there is a touch of vanilla, which immediately becomes mildly evident again on the palate. Here the flavours circulate pleasantly within a rounded structure that develops around silky tannins, and leaves a note of oak at the finish. Also worth trying is the **1999 Haute Carte** Tursan, an equally good dry white wine from the Vignerons de Tursan, costing less than FF 20.

⊶ Les Vignerons de Tursan, 40320 Geaune, tel. 05.58.44.51.25, fax 05.58.44.40.22, e-mail tursan.vin@wanadoo.fr ☒ Y by appt.

Côtes de Saint-Mont AOVDQS

This is a continuation of the Madiran vineyard. The Côtes de Saint-Mont is the most recent of the Pyrenean appellations (1981), producing wines of superior quality. The vineyard covers about 1,000 ha (2,470 acres), and annual production averages 60,000 hl (1,584,000 gal). The main red grape is the Tannat, the whites being made from Clairette, Arrufica, Courbu and the two Manseng varieties. Most of the production is managed by the dynamic Union des Caves Coopératives Plaimont. The red wines are vividly coloured and full-bodied, rapidly becoming round and pleasant. They are drunk with grilled meats and Garbure Gasconne, a local soup. The delicate rosés are appreciated for their fruity bouquet. The whites have a special flavour of the terroir and are dry and lively in character.

LES HAUTS DE BERGELLE 1998*

□ 45 ha 300,000 30–49 F

This dry white wine comes from a judicious blend of Arrufiac, Courbu, Gros and Petit Manseng grapes, and has been matured in barrel for six months. It delighted the jury with its pale gold colour and green highlights, and with its intense nose of exotic fruits with a topping of honey and a toasty aroma in the background. Its round, full-bodied quality on the palate did the rest. It remains fresh as its fruit flavours linger attractively, leaving an excellent feeling of balance.

⊶ Plaimont Producteurs, 32400 Saint-Mont, tel. 05.62.69.62.87, fax 05.62.69.61.68 ☒ Y ev. day except Sun. 9am–12 noon 2pm–6pm; groups by appt.

LES HAUTS DE BERGELLE 1998★

■ 150 ha 1,000,000 30–49 F

The Plaimont cellar produces Tannat, Cabernet Franc, Cabernet Sauvignon and Pinenc wines separately before blending them. The result is a very dark purple wine with an intense aromatic range, which is made up of very ripe dark berries, some herbaceous notes, and aromas of roasted coffee. It is full and round on the palate, where it achieves its balance with firm tannins. This delightfully mature wine shares its success with another red Côtes de Saint-Mont from the same cellar, the **1998 Esprit de vignes**, which has been matured for longer in barrel and doesn't contain any Cabernet Franc.

Plaimont Producteurs, 32400 Saint-Mont, tel. 05.62.69.62.87, fax 05.62.69.61.68 ev. day except Sun. 9am–12 noon 2pm–6pm; groups by appt.

DOM. DE MAOURIES 1999

□ 1 ha 7,800 30–49 F

In Saint-Mont it is unusual to find a winery that is privately owned. There is one, however, at the Maouriès estate which, since 1907, has been cultivating a 22 ha (54-acre) vineyard on very stony, south-facing hillsides, and producing its own wines, such as this Côtes de Saint-Mont. Yellow-green and very clear, it releases discreet aromas of white flowers and fresh fruit. It has a lively attack, and is slightly acid but not without roundness on the palate. A 1999 that is ready to drink.

GAEC Dufau Père et Fils, Dom. de Maouriès, 32400 Labarthète, tel. 05.62.69.63.84, fax 05.62.69.65.49 by appt.

CH. SAINT-GO 1998★

■ 38 ha 180,000 50–69 F

Behind its almost black colour with shades of purple, this Château Saint-Go has an intense, oaky quality; there are smoky fragrances, along with very ripe dark berries. On the palate, it is full-bodied and warm, and has substantial structure. The tannins are still very much in evidence at present, but it has real potential. Another successful red Côtes de Saint-Mont from the Vignoble de Gascogne producers' organisation is the **1998 Thibault de Bréthous Elevée en Fût de Chêne**, which is good value for money (30–49F).

Vignoble de Gascogne, 32400 Saint-Mont, tel. 05.62.69.62.87, fax 05.62.69.61.68 ev. day except Sun. 9am–12 noon 2pm–6pm; groups by appt.

The wines of the Dordogne

The Dordogne vineyard is a natural extension of the Libournais wine-growing area, separated from it only by an administrative boundary. Planted with classic Gironde varieties, the Perigord vineyard is characterised by a very diverse production and a number of appellations. It stretches along slopes on both banks of the Dordogne.

The Appellation Régionale Bergerac comprises whites, rosés and reds. The Côtes de Bergerac offer fuller-bodied white wines with a delicate bouquet, along with reds that are well-structured and round, to be drunk with poultry and meat dishes with sauce. The Appellation Saussignac produces excellent fuller-bodied white wines with an ideal balance between freshness and sugar; they are drunk as aperitif wines, tasting somewhere between a Bergerac and a Monbazillac. Montravel, near Castillon, is the vineyard associated with Montaigne; production is divided into dry white Montravel, readily identifiable because of the Sauvignon, and the Côtes de Montravel and Haut-Montravel, fuller-bodied, elegant and stylish, which make excellent dessert wines. The Pécharmant is a red wine harvested on the slopes of the right bank where the soil, rich in iron, gives it a very distinctive taste of the terroir. A wine to keep, it has a fine, subtle bouquet and is a perfect accompaniment to the classic dishes of the Perigord. The Rosette is a semi-sweet wine, made from the same varieties as the Bordeaux wines, harvested in an enclave on the right bank of the Dordogne around Bergerac.

Known as early as the 14th century, Monbazillac is one of the most famous 'sweet' wines. The vineyard is north-facing on limestone interbedded with molassic sands and marl. The localised micro-climate is particularly good for the development of a particular strain of botrytis, the 'noble rot'. Beautifully golden in colour,

Monbazillac wines have scents of wild flowers and honey and a lingering flavour. They can be drunk as an aperitif, or enjoyed with foie gras, Roquefort cheese and chocolate desserts. They are fleshy and strong and, with age, become great sweet wines with a 'scorched' flavour.

Bergerac

These wines are produced from the 90 communes of the district of Bergerac; the vineyard covers 12,633 ha (31,204 acres). The rosé is fresh and fruity, and is frequently made from Cabernet; the red wine is aromatic and supple, a blend of traditional varieties.

B DE BERGERAC 1998

■ 5 ha 20,000 20–29 F

Previously, Laurent de Bosredon was known as a wine-grower, and now we must expect great things from him as a négociant. One example is the B de Bergerac brand, which has been commended. The nose opens with notes of menthol and spices, and then releases aromas of red berries as the wine swirls around in the glass. The attack on the palate is supple and slightly crisp, with good tannin balance. With a somewhat lighter structure than a classic Bergerac, this wine will be enjoyable to drink with charcuterie.

SCEA Comte de Bosredon, Belingard, 24240 Pomport, tel. 05.53.58.28.03, fax 05.53.58.38.39, e-mail deschard.boisredon@wanadoo.fr B by appt.

CH. BEAUCHAMP 1999

■ 11.5 ha 40,000 20–29 F

This classic, typical Bergerac will appeal to many people. Blackcurrant, bilberry . . . the nose is characterised by notes of berries. Rich at first on the palate, it develops through young tannins that are still a little austere, and ends with another delightful burst of fruit. A structured wine that leaves a good impression.

Union Prodiffu, 17–19, rte des Vignerons, 33790 Landerrouat, tel. 05.56.61.33.73, fax 05.56.61.40.57

BOUTEILLE NOIRE 1998★

■ 3 ha 10,000 30–49 F

Bouteille Noire is made from rigorously selected grapes, and has been matured in barrel for eight months. Its complex, powerful nose combines oaky flavours with dark berry aromas. Structured on the palate by tannins that are noticeable but not at all aggressive, it is a harmonious wine that looks promising for five years to come.

Union de viticulteurs de Port-Sainte-Foy, 78, rte de Bordeaux, 33220 Port-Sainte-Foy, tel. 05.53.27.40.70, fax 05.53.27.40.71 ev. day except Sun. 9am–12 noon 2pm–6pm

CH. BRIAND Elevé en fût de chêne 1998★

■ 7.5 ha 3,000 50–69 F

This estate is still named after a former owner. The oakiness on the nose of this 1998 comes through not just in aromas of vanilla, but in spicy notes as well. It does have some fruitiness, thanks to a hint of prunes. The richness of the raw material is perceptible, and sustained by the flavour of oak, which continues to dominate the fairly supple tannins. A wine that will become more pleasant to drink in two to three years' time. The **1999 Cuvée, Non Boisée** was cited by the jury for its fresh, fruity notes (30–49F).

Gilbert and Kathy Rondonnier, Les Nicots, 24240 Ribagnac, tel. 05.53.58.23.50, fax 05.53.24.94.43 by appt.

CH. BUISSON DE FLOGNY 1999★

■ n.c. n.c. 20–29 F

This somewhat evolved 1999 Bergerac is smooth and fresh, with a nose dominated by notes of blackcurrant and a well-balanced tannic structure. There is a very slight bitterness at the finish, but only because it is a young wine. The **1998 Bergerac Rouge**, which has also been matured in barrels, owes its well-deserved reputation to a very expressive nose centred on ripe fruits, and a good tannic impression, with a discreet oaky flavour that stays in the background and allows the wine to dominate (30–49F).

SCEA Ch. Saint-Méard, Le Buisson, 24610 Saint-Méard-de-Gurçon, tel. 05.53.81.00.87, fax 05.53.80.61.39, e-mail flogny@aol.com by appt.

Marc Bighetti

DUC DE CASTELLAC Vieilles vignes 1998★

■ 6 ha 40,000 20–29 F

There is oakiness here, but not too much: just enough to make this an elegant wine. After an initial sensation of vanilla, aromas of red berries are evident on the nose. It is round and structured on the palate, but not to excess. The overall impression is of softness, harmony and great finesse. The jury also cites the **1998 Pécharmant Noblesse du Périgord**, whose dominant spicy notes give it great elegance (30–49F).

🔑 Producta SA, 21, cours Xavier-Arnozan, 33082 Bordeaux Cedex, tel. 05.57.81.18.18, fax 05.56.81.22.12, e-mail producta@producta.com
Y by appt.

L'ADAGIO DES EYSSARDS 1998★★

■ 1 ha 7,000 70–99 F

The Cuvée du Château, the Adagio, whatever . . . All the des Eyssards wines are highly rated. This one has an intense purple colour, and a complex nose that releases notes of toast and vanilla, mingled with aromas of dark berries. There is a very powerful but elegant attack on the palate, which indicates that the tannins are well-controlled, and the tasting ends on a harmonious note, with dark berry flavours. A mouthwatering wine that can be drunk immediately or kept for four to five years.

🔑 GAEC des Eyssards, 24240 Monestier, tel. 05.53.24.36.36, fax 05.53.58.63.74, e-mail eyssards@aquinet-tm.fr V
Y by appt.

CH. GRINOU Le Grand Vin 1998★★

■ 1 ha 5,000 50–69 F

The Château Grinou's 1998 Grand Vin offers a complex nose of ripe fruits (morello cherries), against an elegant oaky background. It has good structure in the mouth, thanks to round, supple tannins that mingle harmoniously with those it has acquired from oak-ageing. A powerful, concentrated wine that deserves to age for a few years. The **1999 Réserve du Château Grinou** (30–49F) was also awarded two stars, but its tannins are still rather hard and need to round out. Finally, the **1999 Bergerac Sec Réserve** (30–49F) deserves a mention. One taster remarked that it had the style of a New World wine!

🔑 Catherine et Guy Cuisset, Ch. Grinou, 24240 Monestier, tel. 05.53.58.46.63, fax 05.53.61.05.66 V Y by appt.

DOM. DU HAUT-MONTLONG

Cuvée Laurence 1998★★

■ 5 ha 16,000 30–49 F

This Bergerac Cuvée Laurence represents excellent value for money. Its very powerful, mature nose releases aromas of red berries and crystallised fruits, and it has the same power on the palate, where its range of flavours continues harmoniously all the way through to the long finish. A wine for pleasure that is already attractive, but will keep for two to three years. The same estate's **1999 Bergerac Rosé** (20–29F) deserves to be commended for its nose of citrus fruits and its balance of roundness and freshness.

🔑 Alain and Josy Sergenton, Dom. du Haut-Montlong, 24240 Pomport, tel. 05.53.58.81.60, fax 05.53.58.09.42, e-mail sergenton-haut-montlong@wanadoo.fr V
Y ev. day 9am–12 noon 1.30pm–7.30pm; Sat. Sun. by appt.

JULIEN DE SAVIGNAC 1998★

■ 12 ha 98,000 30–49 F

Patrick Montfort has presented an interesting range of wines to the jury. His 1998 Bergerac Rouge stands out from the crowd with a nose of stewed fruits and spices, accompanied by some notes of toast. After a supple attack, it develops on the palate through moderately oaky tannins through to a finish marked by liquorice. Another star goes to the **1999 Bergerac Rosé**, which has citrus-fruit aromas and a beautifully fresh finish. Finally, the **1999 Bergerac Sec** deserves a mention for its very complex nose of bananas, lychees, peardrops, white flowers and crystallised fruits.

🔑 Julien de Savignac, av. de la Libération, 24260 Le Bugue, tel. 05.53.07.10.31, fax 05.53.07.16.41, e-mail julien.de.savignac@wanadoo.fr V
Y ev. day except Sun. 9am–12.15pm 2.30pm–7.15pm

CH. LA BRIE

Cuvée Prestige Vinifié et élevé en fût de chêne 1998

■ 6 ha 10,000 30–49 F

The Château La Brie was acquired in 1960 by the Ministry of Agriculture, and now houses a school of viticulture. With the 1998 vintage, it offers a product that will be an excellent teaching aid for the future winemakers. Despite its very oaky quality, this Bergerac has highly attractive notes of crystallised fruits (prunes). After a fairly supple attack, it moves on to rich tannins that have been slightly hardened by oak-ageing. Best kept for two to three years until it becomes more supple.

🔑 Ch. La Brie, Lycée viticole, Dom. de La Brie, 24240 Monbazillac, tel. 05.53.74.42.46, fax 05.53.58.24.08, e-mail lpa.bergerac@educagri.fr V
Y ev. day except Sun. 10am–7pm; cl. Jan.

DOM. DE LA COMBE 1998★★

■ 1 ha 3,500 30–49 F

A high proportion of Merlot (85%), and 12 months of maturation in oak barrels, are the keys to this remarkable Bergerac. Although very evident on the nose, the oak blends harmoniously with the fruity aromas. The rich tannins on the palate are surprisingly silky, and the oak flavour seems well-integrated into the whole. A thoroughbred, elegant wine, with particularly good length. Best kept for a few years.

🔑 Sylvie and Claude Sergenton, Dom. de La Combe, 24240 Razac-de-Saussignac, tel. 05.53.27.86.51, fax 05.53.27.99.87 V
Y by appt.

CH. DE LA JAUBERTIE

Cuvée Tradition 1999

■ 15 ha 60,000 30–49 F

This estate belonged to Gabrielle d'Estrée. The jury's attention was caught by the Jaubertie red and rosé Bergeracs. The red

wine bears the stamp of Cabernet with its notes of soft fruits and raspberries, after which it fills the mouth and is well sustained by tannins that as yet are a little rustic. Best kept until it becomes more refined. Also commended is the **1999 Rosé**, which has aromas of strawberries and raspberries, and a pleasant, slightly acid quality.
🔑 Ch. de La Jaubertie, 24560 Colombier, tel. 05.53.58.32.11, fax 05.53.57.46.22, e-mail rymanwines@rystone.com ☒
Y by appt.
🔑 S.A. Ryman

DOM. DE L'ANCIENNE CURE

Cuvée Abbaye 1999★★

■ n.c. 15,000 🛢 50–69 F

Christian Roche offers two extremely interesting wines in the Bergerac Rouge range. This remarkable 1999 Cuvée Abbaye has been matured in barrels for 12 months. The nose has aromas of vanilla and oak, accentuated by very pleasant notes of blackcurrant. There is a supple attack on the palate, and the mouth is dominated by roundness. The young structure is still characterised by oak, but should achieve harmony in a few years' time. Next, the **1998 Extase** (100–149F) is a highly successful wine, comparable to the previous one in terms of its aromas. Tannins are still very much in evidence on the palate, but it shows great promise for the future.
🔑 Christian Roche, EARL l'Ancienne Cure, 24560 Colombier, tel. 05.53.58.27.90, fax 05.53.24.83.95 ☒ Y by appt.

CH. DE LA NOBLE

La Noblesse du Château 1998★

■ 2 ha 5,000 🛢 70–99 F

It is said that not far from this estate, from the top of the walls of the Château de Puyguilhem, the first shot was fired from a powder cannon. For Fabien Charron, the 1998 vintage is a trial shot, and also a masterstroke. The ripe fruit that dominates this wine has not been crushed by oak from the barrel-ageing, and its silky, well-harmonised tannins show the quality conferred by 12 months of maturation. The Château de la Noble's **1999 Bergerac**, which is not barrel-matured, is cited here for the same characteristics of fruitiness and balance (20–29F).
🔑 Fabien Charron, La Noble, 24240 Puyguilhem, tel. 05.53.58.81.93, fax 05.53.58.81.93 ☒ Y by appt.

CLOS LA SELMONIE 1998★

■ n.c. n.c. 🛢 50–69 F

The dark red colour of this wine augurs well for its level of concentration. Despite the fact that its powerful nose is still dominated by oak, there are notes of toast as well as blackcurrant aromas that complement each other well. It has a very supple attack, and although it is a little lacking in power as it develops on the palate, oak and vanilla flavours reappear at the end to make for an attractive finish. A wine whose finesse and elegance will be fully appreciated in two to three years' time. From the same producer comes the **1999 Bergerac Rosé**, which the jury particularly wanted to mention for its delightful freshness.

Bergerac

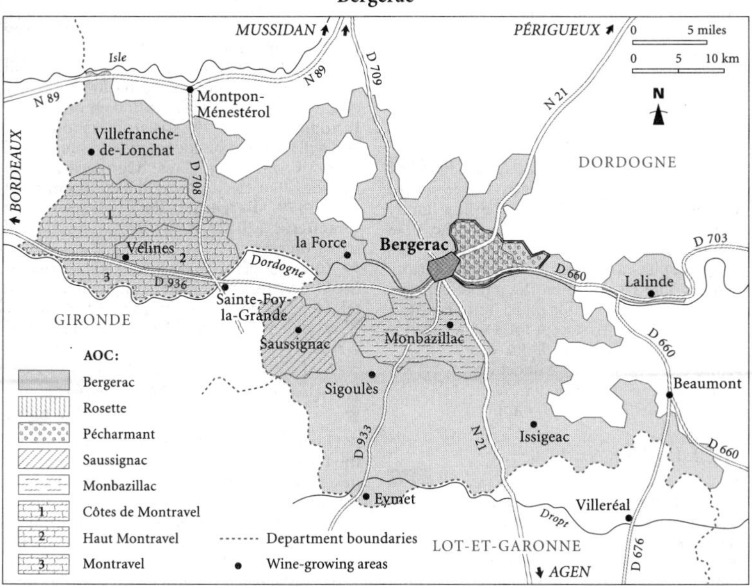

🗝 Christian Beigner, Les Colombes, 24240 Mescoulès, tel. 05.53.58.43.40, fax 05.53.58.49.81 ☑ 𝐘 by appt.

CH. LAULERIE

Vieilli en fût de chêne 1998★

■ 20 ha 120,000 🛢 30-49 F

As with the 1997 vintage, one star is awarded to this 1998 oak-matured wine, which is the product of 20 ha (49 acres) of vines, that is to say, no fewer than 120,000 bottles. The nose is very expressive, and the oak is well-harmonised so that the soft fruit aromas are clearly evident. It is round but not excessively concentrated on the palate, and there is a feeling that the wine's own tannins and those it has taken from the barrel genuinely complement each other. A very elegant wine that can be drunk immediately, but will keep for three years if you can bear to wait. The Château Laulerie's **1999 Montravel** is commended for its Sauvignon flavours and excellent grip.

🗝 Vignobles Dubard, Le Gouyat, 24610 Saint-Méard-de-Gurçon, tel. 05.53.82.48.31, fax 05.53.82.47.64, e-mail vignoblesdubard@wanadoo.fr ☑ 𝐘 ev. day 8am–12 noon 2pm–7pm

CH. LE BONDIEU 1999★

■ 5 ha 30,000 🍷 🌡 30-49 F

A Bergerac doesn't need to be oak-matured to be good . . . The proof is this intense 1999, which has a strong red colour and a nose offering powerful notes of blackcurrant. After a clean attack, it is supported by tannins and fills the palate beautifully, then finishes on a note of fruit. The Château de Bondieu also wins acclaim for its **1999 Montravel**, which is commended for its fruity freshness.

🗝 EARL d'Adrina, Le Bondieu, 24230 Saint-Antoine-de-Breuilh, tel. 05.53.58.30.83, fax 05.53.24.38.21 ☑ 𝐘 by appt.

🗝 Didier Feytout

CH. LE CASTELLOT Cuvée Prestige

Vieilli en fût de chêne 1998

■ 10 ha 7,000 🛢 50-69 F

Not far from the famous tower where Montaigne wrote his *Essais*, the Ley family keeps 55 ha (136 acres) of vines. The 1998 oak-matured Château Le Castellot offers notes of spices and oak, and interesting fruity aromas. The structure on the palate is pleasant, with notes of vanilla and a hint of austerity on the finish. Best kept for a while.

🗝 GFA M. Ley et Fils, Dom. des Templiers, 24230 Saint-Michel-de-Montaigne, tel. 05.53.58.63.29, fax 05.53.58.79.99 ☑ 𝐘 by appt.

CH. LE PAYRAL 1998★★

■ 1 ha 4,000 🛢 30-49 F

This beautifully concentrated wine has spent a year in oak barrels. That has given it a fine, oaky nose that releases notes of prunes as it swirls around in the glass. The first impression on the palate is of roundness and maturity. After that, stewed fruits and prunes came back into evidence, together with well-integrated oak. A well-balanced wine with good ageing potential.

🗝 Thierry Daulhial, 24240 Razac-de-Saussignac, tel. 05.53.22.38.07, fax 05.53.27.99.81, e-mail daulhial@club-internet ☑ 𝐘 by appt.

CH. LES NICOTS 1998★★

■ 7.5 ha n.c. 🛢 30-49 F

The nose of this Bergerac is remarkable for its roasted coffee and chocolate aromas, and for the excellent harmony that exists between the power of the wine and the elegance of the oak. It is mature, fleshy, rich and well-integrated; all the elements have come together to make a great wine that will need to be kept. This wine is not marketed by the producer but by SOVAC, a Bergerac négociant.

🗝 Gilbert Rondonnier, Les Nicots, 24240 Ribagnac, tel. 05.53.57.63.61 ☑ 𝐘 by appt.

CH. LESPINASSAT Vieilles vignes 1998

■ 3 ha 17,000 🍷 🌡 30-49 F

Not only do the grapes here come from old vines grown along the side of an ancient Roman road, they are also hand-picked and rigorously selected, essential factors that contribute to the quality of this 1998. It has a prune aroma on the nose that verges on overripeness. The same sensation of roundness, maturity and richness dominates on the palate. A pleasant wine for drinking young.

🗝 Agnès Verseau, Les Oliviers, 24230 Montcaret, tel. 05.53.58.34.23, fax 05.53.61.36.57 ☑ 𝐘 by appt.

CH. LE TOURON

Cuvée Prestige Elevé en fût 1999★

■ n.c. 15,000 🛢 30-49 F

This wine has long been highly commended. In the 1999 vintage, its nose is still marked by oak, but in the mouth its fruity quality blends well with the flavour of vanilla. In addition to that, the structure is promising, and will become rounder in two or three years' time. From the Cave Coopérative de Monbazillac, the jury would like to commend the **1999 Bergerac Rosé Marquis de Chamterac** (20–29F) for its freshness and fruity flavours.

🗝 Cave coopérative de Monbazillac, rte de Mont-de-Marsan, 24240 Monbazillac, tel. 05.53.63.65.00, fax 05.53.63.65.09 ☑ 𝐘 ev. day except Sun. Mon. 10am–12.30pm 1.30pm–7pm

MIRAGE DU JONCAL 1998★★

■ 1.25 ha 3,000 🛢 70-99 F

One star for the 1997 vintage, two stars for the 1998 . . . We can't wait to see what happens next. The colour is an appealing ruby red, while the very complex nose has an attractive oaky quality, with aromas of toast, grilling, smoke and tobacco. The attack on the palate is somewhat masked by oak, but the fruit flavours – blackcurrant and raspberry – become

apparent at the finish. With its remarkable concentration and well-controlled oakiness, this is guaranteed to be an excellent wine in a few years' time.
🔑 SCEA Le Joncal, Clos Le Joncal, 24500 Saint-Julien-d'Eymet, tel. 05.53.61.84.73, fax 05.53.61.84.73 ☒ Y by appt.

CH. MONDESIR 1999

■ 9 ha 66,000 ▮ 🌡 20–29 F

This Bergerac from the Univitis group is always a highly regarded wine. In the 1999 vintage, the cherry colour is not that strong, but the nose is powerful, with highly distinct notes of ripe fruits. On the palate, the wine takes on a rounder quality, with very harmonious tannins. The taster is left with an impression of fruit aromas and a pleasantly smooth quality that is characteristic of the vintage.
🔑 Closerie d'Estiac, 33320 Sainte-Foy-la-Grande, tel. 05.57.56.02.02, fax 05.57.56.02.22 ☒ Y by appt.

CH. MOULIN CARESSE

Cuvée Prestige Elevé en fût de chêne 1998★★★

■ 7.5 ha 45,000 ⦀ 70–99 F

The Château Moulin Caresse's 1997 Bergerac was very good indeed, but in the case of this 1998 Cuvée Prestige, matured for 18 months in new oak barrels, the judges' verdict is that it is quite exceptional. With a black colour that clings to the glass, it is very much an oaky, toasty wine. Nevertheless, ripe fruit aromas come through as it swirls around, ranging through cherries, grapes and blackcurrants. After a fairly supple attack, there is a superb surge of power on the palate. Following on from liquorice and vanilla, ripe fruits reappear as the wine is savoured. Apart from its concentration, it is the finesse and elegance of this Bergerac that deserve recognition. The work of a goldsmith. Should be kept for five to six years.
🔑 Sylvie and Jean-François Deffarge, Ch. Moulin Caresse, 24230 Saint-Antoine-de-Breuilh, tel. 05.53.27.55.58, fax 05.53.27.07.39 ☒ Y ev. day 9am–12 noon 3pm–7pm; Sat. Sun. by appt.

SEIGNEURS DE BERGERAC 1999

■ n.c. n.c. ▮ 20–29 F

As we can see from the label, this Bergerac celebrates a *langue d'oc* festival that is very typical of the Périgord: the *félibrée*. Its fresh, fruity aromas are accompanied by notes of spice and roasting. It has moderately powerful extract on the palate, at the heart of which fruit flavours linger attractively. A pleasant wine that can be drunk without delay.
🔑 SA Yvon Mau, B.P. 1, Gironde-sur-Dropt, 33193 La Réole Cedex, tel. 05.56.61.54.54, fax 05.56.61.54.61 Y by appt.

CH. TOUR D'ARFON

Vieilli en fût de chêne 1998

■ 0.5 ha 3,000 ⦀ 30–49 F

There is a strong sense here that care has been taken to preserve a balance between wine and oak. Notes of vanilla are followed by intense, complex fruit aromas. The structure on the palate is full and dense. Oak is very much in evidence, but there is a beautiful resurgence of fruits at the finish. Best kept for two to three years.
🔑 H. et F. Ferté, La Tour d'Arfon, 24240 Monestier, tel. 05.53.73.36.49, fax 05.53.73.36.49 ☒ Y by appt.

CH. TOUR MONTBRUN 1999★

■ 1.7 ha 13,300 ▮ 20–29 F

A typical 1999, with plenty of fruit and a pleasant structure which enables it to be drunk quickly. The nose is made up of blackcurrant, raspberry, and various Cabernet aromas. There is a supple attack on the palate, and the tannins are well-integrated. Fruit flavours return at the end to make for a pleasant finish. Drink now.
🔑 Philippe Poivey, Montravel, 24230 Montcaret, tel. 05.53.58.66.93, fax 05.53.58.66.93, e-mail philippe.poivey@wanadoo.fr ☒ Y by appt.

CH. VEYRINES

Cuvée Prestige Vieilli en fût de chêne 1998★

■ 0.5 ha 1,500 ⦀ 30–49 F

This estate was taken over in 1996, and has produced a very successful 1998 wine that has been matured in oak for 12 months. It has a complex, intense range of oak, vanilla and red-berry aromas. After a supple attack on the palate, the tannins become more powerful, and finally the original aromas reappear. It would be advisable to keep this wine for two to three years.
🔑 Eric Lascombes, Veyrines, 24240 Ribagnac, tel. 05.53.73.01.34, fax 05.53.73.01.34 ☒ Y by appt.

DOM. DU VIGNEAUD

La Boissière Vieilli en fût de chêne 1998★

■ 2 ha 10,200 ⦀ 30–49 F

This oak-matured wine is already delightful, but it should become even more interesting once it has aged for a few years. Oaky aromas of vanilla and spices dominate the nose within an overall framework that is very well-balanced and unaggressive. The silky, harmonious tannic structure on the palate leads on to a thoroughbred finish with

excellent length. The ideal accompanient to red meat.
🔑 Serge Lagarde, Dom. du Vigneaud, 24240 Monestier, tel. 05.53.58.80.54, fax 05.53.24.88.56 ☑ Y by appt.

Bergerac Rosé

DOM. DU BOIS DE POURQUIE 1999★★

◪ 1.5 ha 10,700 ▮ ♁ 30–49 F

According to Marlène and Alain Mayet, 'Nothing can be left to chance in the Dordogne' by those who live there. It is certainly not by chance that this rosé has turned out as it has. Its particularly fruity, very complex nose releases notes of bananas, blackcurrants, raspberries and also grenadine. The wine is supple and slightly sweet on the palate, with more attractive blackcurrant flavours at the finish. Enjoy it with an exotic fruit sorbet.
🔑 Marlène and Alain Mayet, Le Bois de Pourquié, 24560 Conne-de-Labarde, tel. 05.53.58.25.58, fax 05.53.61.34.59 ☑ Y ev. day 8am–12 noon 2pm–7pm

DOM. LA TUILIERE 1999★

◪ 2 ha n.c. ▮ ♁ 20–29 F

A very long time ago, the forebears of the current owners made tiles on this estate, as its evocative name suggests. There is a great deal of clay in the soil, which these days is used to develop an excellent Bergerac Rosé with a highly attractive nose of both fruity and flowery aromas, including raspberries and violets. It has a round, supple attack on the palate, on which some residual sugar is evident. The fruit flavours are elegant without being bitter. Best drunk as an apéritif or with dessert.
🔑 SCEA Moulin de Sanxet, Belingard-Bas, 24240 Pomport, tel. 05.53.58.30.79, fax 05.53.61.71.84 ☑ Y ev. day 8.30am–6.30pm; Sunday by appt.

CH. DE PERROU 1999

◪ 10 ha n.c. ⏸ 30–49 F

The nose of this Bergerac is dominated by grenadine and peardrops. It is pleasant on the palate, revealing a slight note of acidity at the finish. A well-made rosé, which can be drunk without delay.
🔑 Armand Loewe, Le Vernajou; 24240 Gageac-et-Rouillac, tel. 05.53.22.92.16, fax 05.53.22.92.16 Y by appt.
🔑 Albano Muller

CH. DU PRIORAT 1999★★

◪ 5.75 ha 40,000 ▮ ♁ 20–29 F

The nose of this rosé is an explosion of red berry aromas (strawberries and raspberries) and peardrops. There is a flavour of crushed strawberries on the palate, where the stucture is powerful and persistent, with a slight note of acidity at the finish. Will go well with a seafood soufflé. The **1999 Bergerac Sec du Domaine** was also cited for its very pronounced Sauvignon flavours.
🔑 GAEC du Priorat, Le Priorat, 24610 Saint-Martin-de-Gurson, tel. 05.53.80.76.06, fax 05.53.81.21.83 ☑ Y ev. day except Sun. 8am–12.30pm 2pm–7pm
🔑 Maury

CH. ROQUE-PEYRE 1999

◪ 5 ha 30,000 ▮ ♁ 20–29 F

In a little over 100 years, the Château Roque-Peyre's vineyard has gone from six to 47 ha (15 to 116 acres), with the result that it now produces some 300,000 bottles. The wine it entered was a rosé with an intense colour and pleasant, slightly acid fruity aromas. It turned out to be well-balanced on the palate, with notes of raspberry, and a resurgence of vigour at the finish. A pleasant wine to drink at the beginning of a meal.
🔑 Vallette Frères-GAEC Roque-Peyre, Ch. Roque-Peyre, 33220 Fougueyrolles, tel. 05.53.24.77.98, fax 05.53.61.36.87 ☑ Y by appt.

DOM. DU SIORAC 1999

◪ 3.7 ha 10,000 ▮ ♁ 20–29 F

The Landat family has opened a new shop, in which it offers a selection of Périgord farm products (foie gras, conserves, nuts, verjuice), and of course its range of wines. This very pale 1999 rosé is almost a Vin Gris. It has both floral and spicy aromas, and although there is quite a high sugar content on the palate (9 g/l), it is nonetheless well-balanced. A wine that gives an overall impression of harmony, and is ready to drink now.
🔑 GAEC du Dom. du Siorac, 24500 Saint-Aubin-de-Cadelech, tel. 05.53.74.52.90, fax 05.53.58.35.32 ☑ Y by appt.

Bergerac Sec

The mixed soils (limestone, gravel, clay, sand, alluvial deposits and stones) give rise to a range of aromas for these wines.

When young, they are fruity and elegant, with a touch of vitality. If they are vinified in wood, it is necessary to wait for a year or two for the flavour of the terroir to become apparent.

CALISTA 1998★★

☐ 0.25 ha 2,100 100–149 F

On a particular type of limestone terroir which can only be found in the communes of Thénac and Port-Sainte-Foy, Charles Martin has produced a few – sadly all too few – bottles of a remarkable Bergerac sec. Its aromas of oak, toast and spices show that it has been matured in barrels. The wine itself comes through in notes of dried flowers, then fills the mouth with a noticeably rich structure that is beginning to get the upper hand over the oak. A wine with fine prospects for the future. In the **Bergerac Rouge** range, the **Carminé** – which won the *coup de coeur* for three years running – won one star for the **1998** vintage. Also cited was the **1999 Bergerac Rouge Château de la Colline**.

Charles Martin, Ch. de la Colline, 24240 Thénac, tel. 05.53.61.87.87, fax 05.53.61.71.09, e-mail charlesm@la.colline.com ☒
by appt.

CH. DE FAYOLLE Elevage sur lie 1999

☐ 3.95 ha 34,000 20–29 F

The famous British brewers Ringwood and Co. bought this vineyard in 1997, that is to say almost 500 years after the English destroyed the castle during the Hundred Years War. In the 1999 vintage they offer a Bergerac sec whose maturation on lees has given it a complex nose of fruit and flower aromas. From the start, it is essentially fruity and rich on the palate and, although not long, is well-balanced.

Ets Ringwood Brewery, Fayolle, 24240 Saussignac, tel. 05.53.74.32.02, fax 05.53.74.32.02 ☒ ev. day 8am–6pm
SARL Marcassin

CH. DE LA GRANDE BORIE 1999

☐ 3 ha 20,000 20–29 F

Made from Sauvignon and matured on its lees, this wine stands out for its excellent maturity. This is conveyed on the nose by notes of citrus and other fruits, and although the attack on the palate has surprising freshness, the returning fruit flavours at the finish are extremely attractive.

EARL des Vignobles Lafon-Lafaye, La Grande Borie, 24520 Saint-Nexans, tel. 05.53.24.33.21, fax 05.53.24.97.74 ☒
by appt.
Claude Lafaye

CH. LA MAURIGNE Elevé en fût 1999

☐ 1 ha 5,000 20–29 F

This Bergerac sec has unusually fine notes of tea and bergamot orange, accentuated by a slight hint of vanilla. There is a taste of peardrops on the palate alongside the oaky aromas. The overall impression is quite lively and makes this a pleasant wine that is ready to drink now.

Chantal and Patrick Gérardin, La Maurigne, 24240 Razac-de-Saussignac, tel. 05.53.27.25.45, fax 05.53.27.25.45 ☒
ev. day 9am–7pm

CH. LA RAYRE 1999

☐ 10 ha 20,000 20–29 F

With a change of owner, the Château La Rayre is in the fore again, which only goes to show that 'a good terroir will out'. As before, there is an explosion of Sauvignon aromas on the nose, and the wine has a pleasant fruitiness on the palate, despite a rather lively finish. Needs to be drunk straight away.

EARL Ch. La Rayre, 24560 Colombier, tel. 05.53.58.32.17, fax 05.53.24.55.58, e-mail vincent.vesselle@wanadoo.fr ☒
by appt.
Vesselle V.

CH. LA TOUR DE GRANGEMONT 1999★

☐ 3 ha 14,000 20–29 F

Whether it be a Côtes de Bergerac Moelleux or a Bergerac Rouge, there is always a fine wine from the Château La Tour de Grangement. This year, it is the 1999 Bergerac sec that wins a star. Forthright and clean, it shows the characteristics of the appellation very well in its typical Sauvignon nose of citrus fruits and lychees, and fresh, even sharp, flavours in the mouth.

EARL Lavergne, Ch. La Tour de Grangemont, 24560 Saint-Aubin-de-Lanquais, tel. 05.53.24.32.89, fax 05.53.24.56.77 ☒ ev. day except Sun. 8am–12 noon 2pm–7pm
Christian Lavergne

CLOS DE MONESTIER 1999★

☐ n.c. 34,375 30–49 F

Built in the 13th century, the Château La Tour once belonged to the estates of the Comte d'Eymet and the Comte de Pellegrue. Later the property was divided up and sold, and now vines are grown there over an area of 17 ha (42 acres). The 1999 Clos de Monestier has slight touches of toast and vanilla on the nose, and equally noticeable floral notes that give it fine aromatic power. On the palate, it has all the assets of a very well-made wine: richness, substance and good, fruity extract. The finish is marked by a hint of bitterness.

SCEA La Tour, 24240 Monestier, tel. 05.53.61.87.87, fax 05.53.61.71.09 ☒
by appt.

MOULIN DES DAMES 1998★

☐ 3.5 ha 15,000 70–99 F

In 1981, Luc de Conti moved into this 12th-century vineyard farmhouse. His Moulin des Dames has a complex nose with a range of citrus-fruit and floral notes, supported by a fine, oaky aroma. Harmoniously balanced on the palate, it is a delightfully curvaceous wine,

SOUTH-WEST

which in two years' time will make a good accompaniment to a fish dish with a creamy sauce.
SCEA de Conti, Les Gendres, 24240 Ribagnac, tel. 05.53.57.12.43, fax 05.53.58.89.49 V Y by appt.

Côtes de Bergerac

This appellation conforms not to a terroir but rather to a set of more restrictive conditions for the harvest, intended to produce rich and well-structured wines. They are sought after for their concentration of flavour and their long-term keeping qualities.

DOM. DE BEAUREGARD

Vieilli en fût de chêne 1998★

■ 1.5 ha 7,500 30–49 F

Once again a star is awarded to the Beauregard estate's oak-matured Côtes de Bergerac. The 1998 vintage has strong aromas of toast and a burnt element on the nose, but fruit comes through when it is swirled in the glass. The tannic structure on the palate is impressive, and takes on a slightly rustic quality. Excellent extraction has produced a wine that will become more refined with time, and should keep for up to five years.
Jean-Marie Teillet, Dom. de Beauregard, 24610 Villefranche-de-Lonchat, tel. 05.53.80.76.34, fax 05.53.80.76.34 V
Y ev. day except Sat. Sun. 10am–12 noon 2pm–4pm

CH. BELINGARD Cuvée Prestige 1998★★

■ 2 ha 7,500 70–99 F

This vineyard once belonged to a monastery, and is set in admirable surroundings. Following on from the 1997 Blanche de Bosredon, the 1998 Cuvée Prestige now wins unanimous acclaim and is awarded the *coup de coeur*. Its powerful nose releases notes of

fruits in brandy and very evident oaky aromas. On the palate, the tannins are softened by a silky texture with no bitterness or acidity. Although this very mature wine can be enjoyed straight away, it will gain from four or five years of ageing. The **1999 Cuvée Comte de Bosredon en AOC Bergerac Rouge** is also cited for its complex, unusual nose, which combines notes of green peppers, hazelnuts, blackcurrants, sloes, and many other aromas besides (20–29F).
SCEA Comte de Bosredon, Belingard, 24240 Pomport, tel. 05.53.58.28.03, fax 05.53.58.38.39, e-mail deschard.boisredon@wanadoo.fr V
Y by appt.
L. de Bosredon

CH. BRUNET CHARPENTIERE

1998

■ 0.58 ha 4,500 20–29 F

Two wines from the Château Brunet Charpentière merit citations. This Côtes de Bergerac has a fine nose combining spices and blackcurrants. Its richness and fullness on the palate are supported by harmonious tannins, after which the finish is long and slightly warm. The tank-matured **1998 Bergerac Rouge** is singled out for its Cabernet aromas (green peppers) and evident tannins, which will need a little more time to age.
Pierrette Descoins, Les Charpentières, 24230 Montazeau, tel. 05.53.27.54.71 V
Y by appt.

CH. COMBRILLAC 1998

■ 3.41 ha 11,600 70–99 F

This wine has been vinified with a view to achieving the best possible tannic structure, which has meant a long, 16-month period of maturation in barrel. It now has a powerful, complex nose of vanilla and ripe fruits. With the same combination of fruit and oak on the palate, it is a full-bodied, balanced wine that will need to be kept for a while.
GFA de Combrillac, Gravillac, 24130 Prigonrieux, tel. 05.53.57.63.61, fax 05.53.58.08.12 Y by appt.

CONSTANT-HERITAGE 1998

■ 1 ha 2,850 30–49 F

Wine production is fairly limited on these Monsaguel and Issigeac limestone soils. Some very good wines are made here, however, such as this Côtes de Bergerac. The nose is dominated by red berries, punctuated by a few floral notes of hyacinth and iris. After a forthright attack on the palate, the tannins contribute to a wine that is structured, but not excessively so. It will be interesting to taste it in two to three years' time.
Steven Atkins, Le Terme, 24560 Monsaguel, tel. 05.53.73.32.12, fax 05.53.73.32.23, e-mail leterme@club-internet.fr V
Y by appt.

CH. COURT-LES-MUTS 1998

■ 8.73 ha 60,000 50–69 F

Somewhat dominated by oak on the day of the tasting, this Côtes de Bergerac has a spicy nose, complemented by slight hints of musk, and a round attack on the palate followed by a full tannic structure. It ends on a rather austere note that tends to mask the final fruit flavours. But there's no need to worry. It should improve with age.

Vignobles Pierre Sadoux, Ch. Court-les-Mûts, 24240 Razac-de-Saussignac, tel. 05.53.27.92.17, fax 05.53.23.77.21 ev. day except Sun. 9am–11.30am 2pm–5.30pm; Sat. by appt.

CH. DAUZAN LA VERGNE Elevé en fût de chêne 1998★

■ 4.16 ha 31,000 50–69 F

This château has won a good triple bet, with three wines each receiving one star. This balanced Côtes de Bergerac shows all the signs of well-handled maturation in cask. Cherry and blackcurrant aromas mingle with spices and liquorice. There is still a strong tannic feel on the palate, but the fruit flavours prevail at the finish. The **1998 Montravel Elevé en Fût de Chêne** shows a good balance between oak and fruit flavours, which means that it should age well. Finally, the vat-matured **1998 Côtes de Montravel Château Pique-Sègue** is delightfully sweet, with a fine surge of power as it finishes on notes of crystallised fruits (30–49F).

SNC Ch. Pique-Sègue, Pique-Sègue, Ponchapt, 33220 Port-Sainte-Foy, tel. 05.53.58.52.52, fax 05.53.63.44.97 by appt.

Philip and Marianne Mallard

CH. FONFREDE 1998★★

■ 5 ha 10,000 30–49 F

This wine has a concentrated nose of dark berries and tobacco, mingled with the spice and vanilla aromas that come from oak. Those fruit aromas remain elegantly in evidence throughout the tasting. The tannins are concentrated yet supple, and the oak flavour is beginning to fade. A wine with excellent prospects, and that should keep for five years. The **1998 Pécharmant du Domaine Puy de Grave**, also from the La Métairie estate, receives one star: it still has a very strong oaky quality, but time should remedy that (70–99F).

SARL Dom. La Métairie, Fonfrède, 24610 Villefranche-de-Lonchat, tel. 05.53.80.09.85, fax 05.53.80.14.72, e-mail metairieetdomaines@wanadoo.fr by appt.

CH. HAUT BERNASSE 1998★★

■ 6 ha 12,600 30–49 F

The quality of this château's red wines and Monbazillacs cannot be unconnected with the fact that it still uses the old vertical hydraulic wine-presses. The proof is this Côtes de Bergerac, whose toast and oak nose is pierced by crystallised fruits. Richness dominates the other sensations on the palate, but the taster is also aware of a fine, complex stucture that balances oak and fruit tannins well. A harmonious, aromatic wine.

Jacques Blais, Ch. Haut Bernasse, 24240 Monbazillac, tel. 05.53.58.36.22, fax 05.53.61.26.40 by appt.

CH. LA BARDE-LES TENDOUX

Vieilli en fût de chêne 1998★★★

■ 7.5 ha 26,000 70–99 F

In order to ensure maximum extraction of the tannins, this wine has had a long period of maceration, during which, significantly, it was pumped over twice a day. The result is an intense vanilla aroma, but also some perceptible notes of cherries and blackcurrants. The structure on the palate is monolithic, enveloped in an oakiness that is intense, fleshy and rich. At the finish the vanilla fades well, and the fruit flavours that have so far hung back now return to the fore. A very great wine, which has a long time ahead of it to achieve perfection.

SARL de Labarde, Ch. de Labarde, 24560 Saint-Cernin-de-Labarde, tel. 05.53.57.63.61, fax 05.53.58.08.12 by appt.

CH. LE CHABRIER

Elevé en fût de chêne 1998★★

■ 12.85 ha 18,000 30–49 F

Given the very low yields (25 hl/ha) from which this wine has been produced, it is not surprising that it has achieved such concentration. It has a nose of spice and toast aromas, while on the palate it is full and structured around tannins that are softened, round and pleasant. The spice and toast flavours dominate, and then give way at the finish to a delightful new note of fruit. A remarkable wine that should be allowed to age for a while. The **1999 Bergerac Sec du Domaine** was cited for its complex nose and richness on the palate, which come from maturation on the lees (20–29F).

Pierre Carle, Ch. Le Chabrier, 24240 Razac-de-Saussignac, tel. 05.53.27.92.73, fax 05.53.23.39.03, e-mail chateau.le.chabrier@wanadoo.fr by appt.

CH. LE RAZ Cuvée Grand Chêne 1998

■ 7.07 ha 48,500 30–49 F

Once the wine has been swirled in the glass, grilled and toasted aromas give way to fruit, and the nose takes on notes of blackcurrant and liquorice. The fine tannic structure is reinforced by oak flavour from the barrels, but the overall impression is not yet harmonious. It will take time before this wine is ready to be enjoyed fully.

Vignobles Barde, Le Raz, 24610 Saint-Méard-de-Gurçon, tel. 05.53.82.48.41, fax 05.53.80.07.47 ev. day except Sun. 8.30am–12.30pm 2pm–7pm; Sat. by appt.

CH. LES GRIMARD

Cuvée spéciale 1998★★

■ 1.5 ha 8,000 ⛁ 30–49 F

Although the Grimard Cuvée Spéciale has been matured in barrel, oak remains unobtrusive throughout the tasting. The nose is dominated by complex soft fruit aromas, accentuated by some spicy notes. There are rich, very evident tannins in the mouth, which will need to fade with time, but the overall impression is harmonious. The vat-matured **1998 Cuvée Classique** is cited for its fruit aromas and freshness on the palate (20–29F).

⊶ J. et P. Joyeux, GAEC des Grimard, 24230 Montazeau, tel. 05.53.63.09.83, fax 05.53.24.90.14 ☒ 🍷 by appt.

CH. LES MARNIERES

Cuvée la Côte fleurie 1998★★

■ 1.55 ha 5,400 ⛁ 70–99 F

After winning a *coup de coeur* from an earlier jury, this Côtes de Bergerac now receives two stars. There are very clear oaky notes of toast, spices and burnt flavours on the nose, followed very quickly by soft fruit aromas. After a clean attack on the palate, the wine has meatiness and structure. The balance is ideal, and the flavours have excellent length, but it will need to be kept for more than five years to be enjoyed at its best. A somewhat less rich but well-structured wine is the **1998 Cuvée Flavie**, of which only 1,200 bottles were produced, and which is awarded a star (100–149F).

⊶ Alain and Christophe Geneste, GAEC des Brandines, 24520 Saint-Nexans, tel. 05.53.58.31.65, fax 05.53.73.20.34 ☒ 🍷 by appt.

CH. LE TAP Cuvée du Grand Chêne 1998★

■ 2.55 ha 7,730 ⛁ 50–69 F

Against a light background of toast, the nose is mainly given over to crystallised fruits and prunes, which is a sign of excellent maturity. After a supple, silky attack on the palate, the taster is impressed by the way in which the tannins fill the mouth. The oaky flavour remains discreet, which makes it easier to appreciate the richness and concentration of the wine. The jury also cited the **1998 Bergerac Sec Elevé en Fût de Chêne** for the finesse of its aromas (30–49F).

⊶ SCEA Ch. Le Tap, Le Tap, 24240 Saussignac, tel. 05.53.27.53.41, fax 05.53.22.07.55 ☒ 🍷 by appt.
⊶ M. Proffit

CH. DE LADY MASBUREL 1998★★

■ 9 ha 23,000 ⛁ 30–49 F

The Château de Lady Masburel and the **1998 Château Masburel** are evenly matched in this selection. The only difference lies in the balance of grape varieties. In the first case, Cabernet is more prominent. The nose is marked by fruit in alcohol (cherries and prunes), and these reappear on the palate over a tannic structure that is rich but a little austere as yet. The second wine (70–99F) contains more Merlot, and is therefore more supple on the palate, but dominated by notes of oak. After a few months of ageing it will delight the lover of wine.

⊶ SARL Ch. Masburel, Fougueyrolles, 33220 Sainte-Foy-la-Grande, tel. 05.53.24.77.73, fax 05.53.24.27.30, e-mail chateau.masburel@accesinter.com ☒ 🍷 ev. day except Sat. Sun. 9am–12 noon 2pm–5.30pm; cl. Nov.–Mar.
⊶ Olivia Donnan

CH. PECACHARD 1998★

■ 1.5 ha 9,000 ⛁ 50–69 F

The Château Pécachard's Côtes de Bergerac Rouge has notes of chocolate and roasted coffee. Revolving around very mature tannins on the palate are lingering flavours of blackcurrants and plumstones, giving an overall impression of balance and harmony. From the same producer, the **1998 Côtes de Bergerac Moelleux Château Singleyrac** (30–49F) also deserves a star. It has an enjoyable complexity of floral and fruity aromas, accentuated by notes of honey, and a perfect balance between richness on the palate and freshness on the finish.

⊶ SCEA Ch. Singleyrac, Le Bourg, 24500 Singleyrac, tel. 05.53.58.41.98, fax 05.53.58.37.07 ☒ 🍷 by appt.

L'EXCELLENCE DU CH. TOURS DES VERDOTS

Les Verdots selon David Fourtout 1998★

■ 2.8 ha 12,000 ⛁ 100–149 F

For the moment the excellent raw material here is masked by oak. The range of aromas flatters the senses with its notes of ripe fruits, blackcurrants and intense hints of vanilla. Although the tannins on the palate are very mature and powerful, they are still finding it hard to emerge from behind the flavour of oak. Nonetheless, the wine has a promising structure that just needs time to harmonise. The **1999 Bergerac Rouge Clos des Verdots** also merits a star for its delightful roundness (30–49F). Finally, the **1998 Bergerac Sec L'Excellence du Château Les Tours des Verdots** is cited for its complex range of fruit and oak aromas (70–99F). A wine that can be drunk immediately.

⊶ GAEC Fourtout et Fils, Les Verdots, 24560 Conne-de-Labarde, tel. 05.53.58.34.31, fax 05.53.57.82.00, e-mail fourtout@terre-net.fr ☒ 🍷 ev. day except Sun. 9am–12.30pm 2pm–7pm

CH. DES VIGIERS

Réserve Jean Vigier 1998★

■ 1.5 ha 8,000 ⛁ 70–99 F

One star is awarded both to the Réserve Jean Vigier and to the **1998 Cuvée Classique**, the first of which is matured in barrel, the other in vat. The Réserve Jean Vigier's aromatic range develops with the greatest finesse through oaky-spicy aromas and notes of musk. After a supple attack on the palate, it moves on to a tannic structure that is powerful and extremely oaky. The Cuvée Classique is easier to drink, offering scents of ripe fruits and a framework of more supple tannins (30–49F).

SCEA La Font du Roc, Ch. des Vigiers, 24240 Monestier, tel. 05.53.61.50.30, fax 05.53.61.50.31 by appt.
Petersson

CLOS D'YVIGNE Le Petit Prince 1998★

■ 4.5 ha n.c. 30–49 F

Last year the Clos d'Yvigne won a star for its 1997 Côtes de Bergerac, and this star for the 1998 vintage confirms its success. The nose has an attractive vanilla quality with a slight hint of menthol, behind which aromas of cherries and bananas are perceptible. The powerful tannins become a litle austere at the finish, but this is a promising wine that will become more harmonious with time.

Patricia Atkinson, Le Bourg, 24240 Gageac-Rouillac, tel. 05.53.22.94.40, fax 05.53.23.47.67, e-mail patricia.atkinson@wanadoo.fr ev. day except Sun. 9am–12 noon 2pm–6pm

Sweet Côtes de Bergerac

These are made from the same varieties as the dry white wines but are harvested when over-ripe to make popular and supple sweet wines with flavours of preserved fruits.

CH. CAPULLE 1998★

□ 2 ha 3,648 –20 F

There is much to be said for the **1998 Côtes de Bergerac Rouge Château Capulle, Vieilli en Fût de Chêne**, which is cited for its roundness and aromas of soft fruits – cherries and blackcurrants (20–29F). Nevertheless, it was the sweet white wine that won the jury's preference. It has notes of honey on the nose, and then hits the palate roundly with fruit and honey flavours which linger attractively on the palate. Its fine, lively character also leaves a feeling of freshness. A highly typical, enjoyable wine.

Jean-Paul Migot, Ch. Capulle, 24240 Thénac, tel. 05.53.58.42.67, fax 05.53.58.39.50 by appt.

CLOS DALMAIN 1999★★

□ 0.5 ha 2,000 30–49 F

Tim Richardson is a producer of whom more will no doubt be heard in the years to come. After living in Bergerac for eight years, he has now harvested his own grapes for the first time, and two of the wines they have yielded have won two stars: a **1999 Bergerac Sec** with a subtle balance of ripe fruit and toasty oak, and this sweet, very rich Côtes de Bergerac with notes of crystallised fruits. With its rich balance, it will become even better if kept for a while.

Tim Richardson, Le Bourg, 24500 Saint-Julien-d'Eymet, tel. 05.53.58.09.72, fax 05.53.58.09.72, e-mail tim.richardson@wanadoo.fr by appt.

HAUTE TRADITION 1998★★

□ 10 ha 18,000 30–49 F

Haute Tradition offers a range of wines, from which the jury singled out not only a sweet white wine but also a **Bergerac Rouge**, the **1998 Cuvée Vieillie en Fût de Chêne**, which has spent 12 months in barrels, and is cited for its especially velvety, supple tannins. To return to this remarkable Côtes de Bergerac Moelleux, however: its aromas of roasting, wax and honey are indicative of overripening. Full and fruity on the palate, it finishes with great vivacity. A very pleasant, harmonious wine.

Cave coop. des producteurs de Montravel et Sigoulès, 24240 Mescoules, tel. 05.53.61.55.00, fax 05.53.61.55.10 ev. day except Sun. 8.30am–12.30pm 2pm–6.30pm

DOM. DE L'ANCIENNE CURE 1999★★

□ 4 ha 25,000 30–49 F

What a well-made, refreshing wine this 1999 Domaine de l'Ancienne Cure is. Its nose is particularly fruity, with a strong emphasis on citrus. It is rich and fat on the palate, which is marked at the same time by flavours of lemon and mandarin. The overall impression is enhanced by freshness on the finish. There is also a citation for Christian Roche's **1999 Bergerac Sec**.

Christian Roche, EARL l'Ancienne Cure, 24560 Colombier, tel. 05.53.58.27.90, fax 05.53.24.83.95 by appt.

CH. LE PARADIS 1999

□ 2.5 ha 2,800 30–49 F

There is already some freshness in the ripe fruit notes of the nose, but the palate is where exotic fruit flavours really explode. Well-balanced and long, this Côtes de Bergerac Moelleux will make a pleasant apéritif.

EARL Tonneau de Conty, Les Mayets, 24560 Saint-Perdoux, tel. 05.53.61.92.00, fax 05.53.73.16.16 by appt.

CH. REPENTY 1999★

□ 1 ha 6,000 30–49 F

After the 1997, it is now the 1999 vintage's turn to receive a star. The very pale colour of this wine gleams with green highlights. The nose conveys an impression of freshness with its notes of white peaches. On the palate, the balance is excellent for a sweet wine, with no excessive acidity, alcohol or sugar. An

SOUTH-WEST

attractive, classic, smooth Bergerac that is ready to drink immediately.
🔑 Jean-Pierre Roulet, Repenty, 24240 Monestier, tel. 05.53.58.41.96, fax 05.53.58.41.96 ☑ Y by appt.

Monbazillac

Extending over 2,500 ha (6,175 acres), the Monbazillac vineyard produces rich wines made from grapes with 'noble rot'. The clay and limestone soils bring intense aromas to the wines as well as a strong and complex structure. In 1999 38,536 hl (1,017,350 gal) were produced.

CH. BELINGARD

Blanche de Bosredon 1998★

☐ 5 ha 7,000 ⅡⅠ 100–149 F

At the time of the tasting this wine was still in barrel; it was nonetheless judged to be excellent. Its aromas of crystallised fruits and apricots were delightful, as were its concentration, fullness and fine length on the palate. A pleasant surprise awaits you in a few years' time.
🔑 SCEA Comte de Bosredon, Belingard, 24240 Pomport, tel. 05.53.58.28.03, fax 05.53.58.38.39, e-mail deschard.boisredon@wanadoo.fr ☑ Y by appt.

GRANDE MAISON

Cuvée Monsieur 1998★★

☐ 8 ha 12,000 ⅡⅠ 100–149 F

The Cuvée Monsieur is of a less sweet but more aromatic type than the Cuvée du Château that has previously been so successful. Its notes of roasting and fragrances of crystallised fruits register against a background of oak. There is the same aromatic expressiveness on the palate, where crystallised fruit flavours linger on a long finish. A rich, concentrated, well-balanced wine that will keep for about ten years.
🔑 SARL Despréś et Fils, Grande Maison, 24240 Monbazillac, tel. 05.53.58.26.17, fax 05.53.24.97.36, e-mail grandemaison@aquinet.tm.fr ☑ Y by appt.

CH. HAUT-THEULET 1998★

☐ 8.4 ha n.c. ⅡⅠ 50–69 F

A large percentage of Sauvignon (30%) has gone into this wine. The result is an astonishing aromatic range, in which the aromas of overripening are preceded by the typical Sauvignon notes of flowers and citrus fruits. The wine has a fresh, lively quality on the palate that dominates its sweetness. A fresh, pleasant, and somewhat atypical Monbazillac.
🔑 GAEC Ch. Caillavel, 24240 Pomport, tel. 05.53.58.43.30, fax 05.53.58.20.31 Y by appt.

CH. LADESVIGNES

Automne Elevé en fût de chêne 1998★

☐ 3 ha 5,000 ⅡⅠ 70–99 F

Still a little immature, this Monbazillac has a nose that releases notes of overripeness against an oaky background. It surprises the taster with its exotic aromas and rich sugars. The structure turns out to be full and long. It would be best to keep this wine for two to three years. There is also a citation for the **1998 Côtes de Bergerac Velours Rouge Vieilli en Fût de Chêne**, which is notable for its fruitiness, despite the continued presence of tannins on the finish (30–49F).
🔑 Ch. Ladesvignes, 24240 Pomport, tel. 05.53.58.30.67, fax 05.53.58.22.64, e-mail chateauladesvignes@wanadoo.fr ☑ Y by appt.
🔑 Monbouché

RESERVE LAJONIE

Vieilli en fût de chêne 1998

☐ 10 ha 10,000 70–99 F

The Réserve Lajonie offers a classic nose of roasting and burnt flavours. It is elegant, rich and round on the palate, where it is still dominated by retronasal aromas of roasting. A Monbazillac to be drunk young. From the same producer, the **1999 Bergerac Sec Château Pintouquet** (20–29F), based on Sauvignon, is cited for its finesse and freshness.
🔑 Gérard Lajonie, Saint-Christophe, 24100 Bergerac, tel. 05.53.57.17.96, fax 05.53.58.06.46 ☑ Y by appt.

DOM. DE L'ANCIENNE CURE

Cuvée Abbaye 1998★★

☐ 5 ha 8,000 ⅡⅠ 70–99 F

The Cuvée Abbaye came very close to winning a *coup de coeur*, and we shall no doubt be returning to it in the years to come. Its nose of overripened fruits, cinnamon, apricots and quince is quite delightful. The flavours on the palate are even more concentrated; apricots and quince are back in evidence, along with figs. A long, lingering flavour of toast at the end adds the finishing touch to this remarkable wine, which will keep for more than 20 years.
🔑 Christian Roche, EARL l'Ancienne Cure, 24560 Colombier, tel. 05.53.58.27.90, fax 05.53.24.83.95 ☑ Y by appt.

CH. LE FAGE Grande réserve 1998★★

☐ n.c. 8,000 ⅡⅠ 70–99 F

This wine has a very oaky quality, but fortunately it is supported by the concentration of its natural fruit. Following on from the aromas of oak, it has notes of apricots and crystallised grapes. Rich and full on the palate, it develops toasty notes and then fruit, and finally more crystallised apricots, which linger on a long, gorgeous finish. It is hard to resist the temptation to savour this wine straight away, but your patience will be rewarded if you wait. Also worthy of note is the attractive **1999 Bergerac Rosé**, which is produced by the *saignée* method, and is cited for its pronouced aromas of soft fruits (30–49F).

François Gérardin, Ch. Le Fagé, 24240 Pomport, tel. 05.53.58.32.55, fax 05.53.24.57.19 ☒ Y ev. day 9am–12.30pm 2pm–7pm; Sat. Sun. by appt.

CH. LE PUCH Cuvée Le Doyen 1998★

☐ 15 ha 8,600 70–99 F

Crystallised apricots are fully evident on the nose of this wine, along with some hints of oak. It has good balance, as well as moderate fullness and richness on the palate. Fruity flavours still dominate here, with the added support of an attractive touch of vanilla. It all adds up to a pleasant, easy-drinking wine.

SARL des Vignobles J.-P. Hembise, Ch. Le Puch, 24240 Monbazillac, tel. 05.53.58.85.85, fax 05.53.61.67.78, e-mail châteaulepuch@wanadoo.fr ☒ Y ev. day 8am–12 noon 2pm–6pm; Sat. Sun. by appt.

CH. MONBAZILLAC 1998

☐ 25 ha 70,000 70–99 F

As much an emblem of the region as of the appellation, the Château de Monbazillac hoists its high walls and crenellated towers above a superb landscape. This 1998 has a brilliant, pale yellow colour and an appealing, ethereal, fruity nose. It is agreeably fresh and lively on the palate. A wine for a thirsty day. Also mentioned is the **Château Septy** (50–69F), which has dominant aromas of honey.

Cave coopérative de Monbazillac, rte de Mont-de-Marsan, 24240 Monbazillac, tel. 05.53.63.65.00, fax 05.53.63.65.09 ☒ Y ev. day except Sun. Mon. 10am–12.30pm 1.30pm–7pm

DOM. DE PECOULA Cuvée Prestige 1998★★

☐ 17 ha 7,200 70–99 F

There was a very close finish between the best three Monbazillacs in this selection. In the end, however, it was this wine that won the hearts of the grand jury, not so much for its richness as for its elegance. It has a nose of medium maturity, with an aroma of quince jelly. On the palate, it releases powerful,

complex flavours of crystallised fruits and vanilla. The slight hint of freshness at the finish is very attractive. Best kept for at least three years to ensure maximum enjoyment. Also worthy of mention is the Domaine de Pécoula's **1999 Bergerac Sec**, whose floral and mineral aromas are typical of the Sauvignon grape (20–29F).

GAEC de Pécoula, 24240 Pomport, tel. 05.53.58.46.48, fax 05.53.58.82.02 ☒ Y by appt.

GFA Labaye

DOM. DU PETIT MARSALET Cuvée Tradition Elevé en fût de chêne 1998

☐ 1.5 ha 1,730 50–69 F

After 12 months of maturation in new barrels, the Cuvée Tradition reveals toasty notes that harmonise well with its dried-fruit aromas. The rich, concentrated structure on the palate takes on accents of crystallised apricots. A hefty sort of wine, but one that can be drunk immediately.

Marie-Thérèse Cathal, Le Marsalet, 24100 Saint-Laurent-des-Vignes, tel. 05.53.57.53.36, fax 05.53.57.53.36 ☒ Y ev. day 8am–12 noon 2pm–7pm

DOM. DU PETIT PARIS Elevé en fût de chêne 1998★★

☐ 3 ha 6,600 100–149 F

Despite its youth, this brilliant gold Monbazillac is remarkably finely developed. After a slightly candied nose which is dominated by vanilla, the impression it leaves on the palate is of richness and finesse, sustained by a good level of oakiness. At this stage of its development it is a little lacking in fruit, but some does appear on the finish, with a variety of notes ranging from dried fruits and pineapple to coconut. A wine to be drunk in two to three years' time.

EARL Dom. du Petit Paris, 24240 Monbazillac, tel. 05.53.58.30.41, fax 05.53.58.30.27, e-mail petit-paris@wanadoo.fr ☒ Y ev. day 8am–8pm

Geneste

CH. THEULET Cuvée Prestige 1998★★

☐ 2.5 ha 4,800 100–149 F

The Château Theulet's range of wines is complete, since in addition to the Monbazillac, it wins one star for its finely oaky **1998 Bergerac Sec Prestige du Theulet** (30–49F), while the **1998 Côtes de Bergerac Rouge Cuvée Antoine Alard** is cited for its good structure, despite an oaky quality that still needs time to fade. Two stars are awarded to the Cuvée Prestige, which has complex aromas of flowers, apricots, crystallised fruits, honey and vanilla. It is rich and fleshy on the palate, where a good balance is achieved between sugar and acid. A highly typical, sound, powerful wine, which should reach its peak in about ten years' time.

SCEA Alard, Le Theulet, 24240 Monbazillac, tel. 05.53.57.30.43, fax 05.53.58.88.28 ☒ Y ev. day except Sun. 8am–12 noon 2pm–6pm

SOUTH-WEST

CH. TIRECUL LA GRAVIERE

1998★★★

☐ 9.19 ha 9,000 100–149 F

A pillar of the appellation receives an exceptionally high rating. The nose is particularly complex, releasing aromas of hazelnuts, gingerbread, lychees, liquorice and honey, with a slight hint of oak in the background. The concentration of sugar is remarkable, and the wine's length on the palate is extraordinary. Best kept for at least ten years to ensure maximum pleasure.

Claudie et Bruno Bilancini, Ch. Tirecul la Gravière, 24240 Monbazillac, tel. 05.53.57.44.75, fax 05.53.24.85.01
by appt.

CH. VARI

Réserve du Château Elevé en fût de chêne 1998

☐ 3 ha 8,000 70–99 F

There is a family resemblance between these two Château Vari wines, which differ only in their concentration. The Réserve du Château has notes of honey and wax on the nose, and then a good balance of sugar and alcohol on the palate, leading to a certain freshness at the finish. Also cited is the **1998 Château Vari** in its classic version (30–49F), which after nine months of maturation in oak barrels is equally harmonious, and represents a certain classical tendency in Monbazillac.

Vignobles Jestin, Ch. Vari, 24240 Monbazillac, tel. 05.53.24.97.55, fax 05.53.24.97.55 by appt.

Montravel

From a vineyard of 1,200 ha (2,964 acres) on the hills from Port-Saint-Foi to Ponchapt, stretching as far as Saint-Michel-de-Montaine, the terroir of Montravel produces dry and sweet white wines noted for their elegance and consistency. In 1999 production of Haut-Montravel reached 2,224 hl (58,714 gal), of which 1,887 hl (49,817 gal) were Côtes de Montravel.

CH. BONIERES

La Dame de Bonières 1999★

☐ 1.3 ha 6,500 70–99 F

La Dame de Bonières wins a star, as it did in the previous vintage. Straw-yellow in colour, it is still dominated by oak on the nose, but the fruit aromas are beginning to come through. Ripe fruit is somewhat more evident on the palate, where there is a great deal of roundness and good acidity at the finish. This wine should be perfect in a year's time.

SCEA Vignobles André Bodin, Ch. Bonières, 33220 Fougueyrolles, tel. 05.53.24.15.16, fax 05.53.24.17.77
by appt.

CHEVALIER DE SAINT AVIT 1999

☐ 6.5 ha 4,000 20–29 F

Brilliant golden-yellow in colour, the Chevalier de Saint Avit has a nose of moderate intensity but great finesse, dominated by floral notes and aromas of lemon. After a fresh, attractive attack on the palate, the fruit flavours are once again evident, despite very pronounced acidity. A classic, well-made Montravel.

Viticulteurs réunis de Saint-Vivien-et-Bonneville, 24230 Saint-Vivien, tel. 05.53.27.52.22, fax 05.53.22.61.12
by appt.

DOM. DE GRIMARDY

Cuvée Marie-Juliette 1998★

☐ 0.4 ha 3,066 30–49 F

Here is an interesting wine, with a clearly fruity quality that prevails over the oak. The nose offers an atttractive mixture of floral notes and aromas of citrus and crystallised fruits. The extract is very evident on the palate, where it displays great freshness. This wine can be enjoyed straight away, either with fish in a sauce or seafood.

Marcel and Marielle Establet, Les Grimards, 24230 Montazeau, tel. 05.53.57.96.78, fax 05.53.61.97.16

CH. LA RESSAUDIE 1999

☐ 2 ha 15,000 20–29 F

The colour is a little surprising, since its straw-yellow quality is quite unusual for a dry white wine. The aromas, on the other hand, are very classical, mainly lemon and other citrus fruits. With a fair amount of roundness and not much acidity, this Montravel offers further attractive fruity notes on the finish. A well-made wine.

Jean Rebeyrolle, Ch. La Ressaudie, 33220 Port-Sainte-Foy, tel. 05.53.24.71.48, fax 05.53.58.52.29 by appt.

Côtes de Montravel

CH. DU BLOY Aquitain 1998★★

☐ 3 ha 6,000 30–49 F

There can be no question that the quality of this straw-yellow Côtes de Montravel depends on noble rot and Muscadelle. The notes of dried fruits and botrytis are clearly apparent on the nose. After that, the dominant impression on the palate is of richness and weight. A well-balanced wine with good length, it may drunk now or can be left to age further.

🔑 Guillermier Frères, Bonneville, 24230 Vélines, tel. 05.53.27.50.59, fax 05.53.27.56.34 ☒ 🍷 by appt.

DOM. DE LA ROCHE MAROT 1998★★★

☐ 0.5 ha 600 50–69 F

The **1998 Montravel du Domaine de la Roche Marot** (20–29F) is cited for its fruitiness and suppleness, but without a doubt it is this Côtes de Montravel which deserves a *coup de coeur*. Powerful, elegant notes of overripe grapes rise from the glass. It has all the fullness on the palate of a great *liquoreux* wine. There are flavours of crystallised fruits, followed by a fresh, lingering finish with citrus accents. A wine to be discovered, and that will charm the most demanding of palates.
🔑 Yves and Daniel Boyer, GAEC de La Roche Marot, 24230 Lamothe-Montravel, tel. 05.53.58.52.05 ☒ 🍷 ev. day 9am–7pm
🔑 Michel Boyer

Haut-Montravel

MALLEVIEILLE

Elevé en fût de chêne 1998★★

☐ 1 ha 1,000 50–69 F

This is the first year in which the Biau vineyards have produced a wine within the Haut-Montravel appellation. They deserve all credit for their achievement. A discreet oaky aroma is dominated by overripe fruit and notes of honey. There is oak again on the palate, but what satisfies most of all is an impression of roundness and fullness. A fresh finish lightens the wine, but also means that it will keep well, for perhaps two to three years.
🔑 Vignobles Biau, La Mallevieille, 24130 Monfaucon, tel. 05.53.24.64.66, fax 05.53.58.69.91, e-mail chateaudelamallevieille@wanadoo.fr ☒ 🍷 ev. day 9am–7pm
🔑 Philippe Biau

PRESTIGE DE MAYAT 1998★★

☐ 0.5 ha 5,000 50–69 F

A little sweeter than Moelleux but not quite Liquoreux, this Haut-Montravel still bears the stamp of ten months' maturation in oak barrels. As a result, the fruit aromas are dominated by vanilla and toast. On the palate, it is full and rich, with flavours that deserve to last longer at the finish. This already remarkable wine will no doubt become even better after two to three years of ageing.
🔑 Francis Lagarde, Dom. de Mayat, 39220 Fougueyrolles, tel. 05.53.58.32.58, fax 05.53.58.32.58 ☒
🍷 ev. day 8am–12 noon 2pm–7pm

CH. PUY-SERVAIN Terrement 1998★★★

☐ 4.5 ha 8,000 100–149 F

Daniel Hecquet is an oenologist, but he does not neglect his vines, as is proved in every edition by his perfect mastery of the subject. No fewer than three grape selections were necessary in order to produce this exceptional wine. The fruit aromas are so much in evidence throughout the tasting that it seems as though one is chewing the grapes themselves. The aromas of ripe fruit and citrus on the nose are complemented by an attractive vanilla flavour on the palate. This is a wine with the potential to age for at least ten years. One star is awarded to the **1998 Bergerac Rouge Vieilles Vignes** (50–69F), which will be at its best once it has matured for a few years.
🔑 SCEA Puy-Servain, Calabre, 33220 Port-Sainte-Foy, tel. 05.53.24.77.27, fax 05.53.58.37.43 ☒ 🍷 ev. day 8am–12 noon 2pm–6pm; Sat. Sun. by appt.
🔑 Hecquet

Pécharmant

On a slope covered with 400 ha (988 acres) of vines, north-east of Bergerac, the 'Pech' produces very rich red wines with good keeping qualities. Often brought on in hogsheads, these wines have considerable complexity and finesse. In 1999 production was 20,133 hl (531,511 gal).

SOUTH-WEST

CH. BEAUPORTAIL 1998★

■ 2 ha 9,000 30–49 F

Mentioned last year for its 1997 vintage, Château Beauportail is awarded a star in the new selection. On the nose, it has aromas of stewed prunes, spicy notes and scents of gingerbread. The attack on the palate is very supple, and within the well-balanced structure there is a great deal of meatiness. Those prune accents return at the finish.

EARL La Truffière Beauportail, Pécharmant, 24100 Bergerac, tel. 05.53.24.85.16, fax 05.53.61.28.63 ☑
Y by appt.
F. Feytout

CH. DE BIRAN

Cuvée Prestige de Bacchus 1998

■ 10.5 ha 8,000 70–99 F

With its mixture of oaky, spicy notes and musky aromas, the nose is characteristic of a barrel-matured wine. After a supple, pleasant attack on the palate, the tannins develop right through to the finish, which is as yet a little firm. This wine has a promising structure, but needs more time to age.

EARL vignobles Biran, Biran, 24520 Saint-Sauveur, tel. 05.53.22.46.29, fax 05.53.27.54.31, e-mail chbiran@aol.com ☑

DOM. BRISSEAU-BELLOC

Elevé en fût de chêne 1998★

■ 5.58 ha 20,000 30–49 F

Two of the Bergerac cellar's Pécharmants are awarded a star by the jury. First up is this Domaine Brisseau-Belloc, which has a nose of vanilla and coffee, accentuated by red berries. Its tannic structure has power and elegance, and the harmony of the tannins shows excellent potential. Next, the **1998 Château Métairie-Haute, Elevé en Fût de Chêne** has a toasty nose with some rather musky, leathery notes. With tannins still very much in evidence on the palate and needing more time to mature, this wine seems to have even greater potential to improve with age than its stablemate.

Union vinicole Bergerac-Le Fleix, bd de l'Entrepôt, 24100 Bergerac, tel. 05.53.57.16.27, fax 05.53.24.57.47 ☑
Y ev. day except Mon. Sun. 8am–12 noon 2pm–6pm

CH. CORBIAC 1998★★

■ 13.5 ha 85,000 50–69 F

This is a wine of remarkable tannic richness. Its nose of soft fruit aromas is still closed, but not without charm. Although the fruity flavour on the palate is dominated by rather young tannins, it has an attractively lingering finish. Best drunk in four to five years' time, perhaps as an accompaniment to game.

Bruno de Corbiac, Ch. de Corbiac, 24100 Bergerac, tel. 05.53.57.20.75, fax 05.53.57.89.98, e-mail corbiac@corbiac.com ☑ Y by appt.

DOM. DES COSTES

Cuvée Prestige 1998★★

■ 1 ha 3,000 70–99 F

This wine came very close to being awarded a *coup de coeur*. At first the nose is complex, toasty and very intense. Spicy aromas rise from the glass. On the palate, the tannic concentration asserts itself very quickly, and the oak is already harmonious enough to let the richness of the grape flavour come through. Although it is a very concentrated wine, the tannins in the classic **1998 Domaine des Costes** (from 50–69F) are even more harmonious, and it has won a star. Two characteristic Pécharmants: aromatic, structured, supple and round.

Nicole Dournel, Les Costes, 24100 Bergerac, tel. 05.53.57.64.49, fax 05.53.61.69.08 ☑ Y by appt.
Lacroix

CH. LA RENAUDIE

Elevé en fût de chêne 1998

■ 36.5 ha 32,000 30–49 F

A truly classic Pécharmant that regularly pleases selectors. Its toasted, charred aromas are coupled with attractive notes of red berries. It has a round, rich attack on the palate, and very assertive structure. The tannins are still very much in evidence on the finish, and it will need to be kept until they soften.

SCEA dom. de La Renaudie, Ch. La Renaudie, 24100 Lembras, tel. 05.53.27.05.75, fax 05.53.73.37.10 ☑
Y ev. day 9am–7pm
Yves Allamagny

CLOS PEYRELEVADE 1998

■ 10 ha 60,000 30–49 F

Three very different wines, all of which are cited. This Clos Peyrelevade has a powerful nose with pronounced aromas of soft fruits. The tannins are beginning to fade on the palate, which is complex and very full. Next, the **1998 Cuvée Veuve Roches** (50–69F), which releases aromas of prunes and dark berries, and then develops a powerful, full-bodied, round structure in the mouth. Finally, the **1998 Domaine du Haut-Pécharmant Prestige, Vieilli en Fût de Chêne** (50–69F) has aromas ranging from green peppers and cherries to blackcurrants and toast. It is very tannic on the palate, and needs time to become more supple.

Michel and Didier Roches, Haut-Pécharmant, 24100 Bergerac, tel. 05.53.57.29.50, fax 05.53.24.28.05 ☑
Y ev. day except Sun. 8am–12 noon 2pm–7pm

CH. DU ROOY 1998

■ 5.75 ha 4,500 30–49 F

Gilles Gérault is a new producer, and 1998 was the year he harvested his first grapes, having taken over the tenancy of a 12 ha (30-acre) vineyard after the previous owner retired. He offers a promising Pécharmant; the nose is still a little immature, but nonetheless it has gorgeous toasty aromas. A sweet, rich attack

on the palate gives way to tannins that are very apparent but harmonious nonetheless, followed by a return to fruit flavours at the finish. A well-balanced wine that can be drunk young.
Gilles Gérault, Rosette, 24100 Bergerac, tel. 05.53.24.13.68 by appt.

CH. TERRE VIEILLE

Vieilli en fût de chêne 1998★★

7 ha 35,000 50–69 F

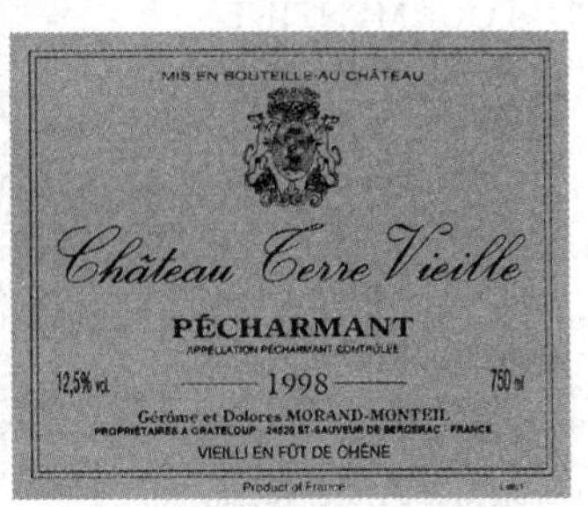

A great wine has balance and harmony, and this one is no exception. It offers a full range of aromas: toast, spices, charred notes and fruits of the forest. After this promising start, the flavours on the palate do not disappoint. The oakiness is very harmonious, and the fruity flavours are long and lingering. The concentration and finesse of this Pécharmant will ensure that it can be kept for about ten years. One star is awarded to the **1998 Cros de La Sal, Vieillie en Fût de Chêne** (30–49F); it has a more discreet oaky flavour that allows the fruit to come through well.
Gérôme and Dolorès Morand-Monteil, Ch. Terre-Vieille, 24520 Saint-Sauveur-de-Bergerac, tel. 05.53.57.35.07, fax 05.53.61.91.77, e-mail gerome-morand-monteil@wanadoo.fr
ev. day except Sun. 9am–7pm

CH. DE TIREGAND

Grand Millésime 1998

2 ha 4,000 70–99 F

In order to achieve better concentration of the grapes and bring out the qualities of the terroir as fully as possible, this vineyard has reorganised its growing methods along high-density lines. The result is this 1998 Pécharmant with an intense nose in which the fruit comes through well, and is accentuated by fine notes of oak. It is clean and forthright on the palate, where the flavour is of fruit as well as the tannins acquired during 18 months of well-managed maturation in oak barrels. A polished wine that would be the ideal accompaniment to an entrecôte steak.
Comtesse F. de Saint-Exupéry, Ch. de Tiregand, 24100 Creysse, tel. 05.53.23.21.08, fax 05.53.22.58.49 ev. day except Sun. 9am–12 noon 2pm–6pm

Rosette

Rosette is the least-known appellation and the best-kept secret of the region. It comes from the clay and gravel soils of hills overlooking the town of Bergerac from the north, and in 1999 production was 607 hl (16,025 gal).

DOM. DE COUTANCIE 1998

3 ha 10,245 30–49 F

No stranger to the jury, the Coutancie estate is one of the all too few remaining producers of Rosette. Its 1998 has a very powerful nose, with pronounced notes of botrytis. It is well-balanced on the palate, which is pleasantly rich and fruity. A Rosette to be served chilled as an apéritif.
Odile Brichèse, Coutancie, 24130 Prigonrieux, tel. 05.53.58.01.85, fax 05.53.58.52.76, e-mail coutancie@wanadoo.fr
by appt.

CH. ROMAIN 1999★

2 ha 4,000 30–49 F

After attracting the jury's approval previously, the Château Romain is now awarded a star in quite a difficult year. Its Rosette has fine aromas of fresh fruits on the nose. Supple and rich on the palate at first, it develops on the palate with freshness and lightness. A very typical 1999.
Colette Bourgès, Les Costes, 24100 Bergerac, tel. 05.53.57.59.89, fax 05.53.24.20.24 ev. day 10am–7pm; Sun. by appt.; cl. Jan. Feb.

Saussignac

Praised in the 16th century in François Rabelais's *Pantagruel* and located in a superb landscape of plateaux and hills, the terroir produces rich, sweet wines of great quality. In 1999 production was 1,680 hl (44,352 gal).

L'ADAGIO DES EYSSARDS 1998★

n.c. 2,000 100–149 F

Although the raw material is the result of excellent concentration, the wine bears the stamp of long maturation in oak, with a nose in which yellow fruits are dominated by toasty notes. This full, rich 1998 will need to be kept for a few years. The **Cuvée Prestige du Château des Eyssards en Bergerac Sec** was also awarded a star. It will only appeal to lovers of oaky white wines. Its flavours of crystallised fruits and orange peel should combine interestingly with a soft cheese (30–49F).

GAEC des Eyssards, 24240 Monestier, tel. 05.53.24.36.36, fax 05.53.58.63.74, e-mail eyssards@aquinet-tm.fr
by appt.

CH. MIAUDOUX Réserve 1998★

☐ 1.5 ha 2,400 100–149 F

Last year Gérard Cuisset received the *coup de coeur* for his 1997. The 1998 vintage has greater richness, but the wine is still masked somewhat by its barrel maturation. On the nose, aromas of oak and toast give way to crystallised fruit with the emphasis on apricots. It is particularly complex on the palate, where there is a great deal of richness and sugar, and a very oaky finish. A powerful wine that will achieve greatness as it ages.

Gérard Cuisset, Les Miaudoux, 24240 Saussignac, tel. 05.53.27.92.31, fax 05.53.27.96.60, e-mail chateau.miaudoux@wanadoo.fr
by appt.

CH. PETITE BORIE 1999

☐ 2.5 ha 30,000 30–49 F

This sweet wine caught the jury's attention by its elegance. Its nose has very intense floral notes of hawthorn and acacia. With strong floral flavours continuing on the palate, this 1999 is characterised above all by its lightness. Just the type of wine that put Saussignac on the map.

Vignobles Pierre Sadoux, Ch. Court-les-Mûts, 24240 Razac-de-Saussignac, tel. 05.53.27.92.17, fax 05.53.23.77.21
ev. day except Sun. 9am–11.30am 2pm–5.30pm; Sat. by appt.

CH. SEIGNORET LES TOURS

Cuvée Coup de Cœur Elevé en fût de chêne 1998

☐ 1.5 ha 3,063 70–99 F

Top of the estate's range is this carefully made wine. Its aromas – not just crystallised fruit, peaches and apricot aromas, but notes of vanilla and honey as well – give it a certain complexity on the nose. The balance on the palate is attractive, despite a finish which is as yet very young. It will need to be kept until the oak has faded.

Serge Gazziola, Ch. Seignoret les Tours, 24240 Saussignac, tel. 06.08.61.58.77, fax 06.53.22.37.79 by appt.

LES VIGNERONS DE SIGOULES

Vendanges d'autrefois 1998★

☐ n.c. 15,000 30–49 F

Another sweet, rich wine that has been produced and matured with the greatest care. Its dominant aromas are of crystallised fruits and honey. It is well-built on the palate, where there are powerful renewed notes of crystallised fruits, along with vanilla and toast flavours, which complete the overall structure. An elegant, harmonious wine. (50 cl bottles)

Cave coop. des producteurs de Montravel et Sigoulès, 24240 Mescoules, tel. 05.53.61.55.00, fax 05.53.61.55.10
ev. day except Sun. 8.30am–12.30pm 2pm–6.30pm

CH. TOURMENTINE

Vendanges tardives 1998★★

☐ 1 ha 3,800 70–99 F

Placed second by the grand jury, this wine deserves its two stars. Its nose is largely dominated by vanilla and oak. It is impressively rich in sugar on the palate, and the fruit and oak are in perfect balance. With its combination of opulence and finesse, this is a wine to be kept. (50 cl bottles) The **1998 Bergerac Rouge Elevé en Fût** received a citation; it has full-bodied tannins that need two or three years to mature (30–49F).

Jean-Marie Huré, Tourmentine, 24240 Monestier, tel. 05.53.58.41.41, fax 05.53.63.40.52 ev. day except Sun. 9am–12 noon 2pm–6pm

CLOS D'YVIGNE

Vendanges tardives 1998★★

☐ 3 ha 3,600 200–249 F

A fight to the finish for Patricia Atkinson's Saussignac, which once again – and without dispute – is awarded a *coup de coeur*! Its aromas of crystallised fruits are in evidence throughout the tasting, and the finish is enhanced by a delicate toasty note. The most remarkable features of this wine, however, are its fullness and power. Elegant and very classy, it still needs time to mature. Don't wait for it to age in the estate's cellars: there isn't very much of it . . . and 65% of it will be going off to Great Britain!

Patricia Atkinson, Le Bourg, 24240 Gageac-Rouillac, tel. 05.53.22.94.40, fax 05.53.23.47.67, e-mail patricia.atkinson@wanadoo.fr
ev. day except Sun. 9am–12 noon 2pm–6pm

Côtes de Duras

The Côtes de Duras vineyard, 2,000 ha (4,940 acres), is the natural extension of the plateau of Entre-Deux-Mers. There is a local story that, after the Revocation of the Edict of Nantes, exiled Gascon Huguenots used to have Duras wine shipped to them in their Dutch retreats. Tulips were planted at the ends of the rows of vines which they reserved for themselves.

Eroded over the ages by the River Dourdèze and its tributaries, the slopes are made up of sandy-clay and limestone soils naturally suited to the Bordeaux varieties. Sémillon, Sauvignon and Muscadelle are used for the white wines; Cabernet-Franc, Cabernet-Sauvignon, Merlot and Malbec for the reds. Also found are Chenin, Odenc and Ugni-Blanc. The real successes are supple sweet whites, with 3,554 hl (93,826 gal) produced in 1999, and, above all, dry whites made mainly from Sauvignon, with 45,678 hl (1,205,899 gal). These are lively wines of pedigree with a specifically identifiable bouquet and are marvellous with seafood and saltwater fish. The red wines, of which 71,485 hl (1,887,204 gal) were produced in 1999; often vinified as varietal wines, are fleshy and round, with a good colour.

DOM. DES ALLEGRETS
Moelleux 1998★★

□ 1 ha 2,400 100–149 F

After much fierce debate, this sweet wine is the winner of the 2001 *coup de coeur*. It already has a beautiful, brilliant gold colour

and long legs on the glass. Its nose has a touch of toast from the barrel, but consists mainly of intense aromas of overripe grapes, honey and beeswax. The balance on the palate plays subtly between sweetness and acidity. The flavours are complex, with notes of crystallised fruits, apricots and figs. On top of all that, there is exceptionally good length. A remarkably elegant wine.

SCEA Francis et Monique Blanchard, Dom. des Allégrets, 47120 Villeneuve-de-Duras, tel. 05.53.94.74.56, fax 05.53.94.74.56 ✓
ev. day 10am–12 noon 2pm–6pm

DOM. DES ALLEGRETS 1998★★

■ 2 ha 10,000 30–49 F

Another accolade for this 15 ha (37-acre) estate, founded in 1984. This wine has a rich, powerful nose characterised by notes of fruits preserved in alcohol. On the palate, it is perfectly balanced, harmonious and long. Best kept for a year or two until it reaches perfection.

SCEA Francis et Monique Blanchard, Dom. des Allégrets, 47120 Villeneuve-de-Duras, tel. 05.53.94.74.56, fax 05.53.94.74.56 ✓
ev. day 10am–12 noon 2pm–6pm

DOM. AMBLARD Sauvignon 1999★

□ 13.4 ha 80,000 20–29 F

This is a Sauvignon with the emphasis on finesse and elegance. It has a full, lingering nose of exotic fruits and citrus. There is a clean, strong attack, and high extract on the palate. The finish is very fresh.

SCEA Dom. Amblard, 47120 Saint-Sernin-de-Duras, tel. 05.53.94.77.92, fax 05.53.94.27.12 ✓ ev. day except Sun. 8am–12.30pm 2pm–7pm
Guy Pauvert

DOM. DU BOURRAN
Vendanges tardives 1998★★

□ 0.25 ha 700 30–49 F

Two wines have been singled out here: one is *liquoreux*, the other more *moelleux*, and based on a different range of grape varieties. The first – an equal blend of Sémillon and Sauvignon – has a nose of white flowers and, oddly, truffles. The attack on the palate is very fine, and there is a perfect balance on the palate of richness, sugar, acidity and fruit-salad flavours. The oakiness has faded too: a remarkable achievement. The second wine is the *1998 Moelleux*, a blend of 10% Sauvignon, 40% Muscadelle and 50% Sémillon, which is more floral on the nose, with a touch of exotic fruits. It has a slightly charred flavour and good balance on the palate, where there is very noticeable freshness at the finish. It receives one star.

Paul McGrane, Le Bourran, 47120 Saint-Jean-de-Duras, tel. 05.53.89.64.31, fax 05.53.89.64.31 ✓

CLOS DU CADARET 1998★★★

■ 2 ha 2,000 100–149 F

Once again, top marks for two exceptional wines from the Clos du Cadaret. This Clos du Cadaret has an expressive nose of ripe fruits with well-integrated aromas of toast. It is quite delightful on the palate; the oaky flavour is clearly evident but not dominant, and it has very good length. The **1998 Cuvée Raoul Blondin en Rouge** offers aromas of ripe fruits and vanilla, on a nose that is intense and complex. Its tannins are astonishingly full and rich, and yet don't mask the fruit flavours. It has a distinctly oaky quality, but because of its concentration, this is not out of place. A wine for keeping.

Corinne and Gérard Le Jan,
Clos du Cadaret, 47120 Loubès-Bernac,
tel. 05.53.94.59.42, fax 05.53.64.34.60,
e-mail cadaret@wanadoo.fr ☒ Y by appt.

DOM. DES COURS Sauvignon 1999★

□ 5 ha 15,000 20–29 F

The fact that this wine is cited by the jury every year as a matter of course shows just how much earnestness and rigour go into producing it. The nose is dominated by broom blossom, blackcurrant buds and exotic fruits; no doubt about it, this is Sauvignon. After a clean, fresh attack, it is soft and round on the palate, with a touch of liveliness at the finish. A characteristic 1999.

Lusoli, Dom. des Cours, 47120 Sainte-Colombe-de-Duras, tel. 05.53.83.74.35,
fax 05.53.83.63.18 ☒ Y ev. day 8am–6pm

DUC DE BERTICOT Elevé en fût de chêne 1998★★★

■ 5 ha 20,000 30–49 F

Here we have two 1998 wines that are particularly worthy of note. The first is this Duc de Berticot, which was selected to go before the grand jury for a possible *coup de coeur*, and has an interesting nose of berries, mingled with slight touches of oakiness. It is mature and very round on the palate, where there are plenty of tannins and further flavours of ripe fruit – a highly successful alliance between the qualities of the terroir and the maturing process. In the same vintage, the **Hauts de Berticot** also has a nose of ripe fruit and toast. Its structure is well harmonised, although the tannins are slightly austere. Two excellent wines.

SCA Vignerons Landerrouat-Duras,
Berticot, 47120 Duras, tel. 05.53.83.75.47,
fax 05.53.83.82.40 ☒ Y by appt.

DOM. DU GRAND MAYNE Sauvignon 1999★

□ 1.1 ha 10,000 30–49 F

The first two wines to catch the jury's attention this year were both dry white, one matured in casks, the other not. The barrel-matured one is based on Sauvignon and has a discreet, oaky nose. The proof of its technical excellence comes on the palate, where it combines notes of vanilla and white fruits. Fruit flavours return in a long finish of remarkable finesse. The **Autre Cuvée** (20–29F) is a blend of 10% Sémillon with Sauvignon, and is produced in stainless steel vats. One more wine deserves a mention here, this time a red: the **1998 Cuvée Elevée en Fût**, a rich, tannic, aromatic wine ideal for long keeping.

SARL Andrew Gordon, Le Grand
Mayne, 47120 Villeneuve-de-Duras,
tel. 05.53.94.74.17, fax 05.53.94.77.02,
e-mail agordon@terre-net.fr ☒
Y ev. day except Sat. Sun. 9am–5pm

CH. LA PETITE BERTRANDE Vendanges tardives 1998★

□ 2 ha 4,000 70–99 F

A rich, well-constructed wine, somewhat dominated at present by an oaky flavour that slightly masks its aromas of almonds and pears. The balance on the palate is pleasant, despite just a tiny touch of bitterness at the finish. It should be kept in the cellar for two to three years until it achieves overall harmony.

Jean-François Thierry, Vignoble Les Guignards, 47120 Saint-Astier-de-Duras,
tel. 05.53.94.74.03, fax 05.53.94.75.27,
e-mail vguignards@aol.com ☒ Y ev. day except Sun. 10am–12 noon 4pm–8pm

Alain Tingaud

DOM. LAS BRUGUES-MAU MICHAU Sauvignon 1999★★

□ 4 ha n.c. 20–29 F

An original wine, rather atypical of the grape variety. It has a complex, intense nose that is both fruity and floral. After a supple attack, it is rich and powerful on the palate, with flavours of very ripe fruit. A touch of carbon dioxide gives it a boost at the finish. Excellent balance.

Prévot, Mau Michau, 47120 Monteton,
tel. 05.53.20.24.51, fax 05.53.20.80.57,
e-mail mprevot@wanadoo.fr ☒
Y ev. day except Sun. 9am–12 noon 2pm–6pm; groups by appt.

DOM. DE LAULAN Duc de Laulan Vieilli en fût de chêne 1998★★

■ 2 ha 14,200 30–49 F

The Duc de Laulan is one of those wines that the *Guide* cannot possibly ignore. It has a remarkable nose of ripe fruits, and is round and rich on the palate, with clearly evident tannins that are slightly marked by oakiness. As yet the finish is a little austere, but the excellence of the raw material bodes well for a great future. The oak-matured **1999 Cuvée Emile Chariot en Blanc Sec** (Sauvignon) is as delightful as ever. Its well-controlled oaky flavour gives it complexity and harmony, and an attractive range of aromas.

EARL Geoffroy, Dom. de Laulan,
47120 Duras, tel. 05.53.83.73.69,
fax 05.53.83.81.54, e-mail
domaine.laulan@wanadoo.fr ☒ Y by appt.

MARQUIS DE BERTICOT

Sauvignon 1999★★

☐ 30 ha 200,000 ▮ 🌡 30–49 F

Two dry white 1999 wines delighted the jury. The Marquis de Berticot has a powerful nose of acacia, broom and citrus fruits. It has a fresh attack on the palate, leading to a long finish with flavours of exotic fruits. The **Cuvée Berticot**, also made exclusively from Sauvignon grapes, has a very fruity nose. Rich and powerful on the palate, it is an aromatic, complex wine.

🔑 SCA Vignerons Landerrouat-Duras, Berticot, 47120 Duras, tel. 05.53.83.75.47, fax 05.53.83.82.40 ☑ 🍸 by appt.

CH. DE PERCEVAL

Vendanges tardives 1998★★

☐ 1 ha 2,500 ⏸ 200–249 F

The château was built in 1690 by the lord of Condom-Perceval, Grand Equerry to the Kings of France. This sweet wine has been matured in oak and acacia barrels. It has a highly intense nose of ripe fruits with notes of toast. After a very fleshy, rich attack on the palate, there is an impression of oak, but this is beginning to become integrated and allow the fruity flavour of the grapes to re-emerge. An elegant wine with remarkable potential.

🔑 SCEA Condom, Ch. Condom Perceval, 47120 Loubes Bernac, tel. 05.53.76.05.02, fax 05.53.76.03.79 ☑ 🍸 by appt.

DOM. DU PETIT MALROME

Cuvée Yvan 1998★★

■ 0.9 ha 4,500 ⏸ 30–49 F

This estate has been converting to organic farming methods since 1997, which has done no harm at all to the quality of its wines. This one has an intense nose characterised by dark berries, strawberries and some notes of vanilla. The attack on the palate is supple and well-balanced. A pleasant oaky flavour on the palate is dominated by fruit. A very rich 1998.

🔑 Alain Lescaut, 47120 Saint-Jean-de-Duras, tel. 05.53.89.01.44, fax 05.53.89.01.44 ☑ 🍸 ev. day except Sun. 10am–12 noon 2pm–7pm

DOM. DU VIEUX BOURG

Cuvée Sainte-Anne 1998★

■ 3 ha 10,000 ⏸ 30–49 F

In addition to the fortified castle whose ruins can be seen here, there also used to be a chapel, after which this wine is named. It starts with aromas of crystallised fruits and quince, then develops smoky notes and hints of undergrowth. Its unexpectedly supple, round attack on the palate is delightful. Although pronounced, the tannins remain velvety and lush; the oakiness has already faded. A wine that will be pleasant to drink quite soon, but will also age well.

🔑 Bernard Bireaud, Dom. du Vieux Bourg, 47120 Pardaillan, tel. 05.53.83.02.18, fax 05.53.83.02.37 ☑

🍸 ev. day except Sat. Sun. 8am–12 noon 2pm–7pm; groups by appt.

THE LOIRE VALLEY AND THE CENTRE

This enormous area is dominated by a single great waterway, the 'royal' Loire. It would justify that epithet on its own merits, though it also became a favoured place of respite for kings and queens, and a cradle of Renaissance arts and culture. The changing countryside of the Loire valley is bathed in a unique light, arising from the subtle marriage of sky and water that enabled the 'Garden of France' to burgeon, and the vine to thrive. From the edge of the Massif Central to the estuary, vineyards stud the landscape along the river and a dozen of its tributaries, creating a vast wine-growing region which encompasses much more than the Loire valley itself, and is generally referred to as 'The Loire Valley and the Centre'. Tourism here is cultural, gastronomic and wine-based, and the roads that follow the river along the heights, or the back roads which run through the vineyards and forests, are unforgettable trails of discovery.

The Loire itself can be narrow and sinuous, or swift-flowing and turbulent, at times imposing and majestic in appearance, at times peaceful. Always the unifying factor in the landscape, it requires attention to its vagaries, particularly when it comes to the wines.

From Roanne or Saint-Pourçain as far as Nantes or Saint-Nazaire, vines grow on the slopes overlooking the banks, braving the nature of the soils and wide differences in climate and local traditions. For some 1,000 km (620 miles), a vineyard area of more than 50,000 ha (135,000 acres) produces greatly varying wines. In 1999, the volume of appellation wines was 2,743,582 hl (72,430,564 gal), that is to say 11.19% of the total production of France. The wines of this vast region share a freshness and delicacy of perfume that are essentially due to the northerly location of most of the producing areas.

All the same, to attempt to group all the different wines produced under the same heading is a little risky, since, even though they are classified as being northern, some vineyards are on a latitude which, in the Rhône valley, enjoys the influence of the Mediterranean climate . . . Mâcon, for example, shares the same latitude as Saint-Pourçain and Roanne the same as Villefranche-sur-Saône. So it is the topography that works on the climate to limit the influence of the prevailing airflow: the Atlantic winds blow west to east along the corridor eroded by the Loire, weakening little by little as they encounter the hills around Saumur and the Touraine.

The wine areas that form identifiable entities are, thus, the Nantes region, plus Anjou and Touraine. However, we have also included the vineyards of Haut Poitou, the Berry, the Côtes d'Auvergne and the Côtes Roannaises; it is important to attach them to a big region, and this is the closest both geographically and as regards the wines that are produced. In general terms, it is appropriate to identify four big groupings, the first three mentioned plus the Centre.

In the lower Loire valley, the Muscadet area and part of the Anjou are on the Massif Armoricain and made up variously of schists, gneiss and other sedimentary rocks, or of outcrops from the Primary era. The soils that have developed on these underlying structures are very well-suited to the vine and the wines produced are of excellent quality. The first entity, the most westerly area, still called the Nantais, has a gentle landscape in which the hard rocks of the Massif Armoricain have been gouged away into almost vertical valley walls by little rivers. The steep valleys have no cultivable slopes and the vines are planted on hillocks on the plateau. The climate is maritime and fairly uniform throughout the year, and the maritime influence diminishes the seasonal variations. The winters are not particularly harsh and the warm summers are often humid; there is a good deal of sunshine, but Spring frosts sometimes disrupt growth.

Anjou is the transitional area between the Nantais region ('le pays Nantais') and the Touraine and, historically speaking, includes Saumur. This wine-growing region lies almost totally within the department of Maine-etLoire but, geographically, Saumur should more appropriately be attached to western Touraine, with which it has more in common so far as terroir and climate are concerned. The sedimentary soils of the Paris Basin covered the Primary formations of the Massif Amoricain from Brissac-Quincé to Doué-la-Fontaine. Anjou falls into several sub-regions: the north-facing Coteaux de la Loire (an extension of the Nantais region) run gently down from the edge of the plateau; the Coteaux du Layon, very steep, on schist soils, together with the Coteaux de l'Aubance; finally, a transitional zone between Anjou and Touraine known chiefly for its rosés.

The Saumur terroir is essentially identified by creamy limestone, or tufa, on beds of chalk; underground, wine being aged in bottles competes with the cultivation of Paris mushrooms (30% of the national crop) in the galleries and cellars dug out of the chalk. The hills provide shelter from the west winds, helping to create a semi-maritime/semi-continental climate. Across from Saumur, on the right bank of the Loire on the slopes outside Tours, you find the vineyards of Saint-Nicolas-de-Bourgueil. East of Tours, and on the same slopes (an extension of those of Saumur and Vienne), Vouvray and Chinon are the leading wines of the Touraine. Azay-le-Rideau, Montlouis, Amboise, Mesland and the Coteaux du Cher are other great names to remember from the 'Garden of France'. The little vineyards of the Coteaux du Loir, the Orléanais, Cheverny, Valençay and the Coteaux du Giennois should be considered with those of the Touraine. It is impossible to decide if you should visit the area for its wines, its châteaux or its goat's cheeses (Saint-Maure, Selles-sur-Cher, Valençay); in that case, why not all at once?

The Berry vineyards make up a fourth region, the Centre, which is quite different in terroir and climate from the other three. Here the soils are essentially Jurassic, as they are in Chablis, Sancerre's neighbour, and in Pouilly-sur-Loire, and the climate semi-continental, with cold winters and hot summers. For ease of presentation, Saint-Pourçain, the Côtes Roannaises and Forez are included in this fourth entity, despite further variations in the soils (primary rock from the Massif Central) and the climate (semi-continental to continental).

This guide follows the same geographic progression to Ÿexamine the specific wine domains. Starting from the Atlantic coast, Muscadet owes its characteristics to a single grape variety (the Melon) producing a unique, dry, irreplaceable wine. In this area, the Folle Blanche variety is the base for another dry white wine, though of lesser quality, Gros-Plant. The region of Ancenis has been 'colonised' by Gamay.

In Anjou, Chenin (or Pineau de la Loire) is the main variety for white wines, although Chardonnay and Sauvignon have more recently been introduced. Chenin is the base for the great rich or, depending on how they develop, sweet wines of the area, as well as for excellent dry and sparkling wines. As for the red varieties the Grolleau Noir, once widely planted, traditionally produces semi-dry rosés, while Cabernet Franc (which used to be called 'Breton') and Cabernet-Sauvignon produce fine, full-bodied red wines with good keeping qualities. The proverbial 'sweetness of the Anjou' arises from a combination of depth, due to its strong acidity, and a soft flavour from the presence of the remaining sugars, and this quality is to be found throughout the sometimes confusing multiplicity of wines produced.

Upstream from the Touraine the main varieties are Chenin, planted in Saumur, Vouvray and Montlouis or on the slopes of the Loir, Cabernet Franc at Chinon, Bourgueil and Saumur, and Grolleau at Azay-le-Rideau. In the eastern region, Gamay for reds and Sauvignon for

The Loire Valley

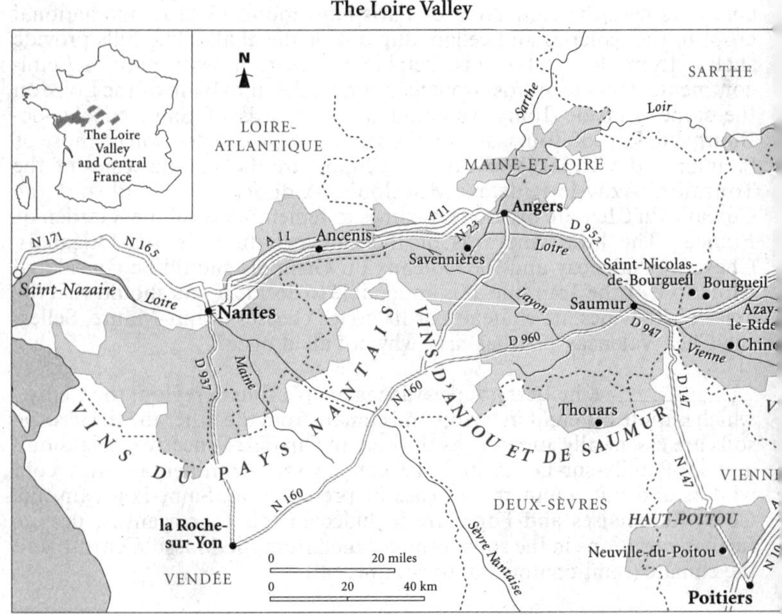

whites produce light, fruity and pleasant wines. Finally, for the sake of completeness, the Pineau d'Aunis from the Coteaux du Loir, which has peppery flavours, should be mentioned, along with the Gris Meunier in the Orléanais.

In the Centre, Sauvignon (making white wines) reigns supreme in Sancerre, Reuilly, Quincy and Menetou-Salon, as well as in Pouilly, where it is still called Blanc-Fumé. There it shares the slopes with the few remaining vineyards of Chasselas, which produce dry, lively wines. As for the reds, the influence of neighbouring Burgundy in the Pinot Noir wines of Sancerre and Menetou-Salon can already be discerned.

To complete this summary of Loire wines, a few words should be added about Haut Poitou, known for lively, fruity Sauvignons, well-structured Chardonnays, and light, robust reds from Gamay, Pinot Noir and Cabernet. Influenced by a semi-maritime climate, Haut Poitou is a zone of transition between the Loire Valley and Bordeaux. Between Anjou and Poitou lies the lesser-known Thouarsais vineyard (AOVDQS). In the Fiefs Vendéens region along the Atlantic coast, an AOVDQS terroir historically known as Vin des Fiefs du Cardinal, the best-known wines are the rosés from Mareuil, made with Gamay and Pinot Noir. The curiosity of the region is the Ragoûtant wine, made from the Négrette variety, but it is difficult to find.

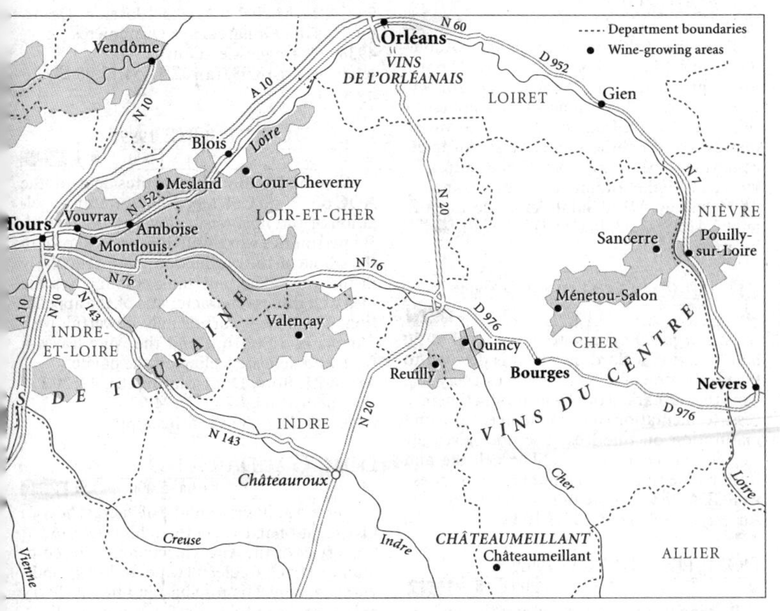

The Loire Valley

The Val de Loire

Rosé de Loire

These wines from the Appellation Régionale, an AOC since 1974, can be produced within the boundaries of the regional AOCs of Anjou, Saumur and Touraine. Cabernet Franc, Cabernet-Sauvignon, Gamay, Pineau d'Aunis and Grolleau are used for making dry rosé wines of which 64,726 hl (1,708,766 gal) were produced in 1999.

DOM. BLOUIN 1999

2.15 ha 5,000 20-29F

This vineyard in the area of Saint-Aubin-de-Luigné, 'the pearl of Layon', is well known for its production of *vins liquoreux*. You will be surprised by the freshness and fruitiness of this rosé. The well-balanced palate leaves an impression of lightness and finesse. An agreeable wine to be drunk from 2000 onwards.

Dom. Michel Blouin, 53, rue du Canal-de-Monsieur, 49190 Saint-Aubin-de-Luigné, tel. 02.41.78.33.53, fax 02.41.78.67.61 by appt.

CH. DE CHAMPTELOUP 1999★

11 ha 67,000 20F+

This *négociant* cultivates a vineyard of 30 ha (74 acres), a third of which is devoted to the production of rosé. It produces a very fine wine that is marked out by its production process: fermentation at a low temperature and maturation on fine lees. The nose gives off sugary and citric aromas. The delicate and fresh palate finishes on a note of red berries.

SCEA de Champteloup, 49700 Brigné-sur-Layon, tel. 02.41.59.65.10

DOM. DE CLAYOU 1999★★

1.5 ha 12,000 20-29F

Proving itself year after year, this domaine is conducting work which is beginning to pay dividends. This wine, so surprising for its appellation, is evidence of this: an intense cherry colour; powerful aromas of red berries with a note of delicate sweetness (pear drops); and a rounded palate which is rich and fruity. A wine of character which can be served with white meat, cold fish, quiches, salad and fruit.

SCEA Jean-Bernard Chauvin, 18 bis, rue du Pont-Barré, 49750 Saint-Lambert-du-Lattay, tel. 02.41.78.42.84, fax 02.41.78.48.52 by appt.

DOM. DU CLOS DES GOHARDS 1999★

4 ha 3,000 20F+

Owned by the same family for four generations, during which time this domaine has grown from 4 to 35 ha (10 to 86 acres). It has a number of old vines producing some little-known wines that do, however, warrant a detour. This one is representative of the appellation. A fine wine, with a pale pink colour, which emits aromas of red berries (strawberry, cherry); the light palate gives the sensation of eating fresh fruit. Delicate and agreeable, this rosé is recommended.

EARL Michel et Mickaël Joselon, Dom. du Clos des Gohards, Les Oisonnières, 49380 Chavagnes-les-Eaux, tel. 02.41.54.13.98, fax 02.41.54.13.98 by appt.

DOM. DU FRESCHE 1999★

0.5 ha 4,000 20-29F

Wine-maker Boré is the president of the AOC of Anjou Coteaux de la Loire, an appellation of *vins liquoreux* enjoying a full revival. He personifies work well done, as is shown in the whole of the production, but particularly in this rosé. The pale pink colour gives the idea of lightness characteristic of the appellation. The nose is surprisingly powerful, with aromas of ripe fruit, and the wine leaves a fresh and delicate feeling on the palate.

EARL Boré, Dom. du Fresche, 49620 La Pommeraye, tel. 02.41.77.74.63, fax 02.41.77.79.39 by appt.

DOM. GAUDARD 1999

1.41 ha 5,000 20-29F

Pierre Aguilas is a bundle of energy: he uses his exceptional drive both on his estate and at the service of the Angevin wine-growing community. His characterful wines reflect his individual energy. His rosé has an intense cherry colour and exudes powerful aromas of flowers and fruit, which are released on airing; the full palate gives a sensation of red berries. Try

the wine with quiche lorraine or a savoury tart at the beginning of a meal.
🗝 Pierre Aguilas, Dom. Gaudard, rte de Saint-Aubin, 49290 Chaudefonds-sur-Layon, tel. 02.41.78.10.68, fax 02.41.78.67.72 ☑ Y ev. day except Sun. 8am–12 noon 2pm–6pm

DOM. DES HAUTES VIGNES

◪ 4 ha 4,000 ▮ ♁ 20–29 F

Founded in 1961 with 2.5 ha (6 acres) of vines, this vineyard has grown to 45 ha (111 acres). The production of the rosé wines involves first taking the free-run juice from pre-fermented red grapes, then adding this to the juice from direct pressing, resulting in a very fine wine with strong notes of red berries. The palate is alluring but leaves a slightly bitter sensation.
🗝 SCA Fourrier et Fils, 22, rue de la Chapelle, 49400 Distré, tel. 02.41.50.21.96, fax 02.41.50.12.83 ☑ Y by appt.

DOM. DE LA DOUNIERE 1999

◪ 2 ha 500 ▮ ♁ 20–29 F

To the north of Deux-Sèvres, this vineyard is in the area of Bouillé-Loretz. You can visit the vineyard house, an old farm building notable for its closed courtyards. This wine, with a clear pink shade and a delicate aroma of flowers and ripe fruit (melon), has captured the jury's attention; the palate is fresh and thirst quenching. A light 99 that is representative of the appellation.
🗝 EARL Lacroix, 107, rue Saint-Vincent, 79290 Bouillé-Loretz, tel. 05.49.67.05.13, fax 05.49.67.11.43 ☑ Y by appt.

VIGNOBLE DE L'ARCISON 1999★★

◪ 2.5 ha 10,000 ▮ ♁ 20–29 F

The acquisition of no fewer than 77 parcels of land at this traditional estate in Anjou, which produces Bonnezeaux, has resulted in the formation of a 7-ha (17-acre) vineyard on Clos du Moulin. This very fine rosé emits an impression of surprising strength. The colour is orangey-pink, and strong aromas of ripe fruit and flowers dominate. A characterful wine.
🗝 Damien Reulier, Vignoble de L'Arcison, Le Mesnil, 49380 Thouarcé, tel. 02.41.54.16.81, fax 02.41.54.31.12 ☑ Y ev. day 9am–12.30pm 2pm–6pm; cl. Oct.

LA TUILIERE 1999★

◪ n.c. 100,000 ▮ ♁ 20 F+

A specialist in rosés and sparkling wines, this *négociant* offers a rosé that is representative of its appellation: pale pink in colour, with delicate aromas of red berries and fresh fruit; the refreshing palate leaves a light impression. A fresh and fruity wine, to be drunk from 2000 onwards.
🗝 De Neuville, rue Léopold-Palustre, 49400 Saint-Hilaire-Saint-Florent, tel. 02.41.53.03.30, fax 02.41.53.03.39 ☑ Y ev. day except Sun. Mon. 9.30am–6.30pm

CH. DE LA VIAUDIERE 1999

◪ 2.8 ha 9,000 ▮ ♁ 20 F+

The current owner of this family business, which has been handed down from father to son for four centuries, is Olivier Gélineau. A lover of words, he writes a poem to his clients every year when the new wines are ready, in March or April. The wine is as agreeable to the eye as to the nose. A similar response is found on the palate, with a supple and fruity first impression. This distinguished representative of the delicate rosés of the Loire Valley has everything in harmony.
🗝 EARL Vignoble Gélineau, Ch. de La Viaudière, 49380 Champ-sur-Layon, tel. 02.41.78.86.27, fax 02.41.78.60.45, e-mail gelineau@wanadoo.fr ☑ Y by appt.

LES TERRIADES 1999★

◪ 12 ha 100,000 ▮ ♁ 20 F+

The Caves de la Loire were created in 1951 and market around 110,000 hl (2,904,000 gal). High-tech equipment and a qualitative process are employed to ensure the wines are typical of their terroir. This rosé leaves a fresh and light impression and the sensation of eating strawberries. An excellent all-round effect is generated by harvesting at a reasonable maturity, but more particularly from good vinification.
🗝 Les Caves de La Loire, rte de Vauchrétien, 49320 Brissac, tel. 02.41.91.22.71, fax 02.41.54.20.36, e-mail loirewines@vapl.fr ☑ Y by appt.

DOM. DES MATINES 1999★★

◪ 3 ha 15,000 ▮ ♁ 30–49 F

Family-owned, this estate owes its celebrity to the personality of the proprietor. The cellar, cut into rock, and the room of old winepress screws are among the curiosities to be discovered. The wine has a beautiful aroma of exotic fruits and flowers, along with sugary nuances. The palate is remarkably well balanced. A characterful and spring-like wine that leaves an impression of freshness and finesse, it is best drunk with white meat.
🗝 Michèle Etchegaray-Mallard, Dom. des Matines, 31, rue de la Mairie, 49700 Brossay, tel. 02.41.52.25.36, fax 02.41.52.25.50 ☑ Y by appt.

DOM. ROMPILLON 1999★

◪ 0.85 ha 7,500 ▮ ♁ 20–29 F

The tourist route of the wine-growing slopes of Layon is the site of this domaine. The production process involves direct pressing of the grapes and fermentation of the must at a low temperature. A pale pink colour, this is a pleasant Loire rosé. The nose gives off aromas of red berries (strawberry, cherry) and flowers, and the palate is supple, pleasant, lively and refreshing.
🗝 Jean-Pierre Rompillon, L'Ollulière, 49750 Saint-Lambert-du-Lattay, tel. 02.41.78.48.84, fax 02.41.78.48.84 ☑ Y by appt.

DOM. DE SAINTE-ANNE 1999★

◪ 5 ha 10,000 ▮ 20–29 F

This estate is on the highest clay-chalk crests of Saint-Saturnin-sur-Loire, a terroir given over to red and rosé wines. The aromatic 99 suggests flowers, pear drops and red berries. The same effect is created on the palate, giving an impression of lightness and freshness. A great success. Would go well with a fruit tart.

🔑 EARL Brault, Dom. de Sainte-Anne, 49320 Brissac-Quincé, tel. 02.41.91.24.58, fax 02.41.91.25.87 ☑ Y ev. day except Sun. 9am–12 noon 2pm–7pm; Sat. 9am–12 noon 2pm–6pm

DOM. DES TROTTIERES 1999★★

◪ 1.8 ha 16,000 ▮ 🌡 20–29 F

Founded in 1905, this domaine covers an area of 110 ha (272 acres), 79 ha (195 acres) of which are planted with vines. A fine maceration of part of the harvests, fermentation at a low temperature and maturation of three months *sur lies fines* all give this wine character, which is further enhanced by well-matured harvests and perfect vinification. A rosé whose full palate evokes tones of red berries. 'It is a Loire Valley rosé particular to the region,' remarked one taster, while another commented: 'To be served at any hour of the day or night.' *Awarded a coup de coeur, regrettably at the time of going to press the label was not available to reproduce here.*

🔑 SCEA Dom. des Trottières, Les Trottières, 49380 Thouarcé, tel. 02.41.54.14.10, fax 02.41.54.09.00, e-mail lestrottieres@worldonline.fr ☑ Y ev. day except Sat. Sun. 8am–12.30pm 2pm–6.30pm

🔑 Lamotte

Crémant de Loire

Here again, the Appellation Régionale can be applied to sparkling wines produced within the boundaries of Anjou, Saumur, Touraine and Cheverny. The Méthode Traditionelle, or Champagne method, works wonders here; the production of these celebration wines went up to 38,080 hl (1,005,312 gal) in 1999. A number of varieties are grown: Chenin (Pineau de Loire), Cabernet-Sauvignon and Cabernet Franc, Pinot Noir, Chardonnay, etc. Even though production is largely of sparkling whites, a few sparkling rosés are also to be found.

CH. DE BELLEVUE 1997★

○ 0.5 ha 3,000 ▮ 🌡 30–49 F

On top of a hillside in the area of Saint-Aubin-de-Luigné, this château hosts the Anjou festival of *vins liquoreux* every year in July. It produces a characterful Crémant that combines lightness and structure. With a pale yellow tint and enlivened by its sparkle, the wine gives off elegant and light aromas of flowers. The fresh palate is well balanced and leaves a harmonious impression.

🔑 EARL Tijou et Fils, Ch. de Bellevue, 49190 Saint-Aubin-de-Luigné, tel. 02.41.78.33.11, fax 02.41.78.67.84 ☑ Y by appt.

🔑 Jean-Paul Tijou

BOUVET Excellence

○ n.c. 66,000 ▮ 50–69 F

Founded in 1851 and specialising in sparkling wines, Bouvet-Ladubay is a well-known vineyard of Saumurois. This particular wine comes from good base wines. The sparkle is lively, bringing herbaceous nuances to the nose. The palate, on the other hand, fills with ripe fruit and ends with great finesse.

🔑 Bouvet-Ladubay, 1, rue de l'Abbaye, 49400 Saint-Hilaire-Saint-Florent, tel. 02.41.83.83.83, fax 02.41.50.24.32, e-mail bouvet-ladubay@symphonie-fai.fr ☑ Y ev. day 9am–12 noon 2pm–6.30pm

MICHEL CONTOUR★

○ 1 ha 6,600 30–49 F

Michel Contour makes a Crémant with a fine and lasting sparkle. Its fruity nose is joined by nuances of almonds; both the harmony and balance are successful.

🔑 Michel Contour, 7, rue La Boissière, 41120 Cellettes, tel. 02.54.70.43.07, fax 02.54.70.36.68 ☑ Y ev. day 8.30am–1pm 2pm–7pm

LES VIGNERONS DES COTEAUX ROMANAIS 1995★

○ 1 ha 7,500 ▮ 🌡 30–49 F

Produced in only small quantities, this wine distinguishes itself among those of this cooperative: a great success, in fact. The sparkle holds up, and the nose gives off aromas of brioche and apple. Supple and harmonious, this Crémant would be a good choice for an apéritif.

🔑 Les Vignerons des Coteaux Romanais, 50, rue Principale, 41140 Saint-Romain-sur-Cher, tel. 02.54.71.70.74, fax 02.54.71.41.75 ☑ Y ev. day except Sun. Mon. 8am–12 noon 2pm–4pm

DIAMANT DE LOIRE★★

○ 1.71 ha 16,000 30–49 F

The Caves de la Loire were founded in 1951 and produce around 110,000 hl (2,904,000 gal). The Crémant is made with only Chardonnay grapes, and the result is extraordinary. With an intense golden-yellow colour, it has an excellent, long-lasting sparkle and complex aromas redolent of white fruit (quince), honey and dried fruit, with a

delicate aftertaste hinting of exotic fruit and brioche. A rich and characterful Crémant, this is the standard-bearer for the quality of work undertaken by the cooperative members.
🔑 Les Caves de La Loire, rte de Vauchrétien, 49320 Brissac, tel. 02.41.91.22.71, fax 02.41.54.20.36, e-mail loirewines@vapl.fr ☑ 🍸 by appt.

GUY DURAND*

○ 0.3 ha 2,000 ▮ 🌡 30–49 F

Guy Durand, on the left bank of the Loire, uses Chenin Blanc (80%) and Chardonnay (20%) grapes to make this golden-yellow wine, enlivened by long-lasting bubbles. The equally intense nose gives off nuances of fresh fruit. This is an open and balanced wine. The producer's **Touraine Amboise Blanc 98** is also a success.
🔑 Guy Durand, 11, Chemin-Neuf, 37530 Mosnes, tel. 02.47.30.43.14, fax 02.47.30.43.14 ☑ 🍸 ev. day 8am–8pm

DOM. DUTERTRE

Cuvée Saint Gilles 1997*

○ 3 ha 20,000 ▮ 🌡 30–49 F

This family estate, well known in the appellation of Touraine-Amboise, also distinguishes itself in Loire Valley Crémant. For proof of this we have this wine, with a colour resembling a Blanc de Noirs. It actually contains 10% of Cabernet Franc and 30% of Pinot Noir to complement the Chenin Blanc and Chardonnay. With a nose giving off aromas of apple, with smoky undertones, it is a fresh, interesting wine.
🔑 Dom. Dutertre, 20–21, rue d'Enfer, 37530 Limeray, tel. 02.47.30.10.69, fax 02.47.30.06.92 ☑ 🍸 ev. day 8am–12.30pm 2pm–6pm; Sun. by appt.

MICHEL FARDEAU 1998*

○ n.c. 13,000 30–49 F

The estate is in the lower regions of the Layon, very close to the convergence of this river and the Loire, at the foot of the Angevin corniche. Its Crémant leaves an elegant impression: delicate bubbles on a base of pale yellow with green tints; fruity and spicy aromas; a refreshing palate and an aftertaste of fresh fruit. Would go with chocolate desserts.
🔑 Dom. Michel Fardeau, Les Hauts Perrays, 49290 Chaudefonds-sur-Layon, tel. 02.41.78.67.57, fax 02.41.78.68.78 ☑ 🍸 ev. day 9am–12 noon 1pm–7pm; Sat. Sun. by appt.

FOUSSY

○ n.c. 30,000 30–49 F

Blanc Foussy is a *négociant* specialising in the development of sparkling wines. Its large cellars, situated in Rochecorbon on the edge of the Loire Valley, are open to visitors, and the whole fermentation process takes place there. This Crémant is now golden and quite lively; its thirst-quenching and rich palate, with aromas of apple, and lightly iodised nature would go well with oysters.
🔑 SA Blanc Foussy, 95, quai de la Loire, 37210 Rochecorbon, tel. 02.47.40.40.20, fax 02.47.52.65.82 ☑

XAVIER FRISSANT

○ 1 ha 4,000 ▮ 30–49 F

Receiving the *Coup de Coeur* in 2000 for his Cuvée Millénnium, this young wine-producer already exports 20% of his product. He is now offering a Blanc de Blancs with slight nuances of honey and almond on a fruity base. An off-dry wine, good for the beginning of a meal.
🔑 Xavier Frissant, 1, chem. Neuf, 37530 Mosnes, tel. 02.47.57.23.18, fax 02.47.57.23.25 ☑ 🍸 ev. day 8am–12.30pm 2pm–7.30pm; Sun. by appt.

GRATIEN ET MEYER Cuvée Royale

○ n.c. 200,000 30–49 F

In 1864, at the age of 23, Alfred Gratien founded his vineyard in Saumur. On his death in 1885, Albert Meyer took over the family business, and his descendants, Alain and Gérard Seydoux, run it today, offering this agreeable Crémant. It emits an impression of fruitiness and freshness. The nose gives off gentle suggestions of fruit and brioche, and the lively palate finishes on lemony nuances. A wine whose acidity would go well with desserts.
🔑 Gratien et Meyer, rte de Montsoreau, B.P. 22, 49401 Saumur Cedex, tel. 02.41.83.13.30, fax 02.41.83.13.49, e-mail contact@gratienmeyer.com ☑ 🍸 by appt.
🔑 Alain Seydoux

CHRISTIANE GREFFE*

○ n.c. 8,000 30–49 F

This Vouvray vineyard has offered a Crémant along with its Vouvray and Touraine for a number of years. Judging from this golden wine, with its gentle sparkle, this has been a great success. There is a pleasant balance with satisfying length along with hints of brioche and quince. This is a Crémant with character.
🔑 Christiane Greffe, 35, rue Neuve, 37210 Vernou-sur-Brenne, tel. 02.47.52.12.24, fax 02.47.52.09.56, e-mail savardja@club-internet.fr ☑ 🍸 ev. day except Sat. Sun. 8am–12 noon 1.30pm–5.30pm
🔑 Jacques Savard

DOM. DE LA DESOUCHERIE 1997*

○ 1.3 ha 9,000 ▮ 🌡 30–49 F

Pale yellow, yet so bright . . . rich and yet so fine . . . soft and yet so refreshing . . . Everything: colour, sparkle, as well as the palate, leads to pleasure. Christian Tessier has succeeded well here.
🔑 Christian Tessier, Dom. de La Désoucherie, 41700 Cour-Cheverny, tel. 02.54.79.90.08, fax 02.54.79.22.48, e-mail christian.tessier@waika9.com ☑ 🍸 by appt.

LOIRE

DOM. DE LA GACHERE 1997★★

○ 1 ha 2,000 30-49 F

The domaine is to the south of the Anjou wine-growing region, in the DeuxSèvres area. Alain and Gilles Lemoine inherited the estate from their father, Claude, and have on their hands a planting of 32 ha (79 acres), with a very good reputation that this remarkable Crémant will do nothing to harm. Because here we have a well-produced Crémant distinguished by long maturation on slats which gives it all its character: lasting sparkle, a pale yellow colour, aromas of brioche and toasted dried fruit, and a full, forthcoming and generous palate with fruity elements. The wine, which has true presence, could be served with white meats or chocolate gâteaux.

GAEC Lemoine, Dom. de La Gachère, 79290 Saint-Pierre-à-Champ, tel. 05.49.96.81.03, fax 05.49.96.32.38, e-mail f.lemoine@wanadoo.fr ev. day except Sun. 9am–12 noon 2pm–6pm

DOM. DE L'ANGELIERE 1997★

○ 1.4 ha 9,000 30-49 F

A vineyard that has been run by the same family for six generations, the Angelière estate has grown from 15 ha (37 acres) to more than 40 ha (99 acres) today. Its vintage Crémant is pale yellow in colour, displaying a fine and lasting sparkle. The same sensation of freshness and lightness is to be found on the nose and palate.

GAEC Boret, Dom. de L'Angelière, 49380 Champ-sur-Layon, tel. 02.41.78.85.09, fax 02.41.78.67.10 by appt.

LES DOUCINIERES Cuvée An 2000

○ 4 ha 8,000 30-49 F

Located near Mesland, this vineyard is biodynamically cultivated. Its Crémant, containing 80% white grapes, has an amber tint and smells of fresh peaches and does not lack suppleness. The pleasant **Touraine-Mesland Blanc 99** also warrants a mention.

Vincent Girault, Ch. Gaillard, 41150 Mesland, tel. 02.54.70.25.47, fax 02.54.70.28.70 by appt.

DOM. MICHAUD★

○ 1.6 ha 13,000 30-49 F

Noyers-sur-Cher is at the eastern extremity of Touraine, on the Tours–Vierzon road, which crosses the wine-growing area. It is here that the producer has developed this wine, composed of 80% white grapes, with a gentle colour and enlivened by fine bubbles. Light hints of brioche are apparent in this well-balanced and elegant blend.

EARL Dom. Michaud, Les Martinières, 41140 Noyers-sur-Cher, tel. 02.54.32.47.23, fax 02.54.75.39.19 by appt.

MONMOUSSEAU 1997

○ n.c. 62,844 30-49 F

Made from 90% white grapes, with Cabernet Franc appearing only as an extra, this Crémant is as gentle on the eye as on the nose (mostly floral aromas). Quite supple, it sits well on the palate.

SA Monmousseau, B.P. 25, 41400 Montrichard, tel. 02.54.71.66.66, fax 02.54.32.56.09, email monmousseau@wanadoo.fr ev. day 10am–6pm; groups by appt.; cl. Sat. Sun. 1st Nov.–31 Mar.

Bernard Massard

MONTCHEAUX★★

○ n.c. 15,000 30-49 F

Montcheaux is a *négociant*, based to the west of the Anjou wine-growing region, specialising in sparkling wines. A fine and lasting sparkle and pale yellow colour with green tints grace this Crémant. The subtle aromas call to mind sweet pastries and dried fruit, while the palate brings freshness with its lemony and fruity finish. An apéritif of high quality.

Cave de La Bouvraie, 6, rue de La Verrerie, 49123 Ingrandes-sur-Loire, tel. 02.41.39.40.44, fax 02.41.39.46.01 ev. day except n. 9am–12 noon 2pm–6pm

DOM. RICHOU 1996★

○ 2 ha 10,000 50-69 F

The Richou estate is one of the leading Anjou vineyards. A name associated with the production of red wine and *vins liquoreux*, their sparkling wines are, however, not to be ignored, as is the case for this Crémant: pale yellow in colour and enlivened by fine, long-lasting bubbles. The aromas, reminiscent of sweet pastries and dried fruit, assert themselves with a certain strength. The harmonious palate leaves a feeling of freshness, which is characteristic of the appellation.

Dom. Richou, Chauvigné, 49610 Mozé-sur-Louet, tel. 02.41.78.72.13, fax 02.41.78.76.05 ev. day except Sun. 8.30am–12 noon 2.30pm–7pm

CH. SOUCHERIE 1996★

○ 1 ha 9,974 30-49 F

The Soucherie château dominates the Layon, occupying a unique mid-slope site. As well as its Coteaux du Layon, Savennières and other Anjous, it produces an elegant Crémant, typical of the appellation. The sparkle leaves a fine and subtle imprint in the pale yellow colour, and on the nose the wine has hints of fruit and sweet pastries, which harmonise with the fresh and well-balanced palate.

⊶ Tijou et Fils, Ch. Soucherie, 49750 Beaulieu-sur-Layon, tel. 02.41.78.31.18, fax 02.41.78.48.29 ☒ Y by appt.

DOM. DES TROTTIERES 1997*

○ 0.59 ha 4,500 30–49 F

The estate covers an area of 110 ha (272 acres), 79 ha (195 acres) of which are in the appellation area on gravelly soil. Its Crémant has been judged to be well balanced at all levels: a fine sparkle, light yellow colour, subtle, flowery aromas, and a delicate and fresh palate. A good representative of the appellation.

⊶ SCEA Dom. des Trottières, Les Trottières, 49380 Thouarcé, tel. 02.41.54.14.10, fax 02.41.54.09.00, e-mail lestrottieres@worldonline.fr ☒ Y ev. day except Sat. Sun. 8am–12.30pm 2pm–6.30pm

The Nantes region

Some two thousand years ago, the Roman legions introduced the vine to the Nantes area, at the crossroads of Brittany, the Vendée, the Loire and the Atlantic coast. After a terrible winter in 1709, when the sea froze solid along the shore and the vines were completely destroyed, the vineyard as a whole was replanted, mainly with the Melon variety from Burgundy.

The Pays Nantais, the area where wines from the Nantes region are produced, today covers 16,500 ha (40,755 acres) to the south and east of Nantes, spilling slightly over the borders of Loire-Atlantique towards the Vendée and Maine-et-Loire. The vines grow on sunny slopes exposed to maritime influences. The soils are rather light and stony, composed of ancient terrain mixed with volcanic rocks. The Nantes region produces four AOC wines: Muscadet, Muscadet des Coteaux de la Loire, Muscadet de Sèvreet-Maine and Muscadet Côtes de Grand-Lieu, as well as the AOVDQS wines, Gros-Plant du Pays Nantais, Coteaux d'Ancenis and Fiefs Vendéens.

Muscadet AOCs and Gros-Plant from the Pays Nantais

Muscadet is a dry white wine that has been an AOC since 1936. It is made from a single grape variety: the Melon. The area of the vineyard covers 13,000 ha (32,110 acres). There are four Appellations d'Origine Contrôlée, identified according to their geographical location, producing 727,150 hl (19,196,760 gal) in 1999: Muscadet de Sèvre-et-Maine, which alone represents 11,000 ha (27,170 acres) and 529,322 hl (13,974,100 gal); Muscadet Côtes de Grand-Lieu (400 ha (988 acres) and 19,130 hl (505,032 gal) in 1999); Muscadet des Coteaux de la Loire (330 ha (815 acres), 13,504 hl (356,506 gal), and Muscadet, 2,270 ha (5,607 acres), 165,195 hl (4,361,148 gal). The Gros-Plant du Pays Nantais, classified AOVDQS in 1954, is also a dry white wine, but made from a different grape variety, the Folle Blanche, from an area of about 2,700 ha (6,669 acres).

Bottling on the lees ('sur lie') is a traditional technique in the region, subject to precise regulations that were made more stringent in 1994. To qualify for the 'sur lie' suffix, the wines must spend no more than one winter in vats or casks, having been matured on the lees and kept in the wine store where they were made until bottling. The wine bottling can take place only during precisely defined periods and in no circumstances before 1 March, and sales are permitted only after the third Thursday in March. These regulations are designed to maximise freshness, finesse and bouquet. In summary, Muscadet is a dry white wine with lively acidity and a generous bouquet, a wine for any occasion. It is the perfect accompaniment for fish, shellfish and seafood, and also makes an excellent aperitif, to be served chilled but not iced at 8–9°C (46.4–48.2°F). Gros-Plant, which should be served at the same temperature, is the ideal wine to drink with oysters.

Muscadet

LE MOULIN DE LA TOUCHE

Sur lie 1999★★

☐ 1 ha 5,500 20-29 F

An eccentric Muscadet, produced very close to the sea, this wine develops on the nose and on the palate with aromas of apple and pear, to which is added a mineral hint. It has a vivid first impression that is confirmed by the powerful and well-structured flavour.

Joël Hérissé, Le Moulin de la Touche, 44580 Bourgneuf-en-Retz, tel. 02.40.21.47.89, fax 02.40.21.47.89 by appt.

DOM. DU RAFOU

Clos des Quinze Sillons 1999

☐ 2 ha 15,000 20-29 F

The unpredictability of the tastings: the second Muscadet retained by the jury is of an origin diametrically opposed to the first one because it comes from Anjou. This one is also classic in its clear colour, and its vivid and structured character is revealed on the palate.

Marc et Jean Luneau, Dom. du Rafou, 49230 Tillières, tel. 02.41.70.68.78, fax 02.41.70.68.78 by appt.

Muscadet des Coteaux de la Loire sur lie

DOM. DU CHAMP CHAPRON

Sur lie 1999

☐ 10 ha 66,000 20 F+

As is suggested by its slight sparkle, this wine opens on the palate with a lively first impression. With a more or less mineral character, it has good length. The estate also produces a **Gros-Plant du Pays Nantais 99** which is a good example of the Folle Blanche grape variety.

SCA Suteau-Ollivier, Le Champ Chapron, 44450 Barbechat, tel. 02.40.03.65.27, fax 02.40.33.34.43 ev. day except Sun. 8am–8pm

DOM. DES GALLOIRES

Sur lie Cuvée de Sélection 1999★★

☐ 1.35 ha 9,000 20-29 F

This estate, cultivated by a family-run GAEC (*groupement agricole*) has produced a wine with a quite unobtrusive apricot nose. It reveals itself more on the palate, which is supple and harmonious, fruity, with nuances of toast, confirming its pleasant nature. The **Coteaux d'Ancenis Rouge 99** from this estate (less than 20F) merits its own star for its nose of violet and liquorice, its supple palate, and its reasonable price.

GAEC des Galloires, La Galloire, 49530 Drain, tel. 02.40.98.20.10, fax 02.40.98.22.06 by appt.

CH. MESLIERE Sur lie 1999

☐ 8.5 ha 30,000 20-29 F

This château takes its name from the Palaeolithic site of Pierres Meslières, where there are two menhirs, the remains of a line of forty megaliths. Its Muscadet Coteaux de la Loire, pale yellow with green tints, has a slight sparkle, and although its nose is somewhat closed, it becomes round and long on the palate and is sustained by a good structure. Also of note, is the **Coteaux d'Ancenis Rouge 99**, which is supple and fruity.

Jean-Claude Toublanc, Les Pierres Meslières, 44150 Saint-Géréon, tel. 02.40.83.23.95, fax 02.40.83.23.95 by appt.

DOM. DE SAINT-MEEN

Sur lie 1999★★★

☐ n.c. 30,000 20-29 F

Pierre Luneau-Papin has extended his activities to Cellier, on the right bank of the Loire. Seductive to the eye, with its lovely slight sparkle and green tints, this wine's qualities are confirmed in a mineral and lemony nose then by its round palate; it has a lively first impression and a long and aromatic finish. To be served with asparagus, smoked salmon and lemon mousse. As to **Muscadet de Sèvre-et-Maine sur lie**, the **Clos des Allées Vieilles Vignes 99** (one star) reveals a very intense and fruity nose with a mineral note. With a well-structured palate, it is also very fresh, thanks to the slight sparkle given by carbon dioxide.

Pierre Luneau-Papin, Dom. Pierre de La Grange, 44430 Le Landreau, tel. 02.40.06.45.27, fax 02.40.06.46.62 by appt.

Pierre Luneau

Muscadet de Sèvre-et-Maine

CH. D'AMOUR Sur lie 1999*

☐ 8 ha 25,000 ▮ 🌡 20–29 F

The cellar of this château once served a romantic purpose, hence its pleasant name. Returned to its wine-making vocation, it produced in 1999 an elegant, very characteristic wine with a complex nose of dried fruit and citrus. With a generous palate, it demonstrates good length along its lightly acidulous finish.

🔑 GAEC Brochard Père et Fils, La Grenaudière, 44690 Maisdon-sur-Sèvre, tel. 02.40.03.80.00, fax 02.40.03.85.13 ☑ Y ev. day except Sun. 8am–7pm

DOM. AUDOUIN Sur lie 1999*

☐ 8 ha 50,000 ▮ 🌡 20–29 F

Coming from gabbro soil, this wine has a discreet nose with a good mineral note. After a clean first impression, the palate opens out roundly, then finishes with a touch of liveliness. Also worth mentioning (without a star) is the Gros-Plant du Pays Nantais **Domaine de la Momenière 99**, which has a very mineral character.

🔑 EARL Audouin, Dom. de La Momenière, 44430 Le Landreau, tel. 02.40.06.43.04, fax 02.40.06.47.89 ☑ Y ev. day 9am–7pm

LE MUSCADET BARRE

Sur lie 1999**

☐ 4.5 ha 30,000 ▮ 🌡 50–69 F

This blended wine represents a certain ideal of Muscadet de Sèvre-et-Maine. Fine and straightforward, it exhibits a wide range of aromas: kiwi, pear and linden flowers on the nose and mostly grapefruit on the palate. It is in addition very smooth. This négociant also offers Muscadet de Sèvre-et-Maine sur lie **Les Printanières 99**, with a powerful nose of exotic fruits, which warrants one star, as well as **Château de la Bretesche**.

🔑 Barré Frères, Beau-Soleil, B.P. 10, 44190 Gorges, tel. 02.40.06.90.70, fax 02.40.06.96.52 ☑ Y by appt.

🔑 P. Guilbaud

DOM. DE BEAU-SOLEIL

Sur lie 1999**

☐ 14 ha 96,000 ▮ 🌡 20–29 F

From a few neglected vines, Jean Macé has, over some 30 years, created a fine estate comprising 20 ha (49 acres) all in one block, which is unusual in this region. His wine exhibits aromas of flowers and pear drops on the nose, followed by more fruity nuances on its long and supple palate.

🔑 GFA J. Macé, Dom. de Beau-Soleil, 1, rue Anne-de-Goulaine, 44430 Le Loroux-Bottereau, tel. 02.40.33.82.16

DOM. BEL AIR Sur lie 1999*

☐ 23 ha 135,000 ▮ 🌡 20–29 F

As with the 1998 vintage, this wine leaves a clear impression of maturity from its very

Pays Nantais

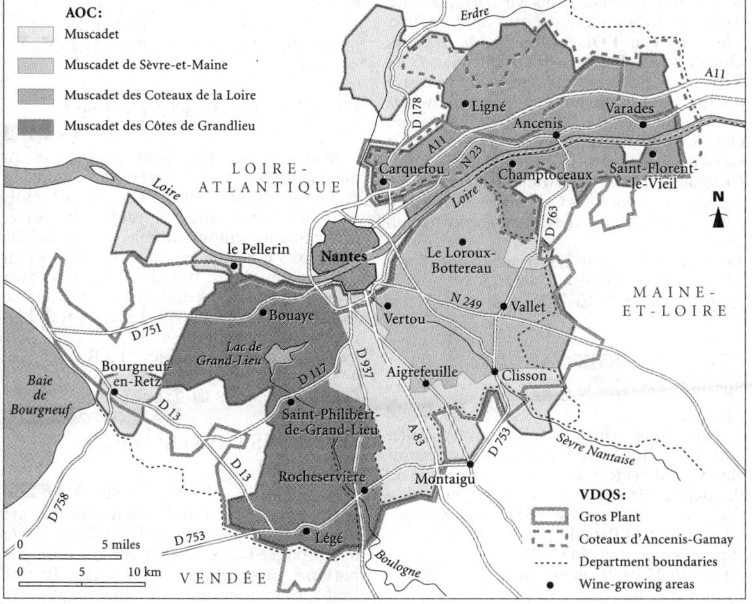

LOIRE

intense nose of liquorice and grilled aromas. Well balanced on the palate, it is nevertheless a typical example of Muscadet de Sèvre-et-Maine.
GAEC Jean-Luc et Emmanuel Audrain, 26, rue de la Caillaudière, 44690 La Haye-Fouassière, tel. 02.40.54.84.11, fax 02.40.36.91.36 ev. day except Sun. 8am–12.30pm 2pm–7.30pm

CLOS DU BIEN-AIME Sur lie 1999★

2 ha 12,000 20-29 F

If you are returning from a trip along the Goulaine marshes, after disembarking at the port of Millau, visit this estate. The jury commends the crystal clearness of this wine, with its intense nose and balanced palate. If it lacks some liveliness, keeping it for a few months will remedy that.
Bernard Gratas, Dom. de La Houssais, 44430 Le Landreau, tel. 02.40.06.46.27, fax 02.40.06.47.25 by appt.

DOM. DU BOIS BRULE Sur lie 1999★

2 ha 12,000 20-29 F

Just to the north of the town of Vallet, this estate produces a wine with quite a sparkle. Although a little vigorous on the palate, this *vin sur lie* is so long, fleshy and rich that it promises a pleasant moment.
Emmanuel Luneau, Bois Brûlé, 44330 Vallet, tel. 02.40.33.91.47 by appt.

DOM. DU BOIS BRULEY

Sur lie 1999★★

9.55 ha n.c. 30-49 F

From a Basse-Goulaine terroir, intense and perfumed on the nose, this wine delights with its perfect balance and strength on the palate. The **Château l'Oiselinière de la Ramée, Grande Vinée de l'Aigle d'Or 98** comes from Vertou and warrants one star. Very expressive on the nose, with aromas veering towards roasted nuances, it is supple on the palate and ends with a mineral finish of gunflint; it would go well with fish. Finally, the famous **Château de Chasseloir, Grande Réserve Comte Leloup Cuvée des Ceps Centenaires 99** is worth a mention (no star): these *centenaires* are still green.
Bernard Chéreau, La MouzièrePortillon, 44120 Vertou, tel. 02.40.54.81.15, fax 02.40.54.81.70 by appt.

CLOS DES BOIS GAUTIER

Sur lie 1999★

n.c. 50,000 20-29 F

This estate, which is split between Vallet and Mouzillon, offers a wine whose terroir character is evident as much on the nose as on the palate. Strong, balanced and long, it is a fine classic of Muscadet de Sèvre-et-Maine.
Christian et Pascale Luneau, Le Bois-Braud, Mouzillon, 44330 Vallet, tel. 02.40.33.93.76, fax 02.40.36.22.73 by appt.

DOM. DU BOIS-JOLY

Sur lie Harmonie 1999★

4.5 ha 30,000 20-29 F

Well known by readers of the *Guide*, this clear-coloured wine attracts with its straightforward nose, with characteristic aromas of citrus and green fruit. Supple and full on the palate, it evokes cheerfulness.
Henri et Laurent Bouchaud, Le Bois-Joly, 44330 Le Pallet, tel. 02.40.80.40.83, fax 02.40.80.45.85 ev. day 9.30am–1pm 3pm–7.30pm

PIERRE-LUC BOUCHAUD

Sur lie Sélection Terroir Le Perd son Pain 1999★

0.73 ha 5,000 20-29 F

With a reputation for barrenness and unprofitability – hence its name – this parcel of land (less than a hectare) is well-suited to the vine. The wine, with a complex nose, green and slightly mineral, exhibits a wellstructured palate, with a slightly sparkling first impression and a warm finish.
Pierre-Luc Bouchaud, La Hautière, 44690 Saint-Fiacre, tel. 02.40.36.95.23, fax 02.40.36.79.56, e-mail pierre-luc.bouchaud@wanadoo.fr by appt.

CH. BRAIRON Sur lie 1999★

1.33 ha 9,000 20-29 F

Serge Méchineau has refitted the château cellars to bring to life this old wine-producing property, which was, not long ago, totally dilapidated. Here, he has produced a wine with a complex nose, whose mineral character is enhanced by hints of smokiness. Rich and long on the palate, it exhibits good terroir characteristics.
Serge et Brigitte Méchineau, Le Châtelier, 44690 Château-Thébaud, tel. 02.40.06.51.21, fax 02.40.06.57.76 by appt.

CUVEE DES BUTTAYS 1999★★

3.15 ha 25,000 20-29 F

Muscadets coming from gabbro soil (a magmatic basic rock typical of the region) are renowned for their finesse. This is true for this well-structured and characteristic wine, thanks to its lemony aromas. An acidulous note gives it all the freshness it needs. From the same producer, two stars have also been given to Gros-Plant du Pays Nantais sur lie **Domaine du Royaume 99**, which is well balanced and minerally.
EARL Philippe Chénard, La Boisselière, 44330 Le Pallet, tel. 02.40.80.98.17, fax 02.40.80.44.38 by appt.

DOM. DES CHATELIERES

Sur lie 1999★

3.5 ha 23,500 20-29 F

On a mica schist and gabbro soil that are typical of the region, the Chatelières estate has produced a wine that is very aromatic both on the nose and on the palate. Its fine first impression and notable length are

memorable. One star also goes to the **Domaine de La Bécassière 99**, a wine, which is not matured *sur lie*, that delivers aromas of lychee, which linger a long time on the palate.
Louis et Denis Luneau, La Bécassière, 44430 Le Loroux-Bottereau, tel. 02.40.33.82.44, fax 02.40.03.76.73 by appt.

DOM. DES CHAUSSELIERES

Sur lie 1999★

☐ 2 ha 14,000 20–29 F

Very close to the Musée du Vignoble de Nantes, which warrants a detour, Chausselières offers this pale yellow wine with a fine and intense nose. Lively and with a slight prickle on the palate, the wine produces mainly fruity aromas of pear and apricot. Not to miss is the Muscadet de Sèvre-et-Maine sur lie **Élevé en Fût de Chêne 98**, which also gains a star. This wine, characterised by wood, exhibits a nose of exotic nuances, spicy and smoky, before revealing a fresh and well-balanced palate (30–49F).
Jean Bosseau, Dom. des Chausselières, 12, rue des Vignes, 44330 Le Pallet, tel. 02.40.80.40.12, fax 02.40.80.46.42 by appt.

CH. DU COING DE SAINT FIACRE

Sur lie 1999★

☐ 6 ha 26,600 30–49 F

The most 'Sèvre-et-Maine' that can be because the château is on the confluence of the Sèvre and the Maine, this Muscadet is still a bit closed on the nose but is fine, fruity and well structured on the palate, and quite full, unveiling a toasty nose, a sign of maturity. From the same producer, **Château de la Gravelle Grande Cuvée Don Quichotte 99** (a reference to the fact that the château is actually a windmill) also gains a star. Clear and well structured, it distinguishes itself with a gassy release, giving it a vigorous palate.
Véronique GüntherChéreau, Ch. du Coing de Saint-Fiacre, 44690 Saint-Fiacre-sur-Maine, tel. 02.40.54.85.24, fax 02.40.54.80.21 by appt.

DOM. DU COLOMBIER

Sur lie Cuvée des deux colombes 1999★★

☐ 3 ha 17,000 20–29 F

This estate is in Maine-et-Loire, at the eastern edge of the Muscadet area. In 1999 it produced a fine, slightly sparkling wine with a subtle, mineral nose and a very polished palate. Rich and distinguished, this Deux Colombes wine is seductive to the last note of its fresh finish. It could be left for two or three years. The estate also offers a very successful **Gros-Plant du Pays Nantais sur lie 99** (less than 20F).
Jean-Yves Bretaudeau, Le Colombier, 49230 Tillières, tel. 02.41.70.45.96, fax 02.41.70.45.96, e-mail bretodo@free.fr by appt.

GILDAS CORMERAIS

Sur lie Prestige Vieilles vignes 1999★★

☐ 2 ha 9,500 20–29 F

Produced between Saint-Fiacre and Maisdon, this Prestige wine does not go unnoticed due to its agreeable nose of mango and its perfectly balanced palate, with fruity and mineral notes. Clean and fresh, it will gain even more with a few months' age.
EARL Gildas Cormerais, La Bretonnière, 44690 Maisdon-sur-Sèvre, tel. 02.40.36.90.13, fax 02.40.36.99.95 by appt.

COUR MAJESTIERE Sur lie 1999★

☐ n.c. n.c. 20–29 F

Majestic though it is, this wine's name is aimed at the mass market. A good choice, as this very mineral Muscadet shows a lot of finesse. With a clean first impression, it also has a pleasing finish.
Félix Loizeau, chem. Vieilles Caves, 44690 Maisdon-sur-Sèvre, tel. 02.40.06.62.80

CHRISTOPHE DROUARD

Sur lie Sélection des Hauts Pémions 1999★

☐ 3 ha 15,000 30–49 F

Christophe and Joseph Drouard's estate is on the left bank of the Sèvre, between Monnières and Saint-Fiacre. These producers offer a typically local wine with a fine, pale colour and quite an intense fruity nose. A gassy peak and an acidulous finish give it an agreeable freshness on the palate.
SCEA Joseph et Christophe Drouard, La Hallopière, 44690 Monnières, tel. 02.40.54.61.26, fax 02.40.54.65.32 by appt.

DOM. DES FEVRIES Sur lie 1999★

☐ 4 ha 10,000 20–29 F

The commune of Maisdon runs between the Sèvre and Maine. The village of La Févrie, at the far north, is allowed the suffix 'sur Sèvre', and it is here that Guy Branger settled in 1974. His Muscadet de Sèvre-et-Maine sur lie, almost white, respects the spirit of the terroir. After an open nose, the first impression is clean and leaves a pleasant touch of acidity on the palate.
Guy Branger, La Févrie, 44690 Maisdon-sur-Sèvre, tel. 02.40.36.90.41, fax 02.40.36.90.41 by appt.

LOIRE

ALAIN FORGET

Sur lie Pierres blanches 1999★★

☐ 2.5 ha 13,000 20–29 F

This Muscadet de Sèvre-et-Maine sur lie, with green tints, comes from 45-year-old vines, planted on an undersoil of gneiss and mica granite. It exhibits the character of its terroir, distinguished by floral and fruity notes on the nose. Complex and well structured, it develops fresh flavours of fruit on the palate and ends with an acidulous finish.

Alain Forget, La Gautronnière, 44330 La Chapelle-Heulin, tel. 02.40.06.75.84, fax 02.40.06.75.84 ev. day 9am–7pm; Sun. by appt.

GADAIS PERE ET FILS

Sur lie La Grande Réserve du Moulin 1999★

☐ 9 ha 60,000 30–49 F

Since windmills abound in the wine-growing areas of Nantes, we should specify that this one is La Faubretière, ideally located on a south-facing hill on the right bank of the Sèvre. This very fruity (citrus fruit, green apple) wine is rounded and well balanced, with a fresh first impression that is echoed in the fine and lively finish. Also worth noting (with no star) is the Muscadet de Sèvre-et-Maine **Domaine de la Tourmaline 99**, whose expressive palate is typical of the region (20–29F).

Gadais Père et Fils, 16 bis, rue du Coteau, 44690 Saint-Fiacre, tel. 02.40.54.81.23, fax 02.40.36.70.25

CLOS DU GAUFFRIAUD

Sur lie 1999★

☐ 0.8 ha 5,000 20 F+

This small parcel of land (less than 1 ha/2.5 acres) used to belong to the Château de Beauchêne, whose crenellated walls can still be seen close by. In 1999 it produced a Muscadet de Sèvre-et-Maine sur lie with good character: tender, fruity and fresh. It should be drunk before the end of 2001.

Jean-Luc Viaud, La Renouère, 44430 Le Landreau, tel. 02.40.06.45.43, fax 02.40.06.45.43 ev. day except Sun. 9am–12.30pm 3pm–7pm; cl. 15–31 Aug.

GRANDE GARDE 1999★

☐ 5 ha 10,000 50–69 F

The Buollaults have, for a long time, been pioneers of Muscadet de Garde. The unanimous decision of the jury: this quality wine, not matured *sur lie*, will benefit from ageing at least two years. Nevertheless, it already shows itself as very structured and rich, revealing on the palate notes of grapefruit and a terroir character.

Boullault et Frères, La Touche, 44330 Vallet, tel. 02.40.33.95.30, fax 02.40.36.26.85, e-mail boullault-fils@wanadoo.fr by appt.

CH. DES GRANDES NOELLES

Sur lie 1999★

☐ 4 ha 30,000 30–49 F

Strategically situated at the meeting of the roads from Saint-Fiacre to Gorges and from Monnières to Maisdon, the Poiron family's estate produces a wine with strawberry notes. The structured 99 wine is typical of the vintage, characterised by a fine first impression and a good length on the palate. It would go well with fish. Although not gaining any stars, the **Muscadet** and the Gros-Plant du Pays Nantais sur lie **Domaine des Quatre Routes 99** (20–29F) warrant a mention.

SA Henri Poiron et Fils, Dom. des Quatre-Routes, 44690 Maisdon-sur-Sèvre, tel. 02.40.54.60.58, fax 02.40.54.62.05 by appt.

GRAND FIEF DE LA CLAVELIERE

Sur lie Grande Réserve 1995★

☐ 2 ha 2,000 30–49 F

At the far southern edge of the appellation, between Aigrefeuille and Saint-Lumine-de-Clisson, the estate of Louis Chatellier and son offers, in small quantities, a wine with a fresh and complex nose, slightly aniseed. Round and supple on the palate, refreshed by a touch of carbonic gas (CO_2), this 95 vintage has still not breathed its last breath.

Louis Chatellier et Fils, La Clavelière, 44190 Saint-Lumine-de-Clisson, tel. 02.40.06.61.40, fax 02.40.06.69.02 by appt.

GRAND FIEF DE L'AUDIGERE

Sur lie 1999★★

☐ 15 ha 80,000 30–49 F

Jean Aubron, an important Vallet producer, has succeeded with this very good Muscadet de Sèvre-et-Maine. The fine, pale yellow colour and especially the complex and pleasant nose, characteristic of the terroir, announce straight away an interesting wine. Very expressive on the palate, it ends with a long and acidulous finish. This is a wine for keeping, which would go well with sea bass with beurre blanc or encrusted in salt. In the same appellation, **La Fleurielle 99** is a great success, its nose of peachy apricot and dried fruit announcing a full and balanced palate.

Jean Aubron, L'Audigère, 44330 Vallet, tel. 02.40.33.91.91, fax 02.40.33.91.91

GREGOIRE

Sur lie 1999★★

☐ 4.5 ha 7,000 20–29 F

The vineyards of this estate stretch over three communes, the length of the banks of the Sanguèze, the third river of Sèvre-et-Maine. Lively on the eye and strong on the nose, this Muscadet de Sèvre-et-Maine sur lie is at the same time elegant and smooth. It follows a supple first impression with jasmine and lemon aromas.

🗝 Pierre-Henri et Patricia Grégoire, SCEA Les coteaux de la Sanguèze, Beauregard, 44330 Mouzillon, tel. 02.40.36.45.64 ☑ Y by appt.

GUILBAUD FRERES

Sur lie Grand Or 1999★★

☐ 40 ha 250,000 ▮ ♁ 20–29 F

Strong and expressive, the chlorophyllous nose foretells a well-structured palate: length and balance without the slightest jolt. Also from Guilbaud Frères, two other Muscadets de Sèvre-et-Maine sur lie deserve a star: **Le Soleil Nantais 99**, for its acidulous nose of green apples and citrus fruit as well as its fresh palate, and **Château de la Pingossière Tête de Cuvée 99**, for its length and minty note (30–49F each).

🗝 Guilbaud Frères, Les Lilas, 44330 Mouzillon, tel. 02.40.36.30.55, fax 02.40.36.36.35, e-mail guilbaud.muscadet@wanadoo.fr ☑ Y by appt.

HAUTE-COUR DE LA DEBAUDIERE Sur lie 1999★★

☐ 10.73 ha 74,000 ▮ ♁ 20–29 F

Above the twists of the Sanguèze, upstream of Mouzillon, Chantal and Yves Goislot have produced a clear and very pale wine. It is characterised by its clean, fruity and mineral nose, and then by its lively and slightly sparkling palate. With no star, **Gros-Plant du Pays Nantais sur lie 99** deserves a mention for its mineral nose and its open fruit on the palate (less than 20FF, bought locally).

🗝 Chantal et Yves Goislot, La Débaudière, 44330 Vallet, tel. 02.40.36.30.73, fax 02.40.36.20.23 ☑ Y by appt.

CH. DU JAUNAY Sur lie 1999★

☐ 21.4 ha 50,000 ▮ ♁ 20 F+

This lovely little neoclassical château, typical of the 19th-century follies of the area, has produced a wine with a fruity nose and rounded palate, which also has good length. Also worth pointing out (without a star) from the same producer is the mineral and fine Gros-Plant du Pays Nantais sur lie **Domaine de la Taraudière 99**.

🗝 GAEC Madeleineau Père et Fils, Dom. de L'Errière, 44430 Le Landreau, tel. 02.40.06.43.94, fax 02.40.06.48.82 ☑ Y by appt.

DOM. DE LA BAZILLIERE

Sur lie Prestige 1999★★

☐ 1.6 ha 10,600 ▮ ♁ 20–29 F

Planted on the southern slopes of Landreau, La Bazillière offers a clear wine, with a complex aroma on the nose as well as on the palate. Strong and well structured, this Muscadet de Sèvre-et-Maine sur lie is ready to drink but could be left for a year or two.

🗝 Jean-Michel Sauvêtre, La Bazillière, 44430 Le Landreau, tel. 02.40.06.40.14, fax 02.40.06.40.14 ☑ Y by appt.

DOM. DE LA BERNARDIERE

Sur lie 1999★

☐ n.c. 12,000 ▮ ♁ 20 F+

Destroyed during the Revolution, La Bernardière survived the Second World War, in thanks for which a grotto in the image of the one at Lourdes was built. This Muscadet is floral, lemony and mineral on the nose and light, pleasing and well balanced on the palate. It's a shame, though, that the flavour does not last a bit longer.

🗝 Dominique Coraleau, 14, rue des Châteaux, La Bernardière, 44330 La ChapelleHeulin, tel. 02.40.06.76.21, fax 02.40.06.76.21 ☑ Y by appt.

CH. DE LA BERRIERE

Sur lie La Cuvée des Rebelles 1997★★

☐ 1 ha 8,000 ⦀ 30–49 F

This Muscadet de Sèvre-et-Maine with a white label, matured in the barrel, is dedicated to the 1793 rebels of Vendée, who fought against the Revolution. Very strong, round and mineral, the wine exhibits a pronounced terroir character. Despite its mature aromas of honey, wax, and breadcrumbs, its strong personality will allow for another few years of ageing.

🗝 SCEA La Berrière, Ch. de La Berrière, 44450 Barbechat, tel. 02.40.06.34.22, fax 02.40.03.61.96 ☑ Y by appt.
🗝 de Bascher

DOM. DE LA BIGOTIERE

Sur lie 1999★

☐ 4.5 ha 28,000 ▮ ♁ 20–29 F

A typical Muscadet de Sèvre-et-Maine sur lie in all regards. Fine and floral on the nose, ample, harmonious and lightly mineral on the palate, it can be left comfortably for a year or two. The La Bigotière estate also produces a very successful **Muscadet de Sèvre-et-Maine Élevé en Fût de Chêne 99**, which is fresh and elegant.

🗝 Pascal Batard, La Bigotière, 44690 Maisdon-sur-Sèvre, tel. 02.40.06.67.02, fax 02.40.33.56.79 ☑ Y by appt.

DOM. DE LA BLANCHETIERE

Sur lie Vieilles vignes 1999★★

☐ 3 ha 5,000 ▮ ♁ 20–29 F

According to a document, the Luneau family cultivated grapes at Blanchetière as early as 1476. The 25-year-old vines produce a clear wine, with a mineral nose characteristic of the terroir. A little austere on the finish, its long palate is nevertheless very well balanced. The estate has also produced a **Gros-Plant du Pays Nantais sur lie 99** which is rich and long and recommended by the jury.

🗝 Christophe Luneau, Dom. de La Blanchetière, 44430 Le Loroux-Bottereau, tel. 02.40.06.43.18, fax 02.40.06.43.18 ☑ Y by appt.

DOM. DE LA BRETONNIERE

Sur lie Cuvée Prestige Vieilles vignes 1999★

☐ 2 ha 10,000 🍷 🌡 20–29 F

These are certainly old vines as they have passed a half-century. Their potential is great, as is shown by this wine with straightforward aromas typical of the terroir, which produces a very good impression on the palate. Long and well structured, this 99 vintage ends on a fine finish.

🔑 GAEC Joël et Bertrand Cormerais, La Bretonnière, 44690 Maisdonsur-Sèvre, tel. 02.40.54.83.91, fax 02.40.36.73.45 ☑ 🍸 ev. day 8am–8pm; Sun. 8am–12 noon

CH. DE LA CANTRIE Sur lie 1999

☐ 15 ha 80,000 🍷 🌡 20–29 F

The soils of La Cantrie, on the left bank of the Sèvre, are among the most uneven of the Nantes wine-growing region. Formed from mica schist and gneiss on certain terraced plantings, they produce a Muscadet de Sèvre-et-Maine with a nose of green apples and a fleshiness that gives a fine first impression and length on the palate.

🔑 Laurent Bossis, 11, rue Beauregard, 44690 Saint-Fiacre-sur-Maine, tel. 02.40.36.94.64, fax 02.40.54.87.60 ☑ 🍸 by appt.

LA CHATELIERE Sur lie 1999★

☐ 71 ha 500,000 🍷 🌡 20 F+

Based at the edge of the Muscadet de Sèvre-et-Maine area, La Chatelière offers this mass-market wine, its strong nose dominated by aromas of exotic fruit. With an especially expressive attack, it has a good structure. Also worth mentioning (without a star) are the Muscadet de Sèvre-et-Maine sur lie **Cave de Val et Mont 99** and the supple and full Gros-Plant du Pays Nantais sur lie **Cave de la Perrière 99**.

🔑 Rolandeau SA, La Frémonderie, B.P. 2, 49230 Tillières, tel. 02.41.70.45.93, fax 02.41.70.43.74

CH. DE LA CORMERAIS

Sur lie 1999★

☐ 17 ha 10,000 🍷 🌡 20 F+

Currently being renovated, this estate was in the Middle Ages the seat of a lord; a moat and drawbridge protected it then. Nowadays it owes its renown to a very aromatic wine. The 99 vintage is lively on the palate, revealing a good balance, and promises to improve after a few months' keeping.

🔑 Thierry Besnard, La Cormerais, 44690 Monnières, tel. 02.40.06.95.58, fax 02.40.06.50.76 ☑ 🍸 by appt.

L'EXCELLENCE DE LA CORNULIERE Sur lie 1999★

☐ 1.5 ha 8,000 🍷 🌡 20–29 F

Halfway between Gorges and Mouzillon, this estate has produced a wine with a nose that, slightly closed at first, opens up on airing to unveil aromas of the terroir. In contrast to the impression on the nose, the palate is harmonious and subtle, full and long. A Muscadet de Sèvre-et-Maine to be drunk until the end of 2001.

🔑 Jean-Michel Barreau, La Cornulière, 44190 Gorges, tel. 02.40.03.95.06, fax 02.40.54.23.13 ☑ 🍸 by appt.

DOM. DE LA COUR DU CHATEAU DE LA POMMERAIE

Sur lie 1999★

☐ 14 ha 90,000 🍷 🌡 20–29 F

After an eventful past, the Château de la Pommeraie has become a professional training centre; its vineyard, which had been broken up for a long time, has been reborn under the leadership of the Poilane family. The 99 vintage, with a very white colour, is expressive on the palate thanks to its length and its slight sparkle. It would go well with seafood and shellfish. One star has also been awarded to the **Gros-Plant du Pays Nantais sur lie 99** from this estate, an almost colourless wine that is fine, fruity and fleshy on the palate.

🔑 Albert Poilane, La Cour du ch. de La Pommeraie, 44330 Vallet, tel. 02.40.33.80.63 ☑ 🍸 by appt.

DOM. DE LA FOLIETTE

Sur lie Vieilles vignes 1999★★

☐ 10 ha 60,000 🍷 🌡 30–49 F

Among the 'follies' (country properties) of Nantes shipowners during the 18th century, some were smaller than others; La Foliette fits into this category. Its Muscadet de Sèvre-et-Maine sur lie exhibits quite an intense nose of peach and exotic fruit. Rich and complex on the palate, it shows full regional character. Its fruity flavours finish with a lengthy charm.

🔑 GAEC Dom. de La Foliette, La Foliette, 44690 La Haye-Fouassière, tel. 02.40.36.92.28, fax 02.40.36.98.16 ☑ 🍸 by appt.

DOM. DE LA FRUITIERE

Sur lie 1999★★

☐ 9 ha 60,000 🍷 🌡 20–29 F

This major family estate is at the western edge of the Muscadet de Sèvre-et-Maine area, on the left bank of the Maine. The 99 vintage aroused the enthusiasm of the jury for its fruity and mineral nose, leaving an impression of undeniable finesse and elegance, a feeling that remains on the palate when flavours of bitter almond appear. Its good structure assures its potential for keeping.

🗝 J. Douillard et J.-M. Boussonnière, Dom. de La Fruitière, 44690 Château-Thébaud, tel. 02.40.06.53.05, fax 02.40.06.54.55 ☑ Y ev. day except Sat. Sun. 8am–12.30pm 2pm–6.30pm; groups by appt.

CH. DE LA GALISSONNIERE

Sur lie Cuvée Prestige 1999★★

☐ 15 ha 100,000 ▮ 🌡 20-29 F

This large estate belonged to Admiral Roland Barin de la Galissonnière, governor of Canada under Louis XV. All that remains of the château, destroyed during the Vendée wars, are the outbuildings. Its Cuvée Prestige is deserving of its name. Typical of the appellation, it exhibits a lot of expression and does not lack finesse and length.

🗝 EARL Vignobles Lusseaud, Ch. de La Galissonnière, 44330 Le Pallet, tel. 02.40.80.42.03, fax 02.40.80.90.27 ☑ Y ev. day 8am–12.30pm 1.30pm–6.30pm

DOM. DE LA GARNIERE

Sur lie Cuvée Vieilles vignes 1999★

☐ 2 ha 12,500 ▮ 🌡 20-29 F

Though the vines from which it comes are 50 years old, this wine was described as 'modern' by one of the tasters. Lively and well balanced, it demonstrates much freshness and elegance on the palate, and a very light sparkle gives it a pleasant liveliness.

🗝 Dom. de La Garnière, la Hautière, 44690 Saint-Fiacre-sur-Maine, tel. 02.40.54.88.07, fax 02.40.54.88.07 ☑ Y by appt.

🗝 Patrice David

LA GOELETTE Sur lie 1999★★

☐ 100 ha 300,000 ▮ 🌡 20-29 F

Year after year the wine-makers of La Noëlle succeed in marrying quantity with quality. La Goélette is in all respects very pleasant: a powerfully aromatic nose, lively and full on the palate, and well balanced. The Muscadet des Coteaux de la Loire **Les Folies Siffait 99** – a well-rounded wine – warrants a star, while the Muscadet Côtes de Grand Lieu **L'Aiguière 99** is also worth a mention. The **Coteaux d'Ancenis, le Gamay Cour de Rohan 99** (one star and less than 20F, bought locally) is certainly more of a classic than the VdL Pineau de la Loire, **Les Champs Jumeaux 99** (mentioned without a star). This last, sold in 50cl bottles (20–29F), would benefit from leaving for a few months.

🗝 Les Vignerons de La Noëlle, bd des Alliés, B.P. 155, 44154 Ancenis Cedex, tel. 02.40.98.92.72, fax 02.40.98.96.70, e-mail vavenel@cana.fr ☑ Y by appt.

DOM. DE LA GRENAUDIERE

Sur lie 1999★

☐ 15 ha 100,000 ▮ 🌡 30-49 F

From the hillsides of the Maine, this pale wine with green tints exhibits a nose of flowers and exotic fruits. Elegant and fine on the palate, it demonstrates true harmony. The estate has also produced a Muscadet de Sèvre-et-Maine which, although not benefiting from bottling *sur lie*, is nevertheless very pleasant (one star); lively and pleasing, it is a café-style Muscadet that should be drunk young.

🗝 GAEC Ollivier Père et Fils, La Grenaudière, 44690 Maisdon-sur-Sèvre, tel. 02.40.06.62.58, fax 02.40.06.66.35 ☑ Y ev. day except Sun. 9.30am–12.30pm 2.30pm–7pm

DOM. DE LA HAIE TROIS SOLS

Fût de chêne 1996★

☐ 1 ha 3,000 ⦀ 30-49 F

Under this label, Dominique and Vincent Richard have produced, in small quantities, this golden wine that exhibits a strong and complex nose. The buttery, grilled and vanilla aromas are evident, particularly after airing, and remain intact on the palate, accompanied by still-present tannins. As for the Muscadet de Sèvre-et-Maine sur lie **Château du Hallay 99** (20–29F), produced by Fabienne Richard, it comes from 9 ha (22 acres) of vines belonging to a château, of which all that remains is a large park surrounded by walls. This wine also gains a star due to its seductive perfumed nose, sweet first impression and full and ample palate.

🗝 SCEA Dominique et Vincent Richard, La Cognardière, 44330 Le Pallet, tel. 02.40.80.42.30, fax 02.40.80.44.37, e-mail fabienne.richard-detournay@wanadoo.fr ☑ Y by appt.

DOM. DE LA HAIE TROIS-SOLS

Sur lie Cuvée des Sages Sélection 2000 1998★

☐ 0.75 ha 4,000 ▮ 🌡 30-49 F

As announced by a fine colour of green with golden tints, the palate opens with a supple first impression then develops complex flavours, notably bitter almond, before a pleasant and fruity finish. The wine can be happily left in the cellar.

🗝 Pierrick et Pierre Lebas, La Haie Trois-sols, 44690 Maisdon-sur-Sèvre, tel. 02.40.54.81.04, fax 02.51.71.60.15 Y by appt.

DOM. DE LA HARDONNIERE

Sur lie 1999★★

☐ 13 ha 30,000 ▮ 🌡 20-29 F

A neighbour of the famous Château de Goulaine, this domaine has produced a fine wine with green tints. With an unobtrusive nose, the hints of lemon are more evident on the palate, where they are enriched by a mineral note. A touch of carbonic gas (CO_2) adds a freshness to the mix.

🗝 Jean-Michel Bouyer, 19, imp. de La Hardonnière, 44115 Haute-Goulaine, tel. 02.40.54.93.16, fax 02.40.54.93.16 ☑ Y by appt.

DOM. DE LA JOCONDE

Sur lie 1999★★

☐ 5 ha 35,000 ▮ 🌡 20-29 F

Situated in the south, above the Sèvre, Le Pé is a small, charming village. This remarkable, slightly sparkling wine is worthy of interest. A pale yellow colour with green tints,

it exhibits a very mineral nose, giving it the terroir character. On the palate, it develops a rich and acidulous flavour.
⊶ Yves Maillard, Le Pé-de-Sèvre, 44330 Le Pallet, tel. 06.08.27.07.64, fax 06.40.80.43.29 ☒ Y by appt.

DOM. DE LA LEVRAUDIERE
Sur lie Vieilles vignes 1999★★

☐	2 ha	12,000		20–29 F

During the 15th century La Levraudière belonged to the Blandin family, whose motto still decorates the monumental fireplace at the residence. Today, it is a fine Muscadet de Sèvre-et-Maine sur lie, complex and full-bloomed, which marks out the estate. Rounded and balanced, it is already very pleasant, but its fruity bouquet will develop even more over a few months.
⊶ Françoise et Alain Gripon, La Levraudière, 44330 La Chapelle-Heulin, tel. 02.40.06.76.38, fax 02.40.06.76.38 ☒ Y ev. day 9am–7pm; Sun. by appt.

DOM. DE LA LEVRAUDIERE
Sur lie Prestige de la Levraudière 1999★★

☐	5 ha	30,000	▮ 🌡	20–29 F

Remarkably consistent (its Cuvée Prestige 98 was highly regarded), this estate, built on the remains of the residence of Breton Count Hoël, founder of La Chapelle-Heulin, offers a wine with a white colour and an agreeable nose of mint and morello cherries. With a fruity palate, strong and even heady, the 99 vintage ends on a fresh finish. Its balance promises a good future. **L'Héritage 96 sur lie** (30–49F), which is characterised by being made from very late-picked grapes and by a long maturation, is worthy of its name, as it demonstrates the Burgundy origins of Muscadet; one star offers a token of esteem for its nose of dried fruit and its lengthy and round palate.
⊶ Bonnet-Huteau, Dom. de La Levraudière, 44330 La Chapelle-Heulin, tel. 02.40.06.73.87, fax 02.40.06.77.56 ☒ Y ev. day 8.30am–12.30pm 2pm–6pm; Sun. by appt.

DOM. DE LA LOUVETRIE
Sur lie Fief du Breil Révélation d'un terroir 1997★★

☐	2 ha	n.c.	▮ 🌡	50–69 F

On the Breil hill, above a twist in the Sèvre, Bernard and Joseph, the sons of Pierre Landron, cultivate a small parcel of land, whose yield is limited to 38 hl/ha (410 gal/acre). They have hereby obtained a fine wine with a steady colour, which exhibits on the nose as well as on the palate the mineral and smoky aromas characteristic of this particular terroir. Full and long, this expressive 97 vintage will continue to develop well over the following years. Another one to keep (with no star) is the **Gros-Plant du Pays Nantais sur lie 99** (20–29F).
⊶ Joseph et Bernard Landron, Les Domaines Landron, Les Brandières, 44690 La HaieFouassière, tel. 02.40.54.83.27, fax 02.40.54.89.82 ☒ Y by appt.

L'AME DU TERROIR Sur lie 1999★★

☐	n.c.	220,000	▮ 🌡	20–29 F

Produced by a *négociant*, this full and round wine, with a pleasant slight sparkle, exhibits a whole range of aromatic nuances (exotic fruit, lime, mineral). On the palate, it proves well balanced by its mineral and lengthy substance. The **Cuvée des 7 Lunes 99** (one star) continues the local wine-making tradition of leaving the Muscadet *sur lie* over a period of seven moons; it is a typical Muscadet, lively and fruity on the palate.
⊶ SA Marcel Sautejeau, Dom. de L'Hyvernière, 44330 Le Pallet, tel. 02.40.06.73.83, fax 02.40.06.76.49, e-mail marcelsautejeau@marcel-sautejeau.fr

DOM. DE LA MORILLERE
Sur lie 1999★★

☐	20 ha	6,000		20–29 F

Behind the famous mound of La Roche, La Morillère produces this well-balanced wine with complex aromas and evocative of a low-temperature fermentation. Moderately long on the palate, but fine and very fresh, it is a wine to be drunk among friends.
⊶ EARL Lechat Fils, La Morillère, 44430 Le Loroux Bottereau, tel. 02.40.33.82.99, fax 02.40.33.82.99 ☒ Y by appt.

CH. LA MORINIERE
Sur lie 1ere cuvée du Château 1999★

☐	13.5 ha	82,000	▮ 🌡	20–29 F

At the eastern edge of the appellation, the major GAEC de la Grande Ragotière has produced a wine with an aromatic nose of white-fleshed peach and the character of the terroir. With good length, the 99 vintage has attained the wished-for balance and finesse. One star also goes to the Muscadet de Sèvre-et-Maine **Collection Privée des Frères Couillaud 97** (from the names of the three proprietors) (30–49F), which is fine, lively and balanced.
⊶ Les Frères Couillaud, GAEC de La Grande Ragotière, 44330 Vallet-LaRegrippière, tel. 02.40.33.60.56, fax 02.40.33.61.89, e-mail frères.couillaud@wanadoo.fr ☒ Y by appt.

DOM. LANDES DES CHABOISSIERES Sur lie 1999★★

☐	14 ha	54,000	▮ 🌡	20–29 F

Perhaps an echo of the controversy that the Chaboissières region was subject to for almost a hundred years up to the mid–19th century: while one taster judged this wine to be merely 'a success', the others found it 'remarkable' for its complex, full, rich and balanced nose and palate.
⊶ Georges et Guy Desfossés, Dom. Landes des Chaboissières, 44330 Vallet, tel. 02.40.33.99.54, fax 02.40.33.99.54 ☒ Y by appt.

DOM. DE LA PAPINIERE

Sur lie Sélection du Moulin 1999★★

☐ 15.5 ha 9,000 20–29 F

On a hill dissected by the Sangèze and the stream La Braudière as well as the Nantes to Cholet road, this major estate produces a well-balanced wine, which should be kept. Signalled by a nose of linden flowers and alcohol, the structure and strength give the wine a great intensity on the palate.

GAEC Cousseau Frères, La Papinière, 49230 Tillières, tel. 02.41.70.46.31, fax 02.41.58.61.51 Y by appt.

DOM. DE LA PROUTIERE

Sur lie Cuvée royale 1999★

☐ 4 ha 15,000 20–29 F

Between Gorges and Mouzillon, the estate of La Proutière has produced a clear wine with a floral and clean, mineral nose. Rounded and strong, with a quite lively finish on the palate, it shows potential.

GAEC Claude Blanchard et Fils, Le Quarteron, 44190 Gorges, tel. 02.40.54.07.82, fax 02.40.36.01.76 Y ev. day except Sun. 8am–1pm 1.30pm–7.30pm

DOM. DE LA ROCHE BLANCHE

Sur lie 1999★

☐ 12.4 ha 30,000 20–29 F

Under the same name, this estate produces a Muscadet sur lie 99 and a Muscadet de Sèvre-et-Maine, which are both a success. The latter is typical of the character of the terroir, and a slight sparkle gives it some liveliness on the palate. Fruity and lengthy, it is pleasant from beginning to end.

EARL Lechat et Fils, 12, av. des Roses, 44330 Vallet, tel. 02.40.33.94.77, fax 02.40.36.44.31 Y by appt.

LA SANCIVE Sur lie 1999★

☐ n.c. 143,200 20–29 F

Drouet Frères, one of the oldest négociants (who also mature the wine) of the Nantes region, export to 56 countries across the world. This wine is a fine ambassador. Its elegant nose unveils hints of exotic fruit and coconut. Well balanced on the nose, it combines suppleness with length, before unmasking a mineral hint. One star also goes to **Le Grand Duc 99** (30–49F), a clean and well-balanced wine, with its character of the terroir intact; it could be kept for a number of years.

SA Drouet Frères, 8, bd du Luxembourg, 44330 Vallet, tel. 02.40.36.65.20, fax 02.40.33.99.78 Y by appt.

DOM. DE LA TOURLAUDIERE

Sur lie Cuvée Vieilles vignes 1999★★

☐ 6 ha 20,000 30–49 F

There are only a few thousand bottles of this cuvée, which comes from 40-year-old vines planted on a mica schist and granite soil. Lengthy and balanced with a pleasant white colour, it reveals plenty of harmony. La Tourlaudière has also produced a **Gros-Plant du Pays Nantais sur lie 99** (20–29F) which is a great success and distinguishes itself with its fine first impression.

EARL Petiteau-Gaubert, La Tourlaudière, 44330 Vallet, tel. 02.40.36.24.86, fax 02.40.36.29.72, e-mail contact@tourlaudiere.com Y ev. day 9am–12.30pm 2pm–7pm

Famille Petiteau

DOM. DE L'AUBINERIE

Sur lie 1999★★★

☐ 2.5 ha 12,000 30–49 F

Mouzillon, the Versailles of Muscadet, hides a miraculous fountain dedicated to Saint Julien. Is Jean-Marc Guérin's 99 vintage miraculous? It is, at the very least, exceptional . . . A small output, but big on quality: this Muscadet de Sèvre-et-Maine sur lie, very clear, reveals a rounded and very polished structure on the palate. It is, at the same time, fine and well balanced. The most elegant shellfish and fish dishes will go well with it.

Jean-Marc Guérin, 26, La Barillère, 44330 Mouzillon, tel. 02.40.36.37.06, fax 02.40.36.37.06 Y by appt.

DOM. DE L'AULNAYE

Sur lie Cuvée Prestige 1999★

☐ 6 ha 20,000 20 F+

Close to the confluence of the Sèvre and Maine, De l'Aulnaye produces a characterful wine, gifted with a sensuous nose of honey and crystallised orange. Supple and rich on the palate, it ends on a note of liquorice following a fine fruity expression.

Pierre-Yves Perthuy, L'Aulnaye, 44120 Vertou, tel. 02.40.34.70.22, fax 02.40.34.70.22

DOM. DE L'EBEAUPIN Sur lie 1999★

☐ 3 ha 25,000 20–29 F

Perched on a granite promontory 40 m (44 yd) above the Maine, this domaine offers a wine of clear and brilliant colour. Quite typical, it delivers lively minty aromas before developing its roundness in a balanced style.

Gilles Poiron, La Bretonnière, 44690 Maisdon-sur-Sèvre, tel. 02.40.36.94.19, fax 02.40.36.71.42 Y ev. day 8am–12 noon 2pm–6pm

LE CLOS ARMAND Sur lie 1998★

☐ 1 ha 5,000 20–29 F

Michel Delhommeau has grown fond of diversifying his range and has obtained some interesting results, regularly mentioned in the *Guide*. This is the case with this Clos Armand, which is very clear, fine and fruity. With a supple first impression, it becomes lively on the palate towards the finish. Also receiving one star is **Les Vignes Saint-Vincent 99**, a Muscadet de Sèvre-et-Maine which is not matured *sur lies*. Its aromas of apple are pleasing and it is also well balanced and representative of the appellation (less than 20F).

🔑 Michel Delhommeau, La Huperie, 44690 Monnières, tel. 02.40.54.60.37, fax 02.40.54.64.51 ☑ 🍷 by appt.

LE FIEF COGNARD

Sur lie Clos de La Bastière Vieilles vignes 1999★

☐ 16 ha 100,000 20 F+

Dominique Salmon has been established, since 1984, at the Château Thébaud, a pretty village raised on a rocky promontory. Coming from 40-year-old vines planted on a gneiss soil on the left bank of the Maine, very close to its confluence with the Sèvre, his rich and aromatic wine with green tints exhibits an acidulous, very pleasing character.

🔑 Dominique Salmon, Les Landes de Vin, 44690 Château-Thébaud, tel. 02.40.06.53.66, fax 02.40.06.55.42 ☑ 🍷 by appt.

LE GRAND R DE LA GRANGE

Sur lie 1999★

☐ 3 ha 15,000 30–49 F

This very professional estate produces Muscadet in different forms, all of which are interesting. With a crystal colour, this well-balanced Grand R is typical of the 99 vintage. Fresh and lengthy on the palate and quite dry, it well expresses the style of the terroir. A star also goes to Gros-Plant du Pays Nantais sur lie **Domaine R de la Grange 99 Vieilles Vignes**, which is fruity and mineral (20–29F).

🔑 Rémy Luneau, La Grange, 44430 Le Landreau, tel. 02.40.06.45.65, fax 02.40.06.48.17 ☑ 🍷 ev. day except Sun. 9am–12 noon 2pm–6pm

LE MOULIN DES BOIS Sur lie 1999★★

☐ 1.5 ha 9,000 20–29 F

Set alight by lightning right in the middle of the 1961 harvest, the windmill has recently been restored to offer a view of the vineyard. Its grapes are the origin of a wine that is remarkable for its balance and harmony. Without excessive roundness or aggressiveness, it has a charming finesse and good length.

🔑 Gilles Savary, Les Bois, 44330 la Chapelle-Heulin, tel. 02.40.06.76.86, fax 02.40.06.76.86 ☑ 🍷 ev. day 8am–8pm; Sun. 8am–1pm

DOM. DE L'EPINAY Sur lie 1999★★

☐ 2.5 ha 10,000 20–29 F

Located between Moine and Sanguèze, this property belonged in the 16th century to a family of Spanish merchants. Nowadays it offers a Muscadet de Sèvre-et-Maine that is very clear and quite characteristic, with a controlled acidity. **L'Espinose 99** (30–49F), a Muscadet de Sèvre-et-Maine whose 96 vintage was higly acclaimed, is matured in oak barrels and is mentioned for its elegant and rich palate.

🔑 EARL Albert Paquereau, L'Epinay, 44190 Clisson, tel. 02.40.36.13.57, fax 02.40.36.13.57 ☑ 🍷 by appt.

CH. LES AVENEAUX Sur lie 1999★

☐ 20 ha 40,000 20–29 F

Between La Chapelle-Heulin and Monnières, Les Aveneaux produces a golden-yellow wine with a strong and agreeable nose of flowers and honey. Clean and round on the palate it is, without a doubt, well balanced.

🔑 Charpentier Fils, Ch. Les Aveneaux, Les Aveneaux, 44330 La Chapelle-Heulin, tel. 02.40.06.74.40, fax 02.40.06.77.72 ☑ 🍷 by appt.

DOM. LES DEUX MOULINS

Sur lie 1999★

☐ 2.35 ha 12,000 20 F+

On a hillside by the Sèvre, between La Bidière windmill and La Justice windmill, Olivier Crémet's vineyard stretches for 12 ha (30 acres). He has produced a 99 vintage with a pale yellow colour. With a rich nose (dried and exotic fruits with a touch of mint) and equally rich on the palate, it finishes on a touch of pear and has a good structure.

🔑 Olivier Crémet, La Hallopière, 44690 Monnières, tel. 02.40.54.66.54, fax 02.40.54.66.54 ☑ 🍷 by appt.

DOM. LES JARDINS DE LA MENARDIERE Sur lie 1999★

☐ 2 ha 10,000 20–29 F

In the commune of Vallet, but equidistant from Pallet and La Chapelle-Heulin, Les Jardins de la Ménardière was born from the regrouping of a number of parcels of land surrounding Benoît Grenetier's cellars. In 1999 he produced a rounded wine with a warm and slightly sparkling first impression, which comes into its own.

🔑 Benoît Grenetier, La Ménardière, 44330 Vallet, tel. 02.40.33.93.30 ☑ 🍷 by appt.

LES JARDINS DES AMIRAUX

Sur lie 1999★★

☐ 25 ha 120,000 20–29 F

Three kilometres (1.8 miles) from Pallet, on the Nantes road, Le Pé-de-Sèvre is a very picturesque village. We would give the village itself two stars, as we have this slightly sparkling wine with green tints. The wine shows a good respect for the terroir. It is well balanced, well structured and opens out with aromas of citrus fruit with a mineral hint. Still somewhat closed, it will benefit from leaving for a few months. To be savoured with sea bass in sorrel.

🔑 GIE Gabare de Sèvre, Le Pé-deSèvre, 44330 Le Pallet, tel. 02.40.80.97.30, fax 02.40.36.29.72 🍷 by appt.

MICHEL LUNEAU ET FILS

Sur lie Clos des Bourguignons 1999★

☐ 4.2 ha 29,000 20–29 F

Since the end of the 17th century (even before the wine-growing disaster of 1709 and the planting of the Melon), Burgundians have lived in the village of Pressoir-Bourguignon in a building that is still visible today. This wine pays tribute to them. Quite

characteristic, it displays suppleness and expression on the palate, with a good balance and lots of body. From the same producer, another Muscadet de Sèvre-et-Maine sur lie warrants a mention: **Vins de Mouzillon 99**. Harmonious and also characteristic, it is the little brother of the former, being a little less fleshy.
🔑 GAEC Michel Luneau et Fils, 3, rte de Nantes, 44330 Mouzillon, tel. 02.40.33.95.22, fax 02.40.33.95.22 ☒ Y by appt.

MARIE-LOUISE Sur lie 1999

☐ 79 ha 537,200 ▮ ♁ 20F+

Coming from the fairly new maturation cellars of Vallée Ligérienne, whose proprietor is Antoine Subileau, this wine with a nose of unripe fruit, still quite fresh and straightforward, manifests a very particular character. To appreciate it at its best, it should be left for a year.
🔑 SA Antoine Subileau, 6, rue Saint-Vincent, 44330 Vallet, tel. 02.40.36.69.70, fax 02.40.36.63.99, e-mail antoine-subileau@wanadoo.fr

DOM. MARTIN-LUNEAU 1999★

☐ 2 ha 10,000 ▮ ♁ 20–29 F

A dynamic and characteristic Muscadet de Sèvre-et-Maine. Green tints enliven the pale, brilliant yellow colour. Next a nose of citrus fruit unveils, underlined by a mineral note. This same freshness is noticeable in the balance of the palate, highlighted by citronella aromas.
🔑 Martin-Luneau, Le Magasin, 44190 Gorges, tel. 02.40.54.38.44, fax 02.40.54.07.23 ☒ Y ev. day except Sun. 8am–12.30pm 2pm–6.30pm; cl. during the grape harvest/picking season

MASTER DE DONATIEN Sur lie 1999★★

☐ 11 ha 80,000 ▮ 20–29 F

Le Master is the standard-bearer of the Donatien Bahuaud company. Its pretty green tints draw the eye and prompt discovery of the very aromatic nose, centred on the fruity (peach and citrus) character. Next, the palate fills with smooth, round flavour, marked out in the finish by a note of toasted almond. The wine is ready to drink.
🔑 Donatien Bahuaud, La Loge, B.P. 1, 44330 La Chapelle-Heulin, tel. 02.40.06.70.05, fax 02.40.06.77.11

LOUIS METAIREAU Premier jour 25 Aug. 1989 Sur lie 1989★★★

☐ 4 ha 27,316 ▮ ♁ 100–149 F

'Quite simply magnificent,' sums up one taster. This legendary Muscadet de Sèvre-et-Maine, originating from the first day of the 1989 harvest (the year of the century, according to many), on the famous Grand Mouton terroir, is not a new discovery. The surprise is that it is still progressing, asserting slightly grilled and polished aromas of ripe fruit. Supple and round on the palate, perfectly balanced, it is still far from uttering its last breath.

🔑 GIE Louis Métaireau, La Févrie, 44690 Maisdon-sur-Sèvre, tel. 02.40.54.81.92, fax 02.40.54.87.83 ☒ Y by appt.

METAIREAU Sur lie Hermine 1999

☐ 4 ha 30,000 ▮ ♁ 30–49 F

Fine and fruity on the nose, smooth on the palate, with a slight sparkle, this wine comes from a village almost at the exact centre of the winegrowing region, between the Sèvre and the Maine. Monnières gained its name from another source: the old milling industry, which the many mills still testify to.
🔑 Hermine et Lionel Métaireau, Coursay, 44690 Monnières, tel. 02.40.54.60.08, fax 02.40.54.65.73 ☒ Y ev. day except Sun. 9am–12 noon 2pm–6pm; cl. 15–30 Aug.

DOM. DE MONTIFAULT Sur lie Elevé en fût de chêne neuf 1997★★

☐ 0.5 ha 1000 ⏸ 30–49 F

At the centre of the Pallet–La Haye Fouassière–La Chapelle-Heulin triangle, Montifault offers, in very small quantities (1,000 bottles), a truly original wine. Very complex after airing, the nose unveils not only grilled and buttery but also herbaceous and vanilla nuances. Generous on the palate, quite astringent and still a little too powerful, this fine Muscadet de Sèvre-et-Maine, though somewhat atypical, is none the less remarkable. It can be left for two or three years. Much more characteristic, the Muscadet de Sèvre-et-Maine sur lie **Clos des Vignes Madame 99**, which is floral and balanced, is recommended.
🔑 Caroline Barré, Montifault, 44330 Le Pallet, tel. 02.40.80.40.62, fax 02.40.80.43.17, e-mail montifault@wanadoo.fr ☒ Y by appt.

DOM. DES MORINIERES Sur lie 1999★

☐ 5.7 ha 40,000 ▮ ♁ 20–29 F

Having received high praise for its 98 vintage, the Domaine des Morinières is still successful with its 99. With a clear pale golden colour, it delivers a good aromatic range, which is apparent both on the nose and on the palate. Its balance creates a wine that is steady from first impression to last. Seafood or fish with beurre blanc will go well with it.

🔑 André Barré, Le Bois, 44330 Vallet, tel. 02.40.36.62.95, fax 02.40.36.31.13 ☑ 🍷 by appt.

DOM. MOULIN DE LA MINIERE

Sur lie Cuvée Prestige 1999★

☐ 2 ha 15,000 ▮ 🌡 20–29 F

At the foot of the mill (without sails), this estate has produced a characterful wine whose nose mixes pineapple with mineral and smoky notes. Quite sparkling on first impression, and still lively and fine on the palate, it is a typical product of the terroir. One star also goes to the Gros-Plant du Pays Nantais sur lie **Moulin de la Minière 99**, which is very well made and extremely pleasing thanks to its fresh and supple palate (less than 20F).

🔑 SC Ménard-Gaborit, La Minière, 44690 Monnières, tel. 02.40.54.61.06, fax 02.40.54.66.12 ☑ 🍷 by appt.

DOM. DES MOULINS D'ASTREE

Sur lie 1999★★

☐ 3 ha 13,000 ▮ 🌡 20–29 F

Situated very close to Sainte-Radegonde church, some of whose Romanesque parts date back as far as the 11th century, this estate produces a very well-made Muscadet, which is gifted with a strong nose of green fruit and a harmonious palate, with a steady length. Will go perfectly with fish.

🔑 Jean-Daniel Bretaudeau, 28, rue de la Poste, 44690 Monnières, tel. 02.40.54.60.04, fax 02.40.54.66.38 ☑ 🍷 by appt.

MOUZILLON IMAGE D'UN TERROIR Sur lie 1999★

☐ n.c. 10,000 ▮ 🌡 20–29 F

For a long time individualistic, the Nantes wine-growing region has here and there some small-sized groups, such as this one, which has 17 members. Mouzillon offers a wine with an agreeable nose, dominated by citrus fruit. Well structured and without the slightest heaviness, this Muscadet de Sèvre-et-Maine sur lie exhibits on the palate a finesse and lively length which allow for appreciation of its mineral nuances.

🔑 GIE Mouzillon Image d'un Terroir, 2, rue des Rosiers, 44330 Mouzillon, tel. 02.40.33.98.88, fax 02.40.36.39.27 🍷 by appt.
🔑 Bordet

DOM. DES NOES Sur lie 1999

☐ 7.68 ha 53,200 ▮ 🌡 20–29 F

This estate, to the north of Pallet, produces a wine with an expressive nose of mineral and fruity notes. With more than a touch of sparkle, it demonstrates length on the palate. Also worthy of mention is the **Muscadet le Fief de la Tégrie 99**, which is of interest for its character of the terroir.

🔑 EARL Dom. des Noës, Bretigné, 44330 Le Pallet, tel. 02.40.80.98.90, fax 02.40.80.48.11 ☑ 🍷 by appt.
🔑 Agoulon

NOUET Sur lie Excellence 1999★

☐ 2.65 ha 18,000 ▮ 🌡 20–29 F

Produced by Jean-Claude and Pierre-Yves Nouet, this wine has come from the same vineyard since 1992. Gentle on the nose, though characteristic for its terroir notes, its complex and mineral qualities are more evident on the palate. The estate has also produced a Gros-Plant du Pays Nantais sur lie **Domaine de la Cognardière 99**, which is very pale with a fine liquorice finish on the palate. It also warrants one star.

🔑 Jean-Claude et Pierre-Yves Nouet, La Cognardière, imp. des Pressoirs, 44330 Le Pallet, tel. 02.40.80.41.72, fax 02.40.80.41.72 ☑ 🍷 by appt.

DOM. DES ORMIERES

Sur lie 1999★★

☐ 2.3 ha 14,000 ▮ 🌡 20F+

On the banks of the Maine, very close to the village of Maisdon, this property has provided a wine with green tints and a complex nose, characteristic of the terroir. If flowers and dried fruit dominate the smelling range, the full palate is more redolent of hazelnut and brioche. A wine to be drunk with shellfish.

🔑 Didier Branger, Le Gast, 44690 Maisdon-sur-Sèvre, tel. 02.40.06.68.06, fax 02.40.03.82.14 ☑ 🍷 by appt.

DOM. DU PARADIS Sur lie 1999★

☐ 15 ha 101,300 ▮ 🌡 20–29 F

A wine from Paradise clearly deserves attention. This particular Paradise is a hamlet to the north of La Haye-Fouassière. With a nose of green apples and its expressive, long palate, this very characteristic Muscadet de Sèvre-et-Maine sur lie is the natural companion to fish with beurre blanc. It could be left in the cellar for a number of years to perfect its already considerable harmony.

🔑 EARL Claude Vicet, Le Paradis, 44690 La Haye-Fouassière, tel. 02.40.36.95.71 ☑ 🍷 by appt.

LAURENT PERRAUD

Sur lie Sélection les Egards 1999★★

☐ 2 ha 7,000 ▮ 🌡 20–29 F

Produced at the very southern edge of the Muscadet de Sèvre-et-Maine area, this Sélection, originating from a renowned hillside, has been well matured. It retains a good terroir character, apparent on a nose of apples and broom flowers, and on its aromatic palate, sustained by a touch of carbonic gas (CO_2). It could be left for two or three years.

🔑 Laurent Perraud, dom. de La Vinçonnière, 44190 Clisson, tel. 02.40.03.95.76, fax 02.40.03.96.56 ☑ 🍷 ev. day 8am–12 noon 2pm–7pm; Sat. Sun. by appt.; cl. 1st Aug.–15 sep.

DOM. DES PETITES COSSARDIERES

Sur lie Sélection vieilles vignes 1999★

□ 3 ha 20,000 ■ ♁ 20–29 F

This small estate, situated at the gates of Landreau, applies classical methods, namely a light pressing of the Melon grape and the use of native yeast. Its perfectly characteristic wine, with elegant aromas, has a slightly sparkling palate; straightforward, balanced and with a quite lively finish. Also mentioned (with no star) is the **Gros-Plant du Pays Nantais sur lie 99**, which is quite acidulous and smells of dried fruit.

🔑 Jean-Claude Couillaud, 17, rue de la Loire, 44430 Le Landreau, tel. 02.40.06.42.81, fax 02.40.06.49.14 ☑ Y by appt.

CH. PLESSIS-BREZOT Sur lie 1999★

□ 20 ha 145,000 ■ ⊕ ♁ 20–29 F

Dominating the Sèvre valley, this beautiful château, which has a number of guest rooms, in 1999 produced a wine with a typically local nose. Its rounded palate is also quite complex, with a buttery note joining the citrus fruit aromas. If you are looking for maturity, you could keep this Muscadet de Sèvre-et-Maine for a year.

🔑 Ch. Plessis-Brézot, 44690 Monnières, tel. 02.40.54.63.24, fax 02.40.54.66.07, e-mail a.calonne@online.fr ☑ Y ev. day 8am–1pm 2pm–8pm

DOM. PLESSIS GLAIN Sur lie 1999★

□ 5 ha 12,000 ■ ♁ 20–29 F

Near the Saint-Barthélemy chapel, built in part with material from the Roman baths that were there before, this estate has produced an extremely aromatic wine which leaves an impression of strength and fruity liveliness on the palate and which has a pleasantly long finish.

🔑 Jean-Paul Pétard, Le Plessis-Glain, 44450 Saint-Julien-de-Concelles, tel. 02.40.03.60.28, fax 02.40.33.34.81 ☑ Y by appt.

DOM. POIRON

Sur lie Cuvée des Vieilles vignes 1999★

□ 20 ha 100,000 ■ ⊕ ♁ 20–29 F

This wine comes from 50-year-old vines planted on crumbly granite soil. Its docile but lengthy nose, its fine first impression and its characteristic palate all go towards making it a very attractive Muscadet de Sèvre-et-Maine sur lie. Somewhat atypical due to its richness and roundness, the Gros-Plant du Pays Nantais **Cuvée Plaisir 99** (less than 20F) also warrants a star.

🔑 Jean Poiron et Fils, L'Enclos, 44690 Château-Thébaud, tel. 02.40.06.51.43, fax 02.40.06.58.02 ☑ Y by appt.

CH. DU POYET

Sur lie Terroir du Poyet 1999

□ 15 ha 26,600 ■ ♁ 30–49 F

Partly destroyed during the royalist uprising stirred up by the Duchess of Berry in 1832, this château offers a wine that well represents the terroir of Poyet. The wine was still fresh during the tasting, but it will become more rounded with time.

🔑 EARL famille Bonneau, Le Poyet, 44330 La Chapelle-Heulin, tel. 02.40.06.74.52, fax 02.40.06.77.57 ☑ Y ev. day except Sun. 9am–12.30pm 2pm–6pm

PRESTIGE DE L'HERMITAGE

Sur lie 1998★

□ 2.9 ha 21,000 ■ ♁ 20–29 F

Located on the Nantes–Aigrefeuille road, this estate offers a 98 vintage that is still full of youth and freshness. Time has added hints of honey to its classical nose of lemon and green apples. After a slightly sparkling first impression, the outburst of aromas gives the palate a terroir character. The fruity and rich **Cuvée Élevée en Fût de Chêne 99** (30–49F) is also worth mentioning (without a star).

🔑 GAEC Moreau, La Petite Jaunaie, 44690 Château-Thébaud, tel. 02.40.06.61.42, fax 02.40.06.69.45 ☑ Y ev. day except Sun. 8am–7pm

DOM. PATRICK SAILLANT

Sur lie 1999★★

□ 5.1 ha 10,000 ■ 20 F+

Does this label tell you something? Unsurprisingly, this estate is very highly rated by the *Guide*. Patrick Saillant is an excellent producer. Take this 99 vintage, for example: well balanced on the palate, elegant, it emits fruity, mineral and even slightly spicy flavours.

🔑 EARL Saillant-Esneu, La Grenaudière, 44690 Maisdon-sur-Sèvre, tel. 02.40.03.80.10, fax 02.40.03.80.10 ☑ Y by appt.

🔑 Patrick Saillant

DOM. YVES SAUVETRE

Sur lie Vieilles vignes 1999

□ 7 ha 20,000 ■ ♁ 20 F+

La Landelle, with its imposing windmill, is to the west of Le Loroux. The wine, less typical than normal, will please enthusiasts of very fruity wines. The result of a modern vinification process, at a controlled temperature, it exhibits a pleasant nose of green fruit and a

LOIRE

balanced palate. The **Gros-Plant du Pays Nantais sur lie 99**, which is also very aromatic but more lively on the palate, is also worthy of note.

🗝 Yves Sauvêtre et Fils, La Landelle, 30, rue de la Durandière, 44430 Le Loroux-Bottereau, tel. 02.40.33.81.48, fax 02.40.33.87.67 ☑ Y by appt.

DOM. DES TROIS VERSANTS
Sur lie La Févrie 1999★

☐ 6 ha 30,000 ▮ 🌡 20-29 F

The vines at this domaine are grown on three hillsides on the left bank of the Sèvre, on gneiss soil. The resulting wine has a marked character of the terroir: warm and rounded, the nose mixes notes of honey and game. It ends on the palate with a finish of liquorice. The **Muscadet de Sèvre-et-Maine 99** (not matured *sur lie*) is mentioned for its fresh scents of green apples and for its fine structure.

🗝 Yves Bretonnière, La Févrie, 44690 Maisdon-sur-Sèvre, tel. 02.40.54.89.27, fax 02.40.54.86.08 ☑ Y by appt.

DOM. DU VAL-FLEURI
Sur lie 1999

☐ 17 ha n.c. ▮ 🌡 20-29 F

Yves and Jacqueline Delaunay have been settled on this 25-ha (62-acre) estate for 7 years. With a fine, green-tinted colour, their wine has a very pleasant scent of broom flowers. Lively and slightly sparkling on the palate, it is also very aromatic and lengthy. 'A straightforward and modern wine,' concluded one taster.

🗝 Yves et Jacqueline Delaunay, Le Val-Fleuri, 44430 Le Loroux-Bottereau, tel. 02.40.33.86.84, fax 02.40.33.88.99 ☑ Y by appt.

DOM. DU VIEUX FRENE
Sur lie 1999★

☐ 1.1 ha 6,000 ▮ 🌡 20-29 F

The Vieux Frêne estate is in Mouzillon, a village rich in prehistoric remains. Stop on the small bridge, dating from Roman times, which spans the Sanguèze, before continuing along the road to the vineyard. On arrival, you will discover this quite fruity wine. Slightly sparkling and rounded on the palate, it develops with a noticeable length and a fine expression.

🗝 Daniel Baudrit, La Récivière, 44330 Mouzillon, tel. 02.40.36.47.70, fax 02.40.36.47.70 ☑ Y ev. day except Sun. 8am–8pm

DOM. DU VIGNEAU Sur lie 1999★★

☐ 10 ha 60,000 ▮ 🌡 20-29 F

In 1999, this fairly new cooperative received national recognition for another of its wines. This one, with a lovely brilliant colour, exhibits a fine and harmonious nose with complex aromas. On the palate the wine is excellent in every respect; round at first, then well balanced and very long. There is another very successful Muscadet de Sèvre-et-Maine

sur lie from these Maîtres Vignerons: the **Cuvée Prestige 99**, characteristic for its mineral nose and well-balanced palate.

🗝 Coop. Les Maîtres Vignerons Nantais, Les Roitelières, 44330 Vallet, tel. 02.40.80.95.64, fax 02.40.80.99.81

Muscadet Côtes de Grand Lieu

DOM. DE BEL-AIR Sur lie 1999★

☐ 1.5 ha 11,000 ▮ 🌡 20-29 F

Very close to the runways of Nantes-Atlantique airport, this domaine has produced, from its 27 ha (67 acres) of vines, a strong and well-balanced wine. It demonstrates a good length and is already beginning to show very well.

🗝 EARL Bouin-Jacquet, Dom. de Bel-Air, BelAir de Gauchoux, 44860 Saint-Aignan-de-GrandLieu, tel. 02.51.70.80.80, fax 02.51.70.80.79 ☑ Y by appt.

DOM. DU HAUT BOURG
Sur lie 1999

☐ 10 ha 30,000 ▮ 🌡 30-49 F

The Haut Bourg estate is in the hills of Herbauge, an area known for its sandy, shingly soil. It produced, in 1999, a pale green wine whose nose exhibits mineral nuances. After a lively first impression, the palate develops roundness on an aromatic and quite gentle basis.

🗝 Michel et Hervé Choblet, Dom. du Haut-Bourg, 11, rue de Nantes, 44830 Bouaye, tel. 02.40.65.47.69, fax 02.40.32.64.01 ☑ Y ev. day except Sun. 9am–12.30pm 2pm–7pm

DOM. DE LA PIERRE BLANCHE
Sur lie 1999

☐ 7.25 ha 14,000 ▮ 🌡 20 F+

Its pale green colour, its grapefruity nose and its light but balanced palate all give finesse to this Muscadet, which comes from the small Vendée enclave in the Côtes de Grand Lieu. Pierre Blanche also deserves attention for its **Gros-Plant du Pays Nantais sur lie 99**.

🔑 Gérard Epiard, La Pierre Blanche, 85660 Saint-Philbert-de-Bouaine, tel. 02.51.41.93.42, fax 02.51.41.91.71 ☑ 🍷 by appt.

CH. DE LA ROULIERE

Sur lie 1999★★

☐	9 ha	8,000	🍾 🌡 20–29 F

All that remains of the original château, found to the south-east of Lake Grand-Lieu, are the moats and the dovecote. It has produced a wine that is strong on the nose and robust and full on the palate. It still needs to mature somewhat but will be perfect in 2001.

🔑 René Erraud, Ch. de La Roulière, 44310 Saint-Colomban, tel. 02.40.05.80.24, fax 02.40.05.53.89 ☑ 🍷 by appt.

LE DEMI BŒUF Sur lie 1999★

☐	10 ha	30,000	🍾 🌡 20–29 F

The label suggest a wine half-beef and half-grape. It is, however, a 100% Muscadet with a pale green colour, a lively and lemony nose and a fine and rounded palate.

🔑 EARL Michel Malidain, 3, Le Demi-Bœuf, 44310 La Limouzinière, tel. 02.40.05.82.29, fax 02.40.05.95.97 ☑ 🍷 ev. day except Sun. 8am–12 noon 2pm–6pm

DOM. LES COINS

Sur lie Vieilles vignes 1998

☐	1 ha	5,000	🍾 🌡 20–29 F

This wine from the banks of the Logne – one of the rivers, along with the Boulogne and the Ognon, that feed Lake Grand-Lieu – comes from 65-year-old vines. Quite pale but very clear, it exhibits a pleasant nose dominated by citrus fruit and green apples. Balanced after a fine first impression, the palate echoes the nose.

🔑 Jean-Claude Malidain, Le petit Coin, 44650 Corcoué-sur-Logne, tel. 02.40.05.95.95, fax 02.40.05.80.99, e-mail jean-claude.malidain@online.fr ☑ 🍷 by appt.

Gros-Plant AOVDQS

Gros-Plant du Pays Nantais is a dry, white wine, AOVDQS since 1954, made from a single variety, Folle Blanche, originally from the Charente, and here called Gros-Plant. The area of the vineyard is 3,000 ha (7,410 acres), producing about 150,000 hl (3,960,000 gal). Like Muscadet, Gros-Plant can be bottled on the lees, and is perfect with seafood in general and shellfish in particular; it should be served chilled but not iced at 8°–9°C (46.4–48.2°F).

DOM. BASSE VILLE Sur lie 1999★

☐	11 ha	35,000	🍾 🌡 20–29 F

This vast estate of 47 ha (117 acres), on a silicon-clay and schistose soil, has been cultivated by the Bossard family for five centuries. It has produced a 99 vintage with a strong nose of fruit, butter and brioche. Light and fresh to the end of the palate, it has a good balance between roundness and acidity.

🔑 Gilbert Bossard, La Basse-Ville, 44330 La Chapelle-Heulin, tel. 02.40.06.74.33, fax 02.40.06.77.48 ☑ 🍷 by appt.

CH. DE BRIACE Sur lie 1999★

☐	0.7 ha	3,000	🍾 🌡 20–29 F

Château de Briacé, which was to a large extent rebuilt in Gothic Revival style during the 19th century, houses the private wine-growing school of the Nantes region. Also a producer, it offers a Gros-Plant that is generally highly regarded. The 99 vintage exhibits an interesting nose composed of hints of ripe fruit, then vegetable touched with a slight smokiness. Quite strong on the palate, it moves on towards crisp green apples. Also worth noting (one star) is a **Muscadet de Sèvre-et-Maine sur lie 99**, which is gently acidulous, lightly mineral, dry and characteristic of the vintage.

🔑 AFG Ch. de Briacé, Lycée agricole de Briacé, 44430 Le Landreau, tel. 02.40.06.43.33, fax 02.40.06.46.15 ☑ 🍷 by appt.

CLOS DES ROSIERS Sur lie 1999★

☐	1.5 ha	3,000	🍾 🌡 20–29 F

Pale yellow with green tints, this wine delivers a fine characteristic nose; floral with a slight touch of greenness. It opens on the palate with a lively first impression of supple substance, without any harshness, which will appeal to Gros-Plant enthusiasts.

🗝 Philippe Laure, Les Rosiers, 44330 Vallet, tel. 02.40.33.91.83, fax 02.40.36.39.28 ☑ 🍷 by appt.

CH. DE FROMENTEAU 1999★

☐ 1 ha 1,200 🍾 🌡 20 F+

This estate, which is reviving the once-prestigious château – whose origins are in the 13th century – also doubles as an educational farm. Produced in small quantities, its Gros-Plant is certainly not the most typical, with its nose of exotic and crystallised fruit and its slightly acidic flavour. It is, nevertheless, a great success.

🗝 EARL Anne et Christian Braud, Fromenteau, 44330 Vallet, tel. 02.40.36.23.75, fax 02.40.36.23.75 ☑ 🍷 by appt.

DOM. DES GRANDS-PRIMEAUX 1999★

☐ 0.3 ha 3,000 🍾 🌡 20 F+

This balanced and persistent wine exhibits aromas of apple enriched by herbaceous and brioche overtones. It is quite characteristic, as is to be expected of a product of the wine-growing village of Le Pé, which rises over the Sèvre. And what does it matter if the **Muscadet de Sèvre-et-Maine sur lie 99** from this producer has been named **L'Original**? It is fruity and lively and lives up to its name.

🗝 Michel Bedouet, Le Pé-de-Sèvre, 44330 Le Pallet, tel. 02.40.80.97.30, fax 02.40.80.40.68, e-mail michel@bedouet ☑ 🍷 by appt.

DOM. DE LA BRETONNIERE Sur lie 1999★

☐ n.c. 23,000 🍾 🌡 20 F+

Very close to the large agricultural college of Briacé, this estate has produced a Gros-Plant that is mineral and fruity and even veers towards pear drops. With a lively first impression, it then reveals fleshiness and body. The estate's **Muscadet de Sèvre-et-Maine 99** also warrants a star for its expressive terroir character.

🗝 GAEC Charpentier-Fleurance, La Bretonnière, 44430 Le Landreau, tel. 02.40.06.43.39, fax 02.40.06.44.05 ☑ 🍷 by appt.

DOM. DE LA CHENAIE Sur lie 1999★★

☐ 2.8 ha 12,000 🍾 🌡 20 F+

Above the Sanguèze bridge, crossing point between Brittany and Anjou, this domaine produces a faultlessly balanced Gros-Plant du Pays Nantais. With great finesse, it offers a characteristically fresh first impression before developing an expressive palate with flavours of peach. From the same producer, the Muscadet de Sèvre-et-Maine sur lie **Cuvée Prestige 99** is remarkable (two stars) for its acidulous character, its length and aromas of fruit and roses (20–29F).

🗝 Dominique Martin, Dom. de la Chenaie, Les Sauvionnières, 44330 Vallet, tel. 02.40.36.23.04, fax 02.40.36.23.04 ☑ 🍷 by appt.

CH. DE LA GRANGE Sur lie 1999★

☐ 10 ha 60,000 🍾 🌡 20-29 F

The château has beautiful gardens dating from the 15th century, in parts altered in the Italian manner acccording to 19th-century Clissonais taste. This Gros-Plant is of brilliant colour, round and fruity, lengthy enough and very pleasing. This grower also makes a slightly sparkling **Muscadet Côtes de Grand Lieu sur lie 99** with a characteristic nose.

🗝 Comte Baudouin de Goulaine, Ch. de La Grange, 44650 Corcoué-sur-Logne, tel. 02.40.26.68.66, fax 02.40.26.61.89 ☑ 🍷 ev. day 2pm–7pm

DOM. DE LA GRANGE Sur lie 1999

☐ 3 ha 6,000 🍾 🌡 20-29 F

With its full colour, its scents of ripe fruit and its rich and ample flavours, this wine evokes maturity. Such characteristics mean it is a good accompaniment to fish.

🗝 Dominique Hardy, La Grange Mouzillon, 44330 Mouzillon, tel. 02.40.33.93.60, fax 02.40.36.29.79 ☑ 🍷 ev. day except Sun. 8am–12 noon 2pm–6pm

DOM. DE LA LANDELLE Sur lie 1999★

☐ 0.6 ha 4,000 🍾 🌡 20-29 F

La Landelle occupies one of the highest points of the Nantes wine-growing region (hence its close proximity to an imposing windmill). Michel Libeau offers a 99 Gros-Plant with good length and a clean mineral character hinting of gunflint both on the nose and the tongue.

🗝 Michel Libeau, La Landelle, 44430 Le Loroux-Bottereau, tel. 02.40.33.81.15, fax 02.40.33.85.37 ☑ 🍷 by appt.

DOM. LA ROCHE RENARD Sur lie 1999★★

☐ 2 ha 5,000 🍾 🌡 20 F+

La Roche Renard encompasses over 26 ha (64 acres) of vines planted on mica-schist soil. It is definitely a remarkable Gros-Plant du Pays Nantais sur lie. A wine notable for its brilliant colour and mineral nose, not devoid of a fresh fruitiness, it is rounded and achieves a true balance between alcohol and acidity.

🗝 EARL Isabelle et Philippe Denis, Les Laures, 44330 Vallet, tel. 02.40.36.63.65, fax 02.40.36.23.96 ☑ 🍷 ev. day except Sun. 10.30am–6pm; cl. weeks 44

DOM. DE LA ROCHERIE Sur lie 1999★★★

☐ 2 ha 6,000 🍾 🌡 20 F+

Cultivating sandy soil typical of Le Landreau, this domaine has produced a lively wine with direct aromas. Its length on the palate leaves plenty of opportunity to appreciate its remarkable richness. Also worth

mentioning is Muscadet de Sèvre-et-Maine sur lie 98 **Vieilles Vignes**, which is very fruity (green apple) and whose fine first impression is echoed in a pleasant finish on the palate (one star).

🔑 Daniel Gratas, La Rocherie, 44430 Le Landreau, tel. 02.40.06.41.55, fax 02.40.06.48.92 ☒ Ɏ ev. day except Sun. 8am–8pm

CH. DE L'OISELINIERE

Sur lie 1998★

☐ 1.5 ha 10,000 20–29 F

Classified as an historical monument, this pretty residence is representative of the Tuscan style that was popular during the reconstruction of Clisson at the beginning of the 19th century. L'Oiselinière is responsible for a Gros-Plant that is extremely rounded and very expressive, which develops marked scents of peach and exotic fruit. Also worth mentioning (no star) is a **Muscadet de Sèvre-et-Maine 99** of the terroir, masculine in character, with light quince aromas.

🔑 SC Aulanier, Ch. de L'Oiselinière, 44190 Gorges, tel. 02.40.06.91.59, fax 02.40.06.98.48 ☒ Ɏ by appt.

Fiefs Vendéens AOVDQS

Historically these domains were the property of the Cardinal, the head of the Roman Catholic hierarchy in France. The name of this appellation is evocative of the history of these wines, replanted in the Middle Ages, as so often, at the instigation of the monks, and later enjoyed by the great Cardinal Richelieu himself. The denomination AOVDQS was granted in 1984 in recognition of the efforts made to improve quality and which continue to be made on the 380 ha (939 acres) planted.

The Mareuil region produces rosés and fine reds with good bouquet and fruit from Gamay, Cabernet and Pinot Noir; the whites are little known. The Brem vineyard, not far from the sea, produces dry whites from Chenin and Grolleau Gris, but also some rosé and red wines. In the area round Fontenay-le-Comte, dry whites (from Chenin, Colombard, Melon and Sauvignon), rosés and reds (Gamay and Cabernet) come from the regions of Pissotte and Vix. The wines should be drunk young to accompany appropriate young dishes.

XAVIER COIRIER

Pissotte Sélection 1999★★

☐ 6 ha 20 000 20–29 F

Near the massive Mervent forest, this estate has combined Chenin Blanc (60%), Chardonnay and Melon to produce a wine typical of the region. With a pretty, clear colour, it develops a nose evocative of exotic fruit and flowers. Lively on the palate at first, it then demonstrates a good balance.

🔑 Xavier Coirier, La Petite Groie, 15, rue des Gélinières, 85200 Pissotte, tel. 02.51.69.40.98, fax 02.51.69.74.15, e-mail vin.pissotte@liberty.surf.fr ☒ Ɏ by appt.

DOM. DES DAMES

Mareuil Les Agates 1999

◪ 4 ha 12,000 20–29 F

Passed down through the women of the family for five generations, Domaine des Dames has produced a pale rosé with an elegant nose of red berries and spice. Light, thirst-quenching and fruity, it is a wine for warm days.

🔑 GAEC Vignoble Daniel Gentreau, Follet, 85320 Rosnay, tel. 02.51.30.55.39, fax 02.51.28.22.36 ☒ Ɏ ev. day except Sun. 9am–12.30pm 2pm–7.30pm; 16 Sep.–14 June by appt.

FERME DES ARDILLERS

Mareuil Collection 1999★

◪ 6 ha 52,000 20–29 F

This old farm, typical of Vendée (although with very modern equipment), offers a rosé with scents of redcurrant underlined by mint. Supple at first, with a round finish and balance, the wine is typical of its type. One star also goes to **Mareuil Rouge Collection 99**, strong and balanced, its tannins promising. Finally, **Mareuil Blanc Collection 99** confirms the success of the estate during the 99 vintage.

🔑 Mourat, Ferme des Ardillers, rte de La-Roche-sur-Yon, 85320 Mareuil-sur-Lay, tel. 02.51.97.20.10, fax 02.51.97.21.58 ☒ Ɏ ev. day except Sun. 8am–12 noon 2pm–6pm

DOM. DE LA VIEILLE RIBOULERIE

Mareuil Cuvée des Moulins brûlés 1999★

■ n.c. 8,000 20–29 F

The highest grounds of Rosnay used to house three windmills, which were burned down during the Revolution. These have now been replaced by vines that have produced this wine, which has violet tints and a nose suggesting blackcurrant and spice. The supple palate finishes on a note of raspberry. We would also mention **Mareuil Rosé Cuvée des Rêves de l'Yon 99** (from the name of the local river), which is straightforward, aromatic and refreshing.

Hubert Macquigneau, Le Plessis, 85320 Rosnay, tel. 02.51.30.59.54, fax 02.51.28.21.80 by appt.

CH. DE ROSNAY

Mareuil Vieilles vignes 1999★★

4 ha 23,000 20–29 F

This château, one of the most important in the Fiefs Vendéens, has produced a slightly sparkling rosé with a salmon-coloured tint. The fine and elegant nose combines red berries, spice and pomegranate. Round and full with a light metallic touch, the wine is characteristic of the appellation. Also worth mentioning (no star) is the **Mareuil Rouge Cuvée Prestige 99**, which is lively and refreshing.

EARL Ch. de Rosnay, 85320 Rosnay, tel. 02.51.30.59.06, fax 02.51.28.21.01 ev. day except Sun. 8am–6pm

Coteaux d'Ancenis AOVDQS

The Coteaux d'Ancenis wine region has been classified AOVDQS since 1954. Four single-variety wines are produced: Gamay (80% of the production), Cabernet, Chenin and Malvoisie. The area of the vineyard is 300 ha (741 acres) and production was about 15,000 hl (396,000 gal) in 1999, of which about 200 hl (5,280 gal) was white.

DOM. DES CLERAMBAULTS

Gamay 1999★

■ 1 ha 7,000 20 F+

In the most southern part of the Coteaux d'Ancenis, this estate has produced a Gamay with a ruby colour, whose nose, at first closed, reveals on airing complex aromas of cherry and raspberry. Still dry on the palate during the tasting, if aged the wine will reach its full maturity in 2001. Also worth mentioning is **Muscadet des Coteaux de la Loire sur lie 99**, which is supple and lively and will also benefit from ageing for a few months.

EARL Pierre Terrien, 30, rue de Verdun, 49530 Bouzillé, tel. 02.40.98.15.38, fax 02.40.98.11.45 by appt.

DOM. DES GENAUDIERES

Malvoisie 1999★

□ n.c. 5,000 30–49 F

On a southern hillside alongside the Loire, this domaine makes a wide range of wines. This one is not the most representative but is alluring for its citrus nose, which precedes its strong, round and full palate. Also of note is **Coteaux d'Ancenis Gamay 99** (20–29FF), which delivers aromas of pear drops; quite supple, it is ready for drinking. Finally, **Muscadet des Coteaux de la Loire sur lie 99** deserves a mention for its floral qualities.

EARL Athimon et ses Enfants, Dom. des Génaudières, 44850 Le Cellier, tel. 02.40.25.40.27, fax 02.40.25.35.61 ev. day except Sun. 9am–12.30pm 2pm–6.30pm

JACQUES GUINDON

Malvoisie 1999★★

□ 1.4 ha 8,000 30–49 F

Presented to the Grand Jury of the *Coups de Coeur*, this Malvoisie missed the supreme accolade by two votes. Those who voted for it were disappointed because it is a true wine-lover's curiosity. Fine, balanced and harmonious, the wine develops aromas of crystallised fruit, ripe quince, pear and beeswax. It would be savoured well as an apéritif or with a dessert of strawberries. The **Coteaux d'Ancenis Gamay 99**, which is quite round, also gets a mention.

Jacques Guindon, La Couleuverdière, 44150 Saint-Géréon, tel. 02.40.83.18.96, fax 02.40.83.29.51 ev. day except Sun. 9am–12 noon 2pm–6pm

DOM. DU HAUT FRESNE

Gamay 1999

1 ha 8,000 20–29 F

Close to Château de la Turmelière, birthplace of Joachim du Bellay, the 16th-century writer and poet, this estate offers a rosé that is gentle but well rounded and balanced. Its **Gamay 99**, characteristic of the terroir, supple and lightly spicy, is also notable.

Renou Frères, Dom. du Haut Fresne, 49530 Drain, tel. 02.40.98.26.79, fax 02.40.98.26.79 ev. day except Sun. 9am–12 noon 2pm–6.30pm

DOM. DE LA PLEIADE

Gamay 1999★★

■ 3 ha 13,000 20F+

In tribute to du Bellay, who liked his '*petit Liré*', this estate has produced a wine with a deep cherry tint, which reveals a great aromatic richness. Cherry, strawberry, blackcurrant and violet all follow each other on the nose, while on the palate a note of the terroir and of liquorice appear. A very harmonious Gamay. **Muscadet des Coteaux de la Loire sur lie 99**, which is lively and long, gains a star.

Bernard Crespin, Dom. de La Pléïade, 49530 Liré, tel. 02.40.09.01.30, fax 02.40.09.07.42 ev. day except Sun. 9am–12 noon 2pm–7pm

Anjou-Saumur

The Anjou and Saumur vineyards occupy Maine-et-Loire, extending a little into the north of the Vienne and the Deux-Sèvres. This undulating landscape, criss-crossed with numerous watercourses, lies at the northern limits of vine cultivation, under the influence of an Atlantic climate.

Vines have always been grown on the slopes of the Loire, the Layon, the Aubance, the Loir and the Thouet. At the end of the 19th century, the vineyard was at its most extensive. Dr Guyot, in a survey for the Minister of Agriculture, reported 31,000 ha (76,570 acres) under vines in MaineetLoire. Phylloxera was to decimate the vineyard, as everywhere else in France. Replanting took place at the beginning of the 20th century, with further efforts in the 1950s and 1960s, though it fell back thereafter. Today, the vineyard covers about 14,500 ha (35,815 acres) and produces from 400,000 to 1 million hl (10,560,000–26,400,000 gal), depending on the weather.

As always, the combination of terroir and climate determines the character of the local wines. However, it is important to identify the clear difference between those grown on 'Anjou Blue' soils, of schists and other primary rocks from the Massif Armorican, and those produced on 'Anjou White', or Saumurois, the sedimentary soils of the Paris Basin, where white, chalky limestone is most in evidence. The rivers and streams of the region have also played an important role in the wine trade: one can still find ruins of the little loading ports on the Layon. Planting density is between 4,500 and 5,000 plants per hectare; pruning, which used mainly to be in goblet or fan shapes, is now more usually in cordons.

Anjou has always been best known for its sweet white wines, those from the Coteaux du Layon being the most highly rated. However, wine styles are changing, moving more towards semi-dry or dry white wines and to red wines. In Saumur, the reds are the most highly regarded, alongside the sparkling wines which have seen a significant increase, particularly the AOC Saumur-Mousseux and Crémant de Loire.

Anjou

The geographical area of this regional appellation, made up of a group of nearly 200 communes, incorporates all the Anjou AOCs. Production is of white wines – 49,336 hl (1,302,470 gal) in 1999 – and reds – 108,000 hl (2,851,200 gal). For many, Anjou wine is synonymous with sweet or medium white wines made with Chenin, also known as Pineau de la Loire. However, in line with the trend towards drier wines, local producers have opted for mixing in Chardonnay or Sauvignon, to a maximum limit of 20%. The much increased production of red wines, from Cabernet Franc and Cabernet-Sauvignon, is in the process of altering the image of the region.

CHARLES BEDUNEAU 1999★

■ 1,5 ha 7,000 30–49 F

The estate is right in the middle of the village of Saint-Lambert-du-Lattay. The Béduneau family receives visitors in a fine wine cellar and is happy to offer its wines for tasting. This Anjou, with a brilliant colour of intense ruby, presents a complex range of red berries, full of youth. On the palate, the rounded structure reveals a good flavour of Cabernet Franc. A balanced and very successful wine.

Dom. Charles Béduneau, 18, rue Rabelais, 49750 Saint-Lambert-du-Lattay, tel. 02.41.78.30.86, fax 02.41.74.01.46 by appt.

CH. DE BOIS-BRINCON

Le Clos Bertin 1997★

■ 2 ha 10,000 50–69 F

Dating from 1219, this vast property of 27 ha (67 acres) is one of the oldest in Anjou. Its grounds are divided among five communes and produce some well-known wines. This wine is a profound garnet-red colour. Complex and impressively intense on the nose, it has hints of black fruit combining with a woody-toasted side resulting from a 12-month maturation in barrels. The rich and voluminous palate is supported by a good tannic presence that gives it its originality. This wine is, without doubt, one to be kept; a success, bearing in mind the vintage.

Xavier Cailleau, Ch. de Bois-Brinçon, 49320 Blaison-Gohier, tel. 02.41.57.19.62, fax 02.41.57.10.46 by appt.

DOM. DE BOIS MOZE 1999★★

■ 8.68 ha 35,000 20–29 F

Previously the property of the Montsabert château, Bois Mozé has been run by the Boury family since the 1920s. In 1999 it produced a very dark wine with aromas of overripe red berries, while on the palate the wine's concentration and complexity prolong the pleasure. Notes of morello and strawberry fit in very well with this ensemble.

Boury Frères, Dom. de Bois-Mozé, 49320 Coutures, tel. 02.41.57.91.28, fax 02.41.57.93.71 by appt.

DOM. DE BRIZE 1999★★

■ 2 ha 8,000 20–29 F

This vast estate of 38 ha (94 acres) deserves a visit for the special taste of its wine. The 99 Anjou, with its very bright purple colour, is far from undeserving of merit. Its nose of overripe grapes evokes crystallised red berries, and its first impression on the palate is very pleasant, with subsequent smoothness, richness and good length reinforcing the pleasure.

SCEA Marc et Luc Delhumeau, Dom. de Brizé, 49540 Martigné-Briand, tel. 02.41.59.43.35, fax 02.41.59.66.90 by appt.

Luc et Line Delhumeau

CH. DE BROSSAY 1999★

■ 10 ha n.c. 20–29 F

In a cellar dating from the 15th century, the Deffois brothers mature the grapes of their 36 ha (89 acres) of vines planted on alluvial-gravelly soil on shale. This wine is a clear ruby colour, with an impression of freshness that reappears after first tasting it. Ripe red berries on the nose are echoed in the elegant and characteristic palate.

Raymond et Hubert Deffois, Ch. de Brossay, 49560 Cléré-sur-Layon, tel. 02.41.59.59.95, fax 02.41.59.58.81, e-mail brossay@groupesirius.com ev. day except Sun. 8am–1pm 2pm–7pm

DOM. DE CLAYOU 1999

□ n.c. n.c. 20–29 F

Saint-Lambert-du-Lattay is proud of being the most vine-laden commune in Anjou. And Jean-Bernard Chauvin, the young president of the appellation, will not dent this pride with the quality of his wine. With light green tints, it is unobtrusive, lively and fresh on the nose with an acidulous side on the palate, which is, nevertheless, well balanced. This is an interesting wine that will go well with seafood.

SCEA Jean-Bernard Chauvin, 18 bis, rue du Pont-Barré, 49750 Saint-Lambert-du-Lattay, tel. 02.41.78.42.84, fax 02.41.78.48.52 by appt.

DOM. DES COQUERIES 1999★

■ 1 ha 6,000 20–29 F

Philippe Gilardeau arrived at this estate, which he subsequently restored, in 1996. His debuts are promising. The intense red of this wine is shaded with ruby. At first, gamey aromas are discernible on the nose, followed by red berries. Well structured and fleshy, the wine's first impression is supple and tender; it balances tannins and finishes with a hint of liquorice.

EARL Philippe Gilardeau, Les Noues, 49380 Thouarcé, tel. 02.41.54.39.11, fax 02.41.54.38.84 by appt.

DOM. DES COTEAUX BLANCS 1999★

□ 2 ha 5,000 20–29 F

Coteaux Blancs has a beautiful view over the Layon river. François Picherit has made a wine with a pale tint and a nose of broom flowers. The 99 vintage results from vinification at a well-controlled temperature, and the inclusion of Chardonnay gives it some very floral notes. Balanced on the palate, the wine is ready for drinking.

François Picherit, Les Coteaux Blancs, 49290 Chalonnes-sur-Loire, tel. 02.41.78.16.83, fax 02.41.74.91.91 by appt.

DOM. COUSIN-LEDUC 1999★★

■ n.c. n.c. 20–29 F

Having returned to traditional methods of cultivation since he took over this estate almost 15 years ago, Olivier Cousin is clearly following the right course, since he has gained two stars for his 99 Anjou. The deep colour is animated by quite visible tints of mauve. Subtly aromatic on the nose, the wine shows a gentle roundness of tannins on the palate after a rich first impression. The wine will improve after ageing for three to five years, when it will reveal all its potential.

🔑 Olivier Cousin, 1, rue du Colonel-Panaget, 49540 Martigné-Briand, tel. 02.41.59.49.09, fax 02.41.59.69.83, e-mail ocousin@wanadoo.fr ☑ 🍷 by appt.

DOM. DITTIERE 1999★★

■ 5 ha 10,000 30–49 F

The Dittière estate is a traditional Anjou domaine. The vineyard is planted on a sandy-gravelly soil typical of the commune of Vauchrétien, which regularly produces expressive wines. This one, very brilliant garnet-red, has a remarkable nose, which is very complex for its nuances of red berries, may blossom and even nutmeg and white pepper. The structured palate has volume and strength from its tannins, which are still very present. Leaving it in the cellar will allow it to develop.

🔑 Dom. Dittière, 1, chem. de la Grouas, 49320 Vauchrétien, tel. 02.41.91.23.78, fax 02.41.54.28.00, e-mail domaine.dittiere@wanadoo.fr ☑ 🍷 by appt.

DOM. DES EPINAUDIERES 1999★★

□ 5 ha 2,000 20–29 F

Roger Fardeau took over the vineyard in 1966 as a *métageur* (sharecropper), before starting to farm it in 1975. In 1991 he went into partnership with his son Paul, and father and son today produce a remarkable Anjou, which is straw-coloured, elegant and fresh. Notes of toasted dried fruits appear on the nose. Since it is made from Chenin Blanc from very ripe harvests, the first impression is one of roundness, and the wine is rich and lightly woody on the palate, the result of two months' maturation in wood. Lively and supple at the same time, the wine will age well.

🔑 SCEA Fardeau, Sainte-Foy, 49750 Saint-Lambert-du-Lattay, tel. 02.41.78.35.68, fax 02.41.78.35.50 ☑ 🍷 by appt.

DOM. DU FRESCHE 1999★

■ 1.5 ha 9,000 20–29 F

The Boré family have been wine-growers – from father to son – for 150 years. Alain maintains the estate's reputation with this bright ruby-coloured wine. The scents of very ripe red berries herald the clean, fresh flavours on the palate, and the wine is well balanced and long-lasting. On the finish, a tannic note is still noticeable, but this will diminish with time.

Anjou and Saumur

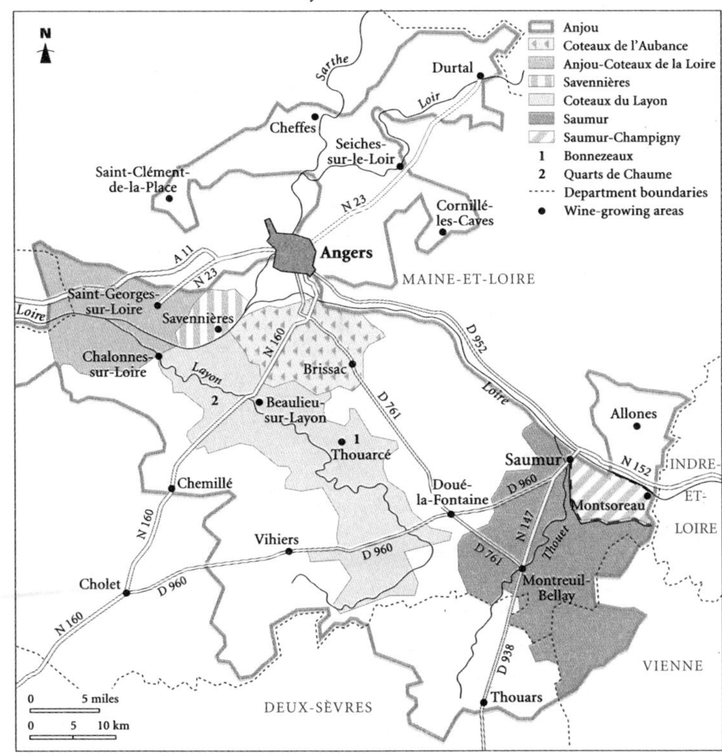

🗝 EARL Boré, Dom. du Fresche, 49620 La Pommeraye, tel. 02.41.77.74.63, fax 02.41.77.79.39 ☑ 🍷 by appt.

DOM. GAUDARD Les Paragères 1999★

□ 1.77 ha 6,000 ■ 🌡 30-49 F

Right in the middle of their vineyard, Pierre and Janet Aguilas have built a vast tasting and reception hall. There you will discover this green-tinted Anjou, its pleasing and lengthy scents giving off generous hints of fresh lemon, with an impression of elegance on the palate, so controlled is the balance. A wine ready to be enjoyed or set aside for future pleasures.

🗝 Pierre Aguilas, Dom. Gaudard, rte de Saint-Aubin, 49290 Chaudefonds-sur-Layon, tel. 02.41.78.10.68, fax 02.41.78.67.72 ☑ 🍷 ev. day except Sun. 8am–12 noon 2pm–6pm

DOM. DE HAUTE PERCHE 1999

□ 2 ha 7,000 ■ 🌡 30-49 F

In 1966 Christian Papin took over a vineyard of 9 ha (22 acres) and totally renovated it and planted it mostly with Chenin Blanc and Cabernet Franc. Presiding over 34 ha (84 acres) today, he has produced a clear yellow wine with green tints. Although not yet totally open on the nose, a brioche character presents itself, auguring well for a palate that reveals itself to be full of quality flavours, which promise to increase.

🗝 EARL Agnès et Christian Papin, 7, chem. de la Godelière, 49610 Saint-Melaine-sur-Aubance, tel. 02.41.57.75.65, fax 02.41.57.75.42 ☑ 🍷 by appt.

DOM. DES HAUTES OUCHES 1999★

■ 15 ha 20,000 20-29 F

The colour is clear and intense, of a fine, natural and clean ruby, and the character of red berries sharpens the smell. This is an elegant wine that does not deceive on the palate: its finesse combines with a good structure. What a beautiful progression through all three parts – eye, nose, palate – of the tasting! The wine is ready for drinking.

🗝 EARL Joël et Jean-Louis Lhumeau, 9, rue Saint-Vincent, Linières, 49700 Brigné-sur-Layon, tel. 02.41.59.30.51, fax 02.41.59.31.75 ☑ 🍷 by appt.

DOM. DE LA BELLE ANGEVINE 1999★

■ 4 ha 11,000 20-29 F

La Belle Angevine, which takes its name from the heroine of a 15th-century legend, is the result of the amalgamation of two properties, one in the commune of Beaulieu-sur-Layon and the other in Saint-Lambert-du-Lattay, where you can visit a charming wine museum. It is seven years since Florence Dufour found herself presiding over some 12 ha (30 acres) of vines. She offers a 99 of full colour with violet tints. Although at the moment unobtrusive on the nose, the wine is none the less pleasant and complex for its fruity-floral hints of iris and peony. On the palate, fruit dominates. The finish is a bit sharp due to its still quite firm tannins, but this element will dissolve perfectly in time. Mentioned by the jury, the **Anjou Gamay 99** is a supple wine, to be served cool.

🗝 Florence Dufour, Dom. de La Belle Angevine, La Motte, 49750 Beaulieu-sur-Layon, tel. 02.41.78.34.86, fax 02.41.72.81.58, e-mail fldufour@club-internet.fr ☑ 🍷 by appt.

DOM. DE LA BERGERIE 1999★

■ 3.5 ha 25,000 ■ 🌡 30-49 F

La Bergerie marries a pretty setting with the 32 ha (79 acres) of its vineyards. With an elegant label, it offers a wine of an intense ruby-red colour. Fresh with notably very ripe red berries (particularly strawberry) on the nose, the wine's flavours are supple, fruity and long-lasting on the palate. Quite a typical Anjou, it is lively and smooth.

🗝 Yves Guégniard, Dom. de La Bergerie, 49380 Champ-sur-Layon, tel. 02.41.78.85.43, fax 02.41.78.60.13, e-mail domainede.la.bergerie@wanadoo.fr ☑ 🍷 ev. day except Sun. 9am–12.30pm 2pm–7pm

DOM. DE LA COUCHETIERE Elevé en fût de chêne 1998★

■ 0.6 ha 4,500 🛢 30-49 F

Although the estate has witnessed the succession of four generations, winegrowing did not take on an important role until after 1944. The vineyard was enlarged during the 1980s. In December 1999 a new tasting cellar was built, where you can discover this intense Anjou, with its violet tints. The strong nose gives off whiffs of stewed cherries and sloes, and the voluminous palate rests on still-present tannins, although fruit is still perceptible. The 98 vintage is successful even if it needs a little time to smooth out.

🗝 GAEC Brault, Dom. de La Couchetière, 49380 Notre-Dame-d'Allençon, tel. 02.41.54.30.26, fax 02.41.54.40.98 ☑ 🍷 ev. day except Sun. 8am–12.30pm 2pm–7pm

DOM. DE LA CROIX DES LOGES 1999★★

■ 15 ha 10,000 ■ 🌡 20-29 F

Situated on the Gennes road, close to the village of Martigné, this 40-ha (99-acre) estate offers a remarkable Anjou with great visual intensity: violet glints shine in the glass. After airing, aromas of red berries and notably of morello appear, followed by hints of liquorice, a sign of a very ripe harvest and well-controlled extraction. The rich palate contributes to the wine's pleasant character.

🗝 SCEA Bonnin et Fils, Dom. de La Croix des Loges, 49540 Martigné-Briand, tel. 02.41.59.43.58, fax 02.41.59.41.11, e-mail bonninlesloges@aol.com ☑ 🍷 by appt.

DOM. DE LA DUCQUERIE

Les Clavières 1999★★

☐	3 ha	24,000	▮ 🌡	20-29 F

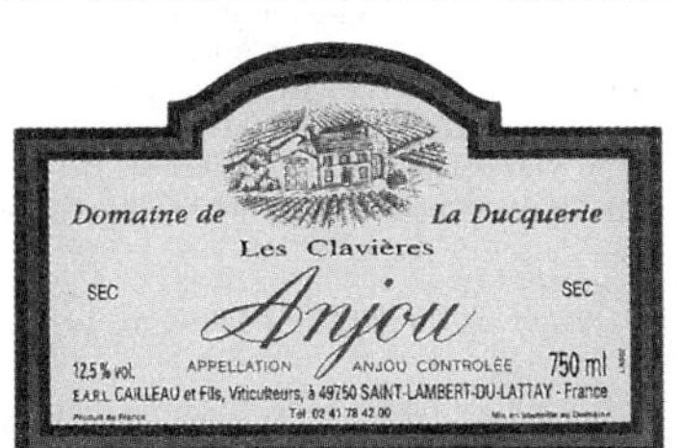

This modern-style estate covers 50 ha (123 acres). Although known for its fabulous Coteaux du Layon vintages, it was this remarkable Anjou that seduced the Grand Jury. Les Clavières attracts the eye with its pale yellow colour, and the nose has an intense range from toasted dried fruit to ripe white fruit. The freshness of the palate is a marvel because it is combined with round and lengthy flavours. Although the wine is ready for drinking, it also promises a very good future.

🗝 EARL Cailleau et Fils, Dom. de la Ducquerie, 2, chem. du Grand-Clos, 49750 Saint-Lambert-du-Lattay,
tel. 02.41.78.42.00, fax 02.41.78.48.17 ☒ Y by appt.

CH. LA FRESNAYE 1999★★

■	6 ha	23,000	▮ ⦀ 🌡	30-49 F

Laure and Philippe Baudin took over the estate of L'Echalier in 1998 and acquired Château de la Fresnaye, along with its 8 ha (20 acres) of vines, a year later. They had to restructure the vineyard in order to keep only Chenin Blanc and Cabernet. Their efforts were not in vain, judging by the colourful and lively hue of this Anjou. The wine gives off lovely aromas of red berries, specifically very ripe cherries, and on swirling the wine in the glass you can actually see the minerality of the schist. The first impression is still somewhat tannic, but the wine has all the potential for improvement if kept for three years. We salute the work of the Coutenceau father and son who have so judiciously combined Cabernet Sauvignon and Cabernet Franc.

🗝 SCEA Ch. de La Fresnaye, 49190 Saint-Aubin-de-Luigné, tel. 02.41.54.78.55, fax 02.41.54.78.55 ☒ Y by appt.

🗝 Laure et Philippe Baudin

DOM. DE LA GRETONNELLE 1999

☐	2 ha	1000	20-29 F

La Gretonnelle is a beautiful residence dating back to the 19th century, built with stone originating in Puy-Notre-Dame. Its Chenin vines are responsible for this bright wine with a quite full yellow colour. Still quite unobtrusive on the nose, although airing releases hints of may blossom and linden flowers, and while the palate is not very full, it nevertheless presents suppleness and balance right up to the long finish.

🗝 EARL Charruault-Schmale, Les Landes, 79290 Bouillé-Loretz, tel. 05.49.67.04.49 ☒ Y by appt.

VIGNOBLE DE L'ARCISON 1999★

■	4 ha	15,000	▮ 🌡	20-29 F

Two-thirds of the wine-growing area of Thouarcé are planted with Cabernet. Damien Reulier offers a good example of the output with this attractive wine of violet colour with scarlet tints. The nose is intense and complex in evoking fresh fruit and overripe fruit punctuated by spicy notes. The wine is sparkling and structured on the palate, and although there is a light tannic point at the end, this will dissipate over time.

🗝 Damien Reulier, Vignoble de L'Arcison, Le Mesnil, 49380 Thouarcé,
tel. 02.41.54.16.81, fax 02.41.54.31.12 ☒ Y ev. day 9am–12.30pm 2pm–6pm; cl. Oct.

LA ROULERIE Le Grand Clos 1999★

☐	3 ha	20,000	⦀	30-49 F

Château de la Roulerie was taken over first by Gaston Lenôtre, then by Bernard Germain, who also owns vineyards around Bordeaux. This Anjou Blanc has a golden-yellow colour. Its range demonstrates notes of over-maturity and a quite ripe harvest. It opens on the palate with a complex first impression, at the same time sweet and fresh, followed soon after by touches of fruit and vanilla.

🗝 Vignobles Germain et Associés Loire, Ch. de Fesles, 49380 Thouarcé,
tel. 02.41.68.94.00, fax 02.41.68.94.01, email loire@vgas.com ☒ Y by appt.

CH. DE LA VIAUDIERE

Cuvée Pierre Blanche 1999★

☐	1.3 ha	5,000	20 F+

The vineyard has been passed from father to son in the Gélineau family for four centuries. A very clear yellow tinge, with green tints, characterises the Pierre Blanche. On the nose the senses are treated to a generous range, combining flowers with overripe fruit. The very aromatic palate continues the same elegant line.

🗝 EARL Vignoble Gélineau, Ch. de La Viaudière, 49380 Champ-sur-Layon,
tel. 02.41.78.86.27, fax 02.41.78.60.45,
e-mail gelineau@wanadoo.fr ☒ Y by appt.

DOM. DE LA VILLAINE 1999★★

■	2 ha	10,000	▮ 🌡	20-29 F

Pascal Batail and Jean-Paul Carré structured their vineyard during the 1970s from a number of small properties. Today, with more than 22 ha (54 acres), they offer a deep and glittering ruby Anjou. Although still closed on the nose, a floral note, characteristically violet, is cleanly expressed. After a smooth first impression there is a veritable explosion of flavours on the palate, and the finish is even more prolonged. The wine-makers have managed to extract the noble constituents without excess to create this fresh and lively wine.

⊶ GAEC des Villains Carré Batail, La Villaine, 49540 Martigné-Briand, tel. 02.41.59.75.21, fax 02.41.59.75.21 ☒ 🍷 by appt.

LE LOGIS DU PRIEURE 1999*

■ 1.5 ha 6,000 30–49 F

Le Logis du Prieuré produces a wide variety of wines in Concourson-sur-Layon. Its Anjou distinguishes itself with its lovely garnet-red colour; it shows off fruity aromas, among which crystallised and ripe cherries dominate. The palate begins with finesse and continues pleasantly as the tannin extraction has been well controlled. A fine wine, representative of the appellation and very successful in this vintage.

⊶ SCEA Jousset et Fils, Le Logis du Prieuré, 49700 Concourson-sur-Layon, tel. 02.41.59.11.22, fax 02.41.59.38.18, e-mail logis-prieure@groupesirius.com ☒ 🍷 ev. day except Sun. 9am–12.30pm 2pm–7pm

DOM. DE MIHOUDY 1999**

■ 5 ha 10,000 30–49 F

The Cochard family's Anjous are always remarkable! The 1999 vintage is a dark red wine, and tilting the glass reveals shades of mauve. The superb nose draws to a close with concentrated, overripe red berries. The palate is supple despite a powerful structure due to the very evident tannins, which will dissipate with time. This Anjou is very promising.

⊶ Cochard, Dom. de Mihoudy, 49540 Aubigné-sur-Layon, tel. 02.41.59.46.52, fax 02.41.59.68.77 ☒ 🍷 by appt.

GILLES MUSSET-SERGE ROULLIER 1999**

■ 2 ha 12,000 20–29 F

1999
Anjou
Appellation Contrôlée
Gilles Musset - Serge Roullier
Vignerons
750 ml
12% vol.

The estate has a wonderful view of the Montjean-sur-Loire church which seems almost to hover over the vineyard. There is a great deal of pleasure in tasting this deep ruby wine with a perfume of stewed cherries: the grapes were certainly ripe. After a supple, round and fruity first impression, the flavours are rich and warm. It is a red Anjou of high quality.

⊶ Vignoble Musset-Roullier, Le Pélican, 49620 La Pommeraye, tel. 02.41.39.05.71, fax 02.41.77.75.76 ☒ 🍷 by appt.

DOM. OGEREAU 1999*

■ 4 ha 13,000 30–49 F

The Ogereau estate is known for its *vins liquoreux* but is gaining a reputation for its red wines, as is proved by this one. Its complex nose breaks down into scents of leather, iris and peony flowers, and strawberry and cherry. Maturity amplifies all these characteristics, because that is where the structure is. A developing wine that has excellent potential.

⊶ Vincent Ogereau, 44, rue de la BelleAngevine, 49750 Saint-Lambert-du-Lattay, tel. 02.41.78.30.53, fax 02.41.78.43.55 ☒ 🍷 by appt.

DOM. PERCHER La Masse 1999

□ 1 ha 4,000 20–29 F

Sparkling wines represent 50% of the bottle sales of this estate: the Percher brothers have matured Saumur Brut using the *méthode traditionnelle* since 1961. This Anjou Blanc, however, is an important part of their range and deserves attention. With a fresh and lively pale yellow colour with sparkling green tints, it delivers quite an intense nose where the mineral side of the Chenin comes across, along with a floral note from the Chardonnay. The ample and well-balanced palate follows with good length.

⊶ SCEA Dom. Percher, Savonnières, 49700 Les Verchers-sur-Layon, tel. 02.41.59.76.29, fax 02.41.59.90.44 ☒ 🍷 ev. day except Sun. 8am–12 noon 2pm–6pm

DOM. DES PIECES MADAME 1999**

■ 5 ha 31,330 20–29 F

This 24-ha (59-acre) vineyard is in the middle of the village of Martigné-Briand. It produces an Anjou with a lovely clean purple colour. With great finesse, the fruity nose reflects the fine maturity of the grape. Along the same lines, the palate leaves a silky impression, as the tannins are enveloped with fleshy fruit. It is a substantial wine that will not disappoint over the next two years.

⊶ EARL de La Gaubretière, 8, rue de La Gaubretière, 49540 Martigné-Briand, tel. 02.41.40.22.71, fax 02.41.40.22.60, e-mail j.verdier@wanadoo.fr

⊶ Joseph Verdier

CH. PIERRE-BISE

Le Haut de la Garde 1998

□ 5.5 ha 17,000 30–49 F

Château Pierre-Bise offers an extraordinary view of the famous hillsides of the Layon. Claude Papin likes to evoke the geological diversity of his region. His Anjou 98 comes from 25-year-old Chenin Blanc vines cultivated on a sandstone, schist and rhyolite soil. Quite golden and shining with amber tints, it has a nose characteristic of a long-awaited, well-controlled and even hand-picked harvest. Aromas of crystallised fruit, quince and very ripe plums are unveiled. A clean and opulent palate completes this thoroughbred wine, which still has a long way to go.

🔑 Claude Papin, Ch. Pierre-Bise, 49750 Beaulieu-sur-Layon, tel. 02.41.78.31.44, fax 02.41.78.41.24 ☑ 🍷 by appt.

CH. DE PIMPEAN

Cuvée du Festival 1999★

■ 13 ha 28,000 30–49 F

Château de Pimpéan was built in 1450; its bas-reliefs that show bunches of grapes are proof of its wine-growing vocation, a vocation the current proprietors are keeping up by investing in the renovation of their heritage. With a ruby colour, the Cuvée du Festival emits its aromas after the glass is swirled. The first impression is attractive, smooth on the palate, with enough fullness from velvety tannins. All that is left for this wine to do is to fill out a little more.

🔑 SCA Dom. de Pimpéan, 49320 Grézillé, tel. 02.41.68.95.96, fax 02.41.45.51.93, e-mail maryset@pimpean.com ☑ 🍷 ev. day 8am–12 noon 1.30pm–5.30pm

🔑 Gilles Tugendhat

CH. DE PUTILLE 1999

□ 2 ha 5,000 20–29 F

Along the road that leads to Château de Putille you come across ruins of ancient lime kilns. Pascal Delaunay, a wine-grower resolutely upholding quality, makes an Anjou that is characteristic of Chenin Blanc and very successful in this vintage. Sparkling tints reinforce the attractiveness of the very clean yellow colour. Although still rather quiet on the nose, there is an appreciable complexity with aromas of ripe fruit, not devoid of freshness. On the palate the richness of the wine is balanced by liveliness.

🔑 Pascal Delaunay, EARL Ch. de Putille, 49620 La Pommeraye, tel. 02.41.39.02.91, fax 02.41.39.03.45 ☑ 🍷 ev. day except Sun. 8.30am–12.30pm 2pm–8pm

MICHEL ROBINEAU 1999★

■ 1 ha 3,000 20–29 F

Michel Robineau threw himself into wine-making in 1990 when he established his vineyard of 7 ha (17 acres). He has succeeded in the 99 vintage with an attractive red Anjou. On the nose, Cabernet Franc appears through characteristically peppery notes, giving a herbaceous tinge that will soften after ageing for a short while. The fruity and softly rich palate is evocative of very ripe grapes. Leaving the wine to breathe will allow it to show even better.

🔑 Michel Robineau, 3, chem. du Moulin, Les Grandes Tailles, 49750 Saint-Lambert-du-Lattay, tel. 02.41.78.34.67 ☑ 🍷 by appt.

DOM. ROBINEAU CHRISLOU 1999★★

■ 4.33 ha 5,000 20–29 F

Louis Robineau took over the family estate in 1991; his wines are always well received, particularly his Anjou Rouge, which, in the 99 vintage, has a very dark violet colour. The strong and complex nose gives off aromas of crystallised fruit, violet and iris. The palate's structure is imposing and voluminous, needing only some development.

🔑 Louis Robineau, 14, rue Rabelais, 49750 Saint-Lambert-du-Lattay, tel. 02.41.78.42.65, fax 02.41.78.42.65 ☑ 🍷 by appt.

DOM. DE ROCHAMBEAU 1999★

■ 3 ha 5,000 20–29 F

The 17-ha (42-acre) vineyard is on the side of a hill and dominates the Aubance. It has produced a dark Anjou Rouge with bright tints. Crystallised overripe morello cherries characterise the nose before a velvety impression invades the palate. Charming and well structured, the wine reveals steady flavours of liquorice, which last a long time at the finish. You can feel that all aspects of the maturation process have been respected.

🔑 EARL Forest, Dom. de Rochambeau, 49610 Soulaines-sur-Aubance, tel. 02.41.57.82.26, fax 02.41.57.82.26 ☑ 🍷 ev. day 6pm–8pm; Sat. 9am–7pm

CH. DES ROCHETTES 1999

□ 2 ha 6,000 20–29 F

The buildings of the château date back, for the most part, to the 19th century, and the old stables act as the winery. This clear, pale yellow Anjou, with green tints, has a woodiness on the nose, although this does not mask the fine fruit of the Chenin Blanc (peach and pear), becoming more pleasing. The structured, rounded palate pulls out a real elegance from the tannins. This wine needs to open out some more to be fully appreciated.

🔑 Jean Douet, Ch. des Rochettes, 49700 Concourson-sur-Layon, tel. 02.41.59.11.51, fax 02.41.59.37.73 ☑ 🍷 by appt.

DOM. DU SABLON 1999★★

■ 1 ha 6,000 20–29 F

Domaine du Sablon has a traditional tufa cellar, completed with a winery in 1999. It integrates perfectly with the troglodytic setting of the village. With a clean and intense ruby colour, shining with violet tints, this is an elegant wine. Fruity and floral on the nose, round, structured and balanced on the palate . . . Nothing can harm the harmony of this fruity, fresh Anjou.

🔑 Jean-Pierre Hélin, Le Sablon, 49320 Grézillé, tel. 02.41.45.57.26, fax 02.41.45.57.26 ☑ 🍷 by appt.

DOM. SAINT-ARNOUL 1999★

□ 1 ha 3,000 20 F+

Since December 1999 Alain Poupard has been in partnership with the oenologist Xavier Maury. Together they have been successful with a pleasant Anjou. Brilliant pale yellow, pointing to a good aromatic intensity, combining notes of honey and lemon. The fresh palate finishes on a lightly bitter taste which, nevertheless, takes nothing away from the charm of this wine. Ready from autumn 2000.

🔑 EARL Poupard et Fils, Sousigné, 49540 Martigné-Briand, tel. 02.41.59.43.62, fax 02.41.59.69.23, e-mail saint-arnoul@wanadoo.fr ☑ 🍸 by appt.

COTEAU SAINT-VINCENT 1999*

■ 5 ha 10,000 🍾 🌡 20–29 F

Michel and Olivier Voisine have installed themselves at the edge of the Coteaux du Layon, Anjou and Anjou-Coteaux de la Loire appellations. They have 19 ha (47 acres) of vines, 5 ha (12 acres) of which are devoted to Cabernet Franc, which, harvested during the first days of October, produced a 99 vintage of clean red and brilliant colour. The complex nose is particularly strong in red berries, and after a softly ripe first impression, a supple structure appears, filled with the freshness and liveliness of the lengthy fruit. A very well-balanced wine.

🔑 Michel et Olivier Voisine, Le Coteau Saint-Vincent, 49290 Chalonnes-sur-Loire, tel. 02.41.78.18.26, fax 02.41.78.18.26, e-mail licheur@infonie.fr ☑ 🍸 by appt.

SAUVEROY Cuvée Iris 1999*

■ 3.32 ha 24,000 🍾 🌡 30–49 F

The Sauveroy estate was created in the 19th century and bought by Francis Cailleau in 1947, when it comprised no more than one hectare of vines. In 1985 Pascal Cailleau took over the vineyard and added to it his area of 28 ha (69 acres). He offers a very full and glittering 99, with an intense and complex nose of liquorice, indicating well-controlled time in the barrel. On the palate the wine unfolds its concentrated flavours, built on finely grained tannins. It is a wine to keep, and would go well with red meat or eel stew.

🔑 Pascal Cailleau, Dom. du Sauveroy, 49750 Saint-Lambert-du-Lattay, tel. 02.41.78.30.59, fax 02.41.78.46.43, e-mail domainesauveroy@terrenet.fr ☑ 🍸 by appt.

DOM. DES VARENNES 1999**

■ 4 ha 5,000 🍾 30–49 F

A lovely dark red colour is a characteristic of this remarkable wine. The warm nose draws out intense scents of crystallised red berries, with cherry dominant. With a clean first impression, the palate is built on tannins that are definitely present around a substance of quality. Very interesting roasted notes are evident on the finish.

🔑 GAEC A. Richard, 11, rue des Varennes, 49750 Saint-Lambert-du-Lattay, tel. 02.41.78.32.97, fax 02.41.74.00.30 ☑ 🍸 by appt.

DOM. VERDIER 1999*

■ 1 ha 5,000 20–29 F

On the nose, this ruby-red Anjou immediately gives out a spicy character, reserving the aromas of red berries until the wine is swirled around the glass. With a straightforward first impression, it gains flesh in the middle of the palate and develops on fine tannins to a great length. An elegant, smooth wine that could be left to age in the cellar for a while.

🔑 EARL Verdier Père et Fils, 7, rue des Varennes, 49750 Saint-Lambert-du-Lattay, tel. 02.41.78.35.67, fax 02.41.78.35.67 ☑ 🍸 ev. day 8am–12.30pm 2pm–7pm; Sun. by appt.; cl. 25 Aug.–3 Sep.

Anjou-Gamay

A single-variety red wine made from the Gamay. When grown on the more schistous soils of the area and well vinified, it can produce an excellent carafe wine. Several growers have specialised in this type of wine, which has no ambition other than seeking to please in its year of harvest. In 1999, production was 18,081 hl (477,338 gal).

DOM. DES BONNES GAGNES 1999*

■ 2 ha 6,000 🍾 🌡 20–29 F

In 1020 the *fief d'Orgigné* – which the Bonnes Gagnes were part of – was rented to the monks of the Ronceray d'Angers abbey to be planted with vines. A separate wine-growing property since 1610, this estate benefits from a rich, clay-chalk soil, which assures good development of the vine. Resulting from this is a 99 vintage with intense colour and violet tints. Although still quiet on the nose, the wine none the less releases complex aromas of flowers and small, delicate red berries. The palate has a prolonged fruitiness on a good balance. This wine will open out more during early 2001.

🔑 Jean-Marc Héry, Orgigné, 49320 Saint-Saturnin-sur-Loire, tel. 02.41.91.22.76, fax 02.41.91.21.58 ☑ 🍸 ev. day 9am–12.30pm 2pm–7pm; Sun. by appt.

DOM. CHUPIN 1999

■ 4.04 ha 20,000 20–29 F

Domaine Chupin is a vast property of around 70 ha (173 acres) of gravelly soil. This wine, with a garnet-red tint, has an intense and complex nose that gives off notes of animal and aromas of grilled, even roasted fruit. The fresh palate is full and contains tannins which will dissipate with time.

🔑 SCEA Dom. Chupin, 8, rue de l'Eglise, 49380 Champ-sur-Layon, tel. 02.41.78.86.54, fax 02.41.78.61.73 ☑ 🍸 by appt.

DOM. DU FRESCHE 1999**

■ 0.6 ha 4,300 🍾 🌡 20–29 F

Of an elegant and scintillating cherry-red colour, this wine delivers an intense, fresh and

sweet nose, quite characteristic of the grape variety. After a fine first impression, the wine appears round, supple and very balanced on the palate. The wine is elegance itself, and the subtle aromatic length makes it even more remarkable.

🔑 EARL Boré, Dom. du Fresche, 49620 La Pommeraye, tel. 02.41.77.74.63, fax 02.41.77.79.39 ☒ 𝐘 by appt.

DOM. DE HAUTE PERCHE 1999★★

■ 1.5 ha 5,000 30–49 F

Agnès and Christian Papin have made a remarkable Anjou-Gamay on the soils of shale-clay of their vineyard. A fine ruby colour, the wine has aromas of just-stewed fruit before taking on a spicy character. Fine, full and generous on the palate at first, then fruit flavours come out, accompanied by quite evident tannins that will tone down after time in the cellar.

🔑 EARL Agnès et Christian Papin, 7, chem. de la Godelière, 49610 Saint-Melaine-sur-Aubance, tel. 02.41.57.75.65, fax 02.41.57.75.42 ☒ 𝐘 by appt.

CH. DE LA GENAISERIE 1999★★

■ 3.09 ha 19,000 20–29 F

Château de la Genaiserie has a reputation for its production of *vins liquoreux*. Their dry wines are no less well made, such as this Anjou-Gamay with quite a full ruby colour. The very expressive nose points, through its intense fruitiness, to a Beaujolais-type vinification. The fresh and lively palate is gifted with a good presence of small red berries along with dissipated tannins. It is a structured, balanced and very long wine.

🔑 SC Ch. de La Genaiserie, 49190 Saint-Aubin-de-Luigné, tel. 02.41.78.33.22, fax 02.41.78.67.78 ☒ 𝐘 by appt.

DOM. DU LANDREAU 1999

■ 2 ha 12,000 30–49 F

Behind its clear colour with ruby sparkles appear floral nuances (especially iris) along with very marked spicy, even gamey notes. The balanced palate has a good presence. A wine to be discovered.

🔑 Raymond Morin, Dom. du Landreau, 49750 Saint-Lambert-du-Lattay, tel. 02.41.78.30.41, fax 02.41.78.45.11 ☒ 𝐘 by appt.

DOM. DE LA POTERIE 1999★★

■ 0.6 ha 1,300 20–29 F

The son of northern farmers whose estate was called La Ferme de la Poterie, Guillaume Mordacq came to Anjou in 1996 to run a 12-ha (30-acre) vineyard using sustainable, eco-friendly organic-style cultivation. His Anjou-Gamay is a dark colour with mauve tones and with violet tints. Its young character is apparent on the nose. After a clean and fruity first impression, silken tannins fill the mouth and contribute to the fine balance of the whole. The fruit has been well extracted.

🔑 Guillaume Mordacq, La Chevalerie, 16, av. des Trois-Ponts, 49380 Thouarcé, tel. 02.41.54.12.29, fax 02.41.52.26.41 ☒ 𝐘 by appt.

DOM. RICHOU

Les Champs de la Pierre 1999

■ 3 ha n.c. 30–49 F

'Maurice Richou, medical doctor, physician in ordinary to the king, winegrower.' Those are the terms of an act of 1550 that attests to the winegrowing line of the Richou family. This wine, of a deep, almost black, colour with violet tints, has a full and well-balanced palate that is well marked by the grape variety, giving a flavour of fine, ripe red berries. Keeping it for a short while would be a good idea.

🔑 Dom. Richou, Chauvigné, 49610 Mozé-sur-Louet, tel. 02.41.78.72.13, fax 02.41.78.76.05 ☒ 𝐘 ev. day except Sun. 8.30am–12 noon 2.30pm–7pm

DOM. VERDIER 1999★★

■ 1 ha 4,000 20–29 F

Domaine Verdier has 22 ha (54 acres) of vines on the schist and clay soil of the commune of Saint-Lambert-du-Lattay. It offers a 99 vintage with an intense ruby colour and clear, violet tints. On the nose the wine has the most elegant, fruity notes. The palate then develops with suppleness, marked by the same fruitiness, and climbs strongly to well-rounded tannins. The lengthy finish is remarkable.

🔑 EARL Verdier Père et Fils, 7, rue des Varennes, 49750 Saint-Lambert-du-Lattay, tel. 02.41.78.35.67, fax 02.41.78.35.67 ☒ 𝐘 ev. day 8am–12.30pm 2pm–7pm; Sun. by appt.; cl. 25 Aug.–3 Sep.

Anjou-Villages

The terroir of this AOC is drawn from a selection of regions within the Anjou appellation. To qualify, soils must be healthy, early-flowering and well exposed. Mainly they lie on schists in various stages of evolution. The ten communes making up the geographical area of the AOC Anjou-Village-Brissac, recognised in 1998, occupy a plateau sloping gently down to the Loire, bordered to the north by the river and to the south by the steep hillsides of Layon. The soils are deep, and the special nature of the terroir is also influenced by the proximity of the Loire, which guards against extreme variations in temperature.

CH. DE CHAMBOUREAU Cuvée d'Avant 1998

■ 1 ha 4 000 30–49 F

Château de Chamboureau gets its reputation from its Savennières. But its red wines also deserve interest. Made and matured in *barrique*, this Anjou-Villages exhibits balance. The ruby colour and aromas of red berries, dried fruit and violets are found again in the pleasant palate, whose freshness is very representative of the vintage.

Pierre Soulez, Ch. de Chamboureau, 49170 Savennières, tel. 02.41.77.20.04, fax 02.41.77.27.78 Y by appt.

DOM. CHUPIN 1998

■ 6.24 ha 45,000 20–29 F

This vast estate of 75 ha (185 acres) practises traditional vinification, with the 'cap' of grape skins being submerged and broken up during a maceration period of 28 days. The 98 vintage has an intense red colour and emits aromas of ripe red berries. This light wine will be pleasant to drink by the end of the year 2000.

SCEA Dom. Chupin, 8, rue de l'Eglise, 49380 Champ-sur-Layon, tel. 02.41.78.86.54, fax 02.41.78.61.73 Y by appt.

DOM. DES EPINAUDIERES 1998

■ 2 ha 6,000 20–29 F

This estate owes much to Roger Fardeau. Paul, who went into partnership with his father in 1991, exhibits the same values. It was not easy to produce a substantial wine in 1998. The result, however, is evident with this Anjou-Villages, which is faithful to the spirit of this estate. Structured and strong, it still has some very young tannins, which will dissipate around Easter 2001.

SCEA Fardeau, Sainte-Foy, 49750 Saint-Lambert-du-Lattay, tel. 02.41.78.35.68, fax 02.41.78.35.50 Y by appt.

DOM. DE LA CROIX DES LOGES 1998★

■ 3 ha 5,000 30–49 F

This Anjou-Villages was the result of quite a long maceration of 22 days and a maturation of 10 months, with 50% of the wine in vat and the other in *barrique*. With its quite light structure, it is representative of its vintage. The developed fruity and liquorice aromas precede a palate balanced by elegant tannins, well controlled during vinification.

SCEA Bonnin et Fils, Dom. de La Croix des Loges, 49540 Martigné-Briand, tel. 02.41.59.43.58, fax 02.41.59.41.11, e-mail bonninlesloges@aol.com Y by appt.

DOM. DU LANDREAU 1996

■ 6 ha n.c. 30–49 F

This wine comes from 30-year-old vines. It attracts with its aromatic richness: notes of quite ripe cherries, tobacco and sloe. After a silky first impression, the tannic structure takes over.

Raymond Morin, Dom. du Landreau, 49750 Saint-Lambert-du-Lattay, tel. 02.41.78.30.41, fax 02.41.78.45.11 Y by appt.

DOM. DE LA POTERIE 1998★

■ 4 ha 2,400 30–49 F

Guillaume Mordacq, who established himself in Anjou in 1996 with 12 ha (30 acres) of vines, is a proponent of sustainable, eco-friendly organic-style cultivation. His structured Anjou-Villages will be fully expressive in a few years: its sombre red colour, its still unobtrusive aromas of oak and stewed fruits, and its strong and compact palate all go together to make it a wine to keep for four or five years.

Guillaume Mordacq, La Chevalerie, 16, av. des Trois-Ponts, 49380 Thouarcé, tel. 02.41.54.12.29, fax 02.41.52.26.41 Y by appt.

DOM. DE LA VILLAINE 1998★

■ 1.7 ha 3,000 20–29 F

This vineyard, created in 1970 from a number of small properties, now extends to more than 22 ha (54 acres). A classical wine-making process and a maceration of 24 days have given this wine a deep red colour which is typical of the appellation. Full of red berries and flowers on the nose, it is rich on the palate, giving the sensation of eating raspberries and cherries. It could be drunk at the end of the year 2000 or kept for up to five years.

GAEC des Villains Carré Batail, La Villaine, 49540 Martigné-Briand, tel. 02.41.59.75.21, fax 02.41.59.75.21 Y by appt.

DOM. LES GRANDES VIGNES Les Cocainnelles 1998

■ 6 ha 27,000 30–49 F

This high-quality vineyard has achieved widespread recognition. Its Anjou-Villages comes from vines under grass and with thinned-out leaves. The 35-day maceration was followed by maturation in tanks with stirring of the lees over three months, then maturation in *barrique* on fine lees. While flavour and structure are not subdued, its intense colour and rich aromas suggest great potential.

GAEC Vaillant, Dom. Les Grandes Vignes, La Roche-Aubry, 49380 Thouarcé, tel. 02.41.54.05.06, fax 02.41.54.08.21 Y by appt.

LES SYLPHIDES 1998

■ 20.21 ha 110,000 ▮ 🌡 20-29 F

La Noëlle cooperative makes mostly Muscadet, but it has acquired a good reputation for red Anjou wines. The weather conditions were not very good for wine in 1998, and creating a wine to keep was a perilous exercise: but a successful one, it would appear. This wine has an intense ruby colour, scents of red berries and acidic fruit (redcurrant), and a palate structured by still-young tannins, which will, however, have softened by the end of the year 2000.

🔑 Les Vignerons de La Noëlle, bd des Alliés, B.P. 155, 44154 Ancenis Cedex, tel. 02.40.98.92.72, fax 02.40.98.96.70, e-mail vavenel@cana.fr ☒ 🍸 by appt.

CH. DES NOYERS 1998*

■ 8 ha 6,000 ▮ ⦀ 🌡 20-29 F

This well-known vineyard occupies a superb 16th-century château with three dry moats and large angled towers. Its wine may surprise with its light structure (quite typical of the vintage); its aromatic nuances are reminiscent of fresh fruit (strawberry, cherry, pomegranate), black fruit (sloe), and mint, which creates a lovely feeling of freshness at the finish.

🔑 SCA Ch. des Noyers, Les Noyers, 49540 Martigné-Briand, tel. 02.41.54.03.71, fax 02.41.54.27.63 ☒ 🍸 by appt.

DOM. OGEREAU 1998**

■ 8 ha 13,000 ▮ ⦀ 🌡 30-49 F

Vincent Ogereau is the master craftsman of the remarkable wines of this estate, which are never less than highly regarded. having produced a fine 97, he repeated his success with the same wine with his 1998, which he receives a *coup de coeur.* The intense garnet-red colour produces strong aromas of ripe fruit, dried fruit and cocoa beans. The dense and rich palate leaves a sensation of stewed fruit at the finish. This wine, matured from a very good grape selection, has been perfectly made.

🔑 Vincent Ogereau, 44, rue de la BelleAngevine, 49750 Saint-Lambert-du-Lattay, tel. 02.41.78.30.53, fax 02.41.78.43.55 ☒ 🍸 by appt.

CH. DE PUTILLE 1998**

■ 5 ha 15,000 ▮ 🌡 30-49 F

If there is a vineyard that has progressed the most over the last five years in the area of

red wines, it has to be Château de Putille. Yields are controlled, harvests undertaken at a good maturity and maturation is well controlled. This wine provides a good representation of the AOC, with its intense ruby colour and aromas of fruit and stewed red berries. The warm, full and rich palate combines substance with elegance. This lovely wine can be drunk now or kept for five years.

🔑 Pascal Delaunay, EARL Ch. de Putille, 49620 La Pommeraye, tel. 02.41.39.02.91, fax 02.41.39.03.45 ☒ 🍸 ev. day except Sun. 8.30am–12.30pm 2pm–8pm

SAUVEROY Cuvée Antique 1998

■ 3 ha 13,300 ▮ ⦀ 30-49 F

The youngest of a family of eight children, Pascal Cailleau took over the vineyard at the age of 19 in 1985. His Cuvée Antique was produced from scrupulously selected vines and is the result of a wine-making process that attempts to extract the best potential from the grapes. This wine surprised the jury with its structure: it will become more ordered with time. It has a sombre, almost black colour, with scents of wood and stewed fruit on the nose. A wine that will be excellent in a few years.

🔑 Pascal Cailleau, Dom. du Sauveroy, 49750 Saint-Lambert-du-Lattay, tel. 02.41.78.30.59, fax 02.41.78.46.43, e-mail domainesauveroy@terrenet.fr ☒ 🍸 by appt.

Anjou-Villages-Brissac

DOM. DE BABLUT 1998*

■ 8 ha 20,000 ▮ ⦀ 🌡 30-49 F

This vineyard has belonged to the same family since 1546, a family that has a strong identity with the region. The strong potential of this dignified Brissac will express itself fully at the end of the year 2000. With a deep red colour, it gives off complex aromas of stewed fruit (mulberry, blackcurrant, raspberry), and the intense palate contains tannins that have softened somewhat but are still present at the finish.

SCEA Daviau, Dom. de Bablut, 49320 Brissac-Quincé, tel. 02.41.91.22.59, fax 02.41.91.24.77 ev. day 8.30am–12.30pm 2pm–6.30pm; Sun. by appt.

CH. DE BRISSAC 1998

10 ha 40,000 30–49 F

Château de Brissac is prominent in France's history. It has always belonged to the family, who built it in the 15th century. Its vineyard, cultivated by C. Daviau, has produced a well-made 98 of an intense red colour. It has aromas of red berries and is well balanced on the palate. It will be ready for drinking at the end of the year

SCEA Daviau, Dom. de Bablut, 49320 Brissac-Quincé, tel. 02.41.91.22.59, fax 02.41.91.24.77 ev. day 8.30am–12.30pm 2pm–6.30pm; Sun. by appt.

Duc de Brissac

DOM. DES CHARBOTIERES

Les Tuloires 1998

1 ha 4,000 50–69 F

Paul-Hervé Vintrou, proprietor of the estate since 1994, originates from a Toulouse family of *négociants*. He was trained as a sommelier, a route that took him to the final of the sommelier contest of 1980. This wine, made from a good base, has been well-extracted. The tannins are dominant at the moment but will soften with age. The promising wine is a beautiful, intense red colour with strong aromas recalling concentrated fruit and red berries.

Paul-Hervé Vintrou, Clabeau, 49320 Saint-Jean-des-Mauvrets, tel. 02.41.91.22.87, fax 02.41.66.23.09, e-mail contact@domainedescharbotieres.com by appt.

DOM. DE HAUTE-PERCHE 1998★★

8.3 ha 32,000 30–49 F

Christian Papin is considered a sage of the Aubance; his personality and his union work make up for a lot of this, but so do his wines, such as the highly praised Anjou-Villages-Brissac 97. The new vintage is in the same spirit as the earlier. All elements of it are remarkable: its intense and sombre red colour, its complex aromas of blackcurrant buds, of ripe cherries, of smoke and of stewed black fruit. The warm and supple palate leads to a finish which, when tasted, was in need of a few months' ageing.

EARL Agnès et Christian Papin, 7, chem. de la Godelière, 49610 Saint-Melaine-sur-Aubance, tel. 02.41.57.75.65, fax 02.41.57.75.42 by appt.

CH. LA VARIERE La Chevalerie 1998

4 ha 12,000 70–99 F

Very close to Château de Brissac, this property includes buildings dating from the 13th and 15th centuries. It is one of the meeting places of enthusiasts of characterful wines, run under the authority of J. Beaujean, called the '*petit maître*'. How can we describe this astonishingly well-built wine marked by its maturation in barrel? Its structure is remarkable for a 98 vintage and its personality will become evident in a few years.

Ch. La Varière, 49320 Brissac, tel. 02.41.91.22.64, fax 02.41.91.23.44, e-mail chateau.la.variere@wanadoo.fr by appt.

CH. LA VARIERE 1998★★★

12 ha 60,000 30–49 F

This wine from Château la Varière has been made in traditional fashion: a long vatting period of 20 days, with a 15-month maturation in vats. The wine excited the tasting jury. Its intense, almost black, ruby colour is splendid. Its subtle aromas of black fruit and red berries anticipate its rich, warm and complex palate. The superb finish ends on a note of fresh fruit. A reference point for the red vines of the 98 vintage.

Ch. La Varière, 49320 Brissac, tel. 02.41.91.22.64, fax 02.41.91.23.44, e-mail chateau.la.variere@wanadoo.fr by appt.

MANOIR DE VERSILLE 1998★

1.3 ha 6,000 30–49 F

This manor is made up of two main buildings at right-angles to each other divided by a square staircase dating from the 16th century. It was acquired in 1998 by Francine Desmet, whose wine, of a light colour, is quite simple, dominated by notes of fresh fruit; it also picks out hints of raspberry and strawberry. It is pleasant, unobtrusive and balanced on the palate. To be drunk very young.

EARL du Manoir de Versillé, Versillé, 49320 Saint-Jean-des-Mauvrets, tel. 02.41.45.22.00, fax 02.41.45.22.00, e-mail manoir.versille@wanadoo.fr by appt.

Francine Desmet

DOM. DE MONTGILET 1998★

3.76 ha 14,677 50–69 F

Montgilet made its name with *vins liquoreux*, and it is also asserting itself in the field of red wines. Coming from slate-shale soil, this wine has been studiously cared for and spends little time in the barrel. The flavours are very imposing and need to be tamed somewhat. Its intense red colour and its strong aromas express themselves on airing. Wait a few years. **Cuvée 98, Vinifiée en Barrique** carries its name well: strength and complexity form a good part of the appeal, but very marked woodiness suggests leaving it

o age a bit. One star (70–99FF).
🗝 Victor et Vincent Lebreton, Dom. de Montgilet, 49610 Juigné-sur-Loire, tel. 02.41.91.90.48, fax 02.41.54.64.25, e-mail montgilet@terre-net.fr ☒ Y by appt.

DOM. DES ROCHELLES

La Croix de Mission 1998★

n.c. 20,000 50–69 F

The Rochelles estate (53 ha/131 acres) has always produced red wines of high quality. This one is particularly successful in the 98 vintage. With an intense, almost black colour, it displays strong aromas of black fruit with nuances of smoke and liquorice and a dense, balanced palate. A wine as secret as a quiet forest, with undergrowth notes that will fully express themselves in a year or two.
🗝 EARL J.-Y. A. Lebreton, Dom. des Rochelles, 49320 Saint-Jean-des-Mauvrets, tel. 02.41.91.92.07, fax 02.41.54.62.63 ☒ Y by appt.

DOM. DE SAINTE-ANNE 1998

2 ha 10,000 30–49 F

The estate is on the highest clay-chalk hill of Saint-Saturnin-sur-Loire, whose particular terroir gives an original style to its red wines. This vintage is described with the words 'tenderness and lightness', quite unusual for wines from this appellation; it seduces with its intense red colour, its aromas of red berries and black fruit, and its palate, with a warm, almost light, first impression. Perhaps to be drunk by the end of the year 2000.
🗝 Dom. de Sainte-Anne, EARL Brault, 49320 Brissac-Quincé, tel. 02.41.91.24.58, fax 02.41.91.25.87 ☒ Y 9am–12pm, 2pm–7pm.

Rosé d'Anjou

As it produces between 140,000 and 195,000 hl (3,696,000–5,148,000 gal) a year, this is the largest of the Anjou appellations by volume. At first, it was very successful at export, yet this medium-dry wine is now harder to sell. The principal variety is Grolleau, which used to be trained in the traditional goblet shape, when it also produced light rosé wines called 'rougets'. It is increasingly being vinified as light red table wine or Vin de Pays.

CH. DE CHAMPTELOUP 1999

14 ha 80 000 20 F+

This grower-distributer cultivates 80 ha (197 acres), 14 ha (34 acres) of which are devoted to the production of Rosé d'Anjou, among which is this really typical wine which gives an impression of lightness, fruitiness and sweetness. Try it with strawberry tart or red berries.
🗝 Dom. de Sainte-Anne, EARL Brault, 49320 Brissac-Quincé, tel. 02.41.91.24.58, fax 02.41.91.25.87 ☒ Y ev. day except Sun. 9am–12 noon 2pm–7pm; Sat. 6pm
🗝 SCEA de Champteloup, 49700 Brigné-sur-Layon, tel. 02.41.59.65.10

DAMES DE LA VALLEE 1999★

n.c. 660,000 20–29 F

Founded in 1855, this family business today sells around 100,000 hl (2,640,000 gal) in the heart of the Loire Valley. Resulting from fermentation at low temperature, this Rosé d'Anjou is pleasant and well balanced; it leaves an impression of freshness, which is enhanced by the presence of light carbonic gas. During the finish, some pleasant notes of fresh fruit appear. A wine that would go well with melon or red berries.
🗝 Rémy Pannier, rue Léopold-Palustre, 49400 Saint-Hilaire-Saint-Florent, tel. 02.41.53.03.10, fax 02.41.53.03.19 ☒ Y ev. day except Sun. Mon. 9.30am–6.30pm

FLANERIE DE LOIRE 1999★★

30 ha 200,000 20–29 F

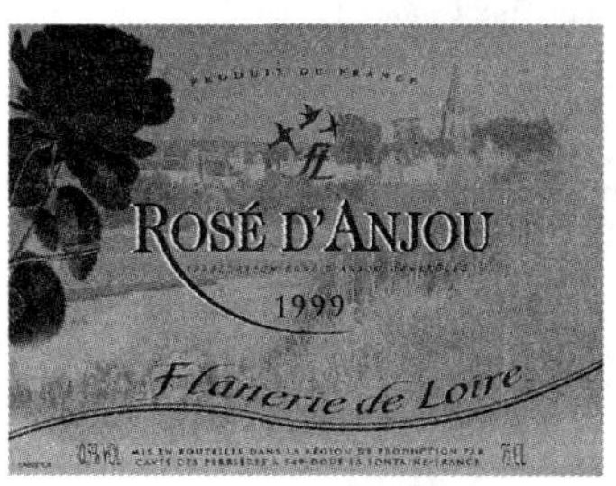

This *négociant* produced around 18,000 hl (475,200 gal) in 1999. It specialises in the production of rosé and sparkling wines. Its Rosé d'Anjou is perfectly typical of the appellation: a delicate salmon colour, with light scents of fruit and a harmonious palate pleasantly combining impressions of freshness and sweetness. A wine that would happily accompany an autumn meal.
🗝 SA Lacheteau, ZI La Saulaie, 49700 Doué-la-Fontaine, tel. 02.41.59.26.26, fax 02.41.59.01.94, e-mail lacheteau.export@symphonie.fai.fr

DOM. DE LA DOUNIERE 1999

1.8 ha 1000 20–29 F

To the south of the Anjou wine-growing region, in the Deux-Sèvres area, and quite representative of Anjou, this vineyard is constantly developing, as is testified by its Rosé

LOIRE

d'Anjou that is very much in the style of the appellation: pale pink in colour, unobtrusive and fine aromas recalling fresh fruit, and a light, fruity and refreshing palate. A wine that will go with a whole meal.
🔑 EARL Lacroix, 107, rue Saint-Vincent, 79290 Bouillé-Loretz, tel. 05.49.67.05.13, fax 05.49.67.11.43 ☑ 🍷 by appt.

DOM. DE L'ANGELIERE 1999★

◪ 7 ha 4,000 ▮ 🌡 20-29 F

Cultivated by the same family for six generations, this domaine has grown from 15 to 40 ha (37 to 99 acres). Its Rosé d'Anjou is produced from Grolleau grapes grown on ancient gravelly soil (a typical terrain for rosé wines). It is pleasant, light and refreshing, with all the characteristics of the appellation. To be drunk by the end of the year 2000.
🔑 GAEC Boret, Dom. de L'Angelière, 49380 Champ-sur-Layon, tel. 02.41.78.85.09, fax 02.41.78.67.10 ☑ 🍷 by appt.

CH. DE MONTGUERET 1999

◪ 6 ha 50,000 ▮ 🌡 20-29 F

André Lacheteau, son of a *négociant*, and his wife Dominique, passionate oenologist, acquired Château de Montguéret in Haut-Layon in 1987. Today, they produce a thirst-quenching wine which is pleasant and light. Pink-orange in colour, it has slightly intense aromas of strawberry and other fruit and a supple and balanced palate.
🔑 SCEA Ch. de Montguéret, 49560 Nueil-sur-Layon, tel. 02.41.59.26.26, fax 02.41.59.01.94, e-mail lacheteau.export@symphonie.fai.fr ☑
🔑 A. et D. Lacheteau

Cabernet d'Anjou

There are some excellent medium-dry rosés made from the Cabernet Franc and Cabernet-Sauvignon varieties in this appellation. Served chilled, they go well with melon as a starter or with desserts that are not too sweet. As they age, the wines take on a tile-red colour and can be drunk as an apéritif. Production was 164,900 hl (4,353,360 gal) in 1999. The best examples come from the fossiliferous sands of the Tigné region and the Layon.

DOM. DE CLAYOU 1999★

◪ 10 ha 55 000 ▮ 20-29 F

In the same family for a number of generations, this domaine evolves over the years: its Cabernet d'Anjou is produced from traditional vinification with maceration of the grape skins. It has an intense pink-orange colour; on the nose small red berries dominate accompanied by hints of aniseed; the balanced palate leaves a pleasant sensation of freshness at the finish. A wine that is typical of its appellation.
🔑 SCEA Jean-Bernard Chauvin, 18 bis, rue du Pont-Barré, 49750 Saint-Lambert-du-Lattay, tel. 02.41.78.42.84, fax 02.41.78.48.52 ☑ 🍷 by appt.

DOM. DES CLOSSERONS 1999★

◪ 4.33 ha n.c. ▮ 🌡 20-29 F

Yves and Jean-Claude Leblanc founded this estate in 1956 and their two sons, Yannick and Dominique, joined them later. The palate of this wine releases flavours of ripe fruit, and as a whole the wine gives a sensation of finesse and elegance.
🔑 EARL Jean-Claude Leblanc et Fils, Dom. des Closserons, 49380 Faye-d'Anjou, tel. 02.41.54.30.78, fax 02.41.54.12.02 ☑ 🍷 by appt.

DOM. DES EPINAUDIERES 1999★★★

◪ 5 ha 7,000 ▮ 🌡 20-29 F

Cabernet d'Anjou is a speciality of Domaine des Epinaudières. This one is a classic of the appellation: pink-orange in colour, with partridge-eye tints; intensely fruity and herbaceous aromas; full and rich on the palate with plenty of red berries. A characterful wine to be drunk as an apéritif or with mixed salad with cold meat.
🔑 SCEA Fardeau, Sainte-Foy, 49750 Saint-Lambert-du-Lattay, tel. 02.41.78.35.68, fax 02.41.78.35.50 ☑ 🍷 by appt.

DOM. DU FRESCHE 1999★

◪ 1 ha 6,000 ▮ 🌡 20-29 F

La Pommeraye is to the west of the Maine-et-Loire region, on the hillsides of the Loire. Its Cabernet d'Anjou is refreshing and can be enjoyed outdoors after a game of tennis, say. It is fresh both of taste and smell, with, on the palate, a sensation of fresh fruit.
🔑 EARL Boré, Dom. du Fresche, 49620 La Pommeraye, tel. 02.41.77.74.63, fax 02.41.77.79.39 ☑ 🍷 by appt.

DOM. DE GATINES 1999

◪ 6 ha 6,000 ▮ 🌡 20-29 F

The estate is known, among others, for its Cabernets d'Anjou, which are characteristic of a particular terroir of Tigné – *faluns*, or sandshell-chalk soil. This wine has a fine, pale and lightly orangey colour. Its more rustic and herbaceous aromas are reminiscent of pepper, but balance is achieved and the finish offers a promising fruity sensation.
🔑 EARL Dessevre, Dom. de Gatines, 12, rue de la Boulaie, 49540 Tigné,

el. 02.41.59.41.48, fax 02.41.59.94.44 ☑ Y v. day except Sun. 8am–12 noon 2pm–.30pm

DOM. DE LA COUCHETIERE 1999*

◪ 4 ha 29,000 ▮ 🌡 20-29 F

This old estate has specialised in wine since 1944. The 1980s saw it grow, and in 1999 a new tasting cellar was built. Its fresh and successful Cabernet d'Anjou is characterised by a fine structure. With a blood-orange colour, it has intense aromas of fruit; the rich palate will become more refined with time. Can be kept for two to five years.

🔑 GAEC Brault, Dom. de La Couchetière, 49380 Notre-Dame-d'Allençon, tel. 02.41.54.30.26, fax 02.41.54.40.98 ☑ Y ev. day except Sun. 8am–12.30pm 2pm–7pm

DOM. DE LA MONTCELLIERE 1999*

◪ 6 ha 8,000 ▮ 🌡 20F+

The family estate was founded in 1879. A Cabernet d'Anjou to be served – according to the opinion of one of the tasters – while playing a game of boules. A light wine that goes down like water and which refreshes with its notes of exotic fruit.

🔑 SCEA Louis Guéneau et Fils, Dom. de La Montcellière, 49310 Trémont, tel. 02.41.59.60.72, fax 02.41.59.66.15 ☑ Y ev. day except Sun. 8am–12.30pm 2pm–7.30pm

DOM. DE LA PETITE ROCHE 1999

◪ 20 ha 10,000 ▮ 🌡 20-29 F

François Regnard has the spirit of the party and of full glasses. It is easy to start a tasting at La Petite Roche, where you will find this light and thirst-quenching wine with fruity aromas that are present both on the nose and on the palate; the finish leaves a very pleasant sensation of freshness.

🔑 François Regnard, Dom. de La PetiteRoche, 49310 Trémont, tel. 02.41.59.43.03 ☑ Y by appt.

DOM. LEDUC-FROUIN

La Seigneurie 1999

◪ 6 ha 10,000 ▮ 🌡 30-49 F

La Seigneurie was the property of the Marquis of Becquedelièvre until 1933, when the Leduc-Frouin family, who had cultivated it since 1873, became the owners. The vineyard, which has been run using natural production methods for four years, offers a Cabernet d'Anjou which is expressive and simple, with a salmon-pink colour, light scents of small red berries and a fresh palate. A well-made, fresh and fruity wine to be drunk from now onwards.

🔑 Mme Georges Leduc, Dom. Leduc-Frouin, Sousigné, 49540 Martigné-Briand, tel. 02.41.59.42.83, fax 02.41.59.47.90, e-mail domaine-leduc-frouin@wanadoo.fr ☑ Y by appt.

DOM. DES NOELS 1999*

◪ 2 ha 7,500 ▮ 🌡 20-29 F

J.-M. Garnier is the president of the powerful Coteaux du Layon union. He took over this estate in 1994. The Cabernet d'Anjou exhibits a very fine balance, with a number of herbaceous notes; the colour is salmon-pink; the aromas pick out notes of fresh fruit and of green pepper; the harmonious palate takes on the same aromatic register as the nose.

🔑 SCEA dom. des Noëls, Les Noëls, 49380 Faye-d'Anjou, tel. 02.41.54.18.01, fax 02.41.54.30.76 ☑ Y by appt.

🔑 J.-M. Garnier

DOM. OGEREAU 1999**

◪ 3 ha 10,000 ▮ 🌡 30-49 F

Vincent Ogereau is head of a line of winemakers from Anjou and regularly appears in leading French wine guides. Yet again, he offers a wine that is surprising for its richness and character: a ripe cherry colour, aromas of concentrated red berries appear on airing, and a full, dense and fruity palate. A high-quality grape selection from the outset is at the origin of this great rosé!

🔑 Vincent Ogereau, 44, rue de la BelleAngevine, 49750 Saint-Lambert-du-Lattay, tel. 02.41.78.30.53, fax 02.41.78.43.55 ☑ Y by appt.

CH. DE PASSAVANT 1999*

◪ 2 ha 10,000 ▮ 🌡 30-49 F

Built by Foulques Nerra, a cruel count but also a major builder of abbeys (972–1040), Château de Passavant was intended to defend the south of Maine-et-Loire. Classified as historical monuments, these medieval buildings include a pavilion from the 18th century, which is very interesting, as are the wines produced here. The mark of the wine-maker is certainly perceptible in this Cabernet d'Anjou; the sugary fermenting aromas recall the strawberry and banana that are present on the nose and on the palate. The wine demonstrates unobtrusive freshness. To be served throughout a meal.

🔑 SCEA David Lecomte, Ch. de Passavant, 49560 Passavant-sur-Layon, tel. 02.41.59.53.96, fax 02.41.59.57.91, e-mail passavant@wanadoo.fr ☑ Y ev. day 9am–12 noon 2pm–7pm; Sat. Sun. by appt.

CH. DE PUTILLE 1999*

◪ 4 ha 10,000 ▮ 🌡 20-29 F

Pascal Delaunay runs his vineyard with conviction and produces a Cabernet d'Anjou that has been described as a party wine: it has a salmon-pink colour, exuberant aromas of ripe fruit, a fresh palate with a sensation of strawberries and raspberries. An excellent lesson in harmony.

🔑 Pascal Delaunay, EARL Ch. de Putille, 49620 La Pommeraye, tel. 02.41.39.02.91, fax 02.41.39.03.45 ☑ Y ev. day except Sun. 8.30am–12.30pm 2pm–8pm

DOM. ROMPILLON 1999★★

◪ 1.16 ha 10,000 ▮ 🌡 20–29 F

The estate is on the tourist route of the wine-growing region, at the foot of the famous Quarts de Chaume hill. Its rosé exhibits notes of ripe fruit (raspberry, strawberry) on the nose as well as on the palate, with a harmonious and unobtrusive finish; it succeeds in establishing a good balance between freshness and strength. Can be served throughout a meal.

🔑 Jean-Pierre Rompillon, L'Ollulière, 49750 Saint-Lambert-du-Lattay, tel. 02.41.78.48.84, fax 02.41.78.48.84 ☑ Y by appt.

Coteaux de l'Aubance

The banks of the little Aubance river are schist slopes planted with old Chenin vines, giving a sweet white wine which improves with age. Production was 5,597 hl (147,761 gal) in 1999. This appellation imposes strict limits on production.

DOM. DE BABLUT Sélection 1998

☐ 13 ha 20,000 ⦀ 50–69 F

Christophe Daviau symbolises the renewal of the Coteaux de l'Aubance appellation. Unappreciated a decade ago, this region's *vins liquoreux* today make up an important part of this prestigious family of wines. It is true that this man's work, particularly on the Bablut estate, is partly responsible for this success: hand selection, slow pressing, fermentation and maturation in barrel have all given this wine a yellow colour with golden tints, aromas of ripe fruit and spices and a balanced palate that leaves a sensation of freshness. To be left for a year or two.

🔑 SCEA Daviau, Dom. de Bablut, 49320 Brissac-Quincé, tel. 02.41.91.22.59, fax 02.41.91.24.77 ☑ Y ev. day 8.30am–12.30pm 2pm–6.30pm; Sun. by appt.

DOM. DE BABLUT Noble 1998★★

☐ 13 ha 5,500 ⦀ 100–149 F

The selection of *grains nobles* (single berries affected by noble rot) were harvested at a natural 17.5% alcohol. This wine has an intense golden colour with orangey nuances. Its aromas have lively hints of ripe fruit, nuts (almond, hazelnut), spices and honey. The strong and rich palate, dominated by notes of crystallised apricot and hand-crafted oak, make an excellent wine, which is among the major *vins liquoreux* of the Loire Valley.

🔑 SCEA Daviau, Dom. de Bablut, 49320 Brissac-Quincé, tel. 02.41.91.22.59, fax 02.41.91.24.77 ☑ Y ev. day 8.30am–12.30pm 2pm–6.30pm; Sun. by appt.

CH. DE BOIS BRINCON 1997★★

☐ 0.4 ha 100 ⦀ 100–149 F

This estate, which dates back to 1219, gained major recognition in 1998, rewarding the work of Xavier Cailleau on the Layon hillside of Faye d'Anjou. His Coteaux de l'Aubance is quite typical of the particularly sunny late season of 1997: its amber-yellow almost caramel colour, its very rich nose with notes of dried and crystallised fruit, its rich sweet and opulent palate, all reveal a wine that has accumulated all the warmth of the vintage and which will keep for decades.

🔑 Xavier Cailleau, Ch. de Bois-Brinçon, 49320 Blaison-Gohier, tel. 02.41.57.19.62, fax 02.41.57.10.46 ☑ Y by appt.

DOM. DE HAUTE PERCHE

Tête de cave 1998

☐ 4 ha 6,600 ▮ ⦀ 🌡 50–69 F

The Haute Perche estate is one of the best vineyards in Aubance. The basic essential work is carried out by the Papins (short pruning, green harvesting, hand picking), with particularly interesting results. This classic wine is fruity and pleasant. It leaves an impression of balance and lightness and offers immediate pleasure. To be drunk at the end of the year 2000 or kept for up to five years.

🔑 EARL Agnès et Christian Papin, 7, chem. de la Godelière, 49610 Saint-Melaine-sur-Aubance, tel. 02.41.57.75.65, fax 02.41.57.75.42 ☑ Y by appt.

MANOIR DE VERSILLE

Cuvée Capucine 1998★

☐ 1.8 ha 2,900 ▮ ⦀ 🌡 30–49 F

This Coteaux de l'Aubance is made for immediate pleasure. Yellow with golden tints, it reveals aromas of exotic and ripe fruits, along with a round and balanced palate with a mineral note at the finish, accompanied by a light taste of bergamot. To be drunk at the end of the year or to be kept for up to five years.

🔑 EARL du Manoir de Versillé, Versillé, 49320 Saint-Jean-des-Mauvrets, tel. 02.41.45.22.00, fax 02.41.45.22.00, e-mail manoir.versille@wanadoo.fr ☑ Y by appt.

🔑 Francine Desmet

DOM. DE MONTGILET

Le Tertereaux 1998★★

☐ 3.56 ha 3,560 ⦀ 100–149 F

The Montgilet estate yet again takes pride of place with the Sélection du Tertereaux. A blue slate clay terrain, late harvests picked by hand, fermentation and maturation in barrel, and a passionate wine-maker, all make up the secret of its success. Amber-yellow, this 98 vintage delivers intense aromas characteristic of overripe grapes (crystallised fruit, honey, quince). The intense and opulent palate is

colourful, like a basket of fruit. A superb bottle. (50cl bottles.)
🗝 Victor et Vincent Lebreton, Dom. de Montgilet, 49610 Juigné-sur-Loire, tel. 02.41.91.90.48, fax 02.41.54.64.25, e-mail montgilet@terre-net.fr ☑ 🍷 by appt.

DOM. DE MONTGILET

Clos Prieur 1998★

☐ 4.5 ha 1,800 🛢 100–149 F

The Clos Prieur is made up of crumbly, sandy shale that has given rise to this very rich wine – almost too rich for some members of the jury. It reaches 161 g/l of residual sugar, and its concentrated aromas, with toasted hints and overripe fruit, are indicators of its surprisingly full palate that leaves a sensation of fruit jelly. To be left for a few years, the wine will appeal to enthusiasts of powerful wines. (50cl bottles.)
🗝 Victor et Vincent Lebreton, Dom. de Montgilet, 49610 Juigné-sur-Loire, tel. 02.41.91.90.48, fax 02.41.54.64.25, e-mail montgilet@terre-net.fr ☑ 🍷 by appt.

DOM. RICHOU Le Pavillon 1998★

☐ 3 ha 5,000 🛢 70–99 F

The family's name is closely associated with red Anjou wines, but the domaine is also very good with *vins liquoreux*. Look for finesse rather than strength in Le Pavillon. Unobtrusive scents of quite ripe pear, quince and dried fruit signal a light and airy palate, which is characteristic of the northern hills bordering the Loire. Very subtle, it is wine for the refined drinker.
🗝 Dom. Richou, Chauvigné, 49610 Mozé-sur-Louet, tel. 02.41.78.72.13, fax 02.41.78.76.05 ☑ 🍷 ev. day except Sun. 8.30am–12 noon 2.30pm–7pm

TERRES D'ALLAUME

Clos des Noëlles 1999

☐ 1.12 ha 4,800 🛢 🛢 🌡 50–69 F

The estate was created in 1992 from a number of small vineyards on the hills bordering the Loire from Rochefort-sur-Loire to Mozé-sur-Louet. The jury confirmed the quality of the maturity in this difficult 99 vintage: notes of ripe and stewed fruit are signs of concentrated harvests; several notes of mushrooms and a light bitterness appear as well during the finish. A good balance on the whole for this wine, which will be ready to drink at the end of the year 2000.

🗝 Eric Blanchard, Le Perray-Chaud, 49610 Mozé-sur-Louet, tel. 02.41.45.76.15, fax 02.41.45.37.79 ☑ 🍷 by appt.

Anjou-Coteaux de la Loire

This appellation is limited to white wines made from Chenin, known here as Pineau de la Loire. Production, which was 1,621 hl (42,794 gal) in 1999, is limited by the size of the area, a dozen communes situated exclusively on schists and limestone at Montjean. Careful picking encourages the grapes to reach over-ripeness, giving the generally medium-dry wines a greener colour than those of Coteaux de Layon. In this region, as elsewhere in Anjou, there is an increasing shift towards the production of red wines.

DOM. DU FRESCHE

Cuvée Vieille Sève 1999★

☐ 2 ha 8 000 🛢 30–49 F

The Anjou-Coteaux de la Loire AOC (of which A. Boré is the President) was little known a number of years ago, but today it occupies its own completely separate place in the family of *vins liquoreux* of the Loire Valley. This one has very good potential. Dominated by noble rot, it delivers notes of ripe yellow fruits (stewed apricot, peach), with an unobtrusive palate that stretches into the finish to recall honey.
🗝 EARL Boré, Dom. du Fresche, 49620 La Pommeraye, tel. 02.41.77.74.63, fax 02.41.77.79.39 ☑ 🍷 by appt.

CH. DE PUTILLE

Clos du Pirouet 1999★

☐ 3.5 ha 9,000 🛢 🌡 30–49 F

Pascal Delaunay has been rewarded in this *Guide* by a *Coup de Coeur* for the Anjou-Villages appellation. Here is a very light wine with plenty of finesse, as much for its pale golden colour as for its subtle hints of exotic fruit (lychees), flowers and ripe fruit. The sweet palate leaves a sensation during the finish of stewed apricots and honey. The wine is ready for drinking but will improve and gain character after ageing for a year or two.
🗝 Pascal Delaunay, EARL Ch. de Putille, 49620 La Pommeraye, tel. 02.41.39.02.91, fax 02.41.39.03.45 ☑ 🍷 ev. day except Sun. 8.30am–12.30pm 2pm–8pm

LOIRE

DOM. DE PUTILLE 1999

☐ 2 ha 2,600 30–49 F

This estate is one of the highest-quality vineyards of Coteaux de la Loire. Unfortunately, Pierre Sécher died during the 1999 harvest and Isabelle Sécher took over. Of a pale golden-yellow colour, the wine is gentle on the nose, with unobtrusive aromas recalling white blossom and honey. The pleasant flavours leave a sensation of freshness. Light and harmonious, it is a good representative of the appellation.

Dom. de Putille, Putille, 49620 La Pommeraye, tel. 02.41.39.80.43, fax 02.41.39.81.91 by appt.

Isabelle Sécher

Savennières

These are dry white wines made from Chenin, mainly produced in the commune of Savennières. The schists and purple sandstone of the area give the wines a particular character which has led them in the past to be defined as part of the Coteaux de la Loire, but they deserve a place in their own right. The wines are a little firm, but full of aromatic flavour, excellent with cooked fish. The production of Savennières and the growths Coulée-de-Serrant and Roche-aux-Moines was 4,725 hl (124,740 gal) in 1999.

DOM. DES BARRES

Les Bastes 1999*

☐ 1.1 ha 4 000 30–49 F

Founded in 1991, this 25-ha (62-acre) vineyard is still family-run. The grapes of this Savennières were collected by hand at slight over-maturity and fermented in part in *barrique*. The very young wine disorientated the jury. Some evident signs of fine flavour from the beginning, like the intense yellow colour or the aromas of ripe white fruit, appear on airing. The palate leaves a sweet sensation. To be left until 2001.

Patrice Achard, Les Barres, 49190 Saint-Aubin-de-Luigné, tel. 02.41.78.98.24, fax 02.41.78.68.37 by appt.

DOM. DES BAUMARD

Clos du Papillon 1997**

☐ 4.21 ha 24,000 70–99 F

The wine-growing family who own this domaine have been settled in Rochefort-sur-Loire since 1634. Clos du Papillon gets its name from the layout of the grounds: tw 'wings' on each side split by a path. This is classic of the appellation as much for its cle golden colour, tinged with grey, as for i quite intense aromas of fern, angelica an ripe fruit. The balanced, elegant and comple palate makes up a wine that is ready to drin but which also has a long future.

Florent Baumard, SCEA Dom. des Baumard, 8, rue de l'Abbaye, 49190 Rochefort-sur-Loire, tel. 02.41.78.70.03, fax 02.41.78.83.82 ev. day except Sun. 10am–12 noon 2pm–5.30pm; cl. 20–30 Dec.

DOM. EMILE BENON

Clos du Grand Hamé 1998**

☐ 5.5 ha 6,000 30–49 F

The Benons established this 12-ha (30 acre) vineyard in 1991. Their Savennière exhibits fullness straight away. Of a supert pale brilliant gold colour, it gives off aroma of grapefruit, pineapple, ripe fruit and flowers along with some mineral notes. The open intense and harmonious palate is very subtle Can be drunk now or kept for a number of years.

Dom. Emile Benon, rte de la Lande, Epiré, 49170 Savennières, tel. 02.41.77.10.76, fax 02.41.77.10.07, e-mail earl.benon@wanadoo.fr ev. day except Sun. 8am–12 noon 2pm–7pm; cl. 15–31 Aug.

CH. DE CHAMBOUREAU 1998**

☐ 11.58 ha 20,000 50–69 F

Château de Chamboureau, dating from the 15th century and altered during the 17th, is a doughty testament to the richness of the Savennières winegrowing tradition, and its vineyard is no exception. This wine combines finesse and richness, as shown in its pale golden colour with light green tints and its complex aromas recalling ripe fruit and grilled pineapple with lengthy mineral notes. The palate is balanced and unobtrusive. **Château de La Bizolière 98**, still not at its peak on the day of the tasting, was judged a great success and will provide a pleasant surprise at the end of the year 2000.

Pierre Soulez, Ch. de Chamboureau, 49170 Savennières, tel. 02.41.77.20.04, fax 02.41.77.27.78 by appt.

DOM. DU CLOSEL

Les Coulées 1999★

☐ 6.5 ha 21,000 50–69 F

Domaine du Closel is one of the most typical vineyards of the appellation. During the 15th century, the property was a religious retreat, and from then on it passed from one owner of note to another, the last being descendants of the Marquis de las Cases, biographer of Napoleon. Today, it is run by talented women. Les Coulées and **Les Caillardières 99** were judged great successes. They offer an aromatic complexity characteristic of the appellation, with austere mineral notes and intense hints of acacia and may blossom and ripe fruit with an opulent and unobtrusive palate, which is rich but also mysterious. To be kept for four or five years.

Mesdames de Jessey, Dom. du Closel, Ch. des Vaults, 49170 Savennières, tel. 02.41.72.81.00, fax 02.41.72.86.00, e-mail domaine.du.closel@wanadoo.fr ev. day 9am–12.30pm 1.30pm–6.30pm; Sun. by appt.

DOM. DU CLOSEL

Clos du Papillon 1998★

☐ 3 ha n.c. 70–99 F

Clos du Papillon is characteristic of the region for its sandy schist intercut with seams of quartz. As always, the wine opens on the palate with a feeling of severity that becomes one of harmony and fullness: aromas dominated by mineral notes give place, bit by bit, to a sensation of ripe apricots and oranges; from a rather reticent beginning, it finishes with an impression of balance and elegance.

Mesdames de Jessey, Dom. du Closel, Ch. des Vaults, 49170 Savennières, tel. 02.41.72.81.00, fax 02.41.72.86.00, e-mail domaine.du.closel@wanadoo.fr ev. day 9am–12.30pm 1.30pm–6.30pm; Sun. by appt.

DOM. DES FORGES

Clos des Mauriers 1999★

☐ 1.5 ha 8,000 50–69 F

Claude Branchereau is a man of conviction who has given his vineyard a solid reputation. He was widely and justly acclaimed for his Savennières 97. Judging the 99 vintage is difficult, as it is still very young. Its clear yellow colour and its aromatic expression are quite typical of the appellation with, at the moment, floral and mineral notes. The harmonious palate is still severe. To be revisited in a year or two, when it will certainly provide a surprise.

Vignoble Branchereau, Dom. des Forges, 49190 Saint-Aubin-de-Luigné, tel. 02.41.78.33.56, fax 02.41.78.67.51 by appt.

NICOLAS JOLY Le Petit Clos 1998★

☐ 3 ha 7,000 70–99 F

An enthusiastic proponent of biodynamic viticulture, Nicolas Joly owns the famous Coulée-de-Serrant. This 98 Savennières seems at first somewhat austere, but this impression dissipates and the mineral and herbaceous aromas develop towards notes of ripe fruit. A sensation of freshness enlivens the palate, where hints of lime are perceptible. This wine will go well with freshwater fish.

Nicolas Joly, Ch. de La Roche-aux-Moines, 49170 Savennières, tel. 02.41.72.22.32, fax 02.41.72.28.68, e-mail couleedeserrant@wanadoo.fr by appt.

DOM. DE LA MONNAIE 1997

☐ 2.5 ha 10,000 30–49 F

The name of this domaine originates in the first purpose of the house, as it was an old tollhouse on the towpath of the Loire. The estate rigorously selects the harvests with hand sorting and conducts the vinification and maturation in *barrique* – something that will either please or displease the jury and consumers. The structure of the 97 vintage has oaky notes and surprises with its aromas of ripe fruit and flowers. Its golden-yellow colour is superb.

Eric Morgat, Dom. de la Monnaie, 49170 Savennières, tel. 02.41.72.22.51, fax 02.41.78.30.03 by appt.

MOULIN DE CHAUVIGNE 1999★

☐ 1.5 ha 10,000 30–49 F

The Chauvigné mill, dating from the 13th century, was bought by Sylvie Termeau, who established this vineyard in 1992. Today, it extends to 8.5 ha (21 acres). This Savennières is quite representative of its appellation, with a first impression of severity and austerity giving place to notes of ripe fruit and a feeling of freshness on the palate. The wine will open out with time and should be left for a year or two.

Sylvie Termeau, Moulin de Chauvigné, 49190 Rochefort-sur-Loire, tel. 02.41.78.86.56, fax 02.41.78.86.56, e-mail lemoulindechauvigne@worldonline.fr by appt.

DOM. DU PETIT METRIS

Clos de la Marche 1999

☐ 2.06 ha 10,000 50–69 F

Family-run for five generations, this domaine has acquired a solid reputation. Its Savennières, still very young, exhibits unobtrusive aromas of white blossom and fern, and leaves a mineral and austere sensation on the palate. It will open out over a year or two and promises a finish in which a touch of bitterness is quite typical of the appellation.

GAEC Joseph Renou et Fils, Le Grand Beauvais, 49190 Saint-Aubin-deLuigné, tel. 02.41.78.33.33, fax 02.41.78.67.77 by appt.

CH. DE PLAISANCE 1999

☐ 1 ha 5,000 50–69 F

Guy Rochais is a colourful wine-maker, producing above all *vins liquoreux*. Today, he also succeeds with Savennières. This one is promising: judged in its youth, it holds all the winning cards for its personality to assert

LOIRE

itself with time. Its pale golden colour; its unobtrusive aromas of white blossom and fruit accompanied by mineral notes; the rounded palate displays, at the finish, a lightly bitter impression that is perfectly classic. A wine to be left for a few years.
Guy Rochais, Ch. de Plaisance, Chaume, 49190 Rochefort-sur-Loire,
tel. 02.41.78.33.01, fax 02.41.78.67.52 by appt.

Savennières Roche-aux-Moines, Savennières Coulée-de-Serrant

It is difficult to distinguish between two growths so similar to each other in character and quality. The Coulée de Serrant is grown on a smaller area (6.85 ha (16.9 acres)), sited on both sides of the valley of the little Serrant river, but mainly on a steep slope with a south-westerly exposure. Totally owned by the Joly family, this appellation has attained the highest reputation at national level for its quality and value for money. It takes five or ten years for the wines to reach their peak. La Roche aux Moines is owned by several growers and covers a declared area of 19 ha (47 acres) (though not all planted), producing an average of 600 hl (15,840 gal). Even though quality is not as consistent, you can find certain vintages of which its namesake would not be ashamed.

Savennières Roche-aux-Moines

CH. DE CHAMBOUREAU
Cuvée d'Avant 1998★
6,35 ha 12 000 70-99 F

The hillside of Roche-aux-Moines has a hard rock spur overhanging the Loire. The château, founded during the 15th century and altered during the 17th, deserves interest as much for its architecture as for its wine. This appellation has been vinified in *barrique* for more than two years, and the very fine 98 vintage needs to be left for a number of years, time for the wood to become less obvious. It offers already a perfect balance, with a palate of notes of apricot, flint, vanilla and linden flowers. It would go very well with lobster.
Pierre Soulez, Ch. de Chamboureau, 49170 Savennières, tel. 02.41.77.20.04, fax 02.41.77.27.78 by appt.

NICOLAS JOLY
Clos de la Bergerie 1998★★
2 ha 6,000 100-149 F

An alley of cypresses leads to Nicolas Joly's beautiful residence that dates from the 13th century. This wine depicts perfectly the beauty and the nature of the soils that bore it, with a first impression of severity with mineral notes that one feels equally when walking these shaly and stony slopes with their sombre colour. But there is also a sensation of harmony and of sweetness, with aromas recalling ripe fruit. This sweet impression on the palate mirrors the feeling one gets when standing before this beauty spot. A vintage that is faithful to the intention of its author.
Nicolas Joly, Ch. de La Roche-aux-Moines, 49170 Savennières,
tel. 02.41.72.22.32, fax 02.41.72.28.68,
e-mail couleedeserrant@wanadoo.fr by appt.

DOM. AUX MOINES 1991★★
n.c. 30,000 70-99 F

This estate was run by a monastery from 1190 to the Revolution, when it was sold as a property of the state. The 91 vintage is surprising for its fullness and balance. A sensation of ripe fruit is constantly present up to a distinguished finish that is as colourful as a basket of fruit. The **Millésime 98** also receives a mention: still closed, it gives way after airing to some floral notes. The wine needs to be left for a year or two.
SCI Mme Laroche, La Roche-aux-Moines, 49170 Savennières,
tel. 02.41.72.21.33, fax 02.41.72.86.55 by appt.

Savennières Coulée-de-Serrant

NICOLAS JOLY 1998★
7 ha 25,000 200-249 F

Nicholas Joly is big in biodynamic viticulture in France, his commitment complying with a philosophy that he puts into practice using a close observation of nature. His

:oulée-de-Serrant 98 has a surprising aro-
1atic expression that comes close to that of *ins liquoreux* grown on the other bank of the ,oire (the Coteaux du Layon wine-growing rea), with notes of ripe fruit (apricot, pear, lum), dried fruit and pastry. On the palate he wine surprises with its lightness and its pparent smoothness. A wine that will assert :self on ageing and needs to be left for at least year or two.

Nicolas Joly, Ch. de La Roche-aux-
Aoines, 49170 Savennières,
el. 02.41.72.22.32, fax 02.41.72.28.68,
-mail couleedeserrant@wanadoo.fr ☒ Y
y appt.

Coteaux du Layon

These are medium-dry, medium-sweet and sweet white wines, of which 52,886 hl (1,396,190 gal) were produced in 1999, from the slopes of 25 communes on the banks of the Layon, from Nueil to Chalonnes. Chenin is the only variety grown. Several villages have a reputation for quality: the best known is Chaume, producing from 78 ha (193 acres). Six other names can also be added to the appellation: Rochefort-sur-Loire, Saint-Aubin-de-Luigné, Saint-Lambert-du-Lattay, Beaulieu-sur-Layon, Rablay-sur-Layon and Fayed' Anjou. They are subtle wines, golden green at Concourson, yellower and stronger downstream, with aromas of honey and acacia from the over-ripe grapes. Their ability to keep is exceptional.

DOM. D'AMBINOS

Beaulieu Sélection de grains nobles 1998★★

☐ 11 ha 2, 500 100–149 F

Widely praised by connoisseurs, Domaine d'Ambinos majors in *vins liquoreux*. This vintage comes from grapes from four hand pickings, each with a natural level of more than 17.5% alcohol. The vinification is carried out in four-to-five year-old barrels. Golden-yellow, the wine delivers intense and complex aromas of pear, peach, honey and wax. Rich and concentrated, with notes of crystallised fruit, the palate is not deficient in freshness characteristic of the *grands liquoreux* of the Loire Valley. A remarkable success, which will not surprise anyone.

Jean-Pierre Chéné, 3, imp. des Jardins,
49750 Beaulieu-sur-Layon,
tel. 02.41.78.48.09, fax 02.41.78.61.72 ☒ Y
by appt.

DOM. BANCHEREAU

Chaume Cuvée Tradition 1999

☐ 2.14 ha 2,300 70–99 F

This traditional estate on the hillsides of the Layon was founded in 1950 and has grown a lot, today extending to 37 ha (91 acres). It enjoys a solid reputation. No fewer than five hand selections have been carried out on this terraced parcel of land that is the origin of this 99 vintage. The result? A pale yellow colour and surprising aromas of eau-de-vie and plum and of fruits marinated in alcohol, as well as a strong and warm palate. An intense wine that will become more refined on ageing.

Dom. Banchereau, 62, rue du Canal-deMonsieur, 49190 Saint-Aubin-de-Luigné,
tel. 02.41.78.33.24, fax 02.41.78.66.58 ☒ Y
by appt.

DOM. DES BARRES

Saint-Aubin Les Paradis 1999★★

☐ 2 ha 3,500 50–69 F

Patrice Achard happily took over the family vineyard (25 ha/62 acres) in 1991 to cultivate high-quality wines. We find again that his Cuvée Les Paradis, given a star for the 97 vintage, definitely deserves its name in the 99 vintage! The jurors pointed out the richness of the harvest, which is indicated by the fine citrus fruit (lemon) aromas and those of fresh fruit, as well as the balance and harmony on the palate. The finish, whose light oakiness indicates well-controlled maturation in the barrel, leaves a very pleasant impression of freshness.

Patrice Achard, Les Barres, 49190 Saint-Aubin-de-Luigné, tel. 02.41.78.98.24,
fax 02.41.78.68.37 ☒ Y by appt.

G. BECLAIR Rochefort 1998★

☐ 1.52 ha 2,500 50–69 F

Five generations have succeeded each other on this vineyard, which today runs to 12 ha (30 acres) of vines. The cellar, dating from the 16th century, was probably originally a grain or salt storeroom, and was transformed during the 18th century into a tannery and leather drying room before finding its vocation at the beginning of the 19th century. Pale yellow in colour, this 98 vintage exhibits fine scents of fresh fruit. Its palate shows more elegance than fullness. Of a quite light, pleasant and well-made type, this wine can be tasted from the end of the year 2000.

G. Beclair, 4, rue Dieuzie-Martreau,
49190 Rochefort-sur-Loire,
tel. 02.41.78.73.25, fax 02.41.78.54.23 ☒ Y
by appt.

M. BLOUIN Chaume 1999

☐ 4.12 ha 8,000 50–69 F

With some 21 ha (52 acres) of vines, this traditional Anjou estate is in Saint-Aubin-de-Luigné, the 'pearl' of Layon. Straw-yellow with golden tints, its Chaume is certainly simple and quite light, but it provides immediate

LOIRE

pleasure with its aromas – still unobtrusive on the day of tasting – of crystallised fruit, and its fresh and balanced palate. A pleasant wine that can be drunk from the end of 2000 and for a few years after that.

Dom. Michel Blouin, 53, rue du Canal-deMonsieur, 49190 Saint-Aubin-de-Luigné, tel. 02.41.78.33.53, fax 02.41.78.67.61 by appt.

DOM. DES BOHUES 1999★★

□ 7.5 ha 5,000 30–49 F

Denis Retailleau has assumed sole responsibility of this 15-ha (37-acre) estate, half of which is devoted to the production of Coteaux du Layon. The jury's accolade for this wine must be good encouragement for him. The wine, though not impressive for its strength, appears to be a remarkable representative of the appellation. The colour is a yellow lightly decorated with green tints, the aromatic quality is well defined, with unobtrusive notes of white blossom, ripe fruit and quince; and the harmonious palate, with a very good balance, is also marked by ripe fruits.

Denis Retailleau, Les Bohues, 49750 Saint-Lambert-du-Lattay, tel. 02.41.78.33.92, fax 02.41.78.34.11 by appt.

CH. DE BOIS-BRINCON

Sélection de grain noble 1997★★★

□ n.c. n.c. 150–199 F

One of the oldest estates of the Anjou region (its existence is documented as far back as the 13th century), this château has managed to milk this fine 97 vintage for all it is worth, since, after its hugely successful Coteaux du Layon Faye, here is a Sélection de Grains Nobles which has been assessed as exceptional. The wine has accumulated all the sun from a remarkable late season, which is testified by its golden amber colour, its intense aromas of crystallised fruit, honey and, on its palate, a veritable basket of fruit. (50-cl bottles.)

Xavier Cailleau, Ch. de Bois-Brinçon, 49320 Blaison-Gohier, tel. 02.41.57.19.62, fax 02.41.57.10.46 by appt.

CH. DU BREUIL

Beaulieu Vieilles vignes 1998★

□ 8 ha 2,500 70–99 F

Château du Breuil (35 ha/86 acres of vines) is on the peak of the hillside of Beaulieu-sur-Layon. Its proprietor, Marc Morgat, is ve active in professional matters. This wine golden-straw colour was produced fro grapes harvested from hundred-year-ol vines and vinified in *barrique* for three to fiv years. Its aromas combine citrus fruit, hone wax and oaky notes; its intense and sweet pa ate leaves at the finish an impression of fres ness. A well-balanced wine that will open ou on ageing.

Ch. du Breuil, 49750 Beaulieu-sur-Layon tel. 02.41.78.32.54, fax 02.41.78.30.03 by appt.

Morgat

CH. DE BROSSAY

Sélection de grain noble 1998★★

□ 2 ha 450 70–99 F

In charge of 36 ha (89 acres) of vines, Raymond and Hubert Deffois have contributed t the fame of the Coteaux du Layon thanks to quality output, of which we have a high opin ion. Their *vins liquoreux* are the product o rigorous hand picking and maturation partl carried out in barrel. Their Sélection d Grains Nobles 98 reveals a remarkable poten tial for the vintage: an intense yellow colou with aromas of ripe fruit, apricot, dried frui and spices, and a strong and concentrated pal ate all point to a wine of character whic needs to be left for a number of years. As fo the **Vieilles Vignes 99** (30–49FF), its aromati complexity is already perceptible and give the palate a sweet and balanced sensatio (mentioned without a star).

Raymond et Hubert Deffois, Ch. de Brossay, 49560 Cléré-sur-Layon, tel. 02.41.59.59.95, fax 02.41.59.58.81, e-mail brossay@groupesirius.com ev. day except Sun. 8am–1pm 2pm–7pm

DOM. CADY

Saint-Aubin Les Varennes 1999★

□ 2.5 ha 8,000 50–69 F

In a pretty village bordering the Layon, the Cady estate is another testimonial to *vins liquoreux*. Les Varennes comes from a hillside where green surface shales rise from the first geological era, a terroir that provides wines of character each year. The 99 vintage distinguishes itself with its very fine expression reminiscent of ripe fruit (pear, peach), which follow right through. The first impression reveals a sweet, delicate and harmonious sensation. Still a bit short, this wine will take on all its dimensions after several years. A **Coteaux du Layon Chaume 99** (70–99F) has received the same mark for its aromas of brioche and dried fruit, and its fresh, fruity and full palate. It can be drunk from the end of the year 2000, but should be kept.

Dom. Cady, Valette, 49190 Saint-Aubin-de-Luigné, tel. 02.41.78.33.69, fax 02.41.78.67.79 by appt.

DOM. CHUPIN 1998

□ 15.23 ha 60,000 30–49 F

Domaine Chupin is a vast vineyard (71 ha/175 acres) in Champ-sur-Layon. Grapes harvested by hand and a fermentation without added yeast, which continued into January, are the basis for this pale yellow 98 tinged with green. It has scents of crystallised fruit, apple and hazelnut, and its light palate gives the impression of eating honeycomb, ending on a note of freshness. To be drunk from the end of 2000.

SCEA Dom. Chupin, 8, rue de l'Eglise, 49380 Champ-sur-Layon, tel. 02.41.78.86.54, fax 02.41.78.61.73 Y by appt.

DOM. DU CLOS DES GOHARDS

1999*

☐ n.c. n.c. 30–49 F

This 35-ha (86-acre) estate has several old Chenin Blanc vines, which, on a gravelly soil, give very good results, as testified by this green-tinted, pale yellow 99 with intense aromas of flowers. Smoky nuances escape on the fruity and sweet palate, with a light vivacity on the finish. A fine representative of the appellation.

EARL Michel et Mickaël Joselon, Dom. du Clos des Gohards, Les Oisonnières, 49380 Chavagnes-les-Eaux, tel. 02.41.54.13.98, fax 02.41.54.13.98 Y by appt.

DOM. DES CLOSSERONS

Vieilles vignes 1999**

☐ n.c. n.c. 50–69 F

Enthusiastic for Coteaux du Layon, Jean-Claude Leblanc and his son have planted some steep slopes. Their wines have been, more than once, described as outstanding, and this one is a testament to their expertise, with its golden-yellow colour, its fine aromas of dried and ripe fruit and wax, and its rich palate, which is at the same time fresh, intense and, nevertheless, unobtrusive. With a remarkable balance, this wine can already be drunk but will open out more with time.

EARL Jean-Claude Leblanc et Fils, Dom. des Closserons, 49380 Faye-d'Anjou, tel. 02.41.54.30.78, fax 02.41.54.12.02 Y by appt.

DOM. DESMAZIERES

Beaulieu Sélection de grain noble 1999*

☐ 3 ha 3,200 70–99 F

Christel and Marc Godeau established themselves at this 17-ha (42-acre) estate in 1987 with the intention of producing high-quality *vins liquoreux*. Watchful for overcropping, they practise hand-picking, rigorous selection of yields, and mature their wine in barrel. Coming from grapes whose natural richness passed 17.5%, this Sélection, with a full golden-straw colour, delivers aromas that are still unobtrusive; after airing, liquorice, ripe apricot, peach and honey are perceptible. The palate is strong and fresh. A wine that will express all its potential when it reaches maturity.

Christel et Marc Godeau, Dom. Desmazières, 27, rue Saint-Vincent, 49750 Beaulieusur-Layon, tel. 02.41.78.41.64, fax 02.41.78.63.35 Y by appt.

DOM. DULOQUET

Cuvée Noblesse 1999**

☐ 6 ha 1,200 100–149 F

Hervé Duloquet, who represents the third generation at this vineyard, took over the reins in 1991. He has provided a new direction, concentrating on high-quality *vins liquoreux*, and he is regularly rewarded with general acclaim for his wines. This one is very representative, with its golden-yellow colour, its aromas of overripe grapes reminiscent of apricot and ripe fruit, its full and extremely sweet palate, marked, at the end, by notes of caramel, citrus fruit and vanilla. **Les Carbonifères 99** (70–99F), dominated at the moment by its youthful aromas (undergrowth, seaweed), needs to age. It gains one star.

Hervé Duloquet, Les Mousseaux, 4, rte du Coteau, 49700 Les Verchers-sur-Layon, tel. 02.41.59.17.62, fax 02.41.59.37.53 Y by appt.

DOM. DES EPINAUDIERES

Saint-Lambert 1999*

☐ 1 ha 4,000 30–49 F

In 1966 Roger Fardeau took over this vineyard as a sharecropper; ten years later he was able to rent the entirety. In 1991 he went into partnership with his son. The vineyard (21 ha/ 52 acres) is today a testament to Anjou. In line with the preceding vintages, this 99 has substance, with its straw colour, scents of concentrated, dried and exotic fruit, and its full, strong and harmonious palate. It will take on fullness with ageing.

SCEA Fardeau, Sainte-Foy, 49750 Saint-Lambert-du-Lattay, tel. 02.41.78.35.68, fax 02.41.78.35.50 Y by appt.

DOM. FARDEAU Vieilles vignes 1999*

☐ n.c. 5,500 50–69 F

This 16-ha (40-acre) estate was restructured a number of years ago. Both the wines presented, of different styles, were both judged very successful. Vieilles Vignes, stronger than the other, leaves a concentrated sensation, with its golden colour, scents of crystallised fruit and unctuous palate. **Cuvée Stéfy Fin de Siècle 99** (70–99F) is lighter and interesting for its aromatic expression of ripe fruit, and for its elegance. Two wines that will improve with age and which will be ready to drink at the end of the year

Dom. Michel Fardeau, Les Hauts Perrays, 49290 Chaudefonds-sur-Layon, tel. 02.41.78.67.57, fax 02.41.78.68.78 Y ev. day 9am–12 noon 1pm–7pm; Sat. Sun. by appt.

DOM. DES FORGES

Saint-Aubin Cuvée des Forges 1999**

☐ 4 ha 4,000 50–69 F

Claude Branchereau is president of the Coteaux du Layon Chaume AOC union. A man of conviction and rigour, he has contributed to the surprising renewal of the winegrowing region of Coteaux du Layon. His output is brilliantly represented in the *Guide*.

LOIRE

This one seduced the jury with its potential. Its aromas of fruit jelly, both on the nose and on the palate, are characteristic of the *grand liquoreux*. A wine that will be talked about as soon as it has achieved maturity.
Vignoble Branchereau, Dom. des Forges, 49190 Saint-Aubin-de-Luigné, tel. 02.41.78.33.56, fax 02.41.78.67.51 by appt.

DOM. GAUDARD Les Varennes 1999*

☐ 2.82 ha 6,600 30–49 F

President of the wine-growing federation of Anjou-Saumur, Pierre Aguilas throws himself with passion into the defence and promotion of the wines of his region. Still young on the day of tasting, his Les Varennes is surprisingly complex with its aromas of crystallised and ripe fruit and spices. The elegant palate combines sweetness with freshness. This Coteaux du Layon will be ready to drink at the end of the year 2000 and will open up even more with time.
Pierre Aguilas, Dom. Gaudard, rte de Saint-Aubin, 49290 Chaudefonds-sur-Layon, tel. 02.41.78.10.68, fax 02.41.78.67.72 ev. day except Sun. 8am–12 noon 2pm–6pm

DOM. DE JUCHEPIE

Faye La Quintessence 1997*

☐ 2 ha 2,000 150–199 F

Previously ironmongers of Belgian nationality, the owner-growers converted to wine-growing, successfully it would appear from their three Sélections du Millésime 97 en Faye d'Anjou, all singled out by the jury for their fine aromas of ripe and crystallised fruit and of quince. The preference is for this Quintessence, with intense golden tints, dense on the palate, and pointing to a concentrated harvest. **Les Churelles** (100–149F), somewhat lighter, leaves an impression of freshness. This is mentioned (without a star), as is **Cuvée Alexander** (150–199F).
Oosterlinck-Bracke, Dom. de Juchepie, 49380 Faye-d'Anjou, tel. 02.41.54.33.47 by appt.

DOM. DE LA BELLE ANGEVINE

Saint-Lambert Bonnes Blanches 1998*

☐ 1.5 ha 4,000 30–49 F

La Belle Angevine is the heroine of a 15th-century legend which is told in Saint-Lambert-du-Lattay. As for the estate, made up of the regrouping of two properties, one in Beaulieu-sur-Layon and the other in Saint-Lambert-du-Lattay, it is generally highly regarded. Hints of undergrowth and iodine, representative of this difficult 98 vintage, appear in the wine, but also aromas linked to the good maturity of the harvest (quince, ripe fruits) and a good balance on the palate. A wine that owes much to the efforts of the wine-maker.
Florence Dufour, Dom. de La Belle Angevine, La Motte, 49750 Beaulieu-sur-Layon, tel. 02.41.78.34.86, fax 02.41.72.81.58, e-mail fldufour@club-internet.fr by appt.

DOM. DE LA BERGERIE

Cuvée Fragrance 1998*

☐ 2 ha 2,800 100–149 F

Well known, particularly for its *vins liquoreux*, this domaine pays particular attention to the management of its vines and practises traditional vinification in barrel. Matured for 18 months in the wood, this Cuveé Fragrance has often been judged remarkable, and even attained an exceptional level in the brilliant 97 vintage. With a straw-yellow colour in the glass, this 98 vintage is intense on the eye, as it is on the nose, which combines scents of ripe fruit (peach, quince), stewed or crystallised fruit, spice and undergrowth. The harmonious and refined palate reveals a touch of bitterness at the end. A Coteaux du Layon that surprised the jury with its length and will fully express its potential in a few years.
Yves Guégniard, Dom. de La Bergerie, 49380 Champ-sur-Layon, tel. 02.41.78.85.43, fax 02.41.78.60.13, e-mail domainede.la.bergerie@wanadoo.fr ev. day except Sun. 9am–12.30pm 2pm–7pm

DOM. DE LA MOTTE

Rochefort Cuvée Cosmos 1999

☐ 1 ha 1,500 70–99 F

Representing the third generation, Gilles Sorin took over the family vineyard (19 ha/47 acres) in 1997. His Cuvée Cosmos is made from scrupulously selected grapes vinified and matured in *barrique*. The maturation is expressed in oaky notes that are still somewhat invasive, but aromas of honey and apricot are also perceptible, indicating a good concentration and good potential. To be left for a while.
Gilles Sorin, 35, av. d'Angers, 49190 Rochefort-sur-Loire, tel. 02.41.78.72.96, fax 02.41.78.75.49 by appt.

CH. DE LA MULONNIERE

Beaulieu 1998**

☐ 18 ha 8,000 50–69 F

B. Marchal-Grossat arrived at the vineyard in 1991 and has managed to give it back its renown: the necessary work undertaken among the vines (controlling the number of bunches, strict hand picking) has allowed the prestigious terroir of La Mulonnière to express itself again. With a golden-straw colour, this 98 delivers intense scents of citrus fruit and quince. The strong and balanced palate reveals a surprising aromatic complexity (hints of citrus, exotic and ripe fruit). Distinguished in character, it is a *grand liquoreux*.
B. Marchal-Grossat, Ch. de La Mulonnière, 49750 Beaulieu-sur-Layon, tel. 02.41.78.47.52, fax 02.41.78.63.63 by appt.

DOM. DE L'ARBOUTE

Cuvée Prestige 1999

☐ 5.47 ha 6,488 30–49 F

Jules Massicot came to this vineyard, established in the 18th century, in 1955, and since 1986 the estate has been run by his son, Yves, and his wife. Their Cuvée Prestige was judged to be characteristic of the appellation. The jury noted a promising aromatic complexity (hints of white blossoms, ripe fruit, dried fruit) and a freshness on the palate which guarantee a good future.

Yves Massicot, L'Arboute, 49380 Faye-d'Anjou, tel. 02.41.54.03.38, fax 02.41.54.40.57 by appt.

VIGNOBLE DE L'ARCISON 1999★

☐ 2 ha 5,000 30–49 F

This 26-ha (64-acre) estate is in the commune of Thouarcé, on the same territory as Cru Bonnezeaux. Its Coteaux du Layon delivers, on airing, scents of ripe fruit, citrus fruit and gingerbread. The palate gives a sensation of freshness and sweetness, indicative of high-quality *vins liquoreux*. To be left for a number of years and to be decanted before drinking.

Damien Reulier, Vignoble de L'Arcison, Le Mesnil, 49380 Thouarcé, tel. 02.41.54.16.81, fax 02.41.54.31.12 ev. day 9am–12.30pm 2pm–6pm; cl. Oct.

DOM. DE LA ROCHE MOREAU

Chaume 1999★

☐ n.c. 3,000 50–69 F

The proprietors of La Roche Moreau are not short of anecdotes about their property, whose output can be discovered in a chalet that dominates the valleys of the Loire and the Layon, in the winery, an ancient classified building dating from the 17th century and in the cellar, previously a coal mine, shut up during the Second World War to conceal the entrance from the occupying forces . . . As for this 99 vintage, it has nothing anecdotal about it: with a full yellow colour, it develops notes of fermentation (pineapple, grapefruit) as well as hints of ripe fruit; the clean and full palate finishes with a fine balance of crystallised fruit. A refined wine that will gain more fullness with time.

André Davy, Dom. de La Roche Moreau, La Haie-Longue, 49190 Saint-Aubin-deLuigné, tel. 02.41.78.34.55, fax 02.41.78.34.55, e-mail davy.larochemoreau@wanadoo.fr by appt.

CH. DE LA ROULERIE Chaume 1998

☐ n.c. n.c. 100–149 F

Château de la Roulerie is at the foot of the Chaume hillside. The vines cross over steep slopes and carboniferous formations. The Coteaux du Layon Chaume 97 was a very successful wine, and the lighter 98 is representative of a difficult vintage. But it exhibits an elegance and finesse fitting for the *grands terroirs*. It has a golden-yellow colour, aromas evocative of crystallised fruit, quince and exotic fruit, and a balanced palate that surprises with its hints of spice and honey. (50cl bottles.)

Vignobles Germain et Associés Loire, Ch. de Fesles, 49380 Thouarcé, tel. 02.41.68.94.00, fax 02.41.68.94.01, email loire@vgas.com by appt.

CH. LA TOMAZE

Faye Sélection de grain noble 1997★★

☐ 2 ha 2,100 100–149 F

The vineyard, which today runs to 40 ha (99 acres), has been in the same family for two centuries. The original part, 20 ha (49.5 acres), was in Rablay-sur-Layon (left bank) and in Faye-d'Anjou (right bank) on hillsides sloping down towards the Layon. As for Château la Tomaze, its owners have just celebrated a hundred years of age. This Sélection de Grains Nobles is remarkable for its balance and elegance. Golden-yellow, it exhibits intense aromas of pears, of wax and of crystallised fruit, along with a delicate hint of oak. The very fine, rich palate, however, remains light and fresh. A wine ready to drink at the end of 2000 that will take on more fullness with ageing. (50cl bottles.)

Vignoble Lecointre, Ch. La Tomaze, 49380 Champ-sur-Layon, tel. 02.41.78.86.34, fax 02.41.78.61.60 by appt.

DOM. LEDUC-FROUIN

Le Grand Clos La Seigneurie 1999★

☐ 3 ha 2,500 50–69 F

This wine is the result of assembling the second passage through the vines and a part of the third, in both cases using botrytised and shrivelled grapes that are left to dry on the vines. Golden-yellow, it combines on the nose the scents of raisins and ripe fruit. Unctuous and sweet on the palate, it is 'a sweetness to be tasted', according to one of the jury.

Mme Georges Leduc, Dom. Leduc-Frouin, Sousigné, 49540 Martigné-Briand, tel. 02.41.59.42.83, fax 02.41.59.47.90, e-mail domaine-leduc-frouin@wanadoo.fr by appt.

DOM. LEROY Vieilles vignes 1999

☐ 4 ha 7,000 30–49 F

In the centre of Aubigné-sur-Layon, in front of the 11th-century church, this family-run domaine offers a 99 vintage deserving of attention. Aromatic notes of ripe fruit reveal that the wine is the result of a mature crop of grapes, and the palate is pleasant, balanced, harmonious and long on the finish. A wine that can be drunk at the end of the year 2000.

Jean-Michel Leroy, rue d'Anjou, 49540 Aubigné-sur-Layon, tel. 02.41.59.61.00, fax 02.41.59.96.47 ev. day except Sun. 8.30am–1pm 2pm–8pm

LES PASTOURELLES 1998

☐ 10 ha 15,000 30–49 F

This cooperative, which produces mainly Muscadet, has also built up a reputation for red Anjou wines. Some efforts have also been made with Chenin vines – control of yields, hand-picking – which have begun to pay dividends. Les Pastourelles, with a pale yellow colour and green tints, delivers aromas of hazelnut and ripe fruit, and its pleasant and balanced palate is a good representative of the appellation.

LOIRE

🔑 Les Vignerons de La Noëlle, bd des Alliés, B.P. 155, 44154 Ancenis Cedex, tel. 02.40.98.92.72, fax 02.40.98.96.70, e-mail vavenel@cana.fr ☑ Y by appt.

DOM. DES MAURIERES

Saint-Lambert Sélection Rive gauche 1997★

☐ n.c. n.c. 100–149 F

This traditional estate, known for its production of *vins liquoreux*, possesses a number of strips of land in the famous Cru Quarts-de-Chaume. The 97 vintage enjoys a great reputation in Anjou due to its particularly sunny and dry late season, which has given the wine a golden-yellow colour tinted with orange. The refined nose gives, after airing, aromas of crystallised fruit and honey. On the full, sweet and concentrated palate, notes of hazelnut, walnuts and caramelised apple appear on the finish. A very rich wine to be served decanted.

🔑 EARL Moron, Dom. des Maurières, 8, rue de Perinelle, 49750 Saint-Lambert-du-Lattay, tel. 02.41.78.30.21, fax 02.41.78.40.26 ☑ Y by appt.

DOM. DE MIHOUDY

Les Valaises 1999★★

☐ 2 ha 5,000 30–49 F

A traditional estate of 45 ha (111 acres), typical of Anjou, this won the prize 'Grappe de Bronze' in the 1997 *Hachette Guide des Vins*. Les Valaises comes from scrupulously selected grapes, vinified and matured in barrel of new oak. The barrels have helped to give it a straw-yellow colour and an oakiness that dissipates delicately. The intense aromas evoke broom flowers, spices and ripe fruit, while the strong palate is remarkably balanced. The wine, which is already excellent, deserves to be kept for a number of years.

🔑 Cochard et Fils, 49540 Aubigné-sur-Layon, tel. 02.41.59.46.52, fax 02.41.59.68.77 ☑ Y by appt.

CH. MONTBENAULT

Faye-d'Anjou Vieilles vignes 1999

☐ 3 ha 4,900 50–69 F

This traditional Anjou estate produces its *vins liquoreux* using the same methods and objectives as it did a decade ago. Faye-d'Anjou Vieilles Vignes has a simple aromatic expression of may blossom, linden flowers and acacia which is characteristic of grapes harvested at maturity but without aiming for a strong concentration. The harmonious and light palate leaves a sensation of freshness at the end.

🔑 Yves et Marie-Paule Leduc, Ch. Montbenault, 49380 Faye-d'Anjou, tel. 02.41.78.31.14, fax 02.41.78.60.29 ☑ Y ev. day except Sun. 9am–12 noon 2pm–7pm

DOM. OGEREAU

Saint-Lambert Cuvée Prestige 1998★★

☐ 6 ha 5,000 70–99 F

Vincent Ogereau has become, through his own efforts, a benchmark for the Anjou wine-growing region as a whole. And this wine, made from scrupulously selected grapes and vinified in part in barrel, is certainly in the style of the estate. Straw-yellow in the glass, it delivers intense scents of ripe fruit, citrus fruit, honey and flowers, to which are added subtle woody notes of vanilla and coconut. The sweet and strong palate remains quite delicate. A wine ready for drinking but which can also be kept for a number of years.

🔑 Vincent Ogereau, 44, rue de la BelleAngevine, 49750 Saint-Lambert-du-Lattay, tel. 02.41.78.30.53, fax 02.41.78.43.55 ☑ Y by appt.

DOM. DE PAIMPARE

Saint-Lambert 1999

☐ 4 ha n.c. 30–49 F

Settled in the most vine-laden commune of Anjou since 1990, Michel Tessier's aim is to produce wines of character. And this is a successful 99 for the vintage; it is certainly light, but balanced and unobtrusive as well. It has a pale yellow colour, aromas evocative of apple and ripe fruit and a harmonious palate dominated by hints of fruit. A wine that can be drunk from the end of 2000.

🔑 SCEA Michel Tessier, 32, rue Rabelais, 49750 Saint-Lambert-du-Lattay, tel. 02.41.78.43.18, fax 02.41.78.41.73 ☑ Y by appt.

DOM. DU PETIT METRIS

Chaume Les Tétuères 1999★

☐ 2 ha 2,500 70–99 F

A family-run estate of 32 ha (79 acres), this is particularly successful with its dry white wines and its *vins liquoreux*. The site of Tétuères is made up of a gravel-shingle soil. This golden-yellow 99 has an unobtrusive nose, that, on airing, develops spicy and grilled hints, along with nuances of undergrowth. The pleasant palate opens out progressively, revealing flavours of ripe fruit, crystallised fruit and almond paste.

🔑 GAEC Joseph Renou et Fils, Le Grand Beauvais, 49190 Saint-Aubin-deLuigné, tel. 02.41.78.33.33, fax 02.41.78.67.77 ☑ Y by appt.

DOM. DES PETITS QUARTS

Faye 1999★

☐ 2 ha n.c. 30–49 F

The Godineau family lived in the village of Bonnezeaux for a long time before settling 800 m (872 yd) further to the west in Faye-d'Anjou. Their vineyard has, however, a strong reputation in Bonnezeaux, which would appear to be fully justified. Its Coteaux du Layon is worthy, though, as testifies this 99, with woody hints of undergrowth and mushrooms, characteristic of the vintage. It distinguishes itself with a very good balance on the palate and with an intense aromatic expression (wax, linden flowers), which reflects the maturity of the grapes. A wine to age to allow it to reveal its potential.

🔑 Godineau Père et Fils, Dom. des Petits Quarts, 49380 Faye-d'Anjou, tel. 02.41.54.03.00, fax 02.41.54.25.36 ☑ 🍷 by appt.

DOM. DU PETIT VAL 1998★

☐ 3.2 ha 8,000 🍾 🌡 30–49 F

This estate, founded in 1950 by Vincent Goizil on an area of 4.5 ha (11 acres) of vines, was taken over by his children in 1988 and today extends to 33 ha (81 acres), half of which is classed as AOC Coteaux du Layon. It offers a particularly pleasant 98 with notes of flowers and hazelnuts and a fresh and fruity palate. The pale yellow colour tinged with green is also a characteristic of wines from this appellation. As for **Cuvée Simon 99** (50–69F), still in its youth, it received a mention.

🔑 EARL Denis Goizil, Dom. du Petit Val, 49380 Chavagnes, tel. 02.41.54.31.14, fax 02.41.54.03.48 ☑ 🍷 by appt.

CH. PIERRE-BISE

Rochefort Les Rayelles 1999★★

☐ 3.57 ha 9,000 🍾 70–99 F

To judge from the praise gathered over the last few years, Château de Pierre-Bise is one of the feathers in the appellation's cap. For the 99, three of its wines were up for a special award. The jury finally gave it to the Rayelles (already crowned during the 97 vintage), the wine that is the most simple and also the most ready. With an intense yellow colour, this wine has a nose of dried apricot, fruit jelly, gingerbread and hazelnut, a full, harmonious and unobtrusive palate: an impression of finesse and elegance remarkable for the year. **Les Rouannières** also should not be missed; it is stronger and more complex, with notes of raisins on the palate. It will express itself fully by the end of 2000.

🔑 Claude Papin, Ch. Pierre-Bise, 49750 Beaulieu-sur-Layon, tel. 02.41.78.31.44, fax 02.41.78.41.24 ☑ 🍷 by appt.

CH. PIERRE-BISE Chaume 1999★★★

☐ 4 ha 6,000 🍾 70–99 F

A surprise awaits enthusiasts in this Coteaux du Layon Chaume. Its flavour and body were judged exceptional by the jury; on the palate, its flavours of exotic, dried and crystallised fruits reflect a *grand terroir* and unrivalled efforts. A star in waiting!

🔑 Claude Papin, Ch. Pierre-Bise, 49750 Beaulieu-sur-Layon, tel. 02.41.78.31.44, fax 02.41.78.41.24 ☑ 🍷 by appt.

CH. DE PLAISANCE Chaume 1999★

☐ 15 ha 30,000 🍾 50–69 F

Guy Rochais cultivates 25 ha (62 acres) of vines in the AOCs Coteaux du Layon Chaume and Coteaux du Layon. The Château de Plaisance is high on the Chaume hill, an exceptional site that has given us a 99 vintage that presents a very fine balance on the palate. The colour is of light gold, and its pleasant aromas combine fruit, spice and bergamot, with concentrated and fresh flavours. A touch of bitterness at the finish will dissipate with time. A promising wine.

🔑 Guy Rochais, Ch. de Plaisance, Chaume, 49190 Rochefort-sur-Loire, tel. 02.41.78.33.01, fax 02.41.78.67.52 ☑ 🍷 by appt.

DOM. DES QUATRE ROUTES

Cuvée Prestige 1999

☐ 0.9 ha 3,500 🍾 30–49 F

Founded in 1976, the vineyard (14 ha/34 acres) is on the Angers–Niort, Tours–Nantes crossroads. The son, Antoine Poupard, returned to the estate for the 99 vintage after a training period of six months at an Australian vineyard. Cuvée Prestige is still in its early youth, with its hints of undergrowth, but will be ready by the end of 2000. Yellow, with golden-green tints, it is beginning to deliver light scents of dried fruit and brioche, with a pleasant, balanced palate hinting of wax and flowers.

🔑 Jean Poupard, Dom. des Quatre Routes, 49540 Aubigné-sur-Layon, tel. 02.41.59.44.44, fax 02.41.59.49.70 ☑ 🍷 ev. day 8am–7pm, Sat. Sun. by appt.

MICHEL ROBINEAU

Saint-Lambert-du-Lattay Sélection de grain noble 1998★★

☐ 2 ha n.c. 🛢 70–99 F

Michel Robineau has thrown himself into a the necessary vineyard work (short pruning, control of yield, strict hand picking) and has, for a number of years, been among a group of wine-makers whose output is awaited with impatience. This 98 vintage has remarkable flavour and still hasn't given its all. On airing, aromas recalling flowers, crystallised fruit, honey and wax appear. The structured and intense palate gives an impression of overripe fruit, characteristic of the *grands liquoreux* of the appellation. The wine should he aged for a few years, decanted and served in a carafe.

🔑 Michel Robineau, 3, chem. du Moulin, Les Grandes Tailles, 49750 Saint-Lambert-du-Lattay, tel. 02.41.78.34.67 ☑ 🍷 by appt.

CH. DES ROCHETTES

Cuvée Sophie 1999★★

☐ 2 ha 4,000 🛢 70–99 F

Run by Jean Douet, this château has been a favourite of connoisseurs over the past few years. This is still the case with his Cuvée Sophie, which surprises with its golden colour, lightly orangey tints and concentrated aromas of overripe grapes, brioche and spices. The powerful palate, impressive for the

vintage, is dominated by notes of honey and crystallised fruit. A remarkable ensemble, as is **Sélection de Vieilles Vignes 99** (50–69F). As for **Cuvée Principale (Moelleux 99)** (30–49F), it offers everything that can be expected of the appellation and gains one star.
🗝 Jean Douet, Ch. des Rochettes, 49700 Concourson-sur-Layon, tel. 02.41.59.11.51, fax 02.41.59.37.73 ✉ 🍷 by appt.

SAUVEROY

Saint-Lambert Cuvée Nectar 1998★

□ 0.65 ha 3,900 70–99 F

This estate, regularly noted by experts, has invested its all in the interests of quality. This Cuvée Nectar is made from scrupulously selected bunches of grapes, at a natural 20%, and fermentation and maturation have been carried out in barrel. Golden-yellow in the glass, it offers aromas of vanilla, flowers and ripe fruit. The harmonious and rich palate gives a sensation of crystallised fruit, citrus fruit and pineapple. It is ready to drink or can be left for a number of years.
🗝 Pascal Cailleau, Dom. du Sauveroy, 49750 Saint-Lambert-du-Lattay, tel. 02.41.78.30.59, fax 02.41.78.46.43, e-mail domainesauveroy@terrenet.fr ✉ 🍷 by appt.

CH. SOUCHERIE

Beaulieu Cuvée de La Tour 1997

□ 4 ha 5,000 70–99 F

This property, bought in 1952 from the Marquis de Brissac, was restored in 1998. A tower, built in the same year, is the origin of the wine's name. With a straw-yellow colour, it has a nose of honey, lemon and wax, with lightly woody notes due to its vinification in barrel. The pleasant and fresh, almost acidulous palate leaves an impression of finesse. A wine that is ready to drink and which will open up over time. From the same estate, **Coteaux du Layon Chaume 99** (50–69F) is mentioned for its aromatic richness, its lightness and its refinement.
🗝 Tijou et Fils, Ch. Soucherie, 49750 Beaulieu-sur-Layon, tel. 02.41.78.31.18, fax 02.41.78.48.29 ✉ 🍷 by appt.

Bonnezeaux

Dr Maisonneuve said in 1925 that this wine was 'inimitable' as an accompaniment for desserts. At the time it was the custom to consume great sweet wines either with dessert, or in the afternoon, socially amongst friends. Nowadays, this very perfumed and vigorous Grand Cru is more generally appreciated as an aperitif. It owes its qualities to an exceptional terroir: the three steep little slopes of schists (La Montagne, Beauregard and Fresles) above the village of Thouarcé.

In 1999, the volume of production reached 2,319 hl (61,221 gal). The area of production includes 130 ha (321 acres) of plantable land. This is a good value, consistently reliable wine that will keep a long time.

CH. DE FESLES 1998★★

□ 14.25 ha n.c. 150–199 F

This wine-growing estate was taken over in 1996 by Bernard Germain and his associates from Gaston Lenôtre, the famous Parisian confectioner: a successful takeover, with a *Coup de Coeur* for a Coteaux du Layon Chaume 97 and the same award for this 98 Bonnezeaux. The golden-yellow colour seduces immediately, and its complex aromas recall honey, exotic fruit, spice and oranges. The palate combines freshness and richness. The finish leaves a sensation of honey, dried flowers and vanilla. Unobtrusive and refined, this château has made a good example of the formidable terroir of Bonnezeaux. (50cl bottles.)
🗝 Vignobles Germain et Associés Loire, Ch. de Fesles, 49380 Thouarcé, tel. 02.41.68.94.00, fax 02.41.68.94.01, email loire@vgas.com ✉ 🍷 by appt.

DOM. DES GAGNERIES

Cuvée Benoît 1999

☐ 2 ha 4,000 70–99 F

Acquired in 1890 by the Rousseau family, this domaine's Bonnezeaux is quite representative of its appellation and vintage, with its elegance and richness; yellow with golden tints, it exhibits complex perfumes of ripe fruit. The palate is concentrated, with notes of ripe fruit, honey and spice, which are indicative of its maturation in *barrique*. A wine that can be drunk at the end of 2000, or kept for up to five years.

EARL Christian et Anne Rousseau, Dom. des Gagneries, 49380 Thouarcé, tel. 02.41.54.00.71, fax 02.41.54.02.62
Y by appt.

DOM. DE LA PETITE CROIX

Vieilles vignes 1999

☐ 3.5 ha 4,000 70–99 F

This traditional estate, offers a Bonnezeaux that leaves an impression of finesse and balance: with a yellow, lightly golden colour, discreet aromas that do not appear until after quite a long airing, a harmonious palate that is not very intense but is fresh and fruity. A wine that can be drunk at the end of the year.

A. Denechère et F. Geffard, Dom. de La Petite Croix, 49380 Thouarcé, tel. 02.41.54.06.99, fax 02.41.54.30.05
Y by appt.

DOM. LES GRANDES VIGNES

Tradition 1998★★

☐ 2.1 ha 4,800 70–99 F

Cultivated by three young brothers and sisters, this domaine has acquired a solid reputation for all its wines. A number of *Coups de Coeur* have been awarded, whether for red wines, dry white wines or *vins liquoreux*. It is difficult to judge fairly this 98 Bonnezeaux as the maturation in *barrique* is still evident. However, hints of ripe and crystallised fruit and a sensation of richness, even opulence, on the palate are signs that rarely lie, characterising a major wine. To be aged for a year or two.

GAEC Vaillant, Dom. Les Grandes Vignes, La Roche-Aubry, 49380 Thouarcé, tel. 02.41.54.05.06, fax 02.41.54.08.21
Y by appt.

DOM. DE MIHOUDY

Vieilles vignes 1999

☐ 1 ha 1,500 100–149 F

Domaine de Mihoudy, a 45-ha (111-acre) estate, has a solid reputation, receiving a *Grappe de Bronze* for this wine, a simple Bonnezeaux, pleasant and well made. Its pale yellow colour and fine and unobtrusive aromas of white blossom and ripe fruits signal a balanced palate, which is quite light and gives a fruity sensation.

Cochard et Fils, 49540 Aubigné-sur-Layon, tel. 02.41.59.46.52, fax 02.41.59.68.77 Y by appt.

DOM. DES PETITS QUARTS

Elevé en fût de chêne 1998★★

☐ 1 ha n.c. 50–69 F

Petits Quarts is a sure bet in the appellation and produces wines of remarkable quality, as testified by this Bonnezeaux. Aged in oak barrels, it has a superb golden-yellow colour, and its strong scents of honey, raisins and gingerbread combine with aromas of maturity and oxidation that are reminiscent of walnuts. The palate is at the same time full and delicate, with notes of dried fruit, orange flower and *rancio*. A very fine wine, not very typical of the appellation due to its immaturity, but still remarkable.

Godineau Père et Fils, Dom. des Petits Quarts, 49380 Faye-d'Anjou, tel. 02.41.54.03.00, fax 02.41.54.25.36
Y by appt.

DOM. DES PETITS QUARTS

Le Malabé 1999★

☐ 3 ha n.c. 70–99 F

Le Malabé 99 is a ravishing straw-yellow colour tinged with orange. Still closed on the nose, it reveals, on airing, aromas of crystallised fruit and honey. The rich palate is reminiscent of ripe apricots. **Cuvée Principale** is also worth noting: simpler, lighter, fresher, it is makes for easy drinking and is representative of its appellation (50–69F).

Godineau Père et Fils, Dom. des Petits Quarts, 49380 Faye-d'Anjou, tel. 02.41.54.03.00, fax 02.41.54.25.36 Y by appt.

DOM. DU PETIT VAL

La Montagne 1999

☐ 2.5 ha n.c. 70–99 F

Founded in 1950 with 4.5 ha (11 acres) of vines, this domaine now has 33 ha (81 acres) and has earned a strong reputation for its *vins liquoreux*. Le Montagne comes from three late selections in the vineyards, the last of which took place on 26 November. Yellow with orange tints, the wine exhibits aromas of undergrowth, humus and ripe fruit, as well as being concentrated and rich on the palate with the bitter sensation representative of this quite difficult vintage. A wine to be aged for a year or two.

EARL Denis Goizil, Dom. du Petit Val, 49380 Chavagnes, tel. 02.41.54.31.14, fax 02.41.54.03.48 Y by appt.

DOM. RENE RENOU

Cuvée Zénith 1998★

☐ 7.36 ha 3,000 300–499 F

René Renou has been president of the INAO since March 1999, a title that brings recognition to the Anjou wine-growing region and its people. Cuvée Zénith comes from rigorously selected grapes over six selections in the vineyards, the last of which took place on 25 November. The wine gives a feeling of richness, finesse, strength and of delicacy, with notes of ripe and dried fruits and spices. A characterful Bonnezeaux that could not have been produced during this difficult vintage

without the rigorous work of the wine-maker.
🔑 Dom. René Renou, pl. du Champ-deFoire, 49380 Thouarcé, tel. 02.41.54.11.33, fax 02.41.54.11.34
☑ 🍷 by appt.

DOM. RENE RENOU

Cuvée Ma Dame 1998★

☐ 7.36 ha 3,000 250–299 F

Cuvée Ma Dame is at the same level as Cuvée Zénith (see preceding entry). Less strong but more expressive, less rich but delicately balanced and aromatic (hints of ripe fruit, peach and pear and linden flowers). A Bonnezeaux that will deliver immediately.
🔑 Dom. René Renou, pl. du Champ-deFoire, 49380 Thouarcé, tel. 02.41.54.11.33, fax 02.41.54.11.34
☑ 🍷 by appt.

Quarts de Chaume

The original nobleman owner kept a quarter ('quart') of the production for himself; naturally, he kept the best, meaning the wine produced on the best soil. The appellation, which covers 40 ha (99 acres) (down to 31 ha/77 acres in 1990), is located on a hump of a hill, facing due south, at Rochefort-sur-Loire. A total of 714 hl (18,850 gal) was produced in 1999.

The combination of old plants, the southerly exposure and the capabilities of the Chenin variety means that only a limited amount of wine is produced, although of very high quality. Selective picking during harvest encourages over-ripening of the grapes, giving a sweet white wine that is firm and full of flavour, and ages well.

DOM. DES BAUMARD 1998★

☐ 5,3 ha 13 000 150–199 F

The Baumard family have, for a long time, been the standard-bearer of this famous Quarts de Chaume wine-growing region. They make a fine wine that leaves an impression of lightness. The golden-white colour, with grey tints, the pleasant aromas of cherry buds, citrus fruit and dried fruit signal a balanced and fresh palate. Of great appeal to connoisseurs.
🔑 Florent Baumard, SCEA Dom. des Baumard, 8, rue de l'Abbaye, 49190 Rochefort-sur-Loire, tel. 02.41.78.70.03, fax 02.41.78.83.82 ☑ 🍷 ev. day except Sun. 10am–12 noon 2pm–5.30pm; cl. 20–30 Dec.

DOM. DE LA ROCHE MOREAU

1999★

☐ n.c. n.c. 100–149 F

Family-run for five generations, this domaine is situated on the Anjou cliff. Lower down, at the edge of the river, is the winery, which occupies a listed building dating from the 12th century. Sections of wall were built in front of the entrance to the cellar during the Second World War to conceal the entrance from the occupying forces. A Quarts de Chaume made from quite a ripe harvest and well vinified. With a golden-yellow colour, fruity (peach) aromas with hints of dried fruit, and a pleasant, supple and characteristic palate, it is a wine that will deliver immediately.
🔑 André Davy, Dom. de La Roche Moreau, La Haie-Longue, 49190 Saint-Aubin-deLuigné, tel. 02.41.78.34.55, fax 02.41.78.34.55, e-mail davy.larochemoreau@wanadoo.fr
☑ 🍷 by appt.

CH. LA VARIERE

Les Guerches 1998★★

☐ 1.5 ha n.c. 100–149 F

Château la Varière is an old wine-growing property that includes buildings that date back to the 13th century. The vinification and maturation in barrel mark for the moment this Quarts de Chaume. But notes of ripe, stewed fruit and a sensation of freshness and unobtrusiveness on the palate rarely lie. This a colourful wine that will express itself fully in a few years. (50cl bottles.)
🔑 Ch. La Varière, 49320 Brissac, tel. 02.41.91.22.64, fax 02.41.91.23.44, e-mail chateau.la.variere@wanadoo.fr
☑ 🍷 by appt.

DOM. DU PETIT METRIS 1999

☐ 1.05 ha n.c. 100–149 F

Owned by the same family for five generations, this domaine has acquired a solid reputation for its white wines. It is not the strength but the finesse that characterises this wine, which has been matured in barrels for eight months. Golden-white in colour, it has unobtrusive whiffs of dried fruit and gingerbread, and the balanced palate is lightly oaky with hints of apricot, hazelnut, citrus fruit and spices. To be kept for two to five years.
🔑 GAEC Joseph Renou et Fils, Le Grand Beauvais, 49190 Saint-Aubin-deLuigné, tel. 02.41.78.33.33, fax 02.41.78.67.77
☑ 🍷 by appt.

CH. PIERRE-BISE 1999

☐ 2.7 ha 6,000 150–199 F

Claude Papin is passionate about his wines. As his Quarts de Chaume is in its early youth, it is difficult to judge the wine fairly, even though hints of ripe fruit and dried fruit are quite evident. There is a flavour of raisins on the palate, a sign of great sweet wines. To be followed closely.

Claude Papin, Ch. Pierre-Bise, 49750 Beaulieu-sur-Layon, tel. 02.41.78.31.44, fax 02.41.78.41.24 by appt.

Saumur

The area of production, 2,735 ha (6,755 acres) covers 36 communes. Here, dry, firm white wines are produced, giving a total 32,733 hl (864,151 gal) in 1999, together with 63,532 hl (1,677,245 gal) of red wines and 106,425 hl (2,809,620 gal) of sparkling wines, from the same grape varieties as the AOC Anjou wines. All keep well.

The vineyards stretch along the slopes overlooking the Loire and the Thouet. The white Turquant and Brézé wines were well thought of in the past; the red wines of Puy-Notre-Dame, Montreuil-Bellay and Tourtenay, among others, have acquired a good reputation. However, the appellation is best known for its sparkling wines, and it is worth stressing how much these have improved in quality. The makers, all of whom are based in Saumur, own cellars hollowed out of the tufa that are well worth a visit.

CH. DE BEAUREGARD*

○ 4 ha 40 000 50–69 F

Beauregard is a vast estate that stretches its 25 ha (62 acres) of vines in front of its neo-Renaissance-style château. Some of the cellars are dedicated to growing mushrooms; others to the maturation of Saumur, two examples of which deserve attention. The first is a sparkling wine which leaves a pleasant sensation of fruit, flowers and lightness on the well-balanced palate. The second is **Saumur Blanc 99** (30–49F), with lively green tinges. Elegant, flowery and smooth on the nose, and balanced on the palate, it warrants a mention.

SCEA Alain Gourdon, Ch. de Beauregard, 4, rue Saint-Julien, 49260 Le Puy-Notre-Dame, tel. 02.41.52.25.33, fax 02.41.52.29.62 by appt.

CH. DE BERRYE 1999**

□ 1.5 ha 6,000 30–49 F

A medieval fortress encircled by moats, Château de Berrye has some fine cellars cut into rock. It offers this equally imposing 99 Saumur. Clear yellow in colour, it delivers an intense and full nose, revealing subtle scents of citrus fruit and passion fruit. The fruity palate stretches out with length and harmony.

Jacques Pareuil, Ch. de Berrye, 86120 Berrie, tel. 01.42.57.65.61, fax 01.47.32.61.14 by appt.

DOM. DU BOIS MIGNON 1999

■ 15 ha 30,000 20–29 F

A very substantial tasting hall, excavated from an old stone quarry, has recently been built at this domaine, which dates from around 1890. There you can sample this Saumur of a fine garnet-red colour with abundant violet tints. The nose is not yet at its optimum, but exposure to air brings out a floral side to the wine. Tannins are quite evident on the palate, as are very aromatic notes of red berries. Balance will appear after a few months.

SCEA Charier Barillot, Dom. du Bois Mignon, 86120 Saix, tel. 05.49.22.94.59, fax 05.49.22.91.54 by appt.

BOUVET Saphir brut vintage 1998**

○ n.c. 170,000 50–69 F

A delicate sparkle animates with length the pale and crystalline yellow colour of this wine. After light and complex aromas of flowers and ripe fruit, the intense and fresh palate opens up. A wine characteristic of the Saumur appellation, which has the finesse and the light and airy quality of the sparkling wines of the Loire Valley.

Bouvet-Ladubay, 1, rue de l'Abbaye, 49400 Saint-Hilaire-Saint-Florent, tel. 02.41.83.83.83, fax 02.41.50.24.32, e-mail bouvet-ladubay@symphonie-fai.fr ev. day 9am–12 noon 2pm–6.30pm

DOM. DE BRIZE*

○ 3 ha 16,000 30–49 F

The Brizé estate produces its sparkling wines entirely on the property. This wine has a strong character: crystalline, pale yellow in colour, aromas of white flowers and dried fruit, a well-balanced palate with notes of freshness and sweetness. The wine has been made from quite ripe grapes along with good vinification. The same balanced impression can be found in the estate's **Saumur Mousseux Rosé**, which seduces in addition with its notes of violet and red berries.

SCEA Marc et Luc Delhumeau, Dom. de Brizé, 49540 Martigné-Briand, tel. 02.41.59.43.35, fax 02.41.59.66.90 by appt.

DOM. DU CAILLOU 1999**

□ n.c. n.c. 20–29 F

You are welcomed with a smile at Domaine du Caillou. The wine here is matured in large wooden casks and in barrel in a cellar that is

typical of Turquant. The 99 vintage is a fine yellow colour, and although still rather weak on the nose, exposure to air reveals complex and concentrated aromas of white flowers. It is a rich and round wine that fills the palate.
Régis Vacher, Dom. du Caillou, 1, rue des Déportés, 49730 Turquant, tel. 02.41.38.11.21, fax 02.41.38.11.21 ☑ Y by appt.

DOM. DES CLOS MAURICE 1999★

■ 4 ha 20,000 ▮ ♁ 20–29 F

In the most vine-laden commune of Saumur, Clos Maurice has produced a fine wine of a dark red colour whose tints sparkle in the glass. Red berries characterise the nose, then a rounded and well-structured palate leaves notes of cherry. A nice wine, typical of well-made Cabernet Franc. The streets of Varrains make a pleasant stroll.
EARL Dom. des Clos Maurice, 10, rue du Ruau, 49400 Varrains, tel. 02.41.52.93.76, fax 02.41.52.44.32 ☑ Y by appt.

COMTE DE COLBERT

Cuvée spéciale★

○ 2.81 ha 16,000 ▮ ♁ 50–69 F

Château de Brézé, whose main building dates from the Renaissance era, is built on foundations that go back to the 11th century and is encircled by dry moats. It has had some famous guests, such as Diane de Poitiers at the beginning of the 16th century, and the Grand Condé during the following century. Its Saumur Mousseux, well made and not too assertive, is pale yellow enlivened by a delicate sparkle. The subtle scents recall linden flowers as well as white flowers, while on the palate the wine leaves an impression of structure and freshness. A wine to be drunk from now onwards.
Comte Bernard de Colbert, Ch. de Brézé, 49260 Brézé, tel. 02.41.51.62.06, fax 02.41.51.63.92 ☑ Y ev. day 8am–11am 1.30pm–4.30pm; Sat. Sun. by appt.

YVES DROUINEAU

Les Beaumiers 1999★★

□ 5 ha 10,000 ▮ ♁ 20–29 F

Yves Drouineau took over this estate, which has been family-run for five generations, from his father nearly 10 years ago. He offers a nicely mature 99, which looks like becoming more and more harmonious with time. The wine shows full colour with golden tints, the nose is elegant and fine. Concentration is evident in its fruity aromas even before complexity and balance hit the palate.
Yves Drouineau, Les Beaumiers, 3, rue Morains, 49400 Dampierre-sur-Loire, tel. 02.41.51.14.02, fax 02.41.50.32.00 ☑ Y ev. day except Sun. 8.30am–12.30pm 2pm–6pm

DOM. DE FIERVAUX

Cuvée Summun 1997★

■ 1.3 ha 5,000 ▮ ♁ 30–49 F

Lines of large barrels make an impressive sight in the 12th-century cellars of Domaine de Fiervaux. Here, it is a Saumur matured in tanks for 18 months which has been singled out. A red-violet colour clothes this wine, while the 'disc' (top of the wine) clings noticeably to the sides of the glass. On sniffing the wine, spicy and roasted scents spring up, signalling that it has already developed. The first impression is still weak, but the flavour increases in the middle of the palate and benefits from a successful balance, although the tannins are somewhat austere. In addition, notes of spice last well on the finish.
SCEA Cousin-Maitreau, 235, rue des Caves, 49260 Vaudelnay, tel. 02.41.52.34.63, fax 02.41.38.89.23, e-mail scea.cousin.maitreau@wanadoo.fr ☑ Y by appt.

DOM. FILLIATREAU

Château Fouquet 1999★

■ n.c. n.c. ▮ ♁ 30–49 F

Château Fouquet 99 is an intense ruby colour, and swirling the glass brings some violet tints to the wine. Still not very intense on the nose, complex notes of red berries (notably strawberry) appear on exposure to air. On the palate, structure and flavour form the backbone of the wine.
Paul Filliatreau, Chaintres, 49400 Dampierre-sur-Loire, tel. 02.41.52.90.84, fax 02.41.52.49.92 ☑ Y ev. day 8am–12 noon 1.30pm–5.30pm; Sat. Sun. by appt.

CH. DE FOSSE-SECHE 1999★★

□ 1.5 ha 6,700 ▮ ♁ 30–49 F

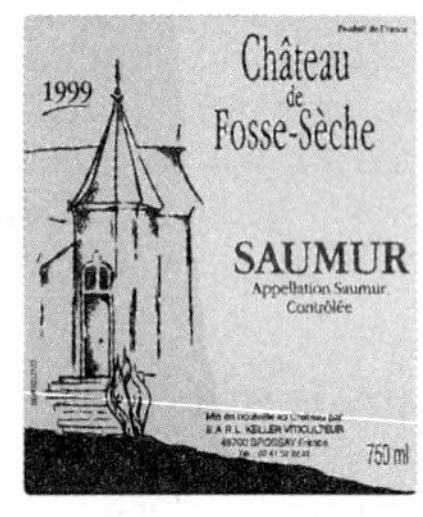

This vineyard was first mentioned in 1238 when it was part of the Montreuil-Bellay priory. Today, with over 17 ha (42 acres) of vines, it is the origin of this remarkable Saumur, which attracts the eye so well with its pale yellow hue and golden tints. The intense nose gives off elegant scents of honey and flowers, which appear again, pleasurably, on the rich and well-structured palate, later creating a sensation of balanced freshness. A well-deserved accolade.
EARL Keller, Fosse-Sèche, 49700 Brossay, tel. 02.41.52.22.22, fax 02.41.67.02.52, e-mail fosseseche@aol.com ☑ Y ev. day 8am–8pm

DOM. DU FUT D'OR 1999★

■ 8 ha 40,000 ▮ 20–29 F

Installed in the grounds of Puy-Notre-Dame, at the very heart of the Saumur appellation, Philippe Elliau cultivates an estate of more than 30 ha (74 acres). The old town prisons of Thouars (15th and 16th century) serve today as cellars. This wine is a very deep violet, and its nose reveals notes of overripe red berries underlined by a lightly gamey quality. The full and well-structured palate benefits from a surprising aromatic freshness. A wine that is already pleasant but which will cope with moderate ageing.

🔑 Philippe Elliau, 225, rue du Château, Sanziers, 49260 Vaudelnay, tel. 02.41.52.29.75, fax 02.41.52.29.75 ☑ 🍸 by appt.

DOM. GERON

Clos de La Tronnière 1997

○ 2 ha 5,000 ▮ 🌡 30–49 F

A pleasant, sparkling wine, well made and light. Behind a classic pale yellow colour are unobtrusive aromas recalling white flowers. Fresh and simple on the palate, this Saumur is ideal as an apéritif or with fish.

🔑 EARL Dom. Géron, 14, rte de Thouars, 79290 Brion-près-Thouet, tel. 05.49.67.73.43, fax 05.49.67.80.89 ☑ 🍸 by appt.

🔑 Samuel Géron

DOM. DES HAUTES VIGNES 1999★

□ 1.5 ha 6,000 ▮ 🌡 30–49 F

Chenin Blanc vines growing in chalky white soil are responsible for this Saumur, which delights the eye with its pale colour tinged with green. Intense aromas evoke fruit and honey, then the palate prolongs the harmonious line thanks to a rich flavour, at once round and fresh. A pleasant and elegant wine that is ready for drinking.

🔑 SCA Fourrier et Fils, 22, rue de la Chapelle, 49400 Distré, tel. 02.41.50.21.96, fax 02.41.50.12.83 ☑ 🍸 by appt.

DOM. DES HAUTS DE SANZIERS 1999★

□ n.c. n.c. 30–49 F

Tessier brother and sister have been at the head of their estate since 1991. They have been successful in the 99 vintage with this wine with a fresh and lively hue enlivened with golden tints. The complex, aromatic palate is of great interest, leaving a honey character. After a strong but balanced first impression, the flavours show liveliness, which indicates good vinification.

🔑 Tessier, 14, rue Saint-Vincent, Sanziers, 49260 Le Puy-Notre-Dame, tel. 02.41.52.26.75, fax 02.41.38.89.11 🍸 by appt.

CH. DU HUREAU 1998★

□ 2.5 ha 9,000 ▮ 🛢 🌡 50–69 F

Philippe Vatan, agricultural engineer, has rejoined his father Georges on this estate. He offers in the 99 vintage a bright straw-yellow wine with a complex and intense nose and a full, rich and equally complex palate. The wine is ready for drinking.

🔑 Philippe et Georges Vatan, Ch. du Hureau, 49400 Dampierre-sur-Loire, tel. 02.41.67.60.40, fax 02.41.50.43.35 ☑ 🍸 by appt.

DOM. JOULIN 1999★

□ 1 ha 800 🛢 30–49 F

The limpidity of this Chenin Blanc is attractive. Hints of vanilla on the nose are accompanied by notes of dried fruit, a sign of time in wood. The palate confirms this impression, its ample flavours working perfectly with the oakiness.

🔑 Philippe Joulin, 58, rue Emile-Landais, 49400 Chacé, tel. 02.41.52.41.84, fax 02.41.52.41.84 ☑ 🍸 by appt.

DOM. DE LA BESSIERE 1996★★

□ 2 ha 2,000 ▮ 🌡 20–29 F

Sights worth looking at in Souzay-Champigny include a 15th-century church and some cave-based homes. To add to them is this remarkable wine, of a clear straw-yellow colour, elegant, subtle, complex and flowery on the nose. Clean, long and fruity on the palate, this is a wine of excellent maturity.

🔑 Thierry Dézé, Dom. de La Bessière, 49400 Souzay-Champigny, tel. 02.41.52.42.69, fax 02.41.38.75.41 ☑ 🍸 by appt.

DOM. LA BONNELIERE 1999★

□ 0.5 ha 1000 ▮ 🌡 20–29 F

One of the two Bonneau sons rejoined the domaine in 1999 and has participated in the production of this quite pale but clear and bright wine. After the glass is swirled, the wine gives off pleasant fruity scents, and the balance on the palate contributes to a very pleasant character in total.

🔑 EARL Bonneau et Fils, Dom. La Bonnelière, 45, rue du Bourg-Neuf, 49400 Varrains, tel. 02.41.52.92.38, fax 02.41.52.92.38 ☑

MLLE LADUBAY

Eclat Jeunes Bois 1998

○ n.c. 80,000 🛢 50–69 F

A traditional vineyard specialising in sparkling wines, this was taken over by the Taittinger group in 1974. The 98 vintage, whose base wine was vinified in oak barrels, is a good representation of the Saumur output. Its pale yellow, green-tinted colour and its fine sparkle create an impression of harmony and delicacy, and scents of flowers and grilling are followed by a clean, fresh palate.

🔑 Bouvet-Ladubay, 1, rue de l'Abbaye, 49400 Saint-Hilaire-Saint-Florent, tel. 02.41.83.83.83, fax 02.41.50.24.32, e-mail bouvet-ladubay@symphonie-fai.fr 🍸 ev. day 9am–12 noon 2pm–6.30pm

DOM. DE LA GIRARDRIE 1999★

☐ 1.5 ha 9,000 20–29 F

Wine fairs and markets have brought the wines of this estate to wider notice. The 99 is a clear wine with a pale yellow colour and an intense nose with notes of fruit. The rich palate, also fruity, lasts a long time. To be drunk from autumn of 2000 onwards.

SCEA Falloux et Fils, Dom. de La Girardrie, 1 rue Fontaine-de-Cix, 49260 Le Puy-NotreDame, tel. 02.41.52.25.10, fax 02.41.38.83.77 Y by appt.

DOM. DE LA GUILLOTERIE 1999

☐ 3 ha 19,000 30–49 F

A clear straw-yellow hue attracts the eye, and the wine's floral character appears cleanly on the nose, while on the palate a freshness is perceptible which, a bit lively on first impression, is soon relieved by a fruity character which lasts to the finish.

SCEA Duveau Frères, 63, rue Foucault, 49260 Saint-Cyr-en-Bourg, tel. 02.41.51.62.78, fax 02.41.51.63.14 Y by appt.

DOM. LANGLOIS-CHATEAU 1999★

■ 10 ha 80,000 30–49 F

This vineyard with a family character was established in 1885. At first specialising in the production of *méthode traditionnelle* wines, it has progressively developed its vineyard and its production of still wines. It is a Saumur with an intense ruby colour, typical of the AOC, that is offered in the 99 vintage. The nose unveils hints of red berries, combined with a spicy character, and the solidly structured palate gives the wine virility.

Langlois-Château, 3, rue LéopoldPalustre, 49400 Saint-Hilaire-Saint-Florent, tel. 02.41.40.21.40, fax 02.41.40.21.49, e-mail langlois.chateau@wanadoo.fr Y ev. day 10am–12.30pm 2.30pm–6.30pm; 1st Nov.–1st Apr. by appt.

DOM. DE LA PALEINE 1999★

■ 3 ha 16,000 30–49 F

The pronounced red colour is adorned with fine violet tints. On the nose, a good intensity is revealed, along with aromas of fruit then of violet. On the palate, the wine is fruity, full and balanced. This is a very successful wine.

Joël Lévi, Dom. de La Paleine, 9, rue de la Paleine, 49260 Le Puy-Notre-Dame, tel. 02.41.52.21.24, fax 02.41.52.21.66 Y by appt.

DOM. DE LA PETITE CHAPELLE 1999★★

☐ 3 ha 10,000 30–49 F

The estate is some 10 km (6 miles) from Fontevraud Abbey, founded at the end of the 11th century and which remains today the most important monastic assembly in the West. La Petite Chapelle is more modest, but its vines nevertheless give rise to this remarkable Saumur. The golden colour of the 99 vintage creates an impression of freshness. The still gentle nose is of grand finesse, liberating a spray of white flowers after airing, and the balanced and full palate leads to a smooth and fruity finish.

Laurent Dézé, 4, rue des Vignerons, Champigny, 49400 Souzay-Champigny, tel. 02.41.52.41.11, fax 02.41.52.93.48 Y by appt.

DOM. DE LA SEIGNEURIE DES TOURELLES 1999★

■ 10 ha 70,660 20–29 F

Dubé father and son have worked in partnership with Joseph Verdier for two years to bring the vinification and marketing of their wines up to standard. Forty per cent of the output is sold abroad. This successful and solid Saumur should also cross borders. With a dark ruby colour, shot with purple tints, it appears concentrated on the nose with very ripe red berries veering towards spicy notes. The palate, also concentrated, is rich and smooth, and benefits from tight tannins that support the aromas.

SCEA Dubé et Fils, Messemé, 49260 Le Vaudelnay, tel. 02.41.40.22.50, fax 02.41.40.22.60, e-mail j.verdier@wanadoo.fr

Joseph Verdier

CH. LA TOUR GRISE

Les Vigneaux 1999★

■ 5.25 ha 36,000 30–49 F

Puy-Notre-Dame is distinguished by its 13th-century church, whose three spires point high up towards the summit of a hill studded with vineyards. Château de la Tour Grise is situated there, with its 23 ha (57 acres) of vines, some of which have produced this Saumur of a fine and intense red colour tinged with blue. The nose evokes dark fruit jam, along with grilled notes. The balanced palate is amplified by concentrated flavours. The still-present tannic structure will dissipate after ageing for around three years.

Philippe Gourdon, Ch. La Tour Grise,1, rue des Ducs-d'Aquitaine, 49260 Le Puy-Notre-Dame, tel. 02.41.38.82.42, fax 02.41.52.39.96 Y by appt.

LOUIS DE GRENELLE

Grande Cuvée★★

○ n.c. 58,000 50–69 F

The Grenelle cellars have made a double impact. Two sparkling Louis de Grenelle Saumurs in effect retained the jury's attention. This one is the Grande Cuvée, made exclusively from Chenin Blanc. It has a marked character with its complex aromas: notes of hay, white flowers and ripe fruit. It is so fresh and long on the palate that it is made to be drunk on its own as an apéritif. As for **Cuvée Louis de Grenelle Classique** (30–49F), it offers a continuous feeling of delicacy, first with its crystalline straw-yellow colour, then its aromas of may blossom, acacia and brioche, and finally with its suppleness and ampleness. An impression of freshness which

will go well with fruit salads or seafood. Very successful.
🗝 Caves de Grenelle, 20, rue Marceau, B.P. 206, 49415 Saumur Cedex, tel. 02.41.50.17.63, fax 02.41.50.83.65 ☑ 🍷 ev. day 9am–12 noon 2pm–5pm; cl. Sat. Sun. 1st Oct.–14 May

DOMINIQUE MARTIN 1999★

■ 1 ha 5,000 ▮ 20–29 F

Dominique Martin is at the head of a family estate of 70 ha (173 acres) whose cellars cut into the rock have sheltered this Saumur of clear garnet-red colour. The good expression on the nose, however, deserves airing in order to unveil all its fruit. The pleasant and balanced palate rests on silken tannins that assures the length of the wine.
🗝 Dominique Martin, 20, rue du Puits-Aubert, 49260 Brézé, tel. 02.41.51.60.28, fax 02.41.51.60.28 ☑ 🍷 by appt.

DOM. DES MATINES 1999

□ n.c. 10,000 30–49 F

A fine golden colour with transparent green tints glistens in the glass. The nose has a remarkable intensity. Very flowery, even honey-like, it finds a fine echo in the first impression on the clean palate, followed by a pleasant sweetness. An attractive wine.
🗝 Michèle Etchegaray-Mallard, Dom. des Matines, 31, rue de la Mairie, 49700 Brossay, tel. 02.41.52.25.36, fax 02.41.52.25.50 ☑ 🍷 by appt.

CH. DE MONTGUERET 1999★

□ 10 ha 70,000 ▮ 🌡 20–29 F

In 1987 André and Dominique Lacheteau succumbed to the charms of Anjou and of this château in the style of Napoleon III, which combines tuffeau, shale and brick. The estate extends to 100 ha (247 acres), 75 ha (185 acres) of which are in upper Layon and the rest in Saumur. The colour of this 99 Saumur is lively, clear and clean. The nose gives off exotic notes, notably of pineapple, and its very balanced palate has kept a point of carbonic gas, which gives the wine liveliness and a certain presence.
🗝 SCEA Ch. de Montguéret, 49560 Nueil-sur-Layon, tel. 02.41.59.26.26, fax 02.41.59.01.94, e-mail lacheteau.export@symphonie.fai.fr ☑
🗝 A. Lacheteau

CH. MONTREUIL-BELLAY 1999

■ 6.5 ha 30,000 ▮ 🌡 20–29 F

Montreuil-Bellay is a charming town with walls that were started in the 13th century and completed 200 years later, narrow streets and ancient houses and, of course, its château, which appears on the label of this Saumur. It is a deep red wine enlivened by violet tints. The aromas are still a bit quiet on the nose, and their expression would be favoured by letting them breathe. Balance is present on the palate, with a long finish of spicy notes.
🗝 Brasier de Thuy, Ch. Montreuil-Bellay, 49260 Montreuil-Bellay, tel. 02.41.52.33.06, fax 02.41.52.37.70 ☑ 🍷 by appt.

DOM. DU MOULIN 1999

□ 1.5 ha 10,000 ▮ 20–29 F

The origins of the windmill, which gives its name to this domaine, date from the 14th century. Damaged during the Revolution, the building was rebuilt in the 19th century and restored in 1985 to serve as a tasting cellar. There you will discover this straw-yellow Saumur, which delivers a rich and complex nose, recalling surprisingly stewed citrus fruit. The ample palate shows a good potential for ageing and promises to find all its harmony in time.
🗝 SCEA Marcel Biguet, 5, pl. de la Paleine, 49260 Le Puy-Notre-Dame, tel. 02.41.52.26.68, fax 02.41.38.85.64, e-mail sbiguet@terre-net.fr ☑ 🍷 by appt.

DOM. DU MOULIN DE L'HORIZON

Cuvée Symphonie 1999

■ 1.6 ha 9,600 ▮ 🌡 20–29 F

December 1999's storm destroyed the windmill that, from the top of its hill, looked over this 30-ha (74-acre) vineyard. Cabernet Franc vines, grown on a clay-chalk soil, produced in 1999 this intense ruby Saumur. Red berries, notably redcurrants, mark the nose, while a spicy note appears on airing. The palate is along the same pleasant lines: redcurrant and pepper finish well in the wine, which is ready to drink.
🗝 Jacky Clée, 1, rue du Lys, Sanziers, 49260 Le Puy-Notre-Dame, tel. 02.41.52.24.96, fax 02.41.52.48.39 ☑ 🍷 by appt.

NEMROD

○ 2 ha 5,000 ▮ 🌡 30–49 F

The first impression of this Saumur is that of exuberance: from the intense yellow colour rise fine and lengthy bubbles that favour the development of the aromas of peach and honey. The palate is more simple, with quite a brief finish, but leaves a pleasant fruity sensation.
🗝 Jean Douet, Ch. des Rochettes, 49700 Concourson-sur-Layon, tel. 02.41.59.11.51, fax 02.41.59.37.73 ☑ 🍷 by appt.

DOM. DE NERLEUX 1999★

□ 10 ha 16,000 ▮ 🌡 50–69 F

Nerleux is a beautiful 18th-century property in the commune of Saint-Cyr-en-Bourg. Régis Neau has produced a 99 wine that shows off its golden-yellow colour to the best effect in the glass. The finely flowery nose is in perfect harmony with the clean, pleasantly-structured palate.
🗝 Régis Neau, 4, rue de la Paleine, 49260 Saint-Cyr-en-Bourg, tel. 02.41.51.61.04, fax 02.41.51.65.34, e-mail rneau@terre-net.fr ☑ 🍷 ev. day 8am–12 noon 14–6pm; except Sat. Sun. 8am–12 noon

DOM. DE ROCFONTAINE 1999★★

□ 1 ha 5,000 ⦀ 20–29 F

Would the ornithologists who come to observe the colonies of laughing gulls and terns on the isle of Parnay let themselves be

distracted by a visit to the Rocfontaine estate? If they did, they could taste this remarkable Saumur. Behind the fine golden tints an intense and full nose appears, composed of scents of fruit and honey. The freshness, balance and length of the palate make this wine an autumnal pleasure.
Philippe Bougreau, Dom. de Rocfontaine, 7, ruelle des Bideaux, 49730 Parnay, tel. 02.41.51.46.89, fax 02.41.38.18.61 by appt.

DOM. DE SAINT-JUST

La Coulée de Saint-Cyr 1999★

3 ha 10,000 70–99 F

After 25 years in the world of finance, Yves Lambert turned himself towards the Saumur wine-growing region and took over the property of his parents-inlaw. With 32 ha (79 acres) of vines, he has produced a clear 99, strawyellow with golden tints. Still unobtrusive, the nose is, nevertheless, pleasant and complex for its floral tones. The fresh first impression gives way on the palate to a structure and balance, contributing to the success of the wine.
Yves Lambert, Dom. de Saint-Just, 12, rue Prée, 49260 Saint-Just-sur-Dive, tel. 02.41.51.62.01, fax 02.41.67.94.51, e-mail domaine-de-saint-just@wanadoo.fr ev. day 9am–12 noon 2pm–5pm

DOM. DES SANZAY 1999★★

0.5 ha 3,000 30–49 F

Varrains has all the charm of wine-growing villages, with its streets bordered by porches. In the Grand-Rue, one can admire a beautiful stone pigeon house with a pyramid-like roof. From there, several paths lead to Didier Sanzay's house. This 99 vintage, with its limpid, pale yellow colour, benefits from an intense and open nose. Its full and elegant palate keeps this same aromatic complexity up to the remarkable finish. An impression of balance characterises the wine.
Didier Sanzay, Dom. des Sanzay, 93, Grand-Rue, 49400 Varrains, tel. 02.41.52.91.30, fax 02.41.52.45.93 by appt.

CAVE DES VIGNERONS DE SAUMUR Réserve des vignerons 1999★

200 ha 1000,000 20–29 F

The impressive cellars of this cooperative, created in 1957, are so vast that tourists travel around them by car. The 99 vintage is marked by a success with the Saumur. Clear cherry-red with bright violet tints, the wine gives a lot of black fruit on the nose, then takes on a smoky character. The balanced palate is prolonged on a thread of melted and silken tannins, up to a fruity and lengthy finish. A very harmonious wine.
Cave des Vignerons de Saumur, rte de Saumoussay, 49260 Saint-Cyr-en-Bourg, tel. 02.41.53.06.06, fax 02.41.53.06.10 by appt.

MICHEL SUIRE 1999★

3.5 ha 7,000 20–29 F

The pale yellow colour of weak intensity appears encircled by a rim of clean and clear green. This Saumur delivers a fresh and lightly acidulous note on the nose, then a pleasant feeling on the palate. Quite intense, it has an interesting structure and stretches out on a good length.
Michel Suire, 12, rue des Perrières, Pouant, 86120 Berrie, tel. 05.49.22.92.61, fax 05.49.22.57.56 ev. day except Sun. 10am–7pm; cl. 15 Aug.–15 Sep.

VEUVE AMIOT Cuvée Haute Tradition

n.c. 123,000 30–49 F

Today an affiliate of the French Compagnie des Grands Vins, Veuve Amiot has been acquired by the Martini group. This pale yellow wine with a tumultuous sparkle has some discreet aromas of hay and white fruits. Pleasant on the palate, the wine on the finish is dominated by notes of flowers. To be served very cold as an apéritif.
SAS Veuve Amiot, B.P. 67, Saint-HilaireSaint-Florent, 49400 Saumur Cedex, tel. 02.41.83.14.14, fax 02.41.50.17.66 ev. day 10am–6pm

DOM. DU VIEUX BOURG 1999

0.92 ha 7,000 30–49 F

Jean-Marie and Noël Girard have made from their Chenin vines planted on clay-sand soil a wine with a clear pale yellow colour, whose fine and unobtrusive nose delivers honeyed notes. Its good structure leaves a pleasant impression of balance on the palate, while the whole still lacks some roundness.
Dom. du Vieux Bourg, 30, Grand-Rue, 49400 Varrains, tel. 02.41.52.91.89, fax 02.41.52.42.43 by appt.

DOM. DU VIEUX PRESSOIR 1999

9 ha 55,000 20–29 F

Domaine du Vieux Pressoir is certainly an asset to Saumur. It offers a Saumur 99 with a red colour and many bluish tinges, recalling peony. Still quite shy, it needs to breathe to reveal its pleasant notes of red berries. The palate opens with a fine flavoury attack, followed by still quite edgy tannins, before ending with fine fruity length.
Bruno Albert, 235, rue du Château-d'Oiré, Messemé-Oiré, 49260 Vaudelnay, tel. 02.41.52.21.78, fax 02.41.38.85.83 by appt.

DOM. DU VIEUX TUFFEAU

Coulée de la Cerisaie 1999★

5.11 ha 7,500 20–29 F

At Vieux Tuffeau, some 10,000 m (10,900 yd) of cellars were excavated some centuries ago. The site is becoming better known today and receives more and more visitors. A nice walk through Puy-Notre-Dame will allow you to discover this very clear ruby Saumur. Fruitiness is the dominant note, still a bit reserved on the nose. From the moment it hits the palate, fresh flavours are perceptible, which develop its aromas well. The finish is still marked by tannins, but these are sure to round off.

Christian Giraud, Les Caves, 212, rue de la Cerisaie, 49260 Le Puy-Notre-Dame, tel. 02.41.52.27.41, fax 02.41.52.26.07 ev. day except Sun. 9am–12.30pm 1.30pm–7pm; groups by appt.

CH. DE VILLENEUVE

Les Cormiers 1998

□ 3 ha 8,000 70–99 F

The 19th-century château is close to a property that was built in the Renaissance era. With a park and a vineyard of 25 ha (62 acres) on the plateau, it offers a vision of peace. The wines go well in this harmonious picture. The lively palate of the 98 vintage offers grilled flavours before leaving the taster with the memory of a long finish.

SCA Chevallier, Ch. de Villeneuve, 49400 Souzay-Champigny, tel. 02.41.51.14.04, fax 02.41.50.58.24 ev. day except Sun. 9am–12 noon 2pm–6pm

Cabernet de Saumur

Even though produced only in small quantities, with 5,623 hl (148,447 gal) in 1999, the Appellation Cabernet de Saumur rosé holds its own due to Cabernet finesse and the limestone terroir.

DOM. DES SANZAY 1999*

0,6 ha 3 500 20–29 F

This vineyard produces principally Saumur-Champigny, but traditionally cultivates a small area of Cabernet for this rosé. This is fortuitous, because it allows for the discovery of a very discreet wine that expresses itself bit by bit on meeting the air. The pale pink colour has the delicacy and lightness of red berry aromas; the palate is pleasant and harmonious. A good representative of its appellation.

Didier Sanzay, Dom. des Sanzay, 93, Grand-Rue, 49400 Varrains, tel. 02.41.52.91.30, fax 02.41.52.45.93 by appt.

TERRASSES DE SAUMUR 1999

6 ha 35,000 20–29 F

A simple, well-made wine, which is refreshing, with a pale pink colour and light aromas of red berries on the balanced and discreet palate. To be drunk with salads.

SA Lacheteau, ZI La Saulaie, 49700 Doué-la-Fontaine, tel. 02.41.59.26.26, fax 02.41.59.01.94, e-mail lacheteau.export@symphonie.fai.fr

Saumur-Champigny

Even though this vineyard, which covers 1,300 ha (3,211 acres), has only recently expanded, the red wines from Champigny have been renowned for many centuries. The area covers nine villages, and the vines are grown on chalk and tufa. In 1999 production was 84,908 hl (2,241,571 gal).

CLOS DU BOIS MOZE

Vieilles vignes 1999

■ 1 ha 4 000 30–49 F

In 1994 Patrick Pasquier took over this 6-ha (15-acre) estate that was founded by his parents in 1955. The 99 vintage comes from 45-year-old vine stock. The clean ruby colour is attractive, and the discreet nose plays on a register of ripe red berries. Although the first impression appears supple and round, the finish on the palate, where you will find ripe fruit, is well structured. A balanced wine.

Patrick Pasquier, 9, rue du Bois-Mozé, 49400 Chacé, tel. 02.41.52.42.50, fax 02.41.52.59.73 by appt.

DOM. DES BONNEVEAUX

Vieilles vignes 1999*

■ 5 ha 30,000 30–49 F

Camille Bourdoux came to the vines a decade ago and, already, the results are showing. This Vieilles Vignes has a beautiful deep colour with lively violet tints. Although the nose is still closed, it gives way to notes of mulberry which can be found again on the palate, a sign of good development. A structured, full and pleasant wine.

Camille Bourdoux, 79, Grand-Rue, 49400 Varrains, tel. 02.41.52.94.91, fax 02.41.52.99.24 by appt.

CH. DE CHAINTRES 1999*

■ 17 ha 100,000 30–49 F

The château, which was a priory in 1675, has a proud allure in its walled vineyard planted with Cabernet Franc and encircled by white walls. The cellars, built on several levels, allow for maturation in the barrel. The quality of the wines corresponds to the imposing character of the site, to judge from the 99 vintage. The colour is a deep garnet-red, and on swirling the wine violet tints plaster the sides of the glass. The nose is still very discreet, but a fruitiness evocative of cherry appears when the wine is allowed to breathe. The first impression appears supple, fresh and without excess, and the lightly tannic finish will become more refined with time.

⊶ SA Dom. viticole de Chaintres, 49400 Dampierre-sur-Loire, tel. 02.41.52.90.54, fax 02.41.52.99.92, e-mail chaintres@wanadoo.fr ☑ Y ev. day 8am–12 noon 2pm–6pm; cl. 25 Dec.–1st Jan.
⊶ M. de Tigny

DOM. DES CHAMPS FLEURIS 1999★★

■ 22 ha 80,000 30–49 F

This charming vineyard (25 ha/62 acres) renovated its vinification cellar five years ago, an investment which has borne fruit. Take this 99 vintage: with a lively and bright purple colour, it is full and intense on the nose with scents of red berries and stewed blackcurrants. Well balanced, it fills the palate with its roundness. Its structure is accompanied by a pleasing fleshy side that leaves a very good final impression. A remarkable success for the vintage.
⊶ Rétiveau-Rétif, 50–54, rue des Martyrs, 49730 Turquant, tel. 02.41.38.10.92, fax 02.41.51.75.33 ☑ Y by appt.

DOM. DES COUTURES 1999★

■ 9.75 ha 15,000 30–49 F

This 15-ha (37-acre) estate has been in the same family for five generations. It offers a 99 vintage with a good style, of a bright, intense, attractive ruby colour. The nose has a lot of fruitiness and freshness. After a very harmonious first impression, the palate appears structured, with full flavous and a very fine tannic finish. An elegant ensemble waiting to be discovered.
⊶ SCA Nicolas et Fils, rue des Martyrs, 49730 Turquant, tel. 02.41.38.11.29, fax 02.41.38.11.29 ☑ Y ev. day except Sun. 8am–1pm 2pm–6pm; cl. 10–31 Aug.

YVES DROUINEAU
Les Beaumiers 1999★

■ 16 ha 60,000 30–49 F

This family domaine of 21 ha (55 acres), whose origins go back to 1722, is regularly mentioned for its Saumur Blanc and Saumur Champigny, and often in the best places. The 99 possesses a fine ruby colour. The nose is elegant, lively with strawberry and cherry fruit coming forward. On the palate it is full, with good length and a balance that makes this wine very attractive.
⊶ Yves Drouineau, Les Beaumiers, 3, rue Morains, 49400 Dampierre-sur-Loire, tel. 02.41.51.14.02, fax 02.41.50.32.00 ☑ Y ev. day except Sun. 8.30am–12.30pm 2pm–6pm

DOM. FILLIATREAU 1999★★

■ n.c. n.c. 30–49 F

Wine-growers from father to son for three generations, the Filliatreau family have often produced a very fine Saumur-Champigny (the 96 caused a sensation). This one, a deep, garnet-red colour with violet tints, immediately makes a good impression. On the nose, stewed fruit with smoky touches are revealed, and the contact with air produces marvels. The first impression is round, full and sumptuous. The evident but subtle tannins last for a long time at the finish. Strength, harmony, softness: the three key words for this wine.
⊶ Paul Filliatreau, Chaintres, 49400 Dampierre-sur-Loire, tel. 02.41.52.90.84, fax 02.41.52.49.92 ☑ Y ev. day 8am–12 noon 1.30pm–5.30pm; Sat. Sun. by appt.

DOM. FOUET 1999★

■ 1.5 ha 10,000 30–49 F

Julien Fouet has worked, for two years, in collaboration with his father Patrice, who has cultivated the family estate for 25 years. Their Saumur-Champigny has an intense ruby to garnet-red colour, and on the nose fruitiness and strawberry are discernible immediately. After this, the palate appears light, followed by a fine progression of ripe tannins covered by fruit. These impressions last for a long time in one of the most harmonious finishes.
⊶ Fouet, 3, rue de la Judée, 49260 Saint-Cyr-en-Bourg, tel. 02.41.51.60.52, fax 02.41.67.01.79 ☑ Y ev. day except Sun. 8am–12 noon 2pm–6pm

DOM. DES HAUTES VIGNES 1999

■ 2.5 ha 20,000 30–49 F

Matured in cellars cut into the chalk, the Fourriers' Saumur-Champigny appears lively on the eye, with a pleasing clear red colour. The light nose is characteristic of Cabernet Franc in this vintage. Pleasant, fine and balanced, without a tannic presence, the palate demonstrates a silken length on the finish.
⊶ SCA Fourrier et Fils, 22, rue de la Chapelle, 49400 Distré, tel. 02.41.50.21.96, fax 02.41.50.12.83 ☑ Y by appt.

CH. DU HUREAU
Cuvée des Fevettes 1999★★★

■ 2 ha 10,000 50–69 F

Philippe and Georges Vatan's cellars are cut into the chalk under the vines on the plateau. They harbour some superb vats which, almost every year, gain a *Coup de Coeur*. This is the case of the Fevettes 99, which proudly follows that of the 96 vintage. Far from being in the image of 'Hureau', the old wild boar that is the mascot of the estate, this deep ruby-coloured 99 with violet sparkles seduced with its extreme delicateness and nose of crystallised red berries. The palate is sumptuous, full, rich and concentrated. An exceptional ensemble.

🔑 Philippe et Georges Vatan, Ch. du Hureau, 49400 Dampierre-sur-Loire, tel. 02.41.67.60.40, fax 02.41.50.43.35
▣ Y by appt.

DOM. DE LA BESSIERE 1999

■ 12 ha 25,000 ▮ ♁ 30–49 F

First, you climb a street flanking the hill-side, dominated by the Renaissance manor of Marguerite d'Anjou, then you penetrate a cellar carved directly in to the hill, a cathedral of tuffeau, (the honey-coloured stone of the region) where the estate's Saumur-Champigny ripens. The 99 vintage presents a light, cherry colour and a fruity nose, characteristic of Cabernet Franc and evocative of ripe red berries with some vanilla nuances. The first impression appears supple, tender, without any apparent tannins, and the fruitiness reappears on the palate flavours. A smooth wine to be served chilled to bring out its fruitiness.

🔑 Thierry Dézé, Dom. de La Bessière, 49400 Souzay-Champigny, tel. 02.41.52.42.69, fax 02.41.38.75.41
▣ Y by appt.

DOM. LA BONNELIERE 1999★

■ 5 ha 20,000 ▮ ♁ 30–49 F

The Caveau Saint-Vincent, created by the Bonneaus, became the Domaine de la Bonnelière in 1995 and has grown considerably since its creation in 1972. In 1999, the year in which they were joined by one of their sons, the estate numbered some 20 ha (49 acres). With a lively, very luminous red, this wine appears light and fresh on the eye. Still quite reticent, the nose reveals fruity notes, and the palate is supple and balanced. The elegance of the reasonably ripe grape is apparent in this very successful wine.

🔑 EARL Bonneau et Fils, Dom. La Bonnelière, 45, rue du Bourg-Neuf, 49400 Varrains, tel. 02.41.52.92.38, fax 02.41.52.92.38 ▣

DOM. DE LA CUNE

Charl'Anne 1999★

■ 3 ha 15,000 ▮ ♁ 30–49 F

The Mary family created this vineyard (14 ha/35 acres) with their own hands. The slopes rise in tiers in front of their property. This Saumur-Champigny reflects the seriousness of their work in the vines. Its deep colour reveals a good extraction of noble composites of berry. The nose has a freshness of red berries. The young but supple tannins provide fine tasting sensations. A balanced and harmonious ensemble.

🔑 Jean-Luc et Jean-Albert Mary, Chaintres, 49400 Dampierre-sur-Loire, tel. 02.41.52.91.37, fax 02.41.52.44.13 ▣ Y ev. day except Sun. 8am–12 noon 2pm–7pm

DOM. DE LA GUILLOTERIE 1999★

■ 25 ha 50,000 ▮ ♁ 30–49 F

J.-C. Duveau is the president of the historical Saumurois union, the Syndicat des Côtes de Saumur. The Saumur-Champigny is the feather in the estate's cap. The wine is a light colour, but sufficient enough to point up its lively and fresh character. Fine, elegant and subtle on the nose, with hints of red woodland berries, on the palate the wine is pleasant with a quite evident tannic structure. Characteristic and well vinified, taking into account the vintage, it leaves a seductive finish.

🔑 SCEA Duveau Frères, 63, rue Foucault, 49260 Saint-Cyr-en-Bourg, tel. 02.41.51.62.78, fax 02.41.51.63.14
▣ Y by appt.

LA SEIGNERE

Clos de la Seignère 1999★★

■ 5.4 ha 25,000 ▮ ♁ 30–49 F

Yves Drouineau acquired La Seignère in 1998, a hillside vineyard of 7.6 ha (18.7 acres). Practising small yields (45 hl/ha/486 gal/acre), he has succeeded remarkably with this wine. The colour is full with bright tints. The nose opens out when the glass is swirled, developing flowery nuances. The first impression is round, supple and unctuous on the palate. A well-balanced wine, with a fine harmony that owes its richness to the terroir.

🔑 EARL Yves Drouineau, La Seignère, 3, rue Morains, 49400 Dampierre-sur-Loire, tel. 02.41.51.14.02, fax 02.41.50.32.00 ▣ Y ev. day except Sun. 8.30am–12.30pm 2pm–6pm

DOM. LAVIGNE Les Aïeules 1999★

■ 5 ha 40,000 ▮ ♁ 30–49 F

At the head of an estate of close to 30 ha (74 acres), Gilbert Lavigne is a regular in the *Guide*, notably for his work on this Les Aïeules. The colour is a clean ruby with garnet-red tints, and the nose, still quite quiet, gives off subtle perfumes of red berries and flowers (iris, peony). The palate is balanced and fresh, and the reasonably ripe Cabernet Franc grape is discernible. Its tannic structure, its richness and its aromas contribute to its harmony. The blending of wines from different parts of the vineyard has been very successful.

🔑 SCA Lavigne, 15, rue des Rogelins, 49400 Varrains, tel. 02.41.52.92.57, fax 02.41.52.40.87, e-mail domaine.lavigne@groupesirius.com
▣ Y by appt.
🔑 Gilbert Lavigne

RENE-NOEL LEGRAND

Les Terrages 1999★★ •

■ 2 ha 12,000 ▮▮ 30–49 F

René-Noël Legrand is an artist of wines who always brings out the unique character of the vintage as determined by the weather of that year. He vinifies very elegant, complex and distinguished Saumur-Champigny. This one, very lively, is a deep garnet-red colour with violet tints. The nose is complex and strong; notes of ripe, jammy red fruits give it a concentrated character. The first impression is unctuous, without vigour, full, with plenty of sweetness. A liquorice finish ends the tasting of this remarkable wine.

LOIRE

🔑 René-Noël Legrand, 13, rue des Rogelins, 49400 Varrains, tel. 02.41.52.94.11, fax 02.41.52.49.78 Y by appt.

LE PETIT SAINT VINCENT 1999★

■ 2.5 ha 14,000 ▮ 30-49 F

Dominique Joseph took over the 12-ha (30-acre) family vineyard in 1990. It is situated on a hillside dominating the Loire Valley. Long recognised by experts for his skill, he has produced this 99 vintage with its very fine colour with garnet-red sparkles. Attractive and strong on the nose, with lots of jammy red fruits, the voluminous first impression is followed by a tannic progression that gives the palate a slightly austere character, something that will dissipate with ageing.

🔑 Dominique Joseph, 10, rue des Rogelins, 49400 Varrains, tel. 02.41.52.99.95, fax 02.41.38.75.76, email djoseph@terre-net.fr ☒ Y ev. day except Sun. 9am–6pm; Sat. by appt.

DOM. LES MERIBELLES

Cuvée Vieilles vignes 1999★

■ 3 ha 20,000 ▮ 30-49 F

Founded in 1984, this vineyard is on the wine tourist route. The wine-maker has produced a wine of suppleness, smoothness and fruitiness, with an attractive colour with garnet-red sparkling tints. It is complex and rich on the nose, with notes of stewed ripe fruit combined with smoked nuances. The first impression is supple and fresh, and the structure is harmonious. A very fruity wine and a good expression of the grape.

🔑 Jean-Yves Dézé, 14, rue de la Bienboire, 49400 Souzay-Champigny, tel. 02.41.67.46.64, fax 02.41.67.73.77 ☒ Y by appt.

CH. DU MARCONNAY 1999

■ 9.47 ha 37,000 ▮ 30-49 F

Hervé Goumain took over this estate from his grandfather in 1997. He has almost 10 ha (25 acres) of vines, a cellar dug into the rock and a cave-based residence dating back to the 15th century. His Saumur-Champigny displays a deep colour with violet tints. The nose delivers intense notes of black fruit. The palate is well structured, gifted with very evident tannins that indicate a good development. The aromas last a long time.

🔑 Hervé Goumain, Ch. du Marconnay, 49730 Parnay, tel. 02.41.50.08.21, fax 02.41.50.23.04, e-mail marconnay@wanadoo.fr ☒ Y ev. day 10am–12.30pm 2.30pm–6pm; 15 Nov.–15 Mar. by appt.

DOM. DE NERLEUX

Les Chatains 1999★

■ 10 ha 30,000 ▮ 30-49 F

It is a pleasure to find oneself facing the beautiful 13th-century property that dominates this estate. This wine is a pleasant colour, sparkling ruby at the rim. The nose, with touches of very ripe Cabernet Franc, violet and iris, reveals a well-cultivated quality grape. The structured palate is concentrated, with tannins in evidence, although these will disappear: the pledge of good longevity.

🔑 Régis Neau, 4, rue de la Paleine, 49260 Saint-Cyr-en-Bourg, tel. 02.41.51.61.04, fax 02.41.51.65.34, e-mail rneau@terre-net.fr ☒ Y ev. day 8am–12 noon 14–6pm; except Sat. Sun. 8am–12 noon

DOM. LES PETITES MARIGROLLES 1999

■ 6 ha n.c. ▮ 🌡 20-29 F

Christian Joseph has built some stainless-steel maceration vats, without neglecting the cellars and the barrels of his ancestors, to produce a consistent and concentrated Saumur-Champigny. His 99 vintage is ruby in colour with tinges of violet. The richness of the nose, evocative of red berries and eau-de-vie, matches the strength on the palate, with a full-bodied tannic structure. A wine to be aged.

🔑 Christian Joseph, 12, rue de la Mairie, 49400 Varrains, tel. 02.41.52.94.43, fax 02.41.52.94.53 ☒ Y by appt.

DOM. DES RAYNIERES 1999

■ 2 ha 14,000 ▮ 20-29 F

J.-P. Rebeilleau has some beautiful vat rooms where he produces Saumur-Champigny with aromas of blackcurrant, raspberry and other red berries, and also casks and barrels in cellars that produce wines with a bouquet of crystallised fruit and plum. This 99 vintage is of the first type: the colour is lively, clear and transparent. The nose, still quite quiet, gives off, after the wine is allowed to breathe, elegant perfumes of red berries. The fine palate reveals a light structure. A wine for the spring which should be drunk cool.

🔑 Jean-Pierre Rebeilleau, SCEA Dom. des Raynières, 33, rue du Ruau, 49400 Varrains, tel. 02.41.52.95.17, fax 02.41.52.48.40 Y by appt.

DOM. DE ROCFONTAINE

Cuvée des vieilles vignes 1999★★

■ 3 ha 13,000 ▮ 🌡 30-49 F

Philippe Bougreau, who took over the family vineyard in 1987, is at the head of 13 ha (32 acres) of vines. His Saumur-Champigny conquered the jury with its intense dark ruby colour and its dense and complex nose, very marked by black fruit. Voluminous and fleshy on the palate, it is chewy and has great length. It is somewhat closed at the moment but has good potential.

🔑 Philippe Bougreau, Dom. de Rocfontaine, 7, ruelle des Bideaux, 49730 Parnay, tel. 02.41.51.46.89, fax 02.41.38.18.61 ☒ Y by appt.

DOM. SAINT-JEAN

Vieilles vignes 1999

■ 2 ha 19,000 ▮ 🌡 30-49 F

This charming family vineyard (24 ha/59 acres) has been passed from generation to generation since the beginning of the 20th century. Its Vieilles Vignes is an intense and deep, clear garnet-red colour. The nose, still quiet, allows scents of red berries to appear, with cherries prevalent. The first impression is light, marked by tannins that are still somewhat astringent, but which are sure to become more refined.

Jean-Claude Anger, 16, rue des Martyrs, 49730 Turquant, tel. 02.41.38.11.78, fax 02.41.51.79.23 by appt.

DOM. DE SAINT-JUST

La montée des Roches 1999★

■ 4 ha 10,000 70–99 F

This family property (32 ha/79 acres) was taken over by Yves Lambert in 1996 after a long financial career. The new wine-maker hopes to make wines of high quality that will improve the image of Saumur. This objective is achieved with the 99 vintage of a fine and luminous intensity, with deep ruby tints. The strong nose evokes red berry jam, and the balanced and smooth palate reveals a silken tannic structure. The finish is harmonious with a smooth oakiness.

Yves Lambert, Dom. de Saint-Just, 12, rue Prée, 49260 Saint-Just-sur-Dive, tel. 02.41.51.62.01, fax 02.41.67.94.51, e-mail domaine-de-saint-just@wanadoo.fr ev. day 9am–12 noon 2pm–5pm

DOM. DES SANZAY 1999

■ 3 ha 20,000 30–49 F

Didier Sanzay, who took over the family estate in 1991, cultivates 27 ha (67 acres) of vines. The colour of his 99 vintage is bright garnet-red, with a lively vivacity. The nose, still quiet, gives off, on airing, aromas full of finesse and elegance. The pleasant and well-balanced palate demonstrates a fullness correct for the vintage.

Didier Sanzay, Dom. des Sanzay, 93, Grand-Rue, 49400 Varrains, tel. 02.41.52.91.30, fax 02.41.52.45.93 by appt.

CAVE DES VIGNERONS DE SAUMUR Lieu-dit Les Poyeux 1999★

■ 14 ha 72,000 30–49 F

You can drive round these impressive cellars by car! The wines here are particularly well cared for, and this one has a deep colour, with very attractive ruby tints. The intense nose combines red berries and flowers (iris and violet), and the supple palate reveals still-grippy tannins. It has good potential for opening out very soon.

Cave des Vignerons de Saumur, rte de Saumoussay, 49260 Saint-Cyr-en-Bourg, tel. 02.41.53.06.06, fax 02.41.53.06.10 by appt.

DOM. DU VAL BRUN

Vieilles vignes Les Folies 1999★

■ 3 ha 10,000 30–49 F

This fine vineyard is in the commune of Parnay, a village that warrants a detour for its alleys and its houses built into the tuffeau rock. Its Les Folies shows intense colour, with lightly violet tints. After swirling the wine in the glass, fruit dominates on the nose. The first taste confirms the fruity character, and the tannins present indicate a wine to be kept. It is to be hoped that they will dissipate with time.

Jean-Pierre et Eric Charruau, 74, rue Valbrun, 49730 Parnay, tel. 02.41.38.11.85, fax 02.41.38.16.22 by appt.

DOM. DU VIEUX BOURG

Vieilles vignes 1999★★

■ 1.8 ha 12,000 50–69 F

A traditional vineyard, run by Jean-Marie and Noël Girard. Vieilles Vignes is a fine scarlet red. On the nose, it is fruitiness that appears cleanly, along with some herbaceous nuances characteristic of pepper. The palate expresses itself fully; it is ample and silken, with a tannic structure clothed with flesh and roundness. A very harmonious ensemble.

Dom. du Vieux Bourg, 30, Grand-Rue, 49400 Varrains, tel. 02.41.52.91.89, fax 02.41.52.42.43 by appt.

DOM. DU VIGNEAU

Vieilli en fût 1999

■ 6.55 ha 10,000 30–49 F

The colour is lovely: ruby, with fine, very pure violet tints. Still gentle on the nose, when the wine is allowed to breathe it takes on a peppery character. The palate is supple and well structured. The wine fills the mouth well, and lacks only secondary aromas, which will be revealed with time.

Camille Mirambaud, 4, pl. de la Paleine, 49400 Souzay-Champigny, tel. 02.41.52.95.74, fax 02.41.52.95.74 by appt.

CH. DE VILLENEUVE

Vieilles vignes 1999★★

■ 3 ha 10,000 50–69 F

The picture is one of peace and harmony: a 19th-century château near a Renaissance building, a park and a vineyard on the plateau. This 99 vintage is an intense ruby colour, and it delivers on the nose notes of grilled, even roasted, dried fruit. The first impression is rich, the structure full and harmonious, and the palate has good length. A characterful and remarkable wine, whose terroir is evident. It should be kept.

SCA Chevallier, Ch. de Villeneuve, 49400 Souzay-Champigny, tel. 02.41.51.14.04, fax 02.41.50.58.24 ev. day except Sun. 9am–12 noon 2pm–6pm

Touraine

The interesting collections housed in the Musée des Vins de Touraine (Touraine Wine Museum) in Tours exhibit the history of advances made in vine-growing and wine in the region. It relates semi-mythical accounts of the life of Saint Martin, the bishop of Tours in 380, and illuminates the 'Golden Legend' with images relating to vine cultivation and wines. By the year 1000, the Abbey at Bourgueil was already cultivating the Breton (Cabernet Franc) variety in its famous enclosed vineyard and, years later, Rabelais, the great French writer, was eloquently singing its praises during the 16th century. History is still much in evidence today along the tourist routes from Mesland to Bourgueil on the right bank (through Vouvray, Tours, Luynes, Langeais), and from Chaumont to Chinon on the left bank (through Amboise and Chenonceaux, the Cher valley, Saché, Azay-le-Rideay and the forest of Chinon).

The Touraine vineyard has been famous for a considerable time, but underwent its most significant expansion at the end of the 19th century. Its present-day area, which is about 13,000 ha (32,110 acres), is actually less than it was before the phylloxera disaster; it lies mainly within the departments of Indre-et-Loire and Loir-et-Cher but, in the north, encroaches into the Sarthe. Tasting very old wines from 1921, 1893, 1874 or even 1858, for example at Vouvray, Borgueil or Chinon, reveals characteristics fairly close to the wines of today. Thus, despite developments in cultivation techniques and the science of wine-making, the 'style' of Touraine wines remains relatively unchanged, probably because each of the appellations is founded upon a single grape variety. The climate also plays its part: maritime and continental influences find expression in the wines, the slopes forming a screen from the north winds. In addition, the east-west valleys of the Loir, the Loire, the Cher, the Indre and the Vienne create a multitude of tufa slopes propitious for vine-growing, enjoying a local climate that shows little variation and maintains a healthy level of humidity. The tufa, a soft, creamy-yellow limestone, is hollowed out into innumerable subterranean caves. In the valleys, clay is mixed with limestone or sand and sometimes silica, while down on the banks of the Loire and the Vienne gravelly soils predominate.

These local variations are reflected in the wines. Each valley corresponds to an appellation, and each year the wines have different individual characteristics depending on the weather. The association of the year of bottling with the description of the cru is thus essential.

In 1989, a hot dry year, the wines were rich and full, with the promise of long life. In 1984, a year when the vines flowered late and the weather was dull, the white wines were drier and the reds lighter, and are only now reaching their full development. Due to these factors, the best vintages from recent decades are as follows: 1959, 1961, 1964, 1969, 1970, 1976, 1981, 1982, 1983, 1985, 1986, 1988, 1989, 1990, 1995 and 1996. Nevertheless, self-evidently, this classification varies between the tannic reds of Chinon or Bourgueil (softer when they are grown on gravelly soils, better structured when they come from the slopes), and the lighter growths from the Appellation Touraine, sometimes sold *en primeur*. There are also variations in the rosés, which are drier or not so dry depending on the amount of sunshine; the same is true of the whites of Azay-le-Rideau or Amboise, and of those from Vouvray and Montlouis, where the styles range from dry to sweet and include sparkling wines. Specific local vinification techniques also play their part. The tufa caves provide an excellent storage environment at a constant temperature of around 12°C (53.6°F), ideal for ageing; in addition, the vinification of the white wines is carried out at a controlled temperature, fermentation sometimes lasting several weeks, or even several months for the sweet wines. The light Touraine reds are produced from short periods of fermentation; with Borgueil and Chinon, however, fermentation is longer: two to four weeks. While the reds undergo malolactic fermentation, the whites and rosés owe their freshness, conversely, to the presence of malic acid. Generally speaking, 55% of the production, which in good years approaches some 700,000 hl (18,480,000 gal), is sold by shippers. Direct sales represent 30% and the co-operatives sell 15%.

Touraine

The Appellation Régionale Touraine covers 5,250 ha (12,967 acres), stretching from the outskirts of Montsoreau in the west as far as Blois and Selles-sur-Cher in the east. It is located principally in the valleys of the Loire, the Indre and the Cher. Tufa emerges rarely; the soils most often overlie clay with silica. The main variety for red wines is Gamay, alongside more tannic varieties such as Cabernet Franc and Cot, depending on the terrain. The majority of red wines, including the light and fruity vins primeurs, are made exclusively with Gamay. Reds made from a mixture of two or three of the main varieties keep well in bottle. The dry white wines are made with the Sauvignon, which in the last forty years has replaced all other varieties (124,706 hl (3,292,238 gal) in 1999). A proportion of the white wines produced (29,780 hl/786,192 gal) in 1999 is made as sparkling wines by the Méthode Traditionelle, or Champagne method. Finally, the rosés (3,758 hl/99,211 gal) in 1999 are always dry, fresh and fruity, made with the red wine grape varieties of the region. Reds and whites together totalled 190,154 hl (5,020,066 gal) in 1999.

It is worth mentioning the historic vineyard to the south of Tours which produces dry rosé Appellation Touraine wines formerly known as Noble Joué, a denomination now revived. The varieties in use here are the three Pinots: Pinot Gris (the majority), Pinot Meunier and Pinot Noir.

DOM. D'ARTOIS

Sauvignon Les Buttelières 1999★

□ 6 ha 45,000 30-49 F

A modern winery, built in the middle of the vines on the Mesland plateau, sheltered this pale-coloured wine, whose complex nose combines mineral and herbaceous scents with fruity (peach) aromas. The quite unctuous but balanced palate finds the same range and finishes with freshness. The **Touraine Les Buttelières Gamay 99** is also a great success.

Dom. d'Artois, La Morandière, 41150 Mesland, tel. 02.54.70.24.72, fax 02.54.70.24.72 Y by appt.

J.-L. Saget

AUGIS

Réserve des Caillouteux Elevé en fût de chêne 1998

■ 1.5 ha 8 500 30-49 F

The property bridges two départements and two appellations, Touraine and the Valençay VDQS. Here it unites Malbec and Cabernet Franc in a wine matured in oak barrels over a year. The oaky character is perceptible but harmonises well on the whole, as the wine has enough body to cope with it.

GAEC Jacky et Philippe Augis, rue des Vignes, Le Musa, 41130 Meusnes, tel. 02.54.71.01.89, fax 02.54.71.74.15 Y by appt.

MARC BADILLER Brut

○ 0.6 ha 4,000 30-49 F

Marc Badiller is settled near Azay-le-Rideau. He mixes Chenin and Grolleau (25%) to make a sparkling Touraine that is intensely fruity and toasty on the nose. This balanced wine is a true, vinous *brut* that fills the palate.

Marc Badiller, 29, Le Bourg, 37190 Cheillé, tel. 02.47.45.24.37, fax 02.47.45.29.66 Y ev. day except Sun. 8.30am–12.30pm 3pm–7pm

CELLIER DU BEAUJARDIN

Gamay 1999

■ 6 ha 35,000 20-29 F

The cooperative of the Cher Valley works for the future of the wine-growing region by persuading young people to settle in the area. It offers a Gamay with a red, purple-violet tone which smells of ripe fruit (cherry). The wine is chewy enough to fill the palate well and ends on a spicy note.

🔑 Cellier du Beaujardin, 32, av. du 11-Novembre, 37150 Bléré, tel. 02.47.30.33.44, fax 02.47.23.51.27 ☑ Y ev. day except Sun. 8am–12 noon 2pm–6.30pm

DOM. BEAUSEJOUR

Les Grenettes 1999

☐ 10 ha 50,000 ▮ 🌡 20–29 F

This family property in Noyers-sur-Cher, to the east of the Touraine region, is regularly mentioned in the *Guide*. Here, it offers a pleasurable wine which is very supple and develops strong notes of banana and pear.

🔑 GAEC Trotignon et Fils, Dom. Beauséjour, 10, rue des Bruyères, 41140 Noyers-sur-Cher, tel. 02.54.75.06.73, fax 02.54.75.06.73 ☑ Y ev. day 8am–12 noon 2pm–7pm

DOM. BELLEVUE Gamay 1999★

■ 5 ha 30,000 ▮ 🌡 20–29 F

The sands on clay and flint of Noyers-sur-Cher work well with Gamay. For proof, here is this 99 vintage, with a deep, cherry-red colour, which discreetly evokes ripe grapes. Quite strong and long on the palate, it is pleasant for the roundness of its tannins.

🔑 EARL Patrick Vauvy, Les Martinières, 41140 Noyers-sur-Cher, tel. 02.54.75.38.71, fax 02.54.75.21.89 ☑ Y by appt.

VIGNOBLE DE BLERE 1998★

■ 8 ha 60,000 ▮ 🌡 20–29 F

This wine from the Bléré cooperative was bottled by the *négociant* Chainier. Behind its bright ruby colour, it has a subtle scent of cocoa and red berries on the nose. The palate, at first unctuous, develops with harmony and strength to the finish.

🔑 Ets Pierre Chainier, ZI La Boistardière, 37400 Amboise, tel. 02.47.30.73.07, fax 02.47.30.73.09 Y by appt.

VIGNOBLES DES BOIS VAUDONS

Côt 1998★★

■ n.c. 9,000 ▮ 20–29 F

On the southern bank of the Cher, this is a family-run business where the new generation has only just settled as a GAEC (*groupement agricole d'exploitation communale*) and has already produced this remarkable Touraine. The eye is attracted by its deep colour with vivid red tints. An unctuous flavour, sustained by rounded tannins, fills the palate. Terroir and grape variety meet harmoniously to assure a good future. *Awarded a coup de coeur, regrettably at the time of going to press the label was not available for reproduction here.*

🔑 GAEC Mérieau, 38, rte de Saint-Aignan, 41400 Saint-Julien-de-Chédon, tel. 02.54.32.14.23, fax 02.54.32.14.32 ☑ Y by appt.

DOM. PAUL BUISSE Sauvignon 1999★

☐ n.c. 30,000 ▮ 🌡 20–29 F

To add to a career as a *négociant*, Paul Buisse acquired this 10-ha (25-acre) estate on the left bank of the Cher in 1989. Ten years later, here is a very successful white Touraine. Pale, with green tints, this Sauvignon Blanc harbours a fine mineral and floral range. On the palate, it leaves a very pleasant impression of fleshiness, roundness and freshness.

🔑 SA Paul Buisse, 69, rte de Vierzon, 41400 Montrichard, tel. 02.54.32.00.01, fax 02.54.32.09.78 ☑ Y ev. day except Sat. Sun. 8am–12 noon 2pm–6pm

DOM. DES CAILLOTS Gamay 1999★★

■ 3 ha 20,000 ▮ 🌡 20–29 F

Above the Cher, on the right bank, the wine-growing plateau of Noyers gives a view of the traffic on the Tours – Vierzon road. Domaine des Caillots has been here for a long time; Dominique Girault's father found some deeds dating back to the 13th century. Modernisation has been deployed from 1983 to 1992, resulting in the expansion of the vineyard (18 ha/44 acres today) and in some remarkable results. The 99 vintage testifies to this. A dark, bright cherry-red colour, it seduces with its fresh and floral bouquet, then ripe red berries dominate. *Awarded a coup de coeur, regrettably at the time of going to press the label was not available for reproduction here.*

🔑 EARL Dominique Girault, Le Grand Mont, 41140 Noyers-sur-Cher, tel. 02.54.32.27.07, fax 02.54.75.27.87 ☑ Y ev. day 8.30am–12 noon 2pm–7pm; Sun. by appt.

DOM. DES CAILLOTS

Sauvignon 1999★★

☐ 6 ha 25,000 ▮ 🌡 20–29 F

What a double success for Dominique Girault! This Touraine Sauvignon Blanc is just as remarkable as the Gamay (see preceding entry) and has a good quality – price ratio. The bright colour, tinted with lime, is not let down in the slightest by aromas of citrus fruits and mineral notes on the nose. On swirling the wine in the glass, floral (broom flowers) perfumes are evident. The palate keeps to the same line, with hints of grapefruit. The first impression is supple, the mouth flavours fresh, lengthy and balanced.

🔑 EARL Dominique Girault, Le Grand Mont, 41140 Noyers-sur-Cher, tel. 02.54.32.27.07, fax 02.54.75.27.87 ☑ Y ev. day 8.30am–12 noon 2pm–7pm; Sun. by appt.

LE CLOS DES CHARTREUX Brut

○ n.c. 11,000 ▮ 30–49 F

In the south of the Touraine region, this vineyard has recently been planted on a property previously belonging to the Liget monastery, founded during the 12th century. This wine, with its fine sparkle, is made from Chenin Blanc and Pinot Noir. Clean and fine, it pleases with its nuances of honey, and with its length.

⊶ Nouveaux Ets Maréchal et Cie, 36, Vallée Coquette, 37210 Vouvray, tel. 02.47.52.71.21, fax 02.47.52.61.05
☑ 𝐘 by appt.

CH. DE CHENONCEAU 1998★

□ 4 ha 20,000 30–49 F

Did you know that Chenonceau has, since it was built at the beginning of the 16th century, been a wine-growing estate where people have been able to take home bottles as a souvenir of their visit? This Touraine, for example. Its strong nose gives off mineral aromas and touches of flowers; its balanced palate then offers a rounded impression which is made even more flavoured by an almond note on the finish.Still on the whites, **Les Dômes de Chenonceau 99** is a wine to be drunk sooner than its senior. Very successful, with a diaphanous colour, it offers an intense and complex bouquet (grilled hazelnut, mineral notes), and has a good balance between freshness and suppleness.

⊶ SA Chenonceau-Expansion, Ch. de Chenonceau, 37150 Chenonceaux, tel. 02.47.23.44.07, fax 02.47.23.89.91
☑ 𝐘 ev. day 11am–6pm; cl. Nov.-mars

DOM. DES CHEZELLES

Sauvignon 1999★

□ 10 ha 80,000 30–49 F

The Marcadet family sells almost one third of their Touraine Blanc production in Belgium and the UK. Their success is justified by this well-presented wine. Complex aromas of flowers and exotic fruits combine on the palate in a balanced ensemble. The finish stretches out on even more fruity note.

⊶ EARL Alain Marcadet, Le Grand-Mont, 41140 Noyers-sur-Cher, tel. 02.54.75.13.62, fax 02.54.75.44.09
☑ 𝐘 ev. day except Sun. 8.30am–12 noon 2pm–7pm

DOM. DES CORBILLIERES 1998★

■ 5 ha n.c. 30–49 F

Two generations of the Barbou family have forged the reputation of this estate, located on a gravelly crest of the Oisly plateau in the Sologne wine-growing area. Deep red in colour, the Touraine Rouge 98 charms with its subtle fruity bouquet. It is sufficiently chewy to give it strength and a good length on the palate, with its hints of red fruit. Also successful, the **Gamay 98** is a full-blooded wine, while the **Sauvignon 99**, supple and fine, leaves a memory of an intense bouquet of white and yellow flowers.

⊶ EARL Barbou, Dom. des Corbillières, 41700 Oisly, tel. 02.54.79.52.75, fax 02.54.79.64.89 ☑ 𝐘 by appt.

REMI COSSON Noble Joué 1999

◪ 2.7 ha 2,500 20–29 F

A promising attempt. This is the first output of Rémi Cosson, working since 1998 on

Touraine

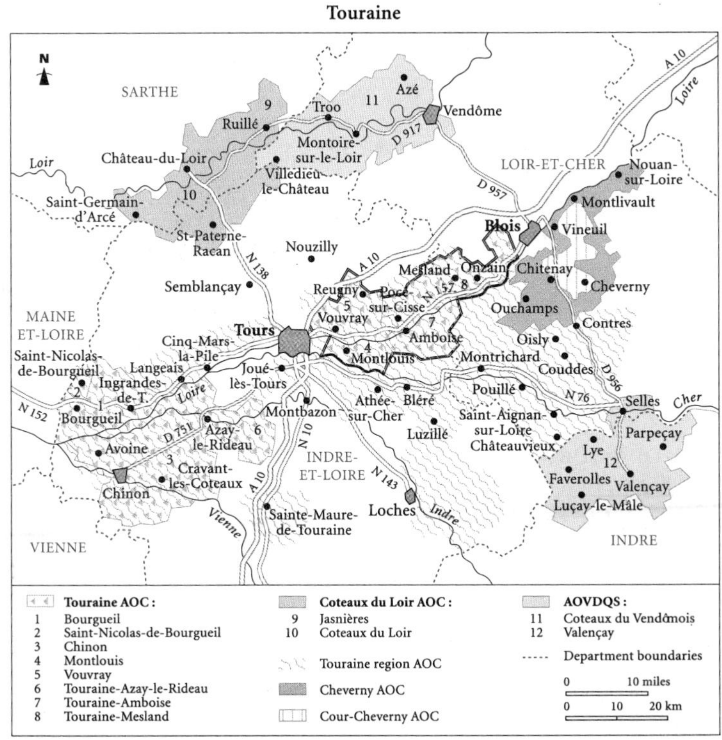

the vines of Noble Joué after a professional course. With a salmon tint, the 99 vintage is a floral wine, enhanced by a sugary note, which has balance and elegance on the palate.
🔑 Rémi Cosson, La Hardellière, 37320 Esvres-sur-Indre, tel. 02.47.65.70.63
☑ 🍷 by appt.

LES VIGNERONS DES COTEAUX ROMANAIS

Sauvignon Cuvée Saint-Vincent 1999

☐ 50 ha 400,000 20–29 F

This cooperative has been completely renovated over the last few years and today collects the fruit of 270 ha (667 acres) of vines. Its Sauvignon 99 is a bright colour with unobtrusive aromas and a good balance on the palate. It is a well-made wine.
🔑 Les Vignerons des Coteaux Romanais, 50, rue Principale, 41140 Saint-Romain-sur-Cher, tel. 02.54.71.70.74, fax 02.54.71.41.75
☑ 🍷 ev. day except Sun. Mon. 8am–12 noon 2pm–4pm

CH. DES COULDRAIES

Gamay 1999*

■ 2.8 ha 2,400 20–29 F

Château des Couldraies is a pretty Renaissance property. Its balanced Touraine Rouge covers the palate and charms with its intense aromas, which are at the same time fruity (cherry, redcurrant) and mineral (gunflint).
🔑 SCEA des Couldraies, Ch. des Couldraies, 41400 Saint-Georges-sur-Cher, tel. 02.54.32.27.42, fax 02.54.32.40.03, e-mail courrier@couldraies.com ☑ 🍷 by appt.
🔑 Pinta

DOM. DE CRAY Sauvignon 1999

☐ 6.2 ha 49,000 20–29 F

This estate was born of the partnership between a Montlouis wine-grower and a British *négociant*, bringing together 60 ha (148 acres), a little more than 6 ha (15 acres) of which is planted with the Sauvignon that is the base for this bright white wine. It opens with freshness before prolonging itself with suppleness on some pleasant notes of exotic fruit. A good wine indeed.
🔑 Boutinot, SARL La Chapelle de Cray, rte de l'Aquarium, 37400 Lussault-sur-Loire, tel. 02.47.57.17.74, fax 02.47.57.11.97
☑

DAME DE TOURAINE

Chenin Vieilles vignes 1998

☐ 4 ha 10,000 30–49 F

In the south of Touraine, in lovely countryside, this estate – cultivating vines since the end of the 19th century – was previously attached to Château de Ris, the old seat of the Baronnie de Preuilly. It offers in the 98 vintage a wine with a mineral nose, accompanied by hints of almonds and butter. The palate, with a sweet first impression, finishes on fruity nuances of apple.
🔑 Dom. de Ris, 37290 Bossay-sur-Claise, tel. 02.47.94.64.43, fax 02.47.94.68.46
☑ 🍷 ev. day except Sun. 5.30pm–7pm; Sat. 10am–12 noon
🔑 Gilbert Sabadie

DANIEL DELAUNAY

Cabernet 1998**

■ 2 ha 5,000 20–29 F

Dominating the Cher on the left bank, La Tesnière is the most vine-laden hamlet in Pouillé. Here you will find this family-run property, which has succeeded in the 98 vintage with this remarkable vivid red Touraine. A smooth first impression introduces a full and fruity (blackcurrant, raspberry) palate, whose length is assured by subtle tannins. Harmonious and typical of its type, this wine has great potential. The **Touraine Blanc 99** is pleasant.
🔑 Daniel Delaunay, 2, rue de la Bergerie, 41110 Pouillé, tel. 02.54.71.46.93, fax 02.54.71.77.34 ☑ 🍷 by appt.

DOM. JOEL DELAUNAY

Gamay 1999*

■ 8 ha 60,000 30–49 F

An air-conditioned winery has been installed at this vineyard, along with a prettily decorated reception/cellar. Visitors are truly welcome here and will discover this very successful wine. With a colour between garnet-red and ruby, it explodes on the nose with spice and fruit. It already seduces with its freshness, roundness and finesse, but will open out between now and 2001. Aged in the barrel, **Saveurs 2000** is interesting.
🔑 Dom. Thierry et Joël Delaunay, 48, rue de la Tesnière, 41110 Pouillé, tel. 02.54.71.45.69, fax 02.54.71.55.97, e-mail joeldelaunay@terre-net.fr ☑ 🍷 ev. day except Sun. 9am–12 noon 2pm–7pm

DOM. DESROCHES Gamay 1999**

■ 3 ha 20,000 20–29 F

The majority of the vines of this family-run estate are planted on sandy and clay-flint soil. This is the case of the 3 ha (7.4 acres) of Gamay which have provided the basis for this ruby-tinted wine. An intense bouquet of red berries and grilling emanate from the glass, and, on the palate, a fine first impression is followed by supple, strong flavours. A successful Touraine.
🔑 Jean-Michel Desroches, Les Raimbaudières, 41400 Saint-Georges-sur-Cher, tel. 02.54.32.33.13, fax 02.54.32.56.31
☑ 🍷 by appt.

DOM. FRISSANT Sauvignon 1999*

☐ 3.5 ha 14,000 30–49 F

Xavier Frissant is a young wine producer whose reputation is growing in the Touraine-Amboise appellation. His vineyard is grouped around the lower slopes and also produces a charming Touraine. This one has perfect balance, giving off aromas of exotic fruit (lychees) and crystallised fruit (apricot), and has good length and lots of finesse.

🔑 Xavier Frissant, 1, chem. Neuf, 37530 Mosnes, tel. 02.47.57.23.18, fax 02.47.57.23.25 ☑ Y ev. day 8am–12.30pm 2pm–7.30pm; Sun. by appt.

DOM. GIBAULT Sauvignon 1999

☐ 10 ha 80,000 20–29 F

Around Martinières, clay and flint carry a sandy covering which is successful with Sauvignon. This lively aromatic wine has certainly benefited: it opens with suppleness and finishes on hints of flowers and yellow fruit.

🔑 EARL Pascal et Danielle Gibault, Les Martinières, 41140 Noyers-sur-Cher, tel. 02.54.75.36.52, fax 02.54.75.29.79 ☑ Y ev. day except Sun. 10am–7pm

CHANTAL ET PATRICK GIBAULT

1999

◪ 2 ha 15,000 20–29 F

Meusnes has an interesting museum built of stone and flint, flint that can also be found at this vineyard, whose clay soils are rich. Chantal and Patrick Gibault can tell you about it over a glass of this Touraine, with a pink colour, which is lively with its notes of fruit and liquorice. Though acidulous, the 99 vintage does not lack body. **Touraine Blanc 99**, evocative of blackcurrant buds, also warrants a mention.

🔑 EARL Chantal et Patrick Gibault, rue Gambetta, 41130 Meusnes, tel. 02.54.71.02.63, fax 02.54.71.58.92 ☑ Y ev. day 8am–7pm; Sun. 10am–12 noon

DOM. DU HAUT PERRON

Vignoble des Perdriettes 1999

■ 3 ha 20,000 20–29 F

Cédric Allion succeeded his father Guy in 1999. Value does not wait for age. The 99 vintage has a fine cherry-red colour, and its unobtrusive nose, mostly floral, finds an echo on the balanced and structured palate. **Touraine Blanc 99** is also pleasant.

🔑 Guy Allion, 15, rue du Haut-Perron, 41140 Thésée, tel. 02.54.71.48.01, fax 02.54.71.48.01, e-mail guy.allion@wanadoo.fr ☑ Y by appt.

DOM. DE LA BERGEONNIERE

Cuvée Olivier 1999

☐ 2 ha 10,000 20–29 F

Jean-Claude Bodin has established himself on the right bank of the Cher; he has invested in stainless-steel equipment for careful vinification. His Touraine Blanc is a lively wine with golden tints. Supple, it is appreciated for its floral nose, centred on acacia and syringa, as well as for its length.

🔑 Jean-Claude Bodin, La Bergeonnière, 41140 Saint-Romain-sur-Cher, tel. 02.54.71.70.43, fax 02.54.71.72.92 ☑ Y by appt.

DOM. DE LA BERGERIE

Sauvignon 1999

☐ 6 ha 30,000 20–29 F

François Cartier is one of the ten or so wine producers installed in the hamlet of La Tesnière in Pouillé. He has produced a Sauvignon that pleases with its freshness. Subtle flavours of citrus fruit are prolonged on the palate with the same scents on the nose.

🔑 François Cartier, 13, rue de la Bergerie, 41110 Pouillé, tel. 02.54.71.51.54, fax 02.54.71.74.09 ☑ Y by appt.

DOM. DE LA CHAISE

Sauvignon 1999

☐ 14 ha 35,000 20–29 F

Saint-Georges-sur-Cher, on the left bank of the river, has more vines than anywhere else in Loir-et-Cher, with more than 400 ha (988 acres) under cultivation. This family-run estate of 53 ha (131 acres), a third of which is situated on an old property of the priory of La Chaise, has renovated its winery and developed direct selling. Here you will find this pale white wine with green tints. With aromas of blackcurrant and exotic fruit, supple and fleshy on the palate, it is a classic of the vintage. The estate's **Gamay 99** is also worth mentioning: its notes of red berries (redcurrant) return with an acidulous side on its well-balanced palate.

🔑 J.-P. et Ch. Davault, Dom. de La Chaise, 37, rue de la Liberté, 41400 Saint-Georges-sur-Cher, tel. 02.54.71.53.08, fax 02.54.71.53.08 ☑ Y by appt.

DOM. DE LA CHARMOISE

Sauvignon 1999★

☐ 17 ha 100,000 30–49 F

Henry Marionnet exports more than a third of his wines, produced from vines grown on the sands of the Sologne wine-growing region, and he has perfect control of the vinification process. The Sauvignon 99, pale in colour with green tints, is not to be ignored: some perceive a herbaceous side (broom flowers), others charming hints of exotic fruit. Everyone is in accord about its body and finesse on the palate. Also mentioned by the jury, the **Gamay 99** has been vinified in the Beaujolais manner; its fine flavour is sure to blossom out.

🔑 Henry Marionnet, La Charmoise, 41230 Soings, tel. 02.54.98.70.73, fax 02.54.98.75.66 ☑ Y ev. day except Sat. Sun. 9am–12 noon 2pm–5pm; cl. Aug.

LOIRE

DOM. DE LA CROIX BOUQUIE

Gamay 1999★

■ n.c. 15,000 30–49 F

Thenay is in the Sologne wine-growing area. Yet again, the Gamay has profited from the clay-sand terrain of the region to give a garnet-red wine with floral nuances. Quite round, this 99 vintage sets off on the palate towards a finish that is still somewhat austere, though rich in mineral, even spicy, impressions. It has character.

🔑 Christian Girard, 1, chem. de la Chaussée, Phages, 41400 Thenay, tel. 02.54.32.50.67, fax 02.54.32.74.17 ☒ Y by appt.

DOM. DE LA GARRELIERE

Cabernet franc 1998★

■ 6.5 ha 15,000 30–49 F

Once the property of Cardinal de Richelieu, this estate of 20 ha (49 acres) sells 30% of its output outside France. Its red Touraine knows how to find a place on people's tables. Its colour is violet and it has character: structure and strength, a certain length that does not, however, preclude immediate attractions, such as its raspberry and spicy notes. The clay-chalk soils of Richelais give, on the other hand, originality to Sauvignon wines. The jury therefore gave the **Touraine Blanc Sauvignon 99** a mention. Its mineral and fruity (quince) aromas are followed by a flavour which is at first fresh, then fills the palate with roundness.

🔑 François Plouzeau, Dom. de la Garrelière, Razines, 37120 Richelieu, tel. 02.47.95.62.84, fax 02.47.95.67.17 ☒ Y by appt.

DOM. DE LA GIRARDIERE

Gamay 1999★

■ n.c. 9,000 20–29 F

The town of Saint-Aignan dominates the Cher with its château and Romanesque church, which appears on the label of Patrick Léger's wines. The Gamay 99 is very successful, with a deep colour. The gentle nose demonstrates complexity with grilled notes, then the wine's full-bodied and harmonious palate is enriched by flavours of red berries. Of the white wines, the **Touraine de Sauvignon 99** is worthy of note for its supple first impression and its pleasing vigour, with herbaceous and mineral notes on the finish.

🔑 Patrick Léger, La Girardière, 41110 Saint-Aignan, tel. 02.54.75.42.44, fax 02.54.75.21.14 ☒ Y by appt.

LES MAITRES VIGNERONS DE LA GOURMANDIERE Gamay 1999★

◪ 30 ha 27,000 20–29 F

This is a major cooperative, which cultivates some 500 ha (1,235 acres) and does not waver in its efforts. Established in Francueil, it is very close to Château de Chenonceau. Its Rosé de Gamay is salmon-pink in colour tinted with vivid red. Floral and fruity (raspberry), it tickles the senses with its freshness, balance and length. Just as good, the **Touraine Mousseux Charlotte de Rostaing** warrants a new star. The **Sauvignon 99** is also worth mentioning; it has mineral and fruity (quince) aromas on a palate that is at once rounded and fresh.

🔑 Les Maîtres Vignerons de La Gourmandière, 14, rue de Chenonceaux, 37150 Francueil, tel. 02.47.23.91.22, fax 02.47.23.82.50, e-mail info@vignerons-gourmandiere.com ☒ Y by appt.

DOM. DE LA GRANDE FOUCAUDIERE

Gamay Tradition 1999★★

■ 4 ha 6,000 20–29 F

The Truets came to the Amboise region in 1992 and have done well in the 99 vintage. They have received a *Coup de Coeur* for the wine, which has a colour between garnet-red and ruby. The strong nose of ripe fruits delighted the tasters, and the balance between freshness and structure enchanted them. Fine nuances of wild strawberry and redcurrant complete this elegant and harmonious wine.

🔑 Lionel Truet, La Grande Foucaudière, 37530 Saint-Ouen-les-Vignes, tel. 02.47.30.04.82, fax 02.47.30.03.55 ☒ Y ev. day 8am–8pm

LA HERPINIERE Cabernet 1998

■ 1.5 ha 6,000 30–49 F

The wines of La Herpinière are matured in a cellar that was cut into the rock during the 15th century and which has more than 3 km (1.8 miles) of galleries. The Touraine Rouge 98, quite light in structure, proves pleasant for its long delivery of red berries (strawberry, raspberry) and black fruit, which is completed by a touch of spice.

🔑 Christophe Verronneau, 16, La Vallée, 37190 Vallères, tel. 02.47.45.92.38, fax 02.47.45.92.39, e-mail laherpiniere@aol.com ☒ Y by appt.

DOM. DE LA MECHINIERE

Sauvignon 1999

□ 5.69 ha 50,000 20–29 F

This property on the left bank of the Cher was taken over by the Forgues family in 1997. Three years later and this is already their second mention in the *Guide*. With a diaphanous hue, this white 99 gives off interesting fruity, herbaceous and floral aromas that appear again, more complex still, on the palate and up to a finish that is full of freshness.

🔑 Valérie Forgues, La Méchinière, 22, rte de Saint-Aignan, 41110 Mareuil-sur-Cher, tel. 02.54.75.41.78, fax 02.54.75.27.61 ☒ Y by appt.

DANIELLE DE L'ANSEE

Sauvignon 1999★

□ n.c. 80,000 20–29 F

Danielle de l'Ansée is a small company founded in 1998 by the wine-grower Pascal Gibault to expand his range for export (50%

of output). The colour of this Touraine shines with all its fire. The bouquet charms with its mineral and fruity notes, while the palate is exhilarated by a touch of carbonic gas (CO_2) which prolongs the aromas well. A very good ensemble.

🗝 Danielle de L'Ansée, Les Martinières, 41140 Noyers-sur-Cher, tel. 02.54.71.09.95, fax 02.54.71.09.95 ▣

🗝 Pascal Gibault

CH. DE LA PRESLE Sauvignon 1999

□ 13.35 ha 90,000 ▮ 30–49 F

The great-great-granddaughter of the purchaser of this estate, in 1885, has settled here with her father. Improvements are assured, as is proved by this 99 vintage with a clear colour and aromas of blackcurrant and dried apricot. It is quite a long wine, pleasing for its refreshing liveliness. The **Touraine Rosé 99** also deserves to be mentioned.

🗝 Dom. Jean-Marie Penet, Ch. de La Presle, 41700 Oisly, tel. 02.54.79.52.65, fax 02.54.79.08.50 ▣ Y ev. day except Sun. 9am–12 noon 2pm–7pm

LES CAVES DE LA RAMEE

Sauvignon 1999

□ 4 ha 4,000 ▮ ♁ 20–29 F

The cellars of La Ramée are not far from the Gallo-Roman ruins of Thésée, a site that can be visited in the tourist season. The 99 vintage is represented here by a bright white wine, with a discreet nose, but a harmonious and quite rich palate. Flavours of ripe fruit are easily perceptible.

🗝 Gérard Gabillet, 31, rue des Charmoises, 41140 Thésée, tel. 02.54.71.45.02, fax 02.54.71.31.48 ▣ Y ev. day except Sun. 8am–12 noon 2pm–7pm

DOM. DE LA RENAUDIE

Sauvignon 1999★

□ 8 ha 60,000 ▮ ♁ 20–29 F

Patricia and Bruno Denis, a young couple of well-trained wine-growers, preoccupy themselves with the quality of their vines and grapes and have produced a very successful Touraine Blanc. Diaphanous on the eye, the 99 vintage has an intense bouquet, mostly of blackcurrant and eucalyptus, and caresses the palate with roundness, almost unctuousness. Note also the **Touraine Rouge de Cot 98**, which has a bouquet of violet, mulberry and spice. The first impression is still severe, but the wine's richness ensures that it will mature well.

🗝 Patricia et Bruno Denis, Dom. de La Renaudie, 115, rte de Saint-Aignan, 41110 Mareuil-sur-Cher, tel. 02.54.75.18.72, fax 02.54.75.27.65, e-mail domaine.renaudie@wanadoo.fr ▣ Y by appt.

DOM. DE LA RENNE Gamay 1999★

■ n.c. 45,000 ▮ ♁ 20–29 F

La Renne is a small river that crosses Saint-Romain before rejoining the Cher, and it is under this name that Guy Lévêque produces his Touraines. The Gamay 99, sombre in colour, opens up with suppleness and opens further with enough tannins. It will mature well and gain finesse.

🗝 Guy Lévêque, 1, chemin de la Forêt, 41140 Saint-Romain-sur-Cher, tel. 02.54.71.72.72, fax 02.54.71.35.07 ▣ Y by appt.

DOM. DE LA ROCHETTE

Gamay Fleur de printemps 1999

■ 20 ha 120,000 ▮ ♁ 20–29 F

Pouillé, on the left bank of the Cher, is a dynamic wine-growing village. François Leclair has made a bright red 99 which has good red berry aromas. Supple and balanced, the wine is pleasant for its youth and smoothness.

🗝 François Leclair, 79, rte de Montrichard, 41110 Pouillé, tel. 02.54.71.44.02, fax 02.54.71.10.94 ▣ Y ev. day 8am–11.30am 2pm–5.30pm; Sat. Sun. by appt.; cl. 24–31 Dec.

DOM. LEVEQUE Sauvignon 1999

□ 8 ha 20,000 ▮ ♁ 20–29 F

Luc and Monique Lévêque's Touraine 99 does not let down its grape of origin – a Sauvignon harvested on 20-year-old parcels of vine. Finesse is certainly present, apparent in the mineral and floral register.

🗝 Luc Lévêque, 41140 Noyers-sur-Cher, tel. 02.54.71.52.06, fax 02.54.75.47.65 ▣ Y ev. day 8.30am–7pm

JACQUELINE LOUET

Sauvignon Cuvée 2000 1999

□ 3 ha 15,000 ▮ ♁ 20–29 F

Château de Chaumont, some ten kilometres (six miles) from the vineyard, appears on the label of this golden-green Touraine. Fruity nuances, reminiscent of Muscat grapes, hit the nose, while on the palate a lively first impression introduces subsequent balanced and refreshing flavours.

🗝 Mme Jacqueline Louet, Cave Pierre Louet, Le Marchais, 41120 Monthou-sur-Bièvre, tel. 02.54.44.01.56 ▣ Y by appt.

DOM. LOUET-ARCOURT

Cuvée Réserve 1998★

■ 1.2 ha 5,000 ▮ ♁ 20–29 F

Monthou-sur-Bièvre is south of Blois, bordering the Touraine and Cheverny appellations. Jean-Louis and Françoise Arcourt have made a ruby-coloured Cuvée Réserve enlivened by purplish highlights. The complex aromas develop through the mineral and floral (violet) ranges. The full, mellow palate finds a harmonious conclusion in a long finish.

🗝 EARL Louet-Arcourt, 1, rue de la Paix, 41120 Monthou-sur-Bièvre, tel. 02.54.44.04.54, fax 02.54.44.15.06 ▣ Y by appt.

LOIRE

JEAN-CHRISTOPHE MANDARD

Sauvignon 1999

☐ 3.5 ha 25,000 20–29 F

Jean-Christophe Mandard is the fourth generation of his family to produce wine on the hillsides on the left bank of the Cher. He has made a bright white Touraine with pleasant white fruit aromas. The wine appeals with its liveliness and its drawn-out floral notes.

Jean-Christophe Mandard, Le Haut-Bagneux, 41110 Mareuil-sur-Cher, tel. 02.54.75.19.73, fax 02.54.75.16.70 by appt.

DOM. DE MARCE Gamay 1999

■ 1.5 ha 5,000 20–29 F

Established at Oisly, between Touraine and Sologne, Daniel Godet markets the whole range of grape varieties in this appellation. The memorable wine here is a Gamay, a bright wine with first vegetal then fruity tones on the nose, and which fills the mouth well after a supple first impression. A spicy hint is discernible too.

GAEC Godet, Dom. de Marcé, 41700 Oisly, tel. 02.54.79.54.04, fax 02.54.79.54.45 ev. day except Sun. 8am–12 noon 2pm–7pm

GUY MARDON L'Elégante 1999★★

☐ 1.8 ha 11,000 30–49 F

Oisly is the cradle of the Sauvignon grape in Touraine. The grapes were harvested slightly overripe from a selection of the oldest vines on the estate (30 years old) to build up this elegant wine. Lemon-yellow glinting with green, its charm lies in its mineral, smoky notes. It opens on the palate with suppleness, then becomes very rich and lingers long on the finish with ripe fruit. This 99 embodies all the potential of the sandy terroir of the Sologne wine-growing area.

Guy et Jean-Luc Mardon, Dom. du Pré Baron, 41700 Oisly, tel. 02.54.79.52.87, fax 02.54.79.00.45 ev. day except Sun. 8am–12 noon 2pm–6.30pm

DOM. JACKY MARTEAU

Gamay 1999★

■ 9.5 ha 40,000 20–29 F

Jacky Marteau, a definite asset to the hamlet of La Tesnière at Pouillé, farms 24 ha (59 acres) of vines planted on the best slopes of the Cher. His Gamay has a dark garnet colour and a scent of red fruit. Structured and well balanced, it lines the palate well. Furthermore, the estate deserves a mention for its thirst-quenching **Sauvignon 99**, which is fine and well marked with its vegetable (blackcurrant bud) and fruity (quince) tones.

Jacky Marteau, 36, rue de La Tesnière, 41110 Pouillé, tel. 02.54.71.50.00, fax 02.54.71.75.83 by appt.

EVELYNE ET FRANCOIS MARTINEAU Gamay 1999★

■ 3.7 ha 25,000 20–29 F

This family winery was established in 1920 on flinty clay soils on the left bank of the Cher. In 1999 it produced a medium-intensity ruby-coloured wine that opens on the nose with spices and red fruit, flavours which are prolonged in a rounded and elegant palate. A moment of pleasure.

François Martineau, 31, rue de la Ferme, 41110 Couffy, tel. 02.54.75.19.71, fax 02.54.75.11.98 ev. day except Sun. 8am–12 noon 2pm–7pm

DOM. MAX MEUNIER Brut★

○ 2 ha 7,000 30–49 F

This wine is the result of mixing 80% white grapes with 20% red. It has a brilliant, golden colour and emits intense aromas of white fruit and almonds. Full and ample, the wine offers balanced flavours, which persist well.

Max Meunier, 6, rue Saint-Gennefort, 41110 Seigy, tel. 02.54.75.04.33, fax 02.54.75.39.69, e-mail maxmeunier@aol.com ev. day 8am–7.30pm; groups by appt.

DOM. MICHAUD Sauvignon 1999★

☐ 6.5 ha 60,000 20–29 F

The Michaud family is one of the go-ahead players in the hamlet of Les Martinières, on the wine-growing hillside of Noyers-sur-Cher. Its 1999 wine has a beautiful pale greeny-gold tint. Emanating from it is a subtle smoky, mineral scent. On the palate, the wine gives a lively first impression and then is pleasantly drawn out. The **Cuvée Rouge Ad Vitam 98** is very successful too.

EARL Dom. Michaud, Les Martinières, 41140 Noyers-sur-Cher, tel. 02.54.32.47.23, fax 02.54.75.39.19 by appt.

MAISON MIRAULT Brut★

○ n.c. 3,000 30–49 F

The label of this sparkling Touraine shows the wine cellars hollowed out of the rock at Maison Mirault. There is no doubt about the speciality of this merchant: sparkling wines. He offers a real *brut* which is worth keeping on the table for an entire meal. A bright straw colour, the wine releases modest fruit aromas, showing effervescence at first and fruit at the end.

Maison Mirault, 15, av. Brûlé, 37210 Vouvray, tel. 02.47.52.71.62, fax 02.47.52.60.90, e-mail maison.mirault@wanadoo.fr ev. day 8am–12 noon 2pm–6.30pm; Sun. by appt.

DOM. DE MONTIGNY Côt 1998★

■ 1 ha 6,000 20–29 F

The vineyard has been taken over by a new generation of wine-makers since the 1998 harvests, but the cellarmaster has not changed: he is a master wine-maker, as evidenced by this ruby Touraine, marked by red fruit (cherry and blackcurrant). It opens roundly on the palate and moves on to very evident tannins that will ensure good development over three or four years.

Annabelle Michaud, Dom. de Montigny, 41700 Sassay, tel. 02.54.79.60.82, fax 02.54.79.07.51 by appt.

CH. DE NITRAY Brut 1998

○ 5 ha 15,000 30–49 F

The Renaissance Château de Nitray houses a vine and wine museum and lends visitors bicycles to ride along the banks of the Cher. Their taste buds are also privileged: this sparkling, straw-coloured Touraine has small bubbles that carry fruity notes of pear and almond. Dry rather than *brut*, it is nevertheless most pleasant.

de L'Espinay, Ch. de Nitray, 37270 Athée-sur-Cher, tel. 02.47.50.29.74, fax 02.47.50.29.61 by appt.

DOM. OCTAVIE Sauvignon 1999

□ 10.37 ha 55,000 30–49 F

Domaine Octavie, family-run since 1885, welcomes visitors in a small wine cellar set up in a well-preserved 17th-century building. In 1999 it produced a very bright wine with a fairly fine nose falling within the registers of floral and mineral. It develops well on the palate. Also worthy of mention is **Fragrance 98**, a balanced Touraine that can age until 2001.

Noë Rouballay, Dom. Octavie, Marcé, 41700 Oisly, tel. 02.54.79.54.57, fax 02.54.79.65.20, e-mail octavie@caves-particulieres.com ev. day 8.30am–12.30pm 2pm–6.30pm; Sun. by appt.

DOM. JAMES PAGET

Cuvée Tradition 1998★

■ 1.5 ha 7,500 30–49 F

The village of Rivarennes is close to Azay-le-Rideau and its château. Here James Paget has made a wine with a sustained colour and a fruity nose. It opens well on the palate and has a supple, rich flavour whose mellowness is indicative of the well-matured grapes used in this harmonious mixture.

EARL James Paget, 13, rue d'Armentières, 37190 Rivarennes, tel. 02.47.95.54.02, fax 02.47.95.45.90 by appt.

CAVES DU PERE AUGUSTE

Côt 1998

■ 6.8 ha 20,000 20–29 F

Most of the vines grow on the hillside facing due south, next to those of Château de Chenonceau. This family-owned estate, where visitors are always most welcome, offers a Malbec wine which is still a little austere but already pleasing for its intense colour, red fruit notes and length. A laying-down period of at least four years is well within reach of this 98 wine.

Famille Godeau, GAEC Caves du Père Auguste, 14, rue des Caves, 37150 Civray-de-Touraine, tel. 02.47.23.93.04, fax 02.47.23.99.58 ev. day 8.30am–7pm; Sun. 10am–12 noon

CH. DE POCE Sauvignon 1999

□ 15 ha 66,000 20–29 F

Above the Renaissance château, the vineyard is farmed by the Chainier house and the grapes are vinified in the Amboise cellars. Here the Sauvignon grapes have given rise to a 99 wine which is pale with green glints. Subtle aromas harmonise well in the well-balanced, rich and rounded flavours.

SCA Dom. Chainier, Ch. de La Roche, 37530 Chargé, tel. 02.47.30.73.07, fax 02.47.30.73.09 by appt.

PRESTIGE DE LA VALLEE DES ROIS

Sauvignon 1999★

□ n.c. 100,000 30–49 F

In 1961 seven wine producers decided to join up to enhance their production, and soon afterwards acquired modern equipment. Bottled in February 2000, its Touraine, greeny-gold in colour, has a fine bouquet with hints of citrus. Its balance and the way in which it lingers on the palate make this wine a pleasure.

Confrérie-Vignerons Oisly-Thésée, Le Bourg, 41700 Oisly, tel. 02.54.79.75.20, fax 02.54.79.75.29 ev. day 9am–12 noon 2pm–6pm

DOM. CHARLY RAVENELLE

Sauvignon 1999★

□ 3 ha 20,000 20–29 F

Soings-en-Sologne used to be known for growing strawberries, but its sandy soils are equally good for growing Sauvignon vines. Round and rich, this 99 appeals for its palette of citrus and apricot scents, then its fruity finish. Serve with chicken in a cream sauce.

Charly Ravenelle, Champdilly, 41230 Soings-en-Sologne, tel. 02.54.98.70.44, fax 02.54.98.70.44 by appt.

DOM. DU RIN DU BOIS

Gamay 1999★

■ 11 ha 80,000 30–49 F

Domaine du Rin is at the edge of a wood in wine-growing Sologne, with part of the vineyard in a clearing. The sandy soils on clay are good for Gamay grapes, as witnessed by this ruby wine with an intense nose of strawberry, cherry and a touch of pepper. It is a supple, smooth and harmonious wine, which you will not tire of.

Pascal Jousselin, Dom. du Rin du Bois, 41230 Soings-en-Sologne, tel. 02.54.98.71.87, fax 02.54.98.75.09, e-mail rin-du-bois@caves-particulieres.com by appt.

LOIRE

ROBERT DE SCHLUMBERGER

Brut★

○ n.c. 25,000 30-49 F

Robert de Schlumberger is the name of an Austrian ancestor of the current owners. It is also the up-market brand of the Blanc Foussy estate. Aged for five years on slats, this wine has a pale gold colour embellished with fine bubbles. It has an intense, well-developed nose of exotic fruit and acacia honey, and forms a strong but still harmonious whole on the palate.

SA Blanc Foussy, 95, quai de la Loire, 37210 Rochecorbon, tel. 02.47.40.40.20, fax 02.47.52.65.82 Y by appt.

CLOS ROCHE BLANCHE

Gamay 1999★

■ 8 ha 40,000 30-49 F

The estate's wine cellar is hollowed out of the rock under the vines. The harvest can thus be taken down to it directly, via a well. The vineyard is run using agrobiology and the yield is controlled. These principles are behind the production of a 99 ruby wine, evocative of spices and red fruit. Structured and long, it finishes powerfully and will hold up well with a meal.

GAEC du Clos Roche Blanche, 19, rte de Montrichard, 41110 Mareuil-sur-Cher, tel. 02.54.75.17.03, fax 02.54.75.17.02 Y by appt.

ROUSSEAU FRERES

Noble Joué 1999★★

◪ 11 ha 47,000 20-29 F

A family of five run this vineyard, on flinty clay and grit, their range of wines based on the Pinot Meunier grape. A fine example of Noble Joué wine, which will shortly obtain its own appellation. A *Coup de Coeur* has to be this good. This rosé, of salmon-pink tints with lively highlights, was unanimously approved by the jury. After a floral (violet) nose comes a full-bodied, fruity palate that develops with suppleness and finesse. This wine 'makes your mouth water', wrote a taster.

Rousseau Frères, Le Vau, 37320 Esvres-sur-Indre, tel. 02.47.26.44.45, fax 02.47.26.53.12 Y ev. day except Sun. 8am–12.30pm 2pm–7pm

DOM. DES SABLONS Cabernet 1998

■ 3.6 ha 30,000 30-49 F

Jacques Delaunay is a skilled wine-maker He has counted on a functional cellar and well-selected vines to make a bright wine that comes within the gamey register embellished by a note of liquorice. Right from the beginning, fullness characterises the palate, whose tannins still need to harmonise.

Jacques Delaunay, Dom. des Sablons, 40, rue de la Liberté, 41110 Pouillé, tel. 02.54.71.44.25, fax 02.54.71.09.25 Y ev. day 8am–7pm; Sun. by appt.

ALAIN ET PHILIPPE SALLE

Sauvignon 1999

□ 11 ha 40,000 20-29 F

A very supple wine is made by these wine-producers in the hamlet of Les Martinières; the family has been established here for many years. The fruitiness of apple and pear is accompanied by vegetal and mineral notes.

EARL Sallé, Les Martinières, 41140 Noyers-sur-Cher, tel. 02.54.75.48.10, fax 02.54.75.39.80 Y by appt.

JEAN-JACQUES SARD

Noble Joué 1999★

◪ 3.8 ha 18,000 20-29 F

Jean-Jacques Sard runs his vineyard on the edge of town, in the suburbs of Tours. Made from more than 50% Pinot Meunier grapes, his rosé has a clear salmon-pink colour. This Noble Joué is balanced, and typical of the 99 vintage in its suppleness. Its fresh and fruity bouquet only adds to the pleasure.

Jean-Jacques Sard, La Chambrière, 37320 Esvres-sur-Indre, tel. 02.47.26.42.89, fax 02.47.26.57.59

DOM. SAUVETE Privilège 1998

■ 2 ha 10,000 50-69 F

Favourably situated on hillsides facing due south, this vineyard specialises in the production of well-structured red wines, and this Touraine conforms to the rule. Almost black, with a powerful nose, it keeps to the style of the house by virtue of its concentration. Open after some years of development in the bottle.

Dom. Sauvète, La Bocagerie, 41400 Monthou-sur-Cher, tel. 02.54.71.48.68, fax 02.54.71.75.31 Y ev. day except Sun. 9am–12 noon 2pm–7pm; cl. 15–31 Aug.

ANTOINE SIMONEAU

Brut Cuvée Millénium

○ 6.23 ha 9,000 30-49 F

You will find Antoine Simoneau's family estate on the road to Château de Monpoupon. This producer, who has been selling direct for six years, has made a golden-yellow Touraine with a pleasant nose of brioche and dry fig. This sparkling wine lingers on the palate with suppleness, on touches of pineapple.

Antoine Simoneau, La Poterie, 41400 Saint-Georges-sur-Cher, tel. 02.54.71.36.14, fax 02.54.32.59.32 Y by appt.

DOM. DES SOUTERRAINS
Gamay 1999★

■ 5 ha 30,000 ▮ ♁ 20-29 F

The wine-producing plateau of Châtillon, at the eastern edge of Touraine, has interesting terroirs. Made in an air-conditioned winery, this luminous red wine offers a bouquet of red fruit. Its lovely flavour has sufficient structure to develop well over time.

🗝 Jacky Goumin, Dom. des Souterrains, 37, rue des Souterrains, 41130 Châtillon-sur-Cher, tel. 02.54.71.02.94, fax 02.54.71.76.26 ☑ Y ev. day except Sun. 8.30am–12 noon 2pm–7pm; cl. 15 Aug.–1st Sep.

DOM. THOMAS Gamay 1999

■ n.c. 8,000 ▮ 20-29 F

The property is at the gates of the Beauval Zoo Park, in the upper part of Saint-Aignan. Below the vineyard, the wine cellar stretches for 2 km (1.2 miles). This 99 wine, a good ruby-red colour, reveals rather spicy and mineral flavours on the palate. It unfurls in suppleness through to a pleasant finish.

🗝 EARL Thomas, Les Ormeaux, 41110 Saint-Aignan, tel. 02.54.75.17.00, fax 02.54.75.16.49 ☑ Y ev. day 8am–12 noon 2pm–7.30pm

FRANCK VERRONNEAU
Cabernet 1998★

■ 2 ha 4,000 ▮ 20-29 F

For ten years Franck Verronneau has held the reins of this family property established by his grandfather in 1935. His 98 Touraine has, behind a deep red colour, a palette of red fruit with a hint of kernel. The tannins are present but supple, and the finish leaves a harmonious impression.

🗝 Franck Verronneau, Beaulieu, Cheillé, 37190 Azay-le-Rideau, tel. 02.47.45.40.86, fax 02.47.45.94.82 ☑ Y ev. day 9am–12 noon 2pm–6pm

DOM. DU VIEUX PRESSOIR
Sauvignon 1999

□ 6 ha 10,000 ▮ ♁ 20-29 F

Domaine du Vieux Pressoir is at Rilly-sur-Loire, between the much-visited châteaux of Chaumont and Amboise. An early 19th-century wine-press marks the entrance. Its Touraine offers an original palette where gunflint mixes with citrus fruit then roses. This is a nice wine, ready to drink.

🗝 Joël Lecoffre, 27, rte de Vallières, 41150 Rilly-sur-Loire, tel. 02.54.20.90.84, fax 02.54.20.99.66, e-mail joel.lecoffre@wanadoo.fr ☑ Y by appt.

Touraine-Amboise

Sited on both banks of the Loire and dominated by the 15th- and 16th-century Château d'Amboise, the vineyard of the Appellation TouraineAmboise, which is (between 150 and 200 ha (370–494 acres) is not far from the Manoir Clos-Lucé, where Leonardo de Vinci spent his last days. Production is mainly of red wines (12,418 hl / 327,835 gal) from Gamay, Côt and Cabernet Franc. These are full wines with only a little tannin; when the Côt and Cabernet are dominant, the wines have some keeping potential. The same varieties also produce dry, charming rosés that are fruity and well defined. The whites, 1,031 hl (27,218 gal) in 1999, are dry or medium-dry, depending on the year, and they, too, may be kept.

DOM. DES BESSONS 1999

◪ n.c. 2,000 ▮ ♁ 20-29 F

Limeray is a wine-growing village where each household has a wine cellar. Walks are organised from the town, leading in particular to Château d'Avizé on the hillside. François Péquin offers for tasting a pale rosé with a pure colour. Modest on the nose, the wine nevertheless fills the mouth well and refreshes with its liveliness.

🗝 François Péquin, Dom. des Bessons, 113, rue de Blois, 37530 Limeray, tel. 02.47.30.09.10, fax 02.47.30.02.25 ☑ Y ev. day except Sun. 9am–7pm

DOM. DUTERTRE
Cuvée Prestige 1998★

■ 4 ha 20,000 ◖◗ 30-49 F

This large family estate has specialised in direct sales for two generations; a quarter of its production crosses borders and oceans. The garnet-coloured Cuvée Prestige, gleaming with purple, has what it takes to seduce. Its aromas of morello cherry and blackcurrant explode on the nose as well as on the palate, sustained by a good network of tannins and an oaky thread resulting from ten months' maturation in barrels. A beautiful balance.

🗝 Dom. Dutertre, 20–21, rue d'Enfer, 37530 Limeray, tel. 02.47.30.10.69, fax 02.47.30.06.92 ☑ Y ev. day 8am–12.30pm 2pm–6pm; Sun. by appt.

XAVIER FRISSANT

Cuvée François Ier 1998★

■ 5 ha 15,000 ▮ ♁ 30-49

Xavier Frissant is a young wine-maker whose family has been growing vines for a long time. He selects the best locations for his plantations. His reputation is growing, and this 1999 works in his favour. Intense purple, it presents non-aggressive tannins. Still very powerful, it makes a good wine for laying down.

🗝 Xavier Frissant, 1, chem. Neuf, 37530 Mosnes, tel. 02.47.57.23.18, fax 02.47.57.23.25 ☑ Y ev. day 8am–12.30pm 2pm–7.30pm; Sun. by appt.

DOM. DE LA GABILLIERE

Moelleux 1998★

□ 2 ha n.c. ▮ ♁ 30-49 F

La Gabillière is the experimental estate of the Amboise School of Wine-Making. On the heights of the town, it has a lovely view of the château and the Chanteloup Pagoda, a notable example of the architecture of the Age of Enlightenment. Its sweet 98, a shade of buttercup, has a lovely smell of acacia honey and apricot. Right to the finish, it lines the palate with its sweetness. A select wine, rare in this vintage, which should be laid down for five to ten years at least.

🗝 Dom. de La Gabillière, 46, av. Emile-Gounin, 37400 Amboise, tel. 02.47.23.35.51, fax 02.47.57.01.76 ☑ Y ev. day except Sat. Sun. 8am–12 noon 1.30pm–5.30pm

DOM. DE LA GRANDE FOUCAUDIERE Clos du Vau 1998

■ 0.3 ha 2,500 ◫ 30-49 F

An ex-railwayman from the Parisian region, Lionel Truet returned to the land in 1992; he built up his estate from scratch by buying vines from a wine-grower in the village and planting them on land belonging to his wife's family. His 98 wine has a beautiful, sustained colour, from which arise nice aromas of morello cherry and blackcurrant. Twelve months' maturation in barrels has left its imprint on the palate.

🗝 Lionel Truet, La Grande Foucaudière, 37530 Saint-Ouen-les-Vignes, tel. 02.47.30.04.82, fax 02.47.30.03.55 ☑ Y ev. day 8am–8pm

DOM. LA GRANGE TIPHAINE

Demi-sec 1999★

◪ 1 ha 4,000 ▮ ♁ 20-29 F

This domaine consists of 30 ha (74 acres) of vines on the heights of Amboise, close to the Mini-Châteaux Park, and commands a pretty view of the real Château d'Amboise. Its lightly tinted rosé is slightly peppery on the nose, and sweetness is noticeable in this pleasing wine, which is full of finesse.

🗝 Jackie Delecheneau, 1353, rue du Clos-Chauffour, 37400 Amboise, tel. 02.47.57.64.17, fax 02.47.57.39.49 ☑ Y by appt.

DOM. DE LA PERDRIELLE

Cuvée François Ier 1998

■ 2.7 ha 20,000 ▮ ♁ 20-29 F

In 2000 Jacques and Vincent Gandon offer a red Touraine-Amboise with a rich, fruity bouquet. Still tannic but very full, this Cuvée François I will evolve favourably over several years' ageing.

🗝 EARL Gandon, Dom. de La Perdrielle, 24, Vauriflé, 37530 Nazelles-Négron, tel. 02.47.57.31.19, fax 02.47.57.77.28 ☑ Y ev. day except Sun. 9am–12.30pm 2pm–7pm

DOM. DE LA PREVOTE

Cuvée François Ier 1998

■ 10 ha 15,000 ▮ ♁ 20-29 F

The estate takes its name from a provost's house (old law courts) of the 11th century, which was bought ten years ago and has since been restored. Here you can sample this very dark red wine, whose pleasant aromas entice you to taste it. Once on the palate, as solid as the law, the wine shows very obvious tannins. Some years are needed before judgement can be passed.

🗝 Dom. de La Prévôté, GAEC Bonnigal, 17, rue d'Enfer, 37530 Limeray, tel. 02.47.30.11.02, fax 02.47.30.11.09 ☑ Y ev. day 9am–7pm; Sun. 9am–1pm

DOM. DE LA RIVAUDIERE 1998★★

■ 2 ha 14,000 ▮ ♁ 30-49 F

This producer's main vineyard is at Vouvray, but here they know all there is to know about red wine. As proof, take this remarkable 98, made with 80% Gamay, which charms instantly with its evocations of ripe fruit. It attacks openly on the palate. Supple, even fresh and fruity, it is nevertheless well structured. Balance and finesse are present, as one would expect from the appellation, and the pleasure lasts and lasts. The **Touraine Rouge and Rosé 99** are no less successful.

🗝 EARL Perdriaux, Les Glandiers, 37210 Vernou-sur-Brenne, tel. 02.47.52.02.26, fax 02.47.52.04.81 ☑ Y by appt.

CELLIER LEONARD DE VINCI

Cuvée François Ier 1998★

■ 8 ha 12,000 ▮ ♁ 20-29 F

This wine cellar, recently modernised, is one of the smallest cooperatives in the département of Indre-et-Loire. It is something of a family affair (115 ha/284 acres

under vines) set up in 1941 by a group of wine-growing friends. Their story is one of success, as witnessed by this deep 98 red, which has been matured in vats for nine months. Gamey notes and a lovely balance are the strong points of this tasting. Serve with *coq au vin*.
Cellier Léonard de Vinci, 11, rte de Saint-Ouen-les-Vignes, 37530 Limeray, tel. 02.47.30.10.31, fax 02.47.30.06.31 ev. day except Sun. 8.15–12 noon 2pm–6pm

ROLAND PLOU ET SES FILS 1999★

3 ha 10,000 20–29 F

This family of wine-makers, established at Chargé on the left bank of the Loire since the 16th century, today own 65 ha (160 acres) of vines and two wine cellars which are open to the public. A bright rosé with a pleasant nose brings it distinction in the 99 vintage. Round and long, this wine is not lacking in finesse.
EARL Plou et Fils, 26, rue du Gal-de-Gaulle, 37530 Chargé, tel. 02.47.30.55.17, fax 02.47.23.17.02 ev. day 9am–1pm 3pm–7.30pm

VIGNOBLE DES QUATRE ROUES

Cuvée François Ier 1998★★

1 ha 4,000 20–29 F

The salamander crest of François I spits fire on the label. A mixture of grapes, as suggested by its name, this 98 wine offers a discreet nose, pleasing and slightly gamey. The well-balanced flavours are structured around supple tannins and fill the mouth well.
Vignoble des Quatre Roues, 27, Fourchette, 37530 Pocé-sur-Cisse, tel. 02.47.57.26.96, fax 02.47.57.26.96 by appt.
C. et F. Catroux

Touraine-Azay-le-Rideau

Grown on 150 ha (370 acres) along both banks of the Indre, the wines here are as elegant as the riverside château of Azay-le-Rideau after which they are named. Half are particularly fine whites - 1,044 hl (27,562 gal) in 1999 – from Chenin Blanc (Pineau de la Loire), which range from dry to soft, and age well. Grolleau (60% minimum of a mixed wine), Gamay and Côt (with a maximum 10% of Cabernets) make very fresh dry, fruity rosés – 1,920 hl (50,688 gal) in 1999.

DOM. DU HAY 1999★

3 ha 7,000 30–49 F

Domaine du Hay owns 15 ha (37 acres) of vines between Azay-le-Rideau and Villandry, oh-so-famous because of their châteaux. Many visitors call in at the wine cellars of the Gallais family. In the 99 vintage, the Touraine-Azay-le-Rideau Rosé is a salmon-pink colour. It offers a bouquet of violet, with even a touch of mineral. It makes a fine first impression, and its liveliness does not exclude fullness. The **Touraine Rouge 98** is pleasant.
EARL Gallais Père et Fils, 5, Le Hay, 37190 Vallères, tel. 02.47.45.39.55, fax 02.47.45.31.27 by appt.

CH. DE LA ROCHE 1998

1.74 ha 6,500 30–49 F

In the Middle Ages La Roche was one of the four strongholds guarding the forest of Chinon. The present château dates from the 16th and 17th centuries. It is not far from the site where a second-century Gallo-Roman wine-press was discovered. This is a bright white wine that caught the tasters' attention. White flowers express themselves on the nose. Beautifully structured, this medium-dry wine should be served with veal or fish.
Ch. de La Roche, La Roche, 37190 Cheillé, tel. 02.47.45.46.05, fax 02.47.45.29.60, e-mail gentil.la-roche@wanadoo.fr ev. day 9am–12.30pm 2pm–7pm
B. Gentil

DOM. JAMES PAGET 1999★★

1 ha 7,500 30–49 F

James Paget has settled at Rivarennes, a commune where you can visit a small Poire Tapée museum (pears soaked in wine then cooked in syrup) and then proceed to taste this speciality, which has been exported to England in the past. From cellars you will appreciate this remarkable rosé with its modest but bright colour. The floral and mineral nose precedes a fine palate that develops with fullness and balance. The finish is refreshing and lasts well. The **Blanc 98** also merits tasting.
EARL James Paget, 13, rue d'Armentières, 37190 Rivarennes, tel. 02.47.95.54.02, fax 02.47.95.45.90 by appt.

PASCAL PIBALEAU Demi-sec 1998★

5 ha 6,000 30–49 F

Pascal Pibaleau is one of the young wine-makers of Azay-le-Rideau. Vinified, then matured for eight months in a 600-litre (40-gal) wooden cask, his lemon-tinted 98 has scents of white flowers on the nose, then opens richly and tenderly on the palate with notes of honey. This lovely wine will improve still further when laid down for two to five years.
EARL Pascal Pibaleau, 68, rte de Langeais, Luré, 37190 Azay-le-Rideau, tel. 02.47.45.27.58, fax 02.47.45.26.18 ev. day except Sun. 8am–12.30pm 1.30pm–7pm

LA CAVE DES VALLEES 1999★

3 ha 6,000 20–29 F

La Cave des Vallées is in the town of Cheillé, almost on the edge of the forest of Chinon. The Badiller family has been growing vines here since 1789. Just a stone's throw away, the village merits a visit for its Roman church. The Touraine-Azay-le-Rideau proffered for tasting has a pretty, sweet pink colour. Winey, floral and mineral, it is pleasing because of its freshness and length.

Marc Badiller, 29, Le Bourg, 37190 Cheillé, tel. 02.47.45.24.37, fax 02.47.45.29.66 ev. day except Sun. 8.30am–12.30pm 3pm–7pm

Touraine-Mesland

The vineyard of this appellation covers 200 ha (494 acres) on the right bank of the Loire, north of Chaumont and downstream from Blois. In 1999, 6,204 hl (163,786 gal) of wine were produced, including 815 hl (21,516 gal) of white. The soils are a mixture of flinty clays covered here and there with Eocene sands and gravel. Production is mostly of red wines, from Gamay mixed with Cabernet or Cot, with good structure and character. Dry whites (mainly from Chenin) and rosés are also produced.

DOM. D'ARTOIS 1999★

8.5 ha 60,000 30–49 F

This wine, with its bouquet of morello cherry and roasted scents, comes from well-equipped cellars in the centre of the wine-growing plateau of Mesland. This harmonious and promising 99 is well served by its tannins. And since you have to pass through Mesland to discover this producer, stop at the village church and admire, among other things, the grotesque masks which ornament the west portal.

Dom. d'Artois, La Morandière, 41150 Mesland, tel. 02.54.70.24.72, fax 02.54.70.24.72 by appt.

BOIS D'ASNIERES 1999★★

5 ha 25,000 30–49 F

Onzain is on the north bank of the Loire. On the other bank, Château de Chaumont is only about 20 km (12 miles) away. Mixing Renaissance influence with Gothic, it looks beautiful surrounded by its park planted with rare species, which welcomes visitors every summer during the Garden Festival. The 99 wine from Les Cailloux is the image of this harmonious edifice. Purplish ruby, it unveils a complex nose of very ripe fruit. Its vanilla flavour on the palate lengthens with lovely balance, underlined by a discreet woodiness. The estate's **Touraine-Mesland Blanc 99** is also very good.

Saunier, Dom. des Cailloux, 7, rue des Fontenelles, 41150 Onzain, tel. 02.54.20.78.77, fax 02.54.33.79.63 by appt.

DOM. DE LA BESNERIE 1999

n.c. 3,300 20–29 F

In this typical Touraine estate, the vines are planted on the hillside, the wine cellars are under the hillside and the buildings are in front of the wine cellars. This is the environment that has given rise to this clear and brilliant 99 wine, eloquent with aromas of honey and flowers. It is rich and mouth-filling.

François Pironneau, Dom. de La Besnerie, rte de Mesland, 41150 Monteaux, tel. 02.54.70.23.75, fax 02.54.70.21.89 by appt.

CLOS DE LA BRIDERIE 1999★★

6.1 ha n.c. 30–49 F

This estate, which sells a quarter of its production for export, is well located on the wine-growing plateau between Monteaux and Mesland. Its vineyard is biodynamically cultivated. With its ruby colour hinting of purple, the 99 vintage contains fruit and tight, elegant tannins. A wine with excellent prospects. What substance! A real thoroughbred. The **Touraine-Mesland Blanc 99** is also remarkable.

J. et F. Girault, Clos de La Briderie, 41150 Monteaux, tel. 02.47.57.07.71, fax 02.47.57.65.70 by appt.

LES VAUCORNEILLES 1999★

0.6 ha 4,000 20–29 F

Gilles Chelin and Jean-Etienne Pigache sign off their second year at the Les Vaucorneilles, crowning it with this successful new rosé. See the pretty salmon-pink glints in the wine, which conforms to the Touraine-Mesland tradition. Floral on the nose, the wine on the palate is tender and well balanced. The **Rouge 99** is also most successful.

GAEC Les Vaucorneilles, 10, rue de l'Egalité, 41150 Onzain, tel. 02.54.20.72.91, fax 02.54.20.74.26 by appt.

Chelin-Pigache

DOM. DE LUSQUENEAU 1999★★

◪ n.c. 13,600 ▮ ♁ 20–29 F

The cellars at Domaine de Lusqueneau are in the very heart of Mesland. Here you will discover a deep-coloured 99 rosé. After a complex palate of very ripe fruit, the wine opens in suppleness then develops at length: a pleasant wine, to drink for itself.

SCEA Dom. de Lusqueneau, rue du Foyer, 41150 Mesland, tel. 02.54.70.25.51, fax 02.54.70.27.49 ▣ Y by appt.

DOM. DU CHEMIN DE RABELAIS 1999★

□ 0.9 ha 2,000 ▮ ♁ 20–29 F

José Chollet has been working with his son since 1999, a collaboration that has resulted in this straw-coloured white with an unassuming nose of white fruit. The balance leans towards suppleness and richness, with such success that the wine caresses the palate.

Chollet, 23, chem. de Rabelais, 41150 Onzain, tel. 02.54.20.79.50, fax 02.54.20.79.50 ▣ Y by appt.

DOM. DES TERRES NOIRES 1999★

■ 1.2 ha 300 ▮ ♁ 20–29 F

The three Rediguère brothers have been working together since 1993, cultivating 12 ha (30 acres) of red grapes growing on sandy clay. The nose of their 99 ruby-coloured wine is characterised by hints of capsicum. Still tannic because of its youth, it promises a pleasant moment in the near future. The **Rosé** of the same year gains a mention.

GAEC des Terres Noires, 81, rue de Meuves, 41150 Onzain, tel. 02.54.20.72.87, fax 02.54.20.85.12 ▣ Y ev. day 9am–7pm

JACQUES VEUX 1999

◪ 1 ha 5,000 ▮ 20–29 F

The vineyard, worked by Jacques Veux since 1974, was started in the 1920s on a sandy clay plateau. In 1999 the Gamay grape has produced a pale salmon-pink rosé, pleasing because of its balance and floral character. Appreciate it with a platter of *charcuteries.*

Jacques Veux, 3 *bis*, Château-Gaillard, 41150 Mesland, tel. 02.54.70.26.27 ▣

Bourgueil

The Appellation Contrôlée Bourgueil area, which covers 1,250 ha (30,875 acres), lies on the right bank of the Loire, west of the Touraine and on the borders of Anjou. In 1999 62,604 hl (1,652,746 gal) of the distinctive Borgueil red wines were produced from the Cabernet Franc variety, also known as Breton. These are thoroughbred wines, graced with elegant tannins, which have undergone a long period of fermentation; those from the yellow tufa slopes have great keeping qualities. The best vintages (1976, 1989 or 1990, for example) continue to develop for decades. Those from the terraces of gravelly and sandy soil are smoother and fruitier in character. A few hundred hectolitres (several thousand gallons) are vinified as dry rosés. It is worth pointing out that the members of the Coopérative de Restignée (a quarter of the Bourgueil growers) often age their wines in their own cellars.

YANNICK AMIRAULT

La Petite cave 1998★

■ 1.5 ha 9,000 ▥ 70–99 F

Yannick Amirauld owns an estate of 16 ha (40 acres) on the boundary of Bourgueil and Saint-Nicolas and produces both these appellations with great success. He presents a Bourgueil for medium-term drinking, with a clean, round first impression, a powerful body and marked tannins. Fruit is plentiful, with an additional note of coffee. The finish is long and slightly woody. From now on the enterprise will welcome its customers at the Grand Clos Pavilion, near the Moulin Bleu.

Yannick Amirault, 5, pavillon du Grand Clos, 37140 Bourgueil, tel. 02.47.97.78.07, fax 02.47.97.94.78 ▣ Y by appt.

HUBERT AUDEBERT

Vieilles vignes 1998★

■ 2 ha 10,000 ▮ ♁ 30–49 F

The Audeberts really do make wine the traditional way in wooden vats, pushing the cap of skins down into the wine with their feet twice a day. Extraction is maximised, and that produces a wine with powerful tannins. Happily, in this 98 vintage, the tannins are accompanied by good flavour, which makes for a pleasing palate. A wine for the future which needs several years' ageing.

Hubert Audebert, 5, rue Croix-des-Pierres, 37140 Restigné, tel. 02.47.97.42.10, fax 02.47.97.77.53 ▣ Y by appt.

DOM. AUDEBERT ET FILS

Vignoble Les Marquises 1998★

■ 1.5 ha 10,000 ▮ ▥ ♁ 30–49 F

In 1996 François Audebert took over most of the 20 ha (49 acres) of vines farmed by the *négociant* of the same name. He offers a lovely wine, round and well balanced, with powerful but non-aggressive tannins and good length, which conjures up red orchard fruit. A bottle that can wait.

🔑 EARL Dom. Audebert et Fils, av. Jean-Causeret, 37140 Bourgueil, tel. 02.47.97.70.06, fax 02.47.97.72.07, e-mail audebert@micro-vidéo.fr ☑ Y ev. day 8am–12 noon 2pm–6pm; Sat. Sun. by appt.

DOM. AUGER 1998

■ 6 ha 35,000 ▮ ♦ 20–29 F

Domaine Auger is a *négociant* with more than 23 ha (57 acres) of vines. It offers a supple 98 vintage, light, elegant and very fruity on the nose as well as on the palate. Drink it quickly so as not to lose its evocations of raspberry and strawberry, which are so pleasant.

🔑 Christophe Auger, 58, rte de Bourgueil, Fougerolles, 37140 Restigné, tel. 02.41.40.22.50, fax 02.41.40.22.60
🔑 Joseph Verdier

CHRISTOPHE CHASLE

Rochecot 1998★

■ 1 ha 6,000 ▮ 50–69 F

Saint-Patrice is the first commune of this appellation which you meet coming from Tours, before the vineyard terrace widens out. The slope is gentle here, and the well-aligned rows of vines reach right up the hill, revealing numerous hamlets built of the local tuffeau stone. In this setting, Christophe Chasle has made this powerful wine, endowed with good tannic support and a promising future. Still closed, this 98 should bloom in a few years' time.

🔑 Christophe Chasle, 28, rue Dorothée-de-Dino, 37130 Saint-Patrice, tel. 02.47.96.95.95, fax 02.47.96.95.95 ☑ Y by appt.

DOM. DU CHENE ARRAULT

Cuvée Vieilles vignes 1998★

■ 1.33 ha 8,000 ▮ ♦ 30–49 F

Domaine du Chêne Arrault was formed in 1990 from an amalgamation of properties belonging to both maternal and paternal grandparents of Christophe Deschamps, and it now covers almost 13 ha (32 acres). Produced on the chalky clay soils of Benais, the wines are generally well structured and meant for laying down. This 98 vintage, with its strong constitution, is a case in point. The palate is full and round, and tannins are evident but tend towards development. A bottle still on the defensive but which time will draw out. Mentioned by the jury, the **Cuvée des Valinières**, lighter and more supple, will help with the wait.

🔑 Christophe Deschamps, 4, Le Chêne-Arrault, 37140 Benais, tel. 02.47.97.46.71, fax 02.47.97.82.90, e-mail domaine.du.chene.arrault@wanadoo.fr ☑ Y by appt.

DOM. DES CHESNAIES

Cuvée Lucien Lamé 1998★

■ 4.2 ha 31,000 ▮ ♦ 30–49 F

The younger generation of the Boucards – Philippe, a technician, and Stéphanie, an œnologist – work closely with their father René, who in his turn worked for many years with his father-in-law, Lucien Lamé. It is to the last that they owe the very distinctive wine-growing and production methods which have assured the fame of the estate's wines, and they have therefore dedicated this wine to him. It is a lovely example of freshness, roundness and length, with very harmonious tannins that give an impression of balance. This 98 vintage is ideal to drink from now onwards.

🔑 EARL Lamé-Delisle-Boucard, 21, rue de la Galotière, Les Chesnaies, 37140 Ingrandes-de-Touraine, tel. 02.47.96.98.54, fax 02.47.96.92.31 ☑ Y by appt.

LYDIE ET MAX COGNARD

Les Tuffes 1998

■ 0.6 ha 4,100 ▮ ♦ 30–49 F

There is a tourist wine cellar which any lovers of Bourgeuil owe it to themselves to visit, and close by Max Cognard's vines grow at the foot of the hill on chalky clay soils. His Les Tuffes stands out in this vintage by virtue of its balance and roundness. The aromas, which make you think of blackcurrant and leather, are pleasing. A nice, light wine, easy to drink.

🔑 Cognard, Chevrette, 37140 Saint-Nicolas-de-Bourgueil, tel. 02.47.97.76.88, fax 02.47.97.97.83 ☑ Y by appt.

DOM. BRUNO DUFEU 1998★

■ 1.5 ha 6,000 ▮ ⅢⅠ 20–29 F

Bruno Dufeu started farming his family's 4 ha (10 acres) in 1995 and swiftly increased them to 9 ha (22 acres), which enabled him to specialise. His 98 vintage, rather developed, is ready to drink. The tannins are very harmonious, and the fruit is at its maximum. It is pleasant and round: drink it on its own.

🔑 Dufeu, Les Neusaies, 37140 Benais, tel. 02.47.97.76.53, fax 02.47.97.76.53 ☑ Y by appt.

LAURENT FAUVY 1998★

■ 3 ha 2,500 ▮ 20–29 F

A very well-made wine, rich, dense and powerful. It reveals roundness and potential. Its aromas, already present, ask only to develop. Already of a good standard, this bottle will gain in elegance and subtlety if you leave it in the cellar for a while. Mentioned by the jury, the **Vieilles Vignes 98** from the same producer (30–49F) is interesting because of its beautiful expression of ripe fruit.

🔑 Laurent Fauvy, 14, rte de Saint-Gilles, 37140 Benais, tel. 02.47.97.46.67, fax 02.47.97.95.45 ☑ Y by appt.

DOM. DES GALLUCHES 1998★

■ 4 ha 12,000 ⅢⅠ 30–49 F

Despite his professional and municipal responsibilities, Jean Gambier ran Domaine des Galluches brilliantly. His nephew James Petit, who took over from him in 1997, offers a beautifully fruity wine, well balanced and elegant. An easy-drinking wine which should evolve well.

James Petit, 37140 Restigné, tel. 02.47.97.30.13 ☑
Jean Gambier

DOM. DES GELERIES

Cuvée Prestige 1998★

■ 1 ha 6,000 30–49 F

Jeannine Rouzier-Meslet, helped nowadays by her son, took over the running of the estate in 1992 on her husband's retirement. Her Cuvée Prestige is beautifully made: aromas of blackcurrant and flowers are persistent, and the initial impression on the palate is supple, becoming firm but not excessively so, and the tannins soften progressively. A wine that is ready to drink but can also wait.

Jeannine Rouzier-Meslet, 2, rue des Géléries, 37140 Bourgueil, tel. 02.47.97.72.83, fax 02.47.97.48.73 ☑ Y by appt.

DOM. DU GRAND CLOS 1998

■ 9 ha 55,000 30–49 F

A prosperous and highly respected firm at Bourgueil. Well distributed in the restaurant trade, offering quality wines, it has done much for the fame of the appellation. It offers a nice wine grown on gravelly soil, light, round and well balanced. Its fruit, dominated by raspberry, is exceptional. The ultimate 'pleasure wine'.

Maison Audebert et Fils, av. Jean-Causeret, 37140 Bourgueil, tel. 02.47.97.70.06, fax 02.47.97.72.07, e-mail audebert@micro-video.fr ☑ Y ev. day 8am–12 noon 2pm–6pm; Sat. Sun. by appt.

ALAIN ET ARNAUD HOUX

Cuvée de La Chopinière 1998★

■ 2 ha 5,000 30–49 F

Four generations of wine-producers have succeeded one another at this 13-ha (32-acre) vineyard on chalky clay soil. Cuvée de la Chopinière has a pretty vivid red colour. The slightly developed nose conjures up capsicum and spices, with a note of coffee. The palate is surprising, with a light freshness and touch of menthol, and it then continues full and round, makes the wine a possibility for laying down.

Alain et Arnaud Houx, 21, le Clos Barbin, 37140 Restigné, tel. 02.47.97.30.95, fax 02.47.97.30.95 ☑ Y by appt.

DOM. HUBERT 1998

■ 8 ha 60,000 30–49 F

Domaine Hubert, owned by the same family since 1730, is entirely in the area of Benais, where the soils (tuffeau and chalky clay) normally have a reputation for producing solid, time-defying wines. That is not the case with this 98 vintage, whose tender first impression, roundness and richness give it a pleasant, nicely balanced character. The tannins are still moderate. The intense fruitiness released on both the nose and the palate confirms that this is a wine very representative both of the appellation and the vintage.

Caslot-Galbrun, La Hurolaie, 37140 Benais, tel. 02.47.97.30.59, fax 02.47.97.45.46 ☑ Y ev. day 9.30am–11.30am 2.30pm–7.30pm; Sun. by appt.

DOM. DE LA BUTTE 1998★

■ 5 ha 8,148 30–49 F

Domaine de la Butte dominates the Bourgeuil vineyards. This choice location, combined with the know-how of two talented wine-makers, has produced a wine with a lovely constitution, fruity, well balanced and sustained by fairly prominent tannins. Harmonious and with good length, its career will be an honourable one. Also of note is **Vieilles Vignes**, from the same producer, which has an equally promising future.

GAEC Gilbert et Didier Griffon, Dom. de La Butte, 37140 Bourgueil, tel. 02.47.97.81.30, fax 02.47.97.99.45 ☑ Y by appt.

DOM. DE LA CHANTELEUSERIE

Cuvée Beauvais 1998★

■ 2 ha 10,000 30–49 F

Thierry Boucard is the seventh generation to farm this 20-ha (49-acre) estate. Rigorously selected, the grapes that produced his Cuvée Beauvais come from tuffeau soil. The wine is the result of a long vatting period and eight months' maturation in wood. Red fruits are very evident both on the nose and palate. The latter, round and full of promise, reveals harmonious tannins. The finish is sufficiently long. A beautiful wine, very representative of the appellation and the vintage, to drink now.

Thierry Boucard, La Chanteleuserie, 37140 Benais, tel. 02.47.97.30.20, fax 02.47.97.46.73, e-mail tboucard@terre-net.fr ☑ Y ev. day except Sun. 8am–12 noon 2pm–6pm

LA CHARPENTERIE

Vieilles vignes Vieilli en fût de chêne 1998★

■ 3 ha 7,000 30–49 F

Just a stone's throw from the Loire is a pretty little Touraine house built of white tuffeau stone. Further from the river, 13 ha (32 acres) of vines grow on siliceous soils. The 40-year-old vine stock has yielded this Vieilles Vignes, which is beautifully fruity, round and well balanced. A little woody finishing touch impedes neither the elegance nor the finesse of the wine, which is ready for drinking. **Cuvée du Même Millésime** also gained a mention by the jury.

EARL Alain-Cyprien Caslot-Bourdin, 21, rue Brûlée, 37140 La Chapelle-sur-Loire, tel. 02.47.97.34.45, fax 02.47.97.44.80 ☑ Y by appt.

DOM. DE LA CHEVALERIE

Cuvée des Galichets 1998★★

■ 4.2 ha 22,000 30–49 F

Descendants of a line of wine-makers which goes back to 1640, the Caslots have inherited a wealth of experience which has certainly contributed to the quality of this superb Bourgeuil (after a 95 which was also highly regarded). The deep vivid red colour sets the tone. Powerful and open on the nose, on the palate the wine reveals a lovely maturity, with rounded tannins enveloped in richness. The balance is remarkable. A wine that can go far. *Awarded a coup de coeur, regrettably at the time of going to press the label was not available for reproduction here.*

🔑 Pierre Caslot, Dom. de La Chevalerie, 37140 Restigné, tel. 02.47.97.37.18, fax 02.47.97.45.87 ☑ Y ev. day 8am–12 noon 2pm–7.30pm; Sun. by appt.

DOM. DE LA GAUCHERIE 1998

■ 2 ha 7,500 30–49 F

With its impressive buildings and machinery, Domaine de la Gaucherie does not go unnoticed when you come into the Bourgeuil vine-growing area from Tours. There you can still see the slate vine stakes that were traditional in the area. Régis Mureau's vines cover the first warm terraces of the appellation and have yielded a beautiful wine, very well balanced, fruity and round, of a light type that will enhance a simple meal. Another wine, **Domaine Régis Mureau 98**, has also gained a mention for its freshness and fruitiness.

🔑 Régis Mureau, La Gaucherie, 37140 Ingrandes-de-Touraine, tel. 02.47.96.97.60, fax 02.47.96.93.43 ☑ Y ev. day except Sun. 9am–12 noon 2pm–6pm

DOM. DE LA LANDE

Cuvée Prestige 1998

■ 2 ha 12,000 30–49 F

This father and son team is already well established and offers a Cuvée Prestige from vines more than 40 years old. The wine opens on the palate with freshness, and it has a powerful body; its tannins still appear a little tight. All these features indicate dependable cultivation and production, but urge you to leave the wine in the cellar to give it time to round out.

🔑 Delaunay Père et Fils, Dom. de La Lande, 20, rte du Vignoble, 37140 Bourgueil, tel. 02.47.97.80.73, fax 02.47.97.95.65 ☑ Y by appt.

DOM. DE LA NOIRAIE

Cuvée Prestige 1998★

■ 4 ha 25,000 30–49 F

This beautiful 18-ha (44-acre) vineyard is run by a well-knit team of two brothers and one wife. Each has his or her role and works according to tradition. Even the horse still has its place here for minor work and pleasure! This Cuvée Prestige is full of charm, with a very open nose and a well-balanced, supple palate. The underlying tannins are fairly obvious but should disappear in the course of time.

🔑 GAEC Delanoue Frères, 19, rue du Fort Hudeau, L'Ereau, 37140 Benais, tel. 02.47.97.30.40, fax 02.47.97.46.95 ☑ Y ev. day 9am–12 noon 2pm–7pm; Sun. 9am–12 noon

VIGNOBLE DE LA RENAISSANCE

Cuvée Vieilles vignes 1998★

■ 0.7 ha 2,000 20–29

Jean-Paul Verneau created this small estate (less than 3 ha/7.4 acres) from nothing and has been farming it for only five years. As in 1999, he has made a very successful wine in 2000, full-bodied and tender. The tannins, tamed, do not encroach on the fruit, which is revealed in a beautiful finish of unusual length. A harmonious, rich bottle, which will please lovers of very oaky wines.

🔑 Jean-Paul Verneau, 7, rue des Brossays, 37340 Cléré-les-Pins, tel. 02.47.24.95.05, fax 02.47.24.95.05 ☑ Y by appt.

VIGNOBLE DE LA ROSERAIE 1998

■ 23 ha 10,000 30–49 F

Joël and Ginette Vallée and their two sons, Eric and Patrick, run this 9.5-ha (23.5-acre) estate. Their Bourgueil reflects the care they have taken over it. It is fresh on the palate, and fruity with redcurrant. The roundness comes afterwards, and you can't miss the slightly developed tannins. You can take advantage of its youth or let it run its course.

🔑 Vignoble de La Roseraie, 46, rue Basse, 37140 Restigné, tel. 02.47.97.32.97, fax 02.47.97.44.24 ☑ Y by appt.

🔑 Vallée

DOM. LES PINS Vieilles vignes 1998

■ 1.5 ha 8,000 30–49 F

A 17th-century building surrounded by the major part of the 18-ha (44-acre) estate; it is invaluable that the same family has cultivated it for five generations. Vieilles Vignes pleased the jury with its fruitiness, elegance and overall harmony. It is a light type of wine that gladdens the heart.

🔑 Pitault-Landry et Fils, Dom. Les Pins, 37140 Bourgueil, tel. 02.47.97.47.91, fax 02.47.97.98.69 ☑ Y by appt.

MICHEL ET JOELLE LORIEUX

Chevrette 1998★

■ 2 ha 5,000 30–49 F

Michel and Joëlle Lorieux are developing a 10-ha (24-acre) estate located at the foot of a hillside, the result of a consolidation of their families' lands. 'Now that's Bourgueil!' said a member of the jury about this wine, an authenticity conferred by its suppleness, fruitiness and length. The tannins, still very evident, also have a part to play.

🔑 Michel et Joëlle Lorieux, Chevrette, 37140 Bourgueil, tel. 02.47.97.85.86, fax 02.47.97.85.86 ☑ Y ev. day except Sun. 9am–12.30pm 2pm–7pm

DOM. LAURENT MABILEAU

1998★★

■ 3.3 ha 25,000 30–49 F

After the disastrous frosts of 1991, Domaine Laurent Mabileau didn't hesitate to equip part of the vineyard with a sprinkler system to counteract frost (this enables the buds to be covered with a protective layer of ice), following the example of the Chablis area: an effective but costly method, justified no doubt by the quality of the wines. It would have been a pity to lose this harvest, with its superb balance, power and length. A very well-turned-out wine, which should preferably be kept out of reach for some time.

🗝 Dom. Laurent Mabileau, La Croix du Moulin-Neuf, 37140 Saint-Nicolas-de-Bourgueil, tel. 02.47.97.74.75, fax 02.47.97.99.81, e-mail laurent.mabileau1@libertysurf.fr ☑ 🍷 ev. day 9am–12.30pm 2pm–7pm

DOM. DES MAILLOCHES

Vieilles vignes sur graviers Cuvée Sophie 1998*

■ 2.5 ha 15,000 30–49 F

Domaine des Mailloches is accustomed to honours: worldwide exhibitions at the end of the 19th century, recognition for outstanding merit at Chicago in 1893 and present on the Elysée table at an official dinner, not to mention numerous plaudits elsewhere. Derived from old vines (more than 50 years old), its Cuvée Sophie opens on the palate with suppleness, revealing power, roundness and harmonious tannins. The whole, well balanced and persistent, develops intense aromas of ripe fruit. A wine that can wait but which can also express itself immediately. **Cuvée Vieilles Vignes sur Tuffeau 98**, which comes from 80-year-old vine stock, is typical and successful.

🗝 Jean-François Demont, Les Mailloches, 37140 Restigné, tel. 02.47.97.33.10, fax 02.47.97.43.43, e-mail infos@domaine-mailloches.fr ☑ 🍷 by appt.

DOMINIQUE MOREAU 1998*

■ 1 ha 3,000 30–49 F

Dominique Moreau is one of the *Guide*'s regulars. His 98 vintage is promising in its richness, balance and fleshed-out tannins that are not yet entirely tamed. However, its aromas of red and stone fruits and its soft attack makes you want to drink it now.

🗝 EARL Dominique Moreau, L'Ouche-Saint-André, 37140 Restigné, tel. 06.61.80.65.85, fax 06.47.96.83.30 ☑

NAU FRERES Les Blottières 1998*

■ 4 ha 23,000 🛢 🌡 30–49 F

The Nau brothers are the sixth generation of wine-makers at Les Blottières, where they cultivate about 20 ha (49 acres). Their Vieilles Vignes 97 was awarded a *Coup de Coeur*, as was a 1993, and now in 2000 they have produced a very beautiful, fruity wine, well constructed with regard to both substance and tannins. It manifests a certain severity that will soften after it has been aged for a while.

🗝 Nau Frères, 52, rue de Touraine, 37140 Ingrandes-de-Touraine, tel. 02.47.96.98.57, fax 02.47.96.90.34 ☑

BERNARD OMASSON 1998*

■ 2 ha 3,000 🛢 🛢🛢 🌡 30–49 F

Traditional in his growing, wine-making and even his labels, Bernard Omasson, farming for 30 years on a small estate with chalky clay soils, still produces solidly structured wines. This one, too, conforms to the rules. It opens subtly and cleanly on a full palate, and is marked by tannins on the slightly woody finish. These qualities combine to make a good wine to lay down that will increase in harmony given time.

🗝 Bernard Omasson, La Perrée, 54, rue de Touraine, 37140 Ingrandes-de-Touraine, tel. 02.47.96.98.20 ☑ 🍷 by appt.

ALAIN OMASSON 1998

■ 1 ha 1,500 🛢 🛢🛢 🌡 20–29 F

Established for the past four years in a small vineyard of 3.5 ha (8.6 acres), Alain Omasson has succeeded in 2000 with a spring-type Bourgueil with lovely flavours that linger on the palate. Supple and well balanced, this is a simple but pleasant wine, which can be served successfully with everyday meals.

🗝 Alain Omasson, 21, rue du Port-Véron, 37130 Saint-Patrice, tel. 02.47.96.90.26 ☑ 🍷 by appt.

DOM. DES OUCHES

Clos Princé 1998*

■ 3.5 ha 18,000 🛢🛢 30–49 F

Paul Gambier was joined by his son Thomas in 1997 and heads this 14-ha (35-acre) estate, which is situated entirely on hillsides on the Ingrandes heights. Its functional winery adjoins a wine cellar hollowed out of the rock. Their Clos Princé wine, aged for ten months in large wooden casks, is quite woody in character. It has substance and potential but also a certain rustic quality due to its youth. Same comments – and same mark – for **Sélection Vieilles Vignes 98**, matured for 11 months in barrels.

🗝 Paul et Thomas Gambier, 3, rue des Ouches, 37140 Ingrandes-de-Touraine, tel. 02.47.96.98.77, fax 02.47.96.93.08 ☑ 🍷 ev. day except Sun. 8am–12 noon 2pm–7pm

DOM. DU PETIT BONDIEU

Cuvée des Brunetières 1998**

■ 1 ha 5,000 🛢🛢 30–49 F

Jean-Marc believes in eco-friendly agriculture, so he treats his vines only when he considers it absolutely necessary. He shuns herbicides and uses only a plough. This is a beneficial return to basics, judging by the quality of this 98 wine, which opens up gently on the palate, with body, richness and length. The tannins are currently austere but will disappear in time. This is a bottle to buy now with confidence, and then allow to age.

🗝 EARL Jean-Marc Pichet, Le Petit Bondieu, 30, rte de Tours, 37140 Restigné, tel. 02.47.97.33.18, fax 02.47.97.46.57 ☑ 🍷 ev. day except Sun. 9am–12 noon 2pm–7pm

DOM. DES RAGUENIERES

Clos de La Cure 1998★

■ 1.1 ha 5,250 30–49 F

Marked by their chalky clay terroir, the wines of Domaine des Raguenières are well constructed and need a short laying-down to round out. This one, already well developed, makes a gentle first impression and is round and fresh on the palate, accompanied by flavours of raspberry, cocoa and tobacco. On the finish it leaves an impression of firmness, which will disappear with time.

Robert Viemont-D. Maître-Gadaix, 11, rue du Machet-Benais, 37140 Bourgueil, tel. 02.47.97.30.16 ev. day 8am–12 noon 2pm–7pm

VIGNOBLE DES ROBINIERES

1998★

■ 3 ha 8,000 30–49 F

This estate has grown over time and now covers 14 ha (34 acres). It has become a real family affair, with the parents and their two sons working happily together. An ideal setting for a round, warm and tender wine, where an expression of stewed fruit is relieved by a little liveliness. A classic Bourgueil, ready to drink.

EARL Marchesseau Fils, 16, rue de l'Humelaye, Les Robinières, 37140 Bourgueil, tel. 02.47.97.82.09 ev. day except Sun. 9am–12.30pm 2pm–7pm

DOM. DU ROCHOUARD 1998★

■ 2 ha 5,000 30–49 F

Dominique Duveau came back to his parents' estate in 1995, bringing with him scientific skills freshly acquired from wine-making college. That is when the estate took the name of Rochouard, making a new start that has been very noticeable. This 98 wine has started out equally well with its aromatic qualities and its promising tannic support. But it is not yet ready: you will need to age it for some time.

GAEC Duveau-Coulon et Fils, 1, rue des Géléries, 37140 Bourgueil, tel. 02.47.97.85.91, fax 02.47.97.99.13 ev. day 8.30am–7.30pm

Guy Duveau

JEAN-MARIE ROUZIER

Cuvée Tradition 1998★★

■ 2 ha 6,000 30–49 F

Jean-Marie Rouzier cultivates 10 ha (25 acres) producing Chinon and Bourgueil. His Cuvée Tradition attracted an avalanche of compliments: its brilliant ruby colour, its intense nose with delicate aromas pierced through with blackcurrant and violet, its rounded first impression, which quickly gives way to a lingering fullness, and its solid but harmonious tannins make it a lovely wine to lay down. It has sufficient flavour to evolve and should develop surprising aromas.

Jean-Marie Rouzier, Les Géléries, 37140 Bourgueil, tel. 02.47.97.74.83, fax 02.47.97.48.73 ev. day except Sun. 9am–12.30pm 2.30pm–7pm

DOM. DES VALLETTES

Vieilles vignes Cuvée An 2000 1998★★

■ 1.5 ha 11,000 30–49 F

Above all a Saint-Nicolas producer who is regularly mentioned in the *Guide*, Francis Jamet also offers Bourgueils from Domaine des Vallettes. The nose of this wine, flavoured lightly with vanilla and oak, is a pleasant surprise. It opens roundly on the palate, followed by a very measured tannic development where oakiness blends harmoniously with fruit. Good persistence encourages this complex aromatic association. A great bottle, drinkable immediately.

Francis Jamet, Dom. des Vallettes, 37140 Saint-Nicolas-de-Bourgueil, tel. 02.41.52.05.99, fax 02.41.52.87.52 by appt.

DOM. DES VIENAIS

Cuvée Prestige 1998★

■ 2 ha 15,000 30–49 F

The soils of Benais are quite stubborn, but have a reputation for yielding well-structured wines. This one, from a chalky clay soil, cannot deny its origins. Its tannins are solid, creating a supple first impression. The flavours are good on a lightly wooded base. A good wine for laying down which will become more refined in time.

Gérard Poupineau, 3, rue des Lavandières, 37140 Benais, tel. 02.47.97.35.19, fax 02.47.97.46.91 by appt.

Saint-Nicolas-de-Bourgueil

The commune of Saint-Nicolas-de-Bourgueil (a single parish that was detached from Bourgueil in the 18th century) has its own appellation, even though the terroir is similar to the neighbouring area of Bourgueil.

At least two-thirds of the slopes are made up of the sandy, gravel terraces of the Loire. At the top, the hill is protected from the north wind by forest and a covering of sand overlies the tufa outcrops. Saint-Nicolas-de-Bourgueil wines are made from a mixture of varieties, and are generally regarded as being lighter than the Bourgueils (not always the case with wine grown on the heights). In 1999, they produced 58,291 hl (1,538,882 gal).

YANNICK AMIRAULT

Les Malgagnes 1998

■ 1.3 ha 6,500 70–99 F

Yannick Amirault still makes his wines the same way: he brings them slowly to maturity. This one, which has a beautiful aromatic, tannic richness, is full of promise, but still seems *brut*; it remains far short of its peak. Have confidence in it and consider it a good long-term investment at three or four years.

Yannick Amirault, 5, pavillon du Grand Clos, 37140 Bourgueil, tel. 02.47.97.78.07, fax 02.47.97.94.78 by appt.

DOM. DES BERGEONNIERES 1998

■ 14 ha 40,000 30–49 F

From 14 ha 34 (acres) out of his total of 16 (39), André Delagouttière has succeeded in producing a homogeneous wine of good quality. Balanced, supple, fresh and fruity, it comes up trumps. A pleasing Saint-Nicolas, 'a good example of this type', concluded the jury. Drink immediately.

André Delagouttière, Les Bergeonnières, 37140 Saint-Nicolas-de-Bourgueil, tel. 02.47.97.75.87, fax 02.47.97.48.47 by appt.

LYDIE ET MAX COGNARD-TALUAU

Cuvée Les Malgagnes 1998

■ 2 ha 6,200 30–49 F

Halfway up the slope, Lydie and Max Cognard's estate covers part of the area known as Les Malgagnes, a good-quality terroir, well known to lovers of Saint-Nicolas. In 1998 they could not attain a very high standard, but this wine does not do badly: a simple nose dominated by fruit, a pleasant first impression followed by a good roundness and pleasing fruitiness, all add up to a nice bottle that will give great satisfaction straight away.

Cognard, Chevrette, 37140 Saint-Nicolas-de-Bourgueil, tel. 02.47.97.76.88, fax 02.47.97.97.83 by appt.

LE VIGNOBLE DU FRESNE 1998*

■ 1.1 ha 7,500 30–49 F

Fresne is full of flowers. The traditional cellars reflect order and method, and the vineyard is kept well. All this indicates a style and a serious approach that reappear in this lovely wine with its nose of capsicum and red fruit mixed with spices. The palate is rounded, with richness and a medium length. A balanced wine, to drink now or to be given a little time.

Patrick Gueneschéau, 1, Le Fresne, 37140 Saint-Nicolas-de-Bourgueil, tel. 02.47.97.86.60, fax 02.47.97.42.53 ev. day 9am–7.30pm; Sun. 9am–12 noon

DOM. DES GESLETS 1998*

■ 3.75 ha 15,000 30–49 F

Vincent Grégoire cultivates 15 ha (37 acres) in the two Bourgueil appellations, and he has really succeeded with his Saint-Nicolas. Its colour is deep, almost black, with violet glints, and a note of coffee pierces the nose of spice and very ripe fruit. The palate is well structured and lingers beautifully, while continuing to show roundness. A lovely bottle to lay down.

Vincent Grégoire, Dom. des Geslets, 37140 Bourgueil, tel. 02.47.97.97.06, fax 02.47.97.73.95 ev. day 9am–6.30pm

GERARD ET MARIE-CLAIRE GODEFROY Vieilles vignes 1998

■ 1.5 ha 10,000 30–49 F

An attractive nose of red fruit with a gamey touch urges you to taste this wine. A little fresh at first, on the palate it gives an impression of lightness, but fullness is not far away. The harmonious tannins together with a pleasant aromatic flavour make this 98 an easy and versatile wine.

Gérard et Marie-Claire Godefroy, 37, rue de la Taille, 37140 Saint-Nicolas-de-Bourgueil, tel. 02.47.97.77.43, fax 02.47.97.48.23 by appt.

DOM. GUY HERSARD

Vieilles vignes 1998

■ 5.5 ha 20,000 30–49 F

At the heart of the appellation, Philippe and Annie Hersard's vineyard covers 10 ha (25 acres) of chalky clay and gravel soil. More than half the area is dedicated to this Vieilles Vignes. The nose, intense and winey, evokes ripe fruit and spice. The initial impression is slightly lively but gives way to a tannic presence, a sign of good potential. An appreciable length and reassuring balance give gravity to the wine, which can wait a while.

Guy Hersard, Le Fondis, 37140 Saint-Nicolas-de-Bourgueil, tel. 02.47.97.76.13, fax 02.47.97.92.06 by appt.

DOM. DE LA CONTRIE 1998

■ 5.61 ha 40,000 30–49 F

From his vineyard of almost 10 ha (25 acres) in the heart of the Saint-Nicolas wine-growing area, Alain Taluau has produced this light 98 vintage, a balanced wine for an every-day meal.

Alain Taluau, 14, dom. de La Contrie, 37140 Saint-Nicolas-de-Bourgueil, tel. 02.47.97.82.26, fax 02.47.97.82.26 ev. day except Sun. 9am–12 noon 2pm–6pm

DOM. DE LA COTELLERAIE-VALLEE

Les Mauguerets 1998**

■ 2.3 ha 8,000 30–49 F

Claude Vallée, who runs 17 ha (42 acres) at his domaine, welcomes people warmly and is happy to chat about his wines. Les Mauguerets is worth lingering over. It is almost black, with purplish hints, and its nose evokes very ripe red fruit. It opens on the palate with suppleness and a rare fullness. The young tannins are discreet but give the wine prolonged interest. A promising wine, not to be drunk too young. A unanimous *Coup de Coeur* from the jury.

LOIRE

Claude Vallée, La Cotelleraie, 37140 Saint-Nicolas-de-Bourgueil, tel. 02.47.97.75.53, fax 02.47.97.85.90 ☒ Y ev. day 9am–12.30pm 1.30pm–7pm

VIGNOBLE DE LA GARDIERE

1998

■ 3 ha 12,000 30–49 F

With a slight oaky touch on a base of tannins, this is a wine that will become more and more interesting as it softens up. It has a lovely colour and well-developed aromas of very ripe red fruit relieved by a note of coffee.

Bernard David, La Gardière, 37140 Saint-Nicolas-de-Bourgueil, tel. 02.47.97.81.51, fax 02.47.97.95.05 ☒ Y by appt.

VIGNOBLE DE LA JARNOTERIE

1998

■ 18 ha 90,000 30–49 F

Jean-Claude Mabileau and his children have continued the work of their predecessors and increased the potential of La Jarnoterie: a flowery welcome, 21 ha (52 acres) of superbly maintained well-aligned vines, a well-equipped cellar, with another cellar for ageing hollowed out of the rock, are so many aces up their sleeves for these growers, who offer a really good 98 wine. A first impression of liveliness and freshness, then supple, harmonious tannins, barely noticeable, make this a true representative of the vintage.

EARL Jean-Claude Mabileau et Didier Rezé, La Jarnoterie, 37140 Saint-Nicolas-de-Bourgueil, tel. 02.47.97.75.49, fax 02.47.97.79.98 ☒ Y by appt.

LES HAUTS-CLOS CASLOT 1998*

■ 6 ha n.c. 30–49 F

A dark garnet colour, with light brick-red touches, makes a good introduction and announces a solid wine. This first impression is not belied by the clean opening on the palate, which is followed by a marked tannic presence lightly pierced by wood. Aromas of stewed fruit and spice mingle on the nose and palate. Leave it for several years to mellow.

EARL Alain-Cyprien Caslot-Bourdin, 21, rue Brûlée, 37140 La Chapelle-sur-Loire, tel. 02.47.97.34.45, fax 02.47.97.44.80 ☒ Y by appt.

DOM. LES PINS 1998

■ n.c. n.c. 30–49 F

Fruitiness, a straightforward opening on the palate, suppleness, harmonious tannins, and fresh and balanced flavours: so many qualities adding up to a successful 98 vintage. Ready to drink, this one would definitely suit lunch with friends.

Pitault-Landry et Fils, Dom. Les Pins, 37140 Bourgueil, tel. 02.47.97.47.91, fax 02.47.97.98.69 ☒ Y by appt.

LES QUARTERONS 1998**

■ 11 ha 54,000 30–49 F

Thierry Amirault succeeded his father at this lovely Saint-Nicolas property in the early 1980s. He increased its area to 25 ha (61 acres) and improved the equipment in the wine cellar. His truly beautiful wine is his hobby-horse. Rich in substance with silky, powerful tannins, the 98 Quarterons evokes red fruit and vanilla. In a year or two, it will be at its peak. **Vieilles Vignes 98**, picked out by the jury, is full of promise.

Clos des Quarterons-Amirault, 37140 Saint-Nicolas-de-Bourgueil, tel. 02.47.97.75.25, fax 02.47.97.97.97 ☒ Y by appt.

Thierry Amirault

PASCAL LORIEUX

Les Mauguerets La Contrie 1998*

■ 3 ha 15,000 30–49 F

Pascal and Alain Lorieux cultivate vines in two AOCs: Chinon and Saint-Nicolas-de-Bourgueil. The two estates share equipment and marketing but make their wine separately. Pascal, who established and maintains the Saint-Nicolas vineyard, offers a well-balanced 98 wine, beautifully coloured and supple, with a note of oakiness. A lovely bottle to lay down, but which can already be appreciated.

EARL Pascal et Alain Lorieux, Le Bourg, 37140 Saint-Nicolas-de-Bourgueil, tel. 02.47.97.92.93, fax 02.47.97.47.88 ☒ Y by appt.

FREDERIC MABILEAU

Les Rouillères 1998

■ 6 ha 50,000 30–49 F

Six of the estate's 8 ha (19 acres) have produced this 98 wine, fairly marked in rich tannins and with strong red fruit aromas. Keep it for hearty meals or leave it for some time to develop.

Frédéric Mabileau, 17, rue de la Treille, 37140 Saint-Nicolas-de-Bourgueil, tel. 02.47.97.79.58, fax 02.47.97.45.19, e-mail mabileau-frederic@wanadoo.fr ☒ Y by appt.

JACQUES ET VINCENT MABILEAU

Cuvée Vieilles vignes 1998

■ 2 ha 8,000 30–49 F

With this 98, Jacques and Vincent Mabileau offer a tannic wine with a strong personality (due allowance being made for the vintage). Wisdom dictates that it should be allowed to evolve, as it will reveal itself little by little.

🔑 EARL Jacques et Vincent Mabileau, La Gardière, 37140 Saint-Nicolas-de-Bourgueil, tel. 02.47.97.75.85, fax 02.47.97.98.03 ☑ 🍸 by appt.

LYSIANE ET GUY MABILEAU

Vieilles vignes 1998

■ 0.63 ha 5,000 30–49 F

Having started with 2.5 ha (6 acres) of vines ten years ago, this wine-growing couple have built up a nice estate of 10 ha (25 acres). Their son has now joined them, forming a determined team which offers two wines selected by the jury from the 98 vintage: a **Cuvée Classique** and this Vieilles Vignes. Well-balanced, fruity and with good persistence, they will make their mark.

🔑 GAEC Lysiane et Guy Mabileau, 17, rue du Vieux-Chêne, 37140 Saint-Nicolas-de-Bourgueil, tel. 02.47.97.70.43, fax 02.47.97.70.43 ☑ 🍸 by appt.

DOM. OLIVIER 1998*

■ 20 ha 150,000 30–49 F

The Oliviers began in 1959 with 1.5 ha (3.7 acres), and the family now owns 28 ha (69 acres). They have made an excellent wine, both on the nose and on the palate. The aromas conjure up very ripe red fruit with touches of smoke and vanilla. The initial impression on the palate is pleasant and is followed by a richness endowed with fine tannins, and then a lingering finish. A harmonious wine which can be kept.

🔑 Dom. Olivier, La Forcine, 37140 Saint-Nicolas-de-Bourgueil, tel. 02.47.97.75.32, fax 02.47.97.48.18 ☑ 🍸 by appt.

LES CAVES DU PLESSIS

Sélection Vieilles vignes 1998

■ 2 ha 16,000 30–49 F

A 24-ha (59-acre) vineyard with a working cellar and another cellar, cut into the rock, for ageing wines; these are a measure of Chantal and Claude Renou's seriousness and ambitions. Their Vieilles Vignes, well structured, has scents of stewed fruit and needs only to fill out.

🔑 Claude Renou, 17, La Martellière, 37140 Saint-Nicolas-de-Bourgueil, tel. 02.47.97.85.67, fax 02.47.97.45.55 ☑ 🍸 by appt.

DOM. PONTONNIER

Cuvée Prestige 1998*

■ 3 ha 15,000 30–49 F

Backed up against the hillside, the vines of Domaine Pontonnier (about 15 ha/37 acres) grow on chalky clay soils, called 'tuf' in this region, and on sand and gravels. The first give the vines firmness; the second confer on them fruitiness characteristic of Saint-Nicolas wines. This Cuvée Prestige is rich and full-bodied, with prominent tannins that are beginning to develop well. This is a nice wine to lay down, promising and worth waiting for.

🔑 Dom. Pontonnier, 4, chem. de L'Epaisse, 37140 Saint-Nicolas-de-Bourgueil, tel. 02.47.97.84.69, fax 02.47.97.48.55 ☑ 🍸 by appt.

JOEL TALUAU Vieilles vignes 1998

■ 4 ha 18,000 50–69 F

The nose, of medium intensity, mingles cherry, morello, redcurrant and undergrowth. The palate is supple, a little fresh and well balanced, with all the necessary tannins. The harmony between strength and roundness leaves a good impression. A wine ready for drinking but which will bring other pleasures with age.

🔑 EARL Taluau-Foltzenlogel, Chevrette, 37140 Saint-Nicolas-de-Bourgueil, tel. 02.47.97.78.79, fax 02.47.97.95.60 ☑ 🍸 ev. day except Sat. Sun. 9am–12 noon 2pm–6pm

DOM. GERALD VALLEE

Le Vau Jaumier 1998

■ 3 ha 15,000 30–49 F

Gérald Vallée, son of Claude Vallée, wanted to spread his wings and started up on the 3 ha (7.4 acres) of Le Vau Jaumier in 1997. He has made a well-balanced, rich wine marked by its time in oak barrels, which has left a trace of vanilla – a style that has its admirers. It needs to be allowed to age to achieve harmony.

🔑 Gérald Vallée, La Cotelleraie, 37140 Saint-Nicolas-de-Bourgueil, tel. 02.47.97.75.53, fax 02.47.97.85.90 ☑ 🍸 by appt.

DOM. DES VALLETTES 1998

■ 14 ha 100,000 30–49 F

Saint-Nicolas used to be part of Bourgeuil but became independent and built its church and town hall during the 19th century. The vines followed the same course, and the appellation was one of the first to be recognised in France, in 1937. It is from this era that Francis Jamet's vineyard dates, 18 ha (44 acres) on deep, healthy, gravelly soil. He has produced a nice wine, all lightness and finesse, deliciously aromatic. It should be appreciated immediately.

🔑 Francis Jamet, Dom. des Vallettes, 37140 Saint-Nicolas-de-Bourgueil, tel. 02.41.52.05.99, fax 02.41.52.87.52 ☑ 🍸 by appt.

Chinon

The AOC Chinon, which covers 2,000 ha (4,940 acres), surrounding the old medieval fort from which it takes its name, lies amid countryside made famous by Rabelais in his epics *Gargantua* and *Pantagruel* (1534). The various terroirs include the ancient gravel terraces of the Véron (a triangle formed by the confluence of the Vienne and the Loire), the low, sandy terraces of the Vienne (Cravant) valley, the higher slopes on both sides of the valley (Sazilly) and chalk (Chinon). Cabernet Franc, known as Breton, makes an average 120,712 hl (3,186,797 gal) of delicious red wines, plus a few thousand hectolitres (hundred thousand gallons) of dry rosé which equal Bourgueil in quality: they have pedigree, elegant tannins and keep well, for several decades in the case of some exceptional vintages! Less known outside the area, but very original, is white Chinon, of which 1,215 hl (32,076 gal) were produced in 1999, a rather dry wine that softens with bottle age.

DOM. DES BEGUINERIES

Vieilles vignes 1998

■ 4.5 ha 15,000 30–49 F

Jean-Christophe Pelletier established himself on a small hillside estate on the edge of the Vienne in 1995. However, he made his debut in 1987 at Château de Saint-Louand. Today, he is still responsible for the winery, while at the same time running his vineyard, which covers almost 10 ha (25 acres). In his Vieilles Vignes, oak does not get the better of red fruit and plum. The palate is light and lively, while the slightly edgy tannins show that the wine needs ageing.

Jean-Christophe Pelletier, Clos de la Rue Saint-Louand, 37500 Chinon, tel. 06.08.92.88.17, fax 06.47.93.37.16 by appt.

DOM. DE BEL-AIR

La Fosse aux Loups 1998★

■ 5 ha 26,000 50–69 F

Forty-year-old vines with a limited yield and stony, gravelly soils are responsible for this wine, which has a beautiful ruby colour. The bouquet is marked by red fruit, with even a note of cocoa with a spicy tinge. Its first impression gives way to a fine, harmonious structure. The wine has already aged well and does not require any laying down. A pleasing bottle.

Jean-Louis Loup, Dom. de Bel-Air, 37500 Cravant-les-Coteaux, tel. 02.47.98.42.75, fax 02.47.93.98.30 by appt.

VINCENT BELLIVIER 1998

■ 0.5 ha 2,000 30–49 F

This Chinon comes from one of the communes in the north-east of the appellation. A very intense, brilliant colour, the wine is rich on the palate, wrapping up the tannins which are quite fine and harmonious. Well balanced, the wine is ready to drink but could also benefit from time in the cellar. A second red wine, **Noune 98**, received similar appreciation from the jury.

Vincent Bellivier, La Tourette 12, rue de la Tourette, 37420 Huismes, tel. 02.47.95.54.26, fax 02.47.95.54.26 by appt.

DOM. DES BOUQUERRIES

Cuvée royale 1998★

■ 2.5 ha 14,000 30–49 F

According to local tradition, this place was given the name of 'Bouquerries' because a butcher used to slaughter billy-goats ('boucs') here at one time. Guillaume and Jérôme Sourdais prefer instead to cultivate this beautiful 27-ha (67-acre) estate, created in 1935 by their grandfather and developed by their father. A deep, natural colour, an open nose with impressions of ripe fruit and jam, and a full, round palate supported by a solid, powerful structure: all contribute to make up a nice, engaging wine. At the finish there is still a slight tannic overflow that will bring itself under control during ageing.

GAEC des Bouquerries, 4, Les Bouquerries, 37500 Cravant-les-Coteaux, tel. 02.47.93.10.50, fax 02.47.93.41.94 by appt.

PHILIPPE BROCOURT

Cuvée Terroir les Coteaux 1998★

■ 5 ha 20,000 30–49 F

The product of a beautiful 17-ha (42-acre) vineyard planted on the terraces of the Vienne, this wine is characterised by a brilliant, very deep colour and aromas of red and stewed fruit, with a slightly smoky aspect. It is assertive on the palate, powerful, concentrated and long, with tannins that are still a little severe but guarantee a promising future.

Philippe Brocourt, 3, chem. des Caves, 37500 Rivière, tel. 02.47.93.34.49, fax 02.47.93.97.40 by appt.

DOM. PASCAL BRUNET

Vieilles vignes Elevé en fût de chêne 1998★

■ 1.5 ha 5,000 30–49 F

This wine-maker started in 1980 with just 1 ha (2.5 acres) of vines and nowadays cultivates 10 ha (25 acres) of new plantings on chalky clay soil. He has produced a Vieilles Vignes of deep ruby colour and an intense nose of red fruit and peony mingled with grilled and woody notes. The opening on the palate is clean, followed by a well-balanced structure. The finish is full of freshness, and an agreeable grapey impression remains at the end. One star, too, for the **Rosé 99**, fruity, floral and elegant all at once.

Pascal Brunet, 11, Etilly, 37220 Panzoult, tel. 02.47.58.62.80, fax 02.47.58.62.80 by appt.

DOM. DES CHAMPS VIGNONS

Cuvée la Jolirie 1998★

■ 4 ha 12,000 30–49 F

These two wine-producers farm 12 ha (5 acres) of vines, which have been passed down through the family for generations. Located in the commune of Ligré, where chalky clay soils have a reputation for producing powerful wines, this vineyard has produced a well-constructed 98 vintage whose structure is not overpowered by tannins. The wine gives a lively and markedly fruity impression, and the body remains supple yet finishes on a reminder of tannins that prevents you from forgetting the wine's origin. A Chinon to lay down, but already pleasing.

M. Thivel et Richard, 2, rue Saint-Martin, 37500 Ligré, tel. 02.47.93.18.48, fax 02.47.98.41.64 by appt.

DOM. DANIEL CHAUVEAU 1998★

■ 2.6 ha 11,000 30–49 F

This wine, with its beautiful expression, slightly gamey, has such structure and intensity that it demands to be aged. These two wine-makers, father and son, who have created a strongly fruity wine, are always delighted to show their impressive collection of corkscrews to visitors.

Dom. Daniel Chauveau, Pallus, 37500 Cravant-les-Coteaux, tel. 02.47.93.06.12, fax 02.47.93.93.06, e-mail domaine.daniel.chauveau@wanadoo.fr by appt.

DOM. DES CLOSIERS DE SAINT HILAIRE Vieilles vignes 1998

■ 2.3 ha 10,000 30–49 F

Unquestionably a wine for laying down. The nose, where raspberry and cherry can be discerned, is dominated by new wood. The wine is structured by tannins, which assert themselves on the palate towards the finish. The whole needs time to harmonise. Come back in two or three years to taste this Chinon on the banks of the Vienne.

François Médard, 10, rue des Lavandières, 37500 Rivière, tel. 02.47.98.42.92, fax 02.47.93.03.01 by appt.

DOM. DU COLOMBIER

Cuvée de La Roche Bobreau 1998★

■ 1.6 ha 7,000 30–49 F

The wine-makers of Chinon are starting to put out sorting tables at harvest time. These enable them to eliminate the grapes that are not fully ripe before putting the rest into vats. This practice is already well established at Yves Loiseau's vineyard, enabling him to attain a good level of quality, notably in Cuvée de la Roche Bobreau. Its nose is discreet but evokes red fruit with grilled and woody hints. On the palate it is fleshy, ample, as full as anyone could wish, and gives the impression that it is ready for drinking, but the finish is still slightly tannic, urging you rather to keep it. The estate's **Rouge Vieilles Vignes 98** warrants a mention too.

EARL Loiseau-Jouvault, Dom. du Colombier, 37420 Beaumont-en-Véron, tel. 02.47.58.43.07, fax 02.47.58.93.99 ev. day except Sun. 8am–12 noon 2pm–7pm

CH. DE COULAINE

Clos de Turpenay 1998★★

■ 1.1 ha 5,000 50–69 F

Located in the Véron region, between the Vienne and the Loire, Château de Coulaine is a very old family estate where the tradition of wine-growing has continued uninterrupted since 1300. From time immemorial, vines have flourished on the chalky soils encircling this impressive property, whose medieval structure shows a strong Italian influence. In 1988 Etienne de Bonnaventure undertook the enlargement of the vineyard, which now comprises 12 ha (30 acres) and is farmed organically. Clos de Turpenay opens on the palate with remarkable fullness. It is very well balanced and as aromatic as anyone could want. You rediscover red fruit and a trace of vanilla which were perceptible on the nose, with an added note of liquorice. The finish is vigorous but still pleasant. This has been made intelligently. Ageing in the bottle is bound to be remarkable. Two other red wines from the same estate gain one star: **La Diablesse** and **Château de Coulaine 98** in its classic version, matured in vats (30–49F).

Etienne et Pascale de Bonnaventure, EARL Ch. de Coulaine, 37420 Beaumont-en-Véron, tel. 02.47.98.44.51, fax 02.47.93.49.15 by appt.

LOIRE

COULY-DUTHEIL

Clos de l'Echo 1998★

■ 30 ha 75,000 30–49 F

This large family estate unites two brothers and their sons: Arnaud, whose father is Jacques Couly-Dutheil, has turned towards the commercial side; Bertrand, Pierre's son, is an oenologist and is responsible for the technical side. It is to him we owe this Clos de l'Echo, named after the vineyard behind the château whose walls return an echo. A warm wine, with red fruit and liquorice at the same time, and dominated by wood, it has spent 12 months in barrels and has a marked oak taste. Give it a long period in which to develop and it will reveal itself. The **Blanc 99** obtained a mention by the jury.

Couly-Dutheil, 12, rue Diderot, 37500 Chinon, tel. 02.47.97.20.20, fax 02.47.97.20.25, e-mail webmaster@coulydutheil-chinon.com by appt.

FRANCIS ET FRANCOISE DESBOURDES L'Arpenty 1998★★

■ 4.5 ha 5,000 30-49 F

It was Francis Desbourdes' grandfather who created the estate of L'Arpenty. The wine cellar has just been renovated, and Francis now runs a lovely unit for the production of quality Chinon. This one presents a full, regular palate with harmonious tannins. It has aromas aplenty: pear, marzipan and peach, with a hint of wild strawberry. This is a very well-balanced wine.

Francis Desbourdes, Arpenty, 37220 Panzoult, tel. 02.47.95.22.86, fax 02.47.95.22.86 by appt.

VIGNOBLE GASNIER

Cuvée Prestige 1998★

■ 1.5 ha 8,000 30-49 F

Fabrice Gasnier represents the fourth successive generation of wine-makers to cultivate this estate. He has made numerous investments in it, the most recent of which is a sprinkler system to counteract frost. The first nose of this Chinon evokes capsicum, the second crystallised red fruit and the third wood. On the palate, exceptional roundness tempers this fairly marked woody aspect, while the finish is supple and mellow, leaving the impression of a happy harmony. A bottle to open from now onwards.

Fabrice Gasnier, Chézelet, 37500 Cravant-les-Coteaux, tel. 02.47.93.11.60, fax 02.47.93.44.83 by appt.

DOM. DES GELERIES

Cuvée Prestige 1998★

■ 1.5 ha 6,000 30-49 F

Primarily a Bourgueil producer, Jeannine Rouzier-Meslet also has a small property in the Chinon appellation which came from her husband: 1.5 ha (3.7 acres) of vines on chalky clay soil, vine stock which has yielded a wine with aromas of ripe fruit, round, and well endowed in terms of substance. The finish is pleasant and light but leaves a slight impression of warmth.

Jeannine Rouzier-Meslet, 2, rue des Gélérles, 37140 Bourgueil, tel. 02.47.97.72.83, fax 02.47.97.48.73 by appt.

DOM. FRANCIS HAERTY 1998

■ 1.5 ha 10,000 30-49 F

The sands and gravels of the Vienne, allied with the know-how of the wine-maker, often produce marvels. It has happened with this Chinon from the Haerty estate. The nose is fairly well developed, fruity with grilled and capsicum notes so typical of Cabernet Franc. Pleasing on the palate, well balanced, with an unbroken finish, it is an honest wine, with a simplicity that enables it to be very versatile.

Francis Haerty, 2, rue des Pêcheurs, 37420 Savigny-en-Véron, tel. 02.47.58.42.74

DOM. DES HARDONNIERES

1998★

■ 3.1 ha 25,000 20-29 F

In 1989 some vineyards grouped together under the name of 'Caves des Vins de Rabelais' in order to get a competitive commercial edge. They have achieved their goal because their products are well distributed, notably abroad, where more than a third are sold. They offer this Domaine des Hardonnières with its ruby colour and very nice nose of stewed fruits. The palate is full, with round, silky tannins and an interesting length. There is a great deal of elegance and quality in the wine, which you can drink immediately but which will also age without a problem. The **Chinon Rouge Pierre Chanau 99**, destined for wide distribution, also earns a star for its harmony.

SICA des Caves des Vins de Rabelais, Les Aubuis, Saint-Louand, 37500 Chinon, tel. 02.47.93.42.70, fax 02.47.98.35.40 by appt.

DOM. CHARLES JOGUET

Clos du Chêne Vert 1998★★★

■ n.c. 13,000 70-99 F

Charles Joguet retired in 1997, but his influence lives on: helping to bring out the character of the terroirs. The bunches of grapes are transported in small boxes as far as the winery, and each lot is then treated separately. Clos du Chêne Vert puts on an exceptional display. Behind the deep garnet colour of the wine, an entire retinue of stewed fruits becomes evident, mingled with undergrowth and that characteristic Cabernet touch, capsicum. It opens cleanly on the palate, and fruit is then again in evidence. Roundness and fullness follow on, to conclude on a velvet finish. The jury was unanimous in awarding this wine the highest mark. It is difficult to say whether to serve it now or save it for later.

Dom. Charles Joguet, La Dioterie, 37220 Sazilly, tel. 02.47.58.55.53, fax 02.47.58.52.22 by appt.

DOM. DE L'ABBAYE 1999

□ 1 ha 6,000 30-49 F

Michel Fontaine founded Domaine de l'Abbaye in 1975 by joining together some small vineyards. You can visit La Devinière, 5 km (3 miles) away, an old farm where François Rabelais was born in about 1495. The 99 wine is well balanced, round and fruity, with an explosive golden-yellow colour. The flavours are composed, pleasantly dominated by citrus fruit, and linger nicely on the palate.

Michel Fontaine, Le Repos-Saint-Martin, 37500 Chinon, tel. 02.47.93.35.96, fax 02.47.98.36.76 by appt.

CH. DE LA BONNELIERE 1998★

■ 6 ha 20,000 30–49 F

The property of the Plouzeau family since 1846, this 15-ha (37-acre) vineyard is on chalky clay soils on the left bank of the Vienne. It is run by the family's youngest son, Jacques. His 98 wine is powerful on the palate, but its measured tannins are treated in such a way that it stays supple and even gives an impression of lightness. The fairly lively finish and intense fruitiness establish the wine as a good example of the vintage. The **Chinon Rosé 99 Rive Gauche** also deserves noting.

Maison Plouzeau, 54, fg Saint-Jacques, 37500 Chinon, tel. 02.47.93.16.34, fax 02.47.98.48.23 Y by appt.

DOM. DE LA CHAPELLE

Vieilles vignes 1998★★

■ 6 ha 15,000 30–49 F

Philippe Pichard inherited this 16-ha (39-acre) estate from his grandparents. There used to be a chapel here, but nowadays only traces of it remain. The winery has modern equipment, and an adjoining wine cellar, hollowed out of the rock, is valuable as a storage area for bottles. Skill is behind this superb, non-aggressive wine, with its power, length and roundness. Balance is already assured, but development would be welcomed.

Philippe Pichard, 9, rue Malvault, 37500 Cravant-les-Coteaux, tel. 02.47.93.42.35, fax 02.47.98.33.76 Y by appt.

DOM. DE LA DOZONNERIE 1998★

■ 4 ha 20,000 30–49 F

The first vines of the estate were planted in 1936, and their harvest was doubtless one of the first to gain the AOC granted to Chinon the following year. In 1990 Jean-François Delalay inherited this property. With its back to the hillside and dominating the plain, it now covers 12 ha (29 acres). This, the estate's main wine, was kept in barrels for six months. It has already developed structure but is still a little biting. Full on the palate, it envelops the tannins nicely. This is therefore a wine with strong potential for ageing, which should not be judged by its current qualities. **Cuvée Vieilles Vignes 98** from the same producer also needs to wait.

Jean-François Delalay, Les Vallées de Basses, 37500 Chinon, tel. 02.47.93.16.72, fax 02.47.93.23.37 Y by appt.

CLOS DE LA GALVAUDERIE

Cuvée des Loges de Vigne 1998★

■ n.c. 6,000 30–49 F

Three months' maturation in vats and then eight months in barrels: that is the norm at La Galvauderie, which produces this wine of special qualities. A clear, limpid ruby colour, a developed nose of red fruit and caramel, and a fruity, supple, balanced palate: it is difficult to ask for more. A most successful, fulfilling Chinon.

EARL Barc, Clos de La Croix Marie, 37500 Rivière, tel. 02.47.93.02.24, fax 02.47.93.99.45 Y by appt.

CH. DE LA GRILLE 1998★

■ 27 ha 160,000 70–99 F

Built on a Roman site, Château de la Grille dates from the 16th century but has been extended more recently; its architecture and dimensions are impressive. It belongs to the Gosset family, who are originally from Champagne, and is surrounded by 58 ha (143 acres) of vines. The winery has modern equipment with an underground section reserved for *barriques*, where the wine stays for a minimum of 15 months. This Chinon unites red fruit and strawberry jam on the nose. Its palate is round and well constructed, leaving an impression of balance. A high-class wine.

Laurent et Sylvie Gosset, Ch. de La Grille, rte de Huismes et Ussé, 37500 Chinon, tel. 02.47.93.01.95, fax 02.47.93.45.91 Y by appt.

CLOS DE LA LYSARDIERE 1998

■ 7 ha 30,000 20–29 F

Established in 1989 to promote the integration of disabled people, this vineyard is 7 ha (17 acres) in area. It is on the chalky clay soils of Beaumont, which are reputed to produce well-structured wines. This 98 wine conforms to the rule, but due allowance must be made for its vintage. The nose of very ripe fruit is fairly expressive, and the wine is full-bodied on the palate, full of elegance and solid flavours, and of good balance. The wine is already pleasing and will also age well.

Vignoble du Paradis, 57, rte du Véron, 37420 Beaumont-en-Véron, tel. 05.49.98.09.09, fax 05.49.98.15.31 Y by appt.

CAT Les Cheveaux Blancs

BEATRICE ET PASCAL LAMBERT

Cuvée Marie 1998

■ 1.8 ha 7,200 50–69 F

Béatrice and Pascal Lambert cultivate a vineyard of more than 9 ha (22 acres) at the foot of the Cravant hillside, and have good wine-making equipment. There are numerous barrels in the store where they age the wine, some of which are new. Its time in wood lasts more than a year and leaves its imprint on the wine. Cuvée Marie is an example of this. While the wine is well made, rich and full-bodied, an oaky presence is still dominant. Ageing is needed to give harmony to the flavours.

Pascal Lambert, Les Chesnaies, 37500 Cravant-les-Coteaux, tel. 02.47.93.13.79, fax 02.47.93.40.97 Y by appt.

PATRICK LAMBERT

Vieilles vignes 1998★

■ 2.5 ha 11,000 30–49 F

Patrick Lambert took over this estate from his parents in 1990 and subsequently enlarged it, taking it to almost 8 ha (20 acres). He is a methodical, traditional wine-maker. His wines spend a long time in wood and generally emerge endowed with a harmonious structure. His Vieilles Vignes is thus long and mellow, although several scattered tannins do

LOIRE

put in an appearance, a sign that it needs more age.

🔑 Patrick Lambert, 6, coteau de Sonnay, 37500 Cravant-les-Coteaux, tel. 02.47.93.92.39 ☑ 🍷 by appt.

DOM. DE LA NOBLAIE 1998★★

■ 11.3 ha 30,000 30–49 F

Pierre Manzagol, who practically created Domaine de la Noblaie on an area of 12.5 ha (31 acres), would be proud of this wine, which his son-in-law Pierre Billard has just produced. Scents abound on the nose: grape, blackcurrant and bilberry. The palate is full, dense and well balanced, with complex fruity notes, and a hint of grilled almond breaking through. The finish lets you catch a glimpse of some fine tannins, which bring a little relief and presage future development. Nevertheless, this Chinon is showing well now. **Chinon Rosé 99** is a very successful fruity and tender wine, and **Blanc 99** earns a mention for its balance.

🔑 SCEA Manzagol-Billard, Dom. de La Noblaie, Le Vau Breton, 37500 Ligré, tel. 02.47.93.10.96, fax 02.47.93.26.13 ☑ 🍷 by appt.

DOM. DE LA PERRIERE

Vieilles vignes 1998★★★

■ 7.5 ha 40,000 30–49 F

Domaine de la Perrière has been in the Baudry family since 1398, a record! Planted on the gravelly terraces of the Vienne, it produces very aromatic wines, often finely structured. This has come from a selection of old vines, several of which are more than 60 years old. A period of eight months spent in wood has given it a certain fullness. The slightly peppery nose is dominated by red fruit and vanilla, with a little touch of wood in the background. The body is round and full, and elegantly structured by unobtrusive tannins. This is a wine that will go far. It was close to receiving the *Coup de Coeur*. Watch out for the highly successful **Chinon Blanc Confidential 98** as well (50–69F).

🔑 Christophe Baudry, Dom. de La Perrière, 37500 Cravant-les-Coteaux, tel. 02.47.93.15.99, fax 02.47.98.34.57 ☑ 🍷 by appt.

DOM. DE LA POTERNE 1998

■ 7 ha 7,000 30–49 F

This is a nice wine, fresh, fruity and round, and it masks its tannins well. The clear ruby colour is in keeping with the notes of red fruit and banana which break through on the nose as well as on the palate. Smooth, tender and aromatic, this Chinon has everything it needs to make an excellent Easter wine. Let us take it as such, and drink it soon with white meat.

🔑 EARL Christian et Robert Delalande, Montet, 37220 L'Ile-Bouchard, tel. 02.47.58.52.54, fax 02.47.58.67.99 ☑ 🍷 by appt.

DOM. DE LA ROCHE HONNEUR

Diamant Prestige 1998★

■ 3 ha 9,000 30–49 F

Domaine de la Roche Honneur, between the Loire and the Vienne on the siliceous, gravelly or chalky clay soils of the Veron, produces wines of different characters. Skilful blending of these produces three improved wines. This one, Diamant Prestige, is the precious baby of Stéphane Mureau: extremely well constructed, it is nicely balanced between flavour and wood. A shade of roundness makes it almost ready to drink, but it could be laid down for a short while. **Cuvée Rubis 98** has already opened out well, and was also noted by the jury as being very successful.

🔑 Dom. de La Roche Honneur, 1, rue de la Berthelonnière, 37420 Savigny-en-Véron, tel. 02.47.58.42.10, fax 02.47.58.45.36 ☑ 🍷 by appt.

🔑 Stéphane Mureau

CAVES DE LA SALLE

Vieilles vignes 1998★★

■ 4 ha 22,000 30–49 F

The house and its outbuildings date from the 18th century, but the farm buildings and winery were built in 1988. The vineyard covers 12 ha (29 acres). Vieilles Vignes, with its bright garnet colour, delivers a nose of rare power, with scents ranging from peach to leather. It opens gently on the palate, followed by a well-balanced structure where richness and tannins get on well together. The long, round finish leaves a clear smoky impression. This is a wine that is full of promise, and it needs to be put on hold for future drinking. From the same vineyard, **Fief de la Rougellerie 98** deserves a mention.

🔑 Rémi Desbourdes, La Salle, 37220 Avon-les-Roches, tel. 02.47.95.24.30, fax 02.47.95.24.83 ☑ 🍷 by appt.

LE CHAMP MARTIN 1998

■ 2.57 ha 11,000 20–29 F

If your journey brings you to Tavant and if you incline towards spiritual nourishment, you could visit the little village church and admire its 12th-century murals. Earthly nourishment comes when you taste this 98 wine with its well-developed nose of peach, apricot, pomegranate and plum. Solid and round on the palate, its balance is good, and it releases flavours of red fruit with grilled notes. This wine is ready to be enjoyed now: with rib of beef, for example.

🗝 Jean-Pierre Crespin, 12, rue Grande, 37220 Tavant, tel. 02.47.97.01.48 ☑ 🍸 by appt.

JACQUELINE LEON 1998

■ 0.8 ha 5,000 ▮ ⦀ 30–49 F

Jacqueline Léon cultivates this small 3.75-ha (9.2-acre) vineyard in the traditional manner. The sandy soils on the banks of the Vienne produce light wines that generally develop a rich bouquet based on raspberry, blackcurrant and redcurrant. This one, with its bright colour, reveals a nose of ripe fruit. The palate, silky and long, could develop further to round off some recalcitrant tannins. However, this wine could already accompany a grill or Saint-Maure *fromage frais*.

🗝 Jacqueline Léon, 2, rue des Capelets, 37420 Savigny-en-Véron, tel. 02.47.58.93.37 ☑ 🍸 by appt.

LE PARADIS 1998★

■ n.c. 30,000 ▮ 🌡 20–29 F

The floral nose develops quickly towards the capsicum which is so characteristic of Cabernet Franc. Harmonious is the word that immediately springs to mind, then together come roundness, fullness and length. A success that will be complete after a year's age.

🗝 Négoce du Paradis, 57, rue du Véron, 37420 Beaumont-en-Véron, tel. 02.49.98.09.09 ☑ 🍸 by appt.

🗝 CAT Cheveaux Blancs

LES CORNUELLES

Vieilles vignes 1998★

■ 6 ha 16,000 ⦀ 30–49 F

'To have been and be able to be again' is Serge and Bruno Sourdais' motivation for running this 40-ha (99-acre) estate created by their family during the 19th century. Six generations have gone by since then, and tradition persists. The wine of Les Cornuelles comes from chalky hillsides with the best possible aspect. After a long time in wood, it is starting to open out into a powerful and warm body with solid tannins. Wait for two or three years.

🗝 Serge et Bruno Sourdais, La Bouchardière, 37500 Cravant-les-Coteaux, tel. 02.47.93.04.27, fax 02.47.93.38.52 ☑ 🍸 by appt.

CH. DE LIGRE

La Roche Saint-Paul 1998★★

■ 5 ha 20,000 ▮ ⦀ 🌡 30–49 F

'Be privy to the secret of soils and wines,' says Pierre Ferrand, a secret he freely and passionately shares as he presents his products. His La Roche Saint-Paul (a Ligré terroir) wine is well made. Its bouquet is divided between blackcurrant, peach and undergrowth. After a well-balanced opening on the palate, there appears a solid concentration of flavour sustained by full-bodied but none the less pleasant tannins. You sense the hands of the wine-maker: art and science at the same time. This wine has a potential laying-down period of ten years, but it can also be appreciated now.

🗝 Pierre Ferrand, Ch. de Ligré, 37500 Ligré, tel. 02.47.93.16.70, fax 02.47.93.43.29, e-mail pierre.ferrand4@wanadoo.fr ☑ 🍸 ev. day 8.30am–12 noon 2pm–6pm; Sat. Sun. by appt.

ALAIN LORIEUX 1998★★

■ 6 ha 35,000 ▮ 30–49 F

Pascal and Alain Lorieux grow both Saint-Nicolas-de-Bourgueil and Chinon grapes. Alain created the Chinon vineyard on an area of 5 ha (37 acres) and it is he who maintains it. The two estates make their wine separately but share equipment and marketing. This 98 wine makes a good impression with its fullness and roundness. A silky tannic structure confers a fairly rare harmony on the whole. As for the aromas, crystallised red fruit invades both the nose and the palate. This wine, after being laid down for two or three years, would go well with pheasant.

🗝 Pascal et Alain Lorieux, Malvault, 37500 Cravant-les-Coteaux, tel. 02.47.98.35.11, fax 02.47.98.36.11 ☑ 🍸 by appt.

DOM. DES MILLARGES

Cuvée de Printemps 1998

■ 2 ha 9,950 ▮ 🌡 30–49 F

The *Centre Viti-Vinicole* at Chinon was set up in 1973 by the county council of Indre-et-Loire and is attached to the Agricultural School of Tours-Fondettes. It trains wine technicians and experiments with cultivation techniques. Its guided tour is richly informative for wine-lovers. The school estate offers a Cuvée de Printemps with a nose of ripe fruit, capsicum and a hint of bracken. It opens on the palate with suppleness; it is well balanced and finishes at some length on an impression of vanilla. A nice wine that will suit all occasions. **Chinon Rouge Elevé en Fût 98** was also singled out by the jury.

🗝 Centre viti-vinicole de Chinon, Dom. des Millarges, Les Fontenils, 37500 Chinon, tel. 02.47.93.36.89, fax 02.47.93.96.20 ☑ 🍸 by appt.

🗝 Lycée agricole

CLOS DE NEUILLY 1998

■ 3 ha 15,000 ⦀ 30–49 F

This Clos de Neuilly comes from 3 ha (7.4 acres) of old vines and 18 months' maturation in large wooden casks. Johann Spelty continues to apply the methods his father introduced with such success. Lucky for him that he does, because this is a pretty wine with aromas of red fruit and violet, and it is supple and long. Drink it with grilled food. Worth letting age a little.

🗝 Johann Spelty, Le Carroi Portier, 37500 Cravant-les-Coteaux, tel. 02.47.93.08.38, fax 02.47.93.93.50 ☑ 🍸 by appt.

DOM. JAMES PAGET

Vieilles vignes 1998★

■ 1.5 ha 6,000 30–49 F

James Paget has professional responsibilities in the Touraine-Azay-le-Rideau appellation, where he has the majority of his vineyards. But in the Chinon area, he cultivates a small property of 1.5 ha (3.7 acres) where the vines are mostly more than 45 years old. Thus, he offers a wine of lovely length, completely harmonious and with scents recalling red orchard fruit. It is a 'pleasure wine', ready to be much appreciated.

EARL James Paget, 13, rue d'Armentières, 37190 Rivarennes, tel. 02.47.95.54.02, fax 02.47.95.45.90 by appt.

DOM. CHARLES PAIN

Cuvée Prestige 1998★★

■ 11 ha 30,000 30–49 F

Domaine Charles Pain covers 20 ha (49 acres) and extends into the three easternmost communes of the appellation. Cuvée Prestige, particularly cherished by its producer, opens up a modest nose which is nevertheless complex and promising. On the palate, in its roundness and silky tannins, you sense a long and successful maturation in oak. The wine has a fine presence, and the jury concluded that it was a good example of the vintage. It has a good capacity for ageing. The **Rouge 98 Classique du Domaine**, round and fruity, was judged to be very successful.

Dom. Charles Pain, Chézelet, 37220 Panzoult, tel. 02.47.93.06.14, fax 02.47.93.04.43 by appt.

PIERRE PRIEUR 1998★

■ 2 ha 10,000 30–49 F

Pierre Prieur's estate comprises a beautiful vineyard of 13 ha (32 acres) on the sands and gravels on the banks of the Loire, complete with a lovely wine cellar in the rock at the bottom of the hill, and here he offers a wine with good potential. The powerful but round tannins are without bitterness and lead into a fairly long finish. The nose emphasises aromas of capsicum, stewed fruit, roasted tones and even coffee. This Chinon will reach its fullness by 2002.

Pierre Prieur, 1, rue des Mariniers, Bertignolles, 37420 Savigny-en-Véron, tel. 02.47.58.45.08, fax 02.47.58.94.56 by appt.

DOM. DU PUY RIGAULT 1998

■ 5 ha 33,000 30–49 F

A purple colour, aromas of crushed raspberry and morello cherry, a good balance on the palate between oak, substance and slightly firm tannins, and you have a nice wine developed by Michel Page at his estate on the banks of the Vienne. Its touch of acidity gives it a freshness which makes it pleasant to drink right away.

EARL Dom. du Puy Rigault, 6, rue de la Fontaine-Rigault, 37420 Savigny-en-Véron, tel. 02.47.58.44.46, fax 02.47.58.99.50 by appt.

Michel Page

DOM. DES QUATRE VENTS

Cuvée Domaine 1998

■ n.c. 10,000 30–49 F

On top of a hillock, this domaine is swept by winds. While the location is not exactly comfortable, it at least spares the vines from spring frosts. The 98 wine is reasonably intense on the nose, dominated by blackcurrant, redcurrant and raspberry with a hint of capsicum. The palate is supple, the flavours sufficient and the finish fresh and fruity. A wine with a good bouquet which will be a perfect accompaniment to grilled foods.

Philippe Pion, La Bâtisse, 37500 Cravant-les-Coteaux, tel. 02.47.93.46.79, fax 02.47.93.99.59 by appt.

JEAN-MAURICE RAFFAULT

Clos d'Isoré 1998★

■ 5 ha n.c. 30–49 F

Jean-Maurice Raffault is one of the leading lights of Chinon viticulture. He has been very militant within the professional organisations, while at the same time building up his 35-ha (86-acre) vineyard in the heart of Véron. Now ably assisted by his son Rodolphe, he makes a Clos d'Isoré wine with a very expressive nose, where raspberry lays down the law. The body is powerful, even impressive, with already-sobered tannins: its time in wood has been skilfully managed. You can drink this Chinon now or keep it for some years. Another red wine, **Les Picasses 98**, was awarded the same mark for its balance and length.

EARL Jean-Maurice Raffault, 31, rue du Bourg, 37420 Savigny-en-Véron, tel. 02.47.58.42.50, fax 02.47.58.83.73, e-mail rodolphe.raffault@wanadoo.fr by appt.

OLGA RAFFAULT 1999★★

□ n.c. n.c. 30–49 F

With its intense golden colour, this Chinon carries the revealing stamp of Chenin: aromas of quince and apricot, complex and sustained. The palate has high-quality, fruity flavours. The finish leaves a most pleasing impression of freshness. The **Rosé 99** is also worthy of mention.

SARL Dom. Olga Raffault, 1, rue des Caillis, 37420 Savigny-en-Véron, tel. 02.47.58.42.16, fax 02.47.58.83.61 by appt.

Jean Raffault

DOM. DU RAIFAULT 1998★

■ 6 ha 32,000 30–49 F

Julien Raffault took over the running of this beautiful 28-ha (69-acre) estate in 1997 and seems to have things well under control. This Domaine du Raifault wine, named after the manor house that dominates the vineyard, is proof of this. The nose has a touch of cocoa with bilberry developing in the background. The palate is full and ferny. The level of tannins says much for ageing possibilities. This is a very nice wine to lay down that will reveal itself in time.

Julien Raffault, 23–25, rte de Candes, 37420 Savigny-en-Véron, tel. 02.47.58.44.01, fax 02.47.58.92.02 ✉ Y ev. day 8am–7pm; Sun. by appt.

DOM. DU RONCEE

Clos des Marronniers 1998★

■ 7.05 ha 22,000 30–49 F

A *clos* is a plot encircled by walls. Vineyards in Touraine were often demarcated thus in the 15th century. Domaine du Roncée reminds of this in the range of its wines. That of the Clos des Marronniers evokes exotic fruit and peony. Its palate, full and supple, is embellished with smoky accents. It is a nice bottle capable of being laid down for ten years or so. The estate's classic **Cuvée Rouge 98** is also very successful in its suppleness and balance.

Dom. du Roncée, La Morandière, 37220 Panzoult, tel. 02.47.58.53.01, fax 02.47.58.64.06, e-mail roncee@club-internet.fr ✉ Y ev. day except Sat. Sun. 9am–12 noon 2pm –6pm

DOM. DES ROUET

Cuvée des Battereaux Vieilles vignes 1998★

■ 3 ha 9,000 30–49 F

Gravelly soils and vine stock of a fair age are the origins of this lovely 98 wine, full of charm and harmoniously balanced. The subtle nose is laden with very ripe red fruit. The level of tannins gives the wine the ability to age well.

Dom. des Rouet, Chézelet, 37500 Cravant-les-Coteaux, tel. 02.47.93.19.41, fax 02.47.93.96.58 ✉ Y by appt.

DOM. WILFRID ROUSSE

Vieilles vignes 1998★★

■ 1 ha 6,000 30–49 F

Wilfrid Rousse's estate consists of 11 ha (27 acres) of vines, the vine stock being 90-year-old Cabernet Franc. This 98 is deep red in colour, and the character of the nose is clearly marked by red fruit and sloe. On the palate the wine is fine and elegant, and the flavours are typical of the vintage. The tannins are still a little raw, but only need maturing. Pleasing now, this Chinon also has good potential for ageing.

Wilfrid Rousse, La Halbardière, 21, rte de Candes, 37420 Savigny-en-Véron, tel. 02.47.58.84.02, fax 02.47.58.92.66 ✉ Y by appt.

GUY SAGET Marie de Beauregard 1998

■ 1.2 ha 6,078 30–49 F

Specialising in white wines, the Saget company now produces reds, notably Chinon. This one, very woody on the nose, is surprising in its supple first impression followed by a fruity palate with a light structure. A wine for those who like simple things and are not put off by oakiness.

SA Guy Saget, La Castille, 58150 Pouilly-sur-Loire, tel. 03.86.39.57.75, fax 03.86.39.08.30 ✉ Y ev. day except Sun. 8am–12 noon 2pm–6pm

CH. DE SAINT-LOUAND

Réserve de Trompegueux 1998★

■ 5.7 ha 25,000 30–49 F

The estate, which nowadays runs to 6.5 ha (16 acres) of vines, was bought in 1935 by Charles Walther, at that time president of the Académie de Médecine. His grandchildren run it now. The term *'trompegueux'*, which is applied to the vine, comes from *'trompes'*, heavy shoes worn by the tramps (*'gueux'*) who used to climb the hillsides. With an intense cherry-red colour, this 98 wine delivers a fruity nose, lightly spiced and oaky. On tasting it, there is a good impression of roundness and length due to velvety flavours. A tinge of oak reappears in the finish. A wine that should stay in the cellar for a little longer.

Bonnet-Walther, Saint-Louand, 37500 Chinon, tel. 02.47.93.48.60, fax 02.47.98.48.54 ✉ Y by appt.

PIERRE SOURDAIS 1999

◢ n.c. 7,000 30–49 F

For the millennium year Pierre Sourdais offers a nice Chinon rosé, very pale but very natural. Brilliant glints are perceptible in the light. After a fairly complex nose, the palate reveals a good structure and long-lasting floral aromas.

Pierre Sourdais, Le Moulin à Tan, 37500 Cravant-les-Coteaux, tel. 02.47.93.31.13, fax 02.47.98.30.48 ✉ Y by appt.

FRANCIS SUARD

Cuvée Prestige Elevé en fût de chêne Vieilles vignes 1998

■ 1.2 ha 5,200 30–49 F

Having a large cellar in the rock with a constant temperature and humidity is an advantage when raising wines in the Chinon area. Francis Suard puts classical methods into practice here, and they seem to succeed for him. His 98 wine gives a luscious, well-balanced impression. Fruity aromas are unobtrusive, but a dominant smoky note breaks loose. The finish is a little severe, indicating that ageing for some years is needed.

Francis Suard, 74, rte de Candes, 37420 Savigny-en-Véron, tel. 02.47.58.91.45 ✉ Y by appt.

CH. DE VAUGAUDRY 1998★

■ 11 ha 40,000 30–49 F

Château de Vaugaudry faces the town of Chinon and its old fortress on the opposite bank. Completely surrounded by walls, the vineyard consists of 12 ha (29 acres) on a terrace with a favourable climate, on the side of a hill on the left bank of the Vienne. The château's wine comes from the main part of the estate and is ruby-coloured with orangey touches. It releases a bouquet with the

Chinon stamp, which leaves an impression of the scent of sloe. On the palate it is supple and balanced, with harmonious tannins finishing on a smoky note. **Clos du Plessis Gerbault 98** was also mentioned by the jury.
SCEA Ch. de Vaugaudry, Vaugaudry, 37500 Chinon, tel. 02.47.93.13.51, fax 02.47.93.23.08 by appt.

DOM. DE VILLEGRON 1998*

9 ha 3,500 20–29 F

A very successful wine, with a brilliant, clear colour that flashes fire. The bouquet is typically Chinon because of its floral scents (iris and violet) and its evocations of red fruit and capsicum. The palate leaves a lingering, velvety impression. At the finish, fruity notes manifest themselves anew. This is a well-built, pleasant Chinon, which will do even better after time in the cellar.
Vincent Bodin, 17, rue de Villegron, 37500 La Roche-Clermault, tel. 02.47.93.24.13, fax 02.47.93.13.75 by appt.

Coteaux du Loir

This AOC and its cru, Jasnières, the only two vineyards in the Sarthe, occupy the slopes of the Loir valley. About twenty-five years ago, Coteaux du Loir was on the verge of extinction, but is now fully revived. The vines are planted on silicious clays over tufa. The wines have great appeal, and include nearly 1,980 hl (52,272 gal) of light, fruity reds (Pineau d'Aunis, mixed with Cabernet, Gamay or Cot) and rosés, together with 1,184 hl (31,258 gal) of dry white (Chenin, known here as Pineau Blanc de la Loire).

DOM. DE CEZIN Pineau d'Aunis 1999*

1.5 ha 5,000 20–29 F

Once again, François Fresneau offers us an attractive Pineau d'Aunis made from grapes grown on flinty clay. A clear salmon-pink colour, his rosé presents an interesting aromatic palette of beeswax and white fruit. The palate, delicately spiced, is sufficiently rich and round. A lovely representative of the type, as is the **Jasnières 99** from the same producer, which is full of finesse.
François Fresneau, rue de Cézin, 72340 Marçon, tel. 02.43.44.13.70, fax 02.43.44.13.70 by appt.

BERNARD CROISARD 1999

1.5 ha 7,000 30–49 F

This wine-grower has brought his wine cellar equipment up to the necessary level, and as a result has produced a pale, very round white Coteaux du Loir. Some of the tasters appreciated its flattering touches of exotic fruit.
Bernard Croisard, La Pommeraie, 72340 Chahaignes, tel. 02.43.44.47.12 by appt.

DOM. DE LA GAUDINIERE 1998

1.1 ha 5,000 20–29 F

Domaine de la Gaudinière is quite close to a dolmen. Garnet-coloured, its rather supple 98 is enjoyable thanks to its bouquet of red berries underlined by a hint of clove and peony.
EARL C. et D. Cartereau, La Gaudinière, 72340 Lhomme, tel. 02.43.44.55.38, fax 02.43.44.55.38 by appt.

LES MAISONS ROUGES 1998*

1.5 ha 4,000 20–29 F

Elisabeth and Benoît Jardin are a friendly couple who reconverted to viticulture five years ago, and have just opened a shop selling products of the terroir. Their 98 Coteau du Loir, somewhere between tile-red and ruby, opens up an intense nose, fruity and grilled. Fine tannins and a good length on the palate make this wine a success in the spirit of the appellation. **Jasnières 99** is also promising.
Elisabeth et Benoît Jardin, Les Maisons rouges, Les Chaudières, 72340 Ruillé-sur-Loir, tel. 02.43.79.50.09, fax 02.43.79.13.95, e-mail benoit.jardin@bull.net by appt.

JEAN-MARIE RENVOISE
Pineau d'Aunis 1998*

1.4 ha 6,000 20–29 F

Jean-Marie Renvoisé settled in the north of the Loir Valley in 1992. His 98 is a very nice wine owing to its palette of black fruit, pepper and coriander. As smooth as anyone could wish for, it is the perfect companion to *charcuterie*.
Jean-Marie Renvoisé, 5, rue Bel-Air, 72340 Chahaignes, tel. 02.43.44.89.37 by appt.

Jasnières

This cru within Coteaux du Loir is precisely delimited on a single south-facing slope, 4 km (2.5 miles) long and only a few hundred metres (yards) wide. In 1999 it produced 2,471 hl (65,234

-gal) of single-variety white Chenin which can be quite sublime in great years. As one authority wrote: 'Three times in a century, Jasnières is the best white wine in the world.' Experts recommend it as an elegant accompaniment for Marmite Sarthoise, a local speciality, as well as for other delicacies of the region, such as chicken and rabbit dishes with steamed vegetables. A rare wine in every sense – a discovery waiting to be made.

DOM. AUBERT LA CHAPELLE

Cuvée Anne-Mathilde 1999

☐ 1.5 ha n.c. 30–49 F

La Chapelle is a house on the largest of the wine-growing plots and was built in 1850 by the parish priest of Marçon. It has given its name to this 12-ha (29-acre) estate, which has produced, in the 99 vintage, an intense yellow Jasnières, matured for six months in barrels. The palate reveals itself as well balanced, endowed with a certain sweetness and discreet, rather floral aromas. A good wine to lay down.

Aubert La Chapelle, La Roche, 72340 Marçon, tel. 02.43.79.17.82, fax 02.43.79.17.82, e-mail j.aubert@lemet.fr by appt.

PASCAL JANVIER 1999

☐ 1 ha 6,500 30–49 F

Pascal Janvier owns a traditional estate of just over 5 ha (12 acres) in the Loir Valley. He has produced a Jasnières with a full colour and aromas of white fruit tinged with smoke. Rich and lively at the same time, the wine will go well with fish . . . from the Loir.

Pascal Janvier, La Minée, 72340 Ruillé-sur-Loir, tel. 02.43.44.29.65, fax 02.43.79.25.25 by appt.

JEAN-JACQUES MAILLET 1999*

☐ 3 ha 13,000 30–49 F

When he settled in Ruillé-sur-Loir in 1972, Jean-Jacques Maillet intended to farm pigs, but he finally chose to replant his grandfather's vines instead. Lucky for us that he did. Bright, very floral, his 99 Jasnières offers an interesting balance. Exotic hints are perceptible on the palate right up to the finish, which is beautiful.

Jean-Jacques Maillet, La Paquerie, 72340 Ruillé-sur-Loir, tel. 02.43.44.47.45, fax 02.43.44.35.30 by appt.

Montlouis

This appellation of 1,000 ha (2,470 acres) of vines including 400 (988 acres) in the AOC Montlouis, is bounded by the Loire to the north, the forest of Amboise to the east and the Cher to the south. The flinty clay soils, with sandy overlays in places, are planted with Chenin (Pineau de la Loire) and produce lively white wines of considerable finesse; they can be dry or sweet, still or sparkling. In 1999 16,103 hl (425,119 gal), including 8,209 (216,717 gal) of sparkling wine, were produced. The dry wines are aged in bottle in tufa cellars, and can be kept for a good ten years.

DOM. AURORE DE BEAUFORT

Brut

○ 3 ha 15,000 30–49 F

The Moyers are the descendants of a noble old Touraine family, the Scourion de Beauforts. Aurore, their daughter, gave her name to the estate, which covers more than 7 ha (17 acres) on the heights of Saint-Martin-le-Beau. This traditional-method *brut* will whet the appetites of the tourists who come to stay in Marie-Claude Moyer's *chambres d'hôte*. The bubbles are light, the first impression is one of roundness, and the aromas of brioche and flowers have a positive presence. An afternoon wine, after a tiring journey, for example.

Jean-Marie Moyer, 23, rue des Caves, 37270 Saint-Martin-le-Beau, tel. 02.47.50.61.51, fax 02.47.50.27.56, e-mail aurore.de.beaufort@wanadoo.fr ev. day except Sun. 8am–8pm

PATRICE BENOIT Sec 1998

☐ 1 ha 2,000 20–29 F

Patrice Benoît, who created this small vineyard in 1985 by amalgamating several plots belonging to different owners, swears by traditional methods. He has made this nice wine, rich in flavour and body and a good example of its type. The nose is a little closed, but a lovely youthful character with honey notes is evident on the palate. This would go really well with Touraine *charcuterie*.

Patrice Benoît, 3, rue des Jardins, Nouy, 37270 Saint-Martin-le-Beau, tel. 02.47.50.62.46 by appt.

DOM. DES CHARDONNERETS

Moelleux 1998

☐ 3 ha 5,000 30–49 F

Daniel Mosny has been cultivating his estate for more than 30 years. But the younger generation is also involved and has taken over

LOIRE

the 14 ha (34 acres) of vines on the banks of the Cher. This sweet wine, which was not easy for this vintage, deserves an entry in the *Guide*. A sweet initial impression, followed by a body that perfectly covers the sugars, then delicacy and a long, refreshing finish. This wine will go a fair distance.
GAEC Daniel et Thierry Mosny, 6, rue des Vignes, 37270 Saint-Martin-le-Beau, tel. 02.47.50.61.84, fax 02.47.50.61.84
ev. day 8am–7.30pm

LAURENT CHATENAY Sec 1998

☐ 1.3 ha 7,000 30–49 F

In 1996 Laurent Chatenay was 37 years old when he took over his parents' 7-ha (17-acre) estate. Equipped with a BTA in viti-oenology, he did not take this decision lightly, proof of which is this appealing Montlouis Sec, with its notes of dried fruit and toast, fresh, well balanced and with a long finish, as well as in the nicely lemony **Montlouis Demi-Sec 98**, which is also worth mentioning.
Laurent Chatenay, 41, rte de Montlouis, Nouy, 37270 Saint-Martin-le-Beau, tel. 02.47.50.65.58, fax 02.47.50.29.90, e-mail laurent.chatenay@wanadoo.fr by appt.

YVES CHIDAINE Demi-sec 1998

☐ 2 ha 10,000 30–49 F

Established in 1936, this estate is on the chalky clay soils of the Loire's northern slopes. A lively first impression, a balanced body and a good finish on the palate are the attactions of this medium-dry wine which still needs to evolve in order to achieve complete harmony.
Yves Chidaine, 2, Grande-Rue, Husseau, 37270 Montlouis-sur-Loire, tel. 02.47.50.83.72, fax 02.47.45.02.16
ev. day 8am–12 noon 2pm–7pm

FREDERIC COURTEMANCHE Sec 1998

☐ 1 ha 2,000 30–49 F

Cultivating a small 5-ha (12-acre) vineyard on the banks of the Cher, Frédéric Courtemanche is a regular in the *Guide*, which is proof of the regularity with which he produces wines of quality. This Montlouis Sec, supple and long, has just the right amount of liveliness to offer a pleasing freshness. Aromas of honey and dried fruit complement this, giving the wine an elegant character. A mention, too, for a sparkling wine: **Montlouis 97**, a good example of this appellation.
Frédéric Courtemanche, 12, rue d'Amboise, 37270 Saint-Martin-le-Beau, tel. 02.47.50.60.89 by appt.

DELETANG 1997★★

○ 2 ha 19,000 30–49 F

Four generations of Deletangs have built up this estate of more than 22 ha (54 acres) of vines, covering the siliceous slopes that lead gently down towards the Cher. South-facing, the vine stock receives generous amounts of sunshine. This traditional-method wine has

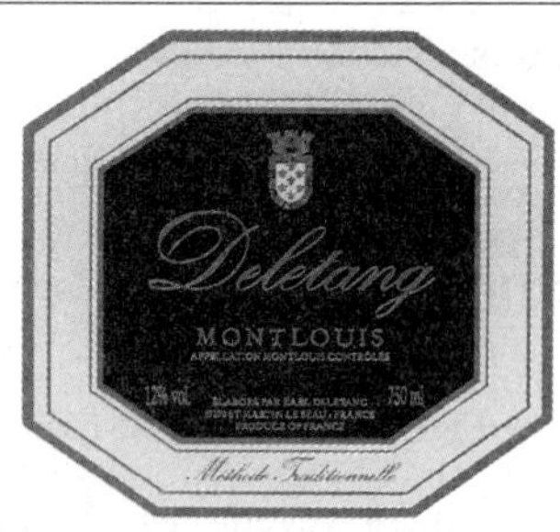

profited greatly from it. The intense nose shows finesse and elegance. It opens on the palate with suppleness and a good effervescence, with a sharp little note that balances it and gives it freshness. Have it as an apéritif, and follow it, with a meal, with a **Montlouis Sec 98**, for which the Deletang estate was awarded a 'remarkable' mention: a fullness all wrapped up in ripe fruit, which would be a good accompaniment for grilled fish.
EARL Deletang, 19, rue d'Amboise, 37270 Saint-Martin-le-Beau, tel. 02.47.50.67.25, fax 02.47.50.26.46, e-mail deletang.olivier@wanadoo.fr
by appt.

JEAN ET CHRISTOPHE GUESTAULT Pigeonnier de Fombèche Sec 1998★

☐ 3 ha 10,000 30–49 F

Jean Guestault is fond of quoting Léon Daudet, who proclaimed, speaking of wines that Ronsard had known: 'The king of white wines is that of Saint-Martin-le-Beau, whose flavour is unique . . .' Unique, too, are the wines that Jean and Christophe produce on an estate of almost 12 ha (29 acres), located between the Loire and the Cher on chalky clay soils. This one – a dry – with strongly dominant floral aromas, has good character, with perfect harmony for a vintage that was difficult to work. The long finish leaves intense notes of ripe fruit. This 98 vintage will gain even more by being kept for a time.
GAEC Jean et Christophe Guestault, Fombèche, 37270 Saint-Martin-le-Beau, tel. 02.47.50.25.52, fax 02.47.50.28.23
ev. day 8.30am–12 noon 2pm–8pm

JEAN-PAUL HABERT Demi-sec 1998★

☐ 0.4 ha 1,800 20–29 F

Before the Revolution, Jean-Paul Habert's wine cellars belonged to the de Beaufort family, among whose members was Gabrielle d'Estrées. But the cellars and their lines of barrels are not all: the 12-ha (29-acre), well-sited vineyard on the hillsides of the Cher also plays its part in the success of the wines. This one, a medium-dry, has a seductive colour glinting with gold, and its enticing nose is full of finesse and elegance. The palate confirms the attraction, thanks to its generosity, mellowness and evocation of ripe fruit. A promising future.

🔑 Jean-Paul Habert, 3, imp. des Noyers, Le Gros Buisson, 37270 Saint-Martin-le-Beau, tel. 02.47.50.26.47, fax 02.47.50.26.47 ☒ Y by appt.

ALAIN JOULIN Demi-sec 1998

☐ 1 ha 5,000 30-49 F

A nice wine from the well-sited Cher hillside that has made the reputation of Saint-Martin-le-Beau wines. The wine-maker's know-how, inspired by tradition, has produced a successful medium-dry. Whiffs of well-selected, fully ripe grapes are apparent on the nose. The palate has character, but in a light style. This is a delightful wine which should be drunk immediately.

🔑 Alain Joulin, 58, rue de Chenonceaux, 37270 Saint-Martin-le-Beau, tel. 02.47.50.28.49, fax 02.47.50.69.73 ☒ Y ev. day except Sun. 8am–12 noon 2pm–8pm

DOM. DE LA MILLETIERE

Les Haies Berthereau Liquoreux 1998*

☐ 3 ha 5,000 70-99 F

Fifteen generations of wine-makers from the same family have followed one another for more than four centuries at Domaine de la Milletière. The traditions of cultivation and wine-making are respected to the letter: working the soil, harvesting by hand with successive pickings, fermenting and maturing in deep wine cellars in oak barrels. Nothing has changed since the time of François I. The palate of this Montlouis is long, well balanced and a good example of its type. Aromas of crystallised fruit and honey revolve all around. The wine is exceptionally sweet and rich, in a year which did not really lend itself to such qualities.

🔑 Jean-Christophe Dardeau, 14, rue de la Miltière, 37270 Montlouis-sur-Loire, tel. 02.47.50.81.71, fax 02.47.50.85.25, e-mail la-milletière@epicuria.fr ☒ Y ev. day except Sun. 9am–12.30pm 2.30pm–7pm

DOM. DE LA ROCHEPINAL

Demi-sec 1998*

☐ 0.8 ha 3,500 30-49 F

Hervé Denis, who has taught at wine-making college, started out in wine-making in 1989. After a difficult start due to the frosts of 1991 and 1994, here he is now, up to cruising speed on 15 ha (37 acres) of vines planted in stony, flint-rich soil facing south. A pretty bright yellow in colour, this medium-dry wine offers a beautiful aromatic range of flowers and dry fruit. These reappear on the full, long palate, which has a perfect acid–sugar balance. A wine that will acquire more fullness and character over the years.

🔑 Hervé Denis, 4, rue de la Barre, 37270 Montlouis-sur-Loire, tel. 02.47.45.16.65, fax 02.47.50.71.70 ☒ Y by appt.

DOM. DE LA TAILLE AUX LOUPS

Cuvée Rémus Sec 1998

☐ n.c. 8,000 50-69 F

Jacky Blot is attentive to the quality of his harvests. He has produced a dry 98, a vintage which did not lend itself to sweetness or richness. Still dominated by 12 months in cask, this wine is not very expressive: oak dominates the powerful nose, while on the palate you notice beautiful flavours, a promise of things to come, but there again oakiness gets the better of the fruit (pear and pineapple). Wait quietly for it to get its stars.

🔑 Dom. de La Taille aux Loups, 8, rue des Aitres, 37270 Montlouis-sur-Loire, tel. 02.47.45.11.11, fax 02.47.45.11.14 ☒ Y ev. day 9am–7pm; cl. Sun. Nov. until Feb.

🔑 Jacky Blot

DOM. DE L'ENTRE-CŒURS

Demi-sec*

○ 1 ha 6,000 30-49 F

Alain Lelarge has made this medium-dry wine in the tradition of the appellation. Result: a straightforward wine, already a little developed, whose aromas of crystallised and exotic fruit form a rich, complex bouquet which is repeated in a long finish.

🔑 Alain Lelarge, 10, rue d'Amboise, 37270 Saint-Martin-le-Beau, tel. 02.47.50.61.70, fax 02.47.50.68.92 ☒ Y by appt.

LES ROCHES BLANCHES

Demi-sec 1998

☐ n.c. 12,000 20-29 F

This company, created in 1997 to make, mature and sell Loire wines, now only really deals with Montlouis wines. It offers a demi-sec with good performance on the palate, where it opens tenderly, and roundness and acidity are balanced within its light structure. The finish carries flavours of apple and citrus fruit. Profit today from its good disposition.

🔑 SARL Les Roches Blanches, 21, rue des Rocheroux, 37270 Montlouis-sur-Loire, tel. 02.47.50.80.70, fax 02.47.50.71.46 ☒ Y by appt.

CLAUDE LEVASSEUR Brut 1996*

○ 2.9 ha 23,000 30-49 F

Claude Levasseur now offers a very elegant traditional-method wine. Fresh and lively, with a bouquet of very ripe grapes, it is made to whet the appetite. Singled out by the jury, the **Montlouis Demi-Sec 98** was awarded a mention for its richness.

🔑 Claude Levasseur, 38, rue des Bouvineries, 37270 Montlouis-sur-Loire, tel. 02.47.50.84.53, fax 02.47.45.14.85 ☒ Y by appt.

DOM. DES LIARDS Brut 1997**

○ 10 ha 55,000 30-49 F

A very well-established house created by two brothers in 1959, and which the younger generation is taking in hand little by little. It is endowed with good equipment and superb wine cellars, and the well-kept vines cover more than 19 ha (47 acres) on the commune's southern slope, which leads gently down towards the Cher. Very experienced in making sparkling wine, Domaine des Liards can be proud of this champagne-style wine, which is remarkable from every point of view. Lovely volume in the mouth, it has freshness, density and balance, which underline the aromas of exotic and dried fruit and quince in a rare and elegant style.

Berger Frères, 70, rue de Chenonceaux, 37270 Saint-Martin-le-Beau, tel. 02.47.50.67.36, fax 02.47.50.21.13 by appt.

DOM. DE L'OUCHE GAILLARD

Demi-sec 1998*

□ 1 ha 2,800 30–49 F

This demi-sec, containing 17 g/l of residual sugar, has been beautifully made: a lot of richness, roundness and harmony. It finishes on a pleasant impression of freshness. Another star is awarded to **Montlouis Méthode Traditionnelle 97**, as evocative of brioche on the nose as it is on the palate.

SCEA Dansault-Baudeau, 94, av. George-Sand, 37700 La Ville-aux-Dames, tel. 02.47.44.36.23, fax 02.47.44.95.30 by appt.

DOM. MARNE Demi-sec*

○ n.c. 2,300 30–49 F

Each generation has participated in the development of this 8-ha (20-acre) vineyard located on the Montlouis heights. The latest, represented by Patrick Marné, has renovated the wine-making plant established in 1979. So good equipment has an important role to play in the production of this traditional-method medium-dry wine, which is very round and will accompany perfectly a sugary dessert providing you make sure there is a good balance between the sugars of the food and the wine.

Patrick Marné, 14, rte du Chapitre, 37270 Montlouis-sur-Loire, tel. 02.47.45.11.32, fax 02.47.45.07.49 ev. day except Sun. 9am–12 noon 4pm–8pm; cl. Aug.

CAVE DE MONTLOUIS-SUR-LOIRE

Cuvée réservée*

■ n.c. n.c. 30–49 F

This is a lovely cooperative undertaking endowed with efficient technical and commercial aids. It plays an important role within the appellation. Run by able technicians and oenologists, it often receives plaudits. Today, it has attracted attention with two traditional-method wines: the first is a very pretty gold, spangled with fine bubbles and emitting scents of liquorice and citrus fruit. Its initial impression is fresh and slightly acid, followed by a round, solid structure, then a long finish. The second wine is also very successful – the cellar's **Cuvée Classique**.

Cave Coop. des Prod. de vin de Montlouis-sur-Loire, 2, rte de Saint-Aignan, 37270 Montlouis-sur-Loire, tel. 02.47.50.80.98, fax 02.47.50.81.34, e-mail cave-montlouis@france-vin.com ev. day 8am–12 noon 2pm–6pm

CH. DE PINTRAY

Cuvée Tradition Demi-sec 1998

□ 5.3 ha 2,200 30–49 F

An elegant 17th- and 18th-century property in parkland: this is the serene setting of Château de Pintray. The vineyard surrounding it (6.5 ha/16-acres) is planted on the flinty clays of the Lussault banks, close to the Loire. Let yourself be charmed by this medium-dry sparkling wine, which makes a pleasant whole, well balanced and full of character. The light finish leaves an impression of harmony.

Marius Rault, Ch. de Pintray, 37400 Lussault-sur-Loire, tel. 02.47.23.22.84, fax 02.47.57.64.27 by appt.

DOM. DES SABLONS

Demi-sec 1996**

○ 0.5 ha 2,500 30–49 F

For a northerner, Gilles Verley has an unshakeable wine-maker's faith. It surfaces in this traditional-method medium-dry wine whose full, round palate makes an impression. The aromas, which are slow to appear on the nose, are compensated for by a long and elegant finish. A bottle of quality, suitable for desserts. The jury also mentioned **Méthode Traditionnelle Brut 96** for its light, well-made structure.

Gilles Verley, Les Sablons, 37270 Saint-Martin-le-Beau, tel. 02.47.50.66.35, fax 02.47.50.60.50 by appt.

DOM. DES TOURTERELLES

Demi-sec 1998

□ 1 ha 2,000 30–49 F

This 98 wine is surprising for the intensity of its floral aromas. On the palate, richness allied to a slightly fresh finish give it an original character that pleases immediately, but the wine will also take a short laying-down period.

Jean-Pierre Trouvé, 1, rue de la Gare, 37270 Saint-Martin-le-Beau, tel. 02.47.50.63.62, fax 02.47.50.63.62 by appt.

Vouvray

Vouvray's full qualities become apparent only after a long time in the bottle. These whites come from an appellation of 2,000 ha (4,940 acres) in the north of the

Loire, stretching across the wide valley of the river Brenne, with the A10 motorway cutting through its northern tip (though the TGV express train goes through a tunnel). Here Chenin (Pineau de la Loire) and Sauvignon made a total in 1999 of 49,797 hl (1,314,641 gal) of still wines, dry or sweet depending on the year, of very high quality. Fizzy or sparkling wines – 76,919 hl (2,030,662 gal) – with a high alcohol content, are also produced. The sparkling wines should be drunk young, while the still wines can be kept for a long time, giving them time to develop aromatic complexity. Fish and goat's cheese go well with some, delicate dishes or light desserts with others, and the wines also make excellent aperitifs.

ALLIAS PERE ET FILS

Brut Pétillant 1997*

○ 6 ha 18,000 30–49 F

A walled estate where, it is said, Balzac stopped to draw inspiration. Run nowadays by Daniel Allias and his son Dominique, who represents the fifth generation, it runs to 12 ha (29 acres) located in the upper reaches of the Coquette valley. This 97 is a *pétillant* with fine bubbles and scents of peach and nectarine which last throughout the tasting. The palate is round, well-balanced and long. Devoid of aggression, the wine makes an excellent apéritif.

GAEC Allias Père et Fils, 106, rue de la Vallée-Coquette, 37210 Vouvray, tel. 02.47.52.74.95, fax 02.47.52.66.38 ev. day except Sun. 8am–12 noon 2pm–7pm

CH. DES ARMUSERIES

Demi-sec Seigneur de Sècheval 1998

□ 2.15 ha 5,250 30–49 F

Château des Armuseries has been owned by the same family since the 12th century. An ancestor, Legras de Sècheval, was mayor of Tours during the Restoration and in that capacity built a canal linking the Cher and the Loire: this saved almost 20 leagues for boats transporting wine to Paris. The 98 Seigneur de Sècheval opens well on the palate and is rich and well balanced in character, all of which denote a wine of quality. In addition there is a very powerful aromatic impression. This bottle would make a successful accompaniment to shellfish terrine or a *flamiche*.

SCEA Ch. des Armuseries, Ch. des Armuseries, D. 77, 37210 Rochecorbon, tel. 02.47.52.57.38, fax 02.47.52.86.06 by appt.

JEAN-CLAUDE ET DIDIER AUBERT

Sec 1998**

□ 4 ha 18,000 30–49 F

Only a stone's throw from the Loire, the house and cellars have seen six generations of the same family. The vineyard – more than 20 ha (49 acres) – spreads out on the hillsides of the Coquette valley, safe from the river's whims. It has produced a wine which offers itself immediately on the nose, opening up scents of wild flowers and ripe fruit. On the palate, the aromatic strength persists with touches of citrus fruit, white peach and quince. The finish holds for a long moment on an impression of freshness. Overall, this is a most elegant wine, and it will enhance fish. From the same estate comes an equally memorable **Méthode Traditionnelle Brut**, which was also mentioned by the jury.

Jean-Claude et Didier Aubert, 10, rue de la Vallée-Coquette, 37210 Vouvray, tel. 02.47.52.71.03, fax 02.47.52.68.38 ev. day 8.30am–12.30pm 2pm–7pm; group by appt.

DOM. DES AUBUISIERES Brut**

○ 7 ha 50,000 30–49 F

Bernard Fouquet was awarded a *Coup de Coeur* in 1998 and three stars in 1999 for sweet wines. Now he appears afresh in the *Guide* with three lovely bottles, starting with this remarkable traditional-method wine. The jurors are still talking of it as an apéritif, each praising its balance, elegance, freshness or aromatic finesse. The jury awarded one star to **Marigny 98** (50–69F), a round, supple **sec** with a bouquet of vanilla, green apple and almond, and a mention to **Cuvée de Silex 98** (30–40F), a charming and pleasing dry wine with good aromatic intensity.

Bernard Fouquet, Dom. des Aubuisières, 37210 Vouvray, tel. 02.47.52.67.82, fax 02.47.52.67.81 by appt.

AUTHENTICITE TERROIR

Demi-sec 1998

□ 1.8 ha 6,500 50–69 F

Thierry Nérisson has just started a small wine business. Harvesting, wine-making and maturing are all undertaken at the grower's property; he follows all these operations very closely and even participates in them. This is the first wine, and it is a success. On the nose, initial vegetal scents evolve into toasted tones, an impression repeated in a well-balanced and very dense palate, where a marked oakiness quickly dominates. A rather atypical style that will find its admirers.

Thierry Nérisson, 1, rue des Hautes-Gâtinières, 37210 Rochecorbon, tel. 02.47.52.53.46, fax 02.47.52.53.46 by appt.

PASCAL BERTEAU ET VINCENT MABILLE Sec 1998

□ 1 ha n.c. 30–49 F

Two young wine-makers who joined together and amalgamated their parents'

LOIRE

farms in 1990. They benefited initially from the retirement of one of their neighbours and now run an estate of close on 20 ha (49 acres). Their know-how finds its expression in this powerful dry wine, round and well-balanced, based on fine-quality grapes, and with good laying-down potential. Two other wines from the estate were awarded the same marks: an aromatic **Demi-Sec 98** and a refreshing **Méthode Traditionnelle Brut**.
GAEC BM, Vaugondy, 37210 Vernou-sur-Brenne, tel. 02.47.52.03.43,
fax 02.47.52.03.43 by appt.

JEAN-PIERRE BOISTARD
Sec 1998★★

□ 0.5 ha 3,000 30–49 F

With an area of 10 ha (25 acres), Jean-Pierre Boistard's vineyard spreads over the hillsides dominating broad stretches of the Loire and so receives an incomparable amount of sunshine, ideal conditions for the production of quality wines. This one is remarkable for its aromas of liquorice, toast and dried fruit. The palate, with its supple first impression, its substance and elegance marked by great freshness, confirms its class. The finish leaves an impression of hazelnut and apricot. A wine of character that will hold its own with cheese. Also from the estate, a fine, elegant **Méthode Traditionnelle Cuvée Prestige 96 Brut** was mentioned by the jury.
Jean-Pierre Boistard, 216, rue Neuve,
37210 Vernou-sur-Brenne,
tel. 02.47.52.18.73, fax 02.47.52.19.95
by appt.

BONGARS Demi-sec 1998

□ 1.2 ha 8,000 30–49 F

Bernard Bongars having retired, it is his wife and daughter who manage this 12-ha (49-acre) estate built up over the years on the hillsides of the Brenne valley. Their 98 is a fairly mineral wine shot through by flavours of plum. With its power, roundness and balance, and taking the vintage into account, it is an entirely honest sweet wine. It could be served with plum tart.
EARL Bongars, 232, coteau de Venise,
37210 Noizay, tel. 02.47.52.11.64,
fax 02.47.52.05.73 by appt.

DOM. BOURILLON-DORLEANS
Moelleux 1998

□ 2 ha 13,000 30–49 F

Cultivating 20 ha (49 acres) of vines, Frédéric Bourillon is an enterprising young wine-grower who has greatly increased his export sales. The majority of his wines have been siphoned away to the UK, United States and Germany. This sweet wine will please for its fruit accented with verbena, lemon and liquorice, and its balance of acids and sugars. Its lovely depth of fruit gives it a full-bodied finish. The estate also produces a **Méthode Traditionnelle 96 Cuvée Hélène Dorléans** which will really whet your appetite. This bottle was also considered worthy of note by the jury.
Frédéric Bourillon, 30 bis, rue de Vaufoynard, 37210 Rochecorbon,
tel. 02.47.52.83.07, fax 02.47.52.82.19 by appt.

MARC BREDIF Brut★

○ n.c. 60,000 50–69 F

Marc Brédif's establishments have been preparing sparkling wines since 1893. They were even the initiators in 1920 of *Pétillant*, a sparkling Vouvray, where pressure in the bottle is only half as high as it is in the traditional method. Nevertheless, the wine he has made is one from the latter category. This *brut* is seductive in the finesse of its approach, with its light, regular bubbles and its floral, slightly minerally nose. The palate is perfectly balanced between liveliness, which gives it a fresh aspect, and vinosity. The finish evokes white flowers. We will be asking for it again ... A *sec*, intense and structured on the palate, **Vigne Blanche 98**, was awarded the same mark.
Marc Brédif, 87, quai de la Loire,
37210 Rochecorbon, tel. 02.47.52.50.07,
fax 02.47.52.53.41, e-mail
bredif.loire@wanadoo.fr ev. day
except Sun. 9am–12.30pm 2pm–6pm
de Ladoucette

YVES BREUSSIN Brut★

○ 3 ha 15,000 30–49 F

Father and son work in tandem to run this 11-ha (27-acre) estate at the edge of the Vaugondy valley. Once again it is a traditional-method wine that brings them to the forefront. A soft yellow, it has notes of lime tree and lilac. Although not very bubbly, the wine gives a sweet, lingering first impression on the palate and finishes on fine, elegant notes. This *brut* is off-dry.
GAEC Yves et Denis Breussin,
Vaugondy, 37210 Vernou-sur-Brenne,
tel. 02.47.52.18.75, fax 02.47.52.13.66
by appt.

VIGNOBLES BRISEBARRE Brut★

○ 8 ha 10,000 30–49 F

A large vineyard on prime Vouvray slopes and time-consuming professional responsibilities occupy wine-maker Philippe Brisebarre. These do not prevent him from taking care of his wine production, as witnessed by this traditional-method *brut* with its yellow colour, intense fruity nose, and supple opening on the palate, where its fruity character returns insistently. A cork you will draw with pleasure.
Philippe Brisebarre, la Vallée-Chartier,
37210 Vouvray, tel. 02.47.52.63.07,
fax 02.47.52.65.59 ev. day except Sun.
8am–12.30pm 2pm–7.30pm; group by appt.

DOM. GEORGES BRUNET
Sec 1998★★

□ 1 ha 3,000 30–49 F

Georges Brunet cultivates 11 ha (27 acres) on the hillsides bordering the Coquette valley. 'Lively, fruity, full of vigour, gold throughout, and with a tremendous freshness', is how

he defines Vouvray. The one he has made corresponds to his definition: an expressive nose of lime tree and vanilla, and a palate which is round, well structured and supple at the same time, and which leaves a long impression of freshly picked green apple. A dry Vouvray to go with grilled fish.
Georges Brunet, 12, rue de la Croix-Mariotte, 37210 Vouvray, tel. 02.47.52.60.36, fax 02.47.52.75.38 by appt.

CHAMPALOU Brut 1998*

○ 4 ha 24,000 30–49 F

Here is Didier Champalou, in the *Guide* again and in a good position with three wines. But the one that is foremost this year is a traditional-method wine. The bubbles are fine and are quite distinctive against the wine's yellow colour. The nose hints of ripe fruit, quince and apricot. Supple on first impression, a pronounced fruity character reappears on the palate. A touch of the terroir gives personality to the wine. **Cuvée des Fondraux 98 en Demi-Sec** is awarded one star (50–69F), while **Champalou Sec 98** is mentioned for its palate, which combines freshness and roundness.
Champalou, 7, rue du Grand-Ormeau, 37210 Vouvray, tel. 02.47.52.64.49, fax 02.47.52.67.99 by appt.

DOM. CHAMPION Sec 1998

□ n.c. 3,500 30–49 F

Here is a well-knit team of father and son running an estate of 13 ha (32 acres) endowed with deep wine cellars where the yeasts work slowly, at a low temperature, to produce wines of great finesse. This one, very expressive on the nose with its notes of toast, flowers and vanilla, reveals a lovely initial freshness on the palate, followed by a solid structure, the toastiness, even impressions of coffee, appearing again. A bottle for seafood. The jury also gave a mention to **Méthode Traditionnelle 96, Réserve de l'An 2000** for its balance and lightness.
GAEC Champion, 57, Vallée-de-Cousse, 37210 Vernou-sur-Brenne, tel. 02.47.52.02.38, fax 02.47.52.05.69 ev. day except Sun. 8am–12.30pm 2pm–7pm

DOM. DU CLOS DES AUMONES

Demi-Sec 1998

□ 2 ha 12,000 30–49 F

This 15-ha (37-acre) estate is on the prime slopes of Rochecorbon, the first village of this appellation that you reach coming from Tours. The chalky clay soil generally gives character to the wine. This one does not show it excessively, owing to its vintage, but harmoniously blends freshness and roundness augmented by grilled, brioche flavours. To prepare your palate before a meal.
Philippe Gaultier, 10, rue Vaufoynard, 37210 Rochecorbon, tel. 02.47.54.69.82, fax 02.47.42.62.01 by appt.

MAISON DARRAGON

Demi-sec Le Haut des Ruettes 1998

□ 2 ha 5,000 30–49 F

Maison Darragon is a good example of family continuity: 'seriousness and tradition' could be its motto. This wine opens freshly on the palate, and its flavour gives it a certain roundness. Its bouquet evokes crystallised fruit, apricot and apple. A successful wine which would make a good accompaniment to *blanquette de veau*.
Maison Darragon, 34, rue de Sanzelle, 37210 Vouvray, tel. 02.47.52.74.49, fax 02.47.52.64.96 by appt.

JEAN-FRANCOIS DELALEU

Sec Clos de Chaillemont 1998

□ 1.5 ha 6,000 30–49 F

Jean-François and Sylvie Delaleu organise reconstructions of old-time harvests with wooden pails, wicker baskets, large casks, horses, carts and period costumes, which amuses the young and quickens the hearts of their elders. This medium-dry will captivate lovers of Vouvray *à l'ancienne* with its aromas of vanilla and quince, its palate full of exotic flavours sustained by a good solid fruit and its stamp of old oak: tradition right to the end!
Jean-François et Sylvie Delaleu, la Vallée-Chartier, 37210 Vouvray, tel. 02.47.52.63.23, fax 02.47.52.69.27 by appt.

MICHEL DUBRAY Brut 1998*

○ 1 ha 6,000 30–49 F

The commune of Vernou is the largest in the Vouvray area. Some of its vineyards dominate the broad stretches of the Loire, while others cover the slopes of valleys that run into the Brenne, a tributary. Michel Dubray's vineyard is in this latter part, on a lovely plateau bathed in sunshine. This location is reflected in this champagne-style wine, which combines quince and dried fruit on the nose. Well balanced, the palate is at first very supple, followed by a return of the same fruity flavours, and the finish, long and lingering, is marked by a pleasing little liveliness. A wine destined by its freshness and aromatic density to be an apéritif.
Michel Dubray, 18, La Rauderie, 37210 Vernou-sur-Brenne, tel. 02.47.52.04.22 ev. day except Sun. 8am–12 noon 2pm–8pm; cl. Aug.

LUC DUMANGE

Brut Cuvée pour l'an 2000 1997

○ 1 ha 8,000 50–69 F

The 'Vignerie du Clos de l'Epinay', another vineyard surrounded by walls, may have belonged to the Duke of Choiseul. The dwelling has 15th-century dormer windows which feature Saint James's cockleshell (a symbol of pilgrimage to Santiago de Compostela in Spain). In fact, Vouvray was a stage on the pilgrims' route. The 17-ha (42-acre) vineyard, on the best slopes of the Loire, has produced this wine for the year 2000. Of a fairly dense straw-yellow colour, it is light on the nose with hints of pears. On the palate, the lightness reappears with fruit and a sugary touch evolving towards a slightly fresh finish. A rather charming **Sec 98** gained a similar mark from the jury.

Luc Dumange, Dom. du Clos de L'Epinay, L'Epinay, 37210 Vouvray, tel. 02.47.52.61.90, fax 02.47.52.71.31, e-mail ldumange@terre-net.fr ☒ Y by appt.

REGIS FORTINEAU

Demi-sec Pétillant 1998

○ 1 ha 5,000 30–49 F

Régis Fortineau offers a *pétillant* Vouvray. It is becoming less and less common, and that is a pity because *pétillant*, with half the pressure in the bottle of a traditional-method wine, enables the fruit to be shown off to better advantage, whereas otherwise it is sometimes flattened by a strong presence of carbon dioxide. But that's the way it goes, the consumer does love to pop the cork! This wine is a good example of its type because of its fruity bouquet. Full and round, it gives an impression of youthfulness which confers on it a pleasant thirst-quenching quality.

Régis Fortineau, 4, rue de la Croix-Mariotte, 37210 Vouvray, tel. 02.47.52.63.62, fax 02.47.52.69.97 ☒ Y ev. day except Sun. 9am–7pm

JEAN-PIERRE FRESLIER

Brut Réserve★★

○ 5 ha 15,000 30–49 F

'Finally, a true traditional-method wine of the terroir!' commented the jury. We have to say that nothing is missing: bright golden-yellow colour, a well-developed nose of ripe, almost crystallised fruit, dense *mousse* and above all a rich, supple palate that lingers almost to infinity. The terroir carries you away on a cloud of fine bubbles to the seventh heaven of ardent Vouvray admirers. Two stars as well for a most beautifully turned out *sec*. Full of quince and ripe pear, this **98** is representative of the vintage without any doubt.

Jean-Pierre Freslier, 92, rue de la Vallée-Coquette, 37210 Vouvray, tel. 02.47.52.76.61, fax 02.47.52.78.65 ☒ Y ev. day 8.30am–12.30pm 2pm–8pm

DOM. GANGNEUX★

○ 7 ha 50,000 30–49 F

Gérard Gangneux cultivates traditions. 'You don't force nature; you help it and direct it.' He sees his efforts rewarded by this traditional-method wine with light bubbles and a fine, elegant *mousse*. An impression of brioche and stewed apple gives its bouquet a distinction which reappears on the palate. A bottle which would honour guests invited for apéritifs. The estate has also been awarded a star for a fresh *sec* dominated by lemon and grapefruit.

Gérard Gangneux, 1, rte de Monnaie, 37210 Vouvray, tel. 02.47.52.60.93, fax 02.47.52.67.66 ☒ Y ev. day except Sun. 8am–12 noon 2pm–7pm

DOM. SYLVAIN GAUDRON

Demi-sec 1998★★

□ 0.5 ha 3,000 30–49 F

Rue Neuve at Vernou would have been travelled long ago by Joan of Arc. It follows a valley lined with wine cellars set up in old quarries, which provided stone to build the châteaux of the Loire. Those of Gilles Gaudron, Sylvain's son, who has been running the estate since 1993, date from the 13th century and are very impressive. It is here that this medium-dry wine was raised, honey and brioche on the nose and a wide-awake palate, generous with flavours of apricot and over-ripe grapes. A wine that would show fruit tarts to good advantage. The same wine-maker gained a star for a **Sec 98** with notes of almond and praline, and a mention for a **Méthode Traditionnelle 97 Brut**, fresh on the palate.

EARL Dom. Sylvain Gaudron, 59, rue Neuve, 37210 Vernou-sur-Brenne, tel. 02.47.52.12.27, fax 02.47.52.05.05 ☒ Y by appt.

Gilles Gaudron

JEAN-PIERRE GILET Pétillant★★

○ 2 ha 10,000 30–49 F

The Abbey of Marmoutier, which maintained a large vineyard, held the manor of Parçay. The monks planted their vines there, knowing the suitability of its soils for wine-growing. Jean-Pierre Gilet has turned this thousand-year-old practice to his advantage in preparing his quality wines. His medium-dry *pétillant* is remarkable. A brilliant yellow, with a persistent 'cordon' of bubbles, it gives off a series of toasted notes, of exotic fruit and grapes. Its fine bubbles and its fruity development on the palate enchanted the jury. A well-made wine, of a well-balanced medium-dry type, to serve with fruit tart. Jean-Pierre Gilet's **Méthode Traditionnelle Brut** (one star) should be drunk as an apéritif.

Jean-Pierre Gilet, 5, rue de Parçay, 37210 Parçay-Meslay, tel. 02.47.29.12.99, fax 02.47.29.07.96 ☒ Y by appt.

DOM. GUERTIN BRUNET Sec 1998★

□ 1.5 ha 4,000 30–49 F

Natural yeasts, fermentation in a stainless-steel vat, nothing but the best on this 12-ha (29-acre) estate. This brilliant pale wine is fairly expressive, but its roundness astonished the Vouvray Sec jury. It is nevertheless pleasing, well balanced and very easy to drink.

Gérard Guertin , 24, rue de la Croix-Mariotte, 37210 Vouvray,
tel. 02.47.52.77.77, fax 02.47.52.65.13
Y ev. day 9.45–7.30pm

DANIEL JARRY Sec 1998

0.4 ha 2,400 20-29 F

A 10-ha (25-acre) vineyard on the heights of the Coquette valley, one of the best terroirs of the Vouvrillon, can yield only good things. That is the case with this dry wine, supple, round and fruity, which would make your day if you drank it with Touraine *charcuterie*.

Daniel Jarry, 99, rue de la Vallée-Coquette, 37210 Vouvray,
tel. 02.47.52.78.75, fax 02.47.52.67.36
Y ev. day 8am–7pm; groups by appt.

DOM. DE LA CROIX DES VAINQUEURS Brut 1998*

7 ha 24,000 30-49 F

The Victors' Cross, or the 'Vingt Coeurs', if you believe the legend which has it as a meeting place of a gallant hunt, consists of 12 ha (29 acres) of vines. You are welcomed in the proprietor's forebears' home, excavated from the living rock and converted in 1740. Here you will find this pale yellow traditional-method wine, brilliant with glints of green and fine bubbles. The scents on the nose recall dried fruit, while on the palate the bouquet is approaching ripe fruit. The attack is lively, and vitality then balances itself with the *dosage*; the wine lingers on the finish with a note of freshness. A nice wine in a bottle with a picture of a little Bacchus.

Francis Denis, 6, rue de la Bergeonnerie, 37210 Chançay, tel. 02.47.52.23.31, fax 02.47.52.23.31 Y by appt.

DOM. DE LA GALINIERE
Brut Cuvée Clément 1997*

5 ha 37,000 30-49 F

Renovated buildings of traditional design and a functional winery are surrounded by 16 ha (39 acres) at this domaine. Pascal Delaleu uses slow fermentations and leaves his sparkling wines on slats for more than two years. This is reflected in this traditional-method wine, round, well balanced and finishing well. Its evident *dosage* will disappoint lovers of real *brut* but will delight others.

EARL Dom. de La Galinière, Vallée-de-Cousse, 37210 Vernou-sur-Brenne,
tel. 02.47.52.15.92, fax 02.47.52.19.50
Y by appt.

DOM. DE LA GAVERIE Brut

1.2 ha 6,000 30-49 F

Domaine de la Gaverie has been in the family since 1850. Nowadays it covers 17 ha (42 acres), with one part next to the Loire, on the best slopes of Rochecorbon. The plots are harvested separately, as they are variously suited to produce dry, medium-dry or sweet wines. The grapes for sparkling wines are picked over the entire estate, chosen for their lightness and aromatic finesse. This traditional-method wine has a beautiful lemony colour glinting with green. Aromas of bread and flowers make the nose pleasing. Lively on the palate, with lots of sparkle, suppleness takes over and gives an impression of harmony. A little lemony note is still there.

GAEC de La Pinsonnière, 13, rue de la Pinsonnière, 37210 Parçay-Meslay,
tel. 02.47.29.14.43, fax 02.47.29.14.43
Y by appt.

Philippe et Vincent Gasnier

JEAN-PIERRE LAISEMENT
Demi-sec 1998

2.1 ha 9,820 30-49 F

Jean-Pierre Laisement has a tasting room where enthusiasts discover his output under the benevolent gaze of Saint Vincent, represented in the centre of a stained-glass window. Here they can drink a wine that is authentic both in its richness and its capacity to develop well. But its freshness urges you to appreciate this 98 wine now, in order not to lose anything of its exotic fruit aromas. **Méthode Traditionnelle 97 Brut** from the same estate also earns a mention.

Jean-Pierre Laisement, 15 et 22, Vallée-Coquette, 37210 Vouvray,
tel. 02.47.52.74.47, fax 02.47.52.65.03
Y ev. day 8am–12.30pm 1.30pm–7pm; Sat. Sun. by appt.

CLOS LA LANTERNE
Sec Cuvée Hadrien 1998**

2 ha 8,000 30-49 F

Wines have been produced at La Châtaigneraie since 1669. The Gautiers have been here since then, and eight generations of wine-makers have succeeded one another on the estate, which now covers almost 16 ha (39 acres). The walled vineyard of La Lanterne, virtually entirely on tuffeau soil, dominates the Loire. It does not escape a single ray of sunshine. It has yielded a wine matured for 12 months whose nose, finely flavoured with vanilla, combines white peaches and praline. The initial impression is fresh, then round, and then aromas of pear, lime tree and once again vanilla appear. With a lovely length, the finish reveals an oaky touch. From the same estate, the jury mentioned a **Méthode Traditionnelle** (champagne style) with a winey character and **Domaine de la Châtaigneraie 97**.

Benoît Gautier, Dom. de La Châtaigneraie, 37210 Rochecorbon,
tel. 02.47.52.84.63, fax 02.47.52.84.65,
e-mail info@vouvraygautier.com Y by appt.

DOM DE LA MABILLIERE
Sec Les Hautbois 1998***

n.c. 900 70-99 F

The proprietors of Domaine de la Mabillière have always been supporters of traditional growing methods and products: Bordeaux mixture, sulphur and mechanical cultivation. Of course, pesticides and herbicides are banned. It is possibly to this return to basics that we owe this exceptional white

LOIRE

wine. The colour is brilliant, bordering on lemon-yellow; the nose opens up scents of vanilla and ripe fruit. After a supple initial impression, on the palate the wine has a pleasant freshness and lovely balance. A sensation of quince and pear appears, prolonged in a charming finish. A superb Vouvray in spite of a difficult year. A good accompaniment to fish.

GAEC Dom. de La Mabillière, 16, rue Anatole-France, 37210 Vernou-sur-Brenne, tel. 02.47.52.10.03, fax 02.47.52.14.98, e-mail domaine-de-la-mabilliere@wanadoo.fr Y by appt.

DOM. DE LA POULTIERE

Brut 1997★

○ 1.5 ha 14,000 30–49 F

With 30 years' experience and a 17-ha (42-acre) vineyard on the best slopes of Vernou, Michel Pinon has no difficulty in succeeding with his traditional-method wines, more especially as he matures them for almost two years on slats. This one has an abundance of bubbles, fine and elegant, which release scents of honey and fruit. The first impression on the palate is lively, but a good roundness quickly takes over, making a harmonious whole. A *brut*, with a fair level of *dosage* which will please delicate palates.

Michel Pinon, 29, rte de Châteaurenault, 37210 Vernou-sur-Brenne, tel. 02.47.52.15.16, fax 02.47.52.07.07 ☑ Y ev. day except Sun. 8am–12.30pm 2pm–7.30pm

DOM. DE LA ROULETIERE Brut

○ 9 ha 55,000 30–49 F

Domaine de la Rouletière is between the Abbey of Marmoutier, founded in 372, and the fortified farm of Meslay, built in 1220. This is an area laden with history where vines and wines have their place. The superb wine cellars, more than 350 m (381 yd) long, are hollowed out of the rock on two levels and have an indisputable role in contributing to quality. The wine is kept there for 24 months on slats. This traditional-method wine has a charming yellow colour with glints of green and a very expressive nose of white flowers and dried leaves. The supple, fresh palate lengthens out in a beautiful balance. A marked *brut*, very pleasant. Also mentioned by the jury was a **Sec 98**, which was also prepared in these deep cellars.

SCEA Gilet, 20, rue de la Mairie, 37210 Parçay-Meslay, tel. 02.47.29.14.88, fax 02.47.29.08.50, e-mail scea.gilet@wanadoo.fr ☑ Y ev. day except Sun. 10am–12 noon 2pm–7pm

DOM. DES LAURIERS Brut 1998

○ 0.9 ha 5,500 30–49 F

At the age of three, Laurent Kraft followed his grandfather into the vines! Having started with a quarter of a hectare (0.6 acres) in 1992, he now cultivates 14 ha (34 acres), well positioned on the sunny hillsides at the edge of the Loire at Vouvray. He makes quite an expressive traditional-method wine, complex and supple, which gives the impression of havin already developed. A *brut* which will find i admirers.

Laurent Kraft, 29, rue du Petit-Coteau, 37210 Vouvray, tel. 02.47.52.61.82, fax 02.47.52.61.82 ☑ Y ev. day 8am–7pm

CAVE DES PRODUCTEURS DE LA VALLEE COQUETTE

Brut Tête de Cuvée★

○ n.c. 200,000 30–4

Established in the heart of the Coquett valley, this cooperative is one of the jewels i the AOC's crown. With its comprehensiv equipment, technicians who are full acquainted with the preparation of qualit wines, and good reception facilities, it con tributes to the reputation of Vouvray. It strong point is the production of traditional method wines, as witnessed by this Tête d Cuvée. Pale yellow with flashes of green, it i beaded with fine bubbles. The nose, with it evocations of fresh fruit, flowers and honey, i very typical of the appellation. A lively palate elegant and harmonious, completes this pic ture of a most successful Vouvray.

Cave des producteurs de Vouvray, 38, Vallée-Coquette, 37210 Vouvray, tel. 02.47.52.75.03, fax 02.47.52.66.41, e-mail cp.vouvray@wanadoo.fr ☑ Y ev. day 9am–12 noon 2pm–6.30pm

DOM. LE CAPITAINE

Demi-sec Cuvée Millenium 1998

□ 2 ha 10,000 30–49 F

The two Le Capitaine brothers get along perfectly together as they pilot this 'vessel' of 18 ha (44 acres) of beautiful vines situated mostly on the very best slopes. Having started with nothing in 1989, they have built up their estate through relentless hard work. Their Cuvée Millennium is a nice wine, a good example of its vintage, where a lack of body is compensated for by an attractive lightness, rendering it subtle and elegant. A finish of mild tobacco gives it a hint of distinction.

Alain et Christophe Le Capitaine, 23, rue du Cdt-Mathieu, 37210 Rochecorbon, tel. 02.47.52.53.86, fax 02.47.52.85.23 ☑ Y by appt.

DOM. LE PEU DE LA MORIETTE

Demi-sec 1998★★

□ 12 ha 40,000 50–69

Jean-Claude Pichot and his son Christophe run a lovely estate of 27 ha (67 acres) well placed on the best Vouvray slopes, not far from the Loire. The winery is made up of quaint cellars hollowed out of the rock in three layers; they harbour a 15th-century winepress. This is the setting that produced this sweet laying-down wine. Its straw colour sets the tone. The powerful nose of citrus fruit and undergrowth, and the palate, with its strong, surprising attack which lingers in unaccustomed density, are good omens for the future. The lusciousness is characteristic of a rich intensity where the sugar is well harmonised. A very beautiful wine from a difficult year. In addition, the **Méthode Traditionnelle Brut Domaine Coteau de la Biche 98** (30–40F), where the components balance well, was mentioned by the jury.

🔑 EARL Jean-Claude et Christophe Pichot, 32, rue de la Bonne-Dame, 37210 Vouvray, tel. 02.47.52.62.55, fax 02.47.52.66.59 ☒ 🍷 by appt.

BERNARD MABILLE Pétillant 1993

○ 2 ha n.c. 30–49 F

Established for more than 40 years, Bernard Mabille is a man of experience. Working a wine and guiding it through its second fermentation by letting it mature on slats for many months no longer hold any secrets for him. With its yellow colour, his *pétillant* already reveals a certain development. This first impression is confirmed on the palate, with flavours going from clove to honey, passing through peach and citrus fruit, with a little touch of freshness on the finish. An unexpected bottle: do not delay drinking it.

🔑 Bernard Mabille, 7, Vallée-de-Vaugondy, 37210 Vernou-sur-Brenne, tel. 02.47.52.10.94, fax 02.47.52.07.32 ☒ 🍷 by appt.

DANIEL MABILLE Brut

○ n.c. n.c. 30–49 F

A traditional-method wine which is already well developed, doubtless stemming from a reserve wine. The result is interesting: a brilliant yellow colour, aromas of dried fruit and a supple initial impression on the palate accompanied by good roundness that lingers pleasantly.

🔑 Daniel Mabille, 25, rue de la Vallée-Chartier, 37210 Vouvray, tel. 02.47.52.75.22 ☒ 🍷 by appt.

FRANCIS MABILLE Sec 1998

□ 0.5 ha 3,492 30–49 F

Francis Mabille represents the fourth generation to work this small family estate of 12 ha (30 acres). Respect for tradition, and also the chalky clay soil, have turned this 98 into quite a structured wine, marked by the terroir. Its characteristic Chenin bouquet is an additional bonus. A powerful bottle to lay down.

🔑 Francis Mabille, 17, Vallée-de-Vaugondy, 37210 Vernou-sur-Brenne, tel. 02.47.52.01.87, fax 02.47.52.19.41 ☒ 🍷 by appt.

DOM. DU MARGALLEAU Brut 1997

○ 2 ha 6,000 30–49 F

Bruno and Jean-Michel Pieaux are two brothers who have been running their 25-ha (62-acre) family estate since 1995. Its vines are distributed over the slopes of the valleys that run into the Brenne, a tributary of the Loire. They offer a traditional-method *brut*, very elegant on the nose with its perfumes of ripe fruit. Initially supple, the palate reveals itself to be round and generally well balanced. Drink this on a lovely day, at the end of the afternoon. A **Méthode Traditionnelle 97 Demi-Sec** of the same medium-dry type also gained a mention by the jury.

🔑 GAEC Bruno et Jean-Michel Pieaux, Vallée de Vaux, rue du Clos-Baglin, 37210 Chançay, tel. 02.47.52.97.27, fax 02.47.52.25.51 ☒ 🍷 by appt.

METIVIER Sec 1998

□ 0.5 ha 2,500 30–49 F

Vincent Métivier has been taking over the reins of the estate little by little since his mother assumed sole charge over ten years ago. Their 13 ha (32 acres) on the Vernou hillsides which dominate the broad expanses of the Loire are an asset that this family team turns to good account. Pale yellow glinting with green, its dry wine charms with its lovely touches of apple, almond and hazelnut. Aromatic sensations, after a clean opening, evolve towards white peach, pear and citrus fruit. A little carbon dioxide teases the palate. A bottle for seafood.

🔑 GAEC Eliane et Vincent Métivier, 51, rue Neuve, 37210 Vernou-sur-Brenne, tel. 02.47.52.01.95, fax 02.47.52.06.01 ☒ 🍷 by appt.

MAISON MIRAULT Brut

○ n.c. 20,000 30–49 F

Owning immense and well-equipped wine cellars tunnelled into the rock, the Maison Mirault has made a speciality out of preparing sparkling wines. It attaches a great deal of importance to the selection of the vines and must; a strictness to which it certainly owes these two mentions in the *Guide*. The first goes to a *brut* whose floral nose mingles with a mineral touch, and which is lively and impressive due to its abundant *mousse*; the second, to a **Demi-Sec**, expressive on the nose, which will improve in the cellar. It would make a good accompaniment to fruit tart.

🔑 Maison Mirault, 15, av. Brûlé, 37210 Vouvray, tel. 02.47.52.71.62, fax 02.47.52.60.90, e-mail maison.mirault@wanadoo.fr ☒ 🍷 ev. day 8am–12 noon 2pm–6.30pm; Sun. by appt.

CH. MONCONTOUR

Brut Cuvée Prédilection 1995★

○ 13 ha 100,000 30–49 F

Built in the 15th century and rebuilt in the 18th, this estate lives on in more than just literary memory (Balzac used it as the setting for *La Femme de Trente Ans*). It comprises more than 140 ha (346 acres) of vines and produces good-quality wines. This Cuvée Prédilection, a traditional-method wine from the 95 harvest, is interesting for its roundness and balance. Endowed with a fine bouquet, it will leave a fresh impression when drunk as an apéritif, leaving the palate ready for a more elaborate sequel. Its sister wine, also **Cuvée Prédilection** but from the 98 harvest, shines by virtue of its rich palate and its youthfulness.

🔑 Ch. Moncontour, 37210 Vouvray, tel. 02.47.52.60.77, fax 02.47.52.65.50, e-mail info@moncontour.com ☒ 🍷 by appt.

🔑 Feray

LOIRE

DOM. D'ORFEUILLES Brut 1996★

○ 2.5 ha 15,000 30–49 F

Located in the ancient outbuildings of a medieval château, Domaine d'Orfeuilles groups together almost 17 ha (42 acres) of vines. The soils, chalky clay by nature, have a strong flint element, which often gives a mineral tone to the wines – they are said to taste of gunflint – although the phenomenon is less marked in the 98 vintage. This traditional-method wine, a *brut*, is well turned out. Lively and well balanced, it leaves a sensation of finesse and elegance. Two other wines from the same producer were singled out by the jury: a nicely fruity **Méthode Traditionnelle Demi-Sec** and a **Sec**, also with a good bouquet, which evokes citrus fruit.

EARL Bernard Hérivault, La Croix-Blanche, 37380 Reugny, tel. 02.47.52.91.85, fax 02.47.52.25.01, e-mail earl.herivault@france-vin.com by appt.

VINCENT PELTIER

Pétillant brut 1996★

○ 1 ha 6,000 30–49 F

The grandfather started on half a hectare (1.2 acres) with a modest cellar. Today, his grandson cultivates 11 ha (27 acres) and has established an impressive winery: a good family history. Vincent Peltier has made a *pétillant* – which unfortunately is less and less frequent in Vouvray – endowed with a bright, limpid straw colour and with a very expressive nose mingling wax, honey and quince. It opens vigorously on the palate, followed by a lightness that develops floral notes with a slight hint of quince on the finish. A harmonious and pleasing bottle. The estate obtained an additional mention for a powerful **Sec 89** (20–29F), pleasantly full-bodied, which will be ready to drink in a few years' time.

Vincent Peltier, 41 bis, rue de la Mairie, 37210 Chançay, tel. 02.47.52.93.34, fax 02.47.52.96.98 ev. day except Sun. 8am–12.30pm 2pm–7.30pm

FRANCOIS PINON

Demi-sec Cuvée Tradition 1998★

□ 3 ha 7,000 50–69 F

Already noted for his skills, François Pinon has distinguished himself in the millennium year with a medium-dry sparkler. Certainly, different vintages don't necessarily resemble each other, but this wine is nothing to be ashamed of. On the contrary: natural and true to type, this 98 wine balances sweetness and flavour, flows over notes of honey and quince and exits the stage with elegance. Consider too a **Méthode Traditionnelle Demi-Sec**, a pleasing wine that can wait, which was mentioned by the jury.

François Pinon, 55, Vallée-de-Cousse, 37210 Vernou-sur-Brenne, tel. 02.47.52.16.59, fax 02.47.52.10.63 by appt.

DOM. DE POUVRAY Brut 1996★

○ 2 ha 3,000 30–49 F

Domaine de Pouvray spreads its rows of vines over more than 20 ha (49 acres), from the Cousse valley to that of Vaugondy. The current proprietor's great-grandfather bought it in 1884. In short, ancestral know-how is behind this traditional-method wine, with its fruitily elegant bouquet. The initial impression is supple, succeeded by a plump, well-balanced structure, with a small accent of the terroir. A bottle that could make a good apéritif. Another **Méthode Traditionnelle Demi-Sec 96** of the same make has also gained a star.

Gilbert Vincendeau, Dom. de Pouvray, 37210 Vernou-sur-Brenne, tel. 02.47.52.02.36, fax 02.47.52.09.82 by appt.

J. G. RAIMBAULT Sec 1998

□ 1 ha 1,700 30–49 F

Managed by a brother and sister, this estate has really lovely wine cellars hollowed out of the rock. They emerge on to a spiral staircase on the hillside, from which you can see a charming Loire landscape. Back in the small tasting cellar, you can sample this freshest dry wine, pleasing in its aromatic development on the palate, where stewed fruit rivals hazelnut and praline. From the same estate, two **Méthodes Traditionnelles**, one *brut* and the other *demi-sec*, were also praised for their lightness.

GAEC Raimbault, 186, coteau des Vérons, 37210 Noizay, tel. 02.47.52.00.10, fax 02.47.52.05.29 ev. day 9am–8pm; Sun. by appt.

DOM. DE VAUGONDY Sec 1998★

□ 3 ha 1000 30–49 F

The hillsides bordering the Vaugondy valley are quite steep and benefit from the best of the sunshine. Philippe Perdriaux, who runs almost 20 ha (49 acres) of vines here, produces very expressive wines that are often noted by experts. This one, a dry wine which a very lemony nose, opens powerfully and with suppleness on the palate, then develops to a harmonious roundness, leaving a most pleasing impression of citrus fruit. A nice wine with the characteristic scents of the terroir.

EARL Perdriaux, Les Glandiers, 37210 Vernou-sur-Brenne, tel. 02.47.52.02.26, fax 02.47.52.04.81 by appt.

DOM. VIGNEAU-CHEVREAU

Demi-sec 1998★★

□ 4 ha 15,000 30–49 F

Jean-Michel Vigneau runs his 23 ha (57-acre) estate biodynamically. It is on the slopes of the Brenne, a tributary of the Loire. Oceanic influences, so important for the maturity of Chenin, a late grape, thus reach as far as his vineyard. This medium-dry (green label) has clearly benefited from them. The nose is all ripe fruit and honey. On the palate, the wine opens pleasantly, followed by a light structure wrapped up in a roundness arising from well-

ripened grapes, with a fruity note of quince in the background throughout. A well-constructed wine of great class. From the same producer, we also chose a **Sec 98** (white label) and a **Méthode Traditionnelle Brut Prestige**, which each gained a star.
🔑 EARL Vigneau-Chevreau, 4, rue du Clos-Baglin, 37210 Chançay, tel. 02.47.52.93.22, fax 02.47.52.23.04
☒ Y ev. day except Sun. 8am–7pm

DOM. DU VIKING 1997*

○ 2 ha 4,000 ▮ 50–69 F

Lionel Gauthier is not from Touraine; he came here from Nantes and has excelled ever since in sparkling wines. He had a good teacher in his father-in-law, who handed the estate, now more than 12 ha (30 acres), over to him. Chenin Blanc speaks nicely in this wine. Scents of menthol, green tea and very ripe grapes open on a fresh, elegant palate, which is succeeded by a perfect balance with a profusion of white peach flavours. A wine 'to drink all night' said a member of the jury, briefly forgetting the need for moderation!
🔑 Lionel Gauthier, Melotin, 37380 Reugny, tel. 02.47.52.96.41, fax 02.47.52.24.84, e-mail viking@france-vin.com
☒ Y by appt.

Cheverny

Classified as VDQS in 1973, Cheverny proceeded to AOC in 1993. The appellation area extends a considerable way along the left bank of the Loire, from Sologne, in the Blésois, to the outskirts of Orléans. Numerous grape varieties are planted in this appellation of 400 hl (10,560 gal) of vineyards in an area of more than 2,000 ha (4,940 acres), where the *terroir* is predominantly sandy (sand on Sologne clay and the terraces of the Loire). The producers have managed to establish a Cheverny 'style' from a mixture of varieties in proportions that vary slightly depending on the terroir. In 1999 13,292 hl (350,909 gal) of red wine were produced, mainly from Gamay and Pinot Noir. They are fruity in youth, later developing an animal muskiness in harmony with the hunting traditions of the region. The Gamay rosés are dry and perfumed. The whites, of which 10,620 hl (280,368 gal) were produced in 1999, and for which a little Chardonnay is added to Sauvignon, are floral and finely made.

The decree of 26 March 1993 recognised AOC Cheverny Rouge, Rosé and Blanc.

PASCAL BELLIER 1999*

□ 9 ha 52,000 30–49 F

This brilliant, pale yellow Cheverny, green glints shimmering in the glass, is a nice wine. The fairly intense floral nose is followed by a palate of great suppleness and good balance, from the heart of which arise flavours of exotic fruit or blackcurrant. Also most successful and fruity, **Cheverny Rosé 99** unites freshness and roundness right through to an elegant finish.
🔑 Les Caves Bellier, 3, rue Reculée, 41350 Vineuil, tel. 02.54.20.64.31, fax 02.54.20.58.19 ☒ Y ev. day except Tue. Thu. Sun. 9am–12 noon 2pm–7pm

ERIC CHAPUZET 1999*

■ 5 ha 25,000 ▮ 🌡 20–29 F

Eric Chapuzet's estate – La Gardette – bears the name of an old walled vineyard belonging to the feudal Château de Fougères-sur-Bièvre, a valuable example of 15th-century military architecture. It is 2 km (1.2 miles) away from this welcoming town. Its vines are responsible for a red wine that is almost cherry-coloured. Its fruity aromas, elegant palate and tannic finesse are beguiling. **Cheverny Blanc 99** also deserves mention: a gracious, well-balanced wine.
🔑 Eric Chapuzet, La Gardette, 41120 Fougères-sur-Bièvre, tel. 02.54.20.27.21, fax 02.54.20.28.34, e-mail e.chapuzet@wanadoo.fr ☒ Y by appt.

CHESNEAU ET FILS 1999

■ 2 ha 15,000 ▮ 20–29 F

Established on about 15 ha (37 acres) of siliceous clay soils, the Chesneau estate offers a pleasant red wine from the 99 vintage. A brilliant colour, this wine draws its originality from a hint of pepper on the well-balanced palate.
🔑 EARL Chesneau et Fils, Le Bourg, 41120 Sambin, tel. 02.54.20.20.15, fax 02.54.33.21.91 ☒ Y by appt.

JEAN-MICHEL COURTIOUX 1999

◪ 2 ha 2,500 ▮ 20–29 F

Made up of equal parts of Pineau d'Aunis and Pinot Noir, this rosé has a clear salmon-pink tone. Its roundness on the palate leaves room for a pleasant freshness on the finish, well suited to crudités or *charcuterie*. Also picked out by the jury, **Cheverny Blanc 99** is a wine full of youthful vigour.
🔑 Jean-Michel Courtioux, Caves à Chitenay, 41120 Les Montils, tel. 02.54.70.42.18 ☒ Y by appt.

DOM. DU CROC DU MERLE 1999★

■ 4 ha 15,000 30–49 F

Domaine du Croc du Merle is used to being praised; its Cheverny Rouge 98 was an outstanding wine. In the 1999 vintage, the jury has once again tasted a most successful wine. The powerful nose releases aromas of red fruit and spices, while a good balance is noticeable on the palate after a clean and fresh attack. Even if Cabernet Franc represents only 5% of the combined total, it stands out in the tasting in a typical way. A star is also given to **Cheverny Rosé 99**, delicately perfumed and orangey in colour, while a mention goes to the **Blanc 99**, which draws appreciation for its bouquet of white flowers and blackcurrant.

Patrice Hahusseau, Dom. du Croc du Merle,38, rue de La Chaumette, 41500 Muides-sur-Loire, tel. 02.54.87.58.65, fax 02.54.87.02.85 ev. day 9am–7pm; Sun. 9am–12 noon; groups by appt.

DOM. DES HUARDS 1999

□ 6 ha 30,000 30–49 F

This pale yellow Cheverny has a good aromatic intensity. A note of blackcurrant buds signals the strong presence of Sauvignon in the mixture (85%), besides Chardonnay. The balance and length on the palate can be appreciated from now onwards. A red to remember is **Le Domaine du Vivier 99** from the estate of Jean-François Deniau et Fils and made by the same producers, which was mentioned by the jury.

Jocelyne et Michel Gendrier, Les Huards, 41700 Cour-Cheverny, tel. 02.54.79.97.90, fax 02.54.79.26.82 by appt.

PATRICK HUGUET 1999

■ 4 ha 14,000 20–29 F

The estate was established in 1873 by Patrick Huguet's grandfather, who started up in wine-growing by renting 2 ha (5 acres) of vines between Romorantin and Tours. At that time the plot belonged to Château de Villesavin. The **Cheverny Rouge** and **Blanc 99** were both singled out by the jury. The former is charming, with its red fruit aromas and fresh, fruity palate. The latter is distinguished by a good aromatic intensity dominated by blackcurrant buds.

GAEC Francis et Patrick Huguet, 12, rue de la Franchetière, 41350 Saint-Claude-de-Diray, tel. 02.54.20.57.36, fax 02.54.20.58.57 by appt.

DOM. DE LA DESOUCHERIE 1999★

■ 9 ha 60,000 30–49 F

Christian Tessier has attracted the jury's attention with two of his wines. **Cheverny Blanc 99** bears his name. Its pale yellow colour, with green tints, denotes careful vinification. Very successful, the red is a lovely bright ruby colour. Its fine nose offers scents of red fruit (raspberry in particular), while the palate is well balanced and brings out very evident tannins on the finish, which will enable this wine to be kept in the cellar for a year to reach its full potential.

Christian Tessier, Dom. de La Désoucherie, 41700 Cour-Cheverny, tel. 02.54.79.90.08, fax 02.54.79.22.48, e-mail christian.tessier@waika9.com by appt.

DOM. DE LA GAUDRONNIERE

Cuvée Laëtitia 1999★

□ 5 ha 20,000 30–49 F

Golden glints enliven the colour of this Cheverny, indicating the perfect maturity of the grapes, harvested on chalky soils around 20 September. The nose is exotic and the palate full and rich, with a good length. Also mentioned by the jury was **Cheverny Rouge Cuvée Elégance 99**, a well-balanced wine, pleasing with its aromas of red fruit underlined by a mineral note.

EARL Christian Dorléans, Dom. de La Gaudronnière, 41120 Cellettes, tel. 02.54.70.40.41, fax 02.54.70.38.83 by appt.

LE PETIT CHAMBORD 1999★

■ 4 ha 25,000 30–49 F

Pretty glints sparkle in the sustained red colour of this wine. While the nose still seems a little timid, aromas of ripe red fruit are conspicuous. The tannins are very supple and confer presence on the wine, together with balance on the palate. **Cheverny Blanc 99** is notable for its evocations of ripe grapes gorged with sunshine.

François Cazin, Le Petit Chambord, 41700 Cheverny, tel. 02.54.79.93.75, fax 02.54.79.27.89 by appt.

JEROME MARCADET

Cuvée de l'Orme 1999

□ 1.5 ha 10,000 20–29 F

Jérôme Marcadet represents the third generation of wine-makers to sell the wines of this estate directly; his earlier forebears used to farm the vines on behalf of other owners. This young wine-grower offers a pale yellow Cheverny with floral aromas. The palate is well balanced, developing towards a refreshing finish of lemon and mulberry.

Jérôme Marcadet, L'Orme Favras, 41120 Feings, tel. 02.54.20.28.42, fax 02.54.20.28.42 ev. day 8am–12.30pm 2pm–6pm

MARQUIS DE LA PLANTE D'OR 1999★

■ 4 ha 1,400 30–49 F

This deep-coloured red Cheverny with violet hints offers scents of redcurrant and mulberry. On the palate, it is round and well balanced. Already pleasing, you can drink it immediately, but it could also wait a few years.

Philippe Loquineau, La Demalerie, 41700 Cheverny, tel. 02.54.44.23.09, fax 02.54.44.22.16 by appt.

DOM. DE MONTCY

Cuvée Clos des Cendres 1999

□ 2.7 ha 16,000 30–49 F

A hundred years ago the vineyard of the present Montcy estate belonged to the Château de Troussay, built in the 15th century for Robert Bugy, controller of the salt store-houses. Today, it has yielded two interesting Cheverny wines. The first, with the pale colour characteristic of the vintage, offers a good balance on the palate and an apprecia-ble length. The red, **La Cuvée Louis de la Saussaye 99**, also deserves a mention for its aromatic intensity and freshness.

R. et S. Simon, 32, rte de Fougères, La Porte dorée, 41700 Cheverny, tel. 02.54.44.20.00, fax 02.54.44.21.00 by appt.

LES VIGNERONS DE MONT-PRES-CHAMBORD 1999★

□ 30 ha 200,000 30–49 F

The jury appreciated this pale yellow, green-tinted wine whose intense nose is marked by white flowers and blackcurrant buds. Well balanced on the palate, it evolves with grace through to a long and generous finish. Also successful and elegant despite a certain timidity, **Cheverny Rouge Terroir et Tradition 99** is charming with its aromas of red forest fruit.

Les Vignerons de Mont-près-Chambord, 816, la Petite-Rue, 41250 Mont-près-Chambord, tel. 02.54.70.71.15, fax 02.54.70.70.65, e-mail cavemont@club-internet.fr ev. day except Mon. Sun. 9am–12 noon 2pm–6pm

DOM. DU MOULIN 1999★

■ 1 ha 3,900 30–49 F

Sustained, intense, balanced: all these define this very successful wine, representa-tive of the appellation. Ardilles wines know how to combine their pretty forest fruit aro-mas with the flavours of fine slices of smoked ham. In the white, the choice is between two wines noted by the jury: **La Bodice 99** and the estate's **Cuvée Principale 99** (20–29F).

Hervé Villemade, Le Moulin Neuf, 41120 Cellettes, tel. 02.54.70.41.76, fax 02.54.70.37.41 ev. day 9am–12 noon 2pm–6pm

JACQUES ROBERT 1999★

◪ 0.5 ha 2,000 20F+

Harvested on the sand and gravel terraces along the Loire, this pale pink wine is made solely from Pinot Noir grapes. Delicate notes of fresh exotic fruit rise from the glass, then a silkiness caresses the palate, all the while leav-ing a pleasing impression of freshness. A distinguished Cheverny.

Jacques Robert, 2, rue de l'Aubergeon, 41350 Saint-Claude-de-Diray, tel. 02.54.20.65.11, fax 02.54.20.65.11 by appt.

DOM. SAUGER ET FILS 1999

■ n.c. 30,000 20–29 F

A sustained red, this Cheverny offers the nose a good aromatic intensity. On the palate, its tannins appear still youthful but promise to supple up during the year. While waiting, you can drink the **Cheverny Blanc 99**, also mentioned by the jury, whose aromas of exotic fruits combine well with those of boxwood.

Dom. Sauger et Fils, Les Touches, 41700 Fresnes, tel. 02.54.79.58.45, fax 02.54.79.03.35 by appt.

DOM. PHILIPPE TESSIER

Le Point du Jour 1999★★

■ 2.5 ha 10,000 30–49 F

Philippe Tessier defends the reputation of Sologne wine-growing remarkably well in his 99 vintage. The red Cheverny was saluted unanimously by the jury, who awarded him a *Coup de Coeur*. Its colour is deep red, with a fresh, clear appearance, and it delivers fine red fruit aromas. The initial impression on the palate is smooth, rich and full, and it finds a lovely echo in a silky tannic network. This is a magnificent wine which will become even better with age. And if you want something to go with goats' cheese from the region, you will have no regrets if you choose the white Cheverny **La Charbonnerie 99**, whose pale golden colour, refined floral scents, supple-ness and balance well deserve their two stars.

EARL Philippe Tessier, 3, voie de la rue Colin, 41700 Cheverny, tel. 02.54.44.23.82, fax 02.54.44.21.71 by appt.

DANIEL TEVENOT 1999

□ 1 ha 5,000 20–29 F

A walk in the Beuvron valley, to the north of Sologne, will doubtless lead you to Daniel Tévenot's 10-ha (25-acre) estate. Its winery, built on the site of an old mill, has been home for the past ten months to this pale yellow wine, a little timid on the nose but typical of the 99 vintage as regards its freshness on the palate.

Daniel Tévenot, 4, rue du Moulin-à-Vent, Madon, 41120 Candé-sur-Beuvron, tel. 02.54.79.44.24, fax 02.54.79.44.24 by appt.

Cour-Cheverny

A decree dated 24 March 1993 recognised Cour-Cheverny as a separate AOC, limited to white wines made using only the Romorantin variety. The area of production comprises the former AOS Cour-Cheverny Mont-Près-Chambord and a few surrounding communes where the variety was maintained. The *terroir* is typical of the Sologne (sand on clay). Production in 1999 totalled 2,005 hl (52,932 gal).

DOM. DE LA DESOUCHERIE 1999★

☐ 3.5 ha 23,000 ▮ 🌡 30–49 F

Christian Tessier's production is regularly represented in the *Guide*. This golden-coloured white wine is a perfect example of what one expects of a Cour-Cheverny. On the one hand, its discreet but elegant nose has floral notes, but, on the other, its fresh, well-balanced palate develops at length on flavours of grapefruit, lemon or mango. A 99 which could be kept.

🗝 Christian Tessier, Dom. de La Désoucherie, 41700 Cour-Cheverny, tel. 02.54.79.90.08, fax 02.54.79.22.48, e-mail christian.tessier@waika9.com ☑ 🍷 by appt.

DOM. DE LA GAUDRONNIERE Mûr Mûr de La Gaudronnière 1999★

☐ 1 ha 6,400 ▮ 🌡 30–49 F

Domaine de la Gaudronnière was bought in 1921 by Marie Dorléans. Nowadays, Christian cultivates 20 ha (49 acres) and has produced from one of his plots a brilliant golden wine which has surprising accents of raisins and fresh fig. Supple and balanced on the palate, this Cour-Cheverny develops a honeyed tone, accompanied by notes of almond which are a good indication of the lateness of the harvests (the end of October). A seductive 99 wine.

🗝 EARL Christian Dorléans, Dom. de La Gaudronnière, 41120 Cellettes, tel. 02.54.70.40.41, fax 02.54.70.38.83 ☑ 🍷 by appt.

DOM. DE L'AUMONIERE 1999★

☐ 3.5 ha 10,000 ▮ 🌡 30–49 F

The Cour-Cheverny walking routes might lead you to the estate of Gérard Givierge, who has produced a successful wine in the 99 vintage, of a very clear yellow glinting with green. A wine of personality, after a discreet but elegant nose, it discloses a fruity-mineral balance then proceeds to a flattering and supple finish.

🗝 Gérard Givierge, Dom. de l'Aumonière, 41700 Cour-Cheverny, tel. 02.54.79.25.49, fax 02.54.79.27.06 ☑ 🍷 ev. day 8am–12.30pm 2pm–8pm; groups by appt.

LE PETIT CHAMBORD 1999★

☐ 4.3 ha 25,000 ▮ 🌡 30–49 F

Thirty-five-year-old vines have yielded a very limpid Cour-Cheverny, which develops aromas of white flowers and honey on the nose. Its supple first impression invites you to appreciate its good development on the palate, where a mineral tone dominates. An elegant wine.

🗝 François Cazin, Le Petit Chambord, 41700 Cheverny, tel. 02.54.79.93.75, fax 02.54.79.27.89 ☑ 🍷 by appt.

DOM. DE MONTCY 1999

☐ 1.7 ha 11,500 ▮ 🌡 30–49 F

Already praised for its 98 vintage, Domaine Montcy has now made a 99 wine which is pale yellow, gleaming green, very clear but still a little timid when analysed on the nose and palate. However, delicate notes of almond, hazelnut and honey are discernible on the nose, and a taste of hawthorn in the mouth. It will be two or three years before this Cour-Cheverny reaches its full potential.

🗝 R. et S. Simon, 32, rte de Fougères, La Porte dorée, 41700 Cheverny, tel. 02.54.44.20.00, fax 02.54.44.21.00 ☑ 🍷 by appt.

LES VIGNERONS DE MONT-PRES-CHAMBORD 1999★

☐ 7 ha 50,000 ▮ 🌡 30–49 F

Golden-yellow, this wine has the characteristic scents of the local Romorantin variety, a mixture of acacia flowers and honey. Already pleasing on the palate with its initial mineral impression and its richness, it will lose its austerity and bloom fully after three years' age.

🗝 Les Vignerons de Mont-près-Chambord, 816, la Petite-Rue, 41250 Mont-près-Chambord, tel. 02.54.70.71.15, fax 02.54.70.70.65, e-mail cavemont@club-internet.fr ☑ 🍷 ev. day except Mon. Sun. 9am–12 noon 2pm–6pm

Coteaux du Vendômois AOVDQS

This unique appellation, between Vendôme and Montoire, produces the highly distinctive Vin Gris de Pineau d'Aunis, noted for its very pale colour and peppery aromas. The whites, made from Chenin, resemble those from the neighbouring AOC Coteaux de Loire and Jasnières, which are grown on similar soils.

The range of red wines is a newer development, in response to consumer demand. The delicately spicy liveliness of the Pineau d'Aunis is combined with Gamay for smoothness, and either improved in finesse by including Pinot Noir or in tannin by using Cabernet.

On average, production is 10,000 hl (264,0000 gal). Visitors can enjoy walking by the Loir and exploring the surrounding hillsides with their 'troglodyte' cave dwellings and cellars carved out of the tufa.

DOM. DU CARROIR Tradition 1999★

■ 4.35 ha 8,000 ▮ 20–29 F

Thoré-la-Rochette has several lovely surprises in store for visitors to the Vendôme area, such as the avenue of plane trees which runs alongside the Loir for 3 km (1.8 miles) and a troglodytic chapel. Jean and Benôit Brazilier offer an interesting range of wines in this commune, one of which is a very successful red. With violet tints, this 99 has a complex palate dominated by spicy aromas associated with scents of very ripe cherry. The palate is rich and rounded right to its elegant, marked liquorice finish. Also noted by the jury was the estate's **Vin Gris 99**, which has a charming corn colour and pleasing body and is slightly peppery on the palate.

⊶ GAEC Jean et Benoît Brazilier, 17, rue des Ecoles, 41100 Thoré-la-Rochette, tel. 02.54.72.81.72, fax 02.54.72.77.13 ☑ Y by appt.

PATRICE COLIN Silex 1999★

□ 2 ha 4,000 ▮ 🌡 20–29 F

This Silex is a pure Chenin Blanc from 2 ha (5 acres) of vines planted on flint soil. It has a lovely golden-yellow colour. On the nose, scents of honey and lime tree make up a complex, very fine mixture. Its balance on the palate is enticing, sustained by good fresh mineral notes. A pleasure in store for late 2000 and for several years to come.

⊶ Patrice Colin, La Gaudetterie, 41100 Thoré-la-Rochette, tel. 02.54.72.80.73, fax 02.54.72.75.54 ☑ Y by appt.

DOM. DU FOUR A CHAUX

Cuvée Tradition 1999★

■ 3 ha 7,000 ▮ 🌡 20–29 F

Very successful, this dark red Coteaux du Vendômois has a complex nose of spices, morello cherry and blackcurrant. Opening with suppleness, it develops on the palate in a consistently full, fruity direction. In addition, Claude Norguet has made a well-balanced **Coteaux du Vendômois Blanc 99**, whose menthol notes underline its pleasing freshness, as well as a harmonious **Vin Gris 99**, which, although still timid on the nose, is already typical of Pineau d'Aunis. These two wines deserve a mention.

⊶ GAEC Norguet, Berger, 41100 Thoré-la-Rochette, tel. 02.54.77.12.52, fax 02.54.77.86.18 ☑ Y by appt.

CHARLES JUMERT Tradition 1999

■ 4 ha 5,000 ▮ ▮▮▮ 🌡 20–29 F

Matured for three months in vats and three months in barrel in wine cellars hollowed straight out of the rock, the wine is clear coloured and elegant. Its distinction persists, thanks to the freshness of its aromas and its balanced structure on the palate. The roundness of the attack contrasts with a mineral note in the impressive finish.

⊶ Charles Jumert, 4, rue de la Berthelotière, 41100 Villiers-sur-Loir, tel. 02.54.72.94.09, fax 02.54.72.94.09 ☑ Y ev. day except Sun. 9am–7pm

DOM. DE LA CHARLOTTERIE

Tradition 1999★

■ 1.61 ha 10,000 ▮ 🌡 20–29 F

From a clear, garnet-red colour tinted with light violet comes scents of red fruit, ripe but still fresh. On the palate, the initial fresh impression gives way to supple, mellow flavours, again rich in red fruit. This harmonious representative of the appellation would make a good accompaniment to red meat.

⊶ Dominique Houdebert, Cave de la Charlotterie, 2, rue du Bas-Bourg, 41100 Villiersfaux, tel. 02.54.80.29.79, fax 02.54.73.10.01 ☑ Y by appt.

LES VIGNERONS DU VENDOMOIS

Gris 1999★

◢ n.c. 120,000 ▮ 🌡 20 F+

Nice work from Les Vignerons du Vendômois in the 99 vintage. This light rosé offers a natural colour and intense aromas, at once fruity and floral. Noticeable on the palate are a real balance and good length. Also very successful, the **Rouge 99** unfurls itself in suppleness after a generous nose of red fruit. Finally, the **Blanc 99** is also worth mentioning (20–29F).

⊶ Cave coop. du Vendômois, 60, av. du Petit-Thouars, 41100 Villiers-sur-Loir, tel. 02.54.72.90.69, fax 02.54.72.75.09 ☑ Y ev. day except Sun. Mon. 9am–12 noon 2pm–6pm

DOM. J. MARTELLIERE

Cuvée Balzac 1999★

■ 0.7 ha 2,000 ▮ 20–29 F

Balzac or Jean Vivien? Both very successful wines are on offer at J. Martellière's estate. With a white label, the Balzac wine is all delicacy. Red fruit aromas mingle with pear drops, then the wine opens with sweetness on the palate and develops richly. With a black label, the **Réserve Jean Vivien 99** (30–49F) is all power. A lovely red in colour, the wine, raised in vats and barrels, opens on notes of oak and very ripe red fruit. While tannins are present on the palate, an assurance that the wine will age well, they are already harmonious.

🔑 SCEA Dom. J. Martellière, 46, rue de Fosse, 41800 Montoire, tel. 02.54.85.16.91, fax 02.54.85.16.91 ☑ 🍷 by appt.

CLAUDE MINIER 1999★

☐ n.c. n.c. 20–29 F

In Ronsard country (Pierre Ronsard was a famous 16th-century French poet), Lunay is a charming staging post which will enable you to discover houses from the 15th and 16th centuries as well as a subterranean chapel whose 12th- and 13th-century frescoes evoke the pilgrims en route to Santiago de Compostela. This white Coteaux du Vendômois releases delicate flavours of bergamot and lime on the nose, while on the palate the full and silky character of this beautiful wine delivers very fruity, slightly acid-drop notes, which contribute to its overall balance.

🔑 GAEC Claude Minier, Les Monts, 41360 Lunay, tel. 02.54.72.02.36, fax 02.54.72.18.52 ☑ 🍷 by appt.

DOM. JACQUES NOURY 1999★

☐ 0.8 ha 6,000 20–29 F

Jacques Noury offers a triad of Vendôme wines from the same vintage and in the same price range. This very successful white presents finesse and a good aromatic intensity. Fresh and full on the palate at the same time, it finishes on honeyed notes. The **Rouge 99**, light to look at, is attractive in its freshness and on the finish. The **Vin Gris 99** plays on its liveliness and good length on the palate. These two wines deserve a mention.

🔑 Dom. Jacques Noury, Montpot, 41800 Houssay, tel. 02.54.85.36.04, fax 02.54.85.19.30 ☑ 🍷 by appt.

Valençay AOVDQS

Bordering Berry, Sologne and the Touraine is an area of mixed agriculture, forestry and husbandry (particularly goat-rearing) in which the vine plays its part. The soils are mainly clay and silica or alluvial clay. There are more than 300 ha (741 acres) under vines, half of which is declared as Valençay, offering wines for early drinking from the classic varieties of this part of the Loire. Sauvignon produces aromatic wines with notes of blackcurrant or broom, and an added fullness when mixed with Chardonnay. The red wines are assembled from Gamay, Cabernet, Côt and Pinot Noir in various proportions. Average production is 10,000 hl (260,000 gal).

The great French statesman Talleyrand (1754–1838) had strong associations with the Valençay region, which is also famous for its goat's cheese, awarded an AOC in 1998. Depending on how mature they are, the little pyramids of goat's cheese will accompany any of Valençay's red and white wines.

JACKY ET PHILIPPE AUGIS 1999★

■ 2 ha 12,000 20F+

Jacky and Philippe Augis' output is as successful as ever . . . Their red Valençay, garnet-red glinting with orange, emits aromas of very ripe red fruit before opening up on the palate on silky, harmonious tannins. The **Blanc 99** (20–29F) is a pale yellow wine, with hints of green, which is pleasing with its fresh, delicate scents, followed by the freshness of a refined palate.

🔑 GAEC Jacky et Philippe Augis, rue des Vignes, Le Musa, 41130 Meusnes, tel. 02.54.71.01.89, fax 02.54.71.74.15 ☑ 🍷 by appt.

DOM. BARDON 1999★

☐ 3 ha 5,000 30–49 F

This straw-yellow Valençay, gleaming with gold, has spent six months in barrel before being released for tasting. It gives a good indication of the grapes' maturity. Scents of vanilla are apparent on the nose, and also citrus fruit. After a round and supple palate, a note of CO_2 brings freshness on the finish.

🔑 Denis Bardon, Le Bourg, 41130 Meusnes, tel. 02.54.71.01.10, fax 02.54.71.75.20 ☑ 🍷 by appt.

CLOS DU CHATEAU DE VALENCAY 1999★

☐ 1.5 ha 10,000 20–29 F

This Valençay is gentle on the nose but already offers all the typical aromas of the appellation's white wines. It is a refreshing wine, cool and easy to drink. Mention should also be made of the **Rouge 99**, which opens firmly on the palate with tannins evident, but the general effect is still balanced.

🔑 SCEV Clos du Château de Valençay, Le Musa, 41130 Meusnes, tel. 02.54.71.00.26, fax 02.54.71.50.93 ☑

CHANTAL ET PATRICK GIBAULT 1999

■ 2.5 ha 15,000 ▮ 20–29 F

While this garnet-red Valençay is still closed on the nose, it can pride itself on having a good structure on the palate. In fact, the opening impression is clean, the body round on fairly evident tannins, and the finish is good.

EARL Chantal et Patrick Gibault, rue Gambetta, 41130 Meusnes, tel. 02.54.71.02.63, fax 02.54.71.58.92 ☒ Y ev. day 8am–7pm; Sun. 10am–12 noon

FRANCIS JOURDAIN

Cuvée Chèvrefeuille 1999★★

□ 1.5 ha 5,000 ▮ ♁ 20–29 F

Francis Jourdain has produced a pale yellow Sauvignon-Chardonnay mix, luminous and unambiguous. This Cuvée Chèvrefeuille calls forth delicacy and finesse, which are well represented by its intense nose of flowers and blackcurrant. Its first impression is supple, the palate balanced, with a good length on the finish.

Francis Jourdain, Les Moreaux, 36600 Lye, tel. 02.54.41.01.45, fax 02.54.41.07.56 ☒ Y by appt.

MONTBAIL 1999

□ 1 ha 8,000 ▮ ♁ 20–29 F

Celebrated for its Montbail Rouge 97, the Garnier estate offers a white Valençay 1999. Brilliant to look at, pale yellow, this one expresses itself well on the palate with flavours of fruit and blackcurrant and reveals a good length on the finish.

Dom. Garnier, Chamberlin, 41130 Meusnes, tel. 02.54.00.10.06, fax 02.54.05.13.36 ☒ Y by appt.

JEAN-FRANCOIS ROY 1999★

■ 6 ha 40,000 ▮ ♁ 20–29 F

Jean-François Roy has scored three succeses in the 99 vintage. In the reds, flavours of very ripe fruit indicate the grapes themselves were fully ripe. His mastery of the wine-making process has enabled him to draw out velvety tannins that will improve still further with time. One star is awarded to the **Cuvée des Pinotes 99**, powerful and complex, mingling red fruits and spices on the nose. Its solid structure makes it a good wine for laying down for up to three years. **Valençay Blanc 99** has a seductive balance on the palate and an enticing, refreshing finish.

Jean-François Roy, 3, rue des Acacias, 36600 Lye, tel. 02.54.41.00.39, fax 02.54.41.06.89 Y by appt.

HUBERT SINSON ET FILS

Closerie de la Maison Blanche 1999★

□ 3 ha 20,000 ▮ ♁ 20–29 F

Hubert Sinson and his sons make a good partnership: you only have to taste their three Valençay wines. The first, with its charming pale yellow gleaming with green, releases elegant scents; its opening in the mouth is supple and its palate balanced. The **Rouge 99**, still timid but very successful, needs a little patience, because it promises flavours of very ripe red fruit. Tannins are evident on the palate and require two years' ageing; it gains a star. Another red wine, **Cuvée Denisot Sinson 99**, is also worthy of note.

GAEC Hubert Sinson et Fils, Le Musa, 41130 Meusnes, tel. 02.54.71.00.26, fax 02.54.71.50.93, e-mail sinson@cavesparticulieres.com ☒ Y by appt.

GERARD TOYER 1999

□ 2.5 ha 12,000 ▮ ♁ 20 F+

A note of blackcurrant combines harmoniously with scents of white flowers in this bright yellow Valençay. Well balanced, the palate finishes as it began, with liveliness and on a lemony note. The red Valençay **Cuvée du Prince 99** is cited for its pretty orange glints and its suppleness on the palate.

Gérard Toyer, 63, Grande-Rue, Champcol, 41130 Selles-sur-Cher, tel. 02.54.97.49.23, fax 02.54.97.46.25 Y ev. day 10am–12 noon 3pm–6pm; Sun. 10am–12 noon

Poitou

Haut-Poitou AOVDQS

In 1865 Dr Guyot reported that the Vienne vineyard covered 33,560 ha (82,893 acres). Nowadays, apart from the vineyard attached to the Saumur area in the north of the department, wine-growing is reduced to the area around the cantons of Neuville and Mirebeau. Marigny-Brizay is the commune with the largest number of individual growers. The others grouped together to set up the Cave de Neuville-de-Poitou. The wines of Haut-Poitou produced 33,346 hl (880,334 gal) in 1998, 17,081 (450,938 gal) of which were whites.

The soils of the Neuville plateau, a mixture of limestone and Marigny clay as well as marl, are well suited to the different varieties of this appellation; the best known of them is Sauvignon (for white wines).

DOM. DU CENTAURE

Sauvignon 1999★

□	1.4 ha	9,000	20 F+

This wine is a beautiful pale yellow colour which flashes with green. On the nose, you notice a very markedly Sauvignon floral aroma. Then the palate, at the same time both supple and lively, opens up many aromas, conferring on the wine a lovely overall harmony. Also successful are the 99 reds, **Pinot Noir** and **Cabernet Franc**. The former is still modest on the nose, but after being allowed to breathe it gives off pleasing floral and fruity notes, accompanied by a light smoky touch. On the palate, it is round and refreshing, very long, with assertive tannins. The latter, clean and complex, with flavours of red fruit (morello cherry and mulberry), show structure.

Gérard Marsault, 4, rue du Poirier, 86380 Chabournay, tel. 05.49.51.19.39, fax 05.49.51.14.25 Sat. 10am–12 noon 2pm–7pm

CAVE DU HAUT-POITOU

Sauvignon 1999

□	158 ha	539,000	20-29 F

The colour of this 99 wine is a very pale yellow. On the nose, Sauvignon is clearly distinguishable. It opens cleanly on the palate, both lively and round at the same time, and the satisfying weight in the mouth leaves an impression of harmony.

SA Cave du Haut-Poitou, 32, rue Alphonse-Plault, 86170 Neuville-de-Poitou, tel. 05.49.51.21.65, fax 05.49.51.16.07, e-mail cave.haut.poitou@gofornet.com by appt.

DOM. DE LA ROTISSERIE

Cabernet 1999★★★

■	3.5 ha	10,000	20-29 F

The road leading to the estate, at Marigny-Brizay, winds between fields of cereals and vineyards. Jacques Baudon has just over 13 ha (32 acres) of vines here, which in 1999 produced this lovely dark red, purplish wine. The intense, expressive nose releases fruity scents reminiscent of morello cherry jam. The full, warm palate is enlivened by notes of blackcurrant. It is well balanced by tannins, which are clearly present but nevertheless harmonious and silky.

Jacques Baudon, 35, rue de l'Habit-d'Or, 86380 Marigny-Brizay, tel. 05.49.52.09.02, fax 05.49.37.11.44 ev. day 8am–12 noon 1.30pm–7pm; Sat. Sun. by appt.

DOM. LA TOUR BEAUMONT

Chardonnay 1999★★

□	1.62 ha	13,500	20-29 F

This estate is a family property which Gilles and Brigitte Morgeau have been running since 1991. The colour of their 99 wine is a lovely clear yellow. Although still timid on the nose, the wine gives off, little by little, lightly spiced, liquoricey scents. Pleasant, well balanced and aromatic, the palate has a very interesting length. Drink it for the pure pleasure of its company.

Gilles et Brigitte Morgeau, 2, av. de Bordeaux, 86490 Beaumont, tel. 05.49.85.50.37, fax 05.49.85.58.13 ev. day except Sun. 2pm–6pm

DOM. DE LA TOUR SIGNY

Cuvée Poitevine 1999★★

■	n.c.	15,000	20-29 F

Christophe Croux has been in charge of the property since 1983. The wines are stored in tuffeau stone wine cellars where all the stages of vinification take place. The Cuvée Poitevine is a very deep lovely purplish ruby colour. You will appreciate delicate aromas reminiscent of strawberry and blackcurrant, then the well-structured palate, which is surprisingly aromatic. **Cuvée Cabernet 99** reveals itself most successfully in gentle floral and fruity aromas. The flavours develop fully and generously on velvety tannins without losing their liveliness. The aromatic length bestows a good general rounded character. Finally, mention must be made of **Haut-Poitou Chardonnay 99**, matured for six months in barrel. Honeyed aromas, underlined by oak, are followed by a long, supple palate.

Christophe Croux, La Tour Signy, rue de Tue-Loup, 86380 Marigny-Brizay, tel. 05.49.55.31.21, fax 05.49.62.36.82 by appt.

DOM. DES LISES Sauvignon 1999

□	0.94 ha	3,000	20-29 F

The daughter of a wine-maker and herself an oenologist Pascale Bonneau returned to vines in 1995, then founded this wine-making and direct sales workshop the following year. She offers a 99 Sauvignon of a clear golden-yellow sparkling with green. Of still only medium strength, the wine releases soft fruity and floral aromas on the nose. The full, round, supple palate leaves a good overall impression. The **Chardonnay 99** is not to be outdone and also deserves a mention.

Pascale Bonneau-Charrais, 21, rue Nationale, 86110 Mirebeau, tel. 05.49.50.53.66, fax 05.49.50.90.50, e-mail pascale.bonneau@libertysurf.fr by appt.

Wines from Central France

From the hills of Forez to the Orléans area, the main wine-growing sectors of the Centre are located on the best exposed sites of hills and plateaux eroded through successive geological eras by the Loire and its tributaries, the Allier and the Cher. These areas, on the hillsides of the Côtes d'Auvergne, in parts of Saint-Pourçain and Châteaumeillant, are located on the eastern and northern flanks of the Massif Central, and yet still open onto the Loire basin.

The vine-growing soils are either silica or limestone, always well situated and exposed, sustaining a limited number of varieties of which the most common are Gamay for red and rosé wines and Sauvignon for white wines. A few special local varieties are grown here and there: the Tressallier at Saint-Pourçain and the Chasselas at Pouilly-sur-Loire for whites; Pinot Noir at Sancerre, Menetou-Salon and Reuilly for reds and rosés, plus the delicate Pinot Gris, again in the latter vineyard; finally, the Meunier which, near Orléans, makes the original Gris Meunier. When all is said and done, it is a notably rich selection.

Whatever the terroir, all the wines made from these varieties share a light, fresh and fruity character which makes them particularly appealing, pleasant and drinkable, especially when matched with the gastronomic specialities of the region. The green, peaceful countryside of the Auvergne, the Bourbonnais, the Nivernais, the Berry or the Orléanais encompasses a region of wide horizons and varied landscapes. The wines are grown in vineyards that are often family-owned and run in traditional ways, and, secure in their roots and traditions, the wine-makers are expert in showing off their worthy wines to best advantage.

Châteaumeillant AOVDQS

Here, the Gamay is raised on *terroirs* of volcanic soils, in an oldestablished wine region. Visitors can find out all about the area's history in an interesting museum devoted to the subject.

The reputation of Châteaumeillant was founded on its famous Gris, a wine made from the first pressing of Gamay grapes, and notable for its remarkable texture, freshness and fruitiness. The reds (which should be drunk young and chilled), combine bouquet, smoothness and sheer drinkability.

DOM. DU CHAILLOT 1999*

◪ 0.4 ha 2,100 ▮ 30–49 F

Pierre Picot has been collecting awards since he started up in 1993. A deep salmon-pink colour, this rosé is not lacking in eloquence and has floral (violet) and fruity (citrus and cherry) scents. It fills the mouth well, linking freshness and length, suppleness and complexity. Beautiful work.

Dom. du Chaillot, pl. de la Tournoise, 18130 Dun-sur-Auron, tel. 02.48.59.57.69, fax 02.48.59.58.78, e-mail pierre.picot@wanadoo.fr ☑ Y by appt.

Pierre Picot

LOIRE

CAVE DES VINS DE CHATEAUMEILLANT Vin gris 1999★

2 ha 17,000 20–29 F

This 99 wine has a pale salmon-pink tint. The nose is fine and elegant, enlivened by floral touches. There is enough suppleness and richness, accompanied by a slight liveliness. A lovely success, and a very good example of the Châteaumeillant type of rosé.

Cave du Tivoli, rte de Culan, 18370 Châteaumeillant, tel. 02.48.61.33.55, fax 02.48.61.44.92 by appt.

VALERIE ET FREDERIC DALLOT 1998

3 ha 4,000 20–29 F

Valérie and Frédéric Dallot began selling their produce under their own name in 1991. Their 98 Châteaumeillant has a yellow tint: garnet glinting with purple. First impressions are enticing, but the finish is still tannic. This wine will benefit from being allowed to breathe, when it will demonstrate richness.

Frédéric et Valérie Dallot, 42, rue Genèst, 18370 Châteaumeillant, tel. 02.48.56.31.84 by appt.

DOM. LANOIX

Cuvée du Chêne Combeau 1999★

8.74 ha 12,000 30–49 F

Patrick Lanoix has applied his motto of 'From the vine to the bottle' to good effect in this wine. Characteristic grapey notes are clearly perceptible on the palate, along with red fruit delicately seasoned with a hint of pepper. Full on the palate, the wine has a great deal of richness and good body. This 99 need not fear the passing of the years.

EARL Dom. Lanoix, Beaumerle, 18370 Châteaumeillant, tel. 02.48.61.39.59, fax 02.48.61.42.19 by appt.

Côtes d'Auvergne AOVDQS

Whether grown on the volcanic hills called *puys*, in Limagne, or on the hills (dômes) on the eastern edge of the Massif Central, all Auvergne wines are made with the Gamay variety, which has been cultivated in the region for centuries. Produced from about 400 ha (988 acres) of vines, these wines have had the right to the denomination AOVDQS since 1977. The unusual rosés and easy-drinking reds (two-thirds of the production) are particularly recommended as companions for the famous local charcuterie and regional dishes. The best growths can acquire surprising character, fullness and personality.

JACQUES ABONNAT Boudes 1999

1 ha 5,000 20–29 F

Violet tinges are noticeable in the pink colour of this wine. Generous on the nose (flowers and passion fruit), it presents agreeable freshness on the palate which carries through to the finish. Drink it with a plate of *charcuterie*.

Jacques Abonnat, 63340 Chalus, tel. 04.73.96.45.95, fax 04.73.96.45.95 by appt.

MICHEL BELLARD Corent 1999

4 ha 12,000 20–29 F

The 25 ha (62 acres) or so of vines belonging to Michel Bellard grow on volcanic ash.

Wines from Central France

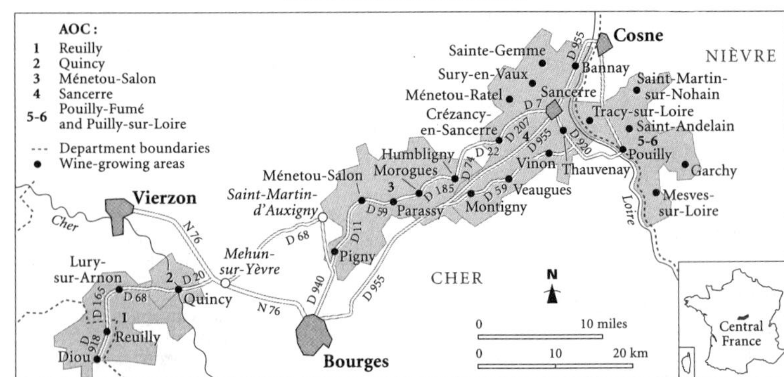

Still timid on the nose, the Corent 99, a bright rosé, shows tenderness on the palate and makes a refreshing wine, which you can enjoy from now onwards.

🔑 Michel Bellard, B.P. 317, 63109 Romagnat Cedex, tel. 04.73.62.66.69, fax 04.73.62.09.22 ☒

HENRI BOURCHEIX 1999

■ 3.23 ha 20,000 🍾 🌡 20-29 F

A lovely purplish-red colour, this is a wine of surprising scents of red fruit acid drops, which recur throughout. Tender on the palate, it had a good length.

🔑 Henri Bourcheix, 4, rue Saint-Marc, 63170 Aubière, tel. 04.73.26.04.52, fax 04.73.27.96.46 ☒ 🍷 by appt.

CHARMENSAT Boudes 1999

■ 7.5 ha 50,000 🍾 🌡 20-29 F

Annie Charmensat has taken up the reins of the estate with the help of her husband, an oenologist. Two of her 99 vintage wines deserve a mention. The first, from old vines planted in terraces on a south-facing hillside, is still reserved on the nose but will soon open out. Its balance and length make it pleasant on the palate here and now. **Côtes d'Auvergne Boudes Cuvée des Grandes Vignes Elevée en Fût de Chêne 99** (30–49F) is interesting for the balance it develops on the palate.

🔑 GAEC Charmensat, rue du Coufin, 63340 Boudes, tel. 04.73.96.44.75, fax 04.73.96.58.04, e-mail charmensat@lokace-online.com ☒ 🍷 by appt.

PIERRE GOIGOUX Châteaugay 1999★

□ 0.7 ha 4,800 🍾 🌡 30-49 F

The 99 vintage marks the tenth birthday of this property at Châteaugay, which has been praised regularly during the past few years. This wine is a pretty golden-yellow, with a nose reminiscent of very ripe fruit and white flowers. Perfectly balanced on the palate, it picks up floral flavours again on the finish. A round, elegant and well-behaved wine.

🔑 GAEC Pierre Goigoux, 22, rue des Caves, 63119 Châteaugay, tel. 04.73.87.67.51, fax 04.73.78.02.70 ☒ 🍷 by appt.

ODETTE ET GILLES MIOLANNE

Volcane 1999★

◪ 1.4 ha 7,800 🍾 🌡 20-29 F

Volcane? Because here the vines grow on a soil of volcanic alluvium. The rosé, with its full, violet-tinged colour, releases strains of very ripe fruit. Powerful on the palate, it is structured enough to make it a good accompaniment to highly seasoned dishes such as grills or Auvergne *charcuterie*. In the red department, **Cuvée Volcane 99** is a round and well-balanced wine deserving of note.

🔑 EARL de La Sardissère, 17, rte de Coudes, 63320 Neschers, tel. 04.73.96.72.45, fax 04.73.96.25.79 ☒ 🍷 by appt.
🔑 Gilles Miolanne

JEAN-PIERRE ET MARC PRADIER

Corent 1999★

◪ 4.5 ha 26,000 🍾 🌡 20-29 F

Orangey tones enliven the colour of this pretty rosé. After an intense nose, it opens on the palate unambiguously, then takes on fullness before a slight tannic hint on the finish. Also very successful, the **Rouge Tradition 99** offers a mixture of very ripe red fruit scents and releases a touch of CO_2 on the palate, an indication of youth.

🔑 GAEC Jean-Pierre et Marc Pradier, 9, rue Saint-Jean-Baptiste, 63730 Les Martres-de-Veyre, tel. 04.73.39.86.41, fax 04.73.39.88.17 ☒ 🍷 Sat. 8.30am–12 noon 2pm–6.30pm

CHRISTOPHE ROMEUF 1999

◪ 3.5 ha n.c. 🍾 🌡 20-29 F

A deep-coloured rosé with purplish touches, this wine is interesting for its intense peppery scents. While it is soft on first impression, a note of CO_2 reinforces its freshness on the finish.

🔑 Christophe Romeuf, 1 bis, rue du Couvent, 63670 Orcet, tel. 06.08.85.01.69, fax 06.73.84.07.83 ☒ 🍷 by appt.

DOM. ROUGEYRON

Châteaugay Cuvée Bousset d'or 1999★

■ 12.03 ha 90,000 🍾 30-49 F

The colour of black cherries, Cuvée Bousset d'Or is fairly intense on the nose, dominated by very ripe red fruit. Unambiguous, straightforward and well balanced on the palate, this is a nice Auvergne wine. **Châteaugay Cuvée Bousset d'Or Rosé 99** is worth noting too.

🔑 Michel et Roland Rougeyron, 27, rue de La Crouzette, 63119 Châteaugay, tel. 04.73.87.24.45, fax 04.73.87.23.55 ☒ 🍷 by appt.

CAVE SAINT-VERNY Corent 1999★

◪ 20 ha 30,000 🍾 🌡 30-49 F

A clear pale pink colour announces the very charming character of this 99 wine. Scents of spices and ripe fruit prevail on the nose, while on the palate the wine gives an impression of sweetness. A slightly tannic note on the finish will go well with *charcuterie*. **Première Cuvée Rouge 99** is mentioned for its supple first impression and its fullness on the palate.

🔑 Cave Saint-Verny, rte d'Issoire, B.P. 2, 63960 Veyre-Monton, tel. 04.73.69.60.11, fax 04.73.69.65.22, e-mail saint.verny@wanadoo.fr ☒ 🍷 by appt.

SAUVAT

Boudes Les Demoiselles oubliées du Donazat Gamay 1999

■ 6.5 ha 47,000 🍾 🌡 30-49 F

While this red wine with sparkling purple tones is still reserved on the nose, it already shows a beautiful harmony on the palate: red fruits fit into a fairly rounded body. In addition, Annie and Claude Sauvat have made a **Côtes d'Auvergne Blanc**, which was also mentioned by the jury: **Boudes Prestige Chardonnay Elevage Bois 99** (50–69F).

Claude et Annie Sauvat, 63340 Boudes, tel. 04.73.96.41.42, fax 04.73.96.58.34, e-mail sauvat@terre-net.fr by appt.

Annie Blot

Côtes du Forez

Great efforts have gone into maintaining this smart and spectacular vineyard, covering 193 ha (477 acres) in 21 communes around Boën-sur-Lignon (Loire).

Nearly all the excellent dry, robust rosé and red wines, made exclusively from Gamay, are grown on Tertiary terrains in the north and Primary soils in the south. Production comes mainly from a splendid Cave Coopérative. These wines which received an AOC in the year 2000, are best drunk young.

LES VIGNERONS FOREZIENS

Richesse du Forez 1999

■ 28 ha 150,000 30–49 F

Vines growing on volcanic soils have produced a medium ruby-coloured wine with a lovely scent of very ripe grapes. Pleasantly structured, aromatic and with a straightforward candour, this 99 wine should be drunk as young as possible.

Les Vignerons Foréziens, Le Pont-Rompu, 42130 Trelins, tel. 04.77.24.00.12, fax 04.77.24.01.76, e-mail vignerons.foreziens@wanadoo.fr by appt.

LES VIGNERONS FOREZIENS

Cuvée Tradition 1999

■ 28 ha 150,000 20–29 F

The wine cellar of Les Vignerons Foréziens, which makes 90% of the appellation's wines, has produced a 99 red which is light and unambiguous, with a fruitiness which is full of freshness. Well balanced, harmoniously aromatic and quite long:, it should be drunk as young as possible.

Les Vignerons Foréziens, Le Pont-Rompu, 42130 Trelins, tel. 04.77.24.00.12, fax 04.77.24.01.76, e-mail vignerons.foreziens@wanadoo.fr by appt.

DOM. DE LA PIERRE NOIRE

Cuvée spéciale 1998*

■ 1 ha 4,000 20–29 F

Nine months of maturation have yielded this *cuvée spéciale* of an enticing purplish-red colour. Semi-intense scents of red fruit and undergrowth hit a structured palate. Aromatic and perfectly balanced, this rich wine can wait another year.

Christian Gachet, chem. de l'Abreuvoir, 42610 Saint-Georges-Hauteville, tel. 04.77.76.08.54 ev. day 9am–12 noon 2pm–6pm

DOM. DE LA PIERRE NOIRE 1999

■ 2 ha 8,000 20–29 F

Now that it is an AOC, the output of this estate has found a standard-bearer in the 99 garnet-coloured red, which releases discreet fruity perfumes underlined by floral and vegetal notes. Nice and plump, structured by marked aromatic tannins, this wine will be ready in 2001.

Christian Gachet, chem. de l'Abreuvoir, 42610 Saint-Georges-Hauteville, tel. 04.77.76.08.54 ev. day 9am–12 noon 2pm–6pm

DOM. DU POYET 1999*

■ 3.5 ha 25,000 20–29 F

A kilometre (0.6 miles) away from Château Sainte-Anne, where there is a raptor centre, this domaine, created in 1995, has produced a wine of an intense purple colour. Voluptuous perfumes of red fruit, peony and undergrowth emanate from this full-bodied 99 vintage. Its young tannic structure reveals a slight bitterness, but this will soften in a few months.

Jean-François Arnaud, Dom. du Poyet, au Bourg, 42130 Marcilly-le-Châtel, tel. 04.77.97.48.54, fax 04.77.97.48.71 ev. day 8am–8pm; groups by appt.

DOM. DU POYET 1999*

◪ 0.5 ha 4,500 20–29 F

The pale salmon-pink colour has a lovely clarity. Delicate scents of apricot, pineapple and grapefruit open out progressively. On the palate, an initial fruity impression is associated with a pleasing freshness. Remaining supple and fine, this excellent representative of Côtes du Forez should be drunk by the end of the year.

Jean-François Arnaud, Dom. du Poyet, au Bourg, 42130 Marcilly-le-Châtel, tel. 04.77.97.48.54, fax 04.77.97.48.71 ev. day 8am–8pm; groups by appt.

Coteaux du Giennois

This appellation, classified as AOC in 1998, covers silicious or limestone soils stretching along the hills of the upper Loire into the Nièvre and the Loiret. In 1999, three traditional varieties, Gamay, Pinot Noir and Sauvignon, produced 8,220 hl (217,008 gal), including 2,926 hl (77,246 gal) of light, fruity white wines with little tannin, expressing the highly distinctive terroir. They can be kept for up to five years and can be drunk with all meat dishes.

Planting is progressing appreciably in the Nièvre and also increasing somewhat in the Loiret, promising continuing good health for this vineyard, which covers 140 ha (346 acres).

JOSEPH BALLAND-CHAPUIS 1999

■ 3.5 ha 25,000 30–49 F

A cherry colour with violet shades shining through, this wine is dominated by scents of ripe red fruit (strawberry jam) on the nose. Still too young, the wine has a very interesting structure that should assert itself more in the months to come. The **Rosé 99** should also be mentioned for the purity of its line.

SCEA Dom. Balland-Chapuis, 6, allée des Soupirs, 45420 Bonny-sur-Loire, tel. 02.38.31.55.12, fax 02.48.54.07.97

DOM. DES BEAUROIS 1999★

□ 2 ha 15,000 30–49 F

Anne-Marie and Bernard Marty's vineyard is in the commune of Beaulieu-sur-Loire, in the Loiret. Their Coteaux du Giennois charms the eye with its golden tone gleaming with silver. The nose, still closed, is all finesse. Freshness and even, on the finish, liveliness, mark the palate without impeding it in any way. A perfect wine for shellfish.

Anne-Marie Marty, Dom. des Beaurois, 89170 Lavau, tel. 03.86.74.16.09, fax 03.86.74.16.09 ev. day 10am–12 noon 2pm–7pm

DOM. COUET 1998

■ 2 ha 9,600 20–29 F

The fifth generation of the Couets at Saint-Père, Emmanuel came to join his father Bernard in 1998. In the 98 vintage he offers a wine of a deep purple colour. More than fruity, the wine falls into a particular range of toasted notes tending towards gaminess on the nose, supple with a hint of bitterness which time will soften. This Coteaux du Giennois will be ready to drink at the end of the year.

Dom. Couet, Croquant, 58200 Saint-Père, tel. 03.86.28.14.80, fax 03.86.28.14.80 ev. day 8am–8pm

DOM. DE LA GRANGE ARTHUIS

Les Daguettes 1999

□ 1.73 ha 11,000 30–49 F

Jean-Luc Pitot, the cellar master on the Grange Arthuis estate, has made a particularly pale Coteaux du Giennois white. Lemony aromas successfully complete sweet notes. On the palate, sweetness and roundness linger in a balanced way. The **Rosé 99** also deserves a mention (20–29F).

Dom. de La Grange Arthuis, 89170 Lavau, tel. 03.86.74.06.20, fax 03.86.74.18.01 ev. day 10am–12 noon 2pm–7pm

François Reynaud

MICHEL LANGLOIS

Champ de la Croix 1998

■ 2.5 ha 20,000 30–49 F

Orange gleams in the colour are a sign of maturity in this wine. It is no surprise, then, to pick up scents of good intensity, recalling grape *marc*. The lightness and tannic grain of the finish characterise the palate. Serve with grilled meat.

Michel Langlois, Le Bourg, 58200 Pougny, tel. 03.86.28.06.52, fax 03.86.28.59.29 ev. day except Sun. 9am–1pm 3pm–7pm

JOSEPH MELLOT

Les Champs de Chaume 1998

■ n.c. 15,000 30–49 F

With its clear, slightly orangey ruby colour, Les Champs de Chaume 98 offers a nose dominated by morello cherries in brandy. Its structure is restrained and well balanced. Of suitable length, this is an ideal type of wine to accompany *charcuterie*.

SA Joseph Mellot, rte de Ménétréol, B.P. 13, 18300 Sancerre, tel. 02.48.78.54.54, fax 02.48.78.54.55, e-mail alexandre@joseph-mellot.fr by appt.

ALAIN PAULAT

Les Belles Fornasses 1998

■ 3.8 ha 20,000 30–49 F

Since 1982 Alain Paulat has been growing his vines using organic viticultural methods. Here is a purple-coloured wine just beginning to evolve on the nose, combining undergrowth and red fruit. Concentrated, with tannins needing several more months to calm down, the wine shows good potential.

Alain Paulat, Villemoison, 58200 Saint-Père, tel. 03.86.26.75.57, fax 03.86.28.06.78 ev. day 8am–12 noon 2pm–7pm

PHILIPPE POUPAT Rivotte 1999★

■ 1.75 ha 14,000 30–49 F

Rivotte is a deep garnet-red. Some grilled notes bring complexity to scents of red fruit

LOIRE

(blackcurrant and raspberry), and balance is achieved on the palate thanks to a fullness which already conceals tannins of good quality, although they still need to be subdued. Wait for it. Also very successful, and awarded a star, is **Trocadéro Rosé 99**, with its intense fruitiness.
🔑 Poupat et Fils, Rivotte, 45250 Briare, tel. 02.38.31.39.76, fax 02.38.31.39.76 ☑ 🍸 by appt.

DOM. DE VILLARGEAU 1999★★

☐ 3 ha 23,000 ▮ 30–49 F

François and Jean-Fernand Thibault have produced this wine with a high-quality nose, intense and pleasing, 'as fine as a white flower in the morning dew'. Rich on the palate, it allows flavours of passion fruit to rise. Fullness gives it a beautiful length. A lovely wine.
🔑 GAEC Thibault, Villargeau, 58200 Pougny, tel. 03.86.28.23.24, fax 03.86.28.47.00, e-mail fthibault@wanadoo.fr ☑ 🍸 by appt.

Saint-Pourçain AOVDQS

Gentle, fertile Bourbonnais boasts a lovely vineyard, in nineteen communes, southwest of Moulins.

Limestone or gravelly slopes and plateaux, skirting the banks of the charming Sioule river, grow Gamay and Pinot Noir which combine to give the red and rosé wines their fruity appeal.

In the past, the native Tressallier variety made remarkable white wines that established Saint-Pourçain's reputation. Today, the original Tressallier is assembled with Chardonnay and Sauvignon to make distinctively aromatic wine worthy of more than a passing comment.

ATLANTIS 1999

☐ n.c. 40,000 ▮ 🌡 20–29 F

This Saint-Pourçain caught the tasters' attention. On the nose, you will notice boxwood aromas with associated grilled notes, and a good attack along with power on the palate.
🔑 Union des vignerons de Saint-Pourçain, rue de la Ronde, 03500 Saint-Pourçain-sur-Sioule, tel. 04.70.45.42.82, fax 04.70.45.99.34 ☑ 🍸 ev. day except Sun. 8.30am–12.30pm 1.30pm–6.30pm; groups by appt.

DOM. DE BELLEVUE

Grande Réserve 1999★

☐ 4.8 ha 40,000 ▮ 🌡 20–29 F

A very nice wine, this is a clear pale yellow 99 whose floral nose powerfully opens out on white flowers and roses. Rich and supple, it offers balance and a good structure. A curiosity, the **Blanc Cuvée Spéciale 94** (30–49F), was judged a success. It is made from 100% Chardonnay, harvested from granitic and stony soils, which doubtless explains its rare longevity in the appellation. Golden in colour, this wine releases a complex nose of aromas of honey and beeswax. It evolves well in the mouth and can be drunk as an apéritif.
🔑 Jean-Louis Pétillat, Dom. de Bellevue, 03500 Meillard, tel. 04.70.42.05.56, fax 04.70.42.09.75 ☑ 🍸 by appt.

DOM. DE CHINIERE 1999

☐ 5.3 ha 30,000 ▮ 🌡 20–29 F

This vineyard, nowadays comprising more than 14 ha (34 acres), has belonged to the same family for two centuries. It has produced this pale yellow wine whose freshness is rediscovered on the palate. It makes a good accompaniment for seafood. (Wine sold at the Saint-Pourçain cooperative wine cellar.)
🔑 Philippe Chérillat, Chinière, 03500 Saulcet, tel. 04.70.45.45.66

CAVE COURTINAT 1999★★

☐ 1.2 ha 7,200 ▮ 🌡 20–29 F

The tasters particularly appreciated the aromatic intensity of this 99 wine, dominated by boxwood notes typical of Sauvignon. Full and fresh on the finish, it possesses remarkable balance. The **Gamay 99**is very successful. While still timid on the nose, it already allows very ripe red fruit to peep through. The initial impression on the palate is clean, and it finishes at some length on spicy flavours.
🔑 Cave Courtinat, Venteuil, 03500 Saulcet, tel. 04.70.45.44.84, fax 04.70.45.80.13 ☑ 🍸 by appt.

BERNARD GARDIEN ET FILS

Nectar des Fées 1999★★

☐ 5 ha 30,000 ▮ 🌡 20–29 F

A bicycle ride in the wood of Villemort and the town of Chassignolles will doubtless take you to the Gardiens' estate. There, Bernard

Gardien and his sons Olivier and Christophe have made the Nectar des Fées, a pale yellow Saint-Pourçain with green glints whose magic has undeniably worked. The intensely mingled, delicate scents of white flowers are succeeded by a harmonious, very long palate. In a rare occurrence, the estate has duplicated its achievement in the same year: **Cuvée du Terroir Rouge 99** is also awarded a *Coup de Coeur*. A deep ruby colour, this was unanimously judged to be remarkable, so full and pleasing were its very ripe fruit aromas and so perfectly balanced its palate.

Dom. Gardien, Chassignolles, 03210 Besson, tel. 04.70.42.80.11, fax 04.70.42.80.93 ev. day except Sun. 8am–12 noon 2pm–7pm

ELIE GROSBOT ET DENIS BARBARA Grande Réserve 1999

■ 1.5 ha 8,000 20–29 F

It was in 1996 that Elie Grosbot and Denis Barbara entered into partnership in the Saint-Pourçain appellation, and their association has yielded good results. As proof, this Grande Réserve was singled out by the jury. It develops scents of black fruit, and it charms on the palate with the lovely balance of its tannins, which are very much present on the finish.

Dom. Grosbot-Barbara, Maupertuis, 03500 Bransat, tel. 04.70.45.26.66, fax 04.70.45.54.95, e-mail cave.barbara@bial.oleane.com ev. day 9am–12 noon 2pm–7pm

DOM. DE LA CROIX D'OR 1999★

□ 3.5 ha n.c. 20–29 F

This estate wins renown with a light yellow white wine, tinged with green. The nose has a good intensity and is marked by white flowers. Gracious and well-balanced on the palate, the wine displays a good length.

Jean-François Colas, La Croix d'Or, 03210 Chemilly, tel. 04.70.42.86.22

NEBOUT 1999★

■ 8 ha 35,000 20–29 F

Here is an enticing wine, with its light red colour. It offers scents of red fruit and flowers on the nose. Very refreshing on the palate, it is ready to drink. Also mentioned by the jury was **Blanc Tradition 99**, which gives off, if you can wait a few minutes, scents of white flowers and honey. It has good balance and length.

EARL Nebout, Les Champions, 03500 Saint-Pourçain-sur-Sioule, tel. 04.70.45.31.70, fax 04.70.45.12.54 ev. day 8am–12 noon 2pm–7pm

FRANCOIS RAY 1999★

◪ 1.5 ha 11,000 20–29 F

This property, which now runs to more than 11 ha (27 acres), was acquired in 1929 by the Ray family. Representing the fourth generation, François makes successful wines of all three Saint-Pourçain colours. The first is a bright and charming rosé. While it releases floral scents on the nose, it reveals itself more powerfully on the palate, and at sufficient length. The **Blanc 99** deserves a mention, with its delicate flowery aromas and a slight bitterness on the finish that will lessen with time, as does the **Rouge 99**, which has a surprising aromatic intensity, small red fruits combining with a note of liquorice, and velvety tannins on the finish.

Cave François Ray, Venteuil, 03500 Saulcet, tel. 04.70.45.35.46, fax 04.70.45.64.96 ev. day except Sun. 9am–12 noon 2pm–7pm; groups by appt.

LES VIGNERONS DE SAINT-POURCAIN Réserve spéciale 1999★

◪ n.c. 100,000 20–29 F

An attractive rosé of full colour gleaming with purple. It registers a good aromatic intensity on the nose, and freshness and a real presence on the palate. In addition, the jury also mentioned **Saint-Pourçain Rouge Réserve Spéciale 99** for its good balance.

Union des vignerons de Saint-Pourçain, rue de la Ronde, 03500 Saint-Pourçain-sur-Sioule, tel. 04.70.45.42.82, fax 04.70.45.99.34 ev. day except Sun. 8.30am–12.30pm 1.30pm–6.30pm; groups by appt.

Côte Roannaise

Volcanic soils on valley slopes in the east, south and south-west create a terroir in which the Gamay is very much at home.

Fourteen communes, covering 176 ha (435 acres) situated on the left bank of the river produce excellent red wines and rather unusual, fresh rosés. Vinification, which totalled 8,891 hl (234,722 gal) in 1998, takes place on the growers' own properties; they create original wines of character appealing to the most prestigious chefs in the region. The area's wine-growing traditions are on show at the Musée Forézien in Ambierle.

Slowly but surely the vineyard is expanding. More important, however, is the attention the shippers and distributors now pay to Côte Roannaise wines, which helps to reinforce the originality and quality of the growth.

Chardonnay is gradually being introduced and makes wines that are bottled as Vin de Pays d'Urfé.

ALAIN BAILLON Montplaisir 1999★★

■ 1 ha 6,000 30–49 F

Eighty-year-old vines are the source of this intense ruby-coloured wine which releases quite full-bodied scents of red fruit and blackcurrant, then faded rose, peony and grilled notes. Its rich, aromatic flavours invade the palate, linked to gentle tannins. This beautiful, well-balanced wine is for drinking in the next three years. Alain Baillon has also made a round, fine **Rosé 99** with notes of ripe red fruit, which fully deserves a mention. Drink it as young as possible.

🔑 Alain Baillon, Montplaisir, 42820 Ambierle, tel. 04.77.65.65.51, fax 04.77.65.65.65 ☒ Y by appt.

CH. DE CHAMPAGNY 1999

■ 4 ha 30,000 20–29 F

This estate produced as many as 4,000 hl (105,600 gal) in the 19th century, but the phylloxera crisis was devastating and it took until 1968, and the arrival of André de Villeneuve, to receive a new impetus. The château's 99 Côte Roannaise has a deep ruby colour and a fairly intense nose of cherry, blackcurrant, violet or peony. The palate, marked by still-young tannins, is full and with good length. Powerful and rich, the wine should be left for another year to reveal its full potential.

🔑 André et Frédéric Villeneuve, Champagny, 42370 Saint-Haon-le-Vieux, tel. 04.77.64.42.88, fax 04.77.62.12.55 ☒ Y by appt.

DOM. DU FONTENAY 1999

■ 3 ha 30,000 20–29 F

This intensely red wine presents moderately developed perfumes of pepper and blackcurrant, then evolves towards the vegetal. After a round, aromatic opening on the palate, light but still rough tannins are evident. A few months should be enough to round them out.

🔑 Dom. du Fontenay, 42155 Villemontais, tel. 04.77.63.12.22, fax 04.77.63.15.95, e-mail hawkins@netsysteme.net ☒ Y by appt.

🔑 Simon Hawkins

DOM. DE LA PAROISSE

Cuvée à l'ancienne 1999★

■ n.c. 5,000 20–29 F

Since 1610, 13 generations of the same family have run this estate. In the last year of the 20th century Jean-Claude Chaucesse has made a dark red wine which, lively but without aggression, opens with peppery notes, smoky aromas and vegetable touches. On the palate, it reveals itself to be aromatic; although well-balanced, it could be a little fuller. Drink within two years.

🔑 Jean-Claude Chaucesse, 121, rue des Alloués, 42370 Renaison, tel. 04.77.64.26.10, fax 04.77.62.13.84 ☒ Y by appt.

DOM. DU PAVILLON 1999

◩ 1 ha 5,000 20–29 F

Salmon-pink, bright and clear, this wine releases very intense scents of strawberry, peach, apricot and apple. Initially lively, on the palate it takes on roundness and a nicely aromatic outline. The strong notes on the nose reappear, intensified, on the palate. A rosé to drink young.

🔑 Maurice Lutz, GAEC Dom. du Pavillon, 42820 Ambierle, tel. 04.77.65.64.35, fax 04.77.65.69.69 ☒ Y by appt.

ROBERT SEROL Les Originelles 1999★★

■ 6 ha 45,000 20–29 F

A *Coup de Coeur* for this Côte Roannaise, which releases well-developed perfumes of rose and peony before opening up on raspberry. Filling the mouth fully and very quickly with its velvety roundness, the wine is nevertheless well structured. A vegetal hint on the finish, combined with fruity aromas, and its harmony is complete. Drink within the next two years.

🔑 Robert Sérol et Fils, Les Estinaudes, 42370 Renaison, tel. 04.77.64.44.04, fax 04.77.62.10.87 ☒ Y ev. day 9am–12 noon 2pm–6pm

PHILIPPE ET JEAN-MARIE VIAL

Découverte 1999

■ 3.5 ha 30,000 30–49 F

Gamay grapes, grown on soils of granitic sand, have produced this purplish-ruby wine with scents of raspberry, kirsch, blackcurrant and peony, a pleasant fruitiness that opens out freshly on the palate. Well structured, fine and pleasing, this wine is for drinking young. From the same producer, the **Rosé 99** deserves a mention, as does **Rouge Bougheran 99**, which bears the name of a hillside reclaimed and cultivated in 1964.

🔑 GAEC Vial, Bel-Air, 42370 Saint-André-d'Apchon, tel. 04.77.65.81.04, fax 04.77.65.91.99 ☒ Y by appt.

L'Orléanais AOVDQS

The wines of Orléans had their moment of glory in medieval times, but the vine still prospers on about 150 ha (370 acres) among the gardens, nurseries and famous orchards of the Orléanais. The tradition was kept going mainly on the sandy, gravelly terraces of the south bank of the Loire between Olivet and Cléry, where the church houses the tomb of Louis XI, who died in 1483.

Pinot Meunier, otherwise mainly used in Champagne, here produces original red and rosé wines. The supple rosés are sometimes described as Vin Gris.

Since the 9th century, the wine-makers have adapted the following varieties, which it is claimed were imported from the Auvergne, but which are identical to the ones in Burgundy: Auvernat Rouge (Pinot Noir), Auvernat Blanc (Chardonnay) and Gris Meunier, to which was added Cabernet (or Breton) with its aromas of red- and blackcurrants. The wines should be drunk with partridge and roast pheasant, game pâtés from neighbouring Sologne and ash cheeses from the Gâtinais. In 1998, the production of red reached 4,593 hl (121,255 gal) from a vineyard of about 150 ha (370 gal); white wine production is more limited at 934 hl (24,658 gal).

VIGNOBLE DU CHANT D'OISEAUX

Gris meunier 1999

■ 2.68 ha 10,000 20–29 F

Jacky Legroux has produced an Orléanais with a very pleasant nose scented with morello cherry. The tannins are still a little young and need a year or two to harmonise totally. Also worth of note is **Rosé Gris Meunier 99**, which leaves an impression of freshness.

Jacky Legroux, 315, rue des Muids, 45370 Mareau-aux-Prés, tel. 02.38.45.60.31, fax 02.38.45.62.35 by appt.

LES VIGNERONS DE LA GRAND'MAISON 1999

□ 19 ha n.c. 20–29 F

White and red, three good wines have been presented by the Vignerons de la Grand' Maison and are mentioned by the jury. The first, a white with a pretty golden straw colour, very round, would be good with fish. **Rouge Gris Meunier 99** is intense on the nose with scents of morello cherry, then becomes fresh and fluid on the palate. The **Rouge Cabernet 99** surprises for its sweetness and harmony.

Les Vignerons de La Grand'Maison, 550, rte des Muids, 45370 Mareau-aux-Prés, tel. 02.38.45.61.08, fax 02.38.45.65.70 by appt.

SAINT AVIT 1999**

■ 2.63 ha 5,000 20–29 F

At the very least, you can say that Javoy Père et Fils have succeeded in their 99 vintage. Purple to look at, the first wine gives off scents of perfectly ripe red fruit, then a fleshy, rich palate sustained by harmonious tannins. Next, one star rewards the **Saint Avit Cabernet 99**, with its aromas of ripe black fruit. Tannins are very evident, ensuring longevity. In the **Blanc 99**, the same mark is awarded to a pale yellow, golden-tinted Orléanais whose floral aromas, while timid, are promising. The palate is round and well balanced, with a note of carbon dioxide bringing freshness.

Javoy Père et Fils, 450, rue du Buisson, 45370 Mézières-lez-Cléry, tel. 02.38.45.66.95, fax 02.38.45.69.77 ev. day except Sun. 8.15–12 noon 2pm–7pm

CLOS SAINT-FIACRE 1999***

■ 5.74 ha 65,000 30–49 F

A jewel in the appellation's crown, this red Orléanais is the epitome of refinement with its perfectly clear ruby colour. On the nose, scents of morello cherry are enhanced by a spicy hint. The initial impression on the palate is clean, firm and straightforward and introduces well-balanced flavours built up on silky tannins. A very good length . . . a treat!

GAEC Clos Saint-Fiacre, 560, rue Saint-Fiacre, 45370 Mareau-aux-Prés, tel. 02.38.45.61.55, fax 02.38.45.66.58 by appt.

Daniel Montigny

CLOS SAINT-FIACRE 1999**

□ 4.92 ha 30,000 30–49 F

Its pale yellow colour shows that this wine was made from well-matured grapes. The nose is all delicacy, the palate all suppleness and unctuousness. A remarkable wine, but even so do not overlook **Cabernet Franc 99 du Clos Saint-Fiacre**, awarded one star. Garnet-coloured, it has a good aromatic intensity of red fruit combined with spice, with silky tannins giving balance. The wine is ready for drinking. The **Rosé 99** is mentioned for its freshness and the youthfulness of its aromas: a fresh and fruity wine, with good length.

LOIRE

GAEC Clos Saint-Fiacre, 560, rue Saint-Fiacre, 45370 Mareau-aux-Prés,
tel. 02.38.45.61.55, fax 02.38.45.66.58
by appt.

Menetou-Salon

Menetou-Salon owes its vinous beginnings to the proximity of the medieval metropolis of Bourges. Unlike many other once-famous wine regions this one has remained a wine-growing area; the present vineyard is of high quality and covers 336 ha (830 acres).

Menetou-Salon's favoured slopes share the same soils as its prestigious neighbour, Sancerre, and grow the same varieties, Sauvignon Blanc and Pinot Noir. From these, the appellation produces fresh, spicy white wines, delicate, fruity rosés, and harmonious, scented reds, all of which should be drunk young. They are the pride of viticulture in Berry and splendidly accompany full-flavoured classic dishes (as an aperitif or with hot starters for the whites; with fish, rabbit or charcuterie for the reds, which should be served slightly chilled). Production reached 23,572 hl (622,301 gal) in 1999, of which 15,046 hl (397,214 gal) were white wines.

DOM. DE BEAUREPAIRE 1999

6 ha 45,000 30–49 F

Discretion and severity characterise this 1999 wine from Domaine de Beaurepaire. It releases some exotic and vegetal (gorse) scents on the nose, and on the palate it evolves from roundness to liveliness. A timid wine which needs time to express itself.

Dom. de Beaurepaire, 18220 Soulangis,
tel. 02.48.64.41.09, fax 02.48.64.39.89
ev. day except Sun. 9am–12 noon 2pm–6.30pm

DOM. DE CHATENOY 1999*

37 ha 315,000 50–69 F

'Silvery-gold: the colour of jewellery', wrote one of the tasters. Blackcurrant buds and peach blossom, a typical Sauvignon nose, one could add. While the opening on the palate is a little lively, balance quickly asserts itself. The wine is ready for drinking and can also be kept for several years. The **Rouge 98**, matured in oak barrels, is worthy of mention too.

SCEA Caves Clément, Dom. de Chatenoy, B.P. 12, 18510 Menetou-Salon,
tel. 02.48.66.68.70, fax 02.48.66.68.71
ev. day except Sun. 8am–12 noon 1.30pm–5.30pm

G. CHAVET ET FILS 1999*

2.17 ha 18,000 30–49 F

The colour of rosés is an important criterion in their analysis; this one is a deep salmon-pink. Pleasant on the nose, with scents ranging from the fruity (cherry) to the floral, the wine's suppleness and depth are good supports for its length. A 'pleasure wine'. The **Blanc 99** obtained a mention.

SARL Chavet et Fils, Les Brangers,
18510 Menetou-Salon, tel. 02.48.64.80.87,
fax 02.48.64.84.78, e-mail
philippe.chavet@wanadoo.fr ev. day except Sun. 8am–12 noon 2pm–6pm

DOM. DE COQUIN 1999**

5 ha 40,000 30–49 F

A hundred and fifty years ago, Jean-Baptiste Audiot exhibited a great passion for wine-making, and today Francis proves that his legacy has not been lost. This 99 wine, with hints of flowers and citrus fruit on the nose, opens on the palate superbly with both balance and substance and already shows concentration by its golden colour. Wisdom dictates that you wait to fully enjoy this lovely, promising wine. The **Rouge 99** receives one star.

Francis Audiot, Dom. de Coquin, 18510 Menetou-Salon, tel. 02.48.64.80.46,
fax 02.48.64.84.51 ev. day 9am–12 noon 2pm–6.30pm; Sun. by appt.

DOM. GILBERT 1999★

■ 13.56 ha 109,000 30–49 F

Wine-makers father and son since 1768, the Gilberts settled a century ago at Les Faucards near Menetou-Salon. Spicy touches and fresh red fruit dominate the scents released by their 99 wine. The tannic structure is of good quality, linking silkiness and solidity. This wine can face the future with confidence. The **Blanc 99** receives one star for its typical aromatic qualities and its texture.

Dom. Gilbert, Les Faucards, 18510 Menetou-Salon, tel. 02.48.64.80.77, fax 02.48.64.82.55 by appt.

LA TOUR SAINT-MARTIN

Morogues 1999★★

□ 6.5 ha n.c. 30–49 F

Silver gleams amid the gold, imparting glamour to this wine. Little honeyed touches enhance richness on the nose, while on the palate the wine is correspondingly rich and round. A lovely wine due to the power of its structure and the delicacy of its aromas. **Rouge 99 Morogues** is awarded a star (50–69F).

Albane et Bertrand Minchin, EARL La tour Saint-Martin, 18340 Crosses, tel. 02.48.25.02.95, fax 02.48.25.05.03, e-mail tour.saint.martin@wanadoo.fr by appt.

LE PRIEURE DE SAINT-CEOLS

Cuvée des Bénédictins 1998★

□ 1 ha 8,000 30–49 F

Maturity is discernible through notes of wax and asparagus on the nose, and hints of white flower and peach-blackcurrant, as well as a lemony freshness, on the palate indicate that this wine will keep well. From the **99** vintage, the **Blanc** and the **Rouge** each deserve a mention.

Pierre Jacolin, Le prieuré de Saint-Céols, 18220 Saint-Céols, tel. 02.48.64.40.75, fax 02.48.64.41.15, e-mail sarl-jacolin@libertysurf.fr ev. day except Sun. 8am–7pm

DOM. DE LOYE 1999

■ 2.47 ha 14,900 30–49 F

This Menetou-Salon's initial impression on the nose is very clearly red fruit in brandy, and letting the wine breathe brings out a vegetal facet. The tannins need time before softening up and delighting our taste buds.

Dom. de Loye, 18220 Morogues, tel. 02.48.64.35.17, fax 02.48.64.41.29 ev. day except Sun. 9.30am–12 noon 2.30pm–6.30pm

Moindrot et Fils

DOM. HENRY PELLE Morogues 1999

□ 15 ha 130,000 30–49 F

As charming as a bouquet of summer flowers, this Menetou-Salon has scents of citrus fruit (lemon and grapefruit) and broom. It reveals a good balance on the palate, firmness translated by flavours of lemon and gunflint. A wine typical of the appellation.

Dom. Henry Pellé, rte d'Aubinges, 18220 Morogues, tel. 02.48.64.42.48, fax 02.48.64.36.88, e-mail domaine.henry.pelle@wanadoo.fr ev. day except Sat. Sun. 8am–12 noon 1.30pm–6pm

Anne Pellé

DOM. JEAN TEILLER 1999★★

□ 6 ha 45,000 30–49 F

A lovely sequence of aromatic tones: first, floral and lemony scents, then discreet grilled touches and finally the vegetal fragrances of broom. The whole is in harmony with the mouth-filling minerality of the palate. Domaine Jean Teiller has also scored a total success with its **99** vintage: the **Rouge** and the **Rosé** have been awarded a star and a mention respectively.

Dom. Jean Teiller, 13, rte de la Gare, 18510 Menetou-Salon, tel. 02.48.64.80.71, fax 02.48.64.86.92, e-mail domaine-teiller@wanadoo.fr ev. day except Sun. 8am–12 noon 2pm–6.30pm

J.-J. Teiller

CHRISTOPHE ET GUY TURPIN

Morogues 1999

□ 6 ha 40,000 30–49 F

This wine resembles a work in the process of creation. The aromas are intensely expressed, reminiscent of the end of alcoholic fermentation (brioche and breadcrumbs). The palate is supple with a hint of bitterness on the finish. Some months of patience should suffice to refine it.

GAEC Turpin Père et Fils, 11, pl. de l'Eglise, 18220 Morogues, tel. 02.48.64.32.24, fax 02.48.64.32.24 by appt.

Pouilly-Fumé and Pouilly-sur-Loire

The delightful vineyard of Pouilly-sur-Loire was first established by Benedictine monks. The Loire pounds against a limestone promontory as it turns north-east, and the soil, less chalky than at Sancerre, provides excellent growing conditions for the south-south-east facing slopes. The main variety is Sauvignon Blanc Fumé, which will shortly have entirely supplanted the traditional Chasselas, previously the source of appealing white wines when cultivated on silica soils. Pouilly-sur-Loire covers

50 ha (123 acres) of which Pouilly-Fumé represents 950 ha (2,346 acres). Total production was 69,478 hl (1,834,219 gal) of a wine that has all the qualities associated with a limestone *terroir*, marked by a freshness, which does not lack a certain structure, and a full array of varietal aromas. It is matured within the area where it is grown according to certain conditions under which the must is fermented.

Pouilly-Fumé

CEDRICK BARDIN 1999

☐ 4,7 ha 25 000 30–49 F

Cédrick Bardin started up in 1991 and cultivates about 10 ha (25 acres) of Sancerre and Pouilly-Fumé. He offers a Pouilly-Fumé with a fine, elegant nose reminiscent of very ripe orange, lemon and white flowers. Sparkling with freshness, lacking neither suppleness nor liveliness, here is an easy wine, all fruit, to drink during the next festive season.

Cédrick Bardin, 12, rue Waldeck-Rousseau, 58150 Pouilly-sur-Loire, tel. 03.86.39.11.24, fax 03.86.39.16.50 ev. day 9am–6pm; Sun. by appt.

DOM. BARILLOT 1999★

☐ 1.6 ha 12,000 30–49 F

The nose has a good aromatic intensity and opens up some grilled notes. The palate is rich and well-balanced; long on the finish, this is a well-prepared Pouilly-Fumé, absolutely true to type.

SCEA Barillot Père et Fils, Le Bouchot, 58150 Pouilly-sur-Loire, tel. 03.86.39.15.29, fax 03.86.39.09.52 ev. day except Sun. 9am–12.30pm 1.30pm–7pm; groups by appt.

DOM. DES BERTHIERS

Cuvée d'Eve Vieilles vignes 1998★

☐ 2.5 ha 15,000 50–69 F

Domaine des Berthiers, close to Pouilly on the Loire hillsides, was taken over in 1995 by the Fournier family from Sancerre. Its Cuvée d'Eve reveals mineral touches of gunflint, drawn from one of the two soils that produced it: flinty clay. It also bears fruity and floral aromas inherited from the other soil: chalky clay. This is a rounded wine which does not disappoint on the palate. From the same estate, **Domaine des Berthiers 99** (30–49F), was mentioned for its balance and potential.

SCEA Dom. des Berthiers, B.P. 30, 58150 Saint-Andelain, tel. 03.86.39.12.85, fax 03.86.39.12.94, e-mail claude@fournier-père-fils.fr ev. day 9.30am–5pm; Sat. Sun. by appt.

J.-C. Dagueneau

GILLES BLANCHET

Les Champs des Plantes 1999★

☐ 0.7 ha 5,000 30–49 F

Running a 6-ha (15-acre) estate since 1991, Gilles Blanchet has established a formidable reputation for his Les Champs des Plantes. Eloquent on the nose, predominantly floral with a slight vegetal hint, the wine is full and rich on the palate, with notes of crystallised fruit and lemon. A pleasant wine.

Gilles Blanchet, Les Berthiers, 58150 Saint-Andelain, tel. 03.86.39.14.03, fax 03.86.39.00.54 by appt.

BOUCHIE-CHATELLIER

Premier millésimé 1999★

☐ 1.3 ha 5,200 70–99 F

There is a superb view from the Bouchié-Chatellier estate which dominates the whole Ligerian wine-growing area, but that is not all you will remember. This Premier Millésimé wine originates from plots with good exposure to the sun, and it is quite obviously made from the ripest grapes, with its intensely fruity pear, quince and citrus fruit. On the palate, everything is as it should be, with freshness and a good length. A classical Pouilly-Fumé.

EARL Bouchié-Chatellier, La Renardière, 58150 Saint-Andelain, tel. 03.86.39.14.01, fax 03.86.39.05.18 by appt.

DOM. DU BOUCHOT 1999★★

☐ 8.5 ha 55,000 30–49 F

The Kerbiquets, father and son, partners in Domaine du Bouchot, know just how to find the right balance between experience and innovation. This balance is also realised in their wines, as witness their 99. Its subtle aromatic freshness, comprised of boxwood, moss and blackcurrant buds, the elegance and fullness of its palate and the lovely marriage of liveliness and richness, make it just the kind of Pouilly-Fumé that we were looking for.

Dom. du Bouchot, B.P. 31, Saint-Andelain, 58150 Pouilly-sur-Loire, tel. 03.86.39.13.95, fax 03.86.39.05.92 by appt.

Kerbiquet

HENRI BOURGEOIS

La Demoiselle de Bourgeois 1999★

☐ 3.8 ha 28,000 70–99 F

This vast estate (60 ha/148 acres) offers a Pouilly-Fumé with a complex nose, where mineral rivals floral and fruity, with a touch of vegetal flavours. The well-structured palate has body, suppleness and liveliness. The finish confirms all the potential of this wine.

Dom. Henri Bourgeois, Chavignol, 18300 Sancerre, tel. 02.48.78.53.20, fax 02.48.54.14.24, e-mail domaine@bourgeois.sancerre.com by appt.

DOMINIQUE BRISSET 1999

☐ 8 ha 40,000 ▮ 30–49 F

This has just what it takes to please. First, Sauvignon grapes burst out on the nose, and, after the wine has been allowed to breathe, these are enriched by slightly grilled tones. It opens gently on the palate, then the wine's liveliness increases, but not excessively, right up to the finish.

⊶ Dominique Brisset, 18, rue des Levées, Bois Fleury, 58150 Tracy-sur-Loire, tel. 03.86.26.16.72, fax 03.86.26.19.87 ☑ Y by appt.

HENRY BROCHARD Sélection 1998

☐ n.c. 30,000 ▮ 50–69 F

This wine-merchant offers a lovely pale golden Pouilly-Fumé containing a few fine bubbles of CO_2. Open on the nose, of good complexity, it releases fruity and smoky notes. Full and well balanced on the palate, this is a wine ready for drinking.

⊶ Henry Brochard, Chavignol, 18300 Sancerre, tel. 02.48.78.20.10, fax 02.48.78.20.19 ☑

DOM. A. CAILBOURDIN

Les Cris 1999★★

☐ 3 ha 20,000 ▮ ♁ 50–69 F

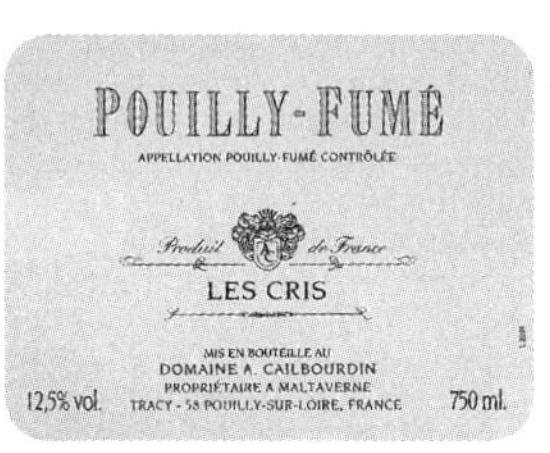

While the aromas of this 99 are still modest, one is nevertheless aware of all its promise. The scents are rather unusual, composed of honey, dried fruit and grilled touches. The wine opens cleanly on the palate, and its flavour is dense and full. In brief, a very beautiful wine, and a *Coup de Coeur* which arrives just in time to celebrate the 20th anniversary of Alain Cailbourdin's starting up. **Cuvée de Boisfleury 99** deserves a mention too.

⊶ Dom. Alain Cailbourdin, R.N. 7, Maltaverne, 58150 Pouilly-sur-Loire, tel. 03.86.26.17.73, fax 03.86.26.14.73 ☑ Y by appt.

JEAN-PIERRE CHAMOUX

Les Chantalouettes 1999

☐ 1 ha 6,000 ▮ ♁ 50–69 F

With a discreet approach, floral touches being followed by notes of pepper and capsicum, this wine is well balanced. Appreciate it in all its simplicity for its freshness, for example with the local fried dish.

⊶ Jean-Pierre Chamoux, 2, pl. de la République, 58150 Pouilly-sur-Loire, tel. 03.86.39.15.58, fax 03.86.39.10.45 ☑ Y by appt.

DOM. CHAMPEAU 1999★

☐ 15 ha 80,000 ▮ 30–49 F

Franck and Guy Champeau took over this lovely family property (close on 17 ha/42 acres) in 1989. Made from a combination of grapes grown on chalky clay and flint, their Pouilly-Fumé is pleasing due to its liveliness and aromas of white flowers mingled with a hint of fern and boxwood. It fills the mouth well thanks to a consistent structure, and it lingers long on the finish.

⊶ SCEA Dom. Champeau, Le Bourg, 58150 Saint-Andelain, tel. 03.86.39.15.61, fax 03.86.39.19.44 ☑ Y ev. day 9am–12 noon 2pm–6pm; Sun. by appt.

⊶ Franck et Guy Champeau

JEAN-CLAUDE CHATELAIN

Les Charmes Chatelain 1999★

☐ 3 ha 24,000 ▮ ⦀ ♁ 50–69 F

A wine-maker and merchant, Jean-Claude Chatelain is heir to a line of wine-growers which stretches back to 1630. The product of maturation half in vats and half in barrels, Les Charmes Chatelain has a seductive finesse. The oakiness from the barrels does not mask the wine's hints of white peach. Tannin is clearly marked on the palate, which is nevertheless full and delicate at the same time. An already-pleasant wine, this needs two or three years before it can be fully appreciated. From the same producer, **Chatelain 99** deserves a mention.

⊶ SA Dom. Châtelain, Les Berthiers, 58150 Saint-Andelain, tel. 03.86.39.17.46, fax 03.86.39.01.13 ☑ Y by appt.

DOM. CHAUVEAU

Les Croqloups 1999★

☐ 0.8 ha 6,500 ▮ ♁ 30–49 F

Benoît Chauveau took over the family estate only in 1998 and here he is in the *Guide* with two wines. Les Croqloups was noticed for the intensity of its perfumes. Aromatic on the palate, it mingles citrus notes (orange peel and lemon) with mango. Supple and pleasing with a mischievous bitterness, you will be delighted by it. **La Charmette 99** (50–69F) is worthy of note too.

⊶ Benoît Chauveau, Les Cassiers, 58150 Saint-Andelain, tel. 03.86.39.15.42, fax 03.86.39.19.46 ☑ Y ev. day 9am–8pm

GILLES CHOLLET 1999

☐ 1.5 ha 13,000 ▮ ♁ 30–49 F

Gilles Chollet has been farming an estate of 10 ha (25 acres) since 1989. In its vegetal scents of asparagus and capsicum, his Pouilly-Fumé stresses one of the many characteristics of Sauvignon. Easy to drink, the wine shows well on the palate, scarcely noticeable but for an attractive freshness.

⊶ EARL Gilles Chollet, 6 bis, rue Joseph-Renaud, Le Bouchot, 58150 Pouilly-sur-Loire, tel. 03.86.39.02.19, fax 03.86.39.06.13 ☑ Y ev. day 9am–12 noon 2.30pm–6.30pm

LOIRE

DOM. PAUL CORNEAU

Cuvée Sélection 1999

☐ 7 ha 40,000 50–69 F

Paul Corneau knows how to make a good wine. This 99 bears the stamp of the Sauvignon grape, with touches of boxwood that are peculiar to it, and the stamp of its vinification in notes of very ripe banana. These sensations are nicely prolonged on the palate, leaving an impression of sweet fullness, embellished on the finish by a lemony freshness.

Paul Corneau, Le Bouchot, 58150 Pouilly-sur-Loire, tel. 03.86.39.17.95, fax 03.86.39.16.32 ev. day 8am–12 noon 2pm–7pm; Sun. by appt.

PATRICK COULBOIS

Les Cocques 1999

☐ 7.4 ha 30,000 30–49 F

Patrick Coulbois' Les Cocques appears regularly in the *Guide*, sometimes among the best-placed wines. Boxwood and blackcurrant buds dominate in the 99 vintage: this is a good example of the Sauvignon grape's vegetal qualities. Floral touches are particularly evident in flavours on the palate, and the acidity is well balanced. A good representative of the appellation.

Patrick Coulbois, Les Berthiers, 58150 Saint-Andelain, tel. 03.86.39.15.69, fax 03.86.39.12.14 by appt.

CAVE DES CRIOTS 1999★

☐ 10 ha 60,000 30–49 F

Bruno Blondelet has been cultivating more than 10 ha (25 acres) of vines since 1979. Characterised by a very fine bouquet, his Pouilly-Fumé attracts attention for its rich, rounded structure. Still reserved at present, it should open out little by little and be sufficiently expressive by the time the *Guide* comes out.

Bruno Blondelet, Cave des Criots, Le Bouchot, 58150 Pouilly-sur-Loire, tel. 03.86.39.18.75, fax 03.86.39.06.65 by appt.

DIDIER DAGUENEAU

En Chailloux 1998★★

☐ 7 ha 40,000 100–149 F

Didier Dagueneau has made two beautiful wines, one of which is his famous **Cuvée Silex 98** (200–249F), rewarded by two stars (complexity enhanced by well-mastered oakiness). The other is Les Chailloux, of a very lovely pale yellow touched with green, and remarkable for its aromas of mango and lychee accompanied by hints of blackcurrant. Supple, enveloping, with a very good length, this is a charming wine.

Didier Dagueneau, Le Bourg, 58150 Saint-Andelain, tel. 03.86.39.15.62, fax 03.86.39.07.61, e-mail Silex@wanadoo.fr by appt.

JEAN DUMONT Les Charmilles 1999

☐ 7.5 ha 65,000 30–49 F

The finish is enough to justify the inclusion of Les Charmilles. Its golden colour is tinted with brown, and while still modest on the nose, playing on citrus fruit, the wine is very pleasing on the palate thanks to its balance between roundness and freshness.

Jean Dumont, R.N. 7, La Castille, 68150 Pouilly-sur-Loire, tel. 03.86.39.56.60

ANDRE ET EDMOND FIGEAT

Les Chaumiennes 1999★

☐ 3 ha 20,000 50–69 F

Les Chaumiennes? A wine of great finesse, with scents of citrus fruit and acacia flowers and lovely elegance that will catch your attention. **Côte du Nozet 99** also gained one star. It has a very pronounced Sauvignon character.

André et Edmond Figeat, Côte du Nozet, 58150 Pouilly-sur-Loire, tel. 03.86.39.19.39, fax 03.86.39.19.00 by appt.

DOM. DES FINES CAILLOTTES

Prestige 1999

☐ 2 ha 17,000 70–99 F

Caillottes are white stones often found in abundance in chalky clay soils. This wine, made by Alain Pabiot, reveals above all the great maturity of the grapes. Fruitiness (plum) gets the better of all the other flavours. The whole is very rounded and full, with a pleasingly long finish.

Jean Pabiot et Fils, 9, rue de la Treille, Les Loges, 58150 Pouilly-sur-Loire, tel. 03.86.39.10.25, fax 03.86.39.10.12 ev. day 8am–12 noon 2pm–6pm

FOURNIER PERE ET FILS

Grande Cuvée Fournier Vieilles vignes 1998★

☐ n.c. 15,000 50–69 F

This family-owned estate, founded in 1850, now consists of 30 ha (74 acres) spread over three areas of the central appellation. Its Grande Cuvée has a seductively rich aromatic palette, very fruity (pineapple and lychee) and elegantly mingled with honey. Supple and dense on the palate, with a spicy hint, this is a wine of class and character. It has not yet reached its peak and could usefully take up some space in your cellar.

Fournier Père et Fils, Chaudoux, B.P. 7, 18300 Verdigny, tel. 02.48.79.35.24, fax 02.48.79.30.41, e-mail claude@fournier-père-fils.fr ev. day 8am–6.30pm; Sat. Sun. by appt.

DOM. DE LA MARNIERE 1999★

☐ 4.65 ha 40,000 30–49 F

This wine carries on a pleasant conversation in all simplicity, on notes typical of this grape variety (boxwood and blackcurrant bud). It continues in a round, supple tone, gliding over a little bitterness, yet the final impression is in no way constrained by it.

Loiret Frères, 44330 Le Pallet, tel. 02.40.80.40.27
Redde-Parisot

LA MOYNERIE 1999

☐ 26 ha 250,000 50–69 F

This family estate runs to 35 ha (86 acres). Its 99 wine gives off the curious but pleasing scents of brioche and acacia honey. Successfully balanced, with roundness on the palate, it is underlined by a certain vigour on the finish. Drink with white meat.

SA Michel Redde et Fils, La Moynerie, 58150 Pouilly-sur-Loire, tel. 03.86.39.14.72, fax 03.86.39.04.36, e-mail thierry-redde@michel-redde.fr by appt.

DOM. LANDRAT-GUYOLLOT

La Rambarde 1999

☐ 12 ha 55,000 50–69 F

This wine opens up agreeable scents of acacia flower tinged with a note of liquorice and mint. A pleasing wine due to its very marked richness – which would be close to heaviness if it were not fortunately revived on the finish by a hint of mandarin.

Dom. Landrat-Guyollot, Les Berthiers, 58150 Saint-Andelain, tel. 03.86.39.11.83, fax 03.86.39.11.65 ev. day 9am–7pm; groups by appt.

LES MOULINS A VENT 1999★★

☐ 6 ha 40,000 50–69 F

These Moulins à Vent wines are products of the Pouilly-sur-Loire cooperative, founded in 1948. The 99 is remarkable for its year. Power and finesse are united in a beautifully complex nose, with accents of blackcurrant buds, citrus fruit and fresh mint with a mineral touch. On the palate the wine is all roundness, voluminous and persistent. It has potential. **Tonelum 98**, matured in barrels, was awarded one star.

Caves de Pouilly-sur-Loire, Les Moulins à vent, B.P. 9, 58150 Pouilly-sur-Loire, tel. 03.86.39.10.99, fax 03.86.39.02.28, e-mail caves.pouilly.loire@wanadoo.fr by appt.

DOM. MASSON-BLONDELET

Villa Paulus 1999

☐ 5 ha 40,000 50–69 F

In 1975 Michelle Blondelet married a lawyer, Jean-Michel Masson. The young couple then started running this estate, which today consists of 19 ha (47 acres) of vines. Their Villa Paulus was a successful in the previous vintage. The 99 version is more modest. The fermentative (banana) and varietal (grapefruit) scents are both classically in evidence on the nose, where there is also a touch of crystallised fruit. On the palate the wine is rich, with a nicely complex fruitiness. The wine deserves to be laid down.

Jean-Michel Masson, 1, rue de Paris, 58150 Pouilly-sur-Loire, tel. 03.86.39.00.34, fax 03.86.39.04.61 by appt.

JOSEPH MELLOT Le Troncsec 1999

☐ 10 ha 84,000 50–69 F

This wine takes its name from a legend: at the time of the Crusades, a dry tree trunk was revived by the relics of Saint Martin which had been deposited in it. The 99 vintage will leave a memory of fine, discreet aromas and, on the palate, lots of richness and fullness. Pike with beurre blanc would make a good match for it.

Vignobles Joseph Mellot Père et Fils, rte de Ménétréol, B.P. 13, 18300 Sancerre, tel. 02.48.78.54.54, fax 02.48.78.54.55, e-mail alexandre@joseph-mellot.fr ev. day except Sat. Sun. 8am–12.15 1.30pm–5.30pm

GUY ET ODILE MICHOT 1999

☐ 3 ha 15,000 30–49 F

Guy and Odile Michot's vineyard is situated partly on chalky clay and partly on flint. This combination has given rise to a wine with a beautiful sensation on the nose. With floral and menthol notes, the flavours are particularly delicate on the palate. A balanced wine in a light style.

Guy et Odile Michot, Soumard, 58150 Saint-Andelain, tel. 03.86.39.13.23, fax 03.86.39.09.25 ev. day 9am–12 noon 2pm–7pm

DOMINIQUE PABIOT

Cuvée Plaisir 1999★

☐ 2.05 ha 10,000 50–69 F

A wine-grower since 1981, Dominique Pabiot formed his own estate in 1997 on the retirement of his father, Jean. Cuvée Plaisir well deserves its name. One is immediately struck by the intensity of the aromas, dominated by evocations of white flowers mingled with a hint of peach and grilled touches. Full and round, with a good length, the palate finishes without any roughness. **Les Vieilles Terres 99** (30–49F) was also awarded a star.

Dominique Pabiot, Les Loges, place des Mariniers, 58150 Pouilly-sur-Loire, tel. 03.86.39.19.09, fax 03.86.39.09.91 ev. day 8am–12 noon 2pm–6pm

DOM. ROGER PABIOT ET SES FILS

Coteau des Girarmes 1999

☐ 12 ha 80,000 30–49 F

Roger Pabiot and his sons farm a trim estate of 21 ha (52 acres). Round and pleasant, with a certain richness, their Coteau des Girarmes presents a genuine liveliness on the finish. Floral, vegetal (broom) and fruity (blackcurrant) notes mingle on the palate. This wine should be served with a freshwater fish such as perch or pike.

Dom. Roger Pabiot et ses Fils, 13, rte de Pouilly, Boisgibault, 58150 Tracy-sur-Loire, tel. 03.86.26.18.41, fax 03.86.26.19.89 by appt.

DOM. RAIMBAULT-PINEAU

La Montée des Lumeaux 1999

☐ 1.64 ha 13,000 50–69 F

This wine, from chalky clay soil rich in *caillottes* (white stones), has a powerful character of an interesting style, but one that still needs to assert itself. The balance is good, with a harmonious quality.

Dom. Raimbault-Pineau, rte de Sancerre, 18300 Sury-en-Vaux, tel. 02.48.79.33.04, fax 02.48.79.36.25 ev. day 9am–12 noon 1.30pm–6pm; Sun. by appt.; cl. 1st–15 Aug. and 8–23 Jan.

J.-M. Raimbault

DOM. DE RIAUX 1999★

☐ 8 ha 40,000 30–49 F

After having been very close to the *Coup de Coeur* with their 98 wine, Bertrand and Alexis Jeannot have produced a promising 99, very much in the style of Domaine de Riaux. The nose is intense, with a fermentation flavour still evident. A youthful vitality, typical of wines from flinty clay, just allows fullness to show through, something that will express itself more openly after a few months' ageing.

GAEC Jeannot Père et Fils, Dom. de Riaux, 58150 Saint-Andelain, tel. 03.86.39.11.37, fax 03.86.39.06.21 by appt.

GUY SAGET Les Logères 1999★★

☐ 8 ha 70,000 30–49 F

All the elements of quality are combined in this wine: flavours on the palate, which should open progressively but already have white flowers and peach bursting through, and richness balanced by vigour. A complete and well-structured wine, this needs to age to reveal itself fully. It should then be served with white meat or perhaps grilled lobster.

SA Guy Saget, La Castille, 58150 Pouilly-sur-Loire, tel. 03.86.39.57.75, fax 03.86.39.08.30 ev. day except Sun. 8am–12 noon 2pm–6pm

OLIVIER SCHLATTER 1999★

☐ 0.72 ha 3,200 30–49 F

Olivier Schlatter was vineyard manager on a Pouilly estate until he established his own vineyard in 1994. He has produced a wine surprising for its original but pleasant evocations of red fruit and a structure that reconciles suppleness and freshness. A well-balanced wine.

Olivier Schlatter, 41, rue des Mardrelles, Boisgibault, 58150 Tracy-sur-Loire, tel. 03.86.26.19.31 by appt.

DOM. HERVE SEGUIN

Cuvée Prestige 1998

☐ 1 ha 6,500 50–69 F

Typical and straightforward, this wine is modest but none the less shows its Sauvignon origins. Its ripe fruit accents underline this. One could expect a little more from the palate, which conveys notes of gunflint and mushrooms, but the colour, still very pale, promises good ageing potential.

Dom. Hervé Seguin, Le Bouchot, 58150 Pouilly-sur-Loire, tel. 03.86.39.10.75, fax 03.86.39.10.26 by appt.

DOM. TABORDET 1999

☐ 5.9 ha 50,000 30–49 F

The Tabordet brothers took over the family farm, which covers almost 10 ha (25 acres), 20 years ago, and, with modern cellar equipment and a great deal of care, they have been successful with this 99 vintage. A very pale gold glinting with light green, it is unobtrusive, with a hint of yeast on the nose, and shows smoothness on the palate. This wine should be reviewed after a few months in the bottle.

Yvon et Pascal Tabordet, Chaudoux, 18300 Verdigny, tel. 02.48.79.34.01, fax 02.48.79.32.69 by appt.

DOM. THIBAULT 1999

☐ 12.51 ha85,000 30–49 F

This large farm of nearly 35 ha (86 acres) offers a 99 wine whose aromas evolve throughout the tasting, passing subtly from vegetal to floral. The structure is well balanced, with a slightly lemony finish. This Pouilly-Fumé will be ready for the year-end festive season.

SCEV André Dezat et Fils, Chaudoux, 18300 Verdigny, tel. 02.48.79.38.82, fax 02.48.79.38.24 by appt.

F. TINEL-BLONDELET

L'Arrêt Buffatte 1999★★

☐ 3.5 ha 28,000 50–69 F

'Making a good wine is not difficult . . . provided that you harvest ripe grapes and make it with care', a philosophy that is behind this Arrêt Buffatte Pouilly-Fumé. Marked by fruitiness and remarkable freshness, it simultaneously exhibits elegance and finesse and is at the same time light and mouth-filling.

Dom. Tinel-Blondelet, La Croix-Canat, 58150 Pouilly-sur-Loire, tel. 03.86.39.13.83, fax 03.86.39.02.94 by appt.

Annick Tinel-Blondelet

HUBERT VENEAU 1998

☐ 8 ha 30,000 50–69 F

With its pale golden colour, this wine is still young but nevertheless is well developed on the nose, which tends towards honey and ripe fruit, and light on the palate. The wine is ready to drink.

SCEA Hubert Veneau, Les Ormousseaux, 58200 Saint-Père, tel. 03.86.28.01.17, fax 03.86.28.44.71, e-mail hubert.veneau@wanadoo.fr by appt.

Pouilly-sur-Loire

DOM. DE BEL AIR 1999*

☐ 0.6 ha 3,000 20–29 F

To the Mauroy-Gauliez family, Pouilly-sur-Loire is part of their heritage and deserves the greatest care. A vegetal hint is discernible on the nose of this 99, which fills the mouth and is lively on the finish with notes of grapefruit and liquorice. A few months longer in the bottle will benefit this very successful wine.

EARL Mauroy-Gauliez, 6, rue Waldeck-Rousseau, Le Bouchot, 58150 Pouilly-sur-Loire, tel. 03.86.39.15.85, fax 03.86.39.19.52 ev. day 8am–12 noon 1.30pm–7pm

GILLES BLANCHET 1999*

☐ 0.7 ha 5,000 30–49 F

The Chasselas grape is evident from the first impression on the nose, through unobtrusive scents of hazelnut and pistachio. Round and rich, almost vinous, this Pouilly-sur-Loire evolves pleasantly and leaves vegetal and fruity (apricot) impressions on the finish. It makes a pleasurable apéritif.

Gilles Blanchet, Les Berthiers, 58150 Saint-Andelain, tel. 03.86.39.14.03, fax 03.86.39.00.54 by appt.

DOM. CHAMPEAU 1999*

☐ 1.8 ha 12,000 30–49 F

A Pouilly-sur-Loire of a typical greeny-gold colour. On the nose the wine gives scents of fresh butter accompanied by light floral touches. On the palate, supple with a touch of richness, it finishes very sweetly.

SCEA Dom. Champeau, Le Bourg, 58150 Saint-Andelain, tel. 03.86.39.15.61, fax 03.86.39.19.44 ev. day 9am–12 noon 2pm–6pm; Sun. by appt.

LA MOYNERIE 1999**

☐ 1 ha 6,500 30–49 F

Michel Redde is passionate about the difficult and sometimes thankless Chasselas grape. On the nose his 99 vintage displays enticing finesse, with scents of fresh hazelnut and wood moss. The structure enchants still further due to its lively freshness, which perfectly balances an astonishing roundness. A really well-made Pouilly-sur-Loire.

SA Michel Redde et Fils, La Moynerie, 58150 Pouilly-sur-Loire, tel. 03.86.39.14.72, fax 03.86.39.04.36, e-mail thierry-redde@michel-redde.fr by appt.

Thierry Redde

DOM. LANDRAT-GUYOLLOT

La Roselière 1999

☐ 1.01 ha 8,000 30–49 F

After being allowed to breathe, this wine's nose opens up to scents between orange fruit and orange blossom. This is an easy wine to drink because of its smoothness and pleasant flavours. It would be a perfect accompaniment to *charcuterie*.

Dom. Landrat-Guyollot, Les Berthiers, 58150 Saint-Andelain, tel. 03.86.39.11.83, fax 03.86.39.11.65 ev. day 9am–7pm; groups by appt.

DOM. ROGER PABIOT ET SES FILS 1999*

☐ 0.4 ha 3,000 30–49 F

This Pouilly-sur-Loire needs to breathe a little in order to release its lovely fruitiness reminiscent of plums. On the palate, it opens with a fanfare, then persists gently. The wine would be very pleasant with fruit or vegetables.

Dom. Roger Pabiot et ses Fils, 13, rte de Pouilly, Boisgibault, 58150 Tracy-sur-Loire, tel. 03.86.26.18.41, fax 03.86.26.19.89 by appt.

GUY SAGET 1999**

☐ n.c. n.c. 30–49 F

Bruno Mineur, oenologist at Guy Saget, can be satisfied with this lively Pouilly-sur-Loire. With a pleasant elegance and a good intensity, the scents on the nose are reminiscent of ripe fruit and fresh undergrowth. The palate confirms the impression; tender, ample and very long, this is a remarkable wine.

SA Guy Saget, La Castille, 58150 Pouilly-sur-Loire, tel. 03.86.39.57.75, fax 03.86.39.08.30 ev. day except Sun. 8am–12 noon 2pm–6pm

Quincy

The vineyards of Quincy and Brinay cover 180 ha (445 acres) on plateaux covered with sand and ancient gravels along the banks of the Cher, not far from Bourges and Mehun-sur-Yèvre, in an area rich in the history of the 16th century.

Quincy wines, of which 9,603 hl (253,519 gal) were produced in 1999, are made only from Sauvignon, and are fresh, fruity and extremely drinkable, with real finesse and personality.

If, as the French wine authority Doctor Guyot wrote, variety determines character, Quincy also provides evidence that the same variety can provide different wines in the same region depending on the structure of the soils. The wine-lover will find this one of the most elegant of the Loire wines, to be drunk with fish and seafood, as well as with the goat's cheeses of the region.

DOM. DES BALLANDORS

Cuvée Chaumoux-Ballandors 1999

☐ 2 ha 45,000 30–49 F

Chantal Wilk and Jean Tatin have made a Quincy derived in equal part from 30-year-old and 8-year-old vines. Pale yellow glinting with green, this 99 vintage releases a lemony freshness on the nose, with a sustained liveliness right through to the finish on the palate. A lovely fruitiness underlines the whole.

Chantal Wilk et Jean Tatin, Le Tremblay, 18120 Brinay, tel. 02.48.75.20.09, fax 02.48.75.70.50 by appt.

DOM. DES BRUNIERS

Vin noble 1999★

☐ 9 ha 45,000 30–49 F

Jérôme de la Chaise is responsible for a wine of character in the 99 vintage. Intense fruit is evident on the nose: yellow peach, lychee, mango and pineapple. The initial impression on the palate is supple and silky, and the whole is invested with a great deal of richness and balance.

Jérôme de La Chaise, Les Bruniers, 18120 Quincy, tel. 02.48.51.34.10, fax 02.48.51.34.10 by appt.

DOM. DES CAVES 1998

☐ 4.36 ha 15,350 30–49 F

Passionate about wines, Bruno Lecomte's dream came true in 1994 when he bought his first plot of AOC Quincy vines. The colour of his 98 vintage has remained a remarkable pale greeny-gold. Intensely floral on the nose, embellished with crystallised fruit, the wine is still firm and performs well on the palate.

Bruno Lecomte, 105, rue Saint-Exupéry, 18520 Avord, tel. 02.48.69.27.14, fax 02.48.69.16.42, e-mail Bruno.Lecomte@wanadoo.fr by appt.

DOM. DE CHEVILLY 1999★★

☐ 5 ha 42,000 30–49 F

What a long way Yves and Antoine Lestourgie have come since 1993, the year they started up in vine-growing. For their seventh vintage they were awarded the *Coup de Coeur*. Their Quincy conveys powerful scents of white flowers (lily of the valley) underlined by a mineral touch. The wine is expressive on the palate: a lively first impression is followed by richness and roundness. The wine has great aromatic persistence, and a memory of it will endure for a long time.

Yves et Antoine Lestourgie, 52, rte de Chevilly, 18120 Mereau, tel. 02.48.52.80.45, fax 02.48.52.80.45 by appt.

DOM. DES COUDEREAUX 1999

☐ 8 ha 60,000 30–49 F

What good intensity on the nose! What a lovely expression of Sauvignon! On the palate the wine seems a little retiring after this initial burst of citrus, passion fruit and apricot, but it will definitely assert itself in the coming months.

SCEA Les Coudereaux, 34, rte de Bourges, 18510 Menetou-Salon, tel. 02.48.64.88.88, fax 02.48.64.87.97 by appt.

DOM. CROIX SAINT-URSIN

Beaucharme 1999

☐ 3.9 ha 30,000 30–49 F

Sancerre wine-growers Sylvain and Jacques Bailly are also interested in Quincy. Their Beaucharme was favourably received by the jury for its particularly complex nose, fruity and floral, with a hint of vegetable, and well-balanced palate, which is pleasant from the outset.

Sylvain Bailly, 71, rue de Venoize, 18300 Bué, tel. 02.48.54.02.75, fax 02.48.54.28.41 ev. day 8am–12 noon 2pm–6.30pm; Sun. by appt.

Jacques Bailly

LES VIGNERONS DU DUC DE BERRY 1999★

☐ 8 ha 60,000 30–49 F

This wine breathes maturity: intensity and aromatic finesse in the contrasting scents of grapefruit as well as – more surprising in Quincy – crystallised fruit and honey. The harmony of the whole is completed on the palate with its roundness and length.

SICA Vignerons du Duc de Berry, 34, rte de Bourges, 18510 Menetou-Salon, tel. 02.48.64.88.88, fax 02.48.64.87.97 by appt.

JEAN-PAUL GODINAT 1999

☐ 8 ha 60,000 30–49 F

It was in 1996 that Jean-Paul Godinat took over this vineyard. His 99 vintage still shows slightly yeasty aromas, marked by citrus fruit and pear drops. The overall structure is well balanced right through to a lemony finish. This wine would suit seafood.

Jean-Paul Godinat, 34, rte de Bourges, 18510 Menetou-Salon, tel. 02.48.64.88.88, fax 02.48.64.87.97 by appt.

DOM. DU GRAND ROSIERES 1999

☐ 3.8 ha 15,000 30–49 F

The wine from Domaine du Grand Rosières appeals more for its typical scents

than for their intensity: the wine is still effectively closed on the nose, with modest mineral notes and touches of boxwood. However, you need only taste to discover, after a lively attack, a very pleasing finish on the palate.
Jacques Siret, Dom. du Grand Rosières, 18400 Lunery, tel. 02.48.68.90.34, fax 02.48.68.03.71 by appt.

DOM. DE MAISON BLANCHE

Vin noble 1999

☐ 6 ha 50,000 30–49 F

This is the first vintage of the new owners of Domaine de Maison Blanche, a group of Quincy wine-makers. While on the palate the wine is still a little timid and needs time to assert itself, on the nose it is delightful, with subtle nuances of freshness.
SCA Dom. de Maison Blanche, 6, chem. des Vignes, 18120 Quincy, tel. 02.48.51.09.45, fax 02.48.51.08.89 by appt.

DOM. MARDON 1999

☐ 11 ha 80,000 30–49 F

Domaine Mardon was established in around 1870. Firmness characterises the 99 vintage on the nose as well as the palate: a young wine, without doubt, even too young when it was tasted. A sustained vigour and mineral aromas lead to the conclusion that time has work to do.
Dom. Mardon, 40, rte de Reuilly, 18120 Quincy, tel. 02.48.51.31.60, fax 02.48.51.35.55 ev. day 9am–12 noon 2pm–7pm; Sun. by appt.

JOSEPH MELLOT Le Rimonet 1998★

☐ n.c. n.c. 30–49 F

This wine comes from vines of 20 to 40 years old. A success! The aromas find their originality in developed notes of butter and hazelnut. The balance on the palate is clearly orientated towards roundness, richness and power. Lovers of the 'old Quincy' style will appreciate this wine.
SA Joseph Mellot, rte de Ménétréol, B.P. 13, 18300 Sancerre, tel. 02.48.78.54.54, fax 02.48.78.54.55, e-mail alexandre@joseph-mellot.fr by appt.

PHILIPPE PORTIER

Cuvée Jean Maxime 1998★

☐ 0.8 ha 3,000 50–69 F

Philippe Portier has dedicated this wine, matured in barrel, to his forefathers. A nose dominated by white flowers and a palate combining a good deal of richness and fruitiness go to make up a wine which is pleasant, not to say seductive. Also picked out by the jury was **Cuvée Principale 99**, which has not been exposed to wood and should be drunk without delay (30–49F).
EARL Philippe Portier, Bois-Gy-Moreau, 18120 Brinay, tel. 02.48.51.09.02, fax 02.48.51.00.96 by appt.

DOM. VALERY RENAUDAT

Vieilli en fût de chêne 1999★

☐ 0.18 ha 1,200 30–49 F

With the 99 vintage, Valéry Renaudat makes his entrance into the world of wine-making and the *Hachette Wine Guide*. Very powerful Sauvignon aromas, suggestions of toast, hazelnut and vanilla (the legacy of six months' maturation in oak barrels), a straightforward attack on the palate, and good roundness . . . in brief, a well-made wine of its kind.
Valéry Renaudat, Seresnes, 36260 Diou, tel. 02.54.49.21.44, fax 02.54.49.30.42 ev. day 8am–12.30pm 1.30pm–7.30pm

DOM. JACQUES ROUZE 1999

☐ 9 ha 50,000 30–49 F

Evocations of citrus (lemon and grapefruit) make up the first impressions on the nose, followed by a rich and fleshy opening on the palate. On the finish the wine is very pleasant, even though it allows a hint of bitterness – a sign of longevity, so they say – to break through.
Dom. Jacques Rouzé, chem. des Vignes, 18120 Quincy, tel. 02.48.51.35.61, fax 02.48.51.05.00 ev. day 9am–12 noon 2pm–6pm

DOM. JEAN-MICHEL SORBE 1999

☐ n.c. n.c. 30–49 F

Power and generosity still appear reserved in this Quincy, which is doubtless too young to be appreciated. Floral and vegetal scents, a firm palate of good length and a great deal of substance make this a promising wine.
Dom. Jean-Michel Sorbe, 9, rte de Boisgisson, 18120 Preuilly, tel. 02.48.51.30.17, fax 02.48.51.35.47 by appt.

DOM. DU TREMBLAY

Gatebourse Vin noble 1999

☐ 1.5 ha 50,000 30–49 F

Touches of flowers and citrus fruit pleasingly join vegetal overtones in this Gatebourse, which has been matured on fine lees with *bâtonnage* – the lees are stirred with a pole. With good firmness for its year, it is round and long. **Assemblage Domaine 99** is also worthy of merit.
Jean Tatin, Le Tremblay, 18120 Brinay, tel. 02.48.75.20.09, fax 02.48.75.70.50 by appt.

DOM. TROTEREAU 1999

☐ n.c. 40,000 30–49 F

Pierre Ragon's Quincy expresses itself here in pure traditional form. The natural qualities of the grape have been preserved during fermentation, giving rise to a clean golden colour, good aromatic intensity, and vinosity and roundness on the palate. The whole seems well-balanced and harmonious.
Pierre Ragon, rte de Lury, 18120 Quincy, tel. 02.48.51.37.37, fax 02.48.26.82.58 by appt.

Reuilly

Steep, sunny hills and remarkable soils make Reuilly a natural environment for the vine.

The appellation covers seven communes in the Indre and the Cher, a charming region crossed by the green valleys of the rivers Cher, Arnon and Théols. It produced 7,991 hl (210,962 gal) of wine in 1999.

Reuilly white wines are dry, fruity Sauvignons, which can achieve notable fullness; production was 4,528 hl (119,539 gal) in 1999. Pinot Gris provides a rosé from direct pressing that is as delicate and distinguished as one might wish. However, the more versatile Pinot Noir, producing fresh, smooth, lustrous rosés and, more particularly, full, complex, fruity reds, is rapidly supplanting this local favourite.

BERNARD AUJARD 1999★★

◢ 0.68 ha 5,000 ▮ ♁ 30–49 F

Pinot Gris is a Reuilly speciality, still relatively under-used, and this is a lovely example, a light rosé of a sort of salmon-pink colour. The first impression on the nose is very intense, very fruity (peach, strawberry and raspberry), with acid drop and mineral tones revealed after the wine has been allowed to breathe. Fresh and supple at the same time, it presents a lovely rich structure on the palate.

🔑 Bernard Aujard, 2, rue du Bas-Bourg, 18120 Lazenay, tel. 02.48.51.73.69, fax 02.48.51.79.74 ☑ Y by appt.

ANDRE BARBIER 1999★★

◢ 0.43 ha 3,500 ▮ ♁ 30–49 F

André Barbier, who set up his estate in 1991, has made a remarkable 99 rosé. Although its pink colour could bother some purists, on the nose the wine is fine and pleasing, with a mineral touch, and on the palate it is lively, with consistent fruitiness. Great harmony in a bottle that could be kept for at least three years.

🔑 André Barbier, Le Crot-au-Loup, 18120 Chéry, tel. 02.48.51.75.81, fax 02.48.51.72.47 ☑ Y by appt.

LES BERRY-CURIENS

Les Chatillons 1999

◢ 0.5 ha 4,000 ▮ ♁ 30–49 F

Some enthusiast of the Berry region and its wines have created Les Berry-Curiens, which owns vines in the Quincy and Reuilly growing areas. Their Reuilly Rosé 99 is characterised by sweet, menthol notes on the nose and well-balanced liveliness on the palate. A fresh wine.

🔑 SCEV des Berry-Curiens, 9, rte de Boisgisson, 18120 Preuilly, tel. 02.48.51.30.17, fax 02.48.51.35.47 ☑ Y by appt.

DOM. HENRI BEURDIN ET FILS

1999★★

□ 7.25 ha 60,000 ▮ ♁ 30–49 F

Terroir, family tradition, professional exactness: Henri Beurdin and his son know how to turn all the wine-growing trumps to their advantage. The result is a floral and fruity 99 vintage with a dash of vegetal flavour. Balance is achieved thanks to a rare alliance of richness, volume and freshness. A fine, complex and harmonious white Reuilly.

🔑 H. Beurdin et Fils, 14, Le Carroir, 18120 Preuilly, tel. 02.48.51.30.78, fax 02.48.51.34.81 ☑ Y by appt.

GERARD BIGONNEAU

Les Bouchauds 1999★

◢ 1 ha 6,000 ▮ ♁ 30–49 F

Pale salmon-pink to look at, this rosé releases peardrop aromas rounded off by strawberry and raspberry. Opening with suppleness on the palate, it then develops richness and a warm finish. A beautiful whole. Another discovery at Gérard Bigonneau's is **Blanc Les Bouchauds 99**, which gained a mention by the jury.

🔑 Gérard Bigonneau, La Chagnat, 18120 Brinay, tel. 02.48.52.80.22, fax 02.48.52.83.41 ☑ Y by appt.

CHANTAL ET MICHEL CORDAILLAT 1999

□ 1.7 ha 12,000 30–49 F

An aromatic expression is already very open here: a real fruit cup of pear, peach, lychee and bergamot. The impressions on the palate evoke suppleness and tenderness. This Reuilly is a good example of the vintage. The **Rosé 99** must also be mentioned.

Chantal et Michel Cordaillat, Le Montet, 18120 Méreau, tel. 02.48.52.83.48, fax 02.48.52.83.09 by appt.

GERARD CORDIER 1999

■ 1.2 ha 5,000 30–49 F

Gérard Cordier represents the ninth generation of wine-makers on the estate, which nowadays covers more than 7 ha (17 acres). In this Reuilly wine, notes of red fruit are already in place. Hints of leather and roasting coffee are more original, and tannins are not excessive. Drink after laying it down for a year.

Gérard Cordier, 6, imp. de l'Ile-Camus, La Ferté, 36260 Reuilly, tel. 02.54.49.25.47, fax 02.54.49.29.34 by appt.

PASCAL DESROCHES

Clos des Lignis 1999★★

◢ 0.65 ha 5,300 30–49 F

A pale whitecurrant-coloured Reuilly with milky first impressions on the nose, which then opens up on muted notes of wild strawberries. The liveliness softens ahead of a pleasant, full-bodied finish. The whole shows a great deal of character and finesse throughout. Congratulations to Pascal Desroches, who has also been most successful in the 99 vintage with his **Close des Varennes Blanc** (one star) and **Close de la Sablière Rouge** (mentioned).

Pascal Desroches, 13, rte de Charost, 18120 Lazenay, tel. 02.48.51.71.60, fax 02.48.51.71.60 by appt.

JEAN-SYLVAIN GUILLEMAIN 1999★

■ 0.86 ha n.c. 30–49 F

Even though the fruitiness of the grape is somewhat masked, the aromatic qualities of this Reuilly are impressive. Scents of coffee and cocoa and notes of leather and undergrowth prevail at this stage of its development. The initial impression on the palate is full and accented, with a finish resting on tannins that really need calming: wait for it.

Jean-Sylvain Guillemain, Palleau, 18120 Lury-sur-Arnon, tel. 02.48.52.99.01, fax 02.48.52.99.09 by appt.

CLAUDE LAFOND La Raie 1999★

□ 6 ha 40,000 30–49 F

According to his motto, Claude Lafond has done in 1999 'Whatever is necessary, adequately, neither more nor less, but just at the right moment'. Three wines offered, three wines selected: the **Rosé**, **La Grande Pièce 99** and the red **Les Grandes Vignes 99** all received citations. The wine which was awarded the highest mark was this white, with its exotic, aniseed nose. After a straightforward opening on the palate, lime aromas fade away progressively, allowing the palate the benefits of increased richness and a good length on the finish. A good example of Reuilly.

Claude Lafond, Bois-Saint-Denis, 36260 Reuilly, tel. 02.54.49.22.17, fax 02.54.49.26.64, e-mail claude.lafond@wanadoo.fr ev. day 8.30am–12.30pm 1.30pm–6.30pm; Sat. Sun. by appt.

ALAIN MABILLOT 1999★★

■ 1 ha 4,000 30–49 F

The intense purplish-red colour is the first indication of good concentration. Liquorice aromas and milky notes retreat subtly after airing to give way to red fruit (strawberry and blackcurrant), and a powerful tannic structure makes the wine very chewy, showing that it has excellent potential for ageing.

Alain Mabillot, Villiers-les-Roses, 36260 Sainte-Lizaigne, tel. 02.54.04.02.09, fax 02.54.04.01.33 by appt.

GUY MALBETE 1999★★

□ 3 ha 25,000 30–49 F

The colour and aromas mark a particular style within the appellation. Very ripe grapes give rise to whiffs of crystallised fruit, honey and almond, and the full, rich palate is in perfect harmony with the nose. A very good wine which can be drunk immediately. The **Rouge 99** receives a star.

EARL Guy Malbète, 16, chem. du Boulanger, Bois-Saint-Denis, 36260 Reuilly, tel. 02.54.49.25.09, fax 02.54.49.27.49 by appt.

DOM. DE REUILLY

Les Pierres Plates 1999★

□ 1.5 ha 9,500 30–49 F

The second year of production and the second year of success for Denis Jamain. Les Pierres Plates, which comes from chalky kimmeridgian soil, is a very pale, crystalline gold. Still not very communicative, and in a mineral style, it is pleasing because of its overall harmony and typical qualities. The estate's **Reuilly Rouge** and **Blanc 99** receive a star and a mention respectively.

SCE Dom. de Reuilly, chem. des Petites-Fontaines, 36260 Reuilly, tel. 02.38.66.16.74, fax 02.38.66.74.69, e-mail denis.jamain@wanadoo.fr by appt.

Denis Jamain

LOIRE

DOM. DE SERESNES 1999★

■ 2.18 ha n.c. 30–49 F

A purple colour shaded with purplish blue, this wine releases scents of red fruit with grilled and smoky hints. The maturity of the grapes shows through the rich and jammy flavours on the palate, and with supple tannins this Reuilly could be drunk fairly soon.

Jacques Renaudat, Seresnes, 36260 Diou, tel. 02.54.49.21.44, fax 02.54.49.30.42 by appt.

JEAN-MICHEL SORBE 1999

3 ha 4,000 30–49 F

Here a salmony-pink tint, veering towards orange, is quite full. You notice a good complexity between milky and vanilla aromas on the nose. Clean and firm on the palate, well balanced and enlivened by a slight sparkle, this is a pleasurable wine for relaxing moments.

Dom. Jean-Michel Sorbe, 9, rte de Boisgisson, 18120 Preuilly, tel. 02.48.51.30.17, fax 02.48.51.35.47 by appt.

JACQUES VINCENT 1999

2 ha 12,000 30–49 F

Produced on an alluvial clay soil, this rosé has a pretty onion-skin tint. It needs a good time to breathe to bring out its fruity scents of peach and apricot. Supple and fresh on the palate, the wine is true to the Jacques Vincent tradition!

Jacques Vincent, 11, chem. des Caves, 18120 Lazenay, tel. 02.48.51.73.55, fax 02.48.51.14.96 ev. day 9am–12 noon 2pm–7pm; Sun. by appt.

Sancerre

The hilltop village of Sancerre, overlooking the Loire, commands a magnificent panorama of well-exposed, sheltered slopes, perfect for winegrowing, stretching over 11 communes. The terroir is composed variously of limestone and chalky marl, which suit the vine and contribute to the quality of the wines. About 2,400 ha (5,928 gal) are planted, and produced 161,505 hl (4,263,732 gal) in 1999, of which 128,995 hl (3,405,468 gal) were white wine.

Two varieties reign supreme in Sancerre: Sauvignon and Pinot Noir, both uniquely capable of expressing the spirit of the terroir to the full. This is amply demonstrated in the wines: fresh, young, fruity whites (the most numerous wines); supple, subtle rosés, and light, perfumed, complex reds.

In addition to this, Sancerre represents, in a unique way, the contribution of wine-growers and wine-makers. It requires great skill and dedication to produce a great wine from Sauvignon, which is a late-ripening variety, so near to the northern limit of vine-growing, and at heights of 200 and 300 metres (656–984 ft). Add to these human challenges the vagaries of the local climate, slopes that are among the steepest in the country, and the fact that fermentation takes place at a critical moment at the end of a late season!

White Sancerre is particularly to be appreciated with dry goat's cheeses, such as the famous Crottin de Chavignol, from a village which itself produces wines. It also goes well with hot starters or fish that are not too strongly seasoned. The reds go well with poultry and the meat dishes of the region.

DOM. JEAN-PAUL BALLAND 1999★

□ 15 ha 100,000 50–69 F

Awarded two stars for his Grande Cuvée 97, Jean-Paul Balland is a definite asset to Sancerre and its terroir. This 99 wine, with its original scents of cloves on the nose, has roundness and depth. The jury was enchanted by its very ripe lemon aspect and aromatic persistence. The **Sancerre Rouge 98** is also worth mentioning. Very characteristic of the grape variety, it is a pleasing wine that would make a good accompaniment to white meat or a plate of *charcuterie* from Lyon.

SA Dom. Jean-Paul Balland, chem. de Marloup, 18300 Bué, tel. 02.48.54.07.29, fax 02.48.54.20.94, e-mail balland.jean.paul@wanadoo.fr by appt.

JOSEPH BALLAND-CHAPUIS

Le Chatillet 1999★★

□ 8.75 ha 60,000 30–49 F

The Joseph Balland-Chapuis estate has successfully produced a nice 99, with an atypical straw-yellow colour and very fine aromas

of grapefruit, heightened by a hint of Muscatel. This wine explodes on the palate with ripe fruit (orange) and leaves the taster in a lasting state of wellbeing, so persistent is its fullness.
🗝 SARL Joseph Balland-Chapuis, La Croix-Saint-Laurent, B.P. 24, 18300 Bué, tel. 02.48.54.06.67, fax 02.48.54.07.97 ☒ Y ev. day except Sat. Sun. 8.30am–12.30pm 1.30pm–5.30pm

CEDRICK BARDIN 1999*

☐ 3.2 ha 18,000 30–49 F

A wine-maker living at Pouilly-sur-Loire, Cédrick Bardin cultivates a few Sancerre vines. This 99 wine distinguishes itself in the vintage by its power. The fat, round palate develops notes of very ripe white fruit right up to its long finish. For lovers of rich, powerful wines.
🗝 Cédrick Bardin, 12, rue Waldeck-Rousseau, 58150 Pouilly-sur-Loire, tel. 03.86.39.11.24, fax 03.86.39.16.50 ☒ Y ev. day 9am–6pm; Sun. by appt.

CLOS DE BEAUJEU 1998*

☐ n.c. 5,000 50–69 F

In 1380 a certain Jehan Boulay was a wine-maker at Chavignol. The tradition has been carefully fostered at Clos de Beaujeu, which is run nowadays by Gérard Boulay. A great deal of freshness is noticeable in the 98 white, where gunflint is softly surrounded by notes of honey. Well balanced and a good example of Sancerre, this wine could be kept for some years.
🗝 Gérard Boulay, Chavignol, 18300 Sancerre, tel. 02.48.54.36.37 ☒

HENRI BOURGEOIS

La Côte des Monts Damnés 1999**

☐ 2 ha 17,640 70–99 F

La Côte des Monts Damnés is a favoured site on the Chavignol hillsides, in the heart of the Sancerre vineyards, and its soil has been wonderfully developed through the work of the Bourgeois estate's vineyard manager. With its intense nose and decided maturity, this elegant wine is powerful on the palate but stays fresh due to intense citrus flavours. The finish is harmonious and as long as one could wish for.
🗝 Dom. Henri Bourgeois, Chavignol, 18300 Sancerre, tel. 02.48.78.53.20, fax 02.48.54.14.24, e-mail domaine@bourgeois.sancerre.com ☒ Y by appt.

DOM. DES BUISSONNES 1999

☐ 10.62 ha 79,000 50–69 F

For ten years, Dominique Naudet and his father-in-law Régis Jouan have been partners in this estate of some 15 ha (37 acres). The former takes care particularly of the vines and the latter of the wine-making. They have produced in this wine a 'white soils' Sancerre. Very ripe citrus fruit, with a hint of tobacco, is apparent on the nose, and after a lovely opening on the palate with flavours of Mediterranean fruit comes a fresh taste, making a good wine with which to discover the Sancerre terroirs.
🗝 SCEA des Buissonnes, Cave Roger Naudet, Maison Sallé, 18300 Sury-en-Vaux, tel. 02.48.79.35.41, fax 02.48.79.34.68 ☒ Y ev. day 9am–12 noon 3pm–7pm

DOM. DU CARROIR PERRIN 1999

☐ 8 ha 50,000 50–69 F

Chaudoux is one of three villages which make up the commune of Verdigny. Here, dynamism and community spirit are acknowledged to be the keys to wine-making success. Pierre Riffault has made a wine which is typical of the appellation. The fine nose releases aromas of white flowers (acacia) and quince jam, and on the palate the wine has a pleasant liveliness, making this Sancerre an engaging wine.
🗝 Pierre Riffault, Chaudoux, 18300 Verdigny, tel. 02.48.79.31.03, fax 02.48.79.35.68 ☒ Y ev. day 8am–12.30pm 2pm–7pm

DOM. DU CARROU 1999*

■ 2 ha 13,000 30–49 F

Domaine du Carrou is under 40% Pinot Noir vines, as opposed to an average of 25% in the rest of the Sancerre area. Cherry, blackcurrant, leather and a grilled touch are discernible on the nose of this 99 vintage, which is sustained by well-structured tannins and a hint of oak, making it a success in what was a particularly difficult year for reds.
🗝 Dominique Roger, 7, pl. du Carrou, 18300 Bué, tel. 02.48.54.10.65, fax 02.48.54.38.77 ☒ Y ev. day 8.30am–12 noon 1.30pm–7pm; Sun. by appt.

DANIEL CHOTARD 1999*

☐ 7 ha 40,000 50–69 F

Daniel Chotard, established in the hamlet of Reigny, in the pretty flowery commune of Crézancy-en-Sancerre, is a wine-maker who has been very conscientious in producing this wine, with its scents of fresh apricots. It has a rounded coherence, with a clean opening on the palate and then an interesting liveliness. It has a certain richness which is rare for the vintage. Recommend it to your friends.
🗝 Daniel Chotard, Hameau de Reigny, 18300 Crézancy-en-Sancerre, tel. 02.48.79.08.12, fax 02.48.79.09.21 ☒ Y ev. day 9am–12 noon 2pm–7pm; Sun. by appt.

DOMINIQUE CROCHET 1998

■ 0.5 ha 4,000 30–49 F

Bué-en-Sancerre is at the bottom of a small valley covered with vines. Dominique and Janine Crochet cultivate 9 ha (22 acres) of vines here and have produced a nice 99 which will help you discover the Sancerre appellation. The finesse of the aromas on the nose elicits a response of lightness and well-integrated tannins on a finish that lets flavours of red fruit re-emerge.

🔑 Dom. Dominique et Janine Crochet, 64, rue de Venoize, 18300 Bué-en-Sancerre, tel. 02.48.54.19.56, fax 02.48.54.12.61 ☑ Y by appt.

ROBERT ET MARIE-SOLANGE CROCHET Le Chêne Marchand 1999*

□ 1.25 ha 5,000 50–69 F

Le Chêne Marchand is famous in Sancerre; this 99 vintage comes from 40-year-old vines. The initial impression on the nose is of fresh bread, opening out to white flowers. Lively, with no roughness on the finish, it will satisfy lovers of real wines.

🔑 Dom. Robert et Marie-Solange Crochet, Marcigoué, 18300 Bué-en-Sancerre, tel. 02.48.54.21.77, fax 02.48.54.25.10 ☑ Y ev. day 9am–7pm; Sun. by appt.

DOM. CROIX SAINT URSIN Prestige 1997*

■ 0.4 ha 2,000 70–99 F

The vineyard goes back to the beginning of the 18th century. Planted on the slopes of the Bué valley, it has given great pleasure to Sylvain Bailly, regularly mentioned in the *Guide*. This 97 Sancerre merits attention. Dark in colour, it releases touches of red fruit and grilled notes on a gamey background. A little tannic, it lingers lengthily, with elegance but without artifice.

🔑 Sylvain Bailly, 71, rue de Venoize, 18300 Bué, tel. 02.48.54.02.75, fax 02.48.54.28.41 ☑ Y ev. day 8am–12 noon 2pm–6.30pm; Sun. by appt.

🔑 Jacques Bailly

DOM. DAULNY 1998

□ 11 ha 80,000 30–49 F

With its golden colour, this 98 wine showers long, overripe aromas on the nose (crystallised fruit and quince) and opens up willingly as soon as it has breathed a little. These aromas are taken up on the palate roundly and at some length. It will be appreciated by lovers of wines made from ripe grapes, picked during the final days of the harvest.

🔑 Etienne Daulny, Chaudenay, 18300 Verdigny, tel. 02.48.79.33.96, fax 02.48.79.33.39 ☑ Y by appt.

DOM. VINCENT DELAPORTE ET FILS 1999*

□ 15 ha 120,000 30–49 F

Imagine the Sancerre hillsides bathed in autumn sunshine. Golden, with marked green glints, this wine conjures up slowly ripened grapes tempting you to eat them: a lovely Sancerre combining freshness and length. Golden-yellow **Maxime 99** (50–69F), from the same domaine, releases marked toastiness, the result of eight months spent in barrel.

🔑 SCEV Vincent Delaporte et Fils, Chavignol, 18300 Sancerre, tel. 02.48.78.03.32, fax 02.48.78.02.62 ☑ Y by appt.

GERARD FIOU 1999*

□ 5.25 ha 30,000 30–49 F

Sancerre wine-maker Gérard Fiou makes visitors feel very welcome at his estate. This 99 vintage is intensely flowery on the nose, finishing on grapefruit, thus fitting in perfectly with the impressions on the palate, which are more citrus-centred, bringing a pleasant hint of vanilla on the finish.

🔑 Gérard Fiou, 13–15, rue Hilaire-Amagat, 18300 Saint-Satur, tel. 02.48.54.16.17, fax 02.48.54.36.89 ☑ Y ev. day 9am–6pm

DOM. FOUASSIER Les Chasseignes 1999

□ 5.99 ha 30,000 50–69 F

Pierre and Jean-Michel Fouassier's three classic 99 wines have been picked out by the jury. From Chasseignes to Romains, passing Clos Paradis, you will discover the plots and their idiosyncrasies: menthol and citronella in **Les Chasseignes**, roundness and citrus fruit in **Le Close Paradis**, gunflint in **Les Romains**. Good diversity, and always quality and originality, are evident.

🔑 SA Fouassier Père et Fils, 180, av. de Verdun, 18300 Sancerre, tel. 02.48.54.02.34, fax 02.48.54.35.61, e-mail fouassier@terre-net.fr ☑ Y ev. day 9am–12 noon 2pm–6pm

DOM. MICHEL GIRARD ET FILS 1999*

□ 9.8 ha 60,000 50–69 F

Touches of mirabelle plum, novel in this appellation, reveal themselves aromatic on the palate. Round and full in the mouth, and centred on rose notes, this wine offers pleasant entertainment, not only to look at.

🔑 Dom. Michel Girard et Fils, Chaudoux, 18300 Verdigny, tel. 02.48.79.33.36, fax 02.48.79.33.66 ☑ Y by appt.

DOM. DES GRANDES PERRIERES 1999

□ 2 ha 17,000 30–49 F

From the road, the view over the picturesque town of Sury-en-Vaux is enchanting, nature at its best. It was in this setting that Jérôme Gueneau started up in 1991. If you like lemon, you will find it in this bottle, sometimes combined with white flowers, sometimes with vanilla. A wine which is a good example of this vintage with its difficult autumn.

🔑 Jérôme Gueneau, Les Grandes-Perrières, 18300 Sury-en-Vaux, tel. 02.48.79.39.31, fax 02.48.79.40.27 ☑ Y ev. day 8am–12 noon 1.30pm–8pm

ALAIN GUENEAU 1999

□ 2 ha 15,000 30–49 F

A pale yellow, this Sancerre offers a good deal of satisfaction, both on the nose (mineral) and the palate, which has a pleasant balance finishing on a lemony hint.

🔑 Alain Gueneau, Maison-Sallé, 18300 Sury-en-Vaux, tel. 02.48.79.30.51, fax 02.48.79.36.89 ☑ 🍷 by appt.

PASCAL JOLIVET

Le Chêne Marchand 1998★★

☐ 1 ha 6,000 ▮ 🌡 70–99 F

Commended by an overwhelming majority of the jury, this 98 white is a pale, clear gold, and on the palate it has a citrus quality that is representative of Sancerre whites. Extremely well balanced, brilliant in the finesse and complexity of its flavours, this wine expresses an unparalleled mastery of and respect for the harvest. What balance and what length! Definitely a **Coup de Coeur*. The white **Les Caillottes 99** is awarded a star. A complete wine, with aromas of ripe orange. **Awarded a coup de coeur, regrettably at the time of going to press the label was not available for reproduction here.*

🔑 Pascal Jolivet, rte de Chavignol, 18300 Sancerre, tel. 02.48.27.28.29, fax 02.48.27.28.20, e-mail info@pascal-jolivet.com ☑ 🍷 by appt.

DOM. DE LA JOLIVE 1999

☐ 1.4 ha 11,000 ▮ 30–49 F

The summer exhibitions at Buranlure are your chance to visit this château, built in the 14th and 15th centuries among the greenery on the valley floor. Domaine de la Jolive is only 10 km (6 miles) away. It offers a harmonious 99 wine, with a strong but slightly vegetal nose. Round and supple, this Sancerre is pleasant and a good example of the vintage. The **Sancerre Rouge 99**, matured in barrels for 15 months, is mentioned for its good balance and very Pinot Noir finish.

🔑 Gérard Terrier, Les Giraults, 18300 Sury-en-Vaux, tel. 02.48.79.35.10, fax 02.48.79.39.98 ☑ 🍷 by appt.

SERGE LALOUE Silex Cuvée réservée 1999

☐ 2 ha 14,000 ▮ 🌡 50–69 F

On a soil which is 80% flinty clay and 20% chalk, Serge and Franck Laloue produce their Silex wine. The 99 vintage is unobtrusive on the nose, with a milky note and aromas of very ripe pineapple. It is firm, and by waiting you will be able to experience its character at its best. In **Rouge**, we should mention the **98**, a powerful wine which releases woody and gamey scents.

🔑 Serge Laloue, Thauvenay, 18300 Sancerre, tel. 02.48.79.94.10, fax 02.48.79.92.48, e-mail laloue@terre-net.fr ☑ 🍷 by appt.

DOM. SERGE LAPORTE 1998

☐ 1.8 ha 7,500 ▮ 50–69 F

At Chavignol, Sancerre wine goes very naturally with the famous *crottins* (named after an ancient round terracotta oil lamp). This wine, enlivened by golden glints, releases scents of honey and crystallised fruit. It has a good structure and evolves harmoniously through to a liquorice finish.

🔑 Dom. Serge Laporte, Chavignol, 18300 Sancerre, tel. 02.48.54.30.10, fax 02.48.54.28.91 ☑ 🍷 by appt.

DOM. DE LA ROSSIGNOLE 1999

☐ 6 ha 40,000 ▮ 🌡 50–69 F

Pierre Cherrier has been involved in the estate since 1984 and his two sons, François and Jean-Marie, increasingly favour eco-friendly farming methods on the 15 ha (37 acres) of vines at Verdigny. They have made a Sancerre which is a good example of the 99 vintage. On the nose it releases scents of Sauvignon grapes with notes of vanilla and white flowers. Here is a full, rounded wine with a pleasant finish on the palate.

🔑 Pierre Cherrier et Fils, Chaudoux, 18300 Verdigny-en-Sancerre, tel. 02.48.79.34.93, fax 02.48.79.33.41 ☑ 🍷 by appt.

DOM. RENE MALLERON 1999

■ 1.59 ha 12,900 ▮ 🌡 50–69 F

Herds of goats are fairly numerous in the hamlets of Crézancy-en-Sancerre, of which Champtin is one. Their cheeses go well with this dark purple Sancerre. Intense on the nose, it evokes fresh grape marc with peppery notes. When this wine was tasted, it still had tannin in the finish which made it a little firm. It will benefit from being matured.

🔑 Dom. René Malleron, Champtin, 18300 Crézancy-en-Sancerre, tel. 02.48.79.06.90, fax 02.48.79.42.18 ☑ 🍷 by appt.

JOSEPH MELLOT La Châtellenie 1999

☐ 20 ha 210,000 ▮ 🌡 50–69 F

The Mellot family has been a name in the Sancerre wine area since 1513. Nowadays the estate is run by Alexandre Mellot, and production is exported to nearly 25 countries. Its 99 is a pleasant wine to taste at the moment because it is very fruity. Initial vegetable notes are substituted by an aroma of fresh grapefruit and a scent of lemon, making the wine a perfect accompaniment to shellfish.

🔑 SA Joseph Mellot, rte de Ménétréol, B.P. 13, 18300 Sancerre, tel. 02.48.78.54.54, fax 02.48.78.54.55, e-mail alexandre@joseph-mellot.fr ☑ 🍷 by appt.

DOM. FRANCK MILLET 1999★

☐ 9 ha 60,000 ▮ 🌡 50–69 F

Franck Millet has produced a very successful 99 Sancerre. Grape – Sauvignon – is immediately evident on the nose, followed by more vegetal (boxwood) touches. The wine is interesting because it allows tenderness and liveliness to appear on the palate at the same time. Although slightly austere on the finish, the wine will round out with age.

🔑 Franck Millet, L'Estérille, rue Saint-Vincent, 18300 Bué, tel. 02.48.54.25.26, fax 02.48.54.39.85, e-mail millet-sancerre.com ☑ 🍷 by appt.

DOM. GERARD MILLET 1999

☐ 11.9 ha 104,000 ▮ 🌡 50–69 F

Gérard Millet was very widely acclaimed in 1999 for his red Sancerre. Since 1979, when he took over the few vines belonging to his grandparents, he has developed his vineyard by planting it on soils rich in *caillottes* – white stones which often occur abundantly in chalky clay soils. Of crystal clarity, his 99 vintage has a good aromatic intensity which will be appreciated by lovers of this specific terroir. With a great deal of fruit on the palate, it entices with its finesse.

🔑 Gérard Millet, rte de Bourges, 18300 Bué, tel. 02.48.54.38.62, fax 02.48.54.13.50, e-mail gmillet@terre-net.fr ☑ 𝕐 by appt.

ROGER MOREUX 1998

■ 2 ha n.c. 50–69 F

A ruby, very slightly amber colour, this red Sancerre, whose perfumes are pleasantly reminiscent of ripe cherry, has a slightly bulky body on the palate. Age will soften the austerity of the finish.

🔑 Roger Moreux, Chavignol, 18300 Sancerre, tel. 02.48.54.05.79, fax 02.48.54.09.55, e-mail moreux912@aol.com ☑ 𝕐 ev. day except Sun. 8am–7pm

DOM. DES CAVES DU PRIEURE 1999

□ 4.5 ha 20,000 30–49 F

With their son, the holder of a BTS in Viti-Oenology who joined them in 1995, Geneviève and Jacques Guillerault cultivate their 15 ha (37 acres) of vines. Their 99 Sancerre is a discreet wine with a good harmony on milky notes and touches of citrus fruit (orange). Good length is evident on the palate, although the finish is a little austere.

🔑 Jacques Guillerault, Dom. des Caves du Prieuré, Reigny, 18300 Crézancy-en-Sancerre, tel. 02.48.79.02.84, fax 02.48.79.01.02 ☑ 𝕐 by appt.

PAUL PRIEUR ET FILS 1999

□ 9.28 ha 80,000 50–69 F

It does you good to walk along the vine paths and little country roads to discover the scenery of the Sancerre hills. Here the Prieurs have a vineyard of more than 14 ha (34 acres). They have produced a nice, traditional Sancerre. On the nose an intense menthol note is enhanced by a buttery scent, and after a fairly lively first impression it has citrus-linked fruitiness and length on the palate.

🔑 Dom. Paul Prieur et Fils, rte des Monts-Damnés, 18300 Verdigny, tel. 02.48.79.35.86, fax 02.48.79.36.85 ☑ 𝕐 ev. day 9am–12 noon 2pm–6pm; Sun. by appt.

DOM. DU P'TIT ROY 1999

■ 2 ha 10,000 30–49 F

Mauvish purple is the sign of excellent concentration, an impression confirmed by astonishing spicy, meaty scents on the nose. These are combined on the palate with tannins that are velvety to the point of astringency. The wine deserves to be aged until 2001.

🔑 Pierre et Alain Dezat, Maimbray, 18300 Sury-en-Vaux, tel. 02.48.79.34.16, fax 02.48.79.35.81 ☑ 𝕐 by appt.

PHILIPPE RAIMBAULT

Apud Sariacum 1999

□ 4.75 ha 38,000 50–69 F

A fossil features on the label of this Sancerre, a reference to the collection that Philippe Raimbault has in his wine cellar. In another connection, the name of this wine recalls the history of the commune of Sury-en-Vaux, which is Gallo-Roman in origin. Of medium intensity, the 99 vintage is redolent of white flowers and combines roundness with finesse. It is ready to drink. The white **Godons 99**, grown on a very beautiful sloping plot in the shape of an amphitheatre, is also worthy of note.

🔑 Philippe Raimbault, rte de Maimbray, 18300 Sury-en-Vaux, tel. 02.48.79.29.54, fax 02.48.79.29.51 ☑ 𝕐 by appt.

ROGER ET DIDIER RAIMBAULT 1999

□ 10 ha 40,000 30–49 F

Pale yellow tinted with gold, this wine, with floral flavours dominating, nevertheless brings out a good volume of mineral notes. The finish conjures up ripe banana and leaves a slightly warm impression. Roger and Didier Raimbault's **Rouge 99** also deserves a mention: its intense cherry scents on the nose will charm lovers of light red wines.

🔑 Roger et Didier Raimbault, Chaudenay, 18300 Verdigny, tel. 02.48.79.32.87, fax 02.48.79.39.08 ☑ 𝕐 ev. day 9am–12 noon 1.30pm–6pm

DOM. RAIMBAULT-PINEAU 1999

□ 8 ha 60,000 50–69 F

We have given up counting how many generations of wine-makers have been at Domaine Raimbault-Pineau. Beneath intense aromas stamped with the Sauvignon grape, mingled with a hint of passion fruit, this Sancerre is a fresh wine which develops richness throughout the tasting. Serve it with white meat.

🔑 Dom. Raimbault-Pineau, rte de Sancerre, 18300 Sury-en-Vaux, tel. 02.48.79.33.04, fax 02.48.79.36.25 ☑ 𝕐 ev. day 9am–12 noon 1.30pm–6pm; Sun. by appt.; cl. 1st–15 Aug. and 8–23 Jan.

PASCAL ET NICOLAS REVERDY 1999★

□ 6 ha 48,000 30–49 F

Two very successful wines from Nicolas and Pascal Reverdy, producers who often appear in the *Guide*. The first is fresh and elegant on the nose, dominated by citrus fruit. The opening impression on the palate is clean, developing fruitiness, with a little austerity on the finish. The **Rouge 99** releases a nose of crushed raspberry. Its straightforward, severe palate is built on silky tannins that allow immediate, full appreciation.

Pascal et Nicolas Reverdy, Maimbray, 18300 Sury-en-Vaux, tel. 02.48.79.37.31, fax 02.48.79.41.48 ☒ Y ev. day except Sun. 2.30pm–7pm

DOM. REVERDY-DUCROUX

Louys Marie Vieilles vignes 1998

■ 0.65 ha 3,500 70–99 F

Forty-year-old vines planted on chalky clay are responsible for this Louys Marie, a very powerful red Sancerre. Although it still bore the flavours of barrel ageing at tasting, it was nevertheless well balanced, and ageing it for a few years will bring out all its subtleties.

Dom. Reverdy-Ducroux, Chaudoux, 18300 Verdigny, tel. 02.48.79.31.33, fax 02.48.79.36.19 ☒ Y by appt.

DOM. BERNARD REVERDY ET FILS 1999

□ 8.6 ha 64,000 50–69 F

An engaging white due to its complex aromatic palette, which combines white flowers and grapefruit. A great deal of fruitiness and a touch of acidity make it a good companion for seafood. The **Rosé 99**, with a clear colour, has an attractive freshness deriving from lemony flavours. It would go well with fish or *charcuterie.*

Bernard Reverdy et Fils, Chaudoux, rte des Petites-Perrières, 18300 Verdigny, tel. 02.48.79.33.08, fax 02.48.79.37.93 ☒ Y by appt.

JEAN REVERDY ET FILS

La Reine Blanche 1999★★

□ 9 ha 70,000 50–69 F

The entire jury was unanimous in its verdict of La Reine Blanche: superb! Jean Reverdy et Fils has a family tradition of producing Sancerre. A beautiful wine, this harmonious 99, always lively and without austerity, opens up menthol notes around blackcurrant and ripe lemon. *Coup de Coeur*!

Jean Reverdy et Fils, 18300 Verdigny, tel. 02.48.79.31.48, fax 02.48.79.32.44 ☒ Y by appt.

CLAUDE RIFFAULT

Les Boucauds 1999

□ n.c. 38,000 30–49 F

An expressive and complex wine with which to discover the appellation. Notes of boxwood then ripe orange are confirmed on the palate with a light hint of acacia. An interesting Sancerre for its vintage. The **Sancerre Rouge 99** is very grapey and very progressive in tannins, which ensures a good aromatic length, and ends with a touch of brandy on the finish.

SCEV Claude Riffault, Maison-Sallé, 18300 Sury-en-Vaux, tel. 02.48.79.38.22, fax 02.48.79.36.22 ☒ Y ev. day 8am–12 noon 2pm–7pm; Sun. by appt.

DOM. DE SAINT-PIERRE 1999★★

□ 12 ha 95,000 50–69 F

One star in 1999 for the 98 vintage, and now two stars for the 99. Lovely work again from this family estate. Very rich on the nose, mingling ripe lemon and orange, the wine evokes crystallised orange on the palate.

SA Pierre Prieur et Fils, Dom. de Saint-Pierre, 18300 Verdigny, tel. 02.48.79.31.70, fax 02.48.79.38.87 ☒ Y ev. day except Sun. 8.30am–12 noon 2pm–6.30pm

DOM. DE SAINT-PIERRE 1999★★

■ n.c. 25,000 50–69 F

A double coup for Domaine de Saint-Pierre because this red Sancerre is every bit as remarkable as the white. A beautiful garnet colour, the top of the glass smells of fresh marc and toast. The bottom is all power and persistence, while still maintaining a fruitiness that will bring joy at Christmas. You will also appreciate the very successful **Maréchal Prieur 98** (70–99F). A deep red, this one shyly releases red fruit aromas characteristic of Pinot Noir. On the palate, power overtakes finesse but removes none of the wine's elegance. Ageing will develop the wine.

SA Pierre Prieur et Fils, Dom. de Saint-Pierre, 18300 Verdigny, tel. 02.48.79.31.70, fax 02.48.79.38.87 ☒ Y ev. day except Sun. 8.30am–12 noon 2pm–6.30pm

LES CELLIERS SAINT-ROMBLE 1999

■ 5.01 ha 35,000 30–49 F

A Sancerre without artifice which will be ready before many wines matured in wood. On the nose are notes of cherries in brandy, and the tannins, never excessive, line the palate well. On the finish the wine is supple, with a certain fullness.

SCEV André Dezat et Fils, Chaudoux, 18300 Verdigny, tel. 02.48.79.38.82, fax 02.48.79.38.24 ☒ Y by appt.

DOM. DE SAINT-ROMBLE 1998★★

■ 1.8 ha 14,000 30–49 F

The jury was unanimous in its verdict of this cherry-red wine. The Pinot Noir grape expresses itself strongly in these Sancerre soils, as witnessed by the red fruit aromas on the nose and the solid but supple body. The balance is excellent and the finish pleasant. Very successful, **Blanc Grande Cuvée Vieilles Vignes 98** is also very pleasing with its Moscatel notes.

🔑 SARL Paul Vattan, Dom. de Saint-Romble, Maimbray, B.P. 45, 18300 Sury-en-Vaux, tel. 02.48.79.30.36, fax 02.48.79.30.41, e-mail claude@fournier-pere-fils.fr ☒ Y ev. day 9am–12 noon 2pm–6pm; Sat. Sun. by appt.

DOM. DE SARRY 1999★

☐ 11 ha 64,000 50–69 F

Michel Brock set up his domaine in 1968 and grows his vines on the famous white soils of Sancerre. A beautiful pale golden colour, his 99 wine is expressive; crystallised fruit, on a note of violet, enhance the character of the palate with finesse, while citrus adds to richness. Also very successful is **Sancerre Rouge 99**, a dark ruby colour, pleasing on the nose with a hint of oak. The palate unveils a certain fullness and a strong but good-quality tannic expression. Wait three to ten years for this wine: it deserves it.

🔑 Dom. Brock, Le Briou-de-Veaugues, rte de Bourges, 18300 Sancerre, tel. 02.48.79.07.92, fax 02.48.79.05.28 ☒ Y by appt.

DOM. TABORDET 1999★

☐ 1.54 ha 13,000 30–49 F

In 1980 the two brothers Yvon and Pascal Tabordet took over the family estate, which today comprises 10 ha (25 acres) on chalky clay soil. Here they have made a successful white Sancerre, with fresh, intense aromas where flowers dominate. The fruit is held in check, and the finish is lovely and persistent, making a very pleasing structure. A wine which is ready for drinking. The **Rouge 99** is a clear expression of Pinot Noir, with a note of aniseed. The wine is round and warm, with fruit surfacing and an aromatic finish. A short time in the bottle would benefit the wine.

🔑 Yvon et Pascal Tabordet, Chaudoux, 18300 Verdigny, tel. 02.48.79.34.01, fax 02.48.79.32.69 ☒ Y by appt.

CH. DE THAUVENAY 1999

☐ 11.5 ha 66,000 50–69 F

A family property since 1810, Château de Thauvenay notably owes its vineyard to the Count of Montalivet, Napoleon's Minister of the Interior and an ancestor of the current proprietor, Georges de Choulot. The latter offers a nice wine of a bright yellow colour and notes of ripe fruit. On the palate, the 99 vintage leads to a well-balanced finish.

🔑 Georges de Choulot, Le Château, 18300 Thauvenay, tel. 02.48.79.90.33, fax 02.48.79.95.67, e-mail chateau-de-thauvenay@terre-net.fr ☒ Y ev. day except Sun. 8.30am–12 noon 2.30pm–6pm

ANDRE THEVENEAU 1998★

■ 11 ha 100,000 30–49 F

The tannins are quite evident but balanced in this dark ruby-coloured wine. Oaky notes get on pleasantly with red fruit. On the palate, morello cherry vies with blackcurrant for star billing. The youthfulness and ardour of the wine should quieten down during the course of a few years in the cellar.

🔑 André Théveneau, Les Chailloux-de-Veaugues, 18300 Sancerre, tel. 02.48.79.09.92, fax 02.48.79.05.28 ☒ Y by appt.

DOM. THOMAS 1999★

◢ 0.8 ha 6,500 50–69 F

Domaine Thomas has had two successes in the 99 vintage. First this rosé, sustained and deep in colour, which releases intense scents of fruit and roses on the nose; it asserts itself on the palate with peach and apricot. The **Sancerre Blanc 99** is a balanced wine, as much on the palate as in its charming, well-developed palette of scents on the nose. A fresh finish provides a lovely expression of the Sancerre terroir and the vintage.

🔑 Dom. Thomas et Fils, Chaudoux-Verdigny, 18300 Sancerre, tel. 02.48.79.38.71, fax 02.48.79.38.14 ☒ Y ev. day 8am–12 noon 1.30pm–6pm

DOM. MICHEL THOMAS 1999★

☐ 10 ha 80,000 50–69 F

A clear and natural gold, this wine will please enthusiasts. Marked by citrus (grapefruit), its scents on the nose are long-lasting, and on the palate liveliness combines with shades of tuberose in perfect balance.

🔑 SCEV Michel Thomas et Fils, Les Egrots, 18300 Sury-en-Vaux, tel. 02.48.79.35.46, fax 02.48.79.37.60 ☒ Y ev. day except Sun. 8am–12 noon 2.30pm–7.30pm

CLAUDE ET FLORENCE THOMAS-LABAILLE

Les Aristides Vieilles vignes 1999

☐ 1.5 ha 8,000 50–69 F

Claude and Florence Thomas-Labaille have been running this 6-ha (15-acre) property since 1994. Les Aristides comes from 45-year-old vines and has been matured half in vats, half in barrels. On the nose, woody notes enhance smokiness with great finesse, whereas on the palate the flavours are subtle and masked by wood. A wine to wait for.

🔑 EARL Thomas-Labaille, Chavignol, 18300 Sancerre, tel. 02.48.54.06.95, fax 02.48.54.07.80 ☒ Y by appt.

DOM. TINET-BLONDELET

La Croix Canat 1999

☐ 2.2 ha 16,000 50–69 F

Slightly vegetal to begin with, this Sancerre emits soft blackcurrant scents after being allowed to breathe. It opens on the palate with suppleness barely marked by a hint of lemony liveliness. A coherent wine.

🔑 Dom. Tinel-Blondelet, La Croix-Canat, 58150 Pouilly-sur-Loire, tel. 03.86.39.13.83, fax 03.86.39.02.94 ☒ Y by appt.

DOM. DES TROIS NOYERS 1999★

☐ n.c. n.c. 50–69 F

Domaine des Trois Noyers has produced a successful Sancerre range in the 99 vintage. A beautiful golden-tinted white, to start with. It releases aromas of blood orange and mint on the nose and opens roundly on the palate, introducing fullness, but the finish is slightly short, suggesting you drink it immediately. The **Rouge 99** opens on a red fruit delight. The tannic network is still a little austere but will round out with time. Finally, the **Rosé 99** astonishingly conjures up candyfloss and orange peel. It is a crisp and pleasant Sancerre.

Reverdy-Cadet et Fils, rte de la Perrière, Chaudoux, 18300 Verdigny, tel. 02.48.79.38.54, fax 02.48.79.35.25 ev. day 10am–12 noon 2pm–6pm; Sun. by appt.

DOM. VACHERON 1998

■ 11 ha 5,000 50–69 F

The cellars of this estate, located under the 'Pitou de Sancerre', harboured a fine 95 vintage red. Another red, the 98, is a pretty cherry colour which harmonises perfectly with aromas of red fruits evolving around kirsch. You will need to wait for the tannins to develop in order to soften the finish, which is still a little austere.

J.-L. et J.-D. Vacheron, rue du Puits-Poulton, 18300 Sancerre, tel. 02.48.54.09.93, fax 02.48.54.01.74 ev. day10am–12 noon 2.30pm–6pm

DOM. ANDRE VATAN

Les Charmes 1999

□ 7.64 ha 67,000 50–69 F

This wine, with its acacia flower tones, starts humbly, then improves progressively thanks to its concentration, so you will find a good length on the finish. This is a Sancerre with character.

André Vatan, Chaudoux, 18300 Verdigny, tel. 02.48.79.33.07, fax 02.48.79.36.30 by appt.

DOM. DES VIEUX PRUNIERS 1999

□ 5.45 ha 45,000 30–49 F

Christian Thirot-Fournier and his wife started up in 1984 on a small vineyard, and their domaine now extends to 9 ha (22 acres) on soil rich in *caillottes* – white stones often abundant in chalky clay soil. The 99 is an attractive wine with a great deal of flavour. Sauvignon aromas express themselves handsomely. It finishes pleasingly and at length with the freshness of a summer's night, making this a convivial Sancerre.

Christian Thirot-Fournier, 1, chem. de Marcigoi, 18300 Bué, tel. 02.48.54.09.40, fax 02.48.78.02.72 ev. day except Sun. 8am–12 noon 1.30pm–7pm

THE RHÔNE VALLEY

As the mighty Rhône races south towards the Midi and the sun, it unites rather than divides the great tracts of country either side of it. Along both its banks stretch vineyards that are among the oldest in France, prestigious in some places, yet unknown in others. In terms of producing fine wines, the Rhône valley is the second largest viticultural area in France, after Bordeaux. In terms of quality it can compete at the highest level with some of the Bordeaux crus and can excite the interest of connoisseurs just as much as some of the most highly prized Bordeaux and Burgundies.

For a long time, however, Côte du Rhône wine was underestimated: it was considered to be a nice, popular little bar wine and, as such, appeared only rarely on dinner tables. It was known as a *vin d'une nuit* (a one-night wine), because its fleeting stay in the vat made it light, fruity and a little tannic, quite at home alongside Beaujolais in the Lyonnais *bouchons* (bars). Nonetheless, true wine-lovers had always appreciated the Grands Crus, tasting a Hermitage with the respect reserved for great bottles. Nowadays, thanks to the efforts of the 12,000 Rhône winegrowers and their professional organisations, along with a constant improvement in quality, the image of the Côte du Rhône wines has improved. While they still flow joyously in bars and bistros, they are also taking their place at the best tables and, while their true richness remains in their diversity, they have reclaimed the success they enjoyed in times past.

Few wine regions are able to lay claim to so glorious a past, and from Vienne to Avignon there is no single village that is not recorded in some of the most memorable pages of French history. The oldest vineyard in the country is said to be on the banks of the Vienne, originally created by Phocaean Greeks who journeyed up from Marseille, and further developed by the Romans. By the 4th century BC, vineyards are recorded in the areas now famous as Hermitage and Côte Rôtie, while those in the region of Die appeared at the very beginning of the Christian era. The Templars, in the 12th century, planted the first vines at Châteauneuf-du-Pape, and the work was continued by Pope John XXII two centuries later. As for the Côte du Rhône wines in the Gard, they used to be very fashionable in the 17th and 18th centuries.

Today, in the southern sector, on the left bank of the river, the medieval château of Suze-la-Rousse has been reconverted to serve the wine industry: the Université du Vin has its headquarters there and organises courses, professional training and various events.

Looking at the valley as a whole, some commentators make a distinction between the wines of the left bank as being heavier and more heady, and the wines on the right bank which are lighter. More generally they distinguish between two main sectors which are clearly differentiated: the sector of the northern Côtes du Rhône, north of Valence, and that of the southern Côtes du Rhône, south of Montélimar, divided from each other by an area about 50 km (31 miles) deep where no vines are grown.

The neighbouring appellations of the Rhône valley should not be left out. Even though they are less well known to the general public, they nonetheless produce original wines of quality. These are the Coteaux du Tricastin in the north, the Côtes du Ventoux and the Côtes du Luberon in the east, and the Côtes du Vivarais in the north-west. There are three further appellations which are geographically more distant still from the valley proper: the Clairette de Die and the Châtillon-en-Dios in the Drôme valley, on the edge of the Vercors, and the Coteaux de Pierrevert, produced in the department of the Alpes-de-Haute-Provence. Finally, it is worth noting the two appellations of Vins Doux Naturels (naturally sweet wines) of the Vaucluse: Muscat de Beaumes-de-Venise and Rasteau (see the chapter on Vins Doux Naturels).

Looking at the variations of soils and climate, it is still possible to identify three sub-groupings within the vast region of the Rhône valley. North of Valence, the climate is temperate with a continental influence, the soils are mostly granites or schists, deposited on hills with very steep slopes; the red wines come from a single variety, Syrah, and the whites from Marsanne and Roussanne, while the Viognier variety is used to make Château-Grillet and Condrieu. In the Dios, the climate is influenced by the mountain relief and the limestone soils are made up of screes at the foot of the slopes, good conditions for the Clairette and Muscat varieties. South of Montélimar the climate becomes Mediterranean and the very varied soils are spread out on a limestone stratum (terraces of rolled pebbles, red clay and sand soils, molasses and sands). Grenache is the main variety here, but the extremes of climate force the wine-growers to use a number of varieties to obtain perfectly balanced wines: these include Syrah, Mourvèdre, Cinsault, Clairette, Bourboulenc and Roussanne.

After a considerable reduction in the planted area in the 19th century, the vineyard of the Rhône valley was extended again, and today it is still expanding. In general terms it covers 59,000 ha (145,730 acres) producing on average 2.9 million hl (76,560,000 gal) a year; nearly 50% of the wine produced in the northern area is sold by shippers, and 70% is sold by cooperatives in the southern area.

Côtes du Rhône

The Appellation Régionale Côtes du Rhône was defined by decree in 1937. In 1996, a new decree set conditions regarding the vine types planted, to be implemented from 2000: for red wines, Grenache should form a minimum proportion of 40%, Syrah and Mourvèdre should also be included. Naturally enough, this arrangement only applies to vineyards south of MontéliTue. White wine varieties will, in future, only be allowed where vines for rosés are grown. The AOC extends into six departments: the Gard, the Ardèche, Drôme, Vaucluse, Loire and Rhône. Produced on 41,000 ha (101,270 acres), nearly all in the southern sector, these wines make 2,200,000 hl (58,080,000 gal), the red wines having the lion's share with 96% of the production, rosés and whites each producing 2%. The 10,000 wine-makers are divided up into 1,610 individual cellars (35% of the volume) and 70 Caves Coopératives (65% of the volume). Out of three hundred million bottles sold each year, 45% are consumed in people's homes, 30% in restaurants and 25% are exported.

Because of the variations in microclimate, the differences in the soil and the vine varieties, these vineyards produce wines that can satisfy every palate. Long-keeping red wines that are rich, tannic and strong, ideal with red meat, are produced in the hotter areas and on the diluvial alpine soils (Domazan, Estezargues, Courthézon, Orange, etc). Fruity, firmer reds are grown on soils that are lighter (Puymeras, Nyons, Sabran, Bourt-Saint-Andéol, etc). Finally, nouveau wines (about 15 million bottles), fruity and smooth and designed to be drunk very young, are released from the third Thursday in November, and are enjoying an ever-growing success.

The Rhône Valley (Northern)

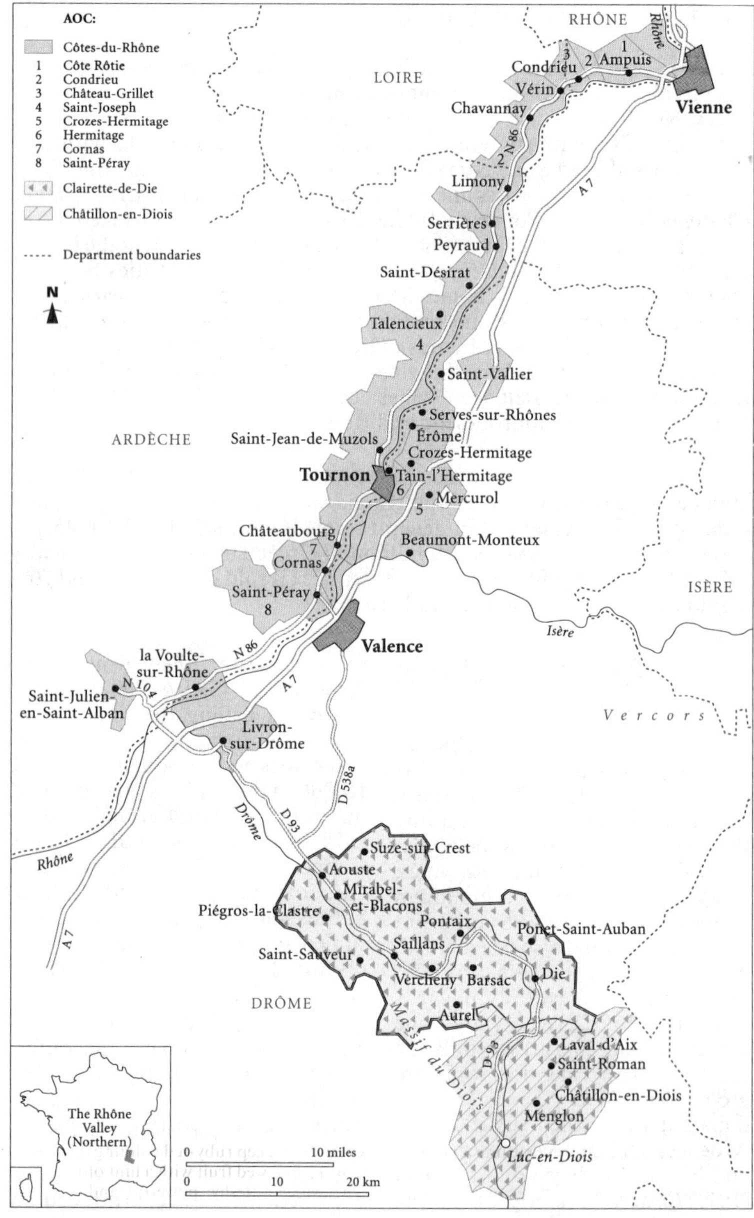

In the case of the whites and rosés, the summer heat promotes a characteristic balance and roundness. Careful cultivation and modern oenological techniques mean that the aromas can be maximised to produce fresh, delicate wines for which demand continually increases. White and rosés should be served respectively with saltwater fish, salads or charcuterie.

CH. DE BASTET Cuvée spéciale 1998★

■ n.c. 100,000 20–29 F

A former silkworm farm, this estate started to grow vines in the 17th century. The vineyard is cultivated biodynamically on a clay and sandy soil, and this wine is produced from equal amounts of Grenache and Syrah. Already tasting very good, it is powerful and distinctive, but easy drinking too. Ready to drink from late 2000 but could be kept longer. It will be enjoyed by one and all. The **La Cuvée Spéciale 99 Blanc** is given the same score. Made entirely from Viognier, the nose has bewitching scents of apples, pears and exotic flowers. Serve with white meat in a sauce. (50–69 F).

Jean-Charles Aubert, Ch. de Bastet, 30200 Sabran, tel. 04.66.89.69.14, fax 04.66.39.92.01 Y by appt.

CH. BEAUCHENE

Grande Réserve 1998★

■ 12 ha 70,000 30–49 F

Michel Bernard's family estate is situated some 5 km (3 miles) from Orange. He has submitted two wines, the **Le Pavillon du Château de Beauchêne 99 Rouge** matured in tank (20–29 F) which was awarded a mention, and this Grande Réserve which spent a year in barrel. The colours are nice and attractive, and the fruity notes on the nose give way to oakiness from the barrel-ageing. Both very well balanced, these wines are the product of high quality grapes and good wine-making.

Michel Bernard, Ch. Beauchêne, rte de Beauchêne, 84420 Piolenc, tel. 04.90.51.75.87, fax 04.90.51.73.36, e-mail chateaubeauchene@worldonline.fr Y by appt.

DOM. BEAU MISTRAL

Grande Réserve Gastronomique 1999

■ 4 ha 10,000 30–49 F

The vineyard of this beautiful 25-ha (62-acre) estate extends over several plots on which the soil varies from brown limestone to red earth over sandstone. This wine, which was from manually harvested and sorted grapes, is typical of the terroir of Rasteau. A warm-climate style, this is a deep-coloured wine with notes of fruit and spice. Both powerful and fine, altogether quite a pleasant wine.

Jean-Marc Brun, Dom. Beau Mistral, Le Village, rte d'Orange, 84110 Rasteau, tel. 04.90.46.16.90, fax 04.90.46.17.30 Y by appt.

DOM. DE BELLE-FEUILLE

Vieilli en Fût de Chêne 1998★

■ 6 ha 15,000 30–49 F

The old village of Vénéjan, just outside Bagnols-sur-Cèze, has a chapel, dating from the 12th century. The chapel is not the least of its attractions, for it is also home to the sizeable 56-ha (138-acre) estate of Belle-Feuille. This wine spent ten months in oak. The intense, dark colour is a good reflection of its forceful personality. The palate has plenty of fruit and richness with hints of well-integrated oak. The jury's verdict: extremely well made.

Gilbert Louche, Dom. de Belle-Feuille, 30200 Vénéjan, tel. 04.66.79.27.33, fax 04.66.79.22.82 Y ev. day except Sun. 8am–12 noon 1pm–7pm

LOUIS BERNARD

Grande Cuvée 1998★★

■ n.c. n.c. 30–49 F

The four red wines submitted by this wine merchant from Orange were enjoyed by the jury. Priced at less than 30 F, the selection **Louis Bernard 99** and the **Réserve du Domaine Bruthel 98** were awarded one star. The former should be kept until spring 2001; the latter is ready now. **Les Pontificales**, half matured in tank and half barrel, was awarded two stars. This Grande Cuvée, a blend of Grenache, Syrah, Mourvèdre and Cinsault, is not great in name alone. Completely oak-aged for 14 months, this wine has an oaky taste that is pronounced yet not overpowering. A well-balanced structure with obvious flavours of ripe and cooked fruit.

Les domaines Bernard, rte de Sérignan, 84100 Orange, tel. 04.90.11.86.86, fax 04.90.34.87.30

DOM. DU BOIS DES MEGES 1999

◪ 0.1 ha 600 20–29 F

This rosé was produced from a short maceration of three grape varieties. Its dazzling salmon pink appearance is visual testimony to its feminine character. Although light in style, the strength of its fruit aromas reveals a tenacious personality, which all combines to place it among the most characteristic of Côtes du Rhône wines.

Ghislain Guigue, Les Tappys, rte d'Orange, 84150 Violès, tel. 04.90.70.92.95, fax 04.90.70.97.39 Y by appt.

DOM. BOUCHE La Truffière 1998★★★

■ 5 ha 26,000 30–49 F

The product of an excellent clay-limestone terroir found near the edge of the ancient and beautiful city of Camaret, this Côtes du Rhône is refined and elegant, showing all the influences of its particularly good soil. A beautifully deep ruby-red colour gives way to a nose of stewed fruit with a hint of liquorice. The wine is fleshy, powerful and well balanced, and should fill out some more with

age, the tannins having already softened. A very harmonious wine, it could be served at the grandest tables without disgracing itself.
🔑 Dominique Bouche, chem. d'Avignon, 84850 Camaret-sur-Aigues, tel. 04.90.37.27.19, fax 04.90.37.74.17, e-mail dbouche@terre-net.fr ☑ 🍷 by appt.

DOM. DU BOULAS 1998*

■ 400 ha 42,000 🍾 🌡 20–29 F

Established in 1925, the co-operative of Laudun has submitted some good quality wines to our jury. This one, with its attractive deep red colour, presents quite a complex character on the nose with fairly persistent fruity notes. The palate is powerful and full with a range of flavours over which spice predominates. The same **Domaine du Boulas 99 Blanc** is ideal with shellfish. It won a mention, as did the **Le Manoir de Figon Rouge 98**, from a vineyard farmed using sustainable agriculture. Drink it right away to best appreciate its fruitiness. Finally, the **Domaine Saint-Léger 98 Rouge** earns a star and should be drunk with friends over a light supper.
🔑 Les Vignerons de Laudun, 105, rte de l'Ardoise, 30290 Laudun, tel. 04.66.90.55.20, fax 04.66.90.55.21 ☑ 🍷 by appt.

DOM. BOULETIN ET FILS 1998*

■ 2 ha 6,000 🍾 🌡 20–29 F

When visiting this region, make sure you stop at the cellars of this estate. You will receive a warm welcome that is in keeping with this Côtes du Rhône. Supple and rich, it has well-made tannins and gamey notes giving way to fruit at the end.
🔑 EARL Bouletin et Fils, quartier les Plantades, 84190 Beaumes-de-Venise, tel. 04.90.62.95.10, fax 04.90.62.98.23 ☑ 🍷 ev. day 9.30am–12.30pm 2pm–8pm

DOM. DES BOUMIANES 1998*

■ 3.5 ha 5,000 🍾 🌡 20–29 F

A stopping-off point on the pilgrimage to Saintes-Marie-de-la-Mer, this estate amounts to about 30 ha (74 acres). The Syrah, Grenache and Mourvèdre varieties were each vinified separately, a wise decision that has produced a well-accomplished wine with well-developed flavours. Swirling it around releases its gamey characteristics. Tannic at first, this is compensated for by a lovely roundness, making this complex wine extremely attractive. Drink in 2002 with game.
🔑 GAEC des Boumianes, Domazan, 30390 Aramon, tel. 04.66.57.02.35, fax 04.66.57.09.48 ☑ 🍷 ev. day except Sun. 9.30am–12 noon 2pm–6pm
🔑 Philippe Meger

CH. DE BOUSSARGUES 1999*

□ 1.5 ha 12,000 🍾 🌡 20–29 F

Boussargues, ancient headquarters of the Knights Templar, rules over a vast estate. Produced in these impressive surroundings, a light-coloured **99 Rosé** gained a mention for its freshness, a perfect companion to Provençal or Italian food. This white wine, an exceptional product of the southern Côtes du Rhône, is fresh, powerful and warming. It shows a good balance of perfect acidity and

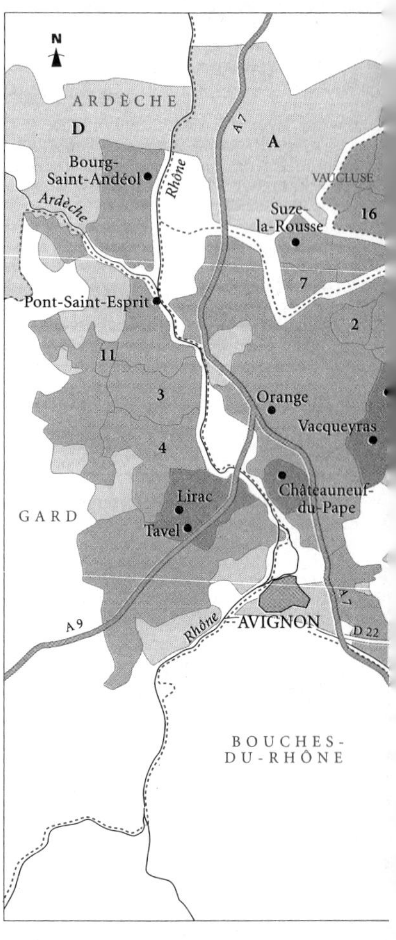

would make an outstanding apéritif as easily as it would accompany seafood or white meat.
🔑 Chantal Malabre, Ch. de Boussargues, 30200 Sabran, tel. 04.66.89.32.20, fax 04.66.79.81.64 ☑ 🍸 ev. day 9am–6pm

LAURENT BRUSSET

Vendange Clavelle 1999★

☐ 2 ha 4,000 50–69 F

The estate was created in 1947 by André Brusset, who passed away in 1999. This wine, made from Viognier, was partially (30%) matured in barrel for six months. Right away the tasters noted: 'an interesting wine with liquorice, pale tobacco and fruity aromas, the palate showing a good alcohol-acid balance'. The Viognier did not seem to typify its variety, but all agreed upon its high quality. The jury recommends serving this wine with chicken dishes or *coquilles Saint-Jacques*.
🔑 SA Dom. Brusset, 84290 Cairanne, tel. 04.90.30.82.16, fax 04.90.30.73.31, e-mail domaine-brusset.fr ☑ 🍸 by appt.

CH. CADILLAC DE MADIERES

1998★

■ n.c. 60,000 20–29 F

Didier and Vinvent Cupissol own this estate in Saint-Gervais, in the Gard, and use Maison Salavert as their distributor. This wine charms the taste buds with its notes of soft red fruit and caramel. The fullness and very soft tannins give it a dense body and a

The Rhône Valley (Southern)

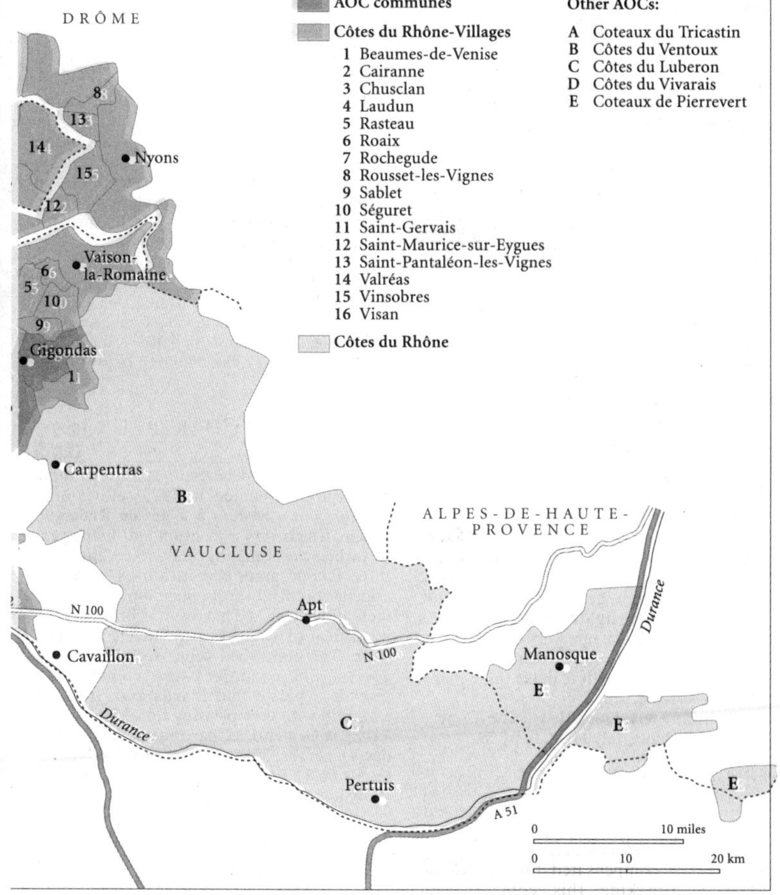

harmony that would be brought out well by hare with wild mushrooms, or warm goat's cheese.
🔑 Caves Salavert, rte de Saint-Montan, 07700 Bourg-Saint-Andéol, tel. 04.75.54.77.22, fax 04.75.54.47.91, e-mail caves.salavert@wanadoo.fr
🔑 GAEC Cupissol

DOM. DE CANTABRIL

Elevé en Fût de Chêne 1998★★

■ 1 ha 4,000 30–49 F

This estate of 42 ha (104 acres) was founded in the 19th century. In addition to the **Domaine Castan 98 Rouge** (20–29 F), which gained one star in this AOC, the jury admired this special selection which is the fruit of nine months' maturation in *foudre* (a large wooden vat), preceded by 21 days of post-fermentation maceration. The result is close to being exceptional. The deep cherry colour heralds primary musky aromas and secondary ones of spice, with hints of oak. The wine fills the mouth with its elegant flavours. Balance and length make this a great amongst the great! Wait two or three years for this one, whereas the former wine is already good to drink.
🔑 GAEC Chantecler, mas Chantecler, 30390 Domazan, tel. 04.66.57.00.56, fax 04.66.57.07.57 ☑
Y ev. day 8am–12 noon 1pm–7pm

LES VIGNERONS DU CASTELAS

1999

□ 30 ha n.c. 20–29 F

Les Vignerons du Castelas, who make wine from 600 ha (1,482 acres), have produced real quality wines in 1999, particularly this very classic white wine with shades of green. Lively and pleasing, and very tasty in the mouth, it should be just right at the end of 2000. It also has a very pretty label.
🔑 Les Vignerons du Castelas, 30650 Rochefort-du-Gard, tel. 04.90.31.72.10, fax 04.90.26.62.64 ☑

DOM. DE CHAMP-LONG

Cuvée Élevée en Fût de Chêne 1998

■ 2 ha 10,000 30–49 F

At the foot of Mont Ventoux in this very typical Provençal cellar, you will be able to sample the whole range from this estate and, in particular, this lightly oaked Côtes du Rhône whose tannins are very much in evidence. Notes of red berry fruit and vanilla allied with a good structure make this a pleasant wine.
🔑 Christian Gély, Dom. de Champ-Long, 84340 Entrechaux, tel. 04.90.46.01.58, fax 04.90.46.04.40, e-mail christian.gely@wanadoo.fr ☑ Y ev. day except Sun. 9am–12.30pm 2pm–7pm

CHANTECOTES 1999★★

◪ 50 ha 30,000 20–29 F

Located three km (two miles) from Suze-la-Rousse, this cooperative, founded in 1972, submitted a fresh and flowery **Chantecôtes 99 Blanc** (one star) and this delicate coloured rosé showing light shades of purple. The scent of pear-drops and the red berry flavours on the nose are intense. It comes together beguilingly in the mouth, the length playing out on a note of liquorice.
🔑 Caveau Chantecôtes, cours Maurice-Trintignant, 84290 Sainte-Cécile-les-Vignes, tel. 04.90.30.83.25, fax 04.90.30.74.53 ☑
Y ev. day 8.30am–12 noon 2pm–7pm

CHARLES DE VALOIS 1998★

■ 4 ha 20,000 30–49 F

A good rabbit stew would help you to appreciate the superb balance of this wine. Patrick Jaume, a producer in Châteauneuf du Pape, knows all about full-bodied wines, but he is able to lend an elegance and depth to his Côtes du Rhône that charms the taste buds.
🔑 Patrick Jaume, Dom. des Chanssaud, quartier Cabrières, 84100 Orange, tel. 04.90.34.23.51, fax 04.90.34.50.20 ☑
Y ev. day 9am–12 noon 2pm–7pm; Sat. Sun. by appt.

CHARTREUSE DE VALBONNE

Cuvée de La Font des Dames 1998★★

■ 2 ha 12,000 30–49 F

The monks created this estate in 1203 and planted vines on some 17 ha (42 acres) of hillside. They were forced to leave Valbonne in 1901. Today, the vineyard is undergoing improvements and the monastery, a listed historic monument, is an occupational help centre. This wine produced by J.-P. Burine is sumptuous. Despite its light colour, it is full and rich with remarkably strong scents of cherry and plum and a well-structured body. The finish is long and pleasant.
🔑 ASVMT, Dom. de la Chartreuse de Valbonne, 30130 Saint-Paulet-de-Caisson, tel. 04.66.90.41.24, fax 04.66.81.76.10 ☑
Y by appt.

CELLIER DES CHARTREUX 1999★

□ n.c. 16,000 30–49 F

The Cellier des Chartreux is a cooperative organisation founded in 1929 selling high quality wines. Besides a **Côtes du Rhône 98 Rouge**, which won a mention and is the perfect wine to accompany steak, this white from three Rhône grape varieties lives up to its appellation. Right from the moment that the meticulously picked harvest was brought in, a great deal of care has been taken with this wine. The controlled cellar techniques and good ageing conditions have combined to provide a palate that is balanced, full and powerful with very pleasing floral aromas.
🔑 SCA Cellier des Chartreux, 216, chem. des Vignerons, 30150 Sauveterre, tel. 04.66.82.53.53, fax 04.66.82.89.07 ☑
Y by appt.

CH. CHEVALIER BRIGAND 1998

■ n.c. 5,000 30–49 F

Situated next to the N 580 which runs from Avignon to Bagnols-sur-Cèze, this tasting cellar will impress you with its welcome. Jean-

Marie Saut, good Provençal man that he is, will enthuse about his wines in the warm accent of the region. You will find the nose on this Chevalier Brigand deep, with gamey notes.

🔑 Jean-Marie Saut, 30200 Codolet, tel. 04.66.90.18.64 ☑
Y ev. day 8am–12 noon 2pm–6pm

CLOS DES MIRAN

Cuvée des Proxumes 1998★

■ 14 ha 19,000 ▮ 30–49 F

Romain Flésia's first vintage coincided with the discovery of an archaeological site next to the estate. The event gave birth to this wine. Meticulous work has yielded a powerful wine with a persistent aroma of wild strawberries. It is rustic, but kept well under control.

🔑 Romain Flésia, clos des Miran, plaine de mas Conil, 30130 Pont-Saint-Esprit, tel. 06.83.23.11.42, fax 04.90.30.86.15 ☑
Y by appt.

CLOS HERMITAGE 1998★

■ 3.5 ha 15,000 ⏸ 50–69 F

The estate is located within the boundaries of the monastery of Villeneuve-lès-Avignon. A third each of Syrah, Grenache and Mourvèdre are blended in a traditional vinification. A garnet colour with a purplish rim, this is a complex wine that gives both elegant notes of game and very ripe berry fruit provided by the Syrah. The Grenache fills it out. Wood notes show through, bringing a hint of astringency that will disappear after a year of ageing.

🔑 Henri de Lanzac, rue de la Fontaine, 30126 Tavel, tel. 04.66.50.07.93, fax 04.66.50.17.02 ☑ Y by appt.

DOM. DE COSTE CHAUDE 1998

■ 1 ha 6,000 ▮ 🌡 30–49 F

The village of Visan still bears relics of the 12th century when it lay within the enclave of the Avignon Popes. It lies in a region, which is widely planted with vineyards, producing this pale-coloured wine. A refined and delicious 98, it will make a beguiling and pleasant accompaniment to a meal with friends. The blend of Grenache and Syrah has resulted in a well-balanced wine. Equally worthy of note is **l'Argentière 98** which gained a mention. (50–69 F).

🔑 SCA Dom. de Coste Chaude, rte de Saint-Maurice, 84820 Visan, tel. 04.90.41.91.04, fax 04.90.41.96.52 ☑
Y by appt.
🔑 Marianne Fues

CAVE COSTES ROUSSES

Lieu-dit Hautes Vouleuyes 1998

■ 50 ha 8,000 ▮ 🌡 20–29 F

This co-operative lies within the commune of Tulette, between Valréas and Orange. Grenache (75%) and Syrah are blended to make a wine that is easy to drink as well as fruity and tannic. This wine's personality has a simple and pleasing balance. Equally worthy of mention is the **Cuvée Guy de Claromane 98 Sélection Vieilles Vignes**, which is a classic Côtes du Rhône.

🔑 SCA Cave Costes Rousses, 2, av. des Alpes, 26790 Tulette, tel. 04.75.97.23.18, fax 04.75.98.38.61 ☑ Y by appt.

LES VIGNERONS DES COTEAUX D'AVIGNON Elevé en Fûts de Chêne 1998

■ 20 ha 130,000 ⏸ 20–29 F

Three cellars which have regrouped to profit from strength in numbers. They submitted a **Cuvée des Vieilles Vignes 98** (30–49 F), which earns a mention but needs to be kept a little longer, although overall an attractive and subtle wine. They also provided this stunningly concentrated wine, blessed with quite a powerful structure, tasting of spice and hints of vanilla, which are characteristic of a carefully controlled maturation period in wood.

🔑 SCA les Vignerons des Coteaux d'Avignon, 583, rte de la Gare, 84470 Châteauneuf-de-Gadagne, tel. 04.90.33.55.20, fax 04.90.33.55.22 ☑
Y by appt.

DOM. COULANGE 1998

■ 10 ha 3,800 ▮ 30–49 F

Father and daughter hold the reins of power at this 34-ha (84-acre) estate. This charming 98 is very fruity due to the presence of 80% Syrah in the blend. The palate is full of the flavours of spring.

🔑 Dom. Coulange, quartier Saint-Ferréol, 07700 Bourg-Saint-Andéol, tel. 04.75.54.56.26, fax 04.75.54.56.26 ☑
Y by appt.

DOM. NICOLAS CROZE

Cuvée Vieillie en Fût de Chêne 1997★

■ 0.7 ha 2,500 ⏸ 30–49 F

The panoramic route along the Ardèche River gorge, with its strategic viewing points looking out over superb countryside, leads to Saint-Martin-d'Ardèche where this estate is situated. With its high proportion of Syrah, this blend has a superb nose with attractive notes of jammy black fruit. A good wine in this delicate vintage, which the jury recommends with Provençal food.

🔑 Dom. Nicolas Croze, 1, rue Max-Ernst, 07700 Saint-Martin-d'Ardèche, tel. 04.75.04.62.28, fax 04.75.04.62.28 ☑
Y by appt.

CELLIER DES DAUPHINS

Grand Millésime 1998

■ 140 ha 900,000 ▮ 🌡 20–29 F

The commune of Tulette, between Sainte-Cécile-les-Vignes and Visan, harbours the biggest union of co-operatives in the region. This wine could be served with an everyday meal. It is a supple Côtes du Rhône, rich in aromas and reflecting the Grenache and Syrah that make up the blend.

🔑 Cellier des Dauphins, B.P. 16, 26790 Tulette,

tel. 04.75.96.20.47, fax 04.75.96.20.12, e-mail cellier.des.dauphins@wanadoo.fr

DOM. JEAN DAVID 1999*

0.5 ha 3,000 30–49 F

Séguret is an artist's village, full of fascinating monuments, gates, fountains and churches, to be rivalled only by the splendour of the countryside that surrounds them. You will be invited by Jean David to sample this very accomplished wine. An intense rosé colour with hints of purple leads on to a pleasant taste in which the fullness does not detract from its freshness. This fruity 99 is the product of organic farming at its most skilled.

Jean David, Le Jas, 84110 Séguret, tel. 04.90.46.95.02, fax 04.90.46.95.02 ev. day except Sun. 9am–7pm

DOM. DE DEURRE

Cuvée des Oliviers 1998

1 ha 2,000 30–49 F

The cellars of the Château De Deurre, which date from the 16th century, were purchased by Jean-Claude Valayer in 1987. In the process of being modernised, these cellars are where he makes the wines from his family's vineyards. With a strong intensity of colour, this dark cherry-red 98 made from 100% Syrah did not disappoint the tasters who found typical musky flavours and red berry fruit. A good balance of acidity will allow three to four years of ageing.

SCEA J.-C. Valayer et Fils, Dom. de Deurre, R.D. 94, 26110 Vinsobres, tel. 04.75.27.62.66, fax 04.75.27.67.24, e-mail valayer.deurre@wanadoo.fr by appt.

DOM. ESTOURNEL 1999

3.15 ha 4,200 30–49 F

This white wine is a Côtes du Rhône from the Gard department. A blend of six grape varieties, it has a lovely light coloured appearance with green hues. The exotic smells and flavours reveal notes of kiwi and grapefruit with an enjoyable palate, both subtle and balanced.

Rémy Estournel, 13, rue de Plaineautier, 30290 Saint-Victor-la-Coste, tel. 04.66.50.01.73, fax 04.66.50.21.85 by appt.

DOM. FOND CROZE

Cuvée la Saint-Romanaise 1998**

1 ha 4,000 50–69 F

This blend, which comes in a screen-printed bottle, emerges from a long period of post-fermentation maceration (20 days) and is put immediately into oak barrels to acquire the characteristic and complex flavours of red berry fruits, liquorice and spices. The members of the jury were united in commending its balance, the subtlety of its tannins and its length. Equally worthy of note is the **Cuvée Classique 98 Rouge**, matured entirely in tank and a very well-balanced wine. It earns a star.

Dom. Fond Croze, Le Village, 84290 Saint-Roman-de-Malegarde, tel. 04.90.28.97.07, fax 04.90.28.94.30 by appt.

DOM. DE FONTAVIN 1999**

0.8 ha 4,000 30–49 F

After studying œnology at Montpellier, Hélène Chouvet took up residence on the family estate in 1998 at a time when Fontavin was already well established. She is doing just as well as previous generations. Take, for example, this remarkable rosé of superb colour with hints of purple. The powerful nose gives floral scents with a dominating accent of violets. Full and rich in the mouth, the wine finishes on a lingering note of red berry fruit. The estate's **Côtes du Rhône 99 Rouge** also wins a mention. Straightforward and very soft, with plenty of fruit.

EARL Hélène et Michel Chouvet, Dom. de Fontavin, 1468, rte de la Plaine, 84350 Courthézon, tel. 04.90.70.72.14, fax 04.90.70.79.39 ev. day except Sun. 9am–12.30pm 1.30pm–7pm

DOM. F DE FONT DE MICHELLE 1999**

n.c. 2,000 30–49 F

The charming village of Bédarrides is located on the *Chemin des Vignes*, a road with several great estates, including this one. Two Côtes du Rhône wines were submitted and two were chosen. This red, a blend of equal amounts of Grenache and Syrah, leans heavily towards ripe red berry fruit. Fairly complex, it has a powerful palate providing musky notes and leather beneath the pervasive black fruit flavours. The combination of intensity with length and persistence was much liked by the jury. This same **Cuvée F 99 Blanc** (50–69 F) is a blend of 80% Viognier with Clairette. It earns a star: bear it in mind to accompany *coquilles Saint-Jacques.*

EARL Les Fils d'Etienne Gonnet, 14, imp. des Vignerons, 84370 Bédarrides, tel. 04.90.33.00.22, fax 04.90.33.20.27, e-mail egonnet@terre-net.fr by appt.

GALLIFFET

Collection privée René Aubert 1999*

n.c. n.c. 70–99 F

This 178-ha (440-acre) estate regularly comes up with great wines and such is the case with this top quality wine, a blend of 20% Grenache Blanc and 80% Viognier. The process of skin maceration has successfully extracted complex aromas of white peach and honey without damaging the wine's richness and full body that shows such beautiful balance.

Vignobles Max Aubert, Dom. de La Présidente, 84290 Sainte-Cécile-les-Vignes, tel. 04.90.30.80.34, fax 04.90.30.72.93 by appt.

René Aubert

CH. GIGOGNAN

Vigne du Prieuré 1999★

□ 2.5 ha 12,500 30-49 F

This young estate, established in 1996, has been chosen by our panel for this very accomplished wine made of 50% Viognier, 25% Roussanne and 25% Clairette. The seductive 99 has a lovely golden colour with green hints. Refined and elegant, it leaves a delicious after-taste of peach, linden flowers and honey. Absolute harmony.

Ch. Gigognan, chem. du Castillon, 84700 Sorgues, tel. 04.90.39.57.46, fax 04.90.39.15.28, e-mail info@chateau-gigognan.fr
ev. day 10am–12.30pm 2.30pm–6pm; Sun. by appt.
Callet

DOM. DU GRAND TINEL 1998

■ 10 ha 60,000 30-49 F

Grenache asserts its presence here in every smell that emanates from this light-coloured wine. Some spicy notes enhance the general sensations on the mouth that marry tannins, acidity and richness. Drink with light and well-seasoned dishes.

Les Vignobles Elie Jeune, rte de Bédarrides, 84230 Châteauneuf-du-Pape, tel. 04.90.83.70.28, fax 04.90.83.78.07
by appt.

DOM. DU GROS PATA

Cuvée Impériale Elevée en Fût de Chêne 1998★

■ 1.54 ha 10,666 30-49 F

This estate, close to Vaison-la-Romaine, a town famed for its archaeological digs, bears a name that harks back to the Middle Ages when you had to pay 'patas' (Provençal currency) to travel from one village to the next. The wine from this family property is both rustic and elegant. The character of the lovely palate, round and robust, is due to the Syrah that constitutes 60% of the blend.

Gérald Garagnon, Dom. du Gros-Pata, rte de Villedieu, 84110 Vaison-la-Romaine, tel. 04.90.36.23.75, fax 04.90.28.77.05
by appt.

GUYOT Cuvée Médaille d'Or 1998

■ n.c. 30,000 20-29 F

This is a blend of the best wine selections from the Orange wine fair. It shows a good balance. Supple and easy to drink, with attractive notes of vanilla and jam, it is a typical Côtes du Rhône.

Guyot, montée de l'Eglise, 69440 Taluyers, tel. 04.78.48.70.54, fax 04.78.48.77.31, e-mail guyotvin@easynet.fr
Thu. Fri. Sat. 8am–12 noon 1.30pm–5.30pm; cl. 15–21 Aug.

CH. D'HUGUES Grande Réserve 1998★

■ 5.68 ha 26,000 30-49 F

Les Chorégies d'Orange (the annual operatic and music festival in Orange) attracts a music-mad audience that is often keen on good wines too. It is just a short distance from Orange to reach this château, whose foundations date back to the 17th century. This *coup de cœur* is produced by a wine-maker who is an amateur painter in his spare time and his artistic skills also find expression in the making of this intense 98, full of red berry fruits. This characterful wine has a powerful palate and good length. A rabbit stew would be a suitable match.

Bernard Pradier, Ch. d'Hugues, 84100 Uchaux, tel. 04.90.70.06.27, fax 04.90.70.10.28 ev. day 9am–12 noon 2pm–7pm; Sun. by appt.

CH. JOANNY Cuvée Prestige 1998★

■ 15 ha 50,000 20-29 F

You will easily find this vast estate which is situated close to the medieval village of Sérignan, on the slopes of the Uchaux mountains. To produce this well-made wine the tanks are set up high to facilitate the techniques of *pigeage* (punching down the cap) and *délestage* (another process of extracting colour and tannins from the skins). Both fine and discreet, the wine shows plenty of fruit, and its elegant structure provides a very beautiful balance. From the same producer, the **Château Carbonel 98 Rouge** and **99 Rosé** both earn a mention. The latter displays a very Provençal character, while the former is both complex and unambiguous.

Famille Dupond, Ch. Joanny, rte de Piolenc, 84830 Sérignan-du-Comtat, tel. 04.90.70.00.10, fax 04.90.70.09.21, e-mail info@bracdelaperriere.com ev. day except Tue. 8am–12 noon 2pm–6pm

LA BASTIDE SAINT-VINCENT 1999

■ 3 ha 14,000 20-29 F

Grenache makes up 70% of this blend that also includes Mourvèdre and Syrah. An attractive wine with glints of red cherry and bluish tinges, it goes on to reveal a discreet but complex nose with attractive notes of undergrowth and fruits macerated in alcohol. The palate has a straightforward balance and pleasing warmth to it. This is a well-knit wine.

Guy Daniel, Bastide Saint-Vincent, rte de Vaison-la-Romaine, 84150 Violès, tel. 04.90.70.94.13, fax 04.90.70.96.13
ev. day 8am–7pm; Sun. by appt.; cl. 1–20 Jan.

DOM. LA BOUVAUDE 1998

■ 1 ha 4,000 30-49 F

After visiting Pègue where students of prehistory will discover an interesting little museum, you will reach the aptly named Rousset-les-Vignes and the 15-ha (42-acre) estate where this dark purplish wine awaits you. This is a light and balanced, pleasant wine with aromas of ripe fruit; despite being from 100% Syrah and having spent 12 months in oak barrels, it remains typical of its Côtes du Rhône appellation.

⊶ Stéphane Barnaud, Dom. La Bouvaude, 26770 Rousset-les-Vignes, tel. 04.75.27.90.32, fax 04.75.27.98.72 ☑
Y ev. day 10am–7pm

DOM. LA CHARADE 1999*

◪ 2 ha n.c. ▮ 🌡 20–29 F

This handsome estate of 50 ha (124 acres), established at the end of the 19th century, submitted a rosé that is the fruit of a long family tradition. It is an astonishing wine, with shades of orange colouration and smells of jam and quince jelly. These develop in the mouth into a dominant flavour of honey enveloped in caramel and orange marmalade. The result is very attractive.

⊶ M. et L. Jullien, Dom. La Charade, 30760 Saint-Julien-de-Peyrolas, tel. 04.66.82.18.21, fax 04.66.82.33.03 ☑ Y ev. day except Sun. 9am–12 noon 2pm–7pm

DOM. DE LA CHARITE 1998

■ 20 ha 80,000 ▮ 🌡 20–29 F

Located in a pretty village in the Gard, this estate offers a warm welcome to enthusiasts. This characteristic, full-bodied and quite well structured wine was grown in clay-limestone soil and comes from Grenache (50%), Syrah (30%) and Mourvèdre, made using carbonic maceration.

⊶ EARL Valentin et Coste, Dom. de la Charité, 5, chem. des Issarts, 30650 Saze, tel. 04.90.31.73.55, fax 04.90.26.92.50 ☑
Y ev. day except Sun. 5pm–7.30pm; Sat. 2pm–7.30pm

DOM. DE LA CROIX-BLANCHE 1999

□ n.c. 2,000 ▮ 🌡 20–29 F

The great surrealist painter Max Ernst lived not far from this estate. Viognier and Marsanne, planted on the limestone slopes of the Ardèche, have produced this attractive wine. You can smell how very ripe the grapes were. Citrus fruits and flowers on the nose, fruit on the palate, this is a fresh and pleasant 99 with a very attractive appearance.

⊶ Daniel Archambault, Dom. de la Croix-Blanche, 07700 Saint-Martin-d'Ardèche, tel. 04.75.04.60.41, fax 04.75.98.77.25 ☑
Y by appt.

CH. LA FRANCE 1998

■ 6 ha 40,000 ▮ ⏣ 🌡 20–29 F

This old 18th-century hunting lodge today presides over a wine estate. The ruby-red 98 has a good intensity of colour. While the nose gives notes of grilled meats and stewed fruit, the initial impression on the palate is more of red berry fruits. A good length and very pleasant aftertaste, the tannins will soften and allow it to be kept for a while.

⊶ Les Grandes Serres, rte de l'Islon, 84230 Châteauneuf-du-Pape, tel. 04.90.83.72.22, fax 04.90.83.78.77 ☑ Y by appt.

DOM. LA GARRIGUE

Cuvée Romaine 1998

■ 2 ha n.c. ▮ 🌡 30–49 F

Albert Bernard's family established themselves amongst the vines of Vacqueyras some 150 years ago. Their motto should be applied with caution: 'Le vin de garrigue jamais ne fatigue!' or 'Wines from the garrigue will never tire you!' This one is well structured with a gamey side that will be appreciated by all those who love substantial and slightly rustic wines. We think a ragout of guinea fowl would do it full justice.

⊶ EARL A. Bernard et Fils, Dom. la Garrigue, 84190 Vacqueyras, tel. 04.90.65.84.60, fax 04.90.65.80.79 ☑
Y ev. day 8am–12 noon 2pm–7.30pm; Sun. by appt.

DOM. DE LA GRAND'RIBE

Les Garrigues d'Eric Beaumard et Christophe Lambert 1998

□ 1.5 ha 9,000 ▮ ⏣ 🌡 30–49 F

A blend of several grape varieties and a few months in barrel have produced a successful and characteristic wine. Its rich balance embellishes the well-developed flavours and there are notes of honey on the finish. Try it with *picodon* (local goat's cheese) or drink it on its own.

⊶ Abel Sahuc, SCEA Dom. de la Grand'Ribe, rte de Bollène, 84290 Sainte-Cécile-les-Vignes, tel. 04.90.30.83.75, fax 04.90.30.76.12 ☑ Y ev. day except Sat. Sun. 10am–12 noon 2pm–6pm

DOM. DE LA JEROME 1998

■ 1.77 ha 12,000 ▮ 🌡 30–49 F

This carefully made wine has a gloriously intense red colour. The initial gamey smell on the nose gives way to an aroma of ripe fruit typical of Grenache. Well-balanced and full-bodied, ready to drink, it could be aged for a further two to three years in the depths of your cellar.

⊶ Sylvette Bréchet, Dom. des Bosquets, rte de Vacqueyras, 84190 Gigondas, tel. 04.90.83.70.31, fax 04.90.83.51.97 ☑
Y by appt.

DOM. LA MONARDIERE

Lou Peyrau 1999**

■ 2 ha 6,500 ▮ 30–49 F

The Vache family acquired this estate in the 19th century and have practically rebuilt it thanks to the recent efforts of Christian and Martine Vache who took over the management in 1987. Lou Peyrau is a superb wine with a brilliant plum colour and a nose that is still slightly closed, but is bursting with the promise of ripe fruit flavours. On the palate the flavours are reminiscent of undergrowth and spices. A remarkable wine with great potential for ageing.

⊶ Dom. la Monardière, Les Grès, 84190 Vacqueyras, tel. 04.90.65.87.20, fax 04.90.65.82.01, e-mail monardiere@wanadoo.fr ☑

Y ev. day except Sun. 10am–7pm
🔑 Christian Vache

DOM. DE LA MORDOREE 1999*

■ 10 ha 40,000 ■ ♁ 30–49 F

This estate submitted their beautifully balanced 99 in which 5% Counoise rounds off the blend of Grenache, Cinsault, Syrah and Carignan: the colour is intense and the aromas combine the floral smells of violet with notes of blackcurrant. The fine tannins are well-balanced and it has good length on the palate.

🔑 Dom. de la Mordorée, chem. des Oliviers, 30126 Tavel, tel. 04.66.50.00.75, fax 04.66.50.47.39 ☑ Y ev. day except Sun. 8am–12 noon 1.30pm–5.30pm
🔑 Delorme

DOM. DE LA PIGEADE 1998*

■ 1.7 ha 12,000 ■ ♁ 30–49 F

This is a 'wine-making facility' established in 1996. Made from 100% Grenache, the tasters could not mistake this Côtes du Rhône 1998. Harvested manually then sorted on a conveyor-belt, this wine can without doubt be judged a great success. Well-balanced with soft tannins, it has an excellent after-taste of very attractive blackcurrant flavours.

🔑 Thierry Vaute, Dom. de la Pigeade, rte de Caromb, 84190 Beaumes-de-Venise, tel. 04.90.62.90.00, fax 04.90.62.90.90, e-mail th.vaute@lapigeade.fr ☑ Y by appt.

DOM. LA REMEJEANNE

Les Chèvrefeuilles 1999*

■ 10 ha 40,000 ■ ♁ 30–49 F

Located five km (three miles) from the village of Sabran, this 30-ha (74-acre) family estate was taken over by Rémy Klein in 1988. Although very young, this wine already combines elegance with power. With an excellent future ahead thanks to its lively but silky tannins, it is very convincing on the palate with characteristic red berry fruits. Some spices also emerge on the aftertaste.

🔑 EARL Ouahi et Rémy Klein, Dom. la Réméjeanne, Cadignac, 30200 Sabran, tel. 04.66.89.44.51, fax 04.66.89.64.22 ☑
Y by appt.

DOM. DE LASCAMP

Cuvée de l'An 2000 Vieilli en Fût 1998**

■ 15 ha 5,000 ⏸ 30–49 F

Very close to being a *coup de cœur*, this is a great vintage for Monsieur Imbert, whose estate is perched on the hillsides of Sabran where his family has been growing vines since 1767. Complex and intense fruit flavours dominate this wine. Very structured yet supple, the palate has quite a long finish.

🔑 EARL Clos de Lascamp, Cadignac, 30200 Sabran, tel. 04.66.89.69.28, fax 04.66.89.62.44 ☑ Y by appt.
🔑 Imbert

DOM. DE LA VALERIANE 1998*

■ 4 ha 15,000 ■ ♁ 20–29 F

Valérie Castan is an œnologist who makes wine on her family estate. She should take a bow for her great success in having all three of her submissions accepted by the *Guide*. The **99 Rosé** could last two years and the **99 Blanc**, which yields a symphony of floral and fruity smells, is an example of a perfect understanding of what a Côtes du Rhône should be. Both received the same score as the wine noted here. Astonishing floral notes embellish this wine's aromas. Red berry fruits emerge on a palate that is full-bodied and warm, with tannins still present, guaranteeing the wine a fine future. These are three elegant wines.

🔑 Mesmin Castan, rte d'Estézargues, 30390 Domazan, tel. 04.66.57.04.84, fax 04.66.57.00.07 ☑ Y by appt.

LA VINSOBRAISE 1999*

◪ n.c. 13,000 ■ ♁ 20 F+

The fruit from close to 2,000 ha (4,940 acres) of vines are vinified by the co-operative of Vinsobres. Their *Rosé de Saignée* (from a short skin maceration) is dominated by soft red fruits, from its morello cherry colour to its finish. Round and rich, it should be drunk by Easter 2001.

🔑 Cave La Vinsobraise, 26110 Vinsobres, tel. 04.75.27.64.22, fax 04.75.27.66.59 ☑
Y by appt.

DOM. LE CLOS DU BAILLY 1999**

■ n.c. 12,000 ■ ♁ 20–29 F

If you are visiting the Pont du Gard, make sure you call in at this estate, which is situated very nearby. Here, in the very centre of the village of Remoulins, you will find a huge range of wines and aperitifs produced by the owner. It was this red 99 that caught the interest of the jury. Recognised as one of the finest of its appellation, it delights the eye and the nose entices with its complex aromas. These recur in a fruity palate structured by fine tannins. 'It comes alive in the mouth', commented one happy taster.

🔑 Soulier Père et Fils, 17, rue d'Avignon, 30210 Remoulins, tel. 04.66.37.12.23, fax 04.66.37.38.44 ☑ Y by appt.

LE CLOS DU CAILLOU 1998*

■ n.c. 20,000 ⏸ 30–49 F

Already well established, this estate's reputation and quality has grown since J.-D. Vacheron settled on the family property. This Côtes du Rhône displays power and amplitude, with scents of spice and vanilla from its six months of maturation in wood. The characteristically floral and complex **Cuvée Bouquet des Garrigues 99 Blanc** was awarded the same mark. Two very elegant wines that are ready now but could be kept.

🔑 J.-D. Vacheron, Clos du Caillou, 84350 Courthézon, tel. 04.90.70.73.05, fax 04.90.70.76.47 ☑ Y ev. day except Sun. 9am–12 noon 2pm–6pm

DOM. LE COUROULOU 1998

■ 2 ha 12,000 20–29 F

Dark purplish-coloured, this wine could accompany a tasty beef dish. With hints of ripe fruit and of cinnamon, the gamey notes on the nose also recur on the palate where the oak flavours show good finesse.

Guy Ricard, Dom. le Couroulou, 84190 Vacqueyras, tel. 04.90.65.84.83, fax 04.90.65.81.25 ev. day except Sun. 9.30am–12 noon 2pm–6pm

LE GRAVILLAS 1999★

■ 8.7 ha 51,000 20–29 F

La Cave Le Gravillas will celebrate its 65th anniversary this year. Located in the magnificent village of Sablet, today it makes wines from 555 ha (1,371 acres) of vineyards. The two wines bearing the cellar's name both earn a star: a **99 Blanc** that is smooth and full bodied, suitable to partner a grilled sea bass in fennel, and this very well structured red wine, which simply requires a little further ageing. The colour, a halo of purplish rings, speaks volumes for its organoleptic qualities. The nose is rich with smells of red berries, and these recur on the palate, which shows good balance.

Cave Le Gravillas, 84110 Sablet, tel. 04.90.46.90.20, fax 04.90.46.96.71 by appt.

DOM. LE PUY DU MAUPAS 1998★

■ 20 ha 5,000 30–49 F

In 1983, Christian Sauvayre decided to completely renovate his winery that had been in ruins for many years. Today, the results are proof that he took the right decision. This dark ruby-coloured Côtes du Rhône is ranked amongst the greats. Spicy, gamey, tannic and full, the structure still displays a firmness that will soften after being kept for a year.

Christian Sauvayre, Dom. le Puy du Maupas, quartier Maupas, 84110 Puymeras, tel. 04.90.46.47.43, fax 04.90.46.48.51 ev. day 9am–12.30pm 2pm–8pm

CH. LES AMOUREUSES

Cuvée Spéciale 1998★★

■ n.c. 15,000 30–49 F

The Ardèche has done itself proud with this remarkable wine. A richly deserved *coup de cœur* has been awarded which acknowledges the achievement of this wine-maker.

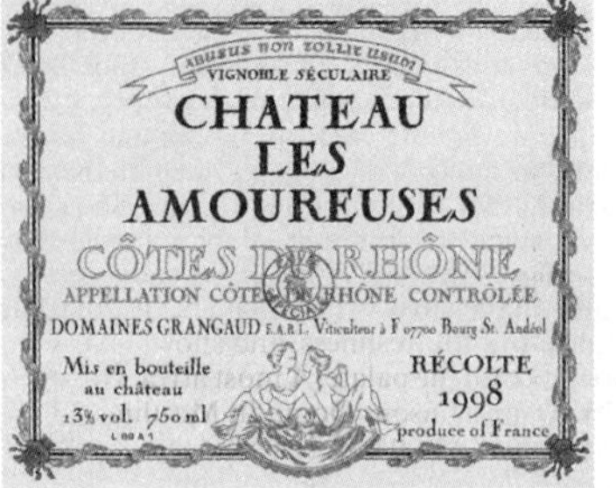

The list of adjectives used by the jury to describe their reactions is impressive – to quote just a few: intense, complex, ripe fruit, strong liquorice, etc. Much attention and a short period in barrel produced this fantastic result. Also note the **Cuvée Principale 98 Rouge**, which was commended by a different jury.

Alain Grangaud, chem. de Vinsas, 07700 Bourg-Saint-Andéol, tel. 04.75.54.51.85, fax 04.75.54.66.38 by appt.

LES ANTIQUES 1998

■ n.c. n.c. 20–29 F

The aromatic richness and supple balance of this wine put it immediately into that class of traditional Rhône valley wines. Simple but very straightforward, it will happily accompany everyday meals.

Maison Thorin, Le Pont des Samsons, 69430 Quincié-en-Beaujolais, tel. 04.74.69.09.10, fax 04.74.69.09.28, e-mail information@maisonthorin.com

LES BROTTIERS 1999★

□ 4 ha 20,000 30–49 F

Châteauneuf-du-Pape has an interesting museum of vine-growers' tools. Laurent Charles Brotte is a wine-merchant and producer whose wines are also to be found in the museum. Amongst the wines to taste is this one from 100% Roussanne ripened on the terroir of Sabran in the Gard. This rounded wine has fruity aromas and a particularly pleasing finish on the palate. Also note the **Cuvée Les Charmilles 99** which blends Grenache Blanc (90%) with Marsanne.

Laurent-Charles Brotte, rte d'Avignon, 84230 Châteauneuf-du-Pape, tel. 04.90.83.70.07, fax 04.90.83.74.34 ev. day 9am–12 noon 2pm–6pm

LES COUDRIERS 1999★★

◪ 10 ha 60,000 20 F+

A *Rosé de Saignée* from the classic blend of Grenache and Cinsault. Perfectly balanced, it displays a round and supple character with nicely judged acidity, making it lively and fresh. The fruity character of the wine charms effortlessly.

Cellier de L'Enclave des Papes, rte d'Orange, 84600 Valréas, tel. 04.90.41.91.42, fax 04.90.41.90.21

LES MENINES 1998

■ n.c. 70,000 30–49 F

From wine-merchants established in 1859, Les Ménines and the **Héritage des Caves des Papes 98 Rouge** are two successful wines. They both come principally from Grenache and Syrah matured in barrel, which provide a complex taste with spicy notes and a dash of liquorice. Both these balanced and rich wines are ready to drink.

Ogier-Caves des Papes, 10, bd Pasteur, 84230 Châteauneuf-du-Pape, tel. 04.90.39.32.32, fax 04.90.83.72.51 ev. day except Sun. 8.30am–6.30pm

DOM. DE MAGALANNE 1998

■ 8 ha 6,000 ▮ ⚲ 20-29 F

Grapes mature very early in these warm Rhône valley vineyards and this is one of the reasons why the wine is always so expressive. Spicy and peppery gamey notes add to its well-made structure.

🔑 SCEA Dom. de Magalanne, rte de Signargues, 30390 Domazan, tel. 04.66.57.02.72, fax 04.66.57.21.58 ☑ Y ev. day 9am–12 noon 2pm–7pm
🔑 Betton et Crouzet

CH. DE MARJOLET 1998

■ 12 ha 65,000 ▮ 20-29 F

Partial carbonic maceration makes this wine fresh and easy drinking. Bernard Pontaud has produced an elegance in the wine that everyone will find approachable. Fruity and supple, it should be drunk very soon, perhaps with grilled lamb chops.

🔑 Bernard Pontaud, Vignobles de Marjolet, B.P. 3, 30330 Gaujac, tel. 04.66.82.00.93, fax 04.66.82.92.58 ☑ Y ev. day except Sat. Sun. 9am–12 noon 2pm–6pm

DOM. MARTIN 1998

■ 25 ha 30,000 ⦀ 30-49 F

Located one km (half a mile) from the Romanesque church of the old 12th-century Travaillan village, this vast estate of 52 ha (128 acres) dates back to 1905. The result of traditional wine-making methods, but with a long post-fermentation maceration period, and matured for 12 months in wood, this wine has terrific depth. Supple and full-bodied, the tannins are very apparent yet already nicely integrated.

🔑 SCEA Dom. Martin, Plan de Dieu, 84850 Travaillan, tel. 04.90.37.23.20, fax 04.90.37.23.20 ☑ Y ev. day except Sun. 8am–12 noon 2pm–7pm

MAS DE LIBIAN 1998

■ 10 ha 10,000 ⦀ 30-49 F

The label is hand-written on this attractively vivid, dark red wine. The intense fruity nose is as good as the colour. The palate is of a similar fruity style enhanced by notes of spice and a powerful structure, with tannins that should soften out by Easter 2001.

🔑 Thibon, Mas de Libian, 07700 Saint-Marcel-d'Ardèche, tel. 04.75.04.66.22, fax 04.75.98.66.38 ☑ Y by appt.

DOM. MIREILLE ET VINCENT

Elevé en Fût de Chêne 1997*

■ 2.3 ha 8,000 ⦀ 30-49 F

There are many good reasons to visit this beautiful region full of lavender and vineyards, not least of which is Valréas with its market, château and Romanesque Provençal church and fine 17th-century organ. The character of the vintage emerges clearly in this lightly oaked and warm 97. Notes of spice on the nose are also present on the palate leaving it with a nicely balanced finish.

🔑 Bernard et Marie-Thérèse Bizard, rte de Taulignan, 84600 Valréas, tel. 04.90.35.00.77, fax 04.90.35.60.06 ☑ Y ev. day 9am–12 noon 2pm–7pm; Sun. by appt.

CH. MONGIN 1998*

■ 6 ha 20,000 ▮ 20-29 F

The work of a group lead by director and œnologist José Carballar, this encouraging wine comes from a rather unusual vineyard, which is part of the agricultural college of Orange. The reward for the students' efforts is this full, fresh wine which shows obvious spicy characters.

🔑 Ch. Mongin, 2260, rte du Grès, 84100 Orange, tel. 04.90.51.48.04, fax 04.90.51.48.20 ☑ Y by appt.

CH. DE MONTFAUCON

Baron Louis 1998*

■ 5 ha 30,000 ▮ ⦀ ⚲ 50-69 F

Rebuilt by Baron Louis in the 19th century, the Château de Montfaucon is an impressive fortress, which appears high up on a peak overlooking a bend of the River Rhône. The estate produces very good wines such as this great Côtes du Rhône, matured for 12 months in oak, giving fine and elegant tannins balancing the flavours of ripe fruit. Keep until 2001 and then drink with meat in a rich sauce. The un-oaked **Cuvée Principale 98 Rouge** is ready now, but likewise looks promising for another two to three years. It also won a star.

🔑 Rodolphe de Pins, 22, rue du Château, 30150 Montfaucon, tel. 04.66.50.37.19, fax 04.66.50.37.19 ☑ Y ev. day except Sat. Sun. 2pm–6pm; groups by appt.

CH. MONT-REDON Viognier 1999**

□ 1.5 ha 5,000 ▮ ⚲ 50-69 F

This estate, well known for its Châteauneuf-du-Pape, proves here that it can give equal quality and care to its other wines. The jury whole-heartedly liked this wine with its powerful aromas, made from 100% Viognier using traditional low temperature vinification. A resounding success.

🔑 Familles Abeille-Fabre, Ch. Mont-Redon, 84230 Châteauneuf-du-Pape, tel. 04.90.83.72.75, fax 04.90.83.77.20, e-mail chateaumontredon@wanadoo.fr ☑ Y by appt.
🔑 Abeille Fabre

DOM. DU MOULIN 1999**

□ 2 ha 5,000 ▮ ⚲ 30-49 F

Since 1984, Denis Vinson has regularly updated his vinification equipment, and in April 2000 he finished building a vaulted underground cellar, providing perfect temperature-controlled maturation conditions. This particular wine is already showing well, with a brilliant straw-yellow colour and an aroma of pale-fleshed fruits and flowers. It combines vivacity with freshness, and shows a very fine balance on the palate. A most attractive wine.

🔑 Denis Vinson, Dom. du Moulin, 26110 Vinsobres, tel. 04.75.27.65.59, fax 04.75.27.63.92 ☑ Y by appt.

DOM. GUY MOUSSET

Cuvée des Garrigues 1998

■ 7 ha 15,000 30–49 F

Intense and stylish, this well-balanced wine is quite rounded with very harmonious tannins. The dark ruby colour verges on black, owing its fine quality to a spell in barrel. It could be a fine accompaniment for *côte de bœuf*.

EARL Vignobles Guy Mousset et Fils, Le Clos Saint-Michel, rte de Châteauneuf, 84700 Sorgues, tel. 04.90.85.56.05, fax 04.90.83.56.06 Y by appt.

ORSAN Les Hautes Planes 1999★

■ 6 ha 6,000 30–49 F

The co-operative cellars of the Rhône have made considerable quality improvements in recent years, selecting specific vineyard plots and grapes, and using careful vinification techniques. The co-operative at Orsan, two km (three miles) from the Caesar's Camp archaeological site, submitted this very successful wine. The nose is complex, fruity and slightly charred, and the same flavours recur on the full-bodied and elegant palate. The **Cuvée Principale 99 Rouge** earned a mention. (20–29 F).

Cave des vignerons d'Orsan, 30200 Orsan, tel. 04.66.90.10.05, fax 04.66.90.00.93 Y ev. day except Sun. 8am–12 noon 2pm–6pm

DOM. DU PETIT-BARBARAS 1999

□ 1 ha 6,000 30–49 F

Two brothers run this estate, which was founded in 1929. The wine is the product of Roussanne (60%) and Marsanne, grown on a clay-limestone soil. An attractive bright colour with shades of green, the chief attraction of this wine lies in its youth. Lively and complex, this fine 1999 would be at its best accompanying fish in sauce.

SCEA Feschet Père et Fils, Dom. du Petit-Barbaras, 26790 Bouchet, tel. 04.75.04.80.02, fax 04.75.04.84.70
Y by appt.

DOM. PIED GIROD 1999

■ n.c. n.c. 20 F+

A perfectly respectable example of the appellation, this pleasant wine shows what one would expect from a local Côtes du Rhône. Well-balanced and blessed with a delicate but reasonably obvious aroma, it will be ideal with grilled meats.

La Compagnie Rhodanienne, chemin Neuf, 30210 Castillon-du-Gard, tel. 04.66.37.49.50, fax 04.66.37.49.51
Y by appt.

DOM. DES QUAYRADES 1998

■ 11 ha 80,000 20–29 F

Made from a blend of traditional Côtes du Rhône grapes, this wine has a lovely texture with a characteristic stewed fruit nose. Simple but well made, it is ready to drink now.

Dom. des Quayrades, La Grand Comtadine, 84190 Vacqueyras, tel. 04.90.65.85.91, fax 04.90.65.89.23
Y by appt.
Patrick Latour

CH. REDORTIER 1998

■ 1 ha 5,000 30–49 F

The limestone craters of the Dentelles de Montmirail, chiselled by erosion, look spectacular. Suzette is situated at an altitude of 419 m (1,374 feet). This handsome Côtes du Rhône has a dazzling ruby-red colour. Powerful and forthcoming, it develops soft tannins and notes of garrigue. It has quite a long finish. Try it as an accompaniment to rabbit in mustard sauce. It could also be drunk right throughout the meal.

EARL Ch. Redortier, 84190 Suzette, tel. 04.90.62.96.43, fax 04.90.65.03.38
Y ev. day 10am–12 noon 2pm–7pm
de Menthon

DOM. RIGOT

Prestige des Garrigues 1998★

■ 14.5 ha 49,000 30–49 F

Jonquières is rich in prehistoric and Roman relics. This estate deserves to be discovered. Made from 60-year-old Grenache (80%) and Syrah (20%) vines, this very aromatic wine is both fine and delicate on the nose. Robust, with attractive peppery notes on the palate, it is a solid and reliable wine that would make a good partner for red meat or game. The **Cuvée Jean-Baptiste Rigot 98 Rouge**, half Syrah, half Grenache, receives a mention.

Camille Rigot, Les Hauts Débats, 84150 Jonquières, tel. 04.90.37.25.19, fax 04.90.37.29.19, e-mail domaine.rigot@wanadoo.fr
Y ev. day 8am–12 noon 3pm–8pm; Sun. by appt.

CH. ROCHECOLOMBE 1998★

■ 9.5 ha 40,000 30–49 F

The Belgium author-composer Robert Herberigs settled here. The property used to grow apricots, but his grandchildren have now converted the land to vines. The characteristic fruit flavours of Côtes du Rhône from the Ardèche come through really well in this charming 98 wine. It will improve with the years, so we leave it to you to discover its full subtlety.

EARL Herberigs, Ch. Rochecolombe, 07700 Bourg-Saint-Andéol, tel. 04.75.34.52.51, fax 04.75.34.35.47
Y ev. day 8.30am–12 noon 1pm–7pm

CAVE DES VIGNERONS DE ROCHEGUDE Cuvée réservée 1999★

◪ 30 ha 16,000 20–29 F

A *Rosé de Saignée* submitted by this young co-operative – young because it's a mere 40 years old. This wine has already developed very pleasant primary fruit aromas, and it should develop interesting secondary aromas over the next year thanks to its rich and complex character. The wine is both soft and powerful with a good length. It will suit all kinds of *charcuterie*.

Cave des Vignerons de Rochegude, 26790 Rochegude, tel. 04.75.04.81.84, fax 04.75.04.84.80

ev. day 9am–12 noon 2pm–6pm

DOM. DE ROCHEMOND

Fût de Chêne 1998★★

n.c. 5,000 30–49 F

This remarkable wine, 100% Syrah, has a dark colour with shades of mahogany and a nose that is both rich and complex. The gamey character shows through the notes of pepper, truffle and undergrowth. The mouth-filling and full-bodied palate is already approachable and gives a warm finish with well-integrated oak, lingering on into a note of plums.

EARL Eric Philip-Ladet, Cadignac-Sud, 30200 Sabran, tel. 04.66.79.04.42, fax 04.66.79.04.42 by appt.

DOM. DE ROQUEBRUNE

Grande Cuvée 1998

2 ha 12,000 30–49 F

The jury reports that this family estate, dating back to the 18th century and with a sandy limestone soil, has produced a wine that is full of personality. Characterised by a good balance, it has a great intensity of colour with scents of stewed fruit. The influence of the soil comes through strongly and leaves a long finish with a touch of chocolate.

Pierre Rique, Dom. de Roquebrune, 30130 Saint-Alexandre, tel. 04.66.39.33.30, fax 04.66.39.23.85 by appt.

DOM. ROUGE GARANCE

Garances 1999★

3 ha 16,000 30–49 F

The name chosen for this estate refers to the role of the French actress, Arletty in *Les Enfants du Paradis* (Garance) as well as to the *garance* (madder) that grows here. This 99 wine is a good ambassador for the Côtes du Rhône. Monsieur Cortellini has managed to bring out unsuspected qualities from the Carignan grape. Accounting for 55% in its mix with Syrah, the *garance* produces a powerful and harmonious wine with persistent, well-balanced and elegant flavours.

SCEA Dom. Rouge Garance, chem. de Massacan, 30210 Saint-Hilaire-d'Ozilhan, tel. 04.66.37.06.92, fax 04.66.37.06.92

by appt.

DOM. DU ROURE 1998

2.5 ha 8,500 20–29 F

Yves Terrasse brought a great deal of energy to the estate when he took over this family property in 1980. The roasted aromas are quite unusual and enrich the harmony of this traditionally made 98. It needs a further year of ageing.

Yves Terrasse, Dom. du Roure, 07700 Saint-Marcel-d'Ardèche, tel. 04.75.04.67.67, fax 04.75.98.75.48 by appt.

CH. DE RUTH 1998★

90 ha 400,000 30–49 F

At the start of the 20th century, Nicolas de Beauharnais, descendant of Joséphine de Beauharnais, owned this vast 110-ha (272-acre) estate. Two of its wines were selected to receive a star. This wine caught our attention for its intense, clean colour and its powerful and spicy nose, with notes of ripe fruit that recur on the palate. A complex wine, characteristic of the regional AOC. The **Cuvée Nicolas de Beauharnais 99 Blanc** has an unusually high proportion of Clairette (50%) in the blend and provides the attractions of richness, balance, acidity and length, as well as citrus fruit on the nose with a touch of cocoa.

Christian Meffre, Ch. de Ruth, 84290 Sainte-Cécile-les-Vignes, tel. 04.90.65.88.93, fax 04.90.65.88.96, e-mail Château.Raspail@wanadoo.fr

ev. day except Sat. Sun. 8am–12 noon 1.30pm–5.30pm; cl. 15–31 Aug.

DOM. SAINT-AMANT

Les Clapas 1998★★

1.5 ha 10,000 30–49 F

This estate was created by a company managing director from Paris who became passionate about the vine. He has decided to work with sustainable viticulture techniques, which are sensitive to the environment, the landscape of terraced hillsides being particularly beautiful here. He calls himself an artisan, and this very promising wine is his just reward. Amongst the many descriptions used by the jury when discussing the wine's potential, the term that stands out was 'promising'. For now, it's still pretty unrefined. However, its richness and body, its aromas and the quality of its tannins make it comparable to the best wines of the Côtes du Rhône.

Dom. Saint-Amant, 84190 Suzette, tel. 04.90.62.99.25, fax 04.90.65.03.56

by appt.

DOM. SAINT-CLAUDE

Prestige Vieilli en Fût de Chêne 1998

1.5 ha 6,000 30–49 F

Vaison was a great Roman town whose relics are still much in evidence. One can also taste some very good wines there. This wine, though not very forthcoming on the nose, does display a beautiful natural ruby-red colour, with brick-red reflections. The aromas of slightly spicy red berry fruits from nine months spent in barrel show through, with some light tannins in the background.

Frédéric Armand, Dom. Saint-Claude, Le Palis, 84110 Vaison-la-Romaine, tel. 04.90.36.23.68, fax 04.90.36.09.16

by appt.

SAINT-COSME 1999★

15 ha 80,000 30–49 F

A 12th-century chapel situated in the heart of the vineyard, and dedicated to Saint-Cosme, patron saint of doctors, gave its name to the estate owned by the Barruol family who operate as wine merchants and producers. Their Côtes du Rhône is really well made: 100% Syrah, it has a blackcurrant and violet nose, and is round and full-bodied on the palate. It should develop well over the next two to three years. Equally successful, the **Cuvée Saint-Cosme 99 Blanc** is a judicious blend of Roussanne, Marsanne and Bourboulenc. A touch of new wood does not spoil the harmony of the flavours. Rich and long, with a stunning after-taste of liquorice, this wine should be delicious with a potato and truffle salad.

Louis et Cherry Barruol, Ch. de Saint-Cosme, 84190 Gigondas, tel. 04.90.65.80.80, fax 04.90.65.81.05 Y by appt.

CAVE DES VIGNERONS DE SAINTE-CECILE-LES-VIGNES

Réserve 1999★

0.7 ha 5,000 20 F+

This co-operative, formed in 1936, has its headquarters on a rocky plain on which there is an abundance of vineyards. In the village are beautiful houses dating back to the 16th century, with a 12th-century church, restored in the 18th century, and dedicated to Sainte-Cécile, patron saint of musicians. This wine would be ideal, served after an enjoyable concert. A lovely clear and bright yellow colour, with a very fine flowery nose. The pleasant palate has good balance showing elegant depth of flavours. Very good value for money.

Cave des Vignerons Réunis de Sainte-Cécile-les-Vignes, 35, rte de Valréas, 84290 Sainte-Cécile-les-Vignes, tel. 04.90.30.79.30, fax 04.90.30.79.39 Y ev. day 8am–12.30pm 2pm–7pm

CH. SAINT-ESTEVE D'UCHAUX

1999

2.8 ha 18,000 30-49 F

Every year in August, Thérèse Français organises a piano festival called 'Liszt in Provence', which takes place on the terraces of the château. Wine is also regarded as one of the fine arts, and the consistent quality from this estate only goes to prove the point. Here is a really well-made 99, a clean white wine with apricot and quince jam smells. Soft acidity places it amongst those white wines that are rich, full-bodied and balanced, and which work well with fish in a cream sauce.

Ch. Saint-Estève d'Uchaux, 84100 Uchaux, tel. 04.90.40.62.38, fax 04.90.40.63.49 Y ev. day except Sun. 9am–12 noon 2pm–6pm

Gérard et Marc Français

DOM. SAINT-ETIENNE

Les Albizzias 1999★

15 ha 100,000 20-29 F

Michel Coullomb has been in charge of this property for the past ten years, and is increasingly the master of his art. He is determined to spend the necessary time in the vineyards to control the quality of the grapes, and the results show. This is a highly concentrated Côtes du Rhône that above all needs time to open out. A connoisseur's wine for those who know how to appreciate it.

Michel Coullomb, Dom. Saint-Etienne, fg du Pont, 30490 Montfrin, tel. 04.66.57.50.20, fax 04.66.57.22.78 Y by appt.

SAINT-MARTIN DE JOCUNDAZ

1999★

0.25 ha 1,300 70-99 F

It was a good decision to make this wine from a plot of Viognier: it has produced a great wine with amazing and slightly menthol aromas. The richness on the palate confers a full-bodied character. Pasta with a truffle sauce or any white meat would match it well.

Jean-Pierre Serguier, Ch. Simian, 84420 Piolenc, tel. 04.90.29.50.67, fax 04.90.29.62.33 Y ev. day except Sun. 8.30am–12 noon 2pm–7pm

CH. SAINT-MAURICE

Sélection Parcellaire 1998★

1 ha 6,000 20-29 F

This vast 100-ha (247-acre) estate selected this wine from a one-ha (2.5-acre) plot. A blend of Grenache Blanc (40%), with Clairette and Roussanne in equal amounts, gives an appealing white wine with aromas of wild flowers and acacia. Light-coloured with tinges of gold, it is sufficiently complex to risk partnering it with truffles. A spicy character, with very good length, the richness and well-balanced acidity will enable it to age for some time.

SCA Ch. Saint-Maurice, R.N. 580, L'Ardoise, 30290 Laudun, tel. 04.66.50.29.31, fax 04.66.50.40.91, e-mail chateau.saint.maurice@wanadoo.fr Y ev. day except Sun. 8am–12 noon 1.30pm–6pm

Valat

DOM. DE SERVANS

Cuvée Tradition Elevé en Fût de Chêne 1998★

1.6 ha 3,000 50-69 F

This 20-ha (49-acre) estate has been selected for a wine that displays the wine-producer's control over every aspect: 50-year-old vines, a blend of 70% Grenache with Syrah, 12 months in barrel. This is a classy wine with dominant oak flavours. Well-balanced and fleshy, it will appeal to lovers of spicy reds, and shows menthol notes mixed with scents of vanilla. Liquorice and cinnamon also come through on the palate, and then jammy fruit. Although as at March 2000 the oak still had the upper hand, the wine should be ready to partner beef fillet or game by December and for some time thereafter. The **Côtes du Rhône 99 Blanc** earns a mention (30–49 F) and is a good match with shellfish.

Pierre Granier, av. de Provence, 26790 Tulette, tel. 04.75.98.31.47, fax 04.75.98.31.47 Y ev. day 9am–8pm

CH. DU TRIGNON 1999★

■ 15 ha 65,000 30–49 F

Owned by the Roux family since 1895 and situated at the foot of the Dentelles de Montmirail, this estate owns state-of-the-art wine-making equipment. The harvest is manual and the grapes are passed along a sorting table. This lovely ruby-coloured wine has an intense nose with a strong red berry influence and a palate that is well structured and pleasant. Can be served until about the end of 2001.

Ch. du Trignon, 84190 Gigondas, tel. 04.90.46.90.27, fax 04.90.46.98.63 ev. day except Sun. 9am–12 noon 2pm–7pm

Pascal Roux

CUVEE DU VATICAN 1999

■ 5.7 ha 40,000 30–49 F

A large Châteauneuf-du-Pape estate, amounting to 53 ha (131 acres). Both powerful and elegant, the Cuvée du Vatican is typical of the vintage. Quite concentrated and warming, the bouquet shows aromas of red berry fruits mixed with smells of vanilla that come from a short period in large oak casks.

SCEA Félicien Diffonty et Fils, 10, rte de Courthézon, B.P. 33, 84231 Châteauneuf-du-Pape Cedex, tel. 04.90.83.70.51, fax 04.90.83.50.36, e-mail cuvéeduvatican@wanadoo.fr ev. day 9am–12 noon 2pm–6pm except Sat. and Sun. 10am–12 noon 2pm–6pm

J. VIDAL-FLEURY 1999★

□ 2.5 ha 15,000 30–49 F

This firm of wine-merchants, founded in 1787, is owned today by Marcel Guigal. We are reminded that Thomas Jefferson visited it before the Revolution during his journey through the vineyards of France. This is a wine most worthy of that prestigious visitor. Made from Viognier, it has a bright yellow colour with quite intense citrus fruits and floral notes on the nose. The palate is fresh with an excellent balance of acidity. Drink it within a year with *coquilles Saint-Jacques*.

J. Vidal-Fleury, 19, rte de la Roche, 69420 Ampuis, tel. 04.74.56.10.18, fax 04.74.56.19.19 by appt.

DOM. DU VIEUX CHENE

Cuvée des Capucines 1998★★

■ 7 ha 26,000 30–49 F

Jean-Claude Bouche is an oenologist who speaks eloquently about his terroir. This Cuvée des Capucines has a very elegant label, but what of the wine? With bright red tinges, this very lovely wine has really fine and complex ripe fruit aromas. On the palate, the well-integrated tannins, together with a full and fruity body, make it a veritable treat. Wait for at least one year, but it could last well beyond five years. Perfect for red meat.

Jean-Claude et Béatrice Bouche, rte de Vaison-la-Romaine, 84850 Camaret-sur-Aigues, tel. 04.90.37.25.07, fax 04.90.37.76.84, e-mail contact@bouche-duvieuxchene.com ev. day except Sun. 9am–12 noon 2pm–6pm

DOM. DU VIEUX COLOMBIER 1997

■ 6.5 ha 10,000 30–49 F

Vines have existed here for over 500 years. This former royal estate, bequeathed to the Chaplins of Bagnols, is run today by Jacques Barrière and his son. They make this Côtes du Rhône in a very traditional way from a base of 60% Grenache. For immediate drinking over a family meal.

Jacques Barrière et Fils, Dom. du Vieux Colombier, 30200 Sabran, tel. 04.66.89.98.94, fax 04.66.89.98.94 by appt.

Côtes du Rhône Villages

Within the Côtes du Rhône area, some communes have terroirs that produce wines with characteristics and qualities that are unanimously acknowledged and appreciated. The conditions of production for these wines, which is about 184,000 hl (4,875,600 gal) are more restrictive than for the Côtes du Rhône, especially with regard to boundaries, yield and alcohol content.

There are two categories of Côtes du Rhône-Villages wines. On the one hand, there are those entitled to included the name of a commune; the 16 names that have been recognised historically are: Chusclan, Laudun and Saint-Gervais in the Gard; Beaumes-de-Venise, Cairanne, Sablet-Séguret, Rasteau, Roaix, Valréas and Visan in the Vaucluse; Rochegude, Rousset-les-Vignes, Saint-Maurice, Saint-Pantaléon-les-Vignes and Vinsobres in the Drôme. These wines comprise 25 communes in all and cover a declared area of 4,400 ha (10,868 acres).

On the other hand, there are the Côtes du Rhône-Villages where no commune name is specified, their territory covering the remainder of all the communes in the Gard, the Vaucluse and the Drôme within the area of the Côtes du Rhône.

Seventy communes have been included. The purpose of defining the territory had the primary objective of making it possible to produce wines that would keep. To date, 3,342 ha (8,255 acres) have been declared.

DOM. D'AERIA

Cairanne Cuvée Prestige 1998★

■ 2 ha 6,000 ▮ 50-69 F

The excellent maturity of the Grenache (60%) and Mourvèdre grapes, grown in a clay-limestone soil, produces a powerful wine with cherry and blackcurrant on the nose. The palate shows spicy notes with a good structure.
🔑 EARL Dom. d'Aéria, rte de Rasteau, 84290 Cairanne, tel. 04.90.30.88.78, fax 04.90.30.78.38 ☑ Y by appt.
🔑 Gap

DOM. DANIEL ET DENIS ALARY

Cairanne La Font d'Estévenas 1998★

■ 2 ha 8,000 ▮ ⫼ 50-69 F

The key wine from this family estate, founded in 1692, La Font d'Estévenas 98 is characterised by very ripe Syrah, which makes up 60% of the blend. Well structured, it shows rich aromas of fruit, spices and notes of game and leather. Its powerful tannins require it to be kept for a year or two.
🔑 Dom. Daniel et Denis Alary, La Font d'Estévenas, 84290 Cairanne, tel. 04.90.30.82.32, fax 04.90.30.74.71 ☑ Y by appt.

DOM. DES AMADIEU

Cairanne 1998★

■ 1.8 ha 8,000 ▮ ♁ 30-49 F

An estate of 7.5 ha (19 acres) that is well known in the United States, so Europe will have to share this wine with the New World. The wine has very developed flavours with a complete range including spices, cocoa and very ripe black fruits. With plenty of body and a good level of tannin, this is a wine that should be kept for two years.
🔑 Marylène et Michel Achiary, Dom. des Amadieu, quartier Beauregard, 84290 Cairanne, tel. 04.90.66.17.41, fax 04.90.66.01.28, e-mail cairanne2000@yahoo.fr ☑ Y by appt.

DOM. D'ANDEZON 1998★★★

■ 3 ha 14,000 ⫼ 30-49 F

Syrah blended with 10% Grenache grown on a fine soil of rounded pebbles produced this magnificent deep purple *Villages*. The nose shows a range of ripe red berry fruit

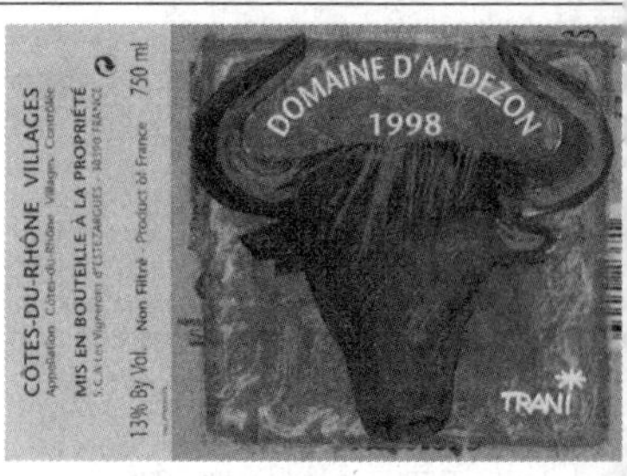

aromas with a whiff of blackcurrant. The palate is remarkably balanced and powerful with an excellent aromatic expression. The wine has a long finish with notes of game, leather and cocoa. The jury marked this as worth keeping for three years.
🔑 Cave des Vignerons d'Estézargues, rte des Grès, 30390 Estézargues, tel. 04.66.57.03.64, fax 04.66.57.04.83, e-mail les.vignerons.estezargues@wanadoo.fr ☑ Y ev. day except Sun. 8am–12 noon 2pm–6pm
🔑 Daniel Lamouroux

CH. BEAUCHENE

Vignoble de la Vialle 1998★

■ 7 ha 45,000 ⫼ 30-49 F

This family estate, which was taken over by Michel Bernard in 1971, comprises 70 ha (173 acres) of which 7 ha (17 acres) are used for this wine. Grenache (60%) and Syrah (30%), with six months' maturation in oak, have produced a wine that is ready to drink now. A cherry-red colour, with a flowery nose, good attack and a fruity palate with appreciable tannins.
🔑 Michel Bernard, ch. Beauchêne, rte de Beauchêne, 84420 Piolenc, tel. 04.90.51.75.87, fax 04.90.51.73.36, e-mail chateaubeauchene@worldonline.fr ☑ Y by appt.

DOM. DE BELLE-FEUILLE 1999★

□ 1.2 ha 4,400 ⫼ 50-69 F

Vénéjan, in the Gard, is a pretty village whose church dates back to the 12th century. Gilbert Louche made his first wine in 1992. Manual harvesting of this 100% Viognier has resulted in a lemon yellow 99 with green tinges. Ageing in barrel for several months gives a touch of vanilla on the palate that complements the aromas of banana and toast. Elegant on the palate, this attractive wine is perfectly fresh and balanced.
🔑 Gilbert Louche, Dom. de Belle-Feuille, 30200 Vénéjan, tel. 04.66.79.27.33, fax 04.66.79.22.82 ☑ Y ev. day except Sun. 8am–12 noon 1pm–7pm

LOUIS BERNARD

Grande Cuvée 1998★★

■ n.c. n.c. ⫼ 50-69 F

Having declared that he was drawing up contracts with his growers to control quality, this merchant now selects only grapes that are harvested when fully ripe. This has

resulted in a *Villages* of very good calibre. The appearance is simply lovely, with an intense colour tinged with purple. The nose provides a mixture of fruit and oak. This elegant 98 is well-balanced with well-integrated tannins and displays an attractive liquorice finish. Worth keeping.
Les Domaines Bernard, rte de Sérignan, 84100 Orange, tel. 04.90.11.86.86, fax 04.90.34.87.30

DOM. BERTHET-RAYNE

Cairanne Tradition 1999★

8 ha 45,000 30–49 F

A consistently good wine that is a credit to the two brothers who produced it. The first reaction of the jury was to note the openness of this wine, the ripeness of the grapes and the quality of the wine-making. The intense garnet-red colour does not disappoint and there are fruity notes present throughout the tasting. Full and rounded with a long-lasting flavour of redcurrants, this wine is enjoyable from now onwards.
Dom. Michel et André Berthet-Rayne, rte d'Orange, 84290 Cairanne, tel. 04.90.30.88.15, fax 04.90.30.83.17 by appt.

DOM. DE BOISSAN

Sablet Cuvée Clémence 1998★

14 ha 8,000 30–49 F

From 60% Grenache and 40% Syrah, matured ten months in barrel, this 98 gives the taster an impression of well vinified, very ripe grapes. Aromas of roasted coffee and cocoa, a powerful, but not aggressive, tannic structure with richness and smoothness on the palate, all promise immediate enjoyment plus the ability to age well.
Christian Bonfils, Dom. de Boissan, 84110 Sablet, tel. 04.90.46.93.30, fax 04.90.46.99.46 by appt.

DOM. BOUCHE Les Garrigues 1998★

5 ha 10,000 30–49 F

An excellent 38-ha (94-acre) estate and two handsome wines. Firstly, the **La Grappe d'Or 99 Blanc**, with its flowery and exotic nose, was considered a great success. Then this red wine, which is made using whole-berry fermentation. Elegance is the one overall abiding impression. Just look at the ruby-red colour, breathe in the nose of soft red fruits and blackcurrant, and marvel at the balanced palate with its fine tannins.
Dominique Bouche, chem. d'Avignon, 84850 Camaret-sur-Aigues, tel. 04.90.37.27.19, fax 04.90.37.74.17, e-mail dbouche@terre-net.fr by appt.

DOM. DES BOUMIANES 1998★

8 ha 4,000 30–49 F

This 30-ha (74-acre) estate was founded in 1920 by the grandfather of Philippe Méger, who has been running it since 1990. Produced from traditional varieties, grown on terraces of rounded pebbles, this wine is rich in red berry fruits with a predominance of very ripe cherry. A well-balanced and warming wine.
GAEC des Boumianes, Domazan, 30390 Aramon, tel. 04.66.57.02.35, fax 04.66.57.09.48 ev. day except Sun. 9.30am–12 noon 2pm–6pm
Philippe Méger

DOM. ANDRE BREMOND

Laudun 1999

6.28 ha 32,000 20–29 F

Submitted by a merchant, this wine needs to be kept for a couple of years in order to reach its potential. At present, it has a powerful tannic structure. Although the nose is closed, the aromas on the palate speak volumes: thyme, rosemary and gamey notes provide a promise of enjoyment in the future.
La Compagnie Rhodanienne, chemin Neuf, 30210 Castillon-du-Gard, tel. 04.66.37.49.50, fax 04.66.37.49.51
by appt.

LAURENT BRUSSET

Cairanne Vendange Chabrille 1998★★

3 ha 14,000 30–49 F

A very balanced and meticulously made 98 has been submitted by this estate. Despite a touch of brick red on the edge of the dark purple colour, the wine is worth keeping. Cherry and ripe fruits marry on the nose, while the palate is more obviously blackcurrant. Structured by fine tannins, this wine is a perfectly balanced example of its appellation. The **Coteaux de Travers 99**, a blend of six white grapes from this AOC, earns one star and is an ideal partner for fish served with sauce.
SA Dom. Brusset, 84290 Cairanne, tel. 04.90.30.82.16, fax 04.90.30.73.31, e-mail domaine-brusset.fr by appt.

DOM. DU CABANON 1998

1 ha 6,000 30–49 F

Carbonic maceration makes this a very pleasant wine that is thoroughly refined with soft tannins, and is already fit to drink. Good acidity with dominant red berry fruit at the start, this is very aromatic and tasty. An easy drinking 98.
Yves Payan, 5, pl. de La Fontaine, 30650 Saze, tel. 04.90.31.70.74, fax 04.90.26.94.62, e-mail domainecabanon@wanadoo.fr
ev. day except Sun. 10am–12 noon 2pm–6pm

DOM. DE CABASSE

Séguret Cuvée de la Casa Bassa 1998★

3 ha 12,000 50–69 F

Two very different labels: one is 'designer' and the other, rather rustic. The latter graces the **Cuvée Garnacho**, a blend of Grenache with Counoise (6%), Cinsault (7%) and Carignan Syrah (6%). Its aromas of fruit macerated in brandy and oak attracted the jury who awarded it one star. A star also goes to this Casa Bassa, which is composed of just Grenache (55%) and Syrah, and which is at its peak. The wine has a clean and bright cherry-

red colour with a well-developed nose of spices, tobacco and plums that recur on the beautifully balanced palate.
🔑 Dom. de Cabasse, 84110 Séguret, tel. 04.90.46.91.12, fax 04.90.46.94.01, e-mail cabasse@avignon.pacwan.net ☑
Y by appt.
🔑 Alfred Haeni

CAVE DE CAIRANNE

Temptation 1998★★

■ n.c. n.c. 30–49 F

A wine museum has been set up in the old keep of Cairanne, which used to be the domain of the Knights Templar. The co-operative submitted two wines. This one has a beautifully intense red colour. Its nose reveals powerful aromas of red berry fruit. Elegance and balance go hand in hand with nicely integrated tannins. The **Cuvée Antique 98** is also very pleasant, but at a higher price. (50–69 F).
🔑 Cave de Cairanne, 84290 Cairanne, tel. 04.90.30.82.05, fax 04.90.30.74.03 ☑
Y by appt.

DOM. DIDIER CHARAVIN

Rasteau 1998★

■ 3 ha 15,000 30–49 F

This estate is known for its **Cuvée des Parpaïouns** (butterflies), and this charmingly structured and typically aromatic 98 (50–69 F), won a mention. Here, we describe the estate's principal wine, ruby-red, tinged with purple and showing cherries on the nose. On the palate, there are obvious but integrated tannins, balanced with a good concentration of fruit. This velvety wine is ready to drink.
🔑 Didier Charavin, rte de Vaison, 84110 Rasteau, tel. 04.90.46.15.63, fax 04.90.46.16.22 ☑
Y ev. day 9am–12 noon 2pm–6pm

DOM. CHAUME-ARNAUD

Cuvée Granges Rouges 1998★

■ 1.5 ha 8,800 30–49 F

Old Carignan (20%) complements the Grenache, both of which were grown in sandy-clay soil. This attractive-looking wine gives floral scents. Straightforward on the palate, the well-integrated, balanced tannins make it ready to partner roast veal.
🔑 Dom. Chaume-Arnaud, Les Paluds, 26110 Vinsobres, tel. 04.75.27.66.85, fax 04.75.27.69.66 ☑ Y by appt.

DOM. CLAVEL Saint-Gervais 1999★

◪ 0.72 ha 4,000 30–49 F

This attractive rosé was made with a short maceration and vinified at low temperature, seemingly a well kept 'chef's secret'. The result, on the other hand, is known to all and the jury loved the mauve-tinged colour and floral bouquet. The palate is lively, well balanced and fresh. *Charcuterie* and barbecued lamb would suit it well, perhaps after a game of tennis or volleyball.
🔑 Denis Clavel, rue du Pigeonnier, 30200 Saint-Gervais, tel. 04.66.82.78.90, fax 04.66.82.74.30 ☑ Y by appt.

DOM. DU CORIANCON

Vinsobres le Haut des Côtes 1998★

■ n.c. 3,000 70–99 F

François Vallot, whose estate amounts to 55 ha (136 acres), created this special selection made from 45-year-old vines (70% Grenache, 20% Syrah and 10% Mourvèdre) grown on a clay-limestone soil. After a long maceration and ageing in barrel, the flavours tend towards cocoa, truffle and prune and show good depth. The colour is an intense garnet. An attractive wine to keep for two to three years, it would be at its best with roast beef, cooked rare.
🔑 François Vallot, Dom. du Coriançon, 26110 Vinsobres, tel. 04.75.26.03.24, fax 04.75.26.44.67, e-mail françois.vallot@wanadoo.fr ☑ Y ev. day except Sun. 9am–12 noon 2pm–7pm

COSTEBELLE

Cuvée Guillaume Magnan 1998

■ 50 ha 16,000 30–49 F

After wandering around Vaison-la-Romaine, you could head towards the cellars of Costebelle at Tulette and taste this very fresh and pleasant Côtes du Rhône *Villages*. Ready-to-drink, the soft red fruits balance well with the tannins. The nose is characterised by notes of leather and flowers.
🔑 Cave Costebelle, 26790 Tulette, tel. 04.75.98.32.53, fax 04.75.98.38.70 ☑
Y by appt.

DOM. DES COTEAUX DES TRAVERS

Cairanne 1998

■ 2 ha 5,000 50–69 F

Grenache (60%), Syrah (10%) and Mourvèdre are de-stemmed to give a dense-coloured wine, enlivened by tinges of garnet. This well-made, full-bodied wine should be ready by the end of 2000.
🔑 Robert Charavin, Dom. des Coteaux des Travers, 84110 Rasteau, tel. 04.90.46.13.69, fax 04.90.46.15.81, e-mail robert.charavin@wanadoo.fr ☑ Y by appt.

CH. COURAC Laudun 1998★★

■ 10 ha 54,000 30–49 F

An excellent wine from this producer who has ceaselessly striven to achieve success. A fruity 98 dominated by Syrah, the wine is characterised by a fine tannic structure, which will allow it to age well without any problem.
🔑 SCEA Frédéric Arnaud, Ch. Courac, 30330 Tresques, tel. 04.66.82.90.51, fax 04.66.82.94.27 ☑ Y by appt.

DOM. DELUBAC

Cairanne Les Bruneau 1997★

■ 3.5 ha 14,000 30–49 F

The three kings of the AOC, Grenache, Syrah and Mourvèdre, combine to make this attractive wine, which has scents of thyme, rosemary and prune on the nose. It has a long post-fermentation maceration period and two years' maturation, giving a concentrated and well-structured palate. In a word, virile, indicating a good wine for ageing. **L'Authentique 98**, matured in oak (70–99 F) was awarded the same marks. Keep it in your cellar for at least two years.

GAEC Dom. Bruno et Vincent Delubac, Les Charoussans, rte de Carpentras, 84290 Cairanne, tel. 04.90.30.82.40, fax 04.90.30.71.18, e-mail vincent.delubac@libertysurf.fr by appt.

DOM. DE DURBAN

Beaumes-de-Venise 1999

17.74 ha 67,000 30–49 F

Despite specialising in Muscat de Beaumes-de-Venise, this estate of nearly 58 ha (143 acres) does not neglect its dry wines. A blend of 75% Grenache, 24% Syrah and 1% Mourvèdre produced this very youthful, bright ruby 99, which has excellent acidity. There is red berry fruit on the nose and a beautiful balance on the palate with a good length of flavour.

SCEA Leydier et Fils, Dom. de Durban, 84190 Beaumes-de-Venise, tel. 04.90.62.94.26, fax 04.90.65.01.85 ev. day except Sun. 9am–12 noon 2pm–6pm

DOM. DE FENOUILLET

Beaumes-de-Venise Cuvée Yvon Soard 1998★

1.9 ha 10,000 50–69 F

The Soard family has been cultivating vines here for the past 150 years. This wine has a delightful, intense colour with tinges of violet. It shows a mixture of stewed fruit and oak aromas. Rich on the palate, with the benefit of lovely, dense well-matured tannins, this charming 98 should be ready to serve within a few months.

GAEC Patrick et Vincent Soard, Dom. de Fenouillet, allée Saint-Roch, 84190 Beaumes-de-Venise, tel. 04.90.62.95.61, fax 04.90.62.90.67 by appt.

DOM. GALEVAN 1997★

3 ha 3,354 30–49 F

A very significant entry in the *Guide* for Coralie Goumarre, who joined her father in 1995 after completing her viticultural and œnological studies. This is a characterful wine, of deep colour and intense bouquet. A powerful wine to lay down.

Coralie Goumarre, 127, rte de Vaison, 84350 Courthezon, tel. 04.90.70.84.26, fax 04.90.70.28.70 ev. day except Sun. 8am–12 noon 2pm–7pm

CH. GIGOGNAN Bois des Moines 1998

23 ha 27,000 30–49 F

Gigognan, a vast estate of 70 ha (173 acres), submitted this Bois des Moines, a beautifully intense ruby-coloured wine. The nose opens up with slightly cooked notes, cinnamon and liquorice. A treat on the palate, this wine shows a lovely length of flavour. It would be excellent with a braised shoulder of lamb.

Ch. Gigognan, chem. du Castillon, 84700 Sorgues, tel. 04.90.39.57.46, fax 04.90.39.15.28, e-mail info@chateau-gigognan.fr ev. day 10am–12.30pm 2.30pm–6pm; Sun. by appt.

CH. DU GRAND MOULAS

Cuvée de l'Ecu Grande Réserve 1998

1 ha 4,000 30–49 F

The village of Mornas includes the ruins of the fortress built in the 12th century by the Count of Toulouse. Marc Ryckwaert made this wine from 95% Syrah. It has a deep colour with a violet rim that betrays its youth. The intense and promising nose shows notes of the garrigue and undergrowth, enhanced by violet. Rather obvious tannins need some time to round out and to further enhance the flavours of game and leather.

Marc Ryckwaert, Ch. du Grand Moulas, 84550 Mornas, tel. 04.90.37.00.13, fax 04.90.37.05.89 by appt.

DOM. GRAND NICOLET

Rasteau 1998★

3 ha 10,000 30–49 F

Made on the estate in the oldest cellar in the village, this Rasteau displays a wonderfully intense cherry-red colour. The powerful nose shows well-developed aromas of crystallised fruit and spices. The full palate plays off red berry fruit and cocoa, balanced by soft tannins.

Nicolet-Leyraud, quartier les Esqueyrons, 84110 Rasteau, tel. 04.90.46.11.37, fax 04.90.46.11.37 ev. day except Sun. 9am–12 noon 2pm–6pm

DOM. GRAND-PERE JULES

Vieilli en fût de chêne 1997

2 ha 4,000 30–49 F

This 97 wine appears youthful after five months' ageing in oak. The palate is still tannic, showing vanilla influences from the oak. The deep red colour is slightly tinged with a note of brick red. Best to serve this wine with meat stew.

Gérard et Xavier Henry, Dom. de La Tuilerie, 84150 Violes, tel. 04.90.70.92.89, fax 04.90.70.97.79 by appt.

DOM. GRAND VENEUR

Les Vieilles Vignes 1998★

5 ha 27,400 30–49 F

This huge 38-ha (94-acre) estate submitted a beautiful wine made from old vines. The jury thought it a very pleasant 98: the tannins, though very apparent, are nonetheless well-balanced. Drink it throughout the meal.

EARL Alain Jaume, Dom. Grand Veneur, rte de Châteauneuf-du-Pape, 84100 Orange, tel. 04.90.34.68.70, fax 04.90.34.43.71 ev. day 8am–12.30pm 1.30pm–6.30pm

DOM. JAUME Vinsobres 1998

■ 4 ha 20,000 30–49 F

An estate of 50 ha (124 acres) that exports 60% of its production to Japan as well as to the United States, and to countries in the European Union. Successful in previous years, this year it submitted a wine that is a blend of 50% Syrah, 35% Grenache and 15% Mourvèdre, matured for 12 months in barrel. It will take some time for its real qualities to become apparent. What we have here is a wine that is rich, generous, warm, tannic, oaky and complex, together with macerated red berry fruit. Once the oak has softened in a year or two, this 98 will be worth a star.

Dom. Jaume, 24, rue Reynarde, 26110 Vinsobres, tel. 04.75.27.61.01, fax 04.75.27.68.40 ev. day except Sun. 8am–12 noon 1.30pm–7pm

DOM. DE LA BICARELLE

Vinsobres 1997

■ 6 ha n.c. 30–49 F

'Lou bicarelo' in the Provençal dialect, means the high grounds, those that dominate the village. This is still a very young 97, showing obvious red berry fruit on the nose as well as on the palate. The very fine tannins do not lack elegance. Ready to drink.

Bouchard de la Bicarelle, la Bicarelle, 26110 Vinsobres, tel. 04.75.27.61.89, fax 04.75.27.67.63 by appt.

LA CHAPELLE NOTRE-DAME D'AUBUNE Beaumes-de-Venise 1998

□ 5.71 ha 20,000 30–49 F

This modern cellar, situated close to the Dentelles de Montmirail, submitted a wine with the name of an 11th-century chapel. This white wine made from 85% Grenache Blanc, Viognier and Clairette, is light and clear with yellow hues. Honey, grilled almonds and apricots vie for prominence on the nose, while the palate displays finesse and balance.

Cave des Vignerons de Beaumes-de-Venise, 84190 Beaumes-de-Venise, tel. 04.90.12.41.00, fax 04.90.65.02.05 ev. day except Sat. Sun. 8.30am–12 noon 2pm–6pm

DOM. DE LA CHARTREUSE DE VALBONNE

Cuvée Terrasses de Montalivet 1999

□ 1.3 ha 6,000 50–69 F

The Charterhouse of Valbonne, a listed monument, was inhabited by the monks until 1901. After visiting this magnificent monastery situated in the middle of the forest, you should call in at the cellars where M. Burrine, the cellar-master, will let you taste this attractive white wine. With a greenish yellow colour, the nose is floral and lively, and the palate sheds notes of apples, pears and exotic fruits. The wine is made from 80% Viognier.

ASVMT, Dom. de la Chartreuse de Valbonne, 30130 Saint-Paulet-de-Caisson, tel. 04.66.90.41.24, fax 04.66.81.76.10 by appt.

LA COMTADINE

Cuvée Le Chasseur 1998*

■ 92 ha 18,673 30–49 F

Cuvée Le Chasseur (the hunter's wine) is well named: notes of undergrowth, game, truffle, blackcurrant and blackberry each contribute to the beautiful range of aromas. It has an intense red colour verging on purple. Full and well structured, the palate is not short of alcohol. Hare in a berry fruit sauce would be a good match.

Cave La Comtadine, 84110 Puyméras, tel. 04.90.46.40.78, fax 04.90.46.43.32 by appt.

DOM. DE LA FERME SAINT-MARTIN

Beaumes-de-Venise Cuvée Saint-Martin 1997

■ 4 ha 15,000 50–69 F

This dark red 97 is well structured and full of character. Very ripe fruit and spices on a quite complex nose. There's an earthy character on the palate, with garrigue and truffle flavours. A full-bodied wine.

EARL Guy Jullien, Dom. de la Ferme Saint-Martin, 84190 Suzette, tel. 04.90.62.96.40, fax 04.90.62.90.84 by appt.

DOM. LA FLORANE Visan 1999*

■ 6.8 ha 33,000 30–49 F

This wine distributed by Gabriel Meffre comes from a vineyard, sited at an altitude of 250 m (820 feet). Dark ruby-coloured, this Visan is still very young. Notes of game and undergrowth, liquorice and red berry fruit are amongst its many virtues. Of a similar style, the **Gabriel Meffre Réserve Clément V 99 Rouge** although still closed, is powerful and well balanced. It will be more enjoyable in a year or two.

Gabriel Meffre, Le Village, 84190 Beaumes-de-Venise, tel. 04.90.12.32.32, fax 04.90.12.32.49

DOM. LA JOUVE

Les Mourizards 1999*

◪ 1 ha 5,600 30–49 F

This estate, an old staging post for ferrymen situated on the edge of the River Rhône, submits a very pleasant wine with redcurrant aromas. Fresh and lively, it has some amylic notes on the nose and a beautiful violet colour.

Richard Gontier, Dom. La Jouve, 84700 Sorgues, tel. 04.90.83.35.57, fax 04.90.39.25.33, e-mail rgontier@terre-net.fr ev. day except Sat. Sun. 8am–12 noon 2pm–6pm

DOM. DE L'AMEILLAUD

Cairanne 1999

■ 8.6 ha 40,000 30–49 F

An intense nose of fruit macerated in brandy gives this wine a warm feel, and this is sustained by its good structure. A wine that needs keeping for a year or two.

■ SCEA de l'Ameillaud, rte de Rasteau, 4290 Cairanne, tel. 04.90.12.32.42, .x 04.90.12.32.49

)OM. LA SOUMADE

asteau Cuvée Prestige 1998★★

■ 8 ha 25,000 70–99 F

André Roméro is one of the reliable talents f the Rhône and of Rasteau, a very fine vil-ıge whose ruins of a 12th-century château nd of the church of Saint-Didier make it orth a detour. Equally worthy is this bal-nced 98 wine. The blackcurrant on the nose ends in well with the cocoa, and the palate hows a perfect rich body, accompanied by erries and vanilla, with obvious but elegant annins. A wine with an excellent future.

André Romero, 84110 Rasteau, l. 04.90.46.11.26, fax 04.90.46.11.69 V
ev. day except Sun. 8.30am–11.30am pm–6pm

ES VIGNERONS DE LAUDUN

audun 1999★

□ 16 ha 17,000 30–49 F

The co-operative of Laudun, who make vine from 770 ha (1,902 acres) of vineyards. ubmitted this white wine, aged from Gre-ache Blanc tempered by 30% Clairette. It is a traightforward and lively wine with flavours f apricot and mango that last right through o the long finish.

Les Vignerons de Laudun, 105, rte de 'Ardoise, 30290 Laudun, el. 04.66.90.55.20, fax 04.66.90.55.21 V
Y by appt.

)OM. CATHERINE LE GŒUIL

Cairanne Cuvée les Beauchières 1998★

■ n.c. n.c. 50–69 F

A lovely wine that is almost black with pur-ple tinges. The very expressive nose at first exudes amylic notes, then after aeration the fruit takes over. The noticeable tannins are beginning to soften and the wine is overall both balanced and round.

Dom. Catherine le Gœuil, Les Sablières, 84290 Cairanne, tel. 04.90.30.82.38, fax 04.90.30.76.56, e-mail cplegoeuil@wanadoo.fr V
Y by appt.

DOM. LE PUY DU MAUPAS 1998★

■ 3.76 ha 5,000 30–49 F

A few kilometres from Vaison-la-Romaine is the village of Puymeras, home of the Puy du Maupas estate, which has been expanding ceaselessly since 1979. The aromas of red berry fruit make this wine seductive to both nose and palate. With its good structure, this wine will keep for several years.

Christian Sauvayre, Dom. le Puy du Maupas, quartier Maupas, 84110 Puymeras, tel. 04.90.46.47.43, fax 04.90.46.48.51 V
Y ev. day 9am–12.30pm 2pm–8pm

DOM. LES GRANDS BOIS

Cairanne Cuvée Maximilien 1998

■ 3.3 ha 10,000 30–49 F

Mireille and Marc Besnardeau have made this wine from very old vines. The red berry fruit on the nose is extremely charming. Solidly built, powerful and warm, this wine really shows great ripeness of fruit. Spice flavours dominate on the finish.

SCEA Dom. les Grands Bois, 55, av. Jean-Jaurès, 84290 Sainte-Cécile-les-Vignes, tel. 04.90.30.81.86, fax 04.90.30.81.86 V
Y ev. day 8am–12 noon
Besnardeau

LES GRANGES Chusclan 1998★

■ 15 ha 55,000 30–49 F

Chusclan lies on the right bank of the Rhône with hillsides that have an ideal expo-sition for vineyards. Its modern co-operative cellars submitted this deep ruby-coloured red wine with fruit compote, wax and nuts on the nose. This seductive wine is powerful on the palate with very ripe black fruit and smooth, elegant tannins. Another Chusclan is the **Les Ribières 98 Rouge**, matured six months in oak. Vanilla, spices and cocoa take over from the fruit, but the silky tannins are already pleasant and the wine deserves its mention.

Cave des Vignerons de Chusclan, rte d'Orsan, 30200 Chusclan, tel. 04.66.90.11.03, fax 04.66.90.16.52, e-mail cave.chusclan@wanadoo.fr V
Y by appt.

LES PARTIDES Cairanne 1998★★

■ 3.75 ha 15,000 50–69 F

Balance and harmony are the key words that apply to this wine. The colour is bright and the flowery nose enchanting. Oak makes its presence felt on the palate with vanilla and liquorice working well with the tannins, which are almost integrated. Life expectancy? Three years.

Vignobles Max Aubert, Dom. de la Présidente, 84290 Sainte-Cécile-les-Vignes, tel. 04.90.30.80.34, fax 04.90.30.72.93 V
Y by appt.
Max René Aubert

CH. LES QUATRE FILLES

Elevé en Fût de Chêne 1998

■ 5 ha 4,500 50–69 F

The château was built using the stones from the old village church. Perhaps that is why the wine seemed austere to the jury — tough and rustic. 'You can almost hear the wood chinking against the glass,' wrote one imaginative taster. You will need to wait for this wine to mature, and then serve with meat casserole.

Roger Flesia, Ch. les Quatre-Filles, rte de Lagarde-Pareol, 84290 Sainte-Cécile-les-Vignes, tel. 04.90.30.84.12, fax 04.90.30.86.15 V Y ev. day 8am–8pm

RHÔNE

DOM. DE LINDAS

Chusclan Cuvée Royale Elevé en Fût de Chêne 1998

■ 1 ha 5,000 70–99 F

Still too young when tasted in March 2000, this wine spent 18 months in barrel. The powerful tannins and obvious oak flavours dominate the fruit. A dash of cherry appears, however, on the nose, surrounded by notes of spices and cocoa. Place your bets: will it open up after two years of ageing?

Jean-Claude Chinieu, rte de Pont-Saint-Esprit, B.P. 25, 30201 Bagnols-sur-Cèze, tel. 04.66.89.88.83, fax 04.66.89.65.70
by appt.

DOM. DE L'OLIVIER 1998★★

■ 2 ha 7,200 30–49 F

His first barrel-matured wine, and yet it was praised by the jury. Eric Bastide has succeeded remarkably well with this wine, a blend of equal amounts of Syrah and Grenache. It has a young, intensely red colour with a purplish rim. The nose, currently tending towards vanilla, does not disguise the oak; just as on the palate vanilla recurs accompanied by other spices. This oaky touch displays great elegance, for the smooth and silky tannins are good quality. Keep for two or three years.

Eric Bastide, EARL Dom. de l'Olivier, 1, rue de la Clastre, 30210 Saint-Hilaire-d'Ozilhan, tel. 04.66.37.08.04, fax 04.66.37.00.46 by appt.

DOM. DE L'ORATOIRE SAINT-MARTIN

Cairanne Réserve des Seigneurs 1998★★

■ 8 ha 35,000 50–69 F

A wine that is true to itself and unpretentious, in which the terroir and the old vines are remarkably expressive. It is cloaked in a brilliant garnet colour with spices and blueberry side by side on the intense and complex nose. Similar notes appear on the full and rich palate, which shows really ripe fruit and great length.

Frédéric et François Alary, Dom. l'Oratoire Saint-Martin, rte de Saint-Roman-de-Malegarde, 84290 Cairanne, tel. 04.90.30.82.07, fax 04.90.30.74.27
ev. day except Wed. Sun. 8am–12 noon 2pm–7pm

DOM. DE L'ORATOIRE SAINT-MARTIN

Cairanne Cuvée Prestige 1998★★

■ 6 ha 17,000 70–99

The eulogies were prolific for this wine: 'A great wine thanks to its charm, its balance, it harmony.' The ruby colour with tinges of violet, the intense aromas of red berry fruit and spices, and the silky tannins are the definitive expression of remarkable skill in using old Grenache and Mourvèdre vines grown on a superb terroir. Expensive? Yes, but worth it.

Frédéric et François Alary, Dom. l'Oratoire Saint-Martin, rte de Saint-Roman-de-Malegarde, 84290 Cairanne, tel. 04.90.30.82.07, fax 04.90.30.74.27
ev. day except Wed. Sun. 8am–12 noon 2pm–7pm

LOU CALIN Visan 1998★

■ n.c. 50,000 30–49

Fifty thousand excellent bottles that come highly recommended by the tasters, who found this wine ready to drink now. The acidity on the palate with added notes of red berry fruit and fine tannins provide this wine with excellence balance.

Cave Les Coteaux, B.P. 22, 84820 Visan, tel. 04.90.28.50.80, fax 04.90.28.50.81, e-mail cave@coteaux-de-visan.fr
by appt.

DOM. MARIE-BLANCHE

Cuvée Crépin Delorme 1998★

■ 10 ha 10,000 20–29 F

Grenache, Syrah and Mourvèdre play an equal role in this intense and brilliant garnet-red 98. The mixture of stewed fruit, violets, garrigue and undergrowth on the nose is very pleasing, as indeed is the well-balanced palate where fruits appear yet again, embellished with spices. Good length.

Jean-Jacques Delorme, Dom. Marie-Blanche, 30650 Saze, tel. 04.90.31.77.26, fax 04.90.26.94.48 ev. day 10.30am–12 noon 4pm–7pm

CH. MONGIN 1998★

■ 4 ha 15,000 30–49 F

The Lycée Viticole d'Orange is situated in the midst of vineyards in a landscape that must inspire the students. As for practical work, you may judge the skills of the masters and pupils from this intense coloured 98 whose still youthful nose shows violets and

…amey notes. The first impression on the palate is good, whilst on the mid-palate tannins become apparent, along with a certain warmth due to the wonderful ripeness of the grapes. You will need to wait until at least mid-2001 for the oak to integrate and to allow the bouquet to open up.

🔑 Lycée viticole d'Orange, 2260, rte du Grès, 84100 Orange, tel. 04.90.51.48.04, fax 04.90.51.48.20 ☑ 🍷 by appt.

DOM. DU MOULIN Vinsobres 1999★★

□ 1.5 ha 8,000 🍾 🌡 50–69 F

Denis Vinson is investing in the construction of a second underground cellar in 2000. He has a real talent for making whites using skin maceration, for once again he has earned two stars for a fine 99 that blends 65% Viognier with Clairette. A superb lemon yellow colour, a lively and exotic nose in which mango co-exists with hints of lemons and apricots. The jury praised the palate for its elegance, balance, and very pronounced floral notes. The **98 Rouge**, in the same *Villages* (30–49 F) displays power and balance. It receives a mention.

🔑 Denis Vinson, Dom. du Moulin, 26110 Vinsobres, tel. 04.75.27.65.59, fax 04.75.27.63.92 ☑ 🍷 by appt.

DOM. DU PARANDOU

Sablet 1998★★

■ 6 ha 6,000 🍾 🌡 30–49 F

Well-exposed terraces on a clay-limestone soil have produced a wine that is typical of its AOC, powerful and generous, with mixed aromas of spices, red berry fruit, violet, leather and liquorice. Its smooth tannins and good length make this an expressive wine that is ready now, but which could also be kept.

🔑 Denis Grangeon, Le Parandou, 84110 Sablet, tel. 04.90.46.90.52, fax 04.90.46.99.05 ☑ 🍷 by appt.

PASCAL Vinsobres 1998

■ 1.5 ha 7,500 🍾 🌡 30–49 F

From a wine-merchant in Vacqueyras, this clear, brilliant red *Villages* shows a flowery nose. Structure and warmth are the chief attributes of this agreeable wine, ready to drink now.

🔑 Pascal, rte de Gigondas, 84190 Vacqueyras, tel. 04.90.65.85.91, fax 04.90.65.89.23 ☑ 🍷 by appt.

DOM. DU PETIT BARBARAS

Sélection 1998★

■ 5 ha 6,000 🛢 30–49 F

Brothers Daniel and Robert run this 48-ha (119-acre) family estate and offer a wine from 75% Syrah blended with Grenache. Twelve months in barrel have given an intensely red wine with a brick-red edge, and an astonishing nose that brings together undergrowth, violet, spices, blackcurrant and a hint of oak. The elegance of the integrated tannic structure beguiled the jury: 'This 98 wine is already enjoyable, but it could grow in stature after a few years of ageing.'

🔑 SCEA Feschet Père et Fils, Dom. du Petit-Barbaras, 26790 Bouchet, tel. 04.75.04.80.02, fax 04.75.04.84.70 ☑ 🍷 by appt.

CLOS PETITE BELLANE

Vieilles Vignes 1999★★

■ 3 ha 10,000 🛢 50–69 F

The juries much enjoyed the two wines submitted by the Clos Petite Bellane. The **Cuvée Principale**, 60% Grenache and 40% Syrah (30–49 F), is a structured and powerful wine, well worth cellaring, It is awarded two stars, as is this perfectly vinified Vieilles Vignes (old vines) selection, made from 100% Grenache and matured in large casks. A very dense red colour heralds a sumptuous nose of ripe fruits and leather. The same aromas are found on the palate, accompanied by notes of grilled meat, undergrowth and a touch of vanilla. Well-balanced, it could be opened in autumn 2001.

🔑 SARL Sté Nouvelle Petite Bellane, rte de Vinsobres, 84600 Valréas, tel. 04.90.35.22.64, fax 04.90.35.19.27 ☑ 🍷 by appt.

🔑 Olivier Peuchot

DOM. DE PIAUGIER Sablet 1999★★

□ n.c. 8,000 🛢 50–69 F

Do not miss this fine estate when you visit the charming Provençal village of Sablet with its church dating back to the 12th and 14th centuries. It submitted two attractive wines. The **Les Briguières 98 Rouge**, made from 80% Grenache and 20% Mourvèdre, is matured for 18 months in barrel. Velvety tannins and scents of raspberries in brandy are appealing, as is this oak-aged white, vinified using skin maceration. With a lemon-yellow colour, it shows a smoky, toasted nose with rose hip and lemon showing through. The full-bodied, rounded palate offers superb notes of apples, pears, spices and citrus fruit. Already excellent, this 99 wine could age until 2005.

🔑 Jean-Marc Autran, Dom. de Piaugier, 3, rte de Gigondas, 84110 Sablet, tel. 04.90.46.96.49, fax 04.90.46.99.48, e-mail piaugier@wanadoo.fr ☑ 🍷 by appt.

CAVE DES QUATRE-CHEMINS

Laudun Elevé en Barrique de Chêne 1997★★

■ 10 ha 10,000 🍾 🛢 🌡 50–69 F

The Cave des Quatre-Chemins, a co-operative on the RN-86, is unusual in having 180 members in the surrounding 22 villages. It submits this intense-coloured red with a complex nose of spices, red berry fruit and nutmeg. After ten months in barrel, liquorice is emerging and the tannins are already velvety. Enjoy this fine and distinguished wine over the next three years.

🔑 Cave des Quatre-Chemins, 30290 Laudun, tel. 04.66.82.00.22, fax 04.66.82.44.26 ☑ 🍷 ev. day except Sun. 8am–12 noon 2pm–6pm

CAVE DE RASTEAU

Rasteau Prestige 1998★★

■ 8 ha 40,000 🍾 🌡 30–49 F

The co-operative at Rasteau makes wine from 750 ha (1,853 acres), *Vins Doux Naturel* in equal proportion to dry wines. This Cuvée Prestige is notable for its finesse, balance and structure. The expressive nose shows red berry fruit in brandy, the palate has evident, yet integrated tannins, rich alcohol and good flavours, all making for a good mix. It is extremely well-made and can be kept for two to three years.

🔑 Cave de Rasteau, rte des Princes-d'Orange, 84110 Rasteau, tel. 04.90.10.90.10, fax 04.90.46.16.65, e-mail rasteau@rasteau.com
🍷 ev. day 8am–12 noon 2pm–6pm

CH. REDORTIER

Beaumes-de-Venise 1999★

◪ 1 ha 3,000 🍾 🌡 30–49 F

Suzette, situated at an altitude of 419 m (1,374 feet), is a small village with a very beautiful view over to the Dentelles de Montmirail. The 35-ha (86-acre) Château de Redortier submits this rosé with all the flavours of Provence: wild flowers, honey and berry fruits. Freshness and balance make this ideal to be enjoyed with barbecued kebabs.

🔑 EARL Ch. Redortier, 84190 Suzette, tel. 04.90.62.96.43, fax 04.90.65.03.38 ☑
🍷 ev. day 10am–12 noon 2pm–7pm
🔑 E. et S. de Menthon

DOM. DES ROMARINS 1998★

■ 10 ha 12,000 🍾 🌡 30–49 F

A blend of 55% Grenache with Syrah, all de-stemmed, has produced this very attractive violet coloured wine. The very young nose is still closed, but the balance and length on the palate with flavours of spices, liquorice and red berry fruits indicate a rich and promising 98.

🔑 SARL Dom. des Romarins, rte Estezargues, 30390 Domazan, tel. 04.66.57.05.84, fax 04.66.57.14.87, e-mail domromarin@aol.com ☑ 🍷 Wed. Fri. Sat. 3pm–7pm; cl. 15 Jan.–15 Feb.

CH. DE ROUANNE Vinsobres 1998★

■ 1.25 ha 6,700 🍾 30–49 F

This is Marc Ferrentino's first bottling: not at all bad, with a ruby red colour, concentrated nose, well-balanced tannins . . . Ready to drink.

🔑 SCEA Ch. de Rouanne, 26110 Vinsobres, tel. 06.83.57.26.61, fax 06.90.46.90.07 ☑ 🍷 by appt.
🔑 Georges Lambert

DOM. SAINTE-ANNE

Cuvée Notre-Dame-des-Cellettes 1999★

■ 4.5 ha 24,000 🍾 🌡 50–69 F

Young, still much too young, this wine from a calcareous sandstone soil needs to be kept in the depths of your cellar for two to three years. The deep colour appears promising, as is the nose, which marries violet, black fruits and a note of liquorice. The powerful tannins do not overwhelm the balance or the presence of fruit. The latter will develop further by the time this 99 wine reaches its best. Quail with grapes will be a good partner.

🔑 EARL Dom. Sainte-Anne, Les Cellettes 30200 Saint-Gervais, tel. 04.66.82.77.41, fax 04.66.82.74.57 ☑ 🍷 ev. day except Sat. Sun. 2pm–6pm; 9am–11am by appt.

CAVE DES VIGNERONS DE SAINTE-CECILE-LES-VIGNES

1999★

◪ 0.6 ha 4,000 🍾 🌡 20–29 F

This co-operative, established in 1936, has produced a pretty **Rosé de Saignée 99**, reminiscent of springtime with aromas of red berry fruit. Drink from the end of 2000 with Chinese food.

🔑 Cave des vignerons réunis de Sainte-Cécile-les-Vignes, 35, rte de Valréas, 84290 Sainte-Cécile-les-Vignes, tel. 04.90.30.79.30, fax 04.90.30.79.39 ☑
🍷 ev. day 8am–12.30pm 2pm–7pm

DOM. SAINT-ETIENNE

Les Galets 1998★★

■ 2 ha 10,000 🍾 🌡 30–49 F

Grenache and Syrah ripen on a pebbly terroir that overlooks the Rhône. This sunny and rich wine has an intense red colour. The nose, also intense, has a dominant note of leather. With a good initial impression, the palate displays tannins that still need to soften, and flavours of red berry fruit. Good balance suggests that this wine will taste excellent in a few months time.

🔑 Michel Coullomb, Dom. Saint-Etienne, fg du Pont, 30490 Montfrin, tel. 04.66.57.50.20, fax 04.66.57.22.78
☑ 🍷 by appt.

LES VIGNERONS DE SAINT-GELY CORNILLON 1998★

■ 0.9 ha 3,500 ⦀ 30–49 F

After a walk in the Cèze valley, make sure you visit the co-operative of Saint-Gely Cornillon, producer of this blend of 78% Syrah and Grenache, matured in barrel for 12 months. This deep ruby *Villages* reveals a nose of grilled meat and spice. Very pronounced tannins support beautiful structure on the palate. With strong vanilla on the finish, this wine requires at least another year's ageing.

🔑 SCA Les Vignerons de Saint-Gely, Saint-Gely, 30630 Cornillon, tel. 04.66.82.21.03, fax 04.66.82.32.94, e-mail contact.st-gely@wanadoo.fr ☑
🍷 by appt.

DOM. DE SAINT-GEORGES 1998

■ 12 ha 30,000 🍾 🌡 30–49 F

André Vignal has run this 30-ha (74-acre) estate since 1960. Made from vines that are half a century old, this very young 98 reveals purple shades of colour and strong aromas of

macerated fruit and spices. Wait two years for the tannins to become rounder and more integrated.
André Vignal, Dom. de Saint-Georges, 30200 Vénéjan, tel. 04.66.79.23.14, fax 04.66.79.20.26 by appt.

CAVE DES VIGNERONS DE SAINT-GERVAIS

Saint-Gervais Prestige 1998★

5 ha 20,000 30–49 F

This co-operative makes wine from 493 ha (1,218 acres) of vines. Like last year, its Saint-Gervais Prestige 98 is ready to drink. Aromas are of fruit in brandy and of coffee. With an overall nice structure, the palate offers good development, balance and a well-made body. Very impressive. From the same village, the **1998 Cuvée de l'An 2000 Blanc** (20–29 F), is awarded the same marks. It provides excellent value for money and is very fresh and complex with notes of apples, pears and beeswax. The same **Cuvée de l'An 2000 99 Rosé** also earned a star. Technically well made, this wine would be ideal drunk with *charcuterie* towards the end of 2000.
Cave des Vignerons de Saint-Gervais, 30200 Saint-Gervais, tel. 04.66.82.77.05, fax 04.66.82.78.85 by appt.

LES VIGNERONS DE SAINT-HILAIRE-D'OZILHAN 1999★

25 ha 130,000 30–49 F

This large co-operative cellar, not far from the Pont du Gard, vinifies wine from 700 ha (1,729 acres) of vineyards. There you will be offered this deep-coloured *Villages* to taste. With a deep colour and a blackcurrant nose, this wine demonstrates good quality on a palate that is dominated by raspberries and blackcurrants once again.
Les Vignerons Producteurs de Saint-Hilaire-d'Ozilhan, av. Paul-Blisson, 30210 Saint-Hilaire-d'Ozilhan, tel. 04.66.37.16.47, fax 04.66.37.35.12, e-mail contact@cotes-du-rhone-wine.com ev. day except Sun. 9am–12.30pm 2pm–6.30pm

DOM. SAINT-LAURENT

Cuvée de la Tamardière 1997★

9 ha 15,000 30–49 F

'We're men of the soil, here', the producer wrote to us. Hardly surprising then that the jury – in a blind tasting, of course – found the wine very 'close to the terroir'. The colour is dark and the nose redolent of the garrigue, of spices and wild fruit. The palate is well structured, virile even, with lovely tannins that blend with the fruit and vanilla oak. Allow it to age for a while.
Robert Henri Sinard, 1375, chem. Saint-Laurent, 84350 Courthézon, tel. 04.90.70.87.92, fax 04.90.70.78.49, e-mail saint-laurent@interlog.fr ev. day except Sun. 9am–12.30pm 2pm–7pm

CH. SAINT-NABOR

Clos de Roman 1997★

2 ha 9,000 30–49 F

A balsamic note is evident at first, but fades in the course of the tasting. From a difficult vintage, we have here a well structured wine demonstrating great wine-making skills in addition to the undeniable merits of its packaging. A lovely bottle in every sense of the word.
Gérard Castor, Vignobles Saint-Nabor, 30630 Cornillon, tel. 04.66.82.24.26, fax 04.66.82.31.40
ev. day 9am–12 noon 2pm–6pm

CAVE DE SAINT-PANTALEON-LES-VIGNES 1999★

n.c. 16,000 20–29 F

Balance and freshness: these are the key words that apply to this pretty rosé for immediate drinking. The colour is pale with mauve hues. The amylic nose is very floral and delicate. Ripeness and red berry fruit are the dominant notes for the palate.
Cave coop. de Saint-Pantaléon-les-Vignes, rte de Nyons, 26770 Saint-Pantaléon-les-Vignes, tel. 04.75.27.90.44, fax 04.75.27.96.43 by appt.

CAVE DES VIGNERONS DE SAINT-VICTOR-LA-COSTE

Laudun Cuvée Vitrail de Saint-Victor 1999★★

8 ha 12,000 20–29 F

Saint-Victor-la-Coste, a medieval village on the crown of the hill, is the headquarters of this co-operative that submitted, under the same label its **98 Rouge**, which won a mention from the jury, and this excellent *Rosé de Saignée*. Elegant and fine with a floral bouquet, it is lively and fresh on the palate, revealing very attractive red berry fruit flavours.
Cave des Vignerons de Saint-Victor-la-Coste, 30290 Saint-Victor-la-Coste, tel. 04.66.50.02.07, fax 04.66.50.43.92
ev. day except Sun. 9am–12 noon 2pm–6pm; Sat. 9am–12 noon

ANDEOL SALAVERT

Rochegude 1998★

n.c. n.c. 20–29 F

The Caves Salavert, a family firm of wine-merchants established in 1840, made an excellent choice with this attractive-looking Côtes du Rhône *Villages*. An intense ruby-red colour with a very subtle, red berry fruit nose, the palate displays spices with a hint of liquorice. Very balanced and excellent value for money.
Caves Salavert, rte de Saint-Montan, 07700 Bourg-Saint-Andéol, tel. 04.75.54.77.22, fax 04.75.54.47.91, e-mail caves.salavert@wanadoo.fr

DOM. DU SERRE-BIAU

Laudun 1998

■ 3 ha 16,600 30–49 F

'Rustic, with plenty of body, tannins and development.' This wine has very rich red berry fruits, with gamey notes and flavours of undergrowth also important.

Faraud et Fils, 4, chem. des Cadinières, 30290 Saint-Victor-la-Coste, tel. 04.66.50.04.20, fax 04.66.50.04.20 ev. day 9am–12 noon 2pm–7pm; Sun. by appt.

DOM. DU TERME Sablet 1999*

□ 1 ha 3,000 30–49 F

In a small cellar within the old ramparts, you can taste this very attractive 99 that has a lively gold colour with a bright green rim. The nose is floral with nuances of citrus fruit, while the palate displays an intense mineral and lemony note, which moves on to an exotic touch on the finish.

Rolland Gaudin, Dom. du Terme, 84190 Gigondas, tel. 04.90.65.86.75, fax 04.90.65.80.29 by appt.

CH. DU TRIGNON Sablet 1998*

■ 15 ha 60,000 50–69 F

Grown on a crumbly sandy-clay soil, this wonderfully intense ruby-coloured wine was made from a selective harvest. Blackcurrant predominates on the nose with gamey notes, which become more apparent on the palate, along with other subtle nuances. This well-balanced 98 has good quality tannins, which require a few months in the cellar.

Ch. du Trignon, 84190 Gigondas, tel. 04.90.46.90.27, fax 04.90.46.98.63 ev. day except Sun. 9am–12 noon 2pm–7pm

Pascal Roux

DOM. DU VAL DES ROIS

Valréas Cuvée Signature 1997

■ 4 ha 15,000 30–49 F

This Val des Rois could as easily have called itself Val des Papes since, like this entire 'enclave', it belonged to the Avignon Popes during the 14th century. Romain Bouchard lives in the pretty Valréas region where you should not miss the church of Notre-Dame de Nazareth, founded in the 11th century, with its organ from the 17th century. The Cuvée Signature has a ruby-red colour with pleasant aromas of stewed fruit and spices. The palate of soft tannins will match lamb well and the wine is ready to drink.

Emmanuel Bouchard, Dom. du Val-des-Rois, 84600 Valréas, tel. 04.90.35.04.35, fax 04.90.35.24.14, e-mail info@valdesrois.com ev. day except Sun. 9am–12.30pm 4pm–7pm

Côte Rôtie

Situated at Vienne, on the right bank of the river, this is the oldest vineyard of the Rhône Valley. It covers a production area of 200 ha (494 acres), spread through the communes of Ampuis, Saint-Cyr-sur-Rhône and Tupins-Sémons. The vines are cultivated on hills that are so steep as to be almost vertiginous. If the Côte Blonde has a separate identity from the Côte Brune it could, according to one story, be in memory of a Maugiron noble who, in his will, divided his lands between his two daughters, a blond and a brunette. It is perhaps worth observing that the wines of the Côte Brune are more full-bodied while the Côte Blonde wines are more delicate.

The soils are the richest in schist in the region. Only red wines are produced, made from the Syrah variety and a proportion of Viognier, which may be added to a maximum of 20%. The Côte Rôtie wine is deep red in colour, its delicate, fine bouquet dominated by aromas of raspberry and spices, with a touch of violet. Well-structured, tannic and richly flavoured, it holds an unchallenged position at the top of the range of Rhône wines, a perfect accompaniment to all dishes that deserve great red wines.

CH. D'AMPUIS 1996*

■ 7 ha 23,000 200–249 F

Marcel Guigal, the new owner of Château d'Ampuis, produced his first vintage in 1995 under that label. Here then is the second, a blend of grapes from the Côte Brune and the Côte Blonde, the Syrah being supplemented with 7% Viognier. This wine reflects perfectly upon the château. Over three years in barrel has given it a fine structure that will equip it for greatness. Concentrated and still closed, you will need to be patient, as this wine will not develop for another three to five years.

E. Guigal, Ch. d'Ampuis, 69420 Ampuis, tel. 04.74.56.10.22, fax 04.74.56.18.76 by appt.

GILLES BARGE Cuvée du Plessy 1997★

■ 4 ha 20,000 🛢 100–149 F

Also tasted last year, this wine has a good deal of character. We said then that it had everything needed to develop well, and so it proved, revealing blackcurrant, spices, liquorice, leather and truffles. Eclectic flavours on a base of noble tannins. Leave it for a year or two.

🔑 Gilles Barge, 8, bd des Allées, 69420 Ampuis, tel. 04.74.56.13.90, fax 04.74.50.10.80 ☑ 🍸 ev. day except Sun. 9am–12 noon 2pm–6pm

PATRICK ET CHRISTOPHE BONNEFOND Les Rochains 1998★

■ 1 ha n.c. 🛢 150–199 F

Brothers Christophe and Patrick took over the running of the family estate in 1990 and have expanded it. Les Rochains is from a single plot of 50-year-old vines. The reader will enjoy the barbecued or roasted nature of this wine that spent 18 months in barrel. The tannins are silky, although it is more robust than concentrated on the palate. A very pleasing and well-balanced 98 that is a good representative of the appellation. It will start to develop in three to four years.

🔑 Patrick et Christophe Bonnefond, Mornas, 69420 Ampuis, tel. 04.74.56.12.30, fax 04.74.56.17.93 ☑ 🍸 ev. day except Sun. 9am–12 noon 2pm–7pm; cl. 1–15 Aug.

DOM. DE BONSERINE La Garde 1998★★

■ 0.22 ha 600 🛢 250–299 F

Five per cent Viognier goes into the making of this wine that beguiled the jury with its intense bouquet of stewed fruit, toast and morello cherry linked with elegant oak flavours. Soft, but pronounced tannins give a deliciously long, liquorice palate. It could be left for five years, or else enjoyed young, depending on the reader's taste. The **Les Moutonnes** selection, from the same vintage, is 100% Syrah and wins a star. Similar to its big sister in make-up, it differs in being still closed. Guaranteed to keep for ten years.

🔑 Dom. de Bonserine, 2, chem. de la Viallière, 69420 Ampuis, tel. 04.74.56.14.27, fax 04.74.56.18.13 ☑ 🍸 ev. day except Sat. Sun. 9am–6pm

DOM. DE BONSERINE Côte Brune 1998★★

■ 1.5 ha 8,000 🛢 100–149 F

The Côte Brune is made up of mica schist that has given the earth a dark colour. The reader would be amazed to see the steepness of these slopes upon which man has worked with such dedication. This dark wine is still so young that the nose shows simply rich roasted notes. Clean, straightforward and well made, it should be kept for two or three years to allow the oak to integrate.

🔑 Dom. de Bonserine, 2, chem. de la Viallière, 69420 Ampuis, tel. 04.74.56.14.27, fax 04.74.56.18.13 ☑
🍸 ev. day except Sat. Sun. 9am–6pm

LAURENT CHARLES BROTTE 1998★

■ n.c. 2,600 🛢 100–149 F

A wine from a Châteauneuf merchant wearing his northern hat. One taster showed his approval by dubbing this Côte Rôtie a promising and original wine; everyone appreciated its lively colour, its personality and potential. One needs simply to wait another three to five years for the oak to soften and for the roasted notes to gain depth from the fruit.

🔑 Laurent-Charles Brotte, rte d'Avignon, 84230 Châteauneuf-du-Pape, tel. 04.90.83.70.07, fax 04.90.83.74.34 ☑
🍸 ev. day 9am–12 noon 2pm–6pm

M. CHAPOUTIER La Mordorée 1998★

■ 3 ha 7,000 🛢 500 F+

The raised marks that you can feel on the labels from this producer are Braille. This is so rarely done that one can do no better than encourage other producers to follow this example. The Braille does not in any sense take away from the aesthetic attraction of the label. Returning to the wine, the intense colour indicates a concentrated body and ample tannins, already silky. The bouquet mixes spices, grilled meat and cherries in brandy. Fleshy and voluptuous, the palate shows how well oak marries with wine. A very interesting 98, still needing five years, but which will be drinkable for 15. Why not try it one Christmas dinner with turkey and chestnut stuffing?

🔑 M. Chapoutier, 18, av. du Dr-Paul-Durand, 26600 Tain-l'Hermitage, tel. 04.75.08.28.65, fax 04.75.08.81.70, e-mail chapoutier@chapoutier.com ☑
🍸 by appt.

EDMOND ET DAVID DUCLAUX 1998★★

■ 4 ha 18,000 🛢 100–149 F

A wine that will grow in power and is a perfect example of a good Côte Rôtie: violets, cocoa, liquorice and cherry make up the aroma, while the palate is given over to ripe fruit. This is backed up with lovely tannins, already silky and of extreme elegance, guarantors of a long life.

🔑 Edmond et David Duclaux, RN-86, 69420 Tupin-Semons, tel. 04.74.59.56.30, fax 04.74.56.64.09 ☑ 🍸 by appt.

PHILIPPE FAURY 1998

■ 0.7 ha 4,000 🛢 100–149 F

Philippe Faury is a producer from Condrieu. He only settled in Côte Rôtie in 1996. You can feel the youth of the vines in this wine, for it lacks the depth of the really great Côte Rôtie wines. But, the cherry and raspberry fruit together with cinnamon flavours give it charm nevertheless.

🔑 EARL Philippe Faury, La Ribaudy, 42410 Chavanay, tel. 04.74.87.26.00, fax 04.74.87.05.01 ☑ 🍷 by appt.

J.-M. GERIN

Champin le Seigneur 1998★★

■ 5 ha 20,000 🛢 100–149 F

They like to say hereabouts that Côte Rôtie was the first place in Gaul where vines were cultivated, when the Romans carved out the hillsides to plant vines. The wine must certainly have been different to this one, which is black, wild and gamey. On the palate, enjoyable flavours of very ripe red berry fruit and spiced cake are present together with just the right degree of acidity to sustain a long life. Leave it for five years.

🔑 Jean-Michel Gerin, 19, rue de Montmain, Vérenay, 69420 Ampuis, tel. 04.74.56.16.56, fax 04.74.56.11.37 ☑ 🍷 by appt.

LAURUS 1998

■ 1 ha 3,000 🛢 150–199 F

This wine was matured in new oak barrels coopered in the traditional way. The oak is certainly very apparent and the tannins really bite! However, one can already discern notes of ripe fruit. Let time do its work.

🔑 Gabriel Meffre, Le Village, 84190 Gigondas, tel. 04.90.12.32.42, fax 04.90.12.32.49, e-mail gabriel-meffre@meffre.com

SAINT-COSME Montsalier 1998★

■ 1 ha 4,500 🛢 100–149 F

This merchant has submitted the only Côte Rôtie in the tasting that is almost ready to drink. The oak is already integrateded and the fine tannins are well rounded, even though the aromas are still dominated by vanilla oak. This will be an appealing wine in a year's time for lovers of very oaky wine.

🔑 Louis et Cherry Barruol, Ch. de Saint-Cosme, 84190 Gigondas, tel. 04.90.65.80.80, fax 04.90.65.81.05 ☑ 🍷 by appt.

DOM. GEORGES VERNAY

Maison Rouge 1997★★

■ 0.5 ha 4,000 🛢 150–199 F

This estate built its reputation upon its Condrieu wines, but is also well known for Côte Rôtie. Ten percent Viognier is added to the Syrah to make this rich and complex 97. Notes of spice, leather, truffles and smokiness join flavours of blackcurrant with violets still lurking behind some attractive oak. With noble tannins and good concentration, perfect cellar techniques have produced a well-balanced wine that is powerful whilst still remaining most agreeable. Not far short of a *coup de cœur*.

🔑 Dom. Georges Vernay, 1, rte Nationale, 69420 Condrieu, tel. 04.74.56.81.81, fax 04.74.56.60.98 ☑ 🍷 by appt.

Condrieu

The vineyard is on granite soils, 11 km (7 miles) south of Vienne, on the right bank of the Rhône. Only wines made exclusively from the Viognier variety are entitled to the appellation which, in seven communes and three departments, covers a mere 102 ha (252 acres). All its characteristics contribute to Condrieu's image as a white wine of very rare quality. Rich in alcohol, fleshy and supple but at the same time fresh, it is highly perfumed, releasing floral aromas – the scent of violets dominates – and notes of apricot. This is a unique wine, exceptional and unforgettable, and while it can be drunk young (with all fish dishes), it can also develop with bottle age. In recent years wines from late harvesting have appeared which are made from successive pickings (sometimes as many as eight times in a harvest).

DOM. DU CHENE 1998★

□ 3.5 ha 3,000 🍾 🛢 🌡 100–149 F

Le Chêne is a 14-ha (35-acre) estate that covers both Saint-Joseph and Condrieu appellations. This wine was matured in barrel. Logical, you might think, given the name. So, provided the wine-maker has controlled the process correctly, you would find similar and appropriate sensations on both nose and palate. And so you do, with stewed apricots and almonds dominating on the excellent palate where richness and length each play their part. One young *sommelière* wrote that she would love to taste this 98 with asparagus. An œnologist commented: 'It's a wine to drink with biscuits.' Another recommended fish in sauce. What a menu to accompany this unique wine!

🔑 Marc et Dominique Rouvière, Le Pêcher, 42410 Chavanay, tel. 04.74.87.27.34, fax 04.74.87.02.70 ☑ 🍷 by appt.

GILBERT CHIRAT 1999★

☐ 0.6 ha 3,500 70–99 F

This clear-coloured wine is already very floral with a good fresh and fruity presence. Nice balance reveals a fleshy, mineral and lightly oaked palate with a long finish. It should give us a delightful wine.

Gilbert Chirat, Le Piaton, 42410 Saint-Michel-sur-Rhône, tel. 04.74.56.68.92, fax 04.74.56.85.28 by appt.

DELAS La Galopine 1998

☐ n.c. n.c. 100–149 F

La Galopine comes from the granite and sandy Verin hillside. Fermented at 16°C (61°F) and matured on its fine lees, its appearance is beyond reproach. At present, peach aromas dominate, together with almonds. With good acidity at the start, the palate displays great warmth and balance, and is quite smooth.

Delas Frères, ZA de l'Olivet, B.P. 4, 07300 Saint-Jean-de-Muzols, tel. 04.75.08.60.30, fax 04.75.08.53.67 by appt.

Champagne Deutz

DOM. FARJON

Les Graines Dorées 1998★

☐ 0.36 ha 250 150–199 F

With a 90 g/l residual sugar level, it was hardly surprising that the jury noted the over-ripeness of the harvest. One taster commented, after having spoken of the aromas of ripe and dried apricots, that he had 'tasted a 1947 Condrieu with something of the same over-ripeness about it, and it was fabulous'. Will this wine survive more than 50 years? We certainly hope so.

Thierry Farjon, Morzelas, 42520 Malleval, tel. 04.74.87.16.84, fax 04.74.87.95.30 by appt.

PHILIPPE FAURY La Berne 1999★★

☐ 0.5 ha 2,500 150–199 F

A selection from the oldest plots went into this superb wine, full of finesse, ideal to accompany the finest gastronomy. Floral notes, hawthorn, grapefruit and lychee are accompanied by touches of broom and honey with superb length. It compares with a very lovely watercolour that never stops giving pleasure. Simpler, the **Cuvée Principale** (100–149 F) does not lack merit and is awarded a star. Of a floral style, it still needs some time.

EARL Philippe Faury, La Ribaudy, 42410 Chavanay, tel. 04.74.87.26.00, fax 04.74.87.05.01 by appt.

PIERRE GAILLARD 1999★★★

☐ 1 ha 4,000 100–149 F

What a perfect coincidence that the label on this vintage shows a bouquet of white flowers, matching the jury's appreciation of the floral intensity on the nose. On the palate the richness and roundness are wonderful, characteristic of Viognier produced on the terroir of Condrieu. Long and smooth, the

wine still shows an elegant and fine oakiness that time will soften. Superb!

Pierre Gaillard, Chez Favier, 42520 Malleval, tel. 04.74.87.13.10, fax 04.74.87.17.66 by appt.

DOM. DU MONTEILLET 1998★

☐ 1.6 ha 3,800 100–149 F

An estate that also devotes itself to breeding goats to make *rigotte de Condrieu* (the local goat's cheese), which they do very well. Enjoy this bright-coloured wine with its bursts of apricot and peach. The palate is full and rich, with a subtler, but still fruity finish.

Vignobles Antoine et Stéphane Montez, Dom. du Monteillet, 42410 Chavanay, tel. 04.74.87.24.57, fax 04.74.87.06.89 by appt.

ANDRE ET JEAN-CLAUDE MOUTON 1998

☐ 1.6 ha 2,600 100–149 F

This 98 wine is still too young with the palate still lacking some character. But what a nose! Worthy of one of Cyrano de Bergerac's eulogies and redolent of white peach.

André et Jean-Claude Mouton, Le Rozay, 69420 Condrieu, tel. 04.74.87.82.36, fax 04.74.87.84.55 ev. day 9am–12 noon 2pm–6pm; cl. Feb.

ANDRE PERRET

Coteau de Chery 1998★★

☐ 3 ha 8,000 100–149 F

André Perret took over the family business in1986. He reaps the benefits of 50-year-old vines on his ten-ha (25-acre) estate. Using only natural yeast this wine was fermented in both oak barrels and stainless steel tanks followed by lees stirring. It is splendid. The whole effect is seductive, right from the clarity of the gold-tinged colour to the finish. Viognier comes through in the floral notes and the intense apricot flavours with almond and lychee are also apparent. Superb balance.

André Perret, Verlieu, 42410 Chavanay, tel. 04.74.87.24.74, fax 04.74.87.05.26 by appt.

ANDRE PERRET

Clos Chanson 1998★

☐ 0.5 ha 2,000 100–149 F

An air-conditioned barrel store, renovated in 1995, with vinification and maturation in

barrel: this Clos Chanson has received meticulous attention. Vanilla and lychee give an exotic feel, while white peach and nutty flavours show the serious side of Condrieu. Serve with *foie gras* on a special occasion.
André Perret, Verlieu, 42410 Chavanay, tel. 04.74.87.24.74, fax 04.74.87.05.26 by appt.

CHRISTOPHE PICHON

Moelleux 1998*

2 ha 8,500 100–149 F

Harvested on 17 October 1998, this clear golden, sweet wine has 34 g/l of residual sugar. It maintains a good balance between the aromas of apricot jam, stewed fruit and sweetness. The jury recommends it with patisseries.
Christophe Pichon, Le Grand Val, Verlieu, 42410 Chavanay, tel. 04.74.87.06.78, fax 04.74.87.07.27 by appt.

HERVE ET MARIE-THERESE RICHARD Le Moelleux 1999*

0.3 ha 2,000 100–149 F

Harvested on 18 October, and left with 30 g/l of residual sugar, the wine is labelled 'late harvest' and lives up to its name. True, the characteristics of the terroir are somewhat erased by the sweetness, but the richness and the aromas of honey, broom and raisins are very appealing and long. A wine that is well worth keeping. Wonderful with *foie gras* and raisins.
Hervé et Marie-Thérèse Richard, Verlieu, 42410 Chavanay, tel. 04.74.87.07.75, fax 04.74.87.05.09 by appt.

DOM. GEORGES VERNAY

Les Chaillées de l'Enfer 1998*

1 ha 4,000 150–199 F

Both **Les Terrasses de l'Empire 98** and **Coteau de Vernon 98** were enjoyed just as much as this Chaillées de l'Enfer, with its brilliant, clear, pale gold colour. The 12 months it spent in barrel (20% new) are hardly perceptible, such is the smell of good quality ripe grapes. The smooth and well-balanced palate is rich in aromas of fruit compote, and these persist on the finish.
Dom. Georges Vernay, 1, rte Nationale, 69420 Condrieu, tel. 04.74.56.81.81, fax 04.74.56.60.98 by appt.

Château-Grillet

This appellation is almost the only one in France to be made by a single estate. It covers 3.5 ha (8.6 acres), spread over two communes, and is one of the smallest Appellations d'Origine Contrôlée. The vines are planted on well-exposed granitic terraces, sheltered from the wind and contained within a hillside basin overlooking the Rhône Valley. This exceptional terroir makes for a highly original white wine made only from the Viognier variety, like Condrieu. Production is 90 hl (2,376 gal). The wine is rich in alcohol, fleshy and lightly acidic, with strong aromas and surprising finesse. It can be drunk young, but if kept it takes on fine aromas which make it a rare classic, ideal with fish.

CHATEAU-GRILLET 1998*

n.c. 10,000 200–249 F

81 82 85 86 **88** |**89**| |90| 92 |**93**| |94| |95| 98

An estate which, with a few other rare monopoly estates, is exceptional in the way it appears on the French AOC listing. One appellation, just one estate. The pale colour differentiates this wine from the preceding ones. Still young, it requires ageing so that its flavours will develop fully. However, one can already discern elegance in its delicate fresh lychee aromas mixed with camomile. The voluptuous palate could almost qualify as being tannic, except that it shows a beautiful fruit-acid balance, which augurs well for the future of this 98 wine.
Neyret-Gachet, Château-Grillet, 42410 Vérin, tel. 04.74.59.51.56, fax 04.78.92.96.10 by appt.
Famille Canet

Saint-Joseph

The appellation stretches over about 900 ha (2,223 acres) along the right bank of the Rhône, in the Ardèche and Loire departments, on steep gravel slopes with beautiful views of the Alps, Mount Pilat and the Doux gorges. Saint-Joseph reds are made from Syrah grapes, and are elegant, relatively light and soft, with subtle aromas of raspberry, pepper and blackcurrant, which open when accompanying grilled chicken and certain cheeses. The white wines, made from the Roussanne and Marsanne varieties, are reminiscent of the Hermitage whites. They are fleshy with a delicate perfume of flowers, fruit and honey, and are best drunk fairly young.

DOM. DES AMPHORES 1998

■ 3 ha 8,000 30–49 F

Established in 1992 with less than one ha (2.5 acres), this estate now has six (15 acres). Its main wine is characterised by lightness on the palate, while blackcurrant and blackberry notes are manifested on the nose, with spices and leather to back them up. The black cherry colour with its bluish tinges is inviting. Should be drunk within two years.

Véronique et Philippe Grenier, Dom. des Amphores, Richagnieux, 42410 Chavanay, tel. 04.74.87.65.32, fax 04.74.87.65.32
Y by appt.

DOM. BOISSONNET

Cuvée de la Belive 1998★

■ 1 ha 2,000 70–99 F

The restored cellars are hidden below this 17th-century house. In one of these recently discovered cellars, a statue of Saint Joseph watches over the barrels, where this wine has been matured for 15 months. Although still closed, the attractive 98 is very full and needs ageing for three or four years. It is worth pointing out that Boissonnet has transformed its vineyards by recreating terraces on the steep hillsides.

Dom. Boissonnet, rue de la Voûte, 07340 Serrières, tel. 04.75.34.07.99, fax 04.75.34.04.55 Y by appt.

BONSERINE Cuvée Petit Pierre 1998★

■ n.c. 2,000 50–69 F

We don't know which vineyard it came from, but this extremely nice wine is from a merchant who certainly knows where to buy from. The tasting was full of interest. From the very start, power, concentration and complexity are revealed. Constantly evolving, we found hazelnuts, over-ripe grapes, crystallised red fruits and a mineral note . . . Something new appears with every mouthful.

Dom. de Bonserine, 2, chem. de la Viallière, 69420 Ampuis, tel. 04.74.56.14.27, fax 04.74.56.18.13
Y ev. day except Sat. Sun. 9am–6pm

BOUCHER Cuvée Panoramique 1998

■ 0.7 ha 2,500 50–69 F

Studies of viticulture and œnology have reunited father and son on this estate at Chavanay, a village where you can still see relics from its medieval past. Their Saint-Joseph is simple and austere, resembling the granite rock on which the grapes grew. The colour is dense, with scents of black fruit, grilled meat and vanilla-oak notes that recur on the substantial palate. It needs time to soften.

GAEC Boucher M.-G.-S., Vintabrin, 42410 Chavanay, tel. 04.74.87.23.38, fax 04.74.87.08.36 Y by appt.

M. CHAPOUTIER

Les Granits 1998★★★

■ 2 ha 5,000 250–299 F

'Les Granits' are of course the wonderful rocks where the finest Saint-Joseph vines grow. Here Syrah is at its best, as demonstrated by this great wine for ageing: good weight and skilful wine-making. 'Well thought out', noted one member of the jury. Another wrote: 'there is something spiritual in this magnificently harmonious wine.' What more can one say? Keep it for two to five years to allow the tannins to integrate. The **Cuvée Deschant 98 Rouge** (70–99 F) receives a star.

M. Chapoutier, 18, av. du Dr-Paul-Durand, 26600 Tain-l'Hermitage, tel. 04.75.08.28.65, fax 04.75.08.81.70, e-mail chapoutier@chapoutier.com
Y by appt.

DOM. DU CHATEAU VIEUX 1998★

■ 0.6 ha 2,400 50–69 F

Triors has a castle built in the 18th century, which is today lived in by the Benedictines. This Château Vieux from Fabrice Rousset evolves consistently throughout the tasting, with blackcurrant and violets, and notes of garrigue together with silky tannins. One female taster described this wine as 'feminine with plenty of character'. Drink it when young or wait six years.

Fabrice Rousset, Le Château Vieux, 26750 Triors, tel. 04.75.45.31.65, fax 04.75.45.31.65 Y by appt.

DOM. COURBIS Les Royes 1998★★

■ 5 ha 13,000 70–99 F

This large 23-ha (57-acre) estate has been cultivated since the 16th century by the same family, who still love the beauty of the steep vine-covered hillsides. Aside from the **Domaine 99 Blanc** (50–69 F), that won a star for the elegance of both the aroma and the palate, this wine thrilled the jury who described it in elegiac terms: 'Extraordinary!' Superb colour and a wonderful nose on which the blackcurrant and blackberry fruit is not obscured by oak, and a mineral note adds to the elegance. The palate is delicious and fresh, full-bodied and well-balanced with all the complexity of a true Saint-Joseph. Serve it in four or five years to partner young rabbit with thyme.

🔑 Dom. Courbis, Les Ravières, 07130 Châteaubourg, tel. 04.75.81.81.60, fax 04.75.40.25.39 ☑ 𝐓 by appt.

PIERRE COURSODON

L'Olivaie 1998★★

■ n.c. 6,000 70–99 F

On 1 February 2000, Pierre Coursodon, the father, and Jérôme, the son, became partners in the company. Despite the rough time they had with frost, their 1998 vintage has scooped up several prizes. Both the red (100–149 F) and the white (70–99 F) **Le Paradis Saint-Pierre** were rewarded with a star for their balance and elegance. As for this wine, L'Olivaie, it elicited much enthusiasm from the jury. Both modern and classic, a straightforward wine and 'vinified and matured with meticulous attention' (wrote one taster). It displays real complexity, mixing notes of blackcurrant, blackberry, liquorice and roasted flavours. Fleshy, powerful, very long, it has the perfect combination of integrated oak and superb fruit.

🔑 EARL Pierre Coursodon, pl. du Marché, 07300 Mauves, tel. 04.75.08.18.29, fax 04.75.08.75.72 ☑ 𝐓 by appt.

DOM. COURSODON 1998★★

□ 1.8 ha 5,000 70–99 F

The prize-giving continues with the main wines from the estate: the **Domaine Coursodon 98 Rouge** (15,000 bottles, 70–99 F) won a star. Still rather tannic, this wine needs to be laid down in the cellar for at least two years. On the other hand, this white Saint-Joseph is already drinkable. Mineral and flowery notes join together with characteristic fruit and good, well balanced acidity ensures balance. An extremely elegant wine.

🔑 EARL Pierre Coursodon, pl. du Marché, 07300 Mauves, tel. 04.75.08.18.29, fax 04.75.08.75.72 ☑ 𝐓 by appt.

DELAS FRERES Sainte-Epine 1997★★

■ n.c. 3,000 100–149 F

With their headquarters at Saint-Jean-de-Muzols, ancient river port of the Greeks and subsequently the Romans, the firm of Delas submitted several Saint-Joseph wines from the 97 vintage. Not a single one was judged worthy of less than a star: one star was awarded to both the **Les Challeys 97 Blanc** (50–69 F) and the **François de Tournon 97 Rouge**, deemed the equal of this Sainte-Epine. Superb colour, a characteristic nose that is still evolving, and a full, rich palate. An excellent ambassador for the AOC, it could partner lamb and *tapenade* now, or be left for two or three years.

🔑 Delas Frères, ZA de l'Olivet, B.P. 4, 07300 Saint-Jean-de-Muzols, tel. 04.75.08.60.30, fax 04.75.08.53.67 ☑ 𝐓 by appt.

🔑 Champagne Deutz

ERIC ET JOEL DURAND

Les Coteaux 1998★★

■ 4.5 ha 10,000 70–99 F

'It holds the road well', wrote one delighted taster who even suggested a *coup de cœur* for it. Everyone gave it two stars and was unanimous about its qualities. A very well-made wine, in which the elegant oak harmonises with fine tannins and red berry fruits behind.

🔑 Eric et Joël Durand, imp. de la Fontaine, 07130 Châteaubourg, tel. 04.75.40.46.78, fax 04.75.40.29.77 ☑ 𝐓 by appt.

DOM. FARJON 1998★

□ 0.26 ha 1,300 50–69 F

A chef for four years, Thierry Farjon switched to the wonderful trade of winemaker in 1989. This wine proves that he knows what wine-making is about: two-thirds Roussanne and one-third Marsanne were vinified in oak barrel and matured *sur lies* (on their lees). This intensely yellow and brilliant 98 displays ripe fruits, citrus character and fine oak on the nose. The well-structured palate shows good length.

🔑 Thierry Farjon, Morzelas, 42520 Malleval, tel. 04.74.87.16.84, fax 04.74.87.95.30 ☑ 𝐓 by appt.

PHILIPPE FAURY

La Gloriette Vieilles Vignes 1998★★

■ 0.7 ha 1,500 70–99 F

A cottage in the middle of the vineyards, the 'Gloriette' used to serve as a hunting lodge or as a place for amorous rendezvous. Since 1997, the name has been used for the wine made from the estate's oldest vines (30 years old). This wine is no less a Saint-Joseph for being extremely fine: intense aromas mix blackcurrant, liquorice, grilled meat and also fruit kernels. Balanced by superb tannins, full-bodied and long on the finish, it is tremendously fresh. The jury liked it as it is now, but it would also be worth keeping. The **99 Blanc**, ten months in barrel, earns a star. A floral, long and elegant 98 that could work well with poultry or fish.

🔑 EARL Philippe Faury, La Ribaudy, 42410 Chavanay, tel. 04.74.87.26.00, fax 04.74.87.05.01 ☑ 𝐓 by appt.

PIERRE FINON 1998★

■ 1.7 ha 7,000 50–69 F

A family vineyard of nine ha (22 acres), with five (12 acres) in Saint-Joseph. The **Les Rocailles 98 Rouge** won a mention (70–99 F) and needs to be kept for two to three years. But the jury's preference was for the intensely fruity estate wine. Some found it a little alcoholic, others balanced, though tannic, with a concentrated weight. What if it were to show both notes at once?

🔑 Pierre Finon, Picardel, 07340 Charnas, tel. 04.75.34.08.75, fax 04.75.34.06.78 ☑ 𝐓 by appt.

GILLES FLACHER

Cuvée Prestige 1998★★

■ 1.5 ha 5,000 70–99 F

A family estate of seven ha (17 acres) established since 1806 on the hills of the AOC. Barrel ageing for 14 months provides the toasty notes that the jury discerned at every stage of the tasting. However, this wine hides nothing: cinnamon and ripe fruit are as obvious on the nose as on the palate, where quite fine tannins give an impression of elegant balance. Grilled chicken could be a good choice, in a year or two.

Gilles Flacher, 07340 Charnas, tel. 04.75.34.09.97, fax 04.75.34.09.96 Y by appt.

PIERRE GONON 1998★

■ 5 ha 18,000 70–99 F

Pierre Gonon matures his wines in *foudres* (large casks) and demi-muids (smaller old casks). His fame has already spread across several continents. An extremely well-made 98, the oak gives toasty notes with very obvious red berry fruits behind. Full of roundness and charm, well-balanced and harmonious, it should be drunk within two years with roast lamb.

Pierre Gonon, 11, rue des Launays, 07300 Mauves, tel. 04.75.08.07.95, fax 04.75.08.65.21 Y by appt.

BERNARD GRIPA 1998★★

■ 6 ha 25,000 50–69 F

Bernard Gripa is a very successful producer. The **98 Blanc** received only one star (although very few of the whites submitted to this tasting came out with any), but your best friends will enjoy it. The red stands out and, according to one taster, in three years' time might accompany venison steak with blueberries. The colour has the mauve rim of promising youth. Gamey flavours, coffee and spices play on the nose. The structure on the palate has a dense body that needs time to soften.

Bernard Gripa, 5, av. Ozier, 07300 Mauves, tel. 04.75.08.14.96, fax 04.75.07.06.81 Y by appt.

DOM. J.-L. GRIPPAT 1998★

□ 1.38 ha 6,200 50–69 F

Jean-Louis Grippat has already conquered the world, since he exports his wine to numerous countries. But, happily for those not familiar with it and who wish to discover an exceptional white Saint-Joseph, there is some of this available. With a promise of greatness in a few years, the complexity should develop more. However, aromas of flowers (acacia) and citrus fruit (grapefruit) already reveal delightful balance.

Jean-Louis Grippat, La Sauva, 07300 Tournon, tel. 04.75.08.15.51, fax 04.75.07.00.97 Y by appt.

J. MARSANNE ET FILS 1998

□ 0.4 ha 1,400 50–69 F

This white has a delicate nose, dominated by sweet floral notes. The palate is warm and ripe.

Jean Marsanne et Fils, 25, av. Ozier, 07300 Mauves, tel. 04.75.08.86.26, fax 04.75.08.49.37 Y by appt.

DOM. DU MONTEILLET

Cuvée du Papy 1998★★

■ 2 ha 5,000 70–99 F

Don't be influenced by the name of this wine (grandpa), for this really is a great wine worthy of drinking with a woodcock. You could serve it to your revered grandfather with utter confidence! Complete destemming, three weeks' maceration with *pigeage* (punching down the cap) and maturation in barrel have given an intensely fruity wine. Magnificent tannins leave a silky sensation on the palate. The **Cuvée Principale 98 Blanc** (50–69 F) wins a star. It is very elegant, and a *rigotte de Condrieu* (the local goat's cheese) – also produced on this estate – would be ideal to accompany it.

Vignobles Antoine et Stéphane Montez, Dom. du Monteillet, 42410 Chavanay, tel. 04.74.87.24.57, fax 04.74.87.06.89 Y by appt.

DIDIER MORION Les Echets 1998★★

■ 0.8 ha 2,000 50–69 F

This wine-maker, who has been in business since 1993 in the Pilat regional park, 20 km (12.5 miles) from Vienne, owns seven and a half ha (19 acres). He submitted a wine named **'D.M.' 98** (mentioned by the jury) that is characteristic, and almost wild beneath the backbone of black fruit and tannin. It's a little more rustic than this wine, Les Echets, whose qualities were described by one taster as follows: 'It has everything. Here is a real Saint-Joseph.' What more can one say? Perhaps that it is very oaky, but that with a very attractive dark colour and excellent weight a remarkably good life is ensured. Wait three to five years before serving it with stuffed quail.

Didier Morion, Epitaillon, 42410 Chavanay, tel. 04.74.87.26.33, fax 04.74.87.26.33 Y by appt.

ALAIN PARET 420 Nuits 1998★★

■ 2 ha 10,000 70–99 F

A regular winner of awards, this wine receives a *coup de cœur.* Would you like to know the secret of such success? Alain Paret discovered this method of vinification written down in his grandfather's journals: 420 days and nights in new oak barrels from different sources. The tasting unfolds to complex gamey aromas, with notes of undergrowth, stewed red berry fruit, spices, cedar and pale tobacco, accompanied by a magnificent use of oak. A huge, weighty wine that needs two or three years and which then will be drinkable for ten years.

🔑 Alain Paret, pl. de l'Eglise, 42520 Saint-Pierre-de-Bœuf, tel. 04.74.87.12.09, fax 04.74.87.17.34 ✉ 🍷 by appt.

ANDRE PERRET Les Grisières 1998*

■ 1 ha 4,000 🛢 70-99 F

While you wander along the Pélussinois way – one of the routes that take you across the Pilat regional park – you should not fail to meet this great man who has become a great wine-producer. At the Chavanay Wine Fair, which takes place during the second weekend of December, you will be able to taste – amongst other wines selected by the *Guide* – this very interesting Saint-Joseph, which shows a most promising dark purple colour. After a tremendously attractive nose where the fruit is not at all submerged by oak, the palate displays a beautiful balance between acidity and richness. This 98 wine could be served with partridge or pheasant.

🔑 André Perret, Verlieu, 42410 Chavanay, tel. 04.74.87.24.74, fax 04.74.87.05.26 ✉ 🍷 by appt.

PHILIPPE PICHON 1998

■ 1 ha 4,500 50-69 F

This is an easy-drinking wine that does not display great length. The fruit is elegant and fine, but ephemeral. It has a light structure that would make it a good partner to white meat. Ready now.

🔑 Philippe Pichon, Le Grandval, 42410 Chavanay, tel. 04.74.87.23.61, fax 04.74.87.07.27 ✉ 🍷 ev. day except Sun. 10am–6pm

DOM. DE PIERRE BLANCHE 1998

■ 1.5 ha 7,000 🛢 50-69 F

Beginning in 1990, Michel and Xavier Mourtier have established this vineyard from scratch on hillsides that used to be fallow. So these are young vines that gave birth to a wine that is not yet very characterised by its terroir. On the other hand, the wine-maker has extracted the maximum from the grapes. Very fashionable! But is it the right way to bring out the soul of the wine? That is the question raised by one taster, and only ageing for two to three years will provide the answer.

🔑 Xavier Mourier, RN-86, Chanson, 42410 Chavanay, tel. 04.74.87.08.39, fax 04.74.87.04.07 ✉ 🍷 by appt.

DOM. DES REMIZIERES 1998**

■ 1.2 ha 5,000 🛢 70-99 F

Last year this estate's Crozes-Hermitage was very successful, this year it earns a *coup de cœur* for a Saint-Joseph. White last year, red this time. This deep-coloured wine, black with bluish tinges, shows wonderful balance and weight. Round and concentrated, the palate demonstrates elegant tannins together with spices, gamey notes, grilled meat and ripe fruit. This wine has the noble character of a great Saint-Joseph and will keep for a long time.

🔑 Cave Philippe Desmeure, rte de Romans, 26600 Mercurol, tel. 04.75.07.44.28, fax 04.75.07.45.87 ✉ 🍷 by appt.

LEON REVOL 1998*

■ 2 ha 8,000 🍾 🛢 50-69 F

This Rhône merchant from Givors knows how to buy good Saint-Joseph, as is evident in this wine. It has been said that: 'this wine dives straight in'. The very concentrated body is ever-present and it will take some time for the weight to allow the tannins to mature.

🔑 Léon Revol, 6, rue Yves-Farges, 69700 Givors, tel. 04.72.49.50.29, fax 04.78.73.16.97 ✉

CAVE DES VIGNERONS RHODANIENS 1998*

□ 2 ha 8,000 🛢 50-69 F

Some of the tasters thought that this was Roussanne. Well no, it's not; in fact, it's 100% Marsanne that has produced this well-made and elegant bright gold wine with a good floral intensity mixed with peach.

🔑 Cave des Vignerons Rhodaniens, 35, rue du Port-Vieux, 38550 Le Péage-de-Roussillon, tel. 04.74.86.37.87, fax 04.74.86.57.95 ✉ 🍷 ev. day except Sun. Mon. 8am–12 noon 2pm–6pm

DOM. HERVE ET MARIE-THERESE RICHARD 1998*

□ 0.7 ha 2,500 🍾 🌡 50-69 F

Founded during the 1950s, this estate grew both fruit and vines until 1989 when it moved to specialise. A **98 Rouge** is quite classical, particularly with a stew. A notch above is this fresh and most vivacious white. The very floral and well-developed nose heralds the

characteristics that appear on the palate.
🔑 Hervé et Marie-Thérèse Richard, Verlieu, 42410 Chavanay, tel. 04.74.87.07.75, fax 04.74.87.05.09 ☑ Y by appt.

CAVE DE SAINT-DESIRAT

Cuvée Côte-Diane Elevé en Fût de Chêne 1998

■ 20 ha 60,000 ⏸ 50-69 F

One can never under-rate how much man fashioned the landscape when he planted vines, nor the importance this has had on preserving the hillsides. The primary role of this co-operative cellar is to make the small plots of vines within the AOC viable. This wine certainly provides a window onto the appellation through which one sees both the severity and the serenity of these places: still closed at present, with oak influences, it will become more expressive in two years' time. Located a few hundred metres from the Romanesque church, the co-operative has opened an attractive tasting cellar.

🔑 Cave de Saint-Désirat, 07340 Saint-Désirat, tel. 04.75.34.22.05, fax 04.75.34.30.10 ☑ Y by appt.

CAVE DE SARRAS

Cuvée Champtenaud Elevé en Fût de Chêne 1997★

■ 7 ha 26,500 ⏸ 50-69 F

The co-operative of Sarras, with 180 vine-growers, has submitted a 1997 with 12 months' barrel ageing. Still young and rather closed, it should be forgotten about in your cellar for two or three years, but no longer. Black fruits macerated in alcohol dominate over oak, but the palate is still tannic, quite mouth-filling and concentrated.

🔑 Cave de Sarras, Le Village, 07370 Sarras, tel. 04.75.23.14.81, fax 04.75.23.38.36 ☑ Y by appt.

CAVE DE TAIN L'HERMITAGE

Les Nobles Rives 1998★

■ n.c. n.c. ⏸ 50-69 F

Founded in 1933, the Tain-L'Hermitage co-operative has already proved itself with its know-how. This wine has a very pretty, typically plummy colour; although the nose is still reticent, the palate has an impressive and substantial structure.

🔑 Cave de Tain-l'Hermitage, 22, rte de Larnage, B.P. 3, 26601 Tain-l'Hermitage Cedex, tel. 04.75.08.20.87, fax 04.75.07.15.16 ☑ Y by appt.

DOM. DU TUNNEL 1998★

■ 0.6 ha 945 ⏸ 50-69 F

Stéphane Robert works alone on this three and a half-ha (nine-acre) vineyard that he has consolidated since 1994. His wines appear on the grandest tables locally and nationally, and he exports 50% of his production. This seductive 98 will have more than one admirer for the very apparent fruit that dominates over the oak. The tannins are integrated but persistent. Drink when young with grilled meat, or wait for a couple of years.

🔑 Stéphane Robert, Dom. du Tunnel, 07130 Saint-Péray, tel. 04.75.80.04.66, fax 04.75.80.06.50 ☑ Y ev. day 2pm–8pm

Crozes-Hermitage

This appellation, which is on land that is easier to cultivate than Hermitage, extends over 11 communes around Tain-l'Hermitage. It is the largest vineyard of the northern appellations: the area of production is 1,238 ha (3,058 acres), and produces 61,000 hl (1,610,400 gal). The soils, which are richer than those of the Hermitage appellation, produce less powerful, fruity wines that are better drunk young. The red wines are fairly supple and aromatic; the whites are dry and fresh, light in colour, with a floral aroma. Like the Hermitage whites, they go splendidly with freshwater fish.

DOM. BERNARD ANGE

Rêve d'Ange 1997★★★

■ 0.8 ha 3,000 ⏸ 70-99 F

What else would an angel dream of but a *coup de cœur*? The angel of 1997 has travelled well and openly displays its virtues: the oak, in which it was matured for 12 months knows its place, allowing the fruit and weight to be fully expressed. Rich and concentrated with pronounced and well-balanced tannins, this wine is very characteristic. Will there be any left for you? The **Cuvée Principale 98** (50–69 F), which is less expressive and less structured, earned a mention. Ask Bernard Ange to show you his barrel cellars that are dug into the foot of a hill. You won't be disappointed.

⊶ Bernard Ange, Pont-de-l'Herbasse, 26260 Clérieux, tel. 04.75.71.62.42, fax 04.75.71.62.42 ▣ Y ev. day except Sun. 9am–12 noon 1.30pm–7pm

BOIS FARDEAU 1998**

■ 4 ha 20,000 30–49 F

Bois Fardeau is produced from a plot of land of the same name, made up of mica schist. Syrah is at its happiest here: this entirely harmonious wine has a great structure together with a very characteristic complexity of flavours. It was one vote away from a *coup de cœur.* This firm has proved its credentials through the number of its wines that were selected by our juries. The **Saint-Joseph Laurus 98 Rouge** (70–99 F) is powerful and wins one star. Keep it for a year. Owned by GAEC Michelas, the **La Combe du Puy 98 Rouge** is distributed by Meffre. Beautifully structured, this wine earned one star (30–49 F).

⊶ Gabriel Meffre, Le Village, 84190 Gigondas, tel. 04.90.12.32.42, fax 04.90.12.32.49, e-mail gabriel-meffre@meffre.com

CUVEE J.-M. CALVET 1998

■ n.c. 18,000 30–49 F

Cuvée Jean-Marie Calvet was created for this vintage through the desire of the great Bordeaux firm to pay homage to its founder who was born at Tain-l'Hermitage. It was there, in 1818, that he established his firm of merchants. Matured in Allier oak, the wine reveals delightful notes of blackcurrant, vanilla, and cinnamon. The tactile sensation is good, and though not completely integrated yet, it should be ready in January 2001.

⊶ Calvet, 75, cours du Médoc, B.P. 11, 33028 Bordeaux Cedex, tel. 05.56.43.59.00, fax 05.56.43.17.78

M. CHAPOUTIER

Les Meysonniers 1998*

■ n.c. 180,000 50–69 F

This well-known merchant chose to submit a wine that is entirely straightforward, supple and balanced. Black fruit and liquorice on the nose recur on a palate dominated by pronounced, but integrated tannins. The finish is just as pleasing. **Les Varonniers 98 Rouge** (250 F) shows great richness but needs a little time. It receives a star. The **Les Meysonniers 99 Blanc** earned a mention (50–69 F). Full of exotic fruit and finely oaked, in all it is simply very good.

⊶ M. Chapoutier, 18, av. du Dr-Paul-Durand, 26600 Tain-l'Hermitage, tel. 04.75.08.28.65, fax 04.75.08.81.70, e-mail chapoutier@chapoutier.com ▣ Y by appt.

DOM. BERNARD CHAVE 1998*

□ 1.44 ha 5,500 50–69 F

Bernard Chave and his son Yann made this attractive 98 blend of 80% Marsanne and Roussanne grown on a clay-limestone soil. Ten percent was matured in barrel. A very appealing nose, on which almonds accompany passion fruit, the wine develops on the palate with a good balance and pleasing length. The **La Tête de Cuvée 98 Rouge** of which 80% is matured in barrel should prove itself after ageing. Charred and noticeably oaked, it receives a mention.

⊶ Yann Chave, La Burge, 26600 Mercurol, tel. 04.75.07.42.11, fax 04.75.07.47.34 ▣ Y by appt.

DOM. LES CHENETS 1998*

■ 6.8 ha 36,000 30–49 F

This estate makes successful AOC wines. The jury stated as much when they wrote 'well-executed maturation'. Indeed, this Crozes was matured 12 months in barrel, 12% of which were new. This level of oak is just what's needed to balance such lovely weight: underlying fruit on the first sniff explodes onto the palate even though the oak has not yet completely lost its hold. Ready in autumn 2001.

⊶ Dom. les Chenêts, Cave Fonfrède et Berthoin, 26600 Mercurol, tel. 04.75.07.48.28, fax 04.75.07.45.60 ▣ Y ev. day except Sun. 8am–12 noon 2pm–6pm

MAXIME CHOMEL

Cuvée Sassenas 1997

■ 1.2 ha 6,000 70–99 F

This small property started with two and a half ha (six acres) of AOC vines and has since grown to ten and a half ha (26 acres). It earns a mention for an almost mature 97. The first impression is of liquorice and red berry fruit and then the palate finishes on an oaky note that still needs time to integrate.

⊶ Maxime Chomel, Les Blancs Chemins des Roches, 26600 Gervans, tel. 04.75.03.32.70, fax 04.75.03.37.58 ▣ Y by appt.

DOM. COLLONGE 1999*

□ n.c. n.c. 30–49 F

Made entirely from Marsanne grown on a soil of clay-limestone mixed with large pebbles, this wine promises a 'loyal' colour – certainly the first time we've seen this expression used on a technical tasting sheet, but it is most apt (editor's note). An intense. very floral nose of 'fleur de lys', we're told, and it certainly has a royal feel to it. The richness, acidity and length combine on the palate to make this an agreeable wine. The **99 Blanc** receives a mention.

⊶ GAEC Collonge, La Négociale, 26600 Mercurol, tel. 04.75.07.44.32, fax 04.75.07.44.06 ▣ Y ev. day 8.30am–12 noon 1.30pm–6.30pm; Sun. 9.30am–12 noon; groups by appt.

DOM. DU COLOMBIER

Cuvée Gaby 1998*

■ n.c. 15,000 70–99 F

This estate submitted its **Cuvée Principale 98 Rouge** (50–69 F) that is already supple and balanced and receives a mention, as well as this special selection whose colour is so dark,

almost black, that it seems to emerge from the granite. The nose, which is very classy, mixes a hint of blackcurrant with spices. The tannins are so silky that they might have travelled from Samarkand. The pronounced fruit character makes this wine a pleasure now.
Dom. du Colombier, 2, rte de Chantemerle-les-Blés, 26600 Tain-l'Hermitage, tel. 04.75.07.44.07, fax 04.75.07.41.43 ☒ Y by appt.

DOM. COMBIER Clos des Grives 1998

■ 9 ha 15,000 70-99 F

This estate has made its wines from organically grown vines for the past 30 years. One would have preferred less oak to allow the red berry fruit at the back to shine through. So, patience will be required, for the body is rich, full and over-powerful now, but the wine is very promising for the future.
Dom. Combier, RN-7, 26600 Pont-de-l'Isère, tel. 04.75.84.61.56, fax 04.75.84.53.43 ☒ Y by appt.

CH. CURSON 1999

□ 2 ha 11,000 70-99 F

The Marsanne grapes, accounting for 60% of the blend, underwent some skin maceration in barrel (70% new) and this may have troubled the tasters. They liked the wine's crystal-clear colour and floral nose, but found that the palate was very muted. This wine should be ready by the end of 2000 to drink with fish in sauce.
Dom. Pochon, Ch. de Curson, 26600 Chanos-Curson, tel. 04.75.07.34.60, fax 04.75.07.30.27 ☒ Y by appt.

DELAS FRERES Les Launes 1997*

■ n.c. n.c. 50-69 F

This merchant has succeeded in making some fine red 1997s. The **Clos Saint-Georges** (70–99 F) was given the same marks as this Les Launes which proved delicious, even if the purists hoped for a longer finish. But don't deny yourself this wine. Everything is there. An interesting colour, close to ink; very ripe fruit; great presence; fine and full-bodied tannins; good balance. Wait two or three years.
Delas Frères, ZA de l'Olivet, B.P. 4, 07300 Saint-Jean-de-Muzols, tel. 04.75.08.60.30, fax 04.75.08.53.67
Y by appt.
Champagne Deutz

DOM. DES ENTREFAUX Les Machonnières 1998**

■ 3 ha 9,000 70-99 F

A 24-ha (59-acre) estate established in 1960 whose name was used from 1979 by the Tardy family. Les Machonnières was made from 30-year old vines planted in a clay-limestone soil with glacial deposits, and matured in barrel. This wine has finesse, body, elegance and restraint. Its oak and menthol notes supply the final touch to this eulogy. Moving on, the **Les Pends 98 Blanc**, which won a star, was vinified in casks with lees stirring. A delicious apéritif wine.
Dom. des Entrefaux, quartier de la Beaume, 26600 Chanos-Curson, tel. 04.75.07.33.38, fax 04.75.07.35.27 ☒
Y by appt.
Tardy

GUYOT Le Millepertuis 1998

■ n.c. 50,000 30-49 F

A 'photofit' of the supple and easy to drink style of Crozes. This merchant went for simplicity and focused on the fruit, though notes of vanilla and roasted flavours are also present.
Guyot, montée de l'Eglise, 69440 Taluyers, tel. 04.78.48.70.54, fax 04.78.48.77.31, e-mail guyotvin@easynet.fr ☒
Y Thu. Fri. Sat. 8am–12 noon 1.30pm–5.30pm; cl. 15–21 Aug.

LES EDILES 1998*

■ n.c. n.c. 30-49 F

The *édiles* are the councillors in charge of a town. It's an unusual name for these wines submitted by this distributor and merchant from Ampuis. Bottled in the Drôme, this wine is good. A brilliant colour, ripe fruit, well balanced and pleasing, it will attract more than one admirer.
Dom. de Bonserine, 2, chem. de la Viallière, 69420 Ampuis, tel. 04.74.56.14.27, fax 04.74.56.18.13 ☒
Y ev. day except Sat. Sun. 9am–6pm

MOILLARD 1998*

■ n.c. 20,000 30-49 F

Moillard, a merchant in Burgundy's Côte d'Or, chose carefully and well in this AOC. Our demanding jury really liked this attractive 98: a brilliant deep colour envelops a beautifully full wine. The slightly jammy black fruits predominate on the very rich palate. A wine to purchase with confidence.
Moillard, 2, rue François-Mignotte, 21700 Nuits-Saint-Georges, tel. 03.80.62.42.22, fax 03.80.61.28.13
Y ev. day 10am–6pm; cl. Jan.

MOMMESSIN Les Epices 1998

■ n.c. n.c. 30-49 F

This very typical Crozes submitted by Jean-Claude Boisset's group provides a nice intensity of fruit and complexity. Well-balanced and warm on the finish, it needs to be served slightly cool.
Mommessin, Le Pont-des-Samsons, 69430 Quincié-en-Beaujolais, tel. 04.74.69.09.30, fax 04.74.69.09.28, e-mail information@mommessin.com
Y by appt.

DOM. DU MURINAIS 1998**

■ 2.5 ha 10,000 30-49 F

In 1998 Luc Tardy established himself here and created a cellar in his old, 17th-century family house. This is his first vintage, and he has immediately won incredible marks in the

Guide. The tasters hailed a real master in the art of barrel maturation. The elements seem well balanced: rounded tannins and complex flavours all come together here. We wish him continued success.
Luc Tardy, quartier Champ-Bernard, 26600 Beaumont-Monteux, tel. 04.75.07.34.76, fax 04.75.07.35.91 ev. day 8am–12 noon 2pm–7pm

LES ALLEGORIES D'ANTOINE OGIER 1998*

2.3 ha 12,000 70–99 F

Matured in *demi-muids* (small oak casks) for 16 months, this wine still needs to assimilate the oak. It is, however, already expressive on the middle palate with fruity notes on top of a lovely fleshy structure. A promising wine that should be kept for a full year.
Ogier-Caves des Papes, 10, bd Pasteur, 84230 Châteauneuf-du-Pape, tel. 04.90.39.32.32, fax 04.90.83.72.51 ev. day except Sun. 8.30am–6.30pm

PASCAL 1998*

3 ha 16,000 30–49 F

A southern Rhône merchant who knows how to buy in the North! This wine was matured for a year in barrel and yet the oak does not dominate. Here is a sign of good wine-making and respect for the raw materials. This is a fine and elegant wine with plenty of character at a good price. What more could one ask?
Pascal, rte de Gigondas, 84190 Vacqueyras, tel. 04.90.65.85.91, fax 04.90.65.89.23 by appt.

CUVEE DES PIONNIERS 1998

n.c. 26,000 50–69 F

The Clairmonts co-operative, which vinifies wine from 102 ha (252 acres) of vines, has done well once again with this quite densely coloured wine, that shows scents of spices and oak. Blackcurrant and stewed fruits are apparent on the palate along with a weightiness that requires a year of ageing.
SCA Cave des Clairmonts, Vignes Vieilles, 26600 Beaumont-Monteux, tel. 04.75.84.61.91, fax 04.75.84.56.98 ev. day except Sun. 9am–12 noon 2pm–6pm; groups by appt.

DOM. PRADELLE 1998

12 ha 50,000 50–69 F

The harvest was 100% de-stemmed and underwent 14 days of maceration followed by malolactic fermentation. Six months in barrel has produced this light but well-balanced wine. Although dominated by blackcurrant, there were obvious toasty notes all the way through, and it finished on a warm note. Drink it with red meat.
GAEC Pradelle, 26600 Chanos-Curson, tel. 04.75.07.31.00, fax 04.75.07.35.34 ev. day except Sun. 8am–12 noon 2pm–6pm

DOM. DES REMIZIERES

Cuvée Christophe 1998**

2 ha 12,000 50–69 F

Everything was put in place to ensure that this Crozes-Hermitage would be a good wine for ageing. Even though the flavours on the palate are still masked by the oak, you can feel the good quality mid-palate, and powerful tannins. A thoroughbred pawing the ground that will finish amongst the winners and last the distance.
Cave Philippe Desmeure, rte de Romans, 26600 Mercurol, tel. 04.75.07.44.28, fax 04.75.07.45.87 by appt.

MESSIRE LOUIS REVOL 1998

2 ha 10,000 30–49 F

This 21st-century wine bears a name that dates back to the 12th century. Possibly a surprising idea, but the wine is nevertheless delicate and characterised by perfectly clean-cut fruit. It has the requisite tannins and weight to make it well-balanced. Drink soon.
Léon Revol, 6, rue Yves-Farges, 69700 Givors, tel. 04.72.49.50.29, fax 04.78.73.16.97

DOM. GILLES ROBIN

Cuvée Albéric Bouvet 1998*

7 ha 30,000 70–99 F

Gilles Robin, great-grandson of a wine-producer, took over this estate in 1996 and has done well. This fine 98 achieves an impression of crunching into a ripe grape. Both powerful and complex, it gives a terrific sensation of freshness.
Gilles Robin, Les Chassis Sud, 26600 Mercurol, tel. 04.75.08.43.28, fax 04.75.08.43.64 by appt.

DOM. DES SEPT-CHEMINS 1998

7 ha 25,000 30–49 F

Phylloxera destroyed this vast estate in the 19th century. It was partially reconstructed and still has a large area of fruit trees. Is it coincidental that the jury liked the jam and stewed fruit nature of this wine? The palate is full-bodied with very agreeable flavours.
Jean-Louis Buffière, Dom. des Sept-Chemins, 26600 Pont-de-l'Isère, tel. 04.75.84.75.55, fax 04.75.84.62.94 by appt.

DOM. DE THALABERT 1998**

40 ha 214,800 100–149 F

Some very attractive wines were submitted by this great Rhône merchant including a

Mule Blanche 98 Blanc (70–99 F) mentioned for the pleasure it already gives when drunk with soft cheeses. A **Domaine Raymond Roure 98 Rouge** (100–149 F), grown on granite hillsides, won two stars, and needs keeping for 18 to 24 months, as does this highly reputed wine. From a glacial alluvial soil, it displays an intense purplish colour, a straightforward attack on the palate and consistent balance all the way through to the slightly tannic finish. Flavours of ripe, confected, concentrated red berry fruits dominate, accompanied by elegant notes of oak.

Paul Jaboulet Aîné, Les Jalets, R.N. 7, 26600 La Roche-de-Glun, tel. 04.75.84.68.93, fax 04.75.84.56.14, e-mail info@jaboulet.com by appt.

THOMAS LA CHEVALIERE 1998★

■ 2 ha 10,000 30–49 F

A pleasant and successful wine. This merchant from the Beaujolais has sought very ripe red berry fruit, freshness, liveliness and boldness. It is ready to provide enjoyable company for a meal with friends and will last until 2002.

Thomas La Chevalière, 69430 Beaujeu, tel. 04.74.04.84.94, fax 04.74.69.29.87 ev. day except Sat. Sun. 8am–12 noon 2pm–5pm

Hermitage

The Hermitage slope is located north-east of Tain-l'Hermitage, with an excellent southerly aspect. Vine cultivation there goes back to the 4th century BC, but the origin of the appellation's name is attributed to the knight Gaspard of Sterimberg who, on his return from the Albigensian crusade in 1224, decided to withdraw from the world. He built a hermitage, cleared the land and planted vines.

The appellation covers about 131 ha (324 acres). To the west, the granite soils of the Tain mountain provide an ideal terrain for producing red wines (Les Bessards). In the south-east, the soils of broken stones and loess (deposits of fine-grained, wind-blown silt and sand) are suited to producing white wines (Les Rocoules, Les Muerts).

The Hermitage red is a very big, tannic wine that is extremely aromatic and needs to be aged from five to ten years, and even up to twenty years, before it develops its bouquet, which is of rare richness and quality. After so long in the bottle, it should be opened well in advance and served at between 16°–18°C (60.8–64.4°F) with game and tasty red meat. The Hermitage white (made from the Roussanne and particularly the Marsanne varieties) is a very fine wine that lacks acidity, but is supple, fleshy and very perfumed. It can be enjoyed from the first year but reaches its full expression after between five and ten years' bottle age. However, for both white and red wines, the great years can be kept for as long as thirty or forty years.

M. CHAPOUTIER Le Méal 1998★

■ 1.5 ha 4,000 500 F+

A very noticeable presence during our tasting. Monsieur Chapoutier, whom we know has worked biodynamically for the past ten years, submitted several wines produced from different terroirs. At more than 500 F and with a star each, there is the **L'Ermite 98 Rouge** from a loess soil, the **Pavillon 98 Rouge** from granite, and this very powerful Méal, which like its brothers needs long ageing before being served with the finest dishes. This Hermitage has a pronounced character of macerated red berry fruit, spices and sandalwood . . . with a very weighty mid-palate whose oaky tannins should integrate in time. The **La Sizeranne 98 Rouge** (200–249 F) is equally successful with an attractive appearance. The wine has already opened up with some discreet oaky notes that will be enjoyed by enthusiasts immediately, but will last six to eight years.

M. Chapoutier, 18, av. du Dr-Paul-Durand, 26600 Tain-l'Hermitage, tel. 04.75.08.28.65, fax 04.75.08.81.70, e-mail chapoutier@chapoutier.com by appt.

M. CHAPOUTIER De l'Orée 1999★

□ 2.2 ha 9,000 500 F+

This white wine is produced from more than 60-year-old Marsanne grown on fluvio-glacial alluvial soil. Slightly disconcerting to members of the jury, who were not able to find any floral notes, they nevertheless enjoyed the scents of exotic and citrus fruits, spices, tobacco and liquorice. The palate is full, well-balanced and long. A very well-made wine, even if it did seem atypical.

🔑 M. Chapoutier, 18, av. du Dr-Paul-Durand, 26600 Tain-l'Hermitage, tel. 04.75.08.28.65, fax 04.75.08.81.70, e-mail chapoutier@chapoutier.com ☑
🍸 by appt.

DOM. BERNARD CHAVE 1998★★

■ 1.14 ha 6,000 ▮ 🌡 150-199 F

'A true wine of the terroir', wrote one jury member. Isn't that the finest compliment one can make about an appellation wine? The quintessence of the environment reproduced by the skill of man. Yann, Bernard's son, has been working on the estate since 1996. He has managed to marry finesse and elegance with concentration of the raw material. Fruit dominates throughout the tasting. A really attractive wine that needs three to five years ageing before being drunk at a grand dinner.

🔑 Yann Chave, La Burge, 26600 Mercurol, tel. 04.75.07.42.11, fax 04.75.07.47.34 ☑
🍸 by appt.
🔑 SCEA Chave Père et Fils

DOM. JEAN-LOUIS CHAVE 1997★★

□ 5 ha n.c. ⦀ 300-499 F

The tasters showered praise on it, but you will have to be patient before opening this bottle, as it will still develop. With a beautiful colour, this superb 97 displays a very fresh nose initially showing menthol then, after aeration, floral notes and ripe fruit, followed by almonds. Although the bouquet is rather ethereal – less honeyed than its elders – the palate shows a great richness with some discreet oak.

🔑 Jean-Louis Chave, 37, av. du Saint-Joseph, 07300 Mauves, tel. 04.75.08.24.63, fax 04.75.07.14.21

DOM. JEAN-LOUIS CHAVE 1997★★★

■ 10 ha n.c. ⦀ 300-499 F

'If perfection is not of this world, then I must already be in heaven!' declared one taster who was enthused by the charm of this clear and deep wine. The jury was unanimous in applauding the lovely ripeness of the grapes and the wine-making, which managed to preserve all the finesse. Everything is right about this wine. A classic and enchanting balance.

🔑 Jean-Louis Chave, 37, av. du Saint-Joseph, 07300 Mauves, tel. 04.75.08.24.63, fax 04.75.07.14.21

DELAS FRERES Les Bessards 1997★★

■ n.c. n.c. ⦀ 300-499 F

Les Bessards comes from a hillside of decomposed granite, situated on the south-western side of the Hermitage hill. This wine, made from very old vines (80 years), is blessed with a splendid deep colour. It may seem surprising to find menthol in a red wine and Hermitage at that, but it did not worry the jury who also found all the classic aromas of the AOC. Concentration and body come together here. This wine is full of character and charm, and will be ready to drink in two or three years.

🔑 Delas Frères, ZA de l'Olivet, B.P. 4, 07300 Saint-Jean-de-Muzols, tel. 04.75.08.60.30, fax 04.75.08.53.67
🍸 by appt.
🔑 Champagne Deutz

PAUL JABOULET AINE La Chapelle 1998★

■ 21 ha 95,900 ⦀ 300-499 F

Jaboulet is a member of the French wine nobility of *négociants-éleveurs* (wine-merchant/producers). A family firm, it owns some of the symbolic locations of the Hermitage AOC, including the 13th-century Saint-Christophe chapel situated at the summit of vineyards. The wine that bears its name is also a monument. It has a substantial structure that time will not perturb. The jury was unanimous in its recognition of the very attractive mid-palate that is dense, full-bodied and classy. Requiring some time to integrate, this very reticent 98 is still guarding the secret of its aromas behind the oak character.

🔑 Paul Jaboulet Aîné, Les Jalets, RN-7, 26600 La Roche-de-Glun, tel. 04.75.84.68.93, fax 04.75.84.56.14, e-mail info@jaboulet.com ☑ 🍸 by appt.
🔑 Famille Jaboulet

PAUL JABOULET AINE Le Chevalier de Stérimberg 1998★

□ 5 ha 61,500 ⦀ 250-299 F

Legend has it that on his return from the Crusades in 1224 and with the permission of Blanche of Castille, the *chevalier* (knight) of Sterimberg decided to retire near a little chapel. He dedicated himself to the contemplative life as well as to the cultivation of vines on this land composed of glacial alluvial deposits. What can we say of this 98? That it is much too young to be fully appreciated. But that it has already acquired great depth, balance, complexity, richness and length. As for the taste of oak, there is the perfect amount. One taster suggested matching it with chicken and truffles in a few years time . . . but do not wait until you return from another hopeless crusade.

🔑 Paul Jaboulet Aîné, Les Jalets, R.N. 7, 26600 La Roche-de-Glun, tel. 04.75.84.68.93, fax 04.75.84.56.14, e-mail info@jaboulet.com ☑ 🍸 by appt.

LES DIONNIERES 1998★★

■ 2 ha 8,400 ⅡⅠ 300–499 F

Quality has no price. This wine seems to confirm the adage since the jury compared it to a work of art. A touch of garnet in the colour envelops red berry fruit, spices (especially pink peppercorns) and even notes of camphor. Rather like a Seurat painting, the pointillist technique creates strong sensations in which size and substance are closely linked.

Ferraton Père et Fils, 13, rue de la Sizeranne, 26600 Tain-l'Hermitage, tel. 04.75.08.59.51, fax 04.75.08.81.59 ☑
Y by appt.

ORATORIO 1998★

■ 0.5 ha 2,400 ⅡⅠ 150–199 F

Ogier, Caves des Papes and Bessac have linked to create a very large *négociant-éleveur* (merchant and producing company) in the Rhône. This Oratorio clearly does not come from the school of Handel, to judge by how closely it follows the modern canons of winemaking. However, the producer has not sought to create a massive opus at any price, but has played instead on the finesse and the fruit.

Ogier-Caves des Papes, 10, bd Pasteur, 84230 Châteauneuf-du-Pape, tel. 04.90.39.32.32, fax 04.90.83.72.51 ☑
Y ev. day except Sun. 8.30am–6.30pm

DOM. DES REMIZIERES

Cuvée Emilie 1998★

■ 2 ha 10,000 ⅡⅠ 100–149 F

The jury believes that for the time being the oak character on this Hermitage is too dominant to make it enjoyable to drink and that long ageing is required. Thereafter it will certainly have its admirers. Currently there are fine and fairly rich tannins with an already expressive palate revealing flavours of quite complex ripe red berry fruit, which show that the wine will balance. Elsewhere, the estate won a mention for its **98 Blanc** produced with some skin maceration in barrel, of which 50% were new. Not surprisingly, this young wine is very oaky. However, there is finesse together with flavours of hazelnut and smoke. 'I would happily drink it with snails', commented one taster.

Cave Philippe Desmeure, rte de Romans, 26600 Mercurol, tel. 04.75.07.44.28, fax 04.75.07.45.87 ☑ Y by appt.

CAVE DE TAIN-L'HERMITAGE

Les Nobles Rives 1997★

■ 25.28 ha n.c. ⅡⅠ 100–149 F

The excellent co-operative at Tain, established in 1933, has submitted a very well-made red 97. With floral scents and attractive spicy notes, the first impression on the palate is bold, and it shows an attractive structure. Worthy of its appellation.

Cave de Tain-l'Hermitage, 22, rte de Larnage, B.P. 3, 26601 Tain-l'Hermitage Cedex, tel. 04.75.08.20.87, fax 04.75.07.15.16 ☑ Y by appt.

Cornas

Lying across the river from Valence, the appellation covers only the commune of Cornas, about 93 ha (230 acres). The granite soils, on fairly steep ground, are held in place by low walls. Cornas is a virile, well-structured wine that must be aged for at least three years (but can often wait a good deal longer) to allow it to express its fruity, spicy aromas. Serve it with red meats and game.

LOUIS BERNARD

La réserve des Pontifes Elevé en Fût de Chêne 1998

■ n.c. n.c. ⅡⅠ 100–149 F

Matured in new barrels, this wine is still dominated by oak: vanilla and spices emerge throughout the tasting. However, the tannins are of good quality and persistence, and allow expression of the underlying fruit that should open up in time.

Les domaines Bernard, rte de Sérignan, 84100 Orange, tel. 04.90.11.86.86, fax 04.90.34.87.30

BIGUET 1998

■ 1 ha 1,500 ▮ⅡⅠ ♁ 70–99 F

With such a gamey nose, we expected the rusticity of a traditional Cornas. Instead we found suppleness and balance together with notes of spices, cocoa and stewed fruit, mixed with vanilla from the oak. Well made, this wine can be drunk from the end of 2001.

Jean-Louis Thiers, EARL du Biguet, Cave Thiers, 07130 Toulaud, tel. 04.75.40.49.44, fax 04.75.40.33.03 ☑
Y by appt.

M. CHAPOUTIER 1998

■ n.c. 16,000 ⅡⅠ 100–149 F

Oak still dominates this wine, which should have been left for a year before presenting it to the jury! The nose has not yet opened despite the presence of some fruity and floral notes. The jury did like the well-balanced structure and its length, which augurs well for the future. For now, the wine will appeal to oak enthusiasts — and they still exist, even if this fashion is waning and becoming dated everywhere in the world.

M. Chapoutier, 18, av. du Dr-Paul-Durand, 26600 Tain-l'Hermitage, tel. 04.75.08.28.65, fax 04.75.08.81.70, e-mail chapoutier@chapoutier.com ☑
Y by appt.

DOM. CLAPE 1998★★★

■ 4 ha 17,000 150–199 F

It is a shame that the estate has run out of this wine. The jury was so thrilled by the 1998 vintage that we can but encourage you to run out and scour the merchants for it. A spell-binding wine! First impressions are of jammy blackberries and gamey notes. Superb richness and concentration. The very pronounced palate has tight-grained and fine tannins, which express the ruggedness of the soil well. Still very youthful, it will gain in stature and become a grand aristocrat. This family estate has always carried the fine reputation of French wines far and wide.

SCEA Auguste Clape,
146, rte Nationale, 07130 Cornas,
tel. 04.75.40.33.64, fax 04.75.81.01.98
by appt.

DUMIEN-SERRETTE

Vieilles Vignes 1998

■ 1.8 ha 3,000 70–99 F

Flavours on the mid-palate perfectly match the intense nose of strawberry and coffee with notes of toast and blackcurrant leaves. The structure is light enough to make one want to enjoy the wine in its youth.

Gilbert Dumien-Serrette,
18, rue du Ruisseau, 07130 Cornas,
tel. 04.75.40.41.91, fax 04.75.40.41.91,
e-mail dumien.serrette@wanadoo.fr
by appt.

ERIC ET JOEL DURAND 1998★

■ 3 ha 11,000 100–149 F

An attractive and very elegant wine. The creators sought refinement and found it, as evidenced by its balance, as well as the subtle mix of flavours with red berry fruits, chocolate, spices and vanilla. This is from the new generation of Cornas.

Eric et Joël Durand, imp. de la Fontaine, 07130 Châteaubourg, tel. 04.75.40.46.78, fax 04.75.40.29.77 by appt.

LA SABAROTTE 1998★★

■ 0.9 ha 4,500 150–199 F

The Courbis estate dates from the 16th century. Today, with 23 ha (57 acres) situated on steep granite hillsides, they manage to appear in the best categories of the *Guide*. Look at this sumptuous, dense-coloured Cornas. The nose thrilled the jury, one of whom noted:

'This wine is a real breakfast'. Cocoa, coffee and toast . . . these flavours appear on a well-balanced palate with powerful weight, accompanied by spices, gamey notes and truffles. *Coup de cœur* was the unanimous popular vote.

EARL Dominique et Laurent Courbis,
Les Ravières, 07130 Châteaubourg,
tel. 04.75.81.81.60, fax 04.75.40.25.39
by appt.

LES EYGATS 1998★★

■ 1.1 ha 4,200 100–149 F

If you ask us what differentiates La Sabarotte and Les Eygats we would answer: the plots of vineyard are different and the Syrah grown is of a different age. These vines are 80 years old, the others 50. But, both wines are superb and elegant. Perhaps there is a note of liquorice here that isn't noticeable on the Sabarotte. Yet, both are concentrated, and well-structured with marvellous flavours. The only drawback is that there is so little. The **Champelrose 98** is slightly shorter on the finish but is awarded one star.

EARL Dominique et Laurent Courbis,
Les Ravières, 07130 Châteaubourg,
tel. 04.75.81.81.60, fax 04.75.40.25.39
by appt.

LES VIGNERONS REUNIS A TAIN-L'HERMITAGE 1997

■ 3 ha n.c. 70–99 F

Blackcurrant and pepper are the aromas. The structure is not exceptional, but still manages to stand out. The jury believes that in two years the wine will be ready . . . and will be good. We would place a small wager on it.

Les Vignerons de Rasteau et de Tain-l'Hermitage, rte des Princes-d'Orange, 84110 Rasteau,
tel. 04.90.10.90.10, fax 04.90.46.16.65,
e-mail vrt@rasteau.com

DOM. DU TUNNEL 1998★★

■ 1 ha 2,738 70–99 F

The **Cuvée Prestige 98** (100–149 F) made from 80-year-old vines is as distinguished as this wine, from 50-year-old vines. An attractive and expressive wine, it has flavours of blackcurrant, leather, spices and chocolate that are powerful yet fine. A touch of vanilla from oak ageing crowns the overall impression. The structure will be in perfect balance in two years' time but those who love young wines will enjoy it now.

🔑 Stéphane Robert, Dom. du Tunnel, 07130 Saint-Péray, tel. 04.75.80.04.66, fax 04.75.80.06.50 ☑ 🍷 ev. day 2pm–8pm

Saint-Péray

Situated on the opposite bank of the river from Valence, the vineyard of Saint-Péray, 62 ha (153 acres), is dominated by the ruined château of Crussol. Saint-Péray has a relatively cooler micro-climate and richer soils than elsewhere in the region, producing white wines that are more acid, drier, and lower in alcohol, but ideal for making sparkling Blanc de Blancs by the Méthode Traditionelle, or champagne method. This, the main type of wine made under this appellation, is one of the best sparkling wines in France.

DOM. CHABOUD 1997

☐ 6 ha 25,000 30–49 F

Established in 1798, the sixth generation of this 12-ha (30-acre) estate has been producing wine since 1997. The mineral character caught the attention of the jury, and there are notes of hawthorn too. This very fresh wine has an attractive pale colour with green hues.

🔑 Dom. Chaboud, 21, rue F.-Malet, 07130 Saint-Péray, tel. 04.75.40.31.63, fax 04.75.40.59.43 ☑ 🍷 ev. day except Sun. 9am–12 noon 2pm–6.30pm

BERNARD GRIPA 1998★

☐ 1 ha 2,500 50–69 F

Of all the Saint-Péray wines that were submitted, only this one had a high percentage of Marsanne (80%). Notes of brioche and apricot are apparent, underpinned by floral scents. The palate is long and characterised by a great deal of suppleness and richness. 'A charmer', wrote one jury member.

🔑 Bernard Gripa, 5, av. Ozier, 07300 Mauves, tel. 04.75.08.14.96, fax 04.75.07.06.81 ☑ 🍷 by appt.

CAVE DE TAIN-L'HERMITAGE 1998

☐ 5 ha 25,000 20–29 F

The nose is so delicate that it was hard to judge this wine. Yet the colour is very simply beautiful, and the palate – surely the most important consideration – is quite characteristic and fine with apple, pear and almonds.

🔑 Les Vignerons de Rasteau et de Tain-l'Hermitage, rte des Princes-d'Orange, 84110 Rasteau, tel. 04.90.10.90.10, fax 04.90.46.16.65, e-mail vrt@rasteau.com

JEAN-LOUIS ET FRANCOISE THIERS 1998

☐ 1 ha 7,000 30–49 F

One young *sommelière* suggested this would be ideal with skate. This bottle displays a real balance between nose and palate, a continuity in its complexity of flavours: linden flowers, hawthorn, peach and pear play their part together with a mineral note that is very characteristic of the AOC. This is what is described as a most typical wine. The jury also mentioned the **Sparkling Brut 97**, noted for its finesse.

🔑 Jean-Louis Thiers, EARL du Biguet, Cave Thiers, 07130 Toulaud, tel. 04.75.40.49.44, fax 04.75.40.33.03 ☑ 🍷 by appt.

DOM. DU TUNNEL 1998

☐ 0.8 ha 2,293 50–69 F

Established in 1994, this three and a half-ha (nine-acre) vineyard is worked by the wine-producer on his own. Throughout the tasting we found that mix of mineral and floral notes so characteristic of this appellation. A classic, lively and fresh Saint-Péray.

🔑 Stéphane Robert, Dom. du Tunnel, 07130 Saint-Péray, tel. 04.75.80.04.66, fax 04.75.80.06.50 🍷 ev. day 2pm–8pm

Gigondas

The famous Gigondas vineyard, at the foot of the breath-taking Dentelles de Montmirail mountains, covers a series of slopes and valleys within the commune of Gigondas itself. Wine-making here is a very ancient tradition, but its real development dates from the 14th century (the vineyards of le Colombier and les Bosquets), greatly assisted by Eugène Raspail. Gigondas was originally classed as a Côtes du Rhône, then in 1966 a Côtes du Rhône-Villages, until it finally obtained its 'letters patent' in 1971, when it became a specific appellation. It covers nearly 1,260 ha (3,112 acres).

Soil and climate combine to make Gigondas red

wines, 44,000 hl (1,161,000 gal) in 1999, very rich in alcohol, powerful, well-structured and well-balanced, with fine aromas of licorice, spices and stone fruits. The wines develop slowly in the bottle and can retain their qualities for many years, making a very suitable accompaniment to game dishes. Gigondas rosés are powerful and heady in character.

LOUIS BERNARD 1998*

■ n.c. n.c. 50–69 F

This fine and elegant Gigondas is really balanced, and according to some tasters, 'ethereal'. Wonderfully intense aromas of red berry fruit, leather and spices, with a touch of fennel, emerge from a warm bouquet. The attractive structure is long-lasting and the wine can be enjoyed from now.

Les domaines Bernard, rte de Sérignan, 84100 Orange, tel. 04.90.11.86.86, fax 04.90.34.87.30

DOM. DES BOSQUETS 1998**

■ 28 ha n.c. 50–69 F

Established in 1644, this estate now amounts to 32 ha (79 acres). An attractive deep colour of ripe red cherries, followed by a wild nose. After a few seconds, your senses are assailed by a flood of nuances: macerated fruit and roasted coffee beans . . . and finally warmth invades the palate. With balance and harmony, you are completely won over. All that remains is to share this pleasurable experience with your best friends regularly over the next three years.

Sylvette Bréchet, Dom. des Bosquets, rte de Vacqueyras, 84190 Gigondas, tel. 04.90.83.70.31, fax 04.90.83.51.97 V
by appt.

DOM. DE CASSAN 1998***

■ 7.5 ha 33,000 50–69 F

This family-owned estate is most successful, as shown by this dark red 98. The olfactory sensations are rich in red and black fruits and leather, embellished by notes of minerals and vanilla. Superb balance complemented by a classic structure make this totally elegant wine a delight to all the senses.

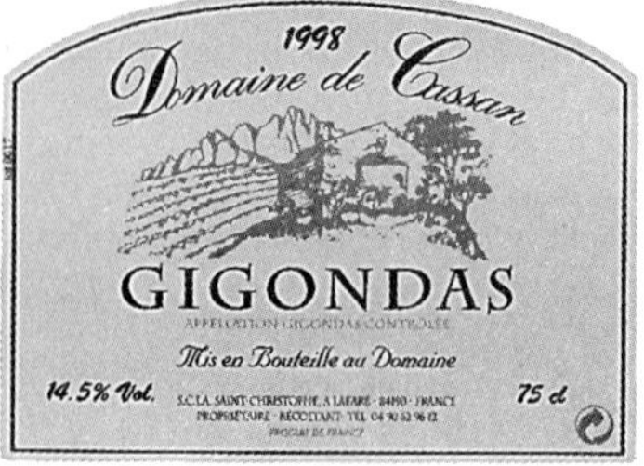

SCIA Saint-Christophe, Dom. de Cassan, 84190 Lafare, tel. 04.90.62.96.12, fax 04.90.65.05.47, e-mail domainedecassan@wanadoo.fr V
by appt.

PIERRE CHANAU 1998

■ 43 ha 200,000 30–49 F

A tasting that flows with complete lucidity. The fine nose reveals mild spices and prune notes. Red berry fruits on the smooth palate prolong the sensations. The well-balanced and elegant tannins make this Gigondas a pleasure. Ready to drink now, it could partner grilled red meat.

Sefivin-H. Bouachon, rte de Châteauneuf, 84230 Châteauneuf-du-Pape, tel. 04.90.83.58.35, fax 04.90.83.77.23, e-mail informatique@caves.saint-pierre.com
by appt.

DOM. CECILE CHASSAGNE 1998*

■ n.c. n.c. 70–99 F

The colour has purplish tinges that show youth, as do the aromas that reveal influences from a spell in new oak. But the powerful red berry and blackcurrant fruits soon take over. Lovely tannins will attract those consumers who enjoy well-structured wines. Drink in a year or two.

Dom. Cécile Chassagne, rte de Vaison, 84110 Sablet, tel. 04.90.46.85.33, fax 04.90.46.85.33

CLOS DU BOIS DE MENGE 1999

■ 15 ha 80,000 30–49 F

A clear-cut colour and a bouquet of red berry fruit are supported by a well-made structure. Certainly, this wine is guilty of the sin of youth, but, after a suitable maturation period, it will become expressive in the nicest possible way.

La Compagnie Rhodanienne, chem. Neuf, 30210 Castillon-du-Gard, tel. 04.66.37.49.50, fax 04.66.37.49.51
by appt.

CLOS DU JONCUAS 1998*

■ 11 ha n.c. 70–99 F

Everything proceeds with perfect style: the fine nose is complex with bay leaf, red berry fruit, blackberry, liquorice and cocoa; a very noble and developed palate shows richness and balance with well-integrated, but noticeable tannins that will guarantee it a good future. A real Gigondas. We note that this estate farms organically.

Fernand Chastan, Clos du Joncuas, 84190 Gigondas, tel. 04.90.65.86.86, fax 04.90.65.83.68, e-mail closjoncuas@cavesparticulieres.com V
by appt.

DOM. DES ESPIERS

Cuvée Tradition 1998*

■ 2.2 ha 11,000 50–69 F

Philippe Cartoux bought his vines in 1989 to establish his estate. The result? This Cuvée

Tradition, in which young red berry fruit is allied with persistent spicy aromas. The jury waxed lyrical about it but was also unanimous. Intense and tannic, yet the wine is also full-bodied. This inspired lengthy discussions, and that's what tastings are all about.
🔑 Philippe Cartoux, Dom. des Espiers, 84190 Vacqueyras, tel. 04.90.65.81.16, fax 04.90.65.81.16 🅥 Y ev. day except Sun. 8am–12 noon 2pm–6pm

DOM. DE FONT-SANE 1998**

■ 10 ha 40,000 ⅢⅢ 50–69 F

Although this estate is run by women, there's nothing 'feminine' about this wine, for finesse and elegance are not the sole preserve of the fairer sex. This Gigondas can cope with the strongest food, especially game. The floral, then more classic spicy nose is complex, as is the superb palate. The excellent quality of the tightly knit tannins takes nothing away from the power that is the essence of this wine.
🔑 Gilbert Peysson et Fille, EARL Dom. de Font-Sane, 84190 Gigondas, tel. 04.90.65.86.36, fax 04.90.65.81.71 🅥 Y by appt.

DOM. GONDRAN 1998

■ 1.4 ha 7,500 ▮ 50–69 F

Spices and roasted aromas mix attractively with dark fruits, especially blueberry and blackberry. Lightness is skilfully linked with opulence, making for an immediate balance.
🔑 Cellier de l'Enclave des Papes, rte d'Orange, 84600 Valréas, tel. 04.90.41.91.42, fax 04.90.41.90.21

DOM. DU GRAND MONTMIRAIL

Le Coteau de Mon Reve 1998**

■ 5 ha 20,000 ▮ 🌡 50–69 F

This was built to last and so to prolong the 'Reverie'. Although in the minority, the Syrah dominates the flavours at present, but with a couple of years of ageing the overall effect will soften, and then you will own a remarkable Gigondas. The intense purplish colour proclaims the powerful structure of this classic wine.
🔑 Dom. du Grand-Montmirail, ferme du Grand-Montmirail, 84190 Gigondas, tel. 04.90.65.00.22 🅥 Y by appt.

DOM. GRAND ROMANE

Sélection de Vieilles Vignes Elevé en Fût de Chêne 1998***

■ 40 ha 40,000 ⅢⅢ 50–69 F

This estate was restructured when the current owner inherited it: he replanted the vines following the contour lines of the hillsides. The vines are 40 years old and grow on a superb clay-limestone soil. What beauty there is in contrast: despite being dark and mature, there are yellow tinges in the colour. The nose shows a youthful fruity character but the wine is robust at the same time. Powerful yet elegant, there is an exceptional synergy between the wine and the oak (both small barrels and large casks) in which the Mourvèdre plays a significant part. While you wait four or five

years, try the oak-aged **Les Espalines 98 Vieilles Vignes, Elevé en Fût**. A Grenache-Syrah blend, in which simplicity equals success, it wins a mention.
🔑 SCEA de Gigondas, Dom. Grand-Romane, 84190 Gigondas, tel. 04.90.65.85.90, fax 04.90.65.82.14, e-mail grand.romane@pierre-amadieu.com 🅥 Y by appt.
🔑 Claude Amadieu

DOM. DU GRAPILLON D'OR

1998*

■ 14 ha 48,000 ▮ ⅢⅢ 50–69 F

Established in 1890, this estate amounts to 28 ha (69 acres) and has submitted a very promising wine from nicely ripened and well-handled fruit. The nose is still somewhat closed. Although at present the notes are gamey and fruity, maturation will reveal other nuances. Attractive notes of truffle appear on a full palate, indicating a good ageing potential. An undeniable success for this family estate.
🔑 Bernard Chauvet, Le Péage, 84190 Gigondas, tel. 04.90.65.86.37, fax 04.90.65.82.99 🅥 Y ev. day except Sun. 9am–12 noon 1.30pm–6pm

DOM. LA BOUSCATIERE 1998**

■ 7 ha 32,000 ⅢⅢ 50–69 F

One guesses at a nascent complexity in the bouquet of red berry fruit, spices and gamey notes. This 98 wine is clearly not ready, and yet it has both great richness and superbly integrated tannins. This most attractive wine, very much in the tradition of great Gigondas, provides an extremely enjoyable palate, part peppery, part gamey.
🔑 Saurel-Chauvet, Dom. la Bouscatière, 84190 Gigondas, tel. 04.90.70.96.80, fax 04.90.70.96.80 🅥 Y by appt.

DOM. DE LA MAVETTE

Cuvée Prestige 1996*

■ 6 ha 4,000 ⅢⅢ 70–99 F

A century spent on these lands has allowed the Lambert family to acquire real savoir-faire. The imprint of time has stamped an expressive face onto this wine and given it a leathery character. Lovely, spicy flavours are revealed on the palate, accompanied by a note of minerals. The silky tannins appear to best effect.

🔑 EARL Lambert et Fils, Dom. de la Mavette, 84190 Gigondas, tel. 04.90.65.85.29, fax 04.90.65.87.41 ☑
Y ev. day 9am–12 noon 2pm–6pm

LAURUS 1998★★

■ 6.5 ha 20,000 ▮ ⊕ ♨ 70–99 F

An impressive number of wines was selected from those submitted by Gabriel Meffre. The accolade goes to the Laurus. It needs time for the oak to integrate, but a lovely sweetness is already developing. Just as good is the **Domaine de la Chapelle 98**, which at present has a more balanced style. Also worth noting is **La Font Boissière 98**, powerful and full-bodied with a good structure, it earns a star.

🔑 Gabriel Meffre, Le Village, 84190 Gigondas, tel. 04.90.12.32.42, fax 04.90.12.32.49, e-mail gabriel-meffre@meffre.com

L'ECHANDOLE 1998

■ n.c. 35,000 ▮ 50–69 F

Established in 1840, this firm of merchants is run by the d'Avout family. A typical Gigondas, spices dominate the flavours, from the first sniff to the finish. Add to that some notes of dried fruit, smoke and leather, and you have a bouquet that is already excellent. The palate is lighter, which makes it possible to serve this wine right away.

🔑 Caves Salavert, rte de Saint-Montan, 07700 Bourg-Saint-Andéol, tel. 04.75.54.77.22, fax 04.75.54.47.91, e-mail caves.salavert@wanadoo.fr

DOM. LE CLOS DES CAZAUX

Cuvée de la Tour Sarrazine 1997★★

■ 15 ha 30,000 ▮ 50–69 F

Undoubtedly it is the high proportion of Mourvèdre that accounts for the very specific smell of smoke on the nose, together with the spices and stewed fruit that are more usual in this appellation. The aromas have a good persistence. The wine has the body of an athlete, and yet it has a suave attractiveness. A good performance in this vintage. Drink it ideally with game, truffles and other regional produce.

🔑 EARL Archimbaud-Vache, Dom. le Clos des Cazaux, 84190 Vacqueyras, tel. 04.90.65.85.83, fax 04.90.65.83.94 ☑
Y ev. day except Sat. Sun. 9am–11am 2pm–6pm
🔑 Maurice Vache

LE DEDUIT DES CHASSES

Grande Réserve 1998

■ 7 ha 30,000 ⊕ 50–69 F

A label reserved for *chasseurs* (hunters). But there is absolutely no 'reserve' in the rich flavours of this wine: spices, coffee, truffles, leather and prunes. Attractive on the palate, a classic Gigondas that should be kept for a year or two.

🔑 Cave des Vignerons de Gigondas, rte de Sablet, 84190 Gigondas, tel. 04.90.65.86.27, fax 04.90.65.80.13, e-mail gigondas.lacave@wanadoo.fr ☑
Y by appt.

LE GRAND MONTMIRAIL 1998★★

■ 12 ha 35,000 ▮ ⊕ ♨ 50–69 F

It labels itself 'grand' and the tasting endorses it: both grand and attractive. The red berry fruit is enhanced by delicate oak flavours. The fullness and structure make a wine designed to age. Weight and velvet go hand in hand. Mentioned by the jury, the **Hauts de Montmirail 98** exudes spicier scents of pepper. A less immediately attractive style, but given time connoisseurs will recognise its qualities (100–149 F).

🔑 SA Dom. Brusset, 84290 Cairanne, tel. 04.90.30.82.16, fax 04.90.30.73.31, e-mail domaine-brusset.fr ☑ Y by appt.

LES CHERS 1998★

■ n.c. 6,000 ▮ 70–99 F

A small and meticulous production which displays attractive aromas of blackcurrant and blueberry fruit, with spices and even a hint of minerals. A good balance based upon powerful and silky tannins, with the same persistent flavours detected earlier on the nose. A certain elegance.

🔑 SA AVF, Les Chers, 69840 Juliénas, tel. 04.74.06.78.00, fax 04.71.06.78.01
Y by appt.

DOM. LES TEYSSONNIERES 1998

■ 9 ha 40,000 ▮ ⊕ ♨ 50–69 F

The spicy aromas accompanied by charred and balsamic notes made this wine stand out. The finesse on the palate endorses that this is a wine to drink immediately. The intense red colour is delightful, and the palate gives a silky impression. Recommended to drink with a roast.

🔑 EARL Franck Alexandre, Dom. les Teyssonnières, 84190 Gigondas, tel. 04.90.12.31.31, fax 04.90.12.31.32 ☑
Y by appt.

CH. DE MONTMIRAIL

Cuvée de Beauchamp 1998★

■ 27 ha 100,000 ▮ ♨ 50–69 F

A family concern that has once again proved its skills. This particularly expressive wine has a nose of great finesse, mixing notes of fruit and aniseed with bay leaf and leather. To complete the picture there is a good attack on the palate and structure to last.

🔑 Archimbaud-Bouteiller, cours Stassart, B.P. 12, 84190 Vacqueyras, tel. 04.90.65.86.72, fax 04.90.65.81.31 ☑
Y ev. day except Sun. 9am–12 noon 2pm–6.30pm

MOULIN DE LA GARDETTE

Cuvée Tradition 1998★

■ 5 ha 20,000 ▮ ⊕ 50–69 F

Fresh aromas of aniseed with red berry fruits at the back recur on the palate with the

unusual addition of rosewood. Concentration and elegance vie for the attention of the taster. Leave this Cuvée Tradition for another three or four years. While you wait, try the **Cuvée Ventabren 97**, which tends more towards morello cherry and spices. It also receives a star (70–99 F).
🗝 Jean-Baptiste Meunier, moulin de la Gardette, pl. de la Mairie, 84190 Gigondas, tel. 04.90.65.81.51, fax 04.90.65.86.80 ☑
Ῑ by appt.

DOM. NOTRE-DAME-DES-PALLIERES

Cuvée bois neuf 1998★★

■ 0.5 ha 1,200 70–99 F

An oratory here was visited in times of great plagues during the Middle Ages. This is an excellent and unusual wine best enjoyed by lovers of oak. The admirable power relies on fine tannins that are already very integrated. The **99 Rosé**, for immediate drinking, shows intense red berry fruit on the nose. A very well-made wine with nice balance, it is warming, round and fleshy, with sufficient acidity. This blend has a high proportion of Cinsault and Mourvèdre, a guarantee of enjoyment (50–69 F).
🗝 GAEC Dom. de Notre-Dame-des-Pallières, rte de Lencieux, 84190 Gigondas, tel. 04.90.65.83.03, fax 04.90.65.83.03 ☑
Ῑ by appt.
🗝 Jean-Pierre et Claude Roux

DOM. PAILLERE ET PIED GU

1998★

■ n.c. 26,000 50–69 F

Distributed by the Mousset firm, this estate has made a Gigondas that deserves four or five years of patient waiting to allow time for the fruity, spicy bouquet to really open up and to reach its peak. The powerful and warm palate is already balanced. Lovely residual notes of leather and the garrigue add to its great qualities.
🗝 SA Louis Mousset, Les Fines-Roches, 84230 Châteauneuf-du-Pape, tel. 04.90.83.59.37, fax 04.90.83.74.79

DOM. DU PARANDOU 1998★

■ 2 ha 8,000 50–69 F

The Grenache vines that make up 80% of the blend are 40 years old, while the Syrah vines are just eight years old. The density of the colour gives an advance indication that there is a wild side to this wine: first some meaty notes on the nose then spice, and finally some leather. Throughout the tasting there is a pleasant sensation of roundness. Better to age this wine for some time, although it is already very characteristic.
🗝 Dom. du Parandou, 84110 Sablet, tel. 04.90.46.90.52, fax 04.90.46.99.05 ☑
Ῑ by appt.

DOM. DU PESQUIER 1997

■ 16 ha 40,000 50–69 F

The pretty intense ruby colour augurs well. Complexity and personality characterise the nose with powerful, expressive gamey and spicy notes. These flavours are joined on the palate by hints of smoke and crystallised fruits with a long finish. Recommended with jugged hare.
🗝 Boutière et Fils, Dom. du Pesquier, 84190 Gigondas, tel. 04.90.65.86.16, fax 04.90.65.88.48 ☑ Ῑ by appt.

DOM. DU PRADAS 1998★★

■ n.c. n.c. 30–49 F

The main characteristic of this wine is the nice combination of concentrated weight and roundness. Twinned fruit and flower flavours persist through to a long finish worthy of the 'greats'. Drinkable now with a rabbit and mushroom stew; however, it will gain in complexity within a year or two.
🗝 Dom. du Pradas, 84190 Gigondas, tel. 04.90.62.94.28 ☑ Ῑ by appt.
🗝 Cottet

CH. RASPAIL 1998

■ 42 ha 80,000 50–69 F

Eugène Raspail discovered a Greek statue in Vaison-la-Romaine, sold it to the British Museum . . . and used the money to build Château Raspail in 1866. This historical estate belongs today to Christian Meffre. The wine already has an appealing bouquet of red berry fruit, liquorice and spices. However, it has not yet reached its peak. The slightly tight structure will mature to create a finer and more agreeable palate that will be ideal with red meat or game.
🗝 Christian Meffre, Ch. Raspail, 84190 Gigondas, tel. 04.90.65.88.93, fax 04.90.65.88.96, e-mail château.raspail@wanadoo.fr ☑
Ῑ ev. day except Sat. Sun. 8am–12.30pm 1.30pm–5.30pm

CH. REDORTIER 1998★★

■ 5 ha 20,000 50–69 F

This old fortified castle was destroyed in the 18th century and replaced by a country house in a lovely setting. It was an agronomist, Etienne de Menthon, who reconstructed the vineyard. Although the blending and wine-making are very traditional, this wine rises above the commonplace with its outstanding class and very fine tannins. The complex nose reveals a delicate note of truffle and the palate is rich, long lasting and very balanced. Added to this, there is a real feeling of warmth. Serve with jugged wild boar.
🗝 EARL Ch. Redortier, 84190 Suzette, tel. 04.90.62.96.43, fax 04.90.65.03.38 ☑
Ῑ ev. day 10am–12 noon 2pm–7pm
🗝 Etienne de Menthon

DOM. SAINT-DAMIEN 1998

■ 12 ha 6,000 30–49 F

Unusual notes of menthol lead on to ripe fruits. Although quite supple, the overall make-up of this wine demonstrates obvious Gigondas characteristics. Ready now.
🗝 SCEA Joël Saurel, Dom. Saint-Damien, 84190 Gigondas, tel. 04.90.70.96.42, fax 04.90.70.96.42 ☑ Ῑ by appt.

DOM. SAINT-GAYAN 1998*

■ 16 ha 70,000 50–69 F

An attractive combination of red berry fruit and spices from the garrigue is revealed on the delicate nose. The powerful and fleshy body makes this Gigondas assertive though approachable at the same time. On the palate, there is a silky feeling right through to the very long finish. Lovers of more oaky wines will certainly prefer the **Fontmaria 98**, which was equally well received (100–149 F).

EARL Jean-Pierre et Martine Meffre, Dom. Saint-Gayan, 84190 Gigondas, tel. 04.90.65.86.33, fax 04.90.65.85.10 ev. day except Sun. 9am–11.45 2pm–6.30pm

DOM. DU TERME 1999

n.c. 3,000 50–69 F

This estate owns a cellar set into the ramparts of the village, where one can not only taste the wines but also visit a small museum of wine-grower's tools. As for this lively pale-coloured 99, the first impression is of its powerful red berry fruit flavours. It has a particularly good balance of alcohol and acidity. Close to the quality of the most impressive wines of the area, this will soon find buyers queuing up for it.

Rolland Gaudin, Dom. du Terme, 84190 Gigondas, tel. 04.90.65.86.75, fax 04.90.65.80.29 by appt.

DOM. DES TOURELLES 1998*

■ n.c. n.c. 50–69 F

Formerly a fortified monastery, whose earliest buildings date from the 17th century, this estate has retained its fine appearance. The altogether balanced 98 lacks any rough edges that might disturb the freshness of the supple string of flavours. A very characteristic Gigondas, which could partner cheese or game according to the occasion.

Roger Cuillerat, Dom. des Tourelles, 84190 Gigondas, tel. 04.90.65.86.98, fax 04.90.65.89.47 by appt.

DOM. VARENNE 1998

■ 5 ha 18,000 50–69 F

Although both the wine-making and blend are entirely 'classical', the intensity on the nose is less so: there is a bouquet of thyme and juniper from the garrigue and of liquorice with fruit and a touch of oak. Straightforward and pleasant on the palate due to the lovely tannins, this wine still has a good future ahead.

Dom. Alain Varenne et Fils, Le Village, 84190 Gigondas, tel. 04.90.65.86.55, fax 04.90.12.39.28 ev. day 10am–12 noon 2pm–6pm

Vacqueyras

The Appellation d'Origine Contrôlée Vacqueyras, made according to conditions of production defined in the decree of 9 August 1990, is the 13th and most recent of the local AOCs of the Côtes du Rhône.

It competes with Gigondas and Châteauneuf-du-Pape in the hierarchy of the Vaucluse department. Lying between Gigondas to the north and Beaumes-de-Venise to the south-east, the territory it covers stretches over the two communes of Vacqueyras and Sarrians. The 1,220 ha (3,013 acres) of vines produced a little more than 46,00 hl (1,214,400 gal) in 1999.

Twenty-three bottlers, a Cave Coopérative and three merchant growers sell 1.5 million bottles of Vacqueyras annually.

The red wines (95% of production), made mainly from Grenache, Syrah, Mourvèdre and Cinsault, are capable of ageing (three to ten years). The rosés (4% of production) are from the same varieties. The whites remain less well known (varieties: Clairette, Grenache Blanc, Bourboulenc, Rousanne).

BOISERAIE 1998**

■ 6 ha 24,000 50–69 F

The colour and nose are correct, but it was the palate that attracted the attention of the jury. Rounded on the middle, a slight oak character appears after some aeration. This attractive wine proves itself to be a characteristic and traditional Vacqueyras.

Ogier-Caves des Papes, 10, bd Pasteur, 84230 Châteauneuf-du-Pape, tel. 04.90.39.32.32, fax 04.90.83.72.51 ev. day except Sun. 8.30am–6.30pm

DOM. CHAMFORT 1998

■ 9.5 ha 40,000 50–69 F

The definitive 'wine for ageing', it needs keeping for about five to seven years. Development will improve it. Complexity and some balanced already exist on the nose together with spices and oak, and these bode well for the future. Don't be put off by the aggressiveness of the tannins at present: the Mourvèdre (20%) will develop. Once the tannins have softened, this will be a true traditional Vacqueyras.

Denis Chamfort, La Pause, 84110 Sablet, tel. 04.90.46.94.75, fax 04.90.46.99.84, e-mail denis.chamfort@wanadoo.fr
by appt.

LA BASTIDE SAINT-VINCENT

1998*

5 ha 12,500 30–49 F

With innumerable delightful villages and impressive landscapes, this region not only attracts tourists from all over the world, but also many lovers of fine wines who come for the excellent vineyards. Guy Daniel is one of those wine-producers that you cannot ignore. Take this wine, for example: its nose seems attractive and ready with notes of red berry fruit. More fruit appears on the palate, but this time it's crystallised or macerated in kirsch, to just the right amount. Do not delay in tasting this already enjoyable 98: make the most of its freshness and vitality.

Guy Daniel, Bastide Sat-Vincent, rte de Vaison-la-Romaine, 84150 Violès, tel. 04.90.70.94.13, fax 04.90.70.96.13
ev. day 8am–7pm; Sun. by appt.; cl. 1–20 Jan.

DOM. DE LA CHARBONNIERE

1998**

4.3 ha 20,000 50–69 F

'Superb', 'fantastic', the jury waxed lyrical about this wine. The complexity on the nose is seductive. There is both balance and finesse on the palate, combined with body, length and an amazing amount of liveliness. Like all great wines, you could enjoy it now, but then you would deprive yourself of all the new flavours that will surely develop once the wine has aged.

Michel Maret, Dom. de la Charbonnière, 84230 Châteauneuf-du-Pape, tel. 04.90.83.74.59, fax 04.90.83.53.46
by appt.

LA FONT DE PAPIER 1998**

5 ha n.c. 50–69 F

A proponent of organic cultivation and a most successful producer, Fernand Chastan has submitted a remarkable Vacqueyras. The floral nose with crushed fruit and leather together with complexity on the palate give great pleasure. Well-made, with plenty of weight, the wine is balanced and satisfying. Ready now, but could be kept longer.

Fernand Chastan, Clos du Joncuas, 84190 Gigondas, tel. 04.90.65.86.86, fax 04.90.65.83.68, e-mail closjoncuas@cavesparticulieres.com
by appt.

DOM. LA FOURMONE

Sélection Maître de Chais 1998*

7 ha 18,000 50–69 F

This region, which is rich in festivals, of both theatre (Avignon) and music (Orange, Aix or even Vaison-la-Romaine), delights the eye with its architecture and landscapes. The wine is part of its charm. A lovely and very fine nose made the tasters' mouths water. Balance and richness come together here. This Sélection Maître de Chais undeniably has the structure of a very attractive Vacqueyras. Wait two to three years before drinking it with roast beef.

Roger Combe et Filles, Dom. la Fourmone, rte de Bollène, 84190 Vacqueyras, tel. 04.90.65.86.05, fax 04.90.65.87.84 ev. day 9.30am–12 noon 2pm–6pm; cl. Feb.

DOM. DES LAMBERTINS 1998*

14 ha 50,000 30–49 F

The 35-year-old vines and six months' maturation in large oak vats have produced a wine whose nose, already open, reveals notes of red berry fruit with tones of morello cherry. To appreciate fully, it would be preferable to wait a little longer for the few blunt edges to soften so that the wine will be ready to partner some good game dishes.

EARL Dom. des Lambertins, La Grande Fontaine, 84190 Vacqueyras, tel. 04.90.65.85.54, fax 04.90.65.83.38
ev. day except Sun. 9am–6.30pm; groups by appt.
Gilles Lambert

DOM. LA MONARDIERE

Cuvée Les Calades 1998**

2 ha 8,000 30–49 F

Purchased in the last century by the Vache family, this estate now amounts to 20 ha (49 acres). The venerable age of the vines accounts in part for the success of the three wines selected. The skills of the wine-maker also make an important contribution. The Cuvée des Calades, very obviously dominated by Grenache, carried off the *coup de cœur*. The terroir character and the development are just right and the nose is very gamey and wild. The texture, richness, perfect structure, harmony and balance are all in place. The **Cuvée Vieilles Vignes 98** (50–69 F) with its silky tannins receives one star. The **Deux Monardes 98** was awarded the same marks. Both have a superb future.

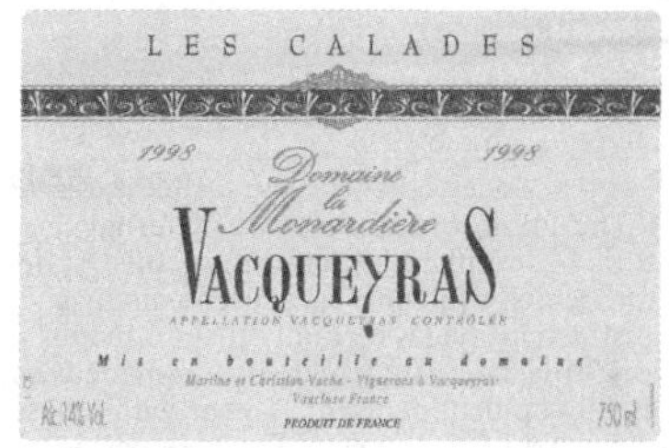

Dom. La Monardière, Les Grès, 84190 Vacqueyras, tel. 04.90.65.87.20, fax 04.90.65.82.01, e-mail monardiere@wanadoo.fr
ev. day except Sun. 10am–7pm
C. Vache

DOM. DE LA TOURADE 1998

6 ha 13,000 30–49 F

Already fit to serve, to judge by this wine's very open bouquet. The palate is altogether fine with a correct structure and an attractive roundness. Note the lovely flavours of crystallised fruit.

EARL André Richard, Dom. de la Tourade, 84190 Gigondas, tel. 04.90.70.91.09, fax 04.90.70.96.31
ev. day 9am–7pm

DOM. LE CLOS DE CAVEAU 1998★

11.8 ha 30,000 30–49 F

What strange alchemy is taking place behind the walls of this Clos? Concentrated macerated fruit is mixed with gamey notes and, more unexpectedly, honey and hazelnuts. Bound by a state of mind, this estate practices organic cultivation and creates a particularly successful alliance between tradition and innovation (both *pigeage* and *délestage* to extract colour and flavour from the skins). Density, roundness and power join together with superb balance.

SCA Dom. le Clos de Caveau, 84190 Vacqueyras, tel. 04.90.65.85.33, fax 04.90.65.83.17 by appt.
H. Bungener

DOM LE CLOS DES CAZAUX

Réserve 1998★★

4 ha 15,000 30–49 F

This successful family estate exports 65% of its production. This Réserve – the yellow label – is remarkable and will live up to the fine reputation of its producers. There is a very open and fine nose of morello cherry. The powerful structure is pleasantly rounded. This is a model Vacqueyras that would benefit from three to four years of ageing before it will express its full potential. The yellow-label **Cuvée Principale 98 Blanc** wins a star. Matured in barrel, it is a blend of Clairette, Grenache Blanc and 25% Roussanne and is both lively and rounded (70–99 F).

EARL Archimbaud-Vache, Dom. le Clos des Cazaux, 84190 Vacqueyras, tel. 04.90.65.85.83, fax 04.90.65.83.94
ev. day except Sat. Sun. 9am–11am 2pm–6pm

DOM. LE COUROULU

Cuvée Classique 1998★

10 ha 40,000 30–49 F

The linking of paternal with maternal vineyards has resulted in the birth of this estate, from which two wines have been equally successful. This one is certainly the product of a very ripe harvest, which has provided an already opulent depth of flavour with a base of ripe fruits and violets. The long period of post-fermentation maceration leaves no margin for error; the raw material must be top quality. A full body and balance confirm this wine's richness. Equally noteworthy is the **Vieilles Vignes 98** (50–69 F) which gains a star and should be laid down for three years.

Guy Ricard, Dom. le Couroulou, 84190 Vacqueyras, tel. 04.90.65.84.83, fax 04.90.65.81.25
ev. day except Sun. 9.30am–12 noon 2pm–6pm

DOM. LE PONT DU RIEU 1998★★

4.5 ha 22,100 30–49 F

A small stream straddled by the Rieu bridge has given its name to the estate, whose wines are distributed by Gabriel Meffre. This is one of the finest representatives of the appellation. Evocative smells conjure up spices and the garrigue. Power and elegance go hand in hand and it shows excellent length on the palate. Mediterranean food would do it justice.

Jean-Pierre Faraud, 84190 Vacqueyras, tel. 04.90.12.32.42, fax 04.90.12.32.49

LES MAGNANS 1998★

12 ha 20,000 50–69 F

Spices and red berry fruits dominate in this Les Magnans from the cooperative of Valréas. A particularly well-balanced palate follows the classic nose. The tannins are pronounced but well integrated, as are the long lasting flavours. This 98 has not yet entirely shown its hand. Also distributed by the same co-operative, the fruity **Domaine de La Cyprière 98** (30–49 F) won a mention. This wine could serve as a good introduction to the Vacqueyras AOC.

Cellier de l'Enclave des Papes, rte d'Orange, 84600 Valréas, tel. 04.90.41.91.42, fax 04.90.41.90.21

DOM. MAS DU SUD 1998★

5 ha 25,000 30–49 F

The very great care taken with the selection of the grapes for the **Laurus 98** (70–99 F) has paid dividends. The new oak and vanilla flavours are still a little over-bearing, but one can guess that underneath the soft tannins is an overall balance that is close to being superb. A more traditional wine, this Domaine Mas du Sud shows a side of the AOC that is full of warmth and, on tasting, provides really nice notes of ripe fruit.

Gabriel Meffre, Le Village, 84190 Gigondas, tel. 04.90.12.32.42, fax 04.90.12.32.49, e-mail gabriel-meffre@meffre.com

CLOS MONTIRIUS 1998★★

8.5 ha 45,000 70–99 F

The name Montirius comes from the erudite contraction of the first names of the three children of the Saurels who, since 1996, have been applying biodynamic methods to the work in their vineyards and winery. It has worked well for this 98 vintage. Two wines have been awarded two stars each. A slight preference was expressed for this wine that

showed a greater influence from Syrah, and which will keep very well: gamey, complex, blessed with excellent weight, ample body and good length. In the meantime, one can enjoy the more floral though equally gamey nose of the **Montirius 98** (50–69 F) that is more influenced by Grenache. It has notable balance and attractive flavours on the finish.
⚷ Christine et Eric Saurel,
Le Deves, 84260 Sarrians,
tel. 04.90.65.38.28, fax 04.90.65.38.28,
e-mail montirius@wanadoo.fr ☑
Y by appt.

CH. DE MONTMIRAIL

Cuvée de l'Ermite 1998★

■ 17 ha 9,000 ▮ ♁ 50-69 F

Maurice Archimbaud and his daughter Monique are perpetuating a very long wine-making tradition on this 50-ha (124-acre) estate. Equal amounts of Syrah and Grenache provide a wine that is powerful, enigmatic and built to last, but you will require patience to appreciate it fully. The nose is fine and complex, combining notes of game and leather in particular – or according to other tasters, spices and liquorice. Scarcity is often synonymous with exceptional quality: the weight of this wine is truly remarkable. The **Cuvée des Deux Frères 98** (30–49 F), made from four varieties but predominantly Grenache (70%), won a mention. It expresses all the power of the terroir and is ready to serve now with red meat.
⚷ Archimbaud-Bouteiller, cours Stassart, B.P. 12, 84190 Vacqueyras,
tel. 04.90.65.86.72, fax 04.90.65.81.31 ☑
Y ev. day except Sun. 9am–12 noon 2pm–6.30pm

DOM. DE MONTVAC 1999

□ 0.7 ha 3,000 ▮▮ 50-69 F

Very expressive on the nose where gamey notes mix with flint, the **98 Rouge**, which won a mention, needs to be left for three to four years. In the meantime, you could try this attractive white wine, slightly oaky and with scents of honey. It is balanced and fresh, and could be drunk with fish in sauce.
⚷ Cécile Dusserre, Dom. de Montvac, 84190 Vacqueyras, tel. 04.90.65.85.51,
fax 04.90.65.82.38 ☑ Y by appt.

PASCAL 1998★★

■ 15 ha 70,000 ▮ ♁ 30-49 F

A wine merchant and producer from Vacqueyras, the firm of Pascal excels in making wines that are real standard-bearers. This wine reveals rich aromas, of course, but also the finesse and elegance found only in the best. It already seems ready to accompany duck, guinea fowl or other game bird. However, the depth of flavours, length and structure suggest that it will taste even better in one or two years' time.
⚷ Pascal, rte de Gigondas, 84190 Vacqueyras, tel. 04.90.65.85.91,
fax 04.90.65.89.23 ☑ Y by appt.

CH. DES ROQUES 1998

■ 24 ha 70,000 ▮ ♁ 30-49 F

This clean-cut and balanced Vacqueyras is a classic of its type. The fine and fruity nose mixes fruit kernel notes with other more gamey ones. The expression of the body, already very enjoyable, is entirely in balance.
⚷ SCEA Ch. des Roques, B.P. 9, 84190 Vacqueyras, tel. 04.90.65.85.16,
fax 04.90.65.88.18 ☑ Y by appt.
⚷ Seroul

VIEUX CLOCHER

Vieilli en Fût de Chêne 1998★

■ n.c. 65,000 ▮ ♁ 30-49 F

Jean-Marie Arnoux together with sons Jean-François and Marc run the company that sells this wine. Red berries and ripe fruits: as much fruit as you like, both on the nose and the palate. The classic Grenache-Syrah blend expresses itself well, and intense warmth pervades this well-crafted and constructed wine.
⚷ Arnoux et Fils, Portail Neuf, 84190 Vacqueyras, tel. 04.90.65.84.18,
fax 04.90.65.80.07 ☑ Y ev. day except Sun. 8am–12 noon 2pm–6pm

Châteauneuf-du-Pape

This appellation, which was the first legally to define its conditions of production in 1931, covers nearly the whole commune from which it derives its name, together with similar terroirs in the neighbouring communes of Orange, Courthézon, Bédarrides and Sorgues, 3,084 ha (7,617 acres). The vineyard is located on the left bank of the Rhône, 15 km (9 miles) north of Avignon. The unique character of its wines comes from a terroir largely composed of vast terraces at different heights, covered with layers of pebbly red clay. The vine varieties are very varied with a predominance of Grenache, Syrah, Mourvèdre and Cinsault. The yield is not greater than 35 hl/ha (378 gal per acre).

The Châteauneuf-du-Pape wines are noted for their intense colour and good keeping qualities, although the time they can be kept varies with the vintage. They are expansive, well-structured, full-bodied wines with a strong, complex bouquet, excellent companions to red meat, game and fermented cheeses. The whites, produced in small quantities, counterbalance their strength with flavour and the finesse of their aromas. The appellation's total annual production is near to 105,000 hl (2,772,000 gal).

ANCIEN DOMAINE DES PONTIFES 1999★

□ 0.3 ha 1,000 70–99 F

This 'ancient' estate was founded at the beginning of the 20th century. The wine is invigorating and does not take itself too seriously. It has a very powerful nose given over to exotic smells of grapefruit and passion fruit. The palate is unusual in that it combines fruit and menthol flavours. Drink it with shellfish or as an apéritif.

Françoise Granier, 13, rue de l'Escatillon, 30150 Roquemaure,
tel. 04.66.82.56.73, fax 04.66.90.23.90
by appt.

DOM. PAUL AUTARD 1998★★

□ 12 ha n.c. 100–149 F

A long family tradition is always an advantage in managing a vineyard: passing on the experiences of successive vintages where each one never resembles the one before. That surely must be one of the secrets of success of Jean-Paul Autard, all three of whose submissions were selected by our demanding tasters. This white 98 is a blend of Grenache Blanc, Clairette and Roussanne half vinified in new barrels. The intense golden colour cloaks an exuberant nose of fruit and thyme. The palate opens cleanly, showing well-integrated oak. There is much finesse in this wine, but it needs two more years of ageing. 'With a *poularde en demi-deuil* (fatted chicken)' was the recommendation of one taster. The **Cuvée Principale 98 Rouge** won a mention (70–99 F), whereas the **Cuvée La Côte Ronde 98** (150–199 F) won a star for the quality of its structure and flavour; the oak still needs time to integrate.

Dom. Paul Autard,
rte de Châteauneuf-du-Pape,
84350 Courthézon,
tel. 04.90.70.73.15, fax 04.90.70.29.59
ev. day except Sun. 9am–12.30pm 3pm–6.30pm

DOM. JULIETTE AVRIL 1998★

■ 21 ha n.c. 50–69 F

An ancestor of Juliette Avril was First Consul of Châteauneuf-du-Pape in the time of the Avignon Popes. This 35-ha (86-acre) estate has inherited long-held skills. The white and red 98 did equally well during this tasting. The first (70–99 F), redolent of hawthorn and almond, would go well with freshwater crayfish or white meat. This red is notable for its finesse and the successful integration of oak and wine. Vanilla appears on the palate, supported by a powerful structure. Ideal for roast lamb, it should be drunk within three years.

Dom. Juliette Avril, 8, av. Pasteur,
84230 Châteauneuf-du-Pape,
tel. 04.90.83.72.69, fax 04.90.83.53.08,
e-mail julietteavril@enprovence.com
ev. day 8.30am–7pm; Sun. 10.30am–7pm
GFA du Majoral

DOM. DE BABAN 1998★

■ 9 ha 30,000 70–99 F

Distributed by Gabriel Meffre, this dark wine leads us through the depths of damp, cool undergrowth. The well-balanced and harmonious palate conceals some substantial tannins. Wait at least two years before serving it with strong characterful cheeses.

SCEA Dom. Riche,
84230 Châteauneuf-du-Pape,
tel. 04.90.12.32.42, fax 04.90.12.32.49

DOM. DU BANNERET 1998

■ 1.77 ha 6,000 70–99 F

The orange-tinged colour introduces us to a world that smells sweetly of apple compote, caramel and quince jelly. The palate remains light and well-balanced. Serve it with any red meat within two years.

Jean-Claude Vidal, 35, rue Porte-Rouge,
84230 Châteauneuf-du-Pape,
tel. 04.90.83.72.04, fax 04.62.24.44.09
ev. day 9am–12 noon 3pm–7pm
J.-C. et M.-F. Vidal

LOUIS BERNARD 1998

■ n.c. n.c. 100–149 F

The colour is very deep and somewhat dull. The oaky nose is embellished with notes of black fruits. It is on the palate that the wine's full power is expressed with tannins that still need to soften. Wait at least two years. It will provide an excellent partner to a rich meat stew or strong cheese.

Les Domaines Bernard,
rte de Sérignan, 84100 Orange,
tel. 04.90.11.86.86, fax 04.90.34.87.30

DOM. DE BOIS DAUPHIN 1999★

□ 2 ha 8,000 70–99 F

A lovely balance is revealed in this wine that is still keeping its cards well hidden. An easy-going mid-palate gives way to notes of honey and vanilla. To the great credit of the wine-maker, the oak appears in delicate harmony. Drink it within three years with a fish in sauce.

EARL Jean Marchand, 21, rte d'Orange,
84230 Châteauneuf-du-Pape,
tel. 04.90.83.70.34, fax 04.90.83.50.83,
e-mail jean.marchand4@wanadoo.fr
by appt.

MAS DE BOISLAUZON 1998★

■ 8 ha 15,000 70–99 F

This is a rich and fine wine that needs more time to fill out. You will enjoy its notes of red berry fruit and spices that delicately flavour the palate. You can keep it for at least three years, and use it to accompany any red meat dish.

Monique et Daniel Chaussy, quartier Boislauzon, 84100 Orange,
tel. 04.90.34.46.49, fax 04.90.34.46.61
ev. day except Sun. 10am–12 noon 1pm–6pm; cl. 15–30 Sep.

BOISRENARD 1998★★

■ 2.5 ha 8,000 150–199 F

This de Beaurenard estate, which came into the Coulon family seven generations ago, is one of the most respected in the AOC because it has always paid attention to vineyard management. And we know that without good grapes there is no great wine. Here they had a very good 1998 vintage. The **Cuvée Principale Rouge** was given a star (70–99 F) and inspires complete confidence. This Cuvée Boisrenard, with a sadly limited production (8,000 bottles only) won the plaudits of the jury. The absence of filtration ensures freer play to the flavours of blueberry and chocolate, and provides the palate with an enjoyably long finish. Already drinkable now, it will reach its best in five year' time. Plan to serve it with game or a good piece of red meat. Also noteworthy is the **Domaine de Beaurenard 99 Blanc** (70–99 F). It was awarded a star for the power and elegance of its aromas. Drink as an aperitif before serving the **coup de cœur* at table. **At the time of going to press, regrettably the label was not available for reproduction here.*

SCEA Paul Coulon et Fils, Dom. de Beaurenard, av. Pierre-de-Luxembourg, 84231 Châteauneuf-du-Pape,
tel. 04.90.83.71.79, fax 04.90.83.78.06,
e-mail paul.coulon@beaurenard.fr
ev. day except Sun. 9am–12 noon 1.30pm–5.30pm; groups by appt.

BOSQUET DES PAPES

Cuvée Traditionnelle 1998★

■ 9 ha 40,000 70–99 F

This cellar is situated 300 m (327 yards) from the château, which was built in the Bosquet district that gave the wine its name. Long post-fermentation maceration (three weeks) was followed by 18 months in oak barrels. A single adjective describes it: robust, even though it gives a subtle first impression on the palate. A superb structure is revealed with flavours of good grapes, prunes, spices and *herbes de Provence*, all associated with delicate oak. You can keep it for a good four or five years, then match it to roast beef with thyme.

M. Maurice Boiron, Dom. Bosquet des Papes, rte d'Orange, 84230 Châteauneuf-du-Pape, tel. 04.90.83.72.33, fax 04.90.83.50.52
ev. day except Sun. 9am–12 noon 1.30pm–7.30pm

LAURENT-CHARLES BROTTE

Vieilles Vignes 1998★★

■ 1 ha 4,000 100–149 F

Charity in exchange for a good wine: the **Cuvée des Hospices 99 Rouge** was awarded a star for its subtlety and the excellent marriage of oak and wine; the producers have donated it in aid of the hospice. This other wine, made from old vines – 88 years old, we're told – fully exploits both the quality of the grapes and the skills of the oenologist. The latter has managed to bring out all the wine's potential. Very attractive, rich and balanced, these were the plaudits of the tasters. Absolutely ready now, but will remain at its peak for about another four to five years.

Laurent-Charles Brotte, rte d'Avignon, 84230 Châteauneuf-du-Pape,
tel. 04.90.83.70.07, fax 04.90.83.74.34
ev. day 9am–12 noon 2pm–6pm

CH. CABRIERES 1998

■ 30 ha 60,000 70–99 F

A pretty château that, before producing wine, supplied bread to the surrounding farms in the 14th century. This finely oaked 98 will thrill enthusiasts: vanilla and grilled meat vie for precedence. The length on the palate is played out on unending liquorice. Well-structured and very characteristic, this wine should be drunk over the next three years with a grilled entrecôte, its flavours consistent with the wine's aromas.

SCEA Ch. Cabrières, rte d'Orange, CD 68, 84230 Châteauneuf-du-Pape,
tel. 04.90.83.73.58, fax 04.90.83.75.55
by appt.

DOM. CHANTE CIGALE 1998★★

■ 30 ha 20,000 70–99 F

Put aside your serious side and allow yourself to be seduced by the velvety notes of red berry fruit in this wine. The palate is round and elegant and you will require several glasses before discovering its many facets. After which, you will be singing its praises for at least five years.

Sabon-Favier, av. Louis-Pasteur, 84230 Châteauneuf-du-Pape, tel. 04.90.83.70.57, fax 04.90.83.58.70
ev. day except Sun. 10am–6pm

MAS CHANTE MISTRAL 1998

■ 2 ha 9,000 50–69 F

At present this wine is still in its hot-headed youth, characterised by gamey notes and spices. The pronounced tannins are sustained by heady alcohol. Wait for two or three years before serving it with roast beef.

Mas Chante Mistral, 1880, rte de Caderousse, 84350 Courthezon,
tel. 04.90.70.72.65, fax 04.90.70.78.10
ev. day 9am–12 noon 2pm–6pm
M. et C. Henri

DOM. CHARVIN 1998★

■ 7.5 ha 20,000 70–99 F

An estate of 22 ha (54 acres) established in 1851. The traditional vinification without de-

stalking requires a longer maturation. But enthusiasts who have the patience to wait for at least five years will not be disappointed. This is a rich wine with scents of thyme, blackcurrant and fruit macerated in alcohol. The length on the palate can compete with the best. Drink with a meat casserole.
🔑 EARL Gérard Charvin et Fils, chem. de Maucoil, 84100 Orange, tel. 04.90.34.41.10, fax 04.90.51.65.59 ☑ Ῑ by appt.

DOM. CHEMIN VIEUX 1998*

■ 10.5 ha 35,000 50–69 F

Much enjoyed for its intensity and freshness, this merchant's wine represents good value for money and should be tried without a second thought. Grilled meat would bring the best out of its balance and length. Ready to drink from now.
🔑 Les Grandes Serres, rte de l'Islon, 84230 Châteauneuf-du-Pape, tel. 04.90.83.72.22, fax 04.90.83.78.77 ☑ Ῑ by appt.

CLEFS DES PRELATS 1998*

■ 4 ha 13,000 70–99 F

A merchant's wine which possesses great olfactory finesse while at the same time being quite heady with notes of crystallised fruit. The rough tannins need around three years to soften.
🔑 Sefivin-H. Bouachon, rte de Châteauneuf, 84230 Châteauneuf-du-Pape, tel. 04.90.83.58.35, fax 04.90.83.77.23, e-mail informatique@caves.saint-pierre.com ☑ Ῑ by appt.

CLOS SAINT-MICHEL 1998

■ n.c. 50,000 70–99 F

A very attractive colour accompanies a gamey nose, with notes of leather. The pronounced tannins on the palate need some time to soften. Reckon on five years before drinking this Clos Saint-Michel with a meat casserole.
🔑 EARL Vignobles Guy Mousset et Fils, Le Clos Saint-Michel, rte de Châteauneuf, 84700 Sorgues, tel. 04.90.85.56.05, fax 04.90.83.56.06 ☑ Ῑ by appt.

CH. DES FINES ROCHES 1999*

□ 4.5 ha 18,000 70–99 F

Louis Mousset bought this impressive fortress before the war. A pale gold that will make you turn pale with pleasure, characterises the colour. The nose is fine and elegant with notes of apricot and exotic fruits acquired through a very cool vinification. An impressive presence that makes a perfect accompaniment to grilled fish or goat's cheese.
🔑 SCEA Ch. des Fines Roches, 1, av. du Baron-Leroy, 84230 Châteauneuf-du-Pape, tel. 04.90.83.51.73, fax 04.90.83.52.77 ☑ Ῑ by appt.

DOM. DE FONTAVIN 1998*

■ 3 ha 14,000 50–69 F

Hélène Chouvet has been cellar-master here since 1998. She has made a very successful wine that is approachable, and characterised by its softness. The nose is a complex mixture of fruit, thyme and spices. The palate is warming with tannins that will integrate in the course of time (reckon on at least three years). A fine example to drink with wild boar.
🔑 EARL Hélène et Michel Chouvet, Dom. de Fontavin, 1468, rte de la Plaine, 84350 Courthézon, tel. 04.90.70.72.14, fax 04.90.70.79.39 ☑ Ῑ ev. day except Sun. 9am–12.30pm 1.30pm–7pm

DOM. FONT DE MICHELLE

Cuvée Etienne Gonnet 1998**

■ 4 ha 16,000 150–199 F

'Font' means a spring. Established on a Gallo-Roman site, Font de Michelle dedicates this lovely wine to the memory of the present owners' father. A light oaky touch brings with it notes of leather and chocolate that vie with those of violets. The very obvious tannins on the palate need simply to soften. You will have to wait five years for that to happen before enjoying the power of this great wine. Then, its character would go well with jugged hare. The estate won a star for the **99 Blanc** (70–99 F). Also full of promise, this wine has achieved a perfect balance between freshness and power.
🔑 EARL Les Fils d'Etienne Gonnet, 14, imp. des Vignerons, 84370 Bédarrides, tel. 04.90.33.00.22, fax 04.90.33.20.27, e-mail egonnet@terre-net.fr ☑ Ῑ by appt.

DOM. DU GALET DES PAPES

Tradition 1998**

■ n.c. 20,000 70–99 F

Managed by the Mayard family since the Second Empire, this estate covers 13 ha (32 acres). The colour has already developed thanks to ageing in oak *foudre* (large casks). One discerns notes of fruit, spices and leather along with great delicacy and much elegance on the palate. Serve it now with small game or delicate cheeses. Take note that the **Cuvée Vieilles Vignes 98**, more powerful and with well-integrated tannins, won a star.
🔑 Jean-Luc Mayard, Dom. du Galet des Papes, 15, rte de Bédarrides, 84230 Châteauneuf-du-Pape, tel. 04.90.83.73.67, fax 04.90.83.50.22, e-mail galet.des.papes@terre-net.fr ☑ Ῑ ev. day except Sun. 9am–12 noon 2.30pm–6.30pm

DOM. GRAND VENEUR 1999**

□ 1.9 ha 8,760 70–99 F

Here is the perfect wine for those who wish to become acquainted with the white wines of Châteauneuf-du-Pape. Characteristic of its appellation and very approachable, it has a lovely gold colour with green tinges. The nose is rich with ripe fruit, quince, honey and spices. The palate in turn is filled with powerful flavours retaining perfect balance. Keep it for two years before serving with fish in sauce. The **Cuvée Les Origines 98 Rouge** (100–149 F) was very appealing with attractive fruit that

does not dominate the oak. Winner of a star, it will improve further.
🔑 EARL Alain Jaume,
Dom. Grand Veneur,
rte de Châteauneuf-du-Pape, 84100 Orange,
tel. 04.90.34.68.70, fax 04.90.34.43.71 V
Y ev. day 8am–12.30pm 1.30pm–6.30pm

LA BASTIDE-SAINT-DOMINIQUE

1999★★

□ 1.5 ha 5,000 70–99 F

This estate, bought in 1976 and comprising 25 ha (62 acres) on sand, clay and pebbles, submitted a special red selection called **Secrets de Pignan 98** (100–149 F) that wins a star. It carries us on a beautifully evocative journey through the garrigue with notes of thyme and resin; very well structured and extremely good. This white is rich and powerful with already attractive notes of flowers and grilled almonds. Providing one has the patience to wait, it is destined for a bright future and should be drunk with fish or white meat in around five years' time.
🔑 SCEA Gérard et Marie-Claude Bonnet,
La Bastide-Saint-Dominique, 84350
Courthézon, tel. 04.90.70.85.32,
fax 04.90.70.76.64 V Y ev. day 8am–12 noon 3pm–7pm

DOM. LA BEGUDE DES PAPES

1998

■ 8 ha 30,000 50–69 F

This light-coloured 98 has a delicate, pleasing nose displaying notes of red berry fruit and quince. However, don't jump too quickly to the conclusion that it lacks character. In reality, the palate is full-bodied and warming, almost fiery. Let it calm down for two to three years before trying it with a game bird.
🔑 Alain Jacumin, 9, chem. du Clos,
B.P. 14, 84231 Châteauneuf-du-Pape,
tel. 04.90.83.78.55, fax 04.90.83.78.55 V
Y ev. day except Sat. Sun. 9am–6pm

DOM. DE LA CHARBONNIERE

Les Hautes Brusquières Cuvée Spéciale 1998★

■ 2.5 ha 10,000 100–149 F

A blend of Grenache (60%) and Syrah, this wine was bottled without filtration. Les Hautes Brusquières is really classy. Of intense colour, it reveals elegant and intense scents of almonds and vanilla. Integrated tannins indicate good ageing potential, certainly ten years. For the less patient, note the **Cuvée Principale 98** which is easier and totally enjoyable (70–99 F).
🔑 Michel Maret,
Dom. de la Charbonnière,
84230 Châteauneuf-du-Pape,
tel. 04.90.83.74.59, fax 04.90.83.53.46 V
Y by appt.

CH. DE LA GARDINE 1998★★

■ 48 ha 200,000 100–149 F

Just as famous abroad as in France, La Gardine offers remarkable wines, such as this example. A wine for long ageing, it does need time to improve. The nose, rich in spices, liquorice and violets, will open little by little. Balanced tannins combine with excellent fruit to give a powerful palate. This is a great Châteauneuf that manages to express its exceptional terroir. Wait five years for it. Also noteworthy is the **Cuvée des Générations 98**, just as remarkable, and from older vines; it is also much more expensive (300–499 F).
🔑 Brunel, Ch. de la Gardine,
rte de Roquemaure,
84230 Châteauneuf-du-Pape,
tel. 04.90.83.73.20, fax 04.90.83.77.24,
e-mail brunel@chateau-de-la-gardine.fr V
Y by appt.

DOM. DE LA JANASSE

Vieilles Vignes 1998★★

■ 2 ha 8,000 200–249 F

This wine attains the very summit in every respect. 70% of the harvest de-stemmed, 26 days maceration, maturation of 60% in traditional large casks and 40% in small oak barrels of which half were new. After 12 months in wood, the oak flavour is pronounced, but allows glimpses of spices and the garrigue. The palate is rounded, full-bodied and heady. You should count on at least five years' ageing. This wine will make a perfect partner to game. If you enjoy fatted chicken, the jury recommends the **Cuvée Prestige 98 Blanc**. Also very oaky, but the balanced and deep palate is enchanting. One star for a price that is as high as for the Vieilles Vignes.
🔑 EARL Aimé Sabon,
27, chem. du Moulin, 84350 Courthézon,
tel. 04.90.70.86.29, fax 04.90.70.75.93 V
Y ev. day 8am–12 noon 2pm–7pm; Sat. Sun. by appt.

DOM. DE LA MORDOREE

Cuvée de la Reine des Bois 1998★★

■ 3.5 ha 14,000 150–199 F

An advocate of small yields to extract the quintessence of the terroir, and accustomed to receiving many awards, the *Guide* has placed this estate at the top of the scoreboard. It demonstrates superb handling of both the raw material and the use of oak barrels. The result is a dark purple wine that is full and elegant. Bay leaf, rosemary, marinated meat, red berry fruit and roasted flavours are marvellously combined. The tannic structure is worthy of the vintage. You will need to wait at least four years to be able to savour this greatly enjoyable wine.
🔑 Dom. de la Mordorée,
chem. des Oliviers, 30126 Tavel,
tel. 04.66.50.00.75, fax 04.66.50.47.39 V
Y ev. day except Sun. 8am–12 noon 1.30pm–5.30pm
🔑 Delorme

CH. LA NERTHE 1998★★

■ 70 ha 230,000 100–149 F

Just to see this magnificent château is worth the trip. It dates from the 16th century but quite probably existed before, for the archives only go back as far as 1560. The cellars are exceptional, but there is never any

wine left in them because this château forms part of France's wine aristocracy. This estate receives the same marks for both red and white. Unanimously loved by the jury for its notes of ripe fruit and cherry in alcohol, this red is particularly expressive on the palate where it reveals all its nobility and magnificence. It can be drunk now, or could be left for a good ten years. Also worth noting is the well-made **Cuvée des Cadettes 97**, one star (150–199 F), which still tastes very oaky.
SCA Ch. la Nerthe, rte de Sorgues, 84230 Châteauneuf-du-Pape, tel. 04.90.83.70.11, fax 04.90.83.79.69, e-mail la.nerthe@wanadoo.fr
ev. day 9am–12 noon 2pm–6pm
M. Richard

CH. LA NERTHE

Clos de Beauvenir 1998★★

□ 1 ha 4,000 150–199 F

If Château la Nerthe is the leading light of the appellation, then its Clos de Beauvenir is the beacon. Rarely can one find so luminous a white or a nose so rich in flowers and fruit. The powerful and fine structure is supported by superb vanilla oak. This wine could be a good partner to grilled fish with fennel. Note also the **Cuvée Principale Château la Nerthe 99 Blanc**, which is very well made and worthy of your attention (100–149 F).
SCA Ch. la Nerthe, rte de Sorgues, 84230 Châteauneuf-du-Pape, tel. 04.90.83.70.11, fax 04.90.83.79.69, e-mail la.nerthe@wanadoo.fr
ev. day 9am–12 noon 2pm–6pm

LA NONCIATURE

Grande Réserve 1998★

□ 1 ha 3,000 100–149 F

After investing one million francs to modernise the barrel store in 1999, a huge effort was made in the vineyard to improve leaf-plucking techniques and harvesting by using successive pickings. Then they established procedures for tracing the wine from the vine to the bottle. This wine is powerful and fleshy. The very obvious oak will please fans: flavours of apricot, flowers and a touch of vanilla provide the wine with exceptional length. Drink within five years with fish in highly seasoned sauces.
Vignobles Max Aubert, Dom. de la Présidente, 84290 Sainte-Cécile-les-Vignes, tel. 04.90.30.80.34, fax 04.90.30.72.93
by appt.
Max et René Aubert

LA PONTIFICALE 1998

■ n.c. 20,000 70–99 F

Finesse and lightness characterise this wine: one is beguiled by the sweetness of the vanilla. To drink soon in relaxed surroundings with grilled lamb chops.
Cellier de l'Enclave des Papes, rte d'Orange, 84600 Valréas, tel. 04.90.41.91.42, fax 04.90.41.90.21
Elie Jeune SA

LAURUS 1998★

■ 3.5 ha 15,000 100–149 F

Two wines from this wine-merchant and producer that are each as successful as the other. The Laurus, with its gamey and grilled meat character, was admired for its good balance. The **Cuvée du Concordat 98** is fruitier with greater finesse (70–99 F). Drink the first with highly seasoned meat and keep the second for more delicate food. Keep for three to five years.
Gabriel Meffre, Le Village, 84190 Gigondas, tel. 04.90.12.32.42, fax 04.90.12.32.49, e-mail gabriel-meffre@meffre.com

COMTE DE LAUZE 1998★

■ 16 ha 71,200 70–99 F

A long maturation of 18 months in small and large casks has given this wine some brown tinges and notes of vanilla and tobacco. Then on the second nosing, spicy cake and honey characters develop. The extremely balanced palate is true to the nose. A full wine that will delight lovers of old oak flavours. Ready from now onwards to drink with grilled red meat.
SCEA Jean Comte de Lauze, 7, av. des Bosquets, 84230 Châteauneuf-du-Pape, tel. 04.90.83.72.87, fax 04.90.83.50.93
ev. day 8am–6pm; Sat. Sun. by appt.

DOM. DE LA VIEILLE JULIENNE

Vieilles Vignes 1998★

■ 1.2 ha 3,600 150–199 F

This very successful blend (80% Grenache, 10% Syrah and 10% Mourvèdre) has spent 12 months in barrel. The colour is dark with purplish highlights. The nose is, of course, oaky. The oak on the palate needs a few years to calm down and to allow the richness and fruity flavours to emerge. Keep it for five years then serve it with a meat casserole.
EARL Daumen Père et Fils, Dom. de la Vieille Julienne, Le Grès, 84100 Orange, tel. 04.90.34.20.10, fax 04.90.34.10.20, e-mail jpdaumen@club-internet.fr
ev. day 9am–12 noon 2pm–7pm; Sat. Sun. by appt.

LE CLOS DU CAILLOU

Réserve 1998★★

■ n.c. 7,000 150–199 F

The Réserve from Clos du Caillou will undoubtedly completely charm you with its stunning power. The tannins do need to soften. Count on at least five years for them to tone down. Although oak is dominant at present, the weight of this wine is so dense and rich that it will assert itself. Enjoy it with a game stew, for example.
J.-D. Vacheron, Clos du Caillou, 84350 Courthézon, tel. 04.90.70.73.05, fax 04.90.70.76.47 ev. day except Sun. 9am–12 noon 2pm–6pm

CH. MAUCOIL 1998*

■ 17 ha 70,000 70–99 F

The Via Agrippa passed close to the edge of Maucoil, once a Roman legionnaire's camp but today a 45-ha (111-acre) estate. Two thousand years on, the vines produce an attractive wine whose colour is showing some evolution from barrel maturation. Crystallised fruit on the nose combines with toasty and vanilla notes. The powerful palate suggests it should partner a fine game stew, but, make sure you wait two to three years.

Ch. Maucoil, B.P. 07, 84231 Châteauneuf-du-Pape, tel. 04.90.34.14.86, fax 04.90.34.71.88 by appt.

Arnaud

DOM. MONPERTUIS 1999*

□ 3 ha 10,000 50–69 F

An estate that really works towards quality: note especially the conscientious sorting of the harvest. This wine reveals itself little by little and only shows all its elegance after some minutes. White peach is the overriding characteristic. Its enjoyable balance would bring out the best from salmon or white meat. Drink within three years.

Vignobles Paul Jeune, 14, chem. des Garrigues, 84232 Châteauneuf-du-Pape, tel. 04.90.83.73.87, fax 04.90.83.51.13, e-mail vignoblespauljeune@wanadoo.fr by appt.

CH. MONT-REDON 1998*

■ 78 ha 370,000 100–149 F

With 100 ha (247 acres) of vines in Châteauneuf-du-Pape and 20 ha (49 acres) in Côtes du Rhône, Mont-Redon is a member of the relatively closed circle of the Grands Crus of the Rhône. This is an ancestral vineyard, with vines of over 40 years old, and exports to 34 countries. The maturation period of the wines is well managed with part in tank and part in barrel. This distinguished 98 has a dark and brilliant colour with a nose marrying vanilla and coffee with blackcurrant. The palate is full, with a beautiful finish of truffle notes. Wait three years to appreciate its richness.

Familles Abeille-Fabre, Ch. Mont-Redon, 84230 Châteauneuf-du-Pape, tel. 04.90.83.72.75, fax 04.90.83.77.20, e-mail chateaumontredon@wanadoo.fr by appt.

DOM. MOULIN-TACUSSEL 1998*

■ 8.5 ha 12,000 70–99 F

One is quickly seduced by the immediate fullness on the palate and the explosion of ripe fruits: blueberry, pear and cherry. This enjoyable and well-balanced wine is drinkable now but could be left for three years. Serve with any red meat.

Dom. Moulin-Tacussel, 10, av. des Bosquets, 84230 Châteauneuf-du-Pape, tel. 04.90.83.70.09, fax 04.90.83.50.92 ev. day 9am–7pm; cl. 21 Dec.-3 Jan.

DOM. DE NALYS 1998*

■ 38 ha 150,000 50–69 F

A very handsome Provençal farmhouse that bears the name of Jacques Nalys, who was Superintendent Farmer of the Avignon Popes. This estate perpetuates the tradition of maturation in *foudre* (large casks) that was very commonplace at the start of the 20th century. It is the *foudres* that give the wine its spicy character, allied with red berry fruits and violets. Well-structured and fleshy, it needs two or even four years to become more refined. Serve with game or meat in a spicy sauce.

SCI Dom. de Nalys, rte de Courthézon, 84230 Châteauneuf-du-Pape, tel. 04.90.83.72.52, fax 04.90.83.51.15 ev. day except Sun. 8am–12 noon 1.30pm–6pm; Sat. by appt.

Groupama

OGIER Cuvée de la Reine Jeanne 1998**

■ n.c. 30,000 70–99 F

A great nobleness is shown by this Cuvée de la Reine Jeanne. The sweetness of the vanilla predominates and the obvious, but good quality tannins have wonderful persistence. This wine still needs three or four years to fully express itself. The patient enthusiast will plan to drink it with spicy food.

Ogier-Caves des Papes, 10, bd Pasteur, 84230 Châteauneuf-du-Pape, tel. 04.90.39.32.32, fax 04.90.83.72.51 ev. day except Sun. 8.30am–6.30pm

DOM. DU PEGAU Cuvée réservée 1998**

■ 17 ha 65,000 100–149 F

An intense, heady wine that exudes aromas of spices, leather and blackberry jam. The palate is round and powerful, with obvious but well-handled oak. Wonderfully characteristic, in other words. Keep it for two or three years to drink with red meat.

Dom. du Pegau, av. Impériale, 84230 Châteauneuf-du-Pape, tel. 04.90.83.72.70, fax 04.90.83.53.02, e-mail pegau@pegau.com by appt.

Ferau

DOM. SAINT-GAYAN 1998

■ 0.77 ha 3,500 70–99 F

The Saint-Gayan estate produces very down-to-earth wines. It is the year of barrel maturation that gives this wine its character: a gamey nose that reveals itself gradually, and noticeable tannins that will soften after four years in a good cellar.

EARL Jean-Pierre et Martine Meffre, Dom. Saint-Gayan, 84190 Gigondas, tel. 04.90.65.86.33, fax 04.90.65.85.10 ev. day except Sun. 9am–11.45 2pm–6.30pm

DOM. DES SENECHAUX 1998*

■ 20 ha 75,000 70–99 F

Bought in 1993 by Pascal Roux (of Château du Trignon at Gigondas), the Sénéchaux was matured partly in wood. With

balance and well-controlled power, this fruity 98 is built for pleasure *par excellence*. To drink over the next three years, it will make an ideal partner to game or red meat dishes.
Pascal Roux, Dom. des Sénéchaux, 3, rue la Nouvelle-Poste, 84231 Châteauneuf-du-Pape, tel. 04.90.83.73.52, fax 04.90.83.52.88 Y by appt.

CH. SIMIAN 1998*

3 ha 14,000 70–99 F

Grenache (70%), Syrah (25%) and 50-year-old Cinsault, all 100% de-stemmed, produced this very attractive, limpid wine. It has retained all the intensity of its red berry fruit. The pronounced tannins, reinforced by 12 months in *foudre* (large oak vats), are of good quality and do not spoil any of the richness. Well-balanced, this wine has a good ageing potential of three to five years.
Jean-Pierre Serguier, Ch. Simian, 84420 Piolenc, tel. 04.90.29.50.67, fax 04.90.29.62.33 Y ev. day except Sun. 8.30am–12 noon 2pm–7pm

DOM. RAYMOND USSEGLIO 1998***

15 ha 10,000 70–99 F

It is rare enough to win the top marks, but to achieve them for two wines is so exceptional as to be worth underlining. So equality reigns on the Raymond Usseglio estate between its main wine and the **Impériale 98** (100–149 F). The first is distinguished by its clarity and fruitiness, the second by its heady and full-bodied palate. One is a blend of three varieties with an average age of 60 years, the other blends grapes from vines nearly 100 years old. Keep for at least five years (ten would be better) as a show of respect for such rare quality.
Dom. Raymond Usseglio, rte de Courthézon, B.P. 29, 84230 Châteauneuf-du-Pape, tel. 04.90.83.71.85, fax 04.90.83.50.42 Y by appt.

DOM. PIERRE USSEGLIO ET FILS 1998**

5 ha 20,000 50–69 F

A wine with a deep, dense colour, powerful and complex, which can compete with the greats. It will live up to its promise. Very pronounced tannins, concentration, charred notes, spices and red berry fruit are all present, together with very attractive weight. Wait for five to ten years, and then serve it with game or some fine red meat.
EARL Dom. Pierre Usseglio et Fils, rte d'Orange, 84230 Châteauneuf-du-Pape, tel. 04.90.83.72.98, fax 04.90.83.72.98 Y by appt.

CH. DE VAUDIEU 1999*

10 ha 12,000 100–149 F

A huge property built in the 18th century by a lieutenant from the Admiralty of Marseilles, today Vaudieu amounts to 70 ha (173 acres) and is run by the daughter and grandson of Gabriel Meffre, who bought it after the Second World War. In addition to a **98 Rouge** (85,000 bottles), a wonderfully light wine, drinkable now, showing red berry fruits, and given a mention by the jury, there is also this very successful white. The crowning effort of the wine-maker, it is dominated by Grenache Blanc and exudes the scents of the garrigue, which also linger on the palate. The lively and elegant balance confers great harmony. Drink within two years with seafood.
Ch. de Vaudieu, 84230 Châteauneuf-du-Pape, tel. 04.90.83.70.31, fax 04.90.83.51.97 Y by appt.
Brechet

DOM. DU VIEUX LAZARET 1998**

10 ha 40,000 70–99 F

A *lazaret* (hospice) from the 18th century gave its name to this estate, owned by the former president of the INAO (controlling body for appellations contrôlées). Two wines were tasted, both of great interest. This wine amazes us with its finesse and richness of flavours. A tendency towards honey and leather is already noticeable, heightened by the balanced oak flavours. It should be drunk within three years with steamed fish. Also worth mentioning, from the same producer, is the **Domaine Duclaux 98**, with more richness and oak; it would make a marvellous accompaniment to fish in sauce.
Vignobles Jérôme Quiot, av. Baron-Leroy, 84230 Châteauneuf-du-Pape, tel. 04.90.83.73.55, fax 04.90.83.78.48, e-mail quiot-vignobles@wanadoo.fr
Y ev. day except Sat. Sun. 8.30am–6pm, groups by appt.

DOM. DU VIEUX TELEGRAPHE La Crau 1998*

50 ha 200,000 100–149 F

A long and meticulous maturation period enables the full potential of the raw material to express itself. The nose is very much given to red berry fruit, whereas the palate shows vanilla and liquorice. The concentration is worthy of the finest wines of the appellation. Leave for at least five years. From the same proprietor we also mention the **Domaine de la Roquette 98**, equally admired, and showing greater delicacy and freshness (70–99 F).
Frédéric et Daniel Brunier, rte de Châteauneuf-du-Pape, 64370 Bédarrides, tel. 04.90.33.00.31, fax 04.90.33.18.47, e-mail vignobles@brunier.fr Y by appt.

Lirac

Lirac has produced quality wines since the 16th century, when the magistrates of Roquemaure authenticated them by burning the letters 'C d R' into the barrels with a red-hot iron. The climate and terroir are nearly the same here, in an area between Lirac, Saint-Laurent-des-Arbres, Saint-Geniès-de-Comolas and Roquemaure, as at Tavel, further north. Since Vacqueyras became an AOC, Lirac is no longer the only southern cru to make three colours of wine. Lirac rosés and whites are full of grace and perfume; they go pleasantly with fish from the Mediterranean nearby and should be drunk young and cool. The reds are strong, with a pronounced terroir character, and offer an ideal accompaniment to red meat. In 1999, Lirac produced 25,600 hl (675,840 gal) from 615 ha (152 acres).

DOM. AMIDO 1998*

■ 6 ha 20,000 30–49 F

An attractive 25-ha (62-acre) estate that has been managed by Christian Amido since 1962. The richness of the Grenache (70%) and the intensity of the Syrah (20%), supplemented by Mourvèdre, have produced a lovely wine. Maturation for 12 months in *foudre* (large casks) has produced spicy aromas of cinnamon, cardamom and vanilla. The soft tannins, good structure and very ripe fruit provide a real impression of fullness. This wine is ready now, but could be kept for two years.

Christian Amido, rue des Carrières, 30126 Tavel, tel. 04.66.50.04.41, fax 04.66.50.04.41 by appt.

CH. D'AQUERIA 1998

■ 13.35 ha 68,000 50–69 F

This château dates back to the 18th century, when the Consuls of Lirac instituted the first regulations ordering inspection of the vineyards before authorising the start of harvest. It submitted a garnet-coloured 98 with red berry fruit and gamey notes joining together on the nose. Good weight on the very flavoursome palate gives a wine for immediate drinking.

SCA Jean Olivier, Ch. d'Aquéria, 30126 Tavel, tel. 04.66.50.04.56, fax 04.66.50.18.46, e-mail contact@aqueria.com
ev. day except Sat. Sun. 8am–12 noon 2pm–6pm

BALAZU DES VAUSSIERES 1998*

■ 1.3 ha 2,500 30–49 F

Carignan (25%), Syrah (20%) and Grenache grown together on clay, sand and pebbles have produced this very well-made Lirac. Silky tannins integrate with notes of ripe fruit and a hint of brandy. Round and fleshy, it will please lovers of subtly oaked wines.

Dom. Christian et Nadia Charmasson, chem. de la Vaussière, 30126 Tavel, tel. 04.66.50.44.22, fax 04.66.50.44.22
Wed. Sat. and Sun. 9am–7pm

CH. DE BOUCHASSY 1999**

2 ha 6,500 30–49 F

The jury really enjoyed the **99 Blanc** with its subtle floral nose. With peach and apricot joining together on the palate, it wins a star, whereas this rosé receives two. There is outstanding freshness and excellent complexity of amylic and fruity aromas in this wine. It shows beautiful balance and great finesse in a joyful union with richness and a touch of blackcurrant.

Gérard Degoul, Ch. de Bouchassy, rte de Nîmes, 30150 Roquemaure, tel. 04.66.82.82.49, fax 04.66.82.87.80
ev. day except Sun. 9am–12 noon 2pm–7pm

PIERRE CHANAU 1998

■ n.c. 100,000 20–29 F

Pierre Chanau is a supermarket brand from the merchant Antonin Rodet, produced by the company Sefivin, situated in Châteauneuf-du-Pape. This firm of merchants makes good selections and has submitted this brilliant ruby-coloured Lirac. The gamey nose reveals additional notes of very ripe red berry fruit, almost jammy. The tannins are reasonably pronounced.

Sefivin-H. Bouachon, rte de Châteauneuf, 84230 Châteauneuf-du-Pape, tel. 04.90.83.58.35, fax 04.90.83.77.23, e-mail informatique@caves.saint-pierre.com
by appt.

DOM. LAFOND ROC-EPINE

■ 4 ha 20,000 30–49 F

Managed since 1990 by Pascal Lafond, this huge 75-ha (185-acre) estate submits a Lirac from 70% Grenache and 30% Syrah, grown on a clay-limestone soil. This beautifully intense, dark red 98 is a wine that will age well. The nose is charred, and the tannins are pronounced, but they should soften given time.

Dom. Lafond Roc-Epine, rte des Vignobles, 30126 Tavel, tel. 04.66.50.24.59, fax 04.66.50.12.42, e-mail lafond.roc-epine@wanadoo.fr
by appt.
Pascal Lafond

DOM. LA GENESTIERE 1998

■ 20 ha 100,000 50–69 F

With a lake in front of the 16th-century country house, this estate, purchased in 1994 by Jean-Claude and Raphaël Garcin, is an attractive place to stop. It submitted a full-bodied and well-balanced wine; the oak is still

noticeable, but the wine should develop well as there is good fruit. Both appearance and nose were more than satisfactory, with pronounced redcurrant and spices underneath the vanilla flavours.
🔑 Jean-Claude Garcin, Dom. la Genestière, 30126 Tavel, tel. 04.66.50.07.03, fax 04.66.50.27.03, e-mail genestiere@paewan.fr ✉
🍷 ev. day except Sun. 8am–6pm

DOM. DE LA MORDOREE

Cuvée de la Reine des Bois 1998★★

■ 5 ha 25,000 50–69 F

A third each of Grenache, Mourvèdre and Syrah were matured in almost equal amounts – in small oak barrels, large casks and tanks. The result is an elegant wine of a beautifully intense garnet colour with purple edges. Spices, cinnamon and cocoa create an expressive range of aromas. The ample, well-structured palate shows great depth of ripe fruit and spices. The **Lirac 99 Blanc** is awarded a star and would go well with goat's cheese.
🔑 Dom. de La Mordorée, chem. des Oliviers, 30126 Tavel, tel. 04.66.50.00.75, fax 04.66.50.47.39 ✉ 🍷 ev. day except Sun. 8am–12 noon 1.30pm–5.30pm
🔑 Delorme

LAURUS 1998★

■ 3 ha 10,000 70–99 F

Matured in barrels of 275 litres coopered in the traditional way and identical to the *demi-queue* of Vaucluse, this is a very well-made wine from a producer who is also a wine-merchant. It has an intense garnet colour with purple hues. Red berry fruit and stewed prunes appear on both nose and palate. There is just the right amount of oak ageing, producing fine tannins and a good balance.
🔑 Gabriel Meffre, Le Village, 84190 Gigondas, tel. 04.90.12.32.42, fax 04.90.12.32.49, e-mail gabriel-meffre@meffre.com

LES LAUZERAIES

Elevé en Fût de Chêne 1998

■ 10 ha 50,000 30–49 F

This wine, which spent seven months in oak, has an intense blackcurrant colour with violet tinges. Vanilla and liquorice occur on both the nose and the palate. It will take time for the wine to open up, but it is built to last.
🔑 Les Vignerons de Tavel, 30126 Tavel, tel. 04.66.50.03.57, fax 04.66.50.46.57, e-mail tavel.cave@wanadoo.fr ✉
🍷 ev. day 9am–12 noon 2pm–6pm

LES QUEYRADES 1997★

■ 4.5 ha 24,000 30–49 F

Franck Popek, cellar-master, and Noël Rabot, consultant œnologist, have made an age-worthy 97. The aromas develop from red berry fruit to crystallised fruit with notes of blackcurrant and blueberry. The complex palate mixes leather and undergrowth. Ready now.
🔑 SCEA Mejan-Taulier, pl. du Président-Le-Roy, 30126 Tavel, tel. 04.66.50.04.02, fax 04.66.50.21.72 ✉ 🍷 by appt.
🔑 André Mejan

DOM. MABY La Fermade 1998★

■ 25 ha 60,000 30–49 F

This old family estate was restructured in 1995. The wine is a blend of Grenache and Mourvèdre (the majority) grown on rounded pebbles and sand. Excellently made with a garnet colour, it reveals a gamey character on the nose. The very expressive and full body with red berry fruit is most characteristic.
🔑 Dom. Maby, rue Saint-Vincent, B.P. 8, 30126 Tavel, tel. 04.66.50.03.40, fax 04.66.50.43.12 ✉ 🍷 ev. day except Sat. Sun. 8am–12 noon 2pm–6pm
🔑 Roger Maby

CH. MONT-REDON 1999★★★

◪ 1 ha 5,600 30–49 F

Mont-Redon has crossed the Rhône in order to complete its range of wines. No one should complain, for this rosé received approval from all the tasters. The colour is quite light, but the aromas are exceptional: broom, linden flowers, peach, and it has wonderful length. Fruit and more fruit . . . a great rosé that is entirely balanced.
🔑 Familles Abeille-Fabre, Ch. Mont-Redon, 84230 Châteauneuf-du-Pape, tel. 04.90.83.72.75, fax 04.90.83.77.20, e-mail chateaumontredon@wanadoo.fr ✉
🍷 by appt.

CH. SAINT-ROCH 1999★★

◪ 2 ha 10,000 50–69 F

After coveting it for some time, the Brunel family, from Château de la Gardine on the other side of the Rhône, purchased Château Saint-Roch in 1998. The estate has begun to increase the planting density by doubling the rows of vines. This bright rose-petal coloured 99 is all that it could have hoped for. Redcurrant, blackcurrant and peach are all found on the nose and there is an attractively fresh palate, with richness and sweetness as well. A hint of the exotic on the finish adds to the lovely balance of this rosé. The very elegant **99 Blanc** won a mention from the jury.
🔑 Maxime et Patrick Brunel, Ch. Saint-Roch, chem. de Lirac, 30150 Roquemaure, tel. 04.66.82.82.59, fax 04.66.82.83.00, e-mail brunel@chateau.saint-roch.com ✉
🍷 ev. day except Sat. Sun. 8am–12 noon 2pm–5pm

CH. DE SEGRIES 1998**

■ 20 ha 80,000 30–49 F

Two or three years are needed before you can appreciate this remarkable wine, which is attractive from the start with a sumptuous scarlet colour. The nose is still slightly reticent but one can detect the violets that indicate the presence of some Syrah. The full-bodied and very fruity palate has excellent weight with plenty of blackcurrant.

Henri de Lanzac, rue de la Fontaine, 30126 Tavel, tel. 04.66.50.07.93, fax 04.66.50.17.02 by appt.

TOUR DES CHENES

Etiquette Fernando Arrabal 1998**

■ 1 ha 5,000 50–69 F

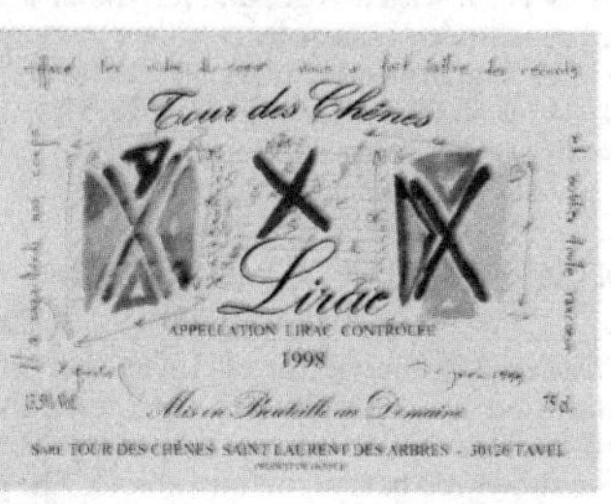

Here is a limited edition of 5,000 that all admirers of the French author, Arrabal should snatch up . . . a collector's bottle with a label penned by this writer devoted to Lirac. But the wine itself justifies such a purchase – note that our jury tastes blind, and did not see the beautiful label. 'Elegant from start to finish', noted one of them. A deep colour, a very distinguished nose of ripe fruits, soft tannins, restrained power; everything seems to express the wonderful terroir.

SCEA Tour des Chênes, 30126 Saint-Laurent-des-Arbres, tel. 04.66.50.01.19, fax 04.66.50.34.69, e-mail tour-des-chenes@wanadoo.fr by appt.

Tavel

Considered by many to be the finest rosé in France, this great wine from the Côtes du Rhône comes from a vineyard situated in the department of the Gard, on the right bank of the river. The vines are grown on land around Tavel, together with a few parcels in the commune of Roquemaure, on 938 ha (2,317 acres) of sand, alluvial clay or smoothed pebbles. Tavel is the only Rhône appellation to produce rosé wines; production is 42,800 hl (1,129,920 gal). A wine of great character, with a floral, then fruity bouquet, Tavel should be served as an accompaniment for fish dishes with sauce, charcuterie and white meats.

CH. D'AQUERIA 1999***

44.23 ha 200,000 50–69 F

One of the jewels of the appellation, Château d'Aquéria has submitted an exceptional wine. With a strong pink colour with bluish tinges, the nose has intense red berry fruit aromas dominated by redcurrants. Power, structure and great depth of flavour are indicative of the perfect wine-making techniques used by this cellar filled with modern equipment. It would be a dream to pair it with a Mediterranean fish stew.

SCA Jean Olivier, Ch. d'Aquéria, 30126 Tavel, tel. 04.66.50.04.56, fax 04.66.50.18.46, e-mail contact@aqueria.com ev. day except Sat. Sun. 8am–12 noon 2pm–6pm

DOM. DES CARABINIERS 1999

5 ha 25,000 50–69 F

For the past two years this estate has been in the process of converting its vineyards to organic cultivation. Its Tavel is salmon-coloured with cherry tinges. The nose marries spices and red berry fruit with a great deal of freshness; the palate follows the same pattern and is beautifully balanced.

Christian Leperchois, Dom. des Carabiniers, 30150 Roquemaure, tel. 04.66.82.62.94, fax 04.66.82.82.15 by appt.

DOM. LAFOND ROC-EPINE

Cuvée Jean-Baptiste 1999**

2 ha 10,000 50–69 F

Tapenade on toast, or chicken with crayfish would make the best partners to this superb wine, according to the tasters. The raspberry colour has shades of very bright purple. The nose is stunning with a whole range of red berry fruits, and notes of spiced cake as well as flowers. The palate appears full-bodied, elegant and smooth.

🔑 Dom. Lafond Roc-Epine, rte des Vignobles, 30126 Tavel, tel. 04.66.50.24.59, fax 04.66.50.12.42, e-mail lafond.roc-epine@wanadoo.fr ✉ 🍷 by appt.
🔑 Pascal Lafond

DOM. LA ROCALIERE 1999*

◪ 23 ha 138,000 30-49 F

A huge 55-ha (136-acre) estate, La Rocalière submits a brilliant and lively redcurrant-coloured 99. The nose is rich, with pronounced red berry fruit that is slightly jammy; there is a lovely alcohol-acid balance on the palate with plenty of weight, fruit and freshness.

🔑 Dom. La Rocalière, Le Palai-Nord, B.P. 21, 30126 Tavel, tel. 04.66.50.12.60, fax 04.66.50.23.45 ✉ 🍷 ev. day 8am–12 noon 2pm–6pm; Sat. Sun. by appt.
🔑 Borrelly-Maby

LES EGLANTIERS 1999*

◪ 6 ha 33,000 30-49 F

A very fine rosé with an attractive nose showing floral and liquorice notes. The full and well-structured palate makes for a pleasant wine to drink with any white meat.

🔑 Laurent-Charles Brotte, rte d'Avignon, 84230 Châteauneuf-du-Pape, tel. 04.90.83.70.07, fax 04.90.83.74.34 ✉ 🍷 ev. day 9am–12 noon 2pm–6pm

DOM. MIREILLE PETIT 1999**

◪ n.c. n.c. 30-49 F

Distributed by a merchant based in Orange, this estate has produced an excellent Tavel. The lively colour is intense, with macerated red berry fruit and a dash of kirsch on the nose. There is a beautiful structure, fruity and long, finishing with a touch of almond.

🔑 Les Domaines Bernard, rte de Sérignan, 84100 Orange, tel. 04.90.11.86.86, fax 04.90.34.87.30
🔑 Mireille Petit

PRIEURE DE MONTEZARGUES 1999*

◪ 34 ha 100,000 50-69 F

Located at the foot of the Montagne Noire, this priory dates from the 12th century. Maceration of skins for 24 hours before running off the juice has produced this magnificent rose-petal coloured wine with raspberry hues. The elegant and fine nose mixes spices and minerals with very ripe raspberries behind. The fresh palate tends towards redcurrant.

🔑 GA du Prieuré de Montézargues, 30126 Tavel, tel. 04.66.50.04.48, fax 04.66.50.30.41 ✉ 🍷 ev. day 10am–12 noon 3pm–6pm; groups and Sat. Sun. by appt.
🔑 Allauzen et Lucenet

DOM. ROC DE L'OLIVET 1999

◪ 2 ha 8,400 30-49 F

This family estate works reverently with its old vines and has submitted a pleasant and sunny rosé. Light-coloured, it displays the same floral and fruity character on both nose and palate. Rich and fairly full-bodied, it is an attractive wine that finishes on notes of jammy fruit.

🔑 Thierry Valente, chem. de la Vaussière, 30126 Tavel, tel. 04.66.50.37.87, fax 04.66.50.37.87 ✉ 🍷 by appt.

LES VIGNERONS DE TAVEL

Cuvée Tableau 1999**

◪ 50 ha 300,000 30-49 F

Congratulations to the co-operative of Tavel for this remarkable rosé that shows shades of purple and morello cherry. The intense nose reveals red berry fruit, almond and citrus fruits. The full-bodied and rounded palate is powerful and rich with notes of red fruits again, with frangipani and marshmallow. Serve it with a vegetable terrine or a veal and mushroom casserole.

🔑 Les Vignerons de Tavel, 30126 Tavel, tel. 04.66.50.03.57, fax 04.66.50.46.57, e-mail tavel.cave@wanadoo.fr ✉ 🍷 ev. day 9am–12 noon 2pm–6pm

DOM. DU VIEUX RELAIS 1999

◪ 9.05 ha 9,600 30-49 F

Situated in the village of Tavel, this estate submitted a deep coloured rosé with lively and intense bluish tinges. The very young nose shows red berry fruit and spices. The palate is as full-bodied as one could wish, with a lovely depth of flavours.

🔑 GAEC Dom. du Vieux Relais, rte de La Commanderie, 30126 Tavel, tel. 04.66.50.36.52 ✉ 🍷 by appt.

Clairette de Die

Clairette de Die is one of the oldest known wines in the world. The vineyard occupies the hillsides of the middle valley of the Drôme, between Lucen-Diois and Aouste-sur-Sye. A sparkling wine is produced mainly from the Muscat variety (75% minimum). The fermentation stops naturally in the bottle, according to ancient Die practice. No 'liqueur de tirage' (a mixture of yeasts, old wine and sugar) is added. Production was 72,926 hl (1,925,246 gal) in 1999.

CLAIRDIE Tradition***

○ 230 ha 1,500,000 30-49 F

The Die co-operative submitted two Clairettes which thrilled the jury: the completely balanced **Cuvée Jadissane**, made from organically grown 100% Muscat grapes,

which won two stars, and this Clairdie, with 20% Clairette added to the Muscat. Gold coloured with green tinges, this wine provides an explosion of sensations (flowers, peach, pineapple and lychee) which last and last . . .
Cave coop. de Die, Union de Producteurs, 26150 Die, tel. 04.75.22.30.00, fax 04.75.22.21.06 by appt.

ALAIN POULET Tradition 1998
○ 9 ha 50,000 30–49 F

Alain Poulet grows 15 ha (37 acres) of vines at the foot of the Vercors Park. His light straw-coloured Clairette explodes with an attractive fine sparkle. Stewed apples and pears appear on a palate that is clean and light. An apricot charlotte would do the trick.
Alain Poulet, la Chapelle, 26150 Pontaix, tel. 04.75.21.22.59, fax 04.75.21.20.95
by appt.

JEAN-CLAUDE RASPAIL
Grande Tradition 1998★★
○ 2.55 ha 17,604 30–49 F

Located between Saillans and Die, the tasting cellar of Raspail, decorated with flowers between March and December, submitted this Clairette bursting with fine bubbles, pale and with green tinges. A rich palate of citrus fruit and flowers accompanies the beautiful richness of this wine. If you come to Saillans, make sure you buy some almond biscuits that are a local speciality and would go perfectly with the Clairette.
Jean-Claude Raspail, Dom. de la Mûre, 26340 Saillans, tel. 04.75.21.55.99, fax 04.75.21.57.57
ev. day 9am–12 noon 2pm–6pm; cl. Jan.

RASPAIL Tradition 1998★
○ 3 ha 23,000 30–49 F

A 'wine craftsman' is how the cellar-master of this well-made Clairette describes himself. Like the smell of roses that characterises the nose, this wine is already very open. The long and powerful palate urges one to enjoy it now with some biscuits.
EARL Georges Raspail, rte du Camping municipal, La Roche, 26340 Aurel, tel. 04.75.21.71.89, fax 04.75.21.71.89
by appt.

Crémant de Die

The AOC Crémant de Die was recognised by decree on 26 March 1993. It is made solely from the Clairette variety by the 'Champagne' method involving secondary fermentation in the bottle.

CAROD 1997★
○ 3.32 ha 27,040 30–49 F

In 1993, a small museum of Clairette was established here. This pale coloured Crémant, with a fine and light bead of bubbles, shows a nose of ripe or even stewed apples and pears. With just the right amount of richness and power, this should be drunk with food.
Carod Frères, R.D. 93, 26340 Vercheny, tel. 04.75.21.73.77, fax 04.75.21.75.22, e-mail info@caves-carod.com
ev. day 9am–12 noon 2pm–6.30pm

CHAMBERAN 1995★
○ 9.4 ha 56,000 30–49 F

Nine growers joined together in 1962 to produce quality wine. This example certainly rewards them for their efforts. Well-made and characteristic of the AOC, pale yellow and embellished with a fine sparkle, this wine is charming and elegant. Very floral, it has a good enough persistence not only to serve as an apéritif, but also to accompany game bird or grilled poultry.
Union des Jeunes Viticulteurs Récoltants, rte de Die, 26340 Vercheny, tel. 04.75.21.70.88, fax 04.75.21.73.73, e-mail ujvr@terre-net.fr
ev. day 8.30am–12 noon 2pm–6.30pm

DIDIER CORNILLON
Brut absolu 1997★★
○ 0.5 ha 4,500 30–49 F

This is what one terms a Brut Zero, with no *dosage* (added sugar). Lemon and grapefruit make the first impression. Then the palate comes into play, revealing a perfect balance with just the right amount of acidity. 'I'm definitely buying some' noted one member of the jury. Another added: 'What richness!' An excellent wine.
Didier Cornillon, 26410 Saint-Roman, tel. 04.75.21.81.79, fax 04.75.21.84.44
ev. day 10am–12.30pm 2pm–7pm; Oct.–Mar. by appt.

FONTAILLY Blanc de blancs★
○ 30 ha 200,000 30–49 F

Grilled almonds, brioche and flowers were part of the range of flavours that immediately attracted compliments. The beautiful balance and length will provide instantaneous pleasure.
Cave coop. de Die, Union de Producteurs, 26150 Die, tel. 04.75.22.30.00, fax 04.75.22.21.06 by appt.

JADISSANE Blanc de blancs

○ 5 ha 25,000 30–49 F

Pliny the Elder, in 77 AD, praised the natural sparkle of the wine made by the Voconces, a Gallic tribe who peopled the present region of Die. Was it to rediscover these ancient tastes that the Jadissane was partly produced from organically grown grapes? A complex wine that shows the influence of ripe apples and quince.

Cave coop. de Die,
Union de Producteurs, 26150 Die,
tel. 04.75.22.30.00, fax 04.75.22.21.06
Y by appt.

Châtillon-en-Diois

The vineyard of Châtillon-en-Diois covers 50 ha (123 acres) on the slopes of the high valley of the Drôme, between Luc-en-Diois, at 550 m (1,804 ft) altitude, and Pont-de-Quart, 465 m (1,525 ft). The appellation produces light and fruity reds (from the Gamay variety), to be drunk young, and whites (from the Aligoté and Chardonnay varieties) that are pleasant and firm. Total production was 3,361 hl (88,730 gal) in 1999.

CLOS DE BEYLIERE 1998

□ 0.4 ha 4,000 30–49 F

The jury tasted 12 wines in this AOC, of which Didier Cornillon, established in 1989, is one of the most respected representatives. Matured in barrel for one year, this pretty pale yellow 98 is as vanilla-flavoured as one could wish. It has an attractive roundness and a quite lively finish ending on a long lingering note of mild spices. This is a very good wine.

Didier Cornillon,
26410 Saint-Roman,
tel. 04.75.21.81.79, fax 04.75.21.84.44 V
Y ev. day 10am–12.30pm 2pm–7pm;
Oct.–Mar. by appt.

COOPERATIVE DE DIE
Cuvée Prestige 1998

■ 1.5 ha 10,000 20–29 F

Between the foothills of the Alps in the Drôme and Provence, a collection of small vineyard plots forms one of the highest altitude vineyard areas (between 500 and 700 m or 1,640 and 2,296 feet). The Die cooperative plays a fundamental role here, and submited an excellent 98. Very attractive spices tantalise the nostrils while the dark mysterious colour arouses your curiosity. The palate is supple to begin with, contrasting with a more virile finish. A blend of Gamay and Pinot Noir to drink with the local lamb.

Cave coop. de Die,
Union de Producteurs, 26150 Die,
tel. 04.75.22.30.00, fax 04.75.22.21.06 V
Y by appt.

Coteaux du Tricastin

This appellation covers 2,000 ha (4,940 acres), in 22 communes on the right bank of the Rhône, from La Baume-de-Transit in the south, through Saint-Paul-Trois-Châteaux, to Granges-Gontardes in the north. The very pebbly ancient alluvial soils and the sandy slopes situated at the limit of the Mediterranean climate produced about 125,000 hl (3,300,000 gal) of wine in 1999. The boundaries of this appellation have recently been redrawn.

LOUIS BERNARD 1999

■ n.c. n.c. 20–29 F

The Bernard estates' brand has talent and style, and this wine is fruity and spicy. The colour is attractive, but the tannins are a touch angular. However, this will enable the wine to survive the passing of time. Serve in 2001.

Les Domaines Bernard,
rte de Sérignan, 84100 Orange,
tel. 04.90.11.86.86, fax 04.90.34.87.30

CELLIER DES DAUPHINS
Hautes Terres 1998

■ 50 ha 300,000 20–29 F

Attractive red berry fruit shows from the start. And yet, it was the palate that the tasters preferred. An obvious amount of quite concentrated Grenache, very pronounced but seemingly supple tannins, and above all, a very loud note of liquorice, which underscored the whole composition.

Cellier des Dauphins,
B.P. 16, 26790 Tulette,
tel. 04.75.96.20.47, fax 04.75.96.20.12,
e-mail cellier.des.dauphins@wanadoo.fr

DELAS FRERES Escarlate 1998*

■ n.c. n.c. 20–29 F

A cherry colour, blackcurrant and blackberry on the nose, with red berry fruit that lasted way beyond the tasting. The nose is embellished with spices and notes of Drôme

garrigue. As for the palate, it has great balance with plenty of velvety tannins and a hint of acidity that lifted the finish.
🔑 Delas Frères, ZA de l'Olivet, B.P. 4, 07300 Saint-Jean-de-Muzols, tel. 04.75.08.60.30, fax 04.75.08.53.67
🍷 by appt.
🔑 Champagne Deutz

DOM. DE GRANGENEUVE
Grande Cuvée Elevée en Fût de Chêne 1998*

■ 4 ha 10,000 50–69 F

Mild spices appear at the very start. The integration of the tannins is exceptionally appealing. An equal amount of Grenache and Syrah is used in this wine, on which one detects some attractive, nicely used oak and, more especially, new barrels. This wine has everything needed to make an excellent Tricastin in a year or two. In the same vein, the **Cuvée Vieilles Vignes** is fruitier but structured to last. If you are an ardent supporter of maturation in oak, then try the **Cuvée de la Truffière 98** that has a particularly powerful and complex nose.
🔑 Domaines Bour, Dom. de Grangeneuve, 26230 Roussas, tel. 04.75.98.50.22, fax 04.75.98.51.09, e-mail domaines.bour@wanadoo.fr
🍷 by appt.

DOM. DE HAUTE CHALERNE
1999

■ 7 ha 45,000 20 F+

A concentrate of blackcurrant liqueur given extra persistence by the fruit: pleasant and long, the **Charte de Qualité 98** is promising. Wait a few months for it to balance. Ready by the end of 2000, the Domaine de Haute Chalerne reveals flavours of raspberry and spices that last all the way through the good finish.
🔑 Cellier de L'Enclave des Papes, rte d'Orange, 84600 Valréas, tel. 04.90.41.91.42, fax 04.90.41.90.21

CH. LA CROIX CHABRIERE
Fruit de l'Ivresse d'un Soir 1997

■ n.c. 1,600 30–49 F

This 20-ha (49-acre) rented estate includes a very attractive group of buildings: the 'château', the cellar, the stables and an orangery. It is also characterised by an irreproachable motto, 'do one's duty', and won two mentions. The wine (in 50 cl screen-printed bottles) with its aromas of fruit, spices and vanilla, is undoubtedly destined for export. The oak ageing has been handled most meticulously. This is also the case for the **Viognier Blanc** (50–68 F) which combines exotic fruits with muscat flavours.
🔑 Ch. la Croix Chabrière, rte de Saint-Restitut, 84500 Bollène, tel. 04.90.40.00.89, fax 04.90.40.19.93 🍷 ev. day 9am–6pm; Sun. 9am–12 noon; groups by appt.
🔑 Patrick Daniel

DOM. DE MONTINE Prestige 1998*

■ 5 ha 10,000 30–49 F

Two wines with two very different styles, but which both found favour with the jury. The Prestige came ahead thanks to its lovely aromas that blend spices and gamey notes with a solidly built structure. It has discreet oak flavours and is of genuine quality. The **Sélection Terroirs 98 Rouge** is fruit-driven with a more supple and lively palate. A characteristic Tricastin, worthy of its name.
🔑 Jean-Luc et Claudy Monteillet, Dom. de Montine, 26230 Grignan, tel. 04.75.46.54.21, fax 04.75.46.93.26
🍷 ev. day 9am–12 noon 2pm–7pm

DOM. SAINT-LUC 1998

■ 25 ha 40,000 30–49 F

Created from several vineyard plots in 1984, this estate submitted a wine whose nose is hard to decipher. On the other hand, the palate is a feast of crushed fruit and long-lasting liquorice. A balanced and classic Coteaux du Tricastin in which there is a high proportion of Syrah.
🔑 Ludovic Cornillon, Dom. Saint-Luc, 26790 La Baume-de-Transit, tel. 04.75.98.11.51, fax 04.75.98.19.22
🍷 by appt.

DOM. DU VIEUX MICOCOULIER
1998*

■ 104 ha 180,000 30–49 F

In 1877 a forbear from the Cévennes established a vineyard in Algeria. Then in 1962, one of his descendants returned here and cleared the land to create a vast wine estate. His attractive 98 has a dark elegant colour that encourages one to inhale the characteristic aromas of fruits and spices. The palate is clean and provides a sensation of sweet liquorice.
🔑 SCGEA Cave Vergobbi, Le Logis de Berre, 26290 Les Granges-Gontardes, tel. 04.75.04.02.72, fax 04.75.04.41.81
🍷 ev. day 9.30am–12 noon 2.30pm–6.30pm; Sun. by appt.

Côtes du Ventoux

This vineyard is at the foot of the limestone Massif du Ventoux, the 'giant of the Vaucluse' (1,912 m/6,271 ft), on soil composed of tertiary sediments, and stretches over 51 communes (6,888 ha/17,013 acres) between Vaison-la-Romaine in the north and Apt in the south. The wines produced are essentially reds and rosés. The climate, cooler than that of the

Côtes du Rhône, causes the grapes to ripen later. The red wines have a lesser alcoholic content, but are fresh and elegant when young; they are better structured in the more westerly communes (Caromb, Bédoin, Mormoiron). The rosé wines are pleasant and need to be drunk young. Total production reached 283,000 hl (7,471,200 gal) in 1999.

DOM. DES ANGES 1998

■ 4.5 ha 20,000 30–49 F

A young Irishman, Ciaran Rooney, bought this estate in 1998 after having worked in South Africa and Australia. With 35% Cinsault there is a light, almost ethereal character. Supple, it leaves an overall balanced and fruity impression.

SCA Dom. des Anges, Dom. des Anges, 84570 Mormoiron, tel. 04.90.61.88.78, fax 04.90.61.98.05, e-mail ciaranr@club-internet.fr
ev. day 8am–12 noon 2pm–6pm

DOM. AYMARD Prestige 1998*

■ 1 ha 3,000 30–49 F

A family business that dates from 1860, the Aymard estate is situated in the heart of the appellation. This Prestige has an agreeable but discreet nose, and a good structure with silky tannins. To sum up, this is a very attractive wine that can be enjoyed from winter 2000 onwards with a meat stew.

Dom. Aymard, Les Galères, Serres, 84200 Carpentras, tel. 04.90.63.35.32, fax 04.90.67.02.79 by appt.

DOM. DE BEAUMALRIC 1999

■ 6 ha 30,000 30–49 F

Pleasant and fruity, this wine will be most appealing in its youth. Both fresh and unctuous, it provides a fruit salad of cherry, strawberry and raspberry flavours, with a touch of pepper and mild spice. This harmonious and well-balanced 99 shows good length.

EARL Begouaussel, Dom. de Beaumalric, B.P. 15, 84190 Beaumes-de-Venise, tel. 04.90.65.01.77, fax 04.90.62.97.28 by appt.

CAVE DE BEAUMONT-DU-VENTOUX

Les Ambrosis 1998

■ 115 ha n.c. 20–29 F

Traditionally vinified from Grenache (85%) and Syrah (15%), this very fruity 98 is a touch light, but easy to drink. Characteristic of the appellation, it can be served right through the meal.

Cave de Beaumont-du-Ventoux, rte de Carpentras, 84340 Beaumont-du-Ventoux, tel. 04.90.65.11.78, fax 04.90.12.69.88, e-mail jacod.michel@wanadoo.fr

DOM. DU BON REMEDE

Cuvée Vincent Vieilli en Fût de Chêne 1998*

■ 1.5 ha 3,200 30–49 F

The vineyard of this estate was planted in 1991, but then restructured in order to offer a balanced mix of grape varieties. From old vines, this Cuvée Vincent has plenty of personality. Very ripe fruits including blackcurrants and wild strawberries dominate the intense nose, while notes of spices and vanilla accompany the fruity character on the palate. This wine is ready to drink, but could also be kept for one or two years.

Frédéric Delay, 1248, rte de Malemort, 84380 Mazan, tel. 04.90.69.69.76, fax 04.90.69.69.76 by appt.

CANTEPERDRIX 1999*

□ n.c. n.c. 20 F+

Perhaps a little 'high tech', this wine from Canteperdrix has a pale yellow colour with green tinges and an intense fresh nose of mainly citrus fruit aromas with floral notes. It is nevertheless a very pleasant wine that should be drunk over the next year with shellfish, grilled fish, or on its own as an aperitif.

Les Vignerons de Canteperdrix, rte de Caromb, B.P. 15, 84380 Mazan, tel. 04.90.69.70.31, fax 04.90.69.87.41
by appt.

DOM. DE CHAMP-LONG 1998

■ 4 ha 25,000 30–49 F

With a beautiful dark ruby colour, this wine has an austere style that requires some time. It is closed and mineral in character, but balanced despite pronounced tannins. You will need to wait a year before it opens up.

Christian Gély, Dom. de Champ-Long, 84340 Entrechaux, tel. 04.90.46.01.58, fax 04.90.46.04.40, e-mail christian.gely@wanadoo.fr
ev. day except Sun. 9am–12.30pm 2pm–7pm

DOM. DE CHANTEGRILLET

Cuvée de l'An 2000 1997*

■ 10.99 ha 2,000 100–149 F

An expensive but lovely looking Cuvée de l'An 2000 that is promising despite its discreet nose that evokes caramel, apples and pears. On the palate, the oaky flavours still dominate over the fruit. A wine for ageing that should be kept for at least two or three years and could be served with truffle-flavoured dishes. By then this will be a souvenir label, since 2000 will be long gone, but the subtle and elegant label alone is worth it.

SCEA Dom. de Chantegrillet, Gourgoumelle, B.P. 6, 84220 Roussillon, tel. 04.90.05.74.83, fax 04.90.06.09.28
by appt.
Guiton

DOM. CHAUMARD 1999*

□ 1.5 ha 5,500 20–29 F

In charge of the property since 1991, œnologist Christine Chaumard has put all her skill into the making of this pale yellow-

coloured wine with its green tinges. With an intense floral and fruity nose, it is an expressive, characterful white and an 'ideal accompaniment to a light meal'. Drink it within the year. Also winner of a star is the **98 Rouge** (30–49 F), which should be left for a year.
🔑 Gilles Chaumard, rte d'Aubignan, 84330 Caromb, tel. 04.90.62.43.38, fax 04.90.62.35.84 ✉ 🍷 by appt.

ETIENNE DE VESC

Elevé en Barrique 1998**

■ 3.8 ha 14,600 🍷 30–49 F

1998
ÉLEVÉ EN BARRIQUES
Cuvée
Etienne de Vesc

To mark the 70th anniversary of the co-operative, an international competition for chamber music composition was launched with the theme, 'Sounds of the Cellar'. The wine shows oaky notes, with quite discreet spice and toast on the nose, and a palate 'with body' that can cope with the wood tannins. Showing the promise of a good future, this was enjoyed by the whole jury, who particularly liked its balanced side and the complexity of its flavours. The **Cuvée Principale 98 Rouge**, aged in tank, won a star for its lovely weight. (20–29 F).
🔑 Cave coopérative Saint-Marc, 84330 Caromb, tel. 04.90.62.40.24, fax 04.90.62.48.83, e-mail cave@saint-marc.com ✉ 🍷 by appt.

DOM. DE FONDRECHE

Cuvée Persia 1999**

□ 1 ha 2,000 🍷 50–69 F

This Cuvée Persia has a lemon colour with green hues and an elegant floral bouquet, accompanied by oaky notes. It is both well-balanced and very integrated, characterised by fine flavours of vanilla, apples and pears. It would make a delicious accompaniment to fish in a cream sauce. The **Cuvée Persia Rouge** (30–49 F) wins a star. Try it in a few months time to accompany duck with truffles.
🔑 Dom. de Fondrèche, quartier Fondrèche, 84380 Mazan, tel. 04.90.69.61.42, fax 04.90.69.61.18 ✉ 🍷 by appt.
🔑 N. Barthélemy et S. Vincenti

DOM. DE FONDRECHE

Cuvée Nadal 1998***

■ 3 ha 16,000 🍷 30–49 F

This Cuvée Nadal, deep garnet with purplish highlights, reveals a complex and powerful nose, mixing accents of the garrigue and liquorice on a base of strawberry jam. Flavours of prunes and caramel add to very rich and remarkably assertive tannins giving a 'lovely compromise between maturation and development'. Recommended with meat casserole or game. It could be left for three to five years. The **Fayard 98 Rouge** wins a star. An easier wine, it is already drinking well.
🔑 Dom. de Fondrèche, quartier Fondrèche, 84380 Mazan, tel. 04.90.69.61.42, fax 04.90.69.61.18 ✉ 🍷 by appt.

DOM. DE LA BASTIDONNE 1998*

■ 3 ha 15,000 ▮ 30–49 F

The Domaine de La Bastidonne is an old 14th-century farm situated on the southern slopes of the Vaucluse mountains. 'A simple but well made and smooth wine,' remarked one jury member, summing up the comments of the tasters regarding this nicely presented 98. The red berry fruit bouquet and suppleness on the palate were unanimously enjoyed.
🔑 SCEA Dom. de la Bastidonne, 84220 Cabrières-d'Avignon, tel. 04.90.76.70.00, fax 04.90.76.74.34 ✉ 🍷 ev. day except Sun. 9am–12 noon 2pm–6pm
🔑 Gérard Marreau

LA GARANCE Saumane 1997**

■ 2.5 ha 5,300 ▮ 30–49 F

A former cellar-master on another estate, Stéphanie Sors rented a vineyard and has produced her own wine under a very attractive label. This is a superb example with a dark purple colour and an open, expressive nose of black fruits and spices. A very well-balanced wine, it is made enjoyable by the tremendous amount of fruit. Taking into account its structure, leave it for two or three years and then drink it with jugged hare or a haunch of venison.
🔑 Stéphanie Sors, Dom. de La Royère, 84580 Oppède-le-Vieux, tel. 04.90.76.87.76, fax 04.90.20.85.37 ✉ 🍷 ev. day except Sun. 9am–12 noon 2.30pm–6.30pm
🔑 Guenoun

LA GARENNE 1998

■ n.c. n.c. ▮ 20–29 F

Jean-Claude Boisset is now in charge of developing Mommessin's business outside of Burgundy. He submits a Ventoux of the kind we love. Fruit married with violets, freshness and balance all make it the perfect wine for a meal outside on the terrace.
🔑 Mommessin, Le Pont-des-Samsons, 69430 Quincié-en-Beaujolais, tel. 04.74.69.09.30, fax 04.74.69.09.28, e-mail information@mommessin.com
🍷 by appt.

DOM. LA TUILIERE

Sélection Vieilles Vignes 1997*

■ 3.5 ha 13,000 ▮ 30–49 F

Domaine La Tuilière used to be a farm where they manufactured tiles for the rooftops of Provence, hence its name. Grenache (50%) and Syrah (50%) are the raw materials for this old-vine wine that has a dark purple colour, and a complex bouquet of spices embellished with toasty notes. The full-bodied and well-balanced palate reveals very fine silky tannins. This wine is ready now and would be marvellous with a stew or a leg of lamb with thyme.

André Ravoire, Dom. La Tuilière, R.D. 60, 84220 Murs, tel. 04.90.05.73.03, fax 04.90.05.78.07, e-mail domaine@la-tuiliere.com
ev. day except Sun. 9am–12 noon 2pm–8pm

DOM. DE LA VERRIERE

Le Haut de la Jacotte Elevé en Fût de Chêne 1998

1.45 ha 7,666 30–49 F

Matured in oak barrels, this 98 sports a lively colour tinged with purple and reveals scents of red berry fruits and spices on the nose. All this indicates a youthfulness that is confirmed on the palate. It needs another year. The **99 Blanc**, also given a mention, is an attractive, fruity wine (20–29 F).

Jacques Maubert, Dom. de La Verrière, 84220 Goult, tel. 04.90.72.20.88, fax 04.90.72.40.33 ev. day except Sun. 9am–12 noon 2pm–6pm

LA VIEILLE FERME 1998*

10 ha 600,000 30–49 F

A silky and elegant wine that offers delicate spicy and red berry fruit aromas on a really beautifully integrated base. The power of the wine is never overplayed but is nevertheless obvious.

Domaines Perrin, quartier La Ferrière, 84100 Orange, tel. 04.90.11.12.00, fax 04.90.11.12.19, e-mail perrin@beaucastel.com ev. day except Sat. Sun. 8am–12 noon 2pm–6pm; cl. Aug.

DOM. LE MURMURIUM 1998*

3 ha 10,000 30–49 F

This ruby-coloured and violet-tinged 98 is dominated by red berry fruits and blackcurrant. An expressive wine, it gives an impression of sweetness and a balance that would go well with a roast rabbit in thyme.

Jean Marot, rte de Flassan, 84570 Mormoiron, tel. 04.90.61.73.74, fax 04.90.61.74.51 by appt.

DOM. LES TERRASSES D'EOLE 1999*

0.8 ha 5,300 30–49 F

In 1998, the son Stéphane moved onto Claude Saurel's family farm. The first vinification on the estate took place in 1999 to produce a pale-coloured wine with pink tinges, a discreet but elegant nose and a well-balanced palate. Extremely carefully made, it will be delicious served very cool from late 2000.

Dom. les Terrasses d'Eole, 468, chem. de Banay, 84380 Mazan, tel. 04.90.69.78.63, fax 04.90.69.78.63, e-mail terrasses.eole@online.fr
ev. day 9am–12 noon 2pm–6pm; cl. 1 Sep.–15 Oct.
M. Saurel

LUMIERES 1998*

3 ha 8,000 20–29 F

Grenache takes pride of place in this wine from Lumières that is characterised by a definite freshness on the nose with raspberry notes. The structure is light and the aromas very clean; this is a really easy-drinking wine, particularly when enjoyed with *charcuterie* or a barbecue. Ready now. The same mark goes to the **Les Quatres Vents 99 Blanc** (less than 20 F), which has good elegance and depth of flavour.

Cave de Lumières, 84220 Goult, tel. 04.90.72.20.04, fax 04.90.72.42.52
by appt.

DOM. DE MAROTTE

Cuvée Prestige 1997*

5.7 ha 7,000 30–49 F

Very open, with pronounced red berry fruit and spices, this elegant 97 is well-balanced and has plenty of richness on the palate. It should be drunk fairly soon with game bird or grilled meat.

EARL La Reynarde, Dom. de Marotte, 84200 Carpentras, tel. 04.90.63.43.27, fax 04.90.67.15.28, e-mail marotte@wanadoo.fr
ev. day except Mon. 10am–1pm 3pm–7pm

LES VIGNERONS DU MONT VENTOUX

Carte Noire Elevé en Fût de Chêne 1997*

5 ha 20,000 30–49 F

The co-operative Les Vignerons de Mont Ventoux, situated at the foot of the 'Giant of Provence' (Mont Ventoux) is a favoured place from which to sell all sorts of quality products. The cellar allows certain amateur painters to exhibit their works. Grenache and Syrah appear in equal proportion in this intense ruby-coloured Carte Noire. It has a subtle and elegant nose with stewed red berry fruits and notes of oak. Well-balanced, full-bodied and powerful, it can be drunk now. Also note the star won by the supple and full-bodied **Domaine Balaquère 98 Rouge** (20–29 F).

SCA Les Vignerons du Mont Ventoux, quartier de la Salle, 84410 Bédoin, tel. 04.90.12.88.00, fax 04.90.65.64.43
by appt.

DOM. PELISSON 1999

3.2 ha n.c. 30–49 F

The product of organic cultivation and low yields, the lovely intense-coloured wine from this estate is now full of youthfulness and spirit. It should settle down soon and has all

the time in the world to become serious. Only consider buying it in a year or two.
🔑 Patrick Pelisson, 84220 Gordes,
tel. 04.90.72.28.49, fax 04.90.72.23.91 ☒
🍷 by appt.

CH. PESQUIE La Quintessence 1998*

■ n.c. n.c. 50–69 F

This country house dating from the 18th century and set in exceptional surroundings is very attractive to visit. And the wine will keep your attention. It is the estate's reds that are best known, in particular this wine, in which Syrah has the virtual monopoly (80%). The scents evoke very ripe red berry fruit, and the flavours are balanced on an expressive palate that reveals the influence of 14 months in new *barrique.* Leave it for two years. The **Cuvée Prestige** has spent just 12 months in barrel and earns the same marks.
🔑 GAEC Ch. Pesquié, rte de Flassan, B.P. 6, 84570 Mormoiron, tel. 04.90.61.94.08, fax 04.90.61.94.13 ☒ 🍷 ev. day 9am–12 noon 2pm–6pm; groups by appt.
🔑 Chaudière et Bastide

DOM. DE TARA 1998*

■ 2 ha 1,000 30–49 F

The estate was only sold in 1999, and is henceforth the property of two women, mother and daughter, Françoise and Frédérique Droux. This intensely coloured 98 has an attractive, fruity nose and pronounced, but not aggressive tannins on the palate. The whole effect is a balanced, well-made wine with plenty of weight. Already pleasant, it will really open up in about a year and will be perfect for a beef Carpaccio with shavings of Parmesan cheese.
🔑 Dom. de Tara, Les Rossignols, 84220 Roussillon,
tel. 04.90.05.74.87, fax 04.90.05.71.35 ☒
🍷 ev. day except Sun. 2pm–6pm
🔑 Droux

DOM. TROUSSEL 1998*

■ 15 ha 20,000 20–29 F

A lively colour with pretty purple highlights, a subtle but clean nose and red fruit flavours with raspberry in particular come together in this beautifully agreeable wine. With a youthful and very attractive character, it should be drunk over the next year to benefit fully from its freshness.
🔑 Dom. Troussel, 2059, rte de Serres, 84200 Carpentras, tel. 04.90.67.28.35, fax 04.90.60.68.99 ☒ 🍷 by appt.

CH. VALCOMBE La Sereine 1998**

■ 4 ha 9,000 100–149 F

La Sereine displays a very intense, almost black colour and ripe fruits with real finesse on the nose. There is plenty of weight and 'a perfect mouthfeel' together with sweetness from the well-integrated vanilla flavours. In short, this is an extremely well made and classy 98.
🔑 Ch. Valcombe, 84330 Saint-Pierre-de-Vassols, tel. 04.90.62.51.29, fax 04.90.62.51.47 ☒ 🍷 by appt.

PAUL VENDRAN E.V. 1998**

■ 1 ha 2,400 70–99 F

It may have a strange name, but this is a superb 98. It reveals a very beautiful intense colour, a complex nose of black fruits, oak and vanilla and is a remarkably well-balanced wine, with plenty of weight and richness, showing good quality oak on the finish. You will need to wait four or five years to fully appreciate it with a meat or game casserole.
🔑 Paul Vendran, la ferme Saint-Pierre, 84410 Flassan, tel. 04.90.61.90.88, fax 04.90.61.89.96 ☒ 🍷 by appt.

Côtes du Luberon

The Appellation Côtes du Luberon was created on 26 February 1988.

The 36 communes included in this appellation extend over the northern and southern slopes of the limestone mountains of the Luberon, and the vineyard covers nearly 3,000 ha (7,410 acres) and in 1999 182,000 hl (4,804,800 gal) were produced. Côtes du Luberon produce good red wines with a marked character from the quality of the varieties used (Grenache, Syrah) and the distinctive terroir on which they grow. The climate is cooler than in the Rhône valley and the late harvests explain the large proportion of white wines (25%) and the acknowledged quality for which they are sought.

CAVE COOPERATIVE DE BONNIEUX Elevé en Fût de Chêne 1998*

■ 20 ha 10,000 30–49 F

Traditionally vinified and grown on clay-limestone soil, this wine has a spicy, oaky nose with nuances of undergrowth. The stewed cherry fruit aromas prove to be elegant. A good example of the appellation that could be aged for two or three years.
🔑 Cave vinicole de Bonnieux, quartier de la Gare, 84480 Bonnieux, tel. 04.90.75.80.03, fax 04.90.75.92.73, e-mail les.vignerons.de.bonnieux@wanadoo.fr ☒
🍷 by appt.

DOM. CHATEAU D'AIGUES 1999★★

10 ha 22,500 20–29 F

This dark red, beautifully presented wine has a very intense vegetal and fruity nose with slight hints of liquorice and spices. The same flavours recur on the palate, which also shows silky tannins and really good length. The wine needs another two or three years of ageing before it can be truly appreciated. Best served with red meat or soft cheeses.

Cellier Val de Durance,
Le Grand Jardin, 84360 Lauris,
tel. 04.90.08.26.36, fax 04.90.08.28.27

CH. DE CLAPIER 1999

1.8 ha 12,000 30–49 F

Long ago this wine estate belonged to Mirabeau's family. Thomas Montagne's ancestors purchased it in 1880. Between the two 1999 Luberon whites submitted, the jury tended to prefer this one, which proclaims the excellent techniques practised by the winemaker. A very young 99, it is lively and flowery. Those who enjoy the flavours of maturation *sur lies* (on the lees) in new oak will prefer the **Cuvée Réservée**, which also won a mention.

Thomas Montagne,
Ch. de Clapier, 84120 Mirabeau,
tel. 04.90.77.01.03, fax 04.90.77.03.26,
e-mail thomas.montagne@chateau-de-clapier.com
Mon. Wed. Sat. 9am–12 noon 2pm–5pm

CH. CONSTANTIN-CHEVALIER
Cuvée des Fondateurs 1998★★★

12 ha 25,000 30–49 F

This Cuvée des Fondateurs was unanimously acclaimed by the jury. It has a very intense and deep colour; the extremely elegant bouquet reveals notes of undergrowth and crystallised fruit, while on the palate superbly fine flavours evoke jam and spices structured by perfect oak. Superlatives are not in short supply: splendid tannins, delicious wine, superb etc.... This magnificent 98 needs three to five years and could be served as an accompaniment to game. The **Cuvée des Fondateurs 99 Blanc** earns a star. Fermentation in new barrels with lees stirring for four months has produced a very pretty wine with elegant oak flavours. An excellent match with fish and crustaceans.

Ch. Constantin-Chevalier et Filles, Ch. de Constantin, 84160 Lourmarin,
tel. 04.90.68.38.99, fax 04.90.68.37.37
by appt.

CLAUDE DIEUDONNE 1998★

15 ha 20,000 20–29 F

Claude Dieudonné has submitted an attractive blend of Grenache with Syrah. This wine has a lovely intense ruby colour with violet tinges, but 'lacks some weight to be truly perfect', according to one member of the jury. A Côtes du Luberon that is characterised by an intense raspberry nose, with balance and suppleness on the palate. This nicely matured wine could accompany a roast lamb and *gratin Dauphinois*.

Claude Dieudonné, Dom. de Régusse,
rte de Bastide-des-Jourdans, 04860
Pierrevert, tel. 04.92.72.30.44,
fax 04.92.72.69.08
ev. day 8am–12 noon 2pm–7pm

DOM. DE FONTENILLE 1999★

18 ha 13,000 30–49 F

Purchased in 1949 by the grandparents of the current owner, Fontenille covers 21 ha (52 acres) of vineyards. This *Rosé de Saignée* has an attractive, intense colour with bluish hues and reveals a fruity nose; the palate is full of flavours, dominated by boiled sweets and fruity nuances. A 'fairly high-tech' wine, it is elegant and well-balanced, showing a good deal of finesse. Mentioned by the jury, the gold and green tinged **99 Blanc** is a very rounded wine.

EARL Lévêque et Fils,
Dom. de Fontenille, 84360 Lauris,
tel. 04.90.08.23.36, fax 04.90.08.45.05,
e-mail fontenille@caves-particulieres.com
ev. day except Sun. 9am–12.30pm
2pm–7.30pm

DOM. DE FONTPOURQUIERE
Cuvée Noël du Villaret 1998★

1 ha 2,000 30–49 F

Syrah dominates this purple-coloured 98 with mauve highlights. It has a powerful nose of red berry fruit, spices and oak. Straightforward, full-bodied, well structured and very well balanced, it is ready to drink now, but equally could be left.

Yves Ronchi, rte de Lumières,
84480 Lacoste,
tel. 04.90.75.80.02, fax 04.90.75.80.02
ev. day except Mon. 9am–12 noon
2pm–6pm

CH. LA CANORGUE 1999★

5 ha 20,000 30–49 F

A very fruity rosé, both on the nose and the palate with an almost synthetic pale pink colour. It has a well-balanced mid-palate with good acidity, in short, an attractive wine that will be enjoyed by rosé enthusiasts. Serve it with a *pissaladière* or canapés.

🔑 EARL J.-P. et M. Margan,
Ch. la Canorgue, 84480 Bonnieux,
tel. 04.90.75.81.01, fax 04.90.75.82.98 ☒
🍷 by appt.

DOM. DE LA CAVALE 1998★

■ 2 ha 11,870 🛢 30–49 F

This wine was made in a traditional way with three weeks of post-fermentation maceration, followed by a period of about eight months in oak. The cherry colour displays an orange rim, the quite intense oaky nose reveals notes of stewed fruit and the well-balanced palate shows hints of pepper on the finish. Serve in two or three years time with a jugged hare or wild boar.

🔑 Paul Dubrule,
rte de Lourmarin, 84160 Cucuron,
tel. 04.90.77.22.96, fax 04.90.77.25.64 ☒
🍷 ev. day except Sun. 9am–12.30pm
2.30pm–6pm

DOM. DE LA CITADELLE 1997★★

■ 5 ha 30,000 30–49 F

Yves Rousset-Rouard bought an old farmhouse and some vines in 1989 and, with the advice of œnologist Noël Rabot, turned it into a pretty 40-ha (99-acre) estate, which he called La Citadelle, an old family name. There he established a corkscrew museum with an extensive collection. Here is a dark, very clear red 97 with a quite powerful bouquet of stewed fruit and jam. The same flavours recur on the palate with pronounced, but not aggressive tannins. Recommended with a rich game stew. Amongst the other wines, the following reds, each received one star: **Cuvée du Gouverneur 97** (70–99 F), having spent 12 months in barrel, has a complex and powerful nose with well integrated tannins; and **Le Châtaignier 99** (30–49 F), which has not seen oak and is fruity and spicy. Well balanced, it would be best decanted. The **Cuvée du Gouverneur 99 Blanc** is a typical example of the AOC.

🔑 Rousset-Rouard,
Dom. de la Citadelle, 84560 Ménerbes,
tel. 04.90.72.41.58, fax 04.90.72.41.59,
e-mail citadelle@pacwan.fr ☒ 🍷 by appt.

DOM. DE LA GARELLE

Cuvée Spéciale 1999

□ 0.5 ha 4,000 🛢 30–49 F

This lemon yellow Cuvée Spéciale is dominated by Vermentino, and reveals a fruity, lightly oaked nose. The subtle palate has plenty of character and needs some aeration. This wine will be appreciated in around a year, and will go particularly well with *coquille Saint-Jacques* in a chive sauce.

🔑 Dom. de la Garelle, quartier des Vallats,
84560 Ménerbes, tel. 04.90.72.31.20,
fax 04.90.72.47.81 ☒ 🍷 by appt.
🔑 Vlasman

DOM. DE LA ROYERE

Cuvée Spéciale 1999★

□ 2.9 ha 4,000 30–49 F

The Domaine de la Royère is situated in a popular tourist area, around 2 km (1 mile) from Oppède-le-Vieux. With a subtle bouquet tending towards flowers, especially lilac, it has attractive length on the palate, very obvious acidity, but plenty of richness. This is a pleasant and beautifully balanced Cuvée Spéciale that can be enjoyed as an aperitif. Also awarded star, the **Cuvée Spéciale 98 Rouge**, from equal amounts of Syrah and Grenache, is very characteristic. Try it with a gratin of aubergines.

🔑 Anne Hugues, Dom. de la Royère,
84580 Oppède,
tel. 04.90.76.87.76, fax 04.90.20.85.37 ☒
🍷 ev. day except Sun. 9am–12 noon
2.30pm–6.30pm; cl. Dec.–Mar.

LA VIEILLE FERME 1999

□ 5 ha 300,000 30–49 F

The area of production for AOC Côtes du Luberon white wines at La Vieille Ferme is located to a large extent in the Luberon regional park, equidistant from Avignon, Aix-en-Provence and Manosque. With a beautiful colour in the glass, this wine has a very fine fruity nose, with an overall reasonable balance, but still needs time to develop. It should be kept for another two years to be best appreciated.

🔑 Domaines Perrin,
quartier La Ferrière, 84100 Orange,
tel. 04.90.11.12.00, fax 04.90.11.12.19,
e-mail perrin@beaucastel.com ☒
🍷 ev. day except Sat. Sun. 8am–12 noon
2pm–6pm; cl. Aug.

DOM. LES VADONS 1999★★

■ 5 ha 7,000 20–29 F

Produced from a stony clay terroir and vinified traditionally, this remarkable wine possesses a powerful nose of red berry fruit, liquorice and spices. The palate is distinguished by an elegant and silky tannic structure with very attractive length. Leave for three to five years. It would go extremely well with stew or jugged hare. Another red, **Cuvée La Melchiorte 99 Rouge** received a star. It was matured for nine months in barrel but the wine still shows through; classic notes of Syrah (30% of the blend) and silky tannins provide an elegant combination.

🔑 EARL Dom. les Vadons, La Resparine,
Saint-Estève, 84160 Cucuron,
tel. 04.90.77.13.40, fax 04.90.77.13.40,
e-mail vadonbreba@terre-net.fr ☒
🍷 by appt.
🔑 Louis-Michel Bremond

CH. DE L'ISOLETTE

Cuvée Prestige Vieilles Vignes 1998★★

■ 20 ha 50,000 🛢 50–69 F

The Domaine de l'Isolette is situated in the commune of Apt, famous for its cathedral. The surrounding villages also provide interest for the tourist: Roussillon for its former ochre quarries, Gordes for the Vasarely Museum and the Sénanque Abbey, Lacoste for the château of the Marquis de Sade . . . And we must not forget this château with its vast 120-ha (296-acre) estate. This Cuvée Prestige is dark garnet-red with a purple rim and it leaves 'numerous legs' down the side of the glass, which may testify to its abundance of glycerol. The intense, very clean and complex nose appears rather musky. Balance prevails on the palate, with a velvety style and very attractive ripe fruity notes. 'I love this rounded and characteristic wine', concluded one jury member.

Ch. de l'Isolette, rte de Bonnieux, 84400 Apt, tel. 04.90.74.16.70, fax 04.90.04.70.73 ev. day except Sun. 8am–12 noon 2pm–5.45pm

EARL Luc Pinatel

CELLIER DE MARRENON 1999*

375 ha 2,000,000 20–29 F

Made from Syrah (30%) and Grenache (70%), this rosé has an intense pink colour with redcurrant tinges. It has a very pronounced bouquet of redcurrant and strawberry with particularly attractive fresh fruity flavours overall. A fairly good example of the appellation, it is for immediate drinking.

Cellier de Marrenon, rue Amédé-Ginies, B.P. 13, 84240 La Tour-d'Aigues, tel. 04.90.07.40.65, fax 04.90.07.30.77, e-mail marrenon@wanadoo.fr ev. day 8am–12 noon 2pm–6pm; Sun. 8am–12 noon

DOM. DE MAYOL 1999**

1.5 ha 6,000 30–49 F

Bernard Viguier owns 30 ha (74 acres) on a terroir that his family has worked since the 15th century. He submits a pale yellow, gold-tinged 99 that has a very pleasant, intense, toasty bouquet and a supple, full-bodied palate. This is an excellent well-balanced wine that one can suggest as an accompaniment for sliced scallops with truffle.

Bernard Viguier, Dom. de Mayol, 84400 Apt, tel. 04.90.74.12.80, fax 04.90.04.85.64, e-mail mayol@wordonline.fr ev. day except Sun. 9am–12 noon 2.30pm–7pm

CH. DE MILLE Blanc de blancs 1999*

6 ha 12,000 30–49 F

Former summer residence of the Avignon Popes, Mille is one of the oldest and most authentic wine châteaux of the Côtes du Luberon. This agreeable 99 is made from equal amounts of Clairette, Roussanne and Bourboulenc and has a beautifully intense bouquet showing amylic and fruity nuances. The subtle flavours, overall balance and roundness produce an extremely nice harmony. Recommended as an aperitif or with fish. In the **99 Rosé** (also one star), Mille personifies all the elegance of a delicate, floral and simultaneously fruity Côtes du Luberon with good length.

Conrad Pinatel, Ch. de Mille, 84400 Apt, tel. 04.90.74.11.94, fax 04.90.74.56.82 ev. day 8am–12 noon 2pm–6.30pm

PAROLE DE TERRE 1998*

8 ha 30,000 20–29 F

This 'wine from organically grown grapes' (as declared on the label) was submitted by Monsieur Pialat, the cellar-master. It is a very agreeable, well-balanced 98 with aromas of leather and prunes. The wine has a good overall harmony with plenty of character and could be served with pheasant casserole.

SCA Cave Lourmarin-Cadenet, montée du Galinier, 84160 Lourmarin, tel. 04.90.68.06.21, fax 04.90.68.25.84 ev. day except Sun. 8am–12 noon 2pm–6pm

CH. SAINT-PIERRE DE MEJANS 1998**

3.5 ha 14,000 30–49 F

The Château Saint-Pierre de Mejans is an old Benedictine monastery from the 12th century that has always owned vines. It is said that in the 15th century the bishop called the monks to order for storing their wines in the church. Brice Doan, the estate director, has made two beautiful 1998 reds: this one, of an intense ruby red, reveals a complex nose of undergrowth, beeswax, truffles and cloves that recur on the well-balanced palate. It can be aged for two to three years before serving with meat casserole. The **Cuvée Vieilles Vignes 98** (also two stars) is just as attractive. With a bouquet of undergrowth, leather and stewed fruit with an elegant palate of pronounced spices, it could be cellared for three to five years. As for the **99 Rosé**, vinified in the *saignée* method (with a short skin maceration), drink it now. A distinctive character won it a mention.

Ch. Saint-Pierre de Mejans, 84160 Puyvert, tel. 04.90.08.40.51, fax 04.90.08.41.96, e-mail tianed@aol.com ev. day 9.30am–12 noon 2.30pm–7pm; cl. Tue. in winter

Laurence Doan de Champassak

CH. VAL JOANIS 1998*

50 ha 160,000 30–49 F

A country house that one can admire, apart from its wines, for the garden on three terraces, one of which has a vegetable garden, full of medicinal plants and many other marvels. Syrah (70%) and Grenache (30%) went into the making of this well-balanced wine whose expressive and intense nose is dominated by red berry fruit and blackcurrants. On the palate, there is an easy-going spicy hint. A touch of acidity on the finish still seems a little sharp. This is a wine with character that should be kept for the best part of a year before serving with red meat or cheese. Also crowned with a star, the **99 Blanc**, made using skin maceration, is very pleasing. The elegant and balanced nutty flavours will partner white meat well.

SC du Ch. Val Joanis, Ch. Val Joanis, 84120 Pertuis, tel. 04.90.79.20.77, fax 04.90.09.69.52, e-mail val-joanis@luberon.com ev. day 10am–12 noon 2pm–6pm

DOM. DES VAUDOIS 1999★

6 ha 5,000 20–29 F

The estate, located in the Vaud area, owns cellars that date from the 17th century. A vaulted troglodyte cave was found here. An intense blue-tinged 99 with a subtle floral bouquet and pronounced red berry fruit flavours. Well-balanced and attractive, this wine can be enjoyed right away with *charcuterie* or chicken.

Aurouze, Dom. des Vaudois, 84240 Cabrières-d'Aigues, tel. 04.90.77.60.87, fax 04.90.77.69.44 by appt.

Coteaux de Pierrevert

Located in the Alpes-de-Haute-Provence department, the appellation lies mostly on the slopes of the right bank of the Durance (Corbières, Saint-Tulle, Perrevert, Manosque, etc), on about 210 ha (519 acres). Climatic conditions restrict cultivation to about ten communes of the 42 legally included in the area of the AOC. The red, rosé and white wines, at 14,000 hl (369,600 gal), are fairly low in alcohol, but lively enough, and are enjoyed by the many who travel through this tourist region. The Coteaux de Pierrevert were recognised as an Appellation d'Origine Contrôlée by the National Committee of the INAO in 1998.

DOM. LA BLAQUE 1999★★

6 ha 28,000 30–49 F

This attractive estate covers 60 ha (148 acres). Made from equal amounts of Vermentino, Grenache Blanc and Roussanne, this very vivid white reveals glints of almond green. The bouquet is quite developed. The palate opens well with good acidity and good balance, despite a hint of alcohol showing through. This Pierrevert would be enjoyable with a fish dish, such as monkfish, or served as an apéritif. The **Rosé de Saignée 99** wins a star. Gilles Delsuc, the chief œnologist, gave it a floral bouquet of violets.

Dom. Châteauneuf, rte de la Bastide-des-Jourdans, 04860 Pierrevert, tel. 04.92.72.39.71, fax 04.92.72.81.26 ev. day except Sun. 8am–12 noon 2pm–6pm

DOM. LA BLAQUE Réserve 1997★★

6 ha 23,000 50–69 F

PRODUIT DE FRANCE
RÉSERVE RÉSERVE
DOMAINE
LA BLAQUE
COTEAUX DE PIERREVERT
13% vol. 75 cl
ALPES DE HAUTE PROVENCE

Made using both carbonic maceration and traditional vinification, this promising 97 won over the entire jury. The colour is deep red with black tinges and the complex nose reveals truffles, spices, red peppers and undergrowth. On the palate there are vanilla-oak flavours with tannins that have not yet integrated. This is a wine that will really open up in about three years' time when it could accompany game or roast turkey with chestnuts. The **Cuvée Collection III 97 Rouge** (70–99 F) from 90% Syrah and 10% Grenache is also matured in barrel and shows plenty of ripe fruit, with notes of leather and undergrowth. It wins two stars.

Dom. Châteauneuf, rte de la Bastide-des-Jourdans, 04860 Pierrevert, tel. 04.92.72.39.71, fax 04.92.72.81.26 ev. day except Sun. 8am–12 noon 2pm–6pm

CAVE DES VIGNERONS DE PIERREVERT

Cuvée du Village d'Or 1999★

n.c. 30,000 20–29 F

Monsieur Silvestre, the director of the co-operative, has made a very successful white 99 that shows attractive aromas of flowers, honey and acacia. It's a warming, well-balanced wine with excellent length, which should be served with shellfish or fish cooked to an exotic, spicy recipe.

Cave des vignerons de Pierrevert, 1, av. Auguste-Bastide, 04860 Pierrevert, tel. 04.92.72.19.06, fax 04.92.72.85.36 ev. day except Sun. 8am–12 noon 2pm–6pm

CH. DE ROUSSET 1999★

10 ha 35,000 20–29 F

This great Provençal estate cultivates both vines and olive trees using growing techniques that respect the environment. Produced by a combination of pressing and *saignée*, this lovely looking rosé 99 is still a little closed at the moment but will be excellent by the end of 2000. On the palate are developed flavours of ripe strawberries. A well-balanced, rounded and rich Pierrevert that would be ideal with Provençal food.

H. et R. Emery, Ch. de Rousset, 04800 Gréoux-les-Bains, tel. 04.92.72.62.49 by appt.

Côtes du Vivarais

At the north-western limit of the southern Côtes du Rhône, the Côtes du Vivarais straddle the departments of the Ardèche and the Gard, covering 577 ha (1,425 acres). The communes of Orgnac (famous for its potholes), Saint-Ramèze and Saint-Montan are authorised to add their name to that of the appellation. These wines, produced on limestone soils, are mainly reds made from Grenache (30% minimum) and Syrah (30% minimum), with some typically fresh rosés, which should be drunk young. This former VDQS was recognised as an AOC in May 1999.

BEAUMONT DES GRAS 1998

■ n.c. 100,000 ▮ 20 F+

A village constructed in the Middle Ages around a Cluniac monastery, Ruoms still retains some interesting remains to show the visitor. The co-operative has established its headquarters here. This wine has particularly attractive aromas: the smells of the garrigue that one might expect on this bleak plateau are mixed with floral nuances and finally some much more unexpected citrus notes, especially grapefruit. The light and easy palate is classic. The jury also mentioned the **Domaine des Bois du Garn 98 Rouge**.

Les Vignerons ardéchois,
B.P. 8, 07120 Ruoms,
tel. 04.75.39.98.00, fax 04.75.39.69.48 ☑
Ɪ ev. day except Sun. 8am–12 noon 2pm–7pm

DOM. DU BELVEZET 1998

■ 7 ha 5,000 ▮ 20–29 F

Established in 1955, this estate submitted a **99 Blanc**, mentioned for its elegance, and this red, mentioned for its clean-cut character. One taster hazarded a guess that Syrah provided the personality, and he was right: 60% of this grape variety adds fruit to the supple tannins that emanate from the 40% Grenache. An easy-drinking wine.

René Brunel, rte de Vallon-Pont-d'Arc,
07700 Saint-Remèze,
tel. 04.75.04.05.87, fax 04.75.04.05.87,
e-mail belvezet.brunel@wanadoo.fr ☑
Ɪ by appt.

DOM. DE COMBELONGE
Cuvée Spéciale 1998

■ 3.5 ha 19,300 ▮ 🌢 20–29 F

Vinezac: the village takes its name from the vineyards that were planted near this market town at the crossroads of history (prehistoric caves, Romanesque churches . . .). This Cuvée Spéciale has a beautiful deep colour and notable influences from Syrah. The fruity and floral nose heralds a fairly classic palate that is rounded, attractive and well balanced. A pleasant wine to enjoy immediately.

Denis Manent, Dom. de Combelonge,
07110 Vinezac, tel. 04.75.36.92.54,
fax 04.75.36.99.59 ☑ Ɪ ev. day except Sun. 9am–12 noon 2.30pm–6.30pm

ALAIN GALLETY Haute Vigne 1998*

■ 6 ha 30,000 ▮ 🌢 30–49 F

This producer has pulled out all the stops in releasing this beautiful wine, which is very worthy of its appellation. Manual harvesting into small boxes and a grape-sorting table are used. The complex nose of flowers and honey is powerful with notes from the garrigue behind. These flavours appear once again on the palate, which is also powerful, though not at all aggressive. You could try this wine with game.

Dom. Alain Gallety, La Montagne,
07220 Saint-Montan, tel. 04.75.52.63.18,
fax 04.75.52.56.18 ☑ Ɪ by appt.

CLOS DE L'ABBE DUBOIS
Saint-Remèze 1998*

■ 3 ha 4,000 ▮ 20–29 F

This wine appears still youthful and bright and presents an invitation to walk in the perfumed and flowery 'clos' where violets dominate. The palate is vivacious with a fine energy on the palate that guarantees enjoyment.

Claude Dumarcher, Clos de l'Abbé
Dubois, 07700 Saint-Remèze,
tel. 04.75.98.98.44, fax 04.75.98.98.44 ☑
Ɪ by appt.

DOM. DE LA BOISSERELLE 1998

■ 4 ha 18,000 ▮ 20–29 F

Now famous for its lavender plantings, Saint-Remèze was formerly renowned for its almond trees and game. The 17-ha (42-acre) estate located here produced a wine in which the majority Syrah (80%) expresses itself in notes of undergrowth and humus. This is a terroir wine with a slight touch of rusticity.

Richard Vigne, Dom. de la Boisserelle,
07700 Saint-Remèze, tel. 04.75.04.24.37,
fax 04.75.04.24.37 ☑ Ɪ by appt.

UNION DES PRODUCTEURS D'ORGNAC-L'AVEN Réserve 1998*

■ 120 ha 60,000 ▮ 🌢 20–29 F

Orgnac is famous for its subterranean grotto, a gigantic pothole accessible by a narrow staircase of 780 steps. After an interesting hour-long visit, you should go to the co-operative (1.5 km or around a mile) to replenish your energy by tasting the three selected wines. This was their last VDQS. With a great depth of colour, the quality of the nose comes from the concentration of floral notes, especially violets, mixed with honey, and these also recur on the palate. This Vivarais red

really owes its success to silky tannins and a full-bodied palate.
🔑 Union des Producteurs d'Orgnac-l'Aven, 07150 Orgnac-l'Aven, tel. 04.75.38.60.08, fax 04.75.38.65.90 ✉ 🍷 by appt.

UNION DES PRODUCTEURS D'ORGNAC-L'AVEN 1999**

□ 10 ha 25,000 ▮ 🌡 20–29 F

The first vintage of the Appellation d'Origine Contrôlée. It's party time at Vivarais. Here is the wine that aroused such eulogies. An intense, complex and expressive nose reveals a range of perfumes followed by flavours of linden flowers, peach, apricot and grapefruit. It displays an overall sense of elegance right through to the long finish, thanks to 80% Grenache Blanc. The **99 Rosé** won a star for its fragrances of blackcurrant, redcurrant and grapefruit, and because it is an ideal wine to drink right through a meal.
🔑 Union des Producteurs d'Orgnac-l'Aven, 07150 Orgnac-l'Aven, tel. 04.75.38.60.08, fax 04.75.38.65.90 ✉ 🍷 by appt.

CAVE DE SAINT-MONTAN

Saint-Montan 1998

■ 20 ha 10,600 ▮ 🌡 20–29 F

An historic label, because this 98 wine is still an AOVDQS and next year it will be an AOC. Tradition is maintained in the blend of Grenache-Syrah with an added 10% Carignan. The aromas are entirely characteristic (floral, with a note of spiciness) as is the palate, which is pleasant though slightly overpowerful. This is a well-made, attractive wine that will liven up hors-d'œuvres or could work right through a meal.
🔑 SCA les Vignerons la Cave de Saint-Montan, 07220 Saint-Montan, tel. 04.75.52.61.75, fax 04.75.52.56.51 ✉ 🍷 by appt.

DOM. DE VIGIER 1999***

◪ 3.5 ha 23,000 ▮ 20–29 F

On the tourist route of the Ibie Valley, not far from Vallon-Pont-d'Arc, is the pretty village of Lagorce. The huge Vigier estate thrilled the jury with its rosé. To all the qualities of the great wines, this 99 wine adds a touch of originality with redcurrant on the nose hiding other subtler aromas. Freshness and immediacy hardly show off the great skill of the wine-producer, but that skill certainly shows through in the elegance and finesse of this excellent 99.
🔑 Dupré et Fils, Dom. de Vigier, 07150 Lagorce, tel. 04.75.88.01.18, fax 04.75.37.18.79 ✉ 🍷 by appt.

VINS DOUX NATURELS (NATURALLY SWEET WINES)

The wine-makers of Roussillon have made highly regarded sweet wines since the 18th century, when Arnaud de Villeneuve perfected the principle of 'mutage'. This involves adding brandy to the must of red or white wines at the moment of full fermentation, a process that prevents further fermentation but preserves a certain quantity of sugar.

The AOC of these sweet wines stretches discontinuously through various parts of southern France: Pyrénées-Orientales, Aude, Hérault, Vaucluse and Corsica – but never too far from the Mediterranean. The principal grape varieties used are the Grenaches (Blanc, Gris and Noir), Macabeu, Malvoisie du Roussillon, also called Tourbat, Muscat à Petit Grains and Muscat d'Alexandrie. Compulsory regulations govern the way the vines are grown and pruned.

The yields are low and, at harvest, the must is required to have a minimum 252 g of sugar per litre. The sugar released at harvest varies depending on the region. Individual wines are accepted only after meeting rather stringent criteria: they must have reached between 15% and 18% alcohol by volume, have a minimum 45 g of sugar per litre (up to more than 100 g per litre for the Muscats), and have a total alcohol level (alcohol content plus strength of alcohol) of at least 21.5%. Some are sold only after three years' ageing in wooden barrels, the traditional method. The level is maintained by topping up with younger wines. Wines aged in this way acquire the particular flavour described as 'rancio', which is a legal definition in wine law. In 1999 total production of these wines was 367,543 hl (9,703,135 gal).

Banyuls and Banyuls Grand Cru

This exceptional terroir is on the extreme east of the Pyrenees, with steeply sloping hills overlooking the Mediterranean. Only the four communes of Collioure, Port-Vendres, Banyuls-sur-Mer and Cerbère are entitled to the appellation. The terraced vineyards (roughly 1,400 ha (3,458 acres)) are on schistous soils with a rocky substratum which, when not immediately visible, is often covered with a thin layer of topsoil. Thus the terroir is poor, often acid, and supports only very ordinary vine varieties, such as Grenache, producing a very low yield, often less than about 20 hl per ha (216 gal per acre). In 1999 production of Banyuls was 24,210 hl (639,144 gal).

On the other hand, the amount of sunshine is maximised by the terraced cultivation (the wine-growers have to maintain the terraces by hand to protect the soil, which can be washed away by the slightest storm). With the additional benefit of proximity to the Mediterranean, the grapes become gorged with sugar and aromatic qualities.

Old Grenache vines predominate. Vinification involves macerating the bunches of grapes; 'mutage' (the addition of brandy) may be carried out at this stage, allowing substantial maceration lasting more than ten days, a method known as maceration in alcohol.

The way in which the wine is brought on plays an essential part. In general, it tends to favour the oxydative development of the wine, either in wood (large barrels of 200–300 hectolitres or wooden casks of 600 litres) or in *bonbonnes* (squat, bulbous containers) exposed to the warmth of the sun under the roofs of the cellars. The different vintages brought on in this way are blended with the greatest care by the cellar-master to create the numerous types of wine that we know. In some contrary cases, the wine is brought on in a way specifically designed to maintain its youthful fruitiness and prevent oxidisation: thus, different wines are obtained with highly specific characteristics; these are called the *rimages* or 'varieties'. To earn the Appellation Grand Cru, wines must brought on in wooden casks for 30 months.

The wines range in colour from ruby to mahogany, and have a characteristic bouquet of dried grapes, cooked fruit, grilled almonds, coffee and prune brandy. The *rimages* retain their aromas of soft fruit, cherry and cherry brandy. Banyuls wines should be served at temperatures from 12–17°C (53.6–62.2°F), according to their age. They may be drunk as an apéritif, with dessert (some consider Banyuls the only wine to drink with a chocolate dessert, for example), with coffee and a cigar, but equally with foie gras, duck with cherries or figs and also with certain cheeses.

Banyuls

CORNET Rimage 1995

■ n.c. 3,100 70–99 F

The secret behind Abbé Rous' Cornet is the concentration in the grapes at harvest-time and the early bottling that is designed to capture the essence of the fruit. Its brick-red colour is attractive, and the nose gives off fruity

Vins Doux Naturels

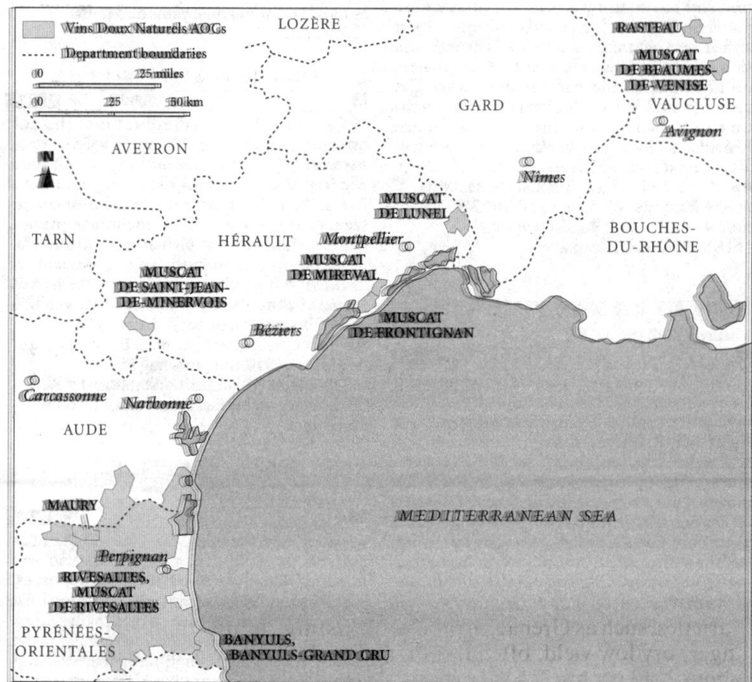

VDN

notes of kirsch with a hint of blackcurrant buds, like grapes close to harvest. This full, generous wine has very sweet balance dominated by ripe cherry, and surprises on the finish with a toasty note.

La Cave de L'Abbé Rous, 56, av. Charles-de-Gaulle, 66650 Banyuls-sur-Mer, tel. 04.68.88.72.72, fax 04.68.88.30.57, e-mail contact@banyuls.com

DOM. DE LA CASA BLANCA

Tradition 1997***

3 ha 8,000 50–69 F

1997 was supposedly a 'bad' year, and yet here are two remarkable wines: a superb **Vintage** and this Tradition, which won universal approval. Congratulations to Laurent Escapa and Alain Soufflet who, with quiet application and good humour, have shared with us their passion for hedonistic wine. The Tradition still has a strong colour. Its intense nose marries red fruits, spices and confectionery in a fine, very characteristic union. The palate is rich and full of sweet strength. The silkiness of the tannins, the harmonious toasty flavours absorbed from the barrel, and the slight touch of cocoa at the finish all evoke dark chocolate. Good for drinking now, but will also keep for several years.

Dom. de La Casa Blanca, rte des Mas, 66650 Banyuls-sur-Mer, tel. 04.68.88.12.85, fax 04.68.88.04.08 by appt.

Soufflet and Escapa

DOM. DE LA MARQUISE

Vintage 1998

n.c. 11,000 50–69 F

The Domaine is a splendid wine-growing environment, where nature has been sculpted by man to protect against fire, an impressive sight with its extraordinary interweaving of low walls and *peu de gall*. The old Grenache vines clinging to the steep slopes yield this purple, fruity wine, whose nose releases notes of leather and prunes. It is a welcoming wine, albeit still a little young and immature, with tannin still evident on the palate, accompanied by flavours of kirsch and stone fruit *eau-de-vie*.

SA Destavel, 7*bis*, av. du Canigou, 66000 Perpignan, tel. 04.68.68.36.00, fax 04.68.54.03.54

Jacques Py

DOM. LA TOUR VIEILLE

Cuvée Francis Cantié**

1.1 ha 4,533 70–99 F

A man of the soil and a woman from the world of communications here link their talents. Demijohns in the sun, vats, barrels – this wine has seen everything. Nonetheless, it retains its red, brick-like hue. It smells of underripe cherries with hints of prune. On the palate, it is rich and complex, its development sweet and strong, falling between fruitiness and toasty notes, and just showing the beginnings of rancio flavours.

Dom. La Tour Vieille, 3, av. du Mirador, 66190 Collioure, tel. 04.68.82.44.82, fax 04.68.82.38.42 by appt.

Cantié et Campadieu

LE DOMINICAIN

Tuilé 6 ans d'âge Vieilli en fût de chêne

80 ha 30,000 50–69 F

Set like a jewel in the cove of Collioure, the Dominican convent, with its painted beams and old Banyuls, is a real treasure. Which to go for: the six-year-old or the **barrel-matured 1990**? The choice between these two Banyuls of equal value was a hard one, but youth carried the day. There was the appeal of its brick-red colour, then the spicy nose with toasty hints, and the velvety, harmonious palate. Candied cherries and charred flavours characterise this well-balanced wine that is ready for drinking.

Cave coopérative Le Dominicain, pl. Orfila, 66190 Collioure, tel. 04.68.82.05.63, fax 04.68.82.43.06, e-mail le.dominicain@wanadoo.fr by appt.

L'ETOILE Extra Vieux 1988***

n.c. 20,000 100–149 F

Jean-Paul Ramio is the director of this co-operative founded in 1921. He offers some superb Banyuls, including a **75ième Anniversaire** wine, which is the equal of this Extra Vieux 1988 with its tawny colour and scents of overripe fruits, including prunes with a whiff of oak. Generous and full, the wine melts in the mouth. The impression of candied fruit yields to notes of very fresh fruit kernels before its remarkable finish, which is full of burnt chocolate flavours.

Sté coopérative L'Etoile, 26, av. du Puig-del-Mas, 66650 Banyuls-sur-Mer, tel. 04.68.88.00.10, fax 04.68.88.15.10 ev. day except Sat. Sun. 8am–12 noon 2pm–6pm

LES CLOS DE PAULILLES

Rimage mise tardive 1995**

2 ha 6,000 70–99 F

After Port-Vendres, the cove of Paulilles unfolds in a landscape that is both wild and inviting, where vines sway in the sea breezes. The **Rimage 1998** and this Mise Tardive 1995 are both equally fine wines. The edge, however, goes to the older wine with its garnet colour and nose of small red berries accompanied by blackcurrant buds. Remarkable for

its balance, this is a wine in its prime: fruit and oak join forces to prepare a splendid future.
🔑 Les Clos de Paulilles, Baie de Paulilles, 66660 Port-Vendres, tel. 04.68.38.90.10, fax 04.68.38.91.33, e-mail jau66@aol.com
☑ Y by appt.
🔑 Famille Dauré

DOM. PIETRI-GERAUD

Cuvée du Soleil 1994*

□ 0.5 ha 1,500 100–149 F

A traditional vineyard and modern cellar together serve the expertise of Laetitia and Maguy Piétri-Géraud, assisted by Hélène. Small wonder that, even after four years in demijohns, the wine retains all its sensitivity. After the welcoming amber colour, the nose sends forth its scents of dried fruits, beeswax and honey accompanied by notes of rancio. Walnut cake, not to mention chocolate cake, would be a choice match for this Cuvée du Soleil.
🔑 Maguy and Laetitia Piétri-Géraud, 22, rue Pasteur, 66190 Collioure, tel. 04.68.82.07.42, fax 04.68.98.02.58 ☑
Y ev. day 10am–12.30pm 3.30pm–6.30pm

CAVE SAINT-LOUIS 1998*

■ 10 ha 5,000 50–69 F

This estate has belonged to the sculptor Maillol's family since 1873. It is listed in the *Guide* for its promising 1998 Banyuls, fortified early in the fermentation. The colour is beautifully deep, and the wine smells of cherries and leather. Evolving as it goes through the mouth, betraying fullness and generosity, it shows expressive spiciness sustained by discreet oak.
🔑 Yvon and Jean-Louis Berta-Maillol, mas Paroutet, 66650 Banyuls-sur-Mer, tel. 04.68.88.00.54, fax 04.68.88.36.96 ☑
Y by appt.

CELLIER DES TEMPLIERS

Rimatge 1998**

■ n.c. 90,000 70–99 F

Rimatge is Catalan for 'vintage'. The fine young wine it labels here is from the not-to-be-missed 'cellar of the Templars'. Its colour is a deep, intense, warm purple. As for the nose, the scent of cherry instantly rises from the body of the wine, borne upon a base of undergrowth characteristic of a good Rimatge. One almost chews the cherry flavour, which is clothed in fine, silky tannin.
🔑 Cellier des Templiers, rte du Mas-Reig, 66650 Banyuls-sur-Mer, tel. 04.68.98.36.70, fax 04.68.98.36.91 ☑ Y by appt.

VIAL-MAGNERES Rivage 1996**

□ 2 ha 8,000 70–99 F

Behind a warm, affable appearance hides a dogged man to whom we owe the existence of Banyuls Blanc, a wine that has enthused France's greatest chefs. His wine is pale gold, tinged with grey, the mark of Grenache Gris. The exotic scent of lychee subtly marries notes of rock-rose and heathland broom. Full and enveloping on the palate, the wine melts in the mouth, sparked at the finish by a surprising hint of tannin that helps to give it even greater length.
🔑 Dom. Vial-Magnères, Clos Saint-André, 66650 Banyuls-sur-Mer, tel. 04.68.88.31.04, fax 04.68.55.01.06, e-mail al.tragou@wanadoo.fr ☑ Y by appt.
🔑 Monique and Bernard Sapéras

Banyuls grand cru

CASTELL DES HOSPICES 1985***

■ n.c. 4,300 150–199 F

CASTELL DES HOSPICES
BANYULS GRAND CRU
1985
VIN DOUX NATUREL

To restore the church at Banyuls, Abbé Rous decided to sell wine. He saw his hopes fully realized, which explains why, although it can't be bought in situ, the wine can be found in wine-shops, delicatessens and restaurants. As soon as it is in the glass, it releases its seductive mix of aromas – sweet oakiness, leather, crystallised prune, and a bewitching scent of the seaside reminiscent of peat. Full, powerful and lively, the wine melts in the mouth, giving overtones of crystallised fruits, spices and cocoa. It needs a Havana cigar, coffee or chocolate to accompany it. Also worthy of mention is the **Reynal 1990**.
🔑 La Cave de L'Abbé Rous, 56, av. Charles-de-Gaulle, 66650 Banyuls-sur-Mer, tel. 04.68.88.72.72, fax 04.68.88.30.57, e-mail contact@banyuls.com

CLOS CHATART 1993**

■ 1.9 ha 3,000 150–199 F

For the visitor who turns his back on Banyuls beach to explore the hinterland, the La Baillaury valley offers a wonderful glimpse of viticultural architecture. Far from the summer din, the 12th-century manse seems to defy time. As soon as one approaches this 1993, the characteristics of its vinification are obvious: the red-brown highlights; the hallmark notes of leather, toast, tobacco and cocoa. But the best is yet to come. The palate reveals astonishing concentration. Candied fruit melts into chocolate, the tannin becomes velvet, and the darkly roasted finish cries out for a Havana cigar.

🗝 Clos Chatart, 66650 Banyuls-sur-Mer, tel. 04.68.88.12.58, fax 04.68.88.51.51 ☑
Y by appt.
🗝 Laverrière

L'ETOILE Doux paillé Hors d'âge***

■ 5 ha 10,000 🍷🛢 150–199 F

The famous Doux Paillé du Président is another marvel. In the manner of Proust's 'madeleine', it will lodge in your memory if you drink it in the village of Banyuls itself, with foie gras and figs! The original deep red has faded, through ageing, to a very pale russet-amber. The nose mixes honey, gingerbread, Virginia tobacco, cut hay and roasted almonds, among other notes. Rich, unctuous and flavoursome, it is certainly a harmonious wine, and on the finish, figs, hazelnuts and dried fruits continuously compete for prominence.

🗝 Sté coopérative L'Etoile, 26, av. du Puig-del-Mas, 66650 Banyuls-sur-Mer, tel. 04.68.88.00.10, fax 04.68.88.15.10 ☑
Y ev. day except Sat. Sun. 8am–12 noon 2pm–6pm

CELLIER DES TEMPLIERS
Cuvée Henri Caris 1988**

■ n.c. 10,150 🍷🛢 150–199 F

In the remarkable setting of the Mas-Reig, the cellar aims to create products that are highly expressive of their environment. Alongside the **Mas de la Serre 1991**, currently in its prime, this Henri Caris 1988 caught the jury's attention. Through keeping, the amber colour has turned closer to mahogany. How enthralling to smell the old cellars in which the casks build these aromas of fruits, leather and coffee! On the silky palate, flavours of prunes, plum *eau de vie* and tobacco soften to a finish of cocoa and cashew. It forms a perfect marriage with all kinds of chocolate.

🗝 Cellier des Templiers, rte du Mas-Reig, 66650 Banyuls-sur-Mer, tel. 04.68.98.36.70, fax 04.68.98.36.91 ☑ Y by appt.

DOM. DU TRAGINER Hors d'âge**

■ 4 ha 3,000 🛢 200–249 F

Ploughing in a Banyuls vineyard is often impossible without the use of a mule. J.-F. Deu practises precisely this sort of cultivation, and is the last to work alongside a muleteer. His Banyuls Grand Cru has stood the test of time, a nuance of red persisting through its brick colour. The intense aromas jostle forth with oak, roasting smells, figs and cocoa. The same aromatic festival continues in the mouth, supported by toasty flavours bestowed by the tannins and the spicy hints that they add to the chocolatey finish.

🗝 J.-F. Deu, Dom. du Traginer, 56, av. du Puig-del-Mas, 66650 Banyuls-sur-Mer, tel. 04.68.88.15.11, fax 04.68.88.31.48 ☑
Y by appt.

Rivesaltes

In terms of area this is the biggest appellation of Vins Doux Naturels, with 14,000 ha (34,580 gal) producing 264,000 hl (6,969,600 gal) in 1995. In 1996 nearly 4,000 ha (9,880 acres) fell victim to frost; production slumped below 200,000 hl (5,280,000 gal), and the Rivesaltes Plan was introduced to re-organise the vineyard, now in economic difficulties, but in 1999 production was 101,532 hl (2,680,445 gal). The terroir of Rivesaltes lies in Roussillon and in a very small part of Corbières, on poor, dry, hot soils that produce well-ripened grapes. Four varieties are permitted: Grenache, Maccabeu, Malvoisie and Muscat, although only small proportions of Malvoisie and Muscat are included. White wines are generally vinified normally, but maceration is also used, especially for the Grenache Noir, to achieve a maximum in colour and tannin.

How the Rivesaltes wines are brought on is crucial in determining quality. Whether brought on in the vat or in wooden casks, they develop very different bouquets. (In difficult years, there is also an option for the wines to be downgraded as Appellation Grand Roussillon.)

The wines range in colour from amber to tile-red, with a bouquet, at its most expressive, recalling roasting coffee, dry fruit or the nutty flavour of rancio. When young, red Rivesaltes have aromas of soft fruit: cherry, blackcurrant or blackberry. They may be drunk as an aperitif or with dessert and should be served at a temperature from 11–15°C (51.8–59°F) depending on their age.

CH. DONA BAISSAS
Ambré Hors d'âge

□ n.c. 15,000 🛢 [illegible]

Estagel is the lung of the Agly valley. Since the tragic floods of November 1999, the village has bound up its wounds and the vignerons have done the same for their vineyards. This Ambré Hors d'Age is very pale, with a surprising glint of gold, and a nose on which notes of marc mingle with those of dried fruit. Supple and warm, the wine is dry and balanced on the palate, and roasted almond flavours compete with lemon on the finish.

🔑 SA Destavel, 7*bis*, av. du Canigou, 66000 Perpignan, tel. 04.68.68.36.00, fax 04.68.54.03.54 V
🔑 G. Baissas

DOM. BERTRAND-BERGE

Ambré Grande Réserve*

□ 2 ha n.c. 50-69 F

This AOC Fitou address has now become AOC Rivesaltes too. With their grey-tinted Ambré redolent of grilling and overripe fruits, the estate seduced the jury. The palate is fat, full, sweet and rich. Flavours of ripe fruit and candied citrus gradually subside towards the finish, to be replaced by a warm, long flavour of walnut.

🔑 Jérôme Bertrand, av. du Roussillon, 11350 Paziols, tel. 04.68.45.41.73, fax 04.68.45.41.73 V Y by appt.

DOM. DE BESOMBES SINGLA

Tuilé Hors d'âge 1991

■ 20 ha 5,000 70-99 F

As the label says, this wine is the product of a centuries-old alliance between one family and the Salses soil, aided and abetted by Grenache. The colour of this wine hesitates between amber and brick-red; the core is russet-amber, and the nose milk and honey. More substantial in the mouth, the wine shows its full and flavoursome character, with notes of gingerbread heralding others of dried fruit, which in turn lend a touch of rancio.

🔑 Damien and Laurent de Besombes-Singla, 4, rue de Rivoli, 66250 Saint-Laurent-de-la-Salanque , tel. 04.68.28.30.68, fax 04.68.28.30.68 V Y by appt.

DOM. JOSEPH BORY

Ambré 25 ans en 2000 1975***

□ 10.19 ha 3,000 100-149 F

Joseph Bory has produced another marvel. His new label evokes the knotty old vines that have given birth to this Ambré, whose strong colour borders on russet with hints of rancio. After 25 years, the wine is ready, gently redolent of figs, prunes, leather and aromas of roasted coffee beans. Remarkably well-balanced, this 1975 has presence; it is supple, with a fruity centre of apricots and currants that evolves to take on notes of roasted hazelnuts and honeyed tobacco.

🔑 Andrée Verdeille, 6, av. Jean-Jaurès, 66670 Bages, tel. 04.68.21.71.07, fax 04.68.21.71.07 V
Y ev. day except Mon. Sun. 3pm–7pm

LES VIGNERONS DE CABESTANY ET D'ALENYA

Cuvée du Cinquantenaire Ambré Elevé en fût de chêne 1995

□ 60 ha 3,300 100-149 F

The name Cabestany means 'lake-head': the terraces of the modern village, a pleasant suburb of Perpignan, overlook the beds of ancient dried-up ponds. This clear, old-gold 1995 Rivesaltes smells of apricot and quince on a base of fruits in *eau-de-vie* and flambéed banana. The wine is very sweet in the mouth from the outset, with flavours of candied fruit and grapes in brandy competing on the finish.

🔑 Les vignerons de Cabestany et d'Alenya, 1, av. du Roussillon, 66330 Cabestany, tel. 04.68.50.48.59, fax 04.68.50.97.80 V
Y by appt.

VIGNERONS CATALANS

Ambré 1995*

□ 50 ha n.c. 30-49 F

The Vignerons Catalans, that institution of the Pyrénées-Orientales, have mainly been known until now for their dry wines. But their members' cellars conceal hidden treasures, like the **Vieil Ambré 1974**, or this young 1995 with its old-gold colour, full of honey and crystallised orange. Still very fruity owing to a touch of Muscat, the palate develops around a dynamic, very fresh balance of bitter orange. Only on the finish does it show its three years in wood.

🔑 Vignerons Catalans, 1870, av. Julien-Panchot, 66011 Perpignan Cedex, tel. 04.68.85.04.51, fax 04.68.55.25.62, e-mail vignerons.catalans@wanadoo.fr
Y by appt.

DOM. CAZES Ambré 1991***

□ 9.07 ha 15,000 70-99 F

With their extraordinary range of wines (whether Vintage, Ambré or Tuilé), the Cazes brothers never cease to surpass themselves in giving ever more pleasure. They inherited this talent from Aimé, who is honoured by the sublime **Aimé Cazes 1975**. The russet-coloured, well-integrated, sweet, smooth Ambré 1991 offers notes of old oak, sliding between citrus and scents of summer scrubland. Bitter orange, gingerbread, cut hay and a touch of verbena yield to a finish of dried fruit. Its lovely complexity would accompany a cheese coated in parsley.

🔑 Sté Cazes Frères, 4, rue Francisco-Ferrer, B.P. 61, 66602 Rivesaltes, tel. 04.68.64.08.26, fax 04.68.64.69.79, e-mail info@cazes-rivesaltes.com V
Y by appt.

DOM. DES CHENES 1992

■ n.c. 2,800 50-69 F

The man from Tautavel had taste when he settled in this valley; it ends in the wild grandeur of the Cirque de Vingrau, where the Razungles, vigneron and oenologist, link their talents. Five years in wood have faded the brick colour, and there is already a hint of

rancio in the well-integrated dried-fruit and toasty aromas. This fine development is confirmed on the palate, which offers a real balance between the sweetness of the fruit and the bitterness of cocoa discernible on the finish.
Razungles, Dom. des Chênes, 7, rue Mal-Joffre, 66600 Vingrau, tel. 04.68.29.40.21, fax 04.68.29.10.91
by appt.

CROIX-MILHAS Grains pourpres*

■ n.c. 30,000 30–49 F

The firm of Cusenier, based in Thuir, is intimately linked with the history of Byrrh invented in 1860 by the Violet brothers. The premises are quite exceptional, comprising an internal station constructed by Eiffel out of 800 beams, and including the world's largest wooden vat. In addition to an excellent **Ambré**, the jury appreciated this young Rivesaltes, which is lively, very fruity and marked by cherry flavours gently evolving towards leather. The model of a fruity young wine.
Cusenier, 6, bd Violet, 66300 Thuir, tel. 04.68.53.05.42, fax 04.68.53.31.00
ev. day 9am–11.45am 2.30pm–5.45pm; cl. Jan.

DOM BRIAL Tuilé 1995**

■ n.c. 20,000 30–49 F

Baixas, capital of the Muscat variety, has a go-ahead cellar that is a shrine to Dom Brial, the enlightened cleric of wit, wisdom and wine. It is rare to find a Tuilé wine that is so subtle and harmonious so young. It is silky, yet has presence, with scents of prunes and roasted hazelnuts. The palate is utterly gorgeous, all the way through to its charred finish. Equally pleasant as an apéritif or with dessert. The **Ambré 1995** is also noteworthy.
Cave des Vignerons de Baixas, 14, av. Mal-Joffre, 66390 Baixas, tel. 04.68.64.22.37, fax 04.68.64.26.70, e-mail baixas@smi-telecom.fr by appt.

LE CELLIER DE LA BARNEDE Tuilé Hors d'âge Rancio 1981***

■ 15 ha 4,000 70–99 F

The wine-making village of Bages displays its wine-growing vocation all along the main street. It's a dynamic way of exorcising an all too easy viticultural past, and demonstrating the present intention to concentrate on the best terroirs. The 20-year-old brick colour of this 1981 wine, admittedly not the brightest around, does nothing to prepare one for the nose, which is that of a great wine, mixing well-integrated oak, wax, roasting, chocolate and a hint of walnut. The palate has breadth and generosity, with the subtlest notes of crystallised fruits and spices, before cinnamon passes the baton to hazelnut on a bed of chocolate. Superb!
SCV Les Producteurs de La Barnède, 5, av. du 8-Mai-1945, 66670 Bages, tel. 04.68.21.60.30, fax 04.68.37.50.13
by appt.

DOM. LAPORTE Ambré 1985

□ 2 ha 5,000 100–149 F

The ancient terraces of the Têt are wonderfully suitable for growing *vins doux naturels*. A stone's throw from the sea, on the historic Ruscino site, these old Ambré wines defy time. The years have turned the amber to mahogany, and the nose releases scents of fig, warm rock-rose and hazelnut. A full, rich, silky wine, in which crystallised fruits blend with toasty notes before a finish of honeyed light tobacco.
Dom. Laporte, Château-Roussillon, 66000 Perpignan, tel. 04.68.50.06.53, fax 04.68.66.77.52, e-mail domaine-laporte@wanadoo.fr by appt.

HENRI LHERITIER Millésime 1998*

■ 1 ha 2,000 70–99 F

Henri Lhéritier is a man of culture, inquisitive and enthusiastic. He puts all his expertise into vat selection from which to make his Grenache wine. First impressions are of intensity, youth, life, and then the wine yields scents of violets, morello cherries and bilberries. Within its richness, the very evident tannin is well balanced by cherry-like sweetness. A wine that can be enjoyed young, but has an even greater future ahead of it.
Henri Lhéritier, av. Gambetta, 66600 Rivesaltes, tel. 04.68.38.56.53, fax 04.68.38.56.52 e-mail domainelheritier@wanadoo.fr
ev. day except Sun. 8am–12 noon 2pm–7pm

DOM. MALER Tuilé Hors d'âge 1992

□ 13 ha 1,400 70–99 F

Tresserre is a village known in Roussillon as much for the conscientious efforts of the technical department of the Comité Interprofessionnel under M Torrès, as for the pagan festival of *bruixes* (witches). It is a monocultural wine village whose example is much followed. This 1992 Tuilé is a well-crafted wine with notes of prune and a touch of cloves. Its well-balanced, dry palate has good tannic presence, developing to flavours of cocoa only just short of dark chocolate.
Pierre and Yolande Maler, 1, rue du Canigou, 66300 Tresserre, tel. 04.68.38.82.61, fax 04.68.38.81.27
by appt.

MAS CRISTINE Ambré 1996*

□ 3.1 ha 10,000 70–99 F

From its first twistings on the rocky hillside, the narrow road snakes up to the manse that suddenly pops out like an oasis in the desert of cork-oak. The gold is in the glass, bright and luminous. The subtly oaky nose of this 1996 Ambré encompasses notes of honey, wax and quince. The palate is in keeping, having a soft, harmonious balance, which evolves to a most attractive finish of dried fruits.

⊶ Mas Cristine, Au ch. de Jau, 66600 Cases-de-Pène, tel. 04.68.38.90.10, fax 04.68.38.91.33, e-mail jau66@aol.com ☒

⊶ Famille Daure

MAS DE LA GARRIGUE

Vieux Récolte 1978★★

■ 19 ha 5,000 ▮ 50–69 F

Given that genuine 1950 Rivesaltes are still on the market, this 1978 version is but a child, the object of all Madame Vila's attentions in her quest for perfection. After 23 years, the brick colour is still firm. The wine is best tasted after a period of air contact. Notes of leather, old oak, eucalyptus, liquorice and burnt flavours escape slowly. Then the palate is mature and solid, evoking crystallised prunes, before liquorice takes over on a finish replete with notes of burnt sugar. Note also the excellent **Vintage 1989**.

⊶ Mme Marcel Vila, Mas de la Garrigue, 17, av. Gal-de-Gaulle, 66240 Saint-Esteve, tel. 04.68.92.06.56 ☒ Y ev. day except Sun. 8am–12 noon 3pm–6pm

CH. MONTNER Ambré 1995★★★

□ 25 ha 50,000 ▮ ⦀ 30–49 F

Against the backdrop of the Canigou, the ancient village of Montner rises amidst the vines, seeming to encourage them to mount an assault on the brown schist terrain of Força Real. The russet-amber colour of this Rivesaltes 1995 is warm and engaging. The wine begins to please with the honeyed scents found in ancient cellars of sweet wine where the toasty aroma of the cask mingles with that of crystallised fruit. Full, forthright, smooth, harmonious, balanced: the palate is perfect. Crystallised apricot takes on a grilled flavour; then almonds appear, and finally honeyed tobacco. Superb!

⊶ Les Vignerons des Côtes d'Agly, Cave coopérative, 66310 Estagel, tel. 04.68.29.00.45, fax 04.68.29.19.80, e-mail agly@little-france.com ☒

Y ev. day except Sat. Sun. 8am–12 noon 2pm–6pm

CH. MOSSE

Vignes des Causses Vieilli en fût de chêne 1995★

■ 10 ha 8,000 ⦀ 50–69 F

A village whose Catalan architecture has been wonderfully restored, Sainte-Colombe is a jewel of the Aspres set in the crown of the Canigou. The limestone *causse* has conferred on this brick-red Grenache, after a short time in oak, notes of honey, leather, crystallised fruits and plum spirit. The palate is at once rich, full and subtle. Crystallised cherry seems surrounded by cinnamon before a finish that is sweet and fresh all at once. Note also the good **Rubis 1996**.

⊶ Jacques Mossé, Ch. Mossé, 66300 Ste-Colombe-de-la-Commanderie, tel. 04.68.53.08.89, fax 04.68.53.35.13 ☒

Y by appt.

DOM. MOUNIE Roc de l'Amor 1986★★

■ 4 ha 3,500 ▮ ⦀ 70–99 F

Tautavel (meaning 'all I want') is famous for its museum of prehistory, and for the compatibility of its terroir for Côtes du Roussillon-Villages as much as for *vins doux naturels*. Six years in vat and seven in barrel have polished this red wine to an engaging brick colour. Its nose evolves from cherry to crystallised fruit, fig and leather. Then the palate is surprising, full and rich: figs appear, accompanied by toasted almonds, before a lengthy finish that is all spice.

⊶ Dom. Mounié, av. du Verdouble, 66720 Tautavel, tel. 04.68.29.12.31, fax 04.68.29.05.59 ☒

Y ev. day 11am–12 noon 3pm–6pm

⊶ Hélène Rigaill

CH. DU PARC

Ancestral Cuvée Henri Jonquères 1969★

□ 30 ha 5,000 ▮ 70–99 F

Which French AOC estate can these days offer wines of ten, 20, or even 30 years of age with as much facility as the Château du Parc? How little understood are these Rivesaltes, Ambré or Tuilé, that recline into old age so happily and only grow more beautiful with it! This 1969 wine is dark, walnut-stained with lights of rancio. The nose is suitably intense: scents of the garrigue are covered by muted hints of soot, old leather and walnut. As for the taste, we are in the world of rancio – an oily and fleshy sensation barely masking a touch of acidity, and above all coffee, caramel, brown tobacco and finally walnut. Note also the well-made **Ave Maria 1995**.

⊶ GAEC Maria-Jonquères, 1, av. Henri-Jonquères, 66300 Ponteilla, tel. 04.68.35.33.32, fax 04.68.35.55.17 ☒

Y by appt.

⊶ X.-L. Maria

LES VIGNERONS DE PEZILLA

Tuilé 1994★

■ 48 ha 10,000 ▮ 30–49 F

The Ribéral (the banks of the Têt) is to arboriculture and market gardening what the terraces and schist soils are to vines – to each its own. When the winery boasts a great president at the cellar and a director who runs marathons, it is small wonder that the wines last the distance. Witness this 1994, the colour of which is still deep, and that evokes cherries and prunes after initial scents of leather and tobacco. A well-balanced wine made from excellent raw material; the tannin on the finish will allow it more life still. Equally noted by the jury is its stablemate, the **Ambré 1994**.

🔑 SCV Les Vignerons de Pézilla, 66370 Pézilla-la-Rivière, tel. 04.68.92.00.09, fax 04.68.92.49.91 ☒ 𝕐 ev. day except Sun. 8.30am–12.30pm 2pm–6.30pm

CH. PRADAL

Elevé en fût de chêne 1997★★

☐ 3 ha 3,000 ▮▮▮ 30–49 F

Encircled by Perpignan, the Pradal district has been resisting the city's spread since 1810, proving with humour the old Catalan adage that translates as 'Better a Malvoisie vine than a bad neighbour (*mauvais voisin*)'. Yet not many vignerons today grow that old variety. Here it accounts for 25% of the wine, leaving its mark on this young Ambré with its fresh scents of bitter orange and grapes in spirit. The subtle, elegant citrus aroma persists. A fresh, supple wine, it is pleasantly endowed on the finish by a touch of honeyed tobacco.

🔑 André Coll-Escluse, Ch. Pradal, 58, rue Pépinière-Robin, 66000 Perpignan, tel. 04.68.85.04.73, fax 04.68.56.80.49 ☒ 𝕐 by appt.

DOM. DE RANCY Hors d'âge 1974★★★

☐ n.c. 1,000 ▮ ▮▮▮ 200–249 F

This is *the* place for old Rivesaltes rancio! Here only sweet wine is produced, with a deep respect for tradition. After 25 years in wood, the amber has become extremely dark, the colour of walnut-stain with characteristic green highlights. The volatile aromas of walnut and oak will not suit every palate, to be sure: only lovers of rancio will find them pleasurable. Its character is evident from the initial attack onward: it is fascinating to encounter the sensation of fatness, of an oily presence seasoned with a touch of acid, before the wine tips towards flavours of roasting, burnt sugar, dried fruits, cocoa and walnut without end . . .

🔑 Jean-Hubert Verdaguer, Dom. de Rancy, 11, rue Jean-Jaurès, 66720 Latour-de-France, tel. 04.68.29.03.47, fax 04.68.29.06.13 ☒ 𝕐 by appt.

ROC DU GOUVERNEUR

Vintage 1995★★

■ n.c. 6,000 ▮▮▮ 50–69 F

The co-operative blends the modern with the traditional, since it is certified ISO 9002 whilst making its wines in a 15th-century château. This dual advantage is exploited fully by the cellar at Salses, as is shown by this still very youthful Rivesaltes, which is ruby-coloured and fruity, poised between blackcurrant, wild strawberry and venison. The palate is full and balanced; wild fruits are embraced by spices before returning on a substantial, lengthy finish.

🔑 Les Vignobles du Rivesaltais, 1, rue de la Roussillonnaise, 66602 Rivesaltes-Salses, tel. 04.68.64.06.63, fax 04.68.64.64.69, e-mail vignobles.rivesaltais@wanadoo.fr ☒ 𝕐 by appt.

CH. ROMBEAU

Grande réserve Hors d'âge 1980★★★

■ n.c. 2,500 ▮▮▮ 50–69 F

Ever-cheery, ever-busy and bursting with ideas, Pierre-Henri de la Fabrègue is a well-known figure in Roussillon. His inn-cellar is a bit of a trap, for to go there is to be beguiled by the place, his personality, and by the wines. The 1980 Rivesaltes is strong brick-red; scents of the garrigue mix with cut hay and the patina of old barrels. It is a surprising wine, what with its integrated character, the sweetness of crystallised fruit, the finesse of roasted hazelnuts, the hint of fresh-roasted coffee and, above all, its length.

🔑 SCEA Dom. de Rombeau, 66600 Rivesaltes, tel. 04.68.64.35.35, fax 04.68.64.64.66 ☒ 𝕐 ev. day 8am–11pm

🔑 de La Fabrègue

SAINT-PAUL

Cuvée Prince de Conti 1984★★★

☐ n.c. 3,000 ▮ ▮▮▮ 100–149 F

The capital of the Fenouillèdes, Saint-Paul is reputed for its *croquants* (almond biscuits), the wild beauty of the landscape and its hills of black marl, ideal soils for *vins doux naturels* of quality. This pale amber 'Prince' has surprising freshness. It seems to have returned from the *maquis* bearing scents of rock-rose and dried fruits. Elegant, subtle, smooth, well-balanced, it marries the bitter freshness of gentian to the roasted aroma of old casks.

🔑 SCV Les Vignerons de Saint-Paul, 17, av. Jean-Moulin, 66220 Saint-Paul-de-Fenouillet, tel. 04.68.59.02.39, fax 04.68.59.07.97 ☒ 𝕐 by appt.

DOM. SARDA-MALET

Le Serrat 1995

☐ 10 ha 6,500 ▮ 30–49 F

At the gates of Perpignan, in the undulating hills of the Serrat d'en Vaquer, Suzy Malet carries on the family tradition with happiness and dedication, as this amber-coloured 1995 wine shows. Notes of gingerbread and crystallised orange herald a full, sweet palate of citrus and candied fruits. The slightly spicy finish recommends it as an accompaniment to blue cheeses.

🔑 Dom. Sarda-Malet, mas Saint-Michel, chem. de Sainte-Barbe, 66000 Perpignan, tel. 04.68.56.72.38, fax 04.68.56.47.60 ☒ 𝕐 by appt.

🔑 Suzy Malet

CH. DE SAU Ambré Hors d'âge★★★

☐ 3.5 ha 5,000 70–99 F

Hervé Passama is deeply devoted to the earth, and is enthused by the notion of terroir. This Ambré Hors d'Age is a blend of several old vintages. Mahogany in colour, it is redolent of peat and flambéed banana. The evident yet well-balanced flavours of dried apricot and ripe banana yield to a finish that is spiced by the sweet bitterness of cocoa.

Hervé Passama, Ch. de Saü, 66300 Thuir, tel. 04.68.53.21.74, fax 04.68.53.29.07, e-mail chateaudesau@aol.com

by appt.

DOM. DES SCHISTES Solera★★★

☐ 5 ha 5,000 70–99 F

Never wholly satisfied, always on the lookout for quality, Jacques Sire is the personification of viticultural passion. He and Nadine offer open house to talk about Solera or offer a taste of his wines that are grown on schist soils. Aromas of tobacco, straw, honeyed flowers and wax escape from this strong amber wine with rancio highlights. Then the Solera coils, coalesces, fills the mouth with its hints of citrus, currants and honey. At the end, roasting hazelnuts and scents of tobacco cry out for a Havana cigar.

Jacques Sire, 1, av. Jean-Lurçat, 66310 Estagel, tel. 04.68.29.11.25, fax 04.68.29.47.17 by appt.

TERRASSOUS Ambré Hors d'âge 1986★

☐ 20 ha 6,000 30–49 F

On the vast viticultural terrace that gave it its name, the village of Terrats, in the heart of the Aspres, seems jealously to guard the terroir that only the Canterrane has dared attack with its winding course. This 1986 wine has taken a decade of vat maturation to attain a clear russet-amber colour and intense aromas of gingerbread, honey and hazelnuts. The palate is appealing for its sweetness, well-integrated character and note of bitter orange. The finish is drier, evoking hazelnuts and hay.

SCV Les Vignerons de Terrats, B.P. 32, 66302 Terrats, tel. 04.68.53.02.50, fax 04.68.53.23.06 ev. day except Sun. 8am–12 noon 2pm–6pm

TORRE DEL FAR 1998★

■ 45 ha 26,000 30–49 F

The Maîtres Vignerons' skill at producing fortified Grenache is beyond dispute. A lengthy maceration of grape and spirit produces a youthful wine with strong colour and a rich nose full of red fruits, dominated by morello cherry and and a suggestion of cherry liqueur. The evident tannins contribute sustaining power of spices and undergrowth. A good wine to accompany a dish of forest fruits.

Les Maîtres Vignerons de Tautavel, 24, av. Jean-Badia, 66720 Tautavel, tel. 04.68.29.12.03, fax 04.68.29.41.81, e-mail vignerons.tautavel@wanadoo.fr

by appt.

CELLIER TROUILLAS

Ambré Elevé en fût de chêne 1986

☐ 80 ha 25,000 30–49 F

Old Grenache Blanc and Macabeu vines produce very versatile raw material. This 1986 wine has been wood-aged, oxidizing slowly, for 13 years! Nothing surprising, then, about this Ambré wine with its aromas of orange-peel and strong, spicy, honeyed orange tones. The softening effect of time is seen on the palate, where the flavours are supple and harmonious, with shafts of gingerbread and honeyed light tobacco, and a finish of the freshest lemon.

SCV Le Cellier de Trouillas, 1, av. du Mas-Deu, 66300 Trouillas, tel. 04.68.53.47.08, fax 04.68.53.24.56

by appt.

DOM. DU VIEUX CHENE

Tuilé Excellence de Haut-Valoir 1977★★

■ 20 ha 2,000 200–249 F

Here is one of the best views of the Roussillon, a splendid setting, a happy marriage between terroirs and a superb cellar: stop at the Vieux Chêne, ten minutes from Perpignan, where this Rivesaltes 1977 awaits you. The mahogany colour testifies to the maturation, which is further confirmed by the intense aromas of dried fig, toast and pre-rancio prune. The palate is very lush and supple; the flavour of chocolate wastes no time blending with that of coffee and tobacco in a harmonious marriage that calls for a coffee or a Havana cigar. Note also the excellent **Vintage 1996**.

Dom. du Vieux Chêne, Mas Kilo, 66600 Espira-de-l'Agly, tel. 04.68.38.92.01, fax 04.68.38.95.79 by appt.

Sarda Bobo

Maury

In 1999 the *terroir* covered the commune of Maury,

north of Agly, together with some of the bordering communes. The vines (Grenache Noir) grow on steep schistous slopes, producing about 24,125 hl (639,900 gal) of wine.

Vinification is often achieved through long maceration, and the way in which the wine is brought on encourages the production of some remarkable vintages.

When young, the wines are garnet in colour, later turning mahogany. The bouquet is initially of soft fruit, developing aromas of cocoa, cooked fruit and coffee with age. Maury wines can be enjoyed as an aperitif or with desserts and sweet foods, but also with spicy dishes.

CHABERT DE BARBERA 1983***

■ 1.65 ha 5,000 50–199 F

1983 CHABERT DE BARBERA MAURY APPELLATION MAURY CONTRÔLÉE

Congratulations on the splendid vinification undertaken under the leadership of Thomas Ferra. This is one of those superb old Maury wines that look rather meagre with their pale brick-red colour and air of rancio, but which burst into life as soon as they are opened with an ambience of roasting coffee, walnuts and wax. A superb wine, fleshy, full and rich, uniting spices, cocoa and walnuts. Sample with a large Havana cigar, after coffee!

🔑 SCAV Les Vignerons de Maury, 128, av. Jean-Jaurès, 66460 Maury, tel. 04.68.59.00.95, fax 04.68.59.02.88 ▼ Y by appt.

DOM. DE LA COUME DU ROY

Vieilli en foudre de chêne 1995

■ n.c. 7,000 70–99 F

Paule is now joined by Agnès, who is taking the reins of this very particular, historic estate. Five years of maturation were required to turn the deep red of this Maury to faded brick. The intense nose evokes the noble cellar with its toasty scents of the wooden casks. A fine, supple palate is impregnated with notes of dried apricot that give way to a finish of toasty dried fruits.

🔑 Paule de Volontat and Agnès Bachelet, 5, rue Emile-Zola, 66460 Maury, tel. 04.68.27.08.14, fax 04.68.59.67.58 ▼ Y by appt.

🔑 GFA de la Coume du Roy

CAVE JEAN-LOUIS LAFAGE

Tradition Vieilli en cuve de chêne 1995**

■ 1.25 ha 2,650 30–49 F

After his *coup de cœur* 1986, Jean-Louis Lafage takes us into another world with this 1995 wine, the product of great savoir-faire and tradition. Its brick-red colour is brilliant. The wine develops in a knowing and expressive way with aromas of candied fruit dressed in leather. Then pure pleasure takes over, as flavours of spices, prunes and grilled dried fruits compete for attention. A remarkable Maury that is ready to drink now.

🔑 Jean-Louis Lafage, 13, rue Dr-Pougault, 66460 Maury, tel. 04.68.59.12.66, fax 04.68.59.13.14 ▼ Y by appt.

DOM. MAS AMIEL Vintage 1998***

■ 55 ha 200,000 70–99 F

With Charles Dupuy gone, Mas Amiel has changed hands. No mean challenge awaits the new person in charge of this Maury institution, yet the wine is as remarkable as ever. This dark red 1998 Vintage reveals its youth. It expresses itself discreetly and slowly through notes of morello cherry in finely spiced *eau-de-vie*. Intense, full and generous, the fine-grained tannin melds with the fruit, which is surprisingly chewy. Ideal with a 'soup' of red fruits.

🔑 SC Charles Dupuy, Dom. Mas Amiel, 66460 Maury, tel. 04.68.29.01.02, fax 04.68.29.17.82 ▼ Y by appt.

LES VIGNERONS DE MAURY

Sélection Devèze 1998*

■ 8 ha 3,000 50–69 F

The terroir of La Devèze, at the foot of Quéribus, is the pride of the Vignerons de Maury. Given due attention, it can produce some very lovely wines, like this 1998 with its slightly fading deep red colour. It is, as the jury says, very 'kirsch-like', with cherry penetrating through the sweet balance. The wine evolves, as the flavour of prune shows itself, stealing a march on the richness of cherry. And then cocoa makes an unexpected, if discreet, appearance, calling for a dessert.

🔑 SCAV Les Vignerons de Maury, 128, av. Jean-Jaurès, 66460 Maury, tel. 04.68.59.00.95, fax 04.68.59.02.88 ▼ Y by appt.

DOM. POUDEROUX 1998*

■ 1.4 ha 6,000 70–99 F

R. Pouderoux grows vines at Corneilla-de-la-Rivière and at Maury, and is particularly sensitive to the notion of terroir, seeking to express it in the best way possible. Hence this red Maury, made in the style of a vintage wine

with maceration after fortification, a short period in oak and then maturation in bottle. Deep and strong, it plays on notes of blackcurrants and vanilla-flavoured prunes. The body of the wine is warm and structured, while appealing tannins accompany the flavours of red fruits. Its future opens before it.
🔑 Dom. Pouderoux, 2, rue Emile-Zola, 66460 Maury, tel. 04.68.57.22.02, fax 04.68.57.11.63 ▣ Ỹ by appt.

Muscat de Rivesaltes

This sweet 100% Muscat can be made anywhere in Rivesaltes, Maury and Banyuls. The area of this vineyard covers more than 4,000 ha (9,880 acres) and produces nearly 140,000 hl (3,696,000 gal). The two varieties permitted are Muscat à Petits Grains and Muscat d'Alexandrie. The first, frequently called Muscat Blanc or Muscat de Rivesaltes, ripens early and is happy in relatively cool soils, preferably limestone. The second, also known as Muscat Romain, is a later-ripening variety which is very resistant to dry conditions.

Vinification is either by direct pressing, or by maceration for a shorter or longer time, according to the wine-maker's judgement. The must is kept in a closed container, to prevent the first aromas released from being oxidised.

The wines are required to have a minimum of 100 g of sugar per litre. They should be drunk young, served at 9–10°C (48.2–50°F), with desserts such as lemon, apple or strawberry tarts, sorbets, ice creams, fruit, touron and marzipan. They are also good with Roquefort cheese.

ARNAUD DE VILLENEUVE 1999*
☐ n.c. 15,000 ▮ 🌡 50–69 F

This vast Rivesaltes co-operative, which handles the harvest of 3,000 ha (nearly 7,500 acres) of vines, makes wine under the labels Arnaud de Villeneuve and Roc du Gouverneur. Once again, the first of these names adorns a sensually pleasing wine. The nose is intense enough, but the palate is an explosion of aromas: peach, violets, crystallised mango and blackcurrant. A long, harmonious wine.
🔑 Les Vignobles du Rivesaltais, 1, rue de la Roussillonnaise, 66602 Rivesaltes-Salses, tel. 04.68.64.06.63, fax 04.68.64.64.69, e-mail vignobles.rivesaltais@wanadoo.fr ▣ Ỹ by appt.

DOM. D'AUBERMESNIL 1999*
☐ 15 ha 30,000 30–49 F

This wine comes from the district of Leucate, remarkable for its limestone cliffs overtopping the sea. Its colour is pale gold with pearly reflections. The aromas are fresh, vegetal, floral and honeyed, and the slightly acid palate reveals notes of aniseed and lemon. A subtle, harmonious ensemble.
🔑 Vignerons de la Méditerranée, 12, rue du Rec-de-Veyret, ZI Plaisance, 11100 Narbonne, tel. 04.68.42.75.00, fax 04.68.42.75.01, e-mail valdorbieu-didierferrier@wanadoo.fr ▣ Ỹ by appt.
🔑 Vignerons du Cap Leucate

CH. AYMERICH 1999*
☐ 2.15 ha 6,000 ▮ 🌡 50–69 F

This estate is located on black schist soils in the Agly valley. Its Muscat is eloquent with notes of exotic fruits, peaches and white flowers (wild rose). The attack is very appealing, the palate harmonious, and the finish subtly bitter.
🔑 Jean-Pierre and Catherine Grau-Aymerich, Ch. Aymerich, 52, av. Dr-Torreilles, 66310 Estagel, tel. 04.68.29.45.45, fax 04.68.29.10.35 ▣ Ỹ by appt.

CH. BELLOCH 1998**
☐ 7 ha 3,000 50–69 F

This estate, dedicated to Saint Germaine, has produced a Muscat that is remarkable for 1998. Its colour is bright old-gold. The aromas appear at once fresh and evolved: blackcurrant, rose, apricot are all present, dominated by quince jelly. The rich, harmonious palate finishes on notes of dried fruits.
🔑 SA Cibaud-Ch. Miraflors et Belloch, 7, rue Béranger, 66000 Perpignan, tel. 04.68.34.03.05, fax 04.68.51.31.70, e-mail vins.cibaud@wanadoo.fr ▣ Ỹ ev. day except Sun. 9.30am–12.30pm 3pm–7pm; cl. Jan.

DOM. BOUDAU 1999
☐ 20 ha 15,000 30–49 F

In the midst of the Rivesaltes district, the Boudau estate's new tasting cellar is particularly aesthetically pleasing. There, they offer this gorgeously fresh Muscat with its aromas of citrus and mint. An unctuous, but well-balanced wine.

VDN

Dom. Véronique et Pierre Boudau, 6, rue Marceau, B.P. 60, 66600 Rivesaltes, tel. 04.68.64.45.37, fax 04.68.64.46.26
ev. day except Sun. 10am–12 noon 3pm–7pm from June–Sep.

DOM. CAZES 1999*

38.06 ha 70,000 50-69 F

Rivesaltes is not simply a good environment for growing Muscat, it is also the Cazes family's backyard. Several generations' expertise went into this bright golden-yellow nectar. Its dense aromas evoke yellow flowers, exotic fruits and verbena. Lots of body, richness and freshness give the palate excellent balance.
Sté Cazes Frères, 4, rue Francisco-Ferrer, B.P. 61, 66602 Rivesaltes, tel. 04.68.64.08.26, fax 04.68.64.69.79, e-mail info@cazes-rivesaltes.com
by appt.

DOM. DES CHENES 1998***

3.5 ha 10,000 30-49 F

DOMAINE DES CHÊNES
MUSCAT DE RIVESALTES
APPELLATION MUSCAT DE RIVESALTES CONTROLÉE
1998
MIS EN BOUTEILLE AU DOMAINE

This vineyard is enclosed within the admirable site of the Cirque de Vingrau. The wine-grower is an oenologist of repute, and the wine is, quite simply, exceptional. Its colour is pure gold with delicate green highlights. On the nose, it shows powerful aromas of crystallised fruit, mimosa, candied pineapple and citrus. The palate has concentration and superb length. Magnificent.
Razungles, Dom. des Chênes, 7, rue Mal-Joffre, 66600 Vingrau, tel. 04.68.29.40.21, fax 04.68.29.10.91
by appt.

CLOS SAINT GEORGES

Cuvée Alexia 1999

5.14 ha 10,000 50-69 F

The colour is light golden and beautifully bright, the nose fine and exotic with nuances of sweet almond and honey. Classic balance: a very generous Muscat.
Ortal, Clos Saint-Georges, 66300 Trouillas, tel. 04.68.21.61.46, fax 04.68.37.52.31, e-mail clortal@club-internet.fr
ev. day 9am–12.30pm 2pm–7pm

HENRI DESBŒUFS 1999*

10 ha 10,000 50-69 F

Henri Desbœufs' Muscats are always a treat (his 1996 was awarded a *coup de cœur*). The Muscat à petits grains variety here expresses all its subtlety with notes of white fleshed fruits, exotic nuances and floral aromas. The elegant palate combines freshness with a delicately liquorous quality.
Henri Desbœufs, 39, rue du Quatre-Septembre, 66600 Espira-de-l'Agly, tel. 04.68.64.11.73, fax 04.68.38.56.34
by appt.

DOM. FONTANEL

L'Age de Pierre 1999

4 ha 8,000

Naturally enough, being located at Tautavel, the Fontanel estate has called one of its wines 'L'Age de Pierre' ('The Stone Age'), though its label is resolutely modern. Its Muscat 1999 is very pale with green-tinged golden highlights. The nose is discreet, but the wine has an expressive palate, releasing notes of honey, mint and crystallised citrus. The balance is sweet and rich, with highly satisfying aromatic persistence.
Dom. Fontanel, 25, av. Jean-Jaurès, 66720 Tautavel, tel. 04.68.29.04.71, fax 04.68.29.19.44 by appt.
Fontaneil

LES VIGNERONS DE FORCA REAL 1999*

n.c. 10,600 30-49 F

The colour is golden with delicate silver highlights. An intense and complex nose releases aromas of exotic fruits, white peach and lily-of-the-valley. The palate has a delicious elegance and impressive length.
SCV les Vignerons de Força Réal, rue Léo-Lagrange, 66170 Millas, tel. 04.68.57.35.02, fax 04.68.57.28.09
ev. day except Sun. Mon. 3pm–6.30pm

LES VIGNERONS DE FOURQUES 1999*

4 ha 4,000 50-69 F

The Fourques cooperative, which makes wine from 430 ha (1,062 acres) of vines, offers a Muscat whose colour is very pale gold, bright and clear. Its powerful nose emits fragrances of exotic fruits (mango, lychee, papaya), white peach and acacia honey. The palate is extremely well-balanced, and finishes on a lively note.
SCV les Vignerons de Fourques, 1, rue des Taste-Vin, 66300 Fourques, tel. 04.68.38.80.51, fax 04.68.38.89.65 ev. day except Sun. 9am–12 noon 2pm–6pm

DOM. GARDIES Flor 1999**

8 ha 12,000 50-69 F

Having run the 45 ha (111-acre) estate since 1990, Jean Gardiés is a wine-grower of real talent. His brilliant pale yellow Muscat has great subtlety. The nose is very fresh, communicating aromas of fruits, white flowers and mint. In the mouth, one is almost chewing the grape itself. The unctuous balance is easy to appreciate, and the finish remarkable.
Dom. Gardiés, 66600 Vingrau, tel. 04.68.64.61.16, fax 04.68.64.69.36
by appt.

CH. DE JAU 1999★★

☐ 25 ha 40,000 50–69 F

With its museum of contemporary art and its bistrot – a good excuse to stop and eat here! – the Château de Jau is a great place to stop within the Roussillon region. There, you can sample a pale golden Muscat at its freshest. Its nose of white flowers, apricots and peaches heralds a full-bodied palate with aromas of honey and acidulated fruits.

Ch. de Jau, 66600 Cases-de-Pène, tel. 04.68.38.90.10, fax 04.68.38.91.33, e-mail jau66@aol.com ☒
ev. day except Sat. Sun. 8am–4pm or 10am–7pm from 15 Jun. until 1 Oct.
Famille Dauré

JEAN D'ESTAVEL Prestige 1998★

☐ n.c. 30,000 30–49 F

This négociant offers a very pretty, light golden-yellow wine. The nose offers evidence of a pleasing, and very traditional, evolution, with notes of crystallised fruits. On the palate, the wine is well-balanced and harmonious, the finish slightly spicy.

SA Destavel, *7bis*, av. du Canigou, 66000 Perpignan, tel. 04.68.68.36.00, fax 04.68.54.03.54 ☒
G. Baissas

DOM. JONQUERES D'ORIOLA 1999

☐ n.c. 25,000 50–69 F

The Jonquères d'Oriola family have been in Corneilla since 1485, in a château built by the Templars at the end of the 12th century. More recently, fencing and horse-riding members of the family have participated in the Olympic Games. Their bright, pale golden Muscat has a nose of fresh fruits (pears and grapes) and citrus. A note of crystallised orange arises in the mouth, giving the finish a flavoursome bitterness. Plenty of qualities, in other words, to help this wine jump the fence!

Jonquères d'Oriola, Ch. de Corneilla, 66200 Corneilla-del-Vercol, tel. 04.68.22.73.22, fax 04.68.22.43.99 ☒
by appt.
Philippe Jonquères d'Oriola

LA CASANOVA 1997★

☐ 10 ha 5,000 50–69 F

The colour of this wine is a very luminous gold. Its aromas are fresh and subtle, evoking linden flowers, the garrigue, mint and citrus. The palate is a good balance of richness and freshness, and the persistent finish has notes of citrus and mint.

Ch. **La Casenove**, 66300 Trouillas, tel. 04.68.21.66.33, fax 04.68.21.77.81 ☒
ev. day except Sun. 10am–12 noon 4pm–8pm
Montes

DOM. LAFAGE 1999

☐ 20.27 ha 60,000 50–69 F

A brilliant, golden colour with green highlights, floral and fruity aromas accompanied by hints of gingerbread, and a subtle, well-balanced palate make this a delightful Muscat, a worthy representative of its appellation.

GAEC Dom. Lafage, mas Llaro, 66100 Perpignan, tel. 04.68.67.12.47, fax 04.68.62.10.99, e-mail enofool@aol.com ☒
by appt.

CH. MONTNER 1999★★

☐ 16 ha 50,000 30–49 F

The Vignerons des Côtes d'Agly are an important co-operative, making wine from some 1,300 ha (3,200 acres) of grapes. There is therefore nothing exclusive about their Muscat, which is good news, since the quality is remarkable. An attractive bright gold in colour, it has a complex range of aromas, allying the freshness of exotic fruits and mint with mature notes (overripe fruits, crystallised orange). Its flavour fills the mouth, and is characterised by an intense emphasis on crystallised fruits, with very good length.

Les Vignerons des Côtes d'Agly, Cave coopérative, 66310 Estagel, tel. 04.68.29.00.45, fax 04.68.29.19.80, e-mail agly@little-france.com ☒ ev. day except Sat. Sun. 8am–12 noon 2pm–6pm

DOM. MOUNIE 1999

☐ 2 ha 6,000 50–69 F

Tautavel is not simply a prehistoric site known the world over, it is also a remarkable location for growing wines, both sweet wines and Côtes du Roussillon-Villages. This Muscat, produced there, shows its youthfulness both in its colour and its aromas. The nose mixes fresh grapes, citronella, citrus and honey, while the palate is full, with a very slight bite of acidity. Excellent balance.

Dom. Mounié, av. du Verdouble, 66720 Tautavel, tel. 04.68.29.12.31, fax 04.68.29.05.59 ☒
ev. day 11am–12 noon 3pm–6pm
Hélène Rigaill

DOM. DE NIDOLERES 1998★

☐ 2.5 ha 3,000 50–69 F

This very ancient family property includes an inn where it is possible to sample typical Catalan cuisine. The Muscat produced on the estate has a good strong gold colour and a complex, highly individual nose that releases overripe notes of honey, orange-peel and caramel. The palate is surprisingly sweet and rich. A rich, lengthy wine.

Pierre Escudié, Dom. de Nidolères, 66300 Tresserre, tel. 04.68.83.15.14, fax 04.68.83.31.26 ☒ by appt.

CH. DE NOUVELLES 1998★

☐ 12 ha 12,000 50–69 F

On this very ancient estate, in the 13th century, the abbé of Lagrasse was already producing highly reputed sweet wines. The Daurat-Fort family is continuing the tradition with this pale gold Muscat, which smells intensely of white flowers and lemon. The 1998 version is very fresh in the mouth, and has a subtle minty note.

🔑 EARL R. Daurat-Fort,
Ch. de Nouvelles, 11350 Tuchan,
tel. 04.68.45.40.03, fax 04.68.45.49.21 ☑
Y by appt.

DOM. PAGES HURE 1999

☐ 10 ha 4,000 30–49 F

In 1991, Jean-Louis Pages gave up the pharmacy in order to care for the family wine estate, which is situated in the terroir of the Albères sihouetted on the labels. This 1999 Muscat is brilliant gold in colour with green highlights. It releases fairly intense aromas of exotic fruits (mango), and is supple, fat and fresh in the mouth.

🔑 SCEA Pages Huré, 2, allée des Moines,
66740 Saint-Génis-des-Fontaines,
tel. 04.68.89.82.62, fax 04.68.89.82.62 ☑
Y by appt.
🔑 Jean-Louis Pages

LES VIGNERONS DE PEZILLA 1999★

☐ 138.4 ha 30,000 30–49 F

The co-operative at Pézilla makes wine from 790 ha (1,950 acres) of vines. Its Muscat makes an immediately favourable impression with its strong golden colour and silvery highlights, and then its intense nose, which evokes fresh fruits (grapes and pears) and roses. After a lively attack, richness and aromatic power develop to give the wine excellent balance.

🔑 SCV Les Vignerons de Pézilla, 66370
Pézilla-la-Rivière, tel. 04.68.92.00.09,
fax 04.68.92.49.91 ☑ Y ev. day except Sun.
8.30am–12.30pm 2pm–6.30pm

DOM. PIQUEMAL 1999

☐ 8 ha 33,000 50–69 F

The production of Pierre and Franck Piquemal is consistently good, whether it be dry wines or *vins doux naturels*. Their Muscat is pale yellow with silvery highlights, and has a fine, floral nose. Its aromas evolve in the mouth, dominated by those of white fruits (pear and peach), honey and fresh Muscat grapes. The palate has a good balance of freshness and roundness.

🔑 Pierre and et Franck Piquemal, 1, rue
Pierre-Lefranc, 66600 Espira-de-l'Agly,
tel. 04.68.64.09.14, fax 04.68.38.52.94 ☑
Y by appt.

CH. PRADAL

La cuvée Centre du Monde 1998★

☐ 8 ha 3,000 100–149 F

Situated well within the urban region of Perpignan, Château Pradal is only a few steps from the railway station – the 'centre of the world', as Salvador Dali put it. (That extremely functional building is represented on the label.) The colour of this Muscat is firm old-gold. Its nose is intense and highly original, characterised by notes of coconut, apricot jam and vanilla. The well-endowed palate has good length. An out-of-the-ordinary wine.

🔑 André Coll-Escluse, Ch. Pradal, 58, rue
Pépinière-Robin, 66000 Perpignan,
tel. 04.68.85.04.73, fax 04.68.56.80.49 ☑
Y by appt.

CH. PRADAL 1999

☐ 8 ha 30,000 30–49 F

The estate's traditional cuvée is bright golden in colour with green highlights. Its intense aromas are dominated by exotic fresh fruits and white flowers. The attack is supple, and the finish shows great freshness.

🔑 André Coll-Escluse, Ch. Pradal,
58, rue Pépinière-Robin, 66000 Perpignan,
tel. 04.68.85.04.73, fax 04.68.56.80.49 ☑
Y by appt.

ROC DU GOUVERNEUR 1999

☐ n.c. 15,000 50–69 F

The colour of this Muscat is a beautiful bright gold. Its nose is a subtle evocation of ripe fruits, with slight vegetal overtones. The balance of the palate is sweet and rich, with notes of aromatic evolution. The finish has good freshness.

🔑 Les Vignobles du Rivesaltais, 1, rue de la
Roussillonnaise, 66602 Rivesaltes-Salses,
tel. 04.68.64.06.63, fax 04.68.64.64.69,
e-mail vignobles.rivesaltais@wanadoo.fr ☑
Y by appt.

CH. ROMBEAU 1999★

☐ 7.33 ha 15,000 30–49 F

Established in 1750, the Rombeau estate of 50 ha (124 acres) is one of the oldest in Roussillon. Pierre Henri de la Fabrègue is a medical doctor whose grandfather did research into *vins doux naturels*. He clearly bequeathed his passion for wine to his grandson, who offers a bright golden-yellow Muscat smelling intensely of flowers, exotic fruits and citrus. The lively, aromatic palate gives the impression of biting into a grape. A wine that can be discovered at the Château Rombeau restaurant.

🔑 SCEA Dom. de Rombeau,
66600 Rivesaltes, tel. 04.68.64.35.35,
fax 04.68.64.64.66 ☑ Y ev. day 8am–11pm
🔑 Pierre-Henri de La Fabrègue

DOM. SALVAT 1999

☐ 8 ha 12,000 50–69 F

The youthful pale golden-green colour is at one with the freshness of the aromas of exotic fruit, grapefruit and linden flowers. The palate is in total harmony, with an appetising hint of acidity.

🔑 Dom. Salvat, Pont-Neuf,
66610 Villeneuve-la-Rivière,
tel. 04.68.92.17.96, fax 04.68.38.00.50 ☑
Y ev. day 10am–6pm; cl. Jan.–Feb.

DOM. SARDA-MALET 1999★

☐ n.c. 5,000 50–69 F

This family estate lies within the commune of Perpignan, and the wines grown on its soil were once appreciated by the Counts of Barcelona. Lightish gold in the glass, where it shows greenish highlights, this Muscat is all

elegance. It evolves aromatically through citrus fruits, rose-petals and exotic fruits. The finish is fresh, subtle and persistent.
Dom. Sarda-Malet, mas Saint-Michel, chem. de Sainte-Barbe, 66000 Perpignan, tel. 04.68.56.72.38, fax 04.68.56.47.60 by appt.
Suzy Malet

TOUR DE TREMOINE 1999

☐ 60 ha 40,000 50–69 F

The tower of Trémoine watches over the vineyard of Planèzes-Rasiguères. This co-operative brings together a hundred growers from three communes, making a total of 600 ha (1,480 acres) of vines. This light golden Muscat has a nose that begins discreetly, and then opens out with notes of roses, honey and citrus. Its balance tends towards sweetness and richness in the mouth, and leaves a meaty impression.
Les Vignerons de Planèzes-Rasiguères, 5, rte de Caramany, 66720 Rasiguères, tel. 04.68.29.11.82, fax 04.68.29.16.45, e-mail rasigueres@little.france.com ev. day except Sun. 8am–12 noon 2pm–6pm

DOM. DU VIEUX CHENE 1999★★★

☐ 28 ha 8,000 50–69 F

The 'Estate of the Old Oak' lies in a superb setting, taking in a view of the Roussillon plain and the miscellaneous colours of the terroirs of Espira de l'Agly. This Muscat, grown on limestone soil, gained the jury's unanimous approval. Its aromas explode in a bouquet of exotic fruits, fresh apricot, citrus and fresh mint. The palate is a sumptuous mixture of liquorousness and freshness.
Dom. du Vieux Chêne, Mas Kilo, 66600 Espira-de-l'Agly, tel. 04.68.38.92.01, fax 04.68.38.95.79 by appt.
Sarda-Bobo

DOM. DU VIEUX CHENE
Haut Valoir 1996★★

☐ 6 ha 6,000 70–99 F

Grown on schist soil and fermented in new oak barrels, the Haut Valoir Muscat from Vieux Chêne has also received much attention. It is solid gold in colour and has a nose of honey, linden flowers and crystallised orange. The wine is powerful on the palate, with lots of richness and aromas of candied fruit. It is a beautifully complex 'old' Muscat of very individual character.
Dom. du Vieux Chêne, Mas Kilo, 66600 Espira-de-l'Agly, tel. 04.68.38.92.01, fax 04.68.38.95.79 by appt.
Sarda-Bobo

Muscat de Frontignan

Here, regulations permit Vins de Liqueur to be made with mutage of the must before fermentation, making for wines that are much richer in sugar (about 125 g per litre). In some cases, bringing on the Muscats in old, large barrels causes a slight oxidisation which gives the wines a distinctive flavour of dried grapes.

CAVE DE FRONTIGNAN
12 ans d'âge Vieilli en fût de chêne★★

☐ 2.5 ha 15,000 100–149 F

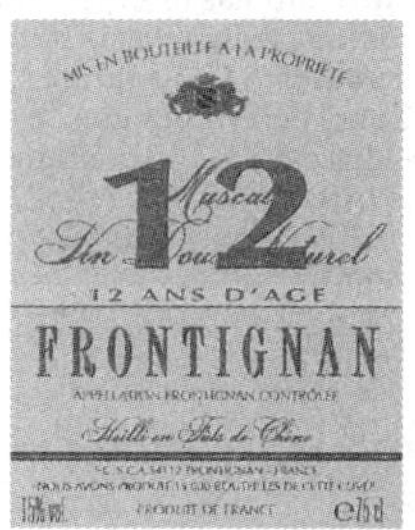

As last year, the Frontignan cellar offers a rare vintage matured for many years in oak casks. After the two stars awarded for the 20-year-old, this 12-year old wine received unanimous approval. The colour is lustrous amber. There is an explosion of aromas on both the nose and palate, comprising orange liqueur, verbena, raisins, liquorice, linden flowers, walnuts and burnt sugar. The finish has remarkable length. A wine to try with orange-flavoured chocolate.
SCA Coop. de Frontignan, 14, av. du Muscat, 34110 Frontignan, tel. 04.67.48.12.26, fax 04.67.43.07.17 ev. day 9.30am–1pm 3.30pm–7pm; groups by appt.

CAVE DE FRONTIGNAN
Premier 1998

☐ 506 ha 1,780,000 30–49 F

Following on from the co-operative's premium cuvée, this is the regular one in the

VDN

twisted bottle. Though this is a high-volume product, nobody should regard this Muscat as a low-class item. Its colour is intense gold. The nose is powerful and slightly evolved, dominated by fading rose and cooked peaches. On the palate, it reveals notes of the garrigue, distilled verbena, citrus zest and crystallised fruits, ending with a subtly acidic finish.
SCA Coop. de Frontignan, 14, av. du Muscat, 34110 Frontignan, tel. 04.67.48.12.26, fax 04.67.43.07.17 ev. day 9.30am–1pm 3.30pm–7pm; groups by appt.

CH. DE LA PEYRADE 1999*

□ 25 ha 40,000 50–69 F

This estate's wines are always remarkably subtle, and this pale golden Muscat is no exception. The nose is floral and the palate lemony, with a honeyed finish. It leaves the palate with an agreeably fresh impression.
Yves Pastourel et Fils, Ch. de La Peyrade, 34110 Frontignan, tel. 04.67.48.61.19, fax 04.67.43.03.31 by appt.

CH. DE MEREVILLE 1998

□ 15 ha 30,000 50–69 F

The estate's 1998 vintage, vinified by the co-operative's cellar, is a pale golden wine with green highlights. Its nose gradually opens out with aromas of crystallised grapes. The full-bodied palate reveals notes of over-ripe and crystallised fruits (grapes, apricots).
SCA Coop. de Frontignan, 14, av. du Muscat, 34110 Frontignan, tel. 04.67.48.12.26, fax 04.67.43.07.17 ev. day 9.30am–1pm 3.30pm–7pm; groups by appt.

Muscat de Beaumes-de-Venise

Located north of Carpentras, beneath the impressive mountains of the Dentelles de Montmirail, the landscape is one of grey limestones and red marls. The terroir is partly composed of sands, marls and sandstone together with weathered, faulted terrain dating from the Triassic and Jurassic eras. Here again, the only grape variety used is the Muscat à Petits Grains, although, on some parcels of land, a mutation has led to pink or red grapes. Muscat de Beaumes-de-Venise wines, of which 13,518 hl (356,875 gal) were produced in 1999, are required to contain a minimum of 110 g of sugar per litre of must; aromatic, fruity and elegant, they are perfect as an aperitif or with cheese.

DOM. DE BEAUMALRIC 1999

□ 8 ha 30,000 50–69 F

The colour of this wine is pale gold with green highlights. Its aromas are light, evoking white-fleshed fruits (pear and peach) and fresh grapes. The balance on the palate is especially good, as between liquorousness on the one hand and liveliness on the other. The finish is slightly bitter, and develops a marc-like note.
EARL Begouaussel, Dom. de Beaumalric, B.P. 15, 84190 Beaumes-de-Venise, tel. 04.90.65.01.77, fax 04.90.62.97.28 by appt.

VIGNERONS DE BEAUMES-DE-VENISE Carte Or 1999

□ 100 ha 200,000 50–69 F

In view of its brilliant colour, Carte Or is well named. This selection wine from the co-operative cellar offers some rather off-beat aromas dominated by the vegetal (black-currant shoots and redcurrant). The wine has a classic, fruity (crystallised apricot) flavour in the mouth, and unctuous balance.
Cave des Vignerons de Beaumes-de-Venise, 84190 Beaumes-de-Venise, tel. 04.90.12.41.00, fax 04.90.65.02.05 ev. day except Sat. Sun. 8.30am–12 noon 2pm–6pm

DOM. BOULETIN 1999

□ 4.8 ha 20,000 50–69 F

This very pale Muscat hits the palate with notes of lemon. Its flavour starts out fresh on the palate, and then becomes silkier, the finish etched in pure Muscat. A very ethereal *vin doux naturel.*
EARL Bouletin et Fils, quartier les Plantades, 84190 Beaumes-de-Venise, tel. 04.90.62.95.10, fax 04.90.62.98.23 ev. day 9.30am–12.30pm 2pm–8pm

DOM. DE FENOUILLET 1999*

□ 7.36 ha 30,000 50–69 F

The Soard family have been working this estate for several generations. Their Muscat is bright gold in colour with pink highlights. The nose displays lightly floral and subtly lemony tones. Citrus is also the keynote on the palate, where the balance is at once lively and warming.
GAEC Patrick et Vincent Soard, Dom. de Fenouillet, allée Saint-Roch, 84190 Beaumes-de-Venise, tel. 04.90.62.95.61, fax 04.90.62.90.67 by appt.

DOM. DE FONTAVIN 1999**

□ 1.69 ha 6,000 50–69 F

Add to an exceptional terroir the talents of a young woman who is both oenologist and

vigneronne, and here you have the secrets of success. The estate receives a *coup de cœur* this year for a Muscat that allies power and subtlety. On the nose, it is floral, fruity and exotic, while the palate is full and round, with a dash of freshness. A superbly balanced whole.

⊶ EARL Hélène and Michel Chouvet, Dom. de Fontavin, 1468, rte de la Plaine, 84350 Courthézon, tel. 04.90.70.72.14, fax 04.90.70.79.39 ☒ Y ev. day except Sun. 9am–12.30pm 1.30pm–7pm

GABRIEL MEFFRE Laurus 1999

☐ 5 ha 10,000 ▮ ♁ 70–99 F

This prestigious wine was assembled by the négociant from selected plots. Pale golden in colour with green highlights, it exudes scents of dried roses and citrus. The palate is intense and warm, with interesting accents of white flowers and citrus zest. A subtle bitterness underpins the finish.

⊶ Gabriel Meffre, Le Village, 84190 Gigondas, tel. 04.90.12.32.42, fax 04.90.12.32.49, e-mail gabriel-meffre@meffre.com

RESERVE J. VIDAL-FLEURY 1999*

☐ 3 ha 12,000 70–99 F

Established in 1781, J. Vidal-Fleury is the oldest firm in the Rhône valley. Since 1986, it has belonged to Marcel Guigal. This bright gold 1999 wine oozes tradition. The aromas are very true to type and have already evolved slightly: crystallised fruits, quince jelly, cooked peaches and linden flowers. The palate is full and concentrated, with notes of dried apricot and burnt sugar.

⊶ J. Vidal-Fleury, 19, rte de la Roche, 69420 Ampuis, tel. 04.74.56.10.18, fax 04.74.56.19.19 ☒ Y by appt.

Muscat de Lunel

A sweet (minimum 125 g of sugar per litre) wine made only from Muscat à Petits Grains. Located around Lunel, the hilltop vineyards sit amid a typical landscape of rolled stones on red clay earth over alluvial folds. A total of 10,125 hl (276,300 gal) was declared in 1999.

CLOS BELLEVUE

Cuvée Vieilles vignes 1999**

☐ 4 ha 9,600 ▮ ♁ 50–69 F

Only a stone's throw from the ancient Via Domitia, Clos Bellevue is made from the estate's oldest vines. The quality of the grapes and the wine-grower's skill have come together to produce a Muscat of great freshness. Its white-fruit aromas evoke pear, peach and more exotic items, while the palate is slightly minty, perfectly balanced, flavoursome and long-lasting. The jury was impressed.

⊶ Francis Lacoste, Dom. de Bellevue, rte de Sommières, 34400 Lunel, tel. 04.67.83.24.83, fax 04.67.71.48.23, e-mail muscatlacoste@dr.com ☒ Y ev. day except Sun. 9am–7pm; groups by appt.

CH. GRES SAINT-PAUL 1998*

☐ 7.15 ha 21,632 ▮ 30–49 F

This property runs to 26 ha (64 acres) and has belonged to the same family since 1831. The 1998 Muscat is bright gold in colour with green highlights. The intense aromas recall eucalyptus, verbena and the herbs of the garrigue, and the finish is pleasantly fresh.

⊶ Ch. Grès Saint-Paul, rte de Restinclières, 34400 Lunel, tel. 04.67.71.27.90, fax 04.67.71.73.76 ☒ Y by appt.

LACOSTE 1999*

☐ 8 ha 26,000 ▮ 50–69 F

The Bellevue manse is not far from the Via Domitia, 3 km (2 miles) from the site of Ambrussum. This 1999 vintage has Francis Lacoste's name stamped all over it. The youthful pale golden colour with green highlights heralds the wine's fresh fruit aromas, and the palate has a matching balance of sweetness and liveliness.

⊶ Francis Lacoste, Dom. de Bellevue, rte de Sommières, 34400 Lunel, tel. 04.67.83.24.83, fax 04.67.71.48.23, e-mail muscatlacoste@dr.com ☒ Y ev. day except Sun. 9am–7pm; groups by appt.

CH. DE LA DEVEZE 1998★

□ 15.12 ha 50,000 30–49 F

The estate's production is vinified by the co-operative cellar at Lunel. The wine has an intense golden hue with green highlights, and an attractively subtle nose characterised by notes of citrus. The palate, too, is very fresh, with citrus zest accompanying a slight savoury bitterness that gives this Muscat lovely balance.

Les Vignerons du Muscat de Lunel, rte de Lunel-Viel, 34400 Vérargues, tel. 04.67.86.00.09, fax 04.67.86.07.52
by appt.

LES VIGNERONS DU MUSCAT DE LUNEL Cuvée Prestige 1998★★

□ n.c. 26,600 30–49 F

This Muscat is bright gold with green highlights, and has gorgeously intense aromas with a Mediterranean dimension, including cypress and crystallised apricot. The wine is full and fresh on the palate, and balanced by its sweetness. A classic within the appellation.

Les Vignerons du Muscat de Lunel, rte de Lunel-Viel, 34400 Vérargues, tel. 04.67.86.00.09, fax 04.67.86.07.52
by appt.

DOM. DE SAINT-PIERRE DE PARADIS Vendanges d'Automne 1998★★

□ n.c. 22,000 50–69 F

The colour of this Muscat is a bright, intense gold. Its complex, evolved nose offers a mixture of aromas, including crystallised fruits, quince jelly, apricots and dried fruits. The wine continues to evolve on the palate with notes of eucalyptus, and a finish evocative of *confiture de lait* (sweet milk concentrated by reduction).

Les Vignerons du Muscat de Lunel, rte de Lunel-Viel, 34400 Vérargues, tel. 04.67.86.00.09, fax 04.67.86.07.52
by appt.

Muscat de Mireval

This vineyard is bordered by the Étang de Vic, and stretches between Sète and Montpellier on the south-facing slope of the Massif de la Gardiole. The soils are of ancient Jurassic alluvium, smoothed stones and the predominant limestone. The single grape variety is Muscat à Petits Grains.

Mutage is carried out fairly early, because the wines must reach a minimum of 125 g of sugar per litre; they are sweet, fruity and rich. In 1999 7,190 hl (189,816 gal) were produced.

DOM. DELTOUR-GROUSSET 1999★★

□ 16 ha 60,000 50–69 F

Legend has it that Rabelais used to enjoy staying at Mireval. How the bard of life's pleasures would have appreciated this 1999 Muscat, with its pale golden colour and scent of new blackcurrant shoots! The wine is both sweet and lively on the palate, finishing on notes of fresh citrus. A treat of a wine, and a *coup de cœur* that does great credit to the producers.

Cave de Rabelais, R.N. 112, B.P. 514, 34114 Mireval Cedex, tel. 04.67.78.15.79, fax 04.67.78.11.71, e-mail cave.rabelais@wanadoo.fr
ev. day except Sat. Sun. 8am–12 noon 2pm–6pm

DOM. DE LA CAPELLE Parcelle 8 1998

□ 5 ha 10,000 100–149 F

This family estate, located several kilometres from the abbey of Maguelonne, has in the last few years taken over some of the neighbouring garrigue. Its Muscat is a bright golden colour, with a subtle, fruity nose showing nuances of overripe grapes. The palate displays similar maturity in the form of cooked peach and burnt sugar flavours, with an accompanying spark of liveliness.

Jean-Pierre Maraval, Dom. de La Capelle, 34110 Mireval, tel. 04.67.78.15.14, fax 04.67.78.58.96 by appt.

Muscat de Saint-Jean de Minervois

This Muscat is produced on parcels of land amid the garrigue, the classic high (average 200 m / 656 ft) – stony moorland of south-west France. It follows that the harvest is late, about three weeks after the other Muscat appellations. Some vines are on primary schist terrain but most grow on limestone interspersed with red clays. Muscat à Petits Grains is the single variety planted; the wines must have a minimum sugar content of 125 g per litre. They are very aromatic with great finesse and characteristic floral notes. This is the smallest Muscat AOC, producing 4,781 hl (126,218 gal) in 1999.

DOM. DE BARROUBIO

Cuvée bleue 1998★

☐ 17 ha 5,000 30–49 F

This estate is one of those that can be relied upon to figure in the *Guide*. Its bright golden-yellow Muscat has a nose that begins discreetly and gradually releases notes of flowers and almonds. Green hazelnuts and crystallised orange register on the palate, and the finish is rounded, offering an appetising hint of bitterness.

Marie-Thérèse Miquel, Dom. de Barroubio, 34360 Saint-Jean-de-Minervois, tel. 04.67.38.14.06, fax 04.67.38.14.06
ev. day 9am–12 noon 3pm–7pm

DOM. DU SACRE-COEUR 1998★

☐ 2 ha 6,500 50–69 F

Although this young estate was established only in 1991, it has for some years played in the big league. Its Muscat is bright gold with delicate green highlights. The aromas of the 1998 are fine, floral, and honeyed, accompanied by a note of verbena, and it leaves the palate with an impression of power and freshness.

GAEC du Sacré-Cœur, Dom. du Sacré-Cœur, 34360 Assignan, tel. 04.67.38.17.97, fax 04.67.38.24.52 by appt.
Marc and Luc Cabaret

LES VIGNERONS DE SEPTIMANIE 1999

☐ 130 ha 130,000 30–49 F

This bright gold 1999 Muscat has an intense nose characterised by aromas of fully ripe pears. The palate amply demonstrates the quality of the terroir, persisting on the finish with hints of *eau de vie*.

SCA Le Muscat de Saint-Jean-de-Minervois, 34360 Saint-Jean-de-Minervois, tel. 04.67.38.03.24, fax 04.67.38.23.38
by appt.

Rasteau

Located in the very north of the Vaucluse department, this vineyard is spread over two distinct geological formations: sand, marl and pebbles in the north, and ancient alluvial terraces left by the Rhône (from the Quaternary era) with smoothed pebbles in the south. The Grenache varieties (Noir, Blanc, Gris) are responsible for all the wines here.

DOM. BEAU MISTRAL

Vieilli en fût de chêne 1998★★

☐ 5 ha 4,000 30–49 F

A harvest born of wind and sun. Rarely here do you get the one without the other. This 1998 pays tribute to the bracing wind that guards the grapes from morning dews and damp autumns. Its firm amber colour is accented by russet highlights. The oak-ageing has certainly done its work. Dried fruits mixed with walnut shells already steal the march on crystallised fruits and hazelnuts, but the palate is very harmonious, supple and velvety. Big old casks have contributed a toasty note, as well as a spiciness that surrounds the long, preserved-fruit finish.

Jean-Marc Brun, Dom. Beau Mistral, Le Village, rte d'Orange, 84110 Rasteau, tel. 04.90.46.16.90, fax 04.90.46.17.30
by appt.

DOM. BRESSY MASSON Rancio★

☐ 3 ha 3,000 50–69 F

Known for its red *vins doux naturels*, this estate also has a way with Rasteau Blanc and Rancio wines. Once again, this light brown wine with coppery highlights demands our attention. Shy at first, it goes on to release notes of roasted almonds, underpinned by beeswax. The balance is good, and the long marriage of wine and oak has produced a rancio with the characteristic notes of walnut.

Marie-France Masson, Dom. Bressy-Masson, rte d'Orange, 84110 Rasteau, tel. 04.90.46.10.45, fax 04.90.46.17.78
ev. day 9am–12.30pm 2pm–7pm

DOM. DES COTEAUX DES TRAVERS 1998★

■ 1 ha n.c. 50–69 F

The AOC Rasteau was for a long time confined to white wine, but is now deservedly applied to reds as well, as this Grenache with its gorgeous ruby colour demonstrates. It is distinctly redolent of red fruits and blackcurrant buds. The still evident tannic core is very fruity, like a charming cherry liqueur. Full integration awaits. In a year or two's time, the wine will go very well with Black Forest gâteau.

Robert Charavin, Dom. des Coteaux des Travers, 84110 Rasteau, tel. 04.90.46.13.69, fax 04.90.46.15.81, e-mail robert.charavin@wanadoo.fr by appt.

DOM. LA SOUMADE Vintage 1998**

5 ha 8,000 70–99 F

A pioneer of Rasteau rouge with a remarkable 1988 a decade ago, André Romero continues to push onward and upward, and now offers this remarkable, beautifully deep red wine that has been fortified on the grapeskins. The nose is discreet, with notes of undergrowth and violets overlaying the red fruits. On the palate, it strikes a lovely balance of cherry and strawberry. A hefty, well-built. wine that would be ideal with a bowl of forest fruits.

André Romero, 84110 Rasteau, tel. 04.90.46.11.26, fax 04.90.46.11.69 ev. day except Sun. 8.30am–11.30am 2pm–6pm

CAVE DE RASTEAU 1997

n.c. n.c. 30–49 F

What a marvellous grape variety is the Grenache. It gives strength and body to a Côtes-du-Rhône red, and sweetness and subtlety to a delicious Rasteau like this. Its amber colour lies somewhere between gold and grey, while the nose mixes mandarin with a soft note of sugared almond. The subtle, sweet balance is nicely integrated with notes of bitter orange. Perfect with a citrus tart.

Cave de Rasteau, rte des Princes-d'Orange, 84110 Rasteau, tel. 04.90.10.90.10, fax 04.90.46.16.65, e-mail rasteau@rasteau.com

Muscat du Cap Corse

The Appellation Muscat du Cap Corse was officially recognised in 1993, the culmination of lengthy efforts made by a handful of wine-makers working on the limestone soils of Patrimonio and the schist soils of the AOC Vin de Corse-Coteaux du Cap Corse. The AOC is located in 17 communes in the extreme north of the islands, and covered 84 ha (207 acres) in 1998.

Since 1993, AOC wines have been limited to Muscat Blanc à Petits Grains and have had to fulfil the stipulated production conditions of Vin Doux Naturels, which require at least 95 grams of residual sugar per litre.

Official recognition for this limited production of 1,983 hl (52,351 gal) in 1999 is well deserved.

NAPOLEON BRIZI 1999

3 ha 10,000 50–69 F

Napoléon Brizi has been working a small family property of 13 ha (32 acres) since 1960, and the succession is assured in the form of his daughter. Their appearance in the *Guide* is with this for a very sweet and rich Muscat, light golden in colour, with the characteristically floral Muscat nose. Drink well-chilled.

Napoléon Brizi, 20217 Saint-Florent, tel. 04.95.37.08.26 by appt.

DOM. DE CATARELLI 1999

2 ha 6,000 50–69 F

The Catarelli estate extends over 11 ha (27 acres) of clay-limestone soil, only one-fifth of which produces Muscat. This 1999 wine is a modern version of the style, with as-yet-reticent aromas of white flowers. The palate is well-balanced, offering delightful notes of almonds and honey.

EARL Dom. de Catarelli, Marine de Farinole, 20253 Patrimonio, tel. 04.95.37.02.84, fax 04.95.37.18.72 by appt.

Laurent Le Stunff

DOM. GENTILE 1999

2.25 ha 9,500 70–99 F

The Gentile estate exports 5% of its wines, some of it to Africa. Imagine tasting this Muscat well-chilled, whilst gazing at the Victoria Falls! Quite an experience! Close your eyes and sample this pretty, pale golden wine. The nose may not be that expressive for the time being, but it has the sweet taste of honey.

Dom. Gentile, Olzo, 20217 Saint-Florent, tel. 04.95.37.01.54, fax 04.95.37.16.69 ev. day except Sun. 8am–12 noon 2pm–6pm; by appt. out of season

DOM. GIUDICELLI 1999**

5.17 ha 16,000 50–69 F

Last year Muriel Giudicelli managed to get noticed with her very first harvest. If you haven't yet sampled her wine, buy some of this little gem straight away: there are only 16,000 bottles on sale. It is no mean achievement to be a grand jury finalist after only your second harvest. The golden-yellow 1999 vintage has intense aromas of honey and orange blossom. Its fine balance of sugar and alcohol in the mouth sustains a freshness that contributes to the wine's aromatic persistence. A very elegant Muscat.

🗝 Muriel Giudicelli, Hameau Paese Novu, 20213 Penta di Casinca, tel. 04.95.36.45.10, fax 04.95.36.45.10 ☑ Y by appt.

DOM. LAZZARINI 1999

☐ 8 ha 15,000 50–69 F

Arriving at Patrimonio, you cannot miss the Lazzarini cellar. Indeed, they may see you first! Among other wines, you will be offered this likeable Muscat, whose golden colour and very evident honey aromas are true to type. You will also be made welcome by this warm and smiling family.

🗝 GAEC Lazzarini, 20253 Patrimonio, tel. 04.95.37.18.61 ☑
Y ev. day 9am–7.30pm; cl. Nov.–Apr.

DOM. LECCIA 1999★★

☐ 1.7 ha 6,500 70–99 F

This superb wine very nearly walked off with a *coup de cœur*! It was a grand jury finalist, having impressed the tasters with its classic character and aromatic complexity. The highly traditional golden colour evokes the colour of grapes roasting in the autumn sun. A wild dance of aromas delights the nose: hints of forest undergrowth, honey and dried fruits all tumble forth, befuddling the senses. As soon as it hits the tastebuds, the dance slows to a harmony of sugar and alcohol to the rhythm of the powerful, complex aromas of crystallised grapes. Drink it now if you must, but it will age most assuredly!

🗝 GAEC Dom. Leccia, 20232 Poggio-d'Oletta, tel. 04.95.37.11.35, fax 04.95.37.17.03 ☑ Y by appt.

CLOS MARFISI 1999★

☐ n.c. 12,000 50–69 F

When you sample this Muscat, share the memories of the Marfisi family gathered in their vineyard, recalling the days of not so long ago, when great and small would tread the grapes with their feet. Their 1999 Muscat is a great success. Its nose is still shy, but will emerge in the coming months. The balance on the palate is excellent. The well-blended aromas of honey, white flowers and fresh Muscat grapes are a source of real pleasure. It is just beginning to drink well.

🗝 Toussaint Marfisi, Clos Marfisi, 20253 Patrimonio, tel. 04.95.37.01.16, fax 04.95.37.01.16 ☑
Y ev. day 9am–12.30pm 2pm–7pm

CLOS NICROSI 1999★

☐ 3.5 ha 6,000 70–99 F

Established on the tip of Cap Corse, where the Libecciu unleashes all its violence, is a really delightful vigneron, Jean-Noël Luigi, who – like his ancestors before him – continues to defy Mother Nature. In some areas, the property is bounded by the Mediterranean, and the land dips into the sea. Doubtless that is the secret of this successful Muscat, whose attractions include its very elegant aspect, its tones of golden-yellow lemon, and intense aromas of buttered white bread, almonds and white flowers. And the taste? Sample its complexity without delay!

🗝 Jean-Noël Luigi, Clos Nicrosi, 20247 Rogliano, tel. 04.95.35.41.17, fax 04.95.35.47.94 ☑
Y ev. day except Sun. 9.30am–12 noon 3.30pm–6.30pm; cl. Oct.-Apr.

ORENGA DE GAFFORY 1999★★

☐ 3.53 ha 11,400 50–69 F

Low yields and perfect mastery of the maturation process are what explain the success of Henri Orenga de Gaffory's latest Muscat. The 1999 version was unanimously approved by the grand jury. This light yellow wine with its bright highlights, expansive and intense nose of white flowers, and balanced palate full of minerally, floral notes, is a very modern wine that could be drunk straight away, but would benefit from a little more time. A magnificent accompaniment to a dessert of dark bitter chocolate.

🗝 Dom. Orenga de Gaffory, Lieu-dit Morta-Majo, 20253 Patrimonio, tel. 04.95.37.45.00, fax 04.95.37.14.25 ☑
Y by appt.

DOM. PASTRICCIOLA 1999

☐ 1 ha 3,500 50–69 F

Three vignerons' sons one day decided to take over an old family estate in their village and found a GAEC. They began enthusiastically in 1989, and their venture this year brings us a beautifully golden, pearl-clear Muscat. It is still immature, but is storing up its mineral notes and taste of gingerbread for bright days ahead.

🗝 Dom. Pastricciola, Maestracci Giovannetti Gilormini, 20253 Patrimonio, tel. 04.95.37.18.31, fax 04.95.37.08.83 ☑
Y ev. day 9.30am–12 noon 3pm–7pm

VDN

DOM. PIERETTI 1999

□ 0.75 ha 3,300 50–69 F

A second successful year for Domaine Pieretti. Muscat is not an easy wine to make; it needs a perfect understanding of grape-ripening and careful fortification to get it right. Evidently no problem for Lina Venturi, whose light golden Muscat has a beautifully balanced palate full of subtle floral aromas.

Lina Venturi-Pieretti, Santa-Severa, 20228 Luri, tel. 04.95.35.01.03, fax 04.95.35.01.03 Y by appt.

DOM. SAN QUILICO 1999

□ 3 ha 12,600 50–69 F

Here is an attractive, crystal-clear wine with scents of the *maquis* and springtime honey. Its balance on the palate will appeal to the sweet of tooth. Drink well-chilled on ice, perhaps with foie gras accompanied by sautéed new potatoes.

Dom. San Quilico, Lieu-dit Morta Majo, 20253 Patrimonio, tel. 04.95.37.45.00, fax 04.95.37.14.25 Y by appt.

VINS DE LIQUEUR

This type of wine is the result of blending must with grape brandy during fermentation. In all cases, wines described as Vins de Liqueur must have between 16% and 22% of alcohol by volume. The addition of brandy to the musts is called mutage; both brandy and must should originate from the same vineyard. The AOC (the equivalent of the EU designation VLQPRD) used to apply only to Pineau des Charentes (apart, in rare instances, from a few Frontignans). However, Floc de Gascogne (classified 27 November 1990) and Macvin du Jura (classified 14 November 1991) have now also joined the Appellation Contrôlée Vin de Liqueur.

Pineau des Charentes

Pineau des Charentes is produced in the Cognac region on an extensive plain sloping gently westwards from a maximum altitude of 180 m (590 ft) towards the Atlantic Ocean. The climate, maritime in character, is typified by a remarkable amount of sunshine and very even temperatures, factors which promote the slow ripening of the grapes.

More than 83,000 ha (205,010 acres) of vines are planted on limestone slopes in a hinterland watered by the Charente river. The grapes are intended mainly for the production of Cognac. Pineau des Charentes is produced by mixing Cognac with partially fermented grape must.

According to legend, a somewhat distracted wine-maker once made the mistake of filling a hogshead that still contained some Cognac with grape must. Noticing that the barrel did not ferment, he left it in the back of the cellar. A few years later, when he was preparing to empty the hogshead, he discovered a clear, delicate liquid with a sweet, fruity flavour: this is said to be the origin of Pineau des Charentes. The legend dates from the 16th century, but the blend is still current today, as is the traditional method of production, because Pineau des Charentes may only be made by wine-growers. Its reputation remained localised for a long time before gradually achieving first national, then international recognition.

The grape musts for white Pineau des Charentes come mainly from Ugni-Blanc, Colombard, Montils and Sémillon, while Cabernet-Franc, Cabernet-Sauvignon and Merlot are used for the rosé. The vines are trained low and cultivated without nitrogenous fertilisers. The grapes have to produce a must of over 10% alcohol by volume. After the blending process, Pineau des Charentes is aged in oak casks for a minimum of one year before bottling.

As is the case with Cognac, it is not the practice to show the vintage. On the other hand, the age of the wine is frequently indicated. The term Vieux Pineau is reserved for Pineau that is more than five years old and Très Vieux Pineau for Pineau that is more than ten years old. In both cases, it must be aged exclusively in the hogshead, and the quality of this ageing process has to be checked by the Commission de Dégustation (the tasting panel). Alcoholic strength must be between 17% and 18% by volume and the content of non-fermented sugar from 125–150 g/l; the rosé is typically sweeter and fruitier than the white, which is firmer and drier. The annual production exceeds 100,000 hl (2,640,000 gal): 55% of it is white, 45% rosé. Five hundred producer-growers and about ten co-operatives make and sell Pineau des Charentes. A hundred shippers are responsible for more than 45% of retail sales.

This is a nectar of honey and fire, its marvellous sweetness camouflaging real power. Pineau des Charentes can be drunk young (after two years) when all its fruit aromas (even fuller in the rosé) are on show. With age, these aromas take on a nutty rancio character. Traditionally, Pineau des Charentes is drunk as an aperitif or with desserts; however, its roundness also perfectly accompanies foie gras and Roquefort. Its sweetness intensifies the natural flavour and sweetness of some kinds of fruit, particularly melon (Charentais melon), strawberries and raspberries. Pineau des Charentes is also used as an ingredient in traditional regional dishes such as mussel stew.

ANDRE ARDOUIN Vieux★★

☐ 1 ha n.c. 70–99 F

This traditional vineyard lies in the north-east of the Cognac region, in an area noted for its architecture; the Romanesque church at Aulnay is greatly admired for its central and southern porches. This Vieux Pineau Blanc is bright and clear, straw-yellow in colour with coppery glints. Its nose is very complex, revealing a subtle succession of many different aromas: hints of walnut, fig, banana, dates, honey, spices and tobacco with a touch of vanilla. In the mouth it is supple and powerful, with long-lingering flavours and a richness balanced by a well-controlled liveliness. Aromas of dried fruits and honey invade the palate. This is a very high-quality wine at a particularly reasonable price.

André Ardouin,
6, rue des Anges, 17470 Villemorin,
tel. 05.46.33.12.52, fax 05.46.33.14.47
by appt.

JEAN AUBINEAU★

☐ 1.37 ha 9,000 50–69 F

Wine-growers from father to son since 1834, the Aubineau family manage a small vineyard with outstanding terroir. This clear Pineau is old-gold in colour flecked with amber, and very aromatic with scents of dried fruits, particularly apricots. The taste is very round with a feeling of great freshness in the mouth, and leaves a very pleasant memory.

Jean Aubineau, 16120 Malaville,
tel. 05.45.97.08.30 by appt.

CLAUDE AUDEBERT Vieux

☐ 6 ha 5,600 70–99 F

Made mainly from the Colombard and Ugni Blanc varieties, and grown on the light chalky soils of the Fins-Bois, this old Pineau Blanc is amber in colour and flecked with gold. While ageing in oak, this rich and intense wine takes on hints of dried and crystallised fruits with aromas of fresh fruit (apricot and grapefruit). Full in the mouth, its sweetness is balanced by a slight sharpness. There is a delightful persistence of aromas of dried fruits and nuts (especially walnuts) and vanilla-flavoured wood.

Claude Audebert,
Les Villairs, 16170 Rouillac,
tel. 05.45.21.76.86, fax 05.45.96.81.36,
e-mail erclaude@wanadoo.fr
ev. day 8am–8pm; groups by appt.

MICHEL BARON Logis de Brissac★★★

☐ 3 ha 20,000 50–69 F

A hunting lodge dating from the time of François I (16th century) dominates a large part of this vineyard in the Borderies. The estate was acquired in 1780 by Léon Alexis de Brémond, Viscount of Ars, before its transfer to the Baron family in 1851. Wondrously straw-gold in colour with multiple glints and smelling richly of dried fruits and wild flowers together with toasty notes, this Pineau is powerful in the mouth, rounded in flavour and long-lasting. There are traces of a promising rancio or nutty aroma. This exceptional Pineau was singled out by the grand jury.

SCEA vignobles Baron, Logis du Coudret, 16370 Cherves-Richemont,
tel. 05.45.83.16.27, fax 05.45.83.18.67,
e-mail veuvebaron@wanadoo.fr
ev. day except Sun. 2pm–6.30pm

HENRI BEGEY★★

☐ 3 ha 20,000 50–69 F

Wine-growers for several generations, the Begeys have been marketing their own production since 1970. Old-gold in colour with plenty of orangey highlights, this Pineau is highly aromatic with enjoyable aromas of spices and crystallised orange. It releases extremely complex notes of citrus fruits in the mouth, and has good length.

Begey et Fils, 17770 Villars-les-Bois,
tel. 05.46.94.91.76, fax 05.46.94.55.00,
e-mail info@begey.com
ev. day except Sun. 8am–8pm

RAYMOND BOSSIS★★★

4 ha 6,000 50–69 F

The Bossis family, who are no strangers to this Guide, have been growing wine on the slopes of the Gironde estuary since 1924. Their exceptional Pineau Rosé, its Merlot clearly predominating over the Cabernet Franc, has a glistening deep ruby colour. Remarkably fruity in character, it offers the nose a broad range of aromas: fresh grapes, blackcurrant, morello cherry, redcurrant and raspberry. These re-emerge in the flavour, which is rich and long with a complex and successful balance between sweetness and acidity. There are discernible roasted or slightly burnt notes, which suggest many good ways to savour it, not simply as an aperitif but also with chocolate desserts.

SCEA Les Groies, Les Groies,
17150 Saint-Bonnet-sur-Gironde,
tel. 05.46.86.02.19, fax 05.46.70.66.85
ev. day 9am–12.30pm 2pm–7.30pm; cl. from 25 Dec. until 01 Jan.
Raymond Bossis

JOAN BRISSON★

1 ha 2,500 50–69 F

Joan Brisson is in Matha, a small town where the remains of two 12th-century churches are worth a visit along with two Renaissance villas belonging to the former château. Botanists will be interested in the 30 varieties of bamboo growing there. Also worth discovering is the Pineau Rosé with its attractive, vivid and very intense colour. The strong presence of the Merlot variety provides its aromas of red and black fruits (cherry and blackcurrant), which develop pleasantly in the direction of kirsch. On the palate it is well-balanced, beginning with cherry and giving way finally to blackcurrant and strawberry.

Joan Brisson, 7, rue Saint-Hérie,
17160 Matha,
tel. 05.46.58.25.07, fax 05.46.58.26.40,
e-mail jbrisson@cer17.cernet.fr
by appt.

CALISINAC Extra vieux

50 ha 2,500 50–69 F

The Liboreau co-operative, founded in 1953, today comprises about a hundred wine-growers cultivating some 230 ha (568 acres) of vines. Golden yellow in colour with glints of ripe wheat and copper, this very old Pineau Blanc has developed an intense nose which is pleasant and supple. Scents of crystallised fruit, peaches, grapes and honey merge delightfully to suggest a light rancio aroma with a well-judged measure of oakiness.

Cave du Liboreau,
18, rue de l'Océan, 17490 Siecq,
tel. 05.46.26.61.86, fax 05.46.26.68.01,
e-mail cave.du.liboreau@wanadoo.fr
by appt.

DOM. DU CHENE★

n.c. 25,000 50–69 F

'A life of passion and a life of patience' is a favourite saying of Jean Doussoux and Jean-Marie Baillif, wine-growers of different generations both fired with the same enthusiasm. The straw-yellow colour and golden lights of their Pineau are followed by enjoyable aromas of white flowers and vanilla, the outcome of a well-regulated ageing process. Good in the mouth, its initial clean taste becomes very full and fruity. This is a well-balanced wine which leaves an excellent impression.

SCEA Doussoux-Baillif, Phiolin,
17800 Saint-Palais-de-Phiolin,
tel. 05.46.70.92.29, fax 05.46.70.91.70
ev. day 8.30am–12 noon 2pm–7pm; Sun. by appt.

DHIERSAT★

5 ha 23,000 50–69 F

This old-established wine-growing family keep vines on the chalky-clay soils of the Fins-Bois. Their mixing of Merlot and Cabernet gives their Pineau a deep mature colour and a definite fruitiness (plum, cherry and ripe quince). In the mouth there is a pleasing balance between sweetness and acidity. The tannins are certainly present, leaving a slightly harsh taste but boding well for the ageing of the wine.

Jean-Claude Dhiersat, Le Breuil,
16170 Rouillac, tel. 05.45.21.75.75,
fax 05.45.96.52.74 ev. day except Sun. 9am–12.30pm 2pm–6pm

DROUET ET FILS X'Cep★

3 ha 1,000 100–149 F

The Drouet et Fils estate has been active since 1968. Today it is run by a young couple who have been marketing their production since 1991. Their Pineau is a many-faceted old-gold in colour. Its aromas of dried fruits with a slight hint of rancio leave an excellent impression. It has an enjoyably fresh taste and the different flavours are perfectly balanced.

Patrick and Stéphanie Drouet, 1, rte du Maine-Neuf, 16130 Salles-d'Angles,
tel. 05.45.83.63.13, fax 05.45.83.65.48
ev. day 9am–12 noon 2pm–7pm; Sun. by appt.

GUILLON-PAINTURAUD★

□ 3 ha 7,000 70–99 F

A wine-growing family since 1610, the Guillon-Painturauds have 18 ha (44 acres). Their Pineau is a very bright golden-yellow in colour with a fine nose and aromas of dried fruits and rancio. The jury enjoyed its pleasing, vanilla-like, rich, lingering taste.

Guillon-Painturaud, Biard, 16130 Ségonzac, tel. 05.45.83.41.95, fax 05.45.83.34.42, e-mail guillon-painturaudepicuria@wanadoo.fr ▼ ev. day except Sun. 9am–12 noon 2pm–6pm

DOM. DE JEREMIE★

□ 5 ha 8,000 30–49 F

Two wine-growing concerns were amalgamated in 1994 to form this estate. The attractive bright and intense colour of the golden-yellow Pineau is matched by an elegant nose that is fruity and floral with suggestions of honey. Generous, with the beginnings of a promising rancio, it is pleasant on the palate. The **Rosé made from old vines**, containing 80% Merlot, has a magnificent bouquet of ripe fruits: redcurrant, blackcurrant and bilberry, together with hints of dried fruits and wood. All of this goes with a quality Cognac. One star (50–69 F).

GAEC Lardière, Jérémie, 17130 Courpignac, tel. 05.46.49.20.14, fax 05.46.49.76.88 ▼ by appt.

JULES GAUTRET Vieux

□ n.c. n.c. 70–99 F

The Jules Gautret label was created in 1847. Since then, this co-operative with headquarters at Jonzac has marketed wines from the Charente vineyards. Golden yellow with old-gold reflections, this Vieux Pineau Blanc is rich in aromas of dried fruits and nuts (walnuts and almonds) and exotic fruits, and also carries hints of acacia flowers and honey. There is a definite oaky taste. Its great persistence in the mouth is due to its excellent balance. Although true to type, it is perhaps a bit lively for a Vieux Pineau Blanc.

Unicognac, 30, av. Foch, 17503 Jonzac Cedex, tel. 05.46.48.10.99, fax 05.46.48.47.70, e-mail rfort@jules-gautret.com ▼ by appt.

DOM. DE LA RAMBAUDERIE★

□ 2.5 ha 8,000 50–69 F

Taken over by the Boucher family in 1931, this vineyard is situated on the slopes overlooking the Gironde. The Pineau has a very clear gold colour, and gives off intense perfumes of dried fruits and a burgeoning rancio aroma. Long-lasting in the mouth, it is highly aromatic; its elegance and richness complement each other well.

Suzette Boucher, Dom. de La Rambauderie, 78, rue des Ajoncs, 17150 Saint-Sorlin-de-Conac, tel. 05.46.86.00.72, fax 05.46.49.06.58 ▼ by appt.

MAURICE LASCAUX★★

□ 4 ha 15,000 50–69 F

This 17th-century dwelling, bought as a ruin by the Lascaux family in 1900, has been restored and converted into a *gîte de France* where the products of the vineyard can be tasted. The straw-yellow Pineau with its glints of old gold breathes scents of honey and espalier-trained peaches. In the mouth it is very rounded and elegant, offering a perfect balance of flavours, and has great persistence.

Maurice Lascaux, Logis du Renfermis, 16720 Saint-Même-les-Carrières, tel. 05.45.81.90.48, fax 05.45.81.98.34 ▼ ev. day 8am–8pm

L'ENCLOUSE DES VIGNES★★

□ 6 ha 12,000 50–69 F

This estate, on the picturesque D 145 linking Royan and Bordeaux, produces an extremely clear Pineau, old-gold in colour with orangey lights and the intense aromas of dried fruits. Well rounded, full and rich, it has a well-balanced taste offering varied flavours with a final slightly oaky note.

L'Enclouse des Vignes, Mageloup, 17120 Floirac, tel. 05.46.90.63.29, fax 05.46.90.60.68 ▼ by appt.

Bourreau

LEYRAT Vieille Réserve

□ n.c. n.c. 100–149 F

The colour of this Pineau is clear and brilliant, touched with golden yellow. Both simple and fine, it displays aromas of dried fruits and vanilla, *pain d'épice* (a kind of spicy loaf) and white flowers along with a well-balanced hint of oakiness. In the mouth it retains its liveliness, with a very slight rancio aroma and notes of dried apricot and honey. It has all the necessary substance, but needs more time to acquire the organoleptic qualities of a Vieux Pineau Blanc.

Leyrat, Dom. de chez Maillard, 16440 Claix, tel. 05.45.66.35.72, fax 05.45.66.48.34, e-mail cognac-leyrat.com ▼ by appt.

CH. DE L'OISELLERIE Pineau Rubis

◪ 5 ha n.c. 50–69 F

Bred and trained for hunting in the 15th century and a symbol of power and majesty, the falcon has become the emblem of the Oisellerie estate. The Pineau has a deep and intense ruby colour. Its nose is delicate, slightly floral and fruity, dominated by raspberry. It has consistency and hits the palate with vigour; its full taste includes fruity, grapey notes with good length.

Lycée agricole Oisellerie, 16400 La Couronne, tel. 05.45.67.36.89, fax 05.45.67.16.51, e-mail expl.legta. angouleme@educagri.fr ▼ by appt.

MAINE LAURE★

□ 10 ha 4,000 50–69 F

When he took over from his father, Olivier Sauvaître chose to rename the estate, and so

'Destrailles' became 'Maine Laure'. This Pineau, intensely straw-yellow in colour with multiple glints, has a pleasing nose with aromas of dried fruits and quince. Delightfully lingering on the palate, it is very full and rich, and finishes on a note of elegant suppleness.
⊶ SARL Maine Laure,
Le Maine Laure, 16360 Le Tatre,
tel. 05.45.78.54.14, fax 05.45.78.53.66,
e-mail sca.r.sauvaitre@wanadoo.fr ☒
Ῑ by appt.
⊶ Olivier Sauvaître

S. MARCADIER ET A. BARBOT*

□ 3 ha 6,000 50–69 F

Four generations have worked on this viticultural property, which is located in the heart of the Grande Champagne. The Pineau is old-gold in colour with orangey lights. It has a very pleasing nose made up of hints of raisins and vanilla. It is fat and rich in the mouth; its freshness and rancio aroma blend well together.
⊶ GAEC La Combe de Bussac,
Le Pible, 16130 Ségonzac,
tel. 05.45.83.41.18, fax 05.45.83.43.21 ☒
Ῑ ev. day 9am–9pm
⊶ S. Marcadier-A. Barbot

MARQUIS DE DIDONNE**

◢ 10 ha 80,000 30–49 F

A label of the Saint-Sulpice-de-Royan cooperative, this 'little marquess' is well-behaved, and wears appropriately ceremonial colours: a slightly modified intense ruby. The scent is of red fruits (strawberry, cherry, redcurrant). In the mouth its well-structured, measured tones of red fruits make a good impression, with the added surprise of a hint of orange peel. This wine has good length and is pleasant to drink straight away.
⊶ Vignerons des Côtes de Saintonge,
B.P. 5, Fontbedeau,
17200 Saint-Sulpice-de-Royan,
tel. 05.46.06.01.01, fax 05.46.06.91.72,
e-mail info@didonne.com ☒ Ῑ ev. day except Sun. 9am–12.30pm 2.30pm–6.30pm

MENARD Très vieux*

□ n.c. 5,000 100–149 F

This Vieux Pineau Blanc has an attractive golden yellow colour with coppery lights. The nose is restrained at first, then develops a fine, broad palette of aromas: cooked fruits, well-ripened apricots and a moderate, subtle rancio. This very successful and well-made product would benefit from further ageing if you are prepared to wait.
⊶ J.-P. Ménard et Fils, 2, rue de la Cure,
16720 Saint-Même-les-Carrières,
tel. 05.45.81.90.26, fax 05.45.81.98.22,
e-mail menard@cognac-menard.com ☒
Ῑ ev. day except Sat. Sun. 8am–12 noon 2pm–6pm

ANDRE PETIT Sélection**

□ 2.5 ha 13,500 50–69 F

There is nothing but good to say of this wine's old-gold colour and multiple glints. It has enjoyable aromas of dried fruits and nuts (fig and walnut in particular). The taste is very full, with a certain freshness showing that the ageing process has been very well controlled.
⊶ André Petit et Fils, Au Bourg,
16480 Berneuil, tel. 05.45.78.55.44,
fax 05.45.78.59.30 ☒ Ῑ by appt.
⊶ Jacques Petit

ALAIN PILLET*

□ 12 ha 10,000 50–69 F

Representing the fifth generation on this old estate, this wine-grower has totally restructured his vineyard on chalky-clay slopes and has been marketing his wines for more than 20 years. Old-gold in colour and extremely bright with multiple facets, this Pineau has a delicate nose of dried fruits. First impressions on the palate are good, revealing a well-rounded and harmonious taste. The final slight rancio flavour is proof of well-controlled ageing.
⊶ Alain Pillet, Chez Bruneau,
17130 Rouffignac, tel. 05.46.49.04.82,
fax 05.46.49.04.82 ☒ Ῑ by appt.

REMY-MARTIN**

□ 50 ha n.c. 50–69 F

Founded in 1724 by a Charente wine-grower, Rémy-Martin is one of the great labels of the Cognac region, presided over by Madame Hériard-Dubreuil. The successful mixing of several grape varieties has produced this old-gold Pineau. Its rich palette of aromas, with hints of flowers and fruits, is apparent both on the nose and palate. The taste is full, characterised by a beautiful rancio flavour that brings harmony to the wine as a whole.
⊶ Remy-Martin, 20, rue de la Société-Vinicole, B.P. 37, 16100 Cognac,
tel. 05.45.35.76.00, fax 05.45.35.02.85
Ῑ by appt.

RENIER Extra vieux*

◢ 2 ha 3.500 100–149 F

A wine-estate where traditionally one expects to find high-quality Vieux Pineaux Rosés. This one is pale pink in colour, clear and coppery with brownish flecks. The subtleties of its smell are complex: the rancio flavour successfully marries with notes of walnut and hazelnut, with scents of macerated cooked fruits and a well-measured touch of oakiness. Rich on the palate, this Pineau is well-balanced and supple; the dominant aromas are those of red cooked fruits and dried fruit with a final rancio.
⊶ SCA du Clos de Mérienne, B.P. 87,
16200 Gondeville, tel. 05.45.81.13.27,
fax 05.45.81.74.30 ☒ Ῑ by appt.
⊶ Charpentron

PAUL VIGIE

◢ 2 ha 3,000 30–49 F

The vineyard stands on flint and clay near the Côte de la Beauté and the Gironde. Vines more than twenty years old, half Merlot and half Cabernet, produce a dark, mature, brick-red rosé. The colour is striking, clear evidence

of a ripe fruit full of blackcurrant, blackberry and bilberry. Blackcurrant remains uppermost in the mouth, giving a refreshingly acidic and fruity taste.
🔑 Dominique Vigié, Roumignac,
17120 Cozes,
tel. 05.46.90.94.66, fax 05.46.90.83.69,
e-mail d.vigie@libertysurf.fr ☑ Y by appt.

Floc de Gascogne

Floc de Gascogne is produced in the same geographical area as the Appellation Bas Armagnac, Ténarèze and Haut Armagnac, as well as in all the communes within the Appellation Armagnac. The wine-growing region is part of the Pyrenean foothills and extends into three departments: the Gers, the Landes and the Lot-et-Garonne. To give themselves extra power, the wine-makers of Floc de Gascogne established a new principle. Instead of describing and defining specific growing areas, as is the case for wines, or a simple geographical area, as for brandies, they propose an annual list of growing areas for approval by the INAO.

The whites are produced from Colombard, Gros Manseng and Ugni Blanc, and, together, these must make up at least 70% of the range of varieties planted. Since 1996, no individual variety can exceed 50%; other varieties included are Baroque, Folle Blanche, Petit Manseng, Mauzac, Sauvignon and Semillon. Rosés are produced from Cabernet Franc and Cabernet-Sauvignon, as well as from Cot, Fer Servadou, Merlot and Tannat, which last may not exceed 50% of the varieties planted.

The regulations laid down by the producers are highly restrictive: a maximum of 3,300 plants per hectare (1,336 per acre), trained *en guyot* or in cordons, the number of buds to the hectare to be fewer than 60,000 (24,291 per acre). Artificial irrigation of the vines is strictly forbidden in any season, and the basic yield from the parcels of land must be less than or equal to 60 hl/ha (648 gal per acre).

Every year, each wine-grower must submit a declaration of intent to make the wines and send it to the INAO, so that the organisation may actually inspect the conditions of production on the ground. The musts harvested may not have less than 100 g/l of must sugar. Once the grapes have been stripped from the stalks and separated from the sediment, they are placed in a receptacle where the must undergoes the beginnings of fermentation. No addition of external products is permitted. The mutage of the must takes place with Eau de Vie d'Armagnac at a minimum of 52% alcohol by volume. The result is left to rest for at least nine months. It may be brought out of the vat room only after 1 September of the year following the harvest. All the lots of wine are tasted and analysed. Given the variations that arise in this type of product, the best of the wine emerges only after ageing in the bottle.

CH. DU BASCOU**

◪ 3.5 ha 6,000 ▮ ♁ 30–49 F

Produced on sandy, gravelly soils, this Floc Rosé has an intense colour with violet lights and is a great delight to nose and tastebuds alike. Its bouquet recalls a basket of red fruits (cherry, plum, blackcurrant) with intense and complex aromas. The taste has the same qualities: even if the wine's fullness tones them down somewhat, this does no harm to its finesse and elegance. Excellent value for money.
🔑 Robert Rouchon, EARL Ch. du Bascou,
32290 Bouzon-Gellenave,
tel. 05.62.09.07.80, fax 05.62.09.08.94 ☑
Y ev. day 9am–12.30pm 3pm–7.30pm;
cl. 1–15 Sep.

BORDENEUVE-ENTRAS*

◪ 1.04 ha 13,500 ▮▮▮ 50–69 F

This vast estate of 36.5 ha (90 acres) has produced two Flocs of quality. The rosé is a real success and has a strong, brilliant red colour. Its nose has intense notes of ripe fruits (morello cherry, blackcurrant, blackberry). Its taste is well-balanced and smooth with a somewhat lively finish due to the Armagnac. The white is pale yellow in colour, with scents of crystallised fruits, and is well-balanced and enjoyable to the taste. It is a fine example of its type.

🔑 GAEC Bordeneuve-Entras,
32410 Ayguetinte, tel. 05.62.68.11.41,
fax 05.62.68.15.32 ✉ 🍷 by appt.
🔑 Maestrojuan

DOM. DE CACHELARDIT★

☐ 0.4 ha 3,000 30–49 F

This producer, from the sixth generation on the property, offers us the pleasures of a beautifully made Floc Blanc. Straw-yellow, fruity and powerful with honeyed touches, this wine creates a happy impression of balance and freshness in the mouth. Best tasted with eyes closed.

🔑 Pierre Philip, Cachelardit,
32100 Cassaigne,
tel. 05.62.28.04.04, fax 05.62.68.24.20 ✉
🍷 ev. day 9am–12 noon 2pm–6pm

DOM. DE CASSAGNAOUS

◪ 3.5 ha 1,494 50–69 F

In the midst of a region much visited by tourists and rich in Gallo-Roman remains, the Zago family has produced two Flocs. First is the rosé, deep red in colour and with a scent of cherry, which is quite complex but a little on the heavy side. The taste develops well with a finish rich in crystallised fruits. The straw-yellow white has a fine nose, a good sweetness in the mouth with a finish marked by the Armagnac. Both are straightforward products well worth inclusion here.

🔑 EARL de Cassagnaous,
Au Cassagnaous, 32250 Montréal-du-Gers,
tel. 05.62.29.44.81, fax 05.62.29.44.81 ✉
🍷 by appt.
🔑 G. Zago

DOM. DE CAUMONT

◪ 1 ha 3,010 50–69 F

Family-owned since 1825, the Caumont estate is frequently mentioned in wine publications, and now offers a pleasant rosé with a slightly pale, brick-red colour, very fruity to the nose and in the mouth. This is a bottle to drink with friends.

🔑 SCEA de Badiole,
32240 Lias-d'Armagnac,
tel. 05.62.09.63.95, fax 05.62.08.70.14 ✉
🍷 by appt.
🔑 Bourdens

DOM. DE CAZEAUX★

☐ 8.51 ha 3,000 70–99 F

Eric Kauffer, at the helm since 1999, here presents the last wine made by his father Michel, who created the Cazeaux estate (the name means 'garden' in Gascon) and with several others established the AOC Floc de Gascogne. The present wine has a fine golden-yellow colour, a somewhat immature nose and a fruity, fat and well-rounded taste, with very expressive notes of oakiness. A very successful product which goes perfectly with foie gras (from the Gers, needless to say). The rosé also wins a mention for its excellent balance and general quality.

🔑 Eric Kauffer, Dom. de Cazeaux,
47170 Lannes, tel. 05.53.65.73.03,
fax 05.53.65.88.95,
e-mail domaine.de.cazeaux@wanadoo.fr ✉
🍷 ev. day 9am–6pm; groups by appt.

LES PRODUCTEURS DE LA CAVE DE CONDOM EN ARMAGNAC

☐ n.c. 20,000 30–49 F

Awarded a *coup de coeur* last year by the jury for a superb rosé, the Condom Co-operative, created in 1950, offers a pale-yellow white with a lovely fruity and flowery nose. Round without being heavy, it gives real pleasure.

🔑 Les producteurs de la Cave de Condom-en-Armagnac,
59, av. des Mousquetaires, 32100 Condom,
tel. 05.62.28.12.16, fax 05.62.28.23.94

DOM. D'EYSSAC★★

☐ 0.5 ha 4,000 50–69 F

Gilles Lhoste has substantially added to the family estate. Since he took over, it has gone from five to 33 ha (12 to 82 acres). His Floc Blanc has a brilliant gold colour, a particularly powerful and complex nose with dried fruits predominant, and a rounded, long, very fruity flavour, and received unanimous approval. The rosé has been selected for its deep red-brown colour and its aromas of red fruits (blackcurrant).

🔑 Gilles Lhoste, Dom. d'Eyssac,
32290 Averon-Bergelle, tel. 05.62.08.52.27,
fax 05.62.61.84.86 ✉ 🍷 by appt.

DOM. DE FARON

◪ 1 ha 7,000 30–49 F

Christian Montelieu has headed this family estate of 52 ha (128 acres) since 1982. His Floc Rosé is ruby-red in colour with a moderately intense nose of flowers (violets) and fruit (blackcurrant). Though initially somewhat sweet on the palate, it has length and is very pleasant. This is a Floc to enjoy in tranquillity.

🔑 Christian Montelieu, Faron, 32800
Bretagne-d'Armagnac, tel. 05.62.09.93.84,
fax 05.62.09.93.84 ✉

FERME DE GAGNET★

◪ 0.6 ha 7,200 50–69 F

In addition to offering canned duck, the Ferme de Gagnet, a *gîte rural*, also has a Floc with a pale, brilliant and clear red colour. Its nose of red fruits (blackcurrant and Morello cherry) is fine and elegant. The same qualities are found in the taste, which has balance and persistence. A good accompaniment to a fruit salad.

🔑 Ferme de Gagnet, Gagnet, 47170 Mézin,
tel. 06.82.36.19.82, fax 06.53.97.22.04 ✉
🍷 ev. day except Sun. 8am–1pm 2pm–9pm
🔑 Tadieu

MICHEL FEZAS Chiroulet★★

◪ 5 ha 16,000 50–69 F

On chalky-clay soils in Ténarèze, in the heart of a tourist region made for lovers of old buildings – don't miss the 13th-century church at Heux, 200 m (218 yd) from the estate – and of the good life, the Fezas family has produced a cherry-red rosé with an intense nose that evokes crystallised red fruits. The initial fruity, well-balanced flavour on the palate, plus its persistence at the finish, is a real pleasure. The Floc Blanc has been selected for its pale yellow colour, fruity nose and a rich flavour tempered by freshness and hints of spices.

Famille Fezas, Dom. de Chiroulet, Heux, 32100 Larroque-sur-l'Osse, tel. 05.62.28.02.21, fax 05.62.28.41.56
by appt.
Michel Fezas

CH. GARREAU Cuvée Royale

12 ha 20,000 50–69 F

One of the founders of the AOC Floc de Gascogne, Monsieur Garreau has become president of the organisation protecting Armagnac, the 'Syndicat de Défense de l'Armagnac'. Two Flocs are on offer. The first is straw-yellow, with a nose of dried and crystallised fruits and a sweet, round taste verging on the overripe. Also worthy of mention is the Cuvée Royale en Rosé. Somewhat reddish in colour, with notes of red fruits in both scent and taste, with an Armagnac character, this wine is supple and without aggressiveness.

Ch. Garreau, Côtes de la Jeunesse, 40240 Labastide-d'Armagnac, tel. 05.58.44.84.35, fax 05.58.44.87.07, e-mail chateau.garreau@wanadoo.fr
by appt.

HAUT BARON

0.36 ha 4,550 50–69 F

Located in the Lower Armagnac region, on the tawny sandy soil on the borders of the Landes and Gers departments, this cellar presented a successful Floc Blanc, the result of a perfect union of Ugni Blanc, Gros Manseng and Armagnac. Rather pale white in colour, it has an expressive floral nose and its aromas persist in the mouth. This is a characteristic and typical Floc.

Cave coopérative deŒ Cazaubon, 32150 Cazaubon, tel. 05.62.08.34.00, fax 05.62.69.50.98 by appt.

DOM. DE LAGUILLE

n.c. 2,400 70–99 F

A new producer of Floc, Guy Vignoli enters the new century with two Flocs, both cited. In the rugby-mad South-West, they call this a converted try! The white, a pale crystal-yellow in colour, has a quite intense nose of citrus fruits and is well balanced and flowery on the palate. The Floc Rosé has a grenadine-red colour with mahogany lights, and is marked by the quality of the Armagnac, which balances the rather muted contribution of the grape.

SCEA La Treille, Laguille Saint-Amand, 32800 Eauze, tel. 05.62.09.77.05, fax 05.62.09.84.77 by appt.

DOM. DE LAUROUX**

0.5 ha 3,600 50–69 F

For the new millennium, Rémy Fraisse presents two Flocs of great quality. The Blanc is remarkable for its light yellow colour and green lights, its fine nose with fruity and floral notes and a hint of Armagnac. It is supple as it crosses the palate, and the taste is balanced and fruity, round and long. The rosé is a vivid red with a flowery, fruity nose, and an impressive freshness. Its fruity length in the mouth makes it a very successful Floc (one star).

Rémy Fraisse, EARL du Dom. de Lauroux, 32370 Manciet, tel. 05.62.08.56.76, fax 05.62.08.57.44
by appt.

CH. DE MONS

1 ha 13,000 50–69 F

Owned by the Chambre d'Agriculture of the Gers since 1963, this château, built in 1285, has stood the test of time throughout its illustrious history. The Mons estate offers two Flocs, both worthy of mention. First, the rosé, a light, brilliant red with an intense nose and a well-mannered fruity taste. Second, the Floc Blanc, which has notes of vanilla and dried fruits and a well-balanced taste. Both are wines for relaxed drinking.

Dom. de Mons, Chambre d'agriculture du Gers, 32100 Caussens, tel. 05.62.68.30.30, fax 05.62.68.30.35, e-mail chateau.mons.cda.32@wanadoo.fr
by appt.

CAVE DES PRODUCTEURS DE NOGARO*

n.c. 50,000 30–49 F

The largest producer of Floc de Gascogne, the Nogaro co-operative cellar offers a beautifully ruby-coloured rosé. The nose, though marked by the spirit, is nonetheless pleasant and fine. Initially fresh in the mouth and then fruity (plum), it has a slightly sharp finish. This is a typical product of the appellation.

Cave des Producteurs réunis, 32110 Nogaro, tel. 05.62.09.01.79
by appt.

DOM. DE POLIGNAC*

3 ha 10,000 50–69 F

The Gratians have considerably enlarged their property from 8 ha in 1981 to 45 ha now (20 to 111 acres). On their stony, chalky, clay soils, they have developed a Floc Rosé that the tasters found noteworthy for its brilliant cherry-red colour, intense nose of red fruits (strawberries) and blackcurrant. Its well-balanced, fresh and fruity flavour has great finesse. As an accompaniment to melon, this Floc cannot fail to give pleasure.

EARL Gratian, Dom. de Polignac, 32330 Gondrin, tel. 05.62.28.54.74, fax 05.62.28.54.86 by appt.

DOM. SAN DE GUILHEM

1.74 ha 11,000 50–69 F

This estate of 54.61 ha (135.9 acres), run by Alain Lalanne since 1974, offers a rosé which is ruby in colour with brick-red nuances, has a nose of ripe red fruits and is well balanced on the palate. Selected for its airy, light, smooth

character, this Floc should be served as an aperitif.
🗝 Alain Lalanne, Dom. San de Guilhem, 32800 Ramouzens, tel. 05.62.06.57.02, fax 05.62.06.44.99 ☑ 𝐘 ev. day 8am–12 noon 1.30pm–6.30pm

CAPITAINE SANSOT

◪ 0.5 ha 1,489 ▮ 30–49 F

The River Baïse lies only half a kilometre (less than a third of a mile) from the estate. Try taking a canoe downstream to see this producer, whose two Flocs have been selected by the jury. One of these is a beautiful cherry-red in colour with a lively but fruity nose. The first impression in the mouth is of freshness, which yields agreeably to hints of chocolate. Also mentioned is the Blanc, which is pale yellow in colour, has a lightly fruity nose and a supple, balanced taste with hints of dried fruits.
🗝 Christophe Mendousse, EARL du Capitaine, 32410 Beaucaire-sur-Baïse, tel. 05.62.68.15.16, fax 05.62.68.14.65 ☑ 𝐘 ev. day 9am–12.30pm 2pm–7pm; cl. Jan.

CH. DU TARIQUET

☐ 5 ha n.c. 50–69 F

In the purest tradition of the Grassa family, this golden- amber Floc Blanc, with its nose of cooked fruits and honey, has a particular character on the palate due to the quality of the Armagnac derived from the Folle Blanche grape variety.
🗝 Ch. du Tariquet, 32800 Eauze, tel. 05.62.09.87.82 ☑ 𝐘 by appt.
🗝 Famille Grassa

Macvin du Jura

This highly distinctive wine could equally well have been called Galant, the name by which it was known in the 14th century, when Marguerite of France, Duchess of Burgundy and wife of Philip the Bold, declared it her favourite wine.

The Macvin — historically Maquevin or Marc-vin — was probably first made in the medieval abbey of Château-Chalon. It was recognised as an AOC under the name of Macvin du Jura by decree on 14 November 1991. The Société de Viticulture began the procedures for AOC recognition in 1976. The inquiry took a long time because agreement had to be reached on a definitive approach to making the wine. Macvin began as a 'cooked' wine, with herbs and spices added to it; it then became Mistelle, a fortified wine made from musts that were concentrated by heating (cooking them), then a Vin de Liqueur muted with eau-de-vie from the Franche-Comté. The last method was the one ultimately agreed upon; for the AOC, this means using a Vin de Liqueur with must that has undergone a very slight initial fermentation, muted with Marc Eau-de-Vie made from wines from the AOC Franche-Comté, which have to come from the same property as the musts. The must should come from vine varieties and a production area with the right to the AOC. The Eau-de-Vie should be *rassise*, that is, aged in an oak cask for a minimum of 18 months.

After this final mixing, the Macvin should rest for a year, without being filtered, in oak casks, since it cannot be sold before 1 October of the year following its harvest.

Production, which is growing, is about 1,700 hl (44,880 gal) from 36 ha (89 acres). Macvin du Jura is enjoying an appreciable development since it is greatly enjoyed, particularly locally, as the aperitif of choice for connoisseurs of Jura wines. It completes the range of appellations in the Comté area and is perfect served with local specialities.

FRUITIERE VINICOLE D'ARBOIS**

☐ 5 ha 25,000 ▮▮ 70–99 F

The co-operative's Macvin has a strong amber colour with mahogany lights. The nose is interesting: marc and must have formed an intimate union and the resulting aromas of apple and honey that result are very pleasing. The finish in the mouth is a trifle warm, but the hints of almond are most agreeable. A fine product with both feminine and masculine qualities, we think it should have a universal appeal.
🗝 Fruitière vinicole d'Arbois, 2, rue des Fossés, 39600 Arbois, tel. 03.84.66.11.67, fax 03.84.37.48.80 ☑ 𝐘 by appt.

CH. D'ARLAY**

☐ 1 ha 4,000 ▮ ◖◗ 100–149 F

The château of Arlay is a listed historic monument, and both the château and park are open to visitors. The estate's Macvin has all the style and class one would expect. The marc spirit has married perfectly with the Chardonnay and Savagnin must. The nose is somewhat influenced by the marc, while the taste subtly reveals the fruitiness of the grape, offering substance, balance and delicious length. A Macvin like this will certainly bring a taste of the château lifestyle to your desserts.

Ch. d' Arlay, rte de Saint-Germain, 39140 Arlay, tel. 03.84.85.04.22, fax 03.84.48.17.96, e-mail chateau@arlay.com ☒ Y ev. day except Sun. 8am–12 noon 2pm–6pm

de Laguiche

BADOZ*

☐ n.c. 1,500 ◖◗ 70–99 F

Pale yellow in colour and with an expressive nose, this wine is both flowery and fruity. The marc is not overwhelming in the mouth; rather, it allows the taste of the grape to come through easily. Balance and finesse meet here in harmony.

Bernard Badoz, 15, rue du Collège, 39800 Poligny, tel. 03.84.37.11.85, fax 03.84.37.11.18 ☒ Y ev. day 8am–8pm

PHILIPPE BUTIN*

☐ 0.2 ha 1,300 ◖◗ 70–99 F

The must used here comes from the Chardonnay variety. This Macvin has a beautiful light-golden colour and a very discreet but enormously pleasing nose, with figs and currants merging harmoniously with the marc. The same partnership continues successfully on the palate.

Philippe Butin, 21, rue de la Combe, 39210 Lavigny, tel. 03.84.25.36.26, fax 03.84.25.39.18 ☒ Y ev. day 8am–7pm

CAVEAU DES BYARDS***

☐ 0.35 ha 3,000 ◖◗ 70–99 F

The colour is brilliant and clear. As one jury member put it, 'The light-yellow colour and green lights are incredibly inviting.' The fresh, fruity nose evokes fruit brandy. It arrives on the palate in a virile but subtle manner, and the taste progresses perfectly, with roundness, fluidity and richness recalling fresh fruits, and then ripe fruits. It is the ultimate in fruit flavour, in total harmony with the marc spirit. It has everything, and in the most precise balance.

Caveau des Byards, 39210 Le Vernois, tel. 03.84.25.33.52, fax 03.84.25.38.02 ☒ Y by appt.

D. ET P. CHALANDARD

■ 0.5 ha 800 ◖◗ 70–99 F

The pale-red colour, almost brick-red but brilliant, may come as a surprise. The nose is moderate in intensity, offering notes of small red fruits and raisins: a very pleasant approach. The flavour is complex and has an astonishingly aromatic character, with blood orange adding itself to the scents already perceived by the nose. This Macvin will not pass unnoticed.

GAEC du Vieux Pressoir, rte de Voiteur, 39210 Le Vernois, tel. 03.84.25.31.15, fax 03.84.25.37.62 ☒ Y by appt.

MARIE ET DENIS CHEVASSU*

☐ n.c. 1,000 ◖◗ 70–99 F

This farm, brimming with flowers, opens its gates on Sundays in August for people to meet and talk about wine. This Macvin has a beautiful golden colour and is well-balanced overall; the spirit makes its presence felt just a little at the finish. A well-made, fine and pleasant wine.

Denis Chevassu, Granges Bernard, 39210 Menétru-le-Vignoble, tel. 03.84.85.23.67, fax 03.84.85.23.67 ☒ Y by appt.

DOM. VICTOR CREDOZ

◪ 0.3 ha 2,400 ◖◗ 70–99 F

Founded by Victor Credoz in 1859, this estate is now in the hands of Daniel and Jean-Claude Credoz. Their Macvin is rose-pink in colour. The taste is balanced and intense, with a long, harmonious finish. Try this wine with a raspberry sorbet for a real taste of *la vie en rose.*

Dom. Victor Credoz, 39210 Menétru-le-Vignoble, tel. 06.80.43.17.44, fax 06.84.44.62.41 ☒ Y ev. day 8am–12 noon 1pm–7pm

RICHARD DELAY*

☐ 0.1 ha 1,200 ◖◗ 70–99 F

Lustrous bronze in colour, this wine has a rich, somewhat candied nose. The flavour is full, supple and balanced, its fine structure conveying a strong impression of harmony.

Richard Delay, 37, rue du Château, 39570 Gevingey, tel. 03.84.47.46.78, fax 03.84.43.26.75 ☒ Y by appt.

DANIEL DUGOIS*

☐ 0.3 ha 2,000 ◖◗ 70–99 F

This wine-grower has already been honoured several times for his Vin Jaune wine. He also knows how to make a Macvin with a very well-balanced nose. The taste is no less mellow: supple and round without being flabby, with developing notes of candied fruit and chocolate. One taster described this Macvin

as 'modern'. Its modernity is nonetheless drawn from the best that tradition can offer.
🔑 Daniel Dugois, 4, rue de la Mirode, 39600 Les Arsures, tel. 03.84.66.03.41, fax 03.84.37.44.59 ☑ Y by appt.

DOM. FORET★★★

☐ n.c. 2,000 🍾 100–149 F

A few bottles from this cellar go to the land of the Rising Sun. With its superb old-gold colour, this is a Macvin ready for adventure. The nose has a good combination of fine aromas of walnut and caramel derived from the ageing process. The taste is encompassing and harmonious, with sugar and alcohol in perfect balance. And what persistence! It cries out for chocolate cake!
🔑 Dom. Foret, 13, rue de la Faïencerie, 39600 Arbois, tel. 03.84.66.23.01, fax 03.84.66.10.98 ☑ Y by appt.

CH. GREA

☐ 40 ha 1,400 🍾 70–99 F

Only Savagnin must is used in the production of this Macvin. The colour is amber with bronze lights. The superb nose is candied, barely caramel. The taste is a little rustic, but some tasters liked it. Best drunk in winter with *pain d'épice* (a kind of spicy loaf), walnuts and honey.
🔑 Nicolas Caire, Ch. Gréa, 39190 Rotalier, tel. 06.81.83.67.80, fax 06.84.25.05.47 ☑ Y by appt.

CAVEAU DES JACOBINS★

☐ 1 ha 6,000 🍾 70–99 F

The marc is very obvious to the nose. The harmonious taste has good persistence with aromas of crystallised fruits and warm apple. A Macvin worthy of Otto III of Pomerania, who built the Church of the Jacobins in 1248.
🔑 Caveau des Jacobins, rue Nicolas-Appert, 39800 Poligny, tel. 03.84.37.01.37, fax 03.84.37.30.47 ☑ Y by appt.

CLAUDE JOLY★★

☐ n.c. 3,500 🍾 70–99 F

The property has been headed by Claude Joly since 1965. They know their Macvin at Rotalier! This one is very pleasant to look at with its light-yellow colour and green lights. The nose is fresh, without any particular scent taking over. Here the harmony is such that, although the marc is discernible, it is discreet. The taste too is very well balanced and remarkably persistent, with fruity notes recalling figs, raisins and apples.
🔑 Claude Joly, chem. des Patarattes, 39190 Rotalier, tel. 03.84.25.04.14, fax 03.84.25.14.48 ☑ Y by appt.

LIGIER PERE ET FILS

☐ 1 ha 2,000 🍾 70–99 F

Savagnin is the grape variety used in the Jura to produce Vins Jaunes. The Ligier family have also opted to use it to advantage in making Macvin. The nose is intense, floral and then fruity. In the mouth, this is a Macvin with a very substantial taste, in which the marc jostles for its place. The finish is agreeable. Think of accompanying it with a slice of chocolate or walnut cake.
🔑 Ligier Père et Fils, 7, rte de Poligny, 39380 Mont-sous-Vaudrey, tel. 03.84.71.74.75, fax 03.84.81.59.82 ☑
Y by appt.

DESIRE PETIT ET FILS★

☐ 0.5 ha 3,700 🍾 70–99 F

Désiré Petit started out on his own with a hectare (2.5 acres) of vines in 1932. His sons Marcel and Gérard have continued their father's work since 1970. Désiré's wine is desirable indeed. First, for its old-gold colour, but also because of its fullness, sensed both in the nose and the mouth, and for the excellent balance between sugar and alcohol. The marc is well integrated and this makes for an excellent final impression.
🔑 Désiré Petit, rue du Ploussard, 39600 Pupillin, tel. 03.84.66.01.20, fax 03.84.66.26.59 ☑
Y ev. day 8.30am–12 noon 2pm–7pm
🔑 Gérard and Marcel Petit

DOM. DE SAVAGNY

☐ n.c. 5,000 🍾 70–99 F

The earthy colour is reminiscent of some of the yellow-ochres found in the Roussillon, though this is a product of the marl-clays of the Jura. The spirit dominates the nose, while the taste is round and offers hints of grapes in brandy and dried fruits. The finish is pleasant and well-balanced.
🔑 Claude Rousselot-Pailley, 140, rue Neuve, 39210 Lavigny, tel. 03.84.25.38.38, fax 03.84.25.31.25 ☑ Y by appt.

ANDRE ET MIREILLE TISSOT

☐ 1 ha 5,000 🍾 70–99 F

'Organic' is the watchword here, conversion to organic methods having begun in 1999. With its old-gold colour and coppery glints, this Macvin has converted us too. The marc is dominant in the nose. When the wine hits the palate, the spirit steals a march on the must, but there are some rather fine fruity aromas at the finish, which has good length.
🔑 André et Mireille Tissot, 39600 Montigny-lès-Arsures, tel. 03.84.66.08.27, fax 03.84.66.25.08 ☑ Y by appt.

JEAN-LOUIS TISSOT

☐ 0.5 ha 1,000 70–99 F

It has a beautiful golden colour and a nose of dried fruits and almonds. How could one resist tasting it? Balance and power are immediately sensed on the palate. If the finish is a trifle oaky, the overall effect is both successful and true to type. A slice of raw ham, a little diced melon, and you have a starter to remember.

Jean-Louis Tissot, Vauxelles, 39600 Montigny-lès-Arsures, tel. 03.84.66.13.08, fax 03.84.66.08.09 ☑

ev. day 9am–12 noon 2pm–6pm; Sun. and groups by appt.

JEAN TRESY ET FILS

☐ 0.3 ha 2,900 70–99 F

Jean Trésy and his son have produced a harmonious Macvin. The nose is a reflection of what follows: notes of marc but also a palette of aromatic fruits and nuts (hazelnuts, figs, apricots and raisins). In the mouth, this wine is round and powerful as it arrives on the palate. It continues in the same vein, rich and beautifully long, with a rather pleasant fruity finish.

Jean Trésy et Fils, rte des Longevernes, 39230 Passenans, tel. 03.84.85.22.40, fax 03.84.44.99.73, e-mail tresy.vin@wanadoo.fr ☑ by appt.

VINS DE PAYS

Although the phrase 'vin de pays' has been in use since 1930, it has only recently been defined officially as 'table wines that are representative of the district, *département* or region from which they originate'. The law passed on 4 September 1979 established basic guidelines for vin de pays production, recommending preferred grape varieties and setting maximum yields. It also stipulated the analytical standards that had to be met by the wines, such as the volume of alcohol, degree of acidity and the quantity of permitted additives. Because of this stringent regulation, the vins de pays are some of the best table wines produced in France. As with AOC wines, they must be approved by a tasting panel. However, while AOC wines are regulated by the INAO, vins de pays are overseen by the Office National Interprofessional des Vins – ONIVINS. Comprised of wine professionals and trade associations charged with maintaining the regional character of each vin de pays, ONIVINS also supervises the marketing of vins de pays, both at home and abroad. Its efforts have made the vins de pays an important component of France's wine exports.

Vins de pays can be categorised in three ways. First, there are the wines that are named after the *département* in which they are produced. The exceptions are those *départements*, namely Jura, Savoie and Corsica, which are also the names of an AOC. A second category is named after a designated zone. The final category is 'regional' vin de pays. There are four large regions, each of which is made up of several *départements*. Vins de pays within a region may be blended in order to produce wines of a consistent style. The regions are: Jardin de France (Val de Loire), Comté Tolosan, Pays d'Oc, and Comtés Rhodaniens. The 1979 law regulates the conditions of production for all three categories of vin de pays. In addition, each zone and region of vin de pays has a directive that sets out more specific, and restrictive, regulations for wine production.

Most of the 7.8 m hectolitres of designated vin de pays produced annually are made by cooperatives. Between 1980 and 1992, vin de pays production almost doubled (from 4 m hl). Of this, 200,000–250,000 hl (5,280,000–6,600,000 gal) are classed as 'nouveau' or 'primeur'. Varietal wines make up another significant proportion of vin de pays production. Most of these (85%) are from vineyards in the Midi. Good ordinary wines with character, vins de pays are best suited to casual drinking. To a wine-lover travelling around France, they provide an insight into regional differences in wine-making style, and make reliable companions to local specialities. Listed below are the zones of production for vins de pays, with regional boundaries as defined by the legislation. These do not correspond to the AOC and AOVDQS wine regions. Note that the directive of 4 May 1995 excluded the Rhône, Bas-Rhin, Haut-Rhin, Gironde, Côte d'Or and Marne *départements* from vin de pays production.

Calvados

ARPENTS DU SOLEIL 1999★★

☐ 0.15 ha 1,300 ▮ 30–49 F

A vin de pays with the name of an AOC? Calvados is better known as an apple brandy appellation. This drink, however, is definitely the product of grapes – Pinot Gris planted in Saint-Pierre-sur-Dives. A pale yellow-gold colour, the 1999 has an intense white-fruit nose of peaches and pears. Its fresh, fine palate boasts a perfectly balanced structure. The original aromas are echoed again on the finish. An attractive wine that could accompany sauced fish dishes.

Gérard Samson, 3, rue d'Harmonville, 14170 Saint-Pierre-sur-Dives, tel. 02.31.20.80.41, fax 02.31.20.29.70

Vallée de la Loire

The wines of the Jardin de France, a regional classification, make up 95% of vin de pays production in the Loire Valley. This vast region is the agglomeration of 13 *départements*: Maine-et-Loire, Indre-et-Loire, Loiret, Loire-Atlantique, Loir-et-Cher, Indre, Allier, Deux-Sèvres, Sarthe, Vendée, Vienne, Cher and Nièvre. In addition, it includes the vins de pays of Retz (south of the Loire estuary), Marches de Bretagne (south-east of Nantes) and the Coteaux Charitols (around Charité-sur-Loire).

At present, the region produces a total of 600,000 hl (15,840,000 gal), made mostly from traditional Loire grape varieties. The whites, 45% of the wine produced, are dry, fresh and fruity. They are made from Chardonnay, Sauvignon Blanc and Grolleau Gris grapes. Gamay, Cabernet and Grolleau Noir are used to make the reds and rosés.

For the most part, vins de pays should be drunk young. The occasional vintage of Cabernet may benefit from cellaring.

Jardin de la France

DOM. DE BEL-AIR

Pays de Retz Grolleau Gris 1999★★

□ 1 ha 6,000 20F+

The estate is located in the heart of the Retz district, a few kilometres from the Grand-Lieu lake. Only one ha of the 27 ha (67 acres) that make up the vineyard is used to grow Grolleau Gris. The 1999 is wonderful. It is fresh on the nose, with intense aromas of white peaches and citrus. Those scents are reiterated by the flavours on the palate, where a light tingle gives the wine a refreshing style. The **Gamay 99** was awarded one star.

EARL Bouin-Jacquet, Dom. de Bel-Air, Bel-Air de Gauchoux, 44860 Saint-Aignan-de-Grand-Lieu, tel. 02.51.70.80.80, fax 02.51.70.80.79 Y by appt.

Dominique Jacquet

BRUNO BIGOT Chardonnay 1999★

□ 0.8 ha 1,000 20–29 F

A Chardonnay that should be ready for drinking from this autumn. Its fruity, slightly buttery nose has finesse and subtlety. The palate strikes a good balance of freshness and richness. An aromatic 1999 with good length.

Bruno Bigot, 1, rue du Châtelet, 41120 Monthou-sur-Bièvre, tel. 02.54.44.05.82, fax 02.54.44.05.82 Y by appt.

DOM. DES BONNES GAGNES

Rouge de Grolleau 1999★★★

■ 5 ha 10,000 20–29 F

'Magnificent!' was the jury's verdict on this wine. It has a rich colour with violet highlights. The spicy nose announces a rounded palate that is both supple and full. This is an estate with a consistent record of quality.

Jean-Marc Héry, Orgigné, 49320 Saint-Saturnin-sur-Loire, tel. 02.41.91.22.76, fax 02.41.91.21.58 Y ev. day 9am–12.30pm 2pm–7pm; Sun. by appt.

CHRISTELLE ET THIERRY BRANGEON Gamay 1999★

■ 2 ha 4,000 20F+

This Gamay with purple highlights has a fine redcurrant and raspberry nose. Those aromas are also present on the palate, where they meld with the supple tannins. A well-made **Cabernet** from this wine-maker was also cited by the jury.

EARL Brangeon-Guinard, La Cour de Blois, 49270 Saint-Christophe-la-Couperie, tel. 02.40.83.77.04, fax 02.40.83.77.05 Y Fri. Sat. 8am–12 noon 2pm–7pm

DOM. DU CELLIER DE LA COCHE

Chardonnay 1999★★

□ 4.2 ha 5,000 20F+

The herbaceous nose (box, broom) leads into a supple and harmonious palate with

floral aromas. A charming, well-balanced Chardonnay that is easy to drink. The **Grolleau 99 Rosé** and **Gamay 99 Rouge**, both well-crafted wines, each received a star.
Emmanuel Guitteny, 19, La Coche, 44680 Sainte-Pazanne, tel. 02.40.02.44.43, fax 02.40.02.44.43, e-mail Eguitteny@hotmail.com
by appt.

CHARDELON 1999★

□ 1.05 ha 8,000 30–49 F

Made from Chardonnay and Melon de Bourgogne grapes, this dry white wine has a light yellow colour and a strong floral nose. On the palate, it displays a style that is both fresh and unctuous. A very balanced wine, it would complement fine fish dishes.
SA Henri Poiron et Fils, Dom. des Quatre-Routes, 44690 Maisdon-sur-Sèvre, tel. 02.40.54.60.58, fax 02.40.54.62.05
by appt.

CHARDET 1999★★

□ 3.5 ha 30,000 30–49 F

A blend of Chardonnay and Melon grapes, this golden wine has an intense nose of flowers and crystallised citrus. The palate is full and well-balanced, with a hint of creamy butteriness. Two other wines by this wine-maker were also cited: the **Domaine Couillaud Chardonnay 99** and the **Domaine Mornière Chardonnay 99**.
Les Frères Couillaud, GAEC de la Grande Ragotière, 44330 Vallet-la-Regrippière, tel. 02.40.33.60.56, fax 02.40.33.61.89, e-mail frères.couillaud@wanadoo.fr
by appt.

CŒUR DE CRAY Chardonnay 1999★

□ 2.5 ha 28,800 20 F+

The Cœur de Cray is a perfect Chardonnay. A straw-yellow colour and potent floral nose introduce a balanced vintage that will be perfect when it has been allowed to age for a while. The **Chardonnay Domaine de Cray 99** was also cited (20–29F).
Boutinot, SARL la Chapelle de Cray, rte de l'Aquarium, 37400 Lussault-sur-Loire, tel. 02.47.57.17.74, fax 02.47.57.11.97

PRIVILEGE DE DROUET Sauvignon 1999★

□ 9 ha 92,000 20–29 F

This well-crafted Sauvignon has an intense aroma of great finesse that carries over from the nose to linger agreeably on the palate. It could be served with crudités, fish or crustaceans.
SA Drouet Frères, 8, bd. du Luxembourg, 44330 Vallet, tel. 02.40.36.65.20, fax 02.40.33.99.78
by appt.

DOM. DU FOUR A CHAUX Sauvignon 1999★★

□ 1.2 ha 5,000 20 F+

Pale yellow with grey highlights, this wine has the characteristic floral notes of a Sauvignon. It strikes the palate with its rich, fleshy presence and a lingering herbaceous flavour, and would best complement seafood. The red **Cot 99** was also cited.
GAEC Norguet, Berger, 41100 Thoré-la-Rochette, tel. 02.54.77.12.52, fax 02.54.77.86.18 by appt.

DOM. DE GATINES Sauvignon 1999★

□ 1.1 ha 3,500 20 F+

Two young brothers manage this 34-ha (84-acre) estate. They have produced a fine Sauvignon with an alluring brilliant yellow colour. The nose is surprisingly complex and delicate. After a vigorous attack, the palate develops powerful, persistent aromas. The **Grolleau Gris 99** was also cited.
Vignoble Dessevre, Dom. de Gatines, 12, rue de la Boulaie, 49540 Tigné, tel. 02.41.59.41.48, fax 02.41.59.94.44
ev. day except Sun. 8am–12 noon 2pm–6.30pm

DOM. DES GILLIERES Marches de Bretagne Melon Cuvée Prestige 1999★

□ 11 ha 120,000 20 F+

A pretty, light yellow colour, this wine, made from Melon grapes, has a lemony nose. It is fresh, elegant and fine. White fruit and citrus flavours linger well on the finish.
Dominique Régnier, Ch. des Gillières, 44690 La Haie-Fouassière, tel. 02.40.54.80.05, fax 02.40.54.89.56
by appt.

DOMINIQUE GUERIN Chardonnay Cuvée Prestige 1999★

□ 3.2 ha 5,000 20–29 F

Carefully controlled fermentation temperatures and the expertise of the wine-maker have resulted in this very good Chardonnay. Pale yellow, it has an intense aroma of white flowers that is echoed on the palate. A gentle tingle on the tongue gives the wine freshness.
EARL Dominique Guérin, Les Corbeillères, 44330 Vallet, tel. 02.40.36.27.37, fax 02.40.36.27.16
ev. day except Sun. 8am–8pm

DOM. DES HAUTES CHARPENTIERES Chardonnay 1999★

□ 2 ha 2,000 20–29 F

The estate is a 17th-century manor with 27 ha (67 acres) of vineyards. Its golden-yellow Chardonnay has a surprisingly intense fruity aroma. The scents begin subtly on the nose and then explode on the palate.
Dominique Chevalet, Les Hautes Charpentières, 37220 Brizay, tel. 02.47.58.30.34, fax 02.47.58.39.79
by appt.

Vins de pays

1 Vin de Pays des Coteaux de Coiffy
2 Vin de Pays de Franche-Comté
3 Vin de Pays des Coteaux de l'Auxois
4 Vin de Pays de Sainte-Marie-la-Blanche
5 Vin de Pays des Coteaux du Cher et de l'Arnon
6 Vin de Pays des Coteaux charitois
7 Vin de Pays du Bourbonnais
8 Vin de Pays d'Allobrogie
9 Vin de Pays d'Urfé
10 Vin de Pays des Balmes dauphinoises
11 Vin de Pays des Coteaux du Grésivaudan
12 Vin de Pays des Coteaux de l'Ardèche
13 Vin de Pays des Collines rhodaniennes
14 Vin de Pays des Coteaux des Baronnies
15 Vin de Pays du Comté de Grignan
16 Vin de Pays des Coteaux du Verdon
17 Vin de Pays de Mont-Caume
18 Vin de Pays des Maures
19 Vin de Pays d'Argens
20 Vin de Pays de la Petite Crau
21 Vin de Pays d'Aigues
22 Vin de Pays de la Principauté d'Orange
23 Vin de Pays des Sables du Golfe du Lion
24 Vin de Pays du Duché d'Uzès
25 Vin de Pays des Cévennes
26 Vin de Pays de la Vistrenque
27 Vin de Pays des Côtes du Vidourle
28 Vin de Pays de la Vaunage
29 Vin de Pays des Coteaux de Cèze
30 Vin de Pays des Coteaux du Pont du Gard
31 Vin de Pays des Coteaux Flaviens
32 Vin de Pays du Val de Montferrand
33 Vin de Pays du Mont Baudile
34 Vin de Pays des Côtes du Ceressou
35 Vin de Pays des Monts de la Grage
36 Vin de Pays des Coteaux d'Enserune
37 Vin de Pays des Coteaux du Libron
38 Vin de Pays de Pézenas
39 Vin de Pays des Coteaux de Murviel
40 Vin de Pays des Coteaux de Laurens
41 Vin de Pays des Côtes de Thongue
42 Vin de Pays de la Bénovie
43 Vin de Pays de Cassan
44 Vin de Pays de la Haute Vallée de l'Orb
45 Vin de Pays des Gorges de l'Hérault
46 Vin de Pays des Coteaux de Bessilles
47 Vin de Pays de l'Ardailhou
48 Vin de Pays des Côtes du Brian
49 Vin de Pays de Cessenon
50 Vin de Pays des Coteaux du Salagou
51 Vin de Pays de la Vicomté d'Aumelas
52 Vin de Pays des Collines de la Moure
53 Vin de Pays de Caux
54 Vin de Pays des Coteaux de Fontcaude
55 Vin de Pays de Bessan
56 Vin de Pays de Bérange
57 Vin de Pays des Côtes de Thau
58 Vin de Pays des Coteaux de Peyriac
59 Vin de Pays de la Haute Vallée de l'Aude
60 Vin de Pays des Coteaux de Narbonne
61 Vin de Pays des Côtes de Prouilhe
62 Vin de Pays de la Cité de Carcassonne
63 Vin de Pays de Cucugnan
64 Vin de Pays du Val de Dagne
65 Vin de Pays des Coteaux du Littoral audois
66 Vin de Pays des Côtes de Pérignan
67 Vin de Pays des Coteaux de la Cabrerisse
68 Vin de Pays des Hauts de Badens
69 Vin de Pays du Torgan
70 Vin de Pays des Côtes de Lastours
71 Vin de Pays du Val de Cesse
72 Vin de Pays de la Vallée du Paradis
73 Vin de Pays des Coteaux de Miramont
74 Vin de Pays d'Hauterive
75 Vin de Pays des Vals d'Agly
76 Vin de Pays des Coteaux des Fenouillèdes
SARTHE
LOIR-ET-CHER
LOIRE-ATLANTIQUE
MAINE-ET-LOIRE
INDRE-ET-LOIRE
VIN DE PAYS DU JARDIN DE LA FRANCE
VENDÉE
INDRE
DEUX-SÈVRES
VIENNE
CHARENTE-MARITIME
HAUTE-VIENNE
80
CHARENTE
DORDOGNE
81
Garonne
LOT-ET-GARONNE
LOT
83
82
84
85
TARN-ET-GARONNE
LANDES
86
VIN DE PAYS DU COMTÉ TOLOSAN
GERS
87
89
90
91
HAUTE-GARONNE
PYRÉNÉES-ATLANTIQUES
92
88
HAUTES-PYRÉNÉES
ARIÈGE

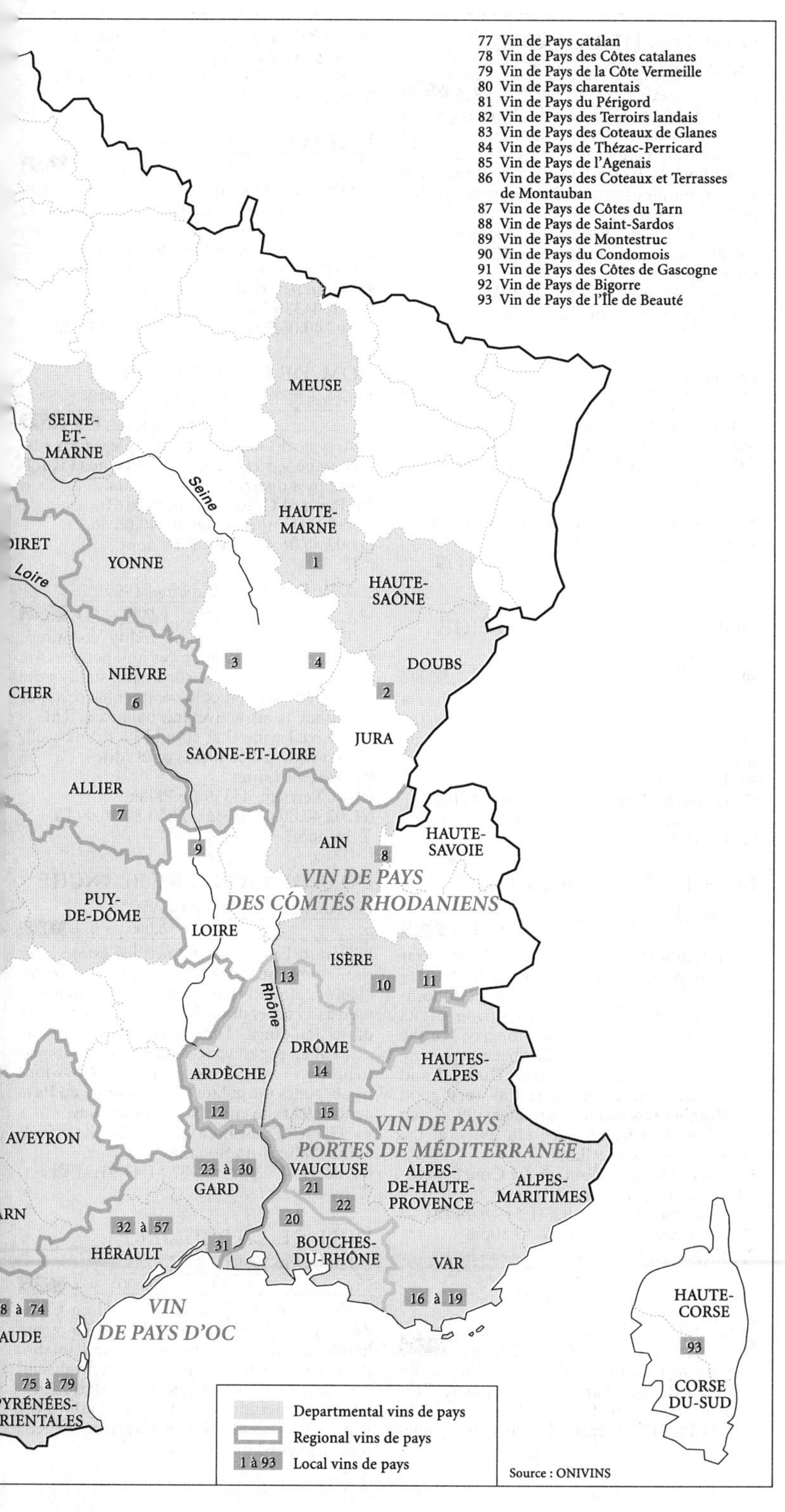
77 Vin de Pays catalan
78 Vin de Pays des Côtes catalanes
79 Vin de Pays de la Côte Vermeille
80 Vin de Pays charentais
81 Vin de Pays du Périgord
82 Vin de Pays des Terroirs landais
83 Vin de Pays des Coteaux de Glanes
84 Vin de Pays de Thézac-Perricard
85 Vin de Pays de l'Agenais
86 Vin de Pays des Coteaux et Terrasses de Montauban
87 Vin de Pays de Côtes du Tarn
88 Vin de Pays de Saint-Sardos
89 Vin de Pays de Montestruc
90 Vin de Pays du Condomois
91 Vin de Pays des Côtes de Gascogne
92 Vin de Pays de Bigorre
93 Vin de Pays de l'Île de Beauté
MEUSE
SEINE-ET-MARNE
Seine
HAUTE-MARNE
YONNE
Loire
HAUTE-SAÔNE
NIÈVRE
DOUBS
CHER
JURA
SAÔNE-ET-LOIRE
ALLIER
AIN
HAUTE-SAVOIE
VIN DE PAYS DES CÔMTÉS RHODANIENS
PUY-DE-DÔME
LOIRE
ISÈRE
Rhône
DRÔME
HAUTES-ALPES
ARDÈCHE
VIN DE PAYS PORTES DE MÉDITERRANÉE
AVEYRON
23 à 30
GARD
VAUCLUSE
ALPES-DE-HAUTE-PROVENCE
ALPES-MARITIMES
32 à 57
HÉRAULT
BOUCHES-DU-RHÔNE
VAR
16 à 19
VIN DE PAYS D'OC
AUDE
75 à 79
PYRÉNÉES-ORIENTALES
HAUTE-CORSE
CORSE DU-SUD
Departmental vins de pays
Regional vins de pays
1 à 93 Local vins de pays
Source : ONIVINS

DOM. DES HERBAUGES

Pays de Retz Grolleau 1999*

◪ 2.6 ha 6,000 20 F+

This year, the Domaine des Herbauges has distinguished itself with a Grolleau rosé. An elegant wine with citrus notes, it is certainly easy to drink. Its freshness makes it the ideal accompaniment for a first course or for grilled meats.

Luc Choblet, Dom. des Herbauges, 44830 Bouaye, tel. 02.40.65.44.92, fax 02.40.32.62.93, e-mail herbauges@libertysurf.fr ☑
Y ev. day except Sun. 9am–12 noon 2pm–6.30pm

DOM. JOLIVET Chardonnay 1999*

☐ 0.5 ha n.c. 20–29 F

The product of silica-clay soils, this Chardonnay has an intensely vegetal nose. The palate is balanced and silky, with a welcome touch of acidity. Already very harmonious, the wine is ready to drink now.

Dom. Jolivet, 31, rue Rabelais, 49750 Saint-Lambert-du-Lattay, tel. 02.41.78.30.35, fax 02.41.78.45.34 ☑
Y by appt.

DOM. DE LA CHARLOTTERIE

Gamay 1999*

■ 1 ha 5,000 20–29 F

This red wine made from Gamay has a clear dark ruby hue. A little closed on the nose, it nonetheless has a full-bodied palate with red berry aromas.

Dominique Houdebert, Cave de la Charlotterie, 2, rue du Bas-Bourg, 41100 Villiersfaux, tel. 02.54.80.29.79, fax 02.54.73.10.01 ☑ Y by appt.

DOM. DE LA COUCHETIERE

Grolleau 1999*

■ 4.5 ha 37,000 20 F+

Although the estate was established four generations ago, it has only focused on wine-making since 1944. In the 1980s, it concentrated on increasing the proportion of its wines sold directly from the property. For the past few years, the estate has been exporting to countries such as the UK, Holland and Switzerland. You may taste this very good **Grolleau 99** red and a **Chardonnay 99**, which was also cited by the jury (20–29F), at the estate's brand new cellars.

GAEC Brault, Dom. de La Couchetière, 49380 Notre-Dame-d'Allençon, tel. 02.41.54.30.26, fax 02.41.54.40.98 ☑
Y ev. day except Sun. 8am–12.30pm 2pm–7pm

DOM. DE LA COUPERIE

Pinot Noir 1999**

■ 1.6 ha 12,000 20–29 F

A strong nose of peardrops is followed by a full-bodied, supple and aromatic palate. This wine is the product of a harvest of high-quality Pinot Noir crafted by an expert wine-maker.

EARL Claude Cogné, La Couperie, 49270 Saint-Christophe-la-Couperie, tel. 02.40.83.73.16, fax 02.40.83.76.71 ☑
Y by appt.

LA DIVA Chardonnay 1999**

☐ n.c. 400,000 20 F+

Donatien Bahaud's 1999 Chardonnay will captivate many wine-lovers. Our tasters enjoyed its intense aromas as well as its complexity. A balanced and very full-bodied wine, it is fully worthy of its two stars.

Donatien Bahuaud, La Loge, B.P. 1, 44330 La Chapelle-Heulin, tel. 02.40.06.70.05, fax 02.40.06.77.11 ☑

DOM. DE LA HOUSSAIS

Marches de Bretagnes Gamay 1999

◪ 0.5 ha 5,000 20–29 F

A typical Gamay that will please fans of this grape variety. The red berry nose is followed by a distinctively fresh palate.

Bernard Gratas, Dom. de la Houssais, 44430 Le Landreau, tel. 02.40.06.46.27, fax 02.40.06.47.25 ☑ Y by appt.

LA PERRIERE Cabernet 1999*

◪ 1 ha 6,000 20–29 F

This Cabernet rosé is richly coloured. Interesting aromas of spices and peppers are present on the nose. A surprising stalky note hints at an overripe, cold-weather harvest, but the palate is attractive and balanced. This is a convivial wine that should be drunk well-chilled with grilled meats or crudités.

Vincent Loiret, Ch. la Perrière, 44330 Le Pallet, tel. 02.40.80.43.24, fax 02.40.80.46.99 ☑
Y by appt.

DOM. DE LA PIERRE BLANCHE

Pays de Retz Chardonnay 1999*

☐ n.c. 6,000 20 F+

Gérard Epiard has named his estate after the numerous white boulders, *pierres blanches*, dotted around it, one of which was used as a cornerstone during the construction of its buildings. The rocky terroir and the skills of an expert wine-maker have combined to produce an exceptional wine. His Chardonnay beguiles the palate. The **Cabernet du Pays de Retz 99** is an equally seductive wine.

Gérard Epiard, La Pierre Blanche, 85660 Saint-Philbert-de-Bouaine, tel. 02.51.41.93.42, fax 02.51.41.91.71 ☑
Y by appt.

DOM. DE LA ROULIERE

Chardonnay 1999*

☐ 7 ha 80,000 20 F+

This estate made a very appealing Chardonnay in 1999. Straw-yellow with green highlights, the wine has a fine and intense floral nose. On the palate, it is fresh, lively and well-balanced. Malolactic fermentation has added an unctuous quality and length to the wine. The **Gamay 99** and **Cabernet 99** reds were also cited by the jury.

René Erraud, Ch. de la Roulière, 44310 Saint-Colomban, tel. 02.40.05.80.24, fax 02.40.05.53.89 by appt.

DOM. DE LA VIAUDIERE

Chardonnay 1999★

□ 2 ha 10,000 20 F+

An attractive Chardonnay with a lively, pale colour and a complex and harmonious nose. On the palate, it is rounded and supple – a distinctive wine that is ready to drink now.

EARL Vignoble Gélineau, Ch. de la Viaudière, 49380 Champ-sur-Layon, tel. 02.41.78.86.27, fax 02.41.78.60.45, e-mail gelineau@wanadoo.fr by appt.

LE FIEF DES TOUCHES

Chardonnay 1999★

□ 4 ha 3,000 20–29 F

Located in the commune of Pallet, this estate cultivates over 17 ha (42 acres) of vines. Its Chardonnay has been aged in oak casks for six months. The resulting wine has lively highlights and a subtle hint of almonds on the nose, while the pleasantly oaky palate shows good balance.

EARL Dom. des Noës, Bretigné, 44330 Le Pallet, tel. 02.40.80.98.90, fax 02.40.80.48.11 by appt.

Agoulon

LE MOULIN DE LA TOUCHE

Pays de Retz Chardonnay 1999★

□ 2 ha 12,000 20–29 F

Wines made by Joël Herrissé are guaranteed to be good value. The jury praised his intense, fruity Chardonnay with its scent of pineapples, bananas and vanilla. Its fruitiness is reaffirmed on the palate, which has a very slight refreshing sparkle. This is a rich and long, well-balanced and attractive 99. The **Grolleau Gris 99** was also cited by the jury.

Joël Hérissé, Le Moulin de la Touche, 44580 Bourgneuf-en-Retz, tel. 02.40.21.47.89, fax 02.40.21.47.89 by appt.

DOM. DE L'ERRIERE

Chardonnay 1999★

□ 0.5 ha 3,000 20 F+

The Domaine de l'Errière has been producing wine in Landreau since the 1930s. It offered the jury a pale yellow Chardonnay with green highlights. Its intense white flower and citrus nose is followed by a rounded palate. A balanced wine that is ready to drink now.

GAEC Madeleineau Père et Fils, Dom. de l'Errière, 44430 Le Landreau, tel. 02.40.06.43.94, fax 02.40.06.48.82 by appt.

DOM. LES HAUTES NOELLES

Gamay 1999★

■ 3.5 ha 30,000 20–29 F

An aroma of red berries and a feeling of freshness on the palate will please Gamay enthusiasts. This wine is so deliciously fruity that it would complement almost any dish.

Serge Batard, La Haute Galerie, 44710 Saint-Léger-les-Vignes, tel. 02.40.31.53.49, fax 02.40.04.87.80 by appt.

LES ROCHERS

Marches de Bretagne Cabernet 1999★★

■ n.c. n.c. 20 F+

Since 1973, Michel Luneau has cultivated Cabernet Franc and Cabernet Sauvignon grapes alongside the Muscadet variety. The vines have yielded some very interesting vins de pays such as this bright red 99, which is redolent of ripe berries. Berry aromas are also present on the palate, where they harmonise with characteristic Cabernet tannins.

GAEC Michel Luneau et Fils, 3, rte. de Nantes, 44330 Mouzillon, tel. 02.40.33.95.22, fax 02.40.33.95.22 by appt.

L'IMAGINAIRE Sauvignon 1999

□ n.c. 500,000 20 F+

The Sauvignon stood out from the many vins de pays made by the Pierre Guéry company. It has a fairly strong fruity aroma (peaches and apricots) with floral overtones. The first impression on the palate is fresh and vigorous. This is followed by a surprisingly rich and full-bodied flavour, adding up to an attractive wine. The **Chardonnay** and the **Pinot Noir 99** from L'Imaginaire also received citations.

Pierre Guéry, La Loge, B.P. 1, 44330 La Chapelle-Heulin, tel. 02.40.06.70.05, fax 02.40.06.77.11

DOM. DU MOULIN

Grolleau Gris 1999★

□ 0.53 ha 1,000 20–29 F

The old mill that gave its name to this 21 ha (52-acre) estate was built in 1814, but winemaking only began on the property in 1960. The Grolleau Gris will please lovers of fruity wines. Both the nose and palate are redolent of yellow fruits, and a degree of acidity is perceptible on the palate.

Michel Figureau, Dom. du Moulin, 5, rue du Plessis, 44860 Pont-Saint-Martin, tel. 02.40.32.70.56, fax 02.40.32.70.56 ev. day 9am–7pm; Sun. 9.30am–11.30am

DIANA ET ALAIN OLIVIER

Cabernet 1997★★★

■ 3 ha 1,400 30–49 F

This richly coloured Cabernet wine has a forceful personality. On the nose, it has aromas of ripe red berries and vanilla. Full and rounded with a hint of oakiness, this is a fine wine that will age well.
🔑 EARL Alain Olivier,
La Moucletière, 44330 Vallet,
tel. 02.40.36.24.69, fax 02.40.36.24.69 ☑
Ɪ ev. day 8am–12.30pm 2pm–7pm

DOM. DU PARC Chardonnay 1999*

□	5 ha	20,000	20–29 F

A Chardonnay of great finesse, the Domaine du Parc has a floral nose with hints of verbena and linden flowers, aromas that are also present on the palate. An attractive and well-balanced wine, it will marry well with fish dishes.
🔑 Pierre Dahéron, Le Parc, 44650 Corcoué-sur-Logne, tel. 02.40.05.86.11, fax 02.40.05.94.98 ☑ Ɪ by appt.

ANTOINE PICHON

Chardonnay Cuvée Laetitia 1999*

□	2.8 ha	1,333	20–29 F

This Chardonnay with green and yellow highlights is powerful and intense on the nose. A frank and supple attack introduces a well-made wine that will develop fully when it has aged a little longer.
🔑 Antoine Pichon, 4, rue Nationale, 41700 Chemery, tel. 02.54.71.80.34, fax 02.54.71.06.15 ☑ Ɪ by appt.

DOM. DES PRIES

Pays de Retz Grolleau 1999**

◪	2.3 ha	8,000	20–29 F

This alluring Grolleau rosé has a raspberryish nose and a rounded and supple palate, where red berry aromas are also evident. It is a balanced and appealing wine. Two fresh and lively white wines from the Pays de Retz were also cited by the jury: a **Grolleau Gris 99**, made in the regional style, and the **Chardonnay 99**.
🔑 Gérard Padiou, Les Priés, 44580 Bourgneuf-en-Retz, tel. 02.40.21.45.16, fax 02.40.21.47.48 Ɪ by appt.

CHRISTOPHE RETHORE

Cabernet 1999**

■	6 ha	9,000	20–29 F

A classic Cabernet, this deep ruby wine has an aroma of red berries with spicy overtones. Very well-structured with silky tannins, it is agreeably round and full-bodied.
🔑 Christophe Réthoré, Les Vignes, 49110 Saint-Rémy-en-Mauges, tel. 02.41.30.12.58, fax 02.41.46.35.44 ☑ Ɪ Fri. Sat. 8am–12 noon 1.30pm–7pm; cl. 2–3 week Aug.

MICHEL ROBINEAU

Sauvignon 1999*

□	0.36 ha	n.c.	20–29 F

Michel Robineau's Sauvignon has been much lauded in previous vintages. This year, the wine has a lime-scented nose, reinforced by its fresh and balanced impression on the palate. A very engaging, typical Sauvignon.
🔑 Michel Robineau, 3, chem. du Moulin, Les Grandes Tailles, 49750 Saint-Lambert-du-Lattay, tel. 02.41.78.34.67 ☑ Ɪ by appt.

DOM. DE SAINTE-ANNE

Sauvignon 1999*

□	2 ha	8,000	20–29 F

Six generations of the Brault family have cultivated this 55 ha (136-acre) estate. The Domaine de Saint-Anne Sauvignon 99 is very well-made. A glittering pale yellow with green highlights, it has a powerful citrus and floral nose. Its pleasantly full first impression leads on to an aromatic palate, and it shows the right degree of acidity on the finish.
🔑 Dom. de Sainte-Anne, EARL Brault, 49320 Brissac-Quincé, tel. 02.41.91.24.58, fax 02.41.91.25.87 ☑ Ɪ ev. day except Sun. 9am–12 noon 2pm–7pm; Sat. 6pm

CLOS SAINT-VINCENT DES RONGERES

Marches de Bretagne Gamay 1999*

■	1 ha	7,000	20–29 F

This red Gamay des Marches de Bretagne has purple highlights. Its nose reveals a complex scent made up of red berries (mulberries and blackcurrants), spices and cocoa. The palate is light and fresh, with great finesse. A balanced, refreshing wine for drinking at any time.
🔑 EARL Yves Provost et Fils, Le Pigeon Blanc, 44430 Le Landreau, tel. 02.40.06.43.54, fax 02.40.06.43.54 ☑
Ɪ ev. day 9am–8pm

DOM. TROIS FRERES

Chardonnay 1999*

□	n.c.	32,000	20–29 F

This Chardonnay is exclusively exported to the United States. It is a blend of grapes from a number of Loire Valley terroirs. As a result, the wine has an attractive and complex balance of flavours: a Chardonnay with potential.
🔑 SARL Chardet Vineyard, La Grande Ragotière, 44330 La Regrippière, tel. 02.40.33.60.56, fax 02.40.33.61.89

MANOIR DE VERSILLE

Cadet de Versillé 1999**

■	1.5 ha	5,000	20 F+

The Manoir de Versillé has made an extraordinary red vin de pays. A richly coloured wine with ruby highlights, it has a complex nose of red berries and spices. On the palate, it is silky and full-bodied, with a fairly solid tannic structure that will allow it to age well.
🔑 Francine Desmet, EARL du Manoir de Versillé, Versillé, 49320 Saint-Jean-des-Mauvrets, tel. 02.41.45.22.00, fax 02.41.45.22.00, e-mail manoir.versille@wanadoo.fr ☑
Ɪ by appt.

Vendée

DOM. DES DEUX LAY 1999★

□ 1.7 ha 3,000 30–49 F

The Domaine des Deux Lay has made a fresh and well-structured white vin de pays. Floral aromas and suppleness lend the wine elegance. From the same estate, it is worth tasting the **Pinot Noir 99**, which was also cited by the jury.

EARL les Deux Lay, 16, rue Marceau, B.P. 41618, 44016 Nantes Cedex 1, tel. 02.40.47.58.75, fax 02.40.89.34.33
by appt.

Cher

ARIELLE VATAN

La Roncière Pinot Noir 1999★

■ 1 ha 9,000 30–49 F

This wine has the complex nose of cherries and blackcurrants that is typical of this variety. After a supple attack, fruity flavours develop on the palate. A very well-made, silky, easy-drinking Pinot Noir, it is ready for drinking now, but would also improve if kept for a while.

Arielle Vatan, Chaudoux, 18300 Verdigny, tel. 02.48.79.33.07, fax 02.48.79.36.30 by appt.

La Vienne

AMPELIDAE Le K 1998★

■ 2 ha 7,000 70–99 F

A deep ruby colour, this wine has a tempting aroma of ripe red berries, given complexity by hints of toast and vanilla. The palate is supple, fleshy and structured with prominent, silky tannins. This is a Cabernet with a great deal of potential, and should be aged for two to five years.

Brochet, Ampelidae, Lavauguyot, 86380 Marigny-Brizay, tel. 05.49.88.18.18, fax 05.49.88.18.85, e-mail ampelidae@amplelidae.com
ev. day 9am–7pm

Coteaux charitois

DOM. DES HAUTS DE SEYR

Le Montaillant Chardonnay 1999★

□ 12.5 ha 100,000 30–49 F

The Cave des Hauts de Seyr is located about ten km (seven miles) from the city of La Charité-sur-Loire, whose church has been classed as a World Heritage Site by UNESCO. The estate comprises 17 ha (42 acres) of vineyards. From it comes this intensely aromatic, buttery Chardonnay. The **Montaillant Pinot Noir Sélection 98**, which has been aged in oak for a year, was also awarded a star.

SA Cave des Hauts de Seyr, Le Bourg, 58350 Chasnay, tel. 03.86.69.20.93, fax 03.86.69.28.57
ev. day except Sat. Sun. 2pm–6pm

Aquitaine et Charentes

Virtually encircling Bordeaux, this region is made up of the Charente, Charente-Maritime, Gironde, Landes, Dordogne and Lot-et-Garonne *départements*. In total, 60,000 hl (1,584,000 gal) of wine are produced here annually. The majority of wines are supple, aromatic reds made in the Aquitaine district using the Bordeaux grape varieties complemented by a few more rustic local grapes (Tannat, Abouriou, Bouchalès, Fer). Charente, Charente-Maritime and Dordogne mostly produce white vins de pays, which may be fine and light (Ugni Blanc, Colombard), rounded (Sémillon blends), or robust (Baroque). Charentais, Agenais, Terroirs Landais and Thézac-Perricard are sub-regional designations; Dordogne, Gironde, and Landes are based on the *départements*.

Charentais

JACQUES BRARD BLANCHARD
1999★

□ 1.76 ha 17,700 20–29 F

Pale yellow with green highlights, this wine has a fruity nose of pears and other white-fleshed fruits. A pleasantly vigorous first impression anticipates a balanced and elegant palate. It will go well with seafood.

GAEC Brard-Blanchard, 1, chem. de Routreau, Boutiers, 16100 Cognac, tel. 05.45.32.19.58, fax 05.45.36.53.21 ev. day except Sun. 9am–12 noon 2pm–6pm; cl. 15 Aug.–1 Sep.

DOM. DU BREUIL
La Côte de Tartillac 1999★

■ 2 ha 10,000 20F+

A blend of Merlot and Cabernet grapes has produced a deep red, almost purple, wine. Its nose displays fine aromas of red berries with overtones of leather. The palate is light and supple, and has good length.

Famille Morandière, 12, rue du Pineau, Le Breuil, 17150 Saint-Georges-des-Agouts, tel. 05.46.86.02.76, fax 05.46.70.63.11
ev. day 9am–7pm

DOM. BRUNEAU Merlot 1999★

■ 4 ha 10,000 20–29 F

Allain Pillet has been making Merlot vins de pays since 1985, and this latest vintage, with its rich red colour, is a resounding success. Red berry aromas, initially perceived on the nose, can be more precisely identified as morello cherries and blackberries as the wine is savoured. A fresh and direct first impression leads on to a rich, well-balanced palate with good length.

Alain Pillet, Chez Bruneau, 17130 Rouffignac, tel. 05.46.49.04.82
by appt.

DOM. GARDRAT Colombard 1999★★

□ 4 ha 45,000 20F+

A watermark on the label of this Colombard gives the year the estate was created, 1894. Jean-Pierre Gardrat has made an attractively coloured wine whose nose is redolent of white flowers. After a forthright entry, floral aromas re-emerge on the palate, enhanced by citrus flavours. The finish is powerful and long. This wine would complement a fillet of sea-bass seasoned with tarragon.

Jean-Pierre Gardrat, La Touche, 17120 Cozes, tel. 05.46.90.86.94, fax 05.46.90.95.22, e-mail jean-pierre.gardrat@wanadoo.fr
ev. day except Sun. 9am–12 noon 2pm–7pm

HENRI DE BLAINVILLE
Cabernet-Sauvignon 1999★

■ 5 ha 30,000 20F+

This ruby-coloured Cabernet Sauvignon has intense aromas characterised by a hint of leather. Its lightness on the palate means that this fresh and fruity wine can be drunk like a rosé. It could be served with grilled meats.

SCA Cave du Liboreau, 18, rue de l'Océan, 17490 Siecq, tel. 05.46.26.61.86, fax 05.46.26.68.01, e-mail cave.du.liboreau@wanadoo.fr
by appt.

DOM. DE LA CHAUVILLIERE
Chardonnay Cuvée Spéciale 1999★

□ 1.5 ha 9,000 30–49 F

Pale green with golden highlights, this wine has a powerful, potent musky nose with hints of dried fruits and toast. Fleshy and rounded, the palate has a slightly smoky flavour and a long finish.

EARL Hauselmann et Fils, Dom. de la Chauvillière, 17600 Sablonceaux, tel. 05.46.94.44.40, fax 05.46.94.44.63
by appt.

LE GOUVERNEUR
Ile de Ré Elevé en Fût de Chêne 1998★★

■ 50 ha 150,000 20–29 F

The wine-makers of Ré have crafted one of the best Vins de Pays de Charente in the *Guide*. A slightly faded red colour, it has a complex aroma of vanilla, leather and green peppers. Quite rounded in texture, the wine has a flavour of ripe black fruits, as well as good length.

Coop. des Vignerons de l'Ile de Ré, 17580 Le Bois-Plage-en-Ré, tel. 05.46.09.23.09, fax 05.46.09.09.26
by appt.

PANORAMIC Colombard 1999★

□ 3 ha 30,000 20F+

Here is a very well-made Colombard. An attractive light yellow-green colour, it contains a few tiny bubbles. The fruity nose suggests peach, possibly pineapple. On the palate, the slight fizz gives the attack extra freshness. This is a well-balanced wine with a supple finish.

La Fiée des Lois, rue Mongolfier, 79230 Prahecq, tel. 05.49.32.15.15, fax 05.49.32.16.05

DOM. PIERRIERE GONTHIER
1999★

■ 2.1 ha 15,000 20–29 F

In 1993, several years after assuming the management of this 20-ha (49-acre) estate, Pascal Gonthier began making vin de pays. The 1999, with its deep, mature colour, has a powerful nose with warm scents of red berries. After a supple attack, the rounded palate also reveals fruity aromas that linger on a fine finish.

🔑 Pascal Gonthier, Nigronde, 16170 Saint-Amand-de-Nouère, tel. 05.45.96.42.79, fax 05.45.96.42.79 ☑ 🍷 by appt.

SORNIN Cabernet 1999★

■ 17 ha 40,000 🍾 🌡 20 F+

This dark red Cabernet has brilliant highlights. The nose is equally attractive with its rich, distinguished aromas of butter and spices. On the palate, it is supple and balanced with a strong flavour of red berries. This wine demands to be served with grilled meat.
🔑 SCA Cave de Saint-Sornin, Les Combes, 16220 Saint-Sornin, tel. 05.45.23.92.22, fax 05.45.23.11.61 ☑ 🍷 ev. day except Sat. Sun. 8am–12 noon 2pm–6pm

Agenais

COTES DES OLIVIERS

Elevé en Fût de Chêne 1998★

■ 0.6 ha 6,000 🛢 20–29 F

Jean-Pierre Richarte produces Agen prunes as well as wine. His 1998 is a very good vintage, with its deep ruby colour and appealing aroma of ripe berries. A supple attack is followed by a balanced and long palate, on which discreet notes of oak and vanilla blend with the berry flavours (50 cl bottle).
🔑 Jean-Pierre Richarte, Les Oliviers, 47140 Auradou, tel. 05.53.41.28.59, fax 05.53.49.38.89 ☑ 🍷 ev. day 9am–7pm

LOU GAILLOT

Cuvée Réserve Vieilli en Fût de Chêne 1998★

■ 1 ha 3,000 🛢 30–49 F

Casseneuil, where the firm of Gilles Pons has its headquarters, was on the waterborne trade route to Bordeaux in the 19th century. Today, the Lou Gaillot estate cultivates 25 ha (62 acres) of vines on one of the few terraced vineyards in the Lot valley. It has produced a bright, clear, ruby-coloured Merlot. Matured for ten months in barrel, the fine, oaky 98 has a supple attack followed by a vanilla-scented, full-bodied and balanced palate. The wine's oakiness is in harmony with the rest of its bouquet. The white demi-sec, **La Cuvée Elégance 99** (20–29F) was also awarded a star. It has the aromatic finesse of a Sauvignon, dominated by a bouquet of white fruits, and the roundness of a Sémillon, all underscored by a well-balanced oakiness with notes of vanilla and toast.
🔑 Gilles Pons, As Gaillots, 47440 Casseneuil, tel. 05.53.41.04.66, fax 05.53.01.13.89, e-mail lougaillot@wanadoo.fr ☑
🍷 ev. day 9am–12 noon 2pm–7.30pm

CAVE DES COTEAUX DU MEZINAIS 1999★

□ 1 ha 6,500 🍾 🌡 30–49 F

The Cave des Coteaux du Mézinais is made up of 36 producers. They make Floc de Gascogne and armagnac as well as vin de pays. Made from Gros Manseng grapes, this 1999 has a bright, clear yellow colour. It is floral and fruity (pears, white peaches), with a touch of honey. Fairly fleshy on the palate, the alcohol, acidity and sweetness are nicely balanced. The aromas of ripe pears lingers on the finish.
🔑 Cave des Coteaux du Mézinais, 1, bd. Colome, 47170 Mézin, tel. 05.53.65.53.55, fax 05.53.97.16.73 ☑ 🍷 by appt.

CAVE DES SEPT MONTS

Instant Choisi 1998★

■ 10 ha n.c. 🍾 🌡 20–29 F

This co-operative wine has earned itself a star. L'Instant Choisi has an orange-tinged ruby colour with bright highlights. The finesse of the nose entices one to discover its supple, rounded and balanced palate.
🔑 Cave des Sept Monts, ZAC de Mondésir, 47150 Monflanquin, tel. 05.53.36.33.40, fax 05.53.36.44.11 ☑
🍷 ev. day 9am–12.30pm 3pm–6.30pm

Thézac-Perricard

VIN DU TSAR

Cuvée du Millénaire 1997★

■ 4.5 ha 34,000 🛢 30–49 F

Cuvée du Millénaire, launched in 1988, does not celebrate the year 2000, but rather refers to the anniversary of the Christianisation of Russia by Prince Vladimir. Matured for six months in barrel, the wine has a rich ruby colour and a fine oaky nose with vanilla overtones. Supple and well-rounded, it is reasonably persistent on the palate, with a hint of vanilla at the finish.
🔑 Les Vignerons de Thézac-Perricard, Plaisance, 47370 Thézac, tel. 05.53.40.72.76, fax 05.53.40.78.76, e-mail info@vin-du-tsar.tm.fr ☑
🍷 ev. day 8.15–12.15pm 2pm–6pm; Sun. 2pm–6pm

Terroirs Landais

BERTRAND ABADIE 1999★

■ n.c. n.c. 20 F+

Bertrand Abadie, an independent winegrower based in Dax, has made a bright ruby wine with an attractive aroma of spices, wood and red berries. After a supple attack, the palate is full-bodied and well-balanced.

🔑 Bertrand Abadie, Pribat, 40180 Benesse-les-Dax, tel. 05.58.98.71.67

HAUT BARON Sables Fauves 1999★★

■ 3 ha 4,110 🍾 🌡 20 F+

Dark-hued with ruby highlights, this wine, made solely from Tannat grapes, has an oaky nose with additional aromas of crystallised ripe red berries. A round, full-bodied wine with good tannins, its balanced palate impressed the jury.

🔑 Cave coop. de Vinification de Cazaubon, rte. de Mont-de-Marsan, 32150 Cazaubon, tel. 05.62.08.34.00, fax 05.62.69.50.98 ☒ Y ev. day 8am–12 noon 2pm–6pm

DOM. DE LABAIGT

Coteaux de Chalosse Moelleux 1999★★

□ 1 ha 10,000 🍾 🌡 20-29 F

Made from Gros Manseng grapes, this sweet vin de pays with a brilliant yellow colour has a complex aroma of passion-fruit, grapefruit and pear. Its fine balance of sugar and acidity, and its good length, constitute a remarkable wine.

🔑 Dominique Lanot, Dom. de Labaigt, 40290 Mouscardès, tel. 05.58.98.02.42, fax 05.58.98.80.75 ☒ Y ev. day except Sun. 8.30am–12 noon 2pm–6.30pm

DOM. DU TASTET

Coteaux de Chalosse Tannat Elevé en Fût de Chêne 1999★★

■ 0.6 ha 4,000 🛢 20-29 F

Six months in barrel have helped refine this dark ruby Tannat. Its fine nose reveals fruits of the forest with oaky overtones. The round, fleshy, well-structured palate stays in the same aromatic register, but adds a hint of liquorice.

🔑 Jean-Claude Romain, Dom. du Tastet, 40350 Pouillon, tel. 05.58.98.28.27, fax 05.58.98.27.63 ☒ Y ev. day 8am–7pm; Sun. 8am–12 noon

Landes

ARC EN CIEL 1999★

■ 1 ha 7,000 🍾 🌡 20-29 F

A Tannat-Cabernet blend, aged for seven months, has produced this very attractive wine. Bright purple, it has a powerful and complex nose of macerated fruit and leather, followed by a rounded palate with good length.

🔑 EARL Dulucq, Château de Perlhade, 40320 Payros-Cazautets, tel. 05.58.44.50.68, fax 05.58.44.57.75 ☒ Y ev. day except Sun. 8am–1pm 2.30pm–7pm

DOM. D'ESPERANCE

Cuvée d'Or 1999★

□ 8 ha 5,000 🍾 🌡 20-29 F

Until the arrival of Jean Louis de Montesquiou in 1990, this 18th-century estate made armagnac. The new owners export 80% of their wine. This rich yellow cuvée has golden highlights. A fine, subtle nose is followed by a lively, long, well-balanced palate with a herbaceous note on the finish. It is a blend of Gros Manseng and Colombard.

🔑 J.-L. de Montesquiou, Dom. d'Espérance, 40240 Mauvezin-d'Armagnac, tel. 05.58.44.85.93, fax 05.58.44.85.93, e-mail espérance@terne.net.fr ☒ Y by appt.

FLEUR DES LANDES

Coteaux de Chalosse Arriloba et Baroque 1999★★

□ 60 ha 150,000 🍾 🌡 20 F+

Arriloba is a grape you may not have heard of. It is the result of a cross between Raffiat de Moncade and Sauvignon, developed in the 1960s by the INRA (National Institute for Agricultural Research) in Bordeaux. Here, it has been blended with Baroque to create a rich golden wine with a ripe fruit nose. Hints of honey and a Muscat-like aroma are also perceptible. Plump and rounded on the palate, this is a harmonious, well-balanced wine.

🔑 Les vignerons des Coteaux de Chalosse, av. René-Bats, 40250 Mugron, tel. 05.58.97.70.75, fax 05.58.97.93.23, e-mail vignerons.chalosse@wanadoo.fr ☒ Y by appt.

GERLAND 1998★

■ 3 ha 18,000 🍾 🌡 30-49 F

The Vignerons du Pays des Landes have blended Tannat and Cabernet to make this wine. Ruby-red with rich garnet highlights, it has a subtle nose of green pepper and red berries. A supple first impression is followed by a rounded, long palate. The finish is warm and still a little austere.

🔑 Armadis, rte. d'Eauze, 40190 Villeneuve-de-Marsans, tel. 05.58.45.21.76, fax 05.58.45.81.92 ☒ Y by appt.

DOM. DE HAUBET

Colombard et Ugni Blanc 1999★

□ 14 ha n.c. 🍾 🌡 20 F+

This 20-ha (49-acre) family estate has made a well-balanced blend of half Colombard and half Ugni Blanc. Fresh and lively (lemony) on both the nose and palate, this bright, pale yellow wine with green highlights is also rich and rounded.

🔑 Philippe Gudolle, EARL de Haubet, 40310 Parleboscq, tel. 05.58.44.35.39, fax 05.58.44.95.99 ☒ Y by appt.

Pays de la Garonne

This region surrounds the city of Toulouse. The Vin de Pays du Comté Tolosan designation includes the following *départements*: Ariège, Aveyron, Haute-Garonne, Gers, Lot, Lot-et-Garonne, Pyrénées-Atlantiques, Hautes-Pyrénées, Tarn and Tarn-et-Garonne. The sub-regional or local designations are: Côtes du Tarn; Coteaux de Glanes (Haut-Quercy, to the north of Lot – reds worth ageing); Coteaux du Quercy (south of Cahors – structured reds); Saint-Sardos (the left bank of the Garonne River): Coteaux et Terrasses de Montauban (light reds); Côtes de Gascogne, Côtes du Condomois and Côtes de Montestruc (the armagnac-producing area of Gers – mostly white wines); and Bigorre. Haute-Garonne, Tarn-et-Garonne, Pyrénées-Atlantiques, Lot, Aveyron and Gers are designations that correspond with the *départements*.

In total, this extremely varied region produces about 200,000 hl (5,280,000 gal) of red and rosé wine, with Gers and Tarn producing 400,000 hl (10,560,000 gal) of white wine. The diverse soils and climate of this region and the Atlantic coastline south of the Massif Central, when combined with an especially wide range of grape varieties, has prompted efforts to produce blended wines made to a consistent style. Since 1982, these have been labelled Vin de Pays du Comté Tolosan. At the moment this accounts for only 40,000 hl (1,056,000 gal) per year.

Comté Tolosan

ARMAND DE TOLOSE

Cabernet Franc 1998★

■ 30 ha 35,000 20-29 F

The Lavilledieu Cellar, which is already highly regarded for its VDQS of the same name, also makes a Vin de Pays du Comté Tolosan. A ruby-coloured wine, it has a powerful, persistent nose and a supple palate with the green pepper aromas characteristic of Cabernet Franc. This is a carefully crafted wine with a very pretty label.

Cave de Lavilledieu-du-Temple, 82290 Lavilledieu-du-Temple, tel. 05.63.31.60.05, fax 05.63.31.69.11 by appt.

Côtes du Tarn

LES RIALS 1999★★

□ 3.3 ha 28,000 20-29 F

A perfect combination of the two main grape varieties of the Tarn region: the aroma and richness of Mauzac and the sinew and vigour of Len de l'El. Together, they result in a crystal-clear, straw-coloured wine with an intense, complex, floral and fruity nose. The full-bodied palate is rich and long. Altogether, this is a very good example of a Vin de Pays des Côtes du Tarn. From the same cellar also comes a **Syrah 99 Rosé** that is equally enjoyable.

Dom. de La Chanade, 81170 Souel, tel. 05.63.56.31.10, fax 05.63.56.31.10 ev. day 9am–12 noon 2pm–7.30pm

DOM. SARRABELLE

Syrah Elevé en Fût de Chêne 1998★★★

■ 0.5 ha 3,000 30-49 F

A great many grape varieties are grown in the vineyards of the Côtes du Tarn. The Domaine de Sarrabelle has succeeded in bringing out the best in its Syrah harvest by carefully ageing it in barrel. Supple and rounded, almost silky, the palate is well-structured and long.

Laurent and Fabien Causse, Les Fortis, 81310 Lisle-sur-Tarn, tel. 05.63.40.47.78, fax 05.63.40.47.78 by appt.

Saint-Sardos

GILLES DE MORBAN 1997★

■ 93.5 ha 68,000 ▮ 20-29 F

The Saint-Sardos cellar chose Gilles de Morban as one of its best wines. The 97 has a subtle, slightly musky nose. Soft tannins contribute suppleness and roundness to the wine.
🔑 Cave des Vignerons de Saint-Sardos, Le Bourg, 82600 Saint-Sardos, tel. 05.63.02.52.44, fax 05.63.02.62.19 V
Y by appt.

Côtes de Gascogne

BORDENEUVE-ENTRAS 1999★

◪ 1 ha 8,000 ▮ 🌡 20-29 F

The appealing pink colour of this wine is an enticement to the taste buds, promising a lively mouthful. Its amylic nose confirms these expectations, as does the fruity, rounded and supple palate. The requisite degree of body and richness are also present.
🔑 GAEC Bordeneuve-Entras, 32410 Ayguetinte, tel. 05.62.68.11.41, fax 05.62.68.15.32 V Y by appt.
🔑 Maestrojuan

DOM. CHIROULET 1998★★

■ 5 ha 25,000 (|) 30-49 F

Although Gascony is known for its white wines, some of its terroirs produce fine reds. The Domaine de Chiroulet has produced a bright, deep garnet wine with ruby highlights from a blend of Cabernet, Merlot and Tannat grapes. On the nose, it has complex, rich aromas of crystallised fruit, toast and prunes. Spicy, balanced tannins and 12 months of judicious barrel-ageing have given the wine body and fullness.
🔑 Famille Fezas, Dom. Chiroulet, Heux, 32100 Larroque-sur-l'Osse, tel. 05.62.28.02.21, fax 05.62.28.41.56 V
Y by appt.

DOM. DE JOY Classique 1999★

□ 25 ha 150,000 ▮ 🌡 20 F+

This estate offers a wine made from the three main grapes cultivated in Gers: Colombard, Ugni Blanc and Gros Manseng. With a fine, fruity nose and a rounded, fleshy palate, the 1999 is full of all the citrus aromas that characterise those varieties.
🔑 GAEC Gessler et Fils, Dom. de Joÿ, 32110 Panjas, tel. 05.62.09.03.20, fax 05.62.69.04.46, e-mail contact@domaine-joy.com V
Y ev. day except Sun. 9am–7pm

DOM. DE LARTIGUE 1998★★

■ 6 ha 10,000 ▮ 20-29 F

This wine's nose is intense and complex, and shows great finesse. Summer berry aromas (blackberries, blackcurrants) are joined by hints of toast, spices and hay with a final note of green pepper. After a soft first impression, the wine is full-bodied and generous on the palate, but its tannins are still a little green and need to age.
🔑 Francis Lacave, Au Village, 32800 Bretagne-d'Armagnac, tel. 05.62.09.90.09, fax 05.62.09.79.60 V Y by appt.

DOM. SAN DE GUILHEM 1999★

□ 31 ha 250,000 ▮ 🌡 20 F+

This is a prototype Vin de Pays des Côtes de Gascogne that has been skillfully made from a blend of Colombard, Ugni Blanc and Gros Manseng. Both the nose and the palate are powerfully aromatic. Complex, supple and well-balanced, this wine will be appreciated by true connoisseurs.
🔑 Alain Lalanne, Dom. San de Guilhem, 32800 Ramouzens, tel. 05.62.06.57.02, fax 05.62.06.44.99, e-mail domaine@sandeguilhem.com V
Y ev. day 8am–12 noon 1.30pm–6.30pm

COTE TARIQUET

Chardonnay et Sauvignon 1999★★★

□ 10 ha 50,000 ▮ 🌡 30-49 F

The Domaine du Tariquet has long been recognised for its varietal wines. For this cuvée, Sauvignon and Chardonnay grapes were blended before fermentation. The Sauvignon is perceptible in the powerful ivy aroma present on both the nose and palate, while the Chardonnay gives the wine richness and weight. It is a perfectly balanced blend, each grape variety being allowed to express its own personality without overwhelming that of the other. An extremely well-made wine.
🔑 Ch. du Tariquet, 32800 Eauze, tel. 05.62.09.87.82, fax 05.62.09.89.49 V
🔑 Famille Grassa

Lot

DOM. DE CAUSE

Bouquet de Cavagnac 1999★★

◪ 0.5 ha 5,400 ▮ 30–49 F

The Lot region is primarily known for its AOC Cahors wines. However, it also produces some excellent white and rosé vins de pays, such as this rosé made from the Cot grape. The wine has all of the youthfulness and vigour promised by its red berry aromas.

🔑 Serge and Martine Costes, Cavagnac, 46700 Soturac, tel. 05.65.36.41.96, fax 05.65.36.41.95, e-mail montalieu@infonie.fr ☑ 🍸 ev. day 9.30am–12 noon 2pm–7pm; Sun. by appt.

Corrèze

MILLE ET UNE PIERRES

Elevé en Fût de Chêne 1998★

■ 11 ha 74,000 ⦀ 30–49 F

The Cave Viticole de Branceilles offers a well-balanced Cabernet Franc-Merlot blend. A deep, bright ruby colour, the wine has a softly oaky scent. On the palate, it is rounded and well-structured with a fairly persistent vanilla flavour.

🔑 Cave Viticole de Branceilles, Le Bourg, 19500 Branceilles, tel. 05.55.84.09.01, fax 05.55.25.33.01 ☑ 🍸 ev. day except Sun. 10am–12 noon 3pm–6pm

Coteaux et Terrasses de Montauban

DOM. DE MONTELS 1999★★

■ 4 ha 20,000 ▮ 🌡 20–29 F

Since taking over the management of this estate from their mother, Phillipe and Thierry Romain have focused on developing both the grape varieties in their vineyards and their wine-making methods. Their 1999, made from Cabernet, Merlot, Tannat and Gamay, is a success. It has a spicy nose and balanced palate with chewy tannins. The **Moelleux 99 Blanc**, made predominantly from Sauvignon grapes, is also appealing.

🔑 Philippe and Thierry Romain, Dom. de Montels, 82350 Albias, tel. 05.63.31.02.82, fax 05.63.31.07.94 ☑ 🍸 ev. day except Sun. 9am–12 noon 2pm–7pm

Pyrénées-Atlantiques

DOM. BORDES-LUBAT 1999

□ 0.84 ha 3,000 ⦀ 20–29 F

It is worth becoming aquainted with the Baroque grape, a variety specific to the Western Pyrenees. Although the floral palate can be a little harsh, it has its own peculiar charm. The wine's bright lemon-yellow colour is also very alluring.

🔑 Francis Lubat, 64330 Taron, tel. 06.11.99.87.48 ☑ 🍸 by appt.

Languedoc et Roussillon

Shaped like a vast amphitheatre overlooking the Mediterranean, the Languedoc-Roussillon region has vineyards stretching from the Rhône down to the eastern Pyrenees.

The largest wine-growing area in France, it produces almost 80% of all vins de pays. Aude, Gard, Hérault and Pyrénées-Orientales are the four designations that take their names from the *départements*. Inland, there are numerous smaller designations. Together, these two categories of vin de pays produce almost 5.5 m hectolitres of wine each year. Finally, there is the Vin de Pays d'Oc regional designation, which produced 2,600,000 hl (68,640,000 gal) in 1996–97 (60% red, 16% rosé, 24% white).

Languedoc-Roussillon vins de pays are made by individually fermenting selected harvests. Traditional grape varieties such as Carignan, Cinsaut, Grenache and Syrah are grown for red wines, with Clairette, Grenache Blanc, and Macabeo for whites. In addition, wine-makers grow some varieties not generally associated with the south of France – Cabernet

Sauvignon, Merlot and Pinot Noir for reds, Chardonnay, Sauvignon, and Viognier for whites.

Oc

DOM. D'ANTUGNAC

Les Grands Penchants 1999★

☐ 8 ha 15,000 30–49 F

Christian Collovrat and Jean-Luc Terrier manage this 50-ha (124-acre) estate. Their vividly coloured wine has a honey-scented buttery nose of great finesse. The palate, which stays in the same register, is rounded, well-balanced and long.

Dom. d'Antugnac, 11190 Antugnac, tel. 04.68.74.00.89, fax 04.68.74.22.60

ARNAUD DE VILLENEUVE

Chardonnay Elevé en Barrique de Chêne 1999★★

☐ 3 ha 20,000 30–49 F

Twenty-five-year-old vines and five months of oak-ageing have produced this exceptional straw-coloured Chardonnay with green highlights. The nose has an attractive mix of aromas, with a fine balance of woody and floral scents. A subtle, delicate oakiness is perceptible on the palate, which is rich and rounded. The components of this wine form a balanced whole that is ready for drinking now.

Les Vignobles du Rivesaltais, 1, rue de la Roussillonnaise, 66602 Rivesaltes-Salses, tel. 04.68.64.06.63, fax 04.68.64.64.69, e-mail vignobles.rivesaltais@wanadoo.fr
by appt.

DOM. DES ASPES Merlot 1998★

■ 5 ha 25,000 30–49 F

A captivating dark colour with violet highlights, this wine has an agreeably powerful nose with an aroma of over-ripe red berries. The balanced palate echoes the nose with flavours of forest fruits. An attractive wine for drinking now.

Vignobles Marcel Roger, Ch. du Prieuré des Mourgues, 34360 Pierrerue, tel. 04.67.38.18.19, fax 04.67.38.27.29, e-mail prieuredesmourgues@wanadoo.fr
by appt.

DOM. DE BARANDON Merlot 1998★

■ 5 ha n.c. 30–49 F

This highly successful dark purple Merlot has a captivatingly ripe, fruity nose of great finesse and complexity. Balance and structure combine on the palate with fine aromatic persistence. A harmonious wine, it is ready to drink now.

Vignerons de la Méditerranée, 12, rue du Rec-de-Veyret, ZI de Plaisance, 11100 Narbonne, tel. 04.68.42.75.00, fax 04.68.42.75.01, e-mail valdorbieu-didierferrier@wanadoo.fr
by appt.

DOM. DE BAUBIAC Merlot 1998★★

■ 1.37 ha 10,600 20–29 F

This Merlot captivated the jury. An attractive deep garnet colour, the wine reveals an aromatic and complex spicy nose. Full and long, the enchanting palate is beautifully structured. A remarkably attractive wine.

SCEA Philip Frères, Dom. de Baubiac, 30260 Brouzet-lès-Quissac, tel. 04.66.77.33.45, fax 04.66.77.33.45, e-mail philip@dstu.univ-montp2.fr
by appt.

DOM. DU BOLCHET

Cabernet-Sauvignon 1998★

■ 1.3 ha 4,000 20–29 F

This estate has been replanted several times. Since 1997, it has been reaping the rewards of its investment, as exemplified by this excellent Cabernet Sauvignon. Ruby, with paler highlights, it has a powerful nose of macerated red berries and slight spicy overtones. These aromas persist on the elegant, full-bodied palate, which has pronounced but soft tannins.

Béatrice Becamel, Ch. Bolchet, 30132 Caissargues, tel. 04.66.38.05.65, fax 04.66.29.14.79 ev. day except Sun. 8.30am–12 noon 2pm–7pm

BORIE LA VITARELE

La Combe 1998★

■ 3 ha 8,000 50–69 F

The motto of the estate, which was established in 1990, is *du soleil dans votre verre* ('sunshine in your glass'). Four grape varieties planted on two different soil types have been blended to create this dark red 98 with bronze highlights. The pleasantly powerful nose has an aroma of undergrowth and old leather. The hefty palate is well-structured and long, with soft tannins and a hint of vanilla.

Jean-François Izarn and Cathy Planes, chem. de la Vernède, 34490 Saint-Nazaire-de-Ladarez, tel. 04.67.89.50.43, fax 04.67.89.50.43 by appt.

THIERRY BOUDINAUD

Merlot Réserve Barriques 1999★★

■ 4 ha 25,000 30–49 F

In 1999, the 'sunny skies' of the Domaine du Soleil saw the production of some fine wines that garnered a crop of stars from the jury: the **Cabernet-Sauvignon 99**, **Chardonnay 99** and **Chardonnay Solstice**, which are all very good, and an exceptional **Solstice Cabernet Sauvignon**, with which one could fittingly celebrate the summer. The Merlot, which is purple with blue highlights, shines in every respect. Its nose is slightly oaky, with hints of spice and vanilla. Full and rounded, the palate has chewy tannins and a similar hint of oak, leading to a long finish.

🗝 Domaines du Soleil,
Ch. Canet, 11800 Rustiques,
tel. 04.90.12.32.41, fax 04.90.12.32.49

DOM. BOURDIC

Syrah Elevé en Fût de Chêne 1998★★

■ 2.63 ha 5,600 50–69 F

This wine, made solely from Syrah grapes, was matured for a year in oak. A charming wine, it appears to be at its peak now. It has a youthful, deep purple colour with blue highlights. Aromas of wild cherries, leather, truffles and vanilla, with a slight toasty overtone, are present on the nose. The palate is full, powerful and concentrated with plenty of soft tannins. A very elegant wine, it could be served now with venison, or kept a little longer.

🗝 Christa Vogel and Hans Hürlimann,
Dom. Bourdic, 34290 Alignan-du-Vent,
tel. 04.67.24.98.08, fax 04.67.24.98.96
Y by appt.

CAMPLAZENS L'ERMITAGE

Elevé en Fût de Chêne 1998★

■ n.c. n.c. 70–99 F

Five varieties (Syrah, Grenache, Carignan, Cabernet and Merlot) have gone into the making of this fine dark red wine with bright violet and brick-red highlights. On the nose, it is spicy with a subtle oakiness. The well-structured, balanced palate has soft tannins and a flavour of liquorice.

🗝 SARL Domaines Camplazens, La Jasse,
34980 Combaillaux, tel. 04.67.87.34.62,
fax 04.67.84.30.51 Y by appt.

DOM. CASTELNAU

Chardonnay 1999★

□ 10.64 ha 20,000 30–49 F

A bright, clear wine with green highlights, this Chardonnay has a powerful nose with obvious finesse. The lively first impression on the palate is succeeded by powerful and persistent floral aromas. This wine is exceptionally well-balanced.

🗝 GFA Dom. de Castelnau-de-Guers, 32,
av. de Pézenas, 34120 Castelnau-de-Guers,
tel. 04.67.98.16.19, fax 04.67.09.43.17
Y ev. day 8am–12 noon 2pm–8pm

DOM. CLAVEL Chardonnay 1999★

□ 0.55 ha 6,600 30–49 F

An appealing Chardonnay made from grapes grown on wind-blown sandy soils in the Cèze Valley microclimate. On the nose, it has fine citrus and floral aromas, while the lively, vigorous palate is equally aromatic. This is a well-balanced wine with a slight hint of spritziness.

🗝 Françoise Clavel, rue du Pigeonnier,
30200 Saint-Gervais, tel. 04.66.82.78.90,
fax 04.66.82.74.30 Y by appt.

DOM. DE CLOVALLON

Les Auriѐges 1998★★

□ 1.5 ha n.c. 70–99 F

This estate is planted on terraced vineyards at the foot of a dolomite cliff. The Les Auriѐges cuvée is a bright golden wine with a potent, complex nose of citrus, ripe berries, tobacco and vanilla. The balanced palate is both lively and well-rounded. An elegant wine that would make a fine accompaniment for fish.

🗝 Catherine Roques, Dom. de Clovallon,
rte Col-du-Buis, 34600 Bédarieux,
tel. 04.67.95.19.72, fax 04.67.95.11.18,
e-mail domaine@clovallon.fr Y by appt.

DOM. COSTEPLANE

Cabernet-Sauvignon et Merlot 1998★

■ 4.53 ha 12,800 30–49 F

This is a rich purple wine made by an estate that has been practising organic viticulture since 1990. The jury was impressed by its aromatic complexity (ripe berries, spices and green peppers), and its fleshy, rich palate with very soft tannins.

🗝 Françoise and Vincent Coste, Mas de
Costeplane, 30260 Cannes-et-Clairan,
tel. 04.66.77.85.02, fax 04.66.77.85.47
Y by appt.

DOM. FERRI-ARNAUD

Chardonnay 1999★

□ n.c. 20,000 30–49 F

It is hard not to be won over by this Chardonnay, with its clear, bright colour, rich floral aroma, and elegant, well-balanced palate. It would complement chicken in a cream sauce.

🗝 EARL Ferri Arnaud, av. de l'Hérault,
11560 Fleury-d'Aude, tel. 04.68.33.62.43,
fax 04.68.33.74.38 Y by appt.
🗝 Richard Ferri

FORTANT DE FRANCE

Chardonnay 1999★

□ n.c. 530,000 20–29 F

Half of the juice used to make this wine was allowed extended contact with the grapeskins, while half was pressed straight through, producing this attractive straw-yellow wine with green highlights. The nose has an aroma of acacia and white blossom, while the palate is lively, balanced and long. The **Grenache Gris 99** was also cited by the jury.

🗝 Les vins Skalli-Fortant de France, 278,
av. du Mal-Juin, B.P. 376, 34204 Sѐte Cedex,
tel. 04.67.46.70.00, fax 04.67.46.71.99,
e-mail info@vinskalli.com Y by appt.

DOM. DU GRAND CHEMIN

Cabernet-Sauvignon 1999★

■ 4 ha 30,000 30–49 F

For five generations, the Floutier family has practised its craft on the Grand Chemin estate, located on the old road between Nîmes and Florac. It is worth stopping by for a taste of this purple Cabernet Sauvignon with violet highlights. The nose has an intense aroma of red berries and strawberries, and introduces a full-bodied, balanced palate with fine tannins. A very good wine that could be aged for a while or served now, perhaps to accompany beef with anchovies.

🔑 EARL Jean-Marc Floutier, Dom. du Grand Chemin, 30350 Savignargues, tel. 04.66.83.42.83, fax 04.66.83.42.83 ☒ 🍷 ev. day 8am–12 noon 2pm–6pm

GRANGE DES ROUQUETTE

Le Pélican 1999★★★

☐ 3.43 ha 6,000 30-49 F

This estate used to grow olive-trees for producing olive oil. After the terrible winter of 1956, it switched to viticulture. Great good has ultimately come from the olive-trees' misfortune in the form of this light wine with glittering golden highlights. Its fine, complex nose has delicate hints of acacia, golden tobacco, citrus and vanilla. The palate has a harmonious balance of fullness and liveliness, and a long, eucalyptus-flavoured finish.

🔑 Vignoble Boudinaud, 30210 Fournes, tel. 04.66.37.27.23, fax 04.66.37.27.23, e-mail boudinaud@infonie.fr ☒ 🍷 by appt.

DOM. DE LA BAUME 1998★

☐ 9.04 ha 9,022 70-99 F

The Viognier (72%) and Chardonnay grapes used in this wine were harvested at night in order to maximise their freshness. The resulting pale-hued wine has golden highlights. Its rich and fine nose is both oaky and floral, and the wine has a lively, well-balanced palate.

🔑 Dom. de la Baume, R.N. 113, 34290 Servian, tel. 04.67.39.29.49, fax 04.67.39.29.40 ☒ 🍷 by appt.

DOM. DE LA DEVEZE

Roussanne Elevé en Barrique de Chêne 1999★

☐ 0.75 ha 2,500 50-69 F

This estate, located in the heart of the Cévennes, was a silk-farm until 1964. Its Roussanne is straw-coloured with golden highlights. It has a powerful floral and mineral nose followed by a well-balanced, aromatic palate that is full-bodied and fleshy. Perfect with strong cheese.

🔑 Laurent Damais, GAEC du Dom. de la Devèze, 34190 Montoulieu, tel. 04.67.73.70.21, fax 04.67.73.32.40, e-mail domaine@deveze.com ☒ 🍷 by appt.

DOM. DE LA JASSE D'ISNARD

Merlot 1998★

■ 3.88 ha 4,000 20-29 F

This estate is currently being run by the fourth generation of the family that has owned it since 1916. Plenty of expertise has gone into the making of this clear dark-coloured wine with its intense, complex nose of ripe berries. The palate is full-bodied and very well-balanced. An extremely attractive wine that would complement meats in sauces.

🔑 F. Michelon, Dom. la Jasse d'Isnard, 30470 Aimargues, tel. 04.66.88.61.98, fax 04.66.88.50.31 ☒ 🍷 ev. day 8.30am–7.30pm

DOM. LALAURIE Merlot 1998★

■ 8 ha 20,000 30-49 F

Jean-Charles Lalaurie, who has run this estate since 1974, is passionate about wine and shows it in the likes of this fine Merlot. It has a youthful, deep cherry-red colour, and an intense and complex nose of leather, menthol and fruit. The well-structured palate has slightly austere, but promising tannins. It could be served now with a platter of cheese or cellared for a while. The **Cabernet Sauvignon 98** from the same estate was also cited.

🔑 Jean-Charles Lalaurie, 2, rue Le-Pelletier-de-Saint-Fargeau, 11590 Ouveillan, tel. 04.68.46.84.96, fax 04.68.46.93.92, e-mail jean-charleslalaurie@libertysurf.fr ☒ 🍷 ev. day 9am–12 noon 3pm–7pm; Sat. Sun. and groups by appt.

DOM. LA MADURA Tradition 1999★

☐ 1.15 ha 5,000 50-69 F

After having been the wine-maker at Château de Fieuzal in Bordeaux, Cyril Bourgne took over this property in Saint-Chinian in 1988. This pale wine with green highlights is the first varietal Sauvignon he has made. The fresh and expressive nose with its herbaceous, lemony aromas is characteristic of the grape, while the lively, rounded palate shows good balance. The finish is very refreshing.

🔑 Nadia and Cyril Bourgne, 61, av. Raoul-Bayon, 34360 Saint-Chinian, tel. 04.67.38.17.85, fax 04.67.38.17.85 🍷 by appt.

DOM. LAMARGUE Merlot 1999★

■ 2 ha 13,000 30-49 F

This young wine has a great deal of potential: an attractive purple colour with violet highlights, and a fine, oaky nose with smoky, balsamic tones. Slightly toasted, oaky aromas are also present on the palate, which is fresh and rich. This well-structured Merlot could be drunk now, but will express itself more eloquently if allowed to age for a while.

🔑 SCI du Dom. de Lamargue, rte. de Vauvert, 30800 Saint-Gilles, tel. 04.66.87.31.89, fax 04.66.87.41.87, e-mail domaine.de.lamargue@wanadoo.fr ☒ Y by appt.
🔑 Bonomi

DOM. DE LA VALMALE

Sauvignon 1999★

☐ 5.04 ha 20,000 ▮ 🌡 20 F+

In the Middle Ages, this estate was a part of the Barony of Coussergues. It has produced a fine golden Sauvignon with a subtle floral nose and lively palate. The white flower and honey flavours have great length. A very balanced wine that lives up to its charming label.
🔑 Alain Clarou, Dom. de la Valmale, 34550 Bessan, tel. 01.43.54.42.49, fax 01.40.46.89.01 ☒ Y by appt.

L'ENCLOS D'ORMESSON

Sauvignon 1999★★

☐ 7 ha n.c. ▮ 🌡 50–69 F

The bright colour of the wine, with its copper highlights, announces a nose of great finesse. The palate is sinewy, rounded and balanced. An exceptional wine that will happily marry with either fish dishes or a platter of cheese.
🔑 Jérôme d'Ormesson, Le Château, 34120 Lézignan-la-Cèbe, tel. 04.67.98.29.33, fax 04.67.98.29.32 ☒ Y ev. day 9am–12 noon 2pm–6pm

DOM. DE L'ENGARRAN 1998★

■ 2 ha 5,000 ⏸ 30–49 F

At the far end of a three-ha (seven-acre) park, you will find a magnificent, listed 18th-century château. While the building will appeal to the aesthetically minded, wine-lovers will also be tempted by this very well-crafted, cherry-red wine. Powerful blackcurrant and citrus aromas are present on the nose. The supple palate, which echoes those berry aromas, does not disappoint.
🔑 SCEA du Ch. de l'Engarran, 34880 Laverune, tel. 04.67.47.00.02, fax 04.67.27.87.89 ☒ Y ev. day 12 noon–7pm; Sat. Sun. 10am–7pm
🔑 Grill

LES COLLINES DU BOURDIC

Viognier 1999★★

☐ 12 ha 50,000 30–49 F

Between 1997 and 2000, the cellar invested a great deal in extensive renovations. It is now reaping the rewards. The **Prestige 98** and the **Pavillon Racine** cuvées were awarded one star each. The Viognier is marvellous. Brightly coloured with green highlights, it has an intense nose of great finesse and complexity, blending floral and fruity notes. These aromas are also present on the palate, which is lively, rounded and perfectly balanced.
🔑 SCA les Collines du Bourdic, chem. de la Gare, 30190 Bourdic, tel. 04.66.81.20.82, fax 04.66.81.23.20 ☒ Y ev. day except Sun. 8am–12 noon 2pm–6pm

DOM. LES FILLES DE SEPTEMBRE

Viognier 1999★

☐ 1.4 ha 5,000 ▮ 🌡 30–49 F

Brothers Roland and Hugues Géraud took over the running of this estate in 1995: Roland manages the vineyards, while Hugues is in charge of the wine-making. Together, they have produced a fine, crystal-clear Viognier with golden highlights. The nose is temptingly intense, fresh and fruity. On the palate, the wine is balanced and full-bodied, with fruity (apricot) flavours and good length.
🔑 EARL Géraud Père et Fils, Dom. les Filles de Septembre, av. G.-Guynemer, 34290 Abeilhan, tel. 04.67.39.01.65, fax 04.67.39.01.65 ☒ Y by appt.

LES VIGNES DE L'ARQUE

Merlot 1999★★

■ 8.3 ha 18,000 ▮ 🌡 20–29 F

Two wine-growers decided to join forces and establish their own cellar, and their wine bears witness to the wisdom of the decision. A deep, bright purple, it has a potent, rich and fruity nose with hints of spice. On the palate, it is fleshy, with well-integrated tannins.
🔑 Les Vignes de l'Arque, 30700 Baron, tel. 04.66.22.37.71, fax 04.66.22.47.49 ☒ Y ev. day 9am–12 noon 2pm–7pm
🔑 Bouveyrolles et Fabre

DOM. LES YEUSES Syrah 1998★★

■ 7.5 ha 10,000 ▮ 🌡 20–29 F

The *yeuses*, or holm-oaks, of the domain's name gave way to vines 20 years ago. Over that time, the estate has modernised its production methods by investing in the latest wine-making technology. The result is this very dark purple Syrah. The ripe fruit nose with hints of spice and undergrowth is exceptional, while the unctuous palate strikes the same aromatic chords and has very supple tannins. A perfectly balanced, elegant wine.
🔑 Jean-Paul and Michel Dardé, Dom. Les Yeuses, rte de Marseillan, 34140 Mèze, tel. 04.67.43.80.20, fax 04.67.43.59.32 ☒ Y ev. day except Sun. 9am–12 noon 3pm–7pm

L'ORANGERIE DE SAINTE-ROSE

Sélection Vieilles Vignes 1998★

■ 20 ha 40,000 ▮ 🌡 30–49 F

This wine has an extraordinary ripe cherry colour, red berries with a hint of plums on the nose, and a full-bodied, well-structured palate. It is a combination that will complement braised meats, venison or cheese. Will improve if kept for a little while.
🔑 Leclercq, Dom. de Sainte-Rose, 34290 Servian, tel. 04.67.39.29.17, fax 04.67.39.29.18, e-mail lvin@club-internet.fr ☒ Y ev. day except Sun. 10am–12 noon 2pm–8pm

HENRI MAIRE Merlot 1999★★

■ n.c. n.c. 20–29 F

The most important *négociant* in the Jura has made a Languedoc wine from a Bordeaux variety! In summarising its allure, the jury declared the result 'extraordinary': a bright, deep ruby colour, powerful fruity and floral nose, rounded, impressive palate and an unctuous finish. It could be served with grilled meat or firm-fleshed fish.

🗝 Henri Maire, Ch. Boichailles, 39600 Arbois, tel. 03.84.66.12.34, fax 03.84.66.42.42, e-mail info@henri-maire.fr

DOM. DE MALAVIEILLE

Chardonnay 1999★

□ 2 ha 2,500 30–49 F

The Domaine de Malavieille, which can be found not far from the red waters of Lake Salagou, has made a lemon-yellow wine from grapes grown on volcanic soils. The fine woody nose, with its hint of vanilla, reflects seven months' maturation in new oak. Fleshy and full-bodied, the palate is well-balanced and has an aromatic finish.

🗝 Mireille Bertrand, Malavieille, 34800 Mérifons, tel. 04.67.96.34.67, fax 04.67.96.32.21 V Y by appt.

MAS MONTEL Chardonnay 1998★★

□ 4 ha 5,000 30–49 F

This remarkable Chardonnay was given a maceration on its skins before fermentation and was then aged on its lees for six months. Golden-yellow in colour, it has a fresh and fruity nose of great finesse. The palate is full, rounded and rich, yet retains a certain vitality. It is a well-balanced, lightly oaky wine that would go well with white meat.

🗝 EARL Granier, Mas Montel, 30250 Aspères, tel. 04.66.80.01.21, fax 04.66.80.01.87, e-mail montel@wanadoo.fr V
Y ev. day except Sun. 9am–7pm

DOM. MAUREL FONSALADE

La Fonsalade Lyre 1998★★

□ 0.47 ha 2,900 30–49 F

This exceptional cuvée is made from a blend of five grape varieties that were given some pre-fermentation skin contact. Training the vines on lyre trellises has paid off in terms of the distinctiveness of the wine. Rich aromas of honey, spices and tropical fruits are present on the nose, while the full-bodied palate shows subtle oak influence. A wine that could be served as an apéritif, with foie gras or with cheese.

🗝 Philippe and Thérèse Maurel, Ch. Maurel Fonsalade, 34490 Causses-et-Veyran, tel. 04.67.89.57.90, fax 04.67.89.72.04 V
Y by appt.

DOM. DE MONT D'HORTES

Cabernet-Sauvignon 1999★★

■ 5.5 ha 40,000 20–29 F

This property, located on the site of a Gallo-Roman villa, has produced an exceptional wine. Its attractive garnet colour has violet highlights. On the nose, it is remarkably intense and concentrated with a mixture of green pepper, spices and scents of the garrigue. The palate, with its soft tannins, is powerful and well-balanced and echoes the original aromas. The **Chardonnay 99** from the same estate is also very good.

🗝 J. Anglade, Dom. de Mont d'Hortes, 34630 Saint-Thibéry, tel. 04.67.77.88.08, fax 04.67.30.17.57 V Y by appt.

OPUS TERRA Merlot et Syrah 1999★

■ 13 ha 120,000 20–29 F

This estate has been in the same family for three generations. As it is on an archaeological site dating back to the first century AD, researchers have been visiting the property to investigate Roman wine-making techniques. This year, it has produced a fine crystal-clear, dark-hued wine with violet highlights. Crystallised fruit aromas dominate the nose, while the palate is well-structured and balanced with flavours of red berries. A wine that could be enjoyed now or laid down.

🗝 Hervé and Guilhem Durand, Ch. des Tourelles, 4294, rte. de Bellegarde, 30300 Beaucaire, tel. 04.66.59.22.69, fax 04.66.59.50.80 V Y by appt.

DOM. DE PIERRE-BELLE

Cuvée Liliane Elevé en Fût de Chêne 1998★

■ 2 ha 10,000 50–69 F

The brilliant purple colour of the Cuvée Liliane is very appealing. Its powerfully aromatic nose has scents of red berries with a hint of vanilla. On the palate, it is rounded, full-bodied and balanced. The **Chardonnay 99** from the same estate was also cited.

🗝 Laguna et Fils – Fernandez et Fils, Dom. de Pierre-Belle, 34290 Lieuran-lès-Béziers, tel. 04.67.36.15.58, fax 04.67.36.15.58, e-mail pierrebelle@mail.chez.com V
Y by appt.

DOM. DE RAISSAC

Chardonnay Le Parc 1999★★

□ 5.5 ha 13,000 30–49 F

The château dates from the 12th century, and has been in the same family for six generations. Today, the estate grows a dozen different varieties of vine on over 90 ha (220 acres). Its Chardonnay has an extraordinary golden colour. The citrus nose is intense and fruity, and the vigorous, well-balanced palate is characterised by great aromatic persistence.

🗝 Jean and Luc Viennet, Ch. de Raissac, rte. de Murviel, 34500 Béziers, tel. 04.67.28.15.61, fax 04.67.28.19.75, e-mail info@raissac.com V Y ev. day except Sun. 9am–12.30pm 2pm–6pm

RESSAC Le Rosé de Syrah 1999★

◪ 25 ha 11,000 ▮ ♁ 20–29 F

This 100% Syrah rosé is richly coloured, with bluish highlights. The wine has been made using the technique of pre-fermentation skin contact. It has a fine, complex nose of ripe fruits with a liquorice overtone. The round, full-bodied and aromatic palate has good length. **Muscat des Garrigues 99**, a second wine put forward by the Cave de Florensac, was also rated highly.

🗝 Cave coop. de Florensac, B.P. 9, 34510 Florensac, tel. 04.67.77.00.20, fax 04.67.77.79.66 ☑
𝕐 ev. day except Sun. 9am–12 noon 2pm–6pm

DOM. ROZES

Cabernet-Sauvignon 1998★

■ 4.01 ha 26,000 ▮ ♁ 20–29 F

This vineyard, which has been in the same family for two centuries, is situated on the alluvial soils of the Agly valley. Its dark purple Cabernet Sauvignon has a fine and complex nose, while the palate is full-bodied and powerful. A fine, well-balanced wine.

🗝 SCEA Tarquin, Dom. Rozès, 3, rue de Lorraine, 66600 Espira-de-l'Agly, tel. 04.68.38.52.11, fax 04.68.38.51.38, e-mail rozes.domaine@wanadoo.fr ☑
𝕐 ev. day except Sat. Sun. 9am–6pm

DOM. DE SAINT-ALBAN

Sauvignon 1999★

□ 1.7 ha 4,800 ▮ ♁ 20 F+

The estate, which is located in the foothills of the Cévennes, has a Norman chapel in its grounds. Its Sauvignon has a bright, attractive colour and a fine, mineral nose with citrus overtones. On the palate, it is lively but also balanced, aromatic and long.

🗝 Jean-Luc Evesque, Dom. de Saint-Alban, 30340 Saint-Privat-des-Vieux, tel. 04.66.86.19.13, fax 04.66.86.84.73, e-mail domaine.st-alban@libertysurf.fr ☑
𝕐 ev. day except Sun. 9am–12 noon 2pm–6.30pm

DOM. SAINT-GEORGES D'IBRY

Merlot 1997★★

■ 4 ha 5,000 ◖▮◗ 30–49 F

The jury was very impressed by two offerings from this estate. The 1997 Merlot with its brilliant brick-red highlights has a well-developed, fine and complex nose with menthol and spice aromas and a hint of toast. Those aromas continue on the palate, which is full-bodied and well-structured. The **Muscat Sec 99** was also judged worthy of two stars.

🗝 Michel Cros, Dom. Saint-Georges-d'Ibry, rte d'Espondeilhan, 34290 Abeilhan, tel. 04.67.39.19.18, fax 04.67.39.07.44 ☑
𝕐 ev. day except Sun. 9.30am–12 noon 2pm–6pm

DOM. SAINT-HILAIRE

La Serpentine Elevé en Fût de Chêne 1998★

■ n.c. 7,000 ◖▮◗ 50–69 F

For the past 25 years, this estate has been diversifying its plantings and renewing its wine-making equipment. This cuvée is just reward for the wine-maker's efforts. Its rich garnet colour with violet highlights is accompanied by a subtle, earthy nose of undergrowth and red berries. The rich, rounded palate is very aromatic. It could be served now with meat or game in sauces, or laid down in your cellar. The white wine from the same estate, **Hommage 98**, is also very good.

🗝 A. N. Hardy, SARL Dom. Saint-Hilaire, 34530 Montagnac, tel. 04.67.24.00.08, fax 04.67.24.04.01, e-mail sthilaire@club-internet.fr ☑
𝕐 ev. day except Sat. Sun. 8am–12 noon 1pm–6pm

DOM. DE SAINT-LOUIS

Cabernet-Sauvignon 1999★

■ 8 ha 20,000 ▮ ♁ 30–49 F

The Gallo-Roman Villa Museum, opened in 2000, is very interesting and well worth a visit. While you are there, you could also drop in on this estate and taste the brilliant purple 1999 Cabernet with its fine, complex nose of fruits and red peppers. The palate is balanced and supple, and has an attractive flavour of cherries.

🗝 Philippe Captier, Dom. de Saint-Louis, 34140 Loupian, tel. 04.67.43.92.62, fax 04.67.43.70.80 ☑ 𝕐 by appt.

HERMITAGE DU DOM. SAINT MARTIN DES CHAMPS

Cabernet-Sauvignon Elevé en Fût de Chêne 1998★

■ 3 ha 20,000 ▮ ◖▮◗ ♁ 30–49 F

In the seventh century, this estate was a hermitage where pilgrims on their way to Saint-Jacques-de-Compostelle could rest. The vineyards themselves date back to the 17th century. Today, they produce wines like this bright, rich red Cabernet that has been matured in oak for 12 months. The nose is subtly oaky with hints of vanilla, cocoa and preserves. Those aromas persist on the palate, which is full-bodied and well-balanced. The **Chardonnay 99** from the same estate is another successful wine.

🗝 Pierre and Michel Birot, Ch. Saint-Martin-des-Champs, 34490 Murviel-les-Béziers, tel. 04.67.32.92.58, fax 04.67.37.84.49, e-mail domaine@saintmartindeschamps.com
☑ 𝕐 ev. day except Sun. 9am–12 noon 3pm–6pm

DOM. SALLE DE GOUR

Sauvignon 1999★★★

□ 6 ha 12,000 20–29 F

The jury was unanimous in awarding a *coup de cœur* to this magnificent Sauvignon. It is a superbly bright wine the colour of old

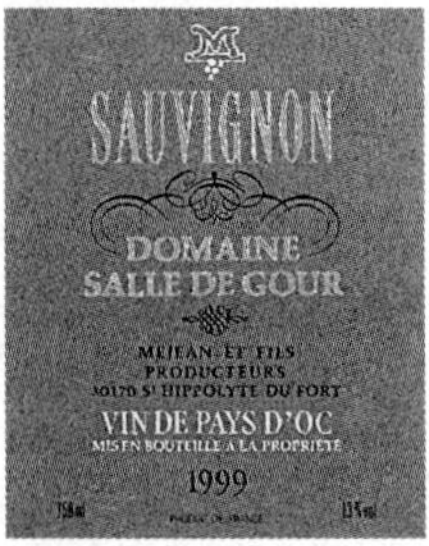

gold. The lustrous colour is matched by the richness and concentration of the nose, which has aromas of tropical fruits and citrus. The palate is full-bodied and rich, yet full of vivacity. The **Merlot 99** from the same producer was also judged to be very good.

M. Méjean, Dom. Salle de Gour, 30170 Saint-Hippolyte-du-Fort, tel. 04.66.77.66.60, fax 04.66.77.94.62
by appt.

DOM. DES SYLPHES

Merlot Elevé en Fût de Chêne 1999**

n.c. n.c. 30-49 F

A rich purple colour, this Merlot has a highly perfumed, balsamic nose. The palate does not let it down; it is rounded, full-bodied and well-structured, with lingering spice and liquorice flavours. This wine will reach its full potential when it has had more time to mature.

Les Domaines Bernard, rte. de Sérignan, 84100 Orange, tel. 04.90.11.86.86, fax 04.90.34.87.30

TERRASSES D'AZUR

Sauvignon 1999*

62.5 ha 300,000 20 F+

This is an attractive lemon-yellow Sauvignon with bright highlights. The fairly intense nose combines box-flower, yeast and tropical fruit aromas, while the palate shows elegance, balance and finesse. A harmonious wine that is ready to drink now. The **Rosé de Cinsault** was also cited by the jury.

Castel Frères, rte. de la Gare, 11590 Sallèles-d'Aude, tel. 04.68.46.60.00, fax 04.68.46.89.59

DOM. DES TERRES NOIRES

Colombard 1999*

3 ha 30,000 30-49 F

Black volcanic soils have produced this brilliant, pale yellow Colombard. The nose has a fruity aroma with a hint of gunflint, and its liveliness on the palate is very appealing. Aromatic, long and wonderfully fresh.

Dominique Castillon, Dom. les Terres Noires, 34450 Vias, tel. 04.67.21.73.55, fax 04.67.21.68.38 by appt.

VILLA APPIANO Chardonnay 1998*

4 ha 34,000 30-49 F

Fifteen-year-old vines were responsible for this fine Chardonnay. Given a short period of skin contact, the wine has an elegant, crystal-clear, rich gold colour. A citrus and white blossom nose leads into a well-balanced, fresh and vigorous palate with great aromatic persistence. A wine to enjoy now.

Méditerroirs, Ch. Cap-de-Fouste, Villeneuve-de-la-Raho, 66100 Perpignan, tel. 04.68.85.69.25, fax 04.68.85.22.26, e-mail mediterroirs@mediterrois.fr
SCV Pia

VIRGINIE Syrah 1999**

70 ha 600,000 20-29 F

This 100% Syrah has a brilliant, rich colour with violet highlights. On the nose, it shows great finesse with oaky, vanilla aromas and fruity nuances. A well-structured, rich, and full-bodied palate follows, all adding up to an extremely balanced wine. The finish is very long. The wine is ready for drinking now, but could be kept for a while. The **Sauvignon 99** and the **Cabernet Sauvignon 99** from the same estate were also judged very good.

Les domaines Virginie, R.N. 13, CS 650, 34536 Béziers Cédex, tel. 04.67.49.85.85, fax 04.67.49.38.40, e-mail mariecabrillac@hotmail.com
P. Degroote

Sables du Golfe du Lion

DOM. DE LA FIGUEIRASSE

Gris de Gris 1999*

3 ha 18,000 20-29 F

Grenache Noir (50%), Grenache Gris and Cinsault have been blended to create an appealing rosé with a youthful, light and elegant colour and a delicate floral nose. On the palate, it is slightly sweet but nonetheless balanced. A harmonious wine that would complement paella.

Robert Saumade, Dom. de la Figueirasse, 30240 Le Grau-du-Roi, tel. 04.67.70.20.48, fax 04.67.87.50.05

Gard

DOM. DES CORREGES Merlot 1998*

35 ha 35,000 20-29 F

This estate, located on the edge of the Camargue, has made a very good Merlot. A bright ruby colour with lively highlights, it has intense aromas of fruit and leather. Fresh and supple, with ripe tannins, the wine is ready for drinking now.

⊶ Antoine and Jean-Luc Barret, Dom. des Corrèges, 30300 Beaucaire, tel. 04.66.01.68.34, fax 04.66.01.17.26 ▼ Y by appt.

DOM. LE PIAN Merlot 1999★

■ 6.2 ha 42,000 ▮ 20-29 F

The name of this estate harks back to the 16th-century Wars of Religion. This enjoyable Merlot has an appealing, crystal-clear, dark red colour, and a fruity nose of great finesse and complexity. On the palate, it is well-balanced and structured, with pleasant tannins and flavours that persist on the finish.

⊶ SCEA le Paradis, Dom. le Pian, 30350 Moulezan, tel. 04.66.77.81.25, fax 04.66.77.89.15 ▼ Y ev. day except Sat. Sun. 9am–12 noon 2pm–6pm

Coteaux de Fontcaude

ROC DELS NOVIS 1998★

□ n.c. 5,800 ▮ ⦀ ⸸ 30-49 F

Half Viognier, half Chardonnay, this wine was grown on marl soils of the Miocene era. The beguiling golden colour is supported by a powerful nose with overtones of jasmine. The lively, well-structured and slightly oaky palate has hints of vanilla and citrus. The **Sauvignon 99 du Domaine du Roueïre** is also a very well-made wine.

⊶ Les Vignerons de Puisserguier, 29, rue Georges-Pujol, 34620 Puisserguier, tel. 04.67.93.74.03, fax 04.67.93.87.73 ▼ Y by appt.

Coteaux de Bessilles

DOM. SAINT-MARTIN DE LA GARRIGUE Cuvée Réservée 1998★

■ n.c. 40,000 ⦀ 30-49 F

Chalky sandstone soils and 12 months in oak have combined to create this impressive cuvée. A very well-made wine with a rich garnet colour and violet highlights, it has a potent nose of forest fruits. Rich, persistent flavours permeate the well-structured, full-bodied palate. A wine that could be kept for a while.

⊶ SCEA Saint-Martin de la Garrigue, Ch. Saint-Martin de la Garrigue, 34530 Montagnac, tel. 04.67.24.00.40, fax 04.67.24.16.15 ▼ Y by appt.

⊶ Umberto Guida

DOM. SAVARY DE BEAUREGARD Cuvée Mathilde 1999★

◪ 10 ha 12,000 ▮ ⸸ 30-49 F

Twenty-year-old vines of Grenache, Cinsault and Syrah have produced this appealing pale rose-coloured wine with silvery highlights. The fresh, powerful and lively nose has an aroma of anise. On the palate, it is exceptionally full and balanced.

⊶ Savary de Beauregard, La Vernazobre, R.N. 113, 34530 Montagnac, tel. 04.67.24.00.12, fax 04.67.24.00.12 ▼ Y ev. day 10am–7pm; Nov.–Apr. 12 noon–5pm

Côtes de Thongue

DOM. DE COSTE ROUSSE Font de Lautre 1999★

□ 3 ha 8,000 ▮ 20-29 F

Font de Lautre is the name of the place where the estate's first vinestock was purchased. It is also the name of this very good, brightly coloured wine. White flower aromas dominate the fine nose. A good attack on the palate is followed by an impression of perfect balance.

⊶ Patrice Taïx, 14, av. de la Gare, 34480 Magalas, tel. 04.67.36.37.95, fax 04.67.36.37.95 ▼ Y by appt.

DOM. LA CONDAMINE L'EVEQUE Viognier 1999★

□ 5 ha 15,000 ▮ ⸸ 20-29 F

This estate, once the summer residence of the Bishops of Agde, has made a bright, straw-yellow wine. Its strong, fresh, buttery nose has aromas of ripe berries. This is a very well-crafted wine that is ready for drinking now, perhaps with oysters.

⊶ SCEA Bascou, Dom. la Condamine l'Evêque, 34120 Nézignan-l'Evêque, tel. 04.67.98.27.61, fax 04.67.98.35.58 ▼ Y by appt.

DOM. DE L'ARJOLLE Méridienne 1999★

◪ 8 ha 20,000 ⦀ 50-69 F

Half Syrah and half Cabernet Franc, Méridienne (the name for an afternoon nap) is a wine to encourage idleness. Its amber-pink colour pleases the eye. The smoky, slightly oaked nose is potent. On the palate, the wine is balanced and long, with an agreeably vigorous character. A very unusual wine

that is definitely worth trying, either before or after your nap. It's up to you.
🗝 Dom. de l'Arjolle, 6, rue de la Côte, 34480 Pouzolles, tel. 04.67.24.81.18, fax 04.67.24.81.90 ☑ 𝐘 ev. day except Sun. 8am–12 noon 2pm–6pm
🗝 Teisserenc

DELPHINE DE MARGON

Chardonnay 1999★

□ 7 ha 60,000 30–49 F

In the summer, you can visit the château and taste this Chardonnay whilst there. It has a brilliant colour with emerald highlights. A concentrated and complex nose with aromas of sweet spices precedes a full, structured palate.
🗝 Delphine de Margon, GAEC de l'Arjolle, 34480 Pouzolles, tel. 04.67.24.81.18, fax 04.67.24.81.90 ☑ 𝐘 ev. day except Sun. 8am–12 noon 2pm–6pm

DOM. DES MONTARELS

Chardonnay Elevé en Fût de Chêne 1998★

□ 20 ha 15,000 30–49 F

This wine is the product of vines planted on marl soils of the Miocene era. A Chardonnay aged for 12 months in barrel, it is pale yellow with green highlights and has a gently oaky nose. The palate is forthright and sinewy, with subtle oak influence. The **Rouge 97 Elevé en Fût de Chêne** from the same estate is equally well-made.
🗝 Cave coop. d'Alignan-du-Vent, rue de La Guissaume, 34290 Alignan-du-Vent, tel. 04.67.24.91.31, fax 04.67.24.96.22 ☑ 𝐘 by appt.

LES VIGNERONS DE MONTBLANC

Chardonnay 1999★★

□ 26 ha 55,000 20–29 F

Albert Lebrun, one of the presidents of the Third Republic, inaugurated this cellar in 1939. It submitted several wines, one of which was this exceptional Chardonnay. It has a light, glittering colour with green highlights. The nose displays a fine, potent array of floral scents. White flower aromas are also present on the rounded and sinewy palate. The **Syrah 99 Rosé** was awarded one star.
🗝 Les Vignerons de Montblanc, av. d'Agde, 34290 Montblanc, tel. 04.67.98.50.26, fax 04.67.98.61.00 ☑

DOM. MONTROSE Salamandre 1999★

□ 3 ha 5,000 50–69 F

An erstwhile silk-farm, this property has just marked its 300th anniversary. In celebration, it has made this charming, bright gold wine. The oaky nose with its vanilla overtones leads on to a round and balanced palate with a hint of honey. White flower aromas emerge on the long finish. The **Les Lézards 98 Rouge** was also judged a very good wine.
🗝 Bernard Coste, Dom. Montrose, R.N. 9, 34120 Tourbes, tel. 04.67.98.63.33, fax 04.67.98.65.27 ☑ 𝐘 by appt.

DOM. DU PRIEURE D'AMILHAC

Cabernet-Sauvignon 1998★★

■ 38 ha 80,000 30–49 F

Limpid but very dark (almost black), this Cabernet has an intense, complex, oaky nose with hints of vanilla, spices and ripe red fruits. On the palate, it is fleshy and well-structured, with a long finish. An exceptionally well-balanced wine.
🗝 SCEA les Domaines Caton, Prieuré d'Amilhac, 34290 Servian, tel. 04.67.39.10.51, fax 04.67.39.15.33, e-mail max.cazottes@online.fr ☑ 𝐘 ev. day except Sun. 8am–12 noon 2pm–6pm

TARRAL Sauvignon 1999★

□ 70 ha 12,000 30–49 F

An appealing rich yellow colour with green highlights, this wine has a very fruity, slightly tropical aroma. The powerful palate shows good balance. A harmonious wine, it is ready for drinking now, perhaps with piperade. The **Chardonnay 99** is also very good.
🗝 UCA le Tarral, av. de Roujan, 34480 Pouzolles, tel. 04.67.98.67.24, fax 04.67.98.67.19 ☑ 𝐘 by appt.

Coteaux de Murviel

DOM. DE CIFFRE Val Taurou 1998★

■ 3 ha 14,000 50–69 F

This dark red wine, with its violet highlights, shimmers in the glass. Two-thirds of the cuvée has been matured in cask for 18 months, which is evident in the spice and vanilla scents and light oakiness of the powerful nose. On the palate, the wine is well-structured. It may be a little young yet, but its aroma and body show a great deal of potential. It should therefore be allowed to age for a while.
🗝 Lesineau, SARL Ch. Moulin de Ciffre, 34480 Autignac, tel. 04.67.90.11.45, fax 04.67.90.12.05, e-mail moulindeciffre@libertysurf.fr ☑ 𝐘 by appt.
🗝 Lesineau

Côtes de Thau

HUGUES DE BEAUVIGNAC

Syrah 1999★

◪ 25 ha 100,000 20–29 F

A flesh-pink pure Syrah, this wine is aromatic both on the nose (peardrops) and the palate. Fresh, round and flavourful, it has a long finish.

🔑 Cave les Costières de Pomerols, 34810 Pomerols, tel. 04.67.77.01.59, fax 04.67.77.77.21 ☑ 🍷 by appt.

Hérault

MAS DE DAUMAS-GASSAC

Haute Vallée de Gassac 1998★★

■	22 ha	109,000	🛢 150-199 F

Situated high up in the Gassac valley, this estate profits from a cool microclimate that is ideal for viticulture. A dozen varieties have been blended to make this wine, but the dominant one is Cabernet Sauvignon (80%). It has a very deep, dark colour enlivened by brilliant highlights. The intense, subtly oaky nose is powerful and complex, with an aroma of spices, undergrowth, leather and overripe fruit. The palate is very full-bodied and well-structured with fine tannins and good length. A very balanced wine. The **Daumas Gassac 99 Blanc** is also very good.

🔑 Véronique Guibert de la Vaissière, Mas de Daumas-Gassac, 34150 Aniane, tel. 04.67.57.71.28, fax 04.67.57.41.03, e-mail contact@daumas-gassac.com ☑ 🍷 ev. day except Sun. 10am–12.30pm 2pm–6.30pm; groups by appt.

DOM. DE MOULINES

Cabernet-Sauvignon 1999★

■	5 ha	40,000	🍾 🌡 20-29 F

The estate was purchased in 1914. In the space of three generations, it has grown from 28 to 55 ha (69 to 136 acres). A brilliant rich colour, the 1999 has a powerful and complex nose. Its well-structured palate is perfectly balanced, if a little youthful. It certainly has potential. The **Prestige** cuvée from the same producer was also cited.

🔑 Michel Saumade, GFA Mas de Moulines, 34130 Mudaison, tel. 04.67.70.20.48, fax 04.67.87.50.05 ☑ 🍷 by appt.

Catalan

MAS CHICHET Cabernet 1997★

■	14 ha	76,000	🛢 30-49 F

This wine's distinctiveness is immediately apparent from its mature colour – brick red with amber highlights. It is confirmed by an intense nose of leather, undergrowth and green pepper. On the palate, the wine is both delicate and balanced. It is ready to enjoy now.

🔑 Jacques Chichet, Mas Chichet, 66200 Elne, tel. 04.68.22.16.78, fax 04.68.22.70.28 ☑ 🍷 ev. day except Sun. 9am–12 noon 2pm–6pm

DOM. DU MAS ROUS

Cabernet-Sauvignon Elevé en Fût de Chêne 1997★

■	2.4 ha	14,000	🛢 30-49 F

During the current proprietor's great-grandfather's time, this estate was known as 'El Mas del Cos', or the blond man's domain. Now it is the domain of the redhead. This garnet-coloured Cabernet Sauvignon with brick-red highlights has a lightly oaked, complex nose with smoky, burnt overtones. Rounded and balanced, the palate is structured by silky tannins.

🔑 Joseph Pujol, Dom. du Mas Rous, 66740 Montesquieu-des-Albères, tel. 04.68.89.64.91, fax 04.68.89.80.88, e-mail joseph.pujol@.fr ☑ 🍷 by appt.

DOM. PAGES HURE

Muscat Sec 1999★

□	2 ha	12,000	🍾 🌡 20-29 F

This is an attractive white wine with straw-coloured highlights. It is intense in every respect. The nose is very musky, exotic and fresh, while the refreshing palate is both aromatic and balanced.

🔑 SCEA Pagès Huré, 2, allée des Moines, 66740 Saint-Génis-des-Fontaines , tel. 04.68.89.82.62, fax 04.68.89.82.62 ☑ 🍷 by appt.

Côtes Catalanes

DOM. CARLE-COURTY 1999★★

□	0.44 ha	900	🍾 20-29 F

Established in 1995, this small 10 ha (25-acre) property managed to survive the frosts of 1998 and the hailstorm of 1999. This year, it surprised the jury with this exceptional wine made from a blend of Grenache Blanc (50%) and Macabéo (50%) grapes grown on brown schist soils. It has a very light, pale colour, while the nose shows powerful, fresh and fruity aromas. Both lively and full-bodied, the palate is well-balanced. This extremely harmonious wine is perfect for serving with a platter of seafood.

🔑 Frédéric Carle, rte. Corneilla, 66170 Millas, tel. 04.68.57.21.79, fax 04.68.57.21.79 ☑ 🍷 ev. day 9.30am–7pm

DOM. PIQUEMAL

Cuvée Pierre Audonnet 1999★

■	5 ha	12,000	🍾 🌡 30-49 F

This vineyard covers 50 ha (124 acres) on the slopes of the Agly valley. A blend of

Merlot, Cabernet and Syrah has produced a beautiful garnet-coloured wine. The nose has a black fruit aroma (blackberry, blackcurrant) with burnt overtones. Sustained tannins and good length complete a well-crafted wine.

Pierre and Franck Piquemal, 1, rue Pierre-Lefranc, 66600 Espira-de-l'Agly, tel. 04.68.64.09.14, fax 04.68.38.52.94 ☒ Y by appt.

Aude

DOM. DE MARTINOLLES

Chardonnay 1999★

□ 12 ha 80,000 30–49 F

The estate is situated on hillsides where, in the 16th century, the monks of the abbey of Saint-Hilaire tended vines, and first produced Blanquette de Limoux (a traditional sparkling wine). The jury liked this pale, brilliant Chardonnay with its extremely fine floral nose. The lively and well-balanced palate, which has aromas of white flowers, also shows great finesse.

Vignobles Vergnes, Dom. de Martinolles, 11250 Saint-Hilaire, tel. 04.68.69.41.93, fax 04.68.69.45.97 ☒ Y ev. day except Sun. 8am–12 noon 2pm–7pm; groups by appt.

Cévennes

DOM. DE GOURNIER

Sauvignon les Vieilles Vignes 1998★★★

□ 1.5 ha 8,000 30–49 F

LES VIEILLES VIGNES
1998
DOMAINE DE GOURNIER
SAUVIGNON
VIN DE PAYS DES CEVENNES
Produit de france
Mis en bouteille au domaine
30190 SAINTE-ANASTASIE FRANCE
12,5% vol 750 ml

A wine like this is a special find. It comes from an estate in the heart of the Cévennes, halfway between Nîmes and Pont du Gard. A glorious golden colour, it glitters with green highlights. The intense, fine nose is redolent of white flowers and tropical fruit, with a touch of smoke. On the palate, it achieves perfect balance – the very definition of elegance. The **Cuvée Templière 98 Rouge** was also cited by the jury.

SCEA Barnouin, Dom. de Gournier, 30190 Boucoiran, tel. 04.66.81.20.28, fax 04.66.81.22.43 ☒ Y by appt.

Coteaux d'Ensérune

LES VIGNERONS DU PAYS D'ENSERUNE Chardonnay 1999★★

□ 20 ha 30,000 20–29 F

This remarkable bright, light-coloured Chardonnay has a fine, floral nose. Its well-balanced, full-bodied palate is aromatic and long. A harmonious wine, it may be enjoyed now.

Les vignerons du Pays d'Ensérune, 235, av. Jean-Jaurès, 34370 Maraussan, tel. 04.67.90.09.82, fax 04.67.90.09.55 ☒ Y by appt.

Cassan

DOM. SAINTE MARTHE

Syrah Elevé en Fût de Chêne 1999★★★

■ 3 ha 15,000 20–29 F

DOMAINE
de
SAINTE MARTHE
VIN DE PAYS DE CASSAN
SYRAH
12,5% vol. Mis en Bouteille à la Propriété 750 ml

Olivier Bonfils has made two excellent Syrah wines. This one, which was matured in oak, sets an extremely high standard. It has a beautiful deep violet colour. The lightly oaked nose blends ripe fruit aromas with burnt notes, while the palate is rich, fleshy and aromatic. Altogether, this is an exceptionally well-balanced wine. It ought to be aged for a while, though, as it would be a pity to drink such a wine before it reached its peak. The **Syrah 99**, which is unoaked, was awarded two stars.

Olivier Bonfils, Dom. de Sainte-Marthe, rte Pouzolles, 34380 Roujan, tel. 04.67.93.10.10, fax 04.67.93.10.05

Haute Vallée de l'Orb

DOM. DE LA CROIX RONDE

Cuvée Spéciale 1998★

■ 1.5 ha 6,000 30–49 F

Regularly praised for its wines, this estate has produced another success with this red cuvée with its brick-coloured highlights. It has a powerful, aromatic, floral nose with a touch of honey. The attractive palate is full-bodied and unctuous with a complex, persistent flavour of the garrigue. A balanced and harmonious wine.

François Pottier, Dom. de la Croix Ronde, 34260 La Tour-sur-Orb, tel. 04.67.95.35.05, fax 04.67.95.37.16 ✓
Y ev. day except Sun. 10am–12 noon 3pm–7pm

Provence, Basse Vallée du Rhône, Corse Provence

The bulk of the wines produced by this vast zone are red; they constitute 70% of the 700,000 hl (18,480,000 gal) yield of the Provence-Alpes-Côte d'Azur administrative region. The rosés (25%) are mostly made in Var, and the whites are the product of Vaucluse and the area north of the Bouches-du-Rhône. Although a wide range of southern grape varieties is grown here, they are rarely made into varietal wines. Depending on soil and climate conditions, they are blended either with unusual, old-fashioned, local varieties such as the Counoise and Roussanne of Var, or with varieties associated with other wine-growing regions such as the Cabernet Sauvignon and Merlot of Bordeaux, to which are added the Syrah grape of the Rhône valley. The following designations are based on the *départements*: Vaucluse, Bouches-du-Rhône, Var, Alpes-de-Haute-Provence, Alpes-Maritimes and Hautes-Alpes. Principauté d'Orange, Petite Crau (south-east of Avignon), Mont Caumes (west of Toulon), Argens (between Brignoles and Draguignan, in Var), Maures, Coteaux du Verdon (Var), Ile de Beauté (Corsica), and the recently recognised Aigues (Vaucluse), are sub-regional or local designations.

Ile de Beauté

A CANTINA 1999

□ 2 ha 2,000 20–29 F

Alain Courrèges has made a wine that is atypical of this region. It has a marked, intense Muscat aroma on both the nose and palate. The wine's richness is balanced by an appropriate degree of acidity.

Alain Courrèges, A Cantina, 20123 Cognocoli, tel. 04.95.24.35.54, fax 04.95.24.38.07 Y by appt.

LES POLYPHONIES DE CEPAGES

Merlot 1999★★

■ n.c. 400,000 20 F+

The 1999 Merlot stands out from the selection of wines made by this co-operative. A very attractive ruby colour, it has a spicy aroma with hints of musk. The palate is velvety, and structured by fine, rounded tannins. It could be drunk now, but will be at its best in a year's time. The **Chardonnay 99** in the same range was also cited.

Union de Vignerons de l'Ile de Beauté, Cave coop. d'Aléria, 20270 Aléria, tel. 04.95.57.02.48, fax 04.95.57.09.59 ✓
Y by appt.

DOM. DE LISCHETTO

Chardonnay 1999★★

□ 60 ha 140,000 20–29 F

This pale Chardonnay has a very aromatic citrus nose. The palate, which is also fruity,

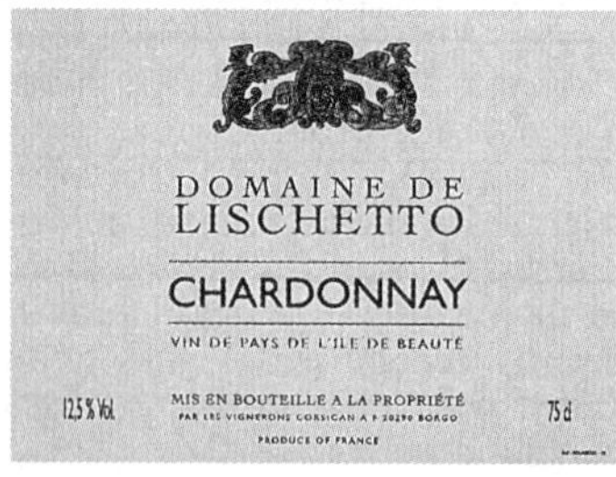

displays an additional flavour of linden flowers. Balanced and rich, it is a wine with fine length. The well-structured **Chardonnay 99 Domaine de Saline**, with its aroma of white flowers and acacia, was awarded one star.
Cave coop. de la Marana, Rasignani, 20290 Borgo, tel. 04.95.58.44.00, fax 04.95.38.38.10

MONTE MARE 1999★

n.c. n.c. 20 F+

This is a pale orangey rosé for the lazy days of an Indian summer. Attractively fruity, it has a well-balanced palate and good length. The equally balanced **Gaspa Mora 99 Rosé**, which is more aromatic on the palate than it is on the nose, was also cited.
Cave de Saint-Antoine, 20240 Ghisonaccia, tel. 04.95.56.61.00, fax 04.95.56.61.60 by appt.

DOM. DU MONT SAINT-JEAN

Aleatico 1999★

7 ha 30,000 20–29 F

This wine provides an opportunity to sample a grape variety rare on Corsica: Aleatico. Cherry-red in colour, it has a flowery, fruity nose and a balanced palate with a very unusual flavour. This is a curiosity that you will either love or hate. It would be the ideal accompaniment to Corsican charcuterie. The **Chardonnay 99** from the same estate was also cited by the jury.
SCA Dom. Mont Saint-Jean, Campo Quercio, 20270 Aléria, tel. 04.95.38.59.96, fax 04.95.38.50.29, e-mail roger.pouyau@wanadoo.fr
Roger Pouyau

DOM. DE PETRAPIANA

Merlot 1998★★

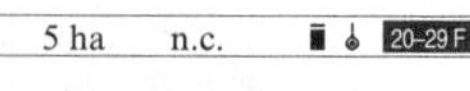
5 ha n.c. 20–29 F

This wine is remarkable in every respect. A beguiling garnet colour, it has a forthcoming, complex nose of red berries with musky, balsamic overtones. The palate is concentrated and well-structured, with powerful tannins that should be allowed to develop and soften.
Poli, Linguizzetta, 20230 San Nicolao, tel. 04.95.38.86.38, fax 04.95.38.94.71
by appt.

TERRA VECCHIA 1999★★

70 ha n.c. 20 F+

A pretty rosé with a fine, delicate, floral and fruity nose, this very elegant wine has an alluring and balanced palate. It is for drinking now. The **Terra Vecchia 99 Rouge**, a blend of Cabernet Sauvignon and Nielluccio, is also notably fruity and balanced with a structured, full-bodied palate (50–69F). The **Terra Vecchia de Vermentino 99** (20–29F) was also cited.
SICA Coteaux de Diana, Les Vins Skalli, Dom. Terra Vecchia, 20270 Tallone, tel. 04.95.57.20.30, fax 04.95.57.08.98 ev. day except Sat. Sun. 9am–1pm 2pm–6pm

Principauté d'Orange

DOM. FOND CROZE Merlot 1999

2 ha 1,200 20–29 F

At present, this wine is a little rough-edged and tannic. However, the jury felt that it had the potential to develop well if laid down for one to two years, and would certainly prove to be worth the wait. Such a powerful wine should only really be served with red meat – perhaps a Provençal daube.
Dom. Fond Croze, Le Village, 84290 Saint-Roman-de-Malegarde, tel. 04.90.28.94.30, fax 04.90.28.94.30, e-mail a-long@cub-internet.fr
by appt.
Daniel and Bruno Long

DOM. DE FONTAVIN 1999

■ n.c. 3,000 20–29 F

This is the Domaine's first bottling of a Grenache-Carignan blend. It is a well-balanced and harmonious wine. The nose is slightly spicy, showing the influence of its 70% Grenache. A very attractive wine that is ready to serve now with grilled meats.

EARL Hélène et Michel Chouvet, Dom. de Fontavin, 1468, rte. de la Plaine, 84350 Courthézon, tel. 04.90.70.72.14, fax 04.90.70.79.39 ev. day except Sun. 9am–12.30pm 1.30pm–7pm

DOM. DE LA BERTHETE 1999

■ 3 ha 25,000 20 F+

Made from a blend of three Mediterranean varieties (Grenache, Cinsault and Syrah), the Domaine de la Berthète is an archetypal vin de pays – pleasant and congenial. It is light, fruity and highly quaffable. Enjoy it with friends around a barbecue or with a platter of charcuterie.

Pascal Maillet, Dom. de la Berthète, rte. de Jonquières, 84850 Camaret, tel. 04.90.37.22.41, fax 04.90.37.74.55 ev. day except Sat. Sun. 10am–12 noon 2pm–6pm; cl. Aug.

DOM. DE LA JANASSE 1998*

■ 5 ha 40,000 50–69 F

This wine has personality. The nose, which is still a little closed, has a meaty aroma suggestive of venison. It is rich and warm on the palate with well-bred tannins. A fine vin de pays, while not at all in the usual easy-drinking style, it should be served with grilled or casseroled meats or with cheese.

EARL Aimé Sabon, 27, chem. du Moulin, 84350 Courthézon, tel. 04.90.70.86.29, fax 04.90.70.75.93 ev. day 8am–12 noon 2pm–7pm; Sat. Sun. by appt.

Mont-Caume

DOM. DU PEY-NEUF 1999*

□ 1 ha n.c. 20–29 F

The tasters were captivated by this wine's intensely aromatic character. Harmonious and balanced, it would have been even more distinguished had it possessed a longer finish.

Guy Arnaud, Dom. du Pey-Neuf, 367, rte. de Sainte-Anne, 83740 La Cadière-d'Azur, tel. 04.94.90.14.55, fax 04.94.26.13.89 by appt.

Maures

DOM. DE REILLANNE

Plan Genet 1999*

◪ 7 ha 60,000 20 F+

This Vin de Pays des Maures is a bright, clear salmon-pink colour. On the nose, it has a fine, delicate citrus aroma. The initial impression of freshness gives way to a balanced, nicely rounded palate, and a lengthy finish completes its appeal. It would complement all Provençal cooking.

Comte G. de Chevron-Villette, Ch. Reillanne, rte. de Saint-Tropez, 83340 Le Cannet-des-Maures, tel. 04.94.50.11.70, fax 04.94.47.92.06 ev. day except Sat. Sun. 8am–12 noon 2pm–5pm

Argens

DOM. LUDOVIC DE BEAUSEJOUR 1999

◪ 2.7 ha 26,000 20–29 F

Try this richly hued salmon-pink rosé with its subtle aroma of toasted brioche. It is the perfect wine for serving with crudités or charcuterie.

Dom. Ludovic de Beauséjour, La Basse Maure, rte. de Salernes, 83510 Lorgues, tel. 04.94.50.91.91, fax 04.94.68.46.53 by appt.

Maunier

Vaucluse

CANORGUE Viognier 1999**

□ 2 ha 9,000 50–69 F

This superb Viognier is worthy of its attractive and distinctive label. Straw-yellow in colour, it has a potent floral (violet) and fruity (apricot) nose. The rich and very full-bodied palate has a good, long finish. A wine like this will make a stunning companion to sweet-and-sour dishes.

EARL J.-P. et M. Margan, Ch. la Canorgue, 84480 Bonnieux, tel. 04.90.75.81.01, fax 04.90.75.82.98 by appt.

DOM. DE COMBEBELLE 1999**

◪ 4 ha 2,500 20–29 F

A 'classic' blend of equal parts Grenache and Cinsault, this wine has clearly been

crafted by an expert. The very powerful nose has a red berry (strawberry) aroma. The palate, which is round and full-bodied, has a persistent flavour of strawberries and raspberries. Well-balanced and long, this is a rosé to serve with lamb cutlets – in the Provençal style, of course.
🔑 Eric Sauvan,
Dom. de Combebelle, 26110 Piegon,
tel. 04.75.27.18.96, fax 04.75.27.15.62 ☑
Y ev. day 9am–12.15 2pm–7pm

DOM. DURIEU 1998

■ 10.74 ha n.c. 20-29 F

Two Bordeaux varieties, Merlot and Cabernet, grown in the land of Châteauneuf-du-Pape, have produced this supple, balanced vin de pays, which has aromas of undergrowth and a hint of liquorice. As it is unlikely to improve with keeping, it should be served now with charcuterie or grilled meat.
🔑 Paul Durieu, 10, av. Baron-le-Roy, 84230 Châteauneuf-du-Pape, tel. 04.90.37.28.14, fax 04.90.37.76.05 ☑ Y by appt.

JOANIS Chardonnay et Ugni Blanc 1999

□ 10 ha 50,000 30-49 F

This two-way blend is very light in colour and has an attractive floral nose. After a positive attack, it is rounded and fleshy on the palate. Persistent aromas of peach linger on through a fairly warm finish. The wine would complement fish or shellfish.
🔑 SC du Ch. Val Joanis,
Ch. Val Joanis, 84120 Pertuis,
tel. 04.90.79.20.77, fax 04.90.09.69.52,
e-mail val-joanis@luberon.com ☑
Y ev. day 10am–12 noon 2pm–6pm

DOM. DE LA BASTIDONNE

Chardonnay 1999*

□ 1.12 ha 2,500 🍷🌡 30-49 F

The style of this Chardonnay charmed the jury. Its elegant nose is a blend of citrus, dried fruit and amber aromas. Unusually in Vaucluse, this Burgundy variety has managed to retain its liveliness. Fine balance and persistent flavours characterise the palate.
🔑 SCEA Dom. de la Bastidonne,
84220 Cabrières-d'Avignon,
tel. 04.90.76.70.00, fax 04.90.76.74.34 ☑
Y ev. day except Sun. 9am–12 noon
2pm–6pm
🔑 Gérard Marreau

DOM. DE LA CITADELLE

Viognier 1999**

□ 1.4 ha 7,300 🍷🌡 50-69 F

This is an exceptionally well-made wine. A typical Viognier, it has a very inviting nose of apricots and citrus. On the palate, it is full, rich and fruity with fine length. Try it with grilled prawns.
🔑 Dom. de la Citadelle, 84560 Ménerbes,
tel. 04.90.72.41.58, fax 04.90.72.41.59,
e-mail citadelle@pacwar.fr ☑ Y by appt.

DOM. LA TUILIERE

Réserve du Chasseur 1998**

■ 3 ha 16,000 🍷 20-29 F

This is an arrestingly dark, richly coloured wine with violet highlights. The scents of liquorice and the garrigue, as well as the balanced, concentrated palate, confirm the promise suggested by its appearance. Rich and velvety, it has pleasantly chewy tannins. The intensity of the wine is the result of well-ripened grapes. It is ready to drink now, but would keep for up to five years.
🔑 Dom. la Tuilière, rte. D.60, 84220 Murs,
tel. 04.90.05.73.03, fax 04.90.05.78.07,
e-mail domaine@la-tuiliere.com ☑
Y ev. day except Sun. 9am–12 noon
2pm–8pm

DOM. DE LA VERRIERE

Viognier Elevé en Fût de Chêne 1999

□ 0.5 ha 3,300 🛢 30-49 F

Yet again, the Domaine de la Verrière has produced a fine wine. This Viognier is lively and full-bodied, but its strong woodiness, with vanilla overtones, needs to modulate so that the varietal character can emerge. Your patience will be rewarded.
🔑 Jacques Maubert,
Dom. de la Verrière, 84220 Goult,
tel. 04.90.72.20.88, fax 04.90.72.40.33 ☑
Y ev. day except Sun. 9am–12 noon
2pm–6pm

DOM. LES TERRASSES D'EOLE

Viognier 1999*

□ 1 ha 6,600 30-49 F

The nose on this Viognier is subtle rather than intense. On the palate, it is appealingly rich and rounded. Its flavours linger on to a forthright, lengthy finish. It may be served as an apéritif or with white meat dishes.
🔑 Dom. les Terrasses d'Eole,
468, chem. de Banay, 84380 Mazan,
tel. 04.90.69.78.63, fax 04.90.69.78.63,
e-mail terrasses.eole@online.fr ☑
Y ev. day 9am–12 noon 2pm–6pm;
cl. 1 Sep.–15 Oct.

DOM. DE MAROTTE 1999

□ 5 ha 35,000 🍷🌡 30-49 F

This pretty, light-gold wine has a complex nose with a dominant note of citrus. The palate is lively and quite aromatic (citrus again). It could be drunk as an apéritif or with grilled fish.
🔑 EARL La Reynarde, Dom. de Marotte,
petit chem. de Serres, 84200 Carpentras,
tel. 04.90.63.43.27, fax 04.90.67.15.28,
e-mail marotte@wanadoo.fr ☑
Y ev. day except Mon. 10am–1pm
3pm–7pm; cl. Jan. Feb.

MAS GRANGE BLANCHE 1999

■ 5 ha 25,000 🍷🌡 20-29 F

This vin de pays has been made from the Provençal trio of Grenache, Cinsault and Syrah. Its vanilla-scented nose and balanced character are appealing in a restrained but appreciable way.

EARL Cyril et Jacques Mousset, Ch. des Fines Roches, 84230 Châteauneuf-du-Pape, tel. 04.90.83.73.10, fax 04.90.83.50.78, e-mail domaines-mousset@enprovence.com
ev. day 10am–6pm; cl. Jan. Feb.

DOM. MEILLAN-PAGES

Sauvignon 1999★★★

1.57 ha 6,000 20-29 F

This is a superb Sauvignon. Very aromatic, it is redolent of elderflowers, citrus and white-fleshed fruits. The perfectly balanced palate is also fruity, echoing the original aromas. It would be an ideal accompaniment to fish or shellfish.

Jean-Pierre Pagès, Quartier la Garrigue, 84580 Oppède, tel. 04.90.76.94.78, fax 04.90.76.94.78
ev. day 10am–12 noon 1.30pm–8pm

LES VIGNERONS DU MONT-VENTOUX Merlot 1998★

1.9 ha 20,000 20-29 F

The jury was impressed by the strong varietal character of this Merlot. It has both elegance and finesse. Devotees of that grape will appreciate its full-bodied palate with fine, silky, perfectly ripe tannins. A wine to serve with grilled red meat.

SCA les Vignerons du Mont Ventoux, quartier de la Salle, 84410 Bédoin, tel. 04.90.12.88.00, fax 04.90.65.64.43
by appt.

JEAN-PIERRE SERGUIER

Numéro 01★

3 ha 20,000 50-69 F

The Numéro 01 is a successful wine-making experiment. The producer blended several varieties from three harvests (1996, 1998 and 1999) in a search for greater complexity. The result is this fine, expressive and well-structured wine, which would go well with roast rib of beef.

Jean-Pierre Serguier, Ch. Simian, 84420 Piolenc, tel. 04.90.29.50.67, fax 04.90.29.62.33
ev. day except Sun. 8.30am–12 noon 2pm–7pm

DOM. DU VIEUX CHENE

Cuvée d'Or 1999★

1 ha n.c. 30-49 F

This daffodil-yellow, green-highlighted Cuvée d'Or has distinct aromatic complexity. On the palate, it is full-bodied and lively. A delicate note of vanilla, derived from oak-ageing, does not obscure the thyme and lime flavours, and the wine ends on a good long finish.

Jean-Claude and Béatrice Bouche, rte. de Vaison-la-Romaine, 84850 Camaret-sur-Aigues, tel. 04.90.37.25.07, fax 04.90.37.76.84, e-mail contact@bouche-duvieuxchene.com
ev. day except Sun. 9am–12 noon 2pm–6pm

Bouches-du-Rhône

DOM. DES GAVELLES 1999

0.95 ha 10,000 20-29 F

Grenache, the dominant variety (80%) in this blend, gives the wine a subtly spicy nose and good roundness on the palate. An attractively supple, well-made wine with a satisfying finish.

Ch. des Gavelles, 165, chem. de Maliverny, 13540 Puyricard, tel. 04.42.92.06.83, fax 04.42.92.24.12, e-mail mail@chateaudesgavelles.com
ev. day 9.30am–12.30pm 3pm–7pm
J. et B. de Roany

DOM. GRAND MAS DE LANSAC 1999★

5 ha 8,000 20 F+

The Montagnier brothers used two Bordeaux grapes, Merlot and Cabernet Sauvignon, to make this richly coloured salmon-pink rosé. A very floral, hawthorn-like nose precedes a seductively round and aromatic palate with floral, honey and acacia notes.

Jean and Michel Montagnier, Dom. du Grand Mas de Lansac, 13150 Tarascon, tel. 04.90.91.35.70, fax 04.90.91.41.18
ev. day except Sun. Mon. 9am–12 noon 2pm–6pm

DOM. LA COSTE Merlot 1999

6 ha 30,000 20-29 F

The nose on this Merlot is still a little closed, and the varietal character is not therefore very obvious. However, the jury's attention was caught by its supple, rounded and balanced style. It is attactively packaged with an unusual label and bottle.

GFA du Ch. la Coste, CD 14, 13610 Le Puy-Sainte-Réparade, tel. 04.42.61.89.98, fax 04.42.61.89.41 by appt.

DOM. DE LANSAC Aubun 1999

◪ 4 ha 2,500 ▮ 20–29 F

Made from an old Provençal variety, Aubun, this dark pink rosé has a subtle aroma of peardrops. On the palate, it is agreeably refreshing and lively. A hint of cherries on the finish completes this likeable wine.

🔑 Eléonore de Sabran-Pontevès, Dom. de Lansac, 13150 Tarascon, tel. 04.90.91.38.38, fax 04.90.91.38.38 ☑

DOM. DE L'ILE SAINT PIERRE Chardonnay 1999★

□ 30 ha 100,000 ▮ 🌡 20–29 F

This is a very enjoyable Chardonnay. It has a pretty colour with green highlights, and a fine, floral nose. On the palate, its refreshing attack is followed by sustained flavours of hazelnuts with a hint of butter. A distinctive and elegant wine.

🔑 Marie-Cécile and Patrick Henry, Dom. de Boisviel-Saint-Pierre, Mas Thibert, 13104 Arles, tel. 04.90.98.70.30, fax 04.90.98.74.93 ☑ 🍷 by appt.

MAS DE REY Caladoc 1999★

◪ 10 ha 20,000 ▮ ⦀ 🌡 30–49 F

Patrick Mazzoleni is particularly interested in crossed Mediterranean grape varieties such as Caladoc, Chasan and Marselan. Among the 1999 vintages, it's the Caladoc (a Grenache Noir-Cot crossing) rosé that appears to have been the most successful. Salmon-pink in colour, it has a reasonably intense nose of redcurrants. The palate is fresh and round, with long-lasting flavours of redcurrant and pomegranate.

🔑 Mazzoleni, SCA Mas de Rey, Trinquetaille, 13200 Arles, tel. 04.90.96.11.84, fax 04.90.96.59.44, e-mail mas.de.rey@provnet.fr ☑
🍷 ev. day 9am–12 noon 2pm–7pm; cl. Sun. Nov.–Mar.

LES VIGNERONS DU ROY RENE Cabernet-Sauvignon 1999★

■ 20 ha 40,000 ▮ 🌡 20 F+

The jury commented that the grapes in this Cabernet had obviously been harvested and vinified at optimum ripeness. The wine's purple colour, potent nose (which doesn't have the usual green pepper aromas), and jammy blackberry and bilberry flavours are all extremely attractive. It would be the perfect accompaniment for a Provençal daube.

🔑 Les Vignerons du Roy René, R.N. 7, 13410 Lambesc, tel. 04.42.57.00.20, fax 04.42.92.91.52 ☑
🍷 ev. day except Sun. 8am–12 noon 2pm–6pm

DOM. DE VALDITION Tête de Cuvée 1999★

□ 4 ha 7,000 ▮ 20–29 F

This is a very attractive wine that is particularly well-balanced. Its acid freshness on the palate is counteracted by ample fullness, and the finish is quite long. As for the nose, it has an aroma of white-fleshed fruit such as peaches.

🔑 Hubert Somm, GFA du Dom. de Valdition, rte. d'Eygalières, 13660 Orgon, tel. 04.90.73.08.12, fax 04.90.73.05.95, e-mail valdition@wanadoo.fr ☑

Var

LE MAS DES ESCARAVATIERS 1999★★

□ 2.51 ha 15,000 ▮ 🌡 20 F+

Must we lose ourselves in adjectives? Let your emotions take over . . . balance, finesse, harmony: this wine will certainly beguile. It would be an obvious partner for seafood, but could also be served as an apéritif.

🔑 SCEA Domaines B.-M. Costamagna, Dom. des Escaravatiers, 83480 Puget-sur-Argens, tel. 04.94.19.88.22, fax 04.94.45.55.83, e-mail escaravatiers@caves-particulieres.com ☑
🍷 by appt.

DOM. DE GASQUI 1999★

■ 5 ha 40,000 ▮ 🌡 20 F+

The jury was charmed by the 'nouveau' style of this wine, evident in the red berry aromas that came through as it was savoured. The nose is floral, and the palate supple and long. It is a well-made wine that you could pick up on the way to visiting the Village des Tortues, a centre for the study of tortoises in Gonfaron.

🔑 SCEA Ch. Gasqui, rte. de Flassans, 83590 Gonfaron, tel. 04.94.78.23.14, fax 04.94.78.27.16 ☑
🍷 ev. day 9am–6pm

DOM. DE TRIENNES Réserve 1996

■ 5 ha 25,000 ▮ ⦀ 50–69 F

This wine, made from 75% Cabernet Sauvignon, has a slightly faded red colour. The nose shows predominantly leathery, animal scents, while the palate has flavours of overripe preserved fruits. It is just a little austere on the finish.

🔑 Dom. de Triennes, R.N. 560, 83860 Nans-les-Pins, tel. 04.94.78.91.46, fax 04.94.78.65.04 ☑ 🍷 by appt.

Hautes-Alpes

LA VALSERROISE Chardonnay 1999

□ 12 ha 80,000 ▮ 🌡 20–29 F

This is a perfectly charming wine to drink as an apéritif with friends, or to serve with seafood. Pretty green highlights, a pronounced floral nose, and a palate with a fine edge of acidity: only a slight lack of length lets it down.

⊶ Cave coop. la Valserroise,
05130 Valserres,
tel. 04.22.54.33.02, fax 04.92.54.31.34 ☒
Y ev. day 8am–12 noon 2pm–6pm

Alpes-Maritimes

GEORGES ET DENIS RASSE

Cuvée Longo Maï Elevé en Fût de Chêne 1997★★

■ 1 ha 2,500 50–69 F

Cuvée Longo Maï is a pleasure from start to finish. Both the nose and palate are marked by the subtle aroma of macerated prunes. A well-judged period of oak-ageing is in complete harmony with the wine's other elements on the palate, and it has good length. This wine could be enjoyed right away, or cellared for a while since it may well improve.

⊶ Georges and Denis Rasse,
Hautes Collines, 800, chem. des Sausses,
06640 Saint-Jeannet,
tel. 04.93.24.96.01, fax 04.93.24.96.01 ☒
Y by appt.

Alpes et Pays Rhodaniens

Stretching from the Auvergne to the Alps, this region includes the eight *départements* of the Rhône-Alpes and the Puy-de-Dôme. The terroirs are therefore particularly varied, resulting in a diverse range of regional wines. Burgundy grapes (Pinot, Gamay, Chardonnay) and southern varieties (Grenache, Cinsault, Clairette) are all present. Then there are the regional grapes – Syrah, Roussanne, Marsanne in the Rhône valley , Mondeuse, Jacquère and Chasselas in Savoie, as well as Etraire de la Dui and Verdesse, curiosities from the Val d'Isère. Bordeaux varieties (Merlot, Cabernet Sauvignon) have also been planted, further extending the vinous range.

Production levels are increasing, approaching 450,000 hl (11,880,000 gal), with Ardèche and Drôme making the majority of the red wines. Generally, each wine is made from just one variety. Ain, Ardèche, Drôme, Isère and Puy-de-Dôme are *département* designations. The eight regional designations are: Allobrogie (Savoie and Ain, 7,000 hl/184,800 gal of mostly white wines), Coteaux du Grésivaudan (central Isère, 2,000 hl/52,800 gal), Balmes Dauphinoises (Isère, 1,000 hl/26,400 gal), Urfé (Loire Valley between Forez and Roannais, 2,000 hl/52,800 gal), Collines Rhodaniennes (10,000 hl/264,000 gal, mostly reds), Comté de Grignan (south-west of Drôme, 25,000 hl/660,000 gal, primarily reds), Coteaux des Baronnies (south-east of Drôme, 35,000 hl/924,000 gal of reds) and Coteaux de l 'Ardèche (320,000 hl/8,448,000 gal of reds, whites and rosés).

In addition, there are two vins de pays designations that cover large zones. The first, Vin de Pays des Comtés Rhodaniens (approximately 25,000 hl/660,000 gal), was established in 1989. It consists of the eight Rhône-Alpes *départements* (Ain, Ardèche, Drôme, Isère, Loire, Rhône, Savoie and Haute-Savoie). The second, Vin de Pays des Portes de Méditerranée, established in 1999, covers seven *départements* (Alpes-de-Haute-Provence, Hautes-Alpes,

Alpes-Maritimes, Ardèche, Drôme, Var and Vaucluse).

Allobrogie

LE CELLIER DE JOUDIN
Chardonnay 1999

□ 1.2 ha 10,000 ▮ ♁ 20–29 F

This viticultural islet at the gateway to the Alps has well-exposed marl soils. Pierre Demeure and his son-in-law combine œnological techniques and vine-growing expertise to achieve the best results. The varietal characteristics of Chardonnay are impressively evident in this fragrant and well-balanced 99.

🔑 Demeure, GAEC le Cellier de Joudin,
73240 Saint-Genix-sur-Guiers,
tel. 04.76.31.61.74, fax 04.76.31.61.74 ☑
Y by appt.

Isère

CAVE DES VIGNERONS RHODANIENS Merlot 1999*

■ 2 ha 5,000 ▮ ♁ 20–29 F

This cellar, established in 1929, restructured its vineyards in the 1960s. It makes vins de pays from vineyards on the pebbly slopes of the left bank of the Rhône. The Merlot 99 has an aroma of liquorice and ripe fruits and a long, velvety palate. It is also worth trying the **Syrah 99**, a **Vin de Pays des Collines Rhodaniennes** that displays all that variety's merits.

🔑 Cave des Vignerons Rhodaniens,
35, rue du Port-Vieux,
38550 Le Péage-de-Roussillon,
tel. 04.74.86.57.87, fax 04.74.86.57.95 ☑
Y ev. day except Sun. Mon. 8am–12 noon 2pm–6pm

Balmes Dauphinoises

DOM. MEUNIER Chardonnay 1998

□ 1.8 ha 17,000 ▮ ♁ 20–29 F

Gilbert Meunier established his vineyard in the northern Isère in 1967. Since then, he has been an outstanding viticultural practitioner. His 1998 Chardonnay is an unusual wine with an aroma of dried fruits. It is ready for drinking now.

🔑 SCEA Dom. Meunier,
38510 Sermerieu, tel. 04.74.80.15.81 ☑
Y by appt.

Coteaux du Grésivaudan

DOM. MAGNE Jacquère 1999**

□ 0.6 ha 5,333 ▮ ♁ 20–29 F

The Coteaux du Gresivaudin is a little-known designation that includes several exciting wines, such as this Jacquère. A lightly sparkling wine with unusual aromas, it is made from an unmistakably Savoyard variety. It may be enjoyed as an apéritif, but would also complement charcuterie such as *jambon cru* or mortadella.

🔑 Michel Magne, Saint-André,
38530 Chapareillan,
tel. 04.79.28.07.91, fax 04.79.28.17.96 ☑
Y by appt.

Coteaux des Baronnies

DOM. LA ROSIERE Viognier 1998**

□ 3 ha 10,000 ▮ ◫ ♁ 30–49 F

For the past 20 years, Serge Liotaud and his son (who has been a partner since 1966) have been reliable producers of wines with character. Their Viognier 98 is a good example. A complex and fine nose of dried apricots and citrus leads seamlessly to a perfectly balanced palate. Fleshy, rounded and distinctly fresh, this wine is definitely one to try. The well-structured **Cabernet Sauvignon 99** was also cited (20–29F).

EARL Serge Liotaud et Fils,
Dom. La Rosière, 26110 Sainte-Jalle,
tel. 04.75.27.30.36, fax 04.75.27.33.69
ev. day 8am–7pm

DOM. DU RIEU FRAIS

Cabernet-Sauvignon Cuvée Alexandre 1997★★

■ 5 ha 18,000 30–49 F

This vineyard, family-owned since 1983, has the perfect conditions for Cabernet Sauvignon to flourish. After 12 months in oak, the Cuvée Alexandre 97, with its liquorice, tobacco, spice and prune nose, has reached its apogee. Enjoy it with game or one of the local cheeses.

Jean-Yves Liotaud,
Dom. du Rieu Frais, 26110 Sainte-Jalle,
tel. 04.75.27.31.54, fax 04.75.27.34.47,
e-mail jean-yves.liotaud@wanadoo.fr
ev. day 8am–12 noon 2pm–7pm

Collines Rhodaniennes

LES EGREVES 1999

■ 4 ha 27,000 20–29 F

A fine blend of mostly Syrah (90%) with a bit of Merlot, this wine has a peony and violet aroma. It would make an enjoyable accompaniment for *caillette de Chabreuil*, the local pork-and-vegetable sausage.

Dom. Pochon, Ch. de Curson,
26600 Chanos-Curson, tel. 04.75.07.34.60,
fax 04.75.07.30.27 by appt.

Coteaux de l'Ardèche

CAVE COOP. D'ALBA

Syrah Cuvée Prestige 1999★★

■ 20 ha 55,000 30–49 F

The Cave d'Alba, which vinifies 610 ha (1,500 acres) of grapes, was recently recognised for its consistent wine-making excellence. It has produced a sumptuous Syrah. Garnet-hued, with powerful spicy and fruity aromas, the wine is full-bodied and well-balanced. In short, it is captivating. The jury also cited a **Pinot 99 Elevé en Fût de Chêne**.

Cave coop. d'Alba, La Planchette,
07400 Alba-la-Romaine,
tel. 04.75.52.40.23, fax 04.75.52.48.76
ev. day except Sun. 9am–12 noon
1.30pm–6pm

LES VIGNERONS ARDECHOIS

Cuvée Privée 1998★★

■ n.c. 30,000 20–29 F

Les Vignerons Ardéchois is the collective name for 25 wine co-operatives in the southern Ardèche region. For 30 years, they have worked together to improve the quality of their wines. An expertly managed blend of several varieties, this Cuvée Privée will appeal to fans of mature, lightly oaked wines. The **Syrah Prestige 98** and the **Chardonnay Prestige 99** were also cited. The **Syrah 99 Rosé** (under 20F) was deemed worthy of a star for its violet colour and flavours of red berries.

Les Vignerons Ardéchois,
B.P. 8, 07120 Ruoms,
tel. 04.75.39.98.00, fax 04.75.39.69.48,
e-mail uvica@uvica.fr
ev. day except Sun. 8am–12 noon
2pm–7pm

DOM. DE BOURNET

Cabernet-sauvignon Elevé en Fût de Chêne 1997★

■ 2.5 ha 8,200 30–49 F

This estate, which has been in the same family for several centuries, has produced a Cabernet Sauvignon that is powerful, elegant and aromatic, with scents of tobacco, smoke and spice. It will go well with game.

Dom. de Bournet,
07120 Grospierres,
tel. 04.75.39.68.20, fax 04.75.39.06.96,
e-mail domaine.debournet@advalvas.be
ev. day 9am–12 noon 2pm–7pm

DOM. DE CHAZALIS

Cuvée Richard Merlot 1999

■ 4.5 ha 45,000 30–49 F

This wine, an oak-aged Merlot, has all the hallmarks of this variety: a complex aroma, good structure and strong tannins. It is ready to beguile your tastebuds now.

Champetier, Dom. de Chazalis,
07460 Beaulieu, tel. 04.75.39.32.09,
fax 04.75.39.38.81 by appt.

DOM. DE COMBELONGE Merlot 1999★

■ 1.74 ha 13,500 20 F+

This estate, situated at the foot of the picturesque village of Vinezac, is a producer of consistently good wines. Its richly coloured Merlot, made from manually harvested

grapes, has a round, soft and supple palate and a long finish.
⊶ Denis Manent, SCEA Dom. de Combelonge, 07110 Vinezac, tel. 04.75.36.92.54, fax 04.75.36.99.59 ☑
Ῑ ev. day except Sun. 9am–12 noon 2.30pm–6.30pm

LOUIS LATOUR

Grand Ardèche Chardonnay 1998★★

☐ 40 ha 150,000 ⦀ 50-69 F

The *négociant* house of Louis Latour was founded in Beaune, Burgundy, in 1797. It began making wines in the Ardèche in 1979, and they have been consistently successful. The richly hued Chardonnay 98 has golden highlights, and a powerful vanilla and mineral nose. On the palate, it is balanced and full-bodied, and has some of the class of a far grander wine.
⊶ Maison Louis Latour, La Téoule, R.N. 102, 07400 Alba-la-Romaine, tel. 04.75.52.45.66, fax 04.75.52.49.19 ☑
Ῑ by appt.

CUVEE TERRE DE GRES

Viognier 1999★

☐ 20 ha 10,000 ▮ 🌡 30-49 F

This Viognier, the product of the sandstone soils of the Cévennes, is a very accomplished wine. It has an extremely complex aromatic bouquet of peaches, dried apricots, tropical fruits and honey, and should be served with either an hors d'oeuvre or a dessert. The **Chatus Cuvée Monnaie d'Or**, made from an old traditional variety, is also worth trying.
⊶ Cave coop. la Cévenole, Le Grillou, 07260 Rosières, tel. 04.75.39.52.09, fax 04.75.39.92.30 ☑ Ῑ by appt.

CAVE DE VALVIGNERES

Viognier 1999

☐ n.c. 10,000 ▮ 🌡 30-49 F

Viognier vines have clearly flourished on this site at the heart of a beautiful valley. A pretty yellow colour, this wine has an aroma of apricots and peaches that is almost fully developed. Rounded and rich, it will go well with hors d'oeuvres.
⊶ Cave coop. de Valvignères, quartier Auvergne, 07400 Valvignères, tel. 04.75.52.60.60, fax 04.75.52.60.33 ☑
Ῑ by appt.

DOM. DES VIGNEAUX

Merlot et Syrah 1998★★

■ 0.6 ha 3,600 ⦀ 20-29 F

This estate, cultivated by three successive generations of the same family, is renowned for its excellent oak-aged wines. This Merlot-Syrah blend has a remarkable purple colour with violet highlights. Its aroma of toast, coffee, spices and prunes dazzles the senses, while the palate is beautifully balanced and rich, with well-integrated tannins.
⊶ GAEC Serre de Gouy, Dom. des Vigneaux, 07400 Valvignères, tel. 04.75.52.51.91, fax 04.75.52.51.91 ☑
Ῑ ev. day 8am–12 noon 1pm–8pm
⊶ Gilbert Comte

Drôme

DOM. DU CHATEAU VIEUX

Cuvée Prestige 1998

■ 0.3 ha 1,800 ⦀ 30-49 F

Established in 1994, this estate is safeguarding the wine-making heritage of the Coteaux de Triors. This pure Syrah has a beautiful, bright, dark red colour and a lightly oaked nose of red berries and spices. It would be the perfect accompaniment for red meat or cheese.
⊶ Fabrice Rousset, Le Château Vieux, 26750 Triors, tel. 04.75.45.31.65, fax 04.75.45.31.65 ☑ Ῑ by appt.

CAVE DE LA VALDAINE

Chardonnay 1999★

☐ 21.15 ha n.c. ▮ 🌡 20-29 F

Located to the east of Montélimar, this co-operative cellar has been undergoing renovation. The welcoming new tasting-room is where you may discover their wines, notably this Chardonnay 99. It has delicate fruity and floral aromas of great finesse, and would be perfect served with fish or crustaceans.
⊶ Cave de la Valdaine, av. Marx-Dormoy, 26160 Saint-Gervais-sur-Roubion, tel. 04.75.53.80.08, fax 04.75.53.93.90 ☑
Ῑ by appt.

The East

In this region, only the remnants of vineyards that were decimated by phylloxera in the 19th century can be found. They produce very small quantities of unusual wines. Before the epidemic, these vineyards basked in the reflected glory of their prestigious neighbours in Burgundy and Champagne. Grape varieties associated with those regions are still cultivated here, complemented by some from Alsace and the Jura. In general, the wines are varietals, and thus express the character of a single grape: Chardonnay, Pinot Noir, Gamay or Pinot Gris (for rosés). The occassional blend may include Auxerrois.

Vins de Pays de Franche-Comté, de la Meuse or de l'Yonne are all agreeable, light, fresh and aromatic wines. Although yields are increasing, at present only 3,000 hl (79,200 gal) are produced each year.

Saône-et-Loire

VIN DES FOSSILES Gamay 1999

■ n.c. 6,000 ▮ 20-29 F

This is an attractive ruby-coloured wine. The nose is a little timid at first, but goes on to develop spicy aromas, while the palate is lively and light. A good quaffing wine. The anise- and liquorice-scented **Auxerrois 99** was also cited.

Jean-Claude Berthillot, Les Chavannes, 71340 Mailly, tel. 03.85.84.01.23 ☒

HAUT-BRIONNAIS Gamay 1999

■ 3.5 ha 26,000 ▮ 20-29 F

This Gamay has a cherry-red colour and aromas of strawberries and raspberries with a vegetal overtone. The palate hints at cherries, and is light, smooth and lively. A somewhat rustic, but unusual and interesting wine.

Cave coop. les Coteaux du Brionnais, 71340 Mailly, tel. 03.85.84.19.21, fax 03.85.84.19.21 Y by appt.

Franche-Comté

VIGNOBLE GUILLAUME

Chardonnay Vieilles Vignes 1998★★

□ 2.5 ha 14,000 30-49 F

The Maison Guillaume's Chardonnay Vieilles Vignes 98 came very close to receiving a *coup de cœur*. It is a distinctive wine with a rich yellow colour. The powerful and complex nose has an aroma of dried fruits and apricots, and the softly oaked palate is very attractive. An extremely fine wine. One juror remarked that it was of remarkable quality for a vin de pays. The fine **Pinot Noir 98** (20–29F) is rounded and well-structured with aromas of red berries, liquorice and spices. The **Pinot Noir Vieilles Vignes 98** was cited for its intense oaky, musky nose and good structure on the palate.

Vignoble Guillaume, Charcenne, 70700 Charcenne, tel. 03.84.32.80.55, fax 03.84.32.84.06 ☒ Y by appt.

Meuse

E. ET PH. ANTOINE 1999★

□ 1 ha 7,000 ▮ 20-29 F

This blend of Auxerrois and Chardonnay has a golden colour and a fruity and floral aroma. On the palate, it is fresh and well-balanced. It would be enjoyable with fish or shellfish. Also cited was the **Gris 99**, made from a blend of Gamay and Auxerrois, which is a lively wine that could be served with a quiche or Lorraine stew.

Philippe Antoine, 6, rue de l'Eglise, 55210 Saint-Maurice, tel. 03.29.89.38.31, fax 03.29.90.01.80 ☒ Y by appt.

DOM. DE COUSTILLE

Chardonnay 1999★

□ 1 ha 6,600 ▮ 20-29 F

Pleasing to both the eye and nose, this is a typically buttery Chardonnay with a well-balanced, full-bodied palate. It is ready for drinking now. The very good **Pinot Blanc 99** is a livelier wine with a powerful scent of apricot. Completing this attractive trio is an **Auxerrois 99**, which received a star.

SCEA de Coustille, 23, Grand-Rue, 55300 Buxerulles, tel. 03.29.89.33.81, fax 03.29.90.01.88 ☒ Y by appt.

LAURENT DEGENEVE

Chardonnay 1999

□ 0.75 ha 7,200 ▮ ♦ 20 F+

Laurent Degenève cultivates a three-ha (seven-acre) vineyard in the charming commune of Creuë, which is located five km (three miles) from Lake Madine. He has made an appealingly light, fresh Chardonnay. We suggest you serve it with a platter of *fruits de mer*.

Laurent Degenève, 7, rue des Lavoirs, 55210 Creuë, tel. 03.29.89.30.67, fax 03.29.89.30.67 ☒ Y by appt.

L'AUMONIERE Chardonnay 1999★

□ 1.3 ha 16,000 ▮ ♦ 20-29 F

There are several places worth visiting in the neighbourhood of this estate. The village of Hattonchâtel, perched on a promontory, has a panoramic view of the Woëvre Plain. It also boasts a 14th-century church and an interesting castle. This wine has a fine, intense nose and well-balanced palate: a good northern Chardonnay.

🔑 GAEC de l'Aumonière, Viéville-sous-les-Côtes, 55210 Vigneulles-les-Hattonchâtel, tel. 03.29.89.31.64, fax 03.29.90.00.92 ☑
Y ev. day 8am–8pm
🔑 Blanpied Frères

DOM. DE MONTGRIGNON

Pinot Noir 1999★

■ 1 ha 4,700 ▮ 20–29 F

1999 was a successful year for these growers, three of whose wines are awarded a star. The Pinot Noir red has a forthright nose and structured tannins that will benefit from a few months' keeping. The **Gris 99** is a Gamay-Pinot Noir blend with a scent of red berries. As for the **Blanc de Pinot Gris 99**, it has a honeyed ripe fruit nose and a rounded palate (the latter two wines are under 20F).

🔑 GAEC de Montgrignon Pierson Frères, 9, rue des Vignes, 55210 Billy-sous-les-Côtes, tel. 03.29.89.58.02, fax 03.29.90.01.04 ☑ Y by appt.

DOM. DE MUZY Gris 1999★

◪ 2 ha 15,000 ▮ 🌡 20–29 F

One of the tasting panel declared that this Gris was one of the best wines in its category. It has a salmon-pink colour, raspberry and redcurrant aroma, and a lively, vigorous palate – a very attractive wine. The fresh, vigorous character of the citrus-scented **Auxerrois 99**, which was also cited, make it a good wine for drinking as an apéritif.

🔑 Véronique and Jean-Marc Liénard, Dom. de Muzy, 3, rue de Muzy, 55160 Combres-sous-les-Côtes, tel. 03.29.87.37.81, fax 03.29.87.35.00 ☑ Y by appt.

Coteaux de Coiffy

LES COTEAUX DE COIFFY

Auxerrois 1999★★

□ 4.05 ha 19,500 ▮ 🌡 20–29 F

This wine has a brilliant, shimmering, pale yellow colour with silver highlights. Its nose is forthright, intense and fruity with notes of pear, plum and citrus. The palate reiterates those aromas. Full and long, it has a slight, refreshing spritz. A wine whose simplicity is a virtue.

🔑 SCEA les Coteaux de Coiffy, 52400 Coiffy-le-Haut, tel. 03.25.90.00.96, fax 03.25.90.18.84 ☑
Y by appt.

Haute-Marne

LE MUID MONTSAUGEONNAIS

Pinot noir Elevé en Fût de Chêne 1998★

■ 0.8 ha 6,500 ⏸ 30–49 F

This is an unusual, carefully crafted wine. It has a fine, intense colour with violet highlights. The nose has a gently oaky aroma of blackcurrant buds while the palate, which echoes those aromas, is full, rich and sinewy. The **Chardonnay 99 Elevé en Fût de Chêne**, which is equally as good, has a caramelly, fruity nose with amylic overtones. Rounded and full-bodied, it is attractively oaky. The **Chardonnay 98**, matured in tank, was also cited.

🔑 SA le Muid Montsaugeonnais, 2, av. de Bourgogne, 52190 Vaux-sous-Aubigny, tel. 03.25.90.04.65, fax 03.25.90.04.65 ☑
Y by appt.

Yonne

DOM. LA FONTAINE AUX MUSES

Chardonnay Moque Grange 1999

□ 0.5 ha 4,000 20–29 F

Pale yellow with green highlights, this Chardonnay has a mineral nose that is paradoxically reminiscent of Sauvignon. The attractive palate has a slight *pétillance* that gives it a refreshing, lively character.

🔑 Vincent Pointeau-Langevin, La Fontaine aux Muses, 89116 La Celle-Saint-Cyr, tel. 03.86.77.40.22

Sainte-Marie-la-Blanche

LES CAVES DE LA VERVELLE

Pinot Noir 1999★

■ 3 ha 29,000 ▮ 🌡 30–49 F

This Pinot Noir has an attractive, deep ruby colour. The forthright, inviting nose has fruity aromas of raspberries and blackcurrants. Its supple palate reflects the original aromas, but develops an additional liquorice note. It has a soft finish highly typical of the variety. The **Chardonnay 99** and the **Rosé de Pinot Noir 99** from the same cellar were also cited.

🔑 Les caves de la Vervelle, Le Château, 21200 Bligny-les-Beaune, tel. 03.80.21.47.38, fax 03.80.21.40.27 ☑
Y ev. day except Sun. 10am–12 noon 2pm–5pm

LUXEMBOURG WINES

The Grand Duchy of Luxembourg is a small, prosperous state in the very heart of the European Union, located at a pivotal point where the Germanic and Latin worlds meet. Since Roman times Vines have been cultivated here on slopes that follow the sinuous course of the Moselle. Today, Luxembourg produces dry, lively and aromatic white wines, and wine consumption in the Grand Duchy approaches the levels recorded in France and in Italy.

The production of wine in Luxembourg is limited to 160,000 hl (4,224,000 gal), in keeping with its modest area of 1,350 ha (3,334 acres). However, wine is taken very seriously, and Luxembourg has its own minister of agriculture and viticulture.

The Moselle vineyard first rose to fame in the 4th century, when Trèves (which is very near to the present border of the Grand Duchy) became an Imperial seat as one of the four capitals of the Roman Empire. Today, from Schengen to Vasserbillig, the slopes on the left bank of the Moselle form a continuous belt of vineyards through the cantons of Remich and Grevenmacher. Facing south and south-east, they benefit from the advantageous influences of the river waters, which moderate the cold airflow from the north and east in spring and the strength of the sun in summer. Because of their northerly latitude (49° north), the Luxembourg vineyards produce almost exclusively white wines. Nearly 35% of the wines come from the Rivaner (or Müller-Thurgau) variety. The Elbling, which is a typical Luxembourg variety (12% of the wine-growing area), makes a light, refreshing wine. Other varieties include Auxerrois, Riesling, Pinot Blanc, Chardonnay, Pinot Gris, Pinot Noir and Gewürztraminer. Co-operatives account for more than two-thirds of the viticultural area. Remich is the headquarters of a research centre and the official viticultural organisation.

The Marque Nationale des Vins de la Moselle Luxembourgeoise, which has official backing, was set up in 1935 with the aims of encouraging improvements in quality and to give the consumer a choice. In 1985 the Appellation Contrôlée Moselle Luxembourgeoise was established. There is also a scale in the classification of the wines (Marque Nationale: Appellation Contrôlée, Vin Classé, Premier Cru and Grand Premier Cru). The originality of the classification system should be emphasised. The wines are marked for quality each year: wines gaining between 18 and 20 points qualify as Grand Premier Cru, those with between 16 and 17.9 points as Premier Cru, those with between 14 and 15.9 points as Vin Classé, those with between 12 and 13.9 points as Vin de Qualité but with no specific description, and under those gaining fewer than 12 points as simple table wines. The Appellation Crémant du Luxembourg was created in 1991.

Moselle Luxembourgeoise

DOM. MATHIS BASTIAN

Wellenstein Foulschette Pinot gris 1998

□ 1.82 ha 4,200 30-49 F

Up on the heights of Remich, Mathis Bastian has been running his business from the heart of the vineyard for nearly 30 years. His Pinot Gris vines, growing on the Keuperian marl soils of Wellenstein Foulschette, have produced a straightforward wine with aromas of linden-blossom, liquorice and apricots. Clean, supple and rich, it fills the mouth with sweet, spicy flavours that have good length and balance. Although it can be enjoyed now, it will develop further in the next two to three years, and will be a good accompaniment to grilled turbot.

Dom. Mathis Bastian, 29, rte de Luxembourg, 5551 Remich, tel. 69.82.95, fax 66.91.18 Y by appt.

DOM. BECK-FRANK

Greiveldenger Primerberg Auxerrois 1998

□ Gd 1er cru 0.35 ha 3,100 20-29 F

Located at the entrance to the village of Greiveldange, this estate has more than seven hectares (17 acres) of Auxerrois vines growing on the clay-limestone soils of Greiveldange Primerberg. They have yielded a wine that is fruity, well-balanced and vinous. With its richness and white peach flavours in the mouth, it is clearly destined for a sweet, harmonious future.

Dom. G. Beck-Frank, 10, Bréil, 5426 Greiveldange, tel. 69.82.92, fax 69.76.07 Y by appt.

CEP D'OR

Brut Crémant de Luxembourg★★★

○ n.c. 6,000 50-69 F

The Cep d'Or estate grows more than 13 ha (32 acres) of vines on clay-limestone soils in the cantons of Remich and Grevenmacher. Since 1995, it has been run by the Vesque family, and offers a vast range of wines from which two have been singled out this year. This Crémat de Luxembourg made the jury's hearts beat faster. Elegant and finely fruity to the last *caudalie*, it also reveals a slightly floral note on the nose, and well-balanced structure on the palate. The **1998 Pinot Gris Grand**

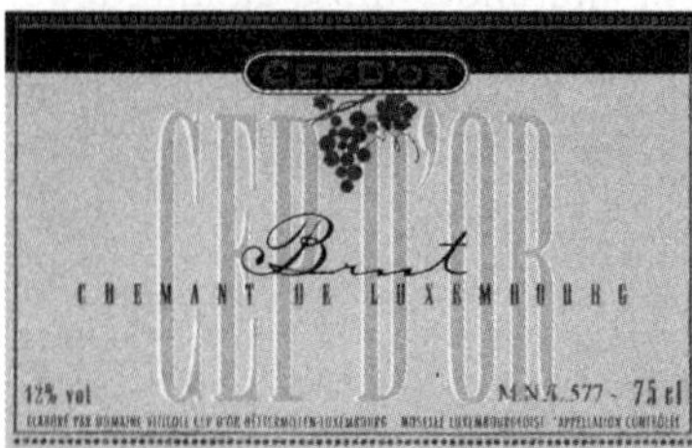

Luxembourg

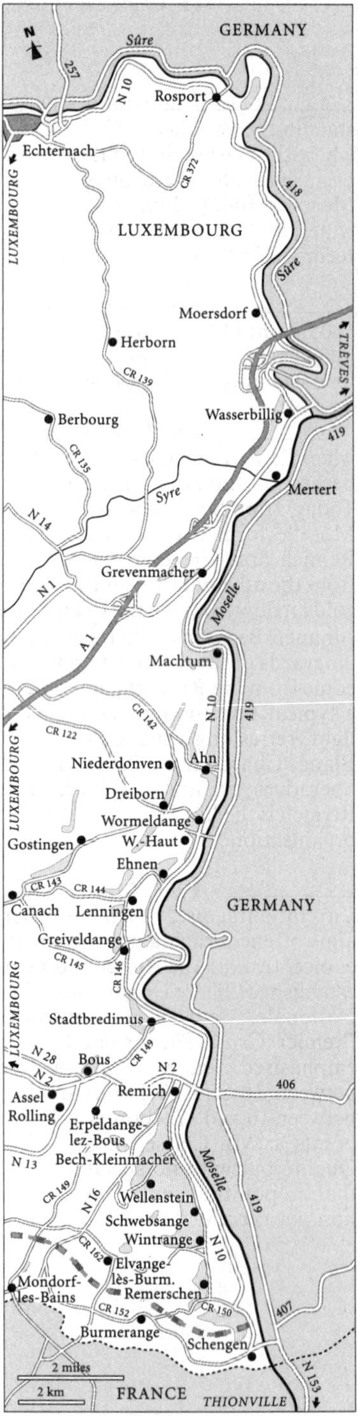

Premier Cru Stadtbredimus Primerberg is also a very good wine; it has a forthcoming nose of apple, liquorice and spice aromas, and is unexpectedly full and substantial on the palate. Worth keeping for four years. Finally, the **1998 Auxerrois Grand Premier Cru Stadtbredimus Primerberg** deserves a commendation (20–29F).

Dom. viticole Cep d'Or, 15, rte du Vin, 5429 Hëttermillen, tel. 76.83.83, fax 76.91.91, e-mail cepdor@pt.lu by appt. Famille Vesque

DOM. CLOS DES ROCHERS

Pinot blanc 1998

☐ 0.5 ha 2,626 30–49 F

This estate has already distinguished itself with a remarkable 1997 Pinot Gris; it now offers a Pinot Blanc that has a clear yellow colour with light green highlights, and gives off discreet notes of white flowers. There is a distinct impression of freshness on the palate, where it lingers elegantly on the finish.

Dom. Clos des Rochers, 8, rue du Pont, 6773 Grevenmacher, tel. 75.05.45, fax 75.06.06, e-mail bermas@pt.lu ev. day 9.30am–6pm; cl. 1 Nov.–1 Apr.

DOM. CHARLES DECKER

Remerschen Kreitzberg Pinot blanc 1998★★★

☐ Gd 1er cru 0.42 ha 4,000 30–49 F

Charles Decker takes the credit here for producing an exceedingly fine example of Pinot Blanc. Its light yellow colour is highlighted with green glints. The nose is already powerful, but even so is not yet revealing all its secrets. After a clean attack on the palate, the richness of the wine fills the mouth completely, along with intense, long-lasting flavours: verbena, oranges, passion-fruit . . . Be patient and keep it for a while, and the pleasure will be all the greater. While you wait, you might try the **Crémant de Luxembourg Millésime 1995** (50–69F), which is cited for its finesse and elegance.

Dom. Charles Decker, 7, rte de Mondorf, 5441 Remerschen, tel. 60.95.10, fax 60.95.20, e-mail deckerch@pt.lu by appt.

DOM. MME ALY DUHR

Crémant de Luxembourg

○ n.c. n.c. 30–49 F

This 8 ha (20-acre) estate, founded in 1872, offers a Crémant with a high reputation. It has a fine, persistent mousse, and offers not only lemony and mineral notes, but also hints of oak, which appear at the retronasal stage. Rich, complex and long on the palate, it displays characteristic flavours of the old Riesling vines from which it comes: a combination of features that is rather atypical of the Moselle, but will suit the English taste in sparkling wine. For drinking now.

Dom. Mme Aly Duhr, 9, rue Aly-Duhr, 5401 Ahn, tel. 76.00.43, fax 76.05.47

CAVES GALES Auxerrois 1998★★

☐ 0.32 ha 2,500 30–49 F

This wine has a perfectly clear, pale yellow colour, and shows a slightly green halo on the side of the glass. Still rather youthful, it gives off aromas of ripe pineapple, honey and malt. It is well-structured on the palate, where its charms include not only a sweet attack on the palate, but also great freshness and balance. With a note of caramel on the finish, this is a modern-style Auxerrois which will be a good accompaniment to a *salade gourmande*, chicken, or sweet and sour dishes.

Caves Gales, B.P. 49, 5501 Remich, tel. 69.90.93, fax 69.94.34 by appt.

A. GLODEN ET FILS

Wellenstein Foulschette Pinot gris 1998★★★

☐ Gd 1er cru 1.2 ha 7,500 30–49 F

The Gloden family has been growing vines at Wellenstein since 1751. It dedicates its hillside Foulschette terroir to producing a quality Pinot Gris, which in the 1998 vintage is of an exceptionally high standard. With its green-yellow highlights and nose of citronella and citrus fruits, it casts a spell from the start. Right from its honeyed attack on the palate, it is clear that this is a rich and complex wine with a highly original, exotic character.

A. Gloden et Fils, 2, Albaach, 5471 Wellenstein, tel. 69.83.24, fax 69.81.32, e-mail a.gloden-fils@village.uunet.lu by appt.

CAVES DE GREVENMACHER

Machtum Göllebour Gewurztraminer 1998★

☐ Gd 1er cru 2.03 ha 15,000 30–49 F

The aromas of this rich, pale Gewurztraminer with green highlights range from notes of wild roses to lychees and white flowers. It has a certain sweetness in the mouth, within a structure that is balanced and rich in exotic flavours (lychees and quince). Also cited is the **1998 Pinot Blanc Grand Premier Cru Machtum Hohfels**, a fresh, fruity wine (with citrus notes) that is typical of the grape variety, and will broaden its range of flavours with time.

Les domaines de Vinsmoselle, Caves de Grevenmacher, 12, rue des Caves, 6718 Grevenmacher, tel. 75.01.75, fax 75.95.13, e-mail info@vinsmoselle.lu ev. day 7am–4.30pm; cl. 1 Nov.–1 May

DOM. HAEREMILLEN

Wormeldange Nussbaum Riesling 1998

☐ Gd 1er cru 0.42 ha 5,400 30–49 F

This is a fine, straightforward wine with a nose of fresh lemon and apples. Its mineral quality on the palate leaves an impression of liveliness, counterbalanced by a certain amount of richness. It is ready to drink now. Also worth a mention is the **1999 Auxerrois d'Ehnerberg**, which has surprising fruitiness and fine mineral balance.

Dom. Haeremillen, 3, Op der Borreg, 5419 Ehnen, tel. 76.84.36, fax 76.91.93 by appt.

CAVES R. KOHLL-LEUCK

Rousemen Pinot gris 1998★

☐ Gd 1er cru 0.3 ha 3,000 30–49 F

Raymond and Cécile Kohll-Leuck have been tending more than 7 ha (17 acres) of vines for almost 30 years, and their son Luc is currently pursuing his viticultural studies. This Pinot Gris has an irreproachably clear, yellow colour and a fresh, fruity nose. On the palate, an impression of very ripe grapes is evident, but it is not the less balanced for that and gives immediate pleasure. The **1997 Crémant de Luxembourg Cuvée Gust Kohll** is also cited for its range of ripe fruit aromas and well-balanced flavours of brioche and toast (50–69F).

Dom. Raymond Kohll-Leuck, 4, an der Borreg, , 5419 Ehnen, tel. 76.02.42, fax 76.90.40

DOM. L. ET B. KOX

Schwebsange Kolteschberg Riesling 1999

☐ 0.6 ha 6,000 30–49 F

Although still a little immature, the nose of this 1999 shows pineapple aromas and mineral notes. It is well-structured, with the balance of a young wine, and releases flavours of lemon and pink grapefruit on the palate. A wine that will go well with seafood dishes.

Laurent et Benoît Kox, 6A, rue des Prés, 5561 Remich, tel. 69.84.94, fax 69.81.01, e-mail kox@pt.lu Y by appt.

DOM. KRIER-BISENIUS

Kourschels Riesling 1998★★

☐ Gd 1er cru 0.27 ha 2,600 30–49 F

This estate scores a double hit in the 1998 vintage, with two remarkable wines being singled out by the jury. This one is both floral and fruity, and is characterised by richness and well-tempered acidity. It fills the mouth with a structure that is round, mature and balanced. The **1998 Auxerrois Grand Premier Cru Foulschette** releases intense, fresh notes of lemon and exotic fruits. It has much power and good length on the palate, with fruity aromas typical of the grape variety.

Dom. Krier-Bisenius, 39, rte du Vin, Bech-Kleinmacher, 5405 Wellenstein, tel. 66.92.06, fax 69.75.25, e-mail krierjp@pt.lu Y by appt.

CAVES KRIER FRERES

Schwebsange Kolteschberg Pinot gris 1999★★

☐ 0.8 ha 10,400 30–49 F

The estate's label shows a view of the Moselle painted by Nico Klopp in the 1920s, when he was a tenant of the Krier family. This Pinot Gris has a clear colour that sparkles with near-green highlights. On the nose, there are pleasant and very persistent notes of blackcurrant and grapefruit. After a sweet attack on the palate, a wide variety of flavours unfolds in the mouth. Also cited is the **1998 Riesling Grand Premier Cru Remich Primerberg**, a fruity, fresh wine that is still young but clearly destined for great things in the future.

Caves Krier Frères, 1, montée Saint-Urbain, B.P. 30, 5501 Remich, tel. 69.82.82, fax 69.80.98 Y by appt.

DOM. KRIER-WELBES

Wintringen Felsberg Riesling 1998

☐ n.c. 2,000 30–49 F

The wine Guy Krier is offering here has a very brilliant, pale yellow colour with green highlights. The nose is delicate and thoroughbred, and it is fresh and lively on the palate, with a certain roundness as well. A powerfully structured wine with some exotic notes.

Dom. Krier-Welbes, 3, rue de la Gare, 5690 Ellange-Gare, tel. 67.71.84, fax 66.19.31, e-mail guykrier@pt.lu Y by appt. Guy Krier

CAVES LEGILL

Schengen Markusberg Riesling 1998

☐ Gd 1er cru 0.25 ha 2,600 30–49 F

Paul Legill has produced very good results in the 1998 and 1999 vintages. This pale wine is developing a slightly lemony nose, shot through with a faint note of green apples. The attack on the palate is clean, after which it has the substantial structure on the palate that typifies a great Riesling. Also cited is the **1999 Pinot Blanc de Schengen Markusberg**, whose very pleasant, rich array of exotic fruit notes lingers both on the nose and on the palate. A good balance of freshness and richness.

Caves Legill et Fils, 27, rte du Vin, 5445 Schengen, tel. 66.40.38, fax 60.90.97 Y by appt.

DOM. MAX-LAHR ET FILS

Crémant de luxembourg

○ 0.6 ha 6,600 50–69 F

This clear, yellow crémant has an attractive floral bouquet of irises and violets, and very persistent bubbles. It is clean and lively on the palate, with plenty of stuffing, marked by notes of citronella and grapefruit. Can be drunk now, or kept for up to three years.

Dom. Max-Lahr et Fils, 4, rue de Niederdonven, 5401 Ahn, tel. 76.00.99, fax 76.92.56 Y by appt. Robert Max

CLOS MON VIEUX MOULIN

Auxerrois 1998

☐ 0.6 ha n.c. 30–49 F

It is nearly 100 years since the old mill stopped turning, but its memory lives on in the name of this property, which was acquired in 1689 by the Duhr brothers' forebears. Their 1998 Auxerrois is a clear wine with aromas of brioche, peach-stones and pineapple. It has good balance on the palate, with a slight hint of spritziness. A wine whose flavours would be enhanced by an exotically flavoured dish. The **1998 Riesling** also deserves commendation for its typically fruity, mineral nose and discreet acidity in the mouth.

Duhr Frères, 25, rue de Niederdonven, 5401 Ahn, tel. 76.07.46, fax 76.85.13 Y by appt.

POLL-FABAIRE Crémant de luxembourg★

○ n.c. 10,000 30–49 F

Poll-Fabaire is one of the brands produced by Les Domaines de Vinsmoselle, a group of co-operatives that produces six wines in each of its cellars. This one comes from the Caves de Stadtbredimus. Its fine, long-lasting mousse gets the tasting off to an inviting start, after which there is an intense nose of floral aromas. Finally, its structure on the palate speaks of the exemplary maturity of the base wines from which it is made.

Les domaines de Vinsmoselle, Caves de Stadtbredimus, Kellereiswe, 5450 Stadtbredimus, tel. 69.83.14, fax 69.91.89 by appt.

CAVES DE REMERSCHEN

Schengen Markusberg Auxerrois Anniversaire 2000 1998

□ Gd 1er cru 18.3 ha 20,000 30–49 F

This pale yellow wine releases a range of fruity aromas, dominated by notes of ripe pineapple. It is marked at first on the palate by an appley rancio flavour, and then develops towards an attractive finish of moderate intensity. The **Crémant de Luxembourg Poll-Fabaire** also deserves a citation for its well-balanced, fairly light citrus and apple aromas.

Les Domaines de Vinsmoselle, Caves de Remerschen, 32, rte du Vin, 5440 Remerschen, tel. 66.41.65, fax 66.41.66, e-mail info@vinsmoselle.lu by appt.

CAVES HENRI RUPPERT

Schengen Markusberg Riesling 1998

□ Gd 1er cru 0.25 ha 2 200 50–69 F

Sold under a European blue label, this Schengen Riesling is a late-harvest wine that is ready to drink. Its fairly well-developed nose is distinctly fruity, but also releases a complex aroma of truffles. It is structured, round and rich in the mouth, with lingering, concentrated, ripe fruit flavours. Also cited is the **Crémant de Luxembourg**, which will keep for three years. It is a straightforward wine with excellent structure and flavours of toast and citronella, which would go well with freshwater fish (cooked in the same Crémant, for example). Finally, the **1998 Pinot Blanc de Schengen Markusberg** receives a citation for its attractive freshness and long finish (30–49F).

Henri Ruppert, 100, rte du Vin, 5445 Schengen, tel. 66.42.30, fax 66.44.83 by appt.

CAVES SAINT-REMY-DESOM

Crémant de Luxembourg★

○ 5 ha 62,000 30–49 F

The 13th-century buildings that now house the Caves Saint-Rémy-Desom were once occupied by the 'weavery' of Edmond de La Fontaine, the Luxembourg poet. From them has emerged this Crémant with its splendid gold colour, a fine topping of mousse, and sparkling, vigorous bubbles. The intense nose gives off notes of toast, brioche and nuts, while the structure on the palate is weighty, rich and elegant. An attractive herbaceous quality and an exceedingly long finish add to the overall balance of this sparkling wine, which would be a good accompaniment to a chicken garnished with truffles and cooked in brioche. Also cited is a wine in a completely different style: the **1998 Pinot Gris Grand Premier Cru Remich Primerberg**, which is already well-balanced but will achieve greater harmony once it has been kept for two to three years.

Caves Saint-Rémy-Desom, 9, rue Dicks, 5521 Remich, tel. 69.87.87, fax 69.93.47 by appt.

CH. DE SCHENGEN

Pinot blanc 1998★★

□ 0.4 ha 2,675 30–49 F

This light yellow Pinot Blanc has lovely pale highlights in the glass and a fine, attractive nose dominated by primary aromas of white fruits, but with some floral notes as well. On the palate, it is extremely fresh and fruity, and shows remarkable balance. Under the same label, which shows a drawing of the château by Victor Hugo, the **1998 Pinot Gris** and the **1998 Riesling** were also cited.

Dom. Thill Frères, 39, rte du Vin, 5445 Schengen, tel. 75.05.45, fax 75.06.06, e-mail bermas@pt.lu by appt.

CAVES JEAN SCHLINK-HOFFELD

Machtum Ongkâf Riesling 1998

□ Gd 1er cru 0.96 ha 5,400 30–49 F

In 1993, René and Jean-Paul Schlink took over from their father on this 11 ha (27-acre) estate. They grow Riesling grapes on the south-facing, limestone Ongkâf terroir at Machtum. This pale 1998 with yellow highlights has the classic Riesling nose: mineral notes, lemon and apples. These continue as flavours on the palate, where a balance is achieved between acidity and residual sugar. Ready to drink now.

Caves Jean Schlink-Hoffeld, 1, rue de l'Eglise, 6841 Machtum, tel. 75.84.68, fax 75.92.62 ev. day except Sun. 8am–6pm; groups by appt. René Schlink

DOM. PIERRE SCHUMACHER-LETHAL ET FILS

Wormeldange Koeppchen Riesling 1998

☐ Gd 1er cru 0.2 ha 1,200 30–49 F

This pale green Riesling's fine, subtle aromatic range is enhanced by a slight mineral quality. Its fruitiness comes through in notes of grapefruit and dried fruits, which make way on the palate for flavours of verbena and pineapple. The structure shows great freshness, good length, and enough richness to achieve elegant balance.

Dom. Pierre Schumacher-Lethal et Fils, 114, rue Principale, 5450 Wormeldange, tel. 76.01.34, fax 76.85.04 ☑ Y by appt.

CAVES DE WELLENSTEIN

Wellenstein Foulschette Pinot gris Terra 1998★

☐ Gd 1er cru 30.9 ha 30,000 30–49 F

Terra is an attractive wine in the Domaines de Vinsmoselle's *Art et Vin* series. It has a light yellow colour and an exquisitely elegant nose. Well-structured on the palate, it lingers powerfully on long, spicy notes – a delightfully well-balanced wine. Equally successful is the **Crémant de Luxembourg Poll-Fabaire** produced at Wellenstein, which is an appealing wine with good length.

Les domaines de Vinsmoselle, Caves de Wellenstein, 13, rue des Caves, 5471 Wellenstein, tel. 66.93.21, fax 69.76.54, e-mail info@vinsmoselle.lu ☑ Y ev. day 7am–4.30pm; cl. 1 Nov.–1 May

CAVES DE WORMELDANGE

Wormeldange Mohrberg Pinot gris 1998

☐ Gd 1er cru 4.98 ha 12,000 30–49 F

After noting its yellow-green colour, the tasters discovered that this wine had a delicately rich nose, and then great maturity, fullness and generosity on the palate, giving an overall impression of fruitiness and balance.

Les Domaines de Vinsmoselle, Caves de Wormeldange, 115, rte du Vin, 5481 Wormeldange, tel. 76.82.11, fax 76.82.15, e-mail info@vinsmoselle.lu ☑ Y ev. day 7am–4.30pm; cl. 1 Nov.–1 May

SWITZERLAND

Compared to its other European neighbours, Swiss vineyards cover the comparatively small area of 14,900 ha (36,803 acres). They extend over the area of three great river basins drained by the Rhône to the west of the Alps, by the Rhine to the north and by the Po to the south of the mountain chain. As a result, they encompass a great variety of soils and microclimates, creating an array of different *terroirs* in spite of their relative proximity. Cultivated by traditional methods on sunny slopes, some steep, some terraced, the vineyards determine the character of the landscape. Three main wine-growing regions can be identified, based on the linguistic divisions of the country. However, they are far from uniform, and the contrasts they display are significant. In the west the vineyards of the Suisse Romande account for more than three-quarters of the whole of Switzerland's wine-growing area. From Geneva they extend into the heart of the Alps in the canton (a Swiss administrative region) of Valais and hug the shoreline of Lake Geneva in the canton of Vaud. Further north they rise above the shores of lakes Neuchâtel, Morat and Bienne (in the canton of Berne) in the foothills of the Jura. The Swiss–German vineyards are much less continuous and account for a total of 17% of the wine-growing area. Starting from Basle, they are dotted along the Rhine valley, following the course of the river into the east of the country and extend equally far into the interior, where they are to be found on the best sites on hills overlooking numerous lakes and valleys. In Italian-speaking Switzerland vine-growing is centred in the southern valley of the Ticino, where natural conditions on the south-facing slopes of the Alps are significantly different from those in other Swiss wine-growing regions. Apart from a whole range of 'specialities', the wine-makers of Swiss Romande traditionally favour the Chasselas variety for whites. The most commonly cultivated red variety is Pinot Noir, followed by Gamay. In the Swiss–German region, Pinot Noir dominates, but is grown side by side with white Müller-Thurgau and various other local varieties, which are much sought after by wine-lovers. In Italian-speaking Switzerland, where white grape varieties are very poorly represented, the best wines – red, white and rosé – are made from Merlot. Finally, a major event in the viticultural life of Switzerland should be mentioned: the Fête des Vignerons de Vevey (Festival of the Wine-growers of Vevey). With its roots in the Middle Ages, this splendid festival brings together the wine-growers and the local population to celebrate their work in the vineyards. The most recent was held in August 1999 and the next is due to be held in 2021 to 2023.

Vaud Canton

In the Middle Ages, Cistercian monks cleared a substantial area of Vaud and planted out the vineyard. By the middle of the 19th century Vaud was Switzerland's primary wine-growing canton (ahead of the Zürich vineyard), but the ravages of phylloxera made complete replanting essential. Today the vineyard covers 3,850 ha (9,510 acres), and ranks second after the Valais.

For more than 450 years, the Vaud has cherished an authentic wine-growing tradition, relying on its châteaux – there are about 50 of them – as much as it does on the experience of the great wine-making and shipping families.

The climatic conditions mark out four large wine-growing zones. The Vaud side of Lake Neuchâtel and the shores of the Orbe produce fruity wines with delicate perfumes. Between Geneva and Lausanne the shores of Lake Geneva produce wines of great finesse. Here the vines are sheltered by the Jura mountains to the north, and benefit from a temperate microclimate influenced by the lake. The vineyards of Lavaux, between Lausanne and Château-de-Chillon, with the terraced vineyards of Dézalay at their heart, benefit from radiated heat from their low-walled enclosures and reflected light from the lake. They produce structured, complex wines often characterised by notes of honey and toasted flavours. Finally, the vineyards of the Chablais are located north-east of Lake Geneva and climb up the right bank of the Rhône. The *terroirs* are typically made up of stony soils, and the climate is much influenced by the Foehn (a hot, dry wind that blows in the Swiss Alps); the wines are strong with flavours of gunflint.

The Vaud vineyard has very good soil for Chasselas (70% of the vines planted), which reaches full ripeness here.

The red varieties represent 27% of the whole (15% of Pinot Noir and 12% of Gamay). These two varieties are frequently blended together, and the wines are known under the name Appellation d'Origine Contrôlée Salvagnin.

A few 'specialities' represent 3% of the wine produced: Pinot Blanc, Pinot Gris, Gewürztraminer, Muscat Blanc, Sylvaner, Auxerrois, Charmont, Mondeuse, Plant-Robert, Syrah, Merlot, Gamaret, Garanoir, and so on.

DOM. DE AUTECOUR

Mont-sur-Rolle Chasselas 1999★★

□Gd cru 11 ha 50,000 50–69 F

Clear and brilliant, this Chasselas is very much in keeping with the style of La Côte wines. Its frank and fresh nose has an aroma of hazelnuts, with a slightly salty overtone. The palate is fresh, fruity and well-structured. A salty aroma is also perceptible on the palate, along with the fine bitterness that is characteristic of this terroir. This wine is ready to drink now, as an apéritif, with white meat or with cheese.

Dom. de Autecour, Obrist SA Vevey, av. Reller 26, 1800 Vevey, tel. 02.19.25.99.25, fax 02.19.25.99.15, e-mail obrist@obrist.ch

Y by appt.

SOCIETE VINICOLE DE BEX

Bex Pinot Noir Elevé en Barrique 1997★★

■ 0.5 ha 3,500 100–149 F

A medium red colour with dark highlights, this wine is beginning to develop an aroma of undergrowth and fruit. Along with its dense tannic structure, the palate has a fine fleshiness and flavours of cherries and undergrowth. The wine's softness and liveliness are well-balanced, and the tannins carry through to a thoroughbred finish. The **Chasselas Sire de Duin de Bex 99** was awarded one star (70–99F).

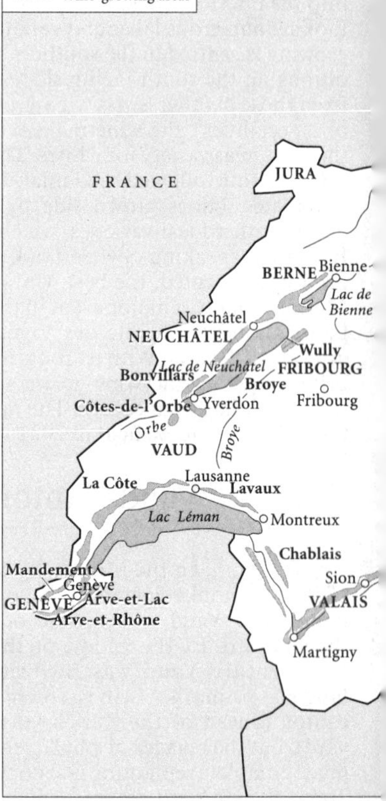

Ste Vinicole de Bex, chem. du Pré-de-la-Cible no4, 1880 Bex, tel. 02.44.63.25.25, fax 02.44.63.32.01, e-mail vinicole@bex.ch
by appt.

CHARLY BLANC ET FILS

Yvorne la Mondeuse Noire 1998★★

■ 0.15 ha 1,200 70–99 F

The Mondeuse is a lively Savoyard variety that is quite tannic, and thus makes wines that age well. This is certainly true of Charly Blanc's Mondeuse Noire. A brilliant rich colour, it has a fruity nose of cherries and blackberries with hints of pepper and cinnamon. The aromatic palate is both fresh and well-rounded. This is an unassertively oaky wine, but its fine tannins need time to soften.

Charly Blanc et Fils, 1852 Versvey, tel. 02.44.66.51.45, fax 02.44.66.51.45, e-mail cropt-blanc@blvewin.ch
by appt.

DOM. BOVY

Saint-Saphorin Chasselas Vieilles Vignes 1999★★

□ 0.6 ha 5,200 70–99 F

The first vines were planted on this 7-ha (17-acre) estate at the end of the 18th century. Vincent and Eric Bovy began managing it in 1998. Light and brilliant, their Chasselas is still a little closed, but well-structured and complex. Its charming palate is fleshy in texture, with a fine hint of mineral bitterness and a long finish. A wine that needs time to develop.

Les Frères Bovy, Dom. Bovy, 15, rue du Bourg-de-Plaît, 1071 Chexbres, tel. 02.19.46.51.25, fax 02.59.46.51.26, e-mail info@domainebovy.ch
ev. day except Sun. 9am–6pm; Sat. 9am–12 noon

SWITZERLAND

Switzerland

CH. DE CHATAGNEREAZ

Mont-sur-Rolle 1999★

■ Gd cru 1.24 ha 16,000 30–49 F

The name of this typical La Côte château derives from the fact that Mont-sur-Rolle was once covered in chestnut trees (*châtaigniers*). The château was donated to the monks of the Abbaye du Lac de Joux in the 12th century. This 1999 has a nose redolent of cherries and violets, with the same fresh tones echoed on a fruity palate that is slightly sweet, with fine tannins. Alcohol and acidity are in good balance, and the finish is clean and distinguished. A fresh and fruity wine that could be kept for another two years or so.

SA Ch. de Châtagneréaz, 1180 Rolle, tel. 02.18.22.02.02 Y by appt.

DOM. DU CHENE

Chardonnay Vendanges tardives 1999★★

□ Gd cru 0.35 ha 900 70–99 F

The 10-ha (25 acres) of vineyards that are cultivated by this estate are situated above the salt-mines of Bex. Chardonnay grapes were harvested at the end of November to produce this remarkably balanced sweet wine. Bright gold in colour, it has intense aromas of crystallised fruit, walnut oil and peppery spice. The palate is very unctuous, but is perfectly counterbalanced by its freshness. The complex aroma and a powerful, long finish are highly seductive. This wine will be enjoyable for another ten years and more.

Dom. du Chêne, 1880 Le-Chêne-sur-Bex, tel. 02.18.25.11.41, fax 02.18.25.47.47 Y by appt.

CLOS DE PEVRET

Pully Chardonnay Elevé en Barrique 1998★★

□ Gd cru 0.25 ha 2,048 70–99 F

The Pully vineyards, which are on the site of a Roman villa, were established in the tenth century by the monks of the Abbaye Clunisienne de Payerne. The Clos de Pevret, to the south of the priory church, is the commune's prize vineyard — it is easy to understand why after tasting this rich Chardonnay with its fine varietal character. Oak is perceptible, but does not overwhelm the elegant fruity aromas of apricot and citrus, tinged with a hint of walnut. Soft and fresh, the palate echoes the original aromas, which linger on to a fresh and fruity finish that is slightly tannic. A structured wine that would complement fish, white meat and cheese.

Commune de Pully, Direction des Domaines, 1, av. Reymondin, 1009 Pully, tel. 02.17.21.35.26, fax 02.17.21.35.15, e-mail domaine@pully.ch Y by appt.

CH. DES CRETES

Montreux Chasselas 1999★

□ 1.5 ha 7,000 50–69 F

It is not just the jazz festival that brings people to Montreux — they make some good wines here too, such as this clear and bright Chasselas from the Château des Crêtes. The 1999 has linden flower aromas and a sweet, velvety palate that bears evidence of some residual sugar. On the finish, it is pleasantly fruity. A wine to drink as an apéritif.

La cave Vevey-Montreux, 28, av. de Belmont, 1820 Montreux, tel. 02.19.63.13.48, fax 02.19.63.34.34 Y by appt.

DOM. DE CROCHET

Mont-sur-Rolle Pinot noir 1998★★

■ Gd cru 0.5 ha 2,500 50–69 F

Pinot Noir grapes grown at 400–450 m (1,300–1,470 feet) above sea-level on the lower slopes of Mont-sur-Rolle have produced a well-structured, rich, deep ruby wine. The nose is complex, but still a little closed. It is very fruity (black cherries) with hints of earthiness. The aromas do not have great persistence, but the palate is nonetheless well-structured and full, with fine tannins that suggest that this wine will keep for at least five years.

Michel Rolaz, 4, chem. de Porchat, 1180 Rolle, tel. 02.18.25.11.41, fax 02.18.25.47.47 Y by appt.

HENRI CRUCHON

Morges Chardonnay Cuvée Gourmande 1998★★

□ 2 ha 16,000 50–69 F

This fine gastronomic wine is pale, clear gold, with the complex, typically fruity Chardonnay aroma of apricots and a distinct hint of the terroir. The elegant palate is rich, velvety and balanced by a fine freshness. The finish is very long indeed.

Henri Cruchon, Cave du Village, 1112 Echichens, tel. 02.18.01.17.92, fax 02.18.03.33.18 Y ev. day except Sun. 8am–12 noon 2pm–6pm; Sat. 8am–12 noon

DE LA TOUR

Dézaley-Marsens Chasselas 1998★

□ Gd cru 3 ha 30,000 100–149 F

A brightly coloured Chasselas, this wine has the rich mineral and floral nose characteristic of this terroir. Its structured, rounded palate echoes the original aromas, which are lifted by a fine bitter after-taste. A slightly sweet wine that would make a good apéritif.

Les Frères Dubois, Le Petit Versailles, 1096 Cully, tel. 02.17.99.22.22, fax 02.17.99.22.54, e-mail office@lfd.ch Y by appt.

CHRISTIAN DUGON

Côtes de l'Orbe Gamaret 1998★★★

■ 0.5 ha 4,150 30–49 F

Christian Dugon richly deserves these three stars. His bright, dark red Gamaret leaves a violet trace in the glass. The rich nose has an aroma of fruit (blackberries), pepper and violets with a hint of oaky vanilla. On the palate, it is elegant and velvety, with dense tannins and an attractive freshness. Fruity, spicy and floral flavours persist through to a complex, clean-tasting finish. A wine that will easily see in the year 2010. The same winemaker has produced an exceptional **Côtes de**

l'Orbe Arpège 98 (50–69F). This is a rich and alcoholic red suitable for cellaring.
Christian Dugon, La Grande-Ouche, 1353 Bofflens, tel. 02.44.41.35.01, fax 02.44.41.35.36 Y by appt.

EN ROSSET Rivaz Chasselas 1999★★

☐ 0.4 ha 4,000 50–69 F

This bright, light Chasselas has an attractive floral aroma. Its rich and full-bodied palate has good tannins that linger to the finish. The characteristics of the Lavaux terroir are clearly apparent in this wine, which will age well.

Alexandre Chappuis et Fils, Bons-Voisins, 1812 Rivaz, tel. 02.19.46.13.06, fax 02.19.46.13.06 Y by appt.

GROGNUZ FRERES

Saint-Saphorin Syrah 1998★★★

■ 0.1 ha 700 100–149 F

The Syrah de Saint-Saphorin's 98 vintage may not quite have been selected as a *coup de cœur*, but it is nonetheless an outstanding wine. Dark violet in colour, it has an intense, fine, very floral nose with a spicy overtone of pepper, cinnamon and a hint of vanilla. The peppery aromas gradually become more dominant on the palate. Balanced by delicate acidity, the wine's velvety palate is supported by dense tannins and complex flavours. A wine suitable for ten years' ageing.

Grognuz Frères et Fils, Cave des Rois, 1844 Villeneuve, tel. 02.19.44.41.28, fax 02.19.44.41.28 Y by appt.

HAUT DE PIERRE

Dézaley Chasselas Vieilles vignes 1998★★

☐ Gd cru 1 ha 4,800 70–99 F

Very pure and mineral, this Chasselas, the product of 30-year-old vines, has an unctuous palate with a subtle flavour of hazelnuts. The terroir has clearly influenced both the wine's nose and its long, attractively bitter finish. Five years' ageing would bring this wine to fruition.

Vincent et Blaise Duboux, Creyvavers, 1098 Epesses, tel. 02.17.99.18.80, fax 02.17.99.38.39, e-mail b.duboux@lavaux.ch Y by appt.

DOM. DE HAUTE-COUR

Mont-sur-Rolle Chasselas 1999★★

☐ Gd cru 7.87 ha 43,000 30–49 F

The Domaine de Haute-Cour has a long history. In the 13th century, the land belonged to the lords of Mont-le-Grand, who then made it over to the monks of Bonmont. Goethe stayed there in 1779. The jury declared this floral (linden flowers), slightly salty, pineapple wine remarkable. Its very fruity palate is a perfect balance of liveliness and roundness, and it has a fine, long, slightly minerally after-taste. An elegant, typical La Côte, it would be excellent served as an apéritif.

SI de Haute-Cour, 1180 Rolle, tel. 02.18.22.02.02 Y by appt.

LA BEGUINE Calamin Chasselas 1999★

☐ Gd cru 0.5 ha 8,000 30–49 F

Jean-Francois and Michel Dizerens own 15 ha (37 acres) of vineyards around Lavaux. The Calamin Chasselas is rich, floral and slightly spicy. It has some residual sugars, which give the palate a velvety character. The wine finishes with an agreeably bitter after-taste that shows the characteristic tone of the terroir.

Jean-François et Michel Dizerens, 31, chem. Moulin, 1095 Lutry, tel. 02.17.91.34.97, fax 02.17.91.24.96, e-mail jmdlutry@swissonline.ch Y by appt.

LA FAVEUR DES MUSES

Ollon Chasselas 1998★

☐ 4 ha 25,000 50–69 F

A clear, bright colour, this Chasselas has an enticing, slightly burnt, floral nose. The round, rich and fruity palate is lifted by a subtle mineral note on the finish.

Association Viticole d'Ollon, rue Demesse, 1867 Ollon, tel. 02.44.99.11.77, fax 02.44.99.24.48, e-mail info@avollon.ch Y by appt.

LA GRUYRE Dézaley Chasselas 1999★★

☐ Gd cru 0.4 ha 5,000 50–69 F

Bright and clear, this Chasselas has a powerful nose full of pure mineral aromas. Its gently textured palate is rounded and sweet, enlivened by a hint of gunflint. The wine has a long finish, characteristic of the terroir. It would go well with Vacherin or Gruyère cheese.

Louis Hegg et Fils, La Mottaz, 1098 Epesses, tel. 02.17.99.14.51, fax 02.17.99.54.04 Y by appt.

LA GUENIETTAZ

Dézaley Chasselas 1999★★

☐ Gd cru 0.45 ha 5,000 30–49 F

The Chappuis family has lived in the commune of Rivaz since 1335. Its vineyards are divided between the Saint-Saphorin and Dézaley appellations. Their Chasselas has the characteristics of its terroir. Rich and tender, it has a subtle burnt aroma on the nose. On

the palate, it is full-bodied and rich, with a hint of gunflint. The long finish is sweet, but with a touch of the bitterness typical of Dézaley wines. Although drinkable now, this wine will also age well.
🔑 Vincent Chappuis et Fils,
en Bons-Voisins, 1812 Rivaz,
tel. 02.19.46.17.57, fax 02.19.46.29.72,
e-mail
cave.vincent.chappuis.et.fils@urbanet.ch
☑ 🍷 by appt.

LA MAISON DU LEZARD

Yvorne Pinot Noir Vinifié et Élevé en Barrique de Chêne 1998★

■ 1.1 ha 8,470 100–149 F

Henri Bacoux has made a distinctive, bright, ruby-coloured wine. His Pinot Noir 98 is fruity (cherries and raspberries) with a hint of vanilla, and a vinous quality that is not at all heavy. The balanced palate, which echoes the original aromas, is fleshy and has fine tannins. On the finish, there is a vanilla-tinged, fruity flavour enlivened by gentle acidity. A wine that will keep for two to four years.
🔑 Henri Badoux,
18, av. du Chamossaire, 1860 Aigle,
tel. 02.44.68.68.88, fax 02.44.68.68.89,
e-mail badoux.vins@bluewin.ch ☑
🍷 by appt.

LA PERLE Epesses Chasselas 1999★★★

□ 0.4 ha 4,000 30–49 F

This Chasselas has beautifully fresh floral aromas with the mineral notes typical of this variety. On the palate, it displays a harmonious balance of vinosity and freshness. As yet, it is by no means the longest or the richest Chasselas, but it is extremely elegant, with the hint of bitterness that is the signature of this great terroir. This wine will age very well, gaining in aromatic complexity over time. The **Chasselas Champ-Noé Villette 99** is very fleshy and rich, with fine linden flower and burnt aromas.
🔑 Jean-Luc Blondel,
12, chem. du Vigny, 1096 Cully,
tel. 02.17.99.31.92, fax 02.17.99.21.92,
e-mail blondel@lavaux.ch ☑ 🍷 by appt.

LE MAGISTRAT

Saint-Saphorin Chasselas 1999★

□ 0.8 ha 6,000 50–69 F

The Saint-Saphorin Chasselas from Le Magistrat is a notably fresh and fruity wine. Its clean, floral and mineral aromas on the nose carry through to the palate, which is slightly sweet and has a nice balance of alcohol and acidity. While it is ready to drink now, the wine may be cellared for a while.
🔑 Jean-François Neyroud-Fonjallaz,
13, rte du Vignoble, 1803 Chardonne,
tel. 02.19.21.71.73, fax 02.19.22.70.17 ☑
🍷 ev. day except Sun. 8am–12 noon
1.30pm–6pm; Sat. 8am–12 noon

LES BLASSINGES

Saint-Saphorin Chasselas 1999★★★

□ 1.8 ha 12,000 50–69 F

Pierre-Luc Leyvraz's estate is a small terraced vineyard on the shores of Lake Léman. His Chasselas 99 is exceptional, boasting a truly complex aroma that is floral and fruity, with mineral and spicy notes. The velvety palate reiterates those aromas with some finesse. They persist through to a slightly bitter finish that is characteristic of the grand terroirs of the Vaud canton. A classy Chasselas that will age perfectly until 2010.
🔑 Pierre-Luc Leyvraz,
4, chem. de Baulet, 1071 Chexbres,
tel. 02.19.46.19.40, fax 02.19.46.19.45,
e-mail pl.leyvraz@freesurf.ch ☑ 🍷 by appt.

LE SECRET D'EPICURE

Vinzel Gamay 1998★

■ 0.1 ha 650 30–49 F

Until 1995, the Domaine Delaharpe only cultivated Chasselas vines. Le Secret d'Epicure, whose label was designed by the painter Gilbert Reinhardt, is their first red wine. The brilliant dark red 98 has an intense, fruity and spicy nose with black cherry, cinnamon and pepper aromas. Its palate is fresh, lively and slightly sweet, but balanced by its tannins. The slightly austere finish suggests that the wine will age well (five years or maybe even longer).
🔑 Gustave et Yann Menthonnex, Dom. Delaharpe, La Tourelle, 1183 Bursins,
tel. 02.18.24.22.30, fax 02.18.24.22.30,
e-mail menthonnex@hotmail.com ☑
🍷 by appt.

LES MENADES

Ollon Chasselas 1999★★

□ 2 ha 10,000 50–69 F

Pierre-Alain Meylan has made two remarkable wines: a **Gamaret d'Ollon 98**

Elevée en Barrique, which is powerful and vinous (100–149F), and this well-structured, thoroughbred Chasselas. The golden-hued 99 has aromas of gunflint and flowers. Rich and velvety, it has excellent acidity that persists through to a long, mineral finish.
Pierre-Alain Meylan, rue de la Chapelle, 1867 Ollon, tel. 02.44.99.24.14
by appt.

LE VIN VIVANT DE BERNARD RAVET

Morges Pinot Noir Elevé en Barrique 1998★★

■ 0.3 ha 1,990 70–99 F

The range of wines bottled as ‘Les Vins Vivant de Bernard Ravet’ is the result of an encounter between the chef of that name and the Uvavins company œnologist. Their Pinot Noir has an expressive, fruity nose of black cherries that is slightly earthy, and also reveals a hint of vanilla. The well-structured palate is similarly fruity and very fresh. This is a distinguished wine that will keep for at least five years. From the same collection, **La Trilogie La Côte 97** (100–149F) was awarded one star. This is a sweet white wine made from Chardonnay, Chasselas and Pinot Gris grapes that were dried on the vine.
Uvavins, Cave de la Côte,
1131 Tolochenaz,
tel. 02.18.04.54.54, fax 02.18.04.54.55,
e-mail uvavins@swissarline by appt.

DOM. DE MARCELIN

Morges Pinot Noir 1998★★★

■ 1.76 ha 10,520 30–49 F

This 7-ha (17-acre) estate, owned by L’Etat de Vaud, has produced two exceptional 1998 red wines in Morges. The young **Assemblage de Cépages Nobles Morges 98** (50–69F) was awarded three stars for its great potential. It will continue to develop until 2010. This Pinot Noir was selected as a *coup de cœur* for its more open, fresh and fruity aromas of cherries and raspberries, which are present on both the nose and palate. The roundness of the palate is in perfect harmony with its alcohol and acidity, and helps to cloak the fine, powerful tannins. A wine that could be enjoyed now or saved for later.
Dom. de Marcelin, av. Marcelin,
1110 Morges, tel. 02.18.03.08.33,
fax 02.18.03.08.36 by appt.
Etat de Vaud

PETIT DUC Epesses Chasselas 1999★★

□ 1.2 ha 10,000 50–69 F

This family vineyard in Lavaux dates back to the 15th century. Today, it covers 4-ha (10-acres) that are mostly planted with Chasselas. This 1999 is a good reflection of its terroir. Full-bodied and velvet-textured, it has a fruity freshness and a long, pleasantly bitter finish. While the wine is certainly captivating now, it has sufficient structure to age well.
Jean-François Chevalley,
Dom. de la Chenalettaz,
1096 Le Treytorrens-en-Dézaley,
tel. 02.17.99.13.00, fax 02.17.99.39.21,
e-mail jf.chevalley@lavaux.ch
by appt.

PIERRE NOIRE

Saint-Saphorin Chasselas 1998★★

□ 2.5 ha 30,000 50–69 F

The **Chasselas Grand Pertuis du Grand Cru Dézaley 98** (70–99F) was declared a very fine wine, but the jury preferred the St-Saphorin. A golden wine, it has intense floral and mineral aromas with hazelnut overtones. The characteristic style of the terroir is evident in the mineral notes that underline the rich, rounded palate, and in the remarkable bitterness of its highly distinguished finish. A complex wine suitable for keeping at least five years.
J.-P. Chaudet et Fils,
Cave du Grillon, 1812 Rivaz,
tel. 02.19.46.11.74, fax 02.19.46.34.35,
e-mail b.chaudet@urbanet.ch by appt.

PLANCHE-CACHE

Villeneuve Pinot Noir 1998★

■ 1.07 ha 10,300 50–69 F

This estate of a little over 4-ha (10-acres) has produced a fine Pinot Noir (blended with a tiny percentage of Garanoir). Shimmering with dark highlights, the 1998 has a slightly spicy aroma of crystallised black fruits. It is tender and full-bodied, with good tannins that linger through to the subtly spicy finish. This wine should be kept for two to four years before drinking.
Louis Amiguet-Schilt, 56, Grand-Rue,
Cave rue des Pressoirs, 1844 Villeneuve,
tel. 02.19.60.28.50, fax 02.19.68.14.06,
e-mail ponverroz@bluewin.ch by appt.

ROBIN DES VIGNES

Vilette Chasselas 1999★

□ 2 ha 20,000 30–49 F

Chasselas grapes harvested from the sloping vineyards of Villette, on the shores of Lake Léman, have produced this wine. It has the fresh, distinctive linden flower aromas characteristic of this variety. Fruity, rich and alcoholic, the palate demonstrates a good balance of fullness and acidity. The impressively long finish is subtly bitter. A wine to serve as an apéritif.

🔑 Association viticole de Lutry, 21, chem. Culturaz 21, 1095 Lutry, tel. 02.17.91.24.66, fax 02.17.91.67.24 ☑ 🍸 ev. day except Sun. 8.30am–6pm; Mon. 1.30pm–6pm; Sat. 8am–12 noon.

JEAN-LUC ROCHAT

Morges Auxerrois 1999**

☐ 0.15 ha 1,100 30–49 F

Soft, fruity and fresh, this Auxerrois would make an excellent apéritif. It is velvety, but not at all heavy, on the palate, where peach flavours echo the aromas of the nose. Ready to drink now.

🔑 Jean-Luc Rochat, Dom. des Chentres, 1163 Etoy, tel. 02.18.08.74.22, fax 02.18.08.74.22 ☑ 🍸 by appt.

CAVE DES ROSSILLONNES

Vinzel Chasselas 1999*

☐ 2.5 ha 16,000 30–49 F

'A very good Dorin from Vinzel.' Dorin is the local name for the white wines of Vaud. This one has a bright and clear colour, and a slightly closed, floral nose with a hint of hazelnut. Structured and velvety, it has well-balanced acidity. Serve it with cheese or white meat.

🔑 Jean-Paul Besson, Cave des Rossillonnes, 1184 Vinzel, tel. 02.18.24.12.46, fax 02.18.24.12.46 ☑ 🍸 by appt.

LOUIS-PHILIPPE ROUGE ET FILS

Dézaley Sous-Marsens Chasselas 1999**

☐ Gd cru 0.55 ha n.c. 100–149 F

This shimmering Dézaley Chasselas has an appealing blend of linden flower and mineral (kerosene) aromas. The tender and unctuous palate has the mineral flavours of the terroir, which persist through to a fine bitter note on the finish.

🔑 Louis-Philippe et Philippe Rouge, Cave de la Cornalle, 1098 Epesses, tel. 02.17.99.41.22, fax 02.17.99.26.64, e-mail rougelpp@worldcom.ch ☑ 🍸 by appt.

SAVEUR DU BRESIL

Bonvillars Pinot Noir – Pinot Gris 1998*

☐ 0.2 ha 700 100–149 F

As the Vaud canton has only recently begun to produce sweet wines, it is difficult to guess how they will develop in the cellar. We have to make an educated guess that this Saveur du Brésil will keep for ten years. Golden yellow, it has an intense and complex bouquet of roses, strawberries and cinnamon. Those aromas are also present on the palate, where sweetness is balanced by fine acidity. The finish is a little austere, though.

🔑 Jacques Bloesch, Dom. la Boulaz, 1427 Bonvillars, tel. 02.44.36.13.80, fax 02.44.36.26.88 ☑ 🍸 by appt.

SIR THOMAS AU CLOS DE SAINT-BONNET

Bursinel 1998**

■ 0.37 ha 1,300 50–69 F

At the end of the 13th century, the land this vineyard is planted on belonged to Thomas de Saint-Bonnet, after whom it is named. The Bursinel vineyard is a well-exposed terrace on the shore of Lake Léman. A blend of Gamaret, Garanoir and Diolinoir has resulted in a dark purple wine. The nose is redolent of blackberries, cherries, pepper, cinnamon and tar. Rich and fruity, the palate is both lively and smooth, with dense tannins and a slight vanilla flavour. An eloquent wine.

🔑 Bernard Steiner, Saint-Bonnet, 1195 Dully, tel. 02.18.24.16.08, fax 02.18.24.16.08, e-mail b-steiner@freesurf.ch ☑ 🍸 by appt.

PHILIPPE STRAUB

Vinzel Chardonnay Elevé en Barrique 1998**

☐ 0.14 ha 600 70–99 F

Phillippe Straub allocates a little over two of his 16 ha (40 acres) of land to vines planted in four appellations. His golden Chardonnay from Vinzel has a remarkably intense, lightly oaked nose with the apricot, citrus and walnut-oil aromas characteristic of the variety. Fresh and fruity, the palate is lively, rounded and well-balanced. This fine food wine is ready to drink now, but could be kept for up to five years.

🔑 Philippe Straub, Dom. de la Tuilerie, 1184 Vinzel, tel. 02.18.24.15.48, fax 02.18.24.15.48 ☑ 🍸 by appt.

DOM. DE TERRE NEUVE

Saint-Prex Gamay 1999*

■ 0.8 ha 5,500 50–69 F

In 1996, David Kind took over the management of this estate in Saint-Prex, which dates back to 1830. His Gamay is nearly always a commendable wine, and the 1999 is very good. Richly coloured with subtle violet highlghts, it has a floral aroma of violets with a hint of pepper. The fresh and fruity palate is well-structured, and combines alcohol, acidity and tannins in perfect balance. The finish is a little tannic, but softened by a slight sweetness. A wine with personality, it is ready to drink now.

🔑 David Kind, Dom. de Terre-Neuve, 1162 St. Prex, tel. 02.18.03.63.44, fax 02.18.03.63.34, e-mail dkind@swissonline.ch ☑ 🍸 by appt.

VEILLON AU CLOITRE

Aigle Chasselas 1999*

☐ 3 ha 25,000 50–69 F

The vineyard lies below the cloisters and Roman church of Saint-Maurice. This wine has a fruity nose with the gunflint note characteristic of Chasselas. On the palate, it is soft and supple with a mineral aroma and a slightly bitter after-taste.

Veillon, av. du Cloître 32, 1860 Aigle,
tel. 02.44.66.23.66, fax 02.44.66.27.81
by appt.

VIGNE EN BAYEL

Féchy Chasselas 1999★★

□ 1 ha 10,000 50-69 F

In the commune of Féchy, between Geneva and Lausanne on the shores of Lake Léman, Raymond Paccot cultivates 10 ha (25 acres) of La Côte wines. Two of these are particularly distinguished. The Féchy is a structured and fresh-tasting Chasselas. Subtly salty and floral, the wine reflects its terroir; it has a balanced, velvety, lively palate. The **Pinot Gris Réserve de La Côte 98** (70–99F), with its pleasant, subtle aromas of flowers, spices and fruit, and its great finesse, was also awarded two stars.

Raymond Paccot, Dom. la Colombe,
1173 Féchy, tel. 02.18.08.66.48,
e-mail raypaccot@freesurf.ch by appt.

CH. DE VUFFLENS

Morges Chasselas 1999★

□ Gd cru 5 ha 30,000 30-49 F

Dating from the 14th century, the Château de Vufflens is an imposing edifice with a red-brick keep overlooking an 8-ha (20-acre) vineyard planted on marl soils. The Chasselas 1999 has a very pure, floral and slightly salty nose. Its fresh and fruity palate, which shows a good balance of acidity, alcohol and a slight sweetness, finishes on a note representative of the terroir, which lends the wine plenty of character.

SA Bolle et Cie, œnothèque la Licorne,
75, rue Louis-de-Savoie, 1110 Morges,
tel. 02.18.01.27.74, fax 02.18.03.00.76,
e-mail bolle@bolle.ch
ev. day except Sun. Mon. 9am–12 noon
2pm–6.30pm; Sat. 2pm–4pm

DOM. DE WURSTEMBERGER

Mont-sur-Rolle Dame de Hautecour Chasselas 1997★★

□ n.c. 2,000 50-69 F

Coraline de Wurstemberger's beautifully matured Chasselas is sold under an elegant label. This bright golden-yellow wine has opened up to reveal a complex bouquet of salty notes, honey, spices (cinnamon and pepper) and peach. Its velvety palate is balanced by attractive freshness, and the wine has sustained aromas of spices and crystallised fruit with a salty undertone.

Coraline de Wurstemberger,
rte. de la Noyère, 1185 Mont-sur-Rolle,
tel. 02.18.26.09.18, fax 02.18.26.01.64,
e-mail coraline@bluewin.ch by appt.

Valais

The valley of the Haute-Rhône is a land of contrasts, fashioned through the millennia by the advance and retreat of the glacier. Many of the vineyards on the steep hills are laid out in terraces.

Valais is like a part of Provence in the heart of the Alps. Close to the eternal alpine snows, vines grow alongside apricot trees and asparagus. On the pathways of the *bisses* (a local name for irrigation channels), a walker will come across almond trees, pheasant's eye, sweet chestnut trees, cactus, praying mantises and scorpions, and find absinthe, wormwood, hyssop and thyme growing along the walls.

More than 40 grape varieties are grown in the Valais, some not to be found elsewhere, including Arvine, Humagne, Amigne and Cornalin. Here, Chasselas is called Fendant and a local cross between Pinot Noir and Gamay creates the Dôle. Both are AOC Crus and, according to the *terroir*, range from fruitiness to a greater elegance in character.

ANTOINE ET CHRISTOPHE BETRISSEY

Syrah de Saint-Léonard Elevé en Fût de Chêne 1998★★

■ 0.2 ha 1,600 70-99 F

The Bétrissy brothers began managing the family estate in 1992. In parallel with their wine-making operation, they run a vine nursery. This Syrah, aged for ten months in oak, has a purple-red colour and powerful, spicy aromas of red fruits and cloves. A well-made wine, it has a lively attack, followed by a well-structured palate with fruity flavours that persist through to a long finish. It should be cellared for four years. The **Pinot Noir de Saint-Léonard Elevé en Fût de Chêne 98** shows well-judged oak-ageing. It was awarded one star (50–69F).

Antoine et Christophe Bétrissey,
rue du Château, 1958 Saint-Léonard,
tel. 02.72.03.11.26, fax 02.72.03.40.26
by appt.

ALBERT BIOLLAZ

Grain Noble 1997★★★

□ 0.2 ha 3,500 100–149 F

The Sylvaner, Marsanne and Pinot Gris grapes used in this wine were raisined on the vine. The resulting *liquoreux* wine has a glittering golden colour and intense aromas of crystallised fruit. Its full-bodied palate shows a harmonious balance of alcohol and acidity, as well as a particularly long finish. The wine should be aged for five to six years. The **La Sirène 99**, a Chardonnay (70–99F), was awarded two stars, while the **Les Riverettes 99** (30–49F) received one.

Les Hoirs Albert Biollaz, 5, rue du Prieuré, 1956 Saint-Pierre-de-Clages, tel. 02.73.06.28.86, fax 02.73.06.62.50, e-mail info@biollaz-vins.ch by appt.

MICHEL BOUEN Dôle 1999★★

■ 1 ha 6,000 30–49 F

Michel Bouen grows 18 different varieties on his 10-ha (25-acre) estate. His rustic, purple-hued Dôle was judged to be particularly successful. The nose has aromas of forest fruits, which are echoed in the persistent wild strawberry and cherry flavours of the rounded, well-balanced palate. The distinguished **Gamay de Chamoson 99** is sustained by fine tannins, and was awarded one star.

Michel Bouen, Cave Ardévaz, 4, Latigny, 1955 Chamoson, tel. 02.73.06.28.36, fax 02.73.06.44.00 by appt.

CAPRICE DU TEMPS

Coteaux de Sierre Humagne Blanc 1999★

□ 0.3 ha 3,000 50–69 F

Hugues Clavien practices organic viticulture on his 3-ha (7-acre) vineyard. Pale yellow and delicately fruity, this wine is seductively vinous. It has a subtly acidic and fruity palate. Although a delicate wine, it reflects the best characteristics of the Humagne grape.

Hugues Clavien et Fils, Cave Caprice du Temps, 3972 Miège, tel. 02.74.55.76.40, fax 02.74.55.76.40, e-mail clavien@bluewin.ch by appt.

JEAN ET FLORENCE CARRUPT

Chamoson Cornalin 1999★

■ 0.2 ha 1,000 100–149 F

Dark ruby in colour, with a fine, elegant nose of morello cherries, this Cornalin is an elegant, rather tannic wine with very attractive red berry and black cherry flavours. Although it is ready to drink now, it could be kept for up to five years, before being served with a game bird.

Jean et Florence Carrupt, La Petite-Cave, rue de Fosseau, 1955 Chamoson, tel. 02.73.06.76.15, fax 02.73.06.76.15 ev. day except Sun. 9am–12 noon 1pm–7pm

PIERRE-MAURICE CARRUZO

Chamoson Humagne Rouge 1999★★

■ 0.25 ha 1,800 50–69 F

This dark ruby wine is fragrant with black fruits and liquorice. Its forthright, lively attack announces a concentrated and elegant palate, structured by supple tannins. The **Malvoisie Flétrie de Chamoson 98** (100–149F), is an equally remarkable *liquoreux* that has been aged in oak for 18 months. Soft but vigorous in style, it has aromas of crystallised fruit, honey, quinces and apricots on the nose, followed by fresh moss and camomile flavours on the palate. Finally, the **Fendant de Trémazière 99** was awarded one star for its fruity and mineral (gunflint) character.

Pierre-Maurice Carruzzo, 24, pré de Monthey, 1955 Chamoson, tel. 02.73.06.37.56, fax 02.73.06.37.46, e-mail vinspmc@bluewin.ch by appt.

CHAMPORTAY

Martigny Gamay 1999★★

■ 2 ha 12,000 50–69 F

Gérard Besse first became involved in wine-making when he bought the terraced vineyard of Champortay 30 years ago. His holdings now cover 14 ha (35 acres). In 1999, he produced three very attractive vat-fermented red wines. The first is a richly coloured Gamay with violet highlights. It is a fleshy, concentrated, very well-structured wine full of spicy black fruit aromas. The second, a rounded, floral **Dôle de Martigny 99**, was awarded one star. The third, a **Pinot Noir 99, Domaine Saint-Théodule**, which has chocolate aromas and elegant tannins, was also declared worthy of a star.

Gérald et Patricia Besse, Les Rappes, 1921 Martigny-Combe, tel. 02.77.22.78.81, fax 02.77.23.21.94 by appt.

CAVE DU CHAVALARD

Johannisberg 1999★★

□ 0.5 ha 2,000 50–69 F

Vincent and Gilles Carron's Johannisberg (aka Sylvaner) is a product of the granite soils of Fully. Golden-yellow in colour, it has an intensely fruity aroma that develops a bitter almond character on the palate. Rich and pleasantly acid, it has a slightly sweet finish. Despite being quite alcoholic, the wine's full body and structure exhibit remarkable finesse. It could easily partner asparagus or cheese.

Vincent et Gilles Carron, Cave de Chavalard, 203, rt. de Martigny, 1926 Branson-Fully, tel. 02.77.46.23.55, fax 02.77.46.30.79, e-mail gc@swissonline.ch by appt.

YVON CHESEAUX

Saillon Cornalin Fût de Chêne 1998★★

■ 0.1 ha 600 100–149 F

In the medieval village of Saillon, Yvon Cheseaux cultivates a tiny vineyard planted on light sandy soils. His intense purple Cornalin is full of fruit, with hints of violet and elderflower. This is a concentrated wine

with great personality. Twelve months of careful maturation in oak have given it a balanced character, but it will develop well over another three to five years.
Yvon Cheseaux,
Cave des Remparts, 1913 Saillon,
tel. 02.77.44.33.76, fax 02.77.44.33.76,
e-mail cavedesremparts@bluewin.ch
by appt.

CAVE CORBASSIERE Gamay 1999**

■ 1 ha 1,500 30–49 F

This powerful wine has inviting aromas of blackcurrant and elderberry. It is well-balanced and long, with fine tannins. The palate is already attractive with its red berry flavours. However, this Gamay will continue to develop until 2004. Meanwhile, the remarkably balanced and long **Dôle 99** from the same estate may be enjoyed over the next two years.
Cave Corbassière, 1913 Saillon,
tel. 02.77.44.14.03, fax 02.77.44.39.20
by appt.

CORNULUS

Clos des Corbassières Fendant 1999***

□ 0.7 ha 6,000 50–69 F

This Valais Fendant is ready to enjoy now. It has a beguiling pale yellow colour with green highlights. Intensely floral (linden flowers), it is very fresh, balanced and extremely fruity – an exceptionally full-bodied and aromatic wine. The sweet, full and balanced **Octoglaive Hermitage Grain Noble 98** (150–199F) is equally outstanding. Finally, the oak aged **Red Humagne Antica 98**(100–149F) was awarded two stars.
Dom. Cornulus, Stéphane, Reynard et Dany Varone, 1965 Saviese,
tel. 02.73.95.25.45, fax 02.73.95.25.45,
e-mail cornulus@bluewin.ch by appt.

CRETE D'OR 1998**

■ 2 ha 10,000 70–99 F

Brightly coloured with purple highlights, this wine is a blend of Pinot Noir, Gamay, Syrah and Diolinoir grapes. Eight months of maturation in oak have added spicy, toasty and vanilla notes to its red berry aromas. On the palate, its rich, powerful attack is balanced by ripe tannins. Generous and well-structured, this wine is ready to drink now with red meat. The **Sion Les Mazots 99 Fendant** (30–49F) was awarded one star for its mineral aromas, characteristic of the terroir, and a good balance of alcohol and acidity.
SA Maurice Gay,
Vignoble de Ravanay, 1955 Chamoson,
tel. 02.73.06.53.53, fax 02.73.06.53.88,
e-mail mauricegay@swissonline.ch
by appt.

DOM. DES CRETES

Fendant de Sierre 1999*

□ 10 ha 12,000 30–49 F

Joseph Vocat and his son Yves cultivate 25 ha (62 acres) of vineyards that undulate over five hills in the village of Sierre. This is a very floral (linden flowers) wine with mineral overtones. On the palate, a soft intial impression precedes a good balance of acidity and body. This harmonious wine has a subtly bitter finish.
Joseph Vocat et Fils,
3976 Noës-sur-Sierre,
tel. 02.74.58.26.49, fax 02.74.58.28.49,
e-mail info@vocatvins.ch by appt.

DOM. CRETTEX A JOSE

Malvoisie Flétrie 1998**

□ n.c. n.c. 100–149 F

Made from late-harvested grapes, this very sweet, straw-yellow wine has an intense aroma of honey and overripe grapes. The palate is long, powerful and velvety. It will continue to be enjoyable until 2005.
Hervé Fontannaz, Cave la Tine,
1963 Vétroz, tel. 02.73.46.47.47,
e-mail doritana@omedia.ch
ev. day except Sun. Mon. 8am–12 noon 1.30pm–6pm; Sat. 8am–12 noon

CHRISTIAN CRITTIN

Cabernet Franc Cabernet-Sauvignon 1997*

■ 0.14 ha 900 70–99 F

This family estate was established in 1888 in Saint-Pierre-de-Clages, a commune famous for its pretty Norman church. Chrisian Crittin has made a rich and complex Cabernet blend. This dark red wine, which was matured in oak for 18 months, has a liquoricey and slightly peppery aroma. Rich and powerful, it could be kept for three to five years.
Christian Crittin, 9, rue Eglise, 1956 Saint-Pierre-de-Clages, tel. 02.73.06.17.34, fax 02.73.06.57.58 by appt.

PHILIPPE DARIOLY

Ermitage Flétri 1998*

□ 0.15 ha 900 100–149 F

Golden-coloured with amber highlights, this *liquoreux* has an aroma of truffles, undergrowth, quince jelly and beeswax. On the palate, it is luscious and rich with smoky overtones. The concentration of the wine is lifted by fine acidity, which leaves an agreeably fresh after-taste. It should be cellared for five to ten years.
Philippe Darioly, Fusion 160, 1920 Martigny, tel. 02.77.23.27.66 by appt.

GILBERT DEVAYES

Leytron Humagne Rouge 1999★★★

■ 0.7 ha 3,000 50–69 F

Gilbert Devayes makes his wines in the vaulted cellars of an 18th-century house. His purple-coloured Humagne Rouge is a velvety yet tannic wine, displaying the rustic character of the variety. The nose has an aroma of forest fruits and spices. In three to five years, the wine will make a fine accompaniment to game.

Gilbert Devayes, Cave la Dôle Blanche, 5, ruelle de la Cotze, 1912 Leytron, tel. 02.73.06.25.96, fax 02.73.06.63.46 Y by appt.

CAVE DUBUIS ET RUDAZ

Marsanne Grain Noble 1997★★

□ 0.35 ha 2,000 100–149 F

Judging by the quality of this *liquoreux*, the Dubuis and Rudaz partnership, which was established in 1986, is a remarkably successful coalition. Their sweet Marsanne has aromas of toast, vanilla and tropical fruits (pineapples), with a hint of white truffle. Balanced and powerful, the palate develops from impressions of sweetness to a hint of salt, the rich flavours lingering for a long time. A wine to be kept for three to four years before drinking.

Cave Dubuis et Rudaz, 1981 Vex, tel. 02.73.21.13.13, fax 02.73.21.13.14, e-mail dubuis.rudaz@bluewin.ch Y by appt.

VINCENT FAVRE-CARRUZZO

Chamoson Fendant 1999

□ n.c. 3,500 50–69 F

This is a very fresh, pale yellow wine with green highlights. It is redolent of linden flowers, with a hint of lavender. A lively attack foreshadows a well-balanced palate and long finish. Ready to drink now.

Vincent Favre-Carruzzo, 1955 Chamoson, tel. 02.73.06.22.65, fax 02.73.06.64.43 Y by appt.

CAVE DU FORUM

Chamoson Pinot Noir 1999★★

■ 2.8 ha 2,500 30–49 F

Henri Magistrini, who also owns vineyards in Vaud, cultivates 12 ha (30 acres) in Valais. He has made a very good **Fendant de Fully 99**, as well as this remarkable, richly ruby-coloured Chamoson Pinot Noir. The undergrowth-scented 1999 is a very expressive wine. Unctuous and powerful, it has soft, ripe tannins that render it ready for drinking now.

Henri Magistrini, Cave du Forum, 36, Deleze, 1920 Martigny, tel. 02.77.22.50.76, e-mail cave-du-forum@bluewin.ch Y by appt.

FRANC TIREUR Païen 1999★★

□ 0.8 ha 7,500 70–99 F

This straw-yellow Païen (Savagnin) shimmers with golden highlights. A fruity aroma with hints of lime and wildflower leads on to a balanced, lemon-scented palate. The wine is both smooth and structured, and will easily keep for ten to 15 years. The rounded, well-built **Red Humagne La Chassenarde 99**, with its intense aromas of fruit, ivy, prunes and undergrowth, was also awarded two stars.

SA les Fils Maye, rue des Caves, 1908 Riddes, tel. 02.73.06.55.86, fax 02.73.06.60.92 Y by appt.

JO GAUDARD

Leytron Chardonnay 1999★

□ 0.1 ha 1,000 50–69 F

This sweet yellow wine, with golden highlights, is balanced and elegant. The nose is a medley of exotic fruit, pear and mango aromas. It leads into a delicate and complex palate with sustained citrus, peach and pineapple flavours.

Jo Gaudard, rte. de Chamoson, 1912 Leytron, tel. 02.73.06.60.69, fax 02.73.06.72.18 Y by appt.

ROBERT GILLIARD Syrah 1998★

■ 1.5 ha 12,200 50–69 F

When it was first established in 1885, this estate only covered 4-ha (10-acres). It now owns 40 ha (100 acres) of vines planted on steep terraces supported by 18-m (59-ft)-high drystone walls. With its purple-red colour, this is a typical Syrah with pepper and blackcurrant aromas and a long palate, structured with good tannins.

SA Robert Gilliard, 70, rue de Loèche, 1950 Sion, tel. 02.73.29.89.29, fax 02.73.29.89.28, e-mail vins@gilliard.ch Y by appt.

FRANCOIS ET DOMINIQUE GIROUD Fendant 1999★

□ 1 ha 5,000 50–69 F

François manages the vineyard and Dominique the wine-making on this 10-ha (25-acre) estate. Together, they produce some very good wines, such as this light yellow Fendant with golden highlights. The floral (linden flowers) and mineral nose is followed by a supple attack. Persistent hazelnut flavours dominate the palate. This wine is ready to drink now.

François et Dominique Giroud, rue du Nasot, 1955 Chamoson, tel. 07.92.20.33.66, fax 07.73.06.10.23, e-mail dominique@giroud-vins.ch Y by appt.

GRAINS DE MALICE

Vendanges tardives Cuvée du Maître de Chai Elevé en Fût 1998★★★

□ 0.75 ha 5,000 150–199 F

The Provins Valais cellar has made four highly rated wines: **Rouge d'Enfer Cuvée du Maître de Chais Elevé en Barrique 98** (100–149F), **Brindamour Malvoisie Vendanges Tardives 98** (100–149F), **Dôle Stockalper 99** (70–99F) and **Tourbillon Ermitage Vendanges Tardives 96** (250–299F). However, the judges preferred this *liquoreux*. A golden wine made

from a blend of Hermitage (Marsanne) and Pinot Gris, it has a lingering, subtle and complex aroma of vanilla-scented crystallised fruit. This is an outstanding wine that is both powerful and elegant. It will easily keep for 20 years.

Provins Valais, 22, rue de l'Industrie, 1950 Sion, tel. 02.73.28.66.66, fax 02.73.28.66.60, e-mail info@provins.ch

DOM. DU GRAND-BRULE

Petite Arvine 1999★★

0.58 ha 3,400 70–99 F

The Bois-Brûlé estate used to be covered in a coppice of Norway pine. Now, it serves as an experimental vineyard for the canton of Valais. Twenty-four varieties are grown here, including the Petite Arvine that was used to make this *moelleux* white wine. Fruity and floral aromas combine on the nose: grapefruit, rhubarb and wisteria. The palate is full, structured and fruity with good acidity. This wine has length and distinction, and will keep for two to five years.

Vignoble de l'Etat du Valais, 1912 Leytron, tel. 02.73.06.21.05, fax 02.73.06.36.05 by appt.

HURLEVENT Pinot Gris 1999★★

1.5 ha 7,420 50–69 F

This *moelleux* may be powerful and concentrated, but it also has an elegant balance of fruit and acidity. The forthright crystallised fruit aromas of the nose continue on the remarkably sustained palate. The wine will keep for a decade. The **Johannisberg Hurlevent 99 Moelleux** was awarded one star.

SA les Fils de Charles Favre, 29, av. de Tourbillon, 1951 Sion, tel. 02.73.27.50.50, fax 02.73.27.50.51 by appt.

DOM. DE LA GLAPIERES

Chamoson Petite Arvine 1999★★

1.2 ha 5,200 70–99 F

René Favre's two sons took over the management of the La Glapières estate in 1988. Petite Arvine grapes grown on shale soils have produced a golden wine with green highlights. The wine leaves a dense bright ring on the rim of the glass. This intense and powerful 99 has aromas of wisteria and rhubarb with a mineral overtone. After a lively and supple first impression, the palate has very well-developed structure. The long lemony finish gives it balance. It should be cellared for five to eight years.

René Favre et Fils, 11, rte. de Collombey, 1956 Saint-Pierre-de-Clages, tel. 02.73.06.39.21, fax 02.73.06.78.49, e-mail renefavrevin@chamoson.ch
ev. day except Sun. 8am–6pm; Sat. 8am–12 noon

CAVE LA MADELEINE

Malvoisie Flétrie sur Souche 1999★★

0.4 ha 2,000 70–99 F

This rich golden wine is redolent of crystallised fruit and quince. An unctuous attack precedes a balanced, powerful, full-bodied and lengthy palate. A *liquoreux* that should last for five, ten, maybe even 15 years. The **Fendant de Vétroz 99** from the same cellar was also judged very good (50–69F).

André Fontannaz, Cave la Madeleine, 1963 Vétroz, tel. 02.73.46.45.54, fax 02.73.46.45.54, e-mail cave.madeleine@vtx.ch
by appt.

LARME D'OR

Petite Arvine Vendange Tardive 1998★★

0.2 ha 850 70–99 F

Thierry Constantin took over the management of this 6.5-ha (16-acre) family estate, located a few kilometres from Sion, in 1995. His rich gold Petite Arvine leaves thick trails on the glass. It has aromas of mango, pineapple, currants and passion-fruit. The tropical fruit aromas continue on the ample and complex palate, which is balanced by good acidity and has a long finish. The **Cornalin Artémis 99** has an equally remarkable structure and fine aromatic complexity (morello cherries). Both are wines for cellaring.

Thierry Constantin, 110, rte des Iles, 1950 Sion, tel. 07.94.33.16.81, fax 07.73.46.60.20, e-mail tyconstantin@tvsznet.ch
by appt.

LA TOURMENTE

Chamoson Humagne Rouge 1999★★★

0.3 ha 1,900 50–69 F

A powerful red wine with dark highlights and a fresh mushroom scent. Fleshy, with complex and intense aromas, the palate is structured by good tannins that sustain a long

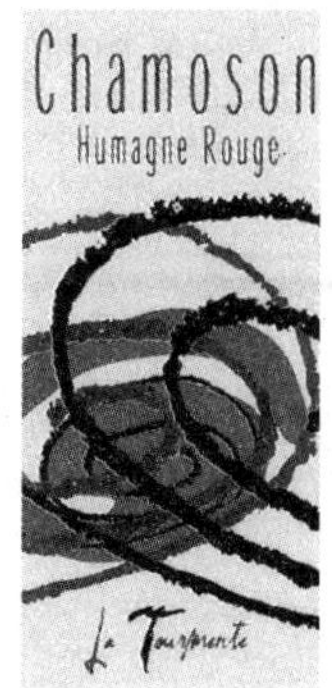

finish and give the wine the potential to last for ten years. Two stars were also awarded to the **Dôle de Chamoson 99** (30–49F) and the **Syrah de Chamoson** (70–99F).
Bernard Coudray et Fils, Cave La Tourmente, 6, Tsavez, 1955 Chamoson, tel. 02.73.06.18.32, fax 02.73.06.35.33, e-mail tourmente.cave@bluewin.ch
by appt.

LA VOUETTAZ

Chamoson Humagne Blanche 1999★★

□ 0.2 ha 1,200 50–69 F

Bertrand and Monique Caloz-Evéquoz use the simplest equipment to vinify the grapes produced on their 4-ha (10-acre) vineyard. Their results are certainly not simple, though. This remarkable wine has a delicate aroma of linden flowers. On the palate, it is intense and complex, with a balanced toasted-almond finish. A wine that displays all the characteristics of the Humagne grape, it is ready to drink now.
Bertrand et Monique Caloz-Evéquoz, 3960 Sierre, tel. 02.74.58.45.15
by appt.

CAVE LE BANNERET

Chamoson Fendant 1999★

□ 1 ha 8,000 30–49 F

This pale yellow Fendant has a strong linden flower aroma. A fresh initial impression develops into a balanced palate with a long finish. A wine to drink with Raclette, a fondue or a piece of Alpine cheese.
Carlo et Joël Maye et Fils, Cave le Banneret, 15, rue de la Crettaz, 1955 Chamoson, tel. 02.73.06.40.51, fax 02.73.06.40.51 by appt.

LE BOSSET Cyhnoir 1998★★★

■ 0.3 ha 2,000 100–149 F

This wine is an outstanding blend of Cabernet Sauvignon, Syrah and Humagne Rouge. The spicy nose has aromas of forest fruits. On the palate, it is round and structured with spicy, feral flavours that meld with finely balanced acidity. A perfectly harmonious, structured and full-bodied wine.
Willy Michellod et Romaine Blaser, Cave Le Bosset, 2, chem. des Ecoliers, 1912 Leytron, tel. 02.73.06.18.80, fax 02.73.06.18.80 by appt.

MABILLARD-FUCHS

Venthône Fendant 1999★★

□ 0.45 ha 4,000 30–49 F

This 4-ha (10-acre) hillside vineyard in Venthône practises organic viticulture. The linden flower-scented Fendant is a wine that is harmoniously fresh and rich with a long finish. The **Red Humagne 99 des Coteaux de Sierre** was also awarded two stars, in recognition of its supple palate and persistent, spicy, wild flavours (50–69F).
Madeleine et Jean-Yves Mabillard-Fuchs, 3973 Venthône, tel. 02.74.55.34.76, fax 02.74.56.34.00 by appt.

ADRIAN MATHIER

Fendant du Ravin 1999★

□ 2 ha 12,000 50–69 F

There have been Mathiers in Salquenen since 1387, but they have only been making wine since the beginning of the 20th century. Fendant, grown in chalky schist soil on a dry, sunny slope, has produced a wine with a sophisticated mineral nose with peach and linden flower overtones. After a forthright and vigorous first impression, the palate develops a balanced richness, with flavours that persist on to a harmonious finish.
Adrian Mathier, Nouveau Salquenen AG, 50, Bahnofstrasse, 3970 Salgesch, tel. 02.74.55.75.75, fax 02.74.56.24.13, e-mail info@nouveau-salquenen.ch
ev. day except Sun. 8am–12 noon 1.30pm–5.30pm; groups by appt.

SIMON MAYE ET FILS

Chamoson Humagne Rouge 1999★★★

■ 0.6 ha 6,000 50–69 F

A number of unusual grape varieties, unique to the region, continue to be cultivated in Valais. Humagne Rouge is a distinctive one. Its characteristics are exceptionally well expressed in this rich red wine. Its nose is an elegant combination of black fruit aromas with mineral overtones and a hint of spiciness. The lively attack develops into a complex palate that is structured with dense tannins. This is a well-balanced wine of good length. It should be drunk over the next three years, perhaps as a partner to a leg of lamb seasoned with rosemary. The **Dôle de Chamonson 99** from the same producer is a very good supple, fruity wine.
Simon Maye et Fils, 3, Collombey, 1956 Saint-Pierre-de-Clages, tel. 02.73.06.41.81, fax 02.73.06.80.02, e-mail simon.maye@swissonline.ch
by appt.

MITIS Amigne de Vétroz 1998★★★

□ 2 ha 10,000 100–149 F

Harvested from schist soils, fermented and matured on the lees in new oak barrels for 21 months, Vétroz Mitis' Amigne is a fine *liquoreux* that has set a high standard in previous vintages. A few green higlights enliven the dark gold colour of the 1998. Complex scents of honey, crystallised peel and saffron comprise a delicious bouquet that is echoed on the palate. The lively attack is balanced by the rich, full and unctuous textures. This is a wine to keep for three to ten years. The *Guide* also awarded two stars to the **Balavaud Dôle de Vétroz 99** (50–69F) and the **Amigne de Vétroz 99** (300–499F), and one star to the **Fendant de Vétroz Les Terrasses 99** (50–69F).

Germanier Bon Père,
Balavaud SA, 1963 Vétroz,
tel. 02.73.46.12.16, fax 02.73.46.51.32,
e-mail wine@bonpere.com by appt.

NOUVEAU SAINT-CLEMENT

Coteaux de Sierre Humagne Blanc 1999★

☐ n.c. 3,600 70–99 F

This is an elegant wine from start to finish. Yellow with green highlights, it has a fruity nose with a hint of hazelnut. The lively palate rests on light tannins, and the wine is ready to drink now. The **Fendant 99** (50–69F) was also judged very good.

SA C. Lamon et Cie, Nouveau Saint-Clément, 3978 Flanthey, tel. 02.74.58.13.32 by appt.

PARADIS Humagne Rouge 1999★★

■ 0.3 ha 3,400 70–99 F

A bright ruby colour, this Humagne Rouge has aromas of wild berries and undergrowth. Forthright and lively at first, the palate develops structure and suppleness, and is balanced by good length. One to keep.

Alex Roten, Cave du Paradis,
135, rte de la Gemmi, 3960 Sierre,
tel. 02.74.55.19.03, fax 02.74.55.19.44,
e-mail roten@cavesduparadis.ch
by appt.

CAVE DU PARADOU

Cornalin 1998★★

■ 0.1 ha 800 70–99 F

Purple-coloured, distinctive and expressive, this wine is redolent of morello cherries, cloves and pepper. It is remarkably well-structured by fine tannins that are soft enough for the wine to be enjoyed right away. Try it with game or red meat. The oak-aged and equally well-structured **Pinot Noir 99** (30–49F) and the **Chardonnay 98** (50–69F) were each awarded one star.

Cave du Paradou, La Villettaz, 1973 Nax, tel. 02.72.03.23.59, fax 02.72.03.60.13 by appt.

DOMINIQUE PASSAQUAY

Gewurztraminer Passerillé 1998★

☐ 0.03 ha 1,000 100–149 F

Made from raisined grapes, this rich, amber-yellow wine has a distinctive nose of mangoes and lychees. Powerful and very aromatic, the palate echoes the nose with just an additional hint of oakiness. The wine will keep for a decade, and would complement blue cheese or foie gras.

Dominique Passaquay, Outre-Vieze,
5, rte. du Montet, 1871 Choex-sur-Monthey,
tel. 02.44.71.18.01, fax 02.44.72.36.22,
e-mail passdom@bluewin.ch by appt.

LES FRERES PHILIPPOZ

Pinot Blanc 1999★★

☐ 2 ha 1,100 50–69 F

The Philippoz brothers specialise in dry white wines. Their Pinot Blanc, with its delicate aroma of acidulated fruit, is very lively on the palate. Fruity and fresh, the wine has a very lemony finish. The **Viognier 99**, with its fine aroma of peaches and plums, and lively, floral, full-bodied palate, was awarded one star (70–99F). Finally, the **Fendant Les Chênes 99** was also awarded a star for its flowery-fruity aroma and delicate freshness.

Philippoz Frères, 13, rte. de Riddes,
1912 Leytron, tel. 02.73.06.30.14,
fax 02.73.06.71.33 by appt.

PIERRE DE SOLEIL Fendant 1999★

☐ 0.25 ha 2,000 50–69 F

A powerful, thoroughbred wine, this Fendant has linden flower aromas and a fresh and balanced palate. Floral and citrus flavours are superseded by a lingering note of gunflint on the finish. A harmonious wine that is worth discovering.

Jérôme Giroud, 4, chem. Proz-chez-Boz,
1955 Chamoson, tel. 02.73.06.20.25,
fax 02.73.06.26.02 by appt.

CAVE DES PLACES

Johannisberg 1999★

☐ 0.3 ha 2,500 50–69 F

This yellow Johannisberg (Sylvaner) with green highlights is very aromatic. Fruity and quite concentrated, it has a blanced and elegant palate with the slightly bitter finish typical of this variety.

Laurent Hug, Les Places, 1971
Champlan-sur-Sion, tel. 02.73.98.31.43,
fax 02.73.98.31.01 by appt.

LA CAVE A POLYTE

Chamoson Pinot Noir 1999★

■ 0.5 ha n.c. 50–69 F

Purple highlights flicker in this ruby-coloured wine. Red berries (particularly raspberries) are apparent on the rounded, rich palate with its fine tannins. A distinguished, well-balanced wine that should be drunk within the next three years.

Jacques Disner, La Cave à Polyte SA,
5, rue de la Place, 1955 Chamoson,
tel. 07.92.20.35.11, fax 07.73.06.26.66,
e-mail disner.j@chamoson.ch by appt.

PRIMUS CLASSICUS

Cornalin 1999★★

■ 2 ha 9,600 100–149 F

The Orsat company was established in 1874. Over the years, it has purchased several estates and currently owns 28 ha (69 acres) of vineyards. As part of its Primus Classicus range, it has made both a red and a white 99. The jury declared the Cornalin, a dark red wine with purple highlights, a remarkable success. It has a spicy morello cherry aroma with subtle overtones of raspberries, and is a structured, velvety and elegant wine. The white

Petite Arvine 99 was awarded one star; a lively and perfumed wine, it has the slightly salty finish characteristic of the variety.
🔑 SA Caves Orsat,
19, rte. du Levant, 1920 Martigny,
tel. 02.77.22.24.01, fax 02.77.22.98.45,
e-mail info@cavesorsat.ch ☑ Y by appt.

QUINTESSENCE Fully Arvine 1998★★

□ 0.17 ha 1,176 70–99 F

The pale yellow Quintessence is slightly sweet. Its fruity and floral (wisteria) aromas have a touch of oakiness, the result of 12 months in barrel, and the fruity, vigorous palate is well-balanced. A touch of saltiness underlying the fruit and flowers is perceptible as the wine is savoured. It has a great future ahead of it.
🔑 Benoît Dorsaz, Cave Coronelle,
chem. du Midi, 1926 Fully,
tel. 02.77.46.11.25, fax 02.77.46.20.45,
e-mail bdorsaz@omedia.ch ☑ Y by appt.

CAVE DE RIONDAZ Syrah 1998★★

■ n.c. n.c. 70–99 F

Full-bodied and well-structured, this wine has liquoricey tannins, and flavours of cloves and pepper. In fact, it is a classic oak-aged Syrah, powerful with concentrated fruit, and should be aged for five to seven years.
🔑 Caves de Riondaz,
38, rte. du Rawyl, 3960 Sierre,
tel. 02.74.55.12.63, fax 02.74.55.31.58 ☑
Y by appt.

RIVES DU BISSE
Humagne Rouge 1998★★

■ 1 ha 10,000 70–99 F

The 10-ha (25-acre) vineyard runs along the banks of the Bisse in the village of Ardon. Thirteen-year-old Humagne vines growing on chalk soils have produced an intense dark red wine that has a characteristic cherry nose with musky overtones. The palate is structured with ripe, fruity tannins. A well-balanced wine.
🔑 SA Gaby Delaloye et Fils, Vins Rives du Bisse, 5, rue de la Fonderie, 1957 Ardon,
tel. 02.73.06.13.15, fax 02.73.06.64.20 ☑
Y by appt.

ROUVINEZ Les Grains Nobles 1998★★★

□ 2 ha 12,000 150–199 F

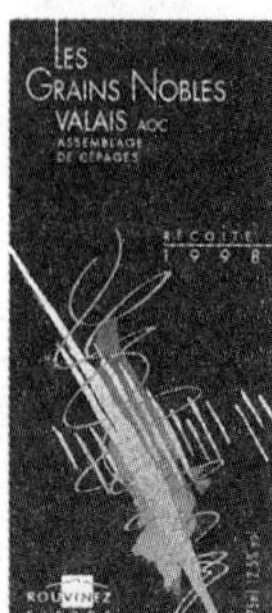

Marsanne and Pinot Gris grapes, harvested on the slopes of Sierre in mid-December 1998, have been made into a rich yellow *liquoreux* with golden highlights. The wine was matured on its lees in oak for 12 months, and stirred at regular intervals. The result is a very complex wine with an aroma of raspberry *eau-de-vie* and white truffles. The palate, which displays an exceptional balance of alcohol and acidity, has flavours of crystallised fruit and truffles. A wine with extremely good potential, it is likely to last for over 20 years. The jury also enjoyed the red **Tourmentin 98** (100–149F), which was awarded two stars, as well as the **Muscat 99** and the **Hermitage 98** (both 70–99F), which were each awarded one star.
🔑 Vins Rouvinez,
Colline de Géronde, 3960 Sierre,
tel. 02.74.55.66.61, fax 02.74.55.46.49,
e-mail info@rouvinez.com ☑ Y by appt.

SAINT-MARTIN Johannisberg 1998★★★

□ 2 ha 4,500 300–499 F

The year that this 20-ha (49-acre) estate was established, 1848, was also the year that the modern Swiss Confederation was formed. Judging from the quality of this sweet Johannisberg, which will easily see out the next two decades, the estate has not wasted the intervening 150 years. A bright golden-yellow, it has an intense and concentrated currant-scented nose. On the palate, it is powerful and unctuous, with a tropical fruit flavour (pineapples, lychees). A robust and thoroughbred finish concludes an elegantly balanced wine that may be enjoyed now, and for many years to come. The sweet **Petite Arvine Sous l'Escalier 98** is a remarkable, complex wine that displays all the characteristics of the grape variety.
🔑 Dom. du Mont d'Or SA-Sion,
Pont-de-la-Morge, case postale 240,
1, 1964 Conthey, tel. 02.73.46.20.32,
fax 02.73.46.51.78 ☑
Y by appt.

CAVE SAINT-MICHEL
Coteaux de Sierre Fendant 1999★

□ 1 ha 10,000 30–49 F

The 3.5-ha (9-acres) of vines owned by this family estate are planted at altitudes of 550–700 m (1,800–2,300 ft), and benefit from a southerly exposure. This is a light, crystal-clear Fendant. Linden-flowers and delicate mineral aromas are present on the nose. The variety's fruitiness is displayed on the palate, which is also full-bodied, lively and long.
🔑 Pierre-Elie Rey et Fils, Cave Saint-Michel, 3960 Corini-Sierre,
tel. 02.74.55.88.52, fax 02.74.56.37.57 ☑
Y by appt.

R. SARTORETTI ET FILS
Johannisberg 1999★

□ 0.5 ha 4,000 50–69 F

This estate celebrated its fiftieth anniversary in 2000. It has produced a Johannisberg with an intense fruit aroma tinged with ginger. The rounded and delicate palate has a

slight bitter almond flavour and good length. The wine is ready to drink now, with asparagus, rainbow trout or crustaceans.
R. Sartoretti et Fils, Cave Crête Blanche, 3977 Granges-Sierre, tel. 02.74.58.11.13, fax 02.74.58.12.13 Y by appt.

SOLEIL DE SIERRE Dôle 1999**

■ 6 ha 50,000 50–69 F

The *soleil* (sun) of Sierre has given rise to a ruby-coloured Dôle with rich violet highlights. The intense, spicy, red berry nose, and full-bodied, balanced and fruity palate make this a hugely enjoyable wine. Wild strawberry and cherry flavours provide a final flourish.
SA Vins Sierre Imesch, 8, place Beaulieu, 3960 Sierre, tel. 02.74.52.36.80, fax 02.74.52.36.89, e-mail imesch.vins@swissonline.ch
Y by appt.
Hoirie Imeschl

ST. JODERNKELLEREI

Visperterminen Heida 1998*

□ n.c. 60,000 50–69 F

Heida is another name for the Païen or Savagnin variety, and Visperterminen is the name of a vineyard planted at 1,000 m (3,300 ft) above sea-level. The co-operative has made a green-yellow wine with a walnut, honey and tropical fruit aroma. Well-structured and distinctive, the palate has a fine balance of fruit and acidity. The finish is long.
St. Jodernkellerei, Unterstalden, 3932 Visperterminen, tel. 02.79.46.41.46, fax 02.79.46.80.76, e-mail info@jodernkellerei.ch Y by appt.

TIMOTHYUS ONE

Chamoson Johannisberg Flétri 1997**

□ 0.4 ha 2,000 100–149 F

Johannisberg grapes were raisined (*flétri*) on the vine for five months before harvesting. The wine was then matured in oak, resulting in a *liquoreux* the colour of golden straw. Pear and currant aromas harmonise on the full and fresh attack. The palate has a good balance of sweetness and acidity, with a gentle flavour of cooked apricots. The long finish hints at bitter almonds, a trait associated with this variety.
Albert Gaillard et Fils, Cave du Vidômne, 8, rue du prieuré, 1956 Saint-Pierre-de-Clages, tel. 02.73.06.27.80, fax 02.73.06.27.02 Y by appt.

VERTIGES Sierre Pinot Noir 1999*

■ 2 ha 20,000 50–69 F

Jean-Louis Mathieu cultivates 12 ha (30 acres) of vines between Sierre and Sion. This rich ruby-coloured Pinot Noir has an aroma of undergrowth and red berries (strawberries, raspberries), with a hint of leather. A full-bodied attack leads on to a fruity palate supported by dense tannins. A wine with sufficient structure to age for two to three years.
Jean-Louis Mathieu, rte. du Téléphérique, 3966 Chalais-Sierre, tel. 02.74.58.27.63, fax 02.74.58.42.44
Y by appt.

FREDERIC ZUFFEREY

Coteaux de Sierre Fendant 1999*

□ 0.5 ha 3,500 30–49 F

This typical Fendant, light yellow with green highlights, has notes of linden flowers on the nose. Fresh and delicate on the palate, it has the slightly mineral taste that is the signature of a limestone terroir. The finish is long.
Frédéric Zufferey, 16, Fond-Villa, 3965 Chippis, tel. 02.74.56.10.59, fax 02.74.55.19.31 Y by appt.

Geneva

Vine-growing in the canton of Geneva dates from before the Christian era, and it survived the vicissitudes of history to flourish to the full after the close of the 1960s.

The Geneva vineyard is divided into 32 appellations, all of which enjoy a temperate climate (due to the proximity of the lake), very good sunshine and favourable soils. Efforts made to improve the potential of the wines include environmentally friendly methods of cultivation and the choice of lower cropping grape varieties suited to a soil that generally has a high limestone content. The results guarantees a wine of high quality. The regulations imposed reflect the determination of both the authorities and the professionals to put on the market wines that will meet the requirements of the AOCs.

The diversity of the grape varieties has widened with the addition of speciality wines to the range. In addition to the main growths from Chasselas for white wines, from Gamay and Pinot Noir for the reds, specialities such as Chardonnay, Pinot Blanc, Aligoté, Gamaret and Cabernet are enjoying great success among knowledgeable wine-lovers.

BACCARAT Prestige Pinot Noir

◑ 0.3 ha 2,000 70–99 F

Bright and clear, this wine is the shade of onion-skin, and has a fresh red berry and floral aroma. The rich and fruity palate is elegantly balanced.

La cave de Genève, 140, rte. du Mandement, 1242 Satigny, tel. 02.27.53.11.33, fax 02.27.53.21.10 by appt.

BARTHOLIE Coteaux de Dardagny★★

◑ 1er cru 1.5 ha 3,000 70–99 F

A blend of Pinot Noir and Pinot Meunier, this sparkling rosé has an elegant nose with aromas that range from brioche to pepper. A hint of liquorice is apparent on the palate, which is rich, fruity and balanced.

Bernard Bosseau, 11, chem. de la Côte, 1282 Dardagny, tel. 02.27.54.12.59, fax 02.27.54.15.59 by appt.

BELLE DE NUIT Avusy Pinot Noir 1998

■ 0.7 ha 4,000 30–49 F

Garnet with orange highlights, this wine has the intense morello cherry and black fruit aromas characteristic of Pinot Noir. Rounded and already quite full-bodied on entry, it exhibits suppleness and balance on a well-structured palate. A slightly burnt taste registers on the finish.

Nicolas Cadoux, 56, rte de Forestal, 1285 Athenaz, tel. 02.27.56.28.81, fax 02.27.56.26.38 by appt.

JACQUES ET CLAUDE BOCQUET-THONNEY

Sézenove Chardonnay 1999★

□ 0.7 ha 4,000 30–49 F

This 5-ha (12-acre) family estate practises organic viticulture. Its bright, clear, straw-coloured Chardonnay shimmers with golden highlights. The fine, complex, floral nose is still a little closed, but on the palate, the wine is full and elegant with an after-taste of ripe fruits.

Jacques et Claude Bocquet-Thonney, 9, chem. des Grands-Buissons, 1233 Sézenove, tel. 02.27.57.45.63, fax 02.27.57.45.63 by appt.

DOM. DU CENTAURE

Dardagny Légende 1998★★

■ 1 ha 7,000 70–99 F

Garanoir and Gamaret are two varieties that were created in 1970 at the Federal Agricultural Research Centre in Changins. The Centaure estate has blended them to make a remarkable wine. Its wild blackberry aroma has overtones of spice and vanilla, showing the influence of oak-ageing. On the palate, the fruit is dominated by oak for the time being, but the wine's balanced structure and fine tannins are nevertheless attractive. A wine to keep.

Claude Ramu, Dom. du Centaure, 480, rte. du Mandement, 1282 Dardagny, tel. 02.27.54.15.09, fax 02.27.54.14.11 by appt.

DOM. DU CREST Jussy 1999★★★

◪ 1.5 ha 10,000 30–49 F

The Château du Crest is associated with the Huguenot poet and humanist Agrippa d'Aubigné, who was condemned in France for publishing *Histoire Universelle*, an account of the religious conflicts between 1553 and 1602. He was in large part responsible for the rebuilding of the château. Today, the estate extends over 13 ha (32 acres), and grows 15 different grape varieties. Pinot Noir and Gamay are blended to make this outstanding wine. A clear pink colour with dark, almost red, highlights, the fragrant 1999 has a fruity nose of ripe strawberries. On the palate, it is as fresh and fruity as it is balanced, and it has impressive structure. The wine is ready to drink now.

G. Béné et J. Meyer, Cave du Ch. du Crest, 40, rte. du Ch. du Crest, 1254 Jussy, tel. 02.27.59.06.11, fax 02.27.59.11.22 by appt.

PIERRE DUPRAZ ET FILS

Coteau de Lully Sauvignon 1999

□ 1er cru 0.7 ha 4,000 50–69 F

Established in 1909, this estate was the first to cultivate the Aligoté variety in the canton of Geneva. It has made a clear and bright Sauvignon with an intense aroma of black-currant leaves. A fresh, fruity and rounded wine, it has a lengthy finish.

Pierre Dupraz et Fils, Dom. des Curiades, 49, chem. des Curiades, 1233 Lully, tel. 02.27.57.28.15, fax 02.27.57.47.85 by appt.

LE PONT DES SOUPIRS

Satigny 1998★

■ 1.3 ha 9,000 100–149 F

This estate, established in 1983, cultivates 20 grape varieties on its 30 ha (74 acres). A deep garnet with violet highlights, Satigny 1998 has a powerful spice and musk nose. Its equally powerful palate is full-bodied and round, with solid tannins. A well-structured wine that will keep.

Roger Burgdorfer, Dom. du Paradis, 275, rte. du Mandement, 1242 Satigny, tel. 02.27.53.18.55, fax 02.27.53.18.55 by appt.

LES HUTINS Gamaret 1999★

■ 1 ha 5,300 50–69 F

Some of the 18 ha (44 acres) that Pierre and Jean Hutin cultivate, following organic principles, is used to grow the Gamaret variety – a red wine variety that is a crossing of Gamay and Reichensteiner. They have made a fine ruby-coloured wine with violet highlights. Its distinctive nose has aromas of red berries and spices. A forthright, supple attack leads on to a palate structured with silky tannins. A harmonious and balanced wine.

Pierre et Jean Hutin, Dom. les Hutins, 8, chem. de Brive, 1282 Dardagny, tel. 02.27.54.12.05, fax 02.27.54.12.27, e-mail domaine.les.hutins@bluewin.ch
by appt.

LES SECRETS DU SOLEIL

Dardagny Chasselas 1999★★★

0.8 ha 5,000 30–49 F

Phillipe Vocat has a 10-ha (25-acre) vineyard in Dardagny, a commune that is well-known for its wines. This Chasselas has an attractive golden colour and a floral nose with subtle mineral overtones. Clean and straightforward, the palate is well-structured and balanced by its freshness. On the finish, the wine has a mineral note characteristic of its terroir.

Philippe Vocat, Dom. Secrets du Soleil, 446, rte. de Mandement, 1282 Dardagny, tel. 02.27.54.13.84, fax 02.27.54.14.10, e-mail philippe.vocat@informaniak.ch
by appt.

GILBERT MISTRAL-MONNIER

Dardagny Muscat 1998★★

0.3 ha 1,500 50–69 F

On sunny limestone vineyards that are located 15 km (10 miles) from Geneva, Gilbert Mistral-Monnier makes fruity, full-bodied wines. This very sweet Muscat is a remarkable example. Its golden straw colour invites us to enjoy the ripe marc-like aromas on the nose. The very complex palate is balanced by good acidity.

Gilbert Mistral-Monnier, 18, chem. des Pompes, 1282 Dardagny, tel. 02.27.54.14.46, fax 02.27.54.19.46 by appt.

MARC RAMU

Dardagny Pinot Blanc 1999★★

0.5 ha 3,000 30–49 F

This family estate, founded at the end of the 17th century, currently extends over 9-ha (22-acres). The bright golden Pinot Blanc 99 is an intensely aromatic wine that has elegant scents of bitter almonds and linden flowers. Supple at first, the wine has a powerful and balanced palate with a long, attractive finish.

Marc Ramu, Clos des Pins, 458, rte du Mandement, 1282 Dardagny, tel. 02.27.54.14.57, fax 02.27.54.17.23
by appt.

BERNARD ROCHAIX

Peissy Pinot Gris Vendanges Tardives 1998

n.c. 600 100–149 F

The colour of straw, this is a powerful Pinot Gris with curranty aromas. Fine freshness balances the palate, which has a flavour of chestnuts and vanilla. While this wine is suitable for drinking now, it would certainly also keep.

Bernard Rochaix, Dom. les Perrières, 1242 Satigny, tel. 02.27.53.90.00, fax 02.27.53.90.09 by appt.

ROUGE-ROUGE★★★

1 ha 3,000 50–69 F

The Cave des Chevalier is a 12-ha (30-acre) estate that makes 14 different wines. The Rouge-Rouge is a wine of designated origin (Category II in the Swiss wine system), made from Gamaret and Pinot Noir grapes. Dark garnet-coloured, it has a black fruit aroma with spicy cinnamon overtones. Its elegant palate is structured with strong tannins that should soften with time. The vanilla flavours on the finish reflect the fact that the wine was matured in oak.

Sébastien Dupraz, 8, chem. de Placet, 1286 Soral, tel. 02.27.56.15.66, fax 02.27.56.43.92, e-mail cdupraz@infomaniak.ch
by appt.

H. SCHUTZ ET R. MOSER

Celigny Pinot Noir 1998★★

3 ha 20,000 70–99 F

This ruby-coloured Pinot Noir has orangey highlights and a black cherry nose. Harmonious and full-bodied, its complex palate is balanced by silky tannins. This well-structured wine is ready to drink now, but could also be cellared for a while.

H. Schütz et R. Moser, Le Clos de Celigny, 38, rte de Celigny, 1298 Celigny, tel. 02.27.76.32.05, fax 02.27.76.07.85
by appt.

DOM. DES TROIS ETOILES

Peissy Merlot 1998★★★

1 ha 8,000 100–149 F

Owing to a delivery error on the part of the vine nursery, this estate became the first to plant Merlot in the Geneva region. It was a happy accident, because the variety has flourished here. This clear and bright 1998 is a ruby-coloured wine with orangey highlights. Elderflower and blackcurrant aromas are joined by a hint of spice on the nose. The well-structured and balanced palate has fine tannins and an attractive vanilla note on the finish. Although the wine is ready to drink now, it also has the potential to age well.

Jean-Charles Crousaz, Dom. des Trois Etoiles, C.P. 32, 1242 Satigny, tel. 02.27.53.16.14, fax 02.27.53.41.55
by appt.

PIERRE ET PHILIPPE VILLARD
Anières Chardonnay 1999★★
☐ 0.6 ha 5,000 30–49 F

This organic family estate cultivates 5-ha (12-acres) of vines on gravelly alluvial soils. Its remarkable Chardonnay beguiled the jury with its clear, bright colour. Very expressive on the nose, the wine has inviting aromas of passion-fruit and citrus, which are echoed on the well-structured palate, and persist through to a long finish.
Pierre et Philippe Villard, 46, rue Centrale, 1247 Anières, tel. 02.27.51.25.56, fax 02.27.51.25.56 by appt.

Neuchâtel

The vineyards of the Neuchâtel canton have a highly privileged position, receiving reflected sun from the lake and shelter from the lower foothills of the Jura. The vines stretch for 40 km (25 miles) along a narrow band between Le Lauderon and Vaumarcus. The dry, sunny climate of the region and the Jurassic limestone soils that predominate have always combined to create excellent conditions for vine cultivation. The first vineyard was officially planted there in 998, a fact that makes wine-making in Neuchâtel over one thousand years old.

In this little wine-growing area, which covers 610 ha (1,507 acres), Chasselas and Pinot rule; there are indeed a few 'specialities' (Pinot Gris, Chardonnay, Gewürztraminer and a Riesling-Sylvaner cross), but cultivation of these varieties covers barely 6% of the area. However, the apparently limited range of vine varieties planted hides a very wide palette of different wines and flavours, thanks to the expertise of the wine-makers and the diverse nature of the *terroirs*.

The reds, from Pinot Noir, are elegant and fruity, often with good keeping qualities. The very typical Oeil-de-Perdrix is a superb rosé, originating from the Neuchâtel vineyards, along with Perdrix Blanche, which is made by being pressed with no maceration. Some growers even make a sparkling wine.

The variety of soils in the canton, from east to west, as well as the personal styles of the wine-makers, result in many different flavours and aromas in the white wines made from Chasselas. These promise an interesting voyage of discovery for the curious, and it is worth highlighting two local speciality wines made from the same variety: the 'non-filtré' Vin Primeur, which cannot be put on sale before the third Wednesday in January, and the 'sur lie' wines, which have been kept on the lees.

Each of the 18 wine-producing communes makes its own appellation, yet the Appellation Neuchâtel can apply to all primary category wines from the canton.

CHAMPREVEYRES Chasselas 1999★★
☐ 0.55 ha 4,000 30–49 F

Champréveyres is a derivation of *champ aux prêtres*, or 'the field of the priests'. Under the terms of a charter of 1143, the estate was donated to the canons of the abbey of Fontaine-André by the Comte de Neuchâtel. In 1999, this prestigious vineyard allowed a young wine-maker, Olivier Lavanchy, to make a fruity and floral Chasselas, with a slight scent of gunflint. This elegant wine is rounded and remarkably balanced on the palate, with an agreeably bitter finish. It would be the ideal accompaniment to the local speciality, fillets of perch from Lake Neuchâtel.
Olivier Lavanchy, 48, rue de la Dîme, 2000 Neuchâtel, tel. 03.27.53.68.89, fax 03.27.53.68.89 by appt.

DOM. GRILLETTE

Œil-de-Perdrix 1999★★

◪ 5 ha 15,000 I ↓ 70–99 F

The Domaine de la Grillette, in the centre of the village of Cressier, has been a part of Neuchâtel's viticultural heritage since 1884. Under the new management of Thierry Lüthi, with Jean-Claude Martin as œnologist, this family enterprise has made a remarkable Œil-de-Perdrix 99 of great finesse and liveliness. It has all the characteristic style of the Pinot Noir grape from which it is made.

Grillette Dom. de Cressier, 2, Molondin, 2088 Cressier, tel. 03.27.58.85.29, fax 03.27.58.85.21 ▣ Y by appt.

J.C. KUNTZER ET FILS

Saint-Sébaste Pinot Noir 1998★★

■ 7 ha 30,000 (I) 50–69 F

This family estate is in the heart of Neuchâtel's viticultural district. Its 1998 Pinot Noir has a ruby colour that is reminiscent of a burgundy. Specially selected harvests from the best terroirs on the estate have produced a wine with a powerfully aromatic nose. Very fine, dense, well-structured tannins distinguish the palate. The wine would be an ideal partner for red meat. It was awarded the highest mark for a red wine by the Neuchâtel jury, and is undisputably deserving of a *coup de cœur.* A true ambassador for the region's wines.

Jean-Pierre Kuntzer, 11, Daniel-Dardel, 2072 Saint-Blaise, tel. 03.27.53.14.23, fax 03.27.53.14.57, e-mail info@kuntzer.ch ▣ Y by appt.

LA FEUILLEE

Cressier Chasselas 1999★★

☐ 4.49 ha 30,000 50–69 F

Jacques Grisoni, the founder of this Cressier company, can be proud of his son-in-law, Christian Jeanneret, who has been running the family business for the past ten years. The cellar's commitment to quality wine-making can be seen in this rich, elegant and appealing Chasselas. A slight fizz gives the wine a very lively character that charmed the jury. On the palate, it is remarkably long and has a pleasantly acid finish. A good apéritif.

Dom. Grisoni, 1, chem. des Devins, 2088 Cressier, tel. 03.27.57.12.36, fax 03.27.57.12.10 ▣ Y by appt.

C. Jeanneret et J. Tatasciore

CAVE DES LAURIERS

Pinot Noir 1998★

■ 2 ha 15,000 (I) 70–99 F

At the foot of the majestic Château de Cressier, another very grand building, built in 1505, houses the Cave des Laurier. Here, wine-making skills have been handed down through five generations of the same family since 1875. In 1998, it produced a remarkable Pinot Noir. An attractive colour, well-developed aromas and promising tannins combine to make this a classy wine. It would particularly complement a grilled steak or one of the local cheeses. The same wine-maker has also made a very good **Œil-de-Perdrix 99**.

Jungo & Fellmann, Cave des Lauriers, 6, rue du Château, 2088 Cressier, tel. 03.27.57.11.62, fax 03.27.57.40.62 ▣ Y by appt.

LES SORCIERES Pinot Noir 1998★★

■ 3 ha 11,000 (I) 70–99 F

The Caves Coopératives de la Béroche specialise in direct sales to the public. One of their member wine-makers is René Felber, a past president of Switzerland. The cooperative, which only vinifies organically grown grapes, has made a remarkable Pinot Noir 1998 Les Sorcières that captivated the jury. It has all the richness and generosity imparted by the sunny Coteaux de la Béroche terroir. This wine would be the ideal accompaniment to red meat or cheese.

Caves de la Béroche, 1–2, Crêt-de-la-Fin, 2024 Saint-Aubin, tel. 03.28.35.11.89, fax 03.28.35.31.80 ▣ Y by appt.

DOM. DE L'HOPITAL DE SOLEURE

Pinot Noir 1998★★

■ 5 ha 11,900 I ↓ 150–199 F

In 1446, the burgesses of the Hôpital de Soleure began to purchase vineyards around Neuchâtel. For the past 500 years, the Hôpital's wines have been enjoyed by the citizens of the fortified 'City of Ambassadors'. Historically, the wines were transported to Soleure by river, and the boatmen certainly did not hesitate to sample their cargo. This Pinot Noir 98 is remarkable both for its richness and for its balanced structure, which is reminiscent of a burgundy. Definitely a wine to keep. As well as the Pinot Noir, the Hôpital has made a remarkable **Chasselas 99** (100–149F), which received the highest marks for a wine made from this variety in Neuchâtel.

Dom. de l'Hôpital de Soleure, 8, Russie, 2525 Le Landeron, tel. 03.27.51.46.01, fax 03.26.23.78.08 ▣ Y by appt.

DOM. E. DE MONTMOLLIN FILS

Œil-de-Perdrix 1999★

◪ 10 ha 15,300 I ↓ 50–69 F

The Montmollin family have been wine-producers since the 16th century. Their 47 ha (116-acre) estate, built up over the centuries, is now the largest in Neuchâtel. The winery is in

the centre of the village of Auvernier. Its Œil-de-Perdrix 1999 is well-structured and long, with an attractive flavour of walnuts. An ideal wine to serve with white meat or fish.
Dom. E. de Montmollin Fils, 3, Grand-Rue, 2012 Auvernier, tel. 03.27.31.21.59, fax 03.27.31.88.06
ev. day except Sun. 8am–12 noon 1.30pm–6.30pm; Sat. 9am–1pm

CAVES DU PRIEURE DE CORMONDRECHE

Œil-de-Perdrix 1999★★

n.c. 7,022 70–99 F

The wines made by the Caves du Prieuré have been highly sought-after for years. The 120-plus growers who deliver their harvests to Cormondrèche are encouraged to produce the best quality grapes. The jury was particularly impressed by the Oeil-de-Perdrix with its subtly balanced and distinctive palate. Although it is very full-bodied and vigorous, the wine has a sweet finish, which makes it suitable for serving at any stage of a meal, including dessert.
Les Caves du Prieuré, 25, Grand-Rue, 2036 Cormondrèche, tel. 03.27.31.53.63, fax 03.27.31.56.13 by appt.

Berne

The wine-growing area in the Berne canton stretches along the shore of Lake Bienne, clinging to the slopes at the foot of the Jura range and surrounding the picturesque villages of the region. Some 55 per cent of the vineyard area is planted with Chasselas, 35% with Pinot Noir and 10% with speciality vine varieties such as Pinot Gris, a Riesling-Sylvaner cross, Chardonnay, Gewürztraminer and so on. The temperate lakeside climate and the shallow limestone soil give the wines finesse and character. The local Chasselas is a light, slightly sparkling white, ideal as an aperitif or to accompany a dish of lake salmon. The Pinot Noir is a light, elegant, fruity red. The wine-growing domains are family concerns of 2–7 ha (5–17 acres), where traditional and modern methods are combined to good effect.

In the other Swiss-German wine-growing cantons, vines grow in northerly locations. Despite the rigour of the climate, these regions produce a majority of red wines (frequently from Pinot Noir), representing 70% of total production. White wines come mostly from a Riesling-Sylvaner cross.

DOM. DE L'HOPITAL DE SOLEURE

Schafiser 1999★

2.3 ha 20,000 50–69 F

Since the 14th century, the Hôpital de Soleure has been vinifying grapes brought to it by boat from the vineyards of Landeron. The wine-making tradition is still in good hands, judging from the finesse of this Chasselas. It is soft, very full-bodied and pleasantly persistent on the palate. The wine is ready to serve now with freshwater fish, or perhaps Raclette or fondue.
Dom. de l'Hôpital de Soleure, 8, Russie, 2525 Le Landeron, tel. 03.27.51.46.01, fax 03.26.23.78.08 by appt.
Fondation Hôpital de Soleure

SCHLOSSLIWY

Schafiser Gutedel 1999★

1.5 ha 10,000 50–69 F

Generations of the Teutsch family have been cultivating this 3-ha (7-acre) vineyard on the chalky banks of Bienne Lake since 1830. Their winery is a handsome listed building, across from the island of Saint-Pierre, that dates from 1570. Heinz Teutsch matures all his wines in oak. He has made a light-bodied wine with a slight spritziness that imparts an appealing impression of liveliness.
Heinz Teutsch, Schafis, 2514 Ligerz, tel. 03.23.15.21.70, fax 03.23.15.22.79
by appt.

PETER SCHOTT-TRANCHANT

Twanner Cuvée Sélectionnée 1999★

0.35 ha 3,000 50–69 F

Visitors are received at the family home, in the centre of the old village of Twann. The charm of the setting is reflected in this well-crafted Chasselas wine. Its fruitiness, which has a tinge of linden flowers, hits the nose in waves. The palate then reveals a good balance of sweetness and acidity, the latter adding a fine touch of bitterness on the finish.
Peter Schott-Tranchant, 117,Dorfgasse, 2513 Twann, tel. 03.23.15.24.86, fax 03.23.15.24.86 by appt.

REBGUT DER STADT BERN

Schafiser Bielersee 1999★

12 ha 100,000 50–69 F

This estate has belonged to the city of Berne since 1528, the year that many of the convents were secularised. It currently owns 20 ha (49 acres) of vineyards planted with Pinot Noir, Pinot Gris, Chardonnay,

Sauvignon Blanc and Chasselas. The Chasselas 99, which is the product of limestone soils, is a fine, attractive, full-bodied wine with mineral flavours; but for all that its finish is a little short.
Jean-Pierre Louis, Dom. de la Ville de Berne, 2520 La Neuveville, tel. 03.27.51.21.75, fax 03.27.51.58.03
by appt.

HARTMANN WEINBAU

Villnachern Argovie Blauburgunder Spätlese 1998★★

n.c. n.c. 70–99 F

A dark ruby colour, this late-harvest Blauburgunder (Pinot Noir) has an oaky nose reflecting its maturation in barrel. Discreet at first, the structured palate displays well-balanced acidity and great persistence on the finish.
Hartmann Weinbau, 17, Rinikerstrasse, 5236 Remigen, tel. 05.62.84.27.43, fax 05.62.84.27.28 by appt.

Argovie

DANIEL FURST-BANZIGER

Hornusser Federweiss Stiftshalde 1999★★

0.6 ha n.c. 50–69 F

This family estate cultivates Müller-Thurgau, Pinot Gris, Dornfelder and Pinot Noir grapes on 3-ha (7-acres). It has produced a remarkable, salmon-pink 99 from Pinot Noir. The intense nose has characteristic varietal aromas, together with a slight amylic note. Rounded and full-bodied, the palate is fruity with well-balanced residual sugars (8 g/l).
Erika et Daniel Fürst-Bänziger, Rebgut Stiftshalde, 5075 Hornussen, tel. 06.28.71.55.61, fax 06.28.71.85.66
ev. day except Sun. 8am–6pm

GEBRUEDER NAUER

Tegerfelder Pinot Noir Prestige Barrique 1998★

1 ha 4,800 70–99 F

This family estate has been making wine in Bremgarten since 1893, using grapes from its own vineyards supplemented by the harvest of other growers. The Pinot Noir has been barrel-aged, giving it a dark red colour. The oakiness on the nose blends well with the fruity Pinot aromas, and the palate is also oaky, with strong tannins that augur well for the wine's future. It boasts a long and elegant finish.
Gebrueder Nauer Ag, Postfach, 5620 Bremgarten 2, tel. 05.66.33.86.33, fax 05.66.31.81.82 by appt.

Grisons

GRENDELMEIER-BANNWART

Zizerser Blauburgunder Auslese 1998★★★

n.c. n.c. 50–69 F

This organic family estate is planted with 4-ha (10-acres) of Pinot Noir, Müller-Thurgau and Chardonnay. The Pinot Noir was fermented in 200-l (53-gallon) oak barrels, resulting in a dark ruby wine with blackcurrant, blackberry and other wild berry aromas. The rich, full-bodied palate is structured by ripe tannins, and there is a fine balance between the wine's tannins, acidity and sweetness. It will keep for three to five years.
Familie Grendelmeier-Bannwart, 7205 Zizers, tel. 08.13.22.62.58, fax 08.13.22.92.66 by appt.

HANS PETER LAMPERT

Maienfelder Blauburgunder Barrique 1997★

n.c. n.c. 70–99 F

Eighty-five percent of this family estate, established in 1983, is planted with Pinot Noir. Fruity, with a slight oakiness, the wine has an agreeably structured palate that displays a good balance of fine tannins and acidity. Although it is ready to drink now, it has the potential to improve in the cellar.
Hans Peter Lampert, 248, Heidelberg, 7304 Maienfeld, tel. 08.13.30.72.05, fax 08.13.30.72.06 by appt.

MARKUS ET SONJA LAMPERT

Maienfelder Blauburgunder Barrique 1997★★

■ n.c. n.c. 70–99 F

Pinot Noir is the most prevalent variety in the German-speaking part of Switzerland. The success of Markus and Sonia Lampert with this variety on their 3-ha (7-acre) estate makes a good case for that predominance. Their 1997 is a remarkably structured wine. Barrel-ageing has imparted oaky flavours to the blackberry and dried fruit nose. Very ripe tannins envelop the palate. This wine is already very attractive, but it will also keep well.

Sonja et Markus Lampert, Lurgasse Torkel, 276, Lurgasse, 7304 Maienfeld, tel. 08.13.30.19.70, fax 08.13.30.19.71, e-mail m.s.lampert@pop.agri.ch
Y by appt.

LIESCH

Malanser Blauburgunder Auslese 1998★★★

■ n.c. n.c. 50–69 F

With the 1998 vintage of their Malanser Pinot Noir, the Liesch brothers have confirmed their lofty reputation. The bottle has a pretty label created by August Rausch, and the equally attractive wine inside has an intense, dark red colour with violet highlights. Its fine, oaky nose has the typical Pinot Noir aroma of concentrated, ripe black fruits (blackcurrants). On the palate, it has a good balance of tannins and acidity that are sustained through to a long finish. Partially matured in barrel, the wine should be cellared for four to five years.

Familien Liesch, Treib, 7208 Malans, tel. 08.13.22.12.25, fax 08.13.30.05.85, e-mail liesch@pop.agri.ch Y by appt.

STUDACH Malanser Pinot Noir 1998★★

■ n.c. n.c. 70–99 F

Barbara and Thomas Studach's have earned two stars for their impressive Pinot Noir. Still youthful, with an intense red colour, the wine nevertheless has a fine nose of raspberries and liquorice. Its fullness and balance on the palate augur well for the future.

Thomas et Barbara Studach, 60, Kirchgasse, 7208 Malans, tel. 08.13.22.25.38, fax 08.13.22.25.38
Y by appt.

Saint-Gall

TRIO CLASSICO

Pinot Noir, Cabernet-Sauvignon, Diolly Noir 1998★★

■ n.c. n.c. 70–99 F

This blend of three varieties, hailing from eastern Switzerland, has been matured in oak for eight months. An intense purple colour, it has a very aromatic nose of wild berries. Velvety, ripe tannins envelop the full-bodied, warm palate, and the wine has a long finish.

Gebrueyer Kuemin, 1, Oechsli, 8807 Freienbach, tel. 05.54.10.31.31, fax 05.54.10.63.67 Y by appt.

Schaffhouse

BAUMANN

Oberhallauer Auslese 1998★★

■ n.c. n.c. 50–69 F

Every Saturday, the Baumann family opens its 7.3 ha (18-acre) estate to visitors for a wine-tasting. They have made this 1998 from late-harvested (*auslese*) Pinot Noir. Matured in tank, it is intensely fruity and robust with very good tannins. The oaky **Cuvée Classique d'Oberhallau 98** is another remarkably successful Pinot Noir, a variety that finds favour in German-speaking Switzerland (from 70–99F). Finally, Rudi Baumann and Michael Meyer have jointly produced a **Pinot Noir Zwaa 98 Osterfing-Oberhallau** (100–149F) that was awarded two stars.

Weingut Baumann, 117, Unterdorf, 8216 Oberhallau, tel. 05.26.81.33.46, fax 05.26.81.33.56 Y by appt.

GRAF VON SPIEGELBERG

Hallauer Beerli Blauburgunder 1998★

■ n.c. n.c. 30–49 F

The harvest festival, which takes place over the first two Sundays in October, is the perfect occasion to sample the wines of the largest cellar in the canton of Schaffhouse. Its owners, Robert and Emil Rahm Hallau, cultivate 10-ha (25-acres) of their own vineyards, but also buy in large quantities of grapes. This is a fruity, raspberry-scented Pinot Noir with fine tannins, which should be drunk within the year. It would make a good partner for poultry dishes.

Rimuss-Kellerei, Postfach, 8215 Hallau, tel. 05.26.81.31.44, fax 05.26.81.40.14
Y by appt.

LANZ & CO WEINKELLEREI

Wilchinger Rötiberg 1997*

■ n.c. n.c. 50–69 F

This family estate, which dates back a very long time, runs its vineyards in Wilchingen on organic lines. Its appealing Pinot Noir has the concentrated aromas characteristic of this variety. Barrel maturation has given the fairly long palate perceptible oakiness.

Lanz Rötiberg-Kellerei & Co, 141, Dorfstrasse, 8217 Wilchingen, tel. 05.26.81.19.21, fax 05.26.81.19.25, e-mail mail@roetiberg.ch Y by appt.

COOPERATIVE LOHNINGEN

Loehninger Auslese Riesling x Silvaner 1999*

□ n.c. n.c. 50–69 F

This late-harvested wine has been made from a crossing of Riesling and Silvaner grapes grown in an area that is largely devoted to this variety. Subtly acidic, intensely fruity and fresh, it is a light yellow wine with light grapey overtones. It is ready for drinking now.

Weinbaugenossenschaft Löhningen, 8224 Loehningen, tel. 05.26.85.23.13, fax 05.26.85.23.13 Y by appt.

MEYER Osterfinger Pinot Blanc 1998**

□ n.c. n.c. 70–99 F

This wine-producer is housed in a beautiful building designed in the style of the Auberge Noble that forms part of the original estate, which dates back to 1472. The Meyers, who have owned the business for the last century, have made a remarkable, pale lemon-yellow Pinot Blanc. The tropical fruit aromas that dominate its complex nose are very inviting while, on the palate, the wine has substantial presence and good acidity. It will age well.

Michael Meyer, Gasthaus & Weingut, Bad Osterfingen, 8218 Osterfingen, tel. 05.26.81.21.21 Y by appt.

PINO'DOR Würenlingen 1998**

■ n.c. n.c. 70–99 F

The Meier familiy have been wine-producers since 1828. It is worth making an excursion to Würenlingen to visit the vine nursery and the restaurant, Zum Sternen. You will also be able to enjoy this blend of Pinot Noir and Dornfelder that combines the raspberry aromas of the first variety with the bilberry aromas of the second. A deep red colour, it has a complex structure, with vanilla flavours that are the result of oak-ageing. The **Chardonnay 98 Würenlingen Wannenberg** was also awarded two stars for its balance of acidity, body and oak. It has the characteristic tropical fruit aromas of Chardonnay with sustained walnut and vanilla overtones.

Andreas Meier, Weingut zum Sternen, 2, Rebschulweg, 5303 Würenlingen, tel. 05.62.81.11.08, e-mail office@weingut-sternen.ch Y by appt.

REGLI

Sonnenspross Hallauer Cuvée 2000 Spätlese 1997*

■ 2 ha n.c. 70–99 F

Since 1931, this family estate has been vinifying both the harvest of its own 2-ha (5-acre) vineyard and that of other Schaffhouse growers. The pure Pinot Noir Cuvée 2000 has a dark red colour and the characteristic aromas of this variety. Its fruity palate, structured by fine tannins, is reasonably long. A *spätlese* (late-harvest) wine that is ready to drink now.

Regli Weine, 498, Sellmattenstrasse, 8215 Hallau, tel. 05.26.81.29.21, fax 05.26.81.42.82 Y by appt.

JUERG SAXER

Neftenbacher Pinot Noir Prestige Barrique 1997**

■ n.c. n.c. 70–99 F

Juerg Saxer manages a 14-ha (35-acre) estate that grows a wide range of grape varieties. The famous Pinot Noir is one of them. This example has dark roast coffee and vanilla aromas that reflect its 12 months of oak-ageing. The palate has very balanced tannins that sustain its lengthy finish. A wine that may be drunk now or aged for a while.

Juerg Saxer, Weingut Bruppach, 8913 Neftenbach, tel. 05.23.15.32.00, fax 05.23.15.32.30, e-mail js@juergsaxer.com Y by appt.

SCHACHENMANN

Gächlinger Riesling x Sylvaner us em Räcketorn 1999**

□ n.c. n.c. 30–49 F

This modern co-operative cellar vinifies classic Schaffhouse grapes such as Pinot Noir, Müller-Thurgau and various other crossed varieties. This is a light yellow wine made from Müller-Thurgau. It has an intense grape and ripe fruit nose that is followed by a very fresh and fruity palate. A well-balanced wine that is ready to drink now.

Gus Schachenmann, 61, Gennersbrunnerstrasse, 8207 Schaffhausen, tel. 05.26.44.28.00, fax 05.26.44.28.01, e-mail weine@gus.ch Y by appt.

Stamm

Thaynger Pinot Noir Spätlese 1998★★★

■ n.c. n.c. 70–99 F

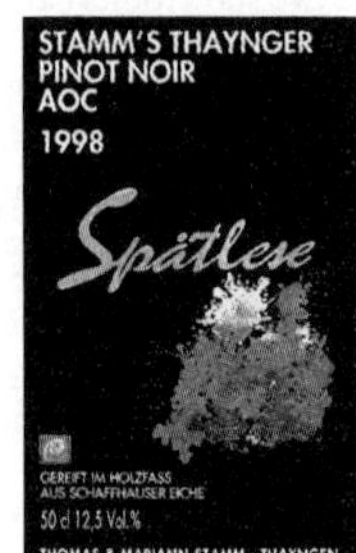

Mariann and Thomas Stamm have been cultivating this 5-ha (12-acre) vineyard for nearly 20 years. They also make their barrels from oak from their own forest. Their late-harvest, oak-aged Pinot Noir 98 is an exceptional wine. A dark red colour with violet highlights, it has a fine aroma of blackcurrants, blackberries and toast. Hefty and powerful on the palate, its luscious warmth is supported by well-structured, ripe tannins and a long finish. The wine could be drunk now or kept, as you wish.

Thomas et Mariann Stamm, 20, Aeckerllstrasse, 8240 Thayngen, tel. 05.26.49.24.15, fax 05.26.49.25.16, e-mail stammson@datacomm.ch Y by appt.

Stamm Eisenhalder Pinot Noir 1998★★

■ n.c. n.c. 50–69 F

The Stamms make fine wines from no fewer than 13 grape varieties. Sometimes, as with this Eisenhald Pinot Noir, the results are remarkable. It has a dark red colour and a beguiling aroma of wild berries and blackcurrants. Robust and well-structured, it has velvety tannins and a long finish that is not over-oaky. Two stars were also awarded to the **Thaynger Cuvée 98** (70–99F), a blend of Pinot Noir, Bianca and Chardonnay matured both in tank and in oak. This white wine has tropical fruit aromas with hints of grapiness and vanilla.

Thomas et Mariann Stamm, 20, Aeckerllstrasse, 8240 Thayngen, tel. 05.26.49.24.15, fax 05.26.49.25.16, e-mail stammson@datacomm.ch Y by appt.

Zahner

Truttker Langenmooser Gewürztraminer 1999★★

□ 0.5 ha n.c. 70–99 F

Established in 1963, this family estate cultivates 7-ha (17-acres) of vines. Thirty percent of the grapes for this wine are fermented in barrel. It has the remarkable rose-petal and fruit aroma that is characteristic of Gewürztraminer. The palate has body and a good balance of acidity and residual sugars, with aromas that persist on to a long finish. A wine to serve with spicy food or desserts.

Familie Zahner, Weinbau, 8467 Truttikon, tel. 05.23.17.19.49, fax 05.23.17.20.95 Y by appt.

Thurgovie

A. et A. Saxer

Kartause Itlingen Warthwingert Müller-Thurgau 1999★★

□ n.c. n.c. 50–69 F

The Saxer estate grows mostly Pinot Noir and Müller-Thurgau on its 8-ha (20-acre) vineyard. This white wine, made from Müller-Thurgau, is light yellow in colour. It is fresh, with good acidity and fruit, and has a delicate sparkle on the palate. A Muscatty hint is perceptible in the delicate flavours, which persist through to a long finish.

A. et A. Saxer, St-Anna-Kellerei, 8537 Nussbaumen, tel. 05.27.45.23.51, fax 05.27.45.27.34 Y by appt.

Zurich

Kumin Rosenberger Räuschling 1999★★

□ n.c. n.c. 70–99 F

Räuschling is a German variety that has been cultivated on the banks of Lake Zürich since the time of the Romans. This 1999 is a very well-made wine. Very fruity, and with the slight sparkle that is typical of this style, it has a refreshing acidity on the palate that makes it suitable for serving with freshwater fish.

Gebrüder Kümin, 1, Oechsli, 8807 Freienbach, tel. 05.54.10.31.31, fax 05.54.10.63.67 Y by appt.

AUGUST PUNTER

Stäfa Chilewägler Clevner 1999★

■ n.c. n.c. 50-69 F

The Pünter family has been cultivating its vineyards in Stäfa, on Lake Zurich, for over 200 years. Its Clevner – another Swiss-German name for Pinot Noir – is a very fragrant wine with raspberry aromas. Its rounded palate has fine tannins.

August et Kathrin Pünter,
53, Glaernischstrasse, 8712 Stäfa,
tel. 19.26.12.24, fax 17.96.36.24,
e-mail puenter-weinbau@dplanet.ch
by appt.

QUERCIBUS

Stammheim Chardonnay 1998★★

□ n.c. n.c. 70-99 F

Quercibus is a brand name for Pinot Noir or Chardonnay wines matured in barrels of Allier oak. This Chardonnay 98 is remarkable, with its fruity nose that shows citrus, coconut and banana aromas with delicate toasty overtones. The well-structured palate has sustained toasty notes and ripe tannins. This balanced wine is ready to drink now.

Volg Weinkellereien,
6, Schaffhauserstrasse, 8401 Winterthur,
tel. 05.22.64.26.26, fax 05.22.64.26.27,
e-mail mailbox@volgweine.ch
by appt.

QUERCIBUS

Rychenberg Winterthur Pinot Noir 1998★★

■ n.c. n.c. 70-99 F

The Pinot Noir is yet another successful Quercibus 98. It has slightly oaky blackberry and clove aromas with a hint of pepper. The influence of oak reappears on the palate as a hint of vanilla. A velvety attack develops into a palate that is structured with rounded, fine tannins that persist on the finish. The very impatient could drink this wine now, but the rest will do well to wait. The **Pinot Noir Quercibus 98 from Malans** in the canton of Grisons is also remarkable, but definitely needs to be kept. Both the **Tegerfelden Pinot Noir 98** (from the Zurich canton), and the **Trimmis** (from Grisons) are fine wines that are ready to drink now.

Volg Weinkellereien,
6, Schaffhauserstrasse, 8401 Winterthur,
tel. 05.22.64.26.26, fax 05.22.64.26.27,
e-mail mailbox@volgweine.ch
by appt.

HERMANN SCHWARZENBACH

Meilener Riesling x Sylvaner Spätlese 1999★

□ n.c. n.c. 50-69 F

In Meilan, on the shore of Lake Zürich, Hermann Schwarzenbach practices organic viticulture, supplemented by modern wine-making equipment. His Riesling-Sylvaner (i.e. Müller-Thurgau) 99 is a harmonious wine with a well-crafted balance of acidity and residual sugar. As well as being generally very fruity, the palate has some Muscat flavours.

Hermann Schwarzenbach,
867, Seestrasse, 8706 Meilen,
tel. 19.23.01.25, fax 19.23.00.37,
e-mail reblaube@bluewin.ch by appt.

STAATSSCHREIBER WEIN

Auslese Cuvée Prestige 1999★★

□ n.c. n.c. 50-69 F

The Rheinau Cloister dates from 876 AD. Taken over in 1862 by the State of Zürich, it is now a wine-making centre, from whose 105-m (114-yard)-long cellars some very good wines are produced. This one certainly has body. Intensely fruity, it is a balanced blend of three varieties (Pinot Noir, Müller-Thurgau and Muscat). The palate is fresh, with good acidity, and the slight residual sugars are just sufficient to give an impression of volume on the palate.

Staatskellerei Zürich,
13–15, Hirschengraben, 8001 Zurich,
tel. 12.51.23.47, fax 12.52.39.44,
e-mail
weinkeller.staatskellerei@moevenpick.ch
by appt.

DOM. ZWEIFEL

Lattenberger Riesling x Gutedel 1999★

□ n.c. n.c. 50-69 F

The Zweifel estate has a century-old tradition of wine-making. It owns vineyards in the cantons of Zürich and Argovie. This very good white wine is made from grapes grown in Zürich. Light yellow in colour, it is fruity and slightly Muscatty. The well-structured palate is full-bodied, with good acidity and a long finish. A wine to drink now.

Dom. Zweifel,
20, Regensdorferstrasse,
8049 Zürich-Höngg, tel. 13.44.22.11,
e-mail info@zweifelweine.ch by appt.

Ticino

The Ticino vineyard stretches from Giornico in the north to Chiasso in the south, covering an area of 900 ha (2,223 acres). Many of the 3,800 wine-growers of the canton own small plots of land, which they cultivate in their leisure time. In the last few years, about 30 of them have specialised in wine-growing, vinifying and selling. About a hundred wine-growers work full time on their vines and sell their grapes to co-operatives. The key variety in the canton is Merlot, originating from Bordeaux, which was introduced into the canton at the beginning of the 20th century. Nowadays, Merlot covers 85% of the wine-growing area of the Ticino and gives white, rosé and red wines. The red Merlot, by far the majority production, can be a light or full-bodied wine, which can be kept, depending on the time it spends in the vat. Some are brought on in hogsheads. The average amount of Merlot produced in Ticino over the last decade has climbed to 55,000 quintals (a local measure equivalent to 100 kg/220 lb).

AMPELIO Merlot del Ticino 1997★★

■ n.c. n.c. 100–149 F

This Bellinzona *négociant's* Merlot Ampelio is always remarkable. An intense ruby colour, it has a delicate fruitiness that is echoed on its full-bodied palate. The tannins may still be a little austere, but they are no less balanced for that. In three years' time, the wine will have rounded out beautifully.

SA Vinicola Carlevaro, 123, via San Gottardo, 6500 Bellinzona, tel. 09.18.29.10.44, fax 09.18.29.14.56, e-mail carlevaro@unitbox.ch Y by appt.

CARATO

Merlot del Ticino Riserva 1997★

■ 2 ha 3,200 200–249 F

Twenty months in oak barrels has left this Ticino Merlot with a concentrated oaky nose and a fruity, slightly tannic palate. This otherwise well-balanced wine is still a little austere, and would benefit from a few years in the cellar. It could then be served with a saddle of venison cooked with chestnuts.

Angelo Delea, 11, via Zandone, case postale 1044, 6616 Losone, tel. 09.17.91.08.17, fax 09.17.91.59.08, e-mail vini@delea.ch Y by appt.

CASTANAR Merlot del Ticino 1998★

■ 0.55 ha 4,100 70–99 F

Roberto Ferrari has used a small percentage of Cabernet Sauvignon to give structure to his Ticino Merlot. Ruby-red with garnet highlights, it has fairly intense, tropical fruit aromas with oaky overtones. On the palate, it is ripe, supple and balanced.

Roberto Ferrari, 6, via Mulino, 6855 Stabio, tel. 09.16.47.12.34, fax 09.16.47.12.51 Y by appt.

COLLE D'AVRA

Merlot del Ticino Riserva Barrique 1997★

■ 4.8 ha 6,500 100–149 F

The *azienda* of Avra has more than 7-ha (17-acres) of vineyards at the bottom of Monte Generoso, not far from the Ours grottoes. It has produced a ruby-coloured wine with garnet highlights that has a discreet, slightly spicy, ripe fruit nose. A subtle hint of vanilla is perceptible on the well-balanced palate, which also displays a surprising level of acidity on the finish.

Azienda Agricola Avra, strada per Avra, 6874 Castel-San-Pietro, tel. 091.646.92.73, fax. 091.646.84.33 Y by appt.

Caspiera SAGL

COMANO

Vigneto ai Brughi Merlot del Ticino 1997★

■ 1.5 ha 6,000 100–149 F

The vineyards around Lugano benefit from a slightly gentler microclimate on account of the lake. The Tamborini estate is located only a few kilometres away from this distinctly Italianate city. Its dark purple Merlot is a powerfully structured, rich and complex wine with very strong tannins and vegetal flavours.

SA Eredi Carlo Tamborini, Strada Cantonale, 6814 Lamone, tel. 09.19.35.75.45, fax 09.19.35.75.49 Y by appt.

Claudio Tamborini

GAUCH

Merlot del Ticino Collina di Sementina Riserva Barrique 1997★

■ 1 ha 4,000 150–199 F

After visiting Bellinzona's three chateaus, it is easy to find your way to Peter Gauch's estate. His 4-ha (10-acres) of vineyards are spread across the slopes of Sementina hill. This Merlot, the product of 30-year-old vines, has a fine, intense colour and a spicy nose with subtle, exotic aromas and a delicate vegetal note. A well-structured wine, it is still slightly bitter on the palate.

Peter Gauch, In Collina, 6514 Sementina, tel. 09.18.57.23.21, fax 09.18.57.03.21 Y by appt.

IL QUERCETO

Merlot del Ticino 1997★★

■ 1.2 ha 10,000 100–149 F

This is the third excellent vintage in a row of Merlot from this estate. An intense ruby colour, the 1997 has a generous and elegant aroma of fruit and spices. The rich palate is structured by strong tannins that should soften with time. Look for the little oak-tree on the label.

SA Terreni alla Maggia, 105, via Muraccio, 6612 Ascona, tel. 09.17.91.24.52, fax 09.17.91.06.54, e-mail terreniallamaggia@swissonline.ch Y by appt.

FATTORIA MONCUCCHETTO

Merlot Lugano Riserva 1998★

■ n.c. 1,500 100–149 F

Niccolo and Lisetta Lucchini are talented wine-makers. Their Merlot Riserva 98 has an oaky, slightly musky nose. Its full-bodied, slightly sweet palate has good tannins.

🔑 Niccolo e Lisetta Lucchini, 30, via Crivelli, 6900 Lugano, tel. 09.19.66.73.63, fax 09.19.22.71.77 V
Y by appt.

MONTAGNA MAGICA

Merlot del Malcantone 1998★★

■ 1.8 ha 5,400 100–149 F

Daniel Huber's wines are of consistently high quality, particularly in the last three vintages. This deep ruby Malcantone Merlot is remarkably well-balanced. Its fresh and fruity nose foreshadows an elegant palate that bears witness to a harvest of fully ripe grapes.

🔑 Daniel Huber, Monteggio, 6998 Termine, tel. 09.16.08.17.54, fax 09.16.08.33.53, e-mail huber.mont@bluewin.ch V
Y by appt.

MONTE CARASSO

Merlot del Ticino Elevé en Barrique 1997★★★

■ n.c. 7,800 70–99 F

Until 1986, Cantina Gagi was a co-operative cellar. Since then, it has operated as a *négociant*, vinifying grapes from around 600 growers into fine wines such as this outstanding Merlot. It has a fragrant, spicy, slightly toasty nose. On the palate, it is robust and long, with silky tannins. A beautifully structured wine that is both modern and yet highly typical.

🔑 SA Cagi-Cantina Giubiasco, 11, via Linoleum, 6512 Giubiasco, tel. 09.18.57.25.31, fax 09.18.57.79.12, e-mail cagi@ticino.com V Y by appt.

PLATINUM Merlot del Ticino 1997★★★

■ 0.5 ha 1,640 250–299 F

This Merlot, from the cellars of Guido Brivio, is appropriately named after a precious metal. After two years in oak, it has an intense purple colour and a delicate, complex, fruity and spicy nose. The rich palate is full-bodied, with great persistence and very fine tannins. A perfectly balanced wine that could be kept for two to three years.

🔑 SA I Vini di Guido Brivio, 3 via Vignoo, 6850 Mendrisio, tel. 09.16.46.07.57, fax 09.16.46.08.05, e-mail brivio@brivio.ch V Y by appt.

ROMPIDEE

Merlot del Ticino Élevé en Barrique 1997★

■ 0.2 ha 13,000 100–149 F

Fabio Arnaboldi has aged this clear, deep ruby Merlot in barrel, which has given it a subtly oaky, fruity nose and a full-bodied palate with good acidity. Although the tannins are a little austere on the finish, this wine could nonetheless be drunk now.

🔑 SA Cantina Chiodi vini, 24, via Delta, 6612 Ascona, tel. 09.17.91.16.82, fax 09.17.91.03.93 V Y by appt.

ROSSO DI CADEMARIO

Malcantone 1998★

■ 1 ha 6,000 100–149 F

Sergio Monti's vineyards are planted on terraces at altitudes of 500–650 m (1,600–2,130 ft). He has made a blend of Merlot (85%) and Diolinoir (11%), with a little Carminoir and Cabernet Sauvignon. The Diolinoir variety, which was created in 1970, is renowned for producing intensely coloured wines that are rich in tannins. This wine's deep ruby colour confirms the variety's reputation. Rich and intense, the spicy aromas of the nose are slightly oaky. The warm and very elegant palate, which is structured with fine tannins, has a slight vanilla flavour. This wine should be kept for another year or two.

🔑 Cantina Monti, Ronchi, 6936 Cademario, tel. 19.19.22.98.22, fax 19.19.22.98.23, e-mail info@montitid.ch V Y by appt.

SINFONIA

Merlot del Ticino Barrique 1997★

■ 4 ha 12,500 100–149 F

Walking down from Bellinzona's three châteaux, one can easily spot this winemaker's headquarters. Its Sinfonia is a highly regarded wine. The 1997 has an intense ruby colour with orangey highlights. Redolent of cocoa and leather, this already mature wine has excellent balance.

🔑 SA Chiericati vini, 10, via Convento, casella postale 1214, 6501 Bellinzona, tel. 09.18.25.13.07, fax 09.18.26.40.07 V
Y by appt.
🔑 Angelo Cavalli

TRENTASEI Merlot del Ticino 1996★★

■ n.c. 2,000 500 F+

Trentasei mesi di barriques . . . Thirty-six months' ageing in oak has produced a ruby-coloured Merlot with garnet highlights. Fine and intense, it has a spicy, subtly vanilla-scented aroma and an elegant, weighty palate. A well-structured and remarkably balanced wine.

🔑 SA Casa Vinicola Gialdi, 3, via Vignoo, 6850 Mendrisio, tel. 09.16.46.40.21, fax 09.16.46.67.06 V
Y by appt.

GLOSSARY

Acerbic. Said of a wine made tart and sour from having far too much tannin and acidity. A very serious defect.

Acidity. In moderation, acidity helps the balance of a wine, giving it freshness and vigour. But if there is too much, it is a defect, making the wine biting and sour. Too little, however, and the wine will be flabby and lacking in grip.

Aggressive. Said of a wine that is too strong (usually in tannins) and attacks the palate in an unpleasant way.

Agreeable. A pleasant, nicely balanced wine in every respect.

Alcohol. The next largest component of wine after water, ethyl alcohol gives wine its warming character. But if there is too much, the wine is said to be hot.

Alcoholic strength. This is generally expressed in degrees or per cent corresponding to the alcoholic content of the wine by volume.

Aligoté. White grape variety used for making Bourgogne Aligoté, a carafe wine to be drunk young.

Altesse. White grape variety used to make very fine Roussette-de-Savoie.

Amber. If white wines are aged for a long time or are oxidised prematurely, they sometimes take on an amber colour.

Ampelography. The study of vine varieties, especially grape vines.

Ample. Said of a harmonious wine which appears to fill the mouth well.

Amylic. Smell of amyl acetate, similar to peardrops, banana or bubble-gum. Usually detected on young white or rosé wines that are made using cool fermentation, or on reds made with carbonic maceration.

Animal. Smells evoking the animal kingdom: musk, venison, leather. Mostly found in old red wines.

AOC. Appellation d'Origine Contrôlée. A regulatory system which guarantees the authenticity of a wine made in a particular area. Almost all the great wines come from AOC regions.

Aroma. In the technical language of winetasting, this term is used for olfactory sensations perceived in the nose and, sometimes, on the palate. It is particularly used for the simple fruit smells of young wines to differentiate from 'bouquet', which is used for smells of more mature wines. The adjective 'aromatic' may describe a generally pleasant smell. See also 'Bouquet'.

Assemblage. Term for the blending of several lots of wine from the same area to obtain the desired final blend. Term used in particular in Champagne for the blending of the base wine *cuvées*, and in Bordeaux for the final blending for the Grand Vin or main Château wine.

Astringency. A rather rough, rasping taste or, technically, a tactile sensation around the gums and on the roof of the mouth. It is often found in young red wines having more tannin than fruit.

Auxerrois. White grape variety used to make Alsace Klevner; the name is also a synonym for the red Malbec variety in Cahors.

Balanced. Said of a wine with a good balance of acidity and sweetness in whites, or tannin and fruit in red wines.

Balsamic. Used to describe smells evoking the world of perfume, including, among others, vanilla, incense, resin and benzine.

Balthasar. Very large bottle containing the equivalent of 16 ordinary bottles (12 litres)

Barrique. Barrel.

Bâtonnage. Stirring the yeast in a barrel with a pole or baton. Particularly used for fine barrel-fermented whites.

Bitartrate deposit. Technical term for the deposit of tartaric acid crystals, often known simply as tartrates and sometimes found in bottled wines.

Bitterness. Caused by tannins overwhelming the fruit. Bitterness can be an advance warning of astringency, which can soften out, while bitterness is an abiding fault.

Blanc Fumé. Name given to Sauvignon at Pouilly-sur-Loire, where the Pouilly-Fumé appellation comes from (not to be confused with Pouilly-Fuissé from Burgundy, which is made from the Chardonnay grape).

Blending. The mixing together of different lots of wines; see also 'Assemblage'.

Body. Characteristic of a well-structured, warming and fleshy wine.

Botrytis cinerea. A fungus which attacks the skins of grapes. Although detrimental to red grape varieties, it can be beneficial for certain whites given certain climatic conditions. In such cases it concentrates the sugars and flavours of the grape enabling the great sweet wines to be made. See also 'Noble rot'.

Botrytised. Grapes that have been affected by *botrytis cinerea* or noble rot.

Bouquet. Smells sensed by the nose while sniffing wine in the glass. Technically used to refer to the smells in more mature wines that emerge as the wine ages. This differentiates it from 'aroma', which is used for smells in younger wines. See also 'Aroma'.

Bourboulenc. Medium-quality white grape variety from the Rhône Valley and Southern France.

Breton. Name given to Cabernet Franc in the Loire Valley.

Brilliant. Said of wine having a very bright or brilliant colour which glints strongly in the light.

Burning. Said of a wine containing too much or an excessive balance of alcohol, leaving a burning sensation in the mouth.

Burnt. Sometimes ambiguous term for smells ranging from caramel to burnt wood, usually associated with ageing in oak.

Brut. Term for dry sparkling wines and Champagnes containing very little sweetness (just enough to temper the wine's acidity); 'Extra Brut' or, in French, *brut zéro* means there is virtually no

added sugar, giving a very dry sparkling wine.
Cabernet Franc. Red grape variety blended with Cabernet-Sauvignon and/or Merlot in Bordeaux, also the main quality red grape in the Loire Valley. It is capable of producing a very fine wine for long-term keeping.
Cabernet-Sauvignon. Noble red grape variety predominant in the Médoc and Graves regions of Bordeaux, also used elsewhere in South-West and Southern France and producing wines for long-term keeping.
Carafe. Semi-ornamental clear-glass bottle or decanter, into which wine is poured to aerate it and/or take it off its sediment.
Carbonic maceration. Method of vinifying red wine by macerating whole grapes in vats saturated with carbon dioxide. It is used mainly to produce wines to be drunk very young (Vins de Primeur) and is widely used in Beaujolais.
Carignan. Red grape variety from Southern France producing very well structured, robust wines.
Casse. Fault in wine caused by oxidation or chemical reduction which makes wine lose its clarity.
Chai. Winery located on the ground floor in regions where they do not dig out underground cellars, especially in the Médoc region of Bordeaux.
Chaptalisation. The addition of sugar to fermenting must to obtain a more robust wine by increasing its richness in alcohol when this is too weak; this process is subject to legal controls.
Chardonnay. Noble white grape variety from Burgundy, also grown in other regions such as Jura. It produces fine wines likely to age well. It is also a key grape variety for Champagne and other sparkling wines.
Chasselas. White grape variety grown chiefly as a table grape but also used for making dry wine (in Switzerland, Alsace and Savoie).
Château. Term often used to describe a wine estate even though – sometimes – it does not contain a real château.
Chenin. White grape variety very common in the Loire Valley, producing fine, balanced wines likely to keep well.
Cinsaut or Cinsault. Red grape variety from the Rhône Valley and South of France which makes very fruity wines.
Clairet. Light, fruity red wine, or rosé wine produced in the Bordeaux.
Clairette. White grape variety from the Rhône Valley and South of France producing fairly fine dry and sparkling wines.
Claret. English term for red wine from Bordeaux.
Clarification. Separating the sediment from grape juice or wine; see also 'Filtration' and 'Fining'.
Clavelin. Unusually shaped bottle holding 62 cl and used for the Vins Jaunes or yellow wines of the Jura.
Climat. In Burgundy, refers to an area characterised by soil type and micro-climate.
Clone. Group of vinestocks grown from cuttings that have been multiplied from a single parent stock.
Clos. Term used in some regions, especially Burgundy, to describe an enclosed vineyard usually surrounded by walls (eg Clos de Vougeot).
Colombard. White grape variety from the South-West of France, producing fairly ordinary, everyday wines.
Cot or Côt. Name given to the Malbec grape variety in the Loire Valley.
Coulure. Poor fruit set following wet or windy weather resulting in the fruit (as small, unformed berries) falling off after flowering.
Corked. A wine suffering from a tainted smell and taste from a faulty cork. The typical smell is musty, mousy or corky.
Crémant. Sparkling AOC wine.
Cru. French term for a vineyard, often translated as 'growth'. The meaning of this term varies from region to region and may be linked to a quality system. See also 'Premier Cru' and 'Grand Cru'. It may also be used to denote certain superior areas of vineyards, eg the Beaujolais crus such as Juliénas or Fleurie.
Cru Bourgeois. Classification for châteaux in the Médoc region of Bordeaux which is below that of the 1855 classification.
Crushing. The process of breaking up the grape skins to extract the juice.
Cuve. Vat, tun or tank used for the fermentation and storage of wine.
Decant. To transfer a wine from its bottle into a carafe or decanter to separate the wine from its sediment and allow the wine to breathe.
Demi-sec. Medium dry, for still wines. For a sparkling wine, the term means medium-sweet.
De-stemming. Removing the stems or stalks from the grapes. If grapes are not de-stemmed, they can give wine a certain astringency.
Deposit. Solid particles in a wine, particularly in old wines, which are removed by decanting before the wine is served.
Disgorgement. The act of expelling the sediment caused by the secondary fermentation in the bottle of sparkling wine. This is followed immediately by topping up and insertion of the final cork.
Dosage. French term for the sweetened wine added to a sparkling wine or Champagne after the yeast deposit has been removed. The level of dosage determines the final style, eg Doux, Demi-sec or Brut.
Doux. Term applied to sweet wines rich in sugar and to highly dosed wines in Champagne.
Dry. In still wines, describes a wine with virtually no residual sweetness (less than 4 grams per litre); on the sweetness scale of sparkling wines, it means having little sugar (between 17 and 35 grams per litre), which gives a medium-dry taste.
Duras. Red grape variety mainly produced in Gaillac in South-West France. (Not to be confused with the appellation of the same name.)
Empyreumatic. Term for smells recalling things burnt, cooked or smoked.
Espalier. Rare method of training vines.
Fat. Synonym for mellow or unctuous.
Feminine. Said of wines suggesting tenderness and lightness.

Fer. Red grape variety used to make wines for long-term keeping in South-West France.

Fermentation. Process by which grape juice becomes wine through the action of yeasts which turn the grape sugar into alcohol.

Fillette. Small bottle holding 35 cl, used in the Loire Valley.

Filtration. The process of filtering out deposits from must or wine to clarify it.

Finesse. Term for a wine that is delicate and elegant.

Fining. Process for clarifying wine by adding a coagulant (egg white, isinglass) which draws off particles still in suspension. These are subsequently filtered out.

Flavour. Overall sensation in the mouth imparted by a wine's taste and its aromas.

Flesh, fleshy. Said of a wine that gives an impression of fullness and density in the mouth, without any roughness.

Folle Blanche. White grape variety producing very fresh, lively wine (Gros Plant).

Foudre. Large barrel.

Foxy. Term for a smell given off by wine made from certain hybrid grape varieties.

Free-run juice. The juice of finished wine that runs freely from the fermenting vat, as opposed to the juice obtained by pressing the skins. (Only applies to red wines.)

Fresh. Said of a wine that is lightly but not excessively acid, and imparts a feeling of freshness or liveliness.

Full. Said of a wine which has the requisite qualities of a good wine and leaves a feeling of fullness in the mouth.

Fût. Small barrel, usually of new oak.

Gamay. Red grape variety, the only one permitted in Beaujolais, also grown widely in the Loire Valley. Makes a very fruity, lively wine.

Garrigue. Scrub or scrubland.

Generic. Term having several applications but often describing a brand-name wine rather than a Cru or Château wine, sometimes directed in a derogatory way at regional appellations such as Bordeaux, Burgundy, etc.

Generous. Said of a wine that is ripe and strong in alcohol but not tiresomely so, as in a heady wine.

Gewurztraminer. Very aromatic white grape variety from Alsace.

Glycerol. A higher alcohol and by-product of fermentation. Present in most wines, it is found in greater concentration in botrytised wines. It adds to the sweetness and oiliness of a wine.

Goût de terroir. Literally the taste from (not of) the soil. The notion of terroir includes soil, climate and exposure. In modern terms, a *goût de terroir* refers to a wine that tastes of where it comes from. See also 'Terroir'.

Grafting. Method used since the phylloxera disaster whereby a vine is grafted onto a rootstock (usually American) resistant to the phylloxera plant louse.

Grand Cru. Literally 'Great Growth', usually left untranslated.

Grand Vin. Term used by the Crus Classés châteaux of Bordeaux to describe the first wine of the château, eg in Margaux, Château Margaux is the Grand Vin of that château and Le Pavillon Rouge de Château Margaux is the second wine.

Gravel. Soil consisting of rounded pebbles and gravel, giving very good drainage. Very suitable for making high-quality red wines and found particularly in the Médoc and Graves areas of Bordeaux.

Green. Said of a wine that is too acidic.

Grenache. Red grape variety grown principally in the Rhône Valley and in some regions of the South such as Banyuls and Languedoc-Roussillon, giving a fruity and very alcoholic wine.

Gris, Vin. Pale rosé wine usually made by direct pressing of red grapes which results in a slightly coloured white wine.

Grolleau. Red grape variety from the Loire Valley used mainly in the production of rosé wines.

Gros Plant. Name given to the Folle Blanche grape variety in the Nantes area of the Loire Valley.

Hard. Said of wine that is too astringent and acid, with too much tannin.

Harmonious. Said of a wine, usually a mature wine, in which the different characteristics are balanced and make a well-rounded whole.

Harshness. A rough, rather biting feeling, caused by far too much tannin.

Heady. Said of a wine that is very high in alcohol and possibly unbalanced.

Heavy. Said of an excessively rich wine.

Herbaceous. Term (often used pejoratively) for aromas recalling grass or vegetation.

Hogshead. Barrel.

Hybrid. Term for grape varieties created from two different species of vine, as distinct from a grape crossing. Hybrids are rarely grown in France today and may only be used for table wines.

INAO. Institut National des Appellations d'Origine. Public body established to administer AOC and AOVDQS wines and regulate their production conditions.

Jacquère. White grape variety found in Savoie which makes a wine to be drunk fairly young.

Jeroboam. Large bottle holding the equivalent of four bottles (three litres) in Champagne and six bottles (4.5 litres) in Bordeaux.

Jurançon. Little-used white grape variety still found in Charente; also a red variety from the South-East used to make fairly ordinary wine. It is also the name for a dry or sweet white AOC wine made from the Gros et Petit Manseng and Courbu varieties in South-West France around the Jurançon commune.

Lactic acid. Acid obtained during malolactic fermentation.

Lees. The natural precipitation of yeast cells and colouring matter that forms as a wine matures in a vat or barrel. When this happens in the bottle, it is called sediment.

Light. Said of a light-coloured wine with little body, but well-balanced and pleasant. In general, a wine to be drunk fairly young.

Limpid. Said of a clear, brightly coloured wine having no sediment.

Liquoreux. Particularly sweet and rich in sugar,

the Vins Liquoreux are made from grapes allowed to develop noble rot and have a generally honeyed bouquet.

Lively. Said of a fresh, light wine, a little bit acid but still pleasant.

Long. Said when the flavours of a wine make a pleasing and persistent impression in the mouth after tasting; wine is also said to have 'length' or 'good length'.

Macabeu. White grape variety from the Roussillon that makes a pleasant wine to be drunk young.

Maceration. When the must and the grapes' solid matter (skins, pips, etc) are still in contact during fermentation.

Maderised. Said of a white wine which is slightly oxidised, taking on an amber colour while ageing and a taste like madeira.

Magnum. Bottle holding the equivalent of two bottles (1.5 litres).

Malbec. Name given in Bordeaux to the Cot grape variety.

Malic acid. Acid naturally present in all wines and which may be turned into lactic acid by malolactic fermentation.

Malolactic fermentation. The transformation, through the action of lactic bacteria, of malic acid into lactic acid and carbon dioxide. It is considered essential for stability in red wines and is sometimes used for whites. Its effect is partly to make the wine less acid, and for whites to develop a generally softer or creamier character.

Manseng. Gros Manseng and Petit Manseng are two of the white grape varieties used to make Jurançon.

Marc. Solid material left over after pressing; also the popular name of the marc brandy made from it.

Marsanne. White grape variety grown in the Hermitage and elsewhere in the Rhône Valley and the South.

Maturation. The period of time the wine spends between the end of the vinification or wine-making process and it being drunk. Maturation may take place in vats or oak barrels, or later in the bottle. The French word *maturation* refers to the ripening process of the grapes, which in English is simply called ripening.

Mauzac. White grape variety cultivated in Southern and South-West France, making a fine wine for early drinking; it is also used as the base for sparkling wines.

Melon de Bourgogne. Originally from Burgundy, Melon is a synonym for the white Muscadet grape grown in the Nantes area of the Loire Valley.

Merlot. Main red grape variety in the Pomerol and Saint-Emilion districts of Bordeaux and blended with the Cabernets.

Methuselah. Name used in Champagne for a large bottle equivalent to eight ordinary bottles (six litres). In Bordeaux, this is also called the imperial bottle.

Mildew. Vine disease caused by a parasitic fungus which attacks the stems and leaves.

Mistelle. Sweet mixture of grape must and alcohol. The fermentation of the must of fresh grapes is stopped by the addition of alcohol. See also 'VDN' and 'VDL'.

Moelleux. Term generally used for very sweet white wines.

Mondeuse. Red grape variety from Savoie which makes a high-quality wine for long-term keeping.

Mourvèdre. Red grape variety from Provence and the Rhône Valley producing fine wines which keep very well.

Mousse. Sparkle or fizziness as seen and tasted in Champagne and other sparkling wines.

Mousseux. French word for sparkling which can be applied to sparkling wines made using all methods.

Muscadelle. White grape variety from Bordeaux which is blended with Sémillon and Sauvignon.

Muscadet. White grape variety grown in the Loire Valley which makes a very fresh wine generally made to be drunk young.

Muscat. A family of grape varieties which all have a similar grapey or floral aroma. The word is also used for wines made from Muscat grapes.

Musky. Said of a smell that recalls musk.

Must. The sugary juice extracted from grapes.

Musty. Said of a wine that has lost some or all of its bouquet through partial oxidation or other faults.

Mutage. Process of stopping the must's alcoholic fermentation by adding wine-based spirit. Mistelle, Vins de Liqueurs and Vins Doux Naturels are made this way.

Nebuchadnezzar. Giant bottle in Champagne, equivalent to 20 ordinary bottles (15 litres).

Négrette. Red grape variety in South-West France giving a rich, strongly coloured wine with little acidity.

Nervy. Said of a lively wine which leaves pronounced flavours and some acidity on the palate, but not too much.

Nielluccio. Red grape variety planted in Corsica, giving high-quality wines for long-term keeping (particularly Patrimonio).

Noble rot. Name given to the action of the *Botrytis cinerea* on white grapes to make the finest sweet white wines.

Nouveau. Wine from the latest harvest to be drunk young. See also 'Primeur'.

Oenology. The scientific study of wine.

Oïdium. Powdery mildew, a fungal disease of the vine which can attack stalks, leaves or grape bunches and leaves a powdery grey residue which severely affects yields; can be treated with sulphur.

OIV. Office International de la Vigne et du Vin. Based in France, this is the inter-governmental body which supervises technical, scientific and economic matters related to growing vines and making wine.

Old. Term with several applications, usually describing a wine which is several years old and has aged in the bottle after its period in the barrel; but may also be said of a wine that is simply past its best.

Onivins. The French Interprofessional Office for Wines. This body succeeded Onivit in its mission to direct and regulate the wine market.

Organoleptic. Describes the qualities and

properties noted by the senses during wine-tasting, eg colour, smell or taste.

Ouvrée. Measurement of land area. 28 ouvrées = 1 hectare.

Oxidation. The action of oxygen (air) on wine. If there is too much, the colour fades and both the smell and taste of the wine are affected.

Pasteurisation. Heat-sterilising process perfected by Louis Pasteur.

Persistence. Length of time that the flavours of a wine remain in the mouth after swallowing. Good persistence, or length, is a positive sign.

Pétillant. A Vin Pétillant is a lightly sparkling wine, less fizzy than Vin Mousseux.

Petit Verdot. In the Médoc district of Bordeaux, a minor red grape variety which may be blended in small quantities with the Cabernets and Merlot.

Phylloxera. Plant louse which between 1860 and 1890 ravaged French vineyards by eating vine roots and thus killing the vines. It is controlled today by grafting vines onto phylloxera-resistant rootstocks. See also 'Grafting'.

Pineau d'Aunis. Minor red grape variety grown in some regions of the Loire Valley and producing a pale-coloured wine.

Pinot Blanc. White grape variety grown mainly in Alsace.

Pinot Gris. High-quality white grape variety grown mainly in Alsace, where it used to be known as Tokay.

Pinot Meunier. Red grape variety which is mainly used in Champagne as part of the blend. It is a hardier and earlier-ripening grape than Pinot Noir, to which it is related.

Pinot Noir. The main red grape variety in Burgundy, where it gives wines with immediate fruitiness which nevertheless keep well. It is also an important part of the blend for Champagne, where it is pressed quickly so as not to extract colour. It is the only permitted red grape in Alsace, and small quantities are grown in the South.

Piquant. Said of a wine with a sharp, acid taste.

Poulsard. Red grape variety grown mainly in the Jura and producing pale-coloured wines sold as rosé or red.

Powerful. Said of a wine which combines a full body with generosity and a rich bouquet.

Premier Cru. Literally First Growth, usually left untranslated.

Pressing. Process of pressing the grapes to extract juice or wine, leaving the skins and other solid matter behind.

Pricked. Property of a wine suffering from acescency, which gives it a sour, vinegary smell.

Primeur. A Vin de Primeur is from the latest harvest and is made to be drunk very young. See also 'Nouveau'.

Racking. Process of transferring a wine from one barrel or vat to another to separate it from the lees or sediment.

Rancio. Some sweet white wines, especially VDN, take on this almost maderised character as they age; it is close to a nutty aroma.

Rasping. Said of a rough, astringent wine.

Ratafia. Vin de Liqueur made in Champagne by mixing grape spirit and fermenting must.

Remuage. Riddling. During the secondary fermentation in the bottle in the traditional (Champagne) method, this is the shaking and turning process by which the remaining sediment is brought down to rest on the cork so that it can be disgorged. Formerly done by hand, it can now be done mechanically with rotating pallets.

Rich. Said of a well-balanced, generous, powerful wine with good colour.

Riesling. White grape variety grown in Alsace and making wines of great distinction.

Roasted. Characteristic taste and aromas of crystallised fruits in sweet wines made from grapes affected by noble rot. Also refers to red wines made from grapes that have been literally 'roasted' by the sun.

Robust. Said of a wine having body.

Rolle. White grape variety from Provence which makes very fine wines.

Romorontain. Rare white grape variety grown in some parts of the Loire Valley.

Rootstock. The part of the vine that is not visible, ie which is below ground. Most European grape varieties are grafted onto American rootstocks, since these are resistant to phylloxera.

Rough. Said of a very astringent, rasping wine.

Round, rounded. Said of a supple, ripe and fleshy wine which leaves a pleasant, harmonious feeling in the mouth.

Roussanne. White grape variety grown mainly in the northern Rhône Valley, a little in the southern Rhône and in small quantities in Savoie, giving a very fine wine for long-term keeping.

Saignée, Rosé de. Rosé wine run off the skins of red grapes after a very short maceration period.

Salmanazar. Very large bottle in Champagne containing the equivalent of 12 ordinary bottles (nine litres).

Sauvignon. White grape variety grown in many regions, but especially in the Loire Valley and Bordeaux, and making a fine wine which keeps well and has a characteristic smoky aroma.

Savagnin. Grape variety from the Jura giving the famous Vin Jaune or yellow wine and making up part of the blend for other Jura white wines. It may be related to the Klevner and Gewurztraminer from Alsace.

Scent. Another word for smell, indicating something scented or perfumed, or delicately aromatic.

Sciacarello. Red grape variety grown in Corsica and giving a fleshy, fruity wine.

Sediment. Solid particles held in suspension in must or wine.

Sémillon. Noble white grape variety grown mainly in Bordeaux and making sweet wines such as Sauternes as well as fine dry wines.

Sensory analysis. Technical term for wine-tasting.

Short. Said of a wine having little length in the mouth after tasting; 'short in the mouth' is also used.

Silky. Said of a supple, mellow, velvety, pleasantly harmonious and elegant wine.

Smoky. Term for a smell like that of smoked

foods, characteristic of, among others, the Sauvignon grape variety (hence the name Blanc Fumé or 'smoky white').
Smooth. A smooth or supple, pleasant wine, easy to drink and which 'slips down well'.
Solid. Said of a well-constituted, well-structured wine.
Sour. Having a highly acid character, accompanied by a smell very like that of vinegar.
Sparkling. Term for wines that have dissolved carbon dioxide, usually the result of a second fermentation.
Stabilisation. All the processes, such as filtration and fining, used before bottling to ensure a wine is kept in good condition. Especially refers to the process of removing tartaric acid crystals before bottling.
Stale. Said of a wine that has lost some or all of its bouquet, usually through oxidation.
Stemming. Alternative term sometimes used for de-stemming. See 'De-stemming'.
Still wine. Non-sparkling wine.
Straightforward. Said of a frank wine with a well-defined character.
Structure. Describes the general form and constitution of a wine, especially its acidity and tannin.
Substantial. Said of a wine that has a strong colour and in the mouth feels rather heavy and thick.
Sulphur. A sulphur solution may be added to must or wine to protect it from faults such as oxidation, or, at the point of fermentation, to kill off certain unwanted yeast strains. Sulphuring refers to the treatment of the vine by spraying with copper sulphate, to prevent fungal diseases.
Supple. Said of a smooth wine, its mellowness prevailing over its astringency.
Sylvaner. White grape variety from Alsace which generally makes straightforward wine for early drinking.
Syrah. High-quality red grape variety mainly planted in the Rhône Valley and Languedoc-Roussillon.
Tannat. Red grape variety grown in the South-West and producing very well-structured fine wines which keep well.
Tannic. A rough, astringent sensation in a wine caused by tannin.
Tannin. Substance found in grape skins, pips and stems which helps wine to keep for a long time and forms part of its structure. Particularly noticeable in young reds.
Tartrates. Tartaric crystals that form in the cask, vat or bottle if the wine has been subjected to intense cold.
Tastevinage. Seal awarded by the Confrérie des Chevaliers du Tastevin to certain Burgundy wines.
Tears. Term for the traces of wine on the glass, sometimes also called 'legs'.
Temperature regulation. Technique for checking and adjusting the temperature in the vat during fermentation and storage.
Terroir. A place where wine is grown. Each terroir has its own physical characteristics (soil, subsoil, exposure, etc) which influence the kind and quality of the wine produced there. See also 'Goût de terroir'.
Tired. Term for a wine that has lost some of its quality. This may be temporary (for example after being transported) and it may just need time to recover.
Tokay. Name given in Alsace to Pinot Gris, a quality white grape variety. No relation to the Hungarian wine of the same name.
Topping up. Process of adding wine to the barrel to keep it full and prevent the wine from coming into contact with air.
Traditional method. Method of making sparkling wines which includes a secondary fermentation in the bottle, as is done for Champagne. Identical to the 'Champagne method'.
Trousseau. Red grape variety from the Jura, producing wine with a darker colour than the Poulsard or Pinot Noir.
Ugni Blanc. White grape variety grown in the South (and in Charente to make Cognac under the name of Saint-Émilion) and giving a fairly acid wine which does not keep well.
Ullage. Space left at the top of a closed bottle. If there is too much ullage, the wine will oxidise. Also refers to the space left in the top of a barrel. See also 'Topping up'.
Unctuous. Said of a wine that is pleasantly mellow, fleshy and full-bodied in the mouth.
VDL. Vin de Liqueur. A sweet wine made by mixing must and alcohol (Pineau des Charentes). These sweet wines do not conform to the legal norms for the VDNs.
VDN. Vin Doux Naturel. A sweet wine made from Muscat, Grenache, Macabeu or Malvoisie grapes. The wine is obtained by stopping the fermentation of the must with the addition of grape spirit, in line with strict conditions about the wine's sweetness and how it is made.
VDP. Vin de Pays. A wine legally belonging to the table wines group, ie below that of AOC and AOVDQS wines, but which carries a mention on the label of the geographical region it comes from. Some VDP may be of high quality.
VDQS. Now AOVDQS: Appellation d'Origine Vin Délimité de Qualité Supérieure. The regional wines in this group are made according to strict regulations.
Vegetal. Said of the bouquet or aromas of a wine (generally a young one) which recall grasses or vegetation.
Venison. Said of the bouquet of a wine which recalls the smell of big-game animals.
Vermentino. White grape variety grown particularly in Corsica where it is known sometimes as Malvoisie. It may be the same as Rolle in Provence.
Villages. Term used in some regions to single out a superior area within a larger appellation (Beaujolais, Côtes du Rhône, Mâcon).
Vinification. The methods and techniques of wine-making.
Vinous. Said of a wine fairly rich in alcohol which seems to sum up neatly the differences between wine and other alcoholic drinks.
Vintage. The year in which the wine was harvested.

Viognier. White grape variety grown in the Rhône Valley and the South and producing a fine, high-quality wine.

Virile. Said of a well-structured, full-bodied and powerful wine.

VQPRD. Vin de Qualité Produit dans une Région Déterminée. This category includes the French AOC and VDQS wines and sets them apart from the table wines category in the European Union.

Warming. Said of a wine conveying an impression of warmth, usually because of its alcoholic strength.

Well structured. Said of a well-constituted wine with plenty of acidity and tannin that will probably age well.

Wine-merchants. In the French wine business, there are straightforward wine-merchants and shippers (*négociants*), but also others (*négociants-éleveurs*) who, especially in the big appellation regions, not only buy and sell wine but take over the maturation of young wine and see it through every stage up to bottling. In Champagne, the *négociant-manipulateur* buys grapes to make his own Champagne wine.

Yeasts. Microscopic single-celled organisms which convert sugar to alcohol during fermentation.

Young. Very relative term, used for a wine in its first year as well as for the taste of an older wine that has not yet developed to its full potential.

INDEX OF APPELLATIONS

INDEX OF COMMUNES

COMMUNES

INDEX OF PRODUCERS

PRODUCERS

PRODUCERS

PRODUCERS

PRODUCERS

PRODUCERS

PRODUCERS

PRODUCERS

PRODUCERS

INDEX OF WINES

WINES

WINES

WINES

WINES

WINES

WINES

WINES

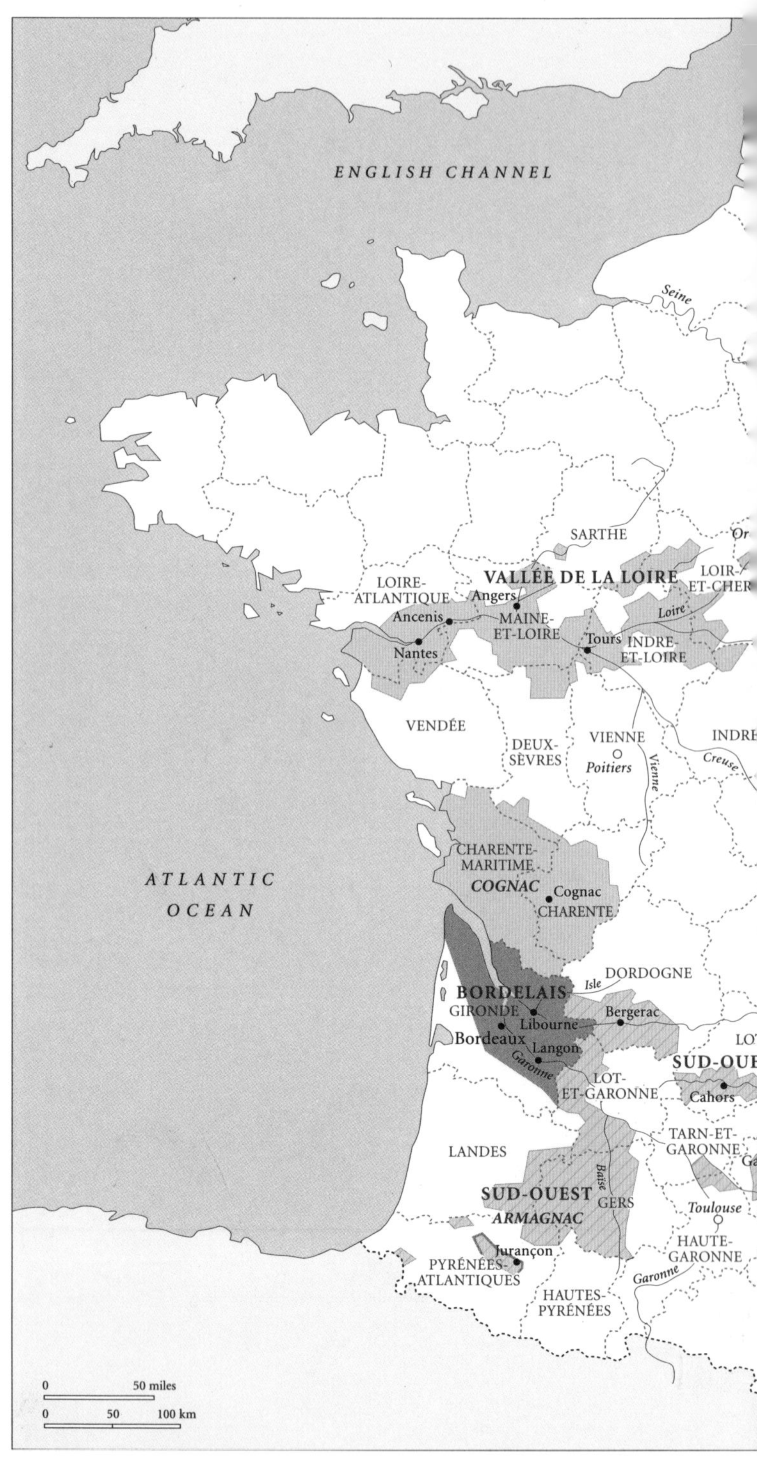

ENGLISH CHANNEL
Seine
SARTHE
VALLÉE DE LA LOIRE
LOIRE-ATLANTIQUE
Angers
LOIR-ET-CHER
Loire
Ancenis
MAINE-ET-LOIRE
Tours
INDRE-ET-LOIRE
Nantes
VENDÉE
DEUX-SÈVRES
VIENNE
Poitiers
Vienne
INDRE
Creuse
CHARENTE-MARITIME
COGNAC
Cognac
CHARENTE
ATLANTIC OCEAN
DORDOGNE
Isle
BORDELAIS
GIRONDE
Libourne
Bergerac
Bordeaux
Langon
Garonne
LOT
SUD-OUE
LOT-ET-GARONNE
Cahors
TARN-ET-GARONNE
LANDES
Baïse
SUD-OUEST
ARMAGNAC
GERS
Toulouse
HAUTE-GARONNE
Jurançon
PYRÉNÉES-ATLANTIQUES
Garonne
HAUTES-PYRÉNÉES
0 50 miles
0 50 100 km